THE ENCYCLOPEDIA

OF

ARCHITECTURE

HISTORICAL, THEORETICAL, AND PRACTICAL

NORTH-WEST VIEW OF BEVERLEY MINSTER, YORKSHIRE.

[Fig. 1218.

THE ENCYCLOPEDIA

OF

ARCHITECTURE

HISTORICAL, THEORETICAL, AND PRACTICAL

BY

JOSEPH GWILT, F.S.A., F.R.A.S.

THIS EDITION, REVISED,
WITH ALTERATIONS AND CONSIDERABLE ADDITIONS

BY

WYATT PAPWORTH

Fellow of the Royal Institute of British Architects

WITH A NEW FOREWORD

BY

MICHAEL MOSTOLLER

Architect, and professor of architecture, Columbia University

BONANZA BOOKS
New York

Library of Congress Cataloging in Publication Data

Gwilt, Joseph, 1784–1863.
    The encyclopedia of architecture; historical,
theoretical and practical.

    Reprint. Originally published: London: Long-
mans, Green, 1867.
    Includes index.
    1. Architecture.   2. Architects—Registers.
I. Papworth, Wyatt Angelicus Van Sandau,
1822–1894.   II. Title.
NA2520.G94   1982b   720   82-1320
ISBN: 0-517-379856   AACR2

    h g f e d c b a

FOREWORD

JOSEPH GWILT'S *Encyclopedia of Architecture* was first published in London in 1842. It comes down to us today as a *tour de force* that only the nineteenth century could produce, a summation of the entire field of endeavor that designed and built a world. To presume to summarize a profession, let alone one that is so comprehensive, seems audacious today. It seemed so even then. In the author's words: "Pythius, the architect of the Temple of Minerva at Priene . . . considered it absolutely necessary for an architect to have as accurate a knowledge of all the arts and sciences as is rarely acquired even by a professor devoted to one." And this encyclopedia fulfills that standard. When the book was first written, the difference between a layman and a professional architect was often slight. In England particularly, the "gentleman architect" was an established position in society. This book enabled that gentleman to merge the swiftly developing technology produced by the Industrial Revolution with more established and traditional concerns. By the end of the century, however, architecture, like many other fields, had become a specialized field of endeavor—still comprehensive, to be sure—but one whose technical, practical, and historical dimensions outstripped the individual. From 1899 on, professional practice was based on a firm employing specialists of all sorts, not an individual utilizing an encyclopedia.

Although not completely unique—in England, Peter Nicolson's *A Theoretical and Practical Treatise* of 1834 and Robert Stuart's *A Dictionary of Architecture* of 1830 preceded it—Gwilt's *Encyclopedia* was both a more complete and more authoritative text than any of its predecessors. It was immediately popular and went through three printings before being updated for this 1867 edition. For the English, it was an important source book for both the practitioner and the layman throughout the nineteenth century.

The book begins with history, proceeding from a description of the "wants of man" and the origins of architecture through the development of design in various countries. The second area of concern, the Theory of Architecture, follows. It is quite down to earth—the sections of explanation deal with "Construction," "Materials," "Use of Materials," and "Mediums of Expression," for example. This is a far cry from what we find in today's Modern-Postmodern theory hothouse—borrowings from esoteric subjects such as semiotics, physics, or linguistics, expressed by terms like "structuralism" and "deconstruction"—each little understood even by specialists but now applied to architecture. It is reassuring to know that an entire century of architects could do without such high-sounding theories and merely build. Gwilt's section on the theory of smithery and ironmongery is certainly old-fashioned, but it is refreshingly direct.

This concentration on pragmatic principles of building in the theory section is followed by the third book—The Practice of Architecture. It begins with a discourse on Beauty! The concepts of order, expression, unity, variety, and others are then discussed. Again, how unlike today, and again, how fresh a viewpoint. Once an understanding of how to build has been reached and how civilizations of the past have done so, the stated goal of architectural practice was to produce a work of art, a thing of beauty. Today, this is no longer true. Beauty is not the goal of practice; practice is merely a means of production, society's way of erecting buildings. A walk through any city in the world confirms this observation: ugly, meaningless buildings have been created for a society that often excludes beauty from practice, relegating it to a theoretical and abstract domain.

In the Practice of Architecture, an examination of building elements follows—the orders of architecture, windows, doors, ceilings, and how to compose them. A section on building types (now also so fashionable) helps the architect in practice come to grips with the general wants of man described earlier, with specific building programs based on social needs and space required.

The work is profusely illustrated. What is illustrated shows, in another way, the power of an inclusive and comprehensive view of what was in fact a lifework, architecture. Architects were assumed to be interested in cathedrals *and* caissons, stones *and* Stonehenge, hinges *and* history. Even methods for the valuation of property and compound interest tables were included—for, after all, even the gentleman architect had to proceed in a capitalist economy.

As would be expected in such an early work, the historical analysis is incomplete in today's terms. For example, the design system articulated in the section on proportion—the "interaxial system"—is an oversimplified view of past examples and less complete than Durand's great work in France.

Yet such a qualification is one of detail not of substance. The book remains a marvelous compendium—the architect's five-foot bookshelf in two inches—that made available to those who were architects (or fancied themselves as such) or to the layman interested in architecture the great body of subject matter that the field embraced at that time. The book's range and depth, its interest in detail, and the all-encompassing view, its amazing stress on beauty as the goal of practice rather than as an esoteric theory—all stand today's architectural world on its head. Yet what is perhaps the most significant aspect of the book is that it puts the entire universe of art and science into the framework of a professional discipline. Consequently, the magic of that discipline—architecture—is excitingly restored to us; for a cathedral and a skyscraper are not only structures, following laws of physics, they are shelters, they provide emotional experiences, and they are "books in stone," images of cities, and signs of culture. Sometimes they are beautiful. This book gives us a remarkable sense of the completeness of architecture, a feeling that architects may generate today, but one that all may share.

NEW YORK CITY   MICHAEL MOSTOLLER
August 1982

PREFACE

THE FIRST EDITION.

An Encyclopædia of any of the Fine Arts has, from its nature, considerable advantage over one which relates to the sciences generally. In the latter, the continual additions made to the common stock of knowledge frequently effect such a complete revolution in their bases and superstructure, that the established doctrines of centuries may be swept away by the discoveries of a single day. The arts, on the other hand, are founded upon principles unsusceptible of change. Fashion may, indeed — nay, often does—change the prevailing taste of the day, but first principles remain the same ; and as, in a cycle, the planets, after a period of wandering in the heavens, return to the places which they occupied ages before, so, in the arts, after seasons of *extravaganza* and *bizzareria*, a recurrence to sound taste is equally certain.

It is unfortunate for the productions of the arts that the majority of those who are constituted their judges are little qualified for the task, either by education or habits ; but on this, as it has been the complaint of every age, it is perhaps useless to dwell. This much may be said, that before any one can with propriety assume the name of architect, he must proceed regularly through some such course as is prescribed in this work. The main object of its author has been to impart to the *student* all the knowledge indispensable for the exercise of his profession ; but should the perusal of this encyclopædia serve to form, guide, or correct the taste even of the mere *amateur*, the author will not consider that he has laboured in vain.

An encyclopædia is necessarily a limited arena for the exhibition of an author's power ; for although every subject in the department of which it treats must be noticed, none can be discussed so extensively as in a separate work. An attempt to produce a *Complete Body of Architecture* the author believes to be entirely original. In his celebrated work, *L'Art de Bâtir*, Rondelet has embodied all that relates to the construction of buildings. Durand, too (*Leçons et Précis d'Architecture*), has published some admirable rules on composition and on the graphic portion of the art. Lebrun (*Théorie d'Architecture*) has treated on the philosophy of the equilibrium, if it may be

so called, of the orders. The *Encyclopédie Méthodique* contains, under various heads, some invaluable detached essays, many of which, however, suffer from want o the illustrative plates which were originally projected as an appendage to them. All these, with others in the French language, might, indeed, be formed into a valuable text-book for the architect ; but no such attempt has hitherto been made. Neither in Germany nor in Italy has any complete work of the kind appeared. In the English, as in other languages, there are doubtless several valuable treatises on different branches of the art, though not to the same extent as in French. In 1756, Ware (London, folio) published what he called *A Complete Body of Architecture*. This, though in many respects an useful work, is far behind the wants of the present day. It is confined exclusively to Roman and Italian architecture ; but it does not embrace the history even of these branches, nor does it contain a word on the sciences connected with construction. The details, therefore, not being sufficiently carried out, and many essential branches being entirely omitted, the work is not so generally useful as its name would imply. From these authorities, and many others, besides his own resources, the author of this encyclopædia has endeavoured to compress within the limits of one closely-printed volume all the elementary knowledge indispensable to the student and amateur ; and he even ventures to indulge the belief that it will be found to contain information which the experienced professor may have overlooked.

Though, in form, the whole work pretends to originality, this pretension is not advanced for the whole of its substance. Not merely all that has long been known, but even the progressive discoveries and improvements of modern times, are usually founded on facts which themselves have little claims to novelty. As a fine art, architecture, though in its applications and changes inexhaustible, is in respect of first principles confined within certain limits ; but the analysis of those principles and their relation to certain types have afforded some views of the subject which, it is believed, will be new even to those who have passed their lives in the study of the art.

In those sciences on which the constructive power of the art is based, the author apprehended he would be entitled to more credit by the use of weightier authorities than his own. Accordingly, in the Second Book, he has adopted the algebra of Euler ; and in other parts, the works of writers of established reputation. The use of Rossignol's geometry may indeed be disapproved by rigid mathematicians ; but, considering the variety of attainments indispensable to the architectural student, the author was induced to shorten and smooth his path as much as possible, by refraining from burdening his memory with more mathematical knowledge than was absolutely requisite for *his* particular art. On this account, also, the instruction in algebra is not carried beyond the solution of cubic equations ; up to that point it was necessary to prepare the learner for a due comprehension of the succeeding inquiries into the method of equilibrating arches and investigating the pressures of their different parts.

In all matters of importance, in which the works of previous writers have been used, the sources have been indicated, so that reference to the originals may be made. Upon the celebrated work of Rondelet above mentioned, on many learned articles in the *Encyclopédie Méthodique*, and on the works of Durand and other esteemed authors, large contributions have been levied; but these citations, it will be observed, appear for the first time in an English dress. In that part of the work which treats of the doctrine of arches, the chief materials, it will be seen, have been borrowed from Rondelet, whose views the author has adopted in preference to those he himself gave to the world many years ago, in a work which passed through several editions. Again, in the section on shadows, the author has not used his own treatise on Sciography. In the one case, he is not ashamed to confess his inferiority in so important a branch of the architect's studies; and in the other, he trusts that matured experience has enabled him to treat the subject in a form likely to be more extensively useful than that of treading in his former steps.

The sciences of which an architect should be cognisant are enumerated by Vitruvius at some length in the opening chapter of his first book. They are, perhaps, a little too much swelled, though the Roman in some measure qualifies the extent to which he would have them carried. "For," he observes, "in such a variety of matters" (the different arts and sciences) "it cannot be supposed that the same person can arrive at excellence in each." And again : "That architect is sufficiently educated whose general knowledge enables him to give his opinion on any branch when required to do so. Those unto whom nature hath been so bountiful that they are at once geometricians, astronomers, musicians, and skilled in many other arts, go beyond what is required by the architect, and may be properly called mathematicians in the extended sense of that word." Pythius, the architect of the temple of Minerva at Priene, differed, however, from the Augustan architect, inasmuch as he considered it absolutely requisite for an architect to have as accurate a knowledge of all the arts and sciences as is rarely acquired even by a professor devoted exclusively to one.

In a work whose object is to compress within a comparatively restricted space so vast a body of information as is implied in an account of what is known of historical, theoretical, and practical architecture, it is of the highest importance to preserve a distinct and precise arrangement of the subjects, so that they may be presented to the reader in consistent order and unity. Without order and method, indeed, the work, though filled with a large and valuable stock of information, would be but an useless mass of knowledge. In treating the subjects in detail, the alphabet has not been made to perform the function of an index, except in the glossary of the technical terms, which partly serves at the same time the purpose of a dictionary, and that of an index to the principal subjects noticed in the work. The following is a synoptical view of its contents, exhibiting its different parts, and the mode in which they arise from and are dependent on each other.

[*A List of the Contents was here inserted.*]

Perfection is not attainable in human labour, and the errors and defects of this work will, doubtless, in due time be pointed out; but as the subject has occupied the author's mind during a considerable practice, he is inclined to think that these will not be very abundant. He can truly say that he has bestowed upon it all the care and energy in his power; and he alone is responsible for its errors or defects—the only assistance he has to acknowledge being from his son, Mr. John Sebastian Gwilt, by whom the illustrative drawings were executed. No apology is offered for its appearance, inasmuch as the want of such a book has been felt by every architect at the beginning of his career. Not less is wanted a similar work on Civil Engineering, which the author has pleasure in stating is about to be shortly supplied by his friend, Mr. Edward Cresy. [*This work has since been published.*]

Without deprecating the anger of the critic, or fearing what may be urged against his work, the author now leaves it to its fate. His attempt has been for the best, and he says with sincerity,

> " Si quid novisti rectius istis
> Candidus imperti ; si non his utere mecum."

J. G.

September 30, 1842.

ADVERTISEMENT.

———◦◇◦———

GWILT'S ENCYCLOPÆDIA, first published in 1842, has now passed through four impressions, having received amendments at the hands of its author, who had noted, in a copy of the last edition, some other useful emendations, which have been adopted.

The continued demand for this work by the public, and by the profession for which it was specially prepared, is sufficient evidence of the extent to which Mr. Gwilt's labours have been appreciated. To keep it worthy of this estimation, the Publishers have deemed it desirable that the book should be accommodated to the present time, and the deficiencies supplied on those points in which recent investigations have given additional information, or have modified previous conclusions.

The preparation, within prearranged limits, of this edition has been entrusted to Mr. Wyatt Papworth, architect, whose additions, beyond the chief alterations about to be named, are indicated by an italic letter following the number of the paragraph.

It was considered preferable to retain Book I., HISTORY OF ARCHITECTURE : with the exception therefore of POINTED ARCHITECTURE, which has been entirely rewritten, and a few pages in extension of ENGLISH ARCHITECTURE, both largely illustrated with new woodcuts, this portion is untouched. The "Supplement" added by Mr. Gwilt on the former subject has been cancelled, but portions of its contents have been inserted in various sections of the work.

In Book II., THEORY OF ARCHITECTURE, the first section on "Arithmetic and Algebra" has been omitted ; this is the only portion absolutely deducted from the late editions. Chapters II. and III. have been considerably enlarged ; many of the sections having been nearly entirely rewritten to include the progress of information on the subjects to which they refer. The chief addition to be named, is the results of recent inquiries into the strength of BEAMS, GIRDERS, and PILLARS, both of timber and of iron. This section, it is believed, will relieve the student of much of the perplexity which he encounters in studying the works of the several authors who have written on the subject, while it will also prepare him for the further study of more scientific

development in those works. Mediæval masonry, carpentry, and joinery, have been dwelt upon at much length ; and many of the subjects, new and old, practically illustrated with new woodcuts.

In Book III., PRACTICE OF ARCHITECTURE, considerable additions have also been made. As the first chapter had treated only the subject of GRECIAN AND ITALIAN ARCHITECTURE, it was deemed desirable to form, within certain limits, a corresponding chapter on MEDIÆVAL ARCHITECTURE, the details of which have been chiefly taken from examples in Great Britain and Ireland. Much of the text with its illustrations previously arranged in the " Appendix" by Mr. Gwilt have been inserted therein, a number of new diagrams being added ; while to secure for reference as large a quantity of illustrations as possible, the chapters on PROPORTION IN ARCHITECTURE have been introduced from the end of Mr. Cresy's *Encyclopædia of Civil Engineering.* That portion of the subject which relates to Mediæval Architecture has been prefaced with a condensed account of the systems of proportion propounded by many investigators.

The chapter on PUBLIC AND PRIVATE BUILDINGS has received a few supplementary sections.

The original APPENDIX has been placed as Book IV., with some additions.

The GLOSSARY has been revised, and the ADDENDA TO THE GLOSSARY of the later editions considerably enlarged. As the " List of Publications " relating to Architecture and its branches, in the former editions, has always been considered of importance, another list, in continuation, has been added in the new GLOSSARY ADDENDUM.

With reference to this new edition, to adopt the words of Mr. Gwilt in his original preface, " No apology is offered for its appearance, inasmuch as the want of such a book has been felt by every architect at the beginning of his career."

Lastly, it is hoped that the short biographical memoir of the author appended to this edition will be of interest to many readers.

PATERNOSTER ROW :
February 1867.

MEMOIR.

—◆◆◆—

The late Mr. Joseph Gwilt, born January 11, 1784, was the second son of Mr. George Gwilt, of some professional celebrity, holding in the year 1770 the appointment of architect and surveyor to the county of Surrey. The eldest son, George, assisted his father, and was known in later life for his able and conscientious restoration of the Lady Chapel and Tower of St. Mary Overy, or St. Saviour's Church, Southwark.

Joseph Gwilt received his earliest instruction at a boarding-school, from which, in 1798, he was removed to St. Paul's School, where he remained two years, and then entered his father's office. In 1801 he was admitted a student of the Royal Academy of Arts in London, and obtained their silver medal for the best drawing of the tower and steeple of the Church of St. Dunstan-in-the-East, on the 10th December of that year. In 1811 he published his first work, *Treatise on the Equilibrium of Arches*, which proceeded to a second edition in 1826 (the edition of 1839 was not sanctioned by him). On March 9, 1815, he was elected a Fellow of the Society of Antiquaries of London. At the end of the following year he visited the principal cities of Italy, in company with his friend Mr. J. S. Hayward. For his own use when abroad he prepared from Milizia's *Lives of Architects* the *Notitia Architectonica Italiana, or Concise Notices of the Buildings and Architects of Italy*, which on his return to England he published, in 1818. This was, in 1822, followed by a *Cursory View of the Origin of Caryatides*; and in the same year, *Sciography, or Examples of Shadows, with Rules for their Projection*, of which a second edition appeared in 1824, and again in 1833.

In the year 1822, also, Mr. Gwilt competed for the new London Bridge, but though twice placed first by the judges, his design was not rewarded by the Committee; he subsequently printed a pamphlet entitled *The Conduct of the Corporation*, etc. Early in 1823 he read *An Historical, Descriptive, and Critical Account of St. Paul's Cathedral*, at the Architects' and Antiquaries' Club, which was printed, and subsequently reprinted with additions in

Brayley and Britton's *Public Edifices of London*, 8vo. 1825–28 ; this work also contains an account with illustrations by him of the staircase in Ashburnham House, Westminster, the reputed design of Inigo Jones.   In 1824 he published a plate showing a comparative view of the four principal modern churches in Europe by means of transverse sections to one scale.   In 1825 he edited an edition, in two volumes, of Sir William Chambers's admirable *Treatise on the Decorative Part of Civil Architecture*, adding an original *Examination of the Elements of Beauty in Grecian Architecture, and an Investigation of its Origin, Progress, and Perfection* ; in 1826, he published the first translation in England of the entire *Treatise on Architecture of Vitruvius* ; and likewise *The Rudiments of Architecture, Practical and Theoretical*, of which other editions appeared in 1835 and 1839.   In 1829 appeared the *Ordinary* to N. H. Nicolas, a *Roll of Arms*.

In 1833 Mr. Gwilt was elected a member of the Royal Astronomical Society, and to the study of this branch of science he later in life further devoted himself, when retired from the profession.   The pamphlet entitled *Observations on the Communication of Mr. Wilkins relative to the National Gallery*, was printed in the same year.   In 1835 appeared a *Treatise on the Art of Music* from his pen, in the *Encyclopædia Metropolitana* ; also *Rudiments of the Anglo-Saxon Tongue*, 8vo. ; in 1837, *Elements of Architectural Criticism, for the Use of Students, Amateurs, and Reviewers*, with an *Appendix* in 1839 ; and in 1838 a pamphlet (in conjunction with his son John Sebastian) relative to *A National Gallery on the Site of Trafalgar Square*. In 1842 he supplied the articles relating to *Architecture* and to *Music*, in Brande's *Dictionary of Science, Literature, and Art* ; and in the same year was published the principal work of his life, the *Encyclopædia of Architecture, Historical, Theoretical, and Practical*, to which in 1845 he added an appendix on *Gothic Architecture*.   In 1848 he edited a new edition of Peter Nicholson's *Principles of Architecture* ; this, with the exception of a few papers which appeared subsequently in some of the periodicals, was his last printed work.

Besides the design for London Bridge, already mentioned, Mr. Gwilt's professional works consisted of the church at Lee, near Blackheath, lately pulled down ; 1819, the land approaches to Southwark Bridge ; 1843, Markree Castle, near Sligo, in Ireland, for E. J. Cooper, Esq. ; and St. Thomas's Church at Charlton, in Kent ; together with numerous other buildings of no important interest, excepting the design for laying out for building purposes the estate of Sir T. M. Wilson at Hampstead : the viaduct there is the only portion of it yet executed.   Until about 1845 Mr. Gwilt held the appointment of Surveyor to the Commissioners of Sewers for the limits extending from East Moulsey, in the county of Surrey, to the river Ravensbourne in Kent, for a period of forty-seven years, having succeeded his father, who held the appointment previously for the space of thirty years.   He was also Architect to the Imperial Fire Assurance Company ; to the Worshipful Company of Wax Chandlers ; as well as to the Worshipful Company of Grocers, the interior of whose Hall he entirely rearranged in 1828, and added the

front towards Princes Street, by the Bank of England, and rebuilt the house of the clerks.

Mr. Gwilt was frequently consulted by the Office of Woods and Forests, and on many occasions gave important evidence before Committees, both of the House of Lords and of the House of Commons, more especially in regard to the Metropolitan Building Act 1855, which he, in conjunction with Mr. Penrose, projected, but was overruled as to many of the clauses. He was a thorough disciple and an ardent admirer of that great Italian architect Palladio; he ever considered the Italian style of architecture as best suited to the climate of this country, and was fearless in expressing his opinions on subjects of art. He made frequent trips to France, Belgium, and Germany, embellishing the remarks which he made in his journal with exquisite pen-and-ink sketches of the objects chiefly interesting him during the journeys.

For many years of his life, being an accomplished musician himself, and on intimate terms with many of the leading professors, Mr. Gwilt was in the habit of holding at his house fortnightly musical soirées, at which were played Mozart's quartetts, Haydn's septetts, and other classical music, his own instrument at these parties being the tenor. At the coronation of the Queen, owing to his musical knowledge, he was selected to act as signal officer to the choir.

After a long, honourable, and arduous career of upwards of fifty years, Mr. Gwilt retired from the active pursuit of his profession, residing, for a few years preceding his death, at South Hill, Henley-on-Thames, at which place he closed his useful life on the 14th September, 1863, in the eightieth year of his age. John Sebastian Gwilt furnished a memoir of his father to the Royal Institute of British Architects, from whose *Transactions*, as well as from the article in the *Dictionary* of the Architectural Publication Society, and the detailed account of Mr. Gwilt's labours in the *Builder* for 1863, page 701, this biographical account has been compiled.

The numerous publications named in the foregoing memoir will not here need any criticism, most of them should be read by the architectural student, especially the *Rudiments*, and the *Elements of Criticism*, with its *Appendix*; the publication of the last-named work was occasioned by the violent attacks which the previous treatise received from reviews. Others of his minor writings have been criticised by Mr. Gwilt himself in the " Preface " to this work. The translation of Vitruvius's *Architecture* is a valuable addition to the library, as such an edition of the whole treatise had not previously been published in England; portions only having been attempted by Newton and by Wilkins. The want of such a " Body " of information as the *Encyclopædia of Architecture* had long been felt by the profession, as it was found that other " Encyclopædias " did not meet the special requirements.

This work has now borne the test of a quarter of a century's use, during which time it has done good service; and more need scarcely now be said of

it than that it is of sufficient merit to have established, without the addition of the other learned writings by this esteemed architect, a reputation for its author as having mastered all the details of numerous branches of Literature and Science. This reputation was enhanced in the eyes of his contemporaries by the manner in which his selections from many of the best native and foreign professional works were placed intelligibly before the architectural student, through the judgment with which Mr. Gwilt not only decided what was theoretically and practically useful in those works, but added to the labours of his predecessors a mass of information entirely due to the store of technical knowledge which he had carefully and laboriously acquired for himself.

WYATT PAPWORTH.

14A GREAT MARLBOROUGH STREET,
    LONDON: *February*, 1867.

CONTENTS.

—◆—

BOOK I.

HISTORY OF ARCHITECTURE.

CONTENTS.

BOOK II.

THEORY OF ARCHITECTURE.

BOOK III.

PRACTICE OF ARCHITECTURE.

BOOK IV.

APPENDIX.

THE ENCYCLOPEDIA

OF

ARCHITECTURE

HISTORICAL, THEORETICAL, AND PRACTICAL

BOOK I.

HISTORY OF ARCHITECTURE.

CHAP. I.

ON THE ORIGIN OF ARCHITECTURE.

SECT. I.

WANTS OF MAN, AND FIRST BUILDINGS.

1. PROTECTION from the inclemency of the seasons was the mother of architecture. Of little account at its birth, it rose into light and life with the civilisation of mankind; and, proportionately as security, peace, and good order were established, it became, not less than its sisters, painting and sculpture, one method of transmitting to posterity the degree of importance to which a nation had attained, and the moral value of that nation amongst the kingdoms of the earth. If the art, however, be considered strictly in respect of its actual utility, its principles are restricted within very narrow limits; for the mere art, or rather science, of construction, has no title to a place among the fine arts. Such is in various degrees to be found among people of savage and uncivilised habits; and until it is brought into a system founded upon certain laws of proportion, and upon rules based on a refined analysis of what is suitable in the highest degree to the end proposed, it can pretend to no rank of a high class. It is only when a nation has arrived at a certain degree of opulence and luxury that architecture can be said to exist in it. Hence it is that architecture, in its origin, took the varied forms which have impressed it with such singular differences in different countries; differences which, though modified as each country advanced in civilisation, were, in each, so stamped, that the type was permanent, being refined only in a higher degree in their most important examples.

2. The ages that have elapsed, and the distance by which we are separated from the nations among whom the art was first practised, deprive us of the means of examining the shades of difference resulting from climate, productions of the soil, the precise spots upon which the earliest societies of man were fixed, with their origin, number, mode of life, and social institutions; all of which influenced them in the selection of one form in preference to another. We may, however, easily trace in the architecture of nations, the types of three distinct states of life, which are clearly discoverable at the present time; though in some cases the types may be thought doubtful.

Sect. II.

ORIGIN AND PROGRESS OF BUILDING.

3. The original classes into which mankind were divided were, we may safely assume, those of hunters, of shepherds, and of those occupied in agriculture; and the buildings for protection which each would require, must have been characterised by their several occupations. The hunter and fisher found all the accommodation they required in the clefts

and caverns of rocks; and the indolence which those states of life induced, made them insensible or indifferent to greater comfort than such naturally-formed habitations afforded. We are certain that thus lived such tribes. Jeremiah (chap. xlix. 16.), speaking of the judgment upon Edom, says, " O thou that dwellest in the clefts of the rock, that holdest the height of the hill ;" a text which of late has received ample illustration from travellers, and especially from the labours of Messrs. Leon de Laborde and Linant, in the splendid engravings of the ruins of Petra (*fig.* 1.). To the shepherd, the inhabitant of the plains wandering from one spot to another, as pasture became inadequate to the support of his flocks, another species of dwelling was more appropriate; one which he could remove with him in his wanderings: this was the tent, the type of the architecture of China, whose people were, like all the Tartar races, *nomades* or *scenites*, that is, shepherds or dwellers in tents. Where a portion of the race fixed its abode for the purposes of agriculture, a very dif-

Fig. 1.   RUINS OF PETRA.

ferent species of dwelling was necessary. Solidity was required as well for the personal comfort of the husbandman as for preserving, from one season to another, the fruits of the earth, upon which he and his family were to exist. Hence, doubtless, the hut, which most authors have assumed to be the type of Grecian architecture.

4. Authors, says the writer in the *Encyc. Methodique*, in their search after the origin of architecture, have generally confined their views to a single type, without considering the modification which would be necessary for a mixture of two or more of the states of mankind; for it is evident that any two or three of them may co-exist, a point upon which more will be said in speaking of Egyptian architecture. Hence have arisen the most discordant and contradictory systems, formed without sufficient acquaintance with the customs of different people, their origin, and first state of existence.

5. The earliest habitations which were constructed after the dispersion of mankind from the plains of Sennaar (for there, certainly, as we shall hereafter see, even without the evidence of Scripture, was a great multitude gathered together), were, of course, proportioned to the means which the spot afforded, and to the nature of the climate to which they were to be adapted. Reeds, canes, the branches, bark, and leaves of trees, clay, and similar materials would be first used. The first houses of the Egyptians and of the people of Palestine were of reeds and canes interwoven. At the present day the same materials serve to form the houses of the Peruvians. According to Pliny (l. vii.), the first houses of the Greeks were only of clay; for it was a considerable time before that nation was acquainted with the process of hardening it into bricks. The Abyssinians still build with clay and reeds. Wood, however, offers such facilities of construction, that still, as of old, where it abounds, its adoption prevails. At first, the natural order seems to be that which Vitruvius describes in the first chapter of his second book. " The first attempt," says our author, " was the mere erection of a few spars, united together with twigs, and covered with mud. Others built their walls of dried lumps of turf, connected these walls together by means of timbers laid across horizontally, and covered the erections with reeds and boughs, for the purpose of sheltering themselves from the inclemency of the seasons. Finding, however, that flat coverings of this sort would not effectually shelter them in the winter season, they made their roofs of two inclined planes, meeting each other in a ridge at the summit, the whole of which they covered with clay, and thus carried off the rain." The same author

afterwards observes, " The woods about Pontus furnish such abundance of timber, that they build in the following manner.   Two trees are laid level on the earth, right and left, at such distance from each other as will suit the length of the trees which are to cross and

Fig. 2.   EARLY TIMBER CONSTRUCTION.

connect them. On the extreme ends of these two trees are laid two other trees, transversely : the space which the house will enclose is thus marked out. The four sides being so set out, towers are raised, whose walls consist of trees laid horizontally, but kept perpendicularly over each other, the alternate layers yoking the angles. The level interstices, which the thickness of the trees alternately leave, is filled in with chips and mud. On a similar principle they form their roofs, except that gradually reducing the length of the trees which traverse from side to side, they assume a pyramidal form.   They are covered with boughs, and thus, after a rude fashion of vaulting, their quadrilateral roofs are formed."   The northern parts of Germany, Poland, and Russia still exhibit traces of this method of building, which is also found in Florida, Louisiana, and elsewhere, in various places. See *fig.* 2.

6. We shall not, in this place, pursue the discussion on the timber hut, which has certainly, with great appearance of probability, been so often said to contain within it the types of Grecian architecture, but shall, under that head, enlarge further on the subject.

SECT. III.

DIFFERENT SORTS OF DWELLINGS ARISING FROM DIFFERENT OCCUPATIONS.

7. The construction of the early habitations of mankind required little skill and as little knowledge.   A very restricted number of tools and machines was required.   The method of felling timber, which uncivilised nations still use, namely, by fire, might have served all purposes at first.   The next step would be the shaping of hard and infrangible stones into cutting tools, as is still the practice in some parts of the continent of America.   These, as the metals became known, would be supplanted by tools formed of them.   Among the Peruvians, at their invasion by the Spaniards, the only tools in use were the hatchet and the adze ; and we may fairly assume that similar tools were the only ones known at a period of high antiquity.   The saw, nails, the hammer, and other instruments of carpentry were unknown.   The Greeks, who, as Jacob Bryant says, knew nothing of their own history, ascribe the invention of the instruments necessary for working materials to Dædalus ; but only a few of these were known even in the time of Homer, who confines himself to the hatchet with two edges, the plane, the auger, and the rule.   He particularises neither the square, compasses, nor saw.   Neither the Greek word πρίων (a saw), nor its equivalent, is to be found in his works.   Dædalus is considered, however, by Goguet as a fabulous person altogether, the word meaning, according to him, nothing more than a skilful workman, a meaning which, he observes, did not escape the notice of Pausanias.   The surmise is borne out by the non-mention of so celebrated a character, if he had ever existed, by Homer, and, afterwards, by Herodotus.   The industry and perseverance of man, however, in the end, overcame the difficulties of construction.   For wood, which was the earliest material, at length were substituted bricks, stone, marble, and the like ; and edifices were reared of unparalleled magnificence and solidity.   It seems likely, that bricks would have been in use for a considerable period before stone was employed in building.   They were, probably, after moulding, merely subjected to the sun's rays to acquire hardness.   These were the materials whereof the Tower of Babel was constructed.   These also, at a very remote period, were used by the Egyptians.   Tiles seem to have been of as high an antiquity as bricks, and to have been used, as in the present day, for covering roofs.

8. The period at which wrought stone was originally used for architectural purposes is

quite unknown, as is that in which cement of any kind was first employed as the medium of uniting masonry. They were both, doubtless, the invention of that race which we have mentioned as cultivators of land, to whom is due the introduction of architecture, properly so called. To them solid and durable edifices were necessary as soon as they had fixed upon a spot for the settlement of themselves and their families.

9. Chaldæa, Egypt, Phœnicia, and China are the first countries on record in which architecture, worthy the name, made its appearance. They had certainly attained considerable proficiency in the art at a very early period ; though it is doubtful, as respects the three first, whether their reputation is not founded rather on the enormous masses of their works, than on beauty and sublimity of form. Strabo mentions many magnificent works which he attributes to Semiramis; and observes that, besides those in Babylonia, there were monuments of Babylonian industry throughout Asia. He mentions λόφοι (high altars), and strong walls and battlements to various cities, as also subterranean passages of communication, aqueducts for the conveyance of water under ground, and passages of great length, upwards, by stairs. Bridges are also mentioned by him (lib. xvi.). Moses has preserved the names of three cities in Chaldæa which were founded by Nimrod (*Gen.* x. 10.). Ashur, we are told, built Nineveh : and (*Gen.* xix. 4.) as early as the age of Jacob and Abraham, towns had been established in Palestine. The Chinese attribute to Fohi the encircling of cities and towns with walls ; and in respect of Egypt, there is no question that in Homer's time the celebrated city of Thebes had been long in existence. The works in India are of very early date ; and we shall hereafter offer some remarks, when speaking of the extraordinary monument of Stonehenge, tending to prove, as Jacob Bryant supposes, that the earliest buildings of both nations, as well as those of Phœnicia and other countries, were erected by colonies of some great original nation. If the Peruvians and Mexicans, without the aid of carriages and horses, without scaffolding, cranes, and other machines used in building, without even the use of iron, were enabled to raise monuments which are still the wonder of travellers, it would seem that the mechanical arts were not indispensable to the progress of architecture ; but it is much more likely that these were understood at an exceedingly remote period in Asia, and in so high a degree as to have lent their aid in the erection of some of the stupendous works to which we have alluded.

10. The art of working stone, which implies the use of iron and a knowledge of the method of tempering it, was attributed to Tosorthus, the successor of Menes. It seems, however, possible that the ancients were in possession of some secret for preparing bronze tools which were capable of acting upon stone. Be that as it may, no country could have been called upon earlier than Egypt to adopt stone as a material, for the climate does not favour the growth of timber ; hence stone, marble, and granite were thus forced into use ; and we know that, besides the facility of transport by means of canals, as early as the time of Joseph waggons were in use. (*Gen.* xlv. 19.) We shall hereafter investigate the hypothesis of the architecture of Greece being founded upon types of timber buildings, merely observing here, by the way, that many of the columns and entablatures of Egypt had existence long before the earliest temples of Greece, and therefore that, without recurrence to timber construction, prototypes for Grecian architecture are to be found in the venerable remains of Egypt, where it is quite certain wood was not generally employed as a material, and where the subterranean architecture of the country offers a much more probable origin of the style.

CHAP. II.

ARCHITECTURE OF VARIOUS COUNTRIES.

SECT. I.

DRUIDICAL AND CELTIC ARCHITECTURE.

11. If rudeness, want of finish, and the absence of all appearance of art, be criteria for judgment on the age of monuments of antiquity, the wonderful remains of Abury and Stonehenge must be considered the most ancient that have preserved their form so as to indicate the original plan on which they were constructed. The late Mr. Godfrey Higgins, a gentleman of the highest intellectual attainments, in his work on the Celtic Druids (published 1829), has shown, as we think satisfactorily, that the Druids of the British Isles were a colony of the first race of people, learned, enlightened, and descendants of the persons who escaped the deluge on the borders of the Caspian Sea; that they were the earliest occupiers of Greece, Italy, France, and Britain, and arrived in those places by a route nearly

along the forty-fifth parallel of north latitude ; that, in a similar manner, colonies advanced from the same great nation by a southern line through Asia, peopling Syria and Africa, and arriving at last by sea through the Pillars of Hercules at Britain ; that the languages of the western world were the same, and that one system of letters — viz. that of the Irish Druids — pervaded the whole, was common to the British Isles and Gaul, to the inhabitants of Italy, Greece, Syria, Arabia, Persia, and Hindostan ; and that one of the two alphabets (of the same system) in which the Irish MSS. are written — viz. the Beth-luis-nion — came by Gaul through Britain to Ireland ; and that the other — the Bobeloth — came through the Straits of Gibraltar. Jacob Bryant thinks that the works called Cyclopean were executed at a remote age by colonies of some great original nation ; the only difference between his opinion and that of Mr. Higgins being, that the latter calls them Druids, or Celts, from the time of the dispersion above alluded to.

12. The unhewn stones, whose antiquity and purport is the subject of this section, are found in Hindostan, where they are denominated " pandoo koolies," and are attributed to a fabulous being named Pandoo and his sons. With a similarity of character attesting their common origin, we find them in India, on the shores of the Levant and Mediterranean, in Belgium, Denmark, Sweden and Norway, in France, and on the shores of Britain from the Straits of Dover to the Land's End in Cornwall, as well as in many of the interior parts of the country. They are classed as follows : — 1. The single stone, pillar, or obelisk. 2. Circles of stones of different number and arrangement. 3. Sacrificial stones. 4. Cromlechs and cairns. 5. Logan stones. 6. Tolmen or colossal stones.

13. (1.) *Single Stones.* — Passages abound in Scripture in which the practice of erecting single stones is recorded. The reader on this point may refer to *Gen.* xxviii. 18., *Judges,* ix. 6., 1 *Sam.* vii. 12., 2 *Sam.* xx. 8., *Joshua,* xxiv. 27. The single stone might be an emblem of the generative power of Nature, and thence an object of idolatry. That mentioned in the first scriptural reference, which Jacob set up in his journey to visit Laban, his uncle, and which he had used for his pillow, seems, whether from the vision he had while sleeping upon it, or from some other cause, to have become to him an object of singular veneration ; for he set it up, and poured oil upon it, and called it " Bethel " (the house of God). It is curious to observe that some pillars in Cornwall, assumed to have been erected by the Phœnicians, still retain the appellation *Bothel.* At first, these stones were of no larger dimension than a man could remove, as in the instance just cited, and that of the Gilgal of Joshua (*Josh.* iv. 20.) ; but that which was set up *under an oak* at Shechem (ibid. xxiv. 26.), was a great stone. And here we may notice another singular coincidence, that of the Bothel in Cornwall being set up in a place which, from its proximi'y to an oak which was near the spot, was called Bothel-ac ; the last syllable being the Saxon for an oak. It appears from the Scriptures that these single stones were raised on various occasions ; sometimes, as in the case of Jacob's Bethel and of Samuel's Ebenezer, to commemorate instances of divine interposition ; sometimes to record a covenant, as in the case of Jacob and Laban (*Gen.* xxxi. 48.) ; sometimes, like the Greek stelæ, as sepulchral stones, as in the case of Rachel's grave (*Gen.* xxxvi. 20.), 1700 years B.C., according to the usual reckoning. They were occasionally, also, set up to the memory of individuals, as in the instance of Absalom's pillar and others. The pillars and altars of the patriarchs appear to have been erected in honour of the only true God, Jehovah ; but wherever the Canaanites appeared, they seem to have been the objects of idolatrous worship, and to have been dedicated to Baal or the sun, or the other false deities whose altars Moses ordered the Israelites to destroy. The similarity of pillars of single stones almost at the opposite sides of the earth, leaves no doubt in our mind of their being the work of a people of one common origin widely scattered ; and the hypotheses of Bryant and Higgins sufficiently account for their appearance in places so remote from each other. In consequence, says the latter writer, of some cause, no matter what, the Hive, after the dispersion, casted and sent forth its swarms. One of the largest descended, according to Genesis (x. 2.), from Gomer, went north, and then west, pressed by succeeding swarms, till it arrived at the shores of the Atlantic Ocean, and ultimately colonised Britain. Another branch, observes the same author, proceeded through Sarmatia southward to the Euxine (Cimmerian Bosphorus) ; another to Italy, founding the states of the Umbrii and the Cimmerii, at Cuma, near Naples. Till the time of the Romans these different lines of march, like so many sheepwalks, were without any walled cities. Some of the original tribe found their way into Greece, and between the Carpathian mountains and the Alps into Gaul, scattering a few stragglers as they passed into the beautiful valleys of the latter, where traces of them in Druidical monuments and language are occasionally found. Wherever they settled, if the conjecture is correct, they employed themselves in recovering the lost arts of their ancestors.

14. To the Canaanites of Tyre and Sidon may be chiefly attributed the introduction of these primeval works into Britain. The Tyrians, inhabiting a small slip of barren land, were essentially and necessarily a commercial people, and became the most expert and adventurous sailors of antiquity. It has been supposed that the constancy of the needle to the pole, " that path which no fowl knoweth, and which the vulture's eye hath not seen,"

was known to the Tyrians ; and, indeed, it seems scarcely possible that, by the help of the stars alone, they should have been able to maintain a commerce for tin on the shores of Britain, whose western coast furnished that metal in abundance, and whose islands (the Scilly) were known by the title of Cassiterides, or tin islands. In this part of Britain there seems unquestionable evidence that they settled a colony, and were the architects of Stonehenge, Abury, and other similar works in the British islands. In these they might have been assisted by that part of the swarm which reached our shores through Gaul ; or it is possible that the works in question may be those of the latter only, of whom traces exist in Britany at the monument of Carnac, whereof it is computed 4000 stones still remain. From among the number of pillars of this kind still to be seen in England, we give (*fig.* 3.) that standing at Rudstone, in the east riding of Yorkshire. It is described by Drake, in his *Eboracum*, as "coarse rag stone or millstone grit, and its weight is computed at between 40 and 50 tons. In form (the sides being slightly concave) it approaches to an ellipse on the plan, the breadth being 5 ft. 10 in., and the thickness 2 ft. 3 in., in its general dimensions. Its height is 24 ft. ; and, according to a brief account communicated to the late Mr. Pegge, in the year 1769

FIG. 3.   PILLAR AT RUDSTONE.

(*Archæologia*, vol. v. p. 95.), its depth underground equals its height above, as appeared from an experiment made by the late Sir William Strickland."

15. (2.) *Circles of Stone.*—The Israelites were in the habit of arranging stones to represent the twelve tribes of Israel (*Exod.* xxiv. 4.), and for another purpose. (*Deut.* xxvii. 2.) And in a circular form we find them set up by Joshua's order on the passage of the Israelites through Jordan to Gilgal (בגלגל) ; a word in which the radical Gal or Gil (signifying a wheel) is doubled to denote the continued repetition of the action. In this last case, Joshua made the arrangement a type of the Lord rolling away their reproach from them.

16. Though traces of this species of monument are found in various parts of the world, even in America, we shall confine our observations to those of Abury and Stonehenge, merely referring, by way of enumeration, to the places where they are to be found. Thus we mention Rolbrich in Oxfordshire, the Hurlers in Cornwall, Long Meg and her daughters in Cumberland, remains in Derbyshire, Devonshire, Dorsetshire, at Stanton Drew in Somersetshire, and in Westmoreland. They are common in Wales, and are found in the Western Isles. There are examples in Iceland, Norway, Sweden, Denmark, and various parts of Germany. Clarke, in his description of the hill of Kushunlu Tepe in the Troad, observes, that all the way up, the traces of former works may be noticed, and that, on the summit, there is a small oblong area, six yards long and two broad, exhibiting vestiges of the highest antiquity ; the stones forming the inclosure being as rude as those of Tiryns in Argolis, and encircled by a grove of oaks covering the top of this conical mountain. The entrance is from the south. Upon the east and west, outside of the trees, are stones ranging like what we in England call Druidical circles. Three circles of stones are known in America, one of which stands upon a high rock on the banks of the river Winnipigon. The stupendous monument of Carnac in Britany, of which we have above made mention, is not of a circular form ; the stones there being arranged in eleven straight lines, from 30 to 33 ft. apart, some of which are of enormous size. They are said to have formerly extended three leagues along the coast. A description of this monument is given in vol. xxii. of the *Archæologia.*

17. Abury, or Avebury, in Wiltshire, of which we give a view in a restored state (*fig.* 4.), is a specimen of this species of building, in which the climax of magnificence was attained. Stukely, who examined the ruins when in much better preservation than at present, says, "that the whole figure represented a snake transmitted through a circle ;" and that, "to make their representation more natural, they artfully carried it over a variety of elevations and depressions, which, with the curvature of the avenues, produces sufficiently the desired effect. To make it still more elegant and picture-like, the head of the snake is carried up the southern promontory of Hackpen Hill, towards the village of West Kennet ; nay, the very name of the hill is derived from this circumstance ;" for *acan*, he observes, signifies a serpent in the Chaldaic language. Dr. S. then goes on to state, "that the *dracontia* was a name, amongst the first-learned nations, for the very ancient sort of temples of which they could give no account, nor well explain their meaning upon it." The figure of the serpent extended two miles in length ; and but a very faint idea can now be formed of what it was in its original state. Two double circles, one to the north and the other to the south of the centre, were placed within the large circle, which formed the principal body of the serpent, and from which branched out the head to Hackpen Hill, in the direction of

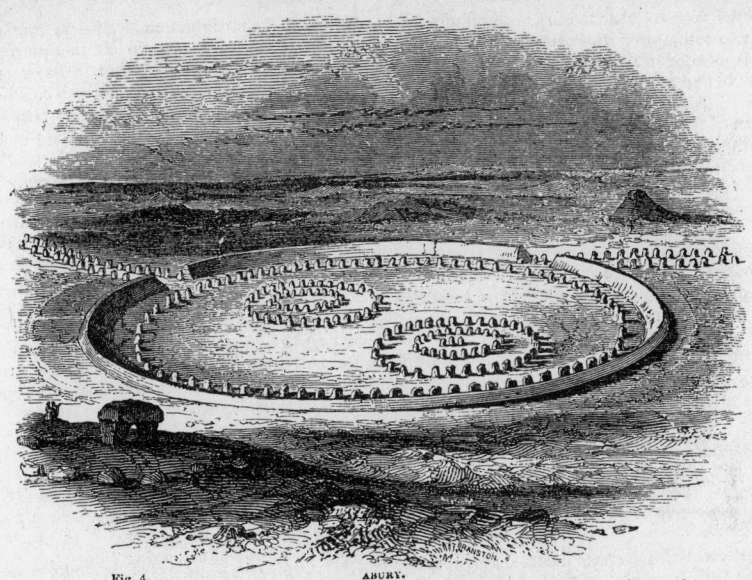

Fig. 4. ABURY.

West Kennet, as one avenue; and the other, the tail, in the direction of Beckhampton. Dr. Stukely makes the number of stones, 652 in all, as under: —

Stones.		Stones.		Stones.
The great circle	100	Central pillar and altar, south		Long stone. Cove jambs . 2
Outer circle north of the centre	30	circle . 2		A stone he calls the ring stone . 1
Inner ditto . 12		Kennet avenue . 200		Closing stone of the tail . 1
Outer circle, south . 30		Beckhampton avenue . 200		
Inner ditto . 12		Outer circle of Hackpen . 40		Total 652
Cove and altar stone, north circle 4		Inner ditto . 18		

Of these, only seventy-six stones remained in the Kennet avenue in 1722. The large circle was enclosed by a trench or vallum upwards of 50 ft. in depth and between 60 and

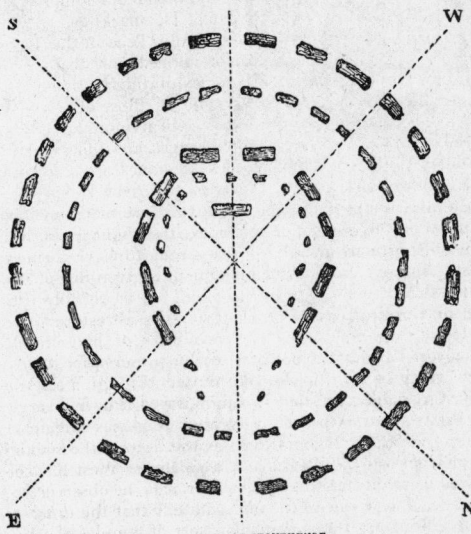

Fig. 5. PLAN OF STONEHENGE.

70 ft. in width, leaving entrances open where the avenues intersected it. The colossal mound, called " Silbury hill," close to the Bath road, was probably connected in some way with the circle we have described, from the circumstance of the Roman road to Bath, made long afterwards, being diverted to avoid it. Dr. Owen thinks that the Abury circle was one of three primary circles in Great Britain, and that Silbury hill was the pile of Cyvrangon (heaping) characterised in the 14th Welsh triad; but the conjecture affords us no assistance in determining the people by whom the monument was raised. If it be in its arrangement intended to represent a serpent, it becomes immediately connected with ophiolatry, or serpent worship, a sin which beset the Israelites, and which would stamp it as proceeding from the central stamen of the hypothesis on which Mr. Higgins sets out. See Observations on Dracontia, by the Rev. John Bathurst Deane, Archæol. vol. xxv.

" Æoliam Pitanen a læva parte relinquit,
Factaque de saxo longi simulacra Draconis,"—Ovid, Met. vii. 357.

which is a picturesque description of Abury.

18. Stonehenge, on Salisbury Plain, about seven miles from Salisbury and two miles

to the west of Ambresbury, is certainly more artificial in its structure than Abury, and its construction may therefore be safely referred to a later date. *Fig. 5.* is a restored plan of this wonder of the west, as it may well be called. The larger circle is 105 feet in diameter, and between it and the interior smaller circle is a space of about 9 feet. Within this smaller circle, which is half the height (8 feet) of the exterior one, was a portion of an ellipsis formed by 5 groups of stones, to which Dr. Stukely has given the name of trilithons, because formed by two vertical and one horizontal stone: the former are from 17 to 18½ feet high, the middle trilithon being the highest. Within this ellipsis is another of single stones, half the height of the trilithons. The outer circle was crowned with a course of stones similar to an architrave or epistylium, the stones whereof were let into or joggled with one another by means of egg-shaped tenons formed out of the vertical blocks. The ellipsis was connected in a similar manner. Within the inner elliptical enclosure was a block 16 ft. long, 4 ft. broad, and 20 in. thick. This has usually been called the altar stone. Round the larger circle, at the distance of 100 ft., a vallum was formed about 52 ft. in width, so that the external dimension of the work was a diameter of 420 ft. The vallum surrounding these sacred places seems to have been borrowed by the Canaanites in imitation of the enclosure with which Moses surrounded Mount Sinai, in order to prevent the multitude from approaching too near the sacred mysteries. The number of stones composing this monument is variously given. In the subjoined account we follow Dr. Stukely: —

	Stones.			Stones.
Great circle, vertical stones	30	Stones within vallum		2
Epistylia	30	A large table stone		1
Inner circle	40	Distant pillar		1
Vertical stones of outer ellipsis	10	Another stone, supposed to have been		
Epistylia to them	5	opposite the entrance		1
Inner ellipsis	19			
Altar	1	Total		140

Northwards from Stonehenge, at the distance of a few hundred yards, is a large single stone, which, at the period of its being placed there, has been by some thought to have marked a meridian line from the centre of the circle.

19. *Fig. 6.* is a view of the present state of this interesting ruin from the west. Mr

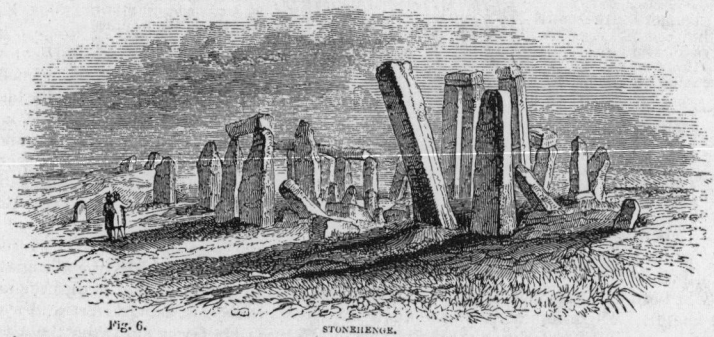

Fig. 6.   STONEHENGE.

Cunnington, in a letter to Mr. Higgins, gives the following account of the stones which remain of the monument: — " The stones on the outside of the work, those comprising the outward circle as well as the large (five) trilithons, are all of that species of stone called '*garsen*' found in the neighbourhood; whereas the inner circle of small upright stones, and those of the interior oval, are composed of granite, hornstone, &c., most probably procured from some part of Devonshire or Cornwall, as I know not where such stones could be procured at a nearer distance."

20. Authors have in Stonehenge discovered an instrument of astronomy, and among them Maurice, whose view as to its founders coincides with those of the writers already cited, and with our own. We give no opinion on this point, but shall conclude the section by placing before the reader the substance of M. Bailly's notion thereon, recommending him to consult, in that respect, authorities better than we profess to be, and here expressing our own belief that the priests of ancient Britain were priests of Baal; and that the monuments, the subjects of this section, were in existence long before the Greeks, as a nation, were known, albeit they did derive the word Druid from δρυς (an oak), and said that they themselves were αυτοχθονες (sprung from the earth).

21. M. Bailly says, on the origin of the sciences in Asia, that a nation possessed of profound wisdom, of elevated genius, and of an antiquity far superior to the Egyptians or Indians, immediately after the flood inhabited the country to the north of India, between the latitudes of 40° and 50°, or about 50° north. He contends that some of the most celebrated observatories and inventions relating to astronomy, from their peculiar character, could have taken place only in those latitudes, and that arts and improvements gradually

travelled thence to the equator. The people to whom his description is most applicable is the northern progeny of Brahmins, settled near the Imaus and in Northern Thibet. We add, that Mr. Hastings informed Maurice of an immemorial tradition that prevailed at Benares, which was itself, in modern times, the grand emporium of Indian learning, — that all that of India came from a country situate in 40° of N. latitude. On this Maurice says, " This is the latitude of Samarcand, the metropolis of Tartary ; and, by this circumstance, the position of M. Bailly should seem to be confirmed. This is the country where, according to the testimony of Josephus and other historians cited by the learned Abbé Pezron, are to be found the first Celtæ, by whom all the temples and caves of India were made. Higgins observes on this, that the worship of the Mithraitic bull existed in India, Persia, Greece, Italy, and Britain, and that the religion of the Druids, Magi, and Brahmins was the same.

22. (3.) *Sacrificial Stones.* — These have been confounded with the cromlech, but the difference between them is wide. They are simple stones, either encircled by a shallow trench (vallum) and bank (agger), or by a few stones. Upon these almost all authors concur in believing that human immolation was practised ; indeed, the name blod, or blood-stones, which they bear in the north of Europe, seems to point to their infernal use. We do not think it necessary to pursue further inquiry into them, as they present no remarkable nor interesting features.

23. (4.) *Cromlechs and Cairns.* — The former of these seem to stand in the same relation to the large circles that the modern cell does to the conventual church of the Catholics. They consist of two or more sides, or vertical stones, and sometimes a back stone, the whole being covered with one not usually placed exactly horizontal, but rather in an inclining

Fig. 7.   KIT'S COTTY HOUSE.

position. We here (*fig.* 7.) give a representation of one, that has received the name of Kit's Cotty House, which lies on the road between Maidstone and Rochester, about a mile north-eastward from Aylesford church, and is thus described in the *Beauties of England and Wales.* It " is composed of four huge stones unwrought, three of them standing on end but inclined inwards, and supporting the fourth, which lies transversely over them, so as to leave an open recess beneath. The dimensions and computed weights of these stones are as follows : — height of that on the south side 8 ft., breadth 7½ ft., thickness 2 ft., weight 8 tons ; height of that on the north side 7 ft., breadth 7½ ft., thickness 2 ft., weight 8½ tons. The middle stone is very irregular ; its medium length as well as breadth may be about 5 ft., its thickness about 1 ft. 2 in., and its weight about 2 tons. The upper stone or impost is also extremely irregular ; its greatest length is nearly 12 ft., and its breadth about 9¼ ft.; its thickness is 2 ft., and its weight about 10½ tons : the width of the recess at bottom is 9 ft., and at top 7½ ft. ; from the ground to the upper side of the covering stone is 9 ft. These stones are of the kind called Kentish rag. Many years ago there was a single stone of a similar kind and size to those forming the cromlech, about 70 yards to the north-west : this, which is thought to have once stood upright, like a pillar, has been broken into pieces and carried away." Another cromlech stood in the neighbourhood, which has been thrown down. The nonsense that has been gravely written upon this and similar monuments is scarcely worth mention. It will hardly be believed that there existed people who thought it was the sepulchral monument of king Catigern, from similarity of name, and others who consider it the grave of the Saxon chief, Horsa, from its proximity to Horsted. Cromlechs are found in situations remote indeed, a specimen being seated on the Malabar coast ; and in the British isles they are so numerous, that we do not think it necessary to give a list of them.

24. The *cairn* or *carn* which we have in this section coupled with the cromlech, perhaps improperly, is a conical heap of loose stones. Whether its etymology be that of Rowland, from the words קרן-כד (kern-ned), a coped heap, we shall, from too little skill in Hebrew, not venture to decide ; so we do not feel quite sure that, as has been asserted, they were raised over the bodies of deceased heroes and chieftains. Our notion rather inclines to their having been a species of altar, though the heap of stones to which Jacob gave the name of Galeed, if it were of this species, was rather a memorial of the agreement between him and Laban. It can scarcely be called an architectural work ; but we should have considered our notice of the earlier monuments of antiquity incomplete without naming the cairn.

25. (5.) *Logan or Rocking Stones.* — These were large blocks poised so nicely on the points of rocks, that a small force applied to them produced oscillation. The weight of the celebrated one in Cornwall, which is granite, has been computed at upwards of 90 tons.

The use of these stones has been conjectured to be that of testing the innocence of persons accused of crime, the rocking of the stone being certain, unless wedged up by the judge of the tribunal, in cases where he knew the guilt of the criminal: but we think that such a purpose is highly improbable.

26. (6.) *Tolmen or Colossal Stones.* — The Tolmen, or hole of stone, is a stone of

considerable magnitude, so disposed upon rocks as to leave an opening between them, through which an object could be passed. It is the general opinion in Cornwall that invalids were cured of their diseases by being passed through the opening above mentioned. " The most stupendous monument of this kind," (see *fig.* 8.) says Borlase, " is in the tenement of Mên, in the parish of Constantine, in Cornwall; it is one great oval pebble, placed on the points of two natural rocks, so that a man may creep under the great one, between the supporters, through a

Fig. 8.   TOLMEN IN CORNWALL.

passage of about three feet wide, by as much high. The longest diameter of this stone is 33 ft., being in a direction due north and south. Its height, measured perpendicularly over the opening is, 14 ft. 6 in., and the breadth, in the widest part, 18 ft. 6 in., extending from east to west. I measured one half of the circumference, and found it, according to my computation, 48½ ft., so that this stone is 97 ft. in circumference, lengthwise, and about 60 ft. in girt, measured at the middle; and, by the best information, it contains about 750 tons." We close this section by the expression of our belief that the extraordinary monuments whereof we have been speaking are of an age as remote as, if not more so than, the pyramids of Egypt, and that they were the works of a colony of the great nation that was at the earliest period settled in central Asia, either through the swarm that passed north-west over Germany, or south-west through Phœnicia; for, on either route, but rather, perhaps, the latter, traces of gigantic works remain, to attest the wonderful powers of the people of whom they are the remains.

Sect. II.

PELASGIC OR CYCLOPEAN ARCHITECTURE.

27. Pelasgic or Cyclopean architecture, (for that as well as the architecture of Phœnicia, seems to have been the work of branches of an original similarly thinking nation) presents for the notice of the reader, little more than massive walls composed of huge pieces of rock, scarcely more than piled together without the connecting medium of cement of any species. The method of its construction, considered as masonry, to the eye of the architect is quite sufficient to connect it with what we have in the preceding section called Druidical or Celtic architecture. It is next to impossible to believe that all these species were not executed by the same people. The nature and principles of Egyptian art were the same, but the specimens of it which remain bear marks of being of later date, the pyramids only excepted. The Greek fables about the Cyclopeans have been sufficiently exposed by Jacob Bryant, who has shown that the Greeks knew nothing about their own early history. Herodotus (lib. v. cap. 57. *et seq.*) alludes to them under the name of Cadmians, saying they were particularly famous for their architecture, which he says they introduced into Greece; and wherever they came, erected noble structures remarkable for their height and beauty. These were dedicated to the Sun under the names of Elorus and Pelorus. Hence every thing great and stupendous was called Pelorian; and, transferring the ideas of the works to the founders, they made them a race of giants. Homer says of Polyphemus, —

Και γαρ θαυμ' ετετυκτο πελωριον, ουδε εωκει
Ανδρι γε σιτοφαγῳ, αλλα ριῳ υληεντι.

Virgil, too, describes him " Ipse arduus, alta pulsat sidera." Famous as lighthouse builders, wherein a round casement in the upper story afforded light to the mariner, the Greeks turned this into a single eye in the forehead of the race, and thus made them a set of monsters. Of the race were Trophonius and his brother Agamedes, who, according to Pausanias (lib. ix.) contrived the temple at Delphi and the Treasury constructed to Urius. So great was the fame for building of the Cyclopeans that, when the Sybil in Virgil shows Æneas the place of torment in the shades below, the poet separates it from the regions of bliss by a Cyclopean wall: —

" —— Cyclopum educta caminis
Mœnia conspicio."

Æn. lib. vi. v. 630

28. The walls of the city of Mycene are of the class denominated Cyclopean, thus denounced for ruin by Hercules in Seneca : —

> " ———— Quid moror ? majus mihi
> Bellum Mycenis restat, ut Cyclopea
> Eversa manibus mœnia nostris concidant."   *Hercules Furens*, act. 4. v. 996.

29. The gate of the city and the chief tower were particularly ascribed to them (Pausanias, lib. ii.) Argos had also the reputation of being Cyclopean. But, to return to Mycene, Euripides, we should observe, speaks of its walls as being built after the Phœnician rule and method : —

> ———— Ὡς τα Κυκλωπων βαθρα
> Φοινικι κανονι και τυκοις ἡρμοσμενα.   *Hercules Furens*, v. 944.

30. *Fig. 9.* is a representation of a portion of the postern gate of the walls of Mycene, for the purpose of exhibiting to the reader the character of the masonry employed in it.

31. The walls of Tiryns, probably more ancient than those we have just named, are celebrated by Homer in the words Τιρυνθα τειχιοεσσαν, and are said by Apollodorus and Strabo to have been built by workmen whom Prætus brought from Lycia. The words of Strabo are, Τιρυνθι ὁρμητηριῳ χρησασθαι δοκει Προιτος, και τειχισαι δια Κυκλωπων᾽ οὑς ἑπτα μεν ειναι, καλεισθαι δε Γαστεροχειρας, τρεφομενους εκ της τεχνης, *Prætus appears to have used Tiryns as a harbour, and to have walled it by the assistance of the Cyclops, who were seven in number, and called Gastrocheirs* (belly-handed), *living by their labour.* "These seven Cyclops," says Jacob Bryant, " were, I make no doubt, seven Cyclopean towers built by the people." Further on, he adds, " These towers were erected likewise for Purait, or Puratheia, where the rites of fire were performed : but Purait, or Puraitus, the Greeks changed to Prætus ; and gave out that the towers were built for Prætus, whom they made a king of that country." The same author says that the Cyclopeans worshipped the sun under the symbol of a serpent ; thus again connecting them with the builders of Abury noticed in page 6. *Fig. 10.* is a view of some portions of the walls of Tiryns, and for others we refer the reader to the *Travels in Albania*, by the late Rev. T. S. Hughes.

Fig. 9.   PART OF THE WALLS OF MYCENE.

Fig. 10.   PART OF THE WALLS OF TIRYNS.

32. Mr. Hamilton (*Archæologia*) divides the specimens of Cyclopean buildings into four æras. In the first he includes Tiryns and Mycene, where the blocks composing the masonry are of various sizes, having or having had smaller stones in their interstices. Second, as at Julis and Delphi, masonry without courses, formed of irregular polygonal stones, whose sides fit to each other. Third, that in which the stones are laid in courses of the same height, but unequal in length of stones ; of this species are specimens in Bœotia, Argolis, and the Phocian cities. Fourth and last, that in which the stones are of various heights, and always rectangular, whereof examples are found in Attica. It may be here mentioned that, in the Etrurian part of Italy we find examples of Cyclopean works of the class, which Mr. Hamilton places in the second æra ; as at Norba in Latium, Cora, Signia, and Alatrium ; in the three last whereof the walls resemble those of Tiryns, Argos, and Mycene ; also at Fiesole, Arezzo, and other places.

33. We shall now return to some further particulars in relation to Tiryns and Mycene, from which a more distinct notion of these fortresses will be obtained ; but further investigation of those in Italy will hereafter be necessary, under the section on Etruscan architecture. The Acropolis of Tiryns, a little to the south-east of Argos, is on a mount rising about fifty

feet above the level of the plain, the foundations of its inclosure being still perfect and traceable, as in the annexed figure (*fig.* 11.).   The ancient city is thought to have sur-

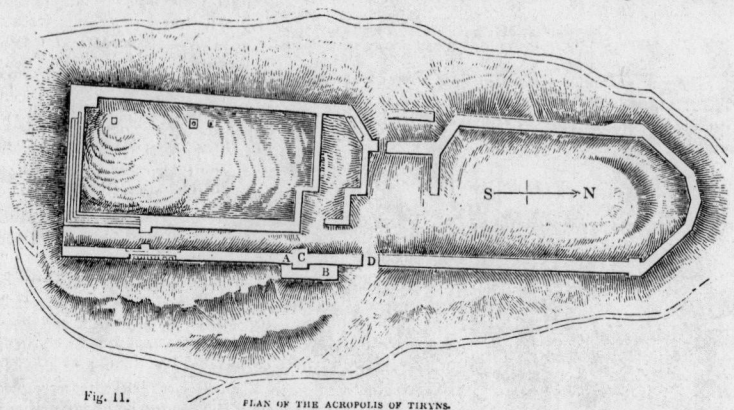

Fig. 11.   PLAN OF THE ACROPOLIS OF TIRYNS.

rounded the fortress, and that formerly the city was nearer the sea than at present. Bryant, with his usual ingenuity, has found in its general form a type of the long ship of Danaus, which, we confess, our imagination is not lively enough to detect. On the east of the fortress are quarries, which furnish stone similar to that whereof it is built. It had entrances from the east and the west, and one at the south-eastern angle. That on the east, lettered A, is pretty fairly preserved, and is approached by an inclined access, B, 15 ft. wide, along the eastern and southern sides of the tower, C, which is 20 ft. square and 40 ft. high, passing, at the end of the last named side, under a gateway, composed of very large blocks of stone, that which forms the architrave being 10 ft. long, and over which, from the fragments lying on the spot, it is conjectured that a triangular stone was placed ; but thereon is no appearance of sculpture. D is the present entrance. The general thickness of the walls is 25 ft., and they are formed by three parallel ranks of stones 5 ft. thick, thus leaving

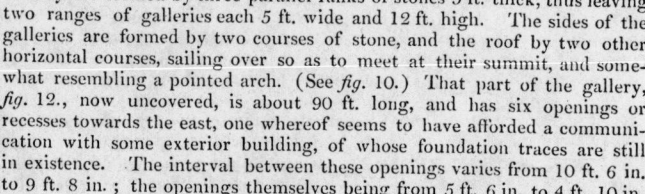

two ranges of galleries each 5 ft. wide and 12 ft. high. The sides of the galleries are formed by two courses of stone, and the roof by two other horizontal courses, sailing over so as to meet at their summit, and somewhat resembling a pointed arch. (See *fig.* 10.) That part of the gallery, *fig.* 12., now uncovered, is about 90 ft. long, and has six openings or recesses towards the east, one whereof seems to have afforded a communication with some exterior building, of whose foundation traces are still in existence. The interval between these openings varies from 10 ft. 6 in. to 9 ft. 8 in. ; the openings themselves being from 5 ft. 6 in. to 4 ft. 10 in.

Fig. 12. GALLERY. wide. It is probable that these galleries extended all round the citadel, though now only accessible where the walls are least perfect, at the southern part of the inclosure. There are no remains of the south-eastern portal. It appears to have been connected with the eastern gate by an avenue enclosed between the outer and inner curtain, of which avenue the use is not known. Similar avenues have been found at Argos and other ancient cities in Greece. The northern point of the hill is least elevated, and smaller stones have been employed in its wall. The exterior walls are built of rough stones, some of which are 9 ft. 4 in. in length and 4 ft. thick, their common size being somewhat less When entire, the wall must have been 60 ft. high, and on the eastern side has been entirely destroyed. The whole length of the citadel is about 660 ft., and the breadth about 180 ft., the walls being straight without regard to inequality of level in the rock.

34. The Acropolis of Mycene was probably constructed in an age nearly the same as that of Tiryns. Pausanias mentions a gate on which two lions were sculptured, to which the name of the Gate of the Lions has been given (*fig.* 13.) These are still in their original position. It is situate at the end of a recess about 50 ft. long, commanded by projections of the walls, which are here formed of huge blocks of square stones, many placed on each other without breaking joint, which circumstance gives it a very inartificial appearance. The epistylium of the gate is a single stone 15 ft. long and 4 ft. 4 in. high. To the south of the gate above mentioned the wall is much ruined. In one part something like a tower is discernible, whose walls, being perpendicular while the curtain inclines a little inward from its base, a projection remained at the top by which an archer could defend the wall below. The blocks of the superstructure are of great size, those of the substructure much smaller. The gates excepted, the whole citadel is built of rough masses of rock, nicely adjusted and fitted to each other, though the smaller stones with which the

interstices were filled have mostly disappeared. The southern ramparts of the citadel and all the other walls follow the natural irregularity of the precipice on which they stand. At

its eastern point it is attached by a narrow isthmus to the mountain. It is a long irregular triangle, standing nearly east and west. The walls are mostly of well-jointed polygonal stones, although the rough construction occasionally appears. The general thickness of the walls is 21 ft., in some places 25 ; their present height, in the most perfect part, is 43 ft. There are, in some places, very slight projections from the walls, resembling towers, whereof the most perfect one is at the south-east angle, its breadth being 33 ft. and its height 43 ft. The size of the block whereon the lions are sculptured is 11 ft. broad at the base, 9 ft. high, and about 2 ft. thick, of a triangular form suited to the

Fig. 13.   GATE OF THE LIONS.

recess made for its reception. This block, in its appearance, resembles the green basalt of Egypt.

35. In this place we think it proper to notice a building at Mycene, which has been called by some the Treasury of Atreus, or the tomb of his son Agamemnon mentioned by

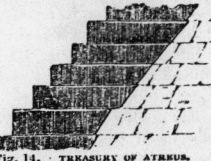

Pausanias. This building at first misled some authors into a belief that the use of the arch was known in Greece at a very early period ; but examination of it shows that it was formed by horizontal courses, projecting beyond each other as they rose, and not by radiating joints or beds, and that the surface was afterwards formed so as to give the whole the appearance of a pointed dome, by cutting away the lower angles (*fig.* 14.). It is probably the most ancient of buildings in

Fig. 14.   TREASURY OF ATREUS.

Greece ; and it is a curious circumstance that at New Grange, near Drogheda, in Ireland, there is a monument whose form, construction, and plan of access resemble it so strongly that it is impossible to consider their similarity the result of accident. A repre-

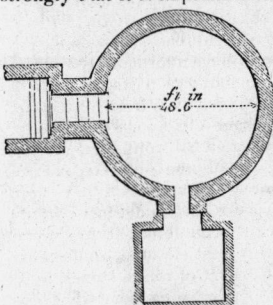

sentation of this may be seen in the work by Mr. Higgins which we have so often quoted, and will, we think, satisfy the reader of the great probability of the hypothesis hereinbefore assumed having all the appearance of truth. By the subjoined plan (*fig.* 15.) it will be seen that a space 20 ft. wide, between the two walls, conducts us to the entrance, which is 9 ft. 6 in. at the base, 7 ft. 10 in. at the top, and about 19 ft. high. The entrance passage is 18 ft. long and leads to the main chamber, which, in its general form, has some resemblance to a bee-hive, whose diameter is about 48 ft. and height about 49. (*fig.* 16) The blocks are placed in courses as above shown, 34 courses being at present visible. They are laid with the greatest precision, without cement, and are unequal in size. Their

Fig. 15.   PLAN OF TREASURY OF ATREUS.

average height may be taken at 2 ft., though to a spectator on the floor, from the effect of the perspective, they appear to diminish very much towards the vertex. This monument has a second chamber, to which you enter on the right from the larger one just described. This is about 27 ft by 20, and 19 ft. high ; but its walls, from the obstruction of the earth, are not visible. The doorway to it is 9½ ft. high, 4 ft. 7 in. wide at the base, and 4 ft. 3 in. at the top. Similar to the larger or principal doorway, it has a triangular opening over its lintel. The stones which fitted into these triangular openings were of enormous dimensions, for the height of that over the principal entrance is 12 ft., and its breadth 7 ft. 8 in. The vault has been either lined with metal or ornamented with some sort of decorations, inasmuch as a number of bronze nails are found fixed in the stones up to the summit. The lintel of the door consists of two pieces of stone, the largest whereof is 27 ft. long, 17 ft. wide, and 3 ft. 9 in. thick, calculated, therefore, at 133 tons weight ; a mass which can be compared with none ever used in building, except those at Balbec and in Egypt. The other lintel is of the same height, and probably (its ends are hidden) of

the same length as the first.   Its breadth, however, is only one foot   Its exterior has two
parallel mouldings, which are continued down the jambs of the doorway.

Fig. 16.   CHAMBER OF TREASURY OF ATREUS.

36. The stone employed is of the hard and beautiful breccia, of which the neighbouring
rocks, and the contiguous Mount Eubora, consist.   It is the hardest and compactest breccia
which Greece produces, resembling the
antique marble called Breccia Tracag-
nina antica, sometimes found among the
ruins of Rome.   Near the gate lie some
masses of rosso antico decorated with
guilloche-like and zigzag ornaments,
and a columnar base of a Persian character. Some have supposed that these
belonged to the decorations of the doorway ; but we are of a different opinion,
inasmuch as they destroy its grand character.   We think if this were the tomb
of Agamemnon, they were much more
likely to have been a part of the shrine
in which the body or ashes were deposited.

37. It is conjectured that the treasury of Minyas king of Orchomenus,
whereof Pausanias speaks, bore a resemblance to the building we have just
described ; and it is very probable that
all the subterranean chambers of Greece,
Italy, and Sicily were very similarly
constructed.   *Fig.* 17. represents the
entrance to the building from the outside. As the architecture of the early
races whereof we have been speaking
will be further discussed in investigating other monuments, we do not

Fig. 17.   TREASURY OF MINYAS.

think it necessary to enlarge further in this place on what we have termed Pelasgic
or Cyclopean architecture.

Sect. III.

BABYLONIAN ARCHITECTURE.

38. The name prefixed to this section must not induce the reader to suppose we shall be able to afford him much instruction on this interesting subject. The materials are scanty; the monuments, though once stupendous, still more so. " If ever," says Keith, in his *Evidence of the Truth of the Christian Religion*, " there was a city that seemed to bid defiance to any predictions of its fall, that city was Babylon. It was for a long time the most famous city in the Old World. Its walls, which were reckoned among the wonders of the world, appeared rather like the bulwarks of nature than the workmanship of man." The city of Babylon is thus described by ancient writers. It was situated in a plain of vast extent, and divided into two parts by the river Euphrates, which was of considerable width at the spot. The two divisions of the city were connected by a massive bridge of masonry strongly connected with iron and lead ; and the embankments to prevent inroads of the river were formed of the same durable materials as the walls of the city. Herodotus says that the city itself was a perfect square enclosed by a wall 480 furlongs in circumference, which would make it eight times the size of London. It is said to have had numbers of houses three or four stories in height, and to have been regularly divided into streets running parallel with each other, and cross ones opening to the river. It was surrounded by a wide and deep trench, from the earth whereof, when excavated, square bricks were formed and baked in a furnace. With these, cemented together through the medium of heated bitumen intermixed with reeds to bind together the viscid mass, the sides of the trenches were lined, and with the same materials the vast walls above mentioned were constructed. At certain intervals watch-towers were placed, and the city was entered by 100 gates of brass. In the centre of each of the principal divisions of the city a stupendous public monument was erected. In one (Major Rennel thinks that on the eastern side) stood the temple of Belus; in the other, within a large strongly fortified enclosure, the royal palace. The former was a square pile, each side being two furlongs in extent. The tower erected on its centre was a furlong in breadth and the same in height, thus making it higher than the largest of the pyramids, supposing the furlong to contain only 500 feet. On this tower as a base were raised, in regular succession, seven other lofty towers, and the whole, according to Diodorus, crowned with a bronze statue of the god Belus 40 feet high.

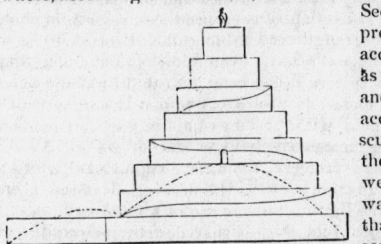

Fig. 18.   TEMPLE OF BELUS.

See *fig.* 18., in which the dotted lines show the present remains, according to Sir R. K. Porter's account in his Travels. The palace, serving also as a temple, stood on an area $1\frac{1}{2}$ mile square, and was surrounded by circular walls, which, according to Diodorus, were decorated with sculptured animals resembling life, painted in their natural colours, on the bricks of which they were depicted, and *afterwards burnt in.* Such was the city of Babylon in its meridian splendour, that city whose founder (if it were not Nimrod, sometimes called Belus,) is unknown. Great as it was, it was enlarged by Semiramis, and still further enlarged and fortified by Nebuchadnezzar. We shall now present, from the account of Mr. Rich, a gentleman who visited the spot early in this century, a sketch of what the city is now. The first grand mass of ruins marked A (*fig.* 19.), which the above gentleman describes, he says extends 1100 yards in length and 800 in its greatest breadth, in figure nearly resembling a quadrant ; its height is irregular, but the most elevated part may be about 50 or 60 ft. above the level of the plain, and it has been dug into for the purpose of procuring bricks. This mound Mr. R. distinguishes by the name of Amran. On the north is a valley 550 yards long, and then the second grand heap of ruins, whose shape is nearly a square of 700 yards long and broad ; its south-west angle being connected with the north-west angle of the mounds of Amran by a high ridge nearly 100 yards in breadth. This is the place where Beauchamp made his observations, and is highly interesting from every vestige of it being composed of buildings far superior to those whereof there are traces in the eastern quarter. The bricks are of the finest description, and, notwithstanding this spot being the principal magazine of them and constantly used for a supply, are still in abundance. The operation of extracting the bricks has caused much confusion, and increased the difficulty of deciphering the use of this mound. In some places the solid mass has been bored into, and the superincumbent strata falling in, frequently bury workmen in the rubbish. In all these excavations walls of burnt brick laid in lime mortar of a good quality are to be seen ; and among the ruins are to be found fragments of alabaster vessels, fine earthenware, marble, and great quantities of varnished tiles, whose glazing and colouring are surprisingly fresh. " In a

hollow," observes Mr. Rich, " near the southern part, I found a sepulchral urn of earthen-

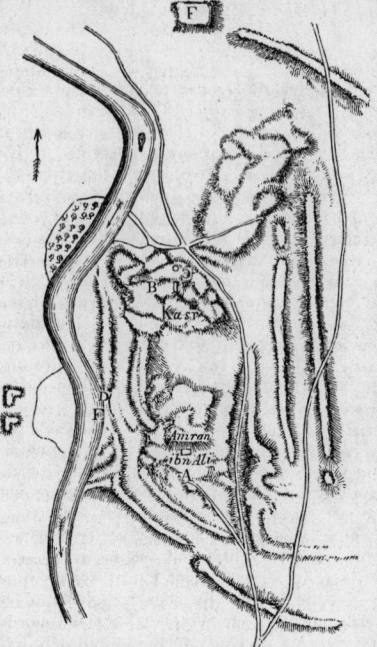

ware, which had been broken in' digging, and near it lay some human bones, which pulverised with the touch." Not more than 200 yards from the northern extremity of this mound, is a ravine near 100 yards long, hollowed out by those who dig for bricks, on one of whose sides a few yards of wall remain, the face whereof is clear and perfect, and appears to have been the front of some building. The opposite side is so confused a mass of rubbish, that it looks as if the ravine had been worked through a solid building. Under the foundations at the southern end was discovered a subterranean passage floored and walled with large bricks in bitumen, and covered over with pieces of sandstone a yard thick and several yards long, on which the pressure is so great as to have pushed out the side walls. What was seen was near seven feet in height, its course being to the south. The upper part of the passage is cemented with bitumen, other parts of the ravine with mortar, and the bricks have all writing on them. At the northern end of the ravine an excavation was made, and a statue of a lion of colossal dimensions, standing on a pedestal of coarse granite and rude workmanship, was discovered. This was about the spot marked E on the plan. A little to the west of the ravine at B is a remarkable ruin called the Kasr or Palace, which, being uncovered, and partly detached from the rubbish, is visible from a considerable distance. It is " so sur-

Fig. 19.   PLAN OF BABYLON.

prisingly fresh," says the author, " that it was only after a minute inspection I was satisfied of its being in reality a Babylonian remain." It consists of several walls and piers, in some places ornamented with niches, and in others strengthened by pilasters of burnt brick in lime cement of great tenacity. The tops of the walls have been broken down, and they may have been much higher. Contiguous to this ruin is a heap of rubbish, whose sides are curiously streaked by the alternation of its materials, probably unburnt bricks, of which a small quantity were found in the neighbourhood, without however any reeds in their interstices. A little to the N. N. E. of it is the famous tree which the natives call Atheli. They say it existed in ancient Babylon, and was preserved by God that it might afford a convenient place to Ali for tying up his horse after the battle Hellah !" " It is an evergreen," says Mr. R., " something resembling the lignum vitæ, and of a kind, I believe, not common in this part of the country, though I am told there is a tree of the description at Bassora." The valley which separates the mounds just described from the river is white with nitre, and does not now appear to have had any buildings upon it except a small circular heap at D. The whole embankment is abrupt, and shivered by the action of the water. At the narrowest part E, cemented into the burnt brick wall, there were a number of urns filled with human bones which had not undergone the action of fire. From a considerable quantity of burnt bricks and other fragments of building in the water the river appears to have encroached here.

39. A mile to the north of the Kasr, and 950 yards from the bank of the river, is the last ruin of this series, which Pietro della Valle, in 1616, described as the tower of Belus, in which he is followed by Rennell. The natives call it, according to the vulgar Arab pronunciation of those parts, Mujelibè, which means overturned. They sometimes also apply the same term to the mounds of the Kasr. This is marked F on the plan. " It is of an oblong shape, irregular in its height and the measurement of its sides, which face the cardinal points as follows: the northern side 200 yards in length, the southern 219, the eastern 182, and the western 136. The elevation of the south-east or highest angle, 141 feet. The western face, which is the least elevated, is the most interesting on account of the appearance of building it presents. Near the summit of it appears a low wall, with interruptions, built of unburnt bricks mixed up with chopped straw or reeds and cemented with clay mortar of great thickness." The south-west angle seems to have had a turret, the others are less perfect. The ruin is much worn into furrows, from the action of the weather, penetrating considerably into the mound in some places. The summit is covered with heaps of rubbish, among which fragments of burnt brick are found, and here and there

whole bricks with inscriptions on them. Interspersed are innumerable fragments of pottery, brick, bitumen, pebbles, vitrified brick or scoria, and even shells, bits of glass, and mother of pearl. The north-

Fig. 20.   NORTHERN FACE OF THE MUJELIBE.

ern face of the Mujelibé (*fig.* 20.) contains a niche of the height of a man, at the back whereof a low aperture leads to a small cavity, whence a passage branches off to the right till it is lost in the rubbish. It is called by the natives the serdaub or cellar, and Mr. Rich was informed that four years previous to his survey, a quantity of marble was taken out from it, and a coffin of mulberry wood, in which was contained a human body enclosed in a tight wrapper, and apparently partially covered with bitumen, which crumbled into dust on exposure to the air. About this spot Mr. R. also excavated and found a coffin containing a skeleton in high preservation, whose antiquity was placed beyond dispute by the attachment of a brass bird to the outside of the coffin, and inside an ornament of the same material, which had seemingly been suspended to some part of the skeleton. On the western side of the river there is not the slightest vestige of ruins excepting opposite the mass of Amran, where there are two small mounds of earth in existence.

40. The most stupendous and surprising mass of the ruins of ancient Babylon is situate in the desert, about six miles to the south-west of Hellah. It is too distant to be shown on the block plan above given. By the Arabs it is called Birs Nemroud; by the Jews,

Fig. 21.   BIRS NEMROUD.

Nebuchadnezzar's Prison. Mr. Rich was the first traveller who gave any account of this ruin, of which *fig.* 21. is a representation; and the description following we shall present in Mr. Rich's own words. " The Birs Nemroud is a mound of an oblong figure, the total circumference of which is 762 yards. At the eastern side it is cloven by a deep furrow, and is not more than fifty or sixty feet high; but at the western it rises in a conical figure to the elevation of 198 ft., and on its summit is a solid pile of brick 37 ft. high by 28 in breadth, diminishing in thickness to the top, which is broken and irregular, and rent by a large fissure extending through a third of its height. It is perforated by small square holes disposed in rhomboids. The fine burnt bricks of which it is built have inscriptions on them; and so admirable is the cement, which appears to be lime mortar, that, though the layers are so close together that it is difficult to discern what substance is between them, it is nearly impossible to extract one of the bricks whole. The other parts of the summit of the hill are occupied by immense fragments of brickwork, of no determinate figure, tumbled together and converted into solid vitrified masses, as if they had undergone the action of the fiercest fire or been blown up with gunpowder, the layers of the bricks being perfectly discernible,—a curious fact, and one for which I am utterly incapable of accounting. These, incredible as it may seem, are actually the ruins spoken of by Pére Emanuel (See *D'Anville, sur l'Euphrate et le Tigre*), who takes no notice of the prodigious mound on which they are elevated." The mound is a majestic ruin, and of a people whose powers were not lost, if the hypothesis brought before the reader in the previous section on Celtic and Druidical architecture be founded on the basis of truth, but shown afterwards, on their separation from the parent stock, in Abury, Stonehenge, Carnac, and many other places. Ruins to a considerable extent exist round the Birs Nemroud; but for our purpose it is not necessary to particularise them. The chance (for more the happiest conjecture would not warrant) of conclusively enabling the reader to come to a certain and definite notion of the venerable city, whereof it is our object to give him a faint idea, is far too indefinite to detain him and exhaust his patience. One circumstance, however, we must not omit; and again we shall use the words of the traveller to whom we are under so many obligations. They are, — " To these ruins I must add one, which, though not in the same direction, bears such strong characteristics of a Babylonian origin, that it would be

improper to omit a description of it in this place. I mean Akerkouf, or, as it is more generally called, Nimrod's Tower; for the inhabitants of these parts are as fond of attributing every vestige of antiquity to Nimrod as those of Egypt are to Pharaoh. It is situate ten miles to the north-west of Bagdad, and is a thick mass of unburnt brickwork, of an irregular shape, rising out of a base of rubbish; there is a layer of reeds between every fifth or sixth (for the number is not regulated) layer of bricks. It is perforated with small square holes, as the brickwork at the Birs Nemroud; and about half way up on the east side is an aperture like a window; the layers of cement are very thin, which, considering it is mere mud, is an extraordinary circumstance. The height of the whole is 126 ft.; diameter of the largest part, 100 ft.; circumference of the foot of the brickwork above the rubbish, 300 ft.; the remains of the tower contain 100,000 cubic feet. (Vide *Ives's Travels*, p. 298.) To the east of it is a dependent mound, resembling those at the Birs and Al Hheimar."

41. The inquiry (following Mr. Rich) now to be pursued is that of identifying some of the remains which have been described with the description which has been left of them. And, first, of the circuit of the city. The greatest circumference of the city, according to the authors of antiquity, was 480 stadia (supposed about 500 ft. each), the least 360. Strabo, who was on the spot when the walls were sufficiently perfect to judge of their extent, states their circuit at 385 stadia. It seems probable that within the walls there was a quantity of arable and pasture ground, to enable the population to resist a siege; and that, unlike modern cities, the buildings were distributed in groups over the area inclosed; for Xenophon reports that when Cyrus took Babylon (which event happened at night) the inhabitants of the opposite quarter of the town were not aware of it till the third part of the day; that is, three hours after sunrise. The accounts of the height of the walls all agree in the dimension of 50 cubits, which was their reduced height from 350 ft. by Darius Hystaspes, in order to render the town less defensible. The embankment of the river with walls, according to Diodorus 100 stadia in length, indicates very advanced engineering skill; but the most wonderful structure of the city was the tower, pyramid, or sepulchre of Belus, whose base, according to Strabo, was a stadium on each side. It stood in an enclosure of two miles and a half, and contained the temple in which divine honours were paid to the tutelary deity of Babylon. The main interest attached to the tower of Belus arises from a belief of its identity with the tower which we learn from Scripture (*Gen.* xi.) the descendants of Noah, with Belus at their head, constructed in the plains of Shinar. The two masses of ruins in which this tower must be sought, seem to be the Birs Nemroud, whose four sides are 2286 English feet in length; and the Mujelibé, whose circumference is 2111 ft. Now, taking the stadium at 500 ft., the tower of Belus, according to the accounts, would be 2000 ft. in circumference; so that both the ruins agree, as nearly as possible, in the requisite dimensions, considering our uncertainty respecting the exact length of the stadium. Mr. Rich evidently inclines to the opinion that the Birs Nemroud is the ruin of this celebrated temple, though he allows " a very strong objection may be brought against the Birs Nemroud in the distance of its position from the extensive remains on the eastern bank of the Euphrates, which for its accommodation would oblige us to extend the measurement of each side of the square to nine miles, or adopt a plan which would totally exclude the Mujelibé, all the ruins above it, and most of those below : even in the former case, the Mujelibé and the Birs would be at opposite extremities of the town close to the walls, while we have every reason to believe that the tower of Belus occupied a central situation."

42. The citadel or palace was surrounded by a wall whose total length was 60 stadia, within which was another of 40 stadia, whose inner face was ornamented with painting, — a practice (says Mr. Rich) among the Persians to this day. Within the last-named wall was a third, on which hunting subjects were painted. The old palace was on the opposite side of the river, the outer wall whereof was no larger than the inner wall of the new one. Above the palace or citadel were, according to Strabo, the hanging gardens, for which, in some respects, a site near the Mujelibé would sufficiently answer, were it not that the skeletons found there " embarrass almost any theory that may be formed on this extraordinary pile."

43. As yet, no traces have been found of the tunnel under the Euphrates, nor of the obelisk which Diodorus says was erected by Semiramis; it is not, however, impossible that the diligence and perseverance of future travellers may bring them to light. Rich believes that the number of buildings within the city bore no proportion to the extent of the walls, —a circumstance which has already been passingly noticed. He moreover thinks that the houses were, in general, small; and further, that the assertion of Herodotus, that it abounded in houses of two or three stories, argues that the majority consisted of only one. He well observes, " The peculiar climate of this district must have caused a similarity of habits and accommodation in all ages; and if, upon this principle, we take the present fashion of building as some example of the mode heretofore practised in Babylon, the houses that had more than one story must have consisted of the ground floor, or *basse-cour*, occupied by stables, magazines, and serdaubs or cellars, sunk a little below the ground, for

the comfort of the inhabitants during the heat; above this a gallery with the lodging rooms opening into it; and over all the flat terrace for the people to sleep on during the summer." In these observations we fully concur with the author, believing that climate and habits influence the arts of all nations.

44. At Nineveh the extraordinary discoveries of Botta and Layard have made us familiar with at least the decorations and arrangement of Assyrian architecture. The city, founded, as supposed, by Ninus or Assur about 2,200 B.C., fell before the rising wealth of Babylon. Here, from the palace of Kouyunjik, Rawlinson establishes the identity of the king who built it with the Sennacherib of Scripture. Its date would therefore be about 713 B.C. The sculptures at this place so much resemble those at Persepolis, and the arrow-headed characters also are so similar to them, as well as those of Babylon, that we may fairly conjecture similarity of habits and taste. Indeed, as the Persian empire grew out of the ruins of the Assyrian empire; and Persepolis, as a capital, succeeded to the capitals of Assyria, we may, without much fear of being wrong, judge by its architecture of that of its predecessors. Greater almost at its birth than ever afterwards, in this part of Asia the art seems all at once to have risen, as respects absolute grandeur, to the highest state of which it was there susceptible; and, degenerating successively under the hands of other people, we may reckon by the periods of its decay the epochs of its duration.

45. No trace of the arch has been found in the ruins either at the Kasr or in the passages at the Mujelibé. Massy piers, buttresses, and pilasters supplied the place of the column. The timber employed was that of the date tree, posts of which were used in their domestic architecture, round which, says Strabo, they twist reeds and apply a coat of paint to them. Thickness of wall was obtained by casing rubble work with fine brick, of which two sorts were made. The one was merely dried in the sun, the other burned in a kiln. The latter was 13 in. square and 3 in. thick, with varieties for different situations in the walls. They are of various colours. The sun-dried is considerably larger than the kiln-dried. There is reason for believing that lime cement was more generally used than bitumen or clay; indeed, Niebuhr says that the bricks laid in bitumen were easily separated, but that where mortar had been employed, no force could detach them from each other without breaking them in pieces.

Sect. IV.

PERSEPOLITAN AND PERSIAN ARCHITECTURE.

46. Persepolis, the ancient capital of Persia, whereof the few ruins now remaining we are about to describe, was seated (lat. about 30° N., long. about 53° E.) in the great plain of Merdasht or Istakhr, one of the most fertile in the world, being watered in all directions by rivulets and artificial drains, which ultimately unite in the Bundemir, the ancient Araxes. The site of this city, destroyed two thousand years since, would, like Memphis, have scarcely left a vestige by which it could have been identified, but for the celebrated ruins of Chel-Minar (*fig.* 22.), which are believed to be the remains of that

Fig. 22.   RUINS OF PERSEPOLIS.

ancient palace of the masters of Asia to which Alexander set fire in a moment of madness and debauch. The information we are about to give on this subject is obtained from De Bruyn, who examined the ruins with great attention in 1704, with some reference also to Niebuhr and Sir R. K. Porter, the latest traveller who has published any account of them.

47. The ruins are situated at the foot and to the west of the mountain Kulirag-met. On three sides the walls are remaining, the mountain to the east forming the other side.

From north to south the extent is 600 paces (1425 ft.), and 390 (802 ft.) from west to east to the mountain on the south side, having no stairs on that side ; average height about 18 ft. 7 in.   On the north side it is 410 paces (926 ft.) from east to west, and the wall is 21 ft. high in some places.   At the north-west corner of the wall, about 80 paces in extent westward, are some rocks before the principal staircase.   On mounting the steps there is found a large platform 400 paces in extent towards the mountain.   Along the wall on three

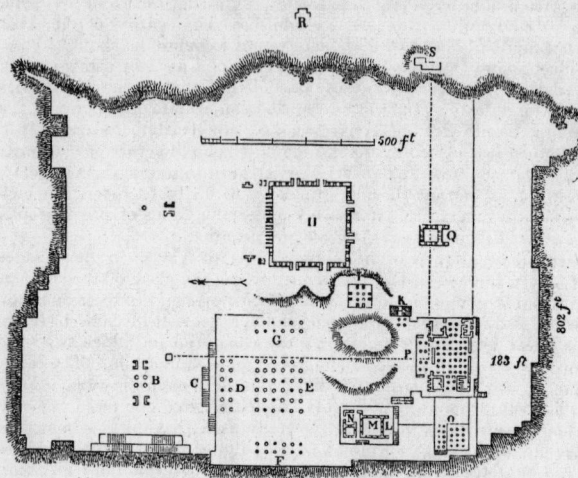

sides a pavement extends for a width of 8 ft.   The principal staircase A (fig. 23.) is not placed in the middle of the west side, but nearer to the north.   It has a double flight, the distance between the flights at the bottom being 42 ft., and the width of them is 25 ft. 7 in.   The steps are 4 in. high, and 14 in. wide.   Fifty-five of them remain on the north side, and fifty-three on the south ; and it is probable that some are buried by the ruins.   The half spaces at the top of the first flight are

Fig. 23.   PLAN OF PERSEPOLIS.

51 ft. 4 in. wide.   The upper flights are separated from the lower by a wall which runs through at the upper landing.   The upper flights are in forty-eight steps, and are cut out of single blocks of the rock.   The upper landing is seventy-five feet between the flights.

48.   Forty-two feet from the landing, at B, are two large portals and two columns (originally four).   The bottom of the first is covered with two blocks of stone, which fill two thirds of the space ; the other third having been destroyed by time.   The second portal is more covered by the earth than the first, by five feet.   They are 22 ft. 4 in. deep, and 13 ft. 4. in. wide.   On the interior side-faces of their piers, and nearly the whole length of them, are large figures of bulls, cut in bas-relief.   The heads of these animals are entirely destroyed ; and their breasts and fore feet project from the piers : the two of the first portal face to the staircase, and those of the other face towards the mountain.   On the upper part of the piers there are some arrow-headed characters, too small to be made out from below.   The remains of the first portal are

39 ft. high, and of the second 28 ft.   The base of the piers is 5 ft. 2 in. high, and projects inwards ; and the bases upon which the figures stand are 1 ft. 2 in. high.   We may here observe that the figures on the further portal have the body and legs of a bull, an enormous pair of wings (fig. 24.) projecting from the shoulders, and the heads looking to the east show the faces of men.   On the head is a cylindrical diadem, on both sides of which horns are clearly represented winding from the brows upwards to the front of the crown ; the whole being surmounted with a sort of coronet, formed of a range of leaves like the lotus, and bound with a fillet carved like roses.   The two columns (at Sir R. K. Porter's visit only one remained) are the most perfect among the ruins, and are 54 ft. high.   At the distance of fifty-two feet south-eastward from the second portico is a water-trough cut out of a single stone 20 ft. long and

Fig. 24.   FIGURE ON A PORTAL AT PERSEPOLIS.

17 ft. 5 in. broad, and standing 3 ft. high from the ground.   From hence to the northern wall of the platform is covered with fragments ; and the remains of one column not channelled as the others are ; this is 12 ft. 4 in. high.

49. At one hundred and seventy-two feet from the portals, southward, is another staircase of two flights (lettered C), one west and the other east. On the top of the ramp of the steps are some foliages, and a lion tearing to pieces a bull, in bas-relief, and larger than nature. This staircase is half buried. The western flight has twenty-eight steps, and the other, where the ground is higher, has only eighteen. These steps are 17 ft. long, 3 in. high, and 14½ in. wide. The wall of the landing is sculptured with three rows of figures, one above the other, and extending ninety-eight feet. The faces of these inner terrace walls

Fig 25.   BAS-RELIEF AT PERSEPOLIS.

are all decorated with bas-reliefs, of which *fig*. 25. is a specimen. On arriving at the top of this staircase, was found another large platform, paved with large blocks of stone; and at the distance of twenty-two feet two inches from the parapet of the landing, are the most northern columns (lettered D), originally twelve in number, whereof in Sir R. K. Porter's time only one remained. At seventy-one feet southward from these stood thirty-six columns more, at intervals of twenty-two feet two inches from each other, whereof only five now remain; the bases, however, of all the others are in their places, though most of them are much damaged. This group of columns is lettered E. To the east and west of the last-named group are two other groups of twelve each marked F and G, whereof five still remain in the eastern one, and four in the western one. The columns of the central group are fifty-five feet high; and those of the other three groups are sixty feet in height. To the south of the three groups of columns is situate the most raised building on these ruins. On the east, towards the mountain, a large mass of ruins is visible (lettered H), consisting of portals, passages, windows, &c. The first are decorated with figures on the interior; and the whole plot on which they stand is 95 paces from east to west, and about 125 paces from north to south. The centre part of the plot is covered with fragments of columns and other stones; and in the interior part there seems to have been a group of seventy-six columns, whereof none are represented by Sir R. K. Porter, nor are they shown in either of Le Bruyn's views. The highest building as to level, marked I, is 118 ft. distant from the columns lettered G. Some foundations are visible in front of this building, to which there is not the slightest trace of a staircase. At fifty-three feet from the façade of it to the right is a staircase of double flight, marked K, where again bassi relievi are to be found, near which are the remains of some portals which Le Bruyn thinks were destroyed by an earthquake. The next ruin (L) is 54½ ft. in extent, and has portals similar to those in other parts of the place. To its north, M exhibits uniform features, with windows, and what travellers have agreed to call niches, which are nothing more than square-headed recesses. Sculpture here again abounds, whereof we do not think a description necessary, as in *fig*. 25. a specimen of it has been given, sufficient to indicate its character. Behind this edifice is another, in some respects similar, except that it is thirty-eight feet longer. It is marked N on the plan. One hundred feet to the south of this last set of ruins (lettered O), Sir R. K. Porter seems to have found traces of columns, which, if we read Le Bruyn rightly, he does not mention. In this, the last-named traveller found a staircase leading to subterranean apartments, as he thought, but nothing of interest was discovered. The general dimensions of the building (P) extend about 160 ft. from north to south, and 190 ft. from east to west. It exhibits ten portals in ruins, besides other remains; and there are traces of thirty-six columns, in six ranks of six each. The spot is covered with fragments, under which have been traced conveyances for water. To the west of the last-named building was another entirely in ruins: to the east of it are visible the remains of a fine staircase, much resembling that first described, and which, therefore, we do not think it necessary to particularise, more than we do the numberless fragments scattered over the whole area, which was equal to nearly thirty English acres! The ruins at Q are of portals. At R and S are tombs cut in the rock, of curious form, but evidently, from their character, the work of those who constructed the enormous pile of building of which we have already inserted a representation. Between the leading forms of the portals of these ruins, or porticoes, as Le Bruyn calls them, and those of the structures of Egypt, there is a very striking resemblance. On comparison of the two, it is impossible not to be struck with the large crowning hollowed member, which seems to have been common to the edifices on the banks of the Nile and those on the plain of Merdasht. In both, this member, forming, as it were, an entablature, is ornamented with vertical ribs or leaves, and the large fillet above the hollow appears equally in each. In the walls of the Persepolitan remains, there is perhaps less real massiveness than in those which were the works of the Egyptians; but the similarity of appearance between them points to the conjecture that, though neither might have been borrowed from the other, they are not many removes from one common parent. The an-

nexed diagram (*fig.* 26.) will give the reader some notion of the style of the architecture of

Fig. 26   ARCHITECTURE OF PERSEPOLIS.

Persepolis. The diagram (*fig.* 27.) exhibits a specimen of a column and capital. *Fig.* 28. is a capital from one of the tombs. The walls forming the revêtement of the great esplanade are wonderfully perfect; and appear still capable of re-sisting equally the attacks of time and barbarism. The surface of the platform, generally, is unequal, and was of different levels: the whole seems to have been hewn from the mountain, from whence the marble has been extracted for con-structing the edifices: hence the pave-ments appear masses of marble, than which nothing more durable or beautiful can be conceived. No cement appears to have been used, but the stones seem to have been connected by cramps, whose removal, however, has neither deranged the courses from which they have been removed, nor affected their nice fitting to each other;

Fig. 28.   CAPITAL FROM A TOMB.

Fig. 27. COLUMN AND CAPITAL. they are, indeed, so well wrought that the joints can scarcely be perceived, so close that the thinnest plate of metal could not be introduced between them.

50. No person can look at the style of composition and details of Persepolis without a conviction of some intimate connection between the architects of Persia and those of Egypt. The principles of both are identical; and without inquiring into the exact date of the monument whose description we have just left, there is sufficient to convince us that the theory started in respect of the Cyclopean architecture, of the arts travelling in every direction from some central Asiatic point, is fully borne out; and that the Egyp-tian style had its origin in Asia. We are quite aware that conjectures, bearing a semblance of pro-bability, have as-signed the erection of this stupendous palace to Egyptian captives, at a com-paratively late pe-riod, after the con-quest of Egypt by

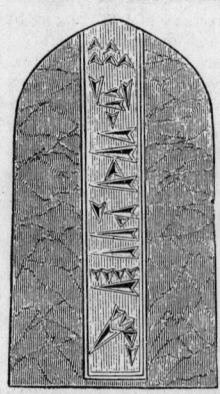

Fig. 29.
ARROW-HEADED CHARACTERS.

Fig. 30.   NAKSHI RUSTAN.

Cambyses; but we think they are answered by the similarity of arrow-headed characters used therein to those of ancient Babylon, whereof an example is here given (*fig.* 29.) from one of the portals of Persepolis. A few miles to the south of Persepolis, the excavated hill of Nakshi Rustán (*fig.* 30.) presents a number of sculptured

tombs, the highest supposed to be coeval with Persepolis, and formed for the sepulture of the early kings of Persia. The lower tombs seem to have belonged to the Parthian Sassanide dynasties.

51a. The early Persians, as we have already noticed, were doubtless indebted to the still earlier Assyrians for the principles on which their art was based. Persepolis lies eastward of Nineveh about 10 degrees, and in a parallel of latitude about 7 degrees south of it. Its remains are such as to afford us a more intimate acquaintance with the details and construction employed. In both places we find the same arrangement of bassi-rilievi against the walls—entrances decorated with gigantic winged animals, bearing human heads—similarity in ornament and costume—processions like those at Nimroud and Khorsabad, with a slight variation of folds in the drapery. The cuneiform character (see the preceding page) has, moreover, in the hands of Major Rawlinson and M. Lassen, become a known language; and from an inscription found on the third terrace, behind the Chel-Minar, the structure is assigned to the time of Darius. Other parts are given to the time of Darius Hystaspes and of Xerxes, 521 to 486 B.C.

51b. The present architecture of Persia much resembles that of other Mahometan countries. The city of Ispahan, in its prosperity, is said to have been surrounded by a wall twenty miles in circuit. The houses are generally mean in external appearance: they commonly consist of a large square court, surrounded with rooms of varying dimensions for different uses, the sides of the area being planted with flowers, and refreshed by fountains. Distinct from this is a smaller court, round which are distributed the apartments belonging to the females of the family; and almost every dwelling has a garden attached to it. The interior apartments of the richer classes are splendidly finished, though simply furnished. Those inhabited by the governor, public officers, and opulent merchants, may almost vie with palaces. Nearly all are constructed with sun-dried bricks, the public edifices only being built with burnt bricks; the roofs, mostly flat, have terraces, whereon the inhabitants sleep during several months of the year. According to Chardin, there were in his time within the walls 160 mosques, 48 colleges, 1802 caravanseras, 273 baths, 12 cemeteries, and 38,000 houses. But the city has since fallen into great ruin. The *Shah Meidan*, however (*figs.* 31.

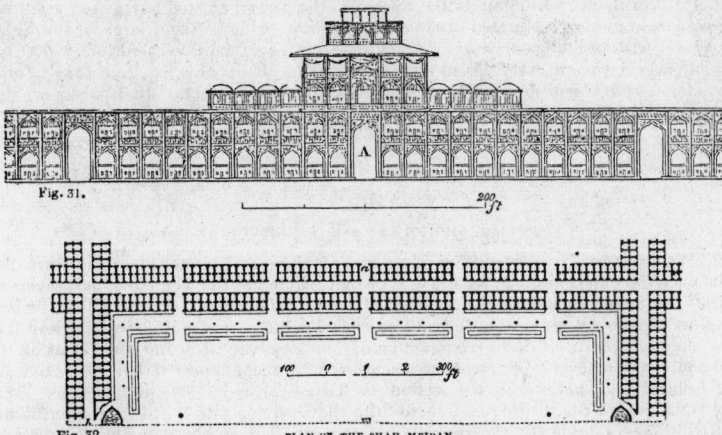

Fig. 31.

Fig. 32.   PLAN OF THE SHAH MEIDAN.

and 32.), or royal square, is still one of the largest and finest in the world. It is 440 paces in length, and 160 in breadth. On its south side stands the royal mosque, erected by Shah Abbas, in the sixteenth century, and constructed of stone, covered with highly varnished bricks and tiles, whereon are inscribed sentences of the Koran. On another side of the Meidan is a Mahometan college called the Medresse Shah Sultan Hossein. The entrance is through a lofty portico decorated with twisted columns of Tabriz marble, leading through two brazen gates, whose extremities are of silver, and their whole surface sculptured and embossed with flowers, and verses from the Koran. Advancing into the court, on the right side is a mosque, whose dome is covered with lacquered tiles, and adorned externally with ornaments of pure gold. This, and the minarets that flank it, are now falling into decay. The other sides of the square are occupied, one, by a lofty and beautiful portico, and the remaining two by small square cells for students, twelve in each front, disposed in two stories. In the city are few hospitals; one stands, however, beside the caravanserai of Shah Abbas, who erected both at the same time, that the revenue of the latter might support the proper officers of the hospital. That the reader may have a proper idea of one of these inns of the

East, if they may be so called, we have here given the plan of that just above named (*fig.*
33.). The palaces of the kings

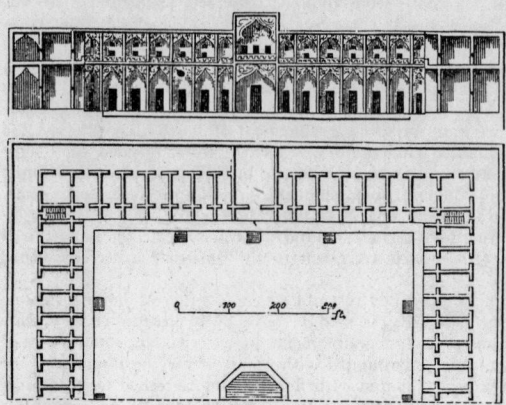

Fig. 33. CARAVANSERAI OF SHAH ABBAS.

are enclosed in a fort of lofty
walls, about three miles in circuit ; in general the front room
or hall is very open, and the
roof supported by carved and
gilded columns. The windows
glazed with curiously stained
glass of a variety of colours ;
each has a fountain in front.
The palace of Chehel Sitoon,
or forty pillars, is placed in the
middle of an immense square,
intersected by canals, and
planted with trees. Towards
the garden is an open saloon
whose ceiling is borne by
eighteen columns, inlaid with
mirrors, and appearing at a distance to consist entirely of
glass. The base of each is of
marble, sculptured into four lions, so placed that the shafts stand on them. Mirrors are
distributed on the walls in great profusion, and the ceiling is ornamented with gilt flowers.
An arched recess leads from the apartment just described into a spacious and splendid hall,
whose roof is formed into a variety of domes, decorated with painting and gilding. The
walls are partly of white marble, and partly covered with mirrors, and are moreover decorated with six large paintings, whose subjects are the battles and royal fêtes of Shah Ismael
and Shah Abbas the Great. Though of considerable age, the colours are fresh, and the
gilding still brilliant. Adjoining the palace is the harem, erected but a few years ago.
The bazaars are much celebrated ; they consist of large wide passages, arched, and lighted
from above, with buildings or stores on each side. One of these was formerly 600 geometrical paces in length, very broad and lofty. From these being adjacent to each other,
a person might traverse the whole city sheltered from the weather. In Ispahan, we must
not forget to notice that some fine bridges exist, which cross the river Zenderond.

Sect. V.

JEWISH AND PHŒNICIAN ARCHITECTURE.

52. We are scarcely justified in giving a section, though short, to the architecture of the
Jews, since the only buildings recorded as of that nation are the Temple of Jerusalem constructed by Solomon, and the house of the forest of Lebanon. The shepherd tribes of
Israel, indeed, do not seem to have required such dwellings or temples as would lead them,
when they settled in cities, to the adoption of any style very different from that of their
neighbours. Whatever monuments are mentioned by them appear to have been rude, and
have been already noticed in the section on Druidical and Celtic architecture. When
Solomon ascended the throne, anxious to fulfil the wish his father had long entertained of
erecting a fixed temple for the reception of the ark, he was not only obliged to send to
Tyre for workmen, but for an architect also. Upon this temple a dissertation has been
written by a Spaniard of the name of Villalpanda, wherein he, with consummate simplicity,
urges that the orders, instead of being the invention of the Greeks, were the invention of God
himself, and that Callimachus most shamefully put forth pretensions to the formation of the
Corinthian capital which, he says, had been used centuries before in the temple at Jerusalem.
The following account of the temple is from the sixth chapter of the First Book of Kings.
Its plan was a parallelogram (taking the cubit at 1·824 ft., being the length generally
assigned to it) of about 109½ ft. by 36½ ft., being as nearly as may be two thirds of the
size of the church of St. Martin's in the Fields. In front was a pronaos, or portico,
stretching through the whole front (36½ ft.) of the temple, and its depth was half its extent.
The cell, or main body of the temple, was 54¾ ft. deep, and the sanctuary beyond 36½
feet, the height of it being equal to its length and breadth. The height of the middle
part, or cell, was 54¾ ft. ; and that of the portico the same as the sanctuary, — that is,
36½ ft., — judging from the height of the columns. In the interior, the body of the temple
was surrounded by three tiers of chambers, to which there was an ascent by stairs ; and the
central part was open to the sky. The ends of the beams of the floors rested on corbels of
stone, and were not inserted into the walls, which were lined with cedar, carved into

cherubims and palm trees, gilt. In the sanctuary two figures of cherubs were placed,
whose wings touched each other in the centre, and extended outwards to the walls. These
were 10 cubits high. In the front of the portico were two pillars of brass, which were cast
by Hiram, "a widow's son of the tribe of Naphtali," whose "father was a *man of Tyre*,"
and who "came to king Solomon and wrought all his work." These two pillars of
brass (1 *Kings*, vii. 14, 15.) were each 18 cubits high, and their circumference was
12 cubits; hence their diameter was 3·82 cubits. The chapiters, or capitals, were
5 cubits high; and one of them was decorated with lilies upon a net-work ground,
and the other with pomegranates. From the representation (*fig.* 34.) here given,
the reader must be struck with their resemblance to the columns of Egypt with
their lotus leaves, and sometimes net-work. In short, the whole description would
almost as well apply to a temple of Egypt as to one at Jerusalem. And this tends,
though slightly it is true, to show that the Phœnician workmen who were employed
on the temple worked in the same style as those of Egypt.

Fig. 34.

53. The house of the forest of Lebanon was larger than the temple, having been 100
cubits in length, by 50 in breadth; it also had a portico, and from the description seems to
have been similar in style.

54. *Phœnician Architecture.* — That part of the great nation of Asia which settled on the
coasts of Palestine, called in scripture Canaanites, or merchants, were afterwards by the
Greeks called Phœnicians. Sidon was originally their capital, and Tyre, which afterwards became greater than the parent itself, was at first only a colony. From what we
have said in a previous section on the walls of Mycene, it may be fairly presumed that their
architecture partook of the Cyclopean style; but that it was much more highly decorated
is extremely probable from the wealth of a people whose merchants were princes, and whose
traffickers were the honourable of the earth. Besides the verses of Euripides, which point
to the style of Phœnician architecture, we have the authority of Lucian for asserting that
it was Egyptian in character. Unfortunately all is surmise; no monuments of Phœnician
architecture exist, and we therefore think it useless to dwell longer on the subject.

Sect. VI.

INDIAN ARCHITECTURE.

55. Whence the countries of India derived their architecture is a question that has occupied
abler pens than that which we wield, and a long period has not passed away since the impression on our own mind was, that the monuments of India were not so old as those of
Egypt. Upon maturer reflection, we are not sure that impression was false; but if the arts of
a country do not change, if the manners and habits of the people have not varied, the admis-

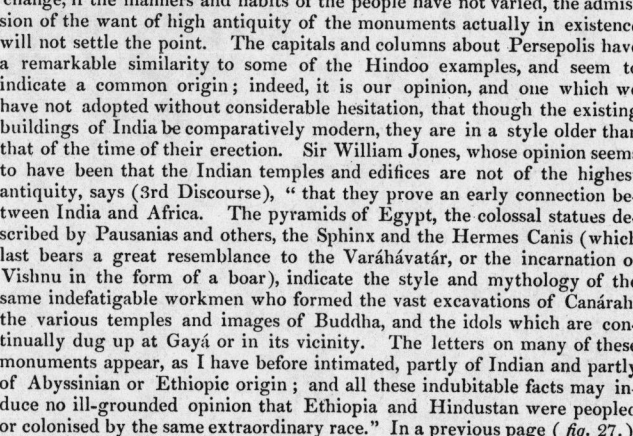

sion of the want of high antiquity of the monuments actually in existence
will not settle the point. The capitals and columns about Persepolis have
a remarkable similarity to some of the Hindoo examples, and seem to
indicate a common origin; indeed, it is our opinion, and one which we
have not adopted without considerable hesitation, that though the existing
buildings of India be comparatively modern, they are in a style older than
that of the time of their erection. Sir William Jones, whose opinion seems
to have been that the Indian temples and edifices are not of the highest
antiquity, says (3rd Discourse), " that they prove an early connection between India and Africa. The pyramids of Egypt, the colossal statues described by Pausanias and others, the Sphinx and the Hermes Canis (which
last bears a great resemblance to the Varáhávatár, or the incarnation of
Vishnu in the form of a boar), indicate the style and mythology of the
same indefatigable workmen who formed the vast excavations of Canárah,
the various temples and images of Buddha, and the idols which are continually dug up at Gayá or in its vicinity. The letters on many of these
monuments appear, as I have before intimated, partly of Indian and partly
of Abyssinian or Ethiopic origin; and all these indubitable facts may induce no ill-grounded opinion that Ethiopia and Hindustan were peopled

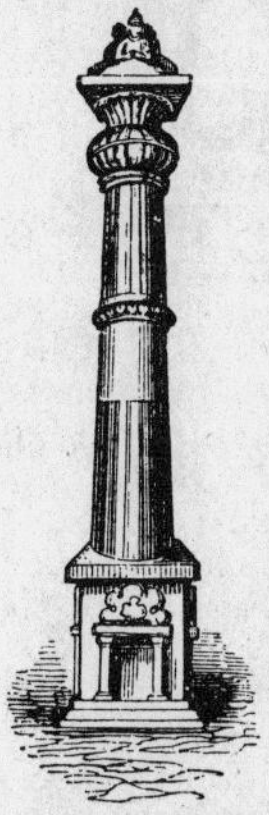

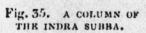

Fig. 35. A COLUMN OF
THE INDRA SUBBA.

or colonised by the same extraordinary race." In a previous page (*fig.* 27.),
the reader will find a Persepolitan column and capital; we place before
him, in *fig.* 35., an example from the Indra Subba which much resembles it in detail, and
at the Nerta Chabei at Chillambaram are very similar examples. Between the styles of
Persepolis and Egypt a resemblance will be hereafter traced, and to such an extent, that
there seems no reasonable doubt of a common origin. The monuments of India may
be divided into two classes, the *excavated* and *constructed*; the former being that wherein a
building has been hollowed, or, as it were, quarried out of the rock; the latter, that built
of separate and different sorts of materials, upon a regular plan, as may be seen in those
buildings improperly called pagodas, which ornament the enclosures of the sacred edifices, of

which they are component parts. The class first named seems to have interested travellers more than the last, from the apparent difficulty of execution ; but on this account we are not so sure that they ought to create more astonishment than the constructed temple, except that, according to Daniel (*Asiat. Res.* vol. i.), they are hollowed in hard and compact granite.

56. The monuments which belong to the first class are of two sorts ; those actually hollowed out of rocks, and those presenting forms of *apparently* constructed buildings, but which are. in fact, rocks shaped by human hands into architectural forms. Of the first sort are the caves of Elephanta and Ellora ; of the last, the seven large pagodas of Mavalipowram. ·It will immediately occur to the reader that the shaping of rocks into forms implies art, if the forms be imposing or well arranged : so, if the hollowing a rock into well-arranged and well-formed chambers be conducted in a way indicating an acquaintance with architectural effect, we are not to assume that a want of taste must be consequent on the first sort merely because it cannot be called constructive architecture. And here we must observe, that we think the writer in the *Encyclopédie Méthodique* (art. Arch. Indienne) fails in his reasoning ; our notion being simply this, that as far as respects these monuments, if they are worthy to be ranked as works of art, the means by which they were produced have nothing to do with the question. It must, however, be admitted, that what the architect understands by ordonnance, or the composition of a building, and the proper arrangement of its several parts, points which so much engaged the attention of the Greeks and Romans, will not be found in Indian architecture as far as our acquaintance with it extends. Conjectures infinite might be placed before the reader on the antiquity of this species of art, but they would be valueless, no certain data, of which we are aware, existing to lead him in the right road ; and we must, therefore, be content with enumerating some of the principal works in this style. The caves at Ellora consist of several apartments ; the plan of that called the Indra Subba (*fig.* 36.) is here given, to show the species of plan which these places

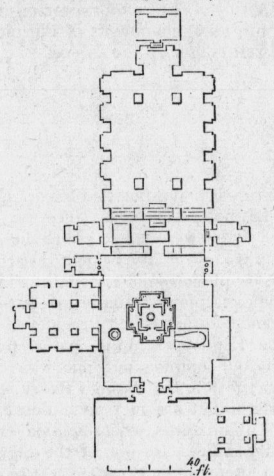

Fig 37.   VIEW INTO THE INTERIOR OF THE INDRA SUBBA.

Fig. 36.   PLAN OF THE INDRA SUBBA.

exhibit ; and *fig.* 37. is a view of a portion of the interior of the same. The group of temples which compose these excavations are as follow : —

	ft.	in.
Temple of Diagannâtha.		
External width of the excavation	57	0
Length (interior)	34	0
Width (ditto)	20	0
Height	13	0
Height of the pillars	11	0
Temple of Parocona.		
Length internally	35	0
Width	25	0
Height	8	0
Temple of Adi — Natha.		
Length	45	0
Height	9	0
Temple of Djenonasla.		
Width	11	0
Height	11	2
Temple of Domma — Leyma.		
Length	55	0
Width	18	6
Height	16	10

	ft.	in
Temple of Indra.		
Length	54	0
Width	44	0
Height	27	0
Height of columns	22	0
Another Temple.		
Length	111	0
Width	22	4
Height	15	0
Temple of Mahadeo.		
Length	68	0
Width	17	0
Height	12	0
Temple of Ramichouer.		
Length	90	0
Height	15	0
Temple of Kailaça.		
Length	88	0
Height	47	0

57. The most celebrated excavated temple is that of Elephanta (*fig.* 38.), near Bombay,
of whose interior composition
the reader may obtain a faint
idea from the subjoined representation (*fig.* 39.). It is
130 ft. long, 110 ft. wide, and
14½ ft. high. The ceiling is
flat, and is apparently supported by four ranks of columns, about 9 ft. high, and
of a balustral form. These
stand on pedestals, about
one third of the height of the
columns themselves. A great
portion of the walls is co-

Fig. 38.   TEMPLE OF ELEPHANTA.

vered with colossal human figures, forty to fifty in number, in high relief, and distinguished by a variety of symbols, probably representing the attributes of the deities

Fig. 39   INTERIOR OF THE TEMPLE OF ELEPHANTA.

that were worshipped, or the actions of the heroes whom they represented. At the end
of the cavern there is a dark recess, about 20 ft. square, entered by four doors, each
flanked by gigantic figures. " These stupendous works," says Robertson, " are of such high
antiquity, that, as the natives cannot, either from history or tradition, give any information
concerning the time in which they were executed, they universally ascribe the formation of
them to the power of superior beings. From the extent and grandeur of these subterraneous mansions, which intelligent travellers compare to the most celebrated monuments of human power and art in any part of the earth, it is manifest that they could not
have been formed in that stage of social life where men continue divided into small tribes,
unaccustomed to the efforts of persevering industry." Excavations similar to those we
have named are found at Canárah, in the Island of Salsette, near Bombay. In these there
are four stories of galleries, leading in all to three hundred apartments. The front is
formed by cutting away one side of the rock. The principal temple, 84 ft. long, and 40 ft.
broad, is entered by a portico of columns. The roof is of the form of a vault, 40 ft. from
the ground to its crown, and has the appearance of being supported by thirty pillars,
octagonal in plan, whose capitals and bases are formed of elephants, tigers, and horses.
The walls contain cavities for lamps, and are covered with sculptures of human figures of
both sexes, elephants, horses, and lions. An altar, 27 ft. high and 20 ft. in diameter,
stands at the further end, and over it is a dome shaped out of the rock. Though the
sculptures in these caves are low in rank compared with the works of Greek and Etrurian
artists, yet they are certainly in a style superior to the works of the Egyptians; and we
infer from them a favourable opinion of the state of the arts in India at the period of their
formation. " It is worthy of notice," observes the historian we have just quoted, " that
although several of the figures in the caverns at Elephanta be so different from those
now exhibited in the pagodas as objects of veneration, that some learned Europeans

have imagined they represent the rites of a religion more ancient than that now established in Hindostan; yet by the Hindoos themselves the caverns are considered as hallowed places of their own worship, and they still resort thither to perform their devotions, and honour the figures there, in the same manner with those in their own pagodas." Mr. Hunter, who in the year 1784 visited the place, considers the figures there as representing deities who are still objects of worship among the Hindoos. One circumstance justifying this opinion is, that several of the most conspicuous personages in the groups at Elephanta are decorated with the *zennar*, the sacred string or cord peculiar to the order of Brahmins, an authentic evidence of the distinction of casts having been established in India at the time when these works were finished.

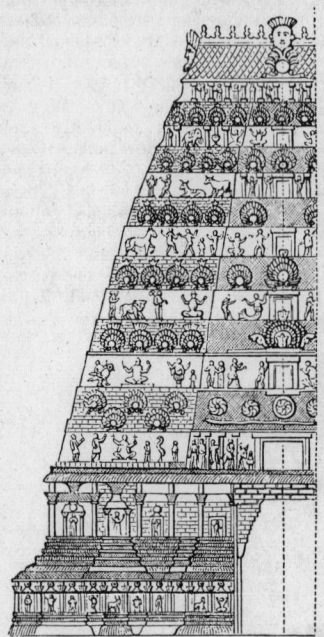

Fig. 40.   PAGODA OF CHILLAMBARAM.

58. The structure of the earliest Indian temples was extremely simple. Pyramidal, and of large dimensions, they had no light but that which the door afforded; and, indeed, the gloom of the cavern seems to have led them to consider the solemn darkness of such a mansion sacred. There are ruins of this sort at Deogur and at a spot near Tanjore, in the Carnatic. In proportion, however, to the progress of the country in opulence and refinement, their sacred buildings became highly ornamented, and must be considered as monuments exhibiting a high degree of civilisation of the people by whom they were erected. Very highly finished pagodas, of great antiquity, are found in different parts of Hindostan, and particularly in its southern districts, where they were not subjected to the destructive fury of Mahometan zeal. To assist the reader in forming a notion of the style of the architecture whereof we are treating, we here place before him a diagram (*fig.* 40.) of part of the pagoda at Chillambaram, near Porto Novo, on the Coromandel coast; one which is, on account of its antiquity, held in great veneration. The monument would be perhaps more properly described as a cluster of pagodas, enclosed in a rectangular space 1332 ft. in length, and 936 ft. in width, whose walls are 30 ft. in height, and 7 ft. in thickness, each side being provided with a highly decorated frustum of a pyramid over an entrance gateway. The large enclosure is subdivided into four subordinate ones, whereof the central one, surrounded by a colonnade and steps, contains a piscina or basin for purification. That on the southern side forms a cloister enclosing three contiguous temples called *Chabei*, lighted only by their doors and by lamps. The court on the west is also claustral, having in the middle an open portico, consisting of one hundred columns, whose roof is formed by large blocks of stone. The last is a square court with a temple and piscina, to which is given the name of the Stream of Eternal Joy. To the temple is attached a portico of thirty-six columns, in four parallel ranks, whose central intercolumniation is twice the width of those at the sides, and in the centre, on a platform, is the statue of the Bull Nundu. It is lighted artificially with lamps, which are kept constantly burning, and is much decorated with sculpture. The central inclosure, on its eastern side, has a temple raised on a platform, in length 224 ft., and in width 64 ft., having a portico in front, consisting of a vast number of columns 30 ft. high; at the end of it a square vestibule is constructed with four portals, one whereof in the middle leads to the sanctuary, named *Nerta Chabei*, or Temple of Joy and Eternity, the altar being at the end of it. The temple is much decorated with sculpture, representing the divinities of India. The pilaster *fig.* 41. is placed at the sides of the door of the *Nerta Chabei*, and is extremely curious; but the most singular object about the building is a chain of granite carved out of the rock, attached to the pilasters, and supported at four other points in the face of the rock so as to form festoons.

Fig. 41.   PILASTER FROM THE NERTA CHABEI.

The links are about 3 ft. long, and the whole length of the chain is 146 ft. The pyramids

above mentioned, which stand over the entrances of the outer enclosure, rise from rectangular bases, and consist of several floors. The passage through them is level with the ground.

59. A very beautiful example of the Indian pagoda exists at Tanjore, which we here insert (*fig.* 42.).

60. One of the largest temples known is that on the small island Seringham, near Trichinopoly, on the Coromandel coast. It is situate about a mile from the western extremity of the island, and is thus described by Sonnerat. It is composed of seven square enclosures, one within the other, the walls

Fig. 42.   PAGODA AT TANJORE.

whereof are 25 ft. high, and 4 ft. thick. These enclosures are 350 ft. distant from one another, and each has four large gates with a high tower; which are placed, one in the middle of each side of the enclosure, and opposite to the four cardinal points. The outward wall is near four miles in circumference, and its gateway to the south is ornamented with pillars, several of which are simple stones, 33 ft. long, and nearly 5 ft. in diameter; and those which form the roof are still larger. In the inmost inclosures are the chapels. About half a mile to the east of Seringham, and nearer to the river Caveri than the Coleroon, is another large pagoda, called Jembikisma, but this has only one enclosure. The extreme veneration in which Seringham is held arises from a belief that it contains that identical image of the god Vishnu which used to be worshipped by Brahma.

61. We shall conclude this section with some observations on Tchoultry (or Iun) at Madurah (*fig.* 43.). Its effect is quite theatrical, and its perfect symmetry gives it the appearance of a work of great art, and of greater skill in composition than most other Indian works. Yet an examination of the details, and particularly of the system of corbelling over, destroys the charm which a first glance at it creates. In it, the ornaments which in Grecian architecture are so well applied and balanced, seem more the work of chance than of consideration. We here insert an external view

Fig. 43.   TCHOULTRY AT MADURAH.

of the temple at this place (*fig.* 44.). The essential differences between Indian and Egyptian architecture, in connection with the sculpture applied to them, have been well given in the *Encyclopédie Méthodique*, and we shall here subjoin them. In Egypt, the principal forms of the building and its parts preponderate, inasmuch as the hieroglyphics with which they are covered never interfere with the general forms, nor injure the effect of the whole ; in India, the principal form is lost in the ornaments which divide and decompose it. In Egypt, that which is essential predominates ; in India, you are lost in the multitude of

Fig. 44.   TEMPLE AT MADURAH.

accessories. In the Egyptian architecture, even the smallest edifices are grand ; in that of India, the infinite subdivision into parts gives an air of littleness to the largest buildings. In Egypt, solidity is carried to the extreme ; in India, there is not the slightest appearance of it.

Sect. VII.

EGYPTIAN ARCHITECTURE.

62. We propose to consider the architecture of Egypt — First, in respect of the physical, political, and moral causes which affected it. Secondly, in respect of its analysis and development. Thirdly, and lastly, in respect of the taste, style, and character which it exhibits.

63. I. In our introduction, we have alluded to the three states of life which even in the present day distinguish different nations of the earth — hunters, shepherds, and agriculturists ; in the second class whereof are included those whose subsistence is on the produce of the waters, which was most probably the principal food of the earliest inhabitants of Egypt. Seated on the banks of a river whose name almost implies fertility, they would have been able to live on the supply it afforded for a long period before it was necessary to resort to the labours of agriculture. In such a state of existence nothing appears more probable than that they should have availed themselves of the most obvious shelter which nature afforded against the extremes of heat and cold, namely, the cavern ; which, consisting of tufo and a species of white soft stone, was easily enlarged or formed to meet their wants. Certain it is, that at a very early period the Egyptians were extremely skilful in working stone, an art which at a later time they carried to a perfection which has never been surpassed. As the Tyrians, Sidonians, and other inhabitants of Palestine were, owing to the material which their cedar forests afforded, dexterous in joinery, so the Egyptians received an impulse in the style of their works from an abundance of the stone of all sorts which their quarries produced. Subterranean apartments, it will be said, are found in other countries ; but they will mostly, India excepted, be found to be the remains of abandoned quarrries, exhibiting no traces of architecture, nor places for dwelling. Egypt, on the contrary, from time immemorial, was accustomed to hollow out rocks for habitation. Pliny (lib. xxxvi. c. 13.) tells us, that the great Labyrinth consisted of immense excavations of this sort. Such were the subterranean chambers of Biban el Melook, those which have in the present day received the name of the Labyrinth, and many others, which were not likely to have been tombs. When the finished and later monuments of a people resemble their first essays, it is easy to recognise the influential causes from which they result. Thus, in Egyptian architecture, every thing points to its origin. Its simplicity, not to say monotony, its extreme solidity, almost heaviness, form its principal characters. Then the want of profile and paucity of members, the small projection of its mouldings, the absence of apertures, the enormous diameter of the columns employed, much resembling the pillars left in quarries for support, the pyramidal form of the doors, the omission of roofs and pediments, the ignorance of the arch (which we believe to have been unknown, though we are aware that a late traveller of great intelligence is of a different opinion),—all enable us to recur to the type with which we have set out. If we pursue this investigation, we do not discover timber as an element in Egyptian compositions, whilst in Grecian architecture, the types certainly do point to that material. It is not necessary to inquire whether the people had or had not tents or houses in which timber was used for beams or for support, since the character of their architecture is specially influenced by the exclusive use of stone as a material ; and however the form of some of their columns may not seem to bear out the hypothesis (such, for instance, as are shaped into bundles of reeds with imitations of plants in the capitals), all the upper parts are constructed without reference to any other than stone construction. It is, moreover, well known that Egypt was extremely bare of wood, and especially of such as was suited for building.

64. The climate of Egypt was, doubtless, one great cause of the subterranean style, as it must be in the original architecture of every nation. Materials so well adapted to the construction it induced, furnishing supports incapable of being crushed, and single blocks of stone which dispensed with all carpentry in roofs or coverings, a purity of air and evenness of temperature which admitted the greatest simplicity of construction from the absence of all necessity to provide against the inclemency of seasons, and which permitted the inscription of hieroglyphics even on soft stone without the fear of their disappearance, — all these concurred in forming the character of their stupendous edifices, and stimulated them in the development of the art.

65. The monarchical government, certainly the most favourable to the construction of great monuments, appears to have existed in Egypt from time immemorial. The most

important edifices with which history or their ruins have made us acquainted, were raised under monarchies; and we scarcely need cite any other than the ruins of Persepolis, of which an account is given in a previous section, to prove the assertion: these, in point of extent, exceed all that Egypt or Greece produced. Indeed, the latter nation sought beauty of form rather than immense edifices; and Rome, until its citizens equalled kings in their wealth, had no monuments worthy to be remembered by the historian, or transmitted as models to the artist.

66. Not the least important of the causes that combined in the erection of their monuments was the extraordinary population of Egypt: and though we may not perhaps entirely rely on the wonderful number of twenty thousand cities, which old historians have said were seated within its boundaries, it is past question that the country was favourable to the rearing and maintenance of an immense population. As in China at the present day, there appears in Egypt to have been a redundant population, which was doubtless employed in the public works of the country, in which the workman received no other remuneration than his food.

67. The Egyptian monarchs appear to have gratified their ambition as much in the provision for their own reception after this life as during their continuance in it. If we except the Memnonium, and what is called the Labyrinth at Memphis, temples and tombs are all that remain of their architectural works. Diodorus says, that the kings of Egypt spent those enormous sums on their sepulchres which other kings expend on palaces. They considered that the frailty of the body during life ought not to be provided with more than necessary protection from the seasons, and that the palace was nothing more than an inn, which at their death the successor would in his turn inhabit, but that the tomb was their eternal dwelling, and sacred to themselves alone. Hence they spared no expense in erecting indestructible edifices for their reception after death. Against the violation of the tomb it seems to have been a great object with them to provide, and doubts have existed on the minds of some whether the body was, after all, deposited in the pyramids, which have been thought to be enormous cenotaphs, and that the body was in some subterraneous and neighbouring spot. Other writers pretend that the pyramids were not tombs, assigning to them certain mystic or astronomical destinations. There are, however, too many circumstances contradictory of such an assumption to allow us to give it the least credit; and there is little impropriety in calling them sepulchral monuments, whether or not the bodies of the monarchs were ever deposited in them. The religion of Egypt, though not so fruitful, perhaps, as that of Greece in the production of a great number of temples, did not fail to engender an abundant supply. The priesthood was powerful and the rites unchangeable: a mysterious authority prevailed in its ceremonies and outward forms. The temples of the country are impressed with mystery, on which the religion was based. Here, indeed, Secresy was deified in the person of Harpocrates; and, according to Plutarch (*De Iside*), the sphinx, which decorated the entrances of their temples, signified that mystery and emblem were engrafted on their theology. Numerous doors closed the succession of apartments in the temples, leaving the holy place itself to be seen only at a great distance. This was of little extent, containing merely a living idol, or the representation of one. The larger portion of the temple was laid out for the reception of the priests, and disposed in galleries, porticoes, and vestibules. With few and unimportant variations, the greatest similarity and uniformity is observable in their temples, in plan, in elevation, and in general form, as well as in the details of their ornaments. In no country was the connection between religion and architecture closer than in Egypt, and as the conceptions and execution in architecture are dependent on the other arts, we will here briefly examine the influence which the religion of the country had upon them.

68. Painting and sculpture are not only intimately connected with architecture through the embellishments they are capable of affording to it, but are handmaids at her service in what depends upon taste, upon the principles of beauty, upon the laws of proportion, upon the preservation of character, and in various other respects. Nature, in one sense, is the model upon which architecture is founded; not as a subject of imitation, but as presenting for imitation principles of the harmony, proportion, effect, and beauty, for which the arts generally are indebted to nature. We think it was Madame de Staël who said that architecture was frozen music. Now, though in architecture, as in the other arts, there is no sensible imitation of nature, yet by a study of her mode of operating, it may be tempered and modified so as to give it the power of language and the sublimity of poetry. In respect of the connection of the art with sculpture, little need be said: in a material light, architecture is but a sculptured production, and its beauty in every country is in an exact ratio with the skill which is exhibited in the use of the chisel. Facts, however, which are worth more than arguments, prove that as is the state of architecture in a country, so is that of the other arts. Two things prevented the arts of imitation being carried beyond a certain point in the country under our consideration; the first was political, the other religious. The first essays of art are subjects of veneration in all societies; and when, as in Egypt, all change was forbidden, and a constant and inviolable respect was entertained for that which had existed be-

fore, when all its institutions tended to preserve social order as established, and to discourage and forbid all innovation, the duration of a style was doomed to become eternal. Religion, however, alone, was capable of effecting the same object, and of restraining within certain bounds the imitative faculty, by the preservation of types and primitive conventional signs for the hieroglyphic language, which, from the sacred purposes for which it was employed, soon acquired an authority from which no individual would dare to deviate by an improvement of the forms under which it had appeared. Plato observes, that no change took place in painting among the Egyptians; but that it was the same, neither better nor worse, than it had been ages before his time. Σκοπων δ' ευρησεις αυτοθι τα μυριοστον ετος γεγραμμενα, η τετυπωμενα (ουχ ως επος ειπειν μυριοστον, αλλ' οντως) των νυν δεδημιουργημενων ουτε τι καλλιονα, ουτ' αισχιω, την αυτην δε τεχνην απειργασμενα. — *De Legibus*, lib. ii.

69. Uniformity of plan characterises all their works; they never deviated from the right line and square. " Les Egyptiens," observes M. Caylus " ne nous ont laissé aucun monument public dont l'elevation ait été circulaire." The uniformity of their elevations is still more striking. Neither division of parts, contrast, nor effect is visible. All this necessarily resulted from the political and religious institutions whereof we have been speaking.

70. II. In analysing the architecture of Egypt, three points offer themselves for consideration, — construction, form, and decoration. In construction, if solidity be a merit, no nation has equalled them. Notwithstanding the continued effect of time upon the edifices of the country, they still seem calculated for a duration equally long as that of the globe itself. The materials employed upon them were well adapted to insure a defiance of all that age could effect against them. The most abundant material is what the ancients called the Thebaic granite. Large quarries of it were seated near the Nile in Upper Egypt, between the first cataract and the town of Assouan. now Syene. The whole of the country to the east, the islands, and the bed of the Nile itself, are of this red granite, whereof were formed the obelisks, colossal statues, and columns of their temples. Blocks of dimensions surprisingly large were obtained from these quarries. Basalt, marble, freestone, and alabaster were found beyond all limit compared with the purposes for which they were wanted.

71. We have already observed, that Egypt was deficient in timber, and especially that sort proper for building. There are some forests of palm trees on the Lybian side, near Dendera (Tentyris); but the soil is little suited to the growth of timber. Next in quantity to the palm is the acacia; the olive is rare. With the exception of the palm tree, there is none suited for architectural use. The oak is not to be found; and that, as well as the fir which the present inhabitants use, is imported from Arabia. Diodorus says, that the early inhabitants used canes and reeds interwoven and plastered with mud for their huts; but he confines this practice to the country away from towns, in which, from fragments that have been found, we may infer that brick was the material in most common use.

72. Bricks dried in the sun were employed even on large monuments; but it is probable that these were originally faced either with stone or granite. The pyramids described by Pocock, called Ktoube el Meuschich, are composed of bricks, some of which are $13\frac{1}{2}$ in. long, $6\frac{1}{2}$ in. wide, and 4 in. thick; others 15 in. long, 7 in. wide, and $4\frac{1}{2}$ in. thick. They are not united by cement, but in some instances cements of a bituminous nature were employed and in others a mortar composed of lime or plaster and sand, of which it would seem that this second was exceedingly powerful as well as durable.

73. The Egyptians arrived at the highest degree of skill in quarrying and working stone, as well as in afterwards giving it the most perfect polish. In their masonry they placed no reliance on the use of cramps, but rather on the nice adjustment of the stones to one another, on the avoidance of all false bearings, and the nice balance of all overhanging weight. Of their mechanical skill the reader will form some idea by reference to volume iii. p. 328. of Wilkinson's *Manners and Customs of the Ancient Egyptians*, from a representation in a grotto at El Bersheh. A colossus on a sledge is therein pulled along by 172 men, but none of the mechanical powers seem to be called in to their assistance. " The obelisks," says Mr. Wilkinson, " transported from the quarries of Syene to Thebes and Heliopolis, vary in size from 70 to 93 ft. in length. They are of one single stone; and the largest in Egypt, which is that at the great temple at Karnak, I calculate to weigh about 297 tons. This was brought about 138 miles from the quarry to where it now stands; and those taken to Heliopolis passed over a space of 800 miles." Two colossi (one of them is the vocal Memnon), each of a single block 47 ft. in height, and containing 11,500 cubic feet, are carved from stone not known within several days' journey of the place; and at the Memnonium is a colossal statue, which, when entire, weighed 887 tons. We consider, however, the raising of the obelisks a far greater test of mechanical skill than the transport of these prodigious weights; but into the mode they adopted we have no insight from any representations yet discovered. We can scarcely suppose that in the handling of the weights whereof we have spoken, they were unassisted by the mechanical powers, although, as we have observed, no representations to warrant the conjecture have been brought to light.

74. In the construction of the pyramids it is manifest they would serve as their own scaffolds. The oldest monuments of Egypt of which we below give a view, and a section of that of the largest, called of Cheops (*fig. 45.*), are the pyramids at Gizeh, to the north of Memphis. Mr. Wilkinson supposes them to have been erected by Suphis and Jeusuphis his brother, 2120 years B. C., that is, previous by nearly 400 years to the entrance of Joseph into Egypt; but the same author admits that, previous to the reign of Osirtasen, 1740 B. C., there is nothing to guide us with certainty as respects dates. The edifices (*fig. 46.*), however, more commonly known by the names of Cheops, Cephrenes, and Mycerinus, are extraordinary for their size and the consequent

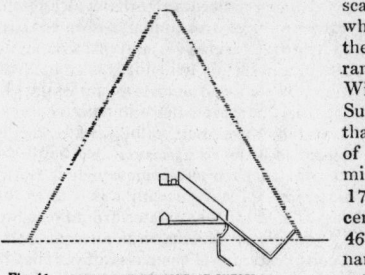

Fig. 45.   SECTION OF PYRAMID OF CHEOPS.

labour bestowed upon them; but as works of the art they are of no further importance than being a link in the chain of its history. They are constructed of stone from the neighbouring mountains, and are in steps, of which in the largest there are two hundred and eight, varying in height from $2\frac{1}{2}$ ft. (French) to 4 ft., decreasing in height as they rise towards the summit. Their width diminishes in the same proportion, so that a line drawn from the base to the summit touches the edge of each step. So great a

Fig. 46.   PYRAMIDS OF GIZEH.

difference in the measures by different authors appears, that we here subjoin those of the pyramid of Cheops: —

Authors.	Length of base.	No. of steps.	Height.	Authors.	Length of base.	No. of steps.	Height.
Herodotus -	- 800 Gr. ft.	-	- 852 Eng. ft.	Thevenot -	- 727 Eng. ft.	208	554 Eng. ft.
Strabo -	- 600 —	-	- 666 —	Niebuhr -	- 757 —	-	- 469 —
Diodorus -	- 700 —	-	- 639 —	Chazelles -	- 751 —	-	- 498 —
Sandys -	- 300 paces			Maillet -	-	-	208
Bellonius -	- 324 —			Pocock -	-	-	212
Greaves -	- 693 Eng. ft.	207	499 —	Belon -	-	-	250
Le Bruyn -	- 750 —	-	656 —	French Engineers	-	-	- 477 —
Prosper Alpinus -	799 —	-	666 —				

Mr Perring, a recent traveller, in respect of the proportions of the great pyramid, has endeavoured to prove that the unit of Egyptian measurement is an ell equal to 1·713 English feet, and that it is expressed a certain number of times without remainder in a correct measurement of the pyramids of Gizeh. Thus, he says, the perpendicular height of the great pyramid is exactly 280 of such ells, the base 448; and that $\frac{1}{2}$ base : perpendicular height :: slant height : base. Upon the top thereof is a platform 32 ft. square, consisting of nine large stones, each about a ton in weight, though inferior in that respect to others in the edifice, which vary from 5 ft. to 30 ft. in length, and from 3 ft. to 4 ft. in height. From this platform Dr. Clarke saw the pyramids of Saccara to the south, and on the east of them smaller monuments of the same kind nearer to the Nile. He remarked, moreover, an appearance of ruins which might be traced the whole way from the pyramids of Gizeh to those of Saccara, as if the whole had once constituted one great city. The stones of the platform are soft limestone, a little harder and more compact than what in England is called *clunch*. The

Fig. 47.   ENTRANCE TO THE SECOND PYRAMID.

pyramids are built with common mortar externally, but no appearance of mortar can be discerned in the more perfect parts of the masonry. The faces of the pyramid are directed to the four cardinal points. The entrance is in the north front, and the passage to the central chamber is shown on the preceding section. That in the pyramid of Cephrenes (*fig. 47.*) is thus described by Belzoni: — The first passage is built of granite, the rest are cut out of the natural sandstone rock which rises above the level of the basis of the pyramid. This passage is 104 ft. long, 4 ft. high, and 3 ft. 6 in. wide; descending at an angle of 26 degrees: at the bottom is a portcullis, beyond which is a horizontal passage

of the same height as the first, and at the distance of 22 ft. it descends in a different direction, leading to some passages below.   Hence it re-ascends towards the centre of the pyramid by a gallery 84 ft. long, 6 ft. high, and 3 ft. 6 in. wide, leading to a chamber also cut out of the solid rock.   The chamber is 46 ft. in length, 16 feet wide, and 23 ft. 6. in. in height, and contained a sarcophagus of granite 8 ft. long, 3 ft. 6. in. wide, and 2 ft. 3 in. deep in the inside.   Returning from the chamber to the bottom of the gallery a passage descends at an angle of 26 degrees to the extent of 48 ft. 6 in., when it takes a horizontal direction for a length of 55 ft. ; it then again ascends at the same angle and proceeds to the base of the pyramid, where another entrance is formed from the outside.   About the middle of the horizontal passage there is a descent into another chamber, which is 32 ft. long, 10 ft. wide, and 8 ft. 6 in. high.   The dimensions of this pyramid, as given by Denon, are a base of 655 ft. and a height of 398 ft.   Those of the pyramid of Mycerinus are a base of 280 ft., and a height of 162 ft.   The pyramids of Saccara, which are as many as twenty in number, vary in form, dimensions, and construction.   They extend five miles to the north and south of the village of Saccara.   Some of them are rounded at the top, and resemble hillocks cased with stone.   One is constructed with steps like that of Cheops.   They are six in number, each 25 ft. high, and 11 ft. wide   The height of one in the group is 150 ft. Another, built also in steps, is supposed to be as high as that of Cheops.   The stones whereof they are composed are much decayed, and more crumbling than those of Gizeh ; hence they are considered older.   One of them is formed of unburnt bricks, containing shells, gravel, and chopped straw, and is in a very mouldering state.   About 300 paces from the

second pyramid stands the extraordinary gigantic statue of the Sphinx (*fig.* 48.), whose length from the fore-part to the tail has been found to be 125 ft.   Belzoni cleared away the sand, and found a temple held between the legs and another in one of its paws. According to Denon, the antiquity of the Egyptian temples may be comparatively determined from their size ; the larger ones being posterior to the smaller.   Since, however, the wonderful insight we have obtained into the meaning of the hieroglyphics, more accurate information than we before possessed may be gained on that point by reference to Mr. (now Sir Gardiner) Wilkinson's works on Egypt and

Fig. 48.   THE SPHINX.

Thebes.   A spirit of simplicity, grandeur, and solidity reigns through the whole of them, and every precaution seems to have been taken to render them eternal.   The walls by which they are enclosed are found sometimes 26 ft. in thickness, and those of the entrance gate of a temple at Thebes are as much as 53 ft. thick at their base, and are composed of blocks of enormous size.   The masonry employed is that called by the Greeks emplectum (εμπλεκτον), all filling in of an inferior or rubble work being discarded.   They are masses of nicely squared and fitted stones, and are built externally with a slope like the walls of a modern fortification.   The columns are absolutely necessary for the support of the ceilings, which consist of large blocks of stone, and are therefore of few diameters in height.   Sometimes they are in a single piece, as at Thebes and Tentyris.   The stones of which the ceilings are composed are usually, according to Pococke, 14 ft. long, and $5\frac{1}{2}$ ft. in breadth, but some run much larger.

75.   Before adverting to the form and disposition of the Egyptian temple, we think it here necessary to notice the recent discovery of an arch in a tomb at Saccara, said to be of the time of Psammeticus II., and of one also at Thebes in the remains of a crude brick pyramid.   (See *Wilkinson's Customs of the Ancient Egyptians*, vol. iii. p. 263. 321.)   That exhibited in the tomb of Saccara, from the vignette given, is clearly nothing but a lining of the rock, and is, if truly represented in the plate, incapable of bearing weight, which is the office of an arch.   That, however, at Thebes, to which Mr. W. assigns the date of 1500 B.C., with every respect for his great information on the subject, and with much deference to his judgment, not having ourselves seen it, we cannot easily believe to be of such antiquity.   Its appearance is so truly Roman, that we must be permitted to doubt the truth of his conjecture.   We are, moreover, fortified in the opinion we entertain by the principles on which the style of Egyptian architecture is founded, which are totally at variance with the use of the arch.   We have ventured to transfer this (*fig.* 49.) to our pages, that the reader may form a judgment on the subject, as well as ourselves.   We will only add, that the reasons assigned by Mr. W. for the Egyptians not preferring such a mode of construction as the arch, because of the difficulty of repairing it when injured, and the consequences attending the decay of a single block, are not of any weight with us, because, practically, there is an easy mode of accomplishing such repair.   And, again, the argument that the superincumbent weight applied to an arch in such a case as that before

us will not hold good, inasmuch as the balance on the back of each course would almost preserve the opening without any arch at all.

Fig. 49.   ARCH AT THEBES.

76. The form and disposition of the Egyptian temple seem to have been founded on immutable rules. The only points wherein they differ from one another are in the number of their subdivisions and their extent, as the city for which they served was more or less rich. Unlike the temples of the Greeks and Romans, whose parts were governed by the adoption of one of the orders, and whose whole, taken in at a single glance, could be measured from any one of its parts, those of Egypt were an assemblage of porticoes, courts, vestibules, galleries, apartments, communicating with each other, and surrounded with walls. Strabo, in his 17th book, thus describes the temples in question. " At the entrance of the consecrated spot the ground is paved to the width of 100 ft. (πλεθρον) or less, and in length three or four times its width, and in some places even more. This is called the court (δρομος, course); thus Callimachus uses the words —

’Ο δρομος ιερος ουτος Ανουϐιδος.

Throughout the whole length beyond this on each side of the width are placed sphinxes of stone, 20 cubits or more distant from one another, one row being on the right, and the other on the left. Beyond the sphinxes is a great vestibule (προπυλον), then a further one, and beyond this another. The number, however, of the sphinxes, as of the vestibules, is not always the same, but varies according to the length and breadth of the course. Beyond the vestibules (προπυλαια) is the temple (νεως), having a very large porch (προναος), which is worthy to be recorded. The chapel (σηκος) is small, and without a statue; or, if there be one, it is not of human form, but that of some beast. The porch on each side has a wing (πτερα); these consist of two walls as high as the temple itself, distant from each other at the bottom a little more than the width of the foundations of the temple, then they incline towards each other, rising to the height of 50 or 60 cubits. These walls are sculptured with large figures, similar to those which are to be seen in the works of the Etruscans and ancient Greeks." This account is not at all exaggerated, as we shall immediately show by the introduction in this place of the plan, section, and elevation of the celebrated temple at Apollinopolis Magna, between Thebes and the first cataract, which, though, as we learn from the deciphering in these days, the hieroglyphics upon it are not of the time of the Pharaohs, seems admirably calculated to give the reader almost all the information necessary for understanding the subject. This will, moreover, so much more fully explain it than words, that we shall not need to do more than afterwards come to some recital of the details.

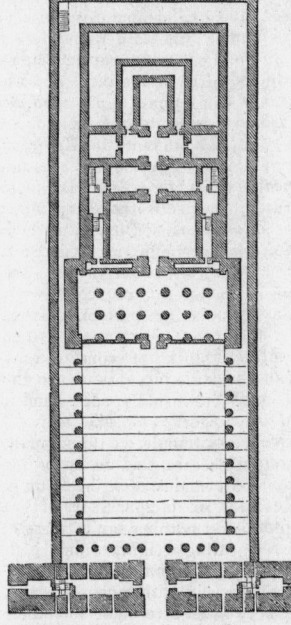

100 ft.

Fig. 50. PLAN OF TEMPLE AT APOLLINOPOLIS MAGNA.

77. This edifice, seated near Edfou, about twenty miles south of Thebes, is one of the largest in Egypt, and is comparatively in good preservation. Its form is rectangular, and its general dimensions 450ft. by 140ft. (fig. 50.) In the centre of one of the short sides is the entrance, which consists of two buildings, each 100 ft. long, and 32 ft. in width; both pyramidal in form, and lying in the same direction, but separated by a passage 20 ft. in width, with a doorway at each extremity. This passage conducts us to a quadrangle 140 ft. long, and 120 ft. wide, flanked by twelve columns on each side, and eight more on the entrance side, all standing a few feet within the walls, and thus forming a colonnade round three sides covered by a flat roof. A view of a portion of it is given in fig. 54. At the further end of the quadrangle (which rises by corded steps) opposite to the entrance, is a portico extending the whole breadth of the quadrangle, and 45 ft. in depth. It has three ranks of columns, containing six in each rank, is covered by a flat roof, and is enclosed by walls on three sides, the fourth, or that opposite the entrance,

being open. This is, however, closed breast high by a species of pedestals half inserted in the columns, and in the central intercolumniation a doorway is constructed with piers, over which are a lintel and cornice cut through. From this portico a doorway leads to an inner vestibule, in which are three ranks of four columns each, smaller than those first described, but distributed in the same way. Beyond this, in Cousin's plan, are sundry apartments, with staircases and passages, whereof the smaller central one was

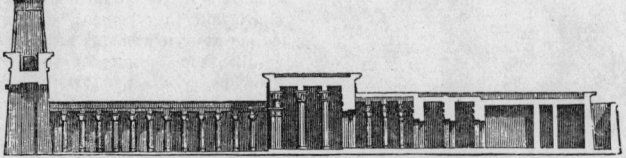

Fig. 51.   LONGITUDINAL SECTION OF TEMPLE AT APOLLONOPOLIS.

doubtless the cell. *Fig. 51.* is a longitudinal section. *Fig. 52.* is the elevation. We

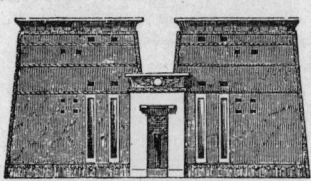

Fig. 52.   ELEVATION.   Fig. 53.   VIEW OF THE TEMPLE.

may here add, that there is so little difference between the earlier and later specimens of Egyptian architecture, that though, as we have hinted, this is of the latter, it

Fig. 54.   VIEW OF THE INTERIOR.

will convey a pretty correct knowledge of all. The general appearance of the temple is given in *fig.*
53., and a view of the interior in
fig. 54. The plan of the Egyptian
temple is always uniform, symmetrical, and rectangular. Its most
brilliant feature is the great number of columns employed, in which
is displayed a prodigality unap-
proached by any other nation. This,
however, was induced by the necessity for employing blocks of stone
for the ceilings or roofs. The
greatest irregularity occurring in any
of the plans known, is in that at the
island of Philæ (see *fig. 55.*), and it
is very evident that the cause was the shape of the ground on which it is placed. The intercolumniations were very small,
rarely exceeding a diameter, or one
diameter and a half of the column.
We know of no specimens of peripteral temples similar to those of
Greece, that is, those in which
the cell is surrounded by columns.
In the elevations of those of Egypt,
the spirit and character of their
architecture is more particularly

Fig. 55.   TEMPLE OF PHILÆ.

developed. But they are monotonous. The repetition of the same forms is carried to
the utmost pitch of tolerance. The pyramidal form prevails in all the combinations, whether
in walls, doors, general masses, or details. In considering the principal parts of the elevations, the first feature that presents itself is the column, which we will notice without its
attendant base and capital. If it were possible to establish a system relative to their invention and subsequent perfection, we might easily arrange them in distinct classes, principally as
respects their decoration ; but as far as regards general form, the Egyptian column may be
reduced to two varieties, the circular and polygonal. The first are of two sorts. Some
are found quite plain or smooth, but ornamented with hieroglyphics (see *fig. 56.*). Some

are composed with ranges of horizontal circles, and look like an assemblage of bundles of rods tied together at intervals The only difference among those columns which are circular and plain is in their having hieroglyphics, or not. Of the second sort there are many varieties, of which we here present three specimens (*fig.* 57.). They have the appearance of being bound together by hoops, like barrels. These are usually in three rows with four or five divisions in each ; but these arrangements seem to have been subject to no certain laws. The species of columns in question is certainly curious, and appears based upon the imitation of stems of trees bound together, so as out of a number to form one strong post. It seems scarcely possible that they could have had their origin in mere whim or caprice. Many polygonal columns are to be found in Egypt. Some square specimens are to be seen in the grottos at Thebes cut out of the rock itself. Similar examples occur at the entrance of the sanctuary of a temple in the same city. Hexagonal ones are described by Norden, and Pocock mentions one of a form triangular on the plan. We do not at present remember any fluted specimen, except in the tombs of Beni-Hassan, of which a representation will be given in the section on Grecian architecture. Their character is shortness and thickness. They vary from three to eleven feet in diameter, the last dimension being the largest diameter that Pocock observed, as in height the tallest was forty feet. Such were some of those he measured at Carnac and Luxor, but this he gives only as an approximation from the circumstance of so much of them being buried in the earth.

Fig. 56.   COLUMNS.

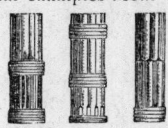

Fig. 57.   SHAFTS.

78. Pilasters, properly so called, are not found in Egyptian architecture. The base of the column, when it appears, is extremely simple in its form. Among the representations in Denon's work is one in which the base is in the shape of an inverted ogee. It belongs to a column of one of the buildings at Tentyris.

79. In their capitals, the Egyptians exhibited great variety of form. They may, however, be reduced to three species, — the square, the vase-formed, and the swelled. The first (*fig.* 58.) is nothing more than a simple abacus, merely placed on the top of the shaft of the column, to which it is not joined by the intervention of any moulding. This abacus is, however, sometimes high enough to admit of a head being sculptured thereon, as in the annexed block. It does not appear, as in Grecian architecture, that in that of Egypt differently proportioned and formed columns had different capitals assigned to them. The notion of imparting expression to architecture by a choice of forms of different nature, and more or less complicated according to the character of an order, was unknown in Egypt. It was an architectural language which the people knew not. The vase-shaped capital (*fig.* 59.) is variously modified : sometimes it occurs quite plain ; in other cases it is

Fig. 58.   CAPITAL.

differently decorated, of which we here give two examples. It certainly has all the appearance of having afforded the first hint for the bell of the Corinthian capital. The third or swelled capital is also found in many varieties ; but if the form be not founded on that of the bud of a tree, we scarcely know wherein its original type is to be sought. Two examples of it are here appended.

Fig. 59.   VASE AND OTHER SHAPED CAPITALS.

80. The entablature, for such (however unlike it be to the same thing in the architecture of Greece) we suppose we must call the massive loading placed on the walls and columns of ancient Egypt, is very little subdivided. The upper part of it, which we may call the cornice, projects considerably, having a large concave member, in some cases consisting of ornaments representing a series of reeds parallel to each other from top to bottom ; in other cases in

Fig. 60.   ENTABLATURE.

groups of three or six in a group, the intervals between them being sculptured with winged globes, as on the portico of the temple at Tentyris, given in *fig.* 60. Sculptures of animals, winged globes, and scarabæi, are the almost constant decorations placed on what may be called the architrave of the Egyptian temple. Of the winged globe, usually found on the centre of it, as also of the great concave cornice, *fig.* 61. is a representation.

Fig. 61.   WINGED GLOBE.

We close our observations on the cornices of the Egyptian temple by requesting the reader, if he have the smallest doubt on the common origin of the archi-

tectures of Egypt and Persepolis, to refer to *fig.* 26., where he will find a precisely similar use of the great cavetto which crowned the buildings of both countries.   The writer who, in the *Description Abrégée des Monumens de la Haute Egypt*, has found that this great curve is borrowed from the bending leaves of the palm tree, has mistaken the elements of decoration for substantial constructive art, and has forgotten that the first object follows long after the latter.   But we doubt if he really meant what his words import.   The ceilings of Egypt are invariably monotonous.   The non-use of the arch, whereon we have touched in a preceding page, and the blocks of stone which the country afforded, allowed little scope for display of varied form.   In the colonnades of the country, architraves of stone rest on the columns (see *fig.* 54.), on which transversely are placed those which actually form the ceilings, just like the floor boards of a modern economical English building.   On them are often found some of the most interesting representations that are in existence : we allude to those of the zodiacal constellations disposed circularly about the centre of the apartments in which they are placed.   Though nothing has been deduced from these to satisfy us on the date of their continent buildings, they are not the less worthy of further investigation, which, however, it is not our province here to pursue.

81. The gates and portals of the Egyptian temples were either placed, as at Carnac and Luxor (*figs.* 62. and 63.), in masses of masonry, or between columns, as already noticed, inclined upwards, having generally a reed moulding round them, and the whole crowned with a large cavetto.   They were plentifully covered with hieroglyphics ; frequently fronted by a pair of obelisks ; and on their sides were placed staircases of very simple construction, leading to platforms on their summits.   It is now difficult to account for the extraordinary labour bestowed on these masses of masonry.   More than pictorial effect must have been the motive.   The reader will, by turning back to *fig.* 52., be equally surprised with ourselves when he contemplates, in the gateway at the Temple of Apollinopolis Magna, such

vast efforts developed on so apparently minor a point.   The masses in these are always pyramidal, and bear great resemblance to the gates of modern fortifications.   Sometimes they are extremely simple, and do not rise so high as the adjacent buildings which flank them.   Their thickness is enormous, some of them extending to the extraordinary depth of fifty feet.

82. Windows were not frequently used.   When they occur they are long small parallelograms, rarely ornamented, but splayed inside.   Many of the apartments were without windows at all.

83. We have, in a previous page, alluded to the Pyramids ; to which we here add, that, whatever might have been their purpose, it is certain that the form adopted in them — one

that, among other people, was devoted to the purposes of sepulture—was of all architectural forms that calculated to ensure durability, and was, moreover, well suited to the views of a nation which took extraordinary means to preserve the body after life, and expended large sums on their tombs.

84. ORNAMENT or DECORATION may be considered under two heads, — that which consists in objects foreign to the forms of the edifices themselves, such as statues, obelisks, &c. ; and that which is actually affixed to them, such as the carving on the friezes, basreliefs, &c.

85. The former of these are remarkable for the size and beauty of the materials whereof they are composed.   First for notice are their statues of colossal dimensions, which are mostly, if not always, in a sitting attitude.   The two here given (*fig.* 64.) are from the Memnonium.

They are generally isolated, and placed on simple pedestals. The use of Caryatides, as

Fig. 64.   COLOSSAL STATUES FROM THE MEMNONIUM.

they are called, perhaps improperly, in Egyptian architecture, if we may judge from remains, does not appear to have been very frequent. In the tomb of Osymandyas, we find, according to Diodorus, that there was a peristylium, 400 feet square, supported by animals 16 cubits high, each in one stone, instead of columns. The same author (vol. i. f. 56. ed. Wesseling), speaking of Psammeticus, says, "Having now obtained the whole kingdom, he built a propylæum, on the east side of the temple, to the God at Memphis; which temple he encircled with a wall; and in this propylæum, instead of columns, substituted colossal statues 12 cubits in height." Statues of sphinxes in allies or avenues were used for ornamenting the dromos of their temples. Of this species of ornament the ruins of Thebes present a magnificent example. They were placed on plinths facing one another, and about ten feet apart. Examples of lions also occur. The form of the Egyptian obelisks is too well known to need a description here. They have been alleged to be monuments consecrated to the sun. From the situation they often occupy, it is clear they were used neither as gnomons nor solar quadrants.

Fig. 65.   PRESENTATION TO OSIRIS.

86. Amongst the ornaments affixed to their buildings, or rather forming a part of them, the most frequent are hieroglyphics and bas-reliefs. The custom of cutting the former upon almost every building was, as we now find, for the purpose of record; but it is nevertheless to be considered as ornamental in effect. The figures that are sculptured on the walls of the temples are mostly in low relief, and are destitute of proportion; and, when in groups, are devoid of sentiment. Painting was another mode of decoration. The grottoes of the Thebaid, and other subterranean apartments, abound with pictures, not only of hieroglyphics, but of other subjects. But the taste of all these, either in drawing, colouring, or composition, is not better than that of their sculpture. (See an example in *fig. 65.*) Yet in both these arts, from the precision with which they are cut and the uniformity of line and proportion they exhibit, a certain effect is produced which is not altogether displeasing.

87. The nymphæa lotus, or water lily, seems to have been the type of much of the ornament used for the purpose of decoration. The leaf of the palm tree was another object of imitation, and is constantly found in the capitals of their columns. The use of the palm leaf in this situation may have been derived from a popular notion mentioned by Plutarch, (*Symposiac.* lib. vi. cap. 4.), that the palm tree rose under any weight that was placed upon it, and even in proportion to the degree of depression it experienced. This supposed peculiarity is also mentioned by Aulus Gellius (lib. iii. cap. 6.). The reed of the Nile, with its head, enters into some combinations of ornament, and moreover fashioned into bundles, seems to have been the type of some of the species of their columns. In their entablatures and elsewhere, animals of all sorts occasionally find a place as ornaments, even down to fishes, which occur in a frieze at Assouan; and, as we have before observed, there are few buildings of importance in which the winged globe does not appear as an ornament.

88. Some observations on the taste, style, and character of Egyptian architecture, will conclude this section. If the type was, as we imagine, derived from the early subterranean edifices of the people, whose customs allowed of no change or improvement, we cannot be surprised at the great monotony that exists in all their monuments. The absence of variety in their profiles, by means of projecting and re-entering parts, of the use of the arch, of the inclined roof, and of all deviation from those shades of different developments, which impart character to a work of art, generated the monotony, the subject of our complaint. It cannot be denied that in those arts which have nature for their model, the artists of Egypt never sought excellence in true representation. Now architecture is so allied to the other arts, that the principles by which they were guided in these latter were carried through in

the former. It was impossible that the abstract imitation of nature, which constitutes almost the essence of architecture, which is founded upon the most refined observations of the impressions of different objects on our senses, which indicates numberless experiments and successive trials, and which therefore requires the independence of the artist, could be developed in a country where the restrictions of religion and the spirit of routine became the dominant genius of all the arts. In positive imitation, whose existence and principles have been already traced from grottoes and hollowed subterranean apartments, the types of Egyptian architecture were unsusceptible of variety, and very remote from that which characterises invention. The monotony thence resulting was attended by another effect, — that of endeavouring to correct it by a profusion of hieroglyphics. As to the other ornaments employed, they seem to have flowed from caprice, both in selection and employment, resting on no fixed principles of necessity or fitness, nor subject to any laws but those of chance. The original forms, indeed, of Egyptian architecture, unfounded, like those of Greece, on a construction with timber, would not suggest the use of ornament. Nothing seemed fixed, nothing determined by natural types. We must, however, except some of their columns, which do appear to have been formed with some regard to imitation.

89. In the architecture of Egypt we find great want of proportion, or that suitable ratio which the different parts of a body should bear to each other and to the whole. In all organised beings, their parts so correspond, that, if the size of a single part be known, the whole is known. Nature has thus formed them for the sake of dependence on and aid to each other. In works of art, the nearer we approach a similar formation, the more refined and elegant will be its productions. Solidity is abused in the works of the Egyptians ; the means employed always seem greater than were necessary. This discovers another cause of their monotony. The masses of material which the country produced measured their efforts and conceptions, and their invention was exhausted by a very restricted number of combinations. Their monuments are doubtless admirable for their grandeur and solidity ; but the preponderance of the latter, when carried beyond certain bounds, becomes clumsiness ; art then disappears, and character becomes caricature. Though we think it useful thus to analyse Egyptian art, it must not be supposed that we are insensible to its imposing, and often picturesque, effect. It can never be revived, and our observations upon it must be understood as in comparison with Greek art, which has proved so susceptible of modification that it is not likely to be abandoned in any part of the world where civilisation has appeared.

90. Though the private dwellings of the Egyptians were not comparable with their public edifices, they were not altogether devoid of splendour. Examples of them from sculptures may be seen in Mr. Wilkinson's work above quoted. In the towns they of course varied in size and plan. The streets were narrow and laid out with regularity ; and the mixture, as frequently met with in eastern towns, of large houses with low hovels, appears to have been avoided. In Thebes, the number of stories were, according to Diodorus, in some cases as much as four and five. Houses of small size were usually connected together, rarely exceeding two stories. They were regular in plan, the rooms usually occupying three sides of a court-yard, separated by a wall from the street ; or on each side of a long passage from a similar entrance court. The court was sometimes common to several houses. Large mansions were detached, having often *different entrances on their several sides*, with portals very similar in form to those of their temples. These portals were about 12 or 15 ft. high, and on each side was a smaller door. Entering through the porch, the passage was into an open court wherein was a receiving room for visitors, and this was supported by columns, and closed in the lower part by intercolumnal panels. On the opposite side of the court was another door, by which the receiving room was entered from the interior. Three doors led from this court to another of larger dimensions, ornamented with trees, communicating on the right and left with the interior parts of the building, and having a back entrance. The arrangement of the interior was the same on each side of the court ; six or more chambers, whose doors faced each other, opened on a corridor supported by columns on the right and left of the area, which was shaded by a double row of trees. A sitting room was placed at the upper end of one of these areas, opposite the door leading to the great court ; and over this and the chambers were the apartments of the upper story. On each side of the sitting-room was a door opening on to the street. Of course there were houses on other plans, which are given by Wilkinson ; but the above conveys a sufficient idea of their general distribution. On the tops of the houses were terraces, serving as well for repose as exercise. The walls and ceilings were richly painted, and the latter were formed into compartments with appropriate borders. Some of their villas were on a very large scale, and were laid out with spacious gardens, watered by canals communicating with the Nile.

91. We close this section with a list of the principal ancient edifices of Egypt (for which we are indebted to the work of Mr. Wilkinson), whose situations are marked on the accompanying map (*fig.* 66.). At Heliopolis (*modern name Matarieh*) (No. 1.), a little to the north of Cairo, the obelisk of Osirtasen I., and the remains of walls and houses. Near

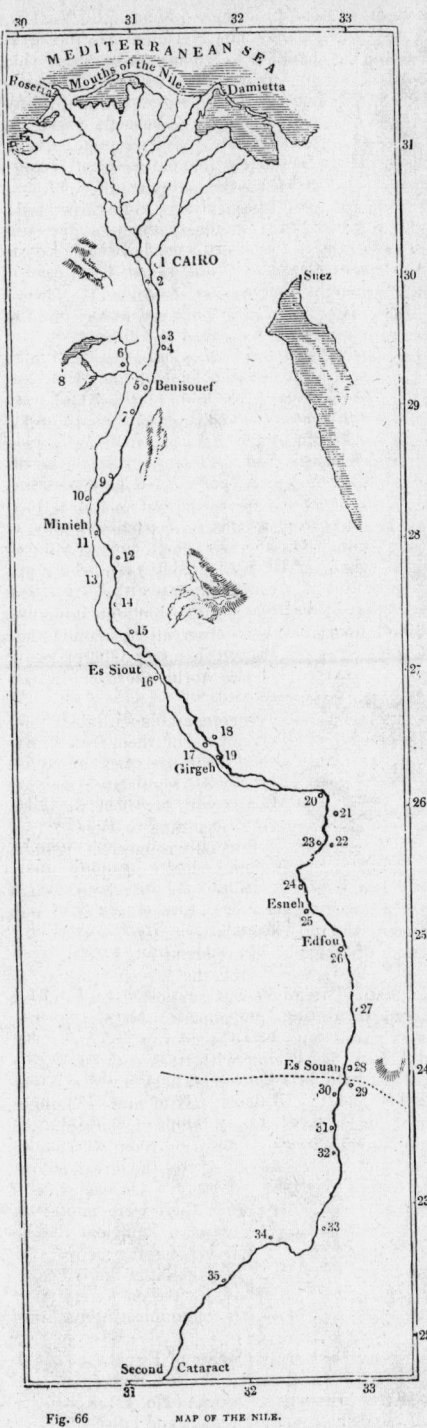

Fig. 66   MAP OF THE NILE.

Cairo, to the south-west, pyramids of
Geezeh (No. 2.), Saccara, and Dashoor.
At Mitraheni (No. 3.), a colossus of
Remeses II. ; the mounds of Memphis,
fragments of statues, and remains of
buildings.   About thirty-eight miles
above Cairo, on the east bank (No. 4.),
are the mounds of Aphroditopolis; and
on the opposite bank a false pyramid.
Three miles further, on the east bank,
the walls of an ancient village called
El Heebec (No. 5.), with some hieroglyphics.   At Benisooef a road leads to
the Fyoom; a brick pyramid at Illa-
houn (No. 6.), another at El Hawara,
and traces of the Labyrinth. An obelisk
at Biggig (No. 7.); ruins near Lake
Mocris and at Kasr Keroun (No. 8.).
From Abou Girgeh (No. 9.), on the
west bank, a road to Oxyrinchery (Bah-
nasa) (No. 10.), where are mounds but
no ruins.   At Gabel e' Tayr, a rock
temple.   Eight miles below Minieh
(No. 11.) is Acoris (Tehneh), on the
east bank, where is a Greek Ptolemaic
inscription on the cliff, tombs in the rock
with inscriptions on the doors, hieroglyphic tablets, &c.   On the east bank,
seven miles above Minieh, Kom Ahmar,
where are the ruins of an old town and
some grottoes.   Nine miles further up
are the grottoes of Beni Hassan (No. 12.);
and about a mile and a half further on
a grotto or rock temple of Bubastis or
Diana.   Antinoe (Shekh Abádeh), west
bank, few traces of the town, a theatre,
principal streets, baths, &c.   Outside the
town, the hippodrome.   At El Bersheh,
a grotto, wherein is a colossus on a
sledge.   Hermopolis, on the west bank
(Oshmounayn) (No. 13.), no remains of
it.   At Gebel Toona are mummy pits,
a tablet of hieroglyphics, and statues in
high relief.   At Shekh Said (No. 14.)
the mountains recede to the eastward,
leaving the river; a little beyond is the
village of Tel eb Amarma, to the north
of which are the remains of a small
town, and to the south the ruins of a
city, which Mr. W. supposes to have
been the Alabastron.   To the east are
grottoes with sculptures; and on the
summit of the mountain an ancient
alabaster quarry.   At El Hargib (No.
15.), the ruins of an old town.   At
E' Sioot (No. 16.) (the ancient Lyco-
polis) are grottoes.   At Gow (Antæo-
polis), a few stones of the temple close
to the river.   At Shekh Heredee, small
grottoes; and a Roman statue at the
base of the mountain cut out of a piece
of the rock.   West of Soohag (No. 17.)
is the old town of Athribis, where is a
Greek inscription in the ruined temple,
and grottoes in the mountain.   On the
east side of the river, opposite, is
E'Khmim (No. 18.) (Parcopolis, Greek

inscription of Temple of Pan, and remains of other stone buildings.   Mensheeh (No. 19.)

Fig. 67   TEMPLE AT TENTYRIS.

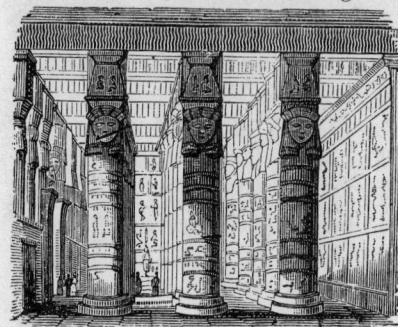

Fig. 68.   INTERIOR OF TEMPLE AT TENTYRIS.

(Ptolemais Hermii), on the west bank, from whence three hours' ride to Abydus (now Arabat el Matfoon), where are two temples and many tombs.   Hou (Diospolis parva), a few remains of Ptolemaic times.   Dendera (No. 20.) (ancient Tentyris) has two temples (*figs.* 67. and 68.), inscriptions, zodiac, &c.   At Qoft (Coptos), ruins of the old town and of a temple; and at the village of El Qala, to the north, a small Roman Egyptian temple.   Qoos (No. 21.) (Apollinopolis parva) no ruins.   At Thebes (No. 22.) (Diospolis magna), on the east bank, Karnac and Lugsor; on the west, tombs of the kings, private tombs, several temples, colossi of the plain, &c.   At Erment (No. 23.) (Hermonthis), west bank, a temple and early Christian church.   At Tofnees and Asfoon (No. 24.) mounds of ancient towns, but no ruins.   Esneh (*fig.* 69.) (Latopolis) (No. 25.) possesses a fine portico, zodiac and quay; sixteen miles from whence is a small stone pyramid.   On the east bank, four miles beyond, is El Kab (Eilethyas), where are ruins of a very ancient town; the temples lately destroyed; grottoes in the mountain;

Fig. 69.   PORTICO AT ESNEH.

and a short distance up the valley three small temples.   Edfu (No. 26.) (Apollinopolis magna) has two temples; and eleven miles above it are the remains of an old town.   At Komombo (No. 27.) (Ombos) are two temples, and an ancient stone gateway in a crude brick wall on the east side of the inclosure of the temples.   At E' Sooan (No. 28.) (Syene), ruins of a small Roman temple, some columns, granite quarries, in one of which is a broken obelisk.   Island of Elephanta, opposite the rocks of E' Sooan, is the Nilometer, with Greek incriptions relating to the rise of the Nile.   A granite gateway bearing the name of Alexander, son of Alexander the Great.   At Philæ (No. 29.) temples and ruins.   On the Island of Biggeh, opposite Philæ to the west, ruined temple, tablets, &c.

92. In Nubia, temples at Dabode (No. 30.) (Paremboli) and Kababshee (No. 31.) (Talmis); to the north of the last a small but interesting temple, called Bayt el Wellea, cut in the rock, and of the time of Remeses II.   A temple at Dandoor (No. 32.), and one cut in the rock, of the time of Remeses II., at Gerf Hossayn (Tutzis).   At Sabooa (No. 33.), a temple of the time of Remeses II., with an avenue of sphinxes, the adytum cut in the rock, the rest built.   At Assaia (No. 34.) or Amada, a temple of Thothmes ancient; and nearly opposite, on the east bank, is Dayr, where is a temple cut in the rock of the date of Remeses II.   At Ypsambool (No. 35.) (*figs.* 70. and 71.), two fine temples

Fig 70.   TEMPLE AT YPSAMBOOL.

Fig. 71.   TEMPLE AT YPSAMBOOL.

cut in the rock of the time of Remeses II., and the finest out of Thebes. Above the last-named place there are no buildings of importance mentioned by our author.

Sect. VIII.

CHINESE ARCHITECTURE.

93. In the first chapter, the reader will remember, we have said that in the tent is to be found the type of this architecture ; and one which, M. de Paw justly observes, cannot be mistaken. We are not aware of the utility of a very minute investigation of its style, which in this country is of no further importance than attaches to the silly decoration of gardens with imitations of its productions ; but as the object of this work would not be fully attained without some account of it, we propose to consider it, firstly, with respect to its principles, character, and taste ; secondly, with respect to its buildings, their parts, and the method of construction adopted in them.

94. (1.) To judge of the arts of a people, we ought to be acquainted with the people themselves, the constitution of their minds, their power, their habits, and the connection of the arts with their wants and pleasures. As one man differs from another, so do these differ among nations. The desire of improving on what has been done before us, no less distinguishes nations than individuals from each other. Whatever may be the cause, this faculty does not seem to be possessed by the Chinese. Unlike their Indian neighbours, amongst whom appears an exuberance of invention, the arts of imitation in China have been bound in the chains of mechanical skill. Their painters are rather naturalists than artists ; and an European, engaged on the foreground of a landscape, tells us that the criticism by a native artist on his work was confined to the observation that he had omitted some fibres and sinkings in some of the leaves of the foliage employed in it. The political and moral subjection of the people seems to have doomed them to remain in that confined circle wherein long habit and repugnance to change have enclosed them.

95. In speaking of the principles of Chinese architecture, the word is used in application to those primitive causes which gave birth to it, and which, in every species of architecture, are the elements of its character and the taste it exhibits. The imitation of the tent, as we have before observed, is the true origin of their buildings ; and this agrees with our knowledge of the primitive state of the Chinese, who, like all the Tartar tribes, were nomadic. On this is founded the singular construction of their dwellings, which would stand were the walls destroyed ; inasmuch as, independent of them, their roofs rest upon timber framing, just as though they had surrounded tents with enclosures of masonry. Indeed, from the accounts of travellers, a Chinese city looks like a large permanent encampment, as well in respect of its roofs as its extent. If, again, we recur to their concave sloped sides, we can arrive at no other conclusion ; and though the carpentry of which they are raised has for ages been subjected to these forms, when we consider the natural march of human invention, especially in cases of necessity, we cannot believe that, in a country where the primitive construction was of timber, the coverings of dwellings would at once have been so simple and so light. Their framing seems as though prepared merely for a canvas covering. Again, we have, if more were wanting, another proof, in the posts employed for the support of their roofs. On them we find resting nothing analogous to the architecture for receiving and supporting the upper timbers of the carpentry ; on the contrary, the roof projects over and beyond the posts or columns, whose upper extremities are hidden by the eaves; thus superseding the use of a capital. A canvas covering requires but a slender support : hence lightness is a leading feature in the edifices of China. The system of carpentry (if such it can be called) thus induced, will be noticed under the second head ; but we must here observe, that lightness is not at all incompatible with essential solidity of construction ; and whilst other materials than those which formed tents have been substituted for them, the forms of the original type have been preserved, making this lightness the more singular, inasmuch as the slightest analogy between those of the original and the copy is imperceptible. This change of material prevents in the copy the appearance of solidity, and seems a defect in the style, unless we recur to the type.

96. A characteristic quality of Chinese architecture is gaiety of effect. Their coloured roofs, compared by their poets to the rainbow, — their porticoes, diapered with variegated tints, — the varnish lavished on their buildings, — the keeping of this species of decoration with the light forms of the buildings, — all these unite in producing, to eyes accustomed to contemplate them, a species of pleasure which they would with difficulty relinquish ; and it seems reasonable that the architecture of Europe must appear cold and monotonous to men whose pleasure in the arts is more dependent on their senses than on their judgment.

97. Taste in art is a quality of vague signification, except amongst those whose lives are

passed in its practice; neither is this the place to say, upon that subject, more than that, in the application of ornament or decoration to architecture, it must depend on the method of construction. This is not found in that whereof we are writing. With the Chinese, the art of ornamenting a building is an application of capricious finery and patchwork, in which grotesque representations of subjects connected with their mythology often prevail: yet, in this respect, they exhibit a fertility of invention, and produce beautiful abstract combinations quite in character with the general forms. Indeed, the parts of their architecture are in harmony with each other. All is based upon natural principles, and is so adapted to the few and simple wants of a nation whose enormous population alone seems to render it independent of every other people, that no period can be assigned to the future duration of an architecture which, we apprehend, has existed amongst them from the earliest date of their dwelling in cities.

98. (2.) Timber is the chief material in use among the Chinese; and that of which the country produces the principal is the *nan-mon*, which, according to some, is a species of cedar; others have placed it among the firs. It is a straight thick tree, and improves with age. De Paw says that it furnishes sticks from twelve to thirteen feet high, of useful wood; but Chambers limits it to a smaller size. Respecting its beauty and duration, all travellers agree. Davis (*Description of the Empire of China*) says that the nan-mo is a description of cedar, which resists insects and lime, and appears to be exclusively used for imperial dwellings and temples. It was an article of impeachment against the minister of Kien-loong, that he had presumed to use this wood in the construction of his private palace. According to Du Halde, the iron-wood, *the-ly-mow*, is as tall as the oaks of Europe, but is less in its trunk, and differs from it in colour, which is darker, and in weight. The author does not tell us whether it is employed for columns. The tse-laù, also called mo-wàng, or king of woods, resembles what we call rosewood; but its use is confined chiefly to articles of furniture. The tchou-tse, or bamboo, grows to a great height in China. Though hollow, it is very hard, and capable of bearing great weight. It is employed for scaffolding and sheds of all kinds; and the frame-work of their matted houses for theatrical exhibitions is carried up with bamboos in a few hours. It is in universal use. The missionaries inform us that brick has been in use with the nation from the earliest period, and of both species, — burnt and merely dried in the sun. Chambers describes the walls of the houses built of this material as generally eighteen inches thick. He says, the workmen bring up the foundations for three or four courses in solid work; after which, as the walls rise, the bricks are used in the alternate courses as *headers* and *stretchers* on the two faces of them; so that the headers meet, and thus occupy the whole thickness, leaving a void space between the stretchers: they then carry up another course of stretchers, *breaking* the vertical joints. Stone and marble are little employed; not on account of their scarcity, for they are abundant, nor on the score of economy, for they are acquainted with the method of working them, as is proved from their use in public buildings and tombs. Neither can it arise from the difficulty or want of acquaintance with the means of transport; for we find in their gardens immense blocks introduced for the purposes of ornament; and in their marble staircases, the steps, whatever the length, are always in a single piece. The fear of earthquakes, moreover, does not appear to have been a motive for their rejection. That is rather to be found in the climate, which, especially in the southern parts, would, from the great heat and moisture, tend to render their houses unwholesome. In the scaffolding they use for the erection of their buildings, security and simplicity are the principal features; not, however, unmixed with skill. It consists of long poles, so inclined as to make the ascent easy, and is executed without any transverse bearing pieces.

99. The police of architecture among the Chinese is, to an European, a singular feature in its practice; and we cannot refrain from presenting to the reader the curious restrictions imposed upon every class in their several dwellings. Police, indeed, may be said to govern the arts of China. Its laws detail the magnitude and arrangement permitted for the *lon*, or palace of a prince of the first, second, or third degree; for a noble of the imperial family, for a grandee of the empire, for the president of a tribunal, for a mandarin, — for, indeed, all classes. They extend, also, to the regulation of the public buildings of capitals, and other cities, according to their rank in the empire. The richest citizen, unless bearing some office in the state, is compelled to restrict the extent of his house to his exact grade in the country; and whatever form and comfort he may choose to give to the interior, the exterior of his dwelling towards the street must be in every respect consistent with these laws. According to the primitive laws on this subject, the number of courts, the height of the level of the ground floor, the length of the buildings, and the height of the roofs, were in a progressive ratio from the mere bourgeois to the emperor; and the limits of each were exactly defined. The ordinary buildings are only a single story high: the climate seems to discountenance many stories. Though Pekin is in the fortieth degree of north latitude, the police obliges the shopkeepers and manufacturers to sleep in the open air under their penthouses in the hottest part of the summer.

100. The *leon* is a building of several stories. Of this sort are almost all the small palaces

built by the emperors in their pleasure gardens.   The taste for this class of building at one period prevailed to such an extent that houses were constructed from 150 ft. to 200 ft. in height, flanked by towers extending to 300 ft.   Though the emperors have, generally, abandoned these enormous buildings, they are still occasionally erected.   Most houses of the country are so slightly built as to be incapable of bearing more than one story.   Indeed, the necessity for making the most of an area by doubling and tripling its capacity, which exists in the capitals of Europe, does not operate in China.

101. The houses of the Chinese are uniform in their appearance.   We here annex the plan and elevation of one (*figs.* 72. and 73.) ; from which it will be seen that a large portion of the area is occupied by courts, passages, and gardens.   Sir W. Chambers describes those of the merchants at Canton as being, generally, a long rectangle on the plan, two stories high, and the apartments divided on the ground floor by a wide passage, which extends through the whole length.   On the side towards the street the shops are placed, beyond which a quadrangular open vestibule leads to the private apartments, which are distributed on the right and left of the passage.   There is a salon, usually about 18 ft. or 20 ft. long, and 20 ft. wide, open towards the vestibule, or with a screen of canework to protect it from the sun and rain.   At the back are doors extending from the floor about half way to the ceiling ; the superior part being of trellis work, covered with painted gauze, which gives light to the bedroom.   The partition walls are not carried higher than the ground story, and are lined with mats to the height of three feet, above which a painted paper is used.   The pavement is of differently coloured stone, or marble squares.   The doors are generally rectangular, of wood, and varnished or painted with figures.   Sometimes the communication between apartments is in the form of an entire circle, which some have compared to the aperture of a bird-cage.   The windows are rectangular, and filled in with framework in patterns of squares, parallelograms, polygons, and circles, variously inscribed in or intersecting each other.   The railwork to the galleries is similarly ornamented.   The compartments of the windows are generally filled in with a transparent oyster shell instead of glass.   The upper floor, which occupies the whole breadth of the

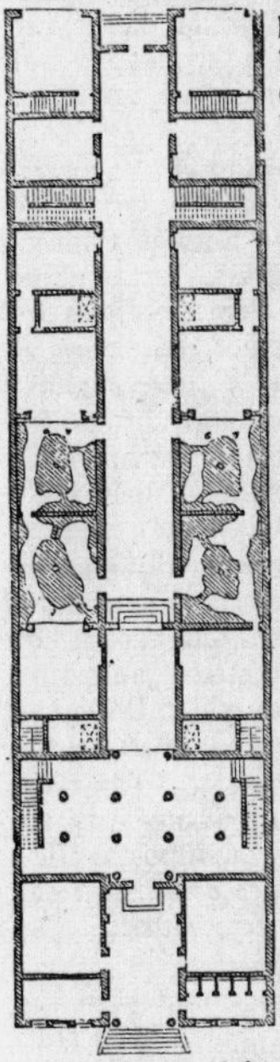

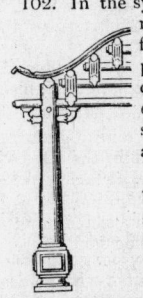

Fig. 72. GROUND PLAN.

Fig. 73.   ELEVATION OF A CHINESE HOUSE.

house, is divided into several large apartments, which are, occasionally, by means of temporary partitions, converted into rooms for visitors, apart from the family.   The sleeping rooms for the people connected with the business are over the shops.   The roof stands on wooden columns ; and its extremities, projecting beyond the walls, are usually decorated with the representation of a dragon.

102. In the system of carpentry practised by the Chinese, the columns and beams look more like the bars of a light cage than the supports and ties of a solid piece of framing, or like a collection of bamboos fastened to one another.   The accompanying diagram (*fig.* 74.) will convey our meaning to the reader.   Their columns vary in their forms and in their proportions from eight to twelve diameters in height, and are without capitals.   They are generally of wood, standing on marble or stone bases, and are occasionally polygonal as well as circular.   Some are placed on moulded bases.

103. The palaces are constructed on nearly the same plan.   Nothing, say the missionaries of Pekin, gives a more impressive idea of a palace and the greatness of its inhabitant, whether we consider its extent, symmetry, elevation, and uniformity, or whether we regard it for the splendour and magnificence of its parts, than the palace of the emperor at Pekin.   The whole, they say, produced an effect upon them for which they were not prepared.   It occupies an area of upwards of 3600 ft. from east to west, and above 3000 ft. from north to south, without including the three fore-courts.   Mr. Barrow, in his *Account of Lord Macartney's Embassy,* describes it as a vast enclosure of a rectangular form, surrounded by double walls, having between them ranges of offices, covered by roofs sloping towards the interior.   The included area is occupied by buildings not more than two stories high, and forming several quadrangular courts of various sizes, in the centres of which are buildings standing on granite platforms, 5 ft. or 6 ft. high.   These are surrounded by columns of wood, which support a projecting roof turned up at the angles.   One of these buildings, serving as a hall of audience, stands like the rest on a platform, and

Fig. 74. COLUMN AND CROSS-PIECE.

its projecting roof is supported by a double row of wooden columns, the intervals between which, in each row, are filled with brickwork to the height of 4 ft. ; the part above the wall being filled in with lattice work, covered with transparent paper. The courts are intersected by canals spanned by several marble bridges. The gateways of the quadrangles are adorned with marble columns on pedestals, decorated with dragons. The courts contain sculptured lions 7 ft. or 8 ft. high ; and at the angles of the building, surrounding each area, are square towers, two stories high, crowned with galleries. The reader will find a delineation of this extraordinary building in Cousin's work, *Du Genie de L'Architecture*, 4to, Paris, 1822, pl. 26. The peristylia of the interior buildings of the palace are built upon a platform of white marble, above which they are raised but a few steps ; but this platform is reached by three flights of marble steps, decorated with vases and other ornaments.

104. It is said that there are 10,000 *miao*, or idol temples in Pekin and its environs. Some of these are of considerable size, others are more distinguished for their beauty ; there is, however, no sufficient account of them, and we shall therefore proceed to those of Canton, which have been decribed by Chambers. He says that in this city there are a great number of temples, to which Europeans usually apply the name of *pagoda*. Some of these are small, and consist of a single chamber ; others stand in a court surrounded by corridors, at the extremity of which the *ting*, or idols, are placed. The most extensive of these pagodas is at *Ho-nang*, in the southern suburb of Conan. Its interior area is of the length of 590 ft., its width 250 ft. This area is surrounded by cells for 200 bonzes, having no light but what is obtained from the doors. The entrance to the quadrangle is by a vestibule in the middle of one of the short sides ; and at the angles are buildings 30 ft. square, in which the principal bonzes reside. In the middle of each of the long sides is a rectangular area, surrounded by cells, one containing the kitchens and refectories, and the other, hospitals for animals, and a burying ground. The great quadrangle contains three pagodas or pavilions, each 33 ft. square on the plan. They consist each of two stories, the lowest whereof is surrounded by a peristyle of twenty-four columns. The basement to each is 6 ft. high, to which there is a flight of steps on each side, and the three basements are connected by a broad wall for the purpose of communication between them, with steps descending into the court. The roofs of the peristylia are concave on the exterior ; and the angles, which are curved upwards, are decorated with animals. The sides of the upper story are formed with wooden posts, filled in with open framework. Round the foot on the exterior is a balcony with a rail in front. The roof resembles that of the peristyle, and has its angles similarly ornamented. The buildings are all covered with green varnished tiles.

105. The Chinese towers, which also Europeans call pagodas, are very common in the country. The most celebrated, whereof a diagram is presented here (*fig.* 75.), is thus

Fig. 75.　　　CHINESE TOWER, OR PAGODA.

described by P. Le Comte. Its form on the plan is octagonal, and 40 ft. in diameter ; so that each side is full 16½ ft. It is surrounded by a wall at a distance of 15 ft., bearing, at a moderate height, a roof covered with varnished tiles, which seems to rise out of the body of the tower, forming a gallery below. The tower consists of nine stories, each ornamented with a cornice of 3 ft. at the level of the windows, and each with a roof similar to that of the gallery, except that they do not project so much, not being supported by a second wall. They grow smaller as the stories rise. The wall of the ground story is 12 ft. thick, and 8½ ft. high, and is cased with porcelain, whose lustre the rain and dust have much injured in the course of three centuries. The staircase within is small and inconvenient, the risers being extremely high. Each floor is formed by transverse beams, covered with planks forming a chamber, whose ceiling is decorated with painting. The walls are hollowed for numberless niches, containing idols in bas-relief. The whole work is gilt, and seems of marble or wrought stone ; but the author thinks it of brick, which the Chinese are extremely skilful in moulding with ornaments thereon. The first story is the highest, but the rest are equal in height. " I counted," says M. Le Comte, " 190 steps, of ten full inches each, which make 158 ft. If to this we add the height of the basement, and that of the ninth story, wherein there are no steps, and the covering, we shall find that the whole exceeds a height of 200 ft. The roof is not the least of the beauties which this tower boasts. It consists of a thick mast, whose foot stands on the eighth floor, and rises thirty feet from

the outside of the building.   It appears enveloped in a large spiral band of iron, clear by several feet from the pole, on whose apex is a gilt globe of extraordinary dimensions.

106.   The word tower has been vaguely applied to all these buildings; but in China there are differences in their application, which are classed under three heads: — 1. *Tai*, or platforms for astronomical or meteorological observations, or for enjoying the air and land-scape.   2. *Hou*, such as that just described in detail, being edifices of several stories, isolated and circular, square and polygonal on the plan, built of different materials in different places. 3. *Ta*, which are sepulchral towers.   These are commonly massive, of strange but simple forms.

107.   The *Pay-leon*, or triumphal arches of the Chinese, are to be found in every city. They are erected to celebrate particular events.   Those at *Ning-po* are with a central and two smaller side openings, and are ornamented with polygonal stone columns, supporting an entablature of three or four fasciæ.   These are usually without mouldings, the last but one excepted, which is a species of frieze filled with inscriptions.   They are crowned with roofs of the usual form, having broad projections, whose angles are turned upwards. The apertures are sometimes square, and sometimes circular headed.

108.   China abounds in bridges; but Du Halde and the missionaries have made more of them in their accounts than they appear to deserve.   What they have described as a bridge of ninety-one arches between Soo-chow and Hâng-chow, was passed by Lord Macartney, and found to be nothing more than a long causeway.   Its highest arch, however, was sup-posed to be between 20 ft. and 30 ft. high, and its length about half a mile.   Some of their bridges, however, as in the case of that observed by the late Sir George Staunton (vol. ii. p. 177.), are skilfully constructed.   They have long been acquainted with the use of the arch composed of wedge-shaped voussoirs, perhaps long before it was known in Europe. Their great wall is one of their most remarkable monuments.   It consists of an earthen mound, retained on each side by walls of brick and masonry, with a terraced platform of square bricks.   Its total height is 20 ft., including a parapet of 5 ft.   The thickness at the

base is 25 ft., and it diminishes to 15 ft. at the platform.   The towers on it, at intervals of about 200 paces, are 40 ft. square at the base, diminishing to 30 ft. at the top; and their height is about 37 ft.   Some of the towers, however, are 48 ft. high, and consist of two stories.   It ex-tends from the province of Shen-Si to the Wanghay, and in a length of 1500 miles is con-ducted over mountains, valleys,

Fig. 76.   'GREAT WALL OF CHINA'

and rivers, often in places inaccessible to an enemy.   (See *fig.* 76.)

Sect. IX.

MEXICAN ARCHITECTURE.

109.   The architecture of the people who had possession of America before its discovery by Columbus has a considerable claim upon our attention.   When a people appears to have had no means of modelling their ideas through study of the existing monuments of older nations, nor of preserving any traces of the style of building practised by the race from which they originated, their works may be expected to possess some novelty in the mode of combination or in the nature of the objects combined; and, in this point of view, American architecture is not without interest.   It is, moreover, instructive in pointing out the bent of the human mind when unbiassed by example in the art.

110.   North America was found by the Spaniards advanced in agriculture and civilisation, and more especially so in the valleys of Mexico and Oaxaca.   These provinces seem to have been traversed by different migratory tribes, who left behind them traces of cultivation.   It is not our intention here to discuss the mode of the original peopling of America; but we must, in passing, observe that the vicinity of the continents of Asia and America is such as to induce us to remind the reader that one of the swarms, which we mentioned in the section on Druidical and Celtic Architecture, might have moved in a direction which ulti-mately brought them to that which, in modern times, has received the name of the New World.   The Toultecs appeared in 648, making roads, building cities, and constructing great pyramids, which are yet admired.   They knew the use of hieroglyphical paintings,

founded metals, and were able to cut the hardest stone. (*Humboldt, New Spain.*) The Aztecs appeared in 1196, and seem to have had a similar origin and language. Their works, though they attest the infancy of art, bear a striking resemblance to several monuments of the most civilised people. The rigid adherence of the people to the forms, opinions, and customs which habit had rendered familiar to them, is common to all nations under a religious and military despotism.

111. The edifices erected by the Mexicans for religious purposes were solid masses of earth of a pyramidal shape, partly faced with stone. They were called *Teocallis* (Houses of God). That of ancient Mexico, 318 ft. at the base and 121 ft. in height, consisted of five stories ; and, when seen at a distance, so truncated was the pyramid that the monument appeared an enormous cube, with small altars covered by wooden cupolas on the top. The place where these cupolas terminated was elevated 177 ft. above the base of the

edifice or the pavement of the enclosure. Hence we may observe that the Teocalli was very similar in form to the ancient monument of Babylon, called the Mausoleum of Belus. The pyramids of Teotihuacan (*fig.* 77.), which still remain in the Mexican Valley, have their faces within 52 minutes of a degree of the cardinal points of the compass. Their interior is clay, mixed with small stones. This kernel is covered with a thick wall of porous amygdaloid. Traces are perceived of a bed of lime, which externally covers the stone.

Fig. 77.　　　　PYRAMIDS OF TEOTIHUACAN.

112. The great pyramid of Cholula (*fig.* 78.), the largest and most sacred temple in

Mexico, appears, at a distance, like a natural conical hill, wooded, and crowned with a small church ; on approaching it, its pyramidal form becomes distinct, as well as the four stories whereof it consists, though they are covered with vegetation. Humboldt compares it to a square whose base is four times that of the Place Vendome

F.g. 78.　　　　GREAT PYRAMID OF CHOLULA.

at Paris covered with bricks to a height twice that of the Louvre. The height of it is 177 ft., and the length of a side of the base 1423 ft.. There is a flight of 120 steps to the platform. Subjoined is a comparative statement of the Egyptian and Mexican pyramids : —

Dimensions.	EGYPTIAN.				MEXICAN.	
	Cheops.	Cephrenes.	Mycerinus.	Saccara (of five stories).	Teotihuacan.	Cholula.
Height in feet - -	448	398	162	150	171	172
Length of base in feet	728	655	280	210	645	1355

The Cholula pyramid is constructed with unburnt bricks and clay, in alternate layers. As in other *Teocallis*, there are cavities of considerable size, intended for sepulchres. In cutting through one side of it to form the present road from Puebla to Mexico, a square chamber was discovered, built of stones, and supported by beams of cypress wood. Two skeletons were found in it and a number of curiously painted and varnished vases. Humboldt, on an examination of the ruins, observed an arrangement of the bricks for the purpose of diminishing the pressure on the roof, by the *sailing over* of the bricks horizontally. The area on the top contains 3500 square yards, and was occupied by the Temple of Quetzalcoatl, the God of Air, who has yielded his place to the Virgin. By the way, we may here mention that tumuli are found in Virginia, Canada, and Peru, in which there are galleries built of stone communicating with each other by shafts ; but these are not surmounted by temples.

113. In the northern part of the intenancy of Vera Cruz, west from the mouth of the Rio Tecolutla, two leagues distant from the great Indian village of Papantla, we meet with a pyramidal edifice of great antiquity. The pyramid of Papantla remained unknown to the first conquerors. It is seated in the middle of a thick forest, and was only discovered by some hunters about thirty-five years ago. It is constructed of immense blocks of stone laid in mortar ; but is not so remarkable for its size as for its form and the perfection of its finish, being only 80 ft. square at the base, and not quite 60 ft. high. A flight of fifty-seven

steps leads to the truncated pyramid. Like all the Mexican teocallis, it is composed of stages, six whereof are still distinguishable, and a seventh appears to be concealed by the vegetation with which its sides are covered. The facing of the stories is ornamented with hieroglyphics, in which serpents and crocodiles, carved in relievo, are discernible. Each story contains a great number of square niches symmetrically distributed. In the first story twenty-four are on each side; in the second, twenty; and in the third, sixteen. The number of these niches in the body of the pyramid is 366, and there are twelve in the stairs towards the east.

114. The military intrenchment of Xochiculco, near Tetlama, two leagues south-west of Cuernavaca, is another remarkable ancient monument. It is an insulated hill, 370 ft. high, surrounded with ditches or trenches, and divided by the hand of man into five terraces covered with masonry. The whole has the appearance of a truncated pyramid, whereof the four faces are in the cardinal points of the compass. The masonry is of porphyry, very regularly cut, and adorned with hieroglyphics; among which are to be seen a crocodile spouting up water, and men sitting cross-legged after the Asiatic fashion. On the platform, which is very large, is a small square edifice, which was most probably a temple.

115. Though the province of Oaxaca contains no monuments of ancient Aztec architecture, which astonish by their colossal dimensions, like the houses of the gods of Cholula, Papautla, and Teotihuacan, it possesses the ruins of edifices remarkable for their symmetry and the elegance of their ornaments. The antiquity of them is unknown. In the district of Oaxaca, south of Mexico, stands the palace of *Mitla*, contracted from *Mignitlan*, signifying, in Aztec, the *place of woe*. By the Tzapotec Indians the ruins are called *leoba*, or *luiva* (burial, or tomb), alluding to the excavations found beneath the walls. It is conjectured to have been a palace constructed over the tombs of the kings, for retirement, on the death of a relation. The tombs of Mitla are three edifices, placed symmetrically in a very romantic situation. That in the best preservation, and, at the same time, the principal one, is nearly 130 ft. long. A staircase, formed in a pit, leads to a subterranean apartment, 88 ft. in length, and 26 ft. in width. This, as well as the exterior part of the edifice, is decorated with fret, and other ornaments of similar character (*fig.* 79.). But the most singular

feature in these ruins, as compared with other Mexican architecture, was the discovery of six porphyry columns, placed for the support of a ceiling, in the midst of a vast hall. They are almost the only ones which have been found in the new continent, and exhibit strong marks of the infancy of the art, having neither base nor capital. The upper part slightly diminishes. Their total height is 19 ft., in single blocks of porphyry. The ceiling under which they were placed was

Fig. 79.   ORNAMENTS AT THE PALACE OF MITLA.

formed by beams of Savine wood, and three of them are still in good preservation. The roof is of very large slabs. The number of separate buildings was originally five, and they were disposed with great regularity. The gate, whereof some vestiges are still discernible, led to a court 150 ft. square, which, from the rubbish and remains of subterranean apartments, it is supposed was surrounded by four oblong edifices. That on the right is tolerably preserved, the remains of two columns being still in existence. The principal building had a terrace, raised between three and four feet above the level of the court, and serving as a base to the walls it surrounds. In the wall is a niche, with pillars, four or five feet above the level of the floor. The stone lintel, over the principal door of the hall, is in a single block, 12 ft. long and 3 ft. deep. The excavation is reached by a very wide staircase, and is in the form of a cross, supported by columns. The two portions of it, which intersect each other at right angles, are each 82 ft. long by 25 ft. wide. The inner court is surrounded by three small apartments, having no communication with the fourth, which is behind the niche. The interiors of the apartments are decorated with paintings of weapons, sacrifices, and trophies. Of windows there are no traces. Humboldt was struck with the resemblance of some of the ornaments to those on the Etruscan vases of Lower Italy. In the neighbourhood of these ruins are the remains of a large pyramid, and other buildings.

116. In the intendency of Sonora, which lies north-west of the city of Mexico, and in the Gulf of California, on the banks of the Rio Gila, are some remarkable ruins, known by the name of the *Casa Grande*. They stand in the middle of the vestiges of an ancient Aztec city. The sides are in the direction of the four cardinal points, and are 445 ft. from north

to south, and 276 ft. from east to west. The materials are unburned brick, symmetrically arranged, but unequal in size. The walls are 4 ft. in thickness. The building was of three stories. The principal edifice was surrounded by a wall with towers in it at intervals. From vestiges which appear, it is supposed the town was supplied with the water of the Rio Gila, by an artificial canal. The plain in the neighbourhood is covered with broken earthen pottery painted in white, red, and blue colours.

117. The capital of Mexico, reconstructed by the Spaniards, is undoubtedly one of the finest cities ever built by Europeans in either hemisphere. Perhaps there scarcely exists a city of the same extent which, for the uniform level of the ground on which it stands, for the regularity and breadth of the streets, and the extent of its great square, can be compared to the capital of New Spain. The architecture is pleasing. Ornament is sparingly applied to it; and the sorts of stone employed, which are a porous amygdaloid called *tetzontli*, and a porphyry of vitreous feld-spath, without any quartz, give to the Mexican buildings an air of solidity, and sometimes even of magnificence. The wooden balconies and galleries which disfigure the European cities in both the Indies are discarded. The balustrades and gates are all of Biscay iron ornamented with bronze; and the houses, instead of roofs, have terraces, like those in Italy and other southern countries. It must, however, be admitted, notwithstanding the progress of the arts there during the last thirty years, that it is less from the grandeur and beauty of the edifices, than from the breadth and straightness of the streets, and their uniform regularity and extent, that Mexico commands the admiration of Europeans.

Sect. X.

ARABIAN, MORESQUE, OR SARACENIC ARCHITECTURE.

118. Before the appearance of Mahomet, in the seventh century, and the consequent establishment of Islamism, the Arabians were by no means celebrated for their skill in architecture. The beautiful country of Happy Yemen, wherein were seated the most ancient and populous of the forty-two cities of Arabia enumerated by Abulfeda, does not appear to have produced what might have been expected from the neighbours of the Egyptians, Syrians, Chaldeans, and Persians. The arts of the surrounding nations seem to have been lost upon them. Though a part of their time and industry was devoted to the management of their cattle, still they were collected into towns, and were employed in the labours of trade and agriculture. The towers of Saana, compared by Abulfeda to Damascus, and the marvellous reservoir of Merab, were constructed by the kings of the Homerites, who, after a sway of two thousand years, became extinguished in 502. The latter, the Meriaba, mentioned by Pliny as having been destroyed by the legions of Augustus, was six miles in circumference, and had not revived in the fourteenth century. "But," says Gibbon, "the profane lustre of these was eclipsed by the prophetic glories of Medina and Mecca." Of the ancient architecture of Arabia there are so few examples remaining, that no satisfactory account can be given of it. Excavations, still seen in rocks, are said to be the houses of the people called Thamud; but the Caaba of Mecca is the only one of the seven temples in which the Arabians worshipped their idols now in existence. It is a quadrangular building, about 36 ft. long, 34 ft. broad, and about 40 ft. high. It is lighted by a door on the east side, and by a window, and the roof is supported by three octangular pillars. Since its adoption by Mahomet, it has been enclosed by the caliphs with a quadrangle, round which are porticoes and apartments for the pilgrims resorting to it. Here were the tombs of the eighty descendants of Mahomet and of his wife; but, in 1803, they were destroyed by the Wahabees, who, however, respected and spared the Caaba and its enclosures.

119. The extraordinary conquests from the Indus to the Nile, under Omar, the second caliph, who, after a reign of ten years, died in A. D. 644, brought the victorious Moslems in contact with nations then much more civilised than themselves. As their empire extended, their love for the arts and sciences increased. The first mosque built out of the limits of Arabia is supposed to be that which was founded by Omar on the site of the ancient temple at Jerusalem. Under the dynasty of the Ommiades, of which race Omar was a member, the cultivation of architecture was carried on with success. The seat of the empire was removed to Damascus, which was considerably enlarged and improved. Among its numerous splendid buildings was the celebrated mosque founded by Alwalid II. It was he who introduced the lofty *minaret*, which, though an innovation at the time, seems, in later years, to have been as necessary a portion of the mosque as the main body of it. This caliph made considerable additions to the mosque at Medina, as he also did to that which had been built by Omar on the site of the Temple of Solomon, above mentioned. His generals and governors of provinces seem to have been equally zealous in the cause of art and the prophet; witness the mosque built by one of the former on taking Samarcand, and

the universal improvement in the provinces under the sway of the latter.   Great as were the works just mentioned, the removal of the seat of the empire to the western frontier of Persia, by the second caliph of the dynasty of the Abassides, gave a lustre to Arabian architecture which almost surpasses belief.   Almansor, the brother and successor of Saffah, laid the foundations of Bagdad in the year 145 from the Héjira (A. D. 762), a city which remained the imperial seat of his posterity during a period of five hundred years.   The chosen spot is on the eastern bank of the Tigris, about fifteen miles above Modain ; the double wall was of a circular form ; " and such," says Gibbon, " was the rapid increase of a capital, now dwindled to a provincial town, that the funeral of a popular saint might be attended by eight hundred thousand men and sixty thousand women of Bagdad and the adjacent villages."   The magnificence displayed in the palace of the caliph could only be exceeded by that of the Persian kings ; but the pious and charitable foundation of cisterns and caravanseras along a measured road of seven hundred miles, has never been equalled.

120. About A. D. 660-5, the prudence of the victorious general Akbah had led him to the purpose of founding an Arabian colony in the heart of Africa ; and of forming a citadel that might secure, against the accidents of war, the wealth and families of the Saracens. With this view, under the modest title of a caravan station, he planted the colony of Cairoan, in the fiftieth year of the Héjira.   " When," observes Gibbon, " the wild beasts and serpents were extirpated, when the forest, or rather wilderness, was cleared, the vestiges of a Roman town were discovered in a sandy plain : the vegetable food of Cairoan is brought from afar ; and the scarcity of springs constrains the inhabitants to collect, in cisterns and reservoirs, a precarious supply of rain water.   These obstacles were subdued by the industry of Akbah ; he traced a circumference of three thousand and six hundred paces, which he encompassed with a brick wall ; in the space of five years the governor's palace was surrounded with a sufficient number of private habitations ; a spacious mosque was supported by five hundred columns of granite, porphyry, and Numidian marble."

121. " In the West, the Ommiades of Spain," says the same author, " supported with equal pomp the title of Commander of the Faithful.   Three miles from Cordova, in honour of his faithful Sultana, the third and greatest of the Abdalrahmans constructed the city, palace, and gardens of Zehra.   Twenty-five years, and above three millions sterling, were employed by the founder : his liberal taste invited the artists of Constantinople, the most skilful sculptors and architects of the age ; and the buildings were sustained by twelve hundred columns of Spanish and African, of Greek and Italian marble.   The hall of audience was incrusted with gold and pearls, and a great bason in the centre was surrounded with the curious and costly figures of birds and quadrupeds."   The streets and houses at this place are hollowed out of the rock, which stands 1200 feet above them.

122. Whether we contemplate the materials furnished by Babylon and its neighbourhood, the dismantled towns of Syria, or the abundant ruins of Egypt, and from Tripoli to the Atlantic, it is curious, as the historian of the western Arabs has remarked, to observe that no people constructed, without recourse to the quarry, so many magnificent edifices.   In Spain, this was most remarkably the case, whereof the reader will be convinced by reference to Murphy's *Arabian Antiquities*, and Laborde's *Voyage Pittoresque de l'Espagne.*

123. From the latter half of the eighth century to nearly the middle of the ninth, the progress of the Arabians in the sciences was wonderful.   Their merit, however, in the art which it is our province to investigate, was of a class inferior to that of the people who invented and carried into execution, though later, the principles which regulated the stupendous monuments of Gothic architecture in Europe.   They certainly understood the science of architecture ; and works on it were written for the benefit of those whose occupations led them to take an interest in the art.

124. We regret that our limits do not permit us to dwell on the progress in the sciences made by the Arabians, though some of them are intimately connected with our subject.   But the information we omit will be much more satisfactorily obtained by the reader consulting the pages of the historian of the decline and fall of the Roman Empire.   Our purpose is now to present a concise view of the architecture of the Arabians from Laborde's *Voyage Pittoresque de l'Espagne* (vol. ii. part 1. xliii. et seq.) ; observing, by the way, that, from our own study of the subject, we are inclined fully to adopt it.   In Spain there is a sufficient number of monuments of architecture to class them chronologically, and to assign an epoch to the different styles they exhibit.   Though the species does not resemble that which has been denominated Gothic, which is clearly not an imitation, the one and the other sprung from the same source.   The point of departure was the architecture of Byzantium, in which city, after the fall of Italy, a totally new style arose, whose development in different modes was the basis of all modern architecture.   As though the Coliseum had furnished the hint, the immense edifices, in the style of the period, were constructed with a multiplicity of stories, — they were heavy without, though lightly and richly decorated within ; the artists employed in their erection seeming to aim at a transference to the architecture and sculpture on which they were engaged of the oriental profusion of ornament visible in the stuffs of India.   This Byzantine school produced the Lombard and

Saxon styles in the North, on which we shall enlarge in the section on Gothic architecture; and, in the South, it produced the Arabian, Saracenic, or Moresque style, by whichever name the reader may choose to distinguish it.   Both were strongly impregnated with the vices and defects into which the Roman architecture of the period had fallen.   For the sake of illustrating what we mean, we refer, as examples, to the Baths of Dioclesian, to that emperor's palace at Salona, and to the buildings of Justinian and Theodosius, — from all which may be learned the abuses and incongruities which attended the fall, not only of architecture, but of all the other arts.   We find in them arches springing from capitals, columns without entablatures, and even zigzag ornaments.   But, with all this perversion of taste, the general form of the plans of the edifices altered not : that of the temples more particularly continued unchanged.   Some great convulsion was necessary before they could undergo alteration, and such was the introduction of Christianity.   Thus, says Saint Isidore, the basilica suffered transformation into the Christian church : — " Basilicæ olim negotiis plenæ, nunc votis pro salute susceptis."   Of this, in a succeeding page, we shall have more to say.   But the change was not confined to the basilica ; the palace and domestic dwelling equally partook of the alteration of wants.   The Romans, whilst masters of the world, were careless in protecting their cities by walls.   Defence was only necessary on their frontiers ; and there, walls and towers were constructed, from which was the first hint for the castle, of which the Roman villa, *fortified*, is the type.   When, however, Italy was invaded, the fate of war soon caused exterior decoration to be sacrificed to internal comfort and luxury ; and even Rome, under Belisarius, was surrounded by walls and towers.   The people, whose prowess made these precautions necessary, soon found the convenience of adopting similar habits and buildings.

125. The Arabians, whose wandering life could scarcely be imagined capable of such a change, ultimately established themselves in Roman castles, and turned the Christian churches, which, at the period, were extremely numerous, into mosques.   For some time, the architecture of the Goths, of the Arabians or Moors, was, as respects plan, the same ; not less so was the character of the ornaments employed by both nations ; but it was not long before these diverged into styles which possessed each its peculiar beauties.   The Christians soon used the pointed arch ; and the style they adopted became slender and tall, whilst that of the Moslems, from the nature of the climate and their peculiar habits, was deficient in elevation, though in the end it acquired a lightness and elegance which it did not at its origin possess.   But it is proper, here, to impress on the mind of the reader that Gothic and Arabian architecture have nothing in common between them, except their origin from a common source.   It is an error to confound them, or to suppose that the pointed arch is found in any strictly Arabian edifices.   That, as far as we can ascertain, did not exist before the eleventh century.   It seems to have been a development in the parts of a style which, as it passed into more northern latitudes, became more acute in the roofs, from the necessity of discharging the rain and snow with greater facility.   This pointed style spread itself over some parts of India ; but, there, none of the examples are older than the fourteenth or fifteenth century.   Except in ornamental detail, whereof we append two specimens (*figs.* 80, 81.) from the Alhambra, the Arabs were not inventive.   It is not

Fig. 80.   PAVEMENT, ALHAMBRA.

unlikely that their skill in geometry greatly assisted them in the extraordinary combination

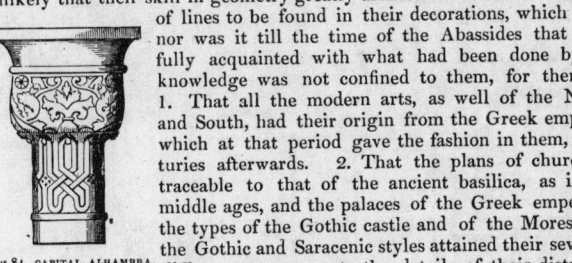

of lines to be found in their decorations, which nothing can surpass ; nor was it till the time of the Abassides that the Arabians became fully acquainted with what had been done by the Greeks. This knowledge was not confined to them, for there is abundant proof, 1. That all the modern arts, as well of the North, as of the West and South, had their origin from the Greek empire at Constantinople, which at that period gave the fashion in them, as did Italy five centuries afterwards. 2. That the plans of churches and mosques are traceable to that of the ancient basilica, as in the citadels of the middle ages, and the palaces of the Greek emperors, are to be found the types of the Gothic castle and of the Moresque alcazar. 3. That the Gothic and Saracenic styles attained their several perfection in very

Fig.81 CAPITAL, ALHAMBRA.

different manners as to the details of their distribution and ornament, and acquired peculiar characters, which in both may be divided into three periods, the last in each being lost in the change that took place in Italy on the revival of the arts. The periods of the Gothic will be noticed under the proper section.

126. The *first period* in the history of Moresque architecture is from the foundation of Islamism to the ninth century, of which the finest example was the Mosque of Cordova in Spain. This was commenced in 770 by Abderahman, and finished by his son and successor, Hisham. Its plan is a parallelogram, whose longest side is 620 ft. by 440, formed by a wall and counterforts, both of which are embattled. The height of the wall varies from 35 to 60 ft., and its thickness is 8 ft. The whole of the quadrangular space is internally divided into two parts, viz. a court of 210 ft. in depth, the mosque itself covering the remainder of the area. The mosque consists of nineteen naves (of a portion of one whereof *fig.* 82. is a

diagram) formed by seventeen ranks of columns, and a wall pierced with arches, from south to north, and thirty-two narrower ranks from east to west. Each of these naves is about 16 ft. wide from north to south, and about 400 ft. long, their width in the opposite direction being less. Thus the intersection of the naves with each other produces 850 columns, which, with fifty-two columns in the court, form a total of upwards of 900 columns. They are about 18 in. in diameter, the mean height of them is about 15 ft., and they are covered with a species of Corinthian and Composite capital, of which there are many varieties. The columns have neither socle nor base, and are connected by arches from one to another. The ceilings are of wood, painted, each range forming, on the outside, a small roof, separated from those adjoining by a gutter. The variety of the marbles of the columns

Fig. 82. MOSQUE AT CORDOVA.

produces an effect of richness which all agree is very striking. They were most probably procured from the Roman ruins of the city. It is impossible to pass over the description of this mosque without calling to mind the resemblance it bears in its arrangement to the basilicas at Rome. The reader who has seen St. Agnese and St. Paolo fuori le mura, we are sure, will think with us. After the conquest of Cordova in 1236, this mosque was converted into a cathedral. In 1528, it was much disfigured by modern erections, which were necessary for better adapting it to the service of the Christian religion. These, however, have not so far ruined its ancient effect as to prevent an idea being formed of it when in its splendour. The decorations throughout are in stucco, painted of various colours, decorated with legends, and occasionally gilt like the churches of the Lower Empire.

127. In the *second period*, the style greatly improved in elegance. It lasted till the close of the thirteenth century, just before which time was founded the royal palace and fortress of the Alhambra, at Granada (*fig.* 83.), perhaps the most perfect model of pure Arabian architecture that has existed. During this period, no traces of the Byzantine style are to be found. An exuberance of well-tempered ornament is seen in their edifices, whose distribution and luxury manifest the highest degree of refinement. Speaking of the interior of the building above mentioned, M. de Laborde says, that it exhibits " tout ce que la volupté, la grâce, l'industrie peuvent reunir de plus agréable et de plus parfait." After passing the principal entrance, you arrive at two oblong courts ; one whereof, celebrated in Arabian history, called the Court of the Lions, is in *fig.* 84. represented on the following page. This court is 100 ft. long and 50 ft. broad, having 128 columns of white marble. Round these two courts, on the ground floor, are disposed the apartments of the palace. Those for state look out towards the country ; the rest, cooler and more retired, have openings for light under the interior porticoes. The whole is on one plane, the walls being placed so as exactly to suit the plateau of the rock ; its entire length is about 2300 ft., and breadth 600 ft. The doors are few and large, and the windows, except on the side where the landscape is most magnificent, are chiefly towards the interior. In one of the apartments, the Arabian architect has, in an inscription, given his reason for this adoption, in the following terms : — " My windows admit the light, and exclude the view of external objects, lest the beauties of

nature should divert your attention from the beauties of my work." The walls are covered with arabesques, apparently cast in moulds, and afterwards joined together. The orna-

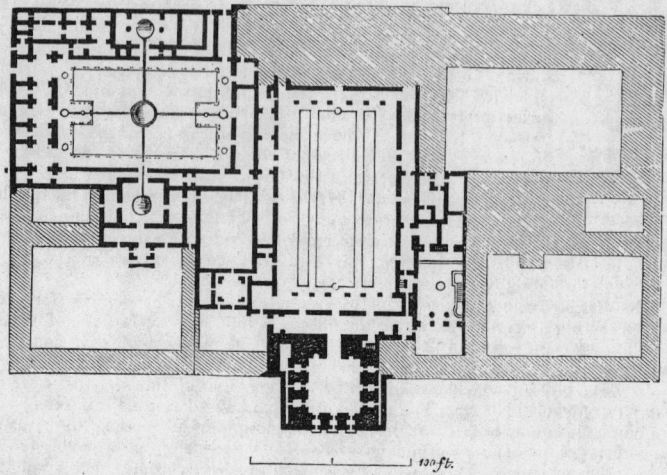

Fig. 83.   PLAN OF THE ALHAMBRA.

ments are in colours of gold, pink, light blue, and a dusky purple, the first colour being nearest the eye, and the last furthest from it; the general surface, however, is white. The

Fig. 84.   COURT OF THE LIONS, ALHAMBRA.

walls, to the height of four feet, were lined with variously figured and coloured porcelain mosaics, as were the floors. The Arabs of the Spanish caliphate appear to have known some mode of preventing the decay of paint and timber, for the paintings, in which the medium for the colour is not oil, retain the original freshness of their colours, and the woodwork of the ceilings presents no symptoms of decomposition. It has been conjectured that the soundness of the wood throughout has arisen from the trees being lanced or drained of their sap at the time of felling; but it may be, that the coating of paint has had some effect in producing the result. Description conveys no notion of this extraordinary edifice: the reader who wishes to obtain one must refer to Murphy's work, already mentioned.

128. The *third period* of Arabian architecture is from the end of the thirteenth century to the decline of the Saracen power in Spain. During a portion of this period, it was used by the Spaniards themselves, and like the Gothic, in the northern and middle parts of Europe, was engrafted on the style which crept from Italy into all countries till the Renaissance. During this period were built the castles of Benavento, Penafiel, and Tordesillas; and the alcazars of Segovia and Seville. The plans continued much the same; but Greek ornaments began to appear, with Moresque arches on Corinthian columns. At this time, also, representations of the human figure are to be seen, which, by the laws of Mahomet, were strictly forbidden. There was a charm about this architecture which makes one almost regret that reason and advance in civilisation have extinguished it.

129. We are not to look to the works of the Arabians for the real grandeur which is exhibited in the works of Egypt, Greece, or Rome. Brick was the material most used. When stone was employed, it was covered with a coating of stucco. In their constructive combinations there is nothing to surprise. The domes which crown their apartments are neither lofty nor large in diameter, neither do they exhibit extraordinary mechanical skill. The Arabian architects seem to have been unacquainted with the science of raising vaults on lofty piers. In the specimen cited at Cordova, the span, from pier to pier is less than 20 ft., which would not have required much skill to vault, yet we find the ceilings of timber. The use of orders was unknown to them; the antique columns which they introduced were employed as they found them, or imitations of them, without an acquaintance with the types from which they were derived, with their principles or proportions. In truth,

their columns are posts. We do not find, in the forms of Arabian art, that character of originality which can be traced from local causes. The Arabians had spread themselves out in every direction, far from their own country, in which they had never cultivated the arts; hence 'their architecture was founded upon the models before them, which the Byzantine school supplied. Of the forms of their arches, some whereof are here exhibited (*fig.* 85.), the most favourite seems to have been the horse-shoe form. They may be ranged into two classes, — that just named, and the other, that wherein the curve is of contrary flexure, and described from several centres. Both classes are vicious in respect of con-

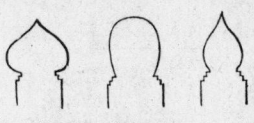

Fig. 85.   ARABIAN ARCHES.

struction, from the impossibility of gaining resistance to thrust at the abutments. In masonry, such arches could not be executed on a large scale. In brick arches, however, the surface of the cement is so increased, that if it be good, and great care be used in not removing the centres till the cement is set, great variety of form in them may be hazarded. If the pleasure — perhaps we may say sensuality— of the eye is alone to be consulted, the Arabians have surpassed all other nations in their architecture. The exquisite lines on which their decorations are based, the fantasticness of their forms, to which colour was most tastefully superadded, are highly seductive. Their works have the air of fairy enchantment, and are only to be compared to that imagination with which the oriental poetry abounds. The variety and profusion wherewith they employed ornament impart to the interior masses of their apartments the appearance of a congeries of painting, incrustation, mosaic, gilding, and foliage; and this was probably much augmented by the Mahometan law, which excluded the representation of the human figure. If a reason be unnecessary for the admission of ornament, nothing could be more satisfactory than the splendour and brilliancy that resulted from their combinations. One of their practices, that of introducing light into their apartments by means of openings in the form of stars, has a magical effect.

130. We have principally confined ourselves, in the foregoing remarks, to the architecture

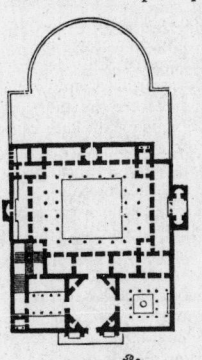

of the Arabians as it is found in Spain, which, it is proper to observe, is only a class of the edifices in the style. There is so close a resemblance between the buildings of that country and those of other places that were, till lately, under the dominion of the Moors,

Fig. 87.   ELEVATION, HOUSE AT ALGIERS.

that, allowing only for difference of climate, we might have left the subject without further illustration, but that we think the representation in *figs.* 86. and 87. of a Turkish house at Algiers, which we have extracted from Durand's *Parallèle des Edifices*, may give a better idea of Arabian architecture than a host of words.

Fig. 86. PLAN, HOUSE AT ALGIERS.

131. In *Mecca*, the city of the Prophet, the houses are of stone, and three or four stories in height. The material employed indicates solidity of construction. The streets are regular. The leading features are — the balconies covered with blinds; fronts of the houses much ornamented; doors, with steps and small seats on both sides; roofs terraced, with very high parapets, opened at intervals by a railing formed of brick, in which holes are left for the circulation of the air, at the same time giving an ornamental appearance to the front; staircases narrow and inconvenient; rooms of good dimensions and well-proportioned, having, besides the principal windows, an upper tier. *Damascus*, of which a slight view (*fig.* 88.) is annexed, has been described as resembling a large camp of conical tents, which, on a nearer approach, are found to be small cupolas to the houses. Brick, sun-dried, is the principal material, and the forms of the roofs mentioned are absolutely necessary to protect against the winter rains. Streets generally narrow, houses well supplied with fountains, and containing a large number of houses that may be ranked as palaces. Mosques, many in number, but presenting none that are very remarkable. The bazaars and baths of considerable size and splendour. In *Bagdad*, there are many large squares. The gates erected by the caliphs are still in existence, and are fine specimens of Arabian art. Its walls of mud are 25 ft. in height, but within them are ramparts, carried on arches. In *Bussorah*, the most remarkable feature is the mode in which they construct their arches, which is effected without centres.

132. We do not think it necessary to detain the reader on the architecture of Moorish or Western Arabia. As in the eastern parts of the ancient empire, the houses usually consist of a court, whereof some or all of its sides are surrounded by galleries. Narrow rooms run generally parallel with the gallery, usually without any opening but the door

opening on to the gallery. Roofs are flat or terraced. Walls variously built, often of lime, plaster, and stones, carried up in a sort of casing, which is removed when the work is set.

Fig 88   VIEW OF DAMASCUS.

From want of good timber, the rooms are narrow. The mosques are by no means worthy of notice. *Fez*, an ancient Arabian city, contains some lofty and spacious houses. Its streets are narrow, and on their first floors have projections which much interrupt the light. In the centre of each house is an open quadrangle, surrounded by a gallery, communicating with a staircase. Into this gallery the doors of the apartments open. The ceilings are lofty, the floors of brick. All the principal houses are supplied with cisterns in the lower parts, for furnishing a supply to the baths, a luxury with which also every mosque is provided. In this town there are nearly two hundred caravanseras or inns, three stories high, in each of whose apartments, varying from fifty to one hundred, water is laid on for ablution. The shops, as in Cairo, are very small; so much so, that the owner can reach all the articles he deals in without changing his posture. In *Tripoli*, the houses rarely exceed one story in height; but we must be content with observing that the character is still the same. " Nec facies omnibus una, nec diversa tamen." Though the late Sultan built a new palace in the Italian style at Constantinople, the Moslems will not easily relinquish a style inti-

Fig. 89.   ENTRANCE TO A RECEPTION ROOM OF THE SERAGLIO.

mately allied to their habits and religion, a style whereof *fig.* 89. will convey some idea to the reader. He is also referred to *figs.* 31, 32, and 33., as examples of the same style in Persia.

Sect. XI.

GRECIAN ARCHITECTURE

133 The architecture of Greece is identical with columnar architecture. Writers on the subject have so invariably treated the hut as the type on which it is formed, that, though we are not thoroughly satisfied of the theory being correct, it would be difficult to wander from the path they have trodden.   In the section on Egyptian architecture, we have alluded to the tombs at Beni-hassan, and we here present a representation of a portion of them from a sketch with which we were favoured many years since by Mr., now Sir Charles,

Fig. 90.   TOMB AT BENI-HASSAN.

Barry (*fig.* 90.).   The reader will perceive in it the appearance of the Doric column almost in its purity.   Wilkinson (*Manners and Customs of the Ancient Egyptians*) is of opinion that the date of these tombs is 1740 B. C., that is, in the time of the first Osirtasen, an antiquity which can be assigned to no example in Greece.   These tombs are excavated in a rock, a short distance from the Nile, on its right bank, about forty-eight French leagues south of Cairo. Two of them have architectural fronts like the above plate.   The columns are five diameters and a half in height.   The number of the flutes, which are shallow, is 20, and the capital consists of a simple abacus. There are no indications of a base or plinth.

Above the architrave, which is plain, there is a projecting ledge of the rock, somewhat resembling a cornice, whose soffit is sculptured, apparently in imitation of a series of reeds, laid transversely and horizontally.   There certainly does, in this, appear some reference to imitation of a hut, and the refinement of the Greeks, in after ages, may have so extended the analogy as in the end to account for all parts of the entablature.   The tradition doubtless existed long before Vitruvius wrote, who gives us nothing more than the belief of the architects of his time.   The point is not, at this time, likely to be answered satisfactorily ; if it could, it might be important, as leading to the solution of some points of detail, which limit the propriety or impropriety of certain forms in particular situations. Having thus cautioned the reader against implicit faith in the system we are about to develope, we shall preface it by the opinion, on this subject, of M. Quatremère de Quincy, an authority of great value in everything that relates to the art.   Carpentry, says that writer, is incontestably the model upon which Greek architecture is founded ; and of the three models which nature has supplied to the art, this is, beyond doubt, the finest and most perfect of all.   And again, he observes, whoever bestows his attention on the subject, will easily perceive that, by the nature of it, it includes all those parts that are effective for utility and beauty, and that the simplest wooden hut has in it the germ of the most magnificent palace.

134. We must here premise that this section is strictly confined to the architecture of Greece and its colonies.   Much confusion has arisen from the want of strict limits to the term *Grecian Architecture*, one which has been indiscriminately applied to all buildings in which the orders appear.   The orders were altered in their profiles, proportions, and details by the Romans ; and though between them and those of the Greeks there is a general resemblance, and their members are generally similar, yet, on a minute examination, great difference will be found.   In the former, for instance, the contour of every moulding is a portion of a circle ; in the latter, the contours of the mouldings are portions of conic sections.   In Roman architecture, we find the dome, which in Greek architecture never occurs.   In the latter, the arch is never seen ; in the former, it is often an important feature.   Indeed, the columnar style, as used by the Greeks, rendered arches unnecessary ; hence, in all imitation of that style, its introduction produces a discord which no skill can render agreeable to the educated eye.   Attempts have been made by the modern German architects to introduce the use of the arch with Greek forms ; but they have been all signal failures, and that because it is incapable of amalgamation with the solemn majesty and purity of Greek composition.   Before such blending can be accomplished with success, the nature of pure Greek architecture must be changed.

135. Following, then, the authors, ancient and modern, on the origin of the art, we now proceed to a development of its origin.   The first trees or posts which were fixed in the earth for supporting a cover against the elements, were the origin of the isolated columns which afterwards became the supports of porticoes in temples.   Diminishing in diameter

as they rose in height, the tree indicated the diminution of the column. No type, however, of base or pedestal is found in trees: hence the ancient Doric is without base. This practice, however, from the premature decay of wood standing immediately on the ground, caused the intervention of a step to receive it, and to protect the lower surface from the damp. Scamozzi imagines that the mouldings at the bases and capitals of columns had their origin in cinctures of iron, to prevent the splitting of the timber from the superincumbent weight. Others, however, are of opinion that the former were used merely to elevate the shafts above the dampness of the earth, and thereby prevent rot. In the capital, it seems natural that its upper surface should be increased as much as possible, in order to procure a greater area for the reception of the architrave. This member, or chief beam, whose name bespeaks its origin, was placed horizontally on the tops of the columns, being destined, in effect, to carry the covering of the entire building. Upon the architrave lay the joists of the ceiling, their height being occupied by the member which is called the frieze. In the Doric order, the ends of these joists were called triglyphs, from their being sculptured with two whole and two half glyphs or channels. These, however, in the other orders in strictly Greek architecture, do not appear in the imitation of the type, though in Roman architecture it is sometimes otherwise, as in the upper order of the Coliseum at Rome, where they are sculptured into consoles. The space between the triglyphs was, at an early period of the art, left open, as we learn from a passage in the Iphigenia of Euripides, where Pylades advises Orestes to slip through one of the metopæ, in order to gain admission into the temple. In after times, these intervals were filled up, and in the other orders they altogether disappear, the whole length of the frieze becoming one plain surface. The inclined rafters of the roof projected over the faces of the walls of the building, so as to deliver the rain clear of them. Their ends were the origin of the mutule or modillion, whereof the former had its under side inclined, as, among many other examples, in the Parthenon at Athens. The elevation, or as it is technically termed, pitch of the pediment, followed from the inclined sides of the roof, whose inclination depended on the climate (See sect. 2030). Thus authors trace from the hut the origin of the different members of architecture, which a consideration of the annexed diagram will make more intelligible to the reader. *Figs.* 91. and 92. exhibit the parts of a roof in elevation and section: a a are the architraves or

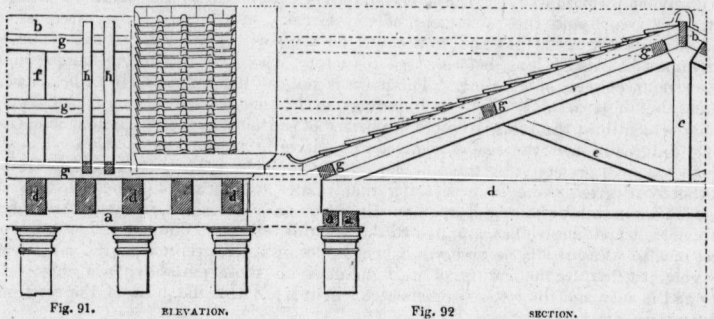

Fig. 91.   ELEVATION.   Fig. 92   SECTION.

trabes; b b the ridge piece or *columen;* c the king-post or *columna* of a roof; d d the tie-beam or *transtrum;* e the strut or *capreolus;* f f the rafters or *cantherii;* g g g g the purlines or *templa;* h h the common rafters or *asseres.* The form of the pediment became an object of so much admiration, and so essential a part of the temple, that Cicero says, if a temple were to be built in heaven, where no rain falls, it would be necessary to bestow one upon it. " Capitolii fastigium illud, et cæterarum ædium, non venustas sed necessitas ipsa fabricata est. Nam cum esset habita ratio quemadmodum ex utraque parte tecti aqua delaberetur utilitatem templi fastigii dignitas consecuta est, ut etiam si in cœlo capitolium statueretur ubi imber esse non potest, nullam sine fastigio dignitatem habiturum fuisse videatur." (*De Oratore*, lib. iii.) The inclination of the pediment will be hereafter discussed, when we speak on the article Roof, in another part of the work. Under the section on Cyclopean Architecture, mention has been made of the works at Tiryns and Mycene. We do not think there is sufficient chain of evidence to connect those ruins with the later Grecian works, though it must be confessed that the temples of Sicily, especially at Selinus, and perhaps those at Pæstum, are connecting links. Perhaps the sculptures at Selinus might be properly called Cyclopean sculpture, in its more refined state.

136. Architecture, as well as all the other arts, could only be carried to perfection by slow steps. Stone could not have been used in building until the mechanical arts had been well known. It is curious that Pliny gives the Greeks credit only for caves as their original dwellings, from which they advanced to simple huts, built of earth and clay. His words are (lib. vii. s. 57.), " Laterarias ac domos constituerunt primi Euryalus et Hyperbias

fratres Athenis : antea specus erant pro domibus." This, perhaps, is no more than a traditionary fable. Fables of this kind, however, often have some foundation in fact. We are not always inclined to discard them, for we have little more than tradition for the early excellence of the Athenians in civilisation, a nation among the Greeks who first became a body politic, and whose vanity caused them to assume the name of Αυτοχθονες, from a belief, almost sanctioned by Plato, that their ancestors actually rose from the earth. How strong the prevailing opinion was of the original superiority of the Athenians, may be gathered from Cicero, in his oration for Flaccus. "Adsunt," he says, "Athenienses, unde humanitas, doctrina, religio, fruges, jura, leges ortæ, atque in omnes terras distributæ putantur : de quorum urbis possessione, propter pulchritudinem, etiam inter deos certamen fuisse proditum est : quæ vetustate eâ est, ut ipsa ex sese suos cives genuisse dicatur." But we shall not attempt, here, an early history of Greece ; for which this is not the place, and, if accomplished, would little answer our views. The Greeks exhibited but little skill in their earliest edifices. The temple of Delphi, mentioned by Homer, in the first book of the Iliad (v. 404. et seq.), which Bryant supposes to have been originally founded by Egyptians, was, as we learn from Pausanias (*Phocic.* c. 5.), a mere hut, covered with laurel branches. Even the celebrated Areopagus was but a sorry structure, as we learn from Vitruvius (lib. ii. cap. 1.), who judged of it from its ruins. The fabulous Cadmus — for we cannot help following Jacob Bryant in his conjectures upon this personage — has been supposed to have existed about 1519 b. c., to have instructed the Greeks in the worship of the Egyptian and Phœnician deities, and to have taught them various useful arts ; but this carries us so far back, that we should be retracing our steps into Cyclopean architecture, if we were here to dwell on the period ; and we must leave the reader — as is our own, and as we apprehend will be the case with all who may succeed us — to grope his way out of the darkness as best he may.

137. The earliest writer from whom gleanings can be made to elucidate the architecture of Greece is the father of poets. To Homer we are obliged to recur, little as we approve of the architectural graphic flights in which the poet is wont generally to indulge. Though the Odyssey may not be of so high antiquity as the Iliad, it is, from internal evidence, of great age, for the poem exhibits a government strictly patriarchal, and it sufficiently proves that the chief buildings of the period were the palaces of princes. We may here, in passing, observe, that in Greece, previous to Homer and Hesiod, the sculptor's art appears to have been unknown, neither was practised the representation of Gods. The words of Athenagoras (*Leg. pro Christ.* xiv.) are — Αἱ δ'εικονες μεχρι μηπω πλαστιχη, και γραφικη, και ανδριαντοποιητικη ησαν, ουδε ενομιζοντο. The altar, which was merely a structure for sacred use, was nothing more than a hearth, whereon the victim was prepared for the meal ; and it was not till long after Homer's time that a regular priesthood appeared in Greece. In Sparta, the kings performed the office. In Egypt, the dignity was obtained by inheritance; as was the case in other places. The Odyssey places the altar in the king's palace ; and we may reasonably assume that the spot was occasionally, perhaps always, used as the temple. From such premises, it is reasonable to conjecture that until the sacerdotal was separated from the kingly office, the temple, either in Greece or elsewhere, had no existence. It may not be without interest to collect, here, the different passages in the Odyssey, which bear upon the nature and construction of the very earliest buildings of importance. Between the αυλη and the δομος there must have been a distinction. The former, from its etymology αω, must have been a *locus subdialis ;* and though it is sometimes used (*Iliad*, Z. 247.) for the whole palace, such is not generally its meaning in the Odyssey. The αυλη was the place in which the female attendants of Penelope were slain by Telemachus (*Odyss.* X. 446.), by tying them up with a rope over the ϑολος or ceiling. Hence we arrive at the conclusion that this ϑολος belonged to the αιθουσα or cloister, supposing, as we have done, that the αυλη was open at top, and the αιθουσα is described (*Iliad*, Υ. 176.) as εριδουπος, that is, sonorous or echoing, and as circumscribing the open part of the αυλη. The ϑολος was supported by κιονες, posts or columns, and in the centre of the αυλη stood the βομος or altar. If our interpretation be correct, the μεσοδμαι in this arrangement must be the spaces between the columns or posts, or the intercolumniations, as the word is usually translated; and the passage in the Odyssey (Τ. 37.), wherein Telemachus is said to have seen the light on the walls, becomes quite clear. The passage is as follows : —

Εμπης μοι τοιχοι μεγαρων, καλαι τε μεσοδμαι,
Ειλατιναι τε δοκοι, και κιονες υψοσ' εχοντες,
Φαινοντ' οφθαλμοις.

There seems no doubt that the word αιθουσα will bear the interpretation given, and the arrangement is nothing more than that of the hypæthral, and even correspondent with the Egyptian temple, particularly that of the temple at Edfou, described by Denon, and represented in his plate 34.

138. Before we quit this part of our subject, let us consider the description which Homer (*Odyss.* H. 81.) gives of the house of Alcinous as illustrative of Greek architecture. This dwelling, which Ulysses visited, had a brazen threshold, ουδος. It was υψερεφης or

lofty-roofed. The walls were brazen on every side, from the threshold to the innermost part. This, however, is rather poetic. The coping Θριγκος was of a blue colour. The interior doors are described as gold. The jambs of them, σταθμοι, were of silver on a brazen threshold. The lintel υπερθυριον was silver, and the cornice κορωνη of gold. Statues of dogs, in gold and silver, which had been curiously contrived by Vulcan himself, guarded the portal. Thus far, making all due allowance for the poet's fancy, we gain an insight into what was considered the value of art in his day, more dependent, it would seem, on material than on form. Seats seemed to have been placed round the interior part of the house, on which seats were cushions, which the women wrought. But we must return to the construction of the αυλη, inasmuch as in it we find considerable resemblance to the rectangular and columnar disposition of the comparatively more recent temple.

139. It would be a hopeless task to connect the steps that intervened between the sole use of the altar and the establishment of the temple in its perfection; though it might, did our limits permit the investigation, be more easy to find out the period when the regular temple became an indispensable appendage to the religion of the country. It is closely connected with that revolution which abolished the civil, judicial, and military offices of kings leaving the sacerdotal office to another class of persons. Though in the palace of the king no portion of it was appropriated to religious ceremony, the spot of the altar only excepted, yet, as it was the depository of the furniture and utensils requisite for the rite of sacrifice, when the palace was no more, an apartment would be wanting for them; and this, conjoined with other matters, may have suggested the use of the cell. Eusebius has conjectured that the temple originated in the reverence of the ancients for their departed relations and friends, and that they were only stately monuments in honour of heroes, from whom the world had received considerable benefit, as in the case of the temple of Pallas, at Larissa, really the sepulchre of Acrisius, and the temple of Minerva Polias at Athens, which is supposed to cover the remains of Erichthonius. The passage in Virgil (*Æn.* ii. v. 74.)-

———— tumulum antiquæ Cereris, sedemque sacratam
Venimus —

is explanatory of the practice of the ancients in this respect; and, indeed, it is well known that sacrifices, prayers, and libations were offered at almost every tomb; nay, the resting-place of the dead was an asylum or sanctuary not less sacred than was, afterwards, the temple itself. From Strabo (lib. ii.) it is clear that the temple was not always originally a structure dedicated to a god, but that it was occasionally reared in honour of other personages.

140. Before proceeding to that which is more accurately known, it may not be uninstructive to the reader to glance at the houses of the Greeks, as may be gathered from passages in the Iliad and the Odyssey. We shall merely remind him that Priam's house had fifty separate chambers, though he lived in a dwelling apart from it. These houses were, in some parts, two stories in height, though the passages supporting that assertion (*Iliad*, B. 514–16. 184.) have been pronounced of doubtful antiquity. There is, however, not the slightest doubt that the dwellings of the East consisted of more than a single story. David wept for Absalom in the chamber *over* the gate (2 *Sam.* xviii. 33.). The altars of Ahaz were on the terrace of the *upper chamber* (3 *Kings*, xxiii. 12.). The summer chamber of Eglon had *stairs* to it, for by them Ehud escaped, after he had revenged Israel (*Judges*, iii. 20.; 1 *Kings*, vi. 8.). In the Septuagint, these upper stories are all represented by the word υπερωον, the same employed by Homer. The Jewish law required (*Deut.* xxii. 8.) the terraces on the tops of their houses to be protected by a battlement; and, indeed, for want of a railing (*Odyss.* K. 552. et seq.) of this sort, Elpenor, one of the companions of Ulysses, at the palace of Circe, fell over and broke his neck. The use of the word κλιμαξ in the Odyssey, connected with the words αναβαινειν and καταβαινειν, and the substantive υπερωον, is of frequent occurrence: it is either a ladder or a staircase, and which of them is unimportant; but it clearly indicates an upper story. To a comparatively late period, the Greek temple was of timber. Even statues of the deities were, in the time of Xenophon, made in wood for the smaller temples (lib. iv. c. 1.), where the revenue of them was not adequate to afford a more expensive material. But time and accidents would scarcely permit their prolonged duration, and none survived long enough to allow of a proper description of them reaching us. The principle of their construction necessarily bore some relation to the materials employed, and the use of stone must have imparted new features to them. In timber, the beam (*epistylium*), which was borne by the columns, would probably extend in one piece through each face of the building. But in a stone construction this could not take place, even had blocks of such dimensions been procurable, and had mechanical means been at hand to place them in their proper position. From this alone follows a diminution of spaces between the columns. The arch, be it recollected, was unknown. It is curious to observe that the relative antiquity of the examples of Grecian Doric may be expressed in terms of the intercolumniations; that is, the number of diameters forming the intervals between the columns. There is, moreover, another point worthy of notice, which is, that their antiquity may be also estimated by the comparison of the heights of the columns compared with their diameters. This, however, will require

further consideration when we come to treat of the orders: here it is noticed only incidentally. Though we are not inclined to place reliance on the account given by Vitruvius of the origin of the orders of architecture, we should scarcely be justified in its omission here. It seems necessary to notice it in any work on architecture; and, after remarking that the age which that author assigns for their origin is long before Homer's time, at which there seems no probability of their existence, from the absence of all reference to them in his poems, we here subjoin the account of Vitruvius (lib. iv. c. 1.):—" Dorus, son of Hellen and the Nymph Orseis, reigned over Achaia and Peloponnesus. He built a temple of this (the Doric) order, on a spot sacred to Juno, at Argos, an ancient city. Many temples similar to it were afterwards raised in the other parts of Achaia, though, at that time, its proportions were not precisely established. When the Athenians, in a general assembly of the states of Greece, sent over into Asia, by the advice of the Delphic oracle, thirteen colonies at the same time, they appointed a governor over each, reserving the chief command for Ion, the son of Xuthus and Creusa, whom the Delphic Apollo had acknowledged as son. He led them over into Asia, where they occupied the borders of Caria, and built the great cities of Ephesus, Miletus, Myus (afterwards destroyed by inundation, and its sacred rites and suffrages transferred by the Ionians to the inhabitants of Miletus), Priene, Samos, Teos, Colophon, Chios, Erythræ, Phocæa, Clazomene, Lebedos, and Melite. This last, as a punishment for the arrogance of its citizens, was detached from the other states in the course of a war levied on it, in a general council, and in its place, as a mark of favour towards king Attalus and Arsinoe, the city of Smyrna was received into the number of the Ionian states. These received the appellation of Ionian, after the Carians and Lelegæ had been driven out, from the name of Ion, the leader. In this country, allotting different sites to sacred purposes, they erected temples, the first of which was dedicated to Apollo Panionius. It resembled that which they had seen in Achaia, and from the species having been first used in the cities of Doria, they gave it the name of Doric. As they wished to erect this temple with columns, and were not acquainted with their proportions, nor the mode in which they should be adjusted, so as to be both adapted to the reception of the superincumbent weight, and to have a beautiful effect, they measured a man's height by the length of the foot, which they found to be a sixth part thereof, and thence deduced the proportions of their columns. Thus the Doric order borrowed its proportion, strength, and beauty from the human figure. On similar principles, they afterwards built the temple of Diana; but in this, from a desire of varying the proportions, they used the female figure as a standard, making the height of the column eight times its thickness, for the purpose of giving it a more lofty effect. Under this new order, they placed a base as a shoe to the foot. They also added volutes to the capital, resembling the graceful curls of the hair, hanging therefrom, to the right and left, certain mouldings and foliage. On the shaft, channels were sunk, bearing a resemblance to the folds of a matronal garment. Thus were two orders invented; one of a masculine character, without ornament, the other of a character approaching the delicacy, decorations, and proportions of a female. The successors of these people, improving in taste, and preferring a more slender proportion, assigned seven diameters to the height of the Doric column, and eight and a half to the Ionic. That species, of which the Ionians were the inventors, has received the appellation of Ionic. The third species, which is called Corinthian, resembles, in its character, the graceful elegant appearance of a virgin, whose limbs are of a more delicate form, and whose ornaments should be unobtrusive. The following is the fabulous account of the origin of the capital of this order. (*Fig.* 93.) A Corinthian virgin who was of mar-

Fig. 93. ORIGIN OF CORINTHIAN CAPITAL.

riageable age, fell a victim to a violent disorder: after her interment, her nurse, collecting in a basket those articles to which she had shown a partiality when alive, carried them to her tomb, and placed a tile on the basket, for the longer preservation of its contents. The basket was accidentally placed on the root of an acanthus plant, which, pressed by the weight, shot forth, towards spring, its stems and large foliage, and in the course of its growth, reached the angles of the tile, and thus formed volutes at the extremities. Callimachus, who, for his great ingenuity and taste in sculpture, was called by the Athenians κατατεχνος, happening at this time to pass by the tomb, observed the basket and the delicacy of the foliage that surrounded it. Pleased with the form and novelty of the combination, he took the hint for inventing these columns, using them in the country about Corinth," &c. Now, though we regret to damage so elegant and romantic a story, we must remind those who would willingly trust the authority we have quoted, that Vitruvius speaks of matters which occurred so long before his time, that in such an investigation as that before us we must have other authentication than that of the author we quote, and most especially in the case of the Corinthian capital, whose type may be referred to in a

vast number of the examples of Egyptian capitals, one of which, among many, is seen in *fig.* 94.

Fig. 94. EGYPTIAN CAPITAL.

141. The progress of the art in Greece, whose inhabitants, in the opinion of the Egyptian priests in the time of Solon, were so ignorant of all science that they neither understood the mythology of other nations nor their own (Plato, in *Timæo*), cannot be satisfactorily followed between the period assigned to the siege of Troy and the time of Solon and Pisistratus, or about 590 B. C. But it is, however, certain that within four centuries after Homer's time, notwithstanding their originally coarse manners, the Grecians attained the highest excellence in the arts. Goguet is of opinion the nurture of the art was principally in Asia Minor, in which country, he thinks, we must seek for the origin of the Doric and Ionic orders, whilst in Greece Proper the advancement was slow. The Corinthian order was, however, the last invented, and it seems generally agreed that its invention belongs to the mother country; but this we shall not stop to discuss here. The Temple of Jupiter, at Olympia, one of the earliest temples of Greece (Pausanias, *Eliac. Pr.* c. 10.), was was built about 630 years before the Christian era; and after this period were reared temples at Samos, Priene, Ephesus, and Magnesia, and other places up to that age when, under the administration of Pericles, the architecture of Greece attained perfection, and the highest beauty whereof it is supposed to be susceptible, in the Parthenon (*fig.* 95.)

Fig. 95.   VIEW OF THE PARTHENON

at Athens. The date of the erection of the temple of Diana, at Ephesus, was really as remote as that of the temple we have just mentioned. If Livy had sufficiently our confidence, and we concede that other writers corroborate his statement (lib. i. c. 45.), its date is as ancient as the time when Servius Tullius was king of Rome. Great, however, as were the works which the Grecians executed, the mechanical powers were, if one may judge from Thucydides (lib. iv.), not then compendiously applied for raising weights.

142. The origin of the Doric order is a question not easily disposed of. Many provinces of Greece bore the name of Doria; but a name is often the least satisfactory mode of accounting for the birth of the thing which bears it. We have already attempted to account for the parts of this order by a reference to its supposed connection with the hut. The writer, in the *Encyclopedie Méthodique*, truly says that if the Doric had an *inventor*, that inventor was a people whose wants were, for a long period, similar, and with whom a style of building prevailed suitable to their habits and climate, though but slowly modified and carried to perfection. At the beginning of this section, we have, however, sufficiently spoken on this matter. But there are some peculiarities to be noticed with respect to the Doric order, which we think will be better given here than in the third book, where we propose to treat of the orders more fully; and these consist in the great differences which are found in its proportions and parts in different examples. For this purpose, several buildings have been arranged in the following table, wherein the first column exhibits the name of the building; the second the height of the column, of the example as a nume-

rator, and its lower diameter as a denominator, both in English feet; the third is the quotient of the second, showing the height of the column, expressed in terms of its lower diameter; the fourth column shows the height of the entablature in terms of the diameter of the column; the fifth column gives the distance between the columns in the same terms; and the sixth shows the height of the capitals also in the same terms : —

Example.	Height divided by lower Diameter in English Feet.	Diameters high.	Height of Entablature in Terms of Diameter.	Interco-lumniations.	Height of Capital in terms of Diameter.
Temple at Corinth - - - -	$\dfrac{23 \cdot 713}{5 \cdot 83}$ =	4·065	. .	1·362	·405
Hypæthral Temple at Pæstum - -	$\dfrac{28 \cdot 950}{7 \cdot 00}$ =	4·134	1·741	1·167	·549
Enneastyle Temple at Pæstum · -	$\dfrac{21 \cdot 000}{4 \cdot 85}$ =	4·329	1·140	1·064	·500
Greater Hexastyle Temple at Selinus -	$\dfrac{32 \cdot 678}{7 \cdot 49}$ =	4·361	2·200	1·490	·490
Temple of Minerva at Syracuse - -	$\dfrac{28 \cdot 665}{6 \cdot 50}$ =	4·410	.	. .	·486
Octastyle Hypæthral Temple at Selinus -	$\dfrac{48 \cdot 585}{10 \cdot 62}$ =	4·572	2·038	1·023	·450
Temple of Juno Lucina at Agrigentum -	$\dfrac{21 \cdot 156}{4 \cdot 59}$ =	4·605	. .	. .	·570
Temple of Concord at Agrigentum -	$\dfrac{22 \cdot 062}{4 \cdot 64}$ =	4·753	1·976	1·071	·487
Hexastyle Temple at Pæstum - -	$\dfrac{20 \cdot 353}{4 \cdot 24}$ =	4·795	1·917	1·111	·564
Temple of Jupiter Panhellenius at Egina -	$\dfrac{17 \cdot 354}{3 \cdot 22}$ =	5·395	. .	1·680	·486
Parthenon - - - - -	$\dfrac{34 \cdot 232}{6 \cdot 15}$ =	5·566	1·977	1·275	·459
Temple of Theseus at Athens - -	$\dfrac{18 \cdot 717}{3 \cdot 30}$ =	5·669	1·964	1·250	·502
Temple of Minerva at Sunium - -	$\dfrac{19 \cdot 762}{3 \cdot 34}$ =	5·899	1·928	1·472	·372
Doric Portico of Augustus at Athens -	$\dfrac{26 \cdot 206}{4 \cdot 33}$ =	6·042	1·724	1·046	·374
Temple of Apollo, Island of Delos - -	$\dfrac{18 \cdot 721}{3 \cdot 0.2}$ =	6·052	1·900	1·500	·555
Temple of Jupiter Nemeus - - -	$\dfrac{33 \cdot 932}{5 \cdot 22}$ =	6·515	1·560	1·348	·383
Portico of Philip of Macedon - -	$\dfrac{19 \cdot 330}{2 \cdot 96}$ =	6·535	1·867	2·700	·480

143. Casting our eye down the third column of the above table, we find the height of the column in terms of its lower diameter varying from 4·065 to 6·535. Lord Aberdeen (*Inquiry into the Principles of Beauty in Greek Architecture*, 1822) seems to prefer the proportion of the capital to the column, as a test for determining its comparative antiquity; but we are not, though it is entitled to great respect, of his opinion, preferring, as we do, a judgment from the height as compared with the diameter to any other criterion; although it must be admitted that it is not an infallible one. The last columns shows what an inconstant test the height of the capital exhibits. There is another combination, to which reference ought to be made, — the height of the entablature, which forms the third column of the table, in which it appears that the most massive is about one third the height of the whole order, and the lightest is about one fourth, and that these proportions coincide with the thickest and the thinnest columns.

144. The entasis or swelling, which the Greeks gave to their columns, and first verified by the observations of Mr. Allason, was a refinement introduced probably at a late period, though the mere diminution of them was adopted in the earliest times. The practice is said to have its type in the law which Nature observes in the formation of the trunks of trees. This diminution varies, in a number of examples, from one fifth to one third of the lower diameter; a mean of sixteen examples gives one fourth. The mere diminution is not, however, the matter for consideration; but the curved outline of the shaft, which is attributed to some refined perception of the Greeks,

relative to the apparent diminution of objects as their distance from the eye was increased, which Vitruvius imagines it was the object of the entasis to correct. It cannot be denied that in a merely conical shaft there is an appearance of concavity, for which it is difficult to account. The following explanation of this phenomenon, if it may be so called, is given by our esteemed and learned friend, Mr. Narrien, in the *Encyc. Metropol.* art. Architecture. " When," he observes, " we direct the axis of the eye to the middle of a tall column, the organ accommodates itself to the distance of that part of the object, in order to obtain distinctness of vision, and then the oblique pencils of light from the upper and lower parts of the column do not so accurately converge on the retina : hence arises a certain degree of obscurity, which always produces a perception of greater magnitude than would be produced by the same object if seen more distinctly. The same explanation may serve to account for the well-known fact, that the top of an undiminished pilaster appears so much broader than the body of its shaft ; to which, in this case, may be added some prejudice, caused by our more frequently contemplating other objects, as trees, which taper towards their upper extremities." Connected in some measure with the same optical deception is the rule which Vitruvius lays down (book iii. chap. 2.) for making the columns, at the angles of buildings, thicker than those in the middle by one fiftieth part of a diameter, — a law which we find followed out to a much greater extent in the temples of the Parthenon and of Theseus, at Athens, where the columns at the angles exceed in diameter the intermediate ones by one forty-fourth and one twenty-eighth respectively. Where, however, the columns were viewed against a dark ground, some artists think that a contrary deception of the eye seems to take place.

145. In the investigation of the Doric order, among its more remarkable features are to be noted the longitudinal striæ, called *flutes*, into which the column is cut ; every two whereof unite, in almost every case, in an edge. Their horizontal section varies in different examples. In some, the flutes are formed by segments of circles ; in others, the form approaches that of an ellipsis. The number all round is usually twenty ; such being the case at Athens ; but at Pæstum the exterior order of the great temple has twenty-four, the lower interior order twenty, and the upper interior sixteen only. It has been strangely imagined, by some, that these flutings, which, be it remembered, are applied to the other orders as well as to the Doric, were provided for the reception of the spears of persons visiting the temples. The conjecture is scarcely worth refutation, first, because no situation for the δουρο-δοκη (place for spears) would have led to their more continual displacement from accident ; and secondly, because of the sloping or hemispherical form in the other orders, the foot of the spear must have immediately slid off. Their origin may probably be found in the polygonal column, whose sides received a greater play of light by being hollowed out, — a refinement which would not be long unperceived by the Greeks.

146. We shall now notice some of the more important Doric edifices, as connected with the later history of the Doric order, which was that most generally used by the European states of Greece, up to their subjugation by the Romans. The temple of Jupiter Panhellenius, at Egina, is probably one of the most ancient in Greece. The story, however, of Pausanias, that it was built by Æacus, before the war of Troy, is only useful as showing us its high antiquity. (*Fig.* 96.) The proportions of its columns and entablature are to be

Fig. 96.   ELEVATION OF THE TEMPLE OF JUPITER PANHELLENIUS.

found in a preceding page. The sculpture with which this building was decorated is now at Munich. Though, perhaps, not so old as the building itself, it is of an antiquity coeval with the Persian invasion. The name of the architect of this temple was Libon, of whom no other work is known; its age is, perhaps, from about 600 years before Christ. The Doric temple at Corinth, of which five columns, with their architrave, are still in existence, is a very early specimen of Grecian architecture. The assertion that it was dedicated to Venus is unsupported by testimony.

147. The Grecian temples in Sicily were erected at periods which it is not easy to fix; and with respect to them, we can only, from circumstances connected with the island, reason on the dates to be assigned to them. The founding of the city of Selinus or Selinuns, on the south-west coast of the island, has usually been attributed to a colony from Megara; but we are of opinion with the Baron Pisani (*Memoria sulle Metope Selinuntine*) that it existed as a Phœnician city long previous to the settlement there by the Megaræans. The style and forms of the sculpture of the Selinuntine temples seem to bear marks of a remoter age than is usually allowed to them, that is, 500 years B. C. Of the means and the circumstances under which they were raised we are ignorant; but their ruins sufficiently indicate the wealth and power that were employed upon them, as well as a considerably advanced state of the art.

148. The temple of Jupiter Olympius, the largest in the island, and one of the most stupendous monuments of antiquity, was, as we learn from Diodorus (lib. xiii. p. 82.), never completed. The Agrigentines were occupied upon it when the city was taken by Hamilcar, in the 93d Olympiad. Its columns were on such a scale that their flutes were sufficiently large to receive the body of a man. The temples of Peace and of Concord, in the few vestiges that remain of them, attest the ancient magnificence of the city of Agrigentum, and are among the most beautiful as well as the best preserved remains of antiquity. A Corinthian colony established itself at Syracuse, as is said, 750 B. C.; but no details of the history of the city furnish us with the means of ascertaining when the first temples there were erected. Its riches and magnificence were, however, such that it soon became an object of temptation to the Carthaginians. Its temple of Minerva is evidently of very remote antiquity.

149. The great Hypæthral temple at Pæstum was probably constructed during the period that the city was under the power of the Sybarites, who dispossessed its original inhabitants, enjoying, for upwards of two hundred years, the fruits of their usurpation. Marks of Greek art are visible in it, and the antiquity of the Hypæthral temple itself is confirmed by the example. The city fell into the hands of the Lucanians about 350 years B. C.; after which, in about 70 years, it was a municipal town of the Roman empire. The following is perhaps the chronological order of the principal buildings of Sicily and Magna Græcia; viz. Syracuse, Pæstum, Selinus, Segesta, and Agrigentum.

150. The dates of the edifices at Athens are, without difficulty, accurately fixed. The Propylæum (*figs.* 97 and 98.) was commenced by Mnesicles about 437 B. C., and, at a great

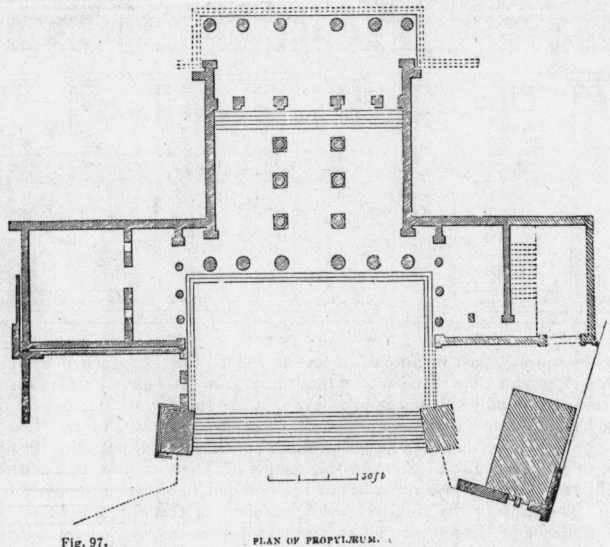

Fig. 97.   PLAN OF PROPYLÆUM.

Fig. 98.   ELEVATION OF THE PROPYLÆUM.

expense, was completed in five years.   It is a specimen of the military architecture of the
period, and at the same time forms a fine entrance to the Acropolis of Athens.   At the rear
of its Doric portico the roof of the vestibule was supported within by two rows of Ionic
columns, whose bases still remain.   By the introduction of these an increased height was
obtained for the roof, the abaci of the Ionic capitals being thus brought level with the ex-

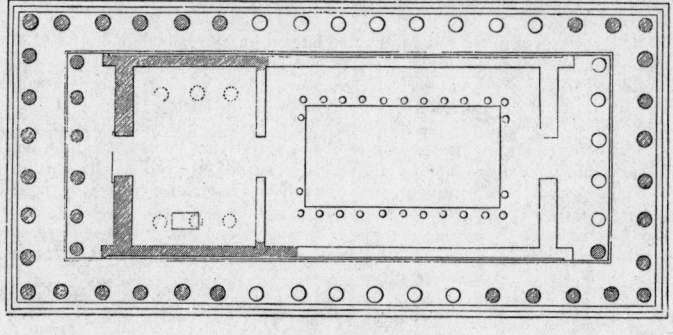

Fig 99.   PLAN OF THE PARTHENON.

terior frieze of the building.   The Parthenon (figs. 99. and 100.) erected a few years later
under the superintendence of Ictinus, is well known as one of the finest remains of antiquity.

Fig. 100.   ELEVATION OF THE PARTHENON.

As well as the building last mentioned, it was reared at the period when Pericles had the
management of public affairs, and was without a rival in Athens.   Phidias was the superintendent sculptor employed ; and many of the productions which decorated this magnificent edifice have doubtless become known to the reader in his visits to the British Museum,
where a large portion of them are now deposited.   Nearly coeval with the Propylæum and
Parthenon, or perhaps a little earlier, is the temple of Theseus (fig. 101.), which was, it
is supposed, erected to receive the ashes of the national hero, when removed from Scyros
to Athens.   The ruins of the architectural monuments of this city attest that the boasted
power and opulence of Greece was not an idle tale.   Pericles, indeed, was charged by his
enemies with having brought disgrace upon the Athenians by removing the public trea-

sures of Greece from Delos, and lavishing them in gilding their city, and ornamenting it

with statues and temples that cost a thousand talents, as a proud and vain woman tricks herself out with jewels. (*Plutarch's Life of Pericles.*) The temple of Minerva, at Sunium, was probably by Ictinus; but one of the happiest efforts of this architect was the temple of Apollo Epicurius, in Arcadia, still nearly entire. The peculiarities found in it we will shortly detail. The front has six columns, and instead of thirteen in each flank (the usual number) there are fifteen. In the interior, buttresses on each side, to the number of six, re-

Fig. 101.   TEMPLE OF THESEUS.

turn inwards from the walls of the cell, each ending in semicircular pilasters of the Ionic order. These seem to have been brought up for the facility of supporting the roof, which was of stone. With the exception of the temple of Minerva at Tegea, its reputation for beauty was such, that it surpassed, if that be a true test, all other buildings in Peloponnesus. Its situation is about three or four miles from the ruins of Phigalia, on an elevated part of Mount Cotylus, commanding a splendid landscape, which is terminated by the sea in the distance.

151. About 370 B.C., Epaminondas restored the Messenians to independence, and built the city of Messene. The ruins still extant prove that the art at that period had not materially declined. Its walls, in many parts, are entire, and exhibit a fine example of Grecian military architecture in their towers and gates. At no distant time from the age in question the portico of Philip of Macedon, at least his name is inscribed on it, shows that the Doric order had undergone a great change in its proportions. This portico must have been erected about 338 B.C., and after it the Ionic order seems to have been more favoured and cultivated. The last example of the Doric is perhaps the portico of Augustus, at Athens.

152. Before proceeding to the investigation of the Ionic order, it may here, perhaps, be as well to speak of the proportions between the length and breadth of temples, as compared with the rules given by Vitruvius (book iv. chap. 4.), that the length of a temple shall be double its breadth, and the cell itself in length one fourth part more than the breadth, including the wall in which the doors are placed. Though in the Greek examples these proportions are approximated, an exact conformity with the rule is not observed in any. The length, for instance, of the temple of Jupiter, at Selinus, is to the breadth as 2·05 to 1; in the temple of Theseus, as 2·3 to 1; and from the mean of six examples of the Doric order, selected in Greece and Sicily, is 2·21 to 1. If the flanks be regulated in length by making the number of intercolumniations exactly double those in front, it will be immediately seen that the proportions of Vitruvius are obtained on a line passing through the axes of the columns. But as in most of the Greek temples the central intercolumniation in front is wider than the rest, the length of the temple would necessarily be less than twice the width. In the earlier specimens of the Doric order the length is certainly, as above mentioned in the temple of Jupiter at Selinus, very nearly in accordance with the rule; but in order to counteract the effect of the central intercolumniation being wider, the number of columns, instead of intercolumniations on the flank, is made exactly double those in front. In the later examples, however, as in the temples of Theseus and the Parthenon, and some others, the number of intercolumniations on the flank was made double the number of columns in the front, whence the number of columns on the flanks was double the number of those in front and one more; so that the proportion became nearly in the ratio of 2·3 to 1. The simplicity which flowed from these arrangements in the Grecian temples was such that it seems little more than arithmetical architecture,—so symmetrical that from the three data, the diameter of the column, the width of the intercolumniation, and the number of columns in front, all the other parts might be found.

153. The Ionic order, at first chiefly confined to the states of Asia Minor, appears to have been coeval with the Doric order. The most ancient example of it on record is the temple of Juno, at Samos. Herodotus (*Euterpe*) says, it was one of the most stupendous edifices erected by the Greeks. In the *Ionian Antiquities* (2d edit. vol. i. c. 5.) is to be found an account of its ruins. It was erected about 540 years B.C., by Rhæcus and Theodorus, two natives of the island. The octastyle temple of Bacchus, at Teos, in whose praise Vitruvius was lavish, shows by its ruins that the old master of our art was well capable of appreciating the beauties of an edifice. Hermogenes, of Alabanda, was its architect, and he seems to have been the promoter of a great change in the taste of his day. Vitruvius

(lib. iv. c. 3.) tells us that Hermogenes, " after having prepared a large quantity of marble for a Doric temple, changed his mind, and, with the materials collected, made it of the Ionic order, in honour of Bacchus." We are bound, however, to observe upon this, that the story is not confirmed by any other writer. It is probable that this splendid building was raised after the Persian invasion; for, according to Strabo (lib. xiv.), all the sacred edifices of the Ionian cities, Ephesus excepted, were destroyed by Xerxes. Besides this octastyle temple, those of Apollo Didymæus, near Miletus, built about 376 B.C., and of Minerva Polias, at Priene, dedicated by Alexander of Macedon, are the chief temples of this order of much fame in the colonies. We shall therefore confine our remaining remarks to the three Ionic temples at Athens, and shall, as in the Doric order, subjoin a synoptical view of their detail.

Example.	Height divided by lower Diameter, in English Feet.	Diameters high.	Height of Entablature in terms of Diameter.	Interco-lumniations.	Height of Capital in terms of Diameter.	Upper Diameter, lower Diam. being 1·000.
Temple on the Ilyssus -	$\frac{14\ 694}{1\cdot783}$ =	8·241	2·265	2·090	0·610	·850
Temple of Minerva Polias -	$\frac{25\cdot387}{2\cdot786}$ =	9·119	2·287	3·500	0·700	·833
Temple of Erectheus -	$\frac{21\cdot625}{2\cdot317}$ =	9·337	. .	2·000	0·773	·816

154. We here see that the Ionic column varies in height from eight diameters and nearly a quarter to nearly nine and a half, and the upper diameter in width between $\frac{85}{100}$ and $\frac{816}{1000}$. The dissimilarity of the capitals renders it impossible to compare them. The mean height of the entablature is about a fourth of the height of the whole order. The height of the Grecian Ionic cornice may be generally considered as two-ninths of the whole entablature.

155. The age of the double temple of Minerva Polias (*fig.* 102.) and Erectheus has

Fig. 102.   TEMPLES OF MINERVA POLIAS AND ERECTHEUS.

not been accurately ascertained. From the earliest times these personages were held in high veneration by the Athenians, and it is more than likely that a confusion has arisen between the ancient and modern edifices. The former was partially destroyed by Xerxes, and there is no certainty that the latter was restored by Pericles.

156. In the bases applied to the order in the Athenian buildings there are two *tori*, with a *scotia* or *trochilus* between them, a fillet below and above the scotia separating it from the tori. The lower fillet generally coincides with a vertical line let fall from the extreme projection of the upper torus. In the temple on the Ilyssus the lower fillet projects about half the distance between the hollow of the scotia and the extremity of the inferior torus. The height of the two tori and scotia are nearly equal, and a bead is placed on the upper

torus for the reception of the shaft of the column.   The temples of Erectheus and that on the Ilyssus have the lower tori of their bases uncut, whilst the upper ones are fluted horizontally.   In that of Minerva Polias, the upper torus is sculptured with a *guilloche*.   The base just described is usually denominated the ATTIC BASE, though also used in the colonies.   The bases, however, of the temples of Minerva Polias at Priene, and of Apollo Didymæus near Miletus, are very differently formed.

157.   The VOLUTE, the great distinguishing feature of the order, varies considerably in the different examples.   In the edifices on the Ilyssus and at Priene, as well as in that of Apollo Didymæus, the volute has only one channel between the revolutions of the spiral; whilst in those of Erectheus and Minerva Polias, at Athens, each volute is furnished with two distinct spirals and channels.   In the temple on the Ilyssus, the capital is terminated a little below the eye of the volute ; in the others it reaches below the volutes, and is decorated with honeysuckle flowers and foliage.   The number of flutes, which on the plan are usually elliptical, is twenty-four, and they are separated by fillets from each other.   In some examples they descend into the apophyge of the shaft.

158.   The tomb of Theron, at Agrigentum, in which Ionic columns and capitals are crowned with a Doric entablature, has, by some, been quoted as an example of the Ionic order ; but we do not believe it to be of any antiquity, and, if it were, it is so anomalous a specimen that it would be useless to pursue any inquiry into its foundation.

159.   In the *antæ* or pilasters of this order, as well as of the Doric, their capitals differ in profile from the columns, and are never decorated with volutes.   Their breadth is usually less than a diameter of the column, and they are not diminished.

160.   The highest degree of refinement of Greek architecture is exhibited in its examples of the Corinthian order, whose distinguishing feature is its capital.   We have, in a preceding page (139), given Vitruvius's account of its origin ; but we much doubt whether Callimachus was its inventor.

161.   The capitals of Egyptian columns are so close upon the invention, that we apprehend it was only a step or two in advance of what had previously been done.   The palm leaf, lotus flower, and even volutes, had been used in similar situations in Egypt, and the contour of the lotus flower itself bears no small resemblance to the bell of the Corinthian capital.

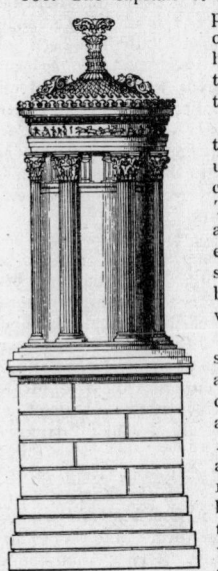

162.   We are inclined to assign the period of the latter part of the Peloponnesian war as that in which the order first came into use.   We find from Pausanias (*Arcad.* c. 45.) that Scopas, the celebrated architect of Paros, rebuilt the temple of Minerva at Tegæa, which was destroyed by fire about 400 years B.C., and that, according to that author, it was the largest and most beautiful edifice in the Peloponnesus.   The cell, which was hypæthral, was surrounded by two ranks of Doric columns, which were surmounted by others of the Corinthian order.   The peristyle of this temple was Ionic.

163.   The delicacy of formation of this order has, doubtless, subjected its examples to earlier destruction and decay than have attended the other orders : hence our knowledge of it is almost confined to the examples we meet of it in the Tower of the Winds, and the Choragic monument of Lysicrates (*fig.* 103.), both at Athens; the former whereof can scarcely be considered Corinthian, and the latter not very strictly so.   It was erected about 330 years B.C., as appears from the inscription on the frieze.   These Choragic buildings, usually of small dimensions, were erected in honour of those who, as choragi or leaders of the chorus in the musical games, were honoured with the prize, which was a tripod.   The following are the proportions observed in the Choragic monument of Lysicrates : —

Fig. 103. CHORAGIC MONUMENT OF
LYSICRATES.

Height of columns in English feet		11·637
Height of columns in terms of lower diameter		10·318
Height of capital in terms of lower diameter		1·216
Upper diameter of shaft in terms of the lower diameter		0·833
Height of the architrave in terms of the lower diameter	0·850	
Height of the frieze in terms of the lower diameter	0·483	
Height of cornice in terms of the lower diameter	0·833	
Total height of entablature in terms of the lower diameter		2·166

From which it appears that the entablature is less than a fifth of the total height of the order.   The intercolumniations are 2·200 diameters.   The base is little different from that used in the Ionic order.

164.   In the ornaments applied for the decoration of the sacred edifices of the Greeks,

they imitated the real and symbolical objects used in their worship. Thus, at the temple of Apollo at Teos, the lyre, tripod, and griffin occur; in the Temple of the Winds at Athens, the winds are personified on the walls; the Choragic monument of Lysicrates exhibits the consequences of a contempt of music; on the temple of Victory, at the entrance of the Acropolis, was recorded, on the very spot, the assault and repulsion of the Amazons; the Lapithæ are vanquished again in the temple of Theseus, the founder of the city; and lastly, in the Parthenon is brought before the eye, on a belt round the cell of the temple, the Panathenaic procession, which, issuing from the door of the cell, biennially perambulated the edifice, whilst its pediment perpetuates the contest between Neptune and Minerva for the honour of naming the city, and calls to remembrance the words of Cicero, " De quorum," (Atheniensium,) "urbis possessione, propter pulchritudinem etiam inter deos certamen fuisse proditum est," &c. In the capitals of the Corinthian examples just noticed the leaves are those of the olive, a tree sacred to the tutelary goddess of Athens, and on that account as well as its beauty of form and simplicity adopted by a people whose consistency in art has never been excelled.

165. Besides the method of supporting an entablature by means of columns, the employment of figures was adopted, as in the temples of Erectheus and Minerva Polias before mentioned (see *fig.* 102.). They were called *Caryatides;* and their origin, according to the account of it by Vitruvius (lib. i. c. 1.), was that Carya, a city of Peloponnesus, having assisted the Persians against the Grecian states, the latter, when the country was freed from their invaders, turned their arms against the Caryans, captured their city, put the males to the sword, and led the women into captivity. The architects of the time, to perpetuate the ignominy of the people, substituted statues of these women for columns in their porticoes, faithfully copying their ornaments and drapery. It is, however, certain that the origin of their application for architectural purposes is of far higher antiquity than the invasion of Greece by the Persians, and in the above account Vitruvius is not corroborated by any other writer. Herodotus (*Polymnia*), indeed, observes that some of the states whom he enumerates sent the required offering of salt and water to Xerxes; but no mention is made of Carya, whose conduct, if punished in such an extraordinary manner, would have been too curious a matter to have been passed over in silence. Whether the use of statues to perform the office of columns travelled into Greece from India or from Egypt, we will not pretend to determine. Both, however, will furnish examples of their application. In the latter country we find them employed in the tomb of King Osymandyas (*Diodorus,* tom. i. f. 56. Wesseling). Diodorus also, speaking of Psammeticus, says that having obtained the whole kingdom, he built a propylæum on the east side of the temple to the god at Memphis, which temple he encircled with a wall; and in this propylæum, instead of columns, substituted colossal statues (κολοττοὺς ὑποστήσας) twelve cubits in height.

166. The application of statues and representations of animals is a prominent feature in the architecture of Egypt, whereof the temple at Ibsambul is a striking example, though in that the figures do not absolutely carry the entablature (see *fig.* 71.). In India many instances of this use of statues occur, as in the excavations of the temple near Vellore described by Sir C. Mallet (*Asiat. Res.* vol. vi.), wherein heads of lions, elephants, and imaginary animals apparently support the roof of the cave of Jugnath Subba; and at Elephanta, where colossal statues are ranged along the sides as high as the underside of the entablature (see *fig.* 39.). But as the settlement of the claims of either of these countries to the invention is not our object, we shall proceed to consider how they obtained in Greece the name that has been applied to them long before the period of which Vitruvius speaks.

167. Καρύα, the nut tree (*Nux juglans*), which Plutarch (*Sympos.* lib. ii.) says received its name from its effect (κάρος, sopor) on the senses, was that into which Bacchus, after cohabitation with her, transformed Carya, one of the three daughters of Dion, king of Laconia, by his wife Iphitea. The other daughters, Orphe and Lyco, were turned into stones for having too closely watched their sister's intercourse with the lover. Diana, from whom the Lacedemonians learnt this story, was on that account, as well perhaps as the excellence of the fruit of the tree, therefore worshipped by them under the name of Diana Caryatis. (*Servius,* note on 8th Ecl. of Virgil, edit. Burman.) Another account, however, not at all affecting the hypothesis, is given of the name of Diana Caryatis in one of the old commentators of Statius (*Barthius,* lib. iv. v. 225.). It is as follows. Some virgins threatened with danger whilst celebrating the rites of the goddess, took refuge under the branches of a nut tree (καρυα), in honour and perpetuation whereof they raised a temple to Diana Caryatis. If this, however, be an allusion to the famous interposition of Aristomenes in protecting some Spartan virgins taken by his soldiers, it is not quite borne out by the words of Diodorus. Salmasius (*Exercit. Plinianæ,* f. 603. et seq.) says, that Diana was worshipped at Carya, near Sparta, under the name of Diana Caryatis; and that at her temple and statue the Lacedemonian virgins had an anniversary festival, with dancing, according to the custom of the country.

168. But to return more closely to the subject, we will give the words of Pausanias (*Laco-*

nics) on the temple to the goddess at Carya. " The third turning to the right leads to Carya, and the sanctuary of Diana; for the neighbourhood of Carya is sacred to that goddess and her nymphs. The statue of Diana Caryatis is in the open air; and in this place the Lacedemonian virgins celebrate an anniversary festival with the old custom of the dance." Kuhnius on the passage in question, after reference to Hesychius, says, " Caryatides etiam dicuntur Lacænæ saltantes, sinistrâ ansatæ, uti solebant Caryatides puellæ in honorem Dianæ."

169. From the circumstances above mentioned, we think it may be fairly concluded that the statues called Caryatides were originally applied to or used about the temples of Diana; and that instead of representing captives or persons in a state of ignominy, they were in fact representations of the virgins engaged in the worship of that goddess. It is probable that after their first introduction other figures, in buildings appropriated to other divinities, were gradually employed; as in the Pandroseum (attached to the temple of Minerva Polias),

for instance, where they may be representations of the virgins called Canephoræ, who assisted in the Panathenaic procession. *Fig.* 104. is a representation of one of those used in the Pandroseum (see also *fig.* 102.); and *fig.* 105. is from the Townley collection, now in the British Museum. Piranesi conjectured that this last, with others, supported the entablature of an ancient Roman building restored by him from some fragments found near the spot where they were discovered, which is rather more than a mile beyond the Capo di Bove, near Rome. Four of the statues were found; and on one of the three, purchased by Cardinal Albani, the following inscription was found: — ΚΡΙΤΩΝ ΚΑΙ ΝΙΚΟΛΑΟΣ ΕΠΟΙΟΥΝ; showing that it was the work of Greek artists.

Fig. 104.   Fig. 105.

170. The republican spirit of Greece tended to repress all appearance of luxury in their private dwellings. The people seem to have thrown all their power into the splendour and magnificence of their temples; and it was not till a late period that their houses received much attention. Except in the open courts of them, it is difficult to conceive any application of the orders. It is certain that they frequently consisted of more than one story; but beyond this all is conjecture. In the time of Demosthenes (*Orat. adv. Aristocratem*) the private houses had begun to be increased in extent; and the description of them by Vitruvius, who knew Athens well, proves that they were then erected on an extent implying vast luxury.

171. Within the last few years discoveries have been made at Athens, which would lead us to the belief that it was the practice of the Greeks to paint in party colours every portion of their temples, and that in violently contrasted colours. This has received the name of *polychrome architecture*. It is rather strange that no ancient writer has spoken of the practice, and the only way to account for the omission is by supposing it to have been so common that no one thought of mentioning it. From the information of M. Schaubert, the government architect at Athens, it appears that every part of the surface of the Parthenon had a coating of paint. That the coffers of the ceiling were painted, and its frieze ornamented with a fret in colours, was, he observes, known; but the whole building, he continues, as well as other temples, was thickly painted, in the metopæ, in the pediment, on the drapery of the figures, on the capitals, and on all the mouldings. So that, as he says with great simplicity, with its mouldings and carvings variously coloured, the simple Doric temple of Theseus was in effect richer than the most gorgeous example of Corinthian; and it would be worth the trouble to restore with accuracy a polychrome temple. From M. Quast (*Mittheilungen über Alt und Neu Athen*, Berlin, 1834), we learn that the colour was not used in a fluid state merely for the purpose of staining the marble, but in a thick coat, so that the material was completely covered; and that in the temple of Theseus this is more traceable than in any other. Though the colours, that of blue smalt more especially, have left but a grey crust, yet their original tone is still apparent. In this building deep blues and reds are the predominant colours, so as to relieve one another. The corona was deep blue, and the guttæ of a brown red; the foliage of the cymatium was alternately streaked with blue and red, the ground being green, which colour is applied to the small leaves on some of the lesser mouldings. Some of the coffers are coloured of a red inclining to purple, on which the ornament is given; others exhibit a blue ground, with red stars. The architrave of the portico was a bright red; the figures in the frieze were painted in their proper natural colours: traces of the colour show that the walls were green. It was not discovered that in the columns more than the arrises of the flutes were painted, although the echinus was. We do not doubt the accuracy of MM. Semper and Quast; but after all it is possible that all this painting may have been executed at a period much later than that of the buildings themselves.

172. The most ancient theatres of Greece were constructed in a temporary manner; but the little security from accident they afforded to a large concourse of persons soon made the Greeks more cautious for their security, and led to edifices of stone, which, in the end, ex-

ceeded in magnitude all their other buildings. Their form on the plan (see *fig.* 106.) was rather more than a semicircle, and consisted of two parts; the σκηνὴ, *scena*, and κοιλον,

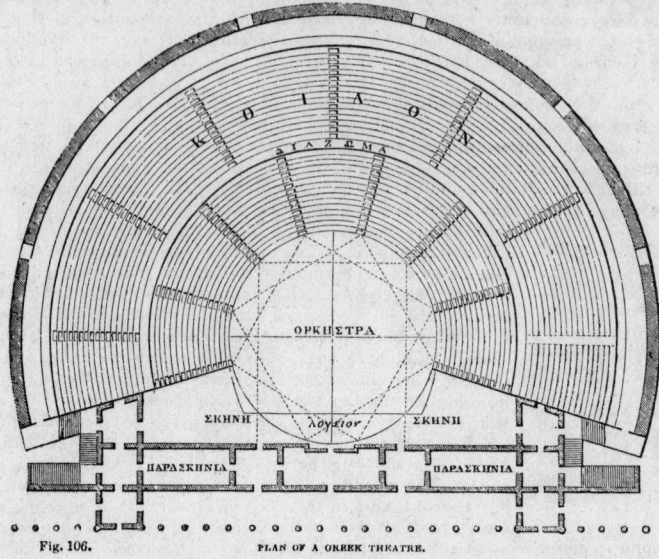

Fig. 106.   PLAN OF A GREEK THEATRE.

cavea. The scena was at first merely a partition for the actors reaching quite across the stage, dressed with boughs and leaves, but in after times was very differently and more expensively constructed. It had three principal gates, two on the sides and one in the centre; at which last the principal characters entered. The whole scene was divided into several parts, whereof the most remarkable were—the βροντεῖον, *brontæum*, under the floor, where were deposited vessels full of stones and other materials for imitating the sound of thunder; the ἐπισκήνιον, *episcenium*, a place on the top of the scene, in which were placed the machines for changing the various figures and prospects; the παρασκήνιον, *parascenium*, which served the actors as a dressing room; the προσκήνιον, *proscenium*, or stage, on which the performers acted; the ορχήστρα, *orchestra*, was the part in which the performers danced and sang, in the middle whereof was the λογεῖον or θυμέλη, *pulpitum*; the ὑποσκήνιον, *hyposcenium*, was a partition under the pulpitum, where the music was placed; the κοιλον, *cavea*, was for the reception of the spectators, and consisted of two or three divisions of several seats, each rising above one another, the lowest division being appropriated to persons of rank and magistrates, the middle one to the commonalty, and the upper one to the women. Round the cavea porticoes were erected for shelter in rainy weather, the theatre of the Greeks having no roof or covering. The theatre was always dedicated to Bacchus and Venus, the deities of sports and pleasures; to the former, indeed, it is said they owe their origin: hence, the plays acted in them were called Διονυσιακὰ, *Dionysiaca*, as belonging to Διονυσος, or Bacchus. Every citizen shared by right in the public diversion and public debate; the theatre was therefore open to the whole community.

173. The Athenian αγοραὶ, or *fora*, were numerous; but the two most celebrated were the old and new forum. The old forum was in the Ceramicus within the city. The assemblies of the people were held in it, but its principal use was as a market, in which to every trade was assigned a particular portion.

174. The supply of water at Athens was chiefly from wells, aqueducts being scarcely known there before the time of the Romans. Some of these wells were dug at the public expense, others by private persons.

175. The first *gymnasia* are said to have been erected in Lacedemonia, but were afterwards much improved and extended, and became common throughout Greece. The gymnasium consisted of a number of buildings united in one enclosure, whereto large numbers resorted for different purposes. In it the philosophers, rhetoricians, and professors of all the other sciences, delivered their lectures; in it also the wrestlers and dancers practised and exercised; all which, from its space, they were enabled to do without interfering with one another. The chief parts (*fig.* 107.), following Vitruvius (lib. v. cap. 11.), are—A, the περιστυλιον, *peristylium*, which included the σφαιριστήριον, *sphæristerium*, and παλαίστρα, *palestra*; 1, 2, 3, are the στοαι, *porticus*, with B B, εξεδραι, *exhedræ*, where probably the scholars used to meet; 4, 4, is the double portico looking to the south; c, εφήβαιον, *ephæbeum*, where the

ephebi or youths exercised, or, as some say, where those that designed to exercise met and agreed what kind of exercise they should contend in, and what should be the victor's reward ; D, is the coryceum ; E, the κονιστήριον, *conisterium*, where the dust was kept for sprinkling those that had been anointed ; F is the cold bath (*frigida lavatio*) ; G, the ελαιοθεσιον, *elæothesium*, or place for

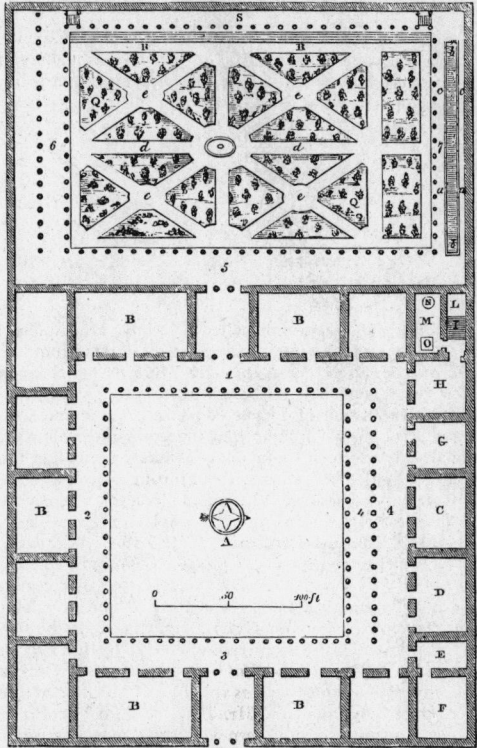

anointing those that were about to wrestle ; H, the *frigidarium*, or cold chamber ; I, passage to the *propigneum*, or furnace ; L, the propigneum ; M, the arched *sudatio*, for sweating ; N, the *laconicum* ; O, the hot bath (*calida lavatio*) ; 5, 7, the two porticoes described as out of the palæstra, of which 7 forms the *xystus*, and 6 a double portico ; *a a*, the *margines*, or *semitæ* of the xystus, to separate the spectators from the wrestlers ; *b b*, the middle part excavated two steps, *c c*, down ; Q Q, gardens ; *d d*, walks ; *e e*, *stationes* for seats ; R R, ξύστα, *xysta*, sometimes called περιδρομιδες, for walking or exercises ; s, the *stadium*, with raised seats round it.

176. The roofs of the edifices of Athens vary from 14½ to 15½ degrees in inclination, a subject which will be hereafter fully considered, when we come to investigate the principles of constructing roofs. In Rome, as will hereafter be seen, the inclination is much more. There is nothing to warrant us in a belief that the arch was known to the Greeks till after the age of Alexander. Indeed, the want of a name for it in a language so generally copious as the Greek, suffices to show that they were unacquainted with it.

Fig. 107.   PLAN OF A GREEK GYMNASIUM.

It was most probably in much earlier use in Italy. The words θολος, αψις, and ψαλις, are not used in a sense that signifies an arch until after the reign of the above-named monarch ; nor is any description extant from which may be conceived the construction of an arch on scientific principles.

177. From the time of Pericles to that of Alexander, all the arts, and most especially that of architecture, seem to have attained a high state of perfection. Every moral and physical cause had concurred in so advancing them. But perfection, when once reached in the works of man, is only the commencement of their falling away from it. Liberty, the love of country, ambition in every department of life, had made Athens the focus of the arts and sciences : the defeat of the Persians at Marathon and other celebrated victories had brought peace to the whole of the states of Greece. In the space of time preceding the Peloponnesian war, there seems to have been, as it were, an explosion of every species of talent, and it was at this period that they set about rebuilding the temples and other edifices that the Persians had thrown down, of which a wise policy had preserved the ruins, so that the contemplation of desolation and misfortune afforded them an eloquent reminiscence of the peril in which they continually stood. It was indeed only after the flight of the general of Xerxes, and the victory gained by Themistocles, that a general restoration of their monuments and the rebuilding of Athens were set about. These were the true trophies of the battle of Salamis. About 335 years B.C. Alexander became master of Greece. Fired with every species of glory, and jealous of leaving to posterity monuments that should be unworthy of his greatness and fame, or other than proofs of the refinement of his taste, this prince gave a new impulse to genius by the exclusive choice that he made of the most skilful artists, and by the liberal rewards he bestowed upon them. The sacking of Corinth by the Romans in less than two centuries (about 146 B.C.) was the first disaster that the fine arts encountered in Greece ; their overthrow there was soon afterwards completed by the country becoming a Roman province. At the former occurrence Polybius

(cited by Strabo) says, that during the plunder the Roman soldiers were seen casting their dice on the celebrated picture of Bacchus by Aristides. Juvenal well describes such a scene (*Satire* xi. 100.) : —

> Tunc rudis et Graias mirari nescius artes,
> Urbibus eversis, prædarum in parte reperta
> Magnorum artificûm frangebat pocula miles.

The well-known story of the consul Mummius shows either that the higher ranks among the Roman citizens were not very much enlightened on the arts, or that he was a singular blockhead. We have now arrived at the period at which Greece was despoiled and Rome enriched, and must pursue the history of the art among the Romans ; incidental to which a short digression will be necessary on Etruscan architecture.

Sect. XII.

ETRUSCAN ARCHITECTURE.

178. The inhabitants of Etruria, a country of Italy, now called Tuscany, are supposed to have been a colony from Greece. They certainly may have been a swarm from the original hive (see *Druidical, Celtic*, 13.; and *Cyclopean Architecture*, 32.) that passed through Greece in their way to Italy. The few remains of their buildings still existing show, from their construction, that they are coeval with the walls of Tiryns, Mycenæ (*figs*. 9. and 10.), and other works of a very early age ; and it is our own opinion that the wandering from that great central nation, of which we have already so much spoken, was as likely to conduct the Etrurians at once to the spot on which they settled, as to bring them through Greece to the place of their settlement. It is equally our opinion that, so far from the country whereof we now treat having received their arts from the Greeks, it is quite as possible, and even likely, that the Greeks may have received their arts from the Etruscans. The history of Etruria, if we consult the different writers who have mentioned it, is such a mass of contradiction and obscurity, that there is no sure guide for us. It seems to be a moving picture of constant emigration and re-emigration between the inhabitants of Greece and Italy. The only point upon which we can surely rest is, that there were many ancient relations between the two countries, and that in after times the dominion of the Etruscans extended to that part of Italy which, when it became occupied by Grecian colonies, took the name of Magna Græcia. The continual intercourse between the two countries lessens our surprise at the great similarity in their mythology, in their religious tenets, and in their early works of art. We are quite aware that the learned Lanzi was of opinion (*Saggio di Lingua Etrusca*), that the Etruscans were not the most ancient people of Italy. We are not about to dispute that point. He draws his conclusion from language ; we draw our own from a comparison of the masonry employed in both nations, from the remains whereof we should, if there be a difference, assign the earliest date to that of Hetruria. This, to be sure, leaves open the question whether the country was preoccupied ; one which, for our purpose, it is not necessary to settle. We have Winkelman and Guarnacci on our side, who from medals and coins arrived at the belief that among the Etruscans the arts were more advanced at a very early age than among the Greeks ; and Dr. Clarke's reasoning tends to prove for them a Phœnician origin.

179. Great solidity of construction is the prominent feature in Etruscan architecture. Their cities were surrounded by walls consisting of enormous blocks of stone, and usually very high. Remains of them are still to be seen at Volterra (*fig*. 108.), Cortona, Fiesole

Fig. 108. WALL AT VOLTERRA.

(*fig*. 109.), &c. " Mœnibus," says Alberti (*De Re Ædific.* lib. vii. c. 2.) " veterum præsertim populi Etruriæ quadratum eumdemque vastissimum lapidem probavêre." In the walls of Cortona some of the stones are upwards of 22 Roman feet in length, and from 5 to 6 ft. high, and in them neither cramps nor cement appear to have been employed. The walls of Volterra are built after the same gigantic fashion. In the earliest

Fig. 109. WALL AT FIESOLE.

specimens of walling, the blocks of stone were of an irregular polygonal form, and so disposed as that all their sides were in close contact with one another. Of this species is the wall at Cora, near Velletri. The gates were very simple, and built of stones of an oblong square form. The gate of Hercules, at Volterra, is an arch consisting of nineteen stones ; a

circumstance which, if its antiquity be allowed to be only of a moderately remote period, would go far to disprove all Lanzi's reasoning, for, as we have noticed in the preceding article, the arch was unknown in Greece till after the time of Alexander. According to Gori (*Museum Etruscum*), vestiges of theatres have been discovered among the ruins of some of their cities. That they were acquainted with the method of conducting theatrical representations is evident from Livy, who mentions an occasion on which comedians were brought from Etruria to Rome, whose inhabitants at the time in question were only accustomed to the games of the circus. The gladiatorial sports, which were afterwards so much the delight of the Romans, were also borrowed from the same people. They constructed their temples peripterally; the pediments of them were decorated with statues, quadrigæ, and bassi rilievi, in terra cotta, many whereof were remaining in the time of Vitruvius and Pliny. Though it is supposed that the Etruscans made use of wood in the entablatures of their temples, it is not to be inferred that at even the earliest period they were unacquainted with the use of stone for their architraves and lintels, as is sufficiently proved in the Piscina of Volterra.

180. The Romans, until the conquest of Greece, borrowed the taste of their architecture from Etruria. Even to the time of Augustus, the species called Tuscan was to be seen by the side of the acclimatised temple of the Greeks.

181. The *atrium* or court, in private houses, seems to have been an invention of the Etruscans. Festus derives its name from its having been first used at Atria, in Etruria : " Dictum Atrium quia id genus edificii primum Atriæ in Etruria sit institutum." We shall, however, allude in the next section to Etruscan architecture as connected with Roman; merely adding here, that in about a year after the death of Alexander the nation fell under the dominion of the Romans.

Sect. XIII.

ROMAN ARCHITECTURE.

182. The Romans can scarcely be said to have had an original architecture ; they had rather a modification of that of the Greeks. Their first instruction in the art was received from the Etruscans, which was probably not until the time of the Tarquins, when their edifices began to be constructed upon fixed principles, and to receive appropriate decoration. In the time of the first Tarquin, who was a native of Etruria, much had been done towards the improvement of Rome. He brought from his native country a taste for that grandeur and solidity which prevailed in the Etruscan works. After many victories he had the honour of a triumph, and applied the wealth he had acquired from the conquered cities to building a circus, for which a situation was chosen in the valley which reached from the Aventine to the Palatine Hill. Under his reign the city was fortified, cleansed, and beautified. The walls were built of hewn stone, and the low grounds about the Forum drained, which prepared the way for the second Tarquin to construct that Cloaca Maxima, which was reckoned among the wonders of the world. The Forum was surrounded with galleries by him ; and his reign was further distinguished by the erection of temples, schools for both sexes, and halls for the administration of public justice. This, according to the best chronologies, must have been upwards of 610 years b. c. Servius Tullius enlarged the city, and among his other works continued those of the temple of Jupiter Capitolinus, which had been commenced by his predecessor ; but the operations of both were eclipsed by monuments, for which the Romans were indebted to Tarquinius Superbus, the seventh king of Rome. Under him the Circus was completed, and the most effective methods taken to finish the Cloaca Maxima. This work, on which neither labour nor expense was spared to make the work everlasting, is of wrought stone, and its height and breadth are so considerable, that a cart loaded with hay could pass through it. Hills and rocks were cut through for the purpose of passing the filth of the city into the Tiber. Pliny calls the Cloacæ, "operum omnium dictu maximum, suffossis montibus, atque urbe pensili, subterque navigatâ." The temple of Jupiter Capitolinus was not finished till after the expulsion of the kings, 508 b. c. ; but under Tarquinius Superbus it was considerably advanced. In the third consulship of Poplicola, the temple was consecrated. As the name, which was changed, imports, this temple stood on the Mons Capitolinus, and embraced, according to Plutarch, four acres of ground. It was twice afterwards destroyed, and twice rebuilt on the same foundations. Vespasian, at a late period, rebuilt it ; and upon the destruction of this last by fire, Domitian raised the most splendid of all, in which the gilding alone cost 12,000 talents. It is impossible now to trace the architecture of the Romans through its various steps between the time of the last king, 508 b. c., and the subjugation of Greece by that people in the year 145 b. c., a period of 363 years. The

disputes in which they were continually engaged left them little leisure for the arts of peace; yet the few monuments with which we are acquainted show a power and skill that mark them as an extraordinary race. Thus in the year 397 B. C., on the occasion of the siege of Veii, the prodigy, as it was supposed, of the lake of Alba overflowing, when there was little water in the neighbouring rivers, springs, and marshes, induced the authorities to make an *emissarium*, or outlet for the superfluous water, which subsists to this day. The water of the lake Albano, which runs along Castel Gondolfo, still passes through it. A few years after this event an opportunity was afforded, which, with more care on the part of the authorities, might have considerably improved it, after its demolition by Brennus. This event occurred 389 B. C., and was nearly the occasion of the population being removed to Veii altogether, a place which offered them a spot fortified by art and nature good houses ready built, a wholesome air, and a fruitful territory. The eloquence, however, of Camillus prevailed over their despondency. Livy (b. vi.) observes, that in the rebuilding, the state furnished tiles, and the people were allowed to take stone and other materials wherever they could find them, giving security to finish their houses within the year. But the haste with which they went to work caused many encroachments on each other's soil. Every one raised his house where he found a vacant space; so that in many cases they built over the common sewers, which before ran under the streets. So little taste for regularity and beauty was observed, that the city, when rebuilt, was even less regular than in the time of Romulus; and though in the time of Augustus, when Rome had become the capital of the world, the temples, palaces, and private houses were more magnificent than before, yet these decorations could not rectify the fault of the plan. Though perhaps not strictly within our own province, we may here mention the temple built in honour of Juno Moneta, in consequence of a vow of L. Furius Camillus when before the Volsci. This was one of the temples on the Capitoline hill. The epithet above mentioned was given to the queen of the gods, a short time before the taking of Rome by the Gauls. It was pretended that from the temple of Juno a voice had proceeded, accompanied with an earthquake, and that the voice had admonished the Romans to avert the evils that threatened them by sacrificing a sow with pig. She was hence called *Moneta* (from monere). The temple of Juno Moneta becoming afterwards a public mint, the medals stamped in it for the current coin took the name of Moneta (money). This temple was erected about 345 years B.C., on the spot where the house of Marcus Manlius had stood.

183. In the time that Appius Claudius was censor, about 309 B. C., the earliest paved road was made by the Romans. It was first carried to Capua, and afterwards continued to Brundusium, a length altogether of 350 miles. Statius calls it *regina viarum*. Paved with the hardest stone, it remains entire to the present day. Its breadth is about 14 ft.; the stones of which it is composed vary in size, but so admirably was it put together that they are like one stone. Its bed is on two strata; the first of rough stones cemented with mortar, and the second of gravel, the thickness altogether being about 3 ft. To the same Appius Claudius belongs the honour of having raised the first aqueduct. The water with which it supplied the city was collected from the neighbourhood of Frascati, about 100 ft. above the level of Rome. The Romans at this time were fast advancing in the arts and sciences; for in about nineteen years afterwards we find Papirius, after his victory over the Samnites, built a temple to Quirinus out of a portion of its spoils. Upon this temple was fixed (*Pliny*, b. vii. c. 60.) the first sun-dial that Rome ever saw. For a long while the Romans marked only the rising and setting of the sun; they afterwards observed, but in a rude clumsy manner, the hour of noon. When the sun's rays appeared between the rostra and the house appointed for the reception of the ambassadors, a herald of one of the consuls proclaimed with a loud voice that it was mid-day. With the aid of the dial they now marked the hours of the day, as they soon after did those of the night by the aid of the clepsydra or water-clock. The materials for carrying on the investigation are so scanty, and moreover, as in the case of Grecian architecture, without examples whereon we can reason, that we will not detain the reader with further speculations, but at once proceed to that period (145 B.C.) when Greece was reduced to a Roman province. Art, in the strict application of that word, was not properly understood by the victorious Romans; and a barrenness appears to have clung about that whereof we treat, even with all the advantages that Rome possessed. It may be supposed that the impulse given to the arts would have been immediate; but, like the waves generated by the ocean storm, a succession of them was necessary before the billows would approach the coast. Perhaps, though it be only conjectural, the first effect was visible in the temple reared to Minerva at Rome, out of the spoils of the Mithridatic war, by Pompey the Great, about sixty years B.C., after a triumph unparalleled perhaps in the history of the world; after the conclusion of a war of thirty years' duration, in which upwards of two millions of his fellow-creatures had been slain and vanquished; after 846 ships had been sunk or taken, and 1538 towns and fortresses had been reduced to the power of the empire, and all the countries between the lake Mæotis and the Red Sea had been subdued. It is to be regretted that no remains of this temple exist. The inscription (*Plin.* lib. vii. c. 26.) was as follows:—

CN . POMPEIUS . CN . F . MAGNUS . IMP .
BELLO . XXX . ANNORUM . CONFECTO .
FUSIS . FUGATIS . OCCISIS . IN . DEDITIONEM . ACCEPTIS .
HOMINUM . CENTIES . VICIES . SEMEL . CENTENIS .
LXXXIII . M .
DEPRESSIS . AUT . CAPT . NAVIBUS . DCCCXLVI
OPPIDIS . CASTELLIS . MDXXXVIII
IN . FIDEM . RECEPTIS .
TERRIS . A . MAEOTI . LACU . AD . RUBRUM . MARE
SUBACTIS .
VOTUM . MERITO . MINERVÆ .

184. The villas of the Romans at this period were of considerable extent; the statues of Greece had been acquired for their decoration, and every luxury in the way of decoration that the age could afford had been poured into them from the plentiful supply that Greek art afforded. To such an extreme was carried the determination to possess every thing that talent could supply, that we find Cicero was in the habit of employing two architects, Chrysippus and Cluatius (*ad Atticum*, lib. iii. epist. 29. and lib. xii. epist. 18.); the first certainly, the last probably a Greek. Their extent would scarcely be credited but for the corroboration we have of it in some of their ruins.

185. Until the time of Pompey no permanent theatre existed in Rome: the ancient discipline requiring that the theatre should continue no longer than the shows lasted. The most splendid temporary theatre was that of M. Æmilius Scaurus, who, when ædile, erected one capable of containing 80,000 persons, which was decorated, from all accounts, with singular magnificence and at an amazing cost. History (*Plin.* xxxvi. 15.) records an extraordinary instance of mechanical skill, in the theatre erected by Curio, one of Cæsar's partisans, at the funeral exhibition in honour of his father. Two large theatres of timber were constructed back to back, and on one side so connected with hinges and machinery for the purpose, that when the theatrical exhibitions had closed they were wheeled or slung round so as to form an amphitheatre, wherein, in the afternoon, shows of gladiators were given. Returning, however, to the theatre erected by Pompey, which, to avoid the animadversion of the censors, he dedicated as a temple to Venus: the plan (*Pliny*, vii. 3.) was taken from that at Mitylene, but so enlarged as to be capable of containing 40,000 persons. Round it was a portico for shelter in case of bad weather: a curia or senate house was attached to it with a basilica or hall for the administration of justice. The statues of male and female persons celebrated for their lives and characters were selected and placed in it by Atticus, for his attention to which Cicero (*Epist. ad Attic.* iv. 9.) was commissioned by Pompey to convey his thanks. The temple of Venus, which was attached to avoid the breach of the laws committed, was so contrived that the seats of the theatre served as steps to the temple; a contrivance which also served to escape the reproach of encountering so vast an expense for mere luxury, for the temple was so placed that those who visited the theatre might seem at the same time to come for the purpose of worshipping the goddess. At the solemnity of its dedication the people were entertained with the most magnificent shows that had ever been exhibited in Rome. We cannot prolong the account of this edifice by detailing them,—indeed that would be foreign to our purpose; but we may add, that such a building presents to us a genuine idea of the vast grandeur and wealth of those principal subjects of Rome, who from their own private revenues could rear such magnificent buildings, and provide for the entertainment of the people shows to which all the quarters of the globe contributed, and which no monarch now on earth could afford to exhibit. This theatre was finished about 54 B.C.

186. In the year 45 B.C. Rome witnessed a triumph not less extraordinary than that we have just recorded,—that of Julius Cæsar on his return from Utica. From the commencement of the civil war that had raged he had found no leisure for celebrating the triumphs which induced the people to create him dictator for ten years, and to place his statue in the Capitol opposite to that of Jupiter, with the globe of the earth under his feet, and the inscription "To Cæsar the Demi-God." We need scarcely remind our readers that his first triumph was over the Gauls; that this was followed by that over Ptolemy and Egypt; the third over Pharnaces and Pontus; and the fourth over Juba. The triumph recorded these appropriately; but we leave that—merely observing, by the way, that the fruit of his victories amounted to 65,000 talents and 2822 crowns of gold, weighing together 20,414 Roman pounds,—to state that on this occasion the Circus was enlarged, a lake sunk for the exhibition of Egyptian and Tyrian galleys, and that in the same year he dedicated a temple to Venus Genetrix, and opened his new forum. Warriors are not often inclined to call in the aid of the arts, except for commemorating their own actions. Not so with Cæsar. In the year 44 B.C., after his triumph over the sons of Pompey, we once more find him engaged in the arts of peace. A temple to Clemency was erected by him, in which his statue was placed near to that of the goddess, and joining hands with her. In the next year he laid

the foundations of what at the time were considered two magnificent edifices for the ornament of the city : a temple to Venus, which for grandeur it is supposed would have surpassed every example of that kind in the world; and a theatre of very gigantic dimensions, —both which were afterwards completed by Augustus. But the projects he conceived were only equalled by those of Alexander.　He began the rebuilding and repair of many towns in Italy; the drainage of the Pontine marshes, the malaria of which is the curse of Rome to the present day ; the formation of a new bed for the Tiber from Rome to the sea, for the purpose of improving the navigation of that river ; the formation of a port at Ostia for the reception of first-rate ships; a causeway over the Apennines from the Adriatic to Rome ; the rebuilding of Corinth and Carthage, whither colonies had been sent by him, a scheme afterwards perfected by Augustus; a canal through the Isthmus of Corinth to avoid the navigation round the Peloponnesus; and lastly, the formation of an exact geographical map of the Roman empire, with the roads marked thereon, and the distances of the towns from each other.　Such was Cæsar, whom to eulogise would be impertinent.

187. Augustus deprived the Romans of their liberty, and in return for the deprivation consoled them with all the gratification the arts could supply.　The victorious Romans had known little of the arts in their highest state of refinement, and the degraded Greeks were constrained to neglect them.　They were in a state of barrenness during a portion of the last age of the Roman republic; nor did they exhibit any signs of fruitfulness until Cæsar had established the empire on the ruins of the expiring republic, and his successor, giving peace to the universe, closed the temple of Janus, and opened that of the arts.　By him skilful artists, pupils of the great masters, were invited from Greece, where, though languishing, they were yet silently working without fame or encouragement.　Some who had been led into slavery, like Rachel of old, carried their gods with them — the gods of the arts.　Encouraged by the rising taste of their masters, they now began to develop the powers they possessed, and their productions became necessary to the gratification of the people.　Thus it was that our art, among the others, born and reared in Greece, made Italy its adopted country, and there shone with undiminished splendour, though perhaps less happy and less durable.　Though the exotic might have lost some beauties in the soil to which it was transplanted, the stock possessed such extraordinary vigour that grafts from it still continue to be propagated in every quarter of the globe.

188. The Greek architects who settled in Italy executed works of surprising beauty : they raised up pupils, and founded a school.　It must be conceded that it was more an imitative than an original school, wherein it was necessary to engraft Roman taste which was modified by different habits and climate, on Greek art.　And here we cannot refrain from an observation or two upon the practice in these days of comparing Greek and Roman architecture.　Each was suitable to the nation that used it ; the forms of Greek columns, their intercolumninations, the inclination of the pediment, were necessarily changed in a country lying between four and five degrees further north from the equator.　But the superficial writers, whose knowledge occasionally appears to instruct the world, never take these matters into their consideration ; and we regret, indeed, to admit that in this country the philosophy of the art is little understood by the public, from the professors being generally too much engaged in its practice to afford them leisure for diffusing the knowledge they possess.

189. The Romans were trained to arms from their cradle; and that they were very averse to the cultivation of the arts by their youth, the passage in the *Æneid* (b. vi. v. 847.), which has been so often quoted, is a sufficient proof : —

> Excudent alii spirantia mollius æra
> Credo equidem; vivos ducent e marmore vultus.
> *　　*　　*　　*　　*　　*
> Tu regere imperio populos, Romane, memento ;
> Hæ tibi erunt artes.

190. They were at all times anxious to subjugate for their own purposes those nations that successfully cultivated the arts ; a motive which, joined to the desire of aggrandisement, induced them at a very early period to carry their arms against the Etruscans, who were in a far higher state of cultivation than themselves.　This was also one motive to their conduct in Sicily and Asia Minor; whence, as well as from Greece, they drew supplies of artists for Rome, instead of employing their own citizens.　Though in Rome architecture lost in simplicity, it gained in magnificence.　It there took deeper root than the other arts, from its affording, by the dimensions of its monuments, more splendour to the character of so dominating a nation.　Its forms are more susceptible of real grandeur than those of the other arts, which are put in juxtaposition with nature herself; and hence they were more in keeping with the politics of the people.　The patronage of the fine arts by Augustus has never before or since been equalled.　They followed his good fortune, they dwelt in the palace, and sat on the throne with him.　His boast was not a vain one, when he asserted that he found his capital built of brick and left it of marble.　By him was reared in the capital in question the temple and forum of Mars the Avenger ; the temple of Jupiter

Tonans, on the Capitol; that of Apollo Palatine, with public libraries; the portico and basilica of Caius and Lucius; the porticoes of Livia and Octavia; and the theatre of Marcellus. " The example," says Gibbon, " of the sovereign was imitated by his ministers and generals; and his friend Agrippa left behind him the immortal monument of the Pantheon."

191. Under Tiberius and Caligula architecture seems to have been in a state of languor, nor do we know of any thing in the reign of Claudius the fifth Cæsar, save the completion of one of the finest aqueducts of Rome, that of *Aqua Claudia*, whose length is 38 miles, in more than seven whereof the water passes over arches raised more than 100 ft. from the surface of the ground. Nero's reign, though his taste bordered more on show than intrinsic beauty, was on the whole favourable to architecture. Much could not be expected of a man who covered with gilding a statue of Alexander, and decapitated fine statues for the purpose of substituting his own head for that of the original. The colossal statues of himself which he caused to be sculptured indicate a mind prone to vice and excess. The same taste for exaggeration was carried into his buildings. His prodigality in every way was inexhaustible; he seems rather to have left monuments of expenditure than of taste. A palace, which from its extraordinary richness has been called the *Domus Aurea*, was erected for him by his architects Severus and Celer, than which nothing could be more brilliant nor gorgeous; beyond it no pomp of decoration could be conceived. In the midst of so much wealth the only object of contempt was its possessor. The reader may form some notion of it when told (*Plin*. lib. xxxvi.) that in finishing a part of it Otho laid out a sum equivalent to near 404,000*l*. sterling.

192. Galba, Otho, and Vitellius scarcely reigned. It was reserved for Vespasian and his son Titus, to astonish the world by masses of architecture such as it may be predicted

will never again be reared. The Coliseum (*figs*. 110. and 129.), named, according to some from its gigantic dimensions, to others from its proximity to a colossal statue of Nero, was commenced by the father and finished by the son. According to Lepsius, the seats held 87,000 persons. Fontana says it was capable of containing 109,000, who could view the sports in the arena. This we think an exaggeration. Taking the clear length at 615 feet, and breadth at 510 feet, we have an area of 246,340 sup. feet, whence deducting 38,842 for the arena, the remainder is 207,498. Now supposing this surface covered with persons standing upright, each occupying only 2·385 sup. feet, we have but 87,000, and in the circuit of the upper portico and parts relied upon by Fontana, 22,000 could not be placed. Hence the estimate of Lepsius seems worthy of confidence. The reader will, from the above description, identify the structure mentioned by Martial:—

Fig. 110.   THE COLISEUM.

Omnis Cæsareo ced t labor amphitheatro,
Unum pro cunctis fama loquatur opus.

" Biennio post ac menses novem amphitheatri perfecto opere," is the expression of Victor in respect to the time employed in its construction. Though the monument itself be astonishing, still more so is it that such a mass should have taken only two years and nine months in building, even with all the means that the emperors had under their power. We shall reserve a more particular description of it for a subsequent page. In spite of the ravages of time, and the hands, ancient and modern, which have despoiled it for its materials, enough still remains completely to exhibit the original plan, and to enable the spectator to form a perfect idea of the immense mass. The Baths of Titus were another of the wonders of the age. The remains of them are not so perfect as others, but they are still majestic. Besides the edifices erected by Vespasian and his son, they made it a part of their duty to take measures for the preservation of those which existed, and were in need of repair and restoration.

193. The last Cæsar, Domitian, was of a disposition too wicked to be of service to his country: his reign was, fortunately for it, but short. In the year 98, on the death of Nerva, Trajan became master of the empire. He had served against the Jews under Vespasian and Titus, and probably acquired from them and their example a great taste for architecture, in which he shed a lustre upon the country as great as his splendid victories over the Persians and Dacians gained for it in the field. Of his works, which, as Gibbon says, bear the stamp of his genius, his bridge over the Danube must have been a surprising effort. According to Dio Cassius, this bridge was constructed with twenty stone piers in

the river, 150 ft. high and 60 feet wide, bearing arches of 170 ft. span. It was destroyed by Hadrian, his successor : some say out of envy ; but the plea was, that it served the barbarians as an inlet to the empire, as much as it facilitated the passage of its troops to keep them in subjection. His triumphal arches, his column (*fig.* 111.), and forum, and other works, attest the vigour and beauty of the art under the reign of Trajan. The forum was a quadrangle surrounded by a lofty portico, into which the entrance was through four triumphal arches, and in the centre was the column. Apollodorus was his principal architect, by whom was erected the column above mentioned, which was not only the chef-d'œuvre of the age, but has never been surpassed. It is 110 ft. high, thus marking the height of the hill that had been cut away to receive the forum. " The public monuments with which Hadrian adorned every province of the empire were executed not only by his orders, but under his immediate inspection. He was himself an artist ; and he loved the arts, as they conduced to the glory of the monarch. They were encouraged by the Antonines, as they contributed to the happiness of the people. But if they were the first, they were not the only architects of their dominions. Their example was universally imitated by their principal subjects, who were not afraid of declaring to the world that they had spirit to conceive and wealth to accomplish the noblest undertakings. Scarcely had the proud structure of the Coliseum been dedicated at Rome, before edifices of a smaller scale indeed, but of the same design and materials, were erected for the use

Fig. 111.   COLUMN OF TRAJAN.

and at the expense of the cities of Capua and Verona. The inscription of the stupendous bridge at Alcantara attests that it was thrown over the Tagus by the contribution of a few Lusitanian communities. When Pliny was entrusted with the government of Bithynia and Pontus, provinces by no means the richest or most considerable of the empire, he found the cities within his jurisdiction striving with each other in every useful and ornamental work that might deserve the curiosity of strangers, or the gratitude of their citizens. It was the duty of the proconsul to supply their deficiencies, to direct their taste, and sometimes to moderate their emulation. The opulent senators of Rome and the provinces esteemed it an honour, and almost an obligation, to adorn the splendour of their age and country ; and the influence of fashion very frequently supplied the want of taste or generosity. Among a crowd of these private benefactors, we select Herodes Atticus, an Athenian citizen, who lived in the age of the Antonines. Whatever might be the motive of his conduct, his magnificence would have been worthy of the greatest kings." We make no apology for so long a quotation from the historian of the *Decline and Fall*, whose expressions are so suitable to our purpose. The family of Herod was highly descended ; but his grandfather had suffered by the hands of justice ; and Julius Atticus, his father, must have died in poverty, but for the discovery of an immense treasure in an old house, the only piece of his patrimony that remained. By the law this would have been the property of the emperor, to whom Julius gave immediate information. Nerva the Just, who was then on the throne, refused to accept it, desiring him to keep it and use it. The cautious Athenian hesitatingly replied, that the treasure was too large for a subject, and that he knew not how to *use it.* The emperor replied, " *Abuse it then,* for 'tis your own." He seems really to have followed the monarch's bidding, for he expended the greatest part of it in the service of the public. This man's son, Herodes, had acquired the prefecture of the free cities of Asia, among which the town of Troas being ill supplied with water, he obtained from the munificence of Hadrian a sum equivalent to 100,000*l.* sterling for constructing a new aqueduct. The work on execution amounted to double the estimate ; and on the officers of the revenue complaining, Atticus charged himself with the whole of the additional expense. Some considerable ruins still preserve the fame of his taste and munificence. The Stadium which he erected at Athens was 600 ft. in length, entirely of white marble, and capable of receiving the whole body of the people. To the memory of his wife, Regilla, he dedicated a theatre, in which no wood except cedar was employed. He restored the Odeum to its ancient beauty and magnificence. His boundless liberality was not, however, confined within the city of Athens. " The most splendid ornaments," says Gibbon, " bestowed on the temple of Neptune in the Isthmus, a theatre at Corinth, a stadium at Delphi, a bath at Thermopylæ, and an aqueduct at Canusium in Italy, were insufficient to exhaust his treasures. The people of Epirus, Thessaly, Eubœa, Bœotia, and Peloponnesus experienced his favours, and many inscriptions of the cities of Greece and Asia gratefully style Herodes Atticus their patron and benefactor."

194. Architecture was still practised with success under the Antonines, the successors of Hadrian, among whom Marcus Aurelius was a great patron of the arts. On these history almost instructs us, that the effect of the individual character of the sovereign, and the general and leading circumstances of his reign, are so influential as to enable us from the two last to estimate the prosperity of the first.

195. The rapidity with which after the time of Commodus, that most unworthy son of a worthy father, the emperors succeeded each other, was as unfavourable for the arts as for their country. A little stand was made against their rapid decline, under Septimius Severus, whose triumphal arch still remains as a link in the chain of their decay, and perhaps the first. It is difficult to conceive how in so short a period from the time of Marcus Aurelius, not thirty years. sculpture had so lost ground. In the arch commonly called that of the Goldsmiths, the form and character of good architecture is entirely obliterated. Its profiles are vicious, and its ornaments debased and overcharged.

196. The art was somewhat resuscitated under Alexander Severus, but it was fast following the fate of the empire in the West, and had become almost lifeless under Valerian and his son Gallienus, whose arch is an index to its state in his reign. The number of competitors for the purple, and the incursions of the barbarians, were felt. Aurelian and Probus suspended its total annihilation; but their reigns were unfortunately too short to do it substantial service. The extraordinary structures at Baalbec and Palmyra have been referred, on the authority of a fragment of John of Antioch, surnamed Malala, to the age of Antoninus Pius; but we are inclined to think the style places them a little later than that period. Baalbec, or, as its Syrian meaning imports, the City of Baal, or the Sun, is situate at the north-eastern extremity of the valley of Becat or Beka, near that place

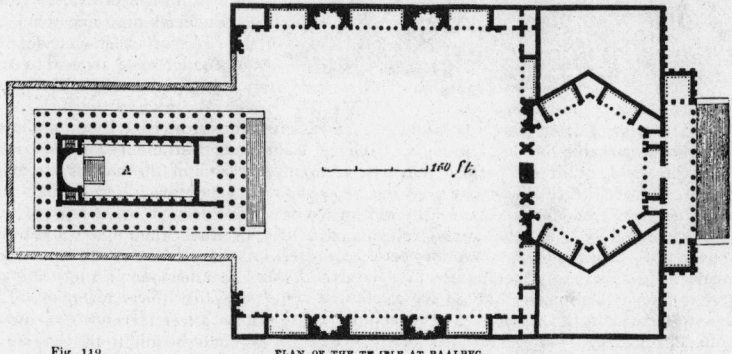

Fig. 112.   PLAN OF THE TEMPLE AT BAALBEC.

where the two Lebanons unite, about fifty miles to the north-west of Damascus. The first traveller who described it with accuracy was Maundrell, in his Journey from Aleppo

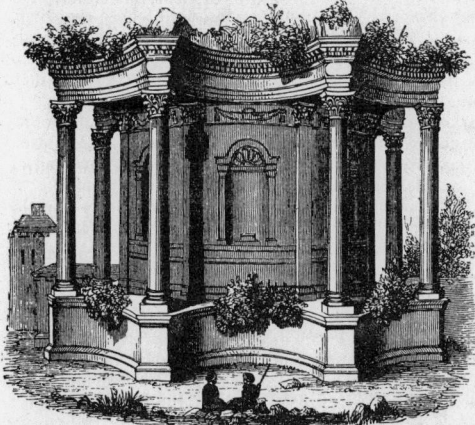

Fig. 113.   CIRCULAR TEMPLE OF BAALBEC.

to Jerusalem, in 1697. It has, however, been since visited, as well as Palmyra, by Messrs. Wood and Dawkins, in 1751, and by M. Volney at a later period. The principal building, the temple, is of a rectangular form, and is seated in the centre of the western extremity of a large quadrangular enclosure, two of whose sides were parallel to those of the temple; and parallel to its front was the third. To this was attached an hexagonal court, serving as a vestibule, in front of which was the grand entrance portico. The length of the quadrangle is about 360 ft. and breadth about 350 ft. (See fig. 112.) The temple, marked A, is, in round numbers, 200 ft. in length, and 100 ft. in breadth; it was dipteral, and had ten columns in front

and nineteen on the sides. That the reader may form some idea of the style, which was to the last degree debased. and would not justify by any utility the extending this ac-

count, we have in *fig.* 113. given the sketch of a circular temple standing near the above. Of Emesa, the other celebrated Cœlo-Syrian city, not a vestige remains.

197. Of Tadmor, or Palmyra, denoting both in Syriac as well as Latin a multitude of palm-trees, Solomon was said to have been the original founder. It lies considerably to the east of Baalbec, and upwards of 200 miles from the nearest coast of Syria. Situate between the Roman and Parthian monarchies, it was suffered to observe a humble neutrality until after the victories of Trajan; when, sinking into the bosom of Rome, it flourished more than 150 years in the subordinate though humble rank of a colony. " It was during that peaceful period," observes Gibbon, " if we may judge from a few remaining inscriptions, that the wealthy Palmyrenians constructed those temples, palaces, and porticoes, whose ruins, scattered over an extent of several miles, have deserved the curiosity of our travellers." The ruins of it were discovered by some English travellers towards the end of the 17th century, and were more lately visited by the Messrs. Dawkins and Wood, already mentioned. The power of Zenobia, who wished to shake off the subjection to Rome, was insufficient to withstand the forces of Aurelian, and Palmyra fell into his hands about the year 237. A slight sketch of the ruins (*fig.* 114.) is here

given. The style of architecture is almost the same as that of Baalbec ; and, like that, so vitiated in almost every profile, that we do not think it necessary longer to dwell upon it, although great the extent of its ruins. In the same way, we must pass over those of Djerash, which were visited by Mr. Barry, and of other considerable cities, though some are said to contain examples in a better and purer style.

Fig. 114.   RUINS OF PALMYRA.

198. The reign of Dioclesian was extended, and was illustrious from his military exploits. It was also remarkable for the wisdom he displayed in dividing with others the discharge of duties he could not himself perform ; as well as, finally, by his abdication and retirement to Spalatro. Architecture was, however, too far sunk for him to raise it ; and, though monuments of great grandeur were reared by him in Rome and his native town of Salona, they were degenerated by innovation and a profusion of ornaments which sometimes proved disastrous to those beneath, upon whom they occasionally fell, but the taste for which, among the Romans, had increased by their intercourse with the East. At a period when no sculptor existed in Rome, this monarch raised the celebrated baths there which bear his name. His palace at Spalatro (*fig.* 115.) covered between nine and ten English acres. Its form was quadrangular, flanked with sixteen towers. Two of the sides were 600 ft., and the other 700 ft. in length. It was constructed of stone little inferior to marble. Four streets, intersecting each other at right angles, divided the several parts of the edifice ; and the approach to the principal apartment was from a stately entrance, still called the golden gate. By comparing the present remains with the Treatise by Vitruvius, there appears a coincidence in the practice here with the precepts of that author. The building consisted of only one story, and the rooms were lighted from above. Towards the south-west was a portico upwards of 500 ft. long, ornamented with painting and sculpture. We do not think it necessary to follow up further the decay of the arts in the West; it is sufficient to add that the fifth century witnessed the contemporaneous fall of them and of Rome itself.

199. Towards the year 330, the seat of the Roman empire was removed to Constantinople, where the reign of Constantine, though brilliant, was unsuccessful in restoring the arts, upon which religious as well as political causes had begun to act. The establishment of Christianity had less effect on architecture than on her sister arts. The new species of worship could be performed as well in the old as in temples of a new form, or the old columns might be employed in new edifices, in which, indeed, they were eminently serviceable ; but statues of the gods were no longer wanted, and the sculptor's art was abandoned. The removal, however, of the government to the Bosphorus retarded the decline of the empire in the East. Byzantium, on whose foundations was placed the city of Constantinople, owed its origin to a colony of Megarians ; and little was it to be imagined that its disasters would have closed in so glorious a termination as occurred to it. The ancient city still continued to possess some splendid productions of the schools of Asia Minor, which it almost touched, and in common with which it enjoyed the arts. Constantine profited by the circumstance, restored the monuments, and transported thither the best examples of sculpture.

200. Architecture was called in by the emperor to aid him in affording security, convenience, and pleasure to the inhabitants of the new metropolis. Vast walls surrounded the city ; superb porticoes, squares of every kind, aqueducts, baths, theatres, hippodromes, obelisks,

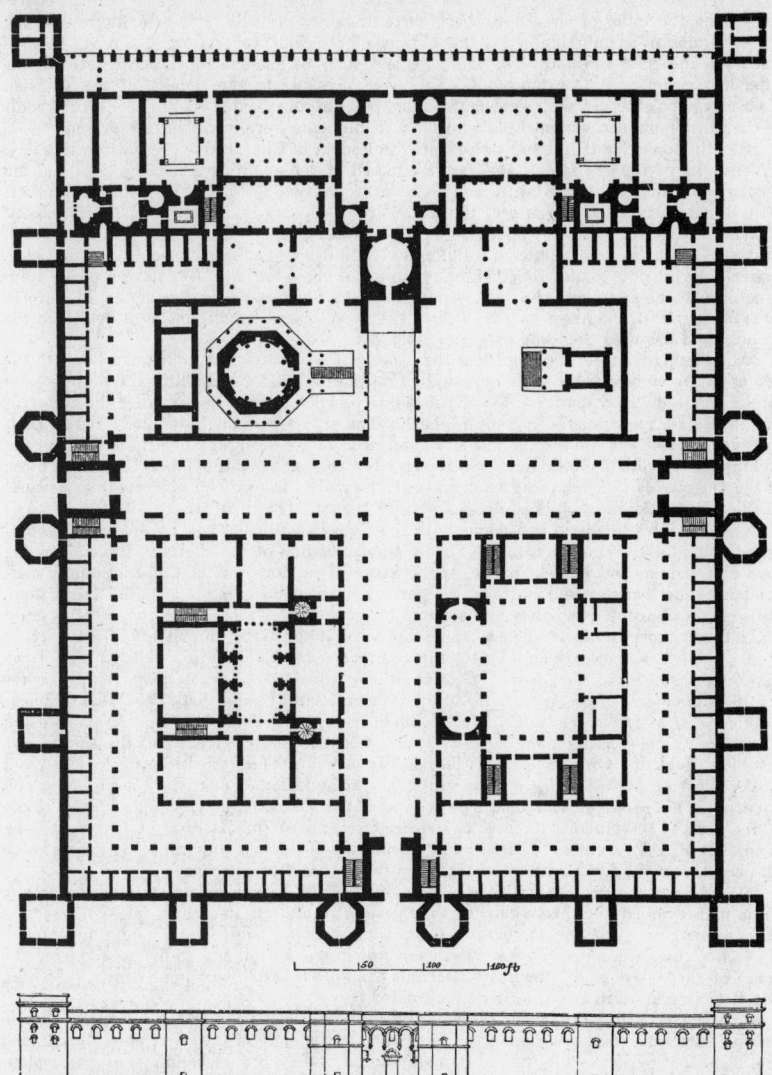

Fig. 115.   PALACE OF DIOCLESIAN AT SPALATRO.

triumphal arches, stately and magnificent temples, were provided for the public. Schools of architecture, which none but persons of good birth were allowed to enter, were established, with professors and prizes for the meritorious. From all this care, one might have supposed a plentiful harvest would have been reaped. But, alas! with all the expense, with all the fine marbles that were employed, with the bronze and gold lavished on the construction and decoration of the edifices erected, the art was not re-established on its true principles. Every thing was rich; but, notwithstanding the exaggerated praises of the ignorant writers of the day, every thing was deficient in real beauty. Richness of material will never compensate for want of elegance in form. " The buildings of the new city," observes Gibbon, " were executed by such artificers as the reign of Constantine could afford , but they were decorated by the hands of the most celebrated masters of the age of Pericles and Alexander. To revive the genius of Phidias and Lysippus surpassed, indeed, the power of a Roman emperor ; but the immortal productions which they had bequeathed to posterity were exposed without defence to the rapacious vanity of a despot. By his

commands the cities of Greece and Asia were despoiled of their most valuable ornaments. The trophies of memorable wars, the objects of religious veneration, the most finished statues of the gods and heroes, of the sages and poets of ancient times, contributed to the splendid triumph of Constantinople, and gave occasion to the remark of the historian 'Cedrenus, who observes, with some enthusiasm, that nothing seemed wanting except the souls of the illustrious men whom those admirable monuments were intended to represent."

201. In Rome, the triumphal arch erected in honour of Constantine presents, to this day, an example of the barbarous and tasteless spirit of the age. It is nothing less than an incongruous mixture, in sculpture and architecture, of two periods remote from each other. But, discordant as the styles are, the absurdity of placing on it part of the triumphs of Trajan, whose arch was robbed for the occasion, is still greater. Not only was Trajan's arch despoiled of its bas reliefs, but the columns and capitals, which the architect, from ignorance, scarcely knew how to put together, were stolen for the occasion. We have used the term ignorance of the architect, who, (if the monument were not standing, the fact could scarcely be credited,) with the finest models before his eyes, placed modillions with dentils in the cornice, and has used the same parts in his impost.

202. The partition of the empire at the death of Constantine was injurious as well to the arts as to the empire; and at its reunion by Constantius in 353, he exhibited but little solicitude about their prosperity. On a visit of thirty days to Rome, he presented the city with the obelisk that now stands in front of the Basilica of S. Giovanni Laterano. It had been intended by Constantine for his new city; and, after being brought down the Nile from the Temple of the Sun at Heliopolis, was conveyed to the banks of the Tiber instead of those of the Bosphorus. After being landed about three miles from the city, it was first elevated in the Circus Maximus. This piece of granite is about 115 ft. in length.

203. Julian's name is in bad odour with the Christian world; but he ought, nevertheless, to have justice rendered to him for his administration of the affairs of the empire, his love of freedom, and his patronage of the arts. This emperor, at Constantinople, constructed some porticoes and improved the port; and, even at so remote a spot as Paris, there still remain the ruins of a palace and baths of his construction; a circumstance which should make his memory an object of respect, perhaps veneration, to the inhabitants of that city.

204. Under Valentinian and Valens the arts received little attention, though the former manifested some care for them. Gratian was entitled to a sort of negative praise for leaving the empire of the West to his brother Valentinian II., and that of the East to Theodosius; who, after the death of the former, held the sway of the whole empire, patronising architecture, and erecting many large edifices in Constantinople. After this the empire was lastingly divided. On the death of Theodosius, Arcadius succeeded him in the East, and in the West Honorius, under whom, whilst he was ingloriously enjoying the pleasures and luxuries of his palace at Ravenna, Alaric, king of the Visigoths, entered and pillaged Rome in the year 410. Honorius raised or repaired several of the Basilicæ at Rome; among them that of S. Paolo fuori le Murà; and, in honour of the two emperors, a triumphal arch was erected in the city in 406, but of this no remains are in existence.

205. After this time, for sixty years the empire of the West was in a state of distraction. Nine princes filled the throne during that period, on and off the stage, rather like actors than monarchs. But the extinction of the Roman name could be no longer protracted. In 455, Genseric, king of the Vandals, gave up Rome for pillage to his soldiers for the space of three days, and some years after, his example was followed by Ricimer. In 476, the Roman empire in the West was annihilated.

206. We have thus, in this and the preceding section, shortly traced the history of Roman architecture from its dawn among the Etruscans to the close of the regal power in Rome; and from that period to the time of its culmination under Augustus, an age of great splendour in the art, comparable even with the best days of Athens, if allowance be made for the respective habits of the nations and the climates under which they were placed. From the zenith we have followed it in its setting under Dioclesian, and after that through its crepusculum, which, in 476, was succeeded by total darkness; a darkness, however, not without meteors and coruscations which occasionally enabled us to enlighten the reader in the journey he has undertaken with us. The revolutions, however, of empires, like those of the globe on its axis, bring other dawns : such is the case with the arts, which follow those revolutions; and we shall hereafter have to record another dawn of them, which, like the light of our great luminary, had its day-spring in the east, whence came the architects of Venice and Pisa. But, before we approach that period, it will be necessary to take a cursory glance at those monuments of Rome and other places under its dominion, in which the ruins alone attest the extraordinary power and magnificence of that State, and to examine the details of their construction as respects what simply presents itself to the eye.

207. We now, therefore, proceed to a view, 1. Of the religious buildings of the Romans in quadrangular and circular temples; 2. Of their public buildings in fora, triumphal arches, bridges, aqueducts, theatres, amphitheatres, and baths and circi; 3. Of their private

houses and tombs; confining ourselves to those ruins in the city, and occasionally the provinces, which best illustrate the subject.

208. *Temples.* — 1. The quadrangular Roman temple partook very much of its Greek, or perhaps Etruscan, original; though occasionally, as in the Temple of Peace, there is a very considerable deviation from the type. But the exceptions to the general rule are very few indeed in number. The most beautiful temple of the Corinthian order that perhaps ever existed in the world was the Temple of Jupiter Stator, in the Campo Vaccino (Forum), at Rome. We adopt the name of Jupiter Stator, because by that, though its propriety cannot be now ascertained, it is generally known. Recent excavations have proved that it was an octastyle peripteral temple, with twelve columns in flank, and that the cell occupied eight columns with their intercolumniations in depth. No Greek work could surpass in elegance and beauty the profile of the Corinthian order employed in this edifice. The capital, whether we consider it in design or execution, is unparalleled. At the same time we must admit that it bears every mark of the improvements that had been effected through the medium of Greek artists. Only three columns of it remain; these are 47·65 ft. high, their lower diameter being 4·84; so that, in terms of the diameter, the columns are 9·8 diameters high. The height of the entablature is a small fraction less than one quarter the height of the column. The intercolumniations are, as nearly as possible, 1·5 diameter of the column; whence the size of the temple will be easily determined.

209. Almost at the foot of the Capitol, not far from the Temple of Jupiter Stator, stands the Corinthian Temple of Jupiter Tonans, reputed to have been built by Augustus, of which, as of the last, only three columns remain. This was an hexastyle peripteral (except on the side towards the rock) temple, 115 ft. long and 92 ft. wide, measured from outside to outside of column. The columns are 47·08 ft. high, and their lower diameter is 4·60 ft.; their height, therefore, in terms of the diameter, is very nearly 10¼ diameters. The height of the entablature is 9·77 ft., or not quite one fifth of the height of the column. The intercolumniations are 1·56 diameter. There is a tale in Suetonius, that Augustus had bells suspended round this temple on the occasion of his dreaming that the god complained of a falling off in the number of his worshippers. Its style is inferior to the one above described, yet it is not without beauty, though the cornice is, as compared with it, deficient in effect. (The description of the different species of temples mentioned by Vitruvius, is given in the Glossary. s. v. Temple.

210. The Temple of Mars Ultor was one of those erected by Augustus. Its profile exhibits a fine and bold example of the Corinthian order. Its whole length was about 116 ft., and its breadth about 73 ft. The cornice of the entablature is wanting. The intercolumniations are about 1½ diameter.

211. In the Campo Vaccino are the remains of a Corinthian temple, built by M. Aurelius in honour of Antoninus, his predecessor, and Faustina, the daughter of that emperor and wife of M. Aurelius. It was prostylos and hexastylos: the columns are 46·10 ft. high; the entablature 11·03 ft.; diameter of the columns 4·85 ft.; and the intercolumniations, except the centre one, which is wider thau the others, are 1½ diameter of the columns. From the above it follows that the columns are 9½ diameters high, and the entablature rather less than one fourth the height of the column. The frieze is ornamented with griffins and candelabra in a very good style of art. It is not our intention to describe more than the principal temples, with their parts, but to afford to the reader in this place a general view of the art; we shall therefore merely mention those of the Maison Carrée at Nismes, and the little edifice at Trevi, which last is erected in a very vitiated style: both are of the Corinthian order, and quadrangular in form.

212. Rome is very poor in examples of Ionic temples, the only two remaining being that of Fortuna Virilis and that of Concord; the first not very pure in its detail, and the latter in the very worst style. The Temple of Fortuna Virilis is of the species called prostyle and tetrastyle; that is, with four columns in front and seven on the sides, whereof the cell occupies four intercolumniations. The height of the columns is 27·35 ft.; the lower diameter of the columns 3·11 ft.; and the height of the entablature 6·78 ft. A peculiarity has been noticed in this example of the different centres of the ornamented members being ranged so as to fall with exactness over the axes of the columns.

213. The Temple of Concord, which is a restoration, as the inscription on it proves, of a former temple that stood on the spot, is most probably of the age of Constantine, and scarcely deserves the notice here taken of it, except as a connecting link in the chain of art. It was hexastyle and peripteral. The eight columns which remain are of red and white granite of different diameters. The bases are Attic, and without plinths, except those of the angular columns. The capitals are inelegant and clumsily sculptured. The mouldings of the architrave have been chiselled away to form a plane surface for containing the inscription. Modillions and dentils are met with in the cornice, and the frieze in the interior was sculptured. The height of the columns is 42·86 ft., and their lower diameter 4·48 ft.; so that they are about 9½ diameters high. The height of the entablature is 7·2 ft., or about one sixth of the height of the column.

214. The circular temples of Rome and its neighbourhood will next be mentioned. Two of them, that of Vesta at Rome and of the Sybil at Tivoli, of the Corinthian order, are of considerable antiquity. Their cells are cylindrical, and are supposed to have been covered with domes resting on the walls, though that is by no means certain. The Temple of Vesta is raised on three steps, whilst that of the Sybil is raised on a circular basement about five feet high. Both the cellæ are encircled about with a colonnade of the Corinthian order. The capitals of the Temple of the Sybil are extraordinary as pieces of effective art. The leaves of the capital, instead of being *appliquées* to the bell, as in other examples, are in this cut into it, and impart a magical appearance to it. The *tout ensemble* of this temple seems to have been conceived with an eye to its situation, and the order seems calculated only for the spot on which it stands (see *fig.* 116.). The circular Temple

Fig. 116.   TEMPLE OF THE SYBIL.

of Bacchus is of a late date. In its exterior there is nothing to remark, except that it has lost a portico at its entrance which originally belonged to it. It consists of a central circular cell, if such it may be called, surrounded by a circular aisle, the former being separated from the latter by twelve pairs of double columns, coupled in the direction of the radii of the plan; from which columns arches spring, carrying a cylindrical wall 39·36 ft. diameter, covered with a hemispherical dome 65·6 ft. high from the pavement. The aisle or corridor is 14·75 ft. wide, surrounding, as we have said, the double colonnade, from which to the exterior wall is a semicircular vault, whose sofite is 32 ft. high from the pavement. The Temple of Minerva Medica is in a very ruined state; little more than half of it is standing. It was, when perfect, of a cylindrical shape, 110 ft. in diameter; but the interior was formed into ten plane vertical faces, each whereof had a semicircular recess open towards the centre of the building. A hemispherical brick dome covered the temple, whose vertex is 113 ft. from the pavement. A semicircular wing, covered by a hemispherically formed vault, stood on each side of the building, but they are now in ruins. *Fig.* 117. shows the ruin as it was in 1816, from a memorandum we then made. A rectangular vestibule with four Corinthian columns formed the

Fig. 117   TEMPLE OF MINERVA MEDICA.

entrance, and was surmounted by a pediment roof.   The temple now stands in a private garden.

215. We have reserved for the last example of a circular temple the celebrated Pantheon, supposed to have formed at one time a portion of the baths of Agrippa ; but whether with truth we must decline investigating, as unconnected with our present purpose.   Our own belief is, that the body of the temple was erected in the time of the republic with simple large niches, as in *figs.* 118. and 119., in the left sides whereof it is shown as originally built,

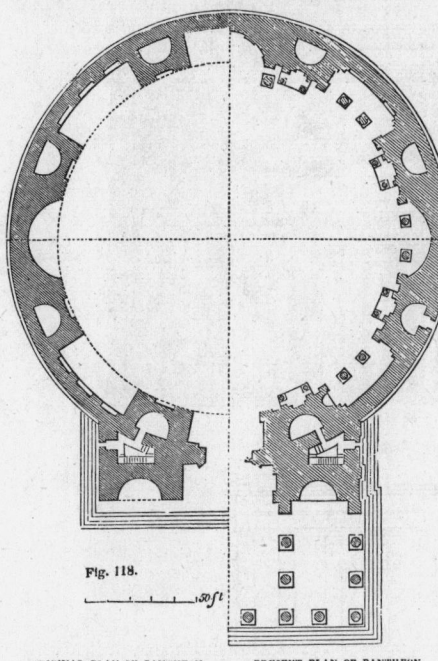

Fig. 118.

|____|____|____|____| 50 ft

ORIGINAL PLAN OF PANTHEON.   PRESENT PLAN OF PANTHEON.

entablature is 10·22 ft., or nearly, not quite a fifth

and on the right sides as now standing, and that the portico was appended by Agrippa about A. D. 14, at which time the columns were added to the niches, and other alterations made, as seen on the right half of the plan and section.   The interior is circular, and about 139 ft. diameter, measuring from inside to inside of the columns, which are about 33 ft. high.   At a height of 75 ft. from the ground in the interior springs the hemispherical dome, which has five horizontal ranks of caissons or panels, the top of the dome being terminated by what is technically termed an *eye*, or circular opening, about 27 ft. diameter.   All that is found in the temple is of the Corinthian order.

(216.) *Fig.* 120. is an elevation of the Pantheon, with the portico of the Parthenon below it, for the purpose of comparing the relative sizes of the porticoes of the two buildings.   The portico, it will be seen, is octastyle, and projects 62 ft. from the circumference of the circular part of the edifice.   The shafts of the columns are plain, and the portico is surmounted by a pediment similar to that on the wall of the building. The columns are 47·03 ft. high, and their lower diameter 4·79 ft.   The of the height of the column.   The profile of the order is bold and well conceived, and the execution in a good style.   It has been stripped of its ornaments, many whereof were bronze, by the cupidity of the possessors of power at various times. Though the present interior is comparatively modern, we think it right to give the following particulars of the order : — The columns are 34·67 ft. high, the lower diameter being 3·64 ft.   The shafts are fluted, and have what are called *cablings* up one third of their height.   It will be seen on inspection of the plan that these columns are placed in front of the great niches.   We are not aware that the circumstance whereto we are about to advert has been heretofore noticed, and we give the result of our

Fig. 119. SECTIONS OF ORIGINAL AND PRESENT PANTHEON.

calculation in round numbers only, as an approximation to the truth.   The rules for lighting apartments will form the subject of a future section.   We shall here merely observe, that the contents of the building, measuring round the inner convexity of the columns, and not calculating the niches, is about 1,787,300 cubic feet, and that the area of the eye of the dome is about 32 square ft., from which it follows that 2226 cubic ft. of space in this building are lighted by 1 foot superficial of light.   The building is neither gloomy nor

dark ; on the contrary a pleasant light is diffused throughout, and darkness is not found in any corner of it.   This is a subject well worthy of consideration, and one which we propose hereafter to turn to practical account.

Fig. 120.   ELEVATION OF PANTHEON.

Fig. 120.   PORTICO OF PARTHENON.

217. The Temple of Peace has been reserved by us to close the notices of the Roman temples, because of its deviation from the general form of other Greek and Roman temples, which in the quadrangular species are so formed on one general plan that *ab uno disce omnes* is the expression applicable to them. The *figs.* 121. and 122. represent the plan and section of this building. The former will be seen to have been rectangular, with a porch extending along the whole breadth of the building in front. This was vaulted, the summit interiorly being 35 ft. high; and in front were seven semicircular-headed apertures serving as entrances. The length of the temple outside, not including the depth of the porch, was 294 ft.; depth of the porch 30 ft.; width of the building 197 ft. The temple was longitudinally divided into three nearly equal parts, whereof the central one was a rectangular *salone* of the whole length of the temple, whose breadth was one third of its length. The roof of this was a vault with three groins, formed by the intersection of semicylindrical vaults at right angles to the central one. The height of the vaulting from the pavement was about 116 ft., and

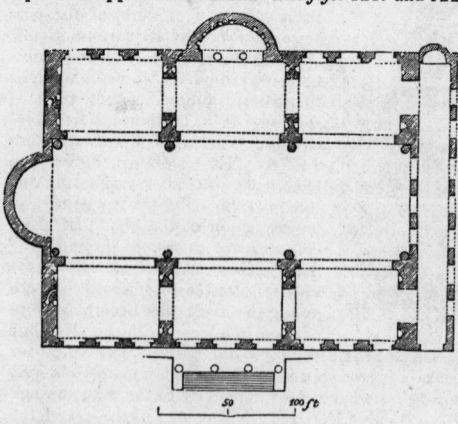

Fig. 121.   PLAN OF THE TEMPLE OF PEACE.

tral one.   The height of the vaulting from the appears to have been decorated with sunk panels. pavement was about 116 ft., and We shall not however pursue the

verbal description of this edifice, which will be much better understood by an inspection of the diagrams. We will only add, that although the columns in the interior are entirely gone, and the building is in a sad state of dilapidation, enough has been discovered to prove

Fig. 122.   TEMPLE OF PEACE.

that the restoration here submitted to the reader is not very far from the truth. In many cases the restorations of Palladio, whose works it is the fashion amongst half-instructed architects and still less informed amateurs to decry, are not to be wholly relied on in his capacity of antiquary, and certainly must not be taken for granted; but his restoration of this temple cannot widely differ from the truth. It appears to have been founded by Claudius, and finished by Vespasian after the conquest of Judea, and seems to have been the depository of the spoils of the temple at Jerusalem. It is uncertain by what accident in the reign of Commodus it was destroyed, but it is conjectured it was restored during his reign. It may not be here altogether out of place to notice that the temple in question seems in some measure to have furnished the hint for the nave of the Italian Duomo with its side aisles. It was but in the addition of the transepts and choir, whose type is indicated even in the basilicæ of the first Christians, that a variation is to be seen. If the cross, however, be not sufficiently apparent in the basilica, it cannot be mistaken in the churches but little later.

218. *Fora.* — 2. The *Forum* of the Romans is described generally in Vitruvius (Book vi. chap. 1.). He directs that it should be a large rectangular area, whose breadth is to be about two thirds of its length. The basilica or court of justice, serving also as an exchange for the merchants, is to be attached to it. The forum in a Roman city was the arena on which business, politics, and pleasure were equally transacted, discussed, and enjoyed. Among the Greeks it was called the αγορα, signifying a place in which the citizens were collected. It is here to be observed, that the fora of the Romans were of two sorts: *Fora Civilia* and *Fora Venalia;* the former whereof were designed as well with the object of ornamenting the cities in which they were erected, as for admitting a site for the public courts of justice, and other public buildings; the latter were intended to provide for the necessities and conveniences of the inhabitants, and no doubt bore a resemblance to our markets. The great Forum at Rome was seated between the Palatine and Capitoline hills. Though its boundary cannot now be satisfactorily traced, there seems little doubt that it included the Arch of Septimius Severus, the Temple of Concord, and the Curia or senate house, as well as the building of the Temple of Jupiter Stator, which has been above noticed. Restorations of this have been imagined by more than one artist, and more particularly by an ingenious French artist of the name of Caristie, who has published a thin folio volume on the subject, well deserving the attention of the architectural student; but as we shall presently place before the reader a forum from Pompeii in which less uncertainty exists, we shall not stop here in our enumeration of the other fora of Rome. The Forum of Nerva is said to have been 367 ft. long, and 164 ft. wide. At one end were five arched entrances, and at the other the Temple of Nerva. The Forum of Trajan, built by the emperor whose name it bears, was erected from the foreign spoils taken by him in his wars. The coverings of its edifices were all of brass, and the porticoes and their columns constructed in an exceedingly splendid style of execution. Ammianus Marcellinus (*Hist.* lib. xvi.) describes, with much force, the delight of Constantius on contemplating it when he made his triumphal entry into Rome. The representations make its length 1150 ft., and its mean breadth about 470 ft. In it was the emperor's magnificent column (*fig.* 111.), at one end was the Temple of Trajan, and at the other his Triumphal Arch. This Forum contained the celebrated and splendid Basilica Ulpiana. The other example we shall mention was at Fano, and we mention it because it contained a basilica by Vitruvius himself. He describes the portico of the Temple of Augustus as joining that side of the basilica which was furthest from the centre of the Forum, and a temple of Jupiter as standing at the opposite end. He goes on to describe the Treasury, Prison, and Curia, as placed on the longer sides of the Forum exteriorly to the shops which surrounded the area. The commentators on Vitruvius have been at considerable pains to make out the plan of the basilica of this building from the verbal description of it by the author, — perhaps none of them with greater success than old Daniel Barbaro.

219. But no words convey the description of a place so well as a diagram of the object under consideration; and as there exists at Pompeii a forum so perfect, that all the rules given by our great master are exemplified in it, we here place the plan (*fig.* 123.) of the forum there before the reader, so that he may have a complete notion of the arrangement. Entering from the gate of Herculaneum, the principal street leads to its north-west corner,

whence the access to it is by a flight of steps downwards, through an arch in a brick wall, still partially covered with stucco. It has been conjectured with probability, that the entrances to it were occasionally closed, from the remains of iron gates having been found at some of them. A smaller passage occurs to the right of the arch just mentioned, and a fountain attached to the wall between them. A is supposed to have been a temple of Venus; B, a public granary; C, a temple of Jupiter; D, probably a Senaculum, or council chamber; E, a temple to Mercury; F, a Chalcidicum; G G, curiæ; H, treasury; I, triumphal arch; K, aræostyle portico with ambulatory above.

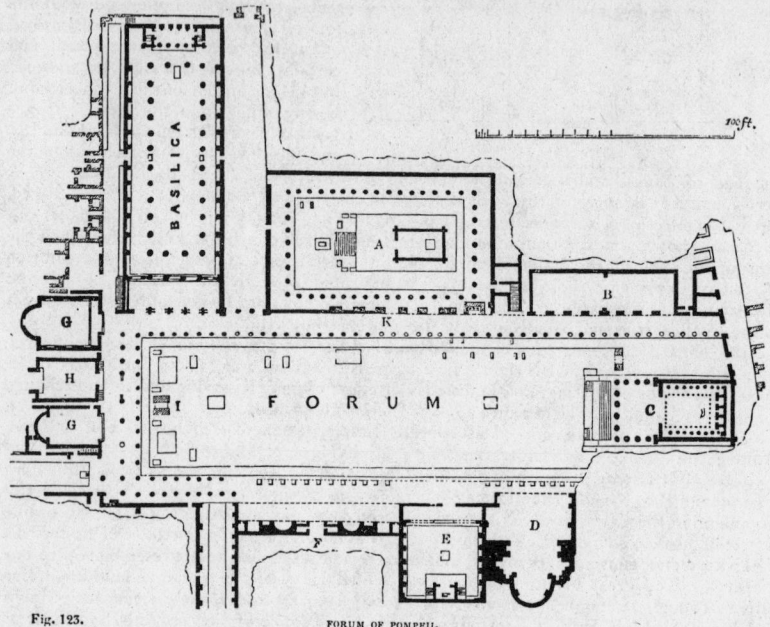

Fig. 123.   FORUM OF POMPEII.

220. *Triumphal Arches.* — The Romans were the first people who erected triumphal arches; their earliest examples being extremely simple and plain. A plain arch with a statue of the victor and his trophies on the summit, was for a long period the only method practised. The arch by degrees expanded in after times, the style became enriched, and the whole was at length loaded with a profusion of every sort of ornament. Latterly they were a rectangular mass (see *fig.* 124. of the arch of Constantine), penetrated by three arches, a central and two smaller side ones. The upper part consisted of a very high attic, frequently covered with inscriptions and bas reliefs, statues, triumphal cars and ornaments of that kind. The keystones were sometimes decorated with figures of victory. Of the triumphal arches that remain there are three classes : — first, those consisting of a single arch, as the arch of Trajan at Ancona, and Titus at Rome; second, those in which there are two arches, as in the example at Verona; third, those with three arches, whereof the central was the principal one, and those at the sides much smaller, as the arches of Constantine, Septimius Severus, &c. The most ancient of the remaining arches is that of Augustus at Rimini. It was erected on the occasion of his repairing the Flaminian way from that town to Rome. The erection of these triumphal arches afforded the means of gratifying the extraordinary vanity of the people with whom they originated. Many of them are in very bad taste; a remark that applies even to the Arch of Titus, which was erected before the arts had more than begun to droop. (See *figs.* in Book III.) The orders applied to them are unnecessary to be described in detail, because inapplicable except under precisely similar circumstances.

221. *Bridges.* — There is perhaps no single point in the history of architecture by which the civilisation of a people is so easily recognised as by that of their bridges. Latterly, in this country, the division of science as well as labour has so changed, that it seems almost necessary to refer to other works for knowledge on this subject; but as this is one in which architecture in all its branches must be considered, we shall here, as in the other sections of this work relating to the point in question, treat it in such manner as to give the reader some notion of the subject. The history of the bridges in every nation is connected with local causes, which have great influence on their construction; and though in other respects a nation may in the arts have attained a high pitch of excellence, yet it is possible that in bridge building their progress may be very limited as respects science. The matter

will depend entirely on the nature of the country. In our view of Grecian Architecture this subject has not been even mentioned. and it is nearly certain that Greece boasts no

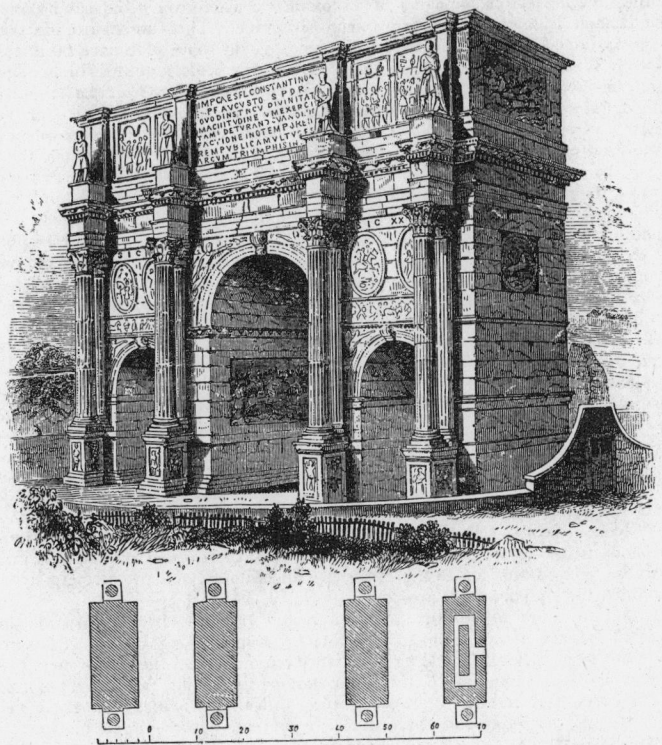

Fig. 124.　　　PLAN AND VIEW OF THE ARCH OF CONSTANTINE.

bridge whose date is anterior to its occupation by the Romans. But, independent of its want of acquaintance with the arch, the circumstance may be accounted for by the country not being intersected by any river of magnitude. Those to which one might be inclined to attach the name of river, are rather mountain torrents than sheets of water rolling their streams down to the ocean. A single arch in most cases would be all that was necessary to connect opposite banks, and the rocks themselves would form abutments for the single arch that was to connect them, without danger of failure.

222. In Italy, however, a country watered by many and considerable rivers, the study of the architecture of bridges was indispensable, as well for the accommodation of the cities with which it abounded, as for the service of the constant military expeditions of the restless and craving people who inhabited its surface. From its very earliest foundation, no city in the world would sooner have been placed in the predicament of requiring bridges than Rome herself; besides which, skill was required in their construction over a river like the Tiber, rapid and liable to be swelled by sudden floods. The earliest bridges of the Romans were of timber : such was that which joined the Janiculum to the Mons Aventinus, called the *Pons Sublicius* from the *sublicæ*, stakes (Liv. i. c. 33.), whereof it was composed. It is not here our intention to enumerate the ancient bridges of Rome; but the ruins of those which have come under our observation exhibit skill and science not inferior to the most extraordinary examples which modern art can exhibit ; witness the Pons Narniensis on the Flaminian way near Narni, about sixty miles from Rome. It was built by Augustus, and at the present day there remains, as though standing to mock modern science, an arch of a span of 150 ft., whose intrados is 100 ft. above the level of the river below. But of the works of this kind executed by the Romans we know of none, either in ancient or modern times, that is comparable with that erected by Trajan over the Danube, whose piers from their foundation were 150 ft. in height, and the span of whose arches was 170 ft., and to the number of twenty. The bridge was 60 ft. in width. This work, whose existence is scarcely credible, putting in the background all that of which in the present day it is our habit to boast, is reputed to have been destroyed by Hadrian, the successor of its founder, under a pretence that if the barbarians became masters of it, it might serve them as well

for making incursions on the empire, as for the empire in repressing those incursions. But other less creditable motives have been attributed to Hadrian for its destruction, one of them the envy he had of the name of its founder. There are still partial remains of an ancient Roman bridge over the Tagus near Alcantara. This consisted of six arches, each 80 ft. span, extending altogether 800 ft. in length, and some of them 200 ft. high above the river. We do not, in closing our brief view of the bridges of the Romans, more than mention the extraordinary temporary bridge which Cæsar threw over the Rhine.

223. *Aqueducts.* — It is obvious that of all the requisites for a city, the supply of wholesome water is only equalled by that of discharging it, which latter we have before seen was well provided for in the Eternal City. The aqueducts by which the Romans supplied their cities with this necessary element, are among the largest and most magnificent of their works. Their ruins alone, without other testimony, supply the means of estimating their extraordinary power, skill, and industry. They are works which sink into nothingness all other remnants of antiquity, not even excluding the amphitheatres, which we shall soon have to notice, because they were for the comfort, not the pastime, of the people. The earliest aqueduct was that of Appius Claudius, which we have above noticed as constructed in the 442d year of the city. It conveyed the Aqua Appia to Rome, from a distance of between seven and eight miles, by a deep subterraneous channel upwards of eleven miles in length. We shall here digress for a moment, by observing that upon the discovery of good water at a distance from the city at a much higher level than the service therein indicated, it was the practice to supply by means of a channel raised at any height as the case needed, through a stone-formed trough raised on the tops of arches as the course of it required over valleys, and otherwise became necessary from the nature of the face of the country, such a quantity as the source would afford. Hence the arcades raised to carry this simple trough of supply were often of stupendous height, and their length was no less surprising. In the present day, the power of steam has afforded other means of supplying a great city with water; but we much question whether the supply afforded by all the concealed pipes of this vast metropolis can compete in refreshment and general utility to its inhabitants with those at the present day poured into Rome, without becoming a burthen to the respective inhabitants, and this principally from the means which their predecessors provided.

224. The aqueduct of Quintus Martius, erected 312 years before Christ, is among the most extraordinary of the Roman aqueducts. Commencing at a spring thirty-three miles distant from Rome, it made a circuit of three miles, and then, after being conveyed through a vault or tunnel of 16 ft. in diameter, continued for thirty-eight miles along a series of arcades 70 ft. in height. It was formed with three distinct channels, one above the other, conveying the water from three different sources. In the upper one was the Aqua Julia, in the next the Aqua Tepula, and in the lowest the Aqua Martia. The Aqua Virginia was constructed by Agrippa, and in its course passed through a tunnel 800 paces in length. The Aqua Claudia, begun by Nero, and finished by Claudius, of which *fig.* 125.

Fig. 125.   AQUA CLAUDIA.

shows several arches, conveyed water to Rome from a distance of thirty-eight miles; thirty miles of this length was subterraneous, and seven miles on arcades, and it still affords a supply of water to the city. The Anio was conveyed to Rome by two different channels: the first was carried over a length of forty-three miles, and the latter of sixty-three, whereof six miles and a half formed a continued series of arches, many of them upwards of 100 ft. in height above the ground on which they stood. At the beginning of the reign of Nerva, there were nine great aqueducts at Rome. That emperor, under the superintendence of Julius Frontinus, constructed five others, and at a later period there were as many as twenty. According to Frontinus (de Aquæductibus) the nine earlier aqueducts supplied 14,018 quinaria daily, which are equal to 27,743,100 cubic ft.; and it has been computed that when all the aqueducts were in delivery, the surprising quantity of 50,000,000 of cubic ft. of water was afforded to the inhabitants of Rome, so that, reckoning the population at one million, which it probably never exceeded, 50 cubic ft. of water were allowed for the consumption of each inhabitant. More magnificent Roman aqueducts are, however, to be found in the provinces than those that supplied the city. That of Metz, whereof many of the arcades remain, is one of the most remarkable; extending across the Moselle, a river of considerable breadth where it crosses it, it conveyed the water of the Gorse to the city of Metz. From the reservoir in which the water was received, it was conducted through subterranean channels of hewn stone, so spacious that in them a man might stand upright. The arches appear to have been about fifty in number, and about 50 ft. in height. Those in the middle of the river have been swept away by the ice, those at the extremities remaining entire. In a still more perfect state than that at Metz is the aqueduct of Segovia,

of which one hundred and fifty of the arches remain, all formed of large blocks unconnected by cement, in two ranks of arcades one above the other.

225. It has been conjectured that the causes for not carrying these aqueducts in straight lines were first to avoid excessive height, where low grounds were crossed, and, secondly, to diminish the velocity of the water, so that it might not be delivered to the city in a turbid state. Along the line of an aqueduct, according to Montfauçon, at certain intervals, reservoirs called *Castella* were formed, in which the water might deposit its silt; these were round towers of masonry raised of course as high as the aqueduct itself, and sometimes highly ornamented. The same author observes that below the general bed of the channel, pits were sunk for the reception and deposit of the earthy particles which the water contained. Vitruvius directs the channels to be covered over to protect the water from the sun's rays, and (lib. viii. chap. 7.) he moreover directs that when water-pipes are passed across a valley, a *venter* should be formed, which is a subterranean reservoir wherein the water may be collected, and by which its expansion may be diminished, so that the hydrostatical pressure will not burst the joints. He also recommends that open vertical pipes should be raised for the escape of the air which accompanies the water, a practice which the moderns have found it necessary to adopt wherever it is necessary to bend pipes upwards, and thus permit the escape of air, which would impede, and even stop altogether, the movement of the water in them. (Some additional details are given in the GLOSSARY.)

226. *Theatres.* — The earliest stone theatre of Rome, as we have before stated (185.), was that of Pompey; but it must be recollected that as there are notices in history of this theatre having been more than once consumed by fire, there can be little doubt that a portion, probably the seats and scenes, were of wood. The second theatre of stone was raised by Julius Cæsar, after which Augustus reared one in honour of Marcellus, the son of his sister. The scanty ruins of this last enable one to do little more than trace its elevation, and from their curve to compute its extent. There was no *essential* difference between the form of the Roman and Greek Theatre, of which latter we have given a diagram in *fig.* 106. We nevertheless think it right here to present the reader with one of the Roman Theatre *fig.* 126.), as nearly as it can be made out from the description of Vitruvius. (Book v.

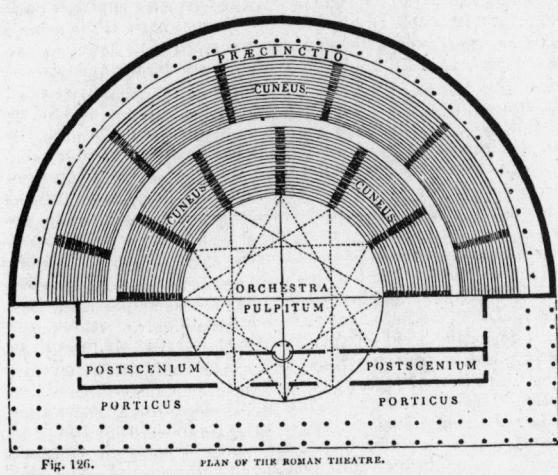

Fig. 126.   PLAN OF THE ROMAN THEATRE.

Chap. 6. "The form of a theatre," according to that author, "is to be adjusted so, that from the centre of the dimension allotted to the base of the perimeter, a circle is to be described, in which are inscribed, at equal distances from each other, four equilateral triangles whose points must touch the circumference of the circle." — "Of these triangles the side of that which is nearest the scene determines the face of it, in that part where it cuts the circumference of the circle. A line drawn parallel to it through the centre will separate the *pulpitum* of the *proscenium* from the *orchestra*. Thus the pulpitum becomes more spacious and convenient that that of the Greeks, because our actors remain chiefly on the *scena*. In the orchestra are assigned seats to the senators : the height of its pulpitum must not exceed 5 ft., so that the spectators in the orchestra may have a clear view of the motions of the actors. The portions between the staircases (*cunei*) of the theatre are to be so divided that the vertices of the triangles, that touch the circumference, may point to the directions of the ascents and steps between the cunei on the first *præcinction* or story. Above these the steps are placed alternately and form the upper cunei in the middle of those below. The angles thus pointing to staircases will be seven in number, and the remaining five will indicate certain points on the scene. That in the centre, for instance, is the situation for the royal door, those on the right and left the doors of the guests, and those at the extremities the points at which the road diverges. The seats (*gradus*) for the spectators are not to be less than 20 in. in height nor more than 22. Their width is not to be more than 2½ ft. nor less than 2 ft." Besides the theatres named, that of Cornelius Balbus, built by him in honour of Augustus, was on a scale of considerable magnificence.

227. The large theatre at Pompeii, as was frequently the case, was formed upon the slope of a hill, the corridor being the highest part, whence the audience descended to their seats, and staircases were saved.   The *gradus* at this theatre were about 1 ft. 3 in. high, and 2 ft. 4 in. wide, and from a part which is divided and numbered off, 1 ft. 3½ in. appear to have been allotted to each spectator.   There still remain some of the iron rings, for the reception of the masts from which the *velarium* or awning was suspended.

228. *Amphitheatres.* — The amphitheatre was unknown to the Greeks. At an early period, however, in Rome, human beings were compelled to fight for the amusement of spectators. The taste for such spectacles increased with its indulgence ; but it was nevertheless not

until the time of the emperors, that buildings were erected solely for exhibition of gladiatorial shows. The principal amphitheatres, of which remains still exist, are one at Alba, a small city of Latium ; another near the Tiber at Otricoli ; one of brick near the banks of the Garigliano ; one at Puzzuoli, wherein parts of the arcades and caves for wild

Fig. 127.   AMPHITHEATRE AT POLA

beasts still remain ; one at Capua ; another at Verona ; a very fine one at Pola in Istria (*fig.* 127.). In France, Arles, Saintes Autun, Nismes, and Nice possessed amphitheatres. In short, wherever the Romans went, they erected those extraordinary monuments of their power and skill. But all that we have enumerated were far surpassed by the Coliseum, which has been already briefly mentioned by us at page 79. The form of this building on the plan is an ellipse, whose transverse exterior axis is 615 ft. and its conjugate 510 ft., covering therefore nearly six English acres of ground. The whole mass is placed on an ascent of six stages, which encircle its whole circumference. In the centre is the *arena*, a name which it received from being strewed with sand, the transverse and conjugate axes whereof are 281 and 176 ft. respectively. Round the arena was a wall on which was the *podium* or fence ; and immediately behind this wall all round was a row of cells in which the beasts were placed preparatory to their entrance into the arena. In the rear of the cells was a corridor from which vaults radiated in directions perpendicular or nearly so to the curve of the ellipse, and serving to support the first *mœnianum* or interior range of seats. In some of these vaults were steps leading to the podium ; others were merely passages between the first corridor and the next towards the interior. The second corridor was lighted by apertures cut through its vault to the *præcinctio* which separated the first and second horizontal division of the seats. In rear of the second corridor, vaults again radiated, in some whereof were steps leading to the second division of the seats, and in others were galleries which led from the corridor to the double arcade, surrounding the whole edifice. The description will be better comprehended by reference to *figs.* 128. and 129., in the latter whereof a portion of the exterior side is removed, to exhibit the section.

229. About the whole exterior of the building, there are three orders of columns rising above each other, and one of pilasters crowning the whole. The columns are of equal diameter, and are filled in between with eighty arcades in each story. The arches of these arcades have all archivolt mouldings round them. Four of the arcades in the lower tier were reserved for the admission of distinguished personages, the remainder for the populace ; these last were called *vomitoria*, serving both for ingress and egress to and from the places of the spectators, by means of steps under the vaults that supported the seats. The piers which support the arches are 7 ft. 4. in. wide ; on each is a half column projecting from the general face of the wall. The opening between the piers is 17 ft. 3$\frac{6}{10}$ in. Impost mouldings are placed at the springing of the arches, and encircle the building except where interrupted by the columns and openings. The lower order resembles the Doric, except that the frieze is without triglyphs and the cornice without mutules. Desgodetz makes the height of the columns 27·63 ft., and their lower diameter 2 91 ft. Their diminution is very small. The height of the entablature is 6·64 ft., and the height, therefore, of the whole order above the pavement is 34·27 ft. The second order is Ionic, and stands on a dado 6 ft. high, broken under the columns to receive their projection from the wall. The columns are 25·73 ft. high. The volutes of the capitals are without ornament ; the eye being merely marked by a circle. The entablature is 6·64 ft. high, and its subdivisions are like that in the order below. There are neither modillions nor dentils in the cornice. The height of the whole order is 38·37 ft. The third order is Corinthian, standing on a dado 6·39 ft. high. The columns are 25·58 ft. high, the entablature 6·59 ft., and the height of the entire order, including the dado, is 38·57 ft.

The upper story is decorated with a series of Corinthian pilasters on subplinths 2·79 ft.
high, placed on a dado of the height of 7 ft.   The height of the pilasters, which are not

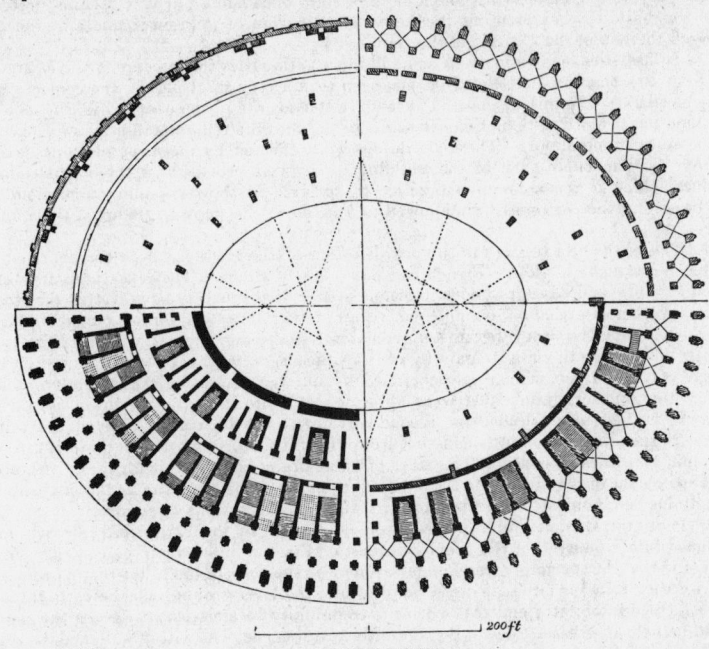

Fig. 128.   PLAN OF COLISEUM.

diminished, is 28 ft., and the height of their entablature is 7·37 ft.   The frieze and architrave are broken vertically in each interpilaster over three corbels, on which it is supposed,

Fig. 129.   SECTION AND ELEVATION OF COLISEUM.

running through the back part of the cornice, poles were placed for holding the *velarium*,
which was occasionally stretched over the building to protect the spectators from the sun
or rain.   The whole height of the façade above the steps was 162 ft.   The columns project
rather more from the walls than their semidiameter; and the faces of the walls are not in
the same vertical plane, but recede from it towards the interior of the building.   The widths
of the piers vary in the different stories, being respectively from the lower part upwards as
8·71, 8·38, and 7·28 ft.   Between the pilasters, in the fourth order, are square windows.
The velarium was attached to the poles round the circumference with a fall towards the
interior, so that the rain was delivered into the arena.   The following has been supposed
as a method of spreading the velarium, of which Fontana gives a representation, but no description.   To a cable placed round and made fast on the edge of the podium, and following its curve, strong ropes were attached in the direction (on the plan) of the radiating walls.
These ropes passed through pullies in the poles, 240 in number, at the top of the building,
which rested on the corbels above mentioned, and thus raised the velarium to the required
height.   It would follow the inclination of the seats, and the cloth, of whatever fabric or
materials it might be, being formed in gores equal on the outer edges to the distance of the
masts from each other, might move on the radiating ropes by rings attached to the edges of

each gore, so as to be moved backwards and forwards by persons stationed on the parapet. Marine soldiers were employed for this purpose. The velarium was sometimes of silk, but more usually yellow or brown woollen cloth. Nero once had a purple velarium stretched across the building, representing the heavens with stars of gold on it, and a design embroidered thereon of the Chariot of the Sun.

230. It has been conjectured by some Roman antiquaries that the arena was boarded; and, from the changes that could be made on it in a very short period, the conjecture is highly probable. Domitian covered it with water for the purpose of exhibiting marine shows and naval fights. Sometimes it was changed into the representation of a forest with wild beasts roaming about. These alterations were effected by means of machines called *pegmata*. In particular parts of the building, pipes were provided for the distribution of perfumes, which it was a common practice to sprinkle in showers; but, on particularly great occasions, the perfumes were allowed to flow down the steps or gradus of the amphitheatre.

231. The conjecture relative to the boarded floor of the arena has been corroborated by the discoveries made while the French had possession of Rome. They excavated the arena, and found vaults and passages under its whole area. It is much to be regretted that these inquiries were not carried on, owing to an accumulation of waters, for which no drainage having been provided, they became unwholesome from stagnancy, and it therefore was necessary once more to close it again by obvious means. Great care was bestowed on the drainage of this edifice, which was encircled by a large sewer for the reception of the water of the interior drains, that were all conducted into it. Another drain, 30 inches wide, was carried round under the second corridor, into which are conveyed the water from the perpendicular conduits and that from the third corridor, whose drain is 3 ft. in depth and 17 inches in width. The sides of these drains are lined with tiles. Another drain runs on the outer side of the third corridor, and is of the same size as the last named. Other drains communicate with these towards the arena in various directions.

232. Paoli thinks that amphitheatres were first used by the Etruscans, and by them introduced into Rome; that the people in question first exhibited their games in narrow valleys, and that the spectators were ranged around on the sides of the hills; that when these sports were exhibited in cities, an arena was dug into the level ground, and the earth thrown out was formed into seats; and that when the community became rich enough, or the games came to be held in greater esteem, the amphitheatre was enclosed with a wall, and the seats formed of wood or stone. It certainly appears to us that Paoli's conjecture is reasonable, and that Etruscan buildings or formations were the original type.

233. The amphitheatre at Nismes was capable of containing 17,000 persons: it was 400 ft. long and 320 ft. broad. That at Verona, upon whose age antiquaries are divided in opinion, some maintaining that it was built in the time of Augustus, and others as late as the time of Maximian, Maffei making somewhat of a mean between the two periods, is of an elliptical form, 508 ft. long and 403 ft. broad. It is in much better preservation than the Coliseum. Its exterior wall has three stories of Tuscan pilasters on the face of the wall, the two upper whereof stand on podia. Between these pilasters are arcades of semi-circular-headed apertures. Maffei says, that allowing a foot and a half of room for each person, this edifice would seat 22,000 spectators. But in this there must be some mistake.

234. *Baths.* — Publius Victor says that the city of Rome contained public and private baths to the amazing number of 850. Some of these we know, from their ruins, were buildings of great extent and magnificence. They were all constructed, we mean the public ones, on plans very similar; and, in order to a description of them, we give in *fig.* 130. a restored plan of the baths of Caracalla, at Rome. Those of Titus and Dioclesian may also be traced; the chief others being those of Agrippa, Nero, and Domitian. The baths of Antoninus Caracalla are thus described by Eustace (vol. i. p. 226.): " Repassing the Aventine Hill, we came to the baths of Antoninus Caracalla, that occupy part of its declivity, and a considerable portion of the plain between it, Mons Cæliolus and Mons Cælius. No monument of ancient architecture is calculated to inspire such an exalted idea of Roman magnificence as the ruins of their thermæ, or baths. Many remain in a greater or less degree of preservation; such as those of Titus, Dioclesian, and Caracalla. To give the untravelled reader some notion of these prodigious piles, I will confine my observations to the latter, as the greatest in extent and as the best preserved; for, though it be entirely stripped of its pillars, statues, and ornaments, both internal and external, yet its walls still stand, and its constituent parts and principal apartments are evidently distinguishable. The length of the thermæ was 1840 ft., its breadth 1476. At each end were two temples; one to Apollo, and another to Esculapius, as the tutelary deities (*genii tutelares*) of a place sacred to the improvement of the mind and the care of the body. The two other temples were dedicated to the two protecting divinities of the Antonine family, Hercules and Bacchus. In the principal building were, in the first place, a grand circular vestibule, with four halls on each side, for cold, tepid, warm, and steam baths: in the centre was an immense square for exercise, when the weather was unfavourable to it in the

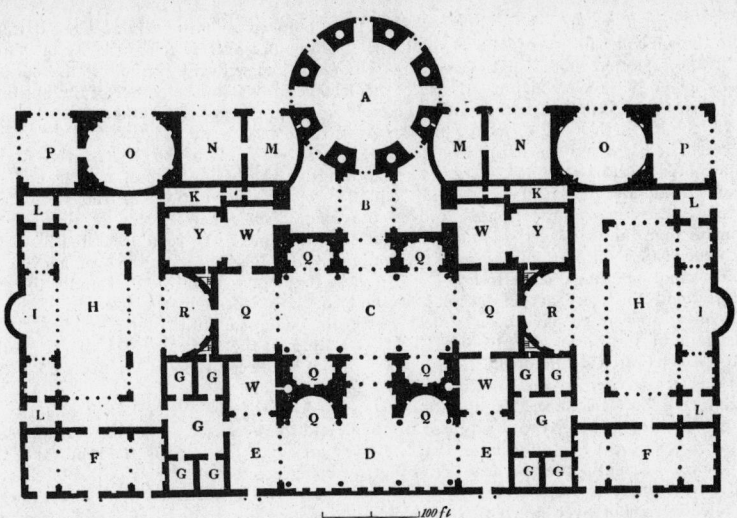

Fig. 130.   BATHS OF CARACALLA.

open air; beyond it a great hall, where 1600 marble seats were placed for the convenience of the bathers: at each end of this hall were libraries. This building terminated on both sides in a court surrounded with porticoes, with a spacious odeum for music, and in the middle a spacious basin for swimming. Round this edifice were walks shaded by rows of trees, particularly the plane; and in its front extended a gymnasium for running, wrestling, &c. in fine weather. The whole was bounded by a vast portico, opening into exedræ, or spacious halls, where the poets declaimed and philosophers gave lectures to their auditors. This immense fabric was adorned within and without with pillars, stucco work, paintings, and statues. The stucco and paintings, though faintly indeed, are yet in many places perceptible. Pillars have been dug up, and some still remain amidst the ruins; while the Farnesian bull and the famous Hercules, found in one of these halls, announce the multiplicity and beauty of the statues which adorned the thermæ of Caracalla. The flues and reservoirs of water still remain. The height of the pile was proportioned to its extent, and still appears very considerable, even though the ground be raised at least 12 ft. above its ancient level. It is now changed into gardens and vineyards; its high massive walls form separations, and its limy ruins, spread over the surface, burn the soil and check its natural fertility."

235. Returning to the plan of the baths in question, we have now to explain that the circular apartment, lettered A, was called the solar cell. It was 111 ft. in diameter, and contained the different *labra* of the baths. This solar cell, Spartianus says, could not be equalled by the best architects of that age. The dome was lined with brass, of which material also were the lattices to the windows. B, the *apodyterium*, or undressing room. C, a *xystus*, or apartment for exercise in unfavourable weather. D contained the piscina, or large reservoir for swimming. E, vestibule for spectators and the dresses of the bathers. F, entrance vestibule of the thermæ, having libraries on each side. G G, rooms wherein the athletæ prepared for their exercises. H, a court, having a piscina for bathing in the centre. I, *ephebeum*, place of exercise for the youth. K K, the *elæotherium*, or apartment for anointing the bathers with oil. L L, vestibules. M, *laconicum*, an apartment so called, as it is said, from the name of the stove by which it was heated, and from the custom of the *sudatio*, or sweating, having originated in Laconia. N, *caldarium*, or hot water bath, which was most frequented. O, *tepidarium*, or tepid water bath. P, *frigidarium*, or cold water bath. Q, *exedræ* for seats for the use of the philosophers and their scholars. W, rooms for conversation. R R, *exedræ*, or large recesses for the use of the philosophers. Y, *conisterium*, or place where, after anointing, the wrestlers were sprinkled with dust.

236. We have just given the common explanation to the word laconicum; but it is right the reader should know that its true meaning is in some doubt. Galiani considers it a great chamber wherein the people underwent sweating. To this Cameron adds, " I for myself hold it certain that the apartment for this purpose has been by some authors improperly termed; the laconicum is nothing more than a little cupola which covered an aperture in the pavement of the hot bath, through which the vivid flame of the hypocaustum, or furnace, passed and heated the apartment at pleasure. Without this means," continues that author, " the hot bath would not have had a greater heat than the other chambers, the

temperature of which was milder.   I have been induced to form this opinion, not only from the ancient paintings found in the baths of Titus, but also by the authority of Vitruvius, who says that the hot bath (*concamerata sudatio*) had within it, in one of the corners, or rather ends, the laconicum.   Now, if the laconicum was in the corner of the hot bath, it is clear that it is not the bath itself, but merely a part of it ; and if, as others have thought, it was the hot bath itself, to what purpose served the concamerata sudatio ? "

237. The baths and thermæ of the Romans, like the gymnasia of the Greeks, were highly ornamented with bassi relievi, statues, and paintings.   The basins were of marble, and the beautiful mosaic pavements were only equalled by the decorations of the vaults and cupolas.   Nothing more strongly proves the magnificence and luxury of the ancient Romans than the ruins of the baths still to be seen in Rome.   Agrippa decorated his baths with encaustic paintings, and covered the walls of the caldarium with slabs of marble, in which small paintings were inserted.   All these luxuries were introduced under the emperors; and the mere act of bathing, as described by Seneca in the instance of Scipio Africanus, appears to have been almost lost in the effeminacy of the later practice.   The splendour of the places may be judged of by calling to the remembrance of the reader that the celebrated statue of the Laocoon was one of the decorations of the baths of Titus, and that of the Farnese Hercules of the baths of Caracalla.

238. We have, in the section on Aqueducts (224.), stated the extraordinary quantity of water with which the city was supplied by them, and there can be no doubt that the baths caused a very great consumption of that necessary article of life.   After the removal of the empire to Constantinople, we hear of no thermæ being erected; and it is probable that at that period many of those in the city fell into decay.   The aqueducts by which they were supplied were, moreover, injured by the incursions of invaders, another cause of the destruction of the baths.   Remains of Roman baths have been discovered in this country, for descriptions whereof the reader is referred to the *Archæologia*.

239. We shall conclude our observations on the Roman baths by the mention of some curious paintings in the baths of Titus, very similar in their features to those found in places on the walls of Pompeii ; we allude to representations of slender twisted columns, broken entablatures, and curvilinear pediments, columns standing on corbels attached to the walls, a profusion of sculpture, with fantastic animal figures and foliage, and many other *estravaganzas*, which found imitators after the restoration of the arts, and, in some cases, with great success.

240. *Circi.* — The circus of the Greeks was nothing more than a plain, or race course ; from its length called Στάδιον (stadium); as also Κιρκος, from its oval figure.   With the Romans it became a regular building of great dimensions and magnificence.   The *Circus Maximus*, constructed originally in a rude manner by Romulus, and afterwards rebuilt by the elder Tarquin, is, in its external dimensions, computed to have been 2000 ft. long and 550 ft. broad, consisting of two parallel walls in the direction of its length, united at one extremity by a set of apartments, called *carceres*, arranged in the form of the segment of a circle of about 430 ft. radius; and, at the opposite short end, by a semicircular enclosure. The carceres contained the chariots ready for starting.   The *arena*, or space thus enclosed, contained a long low wall called the *spina*, 1300 ft. in length, running along its longitudinal axis, and commencing at the centre of the semicircular end, having a *meta*, or goal, at each of its extremities.   Like those of the theatre and amphitheatre, the seats of the spectators were placed round the arena with a podium in front; between which and the spina the races of the chariots were exhibited.   The circus of Nero was nearly of the same form, but neither so long nor so broad, being only 1400 ft. in length and 260 in breadth, and its spina but 800 ft.

241. The remains of the circus of Caracalla, of which Bianconi has given a very good account, are still sufficiently abundant to trace the plan (*fig.* 131.).   It was nearly of the same dimensions as that of Nero.   There are in this building some curious examples of lightening the spandrels of the arches over which the seats were constructed, by filling them in with light vessels of pottery ; a practice which has been partially adopted in some modern buildings, and is still usefully practised on the Continent.   Generally speaking, the circus was a parallelogram, whose external length was from four to five times its breadth. It was surrounded by seats ranged above each other, and bounded by an exterior wall, probably pierced with arcades.   The spina was about two thirds the length of the building, and was ornamented with statues, obelisks, and other ornaments, terminated at each end by the meta, which consisted of three obelisks or columns.   The carceres were closed by gates in front and rear, which were not opened till the signal was given for starting.   In the circus of Caracalla, it will be seen that these carceres were placed obliquely to the long sides of the edifice, so as to equalise the length of their course from the starting point to the goal.   So that it would seem there was as much nicety in a chariot race of old as in a modern horse race.

242. *Private Houses.*—The domestic architecture of the Romans possesses great interest; the general instructions spread over the sixth book of Vitruvius upon their parts and pro-

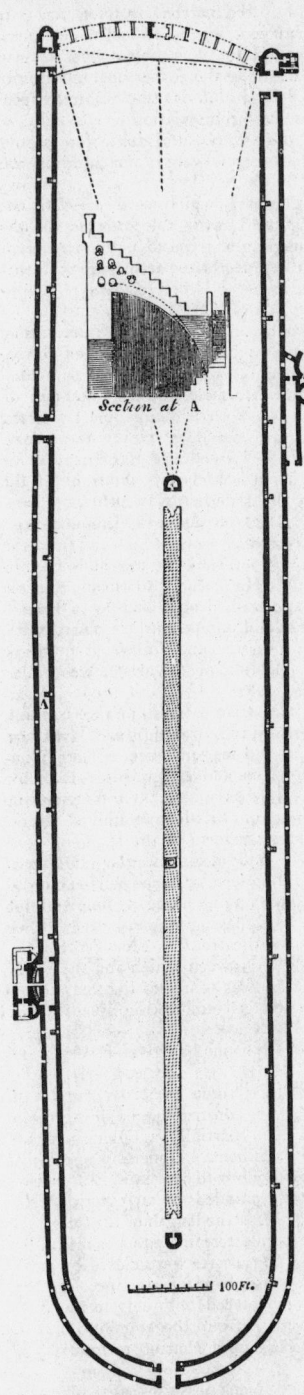

Section at A

Fig. 131.   PLAN OF CIRCUS OF CARACALLA.

100 Ft.

portions have received much illustration from the discoveries at Pompeii; and it is pleasant to find that, following his merely verbal directions, a building might be planned which would correspond as nearly with what we now know was the case, as two houses, even in a modern city, may be expected to resemble one another. In the following observations we have used most abundantly the elegant little work of Mazois (*Le Palais de Scaurus*, 2d ed. 8vo. Paris, 1822), and feel a pleasure in thus acknowledging our obligations to that author; but, before more immediately using his observations on the later habitations of the Romans, we shall premise that until after the war of Pyrrhus, towards the year 280 B.C., the use of tiles as a covering for them appears to have been unknown. Till then thatch or shingles formed the covering of the houses. They consisted of a single story; for, according to Pliny (lib. xxxiv. c. 15.) and Vitruvius (lib. ii. c. 8.), a law was in force forbidding walls of a greater thickness than one foot and a half; whence it is clear they could not have been safely raised higher than a single story with the unbaked bricks then in use. But the space within which the city was confined, with an increasing population, rendered it necessary to provide in height that which could not be obtained in area; so that, in the time of Augustus, the height of a house was limited to 70 ft. (*Aurel. Vict.; and Strabo*, lib. v.)

243. The extraordinary fortunes that were realised in Rome towards the last years of the republic, when the refinements of the arts of Greece were introduced into the city, soon led its more favoured citizens to indulge in architectural splendour. Lucius Cassius had decorated his dwelling with columns of foreign marble; but all other private edifices were thrown into shade by that of Scaurus, in which were employed black marble columns of the height of 38 ft. Mamurra lined his apartments with marble; and, indeed, such was the prodigality, for it deserves that term, of the Romans, that Pliny (lib. xvii. c. 50.) tells us of Domitius Ahenobarbus having offered a sum equivalent to 48,500*l.* sterling (sexagies sestertium) for the house of Crassus, which was refused. Their villas were equally magnificent. Cicero had two of great splendour — his Formian and Tusculan villas; but these were exceeded in beauty by those of Lucullus and Pollio, the latter near Posilippo, where some remains of it are still to be seen. Though Augustus attempted to stop this extraordinary rage for magnificence, he was unsuccessful; and the examples which were afforded by later emperors were unlikely to restrain the practice where the means existed. In the Domus Aurea of Nero, domestic architecture appears, from all accounts, to have reached the utmost degree of splendour and magnificence.

244. In the better class of Roman dwellings, certain apartments were considered indispensable; and these, in different degrees of size and decoration, were always found. There were others which were or were not so found, according to the wealth and fancy of the proprietor. Thus, every private house of any pretension was so planned that one portion was assigned to the reception of strangers, or rather for public resort, and the other for the private use of the family. The public part was destined for the reception of dependants or *clients*, who resorted to the house of their patron for advice and assistance.

The number of these clients was honourable and useful to the patron, as they might, in civil matters, be depended on for their votes. Hence lawyers especially had their houses thronged with them; and it is amusing in the present day to see the term of *client* still kept up among our barristers: for although his state of dependence has lost nothing of its extent, the eminence of the patron is now measured by the quantity and amount of fees his clients enable him to consume. Vitruvius describes the public portion as consisting of the *porticus, vestibulum, cavædium* or *atrium, tablinum, alæ, fauces,* and some few others, which were not added except at the especial desire of the party for whom the building was to be erected.

Fig. 132.   DOOR AND PROTHYRUM, POMPEII.

245. The parts which were sacred to the use of the family were the *peristyle,* the *cubicula* (sleeping apartments), the *triclinium,* the *œci,* the *pinacothecæ,* or picture galleries, the *biblictheca,* or library, baths, *exedræ, xysti,* and others.

246. In the more extended mansions of the Romans was an area, surrounded on two sides by porticoes and shops, and ornamented with statues, trophies, and the like, and on the third (the fourth being open) was the decorated entrance or portico of the house. But in smaller dwellings this entrance or portico was in a line with the front of the houses in the street; the vestibule or *prothyrum* (fig. 132.) being in the Roman houses merely a passage room, which led from the street to the entrance of the atrium. In this vestibule, or rather by its side, the *ostiarius* or porter was stationed, as in French houses we find a *concierge.* When there were two courts, we are inclined to think that the one nearest the street was called the *atrium,* and the farthest from it the *cavædium;* but in many cases we also think that the atrium served equally as a cavædium according to the owner's rank. The explanation of Varro will certainly answer for one as well as the other. It may be that the cavædium was a second atrium of larger size.

247. Of the atrium Vitruvius describes five sorts: 1. The *Tuscan,* wherein the protecting roof was a sort of pent-house on the four sides, supported by beams framed at right angles into each other; the space in the centre forming the *compluvium,* and the basin or area in the centre the *impluvium.* 2. The *tetrastyle* atrium (one with four

Fig. 133.   CORINTHIAN ATRIUM.

columns), which was similar to the Tuscan, except that the angles of the beams of the roof or pent-house rested on four columns. 3. The Corinthian atrium (*fig.* 133.), which differed only from the last in its size, and the number of its columns. 4. The *atrium displuviatum* in which the slope of the roofs was towards the body of the building. 5. The *atrium testudinatum*, which was covered with a ceiling, and with nothing more than an aperture therein to afford light. The compluvium was sometimes (*Plin.* xix. c. i.) provided with a sort of awning. The roof of the four sides of the atrium was covered with ornamental tiles, the eaves' faces whereof were terminated between their sloping junctions with carved faces called *antefixæ*, similar to those in the roofs of the Grecian temples. The atrium was, moreover, frequently embellished with fountains. It was in the atrium that the splendid columns which we have mentioned, as decorating the house of Scaurus, were placed. The walls were either lined with marble or painted with various devices, and the pavement was decorated with mosaic work or with precious marbles.

248. The *tablinum*, which usually opened towards the atrium, seems to have been a sort of levee room, wherein the master of the mansion received his visitors or clients, lists of whom were therein recorded, and where the *maestro di camera* announced their names. Some have thought, and we do not say they are wrong, that this apartment contained (which it might also do without affecting the truth of the first supposition) the family archives, statues, pictures, pedigree, and other appurtenances incident to a long line of ancestors.

249. The apartments on the sides right and left of the tablinum were called, as their name signifies, *alæ*. These were also furnished with portraits, statues, and other pieces relative to the family, not omitting inscriptions commemorative of actions worthy their name.

250. Two corridors, one on each side of the atrium, which led to the interior of the house from the atrium, were called *fauces* (jaws).

251. In houses of moderate dimensions, chambers were distributed round the atrium for the reception and lodging of strangers; but in establishments of importance, wherein the proprietor was a person of extended connexions, there was a separate *hospitium* appropriated to that purpose.

Fig. 134.   PERISTYLE AT POMPEII.

252. We have stated that the peristyle was a portion of the private part of the house. It was mostly, if not always, placed beyond the atrium, with which it communicated by means of the tablinum and fauces. Similar in general form and design to the atrium, for it was surrounded by columns (see *fig.* 134.), it was larger than that apartment. The centre was usually provided with a parterre in which shrubs and flowers were distributed, and in its middle a fish pool. This portion of the peristyle was called the xystus (*Vitr.* lib. vi. c. 10.). In better houses there was an ante-room called *procœton*, to each of the bed-chambers, of whose arrangement very little is known. The triclinium (τρεις κλιναι, three beds), or dining-room, was so called from its having three couches round the table on which the dinner was served; the fourth side being left open for the servants (see *fig.* 135.). It was raised two steps from the peristyle, and separated from the garden by a large window. Winter triclinia were placed towards the west, and those for summer to the east. In large houses there were several triclinia, whose couches would contain a greater or less number of people. The *œci* were large *salons* or halls, of Greek origin, and, like the atria, were of more than one species; as for instance the tetrastyle, the Corinthian, and the Egyptian. " There is this difference," observes Vitruvius (lib. v. cap. 6.), " between the Corinthian and Egyptian œcus. The former has a single order of columns, standing either on a podium or on the ground, and over it architraves and cornices, either of wood or plaster, and a semicircular ceiling above the cornice. In the Egyptian œcus, over the lower column, is an architrave, from which to the surrounding walls is a boarded and paved floor, so as to form a passage round it in the open air. Then, perpendicularly over the architrave of the lower columns, columns one fourth smaller are placed. Above their architraves and cornices, they are decorated with ceilings, and windows are placed between the upper columns. Thus they have the appearance of basilicæ rather than of Corinthian triclinia." The œcus, called Cyzicene by the Greeks, was different to those of Italy. Its aspect was to the north, towards the gar-

Fig. 135.   SMALL TRICLINIUM AT POMPEII.

which was paved with mosaic. B B B B, Tuscan atrium, in whose centre is the compluvium or basin (b) for the reception of the water from the roof.

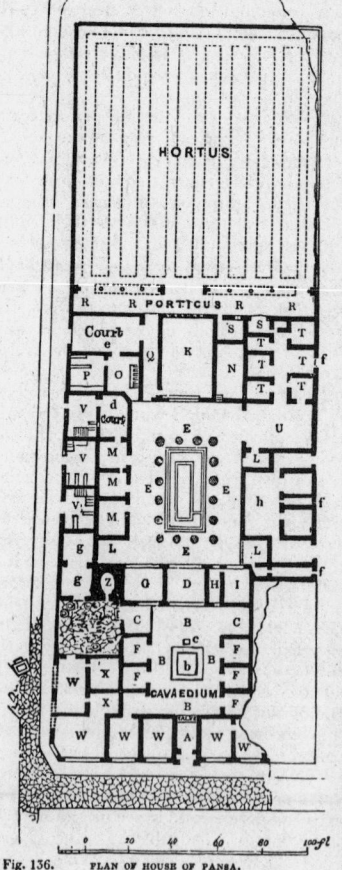

Fig. 136.   PLAN OF HOUSE OF PANSA.

dens, and had doors in the middle. It was made long, and broad enough to hold two triclinia opposite to each other. The Greek œcus was not, however, much used in Italy. The *pinacotheca* (picture room), where possible, faced the north: both this and the *bibliotheca* (library), whose aspect was east, do not require explanation. The *exedræ* of the Roman houses were large apartments for the general purposes of society. The upper stories of the house, the chief being on the ground floor, were occupied by slaves, freedmen, and the lower branches of the family. Sometimes there was a *solarium* (terrace), which was, in fine weather, much resorted to.

253. *Fig.* 136. is a plan of the house of Pansa at Pompeii, by reference to which the reader will gain a tolerable notion of the situation of the different apartments whereof we have been speaking. A is the prothyrum, which was paved with mosaic. One of the proportions assigned to the atrium by Vitruvius is, that the length shall be once and a half the breadth; and here it is precisely such. c, a pedestal or altar of the household god. C C, alæ. They were on three sides surrounded by seats, and, from Sir W. Gell's account, are analogous to similar recesses in the galleries of Turkish houses, with their divans: the thresholds were mosaic. Vitruvius directs them to be two sevenths of the length of the atrium; which is precisely their size here. D, tablinum. It was separated from the atrium by an aulæum, or curtain, like a drop scene. Next the inner court was sometimes, perhaps generally, a window, occupying the whole side. The tablinum was used as a dining-room in summer. E E E E, peristyle, which, in this example, exactly corresponds with the proportions directed by Vitruvius. F F F F were domestic apartments, as penaria, or cubicula, or cellæ domesticæ. G, probably the pinacotheca, or apartment for pictures. H, fauces, or passage of communication between the outer and inner divisions of the house. I, cubiculum. Its use cannot be doubted, as it contains a bedstead, filling up the whole width of the further end of it. K, triclinium, raised two steps from the peristyle, and separated from the garden by a large window. In this room company was received, and chairs placed for their accommodation. L L L, exedræ. M M M, cellæ familiariæ, or family chambers: the further one had a window looking into a court at d. N, lararium or armarium, a receptacle for the more revered and favourite gods. O, kitchen with stoves therein, and opening into a court at e, and an inner room P, in which were dwarf walls to deposit oil jars. Q, fauces conducting to the garden. Along the back front, R R R R, is a portico or pergula, for training vines and creepers on the back front of the house, before the windows of the triclinium. S S: these two rooms, opening into the pergula, were, it is presumed, cubicula. T T, &c.: the apartments thus marked seem to have constituted a distinct portion of the house, and communicated with the street by a separate door. That they were in-

cluded in the establishment of Pansa seems certain, from their being connected with the peristyle by the large apartment U.   On excavating here, four skeletons of females were found marked by their gold ear-rings; also a candelabrum, two vases, a fine marble head of a faun, gold bracelets, rings with engraved stones, &c. &c.   V V V are shops, which appear, by the remains of staircases, to have had apartments above.   They contain dwarf walls for ranging oil jars and other goods against. W W, &c. are different shops.   One is of a baker, and to it the necessary conveniences are appended. X X, apotheca or store-rooms.   Y is the bakehouse, containing the oven Z, the mills, a kneading trough, &c. : it is paved with volcanic stone in irregular polygons. g g, place for the wood and charcoal.   h appears to have been almost a distinct dwelling : two of the apartments had windows to the street, which runs southward to the forum. f f f, entrances from the street to the house of Pansa.   The house was surrounded by streets, or, in other words, was an insula.   We have thus named the principal apartments, and identified them by an example.   In more magnificent houses there were the sacrarium, the venereum, the sphæristerium, the aleatorium, &c. &c.   The painting *fig.* 137. is in the kitchen of the house of Pansa, and represents the worship of the lares, under whose care and protection the provisions and cooking utensils were placed.

Fig. 137.   PAINTING AT POMPEII.

254. *Tombs.*—The Romans were rather given to magnificence in the tombs erected for their dead.   Some of these were public, and others for the interment of individuals or families. The former were often of vast extent, and have been compared to subterranean cities ; the others were pyramids, conical and cylindrical towers, with ranges of vaults in them for sepulture.

255. Perhaps the earliest tomb at Rome is that of the Horatii, which stands on the Appian Way, and was probably constructed by Etruscan workmen.   It has a basement 45 ft. square on the plan, on which stand five masses of rubble or earth, faced with masonry, in the form of frusta of cones, four of which are ten feet diameter at the bottom, and are placed at the four angles of the basement.   The fifth stands in the centre of the whole mass, and is larger than the others.

256. The principal tombs about Rome are, 1. The pyramid of Caius Cestius, whose sides are 102 ft. long, and its height about the same number of feet.   The interior contains in the centre a rectangular cell, 20 ft. long, and 13 ft. broad.   At each external angle of this pyramid stands a Doric column, without any portion of entablature over it.   It is possible these were intended as ornaments, though it has often puzzled us to find out how they ever could have been so thought. 2. The tomb of Adrian, now converted into the Castel St. Angelo, had originally a square basement, whose sides were 170 ft. long.   From this substructure rose a cylindrical tower, 115 ft. diameter, probably at one time encircled by a colonnade.   It is now used as a fortress, and was considerably altered by Pope Paul III. 3. The mausoleum of Cecilia Metella is a circular building, 90 ft. in diameter, and 62 ft. high, standing on a basement of the same form.   Up to the frieze the tomb is of Travertine stone, but the frieze itself is of marble, with sculptured rams' heads and garlands. In what may be called the core is a cell, 19 ft. diameter, to which there is an entrance by a passage on the exterior.

257. We do not, however, think it necessary further to detail the Roman tombs which may be found in Rome or the provinces, but, in lieu of extending our description on this

head, to give the reader a notion of their forms in *fig.* 138. by a group from Pompeii,

among the remains of which city there are a great many and various examples. They are in general of small dimensions, and stand so near one another as to form a street, called the Street of the Tombs. Some of these are decorated very highly, both as respects ornament in the architecture and bassi relievi on the different faces. The Romans were particular in keeping alive the memory of the dead, hence their tombs were constantly looked after and kept in repair; a matter which, in this country of commerce and politics, a man's descendants rarely think of, after dividing the spoil at his death.

Fig. 158.   TOMBS AT POMPEII.

258. *Character of Roman Architecture.*—The character of the Roman architecture in its best period was necessarily very different from the Grecian, on which it was founded. We envy not those who say that they feel no beauties except those which the pure Grecian Doric of the Parthenon possesses. Each style, in every division of architecture, has its beauties; and those, among other causes, arise from each style being suited to the country in which it was reared; neither can we too often repeat the answer which Quatremère de Quincy gives in the *Encyclopedie Méthodique* to the question many years since propounded by the French Academy of Inscriptions and Belles Lettres, " Whether the Greeks borrowed their architecture from the Egyptians ? " The answer of that highly talented writer is, " That there is no such thing as general human architecture, because the wants of mankind must vary in different countries. The only one in which the different species of architecture can approach each other is intellectual; it is that of impressions, which the qualities whose effects are produced by the building art can work upon the mind of every man, of every country. Some of them result from every species of architecture,—an art which sprung, as well from the huts of Greece, as from the subterraneous excavations of Egypt, from the tents of Asia, and from several mixed principles to us unknown. Thus the use of the word architecture is improper. We ought to name the species; for between the idea of architecture as a genus and as a species there is the same difference as between language and tongue; and to seek for a simple origin of architecture is as absurd as a search would be after the primitive language. If so, the hut of Vitruvius would be but an ingenious fable, as some have said; but it would be a ridiculous falsehood if he had pretended that it was the type of *all* architecture." If we must confine ourselves to the simplicity and purity of line which the Greek temple exhibits,—circumstances, be it observed, that no future occasion can ever again effectually call up,—all the admiration of the numberless monuments of the Romans is based upon false data, and we are not among those who feel inclined to set ourselves up against the universal consent of our race. Thus far we think it necessary to observe on the silly rage which a few years ago existed for setting up in this metropolis pure Greek Doric porticoes and pure Greek profiles. What could more exhibit the poverty of an artist's imagination, for instance, if the thing exist, than appending to a theatre the Doric portico of a temple ? But the thing is too ridiculous to dwell on, and we proceed to our purpose. Whether the Romans invented the Tuscan order we much doubt. No example of it exists similar in formation to that described by Vitruvius: it must, however, be admitted that it is a beautiful combination of parts, and worthy so great a people. It seems highly probable that this order was used by the Etruscans, and that to them its origin is attributable. The use of timber in the entablature, which we know was practised by them to a great extent, seems to sanction such an hypothesis. Its detail, as well as that of the other orders of architecture, belong to another part of this work; we shall not therefore further speak of it than in the language of Sir Henry Wotton, who says, with his usual quaintness and simplicity, that it is a sturdy labourer in homely apparel.

259. The Doric order with the Romans was evidently not a favourite. In their hands its character was much changed. The remains of it in the theatre of Marcellus, in the examples at Cora and Pompeii, and the fragment at the baths of Dioclesian, are not sufficient, the case of the first only excepted, to justify us in detaining the reader on the matter. The

lower order of the Coliseum, be it observed, wants the triglyph, the distinguishing feature of the order; so that although in a previous page we have described it as Doric, we scarcely know whether we have not erred in our description. But to approach the subject of the Roman Doric more closely, we will examine the general form of the example which the theatre of ·Marcellus affords. Therein the whole height of the order is 31·15 ft. whereof the entablature is rather more than one fifth, and the columns are 7·86 diameters high. From the intercolumniations nothing can be deduced, because the arcade which separates puts them out of comparison with other examples. Its profile is clearly that which has formed the basis upon which the Doric of the Italian architects is founded; they have, however, generally added a base to it. There is great difference between it and the Grecian Doric, which in its form is much more pyramidal, and would, even in ancient Rome, have been out of character with the decorations applied in the architecture of the city, in which all severity of form was abandoned. The details, however, of the Roman as well as of the Grecian Doric will be given, and, from the representations, better understood by the reader, when we come to treat of the Orders in the third book of this work, where some varieties of it are submitted to the reader.

260. In the examples of Roman Ionic, that of the theatre of Marcellus excepted, there is a much greater inferiority than in the instance of Roman Doric to which we have just alluded; indeed, that of the Temple of Concord is composed in so debased a style, that it ought scarcely to be alluded to. The following table exhibits the general proportions of the four Roman profiles of it:—

	Height divided by lower Diameter in English Feet.	Diameters in Height.	Entablature in Terms of the Diameter.	Intercolumniation.	Height of Capital in Terms of the Diameter.	Upper Diameter of Shaft.
Fortuna Virilis (Temple of) -	$\frac{27\cdot348}{3\cdot109}$ =	8·796	2·182	2·125	·457	·874
Concord (Temple of) -	$\frac{42\cdot861}{4\cdot486}$ =	9·554	1·605	1·807	·500	·325
Marcellus (Theatre of) -	$\frac{23\cdot940}{2\cdot660}$ =	9·000	2·391	- -	·557	·842
Coliseum - - -	$\frac{25\cdot731}{2\cdot91}$ =	8·842	2·280	- -	·466	·833

261. From the above it appears that, except in the case of the Temple of Concord, the entablature is about one fifth of the height of the whole order, and that the column diminishes about $\frac{16}{100}$ of its lower diameter. The capitals of the Roman are much smaller than those of the Grecian Ionic, and their curves are by no means so elegant and graceful. There is no appearance of refinement and care in their composition, for which the rules of Vitruvius give an altogether much more beautiful profile than those examples, we have here quoted, present. In the Temple of Concord, the volutes are placed diagonally on the capital, so that the four faces are similar in form. In the Greek specimens, as also in the Temple of Fortuna Virilis, this is done on one angle only of the capital of the columns, and that for the purpose of again bringing the faces of the volutes on to the flanks of the building, instead of showing the baluster sides of the capitals. On the whole, we think the modern Italian architects succeeded in producing much more beautiful profiles of this order, which never appears to have been a favourite in Rome, than their ancient predecessors.

262. The Corinthian seems to have been greatly preferred to the other orders by the luxurious Romans. There is little doubt that the capitals were generally the work of Greek sculptors, and some of those they have left are exceedingly beautiful; one that we have already mentioned, that of Jupiter Stator, points to sculpture of the highest class. The following table contains the general proportions of six well-known examples in Rome:—

	Height divided by lower Diameter in English Feet.	Diameters in Height.	Entablature in Terms of the Diameter.	Intercolumniation.	Height of Capital in Terms of the Diameter.	Upper Diameter of Shaft.
Pantheon, Portico - -	$\frac{47\cdot029}{4\cdot797}$ =	9·804	2·317	2·092	1·175	·855
Pantheon, Interior - -	$\frac{34\cdot674}{3\cdot642}$ =	9·499	2·251	1·834	1·000	·866
Jupiter Tonans - -	$\frac{47\cdot084}{4\cdot598}$ =	10·241	2·069	1·558	1·167	·867
Jupiter Stator - - -	$\frac{47\cdot648}{4\cdot841}$ =	9·820	2·534	1·575	1·08	·891
Façade of Nero - - -	$\frac{65\cdot5}{6\cdot568}$ =	9·973	2·439	- -	1·269	·883
Arch of Constantine - -	$\frac{28\cdot037}{2\,902}$ =	9·661	2·388	- -	1·095	·882

263. From the above, it appears that a mean of the whole height of the Corinthian order in the Roman examples is 12·166 diameters, and that the entablature is less than a fifth

of the height of the order, being as ·1686 : 1·0000. The diminution of the shaft is not so much as in the Ionic, being only $\frac{124}{1000}$ of the lower diameter. The Temple of the Sybil at Tivoli presents quite a distinct species, and is the romance of the art, if we may be allowed such an expression. The mean height of the columns is 9·833 diameters, being rather slenderer than the height recommended by Vitruvius (Lib. iv. c. 9.). The attic base, which will be considered in another portion of the work, was frequently employed by the Roman artists.

264. The invention of the Composite order is attributed, with every probability, to the Romans. It resembles generally the Corinthian, the main variation consisting in the part above the second tier of leaves in the capital. The following table exhibits the general proportions of three examples : —

Example.	Height divided by lower Diameter in English Feet.	Diameters in Height.	Entablature in Terms of the Diameter.	Height of Capital in Terms of the Diameter.	Diameter at top of Shaft.
Arch of Titus - - -	$\frac{22\cdot065}{2\cdot07}$ =	10·662	2·533	1·287	·887
Arch of Severus - -	$\frac{23\cdot847}{2\,887}$ =	8·260	2·316	1·144	·882
Baths of Dioclesian - -	$\frac{48\cdot476}{4\cdot619}$ =	10·495	2·3	1·181	·802

265. The mean of these makes the entablature a little less than one fifth of the entire height of the order, the ratio being as ·1955 : 1·0000. The diminution of the shaft is $\frac{143}{1000}$ of the lower diameters. The mean height of the columns is 9·806 diameters. A strongly marked feature in Roman architecture is the stylobate or pedestal for the reception of columns, which was not used by the Greeks. In the examples, it varies in height, but, generally speaking, it is very nearly four diameters of the column ; a mean of those used in the triumphal arches comes out at 3·86 diameters. Another difference from Greek architecture is in the form of the Roman pilaster, which was sometimes so strongly marked as to form a sort of square column with capitals and bases similar to those of the columns it accompanies, except in being square instead of circular on the plan. It is diminished in some buildings, as in the portico of the Pantheon, and in that of Mars Ultor, while in others, no such diminution takes place. The reader will recollect that the Greek antæ were never diminished, that their projection was always very small, and that the mouldings of their capitals were totally different from the columns with which they are connected.

266. But the most wonderful change the Romans effected in architecture was by the introduction of the arch ; a change which, by various steps, led, through the basilica, to the construction of the extraordinary Gothic cathedrals of Europe, in its progress opening beauties in the art of which the Greeks had not the remotest conception. These matters will be more entered into in the next section : we only have to observe here, that its importance was not confined to the passage of rivers by means of bridges, but that it enabled the Romans to supply in the greatest abundance to their cities water of a wholesome quality, without which no city can exist. To the introduction, moreover, of the arch, their triumphal edifices were indebted for their principal beauties ; and without it their theatres and amphitheatres would have lost half their elegance and magnificence. Whence the arch came is not known. In the section on Egyptian architecture, the subject has already been noticed. We are not aware of any example ornamentally applied before the time of Alexander.

267. The use of coupled columns and niches exhibits other varieties in which the Romans delighted ; but the former are not found till an age in which the art of architecture had begun to decline.

268. There is still another point to which the reader's attention must be directed, and it is almost a sure test of Roman or Greek design ; namely, the form of the mouldings of an order on their section. In purely Greek architecture, the contours of the mouldings are all formed from sections of the cone, whilst in that of the Romans, the contours are all portions of circles.

269. Under the climate of Rome it became necessary to raise the pitch of the roof higher than was necessary in Greece ; hence the Roman pediment was more inclined to the horizon. As, however, we shall, in another place, when we consider the practical formation of roofs generally, investigate the law which, forced by climate upon the architect, governed the inclination of the pediment ; the reader, for further information, is referred, on that point, to its proper place in this work ; namely, that wherein the subject of roofs is treated of.

Sect. XIV.

BYZANTINE AND ROMANESQUE ARCHITECTURE.

270. We propose in this section to take a concise view of the state of debased Roman architecture, from the year 476, in which the Roman empire in the West was destroyed, to the introduction of the pointed arch at the latter end of the 12th century. It will be necessary to premise that the term Romanesque is very general, and comprises the works of the Lombards as well as those of a later species, which in this country are called Saxon and Norman, for the character of all is the same, and we think much confusion will be prevented by the arrangement we propose. Between the fifth and the eighth centuries, at the beginning of which latter period the whole of Europe formed one great Gothic kingdom, the prospect is over a dreary desert in which the *oases* of our art are few and far between. The constant change of power, the division of the empire, which was so overgrown that it could no longer hang together, the irruptions of the Goths, whose name has been most improperly connected with all that is barbarous in art, make it no easy task to give the unlearned reader more than a faint idea of what occurred in the extended period through which, often in darkness, we must proceed to feel our way. But, previous to this, we shall continue the state of the architecture in the East; because, having already given some account of Saracenic architecture, which had its origin about the seventh century, we shall not again have to divert his attention from the subject until the reader is introduced to the pointed style : an arrangement which, we trust, will assist his memory in this history.

271. The emperor Theodosius, who died A. D. 395, exhibited great talent in arms, and was desirous to extend the benefit of his influence to the arts, in which he did much for the empire. His sons, Arcadius in the city of Constantinople, and Honorius at Rome, were incapable of doing them any service, though by them was raised the famous Theodosian column at the first named city, which was surrounded with bassi relievi, after the fashion of that erected long before in honour of Trajan at Rome. The ascent of Theodosius II. to the throne promised as well for the empire as for the arts. He called architecture to his aid for embellishing the cities of the empire. Under him, in 413, Constantinople was surrounded with a new wall ; some extensive baths, and a magnificent palace for the two sisters of Pulcheria were erected. In 447, an earthquake nearly destroyed the city, which was so admirably restored under this emperor that he might with propriety have been called its second founder. Except some trifling matters under Anastasius II., and Justin his successor, little was done till Justinian, the nephew of the last named, ascended the throne of the East, in 527. By him the celebrated architect Anthemius was invited to Constantinople. Through the genius of this artist, aided by his colleague Isidore the Milesian, on the ruins of the principal church of the city, which, dedicated to Saint Sophia or the Eternal Wisdom, had been twice destroyed by fire, was raised so splendid an edifice, that Justinian is said on its completion to have exclaimed, as Gibbon observes, "with devout vanity : " " Glory be to God, who hath thought me worthy to accomplish so great a work. I have vanquished thee, O Solomon." We shall make no apology for giving the description in the words of the historian we have just quoted; a representation of the building being appended in *figs.* 139. and 140. " But the pride of the Roman Solomon, before twenty years had elapsed, was humbled by an earthquake, which overthrew the eastern part of the dome. Its splendour was restored by the perseverance of the same prince ; and in the thirty-sixth year of his reign, Justinian celebrated the second dedication of a temple, which remains, after twelve centuries, a stately monument of his fame. The architecture of St. Sophia, which is now converted into the principal mosque, has been imitated by the Turkish sultans, and that venerable pile continues to excite the fond admiration of the Greeks, and the more rational curiosity of European travellers. The eye of the spectator is disappointed by an irregular prospect of half domes and shelving roofs : the western front, the principal approach, is destitute of simplicity and magnificence ; and the scale of dimensions has been much surpassed by several of the Latin cathedrals. But the architect who first erected an *aërial* cupola is entitled to the praise of bold design and skilful execution. The dome of St. Sophia, illuminated by four and twenty windows, is formed with so small a curve, that the depth is equal to only one sixth of its diameter; the measure of that diameter is 115 ft.,

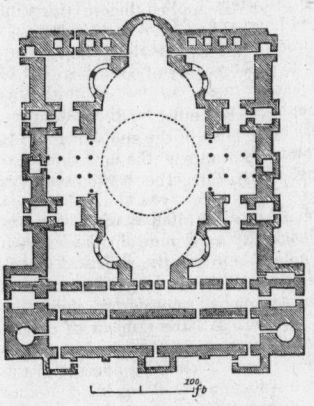

Fig. 139.   PLAN OF CHURCH OF ST. SOPHIA.

Fig. 140.   CHURCH OF SANTA SOPHIA.   ELEVATION AND SECTION.

and the lofty centre, where a crescent has supplanted the cross, rises to the perpendicular height of 180 ft. above the pavement.   The circle which encompasses the dome lightly reposes on four strong arches, and their weight is firmly supported by four massy piles " (piers), "whose strength is assisted on the northern and southern sides by four columns of Egyptian granite.   A Greek cross inscribed in a quadrangle represents the form of the edifice ; the exact breadth is 243 ft., and 269 may be assigned for the extreme length from the sanctuary in the east, to the nine western doors which open into the vestibule, and from thence into the *narthex* or exterior portico.   That portico was the humble station of the penitents.   The nave or body of the church was filled by the congregation of the faithful ; but the two sexes were prudently distinguished, and the upper and lower galleries were allotted for the more private devotion of the women.   Beyond the northern and southern piles " (piers), " a balustrade, terminated on either side by the thrones of the emperor and the patriarch, divided the nave from the choir ; and the space, as far as the steps of the altar, was occupied by the clergy and singers.   The altar itself, a name which insensibly became familiar to Christian ears, was placed in the eastern recess, artificially built in the form of a demi-cylinder, and this sanctuary communicated by several doors with the sacristy, the vestry, the baptistery, and the contiguous buildings, subservient either to the pomp of worship or the private use of the ecclesiastical ministers."   We should be fearful of thus continuing the quotation, but that we prefer the language of Gibbon to our own ; beyond which, the practical knowledge the rest of the description discloses is not unworthy the scientific architect, and the subject is the type of the great modern cathedrals, that of St. Paul, in London, among the rest.   " The memory," he continues, " of past calamities inspired Justinian with a wise resolution, that no wood, except for the doors, should be admitted into the new edifice ; and the choice of the materials was applied to the strength, the lightness, or the splendour of the respective parts.   The solid piles " (piers) " which sustained the cupola were composed of huge blocks of freestone, hewn into squares and triangles, fortified by circles of iron, and firmly cemented by the infusion of lead and quicklime ; but the weight of the cupola was diminished by the levity of its substance, which consists either of pumice-stone that floats in the water, or of bricks from the Isle of Rhodes, five times less ponderous than the ordinary sort.   The whole frame of the edifice was constructed of brick ; but those base materials were concealed by a crust of marble ; and the inside of St. Sophia, the cupola, the two larger and the six smaller semi-domes, the walls, the hundred columns, and the pavement, delight even the eyes of barbarians with a rich and variegated picture."   Various presents of marbles and mosaics, amongst which latter were seen representations of Christ, the Virgin, and saints, added to the magnificence of the edifice, and the precious metals in their purity imparted splendour to the scene.   Before the building was four feet out of the ground its cost had amounted to a sum equivalent to 200,000l. sterling, and the total cost of it when finished may, at the lowest computation, be reckoned as exceeding one million.   In Constantinople alone, the emperor dedicated twenty-

five churches to Christ, the Virgin, and favourite saints.   These were highly decorated, and imposing situations were found for them.   That of the Holy Apostles at Constantinople, and of St. John at Ephesus, appear to have had the church of St. Sophia for their types; but in them the altar was placed under the centre of the dome, at the junction of four porticoes, expressing the figure of the cross.   " The pious munificence of the emperor was diffused over the Holy Land ; and if reason," says Gibbon, " should condemn the monasteries of both sexes, which were built or restored by Justinian, yet charity must applaud the wells which he sank, and the hospitals which he founded, for the relief of the weary pilgrims."   " Almost every saint in the calendar acquired the honour of a temple ; almost every city of the empire obtained the solid advantages of bridges, hospitals, and aqueducts ; but the severe liberality of the monarch disdained to indulge his subjects in the popular luxury of baths and theatres."   He restored the Byzantine palace ; but selfishness, as respected his own comfort, could not be laid to his charge: witness the costly palace he erected for the infamous Theodora, and the munificent gifts, equal to 180,000*l.* sterling, which he bestowed upon Antioch for its restoration after an earthquake.   His care was not limited to the peaceful enjoyment of life by the empire over which he presided ; for the fortifications of Europe and Asia were multiplied by Justinian from Belgrade to the Euxine, from the conflux of the Save to the mouth of the Danube ; a chain of above fourscore fortified places was extended along the banks of the great river, and many military stations appeared to extend beyond the Danube, the pride of the Roman name.   We might considerably extend the catalogue of the extraordinary works of Justinian ; but our object is a general view, not a history of the works of this extraordinary person, of whom, applying the verses architecturally, it might truly be said —

Si Pergama dextra
Defendi possent: etiam hac defensa fuissent ; —

and by whom, if architecture could again have been restored, such a consummation would have been accomplished.

272.   In 565 Justin succeeded to the throne of the East, after whose reign nothing occurs to prevent our proceeding to the Western part of the empire, except the notice necessary to be taken of Leo the Isaurian, who ordered the statues in the different churches to be broken in pieces, and the paintings which decorated them to be destroyed.   Under him Ravenna was lost to the Eastern empire, and under his predecessors Mahomet appeared ; and in his successors originated the Saracenic architecture described in a previous section. It was under Justin, in 571, that the prophet, as he is called, was born, and was in 632 succeeded by Abubekr.

273.   We now return to the empire in the West, whose ruin, in 476, drew after it that of the arts, which had grievously degenerated since the fourth century, at which period their *decadence* was strongly marked.   But we must digress a little by supplying a chasm in the history of our art relative to the ancient basilicæ of Rome, the undoubted types of the comparatively modern cathedrals of Europe ; and within the city of Rome we shall find ample materials for tracing the origin whereof we speak.

274.   The severe laws against the Christians which Severus had passed expired with his authority, and the persecuted race, between A. D. 211 and 249, enjoyed a calm, during which they had been permitted to erect and consecrate convenient edifices for the purposes of religious worship, and to purchase lands even at Rome for the use of the community.   Under Dioclesian, however, in many places the churches were demolished, though in some situations they were only shut up.   This emperor, as if desirous of committing to other hands the work of persecution he had planned by his edicts, no sooner published them, than he divested himself, by abdication, of the imperial purple.

275.   Under Constantine, in the beginning of the fourth century, the Christians began again to breathe ; and though that emperor's religion, even to the period of his death, is involved in some doubt, it is certain that his opinion, as far as we can judge from his acts, was much inclined towards Christianity.   Out of the seven principal churches, or basilicæ, of Rome, namely, Sta. Croce di Gierusalemme, S. Giovanni Laterano, S. Lorenzo fuori le Murà, S. Paolo, S. Pietro, S. Sebastiano, and Sta. Maria Maggiore, all but the last were founded by Constantine himself.   The ancient basilica, which derived its name from βασιλευς (a king), and οικος (a house), was that part of the palace wherein justice was administered to the people.   The building for this purpose retained its name long after the extinction of the kingly office, and was in use with the Romans as well as the Grecians. Vitruvius does not, however, give us any specific difference between those erected by one or the other of those people.   In lib. v. c. 1. he gives us the details of its form and arrangement, for which the reader is referred to his work.   The name of basilica was afterwards transferred to the first buildings for Christian worship ; not because, as some have supposed, the first Christian emperors used the ancient basilicæ for the celebration of their religious rites, but more probably with reference to the idea of sovereignty which the religion exercised, though we do not assert that such conclusion is to be necessarily drawn.

There can be no doubt that the most ancient Christian basilicæ were expressly constructed for the purpose of religion, and their architectural details clearly point to the epoch in which they were erected. These new temples of religion borrowed, nevertheless, as well as their whole as in their details, so much from the ancient basilicæ, that it is not surprising they should have retained their name. We here place before the reader (*fig.* 141.) a plan of

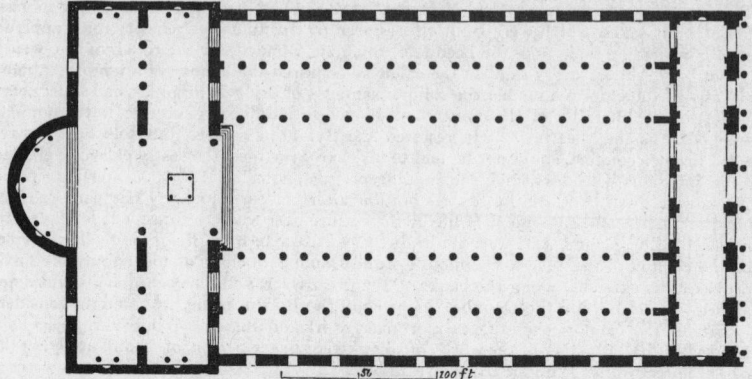

Fig. 141.   PLAN OF THE BASILICA OF ST. PAUL.

the ancient basilica of S. Paolo fuori le Murà, and (*fig.* 142.) an interior view of it, whereby

Fig. 142.   INTERIOR OF BASILICA OF ST. PAUL.

its general effect may be better understood. The latter shows how admirably it was adapted to the reception of an extremely numerous congregation. The numberless columns which the ancient buildings readily supplied were put in requisition for constructing these basilicæ, whereof, adopting the buildings of the same name as the type, they proportioned the elevation to the extent of the plans, and, in some cases, decorated them with the richest ornaments. Instead of always connecting the columns together by architraves on their summit, which might not be at hand, arches were spanned from one to the other, on which walls were carried up to bear the roofing. Though the practice of vaulting large areas did not appear till a considerable time after the building of the first Christian basilicæ, it must be recollected that the Temple of Peace at Rome had previously exhibited a specimen of the profound knowledge of the Romans in the practice of vaulting : in that example, groined vaults of very large dimensions were borne on entablatures and columns. Nor does this knowledge appear to have been lost in almost the last stage of decline of Roman architecture under the emperor Dioclesian. In the baths of this emperor are to be seen not only groined vaults in three

divisions, whose span is nearly 70 ft., but at the back of each springer a buttress, precisely of the nature of a flying buttress, is contrived to counteract the thrusts of the vaulting.

276. In recording the annihilation of the arts on the invasion of Odoacer, at the end of the fifth and during the course of the sixth century, historians have imputed it to the Gothic nations, qualifying by this name the barbarous style which then degraded the productions of the arts. Correct they are as to the epoch of their ruin, which coincided truly enough with the empire of the Goths; but to this nation they are unjust in attributing the introduction of a barbarous style.

277. History informs us, that as soon as the princes of the Goths and Ostrogoths had fixed themselves in Italy, they displayed the greatest anxiety to make the arts again flourish, and but for a number of adverse circumstances they would have succeeded. Indeed, the people whom the Romans designated as barbarous, were inhabitants of the countries to the north and east of Italy, who actually acquired that dominion and power which the others lost. Instructed at first by their defeats, they ultimately acquired the arts of those who originally conquered them. Thus the Gauls, the Germans, the Pannonians, and Illyrians, had, from their submission to the Roman people, acquired quite as great a love for the arts as the Romans themselves. For instance, at Nismes, the birthplace of Antoninus Pius, the arts were in a state of high cultivation; in short, there were schools as good out of as in Italy itself.

278. Odoacer, son of Edicon, the chief of a Gothic tribe, after obtaining possession of Rome in 476, preserved Italy from invasion for six years; and there is little doubt that one of his objects was the preservation of the arts. He was, however, stabbed by the hand, or at least the command, of his rival and successor, Theodoric, in 493. Theodoric, the son of Theodemir, had been educated at Constantinople, and though personally he neglected the cultivation of science and art, he was very far from insensible to the advantages they conferred on a country. From the Alps to the extremity of Calabria, the right of conquest had placed Theodoric on the throne. As respects what he did for the arts, no better record of his fame could exist than the volume of public Epistles composed by Cassiodorus, in the royal name. " The reputation of Theodoric," says Gibbon, " may repose with confidence on the visible peace and prosperity of a reign of thirty-three years; the unanimous esteem of his own times, and the memory of his wisdom and courage, his justice and humanity, which was deeply impressed on the minds of the Goths and Italians." The residence of Theodoric was at Ravenna chiefly, occasionally at Verona; but in the seventh year of his reign he visited the capital of the Old World, where, during a residence of six months, he proved that one at least of the Gothic kings was anxious to preserve the monuments of the nations he had subdued. Royal edicts were framed to prevent the abuses, neglect, or depredations of the citizens upon works of art; and an architect, the annual sum of two hundred pounds of gold, twenty-five thousand tiles, and the receipt of customs from the Lucrine port, were assigned for the ordinary repairs of the public buildings. Similar care was bestowed on the works of sculpture. Besides the capitals, Pavia, Spoleto, Naples, and the rest of the Italian cities, acquired under his reign the useful or splendid decorations of churches, aqueducts, baths, porticoes, and palaces. His architects were Aloysius for Rome, and Daniel for Ravenna, his instructions to whom manifest his care for the art; and under him Cassiodorus, for fifty-seven years minister of the Ostrogoth kings, was for a long period the tutelary genius of the arts. The death of Theodoric occurred in 526; his mausoleum is still in existence at Ravenna, being now called Sta. Maria della Rotunda. That city contains also the church of St. Apollinaris, which shows that at this period very little, if any, change had been made in the arrangement of large churches on the plan of the basilica. The front of the convent of the Franciscan friars in the same town, which is reputed to be the entrance to the palace, bears considerable resemblance to the Porta Aurea of Dioclesian, at Spalatro. These buildings are all in a heavy debased Roman style, and we are quite at a loss to understand the passage quoted by Tiraboschi, from Cassiodorus, who therein gives a particular description of the very great lightness and elegance of columns; thus—" Quid dicamus columnarum junceam proceritatem? Moles illas sublimissimas fabricarum quasi quibusdam erectis hastilibus contineri et substantiæ qualitate concavis canalibus excavatas, ut magis ipsas æstimes fuisse transfusas; alias ceris judices factum, quod metallis durissimis videas expolitum." (Lib. vii. Var. 15.) We know no examples of the period that bear out these assertions of Cassiodorus; on the contrary, what is known of this period indicates a totally different style.

279. If the successors of Theodoric had succeeded to his talents as well as his throne, and if they had been assisted by ministers like Cassiodorus, the arts and letters of Italy might have recovered; but, after the retirement of that minister, from the succession of Vitiges, towards 538, the arts were completely extinct. In 543–7, Rome was taken and plundered by Totila; and afterwards, in 553, this ill-fated city was again united to the Eastern empire by the talents of Belisarius and Narses.

280. From the year 568 up to the conquest of Italy by Charlemagne, in 774, the country was overrun by the Lombards, a people who quickly attained a high degree of civilization,

and were much given to the practice of architecture. Maffei, Muratori, and Tiraboschi have clearly proved that neither the Goths nor the Lombards introduced any particular style, but employed the architects whom they found in Italy.   Fig 143. is the west end

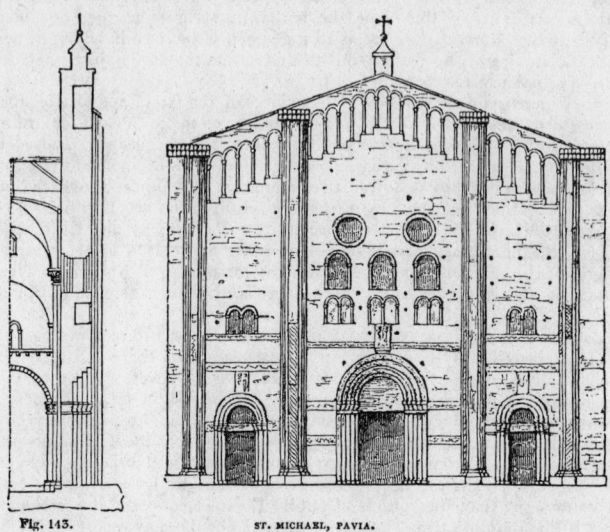

Fig. 143.   ST. MICHAEL, PAVIA.

of the church of St. Michael, at Pavia, a work executed under the Lombards, and, therefore, here inserted as an example of style. The anxiety, however, of the Lombards to preserve the arts was not sufficient to prevent their increasing decay, which daily became more apparent. Not more than the Goths do they deserve the reproach for their treatment of and indifference to them.   Besides fortifications and citadels for defence, they built palaces, baths, and temples, not only at Pavia, the seat of their empire, but at Turin, Milan, Spoleto, and Benevento. Hospitals under them began to be founded. The Queen Theodelinda, in particular, signalised her pious zeal in founding one at Monza, near Milan, her favourite residence, and endowing it in a most liberal manner.

281. In the eighth century the influence of the popes on the fine arts began to be felt. John VI. and Gregory III., at the commencement of the eighth century, showed great solicitude in their behalf. During this age the popes gained great temporal advantages, and their revenues enabled them to treat those advantages so as to do great good for Italy.   In the ninth century Adrian I. signalised himself in this passion to such an extent, that Nicholas V. placed on his monument the inscription,—

Restitult mores, mœnia, templa, Domos.

His works were many and admirable. Among those of great use, he constructed porticoes from the city to San Paolo and S. Lorenzo fuori le Murà.

282. Before we advance to the age of Charlemagne, it will be necessary to notice the church of St. Vitalis, at Ravenna, which we have reserved for this place on account of the singularity of its construction. It was erected, as is usually believed, under the reign of Justinian, in the sixth century. See figs. 144. and 145. The exterior walls are formed in a regular octagon, whose diameter is 128 ft. Within this octagon is another concentric one, 54 ft. in diameter, from the eight piers whereof (55 ft. in height) a hemispherical vault is gathered over, and over this is a timber conical roof. The peculiarity exhibited in the construction of the cupola is, that the spandrels are filled in with earthen vases; and that round the

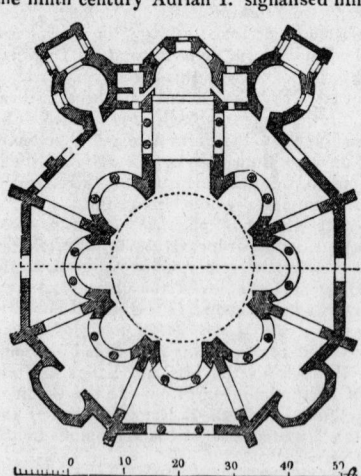

0   10   20   30   40   50   ft.

Fig. 144.   PLAN OF ST. VITALIS, RAVENNA.

Fig. 145.   SECTION OF ST. VITALIS, RAVENNA.

exterior of its base semicircular headed windows are introduced, each of which is subdivided into two apertures of similar forms.   Between every two piers hemicylindrical recesses are formed, each covered by a semidome, whose vertex is 48 ft. from the pavement, and each of them contains two windows subdivided into three spaces by two columns of the Corinthian order, supporting semicircular-headed arches.   Between the piers and the external walls are two corridors, which surround the whole building, in two stories, one above the other, each covered by hemicylindrical vaulting.   The upper corridor above the vault is covered with a sloping or leanto roof.   We have before noticed the introduction of vases in the spandrels at the Circus of Caracalla; and we cannot help being struck with the similarity of construction in the instance above cited.   It fully bears out the observation of Möller (*Denkmahler der Deutschen Baukunst*), " that, though beauty of proportion seems to have been unappreciated in these ages, and architecture was confined within a servile imitation of the earlier forms, the art of compounding cement, the proper selection of building materials, and an intimate acquaintance with the principles of solid construction with which the ancients were so conversant, were fully understood."

283. The æra of Charlemagne, which opened after the middle of the eighth century and continued into the early part of the ninth, gave rise to many grand edifices dedicated to Christianity.   This extraordinary man, rising to extensive dominion, did much towards restoring the arts and civilisation. " Meanwhile, in the south-east," says an intelligent anonymous writer, " the decrepid Grecian empire, itself maintaining but a sickly existence, had nevertheless continued so far to stretch a protecting wing over them [the arts] that they never had there equally approached extinction.   It seems probable that Charlemagne drew thence the architect and artisans who were capable of designing and building such a church as the cathedral of Aix-la-Chapelle, in Germany." " If Charlemagne," says Gibbon, " had fixed in Italy the seat of the Western empire, his genius would have aspired to restore, rather than violate, the works of the Cæsars; but as policy confined the French monarch to the forests of Germany, his taste could be gratified only by destruction, and the new palace and church of Aix-la-Chapelle were decorated with the marbles of Ravenna and Rome." The fact is, that the Byzantine or Romanesque style continued, with various degrees of beauty, over the Continent, and in this country, till it was superseded by the introduction of the pointed style.   Möller, from whom we extract *fig.* 146. which represents the portico of the Convent of Lorsch, situate about two and a half German miles from Darmstadt, considers it as all that remains of the first church built in the time of Charlemagne.   The same learned author observes, that, on comparison with each other of the ancient churches of Germany, two leading differences are discoverable in their styles, of which all others are grades or combinations.   The *first*, or earliest, whose origin is from the South, is, though in its later period much degenerated, of a highly finished character, distinguished by forms and decorations resembling those of Roman buildings, by flat roofs, by hemicylindrical vaults, and by great solidity of construction.   The *second* and later style still preserves the semicircular forms; but the high pitched roof, more adapted to the seasons

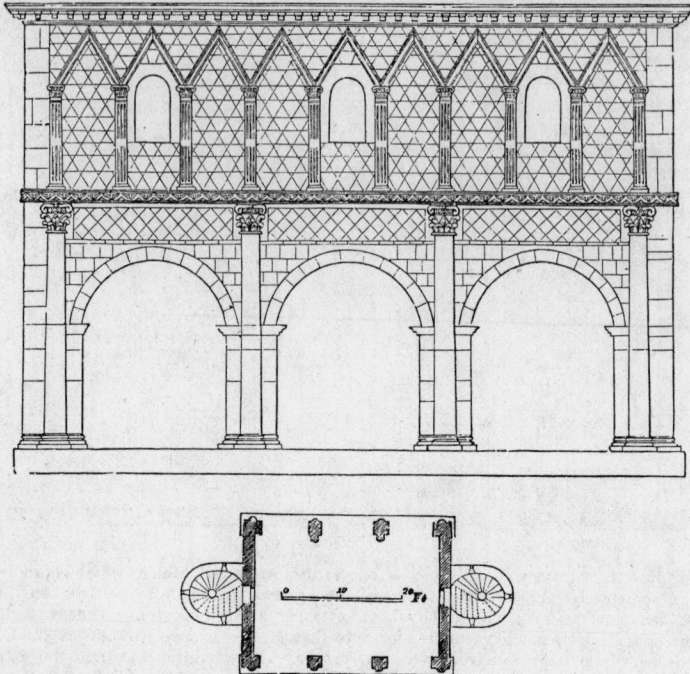

Fig. 146.   PORTICO OF LORSCH.

of a northern climate, begins to be substituted for the flat roof of the South, as at the cathedral of Worms on the west side, the western tower of the church at Gelnhausen, and in
many other examples.

284. We are now approaching a period in which more light can be thrown on our subject than on that we have just quitted. In the ninth century, on, as it is said, the designs of a
Greek artist, rose the cathedral of St. Mark at Venice, the largest of the Italian churches in
the Byzantine style. Its plan is that of a Greek cross, whose arms are vaulted hemicy-
lindrically, and, meeting in the centre of the building, terminate in four semicircular arches
on the four sides of a square, about 42 ft. in length in each direction. From the anterior
angles of the piers, *pendentives* gather over, as in St. Sophia, at Constantinople, and form a
circle wherefrom rises a cylindrical wall or drum in which windows for lighting the interior
are introduced. From this drum, the principal dome, which is hemispherical, springs.
Longitudinally and transversely the church is separated by ranks of columns supporting
semicircular arches. The aisles of the nave and choir, and those of the transepts, intersect
each other in four places about the centre of the cross, over which intersections are small
domes; so that on the roof are four smaller and one larger dome. In the exterior front
towards the Piazza San Marco, the façade consists of two stories, in the centre of the lower
one whereof is a large semicircularly arched entrance, on each side of which are two other
smaller arched entrances of the same form. These have all plain archivolts springing from
the upper of two orders of columns. On each flank of the façade is a smaller open arcade
springing at each extremity from an upper of two orders of insulated columns. A gallery
with a balustrade extends round the exterior of the church, in front whereof, in the centre,
are the four famous bronze horses which once belonged to the arch of Nero. The second
story towards the Piazza San Marco consists of a central semicircular aperture, with two
blank semicircular arches on each side, not quite so high and wide. These five divisions
are all crowned by canopy pediments of curves of contrary flexures, and ornamented with
foliage. Between each two arches and at the angles a turret is introduced consisting of
three stories of columns, and terminated by a pinnacle. The building has been considerably
altered since its first construction; and, indeed, the ornaments last named point to a later
age than the rest of the edifice, the general character of which has, nevertheless, been preserved. There is considerable similarity of plan between this church and that of St.
Sophia.

285. Very much partaking the character of composition of St. Mark, but dissimilar in

general plan, is the church of St. Anthony at Padua, which has six domes over the nave, transepts, centre, and choir. It is, moreover, distinguished by two slender towers or minarets, which impart to it the air of a Saracenic edifice.

286. The Italian architecture in the Byzantine or Romanesque style preserved a very different sort of character from that of the same date in Germany and other parts of Europe. Thus, — taking the cathedrals of Pisa and Worms, whose respective periods of construction are very close together, — the former is separated into its nave and aisles by columns with Corinthian capitals, reminding one very much of the early Christian basilica ; in the latter, the separation of the nave from the aisles is by square piers.   The cathedral at Pisa, with its baptistery, campanile, and the campo santo or cemetery, are a group of buildings of more curiosity than any four edifices in the world, and the more so from being so strongly marked with the distinguishing features of the Byzantine and Romanesque styles.   The cathedral (*fig.* 147.), whose architect was Buschetto of Dulichio, a Greek, was built in the

beginning in the 11th century. It consists of a nave, with two aisles on each side of it, transepts, and choir. Its bases, capitals, cornices, and other parts were fragments of antiquity collected from different places, and here with great skill brought together by Buschetto. The plan of the church is a Latin cross; its length from the interior face of the wall to the back of the recess is 311 ft., the width of the nave and four side aisles 106 ft. 6 in., the length of the transept 237 ft. 4 in., and its width, with its side aisles, 58 ft. The centre nave is 41 ft. wide, and has twenty-four Corinthian columns, twelve on each side, all of marble, 24 ft. 10 in. high, and full 2 ft. 3 in. in diameter.

Fig. 147.   ELEVATION OF CATHEDRAL AT PISA.

From the capitals of these columns arches spring, and over them is another order of columns, smaller and more numerous, from the circumstance of one being inserted over the centre of an intercolumniation below, and from their accompanying two openings under arches nearly equal to the width of such intercolumniations. These form an upper gallery, or *triforium*, anciently appropriated to the use of females. The four aisles have also isolated columns of the Corinthian order, but smaller, and raised on high plinths, in order to make them range with the others. The transepts have each a nave and two side aisles, with isolated columns, the same size as those of the other. The soffit of the great nave and of the transepts is of wood, gilt, but the smaller ones are groined. The height of the great nave is 91 ft., that of the transepts about 84 ft., and that of the aisles, 35 ft. In the centre nave are four piers, on which rest four large arches, supporting an elliptical cupola. The church is lighted by windows above the second order of the interior. The edifice is surrounded by steps. The extreme width of the western front, measured above the plinth moulding, is 116 ft., and the height from the pavement to the apex of the roof is 112 ft. 3 in. The façade has five stories, the first whereof consists of seven arches, supported by six Corinthian columns and two pilasters, the middle arch being larger than the others : the second has twenty-one arches, supported by twenty columns and two pilasters ; the third is singular, from the façade contracting where the two aisles finish, and forming two lateral inclined planes, whence in the middle are columns with arches on them as below. The columns which are in the two inclined planes gradually diminish in height : the fifth story is the same, and forms a triangular pediment, the columns and arches as they approach the angles becoming more diminutive. The two exterior sides have two orders of pilasters, one over the other. The roof of the nave is supported, externally, by a wall decorated with columns, and arches resting on their capitals. The whole of the building is covered with lead. The drum of the cupola is externally ornamented with eighty-eight columns connected by arches, over which are pediments in marble, forming a species of crowns. The principal point of difference in these cathedrals from the old basilicæ, in imitation whereof they were doubtless built, is in the addition of the transepts, by which a cruciform plan was given to these edifices. The style of the building in question is much lighter than most of the buildings of the period. But, whatever the taste

and style, the architect of it was a very skilful mechanic. One of his epitaphs, at Pisa, we subjoin, in proof of what we have stated.

> Quod vix mille boum possent juga juncta movere,
> Et quod vix potuit per mare ferre ratis,
> Buschetti nisu, quod erat mirabile visu,
> Dena puellarum turba levavit onus.

287. In Germany, the 10th and 11th centuries afford some edifices very important in the history of the art. Such are the cathedrals of Spire, Worms, Mayence, and others, still in existence to testify their extraordinary solidity and magnificence. In that country, as Möller remarks, there was a great disparity between its several provinces, as respected their degrees of civilisation. On the banks of the Rhine, and in the south, cities were established when those parts became subject to the Romans, and there the arts of peace and the Christian religion took root, and flourished; whilst, in the north and east, paganism was still in existence. Christianity, indeed, and civilisation gradually and generally extended from the southern and western parts. The clergy, we know from history, themselves directed the building of churches and convents. The buildings, therefore, of these parts are of great importance in the history of architecture. The leading forms of these churches, as well as of those that were built about the same period in France and England, are founded upon the ancient basilicæ; that is, they were long parallelograms with side aisles, and transepts which represent the arms of the cross, over whose intersection with the nave there is frequently a *louvre*. The choir and chancel terminate semicircularly on the plan. The semicircle prevails in the vaultings and over openings. The nave is lofty, frequently covered with groined vaulting, sometimes with flat timber covering; the gables are of small inclination. In the upper parts small short columns are frequently introduced. The prevailing feature in the exterior is horizontality, by which it is distinguished from the style which came into use in the 13th century. The profiles of the mouldings are, almost without exception, of Roman origin; the impost mouldings under the arches are, in this respect, peculiarly striking; and among the parts the Attic base constantly appears. The Roman basilicæ were always covered with flat horizontal ceilings; those of the churches we are speaking of are mostly vaulted. Hence the necessity of substituting pillars or piers for the insulated columns, which had only to carry wooden roofs. There are, however, a few churches remaining, which preserve the ancient type, as a church at Ratisbon, and the conventual churches of Paulinzell and Schwarzach. *Fig.* 148. shows the plan, and *fig.* 149. a sketch of one bay in a

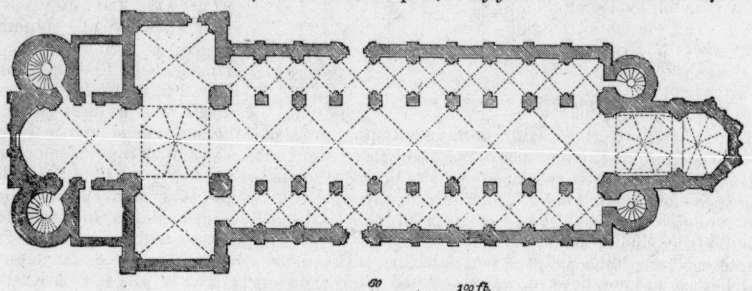

PLAN OF CATHEDRAL AT WORMS.　　　　　　　　Fig 148.

Fig 149. ONE BAY OF NAVE AT WORMS.

longitudinal section of the north side of the nave of the cathedral at Worms, which was commenced in the year 996, and consecrated in 1016. It is one of the most ancient of the German churches, and one of the most instructive. On our examination of it, recently, we were astonished at its state of preservation. The plan, it will be seen, is strongly distinguished by the cross; the square piers are alternately decorated with half columns; and the chancel, at the east end, terminates with a semicircle. The western end of the church, which is octagonal, seems to be more modern than the rest, inasmuch as the pointed arch appears in it. *Fig.* 150. is a view of the edifice.

288. Parts of the cathedral at Mentz are more ancient than any part of that at Worms; hence it may be studied with advantage, as containing a view of the styles of several centuries. The south-eastern gate of the cathedral is given by Möller in his work (Plate VI.).

289. Whittington, a highly talented author, of whom the world was deprived at a very early age (*Historical Survey of the Ecclesiastical Antiquities of France*, 4to. Lond. 1809), observes, that the buildings in France of the 9th and 10th centuries were imi-

Fig. 150.   WORMS CATHEDRAL.

tated from the works of Charlemagne; but that his feeble successors, deficient both in riches and power, were unable to equal them in magnitude or beauty of materials. During a large portion of the 9th century the country was a scene of consternation and bloodshed. The most celebrated, and almost the only foundation of consequence which took place during this dreary period, was the abbey of Clugny. It was built, about 910, by Berno, abbot of Balme, with the assistance of William, Duke of Aquitaine and Auvergne. But there is little doubt that the present church was built in the following century. During the 11th century, the French, relieved from their disordered state, hastened to rebuild and repair their ecclesiastical structures, and their various cities and provinces vied with each other in displays of enthusiastic devotion. Robert the Pious, by his example, encouraged the zeal of his clergy and people; and the science of architecture revived with majesty and effect from its fallen state. Morard, the abbot of St. Germain des Prés, was enabled by this monarch to rebuild the church of his convent on a larger scale. St. Geneviéve was also restored, and a cloister added to it, by his order. He, moreover, made preparations for erecting a cathedral at Paris in a style of as great magnificence as the times would allow. At Orleans, the place of his nativity, he built the churches of Nôtre Dame de bonnes nouvelles, St. Peter, and St. Aignan, which last was consecrated in 1029. But our space does not allow an enumeration of all the works undertaken during his reign. About this time, the cathedral of Chartres was rebuilt by Fulbert, its bishop, whose great reputation, in France and the rest of Europe, enabled him to execute it in a manner till then unknown in his country. Canute, the king of England, and Richard, Duke of Normandy, were among the princes who assisted him with contributions. His successor, Thierri or Theodoric, completed the building. The northern part was afterwards erected in 1060, at the expense of Jean Cormier, a native of Chartres, and physician to the king. The length of the church is 420 ft., its height 108 ft., and the nave 48 ft. wide. The transepts extend 210 ft. The abbey church of Clugny, which succeeded that above mentioned, is one of the largest and most interesting of the ecclesiastical monuments of France, and was begun in the commencement of the 11th century, by the abbot Odilo, and finished by his successor Hugh, in 1069. The ceremony of its dedication did not, however, take place till many years after. The style of architecture in France, in the 11th, was the same as in the preceding centuries; but the churches were larger and more solidly constructed. The oldest buildings of France now existing, with some exceptions, are traceable to this æra; such are the venerable fabrics of St. Germain des Prés, St. Benigne at Dijon, those of Chartres, La Charité sur Loire, Clugny, and others; all remaining to illustrate the history of the arts of this period. But, as we have said before, and to the student the observation cannot be too often repeated, the style which prevailed was no more than a debased and feeble attempt to imitate the ancient architecture of Rome, and its best examples are not, in style even, equal to those of the art in its lowest state under the reign of Dioclesian; indeed the investigation is only important as being one of the means by which we can arrive at a just conclusion on the state of civilisation at different periods. *Mores fabricæ loquuntur* is an expression of Cassiodorus, so true, that to prove it would indeed be lighting the sun with a candle; and we must not trifle with the patience of the reader.

290. The Saxon churches of England, to which and its more modern architecture our succeeding chapter will be entirely devoted, were very inferior in every respect to the Norman churches of France; and these latter differed materially from those in the neighbourhood of Paris, and further to the south. The Norman churches were larger in some examples; but they were more rude in design and execution. The abbey church of St. Stephen, raised at Caen by William the Conqueror, and that founded by his Queen Matilda in the same city in honour of the Holy Trinity, are the chief examples of the peculiar manner of building introduced by the Norman prelates into England at the end

of the 11th century; after which, as we shall presently see, a new and extraordinary style made its appearance in Europe, a style whereof *fig.* 151. will, on inspection, sufficiently give a general notion to the reader.

Fig. 151.   NINTH TO TWELFTH CENTURY.   AFTER TWELFTH CENTURY.

291. Before leaving the subject of this section, we must fall back again upon Italy to notice two or three works intimately connected with this period of the art. We here more particularly allude to the celebrated baptistry and campanile of Pisa, a city which seems to have been a great nursing mother to our art, no less than to those of painting and sculpture. The Campo Santo of that city, of which, from the number of examples to be noticed, we regret we shall be unable to give but a short account, belongs to the next period, and must be noticed after them.

292. Dioti Salvi, whose birthplace even is unknown, commenced, in 1152, the baptistery of Pisa (*fig.* 152.), and after eight years completed it

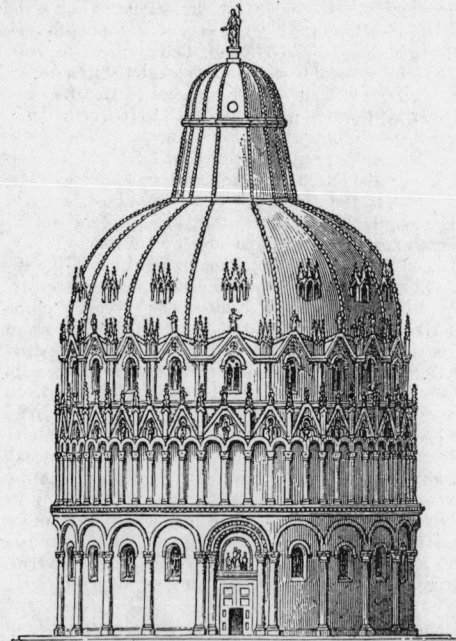

Fig. 152.   BAPTISTERY OF PISA.

It is close to the cathedral of the place, and though on the wall of the inner gallery there be an inscription, cut in the character of the middle ages, " A.D. 1278, ÆDIFICATA FUIT DE NOVO," and it may be consistent with truth that the edifice was ornamented by John of Pisa, there is nothing to invalidate the belief that the building stands on the foundations originally set out, and that for its principal features it is indebted to the architect whose name we have mentioned. It is 100 ft. in diameter within the walls, which are 8 ft. 6 in. thick. The covering is a double brick dome, the inner one conical, the outer hemispherical. The former is a frustum of a pyramid of twelve sides. Its upper extremity forms a horizontal polygon, finished with a small parabolic cupola, showing twelve small marble ribs on the exterior. The outer vault terminates above, at the base of the small cupola, which stands like a lantern over the aperture. From the pavement, the height of the cupola is 102 ft. The entrance is by a decorated doorway, from the sill of which the general pavement is sunk three steps round the building; the space between the steps and the wall having been provided for the accommodation of the persons assembled to view the ceremony of baptism. An aisle or corridor is continued round its interior circumference, being formed by eight granite columns and four piers, from which are turned semicircular arches, which support an upper gallery; and above the arches are twelve piers, bearing the semicircular arches which support the pyramidal

dome. On the exterior are two orders of Corinthian columns engaged in the wall, which support semicircular arches. In the upper order the columns are more numerous, inasmuch as each arch below bears two columns above it. Over every two arches of the upper order is a sharp pediment, separated by a pinnacle from the adjoining ones; and above the pediments a horizontal cornice encircles the building. Above the second story a division in the compartments occurs, which embraces three of the lower arches; the separation being effected by piers triangular on the plan, crowned by pinnacles. Between these piers, semicircular headed small windows are introduced, over each of which is a small circular window, and thereover sharp pediments. Above these the convex surface of the dome springs up, and is divided by twelve ribs, truncated below the vertex, and ornamented with crockets. Between these ribs are a species of dormer windows, one between every two ribs, ornamented with columns, and surmounted each by three small pointed pediments. The total height is about 179 ft. The cupola is covered with lead and tiles; the rest of the edifice is marble.

293. The extraordinary campanile, or bell tower, near the cathedral at Pisa, was built about 1174. It is celebrated from the circumstance of its overhanging upwards of thirteen feet, a peculiarity observable in many other Italian towers, but in none to so great an extent as in this. There can be no doubt whatever that the defect has arisen from bad foundation, and that the failure exhibited itself long before the building was completed ; because, on one side, at a certain height, the columns are higher than on the other; thus showing an endeavour on the part of the builders to bring back the upper part of the tower as vertical a direction as was practicable, and recover the situation of the centre of gravity. The tower is cylindrical, 50 ft. in diameter, and 180 ft. high. It consists of eight stories of columns, in each of which they bear semicircular arches, forming open galleries round the story. The roof is flat, and the upper story contains some bells. The last of the group of buildings in Pisa is the Campo Santo, which, from its style and date (1278), is only mentioned here out of its place in order to leave this interesting spot without necessity for further recurrence to it. It is the public burying place of the city, and, whether from the remains on its walls of the earliest examples of Giotto, and Cimabue, the beauty of its proportions, or the sculpture that remains about, is unparalleled in interest to the artist. It is a quadrangle, 403 ft. in length, 117 ft. in width, and is surrounded by a corridor 32 ft. in breadth. This corridor is roofed, forming a sort of cloister with semicircular-headed windows, which were at first simple apertures extending down to the pavement, but they have been subsequently divided into smaller apertures by columns, which, from the springing of the arches, branch out into tracery of elegant design. The interior part of the quadrangle is open to the sky. Some of the arches above mentioned were completed as late as the year 1464.

The style of the transition to pointed art will be noticed in the section on POINTED ARCHITECTURE at the end of Book I.

SECT. XV.

(a) ORIGIN OF THE POINTED ARCH.

294. About the end of the 12th and the beginning of the 13th century, a most singular and important change took place in the architecture of Europe. The flat southern roof, says Möller, was superseded by the high pitched northern covering of the ecclesiastical edifices, and its introduction brought with it the use of the pointed arch, which was substituted for the semicircular one : a necessary consequence, for the roof and vaults being thus raised, the character of the whole could not be preserved without changing the entire arrangement of the combination of forms. But we have great doubts on Möller's hypothesis; it will, indeed, be hereafter seen we have a different belief on the origin of the pointed arch. Before we at all enter upon the edifices of the period, we think it will be better to put the reader in possession of the different hypotheses in which various writers have indulged, relative to the introduction or invention of the pointed arch; and though we attach very little importance to the discovery, if it could now be clearly established, we are, as our work would be incomplete without the notice, compelled to submit them for the reader's consideration.

295. 1. *Some have derived this style from the holy groves of the early Celts.* — But we can see no ground for this hypothesis, for it was only in the 14th and 15th centuries that ribs between the groins (which have been compared to the small branches of trees) were introduced ; hence it is rather difficult to trace the similarity which its supporters contend for.

296. 2. *That the style originated from huts made with twigs and branches of trees intertwined.* — An hypothesis fancifully conceived and exhibited to the world by Sir James Hall, in some very interesting plates attached to his work. Möller properly observes upon this theory of twigs, that it is only in the buildings of the 15th and 16th centuries that the supposed imitation of twigs appears.

297. 3. *From the framed construction of timber buildings.* — This is an hypothesis which it would be loss of time to examine, inasmuch as all the forms and details undoubtedly arise from the vault and arch; and a close examination of the buildings of the 13th century proves that the ancient ecclesiastical style involves the scientific construction of stone vaulting, all timber construction being limited to the framing of the roof.

298. 4. *From the imitation of the aspiring lines of the pyramids of Egypt.* — This hypothesis is the fancy of Murphy, the ingenious and useful editor of a work on the convent of Batalha, in Portugal, and also of some of the finest edifices of the Moors in Spain. The following is the reasoning of the author : — The pyramids of the Egyptians are tombs ; the dead are buried in churches, and on their towers pyramidal forms are placed ; consequently, the pyramids of the towers indicate that there are graves in the churches ; and as the pyramidal form constitutes the essence of the pointed arch style, and the pyramids of the towers are imitations of the Egyptian pyramids, the pointed arch is derived from the latter. The reader, we are sure, will not require from us any examination of the series of syllogisms here enumerated.

299. 5. *From the intersection of semicircular arches which occurs in late instances of the Romanesque style.* — This was the hypothesis of the late Dr. Milner, a Catholic bishop of great learning and most amiable bearing, and a person so intimately acquainted with the subject on which he wrote, that we regret his reasons for the conjecture are not satisfactory to us, albeit the combination (*fig.* 153.) whereof he speaks is, in the Romanesque style, of frequent occurrence. The venerable prelate seems to have lost sight of a principle familiar to every artist — that in all art the details of a style are subordinate to and dependent on the masses, and that the converse never occurs ; how, then, could the leading features of a style so universal have had their origin in an accidental and unessential decoration, like that of the theory in question? None of the above hypotheses are satisfactory ;

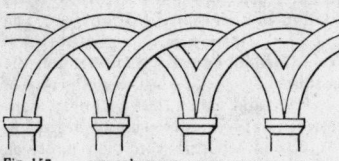

Fig. 153.   MILNER'S ORIGIN OF THE POINTED ARCH.

and Möller well observes, that the solution of the question, whether the pointed style belongs to one nation exclusively, is attended with great difficulties. And it may be said that the problem for solution is not, who invented the pointed arch, but, in what way its prevalence in the 13th century is to be accounted for.

300. We are not of opinion that it is of much importance that this *vexata quæstio* should be settled ; and that it will now satisfactorily be done, we consider very much out of the limits of probability. But we suppose that the reader will be inclined to ask for our own bias on the subject ; and, as we are bound to answer such a question, the reply is, that we are of the faith of the Rev. Mr. Whittington, to whose work we have before referred, that the pointed arch was of Eastern extraction, and that it was imported by the first crusaders into the West. " All eastern buildings," says that ingenious writer, " as far back as they go (and we cannot tell how far), have pointed arches, and are in the same style ; is it not fair to suppose that some of these are older than the 12th century, or that the same style existed before that time? Is it at all probable that the dark ages of the West should have given a mode of architecture to the East?" Lord Aberdeen, whose taste and learning in matters of this nature well qualified him for the posthumous introduction to the public of the author we are using, observes, in his preface to Whittington's work, that, " if we could discover in any one country a gradual alteration of this style [the Romanesque], beginning with the form of the arch, and progressively extending to the whole of the ornaments and general design ; — after which, if we could trace the new fashion slowly making its way, and by degrees adopted by the other nations of Europe ; — the supposition of Mr. Walpole [that it arose from what was conceived to be an improvement in the corrupt specimens of Roman taste then exhibited, and was afterwards gradually carried to perfection] would be greatly confirmed. Nothing, however, of this is the case. We find the Gothic [pointed] style, notwithstanding the richness and variety it afterwards assumed, appearing at once with all its distinctive marks and features, not among one people, but, very nearly at the same period of time, received and practised throughout Christendom. How will it be possible to account for this general and contemporary adoption of the style, but by a supposition that the taste and knowledge of all on this subject were drawn from a common source? and where can we look for this source but to the East, which, during the crusades, attracted a portion of the population, and, in a great degree, occupied the attention, of the different states of Europe?" This was an opinion of Sir Christopher Wren, at least greatly so, his leaning being rather to deducing the origin of the style from the Moors in Spain. It is the fashion of modern half-educated critics to place little reliance on such authorities as Wren. We have, from experience, learned to venerate them. The noble author whom we have been quoting proceeds by stating that " the result receives confirmation from the circumstance of there being no specimen of Gothic [pointed] architecture erected in the West before the period in question." Exception, however, is to be made for the rare occurrence of a very few examples,

whose construction may perhaps be placed higher than the 12th century, and the cause of whose existence may be satisfactorily explained.   " It may be sufficient here to observe, that no people versed in the science of architecture could long remain ignorant of the pointed form of the arch, the most simple and easy in construction, as it might be raised without a centre by the gradual projection of stones placed in horizontal courses ; and, whether produced by accident or necessity, we may reasonably expect to meet with it occasionally in their works." It is certain that, though neglected in their general practice, the ancients were acquainted with this mode of building · and the occurrence of an arch merely pointed and unaccompanied with any other characteristic of the style, is no better evidence of the prevalence of Gothic (pointed) architecture, than that the appearance of Corinthian capitals in Romanesque buildings must give them the right to be called classical edifices.   It is not easy to answer the question, — In what part of the East are we able to point to buildings constructed in the pointed style, of a date anterior to those erected in the West ?   A little reflection, however, will solve the difficulty ; and here we must again trespass on the author we have so copiously used, though our limits will not allow us to follow him in his own words.   It is manifest that the frequent wars and revolutions of the East entailed the same fate on works of art and utility as attended the princes and chiefs of the states subverted.   Thus the number of architectural examples, and especially those of early date, was greatly diminished.   Again, the people of the East with whom we are best acquainted, in a great measure sacrificed their less durable mode of building to that which they found established by the Greeks.   Thus, the church of Santa Sophia was a model, after the conquest of Constantinople, for all the mosques that were erected, with the addition occasionally of minarets more or less lofty, as the piety and magnificence of the sultans might dictate.   Previously to the conquest of the metropolis of the East, such a practice was prevalent, and in the cities of the empire many christian edifices were adapted to the purposes of Mohammedan worship.   Yet, notwithstanding these causes, which form an impediment to full information on the state of the early architecture of the East, there is an abundance of facts to give probability to our notion, except in the eyes of those who view the subject through the medium of prejudice and established system ; at least so we opine.

301. " If a line," says our author, " be drawn from the north of the Euxine, through Constantinople to Egypt, we shall discover in every country to the eastward of this boundary frequent examples of the pointed arch, accompanied with the slender proportions of Gothic [pointed] architecture ; in Asia Minor, Syria, Arabia, Persia ; from the neighbourhood of the Caspian, through the wilds of Tartary ; in the various kingdoms, and throughout the whole extent of India, and even to the furthest limits of China.   It is true that we are unable, for the most part, to ascertain the precise date of these buildings ; but this in reality is not very important, it being sufficient to state the fact of their comparative antiquity, which, joined to the vast diffusion of the style, appears adequate to justify our conclusion.   Seeing, then, the universal prevalence of this mode in the East, which is satisfactorily accounted for by the extensive revolutions and conquests effected by Eastern warriors in that part of the world, it can scarcely appear requisite to discuss the probability of its having been introduced from the West, or, still less, further to refute the notions of those who refer the origin of the style [as some have very ignorantly done] to the invention of English artists.   Had it been adopted from the practice of the West, such a peculiarity of taste and knowledge must have been imparted by some general communication : this has only occurred at one period, during which no building of the species in question existed in Europe.   The inhabitants of the West could not convey a knowledge which they did not possess ; but, as it became pretty general amongst them shortly after the epoch alluded to, it is reasonable to infer that they acquired it from those nations they are said to have instructed.   On the whole, it is probable that the origin of the Gothic style, notwithstanding the occasional imitation of a corrupt and degraded species of Roman architecture, is sufficiently indicated by the lofty and slender proportions, by the minute parts, and the fantastic ornaments of Oriental taste."

302. Möller, a writer for whose opinions we entertain the highest respect, is not, however, of opinion that the pointed arch originated with the Arabs ; and he observes that a scrutiny of their buildings will exhibit nothing that bears upon the Gothic, or pointed, style.   He says that their arches are in the shape of a horseshoe ; that the columns are low, that they stand single, and are not connected in groups ; that the windows are small, the roofs flat, and that the prevalent general forms are horizontal : that, in the ancient churches of the 13th century, the arches are pointed, the pillars high and composed of several columns, windows large, and roofs and gables high.   But at the end of his argument he admits that the solution of the question, " which of the European nations first introduced or improved the pointed style is not so easy, for we find this style of building almost contemporary in all parts of Europe."   Now, though we are not about to use the argument which is not always valid, *post hoc ergo propter hoc*, we must observe, that the introduction of the pointed arch immediately after the first Crusade, and not before, is a most singular occurrence ; and we are inclined to give it the same force as that used by old Bishop

Latimer on the subject of the Goodwin Sands and Tenterden steeple. One of the points of Moller's reasoning we do not think at all fortunate; it is that on the forms of the Moresque arches. Now, it must immediately occur to the reader that one of the forms (as at the side), and that a common one, is to be found in their arches, that of contrary flexure; a form in the architecture of this country in the time of the Tudors universally adopted, though, it must be allowed, much flattened in the application. Another point seems to have been altogether overlooked by Moller, namely, the practice of *diapering* the walls, whereof an instance occurs in Westminster Abbey; and one which has a very strong affinity to the practice of the Moors, who left no space unornamented. The higher-pitched gables of the northern roofs, we admit, fostered the discovery, by the introduction of forms from necessity, which were admirably calculated to carry out to their extreme limits the principles of which the Crusaders had acquired some notion for practice on their return to their respective countries. As to the objection that the Arabs had no original architecture, it is admitted. They must, however, have had that of the tent, whose form inverted would give all that is sought. These observations we do not throw out as partisans; the hypothesis adopted by us is sanctioned, in addition to the learned author upon whom we have drawn so much, by Warburton, and T. Warton, and Sir Christopher Wren; and though none of these had the opportunity of basing their opinions upon the labours of the recent travellers whom we have been able to use, we do not think, upon this mooted question, either of them would be reduced to the necessity of retracting what he has respectively written.

303. In glancing over the many writers on the subject, it is amusing to see the difference of opinion that exists. For instance, twenty are of opinion that it originated in Germany; fourteen, that it was of Eastern or Saracenic origin; six, that it arose from the hint suggested by the intersection of the Norman arches; four, that it was the invention of the Goths and Lombards; and three, that its origin was in Italy. Sprung, however, from whatever place, it appears to have given in every sense an independence to the art not before belonging to it, and to have introduced principles of far greater freedom, in respect of the ratio of points of support to the whole mass, than were previously exhibited or probably known. Those who may feel desirous of consulting these views in detail, will find notices of sixty-six theories in the fifth volume of Britton's *Architectural Antiquities.* Only two of these theories attempt to account for the introduction of the pointed arch on the ground of usefulness; one was put forward by Dr. Whewell as regarded vaulting; the other by Dr. Young and Mr. Weir, who urged that the use of the pointed arch was originally due to a discovery of its diminishing lateral pressure. Mr. Sharpe has advocated the same view. These theories will also be found in Ramée, *Manuel de l'Histoire Générale de l'Architecture,* 1843, ii., 238, 248.

303a. Michelet (*Histoire de France*) observes, "Or, lors de l'apparition de l'ogive en Occident vers 1200, Innocent III est le dernier rayon de cette puissance universelle, le pouvoir de l'Eglise Catholique s'affaiblit. La tentative des ordres des mendiants, des pères prêcheurs est infructueuse. Le pouvoir des prêtres tombe dans la main des laïques. La puissance du droit canonique, de ce robuste auxiliaire de l'Eglise, s'efface en France devant ces lois sages faites par le pieux Roi St. Louis, et ses établissements immortels servent de code nouveau à ses sujets. En Angleterre le Roi Jean-sans-terre donne, en 1215, la grande Charte. En Allemagne, au commencement du treizième siècle, paraît le Sachsenspiegel. Au milieu du quatorzième, où le règne de l'ogive est à son apogée, l'Empereur Charles IV donne la Bulle d'or. Au treizième siècle se terminent les Croisades qui mirent le Pape au dessus des pouvoirs temporels. Ces guerres saintes avaient fait prévaloir l'autorité de l'Evêque de Rome. Mais au treizième siècle l'activité des peuples chrétiens avait prit une autre direction, et ils finirent par secouer toute espèce de domination." It is impossible, in naming the pontificate of Innocent III., to refrain from noticing that it was an epoch, in which such men appeared on the scene as St. Thomas Aquinas, St. Dominic, St. Francis of Assisi, John Gerson, author of the "Imitation of Jesus Christ," a composition that has been oftener printed than any other work; and in literature and the arts, about the same period, are to be found the names of Dante, Robert de Lusarches, Etienne de Bonneveil, Pierre de Montereau, Lapo or Jacopo, besides a host of others.

304. The foregoing remarks comprise a resumé of the early views on this subject, but we must not omit to mention those held by the learned writer, Mr. James Fergusson, who observes that Dr. Whewell, in his *Notes on German Churches,* has very distinctly stated the question of such inquiries:—" These only tend to show how the form itself, as an arch, may have been suggested, not how the use of it must have become universal " (see also 299). Fergusson then (*Builder Journal,* 1849, p. 290, 303, 317), treating the history of the pointed arch succinctly by certain facts, brings forward four sets of pointed arches. I., the ancient buildings extending down to the period of the Roman empire; II., the decline of the Roman influence, extending to the present day, in the countries of the East to which these two classes of arches are confined; III., the arch appearing in the south of France alone, in the age of Charlemagne, extending to the 11th century, when it was superseded by the

round arch style ; and IV., the true Gothic pointed arch, prevailing almost universally over the whole of Europe till the time of the Reformation, in the 16th century. In the East, "arches still are more frequently constructed by placing the stones horizontally than in a radiating position." The history of the subject will never be correctly understood till we take both kinds into account, for the second almost certainly arose out of the first. The first example put forth by him is from the third pyramid at Gizeh, in the roof of the sepulchral chamber (*fig.* 154), consisting

Fig. 154. PYRAMID AT GIZEH.   Fig. 155. CAMPBELL'S TOMB.

only of two stones, showing how early the curvilinear form, with a point in the centre, was used, and consequently how familiar it must have been to the architects of all ages. Another early form is here given from the tomb called "Campbell's Tomb," *fig.* 155. The pyramids at Meröe, in Ethiopia, dating about 1000 to 805 years B.C., at all events being of a period anterior to the age of the Greek and Roman influence, were discovered by Mr. Hoskins. Here, stone arches show both circular and pointed forms (*fig.* 156); and Mr. Layard discovered, at Nimroud, drains with pointed vaults of the same age as those at Meröe. A tumulus near Smyrna, in Asia Minor, presents an example almost a counterpart of that from the third pyramid ; a gateway, near Missolonghi, is formed by the courses of masonry projecting beyond one another till they meet in the centre. Other examples are seen in the tomb of the Atridæ at Mycenæ (*figs.* 14 and 16, tomb called treasury of Atreus); in a city gateway at Arpino, in Italy ; in an aqueduct at Tusculum ; and in a gateway at Assos, in Asia Minor (*fig* 157). This is known from the character of its

Fig. 156. PYRAMID AT MERÖE.   Fig. 157. GATEWAY AT ASSOS.

masonry and other circumstances to belong to the best period of Greek art, in fact to be coeval, or nearly so, with the Parthenon. These examples explain all the peculiarities of this mode of construction.

305. With the appearance of Rome, this form entirely disappears from the countries to which her influence extended, and is supplanted so completely by the circular radiating form, that not a single instance is probably known of a pointed arch of any form or mode of construction during the period of the Roman supremacy. The moment, however, that her power declined, the pointed form reappears in Asia, its native seat ; and we recur to the very few that remain in Syria and Western Asia for examples. The first of these are in the church of the Holy Sepulchre at Jerusalem, built by Constantine the Great, and now known as the Mosque of Omar. Its arches are throughout pointed, but so timidly as to be scarcely observable at first sight. Fergusson also states the reasons for his inability to give other specimens ; and, describes the cathedral of Ani, in Armenia, (see also Donaldson, in the *Civil Engineer, &c. Journal*, 1843, p. 183) which is built with pointed arches throughout, and contains an inscription proving that it was finished in the year 1010 : he quotes M. Texier's assertion (*Descr. de l'Armenie*, fol. 1842) that "it results that, at a time when the pointed arch was altogether unknown, and never had been used, in Europe, buildings were being constructed in the pointed arch style in the centre of Armenia." At Diarbekr, Mr. Fergusson continues, "there is an extremely remarkable building, now converted into a mosque ; the Armenians call it, with much plausibility, the palace of Tigranes; the friezes and cornices are executed according to the principles of Roman art of the 4th century, nevertheless the pointed arch is found everywhere mixed with the architecture, as if it were currently practised in the country." The palace at Modain, the ancient Ctesiphon,

a building of the 6th century, is remarkable for the gigantic portal which has not a pointed but an elliptical arch. The pointed arch, however, was employed in Mesopotamia long before it was known in Europe.

306. In the Roman empire, the aqueducts that supplied Constantinople with water, which were commenced under Constantine immediately after the founding of the city, but completed under Valens, A.D. 364 and 378, exhibit pointed arches, generally in the lowest story, and always in the oldest part, as near Pyrgos—" I would have no hesitation," he says, " in asserting the general use of the pointed arch by the Mahomedans from the earliest years of their existence to the present hour. The Arabs, it must be recollected, when they left their deserts to subdue the world, were warriors and not architects; they consequently employed the natives of the conquered countries to erect their mosques; yet, with scarcely a single exception, all their edifices are built with pointed arches. They are used in the oldest part of the mosque of Amrou, at Old Cairo; this portion was built in the twenty-first year of the Hegira, A.D. 643. Except the two mosques of Amrou, in Egypt, I do not know of any erections of the Saracens anterior to the end of the 7th century. The pointed arch is used throughout the mosque erected by the Calif Walil at Jerusalem, in the year 87, or about A D. 705. The great mosque at Damascus is of the same age; and from that period to the present time there is no difficulty. In Sicily, too, which the Saracens occupied for two centuries preceding 1037, they used the pointed arch in all the monuments they have left there. In Spain, however, although pointed arches occur in the baths at Gerona, at Barcelona, and other places in the north, whose date is tolerably well ascertained to be of the 9th or 10th centuries, as a general rule the Moors used the round or horseshoe arch (see fig. 85), almost universally in their erections in that country. One other example that should be noted, occurs at the celebrated mosque of Kootub, at Delhi. When the Pathans conquered India, in the beginning of the 13th century, they brought with them their own style of architecture. This building, carried out by the Hindoos, was commenced about the year 1230, and completed in about ten years. The principal arch, 22 feet span and about 40 feet high, though of the pure equilateral Gothic form, is erected with horizontal courses to nearly the summit, when courses of stone are placed on their ends, as done in the aqueduct at Tusculum, before mentioned.

307. " With the Western styles, the first series to be noticed is that found in the south of France, comprised by the south of the Loire and the north of the Garonne, extending from the Gulf of Nice to the shores of the Bay of Biscay; being, in date, from about the age of Charlemagne till the middle or end of the 11th century, when it was superseded by the round arch styles. This assertion may startle some readers, but it would long ago have been received as well established facts, had it not been for the preconceived opinion that no pointed arch existed in Europe anterior to the 12th century. One of the best known examples is that of the cathedral at Avignon, where the porch and general details of the church are so nearly classical, that they are usually ascribed to the age of Charlemagne,

and even earlier. At Vaison are two well-known churches, so classical also, that they are often called Roman temples; both are roofed with wagon vaults of a pointed form, and must certainly date before the middle of the 12th century, when Vaison was destroyed and deserted; they are probably of the 9th or 10th centuries. The same remark applies to the churches at Pernes, Souillac (fig. 158), Moissac, Carcassone, and many other churches of that age, all of which are covered with pointed vaults, but of a form extremely different from the true Gothic vaults of the 13th and 16th centuries." The chapel in the castle of Loches in Lorraine is given by Mr. Fergusson in his Handbook, as explaining most of the peculiarities of the style. The original building was founded by the Count of Anjou in the year 962, and the western tower certainly belongs to him. The nave is either a part of the original edifice, or was erected by his son, Foulques Nerra, between 992 and 1040. The supposition that it belongs to the latter receives confirmation from its singularly Eastern aspect,

Fig. 158.   CHURCH AT SOUILLAC.

and the fact that this Count three times visited the Holy Land, and died there in the year above quoted. The churches of Moissac, Souillac, and St. Frond at Périgueux, with several others, are still more eastern in their appearance. This latter building, of which

we give a plan (*fig.* 159), was commenced in the year 984, and was completed in 1047, on the type of, if not copied from, the cathedral of St. Mark, at Venice. A section is given in *fig.* 160, exhibiting the use of the pointed arches in construction only. The choir at Loches was erected between the years 1140 and 1180, and is in the late and elegant Norman style universal in that country, just anterior to the introduction of the true pointed style, which was timidly effected in the *north* of France about the year 1150, being mixed with round arches in all the great cathedrals. and churches erected between 1150 and 1200, at which date the style may be said to have been perfected in all its essential peculiarities.

307*a*. " In England it was in every respect above twenty-five years later. The first really authentic example of its use is in Canterbury Cathedral after the fire in 1175, and was apparently introduced by William of Sens; nearly half a century passed before it can be said to have entirely superseded the Norman arch. In Germany, the introduction was somewhat later, and we know of no authentic specimen of pure Gothic anterior to the commencement of the 13th century, and even then nearly half a century elapsed before it

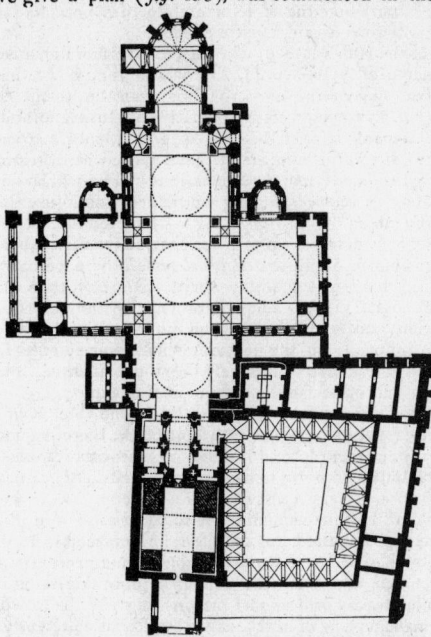

Fig. 159.　　PLAN OF ST. FROND, PERIGUEUX.

entirely superseded the round arch style. During the whole of the first half of that century, we find round arches mixed up with the pointed ones which were then coming into fashion."

307*b*. These views were combated by Mr. E. Sharpe, as noticed in the *Builder*, p. 317, especially as to the first named works being considered as arches at all; and a question arose at the Institute of British Architects, as to the age of the French buildings named; *Transactions*, 1860–61, p. 211, &c., and 115. Mr. Street, in his *Brick Architecture in Italy*, states, (p. 258) that— " The Italians ignored, as much as possible, the clear exhibition of the pointed arch, and, even when they did use it, not unfrequently introduced it in such a way as to show their con-

Fig. 160.　　ST. FROND, PÉRIGUEUX, TRANSVERSE SECTION.

tempt for it as a feature of construction; employing it often only for ornament, and never hesitating to construct it in so faulty a manner, that it required to be held together with iron rods from the very first day of its erection. This fault they found it absolutely necessary to commit, because they scarcely ever brought themselves to allow the use of the buttress."

(*b*) MEDIÆVAL ARTIFICERS.

308. In considering the question of the origin of pointed architecture, those who have hitherto been supposed to have devised the pointed arch itself must not be neglected: and to these persons we are indebted for the gigantic masses of exquisitely decorated composition, to be seen in the structures which they designed and erected. These men are imagined to have belonged to a corporation or guild having authority over all countries, or to a guild in each country, having authority only in its own nation. This so-called confraternity has been known as the Freemasons. In the following account of them we shall much abridge the two papers read before the Royal Institute of British Architects, and given in

the *Transactions* of that society, 1860 and 1861. Before doing so, however, it will be necessary to introduce a few preliminary remarks on the state of architecture previous to the period when the so-called body of Freemasons is said to have arisen.

309. The pontificate, towards the end of the 10th century, of a Benedictine monk, named Gerbert, afterwards known under the name of Sylvester II., and whose life, if Platina (*Lives of the Popes*) may be relied on, was not of the most virtuous character, seems to have induced an extraordinary change in the arts. Gerbert was a native of Auvergne, and, under Arabian masters at Cordova and Granada, applied himself to, and became a great proficient in, mathematical learning. He afterwards appears to have settled at Rheims, and to have there planted a school which threw out many ramifications. The scholars of the period were confined to the clergy, and the sciences, having no tendency to injure the Church, were zealously cultivated by its members.

309a. In the 11th century, architecture, considered as an art, was little more than a barbarous imitation of that of ancient Rome, and in it, all that appears tasteful was, perhaps, more attributable to the symmetry flowing from an acquaintance with geometry, than the result of fine feeling in those that exercised it. It was adapted to religious monuments, with great modifications ; but the materials and resources at hand, no less than the taste of those engaged in it, had considerable influence on the developments it was doomed to undergo. The sculptures of the period were borrowed largely from the ancients, and among them are often to be found centaurs and other fabulous animals of antiquity.

309b. In the 12th century, the *Elements of Euclid* became a text book, and though this country was then behind the Continent, as respected the art of architecture, there is good reason for believing it was by no means so in regard to proficiency in mathematics, inasmuch as the Benedictine monk, Adelard of Bath, is known to have been highly distinguished for his acquirements in them.

310. The crusades had made the people of Europe acquainted with the East, and in the 12th century the result of the knowledge thus acquired was manifest in France, England, and Germany ; it could, however, scarcely be expected that the art would emerge otherwise than slowly under the hands of the churchmen, who were the principal practitioners, as it is generally supposed; but there were undoubtedly professional men, as they may be called, in the 12th century, who undertook the management of work, as we shall notice presently; and it is well authenticated (De Beka, *De Episcopis Ultraject.*) that, in 1099, a certain Bishop of Utrecht was killed by the father of a young freemason, from whom the prelate had extracted the mystery (arcanum magisterium) of laying the foundations of a church. The period at which arose the celebrated *Confraternité des ponts*, founded by St. Benezet, is known to have been towards the latter end of the 12th or the beginning of the 13th century. The association of Freemasons had, however, its types at a period extremely remote. Among the Romans, and still earlier, among even the Greeks, existed corporations (if they may be so called) of artificers and others ; such were Numa's *Collegia Fabrorum* and *Collegia Artificum*, who made regulations for their own governance. These *collegia* were much in favour with the later Roman emperors, for in the third and fourth centuries we find that architects, painters, and sculptors, and many of the useful artificers, were free from taxation. The downfall, however, of the eastern and western empires, involved them in one common ruin, though it did not actually extinguish them.

311. The idea of the early establishment of a superintending body of co-workers such as the Freemasons are said to have been, appears to have originated in the assumption, that as the monuments of the 13th century bear so great a resemblance to each other, no other probable cause could be assigned for their similarity, than the influence of some powerful association of operators. Allowance, however, must, in many cases, be made for the materials at hand in different localities, which, it is hardly necessary to observe, influence style in architecture most perceptibly. Another point too often forgotten in this inquiry, is the gradual progression of the art, and the long transitional periods between each phase of pointed architecture. Some writers on the Freemasons have imagined that the concealment of their modes of arranging arch stones was the chief object of their association, and there can be no doubt that the whole science of construction was studied and taught in the lodges. Others have thought that they inclined to Manicheism, of which the sects were numberless : but we think they had enough to engage their attention, without discussing whether all things were effected by the combination or repulsion of the good and the bad ; or that men had a double soul, good and evil ; or that their bodies were formed, the upper half by God, and the lower half by the devil. Some have considered that though the Freemasons, as a body, were not hostile to the Church, they were inveterate enemies of the clergy and more particularly of the monks. This may be abundantly seen in the ridicule and grotesque lampoons bestowed on them in the sculptures of the 13th century. As an instance of the extreme length to which the ridicule of the priests was then carried, there is at Strasburg the representation of an ass saying mass and served by other animals as acolytes : and this work must have been done under the eyes of the monks themselves !

312. The remarks by the present editor, *On the Superintendents of English Buildings in the Middle Ages* contains the first classified account of the official situations of persons engaged, with some general idea of their duties. This list includes the terms : — 1, Architect ; 2, Ingeniator ; 3, Supervisor ; 4, Surveyor ; 5, Overseer ; 6, Master of the Works ; 7, Keeper of the Works ; 8, Keeper of the Fabric ; 9, Director ; 10, Clerk of the Works ; 11, Devizor ; 12, Master mason ; and 13, Freemason and mason, or inferior workman. It will be impossible here to give more than a brief outline. To commence with the freemasons : — In 1077, Robertus, *cementarius*, was employed at St. Albans, and for his skill and labour, in which he is stated to have excelled all the masons of his time, he had granted to him and his heirs, certain lands and a house in the town. In 1113, Arnold, a lay brother of Croyland Abbey, is designated " of the art of masonry a most scientific master." William of Sens, employed at Canterbury, was a layman and was called " magister " ; the history of his work has been preserved to us in the well written account by the monk Gervase, who details the burning and rebuilding of that cathedral. A number of chosen *cementarii* were assembled at St. Albans in 1200, of whom the chief, magister Hugo de Goldclif, proved to be a " deceitful but clever workman." Very many other names of masons are noticed, but these cannot all be here given. In 1217, a writer uses the synonyms *maszun* for *cementarius* ; *artificer* is a word also used in the same century ; *marmorarius*, or marbler ; and *latomus* or *lathomus*, stone-cutter, also occur. In 1360, a mason *de fraunche pere ou de grosse pere* is named in the Statutes ; while it is not until 1396 that the terms " lathomos vocatos ffremaceons," and " lathomos vocatos ligiers," are used to designate the masons who were called free(stone)masons, and the masons called layers or setters. In the fabric rolls of Exeter cathedral, the term *simentarius* is used before, and the term *fremason* after, the above-named period of 1396. Thus the derivation of the term freemason, from a freestone worker, appears more probable than the many fanciful origins of it so often quoted. What becomes then of the "travelling bodies of freemasons" who are said to have erected all the great buildings of Europe ? Did they ever exist ? The earliest mention of them appears to have been promulgated by Aubrey, some time before 1686, who cited Sir William Dugdale as having told him " many years since, that about Henry III's time (1216-72), the Pope gave a bull or patents to a company of Italian freemasons to travel up and down over all Europe to build churches. From them are derived the fraternity of Adopted Masons." No evidence has been adduced in support of this statement ; searches have been made in the Vatican library without success. Wren's *Parentalia* gives an account of these personages to the same purport, though somewhat enlarged, (*par.* 401), and this has been quoted as an authority. From a careful comparison of circumstances, Dugdale's information to Aubrey most probably referred to the " Letters of Indulgence " of Pope Nicholas III., in 1278, and to others by his successors as late as the 14th century, granted to the lodge of masons working at Strasburg cathedral, as also noticed on page 131 herein.

313. Concerning the *Fratres Pontis*, or the *Confraternité des ponts*, already referred to, (*par.* 310), much has been written during the last one hundred years asserting that this brotherhood had been founded for the express purpose of travelling far and wide to build bridges. Even as regards France, only a notice is found of such a troop having been formed by St. Benezet, for building the bridge at Avignon, and that of St. Esprit, over the Rhone, during the 12th and 14th centuries, (1178-1188 and 1265-1309). In England no such companies are found recorded ; but wherever a bridge was built, a chapel appears to have been founded, to which a priest was attached to pray for the soul of the founder, to receive passage money, and sometimes to pray with the passenger for the safe termination of his journey. Two instances only, of an early date, have been put forward of so called fraternities of masons ; the first is that Godfrey de Lucy, bishop of Winchester, formed in 1202, a confraternity for repairing his church during the five years ensuing. " Such," says Milner, " was probably the origin of the Society of Freemasons." The second, as asserted by Anderson, (*Constitutions of the Free and Accepted Masons*, 1738), but not since authenticated, is that the register of William Molart or Molash, prior of Canterbury cathedral, records that a respectable lodge of freemasons was held in that city in 1429, under the patronage of Henry Chichele, the archbishop, at which were present Thomas Stapylton, master, the warden, fifteen fellowcrafts, and three entered apprentices. It does not then appear to have been known that each cathedral establishment possessed a permanent staff of officers, with certain workpeople, and "took on " additional hands whenever the edifice was to receive additions, or to be rebuilt. The monarch also had an office for carrying out the repairs and rebuildings at the palaces and royal houses. A *guild* of masons was undoubtedly in existence in London, in 1375, 49th Edward III., and in 1376 two companies of masons and of freemasons were in existence. The Masons' Company of London was incorporated in 1411, and Stow says " they were formerly called freemasons." The masons, during the 17th and 18th centuries, often became designers or architects, as witness Nicholas Stone, George Dance the elder, Sir Robert Taylor, and others.

314. At this date of 1375, some writers have placed the origin of that wonderful society, caused, as they urge, by the masons combining and agreeing on certain signs and tokens by

which they might know one another; engaging to assist each other against the then common custom of impressment by the monarch; and further, not to work unless free and on their own terms, especially as the monarch would not pay them as highly as did his subjects. All this appears probable, but there is no sufficient authority for it. The workpeople had at times, as at Stratford-on-Avon, in 1353, special protection until the edifice was completed.

315. But previous to 1375, the date above mentioned, the *Statutes at Large* afford much valuable information, hitherto unquoted, on the subject of the manners and customs of workpeople. In 1349, the Statute 23rd Edward III. relates that " great part of the people and especially of workmen and servants late died of the pestilence, whereby many demand excessive wages and will not work ; " the hours of labour were settled at the same time, because " diverse artificers and labourers, retained to work and serve, waste much part of the day (the manner of doing so is described) and deserve not their wages." Their wages were settled in the year following; while in 1360–1, a Statute declares that " carpenters and masons and all other labourers shall take from henceforth wages by the day and not by the week, nor in any other manner," and continues " that all alliances and covines of masons and carpenters, and congregations, chapters, ordinances and oaths, betwixt them made or to be made, shall be from henceforth void and wholly annulled,"— with other details. This important Act was enforced by many others, and by the well-known Statute of 3rd Henry VI., 1425, passed at the " special request of the Commons," again putting down all chapters and congregations held by masons. In 1436–7, 15th Henry VI., the " masters, wardens, and people of the guilds, fraternities, and other companies incorporate, dwelling in divers parts of the realm," were warned not to " make among themselves unlawful and unreasonable ordinances, for their singular profit and common damage to the people"—their letters patent were to be brought to the justices and others for their approval. Many later Statutes were passed; but they were all at length superseded by the well known Statute of 5th Elizabeth, 1562-3, which continued in force until so late as 1813, when such portion was repealed as forbade exercise of trades by persons not having served, and as regulated the mode of binding apprentices, &c., but at the same time the customs and privileges of cities and boroughs were saved. It is certain, from all these observations, that there were fellowships or guilds of masons existing before the middle of the 14th century; but whether the one in London had any communication with those guilds existing in the other corporate towns, or whether there was a supreme guild which led to a systematic working, is still without elucidation. It has been asserted for years, on the faith of certain manuscript " Constitutions," that a company of Freemasons, formerly existing at York, held a charter of incorporation from King Athelstan, dated in 926, under which they claimed authority over the companies throughout England. As noticed hereafter (*par.* 322a), it is distinctly proved that the Grand Lodge of Masons of Germany was not established until so late as 1452.

316. These guilds or companies had legendary histories, as had probably most of the other building trades. That which belonged to the stonemasons was accepted by the Society of Free and Accepted Masons, when it was established or reestablished in 1722; this last has descended as a highly respected charitable and friendly society to the present day. Of such histories or " constitutions," besides at least six in manuscript, dating about 1646-60, there are two others in the British Museum. The earliest one is presumed to date about the latter part of the 14th century, and has the form of a poem in about 575 lines, entitled *Constitutions of Geometry*; it was first noticed by Mr. Halliwell, and edited by him in 1840. The other manuscript, dating about 1500, has been printed nearly in facsimile by Mr. M. Cooke. They were all undoubtedly compiled for the use of a body of working masons; they refer to yearly assemblies, to a lodge as a workshop, taking apprentices, workmanship, moral conduct, punishment of offenders, and observance of their " articles and points," or bye-laws as they may be termed. No references are made to secret signs or to masonic marks; as regards the latter, a few remarks will be offered subsequently.

317. The masons when about to set to work, had a *lodge* or workshop provided for them, and sometimes had to make it for themselves ; this shed or building also served them occasionally as a residence, or place for eating their meals, as often occurs at the present day. This lodge is noted in an early account as being covered with thatch, while in a much later one it is to be "properly tiled," an expression still in use by the modern society, when the door of their place of meeting is closed. This lodge is adverted to in the manuscripts above mentioned, as also in the Fabric Rolls of York Minster, published in Browne's *History of York Cathedral*, 1838-47, and separately by the Surtees Society, in 1859. These records elucidate many interesting points connected with works and workpeople ; and causes us to regret that the example set in printing them has not yet led other Deans and Chapters to do the like, or to allow them to be published. They show that there was a continuous line of master masons from 1347, the date of the earliest document, who were duly sworn to the office, had a fixed salary, a residence, and if becoming blind (which appears to have been, and is still, very often a result of employment in masonry), or compelled by bodily infirmity to give up the direction of the works, he was pensioned, and sometimes he was bound not

to undertake duties elsewhere while engaged at the cathedral.   The master mason was often succeeded by his junior or assistant; in one instance a fight took place in consequence of a master mason, who was a stranger to the place, having been appointed to the office.   Gowns or robes, the latter sometimes lined with fur, were provided for the master, and tunics for his men, as well as gloves (at $1\frac{1}{2}d$. each) to the masons and carpenters ; also aprons and clogs, and occasional potations and remuneration for extra work.   This officer in the king's household had a livery, as probably had the carpenter and other officers.

318. It is necessary to mention that the trades, from a very early period, appear to have kept themselves to their distinct handicrafts ; thus, while the monasteries had masons and carpenters, and a plumber and his boy, at hand, yet the glazier, bell-founder, painter or decorator, smith, and some others, were residents in the town or some adjoining city.   Only in a few of the monasteries were the monks able to perform some of these duties themselves.   In Italy, however, talented youths were received and educated at such establishments, and became lay brethren, as much for their own safety as out of gratitude to their masters ; the devotion of their time and talents in ornamenting the sacred edifices, has led persons to urge that ecclesiastical buildings were designed, erected, and decorated, by clerical hands.

319. We will now proceed to notice very succinctly the other official titles.   As far as the design of the building was concerned, that labour appears to have been left to the master mason, whatever interest the monarch, the bishop, the abbot, or the prior, may have displayed in giving instructions as to their wishes ; no doubt clever men then, as now, interfered with their architects and induced them to follow special orders, whether correct in taste or otherwise.   The term "Architect" has rarely been found in the middle ages ; perhaps to a certain extent the word " ingeniator," so early as 1199, may have taken its place.   " Supervisor" occurs constantly, soon after the Conquest, and has been translated " surveyor," and sometimes " overseer ; " it is not always clear what is to be understood by the term ; whether actually a " designer " and professional man, as held by some persons in the celebrated example of William of Wykeham, at Windsor Castle ; or merely as a " director," seeing to the orders of others being carried out : as we hold was the position of Wykeham, acting for the monarch, the design being attributable to the master mason. Numerous examples are given in the paper from which we are quoting ; and it likewise contains a searching enquiry into Wykeham's professional capacity, with what result we must beg the reader to judge for himself.   The " Magister Operum " or "master of the works " was an important officer in many monastic establishments ; at Croyland, for instance, he was the first of the six greater officers, and to his superintendence was submitted the construction, reparation, beautifying, and enlarging, of all the buildings belonging to the monastery.   The sacrist often held this office, and many names are known, more especially that of Alan de Walsingham, at Ely monastery, whose history and labours deserve attention.   In the agreement made at York, in 1367, it was arranged that the plumber was to work with his own hand wherever he should be required by the " master of the fabric ; " if his services were not required, he might obtain leave of absence from the chapter, or from the " master of the work," but to return when required by the said master.   At the same period there appears to have been a " keeper of the fabric " who was to settle the amount of the day's work for the plumber and his servants, and to pay salaries.   As the " master of the work," the "keeper of the works," and the " master mason," are all mentioned in one document of the same period, they cannot be considered as one person.   The household of the monarch, as before noticed, comprised an office for carrying out works at the royal palaces.   The earliest list yet found is of the reign of Edward IV. (1461-83) ; in it the " clerk of the works," who is placed first, has a fee of two shillings per day, or 36l. 10s. per annum, a clerk at sixpence per day, four shillings per day for riding expenses, and twenty pence for boat hire.   The next officer in the list is the comptroller, then follow the clerk of the engrossment of the pay-book, the purveyor with an allowance for his horse, the keeper of the store-house, the clerk of the check, the clerk of the comptrollements, the carpenter, the plumber, the mason (in this list is omitted), the joiner, the glazier, the surveyor of the mines, who has also 36l. 10s. per annum, and lastly, the devizor of building, who has the same amount.   It would appear from a passage in the Ordinances published by the Society of Antiquaries, 1790, that this clerk of the works was first instituted by Edward III., and the livery for that officer is known to have been given as early as 1391.   Similar lists occur later ; in Elizabeth's reign, the title becomes that of surveyor and paymaster, or surveyor and clerk ; in one of 1610, containing the household of prince Henry, Inigo Jones is " surveyor of the works ; " Mr. Smith, " paymaster and overseer ; " and Edward Carter, " clerk of the works."   Jones was subsequently " surveyor " of the king's works ; and Denham, Sir C. Wren (who received the fee of 45l. 12s. 6d.), and others, were styled " surveyor-general."   This royal establishment eventually became the Board of Works, then the Office of Works, and is now known as the Commission of Public Works.   It was this Board of Works that served as the school for architects, or to which the best architects were attached, during the 17th and 18th centuries   The earliest instance of the term " clerk of

the works" occurs in 1241, 25th Henry III., for certain works to be done at Windsor; in later times it appears in connection with the palaces at Westminster and elsewhere; and such an appointment it will be remembered was held by William of Wykeham, in 1356, and by Geoffrey Chaucer, in 1389. The "devizor" already named, although it occurs so early as about 1470, is a title to which but one name has been attached, that of John of Padua, on the faith of a passage in Walpole's *Anecdotes.*

320. These careful notices are concluded by the statement that "there is one circumstance respecting nearly all these officers which perhaps needs a passing comment. Very many of them were either ecclesiastics or were rewarded with ecclesiastical preferment. But it must be remembered that, during the period to which our attention has been confined, the *church* was the only field for exertion open to those of the nobility and gentry who were not inclined to embrace the profession of arms; it also afforded a means by which to obtain a livelihood; therefore the clergy, so called, would thus secure the offices at the disposal of the monarch and of the nobility. Some names, however, appear to have been unconnected with the church." It might be added that in late times in France, eminent architects were appointed *abbés,* and from their establishments derived the funds for the remuneration of their services. "It is very difficult to understand the *duties* of these officers. The overseer would be, perhaps, the most easily explained, but his Latin designation as used in the Records, is unknown to us unless the Latin word "Supervisor" has been the one the translators have found. The English word supervisor, if that of steward be questionable, is, perhaps, best kept for those who, acting on behalf of others, as Wykeham for the monarch, have yet no grounds to be considered the designers of the building. The master of the works, as he was called in the monastic establishments, and later in Scotland, held the place of the English king's chief professional man, and was, no doubt, one of the talented advisers of the day. The king's clerk of the works clearly stood in the place of the architect. The master or keeper of the fabric was probably the keeper of the whole structure; and the keeper of the works was, perhaps, only the custodian of the particular works then in progress; the edifice, under those circumstances, being developed by the master of the works or by the master mason. But there is one officer of whom we should desire to know much, but of whom nothing whatever is known; this is the devizor of buildings."

321. We would refer the student to the paper by Mr. Ferrey, read at the same society in 1864, *Some remarks upon the works of the early mediæval architects, Gundulph, Flambard, William of Sens, and others.* The subject will be well concluded by quoting the result of Mr. Street's enquiry into the designers of the buildings in Spain. He states in his *Account of Gothic Architecture in Spain,* 1865, p. 464, that "it is often, and generally thoughtlessly, assumed that most of the churches of the middle ages were designed by monks or clerical architects. So far as Spain is concerned, the result at which we arrive is quite hostile to this assumption, for in all the names of architects that I have noticed there are but three who were clerics. In our own country it is indeed commonly asserted that the bishops and abbots were themselves the architects of the great churches built under their rule. Gundulph, Flambard, Walsingham, and Wykeham, have all been so described, but I suspect upon insufficient evidence; and those who have devoted the most study and time to the subject seem to be the least disposed to allow the truth of the claim made for them. The contrary evidence which I am able to adduce from Spain certainly serves to confirm these doubts. In short, the common belief in a race of clerical architects and in ubiquitous bodies of freemasons, seems to me to be altogether erroneous." This work treats very minutely on the position of the designer of the buildings in Spain.

322. Among other matters connected with the progress of the art, Stieglitz, in 1834, brought to the notice of the public, the marks on courses of stone in many buildings in Germany, and elsewhere, called "mason's marks," which by some have been supposed to be the personal marks of the masters of the works, but which are, in fact, nothing more than directions to the *setters,* and, indeed, are used by masons up to the present hour. Some of these, however, are curious in form and figure, and were most probably determined by the lodges. Their forms are principally rectangular, of forty-five degrees, of the equilateral triangle, of the intersection of horizontal and perpendicular lines, and circular. Some of them have so great a resemblance to Runic characters, that therefore it has been argued the Anglo-Saxons taught the Germans architecture, and that they cultivated the art, and had masonic lodges among themselves, at a very early period; but this seems rather unreasonable; neither is it likely that the natives of this island were the chief artists employed on foreign cathedrals, though some may have been. That these marks, however, were used from some traditional knowledge has also been urged. Thus the mark ⪦, the cruciform hammer of Thor, is found in the minster at Bâle, and repeated in the sixteenth century in the church at Oschatz. This mark abounds in a great variety of phases,—on medals, on annulets, in the museum of the Royal Academy of Copenhagen; and on many Runic monuments, as mentioned by Hobhouse in his illustrations of *Childe Harold.* It is also found on the sacred jar of the Vaishnavas (*Asiatic Researches,* vol. viii.). At the Château de Coucy (13th century) is found ᛋ, the Runic letter S. One mark of frequent recurrence

is ψ, an inverted Runic T. It may be seen at Fribourg, at the beautiful church of St.
Catherine at Oppenheim, and at Strasburg, connected with the letter N. Without founding any hypothesis upon the singular agreement of these marks with the sixteen letters
of the Runic alphabet, it is at least a curious matter for further examination. Hobhouse,
as above mentioned, states, that a character resembling the hammer of
Thor is found in some Spanish inscriptions, and he seems to think it
bears affinity to *fig.* 161. which is often drawn by boys in Italy, though
no meaning is ascribed to it ; just as English shepherds, who never saw
a coin of Antiochus, are in the habit of cutting the pentalpha on the turf.

Fig. 161.

322*a*. The earliest lodge of which we have any authentic knowledge,
was that of Strasburg. Erwin von Steinbach seems to have been at
the head of it ; he appears also to have been the first secular architect
of importance that arose, and to have had privileges of great importance conceded to him by the emperor, Rodolph of Hapsburg. This lodge was
regularly constituted, with power, round a certain extent of territory, to maintain order
and obedience among the workmen under its jurisdiction. In 1278, Pope Nicholas III.
granted to the body a bull of absolution, which was renewed by his successors up to the
time, in the fourteenth century, when Benedict XII. occupied the papal chair. To
Iodoque Dotzinger, master of the works at Strasburg · in 1452, the merit seems attributable of so forming an alliance between the different lodges of Germany, as to induce
a greater uniformity of practice. Whether from the central lodge of Strasburg, whence
certainly branched lodges at Cologne, Vienna, and Zurich, branched also the lodges of
France, England, and Italy, in which last named country one existed at Orvieto, it is now
perhaps too difficult a task to discover.

322*b*. Much stress has been laid upon the *marks*, which are found upon the faces and beds
of stones in nearly all countries. In *fig.* 162. are given several of these fanciful forms, as we

Fig. 162.   MASONS' MARKS ON STONES.

maintain them originally to have been. *a* and *b*, are from the interior and exterior of the
nave of Gloucester cathedral. *c*, Malmesbury abbey church. *d*, Furness abbey. *e*, Poitiers, in France. *f*, St. Radigonde. *g*, Cologne cathedral ; and *h*, Roman altars at Rising-
ham: these are all from Mr. G. Godwin's paper in the *Archæologia*, vol. xxx. *i*, from
Segovia cathedral ; *k*, Tarragona cathedral ; and *l*, Veruela cathedral ; are given, with many
others, by Mr. G. E. Street in his *Gothic Architecture of Spain*. Numerous examples are
given in the *Freemasons' Monthly Magazine*, &c. new series, 1862, and in the *Builder Journal*
for 1863. Perhaps the fact of their occurrence, as in the present day, is simply due to their
being the marks or signs by which each mason recognises the particular stone for the
correct workmanship of which he is answerable. On large works a list is kept of them
by the foreman, and any new man having a mark similar to one already on the list, has to
make a distinctive difference. An eminent practical mason assured us that from the
character of the mark he could tell at once the kind of stone on which it was made.

A general history of Pointed Architecture is placed at page 231; the Practice of
Pointed Architecture is placed in Book III., together with much relative information
and illustration in Principles of Proportion, in the same Book.

Sect. XVI.

ITALIAN ARCHITECTURE.

323. The commencement of a new era in architecture first dawned in Florence, and then
soon spread its meridian light over Italy and the rest of Europe. The French have well
applied the term *renaissance* to its commencement. It is with us denominated that of the
revival of the arts. The Florentines had at an early period, according to Villani, determined to erect in their city a monument which should surpass all that had before
appeared ; and in 1298 Arnolfo di Lapo, according to Vasari, but according to Molini,
Arnolfo di Cambio da Colle, to whom they confided its execution, had so prepared his
plans that its foundations were laid in that year, on the day of the feast of the Nativity,
and the name of Sta. Maria del Fiore was then given to it. This edifice, though com-

menced long before the revival of the arts, seems to have been conceived by its architect in an original style, forming, as it were, a mean between the pointed and ancient style. It is therefore one of particular interest and instruction in the history of architecture, and one wherein we find a construction in which preparation was made for changing the style then prevalent into one sanctioned by the ancient principles of the art; and it is certain that it was the first which gave the hint for the grandest monuments of modern architecture *Fig.* 163. shows the plan, and *fig.* 164. the half section and half elevation of it.   The walls

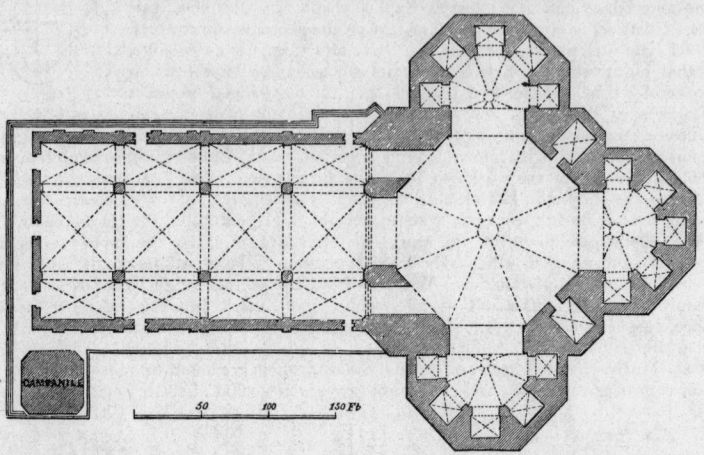

Fig. 163.   PLAN OF SANTA MARIA DEL FIORE AT FLORENCE.

are almost entirely cased with marble.   The whole length of it is 454 feet; from the pavement to the summit of the cross is nearly 387 feet; the transept is nearly 334 feet long; the height of the nave 153 feet, and that of the sides aisles 96½.   Between the period of the beginning of the edifice and that in which its completion was entrusted to Brunelleschi, many architects of great talent had been employed in carrying on the works: among whom we find the names of Giotto; Taddeo Gaddi; Andrea Orgagna, a man of extraordinary powers, as his Loggia in the Piazza at Florence amply testifies; and Filippo di Lorenzo.   The revival of architecture is so connected with the life of Brunelleschi, that a few passages in the latter will assist us in giving information on the former.   He was born in 1377, and by his father Lippo Lippi, a notary of Florence, was intended to succeed him in his own profession; but the inclination of the youth bent towards the arts, and the parent with reluctance yielded to it, and placed him with a goldsmith, an occupation then so connected with sculpture that the greatest artists of the time applied themselves to the chasing and casting ornaments in the precious metals.   Brunelleschi, though skilful as a sculptor, had many rivals; and ambitious, it would seem, to be the first in the art to which he should apply his powers, determined to devote himself entirely to architecture, in which the field was then unoccupied.   In company with Donatello he therefore visited Rome, and applied himself with ardour to the study of the ruins in the Eternal City; and what was said by Constantius on seeing the forum of Trajan, as related by Ammianus Marcellinus, might be truly said of Brunelleschi : — " Hærebat attonitus per giganteos contextus circumferens mentem, nec relatu affabiles, nec rursus mortalibus appetendos."   It was in Rome, though he never communicated his thoughts on the subject to his friend Donatello, that he began to meditate upon the scheme of uniting by a grand cupola the four naves of the Duomo at Florence; a project which till his time was considered almost impossible. During his residence, also, he traced and settled in his mind the proportions of the orders of architecture from the classic examples which the city afforded.   Here it was that he studied the science of construction as practised by the ancients : from them he learnt that perfect accordance which always exists between what is useful and what is beautiful, both of which are reciprocally subordinate to each other.   Here he discovered the principles of that nice equilibrium, equally requisite for the beauty no less than for the solidity of an edifice.   In short, throughout he found "sermons in stones;" and, having thus qualified himself for the great work he sought, returned to Florence in 1407.   In this year the citizens convoked an assembly of architects and engineers to deliberate upon some plan for finishing the Duomo, as Sta. M. del Fiore is usually called; a name given to the cathedrals of the cities of Italy.   To this assembly Brunelleschi was invited, and gave his advice for raising the base drum or attic story upon which the cupola should be placed.   It is not important here to detail the jealousies of rivals which impeded his project; nor, when the

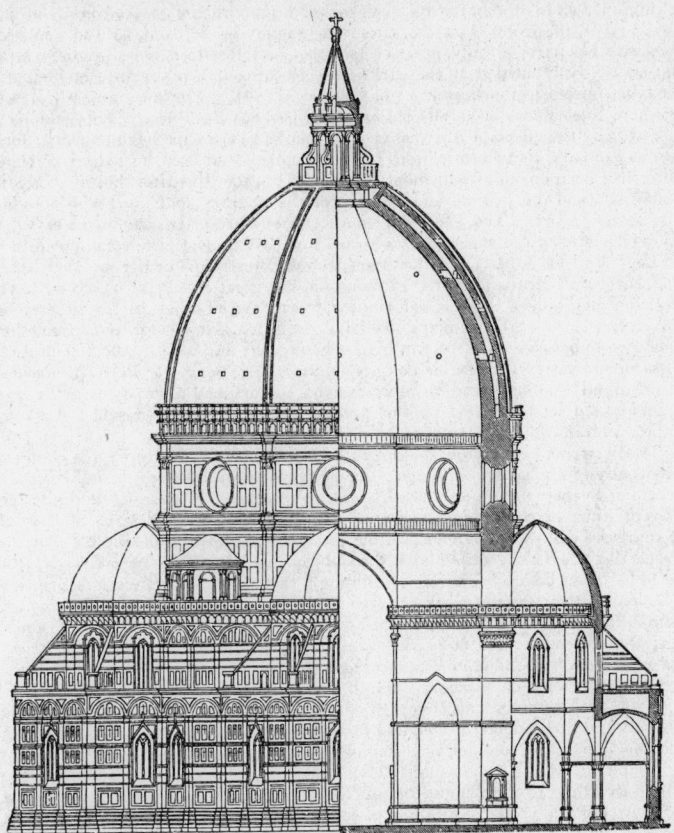

Fig. 164.   HALF ELEVATION AND HALF SECTION OF SANTA MARIA DEL FIORE.

commission was at length confided to him, the disgraceful assignment to him of Lorenzo
Ghiberti as a colleague, whose incapacity for such a task our architect soon made manifest.
Suffice it to say, that before his death he had the satisfaction to see the cupola finished,
with the exception of the exterior of the drum under the cupola ; for whose decoration, as
well as for the lantern with which he proposed to crown the edifice, he left designs, which,
however, were lost.   One of the directions he left on his death particularly insisted upon
the necessity of following the model he had prepared for the lantern, and that it was essential that it should be constructed of large blocks of marble so as to prevent the cupola
from opening ; an advice which experience has since proved in other cases to be far from
sound.   This cupola is octagonal on the plan, as will be seen by reference to the figures,
and is 138 feet 6 inches in diameter, and from the cornice of the drum to the eye of the
dome of the height of 133 feet 3 inches.   Before it nothing had appeared with which it
could be fairly put in comparison.   The domes of St. Mark and that at Pisa are far below
it in grandeur and simplicity of construction.   In size it only yields to St. Peter's at
Rome, for which it is probable it served as a model to Michael Angelo ; for in both, the inner
and outer cupolas are connected in one arch at their springing.   It is moreover well
known that Buonarroti's admiration of it was so great that he used to say that to imitate
it was indeed difficult, to surpass it impossible.   Vasari's testimony of it shall close our
account of this magnificent structure : — " Se puo dir certo che gli antichi, non andarono
mai tanto alto con lor fabriche, ne si messono a un risico tanto grande, che eglino volessino
combattere col cielo, come par veramente ch' ella combatta, veggendosi ella estollere in
tant' altezza che i monti intorno a Fiorenza paiono simili a lei.   E nel vero pare, che il
cielo ne abbia invidia poiche di continuo le saette tutto il giorno la percuotono."   It might
be supposed that such a work was sufficient to occupy the whole of Brunelleschi's time ;
not so : the Duke Filippo Maria engaged him on the fortifications at Milan, besides which

he was employed on several other military works; a proof of the great diversity of talent he possessed. It is, therefore, from the extensive employ he enjoyed, not only in Florence, but in many other parts of Italy, quite certain that he infused a new taste into its buildings, and that he is justly entitled to the title of the Restorer of Architecture in Europe. He died, and was buried in the church he had raised in 1444. He left a number of scholars, among whom Luca Fancelli and Michelozzo were perhaps the ablest. These pupils spread throughout Italy the effects of the vast change that had been thus begun; a taste for architecture was excited; its true principles became known; and in a short space of time, as if the matter had been one of arrangement between them, the illustrious house of Medici, the dukes of Milan, and the princes and nobility of the country contended who should most patronise its professors. The learned began to expound to artists the books of Vitruvius, the only writer among the ancients whose works on that subject have come down to us.

324. Leo Battista Alberti, of the ancient and illustrious family of the Alberti of Florence, succeeded Brunelleschi in carrying on the great change of which we have been speaking, and was, indeed, a great contributor to the art, not only by his literary labours on architecture, in which he displays profound erudition, knowledge of construction, and an intimate acquaintance with the works of the ancients, but also by the distribution, elegance, grace, and variety, which his designs exhibit. His book, *De Re Edificatoriâ*, is the foundation of all that has been since written on the art, and deserves careful perusal by every one who studies for the purpose of practice. We shall here present a short account of it, which, in imitation of Vitruvius, he divided into ten books.

325. The *first* book treats on the origin and utility of architecture; the choice of the soil and situation for placing buildings; the preparation, measurement, and suitable division according to their nature, of the edifices to be erected; of columns and pilasters; of the different kinds of roofs, doors, and windows, their number and size; of the different sorts of staircases and their landings; of the sewage or drains, and of suitable situations for them respectively. In the *second* book the subjects are, the choice of materials; the precautions to be taken before beginning a building; the models, of whatever description, that should be made; the choice of workmen; the trees fit for use, and the season in which they should be felled; the methods for preventing rot, and susceptibility of fire; of stone in its varieties; the different sorts of bricks, tiles, lime, sand, and mortar. The *third* book treats of construction; foundations according to the varieties of soil; encroachments; the carrying up and bond of masonry; rough and rubble work; on the different sorts of masonry; on the inlaying and facing of walls; on beams, joists, and the method of strengthening them; on floors, arches, and vaults; the covering of roofs, pavements, and the season for beginning and completing certain works. The *fourth* book is confined to the philosophy of the art, showing the causes which influence mankind in the adoption of modes of building according to the climate, the soil, and the habits or government of a people. It, however, treats of the proper position of a city; of the size to be given to it; of the form of the walls; of the customs and ceremonies of the ancients as applied to this point; of fortifications, bastions or towers, gates and ramparts; bridges, both of timber and stone; sewers, ports, harbours, and squares requisite in a city. The *fifth* book contains instructions for the erection of palaces for peaceable, and castles for absolute princes; for the houses required by a republic; large and small religious edifices; academies, public schools, hospitals, and palaces for senators. In it are given some hints on military and naval architecture, on farm buildings, and country houses. In the *sixth* book Alberti treats on architectural ornament, columns, and the method of adjusting their proportions. After some observations on the principles of beauty, on taste, and on the mode of improving it, he enters shortly on the history of architecture. These are followed by several chapters on the doctrine of mechanics, machines, the method of raising and working columns, polishing them, imitations in stucco and incrustation in thin layers, and matters of that nature. The *seventh* book continues the discussion on ornaments in architecture, but chiefly in respect of columns, showing the edifices in which the use of them is suitable; and, in imitation of Vitruvius in his directions relative to temples, our author dilates on buildings for ecclesiastical purposes. He shows what sorts of columns and pilasters are best suited to them, how far the employment of statues is proper, and how they should be sculptured. The *eighth* book is on roads and their decorations, tombs, pyramids, columns, altars, epitaphs, &c. In it he turns to the subjects of streets, cities, ornaments appropriate to gates, ports, arches, bridges, crossways, markets, public squares, walks, porticoes, theatres, amphitheatres, circi, libraries, colleges, baths, &c.; and the style in which public buildings should be constructed and decorated. The *ninth* book is a continuation of the preceding one; but in this he speaks in addition of the appropriate decoration of royal palaces, and of the ornaments respectively suitable to city and country dwellings, and of the paintings and sculpture that should be employed in them. In the *tenth* and last book the principal subject is the finding a supply of water for buildings both in town and country, and it closes with some useful hints on the aid of architecture to domestic economy. This truly great man constructed many works in different cities of Italy, some of which still remain to

attest his skill. We are not to examine them with the eye of an architect flourishing even half a century later, though under that category they do him honour, but with the eye of an artist of his own day, and we shall then find our veneration for his memory cannot be too strongly expressed. In Florence he finished the Ruccellai palace, and built the choir of the Annunziata. At Mantua he built a church of singular beauty, consisting of a simple nave, crowned with a vault decorated with *caissons*, which rivals the works of the ancients. The additions he made to the church of St. Francesco at Rimini, a pointed church, though not in the same style, because it then came into disrepute, show an extraordinary aptitude for overcoming the most difficult and repulsive subjects with which an architect has to deal, and that work alone would stamp him as a man of genius. On his other acquirements it is not within our province to dwell; we shall merely sum them up by saying that he was poet, painter, sculptor, philosopher, mathematician, and antiquary. Such was Alberti, in whom was concentrated more refinement and learning than have hardly since appeared in a single individual of our species. The time of his death is not accurately known; some place it at the end of the fifteenth, and others at the beginning of the sixteenth century.

326. About the time that Alberti was engaged on the practice and literature of the art, a very extraordinary volume, written by a member of the Colonna family, was published by Aldus, at Venice, in 1499, folio. Its title is as follows: — *Polyphili Hypnerótomachia; opus italicâ linguâ conscriptum; ubi humana omnia non nisi somnium esse docet.* This work deserves to be better known than we fear its rarity will ever permit. With the singularity of the plan, it unites the advantage of placing before the reader many elevated and elegant ideas, and, under the veil of a fable, of inculcating precepts of the greatest utility to artists and those that love the art. The testimony of Felibien in favour of this work runs so favourably, that we must transcribe it:—" Sans préjudice," says that author, " du grand profit qu'on peut tirer de la lecture de Vitruve, et de l'étude qu'on doit faire de ses principes et de ses règles, il ne faut pas moins examiner les tableaux curieux de plusieurs superbes édifices, monumens ou jardins, que l'imagination riante et féconde de l'auteur du *Songe* a mis sous les yeux de ses lecteurs." When it is recollected that the manuscripts of Vitruvius were extremely rare, and that when Colonna wrote (1467) that author had not been translated, — when we reflect that in his descriptions he rears edifices as magnificent and regular as those which Vitruvius presents to us, we cannot withhold our surprise at the genius and penetration of the author. With him architecture appears in all her majesty. Pyramids, obelisks, mausolea, colossal statues, circi, hippodromi, amphitheatres, temples, aqueducts, baths, fountains, noble palaces, delicious gardens, all in the purest taste and of the most perfect proportion, attend in her train, and administer to the pomp with which the author attires her. With him all these ideal productions of the art were not merely the result of an ardent imagination, but were the fruit of an intimate acquaintance with its rules, which he explains to his reader, and inspires him at the same time with a taste for the subject of his pages. He often breaks out against the gross ignorance of the architects of his day, and endeavours to inculcate in them the sound principles of the art. He demonstrates that it is not enough that an edifice possesses stability and solidity, but that it must be impressed with a character suitable to the purpose for which it is destined; that it is not enough that it be well decorated, but that the ornaments used arise from necessity, or at the least from utility. Architecture thus treated in fiction was much more pleasantly studied than it would have been by mere application to the dry rules of Vitruvius. The impression made by the work was increased by the poetic glow with which the precepts were delivered; the allegories it contained warmed the imaginations of a people easily excited, and Italy soon saw realised what Polyphilus had seen in a dream. This work is decorated with wood engravings of singular beauty, in which the details and accessories are strictly classical; it is written with great spirit and elegance, and we are not amazed at the magical effect which, with the accompaniment of Alberti's book above mentioned, it every where produced.

327. The Italian school, which ultimately appropriated and adapted the ancient Roman orders and their details to comparatively modern habits, was for a long while engrafted on or amalgamated with what is called Gothic. We here (*fig.* 165.) place before the reader an instance of this, in the celebrated Loggia at Florence, designed by Orgagna. The same feeling appears, indeed, in what Brunelleschi did in his Duomo, and in many other buildings in Florence, in Pisa, Sienna, and other cities. Brunelleschi doubtless made a strong effort to emancipate himself altogether from the mixture of two discordant styles, and in some measure succeeded. Still there continued, as is evident in the Ricardi, Strozzi, and other palaces in Florence, a lingering love for the mixture, which the architects had great apparent difficulty in shaking off. It is, however, extraordinary that with all this lingering love for the ancient style, in which there was much littleness, when the architects of this period came to the crowning members of their edifices, they placed on them such massive and finely composed cornices that the other parts are quite lost; and in this member it is evident they were influenced by those feelings of unity and breadth that gave so much value to the best works of the ancients.

Fig. 165.   LOGGIA OF ORGAGNA.

328. The revival of the arts in Italy was vastly assisted by the commerce and riches of the country; and with the decay of that commerce, nearly 300 years afterwards, their palmy days were no more: from that time they have never thriven in the country that gave them birth. It is our intention, in this view of Italian architecture, to consider it under the three schools which reigned in Italy — 1. The Florentine; 2. The Roman; 3. The Venetian.

329. 1. *Florentine School.* — Climate and the habits of a people are the principal agents in creating real style in architecture; but these are in a great measure controlled, or it is perhaps more correct to say modified, by the materials which a country supplies. Often, indeed, these latter restrict the architect, and influence the lightness or massiveness of the style he adopts. The quarries of Tuscany furnish very large blocks of stone, lying so close to the surface that they are without other difficulty than that of carriage obtained, and removed to the spots where they are wanted. This is probably a circumstance which will account for the solidity, monotony, and solemnity which are such commanding features in the Florentine school; and which, if we may judge from the colossal ruins still existing, similarly prevailed in the buildings of ancient Etruria. In later times another cause contributed to the continuation of the practice, and that was the necessity of affording places of defence for the upper ranks of society in a state where insurrection continually occurred. Thus the palaces of the Medici, of the Pitti, of the Strozzi, and of other families, served almost equally for fortresses as for palaces. The style seems to have interdicted the use of columns in the façades, and on this account the stupendous cornices that were used seem actually necessary for the purpose of imparting grandeur to the composition. In the best and most celebrated examples of their palaces, such as the Strozzi, Pandolfini, and others in Florence, and the Picolomini palace at Sienna, the cornices are proportioned to the whole height of the building considered as an order, notwithstanding the horizontal subdivisions and small interposed cornices that are practised between the base and the crowning member. The

courts of these palaces are usually surrounded by columns or arcades, and their interior is scarcely ever indicated by the external distribution.   From among the extraordinary palaces with which Florence abounds, we place before the reader the exquisite façade of the Pandolfini palace, the design whereof (*fig.* 166.) is attributed to the divine Raffaelle d'Urbino.

Fig. 166.   PANDOLFINI PALACE.

In it almost all the requisites of street architecture are displayed.. It is an example wherein the principles of that style are so admirably developed, as to induce us to recommend it, in conjunction with the façade of the Farnese palace hereafter given, to the elaborate study of the young architect.

330. Without further allusion to the double cupola of the Duomo, already noticed, the first of its species, and the prototype of that of St. Peter's at Rome afterwards reared by Michael Angelo, the principles and character of the Florentine school are not so manifest in its churches as in its palaces.   These nevertheless possess great interest; for they were the bases on which those of the Roman school were formed, as well as of those examples which, with different degrees of purity, were afterwards erected in many of the capitals of Europe.   Besides the plan of the Duomo, those of St. Michele, Sta. Maddelina, St. Pancrazio, St. Lorenzo, and St. Spirito, are the key to all excellence in modern art, as respects real church architecture.   It is unfortunate that of this school few of the churches have been finished, so that their façades are generally imperfect.   The interior was properly, with them, a matter to be first considered and brought to perfection.

331. Amongst the many extraordinary architects of the Florentine school, whereof a list will hereafter be given, was Bartolomeo Ammanati, whose bridge, "*della Santissima Trinità*," sufficiently proves that the greatness of the Florentine school does not alone depend on its palaces and churches.   This, one of the most beautiful examples, as well for design as constructive science, in which was obtained for the waters of the Arno a maximum of waterway, combined with a beauty of form inappreciable through graphic means, still strides the river of Florence, to attest the consummate skill of Ammanati. The bridge in question consists of three arches : the middle one is 96 ft. span, and each of the others 86 ft.; the width of the piers is 26 ft. 9 in., and the breadth of the bridge between the parapets is 33 ft.   The arches are very slightly pointed, the cusp being hidden by the rams' heads sculptured on the keystones; their rise above the springing is very little, hence they have been mistaken by some writers for cycloidal arches.   Alfonso and Giulio Parigi, who assisted in constructing the work, left an account of the mode in which it was carried on, and the manuscript is still preserved in the Florentine Library.   More recently, a description of this bridge has been published by Ferroni, under the title of "Della vera Curva degli Archi del Ponte della Santissima Trinità di Firenze."   The Pitti palace had been begun in the time of Brunelleschi, in 1435, for Luca Pitti, a wealthy citizen of Florence. Remaining long unfinished, it was at last sold to Eleonora, wife of Cosmo I., who purchased the adjoining ground, and planted the Boboli Gardens.   About the middle of the 16th century, Nicolo Bracciani, surnamed Tribolo, made designs for finishing the building; and was succeeded by Bernardo Buontalenti.   After him came our Ammanati, who left other designs for finishing, which was accomplished by Alfonso and Giulio Parigi.   It is now the residence of the grand duke, and has served as a model for imitation to many modern architects, though there is in it much to condemn.   The details, however, and proportions of the orders used in it by Ammanati, are very beautiful.   This architect died in 1586, at the age of seventy-five.   He was a pupil of Baccio Bandinelli, and during his life composed a large work, entitled *La Città*, which contained designs for all the fabrics belonging to a regular and well-arranged city, beginning with the gates, then proceeding to the palaces of the prince and magistrates, the churches, the fountains, the squares, the loggia for the

merchants, the bridges, theatres, &c.   This work appears to have been lost, the last possessor of it known having been the prince Ferdinand of Tuscany.   Though in the higher refinement of finished details the Florentine school did not reach the extreme elegance of the Roman and Venetian schools, yet for bold imposing masses of architecture we think no city presents such a collection of highly picturesque architectural examples as Florence. The Pitti palace indeed, just mentioned, is more imposing by its broad parts than almost any other building with which we are acquainted, though it becomes poor when translated into French, as at the Luxembourg.

332. So late as 1454, we find in the Strozzi and other palaces semicircular-headed windows, wherein are half columns at the sides, and a column in the middle, resembling those in the Byzantine or Romanesque edifices.   The two apertures thus formed are crowned by semicircular heads, which are circumscribed by the outer semicircle, and the spandrel formed by the three curves is occupied by a patera.

333. The period of the Florentine school, which must be taken as commencing with Brunelleschi, includes the names of Michelozzo, Leo Battista Alberti, Pollaiuolo (who obtained the soubriquet of Chronaca, from his constant recital of his travels), the architect of the Strozzi palace, Raffaelle Sanzio, Benedetto da Majano, Baccio d'Agnolo, Baccio Bandinelli, Buontalenti, Ammanati, and others: it extends from A. D. 1400 to A. D. 1600. The works of Michael Angelo, though a Florentine, do not belong to this school ; neither do those of San Gallo and some others, who have been improperly classed as Florentine architects.

334. 2. *Roman School.* — Though the city of Rome, during the period of the rise and progress of the Roman school of architecture, was not altogether free from insurrectionary troubles, its palatial style is far less massive than that of Florence.   None of its buildings present the fortress-like appearance of those in the last-named city.   Indeed, the Roman palaces, from their grace and lightness, indicate, on the part of the people, habits of a much more pacific nature, and an advancing state of the art, arising from a more intimate acquaintance with the models of antiquity which were on every side.   The introduction of columns becomes a favourite and pleasing feature, and great care and study appear to have been constantly bestowed on the façades of their buildings; so much so, indeed, in many, that they are but masks to indifferent interiors.   In them the entrance becomes a principal object ; and though in a great number of cases the abuses which enter into its composition are manifold, yet the general effect is usually successful.   The courts in these palaces are most frequently surrounded with arcades, whence a staircase of considerable dimensions leads to the sala or principal room of the palace.   The general character is that of grandeur, but devoid altogether of the severity which so strongly marks the Florentine school.   The noblest example of a palace in the world is that of the Farnese family at Rome, to which we shall afterwards have occasion to return.

335. Bramante, born in 1444 at some place, but which is still in doubt, in the duchy of Urbino, must be considered the founder of the Roman school.   Though educated as a painter under Fra Bartolomeo, and likely to have ranked in that occupation as a master of no ordinary powers, his great love of architecture induced him at an early period to quit painting as a profession.   In Lombardy he wandered from city to city for the purpose of obtaining employment as an architect, but there is no evidence that his exertions in that part of Italy were rewarded with great success.   The dry style which afterwards characterised his works has been said to have had its origin in his protracted stay at Milan, while the works of the Duomo were carrying on there under Bernardino di Trevi, a builder of such skill as to have gained the esteem of Leonardo da Vinci.   Be this as it may, it was in this city his determination to follow our art became irrevocable.   From Milan he went straightway to Rome; where, however, he was obliged to make himself known by some works in his first profession of a painter in the church of St. Giovanni Laterano.   Naturally of hospitable and social disposition, and a lover of expense and luxury, so intense was his ardour to become great in the art he adopted that he refrained from all society, holding commerce only with the monuments of antiquity by which he was surrounded, studying with the utmost diligence, and drawing them for his future application of the principles upon which they were founded.   He even extended his researches to Naples, losing no opportunity of noting all the ruins from which instruction in his art could be drawn.   Oraffa (Cardinal of Naples), who had remarked his zeal, gave him his first commission in Rome, which was the construction of the cloister of the Convent della Pace ; and this, from the intelligence and speed with which he executed the task, brought him at once into repute.   At this period Rome could boast but of few architects, and those that were established there were of small account.   The Florentine school seems to have sprung in the most decided manner from the habits of the people and the massiveness of their materials, modified by some knowledge of the buildings of the ancients : that of Rome seems to have been founded upon the principle of making the ancient architecture of Rome suit the more modern habits of a very different people, though living on the same spot.   To explain more immediately our meaning, we cite the small circular chapel

of St. Pietro in Montorio, wherein we find a jump at once in the adaptation of the circular peripteral temple of the Romans to the purpose of Christian ceremonies.   And again, it is impossible to look at the Palazzo della Cancelleria without being struck by the basement and two orders, which would be suggested by a contemplation of the Colisseum, though afterwards the Roman architects had the good sense to see that the orders of architecture placed against the walls of a building where the use was not required by the interior distribution was a tasteless and useless application of them.   The architect of the Palazzo Farnese only uses them for the decorations of his windows.   In this respect we hope good sense is once more returning to this country ; and that the absurd practice in almost every case of calling in the orders to aid the effect of a façade, will be abandoned for the better plan of obtaining an imposing effect from the simplicity and arrangement of the necessary parts.   We must, however, return to Bramante, whose other employment we pass over to come to his great work, — one which, after the continued labour upon it of his successor Michael Angelo, seems to have exhibited the great canons of art ; one which has regulated all the modern cathedrals of Europe, for they are, in fact, but repetitions of it ; and one, therefore, which requires a lengthened notice in this place, as intimately connected with the rapid progress of the Roman school.   The ancient Basilica of St. Peter had become so ruinous that Pope Nicholas V., a man who delighted in magnificent undertakings, a lover of architecture, and of more than ordinary genius, had conceived the project of rebuilding it, and under the designs of Bernardo Rosellini had actually seen a portion of the design rise from the ground before his death.   The project seemed then to be forgotten and abandoned, until Michael Angelo Buonarroti, seeking a place for the erection of the mausoleum of Julius II., upon which he was engaged, thought that the tribune of Rosellini's projected new basilica would be well suited for its reception, and accordingly proposed it to the pontiff.   Julius, pleased with the suggestion, immediately sent for San Gallo and Bramante to examine into it.   In these cases, one project generally suggests another, and the rearing of a new St. Peter's became a fixed object in the mind of Julius II.   The tribune of Nicholas V. was no longer thought of, except as a space to be included within the new works.   He consulted several architects upon the subject ; but the fact is, that the only real competition lay between Giuliano di San Gallo and Bramante.   The last was the successful artist ; and from a great number of projects the pope at last chose that upon which St. Peter's was afterwards commenced.   The real design of Bramante can scarcely be traced in the basilica of the Vatican as executed.   The changes it was doomed to undergo before completion, more than perhaps any other building was ever subjected to, have been drawn into a history by the Jesuit Bonanni.   When Bramante died, his designs, if indeed he made any, were dispersed ; and for what we do know of them we are indebted to Raffaelle, who took much pains in collecting the ideas of our architect, as they afterwards appeared in Serlio's Treatise on Architecture.   The original plan of Bramante was simple, grand, and in its parts harmonious, and would doubtless have been effective, far beyond the edifice as executed.   It has been well observed by Q. de Quincy, in his Life of Bramante, " Le Saint Pierre d'aujourd'hui paraît moins grand qu'il ne l'est en effet.   Le Saint Pierre de Bramante aurait certainement été plus grand encore en apparence qu'en réalité."   There would moreover have been an accordance between the interior and exterior.   The peristyle was to have three ranks of columns in depth, which would have necessarily had unequal intercolumniations.   The cupola was rather that of the Pantheon, ornamented exteriorly with an order of columns.   Bramante carried his imitation even to the steps round the springing of that monument.   From the medals of the design struck about the period, it seems that the façade was to have been decorated at its extremities with two campanili ; but the authority of a medal may be doubtful.   The idea, therefore, which is said to have originated with Michael Angelo, of placing the dome of the Pantheon upon the vaulting of the Temple of Peace emanated from Bramante, though the honour of actually carrying such a project into execution belongs to Michael Angelo da Buonarroti.   It is not, however, probable that if Bramante had lived he could have strictly executed the design he produced ; for it has been well proved that the piers which carry the dome would not have been sufficiently substantial for the weight to be placed upon them, inasmuch as Bramante's cupola would have been much heavier than that executed by Michael Angelo, and that architect considered it necessary to make his piers three times as thick as the former had proposed for his cupola.   Bramante's general design having been adopted by Julius II., was immediately commenced with a boldness and promptitude of which few but such men as Julius and Bramante were capable.   One half of the ancient basilica was taken down ; and on the 18th of April, 1506, the first stone of the new fabric was laid by the pope in the pier of the dome, commonly called that of Sta. Veronica.   The four piers soon rose ; the centres were prepared for connecting them by vaults, which were actually turned.   The weight and thrust of the vaults, however, bent the piers, and cracks and fissures made their appearance in every direction.   Thus, without more than their own weight, much less that of the cupola, the works threatened ruin.   The great haste used in carrying on the

works had doubtless much contributed to this catastrophe. Bramante in the meantime dying, Raffaelle, Giocondo, and Giuliano di San Gallo, and afterwards Baldazzare Peruzzi and Antonio San Gallo, were engaged on the edifice, and severally used the proper means for remedying the defects that had arisen, and for fortifying the great piers of the dome. To do this, as well as to push forward its completion, Michael Angelo was employed; and the rest of that great man's life was chiefly devoted to carrying on, under his own designs, the works of the fabric. From the death of Bramante in 1513 to 1546, when Antonio San Gallo died, the architects above named, all of whose names are almost sacred, had been more or less employed upon it. It was during this period that Bramante's original plan of a Latin was changed into a Greek cross by Peruzzi. The works had at this time become the source of much jobbing; every body that had any employment on them seemed bent on providing for himself, when Michael Angelo consented, for he was far from desirous of being employed, to superintend the future progress of the fabric. The first use made of his authority by Michael Angelo was that of discharging all the agents and *employés* of the place; he may be said to have again driven the money-lenders out of the temple. That he might have more moral power over this worthless race, he set the example of declining to receive the salary of 600 crowns attached to his appointment as architect, and gratuitously superintended the works during the period of seventeen years,—a disinterestedness that afterwards found a parallel in one of the greatest architects that this or any other country ever saw: we need scarcely mention the name of Inigo Jones. Michael Angelo began by undoing what his predecessor San Gallo had executed; and after having accomplished that, his whole powers were directed towards carrying on the structure to such a point that no change could possibly be made in his plans; so that after having strengthened the great piers, vaulted the naves, and carried up the exterior pedestal of the cupola, at the death of Paul III. in 1549 the form of these parts of the basilica was unchangeably fixed. Under Julius III., the successor of Paul, the intrigues which had always been carried on against Michael Angelo were renewed. He was accused of having contrived the arrangement without sufficient light, and of having changed every thing his predecessors had done. Thus proceeded this great work; but notwithstanding the severe trials he had to undergo from the envy of his contemporaries,—rivals he could not encounter,—Buonarroti steadily pursued his course. He felt that his own destiny and that of the fabric were identical; and, notwithstanding all the disgusting treatment to which he was exposed, determined to stand to his post while life remained. Writing to Vasari, he says, " For me to leave this place would be the cause of ruin to the church of St. Peter, which would be a lamentable occurrence, and a greater sin. As I hope to establish it beyond the possibility of changing the design, I could first wish to accomplish that end; if I do not already commit a crime, by disappointing the many cormorants who are in daily expectation of getting rid of me." And in another letter to Messer Lionardo Buonarrotti, in reply to the pressing instance of the grand duke to have him at Florence, he says, " I would prefer death to being in disgrace with the duke. In all my affairs I have endeavoured to adhere to the truth; and if I have delayed coming to Florence as I promised, the promise should have been construed with this condition, that I would not depart hence until the fabric of St. Peter's was so far advanced as to prevent its being spoiled by others, and my design altered; nor to leave opportunity for those thieves to return and plunder, as has been their custom, and as is still their hope. Thus placed by Divine Providence, I have exerted myself to prevent those evils. As yet, however, I have not been able to succeed in advancing the building to that point which I desire, from want of money and men; and being old, without any one about me to whose care I could leave the work, as I serve for the love of God, in whom is all my hope, I cannot abandon it." At this period, with the letter, to which we have not done sufficient justice in the translation, it is impossible not to sympathise, nor to be unaffected by the simple and unbending honesty of this honour to the race of man, independent of all our admiration of his stupendous power as an artist. At the age of eighty-seven, the pedestal being then ready for the reception of the cupola, he made a small model in clay for that important feature of his work, which was afterwards, to a scale, accurately under his direction, executed in wood; but deficiency in the funds prevented the progress of the building. To the height of upwards of 28 ft. above the exterior attic the cupola is in one solid vault, whose diameter is near 139 ft. at its springing, at which place its thickness is near 10 ft. exclusive of the ribs. As the inner and outer vaults are not concentric, the interval between them increases as they rise. Where they receive the lantern they are 10 ft. 7 in. apart. The construction of this dome proves the profundity of the architect's knowledge as a scientific builder to have equalled his superiority as an architect.

336. After the death of Michael Angelo, this cupola with its lantern was rigorously executed, upon the model he had left, by Jacopo della Porta and Domenico Fontana. His intentions were religiously respected, in the completion of the fabric, until the time of Pirro Ligorio, whom Pius IV. deprived of his situation for attempting to swerve from the model and substitute his own work.

337. Between the foundation of the church by Bramante, and its entire completion by

Carlo Maderno, as seen in *figs*. 167. and 168., a century had elapsed, but during that century

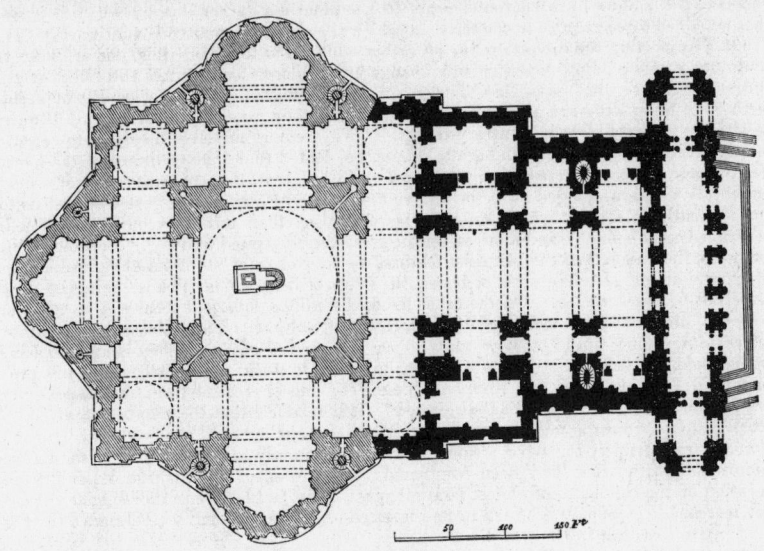

Fig. 167.   PLAN OF ST PETER'S.

Fig. 168.   HALF ELEVATION AND HALF SECTION OF ST. PETER'S.

architectural as well as graphical and plastic taste had undergone great changes; and though the first was still far from the vicious point to which Borromini carried it, the great principles of order and authority, as founded on the models of antiquity, were passed away, and no longer occupied the attention of the architect. The spirit of innovation, too often mistaken for genius, had made such inroads, that regularity of plan, simplicity of form,

and the happy union of taste with common sense had altogether disappeared. The part added to the edifice by Maderno appears in the plan in a darker tint, by which it is seen that he added three arcades to the nave, in which the same ordonnance is continued.

338. Respecting the alteration in, or rather addition to the plan, it is, and is likely to continue, a moot point, whether this change by Maderno has injured the effect of the church. " There are," says De Quincy, "in the method of judging of works of architecture, so many different points of view from which they may be judged, that it is quite possible to approve of even contrary things." We are not ourselves disposed to censure the application of Maderno, though it cannot be denied that the symmetry of the fabric was in some measure destroyed by it. It is possible that the constant habit of seeing cathedrals with a prolonged nave, before we first saw St. Peter's, may have disposed us to look leniently at a point which so many better judges than ourselves have condemned. Michael Angelo's plan was, doubtless, one of great simplicity and unity. According to his intention, the cupola was the principal feature, the four arms of its cross being accessaries which would not interfere with or lessen the effect of its grandeur, whose points of view could not be much varied. On the other hand, the edifice, enlarged according to the first project of Bramante, has acquired an immensity of volume, which, observes the author before quoted, one would be now sorry to see it deprived of. " Ce sont deux grandeurs voisines sans être rivales." In its exterior, however, it must be admitted that the prolongation of the nave has not improved the effect; and that arose from the necessity of strictly conforming to the forms that existed. It is manifest that the number of divisions which resulted from the mixtilinear plan of Michael Angelo would not well sort with the extended mass which the nave created. It was absolutely necessary that it should be conformable with what had been completed; and the effect of this was lessening the elevation of the cupola in an almost fatal manner. The façade of entrance cannot in any way be defended; and it is much to be regretted that the fine entrance designed by the great master was lost to the world.

339. St. Paul's is, perhaps, the only great instance in Europe wherein the design was made and wholly carried into execution by the same architect. Works of this nature usually exceed the span of man's life. St. Peter's was altogether a century and a half in building. The change of architects is not the least inconvenience of such a state of things; for during so long a period such a change of taste arises that the fashion and style of an art are from accident scarcely the same at its commencement and end. Thus the church of the Vatican, which was begun by Bramante in a comparatively pure style, was, in the end, defaced by the vicious bizarreries of Borromini. It was fortunate Michael Angelo, so far foreseeing accidents of this nature, had fixed unchangeably the main features of his composition.

340. That the first idea of this stupendous fabric owes its origin to Bramante cannot be disputed; but its greatness, as conceived by him, is confined to the boast of placing the cupola of the Pantheon upon the vaulting of the Temple of Peace. The sketch of it given by Serlio is nothing like the cupola which was executed. On the other hand, what was executed by Michael Angelo was scarcely new after what Brunelleschi had accomplished at Sta. Maria del Fiore. This, however, was a chef d'œuvre of construction; that of St. Peter's was a chef d'œuvre of construction and architecture combined. What was new in it was, that it was the loftiest and largest of all works, ancient or modern, uniting in its vast volume the greatest beauties of proportion to simplicity and unity of form; to magnificence and richness of decoration a symmetry which gives harmony to the whole, considered by itself, and not less so when considered in relation to the mass of which it is the crown. The great superiority of this cupola over all others is visible in another point of view, which we shall more particularly notice in the account of St. Paul's in a subsequent page: it is, that the same masonry serves for the exterior as well as the interior, whereby an immense additional effect is gained in surveying it from the inside. All is fair; there is no masking, as in other cupolas that followed it.

341. Whatever opinions may be formed on the other works of Michael Angelo, no difference can exist respecting the cupola of St. Peter's. " Si tout," observes De Quincy, " ce qui avait été fait et pensé, ou projeté avant lui, en ce genre, ne peut lui disputer le prix de l'invention et de l'originalité, et ne peut servir qu'à marquer la hauteur de son génie, il nous semble que les nombreuses coupoles élevées dans toute l'Europe depuis lui et d'après lui, ne doivent se considérer encore que comme autant d'échelons, propres à faire mieux sentir et mesurer sa superiorité." The bungling of Carlo Maderno at St. Peter's is much to be regretted. The arches he added to the nave are smaller in dimensions than those which had been brought up immediately adjoining the piers of the cupola; and, what is still more unpardonable, the part which he added to the nave is not in a continued line with the other work, but inclines above 3 ft. to the north: in other words, the church is not straight, and that to such an extent as to strike every educated eye. His taste, moreover, was exceedingly bad.

342. In the principal churches of Rome there is great similarity of plan; they usually consist of a nave and side aisles, in which latter, chapels are ranged along the sides. The separation of the nave and aisles is effected by arcades. The transepts are not much extended, and over the intersection of them with the nave and choir a cupola generally rises. The chapels of the Virgin and of the Holy Sacrament are commonly in the transepts; and the great altar is at the end of the choir, which usually terminates semicircularly on the plan. Unlike those of the Florentine school, the interiors of the Roman churches are decorated to excess. Pictures, mosaics, and marbles of every variety line the walls. A profusion of gilding imparts to them a richness of tone, and the architectural details are often in the highest state of enrichment. They are, indeed, temples worthy of the worship of the Deity. Yet, with all this magnificence, the façades are often mean; and when a display of architecture is exhibited in them, it is produced by abuses of the worst class. They are generally mere masks; for between the architecture of these false fronts and that of the interior there is no architectural connection. In very many instances the sides of the churches are actually hidden by adjacent buildings, so that they are altogether unseen; a circumstance which may have conduced to the repetition of the abuse. Faulty, however, as these edifices are, to them is Europe indebted as models, which have in modern times been more purified. We have not space to enumerate or criticise the churches with which Rome abounds. St. Carlo on the Corso, by Onorio Langhi, is a fine example of them, and gives a fair notion of the general distribution we have described. Those of a later date, especially those by Borromini, may be considered as *indices rerum vitandarum* in architecture; and though we are, perhaps, from the cupidity of upholsterers and house decorators, likely to be doomed to sit in rooms stuffed with the absurdities of the taste prevalent in the time of Louis XV., we can hardly conceive it necessary in these days to recommend the student's abhorrence of such freaks of plan and elevation as are to be found in the church of St. Carlo alle quattro Fontane, by that architect.

343. The palaces of Rome are among the finest architectural works in Europe; and of those in Rome, as we have before observed, none equals the Farnese, whose façade is given in *fig.* 169. "Ce vaste palais Farnese, qui à tout prendre, pour la grandeur

Fig. 169.   FARNESE PALACE.

de la masse, la regularité de son ensemble, et l'excellence de son architecture, a tenu jusqu'ici, dans l'opinion des artistes, le premier rang entre tous les palais qu'on renomme," is the general description of it by De Quincy, upon whom we have drawn largely, and must continue to do so. This edifice, by San Gallo, forms a quadrangle of 256 ft. by 185 ft. It is constructed of brick, with the exception of the dressings of the doors and windows, the quoins of the fronts, and the entablature and loggia in the Strada Giulia, which are of travertine stone. Of the same stone, beautifully wrought, is the interior of the court. The building consists of three stories, including that on the ground, which, in the elevations or façades, are separated by impost cornices. The only break in its symmetry and simplicity occurs in the loggia, placed in the centre of the first story, which connects the windows on each side of it by four columns. On the ground story the windows are decorated with square-headed dressings of extremely simple design; in the next story they are flanked by columns, whose entablatures are crowned alternately with triangular and circular pediments; and in the third story are circular-headed windows, crowned throughout with triangular pediments. The taste in which these last is composed is not so good as the rest, though they were probably the work of Michael Angelo, of whose cornice to the edifice Vasari observes, " È stupendissimo il corniccione maggiore del medesimo palazzo nella

facciata dinanzi, non si potendo alcuna cosa ne più bella ne più magnificà desiderare."
The façade towards the Strada Giulia is different from the other fronts in the centre only,
wherein there are three stories of arcades to the loggia, each of whose piers are decorated
with columns of the Doric, Ionic, and Corinthian orders in the respective stories as they
rise, and these in form and dimensions correspond with the three ranks of arcades towards
the court.   It appears probable that this central arrangement was not in the original
design of San Gallo, but introduced when the third story was completed.   Magnificent as
from its simplicity and symmetry is the exterior of this palace, which, as De Quincy observes,
" est un édifice toujours digne d'être le sejour d'un prince," yet does it not exceed the beauty
of the interior.   The quadrangle of the court is 88 ft. square between the columns of
the arcades, and is composed with three stories, in which the central arrangement above
mentioned towards the Strada Giulia is repeated on the two lower stories, over the upper
whereof is a solid wall pierced in the windows.   The piers of the lower arcade are ornamented with Doric columns, whose entablature is charged with triglyphs in its frieze, and
its metopæ are sculptured with various symbols.   The imposts of the piers are very
finely profiled, so as to form the entablatures when continued over the columns of the
entrance vestibule.   In the Ionic arcade, over this, the frieze of the order is decorated
with a series of festoons.   The distribution of the different apartments and passage is
well contrived.   All about the building is on a scale of great grandeur.   Though long
unoccupied, and a large portion of its internal ornaments has disappeared, it still commands our admiration in the Carracci Gallery, which has continued to serve as a model
for all subsequent works of the kind.   The architecture of the Farnese palace, more
especially as respects the arcades of its court, is the most perfect adaptation of ancient arrangement to more modern habits that has ever been designed.   We here allude more
particularly to the arcades, upon whose piers orders of columns are introduced.   This
species of composition, heavier, doubtless, less elegant, yet more solid than simple colonnades, is, on the last account, preferable to them, where several stories rise above one
another.   The idea was, certainly, conceived from the practice in the ancient theatres and
amphitheatres ; and in its application at the Farnese palace rivals in beauty all that
antiquity makes us in its remains acquainted with.   San Gallo, its architect, died in 1546.

344. It would be impossible here to enumerate the palaces with which Rome abounds ;
but we must mention another, that of St. Giovanni Laterano, by Domenico Fontana,
as a very beautiful specimen of the palatial style. Milizia censures the detail of this edifice,
and there is some truth in his observations in that respect ; but the composition is so simple
and grand, and the cornice crowns it with so much majesty, that the detail is forgotten in
the general effect, and its architect well deserves the rank of a great artist.

345. The villas, *Ocelli d'Italia*, as they have been called, round the suburbs of Rome,
are in a style far lighter than the palaces whereof we have just been speaking.   They are
the original models of the modern country houses of this island, and exhibit great skill in
their plans and elegance in their façades.   Generally they rose from the riches and taste of
a few cardinals, who studded the environs of the Eternal City with some of the fairest gems
of the art.   MM. Percier and Fontaine published a collection of them at Paris, from
which we extract the Villa Pia (*fig.* 170.).   It was designed by Pirro Ligorio, a Neapolitan

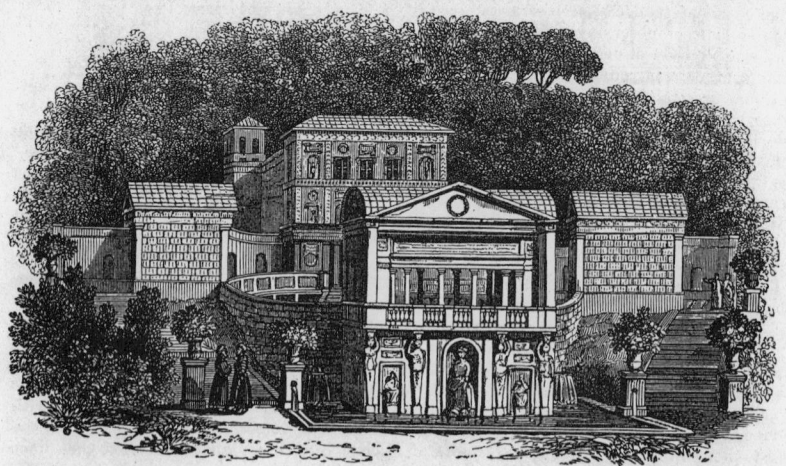

Fig. 170.   VILLA PIA.

architect, who died in 1580, and is thus described by the authors whose view of it we have borrowed. " It was built," say they, " in imitation of the houses of the ancients, which Ligorio had particularly studied. This clever artist, who to his talent as an architect joined the information of a learned antiquary, here threw into a small space every thing that could contribute to render it a delightful dwelling. In the midst of verdant thickets, and in the centre of an amphitheatre of flowers, he constructed an open lodge, decorated with stuccoes and agreeable pictures. The lodge is raised upon a base, bathed by the water of a basin, enclosed with marbles, fountains, statues, and vases. Two flights of steps, which lead to landings sheltered by walls ornamented with niches and seats of marble, offer protection from the sun's rays by the trees that rise above them. Two porticoes, whose interior walls are covered with stuccoes, lead on each side to a court paved in mosaic work. This is enclosed by a wall, round which seats are disposed. Here is a fountain spouting up from the centre of a vase of precious marble. At the end of the court facing the lodge an open vestibule, supported by columns, fronts the ground floor of the principal pavilion ; and is decorated with mosaics, stuccoes, and bassi-relievi of beautiful design. The apartments on the first floor are ornamented with fine pictures. Finally, from the summit of a small tower, which rises above the building, the view extends over the gardens of the Vatican, and the plains through which the Tiber takes its course, and the splendid edifices of Rome." For further information on the Roman villas, we refer the reader to the work we have quoted.

346. The Roman school of architecture, founded by Bramante, includes San Gallo, Buonarroti, Sansovino, Peruzzi, Vignola (whose extraordinary palace at Caprarola deserves the study of every architect), and many others. It ends with Domenico Fontana, the period of its duration being from 1470 to 1607, or little more than 130 years.

347. Before we proceed to the Venetian school, it will, however, be proper to notice two architects, whose works tended to change much for the worse the architecture of their time ; we mean Borromini and Bernini, though the latter was certainly purer in his taste than the former. Borromini, whose example in his art was followed throughout Europe, and who, even in the present day, has his returning admirers, was the father of all modern abuses in architecture ; and the reader must on no account confound his works with those of the Roman school, which had ceased nearly half a century before the native of Bissona had begun to practise. He inverted the whole system of Greek and Roman architecture, without replacing it by a substitute. He saw that its leading forms, sprung from a primitive type, were, by an imitation more or less rigorous, subjected to the principles of the model from which its order and arrangement emanated. He formed the project of annihilating all idea of a model, all principles of imitation, all plea for order and proportion. For the restriction in the art resultant from the happy fiction, or perhaps reality of a type, one whose tendency was to restrain it within the bounds of reason, he substituted the anarchy of imagination and fancy, and an unlimited flight into all species of caprice. Undulating flexibility supplanted all regularity of form ; contours of the most grotesque description succeeded to right lines ; the severe architrave and entablature were bent to keep up the strange delusion ; all species of curves were adopted in his operations, and the angles of his buildings were perplexed with an infinite number of breaks. What makes this pretended system of novelty more absurd is (and we are glad to have the opportunity here of observing that the remarks we are making are applicable to the present fashionable folly of decorating rooms à la Louis XIV. and XV.), that its only novelty was the disorder it introduced, for Borromini did not invent a single form. He was not scrupulous in retaining all the parts which were indicated by imitating the type ; he decomposed some, transposed others, and usually employed each member in a situation directly the reverse of its proper place, and, indeed, just where it never would be naturally placed. Thus, for example, to a part or ornament naturally weak, he would assign the office of supporting some great weight ; whilst to one actually capable of receiving a great load, he would assign no office whatever. With him every thing seems to have gone by contraries; and to give truth the appearance of fiction, and the converse, seems to have been his greatest delight. Out of all this arose a constant necessity for contrivance, which marked Borromini as a skilful constructor, in which respect he attained to an extraordinary degree of intelligence. It seems, however, not improbable that one of his great objects in studying construction was, that he might have greater facility in carrying his curious conceits into execution ; for it may be taken almost as an axiom in architecture, so great is the relation between them, that simple forms and solid construction are almost inseparable ; and it is only necessary to have recourse to extraordinary expedients in construction when our productions result from an unrestrained imagination. Further notice of this architect is not necessary ; one of his most celebrated works is the restoration of the church of St. Giovanni Laterano, — after St. Peter's, the greatest in Rome. His purest work is the church of St. Agnese; whilst that of St. Carlo alle quattro fontane, which we have heretofore noticed, is the most *bizarre*. Borromini died in 1667.

348. Bernini, the other artist whom we have mentioned, was equally painter, sculptor,

and architect; his principal work is the colonnade in front of St. Peter's. He was, notwithstanding the abuses to be found in his works, a man of great talent. In their general arrangement his buildings are good and harmonious; his profiles are graceful; his ornaments, though sometimes profuse, are usually elegant. Bernini, however, was no check upon the pernicious character of his cotemporary Borromini; instead, indeed, of relieving architecture of some of her abuses, he encumbered her with fresh ones. He was also fond of broken pediments, and of placing them in improper situations. He employed undulations, projections innumerable, and intermixtures of right lines with curves; for beautiful simplicity he substituted elegant fancy; and is to be imitated or admired by the student no farther than he followed nature and reason. He made some designs for the Louvre at Paris, which are exceedingly good. His death occurred in 1680.

349. 3. *The Venetian School* is characterised by its lightness and elegance; by the convenient distribution it displays; and by the abundant, perhaps exuberant, use of columns, pilasters, and arcades, which enter into its composition. Like its sister school of painting, its address is more to the senses than is the case with those we have just quitted. We have already given an account of the church of St. Mark, in the 12th century; from which period, as the republic rose into importance by its arms and commerce, its arts were destined to an equally brilliant career. The possession in its provinces of some fine monuments of antiquity, as well as its early acquaintance with Greece, would, of course, work beneficially for the advancement of its architecture. That species of luxury, the natural result of a desire on the part of individuals to perpetuate their names through the medium of their habitations, though not productive of works on a grand or monumental scale, leads, in a democracy (as were the states of Venice), to a very general display of moderately splendid and elegant palaces. Hence the extraordinary number of specimens of the building art supplied by the Venetian school.

350. San Micheli, who was born in 1484, may, with propriety, be called its founder. Having visited Rome at the early age of sixteen for the purpose of studying its ancient monuments of art, and having in that city found much employment, he, after many years of absence, returned to his native country. The mode in which he combined pure and beautiful architecture with the requisites called for in fortifications may be seen displayed to great advantage at Verona, in which city the *Porta dell Pallio* is an instance of his wonderful ingenuity and taste. But his most admired works are his palaces at Verona; though, perhaps, that of the Grimani family at Venice is his most magnificent production. The general style of composition, very different from that of the palaces of Florence and Rome, is marked by the use of a basement of rustic work, wherefrom an order rises, often with arched windows, in which he greatly delighted, and these were connected with the order after the manner of an arcade, the whole being crowned with the proper entablature. As an example, we give, in *fig.* 171., the façade of the Pompei palace at Verona. The genius of

Fig. 171.   POMPEI PALACE, VERONA.

San Micheli was of the very highest order; his works are as conspicuous for excellent construction as they are for convenience, unity, harmony, and simplicity, which threw into shade the minor abuses occasionally found in them. If he had no other testimony, it would be sufficient to say, that for his talents he was held in great esteem by Michael Angelo; and our advice to the student would be to study his works with diligence. San Micheli devoted himself with great ardour to the practice of military architecture; and though the invention was not for a long time afterwards assigned to him, he was the author of the

system used by Vauban and his school, who, for a long period, deprived him of the credit of it. Before him all the ramparts of a fortification were round or square. He introduced a new method, inventing the triangular and pentangular bastion, with plain fossés, flanks, and square bases, which doubled the support; he moreover not only flanked the curtain, but all the fossé to the next bastion, the covered way, and glacis. The mystery of this art consisted in defending every part of the inclosure by the flank of a bastion; hence, making it round or square, the front of it, that is, the space which remains in the triangle, which was before undefended, was by San Micheli provided against. We cannot, however, further proceed on this subject, which belongs to military, which at that period was intimately connected with civil architecture. The *Porta del Pallio* at Verona has been mentioned; that city, however, contains another gate of great architectural merit by this master, the *Porta Nuova*, a square edifice, supported within by a number of piers of stone, with enclosures or apartments for the guards, artillery, &c. The proportions, as a whole, are pleasing; it is of the Doric order, devoid of all extraneous ornament, solid, strong, and suitable to the purposes of the building. Except in the middle gate and the architectural parts, the work is rusticated. The exterior façade stands on a wall, with two large pyramidal pilasters of marble rising from the bottom of the fosse; at the top are two round enclosures approaching almost to towers. In the interior, to the two gates near the angles are two corresponding long passages, vaulted, leading to a number of subterraneous galleries and rooms. For beauty, however, we do not think this gate so beautiful as that of del Pallio, which we here give (*fig.* 172.). But the gem of this great master is the little circular

Fig. 172.   PORTA DEL PALLIO, VERONA.

chapel at San Bernardino, whose beauty, we think, has scarcely ever been surpassed, and which exhibits, in a striking degree, the early perfection of the Venetian school. It was not finished under San Micheli, and blemishes are to be found in it; it is nevertheless an exquisite production, and, in a surprisingly small space, exhibits a refinement which elsewhere we scarcely know equalled. The works which he designed surpass, we believe, in number those of all the masters of Italy, Palladio, perhaps, excepted. He gave a tone to his art in the Venetian states, which endured for a considerable period. His death occurred in 1549.

351. Contemporary with San Micheli, was another extraordinary genius of this school, born at Florence,—Jacopo Tatti by name, but more usually called Sansovino, from the country of his master, Andrea Contucci di Monte Sansovino. Such was the respect for this artist in Venice, his adopted city, that at a moment when it became necessary to raise by means of taxation a large sum on the citizens, the senate made a special exemption in favour of him and Titian. The Roman school might lay claim to him, if the works he executed at Rome, and not his style, would justify it; but that is so marked, so tinctured with the system of arcades with orders, its distinguishing feature, that an inspection of his works will immediately satisfy even a superficial observer. He was a great master of his art; and though he does not in so great a degree appear to have profited by the examples of antiquity as the architect last named, he has left behind buildings, which, for picturesque effect, leave him little inferior in our rating. He was the architect of the library of St. Mark at Venice, a portion whereof is given in *fig.* 173.; a building of noble design, notwithstanding the improprieties with which it is replete. It consists of two orders; the lower one of highly ornamented Doric, and the upper one Ionic and very graceful in effect. Of both these orders, as will be seen in the figure, the entablatures are of inordinate comparative height. The upper one was expressly so set out for the purpose of exhibiting the beautiful sculptures with which it is decorated. The cornice is crowned with a balustrade, on whose piers statues were placed by the ablest scholars of Sansovino. A portico occupies the ground floor, which is raised three steps from the level of the piazza. This portico consists of twenty-one arcades, whose piers are decorated with columns. In the interior are arches corresponding to the external ones, sixteen whereof, with their internal apartments, are appropriated for shops. Opposite the centre arch is a magnificent staircase leading to the hall, beyond which is the library of St. Mark. The

Fig. 173.   LIBRARY OF ST. MARK.

faults of this building, which are very many, are lost in its grace and elegance, and it is perhaps the chef d'œuvre of the master. Whilst Sansovino was engaged on it he propounded an architectural problem, which reminds us very much of the egg of Columbus : " How can the exact half of a metope be so contrived as to stand on the external angle of the Doric frieze ? " The solution, clumsy as that of the navigator with his egg, practised in this building, is, however, a bungling absurdity ; namely, that of lengthening the frieze just so much as is necessary to make out the deficiency. Sansovino was invited to pass into France, where he gave some designs, which tended to the advancement of the art in that country. On his return he built the Zecca, or mint, one of his finest works. Another of his extraordinary productions is the palace of the Comari, on the Grand Canal at San Maurizio. The church of San Fantino, among the finest of Venice, is also by him ; as is that of San Martino and many others. Jacopo was fertile in invention : his architecture was full of grace and elegance ; but he was deficient in a thorough knowledge of construction, which, in the library of St. Mark, brought him into disgrace, of which, from all accounts, the builders ought to have suffered the principal share. He continually introduced the orders, and especially the Doric and Composite. The members of his entablatures were much sculptured ; but his ornaments were extremely suitable and correct. In statues and bassi relievi he greatly indulged, thereby adding considerably to the effect and majesty of his buildings. Scamozzi mentions a work by him on the construction of floors, and particularly describes a method adopted by him for preventing dust falling through the joints of the boards. The work has been lost. Sansovino died in 1570.

352. After such artists as San Micheli and Sansovino, it would have seemed to an ordinary mind difficult to have invented new forms, or rather so to have modified the old ones as to be original. Andrea Palladio, however, not only knew how to be original, but to leave his works as models for the countries of Europe, in which the style which bears his name has had no rival ; so true is it, in all the arts, that there is always room to be found for a man on whom nature has bestowed the faculty of seeing, feeling, and thinking for himself. In the case of the architect something more than genius is necessary : it is requisite that circumstances should exist by which his art may be developed, or, in other words, that what he is capable of producing may at the time be suitable to the wants of society. Such circumstances existed for a long period in Italy, where, up to the time at which we are arrived, the rich and great had been contending with the governments which should be the greatest patrons of the art. Hence sprung the multitude of extraordinary works in the country named, which still point out the greatness in art at which it had arrived, when it was one of the really necessary arts. Neither in the Venetian states, nor at the time when he rose into reputation, which was about the middle of the sixteenth century, had Palladio that opportunity of signalising himself which had occurred to many former masters. Venice had risen into power and wealth by its arms and commerce ; was the natural protectrix of the art ; and although the works she required were not on scales of the grandest dimensions, yet those which her citizens required kept pace in luxury with the increasing wealth of the families by whom they were required. This was the career open to the genius of Palladio. Architecture in these states was not called upon to furnish churches of colossal dimensions, nor palaces for sovereigns, nor immense public monuments left for posterity to finish. The political state of the country, very luckily for his talents, furnished a numerous class of citizens who contended which should procure for himself the aid of this great man in rearing a villa or palace, and which might serve the

double purpose of a present dwelling for, and a future memorial of, his family,— a passion that covered the banks of the Brenta with edifices which, of their class, form a complete school of civil architecture.

353. The taste of Palladio was tempered by the care he bestowed on accommodating exterior beauty to interior convenience, and by suiting the art to the wants of persons with moderate means, through the medium of greatness without great dimensions, and richness of effect without great outlay. In the imitation, or rather appropriation, of the architecture of the ancients, none of his predecessors of any of the schools had so luckily hit on that just medium of exactness without pedantry, of severity without harshness, of liberty without licentiousness, which have since made the architecture of ancient Greece popular, and so modified it as to be practicable and convenient in all countries. We here speak, of course, of the elements, and not the combinations, of Greek art, and of it changed by a passage through an intermediate state during the existence of the Roman empire. No architect can consider himself thoroughly educated who has not studied the works of Palladio. " De fait," says De Quincy, in his Life of this architect, " il n'est point d'architecte qui, après avoir formé ou réformé son style sur les grands modèles de l'art des anciens, et des premiers maîtres de l'Italie moderne, ne se croie pas obligé d'aller encore étudier dans la patrie et les œuvres de Palladio, un genre d'applications plus usuelles, et plus en rapport avec l'état de nos mœurs ; c'est-a-dire, le secret d'accommoder tour-à-tour, et nos besoins aux plaisirs d'une belle architecture, et l'agrément de celle-ci aux sujétions que de nouveaux besoins lui imposent." It was from the peculiar properties of Palladio's taste and style, suited as they are to more moderate fortunes, that they found in England a second native country (if such an expression may be allowed), where Inigo Jones, Wren, Gibbs, Taylor, Chambers, and many others, have naturalised the plans, façades, distribution, and details which were originally planted in the provinces of the Venetian republic. Indeed, the style of Palladio could not be prevented from spreading through Europe, as a mean between the severe use of ancient forms and the licentious style of those who reject all rules whatever. The buildings by him exhibit great good sense, simple means of accomplishing the end, a satisfactory agreement between the demands of necessity and pleasure, and such an harmony between them that it is hard to determine which has submitted to the other. The interior distribution of his palaces and villas in respect of plan would, without considerable modification, be but ill suited to modern habits. We give, in *fig.* 174. (*see next page*), a plan and elevation of the Villa Capra, one of his most celebrated works of that class. Convenience changes as the mode of life varies ; indeed, except in a private building of large extent, the large quadrangular court of the houses of Italy is here unknown. Palladio's plans, however, were convenient to those for whom they were executed ; and in that way they must be judged. With his eyes constantly turned to the practice and detail of the ancients, he acquired a bold, simple, and agreeable style ; and, his churches excepted, the beauties of the master are to be sought in his façades, and the quadrangles of his palaces. Pedestals, either with panels or raisings, were always avoided by him ; his architraves were rarely sculptured ; and the upper ornaments of his entablatures were always carefully centred above each other. His doors, windows, and niches are composed with great simplicity ; and pediments, when used, are unbroken. In the members of his cornices he never lost sight of the character of the order employed, and was extremely particular in duly adjusting its profiles. He, however, did not scruple to vary the proportions of an order according to the nature of the building to which it was applied ; and in the proportions of his churches and apartments he seems to have delighted, as afterwards did Sir Christopher Wren, in arithmetical, geometrical, and harmonic proportions. Though extremely partial to the use of the Ionic order, yet the others were not unfrequently used by him. His Corinthian capital is not to be praised ; it is profiled very clumsily, and ought not to be followed. The domes which he erected are almost invariably hemispherical. It is not to be supposed that his buildings are perfect, though they approach perfection ; but it is more than probable that many of the abuses we see in them arose either from want of sufficient superintendence, the number he designed being very great, or that they were introduced after his death. This, we think, may be safely assumed, because the instructions in his work on architecture are very peremptory on the subject of abuses. So well based upon the practice of the ancients does the style of our master appear to be, that it is, with but few modifications, suited to all nations, and just such as the ancients themselves would have adopted. " Les fermes," observes Le Grand in his parallèle, " que dirigeait Palladio et qu'il couvrait de tuiles on d'un chaume rustique, l'emportent de beaucoup sur les palais somptueux de Borromini, ou sur les riches et bizarres productions de Guarino Guarini." Certain, indeed, it is that simplicity, unity, and style are more powerful means of producing grandeur, than great volume or large masses unskilfully handled. A fine instance of this is seen in the façade of the Thiene palace at Vicenza, *fig.* 175. (*See next page.*)

354. The number of palaces and villas with which Palladio enriched the Venetian and Vicentine territories is almost incredible : the variety of plan and elevation in them seems as inexhaustible as their number. To the buildings above referred to may be added the

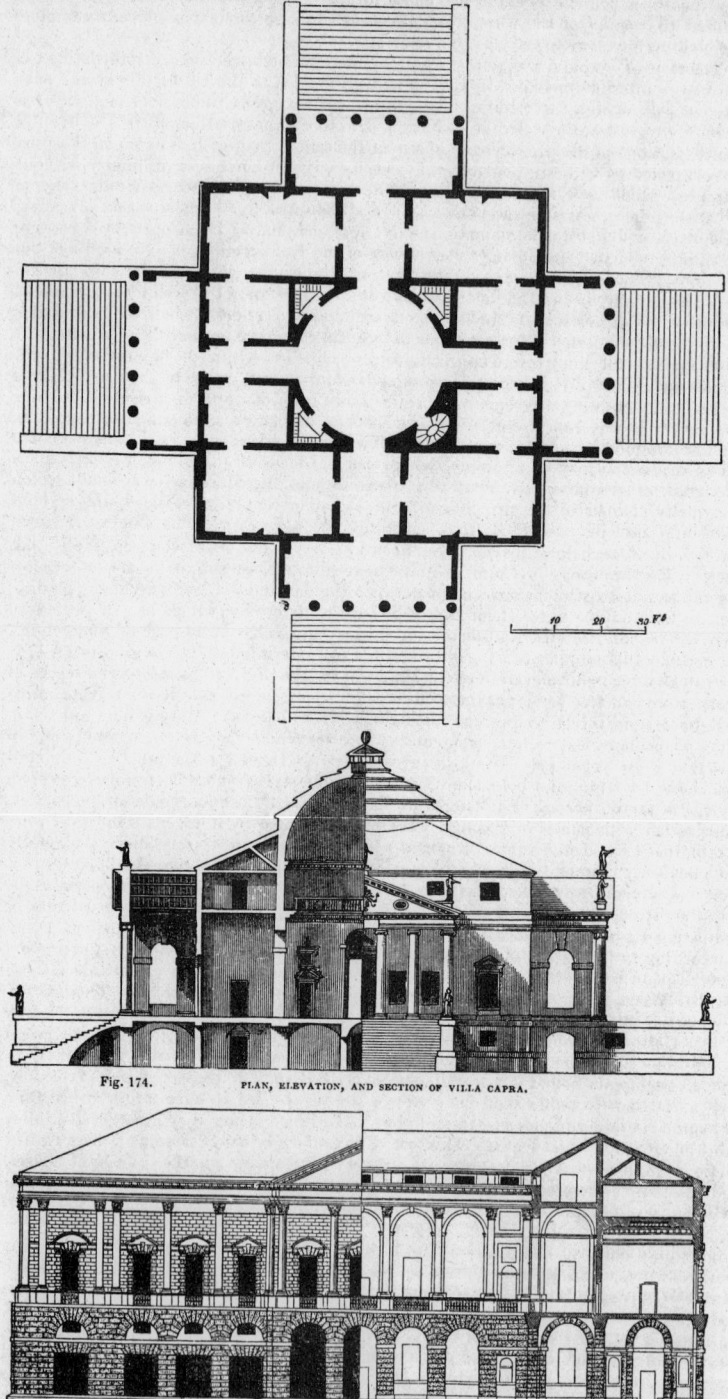

Fig. 174. PLAN, ELEVATION, AND SECTION OF VILLA CAPRA.

Fig. 175. ELEVATION AND SECTION OF PALAZZO THIENE.

Carità at Venice, which is a lovely specimen of his style. His grandest church is that Del Redentore at Venice. Generally in the façades of his churches there are abuses, whereof it is scarcely credible he would have been guilty: such are the two half pediments in the church we have just mentioned. The theatre built upon the ancient model for the Olympic Academy at Vicenza gained great reputation for him. Palladio died in 1580.

355. The last architect of the Venetian school who obtained celebrity was Vincenzo Scamozzi. The son of an architect, and born in a country which had become the nursery of the art, his powers were exhibited at an early age. Like Palladio and other great masters, he selected for his principal guides the antiquities of the Eternal City, and the precepts of Vitruvius, whose work at that period was considered of high importance, as in truth it really was. There is no doubt that Scamozzi was much indebted to the works of Palladio, although he affected occasionally to decry them; but, in opposition to De Quincy, we think that his style is more founded on that of San Micheli or Sansovino. This is, however, of little importance; for his natural talents were of a very high order. At a very early period of his career, so great was his reputation that he was employed by the canons of San Salvadore in opening the lantern to the cupola of their church; a task in which it appears that he acquitted himself with great ability. For the upper order of the Procurazie Nuove at Venice he has often been unjustly reproached, because he did not confine himself to two stories, so as to complete the design of Sansovino. The design of Scamozzi, had it been continued in the Piazza San Marco, would have placed in the back ground every other piazza in Europe. The two lower stories of the Procurazie Nuove are similar in design to the Library of S. Marco; and it is greatly to be regretted that Scamozzi was so much otherwise occupied that he had not the opportunity of watching the whole of its execution, which would have extended to thirty arcades, whose whole length would have been 426 feet. Scamozzi only superintended the first thirteeen; the three built by Sansovino excepted, the rest were trusted to the care of builders rather than artists, and, from the little attention bestowed upon preserving the profiles, exhibit a negligence which indicates a decline in the arts at Venice. Scamozzi is placed in the first rank as an architect by his design for the cathedral at Saltzburg, whither he was invited by the archbishop of the see. This church, which was not completed till after his death in 1616, is 454 ft. long, and 329 ft. wide, being in the form of a Latin cross on the plan, over whose centre a cupola rises. The distribution of the interior is with a nave and two side aisles; the former whereof is 64 ft. wide, and 107 ft. high. Scamozzi's employment was very extended, and his country has to lament it; for fewer commissions would have insured greater perfection in their execution, which, in those that exist, is often unworthy of the name of the master. Scamozzi published a work on the art, which will be found in our list of authors at the end of this work. He died in 1616.

356. Besides Giovanni da Ponte and Alessandro Vittoria, the Venetian school contains the names of few more than those we have named: they appear to have commanded the whole of the employ of the states and neighbourhood of Venice for a period of about 110 years, ending in 1616. When, however, it no longer continued to grow and flourish in its native soil, its scions, grafted throughout Europe, spreading their branches in every country, prospered wherever they appeared. On the former of the two architects just named, a few observations are necessary. He died in 1597, at the age of eighty-five years. Principally occupied in the reparation and re-establishment of the buildings of the city that had fallen into decay, he was nevertheless engaged on some considerable works; among which was the great hall of the arsenal at Venice, 986 feet long, and the more celebrated work of the Rialto Bridge, whence he obtained the sobriquet *Da Ponte*, and for the execution whereof he competed with Palladio and Scamozzi. The span of the single arch of which the work consists is about 72 ft., and the thickness of the arch stones about 4 ft. 4 in. It is segmental, and the height from the level of the water is about 22 ft. 9 in. The width of the bridge is equal to the span of the arch, and this width is divided longitudinally into five divisions, that is, into three streets or passages, and two rows of shops. The middle street or passage is 21 ft. 8 in. wide, and the two side ones near 11 ft. The number of shops on it is twenty-four. The last work of Da Ponte was the construction of the prisons away from the ducal palace. This edifice is a quadrilateral building, with a portico of seven arcades. A story rises out of it pierced by seven great windows decorated with pediments, and it is joined to the palace by the bridge so well known under the name of *Il Ponte dei Sospiri*. The work was not carried to completion during Giovanni's life, but was finished by his nephew Contino. In his church on the Grand Canal, constructed for the nuns of Santa Croce, there is little merit except that of solidity; indeed, he does not appear to have possessed much taste, as may be inferred from the two ranks of columns in the hall of the arsenal above mentioned, which cannot be said to belong to any of the species of columns usually employed. The solid character of the great prison is appropriate, and more in consonance with the rules of the art.

SECT. XVII.

357. The architecture of Europe from the middle of the sixteenth century was founded on that of Italy. Of its value, the French and the English seem to have a stronger perception than the rest of the nations. We shall therefore now consider the architecture of France: that of England from a much earlier date will be separately considered in the succeeding chapter. Philibert Delorme was among the first of the architects of France who promoted a taste for good architecture; and though in some respects he may have been surpassed by other artists of his time, in others, whether connected with theory or practice, he has left his rivals a great distance behind him. Although he might not have had the purity of detail of Jean Bullant, nor the richness of invention and execution of P. Lescot, he has acquired by his talent in construction a reputation which has survived his buildings. The Queen Catherine of Medicis having resolved upon the construction of a palace at Paris, which should far surpass all that had previously been done in France, resolved upon placing it on a spot then occupied by some tile kilns (Tuileries) in the faubourg St. Honoré, and committed the design and erection to Delorme. It is, however, contended by some that Jean Bullant was joined with him in the commission. If that was really the case, it is probable that the labours of the latter were confined to details of ornament and execution, rather than to the general design and disposition. What, if it was so, belonged to each is not now to be discovered; but the genius of Delorme has survived all the revolutions the celebrated building in question has undergone. Catherine seems not to have been satisfied with the works; for she appears to have begun another palace on the site of the Hotel Soissons, that of the present Halle au Bleds, and to have entrusted this to the care of Jean Bullant. That of the Tuileries was in the end continued by Henri IV.; enlarged by Louis XIII. on the same line, after the designs of Du Cerceau, with two main bodies and two composite pavilions; all which were in the time of Louis XIV. afterwards brought together by the designs of Leveau and Dorbay. In the centre pavilion all that now remains of Delorme's work is the lower order of Ionic columns. This morsel of Delorme exhibits a good Ionic profile in the order, and is one of his best works. Generally speaking, the profiles of this master, which Chambrai has admitted into his *Parallèle*, make one acknowledge the justice of that author's observation, that he had " un peu trop vu les plus belles choses de Rome, avec des yeux encore préoccupés du style Gothique. Le talent de cet architecte consistait principalement dans la conduite d'un bâtiment, et de vrai il était plus consommé en la connaissance et la coupe des pierres que dans la composition des ordres; aussi en a-t-il écrit plus utilement et bien plus au long." Delorme was the author of two works on architecture: one, *Un Traité complète de l'Art de Bâtir*, on architecture generally; the other, *Nouvelles Inventions pour bien bâtir et à petits frais.* The last relates more especially to a practice in carpentry, which, on the Continent, has been put into execution with great success, its principle being still constantly applied. The method of carpentry invented by Delorme, and which still goes in France by his name, consists in substituting for the ordinary system of framing and rafters, curved ribs, in two thicknesses, of any sort of timber, three or four feet long, and one foot wide, of an inch in thickness, and which are connected in section and tie according to the form of the curve, whether pointed, semicircular, or segmental. These arches, in order to be strong and solid, should be fixed at their feet on plates of timber framed together, lying very level on the external walls; and the planks which are to form the principal curve are to be placed accurately upright on their ends, in which situation they may be kept by braces morticed into them at convenient distances, and retained in their places by wedges, for it is essential to the strength of this species of carpentry that it should be kept in a vertical position. In this country the species of carpentry just mentioned has never been practised to the extent it deserves. Delorme died in 1570. With him was cotemporary Jean Bullant, whose name has been just mentioned, and who, whilst San Gallo was occupied on the Palazzo Farnese, was raising the Château d'Ecouen, in which the prelude to good taste is manifest, and in whose details are exhibited the work of an architect very far advanced above his time, and capable of raising the art to a much higher pitch of excellence than it enjoyed, had not the habits of the nation restrained him in his useful course. A considerable portion of the façade of the Tuileries towards the Carousel is suspected to have been the work of Bullant; but the château of Ecouen, built, or rather begun, about 1540, for the constable Montmorency, was almost the first step to the establishment of pure architecture in France, and its architect may fairly be named the Inigo Jones of the French

358. By the wars in Italy under Charles VIII., Louis XII., and Francis I., the French had become intimately acquainted with the architecture of Italy, and the taste of the monarch last named induced him to bring from that country some of their most celebrated artists; so that in France there was almost a colony of them. Among them, fortunately

for the quicker working of good taste, was the celebrated Vignola, who resided in France many years; a circumstance which may, with some probability, account for the high esteem in which that great master's profiles have always been held, and indeed in which they are still held there, though, generally speaking, the French have invariably been more attached in their practice to the Venetian than to the Roman school.   Serlio, another Italian architect of note, was employed in the country by Francis, and actually died at Fontainebleau. At the period whereof we are now treating there appears to have been a number of able artists; for to Delorme and Bullant must be added Lescot, who, with Jean Gougeon as his sculptor, was many years employed upon the building usually called the *Vieux Louvre*, to distinguish it from the subsequent additions which have quadrupled the original project of Lescot.   To judge of the works of the French architects of this period, a relative, and not an abstract view, must be taken of them; relative, we mean, to the general cultivation of the arts when any individual artist appears.   In this respect Lescot's works at the Louvre are entitled to the greatest praise; and from the examples he as well as Bullant and Gougeon afforded, it might have been expected that pure architecture would have proceeded without check until it reached a point as high as that to which it had been carried in Italy. Such was not, however, to be the case.   Mary de Medicis, during her regency, having determined on building the Luxembourg palace, was anxious to have it designed in the style of the palaces of Florence, her native city.   Jacques de Brosse, her architect, was therefore compelled to adopt the character required: his prototype seems to have been the Pitti palace, and his version of it is a failure.   The gigantic palaces of Florence well enough bear out against the rustic and embossed work employed upon them; but when their scale is reduced, the employment of massive parts requires great caution.   The palace, however, of the Luxembourg became a model for the fashion of the day, and produced an intermediate style, which lasted many years in France, and arrested the arrival at perfection whereof the above work of Bullant and others had opened a fair prospect.   De Brosse was an able artist, and his design for the façade of St. Gervais of three orders is, under the circumstances, entitled to our praise.   This architect acquired much honour by the aqueduct of Arcueil, the completion whereof, in 1624, it is supposed he did not long survive.

359.   Under Louis XIV. the art remained for the most part in the intermediate state just noticed; and yet that monarch and his minister Colbert lost no opportunity of embellishing the kingdom with its productions.   He employed Bernini to make designs for the palace of the Louvre; and for that purpose induced the artist to visit France, where he was received with the highest respect.   He left a design for a façade of the building in question, which, though in a corrupt style, exhibits nevertheless marks of grandeur and magnificence which would have been worthy of the monarch.   Bernini, disgusted, as he alleged, with the workmen of Paris, departed from the country without leaving any example of his architectural powers.   That he did so France has no reason to lament, since it gave Perrault the opportunity of ornamenting the capital with one of the most splendid monuments of the art which Europe can boast.   To Perrault is the credit due of having given an impulse to French architecture it has never lost, and of having changed the heavy style of his time into the light and agreeable forms of the Venetian school.   The beauties of the façade of the Louvre (*fig.* 176.) are so many and great that its defects are forgotten.   The

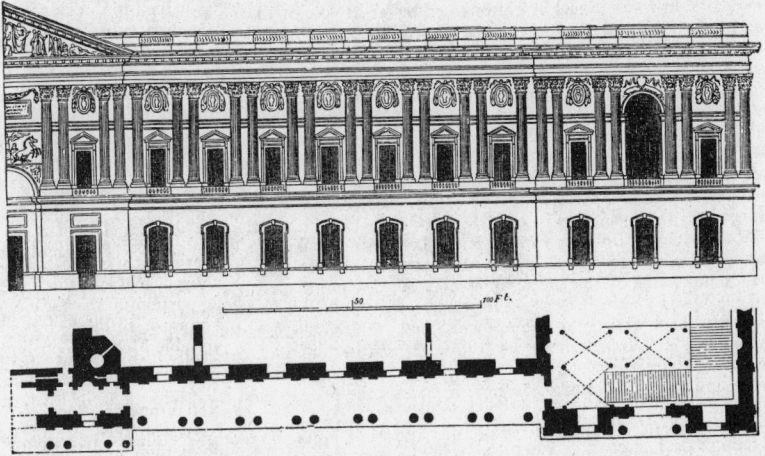

Fig. 176.   HALF FACADE AND HALF PLAN OF LOUVRE.

proportions are so exquisite, that the eye cannot rest on the coupled columns and the arch of the principal gate rising into the story of the colonnade. The original profession of Perrault was that of medicine, which, however, he only exercised for the benefit of his friends and the poor; hence the design he made with others in competition for the above work having been successful, he was associated for its execution with Louis le Veau, the king's principal architect. From the variety of sciences in which Perrault excelled, it is not probable that the assistance of a practical architect was actually necessary; indeed the four volumes which he published under the title *Essais de Physique*, and the collection of machines for raising and removing great weights, which he also published, show that he was, without assistance, quite competent to the charge which was committed to him with others. He built the observatory at Paris, possessing an originality of character which Milizia says is very conformable to its purpose. But however suitable it may have been considered at the time of its erection, and it cannot be denied there is a fine masculine character about it, it is for its purpose in the present age altogether ill adapted for the objects of astronomy. Perrault died in 1688. Cotemporary with him was Le Mercier, the architect of the church de l'Oratoire, in the Rue St. Honoré. Le Mercier died, however, in 1660; eight and twenty years, therefore, before the decease of Perrault. Among the architects whose practice was exceedingly extended was Jules Hardouin Mansart, the architect of Versailles, and the especial favourite of Louis XIV. He was principally employed between the years 1675 and his death in 1708. His ability, as Milizia observes, was not equal to the size of his edifices; though it is hardly fair for that author to have made such an observation on the architect of the cupola of the Invalides at Paris. Of this church and dome De Quincy has most truly stated, that though nothing that can be called classic is to be noticed about it, yet it contains nothing in dissonance with the principles of the art. It is a whole in which richness and elegance are combined; in which lightness and solidity are well balanced; in which unity is not injured by variety; and whose general effect silences the critic, however he may be disposed to find fault. In Versailles, the taste which we have above noticed as introduced by De Brosse is prevalent; but the interior of the chapel displays to great advantage the great genius of Mansart, and shows that he was not incapable of the most refined elegance.

360. Jacques Ange Gabriel was the relation and worthy pupil of Mansart. The colonnades to the Garde Meuble in the Place Louis XV. (now the Place de la Concorde) exhibit a style which, with the exception only of Perrault's façade of the Louvre, not all the patronage of Louis XIV. was capable of eliciting. To Gabriel almost, if not perhaps as much as to Perrault, the nation is under a debt of gratitude for the confirmation of good taste in France. He has been accused of pirating the Louvre; but reflection and comparison will show that there is no real ground for such an accusation. The difference between the two works is extremely wide. The basement of Perrault is a wall pierced with windows; that of Gabriel is an arcade: in the upper stories the columns are not coupled, which is the case at the Louvre. From these circumstances alone the character of the two works is so different, that it is quite unnecessary to enter into other detail. Architecture in France at this period, the commencement of the eighteenth century, was in a palmy state, and has never before or since risen to higher excellence; though the French are still, from the superior method of cultivating the art there, and the great encouragement it receives, the first architects in Europe. The great extent of the Place Louis XV. (744 ft. long, and 522 broad) is injurious to the effect of the Garde Meuble, which, as the reader will recollect, is rather two palaces than one. Its basement is perhaps, speaking without reference to the vast area in front of it, too high, and the intercolumniations too wide, for the order (Corinthian) employed; but it is easier to find fault than to do equally well; and we cannot leave the subject without a declaration that we never pass away from its beauties without a wish to return and contemplate their extreme elegance. They are to us of that class to which Cicero's expression may be well applied: "pernoctant nobiscum, peregrinantur." Gabriel died in 1742. Antoine, the architect of the Mint at Paris, was another of the choice spirits of the period: he continued the refined style whereof we are speaking; and though the age of Louis XV. was not destined to witness the erection of such stupendous edifices as that of Louis le Grand, it displayed a purer and far better taste. This architect was the first who employed in his country the Grecian Doric, which had then become known, though not perfectly, by the work of Le Roy. Antoine used it at *L'Hospice de la Charité;* and De Quincy cites it as a circumstance which called forth the approbation of people of taste, and observes that the attempt would have attracted more followers, if, instead of exciting the emulation of architects in the study of it and its judicious application to monuments, to which the character of the order is suitable, fashion had not applied it to the most vulgar and insignificant purposes. Antoine lived into the present century, having died in 1801, at the age of 68.

361. Louis XV., during a dangerous illness at Metz, is reported to have made a vow which led to the erection of the celebrated church of St. Genevíeve, or, as it has since been called, the Pantheon; the largest modern church in France, and second to none in simplicity,

elegance, and variety.   Another cause may, however, with as much probability, be assigned ;
the inadequacy of accommodation for the religious wants of the population, and especially
of that appertaining to the patroness Saint of Paris.   Many projects had been presented

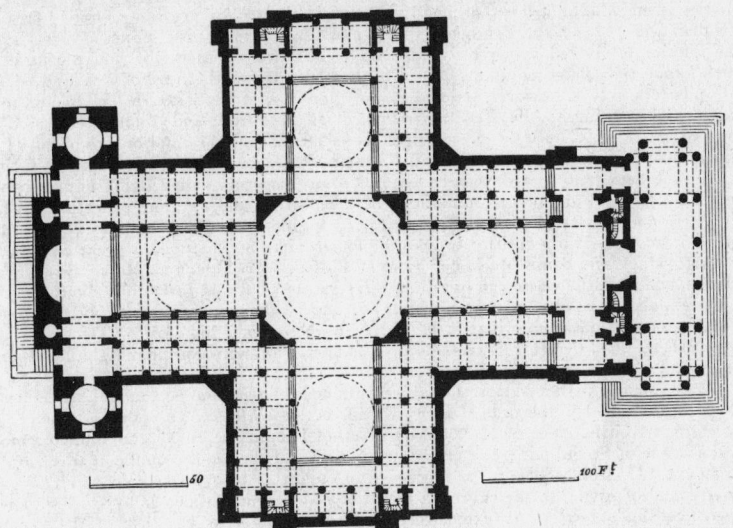

Fig. 177.   PLAN OF PANTHEON, PARIS.

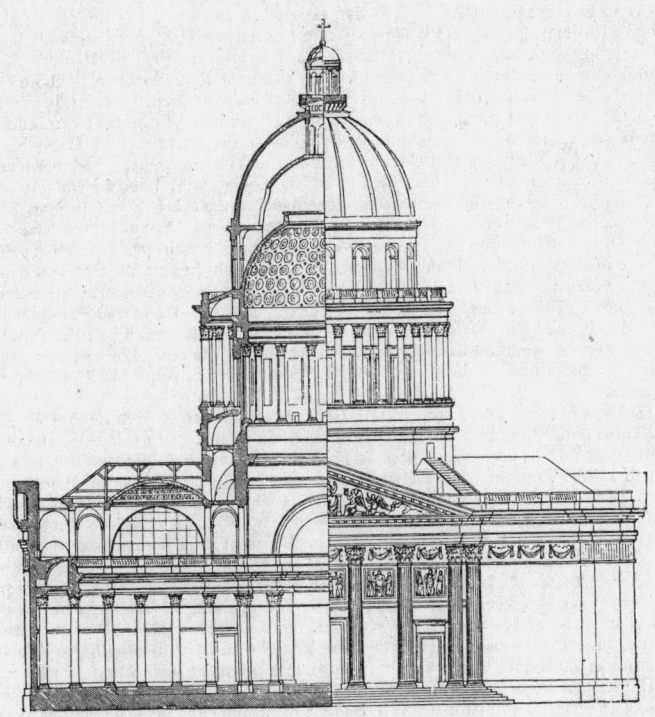

Fig. 178.   ELEVATION AND SECTION OF PANTHEON, PARIS.

for the purpose, but that of Soufflot received the preference. This talented artist, who was born in 1713, at Irancy near Auxerre, after passing some time in Italy, had been settled at Lyons, and there met with considerable and deserved employment. In that city the great hospital had deservedly brought him into notice, for his knowledge in providing against the miseries of mankind, not less than had his beautiful theatre for providing for its pleasures. The plan (*fig.* 177.) of the Pantheon (so it is now usually called) is a species of Greek cross. The interior is divided transversely into two equal parts on each side, and a central one much larger, by isolated columns, instead of the plans previously in use of arcades decorated with pilasters. It is, however, strictly, in its internal as well as external character, to be classed as belonging to the Venetian school. Its west front and transverse section are given in *fig.* 178. The light effect, which is so striking in the interior, produced by the employment of columns instead of the old system of arcades, is extremely pleasing, though, as has often been truly urged, they have no office to perform. Objections, moreover, have been taken to the wide intercolumniations of the portico, and to some other parts, which here it is unnecessary to particularise. It is, notwithstanding all that has been written against it, most certainly entitled to take the fourth place of the modern great churches in Europe; which are, Santa Maria del Fiore at Florence, St. Peter's at Rome, St. Paul's at London, and then the church in question. Its greatest fault is instability about the piers of the cupola, — the old fault, from which not one is altogether free, and one which gave Soufflot so much uneasiness that it is said to have hastened his death. This failure was afterwards rectified by his celebrated pupil Rondelet, who, with consummate skill, imparted perfect and lasting security to the edifice.

362. We ought perhaps before to have mentioned the name of Servandoni, as eminently influencing, in his day, the taste of Paris, which, as the world knows, is that of France. A Florentine by birth, and a scholar of the celebrated Pannini, he, in 1731, exhibited a model for the façade of St. Sulpice ; and after a year's probation before the public, it was adopted. On an extended front of 196 ft. he succeeded in imparting to it, as a whole, an air of great majesty, and of giving to the church a porch of vast extent without injury to the general effect. Servandoni was very extensively employed : his style was that of the Venetian school ; and his death occurred in 1766.

363. To write an history of the modern architecture of France, and at the same time to do its professors justice, would require a much larger volume than that under our pen : we profess to give no more than a bird's-eye view of it, so as to bring the reader generally acquainted with its progress; and it is not without much regret that we propose closing our account of it in the person of Jacques Gondouin, who died at Paris in 1818, at the age of eighty-one; an architect whose veneration for the works of Palladio was so unbounded, that for the study of them exclusively he performed a second journey into Italy : a strange infatuation in a man of great acquirements, if the opinions of some of our anonymous critics are of any value. When Gondouin was employed, the heavy style of Louis XIV. had passed away, and the suitable and elegant style of the Venetian school had been adopted. The pupils of Blondel, among whom he was eminent, were stimulated by the patronage of the whole capital; and even in the present day, so far capable are its inhabitants of appreciating the merits of an architect, regret as we may to record it, that it is from that circumstance alone likely to maintain its superiority over all others in Europe. The most celebrated work of Gondouin is the Ecole de Médecine, whose amphitheatre for lectures, capable of holding 1200 persons, is a model for all buildings of its class, without at all entering on the great merits of the other parts of the building. He was one of those upon whom the effects of the French Revolution fell with particular force, though, upon the re-establishment of order, he in some measure recovered his station in society. He was entrusted with the erection of the column in the Place Vendome, but merely as respected its preparation for the sculpture.

364. In Paris is to be found some of the most beautiful street architecture in Europe. That of Rome and Florence is certainly of a very high class, and exhibits some examples which will probably never be equalled. These, moreover, have associations attached to them which spread a charm over their existence of which it is not easy to divest one's self, and which, perhaps, contain some of the ingredients which enter into our high admiration of them. But, on a great and general scale, the most beautiful street architecture in Europe is to be found in Paris; and so great in this respect do we consider that city, that we are certain the education of an architect is far from complete if he be not intimately acquainted with the examples it affords. In that, as in most of the cities of Europe, the requirements of the shopkeeper interfere with the first principles of the art; but in this the violation of the rules of sound building, so as to connect them with his accommodation, are less felt by the critical observer than elsewhere. The spirit which seems to actuate the French nation is to produce works which may properly be called *monumental ;* in this country, the government has never applied itself to a single work worthy of that epithet. The principal care of an English minister seems to be that of keeping his place as long as the nation will endure him. Commerce and politics are the only subjects which such a personage

seems to think worthy his attention, and the sciences have only been patronised by the government in proportion to their bearing on those two absorbing points. But we shall perhaps revert to this in the following chapter.

Sect. XVIII.

GERMAN ARCHITECTURE.

365. No country exhibits more early, beautiful, or interesting specimens of Romanesque and pointed architecture, than Germany. The Rhine, and the southern parts of it which were under the sway of the Romans, are those, as we have already observed, in which these are principally to be found. Their history, however, has, sufficiently for general purposes, been traced under the sections of Byzantine or Romanesque and Pointed Architecture. The revival of the arts in Italy, as it did in other nations, here equally brought in the styles of the Italian schools, which, as elsewhere throughout Europe, have lasted to the present period ; and will certainly endure until some general change in the habits of its different nations renders necessary or justifies some other style as a worthy successor to them. On this to speculate were a waste of time; though there be some, and those men of talent, who contemplate a millennium of architecture, by making every thing in style dependent on the new materials (cast-iron for instance) which it is now the practice to employ, and often, it must be conceded, most usefully. Whilst the pointed style lasted in Europe, Italy was occasionally indebted to the Germans for an architect. Thus, notwithstanding the denial of Milizia, Lapo, a German architect, was employed in the early stages of construction of Santa Maria del Fiore ; and it is well authenticated that Zamodia a German, Annex of Friburg, and Ulric of Ulm, were employed on the cathedral at Milan. Franchetti (*Storia e Descrizione del Duomo di Milano*, 4to. Milan, 1821) asserts, that the first of these was engaged on it about 1391, the period of the golden age of pointed architecture in Germany; and the reputation of the Germans in this respect was at that time so great, that John and Simon of Cologne were actually carried into Spain for the purpose of designing and carrying into execution the cathedral at Burgos. It is at this period difficult to assign the cause of the nation so completely dropping astern, to use a nautical phrase, in the fine arts, and more particularly architecture. It was most probably the result of their political condition, and the consequent relative position they occupied in the affairs of Europe. But, whatever the cause, it is, in fact, most certain, that from the revival of the arts in Italy until near the end of the 18th century, Germany furnishes the names of few, if any, architects who are known beyond the limits of the country. Italy during the time in question seems to have repaid the nation for the early assistance received from them. At Fulda and Vienna, Carlo Fontana was extensively engaged; Guarini on the church of Santa Anna at Prague ; Scamozzi on the cathedral at Salzburg; Andrew Pozzo, who died at Vienna in 1709, was there employed on several of the churches : Martinelli of Lucca was another of the number that were solicited to decorate the country with their works. Fischers, indeed, was a native ; but his works, and especially his palace at Schönbrun, begun in 1696 for the Emperor Joseph, though not altogether without merit, is but a repetition of the extravagances of the school of Borromini ; and equally so was the palace built by the same artist for Prince Eugene at Vienna, in 1711. (*Essai d'Architecture Historique*, Leipsig, 1725.) Pietro Cart, who built the bridge at Nuremberg, Neuman, Bott, and Eosander of Prussia, are the only native architects of the period recorded by Milizia.

366. But it was not only from Italy that the Germans drew their architects : France contributed a supply to the country in the persons of Blondel, who was there much employed towards the end of the 17th century ; Robert de Cotte and Boffrand in the first part of that following. It is therefore, from what has been stated, impossible to give any independent account of the architecture of Germany. The Germans had none. Whoso were their architects, they were the followers of a style which contemporaneously existed in France and Italy even down to the bizarreries of that which prevailed in the time of Louis XV.; and it is a very curious fact, that whilst Germany was seeking the aid of architects from France and Italy, England could boast of professors of the art whose fame will endure while printing remains to spread knowledge amongst mankind. During the last century, Germany appears to have risen in this respect from its slumber, and to have produced some men of considerable architectural abilities. Of these was Carl Gotthard Langhans who was born in 1732, and built the celebrated Brandenburg gate at Berlin, which, though formed much on the model of the Propylea at Athens, and therefore on the score of originality not entitled to that praise which has been so unsparingly exhausted upon it, proves that a vast change had begun in Germany as respected matters of taste in ar-

chitecture.   Copies prove sad poverty of imagination on the part of the artist copying ; and all, therefore, that can be said in favour of such an expedient as that under consideration is, that better forms being submitted in this example to the Germans, it created a dawn of taste to which they had long been strangers.   The inaccurate work of Le Roy, which had preceded that of Stuart and Revett on the antiquities of Athens, was the means through which Langhans wrought and tried his successful experiment.   In France, as we have already observed, Antoine had tried the employment of the Grecian Doric at Paris, but without the impression produced by Langhans.   This architect died at Berlin in 1808, and is, perhaps, entitled to be considered as the father of good architecture in Germany, where he met the highest patronage and encouragement.   Knoblesdorff, who died in 1753, had, it must be allowed, prepared in some measure the change which was effected ; but neither he nor his successor are known in the world of art beyond the confines of their own country.   The names of Boumann, Goutard, Naumann, and others of much merit, occur to us ; but the examples which they have left are not of the class that justify specimens for presentation to the reader in a general work of this nature.   None of them rise so high as to be put in competition with the examples of the French school ; and from the circumstance of the principal works of Germany at Munich, Berlin, &c. having been executed by artists still living, we feel precluded here from allusion to them ; because, if we were to enter on an examination of them, we must detail their defects as well as their beauties.   An extraordinary species of bigotry has laid hold on some in relation to them, which time will temper ; and the world, as it always does, will ultimately come to a right judgment of the rank they are entitled to occupy as works of art.   In the other branches of the arts the Germans are rising fast ; but there is withal an affectation of the works of the middle ages in their productions, which, impressed as they are with great beauties, are not sufficiently pure to prognosticate the establishment of schools which will sweep all before them, as did those of Italy.

Sect. XIX.

SPANISH AND PORTUGUESE ARCHITECTURE.

367.   What has been said in the preceding section on the architecture of Germany is equally applicable to that of Spain and Portugal, whose architects were educated, if not in the schools of Italy, yet on the principles that guided them.   Still, the pre-eminence in architecture on the revival of the arts must be given to these countries over the contemporaneous buildings erected in Germany, and more especially to those of Spain. Under Ferdinand and Isabella, both greatly attached to the fine arts, the pointed style gave way to the architecture then in esteem in Italy ; and Giovanni de Olotzaga, a native of Biscay, is, we believe, entitled to the merit of having first introduced it in the great college of Santa Croce at Valladolid, which was commenced in 1480, and finished in 1492.   About the same period appeared Pietro de Gumiel, supposed to have been the architect of Santa Engracia at Saragossa ; but known as the artist who designed the college of Alcala, a splendid building in a mixed and impure style.   In this the orders were employed.   The edifice consists of three courts : the first Doric, with an arcade and two orders above, in the lower whereof the Doric was repeated, and the upper was Ionic ; the second court has thirty-two Composite columns, with arcades ; and the third is designed with thirty-six Ionic columns, beyond which is the theatre.   The church is of the Ionic order, and contains the monument of Cardinal Ximenes, the founder, considered one of the finest in Spain.   The names of Giovanni, Alonso, and Fra Giovanni d'Escobado continue in their works the history of the art in Spain, wherein a style between the pointed and Italian prevailed during the greater part of the reign of Charles V.   Giovanni Gil de Hontanon, at the end of the 15th century, appears in Spain as an architect of much celebrity.   He made a design for the cathedral at Salamanca, which was submitted to the judgment of four of the then most eminent architects of the country,— Alonzo de Cobarrubias, the architect of the church at Toledo ; Mastro Filippo of that of Seville ; Giovanni di Badajos of that of Burgos ; and Giovanni Balleso, by whom Hontanon's design was approved and commended.   This church is 378 ft. long, and has a nave and two series of aisles on each side.   The nave is 130 ft. high, and 50 ft. wide.   Rodrigo Gil, son of the above-named architect, had the execution of this church, which commenced in 1513.   It was probably this Rodrigo who, in 1525, erected the church of Segovia, very similar to that of Salamanca, except that it is more simple, and in a purer style.   The cathedral of Segovia, equal in size and grandeur to those of Toledo and Seville, was, after 1577, carried on by Francesco de Campo Aguero, who died in 1660 ; to whom succeeded Biadero, who died in 1678. Respecting Hontanon, Don Ant. Ponz observes, in the 10th volume of his *Travels in Spain,* that he must have been a clever architect, and well acquainted with the Greek and

Roman styles, which in his time were beginning to revive; but that, like many other artists, he was obliged in some measure to humour the taste of those who employed him: he therefore adopted the Gothic style, without the ornaments and details.   The efforts of the architects of this period were not confined altogether to church building; for in 1552 Pietro de Uria constructed a bridge at Almaraz over the Tagus, which may vie with the most extraordinary works of that class.   Two large pointed arches form the bridge, which is 580 ft. long, 25 ft. wide, and 134 ft. high.   The opening of one of the arches is 150 ft., that of the other 119 ft.   The piers are lofty towers, that in the centre standing on a high rock.   An inscription gives the date of erection 1552, and imports that it was constructed at the expense of the city of Placentia.

368.   Alonzo de Cobarrubias, the architect of the church of Toledo, seems to have used in it a Gothic sort of style, though when he flourished the Roman orders had become known and used.   This Alonzo was in considerable employ, as was his assistant, Diego Siloe, who built the church at Granada, with the monastery and church of San Girolamo in that city.   This cathedral has a nave and two aisles; and in it the Corinthian order, though defective in height, is used.   The cupola is well designed.   Both Siloe and his master loaded their buildings with sculptures to excess, from a seeming notion that beauty and richness were the same or inseparable.   Alonzo Berruguette was another architect of the 16th century who was deservedly employed.   He went to Italy in 1500, there to pursue his studies in the arts of painting and sculpture as well as architecture, and was at Florence when Michael Angelo and Leonardo da Vinci exhibited their cartoons. He was the architect of Charles V.; and it is supposed that he designed the palace at Madrid, begun by Henry II., continued by Henry III., and splendidly rebuilt by Charles V., but no longer in existence.   Berruguette erected the gate of San Martino, which is the principal one at Toledo.   It is of the Doric order, with the royal arms on the exterior, and a statue of Santa Leocadia in the interior.   There are great simplicity and elegance in the composition of this work.   The palace of Alcala, the residence of the archbishop of Toledo, is attributed to him; a building not wanting in magnificence, though defective in its detail.   A great portion of the cathedral of Cuença is said to be by Berruguette; but not the façade, which was erected in 1699 by Guiseppe Arroyo, and afterwards continued by Luigi Arriaga.   There is considerable effect about the cloister, which is well and ingeniously decorated.   This architect, it is thought, had some part in the Pardo, which was rebuilt in 1547; where are still allowed to remain,—notwithstanding the additions by Philip II. of the miserable eastern and western façades—the porticoes of Ionic columns, with their low stone arches.   Though the windows are greatly too far apart, and too small in the lower story, the stairs difficult of ascent, yet, upon the whole, the edifice is not ill arranged or executed.   At the period whereof we here speak there was a prodigious passion among the Spaniards for large screens and altars in the churches; in these the taste of Berruguette was most conspicuous.   In the use of the orders, which he fully understood, he was remarkably fond of employing them over one another.   The cathedral at Seville was principally rebuilt by Ferdinando Ruiz, who was much engaged in the city, and especially on enlarging or raising the well-known tower called the Giralda.   This singular edifice was begun in the 11th century, the original idea of it being given by the architect Geber, a native of Seville, to whom the invention of algebra is attributed; and also the design of two other similar towers, one in Morocco, and the other at Rabata. The tower of which we are now speaking was at first 250 ft. high, and 50 ft. wide, and was without diminution as it rose.   The walls are 8 ft. thick of squared stones from the level of the pavement; the rest for 87 ft. is of brick.   In the centre of this tower is a smaller one, the interval between the two towers being 23 ft., which serves for the ascent, one so convenient that two persons abreast can mount it on horseback.   The central tower does not diminish; but as the edifice rises in height the walls gather over, so as to allow the passage of only one person.   Upon the Moors of Seville negotiating their surrender, one of the conditions of it was, that this tower should not be destroyed; to which Don Alphonso, the eldest son of the king, answered, that if a portion of it were touched, not a man in Seville should survive.   In the earthquake of 1395 it was partially injured, and remained in the state of misfortune that then occurred until 1568, when, by the authorities, Ferdinando Ruiz received the commission to raise it 100 ft. higher.   This height he divided into three parts, crowning it with a small cupola or lantern: the first division of his addition is of equal thickness with the tower on a plinth, whence six pilasters rise on each façade, between which are five windows, over which is an entablature surmounted by balustrades; the second division is lower, with the same ornament; and the third is octagonal with pilasters, over which the cupola rises, crowned with a bronze statue of Faith, vulgarly called "La Giralda."   Ruiz by this work augmented his fame; and notwithstanding the earthquakes which have since occurred, it has, fortunately enough, been preserved.   We have, however, to apologise to our readers for this, which is anecdote, and not quite in order to be placed here, because partly connected with a period we have long since left.   Pictorially speaking, the tower of the Giralda is a splendid object, and the

apology was, perhaps, unnecessary. The age of Charles V. in Spain was Augustan for its architecture. By his mandate the palace was raised at Granada, a work of Machuca, another architect of this period. The principal façade is rustic, with three large gates, and eight Doric columns on pedestals sculptured with historical bassi-rilievi. The second story is Ionic with eight columns, over which are pilasters. The internal vestibule is on a circular plan, with a portico and gallery on columns of the same order. Milizia, from whom we have extracted all our notices on the architecture of Spain in this age, regrets that the arches spring from the columns. Though we cannot commend such a practice, we should be sorry, in certain cases, to see a veto put upon it; because the practice is occasionally compatible with fine effect.

369. Towards the end of the sixteenth century appears in Spain an artist, by name Domenico Testocopoli, by birth a Grecian, and a disciple of Tiziano Vecelli. He became, under his master, a good painter; but is known in Spain rather as a celebrated architect in his day. At Madrid, and in Toledo, he executed many works of merit; but his grand work was the church and monastery of the Bernardine monks of San Dominico di Silos, in which he employed his talents in architecture, painting, and sculpture, the whole being from his hand.

370. Garzia d'Emere and Bartolomeo di Bustamente, the latter especially, would require an extended notice in the history of the art in Spain, if our limits permitted us to enter on their merits. The latter was the architect of the hospital of San Giovanni Battista, founded by its archbishop in 1545, near Toledo. We should continue the account if works existed from which a feature different from the contemporaneous works in the rest of Europe could be extracted; but the fact is, that the progress of the art has already been told in other countries, and its success in Spain would be but a repetition in minor degree of what has already been said. Still we consider some notice must be taken of Giovanbatista of Toledo, who died in 1567, an architect and sculptor of surpassing merit; and as he was the architect who gave the designs for the façade of the Escurial, we shall not apologise for transcribing the account of him given by Milizia.

371. Having studied at Rome, he was invited to Naples by Don Pietro di Toledo, then viceroy there, who employed him as architect to the Emperor Charles V. in many important works in that city, whence he was called by Philip II. to become architect of all the royal works ·in Spain, and especially of the Escurial, which that monarch was anxious to erect in the most magnificent style. For this purpose he left Naples, and in 1563 commenced, upon his own design, the Escurial, which he continued to superintend till his death in 1567. In this great undertaking he was succeeded by Giovanni d'Herrera, his pupil, who finished it. Those, therefore, says the author whom we quote, that attribute this work to Luigi de Foix, to Bramante, to Vignola, and other architects who may have given designs for it, are unacquainted with the subject. The wonders related of the Escurial, as to the number of its doors and windows, are not tales to be here recounted; and the attempt, indeed, at exaggeration is vastly silly, because it is on so grand a scale that the simple truth imparts quite sufficient knowledge for conveying an idea of its splendour. The motives of Philip II. in founding this structure were twofold, — first, the injunction of his predecessor Charles V., who was desirous of constructing a tomb for the royal family of Spain; and secondly, of erecting an edifice of colossal dimensions to commemorate the famous victory of S. Quintin, achieved on the festival of San Lorenzo, the saint to whose interposition the king attributed his success. The situation chosen to receive it was beautiful. It is at the distance of a few miles from Madrid, at the foot of the Carpentani mountains, by which the two Castiles are divided. The plan of the edifice is said to resemble a gridiron, the instrument of martyrdom of Saint Lawrence, of which the handle is the projection in the eastern façade; we confess, however, we have some difficulty in tracing the resemblance. It is divided internally into fifteen courts, varying considerably in size; many of them are decorated with porticoes and galleries, and contain in all upwards of eighty fountains. The materials are granite very well wrought; the roofs partly covered with lead and partly with slate. The cupola of the church is stone. The four angles of the main plan are distinguished by towers rising four stories, besides those in the roofs, above the general fronts; besides which there are four others flanking the cupola. Parts of the building are in much better taste than others; but such an enormous pile of building cannot be otherwise than imposing, more especially, too, if there be anything like symmetry and regularity in the parts. Towards the west the principal façade is 740 feet long and 60 feet in height. The towers at the angles just mentioned rise to the height of 200 feet. This façade, like the others, has five stories of windows, which necessarily of themselves, from the way in which they are arranged, have the effect of cutting it up into minute divisions. The central compartment of it is 140 feet in length, and consists of two orders of half columns; the lower has eight semi-columns, which are Doric standing on a plinth, and in the central intercolumniation is the door; the other intercolumniations are filled with niches and windows in three stories. The upper order consists of four Ionic columns on pedestals, and is surmounted by a pediment. This upper

order has two stories of niches in its intercolumniations, in the upper central one whereof is placed the statue of St. Lawrence. The two minor doors in this façade are also made features in the design. The façade towards the east has the projecting handle of the grid-iron to which we have alluded, in which part is contained the palace; and westward of it the great chapel or church, with its cupola rising above the mass, to complete the composition. Towards the south the length is 580 ft., similar to the length on the north. On entering from the central gate of the western façade, the monastery is divided from the college by a large vestibule, from which three large arched openings lead into the king's court: this is 230 ft. long, and 136 ft. wide, surrounded by buildings of five stories, and ornamented with pilasters. At the eastern end of this court is the entrance to the church, over whose vestibule or pronaos are the libraries. To it a flight of seven steps crosses the whole width of the court; and from the landing rises a Doric arcaded porch of five openings, three whereof belong to the central compartment and lead to the church, the other two leading to the monastery and the college. Behind the porch the façade of the church rises, and is flanked by two towers, which respectively belong to the monastery and college, and are ornamented above the general height of the buildings of the court with two orders of pilasters, being terminated by small cupolas. The interior of the church is Doric, and is in plan a Greek cross. The nave is 53 ft. and the aisles are 30 ft. wide. Its whole length is 364 ft., its width 230, and height 170. From the intersection of the nave and transepts the cupola rises, 66 ft. in diameter, and 330 ft. in height from the pavement to the cross. Its exterior is composed with a square *tambour* or drum, if it may be so called, from which the order rises. The choir is only 30 ft. high, and its length but 60 ft. In point of taste and dimensions, the church is inferior to several in other parts of Europe. The presbytery, we should have stated, is raised, so as to form almost another church, and seemingly without relation to the principal one. The staircase which leads to the Pantheon, and which possesses considerable magnificence, is placed between the church and the antesacristy: we are not aware why this name has been given to the sepulchre of the kings of Spain. It is nearly under the high altar. The chamber appropriated to the reception of the kings is 36 ft. diameter, and 38 ft. in height, richly encrusted with various marbles and metals, and ornamented with sixteen double Corinthian pilasters on pedestals, arranged octagonally; and between them are recesses, with the sarcophagi, amounting to twenty-six, that is, four in each of six sides, and two over the entrance which faces the altar of the Resurrection. This is a fair specimen of the style which prevailed in Spain under the reigns of Philip IV. and Charles II. The college, the seminary, and the royal palace occupy the rest of the building. In 1773, many additions were made to the buildings about the Escurial for the Infants Don Antonio and Don Gabriele, by Villaneuva, an Italian architect, and by them the palace was much improved. Giovanni d'Herrera, who died in 1597, besides his employment at the building just described, contributed greatly to the advancement of the art by the execution of the many commissions with which he was entrusted. The bridge of Segovia, at Madrid, is by him; as is the royal pleasure-house at Aranjuez, begun under Philip II. and finished by Charles III., — a work which, though far from pure, exhibits great architectural ability. His successor at the Escurial was Francesco de Mora, by whom, at Madrid, is the Palace de los Consejos, the most splendid edifice which that capital can boast. Instead of a central doorway, it has two at its flanks, of the Doric order, with appropriate decorations. In the beginning of the seventeenth century, the great square of Madrid was erected after the designs of Giovanni Gomez de Mora, and is admirable for its grandeur and symmetry. This architect built at Alcala the church and college of the Jesuits, which, Milizia says, is a magnificent and well-proportioned edifice. It is of two orders, and the material employed in the façade is granite. The royal convent of the Augustins, at Madrid, is also attributed to him.

372. In the beginning of the eighteenth century, Filippo Ivara, a native of Messina, had very great employ, we might almost say throughout Europe. He became the pupil of Fontana, and afterwards, on his visiting Spain, seems to have established a school there. He built the façade of the royal palace of St. Ildefonso, looking towards the gardens. Ivara died in 1735, at Madrid, whither he had been invited by Philip V. to rebuild the palace, which had been consumed by fire. The work was afterwards intrusted to Sacchetti. a pupil of Ivara. It is on a very large scale, and was most solidly constructed.

373. We have thought it necessary to give the above succinct account of the architecture of Spain, which did not, however, produce, after the revival of the arts in Europe, any works, except in respect of dimensions, comparable with those of Italy. The abuses in them are almost universally carried to an extent scarcely credible; it is, therefore, useless to refer the reader or student to them as models. It almost seems as if from Italy pure architecture had not had time to spread itself before it became tinctured with the corruptions of Borromini; which, not only in Spain and Portugal, but throughout Germany, and even France. were diffused with incredible rapidity

The mediæval works have been lately described by Mr. G. E. Street, in *Some Account of Gothic Architecture in Spain*, 1865.

Sect. XX.

RUSSIAN ARCHITECTURE.

374. We scarcely know whether we are justified in making a short section with this heading, inasmuch as there is not known to us, up to the end of the eighteenth century, the name of a single Russian architect. English, French, Italian, and German artists have been employed in the decoration of the city of Petersburg, though we believe that the nation is now beginning to produce persons capable of conducting their public works. Russia has received all its improvement from abroad, and has used every exertion to communicate it to an uncivilised people.

375. The ecclesiastical architecture of Russia is of course coeval with the introduction of Christianity into the country, which was not earlier than the time of Vladimir the Great, although the Princess Olga had been baptized at Constantinople as early as the year 964. Vladimir, to display his zeal in behalf of Christianity, had a church, supposed to be the first built by him, erected at Cherson ; a year after which the church of St. Basil, which, as well as the first named, was of timber, was erected under his command. This prince also built a church at Kief, where, it is said, there were already at the time 500 churches. After Vladimir, Prince Yaroslaf appears to have bestowed great attention on the erection of ecclesiastical edifices. At Kief he founded a church, dedicated to St. Sophia, and at Novogorod another to the same saint : these partly exist in the present day. By him also were reared the convents of St. George and St. Irene. The celebrated convent of Petchorsky, at Kief, was erected in 1075, subsequent to which period the Russian metropolitans continued subject to those of Constantinople till the capture of that city by Mahomet the Second. Between this last capital and Kief the bonds of amity of their rulers were drawn closer by many intermarriages; but in the year 1124 a fire desolated the latter city, which must have risen into great importance, inasmuch as 600 churches and monasteries were destroyed in the conflagration. Afterwards, again, in the civil war under Yisaslaf, Kief was taken and fired; a calamity to which it was again subject at the same period that Constantinople was taken by the Venetians. After this Kief never again recovered its ancient magnificence. In 1154, at which period Moscow is first mentioned in history, it was but an insignificant village. It received great additions under Daniel of Moscow; and in 1304, under John Danielowitz, it became the capital of the empire. On the 4th of August, 1326, the first stone was laid of a church in the Kremlin there in honour of the Assumption of the Virgin. The palace of the Kremlin was a timber structure until the reign of Demetri Donskoi, when it was reconstructed of stone. On the capture of Constantinople by Mahomet the Second, the Russian church ceased to be dependent on that of Constantinople. The palace of the Kremlin, known by the name of the granite palace, rose in 1487; and, in twelve years afterwards, the Belvedere palace was raised. Ivan IV., whose sway was of extended duration, was a great patron of the arts; his decease took place circa 1584. He renewed the laws relative to the paintings in the new churches, whence arises their so close resemblance to each other that it is difficult to judge of the epochs of their execution. The celebrated clock tower Ivan Valiki, at the Kremlin, was erected by the Czar Boris, in 1600, at which time Moscow contained 400 churches, whereof 35 stood in the Kremlin alone. After the time of Peter the Great, a change of style was introduced, (1696–1725).

376. The Church of the Assumption above mentioned, as respects the plan, is an oblong square divided ; the vaulting whereof is supported by six columns in the interior. Though at the first glance it be not perceived, the arrangement of the cupolas soon points to the form of a Greek cross. In the earlier churches the plan was a square, with a porch in front of it ; but, in the Church of the Assumption, the porch is a portion of the church, the arches of the cupolas being placed in the same way as if the church were of the ancient form. The six columns just mentioned divide the church into four parts, — from east to west, and then from north to south. At the eastern sides are three apsides, divided by the width of a column, the middle one being of larger dimensions than the other two; an arrangement which prevails in most of the Greek churches. The apsides contain altars, which are frequent, except in the small chapels. The altar in the Greek church is not exposed to public view ; it is concealed or covered by the iconostasis (image-bearer), a very large screen, which, from occupying the whole width of the church, divides it into two parts. This screen has a central principal and two side smaller doors ; behind which latter, on each side, stands a second and smaller iconostasis, of the width only of the smaller apsis, but whose plan with three doors and an altar behind is similar to the great one. This was the distribution in the early churches; but, in the more modern ones, there are, at nearly the extremity of the edifice, three distinct iconostases. The place for the choristers is on each side in front of the iconostasis, between its principal and side doors. The principal cupola rises in front of the iconostasis; and, in cathedral churches, at the foot of the apsis on the left a canopy is placed for the emperor, opposite whereto is one for the metropolitan.

There is generally one principal and four subordinate cupolas round it, which stand on the four feet of the Greek cross. The iconostasis is a principal object in every church. It is usually in four or five horizontal compartments, each containing an unequal number of pictures of saints painted on tablets or long square panels, whose places are fixed with great precision. In the first story, if we may so call it, are the three doors; the centre one, being in two foldings, is decorated with the subject of the Annunciation, accompanied with the heads of the four Evangelists or their emblems. To the right of the door is a picture of Christ, and of the Madonna on the left. To the right of the Christ is the saint or festival of the church, after which the doors are inserted. Above the doors, on the left hand, is placed a Greek cross; on the right hand the cross of Moses, — as symbols of the Old and New Testaments. The paintings are all on a ground of gold. In the middle of the second story is Christ on a throne; on the right Saint John the Baptist; on the left the Madonna without Child; then, on each side, two archangels and six apostles. In the third story or horizontal compartment, the Madonna is introduced with the Infant on her knees, surrounded on each side by the prophets. In the fourth story is painted God the Father on a throne, with the Infant Jesus, surrounded on each side by patriarchs of the church. Occasionally a fifth story appears, upon which is painted the history or Passion of our Saviour. Paintings on a gold ground abound in the other parts of the church. The exteriors of these churches are extremely simple; cornices or other horizontal crownings are not to found, but the coverings follow the cylindrical forms of the arches to which they are the extradoses, and are variously painted. The Russian churches built in the eleventh century, which from the number of their cupolas resemble, and indeed were imitated from those of the East, give a peculiar effect to the architecture. The forms of these cupolas are varied, but they generally stand on an octagonal *tambour;* some are hemispherical, others in curves of contrary flexure, and a number of other figures.

377. The type of the Russian church, which is on plan a Greek cross, is to be found in Santa Sophia at Constantinople. After the disputes between the Iconoclasts and Iconolaters, which, at the close of the seventh century, ended in the separation of the Eastern and Western churches, sculpture of statues disappeared from the Greek church, statues of angels excepted. Again, at this period, the altars on the side of the principal one were established, not, as in the Catholic churches, at the extremities of the transepts; their place is always in a niche or apsis. This arrangement is found in the churches of the eleventh, twelfth, and thirteenth centuries, at Bari, Trani, Malfetta, Otranto, &c., while the Greek worship existed; and a similar disposition is even seen at Palermo and other places where the worship has been Catholic. In the Catholic churches a sacristy, for the use of the priests in robing, &c., is always provided on the side of the church; in the Greek church, however, the priests robe themselves behind the iconostasis on the left of the altar, another altar being placed on the right for the consecration of the elements; and this arrangement exists in the present day. The Greek church has no gynæceum, or separate place for the women. — For the above we are indebted to the researches of M. Hallmann, an ingenious architect of Hanover.

378. It is in Saint Petersburg principally that we are to look for edifices which deserve mention. The foundation of the city was laid in 1703, by the Czar Peter, when he constructed a fort on an island in the Neva for defence against the Swedes. Buildings, both public and private, were soon erected; and the nobility and merchants being induced to settle there, the place quickly assumed the appearance of a considerable city. In the reigns of Catherine the Second and Alexander it reached a degree of great magnificence, from which it has not declined, but has rather advanced. Magnitude, rather than beauty of form, marks the public buildings of the city. The church of our Lady of Kazan is of great dimensions : for which, and its fifty-six granite columns with bronze capitals, it has obtained more celebrity than it will acquire for the beauty of its composition. Some of the palaces in the city are of colossal dimensions; that of Michailoff, built by Paul, is said to have cost ten millions of rubles. It was under the reign of Peter the Great that the great change took place in the national character of Russian church architecture by the introduction of the classical orders. The bulbous cupola, though at this period not entirely laid aside, fell into comparative disuse, being replaced by a green painted dome of which the Italian form was the model. The tasteless custom of painting the exteriors of buildings with bright and incongruous colours was retained; and, though well enough suited to the barbaric structures of the Muscovite czars, it ill accorded with the purer style of Italy. It is unnecessary further to detain the reader by any observations on the churches of the modern capital. In point of style or of history, they possess little or no interest for an English reader. To those who wish to become better acquainted with the architecture of Russia, we recommend a reference to Geissler's *Tableaux Pittoresques des Mœurs, &c. des Russes, Tartares, Mongoles, et autres Nations de l'Empire Russe;* to Lyall's *Character of the Russians,* &c., 4to, 1823; and Ricard de Montferrand's *L'Eglise de S. Isaac,* fol. 1845. The essay by the late M. Hallmann above noticed, was printed in the *Transactions* of the Institute of British Architects, 1842.

CHAP. III.

ARCHITECTURE OF BRITAIN.

Sect. I.

EARLY HOUSES AND ARCHITECTURE OF THE BRITONS.

379. On the invasion of Britain by Julius Cæsar, in the year 55 b. c., the inhabitants dwelt in houses resembling those of Gaul; and in Kent, and other southern parts of the island, their houses were more substantial and convenient than those in the north. Caves or earth houses seem to have been their original shelter; to which had preceded the wicker enclosure, whose sides were incrusted with clay. These were thatched with straw. The wooden houses of the ancient Gauls and Britons were circular, with high tapering roofs, at whose summit was an aperture for the admission of light and emission of smoke. These, where the edifices were grander than ordinary, were placed upon foundations of stone. There is no instruction to be derived from pursuing this subject further. That the arts at the period in question scarcely existed, is quite certain; and Caractacus may, when carried prisoner to Rome, have well expressed surprise that the Romans, who had such magnificent palaces of their own, should envy the wretched cabins of the Britons.

380. If the Britons were so uninformed in architecture as to be satisfied with such structures for their dwellings as we have named, it will hardly be contended that they were the builders of so stupendous a fabric as Stonehenge. On this subject we have already stated our opinion in Chap. II. From the distant period at which we believe this and similar edifices to have been erected up to that of which we are speaking many centuries must have elapsed, during which the mechanical knowledge which was employed in their erection might have been lost, and indeed must have been, from the condition of the inhabitants, of which mention has been made.

381. The Romans, after their invasion of the island, soon formed settlements and planted colonies; and it is not difficult to imagine the change which took place in its architecture. The first Roman colony was at Camalodunum. This, when it was afterwards destroyed by the Britons in the great revolt under Boadicea, appears to have been a large and well-built town, adorned with statues, temples, theatres, and other public edifices. (*Tacit. Annal.* lib. xiv. c. 32.) In the account given of the prodigies said to have happened at this place, and to have announced its approaching fall, it is mentioned that the statue of Victory fell down without any visible violence; in the hall of public business, the confused murmurs of strangers were perceived, and dismal howlings were heard in the theatre. At Camalodunum the temple of Claudius was large enough to contain the whole garrison, who, after the destruction of the town, took refuge in it; and so strong was it, that they were enabled to hold out therein against the whole British army for a period of two days. London, however, exhibited a more striking example of the rapid progress of Roman architecture in Britain. At the time of the first Roman invasion it was little more than a British town or enclosed forest; and there seems to be ground for supposing that at the time of the second invasion, under Claudius, it was not much improved. But when, about sixteen years afterwards, it came into the possession of the Romans, it became a rich, populous, and beautiful city. Not only did the Romans raise a vast number of solid and magnificent structures for their own accommodation, but they taught the arts to the Britons, and thus civilised them. Agricola, of all the Roman governors, took means for that purpose. That they might become less and less attached to a roaming and unsettled life, and accustomed to a more agreeable mode of living, he took all opportunities of rendering them assistance in erecting houses and temples, and other public buildings. He did all in his power to excite an emulation amongst them; so that at last they were not content without structures for ornament and pleasure, such as baths, porticoes, galleries, banqueting houses, &c. From this time (a. d. 80) up " to the middle of the fourth century," says Henry (*Hist. of England*), " architecture, and all the arts immediately connected with it, greatly flourished in this island; and the same taste for erecting solid, convenient, and beautiful buildings which had long prevailed in Italy, was introduced into Britain. Every Roman colony and free city (of which there was a great number in this country) was a little Rome, encompassed with strong walls, adorned with temples, palaces, courts, halls, basilicæ, baths, markets, aqueducts, and many other fine buildings both for use and ornament The country every where abounded with well-built villages, towns, forts, and stations; and the whole was defended by that high and strong wall, with its many towers and castles, which reached from the mouth of the river Tyne on the east to the Solway Firth on the west.

This spirit of building, which was introduced and encouraged by the Romans, so much improved the taste and increased the number of the British builders, that in the third century this island was famous for the great number and excellence of its architects and artificers. When the Emperor Constantius, father of Constantine the Great, rebuilt the city of Autun in Gaul, A. D. 296, he was chiefly furnished with workmen from Britain, which (says Eumenius) very much abounded with the best artificers. It was about the end of the third century that in Britain, as well as all the other provinces of the Western empire, architecture began to decline.   It may have been that the building of Constantinople drew off the best artists; or that the time left for the peaceful culture of the arts may have been broken in upon by the irruptions of invaders from the north.   According to the Venerable Bede (*Hist. Eccles.*, lib. i. c. 12.), the Britons had become so ignorant of the art before the final departure of the Romans that they, from want of masons, repaired the wall between the Forth and Clyde with sods instead of stone.   Henry observes, however, on this, that " we cannot lay much stress on this testimony; because it does not refer to the provincial Britons, but to those who lived beyond the Wall of Severus, where the Roman arts never much prevailed; and because the true reason of their repairing that wall with turf, and not with stone, was that it had been originally built in that manner.   Besides, we are told by the same writer, in the same place, that the provincial Britons, some time after this, with the assistance of one Roman legion, built a wall of solid stone, 8 ft. thick and 12 ft. high, from sea to sea."

382. The departure of the Romans, and that of the fine arts which they had introduced, were occurrences of almost the same date.   We must, however, recollect that architecture was beginning to decline at Rome itself before the departure in question.   The inhabitants of the country who remained after the Romans were gone had not the skill nor courage to defend the works with which the Romans had provided them; and their towns and cities, therefore, were seized by invaders, who plundered and destroyed them, throwing down the noble structures with which the art and industry of the Romans had adorned the country. The vestiges of Roman architecture still remaining in Britain are pretty numerous; but scarcely any of them are of sufficient interest to be considered as studies of Roman architecture. Even in its best days, nobody would study the works of art in the colonies in preference to those in the parent state.   We have here (*fig.* 179.) inserted a representation of a small portion of the Roman wall at Leicester, as an example of the construction.   Temples, baths, and villas of the time have, moreover, been brought to light not unfrequently.

Fig. 179.   ROMAN WALL, LEICESTER.
(7 ft. 6 ins. to Roman Road, and 3 ft. 6 ins. more to bottom of piers.)

383. The arrival of the Saxons in this country, A. D. 449, soon extinguished the very little that remained of the arts in the island. This people were totally ignorant of art; like the other nations of Germany, they had been accustomed to live in wretched hovels formed out of the earth, or built of wood, and covered with reeds, straw, or the branches of trees. It was not, indeed, until 200 years after their arrival that stone was employed by them for their buildings. Their cathedrals were built of timber.   The Venerable Bede says there was a time when not a stone church existed in all the land; the custom being to build them of wood. Finan, the second bishop of Lindisfarne, or Holy Island, built a church in that island, A. D. 652, for a cathedral, which yet was not of stone, but of wood, and covered with reeds; and so it continued till Eadbert, the successor of St. Cuthbert, and seventh bishop of Lindisfarne, took away the reeds, and covered it all over, both roof and walls, with sheets of lead. Of similar materials was the original cathedral at York, a church of stone being a very rare production, and usually dignified with some special historical record.   Bede, for instance, says of Paulinus, the first bishop of York, that he built a church of stone in the city of Lincoln, whose walls were standing when he wrote, though the roof had fallen down.   Scotland, at the beginning of the eighth century, does not seem to have had a single church of stone. Naitan, king of the Picts, in his letter to Ceolfred, abbot of Weremouth, A. D. 710, intreats that some masons may be sent him to build a church of stone in his kingdom, in imitation of the Romans.

384. We here think it necessary to notice that we have thought proper, under this chapter, to preserve the periods, or rather styles of the periods of architecture, according to their ordinary arrangement in English works, namely, the Anglo-Saxon and Norman, in distinct sections. It is a matter of little importance to the reader how he acquires his knowledge, so that his author do not unnecessarily prolong the acquisition of it. Though, therefore, the Anglo-Saxon and Norman architecture are neither of them anything more than Romanesque or Byzantine, to which we have appropriated rather a long section, we have here separated them into two distinct periods.

385. About the end of the seventh century masonry, as well as some other arts connected with it, was once more restored to England, by the exertions of Wilfred, bishop of York, and afterwards of Hexham, and of Benedict Biscop, the founder of the abbey of Weremouth. The former, who was an indefatigable builder, and one of the most munificent prelates of the seventh century, erected edifices, which were the admiration of the age, at Ripon, York, and Hexham. The cathedral of the latter place obtained great celebrity. Eddius, speaking of it (*Vita Wilfridi*), says, that Wilfrid " having obtained a plot of ground at the place from Queen Etheldreda, he there founded a very magnificent church, and dedicated it to the blessed apostle St. Andrew. The plan of this holy structure appears to have been inspired by the spirit of God; a genius, therefore, superior to mine is wanting to describe it properly. Large and strong were the subterraneous buildings, and constructed of the finest polished stones. How magnificent is the superstructure, with its lofty roof resting on many pillars, its long and lofty walls, its sublime towers, and winding stairs ! To sum all up, there is not on this side of the Alps so great and beautiful a work." Biscop was a zealous cotemporary and companion of Wilfrid, and had also a great love for the arts. He travelled into Italy no less than six times, chiefly for the purpose of collecting books and works of art, and of endeavouring to induce workmen to come over to England. An estate of some extent having been obtained by him from Ecgfrid, king of Northumberland, near the mouth of the river Were, he founded a monastery there in 674. Relative to this monastery of Weremouth, thus writes Bede : — " About a year after laying the foundations, Benedict passed over into France, and there collected a number of masons, whom he brought over with him to build the church of his monastery of stone, *after the Roman manner*, whereof he was a vast admirer. Such was his love for the apostle Peter, to whom the church was to be dedicated, that he stimulated the workmen so as to have mass celebrated in it but a little more than a year from its foundation. When the work was well advanced, he sent agents into France for the purpose of procuring, if possible, glass manufacturers, who at that time were not to be found in England, and of bringing them over to glaze the windows of his monastery and church. His agents were successful, having induced several artisans to accompany them. These not only executed the work assigned to them by Benedict, but gave instructions to the English in the art of making glass for windows, lamps, and other uses."

386. The Bishop Wilfrid, as we learn from William of Malmesbury, with the assistance of the artificers that had been brought over, effected great reparations in the cathedral at York, which was in a decayed and ruinous state. He restored the roof, and covered it with lead, cleansed and whited the walls, and put glass into the windows ; for, before he had introduced the glass makers, the windows of private dwellings as well as churches were filled with linen cloth, or with wooden lattices. It will be observed that the improvements we here mention were introduced by the bishops Wilfrid and Biscop towards the end of the seventh century ; but, from our ancient historians, it would appear that, in the eighth and ninth centuries, stone buildings were rarely met with, and, when erected, were objects of great admiration. The historian Henry observes, that " when Alfred, towards the end of the ninth century, formed the design of rebuilding his ruined cities, churches, and monasteries, and of adorning his buildings with more magnificent structures, he was obliged to bring many of his artificers from foreign countries. Of these (as we are told by his friend Aperius) he had an almost innumerable multitude, collected from different nations ; many of them the most excellent in their several arts. Nor is it the least praise of this illustrious prince, that he was the greatest builder and the best architect of the age in which he flourished." His historian, who was an eyewitness of his works, speaks in the following strain of admiration of the number of his buildings, " What shall I say of the towns and cities which he repaired, and of others which he built from the foundation ? " Henry continues, — " Some of his buildings were also magnificent for that age, and of a new and singular construction ; particularly the monastery of Æthelingay. The church, however, was built only of wood ; and it seems probable that Alfred's buildings were, in general, more remarkable for their number and utility than for their grandeur ; for there is sufficient evidence that, long after his time, almost all the houses in England, and the far greatest part of the monasteries and churches, were very mean buildings, constructed of wood and covered with thatch. Edgar the Peaceable, who flourished after the middle of the tenth century, observed (see *William Malms.* lib. ii. p. 32.), that, at his accession to the throne, all the monasteries of England were in a ruinous condition, and consisted only

of rotten boards." The taste, however, of the Anglo-Saxons was not indulged in magnificent buildings ; and the incursions of the Danes, who destroyed wherever they came, together with the unsettled state of the country, may account for their revenues being expended on mean and inconvenient houses.

387. Under the circumstances mentioned, it may be safely inferred that the art was not in a very flourishing state in the other parts of the island. Indeed, the ancient Britons, after retiring to the mountains of Wales, appear to have lost it altogether ; and, as the Honourable Daines Barrington (*Archæologia*) has thought, it is very probable that few, if any, stone buildings existed in Wales previous to the time of Edward I. The chief palace, called the *White Palace*, of the kings of Wales, was constructed with white wands, whose bark was peeled off, whence its name was derived ; and the price or penalty, by the laws of the country, for destroying the king's hall or palace, with its adjacent dormitory, kitchen, chapel, granary, bakehouse, storehouse, stable, and doghouse, was five pounds and eighty pence, equal, in quantity of silver, to sixteen pounds of our money, or 160*l.* The castles appear also to have been built of timber ; for the vassals, upon whom fell the labour of building them, were required to bring with them no other tool than an axe.

388. Neither do the arts of building appear to have been better understood in Scotland at the former part of the period whereof we are speaking. The church built at Lindisfarne by its second bishop, Finan, in 652, was of wood, —*more Scotorum ;* and it has already been mentioned that, for the stone church which Naitan, king of the Picts, built in 710, he was under the necessity of procuring his masons from Northumberland. In Scotland, there are still to be seen some stone buildings of very high antiquity, which Dr. Henry seems inclined to attribute to this period ; we, however, are inclined to place them in an age far anterior, later (but not much so) than Stonehenge. We have never seen them, and therefore form our opinion from the description given in Gordon's *Itinerarium Septentrionale.* These buildings are all circular, though of two different kinds, so different from each other that they seem to be the works of different ages and of different nations. The four principal ones are in a valley, called Glenbeg. Of a different period, too, we consider the circular towers which are found as well in Scotland as in Ireland. It is true that in both countries these are found in the neighbourhood of churches ; but that does not the more convince us that they were connected with them.

389. Ducarel, in his *Norman Antiquities*, enumerates some of the churches in England which belong to the ages anterior to the Norman conquest. Among them are those of Stukely in Buckinghamshire, Barfreston (*fig.* 180.) in Kent, and Avington in Berkshire. Other examples exist in Waltham Abbey ; the transept arches at Southwell, Nottinghamshire; the nave of the abbey church of St. Alban's, Herts; the nave of St. Frideswide, Oxford, &c. &c. The Anglo-Saxon æra, though it, perhaps, properly comprised the time between A. D. 600 to A. D. 1066 ; that is, from the conversion of the Saxons to the Norman conquest, is not known with any thing approaching to certainty, from the reign of Edgar in 980 to the last-named event ; immediately previous to which Edward the Confessor had, during his lifetime, completed Westminster Abbey in a style then prevalent in Normandy, and with a magnificence far exceeding any other then extant. No less than eighteen of the larger monasteries, all of them Benedictine, had been founded by the Saxon kings in

Fig. 180.   BARFRESTON CHURCH.

their successive reigns; and it is evident that the churches attached to them were the most decorated parts, as respected their architecture. The six principal of these were, St. Germain's, in Cornwall; Colchester, in Essex; Tewkesbury, in Gloucestershire; St. Frideswide and St. Alban's, already mentioned; and Glastonbury, in Somersetshire. King selects the western portion of Tewkesbury as the grandest in England for effect and extent. The characteristics of *Anglo-Saxon Architecture* are detailed in the following subsection.

Fig. 181   SAXON ARCH.

390. *Arches.* — Always semicircular, often plain; sometimes decorated with a variety of mouldings on the sofite as well as on the face, the former being often entirely occupied by them. They are found double, triple, or quadruple, each springing from two columns, and generally cased with a different moulding, which is frequently double, thus making six or eight concentric circles of them; and as each of them projects beyond that under it, a moulding is placed under them, generally the same as that used upon the face. (See *fig.* 181.) *Columns.* — Single, cylindrical, hexagonal or octagonal, on square plinths; very few diameters in height. Shafts often ornamented with spiral or fluted carving, with lozenge, herring-bone, zigzag, or hatched work. (*Fig.* 182.) *Capitals.* — Indented with fissures of different lengths and forms, and in different directions. The divisions thus formed are variously sloped off, or hollowed out towards the top. (See the two examples, *fig.* 183., from the conventual church at Ely.) Occasionally the capitals have rude imitations of some member of a Grecian order, as in the crypt at Lastringham in Yorkshire, where volutes are used. (*Fig.* 184.) In their ornaments much variety is displayed, but the opposite ones are mostly alike. *Windows.* — Semicircular-headed, extremely narrow in proportion to their height, being sometimes not more than six or eight inches wide to a height of more than three feet, and splayed or bevelled off on the inside through the whole thickness of the wall. *Walls.* — Of very great thickness, and Masonry of solid construction. *Ceilings and Roofs.* In crypts, as at York, Winchester, and a few other

Fig. 182.   ARCH, CONVENTUAL CHURCH, ELY.

without any buttresses externally. —Almost always open timbering.

Fig. 183.   TWO CAPITALS, CONVENTUAL CHURCH, ELY.

Fig. 184.   CAPITAL FROM LASTRINGHAM

places, vaulting is to be found. *Ornaments*, except in capitals, in arches and on shafts of columns are very sparingly employed. (See Norman Ornaments also, in the following section on Norman Architecture, subsect. 397.) *Plans.* — Rectangular and parallelogrammic; being usually divided into a body and chancel, separated by an ornamented arch. The *chancel* sometimes of equal, and sometimes of less breadth than

the nave, and terminated towards the east in a semicircle. In larger churches, there is a nave and two side aisles, the latter being divided from the former by ranks of columns; but no transepts appear till towards the latter part of the period. " Whether," observes Mr. Millers, in his account of Ely Cathedral, whose system we adopt, " their churches were ever higher than one tier of arches and a range of windows above (as at Ely), may be questioned. Richard, prior of Hexham, speaks of three stories, which implies another tier of arches; but if he is rightly so understood, this seems an exception from a general rule, for the church at Hexham is spoken of by all writers who mention it, as the glory of Saxon churches in the seventh century. Afterwards, about 970, a considerable change took place ; transepts came into general use, with a square tower at the intersection, rising but little above the roof, and chiefly used as a lantern to give light to that part of the church. Towers were also erected at the west end : the use of them coincides with the introduction of bells, at least of large and heavy ones." The churches of this period were of small dimensions, and the comparative sizes of the Saxon and the Norman churches which followed is almost a criterion of their age.

391. King (*Munimenta Antiqua*, vol. iv. p. 240.) gives three æras of the Saxon style. 1. From Egbert, 598 to 872. 2. From Alfred to Canute and Harold, 1036. 3. To the Norman conquest. He selects no less than thirty-seven examples of Saxon ornaments from mouldings on doorways only. As examples of the periods he adduces, of the *first*, *Barfreston* in Kent; of the *second*, the nave and choir of *Christ Church Cathedral*, Oxford, and Canute's great entrance gate at *St. Edmundsbury*; of the *third*, *Southwell*, Notts, and *Waltham Abbey*, Essex. It has been questioned by antiquaries whether any Saxon remains actually exist in the country; but, admitting their arguments, which are founded on references to records — no mean authorities, — it must be recollected that, on their own showing, some of these trench so close upon the period of the Conquest as to show that the Saxon style might have prevailed in them, for the general change of style in any art is not effected in a day. If we look for examples coeval with the Saxons themselves, and without controversy to be attributed to them, they will, perhaps, be found only in crypts and baptismal fonts ; for many churches were rebuilt by the Normans, who left these parts untouched. The castles of Roman or Saxon foundation were, Richborough, in Kent; Castletown, in Derbyshire; Porchester, in Hampshire; Pevensey, in Sussex; Castor, in Norfolk; Burgh, in Suffolk; Chesterford, in Essex; Corfe, Dorset; Exeter Castle gateway; Dover, in Kent; and Beeston, in Cheshire. For this and the following sections it will be well to refer to the subject *Proportion in Architecture* in Book III.

Sect. II.

NORMAN ARCHITECTURE.

392. From the landing of William in 1066, architecture received an impulse, indicated in various styles, which lasted till the time of the Tudors; when, as we shall hereafter see, it gave way to one altogether different. That called the Norman style, which continued from 1066 to nearly 1200, comprised the reigns of William I., William II., Henry I., Stephen, Henry II., and Richard I. The twelfth century exhibited a rage for building in Britain more violent than has been since seen. The vast and general improvements that were introduced into fabrics and churches in the first years of this century are thus described by a contemporary writer (*Orderic. Vital. Hist. Eccles.*, lib. x. p. 788.) : — " The cathedrals, and abundance of churches, newly built in all parts of the country, the great number of splendid cloisters and monasteries, and other residences for monks, that were there raised, sufficiently prove the happiness of England under the reign of Henry I. Peace and prosperity were enjoyed by the religious of all orders, who lent their whole power to increase the magnificence and splendour of divine worship. The ardent zeal of the faithful prompted them to rebuild their houses, and especially their churches, in a more suitable manner. Thus the ancient edifices raised in the days of Edgar, Edward, and other Christian kings, were taken down, and others of greater magnitude, beauty, and more elegant workmanship, were reared in their stead to the glory of God." As an example of the fervour with which these objects were carried into effect, we cite the following instance, quoting from Dr. Henry, upon whom we have drawn, and shall draw, rather largely. " When Joffred, abbot of Croyland, resolved to rebuild the church of his monastery in a most magnificent manner (A.D. 1106), he obtained from the archbishops of Canterbury and York a bull dispensing with the third part of all penances for sin to those who contributed any thing towards the building of that church. This bull was directed not only to the king and people of England, but to the kings of France and Scotland, and to all other kings, earls, barons, archbishops, bishops, abbots, priors, rectors, presbyters, and clerks, and to all true believers in Christ, rich and poor, in all Christian kingdoms. To make the best use of

this bull, he sent two of his most eloquent monks to proclaim it over all France and Flanders; two other monks into Scotland; two into Denmark and Norway; two into Wales, Cornwall, and Ireland; and others into different parts of England. By this means (says the historian) the wonderful benefits granted to the contributors to the building of this church were published to the very ends of the earth; and great heaps of treasure, and masses of yellow metal, flowed in from all countries upon the venerable abbot Joffred, and encouraged him to lay the foundations of his church. Having spent about four years in collecting mountains of different kinds of marble from quarries, both at home and abroad, together with great quantities of lime, iron, brass, and other materials for building, he fixed a day for the great ceremony of laying the foundation, which he contrived to make a very effectual mean of raising the superstructure; for on the long-expected day, the feast of the holy virgins Felicitas and Perpetua, an immense multitude of earls, barons, and knights, with their ladies and families, of abbots, priors, monks, nuns, clerks, and persons of all ranks, arrived at Croyland to assist at this ceremony. The pious abbot Joffred began by saying certain prayers, and shedding a flood of tears on the foundation. Then each of the earls, barons, knights, with their ladies, sons, and daughters, the abbots, clerks, and others, laid a stone, and upon it deposited a sum of money, a grant of lands, tithes, or patronages, or a promise of stone, lime, wood, labour, or carriages for building the church. After this the abbot entertained the whole company, amounting to five thousand persons, to dinner. To this entertainment they were well entitled; for the money and grants of different kinds which they had deposited on the foundation stones were alone sufficient to have raised a very noble fabric." This spirit extended throughout the island; for, in Scotland, David I. raised thirteen abbeys and priories, some of them on a scale of considerable magnificence, besides several cathedrals and other churches.

393. The common people of the country, and the burgesses in the towns, were not much better lodged than in the previous age; their condition, indeed, was not improved. In London, towards the end of the twelfth century, the houses were still built of timber, and covered with reeds or straw. The palaces, however, or rather castles, of the Anglo-Norman kings, nobility, and prelates, were on a very superior construction. William of Malmesbury says that the Anglo-Saxon nobility squandered their ample means in low and mean dwellings; but that the French and Norman barons lived at less expense, though dwelling in large and magnificent palaces. The fact is, that among these latter the rage for erecting fortified castles was quite as great as that of erecting ecclesiastical buildings among the prelates. The system became necessary, and was induced as well by the previous habits of the country they had left, as by their situation in the island. Surrounded by vassals whom they held in subjection, and whom they depressed and plundered in every way, they were so detested by them that deep fosses and lofty walls were necessary for their security. The Conqueror himself, aware that the want of fortified places had no less assisted his conquest than it might his expulsion, resolved to guard against such a contingency by the strong castles which he placed within the royal demesnes. Matthew Paris observes that William excelled all his predecessors in the erection of castles, in executing which he harassed his subjects and vassals. So much was the practice a matter of course, that the moment one of the nobility had the grant of an estate from the crown, a castle was built upon it for his defence and residence; and this spirit was not likely to be diminished by the disputes relative to the succession in the following reigns. William Rufus, according to the statement of Henry Knighton, was as much addicted to the erection of royal castles and palaces as his father, as the castles of Dover, Windsor, Norwich, and others sufficiently prove; and it is certain that no monarch before him erected so many and noble edifices. Henry I. followed in his taste; but in the reign of Stephen, 1135 to 1154, says the author of the *Saxon Chronicle*, every one who had the ability built a castle, and the whole kingdom was covered with them, no fewer than 1115 having been raised from their foundations in the short space of nineteen years; so that the expression is by no means stronger than is justified by the fact.

394. It will be proper here to give the reader some concise general description of these structures, which served for residence and defence. The situation chosen for a castle was usually on an eminence near a river. Its figure on the plan was often of great extent, and irregular in form; and it was surrounded by a deep and broad ditch, called the *fosse*, which could be filled with water. An outwork, called a *barbican*, which was a strong and lofty wall, with turrets upon it, and designed for the defence of the great gate and drawbridge, was placed before the latter. Within the ditch, towards the main building, was placed its wall, about 8 or 10 ft. thick, and from 20 to 30 ft. high, with a parapet and embrasures, called *crennels*, on the top. At proper intervals above the wall square towers were raised, two or three stories in height, wherein were lodged some of the principal officers of the proprietor of the castle, besides their service for other purposes; and, on the inside, were apartments for the common servants or retainers, granaries, storehouses, and other necessary offices. On the top of the wall, and on the flat roofs of the towers, the defenders were placed in the event of a siege; and thence they discharged arrows, darts,

and stones on their assailants.   The great gate was placed in some part of the wall flanked with a tower on each side, with rooms over the entrance, which was closed with massive oak folding doors, frequently plated with iron, and an iron grate, or *portcullis*. which. by machinery, was lowered from above.   Within this exterior wall, or ballium, was, in the more extensive castles, the outer *ballium*, which was a large open space or court, wherein a church or chapel was usually placed.   Within the outer ballium was another ditch, with wall, gate, and towers, inclosing the inner ballium or court, in which was erected the large tower, or *keep*.   It was a large fabric, some four or five stories high, whose enormously thick walls were pierced with very small apertures, serving barely as windows to the gloomy apartments upon which they opened.   This great tower was the dwelling of the owner of the castle ; and in it was also lodged the constable, or governor.   It was provided with underground dismal apartments for the confinement of prisoners, whence the whole building received the appellation of *dungeon*.   In the keep was also the great hall, in which the friends and retainers of the owner were entertained.   At one end of the great halls of castles, palaces, and monasteries, a low platform was raised a little above the rest of the floor, called the *dais*, on which stood the principal table whereat persons of higher rank were placed.   The varieties which occurred in the arrangement and distribution of castles were, of course, many, as circumstances varied ; but the most magnificent were erected nearly on the plan we have just described, as may be gathered as well from their ruins as from an account by Matthew Paris of the taking of Bedford Castle by Henry III., A.D. 1224.   This castle, we learn from him, was taken by four assaults.   In the first was taken the barbican ; in the second, the outer ballium ; in the third attack, the miners threw down the wall by the old tower, where, through a chink, at great risk, they possessed themselves of the inner ballium ; on the fourth assault, the miners fired the tower, which thereby became so injured and split that the enemy thereon surrendered.   The keeps of which we have spoken are such extraordinary edifices, that we think it right to place before the reader, from the *Discourses upon Architecture* of our late much esteemed and learned friend, the Rev. James Dallaway, the following table of some of the principal ones of the Norman æra.

Internal Square, or Oblong.					
Names.	Length.	Breadth.	Height.	Division of Rooms.	Dates and Founders.
Tower of London -	116 ft.	96 ft.	— ft.	By semicircular arches.	William the Conqueror.
Porchester - -	115	65	—	Four floors.	
Canterbury - -	88	80	50	Two walls continued from the base to the top.	
Rochester - -	75	72	104	By semicircular arches.	Gundulph (Bishop).
Dover - - -	—	—	92		
Colchester - -	140	102	—	Three large rooms on each floor.	
Norwich - -	110	92	70	- - - - -	Roger Bigod.
Ludlow - -	—	—	110	Four stories.	Roger de Laci.
Hedingham - -	62	55	100	Three tiers above basement.	
Guildford - -	42	47	—		
Oxford - -	-	-	-	- - - - -	Robert D'Oiley.
Bamborough - -	-	-	-	- - - - -	1070.
Richmond - -	-	-	-	Vault supported by a single octangular pillar.	1100.
Newcastle upon Tyne	82	62	54	By internal arches and door cases in Norman style.	1080. Robert Curthoise.
Corfe - -	72	60	80		
Round, or Polygonal.					
Arundel - -	69	57	—	Roof open in the centre, straight buttresses.	1070. Roger Montgomeri.
Conisburgh - -	23 diameter.			Three floors, two of them state apartments.	1070. W. de Warren.
York - - -	64	45	-	Four segments of circles	1068. William the Conqueror.
Tunbridge - -	64	50	—		
Berkeley - -	-	-	-	Circular, flanked by four small towers.	1120. Rob. Fitzharding.
Lincoln - -	-	-	—	- - - - -	1086. William the Conqueror.
Oxford - -	-	-	-	Polygon, flanked by three square towers.	
Windsor - -	90	85	—	- - - - -	Rebuilt by Edw. III.
Durham - -	63	61	—	- - - - -	Heightened in 1830.

395.   Gundulph is said to have introduced the architectural ornaments of the Norman style into the interior as well as on the exterior of castles.   The use of battlements, loop-

holes, and open galleries, or machicolations, was certainly, as our author above quoted remarks, known to the Romans.

——— Troes contra, defendere saxis
Perque cavas densi tela intorquere fenestras.   *Æn.* l. ix. 533.

The architects and artificers by whom the Norman works were planned and executed were men of great science and skill, and the names of several have most deservedly obtained a place in history. Gervase of Canterbury records that William of Sens, the architect of Archbishop Lanfranc in building his cathedral, was an artist of great talents; and that he not only made a complete model of the cathedral upon which he was employed, but of all the details of sculpture necessary for its execution, besides inventing machines for loading and unloading the vessels, and conveying the heavy materials, many whereof were brought from Normandy. Of Walter of Coventry, another architect of the age, Matthew Paris speaks in the highest terms, saying that "so excellent an architect had never yet appeared, and probably never would appear in the world." Dr. Henry on this very properly observes, "That this encomium was undoubtedly too high; but it is impossible to view the remains of many magnificent fabrics, both sacred and civil, that were erected in this period, without admiring the genius of the architects by whom they were planned, and the dexterity of the workmen by whom they were executed."

396. Of the twenty-two English cathedrals, fifteen retain parts of Norman erection, whose dates are pretty well ascertained; and by them the Norman manner was progressively brought to perfection in England. We subjoin the following enumeration of Norman bishops, who were either patrons of the art, or practising it themselves.

A. D.	Bishop.	Works.
1059 to 1089	Aldred, Bishop of Worcester.	St. Peter's, Gloucester.
1077 to 1107	Gundulph, of Rochester.	Rochester, Canterbury, and Peterborough.
1086 to 1108	Maurice, of London.	Old St. Paul's Cathedral.
1093 to 1133.	William de Carilepho.	Cathedral of Durham, but completed by Ranulph Flambard.
1080 to 1100	Lanfranc, of Canterbury.	
1107 to 1140	Roger, of Salisbury.	Cathedral at Old Sarum.
1115 to 1125	Ernulf, of Rochester.	Completed Gundulf's works at Rochester.
1123 to 1147	Alexander, of Lincoln.	Rebuilt his cathedral.
1129 to 1169	Henry of Blois, Bishop of Winchester.	Conventual churches of St. Cross and Rumsey, in Hampshire.
1158 to 1181	Roger, Archbishop of York.	

Of Norman architecture the principal characteristics are subjoined in the following subsection.

397. *Arches.*—Generally semicircular, as in the nave of Gloucester, here given (*fig.* 185.).

Of larger opening than the Saxon, and their ornaments less minute; often bounded by a single moulding, though sometimes by more than one; occasionally without any moulding at all; the soffitt always plain. In the second story, two smaller equal arches under one larger, with a column of moderate size, or even comparatively slender, between them. In the third story (see *fig.* 186.), generally three together, the centre one higher and broader than the others, and opened for a window; but the whole three only occupy a space equal to that

Fig. 185.   ARCH FROM NAVE OF GLOUCESTER.

of the lower arch. *Arches of entrance* are profusely decorated (*fig.* 187., from Ely) with mouldings, foliage, wreaths, masks, figures of men and animals in relief, and all the fancies of the wildest imagination, in which every thing that is extravagant, grotesque, ludicrous, nay, even grossly indecent, is to be found. Before the end of the period — and we may almost say early in it — it exhibits examples of *pointed arches.* They are, however, sparingly introduced : one or more tiers appear in the upper stories of a building, whilst all the lower ones are circular. Sometimes they are intro-

Fig. 186.   THREE STORIES OF A NORMAN CATHEDRAL.

duced alternately, sometimes we find one capriciously inserted between several round ones;
these are, for the most part. obtusely pointed, though occasionally they are the reverse.
They are always wide, stand on
heavy columns, or are decorated
with mouldings, or both. The
approaches to the pointed style
were not strongly marked, but
they were indicated; for the
pointed style cannot be pronounced to have commenced
until the sharp-pointed arch
sprung from a slender column
graced with a capital of carved
foliage, and this it is not safe
to place earlier than the reign
of John. The arch which rises
more than a semicircle does
not very often occur; but it
must be mentioned as exhibiting one of the varieties of the
period. *Columns.* — These are
of very large diameter relative
to their heights and intervals.
Their shafts are circular, hexagonal, and sometimes octagonal, on the plan; fluted, lo-
zenged, reticulated, and otherwise sculptured. Sometimes
they are square on the plan,
and then accompanied by portions of columns or pilasters
applied to them. Sometimes
four columns are connected
together, with or without angular pieces. They are much
higher in proportion to their
diameters than the Saxon columns heretofore described ;
and though their capitals are
not unfrequently quite plain,
they are more commonly decorated with a species of volute,

Fig. 187.   PRIOR'S ENTRANCE AT ELY.

or with plants, flowers, leaves, shells, animals, &c. The bases stand on a strong plinth,
adapted on its plan to receive the combined and varied forms of the columns. *Windows,* are
still narrow, and semicircular-headed ; but they are higher, and often in groups of two or three
together. *Ceilings,* usually, if not always, of timber, except in crypts, in which they are
vaulted with stone, with groins mostly plain, yet sometimes ornamented on the edge, but universally without tracery. The White Tower of London, however, exhibits an example of a
centre aisle covered with vaulting. Our belief is, and in it we are corroborated by the Rev.
Mr. Dallaway, whose judgment we hold in no small esteem, that there is no instance of a
genuine Anglo-Norman building which was intended to be covered with a stone roof or
ceiling. This is not only indicated by the detail, but by the circumstance of the walls
being insufficient (thick as they are) in solidity to resist the thrust. Peterborough, Ely,
St. Peter's, Northampton, Steyning, Romsey, &c. are calculated and constructed to receive
wooden roofs only. *Walls,* are of extraordinary thickness, with but few buttresses, and
those of small projection ; flat, broad, and usually without ornament. *Ornaments.*—Among
these must be first named the ranges of arches and pilasters which had nothing to support,
already incidentally mentioned, and which were intended to fill up void spaces, internally
as well as externally, for the purpose of breaking up large masses of surface; they are
very common on the inside of north and south walls. sometimes intersecting each other so
as to produce those compartments that are alleged to have given rise to the pointed arch.
The mouldings of the Saxon period continued much in use, and we ought, perhaps, to
have given some of them, as belonging to the preceding section ; and, indeed, should have
so done, if, in the Norman style, they had not increased in number and variety, and had
not also been employed in profusion about the ornamental arches just named, especially in
conspicuous places on the outside, as in the west front especially. The most usual ornaments (*fig.* 188.) were, 1. The *chevron,* or *zigzag* moulding; 2. The *embattled frette;*

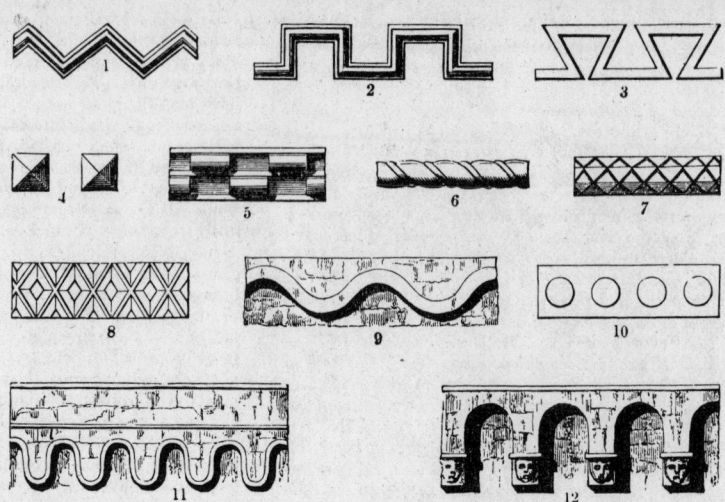

Fig. 188.   NORMAN ORNAMENTS.

3. The *triangular frette*; 4. The *nail head*; 5. The *billet*; 6. The *cable*; 7. The *hatched*; 8. The *lozenge*; 9. The *wavy*; 10. The *pellet* moulding; 11. The *nebule*. The *torus* was used, as was also the *cavetto*, which were both of Grecian extraction. The chief of these ornaments, perhaps all, were used in the Saxon age, besides others which were occasionally employed, and which to designate by name would be difficult; such, for instance, as the *corbel-table* (12), which consists of small ranges of arches, resting on consoles sometimes decorated with carved heads, often introduced along the whole building immediately below the eaves or battlement. Sometimes carved heads are observed in the spandrels of arches, and are also used as capitals of the ornamental pilasters, or as corbels, to support what is called the canopy, or exterior semicircle of moulding on arches of entrance, or above the keystones of those arches. There are instances of whole figures over doors in mezzo-rilievo, which Millers observes was the nearest approach the Normans seem to have made to a statue.   *Plans.* — The churches of this period are always with transepts, and a tower at the intersection, loftier than heretofore, but without spires over them. There are rising from them stories of arches, one above the other; and the eastern ends are semicircular. Though much of the Saxon style is retained, there is, from the larger dimensions of the edifices of this period, a much more impressive air of magnificence than had before appeared. Millers very truly says, that the churches were "in all dimensions much ampler, with a general air of cumbrous massive grandeur. The Normans were fond of stateliness and magnificence; and though they retained the other characteristics of the Saxon style, by this amplification of dimensions they made such a striking change as might justly be entitled to the denomination which it received at its first introduction among our Saxon ancestors, of *a new style of architecture.*" The criterion between the Saxon and Norman styles, of enlarged dimensions, is too vague to guide the reader in a determination of the age of buildings of this period; for it is only in large edifices, such as cathedral and conventual churches, with their transepts, naves, side aisles, and arches in tier above tier, that this can be perceptible. There are many parish churches of this age, whose simplicity of form and small dimensions have been mistaken for Saxon buildings; and which, from not possessing any of the grander Norman features, have been assigned to an earlier age. The distinction ascertainable from heights of columns, — namely, taking the height of the Norman column at from four to six diameters, and that of the Saxon at only two, — will, we fear, be insufficient to decide the question in cases of doubt; but it must be admitted this is one of the means which, in some measure, would lead us to an approximate judgment of the matter, and a careful observation and comparison of specimens would make it more definite. We shall here merely add, that the first Norman architects, by the lengthened vista of the nave, uninterrupted by any choir screen, produced a sublime and imposing effect by the simple grandeur and amplitude of dimensions in their churches.

398. *Examples.*—Examples of Norman architecture in English *cathedral churches* are to be found at *Ely*, in the western towers and nave; at *Bristol*, in the elder Lady Chapel, and Chapter House; at *Canterbury* in the choir, and the round part called Becket's Crown; at *Norwich*.

in the nave and choir ; at *Hereford*, in the transept tower and choir ; at *Wells*, in the nave and choir ; at *Chester*, in the Chapter House ; at *Chichester*, in the presbytery ; at *Peterborough*, in the transept.   In the *conventual churches*, for examples we may refer the reader to *Llantony*, near Monmouth ; the nave and west front of *Fountains*, Yorkshire ; the nave and chapel of *St. Joseph*, at Glastonbury ; the west front at *Selby*, in Yorkshire ; many parts at *St. Alban's;* the choir at *Wenlock*, in Shropshire ; *Cartmell*, in Lancashire ; *Furness ;* West End, at *Byland*, with the wheel window, and the south transept ; parts of *Bolton*, in Yorkshire ; part of *Brinkbourn*, in Northumberland ; part of *Edmondsbury*, in Suffolk ; and *St. John's Church*, at Chester.   For examples of parochial churches, *Melton*, Suffolk ; *Sotterton* and *Sleaford*, Lincolnshire ; *Christchurch*, Hampshire ; *Sherbourn Minster*, Dorset ; *Winchelsea*, *Steyning*, and *New Shoreham*, Sussex ; chancel of *St. Peter's*, Oxford ; *Earl's Barton Tower*, Northamptonshire ; *West Walton Tower*, Norfolk ; *Iffley*, Oxfordshire ; *Castle Rising*, Norfolk ; *St. Margaret's Porch*, at York ; *St. Peter's Church*, Northampton ; besides several round or polygonal bell-towers, both in Suffolk and Norfolk, — may be referred to.   Examples of *military Norman architecture*, from 1070 to 1270, were at *Launceston*, Cornwall ; *Arundel*, Sussex ; *Windsor*, in Berks (rebuilt) ; *Tower of London ;* the square keeps of *Hedingham*, Essex ; *Caerphilly*, Glamorgan ; *Carisbrook*, Isle of Wight ; *Porchester*, Hants (1160) ; *Guildford*, Surrey ; *Bamborough*, Northumberland ; *Kenilworth*, Warwickshire ; *Richmond*, Yorkshire ; *Cardiff*, Glamorganshire ; *Canterbury*, Kent ; *Oxford* (1071) ; *Newcastle*, Northumberland (1120) ; *Gisborough*, Yorkshire (1120) ; *Castle Rising*, Norfolk ; *Middleham*, Yorkshire ; *Cockermouth*, Cumberland ; *Durham* (1153) ; *Lincoln* (1086) ; *Berkeley*, Gloucestershire (1153) ; *Lancaster; Orford*, Suffolk, polygonal (1120) ; *Ludlow*, Salop (1120) ; *Kenilworth*, enlarged (1220) ; *Warkworth*, Northumberland, square, with the angles cut off; *Denbigh ; Beeston*, Cheshire ; *Hawarden*, Pembrokeshire.

Sect. III.

EARLY ENGLISH ARCHITECTURE.

399. The next period of architecture in Britain which comes under our consideration, following, as we consider it, the sensible classification of the Rev. Mr. Millers, is that which he has denominated the *early English style*, whose duration was from about 1200 to 1300 ; extending, therefore, through the reigns of John, Henry III., and Edward I., during which the building of churches and monasteries was still considered one of the most effectual means of obtaining the pardon of sin, and consequently the favour of Heaven.   In the thirteenth and fourteenth centuries, the churches built in Britain were almost innumerable.

400. We have already noticed (chap. ii. sect. xv.) the introduction of the pointed arch into architecture ; a feature which completely changed, from all that previously existed, the character of the edifices to which it was applied. If any service could be rendered to the history of the art, or if the solution of the problem, " who were its inventors ?" could throw any useful light on the manners and customs of the people that first adopted it, we should be the last to relinquish the investigation. The question has furnished employment to many literary idlers, but the labour they have bestowed on the subject has not thrown any light on it ; and excepting the late Mr. Whittington and the present Mr. Willis, of Cambridge, on whose valuable enquiries we cannot sufficiently enlarge, they might have been more usefully engaged. This statement must necessarily be modified in consequence of the publications of the learned labours of Mr. Fergusson, of which we have so largely availed ourselves in the above-named section ; besides those of Thomas Rickman, of Mr. Sharpe, and of other ardent enquirers on this and kindred subjects.

401. During the reign of Henry III. alone, no less a number than 157 abbeys, priories, and other religious houses were founded in England. Several of our cathedrals and conventual churches in a great part belong to this period, in which the lancet or sharp-pointed arch first appeared in the buildings of this country, though on the Continent it was used nearly a century earlier. The great wealth of the clergy, added to the zeal of the laity, furnished ample funds for the erection of the magnificent structures projected ; but it was with extreme difficulty that workmen could be procured to execute them. With the popes it was, of course, an object that churches should be erected and convents endowed. On the subject of the employment of Freemasons we have already expressed our views (*par.* 308, *et seq.*), therefore we cannot coincide with Wren, *Parentalia*, in stating that they ranged from one nation to another, their government was regular, and they made a camp of huts ; a surveyor governed in chief ; every tenth man was called a warden, and overlooked each nine. " Those who have seen the account in records of the charge of the fabrics of some of our cathedrals, near 400 years old, cannot but have a great esteem for their economy, and admire how soon they erected such lofty structures."   It was in the

course of this period that sculpture was first made extensively available for architectural decoration. The cathedral, conventual, and other churches built in Britain, began to be ornamented on the outside with statues of various dimensions in basso and alto rilievo. They were not equal in execution to those of France, which have also had the additional good fortune to have been better preserved, from their exposure to seasons less inclement, and to an atmosphere unimpregnated with the smoke of coal.

402. Great improvements seem to have taken place in the castles of the time ; they still continued to serve for the dwelling and defence of the prelates and barons of the country. The plans of them were generally similar to those already described ; but it must still be conceded that the inhabitants and owners of them sacrificed their convenience to their security, which seems to have been the chief concern in the construction of their castles, whose apartments were gloomy, whose bed-chambers were few and small, whose passages were narrow and intricate, and their stairs steep and dark. The plan, however, as Mr. Dallaway observes, " which allowed of enlarged dimensions, and greater regularity and beauty in the architecture of the towers, owes its introduction into England to King Edward I. We may, indeed, consider his reign as the epoch of the grand style of accommodation and magnificence combined in castle architecture. When engaged in the Crusades, he surveyed with satisfaction the superior form and strength of the castles in the Levant and in the Holy Land." Of the five castles erected by him in Wales, Caernarvon (*fig.* 189.), Conway (*fig.* 190., showing the suspension bridge, and the railway bridge beyond it), Harlech, and Beaumaris still retain traces of their ancient magnificence; but that of Aberystwith has scarcely a feature left. Caernarvon Castle consisted of two distinct parts : one military, and suited to the reception of a garrison; the other palatial. The ground plan was oblong, unequally divided into a lower and an upper ward. Of the towers, which are all polygonal, the largest, from some tradition called the Eagle Tower, has three small angular turrets rising from it ; the others having but one of the same description. " The enclosing walls," continues Mr. Dallaway, " are seven feet thick, with *alures* and parapets pierced frequently with *œillet* holes. A great singularity is observable in the extreme height both of the great entrance gate and that which is called the Queen's. Leland observes of the portcullises at Pembroke, that they were composed *ex solido ferro.* In confirmation of the opinion that the royal founder adopted the form of such gates of entrance from the East, similar ones are almost universal in the castles, mosques, and palaces of the Saracens, which he had so frequently seen during the Crusades. The tower of entrance from the town of Caernarvon is still perfect, and is the most handsome structure of that age in the kingdom. It is at least 100 ft. high ; and the gateway, of very remarkable depth, is formed by a succession of ribbed arches, sharply pointed. The grooves for three portcullises may be discovered : and above them are circular perforations, through which missile weapons and molten lead might be discharged upon the assailants. In the lower or palatial division of the castle stand a large polygonal tower of four stories, which was appropriated to Queen Eleanor, and in which her ill-fated son was born, and another which was occupied by the king, of a circular shape externally, but square towards the court. The apartments in the last mentioned are larger, and lighted by windows with square heads, and intersected with carved mullions. There is a singular contrivance in the battlements, each of which had an excavation for the archers to stand in, pointing their arrows through the slits ; and, a curious stratagem, the carved figures of soldiers with helmets, apparently looking over the parapet. This device is repeated at Chepstow." The ornamental character of the architecture at Caernarvon and Conway is rather ecclesiastical, or conventual, than military. At Conway, as has been well observed by an anonymous author, " what is

Fig. 189.　　　CAERNARVON CASTLE.

Fig. 190.　　　CONWAY CASTLE.

called the Queen's Oriel is remarkable for the fancy, luxuriance, and elegance of the workmanship.   Nor is the contrivance of the little terraced garden below, considering the

Fig. 191.   CAER-PHILLY CASTLE.

history of the times, a matter of small curiosity, where, though all the surrounding country were hostile, fresh air might be safely enjoyed ; and the commanding view of the singularly beautiful landscape around, from both that little herbary or garden, and the bay window or oriel, is so managed as to leave no doubt of its purpose."

403. The model of Conway Castle has little resemblance to that we have just left.   It resembles rather the fortresses of the last Greek emperors, or of the chieftains of the north of Italy.   The towers are mostly circular, as are their turrets, with a single slender one rising from each ; and machicolations, not seen at Caernarvon, are introduced.   The greater part of the castles of Wales and Scotland for the defence of the

Fig. 192.   TREFOIL AND CINQUEFOIL HEADS.

marches were built in the reign of Edward I.   On the subjugation of the former country, and its partition into lordships among Edward's followers, many castles were reared upon the general plan of those he had erected, though varying in dimensions and situation, according to the means of defence proposed to be secured to their founders and possessors. We may here observe, that in the castle at Conway Edward I. erected a hall 129 ft. by 31, and 22 ft. high, which is formed to suit the curvature of the rock ; and that from that period no residence of consequence, either for the nobility or feudal lords,

Fig. 194.   PLAN OF COLUMN.

was erected without one, varying, however, of course, in their minuter parts, according to circumstances, and in degree of magnificence.

404. Caer-Philly Castle, in Glamorganshire (*fig.* 191.), was another

Fig. 193.   COLUMNS OF WESTMINSTER ABBEY.

of the castles of this period.   It was the strong-hold of the De Spencers in the reign of the second Edward.   Its vallations and remains are very extensive.   The hall was much larger than that at Conway.

405. The characteristics of this style are, that the *arches* are sharply (lancet) pointed, and lofty in proportion to their span.   In the upper tiers two or more are comprehended under one, finished in *trefoil* or cinquefoil heads (*fig.* 192.) instead of points, the separating columns being very slender.   *Columns* on which the arches rest (*fig.* 193.) are very slender in proportion to their height, and usually consist of a central shaft surrounded by several smaller ones (*fig.* 194.).   The base takes the general form of the cluster, and the capital (*fig.* 195.) is frequently decorated with foliage very elegantly composed.   The *windows* are long, narrow, and lancet shaped, whence some writers have called this style the *Lancet* Gothic.   They are divided by one plain mullion

Fig. 195.   CAPITAL OF COLUMN.

or in upper tiers by two at most, finished at the top with some simple ornament, as a lozenge or a trefoil.   They have commonly small marble shafts on each side, both internally and externally; two, three, or more together at the east or west end, and tier above tier.   *Roofs* are high pitched and the ceilings vaulted, exhibiting the first examples of arches with cross springers only, which in a short period diverged into many more, rising from the capitals of the columns, and almost overspreading the whole surface of the vaulting.   The longitudinal horizontal line which reigned along the apex of the vault was decorated with bosses of flowers, figures, and other fancies.   *Walls* much reduced in thickness from those of the preceding period: they are, however, externally strengthened with buttresses, which, as it were, lean against them for the purpose of counteracting the thrust exerted by the stone vaults which form the ceilings, and which the walls and piers by their own gravity could not resist.   The buttresses are moreover aided in their office by the pinnacles, adorned with crockets at their angles, and crowned with finial flowers, by which they are surmounted.   *The ornaments* now become numerous, but they are simple and elegant.   The mouldings are not so much varied as in the Norman style, and are generally, perhaps universally, formed of some combination of leaves and flowers, used not only in the circumference of arches, especially of windows, but the columns or pilasters are completely laid down with them.   Trefoils, quatrefoils, cinquefoils, roses, mullets, bosses, pateræ, &c. in the spandrils, or above the keystones of the arches and elsewhere.   The ornamental pinnacles on shrines, tombs, &c. are extremely high and acute, sometimes with and sometimes without niches under them.   In east and west fronts the niches are filled with statues of the size of life and larger, and are crowned with trefoil, &c. heads, or extremely acute pediments, formed by the meeting of two straight lines instead of arcs.   All these ornaments are more sparingly introduced into large entire edifices than in smaller buildings or added parts.   *The plans* are generally similar to those of the second period ; but that important feature the tower now begins to rise to a great height, and lanterns and lofty spires are frequent accompaniments to the structure.   It will naturally occur to the reader, that in the transition from the second to the third style, the architects left one extreme for another, though it has been contended that the latter has its germ in the former.   However that may be, the period of which we are now speaking was undoubtedly the parent of the succeeding styles, and that by no very forced or unnatural relationship.

406. The principal examples of the early English style in the cathedral churches of England are to be seen at *Oxford*, in the chapter-house.   *Lincoln*, in the nave and arches beyond the transept.   *York*, in the north and south transept.   At *Durham*, in the additional transept.   *Wells*, the tower and the whole western front.   *Carlisle*, the choir.   *Ely*, the presbytery.   *Worcester*, the transept and choir.   *Salisbury*, the whole cathedral ; the only unmixed example.   At *Rochester*, the choir and transept.   " It is well worthy of observation," says Mr. Dallaway, " that though the ground plans of sacred edifices are, generally speaking, similar and systematic, yet in no single instance which occurs to my memory do we find an exact and unvaried copy of any building which preceded it in any part of the structure.   A striking analogy or resemblance may occur, but that rarely."

407. The examples of conventual architecture of this period, to which we beg to refer the reader, are those of *Lanercost*, in Cumberland ; *Rivaulx*, Yorkshire ; *Westminster Abbey*. At *Fountains*, the choir and east end ; *Tinterne Abbey*, in Monmouthshire ; *Netley*, Hampshire ; *Whitby*, in Yorkshire ; *Valle Crucis*, in Denbighshire ; *Ripon Minster* and the south transept of *Beverley Minster*, in Yorkshire ; *Milton Abbey*, Dorsetshire ; *part of the nave of St. Alban's ; Tinemouth* and *Brinkbourn*, Northumberland ; *Vale Royal*, in Cheshire ; and the eastern façade of *Howden*, in Yorkshire.

408. Among the examples of parochial churches in this style are *Grantham*, in Lincolnshire, whose tower is 180 ft. high ; *Attelborough*, in Norfolk ; *Higham Ferrars*, in Northamptonshire ; *St. Michael, Coventry ; Truro*, in Cornwall ; *Witney*, in Oxfordshire; *Stratford upon Avon*, in Warwickshire ; *St. Peter Mancroft*, Norwich ; *Boston*, Lincolnshire, remarkable for its lantern tower rising 262 ft. from the ground, and perhaps almost belonging to the succeeding period ; *St. Mary, Edmund's Bury*, Suffolk ; *Maidstone*, in Kent ; and *Ludlow*, in Shropshire.

Sect. IV.

ORNAMENTED ENGLISH ARCHITECTURE.

409. The fourth period in the architecture of Britain is that which Mr. Millers calls the *Ornamented English Style*, which begins about 1300 and lasts till 1460, and comprises, therefore, the latter portion of the reign of Edward I., and the reigns of Edward II., Edward III., Richard II., Henry IV., Henry V., and Henry VI.

410. This æra has by Dallaway and others been subdivided into two parts, viz. first

from 1300 to 1400, which they call that of the Transition Style or pure Gothic, and from 1400 to 1460, called the Decorated Gothic; but the change between the latest examples of the first and the earliest of the last is marked by such nice and almost imperceptible distinctions, that it is next to impossible to mark their boundaries with precision; and we have therefore preferred adhering, as we have in the other ages of the art, to the arrangement adopted by Mr. Millers. In the early part of the period the change, or rather progress, was extremely slow, and marked by little variation, and, indeed, until 1400, the style can scarcely be said to have been perfected; but after that time, it rapidly attained all the improvement whereof it was susceptible, and so proceeded till about 1460; after which, as we shall hereafter see, it assumed an exuberance of ornament, beyond which as it was impossible to advance, it was in a predicament from which no change could be effected but by its total abandonment.

411. Notwithstanding the wars of the rival houses of York and Lancaster, which occupied a considerable portion of the interval whereof we are speaking, and deluged, as the reader will recollect, our land with the blood of the bravest of men, the art did not appear to suffer; a circumstance apparently extraordinary, but satisfactorily accounted for by the zeal of both the contending parties for the religion they in common professed. True it is that the taste for founding and building monasteries and churches was not so universal as in the period last described; the decline, however, of that taste might in some measure have arisen not only from the unhappy state of the country just alluded to, but also from the doubts raised in the minds of many persons of all ranks by Wickliffe and his followers as to the merit attached to those pious and expensive works. " It cannot," says Henry, " be denied that the style of sacred architecture commonly called Gothic continued to be greatly improved, and in the course of this period was brought to the highest perfection." To account in some measure for this, it must be recollected that during the civil wars the superior ecclesiastics were confined to their cloisters, as few of them had taken an active part in the dispute which agitated the realm; and, indeed, some of the finest structures now remaining were reared from the accumulation of wealth amassed by instigating the noble and affluent to contribute to churches built under their own inspection. The choir at Gloucester, a most beautiful example, was completed during these turbulent times by Abbot Sebroke, together with the arcade that supports the magnificent tower of that cathedral.

412. During this period the efforts of painting and sculpture were superadded to those of architecture; and to these must be joined the enchanting effects produced by expanded windows glowing with the richest colours that stained glass could bestow on them. To enter into a history of the rise, progress, and perfection of this art, would here be out of place. A separate work would be required to trace it from its introduction in this country as connected with our art in the reign of Henry III., to that point when it reached its zenith in the fifteenth century. Dallaway observes, with much truth, that it is a vulgar error to suppose the art was ever lost, inasmuch as we had eminent professors of it in the reign of Charles I.

413. In military architecture, from the reign of Edward III. to the close of the contention between the houses of York and Lancaster, many improvements were effected. Within that period a great number of the castellated edifices of which the country could boast were erected or renewed. Their style is marked by turrets and hanging galleries over the salient angles and gateways, of great variety in design. In the fortress at Amberley, in Sussex, built by William Rede, Bishop of Chichester, about 1370, and one of the ablest geometricians of the age, the ground plan is nearly a parallelogram with four large towers at the angles, not projecting externally, but inserted into the side walls. Of this æra is also, at Swansea Castle, the lofty perforated parapet or arcade, through which the water was conveyed from the roof. Upon this plan Henry Gower, Bishop of St. David's, in 1335, improved, in his magnificent castellated palace at Llanphey Court.

414. From the circumstance of the circuit of many of the castles encompassing several acres of ground, the base court was proportionally spacious; hence the halls and other state apartments were lighted by windows, smaller, but similar in form to those used in churches. The rest of the apartments were unavoidably incommodious, defence being the chief consideration. In the castles and palaces of the period, the *halls*, which formed a principal feature in them, require some notice. The earliest whereof mention is made was that built by William Rufus in his palace at Westminster. Hugh Lupus erected one at Chester, and one was executed for Robert Consul at Bristol. Others we find erected by Henry I. at Woodstock and Beaumont in Oxford; probably of rude construction, and divided into two aisles by piers of arcades or timber posts. In the following century, when castles began to be constantly inhabited, and space became requisite for holding the numerous feudal dependents on various occasions, the size of the hall was of course increased, and internal architecture and characteristic ornaments were applied to it. At the upper end, where the high table was placed, the floor was elevated, forming a *haut pas* or *dais*, a little above the general level of the floor. The example afforded by Edward III. at

Windsor was followed during his own and the succeeding reign. The halls of Westminster and Eltham were rebuilt by Richard II. ; Kenilworth by John of Gaunt ; Dartington, in Devonshire, by Holland Duke of Exeter. Crosby Hall, in London, was finished by the Duke of Gloucester, afterwards Richard III. We here subjoin the dimensions of some of the principal halls in castles and palaces before the end of the fifteenth century, ranged in order of their size, as partly revised :—

	Length in feet.	Breadth in feet.	Height in feet.
Westminster (1397) - - - -	238·9	67 to 68	90
Durham Castle - - - 360, now	180	50	36
London, Guildhall - - - -	153	50	60 (Wren's roof)
Conway (roof laid on stone ribs) - -	129	31	22
Bristol (divided by upright beams of timber	108	50	—
Eltham Palace - - - -	101·3	36·3	54
Chester - - - - -	99	45	—
Raby Castle - - - -	90	36	—
Kenilworth Castle (1300) - - -	88·8	45	32·3 walls
Swansea - - - - -	88	30	—
Leicester Castle Hall (oak pillars) - -	78	51	24
Spofforth - - - - -	76	36	—
Dartington (1476) - - - -	70	40	44
Caerphilly - - - - -	70	30	17 walls
Crosby Place (1466–70) - - -	69	17	38·6
Mayfield Hall (stone ribs) - - -	68	38	—
Goodrich Castle - - - -	65	28	—
Warwick Castle - - - -	62	35	25
Berkeley Castle - - - -	61	32	—
Second one at Swansea - - -	58	33	—

415. Generally, in respect of plan, the internal arrangement of these halls was very similar. The high table, as we have observed, was elevated on a platform above the level of the floor, and was reserved for the lord and his family, with the superior guests. Round the walls separate tables and benches were distributed for the officers of the household and dependents. The centre was occupied by the great open fire-place, directly over which in the roof was placed a turret, denominated a louvre, for conveying away the smoke. At Bolton Castle we find the chimneys in the walls ; but, perhaps, those at Conway and Kenilworth are earlier proof of the alteration. The roofs with which some of these halls are spanned exhibit mechanical and artistic skill of the first order. The thrust, by the simplest means, is thrown comparatively low down in the best examples, so as to lessen the horizontal effect against the walls, and thus dispense with considerable solidity in the buttresses. *Fig.* 196. is a section of the celebrated Hall of Westminster, by which our observation will be better understood. These roofs were framed of oak or chesnut. Whether, when of the latter, it was imported from Portugal and Castile, is a question that has been discussed, but not determined, by antiquaries. Large stone corbels and projecting consoles were attached to the side walls, and were disposed in bays called *severeys* between each window. Upon their ends, demi-angels were generally carved, clasping a large escochion to their breasts. Near to the high table, a projecting or bay window, termed an *oriel*, was introduced. It was fully glazed, frequently containing stained glass of the arms of the family and its alliances. Here was the standing cupboard which contained the plain and parcel-gilt plate. The *rere-dos* was a sort of framed canopy hung with tapestry, and fixed behind the sovereign or chieftain. The walls were generally lined to about a third of their height with panelled oak or strained suits of tapestry. It was during this æra that privy chambers, parlours, and bowers found their way into the castle. Adjoining to, or nearly connected with the hall, a spacious room, generally with a bay window, looking on to the quadrangle, was planned as a receiving-room for the guests, as well before dinner as after. This was decorated with the richest tapestry and cushions embroidered by the ladies, and was distinguished by the name of the *presence* or *privy-chamber*. The females of the family had another similar apartment, in which their time was passed in domestic occupations and amusements. This last room was called *my lady's bower* or *parlour*, and here she received her visitors. Bay windows were never used in outer walls, and seldom others, excepting those of the narrowest shape.

416. The dawn of improvement in our domestic architecture opened in the latter part of the period, during which also brick came very much into use in England as a building material. " Michael de la Pole," as we learn from Leland's *Itinerary*, " marchant of Hull, came into such high favour with King Richard II. that he got many privileges for the towne. And in hys tyme the toune was wonderfully augmented yn building, and was enclosyd with ditches, and the waul begun ; and in continuance endid, and made all of brike, as most part of the houses at that time was. In the waul be four principal gates of brike." After

Fig. 196.   SECTION OF WESTMINSTER HALL.

enumerating twenty-five towers, " M. de la Pole," we find from Leland, " buildid a goodlie
house of brike, against the west end of St. Marye's churche, lyke a palace, with goodly
orcharde and garden at large, also three houses besides, every on of which hath a tower of
brik." (*Itin.* vol. i. p. 57.)   This was the first instance of so large an application of brick
in England.

417. One of the most important parts of the castle was the great gateway of entrance,
in which were combined, at the same time, the chief elements of architectural beauty and
military defence.   It usually occupied the central part of the screen wall, which had the
aspect whence the castle could be most conveniently approached.   Two or more lofty towers
flanked either side, the whole being deeply corbelled; a mode of building brought by the
Arabs into Europe, and afterwards adopted by the Lombards and Normans.   The corbel
is a projecting stone, the back part whereof, which lies in the wall, being balanced by the
superincumbent mass, it is capable of supporting a parapet projecting beyond the face of the
wall rising from the horizontal course laid immediately on the corbels, between which the
said horizontal course was pierced for the purpose of enabling the besieged to drop missiles
or molten metal on the heads of the assailants.   The corbel is often carved with the head
of a giant or monster, which thus seems attached to the walls.   In John of Gaunt's entrance
gateway at Lancaster, the arch is defended by overhanging corbels with pierced apertures
between them, and on either side are two light watch-towers crested with battlements.

418. Of the military architecture of this time, a perfect idea may be obtained from
the two remarkable towers of Warwick Castle (*fig.* 197.), which were erected (in
1395) by Thomas de Beauchamp Earl of Warwick.   The taller one rises 105 ft. above
its base, and is 38 ft. diameter, having five stories, which are separated from each other
by groined ceilings.   In the interior, the walls of the state chambers were painted; a practice introduced into England in the beginning of the thirteenth century; and they were

Fig. 197.   WARWICK CASTLE.

sometimes lined with wainscot of curious carved *boisserie* on the panels, which afterwards became more adorned, and were hung with tapestry. At Warwick was a memorable suit of arras whereon were represented the achievements of the famous Guy Earl of Warwick.

419. The period of which we are treating was as celebrated for its bridge as for its military architecture, and exhibits as one of its examples that famed curiosity the triangularly formed bridge of Croyland in Lincolnshire, erected over the confluence of three streams. Bridge architecture was in many instances so necessarily connected with the construction of a fortress, that it may almost, in this age, be taken as a branch of military architecture.

Fig. 198.   ARCH OF YORK MINSTER.

420. This style exhibits *Arches*, less acute and more open (*fig.* 198. from York Minster), the forms varying. *Columns.* — The central and detached shafts now worked together into one, from experience of the weakness of those of the previous style, exceedingly various in their combinations. The *Windows* are larger, divided by mullions into several lights spreading and dividing at top into leaves, flowers, fans, wheels, and fanciful forms of endless variety. These marks are constant, but in the proportionate breadth there is much variation, for after having expanded in the reigns of Edward I. and II., they grew narrower again in proportion to their height in that of Edward III. and also sharper. The head was then formed of lines just perceptibly curved, sometimes even by two straight lines, sometimes just curved a little above the haunches, and then rectilinear to the apex. Eastern and western windows very lofty and ample, and splendidly decorated with painted glass. *Roof or Ceiling.* — The vaulting more decorated. The principal ribs spread from their imposts running over the vault like tracery, or rather with transoms divided into many angular compartments, and ornamented at the angles with heads, orbs, historical or legendary pictures, &c., elaborately coloured and gilded. *Ornaments.* — More various and laboured, but not so elegant and graceful in character, as in the preceding style. Niches and tabernacles with statues in great abundance. Tiers of small ornamental arches are frequent. The pinnacles are neither so lofty nor tapering, but are more richly decorated with leaves, crockets, &c. Sculpture is introduced in much profusion, and is frequently painted and gilt. Screens, stalls, doors, pannelled ceilings, and other ornaments, in carved and painted wood.

421. The principal examples of the ornamented English style in cathedral churches, are at *Exeter*, the nave and choir. *Lichfield*, uniformly. At *Lincoln*, the additions to the central tower. At *Worcester*, the nave. *York*, nave, choir, and western front. At *Canterbury*, transept. At *Gloucester*, transept and cloisters begun. *Norwich*, the spire and tower. *Salisbury*, spire and additions. *Bristol*, the nave and choir. *Chichester*, the spire and choir. *Ely*, Our Lady's Chapel and the central louvre. *Hereford*, the chapter-house and cloisters, now destroyed. In the later part of the period, the choir at *Gloucester ;* the nave at *Canterbury* Bishop Beckington's additions at *Wells*, and from the upper transept to the great east window at *Lincoln*. In conventual churches, for the earlier part of the period, the western façade of *Howden* (1320.), *Chapel of Merton College, Oxford. Gisborne Priory*, Yorkshire. *Chapel at New College, Oxford. St. Stephen's Chapel*, Westminster. The additions to the pediments of the choir at *Kirkstall*, Yorkshire. *St. Mary's* in York. *Kirkham* in Yorkshire, and the *choir of Selby*, in the same county. For the later part of

the period, at *Tewkesbury*, the choir. At *Ely Cathedral*, *St. Mary's Chapel. Croyland* façade in Lincolnshire. *Beverley Minster* in Yorkshire. *Chapel of Magdalen College*, Oxford. *Eton College Chapel*, Bucks. *Chapel on the Bridge at Wakefield* in Yorkshire, built by Edward IV. in memory of his father Edward Duke of York; and the *Beauchamp Chapel* at Warwick. In parochial churches, for the early part of the period, examples may be referred to at *Grantham*, Lincolnshire. *Attelborough*, Norfolk. *Higham Ferrers*, Northamptonshire. *St. Michael*, Coventry. *Truro*, Cornwall. *Witney*, Oxfordshire. *Stratford-upon-Avon*, Warwickshire. *St. Peter Mancroft*, Norwich. *Boston*, Lincolnshire; its remarkable lantern tower, which is 262 ft. high, was begun in 1309, and was in progress of execution during the whole reign of Edward III. The expense of it having been chiefly defrayed by the merchants of the Hanse Towns. *St. Mary, Edmunds Bury*, Suffolk. *Maidstone*, Kent; and *Ludlow*, Salop. For the later part of the period, *St. Mary Overy*, Southwark. *Thaxted* and *Saffron Walden*, Essex. *Lowth* and *Stamford*, Lincolnshire. *Campden*, Gloucestershire. *St. Mary Redcliff* and the *tower of St. Stephen*, Bristol. *Taunton* and *Churton Mendip*, Somersetshire. *Lavenham*, Suffolk. *Manchester College*. *St. Mary's*, Oxford. *Whittlesea*, Cambridgeshire. *Wakefield*, Yorkshire. *Doncaster*, Yorkshire. *Newark-upon-Trent*. *Heckington*, Lincolnshire. *Mould Gresford* and *Wrexham* in Flintshire. *Melton Mowbray*, Leicestershire. *Octangular towers of St. Margaret's*, Norwich, and *All Saints*, York.

SECT. V.

FLORID ENGLISH OR TUDOR STYLE.

422. " There is," as Dr. Henry observes, "a certain perfection in art to which human genius may aspire with success, but beyond which, it is the apprehension of many, that improvement degenerates into false taste and fantastic refinement. The rude simplicity of Saxon architecture was (ultimately) supplanted by the magnificence of the ornamental Gothic; but magnificence itself is at last exhausted, and it terminated during the present period in a style, which some, with an allusion to literature, denominate 'the Florid.' It is a style censurable as too ornamental, departing from the grandeur peculiar to the Gothic, without acquiring proportional elegance; yet its intricate and redundant decorations are well calculated to rivet the eye, and amaze, perhaps bewilder, the mind." The period of the style is from 1460, to the dissolution of the religious houses in 1537, and comprehends, therefore, the reigns of Edward IV. and V., Richard III., Henrys VII. and VIII.

423. The ecclesiastical buildings of this æra are few. Somersetshire, a county devoted to the cause of the House of Lancaster, from the gratitude or policy of Henry VII., boasts perhaps more churches than any other county in the florid style; still they are very few, and the superb chapel which that monarch erected at Westminster is the best specimen that can be adduced for giving the reader a proper and correct idea of the Florid or Tudor style. There is doubtless an abundance of examples in oratories, porches, and small chapels, sepulchral sacella and the like; but beyond them we could cite very few entire sacred buildings; and those will be hereafter appended to this section as in the preceding ones. In civil, or rather domestic architecture, the case was far different: a very great change took place; and we shall endeavour to place a succinct account of it from the Rev. Mr. Dallaway's work, to which we have already been much indebted. The fifteenth century exhibits to us a number of vast mansions of the noble and opulent, wherein the characteristic style of the immediately preceding castles was not entirely abandoned, but superseded and mixed up with a new and peculiar one. The household books of the nobility which have come to our knowledge, indicate a multitudinous set of servants and retainers, for the reception of whom a great area of ground must have been covered, and in which provision, by the number of apartments, was made for a noble display of hospitality. This circumstance, of course, induced a gorgeous style peculiar to the earlier Tudor æra, of most of whose splendid mansions no memorial now exists but in the records of the times. But for the purpose of bringing a view of the whole subject under the eye of the reader, a brief recapitulation will here be necessary. The first palace of the Norman kings was the Tower of London, which was a strictly military residence. At Westminster was a palace of William Rufus, to whom Westminster Hall owes its original foundation. At Oxford a palace was built by Henry I., and at that place he kept his Christmas in 1115, as in 1229 and 1267 Henry III. did in the vicinity at Woodstock. It was at this place that Henry II. built a house of retirement, which has furnished the subject of some well-known legends. Henry III. is said to have refounded the palace at Westminster, which was much enlarged by Edward III. This, from the time of Rufus, its founder, to the reign of Richard II., to whom it owed its completion in the state apartments, with its magnificent hall and bijou of a chapel (St. Stephen's), had attained a greater extent than any contem-

porary palace in Europe. Edward III., besides erecting his suburban palace at Kennington had re-edified and greatly extended Windsor Castle as a habitable fortification. Henry IV. inherited John of Gaunt's castle of Kenilworth and the Savoy in London, to both of which he made great additions. His gallant and victorious son was too much occupied with his military affairs to pay much attention to such matters; but many of his commanders, by the exorbitant ransoms they exacted of their French prisoners, were enabled to construct mansions of vast extent in those counties where their revenues commanded influence. Of these, as signal examples, may be cited Hampton Court in Herefordshire by Sir Rowland Lenthal; and Ampthill, Bedfordshire, by Sir John Cornwal Lord Fanhope. At Greenwich, a palace of great beauty, in the early part of the reign of Henry VI., was built by the regent Humphrey Duke of Gloucester, which, from its superiority over others, was by its founder called *Placentia* or *Plaisance.* This was completed by Edward IV., and is now remembered as the birthplace of Queen Elizabeth. The Lord Treasurer Cromwell expended a large sum on his residence at Tattershall in Lincolnshire, and at Wingfield Manor in Derbyshire, as did Lord Say and Sele, and Lord Boteler, respectively, at Sudley in Gloucestershire, and Hurstmonceaux in Sussex, all of which are now either destroyed or only in ruins. Additions were made by Edward IV. to Nottingham Castle, and by his brother Richard III. to Warwick Castle and that of Middleburg in Yorkshire.

424. Upon the establishment of the Tudor dynasty, Henry VII., on the ruins of a former palace at Shene in Surrey, which after the repairs he bestowed upon it was destroyed by fire, built a palace, whereto he gave the name of *Richmond,* in allusion to his former title, a name which was afterwards given to the beautiful town on the Thames, in its vicinity. The dimensions of the state apartments in this splendid building, whereof not a vestige now remains, are to be found in the Survey of 1649, when it was offered for sale by the Commissioners of Parliament. They abounded with bay windows of capricious formation, with rectangular and semicircular projections, producing a picturesque effect; and to add to its fantastic appearance, there were many octangular towers, surmounted with cupolas of the same plan, whose mitres as they rose were fringed with rich crockets. They were bulbous in their general form, thus bearing a resemblance in contour to the royal crown of the period.

425. The Tudor style, in domestic architecture, is thus divided by Mr. Dallaway. " 1. That just alluded to; 2. The variations under Henry VIII.; 3. The Elizabethan style" (which will form a separate section), " as it admitted of Italian ornament in the designs of John of Padua and his followers, until the time of Inigo Jones.

426. The reign of Henry VIII. supplies numberless instances of the gorgeous expense to which the nobility and gentry proceeded in the productions of our art. The example set by the monarch himself was witnessed in no less than two royal mansions, each large enough to contain his numerous retinue. The following are the palaces that were built or repaired by Henry VIII. : —

1. Beaulieu, or Newhall, Essex.
2. Hunsdon, Herts, originally built by Sir John Oldhall, temp. Edw. IV
3. Ampthill, Bedfordshire.
4. Nonsuch, Surrey.
5. York Place, Whitehall, Westminster.
6. Bridewell and Blackfriars, London, for the reception of the emperor Charles V.
7. St. James's, Westminster.
8. Kimbolton, Huntingdonshire, the jointure of the divorced Queen Catharine of Arragon.
9. Sheriff Hutton, Yorkshire, given for the residence of Henry Duke of Richmond, the king's natural son.
10. King's Langley, Herts.

It was natural that the courtiers of such a monarch should vie with each other in erecting sumptuous houses in the provinces where they were seated. Wolsey, besides the progress he had made, at the time of his fall, in his colleges at Christchurch, Oxford, and Ipswich, had completed Hampton Court, and rebuilt the episcopal residences of York House (afterwards Whitehall), and Esher in Surrey. Edward Stafford, Duke of Buckingham, in his palace at Thornbury, Gloucestershire, almost rivalled the cardinal, and perhaps might have done so entirely if he had not been hurried to the scaffold before his mansion was completed. Grimsthorpe, in Lincolnshire, rose under the orders of the Duke of Suffolk (Charles Brandon). The Duke of Norfolk and his accomplished son, the Earl of Surrey, were, as appears from the descriptions of Kenninghall, Norfolk, and Mount Surrey, near Norwich, magnificent in the mansions they required for their occupation. We shall merely add the following list (which might, if it were necessary, be much augmented) of some other mansions of note. They are — 1. Haddon Hall, Derbyshire. 2. Cowdray, Sussex, destroyed by fire in 1793. 3. Hewer Castle, Kent. 4. Gosfield Hall, Essex, perfect. 5. Hengreave Hall, Suffolk, perfect, and whereof a beautiful work has been published by John Gage, Esq. (now Rookwode), a descendant of its ancient possessors. 6. Layer Marney, Essex, now in ruins. 7. Raglan Castle, Monmouthshire, in ruins. 8. Hunsdon House, Herts, rebuilt. 9. South Wingfield, Derbyshire, dilapidated. 10. Hill Hall, Essex, built by Sir Thomas Smyth, in 1542. 11. Wolterton (see *fig.* 199.)

in East Barsham, Norfolk, in ruins.   12. Harlaxton, Lincolnshire, perfect.   13. Westwood, Worcestershire, perfect.

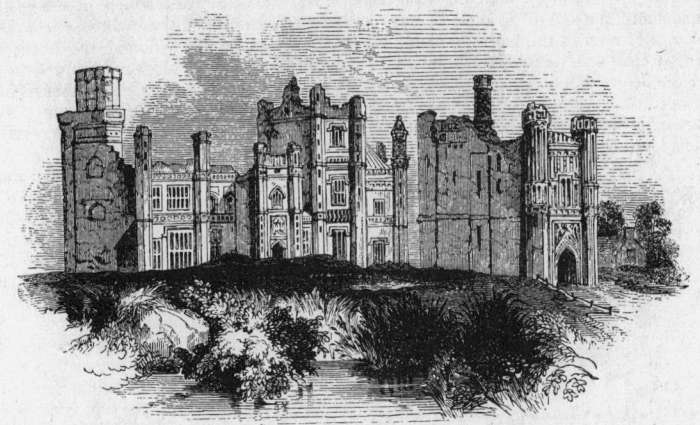

Fig. 199.   WOLTERTON HOUSE.

427. In a very curious tract, entitled, " A Dyetorie or Regiment of Health," by
Andrew Boorde, of Physike Doctor, 8vo., first printed in 1547, the following directions
are given how a man should build his house or mansion; from which it appears that there
were certain leading points for the guidance of the architect, founded, of course, they were
on the habits of the time. " Make," says our friend Andrew, " the hall of such fashion
that the parlor be annexed to the head of the hall, and the buttyre and pantrye at the lower
ende thereof; the cellar under the pantrye sett somewhat at a base; the kechyn sett somewhat at a base from the buttrye and pantrye; coming with an entrie within, by the wall
of the buttrie; the pastrie house and the larder annexed to the kechyn. Then divyde the
logginges by the circuit of the quadrivial courte, and let the gatehouse be opposite, or
against the hall doore; not directly, but the hall doore standyng abase of the gatehouse, in
the middle of the front enteringe into the place. Let the prevye chamber be annexed to
the great chamber of estate, with other chambers necessary for the buildinge; so that
many of the chambers may have a prospecte into the chapell." Some of the principal in-
novations in the early Tudor style, were the introduction of gatehouses, bay windows, and
quadrangular areas, matters rather incompatible with buildings constructed for defence. The
materials of these palaces and mansions were of freestone and brick, according to the facility
with which from the situation they could be procured. Sometimes, indeed often, these
materials were mixed. Moulded brickwork and terra cotta were introduced for ornamental
parts by Trevigi and Holbein towards the end of the period, or, perhaps strictly speaking,
at the end of it. The brickwork was occasionally plastered and pointed as at Nonsuch.
At Layer Marney and other places, bricks of two colours highly glazed were used for
variegating the surface, and were formed into lozenges. The chimney shafts seem to have
exhausted invention in the twisted and diapered patterns into which they were wrought, and
decorated with heads and capitals and cognizances of the founders. The gateways were
prominent features in these edifices, and the most expensive ornaments were lavished on
them. That at Whitehall, designed by Holbein, was constructed with differently coloured
glazed bricks, over which were appended four large circular medallions of busts, still
preserved at Hatfield Peveril, Herts. This gateway contained several apartments, among
which not the least remarkable was the study wherein Holbein chiefly received his sitters.
The gateways at Hampton Court and Woolterton were very similar to this.

428. We will here digress a little on the bay window which, as generally understood,
was simply a projecting window between two buttresses (whence its name, as occupying a
bay of the building), and almost universally placed at the end of the room. It was invented
about a century before the Tudor age, in which it usually consisted on the plan of right
angles intersected by circles, as in the buildings at Windsor by Henry VIII., and at
Thornbury Castle. When placed at the end of a great hall, it extended in height from the floor
to the ceiling, and was very simple and regular in its form. In a MS. at the Herald's College
relating to an entertainment given at Richmond by Henry VII., the following passage
occurs, and may be taken as descriptive of one of the purposes to which it was applied.
" Agaynst that his grace had supped: the hall was dressed and goodlie to be seene, and a
rich cupboord sett thereup in a baye window of IX or X stages and haunces of hight,
furnissed and fulfilled with plate of gold, silver, and regilte." Carved wainscotting in

panels, generally of oak, lined the lower part of the halls with greater unity of design and execution than heretofore; and it now found its way into parlours and presence chambers with every variety of cyphers, cognizances, chimeras, and mottoes, which in the castles of France about the age of Francis I. were called *Boisseries*. Of these some curious specimens still remain in the hall and chambers of the dilapidated mansion of the Lords de La Warre at Halnacre in Suffolk. The area or court was quadrangular, and besides the great staircase near the hall, there were generally hexangular towers containing others: indeed, they were usually to be found in each angle of the great court, rising above the parapets, imparting a pleasant and picturesque effect to the mass of building, and grouping well with the lofty and ornamented chimneys of which we have above spoken.

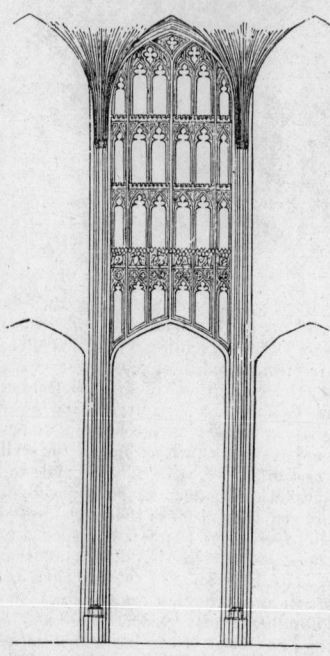

Fig. 200.   TUDOR ARCH, ST. GEORGE'S CHAPEL.

429. It is melancholy to reflect upon the disappearance of these mansions which were once the ornaments of the provinces, and now one by one falling fast away by the joint operation of what is called repair and by decay. Most of their remains have been removed to raise or to be incorporated with other buildings for which they might have well been spared.

430. The characteristics of the style are *arches*, universally flat, and wide in proportion to their height (*fig.*200.). *Windows*, much more open than in the last period, flatter at the top, and divided in the upper part by transoms, which are almost constantly crowned with embattled work in miniature. The *ceilings* or vaultings spread out into such a variety of parts, that the whole surface appears covered with a web of delicate sculpture or embroidery thrown over it; and from different intersections of this ribbed work, clusters of pendant ornaments hang down, as Mr. Millers observes, like "stalactites in caverns." The *flying buttresses* are equally ornamented, and the external surfaces of the walls are one mass of delicate sculpture. The *ornaments*, as may be deduced from the above particulars, are lavish and profuse in the highest degree. Fretwork, figures of men and animals, niches and tabernacles, accompanied with canopies, pedestals, and traceries of the most exquisite workmanship, carried this style to the summit of splendour; and all these combined, had, perhaps, no small share in producing the extinction it was doomed to undergo.

431. Before proceeding to give the examples in this style, to which the reader will be referred, it may be as well to mention that Scotland boasts of many fine specimens of ecclesiastical architecture. The abbeys of Melrose and Kelso, founded by David I., as well as those in Dryburgh and Jedburgh, all in Roxburghshire, prove that the art advanced to as great perfection north of the Tweed, as it did in England. Roslin and Holyrood chapels, the first whereof was erected by Sir William St. Clair, for richness and variety of ornamental carvings cannot be exceeded. Its plan is without parallel in any other specimen of the fifteenth century. The latter was finished by James, the second of that name, in 1440, and is a beautiful example with flying buttresses, which are more ornamented than any even in England.

432. Examples of the Florid Gothic or Tudor style are to be seen at the cathedral churches — of *Gloucester*, in the chapel of Our Lady; at *Oxford*, in the roof of the choir; at *Ely*, in Alcock's chapel; at *Peterborough*, in Our Lady's chapel, and at *Hereford*, in the north porch. In conventual churches, at *Windsor*, St. George's chapel; at *Cambridge*, King's College chapel; at *Westminster*, King Henry VII.'s chapel; at *Great Malvern*, in Worcestershire, the tower and choir; at *Christ Church*, Oxford, the roof of the choir, and at *Evesham Abbey*, in Worcestershire, the campanile and gateway.

433. For parochial churches, except in some very few specimens in Somersetshire, and there perhaps only in parts, we are unable to refer the reader to a complete specimen, in all its parts, of the Tudor style. The pulpit and screen at Dartmouth, in Devonshire, are worthy of his notice.

434. We shall close this section by a tabular view of the founders and dimensions of the different cathedrals of England, extracted from Dallaway and other authors. Since the first edition of 1842, the investigations into their history, causes no little hesitation at again putting forward this tabular view; it is, however, to some extent still useful.

BATH — CONVENTUAL CHURCH OF THE BENEDICTINES.

Dates.	Founders.	Nave.			Choir.			Aisles.			Transept.			Tower.		
		L.	B.	H.	L.	B.	H.	L.	B.	H.	L.	B.	H.	L.	B.	H.
1495 to 1502	Oliver King, bishop -		-		75	35	73		-		46	48	74	20	30	150
1532	Bird Gibbes } priors - }	136	72	78		-		Of the nave. 112 21 38			46	28	74			
1570	Inhabitants of Bath Sir John Harrington and others -		-			-		Of the choir. 80 21 38								
1609	James Montague, bishop	Completed the building														

Building unfinished at the Reformation, and completed by Bishop Montague and the executors of the Lord Treasurer Burleigh. Total length, 210 ft.; breadth, 126 ft.

BRISTOL — CONVENTUAL CHURCH OF ST. AUGUSTINE.

Dates:	Founders.	Nave.			Choir.			Aisles.			Transept.			Tower.
		L.	B.	H.	L.	B.	H.	L.	B.	H.	L.	B.	H.	Height.
1160	Robert Fitzharding													
1230	Robert third Lord Berkeley, Maurice													
1311 to 1332	fourth Lord Berkeley, and Edmund Knowles, abbot -	75	73	43	Originally included.						128	—	43	
1463	Elliot and William Hunt, abbots -		-		100	—	43		-		N. trans.			127
1481 to 1500	John Newland, abbot, completed - -		-		Our Lady's Chapel.									

The church displays two distinct styles. The Chapter House and Elder Lady Chapel were erected at the beginning and close of the twelfth century, and the existing nave and choir in the beginning of the fourteenth. It is probable it was not completed after the plan of the Abbot Knoles. The tower was intended to receive a spire. The aisles and nave are of the same height, which is only 43 ft.

CANTERBURY — CATHEDRAL CHURCH.

Dates.	Founders.	Nave.			Choir.			Aisles.			Transept.			Towers.
		L.	B.	H.	L.	B.	H.	L.	B.	H.	L.	B.	H.	
1070	Archbishop Lanfranc		-			-			-			-		N.W. 100 ft.
1090	Archbishop Anselme													
1100	Ernalphus Conrade } priors -	The second church destroyed by fire in 1174.												
1122	Archbishop W. Corboil.													
1174	W. Senensis archi- W. Anglus tects	Present church. }			150	40	71	Included			Upper 154			
1304	Henry de Estrey, prior.													
1379 to 1431	S. Sudbury W. Courtenay arch- T. Arundel bishops	Improved and ornamented.							-		Lower 124			N.W. spire of lead added 100 ft. high; taken down 1705; S.W. 130 ft.
1449	T. Chittenden T. Goldstone } priors	214	94	80										
1468	W. Sellinge.													
1490	W. Morton, archbishop		-			-			-			-		Central 234 high, 35 diameter.

The original Anglo-Saxon structure of Lanfranc was rebuilt after the canonisation of Thomas à Becket. The very elegant central tower was completed in 1500 by Archbishop Morton. This cathedral

has a lofty crypt of greater extent than, we believe, any other in England. At the eastern end of this cathedral, and projecting eastward of the general line of the plan, is an apartment open to the rest of the church, and consisting of a segment equal to about three fourths of a circle, called "Becket's Crown." The internal length of this church is 514 ft., and breadth 154 ft.

CARLISLE — Cathedral Church.

Dates.	Founders.	Nave.	Choir.	Aisles.	Transept.	Towers.
	Bishops.	L.　B.　H.	L.　B.　H.	L.　B.　H.	L.　B.　H.	Height.
1150 } 1270	Henry Murdac, abbot } of Fountains　　— }	82　—　71 Originally 164	—	Included.		
1353 to 1363	Gilbert de Wilton, } bishop　—　— }	—	137　—　71	71　—　—	124　28　71	
1363 to 1397	T. de Apylby　—　—					
1400 to 1419	Z. de Strickland　　—	—	—	—	—	128 ft.

The total length, 219 ft.; breadth, 124 ft.

CHESTER — Conventual Church of Benedictines.

Dates.	Founders.	Nave.	Choir.	Aisles.	Transept.	Tower.
		L.　B.　H.	L.　B.　H.	L.　B.　H.	L.　B.　H.	Height.
1128	Ranulf Earl of Chester					
1320	—	—	—	—	{ Transept dis- similar. North, a pa- rish church. 180　—　—	
1485	Simon Ripley, abbot } —— Oldham, abbot }	—　73　73	—	—	—	127 ft.
1508	—　—　—	{ The west- ern front }	—	—	{	{ Finished in 1508.

The Chapter House was built by Ranulf Earl of Chester, and in it many of his descendants are interred. A north transept only in this church. Length, 348 ft.; breadth, 180 ft.

CHICHESTER — Cathedral Church.

Dates.	Founders.	Nave.	Choir.	Aisles.	Transept.	Tower.
	Bishops.	L.　B.　H.	L.　B.　H.	L.　B.　H.	L.　B.　H.	
1094	Ralph　—　—　—	First church.				
1125 {	Siffrede　　—　— Abbot of Glastonbury }	105　95　61	—	{ Included —　91　—		
1217	Ralph de Warham　—	—	100　64　61	{ There are four aisles. The only instance in England. }	} North {	95 ft. high W. end.
1282	Gilbert de St. Leofard					
1329	John de Langton　—	—	—	—	{ South, with window.	{ 107 ft. high bell tower ; spire added to tower 271 ft. high.
1520	Robert Sherbourne　—	Repairs and embellishment of the choir, &c.				

It may be right to consider the present church as founded by Siffrede upon that built by Ralph in 1094. Total length, 407 ft.; width, 131 ft

DURHAM — CATHEDRAL CHURCH.

Dates.	Founders.	Nave.	Choir.	Aisles.	Transept.	Tower.
	Bishops.	L. B. H.	L. B. H.	L. B. H.	L. B. H.	
1093	William de Carilelpho -	260 74 69				
1128	Ralph Flambard.					
1230	Richard Poose and -	-	-	Included.	176 57 –	
1233	Melsonby, prior -	-	-	-	- }	Western towers 143 ft.
	Bertram Middleton, and Hugh Darlington, priors - }	-	120 74 71	-	90 18 –	
	Nicholas de Farnham, bishop.					
1295 {	Richard de Houton, prior - }	-	-		- }	Central tower 214.

The Lady Chapel was built in 1390, forming a sort of transept at the end of the choir. This cathedral is remarkable from the pillars of its nave, which are curiously striated. The Galilee, or chapel, at the western end, is 50 ft. by 78 ft., and was finished by Bishop Langley in 1430. Total length of the church, 420 ft.; width, 176 ft.

ELY — CATHEDRAL CHURCH.

Dates.	Founders.	Nave.	Choir.	Aisles.	Transept.	Tower.
	Bishops.	L. B. H.	L. B. H.	L. B. H.	Length.	
1109 to 1133 }	Herney -	-	-	-	N. 178$\frac{1}{2}$	
	Nigillus -	-	Erected the cloisters.			
1174	Id. Geoff. Ridal -	203 – 104	-	-	- {	Centre of West front 210 ft. high.
1235 to 1252 }	Hugh Northwold -	-	Presbytery, which was made the choir in 1769.			
1337	Simon Montacute -	-	Octagon Louvre.			
	I. Wisbich, prior -	-	101 34$\frac{1}{2}$ 70			

A spire of wood was added to the tower by Bishop Northwold, but it no longer exists; a gable built by Eustachius, a Bishop of Ely. The octagon, from which rises the louvre, is 14½ ft. high from the floor, and is 71 ft. 6 in. diameter. It was designed by Alan de Walsingham, a monk of Ely, in 1328. The diameter of the lantern is 30 ft., and its external height 170 ft. Total length, 517 ft.; breadth, 178 ft. 6 in.

EXETER — CATHEDRAL CHURCH.

Dates.	Founders.	Nave.	Choir.	Aisles.	Transept.	Tower.
	Bishops.	L. B. H.	L. B. H.	L. B. H.	L. B. H.	L. B. H.
1100 to 1128 }	W. Warlewast -	-	-	-	-	28 28 145
1280 to 1293 }	Peter Quivil -	-	-	-	140 32 68	
1293 to 1307 }	Thomas Bytton -	180 40 68	-	148 20 35		
1307 to 1318 }	Walter Stapylton -	-	132 34 68	132 20 35		
1340	Edmund Lacy -	Built the chapter house.				

The cloisters, which are only perfect on one side, were added by Thomas Brentinghan. The towers stand at the ends of the transept. The general plan of the church is that designed by Bishop Quivil, from which none of his successors deviated. The total length is 390 ft.; width, 140 ft. Bishop Grandison's screen in this cathedral is celebrated among antiquaries as displaying a series of statues more numerous and entire than are to be found in any other cathedral.

GLOUCESTER — Conventual Church of Benedictines.

Dates.	Founders.	Nave.	Choir.	Aisles.	Transept.	Tower.
		L. B. H.	L. B. H.	L. B. H.	L. B. H.	L. B. H.
1057 to 1089	Aldred, Bishop of Worcester	171 41 67½				
1089	Id.	-	-	N. 171 21 40½		
1310	Abbot, J. Thokey	-	-	S. 171 22 -		
1330	Abbot, J. Wygmore	-	-		S. 66 43½ 78	
1330 to 1357	Adam Staunton to Walter Frocester, and to Thomas Sebroke	Clerestory and vaulting.	140 34½ 86			
1369 to 1375	Ut supra	-	-	-	N. 66 43½ 78	
1457 to 1518	W. Ferleigh to Thomas Bramish, and to W. Parker	-	-	-	-	24 22 224

The Lady Chapel was built by W. Ferleigh about 1498. The western façade and two arches were added to the nave about 1370 by T. Horton. The tower rises from the intersection of the nave and choir with the transepts. The cloisters are the most perfect and beautiful of any in England, and are unusually situated, being on the north side of the church. Total length, 426 ft.; width, 152 ft.

HEREFORD — Cathedral Church.

Dates.	Founders.	Nave.	Choir.	Aisles.	Transept.	Tower.
	Bishops.	L. B. H.	L. B. H.	L. B. H.	L. B. H.	
1079 to 1095	Robert de Losinge	- 144 68 68	-	144 - -	140 - -	
1101 to 1115	Rainelm	-	125 20 64			
1131 to 1148	Robert de Bethune, prior of Llanthony	-		-	Lower. 111 - -	Ancient spire 240 ft. high. West tower was 130 ft.
1200 to 1216	Giles de Bruse	-			-	
1492 to 1502	Edmund Audley	-	-	-	-	The spire, which was taken down in 1790.
			Restored in 1786.			

The great west tower fell in 1786, and destroyed the greater part of the nave and aisles, which were rebuilt shorter by 15 ft. The architecture of the chapter house, which was octagonal, with a single central pillar, and 37 ft. diameter, was unnecessarily taken down by Bishop Egerton. Total length, 325 ft.; width 100 ft.

LICHFIELD — Cathedral Church.

Dates.	Founders.	Nave.	Choir.	Aisles.	Transept.	Tower.
	Bishops.	L. B. H.	L. B. H.	L. B. H.	L. B. H.	
1295 to 1430	Walter de Louton, or Langton - - And his successors -	213 67 67	120 33 67	Included.	88 - -	West spires 183 ft. high.
	William Hewworth, who died in 1447	W. front. 78 - -	} -	-	-	Total of the central spire. 258.

The church is very uniform, having been, like Salisbury and Exeter, completed upon one plan. The arches in the Triforia here show the dog-tooth moulding in great perfection. Total length, 411 ft.; breadth, 88 ft.

LINCOLN — CATHEDRAL CHURCH.

Dates.	Founders.	Nave.	Choir.	Aisles.	Transept.	Towers and Spires.
	Bishops.	L. B. H.	L. B. H.	L. B. H.	L. B. H.	
1184	{ Alexander Nor- mannus - - }	Rebuilt.				
1186 to 1200	} Hugh de Grenoble	240 80 80	140 40 72	Included.		
1240	Robert Grostête	-	-	-	-	Central 288 ft. high W. 260 ft.
1254	Henry Lexington -	-	-	-	-	{
1286 to 1300	} Hugh Burgundus	-	Presbytery.	-	W. 220 63 74	{ W. fron 173 ft. wide 83 ft. high.
1306	John D'Alderby -	-	106 82 72	-	E. 166 63 72	
1438	William Alnewick -	Built the great west window and porch.				

The central spire of this cathedral was higher than that of Salisbury, and was blown down in 1547. The others were removed in 1808. Total length, 498 ft. ; breadth, 227 ft.

LONDON — OLD ST. PAUL'S CATHEDRAL CHURCH.

Dates.	Founders.	Nave.	Choir.	Aisles.	Transept.	Towers.
	Bishops.	L. B. H.	L. B. H.	L. B. H.	L. B. H.	
1086	Mauritius -	- 335 91 102				
1120	Richard de Beaumes -	-	-	Included.	297 - -	
1220	William de St. Maria -	-	163 - 88	-	-	{ Height 260 ft., ditto of spire 274 ft. Burnt down in 1561.

The Chapter House was built by William de St. Maria, and was octangular. The cloisters, which were only 91 ft. square, were erected by Henry de Wingham in 1260 ; and the Lady Chapel by Henry de Lacy, Earl of Lincoln, in 1312. The area which this cathedral covered in 1309 was 3 acres, 3 roods, and 26 perches. The cloisters were removed by the Protector Somerset, to build his palace in the Strand. Inigo Jones commenced his restorations upon the fabric in 1633, and placed, in 1636, a most beautiful but incongruous Corinthian portico at the western end, the expense of which was borne by Charles I. The whole of the church was taken down and removed by Sir Christopher Wren in 1675. The following are the dimensions assigned to the cathedral in 1309 : — Length, 631 ft. ; breadth, 130. The height of the vaulting of the western part, 102 ft. ; of the eastern, 188 ft. : of the tower, 260 ft. : and of the spire, which was timber-framed and covered with lead, 274 ft. Dugdale's history of the church is embellished with numerous plates by Hollar, and is a most interesting work.

MANCHESTER, *see* Addenda to Glossary, s. v. English Cathedrals.

NORWICH — CATHEDRAL CHURCH.

Dates.	Founders.	Nave.	Choir.	Aisles.	Transept.	Tower.
	Bishops.	L. B. H.	L. B. H.		L. B. H.	
1096	Herbert Losinga -	-	-	-	-	Tower.
1171	Eborard - - -	140 71 —				
1197	John of Oxford -	-	165 — —	Included.	191 — —	
1361	{ Ralph Walpole Thomas Percy } -	-	-	-	-	Spire 317 ft.

This church has no Lady Chapel. The cathedral, before 1272, was so dilapidated, that it was nearly rebuilt by succeeding bishops and priors. The cloisters, erected by Bishop Wakering in 1420, are the most spacious in England, being 174 ft. square. Length of cathedral, 414 ft. ; breadth, 191 ft.

OXFORD — CONVENTUAL CHURCH OF ST. FRYDESWIDE AUG. CANONS.

Dates.	Founders.	Nave.	Choir.	Aisles.	Transept.	Tower.
		L. B. H.	L. B. H.		L. B. H.	
1050 1120	{ Guymond, prior of St. Frydeswide }	74 54 41½	80 37 —	Included.		
1122	- - -	-	-	-	102 - -	Tower.
1528	Cardinal Wolsey -	-	-	-		
1545	Robert King, first bishop	-	Clerestory	-	-	Spire.

The Chapter House here is of perfect Anglo-Norman architecture, built in the reign of Henry II. Length of church, 154 ft. ; breadth, 102 ft.

PETERBOROUGH — Conventual Church of the Benedictines.

Dates.	Founders.	Nave.	Choir.	Aisles.	Transept.	Tower.
		L. B. H.	L. B. H.		L. B. H.	
1160 tem. Hen. II.	William de Watteville, 21st abbot - -	-	138 78 78			
1175	Benedict, 22nd abbot -	231 78 —	-	Included.		
1272	Richard de London, 32nd abbot - -	-	-		203 69 78	
1295 1300	William de Parys, prior or W. de Woodford, abbot - - -	-	-	-	-	{ Two spires 156 ft. high.
1330	Geoffry Croyland, 34th abbot - -	-	-	-	-	{ Unfinished tower, 120 ft. { Louvre, 150 ft.
1496	Robert Kirton, 44th abbot, built the chapels at the end of the choir.					

Length, 480 ft. ; breadth, 203 ft.

RIPON, *see* Addenda to Glossary, s. v. English Cathedrals.

ROCHESTER — Cathedral Church.

Dates.	Founders.	Nave.	Choir.	Aisles.	Transept.	Tower.
	Bishops.	L. B. H.	L. B. H.		L. B. H.	
1080	Gundulphus - -	150 75 —	-		122 — —	
1115	Ernulph - - -	-	-	-		
1227	Henry Sanford - -	-	156 — —	Included.	-	Spire, 156 ft.
1270	W. de Hoo, prior, built a chapter house.					

When the choir was rebuilt, in 1227, it was extended to a greater length by several feet than the nave itself. The choirs of Norman churches were all disproportionately short. Total length, 306 ft.; breadth, 122 ft.

SALISBURY — Cathedral Church.

Dates.	Founders.	Nave.	Choir.	Aisles.	Transept.	Tower.
	Bishops.	L. B. H.	L. B. H.		L. B. H.	
1217	Richard Poore - -	229 76 81	-	-	-	To the Parapet, 207 ft.
1230	Robert Bingham -	-	140 — 84	Included.	-	
1274	Robert Wykehampton	-	-	-	230 60 84	Spire, 404 ft.

This is the most uniform of the cathedrals of England. It was ascertained, in 1737, that the roof altogether contained 2641 tons of timber. According to the account delivered to Henry III., it appeared that 40,000 marks (22,666*l.* 13*s.* 4*d.*) had, up to that time, been expended on the fabric. The original plan was given by Bishop Poore, and from it no variation was made by his successors. The church was twice consecrated. The Chapter House is octangular, with a central column, and the cloisters are 160 ft. square. The spire is of masonry only 7 in. thick, and would hence seem to be scarcely adequate to support its own weight. The total length is 474 ft., and the western front is 112 ft. wide. Great repairs were made to it by Sir Christopher Wren.

WELLS — Cathedral Church.

Dates.	Founders.	Nave.	Choir.	Aisles.	Transept.	Tower.
	Bishops	L. B. H.	L. B. H.		L. B. H.	L. B. H
1205 to 1239	Josaline Troteman -	191 67 67	108 67 —	Included.	135 — 67	
1293	W. de March					
1366	John Harwell					
1450	Thomas Beckington -	-	-	-	-	{ Western. 234 - 130
1465	Robert Stillington -	-	-	-	-	{ Central. - - 160

This is a very extraordinary example. Its western façade is decorated with statues in a more perfect state than is seen in any cathedral excepting that of Lincoln. The subjects are kings, bishops,

and warriors. The original plan seems to have been strictly followed to its completion by Bishop Stillington. Speed says that Ralph de Shrewsbury, who died in 1363, was a great benefactor to the church, and prosecuted the original plan. The support of the central tower is assisted by the principle of the inverted arch as at Salisbury, and is a good example of constructive skill. Total length, 371 ft.; breadth, 185 ft.

WESTMINSTER — Conventual Church.

Dates.	Founders.	Nave.	Choir.	Aisles.	Transept.	Tower.
		L. B. H.	L. B. H.	L. B. H.	L. B. H.	
1250	King Henry III. -	166 38 101	155 38 101	166 16 101		Height to the top of the western turrets, addition 102½ ft., 225 ft. in the whole.
1300	King Edward I. -	Extreme breadth of the Nave and Aisles, — 71¾	-	-	136 40 78	
1490	King Henry VII. -	Chapel, 103 ft. long, 35 ft. broad, 60 ft. high; aisles, 62 ft. long, 17 ft. broad.				

The flying buttresses of Henry VII.'s chapel are among the most beautifully decorated in England. The triforia of the church are lighted from a range of windows in the back wall, which are seen externally, each consisting of three circles, inscribed within a triangle, equilaterally composed of three segments of circles.

WINCHESTER — Cathedral Church.

Dates.	Founders.	Nave.	Choir.	Aisles.	Transept.	Tower.
	Bishops.	L. B. H.	L. B. H.		L. B. H.	
1070	Wakelyn - - -	-	-	-	186 — —	150 ft. high.
1190	Godfrey de Laci, the Cloisters					
1350	William de Edynton, the Lady Chapel					
1394	William de Wykeham -	300 86 78	-			
	Cardinal Beaufort -		Presbytery			
1493	T. Langton - -		93 86 78	Included.		

The western front was finished by Edynton. The nave, which was finished by William of Wykeham, is longer than that of York, and considered one of the finest in England. The exterior of the choir is of the finest Gothic of the fifteenth century. The choir, as at Gloucester, is under the tower. Total length, 545 ft.; breadth, 186 ft.

WORCESTER — Cathedral Church.

Dates.	Founders.	Nave.	Choir.	Aisles.	Transept.	Tower.
	Bishops.	L. B. H.	L. B. H.		L. B. H. Lower,	
1218 to 1224	William de Blois -	212 78 72	80 36 61	Included.	128 32 —	
1327	T. Cobham, Lady Chapel					
1372	W. de Lynne -	-	-	-	-	172 ft. high.
1374 to 1380	Henry Wakefield -	-	-	-	Upper, 120 25 —	

The Chapter House here, a decagon 58 ft. diameter, and the cloisters, 120 ft. long and 125 ft. in breadth, were erected in the time of W. de Wynne. The original church was built before 1150, and parts of it may still be traced. The refectory of the convent, 120 ft. by 38 ft., is still perfect. The nave is, for style and proportions, well worthy the attention of the student. The total length of the church is 410 ft.; its breadth, 130 ft.

YORK — CATHEDRAL.

Dates.	Founders.	Nave.	Choir.	Aisles.	Transept.	Tower.
		L. B. H.	L. B. H.	L. B. H.	L. B. H	
	Archbishops.					
1227	Walter Grey - -	-	-	-	222 - 103	
1291	John Romain - -	250 103 92		250 - 47		
	W. de Melton - -	-		-	-	{ Façade and western towers 196 ft.
1361	J. Thoresby - -		150 43 101			
1300 to 1420	J. Birmingham, treasurer, completed the façade -	-	-	-	-	{ L. B. H. Central. 44 42 182

Octagonal Chapter House, erected by W. de Melton. The foundations of the church were laid in 1171, by Roger, then archbishop. The central lantern or steeple, built by Le Romain, was taken down in 1380 by Walter Skirlawe. The aisles surround the church in every part, are of similar dimensions, and were built at the same time. The open central tower, or louvre, is 188 ft. from the floor. The Rose Window, the finest in England, is 22 ft. 6 in. diameter. Total length, 498 ft. ; breadth, 222 ft.

435. The following synoptical view of the general dimensions of the above cathedrals, we think, may prove occasionally useful to the reader, by enabling him to compare the whole of them and their parts with each other. The equality of the proportions is striking ; and, in another part of this work, we hope to place before the reader some principles which tend to prove that there was a much more established practice founded on the laws of statics than has hitherto been conjectured. Dallaway, without the remotest idea of the principles in question, has observed, with his usual sagacity, that there appears in them " a distribution of parts which will hold almost generally, that the width of the nave is that of both the aisles, measured on the plan to the extremity of the buttresses externally ; and that the breadth and height of the whole building are equal. In the more ancient churches, the aisles are usually of the width of the space between the dividing arches." Some idea of the principle is conveyed in the plates of Milan cathedral, curiously introduced into the very early translation of *Vitruvius* by Cæsar Cesarianus, a work of great curiosity, and of which copies are now rarely met with.

A SYNOPTICAL VIEW OF THE LEADING DIMENSIONS OF THE ENGLISH CATHEDRALS.

Cathedral.	Total internal Length.	Naves and Aisles.			Choirs.			Transepts	Spires and Towers.	
		Length.	Breadth.	Height.	Length.	Breadth.	Height.	Breadth.		Height.
Winchester -	545	247	86	78	138	-	73	186		
Ely -	517	327	73	70	101	73	70	178	Tower -	- 210
Canterbury -	514	214	70	80	150	74	80	154	Do. -	- 235
Old St. Paul's	500	335	91	102	165	42	88	248	Spire -	- 534
York -	498	264	109	99	131	-	99	222	Tower -	- 234
Lincoln -	498	-	83	83	-	-	-	227	Do. -	- 260
Westminster -	489	130	96	101	152	-	151	189		
Peterborough -	480	231	78	78	138	-	78	203	Louvre -	- 150
Salisbury -	452	246	76	84	140	-	84	210	Spire -	- 387
Durham -	420	-	-	-	117	33	84	176	Tower -	- 214
Gloucester -	420	174	84	67	140	-	71	144	Do. -	- 225
Lichfield -	411	213	67	-	110	-	86	-	Spire - 258 W.	183
Norwich -	411	230	71	-	165	-	67	-	Do. -	- 317
Worcester -	410	212	78	-	126	-	-	191	Tower -	- 196
Chichester -	401	205	91	61	100	-	74	130	Spire -	- 267
Exeter -	390	173	74	69	131	-	-	131	Tower -	- 130
Wells -	371	191	67	67	106	-	69	140	Do. -	- 160
Hereford, anct.	370	144	68	68	105	-	67	135		
Chester -	348	-	73	73	-	-	64	140	Tower -	- 127
Rochester -	306	150	65	-	156	-	-		Spire -	- 156
Carlisle -	213	-	71	71	137	71	-	122		
Bath -	210	136	72	78	-	-	-		Tower -	- 162
Bristol -	175	100	75	73	100	-	-	126	Do. -	- 127
Oxford -	154	74	54	41	80	-	37½	128 102	Spire -	- 184

To the above we subjoin the correspondent dimensions of the several component parts of some of the cathedral churches enumerated, which we consider useful to the student as well as the general reader.

	Total Length.
Chichester cathedral church - -	410 ft.
Norwich cathedral church - - -	411
Worcester cathedral church - -	410
Durham cathedral church - - -	420
Gloucester conventual church - -	420

	Heights of Naves.	Style.
Salisbury cathedral church	- 84 feet	Pointed arch.
Lincoln cathedral church	- 83 —	Pointed arch.
Canterbury cathedral church	- 80 —	Pure Gothic.
Peterborough conventual church	- 78 —	Norman.
Winchester cathedral church	- 78 —	Pure Gothic.
Durham cathedral church	- 71 —	Norman.
Ely cathedral church -	- 70 —	Norman.
Exeter cathedral church	- 69 —	Pointed arch.
Gloucester conventual church	- 67 —	Norman.
Wells cathedral church	- 67 —	Pointed arch.

Breadths of Naves and Aisles.

Norwich   -   71 ft.

Bristol	- 73	Canterbury	- 74 ft.	Peterborough	78 ft.	Lincoln	- 83 ft.
Chester	- 73	Exeter	- 74	Worcester	- 78	Gloucester	- 84
Ely	- 73	Salisbury	- 76	Durham	- 80	Winchester	- 85

The author just quoted, in reference to the tables here given, says of them, that " the parallel will afford us, at one view, authentic information concerning the proportion of one constituent part to another of every cathedral in England which is worthy the notice of an architect. Such," he continues, " a coincidence of dimensions as that which is found in many of them, can scarcely be supposed to be the effect of chance, especially where the buildings are contemporary and of an exactly correspondent style." It appears that the equality of proportions is confined to each era and style of ecclesiastical architecture in so remarkable a degree as to lead us to conjecture that they might have been designed by the same architect. " The constant rivalry," says Dallaway, " which subsisted between the magnificent prelates, was excited upon the erection of any part of a cathedral of superior beauty, and imitated in those of the same kind which were then undertaken ; and the architect who had once displayed great talents was invited to repeat the more perfect performance, upon which he had rested his professional fame." We have not considered it necessary to devote a special portion of our work to the conventual architecture of England, because it followed the style of the time. It was of great splendour. The ground plans of their habitable portions were usually, though not always, quadrangular, and in the later ages partook of the improvements in domestic architecture, as in the colleges built by Wykham and Waynflete, and many of the episcopal residences. Glastonbury and Reading presented exceedingly fine examples of it ; the former comprised within its walls sixty acres of ground.

Sect. VI.

ELIZABETHAN ARCHITECTURE.

436. The revival of the arts in Italy has furnished the subject of Chap. II. Sect. XVI. It commenced, as we have there seen, with its author Brunelleschi, who died in 1444 ; and it was not till more than a century afterwards that, notwithstanding our constant intercourse with the Continent, its influence began to be felt in this country. The accession of Elizabeth, it will be recollected, took place in 1558.

437. Whilst the art here, though always, as respected its advancing state, much behind that of the Continent, was patronised by the clergy, it flourished vigorously ; but when that body was scattered by the dissolution of the religious houses, no one remained to foster it ; and though Henry VIII. delighted in *spectacle*, and a gorgeous display of his wealth, he was far too great a sensualist to be capable of being trained to refinement in the arts. Neither, moreover, are the English, as a people, susceptible of high feeling in respect of the productions of art. Even to the present hour so low in the scale do they stand, that a lady's cap finds no adoption, receives no sanction among the higher classes, unless moulded and previously sanctioned in the capital of our lively neighbours. In short, the only period in which the arts seemed likely to take root here was under that unfortunate monarch Charles I. ; since whose time they have languished, giving way to politics, which engross the attention of the higher class, and to commerce, which engrosses the attention of the merchants. There is here no general pervading love of the arts, as among all classes on the Continent, though we believe the time for it approaches. The Elizabethan, or, as some have, perhaps more properly, called it, the last Tudor style, is an imperfectly understood adaptation of classic forms to the habits of its day in this country. It is full of redundant and unmeaning ornament, creating a restless feeling in the mind of the spectator, which, in the cinque cento work, the renaissance of Italy, was in some degree atoned for by excellence of design, by exquisite execution of the subject, and by a refinement in the forms which some of the first artists the world ever saw gave to its productions. In Italy, the orders almost

instantaneously rose in their proper proportions, soon leaving nothing to be desired ; but in England they were for a long time engrafted on Gothic plans and forms, producing nothing but heterogeneous masses of absurdity.   It was, nevertheless (strange to say), in this style and the Gothic, that the wisdom of the legislature thought proper to solicit designs from the architects of the country, in the year 1836, for new houses of Parliament, a proceeding which has excited the smiles of the artists of the Continent at our absurdity in matters of art.

438. The work of Andrew Borde has been before mentioned ; but the earliest publication in England relative to practical architecture was, " The first and chiefe Grounds of Architecture used in all the ancient and famous Monyments, with a farther and more ample Discourse uppon the same than has hitherto been set forthe by any other. By John Shute, paynter and architecte." " Printed by John Marshe, fol., 1563." This John Shute had been sent by Dudley, Duke of Northumberland, to Italy, probably with the intention of afterwards employing him upon the works which he was projecting. From this and many other circumstances, it is easy to discover that domestic architecture under Elizabeth had assumed a more scientific character. Indeed, there is ample evidence that no building was now undertaken without the previous arrangement of a digested and regulated plan ; for early in the reign of this sovereign the treatises of Lomazzo and Philibert de Lorme were translated into English ; and in the construction of the palatial houses of the aristocracy, the architects had begun to act upon a system. The principal deviation from the *plans* of the earlier Tudor houses was in the bay windows, parapets, and porticoes, whereof the two latter were intensely carved with all the forms that the most fantastic and grotesque imagination could supply. The exteriors of these porticoes were covered with carved entablatures, figures, and armorial bearings and devices. The galleries were lofty, wide, and generally more than a hundred feet in length ; and the staircases were spacious and magnificent, often occupying a considerable portion of the mansion. Elizabeth herself does not appear to have set, during the passion of the period for architecture, any example to her subjects. She might have thought her father had done sufficient in building palaces ; but, however, be that as it may, she encouraged the nobles of her court in great expenditure on their residences. With the exception of the royal gallery at Windsor, she herself did actually nothing ; whilst on Kenilworth alone, Lord Leicester is supposed to have expended no less a sum than 60,000*l.*, an almost royal sum of money.

439. Before proceeding further, it becomes our duty here to notice a peculiar construction which prevailed in the large manor houses of the provinces, and more especially in the counties of Salop, Chester, and Stafford, the memory of many whereof, though several are still to be seen, is chiefly preserved in engravings ; — we allude to those of timber framework in places where the supply of stone or brick, or both, was scanty. The carved pendants, and the barge-boards of the roofs and gables, which had, however, made their appearance at a rather earlier period, were executed in oak or chesnut with much beauty of design, and often with a singularly pleasing effect. The timbered style reached its zenith in the reign of Elizabeth, and is thus illustrated in Harrison's description of England : — " Of the curiousnesse of these piles I speake not, sith our workmen are grown generallie to such an excellence of devise in the frames now made, that they farre passe the finest of the olde." And, again : " It is a worlde to see how divers men being bent to buildinge, and having a delectable view in spending of their goodes by that trade, doo dailie imagine new devises of their owne to guide their workmen withall, and those more curious and excellent than the former." (p. 336.) The fashion was no less prevalent in cities and towns than in the country ; for in them we find that timber-framed houses abounded, and that they also were highly ornamented with carvings, and exhibited in their street fronts an exuberance of extremely grotesque figures performing the office of corbels. The fashion was imported from the Continent, which supplies numberless examples, especially in the cities of Rouen, Bruges, Ulm, Louvain, Antwerp, Brussels, Nuremburg, and Strasburg, very far surpassing any that this country can boast. We have, however, sufficient remains of them in England to prove that the wealthy burgess affected an ornamental display in the exterior of his dwelling, rivalling that of the aristocracy, and wanting neither elegance nor elaborate finishing, whilst it was productive of a highly picturesque effect in the street architecture of the day. " This manner," says Dallaway, " was certainly much better suited to the painter's eye than to comfortable habitation ; for the houses were lofty enough to admit of many stories and subdivisions, and being generally placed in narrow streets were full of low and gloomy apartments, overhanging each other, notwithstanding that they had fronts, which with the projecting windows and the interstices were filled for nearly the whole space with glass." *Fig.* 201 is a representation of Moreton Old Hall, Cheshire, built circa 1550–59, partly rebuilt 1602.

440. A better idea of the architecture of this age cannot be obtained than by a notice of the principal architects who have furnished materials for the foregoing observations ; and for this purpose we shall use with freedom the notes to Walpole's anecdotes, by our late much valued friend Mr. Dallaway. A MS., belonging to the Earl of Warwick

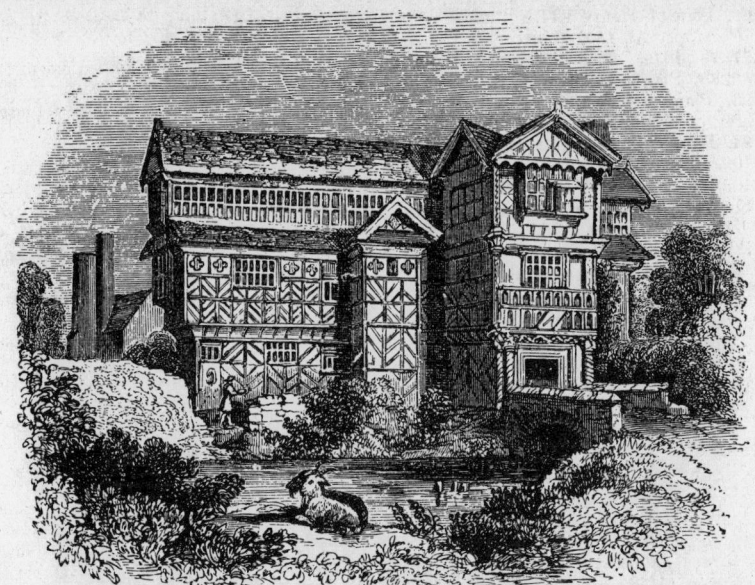

Fig. 201.   TIMBER-FRAMED HOUSE, Moreton Old Hall, Cheshire.

in the time of Walpole, enabled him to bring to the knowledge of the world, and perpetuate the memory of, an artist of no mean powers, whose name, till that author's time, was almost buried in oblivion, though he was the architect of most of the principal and palatial edifices erected during the reigns of Elizabeth, and James, her successor. His name was John Thorpe; and at the sale of the library of the Hon. Charles Greville in 1810, the MS. in question came into the possession of the late Sir John Soane, Professor of Architecture to the Royal Academy. It is a folio, consisting of 280 pages, wherein the plans, often without a scale, are nevertheless accurately executed. Several of the subjects were merely designs for proposed mansions. The elevations are neatly drawn and shadowed. The general form of the plans is that of three sides of a quadrangle, the portico in the centre being an open arcade finished by a turreted cupola. When the quadrangles are perfect, they are, for convenience, surrounded by an open corridor. The windows, especially in the principal front, are large and lofty, and mostly alternated with bows or projecting divisions, and always so at the flanks. Great efforts were made by Thorpe to group the chimneys, which were embellished with Roman Doric columns, and other conceits. Portions of the volume have been engraved by Mr. C. J. Richardson in the first part of his *Architectural Remains of the Reigns of Elizabeth and James I.*, fol. 1838-40. Amongst the contents of Thorpe's volume (which has been collated for this edition, 1866), are:—Outlines of a "jambe mould," "muniell," "rayle mo. for stayre," "corbell table," parapets, &c.; and the five Orders, with rules for drawing them.

Page 19, 20. Plan and elevation, "Buckhurst howse, Sussex." Built, 1565, by Thomas Sackville, Earl of Dorset, Lord High Treasurer to Queen Elizabeth. The front extends 230 ft. The courtyard is 100 ft. by 80 ft., and the hall 80 ft. by 50 ft.

24. "$\frac{1}{2}$ a front or a garden syde for a noble man," dated 1600.

37, 38, 50. "The way how to drawe any ground plot into the order of perspective," with descriptions, the front being parallel with the spectator.

39, 40. Plan, with a courtyard in front. "Sr Geo. Moores howse."

44. Plan. "Cannons, my La: Lakes howse."

48. Plan. "Copthall, 16 fo. 8 ynch. This cort should be 83 (or 88) fo. square." Built for Sir Thomas Heneage. The gallery was 168 ft. long, 22 ft. high, and 22 ft. wide.

49. Elevation. "Woollerton, Sir Fraunc. Willoughby," Nottinghamshire, which has the inscription, "*Inchoatæ,* 1580-1588." Mr. Dallaway notices that the tomb of Robert Smithson, in Wollaton church, calls him "architector and surveyor unto the most worthy house of Wollaton, with divers others of great account. Ob. 1614,' which would appear to invalidate Thorpe's claim; Smithson was probably Thorpe's pupil and successor. The property now belongs to Lord Middleton. (See *fig.* 203.)

54. Plan, rough. "Sr Jo. Bagnall." A gallery 60 ft. long.

57, 58. Two plans. "Burghley juxta Stamford." Built, 1578-80, for William Cecil Lord Treasurer. (See 105.)

67, 68. Two plans. "Thornton Colledg, Sr Vincent Skynners." A gallery 113 ft long, and 25 ft. wide.

69. Plan of Henry VII.'s Chapel. "Capella ista H. 7mi impensis 14,000 lb. adiecit ipse Ao 1502."

77, 78, Plan. Chateau de Madrid, Bois de Boulogne, near Paris, now pulled down.

88, 89, Plan and elevation. Old Somerset House.

93. Plan. "Sr Walter Coap at Kensington, pfected p me J. T." Holland House, finished in 1607, and added to by Inigo Jones and N. Stone.

94. Plan. "Sr George Coppin," Hertfordshire, cir. 1608 (?)

109. Plan. "A London house, La Darby, channell row" (?)

105, 106. Plan. "Duke of Buckingham at Burghley," or Burley-on-the-Hill. (See 57.)

113, 114. Plan. "Wymbleton. An howse standing on the edge of an hie hill." Built, 1588, for Sir Tho. Cecil. Fuller says it was "a daring structure, nearly equal to Nonesuch."

123, 124, 127, 128. Plans. "Queene mother's howse, fabor St. Jarmins, alla Paree, altered p Jo. Thorpe."

136. Plan. "London howse of 3 bredthes of ordy tenemts." Supposed design for Sir Fulke Greville's (Lord Brooke) house, near Gray's Inn.

139, 140. Plan. "Kerby whereof I layd ye first stone, Ao 1570," Northamptonshire, for Lord Chancellor Hatton.

150. Plan. "Richmt. Lodge, Sticles" (?). (Robert Stickles?)

151. Plan. "Sr Peival Hart," Lullingstone, Kent.

Fig. 202.   LONGFORD CASTLE.

155-158. Plan and elevation. "Longford Castle, Wiltshire (fig. 202). A diagram of the Trinity is drawn in the middle of the triangular court. Built for Sir Thomas Gorges and his wife, the Marchioness Dowager of Northampton, in 1591; now the Earl of Radnor's. The plan differs from that given (1766) in Britton's Arch. Antiq.

163. Plan. "Mounsier Jammet in Paris, his howse, 1600.

164. Plan. "Gyddye Hall, 84 fo. square," Essex. Altered for Sir Anthony Coke.

167, 168. Plan. "St. Jarmin's howse, V leagues from Paris, Ao 1600."

203, 204. Plan. "Audley end;" and later, "Audley End in Essex, seat of Lord Suffolk," now the property of Lord Braybrooke. Thorpe's part was completed about 1616.

215, 216. Three plans. Greek cross. Lyveden, co. Northam. (?). Built by Sir T. Tresham.

225. Two plans. "Mr. Tayler at Potter's barr, 1596."

232. Plan, H shape, with a courtyard, "94 fo. square," and a gatehouse. "This plot drawne after 8 fo. 8 inche, p Jo. Thorpe," (? his own drawing).

234. Two elevations. "Heddington Jo Chenyes," (? Tuddington, co. Bedford).

239, 240. Two plans. "Sr Walt. Covert, Sussex," at Slaugham, near Horsham.

267, 272. Two plans. "Ampthill old howse, enlardged p J. Thorpe." "Duke of Bedford" (?). It was the residence of Queen Catherine, first wife of Henry VIII.

265, 266. Plan and elevation. "for Mr. Willm Powell," or Howell; of timber.

Amongst the general designs, which are chiefly plans, are, page 21, "Sir Jo. Danvers, Chelsey;" 28, "Sr Wm. Ruffden"(?); 31, "Mr. Johnson ye Druggyst;" 43, "Sir Walter Rawley—Sir James;" 45, "Sir Tho. Dorrell, Lincolne shire;" 46, and half elevation, "Godstone;" 59, two plans, "Sr George Sct Poole;" 62, a long-fronted house at "Higate;" 65, "Sr James (?) Clifton's howse;" 191, "Mr. Keyes;" 132, "Mr. Denman;" 147, 148, and elevation, "Sr William Haseridge;" 176, "Mr. Panton;" 182, "Holdenby banquetg at 16 fo;" 185, "Mr. Folte"(?); 187, "Mr. W. Fitwilliams;" 199, Sr Hen. Nevile;" 201, 202, "Jo. Clanricard;" 205, "Sr Tho. Holt, 12 pte;" and 253, "Hatfield lodge." 275-278, has a gallery 160 ft. long and about 25 ft. wide; 146

is designed within a circle; and 161, on a triangle with a hexagon interior court; 155 is also a triangular plan, as named. Many of these designs might probably be identified, but it would entail much labour.

441. Walpole, upon *Thorpe's Compositions*, observes, that the taste of this master's mansions was that " bastard style which intervened between Gothic and Grecian architecture, or which, perhaps, was the style that had been invented for the houses of the nobility when they first ventured, on the settlement of the kingdom after the termination of the quarrel between the Roses, to abandon their fortified dungeons, and consult convenience and magnificence." The same author continues, " Thorpe's ornaments on the balustrades, porches, and outsides of windows are barbarous and ungraceful, and some of his vast windows advance outwards in a sharp angle; but there is judgment in his disposition of apartments and offices, and he allots more ample space for halls, staircases, and chambers of state. He appears, also, to have resided at Paris, and even seems to have been employed there." Among the designs he made is that of a whimsical edifice, designed for himself, forming on the plan the initial letters of his name ⊢Г, which are joined by a corridor, the ⎪ being the situation of the offices, and the Т being skilfully distributed into large and small apartments. The epigraph to the design is as follows:—(pages 30 and 50)

> " Thes 2 Letters ⎪ and Т
> ioyned together as you see
> Is ment a dwelling howse for mee
>   JOHN THORPE."

Walpole truly observes of this volume, that " it is a very valuable record of the magnificence of our ancestors, and preserves memorials of many sumptuous buildings of which no other monument remains." We ought, perhaps, to have suffered our account of Thorpe to have been preceded by those of others, but the conspicuous rank he holds in the list of English architects of this period induced us to place him before another, for a little time his predecessor in the works of the country. We allude to the name of Robert Adams, who translated Ubaldini's account of the defeat of the Spanish Armada from the Italian into Latin; a feat which we fear but few architects of the present day would easily accomplish, such is the fall of education for artists, notwithstanding all the boasts of march of intellect. This translation appeared in 4to., 1589. He was surveyor of the queen's buildings, and appears to have been a man of considerable ability. His place of sepulture was in an aisle on the north side of the old church at Greenwich, with this inscription, " Egregio Viro, Roberto Adams, operum regiorum supervisori architecturæ, peritissimo, ob. 1595. Simon Basil, operationum regiarum contrarotulator, hoc posuit monumentum 1601."

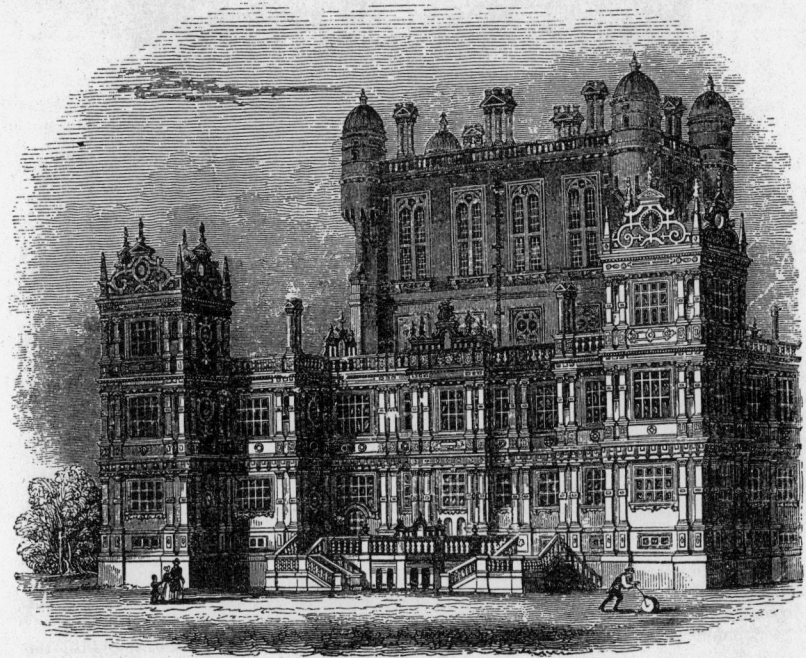

Fig. 205.   WOLLATON HALL.

442. Bernard Adams and Lawrence Bradshaw were also eminent among the architects of the period under our consideration; but we must notice more particularly Gerard Chrismas, who was associated with Bernard Jansen in the erection of Northampton, afterwards Suffolk, and now Northumberland House, not strictly belonging in time, though in style, to the reign of Elizabeth. Both of these architects are considered to have been much employed. In the balustrade and on the street front were the letters H. N. and C. Æ., which no doubt stood for Henric. Howard. Northampton. Comes Ædificavit. Yet C. Æ. has been supposed to denote " Chrismas Ædificavit." Such letters were repeated, a practice then much in vogue, for there are many examples of inscriptions of letters enclosed within the balustrade, as if within lines, and pierced so that the sky seen through them renders them distinct from almost every point of view. Bernard Jansen was probably the architect first employed at the splendid mansion of Audley Inn in Essex, for Thomas Howard, Earl of Suffolk ; and, besides the association with Chrismas above mentioned, was joined with Moses Glover in completing Northumberland House. and was probably the architect who finished Sion House in Middlesex, for Henry Earl of Northumberland, who had at the time expended 9000*l.* in the work.

443. Robert and Huntingdon Smithson, father and son, were engaged on Wollaton Hall (*fig.* 203. at the foot of the preceding page), in Nottinghamshire, as also at Bolsover in Derbyshire. The former died in 1614, at the age of seventy-nine, and the latter in 1648, but it is pretty certain that Thorpe was consulted in this splendid work, for among his designs, as the reader will recollect, are some for Wollaton.

444. Thomas Holt, a native of York, was the architect of the public schools at Oxford

Fig. 204.   PUBLIC SCHOOLS AT OXFORD.

(*fig.* 204.), of which the hint might have been taken from the Campanile of Santa Chiara at Naples, and of the quadrangles of Merton and Wadham colleges. He was the first in this country who introduced the classical orders in series above each other. He evidently borrowed the practice from Philibert Delorme, who had done the same thing at the Chateau d'Anet, near Paris, one of the victim edifices of the Revolution. We apprehend any argument to prove the absurdity of such conceits is unnecessary.

445. Many of the grandest works of what is termed the Elizabethan, or, in truth, the

last Tudor style, were not completed before the middle of the reign of James I. ; so that it may be said to have been practised until the days of Inigo Jones, in whose early works it may be traced. " This fashion," says Dallaway, " of building enormous houses was extended to that period, and even to the civil war. Audley Inn, Hatfield, Charlton, Wilts, and particularly Wollaton, are those in which the best architecture of that age may be seen. Others of the nobility, deserting their baronial residences, indulged themselves in a rivalship in point of extent and grandeur of their country-houses, which was, of course, followed by opulent merchants, the founders of new families. Sir Baptist Hickes, the king's mercer (afterwards ennobled), built Campden House, Gloucestershire, which was scarcely inferior to Hatfield, afterwards burnt down. There is scarcely a county in England which cannot boast of having once contained similar edifices; a very few are still inhabited; others may be traced by their ruins, or remembered by the oldest villagers, who can confirm the tradition; and the sites, at least, of others are pointed out by descriptions as having existed within the memory of man."

446. The following is a list of some of the principal palatial houses finished before 1600. Others of the reign of Elizabeth's successors will hereafter be noticed. Of so many of them are the names of the architects undetermined, though many are assigned to those we have already mentioned, that we shall not attempt to assign a column to the artists in question, for fear of misleading our readers.

Name.	Date about	County.	Founder.	Present State.
Catledge - -	1560	Cambridge	Lord North - -	Taken down.
Basinghouse -	1560	Hants -	Marquis of Winton -	In ruins.
Kelston - -	1587–92	Somerset -	Sir J. Harington - -	Rebuilt.
Gorhambury -	1565	Herts -	Sir N. Bacon - -	In ruins.
Buckhurst -	1565	Sussex -	Lord Buckhurst - -	Destroyed.
Knowle - -	1570	Kent -	Lord Buckhurst -	Perfect.
Penshurst -	1570–85	Kent -	Sir H. Sydney - -	Perfect.
Kenilworth -	1575	Warwick -	Earl of Leicester -	In ruins.
Hunsdon - -	1575	Warwick -	Lord Hunsdon - -	Rebuilt.
Wanstead -	1576	Essex -	Earl of Leicester -	Destroyed.
Burleigh - -	1575–87	Lincoln -	Lord Burleigh -	Perfect.
Osterley - -	1577	Middlesex -	Sir Thomas Gresham -	Rebuilt.
Longleat - -	1579	Wilts -	Sir J. Thynne - -	Perfect.
Stoke Pogis -	1580	Bucks -	Earl of Huntingdon -	Rebuilt.
Toddington -	1580	Beds -	Lord Cheyney - -	Destroyed.
Theobalds -	1570–90	Herts -	Lord Burleigh - -	Destroyed.
Wimbledon -	1588	Surrey -	Sir T. Cecil - -	Rebuilt.
Westwood -	1590	Worcester -	Sir J. Packington -	Perfect.
Hardwick Hall -	1597	Derby -	Countess of Shrewsbury -	In ruins.

447. Relative to Osterley, in the above table, a curious anecdote has been preserved by Fuller, in his *Worthies of Middlesex*. Queen Elizabeth, when visiting its magnificent merchant, the owner, observed to him that the court ought to have been divided by a wall. He immediately collected so many artificers, that before the queen had risen the next morning, says the historian, a wall had been actually erected.

448. Many of these houses possessed terraces of imposing grandeur, which were connected by broad or double flights of steps, with balustrades, whereof, if we may judge from Winstanley's print of Wimbledon, the seat of Sir Edward Cecil, it was a very fine example. The following extracts from the parliamentary survey of it in 1649 will convey some notion of its extent. " The scite of this manor-house being placed on the side slipp of a rising grownde, renders it to stand of that height, that betwixt the basis of the brick wall of the lower court, and the hall door of the sayd manor-house, there are five several ascents, consisting of three score and ten stepps, which are distinguished in a very graceful manner. The platforms were composed of Flanders brick, and the stepps of freestone, very well wrought. On the ground floor was a room called the stone gallery, 108 foot long, pillared and arched with gray marble." The ceiling of the hall " was of fret or parge work, in the middle whereof was fixed one well-wrought landskip, and round the same, in convenient distances, seven other pictures in frames, as ornaments to the whole roome; the floor was of black and white marble."

449. As we have above observed, the Elizabethan style is a mixture of Gothic and Italian. It is characterised by orders very inaccurately and rudely profiled; by arcades whose openings are often extravagantly wide, their height not unfrequently running up into the entablature. The columns on the piers are almost universally on pedestals, and are often banded in courses of circular or square blocks at intervals of their height; when square, they are constantly decorated with prismatic raisings, in imitation of precious stones, a species of

ornament which is of very frequent recurrence. Nothing like unbroken entablatures appear; all is frittered away into small parts, especially in scrolls for the reception of inscriptions, which, at their extremities, are voluted and curled up, like so many pieces of scorched leather. All these eccentricities are so concentrated in their sepulchral monuments, that no better insight into the leading principles of the style can be afforded than an example from Westminster Abbey, here given in the monument of Queen Elizabeth herself (*fig.* 205.). In this it will be seen that the taste is cumbrous and confused; and to add to the anomalies, the figures were coloured, and the different sorts of marbles and alabasters of numberless hues. The general composition consists in a large altar tomb under an open arcade, with a rich and complicated entablature. The columns are usually of black or white marble, of the Doric or Corinthian order. Small pyramidal figures, whose sides were richly veneered with variously coloured pieces, disposed in ornamented squares or circles supporting globes, are of continual occurrence. Armorial bearings in their various colours were introduced to excess. When the monument is placed against a wall, which is more usually the case, the plan was accommodated to it, and the alcove with its columns universally retained. Among the best examples are those of Thomas Ratcliffe Earl of Sussex at Boreham in Essex, to cost 1500*l.*, and of his countess in Westminster Abbey; of Robert Dudley Earl of Leicester at Warwick; and of Henry Carey Lord Hunsdon in Westminster Abbey.

Fig. 205.   QUEEN ELIZABETH'S MONUMENT.

450. It seems droll in this age, when throughout Europe the principles of good taste in architecture are so well understood, that fashion, induced by the cupidity and ignorance of upholsterers and decorators,—the curses of the art,—should again sanction an adoption of the barbarous forms and unmeaning puerilities which it might be supposed Jones and Wren had, by their example, consigned to a merited oblivion. We fear our warning voice will do little to suppress the rage till its cycle is completed. We have, in the prolongation of the subject, sacrificed our own feelings to the rage in the present day for designs of this class, and have assigned to it a far longer description than it deserves. The wretched cockney imitations of it perpetrated for retired shopkeepers in the insignificant villas of the suburbs of the metropolis, and occasionally for the amusement of country gentlemen a little more distant, as well as the use of what is called Gothic, appear to us in no other light than mockeries of a style which is repudiated by the manners of the nineteenth century. The style called Elizabethan we consider quite as unworthy of imitation as would be the adoption in the present day of the model of the ships of war, with their unwieldy and topheavy poops, which encountered the Armada, in preference to the beautiful and compact form of a well-moulded modern frigate.

Sect. VII.

JAMES I. TO ANNE.

451. The first of the reigns that heads this section has, in some measure, been anticipated in our notice of Elizabethan architecture, which it was impossible to keep altogether distinct

from the following reign. The angular and circular bay windows now disappeared entirely, and were supplanted by large square ones, of very large dimensions in their height, unequally divided by transoms, and placed in lengthened rows, so as to form leading features in the several stories of the building. Battlements were now entirely omitted, and the general effect of the pile became one of massive solidity, broken by a square turret loftier than those at the angles. The houses built in the reign of James I. are deficient in the picturesque beauty found in those of his predecessors. Many of them were finished by the architects named in the last section, and they were on a larger scale than even those of the age of Elizabeth. Audley Inn in 1616, Hatfield in 1611, and Charlton House in Wiltshire for Sir Henry Knevett, were, perhaps, the best specimens. The house at Campden, Gloucestershire, built by Sir Baptist Hickes, and which was burned down during the civil wars, consisted of four fronts, the principal one being towards the garden, upon the ground terrace; at each angle was a lateral projection of some feet, with spacious bay windows; in the centre a portico, with a series of the columns of the five orders (as in the schools at Oxford), and an open corridor. The parapet was finished with pediments of a capricious taste, and the chimneys were twisted pillars with Corinthian capitals. A very capacious dome issued from the roof, which was regularly illuminated for the direction of travellers during the night. This immense building was enriched with friezes and entablatures, most profusely sculptured; it is reported to have been erected at the expense of 29,000*l.*, and to have occupied, with its offices, a site of eight acres."

452. The use of the orders became more general. In Glamorganshire, at Beaupré Castle (1600), which has a front and porch of the Doric order, we find a composition including that just named, the Ionic and the Corinthian, wherein the capitals and columns are accurately designed and executed. The following table exhibits some of the principal houses of the period : —

House.	Date.	County.	Founder.	Present State.	Architect.
Holland House	1607	Middlesex	Sir Walter Cope	Perfect	J. Thorpe (?)
Bramshill	1607–12	Hants	Edward Lord Zouche	do.	Uncertain.
Castle Ashby		Northamptn.	Herbert Lord Compton	do.	do.
Summer Hill		Kent	Earl of Clanricarde	do.	do.
Charlton		Wilts	Sir Henry Knevet	Restored	do.
Hatfield	1611	Herts	Robert Earl of Salisbury	Perfect	do.
Longford Castle	1612	Wilts	Sir T. Gorges	do.	J. Thorpe (?)
Temple Newsham	1612–19	Yorkshire	Sir Arthur Ingram	do.	Uncertain.
Charlton	1612	Kent	Sir Adam Newton	do.	do.
Bolsover	1613	Derby	Sir Charles Cavendish	Dilapidated	{ Huntingdon Smithson
Audley Inn	1616	Essex	T. Earl of Suffolk	Perfect	B. Jansen
Wollaton	{ 1580 1588 }	Notts	Sir Francis Willoughby	do.	{ J. Thorpe and R. Smithson

453. Under James, the pride and magnificence of the aristocracy was as equally displayed in the sumptuous monuments erected to the memory of the departed as in their stately palaces; and we can scarcely point to a county in England whose parish churches do not attest the fact by the gorgeous tombs that exist in villages where the mansions of those thus commemorated have not long since passed from the memory of man. A year's rental of an estate, and that frequently under testamentary direction, was often squandered in the sepulchral monument of the deceased lord of a manor.

454. In the reign of James I. properly commences the career of Inigo Jones, to which we hasten with delight, as indicating the dawn of true architecture (for the Gothic had irretrievably passed away) in England. It resembles the arrival of a traveller at an oasis in the desert, after a parching and toilsome journey. "Jones, if a table of fame," says Walpole, "like that in the Tatler, were to be formed for men of real and indisputable genius in every country, would save England from the disgrace of not having her representative among the arts. She adopted Holbein and Vandyck, she borrowed Rubens, she produced Inigo Jones. Vitruvius drew up his grammar, Palladio showed him the practice, Rome displayed a theatre worthy his emulation, and King Charles was ready to encourage, employ, and reward his talents. This is the history of Inigo Jones as a genius." Generally speaking, we are not admirers of Walpole, who often sacrificed truth to fancy, and the character of an artist to a prettily-turned period; hence we are disinclined to concur in his criticisms without many qualifications; but in this case he has so well expressed our own

feelings, that we regret we cannot add force to the observations in which we so fully concur.

455. Inigo Jones was the son of a clothworker, and was born about 1572.   From the most probable accounts he appears to have been apprenticed to a joiner, in which state he was, from some accounts, discovered by the Earl of Arundel, from others by William Earl of Pembroke, and by one or other of these noblemen sent to Italy, rather, however, according to Walpole, to study the art of painting, than that of architecture, for the former of which, the author named says, Nature appears not to have fitted him, inasmuch as " he dropped the pencil, and conceived Whitehall."   But our own belief is, that though he might have afterwards been patronised by both the noblemen above mentioned, he owed this part of his education to neither of them ; for, considering that at his first visit to Italy, before 1605, Lord Pembroke was but just of age, and that Lord Arundel was somewhat younger, there is no great probability that either of them thus assisted him in his studies on the Continent.

456. Of his employment as an architect nothing can be traced previous to the visit of James I. to the University of Oxford, in 1605, at which time he was thirty-three years old ; and then, according to Leland (*Collectanea*, App. vol. vi. p. 647.), " They " (the University) " hired one Mr. Jones, a great traveller, who undertook to further them with rare devices, but performed little to what was expected.   He had for his pains, I have constantly heard, 50*l.* ;" from which it is certain that his earliest visit to Italy was before 1605.   At Venice he became acquainted with the works of Palladio ; and there, as Walpole observes, " learned how beautifully taste may be exerted on a less theatre than the capital of an empire."   In this city his reputation was so great, that Christian IV. appointed him his architect, though of the buildings erected by him in Denmark we know nothing.   In this country's capital, however, he was found by James, and by his Queen (Anne) was removed from Copenhagen to Scotland, in the quality of her architect.   By Prince Henry he was employed in the same capacity, and about this time had the grant in reversion of surveyor general of the works.   On the untimely and lamented death of that prince, he once more visited Italy, where he perfected his taste and ripened his judgment. It appears more than probable that it was previous to his second journey that he designed those of his buildings that partake of a bastard style.   These buildings, however, are such as could, under the circumstances, have been designed only by a great master in a state of transition from one style to another ; such, for instance, are the north and south sides of the quadrangle at St. John's College, Oxford, in which he seems to have copied all the faults of the worst examples of his great master Palladio ; still the composition is so picturesque, that, though reluctantly, we cannot avoid admiring it.   In the garden front of

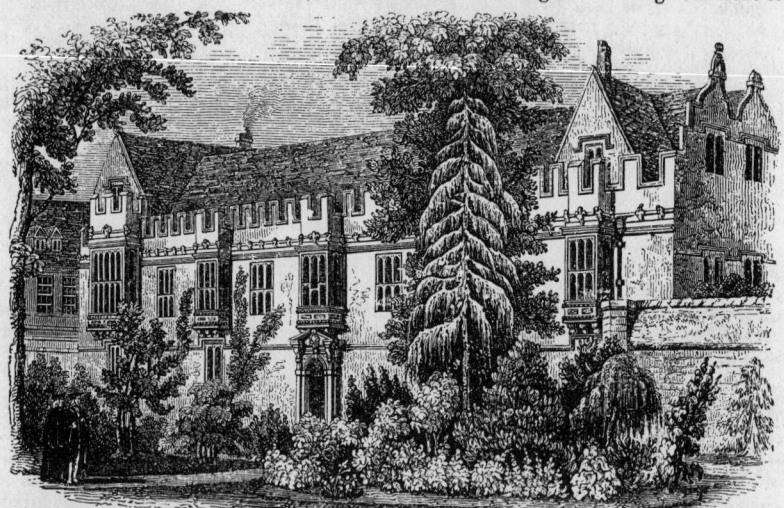

Fig 206.   GARDEN FRONT OF ST. JOHN'S COLLEGE, OXFORD, (1631—5).

the same college (*fig.* 206.), notwithstanding its impurity, there is a breadth and grandeur which subdue criticism, and raise our admiration ; and we by no means subscribe to Horace Walpole's dictum, that " Inigo's designs of that period have a littleness of parts and a weight of ornament."   Previous to his second return to England, the surveyor's place had fallen in, and finding the office in debt, he prevailed, as Walpole observes, with an air of

Roman disinterestedness, and showing that architecture was not the only thing he had learned in Rome, on the comptroller and paymaster of the office, to give up, as he did, all the profits of the office till the arrears were cleared.

457. By the *Fœdera*, vol. xviii. p. 99., we find that there was issued to him, in conjunction with the Earl of Arundel and others, a commission to prevent the building on new foundations within two miles of London and the palace of Westminster; and in 1620 he was, if possible, more uselessly employed by James I. in guessing, for it was no more, who were the builders of Stonehenge. For this last, the necessary preliminary information had not even dawned, although Walpole, in his usual off-hand manner, loses not, in alluding to it, the opportunity of displaying his own dreadful ignorance on the subject. (See Chap. II. Sect. II., where this monument has been examined.) In the year last named, Jones was one of the commissioners for the repair of old St. Paul's, though the repairs were not commenced till 1633, in which year Laud, then Bishop of London, laid the first stone, and Inigo Jones the fourth. Our architect was now too much disinclined to Gothic to bend his genius to

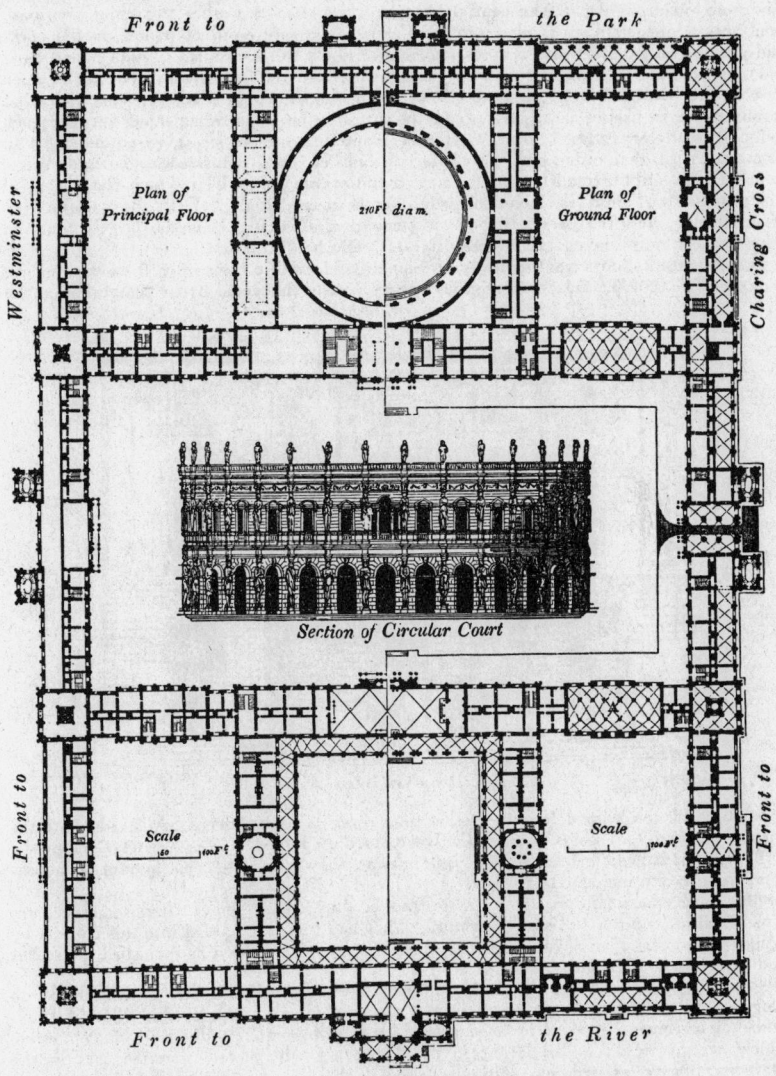

Fig. 207   PLAN OF WHITEHALL.

anything in the shape of a restoration; and though the Roman portico which he placed before the church was magnificent, the application of Roman to Gothic architecture of course ruined the cathedral. The reader will find a representation of this portico in Dugdale's *St. Paul's*. Abstractedly considered, it was a fine composition; and its dimensions, of a length of 200 ft., a depth of 50 ft., and a height of 40 ft., were calculated to give it an imposing effect.

458. The Banqueting House at Whitehall, which we have pride in quoting as one of the most magnificent works in Europe, has generally been supposed to have been erected in the reign of Charles I.; but there is sufficient reason for assigning the period of its execution to the preceding reign. It was begun in 1619, and finished in two years. The designs for the palace of Whitehall, whereof *fig.* 207. at the foot of the preceding page, exhibits a block plan, on which the banqueting-house (at A), it will be seen, forms a very inconsiderable portion, would, had they been executed, have formed, beyond all comparison, the finest in the world. In magnitude it would have exceeded even the palace of Diocletian. The form, as will be observed, was an oblong square, and consisted of seven courts, whereof six were quadrangular. The central one was larger than the other two chief divisions; and these were again subdivided into three courts, the centre one of which, on the north side, had two galleries with arcades, and that on the south a circular Persian court, as it was called, whose diameter was 210 ft. Surrounded on the ground floor by an open arcade, the piers between the arches were decorated with figures of Persians, with what propriety it is useless to discuss; and the upper story was ornamented between each window with caryatides, bearing Corinthian capitals on their heads, surmounted by an entablature of that order, and the whole was finished by a balustrade. Towards Westminster, the front extended 1152 ft.; and that towards the park, in which the length of the banqueting-house is included, would have been 720 ft. With the exception of Westminster Hall, the banqueting-house (now used as a chapel) is the largest room in England, its length being 115 ft., breadth 60 ft., and height 55 ft.

459. In 1632, Jones was employed on Somerset House, to the garden front whereof he executed (*fig.* 208.) a façade of singular beauty, lost to the world by its demolition on the

Fig. 208.   WATER FRONT OF OLD SOMERSET HOUSE.

rebuilding of the edifice for its present purposes. On the ascent of Charles I. to the throne, our architect seems to have been very much employed. As surveyor of the public buildings, his stipend was 8s. 4d. a day, besides an allowance of 46l. per annum for house-rent, a clerk, and incidental expenses.

460. In the passion for masques which prevailed during the reign of Charles I., Jones was a principal contributor to their splendour. They had been introduced into this country by Anne of Denmark; and Walpole gives a list of thirteen to which he furnished the scenes and machinery.

461. They who have seen Wilton can appreciate Inigo's merit for having introduced into England, in the seats of our aristocracy, a style vying with that of the villas of Italy. Some disagreement appears to have arisen between him and Philip Earl of Pembroke, which here it would be irrelevant to dwell on; we will merely mention that in the Harleian library existed an edition of Jones's *Stonehenge*, which had formerly belonged to the nobleman in question; and that its margins are filled by the former

possessor with notes, not on the substance of the work itself, but on its author, and anything else that could be injurious.   He calls him " Iniquity Jones," and says he had 16,000*l.* a year for keeping the king's houses in repair.   The censures were undeserved; and the accusations, unwarranted by facts, are extremely discreditable to the memory of Earl Philip.

Fig. 209.   YORK STAIRS.   (Now considered to be by N. Stone.)

462. The works of Jones were exceedingly numerous; many, however, are assigned to him which were the productions of his scholars.   Such buildings as the Queen's house at Greenwich (much altered, and, indeed, spoiled, of late years, for the purpose of turning it into a public naval school); Coleshill, in Berkshire, built in 1650; Shaftesbury House, in Aldersgate Street; the square, as planned, and Church of St. Paul, Covent Garden; and many other works, are strong proofs of the advancement of architecture during his career.   York Stairs (*fig.* 209.), another of his examples, exhibits a pureness and propriety of character which appears to have been afterwards unappreciated by his successors, with Wren at their head, whose mention by the side of Jones is only justified by the scientific and constructive skill he possessed.

463. Jones was a follower of the Venetian school, which we have described in a previous section.   His respect for Palladio is evinced by the circumstance of a copy of that great master's works being his companion on his travels through Italy.   It is filled with his autograph notes, and is now deposited in the library of Worcester College, Oxford.   Lord Burlington had a Vitruvius noted by him in a similar manner.   It is curious to see the amateurs and pseudo-critics of the present day decry these two authors, whom Jones, a genius of the first order, thought his best instructors.   The class in question are, however, no longer considered worthy of being listened to on matters of the art; and the public taste is, in this respect, turning once more into the proper channel.   Palladian architecture, thus introduced by Jones, would have reached a splendour under Charles I. perhaps equal to that which Italy can boast, had not its progress been checked by public calamities, in which it was the lot of the artist to share the misfortunes of his royal master.   In addition to being the favourite of the king, he was a Roman Catholic; and for this (as it was then curiously called) delinquency, he had to pay 545*l.* in the year 1646.   Grief, misfortunes, and a consequent premature old age, terminated the life of this great man at Somerset House on the 21st of July, 1651.

464. The plans of houses introduced from Italy by this master were not, perhaps, altogether suited to the climate or habits of the English.   One of his greatest faults was that of aiming at magnificence under circumstances in which it could not be attained.   Thus, his rooms were often sacrificed to the show and effect resulting from a hall or a staircase, or both; sometimes, to gain the appearance of a vista of apartments, they were made too small for the scale of the house.   His distribution of windows is purely Italian, and the piers between them consequently too large, so that the light is occasionally insufficient in quantity.   The habits of Italy, which enabled Palladio to raise his principal floor, and to have the farm offices and those for the vintage in the same range of building as the mansion, impart an air of great magnificence to the Italian villa.   Jones saw that this arrangement was not required for English convenience, and therefore avoided the Palladian practice; " but," says Mitford, " the architects who followed him were dazzled, or dazzled their employers.   To tack the wings to the centre with a colonnade became a phrase to express the purpose of plan of the most elegant effect; and the effect, provided the combination be harmonious, will be elegant; but the arrangement is very adverse to general convenience, and especially in the moderate scale of most general use.   Where great splendour is the object, convenience must yield to it.   Magnificence must be paid for in convenience as well as money."   Webb and Carter were the pupils of Jones.   The former will furnish us presently with a few remarks.   During the time of the Commonwealth, the history of architecture in this country is a complete blank.   We know of no public work of consequence that was designed or executed in the interregnum.   On the restoration of

the monarchy, however, the art began to revive; but it was much tinctured with the contemporary French style, which Lord Burlington, on its reappearance many years afterwards, had the merit of reforming, and of bringing back the public taste to the purity which Jones had introduced : but this we shall have to notice hereafter.

465. John Webb was nephew as well as scholar of Inigo Jones, whose only daughter he married. He built a large seat for the Bromley family at Horseheath, in Cambridgeshire; and added a portico to the Vine, in Hampshire, for Challoner Chute, the Speaker to Richard Cromwell's parliament. Ambresbury, in Wiltshire (*fig.* 210.), was only executed

Fig. 210.   AMBRESBURY.   (Before its alterations in 1853.)

by him from the designs of his master, as also the east side of the court of Greenwich Hospital. Captain William Winde, a native of Bergen-op-Zoom, and pupil to Sir Balthazar Gerbier, was, soon after the Restoration, in considerable employ as an architect. He built Cliefden House, Bucks, which was destroyed by fire in 1795 ; the Duke of Newcastle's, in Lincoln's Inn Fields ; Combe Abbey, Warwickshire, for Lord Craven; and for the same peer he finished Hempsted Marshall, which had been begun by his master. But the chief and best work of Winde was Buckingham House, in St. James's Park, on whose site now stands a palace, larger, indeed, but unworthy to be its successor. It is known from prints, and not a few of our readers will probably recollect the building itself. It was erected for John Sheffield, Duke of Buckingham ; and on its frieze was the inscription " SIC SITI LÆTANTUR LARES." The arrears in the payments for this house, according to an anecdote in Walpole, were so distressing, that when it was nearly finished, " Winde had enticed his Grace to mount upon the leads to enjoy the grand prospect. When there, he coolly locked the trap-door, and threw the key to the ground, addressing his astonished patron, ' I am a ruined man, and unless I have your word of honour that the debts shall be paid, I will instantly throw myself over.' ' And what is to become of me,' said the duke ? ' You shall come along with me.' The promise was given, and the trap-door opened (upon a sign made) by a workman in the secret, and who was a party to the plot." We do not vouch for the truth of the tale.

466. An architect of the name of Marsh is said, by Vertue, to have designed the additional buildings at Bolsover, as also to have done some considerable works at Nottingham Castle ; and Salmon, in his account of Essex, mentions a Doctor Morecroft, who died in 1677, as the architect of the manor-house of Fitzwalters. Of the works of the French taste about the middle of the period under discussion, a better notion cannot be obtained than from Montague House, late the British Museum (*fig.* 211.), the work of a Frenchman here whose example had followers; indeed, Wren himself, in some of his works, has caught the vices of the French school of the day, though he was a follower of the Venetian and Roman schools. The fire which destroyed London in 1666, a few years after the death of Jones, brought into notice the talents of Sir Christopher Wren, whose career was opened under

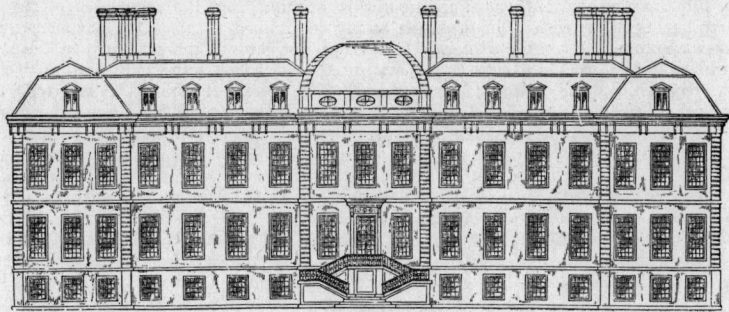

Fig. 211.   BRITISH MUSEUM.

the reign of Charles II.   "The length of his life enriched the reigns of several princes and
disgraced the last of them."   (At the advanced age of 86 he was removed by George I. from
the office of Surveyor General.)   "A variety of knowledge proclaims the universality, a multiplicity of works the abundance, St. Paul's the greatness, of Sir Christopher's genius.   The
noblest temple, the largest palace, the most stupendous hospital, in such a kingdom as
Britain, are all works of the same hand.   He restored London and recorded its fall."   As
the boast of England is the Cathedral Church of St. Paul, it will be necessary to dwell a
little on a description of it.

467. The larger portion of this cathedral stands on part of the site of the old one, as
shown by the annexed diagram (*fig.* 212.), which also exhibits their comparative sizes.   It is

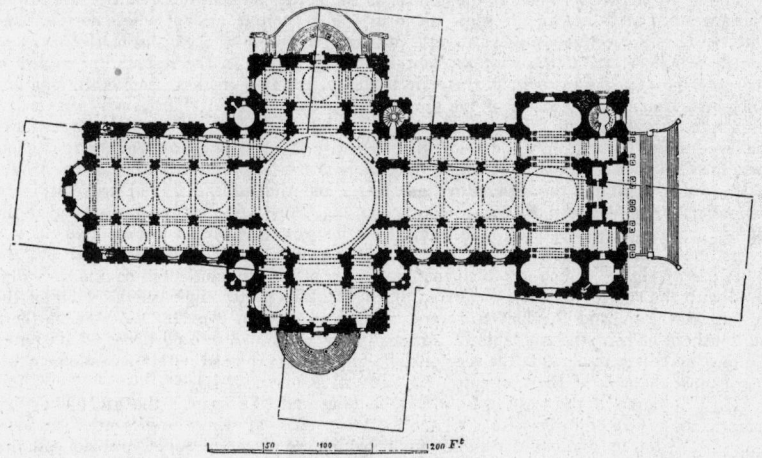

Fig. 212.   PLAN OF OLD AND NEW ST. PAUL'S.

copied from a drawing by Sir Christopher in the library of All Souls College at Oxford.
The instructions to the surveyor, according to the compiler of the Parentalia, were — " to
contrive a fabric of moderate bulk, but of good proportion; a convenient quire, with a
vestibule and porticoes, and a dome conspicuous above the houses:" and in conformity with
them, a design was made which, from various causes, does not appear to have given satisfaction; whereon the compiler observes, that " he endeavoured to gratify the taste of the
connoisseurs and criticks with something coloss and beautiful, with a design antique and
well studied, conformable to the best style of the Greek and Roman architecture."   The
model made from this design is still preserved in the cathedral.   This however was, unfortunately, not approved, and, as our informant continues, " the surveyor then turned his
thoughts to a cathedral form, so altered as to reconcile as near as possible the Gothic to a
better manner of architecture."   These last designs were approved by Charles, who issued
his warrant under privy seal on the 1st of May, 1675, for the execution of the works.

468. Much trouble was experienced in removing the immense ruins of the old church, for
the destruction whereof recourse was had to many expedients.   On the north side, the foundations are placed upon a stratum of hard pot earth about 6 ft. in thickness, but not more

than 4 ft. thick on the south side ; and upon this stratum, from the experience of the old church having firmly rested, the architect wisely determined to place the new one. The work was commenced on the western side, driving eastward to the extremity of the site ; at which, on the northern side, a pit was discovered whence the hard pot earth had been extracted, and the vacuity so made filled up with loose rubbish. The length of this hole in the direction of the foundation was not more than 6 or 7 ft., and from the fear of piles, if driven, becoming rotten, the surveyor determined to excavate through the sand, and to build up from the stratum solid for a depth of 40 ft. The pit sunk here was 18 ft. wide ; in this he built up a pier, 10 ft. square, till it rose to within 15 ft. of the present surface. At this level he introduced an arch from the pier to the main foundation, and on this arch the north-eastern quoin of the choir is founded.

469. On the 21st of June, 1675, the first stone was laid ; and, within ten years, the walls of the choir and its side aisles, and the north and south circular porticoes, were finished ; the piers of the dome also were brought up to the same height. The son of the architect laid the last stone in 1710. This was the highest stone on the top of the lantern. Thus the whole edifice was finished in thirty-five years, under the remarkable circumstances of having only one architect, one master mason (Mr. Strong), and the see being occupied the whole time by one bishop, Doctor Henry Compton. The master builder's name was Jennings.

470. The plan of St. Paul's is a Latin cross, and bears a general resemblance to that of St. Peter's. A rectangular parallelogram, 480 ft. from east to west (measuring from the top of the steps of the western portico to the exterior of the eastern wall of the choir), is crossed by another parallelogram, whose extremities form the transepts, 250 ft. in length from north to south. At the eastern end of the first parallelogram is a hemicylindrical recess, containing the altar, and extending 20 ft. further eastward ; so that the whole length is 500 ft., exclusive of the flight of steps. At the north and south ends of the transepts are porticoes, segmental on the plan, and projecting 20 ft. The centre of the intersection of the parallelograms is 280 ft. from the western front. The width of each parallelogram is 125 ft. At the western end of the edifice, on the north and south extremities, are towers whose western faces are in the same plane as the general front, but whose northern and southern faces respectively project about 27 ft. from the walls of the aisles of the nave ; so that the whole width of the western front is about 180 ft. In the re-entering angles on each side, between the towers and the main building, are two chapels, each 50 ft. long and 20 ft. broad, open to the aisles of the nave at their western end. Externally two orders reign round the building. The lower one Corinthian, standing on a basement 10 ft. above the level of the ground, on the western side, where a flight of steps extending the whole breadth of the front, exclusive of the towers, leads to the level of the church. The height of this order, including the entablature, is 50 ft. ; and that of the second order, which is composite, is one fifth less, or 40 ft. ; making the total height 100 ft. from the ground to the top of the second entablature. The portico of the western front is formed with the two orders above mentioned, the lower story consisting of twelve coupled columns, and the upper one of eight ; which last is surmounted by a pediment, whose tympanum is sculptured with the subject of the Conversion of St. Paul, in pretty high relief. Half of the western elevation, and the half transverse section, is given in *fig.* 213. At the northern and southern ends of the transepts the lower order is continued into porticoes of six fluted columns, standing, in plan, on the segment of a circle, and crowned with a semi-dome abutting against the ends of the transepts.

471. The porch of the western front is 50 ft. long and 20 ft. wide : the great doorway, being in the centre of it, leads to a vestibule 50 ft. square, at whose angles are four piers connected at top by semicircular arches, under which are placed detached coupled columns in front of the piers. The body of the church is divided into a nave and two side aisles, decorated with pilasters supporting semicircular arches ; and on each side of the porch and vestibule is a passage which leads directly to the corresponding aisles. The choir is similarly disposed, with its central division and side aisles.

472. The entrances from the transepts lead into vestibules 25 ft. deep, and the whole breadth of the transept in length, each communicating with the centre by a central passage and its aisles formed between two massive piers and the walls at the intersections of the transepts with the choir and nave. The eight piers are joined by arches springing from one to the other so as to form an octagon at their springing points, and the angles between the arches, instead of rising vertically, *sail* over as they rise and form *pendentives*, which lead, at their top, into a circle on the plan. Above this a wall rises in the form of a truncated cone, which, at the height of 168 ft. from the pavement, terminates in a horizontal cornice, from which the interior dome springs. Its diameter is 100 ft., and it is 60 ft. in height, in the form of a paraboloid. Its thickness is 18 in., and it is constructed of brickwork. From the haunches of this dome, 200 ft. above the pavement of the church, another cone of brickwork commences, 85 ft. high, and 94 ft. diameter at the bottom. This cone is pierced with apertures, as well for the purpose of diminishing its weight as for distributing light between it and the outer dome. At the top it is gathered into a dome, in the

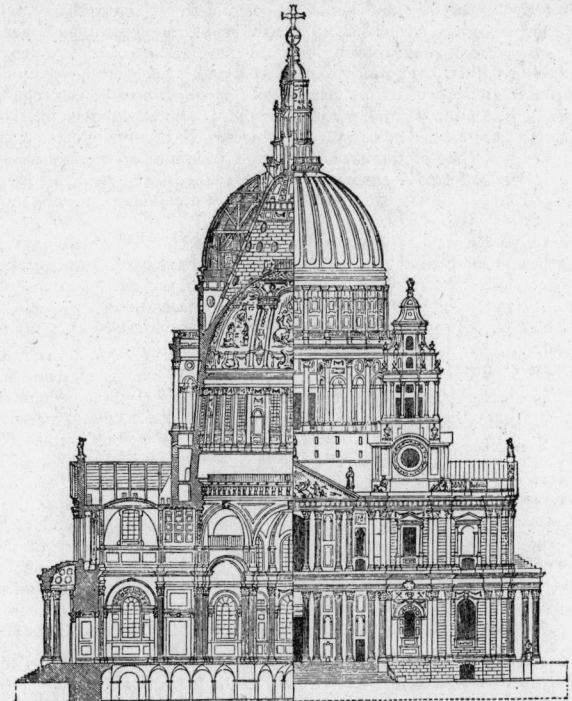

Fig. 213.   HALF ELEVATION AND HALF SECTION OF ST. PAUL'S.

form of a hyperboloid, pierced near the vertex with an aperture 12 ft. in diameter. The top of this cone is 285 ft. from the pavement, and carries a lantern 55 ft. high, terminating in a dome, whereon a ball and cross is raised. The last-named cone is provided with corbels, sufficient in number to receive the hammer beams of the external dome, which is of oak, and its base 220 ft. from the pavement, its summit being level with the top of the cone. In form, it is nearly hemispherical, and generated by radii 57 ft. in length, whose centres are in a horizontal diameter, passing through its base. The cone and the interior dome are restrained in their lateral thrust on the supports by four tiers of strong iron chains, placed in grooves prepared for their reception, and run with lead. The lowest of these is inserted in the masonry round their common base, and the other three at different heights on the exterior of the cone. Externally the intervals of the columns and pilasters are occupied by windows and niches, with horizontal and semicircular heads, and crowned with pediments. In the lower order, excepting modillions under the corona, the entablature is quite plain, and there are also console modillions in the upper order. The edifice, in three directions, is terminated with pediment roofs; and at the extremities, on each of those faces, are acroteria, supporting statues 25 ft. above the roof of the edifice. Over the intersection of the nave and transepts for the external work, and for a height of 25 ft. above the roof of the church, a cylindrical wall rises, whose diameter is 146 ft. Between it and the lower conical wall is a space, but at intervals they are connected by cross walls. This cylinder is quite plain, but perforated by two courses of rectangular apertures. On it stands a peristyle of thirty columns of the Corinthian order, 40 ft. high, including bases and capitals, with a plain entablature crowned by a balustrade. In this peristyle, every fourth intercolumniation is filled up solid, with a niche, and connection is provided between it and the wall of the lower cone. Vertically over the base of that cone, above the peristyle, rises another cylindrical wall, appearing above the balustrade. It is ornamented with pilasters, between which are a tier of rectangular windows above, and one of blanks below. On this wall the external dome is posited. As will be seen by reference to the section, the lantern which we have before noticed receives no support from it. It is merely ornamental, differing entirely in that respect from the dome of St. Peter's.

473. The towers in the western front are 220 ft. high, terminating in open lanterns, covered with domes formed by curves of contrary flexure, and not very purely composed, though perhaps in character with the general façade.

474. The interior of the nave and choir are each designed with three arches longitudinally springing from piers, strengthened, as well as decorated, on their inner faces, by an entablature, whose cornice reigns throughout the nave and church. Above this entablature, and breaking with it over each pilaster, is a tall attic from projections on which spring semicircular arches which are formed into *arcs doubleaux*. Between the last, pendentives are formed, terminated by horizontal cornices. Small cupolas, of less height than their semi-diameter, are formed above these cornices. In the upright plane space on the walls above the main arches of the nave, choir, and transepts, a *clerestory* is obtained over the Attic order, whose form is generated by the rising of the pendentives. The inner dome is plastered on the under side, and painted by Sir James Thornhill, with subjects relating to the history of St. Paul.

475. For external elegance, we know no church in Europe which exhibits a cupola comparable with that of St. Paul's, though in its connection with the church by an order higher than that below it there is a violation of the laws of the art. The cost of the church was 736,752*l*., exclusive of the stone and iron enclosures round it, which cost 11,202*l*. more; in all 747,954*l*. About nine-tenths of that sum were raised by a tax on coals imported into London. As compared with St. Peter's, we subjoin a few of the principal dimensions of the two churches.

Direction of Measure.	St. Peter's in English Feet.	St. Paul's in English Feet.	Excess of the former in Feet.
Length within - -	669	500	169
Breadth at entrance - -	226	100	126
Principal façade - -	395	180	215
Breadth at the cross - -	442	223	219
Cupola, clear diameter -	139	108	31
Cupola, height of, with lantern	432	330	102
Church in height - -	146	110	36

476. If we suppose sections to be made through the transepts of the four principal churches of Europe, we have their relative sizes in the following ratio : —

St. Peter's, Rome -   -   -   -   -   -   - 1·0000
Santa Maria del Fiore, at Florence   -   -   -   - ·5358
St. Paul's, London   -   -   -   -   -   - ·4166
St. Genevieve (Pantheon), Paris   -   -   -   -   - ·3303

477. Notwithstanding its imposing effect as a whole, and the exhibition in its construction of a mechanical skill of the very highest order ; notwithstanding, also, the abstract beauty of the greater number of its parts, it is our duty to observe that many egregious abuses are displayed in the fabric of St. Paul's, the first and greatest whereof is the great waste of interior effect as compared with the total section employed. If we suppose, as before, sections from north to south to be made through the transepts of the four principal churches, the following table will exhibit the proportion of their clear internal to their external areas : —

St. Peter's, Rome -   -   -   -   -   - 8,325 : 10,000
Santa Maria del Fiore, Florence   -   -   -   - 8,855 : 10,000
St. Paul's, London   -   -   -   -   - 6,865 : 10,000
St. Genevieve (Pantheon), Paris   -   -   -   - 6,746 : 10,000

Whence it is seen how highly in this respect the Duomo of Florence ranks above the others. The defect of St. Paul's in this respect is mainly induced by the false dome ; and though we may admire the ingenuity that provided for carrying a stone lantern on the top of a truncated cone, deceitfully appearing, as it does, to stand on the dome from which it rises, we cannot help regretting that it afforded the opportunity of giving the building a cupola, liable to the early attack of time, and perhaps that, more to be dreaded, of fire.

478. In the skill required for raising a building on a minimum of foundation, Sir Christopher Wren appears to have surpassed, at least, those who preceded him. In similarly or nearly so formed buildings, some criterion of the comparative skill employed in their construction may be drawn from comparing the ratio between the area of the whole plan, and that of the sum of the areas of the horizontal sections of the whole of the piers, walls, and pillars, which serve to support the superincumbent mass. The similarity of the four churches already compared affords, therefore, a criterion of their respective merits in this respect. We hardly need say that one of the first qualifications of an architect is to produce the greatest effect by the smallest means. The subjoined table is placed before the reader as a comparison of the four churches in reference to the point in question.

Church.	Whole Area in English Feet.	Area of Points of Support.	Ratio.
St. Peter's at Rome - -	227,069	59,308	1 : 0·261
Sta. Maria del Fiore, Florence	84,802	17,030	1 : 0·201
St. Paul's, London - -	84,025	14,311	1 : 0·170
St. Genevieve (Pantheon), Paris	60,287	9,269	1 : 0·154

The merit, therefore, shown in the *construction* of the above edifices will be nearly as 15, 17, 20, 26, or inversely proportional to the numbers in the last column.

479. We must here mention one of the most unpardonable defects, or rather abuses, which this church exhibits, and which must be learnt from reference to *fig.* 214. There n is

Fig. 214.   ST. PAUL'S. SECTION WITH BUTTRESSES.

given a transverse section of the nave and its side aisles.   From this it will be seen that the enormous expense of the second or upper order all round the church was incurred for no other purpose than that of concealing the flying buttresses that are used to counteract the thrusts of the vaults of the nave, choir, and transepts, — an abuse that admits of no apology. It is an architectural fraud.   We do not think it necessary to descend into minor defects and abuses, such as vaulting the church from an Attic order, the multiplicity of breaks, and want of repose ; the general disappearance of tie and connection, the piercing, as practised, the piers of the cupola, and mitering the archivolts of its great arches, and the like, because we think all these are more than counterbalanced by the beauties of the edifice.   We cannot, however, leave the subject without observing that not the least of its merits is its freedom from any material settlement tending to bring on premature dilapidation.   Its chief failures are over the easternmost arch of the nave, and in the north transept, for the remedy whereof (the latter) the architect left written instructions.   There are also some unimportant failures in the haunches of most of the flying buttresses, which are scarcely worth notice.

480. The wretchedly naked appearance of the interior of this cathedral is a disgrace neither to the architect nor to the country, but to the clergy, Terrick, bishop of London, and Potter, archbishop of Canterbury, who refused to sanction its decoration with pictures, gratuitously proffered by artists of the highest reputation ; and this after the cupola itself had been decorated.   The colour of the sculpture is of no use in heightening the effect of the interior.

481. The *Parentalia* contains a description of the manner in which the walls of the old

cathedral were destroyed, and those of the present one raised; which should be read by all those engaged in the practice of architecture.

482. Wren, having lived to see the completion of St. Paul's, was, as before stated, displaced from the office of surveyor of Crown buildings to make room for an incompetent pretender, named Benson. Pope, in the *Dunciad*, has left a record of the job, in the lines—

> While Wren with sorrow to the grave descends,
> Gay dies unpensioned with a hundred friends.

Wren died at the age of 91 years, and was buried under the fabric, "with four words," says Walpole, "that comprehended his merit and his fame."

"SI QUÆRAS MONUMENTUM CIRCUMSPICE."

483. It will be impossible, consistently with our space, to describe the works of Sir Christopher Wren. One upon which his fame is as justly founded as upon St. Paul's itself, is St. Stephen's Church in Wallbrook, in which, on a plot of ground 80½ ft. by 59½ ft., he has contrived a structure whose elegance is not surpassed by any one we know to have been raised under similar restrictions. The church in question is divided longitudinally into five aisles by four ranks of Corinthian columns standing on pedestals; the places of four columns near the centre being unoccupied; the surrounding central columns form the angles of an octagon, 45 ft. diameter, on which arches are turned, and above which, by means of pendentives, the circular base of a dome is formed, which is in the shape of a segment of a sphere, with a lantern thereon. The ceiling of the middle aisle from east to west is vaulted in groins. The rest of the ceiling is horizontal. The interior of St. James's, Westminster, is another beautiful example of the master, though recently underrated by an ignorant critic.

484. One of the peculiarities remarkable about Wren's period is the investment of the form of the Gothic spire with a clothing of Italian architecture, by which the modern steeple was produced. If any example could reconcile us to such a practice, it might be found in that of Bow Church, another of Wren's works, which rises to the height of 197 ft. from the ground, the sides of the square from which it rises being 32 ft. 6 in. There are in the leading proportions of this tower and spire, some extraordinary examples in relative heights- as compared with widths sesquialterally, which would almost lead one to suppose that, in this respect, our architect was somewhat superstitious.

485. In St. Dunstan in the East, Wren attempted Gothic, and it is the least offensive of his productions in that style. It is an elegant composition, but wants the claim to originality. St. Nicholas, Newcastle, and the High Church, Edinburgh, are its prototypes.

486. The Monument of London is original, notwithstanding columns of this sort had been previously erected. Its total expense was 8856*l.*, and it was commenced in 1671, completed in 1677. The height is 202 ft.; hence it is loftier than any of the historical columns of the ancients. The pedestal is about 21 ft. square, standing on a plinth 6 ft. wider. The lower diameter of the column on the upper part of the base is 15 ft., and the shaft incloses a staircase of black marble, consisting of 345 steps. It was fluted after the work was carried up. The quantity of Portland stone whereof it is composed is 28,196 cubic feet. The Antonine column at Rome is 175, and that of Trajan 147 ft. high. That erected by Arcadius at Constantinople, when perfect, was of the same height as that last mentioned. The structure of which we are speaking loses much by its situation, which has neither been improved nor deteriorated by the streets consequent on the rebuilding of London Bridge: and though it cannot compete with the Trajan column in point of intrinsic beauty, it is, nevertheless, an exquisite and well-proportioned work, and seems much better calculated with propriety to record the object of its erection, than the other is to be the monument of a hero. In these days, it is singular to see that no other mode than the erection of a column could be found to record the glorious actions of a Nelson. Such was the poverty of taste that marked the decision of the committee to whom that object was most improperly entrusted.

487. Among the works of Wren not to be passed without notice is the Library of Trinity College, Cambridge. It is one of his finest productions, and one with which he himself was well satisfied. It consists of two orders; a Doric arcade below, open to a basement supported by columns, which has a flat ceiling, exceedingly convenient as an ambulatory, and itself simple and well proportioned. The principal story is decorated with three-quarter columns of the Ionic order, well proportioned. From their volutes, festoons are pendent, and the key-stones of the windows are carved into cherubs' heads, &c. This is the elevation towards Nevill's Court; that towards the garden has three Doric doors below, but above is without columns or pilasters in the upper stories. Without ornament, it is not the less graceful and imposing. The interior, as a single room, is designed with great grandeur and propriety.

488. We cannot further in detail continue an account of the works of this extraordinary architect, but shall now proceed to submit a list of his principal works, together with a catalogue of those of his principal churches whose estimates exceeded the cost of 5000*l.*

	Begun.	Completed.
Palace at Greenwich, for Charles II.	-	- 1663	
Theatre at Oxford -	-	-	-	- 1668	1669
The Monument	-	-	-	-	- 1671	1677
Temple Bar	-	-	-	-	- 1670	1672
St. Paul's Cathedral	-	-	-	- 1675	1710
Library at Trinity College, Cambridge	-	- 1679	
Campanile at Christ Church, Oxford	-	- 1681	1682
Ashmolean Library	-	-	-	- 1682	
Palace at Winchester	-	-	-	- 1683	Unfinished.
College of Physicians	-	-	·	-	- 1689	
College at Chelsea -	-	-	-	- 1690	
Palace at Hampton Court -	-	-	- 1690	1694
Towers of Westminster Abbey	-	-	- 1696	
Greenwich Hospital	-	-	-	- 1698	1703

Churches : —

	Time of erection	Cost.		
Allhallows the Great	-	-	-	- 1697	5,641l.	9s.	9d.
Allhallows, Lombard Street	·	-	- 1694	8,058	15	6
St. Andrew Wardrobe	-	-	-	- 1692	7,060	16	11
St. Andrew, Holborn	-	-	-	- 1687	9,000	0	0
St. Antholin	-	-	-	-	- 1682	5,685	5	10
St. Bride -	-	-	-	-	- 1680	11,430	5	11
Christ Church, Newgate Street	-	-	- 1687	11,778	9	6
St. Clement Dane's	-	-	-	- 1680–82	8,786	17	0
St. Dionis Backchurch	-	-	-	- 1674–84	5,737	10	8
St. Edmund the King	-	-	-	- 1690	5,207	11	0
St. Lawrence Jewry	-	-	-	- 1677	11,870	1	9
St. James, Garlick Hill	-	-	-	- 1683	3,357	10	8
St. James, Westminster	-	-	-	circa 1689	8,500	0	0
St. Michael Royal -	-	-	-	- 1694	7,555	7	9
St. Martin's, Ludgate	-	-	-	- 1684	5,378	9	7
St. Margaret, Lothbury	-	-	-	- 1690	5,340	8	1
St. Mary, Somerset	-	-	-	- 1695	6,579	18	1
St. Mary, Aldermanbury -	-	-	- 1677	5,237	3	6
St. Mary le Bow	-	-	-	- 1673	8,071	18	1
—————— The steeple	-	-	- 1680	1,388	8	7
St. Nicholas, Coleabbey	-	-	-	- 1677	5,042	6	11
St. Olave Jewry -	-	-	-	- 1673	5,580	4	10
St. Peter, Cornhill -	-	-	-	- 1681	5,647	8	2
St. Swithin's, Cannon Street	-	-	- 1679	4,687	4	6
St. Magnus, London Bridge	-	-	- 1676	9,579	18	10

489. We must here close our account of Wren. Those of our readers who desire further information on the life and works of this truly great man will do well to consult the *Parentalia, or Memoirs of the Family of the Wrens*, compiled by his son; and published by his grandson Stephen Wren. Fol. Lond. 1750.

490. Among the architects of Wren's time, there was a triad of amateurs who would have done honour to any nation as professors of the art. The first of these was Henry Aldrich, D.D., Dean of Christ Church, Oxford, who died in 1710. He was attached to the Venetian school, as we may see in the three sides of Peckwater quadrangle, and the garden front of Corpus Christi College, a façade which for correct taste is not surpassed by any edifice in Oxford. The second of these amateurs was Dr. Clarke, one of the Lords of the Admiralty in the reign of Queen Anne. This distinguished amateur sat for Oxford in fifteen sessions. The Library of Worcester College, to which he bequeathed his valuable architectural collection of books and MSS., was from his design. He built the library at Christ Church. The third was Sir James Burrough, Master of Caius College, Cambridge; by whom, in 1703, the chapel of Clare Hall in that University was beautifully designed and executed.

491. We now approach the works of a man who, whatever some have thought of them, has a stronger claim on our notice as an inventor than any of his predecessors. It must be anticipated that we allude to Sir John Vanbrugh. Upon no other artist has Walpole delivered criticisms more unworthy of himself, nor is there any one of whose genius he had less capacity to appreciate the powers. The singular mind of Vanbrugh was distracted by control : his buildings are the result of a combination of forms and anticipation of effects, originating solely from himself; effects which none before had seen nor

contemplated. As a wit, he was inferior to none that levelled its shafts at him, and hence his novel compositions in architecture became among the professed critics of the day so much the more an object of derision, as, in their puny notions, his only assailable point. Attacked from party feeling, the public allowed itself to be biassed by epigrams and smart verses from the pens of Pope and Swift ; and when the former, in his fourth epistle, in allusion to Vanbrugh's works, exclaims, —

> " Lo ! what huge heaps of littleness around,
> The whole a laboured quarry above ground," —

he little thought he was leaving to posterity a record of his consummate ignorance of art, and of his total insensibility to grandeur, in all that relates to composition in architecture.

492. The opinion of Sir Joshua Reynolds first enlightened the public upon the thitherto condemned works of this extraordinary architect. " I pretend," says Reynolds, in his fifth discourse, " to no skill in architecture. I judge now of the art merely as a painter. When I speak of Vanbrugh, I speak of him merely on our art. To speak, then, of Vanbrugh in the language of a painter, he had originality of invention, he understood light and shadow, and had great skill in composition. To support his principal object, he produced his second and third groups of masses : he perfectly understood in *his* art what is most difficult in ours, the conduct of the backgrounds by which the design and invention is (are) set off to the greatest advantage. What the background is in painting is the real ground upon which the building is erected ; and as no architect took greater care that his work should not appear crude and hard, — that is, that it did not abruptly start out of the ground, without expectation or preparation, — this is the tribute which a painter owes to an architect who composes like a painter." The testimony of Mr. Payne Knight, a person of a taste highly refined and cultivated, in his *Principles of Taste*, is another eulogium on the works of this master. And again we have the concurrence therein of another able writer on these subjects, who, though frequently at variance in opinion with Mr. Knight, thus expresses himself in his *Essay on the Picturesque*, vol. ii. p. 211. : " Sir J. Reynolds is, I believe, the first who has done justice to the architecture of Vanbrugh, by showing it was not a mere fantastic style, without any other object than that of singularity, but that he worked on the principles of painting, and that he has produced the most painter-like effects. It is very probable that the ridicule thrown on Vanbrugh's buildings, by some of the wittiest men of the age he lived in, may have in no slight degree prevented his excellencies from being attended to ; for what has been the subject of ridicule will seldom become the object of study or imitation. It appears to me, that at Blenheim, Vanbrugh conceived and executed a very bold and difficult design, that of uniting in one building the beauty and magnificence of the Grecian architecture, the picturesqueness of the Gothic, and the massive grandeur of a castle ; and that, in spite of many faults, for which he was very justly reproached, he has formed, in a style truly his own, and a well-combined whole, a mansion worthy of a great prince and warrior. " His first point appears to have been massiveness, as the foundation of grandeur : then, to prevent the mass from being a lump, he has made

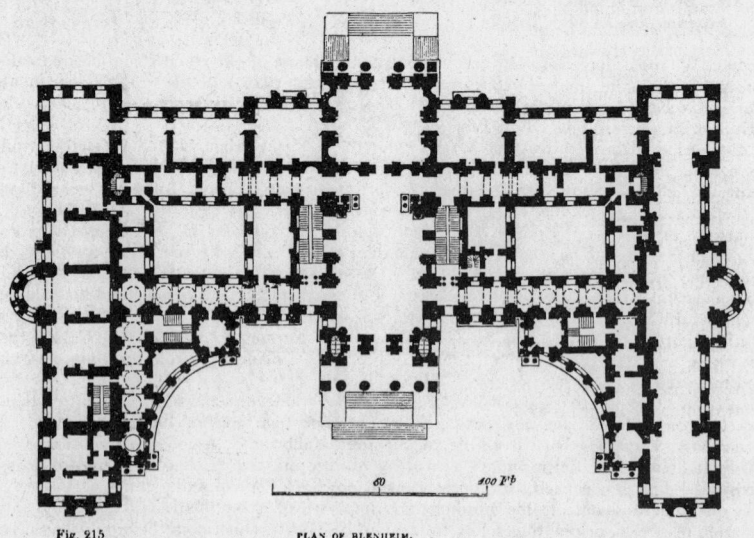

Fig. 215.   PLAN OF BLENHEIM.

various bold projections of various heights, which seem as foregrounds to the main building; and, lastly, having been probably struck with a variety of outline against the sky in many Gothic and other ancient buildings, he has raised on the top of that part where the slanting roof begins in any house of the Italian style, a number of decorations of various characters. These, if not new in themselves, have, at least, been applied and combined by him in a new and peculiar manner, and the union of them gives a surprising splendour and magnificence, as well as variety, to the summit of that princely edifice. The study, therefore, not the imitation, might be extremely serviceable to artists of genius and discernment."

493. Vanbrugh's principal work was Blenheim (whereof we give, in *figs.* 215. and 216.,

Fig. 216.   ELEVATION OF BLENHEIM.

the plan and principal elevation), a monument of the victories of Marlborough raised by a grateful nation. Its length on the north front from one wing to the other is 348 ft. The internal dimensions of the library are 130 by 32 ft. The hall is perhaps small compared with the apartments to which it leads, being only 53 ft. by 44, and 60 ft. high.

494. The execution of his design for Castle Howard, in Yorkshire, was commenced in 1702, and, with the exception of the west wing, was completed by him. The design possesses much greater simplicity than that of Blenheim. There is a portico in the centre, and a cupola of considerable height and magnitude. The galleries, or wings, are flanked by pavilions. The living apartments are small; but for the comfort and convenience of the house, as an habitation, many improvements have been made since the time of Vanbrugh.

495. At Eastbury, in Dorsetshire, he built a spacious mansion for Mr. Doddington. The front of it, with the offices, extended 370 ft. We regret to say that it was taken down by the first Earl Temple, about the middle of the last century.

496. King's Weston, near Bristol, erected for the Honourable Edward Southwell. A beautiful feature in the house is the grouping of the chimneys, in which practice no artist has surpassed, nor perhaps equalled, him. This house is not, however, a favourable specimen of our architect's powers.

497. In the front which he executed to Grimsthorpe, in Lincolnshire, he indulged himself in an imitation of Blenheim and Castle Howard. The hall here is of noble dimensions, being 110 ft. in length, and 40 ft. in height, surmounted by a cupola.

498. Charles Howard, the third Earl of Carlisle, Deputy Earl Marshal in 1703, appointed Vanbrugh, Clarenceux king of arms, over the heads of all the heralds, who remonstrated, without effect, against the appointment. The cause of such an extraordinary promotion is supposed to have had its origin in the Earl's satisfaction with the works at Castle Howard. It was, however, altogether unjustifiable, for Vanbrugh was, from all accounts, totally ignorant of heraldry. He held the situations of surveyor of the works at Greenwich Hospital, comptroller general of the works, and surveyor of the gardens and waters. Though perhaps out of place in a history of architecture, we cannot resist the opportunity of mentioning that our artist was a dramatist of genius. The Relapse, The Provoked Wife, The Confederacy, and Æsop, according to Walpole, will outlast his edifices. He died at Whitehall, March 26. 1726. Vanbrugh can hardly be said to have left a legitimate follower; he formed no school. Archer, indeed, attempted to follow him, and seems the only one of his time that could appreciate the merit of his master. But he was too far behind him to justify our pausing in the history of the progress of British architecture to say more than that his best works are Heythrop, and a temple at Wrest. St. Philip's Church at Birmingham is also by him. " A chef d'œuvre of his absurdity," says Dallaway, "was the church of St. John's, Westminster, with four belfries," a building which has not inaptly been likened to an elephant on his back, with his four legs sprawling in the air.

SECT. VIII.

GEORGE I.

499. Though the example of Wren was highly beneficial to his art, he does not seem to have been anxious to propagate his doctrines by precepts, for he had but one pupil who deserves a lengthened notice. That pupil was Nicholas Hawksmoor, who, at the age of eighteen, became the disciple of Sir Christopher, " under whom," says Walpole, " during life, and on his own account after his master's death, he was concerned in erecting many public edifices. Had he erected no other than the church of St. Mary Woolnoth, Lombard Street, his name would have deserved with gratitude the remembrance of all lovers of the art. This church has recently (on the opening of King William Street) been unfortunately disfigured on its southern side by some incompetent bungler on whom the patronage of the churchwarden lucklessly fell. Such is the fate of our public buildings in this country. The skill displayed by Hawksmoor in the distribution and design of St. Mary

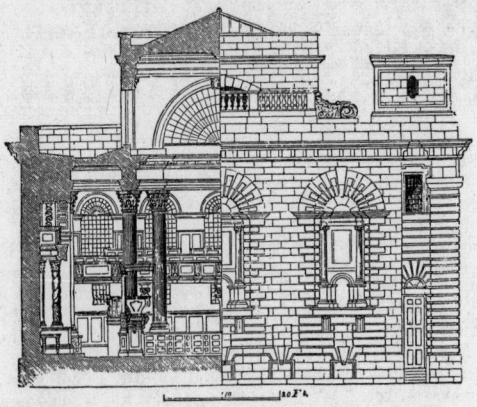

Woolnoth is not more than rivalled by the best productions of his master and instructor. We here give, in *figs.* 217. and 218., a half section, elevation, and plan of it. It was commenced in 1716, and finished in 1719. Not until lately was it seen to advantage. Lombard Street, in which one side still stands, was narrow, and its northern elevation, the only one till lately properly seen, required, from its aspect, the boldest form of detail to give it expression, because of its being constantly in shade, and therefore experiencing no play of light except such as is reflected. This is composed with three large semicircular rusticated niches, each standing on a

Fig. 217.　　HALF ELEVATION HALF SECTION OF ST. MARY WOOLNOTH.

lofty rusticated pedestal, relieved with blank recesses, which are repeated in the intervals below between the niches. The whole rests on a basement, whose openings, of course,

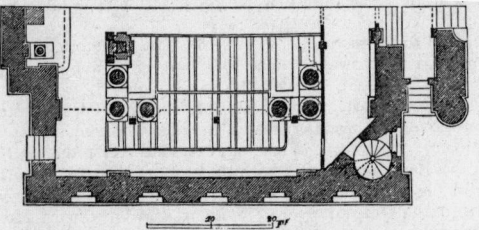

Fig. 218.　　PLAN OF ST. MARY WOOLNOTH.

correspond to those above. The niches in the recesses are decorated with Doric columns on pedestals, and the top of the entablature of the order is level with the springing of each niche head running through on each side, so as to form an impost. The front is crowned with a block cornice, continued round the building, and the central part of the northern front

is surmounted by a balustrade. We are not prepared to maintain that the whole of the details are in the purest taste; but the masses are so extremely picturesque, and so adapted to the circumstances of the aspect and situation, that their faults are forgotten. Not so the interior, which needs no apology. It is a combination of proportions, whose beauty cannot be surpassed in any similar example. The plan is nearly a square, whose north-west and south-west angles are truncated at angles of forty-five degrees, for the introduction of stairs. The leading lines are an inscribed square whose sides are equal to two thirds of the internal width, the remaining sixth on each side being assigned to the intercolumniations between the columns and the pilasters on the internal walls. The columns, twelve in number, are placed within the sides of the inscribed square, and at the angles are coupled at intervals of one diameter. The order is Corinthian; the columns are fluted, and crowned by an enriched entablature one quarter of their height. The space thus enclosed by the columns continues in a clerestory above, pierced on the four sides by semicircular windows, whose diameters are equal to one of the wide intercolumniations below. The height of this, including its entablature, is one half that of the lower order; thus, with its pedestal, making the total height of the central part of the

church, equal to its extreme width. A sesquialteral proportion is thus obtained in section as well as plan. The eastern end is recessed square for an altar piece, and arched with a semicircular ceiling enriched with caissons. The galleries are admirably contrived, and in no way interfere with the general effect, nor destroy the elegance and simplicity of the design. The ceilings throughout are horizontal, and planned in compartments, whose parts are enriched. As regards construction, there is a very unnecessary expenditure of materials, the ratio of the superficies to the points of support being 1:0·263. Hawksmoor was not so happy in the church of St. George's, Bloomsbury, in which he has really made King George I. the head of the church by placing him on the top of the steeple, which we must, with Walpole, term a master-stroke of absurdity. But many parts of the building are highly deserving the attention of the student; and if the commissioners for new churches in these days had been content with fewer churches constructed solidly, like this, instead of many of the pasteboard monstrosities they have sanctioned, the country, instead of regretting they ever existed, which will at no very remote period be the case, would have owed them a deep debt of gratitude. The only gratification we have on this point is, that a century, and even less, will close the existence of a large portion of them. Hawksmoor was deputy surveyor of Chelsea College and clerk of the works at Greenwich, and in that post was continued by William, Anne, and George I., at Kensington, Whitehall, and St. James's. Under the last named he was first surveyor of all the new churches and of Westminster Abbey, from the death of Sir Christopher Wren. He was the architect of the churches of Christ Church, Spitalfields, St. George, Middlesex, and St. Anne, Limehouse; rebuilt some part of All Souls, Oxford, particularly the new quadrangle completed in 1734, and was sole architect of the new quadrangle at Queen's. At Blenheim and Castle Howard he was associated with Vanbrugh, and at the last-named place was employed on the mausoleum. Among his private works was Easton Neston, in Northamptonshire, and the restoration to perpendicularity, by means of some ingenious machinery, of the western front of Beverley Minster. He gave a design for the Radcliffe Library at Oxford, and of a stately front for Brazenose. His death occurred on the 25th of March, 1736, at the age of seventy-five.

500. Those acquainted with the condition of the country will be prepared to expect that the arts were not much patronised by George I. The works executed during his reign were rather the result of the momentum that had been imparted previous to his accession than of his care for them; and it is a consolation that the examples left by Inigo Jones had an effect that has in this country never been entirely obliterated, though in the time of George III., such was the result of fashionable patronage and misguided taste, that the Adamses had nearly consummated a revolution. That reign, however, involved this country in so many disasters that we are not surprised at such an episode.

501. After the death of Hawksmoor, succeeded to public patronage the favourite architect of a period extending from 1720 to his death in 1754, whose name was James Gibbs, a native of Aberdeen, where he first drew breath in 1683. Though he had no claims to the rank of exalted genius, he ought not to have been the object of the flippant criticism of Walpole, whose qualifications and judgment were not of such an order as to make him more than a pleasant gossip. He certainly had not sufficient discernment properly to estimate the talent displayed in Gibbs's works. Every critic knows how easily phrases may be turned and antitheses pointed against an artist whom he is determined to set at nought; of which we have before had an instance in the case of Sir John Vanbrugh; and we shall not here further dilate upon the practice. We will merely observe, that on the appearance of any work of art the majority of the contemporary artists are usually its best judges, and that in ninety-nine cases out of a hundred the public afterwards sanction their decision; and we will add, in the words of old Hooker, that "the most certaine token of evident goodnesse is, if the generall perswasion of all men doe so account it;" and again, "although wee know not the cause, yet this much wee may know, that some necessarie cause there is, whensoever the judgement of all men generally or for the most part runne one and the same way." We do not, therefore, think it useful in respect of an artist of any considerable talent to repeat a criticism more injurious to the writer than to him of whom it was written.

502. The church of St. Martin's in the Fields is the most esteemed work of our architect. It was finished in 1726, as appears from the inscription on the frieze, at the cost of 33,017l. 9s. 3d. The length of it, including the portico, is twice its width, one third whereof, westward, is occupied by the portico and vestibule. The portico is hexastyle, of the Corinthian order, and surmounted by a pediment, in whose tympanum the royal arms are sculptured. The intercolumniations are of two diameters and a half, and the projection of the portico of two. Its sides are flanked by antæ in their junction with the main building, one diameter and a half distant from the receiving pilaster. The north and south elevations are in two stories, separated by a fascia, with rusticated windows in each. Between the windows the walls are decorated with pilasters of the same dimensions as the columns of the portico, four diameters apart; but at the east and west ends these elevations are marked by insulated columns coupled with antæ. The flanks are connected with the

prevailing lines in the portico by columns placed on the walls, recessed for the purpose, and coupled with antæ, whereby a play of light is produced, which imparts great effect to the other parts. The interior is divided into three unequal portions by a range on each side of four Corinthian columns, and two pilasters placed on pedestals, raised to the height of the pewing. From their insulated entablatures rises an elliptical ceiling, covering what may be called the nave. This ceiling is formed by arcs doubleaux, between which the vault is transversely pierced in the spaces above the intercolumniations by semicircular arches springing from the top of the entablature of each column. Over what may be called the aisles, from the entablatures of the columns, semi-circular arches are turned and received northward and southward on consoles attached to the walls, and by their junction with the longitudinal arches from column to column pendentives are evolved, and thereby are generated small flat domes over the galleries. The altar is recessed from the nave in a large niche formed by two quadrants of circles, whose radius is less than one fourth of the whole width of the niche. It is vaulted semi-elliptically. Galleries are introduced on the north, south, and west sides of the church. On the two former sides they extend from the walls to the columns, against which the continuity of their mouldings is broken. The interior is highly decorated, perhaps a little too theatrically for the sombre habits of this country ; but its effect is, on the whole, extremely light and beautiful. The tower and spire are, as in all the English churches of the Italian style, a sad blemish ; but the taste of the day compelled their use, and we regret that the clergy still persist in considering them requisites. The length from the front upper step to the east wall (inclusive) is 159 ft. 6 in., and the breadth from north to south 79 ft. 4 in. The total area of the church is 12,669 ft., whereof the points of support occupy 2803 ft. The ratio, therefore, of the former to the latter is a 1 : 0·220, from which we may infer that the edifice exhibits no very extraordinary constructive skill. The span of the roof (*fig.* 696.), which is of the common king-post form, is 38 ft. Gibbs, unlike Wren, does not appear to have been guided in his leading proportions of this work by a series of ratios. The only point in which we perceive an approximation to such a system is in the length from the plinths of the columns of the portico, being just double the width of the church measured at the same level. The portico is well designed, and hitherto has not been equalled in London.

503. In the church of St. Mary le Strand, Gibbs was not so successful. There is no portion of its space on which the eye rests with pleasure. It is cut up into littlenesses, which, though not individually offensive, destroy all repose or notion of mass in the fabric. He built the new church at Derby, and executed some works at King's College, Cambridge, which last were not calculated to raise his reputation ; but in the senate house of that university, he was more successful. In the Radcliffe Library at Oxford, his fame was maintained. It was completed in 1747, and thereon he was complimented with the degree of Master of Arts. This library is on the plan circular in general form, and rises in the centre of an oblong square, 370 ft. long, by 110 in width. Its cupola is 100 ft. in diameter, and 140 ft. high. It possesses no features of striking beauty, and yet is a most valuable addition to the distant view of Oxford, from whatever point of view it is seen. The interior is pleasing, and the disposition good. The books are arranged in two circular galleries, round a large central area. A description of this celebrated building was published with plans and sections, fol. 1747. Gibbs was the architect also of St. Bartholomew's Hospital. In 1728, he published a large folio volume of designs, including several of his works.

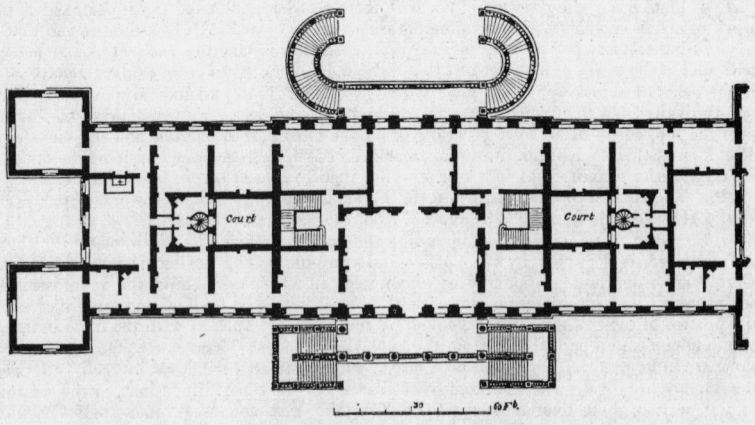

Fig. 219.   PLAN OF WANSTED HOUSE.

504. Some works of considerable importance were erected during the reign of George I., by a countryman of the last-named architect, Colin Campbell, who is, however, more esteemed for three volumes he published of the principal buildings in England, under the name of the *Vitruvius Britannicus*.   Of this work Lord Burlington was the original projector and patron.   Afterwards, in 1767 and 1771, it was continued in two volumes, under the superintendence of Wolfe and Gandon, two architects of considerable reputation. Campbell's talents were not of a very high order, though Mereworth, in Kent, an imitation of the Villa Capra, built for Mildmay Earl of Westmorland, and Wansted House, in Essex, built in 1715, and pulled down in 1815, the latter especially, entitle him to be considered an artist of merit.   Foreigners, whilst this last was in existence, always preferred it to any other of the great mansions of the country.   Gilpin says of it, " Of all great houses, it best answers the united purposes of grandeur and convenience.   The plan is simple and magnificent.   The front extends 260 ft.   A hall and saloon occupy the body of the house, forming the centre of each front.   From these run two sets of chambers.   Nothing can exceed their convenience.   They communicate in one grand suite, and yet each, by the addition of a back stair, becomes a separate apartment.   It is difficult to say whether we are better pleased with the grandeur and elegance without, or with the simplicity and contrivance within.   Dimensions :   Great hall, 51 ft. by 36 ; ball room, 75 by 27 ; saloon, 30 ft. square."   As the building no longer exists, we give, in *figs.* 219. and 220., a

Fig. 220.   ELEVATION OF WANSTEAD HOUSE.

ground plan and elevation of it.   Campbell was surveyor of the works of Greenwich Hospital, and died in 1734.

505. The church at Greenwich, and a very large mansion at Blackheath for Sir Gregory Page, in the latter whereof much is said to have been borrowed from Houghton, but which has many years since disappeared, were, about 1718, erected by John James, of whom very little more is known than these works, and, in London, the churches of St. George, Hanover Square, and St. Luke's, Middlesex, the latter whereof has a fluted obelisk for a steeple. We ought, besides, to mention that he is generally stated to have been employed by the Duke of Chandos, at Canons, in Middlesex, another building no longer in existence, and showing the frail tenure upon which an architect's reputation and fame is held.   At the latter place, however, it may be questioned whether the remark strictly applies, inasmuch as the architect, whoever he may have been, appears to have set taste and expense equally at defiance.

Sect. IX.

GEORGE II.

506. We do not altogether agree with Walpole in the observation that architecture resumed all her rights during this reign, though there is no doubt that the splendid (for the time) publications of Palladio, Jones, and examples of the antique recalled the taste of artists and their patrons the public.   Men of genius were doubtless found to support the arts by their practice, and some high-minded patrons to encourage them in their labours. " Before," observes Walpole, " the glorious close of a reign that carried our arms and victories beyond where Roman eagles ever flew, ardour for the arts had led our travellers to explore whatever beauties of Grecian or Latin skill still subsisted in provinces once subjected to Rome, and the fine additions, in consequence of those researches, have established the throne of architecture in Britain while itself languishes in Rome."

507. Among the earliest of the architects of this reign was Thomas Ripley, a native of Yorkshire, at whom Pope sneers in the lines —

" Who builds a bridge that never drove a pile ?
Should Ripley venture, all the world would smile."
Imit. Horace, Ep. ii. S. 186.

Ripley, it must be confessed, failed at the Admiralty, which was afterwards veiled by Mr. Adam's beautiful skreen since cruelly " cheated of its fair proportions" by the late architect to that Board, in order to make two coach entrances, which might, with the exercise of a little ingenuity, have been managed without defacing the design.   It is difficult, now, to decide the exact share that Ripley had in the house for Lord Orford, at Houghton, for which Campbell appears to have furnished the original design.   Walpole, whom we may presume to have known something about the matter, says they were much improved by Ripley.   He published them in two volumes, folio, 1755—60.   It is to be regretted that scarcely a single line of Pope, in matters of taste relative to the artists of his day, is of the smallest worth, so much did party and politics direct the shafts of the poet's malice.   The plain truth is, that Ripley was the rival of Kent, the favourite of Lord Burlington, whose patronage it was absolutely necessary to enjoy before he could ensure the smiles of Pope. Ripley was comptroller of the Board of Works, and died in 1758.

508. Henry Herbert, Earl of Pembroke, an amateur of this reign, cannot pass unnoticed in the History of its Architecture. He much improved Wilton, where he built the Palladian Bridge ; and it is highly honourable to his memory that, owing to his exertions, the qualifications of Labelye for building Westminster Bridge were acknowledged in opposition to Hawksmoor and Batty Langley, the latter of whom was an ignorant pretender.   Of this bridge Earl Henry laid the first stone in 1739, and the last in 1747.   His works, besides those at Wilton, were, the new lodge in Richmond Park, the Countess of Suffolk's house at Marble Hill, Twickenham, and the Water House at Lord Orford's Park at Houghton.   He died in 1751.

509. Before advancing our history another step, we have to notice another nobleman, whom to enrol among the number of her artists is an honour to England ; and in speaking of Richard Boyle, the third Earl of Burlington and fourth Earl of Ossory, we so entirely agree in Walpole's eulogy of him, that we shall not apologise for transcribing it from that author's pages : — " Never was protection and great wealth more generously and judiciously diffused than by this great person, who had every quality of a genius and an artist, except envy.   Though his own designs were more chaste and classic than Kent's, he entertained him in his house till his death, and was more studious to extend his friend's fame than his own."   Again, he continues, " Nor was his munificence confined to himself and his own houses and gardens. He spent great sums in contributing to public works, and was known to chuse that the expense should fall on himself, rather than that his country should be deprived of some beautiful edifices.   His enthusiasm for the works of Inigo Jones was so active that he repaired the church of Covent Garden, because it was the production of that great master, and purchased a gateway at Beaufort Gardens, in Chelsea, and transported the identical stones to Chiswick with religious attachment. With the same zeal for pure architecture, he assisted Kent in publishing the designs for Whitehall, and gave a beautiful edition of the ' Antique Baths, from the Drawings of Palladio,' whose papers he procured with great cost. Besides his works on his own estate, at Lonsborough, in Yorkshire, he new-fronted his house in Piccadilly, built by his father, and added the great colonnade within the court."   This liberal-minded nobleman gave the credit of this design to Kent, though, as Kent did not return from Italy before 1729, it is certain that architect could have had little to do with it.   His villa at Chiswick, now that of the Duke of Devonshire, was an original design, and not, as is generally supposed, an imitation of Palladio's Villa Capra at Vicenza. It was, however, too much in the Italian taste to be suitable to an English climate or to English comforts ; hence its great external beauty extracted from Lord Chesterfield the well-known verses —

" Possessed of one great house of state,
Without one room to sleep or eat,
How well you build let flatt'ry tell,
And all mankind how ill you dwell."

Lord Hervey also sported his little wit upon this little bijou, which its subsequent additions have not much improved, saying " that it was too small to inhabit, and too large to hang one's watch in."

510. The dormitory of Westminster School, ruined by a late dean, and the Assembly Rooms at York, are beautiful examples of the great powers of Lord Burlington ; but the house for Lord Harrington at Petersham, the Duke of Richmond's at Whitehall (pulled down), and General Wade's house in Great Burlington Street were not well planned, the latter especially, on which it was said by Lord Chesterfield, on account of its beautiful front, that " as the general could not live in it to his ease, he had better take a house over against it, and look at it."   The Earl of Burlington was born in 1695, and died in 1753.

511. William Kent, a native of Yorkshire, where he was born in 1685, if he did not advance the art, was at least far from retarding or checking any progress it seemed likely

to make. Kent was a painter as well as an architect, though as the former very inferior to the latter; and to these accomplishments must be added those of a gardener, for he was the father of modern picturesque gardening. Kent's greatest, and, out of many, also his best work, was Holkham, in Norfolk, for the Earl of Leicester, the plan and elevations whereof were published in folio, 1761, by the late Mr. Brettingham, who had the unparalleled assurance to send them to the world as his own. The noble hall of this building, terminated by a vast flight of steps, produces an effect unequalled by anything similar to it in England. During, and, indeed, previous to, Kent's coming so much into employment, a great passion seems to have existed with the architects for ill-shaped, and, perhaps, almost grotesque, urns and globes, on every part where there was a resting-place for them. Kent not unfrequently disfigured his works in this way, but more especially so at the beginning of his career. The pile of building in Margaret Street, which will shortly have to make way for part of the new parliament houses, now, however, containing the law courts, a house at Esher for Mr. Pelham, the Horse Guards, and other buildings, which it is needless here to particularise, were erected under the designs of Kent, upon whom unbounded liberality and patronage were bestowed by Lord Burlington during the life of this artist, which terminated in 1748.

512. About 1733 appeared, we believe, the last of the stone churches with steeples, which the practice of Wren had made common in this country; this was the church of St. Giles's in the Fields, erected by Henry Flitcroft. The interior is decorated with Ionic columns resting on stone piers. The exterior has a rusticated basement, the windows of the galleries have semicircular heads, and the whole is surmounted by a modillion cornice. The steeple is 165 feet high, consisting of a square tower, the upper part decorated with Doric pilasters; above, it is formed into an octagon on the plan, the sides being ornamented with three quarter Ionic columns supporting a balustrade and vases. Above this rises an octangular spire. Besides this, Flitcroft erected the church of St. Olave, Southwark, and the almost entire rebuilding of Woburn Abbey was from the designs and superintendence of that master, who died in 1769.

513. During the reign under our consideration, the city of Bath may be said to have almost arisen from the designs of Wood, who built Prior Park for Mr. Allen, the friend of Pope, and Buckland was erected by him for Sir John Throckmorton. Wood died in 1754, To him and to his scholars Bath is indebted for the designs of Queen Square, the Parades, the Circus, the Crescent, the New Assembly Room, &c. The buildings of this city possess various degrees of merit, but nothing so extraordinary as to call for more than the mere notice of them. We are by no means, for instance, disposed to agree with Mitford, who reckons the crescent of Bath among "the finest modern buildings at this day existing in the world!"

Sect. X.

GEORGE III.

514. Though the works of the architects about to follow, belong partially to the preceding reign, they are only properly to be noticed under that of George III. Without a lengthened account of them, we commence with the mention of the name of Carr of York, who was much employed in the northern counties, where he built several noble residences, particularly that for Mr. Lascelles, afterwards Lord Harewood, and a mausoleum in Yorkshire for the late Marquis of Rockingham. Paine was engaged at Worksop Manor, Wardour Castle, and Thorndon; and Hiorne, whose county sessions-house and prison at Warwick exhibit considerable genius, was a promising artist, prematurely cut off. His talent was not confined to the Italian style, as may be learnt from reference to the church at Tetbury in Gloucestershire, and a triangular tower in the Duke of Norfolk's park at Arundel.

515. At a early part of the reign of George III., architecture was cultivated and practised here with great success by Robert Taylor, afterwards knighted. His best compositions were designed with a breadth and intimate knowledge of the art, that prove him to have been abundantly acquainted with its principles. That he was not always successful, the wings of the Bank, now removed, were a proof. Of his works sufficient would remain to corroborate our opinion, if only what is now the Pelican Office in Lombard Street existed. We believe it was originally built for Sir Charles Asgill, and ruined by the directors of the Pelican when they took to the place. There are, however, also to attest the ability of Sir Robert Taylor, Sir Charles Asgill's villa at Richmond, and his own house in Spring Gardens. After his visit to Italy he commenced his practice in sculpture, in which branch of the arts he has left monuments in Westminster Abbey and elsewhere; but he afterwards devoted himself to architecture alone. Among his works were a dwelling house for Sir P. Taylor

near Portsdown Hill, a house in Piccadilly for the Duke of Grafton, a mansion in Herts for Lord Howe; Stone Buildings, Lincoln's Inn; Ely House, Dover Street, a very clever composition; Sir John Boyd's at Danson, near Shooter's Hill; the beautiful bridge at Henley on Thames, and Lord Grimstone's at Gorhambury. He had for some time a seat at the Board of Works, was surveyor to the Admiralty, the Bank, and other public bodies. His reputation was unbounded, and met with reward from the public. Sir Robert Taylor died in 1788 at the age of seventy-four.

516. Cotemporary with the last-named artist, was one to whom the nation is indebted for first bringing it to an intimate acquaintance with the works of Greece, to which he first led the way. The reader will, of course, anticipate us in the name of James Stuart, who began his career as a painter. After some time passed in Greece, he, in conjunction with Nicholas Revett, about the year 1762, published the well-known *Antiquities of Athens*, from which he acquired the soubriquet of *Athenian*. The public taste was purified by a corrected knowledge of the buildings of Greece, especially in respect of the form, composition, and arrangement of ornament; but we doubt whether mischief was not for a time induced by it, from the absurd attempt, afterwards, to adapt, without discrimination, the pure Greek porticoes of the temples of Greece to public and private buildings in this country, often with buildings with which they have no more natural relation than the interior arrangement of a church has with that of a theatre. The architects of our own time seem, however, at last to be aware of the impossibility of applying with success the forms of Grecian temples to English habitations; and a better system has been returned to, that of applying to every object a character suitable to the purposes of its destination. We consider Stuart's best work the house, in St. James's Square, which he built for Lord Anson. Among other works, he executed Belvedere, in Kent, for Lord Eardley; a house for Mrs. Montague, in Portman Square; the chapel and infirmary of Greenwich Hospital; and some parts of the interior of Lord Spencer's house, in St. James's Place. Stuart died in 1788, at the age of seventy-five. His *collaborateur*, Revett, shared with him a portion of the patronage of the public. He survived him till 1804, when he died at the advanced age of eighty-two years. He was employed on the eastern and western porticoes of Lord De Spencer's house at West Wycombe, and on some temples. For Sir Lionel Hyde he built the church of Ayot St. Lawrence, Herts, the front whereto is a Doric portico crowned with a low Grecian pediment, and on each side an Ionic colonnade connects the centre with an elegant cenotaph. He also built a portico to the eastern front of Standlinch, in Wiltshire, for Mr. Dawkins.

517. The chasteness and purity which the two last-named architects had, with some success, endeavoured to introduce into the buildings of England, and in which their zeal had enlisted many artists, had to contend against the opposite and vicious taste of Robert Adam, a fashionable architect, whose eye had been ruined by the corruptions of the worst period of Roman art. It can be scarcely believed, the ornaments of Diocletian's palace at Spalatro should have loaded our dwellings contemporaneously with the use among the more refined few of the exquisite exemplars of Greece, and even of Rome, in its better days. Yet such is the fact; the depraved compositions of Adam were not only tolerated, but had their admirers. It is not to be supposed that the works of a man who was content to draw his supplies from so vitiated a source will here require a lengthened notice. Yet had he his happy moments; and that we may do him strict justice, we not only mention, but

Fig. 221.   ELEVATION OF KEDLESTONE.

present to the reader, in *figs.* 221. and 222., the ground plan and elevation of Kedlestone, in Derbyshire, which he erected for Lord Scarsdale. The detail of this is, indeed, not exactly what it ought to have been; but the whole is magnificently conceived, and worthy of any master. Adam died at the age of ninety-four, in 1792; and, besides the Adelphi, in the Strand, which he erected on speculation, he was engaged at Luton Park, in Bedfordshire, for the Earl of Bute; at Caenwood, near Hampstead, for Lord Mansfield; at Shelburne House, in Berkeley Square, now Lord Lansdowne's, well planned, but ill designed, a meagre affair; the disgraceful gateway at Sion, near Brentford; and on part of the Register Office at Edinburgh. None, however, would now do credit to a mere tyro in the art except the first named.

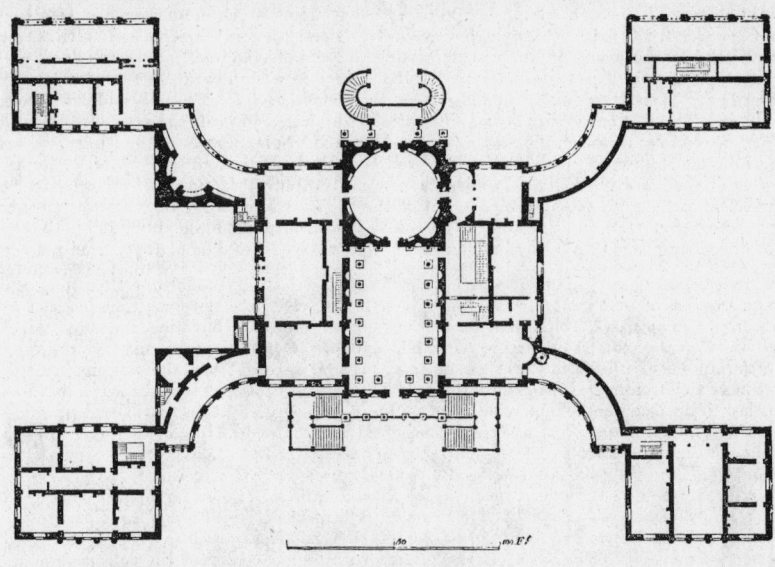

Fig. 222. PLAN OF KEDLESTONE.

518. Previous to the accession of George III. it had been considered by his tutors necessary to complete his education by the study requisite to give him some acquaintance with the art. We venerate the memory of that monarch as an honest good man, but are compelled to say that the experiment of inoculating him with a taste for it was unsuccessful, for during his reign all the *bizareries* introduced by Adam received no check, and seeing that Adam and Bute were both from the north, we are rather surprised that his education was not in this respect committed to the former instead of Sir William Chambers, whom, as one of the first architects of the day, it is incumbent upon us now to introduce. We believe that whatever was done to forward the arts, owes a large portion of its effect to that celebrated man ; and it is probable, with the worthy motives that actuated the monarch, and the direction of his taste by that individual, much more would have been accomplished, but for the heavy and disastrous wars which occurred during his reign, and the load of debt with which it became burthened. The works of Chambers are found in almost every part of England, and even extended to Ireland; but we intend here chiefly to restrict ourselves to a short account of Somerset House, his largest work, in which, though there be many faults, so well did he understand his art, that it is a matter of no ordinary difficulty, and indeed requires hypercriticism, to find anything offensive to good taste in the detail.

519. This work was commenced in 1776, and stands on an area of 500 ft. in depth, and 800 ft. in width. The general interior distribution consists of a quadrangular court, 343 ft. in length, and 210 ft. in width, with a street or wide way running from north to south, on its eastern and western sides. The general termination towards the river is a terrace, 50 ft. wide, whose level is 50 ft. above that of the river, and this occupies the whole length of the façade in that direction. The front towards the Strand is only 135 ft. long. It is composed with a rustic basement, supporting ten Corinthian columns on pedestals, crowned by an attic, extending over the three central intercolumniations, flanked by a balustrade on each side. The order embraces two stories. Nine large arches are assigned to the basement, whereof the three central ones are open for the purpose of affording an entrance to the great court. On each side of them, these arches are occupied by windows of the Doric order, decorated with pilasters, entablatures, and pediments. The key stones are carved in alto-relievo, with nine colossal masks, representing the ocean, and the eight principal rivers of Great Britain. The three open arches of entrance before mentioned lead to a vestibule, which connects the Strand with the large quadrangular court, and serves also as the access to those parts of the building, till lately occupied by the Royal Academy, (1836), and on the eastern side (lately to the Royal Society and) to the Society of Antiquaries, the entrances thereto are within the vestibule. This is decorated with columns of the Doric order, whose entablature supports a vaulted ceiling. We insert a reduced woodcut (*fig.* 223) of Malton's view of this "magnificent Doric arcade leading to the great court, which conveys to the spectator a more ample idea than words can possibly furnish, of this piece of grand and picturesque scenery." The front of this pile of

building towards the quadrangle, is 200 ft. in extent, being much more than the length of that towards the Strand; the style, however, of its decoration is correspondent with it, the principal variation being in the use of pilasters instead of columns, and in the doors and windows. The front next the Thames is ornamented in a similar manner to that already described. It was originally intended that the extent of the terrace should have been 1,100 ft. This last is supported by a lofty arcade, decorated towards the ends with coupled Tuscan columns, whose cornice is continued along the whole terrace. The edifice was at the time the subject of much severe criticism, and particularly from the pen of a silly engraver of the name of Williams, under the name of Antony Pasquin; but the censures he passed on it, the author being as innocent of the slightest knowledge of the art as most of the writing architectural critics of the present day, were without foundation, and have long since been forgotten. At the time, however, they received a judicious reply from the pen of the late Mr. John B. Papworth, which deservedly found a place in our edition of the work by Sir W. Chambers, yet to be noticed.

Fig. 223.　　　　　ENTRANCE VESTIBULE, SOMERSET HOUSE.

520. Malton, in his *London and Westminster*, fol. 1792-7, gives several carefully drawn views of this noble edifice, the design of which he describes as being at that time (1796), " far from complete, and little progress has been made in the building since the commencement of the present war; the exigencies of government having diverted to other uses the sum of 25,000*l.* which for several years had been annually voted for its continuance." Since that period the river frontage has been completed at the east end, by the additions in 1831, under Sir R. Smirke, for King's College: while new offices were skilfully added on the western side, during the years 1852-56, by James Pennethorne.

521. In the year 1759, Sir W. Chambers published a *Treatise on the Decorative Part of Civil Architecture*, in folio; a second edition appeared in 1768; and a third, with some additional plates, in 1791. Two others have since been published, in 1825. This work, as far as it goes, still continues to be a sort of text-book for the student; and much of it has been adopted for that portion of this volume. entitled " Practice of Architecture " Chambers held the office of surveyor-general in the Board of Works, and to him much is owing for the assistance he rendered in establishing the Royal Academy of Arts, in 1768, to which institution he was treasurer. He died in 1796. He had many pupils, several of whom we shall name.

522. Robert Mylne, the descendant of a race of master masons and architects in Scotland, designed Blackfriars Bridge, having been the successful competitor, a preference he obtained while yet unknown and abroad. It was built between the years 1760 and 1768, at an expense of 152,840*l.*, a sum which was said to be somewhat less than his estimate. He was voted an annual salary of 300*l.* and a percentage on the money laid out; but to obtain his commission of 5 per cent. he had a long struggle with the city authorities, his claims not being allowed until 1776. This bridge was pulled down in 1865. At the time when the designs were under consideration, a long controversy arose on the questions of the taste exhibited, and safety in employing elliptic, in place of semicircular, arches, which had been up to that time used in England for bridges. He was surveyor to the dean and chapter of St. Paul's, London, and is said to have placed in that building, over the entrance to the

choir, the memorial tablet with the celebrated inscription (*par.* 482) to the memory of Wren, lately removed. He was appointed, in 1762, engineer to the New River Company; and dying in 1811, was buried in the crypt of the cathedral, near to the grave of Sir C. Wren.

523. George Dance, being nominated, in 1733, by the corporation of the city of London, to the office of clerk of the City Works, and appointed thereto in December 1735, designed St. Luke's Church, Old-Street; St. Leonard's Church; Shoreditch, a bold example of the Doric order; and the Mansion House, or official residence of the Lord Mayor for the time being, during the years 1739-53, at a cost of about 42,639*l.* This edifice has received many alterations, including the removal of the lofty attics in front and rear, which has tended much to deprive the structure of a large share of dignity. Its confined and low situation gives the building an appearance of heaviness; it would be free from this, if placed on an elevated spot, or in an area proportionate to its magnitude. It is substantially built of Portland stone, the material used in most of the erections of this period. The finely designed sculpture in the pediment, above the six columns of the Corinthian order, was well executed by Mr., afterwards Sir Robert, Taylor. Many other buildings in and about the city are attributed to Dance, who died in 1768, and was succeeded in office by his son George Dance, another of the first four architect members of the Royal Academy. He designed Newgate prison, with the Sessions House, &c. It was completed in 1778, at a cost of upwards of 130,000*l.* ; besides being subsequently repaired under his directions,

Fig 224.   NEWGATE PRISON.

after the riots of 1780, when it suffered greatly from fire. This edifice (*fig.* 224.) has become a chief example of the theory of the observation to "apply to every object a character suitable to the purposes of its destination" (*page* 224.). The walls, which are constructed of Portland stone, without apertures, or any other ornaments than rough rustic work and niches, are 50 ft. in height. The principal front is 300 ft. in length. Dance also designed St. Luke's Hospital for Lunatics, Old Street, built in the years 1782-1784, at a cost of about 40,000*l.* It is of brick, with a few plain stone dressings, three stories in height; the spaces between the centre and ends are formed into long galleries—for the females on the western side, for the males on the eastern. The simple grandeur of the design of the façade, the length of which is 493 ft., produces a very agreeable effect of propriety upon the mind. He rearranged the south front of Guildhall in a style of architecture neither Gothic nor Grecian, the capabilities of which his pupil, John, afterwards Sir John, Soane, largely availed himself in after life. He also designed the elegant council chamber attached; together with many country residences for the wealthy citizens and others; and dying in 1825, was buried in the crypt of St. Paul's. Upon the resignation by him of his city appointment in 1816, he was succeeded therein by his other pupil, William Mountague.

524. Henry Holland, in 1763, designed Claremont House, near Esher, for Lord Clive; formed, 1788-90, Carlton House into a palace for the Prince of Wales, afterwards George IV.; designed, in 1791, Drury Lane Theatre; the façade of the East India House, Leadenhall Street; the original 'Pavilion' at Brighton, about 1800; improvements at Woburn Abbey for the Duke of Bedford; and 1786, the vestibule, with its charming portico in the Grecian style, to Melbourne, now Dover House, Whitehall, for the Duke of York. The *fig.* 225 is from Malton's work already mentioned, and is given not only for the intrinsic merit of the design, but because little else now remains, with Claremont, to demonstrate the talents of this fashionable architect of his day. He was the chief introducer of the so-called Greco-Roman style. Holland died in 1806.

525. With these architects should be mentioned Isaac Ware, " of His Majesty's Board of Works," who published, besides other works, a *Complete Body of Architecture,* folio, 1756. This volume, relating to Italian design only, contains much sound information, and is more complete than Sir W. Chambers's publication, but it is not treated so artistically. He designed Chesterfield House, May Fair. Willey Reveley, a pupil of Chambers, followed the steps of Stuart, and visited Athens and the Levant. He was the editor of the third volume of the *Antiquities of Athens,* and died prematurely in 1799. He built the new church at Southampton, and offered some beautiful designs for the new baths at Bath, which, however, were not adopted. Joseph Bonomi, a native of Rome, an associate of the Royal Academy, amongst many large structures composed chiefly in the Grecian style, designed the gallery at Townley Hall, Lancashire, for the collection now in the British Museum ; 1790,

a small church at Packington, Warwickshire, solidly vaulted throughout; Eastwell House, Kent; the mausoleum in Blickling Park, Norfolk, to the memory of John, second Earl of Buckingham; Longford Hall, Shropshire, exhibiting perhaps the earliest adaptation of a portico projecting sufficiently to admit carriages; additions to Lambton Hall, Durham; and, besides many other works, his *chef d'œuvre*, the Italian mansion at Roseneath, Dumbartonshire, for the then Duke of Argyle, between 1803-6, and said to be still remaining incomplete. As will be seen from the perspective view (*fig.* 227.), the entrance portico is remarkable for having a central column; the better to express, as Bonomi stated, that the portico is intended for protecting the visitors from the weather, as the carriages drive, and set down, under it. Thus no central space is required; while the column affords support for any central object which may be placed on the entablature. The apartments are not very large; the music-room, marked *a* on the plan given in *fig.* 226, being only 36 ft. long, and 22 ft. wide. The central passage, *f*, with barely any light except at the two ends, appears a great defect. Plans were subsequently made for a large sunk

Fig. 225.   MELBOURNE, NOW DOVER HOUSE, WHITEHALL.

circular court at each end, from one of which a subterraneous passage led to the sea. The name of Bonomi appears in the best novels of his period as the architect consulted in matters concerning a country residence. He died in 1808.

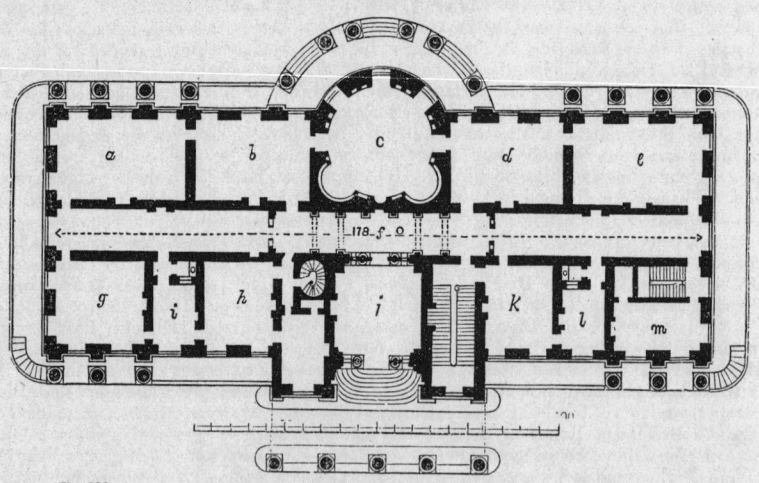

Fig. 226.   PLAN OF ROSENEATH, DUMBARTONSHIRE.

526. Of this period also are the works of James Gandon, a pupil of Sir W. Chambers. His name was first brought before the public, by the publication with John Wolfe of a continuation of Campbell's *Vitruvius Britannicus*, 2 vols fol. 1767 and 1771. The design, by him, for the county-hall and prison at Nottingham, is contained therein. He carried off the first gold medal given for architecture by the Royal Academy, at its foundation in 1768. In 1769 he obtained the third premium for a design for the Royal Exchange in Dublin; and in 1776 one of the premiums for the new Bethlehem Hospital, London; both in competition. At the instance of Lord Carlow, afterwards Lord Portarlington, he made plans for

the new docks, stores, and Custom-House, at Dublin, and proceeded there in 1781 to carry out the works. This building was not completed until 1791 ; it has a front of 375 ft. in length, extending along the quay of the river Liffey, and is 209 ft. in depth. Standing in a fine open *place*, its admirable design and good execution cause it to rank as equal to other works of a like nature, and to be esteemed as a noble pile that would do credit to any city in the world. He was well assisted in the decorative works by a young sculptor named Edward Smith. The great difficulties he experienced during its erection, both from the nature of the soil, as well as from the workpeople, is well described in the memoir of him

Fig. 227.   VIEW OF ROSENEATH, DUMBARTONSHIRE.

prepared by his son, and published by the late T. J. Mulvany, in 1846. To the Houses of Parliament in Dublin he added the side or east portico, with an entrance for the Lords, who agreed to Gandon's desire to have Corinthian columns to this portico, the additional propor-tion in height of which was to make up for the great fall in the ground from the front, where the Ionic is used. This portico entrance he joined with the front by a circular wall *without* columns, so that the two orders should not clash ; the present three-quarter Ionic columns to this circular wall on the one side, and those to the archway on the other side, are the additions by a later hand when the building was adapted for the Bank of Ireland, which has possessed it since 1802. Gandon subsequently added the western portico for the Com-mons' House. A much larger work by him was the edifice for the Four (Law) Courts. The foundation stone was laid March 3, 1786, and was first used at the end of 1796, but the whole was not completed until 1802. The frontage extends along the river quay, and includes, on the east side, the Offices of Records, designed in 1776 by Thomas Cooley, whom Gandon succeeded. The whole extent of ground was but 432 ft., 294 ft. of which being occupied by the offices, left but 140 ft. square for the plan of the Courts, and this had subsequently to be lessened in depth by the portico being set back, to appease the ire of a Right Honourable gentleman whose opinion had been overlooked. This centre building consists of a moderate-sized central hall, 64 ft. in diameter, with a dome which forms exteriorly a marked feature of the design, and one of the most conspicuous objects in the city. This central hall gives access to the four courts. For the same city, he designed Carlisle Bridge and the Inns of Court, but resigned the control over the latter edifice to his pupil, H. A. Baker. He retired in 1808 to his country house near Lucan, and died there as late as 1823, in the eighty-second year of his age.

527. James Wyatt, born about 1743 or 1746, accompanied, at an early age, Lord Bagot to Rome, and applied himself to the study of the ancient monuments in that city and at Venice. After an absence of six years, returning to London, he was employed to design the Pantheon Theatre in Oxford Street, consisting of rooms for public assemblies, &c. This was opened in January 1772, and its completion (*fig.* 228, which shows the interior as arranged for the Handel festival, in May 1784), spreading his fame both far and wide, he was eagerly sought after to superintend numerous public and private buildings in Great Britain and Ireland. Walpole, writing to Mann, in 1771, says of it : — " The new winter Ranelagh in Oxford Road is almost finished. It amazed me, myself. Imagine Balbec in all its glory ! The pillars are of artificial giallo antico. The ceilings, even of the passages, are of the most beautiful stuccos in the best taste of grotesque. The ceilings of the ball rooms and the panels painted like Raphael's loggias in the Vatican. A dome like the Pan-theon glazed. It is to cost fifty thousand pounds." Part only of the Oxford Street front, with the side entrance in Poland Street, now exist of this work, for the interior was gutted by fire soon after its erection. *Fig.* 730 shows the framing of a dome nearly the same as that for this edifice. The drawings he brought home, the knowledge he possessed of the arts in general, and his polished manners, secured for him a host of patrons, and he became the

chief architect of the day. Those critics, amateur or otherwise, who do not choose to make allowances for the state of the knowledge of the arts at the period under notice, hold Wyatt up to the execration of the present generation, for his alterations and restorations of our ancient buildings. Yet,

for King George III., he restored parts of Windsor Castle, to the entire satisfaction of all the connoisseurs of his day, keeping to the original style of the edifice, or as nearly so as the few studies of the style permitted. His Gothic palace at Kew has been pulled down; and the western front of the Houses of Parliament was burnt down; both unregretted. But his houses, villas, and mansions, are amongst the most convenient and tasteful in the country; his own residence in Port-

Fig. 228.   INTERIOR OF THE PANTHEON, LONDON.

land Place, near Langham Church, is a good type. Elmes has elaborately commented upon the peculiarities of Ardbraccan House, near Navan, in Ireland, designed for the Bishop of Meath, as affording the moderate accommodation for a small family, or all the requirements of an Irish ordination, where hospitality has to be afforded to all comers.

528. James Wyatt was among the earliest architects to employ every style of architecture in his designs, yielding all individuality to the passing whims of clients. Among his other buildings usually noticed are Lee Priory, Kent; and Castle Coote, in Ireland, for Viscount Belmont, which for grandeur of effect and judicious arrangement, deserves much commendation. The apartments are upon a moderate scale and well disposed, and the whole designed after a Greek model, in which style he also designed Bowden Park, Wiltshire, for Barnard Dickenson, Esq. (figs. 229 and 230). Another

of his large works is Ashridge, situate in the counties of Buckingham and Hertford, for the Earl of Bridgewater; it is a very extensive and highly decorated mansion designed in the mediæval

Fig. 230.   ELEVATION OF BOWDEN PARK.

castellated style. Fonthill Abbey, Wiltshire, for W. Beckford, Esq., was also another of his edifices in the same style. The exterior measurements are 270 ft. from east to west, and 312 ft. from north to south; the centre tower being 276 ft. high from the floor to the top of the pinnacles. His restorations of our mediæval buildings included that of Henry VIIth's chapel at Westminster Abbey, Thomas Gayfere being the intelligent master mason employed. As so many of his later works belong to the present century, no more will be said here of this influential architect, except that he succeeded Sir W. Chambers as surveyor-general to the Board of Works; that for one year he filled the presidential chair of the Royal Academy; and that, as before stated, he died in 1813, aged sixty-seven, in consequence of

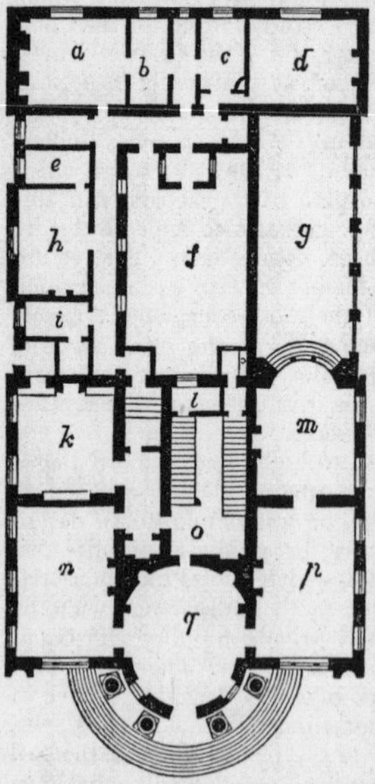

Fig. 229.   PLAN OF BOWDEN PARK.

the overturning of his chariot near Marlborough.

529. This architect must conclude our general view of the history of art in this country to the end of the reign of George III.

CHAP. IV.

POINTED ARCHITECTURE.

530. The history of the pointed styles on the continent of Europe is a matter which may be treated in various ways; but the limit within which this portion of our labour is restricted, in order to render it concordant with the space allotted to other subjects, obliges the choice of the headings France, Belgium, Germany, Spain, and Italy, with as near an approach to a chronological arrangement of the buildings that will serve for examples, as the looseness of annalists and the differences in chronicles will permit. This sequence will give the reader a general view of the subject, which will enable him to understand the irregularity of the progress of pointed art in those countries in comparison with the gradual transition and uniform character which are so generally observable in England; and will prepare him for his own particular study of the characteristics of the schools; these are as numerous as the provinces, almost as numerous as the cities, in the countries to which we refer. He may observe in the following notices several examples of difficulties as to dates; the periods assigned to our examples have been determined by authors who, being natives, may be supposed to have given as much time and learning to the chronology, as English critics have dedicated to the style, of the respective countries.

France.

531. The schools of pointed architecture were confined to certain portions of the country. They arose in the Ile-de-France, Champagne, Picardy, Burgundy and Bourbon, Maine and Anjou, and Normandy, here named in the order in which, before the middle of the 13th century, the new style was adopted. This did not develope itself until a late period in Bretagne, where a character, which corresponds (in the opinion of M. Viollet le Duc) as much to that of England as to that of Maine and Normandy, was always preserved. The style of the royal domain hardly penetrated into Guienne before 1370; and even its official appearance after 1247 at Carcassonne did not procure for it an influence in Auvergne and Provence; they can hardly be said to have ever adopted Gothic architecture. Indeed, the latter district did not belong to France until 1481, and almost passed at once from degenerated romanesque traditions to renaissance art, exhibiting scarcely any mark of the influence of northern Gothic.

532. With regard to ecclesiastical architecture in the south of France, it may be said that the buildings having arches that are positively pointed, date principally in the 14th and two subsequent centuries, as the cathedrals at Alby and Rhodez, the bell-tower at Mende, and the front of the church of St. Maurice at Vienne. In the south, where the climate resembles that of Italy in not requiring high-pitched roofs, the pointed arch seems a foreign element; it is there in body, but not in spirit. The architecture is just as before; the pillars are few and thick; the capitals are square, and have large leaves or scrolls; the ornaments are either barbarous or are imitated from classic works; the towers are few and massive; and the fronts always have a pediment of steeper rake than any antique example can show, under which is a doorway having a round arch, or else one so slightly pointed that the point is only detected by a careful eye.

533. Until the middle of the 12th century (a few cases earlier may be exceptional), the semicircular arch appears to have been almost exclusively employed; but immediately afterwards, the *style romano-ogival* or *style roman de transition*, exhibits the pointed arch, crocket capitals, and groined vaulting with diagonal ribs, on a crowd of civil and ecclesiastical buildings. There are purely romanesque churches, where the small openings have semicircular heads; the four great arches carrying the pendentives of the central lantern or dome, as has already been noticed (*par.* 307.), being pointed. In the centre of France there are churches that are altogether romanesque in plan, in style of decoration, and in form of pillars, that have none but pointed openings, proving that a thoroughly defined architectural system had been slowly constituted, which the architects of the 13th century merely rendered more homogeneous and more perfect; these buildings are romanesque, if style depends upon plan, capitals, and form of mouldings; they are pointed, if it depends upon the form of the arch.

534. Amongst the structures which date in the 12th century may be named St. Pierre-lez-Bitry, with three circular windows in its apse; St. Martin at Cuise, having a square-ended choir like Nôtre Dame at Conchy; and St. Etienne near Pierrefonds; the cathedral at Tulle; St. Julien at Brioude; St. Nectaire, St. Symphorien, and St. Genès at Thiers; St. Nazaire at Carcassonne; with the churches at Mozat, Noirlac, and St. Amand, all being situate in Auvergne; St. Martin at Laon; St. Pierre at L'Assant; St. Pierre at Soissons; and the churches at Braisne and Coucy-le-Chateau. Buildings in

which the pointed arch seems perfectly secondary to its rival, are the portal of the cathedral at Bayeux and the churches at Conchy, Civray, Senlis, and Vézelay, with those of St. Remi at Reims, and of Nòtre Dame at Chartres, Noyon, and Poitiers.

535. The churches which have domical coverings deserve a short notice. They are the cathedral at Cahors, St. Front (*figs.* 159 and 160), and St. Étienne de la Cité, both at Périgueux, the cathedral at Puy, and the churches at Souillac (*fig.* 158.), Angoulême, Le Roulet, and Loches, with the fourteen-sided church at Rieux-Mérinville.

536. A French critic of considerable repute thinks that necessity, facility, and solidity in construction, and a gift of varying the decoration, alone prompted the use of the pointed arch in the south-east of France, where are buildings showing that arch in their lower portions, while the upper parts have semicircular work of the same age. It therefore appears that if the architects in the southern provinces were the first to make the pointed arch, they were also the last to adopt the systematic and absolute use of it; and the usual classifications of the pointed styles cannot serve as perfect indexes to the period of the employment of the subdivisions that have been made, although it might have been supposed that the spirit of methodical order which has eminently distinguished the French nation since 1790 would have shown itself in an analysis of the architecture of their country. The Comité Historique des Arts et Monuments, has issued the following table as in some sort authoritative:—

FIRST PERIOD.

| Architecture with the round arch. | From the fourth to the eleventh century . . . . | *Style Latin.* |
| | Eleventh, and first half of the twelfth, century . . | *Style Roman.* |

SECOND PERIOD.

| Architecture with the round and pointed arch. | Second half of the twelfth century | *Style Romano-ogival* or *Roman de transition.* |

THIRD PERIOD.

Architecture with pointed arches.	Thirteenth century . .	*Style ogival primaire* or *en lancette*
	Fourteenth century . .	*Style ogival secondaire* or *rayonnant.*
	Fifteenth and early part of sixteenth century, till 1480 (De Caumont), pure, afterwards transition .	*Style ogival tertiaire* or *flamboyant.*

537. But this list is not universally used, and in reading the works of any French author on mediæval architecture, it is necessary to ascertain whether he has followed it, or the table propounded by M. De Caumont as here given (with Mr. Poynter's parallel of English periods):—

In France.	A.D.	*In England.*
Romanesque 950 to 1050	1000	Anglo-Saxon 970 to 1066
Transition 1050 to 1150	1100	Norman 1066 to 1189
		Transition 1189 to 1199
Primary (*Gothique*) 1150 to 1250	1200	Early English— First Epoch (*lancet*) 1199 to 1245 Second Epoch 1245 to 1307
Secondary (*rayonnant*)— First Epoch 1250 to 1300 Second Epoch 1300 to 1400	1300	Decorated English 1307 to 1377
Tertiary (*flamboyant*)— First Epoch 1400 to 1460 Second Epoch 1460 to	1400 1500	Perpendicular English or Tudor 1377 to . . . .

For the *château*, M. de Caumont also proposed the subjoined classification:—

1st class. Fifth to tenth century: Primitive Roman.

2nd „ Tenth and eleventh centuries: First secondary.

3rd „ End of eleventh and twelfth century: First tertiary.

4th „ Thirteenth century: Primitive pointed.

5th class. Fourteenth and first half of fifteenth century: Secondary and tertiary pointed.

6th „ Second half of fifteenth and sixteenth century: Quaternary pointed.

538. Before entering into the consideration of the *style ogival*, it will be desirable to explain that *ogive*, also written *augive*, designated originally a diagonal band in groined vaulting formed by the intersection either of barrel vaults or of keel vaults, to both of which the terms *voûte en croisée d'ogives*, or *voûte d'ogives*, were applicable. As equivalent

to a pointed arch, *ogive* is merely the popular confirmation of an error committed by the ignorance of some writers in the present century.

539. Heavy roofs, having few ribs with great width of plain intrados, and carried by

masses of walling, with small openings, are characteristic of Romanesque work. Its successor was exactly the reverse: the subdivision of roofing into a collection of light ribs with no marked intrados, the growth of the engaged or disengaged pillars into the lines of the vaulting, and the carriage of the weight of the ribs by buttresses that form the resisting points of walls which are merely frames to windows, are distinctive features of the Gothic architecture of the 13th century, with the addition of the pointed arch which had previously been employed in ways that tended to the developement of the *style ogival primaire.* As an example of the transitional character of the style in this period, the two bays, *fig.* 231. from the cathedral in Paris, and *fig.* 232. from the church of the abbey at St. Denis, may be compared as having been executed respectively at the beginning and end of the period. The sculptors do not seem to have studied nature beyond exhibiting the costume of their period; and if they chose models at all for their foliage, these were furnished by indigenous plants. The great attention paid in the 11th century to ancient literature is clearly responsible for the centaurs and other fabulous creatures then used for ornament. In like manner, the devo-

Fig. 231. NOTRE DAME, PARIS.

Fig. 232.   ST. DENIS.

tion of the 12th century to the sciences is expressed by the zodiacal signs and emblems of the seasons sculptured on the portals and choirs of churches built in that and the succeed-

Fig. 233.   HOUSES, CAUDEBEC.

ing century. The doorways at Amiens, Autun, Avallon, Nôtre Dame in Paris, St. Denis, and Vézelay, with the choir of the church at Issoire, supply curious examples of this new branch of decoration. This continuation of details, originally belonging to the 12th century, suggests the remark that the edifices constructed by the Gothic school, at the commencement of the 13th century, do not possess features so distinct as to furnish always a means of distinguishing them from those belonging to the period of transition — a remark which may be applied to the two examples of domestic architecture at Caudebec, which form *fig.* 233.

540. Out of the large number of masterpieces in architecture in the 13th century may be selected the cathedrals at Lisieux, Lyon, and Narbonne, executed in the early part of that period; Bordeaux and Châlons-sur-Saône belong to the year 1250; and Coutances dates in the last half of that century. Great part of the cathedrals at Bourges, Dijon, Laon, Nantes, Nevers, Senlis, and Sens; the choir and aisles at Auxerre; the choir and chapels, with the upper part of the nave, at Bayeux; the nave and choir at Séez; the churches at Ourscamp, St. Denis, St. Jean-aux-Bois, and St. Maximin; those of St. Pierre at Avalon, and of St. Victor at Marseilles; the Ste. Chapelle at Paris; the choir of the church at St. Nazaire at Carcassonne; the nave and most of the choir of that of St. Pierre at Lisieux; the chapels, aisles, and choir of that of St. Julien at Mans; the choir of that of St. Nicaise at Rouen; and the Hotel-Dieu at Louvres, were constructed in the course of this period.

541. The cathedrals which are usually taken as affording standards of the style are Chartres, Beauvais, Reims, Paris, Amiens, and Rouen, of which Reims is perhaps more consistent than Amiens. They are universally considered to be two of the finest examples of the style in the world. The former, which was begun 1212, but not quite finished till 1430, is in the form of a Latin cross on the plan (*fig.* 234.); its length from east to west is 492 ft., and its breadth, measured to the extremities of the arms of the

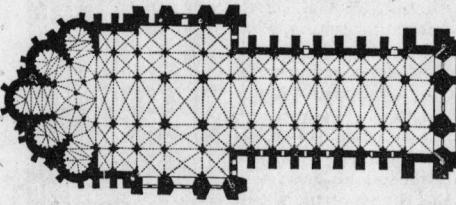

Fig. 254.   PLAN OF REIMS CATHEDRAL.

transepts, is 190 ft. The width of the transepts is 98 ft., and the towers, 270 ft. from the ground, are still imperfect, because their open spires have never been erected

Fig. 235.   CATHEDRAL AT REIMS.

Fig. 256.   CATHEDRAL AT AMIENS.

542. The cathedral of Amiens, begun 1220 by Robert de Luzarches, but continued and completed, 1269, by Thomas and Regnault de Cormont, except the west front that was not finished until the end of the 14th century, is 444 ft. long and 84 ft. wide (*fig.* 237.), and 141 ft. high in the nave. It was commenced within two years of the cathedral at Salisbury. Of the two, Amiens (*fig.*236.) is in a more perfect and advanced state of art than Salisbury, for the French were before us in adding to the simple beauties of the former period many graces not adopted by us until the latter.

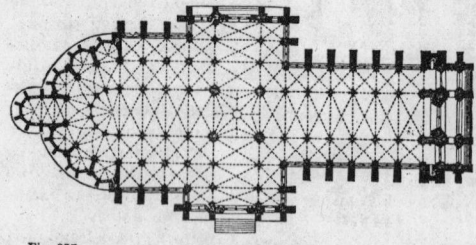

Fig. 257.   PLAN OF AMIENS CATHEDRAL.

543. The *style ogival secondaire* is considered by some architects to be that in which pointed art arrived at perfection; for they deem that an increase of elegance compensates for a loss of severity; but with the latter the purity of the preceding period seems to be wanting. Nevertheless this *style rayonnant* has no absolute character; it is rather, as observed by M. Schayes, a system of transition preserving the elements of the style of the 13th century, but modifying them by greater amount of ornament, and by more expansion and boldness in the curve of the arch, for the *arc en tiers point* is the true arch of the time. This decoration, this arch, and the tracery of the windows, chiefly mark the style: and in regard to the latter point, *figs.* 231 and 232 show the difference between the works of the two periods. The sculptors of the 14th century were more skilful than their predecessors; their carving

shows more delicacy and finish, while their statues are no longer ideali-ties: an important tendency of the period was an attempt at portrait busts, in some cases resulting in an approach to natural simplicity, although the attitude might be stiff and constrained, as was the case in almost all mediæval sculpture. The statues assume greater length in the body, and are dressed in ample dra-pery, cast with some affectation, but still having falling folds slightly bent.

544. The comparison which was recommended between *figs.* 231 and 232, may be paralleled with advan-tage by placing before the reader, *fig* 238, a fair example of the second period, in the choir of St. Ouen at Rouen, and *fig.* 239, an equally modest work of the third epoch from the church of St. Maclou, in the same city.

545. Foreign armies and civil wars caused the usual buildings of the 14th century to be fortified houses and city gateways rather than ec-clesiastical structures. One church, however, that of St. Ouen, at Rouen, 1318-39, (*figs.* 238 and 240), exhi-bits the style in its choir and chapels more perfectly than the ca-thedrals at Clermont-Ferrand, Metz,

Fig. 238. ST. OUEN, AT ROUEN.

Fig. 239. ST. MACLOU, AT ROUEN.

and Perpignan. Other good examples are the transepts at Bayeux, the chapels at Narbonne, and the chapter-house with the cloister at Noyon; besides the churches of the Dominicans and of St. Didier at Avignon; that of St. Jacques at Compiègne, and of St. Nizier at Lyon; the cloister of St. Jean-des-Vignes at Soissons; the palace at Avignon; the hotel-de-ville at St. Omer; the towers of St. Victor at Marseille, and of St. Sernin at Toulouse; and the front of the church of St. Martin at Laon.

546. The third period, the *style ogival tertiaire, fleuri,* or *flamboy-ant,* as it was termed by M. Au-guste le Prévost, used the equi-

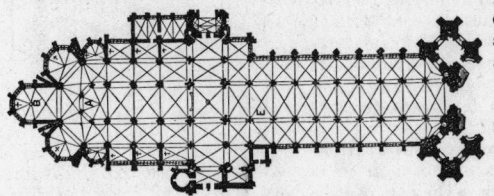

Fig. 240. PLAN OF ST. OUEN, AT ROUEN, (before the front was remodelled by M. Viollet-le-Duc).

lateral arch during the 15th and part of the 16th century; but more commonly one, in some cases stilted, with the radii less than the width of the opening (*ogive surbaissée* or *ogive obtuse*): the elliptic arch (*arc en anse de panier*); the ogee arch (*arc en accolade*); and its reverse (*arc en doucine*), are not uncommon. The pointed arch seems crushed by its canopies and finials; and the system of false-bearing is carried to so great an extent that the buildings might have been intended to defy the laws of equilibrium. There is great skill shown in the *coupe des pierres,* and in working them as decoration with extreme delicacy into petrified leaves of the thistle and curled cabbage, or into imitations of

embroidery. Covered with cusped arches, niches, pinnacles, and tracery, the buildings of the time would be easily recognised even if they were not marked by the wavy or broken lines of the arches; the *moulures prismatiques* or pear-shaped boltels, projecting arrises, and deep hollows, which form the mouldings; and the boldly designed corbelling, pendentives, and vaulting so flat that it resembles a ceiling resting upon extremely thin pillars. In *fig.* 241 we illustrate one of the compartments of the sacristy of the church at Caudebec, which conveys a fair notion of the peculiarity of the style. During this period the sculptors lost much of the simplicity noticed in the preceding century; they evidently copied the living model for at least the head and hands, with great truth and sometimes with happiness in expressing sentiment, but they clothed it in heavy drapery cast with pretension. The grotesque and monstrous figures almost excel the statues, and seem to have some analogy with those which appear in the bassi-rilievi of the 11th century. Such were the last efforts of the pointed style, which owed its principal character to its tendency towards verticality, and finished by seeking horizontality.

547. Amongst the most remarkable works of the 15th century may be mentioned the transepts 1400-39, and the nave 1464-91, obviously modelled upon the previous choir, of St. Ouen at Rouen; the upper part and spire of the north-west tower at Chartres; the central tower, transepts, and chapels at Evreux; Limoges; the northern entrance at Sens; the churches at Notre-Dame-de-l'Épine, St. Quentin, St. Riquier, Than, St. Wulfran at Abbeville; the Celestinians, and St. Pierre at Avignon; St. Jean at Caen; St. Antoine at Compiègne; Ste. Catherine at Honfleur; St. Germain l'Auxerrois at Paris; St. Vincent at Rouen; and St. Pierre at Senlis; the choir and apse of St. Trophime at Arles; the greater part of St. Martin at Avignon; some pure portions (others, *fig.* 242, showing the dying struggles of the style) of St. Jacques at Dieppe; the choir and transepts of St. Remi, at Reims; the pretty Bourbon chapel in the cathedral at Lyon; the *salle des chevaliers* at Mont St. Michel; and the tower of St. Jean at Elbeuf.

548. Among the examples of the style, between the years 1420 and 1531, are the Hôtel des Ambassadeurs at Dijon, about 1420; and the Fontaine de la Croix at Rouen, between 1422 and 1461, lately restored with the greatest success in all its delicate details of ornament and tracery; as well as that which, erected about 1512 opposite the cathedral at Clermont, in Auvergne, was much injured by its renewal in 1799. The palace at Dijon dates about 1467; and in that city are the monuments of the Dukes of Burgundy, Philippe-le-Hardi and Jean-sans-Peur, which were in the church of the Chartreuse. That of the

Fig. 241.   SACRISTY OF THE CHURCH, CAUDEBEC.

last-named was executed by Juan de Huerta, assisted by other artists, about 1475. They are both of the period and are perfect keys to the style that prevailed at the time. At Nancy, the capital of Lorraine, still remains a portion of the ancient palace of its powerful dukes. A representation of its *portail* is given in *fig.* 243. What remains within serves as barracks for the garrison. The date of it is about 1476. The Porte du Cailhau at Bordeaux, 1494, in memory of the battle of Fornovo, shares the fate of the Hôtel de Ville at St. Quentin, with its known date of 1495-1509, in not attracting so much notice as a very peculiar instance of a castle in miniature built by Gerard de Nollent about the end of the 15th century at Caen with four fronts, which from the statues of Neptune and Hercules placed on the battlements, is commonly called the château de la gendarmerie. At Orleans, the Hôtel de Ville, finished in 1498, is now used as a museum. The Château de Blois, with four facades of different design, the eastern work dating about 1498-1515, is too well known to need here any further remark. Ten miles from Caen is situate the Château de Fontaine le Henri; the greater portion is of this period. A part of the west front is given, *fig.* 244, as a characteristic specimen of the residences of the noblesse during

the latter part of
the 15th century, at
which period it evi-
dently was erected.
The well known
Hôtel de Cluny at
Paris, possessing
portions of an ear-
lier date, had the
works resumed in
1490 by Jacques
d'Amboise, Abbé
of Cluny, and after-
wards bishop of
Clermont. This
building now con-
tains the works of
art formerly belong-
ing to M. de Som-
merard. Near St.
Amand is the Châ-
teau de Meillant,
much resembling
the last named edi-
fice, but more orna-
mented.

549. During the
last years of the
15th century, the
campaigns in Italy
by the French made

Fig. 242.   ST. JACQUES, DIEPPE.

them acquainted with the new style, the
imitation of the antique. At first, some
mouldings and some decorations only
were copied. Thus several portions of
the cathedral at Orleans exhibit the essential features of decaded pointed architecture; and while Bullant designed in
the Italian style the château at Ecouen,
he maintained in the appendent chapel
the Gothic taste, as being eminently ecclesiastical, as he did in the parish church
at the same place. In the 16th century
new churches were rare: sumptuous
palaces and pleasure-houses were the chief
works, in which great saloons became the
chief objects; and the middle class also
introduced luxury into their dwellings.
As the main object was the expression
of wealthy ease, not a character of grave
magnificence, the functions of the architect were assumed by the sculptor; and
at the same moment sculpture, no longer
architectural, alike commenced its decadence in France. The chief ecclesiastical
works of the period were the additions of
fronts, or restorations; those done at the
commencement of the epoch form a sort
of transition between the *style fleuri* and
the Italian renaissance employed towards
the end of the reign of Francis I. In
this category may be ranged the churches
of St. Patrice, St. Godard, St. André-
de la-Cité, St. Nicolas, St. Sever, and the
great portal of the cathedral at Rouen;
the church at Brou; and the churches
of St. Etienne-du-Mont and of St. Eus-
tache at Paris. The latter has the

Fig. 243.   PALACE AT NANCY.

general forms of a Gothic building with renaissance details, and as its side entrance was constructed at the same time as the fine flamboyant side entrance to the cathedral at Beau-

Fig. 244.   CHÂTEAU DE FONTAINE LE HENRI, NEAR CAEN.

vais, it is clear that the architectural revolution was not simultaneously effective in all parts of the country.

550. As specimens of civil architecture of the period, may be named the town halls at St. Quentin, Compiègne, and Noyon ; with two of the finest examples of the art of this period, the Palais de Justice and the Hotel de Bourgtheroulde, at Rouen. The first was begun in 1499 and finished in 1508. The plot on which this beautiful work stands, including the court-yard, is about three-fifths of an English acre, and the arrangement of its plan is given, that is, of the ancient part of the building, in *fig.* 245. It is thus described by Dawson Turner :—" The palace forms three sides of a quadrangle " (two of them only are ancient). " The fourth is occupied by an embattled wall and an elaborate gateway. The building was erected about the beginning of the sixteenth century ; and with all its faults " (we are not aware what they are) " it is a fine adaptation of Gothic architecture to civil purposes." " The windows in the body of the building take flattened elliptic heads, and they are divided by one mullion and one transom. The mouldings are highly

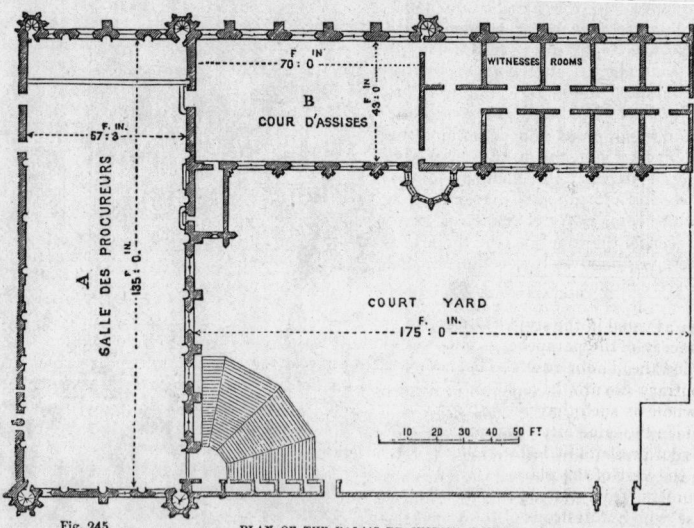

Fig. 245.   PLAN OF THE PALAIS DE JUSTICE, ROUEN.

wrought, and enriched with foliage. The lucarne" (dormer) "windows are of a different design, and form the most characteristic feature of the front; they are pointed, and enriched with

mullions and tracery, and are placed within triple canopies of nearly the same form, flanked by square pillars, terminating in tall crocketed pinnacles, some of them fronted with open arches, crowned with statues. The roof, as is usual in French and Flemish buildings of this date, is of a very high pitch, and harmonises well with the proportions of the building. An oriel, or rather tower, of enriched workmanship projects into the court, and varies the elevations" (an object the designer never once thought about, inasmuch as in all mediæval buildings, the first consideration was convenience, and then the skill to make convenience agreeable to the eye—an invaluable rule to the architect). "On the left-hand side of the court, a wide flight of steps leads to the *Salle des Procureurs*" (marked A on the plan), "a place originally designed as an exchange for the merchants of the city" (*sed quære*), "who had previously been in the habit of assembling for that purpose in the Cathedral." Its dimensions are 135 ft. long, by 57 ft. 3 in. wide. The room B is now the *Cour d'Assises*; the ceiling is of oak, and is arranged in compartments with a profusion of carving and gilt ornaments. The original bosses of the ceiling are gone, as are also the doors which were enriched with sculpture, and the original chimney-piece. Round the room are gnomic sentences, admonishing the judges, jurors, witnesses, and suiters of their duties." The basement story of the *salle* is, or used to be, occupied as a prison. The southern and eastern façades of this elegant edifice have lately (1856) been restored under the direction of M. Grégoire, who probably superintended the internal decorations.

551. *Fig.* 246 is a portion of the south front of the building. The ellipse seems almost to have superseded the pointed arch in the leading forms, over which the crocketed labels or drips, in curves of contrary flexure, flow with surprising elegance. It is only in the lucarnes we find the pointed arch ; and there it is almost subdued by the surrounding accessories. The connection of the lucarnes with the turrets of the façade by means of flying buttresses is most beautiful, and no less ingenious in the contrivance : their height from

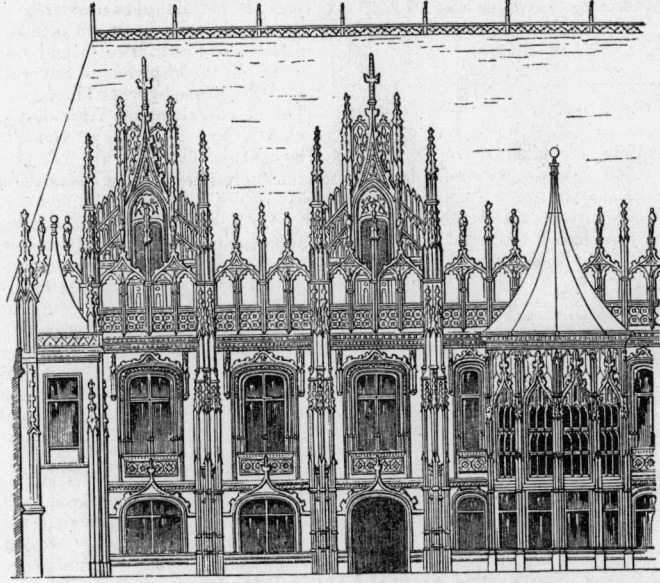

the ground to the top of the finials, is 78 ft. 6 in. The octangular turrets at the end of the salle, next the Rue St. Lo, contain a very pretty example of penetration over the heads of the pointed arch. In the story above the basement, as also in the lucarnes, the soffites of the windows are rounded at the angles, or, as the French call it, have *coussinets ar-*

Fig. 246.　　　ELEVATION OF THE SOUTH FRONT, PALAIS DE JUSTICE, ROUEN.

rondis, as usual in the style, those in the principal story being, besides, slightly segmental. In the tracery of the parapet it is singular to find the quatrefoils centered throughout with what is called the Tudor rose. The arches rising above the parapet, which are crocketed and of contrary flexure, have statues substituted for finials. The richness of the ornamentation of the whole is such that we know no other example, except that of the Hôtel de Bourgtheroulde in the same city that can vie with it. The woodcut, *fig.* 247, is a section of the *salle.* The roof presents little for remark. It is bold and simple, and seems scarcely in harmony with the rest of the place. It is impossible to form an adequate notion of this splendid monument from the figures here given, owing to the necessary smallness of the scale. Those who are desirous of thoroughly understanding its details will be gratified by referring to the plates of it in Britton's *Normandy.*

552. There is no city where the style of the period whereof we are treating can be better studied than Rouen. It possesses, both in secular as well as ecclesiastical architecture,

all that the student can desire. The Hôtel de Bourgtheroulde, in the Place de la Pucelle, is about the same age as the Palais de Justice we have just described, or perhaps three or four years later in the finishing. In some respects it is more elaborate in the ornaments and the abundance of sculpture. The entire front is divided into bays by slender buttresses or pilasters, the spaces between them being filled with bassi-rilievi; every inch of space, indeed, in the building has been ornamented. This building still remains in a most degraded condition.

Fig. 247.   SECTION OF HALL, PALAIS DE JUSTICE, ROUEN.

Belgium.

553. The table of styles given at the commencement of the preceding section applies to the progress of art in this portion of the history. The first appearance of the pointed arch is fixed in the first quarter of the 12th century, by Schayes, *L'Architecture en Belgique*, 1850–53, who notices that the semicircular arch did not disappear until the middle of the 13th, and that only ecclesiastical edifices can be adduced as examples of the *style de transition*. The choir aisles were continued round the chevet, in the churches of Ste. Gudule at Bruxelles, St. Quentin at Tournai, and Pamele at Audenaerde, while Nôtre Dame de la Chapelle at Bruxelles exhibits annulated ribs to the vaulting. The division of the doorway by a post is due to this period; as are gargoyles in decoration; and the introduction, in Flanders, of brickwork.

554. The chief structures are the tower of St. Pierre at Ypres; St. Sauveur at Bruges, 1116-27, the earliest piece of mediæval brickwork in Belgium; St. Nicolas, and St. Jacques, at Gand or Ghent; the abbey church at Afflighem, 1122-44; and the Chapelle du Saint-Sang at Bruges, 1150, despite the decorations added since the 15th century, and the facade reconstructed 1824, being one chapel over another (*fig.* 248.), with a peculiarly shaped tower which is also double, one portion being circular in plan upon a corbel, the other being square in plan at base and attached to it. Probably St. Quentin at Tournai, and St. Martin at Saint Trond, are later. It is remarkable that the blank arcade formed by crossed semicircular arches does not occur in Belgium.

Fig. 248.   CHAPELLE DU SAINT-SANG, BRUGES.

555. Amongst the chief structures in the *style de transition* which were erected during the 13th century, are Nôtre Dame at Ruremonde, 1218-24, which resembles the church of the Apostles at Cologne, and is the first instance of a true cupola in Belgium; the church at Lisseweghe, about 1250; and the Abbey at Villers, which, although in ruins, is a perfect type of the style in the choir and transepts, and moreover retains more of the dependent original buildings than any other establishment in the country; the brewery dates 1197, and the church about 1225; the triforium range of windows to the choir are superposed circles, an idea repeated in the end walls of the transepts; the three-aisled nave has a third triforium and is the most perfect type of the early part of the *style ogival primaire* existing in Belgium, except that of Ste. Pamele; the flying buttresses are remarkable works; the cloister belongs to the 14th and 15th centuries. The chevet, 1220, of Ste. Gudule, and

the contemporaneous choir, with the transepts of Nôtre Dame de la Chapelle at Bruxelles; the Madeleine, about 1250, at Tournai; the choir, 1221, of St. Martin at Ypres, remarkable for the branches of foliage along the strings; the crypt, 1228, of St. Bavon at Gand, which was the last (except one hereafter noticed) that was constructed in the kingdom; Ste. Pamele, built 1235–9, by A. de Bincho, at Audenaerde, which is said to be "le type le plus curieux qu'il soit possible de trouver de ce style;" and St. Jacques at Tournai, which has one triforium over another, and exhibits in the tower a pointed trefoiled arch with columns to support the cusps; are also transitional.

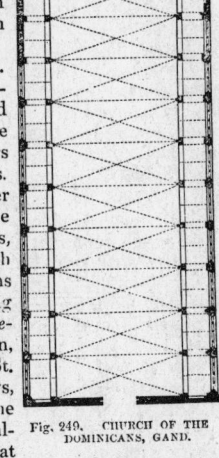

556. The chapel of the castle at Vianden, was about 50 ft. long and 36 ft. wide; its plan was a decagon with one side opening to the castle and another to a pentagonal choir; divided into three portions by columns engaged in square piers; the centre was a hexagonal pit over the dungeons so that the prisoners could hear prayers without leaving their cells; it is now in ruins.

557. To the *style ogival primaire* belong the choir and lower part of the nave of the cathedral of St. Paul at Liége; the choir and chief part of the transepts of Ste. Gudule at Bruxelles, 1250–80; great part of Nôtre Dame at Tongres; the church (*fig.* 249, width between the piers is 53 ft.) of the Dominicans at Gand, 1240–75, with a single nave covered by wooden ceiling (*fig.* 250.), on curves of 60 ft. radius; (both cuts from the *Gentleman's Magazine* for 1862), that of the Dominicans at Louvain, 1230–50, or later; the three-aisled naves and the transepts of St. Martin at Ypres, 1254–66, with one of the few rose windows, existing in Belgium, over the porch to the south transept; the choir of St. Léonard at Leau; Nôtre Dame at Dinant; Ste. Walburge at Furnes; the abbey and hospital called La Byloque at Gand, "with an oaken roof not ceiled where spiders have never come," and with a remarkable brick gable to the refectory; the brick tower of Nôtre Dame at Bruges, 1230–97, said to have been about 420 ft. high, including the spire, till 1818, when 50 ft. were

Fig. 249.   CHURCH OF THE
DOMINICANS, GAND.

removed; the choir of the cathedral at Tournai, 197 ft. long, 121 ft. wide, and 108 ft. (inside) in height, remarkable for its stilted arches and for the means adopted to strengthen their pillars; as well as the choir of St. Bavon at Gand, begun 1275 and not finished in the 13th century, with its opposite clearstories connected by iron ties. In the Netherlands there are a great number of large churches which have a singular identity of appearance in the interior, and at the same time a manifest peculiarity of character. This appears to be due to the employment of plain, well-proportioned cylindrical shafts for their piers; the style in other respects being an elegant Gothic. The principal examples are Nôtre Dame, and the cathedral at Malines; St. Paul at Liége; Nôtre Dame des Victoires, La Chapelle, and Ste Gudule, at Bruxelles; St. Jacques, and the Dominicans, at Antwerp; St. Michel at Gand; and Furnes near Bruges.

558. The *style ogival secondaire* was chiefly employed by the ecclesiastics in finishing structures or in commencing others conceived on so large a scale that their superstructure belongs to a later period. The chief edifices of the style are the five-aisled church of St. Jean at Bois-le-duc, curious for the revolting obscenity of the large statues to the but-

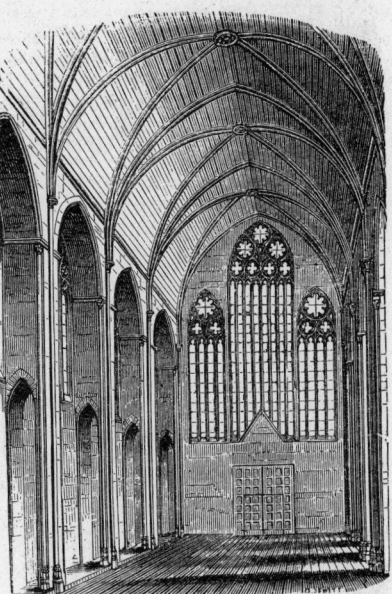

Fig. 250.   CHURCH OF THE DOMINICANS, GAND.

tresses of the choir—it was commenced 1280, but evidently was finished in the latter half of the 15th century; the five-aisled choir of St. Sulpice at Diest; the church of the Grand-Béguinage at Louvain, commenced 1305, noticed for the manner in which the twelve pillars that divide it into three aisles have been strengthened by iron bars; the contemporaneous church of the Béguinage at Diest; the church at Aerschot, built 1331-7 by J. Pickart; and, finest of all, Nôtre Dame at Huy, begun 1311, with a splendid rose window.

To these may be added the cathedral at Saint Rombaut, begun about 1345-50; the nave and southern aisle of Ste. Gudule at Bruxelles; the front of the cathedral at Tournai; and Ste. Croix at Liége, the only church in Belgium, since the destruction of that at Lobes, that has the three aisles of equal height, and from which the architect is reported to have fled rather than superintend the striking of the centering to the vaulting, which in the nave is corbelled out from the pillars.

559. Some of the finest structures belonging to the *style ogival tertiaire* are; great part of Nôtre Dame at Hal, 1341-1409; the porch and towers, completed 1439, to St. Martin at Courtrai, 1390-1439; Ste. Walburge at Audenaerde, rebuilt, except the choir, 1414-1515, with a tower 295 ft. high, by J. van den Eecken; Nôtre Dame at Anvers, the only five-aisled church (except that at Saint-Hubert) in the country, which is really seven-aisled in plan in the nave (the choir belongs to the preceding century, and the completion of the tower, commenced 1422-3, by J. Appelmans, with the cupola and the Lady-chapel, to the first half of the 16th century); St. Gommaire at Lierre, begun 1425, and not less than 250 feet long, with a high tower, finished 1455, but altered 1702; the porch and tower of St. Martin at Ypres, 1434, by M. Utenhove; the chevet of the cathedral at Saint-Rombaut, with 320 ft. of its tower, 1452-1513, which was to have been 600 ft. high, according to the preserved design; Ste. Wandru at Mons, which was building 1450 (with aisles 1525, and nave 1580-9, by J. de Thuin and his son), and is supposed to have been designed by the architect of St. Pierre at Louvain, which was building 1433 with later nave, the design and stone model for the intended colossal triple-towered façade is preserved in the town-hall; St. Michel at Gand, 1440-1515; Nôtre Dame at Malines about 1475-1550; the contemporaneous Nôtre Dame du Sablon at Bruxelles; the upper church at Anderlicht, 1470-82; St. Jacques at Anvers, 1429-1560, with a tower, 1491, by T. de Coffermaker; and the tower, 272 ft. high, of St. Bavon, 1461-1534, by J. Stassins, with that of St. Nicolas, 1406, by T. de Steenhoukebelde, both at Gand.

560. As works of the 15th century must be named, the great entrance and its two towers, with other portions, to Ste. Gudule at Bruxelles; the tower and eastern part of Nôtre Dame at Tongres; the brick tower of St. Jean at Bois-le-duc; and the tower of the church at Aerschot, said to have carried a spire 488 ft. high, that was replaced, 1575, by the present spire, which attains about 320 ft. In the same style are the five-aisled abbey church (see Nôtre Dame at Antwerp) at Saint Hubert, about 1526-64; the brick spire, 1524, of Nôtre Dame at Bruges, which is said to have been 422 ft. high, but lessened, 1818, by 50 ft.; the upper part of the nave, the chapels, and the vaulting of the cathedral of St. Paul at Liége, 1528-9; the nave of St. Bavon at Gand, 1533-53, with an iron railing as triforium, and having the clearstories tied together by iron bars; St. Jacques at Liége, 1513-18, the best specimen of the style; with its rivals, St. Martin in the same city, finished, 1542, by P. de Rickel; the brick church at Hoogstraeten, 1534-46; and the church of the Dominicans at Anvers, 1540-71. The cloisters of St. Paul, St. Barthélemi, and St. Jean-en-Isle at Liége are rather later than that of St. Servais at Maestricht.

561. In the 13th century commences that long series of splendid civil edifices which Belgium possesses in greater number than any other country of its size—viz., the belfrys, the markets, the town-halls, and the club-houses. The most remarkable of the *beffrois* are at Tournai (the oldest), Gand (the original drawing is preserved) 1315-37, Ypres, Bruges, Lierre (1369-1411), Nieuport (1480), and Alost (1487). The enormous *halle*, now hôtel de ville, at Ypres, was commenced 1200, but not completed till 1230 in the right wing, 1285 in the left wing, and 1342 at the back; the *water halle* at Bruges was destroyed 1789, but another, which was attached to it, remains, with a tower, 1284-91, by the priest Simon de Genève; the *halle-aux-draps* at Louvain was commenced, 1317, by J. Stevens, A. Hare, and G Raes, and was given, 1424, to the University that, 1680, added the second story. The *halle*, now *boucherie*, at Diest, dates 1346, and the *halle aux draps* at Gand, 1424, the last in the pointed style. The *boucherie* at Ypres belongs to the 13th century; that at Anvers 1501-3.

562. The hôtel-de ville at Alost has the right flank, built in the year 1200, remaining; that at Bruges, commenced 1377, with its rich ceiling, 1398, was the only edifice of its class raised during the 14th century; that at Bruxelles was begun on the left or east side, 1401-2, by J. van Thienen, the tower was completed, 1448-55, by J. van Ruysbroek, the right side was commenced 1454; that at Louvain was erected 1448-59, by M. de Layens, and is unparalleled in any city; that at Mons was built 1458; the old part of that at Gand was begun, 1481, by E. Polleyt; that at Audenaerde was erected, 1527-30, by H. van Pede, and 1528, a painter and a sculptor were sent from that town to copy, for the use of the architect, the two chimney-pieces and the parapet of that at Courtrai, built 1526-7; and even that at Leau deserves attention. We refer our readers to the end of Book III. for some further remarks on these very important buildings.

563. The *maison des poissonniers* and the *maison des bateliers* at Gand date in the first part of the 16th century. The *poorter's logie* (now école des beaux-arts) at Bruges was erected at the end of the 15th century, or a little later. The *maison du roi* at Bruxelles,

rebuilt 1514–23, by A. D. and R. van Mansdale, D. de Wagemaker, L. van Bendeghem, and H. van Pede, was much injured, 1695; and the *Hôtel du Franc* at Bruges dates 1521–3. The *steen* (prison) at Anvers was built 1520. The episcopal palace at Liége dates 1508–40.

564. According to a tradition preserved at Ypres, the timber of which the wooden houses of the 15th and 16th centuries was built, was procured from Norway; some of these dwellings remain in Anvers and Ypres. Two stone houses of the 13th century exist at Gand, and a couple more dating 1250–1300 at Ypres. One of the 14th is in the Place du Vendredi at Gand, and many brick dwellings of the 15th and 16th may still be seen at Anvers, Ath, Bruges, Gand, Malines, Tournai (*fig.* 251.), Ypres, &c. The Porte de Hal at Bruxelles, 1381; the Porte de Diest at Louvain (1526); the Pont du Broel at Courtrai; the Pont des Trous at Tournai (1290–1300), with the keeps of the châteaux at Sichem and Terheyden close the list of remarkable works of ancient pointed art in this country, with notice of the Chapelle de la Vierge attached, 1649, to the southern or right side of Ste. Gudule at Brussels to balance the chapel, built 1533–7, on the left side.

Fig.251.   HOUSE AT TOURNAI.

Germany.

565. In accordance with the opinion now usually adopted, that Gothic art was received into the north of Europe from France, but that it was altered during the process of naturalisation, the usual division of the styles accords with that used in France. But the periods do not altogether match, inasmuch as while examples of pure first-pointed work occur in the cathedrals at Paris and elsewhere, 1163–1212, the German instances are, like those of Belgium, not earlier than 1225. It is hardly possible, however, to refute the documentary evidence for some buildings being very much in advance of contemporaneous structures in England and France as to style. This seems to be admitted by Dr. Whewell, whose valuable *Architectural Notes on German churches*, 1842, third edition, condenses into a few lines the account of the chief peculiarities of detail in the two classes which he observed in that country. He first suggested the fact that English and German architects, beginning from the same point—the Romanesque, and arriving at the same result—the *complete Gothic*, or decorated period, with geometrical tracery, made the transition each through a separate style; one of these being decidedly Gothic; the other, which he calls early German, rather Romanesque than Gothic. They have in common their slender shafts, clustered and banded, their pointed arches, and their mode of vaulting; but we do not commonly find, in the interior of the transition churches of Germany, the circular cluster of shafts, the arches moulded into a broad and deep mass of small rolls with deep hollows between, the circular abacus with its rounded upper edge, the simple lancet-headed windows, tall and narrow, and the peculiar line of open flowers which is used so profusely in all early English work. Nor do we observe, on the outside, the dripstone to the window, the moulded or shafted window-sides or jambs, the projecting buttress with its chamfered edge and triangular head, or the pyramidal pinnacles of our early cathedrals. Vaulting shafts spring from a corbel, or more usually, from an end hooked into the wall; the arch is often a square-edged opening with no mouldings, though sometimes a rebated edge, sometimes a roll, is seen; the triforium is, in a large district, meant for use as a gallery by the bachelors; the fan-shaped window, a foiled horse-shoe arch; and arch mouldings with three bands, or two bands and a roll at the apex. The difference between early English and early German work is less obvious. The resemblance obtains not only in the general forms of the members and parts, but in the details also—the canopies, bases, profiles of mouldings, &c. The latter style, however, has double planes of tracery—*i.e.*, two frames of tracery, one behind the other, in the same opening. After this general coincidence, the styles seem again to diverge, the later Gothic of Germany being quite different from the contemporaneous or corresponding styles of England, France, and the Netherlands; these again apparently being independent of each other. Nevertheless, a German author would inscribe at the head of this section the following table:—

Early		*Fruehgermanischer styl*				Thirteenth century.
Decorated		*Ausgebildetgermanischer styl*				Fourteenth century.
Late		*Spaetgermanischer styl*				Fifteenth century and later.

566. The earliest truly pointed buildings seem to be, the church of St. Mary at Treves,

1227–44, said to resemble in plan the church at Braine near Soissons; the choir of St. Afra at Meissen, 1235; and the nave of St. Elizabeth at Marburg, 1253–83, which pro-

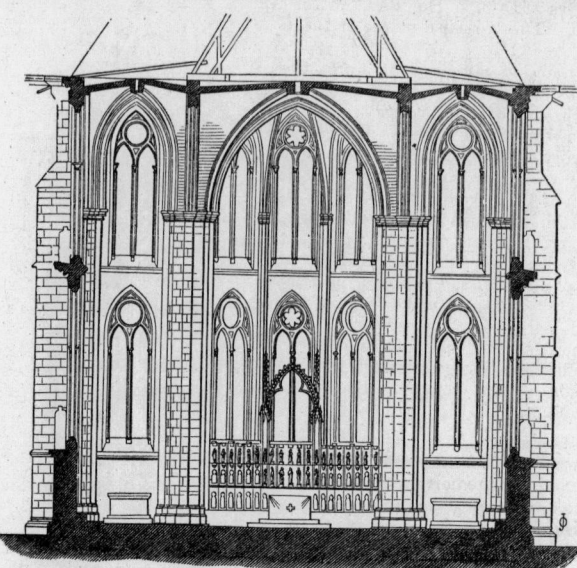

bably was the first instance of the practice of erecting the nave and aisles uniform in height that is so common in Germany (*fig.* 252). The church of the Minorites at Cologne was consecrated 1260, and is said to have been built at over-times by the workmen of the cathedral.

567. The cathedral at Cologne, begun 1248, is held to owe much of the plan to that at Amiens, and of the decoration to the Ste. Chapelle at Paris. The abbey of Altenburg is said to be indebted for its style to Cologne cathedral; the choir at Meissen to that at Naumburg, and Calmar to Strasburg; the churches at

Fig. 252.   SECTION OF THE CHURCH OF SAINT ELIZABETH, MARBURG.

Gruenberg, Nienburg an der Saale, and Wetter, with St. Mary at Frankenberg and at Marburg to that of St. Elizabeth at Marburg. In the 14th century, the five-aisled church at Kuttenberg was indebted to Prague cathedral; the choir of the church of St. Mary at Bamberg to Cologne cathedral, and (for windows) to the church at Oppenheim; and the churches of St. Mary at Rostock and Wismar to Schwerin cathedral. In the 15th century the church at Steier borrowed from Vienna cathedral; St. Mary at Bernburg from St. Nicholas at Zerbst and St. Maurice at Halle; Freiberg cathedral and St. Mary at Zwickau from St. Nicholas at Zerbst; and the church at Elten from St. Algund at Emmerich. These cases of imitation may be deserving of attention.

568. The general character of the work of the first period is very much that of the French buildings of the style: but where the German work is plain, it is much plainer than the French; and where decorated, much richer. Its reminiscences of romanesque art are more obvious in the profiles of mouldings, while the carved work in capitals is almost an exaggeration of the crispness of the French work.

569. Amongst the remarkable buildings erected in the 13th century may be named the

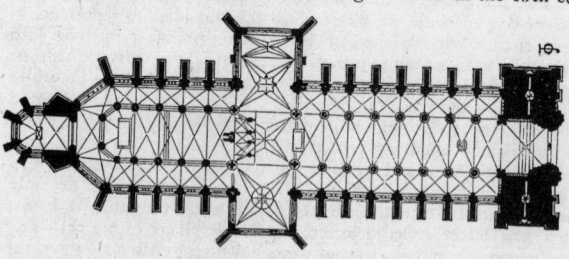

old parish church at Ratisbon, with many romanesque details, 1250–63 or 1290–1300, a difference of nearly half a century, which occurs in the dates given by eminent writers to the whole, or to parts, of many German edifices. The very remarkable cathedral (*fig.* 253), at Halberstadt has the lower part

Fig. 253.   PLAN OF CATHEDRAL, HALBERSTADT.

of the west front older than the rest of the edifice, which dates 1235–1491; its section (*fig.* 254.) is here given as being an instance of elegant proportions that enforce admiration. . The beautiful church at Oppenheim, dedicated to St. Catherine, is a Latin cross on its plan. The chancel is five sides of an octagon. As in many of the churches of Germany, it has a second chancel for the canons at the western extremity, terminating in three sides of an octagon. The entrances are on the north and south sides of the transepts. From a MS. chronicle of the church, quoted by Moller, it is ascertained that the

nave and eastern chancel were begun in 1262, and finished in 1317. The western chancel, now a ruin, was consecrated 1439. The total length of the church, including the two chancels, is 268 ft.; whereof the western chancel, whose breadth is 46 ft., occupies 92 ft. The nave is 102 ft. in length, and its breadth 86, that breadth comprising the two side aisles which are separated from the nave by clustered columns; the aisles have small chapels. The transept is 102 ft. long, and 31 ft. broad. In the western front, at the extremity of the nave, are two towers, standing on square bases, each of four storys, and crowned by an octagonal spire. Over the intersection of the transepts with the nave stands an octagonal tower. This building was erected for Richard of Cornwall, emperor of Germany, and has lately been restored. The church at Wimpfen-im-Thal, 1262–78, is recorded as built by a Parisian " opere francigeno ;" the choir of Meissen cathedral 1274; the simple church of the Dominicans at Ratisbon 1274–77; and the choir of the cathedral in the same city, 1275–80.

570. The western portal of Strasburg cathedral was begun 1277 by Erwin von Steinbach, an architect before mentioned(*par.*

Fig. 254.   SECTION OF CATHEDRAL, HALBERSTADT.

·322a) who died 1318, leaving unfinished part of the second story, which was completed by his son Johann, who died 1339 ; the third story is an addition. The cathedral was carried on under other architects till 1439, since which nothing has been done towards its completion. Among the examples of pointed architecture, this is the most stupendous. There is a similarity of style between it and the cathedrals of Paris and Reims, except that the ornaments are more minute. The plan is a Latin cross, whose eastern end terminates interiorly in a semicircle, but on the exterior in a straight line. The length of the church is 324 ft., that of the transept 150 ft. ; the height of the vault of the nave is 98 ft. The nave has one aisle on each side of it. On the north-west angle of the edifice, rises the spire, whose height has been so variously represented, that some authors have made it 100 ft. higher than others : we believe the correct height to be 466 ft., being greater than that of any church in Europe. To a certain height the tower is square and solid, being formed by one of the vertical divisions of the western façade. Above the solid part, the tower rises to a certain height octangularly, open on all sides, and flanked by four sets of open spiral staircases, which are continued to the line whence the principal tower rises conically in seven stories or steps, crowned at the summit with a species of lantern. John Hültz, sen., Heckler, and John Hültz, jun. continued this fine tower, which was only finished in 1439. In the interior of the church, near one of the large piers of the transept, is a statue of the architect Erwin, in the attitude of leaning over the balustrades of the upper corridor, and looking at the opposite piers. The minster at Freiburg-im-Breisgau, is remarkable as being almost the only large Gothic church in Germany which is finished, and has escaped destruction. It was begun 1152, as appears in the romanesque transepts with their external turrets ; the nave, west front, the tower 380 ft. high, skilfully changed from square to octagon, with open spire, and rich porch below it, date 1236–72 ; the choir (see *fig.* 255.) belongs to the year 1513. The transition, which in France dates 1250, is seen in the west front, 1287, of the cathedral at Agram, where the choir dates 1305–19, with a later nave.

Fig. 255.   NAVE OF MINSTER,
FREIBURG-IM-BREISGAU.

571. In the second period elegance and richness were sought; the latter was obtained, but the former was lost in a manner which may easiest be expressed in the statement that everything seems to be an addition as an after thought Decoration is spread on the work: witness the

crockets and capitals which are only single leaves glued to their places instead of the freely
growing foliage of the previous period.

572. In the 14th century occurred the construction of the nave at Meissen cathedral,
1312-42; the tower and choir of St. Elizabeth at Kaschau, 1321; St. Mary at Prenzlau,

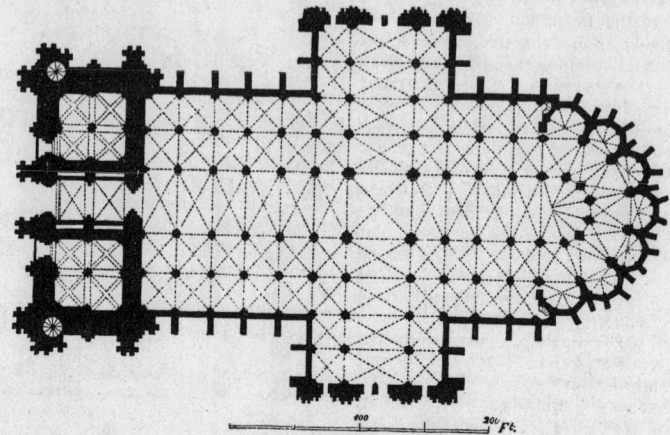

Fig. 256. PLAN OF COLOGNE CATHEDRAL.

1325-40; the church at Friedeberg, 1328; St. Lambert at Muenster, 1335-75; the choir
in St. Mary at Wismar, 1339-54; the five-aisled choir in Prague cathedral, 1343-85; the
choir in the cathedral at Aix-la-Chapelle, 1353; and St. Mary at
Nuremberg, 1354-61, by G. and F. Ruprecht. To the end of
this century belongs the pentagonal church at Kirchheim-im-Ries,
with the convent's choir in the western portion.

573. The plan of the cathedral at Cologne (*fig. 256.*),
exhibits a symmetry not surpassed by the buildings of
ancient Greece and Rome. A church erected on the site of
this cathedral in the time of Charlemagne was destroyed by fire
in 1248, at which time Conrad filled the archiepiscopal throne of
the city. Before fire had destroyed the former cathedral, this

Fig. 257. SOUTH ELEVATION OF COLOGNE CATHEDRAL

prelate had resolved on the erection of a new church, so that in the year following
the destruction of the old edifice, measures had been so far taken, that the first stone

of the new fabric was laid with great solemnity on the 14th of August, being the eve of the Assumption of the Blessed Virgin. Collections were made throughout Europe for carrying on the works, and the wealth of Cologne itself seems to have favoured the hope that its founder had expressed of their continuation. The misfortunes of the times soon, however, began to banish the flattering expectation, that the works would be continued to the completion of the building. The archbishops of Cologne dissipated their treasures in unprofitable wars, and ultimately abandoned the city altogether, for a residence at Bonn. The works do not, however, appear to have been interrupted, though they proceeded but slowly. On the 27th of September, in the year 1322, seventy-four years after the first stone had been laid, the choir was consecrated. The works were not long continued with activity, for about 1370 the zeal of the faithful was very much damped by finding that great abuses had crept into the disposal of the funds. The nave and southern tower continued rising, though slowly. In 1437, the latter had been raised to the third story, and the bells were moved to it. In the beginning of the 16th century, the nave was brought up to the height of the capitals of the aisles, and the vaulting of the north aisle was commenced; the northern tower was carried on to the corresponding height; and everything seemed to indicate a steady prosecution of the work, though the age was fast approaching in which the style was to be forgotten. The windows in the north aisle were decorated, though not in strict accordance with the style, yet with some of the finest specimens of painted glass that Europe can boast, a work executed under the patronage of the archbishop Hermann von Hesse, of the chapter, of the city, and of many noble families who are, by their armorial bearings, recorded in these windows. But with these works the further progress of the building was entirely stopped, about 1509. *Fig.* 257 exhibits the south elevation of the cathedral, in which the darker parts show the executed work. If the reader reflect on the dimensions of this church, whose length is upwards of 500 ft., and width with the aisles 280 ft.; the length of whose transepts is 290 ft. and more; that the roofs are more than 200 ft. high, and the towers when finished would have been more than 500 ft. on bases 100 ft. wide; he may easily imagine, that, notwithstanding all the industry and activity of a very large number of workmen, the works of a structure planned on so gigantic a scale, could not proceed otherwise than slowly, especially as the stone is all wrought. The stone of which it is built is from two places on the Rhine, Koenigswinter and Unckel-Bruch, opposite the Seven Mountains, from both of which the transport was facilitated by the water carriage afforded by the Rhine. The foundations of the southern tower are known to be laid at least 44 ft. below the surface.

574. To King Frederick William III. is due the merit of rescuing it from the state of a ruined fragment. During his reign nearly 50,000l. were laid out upon it, chiefly in repairs; and in that of his successor, Frederick William IV., 225,000l., more than half of which was contributed by the King, the rest by public subscription. In 1842 he laid the foundation of the transept. The choir is now finished. The late architect, Zwirner, estimated the cost of completing the whole at 750,000l. In September, 1848, the nave, aisles, and transepts were consecrated and thrown open; the magnificent south portal was finished 1859, at a cost of 100,000l. The north portal, more simple in detail, is also completed; both are from Zwirner's designs. The iron central spire and iron roof of the nave were added 1860–62, and the whole, except the towers, nearly finished 1865. The faulty stone, from the Drachenfels, on the exterior, has been replaced by another of a sounder texture, of volcanic origin, brought from Andernach and Treves.
The height of the towers when finished will be 532 ft., equal to the length of the church, whose breadth, 231 ft., corresponds with that of the gable at the west end. The choir is 161 ft. high.

575. The cathedral at Ulm (*fig.* 258.) is another of the many celebrated cathedrals of Germany: it was commenced in 1377, and continued, the tower excepted, to 1494. It is about 416 ft. long, 166 ft. wide, and, including the thickness of the vaulting, 141 ft. high. The piety of the citizens of Ulm moved them to the erection of this structure, towards which they would not accept any contribution from foreign princes or cities; neither would they accept any remission of taxes nor indulgences from the pope. The whole height of the tower is 316 ft. 9 in.; it was stopped 1492 because the two pillars under it, on the side next the

Fig. 258.　　ULM CATHEDRAL.

body of the church, gave way. Had it been finished according to the original design (still in existence), it would have been 491 ft. The exterior length is 455 ft.; interior, 391 ft. The nave and choir are partly built of brick. The nave is 146 ft. high, and has twelve

clustered columns bearing lancet pier-arches, without a triforium, flanked by double aisles on slender shafts. The main support of the roof is derived from huge external buttresses. This building does not preserve the regularity of form for which the cathedral at Cologne is conspicuous, but the composition, as a whole, is exceedingly beautiful.

576. Ratisbon cathedral is another fine work, of about the same period (*fig.* 259). It was begun by Andreas Egl, 1275, but left unfinished in the beginning of the 16th century. The west front is in the decorated style of the 15th century, with a triangular portal throwing

out a pier in front so as to form a double archway. The church is 333 ft. long, and 120 ft. high. The transeptal plan is only seen in the clearstory. At Vienna, the cathedral of St. Stephen's exhibits another exquisite example of the style.

577. The history of the collegiate church of St. Victor at Xanten has been tolerably clearly written. It is a five-aisled edifice without transepts, with a romanesque tower dated 1213. The choir was commenced 1263, the sacristy in 1356, by J. von Mainz, who designed, 1368–70, the east part of the north aisle. The buttresses and vaulting were added 1417–37 : a cessation of the work then occurred till 1487, although we find the names of the master-masons T. Moer, 'archilapicida,' 1455 ; H. Blankenbyl, 1470–4 ; and G. von Lohmar, 1483–7, as busy upon the nave; its windows were completed 1487 ; the south side 1492 ; its vaulting 1500 ; its buttresses 1508 ; the great window between the towers 1519, and the north tower, 1525, were designed by Johann von Langeberg of Cologne, 1492–1522; the sacristy

Fig. 259.   RATISBON CATHEDRAL.

and the chapter-house were designed, 1528, by Gerwin from Wesel; and the chapter-house with cloisters was completed, 1550, by H. Maess.

578. In the third period there seemed to be a natural and at first healthy revulsion ; but it ended in being spiky, a term which is more justifiable than prismatic. Every thing that could be curved was bent or twisted; the most tortuous forms of the flamboyant system are common with truncated ends forming stump tracery; interpenetration abounds; and as a last resource of invention, dead branches intertwined take the places of mouldings and of

foliage. So that in the decline and fall of German pointed art, there was as markedly national a character as in that of the French or the English contemporaneous forms.

579. Amongst the structures of the 15th century (excepting St. Mary at Esslingen, which will be hereafter mentioned) were St. Catherine at Brandenburg, 1401, by H. Brunsbergh, with nave and aisles of equal height ; the choir of St. Mary at Coblentz, 1404–31, by Johann von Spey; the church of St. John at Werfen, 1412; that at Weissenfels, commenced 1415 by Johann Reinhard ; the choir of St. Reinold at Dortmund, 1421–50, by Rozier; St. Mary at Ingoldstadt, 1425, with nave and aisles of equal height, by H. Schnellmeier and C. Glaetzel; St. Laurence at Nuremberg, enlarged 1403, with a choir and aisles of equal height, 1439 or 1459–77, by C. Heinzelmann of Ulm, and Johann Bauer of Ochsenfurt, on the plans of C. Roritzer of Ratisbon ; St. Nicolas at Zerbst, 1446–81, with a nave and aisles of equal height, and with a chevet having nine sides externally, by Johann Kuemelke and his son Matthias; the south-west tower of St. Elizabeth at Breslau, 1452–86, with a wooden spire erected in the latter year, by F. Frobel, 'zimmermann;' the church of the hospital at Cues before 1458 ; the nave and choir of the church at Freiburg an der Unstrut, 1499, by P. von Weissenfels; the nave of the church of St. Ulric and St. Afra at Augsburg, 1467–99; the brick cathedral at Munich, with nave and aisles of equal height, 1468–91, by G. Gankoffen ; the choir of the minster (*fig.* 260) at Freiburg-im-Breisgau, 1471–1513, by Johann Niesenberger; and the cathedral at Freiberg, 1484–1500.

Fig. 260.   CHOIR OF MINSTER, FREIBURG-IM-BREISGAU.

580. The church of St. George at Noerdlingen, with its three naves of equal height and

length, and a tower 283 ft. high, is extremely curious, because so many of its architects were engaged at other places. The names are preserved of Johann Felber, 1427–35, of Ulm, who built the outer church at Waiblingen, completed 1488 ; C. Heinzelmann of Ulm, likewise engaged at Waiblingen as well as at Landau, and, 1459–77, with Johann Bauer von Ochsenfurt at the choir of St. Laurence at Nuremberg, designed by C. Roritzer ; N. Eseller and his son of the same name, 1454–59, both of whom were engaged at the church of St. George at Dinkelsbuehl, 1450, as well as at Augsburg and Rothenburg ; C. Hoeflich and Johann von Salzdorf, 1457 ; W. Kreglinger, of Wurtzburg ; and S. Weyrer, who finished, 1495–1505, the vaulting.

581. This passage from one building to another seems to have commenced in Germany during the 14th and 15th centuries. We find B. Engelberger at Heilbronn, 1480, Ulm 1494, and Augsburg 1502–12 ; H. Brunsbergh, of Stettin, 1401, at Brandenburg, Danzig, and Prenzlau ; Paul von Brandenburg at Brandenburg, 1484, and Neuruppin, 1488 ; P. Arler at Colin, 1360, and Prague, 1385 ; M. Boeblinger at Esslingen, 1482, Frankfort, 1483, and Ulm 1492 ; Johann, 1430, at Landshut, Hall, Salzburg, Oetting and Straubing. It is remarkable that in nearly half the cases (and the rest are doubtful) where the name of an architect is recorded, he seems to have come from another town to that in which the building he designed is erected.

582. *Fig.* 261 is a house attached to the *rath-haus* at Münster, and much resembling it in style ; the house dates late in the 15th century, or early in that of the 16th. We give a house in the Altmarkt-platz at Cologne (*fig.* 262.) for its very late date in appearance, but being entirely free from any trace of transition from 11th century work in detail, it is easily attributed to the early part of the 12th century.

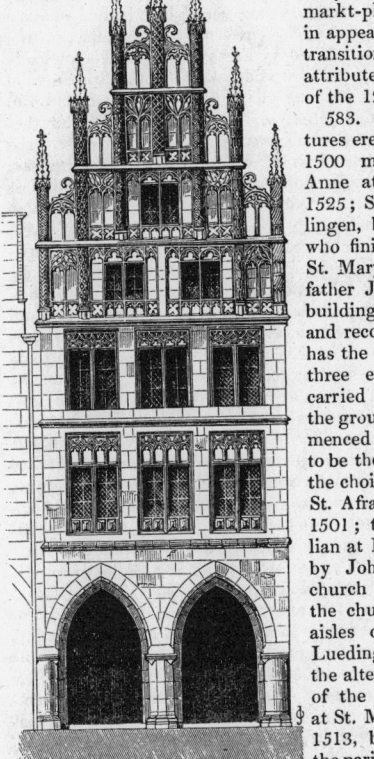

583. Amongst the structures erected about the year 1500 may be named St. Anne at Annaberg, 1499–1525 ; St. Katherine at Esslingen, by M. Boeblinger, who finished the church of St. Mary (left 1482, by his father Johann) ; the latter building was stopped 1321, and recommenced 1406 ; it has the vaulting-ribs of the three equally high naves carried uninterruptedly to the ground ; the tower, commenced 1440, is considered to be the finest in Germany ; the choir of St. Ulrich and St. Afra at Augsburg begun 1501 ; the tower of St. Kilian at Heilbronn, 1507–29, by Johann Scheiner ; the church at Pirna, 1502–46 ; the church with nave and aisles of equal height at Luedinghausen, 1507–58 ; the alterations and vaulting of the romanesque church at St. Matthias near Treves, 1513, by J. von Wittlich ; the parish church at Schneeberg, 1516–40 ; the nave and

Fig. 261.   HOUSE AT MUNSTER.   Fig. 262.   HOUSE AT COLOGNE.

porch of the cathedral at Merseburg, 1500–40 ; the church at Anspach with three western towers, 1530–50 ; St. Mary at Halle an der Saale, completed 1530–54, by N. Hoffmann, with four towers belonging to two earlier churches on the site ; and the vaulting of the nave and refectory at Oliva, 1582–93, by Piper. The church at Freudenstadt, 1601–8 ; and St. George at Coblentz 1618, are specimens of the *zopfstil*, as the German Gothicists designate work of the 17th century, whatever may be its parentage.

Spain.

584. The mediæval architecture of Spain and Portugal will only be divided because the political division exists. It will be necessary to remember that the districts of Aragon

Asturias, Biscay, and North Galicia were never conquered by the Moors; that the cities of Burgos, Leon, Santiago, Segovia, Tarragona, Toledo, and Zamora, were freed from them in the 11th century; Lerida and Zaragoza in the 12th; Seville and Valencia in the middle of the 13th; and Granada on the 2nd January, 1492; that much French influence existed; and that the romanesque buildings of Spain show a large reminiscence of the churches in Northern Italy. But the remarkable similarity between Germany and Spain, in the progress of Gothic art, cannot be attributed to the employment of one or two foreigners. As in Germany, the late romanesque style was retained longer than in France; and in both countries the phase which is termed lancet or early pointed in England and France did not constitute the transition from their romanesque into their decided and well-developed geometrical Gothic.

585. Stone was the usual material employed for ecclesiastical buildings in the really Gothic or even renaissance style. The romanesque and the neo-classic builders employed granite or some of the semi-marbles which the country throughout possesses; where the Moresque traditions of art prevailed, rubble work with brick binding courses and quoins are seen; and the distinctive feature of Spanish brickwork consists in the formation of patterns by recesses and projections in total negligence of terra-cotta or moulded bricks. The diapering of some plastering should be noticed. Few examples of domestic architecture of any importance occur. The window with two or more arches carried on shafts, and forming the *ajimez* or *azimez* of modern builders, is almost universal.

586. Referring to the classification of structures by centuries for examples of the larger works of civil architecture, we regret that little attention has been given to the very interesting class of military buildings, whether fortified houses, peel towers, or small castles, which have escaped demolition. The destruction caused by the generals of Napoleon I. has been followed by the results of the Carlist war of succession, and of the suppression of the monastic establishments; but Spain still possesses one characteristic in construction in the great width of many of the naves. Thus, the church of the dominicans at Palma is 95 ft. wide clear span between the walls; the cathedral at Gerona 73 ft.; that at Coria 70 ft. 8 ins.; that at Toulouse 63 ft., while the churches of Perpignan and Zamora are 60 ft. The width between the centres of the columns of the nave at Palma cathedral is 71 ft.; Manresa collegiate church and Valladolid cathedral (classic) 60 ft.; while Milan cathedral, one of the largest out of Spain, is but 63 ft.

587. Some pure examples of romanesque art date after 1175, such as a church at Benevento and the cathedral at Lugo; but the period of transition to pointed art must be placed much earlier. Thus the cathedral and St. Vicente at Avila, occupying in erection

nearly the whole of the 12th century; the old cathedral, cloister, and chapter-house at Salamanca about 1100–1175; the cathedral at Zamora 1125–75; that at Tudela ten years later; and the cistercian abbey at Veruela 1146–51, lead to such works as the cathedral (except the choir, 1103–23) at Siguenza; the cistercian nunnery of Sta. Maria el Real de las Huelgas, near Burgos, 1180–7; and the eastern portion of the cathedral at Lugo. The cathedral at Tarragona has a positively romanesque apse (perhaps 1130–50), while the rest of the building is early pointed, and may date 1175–1250. The west front (*fig.* 263) is partly middle pointed work. The central portion, dating in style late in the 14th century, although commenced about 1278, stands between the original ends of the aisles, apparently executed as above mentioned. The incomplete false gable might countenance the idea that a foreigner, possibly a German, had been employed; but in 1375 Bernardo de Vallfagona was the architect directing native sculptors.

Fig 263.   CATHEDRAL, TARRAGONA.

588. The cathedrals, commenced, perhaps, 1220 at Burgos, 1227 at Toledo, and 1235 at Leon, are in the advanced pointed style of the 13th century, while the cathedral and cloisters at Lerida, 1203–78, might belong, like the earliest parts of the cathedral at Valencia, 1262, to the previous period. It will not perhaps be ever possible to find documents that will contradict the assertion that the present system of placing the officiating choir in fixed stalls in the nave of the cathedrals was introduced at a late date; but those who hold that it was a very early system may appeal to the plans of the cathedrals, at Tudela, 1135; Toledo, 1227; and Barcelona, 1298. The plans of those at Lerida and Tarragona are very similar to that at Tudela (*fig.* 264, part of the plan given in Mr. Street's *Gothic Arch. in Spain*), which affords a good example of a building arranged accord-

ing to Spanish peculiarities: if the *capilla mayor* or chancel ever contained the choir, the transept must have been blocked up.

589. Amongst the works erected during the 13th century, there are so many which exhibit romanesque work that this period might be said to be merely transitional, as illustrated in the church of S. Pedro at Olite; the large church of the cistercian monastery of Sta. Maria de Val de Dios, 1218, near Villaviciosa; and the bridge 1230, repaired 1449 at Orense in two sections, that nearest the city having three arches, each 36 ft. 8 ins. span; the other, 1213 ft. 6 ins. long, and 16 ft. 6 ins. wide, having seven arches, one of them being 82 ft. 8 ins. wide, and another 143 ft. 6 ins. span, and 124 ft. 6 ins. high. Other works to be noticed are the cathedral, commenced 1199, but continued very slowly until 1258, at Leon; it is dated 1230–40 by Mr. Street, in his work above mentioned, who notices that its construction, in a first-pointed style, was continued until 1303, that it failed, and that the outside or jamb-lights of the clearstory and triforium were filled with masonry, and that the south transept was destroyed for reconstruction about 1860: the fine cathedral, 1248–84, at Badajoz; and

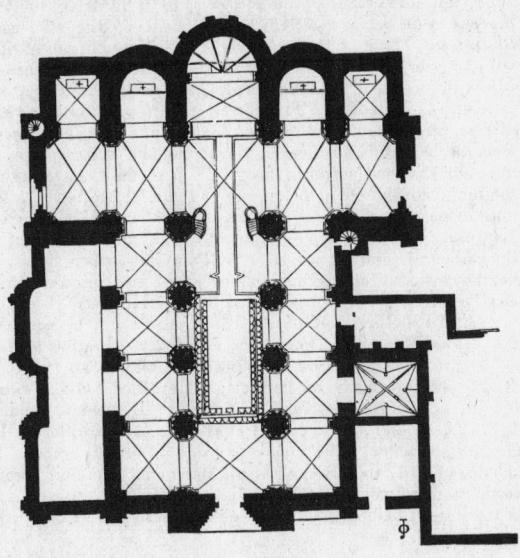

Fig. 261.   PLAN OF CATHEDRAL, TUDELA.

the parish church (not a cathedral) at Figueras near Gerona.

590. The succeeding great division of Gothic art is much more distinctly marked and more uniform throughout Spain, whilst at the same time it is even less national and peculiar. There are very considerable remains of 14th century works, though, perhaps, no one grand and entire example. They are all extremely similar in style, and more allied in feeling and detail to German middle-pointed than to French. Two features deserve record—first, the reproduction of the octagonal steeple, which was a most favourite type of the romanesque builders; and secondly, the introduction of that grand innovation upon old precedents, the great unbroken naves groined in stone and lighted from windows high up in the walls.

591. As an example of the difficulty of classifying the buildings, it may be observed that while the date of 1400 is usually given to the church at Huesca, ascribed to Juan de Olotzaga, it is probable that his name might be attached only to the great portal that is romanesque, and cannot well be dated later than 1290—1300. It is pretty clear that it is almost all a work of the 14th century. The unusually good example of middle-pointed work afforded by the cloisters to the cathedral at Burgos should date 1280–1350 according to Mr. Street, rather than 1379–90, which is the period at which they are said to have been executed. The same author states that the round arches on clustered shafts of the porch or cloister on the south side of the church of S. Vicente at Avila might be supposed to be not later than the 13th century, were it not that a careful comparison of the detail with other known detail proves pretty clearly that they cannot be earlier than about the middle of the 14th century.

592. To the first half of the 14th century are due the west front of the cathedral at Tarragona; the cloisters of the abbey at Veruela; the east end, 1312–46 (decidedly late middle-pointed details) of the cathedral at Gerona; the hieronymite monastery of San Bartolomé, 1330, at Lupiana by Diego Martinez, now private property; and the church of San Justo and San Pastor, 1345, at Barcelona, which is an unbroken chamber 138 ft. by 82 ft. 9 in., and 69 ft. high. The widening, 1298–1329, of the cathedral, built 1058, at Barcelona, seems to have been begun in a first-pointed style, and to have been continued by Jayme Fabre, 1318–88, in a second-pointed style; the vaulting was finished 1448.

593. Among the works dating in the middle of the 14th century, earlier or later, is the church of Sta. Maria de los Reyes, commonly called Sta. Maria del Pino, at Barcelona, which some date 1329–1413, but others 1380–1413. This latter date is possibly that of its tower by Guillermo Abiell; the church Mr. Street considers must have been consecrated

in 1353, not 1453 as stated by Parcerisa. We may also notice at Barcelona the church of Sta. Maria del Mar, begun 1328, and finished 1383 according to Parcerisa, but 1483 according to another authority; the two-storied cloister of the collegiate church of Sta. Anna; and the crypt or *panteon* of Sta. Eulalia, 1339, in the cathedral.

594. During the latter half of the 14th century, mention is made of the chapter house, 1358, and north transept and *cimborio*, 1350–1400, to the cathedral, and the gate called the *puerta* de Serranos, 1349–81, at Valencia; the *casa consistorial*, 1369–78, with a new south front, 1832, at Barcelona; the collegiate church of Sta. Maria de la Seo, 1328–1416, with another church apparently of the same date, but rather later detail, dedicated to Sta. Maria del Carmen, and 47 ft. wide, at Manresa; and the tower, called El Micalete, of the cathedral at Valencia. The tower is here mentioned as having been designed, 1381, and carried up to some height, by Juan Franc and N. Amoros before 1414, when Pedro Balaguer was sent to Lerida, Narbonne, and other places to find the most suitable termination that had yet been designed; it seems to have been completed 1428, and perhaps should be considered as belonging to the next century; as well as the celebrated hieronymite monastery, dated 1389–1413, now a barrack and parish church at Guadalupe near Logrosan, by Juan Alonso; the cathedral, 1353–1462, but altered 1521, at Murcia; and the cathedral, commenced 1397 at Pamplona, where geometrical traceries occur between flamboyant ones, all having somewhat of late middle-pointed character, though the date and the detail class them with the third-pointed style.

595. To the first half of the 15th century may be ascribed the cloisters, 1390–1448, of the cathedral at Barcelona; the university, or rather *les escuelas*, 1415–33, at Salamanca, by Alonzo Rodrigo; the dominican church of San Pablo, 1415–35, at Burgos, by Juan Rodriguez, now a cavalry barrack; the arcaded *patio* or court-yard, 1436, three stories in height, of the *casa de la Diputacion* at Barcelona, modernised 1597–1620; the nave, 1417–58, or later, of the cathedral at Gerona by Guillermo Boffiy (with details of late 14th century character); the *hala dels draps*, 1444, afterwards *Palacio de la Reina* and the residence of the captains-general at Barcelona (the four fronts modernised, 1844); and the towers and spires, 1442–56, by Juan de Colonia, to the cathedral at Burgos. To the century itself belong great parts of the cathedral at Seville, (*fig.* 265.), commenced 1401,

Fig. 265.   CATHEDRAL, SEVILLE.

and attributed either to Alfonso Martinez, architect to the chapter in 1386, or to Pedro Garcia, who held that post 1421. In 1462, Juan Norman was directing the works; but in 1472, they had progressed so slowly that he was superannuated, and his place was supplied by three other artists. Their disputes were referred to an umpire, Jimon, who became sole architect till 1502. The *cimborio* was completed 1507, and fell 1511, but was replaced by the present termination, 1519. The works by Diego de Riaño, 1522, will be mentioned at the end of this notice. The *capilla real* was completed about 1560, and the chapter-house about 1580.

596. To the latter half of the 15th century are due the erection of the *casa de moneda*, 1455, at Segovia; the Castillo de la Mota, 1440–79, at Medina del Campo, by Fernando de Carreño; the church, 1442–88, attributed to Juan and Simon de Colonia, to the dominican monastery of San Pablo at Valladolid; the cathedral, begun 1442, at Plasencia, whose *capilla mayor*, 1498, was designed by Juan de Alava; the Carthusian nunnery, 1454–88, at Miraflores, near Burgos, said to have been designed by Juan de Colonia; the cloisters,

1472, of the monastery at Lupiana ; the hieronymite monastery of Sta. Maria del Parral at Segovia, commenced about 1459 by Juan Gallego, and finished 1475, but the tribune of the *coro* pulled down because too low, and rebuilt 1494 by Juan de Ruesga ; the franciscan monastery of San Juan de los Reyes, finished 1476, and next in architectural importance to the cathedral at Toledo ; the greater part of the cathedral commenced 1471 at Astorga, in the very latest kind of Gothic, with much of the detail, especially on the exterior, renaissance in character ; parts of the cathedral at Burgos, about 1487, such as the range of chapels at the eastern end of the cloisters and of the church, inclusive of the tomb of the constable Pedro Fernandez de Velasco, which is quite flamboyant, and probably executed by Simon de Colonia ; and the *casa del Ayuntamiento*, 1496, at Palencia ; with that, 1499, at Valladolid.

597. Transitional work is observable in the palace, 1461, of Diego Hurtado de Mendoza, duque del Infantado, at Guadalajara ; the Doric columns on the ground floor of the two-storied *patio* seem to have been inserted 1570 ; another transitional building is the dominican college of San Gregorio, 1488–96, at Valladolid, by Macias Carpintero, which has been furnished with sashed windows to render it suitable for the residence of the governor of the province. The octagonal *cimborio*, 1505-20, of the cathedral at Zaragoza has detail that is very renaissance in character ; the cathedral, commenced 1513 at Salamanca by the celebrated architect Juan Gil de Hontañon, is a splendid example of florid Gothic with a leaning to renaissance work ; the first service was performed 1560 : and the same tendency is seen in the *colegio mayor* de Santiago el Zebedeo or del Arzobispo, 1521, at Salamanca, and its chapel by Pedro de Ibarra, which are Gothic, with details verging in character upon its cloister by Ibarra, which is entirely renaissance.

598. For works of the 16th century, it will only be necessary to notice the bridge called the *puente* del Obispo, and the church of San Andres now the Colegiata, 1500, at Baeza ; the *iglesia magistral* de San Justo y San Pastor, 1497–1509, at Alcala de Henares, by Pedro Gumiel ; the *torro nueva* or belfry in the *plaza* de San Felipe, 1504, at Zaragoza, designed 275 ft. high (made 295 in 1749) by Gabriel Gombao and Juan Sariñena, with the Jew Ince de Gali, and the Moors Ezmel Ballabar and Momferriz, erected by Gombao, who, intentionally, after the first 9 ft. from the ground, gave it so much inclination for 100 ft. as to make it incline 8 ft. 9 ins. to the south, the rest being upright ; the chapel and two of the four cloisters, 1504, to the hospital-general at Santiago, by Henrique de Egas ; the cloister finished, 1507, of the cathedral at Siguenza ; the cloisters, 1509, of the cathedral at Badajoz ; the church of San Benito, 1499-1524, at Valladolid, by Juan de Arandia ; the vaulting, completed 1515, to the cathedral at Huesca ; the cathedral commenced at Segovia, 1522, by Juan Gil de Hontañon (who died 1531), and continued, partly under his son Rodrigo, till 1593, which, as may be imagined, is consequently the last really Gothic work in the country ; the church (of the latest Gothic), begun 1524, to the dominican monastery of San Esteban at Salamanca, by Juan de Alava, who succeeded Juan Gil at Salamanca, 1531-37 ; the removal, 1524, of the cloisters of the old cathedral to the site of the new one at Segovia, by Juan de Campero ; the viaduct, 322 ft. long, and 138 ft. high, with five arches, 1523-38, to the dominican monastery and church of San Pablo, of the same date, at Cuenca, by Francisco de Luna ; and the Gothic parish church, 1515–55, at Tudela de Duero.

599. The next change to be indicated would be the expiration of the renaissance style during the period in which some of the preceding examples were executed. But the well authenticated date, 1576, of the church of Sta. Maria Madalena at Valladolid, by Rodrigo Gil de Hontañon, who became maestro mayor, 1538, of the cathedral at Salamanca, and, 1560, of that at Segovia, and died 1577, requires the remark that it does not look so late ; and thus becomes a most useful warning to the student, who may gather another from the remarkable practice, 1530, of Diego de Rianno, architect to the cathedral at Seville, who in that year designed and executed the Gothic *sacristia de los calices*, the plateresque or renaissance *sacristia mayor*, and the modern Italian chapter house.

Portugal.

600. For the reasons given in describing the pointed architecture of Spain, its history in Portugal will require only one introductory sentence. To the rage for rebuilding which was prevalent in that country, and the earthquake of 1755, must be added the destruction caused by the generals of Napoleon I., as reasons why comparatively few are left of those Gothic buildings which arose in the north of Portugal after Lisbon was taken, 1147, from the Moors, and in the south after the conquest, 1223-66, of Algarve. Passing over the remains of pointed arches, which indicate that the country was generally possessed by the Moors, 713-1095, and transitional structures such as the church at San Pedro de Rates, 1095-1112, with its hipped central tower, the cistercian monastery with many additions, begun 1122 and consecrated 1169, at Tarouca, the architect will find a few buildings belonging to the 13th century or rather earlier, such as the bridge at Barcello ; the cloisters and original parts of the modernised cathedral at Oporto ; the church of San Francisco, and part of that of Sta. Maria de Marvilla at Santarem ; and the earliest cloister of the

Templars, with the church of Nossa Senhora dos Olivaes at Thomar; the latter has a detached romanesque tower and windows, filled with pierced slabs of stone.

601. Works which positively belong to the 13th century are the church of San Pedro at Celorico, about 1230; the parallel triapsal church of San Francisco, 1258–80, at Oporto, with its choir-gallery occupying the two western bays of the nave; the walls and towers with castle and church at Freixo d'Espada a Cinta, 1279–1325; the castle at Beja, 1279–1328, which has three (two being vaulted) octagonal stories in a square tower, 120 ft. in height; and the remarkable choir of the church at Thomar, with its altar under an octagonal canopy, and an aisle of sixteen sides, erected before 1279. But above all these is the well known church of the monastery at Alcobaça, which, after its neighbour at Batalha, is usually regarded as the most interesting building in Portugal.

602. The original church built at Alcobaça, in memory of the capture of Santarem, was erected 1147–51, and rebuilt 1578–80; but the celebrated church of the cistercian monastery dates 1148–1222, and is said to resemble so much the church of the abbey at Pontigny as to be manifestly the work of a French architect. In this church, which is 360 ft. long, and at least 64 ft. high, there is neither triforium nor clearstory; the pier-arches are remarkable, therefore, for their height, as also are the aisles, which are as lofty as the nave. The transepts are also aisled; and the presbytery or apse, the Portuguese *charola*, is semicircular, with nine chapels, but was modernised about 1770 by W. Elsden, an Englishman. To the east of this is the sacristy, 1495–1521, which is about 80 ft. long and 38 ft. wide. The western front with two towers was altered in the 16th century; but the original doorway of seven orders remains. The bonfires placed by the French in 1810, round the piers of the church, caused the bases to be reduced to lime for a depth of 6 or 8 ins. The manner in which the restoration of this structure was directed, since 1850, has been commended. In a chapel attached to the south side of the western transept are the tombs of Affonso II. (ob. 1223), and Affonso III. (ob. 1279), with their queens; but those of Pedro I. (ob. 1367) and Ignez de Castro, with straight sided arches, are among the finest specimens of that period. The monastery, almost destroyed 1810, and now principally used as a barrack, was 620 ft. in width, by 750 ft. in depth, and contained five cloisters; the guest-house was at the north-west end; there were seven dormitories. The kitchen was 100 ft. long, by 22 ft. wide, and 63 ft. in height to the vaulting; the fireplace, which stood in the centre, was 28 ft. long and 11 ft. wide, with a pyramidal chimney supported by eight cast-iron columns.

603. The list of works executed during the 14th century is even shorter. It includes, besides the cloisters of the dominican monastery at Guimaraens, the façade of the modern cathedral at Lamego, the magnificent ruins of the castle at Ourem, and (for they may be added here) the triangular castle at Obidos, 1279–1325, the castle at Almeida, 1279–1521, the cistercian nunnery at Odivellas, 1305, the castles at Arrayolos and Estremos, 1306–8, the remarkable fortified tower and church of the formerly double benedictine monastery at Leça do Balio, 1336; the restorations to the cathedral at Lisbon, including the *capella mor* or choir, rebuilt 1344–57, and the western front 1367–83; the church of San Francisco (styled the most beautiful in Portugal) at Abrantes; and the church of Nossa Senhora da Oliveira at Guimaraens, commenced 1387 by João Oare, having a detached tower with a low spire.

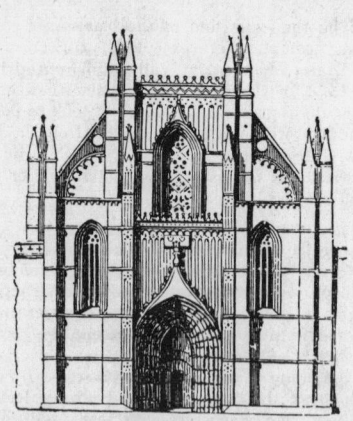 

Fig 266.   CHURCH AT BATALHA; AND   Fig. 267. SOUTH FRONT OF THE MAUSOLEUM OF KING JOHN.

604. To these may be added the work that is usually taken as a type of Portuguese pointed architecture, the dominican monastery at Batalha, founded in memory of the battle of Aljubarrota, 1383. It was commenced 1388, and continued till 1515. The original church (*fig.* 266.), finished before 1416 by D. Hacket, or Ouguet, must be ascribed to

the talents of A. Domingues, who died before 1402. It is 266 ft. long, and 90 ft. high, with no triforium ; the pier arches are 65 ft. high, and the aisles rise to the same height ; the plan may be called cruciform parallel pentapsal. The material is *not* white marble as generally reported, but the local calcareous sandstone, which externally has obtained from the weather a picturesque yellow tinge, but when broken displays its original grey colour. The manner in which the restoration since 1840 was directed has been praised.

605. The *capella do fundador* (*fig.* 267.), or of King John (L on the plan, *fig.* 268.), attributed to D. Hacket, or Ouguet, is 66 ft. square, with a central richly vaulted lantern 40 ft. in diameter, resting on eight arches ; its spire was destroyed in 1745. The tomb of the founder and of his wife, Philippa of Lancaster, which occupies the centre, is less rich than the four canopied recessed tombs of their younger children, 1442–60, on the south side. The small cloister (since part of a barrack) and the elegant chapter-house are ascribed to 1438–81, and may have been designed by M. Vasquez, who died before 1448,

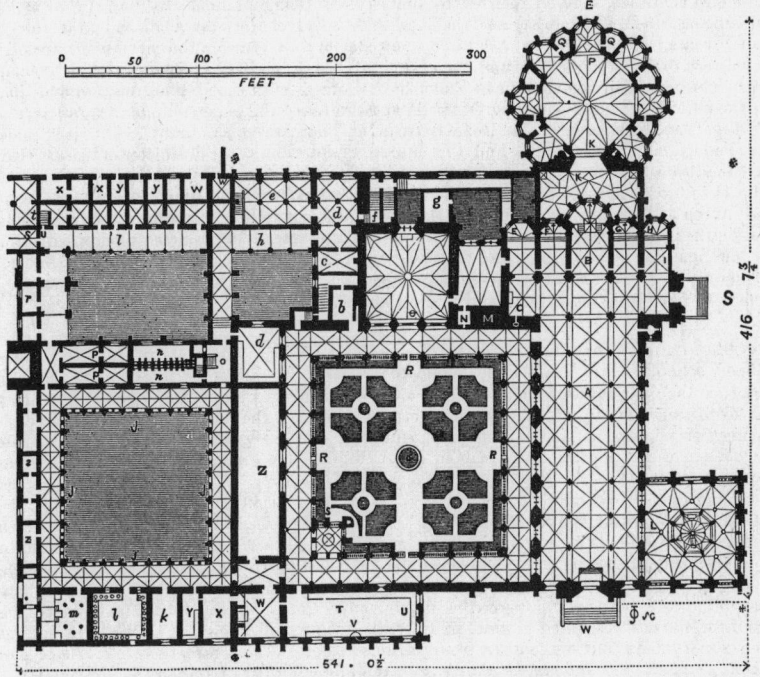

PLAN OF THE DOMINICAN MONASTERY, BATALHA.

or to F. d'Evora, who died after 1473. The chapter-house (o) opens to the great cloister (R) that is considered to have no rival in Europe for richness and variety, or extravagance of the foliage, tracery, and mullions ; these are even exceeded by the three-staged enclosure (s) for the fountain. The cloister is 180 ft. square, and dates 1495–1521 ; it must be ascribed to the elder M. Fernandez, who died 1515, leaving unfinished the *capella* de Jazigo (P), which would have paralleled perhaps internally, the chapel of Henry VII. at Westminster, in purpose, locality, position, completeness of style, and luxuriance of decoration. The chapel is an octagon, with seven oratories, having six-sided closets (Q Q) between them and the entrance (K) to the vestibule : its completion might perhaps have been assured if the king had not found his architect, the younger M. Fernandez, occupied in erecting the clearstory over the entrance doorway (K) with balustrade and semicircular arches. The works were stopped till another flamboyant architect could be found ; they have not yet been resumed. A small spire, at the west corner of the north transept (c) which was destroyed by lightning about 1830, has been rebuilt.

606. "Such is the history and arrangement of this essentially Gothic building, but altogether unlike any particular stage of the northern Gothic, in fact it commingles the features of all its varieties. The pillars are clustered, of the very best early Gothic section, with floriated capitals, but with square bases and abaci. It is a confusion of Gothic forms of all ages and countries ; and yet, if we except the square abaci, every feature is pure, and most of them good, in their respective styles ; and after all there is no such real inconsistency between any two styles of Gothic as to render their mixture offensive to any but a

technical eye. To deny the church of Batalha to be beautiful, because it confuses forms which in France or England belong to different centuries, would be the merest pedantry ; no one but the driest archæologian would quarrel with a building for a skilful application of some incongruous feature, though it might historically belong to some other age or country. At the same time, this very confusion shows a lack of original genius, and proves Batalha to be, what antiquarians are fond of calling modern churches, *imitation Gothic*. It is not the spontaneous effort of native skill, but the mere result of eclecticism." These remarks, taken verbatim from Mr. Freeman, have an important bearing on those sections of this work which are devoted to Italian and Sicilian pointed architecture.

607. If the tower of Don Duarte at Viseu, and the Villa do Infante at Sagres can be placed early in the 15th century, they hardly redeem that age from the charge of exhibiting no structure of importance except Batalha. Even the flamboyant church, 150 ft. long with embattled tower, at Caminha, 1448–1516, and the similar clothing of the romanesque cathedral at Braza, may be referred to that style of King Manoel, 1495–1521 : to which must be ascribed the sacristy at Alcobaça ; the royal chateau at Almeirim ; the fort of San Vicente, and the monastic buildings at Belem ; the restoration of the hieronymite monastery of La Pena at Cintra ; the church of San Francisco at Evora ; the rich façade of the church called the Conceiçao Velha, by J. Potassi, with the restorations and additions to the church of Santa Maria de Marvilla at Santarem ; the octagonal stone spire (rare in Portugal) to the church of San João Battista at Thomar ; the church, 1506, with renaissance additions at Alcantara ; and the church, chapter-house, and cloister of Santa Cruz (ascribed to a French architect), with part of the university and the bridge at Coimbra. The chapel of Santa Caterina with the palace, 1521–57, and the additions, 1495–1578, to the church at Coimbra, exhibiting the richest flamboyant style merging into the renaissance work ; the magnificent dominican monastery at Amarante, 1540, and the modest cathedral at Miranda do Douro, 1545, and Montalegre, 1554, might close the list of structures belonging to the imitation, or rather the adaptation of Gothic architecture, which does not appear to have been more successful in Portugal than in the rest of Southern Europe.

Italy.

608. An attempt has been made to divide the pointed architecture of Italy into well-defined schools : the Venetian is supposed to carry its character in its name, and to influence the district between St. Mark's and Brescia ; the Lombard is styled a pursuit of the exuberant variety of French and German Gothic ; the Tuscan is characterised as having two phases, the earlier simple, and the later extremely beautiful ; and the Genoese is called a direct imitation of Arabian art. Besides this unsatisfactory view, each great monastic order is said to have professed a particular variety, of course differently treated according to each district. To these the singular style peculiar to the Riviera (*e.g.*, the cathedral at Vintimiglia) has to be added. We should prefer to this another system which sees only two schools, one being native simplicity, the other extreme decoration brought from Germany, if there appeared any grounds for believing in this division of a style which, in its early period, is, like the early German, not very definite, and which had no phase resembling the perpendicular or the flamboyant. As a philosophical inquiry into the details of the edifices called Gothic, in Italy, the labours of Professor Willis have not yet been superseded ; but we gather, from various pages of Mr. Street's work, *Brick and Marble Architecture in Italy in the Middle Ages*, the following list of Italian Gothic details :—

609. This consists of the trefoiled arcade used as an ornament for strings, for flat and raking corbel tables, and under sills ; the great projection of the sills ; the marble shafts with square capitals, instead of moulded mullions ; the rows of tufts of drooping foliage (somewhat resembling French and German work) in the capitals ; the classical character of the carving ; the traceried transoms ; the combination of geometrical tracery as well as of trefoiled ogee arches with the semicircular arch ; the use of the keystone, frequently slightly decorated, to pointed arches ; the square-headed panel by which the arches are surrounded ; the use of iron ties instead of the buttress ; the rarity of the dripstone in brickwork ; the peculiar crockets and finials of canopies ; the masses of wall scarcely, if at all, broken ; the buttresses reduced to pilasters ; the single gable to nave and aisles of the churches ; the deep cornices without parapets ; the low relief of tracery and carving ; the squareness, with flatness, of mouldings ; the employment of porches entirely unknown across the Alps ; the use of the glass in wooden frames behind the stone work ; the simplicity of groining ; and the great width of pier arches.

610. It may be said that in Venice, as generally throughout the north of Italy, the pointed arch was first used in construction, and some time later, and very generally, in a modified form for decoration also, yet in that city it is rarely used, constructionally, except in churches ; and even when employed the ogee arch was, from a very early date, preferred wherever the pure pointed arch was not indispensable. This fact is seen in *fig.* 269, which shows the palace called the Ca Contarini Fasan, situated on the grand canal opposite the church of Sta. Maria della Salute ; it is considered to give the only specimen in Venice of a traceried balcony.

611. If there be no discrepancy between their dates and their details, the *broletto* at Como, 1215, and the monastic buildings of San Andrea, with the hospital at Vercelli, founded 1219–24, by Cardinal Guala Jacopo Bicchieri, must be considered to commence the Gothic buildings in Italy.   At Como, however, round arches are seen over pointed ones.   At Vercelli, the exterior of the church is romanesque brickwork with stone dressings, while the interior is decidedly a specimen of early pointed art.   Some writers assume that the design was furnished by the first abbot, Tommaso Gallo, and suppose that he was a Frenchman (*gallus*), taken to Vercelli by the Cardinal, who, having been legate in England, 1216–18, and leaving that country with 12,000 marks, is supposed to have obtained the design there before he negotiated at the German court in the course of his return to Italy ; others say that he sent a model from England.

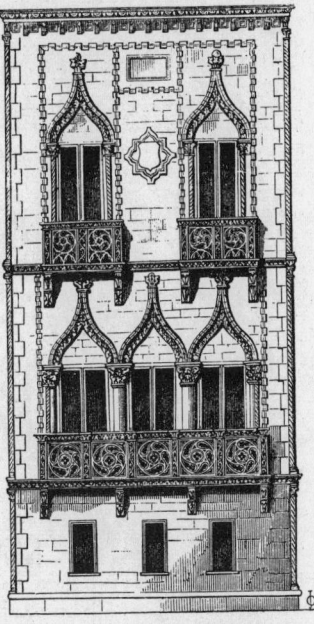

612. The church of San Francesco at Assisi was erected 1228–30, by a German architect named Jacobus ; the aisles being added soon afterwards by F. di Campello.   This structure has attained the character of being the most perfect specimen of Gothic art in Italy, and therefore far superior to Sta. Chiara, erected 1253 by Campello in the same city.   It is one of the most singular churches in Europe, as, in possessing a crypt discovered in 1818, and enlarged, 1820 by Brizi, it forms a sort of three-storied church. The middle church was built 1228–32 ; the upper church, a magnificent work, built 1232–53, is now only used on a few capitular and ferial occasions. The low-pitched roof was placed 1447–70, and the massive buttresses were added 1480 by Pintelli, to prevent the threatened fall of this valuable example of early art.

Fig 269.   HOUSE AT VENICE.

613. Much uncertainty exists in the early dates given to the *broletto* at Monza, 1152–92 ; the *broletto* at Brescia, the end of the 12th century ; the church to San Francesco, 1225, at Coni (or Cuneo) ; the fair example of pointed art, San Francesco at Terni, begun 1218, but not completed until 1265 ; and the yellow brick church of San Antonio at Padua, 1231, with its attempts at domes by N. Pisano.   But in the middle of the 13th century were commenced, by himself or by his school, the brick churches of Santi Giovanni e Paolo, of the Madonna del Orto, and of Sta. Maria Gloriosa de' Frari (the finest of its class) at Venice.   The churches of Sta. Caterina, finished 1272, by G. Agnelli ; and of San Francesco at Pisa ; the imposing specimen of Italian Gothic furnished by the cathedral at Arezzo, contained in the design, 1256, of Jacopo or Lapo, 1275–90, by Margaritone (not Marchione) ; the western front of the church of San Salvatore at Pistoia, 1270 ; the churches of San Domenico, 1250–94, by Maglione, and of San Francesco (apparently called by Professor Willis the Servi), 1286–94, at Arezzo ; the transepts, 1288–1342, by B. Bragerio and G. de Camperio to the cathedral at Cremona, with the upper part, 1284, of its campanile ; the foro de' Mercanti, 1294, at Bologna ; the churches of San Domenico, 1284–1380, and of San Francesco, 1294, at Pistoia ; the church of San Francesco, 1295, and the façade, 1284–90, as well as portions of the cathedral at Siena (which is remarkable for having the baptistery under the choir), date between 1270 and 1300.

614. The style of domestic architecture of the 13th century is seen in many houses at Bracciano, at Corneto, at Frascati, at Galera, and at Lucca ; also the building called La Quarquonia at Pistoia, with two houses of similar date, nearly opposite ; and in the third cloister of

Fig. 270.   HOUSE AT VITERBO.

the monastery of Sta. Scolastica at Subiaco.   The house in *fig.* 270, known at Viterbo as the "palazzetto," belongs to the 12th century, and is here given for comparison with later examples.   The sketch of a house belonging to the 13th, or perhaps even to the 12th

century, at Pisa (*fig.* 271), exhibits the local peculiarity of three stories, composed really, or in appearance, by three piers and two arches. This is common. A fourth story sometimes shows its windows under the arches; but generally is an independent addition

Fig. 271.   HOUSE AT PISA.

Fig. 272.   ELEVATION OF THE PALAZZO BUONSIGNORI, SIENA.

to the design. At the level of each floor are put-log holes for the wooden cantilevers of the balconies, perhaps more properly the *tettoje* or pent-house roofs, which will be noticed in the examples from San Gimignano. The palazzo Buonsignori at the end of the via di San Pietro at Siena belongs to the brickwork of the 13th century; the façade is about 56 ft. long, and consists, on each upper floor, of seven bays, four of which are given in *fig.* 272. A fountain in the piazza Carlano at Viterbo might serve as a type of several others designed in this century.

615. To the end of the 13th and early part of the 14th centuries belongs the cathedral at Orvieto, one of the most interesting examples of Italian Gothic, and an instance of the use, internally as well as externally, of alternate courses of colour, which in this case is produced by black basaltic lava and yellowish-grey limestone. Although the first stone was laid 1290 for the execution of a design by L. Maitani, who had just completed the front of the duomo at Siena and built this cathedral (*fig.* 273.) before his death, 1330, the works were in hand till the end of the 16th century. A list of thirty-three architects has been preserved. The building is 278 ft. long by 103 ft. wide, and 115 ft. high to the plain ceiling, made 1828, which rests on piers 62 ft. high. These piers are fronted by statues of the apostles, 9 ft. 6 in. high, on pedestals that are 5 ft. 6 in. high above the

Fig. 273.   ELEVATION OF THE CATHEDRAL, ORVIETO.

O. JEWITT SC

floor of the nave, which is made of Apennine red marble that has inlaid fleurs-de-lis

before the choir.　The windows have coloured glass in the upper parts, but diaphanous alabaster below it.

616. To the same period belong the church of Sta. Maria sopra Minerva, at Rome, the only pointed edifice which we can name in that metropolis; and the principal examples of pointed art in Florence, such as the church of Sta. Maria Novella, 1278–1357; the church of Sta. Croce, 1294, used 1320, but not consecrated till 1442; the cathedral, 1294, consecrated 1436, with the campanile, designed 1332, by Giotto; the church of San Ercolano, by Bevignate, 1297–1335, at Perugia, with that of Sta. Giuliana, 1292, outside that city; the octagonal baptistery called San Giovanni Rotondo, 1337, and portions of the church of San Francesco, 1294, at Pistoia; and the (then altered) brick and stone church of San Fermo Maggiore, at Verona.　In the first half of the 14th century, the Italian artists exhibited their ideas of Gothic work in the chapel of Sta. Maria dell'Arena, 1303, at Padua; the alterations, 1308–20, of the interior of the cathedral at Lucca; the cathedral, 1312, at Prato, which has the effect of a northern late pointed structure; the fine cathedral, 1325–48, and the church of San Secondo, at Asti; and the church of San Martino, 1332, at Pisa, which is a fair specimen of common late Italian Gothic.

617. The large number of tombs and monuments of this and the next period, with pointed arches, renders difficult any choice of single examples among them; those of the Scaligeri, at Verona, especially that of Mastino II., 1351, contain a history in themselves.

618. To the latter half of the 14th century may be attributed the marble front, in grey and yellow courses, by Matteo da Campione, (a very fine example) before 1396 to the brick cathedral with particularly good detail, more than usually Gothic, built 1290–1390, at Monza; the palazzo della comunita, 1294–1385; and the palazzo pretorio, 1357–77, at Pistoia, which have been highly praised as fine specimens of very perfect Italian Gothic; the cathedral, 1315–1415, at Sarzana; and 1340 to 1369–1423, the upper portion or *sala del consiglio* of the ducal palace at Venice, although another authority considers that the work of this period was the loggia towards the canal and twelve columns on the piazzetta.

619. The general design of the existing cathedral at Milan is also of this period, although extreme doubt exists as to the date of the commencement of the work.　But the statements are clear that the capitals of the great piers were being prepared, 1394–5, and that the piers themselves were being erected 1401.　The records of the wardens of the church are deficient until 1387; in that year an official paper speaks of the building which "multis retro temporibus initiata est et quæ nunc fabricatur."　Chronicles and an inscription concur in fixing March 15, 1386, as the date of commencement; but Simone da Orsenigo, probably an eye-witness of the facts to which he is evidence, stated that the work was begun May 23, 1385, but was destroyed, and that the existing structure was commenced May 7, 1387. He was employed as one of the architects at least as early as December 6, in that year.　So that the date, 1336–87, usually given, as in the previous editions of this book, is possibly the period of attempts to begin the work, and explains the phrase "multis temporibus."　The cathedral has been much praised as an example of northern art modifying itself to suit the southern climate under the hands of a German or, at all events, of a foreigner rather than of a native; but facts seem to destroy this imputed credit.　The official list of the "in-gegneri," as the chief artists who laboured at the duomo were called, shows the earliest employment of foreigners in the case of Nicolas Bonaventure, of Paris, from July 6, 1388, till his dismissal, July 31, 1391; and the same evidence seems to divide the merit of the earliest direction of the works between Marco and Jacopo, both of Campione, a village between the lakes of Lugano and Como.　The first name in the records of 1387 is that of Marco, supposed to be the Marco da Frisone who was buried July 8, 1390, with great honours; Jacopo occurs March 20, 1388, having apparently been engaged from 1378 as one of the architects to the church of the Certosa, near Pavia; he died 1398.

620. The official notes of the disputes that were constantly arising between the contemporaneous "ingegneri-generali" and their subordinates, and the foreign artists, even record the fact that the Italian combatants disagreed on the great question of proportioning the building by the foreign system of squares, or by the native theory of triangles.　If there be any merit in a work that was so clearly the offspring of many minds, much of it must be due to the wardens, who seem to have ordered the execution of little that was not recommended by the majority of their artists, or, in case of an equal division, by an umpire of reputation from some other city.　From 1430, the names of Filippo Brunellesco and six or seven other artists precede the notice, 1483, of Johann von Grätz, who appears to have been invited for the purpose of constructing the central *tiburio* or lantern.　As usual, the foreigner's work was condemned; and April 13, 1490, Giovanni Antonio Omodeo (Heinrich von Gmünden, employed so early as from Dec. 11, 1391, to May 31, 1392, was confused with Omodeo by M. Millin, whence the repute of Heinrich as "Zamodia"), began his long rule over the other artists, which lasted until August 27, 1522, by executing the present work.　It is needless to give the names of his colleagues and successors until the appointment of Carlo Amati, 1806, under whom the completion of the works, including the three pointed windows of the front, was resumed, and of his successor P. Pestagalli, 1813.

621. The cathedral (*fig.* 274,) is constructed of white marble. The plan is a Latin cross, the transepts extending but little beyond the walls of the church. From west to east

Fig. 274.   CATHEDRAL AT MILAN.

its length is 490 ft. and its extreme breadth 295 ft. The length of the five-aisled nave is 279 ft. and its width 197 ft. The transepts are three-aisled. The eastern end of the church is terminated by three sides of a nonagon. The architecture of the doors and windows of the western front is of the Italian or Roman style, and was executed about 1658, for the first three bays of the nave were an addition in front of the original façade, and were not vaulted until 1651–69. About 1790 the wardens determined to make the front Gothic, keeping the doors and windows by Ricchini, from designs by Pellegrini, on account of the richness of their workmanship; its apex is 170 ft. from the pavement. The central buttresses are 195 ft high. The central tower, 1762–72, by F. Croce, rises to the height of 400 ft., being in general form similar to those which appear in the western façade. All the turrets, buttresses, and pinnacles are surmounted with statues. The roof is covered entirely with blocks of marble fitted together with great exactness.

622. The only town in Italy which has preserved so many as twelve of the mediæval domestic towers of great height, is San Gimignano; it possesses, also, several houses that were erected in the 13th and 14th centuries. The casa Buonaccorsi, with a single opening on the ground-floor, is a corner house and is attributed to the earlier period; the casa Boni is next to it, and belongs to the later time; they are shown in *fig.* 275, which is too small to express the bandings of red and white brickwork, and the stucco border to the extrados of each arch; the penthouse roofs, here restored, were suppressed in the 14th century. The village of Coccaglio, between Bergamo and Brescia, is said to contain some valuable remains of domestic architecture. The Venetian palaces of this and the following century have been so efficiently illustrated of late years, that it becomes unnecessary to describe their appearance.

Fig. 275.   ELEVATION OF HOUSE, SAN GIMIGNANO.

623. Many architects have been engaged upon the marble cathedral at Como; from 1396, when L. de' Spazi was employed, down to the last century. The cupola or dome was completed about 1732, by Juvara. The three doors are in the richest Lombard style, and hence the rest of the facade (*fig.* 276.) has been called early Italian Gothic; but it was designed, 1460, by Lucchino da Milano, and completed between 1487 and 1526 by T. Rodario, of Maroggio, whose design for other parts was altered, perhaps not improved, by C. Solaro. The other sides of the exterior are renaissance work by Rodario, who added the canopies for the statues of the two Plinys, in the west front. The transepts and choir internally are renaissance; but the nave and aisles are Italian Gothic.

624 Amongst the structures produced in the 15th century, may be named the church of Sta. Maria della Grazie, 1399–1406, about six miles from Mantua; the beautiful cathedral, 1450. at Prato; the equally fine church of Sta. Anastasia, at Verona, which has been called the noblest of the distinctively Italian pointed churches in the north of Italy; that of San Bernardino, 1452, also at Verona; and the cathedral, 1467, at Vicenza. The church of San Agostino, at Bergamo; the highly interesting, because perfectly untouched, castle at

Bracciano; the façade and *cortile* of the palace of Cardinal Vitelleschi, now the hôtel palazzaccio, at Corneto; the west front of the church of Sta. Maria in Strada, a most elaborate work in brick and terra-cotta, and the church of the dominicans, at Monza; all belong to the last period of Italian Gothic. The nave of the church of Sta. Maria delle Grazie, at Milan, is pointed, and dated 1465, while the transepts and choir are thirty years later, and are renaissance work. The church of Sta. Maria Maggiore, at Città del Castello, belongs to the 15th, but was finished in the 16th, century. The church of San Agostino, at Ancona, is transitional; like that at Montenegro, 1450; and that of the Madonna di Monte Luce, at Perugia. The last idea of Gothic art absorbed by the new style, is seen in the Colleone chapel, 1475; and in the church of Sta. Maria Maggiore, at Bergamo, where the sacristy, 1430, offers one of the earliest dated examples of the modern style. There is scarcely a street in Città della Pieve without numerous cases of pointed doorways and windows walled up

Fig. 276.　　　　ELEVATION OF CATHEDRAL, COMO.

to suit the return to what are commonly, but incorrectly, called classical notions.

625. Such are the chief structures in the northern half of Italy, of which a critic so highly esteemed as Professor Willis does not hesitate to affirm that, "there is in fact no genuine Gothic building." The same author observes that, "it is curious enough that in the Neapolitan territory, in Naples especially, many specimens or rather fragments, of good Gothic buildings are to be found which were executed under the Angevine dynasty, 1266–1435; with this exception I do not believe that a single unmixed Gothic church is to be found in Italy." Others follow his judgment, and accept, as specimens of imitative Gothic art, edifices which they themselves describe as impure and heterogeneous, and impressed with the stamp of classical, romanesque, byzantine, and saracenic influences. To this praise of the churches may be added that of two or three palazzi at Naples; the campanili at Amalfi, and Velletri; the castles at Andria, Castellamare, and Teano, some houses of the 14th and 15th centuries, at Aquila, Popoli, and Solmone, with the aqueduct at the latter place; and the monastery of Sta. Catherina, at Galatino.

626. The cathedral at Trani must be regarded as falling within the ban under which the structures termed "Gothic," in Sicily, are regarded by the purist in archæology. The pointed byzantine style, which is called Siculo-Norman, lasted until 1282; it was transitional in the sense of receiving greater enrichment of a Greek character, until the end of the 14th century; and although further change began in the 15th century, taste did not take any decided direction until the establishment of renaissance art. Mr. Gally Knight, who investigated the indications presented in the great work published by Messrs. Hittorff and Zanth, says that "various novelties were attempted; sometimes the forms were circular, sometimes square, and sometimes elliptic. Amongst other novelties, the pointed style of the north was introduced, with its projecting mouldings and a little of its tracery; but later in Sicily than anywhere else; and though something of its true spirit is caught in the reconstructions of Maniaces, in Syracuse, yet in Sicily, it always appears an exotic." These facts seem, to Mr. Freeman, to prove incontestibly that the pointed style of Sicily, of that portion of western Christendom in which the systematic use of the pointed arch first occurred, is not Gothic even in the sense of being the most distant transition. A few churches and palaces at Palermo, Syracuse, and Taormina, of the 14th century; and in the same cities, with Girgenti and Messina, of the 15th century, would be nearly all that could be named as important examples before the renaissance was employed. The date, 1592, however, appears to be that of the elliptic arches, groined roof, and flamboyant parapet at the entrance to the church of Sta. Maria della Catena, at Palermo.

627–873. We here, with regret, leave the subject, because we have already trespassed beyond the limits prescribed.

BOOK II.
THEORY OF ARCHITECTURE.

CHAP. I.
MATHEMATICS AND MECHANICS OF CONSTRUCTION.

Sect. I.
GEOMETRY.

874 Geometry is that science which treats of the relations and properties of the boundaries of either body or space. We do not consider it would be useful here to notice the history of the science; neither is it necessary to enter into the reasons which have induced us to adopt the system of Rossignol, from whom we extract this section, otherwise than to state that we hope to conduct the student by a simpler and more intelligible method to those results with which he must be acquainted.

The limits of body or space are surfaces, and the boundaries of surfaces are lines, and the terminations of lines are points. Bounded spaces are usually called solids, whether occupied by body or not; the subject, therefore, is naturally divided into three parts,—lines, surfaces, and solids; and these have two varieties, dependent on their being straight or curved.

875. Geometrical inquiry is conducted in the form of propositions, problems, and demonstrations, being always the result of compari. g equal parts or measures. Now, the parts compared may be either lines or angles, or both; hence, the nature of each method should be separately considered, and then the united power of both employed to facilitate the demonstration of propositions. But the reader must first understand these *Definitions*.

1. A solid is that which has length, breadth, and thickness. A slab of marble, for instance, is a solid, since it is long, broad, and thick.
2. A surface is that which has length and breadth, without thickness. A leaf of paper, though not in strictness, inasmuch as it has thickness, may convey the idea of a surface.
3. A line is that which has length, but neither breadth nor thickness. As in the case of a surface, it is difficult to convey the strict notion of a line, yet an infinitely thin line, as a hair, may convey the idea of a line : a thread drawn tight, a straight line.
4. A point is that which has neither length, breadth, nor thickness.
5. If a line be carried about a point A, so that its other extremity passes from B to C, from C to D, &c. (*fig. 223.*), the point B, in its revolution, will describe a curve BCDFGLB. This curve line is called the *circumference* of a circle. The *circle* is the space enclosed by this circumference. The point A, which, in the formation of the circle is at rest, is called the *centre*. The right lines AC, AD, AF, &c. drawn from the centre to the circumference, are called *radii*. A *diameter* is a right line which passes through the centre, and is terminated both ways by the circumference. The line DAL, for example, is a diameter. An *arc* is a part of a circumference, as FG.

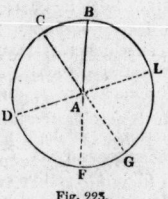

Fig. 223.

6. The circumference of a circle is divided into 360 equal parts, called *degrees ;* each degree is divided into 60 parts, called *minutes*, and each minute into 60 parts, called *seconds*.
7. Two right lines drawn from the same point, and diverging from each other, form an opening which is called an *angle*. An angle is commonly expressed by three letters, and it is usual to place in the middle that letter which marks the point whence the lines diverge; thus, we say the angle BAC or DAF (*fig. 224.*), and not the angle ABC or ACB.
8. The magnitude of an angle does not depend on the lines by which it is formed, but upon their distance from each other. How far soever the lines AB, AC are continued, the angle remains the same. One angle is greater than another when the lines of equal length by which it is formed are more distant. Thus the angle BAL (*fig. 223.*) is greater than the angle CAB, because the lines AB, AL are more distant from each other or include a greater arc than the lines AC, AB. If the legs of a pair of compasses be a little separated, an angle is formed; if they be opened wider, the angle becomes greater; if they be brought nearer, the angle becomes less.

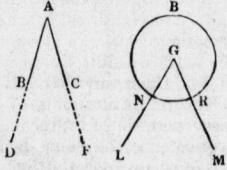

Fig. 224.   Fig. 225.

9. If the point of a pair of compasses be applied to the point G (*fig.* 225.), and a circumference NRB be described, the arc NR contained within the two lines GL, GM will measure the magnitude of the angle LGM. If the arc NR, for example, be an arc of 40 degrees, the angle LGM is an angle of 40 degrees.

10. There are three kinds of angles (*fig.* 226.): a *right* angle (I), which is an angle of 90 degrees; an *obtuse* angle (II), which contains more than 90 degrees; and an *acute* angle (III), which contains less than 90 degrees.

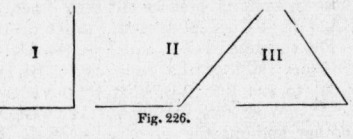

Fig. 226.

11. One line is *perpendicular* to another when the two angles it makes with that other line are equal: thus, the line CD (*fig.* 227.) is perpendicular to the line AB, if the angles CDA, CDB contain an equal number of degrees.

12. Two lines are *parallel* when all perpendiculars drawn from one to the other are equal; thus, the lines FG, AB (*fig.* 228.) are parallel, if all the perpendiculars *cd, cd,* &c. are equal.

13. A *triangle* is a surface enclosed by three right lines, called *sides* (*fig.* 229.). An *equilateral* triangle (I) is that which has three sides equal; an *isosceles* triangle has only two of its sides equal (II); a *scalene* triangle (III) has its three sides unequal.

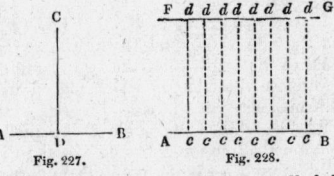

Fig. 227.   Fig. 228.

14. A *quadrilateral* figure is a surface enclosed by four right lines, which are called its sides.

15. A *parallelogram* is a quadrilateral figure, which has its opposite sides parallel; thus,

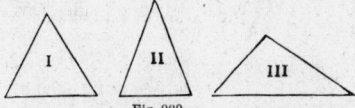

Fig. 229.

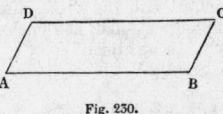

Fig. 230.

if the side BC (*fig.* 230.) is parallel to the side AD, and the side AB to the side DC, the quadrilateral figure ABCD is called a parallelogram.

16. A *rectangle* is a quadrilateral figure all the angles whereof are right angles, as ABCD (*fig.* 231.).

17. A *square* is a quadrilateral figure whose sides are all equal and its angles right angles (*fig.* 232.).

18. A *trapezium* is any quadrilateral figure not a parallelogram.

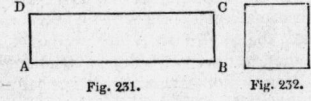

Fig. 231.   Fig. 232.

19. Those figures are *equal* which enclose an equal space; thus, a circle and a triangle are equal, if the space included within the circumference of the circle be equal to that contained in the triangle.

20. Those figures are *identical* which are equal in all their parts; that is, which have all their angles equal and their sides equal, and enclose equal spaces, as BAC, EDG (*fig.* 233.). It is manifest that two figures are identical which, being placed one upon the other, perfectly coincide, for in that case they must be equal in all their parts. It must be observed, that a line merely so expressed always denotes a right line.

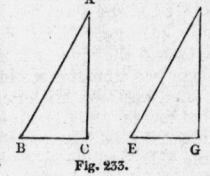

Fig. 233.

AXIOM. Two right lines cannot enclose a space; that category requires at least three lines.

RIGHT LINES AND RECTILINEAL FIGURES.

876. PROPOSITION I. *The radii of the same circle are all equal.*

The revolution of the line AB about the point A (*fig.* 234.) being necessary (Defin. 5.) to form the circle BCDFGLB, when in revolving the point B is upon the point C, the whole line AB must be upon the line AC; otherwise two right lines would enclose a space, which is impossible: wherefore the radius AC is equal to the radius AB. In like manner it may be proved that the radii AB, AF, AG, &c. are all equal to AB, and are therefore equal among themselves.

877. PROP. II. *On a given line to describe an equilateral triangle.*

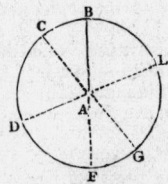

Fig. 234.

Let AB (*fig.* 235.) be the given line upon which it is required to describe a triangle whose three sides shall be equal.

From the point A, with the radius AB, describe the circumference BCD, and from the point B, with the radius BA, describe the circumference ACF; and from the point C, where these two circumferences cut each other, draw the two right lines CA, CB. Then ACB is an equilateral triangle.

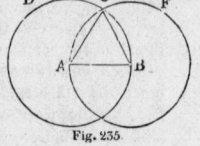

Fig. 235.

For the line AC is equal to the line AB, because these two lines are radii of the same circle BCD; and the line BC is equal to the line AB, because these two lines (Prop. 1.) are radii of the same circle ACF. Wherefore the lines AC and BC, being each equal to the line AB, are equal to one another, and all the three sides of the triangle ACB are equal; that is, the triangle is equilateral.

878. Prop. III. *Triangles which have two sides and the angle subtended or contained by them equal are identical.*

In the two triangles BAC, FDG (*fig.* 236.), if the side DF be equal to the side AB, and the side DG equal to the side AC, and also the angle at D equal to the angle at A, the two triangles are identical.

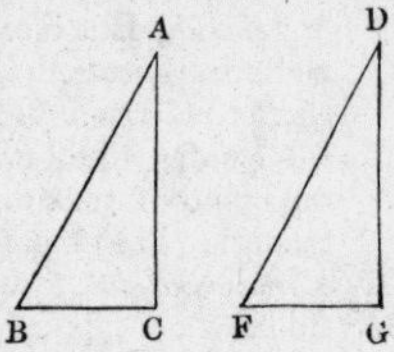

Suppose the triangle FDG placed upon the triangle BAC in such manner that the side DF fall exactly upon the side equal to it, AB. Since the angle D is equal to the angle A, the side DG must fall upon the side equal to it, AC; also the point F will be found upon the point B, and the point G upon the point C: consequently the line FG must fall wholly upon the line BC, otherwise two right lines would enclose a space, which is impossible. Wherefore the three sides of the triangle FDG coincide in all points with the three sides of the triangle BAC, and the

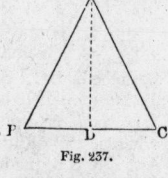

Fig. 236.

two triangles have their sides and angles equal, and enclose an equal space; that is (Defin. 20.), they are identical.

879. Prop. IV. *In an isosceles triangle the angles at the base are equal.*

Let the triangle BAC (*fig.* 237.) have its sides AB, AC equal, the angles B and C at the base are also equal. Conceive the angle A to be bisected by the right line AD.

In the triangles BAD, DAC the sides AB, AC are, by supposition, equal; the side AD is common to the two triangles, and the angles at A are supposed equal. These two triangles,

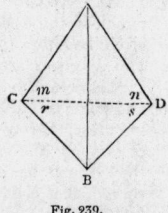

Fig. 237.

therefore, have two sides, and the angle contained by them equal. Hence, they are identical (Prop. 3), or have all their parts equal: whence the angles B and C must be equal.

880. Prop. V. *Triangles which have their three sides equal are identical.*

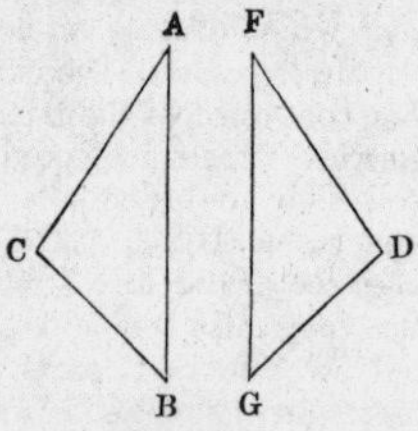

In the two triangles ACB, FDG (*fig.* 238.), let the side AC be equal to the side FD, the side CB equal to the side DG, and the side AB to the side FG; these two triangles are identical.

Let the two triangles be so joined that the side FG shall coincide with the side AB (*fig.* 239.), and draw the right line CD. Since in the triangle CAD the side AC is equal to the side AD,

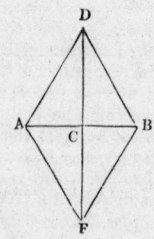

Fig. 238.　　　　Fig. 239.

the triangle is isoceles; whence (Defin. 13.) the angles m and n at the base are equal.

Since in the triangle CBD the side BC is equal to the side BD, the triangle is isosceles; whence (Defin. 13.) the angles r and s at the base are equal.

Because the angle m is equal to the angle n, and the angle r equal to the angle s, the whole angle C is equal to the whole angle D.

Lastly, because in the two triangles ACB, ADB the side AC is equal to the side AD and the side CB equal to the side DB, also the angle C equal to the angle D, these two triangles have two sides, and the contained angle equal, and are therefore (Prop. 3.) identical.

881. Prop. VI. *To divide a right line into two equal parts.*

Let the right line which it is required to divide into two equal parts be AB (*fig.* 240.). Upon AB draw (Prop. 2.) the equilateral triangle ADB, and on the other side of the same line

Fig. 240.

AB draw the equilateral triangle AFB, draw also the right line DF; AC is equal to CB.

In the two larger triangles DAF, DBF the sides DA, DB are equal, because they are the sides of an equilateral triangle; the sides AF, BF are equal for the same reason; and the side DF is common to the two triangles. These two triangles, then, have their sides equal, and consequently (Prop. 5.) are identical, or have all their parts equal; wherefore the two angles at D are equal.

Again, in the two smaller triangles ADC, CDB the side DA is made equal to the side DB, and the side DC is common to the two triangles; also the two angles at D are equal. Thus these two triangles have two sides and the contained angle equal; they are therefore (Prop. 3.) identical, and AC is equal to CB; that is, AB is bisected.

882. PROP. VII. *From a given point out of a right line to draw a perpendicular to that line.*

Let C (*fig.* 241.) be the point from which it is required to draw a perpendicular to the right line AB.

From the point C describe an arc of a circle which shall cut the line AB in two points F and G. Then bisect the line FG, and to D, the point of division, draw the line CD: this line is perpendicular to the line AB. Draw the lines CF, CG.

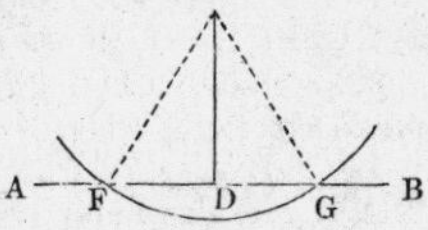

Fig. 241.

In the triangles FCD, DCG the sides CF, CG are equal, because (Prop. 1.) they are radii of the same circle; the sides FD DG are equal, because FG is bisected; and the side DC is common. These two triangles, then, having the three sides equal, are identical (Prop. 5.). Whence (Defin. 20.) the angle CDA is equal to the angle CDB, and consequently (Defin. 11.) the line CD is perpendicular to the line AB.

883. PROP. VIII. *From a given point in a right line to raise a perpendicular upon that line.*

From the point C (*fig.* 242.), let it be required to raise a perpendicular upon the right line AB.

In AB take at pleasure CF equal to CG; upon the line FG describe an equilateral triangle FDG, and draw the line CD; this line will be perpendicular to AB.

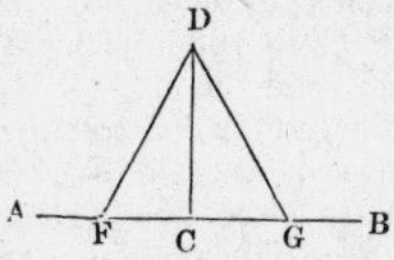

Fig. 242.

In the triangles FDC, CDG the sides DF, DG are equal, because they are the sides of an equilateral triangle; the sides FC, CG are equal by construction; and the side DC is common. These two triangles, then, having the three sides equal, are (Prop. 5.) identical. Therefore (Defin. 20.) the angle DCA is equal to the angle DCB, and consequently (Defin. 11.) the line CD is perpendicular to the line AB.

884. PROP. IX. *The diameter of a circle divides the circumference into two equal parts.*

Let ADBLA (*fig.* 243.) be a circle; the diameter ACB bisects the circumference, that is, the arc ALB is equal to the arc ADB.

Conceive the circle to be divided, and the lower segment ACBLA to be placed upon the upper ACBDA; all the points of the arc ALB will fall exactly upon the arc ADB; and consequently these two arcs will be equal.

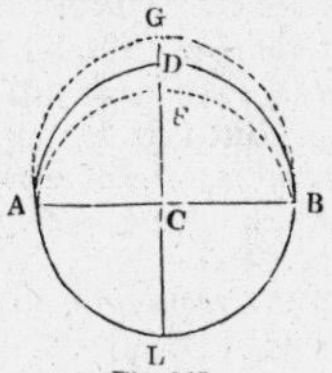

For if the point L, for instance, does not fall upon the arc ADB, it must fall either above this arc, as at G, or below it, as at F. If it fall on G, the radius CL will be greater than the radius CD; if it falls on F, the radius CL will be less than the radius CD, which is (Prop. 1.) impossible. The point L, then, must fall upon the arc ADB. In like manner it may be proved that all the other points of the arc ALB must fall upon the arc ADB: those two arcs are therefore equal.

Fig. 243.

885. PROP. X. *A right line which meets another right line forms with it two angles, which together, are equal to two right angles.*

The line FC (*fig.* 244.) meeting the line DA, and forming with it the two angles, DCF, ACF, these two angles are together equal to two right angles.

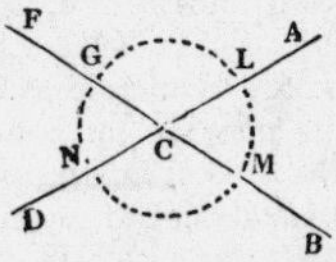

From the point C as a centre describe at pleasure a circumference NGLMN.

The line NCL, being a diameter, divides the circumference (Prop. 9.) into two equal parts. The arc NGL is therefore half the circumference, which contains (Defin. 6.) 180, or twice 90 degrees. Therefore the angles DCF, ACF, which, taken together, are measured by the arc NGL, are twice 90 degrees, that is (Defin. 10.), are equal to two right angles.

Fig. 244.

886. PROP. XI. *A line drawn perpendicularly to another right line makes right angles with it.*

If the line CD (*fig.* 245.) be perpendicular to the line AB, the angle CDA is a right angle, and also the angle CDB.

For the line CD, meeting the line AB, forms with it two angles, which are together (Prop. 10.) equal to two right angles; and these two angles are equal, because CD is perpendicular to AB. Wherefore each angle is a right angle.

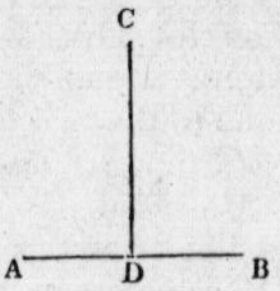

887. PROP. XII. *If two lines cut each other, the vertical or opposite angles are equal.*

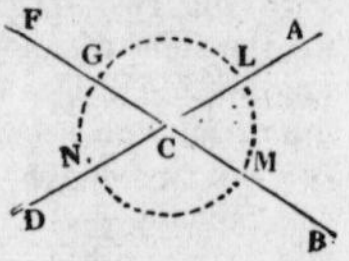

Let the lines AD, BF, (*fig.* 246.) cut each

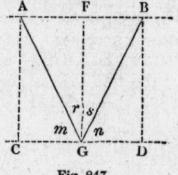

Fig. 245.   Fig. 246.

other at the point C; the angles ACB, FCD, which are called vertical or opposite angles, are equal.

From the point C, as a centre, describe at pleasure a circumference NGLMN.

Since the line NCL is a diameter, the arc NGL is (Prop. 9.) half the circumference; therefore the arcs NGL, GLM are equal. From these two arcs take away the common part GL, there will remain the arc NG equal to the arc LM. Consequently the angles ACB, FCD, which are measured by these two arcs, are also equal.

888. PROP. XIII. *If a line be perpendicular to one of two parallel lines, it is also perpendicular to the other.*

Let AB, CD (*fig.* 247.) be two parallel lines: if the line FG makes right angles with CD, it will also make right angles with AB.

Take at pleasure GC equal to GD; at the points C and D raise the perpendiculars CA, DB, and draw the lines GA, GB.

In the two triangles ACG, BDG, because the line AB is parallel to the line CD, the perpendiculars CA, DB are necessarily equal, as appears from the definition of parallel lines (Defin. 12.); the lines CG, DG are equal by construction; and the angles C and D are right angles. The two triangles ACG, BDG have then two sides and the contained angle equal, they are therefore (Prop. 3.) identical. Whence the side GA is equal to the side GB, and the angle *m* equal to the angle *n*.

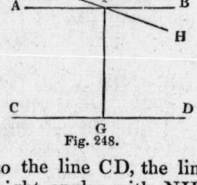

Fig 247.

Again, in the triangles AGF, FGB the side GA is equal to the side GB, as has been proved, and the side GF is common. Moreover, the angle *r* is equal to the angle *s*; for if from the two right angles FGC, FGD be taken away the equal angles *m* and *n*, there will remain the equal angles *r* and *s*. The triangles AGF, FGB have then two sides and the contained angle equal; they are therefore (Prop. 3.) identical. Wherefore the angles GFA, GFB are equal, and consequently are right angles.

889. PROP. XIV. *If one line be perpendicular to two other lines, these two lines are parallel.*

Let the line FG (*fig.* 248.) make right angles with the lines AB and CD; these two lines are parallel.

If the line AB be not parallel to the line CD, another line, as NH, may be drawn through the point F, parallel to the line CD. But this is impossible; for if the line NH were parallel to the line CD, the line FG making right angles with CD would also (Prop. 13.) make right angles with NH; which cannot be, because, by supposition, it makes right angles with AB.

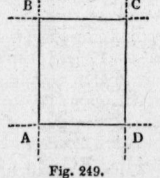

Fig. 248.

890. PROP. XV. *The opposite sides of a rectangle are parallel.*

In the rectangle ABCD (*fig.* 249.) the side BC is parallel to the side AD, and the side AB parallel to the side DC. Produce each of the sides both ways.

The line AB is perpendicular to the two lines BC, AD; the two lines BC, AD are therefore (Prop. 14.) parallel. In like manner, the line AD is perpendicular to the two lines AB, DC; the two lines AB, DC are therefore (Prop. 14.) parallel.

891. PROP. XVI. *The opposite sides of a rectangle are equal.*

Fig. 249.

In the rectangle ABCD (see *fig.* 249.) the side AB is equal to the side DC, and the side BC equal to the side AD. For, since the side BC is parallel to the side AD, the perpendiculars AB, DC are (Defin. 12.) equal; and since the side AB is parallel to the side DC, the perpendiculars BC, AD are equal.

892. PROP. XVII. *A right line falling upon parallel lines makes the alternate angles equal.*

Let the line FG (*fig.* 250.) cut the parallels AB, GD; the angles AFG, FGD, which are called *alternate angles*, are equal. From the point G draw GL perpendicular to the line AB, and from the point F draw FM perpendicular to the line GD.

Since the line GL is perpendicular to AB, it is also (Prop. 13.) perpendicular to the

parallel line GD. Whence the quadrilateral figure GLFM is a rectangle, its four angles being right angles.

In the triangles GLF, FMG the sides LF, GM are equal, because they are opposite sides of the same rectangle; the sides LG, FM are equal for the same reason; and the side FG is common. The two triangles GLF, FMG have then the three sides equal, and consequently (Prop. 5.) are identical. Wherefore the angle LFG opposite to the side LG is equal to the angle FGM opposite to the side FM.

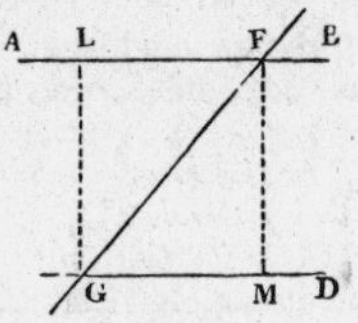

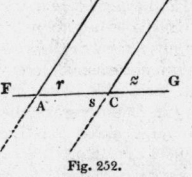

Fig. 250. 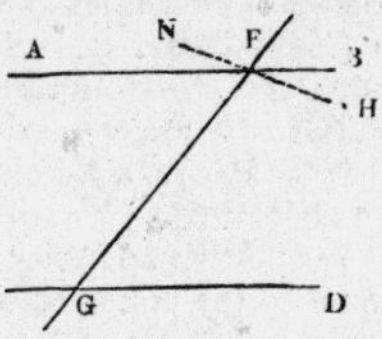   Fig. 251.

Remark. In identical triangles the equal angles are always opposite to equal sides, as by this proposition appears.

893. Prop. XVIII. *If one right line falling upon two others makes the alternate angles equal, these two lines are parallel.*

Let the alternate angles AFG, FGD (*fig. 251.*) be equal; the lines AB, GD are parallel.

If the line AB is not parallel to the line GD, another line, as NH, may be drawn through the point F parallel to GD. But this is impossible; for if the line NH were parallel to the line GD, the angle FGD would be (Prop. 17.) equal to the angle NFG, since these two angles would be alternate angles between two parallel lines; which cannot be, because, by supposition, the angle FGD is equal to the angle AFG.

894. Prop. XIX. *If one right line falls upon two parallel right lines, it makes the interior angle equal to the exterior.*

Let the line FG (*fig. 252.*) meet the parallel lines BA, DC, the interior angle r is equal to the exterior angle z. Produce the lines BA, DC.

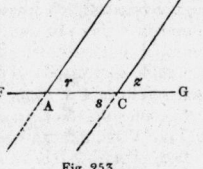

Fig. 252.

The angle r (Prop. 17.) is equal to the angle s, because these are alternate angles, made by a right line falling upon two parallel lines, and the angles s and z are (Prop. 12.) equal, because they are vertical or opposite angles; therefore the angle r is equal to the angle z.

895. Prop. XX. *If one right line falling upon two other right lines makes the internal angle equal to the external, those two lines are parallel.*

Let the internal angle r (*fig. 253.*) be equal to the external angle z, the lines BA, DC are parallel.

The angle r is equal to the angle z by supposition, and the angle z (Prop. 12.) is equal to the angle s, because they are opposite angles. The alternate angles r, s are therefore equal, and consequently (Prop. 18.) the lines BA, DC are parallel.

Fig. 253.

896. Prop. XXI. *Through a given point to draw a line parallel to a given line.*

Let G be the point through which it is required to draw a line parallel to the given line MF.

From any point G (*fig. 254.*) describe, at pleasure, the arc FN; from the point F, in which the arc FN cuts the line MF, with the distance GF describe the arc GM meeting the line MF in M; then make FL equal to GM, and draw the line GL; this line is parallel to the line MF.

Draw the line GF.

The arcs GM, FL are equal by construction; therefore the alternate angles r, s, which are measured by these arcs (Defin. 9.), are equal; and consequently (Prop. 18.) the lines GL, MF are parallel.

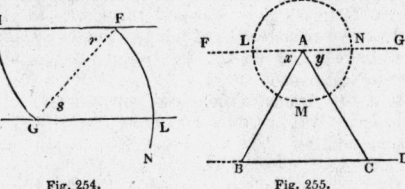

Fig. 254.   Fig. 255.

897. Prop. XXII. *The three angles of a triangle taken together are equal to two right angles.*

In the triangle BAC (*fig. 255.*), the three angles B, A, C are together equal to two right angles.

Produce the side BC both ways; through the point A draw a line FG parallel to BC; and from the point A, as a centre, describe any circumference LMN.

The angle B (Prop. 17.) is equal to the angle x, because these are alternate angles made by a right line falling upon two parallel lines. For the same reason the angle C is equal to the angle y.

Because LAN is a diameter, the arc LMN is half the circumference; therefore the three angles x, A, y, which are measured by this arc, are together equal to two right angles.

But the angle x is equal to the alternate angle B, and the angle y to the alternate angle C.

Therefore, substituting B for x, and C for y, the three angles B, A, C are together equal to two right angles.

CoROLLARY. Hence, if two angles of any triangle be known, the third is also found; since the third angle is that which the other two taken together want of two right angles.

898. Prop. XXIII.　*If two triangles have two angles equal, they have also the third angle equal.*

In the two triangles BAC, FDG (*fig. 256.*), if the angle B is equal to the angle F, and the angle A equal to the angle D, the angle C will also be equal to the angle G.

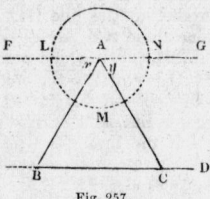

Fig. 256.

Since the angle C (Corol. to Prop. 22.) is that which the angles B and A together want of two right angles; and since the angle G is that which F and D together want of two right angles; the angles B and A being equal to the angles F and D, the angle C must be equal to the angle G.

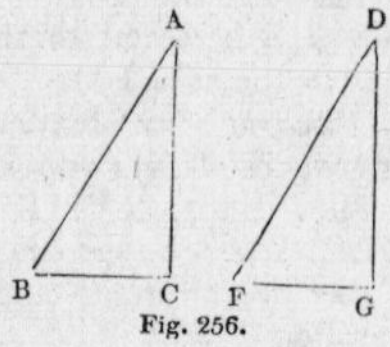

899. Prop. XXIV.　*The exterior angle of any triangle is equal to the two interior and opposite angles taken together.*

In the triangle BAC (*fig. 257.*) produce one of the sides BC; the angle ACD, which is called *exterior*, is equal to the two *interior* and *opposite* angles B and A taken together.

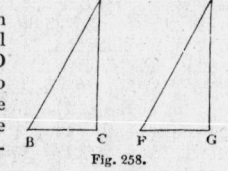

Fig. 257.

The line AC meeting the line BD forms with it two angles, which are together (Prop. 10.) equal to two right angles; the angle ACB is therefore that which the angle ACD wants of two right angles. But the angle ACB is (Corol. to Prop. 22.) also that which the angles B and A together want of two right angles. Wherefore the angle ACD is equal to the two angles B and A taken together.

900. Prop. XXV.　*Triangles which have two angles and the side which lies between them equal are identical.*

In the two triangles BAC, FDG (*fig. 258.*), if the angle F is equal to the angle B, the angle G equal to the angle C, and the side FG equal to the side BC, these two triangles are identical.

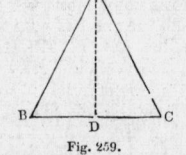

Fig. 258.

Conceive the triangle FDG placed upon the triangle BAC in such a manner that the side FG shall fall exactly upon the equal side BC. Since the angle F is equal to the angle B, the side FD must fall upon the side BA; and since the angle G is equal to the angle C, the side GD must fall upon the side CA. Thus the three sides of the triangle FDG will be exactly placed upon the three sides of the triangle BAC; and consequently the two triangles (Prop. 5.) are identical.

901. Prop. XXVI.　*If two angles of a triangle are equal, the sides opposite to those angles are also equal.*

Conceive the angle A (*fig. 259.*) to be bisected by the line AD.

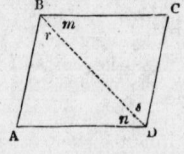

Fig. 259.

In the triangles BAD, DAC the angle B is equal to the angle C by supposition, and the angles at A are also equal. These two triangles have their two angles equal; the third angle will therefore (Prop. 23.) be equal; whence the angles at D are equal. Moreover, the side AD is common to the two triangles. These two triangles, therefore, having two angles and the side which lies between them equal, are (Prop. 25.) identical. Wherefore the side AB is equal to the side AC.

902. Prop. XXVII.　*The opposite sides of a parallelogram are equal.*

In the parallelogram ABCD (*fig. 260.*), the side AB is equal to the side DC, and the side BC equal to the side AD.

Draw the line BD, which is called the *diagonal*.

Because BC is parallel to AD, the alternate angles m and n are equal. In like manner, because AB is parallel to DC, the alternate angles r and s are equal. Also, the side BD is common to the two triangles BAD, BCD. These two triangles have then two angles and the side which lies between them equal, and are therefore (Prop. 3.) identical. Wherefore the side AB opposite to the angle n is (Prop. 26.) equal to the side DC opposite to the angle m; and the side BC opposite to the angle s is equal to the side AD opposite to the equal angle r.

Fig. 260.

Corollary. Hence, the diagonal bisects the parallelogram; for the triangles BAD, BCD, having the three sides equal, are identical.

903. Prop. XXVIII. *Parallelograms which are between the same parallels, and have the same base, are equal.*

Let the two parallelograms ABCD, AFGD (*fig.* 261.), be between the same parallels BG, AM, and upon the same base AD; the space enclosed within the parallelogram ABCD is equal to the space enclosed within the parallelogram AFGD.

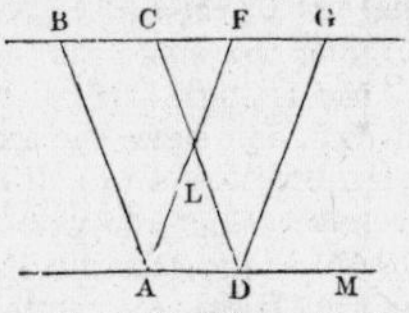

In the two triangles BAF, CDG the side BA of the former triangle is equal to the side CD of the latter, because they are opposite sides of the same parallelogram. For the same reason, the side FA is equal to the side GD. Moreover, BC is equal to AD, because they are opposite sides of the same parallelogram. For the same reason, AD is equal to FG. BC is therefore equal to FG. If to both these CF be added, BF will be equal to CG. Whence the two triangles BAF, CDG, having the three sides equal, are (Prop. 5.) identical, and consequently have equal surfaces.

If from these two equal surfaces be taken the small triangle CLF, which is common, there will remain the trapezium ABCL, equal to the trapezium LFGD. To these two trapezia add the triangle ALD, and the parallelogram ABCD will be equal to the parallelogram AFGD.

904. Prop. XXIX. *If a triangle and a parallelogram are upon the same base, and between the same parallels, the triangle is equal to half the parallelogram.*

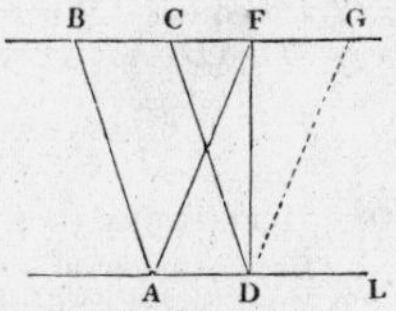

Let the parallelogram ABCD (*fig.* 262.) and the triangle AFD be upon the same base AD, and between the same parallels BG, AL; the triangle AFD is half the parallelogram ABCD. Draw DG parallel to AF.

Because the parallelogram AFGD is bisected by the diagonal FD (Prop. 27. Corol.), the triangle AFD is half the parallelogram AFGD. But the parallelogram AFGD is equal to the parallelogram ABCD, because these two parallelograms are upon the same base, and between the same parallels; therefore the triangle AFD is equal to half the parallelogram ABCD.

905. Prop. XXX. *Parallelograms which are between the same parallels, and have equal bases, are equal.*

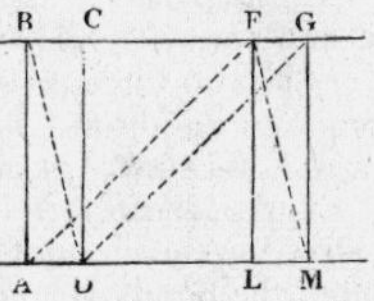

Let the two parallelograms ABCD, LFGM (*fig.* 263.) be between the same parallels BG, AM, and have the equal bases AD, LM; these two parallelograms are equal.

Draw the lines AF, DG.

Because AD is equal to LM, and LM to FG, AD is equal to FG; and they are parallel by construction. Also AF and DG are parallel; for if DG be not parallel to AF, another line may be drawn parallel to it; whence FG will become greater or less than AD. AF and DG are therefore parallel, and AFGD a parallelogram.

Now the parallelogram ABCD is (Prop. 28.) equal to the parallelogram AFGD, because these two parallelograms are between the same parallels, and have the same base AD. And the parallelogram AFGD is equal to the parallelogram LFGM, because these two parallelograms are between the same parallels, and have the same base FG. The parallelogram ABCD is therefore equal to the parallelogram LFGM.

906. Prop. XXXI. *Triangles which are between the same parallels, and have equal bases, are equal.*

Let the two triangles ABD, LFM (see *fig.* to preceding Proposition) be between the same parallels BG, AM, and upon the equal bases AD, LM; these two triangles are equal.

Draw DC parallel to AB, and MG parallel to LF.

The two parallelograms ABCD, LFGM are equal (Prop. 30.), because they are between the same parallels, and have equal bases. But the triangle ABD is (Prop. 29.) one half of the parallelogram ABCD, and the triangle LFM is one half of the parallelogram LFGM; these two triangles are therefore equal.

907. Prop. XXXII. *In a right-angled triangle, the square of the hypothenuse, or side subtending the right angle, is equal to the squares of the sides which contain the right angle.*

In the triangle BAC (*fig.* 264.), let the angle A be a right angle. Upon the hypothenuse BC describe the square BDFC; upon the side AB describe the square ALMB, and upon the side AC the square ARNC; the square BDFC is equal to the two squares ALMB, ARNC taken together.

Fig. 261.

Fig. 262.

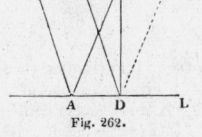
Fig. 263.

Draw the right lines MC, AD, and draw AG parallel
to BD.

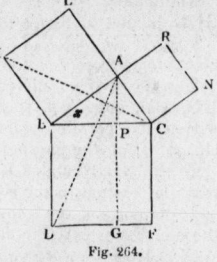

Because the square or parallelogram MLAB and the
triangle MCB are between the same parallels LC, MB, and
have the same base MB, the triangle MCB is (Prop. 29.)
equal to half the square ALMB.

Again, because the rectangle or parallelogram DGPB
and the triangle DAB are between the same parallels GA
and DB, and have the same base DB, the triangle DAB is
(Prop. 29.) equal to half the rectangle DGBP.

Further, since the side MB of the triangle MBC and the
side AB of the triangle ABD are sides of the same square,
they are (Defin. 17.) equal. Also, since the side BC of the

Fig. 264.

first triangle and the side BD of the second triangle are sides of the same square, they are
equal. And because the angle MBC of the first triangle is composed of a right angle and
the angle x, and the angle ABD of the second triangle is composed of a right angle and
the same angle x, therefore these two angles, contained between the equal sides MB, BC
and AB, BD, are equal. Wherefore the two triangles MBC, ABD, having two sides and
the contained angle equal, are (Prop. 3.) identical, and consequently equal.

But the triangle MBC is half the square MLAB, and the triangle ABD is half the
rectangle BDGP; the square and the rectangle are therefore equal.

In the same manner it may be demonstrated that the square ARNC and the rectangle
CFGP are equal. Wherefore it follows that the whole square BDFC is equal to the two
squares MLAB, ARNC taken together.

CIRCLES.

908. DEFINITIONS. — 1. A right line (*fig.* Prop. 33. AB) terminated both ways by the
circumference of a circle is called a *chord*.

2. A line (*fig.* Prop. 39. AB) which meets the circumference in one point only is called
a *tangent ;* and the point T is called the *point of contact.*

3. An angle (*fig.* Prop. 33. ABD) which has its vertex in the circumference of a circle
is called *an angle in the circle.*

4. A part of a circle confined between two radii (*fig.* Prop. 34. ACBFA) is called a *sector.*

5. A part of a circle (*fig.* Prop. 35. AGBDA) terminated by a chord is called a *segment
of a circle.*

909. PROP. XXXIII. *To draw the circumference of a circle through three given points.*

Let there be three given points, A, B, D (*fig.* 265.), through which it
is required to draw the circumference of a circle. Draw the right
lines AB, BD, and bisect them : from the points of the division F, G,
raise the perpendiculars BC, GC ; and at the point C with the radius
CA describe the circumference of a circle ; this circumference will pass
through the points B and D. Draw the lines CA, CB, CD.

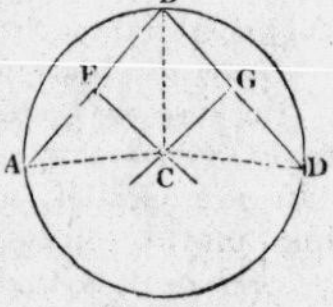

In the triangles CFA, CFB the side FA is equal to the side FB
by construction, the side FC is common, and the two angles at F are
right angles. These two triangles, then, have two sides and the angle
contained by them equal ; they are therefore (Prop. 3.) identical. Consequently the side
CB is equal to the side CA.

Fig. 265.

For the same reason, the triangles CGB, CGD are also identical. Wherefore the side
CD is equal to the side CB, and consequently equal to CA.

And since the right lines CB, CD are equal to the right line CA, it is manifest (Prop. 1.)
that the circumference which passes through the point A must also pass through the
point D.

910. PROP. XXXIV. *If a radius bisect a chord, it is perpendicular to that chord.*

If the radius CF (*fig.* 266.) bisect the chord AB, the angles
CDA, CDB are right angles. Draw the radii CA, CB.

In the triangles CDA, CDB the sides CA, CB, being radii, are equal
(Prop. 1.), the sides AD, DB are equal by supposition, and the side
CD is common. These two triangles, having the three sides equal, are
therefore (Prop. 5.) identical. Wherefore the angles CDA, CDB are
equal, and consequently (Prop. 10.) are right angles.

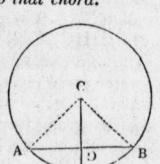

COROLLARY. The two angles at C are also (Prop. 5.) equal.

Hence it appears, that any angle ACB may be bisected by describing
from its vertex C as the centre with any radius AC an arc AFB ; bisect-

Fig. 266.

ing the chord of that arc AB ; and then drawing from the point of division D the right line
CD ; for it may then be shown, as in the proposition, that the triangles ACD, DCB are
identical, and consequently the angles at C equal.

911. Prop. XXXV. *To find the centre of a circle.*

Let the circle of which it is required to find the centre be AGBF. Draw any chord AB

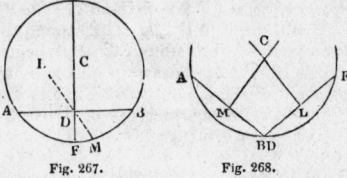

(*fig.* 267.) ; bisect it, and from the point of division D raise a perpendicular FG : this line will pass through the centre, and consequently, if it be bisected, the point of division will be the centre.

If the centre of the circle be not in the line FG, it must be somewhere out of it ; for instance, at the point L. But this is impossible, for if the point L were the centre, the right line LM would be a radius ; and since this line bisects

Fig. 267.   Fig. 268.

the chord AB, it is (Prop. 34.) perpendicular to AB ; which cannot be, since CD is perpendicular to AB.

912. Prop. XXXVI. *To find the centre of an arc of a circle.*

Let ABDF be the arc of which it is required to find the centre. Draw any two chords AB, DF (*fig.* 268) ; bisect them, and from the points of division raise the perpendiculars MC, LC ; the point C, in which these two perpendiculars cut each other, is the centre of the arc.

For (Prop. 35.) the perpendicular MC and the perpendicular LC both pass through the centre of the same circle ; this centre must therefore be the point C, which is the only point common to the two perpendiculars.

913. Prop. XXXVII. *If three equal lines meet in the same point within a circle, and are terminated, they are radii of that circle.*

The lines CA, CB, CD (*fig.* 269.), drawn from the same point C within a circle, and terminated by it, being equal, the point C is the centre of the circle. Draw the lines AB, BD ; bisect them, and let the points of division be F, G ; and draw the lines CF, CG.

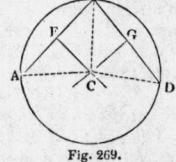

Fig. 269.

In the triangles CFA, CFB, the sides CA, CB are equal by supposition, the sides FA, FB are equal by construction, and the side CF is common. These two triangles, then, have the three sides equal ; they are therefore (Prop. 5.) identical. Wherefore the two angles at F are equal, and the line FC (Defin. 11.) is perpendicular to the chord AB. And since this perpendicular bisects the chord AB, it must (Prop. 35.) pass through the centre of the circle. In like manner, it may be demonstrated that the line GC also passes through the centre. Wherefore the point C is the centre of the circle, and CA, CB, CD are radii.

914. Prop. XXXVIII. *If the radius of a circle be perpendicular to a chord, the radius bisects both the chord and the arc of the chord.*

Let the radius CF be perpendicular to the chord AB (*fig.* 270.) ; the right line AD is equal to the right line DB, and the arc AF equal to the arc FB. Draw the right lines CA, CB.

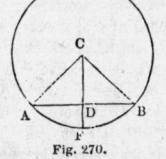

In the large triangle ACB, the side CA (Prop. 1.) is equal to the side CB, because they are radii of the same circle. The angle A is (Prop. 4.) therefore equal to the angle B. The angles at D are right angles, and therefore equal ; and the angles at C are consequently (Prop. 23.) equal. Also the side CA is equal to the side CB, and the side CD is common. These two triangles, then, having two sides and the angle contained by them equal, are (Prop. 3.)

Fig. 270.

identical, whence the side AD is equal to the side DB. Again, since the angles ACF, BCF are equal, the arcs AB, BF, which measure these angles, are also equal. The chord AB and the arc AFB are therefore bisected by the radius CF.

915. Prop. XXXIX. *A right line perpendicular to the extremity of a radius is a tangent to the circle.*

Let the line AB (*fig.* 271.) pass through the extremity of the radius CT in such a manner that the angles CTA, CTB shall be right angles ; this line AB touches the circumference in only one point T. If AB touch the circumference in any other point, let it be D, and draw the line CD.

In the right-angled triangle CTD the square of the hypothenuse CD is equal to the two squares of CT and TD taken together. The square of CD is therefore greater than the square of CT, and consequently the line CD is greater than the line CT, which is a radius. Therefore the point D is out of the circumference. And in like manner it may be shown that every point in the line AB is out of the circumference, except T ; AB is therefore a tangent to the circle.

Corollary. It follows, therefore, that a perpendicular is the shortest line that can be

drawn from any point to a given line; since the perpendicular CT is shorter than any other line which can be drawn from the point C to the line AB.

916. Prop. XL. *If a right line be drawn touching a circumference, a radius drawn to the point of contact will be perpendicular to the tangent.*

Let the line AB (*fig.* 272.) touch the circumference of a circle in a point T, the radius CT is perpendicular to the tangent AB. For all other lines drawn from the point C to the line AB must pass out of the circle to arrive at this line. The line CT is therefore the shortest which can be drawn from the point C to the line AB, and consequently (Corol. to Prop. 39.) is perpendicular to the line AB.

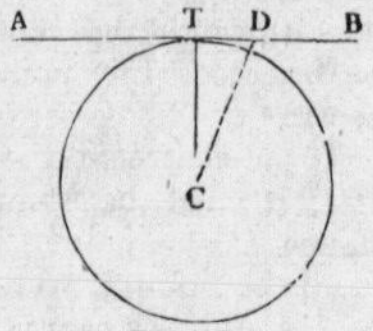

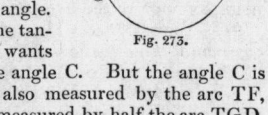

Fig. 272.

917. Prop. XLI. *The angle formed by a tangent and chord is measured by half the arc of that chord.*

Let BTA (*fig.* 273.) be a tangent and TD a chord drawn from the point of contact T; the angle ATD is measured by half the arc TFD, and the angle BTD is measured by half the arc TGD. Draw the radius CT to the point of contact, and the radius CF perpendicular to the chord TD.

The radius CF being perpendicular to the chord TD (Prop. 38.) bisects the arc TFD. TF is therefore half the arc TFD.

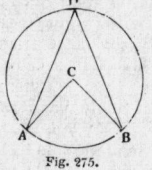

Fig. 273.

In the triangle CML the angle M being a right angle, the two remaining angles are (Prop. 22.) equal to a right angle. Wherefore the angle C is that which the angle L wants of a right angle. On the other side, since the radius CT is perpendicular to the tangent BA, the angle ATD is also that which the angle L wants of a right angle. The angle ATD is therefore equal to the angle C. But the angle C is measured by the arc TF, consequently the angle ATD is also measured by the arc TF, which is half of TFD. The angle BTD must therefore be measured by half the arc TGD, since these two halves of arcs make up half the circumference.

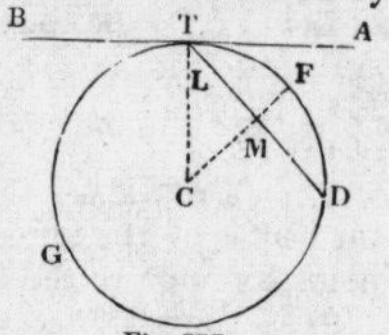

918. Prop. XLII. *An angle at the circumference of a circle is measured by half the arc by which it is subtended.*

Let CTD (*fig.* 274.) be the angle at the circumference; it has for its measure half the arc CFD by which it is subtended.

Suppose a tangent passing through the point T.

The three angles at T are measured by half the circumference (Prop. 22.), but the angle ATD is measured (Prop. 41.) by half the arc TD, and the angle BTC by half the arc TC; consequently the angle CTD must be measured by half the arc CFD, since these three halves of arcs make up half the circumference.

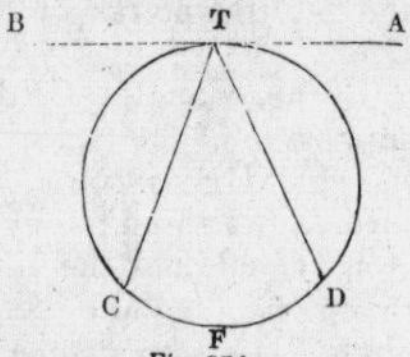

Fig. 274.

919. Prop. XLIII. *The angle at the centre of a circle is double of the angle at the circumference.*

Let the angle at the circumference ADB (*fig.* 275.) and the angle at the centre ACB be both subtended by the same arc AB, the angle ACB is double of the angle ADB.

For the angle ACB is measured by the arc AB, and the angle ADB is (Prop. 42.) measured by half the same arc AB; the angle ACB is therefore double of the angle ADB.

Fig. 275.

920. Prop. XLIV. *Upon a given line, to describe a segment of a circle containing a given angle.*

Let AB (*fig.* 276.) be the given line and G the given angle, it is required to draw such a circumference of a circle through the points A and B that the angle D shall be equal to the angle G.

For this purpose draw the lines AL, BL in such manner that the angles A and B shall be equal to the angle G; at the extremities of LA, LB raise the perpendiculars AC, BC; and from the point C in which these two perpendiculars cut each other, with the radius CA or CB describe the circumference ADB; the angle D will be equal to the angle G.

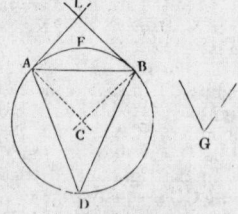

Fig. 276.

The angle LAB, formed by the tangent AL and the chord AB, is (Prop. 41.) measured by half the arc AFB; and the angle D at the circumference is also measured (Prop. 42.) by half the arc AFB; the angle D is therefore equal to the angle LAB. But the angle LAB is made equal to the angle G; the angle D is therefore equal to the angle G.

921. Prop. XLV. *In every triangle the greater side is opposite to the greater angle, and the greater angle to the greater side.*

In the triangle ABC (*fig.* 277.), if the side AB be greater than the side AC, the angle

C opposite to the side AB will be greater than the angle B opposite to the side AC. Draw the circumference of a circle through the three points A, C, B.

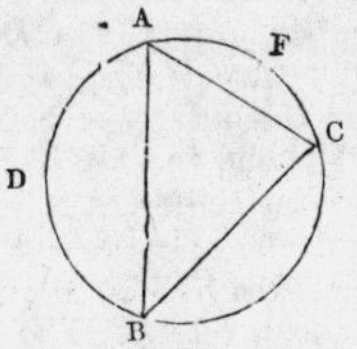

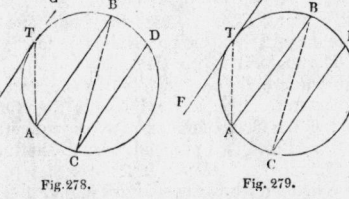

Since the chord AB is greater than the chord AC, it is manifest that the arc ADB is greater than the arc AFC; and consequently the angle at the circumference C, which is measured (Prop. 42.) by half the arc ADB, is greater than the angle at the circumference B, which is measured by half the arc AFC.

Again, if the angle C is greater than the angle B, the side AB opposite to the angle C will be greater than the side AC opposite to the angle B.

Fig. 277.

The angle C is measured (Prop. 42.) by half the arc ADB, and the angle B by half the arc AFC. But the angle C is greater than the angle B; the arc ADB is therefore greater than the arc AFC, and consequently the chord AB is greater than the chord AC.

922. PROP. XLVI. *Two parallel chords intercept equal arcs.*

If the two chords AB, CD (*fig.* 278.) are parallel, the arcs AC, BD are equal. Draw the right line BC.

Because the lines AB, CD are parallel, the alternate angles ABC, BCD are (Prop. 17.) equal. But the angle at the circumference BCD is measured (Prop. 42.) by half the arc AC; and the angle at the circumference BCD is measured by half the arc BD; the arcs AC, BD are therefore equal.

923. PROP. XLVII. *If a tangent and chord be parallel to each other, they intercept equal arcs.*

Let the tangent FG (*fig.* 279.) be parallel to the chord AB; the arc TA will be equal to the arc TB. Draw the right line TA.

Fig. 278.   Fig. 279.

Because the lines FG, AB are parallel, the alternate angles FTA, TAB are (Prop. 17.) equal. But the angle FTA, formed by a tangent and a chord, is measured (Prop. 41.) by half the arc TA, and the angle at the circumference TAB is measured (Prop. 42.) by half the arc TB. The halves of the arcs TA, TB, and consequently the arcs themselves, are therefore equal.

924. PROP. XLVIII. *The angle formed by the intersection of two chords is measured by half the two arcs intercepted by the two chords.*

Let the two chords AB, DF (*fig.* 280.) cut each other at the point C, the angle FCB or ACD is measured by half the two arcs FB, AD. Draw AG parallel to DF.

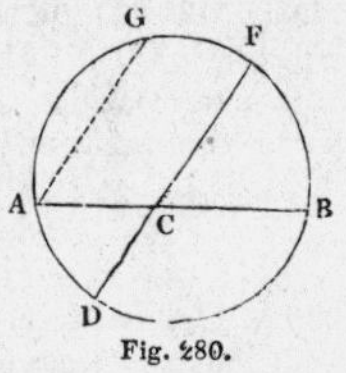

Because the lines AG, DF are parallel, the interior and exterior angles GAB, FCB are (Prop. 19.) equal. But the angle at the circumference GAB is measured (Prop. 42.) by half the arc GFB. The angle FCB is therefore also measured by half the arc GFB.

Because the chords AG, DF are parallel, the arcs GF, AD are (Prop. 46.) equal: AD may therefore be substituted in the room of GF; wherefore the angle FCB is measured by half the arcs AD, FB.

Fig. 280.

925. PROP. XLIX. *The angle formed by two secants is measured by half the difference of the two intercepted arcs.*

Let the angle CAB (*fig.* 281.) be formed by the two secants AC, AB, this angle is measured by half the difference of the two arcs GD, CB, intercepted by the two secants. Draw DF parallel to AC.

Because the lines AC, DF are parallel, the interior and exterior angles CAB, FDB are (Prop. 19.) equal. But the angle FDB is measured (Prop. 42.) by half the arc FB; the angle GAB is therefore also measured by half the arc FB.

Because the chords GC, DF are parallel, the arcs GD, CF are (Prop. 46.) equal; the arc FB is therefore the difference of the arc GD and the arc CFB. Where the angle A has for its measure half the difference of the arcs GD, CFB.

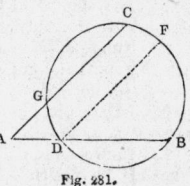

Fig. 281.

926. PROP. L. *The angle formed by two tangents is measured by half the difference of the two intercepted arcs.*

Let the angle CAB (*fig.* 282.) be formed by the two tangents AC, AB; this angle is measured by half the difference of the two arcs GLD, GFD. Draw DF parallel to AC.

Because the lines AC, DF are parallel, the interior and exterior angles CAB, FDB are (Prop. 19.) equal. But the angle FDB, formed by the tangent DB and the chord DF, is measured (Prop. 41.) by half the arc FD. Therefore the angle CAB is also measured by half the arc FD.

Because the tangent AC and the chord DF are parallel, the intercepted arcs GF GD are (Prop. 47.) equal. The arc FD is therefore the difference between the arc GLD and the arc GFD. Therefore the angle CAB, which is measured by half the arc FD, is also measured by half the difference of the arcs GLD, GFD.

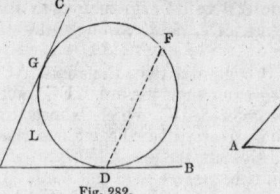 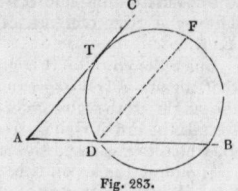

Fig. 282.   Fig. 283.

Corollary. In the same way it may be demonstrated that the angle formed by a tangent ATC (*fig.* 283.) and a secant ADB is measured by half the difference of the two intercepted arcs.

927. Prop. LI. *To raise a perpendicular at the extremity of a given line.*

At the extremity A (*fig.* 284.) of the given line AB let it be required to raise a perpendicular.

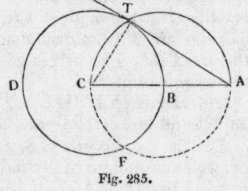

From any point C taken above the line AB describe a circumference passing through the point A and cutting the line AB in any other point, as G. Draw the diameter DG and the right line AD; this line AD will be perpendicular to the line AB.

The angle DAG at the circumference is measured (Prop. 42.) by half the arc DFG, which is half the circumference, because DCG is a diameter. The angle DAG is therefore measured by one fourth

Fig. 284.

part of the circumference, and consequently (Defin. 10.) is a right angle, whence the line AD is (Prop. 11.) perpendicular to the line AB.

Corollary. Hence it follows that the angle at the circumference which is subtended by a diameter must be a right angle.

928. Prop. LII. *From any point without a circle to draw a tangent to that circle.*

From the point A (*fig.* 285.) let it be required to draw a tangent to the circle DTB.

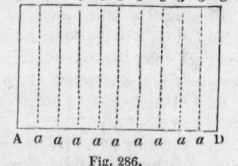

Draw from the centre C any right line CA; bisect this right line, and from the point of division B, as a centre, describe the arc CTA. Lastly, from the point A, and through the point T, in which the two arcs cut each other, draw the right line AT; this right line AT will be a tangent to the circle DTB. Draw the radius CT.

Fig. 285.

The angle CTA at the circumference, being subtended by the diameter CA, is (Corol. to Prop. 51.) a right angle; therefore the line TA is perpendicular to the extremity of the radius CT, and consequently (Prop. 40.) is a tangent to the circle DTB.

SURFACES.

929. Definitions.—1. A *mathematical point* has neither length, breadth, nor thickness. The *physical point,* now for consideration, has a supposed length and breadth exceedingly small.

2. A *physical line* is a series of physical points, and consequently its breadth is equal to that of the physical points whereof it is composed.

3. Since physical lines are composed of points, as numbers are composed of units, points may be called the *units* of lines.

4. As to multiply one number by another is to take or repeat the first number as many times as there are units in the second; so to *multiply one line by another* is to take or repeat the first line as many times as there are units, that is, physical points, in the second.

930. Prop. LIII. *The surface of a rectangle is equal to the product of its two sides.*

Let the rectangle be ABCD (*fig.* 286.). If the physical line AB be multiplied by the physical line AD, the product will be the surface ABCD.

If as many physical lines equal to AB as there are physical points in the line AD be raised perpendicularly upon AD, these lines AB, *ab,* &c. will fill up the whole surface of the rectangle ABCD. Wherefore the surface

B b b b b b b b C

A a a a a a a a a a D

Fig. 286.

ABCD is equal to the line AB taken as many times as there are physical points in the line AD; that is, (Defin. 4.) equal to the line AB multiplied by the line AD.

931. Prop. LIV. *The surface of a triangle is equal to half the product of its altitude and base.*

If from the vertex of any angle A (*fig.* 287.) of the triangle BAC be drawn AD, per-

pendicular to the opposite side BC, this perpendicular is called the *height*, and the side BC
the *base* of the triangle. Now the surface of the triangle is
equal to half the product of the height AD and the base BC.

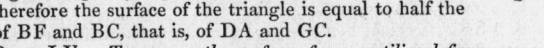

Produce BC both ways; through the point A draw FG
parallel to BC, and raise the two perpendiculars BF, CG.

Because the rectangle BFGC and the triangle BAC are
between the same parallels, and have the same bases, the triangle is (Prop. 29.) half the rectangle. But the surface of
the rectangle is equal (Prop. 53.) to the product of BF and
BC. Wherefore the surface of the triangle is equal to half the
product of BF and BC, that is, of DA and GC.

Fig. 287.

932. Prop. LV. *To measure the surface of any rectilineal figure.*

Let ABCDFA (*fig.* 288.) be the rectilineal figure, whereof it is required to find the
surface.

Divide the whole figure into triangles by drawing the lines
CA, CF. Then, drawing a perpendicular from the point B
to the side CA, multiply these two lines; the half of their product will (Prop. 54.) give the surface of the triangle ABC.
In the same manner let the surfaces of the remaining triangles
ACF, FCD be found. These three surfaces added together
will give the whole surface of the figure ABCDFA.

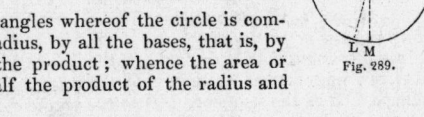

933. Prop. LVI. *The area of a circle is equal to half the product of its radius and circumference.*

If the radius of the circle C (*fig.* 289.) be multiplied by   Fig. 288.
its circumference, the half of the product will give the surface of the circle.

Two physical points being manifestly not sufficient to make a curve line, this must require at least three. If, therefore, all the physical points of a circumference be taken two
by two, these will compose a great number of small right lines. From
the extremities L, M of one of these small right lines if two radii LC
MC be drawn, a small triangle LCM will be formed, the surface of
which will be equal to half the product of its height; that is, the radius
and its base.

To find the surface of all the small triangles whereof the circle is composed, multiply the height, that is, the radius, by all the bases, that is, by
the circumference, and take the half of the product; whence the area or   Fig. 289.
surface of the circle will be equal to half the product of the radius and
circumference.

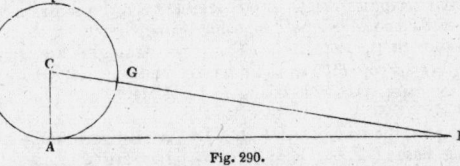

934. Prop. LVII. *To draw a triangle equal to a given circle.*

Let it be required to form a triangle the surface of which shall be equal to that of the
circle AGFDA (*fig.* 290.).

At the extremity of any radius CA of the circle, raise a
perpendicular AB equal to the
circumference AGFD, and draw
the right line CB. The surface of the triangle BCA will
be equal to that of the circle
AGFDA.

Fig. 290.

The surface of the circle is equal (Prop. 56.) to half the product of the radius CA and
the circumference, or the line AB. The surface of the triangle is also equal (Prop. 54.)
to half the product of its height CA, or radius, and its base BA, or circumference. Therefore the surface of the triangle is equal to that of the circle.

PROPORTION.

935. Definitions. — 1. The ratio of one quantity to another is the number of times which
the first contains the second; thus the ratio of 12 to 3 is four, because 12 contains
3 four times; or, more universally, *ratio* is the comparative magnitude of one quantity with respect to another.

2. Four quantities are *proportional*, or *in geometrical proportion*, or two quantities are said
to have the same ratio with two others, when the first contains or is contained in the
second, exactly the same number of times which the third contains or is contained in
the fourth; thus, the four numbers 6, 3, 8, 4 are proportionals, because 6 contains 3 as
many times as 8 contains 4, and 3 is contained in 6 as many times as 4 is contained in
8, that is, twice; which is thus expressed: 6 is to 3 as 8 to 4; or 3 is to 6 as 4 to 8.

936. Prop. LVIII *Parallelograms which are between the same parallels are to one another as their bases.*

Let the two parallelograms ABCD, FGLM (*fig.* 291.) be between the same parallels BL, AM, the surface of the parallelogram ABCD contains the surface of the parallelogram FGLM as many times as the base AD contains the base FM. Suppose, for example, that the base AD is triple of the base FM; in this case the surface ABCD will also be triple of the surface FGLM.

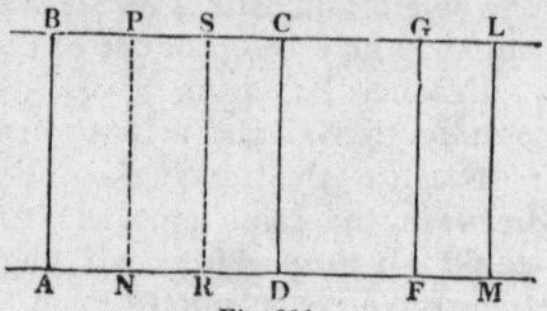

Divide the base AD into three parts, each of which is equal to the base FM, and draw from the points of division the lines NP, RS parallel to the side AB.

Fig. 291.

The parallelograms ABPN, FGLM being between the same parallels and having equal bases, the parallelogram ABPN is (Prop. 30.) equal to the parallelogram FGLM. For the same reason, the parallelograms NPSR, RSCD are also equal to the parallelogram FGLM. The parallelogram ABCD is therefore composed of three parallelograms, each of which is equal to the parallelogram FGLM. Consequently the parallelogram ABCD is triple of the parallelogram FGLM.

937. PROP. LIX. *Triangles which are between the same parallels are to one another as their bases.*

Let the two triangles ABC, DFG (*fig.* 292.) be between the same parallels LF, AG, the surface of the triangle ABC contains the surface of the triangle DFG as many times as the base AC contains the base DG. Suppose, for example, that the base AC is triple of the base DG, in this case the surface ABC will be triple of the surface DFG.

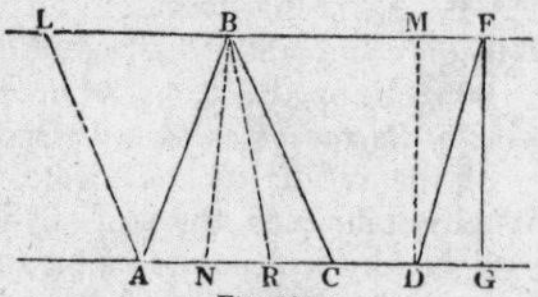

Divide the base AC into three equal parts, AN, NR, RC, each of which is equal to the base DG, and draw the right lines BN, BR.

Fig. 292.

The triangles ABN, DFG being between the same parallels and having equal bases, the triangle ABN is (Prop. 31.) equal to the triangle DFG. For the same reason, the triangles NBR, RBC are each equal to the triangle DFG. The triangle ABC is therefore composed of three triangles, each of which is equal to the triangle DFG. Wherefore the triangle ABC is triple of the triangle DFG.

938. PROP. LX. *If a line be drawn in a triangle parallel to one of its sides, it will cut the other two sides proportionally.*

In the triangle BAC (*fig.* 293.), if the line DF be parallel to the side BC, it will cut the other two sides in such manner that the segment AD will be to the segment DB as the segment AF is to the segment FC. Suppose, for instance, the segment AD to be triple of the segment DB, the segment AF will be triple of the segment FC. Draw the diagonals DC, FB.

The triangles AFD, DFB are between the same parallels, as will be easily conceived by supposing a line drawn through the point F parallel to the side AB. These two triangles are therefore to one another (Prop. 59.) as their bases; and since the base AD is triple of the base DB, the triangle AFD will be triple of the triangle DFB.

Fig. 293.

Again, the triangles BFD, FDC are between the same parallels DF, BC, and upon the same base DF. These two triangles are therefore (Prop. 31.) equal; and since the triangle AFD is triple of the triangle DFB, it will also be triple of the triangle FDC.

Lastly, the triangles ADF, FDC are between the same parallels, as will be easily conceived by supposing a line drawn through the point D parallel to the side AC. These two triangles are therefore to one another (Prop. 59.) as their bases; and since the triangle ADF is triple of the triangle FDC, the base AF will be triple of the base FC.

939. PROP. LXI. *Equiangular triangles have their homologous sides proportional.*

In the two triangles ABC, CDF (*fig.* 294.), if the angle A be equal to the angle C, the angle B equal to the angle D, and the angle C equal to the angle F; the side AC, for example, opposite to the angle B is to the side CF opposite to the angle D as the side AB opposite to the angle C is to the side CD opposite to the angle F. Place the two triangles so that the sides AC, CF shall form one right line, and produce the sides AB, FD till they meet in G.

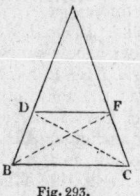
Fig. 294.

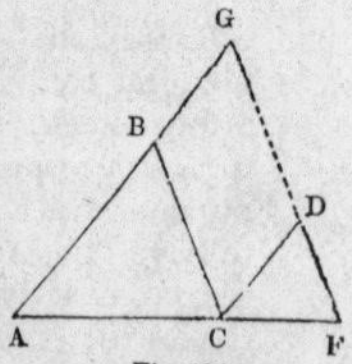

The interior and exterior angles GAF, DCF being equal, the lines GA, DC are (Prop. 20.) parallel. In like manner, the alternate angles GFA, BCA on the same sides being equal, the lines GF, BC are (Prop. 20.) parallel. Wherefore the quadrilateral figure BGDC is a parallelogram, and consequently its opposite sides are equal. In the triangle GAF the line BC, being parallel to the side

FG, cuts (Prop. 60.) the other two sides proportionally; that is, AC is to CF as AB is to BG, or its equal CD.

940. Prop. LXII. *Triangles the sides of which are proportional are equiangular.*

In the two triangles BAC, FDG (*fig.* 295.), if the side AB is to the side DF as the side BC is to the side FG and as the side AC to the side DG, these two triangles have their angles equal.

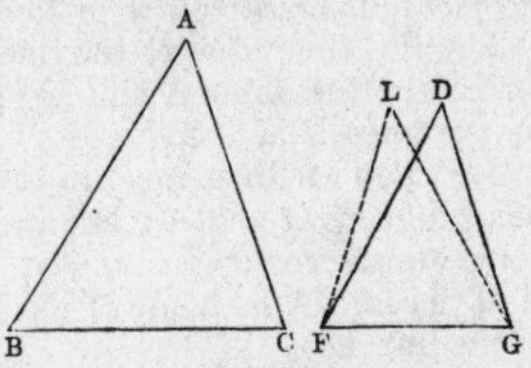

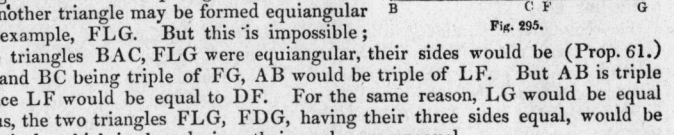

Fig. 295.

Let the side AB be supposed triple of the side DF; the side AC must be triple of the side DG, and the side BC triple of FG.

If the triangle FDG be not equiangular with the triangle BAC, another triangle may be formed equiangular with it; for example, FLG. But this is impossible; for if the two triangles BAC, FLG were equiangular, their sides would be (Prop. 61.) proportional; and BC being triple of FG, AB would be triple of LF. But AB is triple of DF; whence LF would be equal to DF. For the same reason, LG would be equal to DG. Thus, the two triangles FLG, FDG, having their three sides equal, would be (Prop. 5.) identical; which is absurd, since their angles are unequal.

941. Prop. LXIII. *Triangles which have an angle in one equal to an angle in the other, and the sides about these angles proportional, are equiangular.*

If in the two triangles BAC, NMP (*fig.* 296.) the angle A be equal to the angle M, and the side AB be to the side MN as the side AC is to the side MP, the two triangles are equiangular.

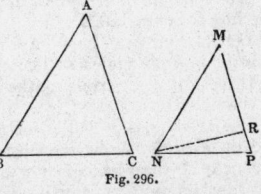

Fig. 296.

If AB be triple of MN, AC must be triple of MP. Now, if the angle MNP, for example, is not equal to the angle ABC, another angle may be made, as MNR, which shall be equal to it. But this is impossible; for the two triangles BAC, NMR, having two angles equal, would be equiangular, and consequently (Prop. 61.) would have their sides proportional; wherefore, AB being triple of MN, AC would be triple of MR, which cannot be, since AC is triple of MP.

942. Prop. LXIV. *A right line which bisects any angle of a triangle divides the side opposite to the bisected angle into two segments, which are proportional to the two other sides.*

In the triangle BAC, let the angle BAC be bisected by the right line AD, making the angle r equal to the angle s. The segment BD is to the segment DC as the side BA to the side AC.

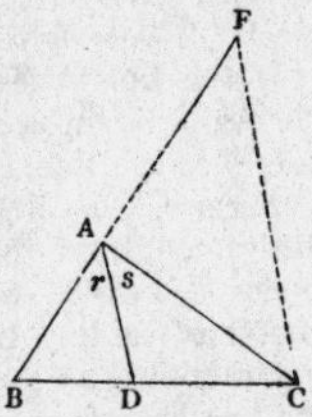

Produce the side BA, and draw CF parallel to DA.

The lines DA, CF being parallel, the interior and exterior angles r, F are (Prop. 19.) equal, and the alternate angles s, C are (Prop. 17.) also equal. And since the angle r is equal to the angle s, the angle F will also be equal to the angle C; and consequently the side AF is equal to the side AC.

In the triangle BFC, the line AD being parallel to the side FC; BD (Prop. 60.) will be to DC as BA is to AF, or its equal AC.

Fig. 297.

943. Prop. LXV. *To find a fourth proportional to three given lines.*

Let the three lines be A, B, C (*fig.* 298.), it is required to find a fourth line D, such that the line A shall be to the line B as the line C is to the line D.

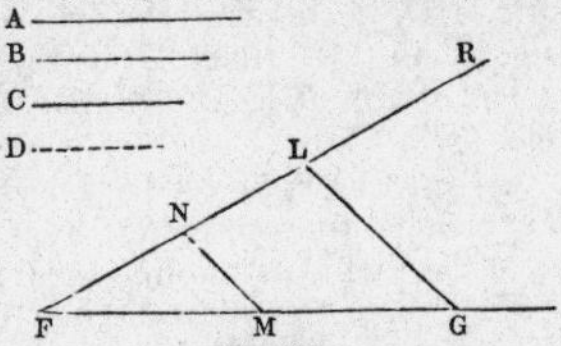

Form any angle RFG, make FM equal to the line A, MG equal to the line B, and FN equal to the line C; draw the right line MN, and through the point G draw GL parallel to MN; NL will be the fourth proportional required.

In the triangle FLG the line NM, being parallel to the side LG, cuts the other two sides (Prop. 60.) proportionally. Wherefore FM is to MG as FN is to NL; that is, A is to B as C is to D.

Fig. 298.

944. Prop. LXVI. *To find a third proportional to two given lines.*

Let the two lines be A, B (*fig.* 299.), it is required to find a third line C, such that the line A shall be to the line B as the line B is to the line C.

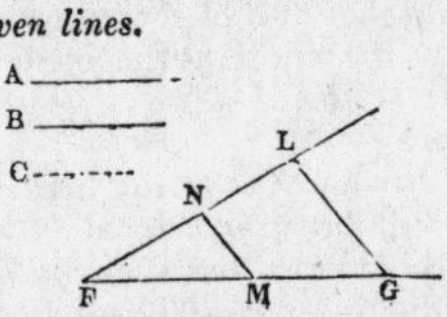

Form any angle LFG, make FM equal to the line A, MG equal to the line B, and FN equal to the line B; draw the right line MN, and through the point G draw GL parallel to MN; NL will be the third proportional required.

In the triangle FLG the line NM, being parallel to the side LG, cuts the other two

Fig. 299.

sides (Prop. 60.) proportionally. Wherefore FM is to MG as FN is to NL; that is, A is to B as B is to C.

945. Prop. LXVII.　*If four lines be proportional, the rectangle or product of the extremes is equal to the rectangle or product of the means.*

Let the line A be to the line B as the line C is to the line D (*fig.* 300.); the rectangle formed by the lines A and D is equal to the rectangles formed by the lines B and C.

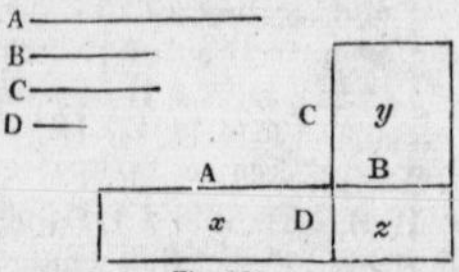

Let the four lines meet in a common point, forming at that point four right angles; and draw the lines parallel to them to complete the rectangles *x, y, z*.

If the line A be triple of the line B, the line C will be triple of the line D.

Fig. 300.

The rectangles or parallelograms *x, z* being between the same parallels, are to one another as their bases. Since the base A is triple of the base B, the rectangle *x* is triple of the rectangle *z*. In like manner, the rectangles or parallelograms *y, z*, being between the same parallels, are to one another as their bases : since the base C is triple of the base D, the rectangle *y* is therefore triple of the rectangle *z*. Wherefore, the rectangle *x* being triple of the rectangle *z*, and the rectangle *y* being triple of the same rectangle *z*, these two rectangles *x* and *y* are equal to one another.

946. Prop. LXVIII.　*Four lines which have the rectangle or product of the extremes equal to the rectangle or product of the means are proportional.*

Let the four lines A, B, C, D (*fig.* 301.) be such that the rectangle of A and D is equal to the rectangle of B and C, the line A will be to the line B as the line C to the line D.

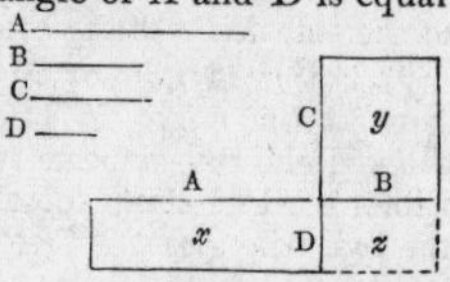

Let the four lines meet in a common point, forming at that point four right angles, and complete the rectangles *x, y, z*.

If the line A be triple of the line B, the line C will be triple of the line D.

Fig. 301.

The rectangles *x* and *z*, being between the same parallels, are to one another as their bases : since the base A is triple of the base B, the rectangle *x* will be therefore triple of the rectangle *z*. And the rectangle *y* is, by supposition, equal to the rectangle *x*; the rectangle *y* is therefore also triple of the rectangle *z*.

But the rectangles *y, z*, being between the same parallels, are to one another as their bases. Hence, since the rectangle *y* is triple of the rectangle *z*, the base C is also triple of the base D.

947. Prop. LXIX.　*If four lines be proportional, they are also proportional alternately.*

If the line A is to the line B as the line C to the line D (*fig.* 302.), they will be in proportion *alternately;* that is, the line A will be to the line C as the line B to the line D.

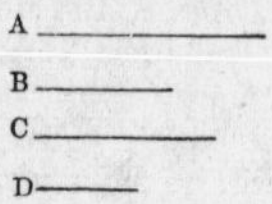

Because the line A is to the line B as the line C is to the line D, the rectangle of the extremes A and D is equal to the rectangle of the means B and C; whence it follows (Prop. 68.) that the line A is to the line C as the line B is to the line D.

Fig. 302

Otherwise, — Suppose the line A to be triple of the line B, the line C will be triple of the line D. Hence, instead of saying A is to B as C to D, we may say three times B is to B as three times D is to D. Now it is manifest that three times B is to three times D as B is to D. Therefore the line A (which is equal to three times B) is to the line C (which is equal to three times D) as the line B is to the line D.

948. Prop. LXX.　*If four lines be proportional, they will be proportional by composition.*

Let the line A be to the line B as the line C is to the line D (*fig.* 303.), they will be proportional by *composition ;* that is, the line A joined to the line B will be to the line B as the line C joined to the line D is to the line D.

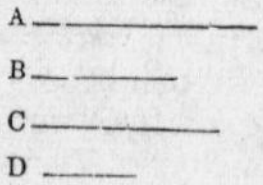

If the line A contain the line B, for example, three times, and the line C contain the line D three times; the line A joined to the line B will contain the line B four times, and the line C joined to the line D will contain the line D four times. Therefore the line A joined to the line B is to the line B as the line C joined to the line D is to the line D.

Fig. 303.

949. Prop. LXXI.　*If four lines be proportional, they will be also proportional by division.*

If the line A is to the line B as the line C is to the line D (*fig.* 304.), they will be proportional by *division ;* that is, the line A wanting the line B is to the line B as the line C wanting the line D is to the line D.

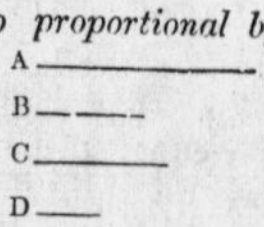

If the line A contain the line B, for example, three times, and the line C contain the line D three times, the line A wanting the line B will contain the line B only twice ; and the line C wanting the line D will also contain the line D

Fig. 304.

twice. Therefore the line A wanting the line B is to the line B as the line C wanting the line D is to the line D.

950. Prop. LXXII. *If three lines be proportional, the first is to the third as the square of the first is to the square of the second.*

If the line CD is to the line cd as the line cd is to a third line x (*fig.* 305.), the line CD is to the line x as the square of the line CD is to the square of the line cd. Take CF equal to the line x, and draw the perpendicular FB.

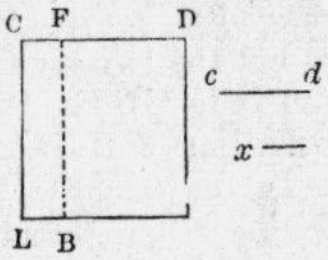

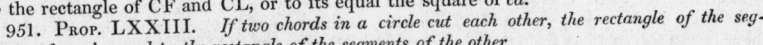

Fig. 305.

Since the line CD is to the line cd as the line cd is to the line CF, the rectangle of the extremes CF, CD, or CL is equal (Prop. 67.) to the rectangle of the means, that is, to the square of cd.

Again, the square of CD and the rectangle of the lines CF, CL, being between the same parallels, are to one another (Prop. 58.) as their bases. Therefore CD is to CF, or x, as the square of CD is to the rectangle of CF and CL, or to its equal the square of cd.

951. Prop. LXXIII. *If two chords in a circle cut each other, the rectangle of the segments of one is equal to the rectangle of the segments of the other*

Let the two chords AB, CD (*fig.* 306.) in the circle cut each other in the point F, the rectangle of AF, FB is equal to the rectangle of CF, FD. Draw the two right lines AC, DB. Because in the triangles CAF, BDF the angles at the circumference A and D are both measured (Prop. 42.) by half the arc CB, they are equal. Because the angles C and B are both measured (Prop. 42.) by half the arc AD, these angles are also equal. And the angles at F are equal, because they are vertical. These two triangles are therefore equiangular, and consequently (Prop. 61.) their sides are proportional. Wherefore the side AF opposite to the angle C is to the side FD opposite to the angle B as the side CF opposite to the angle A is to the side FB opposite to the angle D. Therefore (Prop. 69.) the rectangle of the extremes AF, FB is equal to the rectangle of the means CF, FD.

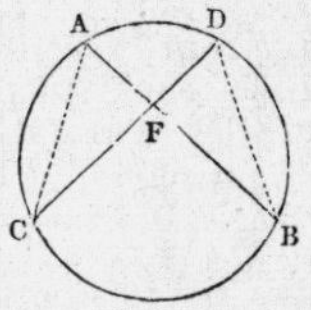

Fig. 306.

952. Prop. LXXIV. *To find a mean proportional between two given lines.*

Let there be two lines A, C (*fig.* 307.), it is required to find a third line B, such that the line A shall be to the line B as the line B is to the line C.

Place the lines A and C in such manner that they shall form one right line DGL, and bisect this right line in the point F. From the point F, as a centre, describe the circumference of a circle DMLN; then, at the point G, where the two lines are joined, raise the perpendicular GM; GM is the mean proportional sought between the lines A and C. Produce MG to N.

Fig. 307.

Because the chords DL, MN cut each other at the point G, the rectangle of the segments DG, GL is (Prop. 73.) equal to the rectangle of the segments MG, GN.

Because the radius FL is perpendicular to the chord MN, FL (Prop. 38.) bisects MN; therefore GN is equal to GM.

Lastly, because the rectangle of the extremes DG, GL is equal to the rectangle of the means GM, GN, or its equal GM, DG is to GM as GM is to GL. Therefore GM is a mean proportional between DG and GL, that is, between the lines A and C.

953. Prop. LXXV. *The bases and altitudes of equal triangles are in reciprocal or inverse ratio.*

Let the two triangles ABC, DFG (*fig.* 308.) be equal; the base AC will be to the base DG, as the perpendicular FM to the perpendicular BL; that is, the bases and altitudes are in *reciprocal* or *inverse* ratio.

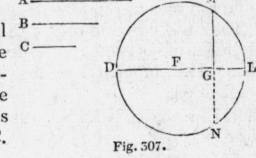

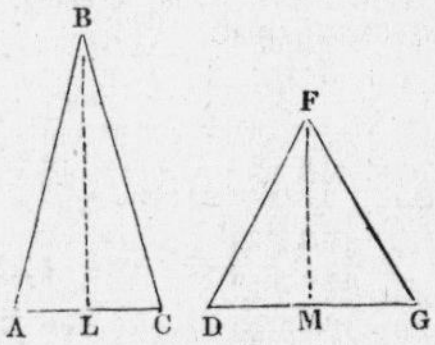

Fig. 308.

The triangle ABC (Prop. 54.) is half the product or rectangle of the base AC and the altitude BL. Again, the triangle DFG is (Prop. 54.) half the product or rectangle of the base DG and the altitude FM. The two triangles being equal, the two rectangles, which are double of the triangles, will therefore also be equal.

Again, because the rectangle of the extremes AC, BL is equal to the rectangle of the means DG, FM; AC (Prop. 68.) is to DG as FM is to BL.

954. Prop. LXXVI. *Triangles the bases and altitudes whereof are in reciprocal or inverse ratio are equal.*

In the two triangles ABC, DFG (*fig.* 309.), if the base AC be to the base DG as the perpendicular FM to the perpendicular BL, the surfaces of the two triangles are equal.

Because AC is to DG as FM is to BL, the product or rectangle of the extremes AC, BL is (Prop. 67.) equal to the product or rectangle of the means DG, FM. The halves (Corol. to Prop. 27.) of these two rectangles, namely, triangles ABC, DFG, are therefore equal.

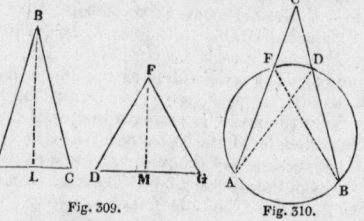

Fig. 309.   Fig. 310.

955. Prop. LXXVII. *Two secants drawn from the same point to a circle are in the inverse ratio of the parts which lie out of the circle.*

Let the two secants be CA, CB (*fig.* 310.); CA is to CB as CD is to CF. Draw the right lines FB, DA.

In the triangles CDA, CFB the angles at the circumference A and B, being both measured (Prop. 42.) by half the arc FD, are equal, and the angle C is common to the two triangles. These two triangles are therefore (Prop. 23.) equiangular and (Prop. 61.) have their sides proportional. Wherefore the side CA of the first triangle is to the side CB of the second triangle as the side CD of the first triangle is to the side CF of the second triangle.

956. Prop. LXXVIII. *The tangent to a circle is a mean proportional between the secant and the part of the secant which lies out of the circle.*

In the circle ABD, CB (*fig.* 311.) being secant, and CA tangent, CB is to CA as CA is to CD. Draw the right lines AB, AD.

The triangles CAB, CDA have the angle C common to both. Also the angle B is measured (Prop. 42.) by half the arc AFD; and the angle CAD formed by the tangent AC and the chord AD is measured (Prop. 41.) by half the same arc AFD. The two triangles CAB, CDA, having their two angles equal, are (Prop. 23.), equiangular, and consequently (Prop. 61.) have their sides proportional. Hence the side CB of the greater triangle opposite to the angle CAB is to the side CA of the smaller triangle opposite to the angle D as the side CA of the greater triangle opposite to the angle B is to the side CD of the smaller triangle opposite to the angle A.

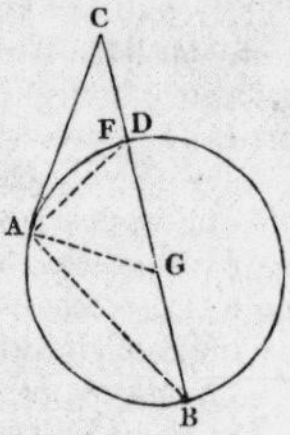

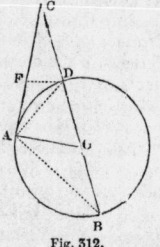

Fig. 311.

Corollary. From this proposition is suggested a new method of finding a mean proportional between two given lines.

Take CB equal to one of the given lines, and CD equal to the other; bisect DB; from the point of division, as a centre, describe the circumference DAB; and draw the tangent CA. This tangent is a mean proportional between CB and CD, as appears from the proposition.

957. Prop. LXXIX. *To cut a given line in extreme and mean ratio.*

Let it be required to divide the line CA (*fig.* 312.) in extreme and mean ratio; that is, to divide it in such a manner that the whole line shall be to the greater part as the greater part is to the less.

At the extremity A of the line CA raise a perpendicular AG equal to half the line CA; from the point G, as a centre, with the radius GA, describe the circumference ADB; draw the line CB through the centre, and take CF equal to CD; the line CA will be divided at the point F in extreme and mean ratio.

Because (Prop. 78.) CB is to CA as CA is to CD, by division, (Prop. 71.) CB wanting CA or its equal DB is to CA, as CA wanting CD or its equal CF is to CD; that is, CD or CF is to CA as FA is to CD or CF; or, inversely, CA is to CF as CF is to FA, or the line AC is cut in extreme and mean ratio.

Fig. 312.

SIMILAR FIGURES.

958. Definitions. — 1. Figures are *similar* which are composed of an equal number of physical points disposed in the same manner. Thus, the figures ABCDF, abcdf (*fig.* 313.) are similar, if every point of the first figure has its corresponding point placed in the same manner in the second.

Hence it follows, that if the first figure is, for example, three times greater than the second, the points of which it is composed are three times greater than those of the second figure.

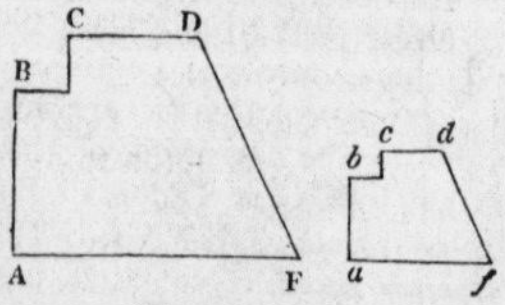

Fig. 313.

2. In similar figures, those lines are said to be *homologous* which are composed of an equal number of corresponding points.

959. Prop. LXXX. *In similar figures the homologous sides are proportional.*

Let the similar figures be ABCDF, *abcdf* (*fig.* 314.), and the homologous lines CA, *ca*, CF, *cf*; CA is to CF as *ca* to *cf*.

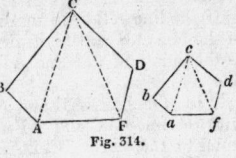

Fig. 314.

Since the lines CA, *ca* are homologous, they are composed of an equal number of corresponding points; as are also the homologous lines CF, *cf*. If, for instance, the line CA is composed of 40 equal points, and the line CF of 30, the line *ca* will necessarily be composed of 40 points, and the line *cf* of 30; and it is manifest that 40 is to 30 as 40 to 30. Therefore CA is to CF as *ca* to *cf*.

960. Prop. LXXXI. *The circumferences of circles are as their radii.*

The circumference DCB (*fig.* 315.) is to the radius AB as the circumference *dcb* is to the radius *ab*.

All circles are similar figures, that is, are composed of an equal number of points disposed in the same manner. They have therefore (Prop. 80.) their homologous lines proportional. Therefore the circumference DCB is to the radius AB as the circumference *dcb* is to the radius *ab*.

961. Prop. LXXXII. *Similar figures are to each other as the squares of their homologous sides.*

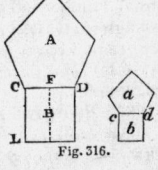

Fig. 315.

Let the two similar figures be A, *a* (*fig.* 316.) Upon the homologous sides CD, *cd* form the squares B, *b*. The surface A is to the surface *a* as the square B is to the square *b*.

Since the figures A, *a* are similar, they are composed of an equal number of corresponding points; and since the homologous sides CD, *cd* are composed of an equal number of points, the squares drawn upon these lines B, *b* are also composed of an equal number of points.

If it be supposed that the surface A is composed of 1000 points and the square B of 400 points, the surface A will be also composed of 1000 points and the square *b* of 400. Now it is manifest that 1000 is to 400 as 1000 to 400. Wherefore the surface A is to the square B as the surface *a* is to the square *b*; and, alternately (Prop. 69.), the surface A is to the surface *a* as the square B to the square *b*.

Corollary. It follows that if any three similar figures be formed upon the three sides of a right-angled triangle, the figure upon the hypothenuse will be equal to the other two taken together; for these three figures will be as the squares of their sides; therefore, since the square of the hypothenuse is equal to the two squares of the other sides, the figure formed upon the hypothenuse will also be equal to the two other similar figures formed upon the other sides.

962. Prop. LXXXIII. *Circles are to each other as the squares of their radii.*

Let two circles DCB, *dcb* (*fig.* 317.) be drawn.

The surface contained within the circumference DCB is to the surface contained within the circumference *dcb* as the square formed upon the radius AB to the square formed upon the radius *ab*.

The two circles, being similar figures, are composed of an equal number of corresponding points, and the radii AB, *ab* being composed of an equal number of points, the squares of these radii will also be composed of an equal number of points.

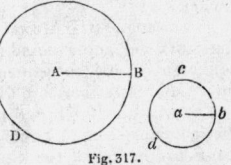

Fig. 317.

Suppose, for example, that the greater circle DCB is composed of 800 points, and the square of the greater radius AB of 300 points, the smaller circle *dcb* will also be composed of 800 points, and the square of the smaller radius of 300. Now it is manifest that 800 is to 300 as 800 to 300. Therefore the greater circle DCB is to the square of its radius AB as the smaller circle *dcb* is to the square of its radius *ab*; and, alternately, the greater circle is to the lesser circle as the greater square is to the lesser square.

963. Prop. LXXXIV. *Similar triangles are equiangular.*

If the two triangles ABC, *abc* (*fig.* 318.) be composed of an equal number of points disposed in the same manner, they are equiangular.

For, since the triangles ABC, *abc* are similar figures, they have their sides (Prop. 80.) proportional; they are therefore (Prop. 62.) equiangular.

964. Prop. LXXXV. *Equiangular triangles are similar.*

If the triangles ABC, *abc* are equiangular, they are also similar. See *fig.* 318.

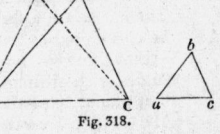

Fig. 318.

If the triangle ABC were not similar to the triangle *abc*, another triangle might be formed upon the line AC; for example, ADC, which should be similar to the triangle *abc*. Now, the triangle ADC, being similar to the triangle *abc*,

will also (Prop. 84.) be equiangular to *abc*; which is impossible, since the triangle ABC is supposed equiangular to *abc*.

965. Prop. LXXXVI. *If four lines are proportional, their squares are also proportional.*

If the line AB be to the line AC as the line AD is to the line AF (*fig.* 319,), the square of the line AB will be to the square of the line AC as the square of the line AD is to the square of the line AF.

With the lines AB and AD form an angle BAD; with the lines AC and AF form another angle CAF equal to the angle BAD, and draw the right lines BD, CF.

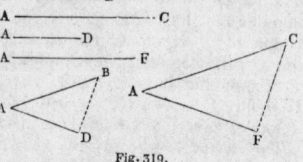

Fig. 319.

Because AB is to AC as AD to AF, and the contained angles are equal, the two triangles BAD, CAF have their sides about equal angles proportional; they are therefore (Prop. 63.) equiangular, and consequently (Prop. 85.) similar : whence they are to one another (Prop. 82.) as the squares of their homologous sides. If, then, the triangle BAD be a third part of the triangle CAF, the square of the side AB will be a third part of the square of the side AC, and the square of the side AD will be a third part of the square of the side AF. Wherefore these four squares will be proportional.

966. Prop. LXXXVII. *Similar rectilineal figures may be divided into an equal number of similar triangles.*

Let the similar figures be ABCDF, *abcdf*, and draw the homologous lines CA, *ca*, CF, *cf*; these two figures will be divided into an equal number of similar triangles.

The triangles BCA, *bca* (*fig.* 320.), being composed of an equal number of corresponding points, are similar. The triangles ACF, *acf* and the triangles FCD, *fcd* are also, for the same reason, similar. Wherefore the similar figures ABCDF, *abcdf* are divided into an equal number of similar triangles.

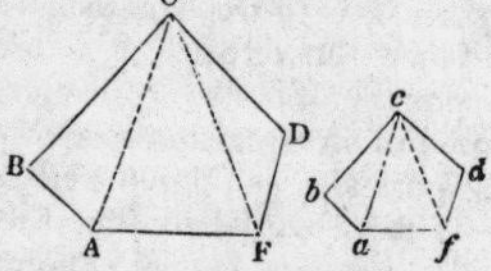

Fig. 320.

967. Prop. LXXXVIII. *Similar figures are equiangular.*

The similar figures ABCDF, *abcdf* (see *fig.* preced. Prop.) have their angles equal. Draw the homologous lines CA, *ca*, CF, *cf*. The triangles BCA, *bca* are similar, and consequently equiangular. Therefore the angle B is equal to the angle *b*, the angle BAC to the angle *bac*, and the angle BCA to the angle *bca*. The triangles ACF, *acf*, FCD, *fcd* are also equiangular, because they are similar. Therefore all the angles of the similar figures ABCDF, *abcdf* are equal.

968. Prop. LXXXIX. *Equiangular figures the sides of which are proportional are similar.*

If the figures ABCDF, *abcdf* (*fig.* 321.) have their angles equal and their sides proportional, they are similar. Draw the right lines CA, *ca*, CF, *cf*.

The triangles CBA, *cba*, have two sides proportional and the contained angle equal; they are therefore (Prop. 63.) equiangular, and consequently (Prop. 85.) similar. The lines CA, *ca* are therefore (Prop. 80.) proportional.

The triangles CAF, *caf* have two sides proportional and the contained angle equal; for if from the equal angles BAF, *baf* be taken the equal angles BAC, *bac*, there will remain the equal angles CAF, *caf*. These two triangles are therefore equiangular, and consequently similar. In the same manner it may be proved that the triangles CFD, *cfd* are similar.

Fig. 321.

The two figures ABCDF, *abcdf* are then composed of an equal number of similar triangles; that is, they are composed of an equal number of points disposed in the same manner, or are similar.

PLANES.

969. Definitions. — 1. A plane is a surface, such that if a right line applied to it touch it in two points it will touch it in every other point. The surface of a fluid at rest, or of a well-polished table, may be considered as a plane.

2. A right line is *perpendicular* to a plane if it make right angles with all lines which can be drawn from any point in that plane. Thus BA (*fig.* 322.) is perpendicular to the plane MLGFPN, because it makes right angles with the lines AM, AL, AG, &c. drawn from the point A.

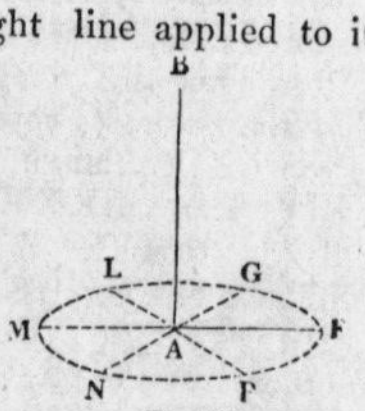

3 Let AB (*fig.* 323.) be the common intersection of two planes.

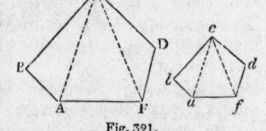

Fig. 322.

If two right lines LM, FG be drawn, in these two planes, perpendicular to the line

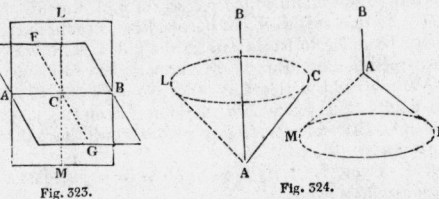

Fig. 323.   Fig. 324.

AB, these will form four angles at the point C, which are called the *inclinations* of the two planes, or the angles formed by the two planes.

4. If the line AB (*fig.* 324.) revolve about itself, without changing its place, the line AC, which makes an acute angle with AB, will describe in the revolution a concave surface LAC; and the line AD, which makes an obtuse angle with AB, will describe in the revolution a convex surface MAD.

5. But the line AF (*fig.* Defin. 2.), which makes a right angle with AB, will describe in the revolution a surface which will be neither concave nor convex, but plane : and the line AB will be perpendicular to the plane MLGFPN, because it will make right angles with the lines AM, AL, AG, &c. drawn from the point A in that plane.

6. Two planes are *parallel* when all perpendiculars drawn from one to the other are equal. See *fig.* 325., wherein AB, CD are equal between the surfaces LM, FG.

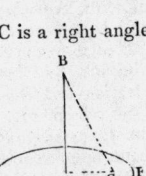

970. Prop. XC. *A perpendicular is the shortest line which can be drawn from any point to a plane.*

Fig. 325.

From the point B (*fig.* 326.), let the right line BA be drawn perpendicular to the plane DF; any other line, as BC, will be longer than the line BA. Upon the plane draw the right line AC.

Because the line BA is perpendicular to the plane DF, the angle BAC is a right angle. The square of BC is therefore (Prop. 32.) equal to the squares of BA and AC taken together. Consequently the square of BC is greater than the square of BA, and the line BC longer than the line BA.

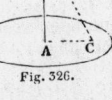

Fig. 326.

971. Prop. XCI. *A perpendicular measures the distance of any point from a plane.*

The distance of one point from another is measured by a right line, because it is the shortest line which can be drawn from one point to another. So the distance from a point to a line is measured by a perpendicular, because this line is the shortest which can be drawn from the point to the line. In like manner, the distance from a point to a plane must be measured by a perpendicular drawn from that point to the plane, because this is the shortest line which can be drawn from the point to the plane.

972. Prop. XCII. *The common intersection of two planes is a right line.*

Let the two planes ALBMA, AFBGA (*fig.* 327.) intersect each other; the line which is common to both is a right line. Draw a right line from the point A to the point B.

Because the right line AB touches the two planes in the points A and B, it will touch them (Defin. 1.) in all other points; this line therefore, is common to the two planes. Wherefore the common intersection of the two planes is a right line.

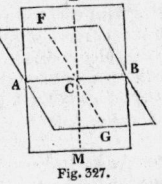

Fig. 327.

973. Prop. XCIII. *If three points, not in a right line, are common to two planes, these two planes are one and the same plane.*

Let two planes be supposed to be placed upon one another, in such manner that the three points A, B, C shall be common to the two planes; all their other points will also be common, and the two planes will be one and the same plane. The point D, for example, is common to both planes. Draw the right lines AB, CD.

Because the right line AB (*fig.* 328.) touches the two planes in the points A and B, it will touch them (Defin. 1.) in every other point; it will therefore touch them in the point F. The point F is therefore common to the two planes.

Again, because the right line CD touches the two planes in the points C and F, it will touch them in the point D; therefore the point D is common to the two planes. The same may be shown concerning every other point. Wherefore the two planes coincide in all points, or are one and the same plane.

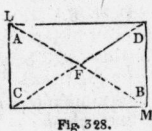

Fig. 328.

974. Prop. XCIV. *If a right line be perpendicular to two right lines which cut each other, it will be perpendicular to the plane of these right lines.*

Let the line AB (*fig.* 329.) make right angles with the lines AC, AD, it will be perpendicular to the plane which passes through these lines.

If the line AB were not perpendicular to the FDCG, another plane might be made to pass through the point A, to which the AB would be perpendicular. But this is impossible; for, since the angles BAC, BAD are right angles, this other plane (Defin. 2.) must pass through the points C, D; it would therefore (Prop. 93.) be the same with the plane FDCG, since these two planes would have three common points A, C, D.

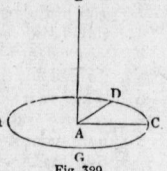

Fig. 329.

975. Prop. XCV. *From a given point in a plane to raise a perpendicular to that plane.*

Let it be required to raise a perpendicular from the point A (*fig.* 330.) in the plane LM.

Form a rectangle CDFG, divide it into two rectangles, having a common section AB, and place these rectangles upon the plane LM in such a manner that the bases of the two rectangles AC, AG shall be in the plane LM, and form any angle with each other; the line AB shall be perpendicular to the plane LM. The line AB makes right angles with the two lines AC, AG, which, by supposition, are in the plane LM; it is therefore (Prop. 94.) perpendicular to the plane LM.

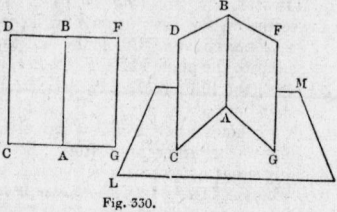

Fig. 330.

976. Prop. XCVI. *If two planes cut each other at right angles, and a right line be drawn in one of the planes perpendicular to their common intersection, it will be perpendicular to the other plane.*

Let the two planes AFBG, ALBM (*fig.* 331.), cut each other at right angles; if the line LC be perpendicular to their common intersection, it is also perpendicular to the plane AFBG. Draw CG perpendicular to AB.

Because the lines CL, CG are perpendicular to the common intersection AB, the angle LCG (Defin. 3.) is the angle of inclination of the two planes. Since the two planes cut each other perpendicularly, the angle of inclination LCG is therefore a right angle.

And because the line LC is perpendicular to the two lines CA, CG in the plane ABFG, it is (Prop. 94.) perpendicular to the plane AFBG.

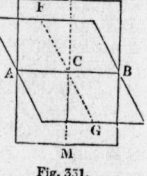

Fig. 331.

977. Prop. XCVII. *If one plane meet another plane, it makes angles with that other plane, which are together equal to two right angles.*

Let the plane ALBM (*fig.* 332.) meet the plane AFBG; these planes will make with each other two angles, which will together be equal to two right angles. Through any point C draw the lines FG, LM perpendicular to the line AB. The line CL makes with the line FG two angles together equal to two right angles. But these two angles are (Defin. 3.) the angles of inclination of the two planes. Therefore the two planes make angles with each other, which are together equal to two right angles.

Corollary. It may be demonstrated in the same manner that planes which intersect each other have their vertical angles equal, that parallel planes have their alternate angles equal, &c.

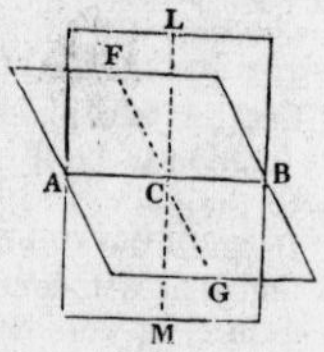

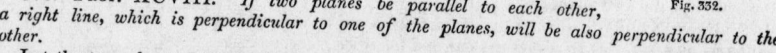

978. Prop. XCVIII. *If two planes be parallel to each other, a right line, which is perpendicular to one of the planes, will be also perpendicular to the other.*

Fig. 332.

Let the two planes LM, FG (*fig.* 333.) be parallel. If the line BA be perpendicular to the plane FG, it will also be perpendicular to the plane LM. From any point C in the plane LM draw CD perpendicular to the plane FG, and draw BC, AD.

Because the lines BA, CD are perpendicular to the plane FG, the angles A, D are right angles.

Because the planes LM, FG are parallel, the perpendiculars AB, DC (Defin. 6.) are equal; whence it follows that the lines BC, AD are parallel.

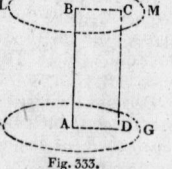

Fig. 333.

The line BA, being at right angles to the line AD, will also (Prop. 13.) be at right angles to the parallel line BC. The line BA is therefore perpendicular to the line BC.

In the same manner it may be demonstrated that the line BA is at right angles to all other lines which can be drawn from the point B in the plane LM. Wherefore (Defin. 2.) the line BA is perpendicular to the plane LM.

SOLIDS.

979. Definitions. — 1. A *solid*, as we have before observed, is that which has length, breadth, and thickness.

2. A *polyhedron* is a solid terminated by plane surfaces.

3. A *prism* is a solid terminated by two identical plane bases parallel to each other, and by surfaces which are parallelograms. (*Fig.* 334.)

4. A *parallelopiped* is a prism the bases of which are parallelograms. (*Fig.* 335.)

5. A *cube* is a solid terminated by six square surfaces : a die, for example, is a cube. (*Fig.* 336.)

6. If right lines be raised from every point in the perimeter of any rectilineal figure, and meet in one common point, these lines together with the rectilineal figure inclose a solid which is called a *pyramid*. (*Fig.* 337.)

Fig. 334.   Fig. 335.

7. A *cylinder* is a solid terminated by two planes, which are equal and parallel circles, and by a convex surface ; or it is a solid formed by the revolution of a parallelogram about one of its sides. (*Fig.* 338.)

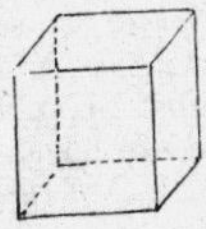

Fig. 336. 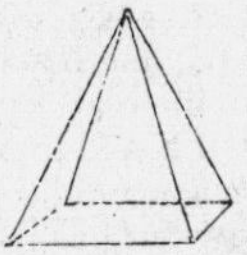   Fig. 337.    Fig. 338.

8. If right lines be raised from every point in the circumference of a circle, and meet in one common point, these lines together with the circle inclose a solid, which is called a *cone*. (*Fig.* 339.)

9. A semicircle revolving about its diameter forms a solid, which is called a *sphere*. (*Fig.* 340.)

10. If from the vertex of a solid a perpendicular be let fall upon the opposite plane, this perpendicular is called the *altitude* of the solid. In the pyramids ACD, A*cd* (*fig.* 341.), AB, *ab* are their respective altitudes.

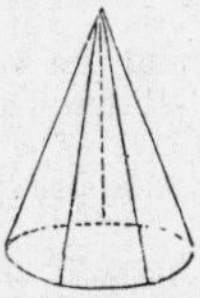

Fig. 339. 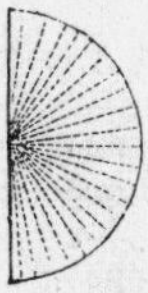   Fig. 340. 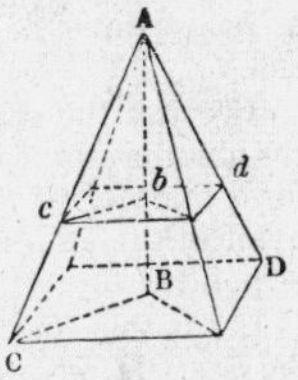   Fig. 341.

11. Solids are said to be *equal*, if they inclose an equal space : thus a cone and a pyramid are equal solids if the space inclosed within the cone be equal to the space inclosed within the pyramid.

12. *Similar solids* are such as consist of an equal number of physical points disposed in the same manner.

Thus (in the fig. Defin. 10.) the larger pyramid ACD and the smaller pyramid A*cd* are similar solids if every point in the larger pyramid has a point corresponding to it in the smaller pyramid. A hundred musket balls, and the same number of cannon balls, disposed in the same manner, form two similar solids

980. Prop. XCIX. *The solid content of a cube is equal to the product of one of its sides twice multiplied by itself.*

Let the lines AB, AD (*fig.* 342.) be equal. Let the line AD, drawn perpendicular to AB, be supposed to move through the whole length of AB; when it arrives at BC, and coincides with it, it will have formed the square DABC, and will have been multiplied by the line AB.

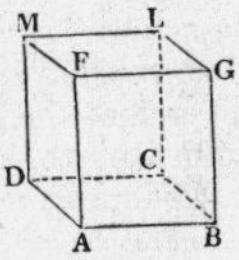

Next let the line AF be drawn equal to AD, and perpendicular to the plane DABC; suppose the plane DABC to move perpendicularly through the whole length of the line AF; when it arrives at the plane MFGL, and coincides with it, it will have formed the cube AFLC, and will have been multiplied by the line AF.

Fig. 342.

Hence it appears, that to form the cube AFLC, it is necessary, first, to multiply the side AD by the side AB equal to AD; and then to multiply the product, that is, the square of AC, by the side AF equal to AD; that is, it is necessary to multiply AD by AD, and to multiply the product again by AD.

981. Prop. C. *Similar solids have their homologous lines proportional.*

Let the two solids A, *a* (*fig.* 343.) be similar ; and let their homologous lines be AB, *ab*, BG, *bg*; AB will be to BG at *ab* to *bg*.

Because the solids A, *a* are similar, every point in the solid A has a point corresponding to it, and disposed in the same

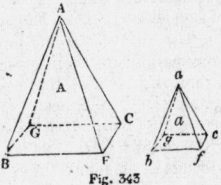

Fig. 343

manner, in the solid *a*. Thus, if the line AB is composed of 20 physical points, and the line BG of 10, the line *ab* will be composed of 20 corresponding points, and the line *bg* of 10. Now it is evident that 20 is to 10 as 20 is to 10 : therefore AB is to BG as *ab* to *bg*.

982. Prop. CI.   *Similar solids are equiangular.*

Let the solids (see fig. to preced. Prop.) A, *a* be similar ; their corresponding angles are equal.

Because the solids A, *a* are similar, the surfaces BAF, *baf* are composed of an equal number of points disposed in the same manner.   These surfaces are therefore similar figures, and consequently (Prop. 88.) equiangular.   The angles B, A, F are therefore equal to the angles *b, a, f*.   In the same manner it may be demonstrated that the other correspondent angles are equal.

983. Prop. CII.   *Solids which have their angles equal and their sides proportional are similar.*

If the solids A, *a* (*fig.* 344.) have their angles equal and their sides proportional, they are similar.

For if the solids A, *a* were not similar, another solid might be formed upon the line BF similar to the solid *a*.   But this is impossible ; for, in order to form this other solid, some angle or some side of the solid A must be increased or diminished ; and then this new solid would not have all its angles equal and all its sides proportional to those of the solid *a*, that is (Prop. 100, 101.), would not be similar.

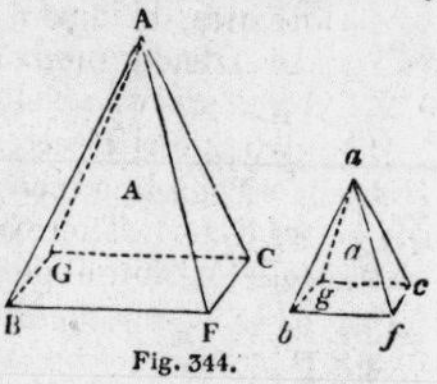

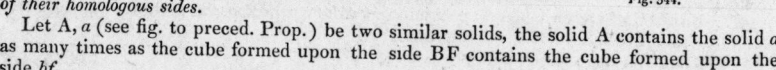

Fig. 344.

984. Prop. CIII.   *Similar solids are to one another as the cubes of their homologous sides.*

Let A, *a* (see fig. to preced. Prop.) be two similar solids, the solid A contains the solid *a* as many times as the cube formed upon the side BF contains the cube formed upon the side *bf*.

Because the solid A is similar to the solid *a*, every point in the solid A has its corresponding point in the solid *a*.   From whence it follows, that if the side BF is composed, for example, of 50 points, the side *bf* will also be composed of 50 points : and consequently the cubes formed upon the sides BF, *bf* will be composed of an equal number of points.

Let it then be supposed that the solid A is composed of 4000 points, and the cube of the side BF of 5000 points ; the solid A must be composed of 4000 points, and the cube of the side *bf* of 5000 points.   Now it is evident that 4000 is to 5000 as 4000 to 5000. Wherefore the solid A is to the cube of BF as the solid *a* to the cube of *bf* ; and, alternately, the solid A is to the solid *a* as the cube of BF to the cube of *bf*.

Corollary.   It may be demonstrated in the same manner that the spheres A, *a* (*fig.* 345.), which are similar solids, are to one another as the cubes of their radii AB, *ab*.

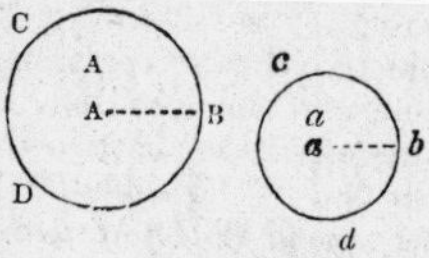

985. Prop. CIV.   *The solid content of a perpendicular prism is equal to the product of its base and height.*

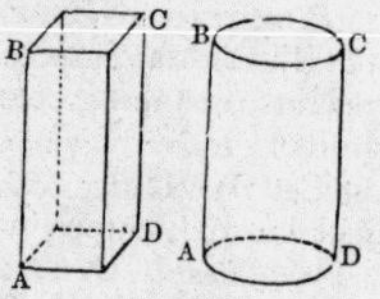

The solid content of the perpendicular prism ABCD (*fig.* 346.) is equal to the product of its base AD, and height AB.

Fig. 345

Fig. 346.

If the lower base AD be supposed to move perpendicularly along the height AB till it coincides with the upper base BC, it will have formed the prism ABCD.   Now the base AD will have been repeated as many times as there are physical points in the height AB. Therefore the solid content of the prism ABCD is equal to the product of the base multiplied by the height.

Corollary.   In the same manner it may be demonstrated that the solid content of the perpendicular cylinder ABCD is equal to the product of its base AD and height AB.

986. Prop. CV.   *The solid content of an inclined prism is equal to the product of its base and height.*

Let the inclined prism be CP (*fig.* 347.), it is equal to the product of its base RP and its height CD.

Conceive the base NB of the perpendicular prism NA, and the base RP of the inclined prism PC, to move on in the same time parallel to themselves ; when they have reached the points A and C, each of them will have been taken over again the same number of times.   But the base NB will have been taken over again (Prop. 104.) as many times as there are physical points in the height CD. The base RP will therefore have been taken over again as many times as there are physical points in CD. Consequently the solid content of the inclined prism CP is equal to the product of its base RP and the height CD.

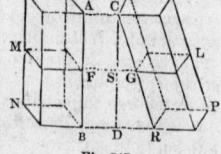

Fig. 347.

987. PROP. CVI. *In a pyramid, a section parallel to the base is similar to the base.*

Let the section *cd* be parallel to the base CD (*fig.* 348.); this section is a figure similar to the base. Draw AB perpendicular to the base CD; draw also BC, *bc*, BE, *bc*.

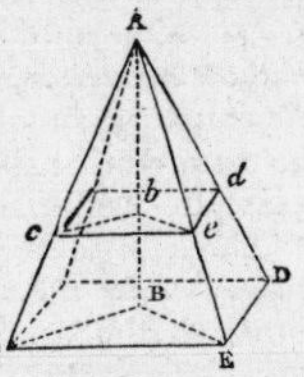

Because the planes *cd* CD are parallel; AB, being perpendicular to the plane CD, will also (Prop. 98.) be perpendicular to the plane *cd*: whence the triangles A*bc*, ABC, having the angles *b*, B right angles, and the angle A common, are equiangular. Therefore (Prop. 61.) A*b* is to AB as *bc* to BC, and as A*c* to AC.

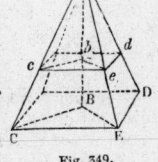

Fig. 348.

In like manner it may be proved that A*b* is to AB as *be* to BE, and as A*e* to AE. Consequently if A*b* be one third part of AB, *bc* will be one third part of BC, *be* the same of BE, A*c* of AC, and A*e* of AE.

Again, in the two triangles *c*A*e*, CAE, there are about the angle A, common to both, two sides proportional; they are therefore (Prop. 63.) equiangular, and consequently (Prop. 61.) have their other sides proportional. Therefore *ce* will be proportional to CE.

The two triangles *cbe*, CBE, having their sides proportional, are therefore (Prop. 89.) similar. The same may be demonstrated concerning all the other triangles which form the planes *cd*, CD. Therefore the section *cd* is similar to the base CD.

REMARK. If the perpendicular AB fall out of the base; by drawing lines from the points *b*, B, it may be demonstrated in the same manner that the section is similar to the base.

988. PROP. CVII. *In a pyramid, sections parallel to the base are to one another as the squares of their heights.*

Let CD *cd* (*fig.* 349.) be parallel sections. From the vertex A draw a perpendicular AB to the plane CD: the plane *cd* is to the plane CD as the square of the height A*b* is to the square of the height AB. Draw BC, *bc*.

The line AB, being perpendicular to the plane CD, will also (Prop. 98.) be perpendicular to the parallel plane *cd*: whence the angle A*bc* is a right angle, and also the angle ABC. Moreover, the angle at A is common to the two triangles A*bc*, ABC; these two triangles, therefore, are equiangular. Therefore (Prop. 61.) the side *cb* is to the side CB as the side A*b* is to the side AB; and consequently the square of *cb* is to the square of CB as the square of A*b* to the square of AB.

The planes *cd*, CD, being (Prop. 106.) similar figures, are to one another (Prop. 82.) as the squares of the homologous lines *cb*, CB; they are therefore also as the squares of the heights A*b*, AB.

Fig. 349.

COROLLARY. In the same manner it may be demonstrated that in a cone the sections parallel to the base are to one another as the squares of the heights or perpendicular distances from the vertex.

989. PROP. CVIII. *Pyramids of the same height are to one another as their bases.*

Let A, F (*fig.* 350.) be two pyramids. If the perpendicular AB be equal to the perpendicular FG, the pyramid A is to the pyramid F as the base CD to the base LM. Supposing, for example, the base CD to be triple of the base LM, the pyramid A will be triple of the pyramid F.

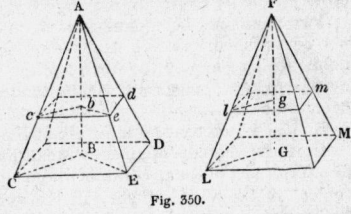

Fig. 350.

Two sections *cd*, *lm*, being taken at equal heights A*b*, F*g*, the section *cd* is (Prop. 107.) to the base CD as the square of the height A*b* to the square of the height AB; and the section *lm* is to the base LM as the square of the height F*g* to the square of the height FG. And because the heights are equal, AB to FG, and A*b* to F*g*, the section *cd* is to the base CD as the section *lm* to the base LM; and, alternately, the section *cd* is to the section *lm* as the base CD is to the base LM. But the base CD is triple of the base LM, therefore the section *cd* is also triple of the section *lm*.

Because the heights AF, FG are equal, it is manifest that the two pyramids are composed of an equal number of physical surfaces placed one upon another. Now it may be demonstrated in the same manner that every surface or section of the pyramid A is triple of the corresponding surface or section of the pyramid F. Therefore the whole pyramid A is triple of the whole pyramid F.

COROLLARY. Pyramids of the same height and equal bases are equal, since they are to one another as their bases.

990. PROP. CIX. *A pyramid whose base is that of a cube and whose vertex is at the centre of the cube is equal to a third part of the product of its height and base.*

Let the cube AM and the pyramid C (*fig.* 351.) have the same base AD, and let the vertex of the pyramid be at the centre of the cube C; this pyramid is equal to a third part of the product of its height and base.

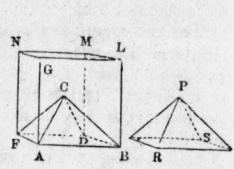

Fig. 351.

Conceive right lines drawn from the centre of the cube to its eight angles A, B, D, F, N, G, L, M, the cube will be divided into six equal pyramids, each of which has one surface of the cube for its base, and half the height of the cube for its height; for example, the pyramid CABDF.

Three of these pyramids will therefore be equal to half the cube. Now the solid content of half the cube is (Prop. 99.) equal to the product of the base and half the height. Each pyramid, therefore, will be equal to one third part of the product of the base, and half the height of the cube; that is, the whole height of the pyramid.

991. Prop. CX. *The solid content of a pyramid is equal to a third part of the product of its height and base.*

Let RPS (*fig.* 352.) be a pyramid, its solid content is equal to a third part of the product of its height and its base RS.

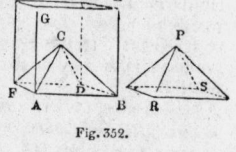

Fig. 352.

Form a cube the height of which BL is double of the height of the pyramid RPS. A pyramid the base of which is that of this cube and the vertex of which is C, the centre of the cube, will be equal to a third part of the product of its base and height.

The pyramids C and P have the same height; they are therefore (Corol. to Prop. 108.) to one another as their bases. If the base AFDB is double of the base RS, the pyramid C will therefore be double of the pyramid P.

But the pyramid C is equal to a third part of the product of its height and base. The pyramid P will therefore be equal to a third part of the product of the same height, and half the base AFDB, or, which is the same thing, the whole base RS.

992. Prop. CXI. *The solid content of a cone is equal to the third part of the product of its height and base.*

For the base of a cone may be considered as a polygon composed of exceedingly small sides, and consequently the cone may be considered as a pyramid having a great number of exceedingly small surfaces; whence its solid contents will be equal (Prop. 110.) to one third part of the product of its height and base.

993. Prop. CXII. *The solid content of a cone is a third part of the solid content of a cylinder described about it.*

Let the cone BAC and the cylinder BDFC (*fig.* 353.) have the same height and base, the cone is a third part of the cylinder.

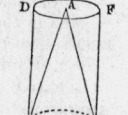

Fig. 353.

For the cylinder is equal to the product of its height and base, and the cone is equal to a third part of this product. Therefore the cone is a third part of the cylinder.

994. Prop. CXIII. *The solid content of a sphere is equal to a third part of the product of its radius and surface.*

Two points not being sufficient to make a curve line, three points will not be sufficient to make a curve surface. If, therefore, all the physical points which compose the surface of the sphere C (*fig.* 354.) be taken three by three, the whole surface will be divided into exceedingly small plane surfaces; and radii being drawn to each of these points, the sphere will be divided into small pyramids, which have their vertex at the centre, and have plane bases.

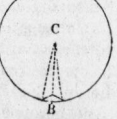

Fig. 354.

The solid contents of all these small pyramids will be equal (Prop. 110.) to a third part of the product of the height and bases. Therefore the solid content of the whole sphere will be equal to a third part of the product of the height and all the bases, that is, of its radius and surface.

995. Prop. CXIV. *The surface of a sphere is equal to four of its great circles.*

If a plane bisect a sphere, the section will pass through the centre, and it is called a great circle of the sphere.

Let ABCD (*fig.* 355.) be a square; describe the fourth part of the circumference of a circle BLD; draw the diagonal AC, through G, the right line FM, parallel to AD, and the right line AL.

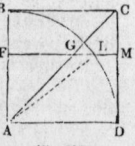

Fig. 355.

In the triangle ABC, on account of the equal sides AB, BC, the angles A and C are (Prop. 4.) equal; therefore, since the angle B is a right angle, the angles A and C are each half a right angle. Again, in the triangle AFG, because the angle F is a right angle, and the angle A half a right angle, the angle G is also half a right angle; therefore (Prop. 26.) AF is equal to FG.

The radius AL is equal to the radius AD : but AD is equal to FM ; therefore AL is equal to FM.

In the rectangular triangle AFL the square of the hypothenuse AL is equal (Prop. 32.) to the two squares of AF and FL taken together. Instead of AL put its equal FM, and instead of AF put its equal FG ; and the square of FM will be equal to the two squares of FG and FL taken together.

Conceive the square ABCD to revolve about the line AB. In the revolution the square will describe a cylinder, the quadrant a hemisphere, and the triangle ABC an inverted cone the vertex whereof will be in A. Also the line FM will form a circular section of a cylinder, the line FL will form a circular section of a hemisphere, and the line FG a circular section of a cone.

These circular sections, or circles, are to each other (Prop. 83.) as the squares of their radii ; therefore, since the square of the radius FM is equal to the squares of the radii FL and FG, the circular section of the cylinder will be equal to the circular sections of the hemisphere and cone.

In the same manner it may be demonstrated that all the other sections or circular surfaces whereof the cylinder is composed are equal to the corresponding sections or surfaces of the hemisphere and cone. Therefore the cylinder is equal to the hemisphere and cone taken together : but the cone (Prop. 112.) is equal to a third part of the cylinder ; the hemisphere is therefore equal to the remaining two thirds of the cylinder ; and consequently the hemisphere is double of the cone. The cone BSC (*fig.* 356.) is (Prop. 111.) equal to a third part of the product of the radius and base BC, which is a great circle of the sphere : the hemisphere ALD is therefore equal to a third part of the product of the radius and two of its great circles ; and consequently the whole sphere is equal to a third part of the product of the radius and four of its great circles.

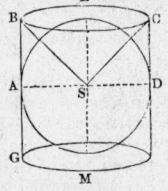

Fig. 356.

Lastly, since the sphere is equal (Prop. 113.) to a third part of the product of the radius and surface of the sphere, and also to a third part of the product of the radius and four of its great circles, the surface of the sphere is equal to four of its great circles.

Sect. II.

PRACTICAL GEOMETRY.

996. Practical Geometry is the art of accurately delineating on a plane surface any plane figure. It is the most simple species of geometrical drawing, and the most generally useful ; for the surfaces of buildings and other objects are more frequently plane than curved, and they must be drawn with truth, and of the required proportions, before they can be properly executed, unless in cases where the extreme simplicity of the form renders it improbable that mistakes should arise. It has been defined as the art which directs the mechanical processes for finding the position of points, lines, surfaces, and planes, with the description of such figures on diagrams as can be intelligibly understood by definition, according to given dimensions and positions of lines, points, &c.

No part of a building or drawing can be laid down or understood without the assistance of practical geometry, nor can any mechanical employment in the building department be conducted without some assistance from this branch of the science. Cases frequently occur requiring a knowledge of very complex problems, as in masonry, carpentry, and joinery ; but these will be given in other parts of this work.

The demonstration of most of the following problems will be found in the preceding section ; we therefore refer the reader back to it for definitions, and for the proof of those enunciations which will follow.

PROBLEMS.

997. Problem I. *To bisect a line* AB ; *that is, to divide it into two equal parts.*
From the two centres A and B (*fig.* 357.) with any equal radii describe arcs of circles intersecting each other in C and D, and draw the line CD. This will bisect the given line in the point E.

998. Prob. II. *To bisect an angle* BAC.
From the centre A (*fig.* 358.) with any radius describe an arc cutting off the equal lines AD, AE ; and from the two centres D, E, with the same radius describe arcs intersecting in F, then draw AF, and it will bisect the angle A, as required.

999. Prob. III. *At a given point* C *in a line* AB *to erect a perpendicular.*

From the given point C (*fig. 359.*) with any radius cut off any equal parts CD, CE of the given line; and from the two centres D and E with any one radius describe arcs intersecting in F. Then join CF, and it will be the perpendicular required.

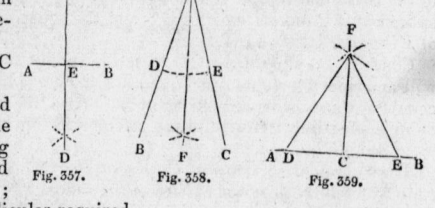

Fig. 357.   Fig. 358.   Fig. 359.

Otherwise — When the given point C is near the end of the line.

From any point D (*fig. 360.*) assumed above the line as a centre, through the given point C describe a circle cutting the given line at E, and through E and the centre D draw the diameter EDF; then join CF, and it will be the perpendicular required.

1000. Prob. IV. *From a given point A to let fall a perpendicular on a line* BC.

From the given point A (*fig. 361.*) as a centre with any convenient radius describe an arc cutting the given line at two points D and E; and from the two centres D and E with any radius describe two arcs intersecting at F; then draw AF, and it will be the perpendicular to BC required.

Otherwise — When the given point is nearly opposite the end of the line.

From any point D in the given line BC (*fig. 362.*) as a centre, describe the arc of a circle through the given point A cutting BC in E; and from the centre E with the radius EA describe another arc cutting the former in F; then draw AGF, which will be the perpendicular to BC required.

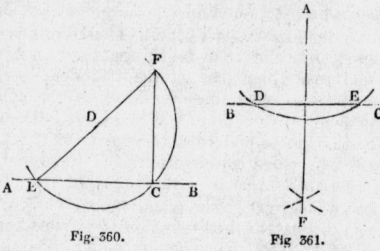

Fig. 360.   Fig 361.

1001. Prob. V. *At a given point* A, *in a line* AB, *to make an angle equal to a given angle* C.

From the centres A and C (*fig. 363.*) with any radius describe the arcs DE, FG; then with F as a centre, and radius DE, describe an arc cutting FG in G; through G draw the line AG, which will form the angle required.

1002. Prob. VI. *Through a given point* C *to draw a line parallel to a given line* AB.

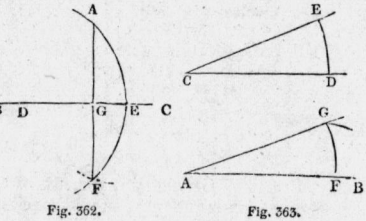

Fig. 362.   Fig. 363.

Case I.

Take any point *d* in AB (*fig. 364.*); upon *d* and C, with the distance C*d*, describe two arcs, *e*C and *df*, cutting AB in *e* and *d*. Make *df* equal to *e*C; and through *f* draw C*f*, and it will be the line required.

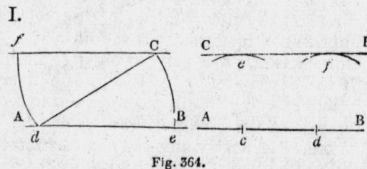

Fig. 364.

Case II.

When the parallel is to be drawn at a given distance from AB.

From any two points *c* and *d* in the line AB, with a radius equal to the given distance describe the arcs *e* and *f*; draw the line CB to touch those arcs without cutting them, and it will be parallel to AB, as required.

1003. Prob. VII. *To divide a line* AB *into any proposed number of equal parts.*

Draw any other line AC (*fig. 365.*), forming any angle with the given line AB; on the latter set off as many of any equal parts AD, DE, EF, FC as those into which the line AB is to be divided; join BC, and parallel thereto draw the other lines FG, EH, DI; then these will divide AB, as required.

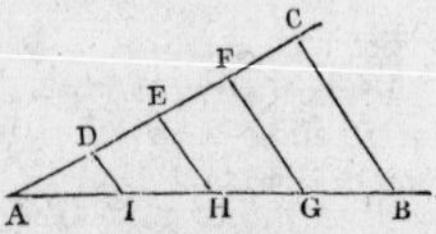

1004. Prob. VIII. *To find a third proportional to two other lines* AB, AC.

Fig. 365.

Let the two given lines be placed to form any angle at A (*fig. 366.*), and in AB take AD equal to AC; join BC, and draw DE parallel to it; then AE will be the third proportional sought.

1005. Prob. IX. *To find a fourth proportional to three lines* AB, AC, AD.

Let two of the lines AB, AC (*fig.* 367.), be so placed as to form any angle at A, and set out AD on AB; join BC, and parallel to it draw DE; then AE will be the fourth proportional required.

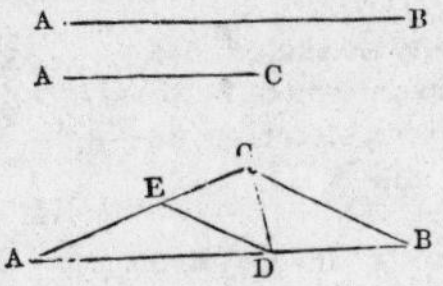

1006. Prob. X. *To find a mean proportional between two lines* AB, BC.

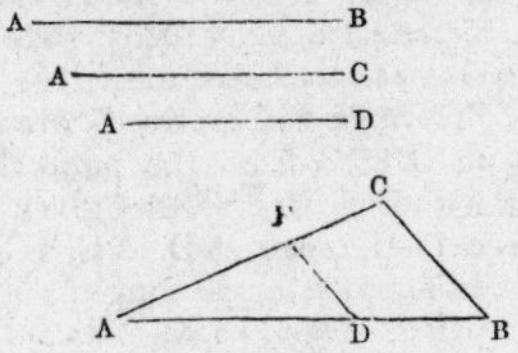

Place AB, BC (*fig.* 368.) joined together in one straight line AC, which bisect in the point O; then with the centre O and radius OA or OC describe the semicircle ADC, to meet which erect the perpendicular BD, which will be the mean proportional between AB and BC sought.

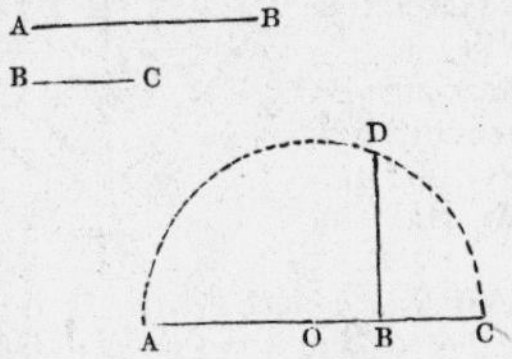

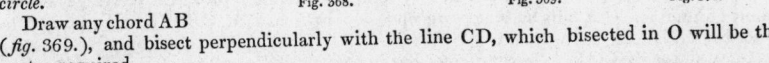

Fig. 366.   Fig. 367.

1007. Prob. XI. *To find the centre of a circle.*

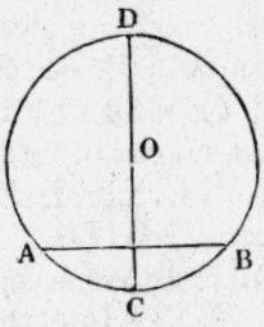

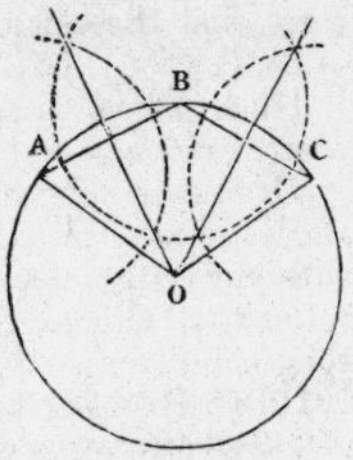

Draw any chord AB (*fig.* 369.), and bisect perpendicularly with the line CD, which bisected in O will be the centre required.

Fig. 368.   Fig. 369.   Fig. 370.

1008. Prob. XII. *To describe the circumference of a circle through three points* A, B, C.

From the middle point B (*fig.* 370.) draw the chords BA, BC to the two other points, and bisect these chords perpendicularly by lines meeting in O, which will be the centre; from the centre O, with the distance of any one of the points, as OA, describe a circle, and it will pass through the two other points B, C, as required.

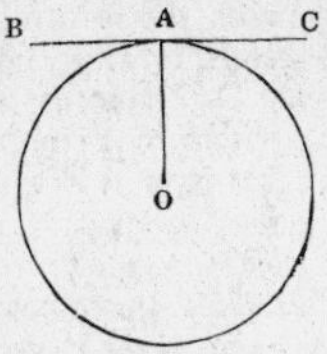

1009. Prob. XIII. *To draw a tangent to a circle through a given point* A.

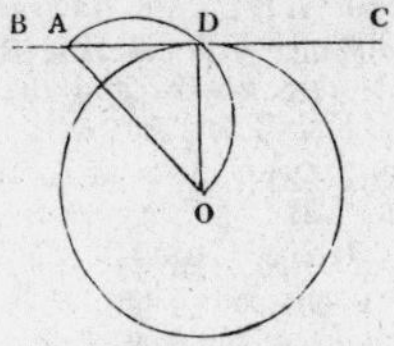

When the given point A (*fig.* 371.) is in the circumference of the circle, join A and the centre O, and perpendicular thereto draw BAC, which will be the tangent required.

If the given point A (*fig.* 372.) be out of the circle, draw AO to the centre O, on which, as a diameter, describe a semicircle cutting the given circumference in D, through which draw BADC, which will be the tangent required.

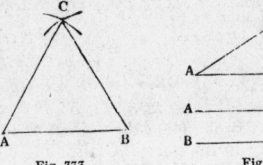

Fig. 371.   Fig. 372.

1010. Prob. XIV. *To draw an equilateral triangle on a given line* AB.

From the centres A and B (*fig.* 373.) with the distance AB describe arcs intersecting in C; draw AC, BC, and ABC will be the equilateral triangle.

1011. Prob. XV. *To make a triangle with three given lines* AB, AC, BC.

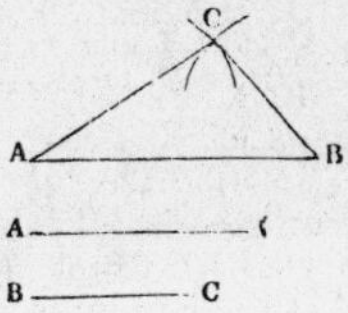

With the centre A and distance AC (*fig.* 374.) describe an arc; with the centre B and distance BC describe another arc cutting the former in C; draw AC, BC, and ABC will be the triangle required.

Fig. 373.   Fig. 374.

1012. Prob. XVI. *To make a square on a given line* AB.

Raise AD, BC (*fig.* 375.) each perpendicular and equal to AB, and join DC; then ABCD will be the square sought.

1013. Prob. XVII. *To inscribe a circle in a given triangle* ABC.

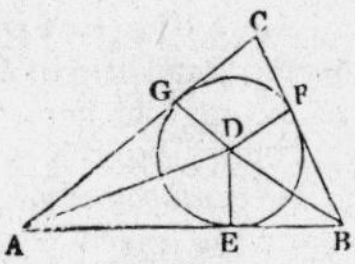

Bisect the angles at A and B with the two lines AD, BD (*fig.* 376.); from the intersection D, which will be the centre of the circle, draw the perpendiculars DE, DF, DG, and they will be the radii of the circle required.

Fig. 375.   Fig. 376.

1014. Prob. XVIII. *To describe a circle about a given triangle* ABC.

Bisect any two sides with two of the perpendiculars DE, DF, DG (*fig.* 377.), and D will be the centre of the circle.

1015. Prob. XIX. *To inscribe an equilateral triangle in a given circle.*

Through the centre C draw any diameter AB (*fig.* 378.) ; from the point B as a centre, with the radius BC of the given circle, describe an arc DCE; join AD, AE, DE, and ADE is the equilateral triangle sought.

1016. Prob. XX. *To inscribe a square in a given circle.* (*Half* AB, BC, &c. *forms an octagon.*)

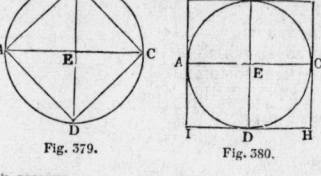

Fig. 377. Fig. 378.

Draw two diameters AC, BD (*fig.* 379.) crossing at right angles in the centre E; then join the four extremities A, B, C, D with right lines, and these will form the inscribed square ABCD.

1017. Prob. XXI. *To describe a square about a given circle.*

Draw two diameters AC, BD crossing at right angles in the centre E (*fig.* 380.) ; then through the four extremities of these draw FG, IH parallel to AC, and FI, GH parallel to BD, and they will form the square FGHI.

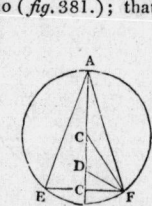

Fig. 379. Fig. 380.

1018. Prob. XXII. *To inscribe a circle in a given square.*

Bisect the two sides FG, FI in the points B and A (see *fig.* 380.) ; then through these two points draw AC parallel to FG or IH, and BD parallel to FI or GH. Then the point of intersection E will be the centre, and the four lines EA, EB, EC, ED radii of the inscribed circle.

1019. Prob. XXIII. *To cut a given line in extreme and mean ratio.*

Let AB be the given line to be divided in extreme and mean ratio (*fig.* 381.) ; that is, so that the whole line may be to the greater part as the greater part is to the less part.

Draw BC perpendicular to AB, and equal to half AB; join AC, and with the centre C and distance CB describe the circle BDF; then with A as a centre and distance AD describe the arc DE. Then AB will be divided in E in extreme and mean ratio, or so that AB is to AE as AE is to EB.

1020. Prob. XXIV. *To inscribe an isosceles triangle in a given circle that shall have each of the angles at the base double the angle at the vertex.*

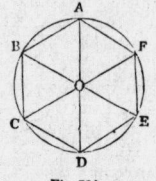

Fig. 381. Fig. 382.

Draw any diameter AB of the given circle (*fig.* 382.), and divide the radius CB in the point D in extreme and mean ratio (by the last problem) ; from the point B apply the chords BE, BF, each equal to the greater part CD ; then join AE, AF, EF ; and AEF will be triangle required.

1021. Prob. XXV. *To inscribe a regular pentagon in a given circle.* (*Half* AD, &c. *is a decagon.*)

Inscribe the isosceles triangle AB (*fig.* 383.) having each of the angles ABC, ACB double the angle BAC (Prob. 24.) ; then bisect the two arcs ADB, AEC, in the points D, E; and draw the chords AD, DB, AE, EC; then ADBCE will be the inscribed regular pentagon required.

1022. Prob. XXVI. *To inscribe a regular hexagon in a circle.* (*Half* AB, &c. *forms a dodecagon.*)

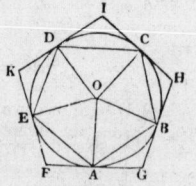

Fig. 383. Fig. 384.

Apply the radius of the given circle AO as a chord (*fig.* 384.) quite round the circumference, and it will form the points thereon of the regular hexagon ABCDEF.

1023. Prob. XXVII. *To describe a regular pentagon or hexagon about a circle.*

In the given circle inscribe a regular polygon of the same name or number of sides as ABCDE (*fig.* 385.) by one of the foregoing problems ; then to all its angular points draw (Prob. 13.) tangents, and these will by their intersections form the circumscribing polygon required.

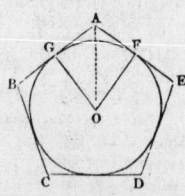

Fig. 385. Fig. 386.

1024. Prob. XXVIII.   *To inscribe a circle in a regular polygon.*

Bisect any two sides of the polygon by the perpendiculars GO, FO (*fig.* 386.), and their intersection O will be the centre of the inscribed circle, and OG or OF will be the radius.

1025. Prob. XXIX.   *To describe a circle about a regular polygon.*

Bisect any two of the angles C and D with the lines CO, DO (*fig.* 387.), then their intersection O will be the centre of the circumscribing circle; and OC or OD will be the radius.

1026. Prob. XXX.   *To make a triangle equal to a given quadrilateral* ABCD.

Draw the diagonal AC (*fig.* 388.), and parallel to it DE, meeting BA produced at E, and join CE; then will the triangle CEB be equal to the given quadrilateral ABCD.

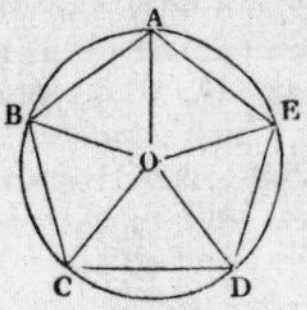

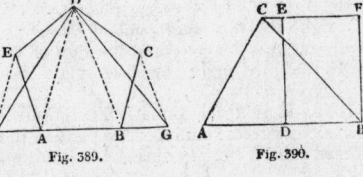

Fig. 387. 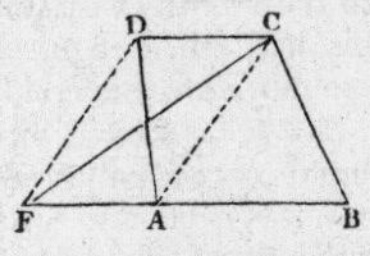   Fig. 588.

1027. Prob. XXXI.   *To make a triangle equal to a given pentagon* ABCDE.

Draw DA and DB, and also EF, CG parallel to them (*fig.* 389.), meeting AB produced at F and G; then draw DF and DG, so shall the triangle DFG be equal to the given pentagon ABCDE.

1028. Prob. XXXII.   *To make a rectangle equal to a given triangle* ABC.

Bisect the base AB in D (*fig.* 390.), then raise DE and BF perpendicular to AB, and meeting CF parallel to AB at E and F. Then DF will be the rectangle equal to the given triangle ABC.

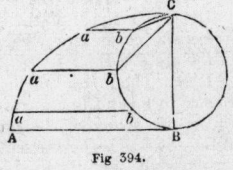

Fig. 389.   Fig. 390.

1029. Prob. XXXIII.   *To make a square equal to a given rectangle* ABCD.

Produce one side AB till BE be equal to the other side BC (*fig.* 391.).   On AE as a diameter describe a circle meeting BC produced at F, then will BF be the side of the square BFGH equal to the given rectangle BD, as required.

1030. Prob. XXXIV.   *To draw a catenary, c* C *d* (*fig.* 392.)

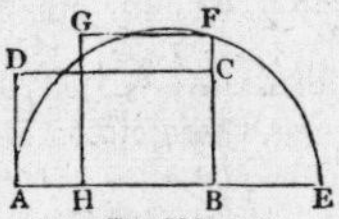

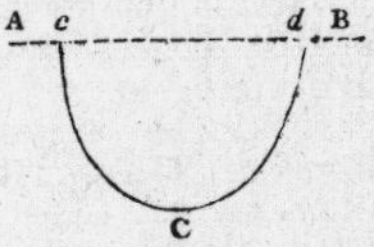

A catenary is a curve formed by a flexible cord or chain suspended by its two extremities.   Let *c, d,* in the line A B (*fig.* 392.) be the two points of suspension, and from them

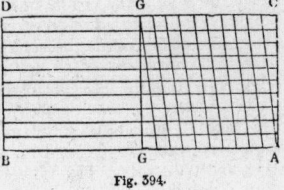

Fig. 391.   Fig. 392.

let the cord or chain be hung so as to touch the point C the given depth.   From this the curve may be traced on the paper.

1031. Prob. XXXV.   *To draw a cycloid.*

Any points *b* (*fig.* 393.) in the circumference of a circle rolled along a right line AB till such point is again in contact with the said line, generate a cycloid.   Let BC be the circle. Then AB is equal to the semi-circumference of such circle, and any chords at whose extremities *b*, lines *ab, ab,* equal to the lengths of arcs they cut off, drawn parallel to AB, will furnish the necessary points for forming the curve.

Fig 394.

1032. Prob. XXXVI.   *To draw a diagonal scale.*

Let it be of feet, tenths and hundredth parts of a foot.   Set off on AB (*fig.* 394.) as many times as necessary, the number of feet by equal distances.   Divide AG into ten equal parts.   On AB raise the perpendiculars BD, GG, and AC, and set off on AC ten equal divisions of any convenient length, through which draw horizontal lines.   Then, from the point G in DC to the first tenth part from G to A in BA draw a diagonal, and parallel thereto the other diagonals required.   The intersections of these diagonals with the horizontal lines give hundredth parts of a foot, inasmuch as each tenth is divided by the diagonals into ten equal parts in descending.

Fig. 394.

Sect. III.

PLANE TRIGONOMETRY.

1033. Plane Trigonometry is that branch of mathematics whose object is the investigation and calculation of the sides and angles of plane triangles. It is of the greatest importance to the architect in almost every part of his practice; but the elements will be sufficient for his use, without pursuing it into those more abstruse subdivisions which are essential in the more abstract relations which connect it with geodisic operations.

1034. We have already observed that every circle is supposed to be divided into 360 equal parts, called degrees, and that each degree is subdivided into 60 minutes, these minutes each into 60 seconds, and so on. Hence a semicircle contains 180 degrees, and a quadrant 90 degrees.

1035. The measure of an angle is that arc of a circle contained between those two lines which form the angle, the angular point being the centre, and such angle is estimated by the number of degrees contained in the arc. Thus, a right angle whose measure is a quadrant or quarter of the circle is one of 90 degrees (Prop. 22. Geometry); and the sum of the three angles of every triangle, or two right angles, is equal to 180 degrees. Hence in a right-angled triangle, one of the acute angles being taken from 90 degrees, the other acute angle is known; and the sum of two angles in a triangle taken from 180 degrees leaves the third angle; or either angle taken from 180 degrees leaves the sum of the other two angles.

1036. It is usual to mark the figure which denotes degrees with a small °: thus, 60° means 60 degrees; minutes are marked thus ': hence, 45' means 45 minutes; seconds are marked thus ", 49" meaning 49 seconds; and an additional comma is superadded for thirds, and so on. Thus, 58° 14′ 25″ is read 58 degrees, 14 minutes, 25 seconds.

1037. The *complement* of an arc is the quantity it wants of 90 degrees. Thus, AD (*fig.* 395.) being a quadrant, BD is the complement of the arc AB, and, reciprocally, AB is the complement of BD. Hence, if an arc AB contain 50 degrees, its complement BD will be 40.

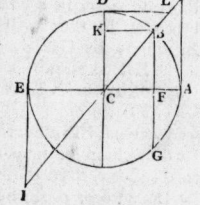

Fig. 395.

1038. The *supplement* of an arc is that which it wants of 180 degrees. Thus, ADE being a semicircle, BDE is the supplement of the arc AB, which arc, reciprocally, is the supplement of BDE. Thus, if AB be an arc of 50 degrees, then its supplement BDE will be 130 degrees.

1039. The line drawn from one extremity of an arc perpendicular to a diameter passing through its other extremity is called a *sine* or *right sine.* Thus, BF is the sine of the arc AB, or of the arc BDE. Hence the sine (BF) is half the chord (BG) of the double arc (BAG).

1040. That part of the diameter intercepted between the arc and its sine is called the *versed sine* of an arc. Thus, AF is the versed sine of the arc AB, and EF the versed sine of the arc EDB.

1041. The *tangent* of an arc is a line which touches one end of the arc, continued from thence to meet a line drawn from the centre, through the other extremity, which last line is called the *secant* of the arc. Thus, AH is the tangent and CH the secant of the arc AB. So EI is the tangent and CI the secant of the supplemental arc BDE. The latter tangent and secant are equal to the former; but, from being drawn in a direction opposite or contrary to the former, they are denominated *negative.*

1042. The *cosine* of an arc is the right sine of the complement of that arc. Thus BF, the sine of AB, is the cosine of BD.

1043. The *cotangent* of an arc is the tangent of that arc's complement. Thus AH, which is the tangent of AB, is the cotangent of BD.

1044. The *cosecant* of an arc is the secant of its complement. Thus CH, which is the secant of AB, is the cosecant of BD.

1045. From the above definitions follow some remarkable properties.

I. That an arc and its supplement have the same sine, tangent, and secant; but the two latter, that is, the tangent and the secant, are accounted negative when the arc exceeds a quadrant, or 90 degrees. II. When the arc is 0, or nothing, the secant then becomes the radius CA, which is the least it can be. As the arc increases from 0, the sines, tangents, and secants all increase, till the arc becomes a whole quadrant AD; and then the sine is the greatest it can be, being equal to the radius of the circle; under which circumstance the tangent and secant are infinite. III. In every arc AB, the versed sine AF, and the cosine BK or CF, are together equal to the radius of the circle. The radius CA, the tangent AH, and the secant CH, form a right-angled triangle CAH. Again, the radius, sine, and cosine form another right-angled triangle CBF or CBK. So also the radius,

cotangent, and cosecant form a right-angled triangle CDL. All these right-angled triangles

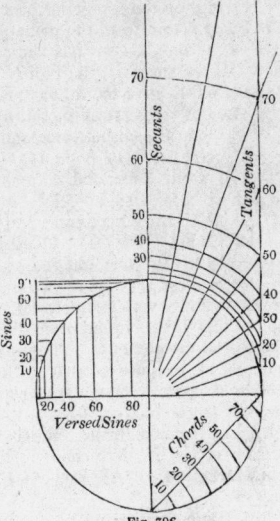

Fig. 396.

are similar to each other.

1046. The sine, tangent, or secant of an angle is the sine, tangent, or secant of the arc by which the angle is measured, or of the degrees, &c. in the same arc or angle. The method of constructing the scales of chords, sines, tangents, and secants engraved on mathematical instruments is shown in the annexed figure.

1047. A trigonometrical canon (*fig. 396.*) is a table wherein is given the length of the sine, tangent, and secant to every degree and minute of the quadrant, compared with the radius, which is expressed by unity or 1 with any number of ciphers. The logarithms, moreover, of these sines, tangents, and secants, are tabulated, so that trigonometrial calculations are performed by only addition and subtraction. Tables of this sort are published separately, and we suppose the reader to be provided with them.

1048. PROBLEM I. *To compute the natural sine and cosine of a given arc.*

The semiperiphery of a circle whose radius is 1 is known to be $3 \cdot 141592653589793$, &c. : we have then the following proportion : —

As the number of degrees or minutes in the semicircle
Is to the degrees or minutes in the proposed arc,
So is $3 \cdot 14159265$, &c. to the length of the said arc.

Now the length of the arc being denoted by the letter a, and its sine and cosine by s and c, these two will be expressed by the two following series, viz. —

$$s = a - \frac{a^3}{2 \cdot 3} + \frac{a^5}{2.3.4.5} - \frac{a^7}{2.3.4.5.6.7} + \&c.$$

$$= a - \frac{a^3}{6} + \frac{a^5}{120} - \frac{a^7}{5040} + \&c.$$

$$c = 1 - \frac{a^2}{2} + \frac{a^4}{2.3.4} - \frac{a^6}{2.3.4.5.6} + \&c.$$

$$= 1 - \frac{a^2}{2} + \frac{a^4}{24} - \frac{a^6}{720} + \&c.$$

Example 1. Let it be required to find the sine and cosine of one minute. The number of minutes in 180 degrees being 10800, it will be, first, as $10800 : 1 :: 3 \cdot 14159265$, &c. : $\cdot 000290888208665 =$ the length of an arc of one minute. Hence, in this case,—

$$a = \cdot 0002908882$$
$$\text{and } \tfrac{1}{6}a^3 = \cdot 000000000004$$

The difference is $s = \cdot 0002908882$, the sine of one minute.

Also from　　1.
take $\tfrac{1}{2}a^2 = 0 \cdot 0000000423079$, &c.
leaves　　$c = \cdot 9999999577$, the cosine of one minute.

Example 2. For the sine and cosine of 5 degrees : —

Here $180° : 5° :. 3 \cdot 14159265$, &c. : $\cdot 08726646 = a$, the length of 5 degrees.
Hence $a = \cdot 08726646$
$$-\tfrac{1}{6}a^3 = \cdot 00011076$$
$$+\tfrac{1}{120}a^5 = \cdot 00000004$$

These collected give $s = \cdot 08715574$, the sine of 5 degrees.

And for the cosine $1 = 1 \cdot$
$$-\tfrac{1}{2}a^2 = \cdot 00380771$$
$$+\tfrac{1}{24}a^4 = \cdot 00000241$$

These collected give $c = \cdot 99619470$, the cosine of 5 degrees.

In the same way we find the sines and cosines of other arcs may be computed. The greater the arc the slower the series will converge ; so that more terms must be taken to make the calculation exact. Having, however, the sine, the cosine may be found from it by the property of the right-angled triangle CBF, viz. the cosine $CF = \sqrt{CB^2 - BF^2}$, or $c = \sqrt{1 - s^2}$. There are other methods of constructing tables, but we think it unnecessary to mention them ; our sole object being here merely to give a notion of the mode by which such tables are formed.

1049. PROB. II. *To compute the tangents and secants.*

Having, by the foregoing problem, found the sines and cosines, the tangents and secants are easily found from the principles of similar triangles. In the arc AB (*fig.* 395.), where BF is the sine, CF or BK the cosine, AH the tangent, CH the secant, DL the cotangent, and CL the cosecant, the radius being CA or CB or CD; the three similar triangles CFB, CAH, CDL, give the following proportions: —

I. CF : FB::CA : AH, by which we find that the tangent is a fourth proportional to the cosine, sine, and radius.

II. CF : CB::CA : CH, by which we find that the secant is a third proportional to the cosine and radius.

III. BF : FC::CD : DL, by which we find that the cotangent is a fourth proportional to the sine, cosine, and radius.

IV. BF : BC::CD : CL, by which we find that the cosecant is a third proportional to the sine and radius.

Observation 1. There are therefore three methods of resolving triangles, or the cases of trigonometry; viz. geometrical construction, arithmetical computation, and instrumental operation. The method of carrying out the first and the last does not need explanation: the method is obvious. The second method, from its superior accuracy in practice, is that whereof we propose to treat in this place.

Observation 2. Every triangle has six parts, viz. three sides and three angles. And in all cases of trigonometry, three parts must be given to find the other three. And of the three parts so given, one at least must be a side; because, with the same angles, the sides may be greater or less in any proportion.

Observation 3. All the cases in trigonometry are comprised in three varieties only; viz.

1st. When a side and its opposite angle are given. 2d. When two sides and the contained angle are given. 3d. When the three sides are given.

More than these three varieties there cannot possibly be; and for each of them we shall give a separate theorem.

1050. THEOREM I. *When a side and its opposite angle are two of the given parts.*

Then — the sides of the triangle have the same proportion to each other as the sines of their opposite angles have. That is,

> As any one side
> Is to the sine of its opposite angle,
> So is any other side
> To the sine of its opposite angle.

For let ABC (*fig.* 397.) be the proposed triangle, having AB the greatest side, and BC the least. Take AD as a radius equal to BC, and let fall the perpendiculars DE, CF, which will evidently be the sines of the angles A and B, to the radius AD or BC. Now the triangles ADE, ACF are equiangular; they therefore have their like sides proportional, namely, AC : CF::AD or BC : DE, that is, the sine AC is to the sine of its opposite angle B as the side BC is to the sine of its opposite angle A.

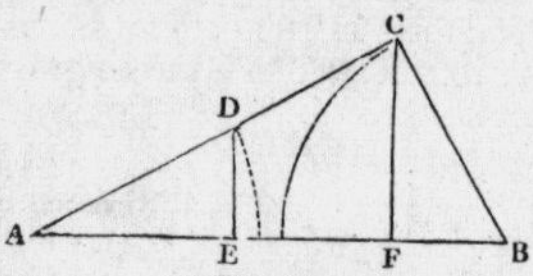

Fig. 397.

Note 1. In practice, when an angle is sought, the proportion is to be begun with a side opposite a given angle; and to find a side, we must begin with the angle opposite the given side.

Note 2. By the above rule, an angle, when found, is ambiguous; that is, it is not certain whether it be acute or obtuse, unless it come out a right angle, or its magnitude be such as to remove the ambiguity; inasmuch as the sine answers to two angles, which are supplements to each other; and hence the geometrical construction forms two triangles with the same parts, as in an example which will follow: and if there be no restriction or limitation included in the question, either result may be adopted. The degrees in a table answering to the sine is the acute angle; but if the angle be obtuse, the degrees must be subtracted from 180 degrees, and the remainder will be the obtuse angle. When a given angle is obtuse, or is one of 90 degrees, no ambiguity can occur, because neither of the other angles can then be obtuse, and the geometrical construction will only form one triangle.

Example 1. In the plane triangle ABC,

> Let AB be 345 feet,
> BC　　232 feet,
> ∠ A　　37° 20′:
> Required the other parts.

First, to the angles at C and B (*fig.* 398.)

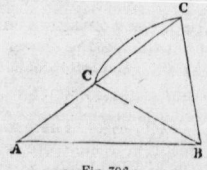

Fig. 398.

As the side   BC = 232   -   -   Log. 2·365488
To sine opp. ∠ A = 37° 20' -   -   9·782796
So side A B   = 345   -   -   2·537819

To sine opp. ∠ C = 115° 36' or 64° 24'   =   9·955127
Add   ∠ A = 37 20   37 20
The sum   = 152 56   101 44
Taken from   180 00   180 00
Leaves ∠ B   27 04   78 16

It is to be observed here that the second and third logarithms are added (that is, the numbers are multiplied), and from the sum the first logarithm is subtracted (that is, division by the first number), which leaves the remainder 9·955127, which, by the table of sines, is found to be that of the angle 115° 36', or 64° 24'.

To find the side AC.
As sine ∠ A   =   37° 20'   -   -   Log. 9·782796
To opp. side BC   = 232   -   -   2·365488
So sine ∠ B   = { 27   04   -   -   9·658037
{ 78   16   -   -   9·990829
To opp. side AC   = 174·04   -   -   2·240729
Or   374·56   -   -   2·573521

Example 2.   In the plane triangle ABC,
Let AB   = 365 yards,
∠ A   =   57° 12'
∠ B   =   24   45
Herein two angles are given, whose sum is 81° 57'.   Therefore 180° − 81° 57' = ∠ C.
As sine ∠ C   =   98°   3'   -   Log. 9·9956993
Is to AB   = 365   -   -   2·5622929
So sine ∠ B   =   24° 45'   -   -   9·6218612

To side AC   = 154·33   -   = 2·1884548

To find the side BC.
As sine ∠ B   =   24° 45'   -   Log. 9·6218612
Is to AC   = 154·33   -   -   2·1884548
So sin. ∠ A   =   57° 12'   -   -   9·9245721

To side BC   = 309·86   -   -   = 2·4911657

1051. Theorem II. *When two sides and their contained angle are given.*
The given angle is first to be subtracted from 180° or two right angles, and the remainder will be the sum of the other two angles.   Divide this remainder by 2, which will give the half sum of the said unknown angles ; and using the following ratio, we have —

As the sum of the two given sides
Is to their difference,
So is the tangent of half the sum of their opposite angles
To the tangent of half the difference of the same angles.

Now the half sum of any two quantities increased by their half difference gives the greater, and diminished by it gives the less.   If, therefore, the half difference of the angles above found be added to their half sum, it will give the greater angle, and subtracting it will leave the lesser angle.   All the angles thus become known, and the unknown side is then found by the former theorem.

For let ABC (*fig.* 399.) be the proposed triangle, having the two given sides AC, BC, including the given angle C.   With the centre C and radius
CA, the less of these two sides, describe a semicircle, meeting
the other side of BC produced in E, and the unknown side AB
in G.   Join AE, CG, and draw DF parallel to AE.   Now
BE is the sum of the given sides AC, CB, or of EC, CB ; and
BD is the difference of these given sides.   The external angle
ACE is equal to the sum of the two internal or given angles
CAB, CBA ; but the angle ADE at the circumference is equal
to half the angle ACE at the centre ; wherefore the same angle ADE is equal to half
the sum of the given angles CAB, CBA.   Also the external angle AGC of the triangle
BGC is equal to the sum of the two internal angles GCB, GBC, or the angle GCB is
equal to the difference of the two angles AGC, GBC ; but the angle CAB is equal to
the said angle AGC, these being opposite to the equal sides AC, CG ; and the angle DAB
at the circumference is equal to half the angle DCG at the centre.   Therefore the angle
DAB is equal to half the difference of the two given angles CAB, CBA, of which it has
been shown that ADE or CDA is the half sum.

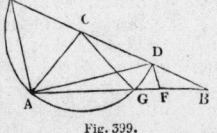

Fig. 399.

Now the angle DAE in a semicircle, is a right angle, or AE is perpendicular to AD; and DF, parallel to AE, is also perpendicular to AD: therefore AE is the tangent of CDA the half sum; and DF, the tangent of DAB, the half difference of the angles to the same radius AD, by the definition of a tangent. But the tangents AE, DF being parallel, it will be as BE : BD :: AE : DF; that is, as the sum of the sides is to the difference of the sides, so is the tangent of half the sum of the opposite angles to the tangent of half their difference.

It is to be observed, that in the third term of the proportion the cotangent of half the given angle may be used instead of the tangent of the half sum of the unknown angles.

Example. In the plane triangle ABC (*fig.* 400.),

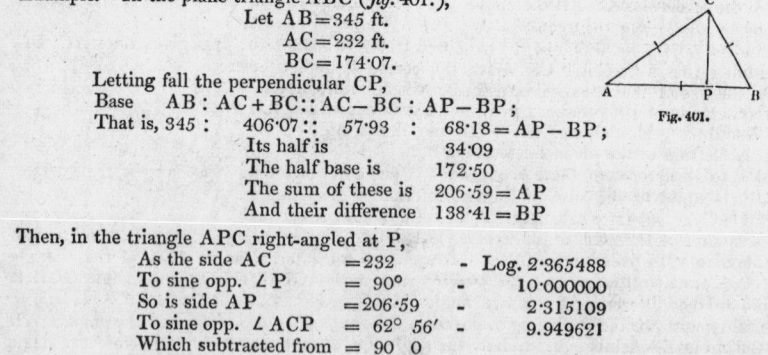

Let AB = 345 ft.
AC = 174·07 ft.
∠A = 37° 20′.

Fig. 400.

Now, the side AB being	345	From	180°	00′
The side AC	174·07	Take ∠A	37	20
Their sum is	519·07	Sum of C and B	142	40
Their difference	170·93	Half sum of do.	71	20

As the sum of the sides AB, AC = 519·07 - - Log. 2·715226
To difference of sides AB, AC = 170·93 - - 2·232818
So tang. half sum ∠s C and B = 71° 20′ - - 10·471298
To tang. half diff. ∠s C and B = 44 16′ - - 9·988890

These added, give ∠C = 115 36′
And subtracted give ∠B = 27 4′

By the former theorem : ⸺

As sine ∠C 115° 36′, or 64° 24′ - - Log. 9·955126
To its opposite side AB 345 - - 2·537819
So sine ∠A 37° 20′ - - 9·782796
To its opposite side BC 232 - - 2·365488

1052. THEOREM III. *When the three sides of a triangle are given.*

Let fall a perpendicular from the greatest angle on the opposite side, or base, dividing it into two segments, and the whole triangle into two right-angled triangles, the proportion will be⸺

As the base or sum of the segments
Is to the sum of the other two sides,
So is the difference of those sides
To the difference of the segments of the base.

Then take half the difference of these segments, and add it to the half sum, or the half base, for the greater segment; and for the lesser segment subtract it.

Thus, in each of the two right-angled triangles there will be known two sides and the angle opposite to one of them, whence, by the first theorem, the other angles will be found.

For the rectangle under the sum and difference of the two sides is equal to the rectangle under the sum and difference of the two segments. Therefore, forming the sides of these rectangles into a proportion, their sums and differences will be found proportional.

Example. In the plane triangle ABC (*fig.* 401.),

Let AB = 345 ft.
AC = 232 ft.
BC = 174·07.

Fig. 401.

Letting fall the perpendicular CP,
Base   AB : AC + BC :: AC − BC : AP − BP ;
That is, 345 :   406·07 :: 57·93 : 68·18 = AP − BP ;
Its half is   34·09
The half base is   172·50
The sum of these is   206·59 = AP
And their difference   138·41 = BP

Then, in the triangle APC right-angled at P,

As the side AC = 232 - Log. 2·365488
To sine opp. ∠P = 90° - 10·000000
So is side AP = 206·59 - 2·315109
To sine opp. ∠ACP = 62° 56′ - 9·949621
Which subtracted from = 90 0
Leaves ∠A = 27 04

Again, in the triangle BPC, right-angled at P,

As the side BC	=174·07	-	Log.	2·440724
To sine opp. ∠ P	= 90° 00′	-		10·000000
So is side BP	=138·41	-		2·141136
To sine opp. ∠ BCP	= 52° 40′	-		9·900412
Which taken from	90 00			
Leaves the ∠ B	37 20			
Also the angle ACP	= 62 56			
Added to the angle BCP	= 52 40			
Gives the whole angle ACB	=115 36			

So that the three angles are as follow, viz. ∠ A 27° 4′ ; ∠ B 37° 20′ ; ∠ C 115° 36.

1053. THEOREM IV. *If the triangle be right-angled, any unknown part may be found by the following proportion :* —

> As radius
> Is to either leg of the triangle,
> So is tangent of its adjacent angle
> To the other leg ;
> And so is secant of the same angle
> To the hypothenuse.

For AB being the given leg in the right-angled triangle ABC, from the centre A with any assumed radius AD describe an arc DE, and draw DF perpendicular to AB, or parallel to BC. Now, from the definitions, DF is the tangent and AF the secant of the arc DE, or of the angle A, which is measured by that arc to the radius AD. Then, because of the parallels BC, DF, we have AD : AB :: DF : BC, and :: AF : AC, which is the same as the theorem expresses in words.

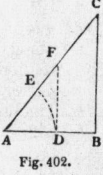

Fig. 402.

Note. Radius is equal to the sine of 90°, or the tangent of 45°, and is expressed by 1 in a table of natural sines, or by 10 in logarithmic sines.

Example 1. In the right-angled triangle ABC,

Let the leg AB =162
∠ A   =53° 7′ 48″

As radius	= tang. 45°	-	Log. 10·000000
To leg AB	=162	-	2·209515
So tang. ∠ A	=53° 7′ 48″	-	10·124937
To leg BC	=216	-	2·334452
So secant ∠ A	=53° 7′ 48″	-	10.221848
To hypothenuse AC	=270	-	2·431363

Note. There is another mode for right-angled triangles, which is as follows : —

ABC being such a triangle, make a leg AB radius; or, in other words, from the centre A with distance AB describe an arc BF. It is evident that the other leg BC will represent the tangent and the hypothenuse AC the secant of the arc BF or of the angle A.

In like manner, if BC be taken for radius, the other leg AB represents the tangent, and the hypothenuse AC the secant of the arc BG or angle C.

If the hypothenuse be made radius, then each leg will represent the sine of its opposite angle; namely, the leg AB the sine of the arc AE or angle C, and the leg BC the sine of the arc CD or angle A.

Fig. 403.

Then the general rule for all such cases is, that the sides of the triangle bear to each other the same proportion as the parts which they represent. This method is called making every side radius.

1054. If two sides of a right-angled triangle are given to find the third side, that may be found by the property of the squares of the sides (Geom. Prop. 32. ; viz. That the square of the hypothenuse or longest side is equal to both the squares of the two other sides together). Thus, if the longest side be sought, it is equal to the square root of the sum of the squares of the two shorter sides; and to find one of the shorter sides, subtract one square from the other, and extract the square root of the remainder.

1055. The application of the foregoing theorems in the cases of measuring heights and distances will be obvious. It is, however, to be observed, that where we have to find the length of inaccessible lines, we must employ a line or base which can be measured, and, by means of angles, which will be furnished by the use of instruments, calculate the lengths of the other lines.

CONIC SECTIONS.

1056. The *conic sections*, in geometry, are those lines formed by the intersections of a plane with the surface of a cone, and which assume different forms and acquire different properties, according to the several directions of such plane in respect of the axis of the cone. Their species are five in number.

1057. Definitions.—1. A plane passing through the vertex of a cone meeting the plane of the base or of the base produced is called the *directing plane*. The plane VRX (*fig.* 404.) is the directing plane,

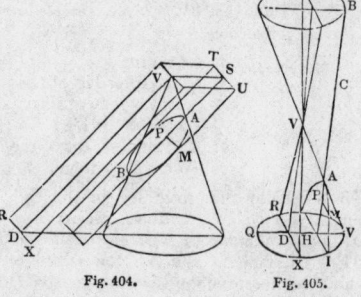

Fig. 404.   Fig. 405.

2. The line in which the directing plane meets the plane of the base or the plane of the base produced is called the *directrix*. The line RX is the directrix.

3. If a cone be cut by a plane parallel to the directing plane, the section is called a *conic section*, as AMB or AHI (*fig.* 405.)

4. If the plane of a conic section be cut by another plane at right angles passing along the axis of the cone, the common section of the two planes is called *the line of the axis*.

5. The point or points in which the line of the axis is cut by the conic surface is or are called the *vertex* or *vertices* of the conic section. Thus the points A and B (*figs.* 404. and 405.) are both vertices, as is the point A or vertex (*fig.* 406.).

6. If the line of the axis be cut in two points by the conic surface, or by the surfaces of the two opposite cones, the portion of the line thus intercepted is called the *primary axis*. The line AB (*figs.* 404. and 405.) and AH (*fig.* 406.) is called the primary axis.

7. If a straight line be drawn in a conic section perpendicular to the line of the axis so as to meet the curve, such straight line is called an *ordinate*, as PM in the above figures.

8. The *abscissa* of an ordinate is that portion of the line of axis contained between the vertex and an ordinate to that line of axis. Thus in figs. 404, 405, and 406. the parts AP, BP of the line of axis are the abscissas AP BP.

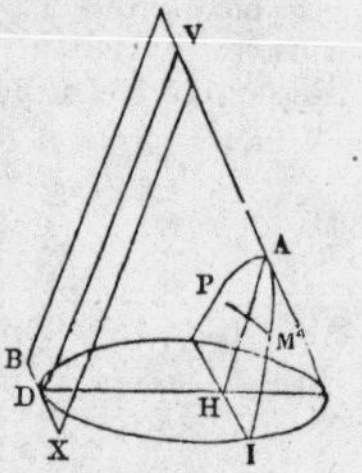

Fig. 406.

9. If the primary axis be bisected, the bisecting point is called the centre of the conic section.

10. If the directrix fall without the base of the cone, the section made by the cutting plane is called an ellipse. Thus, in *fig.* 404., the section AMB is an ellipse. It is evident that, since the plane of section will cut every straight line drawn from the vertex of the cone to any point in the circumference of the base, every straight line drawn within the figure will be limited by the conic surface. Hence the axis, the ordinates, and abscissas will be terminated by the curve.

11. If the directrix fall within the base of the cone, the section made by the cutting plane is called an *hyperbola*. Hence it is evident, that since the directing plane passes alike through both cones, the plane of section will cut each of them, and therefore two sections will be formed. And as every straight line on the surface of the cone and on the same side of the directing plane cannot meet the cutting plane, neither figure can be enclosed.

12. If the directrix touch the curve forming the base of the cone, the section made by the cutting plane is a *parabola*.

OF THE ELLIPSIS.

1058. The primary axis of an ellipsis is called the major axis, as AB (*fig.* 407.); and a straight line DE drawn through its centre perpendicular to it, and terminated at each extremity by the curve, is called the minor axis.

1059. A straight line VQ drawn through the centre and terminated at each extremity by the curve is called a *diameter*. Hence the two axes are also diameters.

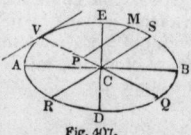

Fig. 407.

1060. The extremities of a diameter which terminate in the curve are called the vertices of that diameter. Thus the points V and Q are the vertices of the diameter VQ.

1061. A straight line drawn from any point of a diameter parallel to a tangent at either extremity of the diameter to meet the curves is called an ordinate to the two abscissas. Thus PM, being parallel to a tangent at V, is an ordinate to the two abscissas VP, PQ.

1062. If a diameter be drawn through the centre parallel to a tangent at the extremity of another diameter, these two diameters are called conjugate diameters. Thus VQ and RS are conjugate diameters.

1063. A third proportional to any diameter and its conjugate is called the *parameter* or *latus rectum.*

1064. The points in the axis where the ordinate is equal to the semi-parameter are called the foci.

1065. THEOREM I.   *In the ellipsis the squares of the ordinates of an axis are to each other as the rectangles of their abscissas.*

Let AVB (*fig.* 408.) be a plane passing through the axis of the cone, and AEB another section of the cone perpendicular to the plane of the former ; AB the axis of the elliptic section, and PM, HI ordinates perpendicular to it ; then it will be

$$PM^2 : HI^2 :: AP \times PB : AH \times HB.$$

For through the ordinates PM, HI draw the circular sections KML, MIN parallel to the base of the cone, having KL, MN for their diameters, to which PM, HI are ordinates as well as to the axis of the ellipse.   Now, in the similar triangles APL, AHN,

$$AP : PL :: AH : HN,$$

And in BPK, BHM,

$$BP : PK :: BH : HM.$$

Taking the rectangles of the corresponding terms,

$$AP \times BP : PL \times PK :: AH \times BH : HN \times HM.$$

By the property of the circle,

$$PL \times PK = PM^2 \text{ and } HN \times HM = HI^2. \quad \text{Therefore,}$$
$$AP \times BP : PM^2 :: AH \times HB : HI^2, \text{ or}$$
$$PM^2 : HI^2 :: AP \times BP : AH \times HB.$$

Coroll. 1.   If C be the centre of the figure, $AP \times PB = CA^2 - CP^2$, and $AH \times HB = CA^2 - CH^2$.

Therefore $PM^2 : HI^2 :: CA^2 - CP^2 : CA^2 - CH^2$.   For $AP = CA - CP$, and $PB = CA + CP$: consequently $AP \times PB = (CA - CP)(CA + CP) = CA^2 - CP^2$; and in the same manner it is evident that $AH \times HB = (CA + CH)(CA - CH) = CA^2 - CH^2$.

Coroll. 2.   If the point P coincide with the middle point C of the semi-major axis, PM will become equal to CE, and CP will vanish ; we shall therefore have

$$PM^2 : HI^2 :: CA^2 - CP^2 : CA^2 - CH^2$$
Now $CE^2 : HI^2 :: CA^2 : CA^2 - CH^2$, or $CA^2 \times HI^2 = CE^2(CA^2 - CH^2)$.

1066. THEOREM II.   *In every ellipsis the square of the major axis is to the square of the minor axis as the rectangle of the abscissas is to the square of their ordinate.*

Let AB (*fig.* 409.) be the major axis, DE the minor axis, C the centre, PM and HI ordinates to the axis AB ; then will

$$CA^2 : CE^2 :: AP \times PB : PM^2.$$

For since by Theor. I., $PM^2 : HI^2 :: AP \times PB : AH \times HB$; and if the point H be in the centre, then AH and HB become each equal to CA, and HI becomes equal to CE ; therefore

$$PM^2 : CE^2 :: AP \times PB : CA^2;$$
And, alternately, $CA^2 : CE^2 :: AP \times PB :: PM^2.$

Coroll. 1.   Hence, if we divide the two first terms of the analogy by AC, it will be $CA : \dfrac{CE^2}{CA} :: AP \times PB : PM^2$.   But by the definition of parameter, $AB : DE :: DE :$ parameter, or $CA : CE :: 2CE :$ parameter $= \dfrac{2CE^2}{CA}$.   Therefore $\dfrac{2CE^2}{CA}$ is the parameter, which let us call P ; then

$$AB : P :: AP \times PB : PM^2.$$

Coroll 2.   Hence $CA^2 : CE^2 :: CA^2 - CP^2 : PM^2$.   For $CA^2 - CP^2 = (CA - CP)(CA + CP) = (AP \times PB)$.

Coroll. 3.   Hence, also, $AB : P :: CA^2 - CP^2 : PM^2$.

1067. THEOREM III. *In every ellipsis, the square of the minor axis is to the square of the major axis as the difference of the squares of half the minor axis and the distance of an ordinate from the centre on the minor axis to the square of that ordinate.*

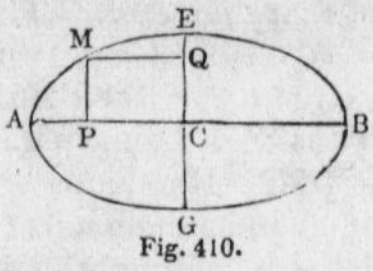

Draw MQ (*fig.* 410.) parallel to AB, meeting CE in Q; then will

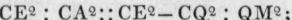

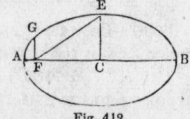

Fig. 410.

$$CE^2 : CA^2 :: CE^2 - CQ^2 : QM^2;$$

For by Cor. 2. Theor. II., $CA^2 : CA^2 - CP^2 :: CE^2 : PM^2$;
Therefore, by division, $CA^2 : CP^2 :: CE^2 : CE^2 - PM^2$.

Therefore, since $CQ = PM$ and $CP = QM$; $CA^2 : QM^2 :: CE^2 : CE^2 - CQ^2$.

Coroll. 1. If a circle be described on each axis as a diameter, one being inscribed within the ellipse, and the other circumscribed about it, then an ordinate in the circle will be to the corresponding ordinate in the ellipsis as the axis belonging to this ordinate is to the axis belonging to the other; that is,

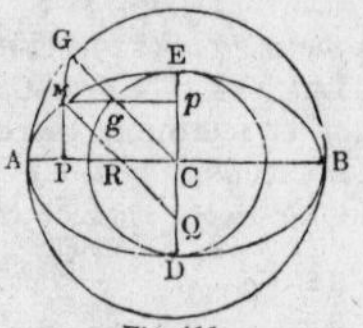

$$CA : CE :: PG : PM,$$
and $CE : CA :: pg : pM$;
and since $CA^2 : CE^2 :: AP \times PB : PM^2$,
and because $AP \times PB = PG^2$; $CA^2 : CE^2 :: PG^2 : PM^2$,
or $CA : CE :: PG : PM$.

Fig. 411.

In the same manner it may be shown that $CE : CA :: pg : pM$, or, alternately, $CA : CE :: pM : pg$; therefore, by equality, $PG : PM :: pM : pg$, or $PG : Cp :: CP : pg$: therefore CgG is a continued straight line.

Coroll. 2. Hence, also, as the ellipsis and circle are made up of the same number of corresponding ordinates, which are all in the same proportion as the two axes. it follows that the area of the whole circle and of the ellipsis, as also of any like parts of them, are in the same ratio, or as the square of the diameter to the rectangle of the two axes; that is, the area of the two circles and of the ellipsis are as the square of each axis and the rectangle of the two; and therefore the ellipsis is a mean proportional between the two circles.

Coroll. 3. Draw MQ parallel to GC, meeting ED in Q; then will $QM = CG = CA$; and let R be the point where QM cuts AB; then, because QMGC is a parallelogram, QM is equal to $CG = CE$; and therefore, since QM is equal to CA, half the major axis and $RM = CE$, half the minor axis QR is the difference of the two semi-axes, and hence we have a method of describing the ellipsis. This is the principle of the trammel, so well known among workmen.

If we conceive it to move in the line DE, and the point R in the line AB, while the point M is carried from A, towards E, B, D, until it return to A, the point M will in its progress describe the curve of an ellipsis.

1068. THEOREM IV. *The square of the distance of the foci from the centre of an ellipsis is equal to the difference of the square of the semi-axes.*

Let AB (*fig.* 412.) be the major axis, C the centre, F the focus, and FG the semi-parameter; then will $CE^2 = CA^2 - CF^2$. For draw CE perpendicular to AB, and join FE. By Cor. 2. Th. II., $CA^2 : CE^2 :: CA^2 - CF^2 : FG^2$, and the parameter FG is a third proportional to CA, CE; therefore $CA^2 : CE^2 :: CE^2 : FG^2$, and as in the two analogies the first, second, and fourth terms are identical, the third terms are equal; consequently

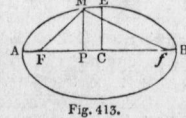

Fig. 412.

$$CE^2 = CA^2 - CF^2.$$

Coroll. 1. Hence $CF^2 = CA^2 - CE^2$.

Coroll. 2. The two semi-axes and the distance of the focus from the centre are the sides of a right-angled triangle CFE, and the distance FE from the focus to the extremity of the minor axis is equal to CA or CB, or to half the major axis.

Coroll. 3. The minor axis CE is a mean proportional between the two segments of the axis on each side of the focus. For $CE^2 = CA^2 - CF^2 = (CA + CF) \times (CA - CF)$.

1069. THEOREM V. *In an ellipsis, the sum of the lines drawn from the foci to any point in the curve is equal to the major axis.*

Let the points F, *f* (*fig.* 413.) be the two foci, and M a point in the curve; join FM and *f*M, then will $AB = 2CA = FM + fM$.

By Cor. 2. Th. II., $CA^2 : CE^2 :: CA^2 - CP^2 : PM^2$,
But by Th. IV., $CE^2 = CA^2 - CF^2$;
Therefore $CA^2 : CA^2 - CF^2 :: CA^2 - CP^2 : PM^2$;

Fig. 413.

And by taking the rectangle of the extremes and means, and dividing the equation by CA^2, the result is—

$$PM^2 = CA^2 - CP^2 - CF^2 + \frac{CF^2 \cdot CP^2}{CA^2}.$$

And because $FP^2 = (CF - CP)^2 = CF^2 - 2CF \cdot CP + CP^2,$

And since $\quad FM^2 = PM^2 + FP^2.$

Therefore $\quad FM^2 = CA^2 - 2CF \cdot CP + \frac{CF^2 \cdot CP^2}{CA^2}.$

Extracting the root from each number, $FM = CA - \frac{CF \cdot CP}{CA}.$

In the same manner it may be shown that $FM = CA + \frac{CF \cdot CP}{CA^2}$; therefore the sum of these is $FM + fM = 2CA.$

Coroll. 1. A line drawn from a focus to a point in the curve is called a radius vector, and the difference between either radius vector and half the major axis is equal to half the difference between the radius vectors. For, since

$$fM = CA - \frac{CF \cdot CP}{CA}; \text{ therefore, by transposition,}$$
$$\frac{CF \cdot CP}{CA} = CA - fM.$$

Coroll. 2. Because $\frac{CF \cdot CP}{CA}$ is a fourth proportional to CA, CF, CP; therefore $CA :$ $CF :: CP : CA - fM.$

Coroll. 3. Hence the difference between the major axis and one of the radius vectors gives the other radius vector. For, since $FM + Mf = 2CA$;

Therefore $FM = 2CA - Mf.$

Coroll. 4.   Hence is derived the common method of describing an ellipsis mechanically, by a thread or by points, thus : — Find the foci Ff (*fig.* 414.), and in the axis AB assume any point G ; then with the radius AG from the point F as a centre describe two arcs H, H, one on each side of the axis ; and with the same radius from the point f describe two other arcs $h,$ $h,$ one on each side of the major axis. Again, with the distance GB from the point f describe two arcs, one on each side of the axis, intersecting the arcs HH in the points HH ; and with the same radius from the point f describe two other arcs, one on each side of the axis, intersecting the arcs described at h, h in the point $h, h.$ In this manner we may find as many points as we please ; and a sufficient number being found, the curve will be formed by tracing it through all the points so determined.

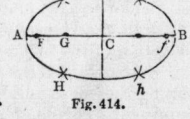

Fig. 414.

1070. Theorem VI.   *The square of half the major axis is to the square of half the minor axis as the difference of the squares of the distances of any two ordinates from the centre to the difference of the squares of the ordinates themselves.*

Let PM and HI (*fig.* 415.) be ordinates to the major axis AB; draw MN parallel to AB, meeting HI in the point N ; then will PM = HN, and MN = PH, and the property to be demonstrated is thus expressed —

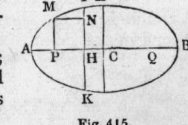

Fig. 415.

$$CA^2 : CE^2 :: CP^2 - CH^2 : HI^2 - HN^2.$$

Or by producing HI to meet the curve in the point K, and making CQ = CP, the property to be proved will be

$$CA^2 : CE^2 :: PH \times HQ : KN.$$

By Cor. 2. Theor. II. $\begin{cases} CA^2 : CE^2 :: CA^2 - CP^2 : PM^2, \\ CA^2 : CE^2 :: CA^2 - CH^2 : HI^2. \end{cases}$

Therefore $\qquad CA^2 - CH^2 : CA^2 - CP^2 :: HI^2 : PM^2$ or HN^2 ;

But, by division, $\qquad CA^2 - CH^2 : CP^2 - CH^2 :: HI^2 : HI^2 - HN^2.$

Alternately, $\qquad CA^2 - CH^2 : HI^2 :: CP^2 - CH^2 : HI^2 - HN^2$;

And, since we have above, $CA^2 - CH^2 : HI^2 :: CA^2 : CE^2,$

Therefore, by equality, $\qquad CA^2 : CE^2 :: CP^2 - CH^2 : HI^2 - HN^2$;

But since $\qquad CP^2 - CH^2 = (CP - CH)(CP + CH) = PH \times QH,$

And since $\qquad HI^2 - HN^2 = (HI - HN)(HI + HN) = NI \times KN,$

Therefore $\qquad CA^2 : CE^2 :: PH \times HQ : NI \times NK.$

Coroll. 1. Hence half the major axis is to half the minor axis, or the major axis is to the minor axis, as the difference of the squares of any two ordinates from the centre is to the rectangle of the two parts of the double ordinate, which is the greatest made of the sum and difference of the two semiordinates.   For KN = HK + HN = HI + HN, which is the sum of the two ordinates, and NI = HI - HN, which is the difference of the two ordinates.

Coroll. 2. Hence, because $CP^2 - CH^2 = (CP - CH)(CP + CH)$, and since $HI^2 - HN^2 =$ $(HI - HN)(HI + HN)$, and because $CP - CH = PH$ and $HI - HN = NI$; therefore $CA^2 : CE^2 :: (CP + CH)PH : (HI + HN)NI.$

1071. **Theorem VII.** *In the ellipsis, half the major axis is a mean proportional between the distance of the centre and an ordinate, and the distance between the centre and the intersection of a tangent to the vertex of that ordinate.*

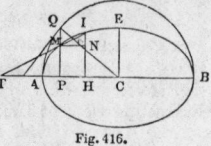

Fig. 416.

To the major axis draw the ordinates PM (*fig.* 416.) and HI, and the minor axis CE. Draw MN perpendicular to HI. Through the two points I,M, draw MT, IT, meeting the major axis produced in T; then will CT : CA :: CA : CP. For,

By Cor. 1. Theor. VI., CE^2 : CA^2 :: (IH + HN)IN : (PC + CH)HP;
By Cor. 2. Th. II., CE^2 : CA^2 :: PM^2 : $CA^2 - CP^2$;
Therefore, by equality, PM^2 : $CA^2 - CP^2$ :: (IH + HN)IN : (PC + CH)HP.
By similar triangles, INM, MPT;   IN : NM or PH :: PM : PT or CT − CP.

Therefore, taking the rectangles of the extremes and means of the two last equations, and throwing out the common factors, they will be converted to the equation

$$PM(CT - CP)(CP + CH) = (CA^2 - CP^2)(IH + HN).$$

But when HI and PM coincide, HI and HN will become equal to PM, and CH will become equal to CP; therefore, substituting in the equation 2CP for CP + PH, and 2PM for IH + HN, and throwing out the common factors and the common terms, we have

$$CT . CP = CA^2$$
$$\text{or } CT : CA :: CA : CP.$$

Coroll. 1. Since CT is always a third proportional to CP and CA, if the points P, A, B remain fixed, the point T will be the same; and therefore the tangents which are drawn from the point M, which is the intersection of PQ and the curve, will meet in the point T in every ellipsis described on the same axis AB.

Coroll. 2. When the outer ellipsis AQB, by enlarging, becomes a circle, draw QT perpendicular to CQ, and joining TM, then TM will be a tangent to the ellipsis at M.

Coroll. 3. Hence, if it were required to draw a tangent from a given point T in the prolongation of the major axis to the ellipsis AEB, it will be found thus : — On AB describe the semicircle AQB. Draw a tangent TQ to the circle, and draw the ordinate PQ intersecting the curve AEB of the ellipsis in the point M; join TM; then TM is the tangent required. This method of drawing a tangent is extremely useful in practice.

1072. **Theorem VIII.** *Four perpendiculars to the major axis intercepted by it and a tangent will be proportionals when the first and last have one of their extremities in the vertices, the second in the point of contact, and the third in the centre.*

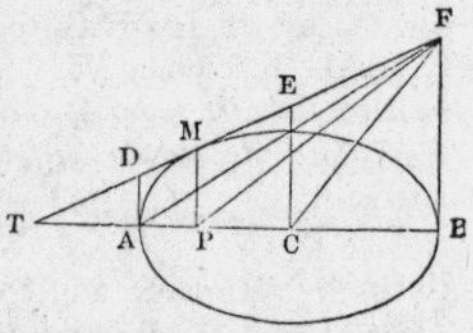

Let the four perpendiculars be AD, PM, CE, BF, of which AD and BF have their extremities in the vertices A and B, the second in the point of contact M, and the third in the centre C; then will

Fig. 417.

                 AD : PM :: CE : BF.
For, by Theor. VII.,   TC : AC :: AC : CP;
By division,   TC − AC : CA − CP :: TC : AC or CB;
That is,   TA : AP :: TC : CB.
By composition,   TA : TA + AP :: TC : TC + CB :
Therefore   TA : TP :: TC : TB.

But by the similar triangles TAD, TPM, TCE, and TBF, the sides TA, TP, TC, and TB are proportionals to the four perpendiculars AD, PM, CE, and BF; therefore

                 AD : PM :: CE : BF.

Coroll. 1. If AM and CF be joined, the triangles TAM and TCF will be similar. For by similar triangles, the sides TD, TM, TE, TF are in the same proportion as the sides TA, TP, TC, TB.

      Therefore   TD : TM :: TE : TF;
      Alternately, TD : TE :: TM : TF: but TAD is similar to TCE;
      Hence   TD : TE :: TA : TC;
      Therefore, by equality, TA : TM :: TC : TF.

Coroll. 2. The triangles APM and CBF are similar;

      For   TA : TP :: TC : TB.
      By division,   TP : TP − TA :: TB : TB − TC;
      That is,   TP : AP :: TB : CB.
      Alternately,   TP : TB :: AP : CB : but TPM is similar to TBF ;
      Consequently,   TP : TB :: PM : BF :
      Therefore, by equality, AP : PM :: CB : BF.

Coroll. 3. If AF be drawn cutting PM in I, then will PI be equal to the half of PM

For, since AP : PM :: CB : BF, and, by the similar triangles API, ABF,

AP : PI :: AB : BF;

Therefore PM : PI :: CB : AB.

But CB is the half of AB ; therefore, also, PI is the half of PM.

1073. **Theorem IX.**   *If two lines be drawn from the foci of an ellipse to any point in the curve, these two lines will make equal angles with a tangent passing through that point.*

Let TM (*fig.* 418.) be a tangent touching the curve
at the point M, and let F, f be the two foci ; join
FM, fM, then will the angle FMT be equal to the
angle fMR.   For draw the ordinate PM, and draw
fR parallel to FM, then will the triangles TFM and
TfR be similar ; and by Cor. Theor. VII.,

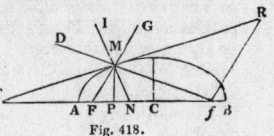

Fig. 418.

By Cor. 2. Theor. V.,

Therefore, by equality,

By division and composition,

That is,

By the similar triangles TFM, TfR;

$$CA : CP :: CT : CA ;$$
$$CA : CP :: CF : CA - FM ;$$
$$CT : CF :: CA : CA - FM.$$
$$CT - CF : CT + CF :: FM : 2CA - FM ;$$
$$TF : T f :: FM : f M.$$
$$TF : T f :: FM : f R.$$

It therefore appears that fM is equal to fR, therefore the angle fMR is equal to the angle fRM : but because FM and fR are parallel lines, the angle FMT is equal to the angle fRM ; therefore the angle FMT is equal to the angle fMR.

Coroll. 1. Hence a line drawn perpendicular to a tangent through the point of contact will bisect the angle FMf, or the opposite angle DMG.   For let MN be perpendicular to the tangent TR.   Then, because the angle NMT and NMR are right angles, they are equal to one another ; and since the angles FMT and fMR are also equal to one another, the remaining angles NMF and NMf are equal to one another.   Again, because the opposite angles FMN and IMG are equal to one another, and the opposite angle fMN and IMD are equal to one another ; therefore the straight line MI, which is the line MN produced, will also bisect the angle DMG.

Coroll. 2. The tangent will bisect the angle formed by one of the radius vectors, and the prolongation of the other.   For prolong FM to G.   Then, because the angles RMN and RMI are right angles, they are equal to one another ; and because the angles NMf and IMD are equal to one another, the remaining angles RMG and RMf are equal to one another.

Scholium. Hence we have an easy method of drawing a tangent to any given point M in the curve, or of drawing a perpendicular through a given point in the curve, which is the usual mode of drawing the joints for masonic arches.   Thus, in order to draw the line IM perpendicular to the curve : produce FM to G, and fM to D, and draw MI bisecting the angle DMG ; then IM will be perpendicular to the tangent TR, and consequently to the curve.

As in optics the angle of incidence is always found equal to the angle of reflection, it appears that the foundation of that law follows from this theorem ; for rays of light issuing from one focus, and meeting the curve in any point, will be reflected into lines drawn from these points to the other focus : thus the ray fM is reflected into MF : and this is the reason why the points Ff are called *foci*, or burning points.   In like manner, a sound in one focus is reflected in the other focus.

1074. **Theorem X.**   *Every parallelogram which has its sides parallel to two conjugate diameters and circumscribes an ellipsis is equal to the rectangle of the two axes.*

Let CM and CI (*fig.* 419.) be two semi-conjugate diameters.   Complete the parallelogram CIDM.   Produce CA
and MD to meet in T, and let AT meet DI in t.   Draw
IH and PM ordinates to the axis, and draw half the minor
axis CE.   Produce DM to K, and draw CK perpendicular
to DK : then will the parallelogram CIDM be equal to the
rectangle, whose sides are CA and CE ; or four times the
rectangle CIDM will be equal to the rectangle made of the two axes AB and GE.

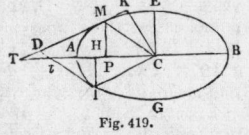

Fig. 419.

By Cor. Theor. VII.,

Therefore

By the similar triangles CtI, TCM,

By equality, therefore,

By the similar triangles CIH, TMP,

Therefore, by equality,

Consequently

But by Theor. VII.,

Therefore, since CT = CP + PT,

$$\begin{cases} CA : CT :: CP : CA, \\ C t : CA :: CA : CH ; \end{cases}$$
$$C t : CT :: CP : CH.$$
$$C t : CT :: CI : TM ;$$
$$CI : TM :: CP : CH.$$
$$CI : TM :: CH : PT ;$$
$$CH : PT :: CP : CH.$$
$$CP \times PT = CH^2.$$
$$CP \times CT = CA^2 ;$$
$$CP^2 + CP.PT = CA^2,$$

And, by transposition,	$CP.PT = CA^2 - CP^2$;
Hence, by equality,	$CH^2 = CA^2 - CP^2$,
Or, by transposition,	$CP^2 = CA^2 - CH^2$.
But by Cor. 2. Theor. I.,	$CA^2 \times HI^2 = CE^2(CA^2 - CH^2)$,
And substituting CP^2 for its equal $CA^2 - CH^2$, we have	$\left.\right\}$ $CA^2 \times HI^2 = CE^2 \times CP^2$;
Therefore	$CA : CP :: CE : HI.$
But again, by Theor. VII.,	$CA : CP :: CT : CA$;
By equality, therefore,	$CE : HI :: CT : CA.$
But by the similar triangles HIC, KCT,	$HI : CI :: CK : CT$;
Therefore	$CE : CI :: CK : CA$:
Consequently	$CE \times CA = CI \times CK.$

The ellipsis is of so frequent occurrence in architectural works, that an acquaintance with all the properties of the curve, and the modes of describing it, is of great importance to the architect. Excepting the circle, which may be called an ellipsis in which the two foci coincide, it is the most generally employed curve in architecture.

1075. PROBLEM I. *To describe an ellipsis.*

Let two pins at E and F (*fig.* 420.) be fixed in a plane within a string whose ends are made fast at C. If the point C be drawn equally tight while it is moved forward in the plane till it returns to the place from which it commenced, it will describe an ellipsis.

1076. PROB. II. *The two diameters* AB *and* ED *of an ellipse being given in position and magnitude, to describe the curve through points.*

Let the two diameters cut each other at

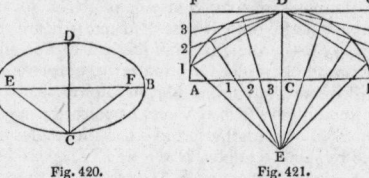

Fig. 420. Fig. 421.

C (*fig.* 421.). Draw AF and BG parallel to ED. Divide AC and AF each into the same number of equal parts, and draw lines, as in the figure, through the points of division; viz. those from the line AF to the point D, and the lines through AC to the point E; then through the points of intersection of the corresponding lines draw the curve AD, and in the same manner find the curve BD; then ADB will be the semi-ellipsis.

It is evident that the same method also extends to a circle by making CD equal to CA; (*fig.* 422.); and it appears that the two lines forming any point of the curve to be drawn will make a right angle with each other. For these lines terminate at the extremities of the diameter ED, and the point of concourse being in the curve, the angle made by them must be a right angle; that is, the angle EAD, or EhD, or EiD, or EkD, is a right angle: and from this property we have the following method of drawing the segment of a circle through points found in the curve.

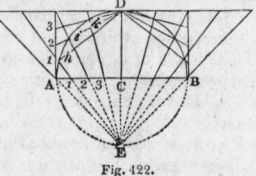

Fig. 422.

Thus, let AB be the chord, and CD be the versed sine of an arc of a circle, to describe the arc. Through D draw HI (*fig.* 423.) parallel to AB; join AD and DB; draw AH perpendicular to AD, and BI perpendicular to BD; divide AC and HD each into the same number of equal parts, and join the corresponding points; divide AF into the same number of equal parts, and through the points of division draw lines to D, and through the corresponding points where these lines meet the former draw a curve AD. In the same manner the other half BD may be drawn.

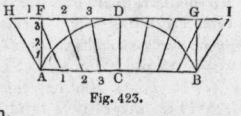

Fig. 423.

1077. PROB. III. *A diameter KH of an ellipsis being given, and an ordinate DL, to find the limits of the other conjugate diameter.*

Bisect KH in I (*fig.* 424.), through I draw EA parallel to DL, and draw DC and KB perpendicular to EA; from the point L with the distance K describe an arc cutting EA at F; join LF, and produce LF to C; make IE and IA each equal to LC; then will EA be a diameter conjugate to KH.

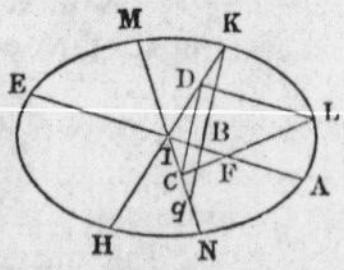

1078. PROB. IV. *A diameter KH and an ordinate DL of an ellipsis being given, to describe the curve.* (*fig.* 424.)

Find the limits E and A of the other conjugate diameter by the preceding construction. Produce KB to q, and make Kq equal to IA or IE, and through the centre I of the curve and the point q, draw the straight line MN. Then, suppose the straight line KBq to be an inflexible rod, having the point B marked upon it. Move the rod round, so that the point q on the rod may be in the line MN, while the point B is in the line EA; then, at any instant of the motion, the place

Fig. 424.

of the point K on the plane whereon the figure is to be drawn may be marked; the points thus found will be in the curve. Instead of a rod, a slip of paper may be used, and in some cases a rod with adjustible points to slide in a cross groove, and a sliding head for a pencil is convenient; and such an instrument is called a *trammel*.

When the diameters KH and EA (*fig.* 425.) are at right angles to each other, the straight line K*q* coincides with the diameter KH, and consequently the line MN, on which the point *q* of the inflexible line K*q* moves, will also fall upon the diameter KH.   Therefore in this case no-thing more is required to find the limits of the other diameter, than to take the half diameters IK, KH of the given diameters, and from the extremity L with that distance describe an arc cutting the unlimited diameter in the point F; then drawing

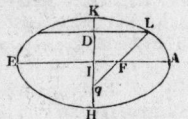
Fig. 425.

LF, and producing it to *q*, and making IE and IA each equal to *q*L, EA will be the other diameter; and since the two diameters are at right angles to each other, they are the two axes given in position and magnitude, and thus the curve may be described as before.

A method of describing the curve from any two conjugate diameters is occasionally of considerable use, and particularly so in perspective.   For, in every representation of a circle in perspective, a diameter and a double ordinate may be determined by making one of the diameters of the original circle perpendicular to the plane of the picture and the other parallel to it; and then the representation of the diameter of the original circle, which is perpendicular to the intersecting line, will be a diameter of the ellipsis, which is the representation of that circle; and the representation of the diameter of the circle which is parallel to the intersecting line will become a double ordinate to the diameter of the ellipsis which is the perspective representation of the circle.

1079. Prob. V.   *Through two given points A and B to describe an ellipsis, the centre C being given in position and the greater axis being given in magnitude only.*

About the centre C (*fig.* 426.) with a radius equal to half the greater axis describe a circle HEDG; join AC and BC; draw AD perpendicular to AC, and BE perpendicular to BC, cutting the circumference in the points D and E; draw also BF parallel to AC, and find BF, which is a fourth propor-tional to AD, AC, and BE; through the point F and the centre C draw FG to cut the circle in H and G, and GH is the major axis of the ellipsis.   By drawing an ordinate B*q*, the curve may be described by the preceding problem, having the axis GH and the ordinate B*q*.

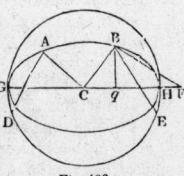
Fig. 426.

1080. Prob. VI.   *Through a given point in the major axis of a given ellipsis to describe another similar ellipsis which shall have the same centre and its major axis on the same straight line as that of the given ellipsis.*

Let ACBD (*fig.* 427.) be the given ellipsis, having AB for its major axis and CD for its minor axis, which are both given in position and magnitude. It is required to draw a similar ellipsis through the point G in the major axis AG.   Draw BK perpendicular and CK parallel to AB, and join KE.   Again, draw GL perpendicular to AB cut-ting EK at L, and draw LH parallel to AB cutting CD in H. On the axis CD make EI equal to EH, and on the axis AB make EF equal to EG.   Then, having the major axis AB, and the minor axis FG, the ellipsis FIGH may be described, and when drawn, it will be similar to the given ellipsis ADBC.

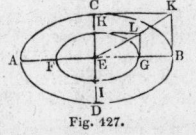
Fig. 427.

1081. Prob. VII.   *Through any given point p, within the curve of a given ellipsis to describe another ellipsis which shall be similar and concentric to the given one.*

Let C (*fig.* 428.) be its centre.   Draw the straight line C*p*P, cutting the curve of the given ellipsis in P.   In such curve take any other number of points Q, R, S, &c., and join QC, RC, SC, &c.; join PQ and draw *pq* parallel thereto cutting *q*C at *q*: join PR and draw *pr* parallel to PR, cutting RC at *r*; join PS and draw *ps* parallel to PS cutting SC in *s*.   The whole being completed, and the curve *p*, *s*, *t*, *u* drawn through the points *p*, *q*, *r*, *s*, &c., the figure will be similar and concentric to the given ellipse P, S, T, U; or when the points at the extremities for one half of the curve have been

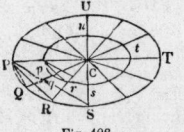
Fig. 428

drawn, the other half may be found by producing the diameter to the opposite side, and making the part produced equal to the other part.

1082. Prob. VIII.   *About a given rectangle ABCD to describe an ellipsis which shall have its major and minor axes respectively parallel to the sides of the rectangle and its centre in the points of intersection of the two diagonals.*

Bisect the sides AD and AB (*fig.* 429.) of the rectangle respectively at L and O;

through L draw GH parallel to AB cutting the opposite side BC of the rectangle in M, and through the point O draw KI parallel to AD or BC cutting the opposite side DC in N. In NK or NK produced, make NQ equal to NC, and join CQ; draw QR parallel to GH cutting CB or CB produced in R; make EH and EG each equal to QC, as also EI and EK each equal to PC; then will GH be the major axis and KI the minor axis of the ellipsis required.

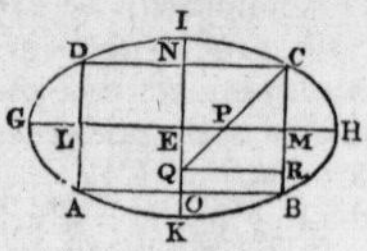

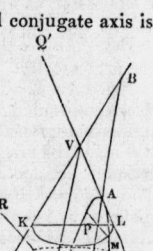

Fig. 429.

The demonstration of this method, in which the line QK has nothing to do with the construction, is as follows : —

By the similar triangles CPM and CQR, we have CP : CM::CQ : CR.

But because MP is equal to MC=EN, and since CR is equal to RQ=EM,

And, by construction, since PC is equal to EI or EK, and QC is equal to EG or EH,

    - EI : EN::EH : EM, or, alternately, EI : EH::EN : EM.

      But EN is equal to MC, and EM equal to NC;

      Whence EI : EH::MC : CN.

But since the wholes are as the halves, we shall have KI : GH::BC : CD.

This problem is useful in its application to architecture about domes and pendentives, as well as in the construction of spheroidal ceilings and other details.

OF THE HYPERBOLA.

1083. The direction of a plane cutting a cone, which produces the form called the hyperbola, has been already described; its most useful properties will form the subject of the following theorems, which we shall preface with a few definitions : —

1. The primary axis of an hyperbola is called the *transverse axis.*

2. A straight line drawn through the centre of an hyperbola and terminated at each extremity by the opposite curves is called a *diameter.*

3. The extremities of a diameter terminated by the two opposite curves are called the *vertices of that diameter.*

4. A straight line drawn from any point of a diameter to meet the curve parallel to a tangent at the extremity of that diameter is called *an ordinate* to the two abscissas.

5. A straight line which is bisected at right angles by the transverse axis in its centre, and which is a fourth proportional to the mean of the two abscissas, their ordinate, and the transverse axis, is called the *conjugate axis.*

6. A straight line which is a third proportional to the transverse and conjugate axis is called the *latus rectum* or *parameter.*

7. The two points in the transverse axis cut by ordinates which are equal to the semi-parameter are called the *foci.*

1084. THEOREM. I. *In the hyperbola the squares of the ordinates of the transverse axis are to each other as the rectangles of their abscissas.*

Let QVN (*fig.* 430.) be a section of the cone passing along the axis VD, the line of section of the directing plane, HB the line of axis of the cutting plane, the directing and cutting plane being perpendicular to the plane QVN. Let the cone be cut by two planes perpendicular to the axis passing through the two points P, H, meeting the plane of section in the lines PM, HI, which are ordinates to the circles and to the figure of the section, of the same time,

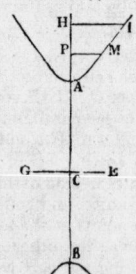

Fig. 430.

By the similar triangles APL and AHN,   AP : PL::AH : HN;

And by the similar triangles BPK and BHQ, BP : PK::BH : HQ.

Therefore, taking the rectangles of the corresponding terms, AP × BP : PL × PK::AH × BH : HN × HQ.

    But in the circle, PL × PK = PM², and HN × HQ = HI² ;

    Therefore   AP × BP : PM²::AH × BH : HI²,

    Or, alternately, PM² : HI²::AP : PB : AH : BH.

1085. THEOREM II. *In the hyperbola, as the square of the transverse axis is to the square of the conjugate axis, so is the rectangle of the abscissas to the square of their ordinate.*

Let AB (*fig.* 431.) be the transverse axis, GE the conjugate axis, C being the centre of the opposite curves; also let HI and PM be ordinates as before; then will

             AB² : GE²::PA × PB : PM².

Or   CA² : CE²::PA × PB : PM².

By Theor. I., PA × PB : HA × HB::PM² : HI² ;

Alternately,   PA × PB : PM²::HA × HB::HI².

But   HA × HB : HI²::AB² : GE² ;

Therefore   AB² : GE²::PA × PB : PM².

Fig. 431.

Coroll.   Hence $AB^2 : GE^2 :: CP^2 - CA^2 : PM^2$ (*fig.* 432.).   For let the cutting plane of the opposite hyperbola intersect two circles parallel to the base in HI and PM, and let the cone be cut by another plane parallel to the base, passing through the centre C of the transverse axis, and let *mn* be the diameter of the circle made by such plane.

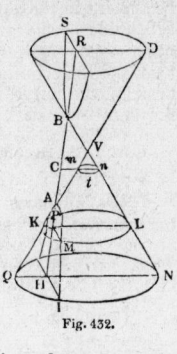

Then   ACm, APK are similar, and AC : Cm :: AP : PK.
And as BCn, BPL are similar,   BC : Cn :: BP : PL.

Therefore, taking the rectangles of the corresponding terms,
$$BC \times AC : Cn \times Cm :: BP \times AP : PL \times PK.$$

But $BC = AC$; $Cm \times Cn = Ct^2$; and $PL \times PK = PM^2$.
Therefore $AC^2 : Ct^2 :: AP \times BP : PM^2$.

Though Ct is not in the same plane, it is what is usually called the semi-conjugate axis, and it agrees with what has been demonstrated in the first part of this proposition.

Fig. 432.

1086.   Theorem III.   *In the hyperbola, the square of the semi-conjugate axis is to the square of the semi-transverse axis as the sum of the squares of the semi-conjugate axis and of the ordinate parallel to it is to the square of the abscissas.*

Let AB (*fig.* 433.) be the transverse axis, GE the conjugate, C the centre of the figure, and PM an ordinate, then will

$$GE^2 : AB^2 :: CE^2 + PM^2 : CP^2.$$
For, by Theor. II., $CE^2 : CA^2 :: PM^2 : CP^2 - CA^2$,
And, by composition, $CE^2 : CA^2 :: CE^2 + PM^2 : CP^2$.

This demonstration may be also applied to what are called conjugate hyperbolas.

1087.   Theorem IV.   *In the hyperbola, the square of the distance of the focus from the centre is equal to the sum of the squares of the semi-axes.*

Let AB (*fig.* 434.) be the transverse axis, CE the semi-conjugate.   In AB, produced within the curve each way, let F be one focus; and f the other, and let FG be the semi-parameter then $CF^2 = CA^2 + CE^2$.

For, by Theor. I., $CA^2 : CE^2 :: FA \times FB : FG^2$;
But, by property of parameter, $CA^2 : CE^2 :: CE^2 : FG^2$.
Therefore $CE^2 = AF \times FB = CF - CA$;
And, by transposition, $CF^2 = CA^2 + CE^2$.

Fig. 433.

Coroll. 1.   The two semi-axes, and the distance of the focus from the centre, are the sides of a right-angled triangle CEA, of which the distance AE is the distance of the focus from the centre.

Coroll. 2.   The conjugate axis CE is a mean proportional between FA and FB, or between fB and fA, for $CE^2 = CF^2 - CA = (CF + CA) \times (CF - CA) = BF \times AF.$

1088.   Theorem V.   *The difference of the radius vectors is equal to the transverse axis.* (*fig.* 435.)

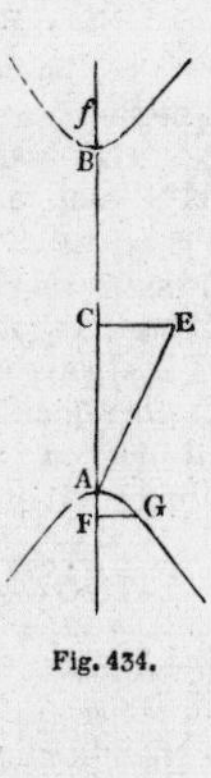

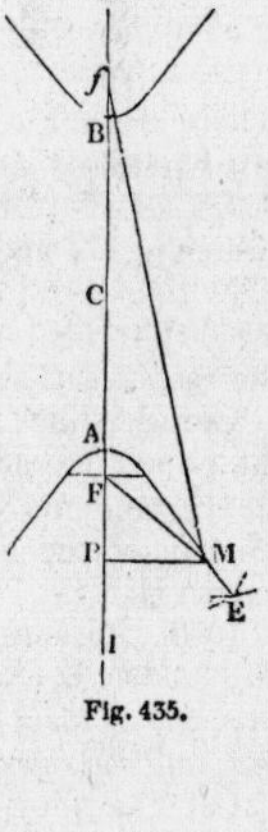

That is, $fM - FM = AB = 2CA = 2CB$.
For $CA^2 : CE^2 :: CP^2 - CA^2 : PM^2$;
And $CE^2 = CF^2 - CA^2$.
Therefore $CA^2 : CF^2 - CA^2 :: CP^2 - CA^2 : PM^2$.

And by taking the rectangle of the extremes and means, and dividing by CA^2,

$$PM^2 = \frac{CF^2 \times CP^2}{CA^2} - CF^2 - CP^2 + CA^2;$$
But $FP^2 = (CP - CF)^2 = CP^2 - 2CP \times CF + CF^2$,
And $FM^2 = PM^2 + FP^2$.

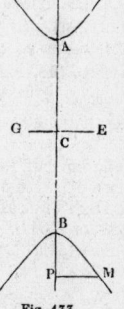

Fig. 434.   Fig. 435.

Therefore $FM^2 = \frac{CF^2 \times CP^2}{CA^2} - 2CP \times CF + CA^2.$

Now each side of this equation is a complete square.

Therefore, extracting the root of each number, $FM = \frac{CF \times CP}{CA} - CA.$

In the same manner we find $fM = \frac{CF \times CP}{CA} + CA$;

And, subtracting the upper equation from the lower, $fM - FM = 2CA.$

Coroll. 1.   Hence is derived the common method of describing the hyperbolic curve mechanically.   Thus : — In the transverse axis AB produced (*fig.* 435.), take the foci F, *f*, and any point I in the straight line AB so produced.   Then, with the radii AI, BI, and the

centre F, f, describe arcs intersecting each other ; call the points of intersection E, then E will be a point in the curve ; with the same distances another point on the other side of the axis may be found.   In like manner, by taking any other points I, we may find two more points, one on each side of the axis, and thus continue till a sufficient number of points be found to describe the curve by hand.   By the same process, we may also describe the opposite hyperbolas.

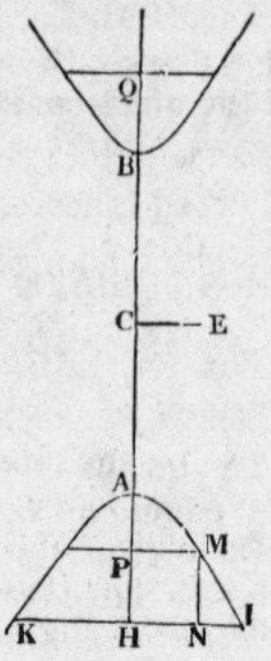

Coroll. 2.   Because $\dfrac{CF \times CP}{CA}$ is a fourth proportional to CA, CF CP, CA : CF :: CP : CA + FM.

1089. Theorem VI.   *As the square of the semi-transverse axis is to the square of the semi-conjugate, so is the difference of the squares of any two abscissas to the difference of the squares of their ordinates.*

By Theor. II.,
$$\begin{cases} CA^2 : CE^2 :: CP^2 - CA^2 : PM^2 \ (fig.\ 436.), \\ CA^2 : CE^2 :: CH^2 - CA^2 : HI^2. \end{cases}$$

Therefore, by equality, $CH^2 - CA^2 : CP^2 - CA^2 :: HI^2 : PM^2$ or HN^2 ;

And, by division, $CH^2 - CA^2 : CH^2 - CP^2 :: HI^2 : HI^2 - HN^2$;

Alternately, $CH^2 - CA^2 : HI^2 :: CH^2 - CP^2 : HI^2 - HN^2.$

But $CH^2 - CA^2 : HI^2 :: CA^2 : CE^2$

Therefore $CA^2 : CE^2 :: CH^2 - CP^2 :: HI^2 - HN^2.$

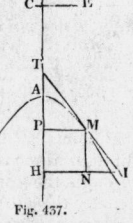

Fig. 436.

Coroll. 1.   If IH be produced to K, and CQ be made equal to CP, then will $CH^2 - CP^2 = (CH + CP)(CH - CP) = (CP + CH)PH$;   and $HI^2 - HN^2 = (HI + HN)(HI - HN) = (HI + HN)NI.$ Therefore the analogy resulting becomes

$$CA^2 : CE^2 :: (CP + CH)PH : (HI + HN)NI.$$

So that the square of the transverse axis is to the square of the conjugate, or the square of the semi-transverse is to the square of the semi-conjugate, as the rectangle of the sum and difference of the two ordinates from the centre is to the rectangle of the sum and difference of these ordinates.

1090. Theorem VII.   *If a tangent and an ordinate be drawn from any point in an hyperbola to meet the transverse axis, the semi-transverse axis will be a mean proportional between the distances of the two intersections from the centre.*

For (*fig.* 437.) $CE^2 : CA^2 :: (IH + HN)IN :: (PC + CH)HP$;

And by Theor. I., $CE^2 : CA^2 :: PM^2 : CP^2 - CA^2$;

By equality, $PM^2 : CP^2 - CA^2 :: (IH + HN)\ IN : (PC + CH)HP$;

And by similar triangles INM, MPT, IN : NM or PH :: PM : PT or CP − CT.

Therefore, taking the rectangles of the extremes and means of the two last equations, and neglecting the common factors, it will be $PM(CP - CT)(CP + CH) = (CP - CA^2)(IH + HN)$; but when IH and PM coincide, IH and HN each become equal to PM, and CH equal to CP: therefore in the equation substitute 2CP for CP + CH, and 2PM for IH + HN, and neglecting the common factors and common terms, the result is $CT.CP = CA^2$, or $CT : CA :: CA : CP.$

Coroll. Since CT is always a third proportional to CP, CA ; suppose the points P and A to remain constant, the point T will also remain constant ; therefore all the tangents will meet in the point T which are drawn from the extremity of the ordinate M of every hyperbola described on the same axis AB.

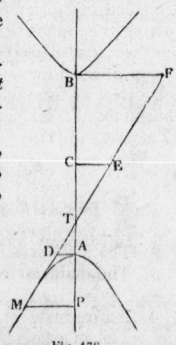

Fig. 437.

1091. Theorem VIII.   *Four perpendiculars to the transverse axis intercepted by it and a tangent, will be proportionals when the first and last have one of their extremities in each vertex, the second in the point of contact, and the third in the centre.*

Let the four perpendiculars be AD, PM, CE, BF (*fig.* 438.), whereof AD and BF have their extremities in the vertices A and B, and the second in the point of contact M of the tangent and the curve, and the third in the centre C.

Then will   AD : PM :: CE : BF.

For, by Theor. VII.,   CT : CA :: CA : CP,

And, by division,   CA − CT : CP − CA :: CT : CA or CB ;

That is,   AT : AP :: CT : CB ;

By composition,   AT : AT + AP :: CT : CT + CB.

Therefore   AT : TP :: CT : BT.

Fig. 438.

But by the similar triangles TAD, TPM, TCE, and TBF, the sides AT, PT, CT, and BT are proportional to the four perpendiculars AD, PM, CE, BF.

$$\text{Therefore } AD : PM :: CE : BF.$$

1092. **Theorem IX.** *The two radius vectors meeting the curve in the same point will make equal angles with a tangent passing through that point.* (*Fig.* 439.)

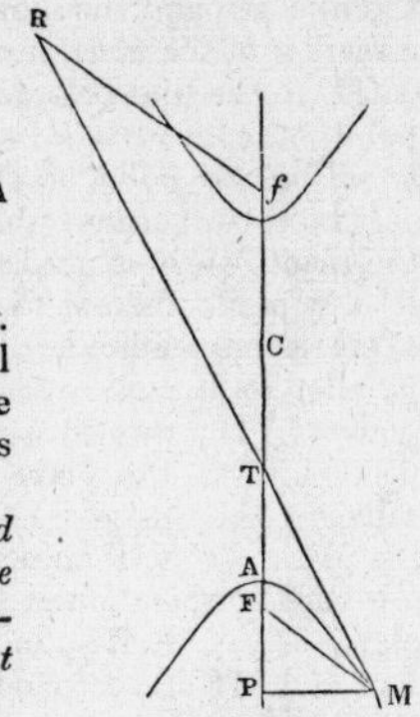

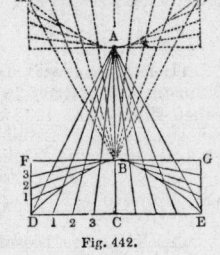

For, by Theor. VII.,   CA : CP :: CT : CA ;
By Cor. 2. Theor. V.,   CA : CP :: CF : CA + FM ;
By equality,   CT : CF :: CA : CA + FM ;
By division and composition, CF − CT : CF + CT :: FM : 2CA
                                                    + FM ;
That is,   FT : fT :: FM : fR ;

And by the similar triangles TFM, TfR, FT : fT :: FM : fR. Therefore fR is equal to fM ; consequently the angle fRM is equal to the angle fMR : and because fR is parallel to fM, the angle FMT is equal to the angle fRM ; therefore the angle FMT is equal to the angle fRM.

1093. **Problem I.** *To describe an hyperbola by means of the end of a ruler moveable on a pin* F (*fig.* 440.) *fixed in a plane, with one end of a string fixed to a point* E *in the same plane, and the other extremity of the string fastened to the other end* C *of the ruler, the point* C *of the ruler being moved towards* G *in that plane.*

While the ruler is moving, a point D being made to slide along the edge of the ruler, kept close to the string so as to keep each of the parts C D, D E of the string stretched, the point D will describe the curve of an hyperbola.

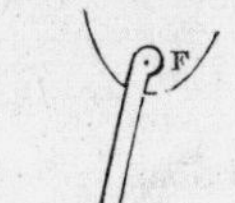

If the end of the ruler at F (*fig.* 441.) be made moveable about the point E, and the string be fixed in F and to the end C of the ruler, as before, another curve may be described in the same manner, which is called the *opposite hyperbola :* the points E and F, about which the ruler is made to revolve, are the foci.

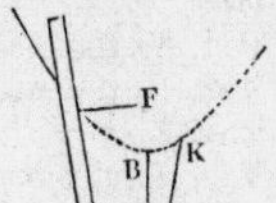

There are many occasions in which the use of this conic section occurs in architectural details. For instance, the profiles of many of the Grecian mouldings are hyperbolic ; and in conical roofs the forms are by intersections such that the student should be well acquainted with the methods of describing it.

1094. **Prob. II.** *Given the diameter* AB, *the abscissa* BC, *and the double ordinate* DE *in position and magnitude, to describe the hyperbola.* (*Fig.* 442.)

Through B draw FG parallel to DE, and draw DF and EG parallel to AB.

Divide DF and DC each into the same number of equal parts, and from the points of division in BF draw lines to B, also from the points of division in DC draw straight lines to A ; then through the points of intersection found by the lines drawn through the corresponding points draw the curve DB. In like manner the curve EB may be drawn so that DBE will form the curve on each side of the diameter AB. If the point A be considered as the vertex, the opposite hyperbola HAI may be described in the same manner, and thus the two curves formed by cutting the opposite cones by the same plane will be found. By the theorists, the hyperbola has been considered a proper figure of equilibrium for an arch whose office is to support a load which is greatest at the middle of the arch, and diminishes towards the abutments. This, however, is matter of consideration for another part of this work.

Fig. 439.

Fig. 440.

Fig. 441.

Fig. 442.

OF THE PARABOLA.

1095. **Definitions.**—1. The parameter of the axis of a parabola is a third proportional to the abscissa and its ordinate.

2. The focus is that point in the axis where the ordinate is equal to the semi-parameter.

3. The diameter is a line within the curve terminated thereby, and is parallel to the axis.

4. An ordinate to any diameter is a line contained by the curve and that diameter parallel to a tangent at the extremity of the diameter.

1096. Theorem I. *In the parabola, the abscissas are proportional to the squares of their ordinates.*

Let QVN (*fig.* 443.) be a section of the cone passing along the axis, and let the directrix RX pass through the point Q perpendicular to QN, and let the

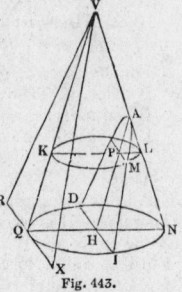

Fig. 443.

parabolic section be ADI meeting the base QIND of the cone in
the line DI, and the diameter QN in the point H; also let KML be
a section of the cone parallel to the base QIN intersecting the plane
VQN in the line KL, and the section ADI in PM. Let P be the
point of concourse of the three planes QVN, KML, AHI, and
let H be the point of concourse of the three planes QVN, KML,
AHI; then, because the planes VRX and ADI are parallel, and
the plane VQN is perpendicular to the plane VRX, the plane ADI
is also perpendicular to the plane VQN. Again, because the plane
QIN is perpendicular to the plane QVN, and the plane KML is
parallel to the plane QIN, the plane KML is perpendicular to the
plane QVN; therefore the common sections PM and HI are perpendicular to the plane VQN; and because the plane KML is parallel to the plane QIN; and these two planes are intersected by
the plane QVN, their common sections KL and QN are parallel. Also, since PM and HI
are each perpendicular to the plane QVN, and since KL is the common section of the
planes QVN, KML, and QN in the common section of the planes QVN, QIN; therefore
PM and HI are perpendicular respectively to KL and QN.

Consequently $AP : AH :: PM^2 : HI^2.$
For, by the similar triangles APL, AHN, $AP : AH :: PL : HN,$
Or $AP : AH :: KP \times PL : KP \times HN.$
But, by the circle   KML, $KP \times PL = PM^2,$
And, by the circle   QIN, $QH \times HN = HI^2.$ But $QH = KP,$
Therefore $KP \times HN = HI^2.$
Therefore, by substitution, $AP : AH :: PM^2 : HI^2.$

Coroll. By the definition of the parameter, which we shall call P,

$$AP : PM :: PM : P = \frac{PM^2}{PA},$$

And $P \times AP = PM^2$, or $P \times AH = HI^2.$
Therefore $P : PM :: PM : AP$, or $P : HI :: HI : AH.$

1097. Theorem II. *As the parameter of the axis is to the sum of any two ordinates, so is
the difference of these ordinates to the difference of their abscissas.*

That is, $P : HI + PM :: HI - PM : AH - AP.$

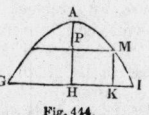

Fig. 444.

For since by Cor. Theor. I. $\begin{cases} P = \dfrac{PM^2}{AP}, \\ P = \dfrac{HI^2}{AH}; \end{cases}$

Multiplying the first of these equations by AP and the second by AH,

they become $\begin{cases} P \times AP = PM^2, \\ P \times AH = HI^2. \end{cases}$

Subtract the corresponding numbers of the first equation, and $P(AH - AP) = HI^2 - PM^2.$
But the difference of two squares is equal to a rectangle under the sum and difference of
their sides.

And $HI^2 - PM^2 = (HI + PM)(HI - PM).$
Therefore $P(AH - AP) = (HI + PM)(HI - PM).$
Consequently $P : HI + PM :: HI - PM : AH - AP.$
Or, by drawing KM parallel to AH, we have $GK = PM + HI$, and $KI = HI - PM$; and
since $PH = AH - AP$; $P : GK :: KI : PH$, or KM.
Coroll. Hence, because $P \times KM = GK \times KI;$
And since $HI^2 = P \times AH;$
Therefore, by multiplication, $KM \times HI^2 = GK \times KI \times AH$, or
                 $AH : KM :: HI^2 : GK \times KI.$
So that any diameter MK is as the rectangle of the segments GK,
KI of the double ordinate GI. From this a simple method has been
used of finding points in the curve, so as to describe it.

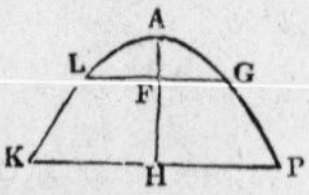

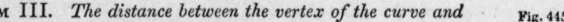

Fig. 445.

1098. Theorem III. *The distance between the vertex of the curve and
the focus is equal to one fourth of the parameter.*

Let LG (*fig.* 445.) be a double ordinate passing through the focus, then LG is the
parameter. For by the definition of parameter $AF : FG :: FG : P = 2FG.$

Therefore $2AF = FG = \frac{1}{2}LG;$
Consequently $AF = \frac{1}{4}LG.$

1099. Theorem IV. *The radius vector is equal to the sum of the distances between the focus and the vertex, and between the ordinate and the vertex.* (*Fig.* 446.)

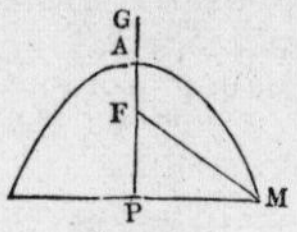

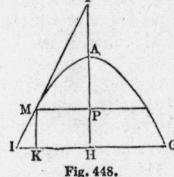

Fig. 446.

That is, $FM = AP + AF.$
For $FP = AP - AF;$
Therefore $FP^2 = AP^2 - 2AP \times AF + AF^2.$
But, by Cor. Theor. II., $PM^2 = P \times AP = 4AF \times AP.$
Therefore, by addition, $FP^2 + PM^2 = AP^2 + 2AF \times AP + AF^2.$

But by the right-angled tringles, $FP^2 + PM^2 = FM^2;$
And therefore $FM^2 = AP^2 + 2AF \times AP + AF^2.$
Hence, extracting the roots, $FM = AP + AF = 2AF + FP;$
Or by making $AG = AF, FM = GP.$

Coroll. 1. If through the point G (*fig.* 447.) the line GQ be drawn perpendicular to the axis, it is called the directrix of the parabola.

By the property shown in this theorem, it appears that if any line QM be drawn parallel to the axis, and if FM be joined, the straight line FM is equal to QM; for QM is equal to GP.

Coroll. 2. Hence, also, the curve is easily described by points. Take AG equal to AF, (*fig.* 447.), and draw a number of lines M, M perpendicular to the axis AP; then with the distances GP, GP, &c. as radii, and from F as a centre, describe arcs on each side of AP, cutting the lines MM, MM, &c. at MM, &c.; then through all the points M, M, M, &c. draw a curve, which will be a parabola.

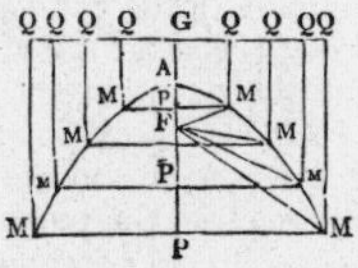

1100. Theorem V. *If a tangent be drawn from the vertex of an ordinate to meet the axis produced, the subtangent* PT (*fig.* 448.) *will be equal to twice the distance of the ordinate from the vertex.*

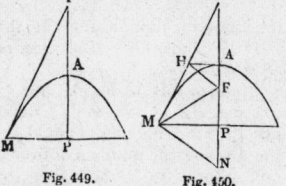

Fig. 447.   Fig. 448.

If MT be a tangent at M, the extremity of the ordinate PM; then the sub-tangent PT is equal to twice AP. For draw MK parallel to AH,

Then, by Theor. II., $KM : KI :: GK :: P;$
And as MKI, TPM are similar, $KM : KI :: PT : PM.$
Therefore, by equality, $P : PM :: GK : PT;$
And by Cor. Theor. I., $P : PM :: PM : AP.$
Therefore, by equality, $AP : PT :: PM : GK.$

But when the ordinates HI and PM coincide, MT will become a tangent, and GK will become equal to twice PM.

Therefore $AP : PT :: PM : 2PM,$ or
$$PT = 2AP.$$

From this property is obtained an easy and accurate method of drawing a tangent to any point of the curve of a parabola. Thus, let it be required to draw a tangent to any point M in the curve. Produce PA to T (*fig.* 449.), and draw MP perpendicular to PT, meeting AP in the point P. Make AT equal to AP, and join MT, which will be the tangent required.

1101. Theorem VI. *The radius vector is equal to the distance between the focus and the intersection of a tangent at the vertex of an ordinate and the axis produced.*

Fig. 449.   Fig. 450.

Produce PA to T (*fig.* 450.), and let MT be a tangent at M; then will $FT = FM.$

For $FT = AF + AT;$
But, by last theorem, $AP = AT;$
Therefore $FT = AF + AP.$
But, by Theorem III., $FM = AF + AP;$
Therefore, by equality, $FM = FT.$

Coroll. 1. If MN be drawn perpendicular to MT to meet the axis in N, then will $FN = FM = FT.$ For draw FH perpendicular to MT, and it also bisects MT, because $FM = FT;$ and since HF and MN are parallel, and MT is bisected in H, the line TN will also be bisected in F. It therefore follows that $FN = FM = FT.$

Coroll. 2. The *subnormal* PN is a constant quantity, and it is equal to half the parameter, or to $2AF.$ For since TMN is a right angle,

Therefore $2AP$ or $TP : PM :: PM : PN.$
But, by the definition of parameter, $AP : PM :: PM : P;$
Therefore $PN = \frac{1}{2}P.$

Coroll. 3. The tangent of the vertex AH is a mean proportional between AF and AP. For since FHT is a right angle, therefore AH is a mean proportional between AF and AT; and since AT=AP, AH is a mean proportional between AF and AP. Also FH is a mean proportional between FA and FT, or between FA and FM.

Coroll. 4. The tangent makes equal angles with FM and the axis AP, as well as with FC and CI.

1102. THEOREM VII. *A line parallel to the axis, intercepted by a double ordinate and a tangent at the vertex of that ordinate, will be divided by the curve in the same ratio as the line itself divides the double ordinate.*

Let QM (*fig.* 451.) be the double ordinate, MT the tangent, AP the axis, GK the intercepted line divided by the curve in the point I; then will GI : IK :: MK : KQ.

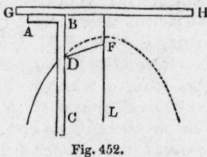

Fig. 451.

For by similar triangles MKG, MPT; MK : KG :: PM : PT, or 2AP;

By the definition of parameter,	P : PM :: PM : 2AP;
Therefore, by equality,	P : MK :: PM : KG;
And again, by equality,	PM : MK :: 2AP : KG;
And by division,	MK : KQ :: GI : IK.

1103. PROBLEM I. *To describe a parabola.*

If a thread, equal in length to the leg BC (*fig.* 452.) of a right angle or square, be fixed to the end C, and the other end of the thread be fixed to a point F in a plane, then if the square be moved in that plane so that the leg AB may slide along the straight line GH, and the point D be always kept close to the edge BC of the square, and the two parts FD and DC of the string kept stretched, the point D will describe a curve on the plane, which will be a parabola.

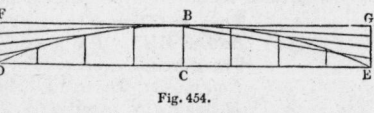

Fig. 452.

1104. PROB. II. *Given the double ordinate DE and the abscissa BC in position and magnitude, to describe a parabola.*

Through B (*figs.* 453, 454.) draw FG parallel to DE, and DF and EG parallel to CD.

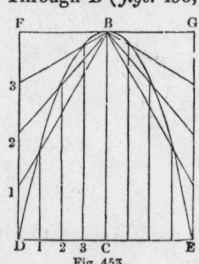

Fig. 453.

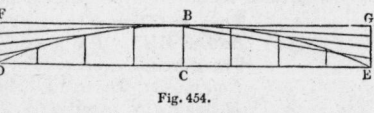

Fig. 454.

Divide DC and DF each into the same number of equal parts. From the points of division in DF draw lines to B. Through the points of division in DC draw lines parallel to BC, and through the points of intersection of the corresponding lines draw a curve, and complete the other half in the same manner; then will DBE be the complete curve of the parabola. The less BC is in proportion to CD, the nearer the curve will approach to the arc of a circle, as in fig. 422.; and hence we may describe the curve for diminishing the shaft of a column, or draw a flat segment of a circle.

1105. PROB. III. *The same parts being given, to describe the parabola by the intersection of straight lines.*

Produce CB to F (*fig.* 455.), and make BF equal to BC. Join FD and FE. Divide DF and FE in the same proportion, or into the same number of equal parts. Let the divisions be numbered from D to F, and from F to E, and join every two corresponding points by a straight line; then the intersection of all the straight lines will form the parabola required.

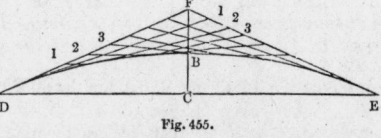

Fig. 455.

1106. PROB. IV. *To draw a straight line from a given point in the curve of a parabola, which shall be a tangent to the curve at that point.*

Let DC (*fig.* 456.) be the double ordinate, cB the abscissa to the parabolic curve DBC, and let it be required to draw a tangent from the point e in the curve. Draw ef parallel to DC, cutting BC in f: produce cB to g, and make Bg equal to Bf, and join ge, then will ge be the tangent required. In the same manner DH will be found to be a tangent at D. If eK be drawn perpendicular to the tangent ge, then will eK be also perpendicular to the curve, and in the proper direction for a joint in the masonry of a parabolic arch.

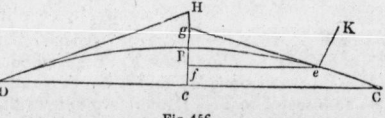

Fig. 456.

1107. The uses of the parabolic curve in architecture are many. The theorists say that it is the curve of equilibrium for an arch which has to sustain a load uniformly diffused over its length, and that therefore it should be included in the depth of lintels and flat arches; and that it is nearly the best form for suspension and other bridges, and for roofs. It is also considered the best form for beams of equal strength. It may be here also remarked, that it is the curve described by a projectile, and that it is the form in which a jet of water is delivered from an orifice made in the side of a reservoir. So is it the best curve for the reflection of light to be thrown to a distance. In construction it occurs in the intersection of conic surfaces by planes parallel to the side of the cone, and is a form of great beauty for the profiles of mouldings, in which manner it was much used in Grecian buildings.

GENERAL METHOD OF DETERMINING AND DESCRIBING THE SPECIES OF CONIC SECTIONS.

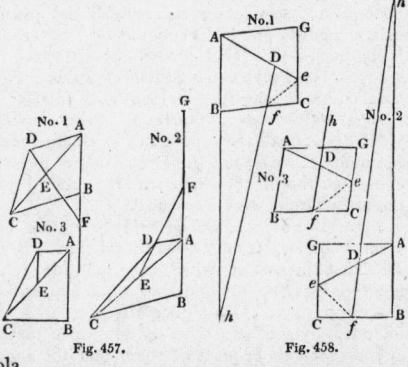

Fig. 457.   Fig. 458.

1108. In a conic section, let there be given the abscissa AB (*fig.* 457.), an ordinate BC, and a tangent CD to the curve at the extremity of the ordinate to determine the species of the conic section, and to describe the figure.

Draw AD parallel to BC, and join AC (Nos. 1. and 2.). Bisect AC in E, and produce DE and AB, so as to meet in F when DE is not parallel to AB; then in the case where DE will meet AB or AB produced in F, the point F will be the centre of an ellipsis or hyperbola. In this case produce AF to G, and make FG equal to FA; then if the ordinate BC and the centre be upon the same side of the apex A, the curve to which the given parts belong is an ellipsis; but if they be on different sides of it, the curve is an hyperbola. When the line DE (No. 3.) is parallel to AB, the figure is a parabola.

1109. In a conic section, the abscissa AB (*fig.* 458.), an ordinate BC, and a point D in the curve being given, to determine the species of the curve, and thence to describe it.

Draw CG parallel to AB (Nos. 1. and 2.), and AG parallel to BC. Join AD, and produce it to meet CG in e. Divide the ordinate CB in f in the same proportion as CG is divided, then will C*f* : *f*B :: C*e* : *e*G. Join D*f*, and produce it or *f*D to meet AB or BA in *h*; then if the points D and *h* fall upon opposite sides of the ordinate BC, the curve is an ellipsis; but if D and *h* fall upon the same side of the ordinate BC, the curve will be an hyperbola. If D*f* (No. 3.) be parallel to AB, the curve will be a parabola. In the case of the ellipsis and hyperbola, A*h* is a diameter; and therefore we have a diameter and ordinate to describe the curve.

SECT. V.

DESCRIPTIVE GEOMETRY.

1110. The term Descriptive Geometry, first used by Monge and other French geometers to express that part of the science of geometry which consists in the application of geometrical rules to the representation of the figures and the various relations of the forms of bodies, according to certain conventional methods, differs from common perspective by the design or representation being so made that the exact distance between the different points of the body represented can always be found; and thus the mathematical relations arising from its form and position may be deduced from the representation. Among the English writers on practical architecture, it has usually received the name of *projection*, from the circumstance of the different points and lines of the body being projected on the plane of representation; for, in descriptive geometry, points in space are represented by their orthographical projection on two planes at right angles to each other, called the *planes of projection*, one of which planes is usually supposed to be horizontal, in which case the other is vertical, the projections being called horizontal or vertical, according as they are on one or other of these planes.

1111. In this system, a point in space is represented by drawing a perpendicular from it to each of the planes of projection; the point whereon the perpendicular falls is the

projection of the proposed point. Then, as points in space are the boundaries of lines, so their projections similarly form lines, by whose means their projection is obtained; and by the projections of points lying in curves of any description, the projections of those curves are obtained.

1112. For obvious reasons, surfaces cannot be similarly represented; but if we suppose the surface to be represented, covered by a system of lines, according to some determinate law, then these lines projected on each of the two planes will, by their boundaries, enable us to project the surface in a rigorous and satisfactory manner.

1113. There are, however, some surfaces which may be more simply represented; for a plane is completely defined by the straight lines in which it intersects the two planes of projection, which lines are called the *traces* of the plane. So a sphere is completely defined by the two projections of its centre and the great circle which limits the projections of its points. So also a cylinder is defined by its intersection (or trace) with one of the planes of projection and by the two projections of one of its ends; and a cone by its intersection with one of the planes of projection and the two projections of its summit.

1114. Monge, before mentioned, Hachette, Vallée, and Leroi, are the most systematic writers on this subject, whose immediate application to architecture, and to the mechanical arts, and most especially to engineering, is very extensive; in consequence, indeed, of which it is considered of so much importance in France, as to form one of the principal departments of study in the Polytechnic School of Paris. A sufficient general idea of it for the architectural student may be obtained in a small work of Le Croix, entitled, *Complément des Elemens de Geometrie*. In the following pages, and occasionally in other parts of this work, we shall detail all those points of it which are connected more immediately with our subject, inasmuch as we do not think it necessary to involve the reader in a mass of scientific matter connected therewith, which we are certain he would never find necessary in the practice of the art whereon we are engaged.

1115. In order to comprehend the method of tracing geometrically the projections of all sorts of objects, we must observe,—I. That the visible faces only of solids are to be expressed. II. That the surfaces which enclose solids are of two sorts, rectilinear and curved. These, however, may be divided into three classes, — 1st. Those included by plane surfaces, as prisms, pyramids, and, generally, similar sorts of figures used in building. 2d. Those included by surfaces whereof some are plane and others with a simple curvature, as cylinders, cones, or parts of them, and the voussoirs of arches. 3d. Solids enclosed by one or several surfaces of double flexure, as the sphere, spheroids, and the voussoirs of arches on circular planes.

1116. *First class, or solids with plane surfaces.* — The plane surfaces by which these solids are bounded form at their junction edges or *arrisses*, which may be represented by right lines.

1117. And it is useful to observe in respect of solids that there are three sorts of angles formed by them. *First*, those arising from the meeting of the lines which bound the faces of a solid. *Second*, those which result from the concurrence of several faces whose edges unite and form the summit of an angle: thus a solid angle is composed of as many plane angles as there are planes uniting at the point, recollecting however that their number must be at least three. *Third*, the angles of the planes, which is that formed by two of the faces of a solid. A cube enclosed by six square equal planes comprises twelve rectilineal edges or arrisses and eight solid angles.

1118. Pyramids are solids standing on any polygonal bases, their planes or faces being triangular and meeting in a point at the top, where they form a solid angle.

1119. Prisms, like pyramids, may be placed on all sorts of polygonal bases, but they rise on every side of the base in parallelograms instead of triangles, thus having throughout similar form and thickness.

1120. Though, strictly speaking, pyramids and prisms are polyhedrons, the latter term is only applied to those solids whose faces forming polygons may each be considered as the base of a separate pyramid.

1121. In all solids with plane surfaces the arrisses terminate in solid angles formed by several of these surfaces, which unite with one another; whence, in order to find the projection of the right lines which represent those arrisses, all that we require to know is the position of the solid angles where they meet; and as a solid angle is generally composed of several plane angles, a single solid angle will determine the extremity of all the arrisses by which it is formed.

1122. *Second class: solids terminated by plane and curved surfaces.* — Some of these, as cones for instance, exhibit merely a point and two surfaces, one curved and the other flat. The meeting of these surfaces forms a circular or elliptical arris common to both. The projection of an entire cone requires several points for the curvature which forms its base, but a single point only is necessary to determine its summit. This solid may be considered as a pyramid with an elliptic or circular base; and to facilitate its projection a polygon is inscribed in the ellipsis or circle, which serves as its base.

1123. If the cone is truncated or cut off, polygons may in like manner be inscribed in the curves which produce the sections.

1124. Cylinders may be considered as prisms whose bases are formed by circles, ellipses, or other curves, and their projections may be obtained in a similar manner : that is, by inscribing polygons in the curves which form their bases.

1125. *Third class : solids whose surfaces have a double curvature.*—A solid of this sort may be enclosed in a single surface, as a sphere or spheroid.

1126. As these bodies present neither angles nor lines, they can only be represented by the apparent curve which seems to bound their superficies. This curve may be determined by tangents parallel to a line drawn from the centre of the solid perpendicularly to the plane of projection.

1127. If these solids are truncated or cut by planes, we must, after having traced the curves which represent them entire, inscribe polygons in each curve produced by the sections, in order to proceed as directed for cones and cylinders.

1128. To obtain a clear notion of the combination of several pieces, as, for instance, of a vault, we must imagine the bodies themselves annihilated, and that nothing remains but the arrisses or edges which form the extremes of the surfaces of the voussoirs. The whole assemblage of material lines which would result from this consideration being considered transparent would project upon a plane perpendicular to the rays of light, *traces* defining all these edges that we have supposed material, some foreshortened, and others of the same size. These will form the outlines of the vault, whence follow the subjoined remarks.

   I. That in order, on a plane, to obtain the projection of a right line representing the arris of any solid body, we must on such plane let fall verticals from each of its extremities.

   II. That if the arris be parallel to the plane of the drawing, the line which represents its projection is the same size as the original.

   III. That if it be oblique, its representation will be shorter than the original line.

   IV. That perpendiculars by means of which the projection is made being parallel to each other, the line projected cannot be longer than the line it represents.

   V. That in order to represent an arris or edge perpendicular to the plane of projection, a mere point marks it because it coincides in the length with the perpendiculars of projection.

   VI. That the measure of the obliquity of an arris or edge will be found by verticals let fall from its extremities.

1129. In conducting all the operations relative to projections, they are referable to two planes, whereof one is horizontal and the other vertical.

PROJECTION OF RIGHT LINES.

1130. The projection of a line AB (*fig.* 459.) perpendicular to a horizontal plane is ex-

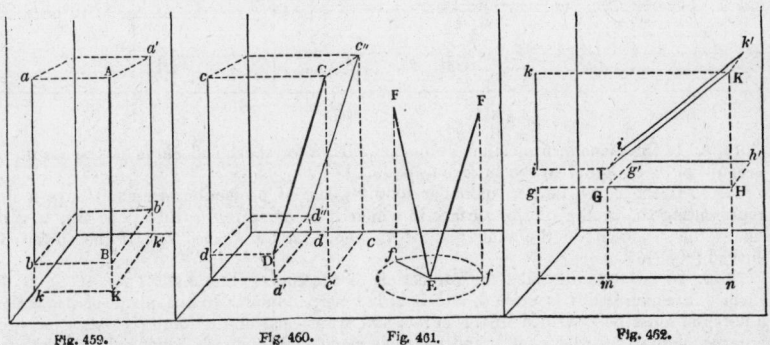

Fig. 459.   Fig. 460.   Fig. 461.   Fig. 462.

pressed on such plane by a point K, and by the lines ab, a'b', equal to the original on vertical planes, whatever their direction.

1131. An inclined line CD (*fig.* 460.) is represented on an horizontal or a vertical plane by cd, c'd', shorter than the line itself, except on a vertical plane, parallel to its projection, on the horizontal plane c''d'', where it is equal to the original CD.

1132. An inclined line EF (*fig.* 461.) moveable on its extremity E, may, by preserving the same inclination in respect of the plane on which it lies, have its projection successively in all the radii of the circle E*f*, determined by the perpendicular let fall from the point F.

1133. Two lines GH, IK (*fig.* 462.), whereof one is parallel to an horizontal plane and the other inclined, may have the same projection m, n, upon such plane. Upon a vertical

plane perpendicular to *mn*, the projection of the line GH will be a point *g*; and that of the inclined line IK, the vertical *ih*, which measures the inclination of that line. Lastly, on a vertical plane parallel to *mn*, the projection *i'k'* and *g'h'* will be parallel and equal to the original lines.

PROJECTION OF SURFACES.

1134. What has been said in respect of right lines projected on vertical and horizontal planes may be applied to plane surfaces; thus, from the surface ABCD (*fig.* 463.), parallel to an horizontal plane, results the projection *abcd* of the same size and form. An inclined surface EFGH may have, though longer, the same projection as the level one ABCD, if the lines of projection AE, BF, DH, CG are in the same direction.

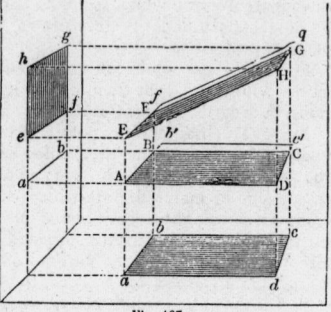

Fig. 463.

1135. The level surface ABCD would have for projection on vertical planes the right lines *ab*, *b'c'*, because that surface is in the same plane as the lines of projection.

1136. The inclined surface EFGH will give on vertical planes the foreshortened figure *hgef* of that surface; and upon the other the simple line *fq*, which shows the profile of its inclination, because this plane is parallel to the side of the inclined surface.

PROJECTION OF CURVED LINES.

1137. Curved lines not having their points in the same direction occupy a space which brings them under the laws of those of surfaces. The projection of a curve on a plane parallel to the surface in which it lies (*fig.* 464.) is similar to the curve.

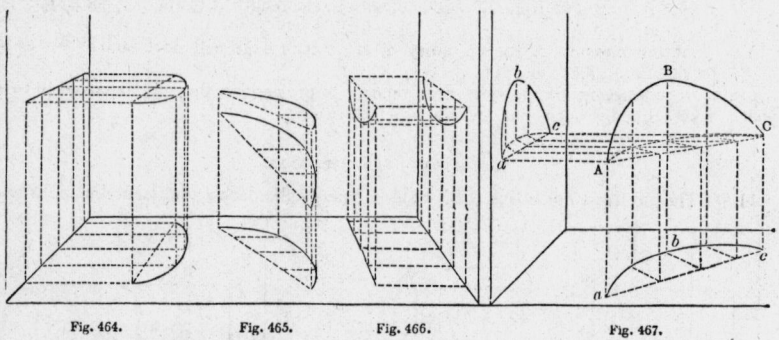

Fig. 464.   Fig. 465.   Fig. 466.   Fig. 467.

1138. If the plane of projection be not parallel, a foreshortened curve is the result, on account of its obliquity to the surface (*fig.* 465.).

1139. If the curve be perpendicular to the plane of projection, we shall have a line representing the profile of the surface in which it is comprised; that is to say, a right line if the surface lie in the same plane (*fig.* 466.), and a curved line if the surface be curved (*fig.* 467.).

1140. In order to describe the projection of the curved line ABC (*fig.* 467.), if the surface in which it lies is curved, and it is not perpendicular to the plane of projection, a polygon must be inscribed in the curve, and from each of the angles of such polygon a perpendicular must be let fall, and parallels made to the chords which subtend the arcs. But it is to be observed, that this line having a double flexure, we must further inscribe a polygon in the curvature which forms the plane *abc* of the surface wherein the curved line lies.

1141. The combination and developement of all the parts which compose the curved surfaces of vaults being susceptible of representation upon vertical and horizontal planes by right or curve lines terminating their surfaces, if what has been above stated be thoroughly understood, it will not be difficult to trace their projections for practical purposes, whatever their situation and direction in vaults or other surfaces.

PROJECTION OF SOLIDS.

1142. The projections of a cube ABCDEFGH placed parallel to two planes, one horizontal and the other vertical, are squares whose sides represent faces perpendicular to these planes (*fig.* 468.), which are represented by corresponding small letters.

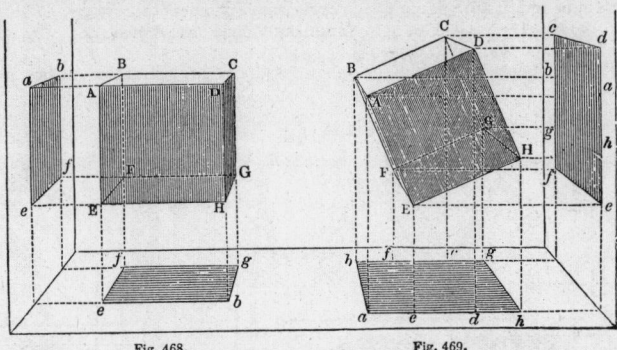

Fig. 468.   Fig. 469.

1143. If we suppose the cube to move on an axis, so that two of its opposite faces remain perpendicular to the planes (*fig.* 469.), its projection on each will be a rectangle, whose length will vary in proportion to the difference between the side and the diagonal of the square. The motion of the opposite arrisses will, on the contrary, produce a rectangle whose width will be constant in all the dimensions contained of the image of the perfect square to the exact period when the two arrisses unite in a single right line.

1144. A cylinder (*fig.* 470.) stands perpendicularly on an horizontal plane, and on such

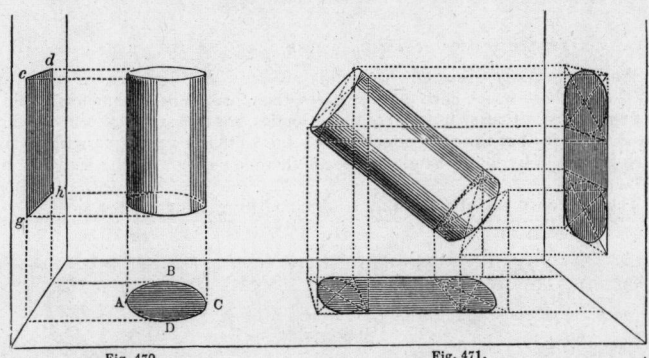

Fig. 470.   Fig. 471.

plane its projection ADBC is shown, being thereon represented by a circle, and upon a vertical plane by the rectangle *gcdh*.

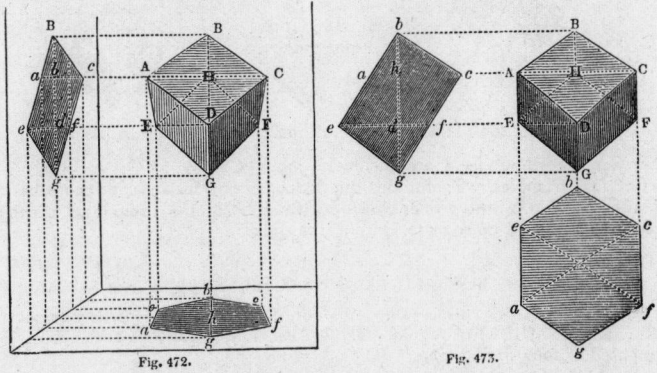

Fig. 472.   Fig. 473.

1145. The projection of an inclined cylinder (*fig.* 471.) is shown on a vertical and horizontal plane.

1146. In *fig.* 472. we have the representation of a cube doubly inclined, so that the diagonal from the angle B to the angle G is upright. The projection produced by this position upon an horizontal plane is a regular hexagon *acbefg*, and upon a vertical plane the rectangle B*egc* whose diagonal B*g* is upright; but as the effect of perspective changes the effect of the cube and its projections, it is represented geometrically in *fig.* 473.

1147. In *figures* 474. and 475. a pyramid and cone are represented with their projections on horizontal and vertical planes.

1148. *Fig.* 476. represents a ball or sphere with its projections upon two planes, one

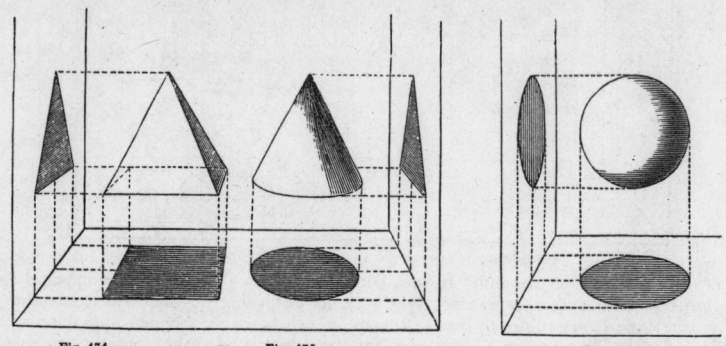

Fig. 474.   Fig. 475.   Fig. 476.

vertical and the other horizontal, wherein is to be remarked the perfection of this solid, seeing that its projection on a plane is always a circle whenever the plane is parallel to the circular base formed by the contact of the tangents.

DEVELOPEMENT OF SOLIDS WHOSE SURFACES ARE PLANE.

1149. We have already observed that solids are only distinguished by their apparent faces, and that in those which have plane surfaces, their faces unite so as to form solid angles. We have also observed that at least three plane angles are necessary to form a solid angle; whence it is manifest that the most simple of all the solids is a pyramid with a triangular base, which is formed by four triangles, whereof three are united in the angles at its apex. (*Fig.* 477.)

1150. The developement of this solid is obtained by placing on the sides of the base,

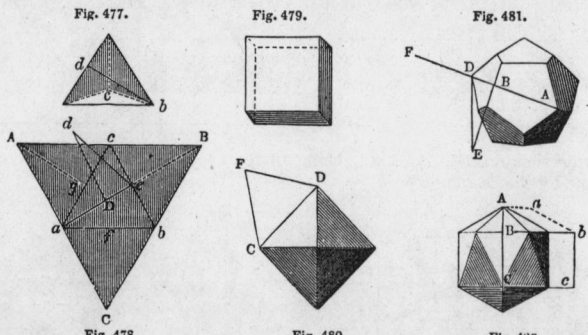

Fig. 477.   Fig. 479.   Fig. 481.

Fig. 478.   Fig. 480.   Fig. 482.

the three triangles whose faces are inclined (*fig.* 478.); by which we obtain a figure composed of four triangles. To cut this out in paper, for instance, or any other flexible material, after bending it on the lines *ab*, *bc*, *ac*, which form the triangle at the base, the three triangles are turned up so as to unite in the summit.

DEVELOPEMENT OF REGULAR POLYHEDRONS.

1151. The solid just described formed of four equal equilateral triangles, as we have seen, is the simplest of the five regular polyhedrons, and is called a *tetrahedron*, from its being composed of four similar faces. The others are —

The *hexahedron*, or cube whose faces are six in number;
The *octahedron*, whose faces are eight equilateral triangles;
The *dodecahedron*, whose faces are twelve regular pentagons;
The *icosahedron*, consisting of twenty equilateral triangles.

These five regular polyhedrons are represented by the *figures* 477. 479, 480, 481, and 482., and their developement by the *figures* 478. 483, 484, 485, and 486.

Fig. 486.

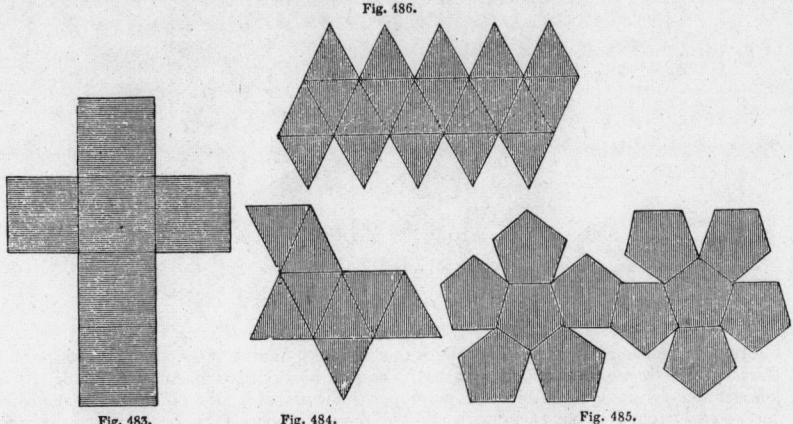

Fig. 483.   Fig. 484.   Fig. 485.

1152. The surfaces of these developements are so arranged as to be capable of being united by moving them on the lines by which they are joined.

1153. It is here proper to remark, that the equilateral triangle, the square, and the pentagon, are the only figures which will form regular polyhedrons whose angles and sides are equal; but by cutting in a regular method the solid angles of these polyhedrons, others regularly symmetrical may be formed whose sides will be formed of two similar figures. Thus, by cutting in a regular way the angles of a tetrahedron, we obtain a polyhedron of eight faces, composed of four hexagons and four equilateral triangles. Similarly operating on the cube, we shall have six octagons, connected by eight equilateral triangles, forming a polyhedron of fourteen faces.

1154. The same operation being performed on the octahedron also gives a figure of fourteen faces, whereof eight are octagons and six are squares.

1155. The dodecahedron so cut produces twelve pentagons united by twenty hexagons, and having thirty-two sides. This last, from some points of view, so approaches the figure of the sphere, that, at a little distance, it looks almost spherical.

DEVELOPEMENT OF PYRAMIDS AND PRISMS.

1156. The other solids whose surfaces are plane, whereof mention has already been made, are pyramids and prisms, partaking of the tetrahedron and cube; of the former, inasmuch as their sides above the base are formed by triangles which approach each other so as together to form the solid angle which is the summit of the pyramid; of the latter, because their faces, which rise above the base, are formed by rectangles or parallelograms which preserve the same distance from each other, but differ, from their rising on a polygonal base and being undetermined as to height.

1157. This species may be regular or irregular, they may have their axes perpendicular or inclined, they may be truncated or cut in a direction either parallel or inclined to their bases.

1158 The developement of a pyramid or right prism, whose base and height are given, is not attended with difficulty. The operation is by raising on each side of the base a triangle equal in height to the inclined face, as in the pyramidal figures 487. and 488., and a rectangle equal to the perpendicular height if it be a prism.

DEVELOPEMENT OF AN OBLIQUE PYRAMID.

1159. If the pyramid be oblique, as in *fig.* 489., wherein the length of the sides of each triangle can only be represented by foreshortening them in a vertical or horizontal projection, a third operation is necessary, and that is founded on a principle common to all projections; viz. *that the length of an inclined line projected or foreshortened on a plane, depends upon the difference of the perpendicular elongation of its extremities from the plane,*

whence in all cases a rectangular triangle, whose vertical and horizontal projections give two sides, the third, which is the hypothenuse, joining them, will express the length of the foreshortened line.

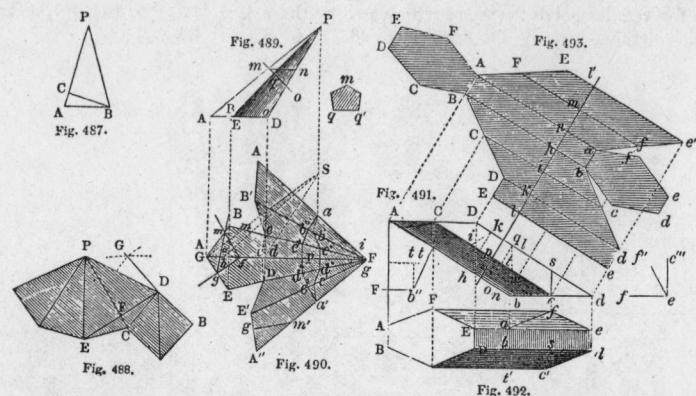

Fig. 487.   Fig. 489.   Fig. 493.   Fig. 491.   Fig. 488.   Fig. 490.   Fig. 492.

1160. In the application of this rule to the oblique pyramid of *fig.* 489., the position of the point P (*fig.* 490.) must be shown on the plan or horizontal projection answering to the apex of the pyramid, and from this point perpendicular to the face CD on the same side the perpendicular PG must be drawn. Then from the point P as a centre describe the arcs B*b*, C*c*, which will transfer upon PG the horizontal projections of the inclined arrisses AP, EP, and DP; and raising the perpendicular PS equal to the height of the apex P of the pyramid above the plane of projection, draw the lines S*a*, S*b*, S*c*, which will give the real lengths of all the edges or arrisses of the pyramid.

1161. We may then obtain the triangles which form the developement of this pyramid, by describing from C as a centre with the radius S*c*, the arc *ig*, and from the point D another arc intersecting the other in F. Drawing the lines CF, DF, the triangles CFD will be the developement of the side DC. To obtain that answering to BC, from the points F and C with S*b* and B*c* as radii, describe arcs intersecting in B′ and draw B′F and CB′: the triangle FCB′ will be the developement of the face answering to the side B*c*.

1162. We shall find the triangle FA′B′, by using the lengths SA and BA to find the points B′ and F, which will determine the triangle corresponding to the face AB, and lastly the triangles FDE′ and FE′A″ corresponding to the faces DE, AE by using the lengths S*b*, DE and SA, AE. The whole developement AEDE′A″F, A′B, CBA being bent on the lines B F*c* F, CD, DF, and EF will form the inclined figure represented in *fig.* 489.

1163. If this pyramid be truncated by the plane *mn*, parallel to the base, the contour resulting from the section may be traced on the developement by producing P*m* from F to *a*, and drawing the lines *ab*, *bc*, *cd*, *de* and *ea″* parallel to A′B′, B′C, CD, DE′ and E′A″.

1164. But if the plane of the section be perpendicular to the axis, as *mo*, from the point F with a radius equal to P*o* describe an arc of a circle, in which inscribe the polygon *ab″c″d″e″a″*. Then the polygon *oqmq′o′* is the plane of the section induced by the line *mo*.

DEVELOPEMENT OF RIGHT AND OBLIQUE PRISMS.

1165. In a right prism, the faces being all perpendicular to the bases which terminate the solid, the developements are rectangles, consisting of all these faces joined together and enclosed by two parallel right lines equal to the contours of the bases.

1166. When a prism is inclined, the faces form different angles with the lines of the contours of the bases, whence results a developement whose extremities are terminated by lines forming portions of polygons.

1167. We must first begin by tracing the profile of the prism parallel to its degree of inclination (*fig.* 491.). Having drawn the line C*c*, which represents the inclined axis of the prism in the direction of its length, and the lines AD, *bd*, to show the surfaces by which it is terminated, describe on such axis the polygon which forms the plane of the prism *h*, *i*, *k*, *l*, *m* perpendicular to the axis. Producing the sides *kl*, *hn* parallel to the axis to meet the lines AD, *bd*, they will give the four arrisses of the prism, answering to the angles *h*, *n*, *k*, *l*; and the line C*c* which loses itself in the axis will give the arrisses *im*.

1168. It must be observed, that in this profile the sides of the polygon *h*, *i*, *k*, *l*, *m* give the width of the faces round the prism, and the lines A*b*, C*c*, D*d* their length. From this profile follows the horizontal projection (*fig.* 492.) wherein the lengthened polygons repre-

sent the bases of the prism.   In order to obtain the developement of this inclined prism, so that being bent up it may form the figure, from the middle of Cc, *fig.* 491. a perpendicular o, p, q must be raised, produced to l, l', *fig.* 493.; on this line must be transferred the widths of the faces shown by the polygon h, i, k, l, m, n, of *fig.* 491. in l, k, i, h, n, m, l', *fig.* 493.: through these points parallel to the axis, lines are to be drawn, upon which qD of *fig.* 491. must be laid from l to E, from k to D, and from l' to E', *fig.* 493.; pC, *fig.* 491., must be laid from i to C, and from m to F in *fig.* 493.

oA, *fig.* 491., is to be laid from h to B and from n to A, *fig.* 493., which will give the contour of the developement of the upper part by drawing the lines ED, DCB, BA, AFE', *fig.* 492.

To obtain the contour of the base, qd of *fig.* 491. must be transferred from l to q, from k to d and from l' to e', *fig.* 493.

pc from *fig.* 491. from i to c and from m to f (*fig.* 493.); lastly, ob of *fig.* 491. must be transferred from h to b and from n to a (*fig.* 493.) and drawing the lines ed, bcd, ba, and afé, the contour will be obtained.

1169. The developement will be completed by drawing on the faces B A and ba, elongated polygons similar to ABCDEF and abcdef' of *fig.* 491. and of the same size.

DEVELOPEMENT OF RIGHT AND OBLIQUE CYLINDERS.

1170. Cylinders may be considered as prisms whose bases are formed by polygons of an infinite number of sides.   Thus, graphically, the developement of a right cylinder is obtained, by a rectangle of the same height, having in its other direction the circumference of the circle which serves as its base measured by a greater or less number of equal parts.

1171. But if the cylinder is oblique (*fig.* 494.), we must take the same measures as for

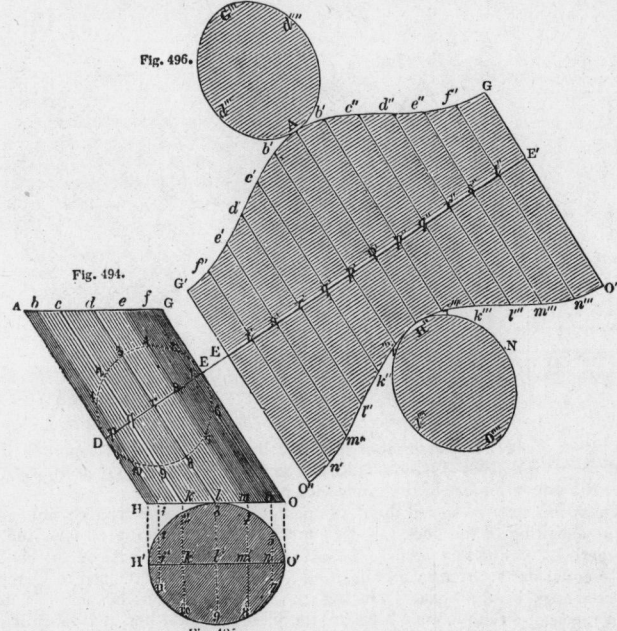

the prism, and consider the inclination of it.   Having described centrally on its axis the circle or ellipsis which forms its perpendicular thickness in respect of the axis, the circumference should be divided into an even number of equal parts, as, for instance, twelve, beginning from the diameter and drawing from the points of division the parallels to the axis HA, bi, ek, dl, em, fm, GO, which will give the projection of the bases and the general developement.

1172. For the projection of the bases on an horizontal plane, it is necessary that from the points where the parallels meet the line of the base HO, indefinite perpendiculars should be let fall, and after having drawn the line H' O', parallel to HO, upon these perpendiculars above and below the parallel must be transferred the size of the ordinates of

the circle or ellipsis traced on the axis of the cylinder, that is, $p1$ and $p10$ to $i'1$, and $i'10 : q2$ and $q9$ in $k'2$ and $k'q$, &c.   In order to avoid unnecessary repetition, the *figs.* 494, 495, 496. are similarly figured, and will by inspection indicate the corresponding lines.

1173. In the last figure the line E'E' is the approximate developement of the circumférence of the circles which follow the section DE perpendicular to the axis of the cylinder, divided into 12 equal parts, *fig.* 494.   For which purpose there have been transferred upon this line on each side of the point D, six of the divisions of the circle, and through these points have been drawn an equal number of indefinite parallels to the lines traced upon the cylinder in *fig.* 494. : then taking the point D' as correspondent to D, the length of these lines is determined by transferring to each of them their relative dimensions, measured from DE in AG for the superior surface of the cylinder, and from DE to HO for the base.

1174. In respect of the two elliptical surfaces which terminate this solid, what has been above stated, on the manner of describing a curve by means of ordinates, will render further explanation on that point needless.

DEVELOPEMENT OF RIGHT AND OBLIQUE CONES.

1175. The reasoning which has been used in respect of cylinders and prisms, is applicable to cones and pyramids.

1176. In right pyramids, with regular and symmetrical bases, the edges or arrisses from the base to the apex are equal, and the sides of the polygon on which they stand being equal, their developement must be composed of similar isosceles triangles, which in their union will form throughout, part of a regular polygon, inscribed in a circle whose inclined sides will be the radii.   Thus, in considering the base of the cone A B (*fig.* 497.) as a

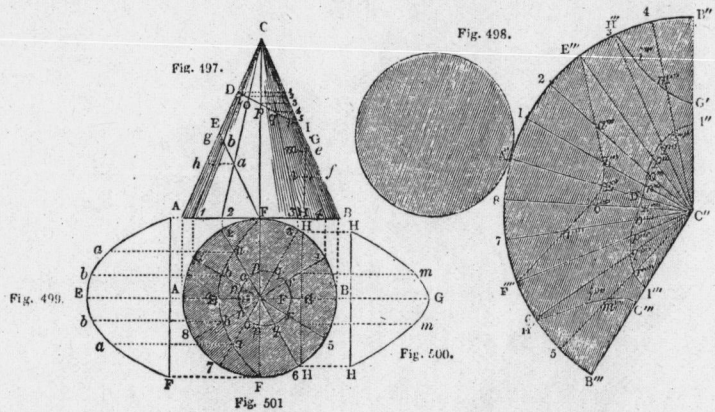

Fig. 498.

Fig. 497.

Fig. 499.

Fig. 500.

Fig. 501.

regular polygon of an infinite number of sides, its developement becomes a sector of a circle A"B"B'''C" (*fig.* 498.) whose radius is equal to the side AC of the cone, and the arc equal to the circumference of the circle which is its base.

1177. Upon this may be traced the developement of the curves which would result from the cone cut according to the lines DI, EF, and GH, which are the ellipsis, the parabola, and the hyperbola.   For this purpose the circumference of the base of the cone must be divided into equal parts ; from each point lines must be drawn to the centre C, representing in this case the apex of the cone.   Having transferred, by means of parallels, to FF, the divisions of the semi-circumference AFB of the plan, upon the line A'B', forming the base of the vertical projection of the cone (*fig.* 497.) to the points 1'2', F3', and 4', which, because of the uniformity of the curvature of the circle will also represent the divisions on the plan marked 8, 7F', 6, and 5; from the summit C' in the elevation of the cone, the lines C'1', C'2', C'F, C'3', C'4' are to be drawn, cutting the plans DI, EF, and GH of the ellipse, of the parabola, and of the hyperbola ; then by the assistance of these intersections their figures may be drawn on the plan, the first in D'p'I'p'* ; the second in FE'F' ; the third in H'GH".

1178. To obtain the points of the circumference of the ellipse upon the developement (*fig.* 498.), from the points n, o, p, q, r of the line DI (*fig.* 497.), draw parallels to the base for the purpose of transferring their heights upon C B' at the points 1, 2, 3, 4, 5.   Then transfer C'D upon the developement, in C"n''', C"o''', C"p''', C'q''', C"r''' ; and in the same order below, C"n'''', C"o'''', C"p'''', C'q'''', C"r'''' ; and CI from C" in I" and I'".   The

curve passing through these points will be the developement of the circumference of the ellipse indicated in *fig.* 497. by the right line DI, which is its great axis.

1179. For the parabola (*fig.* 499.) on the side C′A′ (*fig.* 497.), draw *bg* and *ah*; then transfer C′E on the developement in C″E″; C′*g* from C″ to *b‴* and *b⁗*; C′*h*, from C″ to *a‴* and *a⁗*; and through the points F″, *a‴*, *b‴*, E″, *b⁗*, *a⁗*, F‴, trace a curve, which will be the developement of the parabola shown in *fig.* 497. by the line EF.

1180. For the hyperbola, having drawn through the points *m* and *i*, the parallels *me*, *if*, transfer C′G from C″ to G″, and from C″ to G‴ of the developement, C′*e* from C″ to *m‴* and *m⁗*, C′*f* from C″ to *i‴* and *i⁗*; and after having transferred 3H′ and 6H″ of the plan to the circumference of the developement, from 3 to H‴, and from 6 to H⁗, by the aid of the points H‴, *i″*, *m‴*, G″ and H⁗, *i⁗*, *m⁗*, G‴, draw two curves, of which each will be the developement of one half of the hyperbola represented by the right lines GH and H′H″, *figs.* 497. and 500., and by *fig.* 501.

1181. The mode of finding the developement of an oblique cone, shown in *figs.* 502, 503,

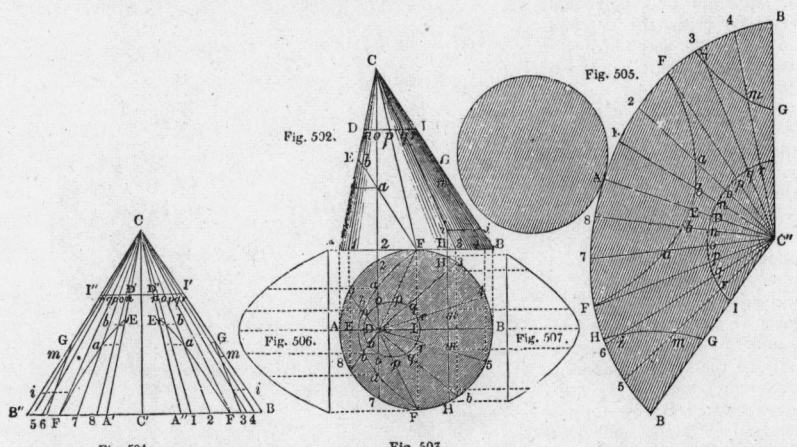

Fig. 502.   Fig. 505.   Fig. 506.   Fig. 507.

Fig. 504.   Fig. 503.

504, 505. differs, as follows, from the preceding. 1. From the position of the apex C upon the plan 503., determined by a vertical let fall from such apex in *fig.* 502. 2. Because the line DI of this figure, being parallel to the base, gives for the plan a circle instead of an ellipsis. 3. Because in finding the lengthened extent of the right lines drawn from the apex of the cone to the circumference of the base, divided into equal parts, *fig.* 504. is introduced to bring them together in order to avoid confusion, these lines being all of a different size on account of the obliquity of the cone. In this figure the line CC′ shows the perpendicular height of the apex of the cone above the plan; so that by transferring from each side the projections of these lines taken on the plan from the point C to the circumference, we shall have CA″, C1, C2, CF″, C3, C4, CB′, on one side, and CA′, C8, C7, CF, C6, C5, and CB″ on the other; lastly, from the point C drawing lines to all these points, they will give the edges or arrisses of the inscribed pyramid, by which the developement in *fig.* 505. is obtained. Having obtained the point C″ representing the apex, a line is to be drawn through it equal to CA″ (*fig.* 504.); then with one of the divisions of the base taken on the plan, such as A1, it must be laid from the point A of the developement of the section; then taking C′1 of *fig.* 504., describe from the point C″ another arc which will cross the former, and will determine the point 1 of the developement. Continuing the operations with the constant length A1 and the different lengths C2, CF, C3, &c., taken from *fig.* 504. and transferred to C″2, C″F, C″3, &c. of the developement, the necessary points will be obtained for tracing the curve B″AB‴, representing the contour of the oblique base of the cone.

1182. We obtain the developement of the circle shown by the line DI of *fig.* 502. parallel to that of the base AB, by drawing another line I′D D′I″ (*fig.* 504.) at the same distance from the summit C, cutting all the oblique lines that have served for the preceding developement; and on one side, CD″, C*n*, C*o*, C*p*, C*q*, C*r*, CI″, must be carried to *fig.* 505., from C″ to D″, *n*, *o*, *p*, *q*, *r*, and on the other from C″ to *n*, *o*, *p*, *q*, *r*, and I‴, on *fig.* 505. The curve line passing through these points will be the developement of this circle.

1183. To trace upon the developement the parabola and hyperbola shown by the lines EF, G3 of *fig.* 502., from the points E*ba*, G*mi* draw parallels to the base AB, which, transferred to *fig.* 504., will indicate upon corresponding lines the real distance of these points from the apex C, which are to be laid in *fig.* 505. from C″ to E, *b*, *a*, *b* and *a* for

the parabola; and from C″ to G, m, i on one side, and on the other to G, m, i, for the hyperbola. Each of these is represented in *figs. 506.* and *507.*

DEVELOPEMENT OF BODIES OR SOLIDS WHOSE SURFACES HAVE A DOUBLE CURVATURE.

1184. The developement of the sphere and other bodies whose surface has a double flexure would be impossible, unless we considered them as consisting of a great number of plane faces or of simple curvatures, as the cylinder and the cone. Thus a sphere or spheroid may be considered, — I. As a polyhedron of a great number of plane faces formed by truncated pyramids whose base is a polygon, as *fig. 508.* II. By truncated cones, forming zones, as in *fig. 509.* III. By parts of cylinders cut in gores, forming flat sides that diminish in width, shown by *fig. 510.*

1185. In reducing the sphere or spheroid to a polyhedron with flat faces, the developement may be accomplished in two ways, which differ only by the manner in which the faces are developed.

1186. The most simple method of dividing the sphere to reduce it to a polyhedron is that of parallel circles crossed by others perpendicular to them, and intersecting in two opposite points, as in the common geographical globes. If, instead of the circle, the polygons are supposed of the same number of sides, a polyhedron will be the result, similar to that represented by *fig. 508.*, whose half ADB shows the geometrical elevation, and AEB the plan of it.

Fig. 508.

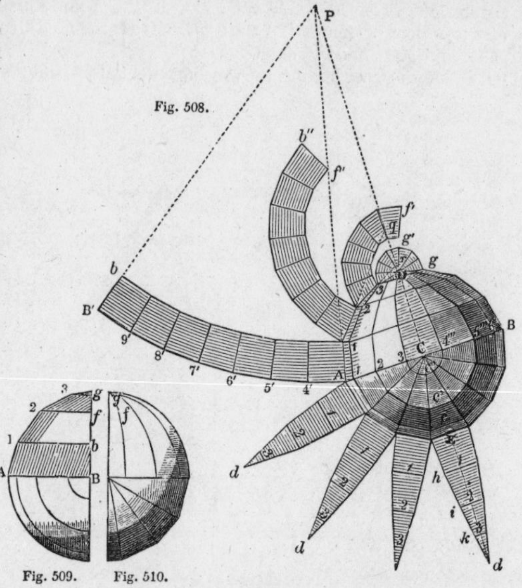

Fig. 509.   Fig. 510.

1187. For the developement, produce A1, 12, 23, so as to meet the produced axis CP in order to obtain the summits P, q, r, D of the truncated pyramids which form the semi-polyhedron ADB; then from the points P, q, r, with the radii PA, P1, q1, q2, r2, r3 and D3, describe the indefinite arcs AB′, 1b′, 1b″, 2f′, 2f″, 3g′, and 3g, upon which, after having transferred the divisions of the demi-polygons AEB, 1e6‴, 2e′5‴, 3e″, 4″, from all the transferred points, as A, 4′, 5′, 6′, 7′, 8′, 9′, B′, for each truncated pyramid draw lines to the summits PqrD, and other lines which will form inscribed polygons in each of the arcs AB′, 1b′, 1b″, &c. These lines will represent for each band or zone the faces of the truncated pyramids whereof they are part.

1188. We may arrive at the same developement by raising upon the middle of each side of the polygon AEB indefinite perpendiculars, upon which must be laid the height of the faces of the elevation in 1, 2, 3, 4; through which points draw parallels to the base, upon which transfer the widths of each of the faces taken on the plan, whereby trapezia will be formed, and triangles similar to those found in the first developement, but ranged in another manner. This last developement, which is called in *gores*, is more suitable for geographical globes; the other method, for the formation of the centres, moulds, and the like, of spherical vaults.

1189. The developement of the sphere by conic zones (*fig. 509.*) is obtained by the same process as that by truncated pyramids, the only difference being, that the developement of the arrisses AB′, 1b′, 2f′, 3g, are arcs of circles described from the summits of cones, instead of being polygons.

1190. The developement of the sphere reduced to portions of cylinders cut in gores (*fig. 510.*) is conducted in the second manner, but instead of joining with lines the points h, i, k, d, (*fig. 508.*) they must be united by a curve. This last method is useful in drawing the caissons or pannels in spherical or spheroidal vaults.

OF THE ANGLES OF PLANES OR SURFACES BY WHICH SOLIDS ARE BOUNDED.

1191. In considering the formation of solids, we have already noticed three sorts of angles, viz. plane angles, solid angles, and the angles of planes. The two first have been

treated of in the preceding sections, and we have now to speak of the third, which must not be confounded with plane angles. Of these last, we have explained that they are formed by the lines or arrisses which bound the faces of a solid ; but the angles of planes, whereof we are about to speak, are those formed by the meeting of two surfaces joining in an edge.

1192. The inclination of one plane ALDE to another ALCB (*fig.* 511.) is measured by two perpendiculars FG, FH raised upon each of these planes from the same point F of the line or arris AL formed by their union.

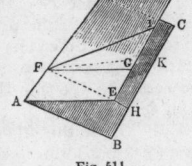

Fig. 511.

1193. It is to be observed, that this angle is the greatest of all those formed by lines drawn from the point F upon these two planes ; for the lines FG, FH being perpendicular to AL, common to both the planes, they will be the shortest that can be drawn from the point F to the sides ED, BC, which we suppose parallel to AL ; thus their distance GH will be throughout the same, whilst the lines FI, FK will be so much the longer as they extend beyond the perpendiculars FG, FH, and we shall always have KI equal to GH, and consequently the angle IFK so much smaller than GFH as it is more distant.

1194. Thus, let a rectangular surface be folded perpendicularly to one of its sides so that the contours of the parts separated by the fold may fall exactly on each other. If we raise one of them, so as to move it on the fold as on a hinge, and so as to make it form all degrees of angles, we shall see that each of the central extremities of the moveable part is always in a plane perpendicular to the part that is fixed.

1195. This property of lines moving in a perpendicular plane, furnishes a simple method of finding the angles of planes of all sorts of solids whose vertical and horizontal projections or whose developements are known.

1196. Thus, in order to find the angles formed by the tetrahedron or pyramid on a triangular base (*fig.* 477.), we must for the angles of the base with the sides, let fall from the angles ABC perpendiculars to the sides *ac*, *cb*, and *ab*, which meet at the centre of the base in D. It is manifest from what has just been said on this subject, that if the three triangles are made to move, their angles at the summit A, B, C will not be the vertical planes shown by the lines AD, DB, DC, and that they will meet at the extremity of the vertical, passing through the intersection of these planes at the point D. Thus we obtain for each side a rectangular triangle, wherein two sides are known, namely, for the side *cb*, the hypothenuse *ed*, and the side *e*D. Thus raising from the point D an indefinite perpendicular, if from the point *e* with *e*B for a radius an arc is described cutting the perpendicular in *d*, and the line *de* be drawn, the angle *de*D will be that sought, and will be the same for the three sides if the polyhedron be regular ; otherwise, if it is not, the operation must be repeated for each.

1197. These angles may be obtained with great accuracy by taking *de*, or its equal *e*B, for the whole sine ; then *de* : *e*D :: sine : sine 19° 28′, whose complement 70° 32′ will, if the polyhedron be regular, be the angle sought. In this case, all the sides being equal, and each being capable of serving as base, the angles throughout are equal. In respect of the cube (*figs.* 479. and 483.) whose faces are composed of equal squares, and whose angles are all right angles, it is evident that no other angles can enter into their combination with each other.

1198. To obtain the angle formed by the faces of the octahedron (*fig.* 480.) from the points C and D : with a distance equal to a vertical dropped upon the base of one of the triangles of its developement (*fig.* 484.), describe arcs crossing each other in F ; and the angle CFD will be equal to that formed by the faces of the polyhedron, and will be found by trigonometry to be 70° 32′. In the dodecahedron (*fig.* 481.), the angle formed by the faces will be found by drawing upon its projection the lines DA, and producing the side B to E, determined by an arc made from the point D with a radius equal to BA. The angle sought will be found to be 108 degrees.

1199. For the icosahedron (*fig.* 482.), draw the parallels A*a*, B*b*, C*c*, and after having made *bc* parallel and equal to BC, with a radius equal thereto, describe an arc cutting in *a* the parallel drawn from the point A ; the angle *abc* will be equal to that formed by the sides of the polygon, which by trigonometry is found to be 108 degrees, as in the dodecahedron.

1200. For the pyramid with a quadrangular base (*fig.* 487.) the angle of each face with the base is equal to PAB or PBA, because this figure, which represents its vertical projection, is in a plane parallel to that within which will be found the perpendiculars dropped from the summit on the lateral faces of the base.

1201. In order to obtain the angles which the inclined sides form with one another, draw upon the developement (*fig.* 488.) the line ED, which, because the triangles PEC, PCD are equal and isoceles, will be perpendicular to the line PC, representing one of the arrisses which are formed. Then from the point D with a radius equal to DF, and

from the point C with a radius equal to the diagonal AD (of the square representing the square of the base) describe arcs intersecting each other. The angle FDG will be the angle sought. We may suppose it taken along the line BC traced in *fig.* 487.

1202. In order to obtain the angles formed by the faces of an oblique pyramid (*fig.* 489.), through some point *q* of the axis draw the perpendicular *mo*, showing the base *oqmq′o′* of the right pyramid *mpo*, whose developement is shown in *fig.* 490., by the portion of the polygon *a, b″, c″, e″, d″, a′* F.

1203. By means of this base and the part developed, proceeding as we have already explained for the right pyramid, we shall find the angles formed by the meeting of the faces, and they will differ but little from those of the little polygon *oqmq′o′*.

1204. In respect to the angles formed by the faces inclined to the base, that of the face answering to the side D*e* of the base is expressed by the angle ADP of the vertical projection, *fig.* 489.

1205. As to the other faces, for instance, that which corresponds to the side AE of the base (*fig.* 490.), through any point *g* draw *gf* perpendicular to it, meeting the line AF, showing the projection of one of the sides of the inclined face; upon the developement of this face, expressed by A″E′F, raise at the same distance from the point E′ another perpendicular *g′m′*, which will give the prolongation of the line shown on the base by A*f*. If we transfer A″*m* of the developement upon A*m*, which expresses the inclination of the arris represented by this line, we shall have the perpendicular height *mf* of the point *m* above the base, which, being transferred from *fm″* upon a perpendicular to *gf*, we shall have the two sides of a triangle whose hypothenuse *gm″* will give *m″gf*, the angle sought.

1206. In the oblique prism (*fig.* 491.), the angles of the faces are indicated by the plane of the section perpendicular to the axis, represented by the polygon *hiklmn*.

1207. Those of the sides perpendicular to the plan of the inclination of the axis are expressed by the angles D*db*, A*bd* of the profile in the figure last named.

1208. In order to obtain the angles formed with the other sides, for instance C*c*D*d* and C*c*A*b*, draw the perpendiculars *csbt*, whose projection in plan are indicated by *s″c′* and *b′t′*, then upon *fc*, drawn aside, raise a perpendicular *c″c′″* equal to *cs* of the profile, *fig.* 491. Through the point *c′″* draw a line parallel to *fc*, upon which, having transferred *c′s′* of the projection in plan (*fig.* 492.), draw the hypothenuse *s″c″*, and it will give the angle *s″e″f* formed by the face C*c*D*d* with the inferior base.

1209. To obtain the angles of the face C*c*A*b*, raise upon F*b″*, drawn on one side, a perpendicular *b″t′″*, equal to *bt* (*fig.* 492.), and drawing as before a parallel to *b″* through the point *t′″*, transfer *b′t′* of *fig.* 492. to *t′″t″*; and drawing *t″b″*, the angle *t″b″*F is that required.

1210. As the bases of this prism are parallel, these faces necessarily form the same angles with the superior base.

1211. An acquaintance with the angles of planes is of the greatest utility in the preparation of stone, as will be seen in chap. iii., and a thorough acquaintance with it will well repay the architectural student for the labour he may bestow on the subject.

Sect. VI.

MENSURATION.

1212. The area of a plane figure is the measure of its surface or of the space contained within its extremities or boundaries, without regard to thickness. This area, or the content of the plane figure, is estimated by the number of small squares it contains, the sides of each whereof may be an inch, a foot, a yard, or any other fixed quantity. Hence the area is said to consist of so many square inches, feet, yards, &c., as the case may be.

1213. Thus if the rectangle to be measured be ABCD (*fig.* 512.), and the small square E, whose side we will suppose to be one inch, be the measuring unit proposed; then, as often as such small square is contained in the rectangle, so many square inches are said to be contained in the rectangle. Here it will be seen by inspection that the number is 12; that the side DC or AB, which is 4 times the length of the measuring unit, multiplied by the number of times 3, which the length of the measuring unit is contained in AD or BC, will give 12 for the product.

1214. Problem I. *To find the area of a parallelogram, whether it be a square, a rectangle, a rhombus, or a rhomboid.*

Multiply the length by the perpendicular breadth or height, and the product will be the area.

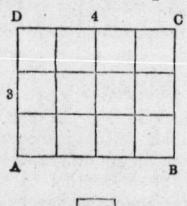

Fig. 512.

Example 1. Required the area of a parallelogram whose length is 12·25 feet, and height 8·5 feet.

$$12\cdot25 \times 8\cdot5 = 104\cdot125 \text{ feet, or } 104 \text{ feet } 1\tfrac{1}{2} \text{ inches.}$$

Example 2. Required the content of a piece of land in the form of a rhombus whose length is 6·20 chains, and perpendicular height 5·45.

Recollecting that 10 square chains are equal to a square acre, we have,

$$6\cdot20 \times 5\cdot45 = 33\cdot79 \text{ and } \frac{33\cdot79}{10} = 3\cdot379 \text{ acres, which are equal to 3 acres, 1 rood,}$$

$20\tfrac{64}{100}$ perches.

Example 3. Required the number of square yards in a rhomboid whose length is 37 feet, and breadth 5 feet 3 inches ($= 5\cdot25$ feet).

Recollecting that 9 square feet are equal to 1 square yard, then we have

$$37 \times 5\cdot25 = 194\cdot25, \text{ and } \frac{194\cdot25}{9} = 21\cdot584 \text{ yards.}$$

1215. PROBLEM II. *To find the area of a triangle.*

Rule 1. Multiply the base by the perpendicular height, and take half the product for the area. Or multiply either of these dimensions by half the other. The truth of this rule is evident, because all triangles are equal to one half of a parallelogram of equal base and altitude. (See Geometry, 904.)

Example 1. To find the area of a triangle whose base is 625 feet, and its perpendicular height 520 feet. Here,

$$625 \times 260 = 162500 \text{ feet, the area of the triangle.}$$

Rule 2. When two sides and their contained angle are given : multiply the two given sides together, and take half their product ; then say, as radius is to the sine of the given angle, so is half that product to the area of the triangle. Or multiply that half product by the natural sine of the said angle for the area. This rule is founded on proofs which will be found in Sect. III., on which it is unnecessary here to say more.

Example. Required the area of a triangle whose sides are 30 and 40 feet respectively, and their contained angles 28° 57′.

By natural numbers : —

First, $\tfrac{1}{2} \times 40 \times 30 = 600$.
Then, 1 : 600 :: ·484046 (sin. 28° 57′) : 290·4276.

By logarithms : —

Sin. 28° 57′ = 9·684887
Log. of 600 = 2·778151
$\overline{}$
2·463038 = 290·4276, as above.

Rule 3. When the three sides are given, take half the sum of the three sides added together. Then subtract each side severally from such half sum, by which three remainders will be obtained. Multiply such half sum and the three remainders together, and extract the square root of the last product, which is the area of the triangle. This rule is founded on one of the theorems in Trigonometry to be found in the section relating to that subject.

Example. Required the area of a triangle whose three sides are 20, 30, and 40.

20 + 30 + 40 = 90, whose half sum is 45.
45 − 20 = 25, first remainder ; 45 − 30 = 15, second remainder ; 45 − 40 = 5, third remainder.

Then, $45 \times 25 \times 15 \times 5 = 84375$, whose root is 290·4737, area required.

1216. PROBLEM III. *To find the area of a trapezoid.*

Add together the parallel sides, multiply their sum by the perpendicular breadth or distance between them, and half the product is the area. (See Geometry, 932.)

Example 1. Required the area of a trapezoid whose parallel sides are 750 and 1225, and their vertical distance from each other 1540.

$$1225 + 750 \times 770 = 1520750, \text{ the area.}$$

Example 2. Required the area of any quadrangular figure (*fig.* 513.) wherein   AP is 110 feet,
                                                       AQ 745 feet,
                                                       AB 1110 feet
                                                       CP 352 feet
                                                       DQ 595 feet.

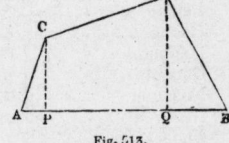

Fig. 513.

Therefore, QB = AB − AQ = 1110 − 745 = 365,
And   PQ = AB − AP − QB = 1110 − 110 − 365 = 635.

For PCDQ, $595 + 352 \times 635 \div 2 = 300672 \cdot 5$
For the triangle ACP, $176 \times 110 = 19360$
For the triangle DQB, $\frac{365 \times 595}{2} = 108587 \cdot 5$

Area $= \overline{428620 \cdot 0}$ feet.

1217. PROBLEM IV. *To find the area of any trapezium.*
Divide the trapezium into two triangles by a diagonal ; then find the areas of the two triangles, and their sum is the area.
Observation. If two perpendiculars be let fall on the diagonal from the other two opposite angles, then add these two perpendiculars together, and multiply that sum by the diagonal. Half the product is the area of the trapezium.
Example. Required the area of a trapezium whose diagonal is 42, and the two perpendiculars or it 16 and 18.
Here, $16 + 18 = 34$, whose half $= 17$; Then, $42 \times 17 = 714$, the area.
1218. PROBLEM V. *To find the area of an irregular polygon.*
Draw diagonals dividing the proposed polygon into trapezia and triangles. Then, having found the areas of all these separately, their sum will be the content required of the whole polygon.
Example. Required the content of the irregular figure ABCDEFGA (*fig.* 514.), wherein the following diagonals and perpendiculars are given.

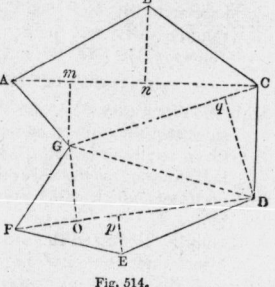

$AC = 55$, $GC = 44$, $Bn = 18$, $Ep = 8$,
$FD = 52$, $Gm = 13$, $GO = 12$, $Dq = 23$.
And $55 \times 9 \quad = 495$
$55 \times 6 \cdot 5 = 357 \cdot 5$
$44 \times 11 \cdot 5 = 506$
$52 \times 6 \quad = 312$
$52 \times 4 \quad = 208$

$1878 \cdot 5$, area required.

Fig. 514.

1219. PROBLEM VI. *To find the area of a regular polygon.*
Rule 1. Multiply the perimeter of the polygon, or sum of its sides, by the perpendicular drawn from its centre on one of its sides, and take half the product of the area ; which is in fact resolving the polygon into so many triangles.
Example. Required the area of the regular pentagon ABCDE (*fig.* 515.), whose side AB or BC, &c. is 25 ft., and perpendicular OP 17·2 ft.
Here $\frac{25 \times 5}{2} = 62 \cdot 5 =$ half the perimeter, and $62 \cdot 5 \times 17 \cdot 2 = 1075$ square feet area required.

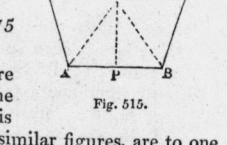

Fig. 515.

Rule 2. Square the side of the polygon, and multiply the square by the tabular area or multiplier set against its name in the following table, and the product will be the area. This rule is founded on the property, that like polygons, being similar figures, are to one another as the squares of their like sides. Now the multipliers of the table are the respective areas of the respective polygons to a side $= 1$; whence the rule is evident. In the table, the apothem of a regular polygon is the line OP.

TABLE OF POLYGONS.

No. of sides	Name of Polygon.	Angle OBP. degrs.	Angle of centre.	Length of Apoth. Rad. = 1	Length of Side. Rad = 1	Length of Rad. Apt. = 1	Length of Radius. Side = 1	Multipliers.
3	Trigon or Equ. Tri.	30	120	·5000	1·732051	2·0000	·5773503	0·4330127
4	Tetragon - -	45	90	·7071	1·414214	1·4142	·7071068	1·0000000
5	Pentagon - -	54	72	·8090	1·175570	1·2360	·8506508	1·7204774
6	Hexagon - -	60	60	·8660	1·000000	1·1547	1·0000000	2·5980762
7	Heptagon - -	$64\frac{2}{7}$	$51 \cdot 25\frac{5}{7}$	·9010	·867767	1·1095	1·1523824	3·6339124
8	Octagon - -	$67\frac{1}{2}$	45	·9239	·765367	1·0823	1·3065628	4·8284271
9	Nonagon - -	70	40	·9397	·684040	1·0642	1·4619022	6·1818242
10	Decagon - -	72	36	·9511	·618034	1·0515	1·6180340	7·6942088
11	Undecagon -	$73\frac{7}{11}$	$32 \cdot 43\frac{7}{11}$	·9595	·563465	1·0422	1·7747324	9·3656399
12	Dodecagon - .	75	30	·9659	·517638	1·0352	1·9318517	11·1961524

Example. Required the area of an octagon whose side is 20 feet.

Here $20^2 = 400$, and the tabular area 4·8284271 ;
Therefore 4·8284271 × 400 = 1931·37084 feet, area required.

1220. **Problem VII.** *To find the diameter and circumference of any circle, either from the other.*

Rule 1. As 7 is to 22, or as 1 is to 3·1416, so is the diameter to the circumference. Or as 22 is to 7, so is the circumference to the diameter.

Example. Required the circumference of a circle whose diameter is 9.

Here $7 : 22 :: 9 : 28\frac{2}{7}$; or, $\frac{22 \times 9}{7} = 28\frac{2}{7}$, the circumference required.

Required the diameter of a circle whose circumference is 36.

Here $22 : 7 :: 36 : 11\frac{10}{22}$; or, $\frac{36 \times 7}{22} = 11\frac{10}{22}$, the diameter required.

1221. **Problem VIII.** *To find the length of any arc of a circle.*

Rule 1. Multiply the decimal ·01745 by the number of degrees in the given arc, and that by the radius of the circle ; then the last product will be the length of the arc. This rule is founded on the circumference of a circle being 6·2831854 when the diameter is 2, or 3·1415927 when the diameter is 1. The length of the whole circumference then being divided into 360 degrees, we have 360° : 6·2831854 :: 1° : ·01745.

Example. Required the length of an arc of 30 degrees, the radius being 9 feet.

Here ·01745 × 30 × 9 = 4·7115, the length of the arc.

Rule 2. From 8 times the chord of half the arc subtract the chord of the whole arc, and one third of the remainder will be the length of the arc nearly.

Example. Required the length of an arc DCE (*fig.* 516.) whose chord DE is 48, and versed sine 18.

Here, to find DC, we have $24^2 + 18^2 = 576 + 324 = 900$,
and $\sqrt{900} = 30 = DC$.

Whence $\frac{30 \times 8 - 48}{3} = \frac{240 - 48}{3} = \frac{192}{3} = 64$, the length of the arc required.

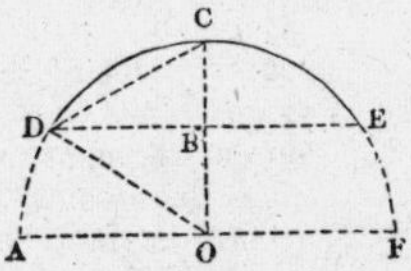

Fig. 516.

1222. **Problem IX.** *To find the area of a circle.*

Rule 1. Multiply half the circumference by half the diameter. Or multiply the whole circumference by the whole diameter, and take $\frac{1}{4}$ of the product.

Rule 2. Square the diameter, and multiply such square by ·7854.

Rule 3. Square the circumference, and multiply that square by the decimal ·07958.

Example. Required the area of a circle whose diameter is 10, and its circumference 31·416.

By rule 1., $\frac{31·416 \times 10}{4} = 78·54.$
By rule 2., $10^2 \times ·7854 = 100 \times ·7854 = 78·54.$
By rule 3., $31·416 \times 31·416 \times ·07958 = 78·54.$

So that by the three rules the area is 78·54.

1223. **Problem X.** *To find the area of a circular ring, or of the space included between the circumferences of two circles, the one being contained within the other.*

Rule. The difference between the areas of the two circles will be the area of the ring. Or, multiply the sum of the diameters by their difference, and this product again by ·7854, and it will give the area required.

Example. The diameters of two concentric circles being 10 and 6, required the area of the ring contained between their circumferences.

Here 10 + 6 = 16, the sum, and 10 − 6 = 4, the difference.
Therefore ·7854 × 16 × 4 = ·7854 × 64 = 50·2656, the area required.

1224. **Problem XI.** *To find the area of the sector of a circle.*

Rule 1. Multiply the radius, or half the diameter, by half the arc of the sector for the area. Or multiply the whole diameter by the whole arc of the sector, and take $\frac{1}{4}$ of the product. This rule is founded on the same basis as that to Problem IX.

Rule 2. As 360 is to the degrees in the arc of the sector, so is the area of the whole circle to the area of the sector. This is manifest, because it is proportional to the length of the arc.

Example. Required the area of a circular sector whose arc contains 18 degrees, the diameter being 3 feet.

By the first rule, 3·1416 × 3 = 9·4248, the circumference.
360 : 18 :: 9·4248 : ·47124, the length of the arc.
·47124 × 3 ÷ 4 = 1·41372 ÷ 4 = ·35343, the area of the sector.

By the second rule, $\cdot7854 \times 3^2 = 7 \cdot 0686$, area of the whole circle.

$$360 : 18 :: 7 \cdot 0686 : \cdot 35343, \text{ the area of the sector.}$$

1225. Problem XII. *To find the area of a segment of a circle.*

Rule 1. Find the area of the sector having the same arc with the segment by the last problem. Then find the area of the triangle formed by the chord of the segment and the two radii of the sector. Take the sum of these two for the answer when the segment is greater than a semicircle, and their difference when less than a semicircle.

Example. Required the area of the segment ACBDA (*fig.* 517.), its chord AB being 12, and the radius AE or CE 10.

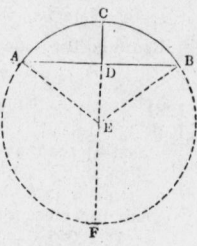

As AE : sin. ∠ D 90° :: AD : sin. 36° : $52\frac{1}{3} = 36\cdot87$ degrees in the arc AC.

Their double 73·74 degrees in arc ACB.

Now, $\cdot7854 \times 400 = 314\cdot16$, the area of the whole circle.

Therefore, $360° : 73\cdot74 :: 314\cdot16 : 64\cdot3504$, area of the sector ACBE.

Again, $\sqrt{AE^2 - AD^2} = \sqrt{100 - 36} = \sqrt{64} = 8 = DE$.

Therefore, $AD \times DE = 6 \times 8 = 48$, the area of the triangle AEB.

Hence the sector ACBE (64·350), less triangle AEB (48) $= 16\cdot3504$, area of segment ACBDA.

Fig. 517.

Rule 2. Divide the height of the segment by the diameter, and find the quotient in the column of heights in the following table. Take out the corresponding area in the next column on the right hand, and multiply it by the square of the circle's diameter for the area of the segment. This rule is founded on the principle of similar plane figures being to one another as the squares of their like lineal dimensions. The segments in the table are those of a circle whose diameter is 1. In the first column is contained the versed sines divided by the diameter. Hence the area of the similar segment taken from the table and multiplied by the square of the diameter gives the area of the segment to such diameter. When the quotient is not found exactly in the table, a proportion is used between the next less and greater area.

Example. As before, let the chord AB be 12, and the radius 10 or diameter 20.

Having found as above $DE = 8$; then $CE - DE = CD = 10 - 8 = 2$. Hence by the rule $CD \div CF = 2 \div 20 = \cdot1$, the tabular height; this being found in the first column of the table, the corresponding tabular area is ·040875; then $\cdot040875 \times 20^2 = \cdot040875 \times 400 = 16\cdot340$, the area nearly the same as before.

AREAS OF THE SEGMENTS OF A CIRCLE WHOSE DIAMETER, UNITY, IS SUPPOSED TO BE DIVIDED INTO 1000 EQUAL PARTS.

Hght.	Area Seg.	Hght.	Area Seg.	Hght.	Area Seg.	Hght.	Area Seg.	Hght.	Area Seg.	Hght.	Area Seg.
·001	·000042	·022	·004322	·043	·011734	·064	·021168	·085	·032186	·106	·044522
·002	·000119	·023	·004618	·044	·012142	·065	·021659	·086	·032745	·107	·045139
·003	·000219	·024	·004921	·045	·012554	·066	·022154	·087	·033307	·108	·045759
·004	·000337	·025	·005230	·046	·012971	·067	·022652	·088	·033872	·109	·046381
·005	·000470	·026	·005546	·047	·013392	·068	·023154	·089	·034441	·110	·047005
·006	·000618	·027	·005867	·048	·013818	·069	·023659	·090	·035011	·111	·047632
·007	·000779	·028	·006194	·049	·014247	·070	·024168	·091	·035585	·112	·048262
·008	·000951	·029	·006527	·050	·014681	·071	·024680	·092	·036162	·113	·048894
·009	·001135	·030	·006865	·051	·015119	·072	·025195	·093	·036741	·114	·049528
·010	·001329	·031	·007209	·052	·015561	·073	·025714	·094	·037323	·115	·050165
·011	·001533	·032	·007558	·053	·016007	·074	·026236	·095	·037909	·116	·050804
·012	·001746	·033	·007913	·054	·016457	·075	·026761	·096	·038496	·117	·051446
·013	·001968	·034	·008273	·055	·016911	·076	·027289	·097	·039087	·118	·052090
·014	·002199	·035	·008638	·056	·017369	·077	·027821	·098	·039680	·119	·052736
·015	·002438	·036	·009008	·057	·017831	·078	·028356	·099	·040276	·120	·053385
·016	·002685	·037	·009383	·058	·018296	·079	·028894	·100	·040875	·121	·054036
·017	·002940	·038	·009763	·059	·018766	·080	·029435	·101	·041476	·122	·054689
·018	·003202	·039	·010148	·060	·019239	·081	·029979	·102	·042080	·123	·055345
·019	·003471	·040	·010537	·061	·019716	·082	·030526	·103	·042687	·124	·056003
·020	·003748	·041	·010931	·062	·020196	·083	·031076	·104	·043296	·125	·056663
·021	·004031	·042	·011330	·063	·020680	·084	·031629	·105	·043908	·126	·057326

Hght.	Area Seg.	Hght.	Area Seg.	Hght.	Area Seg	Hght.	Area Seg.	Hght.	Area Seg.	Hght.	Area Seg.
·127	·057991	·190	·103900	·253	·156149	·315	·212011	·377	·270951	·439	·331850
·128	·058658	·191	·104685	·254	·157019	·316	·212940	·378	·271920	·440	·332843
·129	·059327	·192	·105472	·255	·157890	·317	·213871	·379	·272890	·441	·333836
·130	·059999	·193	·106261	·256	·158762	·318	·214802	·380	·273861	·442	·334829
·131	·060672	·194	·107051	·257	·159636	·319	·215733	·381	·274832	·443	·335822
·132	·061348	·195	·107842	·258	·160510	·320	·216666	·382	·275803	·444	·336816
·133	·062026	·196	·108636	·259	·161386	·321	·217599	·383	·276775	·445	·337810
·134	·062707	·197	·109430	·260	·162263	·322	·218533	·384	·277748	·446	·338804
·135	·063389	·198	·110226	·261	·163140	·323	·219468	·385	·278721	·447	·339798
·136	·064074	·199	·111024	·262	·164019	·324	·220404	·386	·279694	·448	·340793
·137	·064760	·200	·111823	·263	·164899	·325	·221340	·387	·280668	·449	·341787
·138	·065449	·201	·112624	·264	·165780	·326	·222277	·388	·281642	·450	·342782
·139	·066140	·202	·113426	·265	·166663	·327	·223215	·389	·282617	·451	·343777
·140	·066833	·203	·114230	·266	·167546	·328	·224154	·390	·283592	·452	·344772
·141	·067528	·204	·115035	·267	·168430	·329	·225093	·391	·284568	·453	·345768
·142	·068225	·205	·115842	·268	·169315	·330	·226033	·392	·285544	·454	·346764
·143	·068924	·206	·116650	·269	·170202	·331	·226974	·393	·286521	·455	·347759
·144	·069625	·207	·117460	·270	·171089	·332	·227915	·394	·287498	·456	·348755
·145	·070328	·208	·118271	·271	·171971	·333	·228858	·395	·288476	·457	·349752
·146	·071033	·209	·119083	·272	·172867	·334	·229801	·396	·289453	·458	·350748
·147	·071741	·210	·119897	·273	·173758	·335	·230745	·397	·290432	·459	·351745
·148	·072450	·211	·120712	·274	·174649	·336	·231689	·398	·291411	·460	·352742
·149	·073161	·212	·121529	·275	·175542	·337	·232634	·399	·292390	·461	·353739
·150	·073874	·213	·122347	·276	·176435	·338	·233580	·400	·293369	·462	·354736
·151	·074589	·214	·123167	·277	·177330	·339	·234526	·401	·294349	·463	·355732
·152	·075306	·215	·123988	·278	·178225	·340	·235473	·402	·295330	·464	·356730
·153	·076026	·216	·124810	·279	·179122	·341	·236421	·403	·296311	·465	·357727
·154	·076747	·217	·125634	·280	·180019	·342	·237369	·404	·297292	·466	·358725
·155	·077469	·218	·126459	·281	·180918	·343	·238318	·405	·298273	·467	·359723
·156	·078194	·219	·127285	·282	·181817	·344	·239268	·406	·299255	·468	·360721
·157	·078921	·220	·128113	·283	·182718	·345	·240218	·407	·300238	·469	·361719
·158	·079649	·221	·128942	·284	·183619	·346	·241169	·408	·301220	·470	·362717
·159	·080380	·222	·129773	·285	·184521	·347	·242121	·409	·302203	·471	·363715
·160	·081112	·223	·130605	·286	·185425	·348	·243074	·410	·303187	·472	·364713
·161	·081846	·224	·131438	·287	·186329	·349	·244026	·411	·304171	·473	·365712
·162	·082582	·225	·132272	·288	·187234	·350	·244980	·412	·305155	·474	·366710
·163	·083320	·226	·133108	·289	·188140	·351	·245934	·413	·306140	·475	·367709
·164	·084059	·227	·133945	·290	·189047	·352	·246889	·414	·307125	·476	·368708
·165	·084801	·228	·134784	·291	·189955	·353	·247845	·415	·308110	·477	·369707
·166	·085544	·229	·135624	·292	·190864	·354	·248801	·416	·309095	·478	·370706
·167	·086289	·230	·136465	·293	·191775	·355	·249757	·417	·310081	·479	·371704
·168	·087036	·231	·137307	·294	·192684	·356	·250715	·418	·311068	·480	·372704
·169	·087785	·232	·138150	·295	·193596	·357	·251673	·419	·312054	·481	·373703
·170	·088535	·233	·138995	·296	·194509	·358	·252631	·420	·313041	·482	·374702
·171	·089287	·234	·139841	·297	·195422	·359	·253590	·421	·314029	·483	·375702
·172	·090041	·235	·140688	·298	·196337	·360	·254550	·422	·315016	·484	·376702
·173	·090797	·236	·141537	·299	·197252	·361	·255510	·423	·316004	·485	·377701
·174	·091554	·237	·142387	·300	·198168	·362	·256471	·424	·316992	·486	·378701
·175	·092313	·238	·143238	·301	·199085	·363	·257433	·425	·317981	·487	·379700
·176	·093074	·239	·144091	·302	·200003	·364	·258395	·426	·318970	·488	·380700
·177	·093836	·240	·144944	·303	·200922	·365	·259357	·427	·319959	·489	·381699
·178	·094601	·241	·145799	·304	·201841	·366	·260320	·428	·320948	·490	·382699
·179	·095366	·242	·146655	·305	·202761	·367	·261284	·429	·321938	·491	·383699
·180	·096134	·243	·147512	·306	·203683	·368	·262248	·430	·322928	·492	·384699
·181	·096903	·244	·148371	·307	·204605	·369	·263213	·431	·323918	·493	·385699
·182	·097674	·245	·149230	·308	·205527	·370	·264178	·432	·324909	·494	·386699
·183	·098447	·246	·150091	·309	·206451	·371	·265144	·433	·325900	·495	·387699
·184	·099221	·247	·150953	·310	·207376	·372	·266111	·434	·326892	·496	·388699
·185	·099997	·248	·151816	·311	·208301	·373	·267078	·435	·327882	·497	·389699
·186	·100774	·249	·152680	·312	·209227	·374	·268045	·436	·328874	·498	·390699
·187	·101553	·25)	·153546	·313	·210154	·375	·269013	·437	·329866	·499	·391699
·188	·102334	·251	·154412	·314	·211082	·376	·269982	·438	·330858	·500	·392699
·189	·103116	·252	·155280								

1226. Problem XIII. *To find the area of an ellipsis.*

Rule. Multiply the longest and shortest diameter together, and their product by ·7854, which will give the area required. This rule is founded on Theorem 3. Cor. 2. in Conic Sections. (1098, 1100.)

Example. Required the area of an ellipse whose two axes are 70 and 50.

Here $70 \times 50 \times ·7854 = 2748·9$.

1227. Problem XIV. *To find the area of any elliptic segment.*

Rule. Find the area of a circular segment having the same height and the same vertical axis or diameter; then, as the said vertical axis is to the other axis (parallel to the base of the segment), so is the area of the circular segment first found to the area of the elliptic segment sought. This rule is founded on the theorem alluded to in the previous problem. Or, divide the height of the segment by the vertical axis of the ellipse; and find in the table of circular segments appended to Prob. 12. (1224.) the circular segment which has the above quotient for its versed sine; then multiply together this segment and the two axes of the ellipse for the area.

Example. Required the area of an elliptic segment whose height is 20, the vertical axis being 70, and the parallel axis 50.

Here $20 \div 70 = ·2857142$, the quotient or versed sine to which in the table answers the segment ·285714.

Then $·285714 \times 70 \times 50 = 648·342$, the area required.

1228. Problem XV. *To find the area of a parabola or its segment.*

Rule. Multiply the base by the perpendicular height, and take two thirds of the product for the area. This rule is founded on the properties of the curve already described in conic sections, by which it is known that every parabola is $\frac{2}{3}$ of its circumscribing parallelogram. (See 1097.)

Example. Required the area of a parabola whose height is 2 and its base 12.

Here $2 \times 12 = 24$, and $\frac{2}{3}$ of $24 = 16$ is the area required.

MENSURATION OF SOLIDS.

1229. The measure of every solid body is the capacity or content of that body, considered under the threefold dimensions of length, breadth, and thickness, and the measure of a solid is called its solidity, capacity, or content. Solids are measured by units which are cubes, whose sides are inches, feet, yards, &c. Whence the solidity of a body is said to be of so many cubic inches, feet, yards, &c. as will occupy its capacity or space, or another of equal magnitude.

1230. The smallest solid measure in use with the architect is the cubic inch, from which other cubes are taken by cubing the linear proportions, thus, —

$$1728 \text{ cubic inches} = 1 \text{ cubic foot};$$
$$27 \text{ cubic feet} = 1 \text{ cubic yard}.$$

1231. Problem I. *To find the superficies of a prism.*

Multiply the perimeter of one end of the prism by its height, and the product will be the surface of its sides. To this, if wanted, add the area of the two ends of the prism. Or, compute the areas of the sides and ends separately, and add them together.

Example 1. Required the surface of a cube whose sides are 20 feet.

Here we have six sides; therefore $20 \times 20 \times 6 = 2400$ feet, the area required.

Example 2. Required the surface of a triangular prism whose length is 20 feet and each side of its end or base 18 inches.

Here we have, for the area of the base,

$1·5^2 - ·75^2 = (2·25 - ·5625 =) 1·6875^2$ for the perpendicular of triangle of base;

and $\sqrt{1·6875} = 1·299$, which multiplied by $1·5 = 1·948$ gives the area of the two bases;

then, $3 \times 20 \times 1·5 + 1·948 = 91·948$ is the area required.

Example 3. Required the convex surface of a round prism or cylinder whose length is 20 feet and the diameter of whose base is 2 feet.

Here, $2 \times 3·1416 = 6·2832$,

and $3·1416 \times 20 = 125·664$, the convex surface required.

1232. Problem II. *To find the surface of a pyramid or cone.*

Rule. Multiply the perimeter of the base by the length of the slant side, and half the product will be the surface of the sides or the sum of the areas of all the sides, or of the areas of the triangles whereof it consists. To this sum add the area of the end or base.

Example 1. Required the surface of the slant sides of a triangular pyramid whose slant height is 20 feet and each side of the base 3 feet.

Here, 20×3 (the perimeter) $\times 3 \div 2 = 90$ feet, the surface required.

Example 2. Required the convex surface of a cone or circular pyramid whose slant height is 50 feet and the diameter of its base $8\frac{1}{2}$ feet.

Here, $8\cdot5 \times 3\cdot1416 \times 50 \div 2 = 667\cdot5$, the convex surface required.

1233. Problem III. *To find the surface of the frustum of a pyramid or cone, being the lower part where the top is cut off by a plane parallel to the base.*

Rule. Add together the perimeters of the two ends and multiply their sum by the slant height. One half of the product is the surface sought. This is manifest, because the sides of the solid are trapezoids, having the opposite sides parallel.

Example 1. Required the surface of the frustum of a square pyramid whose slant height is 10 feet, each side of the base being 3 feet 4 inches and each side of the top 2 feet 2 inches.

Here, 3 feet 4 inches $\times 4 = 13$ feet 4 inches, and 2 feet 2 inches $\times 4 = 8$ feet 8 inches; and 13 feet 4 inches $+ 8$ feet 8 inches $= 22$. Then $22 \div 2 \times 10 = 110$ feet, the surface required.

Example 2. Required the convex surface of the frustum of a cone whose slant height is $12\frac{1}{2}$ feet and the circumference of the two ends 6 and $8\cdot4$ feet.

Here, $6 + 8\cdot4 = 14\cdot4$; and $14\cdot4 \times 12\cdot5 \div 2 = 180 \div 2 = 90$, the convex surface required.

1234. Problem IV. *To find the solid content of any prism or cylinder.*

Rule. Find the area of the base according to its figure, and multiply it by the length of the prism or cylinder for the solid content. This rule is founded on Prop. 99. (Geometry, 980.). Let the rectangular parallelopipedon be the solid to be measured, the small cube P (*fig.* 518.) being the measuring unit, its side being 1 inch, 1 foot, &c.

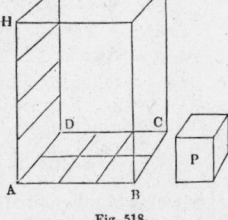

Fig. 518.

Let also the length and breadth of the base ABCD, and also let the height AH, be divided into spaces equal to the side of the base of the cube P; for instance, here, in the length 3 and in the breadth 2, making 3 times 2 or 6 squares in the base AC each equal to the base of the cube P. It is manifest that the parallelopipedon will contain the cube P as many times as the base AC contains the base of the cube, repeated as often as the height AH contains the height of the cube. Or, in other words, the contents of a parallelopipedon is found by multiplying the area of the base by the altitude of the solid. And because all prisms and cylinders are equal to parallelopipedons of equal bases and altitudes, the rule is general for all such solids whatever the figure of their base.

Example 1. Required the solid content of a cube whose side is 24 inches.

Here, $24 \times 24 \times 24 = 13824$ cubic inches.

Example 2. Required the solidity of a triangular prism whose length is 10 feet and the three sides of its triangular end are 3, 4, and 5 feet.

Here, because (Prop. 32. Geometry, 907.) $3^2 + 4^2 = 5^2$, it follows that the angle contained by the sides 3 and 4 is a right angle. Therefore $\frac{3 \times 4}{2} \times 10 = 60$ cubic feet, the content required.

Example 3. Required the content of a cylinder whose length is 20 feet and its diameter 5 feet 6 inches.

Here, $5\cdot5 \times 5\cdot5 \times \cdot7854 = 23\cdot75835$, area of base; and $23\cdot75835 \times 20 = 47\cdot5167$, content of cylinder required.

1235. Problem V. *To find the content of any pyramid or cone.*

Rule. Find the area of the base and multiply that area by the perpendicular height. One third of the product is the content. This rule is founded on Prop. 110. (Geometry, 991.)

Example 1. Required the solidity of the square pyramid, the sides of whose base are 30, and its perpendicular height 25.

Here, $\frac{30 \times 30}{3} \times 25 = 7500$, content required.

Example 2. Required the content of a triangular pyramid whose perpendicular height is 30 and each side of the base 3.

Here, $\frac{3+3+3}{2} = \frac{9}{2} = 4\cdot5$, half sum of the sides;

and $4\cdot5 - 3 = 1\cdot5$, one of the three equal remainders. (See Trigonometry, 1052.) but $\sqrt{4\cdot5 \times 1\cdot5 \times 1\cdot5 \times 1\cdot5 \times 30 \div 3} = 3\cdot897117 \times 10$, or $38\cdot97117$, the solidity required.

Example 3. Required the content of a pentagonal pyramid whose height is 12 feet and each side of its base 2 feet.

Here, $1\cdot7204774$ (tabular area, Prob. 6. 1218.) $\times 4$ (square of side) $= 6\cdot8819096$ area of base; and $6\cdot8819096 \times 12 = 82\cdot5829152$.

Then $\frac{82\cdot5829152}{3} = 27\cdot5276384$, content required.

Example 4. Required the content of a cone whose height is $10\frac{1}{2}$ feet and the circumference of its base 9 feet.

Here, ·07958 (Prob. 9. 1222.) × 81 = 6·44598 area of base,

And 3·5 being $\frac{1}{3}$ of $10\frac{1}{2}$ feet, 6·44598 × 3·5 = 22·56093 is the content required.

1236. Problem VI.   *To find the solidity of the frustum of a cone or pyramid.*

Add together the areas of the ends and the mean proportional between them. Then taking one third of that sum for a mean area and multiplying it by the perpendicular height or length of the frustum, we shall have its content. This rule depends upon Prop. 110. (Geometry, 991.).

It may be otherwise expressed when the ends of the frustum are circles or regular polygons.   In respect of the last, square one side of each polygon, and also multiply one side by the other; add the three products together, and multiply their sum by the tabular area for the polygon.   Take one third of the product for the mean area, which multiply by the length, and we have the product required.   When the case of the frustum of a cone is to be treated, the ends being circles, square the diameter or the circumference at each end, and multiply the same two dimensions together.   Take the sum of the three products, and multiply it by the proper tabular number, that is, by ·7854, when the diameters are used, and ·07958 when the circumferences are used, and, taking one third of the product, multiply it by the length for the content required.

Example 1.   Required the content of the frustum of a pyramid the sides of whose greater ends are 15 inches, and those of the lesser ends 6 inches, and its altitude 24 feet.

Here, ·5 × ·5 = ·25, area of the lesser end,

and 1·25 × 1·25 = 1·5625, area of the greater end:

The mean proportional therefore $\sqrt{·25 \times 1·5625} = ·625$.

Again, $\frac{·25 + ·625 + 1·5625}{3} = \frac{2·4375}{3} = ·8125$, mean area,

and ·8125 × 24 (altitude) = 19·5 feet, content required.

Example 2.   Required the content of a conic frustum whose altitude is 18 feet, its greatest diameter 8, and its least diameter 4.

Here, 64 (area gr. diam.) + 16 (less. diam.) + (8 × 4) = 112, sum of the products;

and $\frac{·7854 \times 112 \times 18}{3} = 527·7888$, content required.

Example 3.   Required the content of a pentagonal frustum whose height is 5 feet, each side of the base 18 inches, and each side of the upper end 6 inches.

Here, $1·5^2 + 1·5^2 + (1·5 \times ·5) = 2·5625$, sum of the products;

but, $\frac{1·7204774 \text{ (tab. area)} \times 2·5625 \text{ (sum of products)} \times 5}{3} = 9·31925$, content required.

1237. Problem VII.   *To find the surface of a sphere or any segment of one.*

Rule 1.   Multiply the circumference of the sphere by its diameter, and the product will be the surface thereof.   This and the rules in the following problems depend on Props. 113. and 114. (Geometry, 994, 995.), to which the reader is referred.

Rule 2.   Square the diameter, and multiply that square by 3·1416 for the surface.

Rule 3.   Square the circumference, then either multiply that square by the decimal ·3183, or divide it by 3·1416 for the surface.

Remark.   For the surface of a segment or frustum, multiply the whole circumference of the sphere by the height of the part required.

Example 1.   Required the convex superficies of a sphere whose diameter is 7 and circumference 22.

Here, 22 × 7 = 154, the superficies required.

Example 2.   Required the superficies of a sphere whose diameter is 24 inches.

Here, 24 × 24 × 3·1416 = 1809·5616 is the superficies required.

Example 3.   Required the convex superficies of a segment of a sphere whose axis is 42 inches and the height of the segment 9 inches.

Here, 1 : 3·1416::42 : 131·9472, the circumference of the sphere;

but 131·9472 × 9 = 1187·5248, the superficies required.

Example 4.   Required the convex surface of a spherical zone whose breadth or height is 2 feet and which forms part of a sphere whose diameter is $12\frac{1}{2}$ feet.

Here, 1 : 3·1416::12·5 : 39·27, the circumference of the sphere whereof the zone is a part;

and 39·27 × 2 = 78·54, the area required.

1238. Problem VIII.   *To find the solidity of a sphere or globe.*

Rule 1.   Multiply the surface by the diameter, and take one sixth of the product for the content.

Rule 2.   Take the cube of the diameter and multiply it by the decimal ·5236 for the content.

Example.   Required the content of a sphere whose axis is 12.

Here 12 × 12 × 12 × ·5236 = 904·7808, content required.

1239. Problem IX. *To find the solidity of a spherical segment.*

Rule 1. From thrice the diameter of the sphere subtract double the height of the segment, and multiply the remainder by the square of the height. This product multiplied by ·5236 will give the content.

Rule 2. To thrice the square of the radius add the square of its height, multiply the sum thus found by the height, and the product thereof by ·5236 for the content.

Example 1. Required the solidity of a segment of a sphere whose height is 9, the diameter of its base being 20.

Here, 3 times the square of the radius of the base $=300$;

and the square of its height $=81$, and $300+81=381$;

but $381 \times 9 = 3429$, which multiplied by ·5236 $= 1795\cdot4244$, the solidity required.

Example 2. Required the solidity of a spherical segment whose height is 2 feet and the diameter of the sphere 8 feet.

Here, $8 \times 3 - 4 = 20$, which multiplied by $4 = 80$;

and $80 \times \cdot5236 = 41\cdot888$, the solidity required.

It is manifest that the difference between two segments in which the zone of a sphere is included will give the solidity of the zone. That is, where for instance the zone is included in a segment lying above the diameter, first consider the whole as the segment of a sphere terminated by the vertex and find its solidity ; from which subtract the upper part or segment between the upper surface of the zone and the vertex of the sphere, and the difference is the solidity of the zone.

The general rule to find the solidity of a frustum or zone of a sphere is : to the sum of the squares of the radii of the two ends add one third of the square of their distance, or the breadth of the zone, and this sum multiplied by the said breadth, and that product again by $1\cdot5708$, is the solidity.

Sect. VII.

MECHANICS AND STATICS.

1240. It is our intention in this section to address ourselves to the consideration of mechanics and statics as applicable more immediately to architecture. The former is the science of forces, and the effects they produce when applied to machines in the motion of bodies. The latter is the science of weight, especially when considered in a state of equilibrium.

1241. The centre of motion is a fixed point about which a body moves, the axis being the fixed line about which it moves.

1242. The centre of gravity is a certain point, upon which a body being freely suspended, such body will rest in any position.

1243. So that weight and power, when opposed to each other, signify the body to be moved, and the body that moves it, or the patient and agent. The power is the agent which moves or endeavours to move the patient or weight, whilst by the word equilibrium is meant an equality of action or force between two or more powers or weights acting against each other, and which by destroying each other's effects cause it to remain at rest.

PARALLELOGRAM OF FORCES.

1244. If a body D suspended by a thread is drawn out of its vertical direction by an horizontal thread DE (*fig.* 519.), such power neither increases nor diminishes the effort

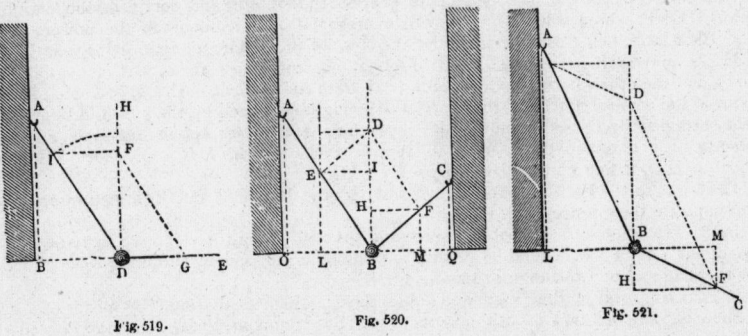

Fig. 519.   Fig. 520.   Fig. 521.

of the weight of the body; but it may be easily imagined that the first thread, by being in the direction AD, will, besides the weight itself, have to sustain the effort of the power that draws it out of the vertical AB.

1245. If the direction of the horizontal force be prolonged till it meets the vertical, which would be in the first thread if it were not drawn away by the second, we shall have triangle ADB, whose sides will express the proportion of the weight to the forces of the two threads in the case of equilibrium being established; that is, supposing AB to express the weight, AD will express the effort of the thread attached to the point A, and BD that of the horizontal power which pulls the body away from the vertical AB.

1246. These different forces may also be found by transferring to the vertical DH (*fig.*519.) any length of line DF to represent the weight of the body. If from the point F the parallels FI, FG be drawn in the direction of the threads, their forces will be indicated by the lines ID, DG, so that the three sides of the triangle DGF, similar to the triangle ADB, will express the proportion of the weight to the two forces applied to the threads.

1247. Suppose the weight to be 30 lbs.: if from a scale of equal parts we set up 30 of those parts from D to F (*fig.* 519.), we shall find DG equal to 21, or the pounds of force of the horizontal line DE, and 35 for the oblique power ID.

1248. If the weight, instead of 30 lbs., were 100, we should find the value of the forces DG and ID by the proportions of $30 : 21 :: 100 : x$, where x expresses the force DG. The value resulting from this proportion is $x = \frac{21 \times 100}{30} = 70$. The second proportion

$30 : 35 :: 100 : y$, where y represents the effort ID, whose value will be $y = \frac{35 \times 100}{30} = 116 \cdot 666$.

1249. If the angle ADH formed by AD and DH be known, the same results may be obtained by taking DF for the radius, in which case $IF = DG$ becomes the tangent, in this instance, of 35 degrees, and ID the secant; whence

$$DF : DI : IF :: \text{radius} : \text{tang. } 35 : \text{sec. } 35.$$

If ID be taken for the radius, we have

$$ID : IF : FD :: \text{radius} : \text{tang. } 35 : \text{sin. } 35.$$

1250. We have here to observe, that in conducting the operation above mentioned a figure DIFG has been formed, which is called the parallelogram of the forces, because the diagonal DF always expresses a compounded force, which will place in equilibrio the two others FI, FG, represented by the two contiguous sides IF, FG.

1251. Instead of two forces which draw, we may suppose two others which act by pushing from E to D (*fig.* 522.) and from A to D. If we take the vertical DF to express the weight, and we draw as before the parallels FG and FI in the direction of the forces, the sides GD and DI of the parallelogram DGFI (*fig.* 519.) will express the forces with which the powers act relatively to DF to support the body: thus $FI = GD$ the weight and two powers which support it will, in case of equilibrium, be represented by the three sides of a rectangular triangle DFI; so that if the weight be designated by H, the power which pushes from G to D by E, and that which acts from I to D by P, we shall have the proportion $H : E : P ::$ $DF : FI : ID$, wherein, if we take DF for radius, it will be as radius is to the tangent of the angle FDI and to its secant.

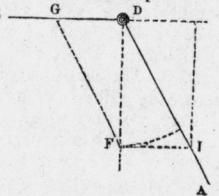

Fig. 522.

As a body in suspension is drawn away from the vertical line in which it hangs by a power higher than the body (*fig.* 520.), it follows that the oblique forces AB and BC each support, independent of any lateral efforts, a part of the weight of the body. In order to find the proportion of these parts to the total weight, take any distance BD on a vertical raised from the centre of the body B to express the weight, and complete the parallelogram DEBF, whose sides EB, BF will express the oblique forces of the powers A and C. These lines, being considered as the diagonals of the rectangular parallelograms LEIB, BHFM, may each be resolved into two forces, whereof one of them, vertical, sustains the body, and the other, horizontal, draws it away from the verticals AO, CQ. Hence IB will express the vertical force, or that part of the weight sustained by the power EB, and HB that sustained by the other power BF: as these two forces act in the same direction, when added together their sum will represent the weight DB. In short, IB being equal to HD, it follows that $BH + BI = BI + ID$.

1252. As to the horizontal forces indicated by the lines LB and BM, as they are equal and opposite they destroy one another.

1253. It follows, from what has been said, that all oblique forces may be resolved into two others, one of which shall be vertical and the other horizontal, by taking their direction for the diagonal of a rectangular parallelogram.

1254. In respect of their ratio and value, those may be easily found by means of a scale if the diagram be drawn with accuracy; or by trigonometry, if we know the angles

ABD, DBC, which AB and BC form with the vertical BD, by taking successively for radius the diagonals BD, BE, and BF.

1255. In the accompanying diagram, the weight, instead of being suspended by strings acting by tension, is sustained by forces which are supposed to act by pushing. But as this arrangement makes no alteration in the system of forces, we may apply to this figure all that has been said with respect to the preceding one. The only difference is, that the parallelogram of the forces is below the weight instead of being above it. Thus ID + IB = BD expresses the sum of the vertical forces which support the weight, and MB and BL the horizontal forces which counteract each other.

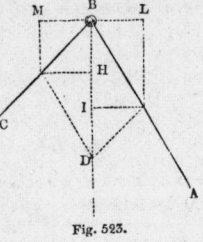

Fig. 523.

1256. In the two preceding figures the direction of the forces which act by tension or compression in supporting the weight form an acute angle. In those represented in *fig.* 521. and the figure at the side (524.), these directions make an obtuse angle; whence it follows that in *fig.* 521. the force C which draws the weight out of the vertical AL, instead of tending to support the weight B, increases its effect by its tendency to act in the same direction. In order to ascertain the amount of this effect upon BD in *figs.* 521. and 524., which represents the vertical action of the weight, describe the parallelogram BADF, for the purpose of determining the oblique forces BA, BF, and then take these sides for the diagonals of the two rectangles LAIB, BHFM, whose sides BI, BH will express the vertical forces, and LB, BM the horizontal ones.

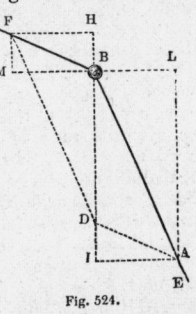

Fig. 524.

1257. It must be observed that in *fig.* 521. the force AB acting upwards renders its vertical effect greater than the weight of a quantity ID, which serves as a compensation to the part BH, that the other force BF adds to the weight by drawing downwards. Similarly, the vertical effect of the force BE (*fig.* 524.) exceeds the expression BD of the weight by a quantity DI, to counterpoise the effect BH of the other power BF, which acts downwards; so that in both cases we have BD only for the vertical effect of the weight. As to the horizontal effects LB and BM, they being equal and in opposite directions in both figures, of course counteract each other.

1258. For the same reason that a force can be resolved into two others, those two others may be resolved into one, by making that *one* the diagonal of a parallelogram whose forces are represented by two contiguous sides. It is clear, then, that whatever the number of forces which affect any point, they may be reduced into a single one. It is only necessary to discover the results of the forces two by two and to combine these results similarly two by two, till we come to the principal ones, which may be ultimately reduced to one, as we have seen above. By such a process we shall find that PY (*fig.* 525.) is the result of the forces PA, PB, PC, PD, which affect the point P.

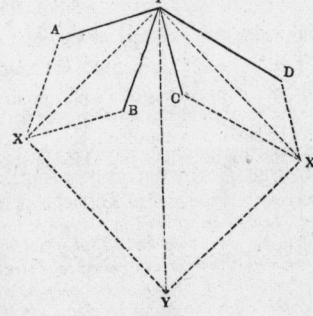

Fig. 525.

1259. This method of resolving forces is often of great utility in the science of building, for the purpose of providing a force to resist several others acting in different directions but meeting in one point.

OF THE PROPERTIES OF THE LEVER.

1260. The *lever* is an inflexible rod, bar, or beam serving to raise weights, whilst it is supported at a point by a *fulcrum*, or prop, which is the centre of motion. To render the demonstrations relative to it easier and simpler, it is supposed to be void of gravity or weight. The different positions in which the power applied to it, and the weight to be affected, may be applied in respect of the fulcrum, have given rise to the distinction of three sorts of levers.

I. That represented in *fig.* 526., in which the fulcrum O is between the power applied P and the weight Q.

II. That represented in *fig* 527., in which the weight Q is placed between the fulcrum

O and the power P, wherein it is to be remarked that the weight and the power act in contrary directions.

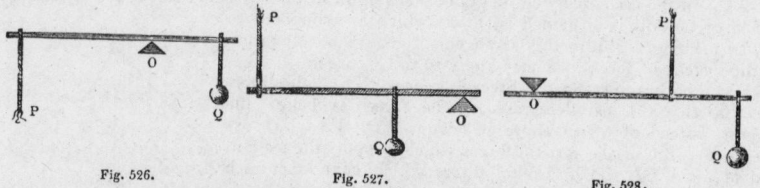

Fig. 526.　　　　　Fig. 527.　　　　　Fig. 528.

III. That represented in *fig.* 528., wherein the power P is placed between the weight and the fulcrum, in which case the power and the weight act in contrary directions.

1261. In considering the fulcrum of these three sorts of levers, we must notice, as a third species of power introduced for creating an equilibrium between the others, 1st, That in which the directions of the weight and of the powers concur in the point R (*fig.* 529.). 2d, That in which they are parallel.

1262. In the first case, if from the point R (*figs.* 529. and 530.) we draw parallel to these directions O*m* R*n*, the ratio of these three forces, that is, the power, the weight, and the fulcrum, will be as the three sides of the triangle O*m*R, or its equal O*n*R; thus we shall have P : Q : R :: *m*R : R*n* : O R ; and as the sides of a triangle are as the sines of their opposite angles, by taking O R as the radius we shall have

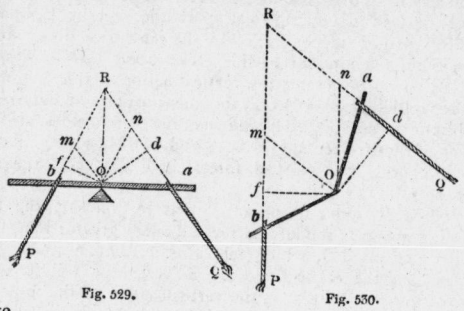

Fig. 529.　　　　　Fig. 530.

$$P : Q :: \sin. OR_n : \sin. OR_m.$$

And if from the point O two perpendiculars be let fall, O*d*O*f*, on the directions RQ, RP,

$$\text{Sin. } OR_n : \sin. OR_m :: O_d : O_f;$$

from which two proportions we obtain

$$P : Q :: O_d : O_f; \text{ whence } P \times O_f = Q \times O_d.$$

This last expression gives equal products, which are called the *momenta, moments,* or quantities of motion of the force in respect of the fulcrum O. This property is the same for the straight as for the angular levers (*figs.* 529. and 530.). As this proportion exists, however large the angles *m*RO and OR*n* of the directions RQ, RP in respect to RO, it follows that when it becomes nothing, these directions become parallel without the proportion being changed ; whence is derived the following general theorem, found in all works on mechanics : — *If two forces applied to a straight or angular lever are in equilibrio, they are in an inverse ratio to the perpendiculars let fall from the fulcrum on their lines of direction : or in other words, In order that two forces applied to a straight or angular lever may be in equilibrio, their momenta in respect of the fulcrum must be equal.*

1263. Since, in order to place the lever in equilibrio, it is sufficient to obtain equal momenta, it follows that if we could go on increasing or diminishing the force, we might place it at any distance we please from the fulcrum, or load it without destroying the equilibrium. This results from the formula $P \times O_f = Q \times O_d,$ whence we have $O_f = \frac{Q \times O_d}{P}.$ Hence the distance O*f* is easily found, to which by applying the known force P, it may counterpoise the weight Q applied at the distance O*d*. In respect of the other points, we have only to know the perpendiculars O*f* and O*d*, for O*a* and O*b*, which are the arms of the real levers, are deduced from the triangles O*f b*, O*d a*, to which they belong.

1264. Suppose two levers (*figs.* 531, 532.), whereof

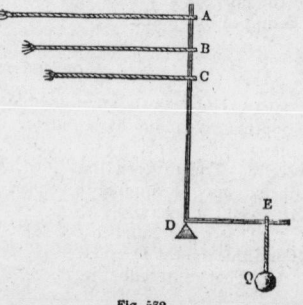

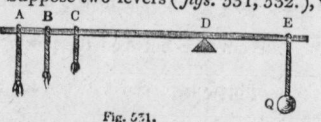

Fig. 531.　　　　　Fig. 532.

one is straight and the other angular, and that the weight Q is 100 pounds, the arm DE of the lever 6 feet; its momentum will be 600. Then if we wish to ascertain at what distance Of a weight of 60 pounds must be placed so that it may be in equilibrio with the first, we shall have

$$Of = \frac{Q \times Od}{P} = \frac{600}{60} = 10 \text{ feet, the distance sought.}$$

1265. Reciprocally, to find the effect of a force P placed at the point C of the other arm of the lever at a known distance from the fulcrum, and marked Of, in order to counter-poise Q placed at the distance Of, we have the formula $P = \frac{Q \times Od}{Of}$; and if we apply this formula to the numbers taken in the preceding example, the question will be, to find a force which placed at the distance of 10 feet from the fulcrum may be in equilibrio with a weight of 100 pounds at the end of the arm of a lever of 6 feet. We must in using the formula divide 600 by 10, and the quotient 60 will indicate the effect with which the force ought to act. If, instead of placing it in C, it is at B, 12 feet from the fulcrum, the force would be $\frac{600}{12}$, which gives 50; and lastly, if we have to place it at a point 15 feet from the fulcrum, the force would be $\frac{600}{15} = 40$. Thus, in changing the situation of the force to a point more or less distant from the fulcrum, we must divide the momentum of the weight which is to be supported by the distance from the fulcrum taken perpendicularly to its direction.

OF THE CENTRE OF GRAVITY.

1266. The centre of gravity of a body is a certain point within it on which the body, if freely suspended, will rest in any position; whilst in other positions it will descend to the lowest place to which it can get. Not only do whole bodies tend by their weight to assume a vertical direction, but also all the parts whereof they consist; so that if we suspend any body, whatever be its form, by means of a string, it will assume such a position that the thread produced to the internal part of the body will form an axis round which all the parts will remain in equilibrium. Every time that the point of suspension of a body is changed, the direction of the thread produced exhibits a new axis of equilibrium. But it is to be re-marked, that all these axes intersect each other in the same point situate in the centre of the mass of the body, supposing it composed of homogeneous parts but sometimes out of the mass of the body, as in the case of bodies much curved, this point is the centre of gravity.

1267. It is therefore easy to perceive that for a body to be in a state of rest its centre of gravity must be supported by a vertical force equal to the resultant of all the forces that affect it, but acting in a contrary direction. So in *figs.* 520. and 523., the weight supported by the forces AB and BC which draw or push, will be equally supported by a vertical force represented by the diagonal DB of the parallelogram which expresses the resultant of the forces.

1268. An acquaintance with the method of finding centres of gravity is indispensable in estimating the resistances, strains, and degree of stability of any part of an edifice. There arise cases in which we may cast aside all consideration of the form of a body, especially too when it acts by weight, and suppose the whole figure collected in the centre of gravity. We may also, for the sake of simplifying operations, substitute a force for a weight.

OF THE CENTRE OF GRAVITY OF LINES.

1269. A straight line may be conceived to be composed of an infinite number of points, equally heavy, ranged in the same direction. After this definition, it is evident that if it be suspended by the middle, the two parts, being composed of the same number of equal points placed at equal distances from the point of suspension, will be necessarily in equi-librium; whence it follows that the centre of gravity of a right line is in the middle of its length.

1270. The points in a curve line not being in the same direction, the centre of its volume cannot be the same as its centre of gravity; that is to say, that a curve suspended by the middle cannot be supported in equilibrio but in two opposite situations; one when the branches of the curve are downwards, and the other when they are upwards, so that the curve may be in a vertical plane.

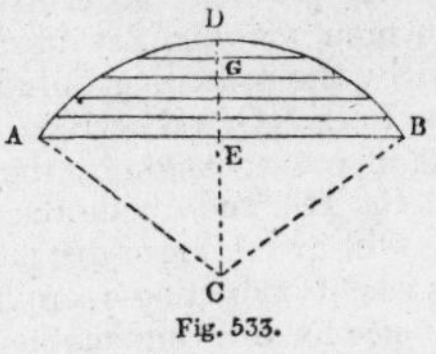

1271. If the curve is the arc of a circle ADB (*fig.* 533.), it is easy to see that from the uniformity of its curvature, its centre of gravity will be found in the right line DC drawn from the centre C to the middle D; moreover, if we draw the chord AB, the centre of gravity will be found between the points D and E.

Fig. 533.

1272. Let us suppose that through all the points of the line DE parallels to the chord AB be drawn, terminated on each side by the curve; and let us imagine that each of these

lines at its extremities bears corresponding points of the curve; then the line DE will be loaded with all these weights; and as the portions of the curve which answer to each parallel AB go on increasing as they approach D, the centre of gravity G will be nearer the point D than to the point E.

1273. To determine the position of this point upon the radius CD which divides the arc into two equal parts, we must use the following proportion : the length of the arc ABD is to the chord AB, as the radius CD is to the fourth term x, whose value is $\frac{AB \times CD}{ABD}$. That is, in order to obtain upon the radius DC the distance CG of the centre of gravity from the centre of the arc of the circle, the chord AB must be multiplied by the radius CD and divided by the length of the arc ABD.

1274. When the circumference of the circle is entire, the axes of equilibrium being diameters, it is manifest that their intersection gives the centre of the curve as the centre of gravity. It is the same with all entire and symmetrical curves which have a centre, and with all combinations of right lines which form regular and symmetrical polygons.

OF THE CENTRE OF GRAVITY OF SURFACES.

1275. In order that a centre of gravity may be assigned to a surface, we must, as in the case of lines, imagine them to be material, that is, consisting of solid, homogeneous, and heavy particles.

1276. In all plane smooth surfaces, the centre of gra-

vity is the same as that of the volume of space; thus the centre of gravity G (*figs.* 534, 535, 536.), of a square of a rectangle, or of a parallelogram, is determined by the intersections of its diagonals AD, BC.

Fig. 534.

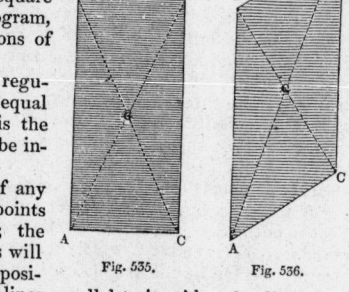

Fig. 535.   Fig. 536.

The centre of gravity of a regular polygon, composed of an equal or unequal number of sides, is the same as that of a circle within which it may be inscribed.

1277. In order to find the centre of gravity of any triangle, bisect each of the sides, and from the points of bisection draw lines to the opposite angles; the point of intersection with each other of these lines will be the centre of gravity sought; for in the supposition that the surface of the triangle is composed of lines parallel to its sides, the lines AE, BF, and CD (*fig.* 537.) will be the axes of equilibrium, whose intersection at G gives the centre of gravity.

We shall moreover find that this point is at one third of the distance from the base of each of the axes ; so that, in fact, it is only necessary to draw a line from the point of bisection of one of the sides to the opposite angle, and to divide it into three equal parts, whereof that nearest the base determines the centre of gravity of the triangle.

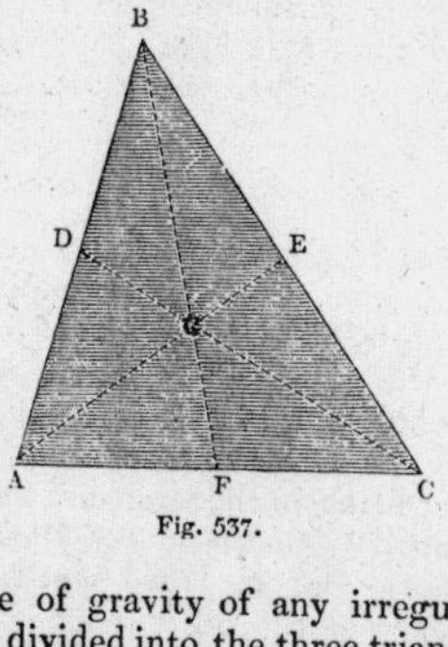

Fig. 537. 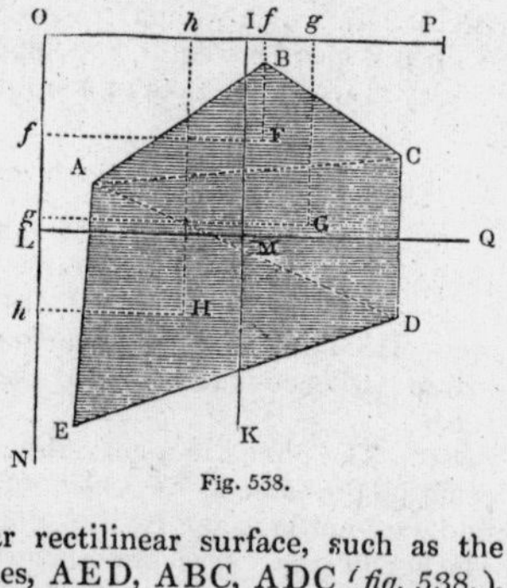   Fig. 538.

1278. To find the centre of gravity of any irregular rectilinear surface, such as the pentagon, *fig.* 538., let it be divided into the three triangles, AED, ABC, ADC (*fig.* 538.), and by the preceding rule determine their centres of gravity F, G, H. Then draw the two lines NO, OP, which form a right angle surrounding the polygon. Multiply the area of each triangle by the distance of its centre of gravity on the line ON, indicated by Ff, Gg, Hh, and divide the sum of these products by the entire area of the pentagon, and this will give a mean distance through which an indefinite line IK parallel to ON is to be drawn. Conducting a similar operation in respect of the line OP, we obtain a new mean distance for drawing another line LQ parallel to OP, which will intersect the first in the point M, the centre of gravity of the pentagon.

The centre of gravity of a sector of a circle AEBC (*fig.* 539.) must be upon the radius CE which divides the arc into two equal parts. To determine from the centre C, at

what distance the point G is to be placed, we must multiply twice the radius CE by the chord AB, and divide the product by thrice the length of the arc AEB. The quotient is the distance CG from the centre C of the circle of the centre of gravity of the sector.

1279. To find the centre of gravity of the crown portion of an arch DAEBF (*fig.* 540.) comprised between two concentric axes, we must —

1. Find the centre of gravity of the greater sector AEBC, and that of the smaller one DFG.

2. Multiply the area of each of these sectors by the distance of their respective centres of gravity from the common centre C.

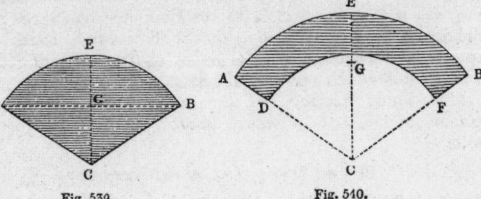

Fig. 539.   Fig. 540.

3. Subtract the smaller product from the greater, and divide the remainder by the area of DAEBF; the quotient will give the distance of the centre of gravity G from the centre C.

1280. To determine the centre of gravity of the segment AEB; subtract the product of the area of the triangle ABC (*fig.* 541.) multiplied by the distance of its centre of gravity from the centre C, from the product of the area of the sector, by the distance of its centre of gravity from the same point C, and divide the remainder by the area AEB; the quotient expresses the distance of the centre of gravity G of the segment from the centre C, which is to be set out on the radius, and which divides the segment into two equal parts.

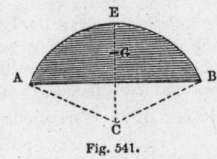

Fig. 541.

It would, from want of space, be inconvenient to give the strict demonstrations of the above rules; nor, indeed, is it absolutely necessary for the architectural student. Those who wish to pursue the subject *au fond*, will, of course, consult more abstruse works on the matter. We will merely observe, that whatever the figure whose centre of gravity is sought, it is only necessary to divide it into triangles, sectors, or segments, and proceed as above described for the pentagon, *fig.* 538.

OF THE CENTRE OF GRAVITY OF SOLIDS.

1281. It is supposed in the following considerations, that solids are composed of homogeneous particles whose weight in every part is uniform. They are here arranged under two heads, regular and irregular.

1282. Regular solids are considered as composed of elements of the same figure as their base, placed one upon the other, so that all their centres of gravity are in a vertical line, which we shall call the right axis. Thus parallelopipeds, prisms, cylinders, pyramids, cones, conoids, spheres, and spheroids have a right axis, whereon their centre of gravity is found.

1283. In parallelopipeds, prisms, cylinders, spheres, spheroids, the centre of gravity is in the middle of the right axis, because of the similarity and symmetry of their parts equally distant from that point.

1284. In pyramids and cones (*figs.* 542, 543.), which diminish gradually from the base to the apex, the centre of gravity is at the distance of one fourth of the axis from the base.

1285. In paraboloids, which diminish less on account of their curvature, the centre of gravity is at the height of one third the axis above the base.

To find the centre of a pyramid or of a truncated cone (*figs.* 542, 543.), we must first multiply the cube of the entire cone or pyramid by the distance of its centre of gravity from the vertex. 2. Subtract from this product that of the part MSR which is cut off, by the distance of its centre of gravity from the apex. 3. Divide this remainder by the cube of the truncated pyramid or cone; the quotient will be the distance of the

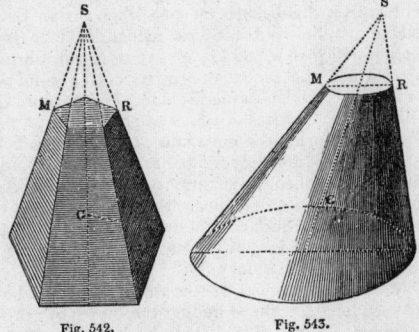

Fig. 542.   Fig. 543.

centre of gravity G of the part of the truncated cone or pyramid from its apex.

1286. The centre of gravity of a hemisphere is at the distance of three eighths of the radius from the centre.

1287. The centre of gravity of the segment of a sphere (*fig. 544.*) is found by the following proportion : as thrice the radius less the thickness of the segment is to the diameter less three quarters the thickness of the segment, so is that thickness to a fourth term which expresses the distance from the vertex to the centre of gravity, set off on the radius which serves as the axis.

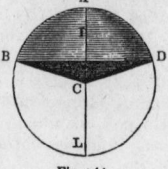

Fig. 544.

1288. Thus, making $r =$ the radius, $e =$ the thickness of the segment, and $x =$ the distance sought, we have, according to La Caille, —

$$3r - e : 2r - \frac{3e}{4} :: e : x, \text{ whence } x = \frac{8re - 3e^2}{12r - 4e}.$$

Suppose the radius to be 7 feet, the thickness of the segment 3 feet, we shall have —
$x = \frac{8 \times 7 \times 3 - 3 \times 9}{12 \times 7 - 3 \times 4}$, which gives $x = 1 + \frac{69}{72} = 1 + \frac{23}{24}$, equal the distance of the centre of gravity from its vertex on the radius.

1289. To find the centre of gravity of the zone of a sphere (*fig. 545.*), the same sort of operation is gone through as for truncated cones and pyramids ; that is, after having found the centre of gravity of the segment cut off, and that in which the zone is comprised, multiply the cube of each by the distance of its centre of gravity from the apex A, and subtracting the smaller from the larger product, divide the remainder by the cube of the zone. Thus, supposing, as before, the radius AC = 7, the thickness of the zone = 2, and that of the segment cut off = $1\frac{1}{2}$, we shall find the distance from the vertex of the centre of gravity of

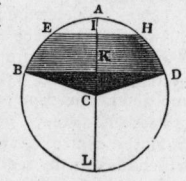

Fig. 545.

this last by the formula $x = \frac{8re - 3ee}{4(3r - e)}$, which in this case gives $x = \frac{4 \times 2 \times 7 \times 1\frac{1}{2} - 3 \times 2\frac{1}{4}}{4(21 - 1\frac{1}{2})}$; and pursuing the investigation, we have $x = \frac{103}{104}$, which will be the distance of the centre of gravity from the vertex A. That of the centre of gravity of the segment in which the zone is comprised will, according to the same formula, be $x = \frac{8 \times 7 \times 3\frac{1}{4} - 3 \times 12\frac{1}{4}}{4(3 \times 7 - 3\frac{1}{2})}$, which gives $x = 2 + \frac{11}{40}$ for the distance of the centre of gravity from the same point A.

1290. The methods of finding the solidities of the bodies involved in the above investigation are to be found in the preceding section, on Mensuration.

OF THE CENTRE OF GRAVITY OF IRREGULAR SOLIDS.

1291. As all species of solids, whatever their form, are susceptible of division into pyramids, as we have seen in the preceding observations, it follows that their centres of gravity may be found by following out the instructions already given. Instead of two lines at right angles to each other, let us suppose two vertical planes NAC, CEF (*fig. 546.*), between which the solid G is placed. Carrying to each of those planes the momenta of their pyramids, that is, the products of their solidity, and the distances of their centres of gravity, divide the sum of these products for each plane by the whole solidity of the body, the quotient will express the distance of two other planes BKL, DHM, parallel to those first named. Their intersection will give a line IP, or an axis of equilibrium, upon which the centre of gravity of the solid will be found. To determine the point G, imagine a third plane NOF perpendicular to the preceding ones, that is, horizontal ; upon which let the solid be supposed to stand. In respect of this plane let the momenta of the pyramids be found by also multiplying their solidity by the distance of their centres of gravity. Lastly, dividing the sum of these products by the solidity of the entire body, the quotient gives on the axis the distance PG of this third plane from the centre of gravity of the irregular solid.

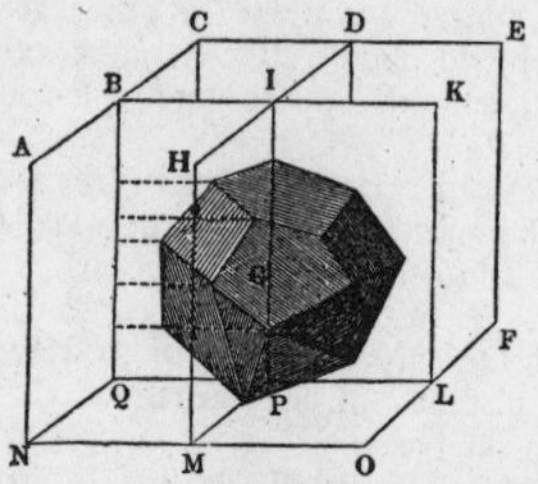

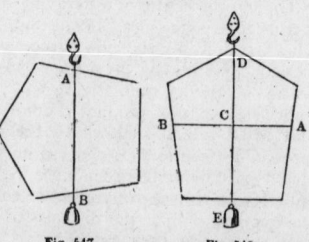

Fig. 546.

Mechanically, where two of the surfaces of a body are parallel, the mode of finding the centre of gravity is simple. Thus, if the body be hung up by any point A (*figs. 547, 548.*), and a plumb line AB be suspended from the same point, it will pass through

Fig. 547.　　　　Fig. 548.

the centre of gravity, because that centre is not in the lowest point till it fall in the plumb line. Mark the line AB upon it; then hang the body up by any other point D, with a plumb line DE, which will also pass through the centre of gravity, for the same reason as before. Therefore the centre of gravity will be at C, where the lines cross each other.

1292. We have, perhaps, pursued this subject a little further than its practical utility in architecture renders necessary; but cases may occur in which the student will find our extended observations of service.

OF THE INCLINED PLANE.

1293. That a solid may remain in a perfect state of rest, the plane on which it stands must be perpendicular to the direction of its gravity; that is, level or horizontal, and the vertical let fall from its centre of gravity must not fall out of its base.

1294. When the plane is not horizontal, solids placed on it tend to slide down or to overturn.

1295. As the surfaces of bodies are more or less rough, when the direction of the centre of gravity does not fall without their base, they slide down a plane in proportion to their roughness and the plane's inclination.

1296. Thus a cube of hard freestone, whose surfaces are nicely wrought, does not slide down a plane whose inclination is less than thirty degrees; and with polished marbles the inclination is not more than fifteen degrees.

1297. When a solid is placed on an inclined plane, if the direction of the centre of gravity falls without its base, it overturns if its surfaces are right surfaces, and if its surface is convex it rolls down the plane.

1298. A body with plane surfaces may remain at rest after having once overturned if the surface upon which it falls is sufficiently extended to prevent its centre of gravity falling within the base, and the inclination be not so great as to allow of its sliding on.

1299. Solids whose surfaces are curved can only stand upon a perfectly horizontal plane, because one of the species, as the sphere, rests only on a point, and the other, as cylinders and cones, upon a line; so that for their continuing at rest, it is necessary that the vertical let fall from their centre of gravity should pass through the point of contact with and be perpendicular to the plane. Hence, the moment the plane ceases to be horizontal, the direction of the centre of gravity falls out of the point or line of contact which serves as the base of the solid, and the body will begin to roll; and when the plane on which they thus roll is of any extent they roll with an accelerated velocity, equal to that which they would acquire in falling directly from the vertical height of the inclined plane from the point whence they first began to roll.

1300. To find the force which is necessary to support a convex body upon an inclined plane, we must consider the point of contact F (*figs. 549, 550.*) as the fulcrum of an an-

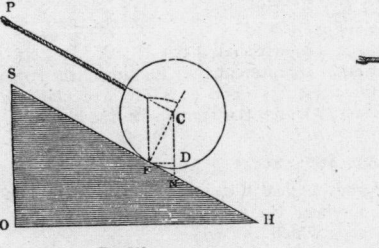

Fig. 549.

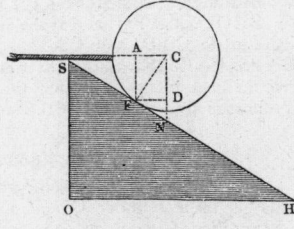

Fig. 550.

gular lever, whose arms are expressed by the perpendiculars drawn from the fulcrum to the direction of the force CP and the weight CD, which in the case of *fig.* 549., where the force which draws the body is parallel to the plane,

$$P : N :: FC : FD.$$

Now as the rectangular triangle CFD is always similar to the triangle OSH, which forms the plane inclined by the vertical SO and the horizontal line OH, the proportion will stand as follows: —

$$P : N :: OS : SH.$$

In the first case, to obtain an equilibrium, *the force must be to the weight of the body as the height* OS *of the inclined plane to its length* SH.

1301. In the case where the force is horizontal (*fig.* 550.) we have, similarly, —

$$P : N :: FA : FD,$$
$$\text{and } P : N :: OS : OH.$$

In this last case, then, *the force must be to the weight of the solid in proportion to the height*

OS *of the inclined plane to its base* OH. In the first case the pressure of the solid on the plane is expressed by OH, and in the second by SH : hence we have —

$$P : N : F :: OS : SH : OH,$$
$$\text{and } P : N : F :: OS : SH : OH.$$

In the first case it must be observed, that the effect of the force being parallel to the inclined plane, it neither increases nor diminishes the pressure upon that plane; and this is the most favourable case for keeping a body in equilibrio on an inclined plane. In the second case, the direction forming an acute angle with the plane uselessly augments the load or weight. Whilst the direction of the force forms an obtuse angle with the inclination of the plane, by sustaining a portion of the weight, it diminishes the load on the plane, but requires a greater force.

1302. The force necessary to sustain upon an inclined plane a body whose base is formed by a plane surface depends, as we have already observed, on the roughness of the surfaces, as well of the inclined plane as of the base of the body; and it is only to be discovered by experiment.

1303. Of all the means that have been employed to estimate the value of the resistance, known under the name of friction, the simplest, and that which seems to give the truest results, is to consider the inclination of the plane upon which a body, the direction of whose centre of gravity does not fall out of the base, remains in equilibrio, as a horizontal plane; after which the degrees of inclination may begin to be reckoned, by which we find that a body which does not begin to slide till the plane's inclination exceeds 30 degrees, being placed on an inclined plane of 45, will not require a greater force to sustain it than a convex body of the same weight on an inclined plane of 15 degrees.

1304. All that has been said on the force necessary to retain a body upon an inclined plane, is applicable to solids supported by two planes, considering that the second acts as a force to counterpoise the first, in a direction perpendicular to the second plane.

1305. When the directions of three forces, PG, QG, GR, meet in the same point G (*fig. 551.*), it follows, from the preceding observations on the parallelogram of forces, that to be in equilibrium their proportion will be expressed by the three sides of a triangle formed by perpendiculars to their directions; whence it follows, that if through the centre of gravity G of a solid, supported by two planes or by some other point of its vertical direction, lines be drawn perpendicular to the directions of the forces, if equilibrium exist, so will the following proportion, viz. P : Q : R :: BA : BC : AC.

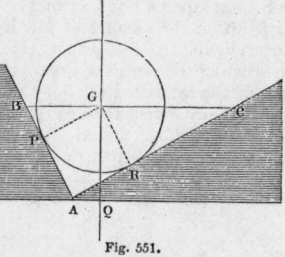

Fig. 551.

1306. Lastly, considering that in all sorts of triangles the sides will between each other be as the sines of their opposite angles, we shall have P : Q : R :: sin. BCA : sin. BAC : sin. ABC; and as the angle BCA is equal to the angle CAD, and CBA to BAE, we shall have P : Q : R :: sin. CAD : sin. BAC : sin. BAE; that is, that the weight is represented by the sine of the angle formed by the two inclined planes, and that the pressures upon each of these planes are reciprocally proportional to the sines of the angles which they form with the horizon.

THE WHEEL AND AXLE.

1307. The wheel and axle, sometimes called the axis in peritrochio, is a machine consisting of a cylinder C and a wheel B (*fig. 552.*) having the same axis, at the two extremities of which are pivots on which the wheel turns. The power is applied at the circumference of the wheel, generally in the direction of a tangent by means of a cord wrapped about the cylinder in order to overcome the resistance or elevate the weight. Here the cord by which the power P acts is applied at the circumference of the wheel, while that of the weight W is applied round the axle or another small wheel attached to the larger, and having the same axis or centre C. Thus BA is a lever moveable about the point C, the power P always acting at the distance BC, and the weight W at the distance CA. Therefore P : W :: CA : CB. That is, the weight and power will be in equilibrio when the power P is to the weight W reciprocally as the radii of the circles where they act, or as the radius of the axle CA, where the weight hangs, to the radius of the wheel CB, where the power acts; or, as before, P : W :: CA : CB.

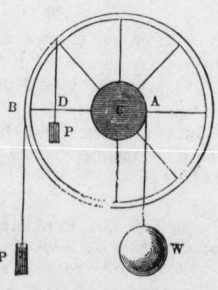

Fig. 552.

1308. If the wheel be put in motion, the spaces moved through being as the circum-

ferences, or as the radii, the velocity of W will be to the velocity of P as CA to CB; that is, the weight is moved as much slower as it is heavier than the power. Hence, what is gained in power is lost in time; a property common to machines and engines of every class.

1309. If the power do not act at right angles to the radius CB, but obliquely, draw CD perpendicular to the direction of the power, then, from the nature of the lever, P : W :: CA : CD.

1310. It is to the mechanical power of the wheel and axle that belong all turning or wheel machines of different radii; thus, in the roller turning on the axis or spindle CE (*fig.* 553.) by the handle CBD, the power applied at B is to the weight W on the roller, as the radius of the roller is to the radius CB of the handle. The same rule applies to all cranes, capstans, windlasses, &c.; the power always being to the weight as is the radius or lever at which the weight acts to that at which the power acts; so that they are always in the reciprocal ratio of their velocities. To the same principle are referable the gimlet and auger for boring holes.

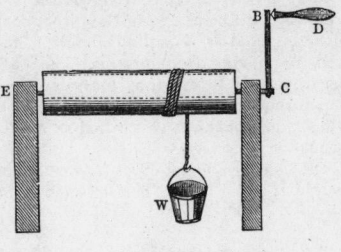

Fig. 553.

1311. The above observations imply that the cords sustaining the weights are of no sensible thickness. If they are of considerable thickness, or if there be several folds of them over one another on the roller or barrel, we must measure to the middle of the outermost rope for the radius of the roller, or to the radius of the roller must be added half the thickness of the cord where there is but one fold.

1312 The power of the wheel and axle possesses considerable advantages in point of convenience over the simple lever. A weight can be raised but a little way by a simple lever, whereas by the continued turning of the wheel and axle a weight may be raised to any height and from any depth.

1313. By increasing the number of wheels, moreover, the power may be increased to any extent, making the less always turn greater wheels, by means of what is called *tooth and pinion* work, wherein the teeth of one circumference work in the rounds or pinions of another to turn the wheel. In case, here, of an equilibrium, the power is to the weight as the continual product of the radii of all the axles to that of all the wheels. So if the power P (*fig.* 554.) turn the wheel Q, and this turn the small wheel or axle R, and this turn the wheel S, and this turn the axle T, and this turn the wheel V, and this turn the axle X, which raises the weight W; then P : W :: CB . DE . FG : AC . BD . EF. And in

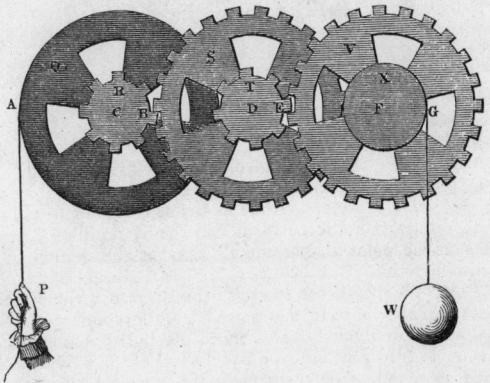

Fig. 554.

the same proportion is the velocity of W slower than that of P. Thus, if each wheel be to its axle as 10 to 1, then P : W :: 1^3 : 10^3, or as 1 to 1000. Hence a power of one pound will balance a weight of 1000 pounds; but when put in motion, the power will move 1000 times faster than the weight.

1314. We do not think it necessary to give examples of the different machines for raising weights used in the construction of buildings: they are not many, and will be hereafter named and described.

OF THE PULLEY.

1315. A pulley is a small wheel, usually made of wood or brass, turning about a metal axis, and enclosed in a frame, or case, called its *block*, which admits of a rope to pass freely over the circumference of the pulley, wherein there is usually a concave groove to prevent the rope slipping out of its place. The pulley is said to be fixed or moveable as its block is fixed or rises and falls with the weight. An assemblage of several pulleys is called a system of pulleys, of which some are in a fixed block and the rest in a moveable one.

1316. If a power sustain a weight by means of a fixed pulley, the power and weight are

equal. For if through the centre C (*fig. 555.*) of the pulley we draw the horizontal diameter AB; then will AB represent a lever of the first kind, its prop being the fixed centre C, from which the points A and B, where the power and weight act, being equally distant, the power P is consequently equal to the weight W.

1317. Hence, if the pulley be put in motion, the power P will descend as fast as the weight W ascends: so that the power is not increased by the use of the fixed pulley, even though the rope go over several of them. It is, nevertheless, of great service in the raising of weights, both by changing the direction of the force, for the convenience of acting, and by enabling a person to raise a weight to any height without moving from his place, and also by permitting a great number of persons to exert, at the same time, their force on the rope at P, which they could not do to the weight itself, as is evident in raising the weight, or *monkey*, as it is called, of a pile-driver, also on many other occasions.

1318. When a pulley is moveable the power necessary to sustain a weight is equal to the half of such weight. For in this case AB (*fig. 556.*) may be con-

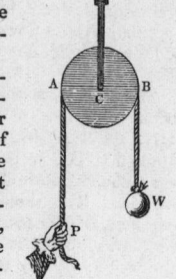

Fig. 555.

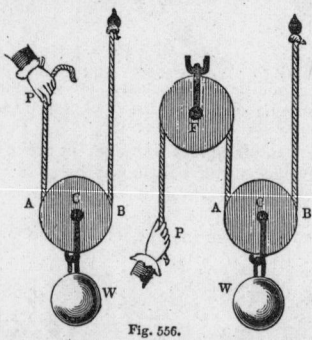

Fig. 556.

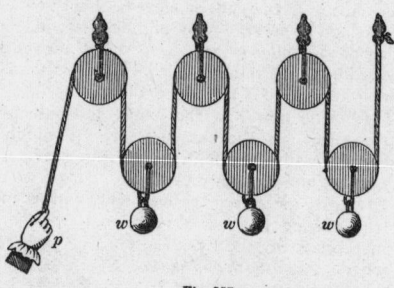

Fig. 557.

sidered as a lever of the second kind, the weight being at C, the power acting at A, and the prop or fixed point at B. Then, because P : W::CB : AB and CB=AB, we have P=½W or W=2P.

1319. From which it is manifest that when the pulley is put in motion the velocity of the power is double that of the weight, inasmuch as the point P descends twice as fast as the point C and the weight W rises. It is, moreover, evident that the fixed pulley F makes no difference in the point P, but merely changes the motion of it in an opposite direction.

1320. We may hence ascertain the effect of a combination or system of any number of fixed and moveable pulleys, and we shall thereby find that every cord going over a moveable pulley doubles the powers, for each end of the rope bears an equal share of the weight, whilst each rope fixed to a pulley only increases the power by unity. In *fig. 557.* P=⅙W, and in *fig. 558.*, $P=\frac{1}{2}w=\frac{w+w+w}{6}$.

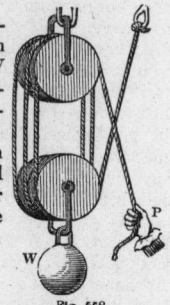

Fig. 558.

OF THE WEDGE.

1321. The wedge is a body in the form of a half rectangular prism, in practice usually of wood or metal. AF or BG (*fig. 559.*) is the breadth of its back, CE its height, CG, CB its sides, and its end, GBC, is the terminating surface of two equally inclined planes GCE, BCE.

1322. When a wedge is in equilibrio, the power acting on the back is to the force acting at right angles to either side as the breadth of the back AB (*fig. 560.*) is to the length of the side AC or BC. For three forces which sustain each other in equilibrio are as the corresponding sides of a triangle drawn perpendicular to the directions in which they act. But AB is perpendicular to the force

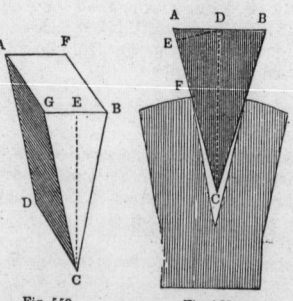

Fig. 559.   Fig. 560.

acting on the back to drive the wedge forward, and the sides AC, BC are perpendicular to the forces acting on them, the three forces are therefore as AB, AC, BC. Thus, the force on the back, its effect perpendicularly to AC, and its effect parallel to AB, are as the three lines AB, AC, and DC, which are perpendicular to them. Hence the thinner the wedge the greater its effect to split any body or to overcome a resistance against the sides of the wedge.

1323. We are, however, to recollect that the resistance or the forces in question are relative to one side only of the wedge; for if those against both sides are to be reckoned, we can take only half the back AD, or else we must take double the line AC or DC. In the wedge the friction is very great, and at least equal to the force to be overcome, inasmuch as it retains any position to which it is driven, whence the resistance is doubled by the friction. But, on the other hand, the wedge has considerable advantage over all the other powers, because of the force of the blow with which the back is struck, a force vastly greater than the dead weight or pressure employed in other machines. On this account it is capable of producing effects vastly superior to those of any other power, such as splitting rocks, raising the largest and heaviest bodies by the simple blow of a mallet; objects which could never be accomplished by any simple pressure whereof in practice application could be made.

OF THE SCREW.

1324. The screw is a cord wound in a spiral direction round the periphery of a cylinder, and is therefore a species of inclined plane, whose length is to its height as the circumference of the cylinder is to the distance between two consecutive threads of the screw. It is one of the six mechanical powers used in pressing or squeezing bodies close, and is occasionally used in raising weights.

1325. The screw, then, being an inclined plane or half wedge, the force of a power applied in turning it round is to the force with which it presses upwards or downwards, without estimating friction, as the distance between two threads is to the circumference where the power is applied. For considering it as an inclined plane whose height is the distance between two threads, and its base the circumference of the screw; the force in the horizontal direction being to that in the vertical one as the lines perpendicular to them, namely, as the height of the plane or distance between two threads, is to the base of the plane or circumference of the screw; the power, therefore, is to the pressure as the distance of two threads is to the circumference. But in the application of the screw a handle or lever is used, by means whereof the gain in power is increased in the proportion of the radius of the screw to the radius of the power, that is, the length of the handle, or as their circumferences. Consequently the power is to the pressure as the distance of the threads is to the circumference described by the power. The screw being put in motion, the power is then to the weight which would keep it in equilibrio as the velocity of the latter is to that of the former; and hence their momenta are equal, and produced by multiplying each weight or power by its own velocity.

1326. Thus it is a general property of all the mechanical powers, that the momentum of a power is equal to that of the weight which would keep it in equilibrio, or that each of them is proportional to its velocity.

1327. From the foregoing observations, we may be easily led to compute the force exerted by any machine whose action is exerted through the means of the screw. In *fig.* 561., representing a press driven by a screw whose threads are each one quarter of an inch apart, let it be turned by a handle or lever 4 feet long from A to B. Then supposing the natural force of a man, by which he can lift, pull, or draw, to be 150 pounds, and that it be required to ascertain with what force the screw will press on the board at D when the man turns with his whole force the handle at A and B; we have AB, the diameter of the power, 4 feet or 48 inches; its circumference, therefore, 48 × 3·1416, or 150⅘ nearly; and the distance of the threads being one quarter of an inch, the power is to the pressure as 1 to 603½. But the power is equal to 150

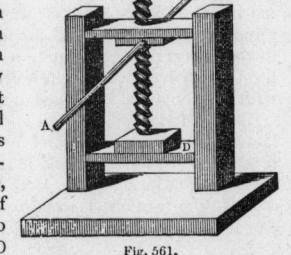

Fig. 561.

pounds; therefore, as 1 : 603½ :: 150 : 90480, and the pressure therefore at D is equal to a weight of 90480 pounds, independent of friction.

1328. In the endless screw AB (*fig.* 562.), turned by a handle AC of 20 inches radius, the threads of the screw are at a distance of half an inch; and the screw turns a toothed wheel E whose pinion L acts in turning upon another wheel F, and the pinion M of this last wheel acts upon a third wheel G, to the pinion or barrel whereof is hung the weight W. If we would know what weight can be raised through the means of this combination by a man working the handle C, supposing the diameters of the wheels to be 18 inches, and those of the pinions and barrel 2 inches, the teeth and pinions being all similar in size; we

have $20 \times 3 \cdot 1416 \times 2 = 125 \cdot 664$, the circumference of
the power; and $125 \cdot 664$ to $\frac{1}{2}$, or $251 \cdot 328$ to 1, is
the force of the screw alone. Again, $18 : 2$ or $9 : 1$,
being the proportion of the wheels to the pinions, and
there being three of them, $9^3 : 1$ or $729 : 1$ is the
power gained by the wheels.

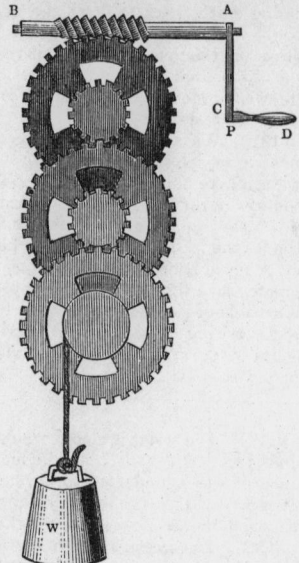

1329. Consequently $251 \cdot 328 \times 729$ to 1, or $183218\frac{1}{9}$
to 1 nearly, is the ratio of the power to the weight
arising from the joint advantage of the screw and the
wheels. The power, however, is 150 pounds; there-
fore $150 \times 183218\frac{1}{9}$ or 27482716 pounds is the weight
the man can sustain, equal to 12269 tons.

1330. It must be observed, that the power has to
overcome not only the weight, but at the same time
the friction undergone by the screw, which in some
cases is so great as to be equal to the weight itself;
for it is sometimes sufficient to sustain the weight
when the power is taken off.

OF FRICTION.

1331. Though in a preceding page we have slightly
touched on the effect of friction, it is to be kept
in mind that the foregoing observations and rules
have assumed the mechanical powers to be without
weight and friction. This is far from the fact; and,
however theoretically true all that has hitherto been
advanced, very great allowances must be made in

Fig. 562.

practice when power is applied to mechanical purposes, in which a great portion of their
effect is lost by friction, inertia, &c. The word friction, properly meaning the act of
one body rubbing on another, is in mechanics used to denote the degree of retardation or
obstruction to motion which arises from one surface rubbing against another. A heavy
body placed upon another is not in a state of equilibrium between all the forces which act
upon it, otherwise it could be moved by the application of the smallest force in a direction
parallel to the plane. This want of equilibrium results from unbalanced force occasioned
by the friction on a level surface. Now if a new force of equal magnitude be applied to
counterpoise such unbalanced force, the body will obey the smallest impulse in such direction, and the force thus employed will exactly measure the retarding force of friction. It
has been well observed, that friction destroys, but never generates motion; being therein unlike gravity or the other forces, which, though they may retard motion in one direction,
always accelerate it in the opposite. Thus the law of friction violates the law of continuity, and cannot be accurately expressed by any geometrical line, nor by any algebraic
formula. The author (Playfair, *Outlines of Natural Philosophy*) just quoted, continues:
" Though friction destroys motion and generates none, it is of essential use in mechanics.
It is the cause of stability in the structure of machines, and it is necessary to the exertion
of the force of animals. A nail or screw or a bolt could give no firmness to the parts of a
machine, or of any other structure, without friction. Animals could not walk, or exert their
force anyhow, without the support which it affords. Nothing could have any stability, but
in the lowest possible situation; and an arch, which could sustain the greatest load when
properly distributed, might be thrown down by the weight of a single ounce, if not placed
with mathematical exactness at the very point which it ought to occupy."

1332. Many authors have applied themselves to the subject of friction, but the most satisfactory results have attended the investigations of the celebrated Coulomb in its application
to practical mechanics; and it is to that author we are indebted for the few following succinct observations.

I. In the friction of wood upon wood in the direction of the fibres after remaining in
contact for one or two minutes, the following mean results were obtained : —

Oak against oak   - $\frac{1}{2 \cdot 34} =$ friction in parts of the weight.

Oak against fir -   - $\frac{1}{1 \cdot 50} =$ ditto.

Fir against fir   -   - $\frac{1}{1 \cdot 78} =$ ditto.

Elm against elm   - $\frac{1}{2 \cdot 18} =$ ditto.

When oak rubbed upon oak, and the surfaces in contact were reduced to the smallest possible dimensions, the friction was $\frac{1}{2 \cdot 36}$, $\frac{1}{2 \cdot 42}$, $\frac{1}{2 \cdot 40}$.

1333. When the friction was across the grain, or at right angles to the direction of the fibres, oak against oak was $\frac{1}{3\cdot76}$. The ratios above given are constant quantities, and not dependent upon the velocities, excepting in the case of elm, when the pressures are very small, for then the friction is sensibly increased by the velocity.

1334. (II.) Friction is found to increase with the time of contact. It was ascertained that when wood moved upon wood in the direction of the fibres, the friction gradually increased, and reached its maximum in 8 or 10 seconds. When across the grain of the wood, it took a longer time to reach its maximum.

1335. (III.) For illustration of the friction of metals upon metals after a certain time of rest, the subjoined experiments were made with two flat rulers of iron, 4 feet long and 2 inches wide, attached to the fixed plank of the apparatus used for the investigation. Four other rulers, two of iron and two of brass, 15 inches long and 18 lines wide, were also used. The angles of each of the rulers were rounded off, and the rubbing surfaces of the rulers were 45 square inches.

With iron upon iron and a pressure of 53 lbs., the friction in parts of the pressure was $\frac{1}{3\cdot5}$.

—   —   453 lbs.,   —   — $\frac{1}{3\cdot6}$.

With iron upon brass and a pressure of 52 lbs., the friction in parts of the pressure was $\frac{1}{4\cdot2}$.

—   —   452 lbs.,   —   — $\frac{1}{4\cdot1}$.

1336. In these experiments each set gives nearly the same result, though the second pressures are nearly nine times the first; from which we learn that, in metals, friction is independent of the extent of the rubbing surfaces. Coulomb, moreover, found that the friction is independent of the velocities. The ratio of 4 to 1 between the pressure of friction, in the case of iron moving upon brass, is only to be considered accurate when the surfaces are new and very large. When they are very small the ratio varies from 4 to 1 to 6 to 1; but this last ratio is not reached unless the friction has been continued more than an hour, when the iron and brass have taken the highest polish whereof they are susceptible, free of all scratches.

1337. IV. In the friction of oak upon oak, when greased with tallow, which was renewed at every experiment, some days were required for obtaining, when the surfaces were considerable, the maximum of friction or adhesion. It was nearly similar to that without grease, sometimes rather greater. For iron or copper with tallow, during rest, the increase is not so considerable as with oak. At first the friction was $\frac{1}{11}$ of the weight, besides a small force of a pound for every 30 square inches independent of the weight. The friction after some time changes to $\frac{1}{10}$ or $\frac{1}{9}$. Olive oil alters the condition of the friction to $\frac{1}{8}$, and old soft grease to about $\frac{1}{4}$.

1338. V. In the case of friction of bodies, oak upon oak for instance, in motion in the direction of its fibres, the friction was nearly constant in all degrees of velocity, though with large surfaces it appeared to increase with the velocities; but when the touching surfaces were very small compared with the pressures, the friction diminished or the velocities increased. For a pressure of 100 to 4000 pounds on a square foot, the friction is about $\frac{1}{9\cdot5}$, besides for each square foot a resistance of $1\frac{2}{3}$ pounds, exclusive of pressure increasing a little with the velocity, occasioned perhaps by a down on the surface. If the surface be very small the friction is lessened. When the narrow surface was cross-grained, the friction was invariably $\frac{1}{10}$. In the case of oak on fir, the friction was $\frac{1}{6\cdot3}$; of fir on fir, $\frac{1}{6}$; of elm on elm, $\frac{1}{10}$, but varying according to the extent of surface; for iron or copper on wood, $\frac{1}{13}$, which was at first doubled by increasing the velocity to a foot in a second, but on a continuance of the operation for some hours it again diminished. For iron on iron, $\frac{1}{3\cdot55}$; on copper, $\frac{1}{4\cdot15}$; after long attrition, $\frac{1}{6}$ in all velocities. Upon the whole, in the case of most machines, $\frac{1}{8}$ of the pressure may be considered a fair estimate of the friction.

1339. In the experiments to ascertain the friction of axles, Coulomb used a simple pulley, where the friction of the axis and that of the rigidity of the rope produce a joint resistance. With guaiacum moving upon iron, the friction was $\frac{1}{5\cdot4}$ or $\frac{1}{6\cdot4}$ of the weight in all velocities exclusive of the rigidity of the rope; the mean was $\frac{1}{6\cdot1}$, or, with a small weight, a little greater. In the cases of axles of iron on copper, $\frac{1}{11}$ or $\frac{1}{11\cdot5}$ the velocity is small; the friction being always somewhat less than for plane surfaces. With grease, the friction was about $\frac{1}{7\cdot5}$. With an axis of green oak or elm, and a pulley of guaiacum, the friction with tallow was $\frac{1}{26}$; without, $\frac{1}{17}$; with a pulley of elm, the quantities in question became $\frac{1}{33}$ and $\frac{1}{20}$. An axis of box with a pulley of guaiacum gave $\frac{1}{23}$ and $\frac{1}{14}$; with an elm pulley, $\frac{1}{29}$ and $\frac{1}{20}$. An axis of iron and a pulley of guaiacum gave, with tallow, $\frac{1}{20}$. The velocity had but small

effect on the rigidity of ropes, except in slightly increasing the resistance when the pressure was small.

1340. The friction and rigidity of ropes was supposed by Amontons and Desaguliers to vary as the diameter as the curvature and as the tension. By Coulomb the power of the diameter expressing the rigidity was found generally to be 1·7 or 1·8, never less than 1·4, and that a constant quantity must be supposed as added to the weight. Wet ropes, if small, are more flexible than such as are dry, and tarred ones stiffer by about one sixth, and in cold weather somewhat more. After rest, the stiffness of ropes increases. A rope of three strands, each having two yarns 12½ lines in circumference, whose weight was 125 grains, being bent upon an axis 4 inches in diameter, required a constant force of one pound (French) and $\frac{1}{54\cdot3}$ of the weight to overcome its rigidity. The same rope tarred, required one fifth of a pound and one fiftieth of the weight. When the strands were of fine yarns, the circumference 20 lines, and the weight 347 grains, the rigidity was equal to half a pound and $\frac{1}{23\cdot1}$ of the weight to move it. With strands of 10 yarns, and a circumference of 28 lines, and a weight of 680 grains to 6 inches, the rigidity of the untarred rope was 2 lbs. and $\frac{1}{13\cdot33}$ of the weight, and the tarred rope of 3·3 lbs. and $\frac{1}{10\cdot34}$ of the weight. Experiments which confirmed the above were made on a roller moving on a horizontal plane, while a rope was coiled completely round it, whence an allowance must be made for the friction of the roller on the plane, which varies as its weight and inversely as its diameter. With a roller of guaiacum or lignum vitæ, 3·6 inches in diameter, moving on oak, it was $\frac{1}{100}$ of the weight; for a roller of elm, ⅔ more.

1341. This subject has, we conceive, been pursued as far as is necessary for the architect; seeing that his further investigation of it, should necessity arise, may be accomplished by reference to the works of Amontons, Bulfinger, Parent, Euler, Bossut, and Coulomb, upon whom we have drawn for the information here given. We shall therefore conclude these remarks by subjoining some of the practical results which experiments on animal power afford, extracted from the celebrated Dr. Thomas Young's *Natural Philosophy*, vol. ii.

1342. In comparing the values of the force of moving powers, it is usual to assume an unit, which is considered as the mean effect of the labour of an active man working to the greatest advantage; this on a moderate calculation will be found sufficient to raise 10 lbs. to the height of 10 feet in one second for 10 hours in a day; or 100 lbs. 1 foot in a second, that is 36,000 feet in a day, or 3,600,000 lbs. 1 foot in a day. The following exhibits a tabular view of the immediate force of men, without deduction for friction. Such a day's work is the measuring unit in the third column of the table.

Operative.	Force.	Continuance.	Day's Work.
A man weighing 133 lbs. French ascended 62 feet French by steps in 34 seconds, but was completely exhausted. *Amontons.* - -	2·8	34 sec.	
A sawyer made 200 strokes of 18 French inches each in 145 seconds, with a force of 25 lbs. French. He could not have continued more than 3 minutes. *Amontons.* - - - -	6·0	145 sec.	
A man can raise 60 French lbs. 1 French foot in 1 second for 8 hours a day. *Bernouilli.* -	0·69	8 hours	0·552
A man of ordinary strength can turn a winch with a force of 30 lbs., and with a velocity of 3½ feet in 1 second for 10 hours a day. *Desaguliers.*	1·05	10 hours	1·05
Two men working at a windlass, with handles at right angles, can raise 70 lbs. more easily than 1 can raise 30 lbs. *Desaguliers.* - - -	1·22	—	1·22
A man can exert a force of 40 lbs. for a whole day with the assistance of a fly, when the motion is pretty quick, at about 4 or 5 feet in a second. *Desaguliers.* But it appears doubtful whether the force is 40 or 20 lbs. - -	2·00	—	2·00
For a short time, a man may exert a force of 80 lbs. with a fly when the motion is pretty quick. *Desaguliers.* - - - - -	3·00	1 sec.	
A man going up stairs ascends 14 metres (35·43 feet) in 1 minute. *Coulomb.* - - -	1·182	1 min.	

OPERATIVE.	Force.	Continuance.	Day's Work.
A man going up stairs for a day raises 205 kilogrammes (451·64 lbs. averd.) to the height of a kilometre (3280·91 feet). *Coulomb.* - -	—	—	0·412
With a spade a man does 12/20 as much as in ascending stairs. *Coulomb.* - - - -	—	—	0·391
With a winch a man does ⅝ as much as in ascending stairs. *Coulomb.* - - - -	—	—	0·258
A man carrying wood up stairs raises, together with his own weight, 109 kilogrammes (240·14 lbs. averd.) to 1 kilometre (3280·91 feet). *Coulomb.* - - - - - -	—	—	0·219
A man weighing 150 French lbs. can ascend by stairs 3 French feet in a second for 15 or 20 seconds. *Coulomb.* - - - -	5·22	20 sec.	
For half an hour 100 French pounds may be raised 1 foot French per second. *Coulomb.* - -	1·152	30 min.	
By Mr. Buchanan's comparison, the force exerted in turning a winch being assumed equal to the unit, the force in pumping will be - - -	0·61		
In ringing - - - - - -	1·36		
In rowing - - - - - -	1·43		

1343. Coulomb's maximum of effect is, when a man weighing 70 kilogrammes (154·21 lbs. avoirdupois), carries a weight of 53 (116·76 lbs. avoirdupois,) up stairs. But this appears too great a load.

1344. Porters carry from 200 to 300 lbs., at the rate of 3 miles an hour. Chairmen walk 4 miles an hour with a load of 150 lbs. each; and in Turkey there are found porters who, it is said, by stooping forwards, carry from 700 to 900 lbs. very low on their backs.

1345. The most advantageous weight for a man of common strength to carry horizontally, is 111 pounds; or, if he return unladen, 135. With wheelbarrows, men will do half as much more work, as with hods. *Coulomb.*

The following table exhibits the performance of men by machines.

OPERATIVE.	Force.	Continuance.	Day's Work.
A man raised by means of a rope and pulley 25 lbs. French, 220 French feet in 145 seconds. *Amontons.* - - - - -	0·436	145 sec.	
A man can raise by a good common pump 1 hogshead of water 10 feet high in a minute for a whole day. *Desaguliers.* - - - - -	0·875	—	0·875
By the mercurial pump, or another good pump, a man may raise a hogshead 18 or 20 feet in a minute for 1 or 2 minutes - - -	1·61	2 min.	
In pile driving, 55¼ French lbs. were raised 1 French foot in 1 second, for 5 hours a day, by a rope drawn horizontally. *Coulomb.* - - -	0·64	5 hours	0·82
Robison says that a feeble old man raised 7 cubic feet of water 11½ feet in 1 minute for 8 or 10 hours a day, by walking backwards and forwards on a lever - - - - -	0·837	9 hours	0·753
A young man, the last-named author says, weighing 135 lbs., and carrying 30 lbs., raised 9¼ cubic feet 11½ feet high for 10 hours a day, without fatigue - - - - -	1·106	10 hours	1·106

1346. In respect of the force of horses, we do not think it necessary to do more than observe that the best way of applying their force is in an horizontal direction, that in which a man acts least to advantage. For instance, a man weighing 140 lbs., and drawing a boat along by means of a rope over his shoulders, cannot draw above 27 lbs.; whereas a horse employed for the same purpose can exert seven times that force.

1347. Generally, a horse can draw no more up a steep hill than three men can carry,

that is, from 450 to 750 pounds; but a horse can draw 2000 pounds up a steep hill which is but short. The most disadvantageous mode of applying a horse's force is to make him carry or draw up hill; for if it be steep, he is not more than equal to three men, each of whom would climb up faster with a burden of 100 pounds weight than a horse that is loaded with 300 pounds. And this arises from the different construction of what may be called the two living machines.

1348. Desaguliers observes, that the best and most effectual action of a man is that exerted in rowing, in which he not only acts with more muscles at once for overcoming resistance than in any other application of his strength, but that, as he pulls backwards, his body assists by way of lever.

1349. There are cases in which the architect has to avail himself of the use of horse power; as, for instance, in pugmills for tempering mortar, and occasionally when the stones employed in a building may be more conveniently raised by such means. We therefore think it proper to observe, that, for effectually using the strength of the animal, the *track* or diameter of a walk for a horse should not be less than 25 to 30 feet.

1350. We close this section by observing, more for the curiosity of the thing than for the service it will be to the architect, that some horses have carried 650 or 700 lbs., and that for seven or eight miles, without resting, as their ordinary work; and, according to Desaguliers (*Experiment. Philos.* vol. i.), a horse at Stourbridge carried 11 cwt. of iron, or 1232 lbs., for eight miles.

Sect. VIII.

PIERS AND VAULTS.

Authors on equilibrium of arches.

1351. The construction of arches may be considered in a threefold respect. I. As respects their form. II. As respects the mode in which their parts are constructed. III. As respects the thrust they exert.

1352. In the first category is involved the mode of tracing the right lines and curves whereof their surfaces are composed, which has been partially treated in Section V. on Descriptive Geometry, and will be further discussed in future pages of this work. The other two points will form the subject of the present section.

1353. The investigation of the equilibrium of arches by the laws of statics does not appear to have at all entered into the thoughts of the ancient architects. Experience, imitation, and a sort of mechanical intuition seem to have been their guides. They appear to have preferred positive solidity to nice balance, and the examples they have left are rather the result of art than of science. Vitruvius, who speaks of all the ingredients necessary to form a perfect architect, does not allude to the assistance which may be afforded in the construction of edifices by a knowledge of the resolution of forces, nor of the aid that may be derived from the study of such a science as Descriptive Geometry, though of the latter it seems scarcely possible the ancients could have been ignorant, seeing how much it must have been (practically, at least) employed in the construction of such vast buildings as the Coliseum, and other similarly curved structures, as respects their plan.

1354. The Gothic architects seem, and indeed must have been, guided by some rules which enabled them to counterpoise the thrusts of the main arches of their cathedrals with such extraordinary dexterity as to excite our amazement at their boldness. But they have left us no precepts nor clue to ascertain by what means they reached such heights of skill as their works exhibit. We shall hereafter offer our conjectures on the leading principle which seems as well to have guided them in their works as the ancients in their earliest, and perhaps latest, specimens of columnar architecture.

1355. Parent and De la Hire seem to have been, at the latter end of the seventeenth century, the first mathematicians who considered an arch as an assemblage of wedge-formed stones, capable of sliding down each other's surfaces, which they considered in a state of the highest polish. In this hypothesis M. de la Hire has proved, in his *Treatise on Mechanics*, printed in 1695, that in order that a semicircular arch, whose joints tend to the centre, may be able to stand, the weights of the *voussoirs* or arch stones whereof it is composed must be to each other as the differences of the tangents of the angles which form each voussoir; but as these tangents increase in a very great ratio, it follows that those which form the springings must be infinitely heavy, in order to resist the effects of the superior voussoirs. Now, according to this hypothesis, not only would the construction of a semicircular arch be an impossibility, but also all those which are greater or less than a semicircle, whose centre is level with or in a line parallel with the tops of the piers; so that those only would be practicable whose centres were formed by curves forming angles with the piers, such as the parabola, the hyperbola, and the catenary. And we may here remark, that in parabolic and hyperbolic arches, the voussoir forming the keystones should be heavier or

greater in height, and that from it the weight or size of the voussoirs should diminish from the keystone to the springing ; the catenary being the only curve to which an horizontal *extrados*, or upper side, can be properly horizontal.   In the *Memoirs of the Academy of Sciences*, 1729, M. Couplet published a memoir on the thrusts of arches, wherein he adopts the hypothesis of polished voussoirs ; but, finding the theory would not be applicable to the materials whereof arches are usually composed, he printed a second memoir in 1730, wherein the materials are so grained that they cannot slide.   But in this last he was as far from the truth as in his first.

1356. M. Danisy, a member of the Academy of Montpellier, liking neither of these hypotheses, endeavoured from experiments to deduce a theory.   He made several models whose extradosses were equal in thickness, and divided into equal voussoirs, with piers sufficiently thick to resist the thrusts.   To ascertain the places at which the failure would take place where the piers were too weak, he loaded them with different weights.   From many experiments, in 1732, he found a practical rule for the walls or piers of a cylindrical arch so as to resist the thrust.

1357. Derand had found one which appears in his *L'Architecture des Voutes*, 1643, but it seems to have been empirical.   It was nevertheless adopted by Blondel and Deschalles, and afterwards by M. de la Rue.   Gautier, in his *Dissertation sur l'épaisseur des Culées des Ponts*, &c. 1727, adopts one which seems to have had no better foundation in science than Derand's.

1358. At the end of a theoretical and practical treatise on stereotomy by M. Frezier, that author subjoined an appendix on the thrust of arches, which was an extract of what had theretofore been published by MM. de la Hire, Couplet, Bernouilli, and Danisy, with the applications of the rules to all sorts of arches.   He seems to have been the first who considerably extended the view of the subject.

1359. Coulomb and Bossut occupied themselves on the subject.   The first, in 1773, presented to the French Academy of Sciences a memoir on several architectural problems, amongst which is one on the equilibrium of arches.   The last-mentioned author printed, in the *Memoirs* (1774 and 1776) of the same academy, two memoirs on the theory of cylindrical arches and of domed vaulting, wherein are some matters relating to the cupola of the Pantheon at Paris, whose stability was then a matter of doubt.

1360. In Italy, Lorgna of Verona considers the subject in his *Saggi di Statica Mecanica applicati alle Arti ;* and in 1785, Mascheroni of Bergamo published, in relation to this branch of architecture, a work entitled *Nuove Ricerche delle Volte*, wherein he treats of cupolas on circular, polygonal, and elliptical bases.

1361. We ought, perhaps, not to omit a memoir by Bouguer in the Transactions of the French Academy of 1734, *Sur les Lignes Courbes propres a former les Voutes en Dome*, wherein he adduces an analogy between cylindrical and dome vaulting ; the one being supposed to be formed by the movement of a catenarian curve parallel to itself, and the other by the revolution of the same curve about its axis.

1362. In this country, the equilibration of the arch, as given by Belidor and others on the Continent, seems to have prevailed, though little was done or known on the subject.   Emerson seems to have been the earliest attracted to the subject, and in his *Treatise on Mechanics*, 1743, appears to have been the first who thought, after the Doctors Hooke and Gregory, of investigating the form of the extrados from the nature of the curve, in which he was followed by Hutton, who added nothing to the stock of knowledge ; an accusation which the writer of this has no hesitation of laying at his own door, as having been the author of a *Treatise on the Equilibrium of Arches*, which has passed through two editions ; but who, after much reflection, is now convinced, that, for the practical architect, no theory wherein the extrados is merely made to depend on the form of the intrados can ever be satisfactory or useful.   It is on this account that in the following pages he has been induced to follow the doctrines of Rondelet, as much more satisfactory than any others with which he is acquainted.

1363. The formulæ of Rondelet were all verified by models, and the whole reasoning is conducted upon knowledge which is to be obtained by acquaintance with the mathematical and mechanical portions of the preceding pages.   It moreover requires no deep acquaintance with the more abstruse learning requisite for following the subject as treated by later authors.

OBSERVATIONS ON FRICTION.

1364. I. In order that the stone parallelopiped ABCD (*fig.* 563.) may be made to slide upon the horizontal plane FG, the power which draws or pushes it parallel to this plane, must not be higher than the length of its base AB ; for if it acts from a higher point, such as C, the parallelopiped will be overturned instead of sliding along it.

1365. As the effects of the powers P and M are in the inverse ratio of the heights at which they act, it follows that a parallelopiped will slide whenever the force which is necessary to overturn it is greater than

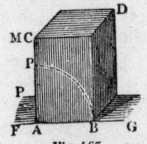

Fig. 563.

that necessary to make it slide, and, reciprocally, it will be overturned when less force is necessary to produce that effect than to make it slide.

1366. II. When the parallelopiped is placed on an inclined plane, it will slide so long as the vertical QS drawn from its centre of gravity does not fall without the base AB. Hence, to ascertain whether a parallelopiped ABCD with a rectangular base (*fig.* 564.) will slide down or overturn ; from the point B we must raise the perpendicular BE : if it pass out of the centre of gravity, it will slide ; if, on the contrary, the line BE passes within, it will overturn.

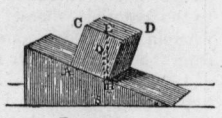

Fig. 564.

1367. If the surfaces of stones were infinitely smooth, as they are supposed to be in the application of the principles of mechanics, they would begin to slide the moment the plane upon which they are placed ceases to be perfectly horizontal ; but as their surfaces are full of little inequalities which catch one another in their positions, Rondelet found, by repeated experiments, that even those whose surfaces are wrought in the best manner do not begin to slide upon the best worked planes of similar stone to the solids until such planes are inclined at angles varying from 28 to 36 degrees.   This difficulty of moving one stone upon another increases as the roughness of their surfaces, and, till a certain point, as their weight : for it is manifest, 1st, That the rougher their surfaces, the greater are the inequalities which catch one another.   2d. That the greater their weight, the greater is the effort necessary to disengage them ; but as these inequalities are susceptible of being broken up or bruised, the maximum of force wanting to overcome the friction must be equal to that which produces this effect, whatever the weight of the stone.   3d. That this proportion is rather as the hardness than the weight of the stone.

1368. In experiments on the sliding of hard stones of different sizes which weighed from 2 to 60 lbs., our author found that the friction which was more than half the weight for the smaller was reduced to a third for the larger.   He remarked that after each experiment made with the larger stones a sort of dust was disengaged by the friction.   In soft stones this dust facilitated the sliding.

1369. These circumstances, which would have considerable influence on stones of a great weight, were of little importance in the experiments which will be cited, the object being to verify upon hard stones, whose mass was small, the result of operations which the theory was expected to confirm.   By many experiments very carefully made upon hard freestone well wrought and squared, it was found, 1st, That they did not begin to slide upon a plane of the same material equally well wrought until it was inclined a little more than 30 degrees. 2d. That to drag upon such stone a parallelopiped of the same material, a little more than half its weight was required.   Thus, to drag upon a level plane a parallelopiped 6 in. long, 4 in. wide, and 2 in. thick, weighing 4 lbs. 11 oz., (the measures and weights are French, as throughout*), it was necessary to employ a weight equal to 2 lbs. 7 oz. and 4 drs. 3d. That the size of the rubbing surface is of no consequence, since exactly the same force is necessary to move this parallelopiped upon a face of two in. wide as upon one of 4.

1370. Taking then into consideration that by the principles of mechanics it is proved, that to raise a perfectly smooth body, or one which is round upon an homogeneous plane inclined at an angle of 30 degrees, a power must be employed parallel to the plane which acts with a force rather greater than half its weight, we may conclude that it requires as much force to drag a parallelopiped of freestone upon an horizontal plane of the same material as to cause the motion up an inclined plane of 30 degrees of a round or infinitely polished body.

1371. From these considerations in applying the principles of mechanics to arches composed of freestone well wrought, a plane inclined at 30 degrees might be considered as one upon which the voussoirs would be sustained, or, in other words, equivalent to an horizontal plane.

1372. We shall here submit another experiment, which tends to establish such an hypothesis.   If a parallelopiped C (*fig.* 565.) of this stone be placed between two others, BD, RS, whose masses are each double, upon a plane of the same stone, the parallelopiped C is sustained by the friction alone of the vertical surfaces that touch it.   This effect is a consequence of our hypothesis ; for, the inequalities of the surfaces of bodies being stopped by one another, the parallelopiped C, before it can fall, must push aside the two others, BD, RS, by making them slide along the horizontal plane of the same material, and for that purpose a force must be employed equal to double the weight sustained.

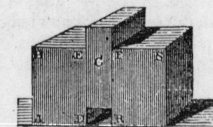

Fig. 565.

* The Paris pound = 7561 Troy grains.
        Ounce =   472·5625.
   Dram or gros =   59·0703.
        Grain =   0·8204.
And as the English avoirdupois pound = 7000 Troy grains, it contains 8538 Paris grains.
   The Paris foot of 12 inches = 12·7977 English inches.
   The Paris line = one-twelfth of the foot.

1373. If to this experiment the principles of mechanics be applied, considering the plane of 30 degrees inclination as a horizontal plane, the vertical faces ED FR may be considered as inclined planes of 60 degrees. On this hypothesis it may be demonstrated by mechanics, that to sustain a body between two planes forming an angle of 60 degrees (*fig.* 566.), the resistance of each of these planes must be to half the weight sustained as HD is to DG, as the radius is to the sine of 30 degrees, or as 1 is to 2.

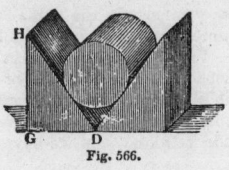

Fig. 566.

EQUILIBRIUM OF ARCHES.

1374. The resistance of each parallelopiped represented by the prism ABDE (*fig.* 565.) being equal to half their weight, it follows that the weight to be sustained by the two prisms should equal one quarter of the two parallelopipeds taken together, or the half of one, which is confirmed by the experiment. This agreement between theory and practice determined Rondelet to apply the hypothesis to models of vaults composed of voussoirs and wedges disunited, made of freestone, with the utmost exactness, the joints and surfaces nicely wrought, as the parallelopipeds in the preceding example.

1375. The first model was of a semicircular arch 9 inches diameter, comprised between two concentric semi-circumferences of circles 21 lines apart. It was divided into 9 equal voussoirs. This arch was 17 lines deep, and was carried on piers 2 inches and 7 lines thick. It was found, by gradually diminishing the piers, which were at first 2 inches and 10 lines thick, that the thickness first named was the least which could be assigned to resist the thrust of the voussoirs.

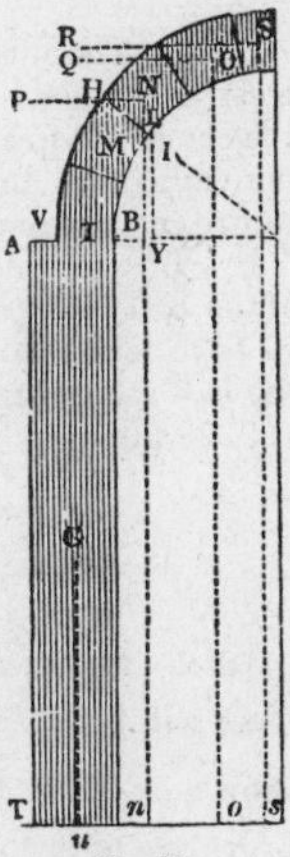

1376. The model in question is represented in *fig.* 567., whereon we have to observe, — 1st. That the first voussoir, I, being placed on a level joint, not only sustains itself, but is able to resist by friction an effort equal to one half of its weight. 2d. That the second voussoir, M, being upon a joint inclined 20 degrees, will also, through friction, sustain itself; and that, moreover, these two voussoirs would resist, previous to giving way on the joint AB, an horizontal effort equal to one half of their weight. 3d. That the third voussoir, N, standing on a joint inclined at 40 degrees, would slide if it were not retained by a power PN acting in an opposite direction. 4th. That taking, according to our hypothesis, an inclined plane of 30 degrees, whereon the stones would remain in equilibrium as an horizontal one, the inclined point of 40 degrees may be considered as an inclined plane of 10 degrees, supposing the surfaces infinitely smooth. 5th. That the effort of the horizontal power which holds this voussoir in equilibrium upon its joints will be to its weight as the sine of 10 degrees is to its cosine, as we have, in the section on Mechanics, previously shown. (1255 et seq.)

Fig. 567.

1377. The model of the vault whereon we are speaking being but 9 inches, or 108 lines in diameter, by 21 lines for the depth of the voussoirs, that is, the width between the two concentric circumferences, its entire superficies will be 4257 square lines, which, divided by 9, gives for each voussoir 473 square lines. Then, letting the weight of each voussoir be expressed by its superficies, and calling P the horizontal power, we have

$$\text{P} : 473 :: \sin. 10° : \cosin. 10°;$$
Or, $\text{P} : 473 :: 17365 : 98481$; which gives $\text{P} = 83\frac{4}{10}$.

The fourth voussoir, being placed upon a bed inclined at 60 degrees, will be considered as standing on a plane inclined only at 30 degrees, which gives, calling Q the horizontal power which keeps it on its joint, —

$$\text{Q} : 473 :: \sin. 30° : \cosin. 30°.$$
Or, $\text{Q} : 473 :: 50000 : 86603 = 273\frac{3}{10}$.

1378. The half-keystones, being placed on a joint inclined 80 degrees, are to be considered as standing on an inclined plane of 50, the area of the half key which represents its weight being $236\frac{1}{2}$. If we call R the horizontal power which sustains it on its joint, we shall have the proportion

$$\text{R} : 236\frac{1}{2} :: \sin. 50 : \cosin. 50;$$
or, $\text{R} : 236\frac{1}{2} :: 76604 : 64279$; which gives $\text{R} = 281\frac{9}{10}$.

1379. Wishing to ascertain if the sum of these horizontal efforts, which were necessary to keep on their joints the two voussoirs N, O, and the half-keystone, was capable of thrusting away the first voussoir upon its horizontal joint AB, the half arch was laid down upon a level place of the same stone without piers, and it was proved that to make it give way an horizontal effort of more than 16 ounces was required, whilst only 10 were neces-

sary to sustain the half-keystone and the two voussoirs N, O. The two halves of the arches united bore a weight of 5 lbs. 2 oz. before the first voussoirs gave way.

1380. To find the effect of each of these voussoirs when the arch is raised upon its piers, let fall from the centres of gravity N, O, S of these voussoirs the perpendiculars Nn, Oo, Ss, in order to obtain the arms of the levers of the powers P, Q, R, which keep them in their places, tending at the same time to overturn upon the fulcrum T the pier which carries the half arch, and we have their effort—

$$P \times Nn + Q \times Oo + R \times Ss.$$

The height of the pier being 195 lines, we have

$$Nn = 244 \cdot 94$$
$$Oo = 256 \cdot 26$$
and $Ss = 260 \cdot 50$, whence we have
The effort $P \times Nn = 83 \cdot 4 \times 244 \cdot 94$, which gives 20427·996
$$Q \times Oo = 273 \cdot 3 \times 256 \cdot 26 \ldots \ldots 70035 \cdot 858$$
$$R \times Ss = 281 \cdot 9 \times 260 \cdot 50 \ldots \ldots 73434 \cdot 950$$

Total effort in respect of the fulcrum, 163898·804

1381. The pier resists this effort, 1st, by its weight or area multiplied by the arm of the lever determined by the distance Tu from the fulcrum T to the perpendicular let fall from the centre of gravity G upon the base of the pier. 2d. By the weight of the half arch multiplied by the arm of its lever VY determined by the vertical LY let fall from the centre of gravity L, and which becomes in respect of the common fulcrum $T = Tt$ or $VB - BY$, in order to distinguish BY, which indicates the distance of the centre of gravity of the half arch (and which is supposed known because it may be found by the rules given in 1275. et seq.) from the width VB that the pier ought to have to resist the effort of the half arch sought. In order to find it, let P, the effort of the arch above found, be 163898·804.

Let the height of the pier $= a$
The width sought $= x$
The weight of the half arch $= b$
The part BY of its arm of lever $= c$

1382. The area of the pier which represents its weight multiplied by the arm of the lever will be $ax \times \dfrac{x}{2} = \dfrac{ax^2}{2}$. That of the half arch multiplied by its arm of lever will be shown by $VB + BY$, where $x + c$ will be $bx + bc$, whence the equation $P = \dfrac{ax^2}{2} + bx + bc$, which we have to solve.

Now first we have $\dfrac{ax^2}{2} + bx = P - bc.$

Multiplying all the terms by $\dfrac{2}{a}$ } $x^2 + \dfrac{2bx}{a} + \dfrac{2p - 2bc}{a}$, an expression in which x is raised to to eliminate x^2, we have the second power; but as $x^2 + \dfrac{2bx}{a}$ is not a perfect square, that is to say, it wants the square of half the known quantity $\dfrac{2b}{a}$ which multiplies the second term; by adding this square, which is $\dfrac{b^2}{a^2}$, to each side of the equation, we have $x^2 + \dfrac{2bx}{a} + \dfrac{b^2}{a^2} = \dfrac{2p - 2bc}{a} + \dfrac{b^2}{a^2}$. The first member by this means having become a perfect square whose root is $a + \dfrac{b}{a}$, we shall have $x + \dfrac{b}{a} + \sqrt{\dfrac{2p - 2bc}{a} + \dfrac{b^2}{a^2}}$, which becomes, by transferring $\dfrac{b}{a}$ to the other side of the equation, $x = \sqrt{\dfrac{2p - 2bc}{a} + \dfrac{b^2}{a^2}} - \dfrac{b}{a}$, in which x being only in the first member of the equation, its value is determined from the known quantities on the other side. Substituting, then, the values of the known quantities, we have

$$x = \sqrt{\dfrac{163898 \cdot 804 \times 2 - 2128 \times 2 \times 12\frac{1}{2}}{195} + \dfrac{2128}{195} \times \dfrac{2128}{195}} - \dfrac{2128}{195},$$

which gives $x = 28\frac{1}{4}$ lines instead of 2 inches and 5 lines, which was assigned to the piers that they might a little exceed equilibrium in their stability.

Proof of the above Method by another Method of estimating Friction.

1383. A proof of the truth of the hypothesis in the preceding section is to be found in the method proposed by Bossut in his *Treatise on Mechanics.*

Let the voussoir N (*fig. 568.*) standing on an inclined plane be sustained by a power Q acting horizontally. From the

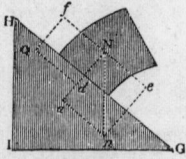

Fig. 568.

centre of gravity let fall the vertical Nn, which may be taken to express the weight of the voussoir. This weight may be resolved into two forces, whereof one, Nc, is parallel to the joint, and the other Na is perpendicular to it. In the same manner the power Q expressed by QN in its direction may be resolved into two forces, whereof Nf will be parallel to the joint and the other Nd perpendicular to it. Producing the line from the joint HG, drawing the horizontal line GI and letting fall the vertical HI, consider the line HG as an inclined plane whose height is HI and base IG. Then the force Nc with which the voussoir will descend will be to the weight as the height HI of the inclined plane is to its length HG. Calling p the weight of the voussoir, we then have N$c = p \times \frac{HG}{HI}$, and the force N$a$ which presses against the plane as the base of the plane IG is to its length, which gives the force N$a = p \times \frac{IG}{HG}$.

1384. Considering, in the same way, the two forces of the power Q which retain the voussoir on the inclined plane, we shall find the parallel force N$f = Q \times \frac{IG}{GH}$, and the perpendicular force N$d = Q \times \frac{IH}{HG}$. The force resulting from the two forces Na, Nd, which press against the joint, will be expressed by $p \times \frac{IG}{HG} + Q \times \frac{H}{GH}$; and as the voussoir only begins to slide upon a plane whose inclination is greater than 30 degrees, the friction will be to the pressure as the sine of 30 degrees is to its cosine, or nearly as 500 is to 866, or $\frac{100}{866}$ of its expression. Calling this ratio n, we shall, to express the friction, have

$$\left(p \times \frac{IG}{GH} + Q \times \frac{IG}{GH} \right) \times n.$$

As the friction prevents the voussoir sliding on its joint, in a state of equilibrium, we shall have the force Nf equal to the force Nc, less the friction; from which results the equation—

$$Q \times \frac{IG}{HG} = p \times \frac{HI}{HG} - \left(p \times \frac{IG}{GH} - Q \times \frac{IH}{HG} \right) \times n.$$

All the terms of which equation having the common divisor HG, it becomes —

$$Q \times IG = p \times HI - (p \times IG - Q \times IH) \times n;$$

and, bringing the quantities multiplied by Q to the same side of the equation, we have

$Q \times IG + (Q \times IH) \times n = p \times HI - (p \times IG) \times n$; which becomes
$Q \times (IG + n \times IH = p \times (HI - n \times IG)$; whence results
$Q = p \times \frac{HI - n \times IG}{IG + n \times IH}$, which is the formula for each voussoir, substituting the values for the expression.

1385. Thus for the third voussoir N (*fig.* 567.) placed on an inclined plane of 40 degrees, HI which represents the sine of the inclination will be 643, and its cosine represented by IG, 766, the expression of the friction n will be $\frac{500}{866}$, or $\frac{15}{26}$ nearly. The weight of the voussoir expressed by its area will be 473, which several values being substituted in the formula, we have

$$Q = 473 \times \frac{643 - \frac{15}{26} \times 766}{766 + \frac{15}{26} \times 643};$$

which gives Q = 83·6, the expression of the horizontal force P, which will keep the voussoir N in equilibrium on its joint instead of 83·4, which was the result of the operation in the preceding subsection.

1386. The same formula $Q = p \times \frac{HI - n \times IG}{IG + n \times IH}$ gives for the voussoir M on an inclined joint of 60 degrees, whose sine HI is 866 and cosine IG 500, $Q = 473 \times \frac{886 - \frac{15}{26} \times 500}{500 + \frac{15}{26} \times 866} = 273·4$; instead of 273·3, which was the result of the operation in the preceding section.

1387. For the half-keystone, the sine HI, being of 80 degrees, will be expressed by 985, and its cosine IG by 174; the half-keystone by 236$\frac{1}{2}$, and the friction by $\frac{15}{16}$.

The formula now will be $Q = 236\frac{1}{2} \times \frac{985 - \frac{15}{16} \times 174}{174 + \frac{15}{16} \times 985}$, which gives Q = 282·2, instead of 281$\frac{9}{10}$ found by the other method. These slight differences may arise from suppressing the two last figures of the sines, and some remainders of fractions which have been neglected. Multiplying these values of the powers which keep the voussoirs in equilibrium upon their beds by the several arms of the levers, as in the preceding calculations, their energy will be as follows : —

For the voussoir N,   83·6 × 244·94 = 20476·98
— O, 273·4 × 256·26 = 70061·48
— S, 282·2 × 260·50 = 73313·10

For the total force in respect of the fulcrum T = 163851·56.

Which is the value of p, and being substituted for it in the formula $x = \sqrt{\frac{2p - 2bc}{a} + \frac{b^2}{a^2}} - \frac{b}{a}$,

as well as the values of the other letters, which are the same as in the preceding example, we have

$$x = \sqrt{\frac{163851\ 56 \times 2 - 2128 \times 2 \times 12\frac{1}{4}}{195}} + \frac{2128}{195} \times \frac{2128}{195} - \frac{2128}{195} = 28 \cdot 16 \text{ lines}$$

for the thickness of the piers, instead of $28\frac{1}{4}$ lines found by the preceding operation.

Application of the Principles in the Model of a straight Arch.

1388. The second model to which the application of the preceding methods was made was a straight arch of the same sort (*fig. 569.*), whose opening between the piers was 9 inches. The arch was 21 lines high and 18 lines thick. It was divided into 9 wedges, whose joints were concentric. To determine the section of the joints, the diagonal FG was drawn on the face of the half arch, and from its extremity F touching the pier, the perpendicular FO meeting O in the vertical, passing through the middle of the opening of the piers, all the sections meeting in this point O. Each of the sections of the piers which support the arch forms an angle of 21° 15′ with the vertical, and of 68° 45′ with the horizon.

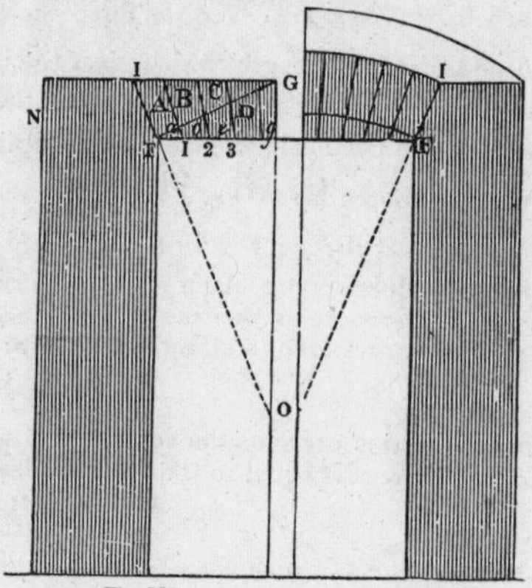

1389. In considering each of the wedges of the half arch as in the preceding method, it will be found that in order to retain the voussoir A on the joint IF (of the pier) which forms with the horizontal line NF an angle of 68° 45′, we have

Fig 569.   Fig. 570.

For the horizontal force	-	-	-	217·50
second B			-	254·33
third C	-	-	-	298·75
fourth D	-		-	354·66
half-keystone	-		-	212·83
		Total	-	1338·07

The height of the piers being 195 lines to the underside of the arch, and 216 to the top of the extrados, it follows that the arm of the lever, which is the same for all the wedges, is $206\frac{1}{3}$, from which we derive for the thrust p of the formula,

$$x = \sqrt{\frac{2p - 2bc}{a} + \frac{b^2}{a^2}} - \frac{a}{b}$$
$$= 1338 \cdot 07 \times 206 \cdot 33 = 276084;$$

b which expresses the area of the half arch $= 1219\frac{1}{2}$; c which expresses the distance of its centre of gravity from the vertical $Fn = 24$, and the height of the pier $a = 216$. Now, substituting these values in the formula, we shall have

$$a = \sqrt{\frac{276084 \times 2 - 2439 \times 24}{216} + \frac{1219\frac{1}{2} \times 1219\frac{1}{2}}{216 \times 216}} - \frac{1219\frac{1}{2}}{216} = 42\frac{1}{3} \text{ lines.}$$

Experiment gives 44 lines for the least width of the piers upon which the model will stand. But it is right to observe that from the impossibility of the joints being perpendicular to the intrados, the forces of the wedges press in a false direction on each other, as will be seen by the lines Fa, 1c, 2e, 3g, perpendicular to the joints against which the forces are directed, so that such an arch will only stand when the perpendicular FG does not fall within the thickness of the arch; and, indeed, this sort of arch is only secure when it comprises an arc whose thickness is equal to the section upon the piers IF, as shown in *fig. 570.*

Observations on the Way in which Stones forming an Arch act to support one another.

1390. Let the semicircular arch AHCDNB (*fig. 571.*) consist of an infinite number of voussoirs acting without friction, and only kept in their places by their mutual forces acting on each other. It will follow —

1. That the first voussoir, represented by the line AB, having its joints sensibly parallel and horizontal, will act with its whole weight in the vertical direction IE to strengthen the pier.

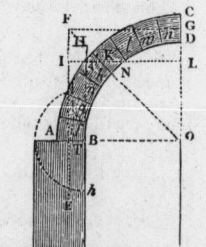

Fig. 571.

2. That the vertical voussoir CD, which represents the keystone, having also its joints sensibly parallel, will act with its whole weight horizontally to overturn the semi-arches and piers which carry them.

3. That all the other voussoirs between these two extremes will act with the compound forces Gn, nm, ml, Kl, Kh, hg, gf, fT, which may each be resolved into two others, whereof one is vertical and the other horizontal: thus the compound force Kh is but the result of the vertical force 4h, and the horizontal force 4K.

4. That the vertical force of each voussoir diminishes from T to G, where, for the keystone CD, it becomes nothing, whilst the horizontal forces continually increase in an inverse ratio; so that the voussoir HN, which is in the middle, has its vertical and horizontal forces equal.

5. That in semi-circular arches whose extradosses are of equal height from their intradosses, the circumference passing through the centre of gravity of the voussoirs may represent the sum of all the compound forces with which the voussoirs act upon one another in sustaining themselves, acting only by their gravity.

6. That if from the points T and G the vertical TF and horizontal GF be drawn meeting in the point F, the line TF will represent the sum of the vertical forces which assist the stability of the pier, and FG the sum of the horizontal forces which tend to overthrow it.

7. That if through the point K the horizontal line IKL be drawn between the parallels FT and CO, the part IK will represent the sum of the horizontal forces of the lower part AHNB of the vault, and KL those of the upper part HCDN.

8. The lower voussoirs between T and K being counterpoised by their vertical forces, the part of the arch AHNB will have a tendency to fall inwards, turning on the point B, whilst the voussoirs between K and G being counterpoised by their horizontal forces, the part HCDN of the arch will re-act upon the lower part by its tendency to turn upon the point A.

9. The horizontal forces of the upper part of the arch shown by KL acting from L towards K, and those of the lower part shown by IK opposite in direction to the former, that is, from I to K, being directly opposed, would counterpoise each other if they were equal, and the arch would have no thrust; but as they are always unequal, it is the difference of the forces which occasions the thrust, and which acts in the direction of the strongest power.

10. If we imagine the width BO of a semi-arch constantly to diminish, its height remaining the same, the sum of the horizontal forces will diminish in the same ratio, so that when the points B and O are common, the horizontal force being annihilated, nothing remains but the vertical force, which would act only on the pier, and tend to its stability, thrust vanishing, because, instead of an arch, it would, in fact, be nothing more than a continued pier.

11. If, on the contrary, the height OD diminishes, the width BO remaining the same, the curve B and D would, at last, vanish into the right line BO, and the arch would become a straight one. In this case, the vertical forces which give stability to the pier being destroyed, all that remains for sustaining the arch are the horizontal forces which will act with the whole weight of the arch; whence this species of arches must be such as exert most thrust, and circular arches hold a middle place between those which have no thrust, and flat arches, whose thrust is infinite, if the stones whereof they are formed could slide freely on one another, and their joints were perpendicular to their lower surfaces, as in other arches.

12. The inconveniences which result from making the joints of flat arches concentric have been before noticed. If the stones could slide freely on one another, as they only act in a false direction, their forces could never either balance or destroy one another.

13. A vast number of experiments made by Rondelet, upon fifty-four models of arches of different forms and extradosses, divided into an equal and unequal number of voussoirs, showed that the voussoirs acted rather as levers than as wedges, or as bodies tending to slide upon one another.

14. As long as the piers are too weak to resist the thrust of the voussoirs, many of them unite as one mass, tending to overturn them on a point opposite to the parts where the joints open.

15. Arches whose voussoirs are of even number exert more thrust than those which are of unequal number, that is, which have a keystone.

16. In those divided into uneven numbers and of unequal size, the larger the keystone the less is their thrust, so that the case of the greatest thrust is when a joint is made at the vertex, as in the case of arches whose voussoirs are divided into equal numbers.

17. A semicircular arch divided into four equal parts has more thrust than one divided into nine equal voussoirs.

18. Arches including more than a semicircle have less thrust than those of a similar span, the intradosses and extradosses being of similar forms.

19. Thrust does not increase as the thickness of an arch increases; so that, *cæteris paribus*, an arch of double the thickness has not double the thrust.

20. A semicircular arch whose extrados is equally distant throughout from, or, in other words, concentric with, the intrados, when divided into four equal parts, will only stand when its depth is less than the eighteenth part of its diameter, even supposing the abutments immoveable.

21. Whenever, in an arch of voussoirs of equal depth, a right line can be drawn from its outer fulcrum to the centre of the extrados of the keystone (*fig.* 572.), fracture does not occur in the middle of the haunches if the piers are of the same thickness as the lower part of the arch.

22. Arches whose thickness or depth diminishes as they rise to the vertex have less thrust than those whose thickness is equal throughout.

23. Semicircular and segmental arches whose extrados is an horizontal line have less thrust than others.

24. As long as the piers in the models were too weak to resist the thrust, it was possible to keep them in their places by a weight equal to double the difference between the thrust and resistance of one pier, acting by a string suspended passing through the joints in the middle of the haunches, or by a weight equal to that difference placed above each middle joint of the arches, as in *fig.* 572.

From these experiments and many others, a formula has been deduced to determine the thickness of piers of cylindrical arches of all species whose voussoirs are of equal depth, whatever their forms; and to this we shall now introduce the reader.

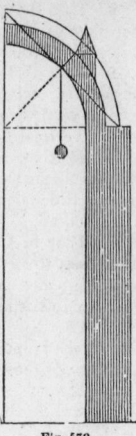

Fig. 572.

Method.

1391. Having described the mean circumference GKT (*figs.* 573, 574.), from the points G and T draw the tangents to the curve meeting in the point F. From this point draw the secan. FO cutting it in the point K. This point is the place of the greatest effort, and of the consequent failure, if the thickness of the piers is too weak to resist the thrust.

1392. Through the point K, between the parallels TF and GO, draw the horizontal line IKL, which will represent the sum of the horizontal forces as will the vertical TF express the vertical forces ; the mean circumference GKT will express the compound forces.

1393. The arches having an equal thickness throughout, the part IK of the horizontal line multiplied by the thickness of the arch will express the horizontal effect of the lower part of either arch, and KL multiplied by the same thickness will express that of the upper part. These two forces

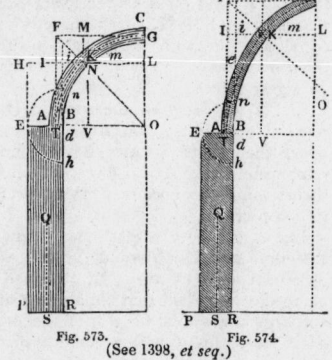

Fig. 573.   Fig. 574.
(See 1398, *et seq.*)

acting in opposite directions will partly destroy each other; thus transferring IK from K to m, the difference mL multiplied by the thickness of the vault will be the expression of the thrust. This force acting at the point K in the horizontal direction KH, the arm of the lever is determined by the perpendicular PH raised from the fulcrum P of the lever to the direction of the thrust, so that its effort will be expressed by mL × AB × PH.

This will be resisted —

1. By its weight represented by the surface EP × PR multiplied by the arm of the lever PS, determined by a vertical let fall from the centre of gravity Q, which gives for the resistance of the pier the expression EP × PR × PS.

2. By the sum of the vertical efforts of the upper part of each arch, represented by MK × AB acting at the point K, the arm of their lever in respect of the fulcrum P of the pier being KH.

3. By the sum of the vertical efforts of the lower part represented by IT multiplied by AB acting on the point T has for the arm of its lever TE.   Hence, if equilibrium exist,

$$m\overline{\text{L} \times \text{AB}} \times \text{PH} = \overline{\text{PE} \times \text{PR}} \times \text{PS} + \overline{\text{MK} \times \text{AB}} \times \text{KH} + \overline{\text{IT} \times \text{AB}} \times \text{TE}.$$

But as in this equation neither PR (= BE) nor PS nor KH nor TE is known, we must resort to an algebraic equation for greater convenience, in which

The effect of the thrust in the expression mL × AB				$= p$
The height of the pier PE	-	-	-	$= a$
EH = TI = KL = KV	-	-	-	$= d$
PH	-	-	-	$= a + d$
EB = PR	-	-	-	$= x$

PS - - - - - - - $= \frac{x}{2}$

The sum of the vertical forces of the upper part or

    MK × AB - - - - - $= m$

The sum of the forces of the lower part IT × AB $= n$

The part iK of the horizontal IKL - - $= c$

TB equal to half the thickness of the arch - $= e$

The arm of the lever KH - - - $= c \times x$

That of TE - - - - - $= x - e$

Thus the first equation becomes $pa + pd = \frac{ax^2}{2} + m\,(c \times x) + n\,(x - e)$,

Or $pa \times pd = \frac{ax^2}{2} + mx + mc + nx - ne.$

Transferring the unknown quantities to the second side of the equation, we shall

have $\frac{ax^2}{2} + mx + nx + = pa + pd + ne - mc.$

Multiply all the terms by 2, and divide by a, in order to get rid of x^2, and we

have $x^2 + \frac{2(m+n)x}{a} = 2p + \frac{2pd + 2nc - 2mc}{a};$

Making $m + n = b$, and adding to each member $\frac{b^2}{a^2}$ for the purpose of extracting

the root of the first member,

We have $x^2 + \frac{2bx}{a} + \frac{b^2}{a^2} = 2p + \frac{2pd + 2ne - 2mc}{a} + \frac{b^2}{a^2}.$

Extracting the root, $x + \frac{b}{a} = \sqrt{2p + \frac{2pd + 2ne - 2mc}{a} + \frac{b^2}{a^2}};$

And lastly, $x = \sqrt{2p + \frac{2pd + 2ne - 2mc}{a} + \frac{b^2}{a^2}} - \frac{b}{a}.$

1394. This last equation is a formula for finding the thickness of all sorts of arches whose voussoirs are of equal depth, which we will now apply to *fig.* 573. The model was 36 inches and 3 lines in span. The arch consisted of two concentric circles, and it was divided into four equal parts, a vertical joint being in the middle, the two others being inclined at angles of 45 degrees. The piers whereon it was placed were 40 inches and 4 lines high, and on a very exact measurement the values were as follow : —

PE (a in the formula) was - - - - - 40·333

EH = TI = KL = KV (d in the formula) - - 13·876

ML × AB (p in the formula) representing the thrust or 8·127 × 3   24·381

2p - - - - - - - 48·762

2pd = 48·762 × 13·876 - - - - 676·621

2MK × AB × KH represented by 2mc (= 5·749 × 3 × 4·249) -   73·282

2ne, which is IT × AB × AB (= 13·876 × 3 × 3) - - 124·824

$b = m + n = $ (MK + IT) × AB (= 19·625 × 3) - - 58·875

a = EP, the height of the pier being 40·333, $\frac{b}{a}$ will be $\frac{58 \cdot 875}{40 \cdot 333}$ or   1·459

$\frac{b^2}{a^2}$ - - - - - - - 2·128

Substituting these values in the formula $x = \sqrt{2p + \frac{2pd + 2ne - 2mc}{a} + \frac{b^2}{a^2}} - \frac{b}{a},$

we have $x = \sqrt{48 \cdot 762 + \frac{676 \cdot 621 + 124 \cdot 824 - 73 \cdot 282}{40 \cdot 333} + 2 \cdot 128} - 1 \cdot 459;$

which gives $x = 5 \cdot 8$, or 5 inches $9\frac{1}{3}$ lines for the thickness of the piers to resist the thrust of the arch, supposing it to be perfectly executed. But, from the imperfection of the execution of the model, it was found that the piers required for resisting the thrust a thickness of 6 inches and 3 lines.

1395. When the piers of the model were made $7\frac{1}{2}$ inches thick the arch on its central joint was found capable of supporting a weight of three pounds, being equal to an addition of 8 superficial inches beyond that of the upper parts of the arch which are the cause of the thrust, and this makes the value of 2p in the formula 56·762 instead of 48·762, and changes the equation to $x = \sqrt{56 \cdot 762 + \frac{787 \cdot 629 + 124 \cdot 828 - 86 \cdot 458}{40 \cdot 333} + 2 \cdot 430} - 1 \cdot 55;$ from which we should obtain $x = 7 \cdot 366$ inches, or 7 inches $3\frac{1}{3}$ lines, exhibiting a singular agreement between theory and practice. Rondelet gives another method of investigating the preceding problem, of which we do not think it necessary to say more than that it agrees with that just exhibited so singularly that the result is the same. It is dependent on the places of the centres of gravity, and therefore not so readily applicable in practice as that which has been just given.

Second Experiment.

1396. *Fig.* 567., in a preceding page, is the model of an arch in freestone, which has been before considered. It is divided into nine equal voussoirs, whose depth to the extrados is 21 lines, and whose interior diameter is 9 inches.

1397. Having drawn the lines heretofore described, we shall find $mL \times AB$ expressed in the formula by

$p = 26 \cdot 7 \times 21$, which gives	-	-	-	560·70
And for $2p$	-	-	-	1121·40
$EH = TI = KL = KV$, expressed by d, will be	-	45·60
Hence $2pd$	-	-	-	5113·584

$2ne$, which is twice the vertical effort of the lower part of the arch, multiplied by $\frac{1}{2}$ AB, will be $45 \cdot 6 \times 21 \times 21$, which gives - - - - 20109·60

$2me$, which indicated twice the vertical effort of the upper part, multiplied by iK, will be $18 \cdot 9 \times 21 \times 2 \times 8 \cdot 4$, which gives - - - - 6667·92

a, which represents the height of the piers, being 195, and $b = m + n = 64 \cdot 5 \times 21 = 1354 \cdot 5$,

$\frac{b}{a}$ will become $\frac{1354 \cdot 5}{195}$ - - 6·94

And all these values being substituted in the formula, will give

$$x = \sqrt{1121 \cdot 40 + \frac{5113 \cdot 584 + 20109 \cdot 6 - 6667 \cdot 92.}{195} + 48 \cdot 163} - 694 = 28 \cdot 62 \text{ lines,}$$

instead of $28\frac{1}{4}$, before found.

Geometrical Application of the foregoing.

1398. Let the mean curve TKG of the arch (whatever its form) be traced as in *figs.* 573, 574., the secant FO perpendicularly to the curve of the arch, and through the point K, where the secant cuts the mean curve, having drawn the horizontal line IKL, and raised from the point B a vertical line meeting the horizontal IKL 'in the point i, make Km equal to iK, and set the part mL from B to h, and then the double thickness of the arch from B to n. Let hn be divided into two equal parts at the point d, from which as a centre with a radius equal to half hn, describe the semi-circumference of a circle which will cut in E the horizontal line BA prolonged. The part BE will indicate the thickness to be given to the piers of the arches to enable them to resist the thrust.

1399. The truth of the method above given depends upon the graphic solution of the following problem: To find the side BE of a square which shall be equal to a given surface $mL \times 2e$; an expression which is equivalent to $2p$, and we have already seen that $x = \sqrt{2p}$ was a limit near enough; hence we may conclude that the thickness BE obtained by the geometrical method will be sufficiently near in all cases.

Experiments on surmounted Arches.

1400. The interior curve of *fig.* 574. is that of a semi-ellipsis 81 lines high; it is divided into four parts by an upright joint in the crown and two others towards the middle of the haunches determined by the secant FO, perpendicular to the interior part of the curve. Having traced the mean circumference GKT, the horizontal IKL, and the vertical Bi, we shall find

KL	-	-	-	-	$36\frac{3}{4}$
IK	-	-	-	-	$21\frac{3}{4}$
iK	-	-	-	-	$17\frac{1}{4}$
IT	-	-	-	-	$66\frac{1}{2}$
MK $= d$	-	-	-	-	19

The effect of the thrust indicated by $KL - iK = mL$ will be $19\frac{1}{2} \times 9$, which gives for the expression p of the formula - 175·5

$2p$ therefore - - - 351·0

d being $66 \cdot 5$, $2pd$ will be $351 \times 66 \cdot 5$, which gives - 23341·5

m, which is KM $\times$ AB, will be 19×9, which gives - 171·0

c, that is, iK, being $17\frac{1}{4}$ lines, we have $2me = 171 \times 17\frac{1}{4} \times 2$, which gives - - - - 5899·50

The height of the piers a - - - 120·00

b, which expresses the sum of the vertical efforts $m + n$, will be equal to MK $+$ IT $\times$ AB or $19 + 66\frac{1}{2} \times 9$, which gives - 769·50

Hence $\frac{b}{a} = \frac{769 \cdot 5}{120}$, which gives - - - 6·41

And $\frac{b^2}{a^2}$ gives - - - - 41·11

Substituting these values in the formula, $x = \sqrt{2p + \frac{2pd - 2mc}{a} + \frac{b^2}{a^2}} - \frac{b}{a}$,

We have the equation $x = \sqrt{351 + \frac{23341 \cdot 5 - 5899 \cdot 5}{120} + 41 \cdot 11} - 6 \cdot 41 = 16 \cdot 77$

lines, or a little more than $16\frac{3}{4}$ lines. The model of this arch would not however stand on piers less than 17 lines thick.

In taking the root of double the thrust the result is $18\frac{3}{4}$ lines, as it is also by the geometrical method.

Application to the Pointed Arch.

1401. The model which *fig. 575.* represents was of the same height and width as the last, and the voussoirs were all of equal thickness. Having laid down all the lines on the figure as before, we shall find iK of the formula to be

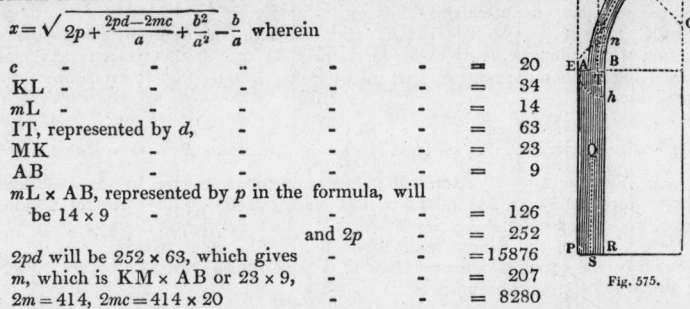

$$x = \sqrt{2p + \frac{2pd - 2mc}{a} + \frac{b^2}{a^2}} - \frac{b}{a} \text{ wherein}$$

c - - - - - - -	=	20
KL - - - - - -	=	34
mL - - - - - -	=	14
IT, represented by d, - - -	=	63
MK - - - - -	=	23
AB - - - - -	=	9

mL × AB, represented by p in the formula, will
be 14 × 9 - - - - - = 126
                                      and $2p$ - = 252
$2pd$ will be 252 × 63, which gives - - = 15876
m, which is KM × AB or 23 × 9, - - = 207
$2m = 414$, $2mc = 414 \times 20$ - - = 8280

Fig. 575.

The height of the pier, represented by a, being 120, we have $\frac{2pd - 2mc}{a} = \frac{15876 - 8220}{120} = 63\cdot8$: b, or FT × AB, will be 86 × 9 = 774; whence $\frac{b}{a} = \frac{774}{120} = 6\cdot45$, and $\frac{b^2}{a^2} = 41\cdot60$. Substituting these values in the formula

$$x = \sqrt{252 + 63\cdot8 + 41\cdot6} - 6.45 = 12\cdot46 \text{ lines for the thickness of the pier.}$$

In taking the square root of double the thrust the thickness comes out 15·88 lines, as it does by the geometrical method. Experiments showed that the least thickness of pier upon which the model would stand was 14 lines.

Application to a surmounted Catenarean Arch.

1402. The lines are all as in the preceding examples (*fig. 576.*). The whole arch acts on the pier in the direction FT, which is resolved into the two forces Tf and Tm, and the formula, as before, is

$$x = \sqrt{2p + \frac{b^2}{a^2}} - \frac{b}{a};$$

thus having found B$m = 22\frac{1}{3}$, we have the value of $p = 22\frac{1}{3} \times 9 = 201$; and $2p = 402$.

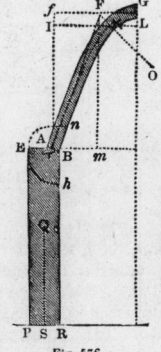

1403. This model was of the same dimensions as the preceding: b, which represents Tf × AB, will be 769·5; $\frac{b^2}{a^2}$ will be 6·41, and $\frac{b}{a} = \frac{769\cdot5}{120} = 41\cdot11$. These values substituted in the formula give

$$x = \sqrt{402 + 41\cdot11} - 6\cdot41 = 14\cdot64 \text{ lines.}$$

1404. Experiment determined that the pier ought not to be less than 16 lines, and the geometrical method made it 20·05.

The following table shows the experiments on six different models.

Fig. 576.

Form of Arch.	Thickness of the Piers.		
	By the formula.	By experiment.	Geometrically.
	Lines.	Lines.	Lines.
The pointed -	12·46	14·00	15·88
The catenary -	14·64	15·00	20·05
The cycloid -	14·66	15·00	17·24
The parabolic -	15·85	16·50	21·30
The elliptic -	16·77	17·00	18·75
The cassinoid -	19·62	21·00	20·79

This table shows that, in practice, for surmounted arches, the limit $x = \sqrt{2p}$, or the thickness obtained for the construction by graphical means is more than sufficient, since it gives results greater than those that the experiments require, excepting only in the cassinoid; but even in the case of that curve the graphical construction comes nearer to experiment than the result of the first formula.

1405. It is moreover to be observed, that the pointed is the most advantageous form for surmounted arches composed of arcs of circles. We have had occasion to speak, in our First Book, of the boldness and elegance exhibited in this species of arches by the architects of the twelfth and thirteenth centuries; we shall merely add in this place that where roofs are required to be fire-proof, there is no form so advantageously capable of adoption as the pointed arch, nor one in which solidity and economy are so much united.

1406. Next to the pointed arch for such purpose comes the catenary (the graphical method of describing which will be found under its head, in the Glossary at the end of the work), and this is more especially useful when we consider that the voussoirs may all be of equal thickness.

Application of the Method to surbased Arches, or those whose Rise is less than the Half Span.

1407. For the purpose of arriving at just conclusions relative to surbased arches, three models were made of the same thicknesses and diameters, with a rise of 35 lines, and in form elliptical, cassinoidal, and cycloidal. We however do not think it necessary, from the similarity of application of the rules, to give more than one example, which is that of a semi-ellipse (*fig.* 577.), in which, as before, the formula is

$$x = \sqrt{2p + \frac{2pd - 2mc}{a} + \frac{b^2}{a^2}} - \frac{b}{a}.$$

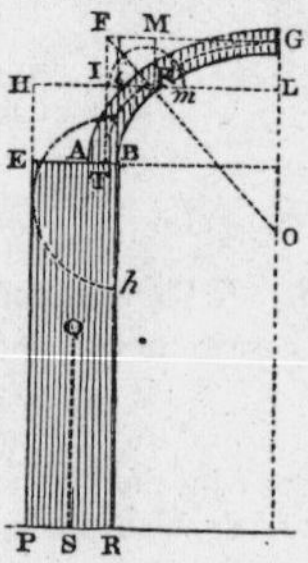

The lines described in the foregoing examples being drawn, we have

$$KL = 45 \cdot 5$$
$$iK = 8 \cdot 5.$$

IT, represented by d in the formula, - - =		24·84
MK - - =		14·66
$mL \times AB$ representing the thrust (37×9) gives the value of p - - - =		333·00
$2p$ therefore - =		666·00
TI, represented by d, being 24·84, we have $2pd$ - - - =		16543·44
m, which is $KM \times AB$, will be $14·66 \times 9$, which gives - - =		131·94
c, representing iK, being 8·5, $2mc$ - - - =		2242·94
b, which expresses the sum of the vertical efforts $m + n (39·5 \times 9)$ - =		355·50
a, being always 120, $\frac{b}{a} = \frac{355·5}{120}$ is - - - - =		2·96
Lastly, $\frac{b^2}{a^2}$ - - - =		8·76

Fig. 577.

Substituting these values in the formula, we have

$$x = \sqrt{666 + \frac{16543·44 - 2242·94}{120}} + 8·76 - 2·96 = 25·22 \text{ lines, or a little less than } 25\tfrac{1}{4} \text{ lines.}$$

1408. In the model it was found that a thickness of 26 lines was necessary for the pier, and the lower voussoirs were connected with it by a cementing medium. Without which precaution the thickness of a pier required was little more than one tenth of the opening. Taking the square root of double the thrust, that is, of 666, we have 25·81, about the same dimension that the graphical construction gives. The experiments, as well as the application of the rules, require the following remarks for the use of the practical architect.

1409. I. The cassinoid, of the three curves just mentioned, is that which includes the greatest area, but it causes the greatest thrust. When the distance between the intrados and the extrados is equal in all parts, it will only stand, supposing the piers immoveable, as long as its thickness is less than one ninth part of the opening.

1410. II. The cycloid, which includes the smallest area, exerts the least thrust, but it can be usefully employed only when the proportion of the width to the height is as 22 to 7 in surbased arches, and in surmounted arches as 14 to 11. The smallest thickness with which these arches can be executed, so as to be capable of standing of themselves, is a little more than one eighteenth of the opening, as in the case of semicircular arches.

1411. III. The ellipsis, whose curvature is a mean between the first and second, serves equally well for all conditions of height, though it exerts more thrust than the last-mentioned and less than the cassinoid.

1412. It is here necessary to remark, that too thin an arch, whose voussoirs are equal in depth, may fall, even supposing the abutments immoveable, and especially when surbased;

because, when once the parts are displaced, the force of the superior parts may lift up the lower parts without disturbing the abutments.

Raking Arches.

1413. Let ACA′ (*fig. 578.*) be the model of a raking arch of the same diameter and thickness as the preceding example, the voussoirs of equal thickness, and the piers of different heights, the lowest being 10 inches or 120 lines in height, and the other $14\frac{1}{2}$ inches or 174 lines. The tangent at the summit is supposed parallel to the raking lines that connect the springing.

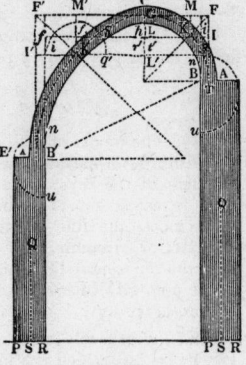

Fig. 578.

1414. This arch being composed of two different ones, the mean circumference on each must be traced, and each has its separate set of lines, as in the preceding examples; the horizontal line KL of the smaller arch is produced to meet the mean circumference of the other in S, and the interior line of its pier in *g*.

1415. The part KLS represents the horizontal force of the part of the arch KGS, common to the two semi-arches; so that if a joint be supposed at S, the part LK represents the effort acting against the lower part of the smaller arch, and LS that against the lower part of the larger arch. These parts resist the respective efforts as follows: the small arch with the force represented by *i*K, and the greater one with the force represented by *g*S. But as *g*S is greater than LS, transfer LS from *g* to *f* to obtain the difference *f*S, which will show how much LS must be increased to resist the effort of the larger half arch; that is, the effort of the smaller one should be equal to L*f*; but as this last requires for sustaining itself that the larger one should act against it with an effort equal to KL, this will be the difference of the opposite effort, which causes the thrust against the lower part of the smaller arch and the pier from whence it springs. Hence, transferring *f*L from L to *q*, taking the half of *iq* and transferring it from L to *h*, the part *h*K multiplied by the thickness AB will be the expression for the thrust represented by *p* in the formula

$$x = \sqrt{2p + \frac{2pd - 2mc}{a} + \frac{b^2}{a^2}} - \frac{b}{a}.$$

Having found $h\mathrm{K} = 30\frac{1}{2}$ and AB = 9, we have for the value of *p* $30\frac{1}{2} \times 9 = 274\frac{1}{2}$, and for that of $2p - 549$, *d* which represents IT, being $29\frac{1}{3}$, $2pd = 16195\frac{1}{4}$. In $2mc$; *m*, which represents MK × AB, will be $12\frac{1}{3} \times 9 = 111$, and $2m = 222$.

c, which represents *i*K, being 8, we have $2mc = 222 \times 8 = 1776$.

The height of the pier represented by *a* being 174, we have

$$\frac{2pd - 2mc}{a} = \frac{16195\frac{1}{4} - 1776}{174} \quad - \quad - \quad - \quad - \quad - \quad - \quad = 82\cdot81$$

The vertical effort represented by *b*, or TF × AB, will be $41\frac{1}{3} \times 9 = 375$,

$$\text{and } \frac{b}{a} = \frac{375}{174} \text{ becomes} \quad - \quad - \quad - \quad - \quad - \quad = 2\cdot15$$

$$\text{and } \frac{b^2}{a^2} \quad - \quad - \quad - \quad = 4\cdot64.$$

Substituting these values in the formula, we have

$x = \sqrt{549 + 82\cdot81 + 4\cdot64} - 2\cdot16 = 23\cdot08$ for the thickness of the greater pier from which the smaller semi-arch springs.

For the half of the greater arch, having produced the horizontal line IK′L′, make K′*r* equal to VL′, and bisect *r*L′ in *t*; the line K′*t* represents the effort of the smaller arch against the greater arch, which resists it with a force shown by *i*′K′: thus making K′*q*′ equal to *i*′K, the effort of the thrust will be indicated by *q*′*t* × AB, whose value *p* in the formula will be

$$20 \times 9 = 180, \text{ and } 2p \quad - \quad - \quad - \quad - \quad = 360$$
d, which is TI, being $69\frac{2}{3}$, $2pd$ will $\quad - \quad - \quad = 25080$
In $2mc$, *m* being $26 \times 9 = 234$, and *c* being $23\frac{1}{6}$, $2mc = 10842$
a, the height of the smaller pier $\quad - \quad - \quad = 120$
We have $\frac{2pd - 2mc}{a} = \frac{25080 - 10842}{120}$, which becomes $\quad = 118\cdot65$
b, which is TF × AB, will be $95\frac{2}{3} \times 9 \quad - \quad - \quad = 861$
$\frac{b}{a} = \frac{861}{120} = 7\cdot175$, and $\frac{b^2}{a^2} \quad - \quad - \quad - \quad = 51\cdot48$

Substituting these values in the formula, we have

$x = \sqrt{360 + 118\cdot65 + 51\cdot48} - 7\cdot175 = 15\cdot855$ lines for the thickness of the smaller pier.

Taking the square root of double the thrust, we should have for the larger pier 23·44 lines, and for the smaller one 19 lines. In the geometrical operation, for the larger pier make Bu equal to hK and Bn equal to 2AB; then upon un as a diameter describe a semicircle cutting the horizontal line BA produced in E. BE will be the thickness of the pier, and will be found to be 23½ lines. For the smaller pier make B'u' equal to $q't$ and B'n' equal to 2A'B'. Then the semicircumference described upon un as a diameter will give 19 lines for the thickness.

1416. By the experiments on the model 22 lines was found to be the thickness necessary for the larger pier, and 18 lines for the smaller one.

Arch with a level Extrados.

1417. The model of arch *fig.* 579. is of the same opening as the last, but with a level extrados, serving as the floor of an upper story. The thickness of the keystone is 9 lines. To find the place of fracture or of the greatest effort; having raised from the point B the vertical BF till it meets the line of the extrados, draw the secant FO cutting the interior circumference at the point K, and through this point draw the horizontal IKL and the vertical HKM

The part CDKF will be that which causes the thrust, and its effort is represented by

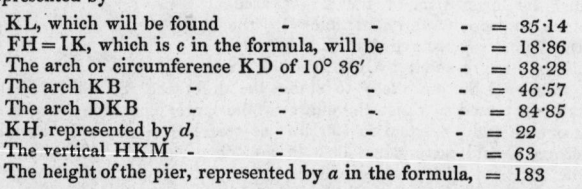

Fig. 579.

KL, which will be found	- - -	= 35·14
FH = IK, which is c in the formula, will be	-	= 18·86
The arch or circumference KD of 10° 36′	-	= 38·28
The arch KB	- - -	= 46·57
The arch DKB	- - -	= 84·85
KH, represented by d,	- -	= 22
The vertical HKM	- - -	= 63
The height of the pier, represented by a in the formula,		= 183

The area of the upper voussoir FKCD = 667·44; but as the load of the haunches is borne by the inferior voussoir, we must subtract the triangle FKH = $\frac{18\cdot26 \times 22}{2}$ = 207·46. The remainder 459·98 multiplied by KL and divided by the arc KD, that is, $\frac{459\cdot98 \times 35\cdot14}{38\cdot28}$ = 422·24, represents the effort of the upper part.

1418. That of the lower part, represented by $\frac{FBKH \times IK}{KB}$, is $\frac{651\cdot07 \times 18\cdot86}{46\cdot57}$, which becomes 263·67. The difference of the two efforts = 158·57 will express the thrust or p of the formula, and we have 2p = 317·14.

1419. The piers being supposed to be continued up to the line EC of the extrados will be greater than the arm of the lever of the thrust which acts at the point K. Thus the expression of the arm of the lever, instead of being $a + d$, as in the preceding examples, will be $a - d$, and the sign of $\frac{2pd}{a}$ must be changed. In numbers, $\frac{317\cdot14 \times 22}{183}$ = 38·12; therefore, in the formula, $+ \frac{2pd}{a}$ becomes $- 38\cdot12$.

1420. In the preceding examples, 2mc, which represented double the vertical effort of the superior voussoir multiplied by the arm of its lever, becomes nothing, because it is comprised in the addition made to the lower voussoir; so that the formula now is

$$x = \sqrt{2p - \frac{2pd}{a} + \frac{b^2}{a^2} - \frac{b}{a}}.$$

b, then, which always expresses the vertical effort of the half arch, is therefore

$\frac{1111\cdot05 \times 63}{84\cdot85}$ = 824·94; and for $\frac{b}{a}$ we have $\frac{824\cdot94}{183}$ = 4·5, and $\frac{b^2}{a^2}$ = 20·25.

Substituting these values in the last formula, we shall have

$$x = \sqrt{319\cdot14 - 38\cdot12 + 20\cdot25} - 4\cdot5 = 12\cdot88 \text{ lines.}$$

Experiment gives 14 lines as the least thickness that can be relied on.

To find the thickness by the geometrical method, make Km equal to IK and Bh equal to mL, Bn to double CD, and upon nh as a diameter describe the semicircumference cutting the horizontal line OB produced in A: then BA = 17¼ lines is the thickness sought.

1421. Rondelet proves the preceding results by using the centres of gravity, and makes the result of the operation 12·74 instead of 12·80, as first found. But the difficulty of finding the centres of gravity of the different parts is troublesome; and with such a concurrence of results we do not think it necessary to enter into the detail of the operation.

A different Application of the preceding Example.

1422. The model (*fig.* 580.) is an arch similar to that of the preceding example, having a story above it formed by two walls, whose height is 100, and the whole covered by a timber roof. The object of the investigation is to ascertain what change may be made in the thickness of the piers which are strengthened in their resistance by the additional weight upon them.

1423. The simplest method of proceeding is to consider the upper walls as prolongations of the piers.

1424. In the model the walls were made of plaster, and their weight was thus reduced to $\frac{3}{4}$ of what they would have been if of the stone used for the models hitherto described. The roof weighed 12 ounces. We shall therefore have that 100, which in stone would have represented the weight of the walls, from the difference in weight of the plaster, reduced to 75. In respect of the roof, which weighed 12 ounces, having found by experiment that it was equal to an area of 576 lines of the stone, both being reduced to equal thicknesses, we have 12 ounces, equal to an area of 13·82 whose half 6·91 must be added to that of the vertical efforts represented by b in $\frac{b}{a}$ and $\frac{b^2}{a^2}$. Changing these terms into $\frac{h}{a}$ and $\frac{h^2}{a^2}$, the formula becomes

$$x = \sqrt{2p - \frac{2pd}{a} + \frac{h^2}{a^2}} - \frac{h}{a}.$$

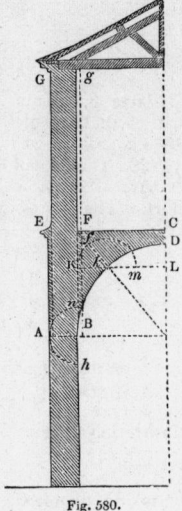

Fig. 580.

The height of the piers or a in the formula = 183 + 75 = 258.

p does not change its value, therefore $2p$ (as in the preceding example) = 265·86.

d, the difference between the height of the pier and the arm of the lever, will = 75.

Hence, $\frac{2pd}{a} = \frac{565·85 \times 75}{258} = 77·28.$

h, becomes 750·69 + 6·91 = 1441·69.

And $\frac{h}{a} = \frac{1441·69}{358} = 5·58.$

Again, $\frac{h^2}{a^2} = 31·22.$

Substituting these values in the formula, we shall have

$$x = \sqrt{265·86 - 77·28 + 31·22} - 5·58 = 9·15.$$

In the model a thickness of 11 lines was found sufficient to resist the thrust, and taking the root of double the thrust the result is 13 lines.

1425. By the geometrical method, given in the last, taking from the result $17\frac{1}{4}$ lines, there found, the value of $\frac{h}{a}$, that is, 5·58, the remainder $11\frac{2}{3}$ lines is the thickness sought.

1426. It may be here observed, that in carrying up the walls above, if they are set back from the vertical BF in *hf*, the model required their thickness to be only 6 lines, because this species of false bearing, if indeed it can be so called, increases the resistance of the piers.

This was a practice constantly resorted to in Gothic architecture, as well as that of springing pointed arches from corbels, for the purpose of avoiding extra thickness in the walls or piers.

Another Application of the Principles to a differently constructed Arch.

1427. The model (*fig.* 581.) represents an arch of 11 voussoirs whereof 10 are with crossettes or elbows, which give them a bearing on the adjoining horizontal courses; the eleventh being the keystone. The opening is 9 inches or 108 lines, as in the preceding examples.

1428. Having drawn the lines BF, FC, the secant FO, and the horizontal line IKL, independent of the five courses above the line FC of the extrados, we have

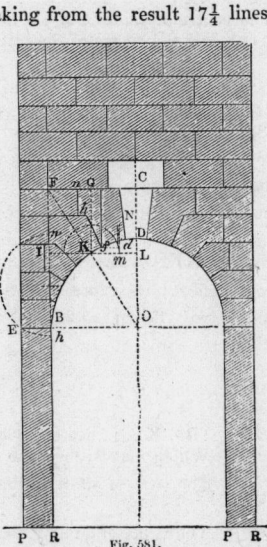

Fig. 581.

$$KL = 30\cdot73$$
$$IK = 23\cdot27$$
$$OC = BF - 78\cdot00$$
$$\text{The arc } KD = 32\cdot70$$
$$\text{The arc } KB = 52\cdot15$$
$$KG = 33\cdot59$$
$$a, \text{ the height of the pier, } = 198\cdot00.$$

The area KFCL of the upper part of the arch will be 1223·10, from which subtracting that of the triangle FKG, which 590·82, the remainder 832·28 being multiplied by 30·73 and divided by 32·7 makes the effort of this part 782·44.

1429. The area of the lower part is 697·95, to which adding the triangle FKG = 390·82, we have 1038·77, which multiplied by 23·27 and divided by 52·15, gives 485·82 for its effort. The expression of the thrust, represented by p in the formula,

$$x = \sqrt{\,2p - \frac{2pd}{a} + \frac{b^2}{a^2}\,} - \frac{b}{a},$$ being equal to the difference of these two efforts,

will be 296·62, and twice p - - = 593·24

d, representing KG, being - - = 33·59

we have $2pd = 19926\cdot93$, and $\frac{2pd}{a}$ - = 100·64

b, representing the sum of the efforts of the semi-arch, will be $\frac{1921 \times 78}{85} = 1762\cdot03$

$\frac{b}{a} = \frac{1762\cdot8}{198} = 8\cdot9$ and $\frac{b^2}{a^2}$ - - - = 79·21

Substituting these values in the formula, we have the equation

$$x = \sqrt{593\cdot24 - 100\cdot64 + 79\cdot21} - 8\cdot9 = 15\cdot01.$$

By taking double the square root of the thrust the result is 23·91, a thickness evidently too great, because the sum of the vertical efforts, which are therein neglected, is considerable.

1430. The geometrical method gives 19 lines. The least thickness of the piers from actual experiment was 16 lines.

1431. Rondelet gives a proof of the method by means of the centres of gravity, as in some of the preceding examples, from which he obtains a result of only 13·26 for the thickness of the piers.

Consideration of an Arch whose Voussoirs increase towards the Springing.

1432. The model (*fig.* 582.) has an extrados of segmental form not concentric with its intrados, so that its thickness increases from the crown to the springing. The opening is the same as before, namely, 9 inches, or 108 lines. The thickness at the vertex is 4 lines, towards the middle of the haunches 7½ lines, and at the springing 14½ lines. The centre of the line of the extrados is one sixth part of the chord AO below the centre of the intrados; so that

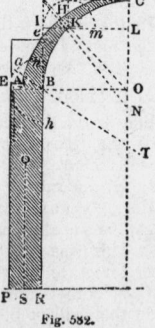

The radius DN = 68·05

KL = 38·18

IK = 15·82

(See 1390, obs. 22, and 1441). The arc BK = KC = 42·43

1433. The area KHDC of the upper part of the arch is 258·75, that of the lower part BAHK 486·5; hence the effort of the upper part is represented by the expression $\frac{258\cdot75 \times 38\cdot18}{42\cdot43} = 232\cdot47.$

1434. The half segment ABe being supposed to be united to the pier; BeHK, whose area is 178, is the only part that can balance the upper effort; its expression will be $\frac{178 \times 15\cdot82}{42\cdot.3\cdot} = 66\cdot24.$ The difference of the two efforts 166·23 will be the expression of the thrust represented by p in the formula

Fig. 582.

$$x = \sqrt{\,2p + \frac{2pd - 2mc}{a} + \frac{b^2}{a^2}\,} - \frac{b}{a}$$

Thus $2p$ - - - = 332·46

IB = KL, indicated by d, - - - = 38·18

Which makes the value of $2pd$ - - = 12693·92

The vertical effort of the upper part indicated by $m = \frac{258\cdot75 \times 1582}{42\cdot43} =$ 96·30

and for $2pm$ - = 192·60

The value of c being 15·82, we have $2mc$ - - = 3046·50

The height of the piers being still 120, we have

$$\frac{2pd-2mc}{a}=\frac{12693\cdot92-3046\cdot5}{120} \quad - \quad - \quad = \quad 80\cdot39$$

b, which indicates the vertical effort of the half arch represented by FB, will be $\frac{745\cdot26\times54}{84\cdot85}$ $\quad - \quad - \quad = \quad 473\cdot48$

$$\frac{b}{a}=\frac{473\cdot48}{120} \quad - \quad - \quad - \quad - \quad = \quad 3\cdot95$$

$$\text{and } \frac{b^2}{a^2} \quad - \quad = \quad 15\cdot56$$

These values being substituted in the formula, will give

$$x=\sqrt{332\cdot46+80\cdot39+15\cdot56}-3\cdot95=16\cdot74 \text{ lines.}$$

1435. The smallest thickness of pier that would support the arch in the model was $17\frac{1}{2}$ lines.

1436. With the geometrical method, instead of the double of CD, make Bh double the mean thickness HK, and Bn equal to mL, and on nh as a diameter describe the semicircumference cutting OB produced in E; then EB$=18\frac{1}{4}$ lines will be the thickness sought.

1437. If the pier is continued up to the point e where the thickness of the arch is disengaged from the pier, the height of the pier represented in the formula by a will be $151\cdot5$ instead of 120, and the difference b, instead of being $\frac{745\cdot26\times54}{85}$, will be only $\frac{436\cdot75\times54}{85}=277\cdot46$.

1438. d, expressed by Ie, will be $6\cdot5$, all the other values remaining the same as in the preceding article, the equation is

$$x=\sqrt{332\cdot46-5\cdot71+4}-2=16\cdot21.$$

1439. Using the method by means of the centres of gravity, Rondelet found the result for the thickness of the piers to be $15\cdot84$. So that there is no great variation in the different results.

1440. In the preceding examples arches have been considered rather as arcades standing on piers than as vaults supported by walls of a certain length. We are now about to consider them in this last respect, and as serving to cover the space enclosed by the walls.

In respect of cylindrical arches supported by parallel walls, it is manifest that the resistance they present has no relation to their length; for if we suppose the length of the vault divided into an infinite number of pieces, as C, D, E, &c. (*fig.* 584. No. 2.), we shall find for each of these pieces the same thickness of pier, so that all the piers together would form a wall of the same thickness. For this reason the surfaces only of the arches and piers have been hitherto considered, that is, as profiles or sections of an arch of any given length. Consequently it may be said that the thickness of wall found for the profile in the section of an arch would serve for the arch continued in length infinitely, supposing such walls isolated and not terminated or rather filled by other walls at their ends. When cylindrical walls are terminated by walls at their extremities, after the manner of gable ends, it is not difficult to imagine that the less distant these walls are the more they add stability to those of the arch. In this case may be applied a rule which we shall hereafter mention more at length under the following section on Walls.

1441. If in any of the examples (*fig.* 582. for instance) PR be produced indefinitely to the right, and from R on the line so produced the length of the wall supporting the arch be set out, and if from the extremity of such line another be drawn, as TB produced through B, indefinitely towards a, and Ba be made equal to the thickness of the pier first found, a vertical line let fall from a will determine the thickness sought. When arches are connected with these cross walls, the effect of the thrust may be much diminished if they are not very distant. If there be any openings in the walls, double the length of them must be added to that of the wall as well as of any that may be introduced in the gable wall.

1442. *Fig.* 583. represents the mode in which an arch fails when the piers are not of sufficient strength to resist the thrust: they open on the lower part of the summit at DM and on the upper part of the haunches at HN; from which we may infer that the thrust of an arch may be destroyed by cramping the under side of the voussoirs near the summit and the upper side of those towards the middle of the haunches; and this method is greatly preferable to chains or iron bars on the extrados, because these have no effect in preventing a failure on the underside. Chains at the springing will not prevent failure in arches whose voussoirs are of equal depth but that too small, inasmuch as there is no counteraction from them against the bulging

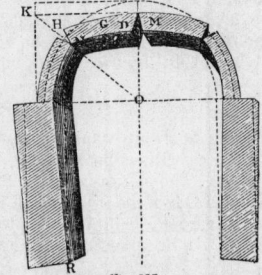

Fig. 583.

that takes place at the haunches, like a hoop loaded when its ends are fixed. The most advantageous position for a chain to oppose the effort of an arch is to let it pass through the point K where the efforts meet. PC is the tangent before failure, and O the centre; R being the inner point of the pier.

OF COMPOUND VAULTING.

1443. M. Frezier, in speaking of the thrust of this sort of arches, proposes, in order to find the thickness of the piers which will support them, to find by the ordinary manner the thickness suitable to each part of the cylindrical arch BN, BK (No. 3. *fig. 584.*) by which the groin is formed, making BE the thickness suitable to the arch BN, and BF that which the arch BK requires; the pier BEHF would thus be able to resist the thrust of the quarter arch OKBN. According to this method we should find the bay of a groined arch 9 inches opening would not require piers more than 21 lines square and 120 lines high; but experience proves that a similar arch will scarcely stand with piers 44 lines square, the area of whose bases are four times greater than that proposed by M. Frezier.

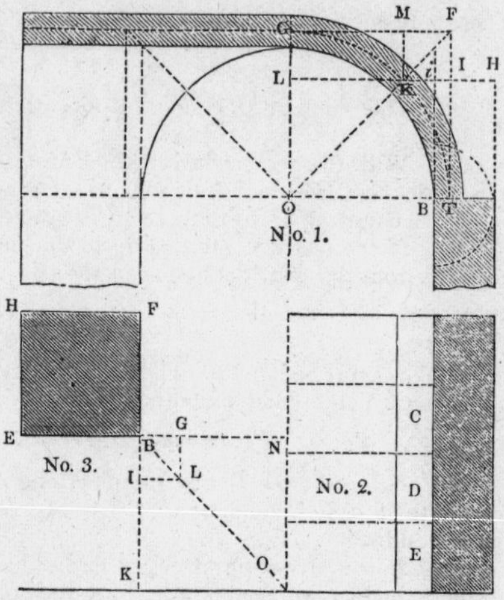

Method for groined Vaulting.

1444. The model in this case (see the last figure) is 9 inches in the opening, voussoirs equally thick, being 9 lines, standing upon four piers 10 inches or 120 lines high.

Fig. 584.

1445. The groin is formed by two cylindrical arches of the same diameter crossing at right angles, as represented in No. 3. of the figure. The four portions of the vault being similar, the calculation for one pier will be sufficient.

1446. On the profile No. 1. of the figure describe the mean circumference TKG, draw the tangents FT and FG, and the secant FO and the horizontal line IKL. Draw the vertical B*i*, and NG and KI on the plan (No. 3.) equal to KL.

1447. In the foregoing examples for arches and cylindrical vaulting there has been no necessity to consider more than the surface of the profiles, which are constantly the same throughout their length; but the species of vault of which we are now treating being composed of triangular gores whose profile changes at every point, we shall be obliged to use the cubes instead of the areas of squares, and to substitute surfaces for lines. Thus in viewing the triangular part KBO, the sum of the horizontal efforts of the upper part of this portion of the vault, represented in the profile by KL, will be represented in plan by the trapezium KILO.

1448. The sum of those of the lower part *i*K in the profile is represented in plan by BIL. The thrust is expressed by the difference of the area of the trapezium and of the triangle multiplied by the thickness of the vault; thus, KB and KO of the plan being 54, the superficies of the triangle BKO will be $54 \times 27 = 1458$; the part BK of the plan being equal to IL, and B*t* to *i*K of the profile $= 12\frac{9}{14}$, the area of the triangle BIL, indicating the sum of the horizontal efforts of the upper part, will be $12\frac{9}{14} \times 6\frac{9}{23} = 79\frac{13}{14}$.

1449. We obtain the area of the trapezium KILO by subtracting that of the small triangle BIL from the greater triangle BKO, that is, $79\frac{13}{14}$ from 1458; the remainder $1378\frac{1}{14}$ gives the horizontal effort of the upper part; lastly, subtracting $79\frac{13}{14}$ from $1378\frac{1}{14}$, the remainder $1298\frac{2}{14}$ will be the expression of the thrust whose value is found by multiplying $1298\frac{2}{14}$ by $9 = 11683\frac{2}{7}$, which is the *p* of the formula.

$$x = \sqrt{2p + \frac{2pd - 2mc}{a} + \frac{b^2}{a^2}} - \frac{b}{a}.$$

Letting *a* always stand for the height, and *d* for TI of the profile, the arm of the lever of the thrust will, as before, be $a + d$, and its algebraic expression be $pa + pd$.

1450. The pier resists this effort by its cube multiplied by the arm of its lever. If the lines KB and OB of the triangle BKO, (which represents the projection of that part of the vault for which we are calculating) be produced, it will be seen that the base of the pier to resist the thrust will be represented by the opposite triangle BHF, which is rectangular and isosceles; therefore, letting *x* represent its side BF, the area of the triangle will be expressed by $\frac{x^2}{2}$, the

height of the pier being a, its cube will be $\frac{ax^2}{2}$. The arm of the lever of this pier will be determined by the distance of the vertical let fall from its centre of gravity on the line $HF = \frac{x}{3}$, which gives for the pier's resistance $\frac{ax^3}{6}$.

1451. This resistance will be increased by the vertical effort of each part of the vault multiplied by the arm of its lever.

That of the upper part will be expressed by its cube multiplied by the vertical KM, and the product divided by the mean arc KG.

The cube of this part will be equal to the mean area; that is, the arc KG multiplied by the thickness of the vault.

1452. To obtain the mean area, multiply KG less KM by the length GO taken on the plan. The length of the arc KG being 46 and KM $17\frac{1}{4}$, we shall have $KG - KM = 28\frac{6}{7}$; GO being 54, the mean area will be $28\frac{6}{7} \times 54 = 1558$. This area multiplied by 9, the thickness of the vault, makes the cube of the upper part $14024\frac{1}{4}$, which multiplied by $KM = 17\frac{1}{4}$ and divided by the arc $KG = 46$, makes $5226\frac{1}{4}$ the value of the vertical effort of the part of the arch m in the formula; and the arm of its lever is $IK + iH$.

1453. IK being $= c$ and $iH = x$, its expression will be $mx + mc$.

The vertical effort of the lower part will be represented by its cube multiplied by TI, and the product divided by the length of the arc TK.

This cube will be found by multiplying the mean area by the thickness of the vault. The area being equal to the arc $TK - TI \times GO$, that is, $46 - 41\frac{5}{14} \times 54 = 250\frac{5}{7}$ for the mean area and $250\frac{5}{7} \times 9 = 2256\frac{2}{7}$ for the cube of the lower part of the vault. This cube multiplied by TI and divided by the arc TK gives $\frac{2256\frac{2}{7} \times 41\frac{5}{14}}{6} = 2028\frac{2}{3}$ for the value of the vertical effort of the part n of the formula. And it is to be observed, that this effort acting against the point B, the arm BF of the lever will be x and its expression nx.

1454. Bringing together all these algebraic values we obtain the equation $pa + pd = \frac{ax^3}{6}$ $+ mx + mc + nx$; and making $m + n$, which multiplies $x = b$, we have $pa + pd = \frac{ax^3}{6} + bx + mc$. Transferring mc to the other side of the equation, we have $pa + pd - mc = \frac{ax^3}{6} + bx$.

Lastly, multiplying all the terms of the equation by $\frac{6}{a}$ for the purpose of eliminating x^3, we shall have instead of the preceding formula $6p + \frac{6pd - 6mc}{a} = x^3 + \frac{6bx}{a}$, which is an equation of the third degree, whose second term is wanting. For more easily resolving this equation, let us find the value of $6p + \frac{6pd - 6mc}{a}$ and that of $\frac{6b}{a}$, by which x is multiplied in the second part of the equation.

p being $11683\frac{2}{3}$, $6p$ will be   - - - - $= 70069\frac{2}{3}$

d being $41\frac{5}{14}$, $6pd$ will be   - - - $= 2899124\frac{2}{3}$

m being $5226\frac{2}{3}$, $6mc$ - - - - $= 537593\frac{1}{7}$

Thus $\frac{6pd - 6mc}{a} = \frac{2361537\frac{7}{9}}{120} = 19679\frac{5}{14}$, and $6p + \frac{6pd - 6mc}{a} = 89779\frac{1}{4}$, which we will call g, for the purpose of simplifying the remainder of the calculation.

b, which represents $m + n$, will be $5226\frac{2}{3} + 2038\frac{2}{3} = 7255\frac{2}{3}$, and $\frac{6b}{a} = \frac{43534}{120} = 362\frac{2}{3}$; this we will call f; so that instead of the equation $6p + \frac{6pd - 6mc}{a} = x^3 + \frac{6bx}{a}$, we have $g = x^3 + fx$, which is thus to be resolved (Bossut, *Élémens d'Algèbre*):—

$$x = \sqrt[3]{\frac{g}{2} + \sqrt[2]{\frac{g^2}{4} + \frac{f^3}{27}}} + \sqrt[3]{\frac{g}{2} - \sqrt[2]{\frac{g^2}{4} + \frac{f^3}{27}}}.$$

Substituting in this formula the values of g and f, we have

$$x = \sqrt[3]{44889\frac{4}{7} + \sqrt[2]{2015073623 + 1767902}} + \sqrt[3]{44889\frac{4}{7} - \sqrt[2]{2015073623 + 1767902}}$$

$= \sqrt[3]{44889\frac{4}{7} + 44909\frac{2}{7}} + \sqrt[3]{44889\frac{4}{7} - 44909\frac{2}{7}}$, from which extracting the cube roots, we have $x = 44\frac{3}{4} - 2\frac{3}{4} = 42$ for the length BF of one of the sides of the triangular pier BAF; the other FA may be determined by the production of the diagonal or line of groin OB.

The part of the pier answering to the part of the vault BNO is determined by drawing from the points B and A the parallels BM and MA to FA and FB. These two triangles will form a square base, each of whose sides will be 42 lines, answering to one quarter of the vault KBNO; thus, to resist the thrust of the vault, four piers, each 42 lines thick, are necessary.

1455. The above result corresponds in a singular manner with the experiments which were made by Rondelet, from which he deduced a thickness of $43\frac{1}{2}$ lines. In his investigation of the example by means of the centres of gravity $40\cdot53$ lines was the result. Our limits prevent further consideration by other examples: we will merely therefore observe, that

the method above given seems to be a safe guide to the architect.   In the case of oblong arches, the results must be obtained for each side.

1456.   In the case of groinings composed of many bays, the chief care necessary is in the external piers, which will require especially to be of sufficient thickness.   Those in the middle, being counterbalanced all round, have only to bear the weights of their respective arches, for which purpose they must have a proportional area and be of such stone as the weight will not crush.   But it ought to be recollected that in good construction the area of the points of support should be so distributed as to establish for each a sufficient strength, because a single weak point will often endanger the whole fabric.

1457.   In practice, a readier method will be wanting than that which has been just discussed; we therefore subjoin one which agrees well enough with theory and experiment, and it is as follows.   Let ABCD (*fig. 585.* No. 1.) be the space to be covered by a

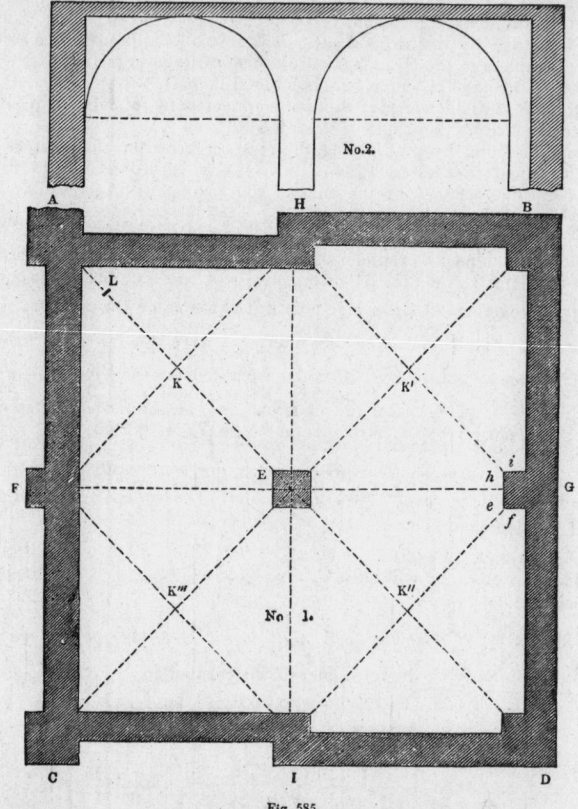

Fig. 585.

groined vault supported in the centre by the pier E.   Dividing each side into two equal parts, draw the lines HI, FG crossing each other in the centre E, and the diagonals AE, EB, EC, ED and HF, HG, IF, IG crossing each other in the points K, K$'$, K$''$, K$'''$. In No. 2. draw the pier its half height to the level of the springing, which half height transfer from K to L, and divide EL into twelve parts.   One of these parts will be a half diagonal of the pier.   For the intermediate piers H, F, I, G, after finding the diagonals of the half piers, produce them outwards to double their projection within, so that altogether their thickness may be once and a half their width.   For the angular piers this method will give an area of base 1½ times greater, which will enable them to resist the thrust they have to sustain.

1458.   When the width of the space to be vaulted is to be divided into three bays, and that of the middle is required to be raised above those of the other two, as in the case of churches with side aisles, the bases of the points of support may be determined in two ways.   That most used, which is borrowed from the Gothic examples, is to give to the areas of the bases of the points of support merely the extent necessary to bear the load they

are to receive, by throwing the strain of the thrust upon the external piers by means of flying buttresses, and giving to their points of support a position and surface of base capable of effectual resistance.

1459. The most simple method derived from the principles of the theory for the first case is as follows : —

Having laid down the plan of the two bays which fall upon the same pier (*fig.* 586. No. 1.), take one half of the sum of the two semi-diagonals A D, A E, to which add one

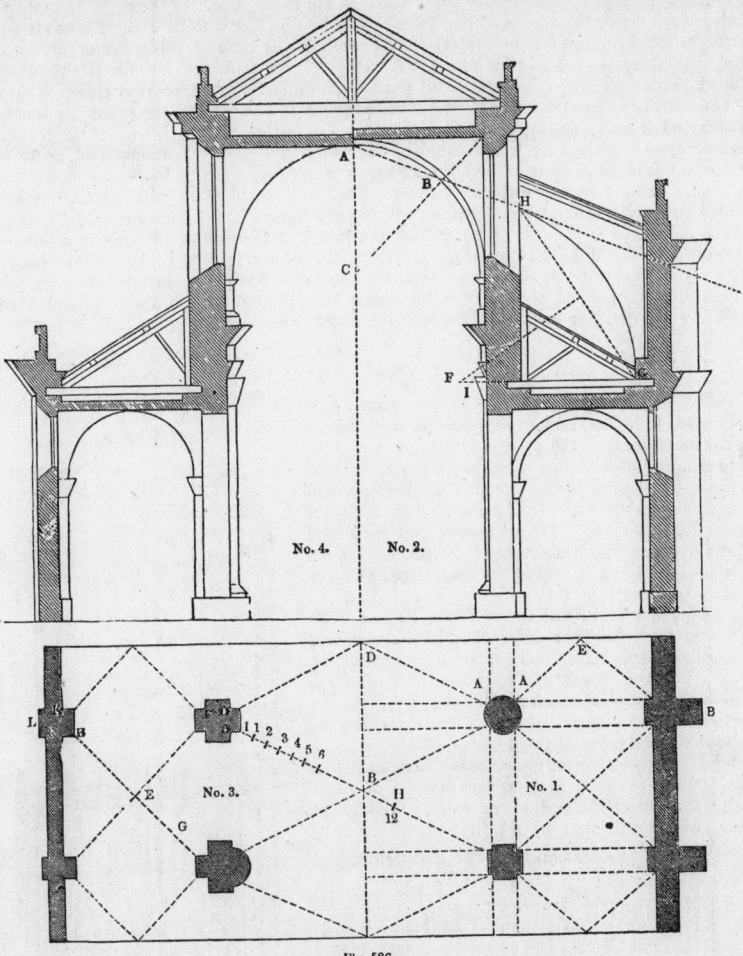

Fig. 586.

half of the height of the point of support, and taking a twelfth part of the whole as a radius, describe a circle as A, No. 1, it will show the surface of the base of the point of support. If it be not circular it must be circumscribed with the form that may be required, so as rather to increase than diminish its solidity. For the exterior point of support B, let a rectangle be formed, having for its width the side of a square inscribed in the preceding circle, and in length double.

1460. Above the roofs of the sides a flying buttress may be carried up, whose pier may be raised on that below, set back one sixth from the exterior face and sloped as much on the interior. The line of summit or tangent of this flying buttress, which should be of the single arc of a circle, will be determined by the chord of the arc of the upper part of the vault produced indefinitely. To find the centre, draw the chord G H (No. 2.), on the middle of which raise a perpendicular, which will cut the horizontal line G F in the point I, which will be the centre of the arc. These raking arches may be connected by

other return arches, which may bear a floor above with a support, upon which a passage round the building may be made, and this may be concealed by an attic order outside.

1461. In the second case, the base of a pier must be found capable of resisting the effort of the great middle vault of the nave, by taking as the height of its pier the distance from its springing from the upper side of the side vaults No. 2., and laying the half of this height from B to H on the plan No. 3. Then having divided IH into twelve equal parts, make IA equal to one of them and AF equal to two. The rectangle made upon the diagonal FI shows the area of the interior pier, to which are to be added, to the right and left, projections to receive the arches of the sides. The length FD is to be divided into six equal parts, whereof two are for the projection of the pilaster or interior half column, upon which the entablature is profiled, three for the thickness of the wall, and one for the pilaster on the side aisles, whose prolongation will form a counterfort above the lower sides.

1462. For the external pier B, as before, one half the height to the springing must be transferred from EG, and $\frac{1}{12}$ of BG from B to L; lastly, $\frac{2}{12}$ from B to K: the rectangle formed upon the diagonal KL is equal to the area of the pier. We must add, as for that in front, the projections to receive the arches or windows, as shown in No. 2.

1463. As long as the intervals between the piers are filled in with a wall, if that be placed flush with the outside, the piers will form pilasters inwards (see *fig.* 585.), as *ihef*, whose projection *ef* is equal to one half of the face *he*; this wall ought to have a thickness equal to *he*; but if it is brought to the inner line of the face of the piers they need be only two thirds of the thickness; so that the piers will form counterforts on the exterior. In conclusion, knowing the effort of the thrust, the calculations will not be attended with difficulty in providing against it by adequate means of resistance.

ON THE MODEL OF A COVED VAULT.

1464. The model (*fig.* 587. Nos. 1. and 2.) is square on the plan, each of its sides is 9 inches internal measure, enclosed by a wall 10 inches high to the springing of the vault. The vault is semicircular in form, the voussoirs throughout 9 lines thick, and it is composed of seventeen parts above the line of greatest effort (see 1391.), as shown in Nos. 1. and 2. in the plan and section. On one of the sides of the first is supposed to be traced the mean circumference TKG, the tangents FT, FG, the secant FO, the horizontal line IKL, and the verticals B*i* and MK. We may now therefore consider this vault as four triangular pieces of cylindrical arches, each resting throughout the length of their base on one of the walls which forms the sides of the square. As the portions of arches or vaults are equal, it is only necessary to take one of them for an example.

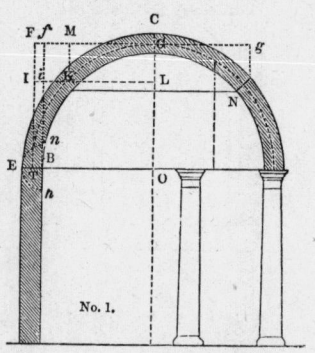

1465. In the last example, cubes are taken instead of the surfaces, and surfaces instead of lines. Thus expressing the length of the wall by *f*, its height by *a*, and its thickness by *x*; the arm of the lever being always $\frac{x}{2}$, its resistance is expressed by $afx\frac{x}{2}$.

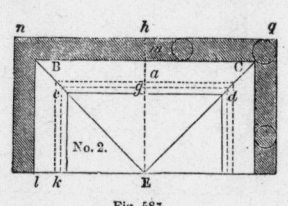

Fig. 587.

Making the thrust - - - - $= p$
EH $=$ TI $=$ KL $=$ KV - - - - $= d$
PH - - - - - $= a + d$
The sum of the vertical efforts of the upper part - $= m$
That of the lower parts - - - - $= n$
The part IK of the horizontal line - - - $= c$
TB $=$ half the thickness of the arch - - - $= e$
The arm of the lever will be - - - $= c + x$
TE - - - - - $= x - e,$

The equation is $pa + pd = \dfrac{afx^2}{2} + (m + n)\,x - ne + mc$;

and making $m + n = b$,

$$\frac{afx^2}{2} + bx = pa + pa + ne - mc$$

Whence $x = \sqrt{\dfrac{2p}{f} + \dfrac{2pd + 2ne - 2mc}{af} + \dfrac{b^2}{a^2f^2}} - \dfrac{b}{af}$

1466. If, however, we suppose the effort to take place at the point B, a supposition hitherto made in the formulæ, we have $e = o$, and the value of x becomes

$$x = \sqrt{\dfrac{2p}{f} + \dfrac{2pd - 2mc}{af} + \dfrac{b^2}{a^2f^2}} - \dfrac{b}{af}.$$

1467. The horizontal effort of the upper part, represented by the line KL, will be expressed by the triangle eEd of the plan; that of the lower part iK in the section will be expressed by the trapezium $eBCd$ on the plan.

1468. The plan of the vault being square, the base ed will be double Eg = KL of the section; and the area of the triangle eEd equal to the square of KL $= 41\frac{5}{14} \times 41\frac{5}{14} = 1710\frac{2}{7}$.

1469. Ea of the plan being equal to the square of 54 less the square of $41\frac{5}{14}$, that is, $1206\frac{2}{7}$, the superior effort being $1710\frac{2}{7}$, their difference is 504, which being multiplied by the thickness of the vault, or 9, is 4536 for the expression of the thrust represented by p in the formula, and for that of

$$2p = 9072 \text{ and } \frac{2p}{f} = 84,$$

d, which represents TI, being $41\frac{5}{14}$, $2pd = 375192$.

1470. To obtain the vertical effort of the upper part of the arch represented by m, its cube must be multiplied by KM, and the product divided by the arc KG.

1471. The cube of this part is equal to the curved surface passing through the middle of its thickness multiplied by the thickness. The mean area is equal to the product of the length nq taken on the plan multiplied by KM.

nq being 117, and KM $17\frac{1}{4}$, the product expressing such mean area is $2005\frac{5}{7}$, which multiplied by 9 makes the cube $18051\frac{1}{4}$. This cube again multiplied by KM $= 17\frac{1}{4}$, and divided by the length of arc KG $= 46$, gives 6727 for the value of m, and for $2m$ 13454; c being $12\frac{9}{14}$, $2mc = 170100\frac{5}{7}$.

$$\frac{2pd - 2mc}{af} = \frac{375192 - 170100\frac{5}{7}}{120 \times 108} = 15 \cdot 82.$$

b, representing the vertical effort of the half vault, will be expressed by the cube multiplied by $Bf = 58\frac{1}{4}$, and divided by the mean circumference TKG $= 92$.

1472. To obtain the cube, the mean superficies, that is, $nq \times Bf$ or $117 \times 58\frac{1}{4}$, is to be multiplied by the thickness AB $= 9$, which gives $6844\frac{1}{2} \times 9 = 61600\frac{1}{2}$.

This cube multiplied by $Bf = 58\frac{1}{4}$ and divided by the mean circumference TKG $= 92$, that is, $61600\frac{1}{2} \times \dfrac{58\frac{1}{4}}{92} = 39169 \cdot 88$, for the value of b, and for that of $\dfrac{b}{a}, \dfrac{39169 \cdot 88}{120 \times 108} = 3 \cdot 02$ and $\dfrac{b^2}{a^2} = 9 \cdot 12$. Substituting these values in the formula,

$$x = \sqrt{\left(\frac{2p}{f} + \frac{2pd - 2mc}{af} + \frac{bb}{a^2f^2}\right)} - \frac{b}{af}.$$

Hence $x = \sqrt{84 + 15 \cdot 82 + 9 \cdot 12} - 3 \cdot 02 = 7 \cdot 41$;

that is, a little less than $7\frac{1}{2}$ lines for the thickness of the walls, which is less than that of the vault; and shows that by giving the walls the same thickness as the vault, all the requisite solidity will be obtained. This is proved by experiments, for in the model the vault was borne equally well on walls of 9 lines in thickness divided into 8 parts, as upon 12 Doric columns whose diameter was 9 lines, four being placed at the angles and eight others under the lower part of the vault.

1473. To find the thickness of these walls by the geometrical method: Take the difference between the area of the triangle BEC and that of the triangle Eed, which divide by the length BC.

Thus, the area of the greater triangle being $\dfrac{108 \times 54}{2} = 2916$; that of the smaller one, $\dfrac{82\frac{5}{7} \times 41\frac{5}{14}}{2} = 1710 \cdot 4$; their difference, $1205 \cdot 6$ divided by $108 = 11 \cdot 16$, which transfer to the profile from B to h, and make Bn equal to the thickness of the vault. Upon nh, as a diameter, describe a semicircle, which at its intersection with the horizontal line BE will determine the thickness of the vault, and be found to be 10 lines.

1474. The small thrust of this species of vaulting occurs on account of the upper part, which causes it, diminishing in volume in proportion as the horizontal effort becomes more considerable, and because the triangular form of its parts and their position give it the advantage of having the larger sides for bases; whilst, in groined vaulting, the triangular parts resting only on an angle, the weight increases as the horizontal efforts.

1475. Moreover, as the return sides mutually sustain each other, a half vault, or even a quarter vault, on a square base, would stand if the walls were 10 lines thick, proving that

the opposite parts, acting little more than against each other, the thrust becomes almost nothing.

1476. By the method of the centres of gravity, Rondelet found a result less than that above given; but that arose from neglecting some points in the calculation which it was difficult to introduce for general practice.

1477. It is obvious that in the above application great allowance must be made when the apartment to be vaulted is not square; that is, its advantages diminish as the two opposite sides become longer than the width, and when the length is twice the width, or even much less, the thrusts must be calculated on the principle of cylindrical vaulting; and as in this species of vaulting the greatest effort occurs in or towards the middle of the sides, opening for doors and windows should there be avoided.

Application of the Method to Spherical (or domical) Vaulting.

1478. The models (*fig.* 588. Nos. 1. and 2. and *fig.* 589. Nos. 1. and 2.) were of the

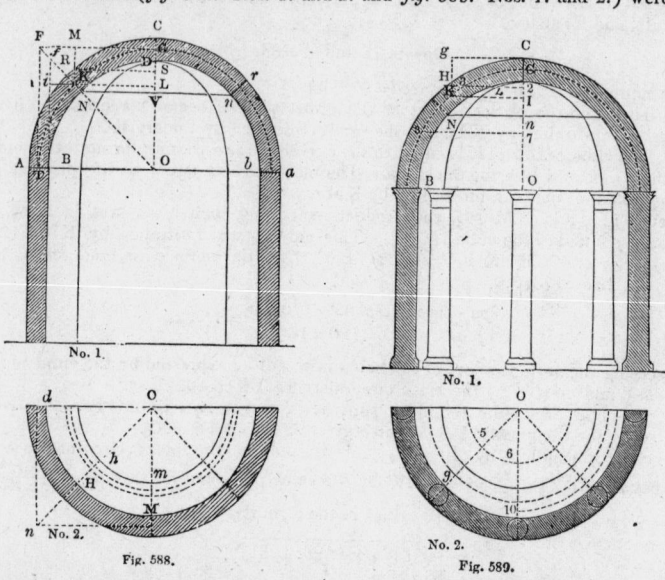

Fig. 588.　　　　　　　　　　　Fig. 589.

same opening as the last mentioned. They are cut into eight equal parts by vertical planes crossing each other in the axis; each of these parts is subdivided by a joint at 45 degrees, altogether forming sixteen pieces. The vault stands on a circular wall of the same thickness divided into eight parts corresponding to those of the vault. All the parts are so arranged as to form continued joints without any bond, in order to give the experiment the most disadvantageous result. Yet it stood firmly, and was even capable of bearing a weight on the top.

1479. If for these eight pieces of circular wall we substitute eight columns of equal height, as in No. 1. *fig.* 589., so that the vertical joints fall over the middle of each column; the vault will still stand, although the cube of these columns, as well as their weight, occupies only one ninth part of the circular wall for which they are substituted.

From this it is evident that spherical vaults, i.e., domes, have less thrusts than coved vaults.

1480. Applying the method of the preceding examples, describe the mean circumference (*fig.* 588. Nos. 1. and 2.), draw the tangents TF, GF, the secant FO, the horizontal line IKL, and the verticals KM and Bi; lastly, calculating for one eighth of the vault, take the sector Ohm to express the horizontal effort indicated by KL, and the part HhMm to express the horizontal effort of the lower part.

1481. The difference of these areas multiplied by the thickness of the vault will be the expression of the thrust p of the formula.

1482. The radius Om of the sector being $41\frac{5}{14}$ and its length $32\frac{1}{2}$, its area will be $672\frac{3}{56}$.

1483. The area of hHMm will be equal to the difference of the two sectors OHM and Ohm, whereof the first is equal to the product of half OM = 27 by the arc HM = $42\frac{3}{4}$, or $1145\frac{4}{7}$, the second $= 672\frac{3}{56}$; whence the difference $= 473\frac{39}{56}$.

1484. The thrust, being equal to the difference between $672\frac{3}{56}$ and $473\frac{39}{56}$, will be $198\frac{15}{48} \times 9$; therefore $p = 786\frac{23}{24}$.

1485. f, representing the developement of one eighth part of the circular wall, will be $42\frac{1}{2}$, whence $\frac{p}{f}=42$. d, the difference between the arm of the lever and the height of the pier, being $41\frac{5}{14}$, we shall have $pd=73897\frac{4}{7}$.

1486. To obtain the value of mc we must first find that of m, which represents the vertical effort of the upper part of the vault, and is equal to the cube of this part multiplied by KM and divided by the arc KG. This cube is equal to the difference of the cube of the sector of a sphere in which it is comprised with that which forms its interior capacity. We will merely recall here to the reader's recollection from a previous page, that the cube of the sector of a sphere is equal to the product of the superficies of the sphere whereof it forms a part by one third of the radius, and that this superficies is equal to the product of the circumference of a great circle by the line which measures its depth. Thus the area of the great sector ORCr (*fig.* 588. No. 1.) is equal to the product of the great circle, whereof Aa is the diameter $=126$, by CS$=18\frac{5}{11}$, which is 7308, and its cube 7308 $\times 21 = 153468$.

1487. The area of the small sector ONDn will be equal to the product of the great circle, whereof Bb is the diameter $=108$ by VD$=15\frac{9}{11}$, which gives $5369\frac{27}{77}$, and its cube by $5369\frac{27}{77}\times 18 = 96648\frac{24}{77}$. Deducting this last cube from that of the great sector already found $=153468$, the remainder 56819 will be the cube of the upper part of the vault forming the cap, whose eighth part $7102\frac{3}{8}$ will be the cube sought, which multiplied by KM$=17\frac{1}{2}$ and divided by the arc KG$=46$, gives $2646\frac{2}{3}$ for the value of m in the formula; c, which represents iK, being $12\frac{9}{14}$, we have

$$mc=33461\frac{3}{7}; \quad pd-mc \text{ will be } 73897\frac{4}{7}-33461\frac{3}{7}=40436\frac{1}{7};$$

$$\text{and for } \frac{pd-mc}{af}, \quad \frac{40436\frac{1}{7}}{120\times 42\frac{1}{2}}=7\cdot 92.$$

1488. In the preceding application to the model of the coved vault, the walls being straight, the distance of their centre of gravity from the point of support was equal to half their thickness; in this, the wall being circular, its centre of gravity is so much more distant from the point of support as it takes in more or less a greater part of the circumference of the circle. By taking it only the eighth part, the centre of gravity falls without the thickness of the walls, by a quantity which we shall call e, so that the arm of the lever, instead of being $\frac{x}{2}$, will be $e+x$, which changes the preceding formula to

$$afx(e+x)+bx=pa+pd-mc;$$

arranging with reference to x, this becomes

$$afx^2+(eaf+b)x=pa+pd-mc;$$

whence we obtain $x^2+(e+\frac{b}{af})x=\frac{pa+pd-mc}{af}$, and making $e+\frac{af}{b}=2h$, we shall have

$$x=\sqrt{-\frac{p}{f}+\frac{pd-mc}{af}+h^2}-h.$$

b expresses the vertical effort of an eighth part of the vault equal to its cube, multiplied by the vertical Bf, and divided by the mean circumference TKG. This cube is equal to an eighth of the sphere, whereof Aa is the diameter, less that of the eighth part of a sphere whose diameter is Bb.

1489. The diameter Aa being 126, the eighth of the circumference of a great circle will be $49\frac{1}{2}$, which, multiplied by the vertical axis, which in this case is equal to the radius or 63, gives for the area of one eighth part of the sphere $3118\frac{1}{2}$, and for its cube $3118\frac{1}{2}\times 21 = 65688\frac{1}{2}$.

1490. The diameter Bb being 108, an eighth part of the circumference of the great circle will be $42\frac{3}{4}$, which, multiplied by the radius 54, gives for the area $2291\frac{1}{7}$, and for its cube $2291\frac{1}{7}\times 18 = 41240\frac{4}{7}$; taking the smaller of these cubes from the greater, the difference $24447\frac{13}{14}$ will be that of this eighth part of the vault, which must be multiplied by B$f=$ $58\frac{1}{2}$, and the product $1430203\frac{33}{28}$, divided by the mean arc TKG$=91\frac{6}{7}$; the quotient 15558 expresses the vertical effort of the eighth part of the vault, represented by b in the formula, whence $\frac{b}{af}=\frac{15558}{5100}=3\cdot 05$.

e being $2\cdot 51$, we shall have for the value of h $2\cdot 78$ and $h^2=7\cdot 72$.

Substituting the values thus found in the formula

$$x=\sqrt{\frac{p}{f}+\frac{pd-mc}{af}+h^2}-h,$$

we have $x=\sqrt{42+7\cdot 92+7\cdot 72}-2\cdot 78=\sqrt{57\cdot 64}-2\cdot 78=4\cdot 72$.

By using the method of the centres of gravity, Rondelet found the result rather less than that just found.

1491. The result of all these calculations induces the following facts: — I. That for a

semicircular cylindrical vault, whose length is equal to its diameter, the area of the two parallel walls is 4698. II. That that of the four square piers supporting a groined arch is 7056. III. That of the four walls of the coved vault, the area should be 3425⅔. IV. That that of the spherical vault is 1238⅙.

1492. In respect of the opening of these vaults, which is the same for all the examples, taking the area of the circular wall for the spherical vault at 1,

That of the walls of the coved vault will be a little less than 3.

That of the cylindrical vault　　-　　-　　less than 4.

That of the groined arch　　　　　-　　　less than 6.

But if we look to the space that each of these vaults occupies in respect of walls and points of support, we shall find that in equal areas the walls of the cylindrical vault will be $\frac{2}{7}$ of such space.

Those of the coved vaulting less than　　-　　$\frac{1}{4}$ of such space.

The piers of the groined arch a little more than　-　$\frac{1}{7}$　——

The circular wall for spherical vault a little more than $\frac{2}{17}$　——

So that, if we suppose the space occupied by each of these vaults to be 400,

The walls of the cylindrical vaulting will be 115

Those for the coved vault　　-　　-　　91

The piers for the groined arch　-　　60

The circular wall for the spherical vault -　48

Which figures therefore show the relative proportions of the points of support necessary in each case.

1493. It is a remarkable circumstance that by the formula the coved and spherical vaults give to the walls a less thickness than that of the arch. But although experiment has verified the formula, we cannot be supposed to recommend that they should be made of less thickness in practice; but we see that, if of the same thickness, considerable openings may be used in them. Irregular as well as regular compound vaults being only an assemblage of the parts of more simple ones, if what has already been said be well understood, and the examples given have been worked out by the student, he will not be much at a loss in determining the efforts of all sorts of vaults.

On the adhesive Power of Mortar and Plaster upon Stones and Bricks.

1494. The power of mortar and plaster will of course be in proportion to the surface of the joints, compared with the masses of stone, brick, or rubble. Thus a voussoir of wrought stone, one foot cube, may be connected with the adjoining voussoirs by four joints, each of 1 foot area, in all 4 feet. But if instead of this voussoir three pieces of rough stone or rubble be substituted instead of 4 feet area of joints, we shall have 8. Lastly, if bricks be employed instead of rubble, we shall want 27 to form the same mass, which gives for the developement of the joints 13 feet. Thus, representing the force which connects the voussoirs in wrought stone by 4, that representing the joints of the rough stones will be 8, and that for bricks 13: whence we may infer that arches built with rough stones will have less thrust than those in wrought stone, and those in bricks more than three times less. From experiments made by Rondelet, he found that at the end of six months some species of mortar showed a capability of uniting bricks with sufficient force to overcome the efforts of thrust in a vault segmental to $\frac{2}{3}$ of a semicircle, 15 feet diameter and 4 inches thick, the extrados being 4 inches concentrically above the intrados. Plaster united a vaulted arch of 18 feet opening, of the same form and thickness. This force is, moreover, greater in arches whose voussoirs increase from the keystone to the springing, and that in proportion to the thickness at the haunches, where fracture takes place; so that whatever the diameter and form of the arch, the strength of good mortar at the end of six months, if the arches are well constructed, is capable of suppressing the thrust as long as the thickness, taken at the middle of the haunches, is stronger than the tenth part of those laid in mortar, and one twelfth of those laid in plaster. Here we have to observe, that arches laid in plaster, as long as they are kept dry and sheltered from the changes of the season, preserve their strength, but, on the contrary, they lose all their stability in seven or eight years, whilst those cemented in mortar endure for ages.

1495. The small quantity of mortar or of plaster used in vaults constructed of wrought stone, in which the joints are often little more than *run*, ought to make an architect cautious of depending merely on the cementing medium for uniting the voussoirs. There are other means which he may employ in cases of doubt, such as *dowels* and *cramps*, means which were much employed by the Romans in their construction; and these are far better than the chains and ties of iron introduced by the moderns.

1495a. Rondelet has stated that hard stones laid dry, commenced slipping at an angle of 30°; and with mortar fresh laid, at angles of 34° and 36°; with soft stones, on mortar fresh laid, at 45°, when the centre of gravity did not fall without the base. In

Barlow's edition of Tredgold's work, from 34° to 36°, is repeated.   G. Rennie, in some careful experiments at London Bridge, found that dressed voussoirs commenced sliding, without mortar, at an angle of 33° 30′ ; and, with mortar fresh laid, at 25° 30′.

1496. Well may it be said that the thrust of an arch is the constant dread of an architect ; but it depends entirely on the method employed in the construction. It is only dangerous where the precautions indicated in the foregoing examples have had no attention paid to them. It has been seen that the least fracture in too thin an arch of equally deep voussoirs may cause its ruin ; and we shall here add, that this defect is more dangerous in arches wherein the number of joints is many, such as those constructed in brick ; for when they are laid in mortar they are too often rather heaped together than well fitted to each other.

1497. Whatever materials are used in the construction of vaults, the great object is to prevent separation, which, if it occur, must be immediately met by measures for making the resistance of the lower parts capable of counterbalancing the effort of the upper parts. Those fractures which occur in cylindrical arches are the most dangerous, because they take place in straight lines which run along parallel to the walls bearing them.   To avoid the consequences of such failures, it is well to fill up the haunches to the height where the fracture is usually to be found, as in K, K′, K″, K‴ (*fig.* 590.) and diminish the thickness towards the key.

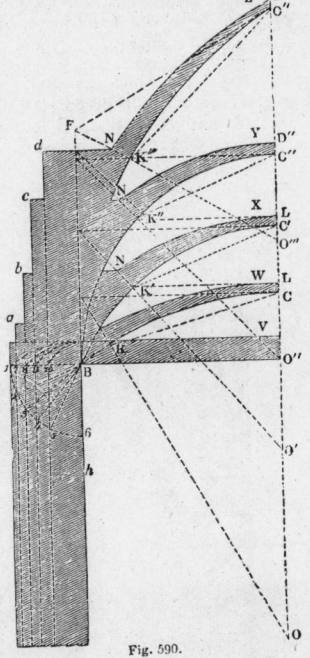

Fig. 590.

1498. Rondelet found, and so indeed did Couplet before him, that the least thickness which an arch of equal voussoirs ought to have, to be capable of standing, was one fiftieth part of the radius.   But as the bricks and stone employed in the construction of arches are never so perfectly formed as the theory supposes, the least thickness which can be used for cylindrical arches from 9 to 15 feet radius is $4\frac{1}{2}$ inches at the vertex if the lower course be laid with a course of brick on edge or two courses flatwise, and 5 inches when the material used is not a very hard stone, increasing the thickness from the keystone to the point where the extrados leaves the walls or piers.   But if the haunches are filled up to the point N (*fig.* 590.), it will be found that for the pointed arch in the figure the thickness need not be more than the $\frac{1}{43}$ of the radius, and for the semicircular arch, $\frac{1}{60}$.   For arches whose height is less than their opening or that are segmental the thickness should be $\frac{1}{8}$ part of the versed sine ; a practice also applicable to Gothic vaults and semicircular cylindrical arches, to which for vaults cemented with plaster one line should be added for each foot in length, or $\frac{1}{14}$ part of the chord subtended by the extrados.   With vaults executed in mortar $\frac{1}{96}$ may be added, the thickness of the arch increasing till it reaches the point N, where the arch becomes detached from the haunches, and where it should be once and a half the thickness of the key. It was in this way the arches throughout the Pantheon at Paris were regulated, and a very similar sort of expedient is practised in the dome of the Pantheon at Rome.   A like diminution at the keystone may be used in groined, coved, and spherical vaults.

1499. For vaultings of large openings, Rondelet (and we fully concur with him) thinks wrought stone preferable to brick or rubble stone, because it has the advantage of being liable to less settlement and stands more independent of any cementitious medium employed.   It is indeed true that this cannot connect wrought stone so powerfully as it does rubble ; but in the former we can employ cramps and dowells at the joints, which are useful in doubtful cases to prevent derangement of the parts.   In many Roman ruins the surfaces of the voussoirs were embossed and hollowed at the joints, for the purpose of preventing their sliding upon each other ; and expedients of the same nature are frequently found in Gothic ruins.

1499a. The figure 590. is one that has been found to perplex students, as it is herein given without much explanation of it.   In Rondelet's work it is engraved for the purpose of elucidating certain tables of thicknesses of the keystones, the parts KN, and the piers, for ready reference in designing arched constructions.   As a proper understanding of the above system is of immense importance to the effective carrying out of buildings, we append an explanation from Rondelet, but in a much abridged form.

1499b. Having laid down the half of the curve required, draw B 4, forming an angle of 45° with the vertical B 6 ; place on this line from B to 4 the thickness shown in the table (in his work) for a cylindrical vault Y, of the diameter and thickness required, and describe the quarter circle 1, 4, 6 ; draw the chord C″B, prolonged to meet the circle at 4 ; then through the point in which it (the chord) will be cut, as 4 ; draw a line parallel to B 6 ; then 4c will represent the thickness required for the wall of the vault. For instance, if in the segmental vault X, its chord C′ B, be prolonged, it will cut the circle at 3 ; through 3 draw the vertical 3b, and it will be the thickness to be given to the wall for such a vault. When the thickness at the key, and towards the middle of the extrados, is required either stronger or weaker than those indicated in the tables, then, if the portion of the extradossed line be of an *equal thickness,* take the square root of the double thickness of this portion, multiplied by mL ; place it from B to 4, and describe the quarter of the circle 1, 4, 6, which will determine, by the length of the chord prolonged beyond the point B, the thickness of the wall pier.

1499c. Take a vault of 30 ft. span ; the extrados being half on a level and half of an *equal thickness,* which it is intended to make only 6 in. thick at the key, instead of 10 in., as indicated in the tables. The radius being 15 ft., we have $KL = \frac{15 \times 70}{99} = 10 \cdot 6$, and $iK = 15 - 10 \cdot 6 = 4 \cdot 4$, which gives $mL = 6 \cdot 2$, which multiplied by 1 foot, or double the thickness of the keystone, will give 6·2, the square foot of which is 2·49, or a trifle under 2 ft. 6 in., instead of 2 ft. 8 in. and 9 lines, marked in the tables. This measure of $2\frac{49}{100}$ ft.,

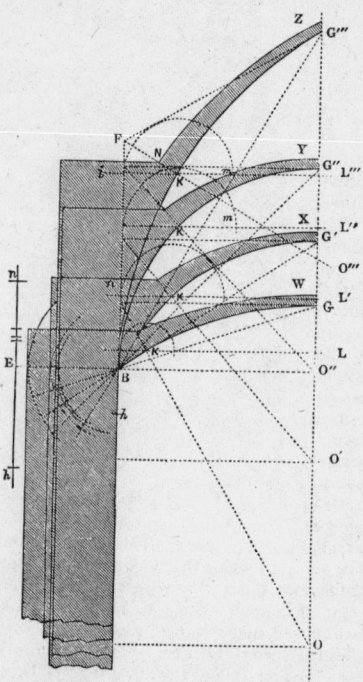

Fig. 590a.

or 2 ft. 6 in., is to be placed from B to 4, and the quarter circle and chord line drawn according to the rise of the arch.

1499d. The geometrical method of drawing it will be to place the double of the thickness of the vault from B to n, and mL from B to h, and describing on nh, as a diameter, a semicircle which shall cut the horizontal BO, giving the thickness to be placed from B to 4 on the chord line ; the remainder of the operation will be as above described.

1499e. If the thickness CD and KN of an extrados portion of a vault, be not the same as indicated in the tables, the sum of the thicknesses intended to be given is to be placed from B to n, and mL from B to h, and then the process goes on as above described. The letters also refer to the preceding diagrams.

1499f. These observations, however, do not apply to *fig.* 590., for it will be observed that the arches therein shown are *not* of equal thickness. On drawing out these arches, according to the directions given (1436, and *fig.* 582.), for an extrados which increases towards the springing (*fig.* 590a.), we find that the chord lines are not properly drawn ; that the thicknesses of the walls vary ; and that the two arches W and X, which are less in height than the semicircular arch Y, are treated in the same manner as Y, instead of the line BF being drawn as a tangent to the curve as directed (1398, and *fig.* 573.) ; this would have caused the walls to be of a *less thickness* the more the arch was depressed, and therefore would evidently have been wrong in principle.

CONSTRUCTION OF DOMES.

1499g. From the *Remarks on Theatres,* 1809, by Samuel Ware, we extract the portion relating to the now little studied subject of construction of domes. " It may with propriety be asked," he writes, " and it is a question of much importance, what are the properties in the construction of a dome, by which its vaulting may have that extreme tenuity, by which its lateral thrust becomes so extremely small in comparison with cylindrical vaulting, while the stone furthest from the supports may be of extraordinary gravity, compared with any other part of the vaulting, or it and any part below it contiguous may be wholly omitted, and yet the equilibrium of the dome be not affected."

1499h. " In analysing a dome, it will be found that it is nothing more than rib-vaulting carried to its maximum, that it consists of as many ribs as there are vertical sections to be made in the dome, or is composed wholly of ribs abutting against each other, in direct opposition, by which the force of each is destroyed. In the ceilings of King's College Chapel, Cambridge, and Henry VII.'s Chapel, London, this most admirable invention is exemplified. The author ventures an hypothesis, that, in an *equilibrated dome*, the thickness of the vaulting will decrease from the vertex to the springing, and assigns the following reason theoretically, and the Gothic vaulting practically, in confirmation.

1499i. " The parts of a circular wall compose a horizontal arch; but the whole gravity of each part is resisted by the bed on which it rests, therefore the parts cannot be in mutual opposition; and, although the parts are posited like those of an arch, a circular wall has not the properties of one. In a semi-spherical dome the first course answers this description, no part gravitating in the direction of its radius. When the beds are oblique on which the parts of the wall rest, each course may then be called an oblique arch, as it then assumes the property of an arch, by having a double action, the one at right angles to, or on the bed, and the other in the direction of the radius; and if this arch be of equal thickness throughout, and has an equal inclination to the horizon, it will be an arch of equilibration. All the courses in a dome are oblique arches of equilibration, of various inclinations, between the horizontal line at the springing, and the perpendicular at its vertex.

1499j. " A dome is comprised of as many vertical arches as there are diameters, and as many oblique arches as there are chords. The actions of the parts of a vertical arch are eccentric, an oblique arch concentric; consequently they will be in opposition, and the greater force will lose power equal to that of the less. An oblique arch bears the same relation to a dome as a voussoir does to an arch; when the vertical arches are not in equilibration, the action is upon the whole oblique arch, not upon the voussoirs separately; although a whole course or oblique arch (which must be the case, or no part of it, admitting that each course in itself is similar and equal throughout) be thrust outwards by the inequilibration of the vertical arches; the incumbent oblique arches will descend perpendicularly, keeping the same congruity of their own parts.

1499k. " As the voussoirs of each oblique arch are in equilibration, no one can approach nearer to the centre of the dome than another, unless the other voussoirs squeeze or crush, which, in investigations of subjects of this nature, are always assumed perfectly rigid; therefore, in their position in the dome, they have obtained their concentration. Hence we obtain the essential distinction between an arch and a dome, that no part of the latter can fall inwardly. Since no part of a dome can fall inwards, it resembles an arch resting on the centre on which it has been constructed, and the resistance which the vertical arch meets with from that centre is similar to the opposition of the oblique arches to the vertical arches. If this deduction be just, the mechanician will be able to describe the extrados of equilibration to a dome and its abutment wall, with the same facility as he may to an arch and its abutment piers."

1499l. Pasley has likewise stated that " as soon as any course is completed all round, the stones or bricks composing it form a circular arch like that of a cone, which cannot by any means fall inwards. Hence there is an important difference between the dome and the common arch, which latter cannot stand at all without its centering, unless the whole curve be completed, and when finished, the crown or upper segment tends to overset the haunches or lower segments. The dome, on the contrary, is perfectly strong, and is a complete arch without its upper segment; and thus, as the pressure acts differently, there is less strain upon the haunches and abutments of a dome, than on those of a common arch of the same curve. Hence a sufficient dome may be constructed with much thinner materials than would be proper for a common arch of the same section. The dome of St. Paul's Cathedral offers a fine specimen of this kind of work." It has been described in *par.* 472.

1499m. The Pantheon, at Paris, has a dome formed of three portions. The first, or interior one, is a regular hemisphere of about 66 ft. $9\frac{1}{2}$ in. span, with a circular opening at top of about 31 ft. $4\frac{1}{4}$ in. in diameter. It is built of cut stones, varying from $18\frac{1}{2}$ in. thick at bottom, to $10\frac{1}{2}$ in. at top. Thus the thickness is only about $\frac{1}{15}$rd part of the span. The intermediate dome is a catenarian curve having a span of about 70 ft. with a rise of 50 ft.; and it has to support considerable weight at top. It has four large openings in its sides to give light, about 37 ft. high by 31 ft. wide, arched at top in a somewhat parabolic form. The outer dome has an external diameter of 78 ft. Its height is not stated, but it appears to be a moderately pointed Gothic arch had it been continued, without forming an opening at top for the sides of a lantern, which it was intended to support. The thickness of the stone at bottom is about 28 in. and 14 in. at top. A great part of the surface is only half the above thickness, as the dome is laid out internally in piers, supporting three tiers of arched recesses, or niches, of less substance, and showing like the panels in joiners' work. (See figs. 177 and 178.)

1499n. Partington, in the *British Cyclopædia*, 1835, expresses the opinion that " the weight of the dome may force out its lower parts, if it rises in a direction too nearly ver-

tical; and supposing its form to be spherical, and its thickness equal, it will require to be confined by a hoop or chain as soon as the span becomes eleven-fourteenths of the whole diameter. But if the thickness of the dome be diminished as it rises, it will not require to be bound so high. Thus, if the increase of thickness in descending begins at about 30° from the summit, and be continued until at about 60°, the dome becomes little more than twice as thick as at first, the equilibrium will be so far secure. At this distance it would be proper to employ either a chain or some external pressure to prove the stability, since the weight itself would require to be increased without limit, if it were the only source of pressure on the lower parts. The dome of the Pantheon, at Rome, is nearly circular, and its lower parts are so much thicker than its upper parts, as to afford a sufficient resistance to their pressure; they are supported by walls of great thickness, and furnished with many projections, which answer the purpose of abutments and buttresses."

1499o. Keeping to the theory of the dome, we must avoid noticing its history, beyond pointing out the papers which have of late years treated on the subject. These are published in the *Transactions* of the Royal Institute of British Architects. The first was by J. Fergusson, *On the Architectural Splendour of the City of Beejapore*, November 1854; the discussion in December following, when J. W. Papworth detailed his interesting and novel theory, to be presently noticed; and two papers by T. H. Lewis, *Some Remarks on Domes*, June 1857; and *On the Construction of Domes*, May 1859, in which, however, great care must be taken by the reader to separate the arch from the dome constructions, as in our opinion they are treated therein as of one principle. The question of a Gothic dome is one on which there has been much discussion in the journals of the period named, without having yet obtained a solution. The subjects of domes and pendentives are illustrated in Fergusson's *Handbook*.

1499p. On the occasion referred to, Mr. Papworth asserted that *a dome was not an arch*, and that domes were not governed by the same laws as vaults. He then entered into calculations on the causes of the stability of domes, showing that in domes of great thickness the upper half of each gore was only about one-third in weight of the lower half, and adduced the possibility of loading the crown to a certain extent. He produced a series of drawings of domes, constructed upon principles which ought theoretically, if they were arches, to lead to their failure, but which had nevertheless proved perfectly sound; his views being fortified by Mr. Fergusson's concurrence as to the absence of examples of failure where the bases were stable. He then alluded to the following arguments of others, and explained his reasons for not agreeing with them. Such as, that the dome of the Pantheon, at Rome, had been built on the principle of a bridge, i.e. of an arch; that it was impossible to plan a large dome without great thickness of walls, i.e. greater than sufficient to bear the weight and its consequences; that it was necessary for the exterior of a dome to stand flush with the wall of the building to which it belonged; that it was desirable to append heavy corbelling to the inside of the wall to counteract the thrust of the dome, with special reference to some circular tambours, of which he exhibited sketches; to the supposed unnecessarily great weight on the top of some examples; and to the supposed beauty of principle exhibited in the dome of Sta. Maria, at Florence, which he characterised as a piece of octagonal vaulting and not a dome. He also explained that domes which had failed had not been supported on a stable foundation; that he saw great beauty in the idea of forming an eye in so large a dome as that of the Gol Goomuz, at Beejapore, where the centre of the curve on each side of the section was in the edge of the eye; that the outer face of the springing of the dome might be within the inside of the square enclosing wall of the building; that if the principles of vaulting were applied, the wagon-headed section of the Gol Goomuz dome would not be expected, theoretically, to stand; and concluded by some observations in explanation of his illustrations, as to the requisite thickness of domes. All writers, so far as he had seen, considered the dome as a case of vaulting on principles deduced from their experiments on arches, which was a mode repudiated by him.

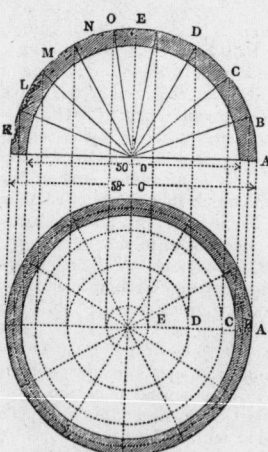

Figs. 590b and 590c.

1499q. The causes of the stability of domes, as thus put forward for the first time, by Mr. Papworth, are the following:—Let the plan (*fig. 590b.*), of a semicircular dome be divided, say, into twelve or more equal parts, and the section (*fig. 590c.*), say, into nine or more. Give a thickness by an inner line for stone or brickwork. Then it will be at once perceived that the lower block K has to support a mass L of less dimensions as to horizontal length; that the

block L supports a still less mass M; that M supports a much less mass N; and that N supports a mass of but a small length in comparison with K, whilst in breadth it diminishes from a few feet to nothing at the apex. If the dimensions of a dome were worked out, say of 50 ft. internal diameter, and of 4 ft. in thickness, it would be found that the block K would be about $413\frac{1}{2}$ ft. cube; L $368\frac{1}{2}$ ft. cube; M $274\frac{1}{2}$ ft. cube; N $146\frac{1}{2}$ ft. cube; and the half block O $22\frac{1}{2}$ ft. cube. The fact has to be remembered, that all domes are built in courses of stones which are bonded one into the other, forming circular rings; and that even if a dome be cut down into four quarters, each quarter will stand of itself.

1499r. Rankine, *Applied Mechanics*, 1858, points out that the tendency of a dome to spread at its base is resisted by the stability of a cylindrical wall, or of a series of buttresses surrounding the base of the domes, or by the tenacity of a metal hoop encircling the base of the dome. The conditions of stability of a dome are ascertained by him in the following manner. Let *fig.* 590*d.* represent a vertical section of a dome springing from a cylindrical wall BB. The shell of the dome is supposed to be thin as compared with its external and internal dimensions. Let the centre of the crown of the dome, O, be taken as origin of coordinates; let *x* be the depth of any circular joint in the shell, such as CC; and *y* the radius of that joint. Let *i* be the angle of inclination of the shell at C to the horizon, and *ds* the length of an elementary arc of the vertical section of the dome, such as

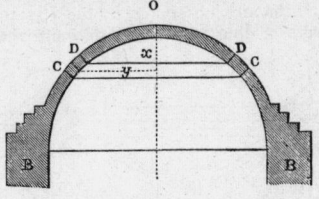

Fig. 590*d.*

CD, whose vertical height is *dx*, and the difference of its lower and upper radii *dy*; so that $\frac{dy}{dx} =$ cotan i; $\frac{ds}{dx} =$ cosec i. Let P_x be the weight of the part of the dome above the circular joint CC. Then the total thrust in the direction of a set of tangents to the dome, radiating obliquely downwards all round the joint CC, is $P_x \frac{ds}{dx} = P_x \cdot$ cosec i; and the total horizontal component of that radiating thrust is $P_x \cdot \frac{dy}{dx} = P_x \cdot$ cotan i. Let p_y denote the intensity of that horizontal radiating thrust, per unit of periphery of the joint CC; then because the periphery of that joint is $2 \pi y$ ($= 6\cdot2832\,y$), we have $p_y = \frac{P_x \,\text{cotan}\, i}{2 \pi y}$.

1499s. If there be an inward radiating pressure upon a ring, of a given intensity per unit of arc, there is a thrust exerted all round that ring, whose amount is the product of that intensity into the radius of the ring. The same proposition is true, substituting an outward for an inward radiating pressure, and a tension all round the ring for a thrust. If, therefore, the horizontal radiating pressure of the dome at the joint CC be resisted by the tenacity of a hoop, the tension at each point of that hoop, being denoted by P_y, is given by the equation $P_y = y p_y = \frac{P_x \,\text{cotan}\, i}{2 \pi}$. Now conceive the hoop to be removed to the circular joint DD, distant by the arc *ds* from CC, and let its tension in this new position be $P_y - dP_y$. The difference, dP_y, when the tension of the hoop at CC is the greater, represents a *thrust* which must be exerted all round the ring of brickwork CC DD, and whose intensity per unit of length of the arc CD is $p_z = \frac{dP_y}{ds} = \frac{1}{2 \pi} \cdot \frac{d}{ds}(P_x \,\text{cotan}\, i.)$

1499t. Every ring of brickwork for which p_z is either nothing or positive, is stable, independently of the tenacity of cement; for in each such ring there is no tension in any direction. When p_z becomes negative, that is, when P_y has passed its maximum and begins to diminish, there is tension horizontally round each ring of brickwork, which, in order to secure the stability of the dome, must be resisted by the tenacity of cement, or of external hoops, or by the assistance of abutments. Such is the condition of the stability of a dome. The inclination to the horizon of the surface of the dome at the joint where $P_z = 0$, and below which that quantity becomes negative, is the angle of rupture of the dome; and the horizontal component of its thrust at that joint, is its total horizontal thrust against the abutment, hoop or hoops, by which it is prevented from spreading. A dome may have a circular opening in its crown. Oval-arched openings may also be made at lower points, provided at such points there is no tension; and the ratio of the horizontal to the inclined axis of any such opening should be fixed by the equation

$$\frac{\text{horizontal axis}}{\text{inclined axis}} = c = \sqrt{\frac{p_y}{p_z \sec i}}.$$

Rankine concludes his investigations with examples of " spherical," and " truncated conical," domes. The whole subject of domical constructions has yet to be investigated theoretically and practically.

1499u. *Cones.*—These are used in tile-kilns, glass-houses, and such like. A building in the shape of a hollow cone forms everywhere a species of circular arch, which may be constructed without centering or support, provided the joints be made to radiate towards the centre. The courses should be laid perpendicular to the sides of the proposed cone. A

rod of variable length, turning on a pivot, must be stretched all round from time to time, upon a moveable centre, rising as the work proceeds, in order to regulate the internal out-line. Such is the strength of this form that the highest kilns are seldom built more than one brick thick, although this dimension would be altogether insufficient for a common wall of the same height. It is, probably, this principle which has conduced to the existence of the Round Towers of Ireland. That of Kilkenny, for example, 100 ft. in height, was built on, or very near, the surface, for at 2 ft. below it, wood coffins with skeletons were found partly under the walls, thus affording an unstable foundation.

Pointed Arch Vaulting.

1499v. We now proceed to enter into a view of the general forms of groining in pointed architecture, observing, by the way, that the groins at the arrises, up to the twelfth century, were seldom moulded with more than a simple torus or some fillets. In the twelfth

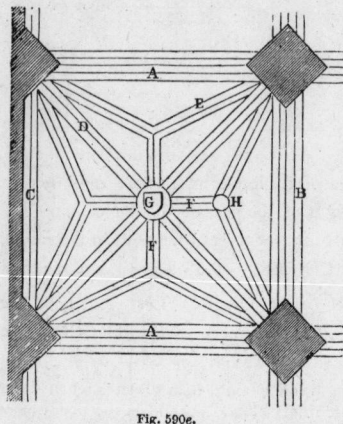

Fig. 590e.

century, however, the torus is doubled, and the doubling parted by a fillet. Towards the end of the twelfth century, three tori often occur; and at the beginning of the thirteenth, the moulded arrises become similar to the moulded archivolts of the arches, both in their form and arrangement. In France, until the middle of the fifteenth century, the arrises of the groins only were moulded; but in this country the practice took place much earlier, for, instead of simple groining, the intro-duction of a number of subdivisions in the soffits of arches had become common. In *fig.* 590e. is given a plan of the soffit of a vault of this kind, in which A is an *arc doubleau* (by which is un-derstood an arc supposited below another at cer-tain intervals, and concentric with the latter); B is an upper arch, called by the French antiqua-ries *formeret*; C, the wall arch, or *formeret du mur;* D is a diagonal rib, or *croisée d'ogive;* E, intermediate rib or *tierceron;* FF, summit ribs or *liernes;* G, the key or boss, *clef de voute.* Mr. Willis has used the French terms here given, and as we have no simple terms to express them in English, it may be convenient to adopt the practice.

1499w. The ribs formed by the intersections of the groins perform the office of supporting

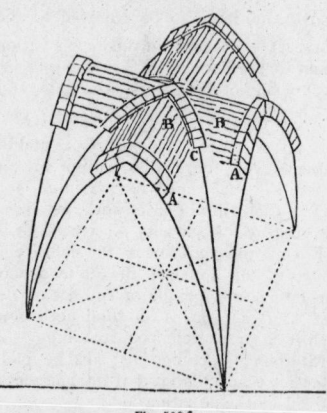

Fig. 590f.

the vaulting which lies upon them, they in their turn being borne by the pillars. Thus, in the simple groin (*fig.* 590f.), the arches AA, and diagonal rib C, carry the vaulting BB, a rebate being formed at the lower part of the ribs on which the vaulting lies. This figure exhibits the simplest form of groining in any species of vaulting, the intersecting arches being of equal height. The contrivance in its earliest state was ingenious, and the study attractive, and we cannot be surprised at Dr. Robison observing, in respect of the artists of the thirteenth and two following centuries, that " an art so multifarious, and so much out of the road of ordinary thought, could not but become an object of fond study to the architects most eminent for ingenuity and invention: becoming thus the dupes of their own ingenuity, they were fond of displaying it where not necessary." This observation would be fully verified had we room for showing the reader the infinite number of devices that ingenuity has created: he will, however, from the few elementary ones that we do give, be enabled to see the germs of countless others.

1499x. Ware, in his *Tracts on Vaults and Bridges*, 1822—a work which, notwithstand-ing the quaint method in which the subject is treated, contains extremely valuable matter, —has made some remarks which we must introduce at length, or justice would not be done to them. "In the vaulting," he says, "of the aisles of Durham and Canterbury cathedrals are to be observed the *arcs doubleaux* and groined ribs in round-headed vaults. In the naves of the same buildings is the same character of vaulting, except that the arch of the vault is pointed. Some vaults of this kind are to be distinguished from others by the

positing of the stones of the vault between the ribs, which, instead of being parallel to each side of the plan, as in Roman groined vaults, take a mean direction between the groined rib and the ribs of the arches over the sides; whence they meet at the vertex at an acute angle, and are received by stones running along the vertex, cut in the form of a ratchet. The advantage of this method consists in requiring less centering, and originates in the position of the ribs at the springing." " From these beginnings vaulting began to assume those practical advantages which the joint adaptation of the pointed arch and ribs was calculated to produce." " The second step differed from the first, inasmuch as at the vertex of the vault a continued keystone or ridge projects below the surface of the vault, and forms a feature similar to the ribs. But here it was necessary that the ridge should be a stone of great length, or having artificially that property, because its suspension by a thinner vault than itself would be unsafe, unless assisted by the rib arches over the diagonals and side, a distance equal to half the width of the vault. To obviate this objection, other ribs were introduced at intervals, which may be conceived to be groined ribs over various oblongs, one side continually decreasing. This practice had a further advantage, as the panels or vaults between the ribs might become proportionally thinner as the principal supports increased. It is now that the apparent magic hardiness of pointed vaulting and the high embowered roof began to display itself; from slender columns to stretch shades as broad as those of the oak's thick branches, and, in the levity of the panel to the rib, to imitate that of the leaf to the branch." " On comparing rib-pointed vaulting with Roman vaulting, it will be invariably found that the rib itself is thinner than the uniform thickness of the Roman vault under similar circumstances; and that the panel, which is the principal part of the vault in superficial quantity, sometimes does not exceed one ninth part of the rib in thickness. The Gothic architects, it has been expressively said, have given to stone an apparent flexibility equal to the most ductile metals, and have made it forget its nature, weaning it from its fondness to descend to the centre."

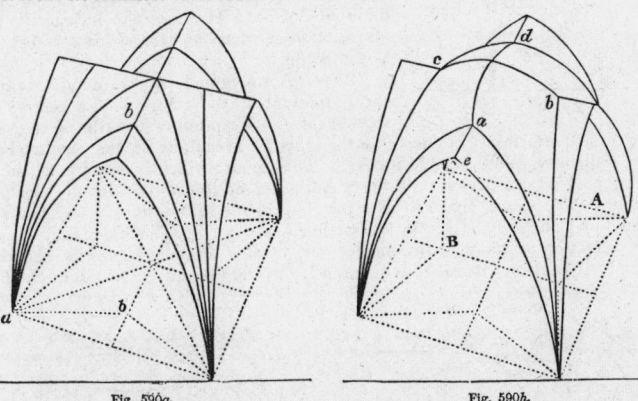

Fig. 590g.   Fig. 590h.

1499y. In the second example (fig. 590g.), another rib, a b, is introduced, which on plan produces the form of a star of four points. The forms of these thus inserted ribs result from curves of the lines on the plan in the space to be vaulted. As many radii are drawn

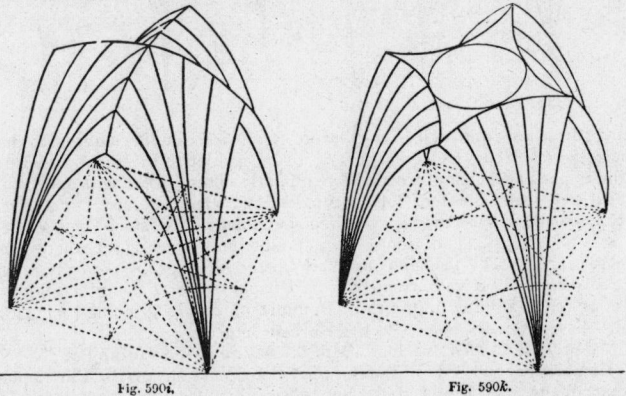

Fig. 590i.   Fig. 590k.

from the angles of the plan as there are ribs intended, until they mutually intersect each other. The curvatures of the ribs will be elongated as they recede from the primitive arch, till they reach the centre on the place where the groins cross, and where of course the elongated curve is a maximum. The ribs thus form, when they are of the same curvature, portions of an inverted conoid.

1499z. In the next example (*fig. 590h.*), the primitive arches are unequal in height, the arch A being higher than B. The plan remains the same as in that immediately preceding; but from the inequality of height, *a d, c b,* must be joined by curved lines, determined on one side by the point *a,* where *e a* intersects the longer arch. A curved summit rib, as well longitudinally as transversely, may occur with equal or unequal heights of primitive arches (as in *fig. 590i.*); but the stellar form on the plan still remains, though differently modified, with the same, or a less or greater, number of ribs on the plan (*fig. 590k.*). By truncating, as it were, the summit ribs, level or otherwise, with the tops of the primitive arches, and introducing on the plan a polygon or a circle touching quadrants inscribed in

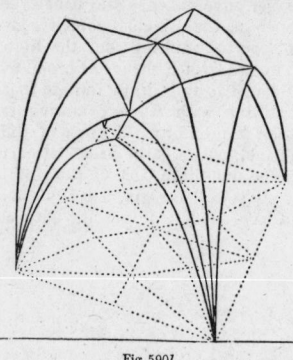

Fig. 590*l.*

the square, we obtain, by means of the rising conoidal quadrants, figures which perform the office of a key-stone. In this, as we have above observed, the construction of the work is totally different from rib vaulting, inasmuch as each course, in rising, supports the next, after the manner of a dome, and is not dependent on ribs for carrying the filling-in pieces. Hence the distinction between fanwork and radiating rib work so judiciously made by Mr. Willis.

1499*aa.* The sixth example (*fig. 590l.*) has primitive arches of different heights, forming an irregular star on plan, that is to say, the points are of different angles. The figure will scarcely need explanation after what has been already said in relation to the subject.

1499*bb.* A polygonal space may be vaulted in three different ways. First, by a central column serving for the reception of the ribs of the vault, the column or pillar performing in such case the office of a wall, as in the chapter-houses of Worcester, Salisbury, Wells, and Lincoln. This mode evidently admits of the largest space being covered, on account of the subdivision of the whole area by means of the central pillar. The second mode is by a pendent for the reception of the arches, as in the Lady Chapel at Caudebec, (given in the section Masonry). This mode is necessarily restricted in practice to small spans, on account of the limits attached to the power of materials; albeit in theory its range is as extensive as the former. The last method is by at

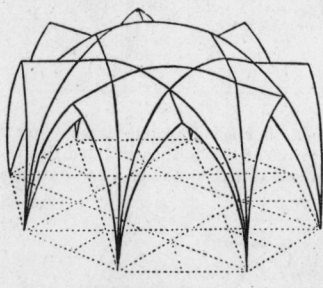

Fig. 590*m.*

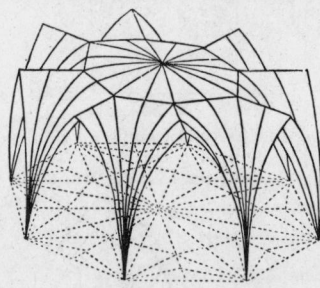

Fig. 590*n.*

once vaulting the space from wall to wall, as in *fig.* 590*m.*, like the vaulting to the kitchen of the monastery of Durham Cathedral, or, *fig.* 590*n.*, similar to the chapter-house at York, of which, the upper part being of wood, Ware quaintly observes, " The people of Yorkshire fondly admire and justly boast of their cathedral and chapter-house. The principle of vaulting at the chapter-house may be admired and imagined in stone; not so the vault of the nave; it is manifestly one of those sham productions which cheat where there is no merit in deceiving." The principle, as Ware justly observes, is perfectly masonic, and might be easily carried out with stone ribs and panel stones, it being nothing more than an extension of that exhibited in the third example of simple groining (*fig.* 590*f.*) above given; and the same remark applies to the Durham kitchen.

1499*cc.* We propose to offer explanations of the nature of the vaulting at King's College Chapel at Cambridge, and the silly story related by Walpole of Sir Christopher Wren, saying, "that if any man would show him where to place the first stone he would

engage to build another" (vault like it). The vault of the chapel in question is
divided into oblong severies, whose shorter sides are placed longitudinally (*fig. 590o.*)

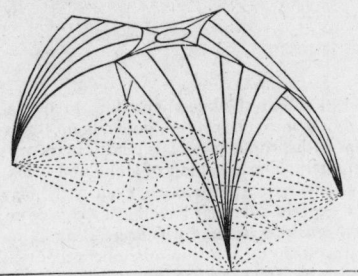

It must be evident that the curves of the
inverted quadrants must intersect each other
previous to the whole quadrant of the circle
being completed. Hence these intersections
form a curved summit line lowest against
the windows or smaller sides of the oblong.
This summit line of the vaulting of the
building in the direction of its length
forms a series of curves, though from the
angle under which it is seen it is scarcely perceptible. Mr. Ware says, " It is observable,
in the construction of this vault, that the principle of using freestone for the ribs, and tufa
for the panels, has not been followed ; but
the whole vault has been *got out* of the same

Fig. 590o.

description of stone, and with an uniform face, and the panels worked afterwards, and reduced to a tenuity hardly credible except from measurement. The artists of this building
might be trusted in the decoration of a vault with what is now called tracery ; they knew
how to render it the chief support, and what was the superfluous stone to be taken away :
every part has a place, not only proper, but necessary ; and in the ribs which adorn the
vault we may in vain look for false positions. This is the ocular music which affords
universal pleasure."

1499*dd*. We now return to the consideration of two more modes of simple vaulting. In
England, the summit ribs of the vault are almost always found running longitudinally and
transversely in the various examples. In Germany the summit ribs are more frequently
omitted than introduced. Thus in the example *fig. 590l*, the scheme is merely a square
diagonally placed within the severy, subdivided into four parts and connected with the base-
points of the groins by ribs not parallel to the alternate sides of the inserted square. This,
however, sometimes occurs in English buildings, as in the monument of Archbishop Stratford,
at Canterbury Cathedral ; though in that the central portion is not domical. It is to be
remarked that the intersecting arches are not of equal height, otherwise the arrangement
could not occur.

1499*ee*. In the example *fig. 590p*, the arrangement
completely assumes what Mr. Willis calls the stellar form.
Here in the soffit a star of six points is the figure on
which the projection depends, the points radiating from
the angles of an hexagon, and thus forming a cluster of
lozenges whose middle longitudinal sides produce another
longitudinal lozenge to connect the centres of the pattern.
The longitudinal arches are, as in the preceding figure,
lower than the transverse arches. Mr. Willis says, " the
principal distinction between these and our own fan-
vaulting is the substitution of lozenge-headed compartments in the fans, for the English horizontal transom
rib. We have also lozenge-headed compartments in our
early vaulting, but they are never so symmetrically
arranged in stars throughout."

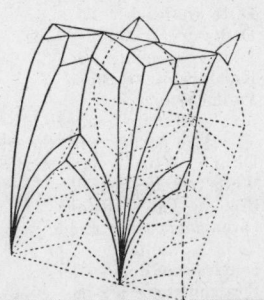

Fig. 590p.

1499*ff*. From the simple lines or principles above
given, it is easy to perceive through what numberless ramifications of form they may be
carried. Another form is that called hexapartite vaulting, where the ribs spring from the
angles, and two others from a shaft placed in the middle of each long side, thus making
six divisions. This is a step beyond the quadripartite groining shown in *fig. 590f*. Examples of hexapartite vaulting are scarce in England, but it may be seen in the chapel of
St. Blaise in Westminster Abbey, the choir of Canterbury Cathedral, and in many parts of
Lincoln Minster.

1499*gg*. It would be difficult to find a system of vaulting more unlike any English
example than that in Anjou generally, of which the Hospital at Angers is a fair specimen.
It is always excessively domical in its sections, both longitudinal and transverse ; and has
eight ribs, the cells being filled in with stones exactly parallel with the centre or ridge of
each cell : the ribs are edge-roll mouldings.

Sect. IX.

WALLS AND PIERS.

1500. The thickness which is to be assigned to walls and points of support, that their stability may be insured, depends on the weight they have to sustain, and on their formation with proper materials ; still more on the proportion which their bases bear to their heights. The crushing of stone and brick, by mere superimposed weight, is of extremely rare occurrence in practice, even with soft stone and with bad bricks. The result of some few experiments that have been made as to the resistance of some of our bricks and stones to a crushing force, by George Rennie, in 1818, are here subjoined. Some later experiments made by the Commissioners mentioned in Book II. chap. ii., and appended to their *Report on Stone*, &c., in 1839; with a few others; as well as some important trials made in 1864 by a committee of the Institute of British Architects, given in *Transactions*, 1863–64, are likewise added.

Table of Crushing Force of Materials, by George Rennie (*Phil. Trans.* 1818).

Materials.		Specific Gravity.	Crushing Weight.
			lbs. Avoir.
Portland stone, 2 inches long, 1 inch square	- -	- -	805
Statuary marble, 1-inch cube	- -	- -	3216
Cragleith stone,　ditto	- -	- -	8688
Chalk	- -	- -	1127
Pale red brick	- -	2085	1265
Roe stone, Gloucestershire	- -	- -	1449
Red brick	- -	2168	1817
Hammersmith brick	- -	- -	2254
Ditto burnt	- -	- -	3243
Ditto fire-brick	- -	- -	3864
Derby grit	- -	2316	7070
Another specimen	- -	2428	9776
Killala white freestone	- -	2423	10,264
Portland stone	- -	2428	10,284
Cragleith white freestone	- -	2452	12,346
Yorkshire paving, with the strata	- -	2507	12,856
Ditto,　ditto,　against the strata	- -	- -	12,856
White statuary marble	- -	2760	13,632
Bramley Fall sandstone	- -	2506	13,632
Ditto, against the strata	- -	- -	13,632
Cornish granite	- -	2662	14,302
Dundee sandstone	- -	2530	14,918
Portland stone, a 2-inch cube	- -	2423	14,918
Cragleith stone, with the strata	- -	2452	15,560
Devonshire red marble	- -	- -	16,712
Compact limestone	- -	2584	17,354
Peterhead granite	- -	- -	18,636
Limerick black compact limestone	- -	2598	19,924
Purbeck stone	- -	2599	20,610
Freestone, very hard	- -	2528	21,254
Black Brabant marble	- -	2697	20,742
White Italian marble	- -	2726	21,783
Aberdeen blue granite	- -	2625	24,556

(Rows from "Chalk" through "Portland stone, a 2-inch cube" are bracketed and marked "One and a half inch cubes." Rows from "Cragleith stone, with the strata" through "Aberdeen blue granite" are bracketed and marked "One and a half in. cubes.")

1501. The above experiments lose much of their practical value from our knowledge that the interior particles in granulated substances are protected from yielding by the lateral resistance of the exterior ones; but to what extent it is impossible to estimate, because so much depends on the internal structure of the body. We are, however, thus far informed, that, taking into account the weight with which a point of support is loaded, its thickness ought to be regulated in an inverse ratio to the crushing weight of the material employed. In Gothic structures we often see, for instance, in chapter houses

with a central column, a prodigious weight superimposed. It is needless to say that, in such instances, the strongest material was necessary, and we always find it so employed. So in the columns, or rather pillars, of the naves in such edifices, the greatest care was usually taken to select the hardest stone. Generally speaking, the thickness of walls and piers should be proportioned rather to their height than to the weight they are to bear; hence often the employment of a better material, though more costly, is in truth the most economical.

1502.   TABLE OF THE WEIGHT REQUIRED TO CRUSH CUBES OF STONE.

Materials.	Specific Gravity.	Cracking Weight.	Crushing Weight.	
		lbs.	lbs.	
I. *Granites* (2-inch cubes):				
Aberdeen (blue) - - - - -	—	—	10,363	B
Dartmoor - - - - - -	—	—	12,175	B
Haytor - - - - - - -	—	—	13,865	B
Herm - - - - - - -	—	—	14,873	B
Penrhyn - - - - - -	—	—	7,728	B
Peterhead (blue) - - - - -	—	—	10,192	B
Ditto (grey) - - - - -	—	—	9,666	B
II. *Limestones* (2-inch cubes) :				
Marble (white) - - - - -	—	—	9.580	
Bolsover - - - - -	2316	19,831	30,147·5	C
Bramham Moor, Smawse - - -	2008	10,666·5	23,649·7	C
Brodsworth - - - - -	2093	7,366·5	18,416·5	C
Cadeby - - - - -	1951	5,666·5	6,516·5	C
Chilmark (three specimens) : - - -	2410	10,285	25,500	C
Hamhill - - - - - -	2260	6,233	16,149	C
Hildenley - - - - -	2098	17,565·5	19,266·5	C
Huddlestone - - - - -	2147	9,633	17,283	C
Jackdaw Craig - - - -	2070	10,666·5	18,903	C
Park Nook - - - - -	2138	7,366·5	17,283	C
Roche Abbey - - - - -	2134	6,800	15,583	C
Totternhoe - - - - -	1891	3,966	7,700	C
III. *Oolites* (2-inch cubes) :				
Ancaster - - - - - -	2182	6,800	9,350	C
Barnack - - - - - -	2090	4,533	7,083	C
Haydor - - - - - -	2040	4,533	7,083	C
Ketton - - - - - -	2645	6,233	10,285	C
Ketton Rag - - - - -	2490	14,166·5	35,983	C
Portland (Waycroft Quarry) - - -	2145	8,500	15,583	C
Box - - - - - -	1839	5,100	5,950	C
IV. *Sandstones* (2-inch cubes):				
Bramley Fall - - - -	2506	—	6,053	
Binnie - - - - - -	2194	10,766·5	20,116·5	C
Craigleith - - - - -	2266	17,000	31,449·5	C
Ditto - - - - - -	2452	—	5,480	C
Darley Dale, Stancliffe - - - -	2628	26,014·5	28,333	C
Derby - - - - - -	—	—	3,110	C
Dundee - - - - - -	—	—	6,490	C
Giffneuch - - - - -	2230	13,698	19,266·5	C
Heddon - - - - - -	2229	7,366·5	15,866	C
Hookstone - - - - -	2253	17,566·5	23,233	C
Kenton - - - - - -	2247	13,698	19,831	C
Mansfield, or C. Lindley's (red) - -	2338	8,038	20,397	C
Ditto, or ditto (white) - -	2277	10,285	20,963·5	C
Morley Moor - - - - -	2053	6,235	19,833	C
Park Spring - - - - -	2321	15,866	30,316	C
Redgate - - - - -	2239	15,383	23,649·7	C
Stanley - - - - - -	2227	10,285	23,883	C

1502a. In the above list B stands for Bramah, and C for the Commissioners' *Report,* &c. It is of very great importance to notice that the size of the cubes experimented upon by the latter, was only two inches; those by Rennie were only one and a half inch cubes. A set of experiments on Portland stone, of the weight sustained up to the point of fracture, i.e. the crushing weight, by accurately cut cubes of two inch faces placed

between perfectly smooth lead surfaces, were carried out with the well-known American mechanical testing machine, by Mr. Abel (*Builder*, 1863, p. 860) :—

War Department Quarry, Vern Hill - - - -	14,795·8	lbs.
Inmosthay Quarry, Whit-bed - - - -	14,591·8	„
Admiralty Quarry, Rough Whit-bed - - - -	14,387·7	„
„ „ Whit-bed - - - -	13,979·5	„
„ „ Base-bed - - - -	13,775·0	„
New Maggott Quarry, Whit-bed - - - -	12,857·1	„
Old Maggott Quarry, LI Whit-bed - - -	12,244·8	„
„ „ „ I T Base-bed - - -	12,857·1	„
„ „ „ L I Base-bed - - -	8,163·2	„
Independent Quarry, Whit-bed - - - -	11,632·6	„
Waycroft Quarry, Base-bed - - - -	11,836·7	„

He also observes that "no definite conclusion can be drawn from the comparative properties of the specimens of stone from one and the same locality, quarried at different periods of time, regarding the influence exerted by exposure, after quarrying, upon the quality of the stone. On the whole, the evidence may be considered as a little in favour of the opinion that an improvement in the strength of the stone is effected, to some extent, by seasoning."

1502b. A very instructive set of experiments on the strength of Portland stone (brown bed), a material now so greatly employed in building, was made by a committee of the Institute, above-mentioned.

TABLE OF THE STRENGTH OF CUBES OF PORTLAND STONE.

Height.	Base.	Cracked.	Crushed.	On square inch.	Remarks.
Inches.	Inches.	Tons.	Tons.	Tons.	
2	2 × 2	- -	3·2	0·8	At once.
	2 × 2	4·0	6·0	1·5	
	4 × 2	- -	20·2	2·5	At once.
	2 × 6	21·0	23·5	1·7	⎫
	4 × 4	8·0	41·0	2·5	⎬ Across the bed.
	6 × 6	64·0	86·0	2·4	⎭
4	2 × 2	- -	3·0	0·75	
	4 × 2	- -	17·0	2·12	
	4 × 4	25·75	29·25	1·82	
	4 × 4	24·25	28·75	1·85	
	4 × 6	31·0	45·0	1·87	a Very slight, external.
	6 × 6	48·0 a	82·0 b	2·27	b Not crushed.
6	2 × 2	2·8	3·4	0·85	
	6 × 2	- -	10·0	0·83	
	4 × 4	18·0	20·45	1·27	⎫
	6 × 4	28·0	32·0	1·33	⎬ At right angles to the bed.
	6 × 6	64·0 c	70·0	1·94	c Very slightly.
	6 × 6	55·0	68·75	1·90	

1502c. C. H. Smith has observed (*Transactions of the Institute of British Architects*, 1860, page 174.), that "the stone which possesses the least cohesive strength, or that which will crush with less pressure than any other, is nevertheless strong enough, when well fixed in a building, for almost all practical purposes. No architectural members have to sustain greater pressure, in proportion to their size, than mullions of large Gothic windows. The tracery in the great north window of Westminster Hall is now executed in Bath stone, which is remarkable for having the least cohesive strength of all the specimens described as experimented upon in the *Report on Stone*, &c. Some of the mullions of that window are less than nine inches wide and more than forty feet high, sustaining not only their own weight, but also that of the whole of the tracery beneath the arch. The eastern window of Carlisle Cathedral, built with a friable red sandstone, is fifty feet high, the mullions are smaller, and the tracery much heavier than in that at Westminster, yet in neither of these examples are there any symptoms of crushing. The cohesive strength of stones is never more severely tested than during their conversion by workmen from the rough state to being fixed in their final situation in a building. During these operations, iron levers, jacks, lewises, and various other implements are applied, frequently with but little regard for the mechanical violence which a stone will safely bear ; and it may, there-

fore, be considered a useful practical rule, that, however soft a stone may be, if it resist the liability of damage until out of the masons' hands, there can be little doubt of its possessing sufficient cohesive strength for any kind of architectural work. If the foundation be insufficient, or any part of the edifice give way, so as to cause an unfair or unequal pressure, a soft stone will, of course, yield sooner than a hard one."

1502d. "Unfortunately," writes Warr, *Dynamics*, 1851, "those experimental results which we possess were obtained without attention to the fact that the specimens should be of a certain height to show a proper compressive strength. The bulk of the examples are with cubes, a fault excusable with those experimenters who made their work public before those peculiarities were well known, but the same cannot be said of the investigations conducted by the Commissioners; these experiments, executed with singular minuteness on some points, would have been useful, from their variety and specification of the localities, but they were made on (2-inch) cubes, at a period when the laws of fracture were as public as at present, and are therefore of limited value."

1502e. Hodgkinson (*Phil. Trans.*, 1840, p. 385), found that in small columns of one inch to one and three-quarters inch square, and from one to forty inches long, a great falling off occurred when the height was greater than twelve times the side of the base. Thus, when the length was—

12 times the size of the base, the strength was	-	-	138
15 „	„	„	„	-	- a little less
24 „	„	„	„	-	-	96
30 „	„	„	„	-	-	75
40 „	„	„	„	-	-	52

He also found that with pillars shorter than thirty times the thickness, fracture occurred by one of the ends failing, and as the longer columns deflected more than the shorter, they presented less of the base to resist the pressure, and therefore more readily gave way. Thus the practical view from these experiments points out an increase of area at the ends as being most economical, and that in proportion to the middle as 13,766 to 9,595 nearly. From the experiments it would appear that the Grecian columns, which seldom had their length more than about ten times the diameter, were nearly of the form capable of bearing the greatest weight when their shafts were uniform; and that columns, tapering from the bottom to the top, were only capable of bearing weights due to the smallest part of their section, though the larger end might serve to prevent lateral thrust. This last remark applies, too, to the Egyptian columns, the strength of the column being only that of the smallest part of the section. (British Association for the Advancement of Science, 15th Report, 1845, p. 27.)

1502f. It might be asked, how does this apply to those small shafts or colonettes so freely used with piers in pointed architecture, and which are generally in height upwards of thirty times their diameter. We would refer the student to the paragraph 1502e., respecting the mullions in windows, and to the circumstance that the small shafts are not pinned-in to the work, but are left free, so that they only apparently carry the weight imposed on their capitals. Where no attention has been paid to this necessary precaution, in modern work, the shaft has fractured when of soft, or shaky, stone.

1502g. Table of the Strength of Shafts 12 inches long, 3 inches diameter,

(Being experiments made by a committee of the Institute, as above-mentioned.)

Materials.	Cracked.	Crushed.	On square inch.	Remarks.
	Tons.	Tons.	Tons.	
Portland stone :				All yielded vertically.
Worked - - -	7·3	10·25	1·48	Bedded in leather.
Rough tooled - -	- -	8·57	1·00	Bedded in plaster.
Devonshire marbles :				
Ipplepen, mottled red -	9·2	10·7	1·37	[with vein.
Poltesco, grey green -	4·3	4·3	0·60	Went across and not
Ditto - - -	- -	6·0	0·84	Went at once.
	- -	33·5	4·73	Went into fragments.
Signal Staff. red and black {	20·0	22·5	3·18	Ditto.
	12·75	16·25	2·29	
Cadgewith, green and black	16·92	17·62	2·49	

1502h. Fairbairn, in a paper read at the Manchester Philosophical Society, and given in vol. xiv. of the Proceedings; and also in his *Useful Information, &c.*, 2nd Series, has detailed the following results of his researches :—

						Crushing Weight in lbs. per sq. in.
Grauwacke from Penmaenmaur	-	-	-	-	-	16,893
Basalt, Whinstone	-	-	-	-	-	11,970
Granite, Mountsorrel	-	-	-	-	-	12,861
Ditto, Argyleshire	-	-	-	-	-	10,917
Syenite, Mountsorrel	-	-	-	-	-	11,820
Sandstone, strong Yorkshire, mean of 9 experiments	-				-	9,824
Ditto, weak specimens, locality not stated				3,000	to	3,500
Limestone, compact, strong	-	-	-	-	-	8,528
Ditto, Magnesian, strong		-	-	-	-	7,098
Ditto, ditto, weak		-	-	-	-	3,050

1502*i*. He further shows that the resistance of strong sandstone to crushing in a direction parallel to the layers, is only six-sevenths of the resistance to crushing in a direction perpendicular to the layers. The hardest stones alone give way to crushing at once, without previous warning. All others begin to crack or split under a load less than that which finally crushes them, in a proportion which ranges from a fraction little less than unity in the harder stones, down to about one half in the softest. The mode in which stone gives way to a crushing load is in general by shearing. The factor of safety in structures of stone should not be less than *eight*, in order to provide for variations in the strength of the material, as well as for other contingencies. In some structures which have stood it is less; but there can be no doubt that these err on the side of boldness, as urged by Rankine, *Civil Engineering*, page 361.

1502*k*.   TABLE OF THE WEIGHTS REQUIRED TO CRUSH BRICKS.

Experiments by T. Cubitt.	Yielded to.	Crushed by.	Remarks.
Good place bricks - -	11 tons	16½ tons	Bedded on plaster.
Ditto - - -	16 ,,	22½ ,,	Ditto.
Two common stocks - -	10 ,,	{ 16 ,, ⟨ 16½ ,,	No plaster.
Good stock - -	30 ,,	34 ,,	
Superior washed stock -	36 ,,	44½ ,,	
Ordinary place brick -	3 ,,	9 ,,	
Ditto - - -	3 ,,	6 ,,	
Common ditto - -	——	5 to 2½ ,,	

A brick made by Beale's machine being placed on bearers seven inches apart, was broken in the middle by the weight of 2,625 lbs. A common hand-made brick was broken by 645 lbs. The hollow or frog formed in the underside of a brick necessarily lessens its resisting power. Young (*Nat. Phil.*) states that the cohesive strength of a square inch of brick is 300 lbs., but the quality is not stated. Other experiments give the following strength of bricks:—

			Cwt.	Tons.	Cwt.
Brick of Huntingdonshire clay, perforated, per square inch -			31	58	18
,, Suffolk clay, solid: (broke across) ,, ,, -			8·75	16	12
,, Made by Prosser's machine, bore ,, ,, -				90	0
,, Arsley, and not crushed ,, ,, -				83	0
,, Ordinary stock, - -				140	0
,, Common fire clay, } per square foot - -				157	0
,, Good ditto, } - -				396	0
,, Used at Edinburgh Gas Works, of fire clay and iron stone, per square foot				400	0

1502*l*. *Brickwork.*—Brick piers 9 inches square, 2 feet 3 inches high, made of good sound Cowley stocks, set in cement, and proved two days afterwards:—

	Cracked at	Broke at
Brick flat, compressed quarter of an inch - - -	25 tons	30 tons
Brick on edge, did not compress - - - -	30 ,,	35 ,,

1502*m*. Mr. L. Clarke's experiments for the works at the Britannia and Conway tubular bridges, on brickwork in cubes, showed that—

9 inches, cemented, No. 1 or best quality, set between deal
    boards, weighing 54 lbs., crushed with 19 tons 18 cwt.
    2 qrs. 22 lbs.   -   -   -   -   - = 551·3 lbs. per square inch.
9 inches, No. 1, set in cement, weighing 53 lbs., crushed with
    22 tons 3 cwt. 0 qrs. 17 lbs.   -   -   - = 612·7 lbs.   ,,   ,,

9 inches, No. 3, set in cement, weighing 52 lbs., crushed with
    16 tons 8 cwt 2 qrs. 8lbs. -   -   = 454·3 lbs. per square inch.

$9\frac{1}{4}$ inches, No. 4, set in cement, weighing $55\frac{1}{2}$ lbs., crushed with
    21 tons 14 cwt. 1 qr. 17 lbs. -   -   = 568·5 lbs.   ,,   ,,

9 inches, No. 4, set between boards, weighing $54\frac{1}{4}$ lbs. crushed
    with 15 tons 2 cwt. 0 qrs. 12 lbs. -   -   = 417·0 lbs.   ,,   ,,
        Mean   -   -   -   -   = 521·0 lbs.   ,,   ,,

The three last cubes continued to support the weight, although cracked in all directions; they fell to pieces when the load was removed. All began to show irregular cracks a considerable time before it gave way. The average weight supported by these bricks was 33·5 tons per square foot, equal to a column 583·69 feet high of such brickwork. (Fairbairn, *Application*, &c., page 192.)

1502n. To crush a mass of solid brickwork 1 foot square, requires 300,000 lbs. avoirdupois, or 134 tons $7\frac{1}{2}$ cwt.

1502o. Besides *compression*, stone is subject to *detrusion* and a *transverse strain*, as when used in a lintel. Of these strengths in stone little is officially known, but we are perfectly aware of the danger of using any kind of stone for beams where there is much chance of serious or of irregular pressures. Its weakness in respect to this strain is manifest from all experimental evidence concerning it. Gauthey states the value of a constant S, for hard limestone = 78 lbs.; for soft limestone = 69 lbs. Hodgkinson, taking the power of resisting a crushing force as = 1000, notices—

	Tensile strain.		Transverse strain.
Black marble - - - - - - -	143	and	10·1
Italian marble - - - - - -	85	,,	10·6
Rochdale flagstone - - - - -	104	,,	9·9
Yorkshire flag - - - - - -	0	,,	9·5
Mean - - - - - - -	104	,,	10·0

Common bricks, S = 64 lbs. (Barlow.)

1502p. The danger above noticed is so great, that it becomes essentially necessary in all rough rubble work to insert over an opening either an iron or timber lintel, or a brick or stone arch, to carry the superincumbent weight, and thus prevent any pressure upon the stone. This must be done more especially when beams or lintels of soft stone are used; the harder stones, as Portland, may in ashlar work support themselves without much danger. In rubble masonry, the stone arch may be shown without hesitation in the face of the work; and also in domestic architecture, the brick arch may exhibit itself in the facework if thought desirable. Portland stone has been constantly used to extend over a comparatively wide opening. All blocks set upon it should have a clear bed along the middle of its length. Thus cills to windows should always be set with clear beds, or, as the new work settles, they are certain to be broken. Lintels over even small openings worked in Bath or some of the softer stones, are very likely to crack across by very slight settlements, especially when supported in their length by a mullion or small pier, as is often introduced. We need hardly add that where *impact* or collision is likely to occur, no lintel of stone should be used.

1502q. Marble mantles may sometimes be seen to have become bent by their own weight. Beams of marble have been employed in Grecian temples as much as 18 feet in the clear in the propylæa at Athens; and marble beams 2 feet wide and 13 inches deep were hollowed out, leaving $4\frac{3}{8}$ inches thickness at the sides and $3\frac{1}{2}$ inches at the bottom; these beams were about 13 feet in the clear in the north portico of the temple at Bassæ near Phigaleia.

1502r. The *cohesive* power of stone is seldom tested. The subject of crushing weights, or the compression of timber and metals, will be treated in a subsequent section (1631e. et seq.); and the strength of some other materials will be given in the chapter MATERIALS.

Of the Stability of Walls.

1503. In the construction of edifices there are three degrees of stability assignable to walls. I. One of undoubted stability; II. A mean between the last; and the III. The least thickness which they ought to possess.

1504. The first case is that in which from many examples we find the thickness equal to one eighth part of the height: a mean stability is obtained when the thickness is one tenth part of the height; and the minimum of stability when one twelfth of its height. We are, however, to recollect that in most buildings one wall becomes connected with another, so that stability may be obtained by considering them otherwise than as independent walls.

1505. That some idea may be formed of the difference between a wall entirely isolated and one connected with one or two others at right angles, we here give *figs*. 591, 592, and 593. It is obvious that in the first case (*fig*. 591.), a wall acted upon by the horizontal force MN, will have no resistance but from the breadth of its base; that in the second

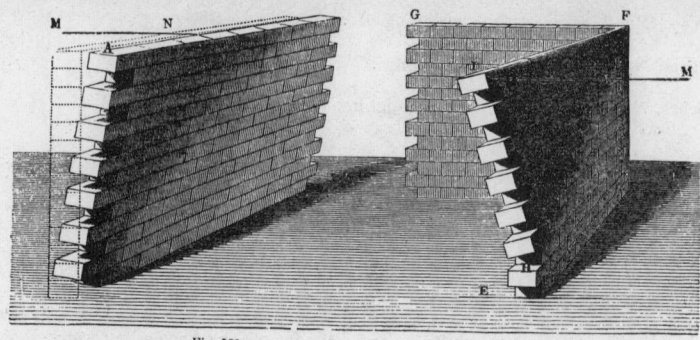

Fig. 591.   Fig. 592.

case (*fig.* 592.) the wall GF is opposed to the force MN. so that only the triangle of it HIF can be detached; lastly, in *fig.* 593. the force MN would only be effective against

Fig. 593

the triangle CGH, which would, of course, be greater in proportion to the increased distance of the walls CD, HI.

1506. In the first case, the unequal settlement of the soil or of the construction may produce the effect of the force MN. The wall will fall on the occurrence of an horizontal disunion between the parts.

1507. In the second case the disunion must take place obliquely, which will require a greater effort of the power MN.

1508. In the third case, in order to overturn the wall, there must be three fractures through the effort of MN, requiring a much more considerable force than in the second case.

1509. We may easily conceive that the resistance of a wall standing between two others will be greater or less as the walls CD, HI are more or less distant; so that, in an extreme approximation to one another, the fracture would be impossible, and, in the opposite case, the intermediate wall approaches the case of an isolated wall.

1510. Walls enclosing a space are in the preceding predicament, because they mutually tend to sustain one another at their extremities; hence their thickness should increase as their length increases.

1511. The result of a vast number of experiments by Rondelet, whose work we are still using, will be detailed in the following observations and calculations.

1512. Let ABCD (*fig.* 594.) be the face of one of the walls for enclosing a rectangular

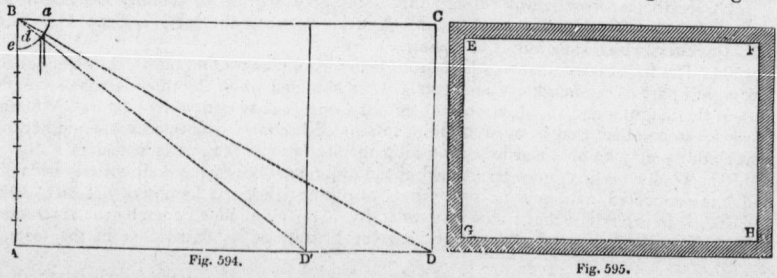

Fig. 594.   Fig. 595.

space, EFGH (*fig. 595.*).   Draw the diagonal BD, and about B make B*d* equal to one eighth part of the height, if great stability be required; for a mean stability, the ninth or tenth part; and, for a light stability, the eleventh or twelfth part.   If through the point *d* a parallel to AB be drawn, the interval will give the thickness to be assigned to the great walls EF, GH, whose length is equal to AD.

1513. The thickness of the walls EG, FH is obtained by making AD′ equal to their length, and, having drawn the diagonal as before, pursuing the same operation.

1514. When the walls are of the same height but of different lengths, as in *fig. 596.*,

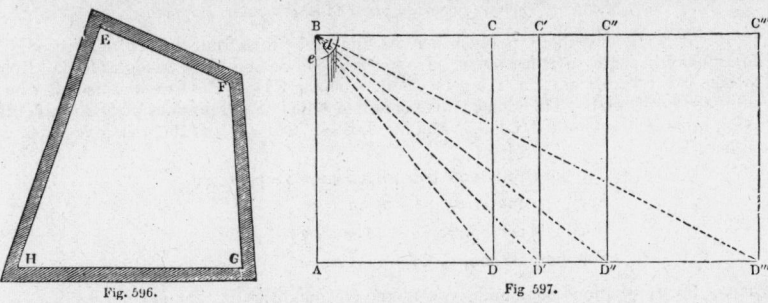

Fig. 596.   Fig. 597.

the operation may be abridged by describing on the point B (*fig. 597.*) as a centre with a radius equal to one eighth, one tenth, or one twelfth, or such other part of the height as may be considered necessary for a solid, mean, or lighter construction, then transferring their lengths, EF, FG, GH, and HE from A to D, D′, D″, and D‴; and having made the rectangles AC, AC′, AC″, and AC‴, draw from the common point B the diagonals BD, BD′, BD″, and BD‴, cutting the small circle described on the point B in different points, through which parallels to AB are to be drawn, and they will give the thickness of each in proportion to its length.

1515. In *figs. 598. to 602.* are given the operations for finding the thicknesses of walls

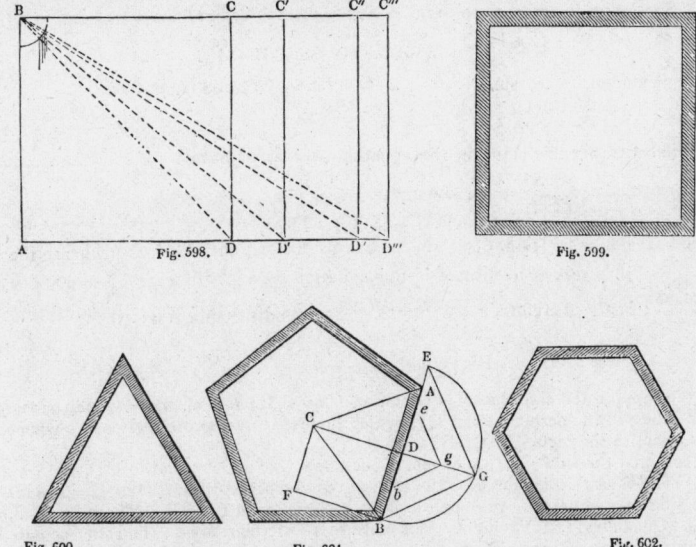

Fig. 598.   Fig. 599.

Fig. 600.   Fig. 601.   Fig. 602.

enclosing polygonal areas supposed to be of the same height; thus AD represents the side of the hexagon (*fig. 602.*); AD′ that of the pentagon (*fig. 601.*); AD″ the side of the square (*fig. 599.*); and AD‴ that of the equilateral triangle (*fig. 600.*).

1516. It is manifest that, by this method, we increase the thicknesses of the walls in proportion to their heights and lengths; for one or the other, or both, cannot increase or diminish without the same happening to the diagonal.

1517. It is obvious that it is easy to calculate in numbers the results thus geometrically obtained by the simple rule of three; for, knowing the three sides of the triangle ABD,

similar to the smaller triangle B*de*, we have BD : B*d* :: AD : *ed*. Thus, suppose the length of wall represented by AD=28 feet, and its height AB=12 feet, we shall have the length of the diagonal =30 feet 5⅓ inches; and, taking the ninth part of AB, or 16 inches, as the thickness to be transferred on the diagonal from B to *d*, we have 30 ft. 6 in. : 16 in. :: 28 ft. : 14 in. : 8 lines (*ed*).   The calculation may also be made trigonometrically; into which there is no necessity to enter, inasmuch as the rules for obtaining the result may be referred to in the section " Trigonometry," and from thence here applied.

Method of enclosing a given Area in any regular Polygon.

1518. It is manifest that a polygon may be divided by lines from the centre to its angles into as many triangles as it has sides.   In *fig.* 601., on one of these triangles let fall from C (which is the vertex of each triangle) a perpendicular CD on the base or side AB which is supposed horizontal.   The area of this triangle is equal to the product of DB (half AB) by CD, or to the rectangle DCFB.   Making DB=x, CD=y, and the area given =p, we shall have,

For the equilateral triangle, $x \times y \times 3 = p$, or $xy = \frac{p}{3}$;

For the square, $xy \times 4 = p$, or $xy = \frac{p}{4}$;

For the pentagon, $xy \times 5 = p$, or $xy = \frac{p}{5}$;

For the hexagon, $xy \times 6 = p$, or $xy = \frac{p}{6}$.

Each of these equations containing two unknown quantities, it becomes necessary to ascertain the proportion of x to y, which is as the sines of the angles opposite to the sides DB and CD.

1519. In the equilateral triangle this proportion is as the sine of 60 degrees to the sine of 30 degrees; that is, using a table of sines, as 86603 : 50000, or 8⅔ : 5, or 26 : 15, whence

$$x : y :: 26 : 15, \text{ and } 15x = 26y; \text{ whence } y = \frac{15x}{26}.$$

Substituting this value in the equation $xy = \frac{p}{3}$, we have

$$\frac{15x^2}{26} = \frac{p}{3}, \text{ which becomes } x^2 = \frac{26p}{45}, \text{ and } x = \sqrt{\frac{26p}{45}}.$$

Supposing the area given to be 3600, we shall therefore have

$$x = \sqrt{\frac{3600 \times 26}{45}} = 45 \cdot 6, \text{ and the side } AB = 91 \cdot 2.$$

For the pentagon, $x : y :: \sin. 36° : \sin. 54°$, or as 58779 : 80902, whence

$$y = \frac{80902x}{58779}.$$

Substituting this value in the equation $xy = \frac{p}{5}$, we have

$$\frac{80902x^2}{58779} = \frac{3600}{5}, \text{ and } x = \sqrt{\frac{58779 \times 720}{80902}};$$

which makes $x = 22 \cdot 87$, and the side $AB = 45 \cdot 74$.

For the hexagon, $x : y :: \sin. 30° : \sin. 60°$, or as 50000 : 86603 :: 5 : 8⅔, whence the value of $y = \frac{26x}{15}$.   This value, substituted in the equation $xy = \frac{p}{6}$, will give $\frac{26x^2}{15} = 600$; whence $x^2 = \frac{600 \times 15}{26}$; lastly, therefore, $x = \sqrt{346 \cdot 15} = 18 \cdot 61$, and the side $AB = 37 \cdot 22$.

Geometrically.

1520. Suppose the case that of a pentagon (*fig.* 601.) one of whose equal triangles is ACB.   Let fall the perpendicular CD, which divides it into two equal parts; whence its area is equal to the rectangle CDBF.

1521. Upon the side AB, prolonged, if necessary, make DE equal to CD, and from the middle of BE as a centre describe the semi-circumference cutting CD in G, and GD will be the side of a square of the same area as the rectangle CDBF.   The sides of similar figures (Geometry, 961.) being as the square roots of their areas; find the square root of the given area and make D*g* equal to it.   From the point *g* draw parallels to GE and GB, which will determine on AB the points *e* and *b*, and give on one side D*b* equal to one half of the side of the polygon sought; and, on the other, the radius D*e* of the circumference in which it is inscribed.   This is manifest because of the similar triangles EGB and *egb*, from which BD : DE :: *b*D : D*e*.

1522. From the truth that the sides of similar figures are to each other as the square roots of their areas we arrive at a simple method of reducing any figure to a given area. Form an angle of reduction (*fig.* 603.) one of whose sides is equal to the square root of the greater area, and the chord of the arc, which determines the size of the angle equal

to the square root of the smaller area. Let, for instance, the larger area =1156, and that of the smaller, to which the figure is to be reduced, =529. Draw an indefinite line, on which make AB=34, the square root of 1156. Lastly, from the point A, as a centre, having described an indefinite arc, with a length equal to the square root 23 of 529, set out B*g*; through *g* draw A*g*, which will be the angle of reduction *g*AB, by means of which the figure may be reduced, transferring all the measures of the larger area to the line AD, with which arcs are to be described whose chords will be the sides sought.

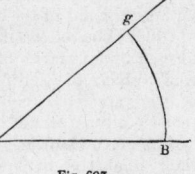

Fig. 603.

1523. If it be not required to reduce but to describe a figure whose area and form are given, we must make a large diagram of any area larger than that sought, and then reduce it.

1524. The circle, as we have already observed in a previous subsection (933.), being but a polygon of an infinite number of sides, it would follow that a circular enclosure would be stable with an infinitely small thickness of wall. This property may be easily demonstrated by a very simple experiment. Take, for instance, a sheet of paper, which would not easily be made to stand while extended to its full length, but the moment it is bent into the form of a cylinder it acquires a stability, though its thickness be not a thousandth part of its height.

1525. But as walls must have a certain thickness to acquire stability, inasmuch as they are composed of particles susceptible of separation, we may consider a circular enclosure as a regular polygon of twelve sides, and determine its thickness by the preceding process. Or, to render the operation more simple, find the thickness of a straight wall whose length is equal to one half the radius.

1526. Suppose, for example, a circular space of 56 ft. diameter and 18 ft. high, and the thickness of the wall be required. Describe the rectangle ABCD (*fig.* 594.), whose base is equal to half the radius, that is, 14 ft., and whose height AB is 18 ft. ; then, drawing the diagonal BD, make B*d* equal to the ninth part of the height, that is, 2 ft. Through *d* draw *ad* parallel to the base, and its length will represent the thickness sought, which is 14¾ inches.

1527. By calculation. Add the square of the height to that of half the radius, that is, of 18 =324, and of 14=196 (=520). Then extract the square root of 520, which will be found =22·8, and this will be the value of the diagonal BD. Then we have the following proportion : 22·8 : 14 :: 2 ft. (⅑ the height) : 14·74.

1528. The exterior wall of the church of *St. Stefano Rotondo* at Rome (Temple of Claudius) incloses a site 198 feet diameter. The wall, which is contructed of rubble masonry faced with bricks, is 2 ft. 4 in. (French) thick, and 22½ ft. high. In applying to it the preceding rule, we shall find the diagonal of the rectangle, whose base would be the side of a polygon, equal to half the radius and 22½ ft. high, would be $\sqrt{49\frac{1}{2} \times 49\frac{1}{2} + 22\frac{1}{2} \times 22\frac{1}{2}} = 54\frac{37}{100}$. Then, using the proportion $54\cdot37 : 49\cdot5 :: \frac{22\frac{1}{2}}{9} : 2$ft. 3 in. and 4 lines, the thickness sought, instead of 2 ft. 4 in., the actual thickness. We may as well mention in this place that a circle encloses the greatest quantity of area with the least quantity of walling ; and of polygons, those with a greater number of sides more than those with a lesser : the proportion of the wall in the circle being 31416 to an area of 78540000 ; whilst in a square, for the same area, a length of wall equal to 35448 would be required. As the square falls away to a flat parallelogram, say one whose sides are half as great, and the others double the length of those of the square, or 17724 by 4431, in which the area will be about 78540000, as before ; we have in such a case a length of walling =44310.

On the Thickness of Walls in Buildings not vaulted.

1529. The walls of a building are usually connected and stiffened by the timbers of the roof, supposing that to be well constructed. Some of the larger edifices, such as the ancient basilicæ at Rome, have no other covering but the roof; others have only a simple ceiling under the roof; whereas, in palaces and other habitations, there are sometimes two or more floors introduced in the roof.

1530. We will begin with those edifices covered with merely a roof of carpentry, which are, after mere walls of enclosure, the most simple.

1531. Among edifices of this species, there are some with continued points of support, such as those wherein the walls are connected and mutually support each other ; others in which the points of support are not connected with each other, such as piers, columns, and pilasters, united only by arcades which spring from them.

1532. When the carpentry forming the roof of an edifice is of great extent, instead of being injurious to the stability of the walls or points of support, it is useful in keeping them together.

1533. Many edifices exist wherein the walls and points of support would not stand without the aid of the carpentry of the roofs that cover them.

1534. The old basilica of *St. Paolo fuori le murà* at Rome was divided into five naves formed by four ranks of columns connected by arcades, which carried the walls whereon the roof rested; the centre nave 73½ ft. (French) wide, and 93 ft. 10 in. high. The walls of it are erected on columns 31 ft. 9 in. high, and their thickness is a little less than 3 ft., that is, only $\frac{1}{33}$ part of their height.

1535. At Hadrian's Villa the most lofty walls, still standing, were but sixteen times their thickness in height, and 51 ft. 9 in. long. The walls were the enclosures of large halls with only a single story, but assisted at their ends by cross walls. And we may therefore conclude that if the walls of the basilica above mentioned were not kept in their places by the carpentry of the great roof they would not be safe. It is curious that this supposition, under the theory, was proved by the fire which destroyed the church of St. Paolo in 1823. The walls which form the nave of the church of Santa Sabina are raised on columns altogether 52 ft. high; they are 145 ft. long, and somewhat less than 2 ft., that is, $\frac{1}{26}$ part of their height, in thickness. They are, therefore, not in a condition of stability without the aid of the roof. In comparing, however, the thickness of these walls with the height only of the side aisles, in the basilica of St. Paolo the thickness is $\frac{1}{17}$, and at Santa Sabina $\frac{1}{13}$. In the other basilicæ or churches with columns, the least thickness of wall is $\frac{1}{2}$ of greater proportion unconnected with the nave, as at Santa Maria Maggiore, Santa Maria in Trastevere, St. Chrysogono, St. Pietro in Vincolo, in Rome; St. Lorenzo and St. Spirito, in Florence; St. Filippo Neri, at Naples; St. Giuseppe and St. Dominico, at Palermo.

1536. We must take into account, moreover, that the thickness of walls depends as much on the manner in which they are constructed, as on their height and the weight with which they are loaded. A wall of rough or squared stone 12 inches thick, wherein all the stones run right through the walls in one piece, is sometimes stronger than one of 18 or 20 inches in thickness, in which the depth of the stones is not more than half or a third of the thickness, and the inner part filled in with rubble in a bad careless way. We are also to recollect that stability more than strength is ofttimes the safeguard of a building; for it is certain that a wall of hard stone 4 inches thick would be stronger than would be necessary to bear a load equal to four or five stories, where a thickness of 18 inches is used; and yet it is manifest that such a wall would be very unstable, because of the narrowness of the base.

1537. From an examination which Rondelet made of 280 buildings in France and Italy, ancient as well as modern, he found that in those covered with roofs of two inclined sides and constructed in framed carpentry, with and without ceilings, and so trussed as not to act at all horizontally upon the walls, the least thickness in brick or rough stones was $\frac{1}{24}$ of the width in the clear.

1538. In private houses, divided into several stories by floors, it was observed, generally, that the exterior walls ran from 15 to 24 inches, party walls 16 to 20 inches, and partition walls 12 to 18 inches.

1539. In buildings on a larger scale, exterior walls 2 to 3 feet thick, party walls 20 to 24 inches, partition walls 15 to 20 inches.

1540. In palaces and buildings of great importance, whose ground floors are vaulted, the exterior walls varied from 4 to 9 feet, and the partition walls from 2 to 6 feet. In many of the examples which underwent examination, the thicknesses of the walls and points of support were not always well proportioned to their position, to the space they enclosed, nor to the loads they bore. In some, great voids occur, and considerable loads were supplied with but slender walls and points of support; and in others, very thick walls enclosed very small spaces, and strong points of support had but little to carry.

1541. For the purpose of establishing some method which in a sure and simple manner would determine the thickness of walls in buildings which are not arched, we have considered, says Rondelet, that the tie-beams of the trusses of carpentry whereof the roofs are composed, being always placed in the direction of the width, as well as the girders and leading timbers of floors, serve rather to steady and connect the opposite walls; but, considering the elasticity and flexibility of timber, it is found that they strain the walls which support them in proportion to the widths of the spaces enclosed, whence it becomes often the better plan to determine the thickness of the walls from the width and height of the apartments requisite. Hence the following rules.

First Rule.

1542. In buildings covered with a simple roof, if the walls are insulated throughout, their height up to the under side of the tie-beams of the trusses, being as shown in *fig.* 604. Having drawn the diagonal BD and thereon made B*b* and D*d*, equal to the twelfth part of the height AB, then through the points *b* and *d*, draw lines parallel to BA and DC, which will bound the thickness of the walls required.

1543. If the height AB and width AD be known, the thickness A*c* may be calculated,

seeing that $BD = \sqrt{AB^2 + AD^2}$; knowing the value of BD, we have that of cA by the proportion $BD : AD :: B b : cA = \frac{AD \times Bb}{BD}$.

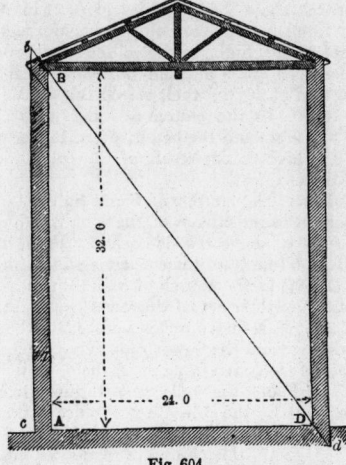

First Example.

1544. Supposing the width AD = 24 ft., and the height AB = 32, we shall have

$\sqrt{AB^2 + AD^2} = \sqrt{24 \times 24 + 32 \times 32}$; whence $BD = \sqrt{576 + 1024} = \sqrt{1600} = 40$ ft.

Bb, which is the twelfth part of AB, or of 32 ft. = 2 ft. 8 in. ; the thickness of the wall expressed by $\frac{AD \times Bb}{BD}$, will be $\frac{24 \times 2\frac{2}{3}}{40} = 1\frac{3}{5}$ ft., or 1 ft. 7 in. 2 lines, for the thickness sought.

1545. If the walls supporting the roof were stiffened by extra means, such as lower roofs at an intermediate height, as in churches with a nave and side aisles, we may make Be in the diagonal BD (*fig.* 605.) equal to one twelfth of the height above the springing of the side roofs, and ef a twenty-fourth part of that height below it, and draw through the point f a line parallel to AB, which will determine the thickness Af' sought ; or, which amounts to the same thing, add together the total height AB of the interior, and that of E B above the point of support, E, whereof take the twenty-fourth part, which will be equal to B$e + ef$.

Fig. 604.

Second Example.

1546. *Fig.* 605. is a section of St. Paolo fuorì le murà, near Rome, as it was in 1816.

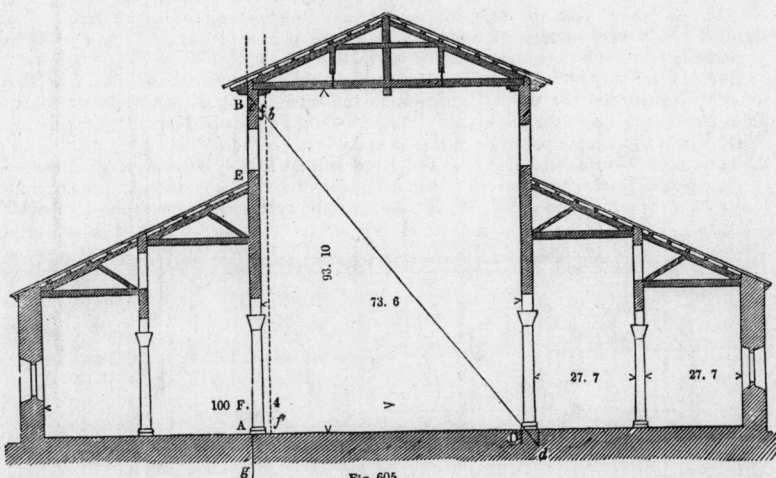

Fig. 605.

The interior height to the under side of the tie-beams is 93 ft. 10 in. (French), whereof 26 ft. 2 in. is the exterior height above the roofs of the side aisles. These two dimensions together make 120 ft., whose twenty-fourth part is 5 ft., to which, on the diagonal BD make Bf equal ; then from the point f letting fall a vertical line, the horizontal line Be will determine the thickness, which will be 3 ft., the width of the nave being 73 ft. 6 in. In figures, as follows : —

$$BD = \sqrt{93 \text{ ft. } 10 \text{ in. } \times 93 \text{ ft. } 10 \text{ in. } + 73 \text{ ft. } 6 \text{ in. } \times 73 \text{ ft. } 6 \text{ in.}} = \sqrt{14207} = 119 \text{ ft. } 2 \text{ in.}$$

1547. For the thickness, eB, as before, $BD : AD :: Bf : Af'$; whence, $Af' = \frac{AD \times Bf}{BD}$

$= \frac{73\frac{1}{2} \times 5}{119 \text{ ft. } 2 \text{ in.}} = 3$ ft. 1 in., instead of 2 ft. 11 in. 9 lines, the actual thickness of the walls.

1548. The same calculation being applied to the walls of the nave of Santa Sabina

(Rome), whose height of nave is 51 ft. 2 in, and width 42 ft. 2 in., with a height of 16 ft. of wall above the side aisles, gives 21 in. 4 lines, and they are actually a little less than 24 in.

1549. In the church of Santa Maria Maggiore, the width is 52 ft. 7½ in., and 56 ft. 6 in. and 4 lines high, to the ceiling under the roof. The height of the wall above the side aisles is 19 ft. 8 in., and the calculation requires the thickness of the walls to be 26¼ in. instead of 28¼ in., their actual thickness.

1550. In the church of St. Lorenzo, at Florence, the internal width of the nave is 37 ft. 9 in., and the height 69 ft. to the wooden ceiling ; from the side aisles the wall is 18 ft. high. The result of the calculation is 21 in., and the actual execution 21 in. and 6 lines.

1551. The church of Santo Spirito, in the same city, which has a wooden ceiling sus‧ pended to the trusses of the roof, is 76 ft. high and 37 ft. 4 in. wide in the nave the walls rise 19 ft. above the side aisles. From an application of the rule the thickness should be 21 in. 3 lines, and their thickness is 22½ in.

1552. In the church of St. Philippo Neri, at Naples, the calculation requires a thickness of 21 in., their actual thickness being 22½ in.

1553. In the churches here cited, the external walls are much thicker ; which was necessary, from the lower roofs being applied as *leantoes*, and hence having a tendency, in case of defective framing of them, to thrust out the external walls. Thus, in the church of St. Paolo, the walls are 7 ft. thick, their height 40 ft. ; 3 ft. 4 in. only being the thickness required by the rule. A resistance is thus given capable of assisting the walls of the aisles, which are raised on isolated columns, and one which they require.

1554. In the church of Santa Sabina, the exterior wall, which is 26 ft. high, is, as the rule indicates, 26 in. thick ; but the nave is flanked with a single aisle only on each side, and the walls of the nave are thicker in proportion to the height, and are not so high. For at St. Paolo the thickness of the walls is only $\frac{1}{24}$ of the interior width, whilst at Santa Sabina it is $\frac{1}{21}$. At San Lorenzo and San Spirito the introduction of the side chapels affords great assistance to the external walls.

Second Rule.
For the Thickness of Walls of Houses of more than one Story.

1555. As in the preceding case, the rules which Rondelet gives are the result of observations on a vast number of buildings that have been executed, so that the method proposed is founded on practice as well as on theory.

1556. In ordinary houses, wherein the height of the floors rarely exceeds 12 to 15 ft., in order to apportion the proper thickness to the interior or partition walls, we must be guided by the widths of the spaces they separate, and the number of floors they have to carry. With respect to the external walls, their thickness will depend on the depth and height of the building. Thus a *single* house, as the phrase is, that is, only one set of apartments in depth, requires thicker external walls than a *double* house, that is, more than one apartment in depth, of the same sort and height ; because the stability is in the inverse ratio of the width.

1557. Let us take the first of the two cases (*fig.* 606.), whose depth is 24 ft. and height

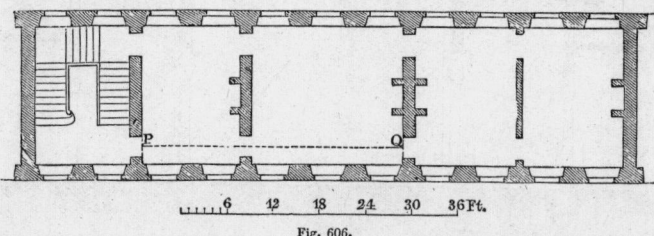

Fig. 606.

to the under side of the roof 36 ft. Add to 24 ft. the half of the height, 18, and take $\frac{1}{21}$ part of the sum 42, that is, 21 in., for the least thickness of each of the external walls above the *set-off* on the ground floor. For a mean stability add an inch, and for one still more solid add two inches.

1558. In the case of a double house (*fig.* 607.) with a depth of 42 ft., and of the same height as the preceding example, add half the height to the width of the building ; that is, 21 to 18, and $\frac{1}{21}$ of the sum $= 19\frac{1}{2}$ is the thickness of the walls. To determine the thickness of the partition walls, add to their distance from each other the height of the story, and take $\frac{1}{36}$ of the sum. Thus, to find the thickness of the wall IK, which divides the space LM into two parts and is 32 ft., add the height of the story, which we will take at 10 ft., making in all 42 ft., and take $\frac{1}{36}$ or 14 in. Half an inch may be added for each story above the ground floor. Thus, where three stories occur above the ground floor, the thickness in

the lower one would be $15\frac{1}{2}$ in., a thickness which is well calculated for bricks and stone, whose hardness is of a mean description.

1559. For the wall AB, which divides the space between the external walls, equal to 35 ft., add to it the height, which is 10 ft., and $\frac{1}{36}$ of 45, the sum of the two; that is, 15 in. is the thickness required for the wall, if only to be carried up a single story; but if through more, then add half an inch, as before, for each story above the ground floor. For the spaces NO, PQ, RS, in this and the preceding figure, the repetition of the operation will give their thicknesses.

1560. To illustrate what has been said, *fig.* 608. is introduced to the reader, being

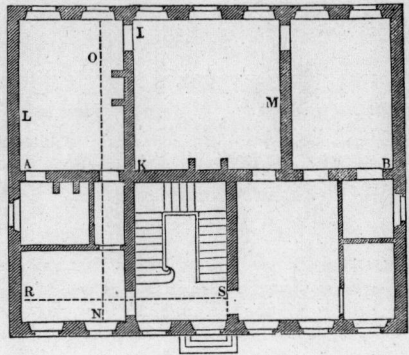

Fig. 607.

the plan of a house in the Rue d' Enfer, near the Luxembourg, known as the Hotel Vendôme,

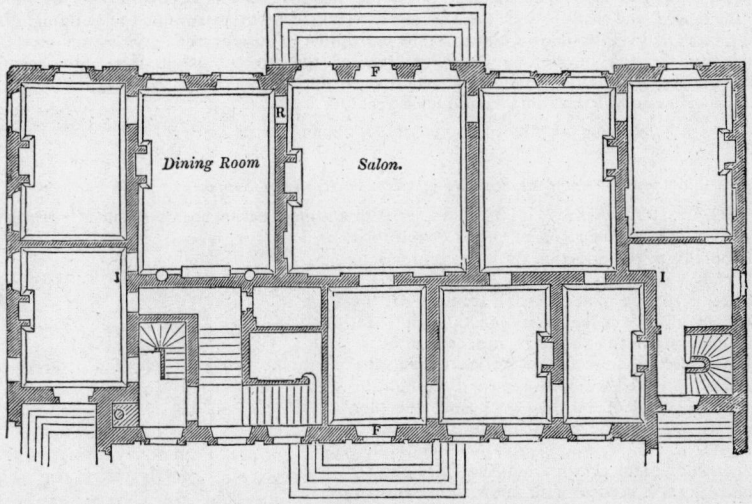

Fig. 608.

built by Le Blond. It is given by D'Aviler in his *Cours d'Architecture.* The building is 46 ft. deep on the right side and 47 ft. in the middle, and is 33 ft. high from the pavement to the entablature. Hence, to obtain the thickness of the walls on the line FF, take the sum of the height and width $=\frac{47+33}{2}=40$ ft., whose twenty-fourth part is 20 in. The building being one of solidity, let 2 in. be added, and we obtain 22 in. instead of 2 ft., which is their actual thickness. For the thickness of the interior wall, which crosses the building in the direction of its length, the space between the exterior walls being 42 ft. and the height of each story 14 ft., the thickness of this wall should be $\frac{42+14}{36}=18$ in. 8 lines, instead of 18 in., which the architect assigned to it.

1561. By the same mode of operation, we shall find that the thickness of the wall R, separating the salon, which is 22 ft. wide, from the dining-room, which is 18 ft. wide and 14 ft. high, should be 18 in. and 6 lines instead of 18 inches; but as the exterior walls, which are of wrought stone, are 2 ft. thick, and their stability greater than the rule requires, the interior will be found to have the requisite stability without any addition to their thickness.

1562. We shall conclude the observations under this head, by reference to a house built by Palladio for the brothers Mocenigo, of Venice, to be found in his works, and here given (*fig.* 609.). Most of the buildings of this master are vaulted below ; but the one in question is not in that predicament. The width and height of the principal rooms is 16 ft., and they are separated by others only 8 ft. wide, so that the width which each wall separates is $25\frac{1}{2}$ ft., and their thickness consequently should be $\frac{25\frac{1}{2}+16}{36}=13$ in. 10 lines. The walls, as executed,

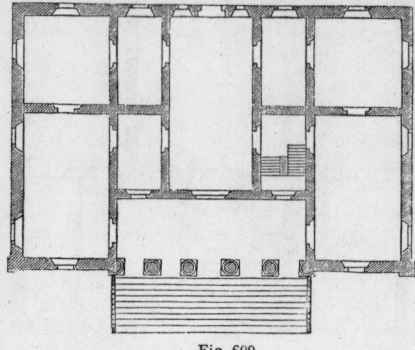

Fig. 609.

are 14 in. in thickness. The exterior walls being 24 ft. high, and the depth of the building 46 ft. Their thickness by the rule should be $17\frac{1}{2}$ in. : they are 18 in.

On passing the Metropolitan Building Act in 1855, previous to which the thicknesses of walls depended on buildings falling within certain classes or rates, we had the satisfaction of advising the Government to adopt the thicknesses of walls now directed to be used. These are based upon rules deduced from sections 1512 *et seq.* Inasmuch, however, as it was thought that builders might be liable to mistakes in extracting the square root of the sum of the squares of the heights and lengths of walls, tables were inserted in the Act to meet all cases.

Generally the formula $t = \frac{hl}{nd}$ will be a useful guide in adjusting the thickness of walls, in which t = thickness, h and l respectively the height and length, d the diagonal formed by the height and length, and n a constant determined by the nature of the building. In the tables for dwelling-houses, the constant multiplier (n) used was 22; for warehouses, 20. And but for the interference in committee of the present Right Hon. Member for Oxfordshire (Mr. Henley), for what scientific reasons it is difficult to say, the constant multiplier for public buildings would have been 18.

When h is less than $\frac{l}{2}$, the constants are 27, 23, and 20 respectively.

Of the Stability of Piers or Points of Support.

1563. Let ABCD (*fig.* 610.) be a pier with a square base whose resistance is required in respect of a power at M acting to overturn it horizontally in the direction MA, or obliquely in that of NA upon the point D. Considering the solid reduced to a plane passing through G, the centre of gravity of the pier, and the point D, that upon which the power is supposed to cause it to turn, let fall from G the vertical cutting the base in I, to which we will suppose the weight of the pier suspended, and then supposing the pier removed, we only have to consider the angular lever BDI or HDI, whose arms are determined by perpendiculars drawn from the fulcrum D, in one direction vertical with the weight, and in the other perpendicular to the direction of the power acting upon the pier, according to the theory of the lever explained in a previous section.

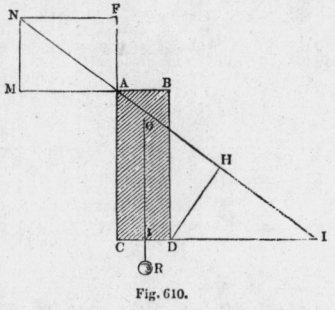

Fig. 610.

1564. The direction of the weight R being always represented by a vertical let fall from the centre of gravity, the arm of its lever ID never changes, whatever the direction of the power and the height at which it is applied, whilst the arm of the lever of the power varies as its position and direction. That there may be equilibrium between the effort of the power and the resistance of the pier, in the first case, when the power M acts in an horizontal direction, we have M : R::ID : DB, whence $M \times DB = R \times ID$ and $M = \frac{R \times ID}{DB}$. If the direction of the power be oblique, as NA in the case of an equilibrium, N : R::ID : DH; hence $N \times DH = R \times ID$ and $N = \frac{R \times ID}{DH}$.

1565. Applying this in an example, let the height of the pier be 12 ft., its width 4 ft., and its thickness 1 ft. The weight R of the pier may be represented by its cube, and is therefore $12 \times 4 \times 1 = 48$. The arm of its lever ID will be 2, and we will take the horizontal power M represented by DB at 12; with these values we shall have M : 48::2 : 12; hence $M \times 12 = 48 \times 2$ and $M = \frac{48 \times 2}{12} = 8$.

That is, the effort of the horizontal power M should be equal to the weight of 8 cube feet of the materials whereof the pier is composed, to be in equilibrium.

1566. In respect of the oblique power which acts in the direction NA, supposing DH $= 7\frac{1}{5}$, we have N : 48::2 : $7\frac{1}{5}$, whence $N \times 7\frac{1}{5} = 48 \times 2$, therefore $N = \frac{48 \times 2}{7\frac{1}{5}} = 13\frac{1}{3}$, whilst the

expression of the horizontal power M was only 8 ft. ; but it must be observed, that the arm of the lever is 12, whilst that of the power N is but $7\frac{1}{3}$ ft. ; but $13\frac{1}{3} \times 7\frac{1}{2} = 8 \times 12 = 96$, which is also equal to the resistance of the pier expressed by $12 \times 4 \times 2 = 96$. It is moreover essential to observe, that, considering the power NA as the result of two others, MA and FA, the first acting horizontally from M against A, tends to overthrow the pier ; whilst the second, acting vertically in the direction FA, partly modifies this effect by increasing the resistance of the pier.

1567. Suppose the power NA to make an angle of 53 degrees with the vertical AF, and of 37 degrees with the horizontal line AM ; then

NA : FA : MA::rad. : sin. 37 deg. : sin. 53 deg. :: 6 : 10 : 8.

Hence, NA being found $= 13\frac{1}{3}$, we have $6 : 10 : 8 :: 13\frac{1}{3} : 8 : 10\frac{2}{3}$.

Whence it is evident that, from this resolution of the power NA, the resistance of the pier is increased by the effort of the power $FA = 8$, which, acting on the point A in the direction FA, will make the arm of its lever $CD = 4$, whence its effort $= 8 \times 4 = 32$.

1568. The resistance of the pier, being thus found $= 96$, becomes by the effort of the power $FA = 96 + 32 = 128$.

1569. The effort of the horizontal power M being $10\frac{2}{3}$, and the arm of its lever being always 12, its effort 128 will be equal to the resistance of the pier, which proves that in this resolution we have, as before, the effort and the resistance equal. The application of this proposition is extremely useful in valuing exactly the effects of parts of buildings which become stable by means of oblique and lateral thrusts.

1570. If it be required to know what should be the increased width of the pier to counterpoise the vertical effort FA, its expression must be divided by ID, that is, 8×2, which gives 4 for this increased length, and for the expression of its resistance $(12 + 4) \times 4 \times 2 = 128$, as above.

1571. If the effort of the power be known, and the thickness of a pier or wall whose height is known be sought so as to resist it, let the power and parts of the pier be represented by different letters, as follows. Calling the power p, the height of the pier d, the thickness sought x; if the power p act in an horizontal direction at the extremity of the wall or pier, its expression will be $p \times d$. The resistance of the pier will be expressed by its area multiplied by its arm of lever, that is, $d \times x \times \frac{x}{2}$; and supposing equilibrium, as the resistance must be equal to the thrust, we shall have the equation $p \times d = d \times x \times \frac{x}{2}$. Both sides of this equation being divisible by d, we have $p = x \times \frac{x}{2}$; and as the second term is divided by 2, we obtain $2p = x \times x$ or x^2; that is, a square whose area $= 2p$, and of which x is the side or root, or $x = \sqrt{2p}$, a formula which in all cases expresses the thickness to be given to the pier CD to resist a power M acting on its upper extremity in the horizontal direction MA.

1572. In this formula, the height of the pier need not be known to find the value of x, because this height, being common to the pier and the arm of the lever of the power, does not alter the result; for the cube of the pier, which represents its weight, increases or diminishes in the same ratio as the lever. Thus, if the height of the pier be 12, 15, or 24 ft., its thickness will nevertheless be the same.

Example. — If the horizontal power expressed by p in the formula $x = \sqrt{2p}$ be 8, we have $x = \sqrt{16} = 4$ for the thickness of the pier. Whilst the power acting at the extremity of the pier remains the same, the thickness is sufficient, whatever the height of the pier. Thus for a height of 12 ft. the effort of the power will be $8 \times 12 = 96$, and the resistance $12 \times 4 \times 2 = 96$. If the pier be 15 ft. high, its resistance will be $15 \times 4 \times 2 = 120$, and the effort of the power $8 \times 15 = 120$. Lastly, if the height be 24 ft., the resistance will be $24 \times 4 \times 2 = 192$, and the effort of the power $8 \times 24 = 192$.

1573. If the point on which the horizontal force acts is lower than the wall or pier, the difference may be represented by f; and then $p \times (d - f) = d \times x \times \frac{x}{2}$;

Which becomes $2pd - 2pf = dx^2$ and $2p - \frac{2pf}{d} = x^2$;

Lastly $x = \sqrt{2p - \frac{2pf}{d}}$.

Suppose $p = 9$. $f = 6$ and $d = 12$,

the formula becomes $x = \sqrt{18 - \frac{18 \times 6}{12}} = \sqrt{9} = 3$, which is the thickness sought.

1574. When the power NA is oblique, the thickness may be equally well found by the arm of lever DH, by resolving it into two forces, as before. Thus, in the case of the oblique power $p = 13\frac{1}{3}$, calling f its arm of lever $7\frac{1}{2}$, we shall have $p \times f = \frac{dx^2}{2}$, which will become $\frac{2pf}{d} = x^2$, whence $x = \sqrt{\frac{2pf}{d}}$; in which, substituting the known values, we have $x = \sqrt{\frac{2 \times 13\frac{1}{3} \times 7\frac{1}{2}}{12}}$ whence $x = \sqrt{16} = 4$, the thickness sought of the pier.

1575. In resolving the oblique effort NA into two forces, whereof one MA tends to overturn the pier by acting in an horizontal direction, and the other fA to strengthen it by acting vertically, as before observed ; let us represent the horizontal effort MA by p; its arm of lever, equal to the height of the pier, by d; the vertical effort fA by n; the arm of lever of the last-named effort, being the thickness sought, will be x; from which we have the equation

$$pd = \frac{dx^2}{2} + nx, \text{ or } 2p = x^2 + \frac{2nx}{d}.$$

1576. As the second member of this equation is not a perfect square, let there be added to each side the term wanting, that is, the square $\frac{n^2}{d^2}$, the half of the quantity $\frac{2n}{d}$, which multiplied x in the second term, whence

$$2p + \frac{n^2}{d^2} = x^2 + \frac{2nx}{d} + \frac{n}{d}.$$

1577. The second member, by this addition, having become a square whose root is $x + \frac{n}{d}$, we shall have $x + \frac{n}{d} - \sqrt{2p + \frac{n^2}{d^2}}$ and lastly $x = \sqrt{2p + \frac{n^2}{d^2}} - \frac{n}{d}$ will be the general formula for finding the thickness x.

Application of the Formula.

1578. Let $p = 10\frac{2}{3}$, $n = 8$, $d = 12$. Substituting these values in the formula, it will become

$$x = \sqrt{10\frac{2}{3} \times 2 + \frac{64}{144}} - \frac{8}{12} = \sqrt{21\frac{1}{3} + \frac{4}{9}} - \frac{2}{3} = \sqrt{21 + \frac{7}{9}} - \frac{2}{3} = 4.$$

1579. If, for proof, we wish to calculate the expression of the resistance, by placing in the equation of equilibrium $2pd = dx\frac{x}{2} \times nx$, the values of the quantities p, d, and x, above found, we shall have

$$10\frac{2}{3} \times 12 = 12 \times 4 \times 2 + 8 = 128, \text{ as was previously found for } FA.$$

1580. From the preceding rules, it appears that all the effects whose tendency is to destroy an edifice, arise from weight acting in an inverse ratio to the obstacles with which it meets. When heavy bodies are merely laid on one another, the result of their efforts is a simple pressure, capable of producing settlement or fracture of the parts acted upon.

1581. Foundations whose bases are spread over a much greater extent than the walls imposed upon them, are more susceptible of settlement or of crushing or fracture. But isolated points of support in the upper parts, which sometimes carry great weights on a small superficies, are susceptible both of settlement and crushing, whilst the weight they have to sustain is greater than the force of the materials whereof they are formed; which renders the knowledge of the strength of materials an object of consequence in construction. Till of late years it was not thought necessary to pay much attention to this branch of construction, because most species of stone are more than sufficiently hard for the greatest number of cases. Thus, the abundant thickness which the ancients generally gave to all the parts of their buildings, proves that with them this was not a subject of consideration ; and the more remotely we go into antiquity, the more massive is the construction found to be. At last, experience taught the architect to make his buildings less heavy. Columns, which among the Egyptians were only 5 or 6 diameters high, were carried to 9 diameters by the Greeks in the Ionic and Corinthian orders. The Romans made their columns still higher, and imparted greater general lightness to their buildings. It was under the reign of Constantine, towards the end of the empire, that builders without taste carried their boldness in light construction to an extraordinary degree, as in the ancient basilicæ of St. Peter's at Rome and St. Paolo fuorì le murà. Later, however, churches of a different character, and of still greater lightness, were introduced by the Gothic architects.

1582. The invention and general use of domes created a very great load upon the supporting piers; and the earlier architects, fearful of the mass to be carried, gave their piers an area of base much greater than was required by the load supported, and the nature of the stone used to support it. They, moreover, in this respect, did little more than imitate one another. The piers were constructed in form and dimensions suited rather to the arrangement and decoration of the building that was designed, than to a due apportionment of the size and weight to the load to be borne ; so that their difference from one another is in every respect very considerable.

The piers bearing the dome of St. Peter's at Rome are loaded with a weight of 14·964 tons for every superficial foot of their horizontal section.

The piers bearing the dome of St. Paul's at London are loaded with a weight of 17·705 tons for every superficial foot of their horizontal section.

The piers bearing the dome of the Hospital of Invalids at Paris are loaded with a weight of 13·598 tons for every superficial foot of their horizontal section.

The piers bearing the dome of the Pantheon (St. Geneviéve) at Paris are loaded with a weight of 26·934 tons for every superficial foot of their horizontal section.

The columns of St. Paolo fuori le mura, near Rome, are loaded with a weight of 18·123 tons for every superficial foot of their horizontal section.

In the church of St. Méry, the piers of the tower are loaded with upwards of 27 tons to the superficial foot. With such a discrepancy, it is difficult to say, without a most perfect knowledge of the stone employed, what should be the exact weight per foot. The dome of the Hospital of the Invalids seems to exhibit a maximum of pier in relation to the weight, and that of the Pantheon at Paris a minimum. All the experiments (scanty, indeed, they are) which we can present to the reader are those given at the beginning of this section. In this country, the government has always been too much employed in considering how long it can keep itself in place, to have time to consider how the services of its members could benefit the nation by the furtherance of science. An exactly opposite conduct has always marked the French government : hence more scientific artists are always found amongst them than we can boast here, where the cost of experiments invariably comes out of the artist's pocket.

Ratio of the Points of Support in a Building to its total Superficies.

1583. In the pages immediately preceding, we have, with Rondelet for our guide, explained the principles whereon depend the stabilities of walls and points of support, with their application to different sorts of buildings. Not any point relating to construction is of more importance to the architect. Without a knowledge of it, and the mode of even generating new styles from it, he is nothing more than a pleasing draughtsman at the best, whose elevations and sections may be very captivating, but who must be content to take rank in about the same degree as the portrait painter does in comparison with him who paints history. We subjoin a table of great instruction, showing the ratio of the points of support to the total superficies covered in some of the principal buildings of Europe. It exhibits also the comparative sizes of the different buildings named in it.

Table showing the ratio of the Walls and Points of Support of the principal Edifices of Europe to the total Area which they occupy.

Names of Edifices.	Total Area of the Building in English superficial feet.	Total Area of the Points of Support in English superficial feet.	Ratio in Thousandths of the Points of Support to the total Area.
The Pantheon at Rome - - -	34,328	7,954	0·232
Temple of Peace at Rome - - -	67,123	8,571	0·127
Great temple at Pæstum - - -	15,353	2,649	0·172
Ancient temple, Galuzzo, at Rome - -	9,206	2,167	0·235
Temple of Concord, Girgenti, Sicily - -	6,849	1,330	0·194
Temple of Juno Lucina, Sicily - -	6,821	1,110	0·163
Central building of the baths of Caracalla -	275,503	48,911	0·176
Central building of the baths of Diocletian -	351,636	58,797	0·167
Temple of Claudius at Rome, now church of S. Stefano - - - - -	36,726	2,051	0·056
Mosque of S. Sophia at Constantinople -	103,200	22,567	0·217
Basilica of S. Paolo fuore le murà (Rome), 1816 - - - - -	106,513	12,655	0·118
Duomo of S. Maria del fiore at Florence -	84,802	17,030	0·201
Duomo of S. Maria del fiore at Milan -	125,853	21,635	0·169
St. Peter's at Rome, as executed -	227,069	59,308	0·261
St. Peter's at Rome, as projected by Bramante	213,610	46,879	0·219
Church of S. Vitale at Ravenna - -	7,276	1,142	0·157
Church of S. Pietro a Vincolà, Rome - -	21,520	3,353	0·155
Church of S. Sabino — destroyed - -	15,139	1,543	0·100
Church of S. Domenico, Palermo - -	34,144	4,988	0·146
Church of S. Giuseppe, Palermo - -	26,046	3,611	0·139
Church of S. Filippo Neri, Naples - -	22,826	2,944	0·129
Church of St. Paul's, London - -	84,025	14,311	0·170
Church of Notre Dame, Paris - -	67,343	8,784	0·140
Hotel of the Invalids, Paris - -	29,003	7,790	0·268
Church of S. Sulpice, Paris - - -	60,760	9,127	0·151
Church of S. Geneviéve, Paris -. -	60,287	9,269	0·154

1583a. It will be manifest, that as these points of support are diminished in area, in respect of the mass, so is a greater degree of skill exhibited in the work. From the following table, it will be seen that, in seventeen celebrated mediæval edifices, the ratio of their points of support to their whole areas varies from ·116 to ·238, nearly double. It is curious to observe the high rank borne in this table by Henry VII.'s chapel ; generally, skill seems to have increased with greater experience : —

TABLE OF POINTS OF SUPPORT.

Building.	Century.	Part of Century.	Ratio of Points of Support to their whole areas.
Henry VII.'s Chapel - -	16	First	0·116
Freiburg Dom - - -	13	Second	0·133
Nôtre Dame, Paris -	13	Second	0·140
King's College Chapel, Cambridge	15	Second	0·152
Milan Duomo - - -	14	Second	0·169
York Cathedral - -	13	Second	0·174
Westminster Abbey - -	13	Second	0·178
Temple Church - -	13	Second	0·185
Ely Cathedral - -	12	Second	0·188
Gloucester Cathedral - -	14	Second	0·188
Salisbury Cathedral -	13	First	0·190
Florence Duomo - -	15	First	0·201
Lincoln Cathedral - -	12	Second	0·202
Worcester Cathedral -	13	First	0·208
Marburg Dom - - -	14	Second	0·218
Canterbury Cathedral - -	12	Second	0·225
Norwich Cathedral - -	12	First	0·238

1583b. Led by Le Brun (*Théorie de l'Architecture*, &c. fol. Paris, 1807.), we were many years ago induced to inquire into the doctrine of voids and solids in the Greek and Roman temples, and though we soon discovered that that author had committed manifest errors in his mode of applying his theory, there could be no doubt that if its principles were properly carried out, they would coincide with the best examples both ancient and modern. The study we have subsequently bestowed upon it has not, we regret, from various pressing occupations, received from us all the attention necessary to reduce the examples within such bounds as to make the matter subject to certain laws, though we think an approximation has been effected towards it.

1583c. It is to be lamented that, among the many and able writers on Gothic architecture, details, more than principles. seem to have occupied their minds.   The origin of the pointed arch seems to have entirely absorbed the attention of a large proportion of them, whilst others have been mainly content with discussions on the peculiarities of style at the different periods, and watching with anxiety the periods of transition from one to another. Foliage, mouldings, and the like, have had charms for others; all, however, have neglected to bestow a thought upon the grand system of equilibrium by which such stupendous edifices were poised, and out of which system a key is to be extracted to the detail that enters into them.   It is, however, to be hoped that abler hands than ours will henceforth be stimulated to the work, such being abundant in the profession whereof we place ourselves as the humblest of its members.

Fig. 610a.

1583d. As on the horizontal projection or plan of a building, the ratio of the points of support have been above considered, so in the vertical projection or section of a building may the ratio of the solids to the voids be compared, as well as the ratio of the solids to the whole area. In *fig.* 610a. the shaded

parts represent the solids, which therefore give boundaries of the voids. Worcester Cathedral is the example shown. In this mode of viewing a structure, as also in that of the points of support, there is a minimum to which art is confined, and in both cases for obvious reasons there are some dependent on the nature of the materials, and others on the laws of statics. Though there may be found some exceptions to the enunciation as a general rule, it may be safely assumed that in those buildings, as in the case of the points of support, wherein the ratios of the solids to the voids in section are the least, the art, not only as respects construction, but also in point of magnificence in effect, is most advantageously displayed. In every edifice like a cathedral, the greater the space over which the eye can range, whether horizontally or vertically, the more imposing is its effect on the spectator, provided the solids be not so lessened as to induce a sensation of danger.

1583e. The subjoined table contains, with the exception of Nòtre Dame de Paris, the same buildings as those already cited. It will be seen that the ratios of the solids to the voids varies from ·472 to 1·118, a little less than half to a little more than a whole. But if in their sections we compare the ratios of the solids to the whole area, there results a set of numbers varying from ·321 to ·528, and that nearly following the order of the ratios of the points of support.

TABLE OF VERTICAL SOLIDS AND VOIDS.

Building.	Century.	Part of Century.	Ratio of Solids to Area.	Ratio of Solids to Voids.
Salisbury Cathedral -	13	First	0·321	0·472
Marburg Dom - -	14	Second	0·335	0·503
Norwich Cathedral -	12	First	0·376	0·603
Worcester Cathedral -	13	First	0·388	0·633
Milan Duomo - -	14	Second	0·393	0·648
Temple Church - -	13	Second	0·395	0·648
Gloucester Cathedral -	14	Second	0·403	0·674
King's College Chapel -	15	Second	0·419	0·722
York Cathedral - -	13	Second	0·421	0·729
Westminster Abbey -	13	Second	0·440	0·980
Henry VII.'s Chapel -	16	First	0·457	0·648
Freiburg Dom - -	13	Second	0·478	0·916
Canterbury Cathedral -	12	Second	0·496	0·904
Ely Cathedral - -	12	Second	0·498	1·000
Lincoln Cathedral -	12	Second	0·499	1·000
Florence Duomo - -	15	First	0·528	1·118

Though the coincidence between the ratios of increase, in the points of support, does not run quite concurrently with the ratios of the solids and the areas in comparing the cathedrals of the different centuries, yet sufficient appears to show an intimate connection between them. Where the discrepancy occurs, the points of support seem inversely set out. Such, for instance, will be seen in Ely Cathedral, wherein, though the ratio of the solids to the voids in section is as high as 1 (or ratio of equality), that of the points of support is as low as 0·182, so that the space, or airiness, which is lost in the former, is compensated by the latter. Generally speaking, however, the points of support diminish as the ornament of the style increases. Thus, in Norwich Cathedral (the nave), of the early part of the twelfth century, the ratio of the points of support is 0·238, that of the solids to the voids being 0·603 ; while at Salisbury (latter part of the thirteenth century) the ratio of the points of support is only 0·190, and that of the solids to the voids, 0·472.

From the foregoing examination, there can scarcely exist a doubt that the first and leading lines of these fabrics were based upon a geometrical calculation of extremely simple nature, but most rigidly adhered to. Thus, taking a single bay in the nave, say, from centre to centre, and ascertaining the area, that has only to be multiplied by the ratio, to give the superficies necessary for the points of support, which, as the tables indicate, were diminished as experience taught they might be. These matters then being adjusted, and falling as they might, the system of ornamentation was applied altogether subsidiary to the great and paramount consideration of stability.

1583f. A very ingenious writer and skilful architect (Mr. Sam. Ware), some years ago, took great trouble to deduce the stability of the buildings in question, from the general mass of the walls and vaulting containing within them some hidden catenarian curve. If such were the case, which can hardly be admitted, in as much as a chain for such purpose might be made to hang in all of them, it is quite certain this property was unknown to those who erected them. Dr. Hooke was the first who gave the hint that the figure of a flexible cord, or chain, suspended from two points, was a proper form for an arch.

Pressure of Earth against Walls.

1584. It is not our intention to pursue this branch of the practice of walling to any extent, the determination of the thickness of walls in this predicament being more useful, perhaps, to the engineer than to the architect. We shall therefore be contented with but a concise mention of it. Rondelet has (with, as we consider, great judgment) adopted the theory of Belidor, in his *Science des Ingenieurs*, and we shall follow him. Without the slightest disrespect to later authors, we know from our own practice that walls of *revête-ment* may be built, with security, of much less thickness than either the theories of Belidor, or, latterly, of modern writers require. We entirely leave out of the question the rules of Dr. Hutton in his Mathematics, as absurd and incomprehensible. The fact is, that in carrying up walls to sustain a bank of earth, nobody, in the present day, would dream of constructing them without carefully ramming down the earth, layer by layer, as the wall is carried up, so as to prevent the weight of the earth, in a triangular section, pressing upon the wall, which is the foundation of all the theory on the subject. With this quali-fication, therefore, we shall proceed; premising, that if the caution whereof we speak be taken, the thickness resulting from the following investigations will be much more than the outside of enough.

1585. Earth left to itself takes a slope proportionate to its consistence; but for our purpose it will sufficiently exhibit the nature of the investigation, to consider the substance pressing against the wall as dry sand or pounded freestone, which will arrange itself in a slope of about $55\frac{1}{2}°$ with the vertical plane, and therefore of $34\frac{1}{2}°$ with an horizontal plane, as Rondelet found to be the case when experimenting on the above materials in a box, one of whose sides was removable. Ordinarily, $45°$ is taken as the mean slope into which earths recently thrown up will arrange themselves.

1586. Belidor, in order to form an estimate for the thrust or pressure into which we are inquiring, divides the triangle EDF (*fig. 611.*) representing the mass of earth which creates the thrust, by parallels to its base ED, forming slices or sections of equal thickness and similar form; whence it follows, that, taking the first triangle aFb as unity, the second slice will be 3, the third 5, the fourth 7, and so on in a pro-gression whose difference is 2.

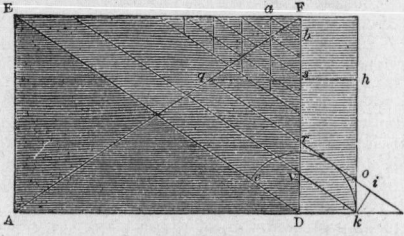

Fig. 611.

1587. Each of these sections being supposed to slide upon an inclined plane parallel to ED, so as to act upon the face FD, if we multiply them by the mean height at which they collectively act, the sum of the products will give the total effort tending to overturn the wall; but as this sum is equal to the product of the whole triangle by the height determined by a line drawn from its centre of gravity parallel to the base, this last will be the method followed, as much less complicated than that which Belidor adopts, independent of some of that author's suppositions not being rigorously correct.

1588. The box in which the experiment was tried by Rondelet was $16\frac{1}{2}$ in. (French) long, 12 in. wide, and $17\frac{1}{2}$ in. high in the clear. As the slope which the pounded free-stone took when unsupported in front formed an angle with the horizon of $34\frac{1}{2}°$, the height AE is $11\frac{1}{3}$, so that the part acting against the front, or that side of the box where would be the wall, is represented by the triangle EDF.

1589. To find by calculation the value of the force, and the thickness which should be given to the opposed side, we must first find the area of the triangle $EDF = \frac{16\frac{1}{2} \times 11\frac{1}{3}}{2} = 93\frac{1}{2}$; but as the specific gravity (or equal mass) of the pounded stone is only $\frac{13}{15}$ of that of the stone or other species of wall which is to resist the effort, it will be reduced to $73\frac{1}{2} \times \frac{13}{15} = 81$. This mass being supposed to slide upon the plane ED, its effort to its weight will be as AE is to ED:: $11\frac{1}{3}$: 20, or $81 \times \frac{11\frac{1}{3}}{20} = 45\cdot9$, which must be considered as the oblique power qr passing through the centre of gravity of the mass, and acting at the extremity of the lever ik. To ascertain the length of the lever, upon whose length depends the thick-ness of the side which is unknown, we have the similar triangles qsr, qho, and kio, whose sides are proportional: whence $qs : sr :: qh : ho$; and as $ko = hk - ho$, we have $qr : qs :: hk - ho : ik$.

Whence, $ik = \frac{(hk - ho) \times qs}{qr}$,

The three sides of the triangle qsr are known from the position of the angle q at the centre of gravity of the great triangle EFD, whence each of the sides of the small triangle is equal to one third of those of the larger one, to which it is correspondent.

Thus, making the side $qr = a$,

$$qs = b,$$
$$rs = c,$$

The unknown side $sh = x$,

$$hk = f,$$

The pressure 45·9 found $= p$,

The height DF $= d$,

We have $b : c :: b + x : \dfrac{bc + cx}{b} = ho$, and $hk - ho$ will be $f - \dfrac{bc + cx}{b}$.

To obtain ik, we have the proportion $a : b :: f - \dfrac{bc - cx}{b} : ik$.

Whence $ik = \dfrac{bf - bc - cx}{a}$; so that the pressure $p \times ik$ is represented by $p\left(\dfrac{bf - bc - cx}{a}\right)$, to which the resistance expressed by $\dfrac{dx^2}{2}$ must equilibrate.

Thus the equation becomes $\dfrac{dx^2}{2} = p\left(\dfrac{bf - bc - cx}{a}\right)$, or $x^2 + \dfrac{2pcx}{ad} = \dfrac{2p(bf - bc)}{ad}$.

For easier solution, make $\dfrac{2pbf - 2pbc}{ad} = 2m$, and $\dfrac{2pc}{ad} = 2n$, and we have $x^2 + 2nx = 2m$, an equation of the second degree, which makes $x = \sqrt{2m + n^2} - n$, which is a general formula for problems of this sort.

Returning to the values of the known quantities, in which

$$a = 6\tfrac{2}{3} \qquad\qquad f = 7\tfrac{5}{8}$$
$$b = 5\tfrac{1}{2} \qquad\qquad p = 45\tfrac{9}{10}$$
$$c = 3\tfrac{3}{4} \qquad\qquad d = 11\tfrac{1}{3}$$

$m = pb \times \dfrac{f - c}{ad}$ becomes $m = 45 \cdot 9 \times 5\tfrac{1}{2} \times \dfrac{7\tfrac{5}{8} - 3\tfrac{3}{4}}{6\tfrac{2}{3} + 11\tfrac{1}{3}} = 12 \cdot 70$ and $2m = 25 \cdot 4$;

$n = \dfrac{pc}{ad}$ becomes $n = \dfrac{45 \cdot 9 \times 3 \cdot 75}{75 \cdot 55} = 2 \cdot 28$ and $n^2 = 5 \cdot 20$.

From the above, then, the formula $x = \sqrt{2m + n^2} - n$ becomes $x = \sqrt{25 \cdot 4 + 5 \cdot 20} - 2 \cdot 28 = 3 \cdot 22$, a result which was confirmed by the experiment, inasmuch as a facing of the thickness of $3\tfrac{1}{4}$ inches was found necessary to resist the pressure of pounded freestone. By Belidor's method, the thickness comes out $4\tfrac{8}{10}$ inches; but it has been observed that its application is not strictly correct. In the foregoing experiment, the triangular part only of the material in the box was filled with the pounded stone, the lower part being supposed of material which could not communicate pressure. But if the whole of the box had been filled with the same material, the requisite thickness would have been found to be $5\tfrac{1}{4}$ inches to bear the pressure.

1590. In applying the preceding formula to this case, we must first find the area of the trapezium BEDF (*fig.* 612.), which will be found $195\tfrac{1}{4}$; multiplying this by $\tfrac{13}{15}$, to reduce the retaining wall and the material to the same specific gravity, we have $169\tfrac{1}{5}$. This mass being supposed to slide upon the inclined plane ED, its effort parallel to that plane will be $195\tfrac{1}{5} \times \tfrac{11\frac{1}{3}}{20} = 95 \cdot 76 = p$. Having found in the last formula that qs is represented by $b = 6 \cdot 93$, sr by $c = 4 \cdot 76$, qr by $a = 8 \cdot 40$, $f = 11 \cdot 3$, $d = 17 \cdot 5$; the thickness of the retaining wall becomes $= sh - x$; $m = pb \times \dfrac{f - c}{ad}$ will become, substituting the values

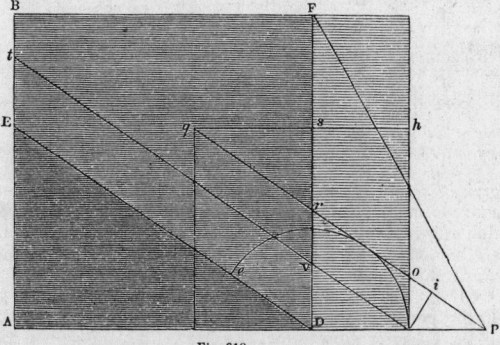

Fig. 612.

$95 \cdot 76 \times 6 \cdot 93 \times \dfrac{11 \cdot 3 - 4 \cdot 76}{8 \cdot 40 \times 17 \cdot 50} = 29 \cdot 52$ and $2m = 59 \cdot 04$. $n = \dfrac{pc}{ad}$ becomes $\dfrac{95 \cdot 76 \times 4 \cdot 76}{8 \cdot 40 \times 17 \cdot 50} = 3 \cdot 1$, and $n^2 = 9 \cdot 61$. Substituting these values in the formula $x = \sqrt{2m + n^2} - n$, we have $x = \sqrt{59 \cdot 04 + 9 \cdot 61} - 3 \cdot 1 = 5 \cdot 2$, a result very confirmatory of the theory.

1591. In an experiment made on common dry earth, reduced to a powder, which took a slope of 46° 50′, its specific gravity being only $\tfrac{3}{4}$ of that of the retaining side, it was found that the thickness necessary was 3 inches $\tfrac{6}{10}$.

1592. It is common, in practice, to strengthen walls for the retention of earth with piers at certain intervals, which are called *counterforts*, by which the wall acquires additional

strength; but after what we have said in the beginning of this article, on the dependence that is to be placed rather on well ramming down each layer of earth at the back of the wall, supposing it to be of ordinary thickness, we do not think it necessary to enter upon any calculation relative to their employment. It is clear their use tends to diminish the requisite thickness of the wall, and we would rather recommend the student to apply himself to the knowledge of what has been done, than to trust to calculation for stability, though we think the theory ought to be known by him.

PRESSURE OR FORCE OF WIND AGAINST WALLS, &c.

1592a. Air rushes into a void with the velocity a heavy body would acquire by falling in a homogeneous atmosphere. Air is 840 times lighter than water. The atmosphere supports water at 33 ft.; homogeneous atmosphere, therefore, is $33 \times 840 = 27,720$ ft. A heavy body falling one foot acquires a velocity of eight feet per second. Velocities are as the square roots of their heights. Therefore to find the velocity corresponding to any given height, expressed in feet per second, multiply the square root of the height in feet by 8. For air we have $V = \sqrt{27,720} = 166,493 \times 8 = 1332$ feet per second: this, therefore, is the velocity with which common air would rush into a void: or 79,920 feet per minute; some say 80,880 feet. (Telford's *Memorandum Book*). Some authors say that the weight or pressure of the atmosphere is equal to the weight of a volume of water 34 ft. in height; or 14·7 lbs. per square inch at a mean temperature; for air and all (?) kinds of gases are rendered lighter by the application of heat, because the particles of the mass are repelled from each other, or rarefied, and occupy a greater space.

1592b. The force with which air strikes against a *moving* surface, or with which the wind strikes against a *quiescent* surface, is nearly as the square of the velocity. If β be the angle of incidence; δ the surface struck in square feet; and v the velocity of the wind in feet per second; then if f equals the force in pounds avoirdupois, either of the two following approximations may be used, viz., $f = \frac{v^2 \delta \sin^2 \beta}{440}$; or, $f = \cdot002288v^2\delta\sin^2\beta$. The first is the easiest in operation, requiring only two lines of short division, viz., by 40 and by 11. If the incidence be perpendicular, $\sin^2 \beta = 1$, and these become $f = \frac{v^2 \delta}{440} = \cdot002288v^2\delta$. (Gregory). The force or pressure per square foot in lbs., is as the square of the velocity multiplied by ·002288.

1592c.   IMPULSE OF THE WIND ON A SQUARE FOOT.

Velocity in Feet Per Second.	Impulse in lbs.	Velocity in Feet Per Second.	Impulse in lbs.	Velocity in Feet Per Second.	Impulse in lbs.
10	0·229	60	8·234	110	27·675
14·67	0·492	66·01	9·963	117·36	31·490
20	0·915	70	11·207	120	32·926
30	2·059	73·35	12·300	130	38·654
36·67	3 075	80	14·638	140	44·830
40	3·660	90	18·526	146·70	49·200
44·01	4·429	100	22·872	150	51·462
50	5·718				

1592d. The resistance of a sphere is stated not to exceed one-fourth of that of its greatest circle. Tredgold, *Carpentry, and Iron*, has minutely examined the effect of the above forces, and the principle of forming the necessary resistance to them in the construction of walls and roofs. See HURRICANES. Where the roofs of buildings, as in the country, are exposed to rude gusts and storms, it is necessary to increase the weight of the ridges, hips and flashings.

1592e. The utmost power of the wind in England is said to be 90 miles per hour, or 40 lbs. per square foot. Tredgold takes the force at 57¾ lbs. per square foot. Dr. Nichol, of the Glasgow Observatory, records 55 lbs. per square foot, or ·382 lbs. per square inch, as the greatest pressure of wind ever observed in Britain (Rankine, *Civil Eng.* 538). During the extremely heavy gale of January 16, 1866, the pressure in London was recorded as 33 lbs. per square foot; at Liverpool it was 30·4 lbs. The velocity of the wind on the south coast of England, during January 11, when it uprooted old elm trees, averaged 65 miles an hour; later in the day it was 90 miles; the latter impetus is equal to the 40 lbs. per square foot, above mentioned.

1592f. Wind exercises a tendency to overthrow a building upon the external edge opposite to the line of its advance, equivalent to the surface of the face receiving the impulsion multiplied by the force of the wind, and by a lever which on the average may be taken to be equal to half the height of the building. To secure the stability of the latter, its

weight multiplied by a lever equal to half the base must exceed the sum of the elements of the wind's action.

1592g. To determine the pressure of wind in pounds per square foot, equal to the stability of a square stalk, multiply the weight of the stalk in pounds, by twice its width in feet at the base, and divide the product by the square of its height in feet, and by the sum of its top and bottom breadths in feet.

Let w = weight of stalk in pounds = 90,000

p = pressure of wind in pounds per square foot equal to stability of stalk

h = height of stalk in feet = 50 feet

b = breadth of stalk at base in feet = 4 feet

c = breadth of stalk at top in feet = 2 feet

Then $\frac{90,000 \times 4 \times 2}{2,500 \ (4 \times 2)} = p = 48$ pounds per square foot. If the stalk be circular, then, to determine the pressure of wind, proceed as before, but replace the breadths by the diameter, and multiply the result by 2. Campin, *Engineers' Pocket Remembrancer*, 1863.

Sect. X.

BEAMS AND PILLARS.

1593. The woods used for the purposes of carpentry merit our attention from their importance for the purpose of constructing solid and durable edifices. They are often employed to carry great weights, and to resist great strains. Under these circumstances, their strength and dimensions should be proportioned to the strains they have to resist. For building purposes, oak and fir are the two sorts of timber in most common use. Stone has, doubtless, the advantage over wood : it resists the changes of moisture and dryness, and is less susceptible of alteration in the mass ; hence it ensures a stability which belongs not to timber. The fragility of timber is, however, less than that of stone, and its facility of transport is far greater. The greatest inconvenience attending the use of timber, is its great susceptibility of ignition. This has led to expedients for another material, and probably it will become greatly superseded by iron.

1594. Oak is one of the best woods that can be employed in carpentry. It has all the requisite properties; such as size, strength, and stiffness. Oaks are to be found capable of furnishing pieces 60 to 80 ft. long, and 2 ft. square. In common practice, beams rarely exceed 36 to 40 ft. in length, by 2 ft. square.

1595. In regard to its durability, oak is preferable to all other trees that furnish equal lengths and scantlings : it is heavier, better resists the action of the air upon it, as well as that of moisture and immersion in the earth. It is a saying relating to the oak, that it grows for a century, lasts perfect for a century, and takes a century to perish. When cut at a proper season, used dry, and protected from the weather, it lasts from 500 to 600 years. Oak, like other trees, varies in weight, durability, strength, and density, according to the soil in which it grows. The last is always in an inverse proportion to the slowness of its growth ; trees which grow slowest being invariably the hardest and the heaviest.

1596. From the experiments made upon oak and other sorts of wood, it is found that their strength is proportional to their density and weight; that of two pieces of the same species of wood, of the same dimensions, the heavier is generally the stronger.

1597. The weight of wood will vary in the same tree; usually the heaviest portions are the lower ones, from which upwards a diminution of weight is found to occur. In full-grown trees, however, this difference does not occur. The oak of France is heavier than that of England; the specific gravity of the former varying from 1000 to 1054, whilst the latter, in the experiments of Barlow, varies from 770 to 920. The weight, therefore, of an English cube foot of French oak is about 58 English pounds. Timber may be said to be well seasoned when it has lost about a sixth part of its weight.

1598. In carpentry, timber acts with an absolute and with a relative strength. For instance, that called the absolute strength is measured by the effort that must be exerted to break a piece of wood by pulling it in the direction of the fibres. The relative strength of a piece of wood depends upon its position. Thus a piece of wood placed horizontally on two points of support at its extremities, is easier broken, and with a less effort, than if it was inclined or upright. It is found that a smaller effort is necessary to break the piece as it increases in length, and that this effort does not decrease strictly in the inverse ratio of the length, when the thicknesses are equal. For instance, a piece 8 ft. long, and 6 in. square, placed horizontally, bears a little more than double of another, of the same depth and thickness, 16 ft. long, placed in the same way. In respect of the absolute force, the difference does not vary in the same way with respect to the length. The following are experiments by Rondelet, to ascertain the absolute force, the specimen of oak being of 861 specific gravity, and a cube foot, therefore, weighing $49\frac{1}{10}$ lbs.

Cohesive Force of Pieces drawn in the Direction of their Length.

First experiment.

A small rod of oak 0·0888 in. (= 1 French line) square, and 2·14
in. in length, broke with a weight of - - - 115 lbs. avoirdupois
Another specimen of the same wood, and of similar dimensions,
broke with - - - - - 105$\frac{8}{10}$
Another specimen - - - - - 110$\frac{1}{10}$
        The mean weight, therefore, was, in round numbers, 110 lbs.
A rod of the same wood as the former, 0·177 inch (=2 French lines)
square, and 2·14 inches long, broke with a weight of - 439$\frac{1}{2}$ lbs. avoirdupois
Another specimen - - - - - 418
Another specimen - - - - - 451$\frac{1}{2}$
        The mean weight, therefore, was 436 lbs. for an area $\frac{35}{100}$ in. (= 4 square lines
        French, or 110 lbs. for each, French line = 0·0888 in. English).

1599. Without a recital of all the experiments, we will only add, that after increasing
the thickness and length of the rods in the several trials, the absolute strength of oak was
found to be 110 lbs. for every $\frac{888}{10000}$ of an inch area (=1 French line superficial).

The Strength of Wood in an upright Position.

1600. If timber were not flexible, a piece of wood placed upright as a post, should bear
the weights last found, whatever its height; but experience shows that when a post is
higher than six or seven times the width of its base, it bends under a similar weight before
crushing or compressing, and that a piece of the height of 100 diameters of its base is
incapable of bearing the smallest weight.   The proportion in which the strength decreases
as the height increases, is difficult to determine, on account of the different results of the
experiments.   Rondelet, however, found, after a great number, that when a piece of oak
was too short to bend, the force necessary to crush or compress it was about 49·72 lbs. for
every $\frac{888}{10000}$ of a square inch of its base, and that for fir the weight was about 56·16 lbs.
Cubes of each of these woods, on trial, lost height by compression, without disunion of
the fibres; those of oak more than a third, and those of fir one half.

1601. A piece of fir or oak diminishes in strength the moment it begins to bend, so that
the mean strength of oak, which is 47·52 lbs. for a cube $\frac{888}{10000}$ of an inch, is reduced to
2·16 lbs. for a piece of the same wood, whose height is 72 times the width of its base.
From many experiments, Rondelet deduced the following progression : —

For a cube, whose height is 1, the strength =1
        —   —   12,   —   =$\frac{5}{6}$
        —   —   24,   —   =$\frac{1}{2}$
        —   —   36,   —   =$\frac{1}{3}$
        —   —   48,   —   =$\frac{1}{6}$
        —   —   60,   —   =$\frac{1}{12}$
        —   —   72,   —   =$\frac{1}{24}$

Thus, for a cube of oak, whose base is 1·066 in. area (=1 square in. French) placed
        upright, that is, with its fibres in a vertical direction, its mean strength is ex-
        pressed by 144* × 47·52 = 6842 lbs.   From a mean of these experiments, the
        result was (by experiment) in lbs. avoirdupois - - - 6853
For a rod of the same oak, whose section was of the same area by 12·792 in. high
        (=12 French in.), the weight borne or mean strength is 144 × $\frac{47·52 \times 5}{6}$ = 5702 lbs.
        From a mean of three experiments, the result was - - - 5735
For a rod 25·584 (=24 French) in. high, the strength is 144 × $\frac{47·52}{2}$ = 3421 lbs. - 3144

For a rod 38·376 (=36 French) in. high, the strength is 144 × $\frac{47·52}{3}$ = 2281 lbs. - 2336

For a rod 51·160 (=48 French) in. high, the strength is 144 × $\frac{47·52}{6}$ = 1140 lbs.

For a rod 63·960 (=60 French) in. high, the strength is 144 × $\frac{47·52}{12}$ = 570 lbs.

For a rod 76·752 (=72 French) in. high, the strength is 144 × $\frac{47·52}{24}$ = 285 lbs.

For a cube of fir, whose sides are 1·066 in. area (=1 square in. French), placed as
        before, with the fibres in a vertical direction, we have 144 × 56·16 = 8087 lbs. - 8089

* The French inch, consisting of 144 lines.

For a square rod, whose base was 1·066 in. area ($=$1 square in. French), 12·792 in.

high, we have $144 \times \dfrac{56\cdot16 \times 5}{6} = 6739$ lbs. -   -   -   - 6863

For a rod 25·584 ($=$24 French) in. high, $144 \times \dfrac{56\cdot16}{2} = 4043$ lbs. -   - 3703

For a rod 38·376 ($=$36 French) in. high, $144 \times \dfrac{56\cdot16}{3} = 2696$ lbs. -   - 2881

For a rod 51·160 ($=$43 French) in. high, $144 \times \dfrac{56\cdot16}{6} = 1348$ lbs.

For a rod 63·960 ($=$60 French) in. high, $144 \times \dfrac{56\cdot16}{12} = 674$ lbs.

For a rod 76·752 ($=$72 French) in. high, $144 + \dfrac{56\cdot16}{24} = 337$ lbs.

The rule by Rondelet above given was that also adopted by MM. Perronet, Lamblardie, and Girard. In the analytical treatise of the last-named, some experiments are shown, which lead us to think it not very far from the truth. From the experiments, moreover, we learn, that the moment a post begins to bend, it loses strength, and that it is not prudent, in practice, to reduce its diameter or side to less than one tenth of its height.

1602. In calculating the resistance of a post after the rate of only 10·80 for every 1·066 superficial line English ($=$1 line super. French), which is much less than one quarter of the weight under which it would be crushed, we shall find that a square post whose sides are 1·066 ft.($=$1 ft. French) containing 22104·576 English lines ($=$20736 French), would sustain a weight of 238729 lbs. or 106 tons. Yet as there may be a great many circumstances, in practice, which may double or triple the load, it is never safe to trust to a post the width of whose base is less than a tenth part of its height, to the extent of 5 lbs. per 1·066 line; in one whose height is fifteen times the width of the base, 4 lbs. for the same proportion; and when twenty times, not more than 3 lbs.

Horizontal Pieces of Timber.

1603. In all the experiments on timber lying horizontally, as respects its length, and supported at the ends, it is found that, in pieces of equal depth, their strength diminishes in proportion to the bearing between the points of support. In pieces of equal length between the supports, the strength is as their width and the squares of their depths. We here continue M. Rondelet's experiments.

1604. A rod of oak 2·132 in. (2 in. French) square, and 25·584 in. (24 in. French) long, broke under a weight of 2488·32 lbs., whilst another of the same dimensions, but 19·188 in. (18 in. French) bore 3353·40; whence it appears that the relative strength of these two rods was in the inverse ratio of their length. The proportion is 19·188 : 25·584 :: 2488·32 : 3317·76, instead of 3353·40 lbs., the actual weight in the experiment.

1605. In another rod of the same wood, 2·132 in. wide and 3·198 deep, and 25·584 in. bearing, it broke with a weight of 5532 lbs. In the preceding first-mentioned experiment it was found that a rod of 2·132 in. square, with a bearing 25·584 in. bore 2488·32 lbs. Supposing the strength of the rods to be exactly as the squares of their heights, we should have 4·54 (2·132²) : 10·23 (3·198²) :: 2488·32 : 5598·7 lbs.; which the second rod should have borne, instead of 5532 lbs. There are numberless considerations which account for the discrepancy, but it is one too small to make us dissatisfied with the theory.

1606. In a third experiment on the same sort of wood, the dimension of 3·198 in. being laid flatwise, and the 2·132 in. depthwise, the bearing or distance between the supports being the same as before, it broke with a weight of 3573 lbs.: whence it follows that the strength of pieces of wood of the same depth is proportional to their width. Thus, comparing the piece 2·132 in. square, which bore 2488 lbs., we ought to have 2·132 : 3·198 :: 2488·32 : 3624·48, instead of 3573 lbs.

1607. From a great number of experiments and calculations made for the purpose of finding the proportion of the absolute strength of oak, to that which it has when lying horizontally between two points of support, the most simple method is to multiply the area of the piece in section by half the absolute strength, and to divide the product by the number of times its depth is contained in the length between the points of support.

1608. Thus, in the experiments made by Belidor on rods of oak 3 French ($=$3·198 English) ft. long, and 1 French ($=$1·066 in. English) in. square, the mean weight under which they broke was 200·96 lbs. avoirdupois. Now, as the absolute strength of oak is from 98 to 110 lbs. for every $\frac{888}{100000}$ in. ($=$1 French line), the mean strength will be 104 and 52 lbs. for its half, and the rule will become (144 lines, being $=$1 French in.) $\dfrac{144 \times 52}{36 \,(\text{F. in.})} = 207\cdot30$ lbs., instead of 200·96 lbs.

1609. Three other rods, 2 French in. square (2·132 Eng.), and of the same length between the supports, broke with a mean weight of 1711·8 lbs. By the rule $\dfrac{576(=144 \times 4) \times 52}{18}$ $= 1658\cdot88$ lbs. avoirdupois. Without further mention of the experiments of Belidor, we

may observe, that those of Parent and others give results which confirm the rule. The experiments, however, of Buffon, having been made on a larger scale, show that the strength of pieces of timber of the same size, lying horizontally, does not diminish exactly in the proportion of their length, as the theory whereon the rule is founded would indicate. It becomes, therefore, proper to modify it in some respects.

1610. Buffon's experiments show that a beam as long again as another of the same dimensions will not bear half the weight that the shorter one does. Thus —

A beam, 7·462 ft. long, and 5·330 in. square, broke with a
weight of - - - - - 12495·06 lbs. avoirdupois.
Another, 14·924 ft. long, of the same dimensions, broke with a
weight of - - - - - 5819.04
A third, 29·848 ft. long, of the same dimensions, bore before
breaking - - - - - 2112·48
By the rule, the results should have been, for the 7·462 ft. beam 12495·60
for that of 14·924 - 6247·80
for that of 29·848 - 3123·90

Whence it appears, that owing to the elasticity of the timber, the strength of the pieces, instead of forming a decreasing geometrical progression, whose exponent is the same, forms one in which it is variable. The forces in question may be represented by the ordinates of a species of catenarian curve.

1611. In respect, then, of the diminution of the strength of wood, it is not only proportioned to the length and size, but is, moreover, modified in proportion to its absolute or primitive force and its flexibility; so that timber exactly of the same quality would give results following the same law, so as to form ordinates of a curve, exhibiting neither inflection nor undulation in its outline: thus in pieces whose scantlings and lengths form a regular progression, the defects can only be caused by a difference in their primitive strength; and as this strength varies in pieces taken from the same tree, it becomes impossible to establish a rule whose results shall always agree with experiment; but by taking a mean primitive strength, we may obtain results sufficiently accurate for practice. For this purpose, the rule that nearest agrees with experiment is —

1st. To subtract from the primitive strength one third of the quantity which expresses the number of times that the depth is contained in the length of the piece of timber.

2d. To multiply the remainder thus obtained by the square of the length.

3d. To divide the product by the number expressing the relation of the depth to the length.

Hence calling the primitive strength - - - $= a$
— the number of times that the depth is contained in the length $= b$
— the depth of the piece - - - $= d$
— the length - - - $= l$

The general formula will be, $\dfrac{a - \frac{b}{3} \times d^2}{b} = \dfrac{ad^2}{b} - \dfrac{d^2}{3}$.

1612. Suppose the primitive strength $a = 64·36$ for each $1·136$ square line ($=1$ line French), we shall find for a beam $5·330$ in. square, by $19·188$ ft. long, or $230·256$ inches, that the proportion of the depth to the length $= \frac{230·256}{5·330} = 43·2 = b$.

1613. The vertical depth being $5·330$ or $63·960$ lines, d^2 will be $4089·88$; substituting these values in the formula $\frac{a \times d^2}{b} - \frac{d^2}{3}$ we have $\frac{64·36 \times 4089·88}{43·2} - \frac{4089·88}{3} = 4067·99$, instead of $4120·20$, the mean result of two beams of the same scantlings in the experiments of Buffon. But as the mean primitive strength of the beams is, according to the second of the following tables, $64·99$, instead of $64·36$, which has been taken for the mean strength of all the pieces given in that table, we ought to have found less. Thus taking $64·99$, we have $\frac{64·99 \times 4089·88}{43·2} - \frac{4089·88}{3} = 4120·20$, as in the experiment.

The scientific world generally, the architect and engineer especially, are indebted to the person from whom the tables which follow have emanated. They are the result of laborious experiments, no doubt, and as such, deserve much consideration. But they must not lead us to ignore the labours in the cause of such men in England as Robison, Young, Bevan, Rennie, Tredgold, Barlow, Hodgkinson, and later, Fairbairn, with others, from some of whose treatises we have adopted passages; nor to speak disparagingly of the results of those who have endeavoured to benefit both the architect and engineer, by bringing the aid of mathematical investigations, to found upon their experiments, safe and general rules for practice.

TABLES OF EXPERIMENTS.

TABLE I.

Experiments on Pieces of Timber 4·264 inches square, supposing the absolute Strength 60·1344.

Length of the Pieces in Feet.	Proportion of Depth to Length.	Weight of the Pieces in Pounds.	Curvature before breaking, in Inches.	Absolute Strength. (From Experiment.)	Relative Strength. (From Experiment.)	Weight in Pounds avoirdupois.	Mean Effort according to Experiment.	Relative Strength according to Calculation.	Breaking Weight calculated on relative Strength.
7·462	21	64·80 60·48	3·721 4·797	60·13	52·57	5778 5697	5768	52·57	5768
8·528	24	73·44 69·04	3·997 4·975	60·29	51·55	4968 4860	4869	51·49	4943
9·594	27	83·16 76·68	5·152 5·863	59·40	49·68	4428 4266	4387	50·41	4301
10·660	30	90·72 88·56	6·218 6·929	62·16	51·36	3715 3884	3946	49·33	3799
12·792	36	108·00 105·84	7·462 7·462	63·28	51·22	3294 3159	3279	47·17	3018

TABLE II.

Experiments on Pieces of Timber 5·330 inches square, supposing the absolute Strength 64·36.

7·462	$16\frac{4}{5}$	101·52 95·58	2·665 2·665	64·37	58·32	12,717 12,177	12,496	58·31	12,496
8·528	$19\frac{1}{5}$	112·32 110·16	2·842 3·109	63·58	56·67	10,692 10,449	10,626	57·34	10,750
9·594	$21\frac{3}{5}$	127·44 125·28 124·20	3·198 3·464 3·731	62·20	54·42	9,072 8,991 8,856	8,635	56·58	9,429
10·660	24	142·56 140·40 138·78	3·375 3·731 4·264	60·40	51·76	7,803 7,614 7,668	7,765	55·72	8,357
12·792	$28\frac{1}{5}$	168·48 166·32	5·886 6·132	63·50	51·54	6,534 6,588	6,644	54·99	6,748
14·924	$33\frac{3}{5}$	192·24 190·08	8·528 8·794	66·42	54·32	5,832 5,616	5,819	52·26	4,600
17·056	$38\frac{2}{5}$	225·72 221·40	8·616 8·705	65·12	51·30	4,779 4,617	4,810	50·53	4,738
19·188	$43\frac{1}{5}$	250·56 249·48	8·528 8·705	64·99	49·44	4,050 3,942	4,120	48·80	4,066
21·320	48	284·04 279·72	9·416 10·660	65·60	48·32	3,537 3,429	3,624	47·08	3,530
23·452	$52\frac{4}{5}$	303·48	11·992	68·34	49·33	3,213	3,364	45·35	3,092
25·584	$57\frac{3}{5}$	334·80 331·56	11·726 14·491	60·76	40·02	2,376 2,295	2,502	43·62	2,726
29·848	$67\frac{1}{5}$	393·12 388·80	19·188 23·452	63·42	39·24	1,944 1,890	2,112	40·16	2,151

TABLE III.

Experiments on Pieces of Timber 6·396 inches square, supposing the absolute Strength 56·88.

7·462	14	138·24 136·62	2·132 2·132	60·44	54·50	20,790 20,142	20,635	51·84	9,196
8·528	16	160·92 157·68	2·487 2·576	57·75	52·28	16,956 16,578	16,804	51·12	16,562
9·594	18	179·28 177·66	2·664 3·020	56·09	49·61	14,526 13,878	14,292	50·40	14,547
10·660	20	203·04 200·88	3·198 3·430	54·23	47·05	12,393 11,907	12,197	49·68	12,877

Table III. — *continued.*

Length of the Pieces in Feet.	Proportion of Depth to Length.	Weight of the Pieces in Pounds.	Curvature before breaking, in Inches.	Absolute Strength.	Relative Strength.	Weight in Pounds avoirdupois.	Mean Efforts according to Experiment.	Relative Strength according to Calculation.	Breaking Weight calculated on relative Strength.
				From Experiment.					
12·792	24	241·92 / 238·68	4·264 / 4·352	54·69	46·05	9,936 / 9,720	9,938	48·24	9,420
14·924	28	275·40 / 274·32	4·797 / 4·441	54·36	44·28	7,766 / 8,100	8,210	46·81	8,666
17·056	32	317·52 / 316·48	5·863 / 6·218	54·86	43·38	6,750 / 6,993	7,030	45·36	7,348
19·188	36	360·72 / 357·48	7·906 / 9·060	54·92	42·96	6,075 / 5,940	6,187	43·92	6,319
21·320	40	407·16 / 405·00	10·126 / 9·416	56·79	42·39	5,427 / 5,259	5,495	42·49	5,506

Table IV.

Experiments on Pieces of Timber 7·462 inches square, supposing the absolute Strength 57·85.

8·528	13⅝	220·32 / 217·62	2·931 / 2·664	59·82	54·88	28,242 / 28,026	28,243	52·92	26,927
9·594	15¾	245·16 / 243·00	3·286 / 3·109	58·59	53·04	27,599 / 23,652	24,260	51·74	23,656
10·660	17½	274·32 / 272·16	2.753 / 3·198	57·60	51·43	21,222 / 20,844	21,169	51·68	21,246
12·792	20⅞	326·16 / 325·08	3·109 / 3·553	58·80	51·41	18,144 / 16,794	17,633	50·49	17,318
14·924	24	379·08 / 379·08	4·441 / 3·997	57·85	49·21	14,688 / 13,878	14,472	49·21	14,470
17·056	27¾	438·48 / 435·24	5·152 / 5·596	56·94	47·07	11,988 / 11,772	12,098	47·98	12,343
19·188	30⅝	491·32 / 491·32	5·863 / 6·218	56·69	45·49	10,106 / 10,152	10,424	46·76	10,693
21·320	34⅞	545·40 / 540·00	8·350 / 9·060	57·09	44·74	8,914 / 8,640	9,208	45·51	9,207

Table V.

Experiments on Pieces of Timber 8·528 inches square, supposing the absolute Strength 55·08.

10·660	15	357·48 / 357·48	3·198 / 2·398	54·46	49·06	30,024 / 29,916	30,148	49·68	30,363
12·792	18	428·76 / 427·14	3·198 / 3·109	56·35	49·87	25,812 / 24,840	25,540	48·60	24,883
14·924	21	497·88 / 495·72	4·086 / 3·375	56·78	49·23	21,654 / 21,060	21,605	47·52	20,854
17·056	24	570·24 / 565·92	5·407 / 6·129	55·42	46·78	18,144 / 17,117	17,968	46·44	17,833
19·188	27	641·52 / 639·64	4·797 / 4·352	52·42	42·70	14,580 / 13,932	14,577	45·36	15,482
21·320	30	717·12 / 712·80	7·995 / 6·396	54·10	43·30	11,717 / 13,176	13,303	44·28	13,593

1614. The five preceding tables give a view of the results of experiments by Buffon upon beams 4·264, 5·330, 6·396, 7·462, and 8·528 inches square, of different lengths, as compared with those found by the modified rule above given (1660.).

1615. The first column shows the length of the pieces in English feet. The second, the proportion of their depth to their length. The third, the weight of each piece in pounds avoirdupois. The fourth, the curvature before breaking. The fifth, the absolute or primitive strength, that is, independent of the length. The sixth, that strength reduced in the ratio of the proportion of the depth to the length of the pieces given in the

second column. The seventh column gives the weight borne before breaking, independent of their own weight. The eighth, the mean effort with which the pieces broke, including half their weight, the other half acting on the points of support. The ninth shows the reduced strength of the pieces in respect of the proportions of the depth to the length, supposing the primitive strength equal for all the pieces in the same table. The tenth column gives the result of the calculation according to the rule above given.

1616. In order to give an idea of the method of representing the strength of wood of the same scantling, but of different lengths, by the ordinates of a curve, we annex *fig.* 613. to explain by it the result of the experiments of Buffon, given in the second table. The ordinates of the polygon N, O, P, Q, &c. represent the results of the experiments made upon beams 5·330 in. square, of different lengths, whose primitive strength varied in each piece.

1617. The ordinates of the regular curve, *m, l, i, h, g, f, e, d, c, b,* Z, show the results of the calculation according to the rule, taking the same primitive strength for each piece.

1618. After what has been said in a preceding page, it is easy to conceive that the primitive unequal strengths would form an irregular polygon, whereof each point would answer to a different curve; whilst, supposing the same primitive strength to belong to each piece, there should be an agreement between the strengths and scantlings which constitute a regular curve.

1619. Thus it is to be observed that the points O and P of the regular polygon only vary from the regular curve, *m, l, k, i,* &c., because the ordinate LO is the product of a primitive strength diminished by the mean primitive strength which produced the ordinate of the curve KP. Hence the point P is above the properly correspondent point *k.*

1620. For the same reason, the point *c* is above its corresponding point X, because the relative ordinate C*c* is the product of a primitive strength greater than the mean which produced the point X.

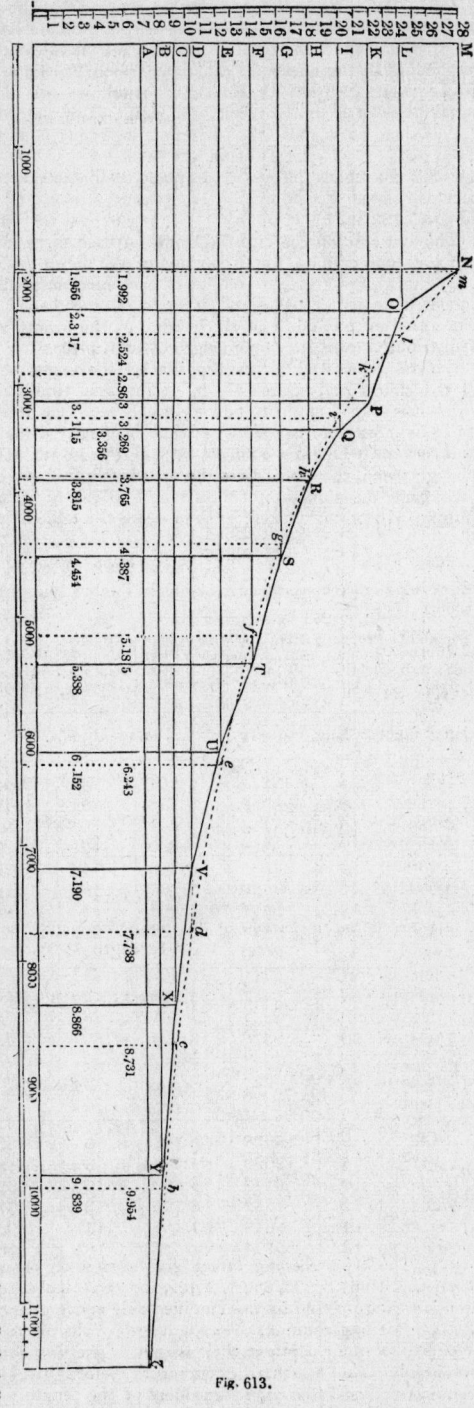

Fig. 613.

1621. Referring to the second table, we find that the primitive strength answering to the point O is but 60·76, and the value of the ordinate LO 2502, whilst that of the point P is 68·34, and the value of the ordinate KP 3364; and as the ordinates L*l* and K*k* corresponding to the curve are calculated upon the same primitive strength of 64·36, which for L*l* gives 2726, and for KP 3092 : it follows that, in considering all these quantities as equal parts of a similar scale, the point P of the polygon should be (3364−3092=) 272 of these parts above the corresponding point *k* of the curve, and the point O 224 of those parts (2726−2502) below the point *l*.

1622. To render the researches made, available and useful, the table which follows has been calculated so as to exhibit the greatest strength of beams from pieces 3·198 in. square, up to 19·188 in. by 26·65 in.

The first column contains the length of each piece in English feet.

The second column, the proportion of the depth to the length; and

The third, the greatest strength of each piece in pounds avoirdupois.

The table is for oak; and it is to be recollected that the weight is supposed to be concentred in the middle of the bearing of the beams, and hence double what it would be if distributed over the whole length of each piece.

Experience, as well as investigation of the experiments, shows, that in order to resist all the efforts and strains which, in practice, timber has to encounter, the weight with which it is loaded ought to be very much less than its breaking weight, and that it ought not to be more than *one tenth* of what is given as the breaking weight in the following table, beyond which it would not be safe to trust it. The abstraction of the last figure on the right hand, therefore, gives the practicable strength by simple inspection. In a subsequent page, the reduction of the strength of oak to fir, which is in more general use in this country, will be introduced, so as to make the table of more general utility.

TABLE VI.

Showing the greatest Strength of Oak Timber lying horizontally, in pounds avoirdupois.

Length of each Piece in English Feet.	Proportion of Depth to Length.	Breaking Weight in lbs. avoirdupois.	Length of each Piece in English Feet.	Proportion of Depth to Length.	Breaking Weight in lbs. avoirdupois.	Length of each Piece in English Feet.	Proportion of Depth to Length.	Breaking Weight in lbs. avoirdupois.
3·198 inches (Eng.) square.			3·198 in. by 5·330 in.			4·264 inches square.		
1·599	6	12245	2·664	6	20418	2·842	8	16224
2·132	8	9068	3·553	8	15109	3·553	10	12728
2·664	10	7163	4·441	10	11934	4·264	12	10469
3·198	12	5889	5·330	12	9815	4·974	14	8696
3·730	14	4980	6·218	14	8303	5·685	16	7645
4·264	16	4290	7·106	16	7167	6·396	18	6702
4·796	18	3771	7·994	18	6283	7·106	20	5951
5·330	20	3247	8·883	20	5578	7·817	22	5333
5·862	22	3000	9·771	22	5010	8·528	24	4820
6·396	24	2711	10·660	24	4519	9·238	26	4386
6·928	26	2447	11·548	26	4111	9·949	28	4014
7·462	28	2257	12·436	28	3758	10·66	30	3686
7·994	30	2076	13·324	30	3459			
3·198 in. by 4·264 in. wide. deep.			3·198 in. by 6·396 in.			4·264 in. by 5·330 in.		
2·132	6	16326	3·198	6	24489	3·553	8	16224
2·842	8	12090	4·264	8	18136	4·441	10	12730
3·553	10	9547	5·330	10	14321	5·330	12	10469
4·264	12	7852	6·396	12	11778	6·218	14	8856
4·974	14	6642	7·462	14	9963	7·106	16	7645
5·685	16	5724	8·528	16	8761	7·994	18	6702
6·396	18	5027	9·594	18	7540	8·883	20	5951
7·106	20	4462	10·660	20	6694	9·771	22	5333
7·817	22	4000	11·726	22	6001	10·66	24	4820
8·528	24	3615	12·792	24	5422	11·55	26	4396
9·238	26	3289	13·858	26	4934	12·44	28	4013
9·949	28	3010	14·924	28	4514	13·32	30	3766
10·660	30	2767	15·990	30	4150			

4·264 in. by 6·396 in.

Length of each Piece in English Feet.	Proportion of Depth to Length.	Breaking Weight in lbs. avoirdupois.
4·264	8	20152
5·330	10	16913
6·396	12	13086
7·462	14	11071
8·5z8	16	9557
9·594	18	8379
10·66	20	7438
11·73	22	6668
12·79	24	6023
13·86	26	5482
14·92	28	5017
15·99	30	4613

4·264 in. by 7·462 in.

Length of each Piece in English Feet.	Proportion of Depth to Length.	Breaking Weight in lbs. avoirdupois.
4·974	8	28224
6·218	10	22277
7·462	12	18321
8·705	14	15499
9·949	16	13379
11·19	18	11730
12·44	20	10413
13·68	22	9334
14·92	24	8427
16·17	26	7675
17·41	28	7022
18·65	30	6457

4·264 in. by 8·528 in.

Length of each Piece in English Feet.	Proportion of Depth to Length.	Breaking Weight in lbs. avoirdupois.
5·685	8	22242
7·106	10	25460
8·528	12	21942
9·949	14	17713
11·37	16	15291
12·79	18	13410
14·21	20	11902
15·63	22	10677
17·06	24	9562
18·48	26	8772
19·90	28	8026
21·32	30	7480

5·330 inches square.

Length of each Piece in English Feet.	Proportion of Depth to Length.	Breaking Weight in lbs. avoirdupois.
4·441	10	19890
5·330	12	16359
6·218	14	13889
7·106	16	11946
7·994	18	10473
8·863	20	9298
9·771	22	8334
10·66	24	7531
11·55	26	6863
12·44	28	6270
13·32	30	5765

5·330 in. by 6·396 in.

Length of each Piece in English Feet.	Proportion of Depth to Length.	Breaking Weight in lbs. avoirdupois.
5·330	10	23869
6·396	12	19630
7·462	14	16374
8·528	16	14294
9·594	18	12568
10·66	20	11157
11·73	22	10001
12·79	24	9037
13·86	26	8223
14·92	28	7524
15·99	30	6918

5·330 in. by 7·462 in.

Length of each Piece in English Feet.	Proportion of Depth to Length.	Breaking Weight in lbs. avoirdupois.
6·218	10	27847
7·462	12	22901
8·705	14	18373
9·949	16	16724
11·19	18	14663
12·44	20	13017
13·68	22	11667
14·92	24	10544
16·17	26	9595
17·41	28	8778
18·65	30	8072

5·330 in. by 8·528 in.

Length of each Piece in English Feet.	Proportion of Depth to Length.	Breaking Weight in lbs. avoirdupois.
7·106	10	32225
8·528	12	26174
9·949	14	22141
11·37	16	19106
12·79	18	16757
14·21	20	14877
15·63	22	13338
17·06	24	12057
18·48	26	10965
19·90	28	10053
21·32	30	9225

5·330 in. by 9·594 in.

Length of each Piece in English Feet.	Proportion of Depth to Length.	Breaking Weight in lbs. avoirdupois.
7·994	10	35803
9·594	12	29445
11·19	14	24919
12·79	16	21493
14·39	18	18853
15·99	20	16737
17·59	22	15002
19·19	24	13556
20·78	26	12336
22·39	28	11287
23·98	30	10378

5·330 in. by 10·660 in.

Length of each Piece in English Feet.	Proportion of Depth to Length.	Breaking Weight in lbs. avoirdupois.
8·883	10	39782
10·66	12	32717
12·44	14	27677
14·21	16	23888
15·99	18	20648
17·77	20	18595
19·54	22	16669
21·32	24	15063
23·10	26	13706
24·87	28	12551
26·65	30	11531

6·396 inches square.

Length of each Piece in English Feet.	Proportion of Depth to Length.	Breaking Weight in lbs. avoirdupois.
5·330	10	28643
6·396	12	23556
7·462	14	19927
8·528	16	17191
9·594	18	15082
10·66	20	13389
11·73	22	12001
12·79	24	10844
13·86	26	9857
14·92	28	8710
15·99	30	8302

6·396 in. by 7·462 in.

Length of each Piece in English Feet.	Proportion of Depth to Length.	Breaking Weight in lbs. avoirdupois.
5·218	10	33400
7·462	12	27482
8·705	14	23244
9·949	16	20067
11·19	18	17596
12·44	20	15321
13·68	22	13986
14·92	24	12652
16·17	26	11572
17·41	28	10534
18·65	30	9668

6·396 in. by 8·528 in.

Length of each Piece in English Feet.	Proportion of Depth to Length.	Breaking Weight in lbs. avoirdupois.
7·106	10	38158
8·528	12	31407
9·949	14	27341
11·37	16	22936
12·79	18	20110
14·21	20	17852
15·63	22	16001
17·06	24	14460
18·48	26	13158
19·90	28	12425
21·32	30	11070

6·396 in. by 9·594 in.

Length of each Piece in English Feet.	Proportion of Depth to Length.	Breaking Weight in lbs. avoirdupois.
7·994	10	42964
9·594	12	35334
11·19	14	29891
12·79	16	25791
14·39	18	22623
15·99	20	20084
17·59	22	18002
19·19	24	16267
20·79	26	14802
22·39	28	13544
23·98	30	12453

6·396 in. by 10·66 in.

Length of each Piece in English Feet.	Proportion of Depth to Length.	Breaking Weight in lbs. avoirdupois.
8·883	10	47738
10·66	12	39261
12·44	14	33212
14·21	16	28670
15·99	18	25135
17·77	20	22315
19·54	22	19973
21·32	24	18075
23·10	26	16447
24·87	28	15050
26·65	30	13638

6·396 in. by 11·726 in.

Length of each Piece in English Feet.	Proportion of Depth to Length.	Breaking Weight in lbs. avoirdupois.
9·771	10	52512
11·72	12	43176
13·68	14	36533
15·63	16	31537
17·59	18	27631
19·54	20	24546
21·50	22	22003
23·45	24	19883
25·41	26	18092
27·36	28	16554
29·31	30	15221

6·396 in. by 12·792 in.

Length of each Piece in English Feet.	Proportion of Depth to Length.	Breaking Weight in lbs. avoirdupois.
10·66	10	57285
12·79	12	47083
14·92	14	37854
17·06	16	34404
19·19	18	30164
21·32	20	26719
23·45	22	24003
25·58	24	21689
27·72	26	19377
29·85	28	18060
31·98	30	16000

7·462 inches square.

Length of each Piece in English Feet.	Proportion of Depth to Length.	Breaking Weight in lbs. avoirdupois.
6·218	10	35746
7·462	12	31911
8·705	14	27123
9·949	16	23413
11·19	18	20530
12·44	20	18224
13·68	22	16335
14·92	24	14761
16·17	26	13436
17·41	28	12637
18·65	30	10940

7·462 in. by 8·528 in.

Length of each Piece in English Feet.	Proportion of Depth to Length.	Breaking Weight in lbs. avoirdupois.
7·106	10	44577
8·528	12	36643
9·949	14	29806
11·37	16	26746
12·79	18	24060
14·21	20	21838
15·63	22	18667
17·06	24	16870
18·48	26	15418
19·90	28	14046
21·32	30	12915

7·462 in. by 9·594 in.

Length of each Piece in English Feet.	Proportion of Depth to Length.	Breaking Weight in lbs. avoirdupois.
7·994	10	50125
9·594	12	41221
11·19	14	35644
12·79	16	30103
14·39	18	26394
15·99	20	23432
17·59	22	21003
19·19	24	18979
20·79	26	17270
22·39	28	15802
23·98	30	14530

7·462 in. by 10·66 in.

Length of each Piece in English Feet.	Proportion of Depth to Length.	Breaking Weight in lbs. avoirdupois.
8·983	10	55738
10·66	12	45804
12·44	14	38757
14·21	16	33449
15·99	18	29226
17·77	20	26142
19·54	22	23325
21·32	24	21087
23·10	26	19139
24·97	28	17557
26·65	30	16144

7·462 in. by 11·726 in.

Length of each Piece in English Feet.	Proportion of Depth to Length.	Breaking Weight in lbs. avoirdupois.
9·771	10	60264
11·73	12	49384
13·68	14	42622
15·63	16	36792
17·59	18	31808
19·54	20	28637
21·50	22	24719
23·45	24	23196
25·40	26	21307
27·36	28	18928
29·31	30	17758

7·462 in. by 12·792 in.

Length of each Piece in English Feet.	Proportion of Depth to Length.	Breaking Weight in lbs. avoirdupois.
10·66	10	66832
12·79	12	55964
14·92	14	46497
17·06	16	40138
19·19	18	34992
21·32	20	31241
23·45	22	28003
25·58	24	25305
27·72	26	23068
29·85	28	21070
31·98	30	18373

7·462 in. by 13·858 in.

Length of each Piece in English Feet.	Proportion of Depth to Length.	Breaking Weight in lbs. avoirdupois.
12·61	10	72403
13·86	12	59546
16·17	14	50371
18·48	16	43483
19·72	18	38124

8·528 inches square.

Length of each Piece in English Feet.	Proportion of Depth to Length.	Breaking Weight in lbs. avoirdupois.
7·106	10	50921
8·528	12	41878
9·949	14	35426
11·37	16	30581
12·79	18	26812
14·21	20	23803
15·63	22	21342
17·06	24	19280
18·48	26	17345
19·90	28	16051
21·32	30	14760

8·528 in. by 9·594 in.

Length of each Piece in English Feet.	Proportion of Depth to Length.	Breaking Weight in lbs. avoirdupois.
7·994	10	57285
9·594	12	47093
11·19	14	39854

Length of each Piece in English Feet.	Proportion of Depth to Length.	Breaking Weight in lbs. avoirdupois.
12·79	16	34403
14·39	18	30170
15·99	20	26773
17·59	22	24003
19·19	24	21690
21·95	26	19737
23·45	28	17960
25·05	30	16605
8·528 in. by 10·66 in.		
8·883	10	62651
10·66	12	52348
12·44	14	44283
14·21	16	38227
15·99	18	33516
17·77	20	29754
19·54	22	26669
21·32	24	24100
23·10	26	21930
24·87	28	20066
26·65	30	18444
8·528 in. by 11·726 in.		
9·771	10	69975
11·73	12	57582
13·67	14	48711
15·63	16	42049
17·59	18	36668
19·54	20	32729
21·50	22	29337
23·45	24	26017
25·40	26	24124
27·36	28	22073
30·20	30	20295
8·528 in by 12·792 in.		
10·66	10	76381
12·79	12	62817
14·92	14	53139
17·06	16	45872
19·19	18	40219
21·32	20	35715
23·45	22	32004
25·58	24	28920
27·72	26	26356
29·85	28	24851
31·98	30	22149
8·528 in. by 13·858 in.		
11·55	10	82746
13·86	12	68052
16·17	14	57576
18·48	16	49627
20·79	18	43628
8·528 in. by 14·924 in.		
12·44	10	89111
14·92	12	73279
17·41	14	61996
19·90	16	53517
22·39	18	46923
9·594 inches square.		
7·994	10	64447
9·594	12	52992
11·19	14	45402
12·79	16	38704
14·39	18	33935
15·99	20	30125
17·59	22	27003
19·19	24	24401
20·79	26	22205
22·39	28	20317
23·98	30	18681
9·594 in. by 10·66 in.		
8·983	10	71607
10·66	12	58891
12·44	14	49818
14·21	16	43010
15·99	18	37705
17·77	20	33473
19·54	22	30003
21·32	24	27112
23·10	26	24671
24·87	28	22574
26·65	30	20756
9·594 in. by 11·726 in.		
9·771	10	78848
11·73	12	64780
13·68	14	54800
15·63	16	47305
17·59	18	41476
19·59	20	36820
21·50	22	33004
23·45	24	29825
25·40	26	27138
27·36	28	24830
29·21	30	22832
9·594 in. by 12·792 in.		
10·66	10	85929
12·79	12	70670
14·92	14	59782
17·06	16	51406
19·19	18	45247
21·32	20	40167
23·45	22	36004
25·58	24	32535
27·72	26	29606
29·85	28	27090
31·98	30	24908
9·594 in. by 13·858 in.		
11·55	10	93089
13·86	12	76458
16·17	14	64763
18·48	16	55906
20·79	18	49117
9·594 in. by 14·924 in.		
12·44	10	100250
14·92	12	82447
17·41	14	69745
19·90	16	60207
22·39	18	52771
10·66 inches square.		
8·883	10	79564
10·66	12	65435
12·44	14	55453
14·21	16	47783
15·99	18	41895
17·77	20	37192
19·54	22	33337
21·32	24	30125
23·10	26	27412
24·87	28	24083
26·65	30	23061
10·66 in. by 11·726 in.		
9·771	10	87520
11·73	12	71978
13·67	14	60889
15·63	16	52548
17·59	18	45985
19·54	20	40911
21·50	22	36671
23·45	24	33138
25·40	26	30155
27·36	28	27491
29·21	30	25369
10·66 in. by 12·792 in.		
10·66	10	95476
12·79	12	78521
14·92	14	66424
17·06	16	57340

Length of each Piece in English Feet.	Proportion of Depth to Length.	Breaking Weight in lbs. avoirdupois.
19·19	18	50274
21·32	20	44631
23·45	22	40005
25·58	24	36151
27·72	26	32896
29·85	28	30100
31·98	30	27676

10·66 in. by 13·858 in.

11·55	10	103633
13·86	12	85065
16·17	14	72037
18·48	16	62118
20·79	18	54463

10·66 in. by 14.924 in.

12·44	10	111389
14·92	12	91609
17·41	14	77495
19·90	16	66896
22·39	18	58653

10·66 in. by 15·990 in.

13·32	10	119345
15·99	12	98152
18·65	14	83030
21·32	16	71675
23·98	18	62841

11·726 inches square.

9·771	10	96272
11·73	12	79174
13·67	14	66978
15·63	16	57818
17·59	18	51493
19·54	20	45002
21·50	22	40338
23·45	24	36407
25·40	26	33087
27·36	28	30350
29·21	30	27906

11·726 in. by 12·792 in.

10·66	10	105023
12·79	12	·86374
14·92	14	73067
17·06	16	63074
19·19	18	55301
21·32	20	49093
23·45	22	44006
25·58	24	38765

27·72	26	36185
29·85	28	33109
31·98	30	30443

11·726 in. by 13·858 in.

11·55	10	113776
13·86	12	93572
16·17	14	79155
18·48	16	68328
20·79	18	60910

11·726 in. by 14·924 in.

12·44	10	122528
14·92	12	100769
17·41	14	85244
19·90	16	73576
22·39	18	64518

11·726 in. by 15·99 in.

13·32	10	131280
15·99	12	107968
18·65	14	91333
21·32	16	78842
23·98	18	69126

11·726 in. by 17·056 in.

14·21	10	148784
17·06	12	122362
19·90	14	103511
22·74	16	89355
25·58	18	78344

11·72 in. by 18·122 in.

15·10	10	157537
18·12	12	129561
21·14	14	109600
24·16	16	94611
27·18	18	82350

12·792 inches square.

10·66	10	115572
12·79	12	89826
14·92	14	79709
17·06	16	68708
19·19	18	60329
21·32	20	53557
23·45	22	48006
25·58	24	43380
27·72	26	39475
29·85	28	36119
31·98	30	·33211

12·792 in. by 13·858 in.

11·55	10	124119
13·86	12	102078
16·17	14	86351
18·48	16	74542
20·79	18	65356

12·792 in. by 14·924 in.

12·44	10	133667
14·92	12	110930
17·41	14	92994
19·90	16	80275
22·39	18	70384

12·792 in. by 15·99 in.

13·32	10	143214
15·99	12	117783
18·65	14	99636
21·32	16	86010
23·98	18	75411

12·792 in. by 17·056 in.

14·21	10	152762
17·06	12	125634
19·90	14	106279
22·74	16	91744
25·58	18	76238

12·792 in. by 18·122 in.

15·10	10	162310
18·12	12	123487
21·14	14	112921
24·16	16	97479
27·18	18	85461

12·792 in. by 19·188 in.

15·99	10	171857
19·19	12	141340
22·37	14	119565
25·58	16	103212
28·78	18	88894

12·792 in. by 20·254 in.

16·88	10	181405
20·25	12	149191
23·63	14	126207
27·00	16	108946
29·38	18	·95521

Length of each Piece in English Feet.	Proportion of Depth to Length.	Breaking Weight in lbs. avoirdupois.	Length of each Piece in English Feet.	Proportion of Depth to Length.	Breaking Weight in lbs. avoirdupois.	Length of each Piece in English Feet.	Proportion of Depth to Length.	Breaking Weight in lbs. avoirdupois.
13·858 inches square.			13·858 in. by 21·326 in.			14·924 in. by 20·254 in.		
11·55	10	134463	17·77	10	205531	16·88	10	212547
13·86	12	110584	21·32	12	170130	20·25	12	174057
16·17	14	93547	24·87	14	144920	23·63	14	147331
18·48	16	80754	28·43	16	124237	27·00	16	127104
20·79	18	70802	31·98	18	108951	29·38	18	111441
13·858 in. by 14·924 in.			13·058 in. by 22·386 in.			14·924 in. by 21·326 in.		
12·44	10	144806	18·65	10	217210	17·77	10	212776
14·92	12	119092	22·38	12	178637	·21·32	12	173218
17·41	14	100813	26·12	14	151115	24·87	14	150991
19·90	16	86966	29·85	16	130049	28·43	16	133733
22·39	18	76249	33·58	18	114374	31·98	18	117306
13·858 in. by 15·99 in.			14·924 inches square.			14·924 in. by 22·386 in.		
13·32	10	154825	12·44	10	155944	18·65	10	233917
15·99	12	127598	14·92	12	128092	22·38	12	192378
18·68	14	107939	17·41	14	108493	26·12	14	162737
21·32	16	93177	19·90	16	93655	29·85	16	140483
23·98	18	81755	22·39	18	82114	33·58	18	112372
13·858 in. by 17·056 in.			14·924 in. by 15·990 in.			14·924 in. by 23·452 in.		
14·21	10	164426	13·32	10	167083	19·54	10	246136
17·06	12	136153	15·99	12	137213	23·45	12	201540
19·90	14	114364	18·65	14	116242	27·36	14	170490
22·74	16	99396	21·32	16	100354	31·27	16	147173
25·58	18	91941	23·98	18	87980	35·18	18	129037
13·858 in. by 18·122 in.			14·924 in. by 17·056 in.			15·99 inches square.		
15·10	10	175836	14·21	10	178223	13·32	10	179009
18·12	12	144611	17·06	12	146674	15·99	12	147229
21·14	14	121332	19·90	14	123993	18·65	14	124547
24·16	16	105601	22·74	16	107034	21·32	16	107513
27·18	18	92588	25·58	18	93845	23·98	18	94164
13·858 in. by 19·188 in.			14·924 in. by 18·122 in.			15·99 in. by 17·056 in.		
15·99	10	141179	15·10	10	189362	14·21	10	190953
19·19	12	153115	18·12	12	155735	17·06	12	160244
22·37	14	129528	21·14	14	131741	19·90	14	132849
25·58	16	111813	24·16	16	113764	22·74	16	114680
28·78	18	98935	27·18	18	99711	25·58	18	100548
13·858 in. by 20·254 in.			14·924 in. by 19·188 in.			15·99 in. by 18·122 in.		
16·88	10	196522	15·99	10	200501	15·10	10	202888
20·25	12	161624	19·19	12	164895	18·12	12	166859
23·63	14	136724	22·37	14	139492	21·14	14	141153
27·00	16	118026	25·58	16	120415	24·16	16	121848
29·38	18	103481	28·78	18	105575	27·18	18	106832

Length of each Piece in English Feet.	Proportion of Depth to Length.	Breaking Weight in lbs. avoirdupois.	Length of each Piece in English Feet.	Proportion of Depth to Length.	Breaking Weight in lbs. avoirdupois.	Length of each Piece in English Feet.	Proportion of Depth to Length.	Breaking Weight in lbs. avoirdupois.
15·99 in. by 19·188 in.			**17·056 in. by 18·122 in.**			**17·056 in. by 25·584 in.**		
15·99	10	214823	15·10	10	216412	21·32	10	305525
19·19	12	176584	18·12	12	177983	25·58	12	251360
22·37	14	149456	21·14	14	150563	29·85	14	212559
25·58	16	129015	24·16	16	129970	34·11	16	183421
28·78	18	113118	27·18	18	113954	38·37	18	160277
15·99 in. by 20·254 in.			**17·056 in. by 19·188 in.**			**18·122 inches square.**		
16·88	10	226757	15·99	10	229144	15·10	10	229907
20·25	12	186490	19·19	12	188456	18·12	12	187107
23·63	14	157759	22·37	14	158439	21·14	14	159973
27·00	16	136183	25·58	16	137617	24·16	16	142094
29·38	18	119401	28·78	18	120659	27·18	18	121077
15·99 in. by 21·326 in.			**17·056 in. by 20·254 in.**			**18·122 in. by 19·188 in.**		
17·77	10	238692	16·88	10	241875	15·99	10	243465
21·32	12	196365	20·25	12	197322	19·19	12	200131
24·87	14	166062	23·63	14	168276	22·37	14	169383
28·43	16	143350	27·00	16	145261	25·58	16	146217
31·98	18	125686	29·38	18	127341	28·78	18	128199
15·99 in. by 22·386 in.			**17·056 in. by 21·326 in.**			**18·122 in. by 20·254 in.**		
18·65	10	250626	17·77	10	254605	16·88	10	257091
22·38	12	206127	21·32	12	209391	20·25	12	211356
26·12	14	174365	24·87	14	177132	23·63	14	178793
29·85	16	150517	28·43	16	152807	27·10	16	154340
33·58	18	131770	31·98	18	134112	29·38	18	135261
15·99 in. by 23·452 in.			**17·056 in. by 22·386 in.**			**18·122 in. by 21·326 in.**		
19·54	10	262561	18·65	10	267334	17·77	10	270317
23·45	12	215935	22·38	12	219861	21·32	12	222479
27·36	14	182668	26·12	14	184989	24·87	14	188203
31·27	16	157685	29.85	16	160552	28·43	16	162463
35·18	18	138254	33·58	18	140768	31·98	18	142443
15·99 in. by 24·518 in.			**17·056 in. by 23·452 in.**			**18·122 in. by 22·386 in.**		
20·43	10	274495	19·54	10	280064	18·65	10	284043
24·52	12	225750	23·45	12	230330	22·38	12	233603
28·60	14	190751	27·36	14	190846	26·12	14	197611
32·69	16	164852	31·27	16	168772	29·85	16	170275
36·78	18	144538	35·18	18	147471	33·58	18	149566
17·056 inches square.			**17·056 in. by 24·518 in.**			**18·122 in. by 23·452 in.**		
14·21	10	203684	21·32	10	292795	19·54	10	297569
17·06	12	167513	25·58	12	240800	23·45	12	244727
19·90	14	141706	29 85	14	203702	27·36	14	207023
22·74	16	122967	34·11	16	175842	31·27	16	188710
25·58	18	107251	38·37	18	154174	35·18	18	156688

18·122 in. by 24·518 in. | 19·188 in. by 21·326 in. | 19·188 in. by 25·584 in.

Length of each Piece in English Feet.	Proportion of Depth to Length.	Breaking Weight in lbs. avoirdupois.	Length of each Piece in English Feet.	Proportion of Depth to Length.	Breaking Weight in lbs. avoirdupois.	Length of each Piece in English Feet.	Proportion of Depth to Length.	Breaking Weight in lbs. avoirdupois.
20·48	10	310771	17·77	10	286430	31·32	10	343716
24·52	12	255851	21·32	12	235565	25·58	12	282679
28·60	14	216434	24·87	14	196074	29·85	14	140130
32·69	16	186833	28·43	16	171010	34·11	16	207092
36·78	18	163810	31·98	18	150823	38·37	18	180987

18·122 in. by 25·584 in. | 19·188 in. by 22·386 in. | 19·188 in. by 26·65 in.

Length	Proportion	Breaking Weight	Length	Proportion	Breaking Weight	Length	Proportion	Breaking Weight
21·32	10	324621	18·65	10	300763	22·21	10	358037
25·58	12	256975	22·38	12	247344	26·65	12	294458
29·85	14	225844	26·12	14	209238	31·09	14	249092
34·11	16	194956	29·85	16	180621	35·53	16	216026
38·37	18	170933	33·58	18	158364	39·97	18	188529

19·188 inches square. | 19·188 in. by 23·452 in. | 20·254 inches square.

Length	Proportion	Breaking Weight	Length	Proportion	Breaking Weight	Length	Proportion	Breaking Weight
15·99	10	257787	19·54	10	315073	16·88	10	287226
19·19	12	212107	23·45	12	259122	20·25	12	236220
22·37	14	179347	27·36	14	219101	23·63	14	199827
25·58	16	150818	31·27	16	189222	27·10	16	172498
28·78	18	135741	35·18	18	165905	29·38	18	151242

19·188 in. by 20·254 in. | 19·188 in. by 24·518 in. | 20·254 in. by 21·320 in.

Length	Proportion	Breaking Weight	Length	Proportion	Breaking Weight	Length	Proportion	Breaking Weight
16·88	10	272108	20·43	10	329395	17·77	10	292343
20·25	12	223788	24·52	12	270901	21·32	12	248653
23·63	14	189310	28·60	14	229165	24·87	14	200345
27·00	16	163419	32·69	16	197824	28·43	16	181577
29·38	18	143281	36·78	18	173446	31·98	18	159202

1623. The table from which the above has been reduced to English measures, is extended to pieces of 31·980 in. square, and 47·97 ft. long; but as such scantlings rarely if ever occur in practice, unless strengthened by means of trussing, we have not considered it necessary to proceed beyond the scantling of 20·25 in. by 21·320 in., and 32 ft. long.

1624. Though the table is founded upon experiments on oak, it will serve for all sorts of wood, whose primitive strength is known, and the proportion they bear to oak. In order to facilitate calculations of that nature, the following table has been constructed, in which will be found the absolute and primitive strengths of the several sorts of timber, ordinarily used in carpentry, as also of some few others.

TABLE VII.

For applying the preceding Table to the Woods undermentioned. The primitive horizontal or transverse Strength of Oak is taken at 1000; its supporting or primitive vertical Strength at 807; and its cohesive or absolute Strength at 1821; being deduced from Pieces 19·188 lines English square.

Species of Wood.	Primitive horizontal Strength.	Primitive vertical Strength.	Absolute cohesive Strength.	Species of Wood.	Primitive horizontal Strength.	Primitive vertical Strength.	Absolute cohesive Strength.
Acacia (yellow)	780	1228	1560	Fir -	918	851	1250
Ash -	1072	1112	1800	Oak -	1000	807	1821
Beech -	1032	986	2480	Pine-tree -	882	804	1141
Birch -	853	861	1980	Poplar -	586	680	940
Cedar -	627	720	1740	Service-tree -	965	981	1642
Cherry tree	961	986	1912	Sycamore -	900	968	1564
Chestnut -	957	950	1944	Yew-tree -	1037	1375	2287
Elm -	1077	1075	1980	Walnut -	900	753	1120

Method of using the above Table for Horizontal Timbers.

1625. To find the strength of a beam of fir 23·98 ft. long and 5·330 by 9·594 in. Against these dimensions in the Table VI. we find 10378 as the breaking weight. In the Table VII. we find the primitive horizontal strength of oak is to that of fir as 1000 to 918. Hence 1000 : 918 :: 10378 to a fourth term which = 9527 ; which expresses the greatest strength of such a beam of fir, or that which would break it. Cutting off the last figure on the right hand, that is, taking one tenth, we have 952 for the greatest weight with which such a beam should be loaded.

1625a. If the beam be of chesnut, whose primitive strength is 957, the proportion becomes 1000 : 957 :: 10378 : 9931 = the greatest strength of such a piece, and $\frac{9931}{10}$ the greatest weight with which it should be loaded.

Method of Application for the vertical bearing Strength.

1626. To find the vertical strength of an oak post 9·594 in. square, and 9·594 ft. high, we shall find in Table VII. for the primitive vertical strength, 807 for 19·188 lines English superficial. But as this strength diminishes as the relative height of the post increases, which in this cases is 12 times, we must (1601.), take only $\frac{5}{6}$ of 807, according to the progression there given, that is, $672\frac{1}{2}$.

1626a. The post being 9·594 in. square, its area will be $\overline{9\cdot594 \times 12}|^2 = 13254\cdot756$, and $\frac{13254\cdot756}{19\cdot188} = 692\cdot34$, and $692\cdot34 \times 672\cdot5 = 465000$, which divided by 10 = 46500 ; is the weight with which without risk the post may be loaded.

1626b. If the post be of fir, whose primitive vertical strength to that of oak is as 851 to 807, we have only to use the proportion 807 : 465000 :: 851 : 490980, which divided by 10 = 49098 ; the greatest weight with which it should be loaded.

Method for obtaining the absolute or cohesive Strength.

1627. In respect of this species of strength, which is that with which timber resists being drawn asunder in the direction of its fibres by weights acting at its end, it is only necessary to multiply the area of the section of the piece reduced to lines by the tabular number 1821, if it be oak, and divide the product by 19·188, and the quotient will show the greatest effort it can bear.

1627a. Thus for a piece of oak 9·594 in. square, we have $\frac{13254\cdot75 \times 1821}{19\cdot188} = 1260700$ (in round numbers), which divided by 10 gives the greatest weight that should be suspended to the piece.

1627b. From Table VII. it will be seen that in the direction of the absolute strength, beech is the strongest wood, and that strength will be $\frac{13254\cdot75 \times 2480 \text{ (the tabular number)}}{19\cdot188} =$ 1363850, which will give 136385 for the greatest weight to be attached.

Of the Strength of Timbers in an inclined Position.

1628. If we suppose the vertical piece AB to become inclined to the base, experiment proves that its strength to resist (*fig.* 613a) a vertical effort diminishes as its inclination increases ; so that, if from the upper part in D a vertical D*f* be let fall, and from the points of the base the horizontal line BC be drawn, the strength of the piece diminishes as B*f* increases : whence, I. The strength of a vertical piece is to that of an inclined piece of the same length and scantling as the length AB is to B*f*, or as the radius is to the sine of the inclination of the piece. II. Vertical pieces have the greatest strength to resist a weight, and the weakest are pieces which lie horizontally.

1628a. The first of these results furnishes an easy method of finding, by the aid of the last table, the strength of a piece of timber whose length and inclination are known. Thus, suppose a piece of oak inclined 4·692 ft. and 9·594 ft. long ;

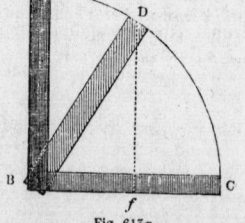

Fig. 613a.

its size being 8·528 by 9·594 ins., whose area, therefore, is 11781·74 lines. This must be divided by the tabular number 19·188, and the quotient will be 614. In table VII., 807 is the primitive vertical strength of oak for 19·188 lines superficial of section ; but as the piece is more than 12 times the width of its base, we are, as before observed, to take only $\frac{5}{6}$ of 807, or 672·5, which is to be multiplied by 614, and the product is 412915. Then the proportion 9·594 : 4·692 :: 412915 : 843400 is the strength, which divided by 10 = 84340, is the greatest load to which the inclined piece ought to be subjected.

1628b. In Practical or Constructive CARPENTRY, Chap. III. Sect. iv., tables of scantlings for timbers are given more immediately useful to the practical architect than those deducible from the above rule. These tables and rules, however, have been approved by others,

especially by Cresy in his *Encyclopædia of Civil Engineering*; but in consequence of the very large amount of information obtained, since the first edition of this work, resulting from the investigations of scientific and practical experimentalists, the following condensed summary of the new ideas on the strength of BEAMS, GIRDERS, and PILLARS, both in *timber* and *iron*, must necessarily be submitted for the consideration of the reader and student.

1628c. The term *beam* is applied herein to large rectangular sections; that of *girder*, to large irregular shapes; and those of *bar* and *irons*, to small rectangular and irregular forms.

1628d. Beams and girders are calculated for the following classes of buildings:—

I. Light workshops and factories, public halls, churches, and other buildings in which people only accumulate, with warehouses for light goods. For all these an allowance of $1\frac{1}{2}$ cwt., or 168 lbs. per square foot of floor surface, will include the weight of the joisting, the flooring, and the load upon it.

II. Storehouses for heavy goods, or factories in which heavy machinery and goods are placed. For these an allowance of $2\frac{1}{2}$ cwt. or 280 lbs. per square foot of floor surface will include the same weights.

III. Ordinary dwelling houses. For these an allowance of $1\frac{1}{4}$ cwt, or 140 lbs. per square foot, will include the same weights.

IV. Tredgold calculates 40 lbs. per square foot for the weight of a ceiling, counter floor, and iron girders, with 120 lbs. per foot more, supposing the floor to be covered with people at any time, making together a weight equal to 160 lbs. as the least stress that ought to be taken. Partitions, or any other additional weights brought upon the floor, must also be taken into consideration. (See further s. v. Weight, in GLOSSARY, Addendum.)

V. The weight of the load to be carried must always include that of the girder itself.

STRAINS ON BEAMS AND GIRDERS.

1628e. These we shall consider under the heads I. TRANSVERSE STRAIN (1628g.), which consists partly of the action of *Tension* as well as of *Compression*, each of them being dependent upon the *Cohesion* of the material. Under II. TENSION (1630c.), will be considered the *neutral axis* (1630c.), *deflection* of beams (1630e.), with the *modulus of Elasticity* (1630i.), *impact* or *collision* (1630o.), and the *tensile strength* (1630p.). Under III. COMPRESSION (1630w.) is considered *Deflection* of pillars, and *Detrusion* (1631n.). The subject IV. TORSION (1631x.) closes this section.

1628f. Timber is permanently injured if more than even $\frac{1}{4}$ of the breaking weight is placed on it. Fairbairn states that for bridges and warehouses, cast iron girders should not be loaded with more that $\frac{1}{5}$ or $\frac{1}{6}$ of the breaking weight in the middle. For ordinary purposes, $\frac{1}{3}$ for cast iron is allowed for the permanent load (Barlow). A little more than $\frac{1}{3}$ can be allowed for wrought iron beams, as that material, from its extensile capability, does not suddenly give way (Warr); but they should never be loaded with more than $\frac{1}{4}$th. (Fairbairn). Girders, especially those of cast iron, which are liable to be less strong than intended from irregularity in casting and cooling, should be proved before use to a little more than the extent of the safe load; this proof, however, should never exceed the half of the breaking weight, as the metal would be thoroughly weakened. Tredgold observes that a load of $\frac{1}{5}$ of the breaking weight causes deflection to increase with time, and finally to produce a permanent set. The Board of Trade limits the working strain to 5 tons or 11,200 lbs. per square inch, on any part of a wrought iron structure.

TRANSVERSE STRAIN.

1628g. The strength of beams in general is, directly as the breadth, directly as the square of the depth, and inversely as the length; thus $\frac{\text{breadth} \times \text{depth}^2}{\text{length}}$. But a certain supposed quantity must, however, be added to express the specific strength of any material, a quantity only obtained by experiments on that material. This supposed quantity is represented by S. We then obtain $\frac{\text{breadth} \times \text{depth}^2 \times \text{S}}{\text{length}} = $ breaking weight. Therefore, in experiments, a simple transposition of the quantities evolves the value of S, thus $\frac{\text{length} \times \text{breaking weight}}{\text{breadth} \times \text{depth}^2} = \text{S}$, which S then becomes a constant. As regards the usual form of a cast-iron girder, using C as a constant for a signification in a *girder*, similar to that of S in a *beam*, the formula $\frac{\text{area of section} \times \text{depth}^2 \times \text{C}}{\text{length}} = $ breaking weight. The values of S and C are only applicable to a beam or girder of a similar sectional form to that from

which the value was derived, since this *constant* expresses the specific strength of that form of section.

1628h. Another formula for estimating the strength of beams rests on the knowledge of the resistance (or *r*) offered by any material to fracture by a tensile or crushing force, and the depth of the neutral axis (or *n*) of this area in the beam; the latter, of course, cannot be calculated, except from experiment. The rule is $\frac{r \times \text{breadth} \times \text{depth}^2}{n \times \text{length}}$ = breaking weight. See RESISTANCE, in Glossary.

1628i. TABLE OF THE TRANSVERSE STRENGTH OF TIMBER : 1 Inch Square, 1 Foot Long.

Name.	Specific Gravity.	Warr. Value of S.	Value of S of others.	Barlow. Value of S.	Tredgold Value of S.	Hurst. 1865 Value of S.	Molesworth. 1865 Value of S.
				lbs.	lbs.	lbs.	lbs.
Ash, English	·760	506	518	675	656	560	672
Beech, ,,	·696	390	- -	- -	677		
,, Amer. White	·711	345					
,, ,, Red	·775	435					
,,		- -	- -	519	- -	448	504
Poplar	- -	- -	- -	- -	327		
Birch, Common	·711	482	- -	607			
Elm, English	·579	200	595	338	540	336	336
,, American	- -	- -	631·5	611			
Oak, English	·829	424	- -	400	710		
,, ,,	- -	- -	- -	470	400	560	560
,, ,,	- -	- -	- -	557			
,, African	·988	630	869·5				
,, Adriatic	- -	- -	- -	461	448		
,, Amer. White	·779	433					
,, ,, Red	·952	422	653·5				
,, Canadian	- -	- -	- -	588			
,, Dantzic	·720	377	- -	486			
,, Memel	·727	416	444				
,, Riga	- -	- -	- -	- -	714		
Pine, Amer. White	·432	307					
,, ,, Red	·576	382	467	447	- -	448	448
,, ,, Yellow	·508	300	358·5	- -	658		
,, Pitch	·740	432	629	544	560	560	
,, Dantzic	·649	356					
,, Memel	·601	334	- -	577	545		
,, Riga	·654	346	- -	376	530	336	
,, ,,	- -	- -	- -	359			
Fir, Spruce	·503	336					
,, ,, American	·772	260	- -	- -	570		
,, Mar Forest	·698	308	- -	381	315		
,, ,,	- -	- -	- -	{ 415 / 408			
,, Scotch	- -	- -	- -		582		
,, New England	- -	- -	- -	367			
,, Yellow	- -	- -	- -	- -		336	
Deal, Christiania	·689	400	- -	521	686		
Larch	·505	256	- -	280	557	336	336
,, Amer. Tamarac	·433	230					
Walnut	- -	- -	- -	- -	500		
Spanish Chesnut	- -	- -	- -	- -	610		
Mahogany, Nassau	·668	430	673·5				
,, Honduras	- -	- -	- -	- -	637		
,, Spanish	- -	- -	- -	- -	425		
Teak	·729	527	- -	820	717		
Poon	- -	- -	- -	740	590		
Mora	- -	- -	691				
Sabicu	- -	- -	854·25				
Green-heart	- -	- -	1,079·5				
Cowrie	- -	- -	- -	- -	610		

1628k. The results of Barlow, Nelson, Moore, Denison, and some others, are collected in the above table, which gives a *mean* of the whole (Warr); Barlow's values are also noted separately, being those usually supplied in the Handbooks; and obtained by Barlow's formula $\frac{l \times \mathrm{B\,W}}{4\,a\,d^2} = \mathrm{S}$, from experiments on a projecting beam or arm : or from the formula $\frac{l \times \mathrm{B\,W}}{a\,d^2} = \mathrm{S}$, when a beam supported at the ends is under trial. A measureable set is produced by a straining force very much less than that to which the material will be likely to be exposed in practice. Without having this principle in mind, the differences between the actual breaking weight and the permanent set weight of some writers will be misunderstood. The practical man, however, will use one third or some other proportion of these values, as noticed in *par.* 1628f.

1628l. TABLE OF THE TRANSVERSE STRENGTH OF METALS: 1 Inch Square, 1 Foot Long.

Name.	Barlow.		Tredgold* (Safe Weights); and others.	Hurst.	Molesworth.
	Breaking Weight.	One-third for set.		Breaking Weight.	
	lbs.	lbs.	lbs.	lbs.	lbs.
Wrought iron, good English -	8550?	2850	*952 2048	2800	3024
„ „ - - -	- - -	- - -	2048		
„ „ best Derbyshire and Staffordshire - }	- - -	- - -	2500		
			1700 to 1900	Dobson.	
„ „ Scotch hot blast -	- - -	- - -	*2290		
Cast iron - - - - -	7644	2548	*850 2000	2016	2016
„ „ - - -	- - -	- - -			
Brass, cast - - - -	- - -	- - -	*890	896	896
Lead, cast - - - -	- - -	- - -	*196		
Tin, cast - - - - -	- - -	- - -	*372	784	
Zinc, cast - - - - -	- - -	- - -	*746	784	728

1628m. Fairbairn's experiments on *cast irons* obtained from the principal iron-works, and made into bars 1 inch square and 5 feet long, proved that the longer beams are weaker than the shorter in a greater proportion than their respective lengths; that the strength does not increase quite so rapidly as the square of the depth; that the deflection of a beam is proportional to the force or load; and that a set occurs with a small portion of the breaking weight.

In 59 experiments, the strongest; Ponkey No. 3, cold blast   -   -   - } Spec. Grav. 7·122   Break. Wt. 578 lbs.   Ult. deflect. 1·74, hard.

In 59, experiments, the weakest; Plaskynaston, No. 2, hot blast   -   -   - } 6·916   357 lbs.   1·36, soft.

Mean value 440 lbs., affording for the specific strength, S = 1980 lbs., or = ·884 tons. For the rule including *n*, a comparison of two specimens gave $n = 2·63$.

1628n. Morries Stirling has considerably strengthened *cast iron* by adding a portion of malleable cast iron. Four experiments, by Hodgkinson, gave the following results :—

No. 2 quality (20 per cent. scrap), bars 9 ft. long, 2 ins. square   -   S = 2248
No. 3   „   (15 per cent. scrap),   „   „   „   „   -   S = 1682
No. 2   „   „   „   „   bars 4 ft. 6 ins. long, 1 in. square   S = 2803
No. 3   „   „   „   „   „   „   „   „   -   S = 1996

His irons are also stronger under compression and tension.

Tensile power, No. 2 -   11·50 tons. | Compressive power, No. 2 -   54·62 tons.
„   „   No. 3 -   10·47 „ | „   „   No. 3 -   64·41 „

1628o. Hodgkinson also found the average breaking weight in pounds of a bar of *cast iron*, 1 inch square and 4 feet 6 inches long between the supports, to be as follows :—

Average of 21 samples of *hot blast* iron   -   -   - 445·5714 pounds
Average of 21 samples of *cold blast* iron   -   -   - 456·9090 pounds

The superior transverse strength of *cold blast* iron equals nearly 2½ per cent. R. Stephenson experimented, in 1846 and 1847, on bars of different kinds of cast iron, 1 inch square and 3 feet bearing. The results are given in the *Civil Engineer*, 1850, pp. 194–9.

SHAPES OF BEAMS AND GIRDERS.

1628p. "Calculation affords the following *shapes for iron beams*, as being enabled to do the most work with the least expenditure of substance. *Beams supported at one end* : I.

If the load be terminal and the depth constant, the form of the beam in breadth should be wedge-shaped, the breadth increasing as the length of the beam (the latter measured from the loaded end). II. If the breadth be constant, the square of the depth must vary as the length, or the vertical section will be a parabola. III. When both breadth and depth vary, the section should present a cubical parabola. IV. When the beam supports only its own weight, it should be a double parabola, that is, the upper as well as the lower surface should be of a parabolic form, the depth being as the square of the length. V. When a beam is loaded evenly along its surface, the upper surface being horizontal, the lower one should be a straight line meeting the upper surface at the outer end, and forming a triangular vertical section; the depth at the point of support being determined by the length of the beam and the load to be sustained. VI. If an additional terminal load be added to such a beam, the under surface should be of a hyperbolic curvature. VII. And in a flanged beam, the lower flange should describe a parabolic curve (as in example IV.).

1628q. "*Beams supported at both ends.* I. A beam loaded at any one point, as scale beams and the like, should have a parabolic vertical section each way from the loaded point,

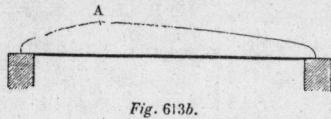

Fig. 613*b.*

A, *fig.* 613*b.* II. In *flanged beams*, the lines may be nearly straight, and approach the straight lines more as the flanges are thinner. III. A beam loaded uniformly along the whole of its length, should have an elliptic outline for the upper surface, the lower one being straight. This form applies to girders for bridges and other purposes where the load may be spread. IV. With thin flanges, a beam so circumstanced should be of a parabolic figure. V. If a flanged beam have its upper and lower sides level, and be loaded uniformly from end to end, the sides of the lower flange should have a parabolic curvature." (Gregory.) VI. In the case of example III., Fairbairn observes that the greatest strength will be attained, while the breadth and depth is allowed to be diminished

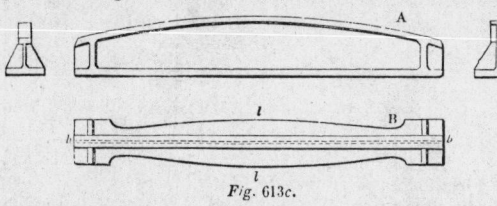

Fig. 613*c.*

towards the ends. This diminution should take place in curved lines which are strictly parabolic. The most convenient way of doing this is by preserving a horizontal level in the bottom flange, diminishing its width, as well as the height of the girder, as *fig.* 613*c.* Thus the spaces *bb* should be square on plan for the bearings on the wall, &c., and equal to the width of the bottom flange at the centre; the intermediate length *l* to be curved to the form prescribed. The width of the bottom flange is to be reduced near the ends to one half of its size in the middle, and the total depth of the girder reduced at the ends in the same proportion. At the middle of the bearing, a flange may be cast on to connect the upper and lower flanges, and this will give additional stiffness to the girder.

1628r. Gregory further remarks on this subject : when *the depth of the beam is uniform*, and (VII.) the whole load is collected in one point (as A, *fig.* 613*d.*) the *sides* of the beam

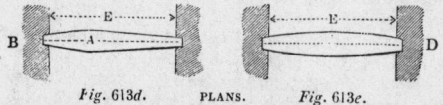

Fig. 613*d.* PLANS. *Fig.* 613*e.*

should be straight lines, the breadth at the ends, B, being half that where the load is applied.

VIII. When the load is uniformly distributed (*fig.* 613*e.*) the *sides* should be portions of a circle, the radius of which should equal the square of the length of the beam divided by twice its breadth. When the *breadth of the beam is uniform* and (IX.) the load is collected in one point, the extended (under) side should be straight, the depth at the point where the load is applied twice that at the ends, and the lines connecting them straight (*fig.* 613*b.*) See example I. When the load is uniformly distributed, X. the extended (under) side should be straight, and the compressed (upper) side a portion of a circle whose radius equals the square of half the length of the beam divided by its depth. See examples III. and VI. When the *transverse section* of a beam is a similar figure throughout its whole length; XI. if the load be collected at one point, the depth at this point should be to the depth at its extremities as 3:2: the sides of the beam being all straight lines. XII. When the load is uniformly distributed, the depth in the centre should be to the depth at the end as 3 : 1, the sides of the beam being all straight lines.

Various Laws affecting Beams and Girders.

1628s. The principles on which the rules subjoined are founded may be seen in Gregory, *Mechanics, &c.* and Barlow, *Strength of Materials*, but divested, certainly, of the refine-

ment of Dr. T. Young's *Modulus of Elasticity*, and some other matters, which we cannot help thinking unnecessary in a subject where, after exhausting all the niceties of the question, a large proportion of weight is considered too much for the constant load.

1628*t*. The *transverse strength* is that power, in the case of a beam, exerted in opposing a force acting in a direction perpendicular to its length. The following formulæ and rules apply to the various positions in which a beam or girder is placed.

	Girder.	Beam.
I. If a beam be loose (or supported) at both ends, and the weight be applied in the middle - - -	$\dfrac{C a d^2}{l} = W$	$\dfrac{S b d^2}{l} = W$
II. If a beam be loose at both ends, and the weight be applied uniformly along the same length, it will bear twice the load placed in the middle - - - -	$\dfrac{2C a d^2}{l} = W$	$\dfrac{2 S b d^2}{l} = W$
III. If a beam be loose at both ends, and the weight be applied at an intermediate point; the spaces m with $n = l$ -		$\dfrac{S b d^2 l}{4 m n} = W$
IV. If a beam be fixed at both ends, and the weight be applied in the middle, it will bear one half more than if both ends be loose (I.) - - - - - -	or	$\dfrac{1\cdot5 S b d^2}{l} = W$ $\dfrac{3 S b d^2}{2 l} = W$
V. If a beam be fixed at both ends, and the weight be applied uniformly along the same length, it will bear three times more than the load in the middle of No. 1, than if both ends be loose - - - - -		$\dfrac{3 S b d^2}{l} = W$
VI. If a beam be fixed at both ends, and the weight be applied at an intermediate point - - - -		$\dfrac{3 S b d^2 l}{8 m n} = W$
VII. If a beam be fixed at one end, and the weight be applied at the other end, it will bear only one fourth of the weight carried by beam No. 1, of the same length -		$\dfrac{S b d^2}{4 l} = W$

VIII. If a beam be fixed at one end only, and the weight be applied in the middle, it will bear half as much again as at the end.

IX. If a beam be fixed at one end, and the weight be applied uniformly along its length, it will bear double the load at the end.

X. If a beam be fixed at one end only, it is as strong as one of equal breadth and depth, and twice the length which is fixed at both ends.

XI. If a beam be supported in the middle and loaded at each end, it will bear the same weight as when loose at both ends and loaded in the middle (as I.)

XII. If a beam be continued over three or four points and the load be uniformly distributed, it will suffice to take the part between any two points of support as a beam fixed at both ends.

XIII. If some of the parts have a greater load than the others, it will be near enough in practice to take the parts so loaded as supported at the ends only.

XIV. If a beam be *inclined* and *supported* at both ends, it has its breaking weight equal to that of the same beam when horizontal, multiplied by the length of the inclined beam and divided by the horizontal distance (*fig.* 613*u.*).

NOTE.—In calculating for the strength of a beam or of a girder, it is usual to reckon on the ends being loose, from the difficulty of fixing the ends in a sufficient manner to warrant the rule in that case being followed: and when the ends are solidly embedded, they should penetrate the wall for a distance equal to at least three times the depth of the beam or girder (*par.* 1630*m.*); but this precaution is seldom carried out in practice.

1628*u*. For the effect of running loads over bars, we must refer to Professor Willis's experiments at Cambridge, given at the end of Barlow's *Strength of Materials*, &c., 1851.

1628*v*. Two geometrical methods of finding the *best* proportion of a beam to be cut out of a given cylinder have been propounded. The *stiffest* beam, says Tredgold, that can be cut out of a round tree, is that of which the depth is to the breadth as $\sqrt{3}$ to 1, or nearly as $1\cdot7320508$ to 1; this is in general a good proportion for beams that have to sustain a considerable load. The required proportions are obtained by dividing a diameter as *ab* in *fig.* 613*f.*, into two equal parts, *ac* and *cb*, then drawing with *a* and *b* as centres two arcs through *c* to cut the circle in *e* and *f*; the points *aebf* being joined, the figure is that of the *stiffest* beam that can be cut out of a cylinder, to resist a perpendicular strain. It is also observed by Tredgold that the *strongest* beam which can be cut out of a round tree is that of which the depth

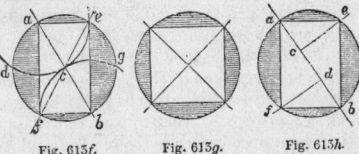

Fig. 613*f*.   Fig. 613*g*.   Fig. 613*h*.

is to the breadth as $\sqrt{2}$ is to 1, or nearly as 1·4142136 to 1; or as 7 to 5. Its two sides must be to the diameter of the tree as the $\sqrt{\frac{1}{3}}$ and $\sqrt{\frac{2}{3}}$ to 1. The required proportions are obtained by dividing a diameter ab, *fig.* 613h., into three equal parts ac, cd, db, and drawing the lines ce and df at right-angles to ab; the points $aebf$ being joined, the figure is that of the *strongest* beam that can be cut out of a cylinder. The strength of a *square* beam, *fig.* 613g., cut from the same cylinder, is to the strength of the strongest beam nearly as 101 to 110, although the square beam would contain more timber nearly in the ratio of 5 to 4·714. The stiffest beam is to the strongest as 0·97877 to 1, as regards power of bearing a load; but as 1·04382 to 1 as regards amount of deflection, in equal lengths between the supports.

1628w. Buffon, during his extensive series of experiments on oak timber, from 20 to 28 feet in length, and from 4 inches to 8 inches square in section, found that the heart-wood which was densest was also strongest, and the side on which the beam was laid also affected the strength; for when the annual layers were horizontal, and the strength 7, the layers laid vertically gave a strength of 8. He also found that beams which had each supported, without breaking, a load of 9,000 lbs. during one day, broke at the end of five or six months with a weight of 6,000 lbs., that is to say, they were unable to carry for six months two-thirds of the weight they bore for one day.

TRANSVERSE SECTIONS.

1628x. The transverse section of a cast iron girder previous to Hodgkinson's experiments was that of Tredgold, consisting of equal flanges at top and bottom, as A, *fig.* 613i; and that of Lillie and Fairbairn, in 1825, with a single flange, as B; Hodgkinson deduced a section of greatest strength having areas of flanges as 6 to 1, as C. Taking this form as unity, the ratios will stand:—

For Hodgkinson and Fairbairn, as - - - 1 : ·754
For Hodgkinson and Tredgold, as - - - 1 : ·619
For Fairbairn and Tredgold, as - - - 1 : ·820

(Fairbairn, *Application*, &c. p. 25: Tredgold, *Cast Iron*, 1824, p. 55, describes the advantages of his own form of section.)

1628y. Hodgkinson's complete section for a *cast iron* girder is shown in *fig.* 613j. Its chief principle is, that the bottom flange must contain six times the area of the top flange. The several dimensions are taken thus:—I. For the depth, the total dimension D. II. For the bottom flange, the width B, and for the two thicknesses, one is taken at the centre bb; the other b at the end. III. For the top flange, the width T, and for the two thicknesses, one is taken at the centre tt, the other t at the end. In this manner the dimensions of the flanges are quite independent of the thickness of the rib. IV. For the rib the two dimensions r and rr are measured as continued to the extreme top and bottom surfaces of the girder, with the same view of making these dimensions independent of those of the flanges, and promoting exactness in defining the entire section. Hodgkinson's complex rule for obtaining the weight a girder will carry, is $\frac{2}{3\,d\,l}\big\} b\,d^3 - (b - b_1{}^3)\,d_1{}^3 = W$. Here W = tons, or breaking weight; l feet, or length between supports; d whole depth; d_1 depth to bottom flange; b breadth of bottom flange; and b_1 thickness of vertical rib. The simpler rule usually employed, as $\frac{a \times d \times C}{l\ \text{feet}} = W$ tons, or the permanent load distributed, allowing that load to be $\frac{1}{4}$ of the breaking weight; and it gives a result less by 7 per cent. than the complex rule above described, therefore an excess of strength is obtained.

1628z. The proportions of the rib are undetermined, but it is evident that they should bear some ratio to those of the flanges. It must be sufficiently rigid to prevent lateral weakness. Moreover the very theory which maintains the principle of the *neutral axis* (*par.* 1630c) also recognises the increase of the forces of compression and extension upward and downward from the *neutral axis*, and would therefore lead to the adoption of a rib tapered in both directions. In practice it is found desirable to taper the rib so as to meet each of the flanges with a thickness corresponding to that of the flange, for if any very great disproportion exists, the operation of casting the beam cannot be so perfectly performed, from unequal shrinkage of the metal, and an imperfect casting or one having flaws in it, renders futile all calculations of strength.

1629. Hodgkinson gradually varied the form of section of girder in his experiments until the widths and depths of the flanges were as follows:—Top flange 2·33 inches wide, 0·31

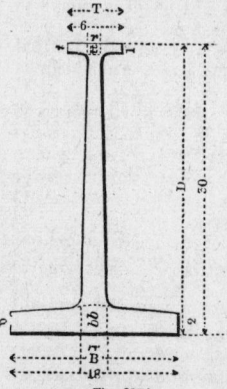

Fig. 613i.

Fig. 613j.

inch deep; bottom flange 6·67 inches wide, 0·66 inch deep; the areas being ·720 and 4·4 inches. The rib was ·266 inch thick, and the total depth $5\frac{1}{8}$ inches. The constant or C was found to be 514 for cwts., or 26 for tons. (Warr.)

1629a. It will scarcely be within our province to describe all the forms of sections, and the results of the experiments made by Fairbairn in obtaining his *box beam* or *plate girder* in *wrought iron*, but it is to be noted that all the cylindrical tubes broke by extension at the rivets before the tube could fail by compression. Fairbairn in his *Application of Cast and Wrought Iron to Building Purposes*, edit. 1857–8, p. 80, notices that although the *plate girder* be inferior in strength to the *box beam*, it has nevertheless other valuable properties to recommend it. On comparing the strength of these separate beams, weight for weight, it will be found that the box beam is as 100 : 93. The plate beam is in some respects superior to the box beam; it is of more simple construction, less expensive, and more durable, from the circumstance that the vertical plate is thicker than the side plates of the box beam. It is also easier of access to all its parts for the purposes of cleaning, &c.

1629b. Fairbairn has formed a comparison between a *wrought iron* and a *cast iron* girder for a span of 30 feet. The *plate girder, fig.* 613k, would be 31 feet 6 inches in length, and would be composed of plates 22 inches deep and $\frac{5}{16}$ths thick; with angle iron $\frac{3}{4}$ths thick, riveted on both sides at the bottom of the plate, and angle iron $\frac{1}{2}$ inch thick at the top, the width over the top being $7\frac{1}{4}$ inches, and the bottom $5\frac{1}{2}$ inches. The breaking weight of this beam, taking the constant at 75, would be $\frac{a\,d\,C}{l} = W$; or $\frac{6 \times 22 \times 75}{360}$ = 27·5 tons in the middle, or 55 tons distributed equally over the surface. In the edition of 1857–8, the angle irons are described as 3 inches by 3 inches, $\frac{1}{2}$ inch thick for the bottom, and 4 inches by 4 inches, $\frac{1}{2}$ inch thick at the top; it would, therefore, be $8\frac{1}{2}$ inches over at the top, and about $6\frac{1}{2}$ inches at the bottom. Now a *cast iron* girder of the best form and strongest section and calculated

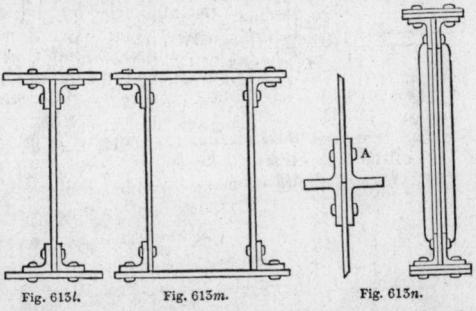

Fig. 613k.

to support the same load, would weigh about 2 tons, the plate beam about 18 cwts., or less than one half. To secure uniformity of strength in a rectangular box beam, the top is required to be about twice the sectional area of the bottom; hence resulted the use of cells in that portion.

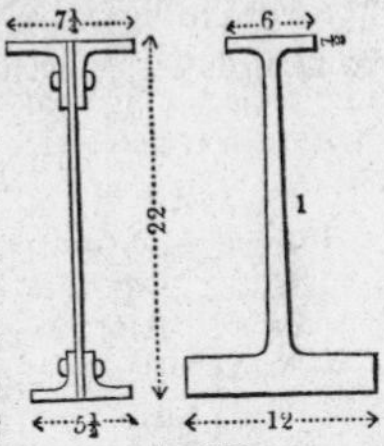

1629c. *Fig.* 613l. is a *plate beam* having a single plate for the vertical web, while each of the flanges consists of a flat bar and a pair of angle irons riveted to each other and to the vertical web. *Fig.* 613m. is a *box beam*, in which there are two vertical webs. *Fig.* 613n. is a *plate girder* of greater dimensions than *fig.* 613l.; the flanges contain more than one layer of flat bars, and the web, which consists of plates with their largest dimensions vertical, is stiffened by vertical T iron ribs at the joints of those plates, as shown in the plan or horizontal section lettered A. The pieces should abut closely and truly against each other, having end surfaces made exactly perpendicular to the axis of the

Fig. 613l.   Fig. 613m.   Fig. 613n.

beam. The thickness of the web is seldom made less than $\frac{3}{8}$ths inch, and except for the largest beams, this is in general more than sufficient to resist the shearing stress. Above each of the points of support, the vertical ribs must be placed either closer or made larger, so that they may be jointly capable of safely bearing as pillars the entire share of the load which rests on that point of support. A pair of vertical T iron ribs riveted back to back through the web plates (as A, *fig.* 613n.) may be held to act as a pillar of cross-shaped section.

1629d. The rib or web of a plate beam, as fig. 613l, having little or nothing to do with the pressure directly, has been replaced in some cases by simple upright struts or diagonal braces between the flanges, which in cast iron girders are in one casting, but experience has proved this not altogether politic, particularly in cast iron. Hodgkinson remarked that such beams were weaker than those with a solid rib. Rankine observes that transverse ribs or feathers on cast iron beams are to be avoided, as forming lodgments for air bubbles, and as tending to cause cracks in cooling. Open work in the vertical web is also to be avoided, partly for the same reasons, and partly because it too much diminishes the resistance to distortion by the shearing action of the load.

1629e. "Where the span renders it impracticable to roll a beam in one piece," Fairbairn, page 91, notices that "convenient weights might be rolled into sections of the proper form — and being united by properly proportioned covering plates at top and bottom, and to

the joints (*par.* 1630*y.*), and all the riveting be well executed, the beam will be equal in strength to one" of an entire length. "This construction may be carried to a span of 40 to 50 feet. In practice it is found necessary to confine the use of cells to spans exceeding 100 or 150 feet: within these limits the same objects are most economically obtained by the use of thicker plates (page 215). "The more nearly the bottom approximates to a solid homogeneous mass, the better it is calculated to resist a tensile strain" (see pages 248 to 256 for full instructions as to riveting plates; and Kirkaldy, *Experiments, &c.*, page 196, for comparison of strength). As the bending moment of the load on a girder diminishes from the middle towards the ends, and the shearing force from the ends towards the middle, it follows that the transverse sections of the bottom plates may be diminished from the middle towards the ends, and that of the vertical web from the ends towards the middle, so as to make the resistance to bending and shearing respectively vary according to the same law. Consequently, towards the centre of a girder for a large span, the bottom plate is usually increased by additional plates to secure the requisite strength in the sectional area, giving the underside of the plate a bellied form.

1629*f.* The results of various testings of a new manufacture of girder patented by Messrs. Phillips have just been reported. A double weight in a cast iron girder is required to give equal strength with one of wrought iron. A riveted plate girder is not always adaptable for general purposes. The present sections of rolled irons are so limited in depth that they have been hitherto only valuable where light loads and limited spans occur. The new system consists in riveting plates to the top and bottom flanges of rolled

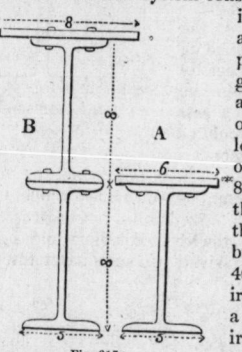

iron beams, and so strengthening them as to obtain results apparently disparaging to ordinary plate girders. The experiments noticed here in an abridged form were on a patent girder of 22 lbs. per foot run, with a web plate, as A, *fig.* 613*o.*, and 20 feet bearing, as compared with a riveted plate girder of 9 in depth, it gave a breaking weight of 7 tons and a safe load of 4 tons; the formula for the breaking weight of an ordinary plate girder would give 3½ tons. When two of the 8-inch rolled girders were riveted together, with a plate on the top, as B, the metal being about 40 lbs. per foot run, the girder was found to resist 20 tons, even then not breaking, but becoming twisted. An ordinary riveted plate girder of 40 lbs. per foot run, with a web of 12 inches with double angle irons of 3 inches by 3 inches and ½ inch thick, would break with a strain of 9 tons. A simple web plate girder, with angle irons top and bottom (*fig.* 613*k.*) gives C = 60; a plate on top and bottom in addition (*fig.* 613*l.*) gives C = 75; and a box

Fig. 613*o.*

beam (*fig.* 613*m.*) gives C = 80. The rolled girders made by the Butterley Company give C = 57 to 88. The example A gives C = 210; and the example B, 300. Other experiments are required fully to prove the superiority of the new system over the beams and girders of the old sections. The details of the above testings are given in the *Builder*, p. 148; *Mechanics' Magazine*, p. 129; *Engineering*, p. 139; &c., all for the year 1866.

Condition of Breaking Weight in the Middle.

A　　B　　C　　D　　E　　F　　G　　H　　I　　K

Fig. 613 *p.* VARIOUS FORMS IN USE FOR BEAMS, GIRDERS, AND IRONS.

1629*g.* PROBLEM I.—To find the breaking weight of a *beam*, the load being in the middle and all the dimensions known. The ends loose or supported.

For **A**, *Timber beams* :—

$$\frac{b\,d^2\,\text{S lbs.}}{l\,\text{feet}} = \text{W lbs.} \quad \Big| \quad \frac{b\,d^2\,\text{S cwt.}}{l\,\text{feet}} = \text{W cwt.} \quad \Big| \quad \frac{b\,d^2\,\text{S tons}}{l\,\text{feet}} = \text{W tons.} \quad \Big| \quad \frac{a\,4\,d\,\text{S}}{l\,\text{ins.}} = \text{W lbs.}$$

Here S, in the first formula, represents the value of the breaking weight in *pounds* in the middle, taken from the preceding table: in the other two it would be deduced from it; thus taking Riga fir $\frac{359\,\text{lbs.}}{112\,\text{lbs.}} = 3\cdot21$ for cwt.; and $\frac{3\cdot21}{20\,\text{cwt.}} = \cdot160$ for tons: *b* breadth in inches; *d* depth in inches; *l* distance between the points of support, in feet; *a* area of section. These letters will be continued in these problems, until other values are attached to them. W will always represent the breaking weight.

1629*h.* For **B**, *wrought or cast iron rectangular beams* :—

$$\frac{b\,d^2\,\text{S lbs.}}{l} = \text{W lbs.} \quad \Big| \quad \frac{b\,d^2\,\text{S cwt.}}{l} = \text{W cwts.} \quad \Big| \quad \frac{b\,d^2\,\text{F}}{6\,l} = \text{W lbs.}$$

Here F represents the weight in pounds borne by a rod 1 inch square, when the strain is as great as the rod will bear without destroying part of its elastic force, $= 15,300$ for cast iron. From a mean of 265 experiments by Hodgkinson and Fairbairn, it appears (by Gregory) that a weight of 454·4 pounds in the middle of a bar of cast-iron, 1 inch square and 4·5 feet bearing, produced fracture. Therefore, for a bar of any other dimensions, we have:—

$$\frac{b\,d^2\,\mathrm{C}=2045}{l}=\mathrm{W\ lbs.} \quad \Big| \quad \frac{b\,d^2\,\mathrm{C}=18\cdot25}{l}=\mathrm{W\ cwts.} \quad \Big| \quad \frac{b\,d^2\,\mathrm{C}=\cdot912}{l}=\mathrm{W\ tons.}$$

1629i. For **C**, *cast iron girder* ; (Tredgold's section).

$\dfrac{b\,d^2\,\mathrm{F}}{6l} \times (1-q \times p^3)=\mathrm{W\ lbs.}$ Here q difference between the breadth in the middle and the extreme breadth $= \cdot625$ as found to answer in practice ; and p, depth of the narrow part in the middle $= \cdot7$ as found to answer. When the middle part of the beam is omitted, except sufficient uprights to connect the top and bottom bars, then $\dfrac{b\,d^2\,\mathrm{F}}{6l} \times (1-p^3)=\mathrm{W\ lbs.}$ Here d whole depth ; and p depth of part omitted. If the thickness of the web be about $\frac{1}{12}$th or $\frac{1}{15}$th of the depth of the beam, then—

$$\frac{a\,d\,\mathrm{C}=514}{l\text{ inches}}=\mathrm{W\ cwts.} \quad \Big| \quad \frac{a\,d\,\mathrm{C}=26}{l\text{ inches}}=\mathrm{W\ tons.} \quad \Big| \quad \frac{a\,d\,\mathrm{C}=2\cdot166}{l\text{ feet}}=\mathrm{W\ tons.}$$

Here 514 cwts. may be used for side castings, or 536 cwts. for erect castings. The other quantities are obtained thus : $\frac{514\text{ cwts.}}{20\text{ for tons}}=25\cdot7$, called 26 tons ; $\frac{536}{20}=26\cdot8$, called 27 tons. When l is used in feet, $\frac{26}{12}=2\cdot166$: a represents area of bottom flange in inches.

1629k. For **D**, *cast iron girder* (Hodgkinson's pattern):—

$$\frac{a\,d\,\mathrm{C}=514}{l\text{ inches}}=\mathrm{W\ cwts.} \Big| \frac{a\,d\,\mathrm{C}=26}{l\text{ inches}}=\mathrm{W\ tons.} \Big| \frac{a\,d\,\mathrm{C}=2\cdot14}{l\text{ feet}}=\mathrm{W\ tons.} \Big| \frac{2\,a\,d}{l\text{ ft.}}=\mathrm{W\ tons.} \Big| \frac{a\,d}{l\text{ ft.}}=\mathrm{P\ tons.}$$

Here a and d as before ; P permanent load distributed, or about one-fourth of the breaking weight distributed ; and multiplied by 2 when the ends are fixed = one-half BW. From the experiments above quoted from Gregory, we obtain—

$$\frac{a\,d\,4852}{l}=\mathrm{W\ lbs.} \quad \Big| \quad \frac{a\,d\,43\cdot33}{l}=\mathrm{W\ cwts.} \quad \Big| \quad \frac{a\,d\,2\cdot166}{l}=\mathrm{W\ tons.}$$

1629l. Gregory's work also states an arbitrary formula given by Mr. Dines, which he found to be tolerably correct in all cases where the length of the girder did not exceed 25 feet ; its depth in the centre not greater than 20 inches ; the breadth of the bottom flange not less than one-third, or more than half, the depth ; the thickness of the metal not less than $\frac{1}{16}$th of the depth. Then—

$$\frac{1792}{l}[b\,d^2-(b-b_2)d_2{}^2]=\mathrm{W\ lbs.} \quad \Big| \quad \frac{16}{l}[b\,d^2-(b-b_2)d_2{}^2]=\mathrm{W\ cwts.}$$
$$\frac{0\cdot8}{l}[b\,d^2-(b-b_2)d_2{}^2]=\mathrm{W\ tons.}$$

Here b entire breadth of bottom flange ; b_2 thickness of the vertical part ; d depth of whole girder ; d_2 depth without the lower flange, all in inches ; l length in feet.

1629m. Hurst, *Handbook*, notices that the area of the top flange should be $\frac{1}{3}$ of that of the bottom flange when the load is on the top ; and $\frac{1}{8}$ when the load is on the bottom flange : Molesworth, *Formulæ*, has $\frac{1}{2}$ for the latter ; he notes that if the depth of the girder be $\frac{1}{12}$ of the span, then $a\,4\cdot17=\mathrm{W}$ tons, the weight being distributed. When the depth is $\frac{1}{10}$, $a\,5=\mathrm{W}$ tons, the weight being distributed. The depth at the ends may equal $\frac{2d}{3}$. Approximate rules for these girders have been given in the *Pocket-book* for 1865, as $l \times \mathrm{P}=d \times a$, $\frac{d \times a}{l}=\mathrm{P}$, $\frac{l \times \mathrm{P}}{d}=a$. Here l feet ; P tons distributed ; d depth of girder ; a area of bottom flange, both in inches.

1629n. For **E**, *wrought-iron tube or beam, or box-beam* :—

$$\frac{a\,d\,\mathrm{C}=80}{l\text{ inches}}=\mathrm{W\ tons.} \quad \Big| \quad \frac{a\,d\,\mathrm{C}=6\cdot66}{l\text{ feet}}=\mathrm{W\ tons, when }d\text{ is more than }\frac{l}{14}.$$

Here a area of the whole cross section ; C coefficient determined for this *particular form* of tube. In the table given by Fairbairn (pp. 116–17), the constant $\mathrm{C}=17\cdot8$ tons, for a tube having the top flange $= \cdot142$ thick, twice the area of the bottom one ; the tube being 9·6 inches square, and 17·5 feet long between the supports. Such a beam deflected 1·88 inches with the breaking weight of 7,148 lbs.

1629o. Hurst states it is usual to camber a riveted girder, so that on receiving the permanent load it may become nearly horizontal. If the required rise or camber equals e in the middle in inches, d being in inches and l in feet, we have $\frac{l^2}{d}\mathrm{K}=e$. For girders uniformly loaded and of uniform section throughout the length, $\mathrm{K}=\cdot018$. When the section is also made to vary so that the girder will be of equal strength throughout, $\mathrm{K}=\cdot021$. Molesworth notes the area of top flange as $a\,l\,1\cdot18$; Hurst says $a\,l\,\cdot75$. If the depth of the girder be $\frac{1}{12}$ of the span, then $\mathrm{W}=13\cdot3a$ tons ; if $\frac{1}{13}$, then $\mathrm{W}=16a$ tons. The rivets to be $\frac{3}{4}$ inch and inch in diameter, placed 3 inches apart in the top, and 4 inches apart in the bottom, flange.

1629p. For **F**, *Wrought-iron plate girder* :—

$\dfrac{a\,d\,C=1500}{l\text{ inches}} = W$: the area of the top flange being $\frac{1}{3}$ greater than the bottom flange, and the thickness of the web about $\frac{1}{24}$ or $\frac{1}{30}$ of the depth of the beam. $\dfrac{a\,d\,C}{l\text{ inches}} = W$ tons, in which case C = 75 for deep plates as 22 inches; or = 60 for less depth as 7 inches. $\dfrac{a\,d\,C=6\cdot25}{l\text{ feet}} = W$ tons, when d is more than $\frac{l}{14}$, and the area of the top flange is 1·75 of the bottom flange. Here a area of bottom flange in inches; some calculators deduct the rivet holes from its total width. For depths under 12 inches, the width of the top flange should be half the depth; and when over 12 inches, one-third. With the latter proportion, feathers or stiffening pieces should be used to supply the deficiency in lateral stiffness occasioned by the reduced width of flange (*par.* 1629c.). The usual thickness of web for all depths under 3 feet, is $\frac{3}{8}$ inch. Fairbairn (*Tubular Bridges*, p. 247.), discovered that the *top* flange should have an area double that of the *lower* one to give the strongest form of *wrought iron* beam, a contrary principle to that obtained in cast iron.

1629q. To find the area of either of the flanges at the centre of a girder supported at both ends, the formula is $\dfrac{W\,l}{8sd} = a$. Here W represents live and dead loads uniformly distributed in tons; l span in feet; d depth in inches; and s safe strain per square inch of metal on the flange, in tons. Therefore, say $\dfrac{W=150\times l=100}{8\times s=5\times 8\cdot33\text{ sect. area}} = 45$ square inches, excluding rivet holes in the bottom flange. This formula is the equivalent of $\dfrac{W=\text{weight per foot run}\times l^2}{8sd} = a$. When the sectional area of the top flange is to be greater than that of the bottom flange, multiply the latter area by 1·2. The average sectional area of a theoretically proportioned flanged girder may be taken at $\frac{2}{3}$rds of the central sectional area. To find the sectional areas of either flange at any point along the whole length of the girder, the formula is $\dfrac{W\,x}{2sd}(l-x) = a$, excluding rivet-holes in bottom flange. Here W weight per foot run in tons; x lesser segment into which the span is divided; $l-x$ greater segment; s and d as before. To find the sectional area at any length of the web, the formula is $\dfrac{W\,x}{s} = a$ square inches. Here x is the distance from the centre; W and s as before. The vertical strain, at the centre of the beam, when one-half of the girder is fully loaded, is equal to $\frac{1}{8}$ of the fully loaded beam, that is $\frac{1}{8}W\times l$. At the ends or pillars, the vertical strain is greatest and is equal to $\frac{1}{2}W\times l$. The strain at the centre, when the load is uniformly distributed, is obtained from the formula $\dfrac{W\,l}{8d} = s$. Here W distributed load in tons; l length in feet; d depth in feet; s strain in tons of compression in the top flange and tension in the bottom flange. Half the load collected at the centre of a girder being equal to the load distributed, the above formula becomes $\dfrac{W\,l}{4d} = s$. At any other point, ratios of strain will be as the square of half the span to the square of the segments into which a given point divides the span. The approximate strain at the centre, per square inch, on any beam, may be obtained from the formula $\dfrac{W\,l}{8a} = s$. Here W distributed load in tons; l length in terms of the depth; a sectional area in square inches; and s strain in tons per square inch. To find the sectional area of a flange for a plate girder fixed at one end and free at the other, the formula is $\dfrac{W\,x}{ds} = a$ exclusive of rivet holes in the top flange; W weight in tons at the end of the girder; x length in feet from loaded end to the point where the sectional areas are required; d depth in feet; s safe strain per square inch in tons. When the load is uniformly distributed, using the same notations as before, except that W in tons is the load per foot run, the formula is $\dfrac{W\,x^2}{2sd} = a$. (*Engineers, Architects, &c. Pocket-book*, 1865.)

1629r. For **G**, *Rolled irons or bars* :—

$\dfrac{a\,d\,C=6}{l\text{ feet}} = W$ tons. Here a area of bottom flange includes to above the upper part of the swelling for flange, as $b\,c$ (*fig.* 613q); or to the whole of the angle, in plate girder **F**. A railway bar is often useful in country places; the intricate formulæ for the strengths of the various parts will be found in Barlow; and in the *Engineers, &c., Pocket-book for* 1861.

Fig. 613q.

1629s. For **H**. *Tee irons, or Rolled* **T** *irons* :— $\dfrac{a\,d\,C=4}{l\text{ feet}} = W$ tons.

1629t. For **I**, *Reversed Tee irons* :—

When x is one-fourth of the table or flange $b\,c$, and the form as 5 : 12 of a rectangle, then $\dfrac{b\,d^2\,F}{6\times 2\cdot4l} = SW$. It was stated in the *Oldham Mill Report*, that this form of beam, which might be considered to support a weight of say 1,000 lbs., may be broken if reversed, that is, the flange placed uppermost, as **T**, with a weight of say 340 lbs. Hodgkinson experi-

mented on two bars 4 feet 3 inches long, the flange 4 inches wide, rib $1\frac{1}{10}$ inches deep, with a thickness of metal of about $\frac{1}{4}$ inch. One bar was tried with the flange uppermost, the other bar with the flange downwards. The former broke with $2\frac{1}{2}$ cwt., the latter with 9 cwt. Experiments on three girders of this shape, the web being 2 inches high and $\frac{1}{4}$ inch thick; the flange 2 inches wide by $\frac{1}{4}$ inch thick, and 24 inches long, were made by Cooper of Drury Lane. He stated that the gain in strength over a flitch ⊓ 2 inches by $\frac{1}{4}$ inch, was 25 per cent.; the loss in stiffness being 30 per cent. The strength arising from the accumulation of the quantity submitted to tensile action, bears out an adequate result, or 580 times its own weight, instead of 400, as ⊓ 2 inches by $\frac{1}{2}$ inch, and ⊓ ⊓ 2 inches by $\frac{1}{4}$ inch each, placed $\frac{1}{2}$ inch apart, showing over them an increase of strength of nearly 50 per cent. In using this form of section, it makes no difference whether the load be placed wholly on the top of the vertical web, or on the lower flange; the result obtained in either case was the same.—*Builder*, 1845, vol. iii. p. 593. The results of some other experiments on this useful form of iron are given in the *Engineers' Pocket-book for* 1861, p. 205.

The formula $\frac{a\,d\,C=6}{l\ \text{feet}} = \text{W}$ tons, is also applicable to the trough-shaped section, as N (*fig* 613r), as to the inverted Tee or ⊥ shape M, taking the two vertical ribs to be equivalent to one rib of the same depth and double the thickness. The thickness of the horizontal and vertical parts of these girders should be equal, or nearly equal, so as to obtain as near an equality in cooling as possible. Rolled malleable iron joists and girders are ordinarily to be obtained of various sizes up to 12 inches deep, with top and bottom flanges 5 inches wide, rolled up to 30 feet in length, They can be produced 18 inches deep if required. Messrs. Moser, of Birmingham; Messrs. Moore and Manby, of Dudley; Messrs. Mather, Ledward, and Co., of Liverpool; and Messrs. Phillips, of London; have lately issued tables of values of strength to accompany their engraved sheets of sections.

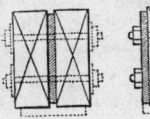 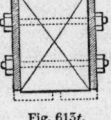

Fig. 613r.

1629u. For **K**, Mixed beams; *Flitch beams and double flitch beams* :—These beams are composed of an iron plate (cast or wrought) placed between two pieces of fir timber, *fig*. 613s; or of a plate placed on each side of the solid timber beam, *fig*. 613t. These plates again may have a table or flange, as in the case of the single plate; or of a half flange, as in the case of the plates on each side of the beam. All these should be bolted, or otherwise secured together, to render them as homogeneous as possible. Hurst gives the formula

Fig. 615s.   Fig. 615t.

$\frac{d^2}{l\,\text{inches}}(Cb + 30t) = \text{W}$ in cwts. Here t breadth of the one, or two, *wrought iron* flitches; b breadth of the timber; C, coefficient = 4 teak, 3 oak, 2·5 fir, and 2·0 elm. Fairbairn considers that " the addition of the timber on each side of the plate gives increased stiffness, and renders it less liable to warp under strain. It is called a sandwich beam." He states this beam "to be weak, comparing the results with those of the simple plate girder; and its elasticity, although considerable, is nevertheless so imperfect as to render it inadmissible for the support of *great loads*, whether proceeding from a dead weight, or one in motion over its surface. With riveted angles or flanges, the timbers on each side might have been useful in preventing lateral flexure, but they would not have contributed, in any great degree, to the vertical bearing powers of the beam."—(*Application*, &c., p. 284–5.) Rolled flat irons can now be obtained about 13 to 14 inches deep, from $\frac{1}{2}$ inch to an inch in width, up to 30 feet in length, and for special cases somewhat longer.

1629v. The method of *trussing* a beam is explained in CARPENTRY (*par.* 2021, *et seq.*).

1629w. The formulæ for finding the strength for the examples IV and V, *fig*. 675, are $\frac{\text{W}\,l}{8d} = h$; and $\sqrt{h^2 + \frac{\text{W}^2}{16}} = s$. Here l length in feet; d depth in feet—both measured from the points of intersection of the stay, tension rod, and top beam; W load in tons uniformly distributed; h horizontal thrust on beam in tons; and s strain on inclined part of tension rod in tons. When the truss has more than one stay, h, l, and d will represent the same; and h_1 tensile strain on the horizontal portion of the rod. The strain on the inclined tie rod will be $\frac{\text{W}}{8d}\sqrt{l^2 + n^2 d^2} = s$; n the number of times that the horizontal distance between the pier and the nearest stay is contained in l. If any load be placed on the middle, the strain h will be doubled. If any load be placed on each of the stays, then l will represent the distance of each loaded stay from the nearest pier; d depth as before; h horizontal thrust on the part next the pier; s tension on each of the inclined ties. Then $\frac{\text{W}\,l}{d} = h$; and $\sqrt{h^2 + \text{W}^2} = s$. To resist the strains of the inclined tie rods with safety, allow an inch of sectional area in the tie rod for every 5 tons of strain. The stay, being in compression, should be calculated as a column capable of supporting the load if in the middle, or one half if distributed. The beam, though in compression, should be capable of supporting the

load between the stays, as a beam exposed to transverse strain, according to the rules before given. Tie rods, when exposed to great strains, are not generally of much value, because the iron stretches.

1629x. Mr. Cubitt experimented on an equal flanged cast iron girder, 27 feet long, 10 inches deep, and 4 inches broad across the flanges; the rods were 1 inch diameter. When the ends of the rods were placed above the beam, it was found to be weaker than having no rod at all. When the fastening was made at the upper end of the girder, and giving a distance to the rod of $6\frac{1}{4}$ inches below the girder instead of an inch, an increased stiffness was obtained of above a ton (Warr, p. 259). Some experiments are recorded in the *Builder*, 1857, on two beams of Dantzic timber, each 28 feet long, 14 inches square, with and without a tie rod. Barlow records an experiment (p. 158) on four beams, two being trussed similarly to the figure on plate xxxix. of Nicholson's *Carpenters' New Guide*. Mr. Cooper's experiments on trussed beams are given in the *Builder*, 1845, p. 612. For *Trellis girders*, another mode of trussing a beam, Fairbairn, p. 129, uses the same formula as for the plate girder F, but with the constant 60. For this, the student is referred to the *Application &c. of Iron*, enlarged edition, 1864.

Other conditions than that of the Weight in the Middle.

1629y. To find the ultimate strength of a beam (section **A** or **B**), when a weight
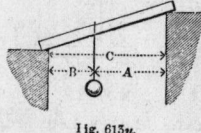
is placed somewhere between the middle and the end. Rule— Multiply twice the length of the longer end, A, fig. 613u, by twice the length of the shorter end B, and divide the product by the whole length C, which will give the *effective length* to be used as the divisor for the calculation of strength under the conditions of the beam:—Thus say a beam is—

Fig. 613u.

$$\frac{2\times10)\times(2\times5)}{15 \text{ long}} = 13\cdot33 \text{ effective length; and } \frac{(S=2548 \text{ cast iron})\times2\times6^2}{13\cdot33} = 13{,}762\cdot64 \text{ lbs. weight.}$$

Hurst puts it as, $\dfrac{(\frac{1}{2}l)^2 \times W}{\text{product of two lengths from each end.}}$

1629z. Barlow (p. 39–40) has stated a case where a beam has to support *two equal weights* between the points of support, FF', as at D and E, Example I. *fig.* 613v, then since $IC = iC = \frac{1}{2}Ii$, and $W = W^1$, the general expression becomes $\frac{(ID+iE),iC,W}{Ii} = \frac{ID+iE}{2} \times W = f$. And if we suppose further $ID = iE$, then it becomes simply $ID.W = f$.

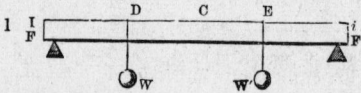

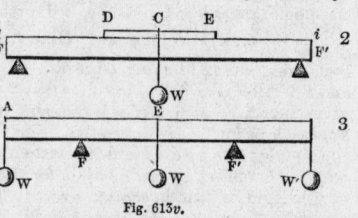

Fig. 613v.

Now, if both weights act at the centre, it appears from the preceding investigation, that $\frac{1}{4}Ii. (2W) = \frac{1}{2} Ii.W = IC.W = f$. Whence the strain in the two cases will be to each other as ID to IC; and hence the following practical deduction:—
When a beam is loaded with a weight, and that weight is appended to an *inflexible bar*, or bearing, as DE, in Ex. 2, the strain upon the beam will vary as the distance ID, or as the difference between the length of the beam and the length of the bearing; for the bearing DE being inflexible, the strains will be exerted in the points D and E, exactly in the same manner as if the bearing was removed, and half the weight hung on at each of these points. This remark may be worth the consideration of practical men in various architectural constructions. He also puts the case of a beam, which, instead of being fixed at each end, merely rests on two props, and extends beyond them on each side equal to half their distance, as Ex. 3: if the weights W W' were suspended from these latter points, each equal to one-fourth of the weight W, then this would be double of that which would be necessary to produce the fracture in the common case; for, dividing the weight W into four equal parts, we may conceive two of these parts employed in producing the strain or fracture at E, and one of each of the other parts as acting in opposition to W and W', and by these means tending to produce the fractures at F and F'. This is the case which has been erroneously confounded with a former one (fixed at each end), but the distinction between them is sufficiently obvious; because here the tension of the fibres, in the places where the strains are excited, are all equal; whereas in the former the middle one was double of each of the other two.

1630. Experiments are recorded in the *Civil Engineer Journal*, 1849, xi, page 44, on parallel bars of cast iron, 4 feet $8\frac{1}{2}$ inches long and 4 inches square, placed on two

supports CC (*fig.* 613*w.*). Weights were placed at each end at equal distances from the supports, and the weights being gradually increased, the bar broke simultaneously through at EE. On another trial, a bar broke only in one point F, being a little nearer to the middle. This was considered a sufficient proof that a portion of the metal might be removed from the middle of the bar without diminishing its lateral strength, and that by adding this metal about the points EE, the lateral strength would be increased.

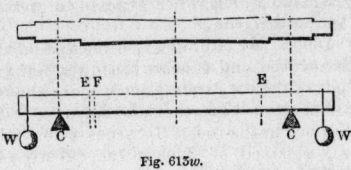

Fig. 613*w.*

Various Problems.

1630*a*. I. When a beam (as sections **A** and **B**), with the ends supported, is to be calculated to support a permanent weight in the middle, the formulæ for obtaining the breadth and depth are $\frac{l\text{ feet W lbs}}{S \div 3d^2} = b$, and $\frac{l\,W}{S \div 3\,b} = d^2$. W weight to be supported, S safe weight, or $\frac{1}{3}$ of the ultimate strength of an inch bar; b and d in inches.

II. When a similar beam for obtaining the breadth and depth had the ends fixed, the formula for the breadth is $\frac{l\,W}{S\,3\,d^2\,1\cdot5} = b$.

III. When a similar beam projects from a wall, and is loaded at the ends, the formula for the depth is $\frac{l\,W}{S \div 3\,b\,\cdot 25} = d^2$.

IV. When a similar beam has to support a load placed at some distance from the end (*fig.* 613*u*), the effective length must first be obtained by the rule, *par.* 1629*y*. Then the formula for the depth is $\frac{\text{Effect. } l\,W}{S \div 3\,b} = d^2$.

To find the *diagonal* of a uniform square cast iron beam, to support a given strain in the direction of that diagonal, when the strain does not exceed the elastic force of the material (Tredgold):—

V. When the beam is supported at the ends, and loaded in the middle, the formula is $\frac{l\,W}{212 \text{ for cast iron}} = \sqrt[3]{\ } \text{ diagonal in inches.}$

VI. When a similar beam has not the strain in the middle of the length $\frac{W \times B \times A}{l\,53}$ $= \sqrt[3]{\ } \text{ diagonal in inches.}$ Here A and B refer to *fig.* 613*u*.

1630*b*. To obtain dimensions, &c. of beams and girders :—

I. To find the *depth* of a beam, the length, breadth, and weight being given. For **A** and **B**, $\sqrt[2]{\frac{l \text{ feet W lbs.}}{s\,b}} = d$ inches. If no breadth or depth be given, let $n =$ any number, then $\sqrt[3]{\frac{n\,l \text{ feet W lbs.}}{s}} = d$, and $b = n$th part of d.

For **C**, $\sqrt[2]{\frac{l \text{ W not exceeding the elastic force}}{(850 \text{ or } SW)\,b\,(1 - \cdot73 \times \cdot625)}} = d$ inches. For **D**, $\frac{l\,W}{ } = d$. For **E**, $\frac{l}{16} = d$.

II. To find the *breadth* of a beam, the depth, length, and weight being given. For **A** and **B**, $\frac{l \text{ feet W lbs.}}{s\,d^2} = b$ inches. For **D**, $\frac{l\,W}{C\,d^2} = b$.

The proportion between the breadth and depth which will afford the best result is 6 : 10 depth, in timber. The formula for the least breadth a beam for a given bearing should have, is $\frac{l \text{ feet}}{\sqrt{d} \text{ inches} \times 0\cdot6} = $ breadth.

III. To find the *length*, the weight, depth, and breadth being given:— For **A** and **B**, $\frac{S\,b\,d^2}{W} = l$.

IV. To find the *constant* S, the length, depth, breadth and breaking weight per foot in length, inch square, being given, For **A** and **B**, $\frac{W \text{ lbs. } l \text{ feet}}{b\,d^2} = S$.

V. To find the *area* of the bottom flange, the length, load, and depth being given. For **D**, $\frac{l \text{ feet permanent load in tons distributed}}{d \text{ inches}} = a$ inches. For **E**, tension $= 2$ load $+$ beam, or tension not more than 5 tons per square inch.

VI. To find the *multiple of depth and area of the bottom flange*, the length and load being given. For **D** girder, $l\,P = d \times a.$

VII. To find the *area* of the top flange. For **E** girder, bottom $+ \frac{1}{4}$.

VIII. To find the *area* of the side plates. For **E** girder, $\frac{1}{2}$ area of bottom.

Tension, etc.

1630*c*. *The neutral axis.* A timber beam supported at the ends and pressed down in the middle by a weight, will have its lower fibres extended, while the upper fibres are

pushed together. Since there are these two strains, there will be some line or point in the depth which is labouring under neither the one nor the other; this is the neutral axis. The further the fibres are from the neutral line, the more they will resist deflection from the load. It might be inferred that the material should be placed so far above and below the neutral line as other circumstances will allow, in order that they may be in a position to exercise the greatest power. The most simple application of these views is shown in Laves's girder (described in Carpentry). " As cast iron resists fracture about six times more powerfully under compression than under tension, it is useless to give as much area of material in the upper or compressed, as in the lower or extended, flange of a cast iron beam." Hodgkinson (*Experimental Researches*, 1846, p. 484-94) states that the position of the neutral axis in cast iron rectangular beams, at the time of fracture, is situated at about $\frac{1}{7}$ of the whole depth of the beam below its upper surface. The sectional area of the top flange of a cast iron girder must be rather more than $\frac{1}{6}$ of the bottom flange, to keep the position of the neutral axis at $\frac{1}{7}$ of the depth. In sudden fractures it was from $\frac{1}{5}$ to $\frac{1}{6}$ of the depth.

1630d. Tredgold, *Iron*, 1st edit. 1822, p. 53, considered the line of neutral axis in this section to be in the middle of the depth. He notices the curious fact put forth by Du Hamel, who cut beams one-third, one-half, and two-thirds through, and found the weights to be borne—by the uncut beam 45 lbs.; and by those cut 51 lbs., 48 lbs., and 42 lbs. respectively, which would indicate that less than half the fibres were engaged in resisting extension, although it does not prove that two-thirds of the thickness contributed nothing to the strength, as Robison imagines. Barlow found that in a rectangular beam of fir, the neutral axis was about five-eighths of the depth, as shown by the section of fracture. Warr gives for cast iron, the value of *n* or neutral axis 2·63; $n=6$ when the line may come in the middle. Attention should be given to the highly valuable paper by the Astronomer Royal (Prof. Airy), *On the Strains in the Interior of Beams and Tubular Bridges*, read in 1862 before the British Association at Cambridge. It is given in the Athenæum for October 11; and its further elucidation in the last edition (1864) of Fairbairn's *Application of Cast Iron, &c.*

1630e. *Deflection.* The deflection of a beam supported at the ends and loaded in the middle, is directly as the cube of the length, inversely as the cube of the depth, and inversely as the breadth; therefore, $\frac{\text{load} \times \text{length}^3}{\text{breadth} \times \text{depth}^3} = $ deflection. Beams have been said to bear considerable deflection without any injury to the elasticity of the material. Buffon and Tredgold considered the elasticity to remain perfect until one-third of the breaking weight is laid on. Hodgkinson was perhaps the first who practically showed that in a cast iron beam, a $\frac{1}{33}$nd part of the breaking weight caused a visible set after that weight was removed; while another beam took a visible set with $\frac{1}{80}$th part of its breaking weight. He found the *permanent set* in cast iron beams to be as the square of the load applied. He also found that cast iron beams bore two-thirds, and even more, of their breaking weight for long periods, without any indication of failing. Gregory (*Mechanics for Practical Men*, 4th edit. 1862) considers that, though the above rule may be correct for beams about 5 feet in length, it does not apply when they are much longer. Thomas Cubitt found by his experiments that, when the length became about 20 feet, the set was only as the weight; and that with larger beams the set was still less. Fairbairn found the impropriety of adopting any rule founded on elastic limits, since it was evident that, while the elasticity of a bar is injured as soon as a weight was applied, the particles or fibres take up fresh positions until the antagonistic forces in the beam are brought nearly to equality, when one-third or two-thirds of the breaking weight will affect the subsequent deflection of the beam.

1630f. For a rectangular beam of cast iron supported at both ends and loaded in the middle to the extent of its elastic force, $\frac{l^2 \text{feet} \cdot 02}{d \text{ inches}} = $ deflection. For similar beams, loaded uniformly, multiply by ·025 in place of ·02. (Tredgold.) It has been stated that the ultimate strength of a girder of the usual proportions may be approximately ascertained from its deflection under proof, on the assumption that a load equal to half the breaking weight will cause a deflection of $\frac{1}{40}$ of its length (Dobson). The proportion of the greatest depth of a beam to the span is so regulated, that the proportion of the greatest deflection to the span shall not exceed a limit which experience has shown to be consistent with convenience. That proportion, from various examples, appears to be for the working load, $\frac{\text{defl.}}{l} = $ from $\frac{1}{600}$ to $\frac{1}{1500}$; for the proof load, $\frac{\text{defl.}}{l} = $ from $\frac{1}{200}$ to $\frac{1}{800}$ (Rankine).

1630g. Mr. Dines, when superintending upwards of two hundred experiments for Mr. Cubitt, on cast-iron girders (as section D) whose dimensions are limited, found that when the load in the centre is taken as $\frac{2}{3}$ths of the breaking weight, the following formulæ may be used, (*d* depth in centre; *l* length in feet) :—I. When the top and bottom flanges are

equal, and the girder parallel, or equal depth throughout, $\frac{l^2}{40\,d}$ = deflection.   II. When the flanges are not equal, and the girder is not parallel, $\frac{l^2}{35\,d}$ = deflection.   III. When the beam has no top flange, and the depth varies, $\frac{l^2}{30\,d}$ = deflection (Gregory).

1630h. The formulæ given by Hurst, *Handbook, &c.* for finding deflection, which occur under *Stiffness of beams,* are, I. When supported at the ends and loaded in the middle, $\frac{l\,\text{feet}^3\,\text{W cwts. C}}{40\,b\,\text{inches}\ d^3\,\text{inches}}$ = deflection inches.   II. For cylinders, $\frac{l^3\ \text{W C}}{24\,d^4\ \text{or diam. inches}}$ = deflection inches. III. If the beam be fixed at one end and loaded at the other, the deflection = 16 times the product.   IV. If fixed at one end and uniformly loaded, 6 times.   V. If supported at both ends and uniformly loaded, $\frac{5}{8}$ths.   VI. If fixed at both ends and loaded in the middle, $\frac{1}{4}$th. VII. If fixed at both ends and uniformly loaded, $\frac{3}{10}$ths.   He gives the following :—

TABLE OF THE RELATIVE STRENGTH OF BODIES TO RESIST DEFLECTION = C.

Wrought iron -	·067	Baltic oak -	1·120	Ash - -	1·176
Cast iron - -	·112	Yellow fir -	1·120	Beech - -	1·434
Teak -	·851	Memel fir -	1·008	Elm - -	1·904
English oak -	1·344	Red pine - -	1·232	Mahogany -	1·300
Canadian oak -	1·008	Yellow pine -	1·254		

VIII. The deflection of a rectangular beam is to a cylindrical one, as 1 to 1·7.   IX. When the deflection is taken as $\frac{1}{40}$th of an inch per foot in length (which is considered to be safe under a proof of $\frac{1}{3}$ of the breaking weight) then for a beam supported at both ends and loaded in the middle, $\frac{l^2\,\text{W C}}{d^3} = b$; $\sqrt[3]{\frac{l^2\,\text{W C}}{b}} = d$; $\frac{b\,d^3\,\text{C}}{l^2} = \text{W}$; $\sqrt[2]{\frac{b\,d^3\,\text{C}}{\text{W}}} = l$; $\frac{l^2\,\text{W}}{b\,d^3} = \text{C}$; but $\frac{\text{C}}{2}$ for $\frac{1}{20}$ or 2C for $\frac{1}{80}$.   XI. For cylinders, $\sqrt[3]{1\cdot7 l^2}\text{WC}$ = diameter.   XI. For an uniform load take $\frac{5}{8}$ths, as before.

1630i. The *modulus of elasticity,* or resistance of materials to stretching, is the term given to the ratio of the force of restitution to the force of compression.   It is the measure of the elastic force of any substance.   By means of it, the comparative *stiffness* of bodies may be ascertained.   Thus from the following table it will be perceived that a piece of cast iron is 10·7 times as stiff as a piece of oak of equal dimensions and bearing. *Resilience,* or *toughness of bodies,* is strength and flexibility combined ; hence any material or body which bears the greatest load, and bends the most at the time of fracture, is the toughest. The modulus is estimated by supposing the material to present a square unit of surface, and by any weight or force to be extended to double, or compressed into one-half the original length ; such a weight will represent the modulus.

TABLE OF THE MODULUS OF ELASTICITY ; WITH THE PORTION OF IT (LIMITING THE COHESION OF THE MATERIAL, OR) WHICH WOULD TEAR THEM ASUNDER LENGTHWISE.

LESLIE.			BEVAN.		
	Feet.	Part.			Feet.
Teak - -	6,040,000 or	168th	Fir, bottom, 25 } years old -	- -	7,400,000
Oak - - -	4,150,000 ,,	144th			
Beech - -	4,180,000 ,,	107th	Petersburgh Deal -	-	6,000,000
Elm - - -	5,680,000 ,,	146th	Yew - - -	-	2,220,000
Memel Fir -	8,292,000 ,,	205th	*Stones, &c.*		
Christiania Deal -	8,118,000 ,,	146th	Dinton - -	- -	2,400,000
Larch - -	5,096,000 ,,	121st	Ketton - -	- -	1,600,000
			Jetternoe -	-	635,000
BEVAN.			Reigate - -	-	621,000
			Yorkshire paving -	-	1,320,000
		Feet.	Portland stone -	-	1,570,000
Yellow Pine -	-	9,150,000			
,, ,,	-	11,840,000	Slate, Leicester -	-	7,800,000
Finland Deal -	-	6,000,000	Glass-tubes - -	-	4,440,000
Teak - -	-	4,780,000	Ice - - -	-	6,000,000
Mahogany -	-	7,500,000	White marble - -	-	2,150,000
Dry Oak - -	-	5,100,000	*Metals.*		
Oak - - -	-	4,350,000	Steel - - -	-	9,300,000
Lincolns. Bog Oak -		1,710,000	Bar iron - -	-	9,000,000
Lance-wood -	-	5,100,000	,, ,, - -	-	8,450,000

TABLE OF THE MODULUS OF ELASTICITY, &c.—*continued.*

TREDGOLD AND OTHERS.		TREGOLD AND OTHERS.	
	lbs. avoir. per sq. inch.		lbs. avoir. per sq. inch.
Beech - - -	{ 1,350,000 R	Oak, Adriatic - -	974,400
	1,345,000	„ Canadian - -	2,148,800
Elm - - - -	{ 700,000 R	„ African - -	{ 1,728,000
to	1,340,000		2,282,300
Larch - - -	{ 1,363,500	„ Riga - -	1,610,500
	1,740,000	„ Dantzic - -	1,998,000
„ - - -	{ 900,000 R	American Red Oak -	{ 2,150,000 R
to	1,360,000		1,958,700
Fir, Red or Yellow -	2,016,000	Saul - - - -	2,420,000 R
„ White - - -	1,830,000	Teak, Indian - -	{ 2,167,074
„ Yellow American -	1,600,000		2,414,400 R
„ Mar Forest - -	845,066	Poon - - -	1,689,800
„ Scotch - -	951,750	Cowrie - - -	1,982,400
„ Riga - -	{ 1,687,500	*Metals.*	
	1,328,800	Cast steel - -	13,680,000
„ Memel - -	1,957,750	Best shear steel, not hardened - - }	29,000,000
„ „ - -	1,536,200		
Birch - - -	1,645,000 R	Cast brass - -	8,930,000
Chesnut - - -	1,140,000 R	„ „ - -	9,170,000 R
Walnut - - -	1,432,000	Cast iron - -	{ 18,400,000
Cedar - - -	486,000	average	17,000,000 R
Red Pine - -	{ 1,460,000 R	Cast lead - -	720,000
to	1,900,000 R	Cast tin - - -	4,608,000
Spruce Fir - -	{ 1,400,000 R	Zinc - - -	13,680,000
to	1,800,000 R	Gun metal - -	9,873,000
Christiania White Deal	{ 1,672,000	Brass wire - -	14,230,000 R
	1,804,000	Copper wire, (2) -	17,000,000 R
American White Spruce	1,244,000	Iron wire - -	25,300,000 R
Weymouth or Yellow Pine	1,633,500	*Stones, &c.*	
Pitch Pine - -	{ 1,252,200	Portland stone - -	1,530,000
	1,225,600	Slate, Welsh, average -	15,800,000
Mahogany - -	{ 1,255,000 R	Window glass - -	8,580,000
to	1,596,300	„ „ - -	8,000,000 R
Good English Oak -	1,700,000	White marble - -	2,520,000
Oak - - -	{ 1,200,000 R		
to	1,714,500	R, from Rankine, *Civil Engineering.*	

1630*k*. Hence, the modulus of elasticity being known for any substance, the weight may be determined which a given bar, nearly straight, is capable of supporting. For instance, in fir, supposing its height 10,000,000, a bar one inch square and 10 feet long may begin to bend with the weight of a bar of the same thickness, equal in length to ·8225 × $\frac{1}{120 \times 120}$ × 10,000,000 feet = 571 feet, that is, with a weight of about 120 lbs; neglecting the effect of the weight of the bar itself. If we know the force required to crush a bar or column, we may calculate what must be the proportion of its length to its depth, in order that it may begin to bend rather than be crushed. (Gregory, p. 382.)

1630*l*. For a rectangular beam supported at both ends and the weight applied in the middle, Gregory, p. 388, gives the formula $\frac{432\,l^3\,W}{M\,b\,d^3}$ = deflection in inches in the middle. Here M modulus of elasticity in pounds; *l* length in feet; W weight in pounds; *b* breadth and *d* depth both in inches. Fenwick, *Mechanics of Construction*, gives the formula $\frac{4\,W\,l^3}{M\,b\,d^3}$ or $\frac{W\,l^3}{48\,M\,I}$ = deflection. Here *l* length is in inches; and I moment of inertia of the section, which for a rectangle, = $\frac{1}{12}\,b\,d^3$.

1630*m*. As it may often be necessary to calculate the deflection for an arm from that of a beam, or *vice versâ*, we notice the statement made by Barlow, edit. 1837, that "the deflection of a beam fixed at one end in a wall and loaded at the other, is *double* that of a beam of twice the length, supported at both ends, and loaded in the middle with a double weight." But by his editor in 1851, the word *double* was altered to *equal*. Certain experiments made by us on both the beam and the arm, tended to prove that the former was correct (*Builder*, 1866, p. 124); but scientific investigations show that mathematically the latter is correct;

but as they mainly depend upon the perfect manner in which the tail of the arm is secured, the former, or *double* deflection, is recommended to be anticipated in practice.

1630*n*. There is no such thing as permanent elasticity in any rigid material, and the only possible way of constructing a beam which will return to its original form after the load is removed, is a compound or *trussed beam*, put together in such a way that the permanent alteration of one material counterbalances that of the other. All beams, without exception, will settle in the course of time, even with the lightest load. Not only the load, but the changes of temperature afford a permanent cause of this settling. Facts on this point are difficult to obtain, as the experiments require to be extended over years, and on the same piece of material. *Iron rods*, one inch square, which may carry 60,000 lbs. before they are torn, stretch permanently by a load of less than 20,000 lbs. The best wrought iron cannot bear more than *one-sixth* of its load, without being permanently altered. These data apply only where the material is permanently at rest; if motion or accidental increase of burden happens, the above rules and numbers are considerably modified. As elasticity in material varies as much as its strength, and does not follow the same rules as cohesion, it is advisable to make experiments in each particular case where important structures are to depend upon the smallest quantity of material. (Overman).

1630*o*. *Impact or Collision.* A second force, after direct pressure, is that of *impact*, says Fairbairn, involving a proposition on which mathematicians are not agreed. For practical purposes, we may suppose a heavy case equal to 2,240 lbs. or one ton, falling from a height of 6 feet upon the floor. According to the laws of gravity, a body falling from a state of rest obtains an increase of velocity in a second of time equal to $32\frac{1}{5}$ feet and during that period falls through a space of $16\frac{1}{10}$ feet. This accelerated velocity is as the square roots of the distances; and a falling body having acquired a velocity of 8·05 feet in the first foot of its descent, and 6 feet being the height from which a weight of one ton is supposed to fall, we have $\sqrt{6} \times 8·05 = 2·449 \times 8·05 = 19·714$ for the velocity in a descent of 6 feet. Then $19·714 \times 2240 = 44,159$ lbs. or nearly 20 tons, as the momentum with which the body impinges on the floor. In the present state of our knowledge, this momentum may probably be taken as the measure of the *force of impact*.—" On the effects of impact, the deflections produced by the striking body on wrought iron are nearly as the velocity of impact, and those on cast iron greater in proportion to the velocity. The experiments and investigations made for the Commissioners on Railway Structures are extremely valuable. Their results showed that "the power of resisting impact increases with the permanent load upon the beam; the greater the weight at rest upon the beam, the greater must be the momentum of a striking body in order to break it. This is satisfactory, as it diminishes the risk from falling weights in warehouses: the more nearly the weight upon the floors approaches the point at which danger begins, the greater is their power of resisting sudden impacts. Comparing the mean results of the experiments on bars not loaded, " we find that the transverse is to the impactive strength as 2685 : 3744, or as 1 : 1·39. Similarly, when the bar is loaded with 28 lbs. in the centre, the transverse is to the impactive strength as 2685 : 4546, or as 1 : 1·69; and when 391 lbs. is spread uniformly over the bar, the transverse is to the impactive strength as 2685 : 5699, or as 1 : 2·12."—(Fairbairn, p. 228).

1630*p*. *Tensile strength* is that power of resistance which bodies oppose to a separation of their parts when force is applied to tear asunder, in the direction of their lengths, the fibres or particles of which they are composed. Tredgold's assertions of the principles have been combated by Gregory, to whose work we must refer the student for the reasons he gives. If a piece of No. 10 iron wire bears a tension of 2,000 lbs. before it breaks, ten wires will bear ten times 2,000 lbs. If the sections of 50 wires of this number, form the contents of one square inch, then it will bear a stress of 50×2000 lbs. before it is torn asunder, provided the wires are so arranged that each will carry its full weight. But it does not follow that a *bar* of wrought iron of one square inch will carry an equal weight, not even if the iron be of the same quality. If a solid iron rod of one square inch will carry 50,000 lbs., it does not follow that a rod of 10 square inches in section will carry ten times as much. When welded together, the capacity for resistance appears to be weakened. This observation applies to almost every kind of material, and varies only in degree. The tables of cohesion are generally computed to the tearing of the material, but our calculations should never go beyond the excess of elasticity, for fear of injuring the material. (Overman.)

1630*q*. If the strain upon a rod or strut be greatest on any one side, that side must sustain the whole force or break. This consideration is of great practical moment in estimating the value of all kinds of ties, as king and queen posts, &c.—(Tredgold).

1630*r*. The formula for the strength of tie-rods, suspension bars, &c. is C tons × area of section in inches = W tons—a quarter to be taken for safe weight—or C lbs. × area of section in inches = W lbs. : C being obtained from one of the columns in Tables I and II.

If the weight to be sustained be given, and the sectional dimensions of the bar be required, divide the weight given by one-third or one-quarter of the cohesive strength, and the square root of the quotient will be the side of the square. If the section be rectangular, the quotient must be divided by the breadth.

TABLE I., OF THE ABSOLUTE COHESIVE POWER (OR BREAKING WEIGHT) OF METALS: Sectional area, 1 inch square, 1 foot in length.

METALS. Rennie, 1817, and others.	Cohesive Power. lbs.	Cohesive Power. Tons.
Bar Iron, Swedish - - -	65,000	29·20
" " " rolled -	72,064	
" " " - - R	{ 41,251 / 48,933	
" " Russian - - -	59,470	26·70
" " " - - R	{ 49,564 / 59,096	
" " English	55,872	24·93
" " Mean strength,- R	- -	27·00
" " Charcoal, R - -	63,620	
" " Lancashire, - R	{ 53,775 / 60,110	
" " " " - R	64,200	
" " Low Moor, - R	52,490	
" " " crosswise -	{ 60,075 / 66,390	
" " Welsh - - -	16,255	
" " Staffordshire, - R	{ 56,715 / 62,231	
" " Lanarkshire, - R	{ 51,327 / 64,795	
Bridge Iron, Yorkshire, - R	49,930	
" " " crosswise	43,940	
" " Staffordshire, R -	47,600	
" " " " crosswise	44,385	
Rivet Iron, Low Moor } R and Staffordshire, }	59,740	
Bushelled Iron from Turnings	55,878	
Scrap, Hammered - - -	53,420	
Angle Iron, various Districts -	{ 50,056 / 61,260	
Strap " " - -	{ 41,386 / 55,937	
Plates :— (Rankine)		
" Yorkshire - -	{ 52,000 / 58,487	
" Bessemer, rolled, M	70,000	
" " " - -	72,643	
" " boiler - R	68,319	
" Staffordshire - - -	{ 46,404 / 56,996	
" " crosswise -	{ 44,764 / 51,251	
" " BB, charcoal	45,010	
" " crosswise -	41,420	
" " BB	49,945	
" " " crosswise	{ 59,820 / 54,820	
" " " crosswise	46,470	
" " Best - -	61,280	
" " " crosswise	53,820	
" " Common -	50,820	
" " " crosswise	52,825	
" Lancashire - - -	{ 43,433 / 53,849	
" " crosswise -	{ 39,544 / 48,848	
" Durham - -	51,245	
" " crosswise -	46,712	
Steel and Steely Iron :—		59·93
Bars, cast - - -	134,256	59·43
" Blistered - - -	133,152	56·97
" Shear - - -	127,632	
Plates, average - - R	80,000	
Bars, Cast, Rolled, and Forged	{ 92,015 / 132,909	
" " " " -	130,000	

METALS. Rennie, 1817, and others.	Cohesive Power. lbs.	Cohesive Power. Tons.
Bars, Cast, Blistered, Rolled, } and Forged - }	104,298	
" " Shear, Rolled, } and Forged - }	118,468	
" " Bessemer's, Rol- } led and Forged }	111,460	
" " Bessemer's, Cast } Ingots - - }	63,024	
" " Bessemer's, Ham- } mered or Rolled }	152,912	
" " Spring, Ham- } mered or Rolled }	72,529	
Homogeneous Metal :—		
Bars, Rolled - - - -	90,647	
" " - - - -	93,000	
" Forged - - -	89,724	
Puddled Steel :—		
Bars, Rolled and Forged - -	{ 62,768 / 71,484	
" " " -	90,000	
" " " -	94,752	
Plates :—Cast Steel - -	{ 75,594 / 96,280	
" " crosswise -	{ 69,082 / 97,150	
" " hard - -	102,900	
" " soft - - -	85,400	
Homogeneous Metal, First Quality - - - -	96,280	
" " crosswise -	97,150	
" Second Quality -	72,408	
" " crosswise -	73,580	
Puddled Steel - - - -	{ 71,532 / 102,593	
" " crosswise -	{ 67,686 / 85,365	
" " "	93,600	
Iron, Cast - - - -	17,628	7.87
" " - - - -	19,488	
" " horizontal - G	19,096	
" " vertical - G	18,656	
" Carron, No. 2, cold Blast	19,488	
" Bessemer, - - M	16,683	Tate
" Ingot } R (see also in text) }	41,000 / 41,242	
Gun Metal, hard - -	36,368	16·23
" " Mushets - R	103,400	
Copper, Wrought - - -	33,892	15·08
" Cast - - -	19,096	
" Sheet - - R	30,000	
" Bolts - - R	36,000	
" Wire - - R	60,000	
Brass, Yellow Cast - -	17,958	
" Wire - - T	49,000	
Zinc - - - R	7 to 8,000	
Tin, Cast - - - R	4,736	2·11
" " - - -	4,600	
Bismuth, Cast - - -	3,250	1·45
Lead, Cast - - - -	1,824	0 81
" Sheet, - - R	3,300	
Iron Wire, English, 1-10th. } diameter - - }	- -	36· 0
" " Telford -	- -	38· 4
" Russian, 1-20th in. } diameter - - } T	- -	60· 0

Tables I. and II. are derived chiefly from the summary in Rankine's *Civil Engineering*, p. 511, obtained from the experiments of Clay, Fairbairn, Hodgkinson, Mallet, Morin, Napier, Napier and Sons, Rennie, Telford, and Wilmot. Most of the remainder are from Rennie and other authorities.

1630*s*. English boiler-plates are stated to be of two classes: Yorkshire, and the manufacture of other districts, classed as Staffordshire.

TABLE II., OF THE ABSOLUTE COHESIVE POWER (OR BREAKING WEIGHT) OF THE TIMBERS USUALLY EMPLOYED. Sectional area, 1 inch square, 1 foot in length.

TIMBER. Rennie, 1817, and others.	Cohesive Power.	Cohesive Power.	TIMBER. Rennie, 1817, and others.	Cohesive Power.	Cohesive Power.
	lbs.	Tons.		lbs.	Tons.
Turtosa, or African Teak L	17,200	7·58	Deal, Christiania - - L	12,346	
Teak, or Indian Oak - -	14,500	6·47	„ middle - - - T	12,400	
„ „ „ - B	15,000		Oak - - - - - -	11,592	
„ „ „ - L	12,915		„ - - - - - B	10,000	
Ash - „ - - - L	15,780	7·04	„ - - - - - L	11,880	
„ - - - - L	14,130		„ Dantzic - - - L	12,780	
„ - - - T and B	17,207		„ Riga - - - - L	12,888	
Beech - - - - L	12,000	5·35	„ „ - - - - T	12,857	5 17
„ - - - - T	17,850		„ English - - - T	10,853	
„ - - - - B	11,500		„ American Red - R	10,250	
„ - - - - L	12,225		Cedar - - - - L	7,420	
Poona or Peon - - L	12,350	5·51	„ - - - - -	11,400	
Cowrie - - - L	10,960		Elm - - - - -	11,500	5·13
Saul - - - - R	10,000		„ - - - - - L	9,720	
Fir or Pine, American -	11,800	5·26	Chesnut, Spanish - -	10,800	4·82
„ New England - - T	13,489		„ „ - - R	13,000	
„ „ „ - - B {	10,400 / 12,000		Larch - - - - -	9,500	4·24
„ Spruce - - - R	12,400		„ - - - - - L	12,240	
„ American, white - L	10,296		Mahogany, Honduras - L	11,475	5 12
„ Red Pine - - - R {	12,000 / 14,000		„ Spanish - - L	7,560	3·37
„ Weymouth or Yellow L	11,835		„ „ - - B	8,000	
„ Pitch - - - L	9,796		Walnut - - - - -	7,740	3·45
„ Mar Forest - - L	7,323		„ - - - - L	8,800	
„ Scotch - - - L	7,110		Hempen Rope, 1 sq. in., sec-tion, 1 foot=·578 lbs. - / 1 in.circumf.=·046 lbs. T }	6,400	
„ Memel - - - L	9,540		Ditto, Cables - - - R	5,600	

1630t. The *tensile* strength of cast iron was long very much overrated when Tredgold estimated it at 20 tons. Captain Brown, however, put it at 7·26 tons; G. Rennie (*Phil. Trans.* 1818) obtained 8·52 and 8·66 tons; Barlow conjectured at least 10 tons from theoretical principles; Hodgkinson made the following experiments more recently;

Name and Quality of Iron.	Hot Blast Iron.			Cold Blast Iron.		
	Weight, lbs.	Mean.	Tons cwt.	Weight, lbs.	Mean.	Tons cwt.
Carron, No. 2 - -	13,892 / 12,993 / 13,629 }	13,505 =	6 0$\frac{1}{2}$	16,772 / 16,594 }	16,683 =	7 9
„ No. 3 - -	16,840 / 18,671 }	17,755 =	7 18$\frac{1}{3}$	13,984 / 14,417 }	14,200 =	6 7
Devon (Scot.), No. 3 -	21,907		9 15$\frac{1}{2}$			
Buffery, No. 1 - -	13,434		6 0	17,466		7 16
Coed Talon (N.Wales) No. 2	16,279 / 17,074 }	16,676 =	7 9	19,610 / 18,100 }	18,355 =	8 4
		Mean	7 4$\frac{2}{3}$		Mean	7 14

Low Moor, (Yorkshire,) No. 3, bore 6$\frac{1}{2}$ tons.
A mixture of irons, a mean of four experiments, gave 7 tons 7$\frac{3}{4}$ cwt.

1630u. The mean of several experiments on the ultimate cohesive strength of a *wrought iron bar*, 1 inch square section, was :—

No. 11 experiments by Captain Brown, gave   -   - 56,000 lbs. =25·00 tons.
No. 9   „   by Telford,   „   -   -   - 65,520 „ =29·25 „
No. 10   „   by Brunel,   „   -   -   - 68,992 „ =30·80 „
No. 4   „   by Barlow,   „   -   -   - 56,560 „ =25·25 „

Mean 61·768 lbs. =27·575 tons.

No. 3 experiments by Brunel, on hammered iron, gave 30·4, 32·3, and 30·8 tons respectively.

Several experiments by Cubitt, gave   -   -   - 58,952 lbs. =26 tons 6·3 cwt.

	Highest lbs.	Lowest lbs.	Mean lbs.	Breaking Weight. Tons.
188 bars, rolled, experimented upon by Kirkaldy,	68,848	44,584	57,555	=25$\frac{3}{4}$
72 angle irons „ „ „	63,715	37,909	54,729	=24$\frac{1}{2}$
167 plates, lengthways „ „ „	62,544	37,474	50,737 }	=21$\frac{3}{4}$
160 plates, crossways „ „ „	60,756	32,450	46,171 }	

He states that 25 tons for bars and 20 tons for plates, are the amounts generally assumed

1630v. The detailed experiments by Messrs. Clarke and Fairbairn, on the strength of *iron plates*, are given in the work by the latter, and in the *Engineers' Pocket Book* for 1861 and 1865. Clarke assumes the ultimate tensile strength of wrought iron plates at 20 tons per square inch, and of bars at 24 tons, and that within this former limit, its extension may be taken at $\frac{8}{100,000}$ of the length, per ton, per inch square of section.

The ultimate strength of plates drawn in direction of the fibre } experiment 1, 19·66 tons.
„ 2, 20· 2 „
„ „ „ „ broken across the } „ 1, 16·93 „
fibre } „ 2, 16· 7 „

The ultimate *extension* was twice as great when the plate was broken in the direction of the fibre. The best scrap rivet iron, made by Messrs. Mare at their London works, broke on an average with 24 tons per square inch; the mean ultimate extension, which was uniform, was ⅛ of the length.

COMPRESSION, &c.

1630w. *Compression* is the second of the forces under which TRANSVERSE STRAIN is comprised. The following facts appear to be well established as to materials under a crushing force. I. The strength is as the transverse area or section. II. The plane of rupture in a crushed body is inclined at a constant angle to the base of the body. III. The measure of compression-strength is constant only within certain proportions of the height and diameter in any specimen. Hodgkinson found that twelve cylinders of teak wood furnished the following results:—

	½ inch diam.	inch diam.	2 inch diam.
Crushing weight - - - -	2439 lbs.	10,171 lbs.	40,304 lbs.
Proportion of weights - - -	1 „	4·17 „	16·5 „

The areas being as the squares of the diameters an exact proportion would have been 1, 4, and 16; but some materials may possibly be found to have an increased apparent strength.

TABLE I., OF EXPERIMENTS ON TIMBER PILLARS, made by the Committee of the Institute of British Architects, 1863–64.

Wood.	Crushed at	Per square inch.	Remarks.
4 inch cube.	tons.	tons.	
Moulmein Teak - - -	50· 8	3·17	Crushed endways; fibres torn
Archangel Deal - - -	28· 8	1·11	apart.
Shafts, 12 ins. long, 3 ins. diam.			
Moulmein Teak - - -	18·25	2·58	{ Lost ⅛ of its length. Point of
„ same piece with 6 ins. sawn off	18· 7	2·64	{ yielding ₅⁄₁₂ of its length.
Moulmein Teak - - -	16· 0	2·26	Ditto.
„ same piece, ditto	17·75	2·50	
Deal, Archangel - - -	19· 1	2·70	{ Lost ₃⁄₁₆ of its length. Point of
„ same piece, ditto -	19· 3	2·73	{ yielding ₅⁄₁₂ of its length in both.
„ Archangel - - -	16· 3	2·30	
„ same piece, ditto -	19· 4	2·74	

TABLE II., OF COMPRESSION OF TIMBER.

Wood.	Crushing Strength.	Wood.	Crushing Strength.	Wood.	Crushing Strength.
Christiania white Deal - }	lbs. 6,000	American white Spruce }	lbs. 6,844	Cedar - -	lbs. 5,768
English Oak	9,509	Walnut - -	6,645	Blue Gum -	
Quebec Oak	5,982	Red Deal -	6,167	West India Ebony	
American red Oak - }	6,000	Yellow Pine -	5,375	Morra - -	
		Elm - -	10,331	Indian Teak or }	12,100
American Fir and Pine }	5,430	Larch - -	5,568	Moulmein Teak }	
		Spanish Mahogany	8,198		

Rondelet gives the power of Oak as 6,853 lbs., and of Fir as 8,089 lbs. (See *par.* 1601.) Rennie (inch cube, crushed) English oak, 3,860 lbs.; a piece 4 inches high, 5,147 lbs. Elm, 1,284 lbs.; White Deal, 1,928 lbs.; American Pine, 1,606 lbs.

Table III. of Compression of Timber. (Hodgkinson and others).

Wood.	Damp, 2 ins. high and inch diam.	Dry, Inch high generally.	Wood.	Damp, 2 ins. high and inch diam.	Dry, Inch high generally.
	lbs.	lbs.		lbs.	lbs.
Alder -	6,831	6,960	Oak, Dantzic -	- -	7,731
Beech -	7,733	9,363	„ English -	6,484	10,058
American Birch	- -	11,663	„ Quebec -	4,231	5,982
English Birch -	3,297	6,402	Pine, Pitch -	6,790	6,790
Cedar -	5,674	5,863	„ Yellow, full ⎱ of turpentine ⎰	5,375	5,445
Red Deal -	5,748	6,586			
White Deal -	6,781	7,293	„ Red -	5,395	7,518
Elm - -	- -	10,331	Teak - -	- -	12,101
Spruce Fir -	6,499	6,819	Larch - -	3,201	5,568
Mahogany -	8,198	8,198	Walnut - -	6,063	7,227

1630*x*. It is now a well ascertained circumstance that the crushing strength of a body varies according to its relative height and breadth. Hodgkinson remarks, " When bodies are crushed they give way by a wedge sliding off in an angle dependent on the nature of the material; and in *cast iron* the height of this wedge is about 1⅓ of the diameter or thickness of the base of the wedge." Gregory puts the angle of this wedge at 34°. If the body to be crushed is shorter than would be sufficient to admit a wedge of the full length to slide off, then it would require more than its natural degree of force to crush it ; because the wedge itself must either be crushed, or slide off in a direction of greater difficulty. If, on the other hand, the height of the body to be crushed be much greater than the length of the wedge, then the body will sustain some degree of flexure, and fracture will be facilitated in consequence. *Phil. Trans.*, 1840, cxxx. page 419. Warr says, "It is highly probable that none of Hodgkinson's values would agree with the most careful trial on any similar woods." See 1502*d, et seq.*

1630*y*. The power of resistance to compression of cast-iron was heretofore very much overrated. It has now been well ascertained by experiment that a force of 93,000 lbs. upon an inch square will crush it; and that it will bear 15,300 lbs. upon an inch square without permanent alteration.

Table of the Compression of a Cast Iron Bar (as a pillar), 10 feet long and 1 inch square.

Tons.	Compression per Ton.	Total Compression.	Total Permanent Set.	Tons.	Compression per Ton.	Total Compression.	Total Permanent Set.
	Inch.	Inch.	Inch.		Inch.	Inch.	Inch.
1	·020330	·020338	·000510	9	·022374	·201373	·024254
2	·021038	·042077	·002452	11	·022567	·248237	·032023
3	·021618	·064855	·004340	13	·023014	·299187	·043318
5	·021594	·107872	·009188	15	·023539	·353092	·060905
7	·021950	·153654	·015243	17	·024805	·421695	·086298

1630*z*. Hodgkinson's experiments in 1851 on the ultimate strength of cast iron, the pieces being placed in an iron box or frame, gave a mean in 81 trials of 107,750 lbs. per square inch, or 48 tons 2 cwt. ; and the crushing force to the tensile, as 6·507 to 1. Rennie's calculations gave only 40 tons per square inch for the lowest estimate.

Table of the Crushing of Cubes of Iron.

Materials.	Crushing Weight.	Square inch.	Materials.	Crushing weight.	Square inch.
	lbs.	lbs.		lbs.	lbs.
A cube of ⅛ inch side Soft cast iron . . .	1,439	92,138	Cubes of ¼ inch side	9,773	156,368
ditto, 2 heights .	2,116	135,424	Horizontal casting	10,114	161,824
ditto, 3 or more .	1,758	112,524	Vertical casting	11,110	177,760
(Overman)			Directly cast, not cut from a larger piece		219,490
Cubes of ¼ inch side :—					
Cast copper . . .	7,318		Same iron, but twice melted, once in the cupola, and once in the reverberatory furnace, and cast in cube		262,675
Cast tin	966				
Cast lead	483				
		(Rennie)			(Rennie)

1631. Hodgkinson, " considering the pillar as having two functions, one to support and the other to resist flexure, it follows that when the material is incompressible (supposing such to exist), or when the pressure necessary to break the pillar is very small on account of the greatness of its length compared with its lateral dimensions, then the strength of the whole transverse section of the pillar will be employed in resisting flexure ; when the breaking pressure is one-half of what would be required to crush the material, one-half only of the strength may be considered as available for resistance to flexure, whilst the other half is employed to resist crushing; and when, through the shortness of the pillar, the breaking pressure is so great as to be nearly equal to the crushing force, we may consider that no part of the strength of the pillar is applied to resist flexure." Thus he assumed that the real breaking weight would be equal to the breaking weight as obtained for the long columns, multiplied by the force requisite to crush it without flexure; and divided by the same two quantities added together, minus the pressure which it would support as flexible, without being weakened by crushing. The formula thus found for calculating the strength was $\dfrac{Wc}{W+3c}$.

Here W breaking weight of long pillars, and c crushing force of the iron. (Warr and Gregory.)

1631a. Euler, treating on the strength of pillars purely on theoretical grounds, showed that the strength varied as the fourth power of the diameter, and inversely as the square of the length of the pillar. The strength of similar pillars increases as the square of their diameter; and as the area is as the square of the diameter, the strength increases as the area of the pillar (Warr.)

1631b. The strength of a pillar or a column, or the power of resistance to compressive force, is obtained by the law that the resistance to crushing is as the cube of the thickness multiplied by the width, and this divided by the square of the length. Therefore in columns of equal length and thickness, the resistance is as their width ; and in equal lengths and widths, it is as the cube of the thickness. If the width and thickness be equal, or if the pillar be square, the resistance is inversely as the square of its length.

Ia. The formula for a rectangular *pillar* of oak, is $\dfrac{R b d^3}{4 d^2 + \cdot 5 l^2} = $ W lbs. R = 3,960.

Ib.   „   „   cast iron, is $\dfrac{R b d^3}{4 d^2 + \cdot 18 l^2} = $ W lbs. R = 15,300.

Ic.   „   „   wrought iron, is $\dfrac{R b d^3}{4 d^2 + \cdot 16 l^2} = $ W lbs. R = 17,800.

IIa.   „   solid *cylinder* of oak, is $\dfrac{R d^4}{4 d^2 + \cdot 5 l^2} = $ W lbs. R = 2,470.

IIb.   „   „   cast iron, is $\dfrac{R d^4}{4 d^2 + \cdot 18 l^2} = $ W lbs. R = 9,562.

IIc.   „   „   wrought iron, is $\dfrac{R d^4}{4 d^2 + \cdot 16 l^2} = $ W lbs. R = 11,125.

Here l length in feet ; b breadth in inches ; d diameter in inches ; R resistance to compressive force ; W breaking weight of the pillar or cylinder. (Tredgold, *Cast Iron*.)

1631c. The relative strengths of long columns of different materials, but of the same dimensions, are as follows :—

Cast iron.	Cast steel.	Wrought iron.	Dantzic oak.	Red deal.			
1,000	2,518	1,745	108·8	78·5	(Gregory)		
			English oak.	Red Pine.	Teak.	Larch.	Elm.
100	180	79	18	15	19	12	10 (Hurst.)

1631d. Hodgkinson, *Cast Iron*, 1846, states that there are general properties common to wrought iron, steel and wood. It appeared from experiments that long (solid) pillars break first at, or near to, the middle; this occurred in all cases. Pillars were, therefore, tried, having a middle diameter of from $1\frac{1}{4}$ to 2 inches, the ends being 1 inch. The strength was not increased according to the increase of the middle diameter, but appeared to be from $\dfrac{1}{6\cdot62}$ to $\dfrac{1}{8\cdot05}$, or from one-seventh to one-eighth ; they did not, however, fracture in the middle, as did those of uniform diameter. He found that—

The strength, as dependent on the diameter, was on the mean - 3·736
    „   „   „   length,   „   „   - 1·7

I. The formula given by him for *long* solid cylindrical pillars (when l exceeds 30 d) with flat ends and fixed, is $\dfrac{44\cdot16 \text{ tons } d^{3\cdot35}}{l^{1\cdot7}} = $ W tons, or (33,379 lbs. = 14·901 tons). The formula for ditto with rounded ends (or when l is less than 30d and exceeding 15d, is $\dfrac{14\cdot9 \text{ tons } d^{3\cdot76}}{l^{1\cdot7}} = $ W tons, or (98,922 lbs. = 44·16 tons). Here d external diameter inches; l length feet ; $\frac{1}{10}$ of W to be taken for safe weight.

II. For *short pillars*, below 30 times their diameter in height with flat ends, or 15 times their diameter in pillars with rounded ends, the above formulæ do not apply.

III. For *solid columns*, when the length is less than 30d, the formula is $\frac{49\,\text{W}\,a}{\text{W}+37\,a}=\text{W}^1$. Here W¹ crushing weight of short column in tons; a sectional area of solid part of columns inches. In *hollow columns* the thickness of metal should not be less than $\frac{d}{12}$. $\frac{\text{W C}}{.\text{W}+\frac{3}{4}\text{C}}=\text{W}^1$ tons. Here W as found above for long columns; C crushing force of material × sectional area of column; and W¹ crushing weight of short columns.

1631e. The formula for a rectangular pillar of timber, fixed at both ends $\frac{7.200\,a}{1+\frac{l^2}{250\,h^2}}=\text{W lbs.}$

„ cylindrical pillar of cast iron „ $\frac{80,000\,a}{1+\frac{l^2}{400\,h^2}}=\text{W lbs.}$

„ rectangular strut of wrought iron „ $\frac{36,000\,a}{1+\frac{l^2}{3,000\,h^2}}=\text{W lbs.}$

A pillar rounded or jointed at both ends $\frac{80,000\,a}{1+4\times400\,h^2}\,l^2=\text{W lbs.}$; or 36,000, or 7,200, as the case may be. (Rankine, from Gordon, and Hodgkinson.)

1631f. The formula for a circular post or pillar $\frac{\text{C }d^4 \text{inches}}{l^2 \text{ feet}}=\text{W tons, or safe load}=\frac{1}{10}\text{ W.}$

„ square pillars $\frac{1\cdot7\,\text{C}\,s^4}{l^2}=\text{W}$ „ „

„ rectangular column $\frac{1\cdot7\,\text{C}\,b\,t^3}{l^2}=\text{W}$ „ „

Here b breadth ; t least thickness in inches; s side in inches; d diameter; and C Teak 15 ; English oak 14; Canadian oak 13; Baltic oak 12; Red pine 12 ; Riga fir 11; Ash 12 ; Beech 11; Larch 9 ; and Elm 8. (Hurst.)

1631g. In order to give lateral stiffness to a flat-ended pillar, its ends should be spread so as to form a capital and base, whose abutting surfaces should be "faced" in the lathe, or planed, to make them exactly plane and perpendicular to the axis of the pillar. For the same reason, when a cast iron pillar consists of two or more lengths, the ends of those lengths should be made truly plane and perpendicular to the axis of the pillar by the same process, so that they may abut firmly and equally against each other ; and they should be fastened together by at least four bolts passing through projecting flanges. (Rankine.)

1631h. *Hollow Columns.*—With an equal quantity of metal, a round column cast hollow is far stronger than one cast solid. The best form for cast iron columns is to make the inner diameter five-eighths of the size of the exterior diameter. The ring thus formed of the section of the column increases in strength according to the thinness, but the size of it must be kept within practical limits. If, in casting a hollow column, the core is driven to one side, the column of course cannot be loaded to its full resistance ; it will not carry more than the thinnest part of it is strong enough to bear. Hollow columns, therefore, require particular care in casting them. Hodgkinson noticed in hollow pillars above 30 times as long as their diameter, that although the pillars were generally thicker on one side than the other, yet in bending, the compressed was always the thinner side ; and as cast iron resists compression with above six times the force with which it sustains tension, *no danger resulted* from this almost unavoidable difference of thickness.

I. The formula given by him for a *hollow cylinder* not less than 15 times its diameter in height, with rounded ends, is $\frac{13\cdot0 \text{ tons } d^{3\cdot76}-d_1^{3\cdot76}}{l^{1\cdot7}}=\text{W tons.}$

II. For the same when not less than 30 times its height, with flat ends and fixed by discs, is $\frac{44\cdot3 \text{ tons } d^{3\cdot35}-d_1^{3\cdot55}}{l^{1\cdot7}}=\text{W tons.}$

III. When the length is equal to 20 diameters, the value of W is $=77,817$ lbs. or $34\cdot7$ tons.

Gregory has adopted an average of $d^{3\cdot6}$ in both of these formulæ.

IV. For *short pillars*, below those lengths, the formulæ do not apply, as the strength of the column becomes modified in consequence of its being then partially crushed as well as bent.

Stancheons and Struts.

1631i. Gordon's formula for the ultimate strength of *wrought iron struts* of a solid rectangular section fixed at the ends, as deduced from Hodgkinson's experiments, is $\frac{36,000}{l+3000\,l^2}\Bigg/b^2=\frac{\text{W or load}}{a \text{ or sect. area}}$. (b least thickness). For other forms of cross section, approximate rules have been given. But it may be, in many cases, more satisfactory to take into account the least "radius of gyration" of the cross section ; and for that purpose the formula may be put in the following shape : $\frac{36,000}{1+\frac{l^2}{36,000\,r^2}}=\frac{\text{W}}{a}$. Here r^2 is the mean of the

squares of the distances of the particles of the cross section from a neutral axis traversing its centre of gravity in that direction which makes r^2 least. For hinged ends, take $\frac{1}{4}$, or 9,000 is to be substituted for 36,000. The value of r^2 for a solid rectangle, least dimension $= b$, then $\frac{b^2}{12}$. For a thin square cell, side $= b$, then $\frac{b^2}{6}$. For a thin rectangular cell, breadth $= b$, depth $= h$, the $\frac{12}{h^2} \cdot \frac{h+b}{h+3b}$. For a solid cylinder, diameter $= b$, then $\frac{b^2}{16}$. For a thin cylindrical cell, diameter $= b$, then $\frac{b^2}{8}$. For an angle iron of equal ribs, breadth of each $= b$, then $\frac{b^2}{24}$. For an angle iron of unequal ribs, greater $= b$, lesser $= h$, then $\frac{b^2 h^2}{12(b^2 + h^2)}$. For a cross of equal arms $\frac{b^2}{24}$. For H iron, breadth of flanges $= b$, their joint area $=$ B, area of web $=$ A, then $\frac{b^2}{12} \cdot \frac{A}{A+B}$. (Rankine, who follows out the subject further.)

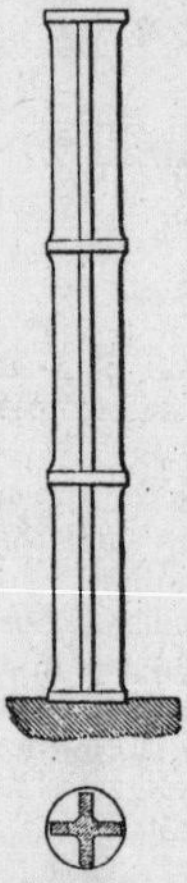

1631k. *Stancheons* of cast iron are recommended to be used in lieu of cast iron *columns*.

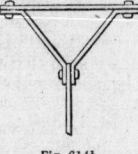

The form shown in *fig.* 613x. is generally considered as the best for use; the flanges which divide the length into three equal parts, are found to add considerably to the strength of the casting in resisting the tendency of its load to produce deflection from the vertical position. Hodgkinson's experiments show that while *cast iron* is the better material for a pillar whose length does not exceed 26 times the diameter, *wrought iron* is the better material when the length exceeds that limit. For pillars with hinged ends, about 13 times is the limit, but these results are roughly approximate only. In order to stiffen *wrought iron* struts, they are made of various forms in cross section, such as angle iron, T iron, double T iron, channel iron, &c. The cross is a very convenient form as in cast iron; it is generally built by riveting bars of simple forms together. Thus it may be made up of T irons riveted back to back, or four angle irons riveted back to back; or by one flat bar, two narrower flat bars, and four angle irons, all riveted together, as *fig.* 613y., and as used for the strut diagonals of the Warren girders in the Crumlin viaduct. The stiffest form for a wrought iron strut is that of a cell or built tube,

Fig. 613x.   Fig. 613y.   Fig. 614a.   Fig. 614b.

fig. 614a., which may be cylindrical, rectangular, or triangular, as *fig.* 614b. When a wrought iron strut is considered as hinged at the end, that is generally effected by its abutting at each end against a cylindrical pin, by which it is connected with some other piece of the frame-work, in the manner already described for tie-bars. To fix its ends in direction, as it seldom has large abutting faces, it is in general necessary to fasten it to the adjoining pieces of the structure by several bolts or rivets.

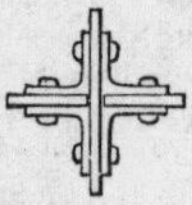

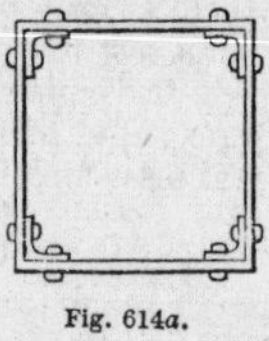

1631l. Cast iron, from its great resistance to crushing, is peculiarly well suited for struts, especially those of moderate length. The best form containing a given quantity of metal is that of a hollow cylinder (*fig.* 614c.); the thickness of metal is seldom less than $\frac{1}{12}$ of the diameter. I. The formula for the *cylinder* has already been given; II. for a cast iron strut of a cross shape (*fig.* 614d.) the whole width being d, then $\dfrac{80,000}{1 + \dfrac{3l^2}{400d^2}} =$ W lbs. per square inch of sectional area. III. For a hollow square (*fig.* 614e.), $d =$ diagonal, $\dfrac{80,000}{1 + \dfrac{3l^2}{800d^2}} =$ W, as before.

IV. For a hollow cylinder (*fig.* 614f.), $d =$ diameter $\dfrac{80,000}{1 + \dfrac{l^2}{400d^2}} =$ W, as before. These formulæ refer to struts fixed at both ends. V. When they are hinged at the ends, the second term of each division is to be made four times as great.

1631m. With the ends fixed; I. the formulæ for a hollow tube (*fig.* 614c.) $a = 3000$, then

$$\dfrac{16s \text{ (or sectional area inches)}}{1 + \dfrac{l^2 \text{ inches}}{a\,\text{D}^2 \text{ or (diam. inches)}}} = \text{W tons.}$$

 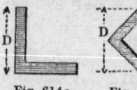

Fig. 614c.   Fig. 614d.   Fig. 614e.    Fig. 614f.

II. The formulæ for a cross with equal arms (*fig.* 614d) $a = 1000$.

III. The formulæ for an angle with equal sides (*fig.* 614e) $a = 1000$.

IV. When hinged at the ends, take $\frac{a}{4}$.

1631n. *Detrusion, or shearing*, denominates that kind of fracture, which would occur in the use of shears if their edges were blunt; or when the punch of a punching machine

makes a hole in a plate. Fairbairn has deduced the following laws from his experiments : I. That the ultimate resistance to shearing in any bolt or rivet, is proportional to the sectional area of the bar torn asunder. II. That the ultimate resistance of any bar to a shearing strain is nearly the same as the ultimate resistance of the same bar to a direct longitudinal tensile strain.

TABLE OF THE RESISTANCE OF MATERIALS TO SHEARING AND DISTORTION.

Materials.	Resistance to Shearing, per square inch.	Transverse Elasticity, or Resistance to Distortion, per square inch.
	lbs. avoirdupois.	lbs. avoirdupois.
Brass wire, drawn -	- -	5,330,000
Copper - - -	- -	6,200,000
Cast iron - - -	27,700 to 32,500	2,850,000
Wrought iron - -	50,000	8,500,000 to 9,500,000
Pine, red - - -	500 to 800	62,000 to 116,000
Fir, Spruce - - -	600	—
Larch - - - -	970 to 1,700	—
Oak, English - -	2,300	82,000
Poplar - - -	1,800	—
Ash and Elm - -	1,400	76,000
Deal - - - -	592	
Cast iron - - -	73,000 ? } Warr.	Rankine.
Wrought iron - -	45,000 to 53,000	

1631*o*. To find the length between the end of a beam and the foot of a strut or of a rafter, necessary to resist the thrust of the latter, so as to prevent the detrusion of the beam, the formula to be used is $\frac{4h}{bS} =$ the length in inches. Here b the breadth of the beam in inches ; h horizontal thrust in pounds; and S, the cohesive strength in pounds of a square inch of the material. Tredgold states that 4 is a sufficient value for a factor of safety in this case ; S = 600 lbs. per square inch for fir, and 2,300 lbs. for oak. The strap or bolt usually employed to bind the rafter and beam together, should be at as acute an angle as possible, and holds the rafter in its place should the end of the beam give way.

1631*p*. *Iron fastenings to joints.* In forming eyes by welding, at the end of iron bars for chain links and other purposes, the bar is found to be weaker than in its plain form. In iron plate work, the joints are made by riveting on which the whole efficacy of the built-up plate work depends. Taking the strength of the plain plate as 100, a double-

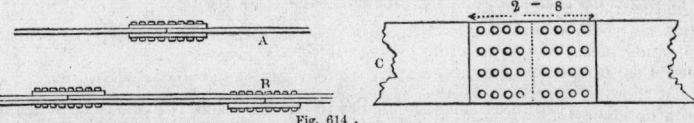

Fig. 614 .

riveted plate will be 70; and a single-riveted, 56. Again, with *single plate jointings* having a top and bottom covering plate over the joint, and with half-inch rivets, as A, *fig.* 613*x*, the plates were torn asunder through the rivet-holes, with 24·41 tons in the square inch. With a *double plate*, having a single covering plate on the side of the joint, as B, the plates broke asunder by shearing off the rivets close to the plate, with 18·73 tons per square inch ; but the rivets having been made larger, a similar strength to the previous experiment was realised. A plain plate broke with 22·78 tons mean value.

1631*q*. Fairbairn recommends the flanges or double plates to be used as long as possible, and the joints to be carefully united by covering plates, *chain-riveted*, as C, with three or more rows of rivets according to the widths of the plates. Eight rivets are required in each of the lines, four on each side of the joints, to give sufficient strength, and the area of the rivets collectively should be equal to the area of the jointed plates taken transversely through one line of the rivets, the area of the parts punched out in that line being deducted. These proportions give the required security to the joint, and afford nearly the same strength to a tensile strain as the solid plate ; that is, if the covering plates be as much thicker as will give the same area of section through the rivet-holes as the unperforated double plate. (*par.* 1629*e*.)

1631*r*. Rivets are made of the most tough and ductile iron. It is essentially necessary that the rivet should tightly fit its hole ; and the longitudinal compression to which rivets are subjected during the formation of its head, whether by hand or machinery, tends to produce that result. The diameter of a rivet for plates less than half an inch thick, is

about double the thickness of the plate. For plates of half an inch thick and upwards, about once and a half the thickness of the plate. The length of the rivet before clenching (which is effected whilst the rivet is red hot), measuring from the head, equals the sum of the thickness of the plates to be connected, added to $2\frac{1}{2}$ inches multiplied by the diameter of the rivet.

1631s. Steel rivets, fully larger in diameter than those used in riveting iron plates of the same thickness, being found to be greatly too small for riveting steel plates, the probability is suggested that the proper proportion for iron rivets is not, as generally assumed, a diameter equal to the thickness of the two plates to be joined. The shearing strain of steel rivets is found to be about a fourth less than the tensile strain. (Kirkaldy).

1631t. In the bridge over the Thames for the Charing Cross Railway, the holes were drilled and not punched. This is a point upon which engineers differ considerably; but most firms punch the holes. At Fairbairn's works at Manchester, drilling holes was considered to be more expensive without adding to the strength. Mr. Parkes thinks that the punching injured the iron considerably, and thought Fairbairn's experiments went to show it. (Society of Engineers, *Transactions*, 1865).

1631u. *Pins, keys, and wedges* are exposed, like rivets, to a shearing stress. The formula for finding their proper sectional area is the same. They must be held tightly in their seats; and in order that a wedge or key may not slip out of its seat, its angle of obliquity ought not to exceed the angle of repose of iron upon iron, which, to provide for the contingency of the surfaces being greasy, may be taken at about 4°. (Rankine).

1631v. If a *bolt or screw* has to withstand a shearing stress, its diameter is to be determined like that of a cylindrical pin. If it has to withstand tension, its diameter is to be determined by having regard to its tenacity. In either case the effective diameter of the bolt is its least diameter; that is, if it has a screw upon it, the diameter of the spindle inside the thread. The projection of the thread is usually one-half of the pitch; and the pitch should not in general be greater than one-fifth of the effective diameter, and may be considerably less. In order that the resistance of a screw or screw-bolt to rupture, by stripping the thread, may be at least equal to its resistance to direct tearing asunder, the length of the nut should be at least one half of the effective diameter of the screw; and it is often in practice considerably greater; for example, once and a half that diameter. The head of a bolt is usually about twice the diameter of the spindle and of a thickness which is usually greater than $\frac{5}{8}$ths of that diameter. (Rankine).

1631w. *Washers* are flat plates of iron, placed at the sides of timbers to secure them against the crushing action of the head and nut of a bolt whilst being screwed up. For fir, the diameter of the washer is made about $3\frac{1}{2}$ times that of the bolt; and for oak, about $2\frac{1}{2}$ times. When a bolt is placed oblique to the direction of the beam which it traverses, a notch should be cut in the timber perpendicular to the bolt, to receive the pressure of the washer equally, or notched to receive a bevelled washer of cast iron, one side of which fits the wood, and the other fits the axis of the bolt.

Torsion.

1631x. *Torsion*, or the resistance of bodies to being twisted, is found: I. When a body is fastened at one end and a force is applied at the other. II. When the force at one end is greater than at the other end. III. When the forces at the ends are in opposite directions, and are so applied as to twist the body. As this fact chiefly, if not entirely, concerns machinery in motion, we refer the student for more specific details to Warr, *Dynamics*, p. 269, who gives a table of "modulus of torsion" of various timbers and metals, derived from experiments made by Bevan, in *Phil. Trans.* 1829, p. 128. Approximate formulæ are given by Hurst:—

I. When the shaft is circular, $\sqrt[3]{\dfrac{W l}{C}} = d$. And $\dfrac{C d^3}{l} = W$. II. When the shaft is square,

$\sqrt[3]{\dfrac{4 W}{5C} l} = s$. Here d diameter inches; W weight pounds permanently sustained by the shaft; l length of lever in feet, at the end of which W acts; s side in inches; and C, cast steel 590; wrought iron 335; cast iron 330; gun metal 170; brass 150; copper 135; lead 34.

1631y. In the *Artizan* for 1857 and 1858 is an instructive *Enquiry into the Strength of Beams and Girders*, by S. Hughes, deserving attention. The chief authorities for the data contained in that article, and also in this section, are quoted herein.

CHAP. II.

MATERIALS USED IN BUILDING.

Sect. I.

STONE.

1636. It is not our intention to advert to the stone which the Continent affords for building purposes; a knowledge of the different kinds there found would be of no use to the English architect, and would occupy too much of our space as mere information. It is almost superfluous to say that the choice of stone for a building intended to be durable is of the very highest importance. "In modern Europe," it has been observed, "and particularly in Great Britain, there is scarcely a public building, of recent date, which will be in existence a thousand years hence. Many of the most splendid works of modern architecture are hastening to decay in what may be justly called the infancy of their existence, if compared with the dates of public buildings that remain in Italy, in Greece, in Egypt, and the East."

1637. The various sorts of stone take their names either from the places where they are quarried or from the substances which principally enter into their composition. The term "Freestone," which is used in a very arbitrary way, is, as its name implies, that sort which can be wrought with the mallet and chisel, or cut with the saw, an operation which cannot be performed upon granite, whose hardness requires it to be dressed with pointed tools of different weights and sizes. It includes the two great general divisions of Limestone and Sandstone. The limestone of Portland is that which has for many years past been chiefly used in the metropolis. Latterly, other sorts have found their way in from the provinces; and though, from many circumstances, we do not think it likely that Portland stone, from its facility of transport and other causes, will be altogether superseded, there is no doubt that its use is on the wane from the introduction of provincial sorts.

1638. We shall proceed, after some preliminary observations, to give, from the Report addressed in 1839 to the Commissioners of Woods and Forests on the occasion of selecting the stone for building the new Houses of Parliament, a view of the principal sorts of stone found and used in the island. A new edition was printed in 1845.

1639. The qualities requisite for a building stone are hardness, tenacity, and compactness. It is not the hardest stone which has always the greatest tenacity or toughness; for limestone, though much softer, is not so easily broken as glass.

1640. The *decay and destruction* of stone are accelerated by nearly the same causes as those which destroy rocks themselves on the surface of the globe. Such causes are of two kinds: those of decomposition and those of disintegration. The former affects a chemical change in the stone itself, the latter a mechanical division and separation of the parts. The effects of the chemical and mechanical causes of the decomposition of stone in buildings are much modified, according to their situation, as in the town or country. In populous and smoky towns the state of the atmosphere accelerates decomposition more than in those placed in the open country. (par. 1667.)

1641. "As regards the sandstones that are usually employed for building purposes, and which are generally composed of either quartz or siliceous grains, cemented by siliceous, argillaceous, calcareous or other matter, their decomposition is effected according to the nature of the cementing substance, the grains being comparatively indestructible. With respect to limestones composed of carbonate of lime, or the carbonates of lime and magnesia, either nearly pure or mixed with variable proportions of foreign matter, their decomposition depends, under similar circumstances, upon the mode in which their component parts are aggregated, those which are most crystalline being found to be the most durable, while those which partake least of that character suffer most from exposure to atmospheric influences.

1642. "The varieties of limestones termed Oolites (or Roestones) being composed of oviform bodies cemented by calcareous matter of a varied character, will of necessity suffer unequal decomposition, unless such oviform bodies and the cement be equally coherent and of the same chemical composition. The limestones which are usually termed 'shelly,' from being chiefly formed of either broken or perfect fossil shells cemented by calcareous matter, suffer decomposition in an unequal manner, in consequence of the shells, which, being for the most part crystalline, offer the greatest amount of resistance to the decomposing effects of the atmosphere.

1643. "Sandstones, from the mode of their formations, are very frequently laminated,

more especially when micaceous, the plates of mica being generally deposited in planes parallel to their beds. Hence, if such stone be placed in buildings with the planes of lamination in a vertical position, it will decompose in flakes, according to the thickness of the laminæ; whereas, if it be placed so that the planes of lamination be horizontal, that is, most commonly upon its natural bed, the amount of decomposition will be comparatively immaterial.

1644. " Limestones, such at least as are usually employed for building purposes, are not liable to the kind of lamination observable in sandstones; nevertheless, varieties exist, especially those commonly termed *shelly*, which have a coarse laminated structure, generally parallel to the planes of their beds, and therefore the same precaution in placing such stone in buildings so that the planes of lamination be horizontal, is as necessary as with the sandstones above noticed.

1645. " The chemical action of the atmosphere produces a change in the entire matter of the limestones, and in the cementing substance of the sandstones according to the amount of surface exposed to it. The mechanical action due to atmospheric causes occasions either a removal or a disruption of the exposed particles, the former by means of powerful winds and driving rains, and the latter by the congelation of water forced into or absorbed by the external portions of the stone. These effects are reciprocal, chemical action rendering the stone liable to be more easily affected by mechanical action, which latter, by constantly presenting new surfaces, accelerates the disintegrating effects of the former.

1646. " Buildings in this climate are generally found to suffer the greatest amount of decomposition on their southern, south-western, and western fronts, arising doubtless from the prevalence of winds and rains from those quarters; hence it is desirable that stones of great durability should at least be employed in fronts with such aspects.

1647. " Buildings situated in the country appear to possess a great advantage over those in populous and smoky towns, owing to lichens, with which they almost invariably become covered in such situations, and which, when firmly established over their entire surface, seem to exercise a protective influence against the ordinary causes of the decomposition of the stone upon which they grow.

1648. " As an instance of the difference in degree of durability in the same material subjected to the effects of the atmosphere in town and country, we may notice the several frusta of columns and other blocks of stone that were quarried at the time of the erection of St. Paul's Cathedral in London, and which are now lying in the island of Portland, near the quarries from whence they were obtained. These blocks are invariably found to be covered with lichens, and although they have been exposed to all the vicissitudes of a marine atmosphere for more than 150 years, they still exhibit, beneath the lichens, their original forms, even to the marks of the chisel employed upon them, whilst the stone which was taken from the same quarries (selected, no doubt, with equal, if not greater, care than the blocks alluded to) and placed in the cathedral itself, is, in those parts which are exposed to the south and south-west winds, found in some instances to be fast mouldering away. Colour is of more importance in the selection of a stone for a building to be situated in a populous and smoky town, than for one to be placed in an open country, where all edifices usually become covered, as before stated, with lichens; for although in such towns those fronts which are not exposed to the prevailing winds and rains will soon become blackened*, the remainder of the building will constantly exhibit a tint depending upon the natural colour of the material employed.

1649. " Before we proceed to adduce a few examples of the present condition of the various buildings we have examined, we would wish to observe that those which are highly decorated, such as the churches of the Norman and pointed styles of architecture, afford a more severe test of the durability of any given stone, all other circumstances being equal, than the more simple and less decorated buildings, such as the castles of the fourteenth and fifteenth centuries, inasmuch as the material employed in the former class of buildings is worked into more disadvantageous forms than in the latter, as regards exposure to the effects of the weather; and we would further observe, that buildings in a state of ruin, from being deprived of their ordinary protection of roofing, glazing of windows, &c., constitute an equally severe test of the durability of the stone employed in them.

1650. " As examples of the degree of durability of various building stones in particular localities, the following may be enumerated. Of the sandstone buildings which we examined, we may notice the remains of Ecclestone Abbey, of the thirteenth century, near Barnard Castle, constructed of a stone closely resembling that of the Stenton quarry in the vicinity, as exhibiting the mouldings and other decorations, even to the dog's-tooth ornament, in excellent condition. The circular keep of Barnard, apparently also built of the same material, is in fine preservation. Tintern Abbey may also be noticed as a sandstone

---

* We must take leave to question this statement; as, for instance, in St. Paul's Cathedral we find the northern front peculiarly black, whilst the south front and south-western angle are comparatively white. This we have always considered to have arisen from the more constant action of the sun's rays upon them.

edifice that has to a considerable extent resisted decomposition; for although it is decayed in some parts, it is nearly perfect in others. Some portions of Whitby Abbey are likewise in a perfect state, whilst others are fast yielding to the effects of the atmosphere. The older portions of Ripon Cathedral, constructed of sandstone, are in a fair state of preservation. Rivaulx Abbey is another good example of an ancient sandstone building in a fair condition. The Norman keep of Richmond Castle in Yorkshire affords an instance of a moderately hard sandstone which has well resisted decomposition.

1651. "As examples of sandstone buildings of more recent date in a good state of preservation, we may mention Hardwicke Hall, Haddon Hall, and all the buildings of Craigleith Stone in Edinburgh and its vicinity. Of sandstone edifices in an advanced state of decomposition we may enumerate Durham Cathedral, the churches at Newcastle upon Tyne, Carlisle Cathedral, Kirkstall Abbey, and Fountains Abbey. The sandstone churches of Derby are also extremely decomposed; and the church of St. Peter at Shaftesbury is in such a state of decay that some portions of the building are only prevented from falling by means of iron ties.

1652. " As an example of an edifice constructed of a calciferous variety of sandstone, we may notice Tisbury Church, which is in unequal condition, the mouldings and other enrichments being in a perfect state, whilst the ashler, apparently selected with less care, is fast mouldering away.

1653. " The choir of Southwell Church, of the twelfth century, may be mentioned as affording an instance of the durability of a magnesio-calciferous sandstone, resembling that of Mansfield, after long exposure to the influences of the atmosphere.

1654. " Of buildings constructed of magnesian limestone we may mention the Norman portions of Southwell Church, built of stone similar to that of Bolsover Moor, and which are throughout in a perfect state, the mouldings and carved enrichments being as sharp as when first executed. The keep of Koningsburgh Castle, built of a magnesian limestone from the vicinity, is also in a perfect state, although the joints of the masonry are open in consequence of the decomposition and disappearance of the mortar formerly within them. The church at Hemmingborough, of the fifteenth century, constructed of a material resembling the stone from Huddlestone, does not exhibit any appearance of decay. Tickhill Church, of the fifteenth century, built of a similar material, is in a fair state of preservation. Huddlestone Hall, of the sixteenth century, constructed of the stone of the immediate vicinity, is also in good condition. Roche Abbey, of the thirteenth century, in which stone from the immediate neighbourhood has been employed, exhibits generally a fair state of preservation, although some portions have yielded to the effects of the atmosphere.

1655. " As examples of magnesian limestone buildings in a more advanced state of decay, we may notice the churches at York, and a large portion of the Minster, Howden Church, Doncaster Old Church, and others in that part of the country, many of which are so much decomposed that the mouldings, carvings, and other architectural decorations are often entirely effaced.

1656. "We may here remark, that, as far as our observations extend, in proportion as the stone employed in magnesian limestone buildings is crystalline, so does it appear to have resisted the decomposing effects of the atmosphere; a conclusion in accordance with the opinion of Professor Daniell, who has stated to us that from the results of experiments, he is of opinion ' the nearer the magnesian limestones approach to equivalent proportions of carbonate of lime and carbonate of magnesia, the more crystalline and better they are in every respect.'

1657. " Of buildings constructed of oolitic and other limestones, we may notice the church of Byland Abbey, of the twelfth century, especially the west front, built of stone from the immediate vicinity, as being in an almost perfect state of preservation. Sandysfoot Castle, near Weymouth, constructed of Portland oolite in the time of Henry VIII., is an example of that material in excellent condition; a few decomposed stones used in the interior (and which are exceptions to this fact) being from another oolite in the immediate vicinity of the castle. Bow and Arrow Castle, and the neighbouring ruins of a church of the fourteenth century, in the Island of Portland, also afford instances of the Portland oolite in perfect condition. The new church in the island, built in 1766, of the variety of the Portland stone termed *roach*, is in an excellent state throughout, even to the preservation of the marks of the chisel.

1658. " Many buildings constructed of a material similar to the oolite of Ancaster, such as Newark and Grantham Churches, and other edifices in various parts of Lincolnshire, have scarcely yielded to the effects of atmospheric influences. Windrush Church, built of an oolite from the neighbouring quarry, is in excellent condition, whilst the Abbey Church of Bath, constructed of the oolite in the vicinity of that city, has suffered much from decomposition; as is also the case with the cathedral, and the churches of St. Nicholas and St. Michael in Gloucester, erected of a stone from the oolitic rocks of the neighbourhood.

1659. " The churches of Stamford, Ketton, Colley Weston, Kettering, and other places

in that part of the country, attest the durability of the Shelley oolite, termed *Barnack Rag*, with the exception of those portions of some of them for which the stone has been ill-selected. The excellent condition of those parts which remain of Glastonbury Abbey show the value of a shelly limestone similar to that of Doulting, whilst the stone employed in Wells Cathedral, apparently of the same kind, and not selected with equal care, is in parts decomposed. The mansion, the church, and the remains of the abbey at Montacute, as also many other buildings in that vicinity, constructed of the limestone of Ham Hill, are in excellent condition. In Salisbury Cathedral, built of stone from Chilmark, we have evidence of the general durability of a siliciferous limestone; for, although the west front has somewhat yielded to the effects of the atmosphere, the excellent condition of the building generally is most striking.

1660. " In the public buildings of Oxford, we have a marked instance both of decomposition and durability in the materials employed; for whilst a shelly oolite, similar to that of Taynton, which is employed in the more ancient parts of the cathedral, in Merton College Chapel, &c., and commonly for the plinths, string-courses, and exposed portions of the other edifices in that city, is generally in a good state of preservation, a calcareous stone from Heddington, employed in nearly the whole of the colleges, churches, and other public buildings, is in such a deplorable state of decay, as in some instances to have caused all traces of architectural decoration to disappear, and the ashler itself to be in many places deeply disintegrated.

1661. " In Spofforth Castle we have a striking example of the unequal decomposition of two materials, a magnesian limestone and a sandstone; the former employed in the decorated parts, and the latter for the ashler or plain facing of the walls. Although the magnesian limestone has been equally exposed with the sandstone to the decomposing effects of the atmosphere, it has remained as perfect in form as when first employed, while the sandstone has suffered considerably from the effects of decomposition.

1662. " In Chepstow Castle, a magnesian limestone in fine preservation, and a red sandstone in an advanced state of decomposition, may be observed, both having been exposed to the same conditions as parts of the same archways; and in Bristol Cathedral there is a curious instance of the effects arising from the intermixture of very different materials, a yellow limestone and a red sandstone, which have been indiscriminately employed both for the plain and decorated parts of the building; not only is the appearance in this case unsightly, but the architectural effect of the edifice is also much impaired by the unequal decomposition of the two materials, the limestone having suffered much less from decay than the sandstone.

1663. " Judging, therefore, from the evidence afforded by buildings of various dates, there would appear to be many varieties of sandstone and limestone employed for building purposes which successfully resist the destructive effects of atmospheric influences; amongst these the sandstones of Stenton, Whitby, Tintern, Rivaulx, and Cragleith, the magnesio-calciferous sandstones of Mansfield, the calciferous sandstone of Tisbury, the crystalline magnesian limestones, or *Dolomites* of Bolsover, Huddlestone and Roche Abbey, the oolites of Byland, Portland, and Ancaster, the Shelly oolites and limestones of Barnack and Ham Hill, and the siliciferous limestone of Chilmark appear to be amongst the most durable. To these, which may all be considered as desirable building materials, we are inclined to add the sandstones of Darley Dale, Humbie, Longannet, and Crowbank, the magnesian limestones of Robin Hood's Well, and the oolite of Ketton, although some of them may not have the evidence of ancient buildings in their favour." The Report upon which we have drawn so largely, and from which we shall extract still larger drafts, then proceeds to close by a preference to limestones on account " of their more general uniformity of tint, their comparatively homogeneous structure, and the facility and economy of their conversion to building purposes," of which it prefers the crystalline; on which account, and its combination with a close approach to the equivalent proportions of carbonate of lime and carbonate of magnesia, for uniformity in structure, facility and economy in conversion, and for advantage of colour, the parties to the Report prefer the magnesian limestone or dolomite of Bolsover Moor and its neighbourhood. The Report deserves every commendation; upon the whole it has been well done, and is the first scientific step the government of this country has ever taken in respect of practical architecture. It, moreover, only cost the moderate sum of £1,400, including the many collections of specimens deposited in various institutions for reference.

1664. The following table presents a synoptical, and, to the architect, important view of the relative value, in every respect, of the principal species of stone which the various provinces of England afford for building purposes. It is taken from the Report so much quoted, the list of stones being considerably abridged. We should direct attention to the fact that facilities of conveyance have greatly modified the cost of each stone in London. It will be well also to notice the valuable " Quarry Returns" of building and other stones, the produce of the United Kingdom of Great Britain and Ireland, published in the *Memoirs of the Geological Survey of Great Britain*, &c., and edited by Robert Hunt, being Part II. for 1858, but published in 1860.

SANDSTONES.

Name of Quarry, and where situated.	Proprietor of Quarry.	Component Parts of Stone.	Colour.	Weight of a Cubic Foot in its ordinary State.	Weight of Block, and the Thickness procurable.	Price per Cubic Foot at the Quarry.	Price per Cubic Foot, delivered in London.	Where used.
				lb. oz.		s. d.	s. d.	
Abercarne and New-bridge, near Newport, Monmouth-shire	Sir B. Hall, Bart.	Quartz and siliceous grains, moderately fine, with argillo-siliceous cement; micaceous, and with remains of fossil plants	Dark bluish grey.	167 15	1 to 10 tons, in thicknesses of 5 feet.	4½d., or 5s. per ton	1 5	Old churches and modern buildings in vicinity; new Docks at Newport and Cardiff.
Ball Cross	- -	Siliceous grains with argillo-siliceous cement; occasionally micaceous, ferruginous.	Ferruginous brown striped, and zoned in deeper tints.	- -	- -	- -	- -	At Chatsworth and Bakewell.
Barbadoes, Tintern, Monmouth-shire.	Duke of Beaufort.	Fine and coarse quartz, and other siliceous grains, with argillo-siliceous cement, ferruginous spots, and plates of mica.	Light greyish brown.	146 12	1 to 10 tons, thickest bed 10 to 12 ft.	10d. to 1s.	- -	Tintern Abbey.
Binnie, Up-hall, and in Linlithgow-shire.	Earl of Buchanan.	Fine quartz grains, with argillo-siliceous cement, micaceous, chiefly in planes of beds.	Brownish grey.	140 1	Bands 14 to 18 ft. thick (3 in number).	1s. 1d. to 2s. for largest blocks.	2 9 to 3 8	New club-house in Prince's Street, Edinburgh, and numerous private houses there and in Glasgow.
Bolton's Quarry, Aislaby, Yorkshire.	Messrs. Elgie and Lawson, as executors of the late Mr. Noble, of York.	Moderately fine siliceous grains, with argillo-siliceous cement, plates of mica, and spots of carbon disseminated.	Warm light brown.	126 11	100 ft. cube; top beds for house building, bottom beds for docks. Beds 3 to 8 ft. thick.	10d. to 1s.	1 9 to 2 1	Whitby Abbey, New University Library at Cambridge, Scarborough and Bridlington Piers, Sheerness and St. Katharine's Docks, &c.
Bramley Fall (Old Quarry), near Leeds, Yorkshire.	Earl of Cardigan.	Quartz grains (often coarse), and decomposed felspar, with argillo-siliceous cement. Mica rare. Small ferruginous spots disseminated.	Light ferruginous brown.	142 3	Up to 18 tons.	- -	- -	In numerous bridges, waterworks, &c.
Calverley, Tunbridge Wells, Kent.	John Ward, Esq., Holwood Park, Bromley, Kent.	Fine siliceous grains, with a slightly calcareous cement.	Variegated browns.	118 1	70 or 80 ft., and upwards to 500. Beds to 3½ ft.	4d. to 6d.	1 2 to 1 4	Upper part of new church at Tunbridge Wells; Catholic Chapel, the Calverley Hotel, new Market House, and Victoria National School, and about 100 houses, &c., at Tunbridge Wells and its vicinity.

SANDSTONES — *continued.*

Name of Quarry, and where situated.	Proprietor of Quarry.	Component Parts of Stone.	Colour.	Weight of a Cubic Foot in its ordinary State.	Weight of Block, and the Thickness procurable.	Price per Cubic Foot at the Quarry.	Price per Cubic Foot, delivered in London.	Where used.
				lb. oz.			s. d.	
CRAIGLEITH, Craigleith Hill, near Edinburgh.	W. R. Ramsay, Esq., of Barnton.	Fine quartz grains, with a siliceous cement, slightly calcareous, occasional plates of mica.	Whitish grey.	145 14	Any practicable length and breadth, from 6 in. to 10 ft. thick.	9d. to 2s. 6d., according to quality.	1 10½ to 3 7½	Used extensively in public buildings in Edinburgh; the College (1580), Registry (1774), courts of law, Custom House, Royal Exchange, National Monument, and numerous churches, and now using for repairs at Blackfriars Bridge.
CRAWBANK, Borrowstones, Linlithgowshire.	Duke of Hamilton.	Fine quartzose grains, with an argillo-siliceous cement, somewhat ferruginous; disseminated mica.	Light ferruginous brown.	129 2	5 ft. thick, 6 ft. broad; 10 ft. long.	1s. for blocks of not more than 5 cubic ft.	2 2	A Roman bridge (A. D. 140.), old church of Kinneil, of the twelfth century.
DUFFIELD BANK, Duffield, Derbyshire.	Mrs. Strathan.	Quartz grains of moderate size, and decomposed felspar, with an argillo-siliceous cement, ferruginous spots, and occasionally plates of mica.	Light brown with dark brown and purplish tints.	132 14	150 ft.; thickest beds about 4 ft.; half the depth brown, half white.	1s. 1d. the white stone, 9d. the brown stone.	- -	St. Mary's Bridge, Reporter Office, Mechanics' Lecture Hall, and Bishop Ryder's Church now building (Derby); also Duffield Bridge and chimney shafts to Grammar School, Birmingham.
DUKE'S QUARRIES, Holt Stanwell Bridge, Derbyshire.	Duke of Devonshire.	Quartz grains, generally coarse, with decomposed felspar, and an argillo-siliceous cement; ferruginous spots.	Red, varied with green, brown, and grey.	144 8	- -	7d.	2 8	Penitentiary at Millbank, and the filling in parts of Waterloo Bridge, London.
ELLAND EDGE, near Halifax, Yorkshire.		Fine quartz grains, with an argillo-siliceous cement, micaceous in planes of beds.	Light grey brown.	153 4				
GATHERLEY MOOR, near Richmond, Yorkshire.	John Warton, Esq. Gisborough.	Quartz grains of moderate size, and an argillo-siliceous cement; ferruginous spots and plates of mica.	Cream.	135 13	1 to 3 tons, a bed 12 ft. deep.	8d. for the 12 ft. bed.	2 1	Aste Hall near Richmond, and Caterick bridges over the Swale; Purse Bridge over the Tees; Skelton Castle, Darlington Town Hall, Lockburn Hall, and numerous modern buildings.

SANDSTONES — *continued.*

Name of Quarry, and where situated.	Proprietor of Quarry.	Component Parts of Stone.	Colour.	Weight of a Cubic Foot in its ordinary State.	Weight of Block, and the Thickness procurable.	Price per Cubic Foot at the Quarry.	Price per Cubic Foot, delivered in London.	Where used.
				lb. oz.		s. d.	s. d.	
GATTON, Gatton, Surrey.	Lord Monson.	Fine siliceous grains, with a calcareo-siliceous cement, containing green silicate of iron and plates of mica.	Greenish light brown.	103 1	35 to 60 ft. cube, from 4 to 10 ft. long.	1 4 to 1 6	- -	Hampton Court and Windsor Castle, &c.; many churches in Surrey; Town Hall and Almshouse Establishment at Croydon; and several modern buildings in the parish of Gatton.
GLAMMIS, Forfarshire.	Earl of Strathmore's trustees.	Siliceous grains of moderate size; cement slightly calcareous; mica abundant in planes of beds.	Purple grey.	161 2	Any practicable size; thickest bed 6 ft.	0 7 to 1 0	about 19s. per ton.	Glammis Castle and Inverquharity Castle, supposed of the tenth century; Cortachy Castle; and in modern buildings; Lendertis House, &c.
HEDDON, near Newcastle, Northumberland.	Mrs. Bewick, near Newcastle upon Tyne.	Coarse quartz grains, and decomposed felspar, with an argillo-siliceous cement, ferruginous spots.	Light brown ochre.	130 11	Beds 4 to 12 ft. thick.	0 6 to 0 10	1 8 to 2 0	Church at Heddon, steeple, 1764; Norman chancel; columns of portico to theatre, and Grey Monument at Newcastle; and nearly all the buildings, ancient and modern, in and about Newcastle.
HOLLINGTON, Staffordshire.	Sir J. Gibbons, Bart., near Staines, Middlesex.	Quartz grains of moderate size, with an argillo-siliceous cement; plates of mica.	Light brownish grey.	133 1	30 to 40 ft. square, and 8 ft. thick.	0 7 to 1 0	2 6	Trentham Hall, Drayton Manor, Heathhouse, and various public and private buildings in Staffordshire; Town Hall, Derby; Mear Hall, Cheshire, &c.
HUMBIE, Humbie, Linlithgowshire.	Earl of Hopetoun.	Fine quartz grains, with siliceous cement; slightly calcareous; mica chiefly in planes of beds.	Pale grey and light brown.	White 140 3 grey 135 13	90 cubic ft. and upwards, if required; thickest bed 8 ft.	1 0 to 1 10	2 6 to 3 2	Newliston House, Kirkliston; Dundas Castle; additions to the Royal Institution; front of Surgeons' Hall, spire of Tron Church, and various other public buildings in Edinburgh; also in Glasgow.
LONGANNET, near Kincardine, in Perthshire.	Trustees of late Lord Keith.	Fine quartz grains, with siliceous cement, containing oxide of iron; a few plates of mica.	Light ferruginous brown.	131 11	4 to 5 tons; thickest beds 5 ft.	0 8 to 2 6	1 8 to 3 6	Staadt House, Amsterdam; Exchange, Edinburgh; Tulle Mare Castle, Perthshire; and part of a street in Perth.

SANDSTONES — *continued.*

Name of Quarry, and where situated.	Proprietor of Quarry.	Component Parts of Stone.	Colour.	Weight of a Cubic Foot in its ordinary State.	Weight of Block, and the Thickness procurable.	Price per Cubic Foot at the Quarry.	Price per Cubic Foot, delivered in London.	Where used.
				lb. oz.		s. d.	s. d.	
MUNLOCHY, in Ross-shire.	John Matheson, Esq., of Bennetsfield.	Fine siliceous grains, with an argillo-siliceous cement; micaceous.	Red and variegated.	160 9	Of large size; beds 2½ to 6 ft. thick.	0 5 to 0 5½	- -	Cathedral Church of Ross at Fortrose, A.D. 1124; Inverness Old Bridge, Cromwell Court, &c.
MYLNEFIELD, or RINGOODIE, near Dundee, in Perthshire.	James Mylne, Esq.	Fine siliceous grains, with a calcareo-argillo-siliceous cement; micaceous in planes of beds.	Purplish grey.	160 0	Any practicable size.	0 9 to 1 5	- -	Old steeple of Dundee, 12th century, well preserved; Royal Asylum of Dundee, &c.; Bell Rock Lighthouse, Royal Asylum of Perth, Kinfauns Castle, Castle Huntley, &c. &c.
PARK SPRING, near Leeds, Yorkshire.	Earl of Cardigan.	Fine quartz grains, and decomposed felspar, with an argillo-siliceous cement; mica chiefly in planes of beds.	Light ferruginous brown.	151 1	10 to 12 ft. long; thickest bed 2 ft. 4 in.	0 7	2 1½ to 2 5	Commercial buildings at Leeds, from the old quarry, which is of exactly similar stone to that of this quarry.
PENSHER, near Houghton-le-Spring, Durham.	Marquess of Londonderry.	Coarse quartz grains, with an argillo-siliceous cement; plates of mica.	Pale whitish brown.	134 5	Any practicable size; thickest bed 20 ft.	0 8¾	1 7	Pensher Chapel; Scotch Church, Sunderland; Sunderland Pier, Seaham Harbour, Victoria Bridge, on the Wear, &c.
PYOTDYKES, near Dundee, Forfarshire.	Alexander Clayhills, Esq., Innergowrie.	Siliceous grains of moderate size, with a calcareo-argillo-siliceous cement; micaceous.	Purplish grey.	162 8	Thickest bed 3 to 4 ft.	0 10 to 1 2	2 1 to 2 5	Extensively for the works at Dundee Harbour, &c.
SCOTGATE HEAD, Huddersfield, Yorkshire.	The freeholders of Onley.	Quartz grains, of moderate size, with an argillo-siliceous cement; mica in planes of beds, and occasional specks of carbon.	Light greenish grey.	158 0	Thickest bed 3 ft. 6 in.	0 8	1 2	York Castle; Bath Hotel, at Huddersfield.
STANCLIFF, or DARLEY DALE, near Bakewell, Derbyshire.	A. H. Heathcote, Esq., Blackwell.	Quartz grains of moderate size, and decomposed felspar, with an argillo-siliceous cement, ferruginous spots, and plates of mica.	Light ferruginous brown.	148 3	Of very large size.	1 5	3 3	Abbey in Darley Dale; Stancliff Hall, Birmingham; Grammar School, Birmingham; and Nottingham Railway Station Houses.
STENTON, near Barnard Castle, Durham.	Duke of Cleveland.	Fine quartz grains, and decomposed felspar, with an argillo-siliceous cement, ferruginous specks, and some plates of mica.	Ferruginous light brown.	142 8	15 to 20 ft. long, 2 ft. to 8 ft. in thickness.	0 5½	1 5	The Round Keep of Barnard Castle; Joint Stock Bank, and Market House, Barnard Castle.

SANDSTONES — *continued.*

Name of Quarry, and where situated.	Proprietor of Quarry.	Component Parts of Stone.	Colour.	Weight of a Cubic Foot in its ordinary State.	Weight of Block, and the Thickness procurable.	Price per Cubic Foot at the Quarry.	Price per Cubic Foot, delivered in London.	Where used.
				lb. oz.		s. d.	s. d.	
WHITBY COMPANY'S AISLABY, near Whitby, Yorkshire.	Mrs. Helen Noble, York.	Siliceous grains of moderate size, with an argillo-siliceous cement ; some plates of mica and spots of carbon disseminated.	Light brown.	126 11 * 123 2	40 × 25 ft.	0 10	1 8	Some parts of Whitby Abbey ; New Library at Cambridge ; Baths and Town Hall at Whitby ; cemetery at Highgate ; Hungerford Market, &c.
WHITBY COMPANY'S EGTON QUARRIES, being *Arncliffe, Julian Park, Proddams,* and *Lease Rigge,* near Whitby.	Robert Cary Elwes, Esq., Great Billings, Northamptonshire.	- - - - *	Pale, to dark brown.	- - 127 14	Arncliffe, 15 × 10 × 9 Proddams, 10 × 8 × 8 Lease Rigge, 10 × 6 × 5	0 11½	1 9½	Grosmont Abbey and Bridge ; Egton Bridge ; London and Birmingham Railway ; Whitby and Pickering Railway.
WHITBY COMPANY'S SNEATON, near Whitby.	Charles Saunders, Esq., Sneaton Castle.	- - - *		134 13	24 × 9 × 3½	1 1	1 11	Parts of Whitby Abbey, and a portion of the parapet of old Blackfriars Bridge, London.
WHITBY COMPANY'S NEWTON DALE, near Whitby.	R. W. Skelton, Esq., near Pickering.	- - - *		131 11	6 ft. by 4 ft. and 18 in.	0 10	1 8	Lewisham Church.

LIMESTONES.

Name of Quarry, and where situated.	Proprietor of Quarry.	Component Parts of Stone.	Colour.	Weight of a Cubic Foot in its ordinary State.	Weight of Block, and the Thickness procurable.	Price per Cubic Foot at the Quarry.	Price per Cubic Foot, delivered in London.	Where used.
				lb. oz.		s. d.	s. d.	
BEER, near Axminster, Devonshire.	Lord Rolle.	Chiefly carbonate of lime, friable, and with partial indurations.	Light tint of brown.	131 12	6 to 7 ft. long, 3 ft. wide, and 2 ft. thick.	- - -	- - -	In the churches of the vicinity ; St. Peter's Church, Exeter, in exposed parts ; Colyton Church, Charmouth, &c.&c.
CHILMARK, near Salisbury, Wiltshire.	Earl of Pembroke.	Carbonate of lime, with a moderate proportion of silica, and occasional grains of silicate of iron.	Light greenish brown.	153 7	10 cwt. to 3 tons. Several beds ; thickest bed about 3 ft.	1 6 to 2 0	4 10 to 5 4	Salisbury Cathedral, Wilton Abbey, and many other ancient and modern buildings in the vicinity.
HOPTON WOOD, near Wirksworth, Derbyshire.	Philip Gall, Esq., Hapton Hall, near Wirksworth.	Compact carbonate of lime, with encrinal fragments abundant.	Warm light grey.	158 7	100 feet cube ; beds vary in thickness from 3 to 10 ft.	3 0 to 4 0	4 10 to 5 10	At Chatsworth, Belvoir Castle, Trentham Hall, Drayton Manor, Birmingham Grammar School, &c.

* From my own experiments.

LIMESTONES — *continued.*

Name of Quarry, and where situated.	Proprietor of Quarry.	Component Parts of Stone.	Colour.	Weight of a Cubic Foot in its ordinary State.	Weight of Block, and the Thickness procurable.	Price per Cubic Foot at the Quarry.	Price per Cubic Foot, delivered in London.	Where used.
				lb. oz.		s. d.	s. d.	
SEACOMBE, near Corfe Castle, Dorsetshire.	William John Bankes, Esq.	Semi-compact carbonate of lime, with fragments of shells.	Light brown.	151 0	The largest 6 to 8 ft., by 2 to 3 ft. by 3 to 4 ft.	1 2½	1 9¼	Lighthouse at Margate; the Clockhouse, Dover Pier; prison at Winchester; at the West India Docks, forty years since; lighthouse now building on the Isle of Wight, &c.
SUTTON, near Bridgend, Glamorganshire.	The Crown, and others.	Compact-carbonate of lime, highly crystalline.	Very light cream.	136 0	6 tons, and upwards; thickest bed 12 ft.	- -	- -	Dunraven Castle, Ogmond Abbey, St. Donats Corty, Neath Abbey, and very ancient buildings in the adjoining counties.
TOTTERNHOE, near Dunstable, Bedfordshire.	James Jaly Wing.	Calcareous and argillaceous matter in about equal portions; structure fine.	Greenish white.	116 8	40 cubic ft. or upwards; 5 to 6 ft. long.	1 3	2 5	Dunstable Priory Curch, Luton, and many other churches in Bedfordshire and Hertfordshire; Woburn Abbey, Fonthill House, Ashridge, &c.

MAGNESIAN LIMESTONES.

Name of Quarry, and where situated.	Proprietor of Quarry.	Component Parts of Stone.	Colour.	Weight of a Cubic Foot in its ordinary State.	Weight of Block, and the Thickness procurable.	Price per Cubic Foot at the Quarry.	Price per Cubic Foot, delivered in London.	Where used.
				lb. oz.		s. d.	s. d.	
BOLSOVER, near Chesterfield, Derbyshire.	Earl Bathurst.	Chiefly carbonate of lime and carbonate of magnesia; semi-crystalline.	Light yellowish brown.	151 11	56 ft. cube, in beds from 8 in. to 2 ft. thick.	0 10	2 0	Southwell Church, and numerous buildings in the vicinity.
BRODSWORTH, near Doncaster, Yorkshire.	Lord Rendlesham.	Chiefly carbonate of lime and carbonate of magnesia, with sub-oolitic grains; friable.	Light brown tint.	133 10	Thickest bed 3 ft. 6 in.	- -	- -	Doncaster Old Church and Mansion-house, Brocklesby Hall, &c.
CADEBY, near Doncaster, Yorkshire.	Sir Joseph Copley, Bart.	Chiefly carbonate of lime and carbonate of magnesia, with sub-oolitic and irregularly formed oolitic grains; friable.	Cream.	126 9	Central beds (the best) 4 ft. thick.	- -	1 10	Day and Martin's, in High Holborn; almshouses at Edgware, &c.

MAGNESIAN LIMESTONES — *continued.*

Name of Quarry, and where situated.	Proprietor of Quarry.	Component Parts of Stone.	Colour.	Weight of a Cubic Foot in its ordinary State.	Weight of Block, and the Thickness procurable.	Price per Cubic Foot at the Quarry.	Price per Cubic Foot, delivered in London.	Where used.
				lb. oz.		s. d.	s. d.	
HUDDLE-STONE, near Sherburne, Yorkshire.	Oliver Gascoigne, Esq., near Abberford.	Chiefly carbonate of lime and carbonate of magnesia, semi-crystalline.	Whitish cream.	137 13	50 to 250 cubic ft. Beds have been met with 4ft. thick.	2 0	3 0	York Minster, Selby Cathedral, Huddlestone Hall, Sherburne Church, Westminster Hall, Galeforth Hall, &c.
JACKDAW CRAIG, near Tadcaster, Yorkshire.	Sir Edward Vavasour, Bart.	Chiefly carbonate of lime and carbonate of magnesia.	Dark cream.	- -	Beds irregular, from a few inches to 3 feet.	- -	- -	York Minster, and probably most of the churches in York; also for the late restorations of York Minster.
ROCHE ABBEY, near Bawtry, Yorkshire.	Earl of Scarborough.	Chiefly carbonate of lime and carbonate of magnesia, with occasional dendritic spots of iron or manganese, semi-crystalline.	Whitish cream.	139 2	8 or 10 tons, thickest bed will work 2ft. 6 in.	0 8 to 1 6	2 1½ 2 11½	Roche Abbey Church, Tickhill Castle, and Church and Bridge, Sandbeck Hall, Selby Hall, two churches at Retford, Bawtry Church, and numerous churches in Yorkshire and Lincolnshire.
SMAWSE, near Tadcaster, Yorkshire. (Bramham Moor).	Thomas Perrott, Esq.	Chiefly carbonate of lime and carbonate of magnesia, slightly crystalline.	Light yellowish brown.	127 8	Largest obtained 8·0 x 3·0 × 30.	0 7	2 1½	Hull Old Church, Ripon Minster, St. Mary's Church and the minster at Beverley, the minster and several churches at York, and a new church at Appleby, in Lincolnshire.

OOLITIC STONES.

Name of Quarry, and where situated.	Proprietor of Quarry.	Component Parts of Stone.	Colour.	Weight of a Cubic Foot in its ordinary State.	Weight of Block, and the Thickness procurable.	Price per Cubic Foot at the Quarry.	Price per Cubic Foot, delivered in London.	Where used.
				lb. oz.		s. d.	s. d.	
ANCASTER, near Sleaford, Lincolnshire.	Mrs. Myers, Grantham.	Fine oolitic grains, cemented by compact, and often crystalline, carbonate of lime.	Cream.	139 4	3 to 5 tons, beds, 18 inches.	0 9 to 1 5	2 7	Wollaton Hall, Belvoir Castle, Belton House, and numerous mansions and churches in Lincolnshire.
BARNACK MILL, near Stamford, Northamptonshire.	Mr. John Martin, Ufford, near Stamford.	Carbonate of lime, compact and oolitic, with shells, often in fragments, coarsely laminated in planes of beds.	Light whitish brown.	136 12	Up to 30 ft., beds, 9 to 18 in.	1 0	2 3	Burleigh House, Peterborough Cathedral, Croyland Abbey, and the greater proportion of churches in Lincolnshire and Cambridgeshire.

OOLITIC STONES — *continued.*

Name of Quarry, and where situated.	Proprietor of Quarry.	Component Parts of Stone.	Colour.	Weight of a Cubic Foot in its ordinary State.	Weight of Blocks and the Thickness procurable.	Price per Cubic Foot at the Quarry.	Price per Cubic Foot, delivered in London.	Where used.
				lb. oz.		s. d.	s. d.	
Bath Lodge Hill, Combe Down, near Bath, Somersetshire.	W. V. Jenkins, Esq., Combe Grove House, Bath.	Chiefly carbonate of lime, in oolitic grains.	Cream.	116 00	12 to 96 ft. cube. Thickest bed, 4½ ft.	0 6	- -	Restoration of Henry VII.'s chapel, twenty years since. Kennet and Avon Canal, and other works.
Bath Baynton Quarry, Box, near Chippenham.	Thomas Strong, of Box, near Chippenham.	Chiefly carbonate of lime, in moderately fine oolitic grains, with fragments of shells (weather bed).	Cream.	123 00	Up to 10 tons. Thickest bed, 5 ft.	0 7	1 11	Laycock Abbey, Longleat, Bowood, south front of Wilton House, Windsor Castle, &c.
Bath (Drewe's Quarry), Monkton Farleigh, near Bath.	Wade Brown, Esq., Monkton Farleigh.	Chiefly carbonate of lime, in oolitic grains of moderate size.	Cream.	122 10	120 to 125 ft. Several beds, the deepest about 4 ft. 2 in. thick.	0 6	1 10	Buckingham New Palace; St. James's Square, Bath.
Cranmore, near Doulting, Wiltshire.	- -	Carbonate of lime, with a few oolitic grains, and an abundance of small shells, commonly in fragments, often crystalline.	Light brown.	134 4	Of large size. The thickest beds will work 20 in.	0 7	- -	Cathedral of Wells, Glastonbury Abbey, &c.
Haydor, near Grantham, Lincolnshire.	John Archer Houblon, Esq., near Bishop's Stortford.	Carbonate of lime, with oolitic grains, often crystalline.	Brownish cream.	133 7	14 ft. × 3 ft. × 4 ft.	0 8	2 4	Lincoln Cathedral, Boston Church, Grantham Church, Newark Church, and most of the churches in the neighbourhood, and in the lower part of Lincolnshire; Culverthorpe House, Belvoir Castle, &c.
Ketton, in Rutlandshire, near Stamford.	Lord Northwick.	Oolitic grains of moderate size, slightly cemented by carbonate of lime.	Dark cream colour.	128 5	Up to 100 ft., beds vary very much: one 3 ft. 6 in. thick, called rag.	1 9	3 4	Cambridge, Bedford, Bury St. Edmund's, Stamford, London, &c.; many of the ancient and modern buildings at Cambridge; also in the modern works of Peterborough and Ely Cathedral, and at St. Dunstan's New Church, in London.
Portland (Trade Quarry), Island of Portland.	Messrs. Weston.	Oolitic carbonate of lime, with a few fragments of shells	Whitish brown.	- -	Any practicable size.	1 4½	2 3	Various public buildings in London.

OOLITIC STONES—continued.

Name of Quarry, and where situated.	Proprietor of Quarry.	Component Parts of Stone.	Colour.	Weight of a Cubic Foot in its ordinary State.	Weight of Block, and the Thickness procurable.	Price per Cubic Foot at the Quarry.	Price per Cubic Foot, delivered in London.	Where used.
				lb. oz.		s. d.	s. d.	
PORTLAND (KING BARROW EAST END QUARRY) adjoining WAYCROFT, Island of Portland.	Messrs. Weston.	Oolitic carbonate of lime, with a few fragments of shells.	Whitish brown.	- -	Any practicable size.	1 4½	2 3	Various public buildings in London.
PORTLAND (VERN-STREET QUARRY), Island of Portland.	Messrs. Weston.	Oolitic carbonate of lime, with a few fragments of shells.	Whitish brown.	134 10 top bed.	Any practicable size.	1 4½	2 3	Various public buildings in London.
PORTLAND (CASTLE'S QUARRY), Island of Portland.	Messrs. Weston.	Oolitic carbonate of lime, with a few fragments of shells.	Whitish brown.	- -	Any practicable size.	1 4½	2 3	Various public buildings in London.
PORTLAND (WAYCROFT QUARRIES), Island of Portland.	The Crown, on lease to Messrs. Stewards and Co.	Oolitic carbonate of lime, with disseminated fragments of shells.	Whitish brown.	135 8 top bed.	Any practicable size.	1 4½	2 3	Goldsmiths' Hall, Reform Club House, and other public buildings in London.
PORTLAND (MAGGOTT QUARRY).	The Crown, on lease to Messrs. Stewards and Co.	Oolitic carbonate of lime, with fragments of shells.	Whitish brown.	- -	Any practicable size.	1 4½	2 2	Various public buildings in London.
PORTLAND (GOSLING'S QUARRY).	Messrs. Stewards and Co.	Oolitic carbonate of lime, with fragments of shells.	Whitish brown.	126 13 Roach	Any practicable size.	1 4½	2 3	Several public buildings in London.
PORTLAND (GROVE QUARRY BOWERS).	Messrs. Stewards and Co.	Oolitic carbonate of lime, with numerous fragments of shells.	Whitish brown.	147 10 best bed. 145 9 carf.	Any practicable size.	1 4½	2 3	St. Paul's Cathedral, and several churches in London, built during the reign of Queen Anne.
PORTLAND (GROVE QUARRY, REDCROFT).	Messrs. Stewards and Co.	Oolitic carbonate of lime, with a few fragments of shells.	Whitish brown.	- -	Any practicable size.	1 4½	2 0	St. Paul's Cathedral, and many churches in London, of Queen Anne's reign.

Of the Portland stones, it is to be observed generally, that the dirt bed is full of fossil roots, trunks, and branches of trees, in the position of their former growth. The top cap is a white, hard, and closely compacted limestone. The skull cap is irregular in texture, and is a well-compacted limestone. The roach beds are always incorporated with the freestone beds, that invariably lie below them, and are full of cavities formed by the moulds of shells and the like. The top bed is the best stone, the bottom one ill cemented, and will not stand the weather. A middle or curf bed occurs only in the southernmost quarries on the east cliff; it is soft to the north, and hard to the south. The good workable stone in the east cliff quarries is generally less in depth than in the same bed in the west cliff quarries, but the east cliff stone is harder, more especially to the south of the island. The stone, even in the same quarries, varies considerably. That which contains flints will not stand the weather. The bottom bed on the west cliff is not a durable stone, though sold as a good stone in the London market. The best stone is in the north-eastern part of the island; the worst in the south-western part. The annual consumption of the whole of the quarries in the island is equal to an area of one acre of the good workable stone, or about 24,000 tons. The entire area unworked is about 2000 acres. There are 56 quarries in the island, and about 240 quarrymen employed, of which number Messrs. Stewards employ usually about 138. (See Subsection 1666f. et seq.)

OOLITIC STONES — *continued.*

Name of Quarry, and where situated.	Proprietor of Quarry.	Component Parts of Stone.	Colour.	Weight of a Cubic Foot in its ordinary State.	Weight of Block, and the Thickness procurable.	Price per Cubic Foot at the Quarry.	Price per Cubic Foot, delivered in London.	Where used.
				lb. oz.		*s. d.*	*s. d.*	
TAYNTON, or TEYNTON, near Burford, Oxon.	Lord Dynevor.	Carbonate of lime, partly oolitic and friable, with very small fragments of shells, irregularly laminated.	Streaky brown.	135 15	Any practicable size. Thickest bed, about 7 ft.	0 10 to 1 0	2 4	Blenheim, Cornbury Park, Barrington Park, the interior of St. Paul's and many other churches in London and Oxford, and in various bridges in Oxfordshire.
WASS, near Thirsk, Yorkshire.	Martin Stapleton, Esq.	Compact carbonate of lime, with oolitic grains and an argillo-calcareous cement; carbon disseminated.	Brown.	141 11 soft. 162 8 hard.	Beds variable, about 16 in.	- - -	- - -	West front and a large proportion of Byland Abbey.
WINDRUSH, near Burford, Gloucestershire.	Lord Shelburne.	Fine oolitic grains, with calcareous cement, and a few fragments of shells.	Cream.	118 2 soft. 135 15 hard.	5 to 40 ft. Thickest bed, 2 ft. 6 in.	0 8	2 7	Windrush Church, Barrington House, and all the old buildings within many miles of the quarry.

1665. The following very useful enumeration of the stones used in buildings of the island, arranged under that head, and divided into the sorts of stone employed in them, we add, *verbatim*, from the Report which we have so much used. The heads are under SANDSTONE buildings, LIMESTONE buildings, and MAGNESIAN LIMESTONE buildings.

SANDSTONE BUILDINGS.

BAKEWELL, Derbyshire. The houses generally are of sandstone, and in fair condition. A new bank now erecting of sandstone from Bakewell Edge.

BAKEWELL CHURCH (14th century), of a sandstone of the vicinity, very much decomposed.

BARNARD CASTLE, Durham (14th century). Circular keep, apparently of Stenton stone, in excellent condition. In modern works, the Joint Stock Bank and Market-house of Stenton stone, in good condition.

BELPER NEW CHURCH, Derbyshire. Built 10 years since, of sandstone from Hungerhill, in an incipient state (in parts) of decomposition.

BLANDFORD PARISH CHURCH, Dorsetshire (1769). Of a green siliceous fine-grained sandstone, the dressings being of a stone similar to the Portland oolite; the former much decomposed; the latter in very good condition. Town Hall, about 80 years old, of stone similar to the Portland oolite, in good condition.

BRANCEPETH CASTLE, Durham. Of ancient date, of sandstone of the vicinity; recently restored extensively; older parts in various states of decomposition.

BRIAVEL'S, ST., CASTLE, Glocestershire. In ruins (13th or 14th century). Entrance gateway (the chief remains of the castle) built of red sandstone, decomposed.

BRISTOL CATHEDRAL (13th and 14th centuries). Built of red sandstone and a yellow limestone (magnesian ?) strangely intermixed; the red sandstone in all cases decomposed, the limestone more rarely decayed; the tracery, &c. of the windows, which are of the limestone, are in good condition; but the pinnacles and other dressings, which are of the same material, are much decomposed. The east end of the cathedral is a remarkable instance of the decay and preservation of the two stones employed. Norman gateway, west of the cathedral (the upper part of the 15th century); the Norman archway and its enrichments, which are of a very florid character, built of yellow limestone (magnesian ?), in excellent condition.

BYLAND ABBEY (12th century). In part of a siliceous grit (principally in the interior), and in part (chiefly on the exterior) of a compact oolite, from the Wass quarries in the

vicinity. The west front, which is of the oolite, is in perfect condition, even in the dog's-teeth and other florid decorations of the doorways, &c. This building is *covered generally* with lichens.

CARLISLE. Ancient buildings: Cathedral (13th century), of red sandstone, in various states of decomposition. Modern buildings: Many of red sandstone, more or less in a state of decomposition.

CASTLE HOWARD, Yorkshire. Built generally of a siliceous fine-grained sandstone from the park; generally in good condition, but in some parts, such as the parapets, cupolas, and chimney shafts, much decomposed. The pilasters of the north front from a quarry at Appleton; in good condition, except where subjected to alternations of wet and dry, as in the plinths, where there are signs of decomposition. The stables are of Appleton stone, and in good condition.

CHATSWORTH HOUSE, Derbyshire. Original house built of Bell Crop sandstone from Bakewell Edge, not in very good condition, particularly in the lower parts of the building. In the recent additions the same stone is employed, together with that of Bailey Moor and Lindrop Hill.

CHEPSTOW CASTLE, Monmouthshire (11th and 12th centuries, with additions of the 14th century). Of mountain limestone and old red sandstone; the former in good condition; the latter decomposed. Dressings of doors, windows, archways, and quoins are for the most part of magnesian limestone, in perfect condition; the remainder is of red sandstone, and is generally much decomposed. Chapel (of the 12th century); mouldings and carvings of the windows, &c., which are of magnesian limestone, are in perfect condition.

COXWOLD CHURCH, Yorkshire (15th century). Generally of fine siliceous grit of the vicinity, and in part of a calcareous nature. Tower in good condition; porch decomposed; lichens abundant on the north side.

DERBY. St. Peter's Church (13th century), of the variegated coarse sandstone of the vicinity, similar to that of Little Eaton. The whole in bad condition; but the red stones less so than the grey or white. St. Almund's Church (of the 14th century), of a coarse sandstone of the vicinity, in a very decomposed state, to the obliteration of the mouldings and other details; it has lately been scraped and painted, to preserve it from further destruction. All Saints Church (tower of the 15th century), of sandstone, similar to that of Duffield Bank, partly in fair condition, and partly much decomposed, particularly the great western entrance. The body of the church, built 110 years since, of sandstone, in part decomposing. Modern buildings: Town Hall, of sandstone from Morley Moor, built a few years since, in very good condition.

DURHAM CATHEDRAL (11th and 12th centuries). Of a sandstone of the vicinity, elected indiscriminately, and in all stages of decomposition; few stones are quite perfect. CASTLE (of the 11th century). Of similar stone, and in a similar state.

EASBY ABBEY, Yorkshire (13th and 14th centuries). Of sandstone of the vicinity; mouldings and carvings decomposed and in part obliterated. Walls built very rudely, and in various states of decomposition; some parts, however, maintain their original surface.

ECCLESTON ABBEY, Yorkshire (13th century). Of stone similar to that of the Stenton quarry. The mouldings and other decorations, such even as the dog's-teeth enrichments, are in perfect condition.

EDINBURGH. Ancient buildings: Holyrood Chapel (12th century), of sandstone from the vicinity, in part much decomposed; in other parts, such as the west door, almost perfect. The palace (built in the 16th and 17th centuries) of similar stone, generally in good condition, the older parts being slightly decomposed. The oldest part of the Tron Church (1641), of sandstone, much decomposed. A house on the Castle Hill (1591), of sandstone, only slightly decomposed.

Modern buildings, wholly erected of sandstones from the Cragleith, Red Hall, Humbie, and Binnie quarries, for the most from the first-mentioned quarry. None of them exhibit any appearance of decomposition, with the exception of ferruginous stains, which are produced upon some stones. Among the oldest is the Registry Office, which is of Cragleith stone, and built above sixty years since; it is in a perfect state.

FOUNTAIN'S ABBEY, Yorkshire (11th and 12th centuries, with additions of the 16th century). Of coarse sandstone of the vicinity, generally in bad condition, particularly the west front, which is much decomposed. The nave and transept, which are the earliest portions of the building, are the best preserved.

FOUNTAIN'S HALL, Yorkshire (1677). Of sandstone of the vicinity, and magnesian limestone in the dressings. The whole in fair condition.

FOREST OF DEAN, Gloucestershire. Park End new church, built fifteen years since, of sandstone, similar to that of Colford. No appearance of decomposition.

GLASGOW. Ancient buildings: High Church (12th century), sandstone of the vicinity, generally very much decomposed, particularly on the south side Old quadrangle of the College (James II.), of sandstone, decomposed.

Modern buildings: Hunterian Museum (1804); superstructure said to be of stone from the President quarry; slight traces of decomposition on the south-west front. The basement of another sandstone, in a more advanced state of decomposition; other parts of the building are in an almost perfect state. The other buildings are generally erected of stone from the Giffneuch and other quarries in the immediate neighbourhood, except the new Exchange buildings, which are of stone from the Humbie quarry, thirty miles from Glasgow, recently erected, in which there are not any apparent symptoms of decomposition.

GLOUCESTER CATHEDRAL (Norman for the greater part, altered and cased in the 15th century), built of a fine-grained and ill-cemented oolite, a shelly oolite, and a red sandstone (north side) intermixed, of which the former constitutes the greater portion. The tower (15th century), of shelly oolite, in perfect condition. The early turrets of the south transepts are also in good condition. The body of the building is much decomposed. The great cloister is built of the same materials as the cathedral. The moulded and decorated work is in good condition, the other parts are more or less decomposed. The small cloister is built of a fine oolite with a compact cement, and is in good condition. THE NEW BRIDGE, of Whitchurch sandstone, parapets of Ruordean fine-grained sandstone, in good condition.

HADDON HALL, Derbyshire (15th and 16th centuries). Of a fine-grained sandstone, similar to that of Lindrop Hill. The dressings, parapets, chimney shafts, quoins, &c. are wrought and rubbed; the remainder of the walls is of rough walling. The whole in fair condition.

HARROWGATE. Cheltenham Pump Room, of sandstone from Woodhouse, near Leeds. Built recently. In good condition. Swan Hotel and other modern buildings, of a coarse sandstone of the vicinity; generally in good condition.

HARDWICKE HALL, Derbyshire. (1597.) Of a fine-grained sandstone, chiefly from a quarry in the hill on which the house is built, intermixed with a calciferous grit, similar to that of Mansfield; generally in good condition. The ashler is in parts decomposed, especially where it is set on edge.

HOWDEN CHURCH, Yorkshire (15th century); partly of magnesian limestone, of a deep yellow colour, and partly of a coarse siliceous grit, of a ferruginous colour. Dressings and enrichments and the central tower are of the former stone; generally decomposed, particularly at the top of the tower. The other parts of the building, which are of the grit, are very much decomposed.

KIRKSTALL ABBEY, Yorkshire (11th century). Of coarse sandstone of the vicinity, in various stages of decomposition according to the aspect. The east side is in fair condition; some of the zig-zag enrichments and early capitals and other enrichments of mouldings are in perfect condition. The windows of the chancel and tower (inserted in the 16th century) of a yellow sandstone, are for the most part gone, and what remains is much decomposed.

MANSFIELD TOWN HALL, Nottinghamshire. Built three years since, of magnesio-calciferous sandstone from Mansfield: no appearance of decomposition.

NEWCASTLE-UPON-TYNE. Ancient buildings: St. Nicholas' Church (14th century), of sandstone of the vicinity, similar to that of the Heddon Quarry, very much decomposed. Parts restored within the last century, with the same stone, now decomposing. The upper part of the tower and spire restored within the last five years, and painted to preserve the stone from decay. Other ancient buildings, of the same stone, more or less in a state of decomposition, according to the date of their erection.

Modern buildings, built within the last 25 years, of sandstone from the Felling and Church quarries at Gateshead and the Kenton quarry: parts already show symptoms' of decomposition.

PONTEFRACT CASTLE, Yorkshire (14th century). Built generally of a coarse grit, of a dark brown colour, occasionally mixed with an inferior magnesian limestone. The whole in a very decomposed state, more particularly the sandstone, in which all traces of the original surface are effaced. Fragments of magnesian limestone are embedded in several parts of the walls, with mouldings of the 12th century, in perfect condition.

RABY CASTLE, Durham (14th century). Of sandstone of the vicinity: parts in a perfect state, others slightly decomposed.

RICHMOND CASTLE, Yorkshire (11th century). The keep, of sandstone, similar to that of Gatherly Moor, generally in good condition; mouldings and carvings in columns of window in a perfect state.

RIPON, Yorkshire. An obelisk in the market-place (1781), of coarse sandstone, much decomposed in laminations parallel to the exposed faces.

RIPON CATHEDRAL. Lower part, east end, and south-east angle (Norman), of coarse sandstone of the vicinity, in good condition. The west front, the transepts, and tower (of the 12th and 13th centuries), of the coarse sandstone of the vicinity, in fair condition. The mouldings, although generally decomposed, are not effaced. The dog's-teeth ornaments in most parts nearly perfect. The aisles of the naves, the clerestory, and the choir (of the 14th and 15th centuries), of coarse sandstone and magnesian limestone intermixed, not in good condition; the latter stone, on the south side, often in fair condition. The lower parts of the building generally, but particularly the west fronts, which are of coarse sandstone, are very much decomposed.

RIVAULX ABBEY, Yorkshire (12th century). Of a sandstone at Hollands, one mile from the ruins; generally in excellent condition. West front slightly decomposed; south front remarkably perfect, even to the preservation of the original toolmarks.

SHAFTESBURY, Dorsetshire. St. Peter's Church (15th century). Of a green siliceous sandstone, from quarries half a mile south of the church. The whole building much decomposed. The tower is bound together by iron, and is unsafe, owing to the inferior quality of the stone.

SPOFFORTH CASTLE, Yorkshire (14th century). Of coarse red sandstone; more or less, but generally much, decomposed. The dressings of the windows and doors, of a semi-crystalline magnesian limestone, are in perfect state, the mouldings and enrichments being exquisitely sharp and beautiful.

TINTERN ABBEY (13th century). Considerable remains of red and grey sandstones of the vicinity, in part laminated. In unequal condition, but for the most part in perfect condition; covered with grey and green lichens.

TISBURY CHURCH (13th and 14th centuries; the lower part of the tower of the 12th century). Of calciferous limestone from Tisbury. The dressings are composed of stone throughout, in perfect condition. The ashlar variable; in part much decomposed; the undecomposed portions are covered with lichens. Tombstones in the churchyard generally in good condition, some being more than a century old. The houses of the village built generally of the Tisbury stone, and are in very good condition. The whole covered with lichens.

WAKEFIELD PARISH CHURCH, Yorkshire (tower and spire of the 16th century). Of sandstone, much decomposed. The body of the church, of recent date, of sandstone strongly laminated, and generally decomposed between the laminæ.

WHITBY ABBEY (13th century). Of stone similar to that of Aislaby Brow, in the vicinity; generally in good condition, with the exception of the west front, which is very much decomposed. The stone used is of two colours, brown and white; the former, in all cases, more decomposed than the latter. The dog's-teeth and other enrichments in the east front are in good condition.

LIMESTONE BUILDINGS.

BATH. Abbey church (1576), built of an oolite in the vicinity. The tower is in fair condition. The body of the church, in the upper part of the south and west sides, much decomposed. The lower parts, formerly in contact with buildings, are in a more perfect state; the reliefs in the west front of Jacob's ladder are in parts nearly effaced. Queen's Square, north side, and the obelisk in the centre, built above 100 years since, of an oolite with shells, in fair condition. Circus (built about 1750), of an oolite in the vicinity, generally in fair condition, except those portions which have a west and southern aspect, where the most exposed parts are decomposed. Crescent (built above 50 years since), of an oolite of the vicinity, generally in fair condition, except in a few places, where the stone appears to be of inferior quality.

BRISTOL CATHEDRAL (of the 13th and 14th centuries). Built of red sandstone and apparently a yellow limestone (magnesian?) strangely intermixed. The red sandstone in all cases decomposed; the limestone more rarely decayed. The tracery, &c. of the windows, which are of the limestone, are in good condition, but the pinnacles and dressings of the same material much decomposed. The east end of the cathedral is a remarkable instance of the decay and preservation of the two stones employed. Norman gateway, west of the cathedral (the upper part of the 15th century), the Norman archway and its enrichments, which are of a very florid character, built of yellow limestone (magnesian?), in excellent condition.

———, ST. MARY REDCLIFFE (tower of the 12th century; body of the church of the 15th century). Of oolitic limestone, from Dundry; very much decomposed.

BURLEIGH HOUSE (15th century). Of a shelly oolite (Barnack rag), in excellent condition throughout. The late additions are of Ketton stone.

BYLAND ABBEY, Yorkshire (12th century). In part of a siliceous grit (principally in the interior), and in part (chiefly on the exterior) of a compact oolite, from the Wass quarries in the vicinity. The west front, which is of the oolite, is in perfect condition,

even in the dog's-teeth and other florid decorations of the doorways, &c. This building is generally covered with lichens.

COLLEY WESTON CHURCH, Northamptonshire (14th century). Of a shelly oolite (Barnack rag), in perfect condition throughout.

DORCHESTER. St. Peter's Church (15th century). Of laminated oolite, somewhat similar to that of Portland, and of a shelly limestone, somewhat resembling that of Hamhill. The latter used in pinnacles, parapets, and dressings. The whole in a decomposed state.

GLASTONBURY — Abbey. Joseph of Arimathea's Chapel. Considerable ruins; Norman, of shelly limestone, similar to that of Doulting; generally in good condition; the zig-zag and other enrichments perfect; the capitals of the columns, corbels, &c. are of blue lias, much decomposed, and in some cases have disappeared. The *Church.* Considerable remains of the choir, and a small portion of the nave (11th century), of shelly limestone, similar to that of Doulting, in good condition. *St. Benedict's Parish Church* (14th century). Of limestone, similar to that of Doulting, in good condition. *St. John the Baptist's Parish Church* (15th century). Of stone similar to that of Doulting, generally in fair condition.

GLOCESTER — Cathedral, (Norman for the greater part, altered and cased in the 15th century). Built of a fine-grained and ill-cemented oolite, a shelly oolite, and a red sandstone (north side) intermixed, the former constituting the greatest portion of the edifice. The tower (15th century), of shelly oolite, in perfect condition. The early turrets of the south transept are also in good condition. The body of the building is much decomposed. The great cloister is built of the same materials as the cathedral. The moulded and decorated work is in good condition; the other parts are more or less decomposed. The great cloister is built of a fine oolite, with a compact cement, and is in good condition. *St. Nicholas's Church* (body Norman; tower and spire, 15th century), of a shelly and inferior kind of oolite intermixed, and in unequal condition. *St. Michael's Church* (15th century), built of same stone as that of St. Nicholas, and in the same condition.

GRANTHAM CHURCH (13th century). Lofty tower and spire at the west end. Built of an oolite, similar to that of Ancaster, in good condition, more especially the tower, except as to some portions of the base mouldings.

KETTON CHURCH, Rutlandshire. (West entrance door, Norman; tower of the 12th or 13th century; nave, aisles, and chancel of the 14th century). Of a shelly oolite (Barnack rag), in good condition. Dog's-teeth, carved corbels, and other enrichments in a perfect state.

KETTERING CHURCH (14th and 15th centuries). Of a shelly oolite, fine-grained, the greater portion resembling Barnack rag. The tower and spire in perfect condition. The body of the church in parts slightly decomposed.

KIRKHAM PRIORY, Yorkshire (13th century). Inconsiderable remains. The western front and great entrance slightly decomposed throughout; the portions which remain of the body of the church very perfect, but many of the stones are much decomposed. The stone is very similar to that of the Hildenly quarry. The whole is covered with lichens.

LINCOLN CATHEDRAL (the minster generally of the 12th and 13th centuries). Of oolitic and calcareous stone of the vicinity; generally in fair condition, more especially the early portions of the west front. The ashler and plain dressings of the south front are, however, much decomposed. The mouldings and carvings of the east front are in a perfect state. *Roman Gate,* of a ferruginous oolite, in fair condition. *The Castle Gateway* (13th century), of an oolitic limestone; ashler much decomposed, dressings perfect.

MELTON OLD CHURCH, Yorkshire (12th century). Light semi-compact limestone, similar to that of the Hildenly quarry; generally in good condition, particularly the great west door (of the 11th century), where the zig-zag and other enrichments are perfect. Some stones are much decomposed.

MONTACUTE, Somersetshire — Parish Church (15th century). Of Hamhill stone, in perfect condition, covered with lichens. The Abbey (15th century). Supposed abbot's house and gateway, of Hamhill stone, in good condition. *Montacute House* (17th century), of Hamhill stone, in excellent condition.

MARTOCK CHURCH, Somersetshire (15th century). Of a shelly ferruginous brown limestone from Hamhill, in good condition, except the plinth and base mouldings, which are much decomposed. Covered with lichens.

NEWARK CHURCH (15th century; the tower, in part, of the 12th century). Of an oolite, similar to that of Ancaster; generally in fair condition, with the exception of parts of the base mouldings. The building is covered with a grey lichen. *The Castle* (Norman, with additions in the 15th century). Chiefly of sandstone of the vicinity; in unequal condition. A large portion of the dressings of the windows, &c. are of oolite,

probably from Ancaster. *Town Hall* (50 or 60 years old). Built of the Ancaster oolite; in good condition; in some blocks, however, there is an appearance of lamination, where decomposition has to a slight extent taken place.

Oxford Cathedral, Norman (12th century). Chiefly of a shelly oolite, similar to that of Taynton; Norman work in good condition, the latter work much decomposed. *Merton College Chapel* (13th century). Of a shelly oolite, resembling Taynton stone; in good condition generally. *New College Cloisters* (14th century). Of a shelly oolite (Taynton), in good condition. The whole of the colleges, churches, and other public buildings of Oxford, erected within the last three centuries, are of oolitic limestone from Heddington, about one mile and a half from the university, and are all, more or less, in a deplorable state of decomposition. The plinth, string-courses, and such portions of the buildings as are much exposed to the action of the atmosphere, are mostly of a shelly oolite from Taynton, fifteen miles from the university, and are universally in good condition.

Paul's, St., Cathedral, London (finished about 1700). Built of Portland oolite, from the Grove quarries on the east cliff. The building generally in good condition, especially the north and east fronts. The carvings of flowers, fruit, and other ornaments are throughout nearly as perfect as when first executed, although much blackened; on the south and west fronts, larger portions of the stone may be observed of their natural colour than on the north and east fronts, occasioned by a very slight decomposition of the surface. The stone in the drum of the dome, and in the cupola above it, appears not to have been so well selected as the rest; nevertheless scarcely any appreciable decay has taken place in those parts.

Pickering Church, Yorkshire (13th and 14th centuries). Oolite rock of the neighbourhood; very much decomposed; the windows, mullions, and buttress angles obliterated.

Pickering Castle (14th century). The walls of the oolite of the neighbourhood, and the quoins of a siliceous grit. The whole in fair condition.

Portland, Dorsetshire — New Church (built 1766), of Portland oolite, fine roach; in a perfect state, still exhibiting the original tool marks. Wakeham Village, Tudor House, of Portland oolite, in excellent condition. *Old Church*, in ruins, near Bow and Arrow Castle (15th century), of Portland oolite, resembling top bed; in very good condition; original chisel marks still appear on the north front. *Bow and Arrow Castle.* Considerable remains of the keep, many centuries old, of Portland oolite; the ashlar resembles the top bed, and is in perfect condition; the quoins and corbels of the machicolated parapet appear to be of the cap bed of Portland oolite, and are in good condition.

Salisbury Cathedral (13th century). Of siliciferous limestone from Chillmark quarry. The entire building is in excellent condition, except the west front, which in parts is slightly decomposed. The building generally covered with lichens.

Sandysfoot Castle, near Weymouth (temp. Hen. VIII.). Considerable remains of keep, chiefly of Portland oolite, partly of the top bed and partly of the fine roach; generally in excellent condition, with the exception of a few and apparently inferior stones. The inside ashlar of the walls is of large-grained oolite, apparently from the immediate vicinity of the castle, much decomposed.

Somerton Church, Somersetshire (14th century). Built chiefly of blue lias; the quoins, buttresses, parapets, and other dressings of a coarse ferruginous shelly limestone, in various stages of decay. The parapet of the clerestory of a lighter-coloured stone, in good condition.

Stamford — St. Mary's Church (13th century). Of a shelly oolite (Barnack rag), in fair condition. *St. John's Church* (14th century). Of similar stone, ill selected, and consequently decomposed in parts and in laminations, according to the direction of the beds of shells. *St. Martin's Church* (14th century). Of similar stone, in good condition. *All Saints* (lower part of the body of the church 13th century; the remainder 15th century). Tower and spire in fine condition; body of the church decomposed. *Standwell's Hotel*, built twenty-four years since of an oolite similar to that of Ketton; in perfect condition. *St. Michael's New Church.* Built four years since; no appearance of decomposition.

Wells, The Cathedral. West front (13th century), upper part of tower (14th century), of shelly limestone, similar to that of Doulting, generally decomposed, but not to any great extent. North flank (porch and transept 13th century, the remainder of the 14th century), of similar stone, in good condition, except lower part of flank and west tower. The central tower (of the 14th century) in very good condition. South side of the cathedral generally in good condition. *Chapter House* (13th century, with additions of the 15th century). The whole in good condition excepting the west front of the gateway, which is decomposed. Close gates (15th century) much de-

composed, but especially on the south and south-west. The cloisters (15th century) generally decomposed, particularly the mullions and tracery.

WESTMINSTER ABBEY (13th century). Built of several varieties of stone, similar to that of Gatton or Ryegate, which is much decomposed, and also of Caen stone, which is generally in bad condition; a considerable portion of the exterior, especially on the north side, has been restored at various periods, nevertheless abundant symptoms of decay are apparent. The cloisters, built of several kinds of stone, are in a very mouldering condition, except where they have been recently restored with Bath and Portland stones. The west towers, erected in the beginning of the 18th century with a shelly variety of Portland oolite, exhibit scarcely any appearance of decay. Henry the Seventh's Chapel, restored about twenty years since with Combe Down Bathstone, is already in a state of decomposition.

WINDRUSH CHURCH (15th century). Of an oolite from the immediate vicinity; in excellent condition. A Norman door on the north side, enriched with the bird's-beak and other characteristic ornaments, is in perfect condition. Tombstones in the churchyard, very highly enriched and bearing the dates of 1681, 1690, apparently of Windrush stone, are in perfect condition.

WYKE CHURCH, Dorsetshire (15th century). Of oolite, similar to Portland, the whole in good condition, except the mullions, tracery, and dressings of doors and windows, which are constructed of a soft material, and are all decomposed. On the south side, the ashler is in part covered with rough-cast. The entire building is thickly covered with lichens.

MAGNESIAN LIMESTONE BUILDINGS.

BEVERLEY, Yorkshire. The minster (12th, 13th, and 14th centuries), of magnesian limestone from Bramham Moor, and an oolite from Newbold; the former, which is used in the west tower, central tower, and more ancient parts of the minster, generally in good condition; but in other parts of the building the same material is decomposed. The Newbold stone, chiefly employed on the east side, is altogether in a bad condition. Some of the pinnacles are of Oulton sandstone, and are in bad condition. The building is partly covered with lichens. *St. Mary's Church* (14th century), now in course of restoration, of magnesian limestone and oolite, supposed to be from Bramham Moor and Newbold, respectively. The ancient parts are in a very crumbling state, even to the obliteration of many of the mouldings and enrichments.

BOLSOVER CASTLE, Derbyshire (1629). Mostly in ruins; of magnesian limestone of several varieties, and of a calcareous fine-grained sandstone. The dressings, which are generally of sandstone, are much decomposed, in some instances to the entire obliteration of the mouldings and other decorations, and to the destruction of the form of the columns, rustications, &c. Most of the string courses, a portion of the window dressings, and the ashler, which are of magnesian limestone, are generally in excellent condition.

BOLSOVER CHURCH, Derbyshire (15th century). Of a magnesio-calciferous sandstone, more or less in a decomposed state throughout.

CHEPSTOW CASTLE, Monmouthshire (11th and 12th centuries, with additions of the 14th century). Of mountain limestone and old red sandstone; the former in good condition, the latter decomposed. Dressings of door, window, archway, and quoins are for the most part of magnesian limestone, and in perfect condition. The remainder is of red sandstone, and is generally much decomposed. Chapel (of the 12th century), mouldings and carvings of windows, &c., which are of magnesian limestone, in perfect condition.

DONCASTER (OLD) CHURCH (15th century). Of an inferior magnesian limestone, generally much decomposed, more especially in the tower, and on the south and west sides; now under general and extensive repair.

HEMINGBOROUGH CHURCH, Yorkshire (15th century). Of a white crystalline magnesian limestone. The entire building is in a perfect state, even the spire, where no traces of decay are apparent.

HOWDEN CHURCH, Yorkshire (15th century). Partly of magnesian limestone of a deep yellow colour, and partly of a coarse siliceous grit of a ferruginous colour. Dressings and enrichments, and the central tower, are of the former stone, generally decomposed, particularly at the top of the tower. The other parts of the edifice, built of the grit, are very much decomposed.

HUDDLESTONE HALL, Yorkshire (15th century). Of semi-crystalline magnesian limestone from the neighbouring quarry. In excellent condition, even to the entire preservation of the mouldings of the chapel window in the south-west front. The outer gate piers in the fence wall, also of magnesian limestone, very much decomposed.

KNARESBOROUGH CASTLE, Yorkshire (12th century). Magnesian limestone, carious in part;

generally in very good condition, except on the south and south-west portions of the circular turrets, where the surface is much decomposed. The mouldings generally are in a perfect state. The joints of the masonry, which is executed with the greatest care, are remarkably close. The stone of the keep, which is of a deep brown colour, and much resembles sandstone, is in good condition, especially on the south-west side.

KONINGSBOROUGH CASTLE, Yorkshire (Norman). Coarse-grained and semi-crystalline magnesian limestone, from the hill eastward of the castle; in perfect condition. The masonry is executed with great care, the joints very close, but the mortar within them has disappeared.

RIPON CATHEDRAL. Lower part, east end, south-east angle (Norman), of coarse sandstone from the vicinity, in good condition. The west front, the transepts, and tower (of the 12th and 13th centuries), of coarse sandstone of the vicinity, in fair condition. The mouldings, although generally decomposed, are not effaced. The dog's-teeth ornament in most parts nearly perfect. The aisles of the nave, the clerestory, and the choir (of the 14th and 15th centuries), of coarse sandstone and magnesian limestone intermixed, not in good condition. The latter stone, on the south side, often in fair condition. The lower parts of the building generally, particularly the west fronts, which are of coarse sandstone, are much decomposed. An obelisk, in the market-place (1781), of coarse sandstone, is much decomposed, and in laminations parallel to the exposed faces.

ROBIN HOOD'S WELL, Yorkshire (1740). A rusticated building, of magnesian limestone, in perfect condition.

ROCHE ABBEY, Yorkshire (12th century). Inconsiderable remains, of semi-crystalline magnesian limestone from the neighbouring quarry, generally in fair condition. The mouldings and decorated portions are perfect. Gate-house (12th century) generally decomposed, with the exception of the dressings and mouldings, which are perfect.

SELBY CHURCH, Yorkshire (nave and lower part of the tower of the 11th century; the west front and aisles of the 12th century; and the choir with its aisles of the 14th century). The Norman portion of the building, which is of grey magnesian limestone, is in excellent condition, particularly the lower part. The early English portions of the building are also of magnesian limestone, and in a partially decomposed state. The later portions of the building, which also are of magnesian limestone, are much decomposed and blackened.

SOUTHWELL CHURCH, Notts (of the 10th century). Of magnesian limestone, similar to that of Bolsover Moor, in perfect condition. The mouldings and enrichments of the doorway appear as perfect as if just completed. The choir, which is of the 12th century, and built of a stone similar to that of Mansfield, is generally in good condition.

SPOFFORTH CASTLE, Yorkshire (14th century). Of coarse red sandstone, generally much decomposed. The dressings of the windows and doors, of a semi-crystalline magnesian limestone, are in a perfect state, the mouldings and enrichments being eminently sharp and beautiful.

STUDLEY PARK, Yorkshire. Banquetting house, about 100 years old, of yellowish magnesian limestone, in perfect condition.

THORPE ABBEY VILLAGE. The houses generally of this village are built of magnesian limestone from the vicinity; they are in excellent condition, and of a very pleasing colour.

THORPE SALVIN, near Worksop. Manor-house (15th century), in ruins. Of a siliciferous magnesian limestone and a sandstone, in unequal condition; the quoins and dressings are generally in a perfect state. Parish Church (15th century), also of a siliciferous variety of magnesian limestone and a sandstone, in unequal but generally fair condition. A Norman doorway under the porch is well preserved.

TICKHILL CHURCH, Yorkshire, (15th century). Of magnesian limestone, in excellent condition. The lower part of the tower (of the 12th century) also in fair condition.

YORK. Ancient Buildings: CATHEDRAL (transepts, 13th century; tower, nave, &c., 14th century). Of magnesian limestone, from Jackdaw Craig. West end and towers restored thirty years since; they are generally in fair condition, but some of the enriched gables and other decorations are obliterated. The transepts are in many places much decomposed, especially in the mouldings and enrichments. The central tower is generally in good condition, but several of the enriched parts are decomposed. St. Mary's Abbey (12th century), of magnesian limestone. West front of the church generally much decomposed; the north flank in better condition, but in parts much decomposed. The gateway, which is of Norman origin, is in fair condition. Roman Multangular Tower. Built of small stones; such as are of magnesian limestone are in good condition. St. Denis's Church. Norman doorway, of magnesian

limestone; south side highly enriched with zig-zag and other ornaments; the columns are gone; the parts which remain are in good condition. *St. Margaret's Church* (15th century), of magnesian limestone; east front much exposed, and in good condition. The porch is of Norman date, and has been reconstructed; four bands of enrichment in the head, in tolerably fair condition, but many stones, particularly those of a deep yellow brown colour, are much decomposed. *The other churches of York* (which are of the 14th and 15th centuries) are built of magnesian limestone, and are generally in an extremely decomposed state; in many instances all architectural detail is obliterated. *Modern Buildings:* The Museum, of Hackness sandstone, built nine years since, much decomposed wherever it is subject to the alternation of wet and dry, as at the bottom of the columns of the portico, plinth, &c. The Castle (recently erected); the plinth of the boundary wall (which is of Bramleyfall sandstone) already exhibits traces of decomposition. *York Savings Bank.* Huddersfield stone (?), in good condition.

Worksop Church (principally of the 13th century), of a siliciferous variety of magnesian limestone and of a sandstone; in very unequal condition. Some parts are very much decomposed, whilst others are in a perfect state.

Table of the Chemical Analysis of Sixteen Specimens of Stone.

	Sandstones					Magnesian Limestones				Oolites				Limestones		
	Cragleith	Darley Dale (Stancliffe)	Heddon	Kenton	Mansfield, or C. Lindley's Red	Bolsover	Huddlestone	Roach Abbey	Park Nook	Ancaster	Bath Box	Portland	Ketton	Barnack	Chilmark	Ham-hill
Silica	98·3	96·40	95·1	93·1	49·4	3·6	2·53	0·8	0·0	0·0	0·0	1·20	0·0	0·0	10·4	4·7
Carbonate of lime	1·1	0·36	0·8	2·0	26·5	51·1	54·19	57·5	55·7	93·59	94·52	95·16	92·17	0·0	79·0	79·3
Do. of magnesia	0·0	0·0	0·0	0·0	16·1	40·2	41·37	39·4	41·6	2·90	2·50	1·20	4·10	93·4	3·7	5·2
Iron alumina	0·6	1·30	2·3	4·4	3·2	1·8	0·30	0·7	0·4	0·80	1 20	0·50	0·90	3·8	3·7	5 2
Water and loss	0·0	1·94	1·8	0·5	4·8	3·3	1·61	1·6	2·3	2·71	1·78	1·94	2·83	1·5	2·0	8·3
Bitumen	0·0	0·0	0·0	0·0	0·0	0·0	0·0	0·0	0·0	A trace.	Do.	Do.	Do.	A trace.	4·2	2·5
Specific Gravities.																
Of dry masses	2232	2628	2229	2247	2338	2316	2147	2134	2138	2182	1839	2145	2045	2090	2481	2260
Of particles	2646	2993	2643	2625	2756	2833	2867	2840	2847	2687	2675	2702	2706	2627	2621	2695
Cohesive Powers.																
	111	100	56	70	72	117	61	55	61	33	21	30	36	25	101	57

1666. In the above table the names of the quarries are inserted under the general divisions of the different species of stone, and the specimens were considered as fair average samples of the workable stone in such quarries. The experiments were conducted by Messrs. Daniel and Wheatstone. As a conclusion to the report, it may be satisfactory to name the actual stones used in the construction of the first portions (1840) of the Houses of Parliament. The foundation was laid with Penryn granite, rising to the level of the ground, therefore but little seen. Above it is Fog-tor granite from Dartmoor. A small portion only of the superstructure, to the top of the basement windows, was built with Bolsover Moor stone from near Chesterfield; after which Anston stone was used for the remainder of the outside works. In the interior, Painswick and Caen stones have been employed; St. Stephen's crypt is of Beer stone. It has been asserted that had Government employed a supervision at the quarries to prevent imperfect blocks being sent up to London, the present unsightly appearance of many parts of the building would not have resulted.

1666a. In *par.* 1500 is already supplied tables of the *crushing weights* of many of the stones herein mentioned. Hereto is added a further table of the *weights* of a large number of building stones, taken from the one prepared by the late C. H. Smith for R. Hunt's *Mineral Statistics of the United Kingdom, &c.* Part II. for 1858, published 1860; it was also given in the *Transactions* of the Institute of British Architects, 1859–60.

1666b.   TABLE OF THE WEIGHTS OF BUILDING STONES, (IN CONTINUATION).

Name of Quarry.	Post Towns.	Weight per cubic foot avoirdupois.
		lb. oz.
Tisbury	Tisbury, Wilts	111 2
Farleigh Down	Bath, Somerset	122 10
Box Hill	Chippenham, Wilts	123 0
Park Quarry	Tixall, Stafford	124 9
„ „	Corby, Lincoln	125 11
Dundry Hill	Bristol, Somerset	126 2
Steetley (white)	Worksop, Notts	128 3
Doulting, Old Down	Shepton Mallet, Somerset	130 4
Morley Moor	Derby	130 8
Steetley (yellow)	Worksop, Notts	130 9
Dunmore Stable	Falkirk, Stirling	132 2
Gosling's Portland (bottom bed)	Weymouth, Dorset	132 5
Castle's Portland	„ „	133 6
Moakery	Corby, Lincoln	133 8
Hunger Hill	Belper, Derby	135 15
Park Nook	Doncaster, York	137 3
Duke of Hamilton's	Linlithgow	137 4
Hildenley	Malton, York	137 10
Hawksworth Wood	Leeds, York	137 14
Duke of Hamilton's	Linlithgow	138 2
Redgate	Wolsingham, Durham	139 9
Meanwood	Leeds, York	139 14
Scullcap, Portland	Weymouth	140 1
Stanley	Bewdley, Shropshire	141 7
Cateraig	Borrowstoness, Linlithgow	141 11
Craigleith (bed rock)	Edinburgh	141 12
Ham Hill	Yeovil, Somerset	141 12
Hookstone	Harrowgate, York	142 10
Westwood	Leeds, York	143 0
Giffneuk	Glasgow, Lanark	143 14
Anston, Norfall Quarry	South Anston, York	144 0
„ Stone-Ends Quarry	„ „	144 3
Kenton	Newcastle-on-Tyne	145 1
Victoria	Leeds, York	145 3
Woodhouse	Mansfield, Notts	145 12
Gun Barrel	Bewdley, Shropshire	146 0
Mansfield (white)	Mansfield, Notts	146 9
Corby	Corby, Lincoln	146 11
New Leeds	Leeds, York	147 8
Warwick	Huddersfield, York	148 10
Mansfield (red)	Mansfield, Notts	148 10
Amygdaloid	Crediton, Devon	149 9
Talacre	Holywell, Flint	150 4
Chilmark (Trough bed)	Salisbury, Wilts	151 6
„ (Penney bed)	„ „	151 9
Hoyle House (clough)	Huddersfield, York	151 7
Longwood Edge	„ „	153 7
Crossland Hill	„ „	155 4
Ketton (Rag bed)	Ketton, Rutland	155 10
Viney Hill	Colford, Gloucester	155 11
Chilmark (hard white bed)	Salisbury, Wilts	157 6
Lochee	Dundee, Forfar	158 11
Auchray	„ „	158 14
Lioch	„ „	159 3
Knockley	Colford, Gloucester	159 5
Dylais	Swansea, Glamorgan	166 3
Kentish Rag	Maidstone, Kent	166 9
Trebaunws	Swansea	168 1
Red Jacket	„	168 2
Cenfas	„	170 2
Mumble	„	170 7

1666c. In the year 1858, the present editor contributed to the *Builder Journal* (pp. 632–3) a list of the *Building Stones used externally in and near the Metropolis*, with the names and dates of erection of the buildings in which they had been used. This list cannot be here inserted, but the following are the stones named:—Anston, Aubigny, Bargate, Bath, Bramley Fall, Broomhill, Cadeby, Caen, Chapel Town (near Leeds) rubble, Craigleith, Godstone, Great Barrington, Harehill, Kentish rag, Yorkshire stone (hammer-dressed face), Ketton, Portland, Prudholme or Prudham, Reigate, Roche Abbey, Sneaton rag (from Whitby), Steetley, Swanage or Purbeck, and Whitby (Egton Quarries) stones, besides Granite, and Flint; we consider it desirable, however, to notice a few of the leading stones now employed in London.

1666d. The North Anston stone of Yorkshire, not mentioned in the preceding *Report*, belongs to the magnesian limestone formation, and is of a yellowish brown colour. As examples of its use we point to the Museum of Practical Geology in Jermyn Street, Pall Mall, in the façades of which there is scarcely a bad stone to be seen. This well conceived structure was erected from the design of James Pennethorne during the years 1837 to 1848. At the New Hall and Library, Lincoln's Inn, designed 1843–45 by P. Hardwick, R.A., this stone is in a lamentable state of decay, occasioned (as is reported in the discussion on G. R. Burnell's paper, *On Building Stones, &c.*, read at the Society of Arts in 1860), by the use of two particular beds, the blocks of which were in a state of decay before they left the quarry, and supposed to have been selected by the builder as yielding him the best profit. The labour upon Anston stone is intermediate between Yorkshire and Portland stones; it can be obtained of any required dimensions. The office of the Amicable Life Assurance Company, in Fleet Street, was erected 1843, with the Mansfield Woodhouse or Bolsover stone, in the façade of which there is scarcely any trace of decay.

1666e. From the Mansfield quarries are now sent up the red Mansfield stone, the white Mansfield stone, and the yellow magnesian or Bolsover limestone. The former is much introduced for colonnettes, short shafts, and bands in coloured coursed ashlar work. For similar decorative work, the following stones have been used (1865) at the new offices of the Crown Assurance Company in Fleet Street; namely, Portland stone in the piers and caps; Forest of Dean, red Mansfield, and blue Warwick, in other portions of the front; and Sicilian marble over the arches.

1666f. In consequence of the reintroduction of Portland stone of late years, we would refer, in addition to what has been stated on p. 467, as to the quarries of Portland stone, to the article *Lithology*, written by the late C. H. Smith, and published in the *Transactions* of the Institute of British Architects, 1842. Also to a report, published in the *Builder* of 1863, p. 859, by F. A. Abel, being the result of his examination into the comparative qualities and fitness for building purposes, of samples of stone from different quarries, and made under the direction of the Inspector General of Fortifications.

1666g. These results " show that all the superior descriptions of ' whit bed ' stone combine strength and compactness in a considerably higher degree than the varieties of ' base-bed ' stone. Some kinds of the ' whit-bed ' stone, however (i.e. those from the New Maggot and Inmosthay quarries), though ranking with the best as regards strength, exhibit a greater degree of porosity. Again, other ' whit-bed ' stones (from Old Maggot, Waycroft, and Independent quarries) exhibit but little superiority, in point either of strength or compactness, over the generality of the ' base-bed ' stones, and are, indeed, inferior to the best ' base-bed ' variety."

1666h. " The ' base-bed ' stones are, undoubtedly, more generally uniform in structure than those of the ' whit-bed; ' this being mainly due to the comparative freedom of the former from distinct petrifactions. Though such petrifactions were shown, by the results of experiments, to impart, in many instances, great additional strength to the stone, they frequently give rise by their existence to cavities sometimes of considerable size, which not only serve to weaken those particular portions of the stone, but may also, if they exist in proximity to exposed surfaces of a block of stone, promote its partial disintegration by the action of frost. Greater care is, therefore, unquestionably required in the selection of ' whit-bed ' stone than need be employed in the case of all the better varieties of ' base-bed ' stone." The results of my experiments lead me to the following conclusions regarding the comparative merits of the various descriptions of Portland stone in question, for building purposes:—

" For *External* work, in the order of their merit:—I. Stone from War Department quarry, Vern Hill; and ' whit-bed ' stone, Admiralty quarry.

II. ' Whit-bed ' stone, New Maggot quarry; ' base-bed ' stone, Admiralty quarry (this may be considered quite equal in quality to ' whit-bed ' stone); and ' whit-bed ' stone, Inmosthay quarry (particularly adapted from its texture and uniformity for ornamental work).
III. ' Whit-bed ' stone, Old Maggot quarry: *a* marked LI; and *b* marked IT and IE. The ' roach ' stone, from War Department quarry, is an invaluable stone for external work in localities where any considerable strength and power of resisting mechanical wear are

required, as in connection with those portions of work which may become exposed to the continual abrasive action of water. The rough 'whit-bed' stone from Admiralty quarry, is also a highly valuable stone for work of a similar kind, where great strength is required, and particularly where the numerous irregularities in the 'roach' stone may be objectionable.

For *Internal* work, the following rank highest, on account of uniformity and comparative strength :—'base-bed' stone, Old Maggot quarry IT; 'whit-bed' stone, Independent quarry; 'base-bed' stone, Waycroft quarry; and 'base-bed' stone, New Maggot quarry. The following are inferior to those just named, both in texture and uniformity :—'Whit-bed' stone, Waycroft quarry; 'base-bed' stone, Old Maggot quarry, IE; and 'base-bed' stone, Inmosthay quarry. The 'base-bed' stone, from Old Maggot quarry, marked LI, and that from Independent quarry, are of low quality, as compared with the remainder; and no reliance can be placed on the durability of the 'roach' stone from Independent quarry, judging from the specimens received."

1666*i*. *Hopton Wood stone* is obtained from quarries situated near Middleton and Wirksworth, in Derbyshire, in the mountain limestone districts of that part of the country. An analysis of it gives :—lime 55·09, magnesia ·17, carbonic acid 44·30, water ·16, organic matter ·05, silicious matter insoluble in acids ·15, oxide of iron ·10, alumina a trace, and silica soluble in acids, a minute trace = 100·02. It is well adapted for paving purposes, owing to the closeness and evenness of the grain; these properties give this stone its principal recommendation; its durability does not depend, apparently, upon any necessity for placing it on its quarry bed. The late Mr. C. H. Smith has stated in the *Builder*, 1864, p. 912, that "these extensive quarries have been worked from time immemorial; the material is decidedly *marble*, for it is fine grained, compact in texture, and quite hard enough to take a brilliant polish. The colour is a pale brownish white, certainly as white as Sicilian marble, which approaches to a bluish grey. It is much heavier than Portland stone, but lighter than Carrara marble. Blocks of very large dimensions may be obtained free from serious defects; and as it is an aqueous formation, hard, and well crystallized, there is no doubt of it standing weather extremely well. Both material and workmanship are less than those of Sicilian marble. In London, where it has not yet been used for building, a large quantity of it was laid down as paving about 1854, for foot-pavements, close to the Parliament Houses in Old Palace-yard, and part of Abingdon Street; and, though in constant use, no symptoms of decay, or of the surface wearing away, are perceptible." It has been stated that the price of it would always oppose its introduction into the London market; and that the labour of the stone is about half as expensive again as that of Portland; but, probably, as the price at the quarries has lately been reduced, the first named disadvantage may be found no longer to exist. This stone is noticed for its many advantages, and as it is but little known to the profession.

1666*j*. We do not purpose to enter into a description of quarrying stone; but, besides the useful treatise by Burgoyne, published among Weale's Elementary Treatises, we would refer to the detailed mode of working at the Bath quarries, published in the *Builder* in 1862, p. 613.

French Building Stones.

1666*k*. Of the foreign building stones imported into the London market, it will suffice to name two of them :—the Caen, and the Aubigny, stones. The latter material is stated to be obtained from quarries situated at St. Pierre Canivet, a short distance from Falaise, in Normandy. It is probably of the same nature as Caen stone, namely, oolitic, but much more crystalline in its structure, with semi-transparent crystals, showing no appearance of ova; very fine grained; as hard or harder than Anston stone; nearly as heavy as granite; and able to support a greater crushing weight than Caen stone; when worked it requires to be sawn wet with sand. There are two workable beds, one averaging 24 inches, the other 15 inches, in thickness. G. R. Burnell, (in his remarks on the works at Bayeux cathedral, read at the Institute of British Architects, 1861, p. 257), stated that he was convinced the use of Aubigny stone in London would be attended with danger. M. Flachat chose this stone because it yielded more satisfactory results under the trials to which he exposed the various local stones, so far as their resistances to crushing weights were concerned; but his assistants expressly state in their published account of the works at Bayeux, that the Aubigny stone yielded easily under the action of frost, if used exteriorly. Any one who may have examined the mediæval buildings in Falaise must also be convinced that the Aubigny stone used there has decayed in a frightful manner. I am, however, disposed to believe that even when used in the exterior (query, interior) of a building, this stone is exposed 'to take on' a decay somewhat analogous to the mysterious decay which we know affects Purbeck or Petworth marbles in our own cathedrals. I fear that the edges of the various courses will ultimately, crumble away like those of Purbeck marble. It may, however, be centuries before this effect is produced." Perhaps the only building erected with this stone in London, is that part of the old Schomberg House, Nos. 81 and 82, Pall Mall, which was rebuilt in 1851.

1666*l*. *Caen stone* is obtained from the great oolitic formation in Normandy, and has

been imported into England from a very early period; but it first appears to be named in documents after the year 1300. There was a cessation of its use after 1448, when Normandy was lost to this country; and it is not until the commencement of the present century that its employment here was resumed. This stone is now generally obtained from quarries situated at Allemagne, a small village on the right bank of the Orne at the gates of Caen, or from those of St. Germain de Blancherbe, commonly called La Maladrerie, the commune immediately adjoining that city, on the left bank.

1666m. The Caen stone of commerce is of a pale yellow colour and of a loose open grain, which when freshly quarried, soils the fingers like chalk, and is very friable. In many places it appears to have lost its oolitic character; and in others it is harder and more compact, being entirely formed of a species of lamellous spath, without any trace of oolites; the latter appearance is, however, principally to be observed in the beds which are worked between Caen and Falaise; at Allemagne and La Maladrerie the former prevails. Neither of these two latter quarries appear to have been opened for any great length of time, the stone used in the old city having been chiefly got on its site; and it is remarkable that the portions of the public buildings which required stones of larger dimensions than could be obtained from the upper beds of the oolitic formation immediately around the town, were executed in the Creuilly, Ranville, or Fontaine Henri stones, never in the stone obtained from the beds now worked exclusively for both the French and the English markets, and which beds have been rendered available with the advance of mechanical science. The upper beds, called the *bancs de bittes*, which yielded the stone in olden times, is generally speaking of a harder character, of a finer grain, and presenting a more crystalline appearance than that obtained from the lower beds; but even in these upper beds care is required in the selection, for the texture is far from uniform; while the small size of the stones is too often considered an objection to it, as the eight layers, between each of which occurs a bed of flint 2 inches in thickness, are of variable depth (between 11 inches and 26 inches), being about 18 inches on the average.

1666n. The lower beds comprise the *banc de chambranle*, 16 inches thick; the *banc de deux pieds un quart*, about 30 inches English thick, yielding a good stone, disfigured unfortunately by the fossils it contains; the *banc rouge*, 22 inches thick, of very bad quality and stained by ochreous iron ore, besides being traversed by numerous vertical vents; then the *gros banc*, 40 inches thick, a very good stone, but likewise disfigured by fossils; the *banc de fond*, usually from 18 inches to 30 inches thick, of a closer and finer grain than the last named; and then the *banc de 81 centimetres*, of very inferior quality, worked only for the immediate neighbourhood.

1666o. Experience proves that Caen stone will not resist the dissolving power of water charged with carbonic acid gas; and as the rain water of our large towns contains a considerable quantity of that gas, it is not expedient to employ this stone in any situation where water is likely to lodge or even to be taken up by capillary action, unless, indeed, the projecting parts be protected by metal. In upright walling above the plinths, and in the sheltered portions of cornices, it can be employed when judiciously selected; and in internal work, with safety and economy. The bedding of the stone should be observed. From the state of some buildings at Hâvre, it is considered that the sea air is particularly destructive to this stone; and it is generally believed that the stone from La Maladrerie is inferior to that from Allemagne. In Caen itself, the plinths or basements of houses are executed in granite, or in the Ranville, Cherence, or Creuilly, stones, which are practically non-absorbent; and, moreover, the Creuilly stone is used in the best buildings for the exposed portions of the elevation, although, of course, "Caen stone" is found at the very gates of the town.

1666p. More lengthened notices will be found in the accounts given in the *Builder*, vols. vi. and vii., entering into the qualities of the stone, from personal surveys of the quarries. When freshly quarried, this stone can be cut with the toothed saw, and carved with ordinary chisels, even more easily than Bath stone.

1666q. TABLE OF THE WEIGHTS OF SOME FRENCH STONES.

Bed or Quarry.	Weight per cubic foot, avoirdupois.		
	lbs.	oz.	dr.
Caen, Franc banc bed - - - - - - -	116	2	0
„ Banc de quatre pieds - - - - -	118	0	8
„ Gros Banc - - - - - - -	122	0	8
„ Pierre franche - - - - - -	123	3	0
„ Piere de trente pouces - - - -	128	5	0
Ranville, near Caen - - - - - -	142	6	0
Aubigny, near Falaise - - - - - -	150	6	8

1666*r*. The new façade of Buckingham Palace, erec:ed in 1846–7, is perhaps the most remarkable failure of Caen stone.   Mr. H. T. Hope's house, in Piccadilly, built 1849–50 has been considered one of the best specimens of its employment in London, as it has stood well.   The projections were protected by lead or by slates.   The crushing weight of Caen stone is about 2000 lbs. per inch superficial.

1666*s*. The *Kentish ragstone* is a limestone with a very small proportion of earthy matters, frequently subcrystalline, but ordinarily of a confused texture.   When well chosen it is very hard and dense, and the labour upon it so expensive that it is very rarely used for anything but rubble masonry in districts remote from the quarries.   The custom has been, therefore, to execute all the moulded or carved portions of the buildings in Caen or Bath stones, and even to carry up the quoins and jambs in those materials, whilst the intervening spaces, or the wall, are filled in with the rag.   The colour varies from a lightish green to a deep blue, and although the colour of the two materials is at first very different, a few years' exposure causes them to harmonise in tint.

1666*t*. The district in which ragstone is quarried extends about thirty miles east and west through the central part of Kent, and averages from four to ten miles in breadth, comprising the towns of Sevenoaks, Maidstone, Lenham, &c.   Reigate or firestone, and Tunbridge sandstone, are also afforded by the same formation, greensand.   The ragstone is found in beds varying from six inches to three feet in thickness, alternated with fine sand known as *Hassock*, which in some beds becomes so consolidated as to form an occasional useful auxiliary to the ragstone, in buildings.   The quality of the rag differs very greatly, according to the place in which it is quarried ; some quarries only yielding stone of a hard flinty nature, almost unfit for building, while the stone obtained from others is almost as free working as Portland stone.   The finest qualities are at present obtained from quarries situated at Boughton, near Maidstone, where they have been worked for several centuries. A section of them is given by J. Whichcord, in his pamphlet on the subject, published in 1846 ; wherein also are given the local names of the various beds.

1666*u*. *Flint work.*   This material, as used for a description of rubble work, was formerly much employed in the counties of Cambridge, Norfolk, Suffolk, Sussex, and Kent, where the chalk formation abounds, and is still used for the purpose in such localities.   Flint is the name accorded to the nearly pure silicious earth, which by the action of fire becomes opaque and white, and is harder than quartz, which it scratches.   The colour is usually grey, of various shades ; but is sometimes black, brown, red, and even yellow.   Flint is fragile, with a perfect and large conchoidal fracture, and being rarely laminated, it is broken with equal facility in almost every direction ; the fragments are sharp.   In the chalk formation it occurs in regular beds, consisting either of nodules or of flat tabular masses.

1666*v*. At Brandon, in Suffolk, one of the places where flint forms an article of commerce, it is obtained from pits sunk in the chalk, which is within 6 feet of the surface. The first stratum is found in the clay overlying the chalk ; when this has been removed, a shaft is sunk 6 feet in depth ; if no flint is there found, a tunnel is driven for three feet horizontally, and another shaft is sunk ; and so on alternately with tunnel and shaft till a depth of 40 feet is reached.   The flint is found in *floors* about 8 feet below each other, and is obtained by tunnels being driven sometimes a furlong in length under each floor, and the flint broken down by crowbars.   The small tunnels in the shaft form tables, upon which men stand and hand up the flint to each other from below to the surface ; no machinery or tackling is used.

1666*w*. Flint is split upon the workman's knee, by sharp blows from a hammer with an oblate face, and squared upon a steel stake let into a wood block, with a blunt axe formed by passing a handle through an old flat file about a foot long, the cutting edge being $1\frac{3}{4}$ inches wide by $\frac{1}{12}$ of an inch thick.

Decay of Stone.

1667. In the paragraphs 1640 to 1648 have already been quoted some of the causes of decay and decomposition in stones, as stated in the Report of the Commissioners, and after the lapse of nearly thirty years since its publication, but few additional facts have been obtained on the subject.   One of the most commendable essays relating to it is that by G. R. Burnell, read at the Society of Arts, in March 1860, which is likewise useful for the discussion thereon by some of the members learned in chemistry.   We quote a few of the paragraphs for further elucidating some points important to those who have good building under consideration.

1667*a*. " Atmospheric moisture, when absorbed into building stones, acts upon them quite as much through the changes in its own volume.   When the stone is placed in such a manner as that water can accumulate in any perceptible quantities between its various layers, and the position of those layers be such that the expansion of the water in freezing cannot take place freely, the respective layers containing the water will be violently de-

tached from one another. This is a more important consideration in the case of the *bedding* of stones, and it is unfortunate that the system of competition throws so great a temptation in the way of the practical builder as to render it a mere matter of chance whether this constructive law be observed or not, unless a costly system of supervision be organised, and thus the precautions often taken by the stone merchant to indicate the upper bed of the material he delivers, are defeated.

1667b. The chemical reactions which take place in building stones are mainly those arising from the oxygenation, or the hydration of the various ingredients of which those stones are composed. These reactions are independent of those resulting, in the interior of the country, from the agents directly presented by atmospheric moisture in the form of carbonic acid gas, sulphur, and ammonia ; or upon the sea-shore, in the form of hydro-chloric acid, or of common salt itself, in minute particles. Thus, if the oxide of iron be present in any notable proportions, it is likely to undergo changes of a nature to disturb the stability of the compound, and even the crystalline sulphates of lime are exposed to chemical decomposition, in consequence of the liberation of the sulphuric acid gas they contain. The other mineral salts, such as the silicates and the sulphates of iron, so often met with in building stones, are at times susceptible of very injurious decomposition ; and the soda, potassa, or the organic matters the stones may contain, frequently give rise to the formation of new salts ; mainly under the action of atmospheric moisture, it is true, but also under the influence of the partial decomposition which take place around them. It is to be observed, however, that the danger to building stones from this peculiar class of influences, is very small and very slow in its action, compared with the dangers arising from the mechanical disintegration produced by atmospheric causes : and that, with the exceptions of the actions of free carbonic acid upon the felspar of granites, the changes of state produced in limestones by the same agent, and the modifications of the abundant salts of iron in some peculiar stones, there is little practical necessity for dwelling upon this interesting but obscure branch of applied chemistry.

1667c. The actions capable of affecting the stability of the composition of ordinary building stones, by reason of the new forms of matter they superinduce, may principally be considered to be those resulting from the absorption of the gases of the atmosphere, and especially the process known by the name of *saltpetring*, or more correctly, of nitrification. This process displays itself in the formation of minute crystals, efflorescing from the interior to the exterior of the stone, and it leads to the destruction of the exposed surfaces of the latter, through the gradual removal of the minute particles, in consequence of the disintegration produced by the expansive action of the crystals in process of formation.

1667d. It is supposed that the organic matter diffused through nearly all stratified deposits gives rise to the formation of certain nitrates, such as the nitrate of lime and nitrate of soda, under the influences of damp, of air, and of light of certain descriptions —for nitrification certainly takes place most abundantly near damp ground, rising in a wall *pari passu* with the range of the capillary attractions of its materials, and upon the northern or shaded faces of the said walls. Not only does this nitrification throw off the minute and less adherent particles of the building materials themselves, whether they be of *stone* or *brick*, but it is also able to detach any protecting coat which may be put upon them, if the adhesion of that coat to the subjacent material should not be of a very ener-getic nature. Let the adhesion, however, be ever so energetic, if once the action of nitrifi-cation should have been established, it must run its course, and the amount of evil it is capable of producing will simply depend upon the quantity of organic matter originally contained in the materials, or susceptible of being absorbed by them from the atmosphere.

1667e. The secondary limestones which have not been affected by plutonic action, the loamy clays, some kinds of pit sand, sea sand, and some descriptions of natural cements, are particularly exposed to the danger of nitrification in damp situations, rendering it in vain to expect to be able to preserve any mural paintings, or even any sculpture of a delicate character.

1667f. Practically, then, the great agent of destruction of building stones, in any of its modes of exhibition, is the damp, or the water supplied by the atmosphere, directly or indirectly ; the efforts of those who seek to prevent this destruction must be directed to combating this primary source of evil. Fortunately the precautions to be observed for this purpose are very simple, and they only require a little common sense on the part of the builders charged with their application, to the materials at least, which have been long before the public. The first and foremost rule is never to employ a porous absorbent stone in the ground, or in elevation ; unless, in the former case, it be maintained constantly wet ; or, in the second case, the absorption of moisture from the ground be prevented by the interposition of some impermeable material. Porous stones should not be used for the copings, parapets, window-sills, weather-beds of cornices, plinths, strings, or other parts of a building where water may lodge. Care must also be taken to bed such stones with mortars which are not exposed to develope in themselves, or are not likely to excite

in the stones, the efflorescence of any of the nitrates of soda, potassa, or of lime. If porous stones be used, it will be found that decay will commence, and be most apparent in the zone of alternate dryness and humidity, or as the workmen say, "between wind and water." The stonework about that part should therefore be executed in such a manner as to allow of its being easily replaced, if necessary ; and in case the decay exhibits towards the interior, (as it will do when the exterior surface is covered with a coating impervious to the air), care must be taken to isolate the decorative plastering or wall linings from the surfaces which are likely to be covered by efflorescence.

1667*g.* A committee appointed by the First Commissioner of Public Works and Buildings, on the 23rd March 1861, "to enquire into the decay of the stone of the New Palace of Westminster and into the best means of preserving the stone from further injury," reported on—I. The extent and position of the decay. II. The causes to which it is attributable, taking into consideration the composition of the stone, and the influence exerted upon it by moisture, and by the acids diffused in the London atmosphere. III. The best means of preserving the stone from further injury. IV. The qualities of the stones to be recommended for future use in public buildings to be erected in London." This report was ordered to be printed 1st August 1861. It is also given in Adcock's *Engineers' Pocketbook* for 1862, p. 205-211.

Preservation of Stone.

1667*h.* Even when all the best precautions, as above detailed, have been taken, it is occasionally found necessary to protect the exposed surfaces of the soft and absorbent, or hygrometric, stones, with some coating which shall prevent their absorbing the injurious atmosphere. This is done in various ways.

1667*i.* I. *By painting*:—The objection to this process consists in the fact that, as the oil evaporates, the stone becomes again exposed, and even the absorbent powers of the stone itself contribute to this action ; thus this costly palliative has to be often repeated, to the destruction of any delicate moulded work.

1667*j.* II. *By the injection of oleaginous, fatty, or waxy matters*:—These, it must be evident, can only act mechanically by closing the pores of the stone, and therefore, unless the surfaces be protected from the extremes of heat and cold, the heterogeneous materials thus affected must be acted upon in very different manners. Experience has confirmed this theoretical inference, and it has been found in practice that the protecting coats of any of the materials alluded to are gradually detached from the stone, and that they require to be renewed quite as frequently as does oil painting itself.

1667*k.* III. *By washing the face with a solution able to convert the material into an insoluble non-absorbent substance*:—This is the process introduced by M. Kühlmann, in which the carbonates of lime are washed with a solution of an alkaline silicate, as silicate of soda, or potassa, or "water glass" as he called it, with a view to converting them into silicates of lime through the elective affinities of the lime and the silica. In some cases this system has succeeded, and very great hardness, very great resisting powers, have been communicated to the stones operated upon. But unfortunately, the action of the silicic acid is a very slow one, and when the surfaces washed in the manner described are exposed to rain, it is by no means rare to find the solution carried away. Another objection is, that when the alkaline silicate acts upon the stone, the soda and potassa generally used are left free, and in efflorescing they are likely to carry away the finer details of the sculpture ; at the same time as they form to some extent deliquescent salts upon the face of the stone, they attract to it a dangerous amount of humidity. This process is only applicable to the preservation of the stones in which the carbonates of lime predominate.

1667*l.* IV. *By filling in the pores of the stone with an insoluble material which should effectually exclude water*:—This may be said to have been effected by the process patented by Mr. Ransome. The stone is first cleaned carefully from dust or other extraneous matters ; then it is made to absorb as large a quantity as possible of the silicate of soda or potassa. When this solution has dried into the stone, a second wash is applied, consisting of the chloride of calcium or of baryta. The silicate of soda and the chloride of calcium are most frequently employed ; and the effect of the respective applications is, that a double decomposition takes place in the washes, giving rise to the precipitation of a finely crystallised silicate of lime or of baryta in the pores of the stone, and an efflorescence of extremely soluble salts of the chlorides of soda or of potassa. The former remain in the pores, the latter are speedily washed away by rain. As the rate of contraction and expansion of the silicate of lime is, as nearly as may be, the same as that of the stone it is intended to protect, there is no danger of the precipitate being detached by this cause. This process, in contradistinction to that of Kühlmann's, is applicable to limestones, sandstones, bricks, plasters, and cements. It has even been suggested that it may be advantageously applied to chalk.

1667*m.* It must not be forgotten, however, that it is as important to prevent a stone from decaying, as it is to afford a protection to it when that effect has commenced. If

any internal decay or any organic decomposition, so to speak, be once allowed to establish itself in a building stone, it will be imposible effectually to arrest its progress. Efflorescence, for instance, will continue, however effectually the exposed surface of the stone may be closed by a mechanical or a chemical deposit, and thus even some of the results of Mr. Ransome's process appear equivocal. The student should make himself master of the attempts lately made to discover an universal remedy for protecting the surfaces of various materials; the following list of their authors were detailed by Mr. W. Tite, M.P., at the Institute of British Architects, January 1861 :—I. Bethell's patent, 1838, perhaps never applied to stone. II. Hutchinson's, 1847, which has been chiefly applied to the Calverley stone of Tunbridge. III. Daines's, 1854. IV. Szerelmey's, 1857. V. Newton's, 1841. And VI. Ransome's, 1856. We consider it needless to notice here the inventions in detail. It is difficult to pronounce on their respective merits, but Ransome's perhaps promises the best results; it is mentioned in a subsequent paragraph.

1667n. Sylvester, in 1846, suggested the following very useful and simple recipe for protecting stone or brickwork from the absorption of water; it has been repeatedly tried and answers well in exposed situations, but requires a fresh application about every three or four years. Mix $\frac{3}{4}$ lb. of mottled soap in a gallon of nearly boiling water, and apply it in a boiling state over the surface of the work, steadily and carefully, with a large flat brush, making no lather, and filling up the crusty surface of the work, either of brick or stone. This is to remain for twenty-four hours to become dry and hard. Then $\frac{1}{2}$ lb. of alum is to be mixed with four gallons of water and left standing for about twenty-four hours, so that the alum may be completely dissolved; this solution is to be applied in the same manner. Mr. G. G. Scott has used for the internal work at Westminster Abbey a solution of shell-lac in spirits of wine, which squirted into the stone work, appears to answer perfectly in securing the face from further decay arising from damp only. He also found it of some effect in the open air where defended from rain, but it failed when exposed to its action.

Artificial Stone.

1667o. The term is sometimes made to comprise not only *Terra Cotta*, which is noticed in this work in the section BRICK, but also the many *Concretes*, which are described in the section LIME, &c. Those mixtures or concreted masses, having more affinity to the original they profess to imitate, are here described.

1667p. *Austin's artificial stone* was invented about fifty years since, during which period it has been well tested. It is used chiefly in the manufacture of statues, garden ornaments, chimney shafts, and the like. This material is generally considered to be little else than ordinary cement, but it is plain there is much more ingenuity in the matter; at all events, it is evidently a concrete of sand and so on, cemented by lime; it is not burnt as is often supposed, and much of its value is no doubt due to the manipulation of the materials.

1667q. *Ransome's silicious stone* was patented in 1844. Calcined flints ground to a fine powder were mixed with common soda (sub-carbonate of soda) rendered caustic, and water, the mixture being boiled under steam pressure; he thus obtained the silicate of soda in a liquid form. To one part of this *water glass* he added ten parts of sand, a little pounded flint, and a little clay; mixed the whole to a putty; made castings of the desired form under compression; dried these, *burnt* them in a kiln to a bright red heat, and so made them into blocks of stone. The chemical question was this :—the alkali of the soluble silicate of soda combined with a portion of the natural silica or sand, and thus formed an insoluble silicate or glass, as a cement, wherewith the remainder of the sand became concreted together. A sandstone was produced, and technically one of a silicious type; but its connecting medium was not crystalline as in nature, but as an equivalent, professedly vitreous. This vitreous element, however, was always seen to be its blemish, and the manufacture is now discontinued for the following more recent invention by the same patentee.

1667r. During the experiments made for obtaining a liquid or liquids wherewith to wash the surface of stone after it has been worked, Ransome selected and applied the silicate of soda, and upon the saturated surface a solution of chloride of calcium. A double decomposition then follows, not slowly but instantly, and the silicate of soda and chloride of calcium, the one, an insoluble substance filling the pores of the stone, and the other, common salt to be washed out by the weather. Pieces of the putty out of which the previously described silicious stone was daily made, *i.e.* sand mixed up with silicate of soda, were dipped in chloride of calcium, out of which it came changed to a hard and solid stone. This rather unexpected result led to the formation of an entirely new species of artificial stone, in a manner which was related by Professor Kerr at a meeting of the Institute of British Architects in 1863, from whose account we have been quoting.

1667s. *Ransome's Concrete stone* is the name given to this new material, invented in 1861. The process of manufacture now followed is first to dissolve flints in caustic alkali at a temperature of 350° Fahr., leaving them in a boiler for twenty-four hours. The liquid then produced, consisting of silicate of soda, is drawn off, and is allowed to evaporate until it becomes a thick matter like treacle. It is next mixed with clean pit sand incor-

porated with five to ten per cent. of chalk in a pug mill, and in four to five minutes this mixture is formed into a stiff putty. It is then pressed into a mould and afterwards either saturated with, or immersed in, a solution of chloride of calcium, which being rapidly imbibed, the formation of an insoluble silicate of lime and a soluble chloride of sodium or common salt results. This latter (about three per cent.) has to be removed by washing, to effect which it is placed in a hot-water bath for many hours. The employment of this new material as stone in building is gaining ground; for cast ornaments and moulded work it has been longer used, and probably it may yet be brought to serve for the chisel of the carver.

1667t. The committee of the Institute experimented on this material in 1864. Four-inch cubes were made of equal parts of sand and coarse ballast, with a quarter part of clay; on the third day a cube crushed with a weight of 9·35 tons; on the tenth day with 15·25 tons. With six parts of sand to one of chalk, on the third day a cube crushed with 6 tons; at ten days old, 9·40 and 13·25 tons. Other samples, however, proved to be weaker, as at eight and thirty-six weeks old, they crushed with 8·4 and 8·4 tons respectively, yet one of twenty-eight weeks crushed with 14 tons, apparently depending on the depth of the induration which in the weaker samples was only from 1 to 3 inches. A block formed of five parts of sand to one of fine silex bore 30 tons when three weeks old, with-out showing the least effect; it had been previously tested up to 20 tons. It will be well to contrast another sample formed of "all road scrapings from the neighbourhood of Ipswich" which at only *three days* old crushed with 28 tons; this was probably due to the silex contained in it. As another proof that its strength is entirely due to the com-plete induration of the material, a nine-inch brick made of four parts of sand, four of fine sand, and one of chalk, cracked when thirteen weeks old with 14 tons and crushed with 35 tons; this specimen was gradually filled with chloride of calcium being *poured* over it, and took fifteen minutes to saturate. Another at eight weeks with 4·2 and 30·0 tons; another with 20·15 and 38·8 tons; while a fourth cracked at 6 tons and crushed with 6·65 tons; these were *soaked* in the chloride of calcium, The tensile strength at twenty-eight weeks old varied as 47, 74 and 67 lbs. per square inch; while two specimens made of road scrapings, only three days old, broke with 101 and 97 lbs. per square inch, a strength also, no doubt, due to the silex contained in it.

1667u. A gallon of each solution is sufficient to produce a cubic foot of stone of the finer quality; but the cost of a block of coarser quality would be less than about half what the other would be. To render this concrete stone perfectly non-absorbent, the surface of the stone, after it is formed into blocks, is treated a second time with a wash of the silicate of soda, and a second application of the solution of chloride of calcium. These solutions are also applied for the preservation of other stones, or of brickwork; the silicate being diluted with water in proportions according to the absorbent character of the material, which must be clean and thoroughly dry before being operated upon. Tinting solutions are also supplied for harmonising with the natural colour of the stones. About four gallons of each solution will be, under ordinary circumstances, sufficient for each 100 yards superficial of surface.

1667v. Experiments conducted by G. R. Burnell, and reported upon by Professor Ansted in a paper read at the British Association at Cambridge, 1862, showed that the transverse strength of a beam 4 inches square resting one inch at each end, with 16 inches clear span, sustained a weight of 2,122 lbs. or 132 lbs. per inch superficial; whilst a similar bar of Portland stone broke with 759½ lbs., or nearly 42 lbs. per inch. The adhesive or tensile strength was proved by pieces of stone notched for the purpose, the sectional area at the weakest part being 5½ inches.

The patent concrete stone sustained	-	-	1980 lbs.	= 360 lbs.	per inch.
Portland stone broke with	-	-	1104 lbs.	= 200 lbs.	,,
Bath stone ,, ,,	-	-	796 lbs.	= say 150 lbs.	,,
Caen stone ,, ,,	-	-	768 lbs.	= say 150 lbs.	,,

A 4-inch cube of the patent stone sustained a weight of 30 tons, nearly 2 tons per inch, before it was crushed.

1667w. The following result of chemical tests of this artificial stone, as compared with natural ones, will be found instructive. They were made by Mr. E. Frankland at St. Bartholomew's Hospital in December 1861. " The experiments were made in the follow-ing manner. The samples were cut as nearly as possible of the same size and shape, and were well brushed with a hard brush. Each sample was then thoroughly dried at 212°, weighed, partially immersed in water until saturated, and again weighed; the *porosity* or absorptive power of the stone was thus determined. It was then suspended for forty-eight hours in a very large volume of each of the following acid solutions, the alteration in weight after each immersion being separately estimated. The sample was then boiled with water until all acid was removed, and again weighed. Finally, it was dried at 212°, brushed with a hard brush, and the total degradation or loss since the first brushing was ascertained. The following numbers were obtained."

Name of Stone.	Porosity. Water absorbed by dry Stone. per cent.	Alteration in weight by immersion in dilute acid.						Loss by action of acid and boiling in water. per cent.	Further loss by brushing.	Total degradation from all causes.
		of 1 per cent.		of 2 per cent.		of 4 per cent.				
		Loss	Gain	Loss	Gain	Loss	Gain			
Bath - - -	11·57	1·28	—	2·82	—	2·05	—	5·91	·26	6·17
Caen - - -	9·86	2·13	—	4·80	—	·67	—	11·73	1·60	13·33
Aubigny - -	4·15	1·18	—	4·00	—	—	1·04	3·56	·29	3·85
Portland - -	8·86	1·60	—	1·10	—	1·35	—	3·94	·24	4·18
Anston - -	6·09	3·52	—	3·39	—	3·11	—	11·11	·27	11·38
Whitby ' - -	8·41	1·07	—	—	·53	none	none	1·25	·18	1·43
Hare Hill - -	4·31	·75	—	—	·60	none	none	·98	·15	1·13
Park Spring -	4·15	·71	—	—	·10	·15	—	·81	none	·81
Ransome's - -	6·53	—	·95	none	none	none	none	·63	·31	·94

" Whilst Portland, Whitby, Hare Hill, and Park Spring stones, are thus pointed out as the natural stones best adapted to withstand the influences of town atmospheres, they also indicate that Ransome's patent concrete stone will be found equal to the best of these, and there is nothing in the composition which would lead one to anticipate that it would suffer from exposure to the saline influences of the atmosphere upon the sea coast."

1667x. Bousfield's patent, 1856, consists of 80 or 85 parts of chalk and 15 or 20 of slaked lime, mixed together, moulded under pressure, and dried in the open air, when the blocks, says the patentee, " will be found to possess a degree of compactness and firmness resembling stone, which increases indefinitely with age, and if the ingredients are pure, will rival marble in whiteness and beauty." Barff's patent for an artificial stone was obtained in 1861. He takes 1 part of an aqueous aluminate of potash, with 3 parts of an alkaline silicate, or water glass (silicate of potash, however, not of soda), which will in a few hours set into a sort of dull glass, an artificial felspar in fact, perfectly brittle and of no very great tenacity, but altogether insoluble in water. With this silicate of alumina while in a liquid state, he makes up sand or any dust (as pounded stone) into a paste, moulding it into blocks, and drying them in the open air, until they have set hard. Silicate of soda and potash are extremely viscid, and anything mixed up or coated by them is rendered thereby impermeable; to get another solution into such silicates, much less behind it, to effect their decomposition, is considered impossible, the only alternative, therefore, is to put on the two solutions as one. Decomposition then setting in, mere dryness is all that is necessary to produce the material; but if the silicate of potash and the aluminate of potash be mixed up in a liquid, they remain liquid for any period within reason, and they may be mixed up with any materials selected, or washed over their surface. When put into stone it hardens and produces an artificial stone, without heat or further process. A previous patent, dated 1860, describes that silicate of soda or silicate of potash may be combined with, or decomposed by, carbonate of lead, carbonate of zinc, or other suitable material insoluble in water, which will decompose or chemically unite with the said silicates; proportionate quantities of chalk, sand, or other similar substance may also be incorporated with the compound, and thus enable it to be obtained at less cost, in accordance with the nature or description of the work to which it is intended to be applied. A piece of stone manufactured with carbonate of lead, powdered pumice stone, and silicate of soda, in proportions stated in the specification, produces a very hard stone, without the application of any heat.

1667y. Fluo-Silicic acid and silicate of potash are also applied to the surfaces of stones.

Sect. II.

GRANITE.

1668. Among the primitive rocks of the globe, whose period of creation is considered by geologists as antecedent to that of organic beings, is that of granite, whose use in architecture seems to bid defiance to time itself. The term granite appears to be a corruption of the Latin word *geranites*, used by Pliny to denote a particular species of stone. Tournefort, the naturalist, in the *Account of his Voyage to the Levant* in 1699, is the first of modern writers who uses the name. The word seems to have been applied by antiquaries to every granular stone susceptible of use in architecture or sculpture, in which vague sense it was used by mineralogists, until about fifty years since, when true granite was classed as a particular mountain rock. Its constituent parts are concretions of felspar, quartz, and mica, intimately joined together, but without any basis or ground. These parts are variable in quantity, so that sometimes one, sometimes the other, and frequently

two of them, predominate over the third. The felspar is, however, generally in excess, as mica is the least considerable ingredient of the rock. In some varieties the quartz is wanting, in others the mica; but where these peculiarities occur, the granites must be considered as varieties, not as distinct species.

1669. The constituent parts differ in their magnitude, alternating from large to small and very fine granular. The colour, moreover, is very variable, depending principally on the predominating ingredient—the felspar, the quartz, and the mica having usually a grey colour. The felspar is mostly white, inclining to grey and yellow, sometimes red, and even grey, seldom milk-white, and always translucent. The mica is usually grey, and sometimes nearly black. The felspar in granite has usually a vitreous lustre, and of perfectly foliated fracture; yet in some varieties it becomes quite earthy, with the loss of its hardness and lustre; in other words, it has passed into porcelain earth. The appearance in question is sometimes produced by the weathering of the felspar, and sometimes it appears to be in its original state. When pyrites are found in the veins which traverse granite, the vicinous felspar and mica are converted into a species of steatitical matter by the action of the sulphuric acid formed during the decomposition of the pyrites. In Cornwall, there is a considerable portion of its granite in which earthy felspar is found. When felspar occurs in abnormal quantities, the granite becomes porphyritic, as the Devonshire granite, and that of St. Honorine (Calvados): the name being derived from the colour, which is purple. Schorl takes the place of the mica in some parts of Devonshire; and even the quartz is sometimes wanting, as is often the case in the elvans or courses laden with mineral matters in that district. When hornblende occurs instead of mica, the granite becomes syenite, as at Malvern, and at Syene, in Egypt; and when present with mica in about equal quantities, the material is called Syenitic granite. When mica is present in such quantities as to cause the rock to assume a slaty cleavage, it is called gneiss.

1670. Granite is not decomposed by acids, and is only imperfectly and slowly calcinable in a great heat. Those species which contain much white felspar, and only a small portion of quartz, like the greater part of the granites of Cornwall and Devonshire, are liable to decomposition much sooner than many of the Scotch granites, in which the quartz is more abundant, and equally disseminated. In the selection of the Cornish and Devon granites, those are to be preferred which are raised in the largest blocks and are easiest worked, which, for common purposes, answer well enough, such as for paving-stones and the like; but harder granite must be sought for than Devonshire or Cornwall produces, where the construction is of importance; for the masses in these counties are mostly in a condition of rapid disintegration and decay, which seems chiefly attributable to their containing a large portion of potassa. The Naval Hospital at Plymouth is built of a granite whose parts appear to have been well selected. It was erected between the years 1756 and 1764, and, except in the columns of the colonnades, does not exhibit symptoms of decay. In these, on their more exposed sides, the disintegration of the felspar has commenced, and lichens have already attached their roots to some parts of the surfaces.

1670a. The cause of the *decomposition* of granite is a point yet unsolved by chemists. Some state that the felspar, being acted upon by the carbonic acid in rain water, becomes decomposed, and is then easily removed, leaving the mica and the quartz in relief without any cementing material; and that the decay of the felspar does not take place by any known rules, for the more crystalline it may be, more perfectly does it resist the decomposing action of atmospheric agents. Other scientific men are of opinion that the felspars containing soda generally decompose, whereas those which contain potash do not decay. It has also been considered that the kaolin or China clay was produced by the decomposition of the felspar with the granite; but it has been stated that so far as human observation could go, China clay never was true granite, and that atmospheric decomposition acting upon felspar, had never gone to the depth of 300 feet, at which depth finer China clay was found than nearer the surface: miles of country could be shown strewed with felspar; the quartz was gone, but the felspar remained. We must leave the decision in far more able hands.

1671. Red granite, sometimes yellowish, and generally interspersed with black mica, is found in Devonshire; at Mount Edgcombe there are tables of it equal to the finest oriental granite, and it is found in other parts of England. For hardness, and in works where durability is indispensable, the granites from Mount Sorrel, in Leicestershire; Aberdeen and Dundee, in Scotland; and the Cheesewring of Cornwall, are to be preferred by the architect. These take an admirable polish, and are superior to all others which this island produces. The increasing demand of late years for this material, has caused many new quarries to be opened up in various localities. The red is generally harder than the grey sorts, and more difficult to work. The Peterhead, from the vicinity of Aberdeen, is perhaps the best, and it is, moreover, in appearance the most beautiful which Scotland affords; indeed, in point of beauty, it is only surpassed by the oriental granites.

1671a. Dartmoor granite is, in general, coarse grained, varying much in colour. The grey

sort is chiefly quarried and worked at Hay Tor on the east side, shipped at Teignmouth; and at King Tor and Rigmoor Down, on the west side, shipped at Plymouth. The Brown Willy district, worked at the Cheesewring quarries, near Liskeard; the granite is of a light grey colour, and was used in the piers of the new Westminster bridge. The granite of the eastern portion of the Hensbarrow district, near St. Austell, worked above Par, is of good quality; it is shipped from that port, and known as Lostwithiel granite: the western portion is remarkable for its liability to decomposition, and is worked for kaolin clay. The Carn Menelez district supplies the granite generally known as Cornish, shipped from Penryn and Port Navis: blocks of several hundred tons are often raised, varying from 20 to 70 feet in length, and of proportionate breadth and thickness. The finest grain is obtained in the Carnsew quarries, from whence were got the stone for the lodges and piers at the British Museum, the plinth to the Royal Exchange, the pedestal for the statue to Lord Clive at Shrewsbury, and that for the statue of Carlo Alberto at Turin. The columns at the entrance of the royal mausoleum at Frogmore are from Lamorna, south of Penzance; which, with Boswarvah and New Mill, to the west, have, with those at Penryn, supplied granite to most public works. Fremator granite, largely used at the steam dock yard at Keyham, is white in colour, and being very close grained, it can be brought to a highly finished surface, and is said to be very durable.

1671b. Hay Tor granite company supplies a granite of a very fine grain, hard, of unquestionable durability, and generally of a beautiful blue or grey colour; it can be obtained in blocks of any size that is capable of being removed with existing machinery. The quarries have supplied the Nelson column and its pedestals; the granite plinth and steps of the Royal Exchange; the statue and pedestal of King William IV.; part of the river wall of the Houses of Parliament; the plinth of the Sun Fire Office, &c.; the large landings and steps of the terraces at the Crystal Palace; the graving docks at all HM. Dockyards, as well as the ashlar steps and landings for the royal mausoleum at Frogmore. Grey granite from Lundy island, off the coast of Devonshire, is supplied for the first section of the Thames embankment.

1671c. The Port Nant granite, in Carnarvon bay, near Port Dinllaen, has been used at Liverpool for paving, for some years; for the tramway on Westminster bridge; for the Metropolitan drainage outfalls, and for the foundation works and pavement of the Thames embankment.

1671d. Granite is supplied from a comparatively limited extent in the north-eastern part of Aberdeenshire. The first or central portion is somewhat circular in form, having a diameter of about six miles, within which the rocks are of red granite of different varieties, typified by the fine warm coloured Stirling Hill stones; and secondly, of an annular space surrounding this nucleus, in which the grey and blue granites abound. Of these, the Cairngall is close-grained, hard and dense, and as obdurate as any of the red granites. At Pitsligo is obtained a light coloured bluish-white stone, which when fresh from the quarry, is wrought with greater facility than even some of the Scottish sandstones. It stands the weather well; but the want of railway communication prevents its being used at any distance from its own locality.

1671e. Rubislaw quarry was the first known quarry in Aberdeenshire, about two hundred and fifty years since, and furnished stones for paving London, and later for works at Portsmouth Docks and the Bell Rock Lighthouse. Since its introduction about 1820, various quarries have supplied granite for works at Waterloo Bridge (the balustrading), Sheerness Docks, upper side of London Bridge, &c. About 1822 Mr. A. Macdonald, of Aberdeen, reduced to practice the difficult problem of giving any required form to so stubborn a material, and communicating to its surface an enduring polish, which it is said, is retained under all atmospheric changes; nor does the material contract any stain with vegetation. The red granite quarries of Stirling Hill, near Peterhead, about thirty miles from Aberdeen, supplied the shaft of the Duke of York's column; the pillars in Fishmongers' Hall; the columns in the king's library in the British Museum about 1830; the pedestals for the statues in the same building; the columns at St. George's Hall, Liverpool, 25 feet in length in one block; and is now used in numerous buildings in nearly all the cities in Great Britain.

1671f. Grey or blue granite is supplied from the quarry of Rubislaw, but principally from Cairngall, which is more of a syenite than a granite, a clear blue finely-grained material, used for the finest work. This has been employed for portrait statues, as at Aberdeen, at Portsmouth, &c.; for the sarcophagus for the Duchess of Kent, and for that of the Prince Consort, both at Frogmore.

1671g. Argyleshire has only within the last twenty years been opened up for granite. Furnace quarry, near Inverary, is more of a Syenitic or porphyritic character than that of true granite, and is remarkably hard, in fact harder than that of Aberdeen. It is used chiefly for paving the streets of Glasgow. Bonaw Island quarry, near Oban, gives an excellent large-grained grey granite; it has been used in the harbour works, the flight of steps at the West End Park, &c., all at Glasgow, being obtainable in large blocks. Bonaw

Causeway quarry, near the above, though fine grained, does not supply large blocks; it is used for paving stones. Ardsheal quarry, north-east of Oban, has a good grey granite for general purposes. It is easily quarried in layers of any required length or breadth, and varies in thickness from 6 inches up to 3 feet. It is said to be less noisy and more safe as a paving stone than the generality of granites employed for that purpose.

1671*h*. The Ross of Mull quarries, in the island of the same name, supply granite of two sorts, red and pink, the felspar being in the former of a brilliant red, and in the latter of a delicate pink, tint. In its physical character it resembles the Aberdeen granite. It is now sent in large quantities to the polishing works at Aberdeen, and, moreover, these quarries can supply larger blocks than can those of Peterhead. Both the red and pink varieties, after having been polished at Mr. Sim's works at Glasgow, were used in the Prince Consort's mausoleum at Frogmore; at the Skerryvore lighthouse; the Liverpool Docks; the Londonderry Docks; the Glasgow Water Works, &c.; and the pink granite in the foundations of the early work at the new Westminster Bridge: the Tormore or red granite being used for the curb to the footways.

1671*i*. The only quarries in the south-west of Scotland are Kirkmabreck quarry, near Creetoun, Wigtown Bay, which furnishes a silver-grey granite, used for the obelisk sent by Mr. Sim to the Exhibition of 1862; and used for many years in the Liverpool Docks. Blocks of any size are readily attainable. Dalbeattie quarry, near Dumfries, has a large-grained grey granite, taking a high polish; there is a difficulty in getting large blocks free from black marks, but it is largely worked for general purposes, kerbing, &c., and for ornamental purposes.

1671*j*. The granites of Ireland are in general a speckled grey, inclining to white, as those of Wicklow, Dublin, &c.; also greenish from hornblende, as Mourne, Newry, &c.; reddish, as Galway. The granite of the Wicklow range is used more extensively than that of any other district in the island. It varies considerably even within a limited distance. Near Kingstown it is very hard, the quartz predominating; this is only used for plain heavy work. For more ornamental purposes granite is brought from Ballyknocken, or Golden Hill, about twenty miles distant. It contains a larger proportion of felspar and less quartz than that of Kingstown, and is therefore more easily worked, and is of a lighter and more uniform and handsome colour, though less durable. Granite of the Carlow portion of the same range is similar. Granite of Down is generally of a darker colour, and more finely crystallized; it is quarried at several places, especially at Newry, from whence it is conveyed by water to several parts of the north of Ireland; it can be worked into fine mouldings, and is of a dark speckled colour. Galway granite is commonly of a reddish colour, containing large crystals of flesh-red felspar; occasionally it has a bluish tint. To the west of Clifden blocks of a moderate thickness, but of great length and width, can be obtained. Granite to the west of Mayo is similar, but the greater part of it in that county is of a dark bluish-grey colour, difficult to work and seldom used. In Donegal and Tyrone it is gneissose, and of the same character, and reddish. Cavan granite is similar to that of Down, and but little employed. In the counties of Kilkenny and Wexford it generally resembles that of the great Carlow range before noticed.

1671*k*. The Bagnalstown quarries, in Carlow, supply four different qualities of granite; I. For plain work, portions being soft, others hard; some fine-grained, and others coarse; and red, blue, grey, and brown in colour; all are obtained from the surface of the land. II. A fine grit, employed for ornamental work even in the Gothic style, is very durable, and of a very white colour. III. Not quite so fine, but much used for buildings and ornamental work, being very white in colour. It lies in horizontal beds of about 1 foot to 15 feet in thickness, and from 15 to 20 feet in length; some beds run 40 feet long. In the hall of the Oxford University Museum is a slab of it, about 10 feet long, 5 feet wide, and 7 inches thick. IV. A very hard granite used for street crossings in and near Cork, not slippery. All these granites are approved for terrace steps, from 6 to 15 feet in length; for floors in stores, porches and halls, as in damp weather it absorbs the moisture from the atmosphere.

1672. Granite used for *paving* purposes is imported for *curbs and trams*, from Guernsey, Jersey, Aberdeen, and Devonshire. For *pitching and macadam*, from Aberdeen; Mount Sorrel, Markfield, and Grooby, all in Leicestershire; Guernsey; and a small quantity from Wales. Mount Sorrel granite is red in colour, and was employed for the altar steps in St. Paul's Cathedral. Granite from the Furnace quarries, at Inverary, as before noticed, is much used in the streets at Glasgow. Markfield and Grooby granites are dark green. The granite from the island of Herm, near Guernsey, was used for the steps to the Duke of York's column, but the cost of working and difficulty of shipping it at the quarry, have led to much discontinuance of its use.

1672*a*. Aberdeen granite is most extensively employed for *curbs, trams, and pitching*; the latter in thin cubes about 9 inches in depth, 3 inches in thickness, and not exceeding 18 inches in length, fair dressed throughout, it being considered the best granite adapted for the traffic of London, as it is very durable and less slippery than most other granites,

such as that of Guernsey, for instance, which is therefore now seldom adopted. The Welsh granite has the same fault, for, with a large amount of traffic in dry weather, it becomes necessary to throw gravel over it. Guernsey macadam, broken to pass through a 2½ inch mesh at the largest, is found to be by far the best material for the purpose, one coat properly applied outlasting two of any other granite. The Devon granite being coarse in grain, is used only in curbs for second-rate streets, while for pitching it is not to be compared in price or quality with that of Aberdeen. Blue Bombay, and blue Port Philip, granites, are hard and tough, and make good second-class roads; while grey China granite is soft and friable, and only good for the foundation of a new road.

1672b. We are indebted for several of the details here given on this subject, to the article in the *Dictionary of Architecture* of the Architectural Publication Society. The *Builder* for 1866 has also entered on the merits of Scottish granites.

1672c.　　　　　　　Table of the Weights of Granites.

Name.	Country.	Weight per cubic foot, Avoirdupois.		
		lbs	oz.	dr.
Stirling Hill - - -	Stirling - -	165	14	5
High Rock, Breadalbane -		166	0	9
Black Hill - - -	Stirling - - -	166	10	4
Dalkey - - -	Dublin - - -	169	9	7
Bars, Breadalbane - -	- - -	169	11	5
Hay Tor - - -	Devonshire - -	165	3	0
Blue, Penmaenmawr (Grauwacke)	Carnarvonshire - -	160	1	0
Aberdeen grey - -	Aberdeenshire - -	166	8	0
„　red - - -	„　 - -	165	4	0
Cornish grey - - -	Cornwall - - -	166	12	0
„　red - - -	„　 - -	164	0	0

Sect. III.

MARBLE.

1673. With the architect and sculptor the name of marble is applied to all stones, harder than gypsum, that are found in large masses, and are susceptible of a good polish. On this principle, under the head of marble, are included many varieties of limestone, porphyry, and even granite and fine-grained basalts. But with mineralogists the word is used in a much more restricted sense, and is confined to such varieties of dolomite, swinestone, and compact and granularly foliated limestone as are capable of receiving a good polish.

1674. The *external characters* are as follows: colours white, grey, red, yellow, and green. Has generally but one colour, though it is often spotted, dotted, striped, and veined. Occurs massive, and in angulo-granular distinct concretions. Internally it alternates from shining to glistening and glimmering; lustre intermediate between pearly and vitreous. Fracture foliated, but oftentimes inclining to splintery. Fragments indeterminate, angular, and rather blunt-edged. More or less translucent. Brittle, and easily frangible. Its *chemical characters* are, that it generally phosphoresces when pounded, or when thrown on glowing coals. It is infusible before the blow-pipe. Dissolves with effervescence in acids.

　　　　Constituent parts, Lime - - - - 56·50
　　　　　　　　　Carbonic acid - - - 43·00
　　　　　　　　　Water - - - - 0·50
　　　　　　　　　　　　　　　　　　　─────
　　　　　　　　　　　　　　　　　　　100·00

1675. All the varieties may be burnt into quicklime; but it is found that in many of them the concretions exfoliate and separate during the volatilization of their carbonic acid, so that by the time that they become perfectly caustic, their cohesion is destroyed, and they fall into a kind of sand, a circumstance which renders it improper to use such varieties in a common kiln.

1676. The varieties of marble are almost infinite, and their classification would be perhaps useless here. Those employed by the ancients, as well as porphyry, are noticed in the Glossary. Parian marble consists almost entirely of carbonate of lime; that of Carrara, in Italy, is often mixed with granular quartz in considerable proportion. Dr. Clarke says that while ancient works in Parian marble remain perfect, those in Pentelic marble have become decomposed, and sometimes exhibit a surface as earthy and rude as that of common limestone. This is considered to be principally owing to veins of ex-

traneous substances which intersect the Pentelic quarries, and which appear more or less in all the works executed in this kind of stone. Parian marble has a waxy appearance when polished; it hardens by exposure to the air; and must be held in estimation even now, as the material from which were formed the Venus di Medici, the Diana Venatrix, the colossal Minerva Pallas of Velletri, and the Capitoline Juno. A green and a red marble are sent from Greece. The marbles known as Verde antico and Verde di Corsica are composed of limestone, calcareous spar, serpentine, and asbestos.

1677. The principal part of the supply to England of foreign marble is from Carrara, a small town or village of Tuscany, in Italy. The quarries at this place were celebrated from an early period, and spots are still shown about them whence they dug the marble for the Pantheon. Masses of marble are sometimes procured there nine feet in length and from four to six in breadth. The quarries are the property of the principal inhabitants of the town, who carry on an extensive trade in the article; but the difficulty of choosing the marble has induced artists to settle there for the execution of their works, and the consequence is, that sculpture abounds and flourishes in the town. The white or Statuary, Italian-veined, Dove-coloured, Pavonazzo or purple veined, and Ravaccione (called Sicilian, supposed to have obtained its name from early ship loads of it having been reshipped or sent on from some port in Sicily, at which the vessel touched in its voyage) marbles, are but very slight variations of the same substance; the Dove and " Sicilian" have a little more carbonaceous matter in their composition; but they are all procured from quarries in the immediate neighbourhood of Carrara. Serravezza in Lucca, produces Statuary, Ravaccione, veined or Bianco chiaro, Mischio di Serravezza, Bardiglio, and Bardiglio fiorito.

1677a. All varieties of Carrara marble have perishable qualities, which ought to preclude them from being ever applied to external purposes in this country. After exposure to the weather for thirty or forty years, disintegration through its entire mass, but mostly on or near the surface, evidently takes place; after the lapse of about a century, more or less, according to the quality of the marble, the entire substance falls into a kind of sparkling sand. The group of Queen Anne, &c., in front of St. Paul's Cathedral, sculptured by Francis Bird, in the beginning of the last century, has long since been painted, in order to preserve it a little longer from total ruin. Even the statue of King George III., by J. Wilton, placed under cover, at the old Royal Exchange, but exposed to the atmosphere, when taken down to be repaired about 1825, was found to be too much decomposed to be put up again; it has long since crumbled to dust. A mural monument by J. Nollekens, erected about 1780 over the centre door within the portico of Bloomsbury Church, fell on to the pavement during the winter of 1837-8, so thoroughly pulverized as to resemble a fall of snow rather than bits of marble. Milan Cathedral is built of the white marble of Monte Candoglio or Candido, on the Toce, a tributary of the Lago Maggiore, selected as better fitted to stand the atmosphere than Carrara marble, of which it is usually said to be built: the " 4,000 statues " are most probably all of the latter material.

1677b. The Ravaccione, or so called " Sicilian" marble, is expected to resist the action of an English atmosphere longer than Italian veined, or white Carrara marble. On examination, however, it will be found that its chemical and mineralogical character scarcely differs from them, except in weight, hardness, and as containing a little more carbonaceous matter. The Marble Arch, erected 1825-7 in front of Buckingham Palace, was removed to its present site 1850-1, when it was found necessary to rub the exposed surfaces with sand and stone, as they were in a state of disintegration. Perhaps the tomb by Sir F. Chantrey, executed about 1820 in the burial-ground of St. John's Wood Chapel, is the oldest specimen in London, if not in England. The surface may now be abraded with the fingers, like sand. This material has of late years been extensively used in the cemeteries round London. But on a careful inspection of stones of three years' date, it will be found that the polish is nearly gone; and even the paint of the lettering has entirely disappeared. Frequent changes of temperature also tend to destroy Carrara marble more rapidly than atmospheric influences; thus the mantel of a chimneypiece is invariably disintegrated long before any other part. These useful practical remarks have been mostly derived from a paper by the late C. H. Smith, given in the *Builder* of 1864, who in conclusion strongly urged the employment of Hopton Wood stone (par. 1666i.) in lieu of it, for all out-door works.

1678. There is a beautiful species of yellow marble obtained from the quarries near Siena, in Italy, and known in England as Siena marble; but the quantity now imported is not very great, and what is introduced is very poor in colour. A good quality, both in colour and vein, can, however, be procured at the quarries by special orders.

1678a. The marbles of Sicily, little, if at all, employed in this country, are enumerated as follows:—Marmo di Trapani, of a grey colour; M. di Castelnuovo, of a yellow colour; M. di Segesta, of a yellow colour; M. di Taormina, of a red colour; M. di Parco, of a yellow colour; M. d'Ogliastro, of a red colour; and M. di Castelaccio, of a grey colour. The two last-named marbles are readily obtainable in blocks 12 or 13 feet

long. Specimens of some, if not all of these, are included in the fine collection of polished marbles made by the learned Corsi of Rome, an account of which he published : the collection was subsequently brought to England, and is believed to exist at Liverpool. Each specimen it contained is no less than 8 inches Italian long, 4 inches wide, and 2 inches thick, and highly polished on all sides.

1679. Many of the marbles of France and Belgium are extremely beautiful. They are chiefly used in this country for chimney pieces. The following is a list (including others) of those so worked, supplied from one of the Belgian workshops:—Rouge royal ; Bleu Belge ; Rouge Griotte ; French red ; Saint Anna ; Noir Belge ; Noir Belge, second quality ; Breccia (Brèche) ; Breccia and black ; Breccia Romana ; Breccia rose ; Saint Gerard ; Sicilian ; Sicilian, white veined ; Pavonazzo ; Statuary ; Statuary, second quality ; Malachite ; Ver de Mer ; Black and green ; Porphyry ; Brocatello ; Siena ; Siena, second quality ; Italian Griotte ; Black and gold ; Black and gold, second quality ; Bardilla ; and Sarracolin. Another marble, named Saint Mont Clarie, is a pure black.

1680. The marbles of Spain are likewise very fine, but are not exported. A specimen of the " Emperor's Red," of unusually fine quality, was presented to the Queen by the late Don Pedro, King of Portugal, for the royal mausoleum at Frogmore.

1681. The marbles of the British Islands deserve more notice from the English architect than they have hitherto received. In England there are but few as yet quarried of granular foliated limestone, the greater number of varieties of them belonging to the floetz or secondary limestone. The most remarkable, and perhaps most beautiful, of the English marbles, is that of Anglesea, called *Mona marble*, and much resembling Verd antique. Its colours are greenish black, leek green, and sometimes purple, irregularly blended with white, but they are not always seen together in the same piece. The white part is limestone, the green shades are said to be owing to serpentine and asbestus. The Isle of Man marbles are—I. Black flagstone (Posidonia schist) from Poolvash, the quarries of which have been worked for upwards of two hundred years ; and furnished the steps in St. Paul's Cathedral, presented by Bishop Thomas Wilson. II. Grey marble (encrinital and shelly limestone) from Poolvash, used for tables and chimney ornaments. III. Black marble (lower carboniferous) limestone, from Port St. Mary, extremely hard and durable, taking a good polish ; raised in blocks and flags of great size, and used for piers, floorings, and tombstones. IV. Pale marble (carboniferous limestone (from Scarlett. Castle Rushen, nine hundred years old, and other places, are built with this most durable material. V. Spanish Head flagstone (clay schist), Port St. Mary ; is a durable material, and used for lintel and gate posts ; it is slightly elastic when in thin flags, and can be raised in square slabs of 16 feet. VI. Peel freestone (old red sandstone), from Craig Millin ; of this stone a large portion of Peel Cathedral was built in 1226. (Cumming, *Isle of Man, &c.*)

1681a. The ornamental marbles of Derbyshire are mostly confined to the 1st, 2nd, and 3rd classes of limestones, which are separated from each other by the *toadstone*, an amygdaloidal trap rock. These marbles are usually distinguished by their colour, as white, grey, dove, blue, black, and russet ; or by physical peculiarities, depending mostly on their fossil contents, as bird's-eye, dog-tooth or muscle, entrochal, shelly, and breccia marbles. Quarries of *black marble* are situated near Ashford, where machinery for cutting and polishing these marbles was first used in 1748. The beds of black marble seldom exceed 7 or 8 inches ; it is difficult to be obtained of any considerable surface free from " shakes," or small veins of white spar. It is also procured at Matlock and Monsaldah. A brown marble, in thin bands of various depths of colour, is called " rosewood," as it presents the appearance of it when polished. It is one of the hardest and most durable of the Derbyshire marbles. A red marble, resembling Rosso antico, is found chiefly near Newhaven, in lumps of no great size. These and other Derbyshire marbles are principally used for inlaying work, as vases, tables, &c., but chimney pieces, columns, &c., are now made at Ashford, Bakewell, Buckland Hollow, and at Derby. This Florentine work, as it is called, is remarkable for fineness of execution and beauty of design, and is almost confined to the county.

1681b. A beautiful greyish-black coralloid marble is also found in Derbyshire and in Wales. The corals it contains are of the porous kind, of the most elegant species, lodged at all angles and in all directions, and are in general about one inch and a half long and three quarters of an inch broad. The other species of coralloid marble is equally beautiful and compact, fine, even texture, very hard, of a deep jet black, and capable of a very high polish. It is variegated with species similar to the above, but smaller, and of a less elegant texture ; among these it has usually a great number of sea shells, both turbinated and bivalve, the coral and shells being of a pure snow white.

1681c. The North Devonshire marbles are abundant and diversified. There are varieties of black and white, from Bridestow, South Tawton, and Drewsteignton. Some of the Chudley, Staverton, and Berry Pomeroy, marbles, have a black ground with large veins of calcareous spar traversing it in all directions. The variegated marbles are gene-

rally reddish, brownish, and greyish, variously veined with white and yellow, and the colours are often intimately blended.   The South Devonshire marbles, now chiefly worked at St. Mary Church, Torquay, from the Babbacombe limestone, are called after the name of the estate or quarry from whence they are taken, such as the Petiton, Ogwell, Ashburton, Babbacombe, &c.   The colours are red, grey, and variegated, of almost every tint.   The sizes of the blocks vary from 1 to 10 tons ; the ordinary length runs from 4 to 5 feet ; 7 to 8 feet is considered as a good length.   At Ipplepen are reddish varieties that are extremely handsome.   They are of different qualities, as compact, porcellanic, granular, crystalline, shelly, magnesian, pozolanic or water, stinking or swine.   The Bartons quarry at Ipplepen, belonging to Mr. Field, of Parliament Street, is worked at 80 to 100 feet in depth ; the lowest beds are about 8 feet thick, and of a mottled character, being dark red and white in colour; the deposit over it is streaky and lighter in colour.   Blocks of 18 feet square are now conveyed to London.   This quarry has lately supplied the mono-lithic polished shafts for the forty columns (18 out of one block), each 12 feet 3 inches in length, and $18\frac{1}{2}$ inches diameter on the fillet, with many others, for the new building of the National Provincial Bank of England, in Bishopsgate Street.   The bases are of Irish black marble, and the caps of the cream-coloured Huddlestone stone.   In the corridor of the new Freemasons' Hall are four columns, two being from the Bartons quarries, and two of Languedoc marble : eight others are placed in the coffee-room of the Charing Cross Hotel.   The limestones of Plymouth are not so fine.   They are of two sorts; one, an ash colour shaded with black veins ; the other blackish grey and white, shaded in concentric spots interspersed with irregular red spots; or black with white veins about a quarter to an inch in width.

1681d.   Serpentine, "beyond all question, the most beautiful of the ornamental stones of this country " (Hunt), is chiefly found in the sea-bound peninsula called the Lizard, the most southerly land in Great Britain.   This rock, with another called diallage, con-stitute nearly half of the Lizard peninsula.   Serpentine has evidently been under the influence of heat.   At one spot it seems to shade off into the hornblende slate in which it is embedded ; at another, it has every appearance of having been thrust up among the hornblende slate. Sir Henry de la Beche wrote, many years since, that serpentine *ought* to be employed for decorative purposes.   He named Landewednack, Cadgwith, Kennack, Cove, and Goosehilly Downs, as four sites whence beautiful specimens might be obtained, vary-ing in colour, as, an olive green base striped with greenish-blue steatite veins ; another specimen, very hard, with a reddish base studded with crystals of the mineral called *diallage*, which when cut through and polished, gives forth a beautiful metallic green glitter, heightened still further by the reddish tint of the mass in which it is embedded.   To the Exhibition of 1851, Penzance sent fine specimens in all kinds of ornaments.   The blocks are small, but sometimes they have been obtained 7 feet in length and 4 or 5 tons in weight; the largest was 8 feet long, 3 feet wide, and $2\frac{1}{2}$ feet thick; from 2 to 3 feet long is the usual size.   The best blocks are worth from 5 to 10 guineas per ton, according to their weight, the larger the size the higher is the value in an increasing proportion. Chemically, steatite and serpentine differ little from each other, and as they are quarried in juxtaposition, specimens of both kinds are selected for use ; but serpentine being much harder and more richly coloured, is appropriated to the larger articles.

1681e.   In the *Builder* of 1865, p. 877, it is stated that serpentine is not a marble, but a talc containing a tolerable quantity of chromate of iron.   It is sometimes good for external ornamentation, but never when it has the white streaks so commonly seen in it.   Hunt's *Handbook to the* 1851 *Exhibition*, gives the following analysis of serpentine obtained at the Lizard:—Magnesia, 38·68 ; silica, 42·50 ; lime and alumina, 2·10 ; oxide of iron, 1·50 ; oxide of manganese, 1·0; oxide of chromium, 0·30; the colouring matter is probably a combination of chromium, iron, and manganese.   In his *Handbook to the* 1862 *Exhibition*, it is called a hydrated silicitate of magnesia, composed of silica, 43·64 ; magnesia, 43·35 ; and water, 13·01 = 100.   Besides the supply from the Lizard, it is obtained in Anglesea, Portsoy in Banffshire, Unst and Fetlar in Scotland.   The "green marble," or serpentine, of Connemara, is noticed among the Irish marbles.   This material is sawn by steam power with sand and water ; and when brought into the form required, it is ground, turned, rubbed, and polished until it presents a beautiful glossy surface, said to be capable of resist-ing grease and acids, which is not the case with marble in general.

1681f.   It is said that two brackets of old monuments in Westminster Abbey ; the panel-bordering of the monument erected to the memory of Addison ; the brackets of a chimney-piece at Hampton Court, are all carved in serpentine, and the present condition of these specimens shows the durability of it.   " Equal to granite in durability," is the statement made in advertisements, but probably some further time must elapse before such a statement can be endorsed, though it may be allowed that it appears to stand atmospheric influences remarkably well.   Experiments on the strength of serpentine have been noticed in par. 1502g.   Therein is mentioned a shaft of Poltesco grey-green Devonshire serpentine, one of the weakest examples, which went across and not with the vein : the latter running

in the line of the diameter. The green serpentine has been used lately on the outside of some offices in Cornhill; and the red quality in 1853 in Leicester Square.

1681*g*. Purbeck, Petworth, or Sussex marble, is the name of a material common to Derbyshire, Dorsetshire, the Isle of Wight, Kent, Surrey, and Sussex. It is found at Dinton, near Aylesbury, and it occurs at Boulogne and at Beauvais, in France. In some places, as in the most westerly quarries near Corfe Castle, and at the top of the Isle of Portland, the Purbeck stone is so highly coloured and fine-grained, that it is chiefly identified as belonging to the fresh water deposits by the fossils it contains. In general, the stone may be said to be fine grained in the quarries north and west; while in those approaching the east the pattern is larger, the shells well defined, and scarcely any of them broken; the marble from this district is therefore handsomer, and more in request for ornamental purposes. Purbeck was well known for its quarries during the middle ages, when the marble was in great request for decorating the clustered shafts and sepulchral tombs, and for pavements, in churches. At the present time, there is scarcely sufficient demand to keep more than a few men at work, and this at Woody-hyde, near Corfe Castle, where the genuine material or Purbeck marble can be obtained, and that quarry is a *hole* more than a quarry. It has been stated that, during the middle ages, this material was also obtained from quarries at Parham Park, six miles north-east of Arundel, but there are now no traces of it left on the surface.

1681*h*. All varieties of Purbeck marble contain a large proportion of clay in their composition, which is one chief cause of their perishable nature. In the interior of buildings the moisture in the air will be condensed, and absorbed into the argillaceous portion of the marble. While this process is going on, the lustre of the polish is gradually diminished, the colour is altered, its hardness and cohesion destroyed, until the surface is completely changed to a dull earthy appearance, and decay results, which will be facilitated in proportion to the amount of clay contained in a given mass. When, as in small columns, this material is placed with the planes of lamination in a vertical position, there results another and a greater tendency to decay. The clustered columns in the Temple church, though renewed in 1840–42, had already lost much of their polish in 1853, a preliminary stage towards decay. The large ancient columns supporting the clere-story at Westminster Abbey, have now scarcely a trace left of their original surface. (C. H. Smith, *Transactions*, Institute of British Architects, 1853). As already stated, this sort of marble is obtained in Kent, where it is also known as Bethersden marble, and likewise as Lovelace marble, obtained near Ashford. In the east and west sides of the new quadrangle of St. John's College, Oxford, are sixteen entire columns of " Bletchingden marble," which were put up in 1631–35. It may be seen in Hythe Church and in some of the neighbouring churches, where it is often varnished in lieu of being polished. The Purbeck marble columns used in Lincoln Minster, in 1186–1200 are asserted to have been worked up by vinegar.

1682. Of the Scotch marbles the principal are the *Tiree*, of which there are two varieties, red and white. The *Iona*, whose colours are a greyish white and snow white, sometimes intermixed with steatite, giving it a green or yellow colour in spots and known under the name of Iona or Icolmkill pebbles. It does not take a high polish. The *Skye* marble, of greyish hue, with occasionally various veins. The *Assynt* varieties of white, of grey, and dove colour. *Glen Tilt* marble, white and grey, with occasionally yellow and green spots. Marble of *Balliculish*, of a grey or white colour, and capable of being produced in considerable blocks. *Boyne* marble, grey or white, and taking a good polish. *Blairgowrie*, in Perthshire, of a pure white colour, fit, it is said, to be employed in statuary and for architectural purposes; and *Glenavon*, a white marble, said by Williams (*Natural History of the Mineral Kingdom*) to be a valuable marble, is not used, from the remoteness of its situation and the difficulty of access to it.

1683. Ireland is rich in marbles. The dark colours vary from jet black to dark dove colour, purple, blue, and grey; the light colours, from the pure snow white to the celined, cream coloured, pink, and light grey. The variegated consist of the serpentine, black and white veined, mottled, and those marked with fossil organic remains. The black marbles, which are those of most value in Ireland, are extensively met with, and belong to the lower limestone. The merchantable beds of the best quality, which have been extensively worked, are met with in the counties of Galway, Limerick, Carlow, and Kilkenny. It is also found in the counties of Mayo and Waterford. The best quarries are considered to be those close to the town of Galway, near the bank of Lough Corrib. It occurs in three beds, varying from about 9 to 12 inches in thickness. One is called the " London bed," as it supplies most of the black marble exported to London. Blocks are raised of an average size of about 5 to 10 feet in length, and 4 to 5 feet in width; others 20 feet in length can be obtained. Some blocks 16 feet in length were sent over for a staircase for the Duke of Hamilton's seat in Scotland, who was also furnished with landings and solid balustrades worked to a fine polish. Angliham and Merlin Park quarries supply black marble of the very finest description, and capable of receiving a very high polish. Steps of this material were supplied for the staircases at Marlborough House, Hampton Court, and Kensington Palace, under Sir C. Wren, cir. 1700. At Oughterard, the beds contain more

or less silica, rendering them not so valuable.   At Kilkenny, it abounds with shells, which
become more conspicuous as the marble dries   Kilkenny marble was once extensively
employed in Ireland, but the black is now preferred.   The polish of black marble, while it
is considerably affected by dampness, is much improved and preserved by being kept dry.

1683*a.* Dark grey and dark mottled grey marbles are met with chiefly in King's county
and in several parts of the county of Cork.   Near Tullamore, marble is obtained in large
blocks capable of receiving a fine polish, and is much used for chimney-pieces and ornamental works.   The limestone around Cork produces easy working marble of a light
grey or dove colour, and more or less mottled, receiving a good polish.   In the primary
districts of Donegal, a light grey and bluish grey coloured marble of close grain is found
to a great extent ; most of it, however, is hard to work from the quantity of silex it contains.
The same kind of a bluish tint is very frequent in Connemara.   It is compact in texture,
but does not always produce a satisfactory polish.   *White marble* occurs in the western
portion of county Donegal, differing much from that of Connemara.   It is of comparatively
easy conversion, and can be obtained in cubical blocks in great quantities; its very coarsely
granular texture, however, is prejudicial to it for many purposes; for boldly executed
works in sculpture, where the expense of carriage would be avoided, it might be advantageously employed for many purposes ; but it will not vie with the marble of Carrara.
The Connemara white marble is hard and fine, and the strongest yet found; it cannot,
however, be procured in large blocks free from streaks, which pass through the blocks
parallel with the beds.   At Chevy, near Dungannon, county Tyrone, a very delicate cream
coloured marble is obtained, very compact in texture, receiving a high degree of polish, and
blocks of great length can be procured.   The coarsely crystalline and fossiliferous limestone
at Ardbraccan produces light coloured marble of easy conversion.

1683*b.* Of the variegated marbles, the *Siena* of the best quality is perhaps the most
beautiful.   It is obtained in several places in King's county ; but the best, the veined or
mottled Siena, is found near the Seven Churches.   It is susceptible of a high polish, and
exhibits many bright and distinct colours.   Marble of the same character also prevails,
having a dove coloured ground, varied or mottled with Siena colour.   In the county of
Armagh, a Siena, or rather a brownish red marble, is found, containing a great number of
fossil shells ; several varieties of colour, from a very light reddish brown to a rather dark
red, are also met with, more or less marked with shells.   At Pallaskenry in the county of
Limerick, a dark red and mottled marble is abundant, and has been much used.   A red
coloured marble, of a compact but slaty texture, occurs in the county of Cork, extending
from the city in a narrow seam, for a distance of several miles.   It is hard to work and dull
in colour : at one time it was extensively used.

1683*c.* The serpentine, or *green marble,* as it is usually called, of Connemara, in county
Galway, is of a dull green colour.   Blocks are raised of considerable size, from which slabs
can be obtained, at Barnanoraun quarry, near that at Recess; and at Letternaphy quarry,
near Clifden ; the latter being rather coarse in quality ; while at Tievebaun quarry, near
Recess, the marble is dark green, very sound, and free from shakes of any kind.   Black
and white marble, and that of a mottled character, occur near Cork, in the counties
of Waterford, Longford, and Kerry; some of the varieties are very fine; that obtained
near Mitchelstown is well marked and receives a high polish.   The limestone obtained
near the Seven Churches in King's county, when polished, produces a good marble
of an even grey colour.   It is strongly mottled with very numerous fossil organic
remains.   It is easily worked, and raised from the quarries in thin beds.   This marble, in a
polished state, has been used in the construction of one of the principal ruins at the Seven
Churches; some of the stones retain their polish to this time, while others exhibit decay.
(Wilkinson, *Geology, &c. of Ireland,* 1845).   A fine purple marble is found at Lough-
lougher in county Tipperary, which is said to be beautiful when polished.   Some of a
purple colour, and purple and white intermixed with yellow spots, were to be procured in
the islands near Dunkerron in the river Kenmare.

1683*d.*   Table of the Weights of Marbles.

Name.	County or Country.	Weight per cubic foot, avoirdupois.		
		lbs.	oz.	dr.
Black - - - -	Kilkenny - - -	171	6	0
Tiree - - - -	Hebrides, Scotland - -	172	5	0
Carrara, Statuary - -	Tuscany - - -	168	10	5
„ Ravaccione - -	„ - - -	169	2	8
Ipplepen, Bartons quarry -	Devonshire - - -	163	6	0

Its tenacity is stated at 6,000 lbs. per square inch, and its crushing weight is also put at
6,000 lbs. per square inch.   (Hunt.)

Sect. IV.

TIMBER.

1684. The information we propose here to lay before the reader relative to the different species of timber is extracted from Miller's *Gardener's Dictionary*, Rondelet's *Art de Bâtir*, Rees's *Cyclopædia*, and Hunter's edition of Evelyn's *Sylva*. To give any thing like the information that would satisfy the botanist would be out of place in an architectural work; and we therefore confine our observations to those which will be useful to the student.

1685. Oak. Of this most valuable timber for building purposes Vitruvius (lib. ii. cap. ix.) enumerates five species, which it would now be difficult to identify. That some species of the Quercus of the botanists are more valuable for building purposes than others no doubts exist. Evelyn seems to commend especially the Irish oak, because of its withstanding the efforts of the worm; but it is not easy to ascertain the particular species to which he alludes. In the present day the Sussex oak is esteemed the most valuable; a value, according to some authors, derived from the nature of the soil and from good management in the culture, which is an object of no small importance.

1686. Generally, it has been usual to consider England as producing, without difference in quality, but one species of oak; but two sorts are well known to the English botanist, the *Quercus Robur* and the *Quercus Sessiliflora*. The former is found throughout the temperate parts of Europe, and is that most common in the southern parts of England. Its leaves are formed with irregular sinuosities, and their footstalks are short, occasionally almost without any at all. It attains a very large size, and the wood is tolerably straight-grained and pretty free from knots, in many instances resembling the German species called wainscot. It is easily split for making laths for plasterers and slaters, and is beyond doubt the best sort for joist, rafters, and other purposes where stiff and straight-grained timber is a desideratum. In the Quercus Sessiliflora, which, though found about Dulwich and Norwood, according to Miller, appears to be the common oak of Durham, and perhaps of the north of England, the leaves have long footstalks, frequently an inch in length, and their sinuosities are not so deep, but are more regular than those of the Robur just described. The acorns are so close to the branches as to have scarcely any stalks. The wood is of a darker hue, and the grain is so smooth that it resembles chesnut. Than the Robur it possesses more elasticity, hardness, and weight, but in seasoning it is subject to warp and split; hence unfit for laths, which in the north of England are rarely of oak. There is no reason for supposing, as has been conjectured, that the oak of the Gothic roofs of the country is of this species, though we are aware of the great durability of the oak in the buildings in the northern part of the island.

1687. The specific gravity of the species first named, that is, the Quercus Robur, may be taken at about ·800, and the weight of a cube foot 50·45 lbs. That of the last-named at ·875, and the weight of a cube foot at about 55·00 lbs. Their cohesive force and toughness are proportionable.

1688. The American species scarcely claim a notice here, because their use in England is, from every circumstance, out of the question. Of the red oak of Canada (Quercus rubra), the only one of which the use could be contemplated, we merely observe, that it is a light, spongy, and far from durable wood, though, in the country, in many instances useful. Its growth is rapid, and it rises to the height of 90 or 100 feet.

1689. There is a species of oak imported from Norway, which has received the name of *clapboard*, and another imported from Holland, known under the name of *Dutch wainscot*, though grown in Germany, whence it is floated down the Rhine for exportation. The latter is destitute of the white streaks which cross the former, and is thereby distinguished from it. The use of these woods has latterly much diminished in England. They are both softer than common oak, and the clapboard far inferior to wainscot. They are more commonly used for fittings and fixtures, whereto they are well adapted. In damp situations, oak decays gradually from its external surface to the centre of the tree; the ring on the outside, which it acquired in the last year of the growth of the tree, decaying first; but if the tree be not felled till past its prime, its decay is reversed by its commencement at the centre. An oak rarely reaches its prime under the age of an hundred years; after that period, which is that of its greatest strength, it cannot be considered as fit for building purposes; and, indeed, it may be taken as a rule, that oak before arriving at its maturity is stronger than that which has passed it.

1690. If the architect has the opportunity of selecting the timber whilst in a state of growth, he will, of course, choose healthy, vigorous, and flourishing trees. Those in which the trunks are most even are to be preferred. A mark of decay is detected in any swelling above the general surface of the wood. Dead branches, especially at the top of the tree, render it suspicious, though the root is the best index to its soundness. The notion of Alberti (*De Re Ædificatoria*), of using all the timber in the same building from

the same forest, is a little too fanciful for these days, though we confess we have some mis-givings in impugning an authority which, in most other respects, we are inclined to receive with the highest veneration.

1691. In felling not only the oak, but all other large trees, the great branches should be first cut off, so that the tree may not be injured or strained in its fall; and the trunk, moreover, must be sawed as close to the ground as possible. When felled, but not before, it is to be barked, trimmed of its branches, and left to season. Before, however, leaving it for this purpose, it is considered by workmen better to square it, which, it is thought, prevents its tendency to split. If to be employed for posts or bearing pieces, boring it has been employed with success; but it is needless to observe, that in pieces subject to transverse strains such a practice is not to be recommended.

1692. The pieces selected for building must be chosen with the straightest grain; but there are pieces which are occasionally employed, as for knees and braces, wherein a curvilinear direction of the fibres of the timber is extremely desirable. It may, however, be generally stated, that, in the case of two equal-sized and seasoned pieces, the heavier is the piece to be preferred.

1693. In oak, as in all other woods, the boughs and branches are never so good as the body of the tree; the great are stronger than the small limbs, and the wood of the heart stronger than all. When green, wood is not so strong as when thoroughly dry, which it rarely is till two or three years after it is felled. It is scarcely necessary to say, that, con-taining much sap, it is not only weaker, but decays sooner. It is weakened by knots, at which, in practice, it is found that fractures most frequently occur; and it is important to the architect to recollect that he should always reject cross-grained pieces.

1694. The great use of oak in this country is more for ship-building purposes than for architectural, its use, except in the provinces, being principally confined to pieces which are much liable to compression, or where great stiffness is required, or in pieces like sills to windows and door-cases, where there is much alternation of dryness and damp. So early as 1788, the consumption of oak for ship-building purposes was, in that year upwards of 50,000 loads.

1695. When of good quality, it is more durable than any other wood which is procur-able of a like size. In a dry state, it is ascertained to have lasted nearly a thousand years. The open-fibred porous oak of Lincolnshire, and some other places, is a bad sort. The best is that with the closest grain and the smallest pores. The colour, as is well known, is a fine brown; that which partakes of a reddish hue is not so good as the other. The smell of it is peculiar; it contains gallic acid, and it assumes a black purple colour when damp, by contact with iron. It warps and twists much in seasoning, and shrinks in width about one thirty-seventh part.

1696. Chesnut. One of the finest of the European timber trees, the *Fagus castanea* of botanists, was heretofore so common in this country, that Fitzstephen, in his description of London about the time of Henry II., mentions a fine forest of chesnuts as growing on the northern side of the city. It is stated to have been used in the buildings of our ancestors, but it is very doubtful if it was so employed. The young tree vies with the oak in durability, from the small proportion of sapwood it contains. Of its durability, the roofs of Westminster Hall, that of King's College, Cambridge, and that of Notre Dame, at Paris, are cited as examples, though the fact of the latter being of chesnut is doubted by Rondelet, who says that Buffon and D'Aubenton thought it a species of oak, which is now well known to be the case in the roof first named.

1697. Chesnut, however, is not to be trusted like oak. As Evelyn observed, it is often well-looking outside, when decayed and rotten within. Belidor says it soon rots when the ends of timbers of it are closed round in a wall.

1698. It is, perhaps, from the circumstance of its colour so nearly resembling that of oak, that one timber has so often been mistaken for the other. The difference, however, is, that the pores of the sapwood of the oak are larger and more thickly set and easily distinguished, whilst those in the chesnut require magnifying powers to be distinguished. But a more decided difference is, that the chesnut has no large transverse septa. It is far easier to work than oak, and is not very susceptible of swelling and shrinkage. From what has been mentioned above, it may be inferred that the wood, though tough and com-pact, is, when young, hardest and most flexible, the old wood being often shaky and brittle.

1699. Water pipes of this tree endure much longer than those of elm; and for tubs and vessels to hold water, it is superior to oak; for when once thoroughly seasoned, it will neither shrink nor swell, on which account it is used by the Italians for wine tuns and casks. It will thrive on most soils, but rather delights in a rich loamy land, succeeding well, also, on that which is gravelly, clayey, or sandy. Mixed soils are suitable to it, and it is found in the warmer mountainous situations of most parts of Europe.

1700. From the experiments, the cohesive force of a square inch of chesnut, when dry, varies from 9570 to 12,000 lbs., and the weight of a cubic foot, when dry, is from 43 to 55 lbs.

1701. Beech (*Fagus Sylvatica*). A beautiful tree, growing to a considerable height, and carrying a proportionable trunk. It flourishes most in a dry warm soil, and grows moderately quick. The wood is hard, close, has a dry even grain, and, like the elm, bears the drift of spikes. The sorts of beech are the brown or black, and the white beech. It is common throughout Europe. In the southern parts of Buckinghamshire, where the soil is chalky, it is particularly abundant; and such is the case near Warbleton, in Sussex, on the southern range of chalk hills, where the beeches are very fine.

1702. Constantly immersed in water, the beech is very durable; such also is the case with it when constantly dry; but mere damp is injurious to it, and it is very liable to injury by worms, though to these Duhamel considers it much less liable when water-seasoned, than when seasoned in the common way. To render it less liable to the worm, it has been recommended to fell it about a fortnight after Midsummer, to cut it immediately into planks, which are to be placed in water about ten days and then dried. Beech is little used in building, except for piles, in which situation, if constantly wet, they are very durable. From its uniform texture and hardness, it is a good material for tools and furniture, and of it, in boards and planks, large quantities are brought to London. It is without sensible taste and smell, easy to work, and susceptible of a very smooth surface. The white sort is the hardest, though the black is tougher, and, according to Evelyn, more durable. The weight of a cube foot varies from 43 to 53 pounds.

1703. Walnut (*Juglans, quasi Jovis glans*) is of several sorts. The Juglans Regia, or common walnut, was formerly much cultivated in this island, as well for the sake of its timber as of its fruit. On the former account the importation of mahogany has long since rendered its cultivation less common. It flourishes better in a thin limestone soil, than in one that is rich and deep, and, if raised for timber, should not be transplanted, but remain in the place where it is sown. For furniture, from its rich brown colour, it is by many persons preferred to mahogany. Its scarcity renders its employment rare for building purposes, though by the ancients it was so employed. One of its properties is, that it is less liable to be affected by worms than any other timber, cedar only excepted; but from its brittle and cross-grained texture, it is not generally useful for the main timbers of a building.

1704. The heart-wood is of a greyish brown with dark brown pores, often veined with darker shades of the same colour, which are much heightened by oiling. The texture is not so uniform as that of mahogany, nor does it work so easily, but it may be brought to a smoother surface. The weight of a cubic foot is about 45 pounds.

1705. Cedar (*Pinus Cedrus*) is an evergreen cone-bearing tree, of which though several have been grown in this country, it is too scarce to be employed in building. Its durability is very great; such, indeed, that Pliny states cedar to have been found in the Temple of Apollo at Utica, which must have been 1200 years old. Its colour is a light rich yellow brown, with the annual rings distinct. It is resinous, and has a powerful smell. The taste is slightly bitter, and it is not subject to worms. It is very straight in the grain, works easily and splits readily. Weight of a cubic foot from 30 to 38 pounds.

1706. Fir (*Pinus Sylvestris*). The red or yellow fir is produced on the hills of Scotland; but the forests of Russia, Denmark, Norway, Lapland, and Sweden produce the finest timber of this species. It is imported, under the name of red wood, in *logs* and *deals*. From Norway the trees are never more than 18 inches diameter, whence there is much sap-wood in them; but the heart is a stronger and more durable wood than is had from larger trees of other countries. From Riga a great deal of timber is received under the name of *masts* and *spars:* the former are usually 70 or 80 feet in length, and from 18 to 25 inches diameter; when of less diameter they take the latter name. Yellow deals and planks are imported from Stockholm, Frederickshall, Christiana, and various other parts of Sweden, Russia, Norway, and Prussia. Of the pine species the red or yellow fir is the most durable; and it was said by the celebrated Brindley, that red Riga deal, or pine wood, would endure as long as oak in all situations. In Pontey's *Forest Pruner*, on the authority of Dr. Smith, an instance is given of the durability of natural-grown Scotch fir. It is therein stated, that some was known to have been 300 years in the roof of an old castle, and that it was as fresh and full of sap as timber newly imported from Memel, and that part of it was actually wrought up into new furniture. It is to be observed, that foreign timber has an advantage too seldom allowed to that which is grown at home, the former being always in some degree seasoned before it arrives in this country, and therefore never used in so unseasoned a state as the latter timber usually is.

1707. From its great lightness and stiffness it is superior to any other material for beams, girders, joists, rafters, and framing in general. In naval architecture it is used for masts and various other parts of vessels. In joinery, both internal and external, it stands better, is nearly as durable as oak, and is much cheaper.

1708. There is great variety in the colours of the different sorts of this fir: it is generally of a red or honey yellow of different degrees of brightness, and consists in section of hard and soft circles alternately, one part of each annual ring being soft and light coloured, the

other harder and dark coloured, and possessing a strong resinous taste and smell. When not abounding in resin it works easily. That from abroad shrinks in the log, from seasoning, about one thirtieth part of its width.

1709. The annual rings of the best sort of this timber do not exceed one tenth of an inch in thickness, their dark parts are of a bright red colour. That from Norway is the finest of the sort, to which the best Riga and Memel are much inferior. The inferior timber of this kind, which is not so durable nor so capable of bearing strains, has thick annual rings, and abounds with a soft resinous matter, which is clammy and chokes the saw. Much of the timber of this sort is from Sweden, but it is inferior in strength and stiffness. That which is produced in the colder climates is superior to that which is the product of warmer countries, the Norway timber being much harder than that of Riga. The weight of a cubic foot of this fir, when seasoned, varies from 29 to 40 pounds. That of English growth, seasoned, from 28 to 33.

1710. WHITE FIR (*Pinus abies*), commonly called the spruce of Norway, whose forests produce it in abundance. This is the sort which in deals and planks is imported from Christiana, in which condition it is more esteemed than any other sort. The trees from which these are generally obtained are of 70 or 80 years' growth, and are usually cut into three lengths of about 12 feet each, which are sawn into deals and planks, each length yielding three deals or planks. Their most usual thickness is 3 inches, and they are generally 9 inches wide. In this country they are sold by the hundred, which in the case of white as well as yellow deals, contains 120 deals, be their thickness what it may, reduced to a standard one of an inch and a half, a width of 11 inches, and a length of 12 feet. What is called whole deal is an inch and a quarter thick, and slit deal is one half of that thickness. It unites better by means of glue than the yellow sort, is used much for interior work in joinery, and is very durable when in a dry state.

1711. The colour of the spruce fir is a yellow or rather brown white, the annual ring consisting of two parts, one hard, the other softer. The knots are tough, but it is not difficult to work. Besides the importation above named, there is a considerable quantity received from America. Of the Christiana fir a cubic foot weighs from 28 to 32 pounds when seasoned. That from America about 29 pounds; and the Norway spruce grown in Britain about 34 pounds. In seasoning it shrinks about a seventieth part, and after being purchased as dry deals at the timber yards, about one ninetieth.

1712. AMERICAN PINES. The *Pinus Strobus*, or what is called the Weymouth or white pine, is a native of North America, imported in logs often more than 2 feet square and upwards of 30 feet in length. It is an useful timber, light and soft, stands the weather tolerably well, and is much used for masts. For joiners' work it is useful from its clean straight grain. But it should not be used for large timbers, inasmuch as it is not durable, and is moreover very susceptible of the dry rot. Its colour is a brown yellow, and it has a peculiar odour. The texture is very uniform, more so, indeed, than any other of the pine species, and the annual rings are not very distinct. It stands well enough when well seasoned. A cubic foot of it weighs about 29 pounds.

1713. The yellow pine, or *Pinus variabilis*, is imported into England, but it is not much used; it is the produce of the pine forests from New England to Georgia.

1714. The pitch pine (*resinosa*), remarkable for the quantity and fragrance of the resin it produces, is a native of Canada. It is brittle when dry, and, though heavy, not durable. It is of a much redder hue than the Scotch pine, and from its glutinous property difficult to plane. The weight of a cubic foot is 41 pounds.

1715. The silver pine (*picea*) is common in the British plantations. This species of timber is produced in abundance, and is much used on the Continent both for carpentry and ship-building. It is light and stiff, and according to Wiebekin, lasts longer in air than in water. A cubic foot weighs about 26 pounds.

1716. The Chester pine (*pinaster*) is occasionally cultivated in the British plantations. It is better suited to water than exposure to the air, and has a finer grain, but contains less resin, than the pine or silver fir. A cubic foot weighs about 26 pounds.

1717. LARCH (*Pinus Larix*). A timber tree only lately to any considerable extent adopted in the plantations of Great Britain, among whose cultivators the Duke of Athol has been one of the most ardent and successful. It grows straight and rapidly, is said to be durable in all situations, and appears to have been known and appreciated by Vitruvius, who regretted the difficulty of its transport to Rome, where, however, it was occasionally used. Wiebekin prefers it to the pine, pinaster, and fir, for the arches of timber bridges. To flooring boards and stairs, where there is much wear, it is well suited, and when oiled assumes a beautiful colour, such, indeed, that when used for internal joinery, a coat of varnish gives it a more beautiful appearance than it could receive from any painting. The American larches do not produce turpentine; but the timber has been considered equal to the European sorts. It is of a honey yellow colour, and more difficult to work than the Riga or Memel timber, though, when obtained, the surface is better. It bears the driving

to nails and bolts, and stands well if properly seasoned.   A cubic foot weighs from 30 of 40 pounds.

1718. Poplar. The *Populus* of botanists, whereof five species are grown in England: the common white poplar, the black, the aspen or trembling poplar, the abele or great white poplar, and that of Lombardy. The wood of this tree is only fit for the flooring of inferior rooms where there is not much wear. Evelyn attributes to this wood the property of burning " *untowardly*," rather mouldering than maintaining any solid heat. Its colour is a yellow or brown white. The annual rings, whereof one side is a little darker than the other, making each year's growth visible, are of an uniform texture. The best sorts are the Lombardy, the black, and the common white poplar. Of the Lombardy poplar, the weight of a cubic foot is about 24 pounds; of the aspen and black poplar, 26 pounds; and of the white poplar, about 33 pounds.

1719. Alder (*Betula alnus*). A tree delighting in wet places by the banks of rivers, and which furnished the material, says Vitruvius, for the piles whereon the whole of the buildings of Ravenna stand. In a dry situation it is unfit for employment, on account of its early rot when exposed to the weather or to mere damp, and its susceptibility of engendering worms. Evelyn says that it was used for the piles upon which the celebrated bridge of the Rialto at Venice was founded in 1591; but we have no certain data by which such assertion can be maintained. There is, however, no doubt that it may be advantageously employed in situations where it is constantly under water.

Its colour is of a red yellow, of different shades, but nearly uniform; which latter quality is exhibited in its texture.

From its softness it is easily worked, and seems adapted, therefore, for carving. In a dry state the weight of a cubic foot varies from 36 to 50 pounds.

1720. Elm (*Ulmus*). In Great Britain five species of this tree abound, whereof the *Ulmus campestris*, common in the woods and hedges of the southern parts of England, is a hard and durable wood, but is rarely used except for coffins. The *Ulmus suberosa*, or cork-barked elm, is an inferior sort, and is very common in Sussex.

1721. The *Ulmus Montana* is the most common species in Europe, and particularly in the northern counties of England. It is more generally known by the name of the broad-leaved elm or wych hazel. Without enumerating the other varieties, whereof the Dutch elm (*Ulmus major*) is good for nothing, we shall merely observe, that the *Ulmus glabra*, common in Herefordshire, Essex, and the north and north-eastern counties of England, grows to the largest size and is most esteemed, whilst the Dutch elm is the worst. The elm is a durable timber when constantly wet, as a proof whereof we have only to mention that it was used for the piles on which the old London Bridge stood. Indeed, its durability under water is well known; but for the general purposes of building it is of little value, and it rarely falls to the lot of the architect to be obliged to use it.

1722. The colour of the heart-wood is darker than that of oak, and of a redder brown. The sapwood is of yellow or brown-white colour. It is porous, cross and coarse grained, has a peculiar smell, twists and warps very much in drying, and shrinks considerably in breadth and length. Though difficult to work, it bears the driving of bolts and nails better than most other sorts of timber. The weight of a cubic foot, when dry, varies from 36 to 48, seasoned from 37 to 50 pounds. From experiment it seems that in seasoning it shrinks one forty-fourth part of its width.

1723. Ash (*Fraxinus excelsior*). This, the most valuable of the genus, is common throughout Europe and the northern parts of Asia. It grows rapidly, and of it the young is more valuable than the old wood. It is much affected by the difference of the soils in which it grows. It will not endure when subject to alternations of damp and moisture, though sufficiently durable when constantly in a dry situation. Its pores, if cut in the spring, are of a reddish colour, and it is improved by water-seasoning. Evelyn says, that when felled in full sap, the worm soon takes to it; and therefore recommends its being felled in the months from November to February. The texture is compact and porous, the compact side of the annual ring being dark in colour, whence the annual rings are distinct. The general colour is brown, resembling that of oak; but it is more veined, and the veins darker than those of oak. The timber of the young tree is a white, approaching brown, with a greenish hue. It has no peculiar taste or smell, is difficult to work, and is too flexible for use in building, beside the important want of the character of durability. The weight of a cubic foot varies from 35 to 52 pounds; and it is to be observed, when the weight is much less than 45 pounds the timber is that of an old tree.

1724. Sycamore (*Acer pseudo-platanus*), usually called the plane tree in the northern part of the island, is common in Britain and on the mountains of Germany. It is rapid in growth, and the wood is durable when it escapes the worm, to which it is quite as liable as beech. The use of it in buildings is not common, but for furniture it is valuable. The colour is a brown white, yellowish, and sometimes inclining to white. Texture uniform; annual rings indistinct. It is not so hard as beech, brittle, and generally easy to work. A cubic foot, when seasoned, weighs from 34 to 42 pounds. Ware says that there are old

houses in this country floored with sycamore and wainscoted with poplar. It seems well enough calculated for floors.

1725. BIRCH. *Betula alba*, or common birch, is a species of alder, to which article the reader is referred (1719). The American birch, from Canada, is but little superior to the European birch. The Russian birch, on account of its clean light colour and silvery grain, has been for many years extensively employed for bedroom furniture.

1726. A description of fir (*Wellingtonia gigantea*) has been lately introduced from our colony of Victoria, in Vancouver's Island, on the western side of North America. It is sent in logs, deals, and planks. Instead, however, of being only 14 to 16 inches square, and 60 feet long at the maximum, as in the case of Baltic timber, one stick of this timber has been sent not less than 127 feet long, and about 42 inches square at one third of the height measuring from the butt end, which end was about 50 inches square. It contained 1307 cubic feet of timber ; this is not an exceptional size. A tree is reported to have been cut down lately, the circumference of which was 90 feet, and its height 325 feet ; the bark was in some places 4 feet thick. The tree, sound and solid, contained 250,000 feet of timber. It was supposed to be 3,100 years old. G. R. Burnell states the tenacity of this timber to be greater than, and its resistance to a crushing weight apparently superior to, Baltic timber. When loaded in the centre to the point of instantaneous rupture, the Vancouver's island wood bore weights which were to those borne by English oak as 13 to 12, and to those borne by the Baltic fir as 13 to 8. Three-inch cubes of the three woods were subjected to weights of 45 tons each, or 5 tons (11,240 lbs.) on the inch superficial, when the permanent elasticity of oak was not affected, that of the fir only slightly so, whilst the Baltic timber was permanently and perceptibly compressed.

1726a. For joiner's work, the straightness, freedom from knots, deep warm colour, and beauty of the grain, places this timber above any other of the fir or pine woods ; whilst its greater hardness would in staircases, floors, &c., compensate for any slight increase in the price of labour for working it. It has been employed by Mr. Burnell in the joiner's work of an office in Lincoln's Inn Fields. It seems to affect iron somewhat as does oak.

1727. MAHOGANY (*Swietenia Mahogoni*) is a native of the West Indies and the country round the Bay of Honduras. The tree is said to be of rapid growth; its trunk often exceeds 40 feet in length and 6 feet in diameter. Its Spanish name is *caôba*. *Spanish* mahogany is imported from Cuba, Jamaica, Hispaniola, St. Domingo, and some other of the West India Islands and the Spanish Main. The best quality is considered to come from the sea-board on the south part of the island of San Domingo or Hayti. The logs are from 20 to 26 inches square, and about 10 feet in length. It is close grained, hard, sometimes strongly figured, and generally of a rich brown colour, darker than Honduras; but its pores frequently appear as if chalk had been rubbed into them. It takes a very high polish with hand labour; and French polishing brings out its flower with great lustre.

1727a. *Honduras* mahogany is imported in logs of larger size than the above, that is, from 2 to 4 feet square, and from 12 to 18 feet in length ; logs 40 feet in length have been obtained ; planks 6 to 7 feet wide are occasionally imported; but 5 feet square and 15 feet long are the more ordinary dimensions. It is so distinctly inferior to the Spanish quality, that no ordinary judge can possibly be mistaken in the normal samples. In weight it is lighter ; and it is of a straighter and more open or spongy grain, without much flower, and therefore little sought after by cabinet-makers. The worst kinds are those most filled with grey specks, from which Spanish mahogany, except the Cuba, is comparatively free.

1727b. Spanish mahogany is in this country far too valuable to be used in common building. It sometimes sells for as much as 6l. per foot cube, when good fir, of nearly equal value for such purposes, would only cost 2s. at the maximum. In Jamaica, mahogany has been frequently employed for floors, joists, rafters, shingles, &c. ; and ships have been built of it ; for which last purpose, the circumstance of its allowing shot to be buried in it without splintering, makes it peculiarly suitable. Soon after its introduction into this country in 1724, when a specimen was sent to Dr. Gibbons by his brother, a West India captain, it was employed for doors, as at the Treasury, by W. Kent, in 1733. The better qualities are reserved for small articles of cabinet-work and furniture, the best being employed in the form of veneers, of which twenty-one cuts are now got out of an inch thickness. Solid work for more general purposes, such as handrails of stairs, sashes, sash-doors, and ordinary counting-house and office fittings, &c., is worked out of Honduras mahogany, which is also employed as the groundwork for veneers of the finer quality.

1727c. It is generally sold at per foot superficial, one inch thick ; the common qualities at 5s. to 5s. 6d. per cubic foot. It holds with glue better than any other wood. Of Honduras mahogany, the quality called 'common southern' weighs about 26 lbs. ; 'superior northern' about 42½ lbs. ; 'good northern' about 32 lbs. ; and 'common northern' about 36 lbs., per cubic foot. All these qualities are used in shipbuilding, the lightest, for furniture. Spanish mahogany weighs 48 lbs. 6 oz., the best from 50 lbs. to 54 lbs. per cubic foot. All kinds of this timber are said to be very durable, and free from the attack of worms when kept constantly dry. They do not warp or crack under the influence of

the sun, but they do not resist alternations of great wetness and dryness. They shrink but little in drying, and twist and warp less than any other wood.

1727*d. African* mahogany (*Swietenia* or *Khaya Senegalensis*), from Gambia, is a more recent importation ; it twists much more than either of the above, and is decidedly inferior to them in all respects except hardness. Small quantities of mahogany are also received from Jamaica and the other West India islands, but they are of a quality so inferior even to the Honduras variety, that they are practically unknown to timber merchants. Florida *cedar* and other varieties are frequently made to pass as mahogany in cheap works.

1728. TEAK (*Tectona grandis*), has of late years formed a valuable timber for ship-building ; and to a small extent in house, and even carriage, joinery. The best varieties are obtained,from the ports of Rangoon or Moulmein (called Moulmein teak), and from the coast of Malabar (called East Indian teak). It is by no means rare to meet with sticks of perfectly straight teak 60 or 70 feet long, and about 24 to 30 inches square. The wood is of a light brown colour, porous, very hard, tough, and when sound, of great strength and tenacity. It derives much of its value from the aromatic oily substance with which it is more or less saturated in the fresh state ; but this does not prevent its attack by insects whilst in the forest, consequently the trees turn out to be very defective. The wood works well ; takes a good polish, and though porous, it is very durable in exposed situations : it is considered that its oily properties render it less injurious to iron than oak. The tenacity of Moulmein teak is 15,000 lbs. per superficial inch. Some fine planks from Rangoon were nearly 3½ feet wide.

1728*a.* MORUNG SAUL (*Shorea robusta*), of Nepaul, in the East Indies, is in great repute for shipbuilding. It is a heavy, close-grained, light brown wood. This timber is considered to be the most valuable and extensively used of all the trees of India, but the value of it is much diminished from the injudicious mode in which it is squared. The *saul* or *sál* timber brought to Calcutta is seldom more than 30 feet in length. In strength and tenacity it is considerably superior to the best teak, compared with which, Captain Baker's experiments prove that its strength is about as 1121 to 869. From Major H. Campbell's experiments, unseasoned saul broke with a weight of 1308 lbs. ; seasoned saul with 1319 lbs. ; and teak wood with 1091 lbs. Considered as a building wood, it is somewhat apt to shrink unless very well seasoned, (*Juror's Reports*, 1851).

1728*b.* MORRA (*Mora excelsa*), sometimes called Demerara locust, is sent from Demerara in South America. It is a valuable timber for shipbuilding.

1728*c.* GREENHEART (*Laurus chloroxylon*, or *Nectandra rodiæi*), imported from the English colony of British Guiana, and Brazil, possesses the reputation of immunity from the attacks of marine boring worms; and for this reason it is now largely used in hydraulic works. Mr. Burnell has stated his conviction from what he saw, especially of two logs, in the West India Docks in 1860, that this timber does suffer from the attacks of land insects ; and he was at that time in possession of a piece of the timber from Victor Bay, Panama, which was completely riddled by the *Teredo navalis*. A writer, commenting on this statement, says that " his experience proves that greenheart is exempt from the therosion by the *teredo*, but that a mollusc is found alive in it when arriving here from the West Indies. The worm is found in sizes from the *lymexylon* to the *teredo*, but it is of a different species, and seems not to live when this wood is used in such constructions as dock gates, in this country." The timber squares from 18 to 24 inches, but usually arrives about 16 inches square and 70 feet in length. It is a hard, heavy, fine, but not even-grained wood; it proves strong and durable in positions that are alternately wet and dry.

1728*d.* Among the other useful hard woods are :—I. The PEON, or *Poon wood*, an Indian wood of Travancore, East Indies, formerly imported to some extent, from 2 to 4 feet in circumference and 80 feet in length ; but latterly it has been regarded with such disfavour that it is now hardly ever imported. II. The KOWRIE, a New Zealand wood. III. The Australian RED CEDAR. IV. The SABICUE, from Cuba, which was used for the steps of the stairs in the Great Exhibition building of 1851, and are now in the Crystal Palace at Sydenham. It makes excellent beams and planks. A heavy specimen obtained of this wood was " a portion of a large beam, which broke merely in falling from a truck ! " V. The IRON BARK, of Van Diemen's Land, Australia, is a very hard and compact wood, with a specific gravity heavier than water. VI. BORNEO WOOD, imported from Sarawak, was used in 1865 for the floors and staircase in a warehouse in Gresham Street West. It is of so peculiar a character that it broke nearly all the saws used to reduce it to battens : it is light brown in colour, with a texture very similar to teak. It may probably be the *Bilian*, or iron wood of that country, said to be impervious to the attacks of the white ant. It has not been known to decay when immersed either in fresh or salt water. An engineer who had resided in Borneo for five years, states he had never seen a rotten piece of *Bilian* wood.

1728*e.* Besides the weights of various woods given in the text (as marked *) the subjoined list of the weight per foot cube in pounds avoirdupois, may be useful.

TABLE OF THE WEIGHTS OF TIMBERS.

Timber.	Rondelet.	Tredgold.	Others.	Burnell.
Acacia - - - - - - -	47·74			
*Alder - - - - - - -	39·74			
Almond tree - - - - - -	66·74			
*Ash - - - - - - -	47·52	52 81	41·81	
*Beech - - - - - - -	43·63	53·25		
*Birch, common - - - - -	42·55			
Box - - - - - - -	55·55	{ 83·00 / 57·00 }		
*Cedar of Lebanon - - - -	36·50	35·06		
Chesnut, wild (*Chataignier*) - - -	41·47			
* „ sweet (*Marronier*) - - -	43·73	37·75		
Cork - - - - - - -	-	15·00		
Cypress, pyramidal - - - - -	39·74			
Ebony of the Alps - - - -	63·72			
*Elm - - - - - - -	42·00	42·06		
„ English - - - - - -	-	-	37·31	
„ American - - - - - -	-	-	45·31	
*Fir - - - - - - -	31·92			
„ Christiania, white deal - - -	-	34·43		
„ Memel - - - - -	-	37·00		
„ Wellingtonia gigantea - - -	-	-	-	42·00
*Larch, English - - - - -	-	33·02	32·56	
Linden - - - - - - -	34·13			
*Mahogany, Spanish - - - - -	·	66·43		
*Oak, common of Canada - - - -	51.18			
„ Virginia red - - - -	35·42			
„ Common - - - - -	54·69			
„ American - - - - -	-	-	44·87	
„ African - - - - -	-	-	51.44	
„ English - - - - { fresh / - }	- / -	{ 69·56 / 46·43 }	53·31	
*Pine, Northern - - - - -	37·17			
„ Yellow - - - - - -	-	-	25·69	
„ Baltic - - - - - -	-	-	29·06	
„ Red - - - - - -	-	41·06	33·44	
„ Pitch - - - - - -	-	-	45·75	
„ Weymouth or Yellow - - -	-	40·76		
Plane - - - - - - -	37·58			
*Poplar, of Italy - - - - -	24·25			
„ - - - - - - -	-	23·93		
Service tree (*Cormier*) - - - -	55·07			
*Sycamore - - - - - -	38·88	37·75		
*Walnut - - - - - - -	41·04	41·93		
„ American - - - - -	41·90			
Yew - - - - - - -	47·09			
Teak, African - - - - -	-	-	60·56	
„ Indian - - - - - -	-	46·87	38·12	
„ Moulmein - - - - -	-	-	-	32·00
„ Malabar - - - - -	-	-	-	38·00
Morra - - - - - - -	-	-	71·25	{ 55·75 / 57·80 }
Sabicue - - - - - - -	-	-	{ 59·69 / 61·60 }	{ 57·31 / 63·63 }
Greenheart - - - - - -	-	-	69·75	
Iron wood - - - - - -	-	-	73·50	
Cowrie - - - - - - -	-	36·00		
Morung Saul - - - - - -	-	-	-	{ 43·87 to / 45·87 }
Indian Saul - - - - - -	-	-	-	52·63
Iron Bark - - - - - -	-	-	-	65·60

1728*f*. The chief woods employed in shipbuilding and acknowledged as "first-rate" by the authorities at Lloyds, are eight in number. These are, I. English oak; II. American live oak; III. African oak; IV. Morung Saul; V. East Indian Teak; VI. Greenheart; VII. Morra; and VIII. Iron Bark.

1729. In timber yards, deals are sold by the long hundred or six score; thus the "standard" of deals is reckoned as 120—12 ft. × 1½ in. × 11 ins., but varying lengths and thicknesses are imported (See par. 2362 and 2363).

Names.	No.	Ft. long.	Ins. thk.	Wide.	Sup. ins.	Cube ft.
Petersburg deals - -	120	12	1½	11	1980 of 1″	165
„ battens -	120	12	2½	7	- -	175
Dantzig deals - -	120	12	1½	12	- -	180
Norway „ - -	120	12	3	9	3240	270
Sweden „ - -	120	14	3	9	- -	315
Baltic deck deals - -	-	40	3			
Christiania standard -	120	11	1¼	9	1237½ of 1″	103⅛
Drammen - - -	120	9	2½	6½		
Ditto - - - -	120	13	1¼	9	1462 of 1″	121⅚
Quebec, long - -	100	12	1½	11		
Ditto, short - -	120	10	3	11	2750 of 1″	229⅙
London and Dublin -	120	12	3	9	3240 of 1″	270

The measurements have been reduced to one standard of 12 ft. long, 3 in. thick, and 9 in. wide. Two of the latest works for calculating deals according to this, the Petersburg standard hundred, are, J. Smith, *Companion to Hoppus; Handbook of Tables for the use of Timber Merchants, &c.*, London, 1860; and Grandy, *Timber Importers', &c. Standard Guide*, 8vo., London, 1865, to which latter work we are glad to refer the student, and from which we select the following extracts:—

1729*a*. "American Ports.—At *Quebec*, there are three qualities of spruce deals, 1st, 2nd, and 3rd. Irregular size scantlings are scarcely ever shipped from this port, the general run being battens, 7 × 3; deals, 9 × 3; and planks, 11 × 3, 7 × 2, 9 × 2, and 11 × 2; general lengths from 8 to 14 feet. All under 8 feet are classed as "ends." Yellow pine battens, deals, and planks are shipped as 1st, 2nd, and 3rd qualities. Battens are not so valuable as deals and planks, some of the latter running 11 to 30 inches; the finer qualities bear a high rate.

1729*b*. *St. John's* deals rank after those of Quebec in quality. Battens, deals, and planks run from 8 to 26 feet; all lengths under 8 feet being classed as ends. All deals are scarcely ever classed into 1st, 2nd, and 3rd, but taken by the run; the sizes 7 × 3, 9 × 3, and 11 × 3, being the highest in price. Irregular scantlings, such as 3 × 3, 4 × 3, 6 × 3, 5 × 2½, &c., are less per thousand.

1729*c*. *Pugwash, Miramichi, and other Lower Ports.* Battens, deals, and planks are obtained as at St. John's. The deal is a closer grain, but coarser, and hence not so valuable. The lengths run from 8 to 14 feet, all under 8 feet being 'ends.' Scarcely any irregular scantlings are shipped from these ports. The square timber at the American ports is generally purchased by the cubic foot.

1729*d*. Baltic Ports.—*Memel.* Battens and deals are scarce; planks form the bulk of the timber imported. They all run from 8 to 20 feet. They are generally sold by 720 feet run of 11 × 3, = 1 Petersburg standard. Battens and deals run 7 × 3 and 9 × 3. *Christiania.* Battens and deals, and *Drammen* deals run 9 × 3, 7 × 3, or 7 × 2½. *Crown Memel.* Square timber is generally sold by the 50 running feet, as 1st middling, and 2nd middling. But "undersized" timber, that is, under 12 inches square, is sold by 50 cubic feet, or by 50 running feet. There are also "short lengths of undersized" timber.

1729*e*. Home Trade.—At *London*, pine deals are sold by the Petersburg, and spruce deals by the London, standard. Square timber is sold by the load, or 50 cube feet, or by the cube foot, calliper measurement. At *Liverpool and Bristol*, deals are sold by the Petersburg standard; square timber by the load or foot, string measurement. At *Glasgow*, deals are sold by the cube foot; square timber by the cube foot, string measurement. At *Dublin*, deals are sold by the London or Dublin standard of 120, 12 × 9 × 3; square timber by the ton of 40 feet, string measurement."

1729*f*. These timbers are used in building for the undermentioned purposes:—
Joists and main timbers: The largest, of Dantzic, Memel or Riga, fir; those of 10 or 12 inches square, from Sweden; those of 8 inches square, from Norway.

Partitions and minor timbers: American red wood or red pine, which not being so strong as that from the Baltic, must be cut to a little larger size.

Sleepers, window sills, and some parts of the roof: Oak.

Framing: Norway and Christiania white deals; Christiania yellow deals are sappy; Swedish deals are bad, as they warp much.

Panelling: Christiania white pine; or American yellow pine.

Best ordinary floors: Drammen and Christiania white deals; American pitch pine; American deals are bad for floors, as they are a softer wood.

Ground floors: Stockholm and Gefle yellow deals.

Warehouse floors, and Staircases: Archangel and Onega planks, and American pitch pine.

Best floors: Petersburgh, Onega, and Christiania battens.

Interior finishings generally: Baltic red and white wood, and American red and yellow pine.

1729g. Memel timber is generally considered the most convenient for size, and is superior in strength to the Swedish, or Norwegian; Riga, the best in quality; Dantzic, when free from large knots, the strongest; and the Swedish, the toughest, but weakest. Riga can always be depended upon, and although the dearest in price, is the cheapest in the end.

1730. We shall now place before the reader, observations on timber made by the celebrated Evelyn though perhaps at the risk of repetition in what follows after them.

1731. " Lay up your timbers very dry, in an airy place, yet out of the wind or sun, and not standing very upright, but lying along, one piece upon another, interposing some short blocks between them, to preserve them from a certain mouldiness which they usually contract while they sweat, and which frequently produces a kind of fungus, especially if there be any sappy parts remaining.

1732. " Some there are yet who keep their timber as moist as they can by submerging it in water, where they let it imbibe, to hinder the cleaving; and this is good in fir, both for the better stripping and seasoning; yea, not only in fir, but other timber. Lay, therefore, your boards a fortnight in the water (if running the better, as at some mill-pond head); and there, setting them upright in the sun and wind, so as it may freely pass through them (especially during the heats of summer, which is the time of finishing buildings), turn them daily; and thus treated, even newly sawn boards will floor far better than many years' dry seasoning, as they call it. But, to prevent all possible accidents, when you lay your floors, let the joints be shot, fitted, and tacked down only for the first year, nailing them for good and all the next; and by this means they will lie staunch, close, and without shrinking in the least, as if they were all one piece. And upon this occasion I am to add an observation, which may prove of no small use to builders, that if one take up deal boards that may have lain in the floor a hundred years, and shoot them [plane their edges] again, they will certainly shrink (toties quoties) without the former method. Amongst wheelwrights the water seasoning is of especial regard, and in such esteem amongst some, that I am assured the Venetians, for their provision in the arsenal, lay their oak some years in water before they employ it. Indeed, the Turks not only fell at all times of the year, without any regard to the season, but employ their timber green and unseasoned; so that though they have excellent oak, it decays in a short time, by this only neglect.

1733. " Elm felled ever so green, for sudden use, if plunged four or five days in water (especially salt water), obtains an admirable seasoning, and may immediately be used. I the oftener insist on this water seasoning, not only as a remedy against the worm, but for its efficacy against warping and distortions of timber, whether used within or exposed to the air. Some, again, commend burying in the earth; others in wheat; and there be seasonings of the fire, as for the scorching and hardening of piles, which are to stand either in the water or in the earth.

1734. " When wood is charred it becomes incorruptible; for which reason, when we wish to preserve piles from decay, they should be charred on their outside. Oak posts used in enclosures always decay about two inches above and below the surface. Charring that part would probably add several years to the duration of the wood, for that to most timber it contributes its duration. Thus do all the elements contribute to the art of seasoning.

1735. " Timber which is cleft is nothing so obnoxious to reft and cleave as what is hewn; nor that which is squared as what is round: and therefore, where use is to be made of huge and massy columns, let them be bored through from end to end. It is an excellent preservative from splitting, and not unphilosophical; though to cure the accident painter's putty is recommended; also the rubbing them over with a wax cloth is good; or before it be converted the smearing the timber over with cow-dung, which prevents the effects both of sun and air upon it, if of necessity it must lie exposed. But, besides the former remedies, I find this for the closing of the chops and clefts of green timber, to anoint and supple it with the fat of powdered beef broth [we do not quite agree with our author here], with which it must be well soaked, and the chasms filled with sponges dipped into it. This to be twice done over.

1736. " We spake before of squaring ; and I would now recommend the quartering of such trees as will allow useful and competent scantlings to be of much more durableness and effect for strength, than where (as custom is and for want of observation) whole beams and timbers are applied in ships or houses, with slab and all about them, upon false suppositions of strength beyond these quarters.

1737. " Timber that you have occasion to lay in mortar, or which is in any part contiguous to lime, as doors, window cases, groundsils, and the extremities of beams, &c., have sometimes been capped with molten pitch, as a marvellous preserver of it from the burning and destructive effects of the lime; but it has since been found rather to heat and decay them, by hindering the transudation which those parts require; better supplied with loam, or strewings of brick-dust or pieces of boards; some leave a small hole for the air. But though lime be so destructive, whilst timber thus lies dry, it seems they mingle it with hair to keep the worm out of ships, which they sheathe for southern voyages, though it is held much to retard their course.

1738. " For all uses, that timber is esteemed the best which is the most ponderous, and which, lying long, makes the deepest impression in the earth, or in the water being floated ; also what is without knots, yet firm and free from sap, which is that fatty, whiter, and softer part called by the ancients *albumen*, which you are diligently to hew away.　My Lord Bacon (Exper. 658.) recommends for trial of a sound or knotty piece of timber, to cause one to speak at one of the extremes to his companion listening at the other ; for if it be knotty, the sound, says he, will come abrupt."

PRESERVATION OF TIMBER.

1739. The preservation of timber, when employed in a building, is the first and most important consideration.　Wherever it is exposed to the alternations of dryness and moisture, the protection of its surface from either of those actions is the principal object, or, in other words, the application of some substance or medium to it which is impervious to moisture ; but all timber should be perfectly dry before the use of the medium.　In Holland the application of a mixture of pitch and tar, whereon are strewn pounded shells, with a mixture of sea sand, is general ; and with this, or small and sifted beaten scales from a blacksmith's forge, to their drawbridges, sluices, and gates, and other works, they are admirably protected from the effects of the seasons.　Semple, in his work on aquatic building, recommends, that "after your work is tried up, or even put together, lay it on the ground, with stones or bricks under it to about a foot high, and burn wood (which is the best firing for the purpose) under it, till you thoroughly heat, and even scorch it all over ; then, whilst the wood is hot, rub it over plentifully with linseed oil and tar, in equal parts, and well boiled together, and let it be kept boiling while you are using it; and this will immediately strike and sink (if the wood be tolerably seasoned) one inch or more into the wood, close all the pores, and make it become exceeding hard and durable, either under or over water." Semple evidently supposes the wood to have been previously well seasoned.

1740. Chapman (on the preservation of timber) recommends a mixture of sub-sulphate of iron, which is obtained in the refuse of copperas pans, ground up with some cheap oil, and made sufficiently fluid with coal-tar oil, wherein pitch has been infused and mixed.

1741. For common purposes, what is called *sanding*, that is, the strewing upon the painting of timber, before the paint dries, particles of fine sand, is very useful in the preservation of timber.

1742. Against worms we believe nothing to be more efficacious than the saturation of timber with any of the oils ; a process which destroys the insect if already in the wood, with that of turpentine especially, and prevents the liability to attack from it.　Evelyn recommends nitric acid, that is, sulphur immersed in aquafortis and distilled, as an effectual application.　Corrosive sublimate, lately introduced under Kyan's patent, has long been known as an effectual remedy against the worm.　Its poisonous qualities of course destroy all animal life with which it comes in contact; and we believe that our readers who are interested in preserving the timbers of their dwellings may use a solution of it without infringing the rights of the patentee.　But the best remedy against rot and worms is a thorough introduction of air to the timbers of a building, and their lying as dry and as free from moisture as practicable.　Air holes from the outside should be applied as much as possible, and the ends of timbers should not, if it can be avoided, be bedded up close all round them.　This practice is, moreover, advisable in another respect, that of being able, without injury to a building, to splice the ends of the timbers should they become decayed, without involving the rebuilding of the fabric ; a facility of no mean consideration.

1743. The worm is so destructive to timber, both in and out of water, that we shall not apologise for closing this part of our observations with Smeaton's remarks upon a species of worm which he found in Bridlington piers.　" This worm appears as a small white soft substance, much like a maggot ; so small as not to be seen distinctly without a magnifying glass, and even then a distinction of its parts is not easily made out.　It does not attempt

to make its way through the wood longitudinally, or along the grain, as is the case with the common ship worm, but directly, or obliquely, inward. Neither does it appear to make its way by means of any hard tools or instruments, but rather by some species of dissolvent liquor furnished by the juices of the animal itself. The rate of progression is, that a three inch oak plank will be destroyed in eight years by action from the outside only." For resisting the effects of these worms, Smeaton recommends the piles to be squared, to be fitted as closely as possible together, and to fill all openings with tar and oakum, to make the face smooth, and cover it with sheathing.

1744. The destructive effects of the white ant are so little known here, that it is unnecessary to make further mention of them, than that in India they are the most inveterate enemies with which timber has to contend. From Young's *Annals* we extract the following curious statement of experiments made upon inch and a half planks, from trees of thirty to forty-five years' growth, after an exposure of ten years to the weather.

Cedar was perfectly sound.	Chesnut, very sound.
Larch, sap quite decayed, but the heart, sound	Abele, sound.
	Beech, ditto.
Spruce fir, sound.	Walnut, decayed.
Silver fir, in decay.	Sycamore, considerably decayed.
Scotch fir, much decayed.	Birch, worthless.
Pinaster, in a perfectly rotten state.	

Whence we may be led to some inference of the value of different sorts of timber in resisting weather; though we must not be altogether guided by the above table, inasmuch as it is well known that the soil on which timber is grown much increases or deteriorates its value, and that split timber is more durable and stronger than that which is sawn, from the circumstance of the fibres, on account of their continuity, resisting by means of their longitudinal strength; whereas when severed by the saw, the resistance depends more on the lateral cohesion of the fibres. Hence whole trees are invariably stronger than specimens, unless these be particularly well selected, and of a straight and even grain; but in practice the results of experiments are on this account the more useful.

DECAY OF TIMBER.

1745. If timber, whatever its species, be well seasoned, and be not exposed to alternate dryness and moisture, its durability is great, though from time it is known to lose its elastic and cohesive powers, and to become brittle if constantly dry. On this account it is unfit, after a certain period, to be subjected to variable strains: however, in a quiescent state it might endure for centuries. Dryness will, if carried to excess, produce this category. The mere moisture it absorbs from the air in dry weather is not sufficient to impair its durability. So, also, timber continually exposed to moisture is found to retain for a very long period its pristine strength. Heat with moisture is extremely injurious to it, and is in most cases productive of rot, whereof two kinds are the curse of the builder, the *wet* and the *dry* rot, though perhaps there be but little difference between the two. They appear to be produced by the same causes, excepting that the freedom of evaporation determines the former, and an imperfect evaporation the latter. In both cases the timber is affected by a fungus-like parasite, beginning with a species of mildew; but how this fungus is generated is still a *vexata quæstio;* all we know is, that its vegetation is so rapid, that often before it has arrived at its height, a building is ruined. From our inquiries on the Continent, we believe the disease does not occur to the extent that it does in this country; a fact which we are inclined, perhaps erroneously, to attribute to the use of the timber of the country, instead of imported timber. Our opinion may be fanciful, but there are many grounds on which we think that is not altogether the case. Our notion is, that our imported timber is infected with the seeds of decay long before its arrival here (we speak of fir more especially), and that the comparative warmth and moisture of the climate bring more effectually the causes of decay into action, especially where the situation is close and confined. Warmth is, doubtless, known to be a great agent in the dry rot, and most especially when moisture co-operates with it, for in warm cellars and other close and confined situations, where the vapour which feeds the disease is not altered by a constant change of air, the timbers are soon destroyed, and become perfectly decomposed.

1746. The lime, and more especially the damp brickwork, which receive the timbers of a new building, are great causes of decay to the ends of them; but we do not think that the regulations of the 19 Car. II. cap. 3., which directed the builders after the fire of London, to bed the ends of their girders and joists in loam instead of mortar, would, if followed out in the present day, be at all effective in preventing the decay incident to the ends of timbers. Timber, in a perfectly dry state, does not appear to be injured by dry lime; and indeed, lime is known to be effectual in the protection of wood against worms. Timber in contact with masonry is constantly found to decay, when the other parts of the

beam have been sound. This will be entirely obviated by inserting the wood in an iron shoe, or by placing a thin piece of iron betwixt the wood and the stone. Cases are known in which the iron shoe appeared to have proved a complete protection against dry rot and decay ; a hard crust being formed on the timber in contact with the metal. The system of grouting must contribute to the early decay of wood bond ; but at Manchester, where it was used very generally, it appeared to answer well, for the high temperature kept up in the buildings may cause the walls to dry very soon. Sea-sand, used for outside and in-side purposes, in a spirit of economy, soon shows the result by inducing the appearance of rot in timber. Wood laid in sandy soil is well preserved, as was found to be the case in the specimens lately dug up at Birkenhead from depths varying from 8 feet to 32 feet ; they were considered to have been buried for centuries.

1747. Nothing is more injurious to the floors of a building than covering them with painted floorcloth, which entirely prevents the access of atmospheric air, whence the dampness of the boards never evaporates ; and it is well known that oak and fir posts have been brought into premature decay by painting them before their moisture had evaporated ; whilst in the timber and pewing of old churches, which have never been painted, we see them sound after the lapse of centuries. Semple, in his *Treatise on Building in Water*, notices an instance of some field gates made of the fir of the place, part whereof, near the mansion, were painted, and had become rotten, while those more distant from the mansion, which had never been painted, were quite sound.

1747a. According to Baron Liebig, the decay of wood takes place in the three following modes :—I. The oxygen in the atmosphere combines with the hydrogen of the fibre, and the oxygen unites with the portion of carbon of the fibre, and evapo-rates as carbonic acid ; this process is called decomposition. II. The actual decay of the wood which takes place when it is brought in contact with rotting substances. And III. The inner decomposition of the wood in itself, by losing its carbon forming carbonic acid gas, and the fibre under the influence of the latter is changed into white dust ; this is called putrefaction.

PREVENTION OF DECAY.

1748. After timber is felled, the best method of preventing decay is the immediate re-moval of it to a dry situation, where it should be stacked in such a manner as to secure a free circulation of air round it, but without exposure to the sun and wind, and it should be rough squared as soon as possible. When thoroughly seasoned before cutting it into scantlings, it is less liable to warp and twist in drying. The ground about its place of de-posit should be dry and perfectly drained, so that no vegetation may rise on it. Hence a timber yard should be strewed with ashes, or the scales from a foundry or forge, which supply an admirable antidote to all vegetation. It is thought that the more gradually timber is seasoned the greater its durability ; and as a general rule, it may be stated, that it should not be used till a period of at least two years from its being felled, and for joiners' work at least four years. Much, however, is dependent on the size of the pieces. By some, water seasoning has been recommended ; by others the steaming and boiling it ; smoke-drying, charring, and scorching have also been recommended. The latter is, perhaps, the best for piles and other pieces that are to stand in the water or in the ground. It was prac-tised by the ancients, and is still in use generally for the posts of park paling and the like.

1749. In Norway the deal planks are seasoned by laying them in salt water for three or four days, when newly sawed, and then drying them in the sun, a process which is con-sidered to be attended with advantage ; but it does not prevent their shrinking. Mr. Evelyn recommends the water seasoning for fir.

1749a. The effectual seasoning obtained by Davison and Symington's patent process of forcing heated air in a continued current through timber under pressure, effectually dries it, and coagulates the albumen. The timbers for the flooring of the Coal Exchange at London have been so treated, and show no signs of shrinkage. The wood was taken in its natural state, and in less than ten days it was thoroughly seasoned ; in some cases from 10 to 48 per cent of moisture was taken out of it. The air when heated to about 110° or 120° is sent through the timber at a rate of about 48 miles per hour ; the heat being regulated according to the quality of the timber. Honduras mahogany exposed to a heat of 300°, would have the whole of the moisture taken from it in 48 hours. This process, however, sometimes splits the timber. Out of a hundred specimens of wood experimented upon, varying from one inch to twelve inches square, not one of them split : even some openings which were visible before the process was applied, were found to be closer after it. Perhaps 9 inches square is the limit to which the operation can be successfully applied.

1750. Notwithstanding, however, all care in seasoning, when timber is employed in a damp situation it soon decays ; and one of the principal remedies against that is good drainage, without which no precautions will avail. It is most important to take care that earth should not lie in contact with the walls of a building, for the damp is quickly com-municated, in that case, by their means to the ends of timbers, and rot soon follows. No expedient to guard against this contingency is so good as what are called air drains.

1751. When the carcass of a building is complete, it should be left as long as possible to dry, and to allow to the timbers what may be called a second seasoning. The modern practice of finishing buildings in the quickest possible period, has contributed more to dry rot than perhaps any other cause; and for this the architect has been blamed instead of his employer, whose object is generally to realize letting or to enjoy occupation of them as early as possible. After the walls and timbers of a building are once thoroughly dry, all means should be employed to exclude an accession of moisture, and delay is then prejudicial.

1752. Among the many inventions to preserve wood from decay, those of England have proved the most successful. In 1737 a patent was granted to Mr. Emerson to prepare timber with hot oil. This was followed by various recommendations early in the present century; those of later date consist of :— I. Kyan's process, 1832, who steeped the timber in a solution of *bichloride of mercury*, known as corrosive sublimate (*par.* 1742.) It appears to penetrate fir less than some other woods (Faraday). The wood thus treated becomes of less specific gravity, less flexibility, and more brittle. II. Sir William Burnett's patent of 1836, was for using the chloride of zinc. III. M. Bréant in 1837 suggested sulphate of iron, which was found not to alter the qualities of the timber as did the corrosive sublimate. IV. Margary's patent, 1837, is for steeping timber in a solution made of one pound of sulphate of copper with eight gallons of water. Wood impregnated with sulphate of copper (blue vitriol) will not last longer in sea water than any other wood. But wood so treated will last longer in the soil than if either tarred or charred. Its application for the prevention of rot is beneficial, and it might be used where not exposed to the action of water, on account of the solubility of the salts. The proportion of the sulphate should be one pound to four gallons of water; we have also met with the proportion of one pound to two gallons; perhaps the strongest is the best (*par.* 1752b.) V. Payne, 1841, patented a system for using two solutions; first, sulphate of iron, which would form an oxide of iron in the cells; and secondly, carbonate of soda : some very good results were obtained, but the process must be done under pressure and with the greatest care.

1752a. VI. Bethell's patent, 1838, consists in the injection of oil of tar, containing creasote and a crude solution of acetate of iron, commonly called pyrolignite of iron, after the air in the wood has been extracted. This process is effective to a great extent, and full particulars are given by G. R. Burnell in his paper read before the Society of Arts 1860, from which we have been quoting. It, however, can only be recommended for railways and other large works; the offensive smell and increased danger by fire should deter its use in house building. In the best creasoting works, the oil is injected at a temperature of 120° and under a pressure of 150 lbs. on the square inch, so that ordinary fir timber absorbs 10 lbs. weight of the creasote per cubic foot; the wood should be weighed to ascertain that it did absorb that quantity. For all engineering purposes, fir timber thus treated is far more durable than the best oak, teak, or other hard woods, and the cost of the operation is very small. Timber which has just been taken out of water contains so large a quantity that it resists the entrance of the oil ; unless time, therefore, be given for it to be first dried, it would necessarily be badly prepared.

1752b. VII. Dorsett and Blythe, 1863, patented the injection of heated solutions of sulphate of copper (*par.* 1752, IV.), a process said to have been adopted by French, Spanish, Italian, and other railway companies. Amongst its advantages, they state that wood so prepared is rendered to a great extent incombustible; and that for out-door purposes it has a clean yellowish surface, without odour, requires no painting, remaining unchanged for any length of time. Experience of the English processes shows that creasoting is the most generally successful; the application of the sulphate of copper is satisfactory in many cases; while the other processes, although no doubt of occasional value, have been practically abandoned. They all depend for their success upon the skilful and conscientious manner in which they are applied; for as they involve chemical actions on a large scale, their efficiency must depend upon the observation of the minute practical precautions required to exclude any disturbing causes.

CURE OF DRY ROT.

1753. It is no easy matter to cure the dry rot where it has once taken root. If it be found necessary to substitute new timbers for old ones, every particle of the fungus, known as the *Merulius lacrymans*, must be removed from the neighbourhood of such new timbers. After scraping it from the adjoining walls and timbers, perhaps no better application than one of the washes above mentioned can be employed, inasmuch as they can always be with safety applied to the parts. An extraordinary degree of heat, about 300°, would effect the same purpose, but this, especially in the case of floors, is difficult in application. Coal tar has been found useful, but its extremely unpleasant odour, which always arises at a moderate degree of heat, is an objection to its use in houses of any class. We have also ourselves found that a weak solution of vitriolic acid with water will generally stop the rot if it have not gone too far. Pyroligneous acid is recommended, and, we think, very usefully, as a remedy for preventing the spreading of the disease. The precautions indicated above for the prevention of decay, although not always successful, must be deemed preferable to the application of after remedies.

1754. Iron is a metal found in almost all parts of the world, and though not mentioned by Homer, and hence, we may suppose, in his time extremely scarce, it is now more abundant than any of the other metals, and is, at the same time, the most useful. Although, with the exception of tin, it is the lightest of all metals; yet it is, when pure, very malleable and extremely hard. Its malleability is increased by heat, whereas most other metals, as they are heated, become more brittle. It is the only known substance whereon the loadstone acts, and its specific gravity to water is as 7632 to 1000.

1755. The iron manufactured in Great Britain is obtained from three species of the ore. The *Lancashire*, which is very heavy, fibrous in texture, and of a dark purple colour inclining to black, and lodged in veins. The *Bog ore*, which has the appearance of a deep yellow clay, and is found in strata of from twelve to twenty inches in thickness. And lastly, *Iron stones*, of an irregular shape, frequently in beds of large extent, similar to other stony masses, and often intersected with seams of pit coal. It is principally from the argillaceous ore or clay iron-stone that iron is extracted in this country.

1756. After raising, the ores are selected and separated as much as possible from heterogeneous substances. They are then roasted in large heaps in the open air, for the purpose as well of freeing them from the arsenic and sulphur they contain as to render them friable or easy of reduction to a powder. The roasting is performed by means of bituminous coal, and the result is a substance full of fissures, friable, and a deprivation of all vitreous lustre. After this it is transferred to the crushing mill for complete pulverization, whence it is carried to the smelting furnace for conversion into iron. Herein it undergoes two separate processes: first, the reduction of the oxide to a metallic state; second, the separation of the earthy particles in the form of scoria. These operations are conducted by submitting the ore, ordinarily mixed with certain fluxes, to the action of carbon at a very high temperature, in what are called blast furnaces, which vary in height from twelve to sixty feet, and are of the form of truncated cones, sometimes however of pyramids, terminating usually in cylindrical chimneys, whose internal diameter is from four to six feet. The interior of these furnaces is usually of a cylindrical form, whose internal diameter is from four to six feet. Their cavity is usually of a circular form, except at the *crucible* or *hearth*, where it becomes a right rectangular prism, oblong in a direction perpendicular to the blast orifices or *tuyeres* of the bellows. The sides of the crucible are most commonly formed of gritstone. The *boshes*, which are in the form of an inverted quadrangular pyramid approaching a prismatic shape, are placed above the crucible, and above them rises the conical body of the furnace, which is lined with fire-bricks, and, in ascending, is contracted similarly to the narrow end of an egg, until it terminates in the chimney. The furnace is of course constructed in the most solid manner, and strengthened by iron bands and bars. The bellows employed are mostly of a cylindrical form, and their pistons worked either by water or steam. The blast holes, which are in the upper part of the crucible, and frequently placed on opposite sides, but so that the two opposite currents may not impinge upon one another, are two in number. Openings are provided at the lower part of the crucible for the discharge of the metal and scoria, and are kept stopped by clay and sand upon the exterior when the furnace is in operation. The reduction is commenced by gradually heating up the furnace until capable of being entirely filled with fuel, and then, as its contents begin to sink, alternate changes of ore, mingled with *flux*, and of charcoal and coke, are added. The blast is now let on, and the metal in the ore, parting with its oxygen, flows by degrees, subsiding to the bottom of the crucible, covered with a melted *slag*, which is occasionally let off by removing the clay from one or more, if necessary, apertures in the crucible; and on the bottom of the furnace becoming filled with the metal, which generally occurs after nine to twelve hours, the iron itself is discharged by one of these openings into a fosse of sand mixed with clay. When the iron has flowed out the aperture is again closed, and by this method the furnace is kept in constant action.

1757. Limestone of the best quality is employed as a flux to assist the fusion of the ore, which it accomplishes by vitrefying the earths wherewith it is mixed up with the oxide of iron. The iron when run out from the blast furnace in the state of cast iron is far from being in a pure state, having a coarse grain, and being brittle. In its conversion to bar iron, it undergoes one of the two following processes, as charcoal or coke may be employed. In the former case a furnace much resembling a smith's hearth is used, having a sloping cavity sunk from ten to twelve inches below the blast pipe. After the cavity has been filled with charcoal and scoria, a pig of cast iron, well covered with hot fuel, is placed opposite the blast pipe. The blast being introduced, the pig of iron lying in the very hottest part soon begins to melt, and runs down into the cavity below, where, being out of the influence of the blast, it becomes solid, and is replaced in its former position, and the

cavity is again filled with charcoal. It is there again fused, and so on a third time, all these processes being accomplished in three or four hours. The iron, thus again solid, is taken out, and very slightly hammered, to free it from the attached scoria; after this it is returned to the furnace, in a corner whereof it is stacked, out of the action of the blast, and well covered with charcoal, where it remains gradually to cool until sufficiently compact to bear the *tilt* or *trip hammer* (to be *shingled*, to force out the cinders), which is moved by machinery, and whose weight is from 600 to 1200 lbs. Thus it is beaten till the scoriæ are forced out, and the particles of iron welded together, when it is divided into several portions, which by repeated heating and hammering are drawn into bars, in which state it is ready for sale.

1758. There are various methods of procuring the blast; the first, and most ancient, is by means of bellows; the latest, which has been found in the mining districts to be a contrivance of great importance, is the placing a series of vanes attached to an axis, which, by machinery, are made to revolve in a box with great rapidity. A pipe passing from the outside of the box to the furnace conveys the air to it as the vanes revolve, a new portion continually entering by a hole at the axis. The air thus driven through at its natural temperature constitutes a *cold blast* in contradistinction to air heated by artificial means or *hot blast*. This latter system was discovered by J. B. Neilson, of Glasgow, about the year 1826; his patent expired in 1842. At the present day air is forced into the furnaces at a temperature of 600°, and even of 800° Fahr., although at the commencement it was rarely used above 300°. The irons obtained from the former process are considered to be tougher and stronger than those obtained from the latter process, and present a closer texture and a smaller crystallization than the latter irons. The Blaenavon, Coed Talon, Lowmoor, and Muirkirk irons are amongst the most esteemed varieties. Perhaps it may be laid down as a general principle that where pig-iron is remelted with coke in the cupola furnace, for the purposes of the ironfounder, or refined with coke in the conversion of forge pig into bar iron, it is of little consequence whether the reduction of the ore has been effected with the *hot* or the *cold* blast; but where large castings have to be run directly from the smelting furnace, the quality of the metal will, no doubt, suffer from the use of the hot blast.

1759. The proportion of pig or cast iron from a given quantity of ore varies as the difference in the metallic contents of different parcels of ore and other circumstances, but the quantity of bar obtained from pig iron is not valued at more than 20 per cent.

1760. The other process for manufacturing bar iron, which is that chiefly employed in this country, is conducted in reverberatory furnaces, usually called *puddling furnaces*. The operation begins with the fusion of the cast iron in refinery furnaces, like the one above described. When the iron is fully melted, a tap-hole is opened in the crucible, and the metal and slag flow out together into a fosse covered with clay well mixed with water, by which a coating is formed that prevents the metal from sticking to the ground. The finer metal forms a slab about ten feet long, three feet broad, and from two to two and a half inches in thickness. For the purpose of slightly oxidizing it, and to make it brittle, it is much sprinkled over with cold water. In this part of the process it loses in weight from 12 to 17 per cent. After this, it is broken up into pieces, and placed on the hearth of a reverberatory furnace, in portions heaped up to its sides in piles which rise nearly to the roof, leaving a space open in the middle to give room for puddling the metal as it flows down in streams. When the heat of the furnace has brought it to a pasty state, the temperature is reduced, a little water being sometimes thrown on the melted mass. The semi-liquid metal is stirred up by the workman with his *puddle*, during which it swells, and parts with a large quantity of oxide of iron, which burns with a blue flame, so that the mass appears ignited. As it refines, the metal becomes less fusible, or, as the workmen say, it begins to *dry*. The puddling goes on until the whole charge assumes the form of an incoherent sand, when the temperature is gradually increased to give it a red white heat, at which period the particles begin to agglutinate, and the charge, in technical language, *works heavy*. The refining is now considered finished, and the metal has only to be formed into balls, and condensed under the rolling cylinder. From this state it is brought into *mill bar iron*. After this last operation, several pieces are welded together, from which it acquires ductility, uniformity, and cohesion. A lateral welding of four pieces together now follows, and the mass passes through a series of cylinders as in the first case, and becomes English bar-iron.

1761. The lamination of iron into sheets is by a refinery furnace, with a charcoal instead of a coke fire.

1762. Malleable iron is often obtained from the ores directly, by one fusion, if the metallic oxide be not too much mixed with foreign substances. It is a mode of working much more economical than that above described, and from the circumstance of its having been long known and used in Catalonia, it is known by the name of the *method of the Catalonian forge*. The furnace employed is similar to the refiner's forge already described. The crucible is a kind of semicircular or oblong basin, eighteen inches in diameter, and

eight or ten in depth, excavated in an area, or small elevation of masonry, eight or ten feet long, by five or six broad, and covered in with a chimney. The tuyere is placed five or six inches above the basin, inclining a little downwards, and the blast is received from a water blowing machine. The first step consists in expelling the water combined with the oxide, as well as the sulphur and arsenic when these are present. This, as usual, is done by roasting in the open air, after which it is reduced to a tolerably fine powder, and thrown at intervals by shovels-full upon the charcoal fire of the forge hearth, the sides and bottom of the basin being previously lined with *brasques* (coats of pounded charcoal). It gradually softens and unites into lumps more or less coherent, which finally melt and accumulate in the bottom of the crucible or basin. A thin slag is occasionally let off from the upper surface of the melted metal in the basin through holes which can be closed and opened at the discretion of the workman. The melted iron preserves a pasty condition owing to the heat communicated from above. When a mass sufficiently great has accumulated, it is removed, put under the hammer, and forged at once. A lump, or bloom, of malleable iron is thus produced in the space of three or four hours. Four workmen are employed at one forge, and by being relieved every six hours, they are enabled to make 86 cwt. of iron per week. In the Catalonian forge, 100 lbs. of iron are obtained from 300 lbs. of ore (a mixture of sparry iron, or carbonate and hematite), and 310 lbs. of charcoal, being a produce of 33 per cent.

1763. A visit to some of the iron districts is necessary fully to understand the processes we have above shortly described ; but the founding of iron may be well enough observed in the metropolis, though not on so large a scale as in some of the provinces. A succinct description, however, is given under the heading Foundry, Chap. III. Sec. xi.

1764. We here subjoin a summary of the modern observations on iron (collected from various authorities) as given in Rankine's *Civil Engineering*. The metallic products of the iron manufacture are of three kinds : I. Malleable or wrought iron ; II. Cast iron ; and III. Steel : both the latter being certain compounds of iron with carbon. Some investigators affirm that nitrogen is one of the essential constituents of steel, but this requires confirmation. The strength and other good qualities of these products depend mainly on the absence of impurities, and especially of certain substances which are known to cause brittleness and weakness, of which the most important are sulphur, phosphorus, silicon, calcium, and magnesium. Sulphur, and (according to Mushet) calcium, and probably also magnesium, make iron what is termed *red short*, that is, brittle at high temperatures. Phosphorus and (according to Mushet) silicon make it *cold short*, that is, brittle at high temperatures. These are both serious imperfections, but the latter is the worst defect.

1764a. Wrought or malleable iron in its perfect condition is pure, or nearly pure, iron ; its strength is in general greater or less according to the greater or less purity of the ore and fuel employed in its manufacture. Malleable iron is distinguished by the property of *welding*. Two pieces, if raised nearly to a white heat and pressed or hammered firmly together, adhering so as to form one piece. It is essential that the surfaces to be welded should be perfectly clean and free from oxide of iron, cinder, and all foreign matter. Where several bars are to be faggoted or rolled into one, they require careful *piling*, so as to ensure the pressure exerted by the hammer or the rollers being transmitted through the whole mass ; otherwise the finished bar or piece may show flaws marking the divisions between the bars of the pile. Wrought iron, although it is at first made more compact and strong by *reheating* and hammering, or otherwise working it, soon reaches a maximum strength, after which all reheating and working rapidly makes it weaker. Good *bar iron* has in general attained its maximum strength, and therefore, in all operations of forging it, the desired size and figure ought to be given to it with the least possible amount of reheating and working. In large forgings, the tenacity is only about *three fourths* of that of the bars from which the forgings were made, and sometimes even less.

1764b. It is still a matter of dispute to what extent and under what circumstances wrought iron loses its *fibrous* structure and toughness, and becomes *crystalline* and brittle. By some authorities it is asserted that all shocks and vibrations tend to produce that change ; others maintain that only sharp shocks and vibrations do so ; and others that no such change takes place ; but that the same piece of iron which shows a *fibrous* fracture, if *gradually broken* by a steady load, will show a *crystalline* fracture, if *suddenly broken* by a *sharp* blow. It is certain, at all events, that iron, whether cast or wrought, ought to be as little as possible exposed to sharp blows and rattling vibrations. Kirkaldy, *Wrought Iron and Steel*, 1863, p. 52, and in his concluding observations (p. 92), states further, that " the appearance of iron may be changed from fibrous to crystalline by merely altering the shape of the specimen so as to render it more liable to snap," and that " iron is less liable to snap the more it is worked and rolled. In the fibrous fractures the threads are drawn out, and are viewed externally, whilst in the crystalline fractures the threads are snapped across in clusters, and are viewed externally or sectionally, In the latter cases

the fracture of the specimen is always at right angles to the length; in the former it is more or less irregular."

1764c. The *continuity of the fibres* near the surface should be as little interrupted as possible. For example, projections formed out of a block by turning, rolling, and hammering, were broken off by blows with a 6 lb. hammer, with the first, fifth, and eighth blows respectively (Rankine, *Proceedings of Inst. of Civil Engineers*, 1843). In iron work which is to sustain shocks and vibrations abrupt variations of dimensions and angular figures must be avoided as much as possible, especially those with reentering angles; for at those points fractures are apt to commence. If two parts of a beam are to be of different thicknesses, they should be connected by means of curved surfaces.

1764d. The fibres of wrought iron are always an indication of its strength, but in the application of such iron we are to be cautious. If the iron be impure in its elements, or has been badly worked, it may be very fibrous and also strong, but in exposing it to a welding heat it loses all its fibre, and is converted into brittle *granulated iron.* This happens frequently with puddled iron and sometimes with charcoal iron. It follows, therefore, that iron which does not retain its fibre after receiving a welding heat is not to be trusted. Only good charcoal iron should be used where strength is required, in case any smithing is to be done to the iron before it is put to use. Where iron is exposed to heat, the very purest and best kinds only should be used: with constant heat, even of low temperature, wrought iron, if not very pure, becomes *granulated.* Very fibrous puddled iron may carry 80,000 lbs. per inch square, when newly made, but it may in a short time be converted into granular iron, and reduced to 20,000 lbs., and be inferior in strength to cast iron. Where this change in the iron would be detrimental to the work steel should be substituted, as its strength is not impaired by any degree of heat beyond a red heat.

1764e. The quality of iron for boiler plates must be attended to from the first stages of its manufacture from the ore, which should be of good quality: even then it may be spoiled in the furnaces. Above all things, states Overman, (whom we are now quoting), hot blast ought to be excluded in these cases; it ought to be a criminal offence to employ hot blast iron for boiler plates. Iron may be fibrous, and when cold very tenacious; but the test consists in heating it red hot and cooling it in cold water. If it continues tenacious it may be considered good; if not it is bad, and unfit for boiler plate.

1764f. Strength and toughness in *bar iron* are indicated by a fine, close, and uniform fibrous structure, free from all appearance of crystallization, with a clear bluish grey colour, and a silky lustre on a torn surface where the fibres are shown. *Plate iron* of the best kind consists of alternate layers of fibres crossing each other, and ought to be nearly of the same tenacity in all directions. The breaking strain and contraction of area of puddled *steel plates*, as in iron plates, are greater in the direction in which they are rolled; whereas in cast steel they are less. (Kirkaldy.)

1765. CAST IRON is the product of the process of smelting iron ores. The total quantity of carbon in *pig iron* ranges from 2 to 5 per cent. of its weight. Different kinds of pig iron are produced from the same ore in the same furnace, under different circumstances as to temperature and quantity of fuel. A high temperature and a large quantity of fuel produce *grey* cast iron, which is further distinguished into Nos. 1, 2, and 3, and so on; No. 1 being that produced at the highest temperature. A low temperature and a deficiency of fuel produce *white* cast iron. *Grey* cast iron is of different shades of bluish grey in colour, granular in texture, softer and more easily fusible than *white* cast iron, which latter is silvery white, either granular or crystalline, comparatively difficult to melt, brittle, and excessively hard. It appears that the differences between these kinds of irons depend on the proportions of carbon in them. Thus *grey* cast iron contains 1 per cent., and sometimes less, of carbon in chemical combination with the iron, and from 1 to 3 or 4 per cent. of carbon in the state of plumbago in mechanical mixture; while *white* cast iron is a homogeneous chemical compound of iron with from 2 to 4 per cent. of carbon. Of the different kinds of *grey* cast iron, No. 1 contains the greatest proportion of plumbago (which renders iron comparatively weak and pliable), No. 2 the next, and so on.

1765a. There are two kinds of *white* cast iron, the granular and the crystalline. The granular sort can be converted into *grey* cast iron by fusion and slow cooling. *Grey* cast iron can be converted into granular *white* cast iron by fusion and sudden cooling. This takes place most readily in the best iron. Crystalline *white* cast iron is harder and more brittle than granular, and is not capable of conversion into *grey* cast iron by fusion and slow cooling. It is said to contain more carbon than granular *white* cast iron; but the exact difference in their chemical composition is not yet known. *Grey* cast iron No. 1 is the most easily fusible, and produces the finest and most accurate castings; but it is deficient in hardness and strength.

1765b. The order of strength of cast iron among different kinds from the same ore and fuel is as follows:—Granular *white* cast iron, *grey* cast iron No. 3, No. 2, and No. 1. Crystalline *white* cast iron is not introduced into this classification, because its extreme brittleness makes it unfit for use in engineering structures. Granular *white* cast iron also,

although stronger and harder than *grey* cast iron, is too brittle to be a safe material for the entire mass of any girder, or other large piece of a structure. It is used to form a hard and impenetrable *skin* to a piece of *grey* cast iron by the process called *chilling*. This consists in lining the portion of the mould where a hardened surface is required with suitably shaped pieces of iron. The melted metal, on being run in, is cooled and solidified suddenly where it touches the cold iron; and for a certain depth from the chilled surface, varying from about $\frac{1}{8}$ to $\frac{1}{2}$ inch in different kinds of iron, it takes the *white* granular condition, while the remainder of the casting takes the *grey* condition. Even in castings which are not chilled by an iron lining to the mould, the outermost layer, being cooled more rapidly than the interior, approaches more nearly to the *white* condition, and forms a skin harder and stronger than the rest of the casting. The best kinds of cast iron for large structures are No. 2 and No. 3; because being stronger than No. 1, and softer and more flexible than *white* cast iron, they combine strength and pliability in the manner which is best suited for safely bearing loads that are in motion. A strong kind of cast iron called *toughened cast iron*, is produced by the process, invented by Morries Stirling, of adding to the cast iron, and melting amongst it, from one-fourth to one-seventh of its weight of wrought iron scrap.

1766. Soft grey cast iron is the best sort; it yields easily to the file when the external crust is removed, and is slightly malleable in a cold state. It is, however, more subject to rust than the white cast iron, which sort is also less soluble in acids. Grey cast iron has a granulated fracture with some metallic lustre. White cast iron in a recent fracture has a white and radiated appearance, indicating a crystalline structure.

1767. The most certain test of the goodness of a piece of cast iron is by striking the edge with a hammer, which if it make a slight impression, denoting some degree of malleability, the iron is of a good quality, provided it be uniform; if fragments fly off, and no sensible indentation be made, the iron will be hard and brittle. The difference between good and bad iron is shown mainly by the breaking; good iron breaks like a piece of good fir timber; bad iron will break like a carrot, it snaps in two. Cast iron, when at a certain degree of heat, may be cut like a piece of wood with a common saw. This discovery was announced in a letter from M. Dunford, director of the iron works at Montalaire, to M. d'Arcet, and published in the *Annales de Chimie*. The experiment was tried in 1813 by a gentleman of the Philosophical Society at Glasgow, who with the greatest ease cut a bar of cast iron, previously heated to a cherry red, with a common carpenter's saw, in the course of less than two minutes. The saw was not in the least injured by the operation.

1768. The security afforded by iron for supporting weight, and against fire, has, of late years, very much increased the use of it, and may in many cases entirely supersede the employment of timber. Again, it is valuable from its being not liable to sudden decay, nor soon destroyed by wear and tear, and, above all, from its plasticity.

1769. STEEL, the hardest of the metals and the strongest of known substances, is a compound of iron with from 0·5 to 1·5 per cent. of its weight of carbon. These, according to most authorities, as noticed by Rankine, are the only essential constituents of steel. Impurities of different kinds affect steel injuriously in the same way with iron. A very small part of its weight, $\frac{1}{2000}$th, of silicon, causes steel to cool and solidify without bubbling or agitation; a larger proportion would make the steel brittle. Manganese improves the steel by increasing its toughness, and making it easier to weld and forge.

1769a. The term *steely iron*, or *semi steel*, may be applied to compounds of iron with less than 0·5 per cent. of carbon. They are intermediate in hardness and other properties between steel and malleable iron. In general, such compounds are the harder and the stronger, and also the more easily fusible, the more carbon they contain; those sorts which contain less carbon, though weaker, are more easily welded and forged, and from their greater pliability are the fitter for structures that are exposed to shocks.

1769b. Steel is distinguished by the property of *tempering*, that is to say, it can be hardened by sudden cooling from a high temperature, and softened by gradual cooling; and its degree of hardness or softness can be regulated with precision by suitably fixing that temperature. The elevation of temperature previous to the *annealing* or gradual cooling is produced by plunging steel into a bath of a fusible metallic alloy, ranging from 430° to 560° Fahr.

1770. *Steel* is made by various processes which have of late become very numerous. They may all be classed under two heads, viz., *adding* carbon to malleable iron, used in making steel for cutting tools and other fine purposes; the other, *abstracting* carbon from cast iron, used for making great masses of *steel* and *steely iron* rapidly and at a moderate expense. Among the processes are the following:—

1771. I. *Blister steel* is made by *cementation*, by embedding bars of the purest wrought iron in a layer of charcoal and subjecting them for several days to a high temperature. Each bar absorbs carbon, and its surface becomes converted into steel. *Cementation* may also be performed by exposing the surface of the iron to a current of carburetted hydrogen gas at a

high temperature. *Cementation* is also applied to the surfaces of articles of malleable iron in order to give them a skin or coating of steel, and is called *casehardening*.

1772. II. *Shear steel* is made by breaking bars of blister steel into lengths, faggoting them, and rolling them out at a welding heat; repeating the process until a near approach to uniformity of composition and texture has been obtained. It is used for tools and cutting implements.

1773. III. *Cast steel* is made by melting bars of blister steel with a small additional quantity of carbon (in the form of coal tar), and some manganese. It is the purest, most uniform, and strongest, steel, and is used for the finest cutting implements. Another process requiring a higher temperature, is to melt bars of the purest malleable iron with manganese and with the whole quantity of carbon required in order to form steel. The quality as to hardness is regulated by the proportion of carbon. A sort of *semi steel* or *steely iron*, made by this process and containing a small proportion of carbon only, is known as *homogeneous metal*.

1774. IV. *Steel made by the air blast* is produced from molten pig iron by Bessemer's process, wherein the molten pig iron, having been run into a suitable vessel or *converter*, has jets of air blown into it through tubes as the liquid is poured in. The oxygen of the air combines with the silicon and the carbon of the pig iron, and in so doing produces enough of heat to keep the iron in a melted state till it is brought to the malleable condition; it is then run into large ingots, which are hammered and rolled in the usual way. About two hours suffice to convert cold iron into pure steel.

1775. V. *Puddled steel* is made by puddling pig iron, and stopping the process at the instant when the proper quantity of carbon remains. The bloom is shingled and rolled like bar iron. VI. *Granulated steel*, the invention of Capt. Uchatius, is made by running melted pig iron into a cistern of water over a wheel, which dashes it about so that it is found at the bottom of the cistern in the form of grains or lumps of about the size of a hazel nut. These are imbedded in pulverized hæmatite or sparry iron ore, and exposed to a heat sufficient to cause part of the oxygen of the ore to combine with, and extract, the carbon from the superficial layer of each of the lumps of iron, each of which is reduced to the condition of malleable iron at the surface, while its heart continues in a state of cast iron. A small additional quantity of malleable iron is produced by the reduction of the ore. These ingredients being melted together produce steel.

1776. Kirkaldy observes that "Steel invariably presents, when fractured slowly, a silky fibrous appearance. When fractured suddenly, the appearance is invariably granular; in which case also the fracture is always at right angles to the length. When the fracture is fibrous, the angle diverges always more or less from 90°. The granular appearance presented by steel suddenly fractured is nearly free of lustre, and unlike the brilliant crystalline appearance of iron suddenly fractured; the two combined in the same specimen are shown in iron bolts partly converted into steel. Steel which previously broke with a silky fibrous appearance is changed into granular by being hardened. Steel is reduced in strength by being hardened in water, while the strength is vastly increased by being hardened in oil. The increase of strength is greater the higher steel is heated (not being burned) and so treated."

1777. "In a highly converted or hard steel the increase in strength and in hardness is greater than in a less converted or soft steel. Steel plates hardened in oil and joined together with rivets are fully equal in strength to an unjointed soft plate; or the loss of strength by riveting is more than counterbalanced by the increase in strength by hardening in oil. The most highly converted steel does not, as some may suppose, possess the greatest density. In cast steel, the density is much greater than in puddled steel, which is even less than in some of the superior descriptions of wrought iron."

1778. This subject may, perhaps, be considered of greater importance to the architect and engineer, if those experienced scientific men be right, who predict that the time is not far hence when there will be no such metals as either wrought or cast iron; steel taking the place of both for all practical purposes. As one instance among many, it has been urged that the absolute strength of any cast iron girder may be doubled by the judicious use of a very few pounds of steel, costing but a trifle.

Corrosion and Preservation of Iron.

1779. Cast iron will often last for a long time without rusting, if the skin be not injured, which is coated with a film of the silicate of the protoxide of iron, produced by the action of the sand of the mould on the iron. Chilled surfaces of castings are without this protection, and therefore rust more rapidly. The corrosion of iron is more rapid when partly wet and partly dry, than when wholly immersed in water or wholly exposed to the air. It is accelerated by impurities in water, and especially by the presence of decomposing organic matter, or of free acids. It is also accelerated by the contact of the iron with any metal which is electro-negative relatively to the iron, or in other words, has less affinity for oxygen, or with the rust of iron itself. If two portions of a mass of iron are in different

conditions, so that one has less affinity for oxygen than the other, the contact of the former makes the latter oxidate more rapidly. In general, hard and crystalline iron is less oxidable than ductile and fibrous iron. Cast iron and steel decompose rapidly in warm or impure sea water. The purest and the most malleable irons are the most easily attacked by sea water, *when used alone;* for it is to be observed that the fine grained, crystalline, white and brittle metal, which usually resists the action of air and water most successfully, is also the most easily attacked by the dilute acids present in the woods so often used in connection with iron in ship building, or in timber structures in sea water. The most extreme care, and the greatest practical skill, are therefore required in the selection of the irons to be used in certain positions. To R. Mallet we are indebted for a valuable communication to the Institute of Civil Engineers in May 1840, *On the Corrosion of Cast and Wrought Iron in Water,* under protected and unprotected states : an abstract is given in the *Civil Engineer Journal,* iii. p. 424, from the Proceedings of the Institute.

1779a. In the Reports of the British Association, 1843 and 1849, Mallet, *On Corrosion of Iron,* further states that iron kept constantly in a state of vibration oxidates less rapidly than that which is at rest. Thus the rails of a railway on which a constant traffic runs, do not rust so quickly as those on which there may be no traffic.

1779b. Spencer, *Iron, its active and inactive states,* read before the Liverpool Polytechnic Society, stated that " It required a mixture of air and water, or what is usually termed dampness, to produce rust on iron—one without the other would not do it. Steel filings became rusty in water, because they absorbed the oxygen in the water ; if a second quantity of filings be put in, they would not rust, as there was no more oxygen. A coating of carbon effectually prevents iron from oxidation, and it can protect it from a body so strong as even aqua-fortis itself. If the aqua-fortis be diluted with water, the protective power no longer exists. The slightest scratch or abrasion on the surface of the metal also prevented the action of the protecting influence. A piece of solid carbon also imparts a protective property to iron, little short of that given to it by platinum."

1779c. Sugar exercises a material influence on iron and other metals : *Athenæum,* Sept. 1853 and May 1854.

1779d. The iron wire suspension bridges of France, which have fallen within the last few years, appear to have done so principally through the oxidation of the wires in the portion passing into the anchoring wells : this was notoriously the case with the bridge at Angers. The constant state of humidity prevailing in these wells must sooner or later have rusted the wires, and although the precaution, recommended by Vicat, of surrounding the cables with rich lime had been adopted, the vibration of the bridge had detached the cables from their supposed protecting case, and the spaces between the wires allowed moisture from the exterior to permeate the interior of the cable ; at Angers the cables were thus almost entirely rusted through. In such places it is better to employ bar chains.

1780. The following recommendations have been made for preserving iron. I. Boiling the iron in coal tar, especially if the pieces have first been heated to the temperature of melting lead. II. Heating the pieces to the temperature of melting lead and smearing their surfaces whilst hot with cold linseed oil, which dries and forms a varnish. This is recommended by Smeaton ; and is a good preparation for painting upon.

1780a. III. Painting with white lead in oil, which must be renewed from time to time. Mr. John Braithwaite has stated that his father had used red lead for fifty years with good result ; white lead was of no use, as the acid used in the preparation of it produced swelling effects. He had placed rods in a well 200 feet deep, forty-five years since, having painted them with pure red lead, and on taking them up in 1863 he found that their weight was precisely the same. Red lead and one-third litharge made into paint with nut oil will last longer than when mixed with linseed oil. Iron heated and covered with mineral bitumen or asphaltum in the solid state had resisted a moist atmosphere for fifteen years ; the natural asphaltum was the best, the liquid asphalte not answering so well; with all other materials the rust had penetrated beneath. C. H. Smith, in a communication to the *Builder,* 1864, p. 318, brought forward the advantages of lime whiting as a preservative of iron from rust. In support of the use of lime, he notices that polished steel goods may be preserved by beating a little powdered lime upon them ; and that bricklayers always smear their bright trowels even with damp mortar when leaving work.

1780b. IV. Coating with a metal, commonly called *galvanizing.* Zinc is efficient, provided it is not exposed to the acids capable of dissolving it ; but it is destroyed by sulphuric acid in the air of places where much coal is burnt ; and by muriatic acid in the neighbourhood of the sea. All attempts to use galvanized iron for roofs in large towns or smoky districts have failed. The use of this material will be noticed in the section on ZINC. Tinned iron does not now answer so well even as good zinc. It is known that during the medieval period, iron nail-heads, anchors, dogs, and such like articles were tinned over, no doubt to prevent oxidation ; and tinned iron is greatly used for the covering of houses in America. In St. Petersburg and in Moscow, iron is mostly used, but it requires painting. The coppering of iron has failed unless it was done in so expensive a manner as

not to be practicable in any extended employment of it. A coating of lead, or of lead and antimony, is wanted to iron, so as to combine the stiffness and cheapness of iron with the durability of lead. Messrs. Morewood have recently introduced metal plates covered with a uniform coating of lead. These plates are supposed to possess all the advantages of sheet lead, and they can be rendered serviceable at a considerably reduced cost (Hunt, *Handbook*, 1862). Enamelled iron is a late invention, and one tending to be very serviceable.

Sect. VI.

LEAD.

1781. Lead, the heaviest of the metals except gold and quicksilver, is found in most parts of the world. It is of a bluish white when first broken, is less ductile, elastic, and sonorous than any of the other metals : its specific gravity is from 11,300 to 11,479, and a cubic foot, therefore, weighs about 710 lbs. It is soluble in all acids and alkaline solutions, fusible before ignition, and easily calcined. The ore, which is easily reduced to the metallic state by fusion with charcoal, is found mineralised with sulphur, with a slight mixture of silver and antimony, in diaphanous prismatical crystals, generally hexagonal, white, yellowish, or greenish, in Somersetshire, about the Mendip Hills. About Bristol, and in Cumberland, it takes the form of a white, grey, or yellowish spar, vithout the least metallic appearance : in some places it is in a state of white powder or native ceruse ; and in Monmouthshire it has been found native, or in a metallic state.

1782. Exposure to air and water does not produce much alteration in lead, though it quickly tarnishes and acquires a white rust, by which the internal parts are defended from corrosion. Pure water, however, does not alter it ; hence the white crust on the inside of lead pipes through which water flows must probably be owing to some saline particles in the water. Lead will form an union with most other metals : one exception, however, is iron. Next to tin, it is the most fusible of metals. It is run from the furnace into moulds ; the main form is called a *sow*, the smaller ones *pigs* : from these it is run into sheets, pipes, &c.

1783. Sheet lead is of two sorts, *cast* and *milled*. The thicker sort of the former, or the common cast sheet lead, is manufactured by casting it on a long table formerly made of wood but now of cast iron, (with a rising edge all round it) from 16 to 20 feet in length, and 6 feet in width, which is covered with fine pressed sand beaten and smoothed down with a strike and smoother's plane. The pig lead is melted in a large vessel, near this table, and is ladled into a pan of the shape of a common triangular prism, whose length is equal to the width of a sheet, from which pan it is poured on to the table or mould. Between the surface of the sand and the *strike*, which rides upon the edges of the table, a space is left which determines the thickness of the sheet. The strike bears away the superfluous liquid lead before it has time to cool, as it moves by hand along the edges of the table before mentioned. When lead is required to be cast thin, a linen cloth is stretched on an appropriate table over a woollen one ; in which case the heat of the lead, before spreading it on the cloth, must be less than will fire paper, or the cloth would be burnt. The strike must for the purpose be passed over it with considerable rapidity.

1784. In manufacturing milled lead, it is usual first to cast it into sheets from 8 to 10 feet long according to circumstances, but the width is regulated by the length of the rollers through which it is to be passed in milling ; the thickness varies from 2 to 5 inches. By a mechanical action it is made to pass through rollers whose distance from each other is gradually lessened until the sheet is reduced to the required thickness. For a long time a great prejudice prevailed against milled sheet lead ; but it is now generally considered that, for the prevention of leakage, milled is far superior to cast lead, wherein *pin holes*, which have naturally formed themselves in the casting, often induce the most serious consequences. The sheets rolled out are about 30 feet long and 6 feet 6 inches in width. The lead from the mines of Walter Beaumont, M.P., in Northumberland, when manufactured for the market is known as " W.B. lead," and is considered the best in quality. Lead melts at a temperature of about 612° to 630° Fahr. The tenacity of sheet lead is 3,300 lbs ; and the modulus of elasticity 720,000 lbs.

1785. In *distilled* water which has been freed and kept from the contact of the air, lead undergoes no change ; but if the lead be exposed to air and water, it is oxidized and converted into a carbonate with considerable rapidity. This carbonate has the appearance of shining, brilliant scales. The presence of saline matter in the water very much retards the oxidation of the lead. So small a quantity as a 30,000th part of the phosphate of soda or iodide of potassium in distilled water, prevents lead from being much corroded, the small deposit which is formed preventing the further corrosion of the metal.

1785a. The danger of using water from leaden pipes or cisterns was known even to the Romans. The rarity of any fatal results shows that the risk has been much overrated. This is sufficiently explained by the protecting power of the insoluble salts of lead, formed by the action of the ingredients of the water on the lead, hindering the subsequent supplies of

water from coming in contact with the metal. Distilled waters and waters which are remarkably *pure* dissolve lead, and become impregnated with it. The more *impure* the water, such as Thames water, the more it will form a protecting incrustation. A new cistern should be allowed to form this coating, by the water standing in it for some time without being renewed. To expedite the action a little phosphate of soda, or iodide of potassium, or a few drops of sulphuric acid may be added. The lid or cover of cisterns should not be of lead, as the vapour condensing in it possesses all the solvent power of distilled water. Water which has flowed over leaden roofs, more particularly in towns, carries with it from the surface some soluble salt. The holes with which lead is often riddled are caused by the larva of an insect, the *Callidium bajulus*, in the stomach of which lead is often found (Kirby and Spence, *Entomology*, i. p. 235). A pipe conveying water impregnated with sulphur salts, has after a time been coated with a sulphate or sulphide, and this sulphide being perfectly insoluble in pure water, and equally so in water not too excessively charged with foreign matters to be potable, renders the leaden vehicle perfectly harmless. Dr. Schwarz, a chemist of Breslau, has stated that by passing a hot solution of sulphide of potassium through leaden pipes, the face is transmuted from the metallic state to that of a sulphide in a few minutes, at a cost too insignificant to mention. It is said that water in the mines of galena, the sulphide of lead, can be drank with impunity.

1786. *Wetterstedt's patent marine metal* for roofing and other purposes is the invention of a native of Germany, introduced into England in 1837 by Messrs. Young, Dowson, and Co., and manufactured by Messrs. Johnson, both of Limehouse. It is composed of lead and antimony, and is adapted to all purposes to which lead is usually put. Its advantages are its malleability, its great tenacity, elasticity and durability, and resistance to acids, oxidation, and the action of the sun and atmosphere. It does not lose in weight. It is manufactured in sheets:—I. 9 feet by 3 feet, at 3 lbs. and 2 lbs. per square foot; II. 8 feet by 2 feet 9 inches at 1½ lbs. and 1 lb. per square foot; and III. 8 feet by 2 feet 6 inches, at 8 ounces per square foot. No. I. sizes are employed for flats, large roofs, covering to stairs, and small sloping and curb roofs. No. II. sizes for verandahs. No. III. for lining damp walls; it should be fixed with wrought copper nails. The roof of the Royal Polytechnic Institution was covered with this patent metal in 1838; it is still in a perfect condition. In price it is somewhat under that of lead per cwt., but a much less weight per foot superficial than of that material is used. The *patent metallic canvas*, is a combination of Wetterstedt's patent metal No. III., with canvas of various substances and strength, as calico, japanned cloth, woollen, &c., varying according to the purposes to which it is to be applied. By this combination, sufficient strength is given to a metal weighing only eight ounces per foot to enable it to be used as a perfectly waterproof and secure covering. When used to damp walls, the calico is placed outside, forming a good surface for papering, painting, &c. The cement with which the combination is effected is stated to be elastic and impervious to damp, and a thorough disinfectant.

Sect. VII.

COPPER.

1787. Copper, among the first of the metals employed by the early nations of the world, is neither scarce nor difficult to work and extract from its ore. When pure it is of a pale red colour; a cubic foot of cast copper will weigh 537 lbs., in sheet 549 lbs., and when hammered 556 lbs.; the weight of a bar 1 foot long and 1 inch square varies from 3·63 lbs. to 3·81 lbs.; all the weights depending upon the copper being more or less hammered. Its elasticity and hardness are very considerable, and it is so malleable that it may be hammered into fine leaves. It is also very tenacious, a wire of a tenth of an inch in diameter being capable of sustaining 360 lbs. The tenacity of cast copper is 19,000; in sheet, 30,000; in bolts, 36,000; and in wire, 60,000. The modulus of elasticity or resistance to stretching, being 17,000,000. The transverse elasticity or resistance to distortion is 6,200,000 lbs. Copper is diminished to about two-thirds by a temperature of 600° Fahr.

1788. The sixteen copper smelting works at Swansea and Neath are supplied with ore from Cornwall, Devonshire, Ireland, and from some foreign and colonial sources. There are six smelting establishments at Liverpool and St. Helens, which obtain their ore from the Cumberland mines, from Alderley Edge, and such ores as arrive at the port of Liverpool. The single works at Cheadle produce a very fine copper, which is used in the manufacture of brass wire; the ore is selected carefully from different mines somewhat widely scattered. The Mona smelting works obtain the ores from the Mona and Pary's mines in Anglesea and from those in North Wales. The "once famous" mines in Pary's mountain formerly yielded the yellow sulphuretted ore of copper, to an annual amount of from 40,000 to 80,000 tons. This ore usually contains from one and a half to twenty-

five per cent. of copper, and is partly dug in what are called *packages*, and partly blasted by gunpowder, and then broken into small pieces previous to its being roasted.   This operation is performed in kilns, whose shape has a resemblance to lime-kilns, in which expedients are used for removing the ore as it is roasted, and adding fresh ore.   The kilns are arched level with the upper surface of the ore, and adjoining and communicating with the kiln is the floor of a condensing chamber to receive the sulphureous vapours generated in the kiln, which fall down in the form of the finest flowers of sulphur.   Several hundred tons at one time are put into the kiln, and for completing the operation six months are required.   The ore is reduced to one fourth of its previous quantity by roasting, and is then washed and pressed to remove the impurities. The richer ores are then dried, and removed for smelting and refining in reverberatory furnaces from which it is at length produced in short bars or pigs.   The water which filters through the fissures is often highly impregnated with sulphate of copper, and this water is pumped up into rectangular pits about thirty feet long, twelve broad, and two deep, to mix with that in which the roasted ore has been washed ; and in it are immersed pieces of iron, which, combining with the sulphuric acid, precipitate the copper in the form of a red-coloured powder slightly oxidated.   The precipitate thus obtained very frequently gives above 50 per cent. of pure copper, and is even more profitable to the worker than the metal produced from the crude ore.

1788a. In the process of copper smelting the specimens produced are—I. Calcined ore, or copper ore after the extraction of the sulphur.   II. Coarse metal, obtained by the second process of smelting, producing about 40 per cent. of copper.   III. Calcined coarse metal, for extracting the sulphur from II.   IV. Metal "brych," producing about 65 per cent. of copper.   V. Close regule, producing about 70 per cent.   VI. Spongy regule, producing about 80 per cent.   VII. Blister copper, producing about 95 per cent.   VIII. Select ingot, the fine metal as prepared for market.   IX. Tough ingot, ready for market. X. Tough cake, hammered out by hand.   XI. Tough bar copper, as prepared for the manufacture of wire.

1789. Sheet copper was formerly much used for its lightness to cover roofs and flats ; but it is almost superseded now by the use of zinc, which is much cheaper, and nearly if not quite as durable ; and which, moreover, is not so liable to be corrugated by the action of the sun.   Copper is reduced to sheet by being passed through large rollers, by which it can be rendered very thin. The thickness generally used is from 12 to 18 ounces to the foot superficial.   Exposed to the air its lustre is soon gone ; it assumes a tarnish of a dull brown colour, gradually deepening by time into one of bronze ; and, lastly, it takes a green rust or calx, called *patina* by the antiquaries, which, unlike the rust of iron, does not injure and corrode the internal parts, confining itself to the surface, and rather preserving than destroying the metal.   Hence one of the most important applications of copper is in cramps for stone work, especially when they are exposed to the air, when its cost, which is about six or eight times that of iron fastenings, can be afforded.   It may be here well to observe, that if water is collected from roofs for culinary purposes, copper must not be used about them, neither should any reservoirs for collecting and holding it be made of that metal, as on the surface is formed a film of verdigris, which is poisonous.

1790. Alloyed with zinc, it forms *brass* for the handles of doors, shutters, locks, drawers, and the furniture generally of joinery.   The usual proportion is one part of zinc to three of copper ; than which it is more fusible, and is of a fine yellow colour, less liable to tarnish from the action of the air, and so malleable and ductile that it can be beaten into very thin leaves and drawn into very fine wire.   The extremes of the proportions of zinc used in it are from 12 to 25 per cent. of the whole.   Even with the last, if well manufactured, it is quite malleable, although zinc by itself scarcely yields to the hammer.   The appearance of brass is frequently given to other metals by washing them over with a yellow lacquer or varnish.

1791. Copper with *tin* (which last melts at 426° Fahr. and resists oxidation better than any of the more common metals) in the proportion of one tenth to one fifth of the whole forms a composition called bronze or bell-metal, used in the foundery of statues, bells, cannons, &c.   When tin forms nearly one third of the alloy, a beautiful white close-grained brittle metal is formed, susceptible of a very high polish, which is used for the specula of reflecting telescopes.

SECT. VIII.

ZINC.

1792. Zinc is found in all quarters of the globe.   In Great Britain it is abundant, though therein never found in a native state.   It usually contains an admixture of lead and sulphur.   When purified from these, it is of a blue light colour, between lead and tin,

inclining to blue. The ore, after being hand-dressed to free it from foreign matter, is first calcined, by which the sulphur of the calamine and the acid of the blende are expelled. The product is then washed to separate the lighter matter, and the heavy part which remains, being ground in a mill, is mixed with one eighth of its weight of charcoal, or with one third of its bulk of powdered coal. This mixture is placed in pots, resembling oil jars, to be smelted. A tube passes through the bottom of each, the upper end being terminated by an open mouth near the top of the pot, and the lower end going through the floor of the furnace into water. By the intense heat of a furnace the ore is reduced, the zinc is volatilized, escaping through the tube into the water, wherein it falls in globules, which are afterwards melted and cast into moulds. Thus procured, however, it is not pure, as it almost invariably contains iron, manganese, arsenic, and copper. In order to free it from these, it is again melted and stirred up with sulphur and fat, the former whereof combines with the heterogeneous metals, leaving the zinc nearly pure, and the latter preventing the metal from being oxidated. At the Vieille Montagne Zinc Company's Works, the pots are placed in the furnaces at six o'clock every morning; at six o'clock in the evening the smelting is complete; the metal is then drawn out and run into metal moulds, after which it passes into the rolling house, and is again melted and recast in a metal mould to produce ingots of the proper size and weight for the required gauge of the sheets to be rolled; this second melting is also desirable to obtain proper purity.

1793. Under rollers at a high temperature, zinc may be extended into plates of great tenuity and elasticity, or drawn into wire. These rollers are from 2 feet 8 inches to 6 feet in length, and the original thickness of the plate subjected to them is about 1 inch. A wire, one tenth of an inch diameter, will support 26 pounds. If zinc be hammered at a temperature of 300°, its malleability is much increased, and it becomes capable of much bending. Its fracture is thin, fibrous, and of a grain similar to steel. It can be drawn into wire $\frac{1}{200}$th of an inch in diameter, which is nearly as tenacious as that of silver. The specific gravity is somewhat below 7·0, but hammering increases it to 7·2. When heated, it enters into fusion at a heat of about 680° or 700°: at a higher temperature it evaporates; and if access of air be not permitted, it may be distilled over, by which process it is rendered purer than before, although then not perfectly pure. When heated red hot, with access of air it takes fire, burns with an exceedingly beautiful greenish or bluish flame, and is at the same time converted into the only oxide of zinc with which we are acquainted, consisting of 23·53 parts of oxygen combined with 100 of metal.

1794. Zinc, though subject to oxidize, has this peculiarity, that the oxide does not scale off as that of iron, but forms a permanent coating on the metal, impervious to the action of the atmosphere, and rendering the use of paint wholly unnecessary. Dr. von Petenkoffer, however, has stated that zinc is oxidized to the extent of 130 grains per square foot in twenty-seven years, about two-fifths of the oxide being removed by the moisture of the atmosphere. Its expansion and contraction are greater than those of any other metal: thus, supposing 1·0030 to represent the expansion, 1·0019 is that of copper, and 1·0028 that of lead; but the thicker the zinc, the less its contraction and expansion. The tenacity of zinc is from 7,000 to 8,000. The weight of a cubic foot varies from 424 lbs. to 449 lbs. The tenacity of zinc to lead is as 16·616 to 3·328, and to copper as 16·616 to 22·570; hence a given substance of zinc is equal to five times the same substance in lead, and about three-fourths of copper.

1795. On the first introduction of zinc into this country as a material, the trades with which it was likely to interfere used every exertion to prevent its employment; and, indeed, the workmen who were engaged in laying it, being chiefly tinmen, were incompetent to the task of so covering roofs as to secure them from the effects of the weather. Hence, for a considerable period after its first employment, great reluctance was manifested by architects in its introduction. A demand for it has, however, gradually increased of late, and the comparatively high prices of lead and copper will not entirely account for the disparity of consumption. The Vieille Montagne Zinc Mining Company, about the year 1861, took steps to improve the quality of the zinc for use in this country, the mode of laying zinc roofs, and for the prevention of the use of thin gauges of sheets which are unfit for the purpose. Their zinc possesses a reputation for its purity and excellence. The result of this care, and the better understanding of the merits of the material, has caused it to be now extensively used for purposes which are noticed in the following chapter.

1795a. A sheet of pure zinc, as stated by J. Edmeston in his Report on Zinc, will be of an even colour, without black spots or blotches; it will be very ductile, bending readily backwards and forwards in the hand; and it will not easily break. If impure, it will be the opposite of all this. If there be any iron in it, it will be worthless; if it contain any lead, it will still, though to a less extent, contain the germs of destruction within itself.

1795b. Common zinc is destroyed by the sulphuric acid in the atmosphere where much coal is burned; and by muriatic acid in the neighbourhood of the sea. Cement does not injure zinc; but lime, and calcareous waters destroy it; and zinc pipes to flues over wood fires are destroyed by them.

1796. GALVANIZED IRON is a designation misapplied to that iron which may have received a coating of zinc ; it should be called *zinked iron*. The metal is first cleaned perfectly by the joint action of dilute acid and friction, and then plunged into a bath of melted zinc, covered with sal ammoniac, and stirred until the iron is sufficiently coated with zinc.   No galvanic action whatever occurs between the metals ; it is simply a coating. This process, it is stated, was invented in France by Maloin, in 1742, but not patented until 1836 by Sorel.   The efficacy of the process depends upon the skill employed in removing every trace of the scales of the hydrous oxide of iron, and in its further treatment.   The coating must not become loosened, or any hole be made through it, as moisture obtaining access to the iron will rapidly extend, and the scales of the oxide of iron will force up the slight zinc covering, when the iron will be gradually destroyed, unless it be at once painted.   When well executed it may perhaps be durable for a lengthened period, but when badly prepared it is not so valuable as iron well painted (*par.* 1779*b*.).   At the Houses of Parliament, where the iron roofing plates were galvanized, it was found necessary from 1860 to commence coating them with paint or some other material.

1796*a*. The other process, which might be properly called *zinked-tinned iron*, is thus performed :—The sheets of iron are pickled, scoured, and cleaned, as for ordinary tinning.   A wooden bath is half filled with a solution—the proportion of 2 quarts of muriate of tin with 100 quarts of water.   Over the bottom of the bath is spread a thin layer of finely granulated zinc, then a cleaned plate, and so on alternately ; the zinc and iron and the fluid constitute a weak galvanic battery, and the tin is deposited from the solution so as to coat the iron, in about two hours, with a dull uniform layer of metal.   The iron in this state is then passed through a bath containing fluid zinc covered with sal ammoniac mixed with an earthy matter, to lessen the volatilization of the sal ammoniac, which becomes as fluid as treacle.   Two iron rollers are driven by machinery to carry the plates through the fluid at any velocity previously determined ; the plates thus take up a very regular and smooth layer of zinc, which owing to the presence of the tin beneath, assumes its natural crystalline character.   This is said to be the process adopted by Messrs. Morewood and Rogers, whose patents date in 1846 and 1850.   It is asserted that iron thus prepared does not warp or buckle ; that the plate is not affected by the heat of the zinc, whereas thin sheet iron, kept in molten zinc for a few minutes, becomes so brittle that it will not bear folding or grooving ; that the plate is equally covered with zinc, whereas by the dipping process the lower half receives more than the upper : and that zinc is not contaminated by iron as when dipped, the contamination increasing with each dipping until the zinc in the bath becomes so injured as to be worthless, it being well known that the alloy of zinc and iron is more oxidizable than zinc alone, or than zinc and tin.   Professor Brande has stated that in common tinned plate, the combination is such that the oxidization of the iron is accelerated by the tin, so that the iron is the protecting, and the tin the protected, metal, but in this case the reverse effect ensues, the iron is the protected metal, and the zinc the protector.

1796*b*. Time has proved that galvanized iron has corroded after *seven years* in a roof-gutter ; and the state of most of the roofs to railway sheds and stations and such like places, proves that at least some sorts of galvanized iron will decay ; the difficulty always is to ascertain what description of coating the iron has undergone.   Galvanized iron bolts do not act upon oak either in sea or in fresh water, when care has been taken not to remove the zinc in driving them.

1796*c*. Galvanized iron is said to be nearly the same cost as zinc, and to be less than one quarter as liable to expansion or contraction : to be equally as durable as lead ; less in first cost, and not to require boarding ; to be not quite one-third the price of copper, and to be equally as durable ; and as compared with plain iron, the cost is increased about two-thirds, but that it increases the strength and durability of the iron.

1797. The soldering used is composed of spirits of salts killed by putting about three ounces of zinc to a pint of spirit ; care must be taken that this solder soaks well between the laps.

Sect. IX.

SLATE.

1798. Slate is a species of argillaceous stone, and is an abundant and most useful mineral. This material is so soft, that the human nail will slightly scratch it, and is of a bright lamellated texture.   Its constituent parts are argill, earth, silex, magnesia, lime, and iron ; of the two first and the last in considerable proportion.   The building slate is the *schistus tegularis*.

1799. *Mica slate* is a species of gneiss, distinguishable by containing little or no felspar, so that it consists chiefly of quartz and mica. It has a laminated or slaty structure, with the silky lustre of mica; it is a tough material in directions parallel to its layers, but is more perishable than gneiss. In thin layers it may be used for roofing purposes. *Chlorite slate* is also laminated, soft, and easily cut, but more opaque than talc, and is sometimes used for roofing purposes. It has a green or greenish grey colour and silky lustre. *Hornblende slate* is hard, tough, durable, and impervious to water, and is used for flagstones. *Grauwacke slate* is a laminated claystone, containing sand and sometimes fragments of mica and other minerals. It is used for roofing and flag stones. All these descriptions of slate are inferior to the ordinary *clay slate.*

1800. Slate quarries usually lie near the surface; and, independent of the splitting grain, along which they can be cleft exceedingly thin, they are mostly divided into *stacks*, by breakings, cracks, and fissures. Slate is separated from its bed, like other stones, by means of gunpowder, and the mass is then divided into scantlings by wedges, and, if necessary, sawn to its respective sizes by machinery. The blue, green, purple, and darker kinds are most susceptible of thin cleavage, the lighter-coloured slates being coarser. The instruments used in quarrying and splitting slates, are slate knives, axes, bars, and wedges.

1801. The tenacity of slate is from 9,600 to 12,800. The modulus of elasticity varies from 13,000,000 to 16,000,000. The resistance to rupture is 5000. The weight of a cubic foot is from 175 lbs. to 181 lbs. The transverse strength of Welsh slate is greater than any other mineral product of the stone kind. For such qualities as strength, space, and cleanliness, no other material is so cheap as slate.

1802. The slates used about London are brought chiefly from Bangor in Carnarvonshire. The slate quarries of North Wales are the most important in this country. The chief works are situated as follows, and belong respectively to the geological formations named:—

Penrhyn, Bangor } Cambrian. Llanberis, Dinorwic }		Llangollen, Llangollen : Upper Silurian. Machynlleth, Aberdovey, Lower Silurian.
Ffestiniog, Port Madoc : Lower Silurian.		Royal Slate, Bangor : Cambrian.

The large quarries at Penrhyn near Bangor, belonging to Colonel Pennant, and from which the best Bangor slates are obtained, are worked in successive terraces; the slate is obtained in immense masses by blasting, therefore the waste is enormous, but being got rid of without difficulty, the price is kept moderate. These quarries have been variously estimated as yielding from 30,000*l*. to 40,000*l*. worth of slates per annum. Many smaller ones have lately been opened near Bangor, all supplying "best Bangor" slates, without affecting the produce of the well-established works at that place. The Llangollen quarries are remarkable for the size of the slates they can obtain.

1803. The Delabole quarries in Cornwall have been worked for a considerable period; these slates are shipped from Tintagel and Boscastle. This grey-blue slate, confined till lately to the western counties, is now obtained in London; the Wellington College at Sandhurst, Berkshire, is roofed with them. The Tavistock slates from Devonshire were at one period in considerable demand. One of the most esteemed slates is of a pale blue-green, brought from Kendal in Westmoreland, and called Westmoreland slate. There are quarries in the neighbourhood of Ulverstone, in Lancashire; and the Cumberland sea-green slate works are at Maryport.

1804. The extended use of this material for paving, shelving, cisterns, &c., has caused numerous companies to be formed for the working of old, and of many new, quarries, chiefly in North and South Wales. Amongst the companies putting forth peculiarities of slate, are the Dorothea West, Green, Blue, and Red, Slate Company, situate in Carnarvonshire, which supplied the pale green slates for the Charing Cross Railway Hotel, the London Bridge Hotel, and the Star and Garter Hotel at Richmond. The Llanfair Green and Blue Slate Company is also to be noticed.

1805. The slates of Scotland are not in much repute. The Balahulish quarries in the north of Scotland are very extensive, as between five and seven millions of roofing slates are quarried annually. The weight of this number would be about 10,000 tons, and the quantity of rubbish being generally five or six times as much as the slates, some 50,000 or 60,000 tons of refuse have to be disposed of, which in this case are thrown directly into the sea, securing an immense saving of expense.

1806. The more important slate quarries in Ireland are in the southern division of the country, viz., Killaloe, county Tipperary; Valentia, county Kerry; Benduff, near Glandore Harbour, county Cork; and near Ashford Bridge, county Wicklow. The chief one is at Curraghbally, situate about six miles from Killaloe. The colour of the slates is a dull bluish grey, preferred by many to the decided blue of the Bangor quarries; they are greatly used in the west of Ireland, where they have superseded the Welsh slates. The colour of the Valentia slates is rather greener than those above mentioned. They are generally thicker and more uneven on the surface, and so are better suited for the exposed

aspects of buildings in the western counties. This quarry has more capabilities for sawn flags and slabs, of which a large amount is now exported to England for cisterns, baths, urinals, &c. The Banduff quarry is nearly given up. The slates from Ashford Bridge both in colour and quality closely resemble the Bangor slates. (Wilkinson, *Geology, &c. of Ireland*, 1845.)

1807. A fine sound texture is the most desirable among the properties of a slate; for the expense of slating being greatly increased by the boarding whereon it is placed, if the slate absorbs and retains much moisture, the boarding will soon become rotten. But a good slate is very durable. Its goodness may readily be judged by striking it as a piece of pottery is struck; a sonorous, clear bell-like sound is a sign of excellence; but many pieces of the slate should be tried before a conclusion can be arrived at. It is thought to be a good sign, if, in hewing, it shatters before the edge of the *zax*. The colour, also, is some guide, the light blue sort imbibing and retaining moisture in a far less degree than the deep black-blue sort. The feel of a slate is some indication of its goodness: a good one has a hard and rough feel, whilst an open absorbent slate feels smooth and greasy. The best method, however, of testing the quality of slates is by the use of water, in two ways. The first is, to set the pieces to be tried edgewise in a tub of water, the water reaching above half way up the height of the pieces: if they draw water, and become wet to the top in six or eight hours' time, they are spongy and bad; and as the water reaches less up them, so are the pieces better. The other method is, to weigh the pieces of slate, and note their weights. Let them then remain for twelve hours in water, and take them out, wiping them dry. Those that on re-weighing are much heavier than they were previous to their immersion should be rejected. Where the character of a slate quarry is not previously known, experiments of these sorts should never be omitted.

1808. The following comparison of the advantages of slates over tiles is given by R. Watson, former Bishop of Llandaff. That sort of slate, other circumstances being the same, is esteemed the best which imbibes the least water; for water not only increases the weight of the covering, but in frosty weather, being converted into ice, swells and shivers the slate. This effect of frost is very sensible in tiled houses, but is scarcely felt in those which are slated, for good slates imbibe but little water; though tiles, when well glazed, are rendered in some measure similar to slate in this respect. The bishop took a piece of Westmoreland slate and a piece of common tile and weighed each of them carefully. The surface of each was about thirty square inches. Both the pieces were immersed in water about ten minutes, then taken out and weighed as soon as they had ceased to drip. The tile had imbibed about a seventh part of its weight of water, and the slate had not imbibed a two-hundredth part of its weight; indeed, the wetting of the slate was merely superficial. He placed both the wet pieces before the fire; in a quarter of an hour the slate was perfectly dry, and of the same weight as before it was put into the water; but the tile had lost only about twelve grains it had imbibed, which was, as near as could be expected, the very same quantity that had been spread over its surface; for it was the quantity which had been imbibed by the slate, the surface of which was equal to that of the tile. The tile was left to dry in a room heated to sixty degrees, and it did not lose all the water it had imbibed in less than six days.

1809. Professor Ansted states that the best slates are those which are most crystalline, and which, when breathed upon, give out a faint argillaceous odour; when this was given out strongly, then the slates would readily decompose.

1810. The largest slab of slate, perhaps, ever as yet obtained, was the one sent by the Llangollen Slate Company to the International Exhibition of 1862. It was 20 feet long, 10 feet wide, and weighed 4½ tons; the thickness, however, was not named. The Welsh Slate Company, whose quarries are at Festiniog, in Merionethshire, sent several slabs averaging 14 feet by 7 or 8 feet. All the slate from this neighbourhood possesses the remarkable quality of splitting with great facility, and with wonderful accuracy of surface, into thin laminæ or sheets. Some of these thinly divided sheets are obtained 5 to 10 feet long from 6 to 12 inches wide, and not more than the sixteenth of an inch in thickness. They are so elastic as to bend like a veneer of wood. (Hunt, *Handbook*, 1862.)

Sect. X.

BRICK AND TILE.

1811. A brick is a factitious sort of stone, manufactured from argillaceous or clayey earth, well tempered and squeezed into a mould. When so formed, bricks are stacked to dry in the sun, and finally burnt to a proper degree of hardness in a clamp or kiln. The use of bricks is of the highest antiquity. They are frequently mentioned in the historical

books of the Old Testament; but whether they were merely sun-dried or burnt in a kiln seems uncertain. We are inclined to doubt the burning of them at a very remote period. It will immediately occur to the reader that the making of bricks was one of the tasks imposed upon the Israelites during their servitude in Egypt. Though the oldest remains in Egypt are of stone, Pococke describes a pyramid of unburnt bricks, which are composed of a black sandy earth, intermixed with pebbles and shells, the sediment deposited by the overflowing of the Nile. This species of bricks is still common in Egypt and many other parts of the East. By the ancient Greeks and Romans, both burnt and unburnt bricks were used; the method of making the latter whereof is thus described by Vitruvius, in the third chapter of his second book : " I shall first," says that author, " treat of bricks, and the earth of which they ought to be made. Gravelly, pebbly, and sandy clay are unfit for that purpose; for if made of either of these sorts of earth, they are not only too ponderous, but walls built of them, when exposed to the rain, moulder away, and are soon decomposed; and the straw, also, with which they are mixed, will not sufficiently bind the earth together, because of its rough quality. They should be made of earth, of a red or white chalky, or a strong sandy nature. These sorts of earth are ductile and cohesive, and not being heavy, bricks made of them are more easily handled in carrying up the work. The proper seasons for brick-making are the spring and autumn, because they then dry more equably. Those made in the summer solstice are defective, because the heat of the sun soon imparts to their external surfaces an appearance of sufficient dryness, whilst the internal parts of them are in a very different state; hence, when thoroughly dry, they shrink and break those parts which first dried; and thus broken, their strength is gone. Those are best which have been made at least two years; for in a period less than that, they will not dry thoroughly. When plastering is laid and set hard on bricks which are not perfectly dry, the bricks, which will naturally shrink, and consequently occupy a less space than the plastering, will thus leave the latter to stand of itself. From its being extremely thin, and not capable of supporting itself, it soon breaks to pieces; and in its failure, involves sometimes even that of the wall. It is not, therefore, without reason that the inhabitants of Utica allow no bricks to be used in their buildings which are not at least five years old, and also approved by a magistrate.

1812. " There are three sorts of bricks: the first is that which the Greeks call *Didoron* (διδῶρον), being the sort we use; that is one foot long and half a foot wide. The other two sorts are used in Grecian buildings; one is called *Pentadoron*, the other *Tetradoron*. By the word *doron*, the Greeks mean a palm, because the word δῶρον signifies a gift which can be borne in the palm of the hand. That sort, therefore, which is five palms each way, is called Pentadoron; that of four palms, Tetradoron. The former of these two sorts is used in public buildings, the latter in private ones. Each sort has half bricks made to suit it, so that when a wall is executed, the course on one of the faces of the wall shows sides of whole bricks, the other face of half bricks; and being worked to the line on each face, the bricks on each bed bond alternately over the course below." Vitruvius concludes the chapter with the mention of the bricks made at Calentum in Spain, at Marseilles in France, and Pitane in Asia, which are specifically lighter than water.

1813. It is to be regretted that plastering with cement, a practice which is more to the interest of the brickmaker and bricklayer than to the consumer, has become so prevalent in this country. These tradesmen thus get rid of their worst bricks, which are hidden by a coat of plaster; the building soon decaying when the heart of the wall is bad. Colour seems to be the objectionable quality about this material, the commonplace architect forgetting that form is much more essential to beauty than colour. In the times of Jones and Wren, red brick was beautifully wrought into architectural forms, of which a few examples still remain in the metropolis : and by Palladio, bricks were occasionally used for columns without smearing them over with plaster.

1814. In England, the best earth for making bricks is a clayey loam, neither abounding with too much sand, which renders them brittle, nor with too large a portion of argillaceous matter, which causes them to shrink and crack in drying. It should be dug at the least a year before it is wrought, that by exposure to the atmosphere it may part with all extraneous matter which it possessed when first dug. The general practice is, however, to dig it in the autumn, and allow it to remain through the winter to mellow and pulverize, by which the operation of tempering is greatly facilitated. Upon this operation the quality of the brick mainly depends, and great attention should be bestowed upon performing this part of the process in a proper manner. This branch of the manufacture was formerly executed by throwing the clay into shallow pits, and subjecting it to be trodden by men and oxen; a method which has been advantageously superseded by a clay or pugmill, with a horse track.

1815. As soon as the clay has been thoroughly tempered by one of the methods above named, it is taken to the moulder's bench, where it is cut by the moulder's assistant, generally a woman or a lad, into pieces rather larger than the mould, which are passed on to the moulder, who throws it with some force into the mould, which has been previously

dipped in sand. He presses it down, so that it may fill the whole of the cavity, striking off the superfluous clay with a flat wooden rule. The newly-formed brick is then turned out of the mould on to a thin board, somewhat larger than a brick, and it is removed by a boy to a latticed wheelbarrow, and conveyed, covered with fine dry sand, to the *hack*. A handy moulder, working fifteen hours, will mould 5000 bricks. In the hacks, which are eight courses in height, the bricks are arranged diagonally above each other, with a passage between each for the circulation of air round them. The time required for drying in the hacks will of course depend on the fineness of the weather; it is but a few days if the season be propitious; and they are then turned and reset wider apart, after which, in about six or eight days, they are ready for the clamp or kiln. If the weather be rainy, the bricks in the hack must be covered with wheat or rye straw; and as they ought to be thoroughly dry before removing to the clamp or kiln, a few are generally selected from different parts, and broken, to ascertain if the operation of drying has been well performed. The moisture arising from bricks when burning is very injurious to their soundness.

1816. The quantity of clay necessary to make 1000 bricks will be somewhere about 54 cube feet, which allows about 5 feet for shrinkage in drying and burning; for $1000 \times 8\frac{1}{2}$ in. $\times 2\frac{1}{2}$ in. $\times 4$ in. $= 49 \ 2 \ 3'' \ 4'''$. The cost of making 1000 bricks, in the neighbourhood of London, is nearly as follows:—

Digging, wheeling, carting, &c.	-	-	-	-	-	-	0	1	6
Moulding, stacking, &c.	-	-	-	-	-	-	0	11	6
Sand, one-sixth of 2s.	-	-	-	-	-	-	0	0	4
Straw for hacks	-	-	-	-	-	-	0	0	9
Barrows, moulds, planks, &c.	-	-	-	-	-	-	0	0	6
Fuel 9 cwt. per 1000	-	-	-	-	-	-	0	10	6

$$= £1 \ 5 \ 1$$

1817. In the brickfields about London, bricks are mostly burnt in what are called *clamps*. These are generally oblong in form, and their foundations are made with the driest of the bricks from the hacks, or with common worthless bricks, called place bricks. The bricks for burning are then arranged, tier over tier, to the height assigned to the clamp, according to the quantity to be burnt, and a layer of breeze or cinders, two or three inches deep, is placed between each course of bricks, and the whole, when built up, covered with a thick stratum of breeze. On the western face of the clamp a vertical fireplace is formed, about 3 feet in height, from which flues are driven out by arching the bricks over, so as to leave a space about one brick wide. The flues run in a straight direction through the clamp, and are filled with a mixture of coals, breeze, and wood, closely pressed together. If the bricks are required to be burnt quickly, the flues should not be more than 6 feet apart; but if time do not press, the flues need not be nearer than 9 feet to each other, and the clamp is allowed to burn slowly. It is possible, if required, to burn a clamp in a period of from 20 to 30 days, according to the dryness of the weather. The practice of steeping bricks in water after they have been burnt, and then again burning them, has been found to have the effect of considerably improving their quality.

1818. A new mode of burning bricks in clamps has been patented by Robert White at Erith, wherein the advantages are stated to be that, 1st, nearly all the bricks are burnt into stocks, and the yield of inferior bricks is reduced from 35 to about 10 per cent. of the total make; and, 2ndly, the bricks are so much improved in colour and soundness as to give them a considerable additional value in the market over common stocks.

1819. The *kilns* which are used for burning bricks are usually 13 feet long, by 10 feet 6 inches in width, and 12 feet in height. The walls are one brick and a half thick, and incline inwards as they rise. A kiln is generally built to contain 20,000 bricks at each burning. The fireplace consists of three arches, which have holes at top for distributing heat to the bricks. These are placed on a lattice-like floor, and first undergo a gentle action of the fire for two or three days, in order to dry them thoroughly. As soon as they thus become ready for burning, the mouth of the fireplace is dammed up with what is called a *shinlog* (which consists of pieces of brick piled against each other, and closed with wet brick earth), leaving about it sufficient room to introduce a faggot. The kiln is then supplied with brushwood, furze, heath, faggots, &c., and the fire is kindled and kept up until the arches assume a white appearance, and flames appear through the top of the kiln. The fire is then slackened, and the kiln gradually cooled. This process of alternately raising and slacking the heat of the kiln is repeated till the bricks are thoroughly burnt, which is usually accomplished in about eight and forty hours.

1820. The malm or marl stock, which is of a bright yellowish uniform colour and texture, is not always to be had, especially in the London districts; in consequence of which, several years ago, it was discovered that chalk mixed in certain portions with loam, and treated in the usual manner, proved an excellent substitute for it. It not only was found to improve the colour, but to impart soundness to the brick; and the practice is now generally adopted about London. At Emsworth in Hampshire, and also at Southampton,

ooze, or sludge, from the sea-shore, containing much saline matter, is used for a similar purpose: these bricks, however, have not the rich brimstone colour of the London malm stock, nor the regular stone-coloured hue of the Ipswich or Suffolk bricks.

1821. The finest marl stocks, which are technically called *firsts*, or *cutters*, are principally used for arches of doorways and windows, quoins, &c., for which purposes they are rubbed and cut to their proper dimensions and form. There is also a red cutting brick, whose texture is similar to the malm cutter, which must not be confounded with the red stock. The next best, which are chiefly used for principal fronts, are called *seconds*; they are not quite so uniform in colour, nor so bright as the last, but are, nevertheless, a handsome and durable brick.

1822. *Stocks* are red and grey, both sorts being equal in texture. The red sort are burnt in kilns. The grey stocks are less uniform in their colour than seconds, and are of rather an inferior quality. They are used for common fronts, and walls.

1823. *Place bricks*, or *peckings*, sometimes also called *sandel*, or *samel bricks*, are those which, having been outermost or furthest from the fire in the clamp, or kiln, have not received sufficient heat to burn them thoroughly. They are consequently soft, uneven in texture, and of a red colour. These should never be used in a building where durability is required. The name was formerly applied to the second quality of bricks, and these are still so called in Ireland, being used for inside walls: the Irish harder burnt brick, having a semi-glazed surface, is called *fire brick*, and is used for exterior work where expense is not an object; of course it lasts much longer than the other sorts.

1824. *Burrs* and *clinkers* are such bricks as have been violently burnt, or masses of several bricks run together in the clamp or kiln.

1825. The red bricks derive their colour from the nature of the soil whereof they are composed, which is generally very pure. The best of them are used for cutting-bricks, and are called red rubbers. In old buildings they are frequently found set in lime putty, and often carved into ornaments over arches, windows, doorways, &c.

1826. *Firebricks*, so called from their capability of resisting the most violent action of the fire, are of a dark red colour, and of very close texture; they are made about 9 inches long, 4½ inches broad, and 1½ inches thick. The loam of which they are made is yellow, harsh to the touch, and contains a considerable portion of sand. Their quality renders them highly serviceable in furnaces and ovens. The greatest part of those used about London were formerly brought from Hedgerly, a village near Windsor, whence they obtained the name of Windsor bricks. This sort of brick is made also in various parts of Wales, whence they are called *Welsh lumps*; also at Newcastle; at Poole in Dorsetshire; at the Hurlford works near Glasgow; and at Stourbridge; the latter supplies chiefly the London market, but the material is one of the dearest. Fire clay, and flue linings for furnaces, are extensively used. The Dinas brick, manufactured by the Ynisymudu Company, near Swansea, stands a heat that will melt the Stourbridge brick.

1827. *Paving bricks* are for the purpose which their name implies, and their dimensions are the same as those of the foregoing sort.

1828. *Dutch clinkers* and *Flemish bricks* vary little in quality; they are exceedingly hard, and are used for the paving of stables, yards, &c., though they are by some objected to, as being too hot for the horses' feet. The former are 6 inches long, 3 inches broad, and 1 inch thick, and are often laid on edge in various fanciful forms, as the herring-bone, &c.

1829. *Compass bricks* are circular on the plan, and are chiefly employed for *steyning*, or walling round wells.

1830. *Concave* or *hollow bricks* are made like common bricks, but hollowed on one side in the direction of their length, and are adapted to the construction of drains and watercourses. Other *hollow* bricks are noticed in *par.* 1831c.

1831. Amongst the many qualities and varieties of bricks now in use in the metropolis, the following may be enumerated in addition to those already mentioned. The *Cowley*, *Essex and Kent bricks*. From Cowley are sent stocks, best yellow, and white cutters; yellow and white seconds, paviours, pickings, &c. The *Aylesford and Burham* works, near Maidstone, on the river Medway, formerly the property of the late Thomas Cubitt, produce *gault* bricks of good quality. (See *par.* 1831f.)

1831a. The *Suffolk bricks*, called white Suffolks, are of two or more qualities, expressly made for facings, and are expensive; the *best* are rarely to be obtained in London, being sold in the locality of their manufacture. They have a disagreeable cold hue, rendered still more dull after a few years' wear in the smoky atmosphere even of a provincial town. They are not so well burnt as those which are somewhat of a light pink or salmon tint. These latter are to be bought at the kiln at about 17s. per thousand, and by some persons are thought to make better brickwork than those which fetch 60s. or more per thousand in London. The works supply superior white and red (kiln burnt) *Suffolk* facings, splays, door-jambs, coping bricks, stable clinkers, &c.; dark red facings, rubbers, splays, paving bricks, &c.; bright yellow malm facings, and cutters of best quality. Mean quality, and pale malm seconds, pickings, paviours, &c. A dark-coloured brick from *Huntingdon* is

of a finer colour, uniform, much smoother than ordinary, and equal to those made in Kent.

1831b. *South Staffordshire* supplies a blue vitrified sewerage and paving brick (as used on Charing-cross suspension bridge, 1856, and on Chelsea new bridge), and a channeled stable brick. It is stated that the *Tipton blue brick*, when used for facings, lets in the wet most thoroughly, either through the brick or through the mortar joints, so that walls of this material should be built hollow. The construction of the work was questioned, as 9 and 14 inch walls have been erected with these bricks with success: as they are scarcely absorbent, mortar does not thoroughly adhere to them; this want of adhesion might be remedied by well soaking the bricks before using them.

1831c. *Hollow* and *pierced bricks* of several shapes and sizes are supplied by various manufacturers. A *beaded brick*, drilled with holes, for garden walls, to avoid the necessity of nailing in training trees, are made at Stony Stratford, in Northamptonshire.

1831d. *Black bricks* are obtained from Cowbridge in South Wales; these were used at All Saints' Church, Margaret Street, and cost £4 per thousand. The Ballingdon or Ewell deep black rubbing and building bricks, probably so rendered by manganese, are soft in make, and dead-looking in colour. The same factory, and Chalfont, supply dark, and bright, red rubbers; with black headers, glazed and unglazed. Red and black bricks are sent from Burgess Hill, Sussex; and from Maidenhead, in Berkshire.

1831e. *White glazed bricks* are useful for cleanliness, and for obtaining reflected light. Best white, and buff, silica pressed facing bricks, are also to be obtained.

1831f. *Beart's patent bricks* are made at Arsley near Hitchin, on the Great Northern Railway, of the following qualities, ranged according to price:—White rubbers; hand made moulded solid brick, equal to the best Suffolks; No. 1 best selected white facing brick (pierced); and ordinary; these two are of uniform colour, hard and well burnt, and used extensively for facings; No. 2 mingled, red and pink, vary from the above only in colour, and are equal in every respect to the best made stock bricks. These bricks are made from the *Gault* clay, one of the subcretaceous formations interposed between the chalk and the wealden deposits, or between the chalk and the upper oolite. The composition varies, for although it is of a tolerably uniform dark blue colour, it sometimes contains large quantities (comparatively) of the hydrous oxide of iron; and in others it contains much of the bicarbonate of lime, in combination. The former burn in the kiln into a deep red brick or tile of rather inferior quality; the latter are used for the pierced hard white bricks above described. It is stated that these bricks are required to be burnt with great care, for if the calcination of the lime should take place under such conditions as to leave the lime in a caustic state, it will slack on exposure to the weather, or when moisture is applied to it. There is some difference of opinion as to whether mortar can be made to adhere to the smooth hard face of these bricks to make sound and strong work.

1832. By the 17th Geo. III. cap. 42. all bricks made for sale were directed, when burnt, to be not less than $8\frac{1}{2}$ inches long, $2\frac{1}{2}$ inches thick, and 4 inches wide. This statute, which was enacted for the purpose of levying a duty, is now no longer in force, and the manufacturer is at liberty to make bricks and tiles of whatever size and form may be best suited to the work for which they are used. This act having been rescinded, has led to the introduction of *moulded* and *ornamented* bricks to a vast extent, which will probably be still further extended as brickmaking machines become more useful and certain in their operations. The patents for them are now very numerous: some of them are stated to make up to 20,000 per day, as may be required. The size of the brick, however, has been retained, and habit will, no doubt, continue it in favour, especially for repairs.

1832a. Bricks laid in the summer season should be well saturated with water previous to laying; and if the work be left for a day only, the walls should be as carefully covered up as in the winter, for in hot weather the mortar sets too rapidly, and hence the necessary cohesion is destroyed; an evil much aggravated by the dust constantly hanging about the bricks, more especially at that season of the year.

1833. A valuable paper, *On the transverse strength of bricks*, was delivered by Mr. W. Hawkes at the Institute of British Architects, January 1861. He stated that he had always tested bricks by their transverse power in preference to the crushing weight which was but seldom called in question, as it tells nothing if the bricks will resist from 30 to 100 tons dead weight. It would often be useful to know if in a 9 inch wall we could distribute a weight, say of 13 tons, over an opening 90 inches wide, having only 40 inches depth; supposing that the bricks be of moderate strength and the mortar be as strong as the bricks. The pressure and weights were applied in each case in the centre of the brick.

1833a. He experimented on *Dutch clinkers* (made at Moor, near Gouda, in South Holland, from the slime deposited on the banks of the river Yssel; and formerly from that of Haarlem Meer; the clay or slime is washed to get rid of the earthy matter before being moulded; the colour is lightish yellow brown); Tipton blue bricks; Birmingham, hand and machine made; Leeds, ditto; Bridgewater; Colchester; Oxford; and London, &c.; with *tiles* of various kinds. As, however, these experiments were made to a calculated standard size of 7 inches long, 4·5 inches wide, and 3 inches thick, the results are

not generally useful for a work of this description. But we give the few actual weights borne by certain bricks. Thus the 9 Leicester bricks carried at the ordinary size 1,462 lbs., 1,392 lbs., 1,252 lbs., 1,132 lbs., 1,052 lbs., 1,002 lbs., 902 lbs., and 892 lbs. The 9 from Rugby carried 1,222 lbs., 1,022 lbs., 1,012 lbs., 862 lbs., 822 lbs., 552 lbs., 422 lbs., and 362 lbs. The 7 London bricks carried 1,142 lbs., 1,042 lbs., 952 lbs., 662 lbs., 652 lbs., 422 lbs., all being *stocks*; the last, a *place* brick, carried 270 lbs. The 7 London bricks (second set) carried 970 lbs., 690 lbs., 580 lbs., 400 lbs., all *stocks*; and 650 lbs., 490 lbs., 340 lbs., all *place*; the *frog* was not allowed for in the calculation.

1833b. The following are the ascertained weights of bricks of the sizes stated:—

	ins.	ins.	ins.	lbs.	cwts. per 1000.
London stocks	$8\frac{3}{4}$	$\times 4\frac{1}{4}$	$\times 2\frac{3}{4}$	$= 6\cdot81$	$= 60\frac{3}{4}$
Red kiln	$8\frac{3}{4}$	$\times 4\frac{1}{4}$	$\times 2\frac{3}{4}$	$= 7\cdot00$	$= 63$
Welsh fire	9	$\times 4\frac{1}{2}$	$\times 2\frac{3}{4}$	$= 7\cdot84$	$= 65$ to 75
Paving	9	$\times 4\frac{1}{2}$	$\times 1\frac{3}{4}$	$= 5\cdot00$	$= 45$
Dutch clinkers	$6\frac{1}{4}$	$\times 3$	$\times 1\frac{1}{4}$	$= 1\cdot55$	$= 14$
Irish fire	$8\frac{3}{4}$	$\times 4\frac{1}{8}$	$\times 2\frac{5}{8}$		$= 67$
Worcestershire, solid, machine made				$8\cdot75$	
Ditto, perforated				$6\cdot00$	
Staffordshire, solid, hand made				$9\cdot50$	
London stock, hand made				$5\cdot75$	

1833c. Brickwork expands with great heat. Mr. Hawkes's experiments, already noticed, on a furnace chimney, 54 feet 7 inches in height, showed that the result of six trials was an elongation of 1·425 inches. The great heat of the furnace chimney for melting iron is never reached in house flues, but since the introduction of hot air cockles and hot water furnaces, particularly the high-pressure, the heat of these flues is increased fivefold compared with flues from open fireplaces. An iron bar might perhaps be heated to redness in some of the furnace flues. In another chimney, at Thames Bank, in a height of 80 feet, the brickwork showed an expansion at times of $\frac{5}{8}$ of an inch.

1834. Tiles, which in their constituent parts partake much of the nature of bricks, are plates of clay baked in a kiln, and used instead of slates, or other covering of the roofs of houses. The clay whereof tiles are formed will always make good bricks, though the converse does not hold, from the toughness required on account of their being so much thinner than bricks. The common kinds are made of a blue clay, found in many parts about London, and mostly deeper seated than brick earth. The best season for digging it is in September and October, and it should then lie exposed during the winter. It may, however, be turned up in January, and worked in February; and, as in brick, so in tile-making, the more care bestowed on beating and tempering the clay, the better will be the tiles. Tiles are burnt in a kiln constructed on the same principles as the brick-kiln, but with the addition of a cone, having an opening at top round the chamber of the kiln. They require much care in burning. If the fire be too slack, they will not burn sufficiently hard; and if too violent, they glaze, and suffer in form.

1835. *Plain* or *crown tiles* are such as have a rectangular form and plane surface. They were made $10\frac{1}{2}$ inches long, $6\frac{1}{4}$ inches broad, and $\frac{5}{8}$ of an inch thick, by the statute. They are manufactured with two holes in them, through which, by means of oak pins, they hang upon the laths. In using all coverings of this species, one tile laps over another, or is placed over the upper part of the one immediately below; that part of the tile which then appears uncovered is called the *gauge* of the tiling. *Terro-metallic* tiles for roofs, with two projections at the back to catch on the laths in lieu of pegs, are now in use. *Italian tiles*, which were made about 1840, by Brown of Surbiton, differ somewhat from their first prototype, as instead of being flat, they are slightly curved, fit easily one into the other, with a horizontal indentation across the upper part, to prevent the wind drifting the rain over the tile head; they have either wide or narrow vertical rolls. Such tiles are usefully employed in picturesque buildings in the country. Taylor's *new roofing tiles* have a plane surface and a slight turned up edge at the sides, a lump on the surface near the upper edge prevents the upper tile slipping; a cover tile is of a similar size and form; these tiles have been lately used, as at the new railway station in Liverpool Street. They are recommended as being half the weight of ordinary plain tiling, each tile weighing under 4 lbs.; and as light as slating; they may be laid to as flat a pitch as slates; and that 180 will cover a square of roofing.

1836. *Ridge roof* and *hip tiles* are formed cylindrically, to cover the ridges of houses. They should be 13 inches long, and girt about 16 inches on the outside. Weight about 5 lbs. Ridge tiles, plain, and with cresting, are now introduced in red, blue, black, and green ware. Plain, flanged, rolled top, and ornamental groved ridging tiles, are commonly seen.

1837. *Gutter tiles* are about the same weight and dimensions as ridge tiles, though differing in form, and are for the valleys of a roof. They are now rarely used, their place having been supplied by lead, and lately by zinc in common work.

1838. *Pan* or *Flemish tiles* have a rectangular outline, with a surface both convex and concave, thus 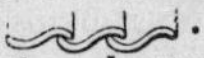. They have no holes for pins, as plain tiles have, but are hung on to the laths by a knot of their own earth on their underside, nearest the ridge, formed when making. They are often glazed, and should be 14½ inches long and 10½ inches broad. The *Bridgewater double roll tiles* are shown in fig. 614*a*. Three stubs are formed on the back to catch the lath. They lap over two inches, and afford good ventilation for farm buildings, with good protection from rain and snow.

Fig. 614a.

1839. The following are the *weights* of the undermentioned sizes of tiles used for various purposes:—

Paving tiles at per 100.

		cwts.	qrs.
9 × 9 × 2¼	=	0	13 2
9 × 9 × 1¾	=	0	9 2
9 × 9 × 1¼	=	0	7 3
9 × 9 × 1½	=	9 lbs. each	
12 × 12 × 1½	=	16 "	
12 × 12 × 2	=	22 "	
14 × 14 × 2⅜	=	35½ "	
16 × 16 × 2⅜	=	44 "	
18 × 18 × 2½	=	64½ "	
20 × 20 × 2⅝	=	84 "	
22 × 22 × 2⅞	=	104 "	
24 × 24 × 3	=	133 "	
Ridge tiles 18 in., about		15 "	

10 to 14 cwts. per 100.
" rolled, 18 to 24 in.
23 to 29 lbs. each.
12 to 18 cwts. per 100.

Malt kiln tiles
12 × 12 × 2 = 16 lbs. each
Hothouse flue tiles
12 × 12 × = 13 "

	lbs. each	cwts. per 1000
Plain tiles		
11¼ × 6½ × ½ =		
10½ × 6½ × ⅝ =	2·51 =	22¼
11 × 7 × ⅝ =	2·90 =	26¼
Pan tiles		
13½ × 9½ × ½ =	5·25 =	47
Bridgewater double roll tiles		
16½ × 14 × ½ to ⅝ =	8·80	
Paving tiles, squares		
6 × 6 × 1 =	2·16 =	19¼
9¾ × 9¾ × 1 =	5·70 =	50
11¾ × 11¾ × 1½ =	12·42 =	111
Ditto, hexagons		
6 × 6 × ⅞ =	1·63 =	14½
6 × 6 × 1 =	1·86 =	16½

1839*a*. The Terro-Metallic manufacture provides red, blue, and buff paving tiles. The *Adamantine clinker* is noticed in the next chapter. *White glazed* tiles of Dutch and English manufacture are used for lining the walls of baths, larders, dairies, butchers' and other shops, kitchen ranges, areas for reflected light, and other such like purposes. *Mathematical* tiles are employed for covering the vertical surfaces on the outside of walls, in imitation of brickwork, and to prevent wet being absorbed.

1839*b*. *Ornamental Pavements*. The use of hardened clay for pavement is of the highest antiquity. Our own country furnishes numerous examples of the varieties employed by the Romans. The tiles are usually made of the clay found in the immediate neighbourhood in which they have been used; and ornamented, sometimes with colour, but more frequently with merely an impressed or raised design. During the Mediæval age, encaustic and other tiles were largely employed. Many varieties of plain and ornamental tiles are now made in the Potteries, as at Broseley; also at Poole in Dorsetshire. The coarser kinds, for streets and doorways, have a red, or a buff, colour, and are prepared from the Staffordshire clay, which is found associated with coal. By mixing metallic oxides with the finer clays, blue and other colours are produced. The manufacture consists in bringing the clay into a state of fine powder, containing a certain amount of moisture; the mass is then placed in a mould of iron which it completely fills, when the ram of an hydraulic press, exactly fitting the mould, gives a pressure of from 150 to 200 tons, compressing the clay into a comparatively very small space; on being removed from the mould it is polished or smoothed off on the surface, and then it is ready for being baked in the kiln. The *encaustic* or variegated tile is composed, in the body, of ordinary red or buff clay; it is pressed in a mould under a common screw press, the mould not only producing the outer form of the tile, but also certain impressions on the face of the clay, about a quarter of an inch in depth. It is then taken out of the mould, and allowed to acquire a certain state of dryness. Devonshire or Cornish clay, coloured, is then poured over the whole surface filling the impressions, in the state of a very thick *slip*; when this has been dried to a certain extent, the slip is scraped until the face of the common clay or body is seen, the impressed spaces only being filled with the coloured matter. A layer of clay is also applied to the back, and is sometimes pierced with holes to prevent the bending of the tiles in the process of baking.

1839*c*. The *Tesseræ* are manufactured by a similar process. In Lambeth, clay being properly prepared and stained of the desired colour, as black, red, blue, &c., is made into long narrow ribbons, by means of a squeezing machine. These ribbons are cut into squares, which are placed one on another, 15 or 20 high, previously oiled to prevent adhesion. These piles are then placed upon a frame sliding in two perpendicular grooves, with fine steel wires stretched tightly across, so that by pressing the frame downwards, the wires

subdivide the slices into the square, oblong, triangular, or other shaped tesseræ required; these are then dried and baked in the ordinary way. Messrs. Minton manufacture their tesseræ by pressure as for making tiles.

1839d. The mode of forming tesseræ into *mosaic paving slabs* is as follows:—The tesseræ are laid face downwards on a perfectly flat slate, in the pattern or design required. The size and shape of the slab is given by strips of wood or slate fastened round the tesseræ. Portland cement is poured on the backs of the tesseræ, and two layers of common red tiles are added in cement; thus forming a flat and strong slab, which is fitted for laying down as pavement. (Hunt, *Handbook*, 1851.) The better tiles, and the larger tesseræ for pavements, are laid separately on a carefully prepared foundation of fine concrete, and then set in fine sand. The durability of a tesselated pavement consists greatly in the solidity of the foundation given to it. With a floor subjected to vibrations such a work will go to pieces. The encaustic tiles with raised patterns should only be used as wall linings, as at Granada, and never for pavements, as is sometimes done.

1839e. TERRA-COTTA. This term has become generic for articles of an artistic character, made of clay and burnt, or of a composition in which clay forms the chief substance. The best materials are akin to those used in porcelain; but the substance burnt is quite unlike it. The clays are generally red, brown, buff, and a dull white, in colour. They may be mixed with manganese, ochres, and cobalt. Old stoneware, ground to powder, and combined with the new clays, tends to prevent large lumps of clay from warping and twisting in the drying and burning, so that, with careful management, blocks with a moulded surface 20 feet cube can be burnt of perfect form. By the mixture of felspar, ground glass, and other bodies with the clay, the fire partially vitrifies the mass, and renders it proof against the weather, and against acids and alkalies. Great care is necessary in baking the terra-cotta; for if the heat be applied too rapidly, the material cracks and the design is spoiled. The fire is, therefore, kept low at first, and gradually increased, not reaching its maximum for eight or ten days. This description of pottery is unglazed. Before the material goes into the ovens, it is in such a hard, close, and compact condition that it can be turned in a lathe, and is thus adapted to the most delicate forms which can be desired. After they are baked, the forms hold as exactly, and nearly as purely, as if they had been worked out of stone by hand. The manufacture of terra-cotta for decoration is brought at the present time to great perfection, and it possesses capabilities for being introduced to an enormous extent, but the dread of the resultant twisting of the material, if it be not properly manufactured, will always cause a preference for carved work.

1839f. STONEWARE is a dense and highly vitrified material, impervious to the action of acids, and of peculiar strength. Until about 1836, when the duty was taken off, this material was chiefly used for common spirit bottles, oil jars, &c. The clay used is found near the coast in Devonshire and Dorsetshire. It is dug in square lumps of about 40 lbs. each, and transported in ships to London. After being perfectly dried it is ground to a powder, mixed with water, and, after being allowed to become of uniform consistency, the mass is passed through pug mills, and taken to the workmen. For making large articles, portions of the burnt material, finely ground, are mixed with the new clay; also some white sand found in the neighbourhood of Woolwich and Reigate.

1839g. Almost all round articles are formed by the potter, on wheels turning with the required rapidity. For articles of other shapes, the composition in a soft and plastic state is laid in plaster of Paris moulds; the porous plaster gradually absorbs the moisture from the clay, and when sufficiently firm it is removed. Some thousand articles are frequently made from one mould before it is destroyed. When thoroughly dry, the ware is placed in ovens or kilns, and exposed to a gradually increasing heat, so intense as to become, before finishing, quite white; salt is then thrown in, and being decomposed, the fumes act chemically on the surface of the ware, and fuse the particles together, giving the glaze so well known. *Stoneware* differs from all other kinds of *glazed earthenware* in this important respect, that the *glazing* is the actual material itself fused together; in other kinds of ware it is a composition in which the article is dipped while in what the potters call the *biscuit*, or half burnt state. Hunt, *Handbook*, 1851.

1839h. BURNT CLAY BALLAST. This is now extensively used for forming the foundations of the new formed roads round the metropolis, and for footpaths in the suburban gardens. The clay obtained in making the excavations for the new houses is run to a convenient locality adjacent; a log of old timber is fixed upright in the ground; a horizontal flue 6 or 8 feet long is formed with bricks on edge, with an opening on the top near the log. Shavings are laid round the post and in the flue, outside of which pieces of timber are piled in a conical form about 8 feet wide and 5 feet high; and then coated with about half a ton of coal, which is covered with the newly excavated clay to a convenient thickness. The shavings are then lighted, if the wind suit; and in a short time the top of the heap falls in, lumps of coal are then thrown in, and on them more lumps of clay. The object to be attained is to have a mass of red hot fire in the middle of the heap. For a heap of about 100 solid yards of clay, about 11 loads of breeze or ashes, and 4 tons of slack or fine coal will be needed. The heap, once fairly alight, is covered with clay. The tendency of

the fire being to burn upwards, the fireman, with a long rake, drags the outer surface downwards every time the burning heap is fed ; this is done by scattering the slack over it with a shovel to quicken the fire, and the breeze is then laid on to retain it; while a fresh layer of clay is subsequently put on all over the heap.   When this clay is nearly burnt through, the operation is repeated.   When there is a gentle smoke all over the heap the fire is going on properly ; if too little, an iron rod is pushed in to stir it up ; if too much, shields must be put up to break the wind.   The general form of the heap, which is cone-shaped at starting, becomes of a flattened circular top in course of being worked.   It should not be made too high, as that increases the labour of wheeling the clay.   When all the clay is used, such portions as are not sufficiently burnt are raked off and thrown up to the top to the greater heat: the heap is then trimmed off and left to cool.

1839*i.* When *well burnt*, the ballast may be worth the trouble ; when badly done, as is usually the case, it is not much better than rubbish, in fact not nearly so good as the usual dry brick rubbish of which roads should be made.   When well burnt, ground fine, and mixed with an equal portion of sand, and a less than the ordinary proportion of good lime, it makes a mortar which will set as hard as cement.   The ballast may also be sifted through a 65 or 70 wire sieve, and the fine stuff, hard and clean, used for mortar or for the plasterer ; the coarse and the rough, for concrete in addition to gravel.   When used as *core* for a road, it should be at once covered with the Cowley or other gravel, or the clay beneath it rises up with traffic, and much rain will soon render the road as bad as though the soil had not been covered ; in fact it turns into mud, and the scamping builder finds it pays to mix his bad lime in the roadway dirt, and to use the mixture for mortar.

Sect. XI.

LIME, SAND, WATER, MORTAR, CONCRETE, AND CEMENT.

1840. Lime has not been found in a native state ; it is always united to an acid, as to the carbonic in chalk. By subjecting chalk or limestone to a red heat it is freed from the acid, and the lime is left in a state of purity, and is then called caustic or quicklime, which dissolves in 680 times its weight of water.   It is not our intention here to enter into any account of either of the theories relative to the formation of lime, facts being of more importance to the architect in its employment than the refined fancies of the scientific chemist.   The calcareous minerals are mostly distinguished by their effervescing with, and dissolving in, an acid, as also by their being easily scratched or cut with a knife.   In respect of the lime obtained from chalk, Dr. Higgins (in his work on *calcareous cements,* Lond. 1780) says, " It should be observed, that the difference between chalk lime and the lime obtained from the various limestones, chiefly consists in the greater retention or expulsion of the carbonic acid gas contained in them."

1841. An account of the stone from which lime may be obtained in the different counties of England would unnecessarily extend this article ; we shall, therefore, after observing that the use of marble for burning to lime would be too expensive, state the varieties of limestone as, 1. the compact; 2. the foliated ; 3. the fibrous ; and, 4. the peastone. The compact limestones are of various colours, in hues inclining to grey, yellow, blue, red, and green, and to a smoky sort of colour besides. It is usually found massive, often compounded with extraneous fossils, particularly shells.   Its internal appearance is dull, the texture is compact, the fracture small, fine, and splintery ; fragments indeterminately angular, more or less sharp-edged ; semi-hard, sometimes soft, brittle, and easily frangible. Specific gravity varies from 2500 to 2700, and it is composed of lime, carbonic acid, and water, mostly with a portion of argyl and oxide of iron, and sometimes of inflammable matter.

1842. The foliated limestones are such as calcareous spar, statuary marble, &c. ; the fibrous limestones, such as satin spar ; and the peastone, another species of spar. It may be remarked, that the various sorts of marble, chalk, and limestone may be divided into those which are nearly pure carbonate of lime, and those containing in addition from one twentieth to one twelfth of clay and oxide of iron.   " Though the best limestones are not such as contain the greatest quantity of clay, yet," observes Mr. Smeaton, " none have proved good for water building, but what, on examination of the stone, contained clay; and though," he continues, " I am very far from laying down this as an absolute criterion, yet I have never found any limestone containing clay in any considerable quantity, but what was good for water works, the proportion of clayey matter, being burnt, acting strongly as a cement; and limes of this kind all agree in one more property, that of being of a dead frosted surface on breaking, without much appearance of shining particles."

1843. Among the strongest limes, such as will set under water, those most in use in the metropolis are called *grey stone limes,* and are procured from Dorking, Merstham, and the vicinity of Guildford in Surrey. The Dorking and other limes of that part are burnt from

a chalk formation so extremely hard that it is quarried even for the purposes of masonry. Those of Merstham particularly are obtained from an indurated chalk marl (clay and chalk) which is so hard that it partakes of the nature of stone.

1843a. The known property of the *blue lias* formation for setting under water renders it an invaluable material in the hands of the architect. In the neighbourhood of Bath it is called Bath brown lime, and when prepared for cementing with metallic cement, is said to be *wind slaked*; that is, after burning, it is placed in roofed sheds open at the sides, and the atmosphere is thus introduced to act upon it. The colour of the *lias*, previous to burning, is blue; after it has passed the kiln, it is of a rich brown colour.

1843b. It is extremely difficult to give any quantitative analysis of the *blue lias*. Every layer in a quarry will be found to differ more or less decidedly from those above or below it. The beds extracted for burning into lime may be said to consist principally of carbonate of lime (perhaps as much as 90 per cent.) in combination with silicate of alumina, some oxide of iron, potash, and a small quantity of sand, in mechanical mixture; but the ingredients insoluble in nitrous acid, such as silicate of alumina and sand, vary in every imaginable proportion between 5 and 18, or at times 20, per cent. The best blue lias lime is obtained from the beds of calcareous marl which contain about 16 per cent. of silicate of alumina; such as is brought from Aberthaw in South Wales, Watchet in Somersetshire, and Barrow, in Leicestershire: the limes from Whitby, in Yorkshire, and from Lyme Regis, in Dorsetshire, are nearly equal to them. The principal objection to this lime as used in London is founded upon the large proportion of underburnt or unburnt stone or *core* left in it. The weight of an imperial bushel of Aberthaw lime of a superior quality is 85 lbs.

1843c. The magnesian limestone of Sunderland lies north-west of the red sandstone. In the vicinity of South Shields, in the county of Durham, the formation becomes extensive, and is to be traced to the Tees below Winston Bridge. The Whitby quarry near Callercoats has been described in the 4th volume of the *Geological Transactions*. The Sunderland limestone is of a bronze colour, and from containing inflammable matter, does not require so much fuel to convert it into lime. The naturally hydraulic limestone of Arden, found near Glasgow, in Scotland, has been largely used in the local dock works, in the proportion, for concrete, of one part of ground lime, one part of iron mine dust, one part of sand, and four and a half parts of gravel and quarry chips. Pure hydraulic lime, as it is called, manufactured (in Flintshire) from the best Halkin Mountain limestone, is much used in the dock works at Liverpool and Birkenhead.

1843d. *Hydraulic limes* have been thus classed:—If they harden under water in periods varying from fifteen to twenty days after immersion, they are slightly hydraulic; if from six to eight days, simply hydraulic; if from one to four days, eminently hydraulic. Hydraulic works frequently burst from the *slaking* of the lime which has not been properly prepared for its office. It should be all hydrated before placing, and this requires more time than the slaking of ordinary lime; the heat developed is much less than in any other lime.

1844. Before limestone is burnt it seems to possess no external character by which a distinction can be made between the simple and the argillo-ferruginous limestones; whatever the colour of the former, they become white when burnt, whilst the latter partake more or less of a slight ochrey tint. Brown lime is the most esteemed for all sorts of cements, whilst for common purposes the white sorts, which are more abundant, are sufficiently useful. In England, the limestones in colour generally incline to a red or blue, and those which are found firm, weighty, and uniform in texture are to be preferred. Masses broken from large rocks and beds on the sides of hills, and those when newest taken and deepest dug, are most to be valued.

1845. The process of analysing limestones is so eminently useful to all concerned in building, that we cannot refrain from transcribing the method used by Smeaton in his own words. " I took about the quantity of five pennyweights (or a guinea's weight) of the limestone to be tried, bruised to a coarse powder, upon which I poured common aquafortis, but not so much at a time as to occasion the effervescence to overtop the glass vessel in which the limestone was put, and added fresh aquafortis after the effervescence of the former quantity had ceased, till no further ebullition appeared by any addition of the acid. This done, and the whole being left to settle, the liquor will generally acquire a tinge of some transparent colour; and if from the solution little or no sediment drops, it may be accounted a pure limestone (which is generally the case with white chalk and several others), as containing no uncalcareous matter in its composition. When this is well settled, pour off the water, and repeatedly add water in the same way, stirring it, and letting it settle till it becomes tasteless. After this, let the mud be well stirred into the water, and without giving it time to settle, pour off the muddy water into another vessel, and if there be any sand or gritty matter left behind (as will frequently be the case), this collected by itself will ascertain the quantity and species of sabulous matter that entered into the texture of the limestone. Letting, now, the muddy liquor settle, and pouring off the water till no more can be got without an admixture of mud, leave the rest to dry, which,

when of the consistence of clay, or paste, is to be made into a ball, and dried for further examination."

1846. There are many sorts of kilns for burning limestone, varying in form with the fuel employed, and the combination of the process itself with some other, such, for instance, as making coke, and sometimes bricks. The limestone, however, is generally burnt in kilns whose plans are circular and section resembling an inverted truncated cone; of late more frequently made spheroidal. The heat is in either case obtained from a fireplace under the limestone, which rests on bars, that can, when the kiln is a perpetual one, egg-formed, or a draw kiln, be removed to let out the lime as it is burnt, whose deficiency, on extraction, is supplied by fresh stone at the top of the kiln. *Sod kilns* are sometimes used for lime burning. These are formed by excavating the earth in a conical form, and then building up the sides as the earth may require. In using these the limestone is laid in with alternate layers of fuel to the top of the kiln, and the top being covered with sods, so as to prevent the heat from escaping, the fire is lighted and the process effected. The lime is not removed till it is thoroughly cool. This mode is a tedious operation, and, because of the quantity of fuel consumed, far from economical. In the common lime-kiln, the fire is never suffered to go down, but as the well-burnt lime is removed, fresh lime is supplied. There is a species of kiln called a flame-kiln, in which the calcination is effected with peat. In this kiln the process of burning bricks is carried on at the same time. The loss of limestone by burning is about four-ninths of its weight, shrinking, however, but little. When completely burnt, it falls freely, in slaking, into powder, and then occupies about double its previous bulk.

1847. Lime burners have made the important observation, that the quantity of stone calcined and the quantity of fuel expended depend on the quality of the fuel. Hence the kiln is constructed with reference to the fuel, rather than to the nature of the stone to be calcined. Limestone, taking an average time, requires burning about sixty hours to reduce it to lime, when the heat is strong and well regulated: but of course no general rule can be laid down, as different species will require different periods of time. The principal object to be accomplished is the expulsion of the carbonic acid gas which enters into its composition.

1848. The lime generally most esteemed is that which heats most in slaking, and slakes the quickest, falling into a fine powder. If there be among it coarse unslakable lumps called *core*, that will not pass through the screen, either the stone has not been sufficiently burnt, or it originally contained extraneous matter; this not only indicates defect in quality, but that it will be, as they more or less abound, more costly in use. Lime in slaking absorbs a mean of 2·5 times its volume; and 2·25 its weight of water. The hydraulic limes absorb less water than the pure limes, and only increase in bulk from 1·75 to 2·5 times their original volume. Slaked lime is a hydrate of lime.

1849. From the experiments of Mr. Smeaton and of Dr. Higgins, it is sufficiently proved that, when chalk or stone lime is equally fresh when used, the cementitious properties of both are nearly, if not quite, equal; but from the circumstance of quicklime absorbing carbonic acid more or less in proportion as its texture is solid or spongy, so it gradually parts with its cementing nature, becoming at length altogether unfit for the purposes of mortar. Thus, though each of the sorts may be equally good, if properly burnt and quite fresh from the kiln, yet from the chalk lime so much more easily and rapidly taking in the carbonic acid than stone lime does, it is not so fit for general use; and, indeed, now the metropolis is so well supplied with the harder chalk and stone limes, there is no excuse for its use, and it should in sound building be altogether banished.

1850. The following table, from Smeaton, contains a list of the limestones he examined on the occasion of building the Eddystone Lighthouse:—

Species of Stone.	Proportion of Clay.	Colour of the Clay.	Reduction of Weight by burning.	Colour of Brick made of such Clay.
Aberthaw, on the coast of Glamorganshire	$\frac{3}{23}$	Lead colour	4 to 3	Grey stock brick.
Watchet, small sea-port in Somersetshire	$\frac{3}{23}$	Do.	4 to 3	{ Light colour, reddish hue.
Barrow, Leicestershire	$\frac{3}{11}$	Do.	3 to 2	Grey stock brick.
Long Bennington, a village in Lincolnshire	$\frac{3}{22}$	Do.	- -	Dirty blue.
Sussex Church, near Lewes in Sussex	$\frac{3}{16}$	Ash colour	3 to 2	Ash colour.
Dorking, Surrey	$\frac{1}{17}$	Do.		
Berryton grey lime, near Petersfield, Hants	$\frac{1}{12}$	Do.		
Guilford, Surrey	$\frac{2}{19}$	Do.		
Sutton, Lancashire	$\frac{3}{16}$	Brown		

1851. SAND should by all means, if possible, be procured from a running clear stream, in preference to that obtained from pits. It is cleaner and not so connected with clayey or muddy particles. About the metropolis it is the practice to use (and an admirable material it is) the sand of the Thames procured from above London Bridge. This sand has acquired a deserved reputation among the architects and builders of the capital. It contains, however, a vast portion of heterogeneous matter, such as calcareous fossil, quartzose, and flint sands, particles of coal alluvium, and much iron. The sharp drift sand of the Thames, therefore, before mixing with the lime, should be well screened and washed.

1852. If *pit sand* only can be procured, it should be repeatedly *washed*, to free it from the earthy and clayey particles it contains, until it becomes bright in colour, and feels gritty under the fingers. Smeaton has stated that clay, even in very small quantities, materially interferes with the hardening of mortar, and disposes it to perish in a few years. When the architect is obliged to use *sea sand*, it must be well washed in fresh water until the salt is entirely removed ; otherwise the cement for which it is used will never dry. So small a quantity as 3 per cent. of salt causes great inconveniences. Whenever the weather is dry, the walls will show an efflorescence on the inside or outside. This, when there is damp in the atmosphere, will collect moisture, causing the wall to look wet, and will throw off any paper placed on it. In one case where a builder, being in close proximity to the seaside, indiscriminately employed sea sand for outside and inside purposes, the saline property soon told its own tale by introducing the rot to all adjoining timber.

1852a. It will be well to notice here that Professor Wilson, of the Edinburgh Laboratory, made in 1848 a report on the use of *sea sand* in mortar in a house, No. 10 Randolph Crescent, which was said to be damp from the use of it. On analysis he found that the mortar contained only 1-10,000th part of its weight of the chloride of magnesium, a highly deliquescent attracting substance. But he considered that the setting of the mortar mechanically enveloped and locked up within its mass the substance in question ; and further, that it might chemically combine with the lime of the mortar to form a compound not readily to be dissolved in water. It was also thought that in consequence of a chemical action taking place between the lime in the mortar and the chlorine derived from the sea water contained in the sand, chloride of calcium (muriate of lime) would be produced, and this being a deliquescent substance, would attract moisture and render the walls damp. The amount, however, of chlorine in specimens of sea sands, was found to vary from a 2,174th to a 549th part of their weights ; the mean amount was a 1,204th part. The quantity in the mortar was so minute that it could not sensibly produce the effects of damp. The mechanical envelopment of the chloride of calcium in the mortar would also shut up this deliquescent substance from moisture, and conduce to dryness. A further substance in sea sand, is chloride of sodium (common salt), and if the chlorine of this be transferred to the lime to form chloride of calcium, the sodium will become converted into carbonate of soda. These substances may co-exist in the mortar, but as soon as they are separated from it, and diffused through the stone, or brought to its surface, the carbonate of soda will convert the chloride of calcium into carbonate of lime (chalk) and become itself chloride of sodium (common salt). A consideration of these facts led the analyst to affirm that the apprehension that chloride of calcium, as derived from sea sand, would render the house damp, was altogether chimerical. On an analysis of some of the pit sands in the neighbourhood, he found that one of them contained almost the same quantity of chlorine as in the sea sand, although no charge was made against it. It does not admit of doubt, he reported, that, other things being equal, sea-sand mortar will dry more quickly and keep more thoroughly dry than will pit-sand mortar ; this sand, it must be noticed, contained about 13 per cent. of earthy matter, and was therefore not so *pure* as the sea sand.

1852b. Although all the professional publications of late years have described the bad effects likely to result from the use of unwashed *pit sand*, builders in the outskirts of the metropolis have taken to use road sweepings in lieu of sand, and this even without having washed it to free it from those impurities not only detrimental to its making good mortar, but also to the building itself, as it may be the cause of introducing the dry rot. Lately we have noticed a case in the professional journals where the lime, such as it was, was "mixed with a large proportion of garden mould and mud, the bricks being of an inferior quality and insufficient strength." We have already noticed the use of road dirt (*par.* 1839i.) In another case "the composition with which the portions of bricks were held together consisted of soap lees with a few small limestones and dirt." The interests of the poorer classes should be better protected.

1852c. *Metallic sand* for cement was introduced about 1843. It was sold in coarse or fine powder as required, to be mixed up with blue lias lime for joining bricks and stone, for concretes, for face work, or for moulded work. 1 measure of the sand, 1 of lime, and 6 of gravel were the proportions used in the foundations of the new Houses of Parliament, and at the great tunnels of the Birmingham railway. It has also been used for malt-house

steeping troughs, and floors; for the latter purpose it can be polished. For exterior facings, as stucco, it was used at 57 Coleman Street; and at the Alfred Insurance Office, Lothbury: the latter building has lately (1866) been pulled down. The marine turret at Herne Bay was also coated with it.

1853. Water. Dr. Higgins recommends the use of lime-water for the composition of mortar. This, in practice, would be impossible. The water used, however, for the incorporation of the lime with the sand should be soft and pure. Mortar and concrete have both been recommended to be made up with *hot* water; with the latter especially, when it is desirable that it should set immediately: concrete thus made has been found exceedingly hard. Its employment with mortar dates from before 1520. It is probable that water charged with iron, as at Tunbridge Wells; a solution of chalk, as in Hertfordshire; sulphuretted hydrogen, as at Harrowgate; and salts, as at Epsom and elsewhere; may all affect lime when combined with it. Smeaton stated that he could not discover any difference in the strength of mortar, whether it were made with sea, or with fresh, water.

1854. In forming mortar from lime, it must, when slaked, be passed through a sieve leaving only a fine powder, an operation usually performed with a quarter inch wire screen set at a considerable inclination to the horizon, against which the lime is thrown with a shovel after slaking. That which passes through is fit for use; the core falling on that side of the screen against which the lime is thrown, being entirely rejected for the purpose in question, though it is an excellent material for filling in the sides of foundations under wood floors where they would otherwise be next the earth, and the like. The sifted or screened lime is next to be added to the sand, whose quantity will vary as the quality of the lime, of which we shall presently speak. In making mortar, there is no point so important, as respects the manufacture itself, as the well tempering and beating up the lime with the sand after the water is added to them. In proportion, too, as this is effectually done, will a small proportion of lime suffice to make a good mortar. The best mode of tempering mortar is by means of a pug-mill with a horse-track similar to the clay-mills used for making bricks. But if such cannot be had, the mortar should be turned over repeatedly, and beaten with wooden beaters, until it be thoroughly mixed. That this process should be carefully performed, will appear of the more importance when it is considered that it thereby admits a greater proportion of sand, which is not only a cheaper material, but the presence of it renders a less quantity of water necessary, and the mortar will consequently set sooner: the work, too, will settle less; for as lime will shrink in drying, while the sand mixed with it continues to occupy the same bulk, it follows that the thickness of the mortar beds will be less variable.

1855. Vitruvius recommends that mortar should be beaten with wooden staves by a number of men before being used. Smeaton reckoned it a fair day's work for a labourer to mix and beat up two or three hods of mortar for use. The pug-mill does this now in two or three minutes. Pliny expressly states that " in ancient specifications for buildings it was provided that no slaked lime less than three years old should be used by the contractor." Covent Garden Theatre was built in 1808–9 with lime while still hot from the kiln: when the walls were demolished a few years since, the mortar was found to be hard and solid. It was so used at Tothill Fields prison. At the new Royal Exchange, the lime was to be thoroughly and freshly burnt, to be kept in an enclosed shed, and no more mortar to be made than was sufficient for each day's consumption.

1856. In most of the public works executed in Great Britain of late years, the proportion of lime to sand is as 1 to 3; and when the former is made from good limestone, the sand is by no means too much in proportion. Dr. Higgins, in his experiments, has gone so far as to recommend 7 parts of sand to 1 of lime, which, for mortar, is perhaps carrying the point to the extreme. It may be taken as an axiom, that no more lime is necessary than will surround the particles of sand. C. H. Smith has stated, (*Builder*, 1865, p. 41), that if each particle of sand be covered with lime about the thickness of an ordinary coat of paint, he should be disposed to consider such an amount as very near the perfection of quantity. A superabundance of lime or sand, no matter how good it may be, is, under any circumstances, objectionable.

1857. Various opinions have long been entertained by chemists and others respecting the effect of sand and lime upon each other in the formation of mortar. The general impression is, that the slaked lime and sand in contact have a chemical affinity for each other; that the lime decomposes the surface of the sand, and the atoms or molecules interpenetrate each other, forming a sort of silicate of lime. This is an extremely ingenious theory, says C. H. Smith, but it has never been proved. It has been stated, he also adds, that the hardening of mortar arises from the presence of carbon and oxygen formed into carbonic acid, which is absorbed by the lime; but the source from whence the carbon is obtained is at present a mystery. Oxygen is abundant in the composition of water and atmosphere, and that quicklime has an astonishing affinity for it, is evinced by the practice of dusting steel goods with it when not in use, to prevent their rusting; or that of placing a small lump of it in any box or case containing such goods. Bricklayers

smear their trowels with the mortar before leaving off work ; and in the *Parentalia*, it is noticed that "in taking out cramps from stonework at least 400 years old, which were so bedded in mortar that all air was perfectly excluded, the iron appeared as fresh as from the forge."

1858. Various additions are made to mortar, in order to increase its hardness and tenacity ; such as coal and wood ashes, forge scales, roasted iron ore, puzzuolana, and the like. The property of hardening under water or when excluded from the air, conferred upon a paste of lime, is effected by the presence of certain foreign substances, as silicon, alumina, iron, &c., when their aggregate presence amounts to one tenth of the whole. Artificial hydraulic limes do not attain, even under favourable circumstances, the same degree of hardness and power of resistance to compression as the natural limes of the same class.

1858a. As Burnell, in *Limes, Cements, &c.*, 1857, p. 71, says—"It is often a matter of importance to know the power of resistance of mortars; but as they differ within a very large range, it is not easy to state it very precisely. The best experiments, however, show that we may safely calculate upon a resistance of 14 lbs. per inch superficial for its cohesive force; of 42 lbs. to a crushing force; and of 5¼ lbs. to a force tending to make the particles slide upon one another. It would not be safe to expose new works to greater efforts than those which could be included within the above limits." In the construction of a wall, whether of brick or rough stone, it should be clearly understood that there is an important distinction between mere drying and the ultimate process of induration. The mortar may become sufficiently set, dry, and solid, in a few days or weeks, to enable the wall to bear a very considerable weight and pressure ; but it does not acquire the maximum degree of hardness till after the lapse of many years and even of centuries. All cements and limes tend to reassume a state of carbonization similar to that in which they existed in the stones from whence they were extracted ; they only do so to a very imperfect degree. The saying that lime at a hundred years is but a child, is perfectly true. Cements on the contrary harden very rapidly, but we have no instances of their acquiring the strength of the original stone.

1859. The *cendre de Tournay* is used in the Low Countries. This is an article procured from the lime-kilns bordering the Scheldt. The lime of this district contains a considerable portion of clay mixed with iron ; and the pit-coal with which it is burnt contains a large quantity of an argillaceous schist, impregnated with iron. After the lime is taken out of the kilns, there remains the *cendre*, about one fourth of which consists of burnt lime-dust, and three fourths of coal-ashes. This material is sprinkled with water to slake the lime, and well mixed together, and put into a proper vessel and covered over with wet earth. In this state it is kept for a considerable time ; and when taken out, and strongly beaten up for half an hour with an iron pestle in a wooden mortar or trough, it is reduced to a soft pasty consistence ; it is then spread out for several days in a shady place, and the operation of beating repeated : the oftener this is done the better, except it should become unmanageable from being too much dried. In a few minutes, this cement, when applied to brick or stone, adheres so firmly that water may be immediately poured over it ; and if kept dry twenty-four hours, it afterwards receives no injury even from the most violent action of a flowing stream.

1859a. In London, a mortar made of lime with sea-coal ashes from a smith's forge mixed with the iron scales, and called *blue* mortar, is used for covering parts of buildings much exposed to the weather ; and if prepared with similar labour and attention, it might, in a great degree, possess the valuable properties of the mortar of the Scheldt, just mentioned.

1859b. Common *ashes* mortar is made by mixing two bushels of newly slaked lime and three bushels of wood ashes, which, when cold, must be well beaten, in which state it is usually kept for a considerable time, and indeed it improves by keeping if beaten two or three times previous to using it. This mixture is superior to terras mortar in resisting the alternate effects of dryness and moisture, but not comparable with it under water.

1859c. *Brick* and *tile* and *burnt clay ballast*, each well burnt and ground to a powder, combined with rich lime, possesses hydraulic energy. *Pulverised silica* burned with rich lime produces hydraulic lime of excellent quality. In some experiments made by MM. Chatonoy and Rivot, this lime hardened under water in from three to four days, and acquired in twenty-two months a hardness superior to Portland cement. The weight of the powdered lime never exceeded four times, and was never less than one half that of the powdered silica. Brick-dust mortar used to be considered in some cases better than mortar made of terras, for unless the terras was always wet it was not thought better than common mortar made of lime and sand ; 2 bushels of hot lime, i.e., fresh slaked lime, added to 1 bushel of brick-dust made from red stock bricks, was to be well beaten and worked up before using, with but little water: the longer it was beaten the better it became. The dry brick rubbish of old walling broken down and *sifted*, was considered better than sand, as less sand is required, and it might be safely used in frosty weather. A tract on Old Charing Cross, mentions that it was "so cemented with mortar made of purest lime,

callis sand, white of eggs, and the strongest wort, that it defied all hammers and hatchets whatsoever." The mortar used in bishop Gundulph's works at Malling and Rochester is described by B. Ferrey as consisting of a sort of tufa found only in the cliffs at Dover, which appears to have been exclusively used in his works.

1859d. *Slag* is applied to the vitrified earths left in furnaces, either for glass or iron. *Scoriæ* are the lighter, more porous, and less vitrified earths arising from the puddling and refining of iron. The *cinders* used are the earthy residues derived from the combustion of coal. When ground into powder, the two former, which contain a large proportion of the mineral oxides, make very good mortars if mixed with middling or perfectly hydraulic limes. Cinders appear to render the rich limes moderately hydraulic when properly mixed. They require a large quantity of water to render perfect the crystallization of the hydrate of lime. All these mortars may be usefully employed for works out of water.

1859e. The stones whereof the *Dutch terras* is made are found in the neighbourhood of Liege, and also, we believe, at Andernach on the Rhine, from the size of a pea to that of a middle-sized turnip. From their being brought down the rivers to Holland the cement has been called Dutch ; the only operation they undergo in that country is the reduction of them to a coarse powder by means of mills. They are beaten by iron-headed stampers on an iron bed till they will pass through a sieve whose wires are about one eighth of an inch apart. This cement is sent from Holland in casks. *Trass, terras*, or *tarras*, is a blue-black trap. It is obtained from pits of extinct volcanoes, and has nearly all the distinguishing elements of puzzuolana, resembling it in composition, and in the requirements of its manipulation, having to be pulverised and added to rich lime to develope its hydraulic properties.

1859f. The *Puzzuolana*, or *terra Puteolana* of the Italians, which, as well as the last-named cement, has been almost if not quite superseded by the introduction of the Roman cement, is brought from Civita Vecchia. Its name is however derived from Puzzuoli, where it is principally found, though produced in other parts of Italy, in the neighbourhood of extinct volcanoes. It suddenly hardens when mixed with one third of its weight of lime and water, forming a cement more durable under water than any other. Bergman found 100 parts of it to contain 55 to 60 parts of siliceous earth, 20 of argillaceous, 5 or 6 of calcareous, and from 15 to 20 of iron; this last constituent is considered to be the cause of its property of hardening under water. The iron decomposes the water of the mortar, and thus in a very short time a new compound is formed. According to Vitruvius, when used for buildings in the water, 2 parts of puzzuolana were mixed with 1 of mortar. Artificial puzzuolana may be made by slightly calcining clay, and driving off the water of combination at a temperature of $1,200°$.

1859g. Subsequently to the use of this material from Puzzuoli, a similar material has been found near Edinburgh ; and in the Vivarais, a site of extinct volcanic action in the centre of France. Its aspect and colour, however, vary very much even in the same locality. Berthier gives the following analysis of two of these materials: —

	Puzzuolana from Civita Vecchia.	Terras from Andernach.
Silica	·445	·570
Alumina	·150	·120
Lime	·088	·026
Magnesia	·047	·010
Oxide of Iron (in a slight state of magnetism)	·120	·050
Potash	·014	·070
Soda	·040	·010
Water	·092	·096
	0·996	0·952

1859h. In the use of *blue lias* lime for mortar, workmen ignorant of its qualities invariably spoil it. In important works the lime should be supplied in an unground state, to prevent the *core* being mingled with the good lime. In slaking, the lumps should be broken into pieces of about the size of a nutmeg; then immersed upon a sieve in water, and kept therein until air bubbles freely rise to the surface : the lime so wetted is to be left in a heap, and covered with damp sand, for twenty-four hours. At the expiration of that time it should be screened and mixed with sand and the least possible quantity of water. When slaked, it does not sensibly increase in bulk, unlike the ordinary chalk or stone lime of the neighbourhood of London. The best descriptions of blue lias lime will not bear more than $1\frac{1}{2}$ parts of sand to 1 of lime. Wood, of Bath, in his work on *Cottages*, 1788, has stated that "blue lias lime mixed with coal ashes in the manner prescribed by M. Loriot, will make the hardest cement I ever saw, as I have found by various experiments; it will hold water, resist frost, harden in a few hours in water, and will bear a very

good polish. Coach or carriage ways are laid, or pitched with blue lias, which wears very well, though it will not bear the frost."

1859*i.* A very useful *hydraulic mortar* for executing sea-walling, consists of 1 part of chalk lime, or of Halkin lime, with one part of puzzuolana from Civita Vecchia, and 1½ parts of sand; but the value of this mixture depends upon the influence exercised by the puzzuolana on the setting of the lime. A mixture of the natural calcareous cements, or of Portland cement with sand, is another good mortar. The presence of sulphate of lime in any composition intended to resist the action of sea water would be fatal, as it crystallises at a different rate of rapidity, and it is more easily soluble than the carbonate of lime. French authorities lay particular stress on the following qualities for the formation of good hydraulic mortar: I. It is essential that the materials should be perfectly pulverised before mixing, so that the combination may be as perfect as possible. II. Sufficient free lime must be present to allow the carbonic acid in the water to combine with it, and form a protective coating of carbonate. III. Long soaking of the materials is advisable, in order that the chemical combinations necessary for the ultimate stability of the mortar may take place before it is actually used.

1859*k.* Mr. Smeaton discovered, by a course of experiments, that the scales (grey oxide of iron) that fly off under the forge hammer from red hot iron, pulverised, sifted, and mixed with lime, form an admirable cement, equal to puzzuolana. He found, in pursuing his experiments, that roasted iron ore produced an effective water cement, by using a greater proportion of it than either terras or puzzuolana. Equal quantities of iron scales and argillaceous lime, with half the quantity of each of these of sand, produced a cement in every respect equal to terras mortar. If pure carbonate of lime be used, equal parts of each of the ingredients ought to be incorporated. We do not think it necessary here to give any account either of Loriot's cement, or that proposed by Semple: neither are to be depended on: indeed the first, as a water cement, is of inferior utility, and very little better than common mortar dried before the admission of water upon it.

1860. *Grout,* or *liquid mortar,* is nothing more than common mortar mixed with a sufficient quantity of water to make it fluid enough to penetrate the interstices and irregularities of the interior of brick walls, which common mortar will not reach. The mortar whereof it is made will bear 4 of sand to 1 of lime, but it should be thoroughly beaten. It may be kept a little longer, whereby its quick setting will be facilitated.

1861. CONCRETE is a compound of ballast, or stone chippings, and lime mixed together. It is so called from the speedy concretion that takes place between these particles. If, however, *gallots* or small stone chippings are used, sand in a large proportion to the lime must be used. The use of concrete was well known at an early period; it is mentioned by De Lorme in his work published in 1568; and it is by no means, therefore, a discovery of modern days. Wherever the soil is soft, and unequal for the reception of the foundations of a building, the introduction of concrete under them is an almost infallible remedy against settlement. The Thames ballast, commonly used for concrete, is a mixture of sand and small stones. With this, and lime in the proportion of never less than 4 to 1, and never properly exceeding 9 to 1, of stone lime, or such as is known to set hard in water, a mixture is made. The lime is generally used in powder, and the whole being shovelled together, it is wheeled in barrows to a stage over the spot where it is to be used, and let fall into the trench dug out for the reception of the foundation. The greater the height the concrete is made to fall, the sounder and stronger it becomes. It must always be recollected that no more lime is necessary than with the thinnest coat to surround the particles of the ballast, and that therefore the size of the pebbles or stones should influence the quantity of the lime. As the ground is more or less to be trusted, the thickness of the concrete must be regulated; when used on the best ground, a foot in thickness will be sufficient; while on the worst, as many as four feet or more may be required. The upper surface being levelled, it is usual to lay on it a tier of Yorkshire stone landings, for the reception of the brick-work or mason's work: in some cases, after carrying the wall a certain height, a second tier of landings has been introduced. When the soil is watery, no water should be put to the concrete, but the ballast and lime merely mixed and tumbled in. The usual practice of making concrete as above stated, is objected to by many practitioners, who recommend that the French method of making *béton* should be followed in lieu of it.

1862. In forming concrete, the stones or pebbles used should never exceed the size of a hen's egg, of which 2 parts may be combined with 1 part of the smaller substances used; this makes it about equal to Thames ballast. It has been calculated, that as the lime absorbs the water, and with the sand fills up the interstices of the larger material, if the proportion of the lime be about one eighth of the ballast, then $3\frac{3}{4}$ cubic feet of ground lime, and 30 cubic feet of ballast, with a sufficient quantity of water to effect the admixture (and this is generally rather less than a gallon to a cubic foot of ballast, or than equal measures of water and lime), will be required to make 27 cubic feet of concrete; that is, there is a loss of bulk equal to all the lime, and of about 10 per cent. of the ballast. But some experiments made in 1857–8, in which the present editor assisted, showed that the same measure

which gave a cubic yard of ballast, held precisely the same ballast *with the addition* of one sixth in bulk of ground stone lime made with it into concrete, besides about fourteen pails of water ; and likewise tended to disprove the assertion that concrete swells in setting. This cubic yard of concrete weighed 27 cwt. In estimating, allowance must be made for the loss of material.

1862a. Expansion taking place in concrete made of *unground* lime, during its slaking, has been taken advantage of by G. L. Taylor in the underpinning of some walls at Chatham, as detailed in the *Transactions* of the Institute of British Architects, 1835. This expansion has been found to average about ⅜ of an inch for each foot in height, and the size thus gained the concrete never loses. Care must be taken when using it for floors and for the spandril of arches, to allow sufficient space, and to lay it in such a way that this increase may take place without thrusting out the walls, as has occasionally happened. In old malt houses in the West of England, with concrete floors 5 to 6 inches thick, stone walls 2 feet 6 inches to 3 feet thick have bulged out 3 or 4 inches on each side by the expansion of the concrete, as also noticed in the *Transactions* of the above named society, 1854, p. 74. When *ground* lime is used the assertion that concrete swells is very questionable, as stated in the previous paragraph.

1862b. For water works required to set rapidly, an excellent concrete may be made by a mixture, the proportions of which were found by Treussart as follows :—30 parts of hydraulic lime, very energetic, measured in bulk, and before being slaked ; 30 parts of terras of Andernach ; 30 parts of sand ; 20 parts of gravel ; and 40 parts of broken stone, a hard limestone. These proportions diminish one fifth in volume after manipulation ; the mortar is made first. When the Italian puzzuolana is used, the proportions should be 33 parts of lime, as before ; 45 parts of puzzuolana ; 22 parts of sand ; and 60 parts of broken stone and gravel. The first of these concretes should be employed immediately it is made ; the second requires to be exposed about twelve hours before it is put in place. When burnt clay or pounded bricks are used, 30 parts will suffice, but this mortar must not be used in sea water. If only rich, instead of hydraulic, limes be used, the quantity of the natural or artificial puzzuolanas must be increased, and that of the stones and gravel be decreased. (Burnell, *Limes, &c.*)

1862c. After many experiments M. Kuhlmann recommends a cement composed of 30 parts of rich lime, 50 of sand, 15 of uncalcined clay, and 5 of powdered silicate of potash, as having all the requisite hydraulic properties, especially for cisterns intended for spring water. In marine constructions care should be taken to add an excess of silicate to those portions of cement which are exposed to the immediate contact of the sea.

1862d. The object to be aimed at in making *hydraulic concrete*, is to give such a sufficiency of mortar as will produce the aggregation of the whole mass of rough rubble materials. In Portland cement concrete for instance, the proportions for the mortar may be 1 of cement to 3 of sand, and this mortar may then be mixed with 6 parts of ballast or shingle. In blue lias lime concrete, the proportions may be 1 of unground lime to 2 or 2½ of sand, and this mortar may be mixed with 3 or 4 parts of ballast ; and it must be understood in all cases that the mortar must be made first, and that it then should be thoroughly incorporated with the ballast or shingle. This concrete as used at the recent extension of the London Docks by Mr. Rendel, consisted of 1 part of blue lias lime with 6 parts of gravel and sand. The proportions for the blocks of the mole at Marseilles, were 3 parts of Theil lime to 5 parts of sand mixed up into mortar, and then added to 2 parts of broken stone.

1862e. *Béton*, or concrete, as made in France, is invariably composed as follows:— I. The mixture of lime and sand, either by hand or by a pug-mill, as for ordinary mortar. Great importance is attached to the choice of the lime and to the mode of slaking it ; and if a sufficiently good one cannot be obtained, artificial puzzuolanas are introduced. The *mode of slaking* is prescribed in the specification according to the nature of the lime, instead of being left to the choice of the workmen. II. The *mortar* so prepared is then well mixed by rakes with broken stones or ballast in such proportions as shall ensure its filling up the intervals between them ; the volume having been ascertained by immersing the stones in a known quantity of water. These spaces are equal to about 0·38 to 0·46 of the cubical contents of the vessel ; but in practice, about one fourth more mortar is added than necessary to ensure solidification of the mass, especially when the *béton* is intended to resist water pressure. III. The material is then wheeled to its situation and rammed down carefully until the mortar begins to work up to the surface.

1862f. In an English patent, 1859, No. 2757, M. Coignet, of Paris, argues that the tenacity of mortar is not produced as hitherto supposed by the formation of silicate of lime and alumina, but by the crystallisation of lime. His concrete, called *Béton Aggloméré*, consists of about 180 parts of sand, 44 of lime produced by slaking, 33 of Portland cement, and 20 of water, combined by a process of two main operations : I. A complete consolidation of the materials with little water ; and II., the steady but not violent compression of the consolidation in moulds. The cement is mixed with the sand and lime, and sprinkled whilst mixing with a *little* water. This mixture is thrown into a machine,

formed like an endless screw enclosed in a cylinder, at the rate of two shovelfuls followed by about a quart of water, until the cylinder is full.   The screw, turned by two men, delivers the mixture through a series of holes in the bottom of the cylinder; but on a large scale, a machine is used of 10 to 15 horse power.   This mixture, after its delivery from the machine, is put by degrees into moulds, and each layer is rammed in by workmen.   In reply to questions put to the inventor by the Committee of the Institute already mentioned, he stated that chalk lime was not sufficiently hydraulic for the purpose : that ground lime as delivered had always *core* in it, and therefore had to be slaked with one fifth of its bulk of water for forty-eight hours before employment ; such mixture was equal in effect to two of common ground lime : that when very hard mortar was required it was necessary to use less water and more sand than usually adopted : that water evaporated from mortar as usually made, leaves it full of minute holes, and that the more water, the less is the crystallisation : that in the proportions above given, if cement be used as a twentieth part, it requires to be twice passed through the large machine, but if used as a thirtieth part, only once : that he found by experience that the purer the lime the quicker was the crystallisation; and that, although pure hydrate of lime will take carbonic acid, silicate of lime and alumina will not take it, because silicic acid took the place which carbonic acid did with the pure lime ; and frankly admitted that his first experiments in 1855, in marine works, had not entirely succeeded, but claimed perfect success for those at Marseilles since 1859, and for those now (1864) executing in Paris and elsewhere.

1862*g*. The resistance of *béton* and *concrete* should never be regarded as being superior to those given for limes, if the superstructure be commenced upon them immediately.   In both cases the resistances are found to increase with comparative rapidity during the first six or seven months.

1863. Among the CEMENTS used in England, *Parker's*, also called *Roman* cement (1796), is manufactured principally from stone found in the Isle of Sheppey, and at Harwich, being *septaria* from the London clay, and properly classed among the limestones indigenous to this country.   It consists of ovate or flattish masses of argillaceous limestone arranged in nearly horizontal layers, chiefly found imbedded in the clay.   The substance being coated with a calcareous spar or sulphate of barytes, forms the basis of the cement.   That now in use we do not think at all equal to the material originally employed. About 1810–15 it was possible to use it in the depth of winter ; which, we apprehend, would be a hazardous thing to do with the cement at present made.   Whether the inferiority arises from adulteration, bad manufacture, or the material being worse, we cannot pretend to say ; we, however, do not believe that it arises from the badness of the raw material.   If this cement be of extremely good quality, 2 parts of sand to 1 of the cement may be used.   The cement itself is a fine impalpable powder ; yet when wetted it becomes coarse, and, unless mixed with great care, it will not take a good surface. When mixed with the sand and water, it sets very rapidly ; it is necessary, therefore, to avoid mixing much at a time, or a portion will be lost.   The colour of this cement, when finished, is an unpleasant dark brown, and the surface requires frequent colouring.   The great value of Parker's cement is its being impervious to water almost the moment it is used ; hence it becomes highly serviceable on the backs of arches under streets, for the lining of cisterns, and for carrying up in it, or coating with it, damp walls on basement stories.   It will not resist fire so well ; and it should therefore never be employed for setting grates, ovens, coppers, or furnaces.

1864. *Atkinson's* cement is a good material, preferable in colour to the last named, but, as we think, inferior in quality.   It takes a much longer time to set than Parker's cement, than which it absorbs more moisture.   It answers well enough in dry situations.   Vicat formed a factitious Roman cement ; but its efficacy was doubtful, though it had, for want of a better substitute, been much employed at Paris.

1864*a*. *Portland cement*, the latest (about 1843) of all these cements, is made from limestone and clay.   The mud of the river Medway, corresponding to the argillo-calcareous stone of Roman cement, is mixed with chalk and ashes from former makings, and calcined at a heat amounting almost to that of vitrification.   A larger quantity of sand may be mixed with it than with Roman cement, to which it is superior in colour and hardness of setting. The heaviest, considered the best in quality, weighs 110 lbs. per striked bushel.

1864*b*. The distinguishing peculiarities which should render *Portland* cement a permanent substitute for *Roman* cement, have been explained by a London manufacturer of both materials (*Builder*, 1863, p. 761). It may be condensed into the statement:—That the stone from which Roman cement is made, though composed of lime and the silicate of alumina, yet the proportion of the latter preponderates to such an extent as to prevent a perfect amalgamation of the ingredients in burning.   The result is a cement loose in its texture, because containing inert foreign matter, which is retentive of moisture, and consequently attackable by frost and vegetable growth.   In Portland cement the case is otherwise. The dose of lime to clay is in the ascertained correct proportion of two to one, and with this condition there is the power thoroughly to combine the ingredients by burning, and thus to give a density and compactness to the product, which in enabling it to resist water, frost,

and other decomposing agencies, are the elements of its durability and of its superiority to the natural cements.   Carelessness, or want of proper knowledge in its manufacture; an improper mixture of the ingredients; an imperfect calcination; its bad manipulation; and unfair handling when used as a cement, are all likely to result in disastrous effects on being used.   When employed as a mortar or as a concrete, it has seldom been known to fail.

1864c. It is usual for the manufacturer to grind the cement after burning it.   It is then placed in well-closed casks which should not exceed 6 cwt. each, when the cement may be preserved for some time; but contact with the atmosphere rapidly deteriorates its quality, as it absorbs humidity and carbonic acid from it, and thus becomes useless.   It should be ground very fine.   For the sieve in sifting it, the French engineers require 185 meshes to the square of 4 inches on a side.   One-third of the volume of the cement for the quantity of water is the best proportion, and the more that the cement is beaten up, the harder it becomes.   The best cement will harden in about five or six minutes, and under water in about an hour: when mixed with sand it takes a little longer.   When mixed with sea-water, and used in sea-water with a large quantity of sand, it may take even twenty-four hours before setting.

1864d. The resistance to rupture of pure cement after 20 days' exposure to the air, is about 54 lbs. per inch square; if sand be added in the proportion of $\frac{1}{2}$ to 1 of cement, it falls to 37 lbs.; and if it be in equal proportions, it falls to 27 lbs.   The permanent load in any large works should never be more than one-sixth of that required to produce rupture: and if small materials be employed, only one-fifteenth should be calculated upon.   The strength of Portland cement has been tested for drainage works by John Grant, as described at the Institution of Civil Engineers, December 1863, giving it as 500 lbs. upon an area of $1\frac{1}{2}$ inches square, equal to $2\frac{1}{4}$ square inches.

1865. *Hamelin's mastic* cement, though patented of late years, is an invention of P. Loriot, a century old; the medium for mixing the pounded brick-dust, limestone and sand, is oil instead of water.   It is much more difficult to use than the other cements, and requires great experience and care.   A coat of it should never exceed one quarter of an inch in thickness; hence it is totally unfit for working mouldings in the solid.   In the metropolis it is generally used in a very thin coat over a rough coat of Roman cement, in which case it is rarely more than an eighth of an inch thick.   Thus used, it not only presents a beautiful surface, but is extremely durable, but it requires to be constantly painted to resupply the oil that has evaporated, or been taken up by the atmosphere.

1866. *Keene's* cement is obtained by soaking plaster in alum water after a first calcination: it is then kiln-burnt a second time and ground.   It is in reality only a plaster, and is capable of being worked to a very hard and beautiful surface.   *Martin's* patent fireproof and ornamental cement is a plaster of somewhat similar make, and equally good-looking.   It is manufactured in three qualities, coarse, fine, and superfine.   It is said to be used with greater facility by workmen than any other cement yet produced, requiring only about an hour to set, which is less by one-half the time of other cements.   It appears to be chiefly prepared at Derby.   *Parian* cement (Keating's patent) is also composed of gypsum, but mixed with borax (borate of soda) in powder, and the mixture calcined and ground.   A fine quality produces a hard scagliola imitation of marble.   When applied to old brick or plastered work, as in repairs, these cements may be papered, or painted upon, in about 18 to 24 hours after execution.   But on new work time must be given for any efflorescence to disengage itself.

1866a. *John's patent permanent stucco wash, stucco cement, and stucco paint,* were introduced about 1843.   As a paint it is cheap, durable, agreeable in colour, and finishes without a gloss.   It gives out no deleterious exhalations or odour in drying, and it is stated that as the oil cannot evaporate (?), but is held in intimate and indissoluble union with the other materials, there can be no decay, an objection to which oil mastic is so liable.   It requires no driers or turpentine, and is applicable both for outside and inside work.   The cement, which is stated not to deteriorate with age, is packed in casks, and requires to be mixed with 3 parts of good, sharp, clean sand to make a stucco, its application for which is the same as for any other stucco.   It adheres well to glass, iron, slate and tiles in roofing, wood, old plaster, or Roman cement.   When set it is hard, and impervious to wet and damp.   One coat of its own paint, which it will take after twenty-four hours, is sufficient.   Mouldings may be run in it, and castings made.

1866b. A cement which will withstand a moist climate, is stated to be composed of one bushel of lime with 15 gallons of water and half a bushel of fine gravel sand, mixed with $3\frac{1}{2}$ lbs. of copperas dissolved in hot water, and kept stirred while being incorporated and in use.   Sufficient should be made for the day during which it is to be used, as the colour is not easily matched.

1866c. GYPSUM, better known as *Plaster of Paris*, is a sulphate of lime.   It is found at Alston, in Cumberland; at Shotover Hill, Oxfordshire; at Orston, near Grantham; in Nottinghamshire, in Derbyshire, and in Cheshire; in France, in the neighbourhood of Paris, chiefly at Montmartre; and in the departments of the Saone, Loire, of the Rhone,

and of many others; and in Tuscany, Savoy, Spain and Switzerland; in some parts of the British Colonies of North America, wherefrom it is exported principally to the United States. The stone is broken into small blocks, and burnt in a walled space with openings in the tiled roof to let out the steam. After its water of crystallization is driven off, it becomes pulverulent and like flour. On fresh water being added, it combines with the normal quantity of water, and reassumes the form of a hydrate, recovering its original density and strength to a very great degree. A heat of about 200° centigrade is sufficient. The London manufacturers adopt a kind of oven for burning the stone, which prevents the smoke from injuring the plaster. In France it has been proposed to throw a jet of steam heated above 400° Fahr. over the stone, which is broken very much smaller than usual: this jet takes up all the water present, and leaves the plaster in the state of a pure anhydrous sulphate of lime. The plaster obtained from Paris is considered the best of all in quality, probably arising from the fact that the stone is the hardest. Gypsum swells in setting in contradistinction to the cements, which generally shrink. The specific gravity of pure gypsum may be taken at 2·322 ; and its constituent parts to be sulphuric acid 46, lime 32, and water 21. (See GLOSSARY, s. v.)

1867. The best *bituminous cements* are obtained from the natural *asphalte*, which is found in large quantities on the shores of the Dead Sea; in Albania; in Trinidad ; at Lobsann, and Bekelbronn, in the department of the Bas Rhin; in the department of the Puy de Dôme ; at Gaugeac in that of the Landes, &c. The asphalte which is found in inexhaustible quantities at Pyrimont Seyssel, in the Jura Mountains, in the department of the Aire in France, was introduced into England about 1838, under Claridge's patent. The principal ingredient in its composition is a bituminous limestone, of a rich brown colour. After it has been reduced to a fine powder, a certain portion of grit is mixed with it; it is then placed in cauldrons heated by strong fires with a sufficient quantity of *mineral tar* to prevent the asphalte from calcining. The whole mass is thoroughly incorporated and reduced to a mastic, in which state it is run into moulds to form blocks, each 1 foot 6 inches square, 6 inches in depth, and weighing 125 lbs.

1867a. The mastic is of three qualities, fine, gritted, and coarse gritted. The first, being without any admixture of grit, is used for magazine floors, and as a cement for making, in special cases, very close joints in brickwork. II. The fine gritted is used for covering terraces, roofs and arches, lining of tanks, and as a cement for brickwork, and for running the joints of stones. III. The coarse gritted is used for paving and flooring, and where great strength of work is desirable, such as gun-shed floors, tun-room floors, and margins of stable floors ; while in gateways for heavy carriage traffic, small pieces of granite chippings are introduced. These mastics, and more particularly the first two, being ductile and readily yielding to any change that may take place on the surfaces upon which they are laid, require a proper foundation to be prepared.

1867b. When required for use, an iron cauldron having been prepared, 2 lbs. of mineral tar are put in, and then 56 lbs. of asphalte broken into pieces of not more than 1 lb. in weight. These are mixed together until the asphalte becomes soft. After a quarter of an hour the stirring is repeated, and another 56 lbs. of asphalte added, and so on until a proportion of 112 lbs. of asphalte to each 1 lb. of tar, under ordinary circumstances, fills the cauldron and the whole is thoroughly melted. When fit for use the asphalte will emit jets of light smoke, and freely drop from the stirrer.

1867c. It will be well to note that it is stated asphalte never flames, but merely passes into a state of fusion. At the fire at Hamburg in 1842, it was remarked that when asphalted roofs fell in, " the asphalte, in which a sort of rubble is mixed up, was found to have resisted the effects of the heat, and, like a mass of dirt, served rather to smother the flames than to give them increased vitality." A like result is recorded of a fire that took place at the Bazaar Bordelais, at Bordeaux, in 1835 ; of another in Stangate, London, in 1855 ; and experiments were made by order of the authorities of the British Museum before this material was allowed to be applied to the snow gutters of the dome of the new Reading Room and other roofs, with a satisfactory result. Notice is not generally taken of the fact that if in works, asphalte or tar be used in places where it may be affected by heat, a smell arises which is very prejudicial to the comfort of the occupiers of the building.

1867d. The term asphalte has also been given to several compositions formed by the admixture of chalk, lime, gas tar, and other substances for cheapness. The *coal tars,* and vegetable pitch, although not so good as the bitumens, are fairly good substitutes in many cases, as in coating vaults, or walls exposed to the dampness of earth. The proportions in which to mix powdered calcareous stone must be regulated by practice, as also the heat, that the stone be not converted into quicklime, perhaps from 6 to 7 of the pitch in volume to 1 of limestone will suffice ; and it is recommended to use these in greater thickness than the asphalte, being about half an inch for the latter material.

Sect. XII.

GLASS.

1868. Glass is a combination of silex with fixed alkali, generally soda. The mixture when calcined receives the name of *frit*, which after the removal of all its impurities, is conveyed to the furnace and melted in large pots or crucibles till the whole mass becomes beautifully clear, and the dross rises to the top. After being formed into the figures required, it is annealed or tempered by being placed in an appropriate furnace. The fineness depends on the purity and proportion of the ingredients. An extremely fine crystal glass is obtained from 16 parts of quartz, 8 of pure potash, 6 of calcined borax, 3 of flake white, and 1 of nitre. The specific gravity of glass is about 2600; of French plates, 2840; of English flint glass, 3320. Glass is extremely elastic, and less dilatable by heat than metallic substances.

1868a. Four pieces of the common sort of glass being cut from one strip, each piece was 5 inches wide, 6 inches long, and 4 inches thick. In the trial of strength they were calculated out at a standard size, and gave 17,208 lbs., 15,435 lbs., 14,931 lbs., and 11,385 lbs.; the mean being 14,931 lbs. This great difference is the more singular from the circumstance of all the pieces being cut from the same plate. The weight of the glass at a size of $9.0 \times 4.5 \times 3$, all in inches, would be 11·12 lbs. *Sheet* glass is stated to be stronger than *plate* or *crown* glass, but less flexible. The compressive strength of glass is about $12\frac{1}{4}$ tons per square inch. The resistance of glass to a crushing force is about 12 times its resistance to extension.

1869. Pliny gives the following account of the discovery of manufacturing glass, which was well known in Aristotle's time, 350 B.C. "A merchant vessel, laden with nitre or fossil alkali, being driven on the coast of Palestine, near the river Belus, the crew accidentally supported the kettles on which they dried their provisions on pieces of the fossil alkali ; the sand about it was vitrified by its union with the alkali, and produced glass." Though, according to Bede, artificers skilled in making glass were brought into England in 674, glass windows were not generally used here till 1180, and were for a considerable time esteemed marks of great magnificence.

1870. The manufacture of window glass during the last thirty years has undergone entire alteration, especially since the abolition of the excise duty in 1845. There are now three special kinds of glass used for glazing purposes, and several varieties of them :

1870a. I. *Crown* glass, which is blown into large globes and opened out into circular flat tables. II. *Sheet* glass, which is blown into long cylinders or *muffs*; then split down and flattened. III. *Plate* glass, which is either cast on iron tables for large purposes, and polished; or for smaller masses, blown into a cylinder and polished.

1871. *Crown* glass, the commonest window glass, differs from flint glass in its containing no lead or any metallic oxide except manganese, and sometimes oxide of cobalt, in minute portions, for correcting the colour, and not as a flux. It is compounded of sand, alkali, either potash or soda, the vegetable ashes that contain the alkali, and generally a small portion of lime. To facilitate fusion, a small dose of arsenic is frequently added. Zaffre or oxide of cobalt, in the proportion of 1 ounce for 1000 pounds, is added to correct the colour; but when the sand, alkali, and lime are very fine, and no other ingredients are used, zaffre is not required. Its manufacture is conducted differently from that of flint-glass articles, the object being to produce a large flat thin plate, which is afterwards by the glazier's diamond cut into the requisite shape. It is blown in circular plates, varying from 3 feet 6 inches to 4 and 5 feet diameter: the process is as follows:—The workman, having a sufficient mass of melted metal on his blowpipe, rolls it on an iron plate, and then, swinging it backwards and forwards, causes it by its own gravity to form into a globe, which is made and brought to the required thinness by blowing with a fan of breath, which persons accustomed to the work know how to manage. The hollow globe is then opened by holding it to the fire, which expanding the air confined within it (the hole of the blowpipe being stopped), bursts it at the weakest part, and while still soft it is opened out into a flat plate by centrifugal force ; and being disengaged from the rod, a thick knob is left in its centre. It is then placed in a furnace, or in a certain part of the furnace to undergo the process of annealing. When the table is cut for use, the centre part in which the knob remains is called *knob-glass*, and is used only for the very commonest purposes. Tables are now made of such a size that squares may be procured 38 inches by 24 inches as extra sizes.

1871a. The qualities of crown glass in common use are called best, seconds, thirds, and fourths or coarse ; with two still coarser. The last is of a very green hue, and only used for inferior buildings. They were sold by the *crate*, at the same price, the difference being made up by varying the number of the tables contained in it. Thus a crate of best crown glass contained twelve tables ; of seconds, a crate contained fifteen; and of thirds, eighteen tables. They are now sold (by Messrs. Hartley) in crates of eighteen tables of the usual

thickness averaging 53 inches ; and in crates of twelve tables of extra thickness averaging 52 inches. Flattened slabs of the same qualities are sold in crates of thirty-six slabs of the usual thickness, and in crates of twenty-four slabs of extra thickness, each averaging 24 inches, 22¾ inches, and 21½ inches. The flattened slab is also made as 'obscured' glass. The sizes of both qualities vary from 'quarries'; under 9 by 7; up to, above 4½ feet, and not above 5 feet superficial. Taking the usual thickness of

Best	as	00	extra thickness	150
Seconds	„	90	„	135
Thirds	„	65	„	110
Fourths	„	50	„	85
CC and CCC	„	43 and 40	„	63 and 50 (Adcock).

1872. *Sheet* glass has been manufactured in England with great improvements since 1832 to 1838 by Messrs. Chance and Hartley, with the co-operation of M. Bontemps, of Paris. Though inferior in colour, this glass is in other points generally superior to that of the foreign manufacture. It is composed of the same or similar materials to the above, in well ascertained proportions, and with sulphate of soda to give whiteness. In the manufacture of sheet glass a sufficient quantity of the metal is collected at the extremity of a blow-pipe, and then lengthened by swinging and blowing, till it acquires the form of a hollow cylinder, which is then detached, the neck being cut off with a thread of hot glass; and one side of the cylinder is cut down lengthwise with a heated iron or diamond. It is then taken to the flattening kiln, where the heat causes it gradually to open nearly flat on a bed called *largre*, where it is rubbed down by means of a block of wood called a *polissoir*, and then becomes *flattened sheet*. After this operation it is placed in the annealing oven to cool gradually. This operation is referred to by the monk Theophilus, who wrote about the end of the twelfth century or later, as in use in his time. The method was also employed by the Venetians especially for coloured glass, as it secured uniformity. But on the cessation for its demand, the employment of the cylinders was entirely superseded in France, England, and the North of Germany, for the rotary principle.

1872a. The great advantage of *sheet* glass is that of affording plates of larger dimensions, and not only of avoiding the waste arising from the circular form of the *crown* tables, but also from the knob or bull's eye in the centre. The surface, however, is much less brilliant than that of crown glass, and is more wavy and undulated. Messrs. Chance, in 1838, introduced a thicker quality of sheet glass, which was at the same time of a better surface, and since then its use has become general.

1872b. In 1840 the same firm introduced a new variety of window glass under the name of *patent plate*, which they obtained from a thick sheet glass by a new process of grinding and polishing. They made plates of several degrees of thickness, and of sizes containing from 8 to 12 feet superficial. The surface of the glass obtained by this process, though not perfectly true, is very nearly so; and in brilliancy it is unsurpassed even by cast plate. For glazing sashes it has nearly superseded crown and sheet glass. But for squares of somewhat large dimensions, it may be calculated whether *plate* glass will not be as cheap or cheaper.

1872c. As will be perceived by the above short account of the mode of manufacture of *sheet* glass, its size is almost only limited by the strength of the workman. It is chiefly sold in crates as manufactured, in sheets of not less in width than 28 inches, and not less than 9 feet superficial area; with a limit of width not exceeding 45 inches, and a limit of length not exceeding 75 inches; but these extremes of width and length cannot be combined in the same sheet. Thus in glass of 15 ounces to the foot, the dimensions 55 by 36 inches, or 12½ feet in area, is the largest plate. In 21 ounce glass, 75 by 45 inches, or 18 feet area: in 26 ounce glass, 75 by 45 inches, or 17 feet area: in 32 ounce glass, 65 by 44 inches, or 15 feet area: in 36 ounce glass, 60 by 42 inches, or 12½ feet area: and in 42 ounce glass, 55 by 38 inches, or 11 feet area. The four first weights are made in qualities of best, seconds, thirds, and fourths; and the two first have two qualities A and B for pictures. There is no fourth quality to the two last named weights. All these sorts are cut into squares for glazing.

1872d. *Fluted sheet* glass of 15 ounce and 21 ounce is usually supplied in crates not above 43 inches long; but it is made up to 50 inches in length. *Obscured sheet glass* is supplied in all substances.

1873. *Patent plate* glass, already described (*par.* 1872b.) is made in three qualities, B or best, C or second, and CC or third, quality. Each of these are of four kinds, known as No. 1, which is of an average thickness of $\frac{1}{8}$th of an inch, and is of an average weight of 13 ounces to the foot; No. 2 is $\frac{1}{12}$th thick, and 17 ounces; No. 3 is $\frac{1}{10}$th, and 21 ounces; and No. 4 is $\frac{1}{8}$th, or 24 ounces to the foot. No. 4 B is thus the very best quality made; the prices for the size required vary but about one or two pennies per foot in each kind; and from threepence to sevenpence in each quality. They are manufactured in sizes from 4 to 13 feet in area, not above 50 inches long, or 36 inches wide.

1874. *German sheet*, or *Belgian sheet* glass, as it is sometimes called, was formerly in much demand in England; and is still used for cheapness. Its appearance is more wavy

and speckled than the English manufacture. *Crystal white sheet* glass, for glazing pictures and prints, is imported from Florence in cases of 100, 200 and 300 feet, in first, second and third qualities, and appears superior to other glass in whiteness, but it has the defect of 'sweating.' Similar named glass for such purposes made by Messrs. Chance, appears to us to be very green, and therefore detrimental to prints and pictures; but on the other hand it does not sweat.

1875. *Plate* glass is so called from its being cast in large sheets or plates. Its constituent parts are white sand, cleansed with purified pearl-ashes, and borax. If the metal should appear yellow, it is rendered pellucid by the addition, in equal small quantities, of manganese and arsenic. It is cast on a large horizontal table, and all excrescences are pressed out by passing a large roller over the metal. To polish it, it is laid on a large horizontal block of freestone, perfectly smooth, and then a smaller piece of glass, fastened to a plank of wood, is passed over the other till it has received a due degree of polish. For the purpose of facilitating the process, water and sand are used, as in the polishing of marble; and lastly, Tripoli, smalt, emery, and putty, to give it lustre; but to afford the finishing polish the powder of smalt is used. Except in the very largest plates, the workmen polish their glass by means of a plank having four wooden handles to move it, and to this plank a plate of glass is cemented.

1876. In the Glossary, s. v. Glass, plate, will be found the tariff of the Thames Plate Glass Company in London, for unsilvered plates for mirrors, of which there are two qualities, second and best. The Paris factory supplied in 1865 two looking glasses for the Mayor's room in the Town Hall at Liverpool, each 15 feet by 10 feet. *Polished plate* glass is manufactured for general glazing purposes up to about 80 feet superficial, of two qualities, usual and best. The usual thickness is a quarter of an inch: higher prices are charged for glass selected to be cut above $\frac{3}{16}$ths., $\frac{5}{16}$ths., and $\frac{3}{8}$ths. thick; while for above $\frac{3}{8}$ths. thick, special prices are charged. The best quality is declared to be of the very purest colour, free from specks, and not subject to dampness or sweating.

1877. *Rough plate* glass, cast, is used for roofing, in skylights, windows, &c., in plates from not above 20 inches long, to above 120 inches long, in thicknesses of $\frac{1}{4}$, $\frac{3}{8}$, $\frac{1}{2}$, $\frac{3}{4}$, inch, $1\frac{1}{4}$, and $1\frac{1}{2}$ inch; but these thicknesses have certain limited lengths. The widths are the same as for plate glass. This glass is not ground or polished, but rough from the table, and showing the table marks on its underside.

1878. The *patent rough plate* glass, which is also cast, must not be confounded with the above. It is extensively used for ridge and furrow roofs, conservatories, manufactories, skylights, workshops, and other places where "obscured" glass is required to intercept the vision without diminishing the light. Blinds are unnecessary, and when it is used in greenhouses, no scorching of the plants occurs. The quality known as $\frac{1}{8}$th. of an inch thick, weighing about 2 lbs., or 32 ounces to the foot, is usually provided for these purposes, and is no more, weight for weight, than common crown glass. When greater strength is required, $\frac{3}{16}$ths. and $\frac{1}{4}$ inch thick is said to be cheaper and of a finer quality than the common rough plate; but we demur to this statement, as of late years the manufacture appears to have decreased in strength from the greater use of sand for cheapness; in moveable window frames in warehouses, a lamentable quantity of broken squares is to be seen almost before the floors are occupied.

1878a. This glass is made of two kinds; I. Plain, which is merely marked by the fine grain of the casting table, and is that above noticed; and II. Fluted, of two sorts, No. 1, large pattern, having $3\frac{1}{2}$ flutes to the inch; and No. 2, small pattern, having 12 flutes to the inch. Both the plain and the fluted kinds are made $\frac{1}{8}$th. $\frac{3}{16}$ths. $\frac{1}{4}$. $\frac{3}{8}$ths. and $\frac{1}{2}$ inch in thickness. The width is about 3 feet, and the length usually not above 70 inches; but 75, 90, and 100 inches long, are also made. When a clear glass and much non-transparency are required, No. 2 fluted is the best.

1879. *Quarry* glass is also made in this material; No. 1 being 6 inches by $4\frac{1}{8}$th inches from point to point; No 2 being 3 inches by $2\frac{1}{16}$ inch. A *stained ornamented patent quarry rough plate* is made for churches, chapels, schools, &c. A *patent diamond rough plate* glass is also manufactured. A patent rough plate, and sheet, *perforated* glass, polished or unpolished, for ventilation, can be obtained in sizes, which require consideration in arranging, on account of the length of the slits or perforations. It is usually made in columns $1\frac{1}{2}$ inches wide, and $2\frac{1}{2}$ inches apart; the space between each slit vertically being $1\frac{1}{2}$ inches. Larger sizes, or the columns wider apart, can be obtained from various manufacturers, or to order.

1880. Many other applications of glass will be noticed in the ensuing chapter. We must here state that the details given in this section are founded upon the price list issued by Messrs. Hartley, of Sunderland, and would state our regret that the manufacturers have not deemed it advisable for their own interests, to provide some place in London, and in other large towns, where the architect can call and compare the qualities of glass supplied under his specification with standards there placed. It was comparatively easy in former years to judge of good glass; now it is almost impossible.

CHAP. III.

USE OF MATERIALS, OR PRACTICAL BUILDING.

Sect. I.

FOUNDATIONS AND DRAINS.

1881. In the previous chapter, we have enumerated the principal materials used in building; we shall now proceed to show how those materials may be most advantageously employed; but we shall not, in the various branches of the practice, again touch on the materials themselves, which have been, we conceive, already sufficiently described. But previous to entering upon the different branches of practical building, we think it right to submit to the reader a few observations on that most important of all considerations—a due regard to the security of the foundations on which a building is to stand, as a preliminary to the works of the bricklayer and mason, as the case may be. No advance or improvement has been made in this branch of architecture, as a science, since the time of the ancients. The advice of Vitruvius may still be followed with safety. In England, the recent introduction of concrete (no modern invention) has superseded the use of wood under walls in the earth; and piles are now quite exploded, except for the piers of bridges and other situations in which they can constantly be kept wet.

1882. The best soils for receiving the foundations of a building are rock, gravel, or close-pressed strong sandy earth; "but," says L. B. Alberti, "we must never trust too hastily to any ground, though it may resist the pick-axe, for it may be in a plain, and be infirm, the consequence of which might be the ruin of the whole work. I have seen a tower at Mestre, a place belonging to the Venetians, which, in a few years after it was built, made its way through the ground it stood upon, which, as the fact evinced, was a loose weak soil, and buried itself in earth up to the very battlements. For this reason, they are very much to be blamed who, not being provided by nature with a soil fit to support the weight of an edifice, and lighting upon the ruins or remains of some old structure, do not take the pains to examine the goodness of the foundation, but inconsiderately raise great piles of building upon it, and out of the avarice of saving a little expense, throw away all the money they lay out in the work. It is, therefore, excellent advice, the first thing you do, to dig *wells*, for several reasons, and especially in order to get acquainted with the strata of the earth, whether sound enough to bear the superstructure, or likely to give way." It is important, previous to laying the foundations, to drain them completely, if possible, not only from the rain and other water that would lie about, but from the land water which is, as it were, pent up in the surrounding soil. In soft, loose, and boggy ground, the use of concrete will be found very great; and in these soils, moreover, the width and depth it should be thrown in, should, as well as the lower courses of the foundation, be proportioned inversely to the badness of the soil. Clay of the plastic kind is a bad foundation, on account of the continual changes, from heat and moisture, to which it is subject, and which often cause it so to expand and contract as to produce very alarming settlements in a building. The best remedy against this inconvenience is to tie the walls together by the means of chain plates, buried in the centre of the footings, and on the top of the landings that rest on the concrete; these plates to be, of course, connected at the returning angles, so as to encompass the whole building. In these cases, the clay must be excavated to make room for the concrete. This will be found an effectual remedy in clay soils.

1883. If the soil be a sound gravel, it will want little more than ramming with heavy rammers; and if the building be not very heavy, not even that.

1884. Where vaults and cellars are practised, the whole of the soil must, of course, be excavated; but where they are not required, trenches are dug to receive the walls, which, in both cases, must be proportioned in strength to the weight of the intended superstructure and its height. In general terms, we may direct the depth of foundations to be a sixth part of the height of the building, and the thickness of the walls twice that of those that are raised upon them. Care must be taken that that which is to receive the footings of the walls be equable; otherwise, where external and internal walls are connected together, the former, being the heaviest, may settle more than the latter, thereby causing fractures, which, though not, perhaps, dangerous, are extremely disagreeable in appearance. The lower courses, which are called the footings of the wall, are often laid dry; and, perhaps, at all events, a sparing use of mortar in a spot loaded with the greatest pressure should be preferred. If the footings be of stone, very particular attention should be bestowed on

placing the stone in the courses in the same direction or bed as it lay in the quarry, to prevent its splitting.

1885. In foundations where, from columns or small piers pressing upon particular parts, there would be a liability, from uneven bearing, to partial failure, it has been the practice from a very early period, to turn inverted arches (see *fig.* 615.) to catch on their springing the weight to be provided against, by which means such weight is equally distributed throughout the length of the foundation. "Standing thus," says our master Alberti, "they (the columns or weights) will be less apt to force their way into the earth in any one place, the weight

Fig. 615.

being counterpoised and thrown equally on both sides on the props of the arches. And how apt columns are to drive into the ground, by means of the great pressure of the weight laid on them, is manifest from that corner of the noble temple of Vespasian that stands to the north-west; for, being desirous to leave the public way, which was interrupted by that angle, a free and open passage underneath, they broke the area of their platform, and turned an arch against the wall, leaving that corner as a sort of pilaster on the other side of the passage, and fortifying it as well as possible with stout work, and with the assistance of a buttress. Yet this, at last, by the vast weight of so great a building, and the giving way of the earth, became ruinous."

1885a. A method of forming foundations has lately come into vogue for bridges and other hydraulic constructions by the use of *cylinders* or other shaped air-tight cases. In India the system of founding large masses of masonry on cylindrical piers built in the interior of wooden curbs, has prevailed for a long period. The method of constructing the piers is the same as that used in England in sinking the steining for ordinary wells; and when sunk the interior is filled up with concrete or rubble masonry. Some of the iron bridges lately erected over the River Thames and elsewhere have been placed on foundations formed by cast iron cylinders filled in with concrete. Further details must be sought in works devoted to *Civil Engineering*, as the system will seldom be applicable in strictly architectural constructions.

1886. It is most important, when the walls are raised on the foundations, and brought up a little above the level of the earth, to take care that the earth, most especially if moist, should not lie against them; for if walls, before they are dry and settled, imbibe moisture, they rarely ever part with it, and thence gradually impart rot to the timbers throughout the house. In all buildings, it is an object to have a second thin wall outside the basement walls, so as to leave between it and them a cavity for the circulation of the air, such cavity being technically called an *air-drain*. This is in all cases desirable, but in moist and loose soils it is essentially necessary for the durability of the building, as well as for the health of those who are to dwell in it.

1886a. It is important that the *air-drain* or *dry area* should commence at least as low as the foundations of the building; in very wet situations it should be provided with pipes connected with the main drains of the building, to carry off the superabundant moisture. Even when provided, the usual precautions to prevent damp arising in the main walls must not be neglected. The *air drain*, which should never be less than 8 inches wide, or more if possible, is commonly covered with a half-brick arch, or with stone, slate, or tile, *below* the surface of the ground. This entirely does away with the benefit anticipated by its formation, because the surface drainage descends and injures the main wall even when cemented above the covering; this should be placed some inches *above* ground. It also often degenerates into a hole for dirt and vermin. The best arrangement is to make a *dry area*, or a space wide enough to be easily cleared out, and to which a cat or dog can have access, and to cover it with stone with moveable gratings at convenient distances; the expense will not be much greater, while the result will be very effective. The most secure arrangement, however, is to form an open area all round the building. The want of such a precaution in the houses in the suburbs of London renders a large majority of those having basements nearly uninhabitable from the disagreeable consequences of damp walls.

1886b. *Damp courses.* This simple provision to prevent wet which is likely to get into walls, from rising in them by capillary attraction, is too often neglected, especially in cheap work, for the present saving of a pound or two; but at the ultimate expenditure of many pounds. The simplest plan has generally been to work three courses of the brickwork above the footings and below the ground floor, in cement. Messrs. Smith of Darnick state that a coating of cement, done in a very substantial manner, did not appear to have the smallest effect, as the wall was as damp above it as below. For *small* cottages they found an effective plan was to build all the parts of the wall underground quite *dry*, and

not to use any mortar until clear of the earth. This left the walls quite dry above. The next method is to bed a course of sound whole slate slabs, a quarter of an inch thick, in cement. When the soil is very damp, two or even three courses of ordinary slates may be laid in and well bonded, not only in the main walls, but in all cross partitions and dwarf walls. For some reason, probably that of the slates and cement having separated or crushed with the weight of the walls, allowing the damp to pass through, this method has fallen into disuse. As Portland cement will adhere to slate, probably in solid works, if used instead of Roman cement, the result would be more satisfactory.

1886c. Sheet zinc bedded in loam has been found to decay. In extensive works, fine-gritted asphalte, applied in a hot state, is introduced as a layer, about half an inch in thickness. This material is stated, in the Appendix to the *Report of the Fine Arts Commissioners*, to have kept out the effects of damp, which would have shown themselves, as the foundations of the building referred to were always in water about 20 inches below the level of the ground floor. The brickwork should be dry and protected from rain during the operation, to prevent the asphalte becoming honeycombed. In buildings already erected, the walls can be underpinned to introduce the material. At the New Palace at Westminster the joints are only half filled with mortar, the asphalte filling the remainder when poured over the bricks. The bricks for the next course, having been heated at a coke fire, were placed on the asphalte in its fluid state, and the joints half flushed up. The outer courses, however, should be first laid for short distances, that they may set before the middle is filled in. In rubble masonry, it will be necessary to fill up all inequalities on the surface with fine concrete; when this has set sufficiently, the asphalte is to be laid as described for brickwork. Gas tar mixed with lime is said to be impervious to wet.

1886d. Two centuries ago, thin sheet lead was laid on the top course of a wall to prevent damp coming down it from the gutters; of late years, a layer of 4 lb. milled lead has been proposed to prevent it rising; no doubt the best and most efficacious remedy, but the cost would be greater than usually allowed. But the best invention, having price also in its favour, is the *damp-proof course*, formed of brown stoneware, perforated through-

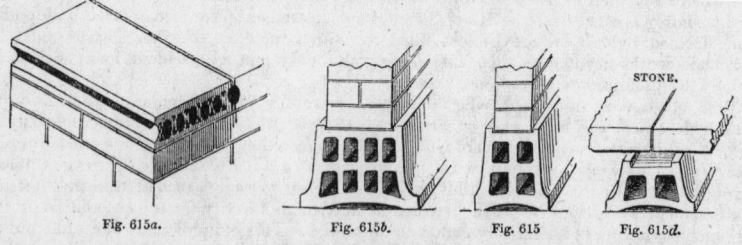

Fig. 615a.   Fig. 615b.   Fig. 615   Fig. 615d.

out its entire width, with a half air space, which remains open after the mortar beds are laid, on each side of the slab. In an executed work, a course of bricks can be cut out and the stoneware be inserted. This is one of the many building inventions of Mr. John Taylor, junior. *Fig. 615a.* shows one for an 18-inch wall; other sizes as well as angle blocks are provided. Each foot superficial is stated to be equal to the support of 25 tons or 600 feet of vertical brickwork. Jennings has patented earthenware *sleeper blocks*, "non-conductors of damp and a cheap substitute for brick sleeper walls;" they are also useful for carrying stone paving: *Figs.* 615b., 615c., and 615d. describe themselves.

1886e. Precautions are also necessary to prevent the access of damp from the surface of the ground next the outside face of the wall. If the dry area be carried up sufficiently high, the two measures are effected at once. If not, a facing of stone or slate is the best remedy. The former need not be very thick; but it is well for both to be from two to three feet high. If a small interval be left between this facing slab and the outside surface of the wall, it will provide for a circulation of air being kept up in the space. By this provision, although the facing slabs may be temporarily damped by rain, they will soon be again dried without having communicated the damp to the body of the wall.

1886f. A preventive against the effects of damp in the inside of the building is to cover the whole area within the walls with a layer of *concrete*, about 4 to 6 inches thick (from 6 to 9 inches is better); but as concrete is of a honey-comb character even when fixed or set, being full of little fissures or holes, there is some danger in placing it in *wet* soils, for it will often weep, and if cut, water will be seen to ooze through the joint. Also, when placed under the basement floor to keep out damp, water will invariably find its way through if there be any pressure, as from springs. To prevent vapours rising from decomposed matter in the soil, a good practice, even in dry localities, is to cover the soil before the floor boards are laid, with a layer of two inches of unslaked lime, which on slaking with damp or damp air destroys any vegetation that may have been left on the surface.

1887. We, perhaps, might have more properly spoken first of the subject of DRAINAGE and SEWERS, whereof it now becomes our duty to give some information, inasmuch as before a brick or stone of any building be laid, the architect neglects his duty if he has not provided for perfect drainage in the lowest parts of the structure. This must not be by the aid of a small stagnant tank, called a *cesspool*, often the cause of much disease in a family; but by means of a drain into some running stream at a distance from the building, or, if that be not practicable, into some far removed pond, whose exhalations shall not be blown by the prevalent winds of the spot back upon the place where they were generated, in a different form. Neither does the health alone of the family whose comfort is to be provided for, demand this consideration of drainage; for the durability of the structure is quite as much involved in good drainage as is the health of the family whose dwelling-place the house is to become: hence we are the more earnest in pressing the point. In cities, the architect cannot always accomplish this important object; but in the country he is unpardonable if he neglect it. London with its suburbs is now probably the best drained capital in Europe. The lines of sewers forming the main drainage may be deemed completed, and to have relieved the noble river of nearly all the sewage matter. Every street has its public sewer, acting more or less perfectly, and nearly every house its separate drain into the sewer, although for a time, a few years back, this rule of a separate drainage, which had long been in force, was annulled.

1888. The main drain necessary for the service of the largest house (we suppose the case of one in the country), if the fall be even but moderate, requires no large dimensions. When we see a small river draining considerable tracts of country, often in section only 8, 9, or 10 feet superficial; it may easily be conceived that the surplus water from, and rain falling on, a mansion is a quantity, even in pressing times, that exacts no large area of discharge to free the place from damp. There are few cases in which the greatest mansion would demand an area exceeding 5 feet, which a sewer 2 ft. by 2 ft. 6 in. would afford, supposing it to have a parallelogrammic section; but of course when the fall permits, a greater height would be preferable. Drains should, as well for their durability as on other accounts, be constructed with curved bottoms, but not with the lower part egg-shaped; for instance, as respects flat bottoms, take the lower parts of two drains, whose depth of running water is 1 foot, one whereof is formed with a semicircular bottom, 2 feet wide. The area of the column of water will, therefore, be 1·5708, and the length of the half curve will be 3·1416. To obtain with one foot depth of water, the same area in a drain whose bottom is flat and sides upright, we must have the width 1·5708, and the sum of the three sides touched by the water will be 3·5708. Then 3·5708 − 3·1416 = ·4292 represents roughly the difference of friction or impediment in favour of the semicircular bottom in the case stated, nearly $\frac{13}{100}$ of the power being lost by the use of a flat bottom.

1888a. Since the introduction, about 1845, of pipes into the sewerage and drainage systems, brick drains have been discarded. But easy as it may appear to lay down pipes, unless it be done under careful supervision, the fall may hereafter be found insufficient; the fall perhaps reversed; the effective drainage stopped by carelessness in forming the joints; and so on. The chief point to be here noticed respecting this familiar subject is, that great difference exists between the vitrified stoneware pipe drains, and the glazed or unglazed earthenware pipe drains, substituted for cheapness. The sewage in the latter soon corrodes the glazing, which being removed, the half burnt earthenware sucks in the foul water and decays. Nor is it nearly so strong as the stoneware article.

1888b. Great diversity of opinion exists as to the effective size of a pipe required for a building. One person urges that his ten roomed house and outbuildings have never been inconvenienced by the use of a 3 inch drain, whilst other houses, with 6 inch and even 9 inch drains, have been seriously affected. Much depends, as noticed in the previous paragraph, on the fall, and on the careful laying of the pipes, and something on the quantity of water used for household purposes. Where a water closet is placed at or near the head of a drain, a stoppage of its pipe often occurs; while grease from the kitchen sink incrusting in the pipe, for want of occasional flushing with hot water, is another frequent cause. Sewers also occasionally require that assistance by flushing them from their head. One of the best arrangements proposed is that of an iron tilting cistern, to hold about 90 gallons, inserted in a brick pit at the head of a pipe sewer. This cistern with its brass bearings and plates, brickwork, stone cover, and water tap, costs about nine pounds, and if one were placed at the head of each pipe sewer in a town, and all were turned off at the same time, a material assistance in keeping the main line also clear, would be found.

1888c. Various arrangements are advertised for obtaining access to drains for inspection, without the necessity for breaking into them. A velocity of 2 feet per second is the least which will keep sewers clear of all ordinary obstructions; while house drains and small pipes require a velocity of 3 feet per second to keep them clear (Hurst). No new sewer can now be made in London without the previous approval of the Metropolitan Board of Works; and no drain can be laid into a sewer without the previous approval of the vestry

or district board, which has to apply to the Metropolitan Board of Works for their sanction in both cases.   Many towns in England have now their Board of Health supervising
the drainage of the streets and houses, pursuant to " The Public Health Act, 1848," and
" The Local Government Act, 1858."

SECT. II.

BRICKLAYING AND TILING.

1889. Bricklaying, or the art of building with bricks, or of uniting them by cement or
mortar into various forms, includes, in the metropolis, and mostly in the provinces, the business of walling, tiling, and paving with bricks or tiles, and sometimes plastering ; but this
last is rarely, if ever, undertaken by the London bricklayer ; though in the country the
trades of bricklaying and plastering are usually united, and not unfrequently that of masonry also.   The materials used have been described in a previous part of the work, to
which the reader is referred (1811. *et seq.*).

1890. The tools used by the bricklayer, who has always an attendant labourer to supply
him with bricks, mortar, &c., are — 1. A *brick trowel*, for taking up and spreading the
mortar, and also for cutting the bricks to any required length.   2. A *hammer*, for cutting
holes and chases in brickwork.   3. The *plumb rule*, being a thin rule, 6 or 7 inches wide,
with a line and plummet swinging in the middle of it, in order to ascertain that the walls
are carried up perpendicularly.   4. The *level*, which is about 10 or 12 feet long, with a
vertical rule attached to it, in which a line and plummet are suspended, the use whereof is
to try the level of the walls at various stages of the building as it proceeds, and particularly
at the window cills and wall plates.   5. The *large square*, for setting out right angles.
6. The *rod*, for measuring lengths, usually 5 or 10 feet long.   7. The *jointing rule*, about
8 or 10 feet long, as one or two bricklayers are to use it, and 4 inches broad, with which
they *run* or mark the centre of each joint of the brickwork.   8. The *jointer*, which is of
iron, shaped like the letter S.   9. The *compasses*, for traversing arches and vaults.   10. The
raker, a piece of iron having two knees or angles, dividing it into three parts at right
angles to each other, the two end parts being pointed and equally long, and standing upon contrary
sides of the middle part.   Its use is to rake out decayed mortar from the joints of old walls
for the purpose of replacing it with new mortar, or, as it is called, *pointing* them.   11. The
hod, which is a wooden trough shut close across at one extremity and open at the other.
The sides consist of two boards at right angles to each other, from the meeting whereof a
handle projects at right angles to their union.   It is used by the labourer for conveying
bricks and mortar to the bricklayer ; for which purpose, when he has the latter office to
perform, he strews dry sand on its inside, to prevent the mortar from sticking.   12. The
line pins, which are of iron, for fastening and stretching the line at proper intervals of the
wall, that each course may be kept straight in the face and level on the bed.   The pins have
a line attached to them of 60 ft. to each pin.   13. The *rammer*, used for trying the ground,
as well as for beating it solid to the utmost degree of compression.   13. The *iron crow* and
pick axe, for breaking and cutting through walls or moving heavy weights.   14. The *grinding stone*, for sharpening axes, hammers, and other tools.   The following ten articles relate
entirely to the preparation and cutting of guaged arches.   15. The *banker*, which is a bench
from 6 to 12 ft. long, according to the number of workmen who are to work at it.   It is
2 ft. 6 in. to 3 ft. wide, and about 2 ft. 8 in. high.   Its use is for preparing the bricks
for rubbed arches, and for other guaged work.   16. The *camber slip*, a piece of wood
usually about half an inch thick, with at least one curved edge, rising about 1 inch in
6 feet, for drawing the sofite line of straight arches.   When the other edge is curved, it
rises about half that of the other, that is, about half an inch in 6 feet, for the purpose of
drawing the upper line of the arch, so as to prevent it becoming hollow by the settling of
the arch.   The upper edge is not always cambered, many preferring it straight.   The slip
being sufficiently long, it answers the width of many openings ; and when the bricklayer has
drawn his arch, he delivers it to the carpenter to prepare the centre for it.   17. The *rubbing
stone*. This is of a cylindrical form, about 20 inches diameter, but may be less.   It is fixed at
one end of the banker, upon a bed of mortar.   After the bricks for the guaged work have
been rough-shaped by the axe, they are rubbed smooth on the rubbing stone.   The headers
and stretchers, in return, which are not axed, are called *rubbed returns* and rubbed headers
and stretchers.   18. The *bedding stone*, which is a straight piece of marble 18 or 20 inches in
length, of any thickness, and about 8 or 10 inches wide.   It is used to try the rubbed side of a
brick, which must be first squared to prove whether its surface be straight, so as to fit it
upon the leading *skew back*, or leading end of the arch.   19. The *square*, for trying the
bedding of the bricks, and squaring the sofites across the breadth of the bricks.   20. The
bevel, for drawing the sofite line on the face of the bricks.   21. The *mould*, for forming the

face and back of the brick, in order to reduce it in thickness to its proper taper, one edge of the mould being brought close to the bed of the brick when squared. The mould has a notch for every course of the arch. 22. The *scribe*, a spike or large nail, ground to a sharp point, to mark the bricks on the face and back by the tapering edges of the mould, for the purpose of cutting them. 23. The *tin saw* used for cutting the sofite lines about one eighth of an inch deep, first by the edge of the level on the face of the brick, then by the edge of the square on the bed of the brick, in order to enter the brick axe, and to keep the brick from spalting. The saw is also used for cutting the sofite through its breadth in the direction of the tapering lines, drawn upon the face and back edge of the brick; but the cutting is always made deeper on the face and back of the brick than in the middle of its thickness, for the above-mentioned purpose of entering the axe. The saw is also used for cutting the false joints of headers and stretchers. 24. The *brick axe*, for axing off the sofites of bricks to the saw cuttings, and the sides to the lines drawn by the scribes. The bricks being always rubbed smooth after axing, the more truly they are axed the less labour will be requisite in rubbing them. 25. The *templet*. This is used for taking the length of the stretcher and width of the header. 26. The *chopping block*, for reducing the bricks to their intended size and form by axing them. It is made of any piece of wood that comes to hand, from 6 to 8 inches square, and generally supported upon two 14-inch brick piers, if only two men work at it; but if four men, the chopping-block must be lengthened and supported by three piers, and so on according to the number employed at it. It is about 2 ft. 3 in. in height. 27. The *float-stone*, which is used for rubbing curved work to a smooth surface, such as the cylindrical backs and spherical heads of niches, to take out the axe marks. It is, before application to them, made of a form reversed to the surface whereon it is applied, so as to coincide with it as nearly as possible in finishing.

1891. Before adverting to the *bond*, as it is technically called, of brick walling, which is the form of connection of the bricks with each other, we will stop to observe, that in working walls, not more than 4 or 5 feet should be brought up at a time; for as, in setting, the mortar shrinks and a general subsidence takes place, the part first brought up, if too large in quantity, will have come to its bearing before the adjacent parts are brought up, and thus fissures in the work and unequal settlements will take place. In carrying up any particular part above another, it should always be regularly sloped back to receive the adjoining parts to the right and to the left. On no account should any part of a wall be carried higher than one scaffold, except for some very urgent object.

1892. Previous to the reign of William and Mary, all the brick buildings in this island were constructed in what is called *English bond*; and subsequent to the reign in question, when, in building as in many other cases, Dutch fashions were introduced, we regret to say, much to the injury of our houses' strength, the workmen have become so infatuated with what is called *Flemish bond*, that it is difficult to drive them out of it. To the introduction of the latter has been attributed (in many cases with justice) the splitting of walls into two thicknesses; to prevent which, expedients have been adopted, which would be altogether unnecessary if a return to the general use of English bond could be established.

1893. In chap. i. sect x. of this book (1550. *et seq.*) we have spoken generally on walls; our observations here, therefore, in respect of them, will be confined to brick walls and their bond.

1894. *English bond* is that disposition of bricks in a wall in which (except at the quoins) the *courses* are alternately composed of *headers* and *stretchers*. In brick walling, and indeed in stone walling also, a *course* means the horizontal layer of bricks or stones whereof the wall is composed, being contained between two faces parallel to the horizon, and terminated on each side by the vertical face of the wall. The mass also formed by brick or stones in an arch are also termed courses, but receive the name of concentric courses. The term header is applied to a brick or stone whose small head or end is seen in the external face of the wall; and that of stretcher, to a brick or stone whose length is parallel to the face of the wall. We are therefore to understand by English bond, a continuation either of header or stretcher, continued throughout in the same course or horizontal layer, and hence we have described it as consisting of alternate layers of headers and stretchers (*fig.* 616.), the former serving to bind the wall together in a transverse direction or widthwise, and thus prevent its splitting, whilst the latter binds it lengthwise, or in a longitudinal direction. None but the English bond prevents the former occurrence, as work executed in this way, when so undermined as to cause a fracture, separates, but rarely breaks through the solid brick, as if the wall were composed of one entire piece.

1895. The ancient Roman brickwork was executed on this

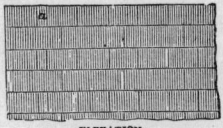

ELEVATION.

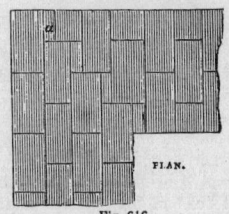

PLAN.

Fig. 616.

principle; and its extraordinary durability is as much to be attributed to that sort of work being used for bonding it together, as to its extraordinary thickness.

1896. In this, as well as Flemish bond, to which we shall presently come, it will be observed, that the length of a brick being but 9 inches, and its width 4½ inches, in order to *break* the joints (that is, that one joint may not come over another), it becomes necessary near the angles to interpose a quarter brick or *bat, a*, called a *queen closer*, in order to preserve the continuity of the bond in the heading course. The bond, however, may equally be preserved by a three-quarter bat at the angle in the stretching course, in which case this last bat is called a *king closer*. In each case an horizontal lap of two inches and a half is left for the next header. The figure above given is that of a two-brick or 18-inch wall, but the student will have no difficulty in drawing, on due consideration of it, a diagram of the bond for any other thickness of wall; recollecting, first, that each course is formed either of headers or stretchers. Secondly, that every brick in the same course and on the same face of the wall must be laid in the same direction, and that in no instance is a brick to be placed with its whole length against the side of another, but in such way that the end of one may reach to the middle of the others that lie contiguous to it, excepting in the outside of the stretching course, where three-quarter bricks, or king closers, will of course be necessary at the ends, to prevent a continued upright joint in the face of the work. Thirdly, that a wall crossing at right angles with another will have all the bricks of the same level course in the same parallel direction, whereby the angles will be completely bonded. We shall close these observations with a recommendation to the young architect, founded on our own experience, on no account, in any building where soundness of work is a desideratum, to permit any other than English bond to be executed under his superintendence.

1897. *Flemish bond* is that wherein the same course consists alternately of headers and stretchers, which, in appearance, some may fancy superior to that just described. Such is not our opinion. We think that the semblance of strength has much to do with that of beauty in architecture. But there is in the sufferance of Flemish bond a vice by which strength is altogether lost sight of, which we shall now describe. It was formerly, though now partially, the practice to face the front walls of houses with guaged or rubbed bricks, or with at least a superior species of brick, as the malm stock; in the former cases, the bricks being reduced in thickness, and laid with a flat thin joint frequently, what the workmen call a *putty joint*, for the external face, the outer and inner work of the same courses in the same wall, not corresponding in height, could not be bonded together except where occasionally the courses fell even, where a header was introduced from the outside to tie or bond the front to the internal work. Hence, as the work would not admit of this, except occasionally, from the want of correspondence between the interior and exterior courses, the headers would be introduced only where such correspondence took place, which would only occur in a height of several courses. Thus a wall two bricks in thickness, if faced on both sides, was very little indeed better than three thin walls, the two outer half a brick thick, and the middle one a brick or 9 inches thick. Bricklayers having little regard for their character will, if not prevented by the architect, not only practise this expedient, but will also, unless vigilantly watched, when a better sort of brick is used for the facing, cut the headers in half to effect a paltry saving of the better material. In walls of one brick and a half in thickness, the strength of the wall is not diminished by the use of Flemish bond so much as in those of greater thickness, as may be seen by the diagram (*fig.* 617.). Many expedients have been invented to obviate the inconveniences of Flemish bond; but we think it rather useful to omit them, lest we should be considered as parties to a toleration of its use, for the continuation whereof no substantial reason can be assigned. As we have before observed, all that can be alleged in its favour is a

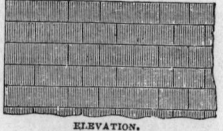

ELEVATION.

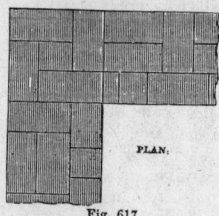

PLAN.

Fig. 617

fancy in respect of its appearance: but were the English mode executed with the same attention and neatness bestowed on the Flemish method, we should say it was equally beautiful; and therefore we shall thus close our notice of it.

1898. The two principal matters to be considered in brick walling are, first, that the wall be as strong as possible in the direction of its length. Secondly, that it be so connected in its transverse direction that it should not be capable of separating in thicknesses. To produce the first, independent of the extraneous aid of bond timbers, plates, &c., it is clear that the method which affords the greatest quantity of longitudinal bond is to be preferred, as in the transverse direction is that which gives the greatest quantity of bond in direction of the thickness. We will, to exemplify this, take a piece of walling 4 bricks long, 4 bricks high, and 2 bricks thick, of English bond: in this will occur 32 stretchers, 24 headers, and 16 half headers to break the joint, or prevent one joint falling over another. Now, in an equal piece of walling constructed in Flemish bond, there will occur only 20

stretchers and 42 headers; from which the great superiority of English bond may be at once inferred.

1899. *Bond Timber* should be used in pieces as long as circumstances will admit. In walls where the thickness will allow of it, some prefer that the timber should be laid in the centre, so that when it decays no material damage is done. Also that in case of fire, the bond timber is not affected by it. If so placed, when dressings of wood are required, wooden plugs must be provided to which to secure them. When a fire occurs and the bond is next the inside face, it is burnt out, and the strength of a thin wall, say 9 or 14 inches thick, is seriously affected thereby. Two or three tiers in the height of the room are usually employed.

1899a. However useful timber may be in bonding thin walls whilst the brickwork is yet green, it has for some years been entirely superseded by *hoop iron bond.* This consists of narrow and thin strips of iron (see SMITHERY) laid between two courses of bricks. The iron should be tarred and sanded, the former as a preservative from rust, the latter to afford a firmer hold to the mortar. Some authorities go so far as to state that hoop iron bond, unless it is set in a cement course, is not so efficient as wood bond. A tier of bond is placed in each three feet of height, one strip of iron to each half brick. In extensive works, or in special cases, two, three, or more, tiers are recommended. In addition to the use of concrete on clay soils, it may be occasionally useful to build all the footings for four or six courses in height of brickwork in cement, each course well bonded with hoop iron, laid both longitudinally and diagonally; it is perhaps better than a course of Yorkshire stone (par. 1882.) as the bond is continuous. During the execution of the works, the iron is continued through all openings as with wood bond; the latter is cut away when requisite, but the former should be turned down against the brickwork. The laps at a junction should be carefully made to secure the continuity of the tie. An addition to the plain band of iron has been introduced, and *Tyerman's patent notched hoop iron bond* has been extensively employed. It consists in forming a slight notch at intervals of 11¾ inches on both sides alternately, and turning it up in succession, in contrary directions, forming a triangular piece, whereby a better key is obtained upon the bricks and mortar.

1900. *Mortar joints.* The propriety of using mortar beds as thin as possible, has been inculcated in this work, and most specifications state that four courses of brickwork formed of the ordinary sized bricks are not to rise more than 11¾; sometimes 12 inches is named, as the joints should not exceed ⅔ths of an inch. When good mortar is used that sets rapidly, the joint might be thicker than thus allowed. In Roman and most Eastern work, the joint was usually 1 and 1¼ inches thick, and where the mortar has been good, such buildings so executed are sound after centuries of wear. "In modern practice, in all masonry and brickwork where strength is required rather than ornament, thick beds and joints of good mortar will be useful. Thin bricks or tiles will also be better than thick bricks, as the material will be better burned, and consequently more enduring. More good mortar can also be used, which in such work gives strength." Such is the practical opinion of R. Rawlinson (*Builder*, xxi. page 152), who declares that "the proportion of mortar to rubble stonework should be about 1 to 3, that is, in 4 cubic yards of rubble wall there should not be less than 1 cubic yard of mortar. In brickwork (ordinary bricks) the proportion will be 1 to 4. If thin bricks be used, or if very small stone be used for rubble-work, the proportions may be as 1 to 1." It has been urged that the peculiarity of early Norman masonry, even of the period of bishop Gundulph, is that of very thick beds of mortar. Mr. Rawlinson further adds, " As a general rule, buildings whether of marble, limestone, sandstone, or of brickwork alone, or of brick and terracotta combined, which are ornamental in character, must all have *thin* joints and beds. Thick beds and joints of mortar would destroy the harmony of design by deteriorating the appearance of labour bestowed on the rich materials in such buildings."

1900a. The fine joints of rubbed brickwork are formed by lime putty, being mortar reduced to the consistency of cream; the bricks are dipped into it to take up a coating, and then driven close upon each other. Ashlar work is usually set in a putty formed of lime, white lead, and a small quantity of very fine sand.

1900b. A defect in the solidity of work arises from the use of many of the hollow, perforated, and machine made, bricks, in that their surfaces are so hard as to prevent the mortar sticking, unless they be first coated with sand. Many walls on being pulled down have shown that the mortar had had no hold upon the bricks, a key had been formed between two bricks by the holes at their ends, but no proper adhesion had taken place. A wall built in first-rate work, could be easily shaken to pieces even after it had been built four or five years. In all brickwork, especially in hot weather, the bricks should be soaked in water (par. 1832a.); and even some of the courses of bricks be sprinkled with water from a rose watering pot. This precaution tends to prevent the absorbent material brick withdrawing all moisture from the mortar before the lime has had time to crystallize. The defect, however, of so doing is, that the walls take longer to dry (par. 1832.); as is also the case when grouting (par. 1860.) is employed.

1900c. The mortar or cement should be such as will quickly set, to prevent the super-incumbent weight pressing the joints closer, and thereby causing settlements, which even with the greatest care, often take place unequally. As often as it is conjectured, from the nature of the soil, or from the foundation being partly new and partly old, that the work will not come to its bearing equally, it is better to carry up the suspected parts separately, and to leave at their ends what are called *toothings*, by which junctions may be made when the weaker parts have come to their regular sound bearing.

1900d. The thickness of walls has furnished the subject of previous pages : we shall therefore only add, that too much care cannot be bestowed on strengthening all angles as much as possible, and well connecting the return of one wall into another ; that piers or pilasters are exceedingly useful in strengthening walls, inasmuch as they act by increasing the base whereon the whole stands ; and, lastly, that in carrying up walls to any considerable height, it is usual to diminish their thickness by *sets off* as they rise.   In houses, above the ground-floor, the sets off are usually made on the inside, having the outside in one face ; but, if it be possible, it is better to set off equally from both faces, because of the better balance afforded.

1900e. *Joints* in brickwork are finished on the face in several ways.   The most common are the 'struck joint,' which is merely finishing the joint by drawing the point of the trowel along it : or 'jointed,' as done by a tool called a *jointer* (par. 1890, art. 8), so as to leave a line impressed on the mortar : or 'flush joint,' in which case the joint is drawn at top and bottom with the trowel when the brick is laid, and afterwards when the mortar is partially set, the middle of the joint is flushed flat with the 'jointer ;' this is sometimes called a 'high joint.'

1901.   A bricklayer, with the assistance of one labourer, can, if he be so inclined, lay in one day about 1000 bricks in common walling ; but the trades unions now prevent him from laying more than about one-third that number.   Occasionally, for a higher remuneration some non-union man may be found to lay near the former number, and then he would complete a rod of brickwork in four days and a half, its area being $272\frac{1}{4}$ feet superficial of the thickness of one brick and a half. When, however, there are many apertures or other interruptions to his work, he will be proportionably longer over it.   The weight of a rod of brickwork is about 13 tons.   Generally it may be taken as consisting of from 4300 to 4500 stock bricks, allowing for waste according to the quality of the bricks, 27 bushels of chalk lime, and 3 single loads of drift sand, or 18 bushels of stone lime and $3\frac{1}{2}$ single loads of sand.   In cement, of 36 bushels, and the same quantity of sharp sand. A rod of brickwork laid dry contains 5370 bricks.   A cubic yard contains 384 bricks, and requires about $6\frac{1}{2}$ cubic feet of sand and $2\frac{1}{2}$ of lime.   A ton of bricks contains about 373 on an average.   330 well burnt bricks weigh generally about 20 cwt., so that a cubic foot weighs about 125 lbs.

1902. *Brick-nogging* is a method of constructing a wall or partition with a row of posts or quarters 3 feet apart, whose intervals are filled up with occasional plates of wood with brickwork between.   It is rarely more than the width of a brick in thickness, and the bricks and timbers on the faces are flush.   It should never be used where thickness can be obtained for a nine-inch wall.   A half brick-nogged partition will require about 500 bricks ; a whole brick-nogged partition about 1000 bricks ; and with brick on edge about 340.

1902a. A *half-brick partition* built in mortar is now adopted in many of the model lodging houses, sometimes with an occasional hoop-iron bond.   These are built four, five, and six stories in height, the joists of the floors steadying them as they are carried up.   Of course the apartments in such places are small in all their dimensions, being about 12 feet long, 9 feet wide, and from 9 to 9 feet 6 inches in height.   A half-brick wall of greater dimensions may be built in cement, and when the floor joists are laid upon it, it becomes very steady, strong, and little likely to be injured by a fire.   Thin slabs of stone have been used as partitions in small houses near a quarry.   Tiles in cement with wood plugs inserted for the dressings, make a sound partition, and when plastered direct upon the tiles, it takes up much less room than a one-brick wall.

1902b. Many varieties of *hollow bricks* are made for a similar purpose.   The " patent bonded hollow bricks or rebated tiles " (*fig.* 617a.) of Hertslet and Co., were employed in 1846–7, by Henry Roberts in the model lodging house in George Street, St. Giles's ; as also in the so-called Prince Albert's model houses, erected in Hyde Park in 1851, and removed to Kennington Park.   A is a bond stone ; B concrete, C floor boards, and D a tie rod. When used for partitions, or for roof and floor arches, these hollow bricks are fireproof, deaden sound more effectually, and are considerably ligher, than solid brickwork.   Such bricks as a lining to stone or flint walls, supersede the necessity for battening.   They are also well adapted for cottage floors. *Hollow bricks* can be made by any good tile machine,

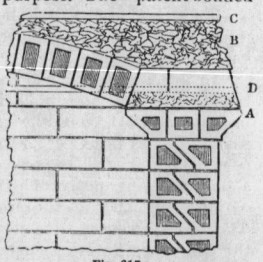

Fig. 617a.

in the same manner as ordinary drain-pipes. They are more compressed, require less drying, and are generally better burned than ordinary bricks. An interesting and complete paper on the subject, with illustrations on the English and French systems of making hollow bricks, is given in the *Building News* for 1858.

1902c. HOLLOW WALLS, formed of ordinary stock bricks, were employed for two-story cottages early in this century. Three methods are usually adopted in the construction of a wall. I. All the bricks placed on edge, as *fig.* 617b, the stretchers and headers breaking joints, and the headers forming the bond. Many persons consider that this arrangement produces a disagreeable appearance on the outside face. II. All the bricks laid flatways, but the stretchers are sawn in half, so as to leave a space of 4½ ins. between them; and in laying the headers, as *fig.* 617c. care must be taken only to fill up with mortar the joints

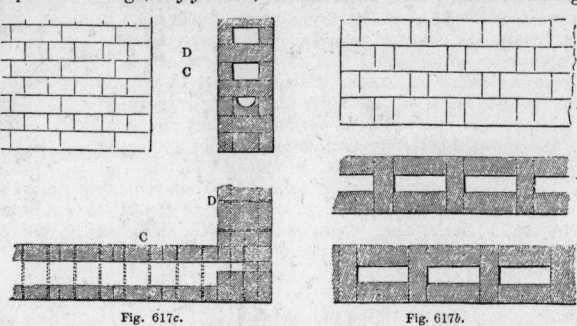

Fig. 617c.   Fig. 617b.

over the half brick on edge, so as to leave the middle of the joint open. III. To lay all the bricks flat in the usual English bond, leaving a space of about 2 inches between each face, and to make up the thickness thus caused, viz. 11 or 11½ inches, by a bat to each header. This may be varied by using a less number of headers, and placing two or three stretchers together, according to the strength of the work required. At Southampton, and perhaps elsewhere, headers are not used, the two faces being bonded together by hoop-iron cramps (*fig.* 617d.), with forked ends, 1¾ths by 1/10th inch, tailing into the frogs of the brick (*fig.* 617e.), and having a bend in the middle of its length partly as a strut to the inside, and partly to prevent any moisture

Fig. 617f.   Fig. 617d.   Fig. 617e.

running along it to the inside face. A cast iron cramp (*fig.* 617f.) is also made, ½ inch by 3/16ths in. thick. Jennings has adopted *bonding bricks* of stoneware for hollow walls. *Fig.* 617g. shows the application of the three sizes; A is 13¼ inches long, to be used in garden walls and other places where an uniform face is not required; B is 11¼ inches long,

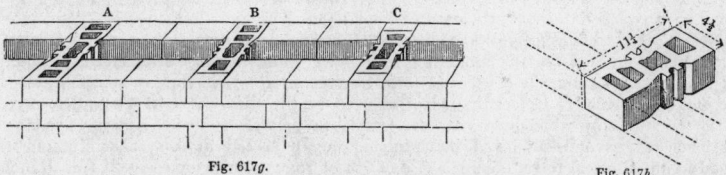

Fig. 617g.   Fig. 617h.

where but one uniform face is required (the brick is shown to a larger size in *fig.* 617h.) the end of the bond brick being faced with a closure of the same material as the wall; and C is a brick 9 inches long, when both faces are to be uniform, closures being used at both ends of it. A 16 inch hollow wall can be built with a 9 inch inside wall, a 2 inch space, and a 4½ inch wall outside. Such a wall is of very common erection in North America, and it is found to stand very well for country villas of good dimensions.

1902d. Much diversity of opinion exists as to whether the space so left should be ventilated by air gratings just above the ground, and also by others under the coping, to obtain a current of air and secure dryness if water be blown through the outer brickwork. In exposed situations, especially on the sea-coast, if hollow walls are not built, either the wall has to be slated on the outside; or it has to be battened on the inside, even when cemented on the outside, to prevent damp showing on the interior surface. Hollow cement blocks have lately been introduced in France, and are said to be cheap, as durable as stone, ventilation easily secured, and provide for the ready formation of shafts for warm air or for flues. The blocks have a resistance of 430 lbs. to the square inch, and are adapted to walls about 20 inches thick as well as to partitions of less width.

1902e. Mr. Taylor has adopted an arrangement of an interior face of common bricks B, with an exterior *facing block* of a better manufactured brick A, in the shape of the letter

L, leaving a cavity of 2 or more inches between them, (*fig.* 617*i*).

1903. GROINED ARCHES. A groin is the angular curve formed by the intersection of two semi cylinders or arches. The centering for raising the more simple groins that occur in using brick arches, belongs to the section CARPENTRY. . The turning a simple arch on a centre only requires care to keep the courses as close as possible, and to use very little mortar on the inner part of the joints. In executing a brick groin, the difficulty arises from the peculiar mode of making proper bond, at the intersection of the two circles as they gradually rise to the crown, where they form an exact point. At the intersection of these angles, the inner rib should

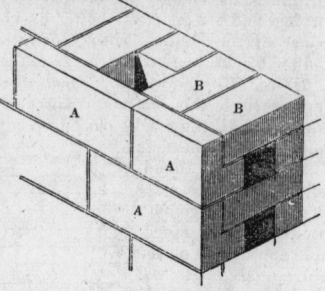

Fig. 617*i*.

be perfectly straight and perpendicular to a diagonal line drawn on the plan. After the centres are set, the application of the brick to the angle will immediately show in what direction it is to be cut. With respect to the sides, they are turned as for common cylindric vaults. Mr. George Tappen, an architect of great practical skill, introduced a method of constructing groins rising from octangular piers, which had the advantage of not only imparting strength to the angle, which in the common groin is extremely deficient, but of increasing the space for the stowage or removal of goods, and further, of strengthening the angles of the groin in this construction by carrying the band round the diagonals (*fig.* 618.) of equal breadth, and thus affording better bond to the bricks.

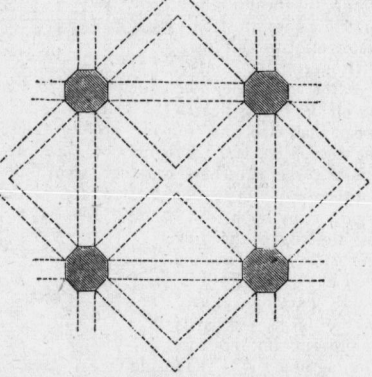

Fig 618.

1903*a*. The Metropolitan Building Act, 1855, requires that *under* a public way, an *arch*, if it be employed, of a span of not more than 10 feet, is to be at least 8½ inches thick; when not exceeding 15 feet, it must be 13 inches at least; and beyond that width the thickness requires special approbation. If of iron construction or other incombustible material, it must be built in a manner approved by the district surveyor. An arch *over* a public way must be formed in the above manner, but a span not exceeding 9 feet must be 8½ inches thick at least. A like special approval is required if the arch or floor be of iron.

1903*b*. *Light arched flat floors,* composed of bricks cemented with gypsum or plaster, have been in common use in Roussillon from time immemorial. Rondelet is of opinion that the segment of a circle is a better form for such arches than the low semi-ellipse. He describes apartments of 18 feet by 25 feet, as used at the War Office at Versailles, covered with brick arches of which the rise was only $\frac{1}{15}$th part of the span and in five stories. The coach-houses and stables of the Marshal de Belle Isle at Bisy near Vernon, were arched in an elliptical form, having a rise of $\frac{1}{8}$th of their span, which was 32 feet 9¾ inches. They were not finished until a year after the walls and roof had been completed. The walls were built of rubble-work having chains of cut stone at intervals of about 16 feet. They were 2 feet 8½ inches thick, being about equal to $\frac{1}{12}$th part of the span. These arches were formed of a double thickness of bricks laid flat, and in plaster, built in succession, with the vertical joints broken. The haunches were filled up with rubble stone in plaster. The springing was formed by notches in the wall, above which the regular courses of stone projected inwards as gathering courses. Above all, a third course of flat bricks was laid horizontally, forming a pavement. Rondelet considers that arches of small and light materials cemented by gypsum become as it were one body, and exert little or no lateral pressure upon the abutments excepting at first, because that cement has a tendency to swell in setting. Rondelet relates that a stone of 4000 lbs. or 5000 lbs. weight was dropped upon one of these arches from a height of 4 or 5 feet, which made a large hole through the arch, without doing any further injury. If mortar be used the parts must be thicker, and the centering left, until the work has set. Portland and Roman cement might be better than gypsum for work in England. Rondelet also states that it is better to use coved arches springing from the four walls, than a common arch springing from two opposite walls only.

1903*c*. The *arched brick floors,* used in the dwellings for workmen at Birkenhead, by the architect C. E. Lang, were 7 feet in span, worked in half brick except at the springing

and the skew-backs, with a few three-quarter and other parts of bricks inserted, so as to form a toothing or vertical bond with the concrete with which the spandrels were filled. The six or seven courses at the crown were wedged in with slate while the mortar was wet, and in no instance did the least subsidence take place at the crown, although subjected to very severe trials, such as that of men jumping from the walls upon the arches. The span of 7 feet is perhaps the limit of a half-brick arch turned in mortar with the ordinary rough brick. The arches rise about one inch to every foot in span. Tiles were laid in mortar on the concrete, which made the thickness of the floor at the crown of the arch 5¾ inches. There were altogether about 1200 arches of this kind turned, and without the slightest accident. This explains the usual method of forming fireproof floors, by turning brick arches between iron girders, which are in large spans tied together at the springing by iron tie rods; a subject which has been so often considered and discussed, and nowhere more so than at the Institute of Architects, as detailed in their *Transactions*.

1903*d*. The *Dennett arch*. A fireproof system, invented by Messrs. Dennett, of Nottingham, and used for the last twelve years. They execute a groin, dome, or circular ceiling of any length, width, or height, without tie rods or intermediate supports, at much less cost than can be done by any other fireproof material: circular ceilings of 36 feet diameter, with coffers in them, or any amount of decoration can be executed on the soffits, and the upper surface can be finished smooth in itself, or with stone, wood, tiles, cement, or asphalte, and a current of air ensured underneath. Very few iron girders are required. For floors, although in an arched shape, it is in reality a beam, as a complete floor can be turned from wall to wall, resting on a projection of brickwork, and the material be left without any abutment. Its durability equals stone; and its strength is equal to brickwork. The floors are bad conductors of heat; leave no harbour for vermin; ventilating pipes may be laid in them, and also flues. The material can be used for a sound proof construction, when laid in the old method between wood joists.

1903*e*. Three courses of plain tiles laid in cement and well bonded have been for many years employed for slightly curved roofs to form terraces; roofs for cellars under paving; as roofs over small back buildings, and for similar purposes. Where the walls are well backed up, tie rods may not be necessary. It has been asserted that the tiles should *not* be covered with the cement. Portland or other cements laid on brick arches, or on tile, or on a flat concrete roof supported by iron joists; also asphalted roofs; all generally crack and let in wet, especially where there is any traffic on them, or their foundations are not perfectly stable. At Austin and Seeley's artificial stone works, New Road, flat roofs, floors and steps are formed in their material. The terrace roofing is formed of plain tiles in three courses, rendered on the top to the thickness in all of about 4 inches, carried over by arches slightly cambered, springing from small brick piers, and tied by light iron rods, which form their chord line. These flats have an immense weight upon them, and are cast in one piece, as it were, there being no perceptible joint; they are completely water-tight, and can be easily cleaned.

1903*f*. Light arches may likewise be formed by placing thin *iron plates* between joisting of iron or wood, bending them to a slight curve, and filling in above them with concrete to form solid work. *Mallet's buckled wrought iron plates*, are usually made in square or oblong shapes, having a slight convexity in the middle, and a flat rim round the edge, called the *fillet*. These plates are considered the best form yet devised for the iron covering of a platform, and are usable for the above purposes. They are often placed so that the convex part is compressed, and the flat fillet stretched; when they give way under an excessive load, it is usually by the crushing or crippling of the convex part. The safe loads given in the tables published by the inventor, for a plate 3 feet square, ¼ inch thick, and with 1·75 inch of curvature, are 4·5 tons for a steady load, and 3 tons for a moving load. The square form, supported and fastened at all the four edges, is the most favourable to strength. The buckled plates used by Mr. Page for the platform of new Westminster bridge measure 84 inches by 36 inches, with a curvature of 3¼ inches, and thickness of ¼ inch; they bear 17 tons on the centre without giving way (Rankine, *Civil Engineering*).

1903*g*. In India, where all buildings of any importance have *flat roofs*, the long established practice is to form them of tiles, mostly 12 inches square and 1½ inches thick; in Calcutta they are generally 18 inches square and 2 inches thick. These tiles are made with great care: they are burnt the same as pottery, and are used both for roofing and for flooring. In roofing a room of 20 feet span, it is first covered with teak beams 12 inches deep by 8½ inches broad, placed 3 feet apart, which carry *burgahs* or joists, 3 inches square, fixed 1 foot apart, and on these the tiles are placed in two layers carefully jointed with each other. Above them is laid 6 inches of concrete, formed of broken bricks and lime, spread evenly and beaten down to 4 inches, and beaten until the mass is dry; finally it is plastered, and rubbed or polished. If well made and of good materials, it is impervious to wet, and will last as long as the timber under it.

1903*h*. A floor, or even a flat roof, patented by Bunnett in 1858, is formed of hollow bricks having the two sides each composed of two parallel inclines, and each about half the depth of the block, connected by a horizontal or nearly horizontal plane, and the two

inclines on one side are parallel with those on the opposite side. Through these bricks, tie rods are passed and secured at each end to wall plates formed of angle iron ; the whole is then screwed up, when the bricks form a slight curved arch in section, and from the inclined sides they over and underlap one another and mutually give and receive support from the neighbouring blocks. This invention has been carried to 21 feet span with a rise of about $2\frac{3}{4}$ inches, and about 13 feet wide. Other arches have been constructed for the purpose of testing its bearing powers. One of the latter, 15 feet between the bearing walls, and 2 feet 3 inches wide, was loaded with 4 tons 10 lbs. (or 267 lbs. to the square foot), and was quite elastic. The deflection was about $\frac{9}{16}$ths of an inch. The bricks are put together with Portland cement and sand. Each brick is $10\frac{3}{8}$ inches long, by $9\frac{3}{8}$ inches wide, and 6 inches thick ; and weighs 21 lbs. 100 square feet comprise: —

	ton.	cwt.	qrs.	lbs.
145 bricks, weighing - - - - - - -	1	7	0	21
Cement and sand - - - - - - - -	0	2	3	19
Angle iron and tension bars (bars being 4 feet apart) -	0	2	2	5
Total weight per square - - - - - -	1	12	2	17

1903*i*. Pots and jars and hollow bricks have all been used in arched work to reduce its weight. Sir John Soane employed jars in the dome of the Rotunda at the Bank of England, which is about 65 feet in diameter. In floors of arched work either iron ties must be used to prevent the walls being forced out, or iron girders employed, thus subdividing the length, and the work arched across the length, i. e. between each girder. The *Builder* of 1849 records the use of hollow bricks in the vaulting of St. George's Hall, at Liverpool ; and Daly's *Revue Générale* for the same year, the use of such bricks in walls.

1903*k*. The Indians about Nagpore, build their *stone vaults* in a peculiar method, which might be followed with advantage in some cases in this country. At the springing, stones of a considerable depth are used, having the intrados cut to the form of the curve, six courses are laid, the upper one having a groove five inches wide and two deep. Then stones of a smaller depth are laid, each having a groove cut in one face, 2 inches in depth and 4 inches in breadth, with a corresponding projection in their other face, the groove being on the upper side to receive the projection formed in the next course. About eight courses having been laid, it then becomes necessary to prevent the work from falling inwards. At every 10 feet in length two strong rods are placed horizontally across the chasm, and the ends are forced into the grooves. From these courses as from a new base, similar grooved stones to those already described are continued, the length of each course contracting until the key course is inserted. When this last course is completed, the rods are sawn across at either end of the finished vault, and the work continued. When the arch or vault is of considerable span, a series of bases may be adopted, each at higher points than the other, until one part is keyed. A slight scaffolding supports the workman, but no frame or centering is used.

1903*l*. CONCRETE AND CEMENT BLOCKS. Blocks formed of Roman cement, puzzuolana, lime, and sand, were soon suggested for such a purpose. Those made without the cement were found to be longer in setting, but eventually became the strongest. To these combinations, potsherds were added, as Pliny relates was in use in the time of the Romans, increased toughness resulted. The late Mr. Walker, engineer, possessed specimens of Dutch terras, which had been used in Woolwich dockyard in the reign of George III. These were of very great hardness ; in fact, gunpowder had to be used in breaking up the dock where it had been employed. For concrete and mortar for the river wall of the Houses of Parliament he used 2 measures of sand, 1 of puzzuolana, and 1 of lime. Mr. Lee used Portland cement, Portland stone chippings, sand, and shingle, in blocks in cubes of 16 feet and upwards, made in moulds, for the breakwater at Dover. Mr. Blashfield had made experiments for that work, with Lancashire terras mixed with broken tiles and sand ; but it was not deemed equal in hardness to the Portland cement concrete blocks.

1903*m*. The use of *concrete* has extended from the foundations of buildings, backings of wharfs and retaining walls, to the employment of it for the backing of vaults to produce a level surface ; for the substance of fireproof floors ; for the base of floors, pavements, and roads ; for backing to the abutments of arches ; and in the shape of pisè work for the walls, floors, &c. of houses, bridges, and moles, by French, if not, as in some cases, by English, engineers.

1903*n*. *Atkinson's* or *Mulgrave cement* was used by its patentee for concrete blocks of shingle, sand, and cement, used as ashlar stone, in the case of a house at the corner of Mount Street, Grosvenor Square, still standing in a substantial condition. Concrete in small blocks, known as *Ranger's patent artificial stone*, has been used to a limited extent in the construction of domestic buildings. It was employed in the additions to the College of Surgeons, Lincoln's Inn Fields, 1835-6 ; a guard-house in St. James's Park ; the Imperial Assurance Office, in Pall Mall ; and in a row of houses in the Western Road, at Brighton, partly in blocks and partly in moulds as pisè work. This process is not continued, probably from the mortar not being properly mixed in the first instance, and the

concrete being exposed too soon to the action of the weather, for it dries unevenly and cracks in all directions.

1903o. *Buckwell's Granitic Breccia stone* was patented about 1858 to compete with brick-work in price; its strength and durability being greater, and its bulk and weight considerably less. It was impermeable to wet and never vegetated, so that for pavements, and linings for tanks, it appears to have answered well; but for some reason not ascertained, the manu-facture of it was lately given up. It could have been manufactured in a single piece, of a weight varying from 1 cwt. to 60 tons or more; also in slabs from 5 feet to 100 feet super-ficial; and to any contour. *Wheeble's Reading Abbey patent concrete stone*, formed with Bridge-water stone lime, when made into a brick, was found to be equal in strength to a common stock. Some specimens never attained the strength of concrete except in a case where large gravel or flint was the chief ingredient. *Messrs. Bodmer's patent compressed stone bricks,* compounded chiefly of 1 part of hydraulic lime and 7 of siliceous sand, well mixed, are subjected to great pressure in moulds. Upon removal, the bricks are piled up in the open air, when induration commences, and the material is converted into stone. They appear to be ready for use after six weeks' to two months' exposure, and experiments show a steady progressive increase in strength as they advance in age. When eleven days old they crushed at 3·77 tons; at twenty-two weeks from 5·4 to 6·95 tons; and at sixty-three weeks a pressure of upwards of 8 tons was reached without effect.

1903p. *Coignet's Béton Agglomeré* has been employed in France in the construction of a church in the park of Vésinet near St. Germain, from the designs of M. Boileau, and into the construction of which he has also introduced cast and wrought iron. The *béton* is formed with all the mouldings of Gothic architecture both externally and internally. It was built similarly to pisè work, though it is also applicable for blocks, like stone, in which manner he has lately executed some bridges of 140 feet span. The very hard frosts of January 1865 had not appeared to have had any effect on the *béton* at the church, which was being executed at the time, and is described in the *Builder* for November 1864; views are also given in the volume for 1865. It is stated that such structures cost only about one-half or perhaps one-third of the expense of a stone building, with greater decoration.

1904. Many ornamental brick cornices may be formed by but little cutting, and chang-ing the position of the bricks employed, and several, indeed, without cutting, by chamfer-ing only. Of late years the machines for making bricks have permitted the extensive use of moulded bricks of different forms, which have entirely superseded the more artistic advantages of cut brickwork to required outlines or ornamental details.

1905. *Niches* may be formed in brickwork. They constitute the most difficult part of the bricklayer's practice. The centre will be described under the section CARPENTRY. The difficulty in forming them arises from the thinness to which the bricks must be reduced at the inner circle, as they cannot extend beyond the thickness of one brick at the crown or top, it being the usual as well as much the neatest method to make all the courses standing.

1906. TILING is the operation of laying the tiles on a roof for the covering of the building, and is effected with either plain or pan tiles; the former is the most secure description. Plain tiles are laid at different gauges, (see par. 2301). 210 plain tiles laid flat will cover a square of tiling which can be laid in a day by a man and his assistant. As old tiles are of a much better consistency than those now made, it may be desirable to re-use the best of them with new tiles to fill in; in which case the old ones are laid with the best effect in courses, say three or four rows of new tiles and two of old tiles; or laid in a diapered pattern, according to the quantity. Pan tiles are generally pointed in mortar, which if it be not very strong will not stick; in consequence of this, tile roofs require fresh pointing every few years, especially in exposed situations. A practice has obtained of late years, when plain tiles are set in mortar, not to peg more than about one tile in ten; this should not be permitted, as with the decay of the mortar the tiles slip down. An ancient custom pre-vailed, to bed the tiles in hay or moss, and when the roof is of the *full pitch* this suffices without mortar; they may even then be laid dry. But with any less pitch, some precau-tion must be used to keep out drifting snow, and such wet as may be blown up between the tiles lifted by the force of the wind. In lieu of oak pegs, extra large flat headed wrought nails, made of pure zinc or of zinc and copper, have been used, and it has the advantage of allowing a tile to be replaced from the *inside* of the roof, by lifting up the others to place in the tile and drop in the nails in a few seconds. The utility of the mortar is questioned in the *Builder* for 1865.

1907. Pan tiling is laid to a 10 inch gauge; and 180 pan tiles will cover a square. From the frequent repairs necessary to tiled roofs, slating has become the most useful covering, and is generally employed, except for the most common buildings. See par. 2301.

1908. The tiler's tools are—the *lathing hammer*, with two gauge marks on it, one at 7 ins., the other at 7½ inches. The *lathing staff*, of iron, in the form of a cross, to stay the cross laths and clinch the nails. The *tiling trowel*, to take up the mortar and lay it on the tiles: it differs from the brick trowel, in being longer and narrower. The *bosse*, made of wood, with an iron hook, to hang on the laths or on a ladder, for holding the mortar and tiles. The *striker*, a piece of lath about 10 inches long, for separating and taking away the

superfluous mortar at the feet of the tiles. The *broom*, to sweep the tiling after it is struck.

1908*a*. The bricklayer has often to provide temporary COVERINGS to buildings whilst his or other operations are being performed. The commonest method is that of merely nailing old boards laid weather-board fashion to any slope that may be desirable. The next is the use of tarpaulins supported by open boarding, and secured to posts or scaffolding rigged up for the purpose; this must be efficiently done, as in case of high winds the whole may be carried away. Felt is also used for temporary roofs, for which purpose, likewise, Messrs. Rigg and Co. have a new material composed of canvas covered with a water-proofing substance having vegetable oil as a basis, and consequently not liable to the desiccating action of the rays of the sun.

1908*b*. PAVING. When neither slate, granite, Yorkshire or other stone, flint, nor shells, are used for paving, recourse is had to bricks, tiles, and asphalte. A yard superficial of *brick paving* requires 32 to 36 stocks laid flat; 48 to 52 laid on edge; 36 paving bricks laid flat, 82 on edge; 140 Dutch clinkers on edge; 9 twelve inch tiles; and 13 ten inch tiles. Brick paving is laid *flat* in sand; jointed in mortar; jointed in cement; and laid *on edge*, in the same manner. Tile paving is generally laid in sand or mortar, (par. 2282). Besides the ordinary brick, some others have been introduced, especially for stables and yards, such as the *Terro metallic grooved bricks*; and the *Adamantine clinker*, which is said to be superior to the *Dutch clinker* in shape, colour, density, and wear (par. 1830). The second is made near Little Bytham Station, on the Great Northern Railway. The clay contains the unusually high proportion of 69 per cent. of silica.

1908*c*. Ordinary *tile paving* is made of about 8, 9, 10, 11, or 12, inch tiles of a hard and well burnt clay. The 11 inch tiles used in the footpaths, which are each 14 feet 6 inches wide, of new Westminster bridge, were made by Blashfield, and are laid diagonally, (par. 1839). The Staffordshire paving tiles, in blue, red, and buff, are very durable, and for general purposes as effective as the more expensive qualities for inlaid purposes. It will be sufficient here to notice the use of encaustic or inlaid tiles for paving, and of mosaic tiles for the same purpose; and of tesseræ for mosaic work, whether for pavements or for wall decorations.

1908*d*. ASPHALTE has now taken the place of most other sorts of manufactured pavements of the same character. A solid foundation is prepared by a bed of concrete of hydraulic lime and gravel, with a layer of finer concrete over it, to fill up the vacuities. When dry, the asphalte is put on, of a thickness for private purposes of about $\frac{2}{3}$ths. of an inch; for public purposes, one inch is not too much : it should be applied as hot as possible. A small quantity of pure quick lime is added to the asphalte when in ebullition, to prevent it melting by the heat of the sun. This material has been much used for thrashing floors of barns, for malt-houses, armouries, tun rooms, (sometimes from 2 to $2\frac{1}{4}$ inches thick), dissecting rooms, dog kennels, exercising yards, mills of many kinds, granaries, verandahs, and numerous factories and buildings. For carriage traffic, the asphalte is embedded with small Guernsey granite chippings. This material is *not* suitable for any floor where oil, tallow, or other greasy matter is employed. All the public paving laid in asphalte in London has been removed as unsatisfactory, the causes of which we are not fully informed : the public generally complain of the heaviness which is felt when walking over it, whereas stone gives a springing motion to the feet. The Polonceau and Seyssel Asphalte Company indent the surface into small squares affording a foothold for horses in a stable; this is also considered useful for flat roofs and paving generally. Wright's *marble tar pavement* for yards, play-grounds, &c. has been used for the platforms of the Windsor, and the Waterloo stations, and in the middle part of the quadrangle of Somerset House.

SECT. III.

MASONRY.

1909. Masonry is the science of preparing and combining stones so as to tooth, indent, or lie on each other, and become masses of walling and arching for the purposes of building. The tools of the mason vary as the quality of the stone upon which they are to act. About the metropolis the value of stone is considerable; and it is accordingly cut into slips and scantlings by a saw moved horizontally backwards and forwards by a labourer. In those parts where stone is abundant, it is divided into smaller scantlings by means of wedges. The principal tools of the mason are the *mallet* and *chisels*, the latter being formed of iron, except at the steel end, and the cutting edge being the vertical angle. The end of the chisel struck by the mallet is a small portion of a spherical surface, and projects on all sides beyond the adjoining part or hand hold, which increases in magnitude towards the middle of the tool, to the entering or cutting edge. The other tools of the mason are a

level, a plumb-rule, a square, a bevel, with straight and circular rules of divers sorts, for trying surfaces in the progressive states of the work.

1910. In London, the tools used to work the face of a stone are, successively, the *point*, the *inch tool*, the *boaster* (the operation of working with which is called *boasting*, as that with the point is called *pointing*), and the *broad tool*. The use of the point leaves the stone in narrow furrows, with rough ridges between them, which are cut away by the inch tool, and the whole made smooth by the boaster. The point is from $\frac{1}{8}$ to $\frac{3}{8}$ of an inch broad, the boaster is 2 inches wide, and the broad tool $3\frac{1}{2}$ inches at the cutting edge, which in use is always kept perpendicular to the same side of the stone. It performs two sorts of operations. Thus, imagine the impression made by the whole breadth of the tool at the cutting edge, to be called a cavity; in one operation, the successive cavities follow one another in the same straight line; until the breadth or length of the stone is exhausted; successive equidistant parallel lines are then repeated in the same manner, until the tool has passed over the whole surface. This operation produces a sort of fluted surface, and is called *stroking*. In the other operation, each successive cavity is repeated in new equidistant lines throughout the length or breadth of the stone; then a new series of cavities is repeated throughout the length and breadth of the stone; and thus until its whole length or breadth is gone through. This operation is called *tooling*. The tools for working the cylindrical and conical parts of mouldings are of all sizes, from $\frac{1}{8}$ of an inch upwards. Those for working convex mouldings are not less than half an inch broad, except the space be too confined to admit of such breadth.

1911. A stone is taken out of winding principally with points, and finished with the inch tool. In London, the squared stone used for facing buildings is usually stroked, tooled, or rubbed.

1912. In those parts of the country where the stone saved by the operation of sawing is not enough to compensate for the labour, the operation is altogether performed with the mallet and chisel.

1913. When stones, previous to the operation of hewing, are very unshapely, a *stone axe*, *jedding axe*, *scabbling-hammer*, or *cavil*, is used to bring the stone nearly to a shape; one end of the jedding axe is flat, and is used for knocking off the most protuberant angular parts, when less than right angles; the other end is pointed for reducing the different surfaces to nearly the intended form.

1914. In Scotland, besides the above described sorts of work, there are some other kinds, termed *droved*, *broached*, and *striped*. Droving is the same as that called random tooling in England, or boasting in London. The chisel for broaching is called a *punch*, and is the same as that called a point in England. Broached work is first droved and then broached, as the work cannot at once be regularly done with the punch. Striped work must also be first droved and then striped. If broaching is performed without droving, which is sometimes done, it is never so regular, and the surface is full of inequalities. Of the three kinds of surfaces obtained, the droved is the cheapest.

1915. It is, however, to be observed, that the workmen will not take the same pains to drove the face of a stone which is to be afterwards broached, as in that of which the droving is to remain the final finish. When the surface of stone is required to be perfectly smooth, it is accomplished by rubbing with sand or gritstone, and it is called rubbed work.

1915a. Some useful practical remarks for obtaining the face to stone in mediæval work, is given in Denison's *Lectures on Church Building*, 1856, p. 216. " The mode of working mouldings depends a good deal upon the kind of stone used. In that from Steetly near Worksop, employed almost exclusively outside the new church at Doncaster, and in the Ancaster stone, used for pieces of window tracery and mullions too large for the blocks that can be got from Steetly, and in the Brodsworth stone, the mouldings are all completed with a *drag*. I do not use the word ' finished,' because that means going over the work to put a particular kind of surface upon it after it is really completed. On the other hand, the Crookhill stone, of which all the pillars and a few other parts are made, would utterly defy any such small tooth-comb work, as a drag; nothing under a chisel with a heavy hammer will touch it. Again, some stone from Huddlestone is too tough and cheese-like for dragging, and the mouldings in it are completed by shaving them with a chisel, something like wood carving. The effect of that is very good, because a chisel run along in that way will always make a rather undulating surface, though smooth enough to the touch, even to please the finger of a clerk of the works. In some real Norman arches, which had been covered with plaster for centuries, the mouldings showed that the drag or tool had never been allowed to make the marks directly across; generally they are oblique and sometimes parallel to the direction of the moulding. Worked in this way, the stones will be sure to show themselves distinctly, and the effect of the mortar staining the stones for a little distance from the joints, produces anything but a bad effect. Tuck-pointing, to rather rough masonry especially, *i. e.*, making prominent joints in mortar, with the edges cut quite straight and square, is another chance of spoiling work. After a few years this generally splits off," and the building may look at last as it should have done at first. The mortar should be finished within the face of the stone.

1915b. Grey granite, or moorstone as it is called in Cornwall, is got out in blocks by splitting it with a number of wedges applied to notches *pooled* in the surface of the stone, about four inches apart. The *pool holes* are sunk with the point of a *pick*, much in the same way as other hard quarry stones are split. The harder the moorstone the nearer it can be split to the scantling required. Generally speaking, granite has no planes of stratification, and it works or cleaves equally well in every direction; but in the porphyritic varieties there is a rough kind of arrangement of the crystals; and in gneiss there is a species of layer, formed by plates of the mica, which is plainly discernible. When brought to near the size required, it is first *scabbled* by a hammer with a cutting face 4½ inches long by 1½ inches wide, weighing 22 lbs.; then brought to a *picked face* with a pick or pointed hammer weighing 20 lbs., formed by two acute angled triangles, joined base to base by a parallelogram between them thus ◁ o ▷ ; and if to be *finely wrought or fine picked*, it is further dressed with a similar pointed hammer, reducing the roughness to a minimun. The finer finish or *fine axed face* is produced by a hammer or axe with a sharp edge on both sides, weighing 9 lbs.; for *fine work* the "patent axe" is also used, which is a hammer formed of several parallel blades screwed together, capable of being taken to pieces when required to be sharpened. Polishing can then be done by machinery, the granite being rubbed by iron rubbers with fine sand and water, and finished with other materials.

1915c. Aberdeen red granite possesses the property common to all granites, that of a distinct plane of cleavage, which, though not perceptible to the eye, is at once recognisable under the hammer of the workman, and of course can be wrought with much greater precision and effect with the bed, than transversely to it. This bed bears no traceable relation to the natural joints of the rocks, which are indefinite in their directions; and still less so to their stratification. The grey granites are but slightly affected with cleavage, being capable of being *blocked* with the hammer with about equal facility in every direction. The local varieties of worked granite differ somewhat from those used in England, and are, I. *Hammer-blocked*, as in foundations, plinths, &c. II. *Scappled blocks*, squared with the heavy pick, as in docks and heavy engineering works. III. *Picked*, a better finish than No. II. IV. *Close picked*, the bed and arrises made fair, and the outer surfaces made as fine as the pick will make them; used in ashlar work, &c. V. *Single axed*, a finer finish than No. IV., and used in quoins, rebates, cornices, &c., in house building. And VI. *Fine axed*, the finest finish before polishing, given to dressed granite by means of the *patent axe*, used in the best work in house building, cemetery memorials, and as a finish to contrast with polished work.

WALLING.

1916. In stone walling the bedding joints are usually horizontal, and this should always, indeed, be so when the top of the wall is terminated horizontally. In building bridges, and in the masonry of fence walls upon inclined surfaces, the bedding joints may follow the general direction of the work.

1916a. Footings of stone walls should be built with stones as large as may be, squared and of equal thicknesses in the same course, and care should be had to place the broadest bed downwards. The vertical joints of an upper course are never to be allowed to fall over those below, that is, they must be made, as it is called, to *break joints*. If the walls of the superstructure be thin, the stones composing the foundations may be disposed so that their length may reach across each course from one side of the wall to the other. When the walls are thick, and there is difficulty in procuring stones long enough to reach across the foundations, every second stone in the course may be a whole stone in breadth, and each interval may consist of two stones of equal breadth, that is, placing header and stretcher alternately. If those stones cannot conveniently be had, from one side of the wall lay a header and stretcher alternately, and from the other side another series of stones in the same manner, so that the length of each header may be two thirds, and the breadth of each stretcher one third of the breadth of the wall, and so that the back of each header may come in contact with the back of an opposite stretcher, and the side of that header may come in contact with the side of the header adjoining the said stretcher. In foundations of some breadth, for which stones cannot be procured of a length equal to two thirds the breadth of the foundation, the works should be built so that the upright joints of any course may fall on the middle of the length of the stones in the course below, and so that the back of each stone in any course may fall on the solid of a stone or stones in the lower course.

1917. The foundation should consist of several courses, each decreasing in breadth as they rise by sets off on each side of 3 or 4 inches in ordinary cases. The number of courses is necessarily regulated by the weight of the wall and by the size of the stones whereof these foundations or footings are composed.

1918. Walls are most commonly built with an ashlar facing, and backed with brick or rubble-work. In London, where stone is dear, the backing is generally of brick-work, which does not occur in the north and other parts, where stone is cheap and common. Walls faced with ashlar, and backed with brick or uncoursed rubble, are liable to become

convex on the outside from the greater number of joints, and, consequently, from the greater quantity of mortar placed in each joint, as the shrinking of the mortar will be in proportion to the quantity ; and therefore such a wall is inferior to one wherein the facing and backing are of the same kind, and built with equal care, even supposing both sides to be of uncoursed rubble, than which there is no worse description of walling. Where a wall consists of an ashlar facing outside, and the inside is coursed rubble, the courses at the back should be as high as possible, and the beds should contain very little mortar. In Scotland, where there is abundance of stone, and where the ashlar faces are exceedingly well executed, they generally back with uncoursed rubble ; in the north of England, where they are not quite so particular with their ashlar facings, they are much more particular in coursing the backings. Coursed rubble and brick backings admit of an easy introduction of bond timber. In good masonry, however, wooden bonds should not be continued in length ; and they often weaken the masonry when used in great quantity, making the wall liable to bend where they are inserted. Indeed, it is better to introduce only such small pieces, and with the fibres of the wood perpendicular to the face of the wall, as are required for the fastenings of battens and dressings.

1919. In ashlar facing, the stones usually rise from 28 to 30 inches in length, 12 inches in height, and 8 or 9 inches in thickness. Although the upper and lower beds of an ashlar, as well as the vertical joints, should be at right angles to the face of the stone, and the face and vertical joints at right angles to the beds in an ashlar facing ; yet, when the stones run nearly of the same thickness, it is of some advantage, in respect of bond, that the back of the stone be inclined to the face, and that all the backs thus inclined should run in the same direction ; because a small degree of lap is thus obtained in the setting of the next course, whereas, if the backs are parallel to the front, no lap can take place when the stones run of an equal depth in the thickness of the wall. It is, moreover, advantageous to select the stones so that a thicker one and a thinner one may follow each other alternately. The disposition of the stones in the next superior course should follow the same order as in the inferior course, and every vertical joint should fall as nearly as possible in the middle of the stone below.

1920. In every course of ashlar facing in which the backing is brick or rubble, *bond*, or, as they are called in the country, *through* stones should be introduced, their number being proportioned to the length of the course ; every one of which stones, if a superior course, should fall in the middle between every two like stones in the course below. And this disposition should be strictly attended to in all long courses. Some masons, in carrying up their work, to show that they have introduced a sufficient number of bond stones into their work, choose their bond stones of greater length than the thickness of the wall, and knock or cut off their ends afterwards. But this is a bad practice, as the wall is liable to be shaken by the force used in reducing, by chiselling or otherwise cutting away the projecting part, and sometimes with the chance even of splitting the bond stone itself.

1921. In piers, where the jambs are coursed with ashlar in front, every alternate jamb stone should go through the wall, with its bed perfectly level. If the jamb stones are of one entire height, as is often the case when architraves are wrought upon them, and also upon the lintel crowning them, of the stones at the ends of the courses of the pier which are to adjoin the architrave jamb, every alternate stone should be a bond stone ; and if the piers be very narrow between the apertures, no other bond stones will be necessary in such short courses. When the piers are wide, the number of bond stones is to be proportioned to the space. Bond stones, too, must be particularly attended to in long courses above and below windows. They should have their sides parallel, and of course perpendicular to each other, and their horizontal dimension in the face of the work should never be less than the vertical one. The vertical joints, after receding about three quarters of an inch from the face of the work with a close joint, should widen gradually to the back, so as to form hollow wedge-like figures for the reception of mortar and *packing*. The adjoining stones should have their beds and vertical joints filled with oil-putty, from the face to about three-quarters of an inch inwards, and the remaining part of the beds with well-prepared mortar. Putty cement is very durable, and will remain prominent when many stones are in a state of dilapidation, through the action of the atmosphere upon them. The use of the oil-putty is at first disagreeable, from the oil spreading over the surface of the contiguous stones ; but after a time this unpleasant look disappears, and the work seems as though of one piece.

1922. All the stones of an ashlar facing ought to be laid on their natural beds. From inattention to this circumstance, the stones often flush at the joints ; and, indeed, such a position of the lamina much sooner admits the destructive action of the air to take place. Methods of building in cement and concrete blocks, are noticed in the previous section.

1922a. RUBBLE-WORK. A wall consisting of unhewn stone is called a *rubble* wall, whether or not mortar is used. This species of work is of two kinds, coursed and uncoursed. In the former, the stones are gauged and dressed by the hammer, and thrown into different heaps, each

containing stones of the same thickness. The masonry is then laid in horizontal courses, but not always confined to the same thickness. The uncoursed rubble wall is formed by laying the stones in the wall as they come to hand, without gauging or sorting, being prepared only by knocking off the sharp angles with the thick end of the scabbling hammer.

1922b. Apparently, wherever there was any difficulty in obtaining stone, the mediæval builders employed the worst of all methods of construction in walling, viz., concrete or rubble-work between the two faces of squared stone. In the early period of mediæval art, flint or rough rubble, with "short and long work" to the quoins, seems to have been very general; this "short and long work" was also used in faced walls; in both cases the short work consists of stone upon its bed, and alternates with the long work or stone upright: the short work ought to serve as bond throughout the walls. In the 12th century the use of rubble in conjunction with worked stone became frequent. The chief defect, frequently considered one of the merits, of this system, consists in the omission of sufficient bond both in piers and walls; the occurrence of joints in angles is too frequent; in fact, any expedient seemed better than the trouble of making a back-joint.

1922c. KENTISH RAGSTONE. This material, now so extensively employed for mediæval work in the metropolis and suburbs, is never used internally, as it sweats, that is, the condensed moisture from the atmosphere is not absorbed, and will show itself even through two coats of plastering. Hassock stone, however, which is the sandstone separating the beds of the ragstone, the sand being sufficiently agglutinated to allow of its being raised in blocks, must never be used externally. It is easily worked, and makes a good lining for ragstone walls, as it does not sweat. It should be roughly squared, for if not done, the crumbling nature of the stone would endanger the security of the work, should it be exposed to any unequal pressure: it must not be placed where it would be exposed to very great pressure, as in arches, jambs, &c. Hassock may be procured in London at from 6s. to 7s. per cord (3 feet cube), in roughly squared pieces; while rough rag is about 5s. per ton, and rag headers about 12s. 6d. per ton.

1922d. Sunk and moulded work in so hard a material is to be avoided, and so much wrought surface would cause decay. In using ragstone ashlar, it must be laid upon its natural bed, otherwise rapid decay will almost certainly follow, arising from the thinness of the strata, for blocks of a large size can seldom be entirely freed from hassock; and even what appears to the eye as blue stone, retains for a considerable distance inward the perishing nature of its enveloping crust. A block of ragstone, if the face be worked, will present in damp weather an appearance precisely similar to the heart and sap of timber. In the case of copings, &c., where one bed is exposed, the stone should be skiffled (or knobbled) as much as possible from the upper side, so as to expose only the soundest portion of the stone to the action of the atmosphere. In some situations, as mullions, door and window jambs, an unsightly appearance would be produced by too exact an attention to the beds of the stone, as the ashlar is generally too small to range with more than one course of headers. In these cases the old masons seem to have departed from their usual rule, and to have set the blocks on end, so as to embrace two or three courses; but as the depth of the block required to work an ordinary jamb or mullion is not very great, it is not difficult to get the whole thickness required out of the heart of the stone.

1922e. Stone of the smaller layings are generally worked into headers; it is common to work one side of the stone to a rough face with parallel sides, without paying much attention to the beds and joints, which often recede at an acute angle with the face, so as to bring the stones, when laid, to a closer joint. Such stones, however, must be properly pinned in behind, and carefully bonded with the work at back. Headers are generally knocked out to six, seven, eight, or nine inch gauge for the height; the length and tail being determined by the size of the stone: on the face they do not vary much from the square form. Formerly headers were set on their natural bed, therefore it is not unusual to find stones in an old wall entirely gone from this cause.

1922f. In the Whitelands bridge bed, a very free working stone of a bluish colour can be got 12 feet long with certainty, and the Horsebridge bed yields a good stone to a length of 15 feet. The white rag, the lowest of the beds in the quarry, tumbles to pieces on exposure to the air (Whichcord, Kentish Ragstone, 1846).

1922g. In its mechanical properties, ragstone possesses some of the qualities of granite, though in an inferior degree. In respect to resistance to pressure, it stands next to granite in the list of British stones; but when loaded for a transverse strain, the numerous vents to which even the best layings are liable, renders it untrustworthy for lintels, or in a suspended position, without much precaution. In the former case of lintels and architraves, three stones, arch jointed, gives the requisite security.

1922h. WHINSTONE, a material, in one form or another, found almost over all Scotland, makes a very durable arch for bridge work, when well built with good mortar, the stone being in its nature weather proof. In the neighbourhood of Edinburgh, whinstone arches have been erected since about 1770, the greatest span being about 60 feet. The Messrs.

Smith, of Darnick, stated, in the *Transactions* of the Institute of British Architects, that they had erected bridges with semi-elliptical arches of the spans of 51 feet, and of 62½ feet, of whinstone faced with hewn stone. A bridge, almost entirely of whinstone, having an arch 63½ feet span, the depth of the masonry being 2½ feet on the average, was erected in 1833 ; while another, 76 feet 4 inches span, at Falshope, was entirely of whinstone, with a rise of about 18 feet. It sunk about seven inches when the centre was struck, but no broken stone was observed. The depth of the arch, requiring three breadths of stone to make it up, was 3 feet; their average thickness was 3½ inches ; but it varied from 1½ to 6 inches. The stones were laid as close as possible, and in crossing the bond the work was made firm, but the stones were not dressed straight upon the beds. Its cost was 360*l.* exclusive of the digging for the foundations.

1922*i*. The most annoying part in the building of rubble arches, is the slowness of the setting or drying of the mortar, as until the mortar is able to bear considerable resistance the arch is extremely supple, and easily bent out of its proper curve when the centre is struck. This bridge stood five weeks before that measure was considered advisable. Cement would perhaps be best for large rubble arches, and even if expensive, the whole cost would be cheaper than a bridge of hewn stone. With cement, almost any kind of stone, even the refuse of a slate quarry, might be worked into an arch of almost any extent.

1922*k*. Flintwork.—In the chalk districts, the houses of the fifteenth century are frequently faced with flints, cut and trimmed, and arranged with great skill and effect. One of the best examples is a house in St. Andrew's, at Norwich, next the cemetery, a fragment of the decorated period of Gothic architecture, in which the flint work is so delicately finished that a penknife can scarcely be inserted in the interstices.

1922*l*. As flint itself is practically imperishable, and as flintwork becomes, when perfectly set, a mass of concrete, it produces substantial work, if great care be taken in its manipulation. But flint walls frequently fail, by bulging while they are in course of construction, and splitting when they are old. On any sufficient natural cause, as the giving way of the foundation, they are riven into immense masses ; hence a flint building gets out of repair less readily than a stone one, but if it suffer at all, it is very apt to become a complete ruin.

1922*m*. Flint walls intended for durability should not be less than two feet in thickness, built slowly and solidly, flushed up with stiff strong mortar compounded of quick-setting stone lime and coarse sharp sand free from loam. As flint is a non-absorbent, bricks and tiles are often worked into the middle of the walls to assist in the induration of the mortar ; but for the sake of economy, lumps of hard chalk, pebbles, and flat-bedded stones are frequently used as the principal components of the *core* or middle of the wall. The work must be kept as dry as possible during its erection, as well as subsequently ; frost is found soon to level the work while saturated with water.

1922*n*. Flint walls are strengthened by *lacing courses*, formed of bricks three or four courses deep, not generally showing outside. At Cambridge, Brandon, and elsewhere, they do show, and are used every two or three feet. The object is not only to get a continuous bond, but to bring the work to a level bed, and again start fair. When round flints are split, and the thicker portion is kept, as usual, at the face of the wall, driving rains are readily conducted by the inclination of the upper bed of each course to the middle of the wall, and by keeping it damp conduce to its decay ; but as flints are seldom split at right angles to their axis, they can be so laid in the work as to be flush on the face as well as level, and the lower bed must be firmly pinned up with fragments. It is desirable that cavities for drainage, with exit holes at the plinth level, be formed in the middle of the wall by building in rods of wood or iron vertically, and drawing them up as the work progresses. The face is sometimes finished by inserting in the mortar joints *gallets*, or the sharp fractured bits of flint, when the work is called *galleted* or *garreted* (*Dictionary of Architecture*).

1922*o*. Amongst examples of a systematic parsimony of labour and material in mediæval art, may be noticed the characteristic *tables* or courses, where each projection

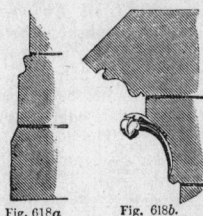

is taken out of a separate course of stone or out of the smallest stone adjoining to it. The base (*fig.* 618*a.*) and the capital (*fig.* 618*b.*) of a shaft are kept so small as to be got out of single blocks; the astragal belongs to the capital, and not, as in Roman work, to the shaft; the bell is in one stone, the abacus in another (*fig.* 618*d.*); each *order* of an arch is an independent range of stones; the hoodmould is self-existent ; the sills are not dished, and the buttresses are toothed rather than bonded. In two cases, however, the use of large stones prevailed, viz., in shafts of the 13th century (in France, 1160–1230), which are long rods of stone 6, 4, or 3 inches in diameter

Fig. 618*a*   Fig. 618*b.*

and incapable of bearing any great weight, unless banded or bonded to the nearest wall or

pillar, and in the springing stones of vaulting, which are worked with level beds. (See par. 2002*f.*) The horizontal courses at the bottom of the arch are also seen in the construction of large horse-shoe arches. With the 13th century, also came the decided distinction between decoration and mere construction, which employed stone vertically, not only for shafts of columns, but for mullions and tracery of windows and dwarf walls, such tracery being cut out of slabs and confined by grooves or similar means.

1923. Where walls or insulated pillars of very small dimensions are to be carried up, every stone should be carefully bedded level, and be without concavity in the middle. If the beds should be concave, as soon as the superimposed weight comes to be borne by the pier or pillar, the joints will in all probability begin to flush ; and it is, moreover, better, if it be possible, to make every course in the masonry of such a pier or pillar in one stone.

COLUMNS.

1924. When large columns are obtained in a single block, their effect, from that circumstance alone, is very striking ; but as this is not very often to be accomplished, the next point is to have as few and as small joints as possible ; and the different stones, moreover, ought to be selected with the view, as much as possible, of concealing the joints, by having the blocks as much of the same colour as possible. It will immediately, of course, occur to the reader that vertical joints in columns are inadmissible, though in many of the great edifices at Paris such do occur, much to their detriment.

1925. The stones for an intended column being procured, and the order in which they are to be placed upon one another having been determined, we must correctly ascertain the exact diameter for the two ends of each of them. To effect this, draw an elevation of the column proposed to its full size, divide it by lines parallel to the base into as many heights as the column is intended to contain stones, taking care that none of the heights exceed the lengths the stones will produce ; the working of the stones to the diameters thus obtained then becomes easy. The ends of each stone must first be wrought so as to form exactly true and parallel planes. The two beds of a stone being thus formed, find their centres, and describe a circle on each of them ; divide these circles into the same number of equal parts, which may, for example, amount to six or eight ; draw lines across each end of the stone, so that they will pass through the centre and through the opposite divisions of the same end. The extremities of these lines are to regulate the progress of the chisel along the surface of the stone ; and, therefore, when those of one end have been drawn, those of the other must be made in the same plane or opposite to them respectively. The cylindrical part of the stones must be wrought with the assistance of a straight-edge ; but for the swell of a column, a diminishing rule, that is, one made concave to the line of the column, must be employed. This diminishing rule will also serve to plumb the stones in setting them. If it be made the whole length of the column, the heights into which the elevation of the column is divided should be marked upon it, so that it may be applied to give each stone its proper curvature. But as the use of a very long diminishing rule is inconvenient when the stones are in many and short lengths, rules or rods may be employed corresponding in length to the different height.

1925*a.* The method of setting the blocks or *frustra* by the ancients, was to *dish out* the beds to obtain a truly fine joint. In the Parthenon, an outer space of 7 inches in width all round the drum, was left a perfectly level and smooth bed for actual contact. The next space, of 1 foot in width, was very slightly tooled or scratched over. The next, 9 inches in width, was made still lower by being tooled over very roughly. The remaining portion round the centre was left smooth, but was made as low as the surface of the second space. A square hole, worked at the quarry, in the centre of the shaft, was filled with a cube of hard wood, in which was a hole to receive the half of a circular pin, also of wood, suggesting the idea that when the marble *frustra* were set, they were rubbed against each other. The first drum, at the temple of Hercules at Agrigentum, when placed on the stylobate, was turned round until it had been well ground down. (*Civil Engineer, &c.* vii. p. 241.) The practice of late years, for large columns, has been to place a plate of thin lead between the beds of stone, so as to secure an equal bearing and prevent the edges flushing, any space being filled in with putty or cement. At Paris, in many of the porticoes, the columns have very deep thin rustics (*fig.* 618*c.*), which would effectually prevent any broken edges from being observed. The effect is peculiar, especially in strong sunlight. The height of the face of the stone is ·385 of a metre ; the height of the channel, including the founded arrises, is ·40, and the depth of the channel is ·85.

Fig. 618*c.*

1925*b.* Besides the usual mode of drawing a volute, described in par. 2576, we insert a method recommended by Mr. Gwilt for adoption. A general method of inscribing a spiral in a rectangular quadrilateral, A B C D :—Multiply the given height by the given

breadth, and divide the product by the sum of the height and breadth. Then subtract the quotient from the height. The remainder is the radius of the first quarter revolution of the spiral : The formula is

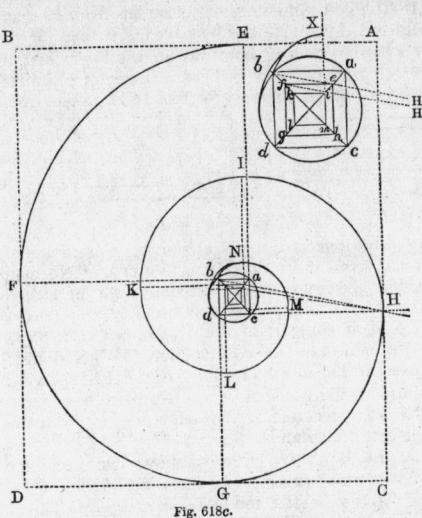

Fig. 618c.

$h - \dfrac{h \times b}{h + b} = r \ (= BE, b\,a \text{ or } F\,a)$. Subtract the radius aF so found from the height BD and the remainder FD will be the radius of the second quarter of the revolution, and is to be set from F to b. The difference $a\,b$ between a F and b F will form one side of the quadrilateral $abcd$. Subtract the radius Fb from the width CD and the remainder GC will give bd the other side of the quadrilateral $abcd$ (which points will be the centres for the portions of the first revolution), and will be a figure similar to, or of the same proportions as, the given quadrilateral ABCD. Then dG will be the radius of the third quarter of the revolution and Hc the radius of the fourth quarter. In the quadrilateral or parallelogram $abcd$, draw the diagonals ad, bc, and draw bH, cutting the diagonal ad in e, then will e be a point for the formation on the diagonals of another parallelogram $efgh$, whose angles (as in that first made) will be the centres for the radii of the second revolution. By again drawing Hf to cut the diagonal ad, another parallelogram may be formed, and so on to bring out the spiral. X is the centre part to a larger scale (*Builder*, xviii. p. 364).

1925c. From the nature of the formula it is evident that when $h : b$ is but by a trifle in a greater ratio than 1·61 : 1 the first radius will be greater than the breadth of the quadrilateral, and the spiral cannot be described within the figure. Also that when h and b are equal, the spiral vanishes, for the formula becomes $h - \dfrac{h^2}{2h}$ and the first radius is equal to half the side of the circumscribing square. Hence a circle is inscribed. Also that as the height and breadth approach equality the number of revolutions increases. In the diagram the height is taken at 27 equal parts and the breadth at 23 of such parts. Upon trial it will be found that the exact proportion of the height to the breadth to bring out a spiral within the given quadrilateral lies between 1·61 : 1 and 1·62 : 1.

1925d. When a *pier* was to stand upon the head of a pillar, the early mediæval builders avoided an error which their ancestors often committed. Instead of turning the arches and filling up the space at the springing until there was a clean base for the pier (*fig.* 618d.), they built some courses of the arch-stones in single blocks exceeding the width of the pillar. When these had risen so high that the base of the pier would not interfere with the

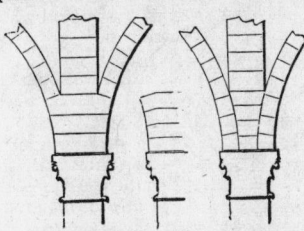

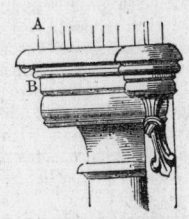

Fig. 618d.   Fig. 618f.   Fig. 618e.   Fig. 618g.   WESTMINSTER ABBEY.

Fig. 618h.

arch-stones, these horizontal courses were discontinued (*fig.* 618e.). A modern folly (*fig.* 618f.) was unknown to them. A similar system dictates the construction of a corbelled foundation for any work standing free from the general thickness of the wall. In early pointed work the intrados of an arch (as A in *figs.* 618g. and 618h.) was plumb with the face of the square block B, forming part of the capital ; and equally the front of a shaft over a capital is plumb with the same square block.

1925e. JOGGLING. Lintels or flat arches, stone architraves, chimney mantels, and such like, when formed of small stones, are secured by joggling the joints of adjacent stones so as to form a continuous beam, the strength depending upon the solidity of the abutments. The gauged arches formed of cut bricks and used as heads to openings, are similar in

effect, but as they have neither joggles nor dowels, they are now sometimes assisted, especially in uncertain foundations, by placing under them a thin flat bar of wrought iron. Bartholomew, in his *Specifications*, 1840, gives some ancient specimens from Roman sepulchres, the three lower courses being prevented from sliding by a wedge-shaped joggle formed on the top bed of one stone, and a corresponding hole cut in the lower bed of the next stone, to receive it. *Fig. 618i.* is perhaps the earliest instance of a similar contrivance, and shows the oversailing portions (French *crossettes*). It is taken from

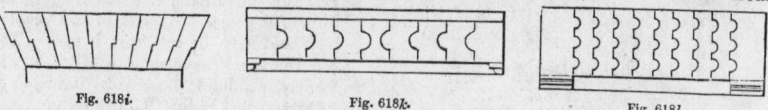

Fig. 618i.   Fig. 618k.   Fig. 618l.

Diocletian's palace at Spalato, a building often referred to as exhibiting the germs of several of the peculiar ornaments afterwards prevalent in the Romanesque and Norman styles of art (par. 198). The same principle is seen in a semicircular arch of eleven voussoirs in the lower story of the reputed tomb of Theodoric at Ravenna ; in a chimney-piece at Conisborough Castle, Yorkshire ; and at the gate of the Alhambra. Murphy's *Batalha*, gives, in plate 2, two instances of the same kind of construction. With double set-offs, an example is found in the upper part of Theodoric's tomb. *Fig. 618k.*, showing the introduction of tenons of a circular form, is the transom of the Norman west door-way of Rochester Cathedral. *Fig. 618l.* having three tenons to each stone, is from the mantel of a fireplace in Edlingham Castle, Northumberland.

1925f. Serlio, in his *Opere d'Architettura*, in Book iv. chap. v., shows two excellent modes for relieving the weight from a lintel over an opening, *figs. 618m.* and 618n. *Fig.*

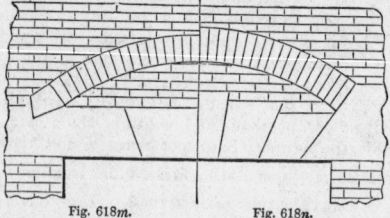

Fig. 618m.   Fig. 618n.

618o. is the mode adopted by Mylne, in erecting Blackfriars Bridge, where each joggle consists of a cube foot of a hard stone. During the repairs of this structure in 1833, the decayed or broken stones were cut out, and new blocks inserted by the in-genious arrangement shown in *fig. 618p*. A represents the new block let in, in two parts. B is first fixed, having a hole cut to receive a plug C, which is placed in a hole in the half D ; on this block being inserted in place, the plug C drops half its length into the hole in B and secures the portion D. Channels were also cut through the blocks, through which wires were placed attached to the plug to insure its sliding into its place. These were cemented up subsequently. In small works, copper plugs, or dowels would be more proper than the large blocks shown in *fig. 618o.*, as they require the removal of less of the substance of the arch stones as necessary for admitting joggles. Cubes, and dowels, of slate are now very much employed.

1925g. Another method much practised consists in joining, by an elbow to each voussoir, a portion of the neighbouring horizontal course of the work. This arrangement will be understood at once by reference to *figs. 956* and 957 ; but, however good it may appear at first sight, it is liable to split at the junction of the horizontal portion with the radial parts, if any irregular settlement takes place. The rustic channels of arcades wrought in this form have, however, a good effect.

1925h. From Viollet le Duc, *Dictionnaire*, we obtain the use of the *crossettes* as exemplified in a chimneypiece (*fig. 618q.*). *Fig. 618r.* is the lintel to the door on the north side of the Church of St.

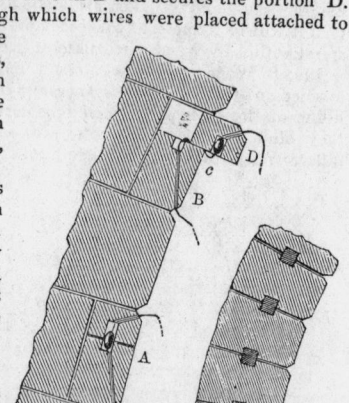

Fig. 618p. BLACKFRIAR'S BRIDGE. Fig. 618o.

Etienne at Beauvais; and *fig. 618s.* that of the Church of Villers Saint Paul. *Fig. 618t.* shows the system described by Rondelet, in plate 27 of his valuable publication, for ob-taining the requisite proportion of strength in such flat arches, as they are called. Who-ever may be interested in the method of supporting and tying together by rods and bars, the stones of architraves, as formerly practised by the eminent architects of France, must be referred to the publications of Rondelet, Patte, D'Aviler, Blondel, and others of that period; in fact, the system is still introduced in the modern publications on con-struction, in the French school of architecture.

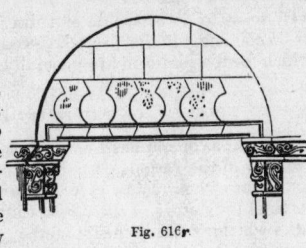

1925i. To tie in ashlering to the brick wall, cramps are used, either of cast iron, wrought iron, copper, or bronze. The two latter are of course the best; the two former exfoliating by air and damp, and splitting the stone, unless perfectly

Fig. 616r.

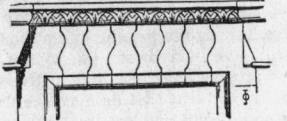

Fig. 618s.

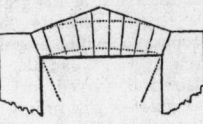

Fig. 618t.

Fig. 618q.

secured. During the restorations at Cologne Cathedral, the cornice (above the 55 feet high windows) is 3 feet 7 inches high, and in order to connect the stones, iron hooks were put hot into the holes, which were then filled up and surrounded with asphalte. By this proceeding the iron is for ever preserved from oxidation; it has proved itself the best system, because the applications of mortar, gypsum, sulphur and lead, have all failed. On the exterior, bronze surrounded with lead has been used, which has hitherto proved satisfactory. Cramps are also now set in Portland cement.

STAIRS.

1926. Nothing to perplex will occur in carrying up stairs which are supported by a wall at both ends, because the inner ends of the steps may either terminate in a solid *newel*, or be tailed into a wall surrounding an open newel. Where elegance is not required, and where the newel does not exceed 2 feet 6 inches, the ends of the steps may be conveniently supported by a solid pillar; but when the newel is thicker, a thin wall surrounding the newel would be cheaper. In stairs to basement stories, where geometrical stairs are used above, the steps next to the newel are generally supported upon a dwarf wall:

1927. In *geometrical stairs*, the outer end of each step is fixed in the wall, and one of the edges of every step supported by the edge of the step below, and formed with *joggled* joints, so that no step can descend in the inclined direction of the plane nor in a vertical direction; the sally of every joint forms an exterior obtuse angle on the lower part of the upper step, called a back rebate, and that on the upper part of the lower step of course an interior one, and the joint formed of these sallies is called a *joggle*, which may be level from the face of the risers to about one inch within the joint. Thus the plane of the tread of each step is continued one inch within the surface of each riser; the lower part of the joint is a narrow surface, perpendicular to the inclined direction or soffit of the stair at the end next to the newel.

1928. With most sorts of stone the thickness of every step at the thinnest place need not exceed 2 inches for steps of 4 feet in length; that is, measuring from the interior angle of every step perpendicular to the rake. The thickness of steps at the interior angle should be proportioned to their length; but allowing that the thickness of the steps at each of the interior angles is sufficient at 2 inches, then will the thickness of them at the interior angles be half the number of inches that the length of the steps is in feet; for instance, a step 5 feet long would be 2½ inches at that place.

1929. The stone platforms of geometrical stairs, that is, the *landings, half paces,* and *quarter paces,* are constructed of one or more stones, as they can be procured of sufficient size. When the platform consists of two or more stones, the first of them is laid on the last step that is set, and one end tailed in and wedged into the wall; the next stone is joggled or rebated into the one just set, and the end also fixed into the wall, as that and the preceding steps also are; and every stone in succession, till the platform is completed. When another flight of steps is required, the last or uppermost platform becomes the spring stone for the first step of it, whose joint is to be joggled, as well as that of each succeeding step, similarly to those of the first flight. The principle upon which stone geometrical stairs are constructed is, that every body must be supported by three points placed out of a straight line; and therefore, that if two edges of a body in different directions be secured to another body, the two bodies will be immoveable in respect to each other. This last case occurs in the geometrical staircase, one end of each stair stone being tailed into the

wall so as to be incapable of tilting, and another edge resting either on the ground itself, or on the edge of the preceding stair stone or platform, as the case may be. The stones which form a platform are generally of the same thickness as those forming the steps.

ON THE SCIENTIFIC OPERATIONS OF STONE CUTTING.

1930. The operations by which the forms of stones are determined, so as to combine them properly in the various parts of an edifice, are founded on strictly geometrical principles, and require the greatest care and exactness in execution. It is only by a thorough knowledge of the nature of these operations that the master mason is able to cut and carve the parts which, when joined together, compose the graceful arch, the light tracery of the Gothic vault, or the graceful and magnificent dome. The method of simple walling, and its general principles, have been given in this book, chap. i. sect. x. In what follows we propose to confine ourselves, 1st, to the leading operations necessary to *set out* the simple arch or vault, and the groins formed by it; 2d, to the forms produced by vaults with plain and curved surfaces intersecting; 3d, and lastly, to dome vaulting; giving such examples as will so initiate the student that he may, we trust, have little, if any, difficulty in resolving any case that may occur, and reminding him that if he well understand the section already submitted to him on Descriptive Geometry, his labour will be much abridged, not only in what immediately follows, but in that section which treats hereafter on Carpentry.

1931. I. Of the Construction of Arches and simple Vaults, and the Groins formed by their Intersection. In arches and simple vaults we have to ascertain the exact form of the arch in all its parts, and the direction of its joints; both which points are dependent on the geometrical properties of the curve used for the arch.

1932. *To find the joints of a flat arch without using the centre of the circle of which the arch is a part.* Divide the arch AB (*fig.* 619.) into as many equal parts as there are intended to be arch stones, at the points 1, 2, 3, &c. From A, with any convenient radius, describe an arc at *a*, and from 2, with the same radius, describe another arc, crossing the first at *a*, and join *a*1; then 1 is the first joint from A. To find the joint

Fig. 619.

passing through 2; with the same radius as before, from the joints 1 and 3 as centres, describe arcs cutting each other at *b*, and draw 2*b*; then 2*b* is the second joint. In the same manner all the other joints between A and B will be found. To find the *skew backs,* or abutting joints AC and DB; with a radius equal to 1*a*, from the centre A describe an arc at C; from the centre 1, with the radius A*a*, describe an arc cutting the former at C, and draw the line AC, which will be the springing bed of the arch. In the same manner the joint BD may be found.

1933. The joints of any arch may be drawn with considerable accuracy by setting off at equal distances a point in the curve on each side of the place for the joint, and from these points, as centres, with any radius, arcs to intersect, through whose intersections lines being drawn, will give the directions of the joints.

1934. *To draw an elliptical arch to any two dimensions by circular arcs.* Draw the straight line AB (*fig.* 620.). Bisect AB in C by the perpendicular D*g*, make CA and CB each

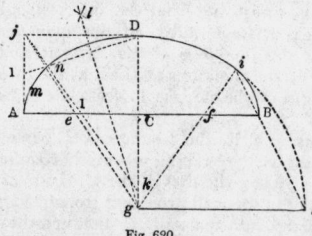

Fig. 620.

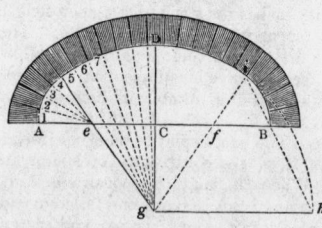

Fig. 621.

equal to half the span of the arch, and make CD equal to the height, and A*j* parallel and equal to CD. In C*g* make C*k* equal to CD. Divide A*j* and AC each into two equal parts. Through 1 in AC draw *kn*, and through 1 in A*j* draw 1D, cutting *kn* at *n*. Bisect *n*D by the perpendicular *lg*, and from *g* with the radius *gn* or *g*D describe the arc *n*D*ih*. Draw *gh* parallel to AB, and join *h*B, and produce *h*B to meet the arc *n*D*ih* in *i*. Join *gi* cutting AB in *f* and make C*e* equal to C*f*. Join *ge*, and produce it to meet the arc *n*D*h* in *n*. From *f* with the radius *fi* describe the arc *i*B, and from *e* with the radius *e*A describe the arc A*mn*. Then A*m*D*i*B is the arch required.

1935. *An elliptical arch* ADB (*fig.* 621.) *being given, to draw the joints for a given number*

of arch stones. Find the centres *e, f, g* in the same manner as if the arch were to be drawn; join *ge* and produce it to meet the arch; also join *g, f* and produce it to meet the arc in *i.* Divide the elliptical curve ADB into as many equal parts as the number of arch stones. From the centre *e* draw lines through the points of division in the curve between A and

where *ge* meets the curve, and from the centre *g* draw lines through all the intermediate points between *ge* and *gf*, and lastly draw lines from *f* through all the intermediate points between *i* and B, and the parts of the lines thus drawn on the outside of the curve will be the joints of the arch stones.

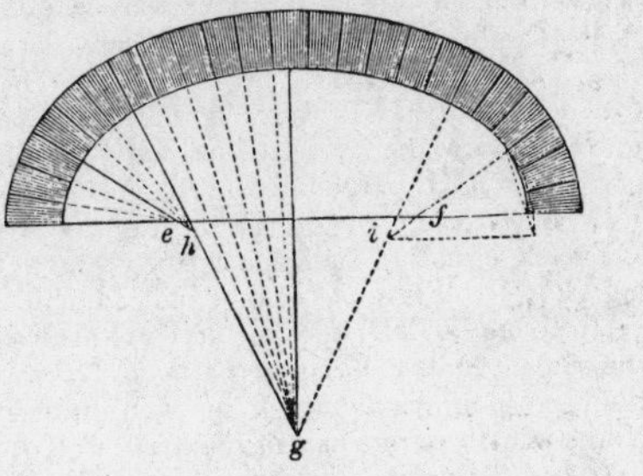

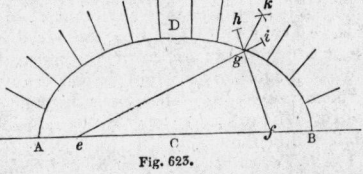

1936. In very large arches it will be desirable to find five centres, as in *fig.* 622., and these will be obtained by finding two intermediate points in each half of the curve instead of one; then bisecting each pair of adjacent points by a perpendicular, we shall have the centres *e, h, g, i, f*, to be used for drawing the joints in the same manner as in the preceding figure.

Fig. 622.

1937. The above methods are sufficient for ordinary purposes; but where strict accuracy is required, the following method is mathematically true. Suppose any joint, as *gk*, is required to be drawn (*fig.* 623.), and that the point D is the middle of the arch and the point C the middle of the springing line; then with the distance CA or CB, from the point D describe an arc at *e* and another at *f* to cut AB at *e* and *f*. Draw *eg* and *fg*; produce *eg* to *i* and *fg* to *h*, bisect *hgi* by the straight line *gk*, which will be the joint required. In the same manner, by drawing

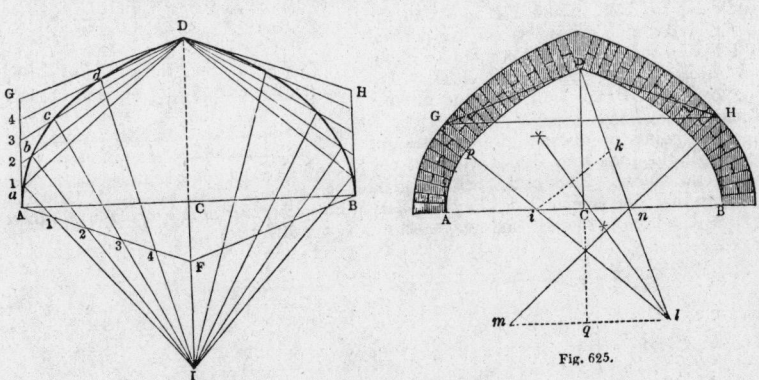

Fig. 623.

lines from *e* and *f* to each point of division, and bisecting the angle, lines for the other joints may be drawn.

1938. *To draw a Gothic arch to any given dimensions* (*fig.* 624.). Draw the straight line

Fig. 624.   (CI is made equal to BC.)

Fig. 625.

AB equal in length to the span of the arch. Bisect AB in C by the perpendicular DI, and draw AG and BH parallel to DI. Make CD equal to the height of the arch, and the angles CDG and CDH each equal to half the vertical angle; make CF equal to the difference between CD and AG and join FA and FB. Divide AG and AF each into the same number of equal parts, counting each from the point A. Through the points 1, 2, 3, 4 in AF draw I*a*, I*b*, I*c*, I*d*, and through the points 1, 2, 3, 4 in AG draw 1D, 2D, 3D, 4D cutting I*a*, I*b*, I*c*, I*d* at the points *a, b, c, d*, then through the points A*abcd*D draw a curve; which will be half of the Gothic arch required. (Other methods, *par.* 1943*a.*, *et seq.*)

1939. *To draw the joints of the arch stones of a Gothic arch* (*fig.* 625.). Having formed the angles CDG and CDH as before, make A*i* equal to AG and draw D*l* perpendicular to DG. In D*l* make D*k* equal to A*i* and join *ik*. Bisect *ik* by a perpendicular meeting D*l* in *l*. Produce *li* to *p*. Divide the curve into as many equal parts as the arch stones are to be in number. Then *i* will be the centre of the joints which pass through all the

points between A and p, and l will be the centre for drawing the joints of the arch stones which pass through all the points between p and D.

1940. The reason for the foregoing rule is obvious; for the joints are merely made to radiate to the centres of the arcs of circles whereof the arches themselves are formed; as in subsections 1934, 1935, they were drawn to the centres of the approximating circles wherefrom the elliptical curves were struck.

1941. *To describe a parabolic curve for a pointed or Gothic arch by means of a series of lines touching the curve, the dimensions of the arch and the angles it forms at the crown being given.* Draw the straight line AB (*fig.* 626.) and draw CD perpendicular to AB. Make CD equal to the height of the arch, CA and CB each equal to half the span. Make the angles CDe and CDf each equal to half the vertical angle. Divide Ae and eD each into the same number of equal parts, and through the corresponding points of division draw lines which will form one half of the arch: the other half DB may be found in the same manner.

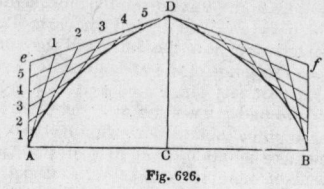

Fig. 626.

1942. *To draw the joints of the arch stones to the above sort of arch.* Draw the chords AD, DB for each half of the arch (*fig.* 627.); divide the arch into as many equal parts as there are to be arch stones. Let it now be required to draw a joint to any point h: bisect AD in k, and join ek cutting the curve in l. Draw hg parallel to Ak, cutting ek in g, and in el make li equal to lg. Join hi and draw hm perpendicular to hi. Then hm is the joint required. In the same manner all the remaining joints will be found.

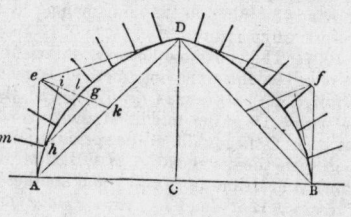

Fig. 627.

1943. *To describe a rampant pointed arch, whose span, perpendicular height, and the height of the ramp are given.* Draw the straight line AB (*fig.* 627.), and make AB equal to the span of the arch. Draw BC perpendicular to AB, and make BC equal to the height of the ramp. Bisect AC in D, and draw DE perpendicular to AB. Make DE equal to the height of the arch; draw Af and Cg parallel to DE, and make Af and Cg equal to about two thirds of DE. Join fE and Eg. Divide Af and fE each into the same number of equal parts, and through each two corresponding points of division draw a straight line. All the lines thus drawn will give one half of the curve. The other half may be drawn in the same manner. *To find the joints of the arch-stones to this sort of arch*, proceed as for a plain arch in the last example, as shown by *fig.* 629.

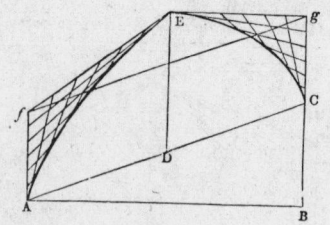

Fig. 628.

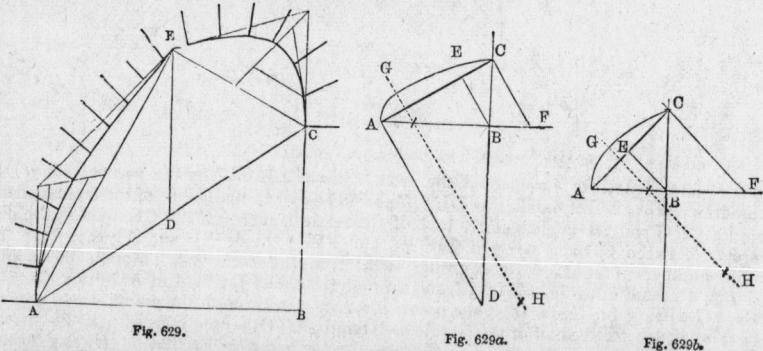

Fig. 629.   Fig. 629a.   Fig. 629b.

1943a. Besides the rule given in *par.* 1938, *To draw a Gothic arch to any given dimensions*, the following plan has been put forward for finding the curves of arches and ribs. The fundamental rule that the curves should spring from the line of the impost has been abandoned by many; one centre was to be taken a little above this line, another a little below it, and so on. The following rule furnishes a principle which gives the centres of all these curves with perfect certainty and perfect harmony, at the same time furnishing

what is a further requisite, an independent projection for each rib. The author insists that these curves were always elliptical. If the arch to be drawn be *less* in height than the half width, let AB, (*fig.* 629*a.*) be the half width; BC the height; join AC; draw lines from B and A perpendicular to AC, and the points E and D are those required. Then EC will be the smaller radius, and EC added to AD will be the longer radius. For arches whose height is *greater* than their half width (*fig.* 629*b.*), draw CF and BE perpendicular to AC, then EC will be the smaller radius; and EC added to CF will be the longer radius. The author of this theory is Thos. L'Aker, as read at the Liverpool Arch. Society, 16th October, 1850, and printed in the *Civil Engineer*, vol. xiii. p. 365. See *par.* 2002*d.*

1943*b.* Although the term *arc en tiers point* is still used in France for an arch enclosing an equilateral triangle, as it was in the time of De Lorme, that architect, in his work entitled *Nouvelles Inventions pour bien bastir*, published in 1578, showed that the *arc en tiers point* was obtained by division of the space into three equal portions, of which two gave the radius. The *arc en quatre points* was obtained by division into four, three of them giving the radius. This mediæval mode of determining some of the shapes of pointed arches, was noticed by Professor Willis in his elucidation of Wilars de Honecort's *Sketch-book*, 1859, p. 138–40. He is disposed to call the equilateral arch, the arch of two points; mentions arches of six points; and instances cases with a radius of five-sevenths and a radius of five-eighths, besides the occurrence of a centre placed to the extent of half the span outside the springing point. The same authority observes that the true method was forgotten soon after the disuse of mediæval art, as Viola Zanini, in his book *Della Architettura*, published 1629, defines the *terzo acuto* as the arch on an equilateral triangle, the *quarto acuto* as the arch on a square with the diameter for radius, and the *quinto acuto* on a pentagon : these last are respectively rather higher and lower than the true arch of four points. The term *point* is here used as meaning a division, and not a puncture.

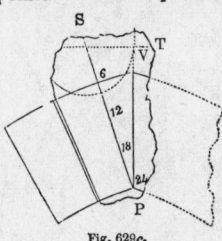

1943*c.* The Professor has also explained, p. 141, that to know the extra length of a voussoir at the top of an arch of 2, 3, 4, or 5 points, the radius may be prolonged through the point P (*fig.* 629*c.*) of the arch to any extent S; then PS being divided into twenty-four parts, a line from S may be drawn parallel with the springing line to T, and respectively 12, 6, 8, or 9 of those parts in length; which will give a point V, so that PV will be the line of the central point.

1943*d.* The construction of *ogee arches* is very simple; but as will presently be shown, the rule is open to judicious variation. The general principle is to draw the line of the nose Z, (*fig.* 629*d.*) of the hoodmould ; to take a point upon

Fig. 629*c.*

that line ; to draw from the springing a line through that point to the centre line, to accept the place where the centre line is cut as the height of the ogee, and to find in the usual manner the centre for the upper part of the ogee. The following directions are chiefly taken from Viollet le Duc, *Dict.*

1943*e.* *To draw an ogee arch of one point* (*fig.* 629*d.*). Bisect the span in D, draw the

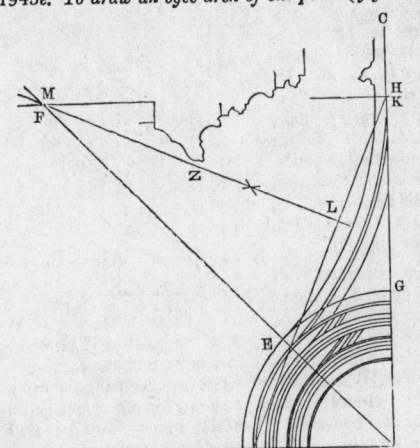

centre line CD, describe the arc AG, bisect AG in E, and through E from A draw a line cutting the centre line in H ; through H draw FK parallel to the springing line, and through E from D draw a line cutting FK at M, which will be the centre for the upper part of the ogee arch. In some cases, as in the figures 629*e, f,* and *h,* the three points KMN form an equilateral triangle.

1643*f.* *To draw an ogee arch of two points* (*fig.* 629*e.*). Bisect the span AB, draw the centre line, and describe the arcs AGB; then divide GB into five parts G1, &c., and proceed as before.

1943*g.* *To draw an ogee arch of three points* (*fig.* 629*f.*). Repeat the above operations, observing to divide the span AB into three parts, AE, EF, FB, and to divide GB into four parts, G1, &c. It will be observed that in *fig.* 629*g.* (from Pugin), AB is divided into three parts, and the centres E with

Fig. 629*d.*

F serve to describe the arcs on their own sides of the centre line ; that the distances AI, II, and IB are equal, and that EH is equal to EI.

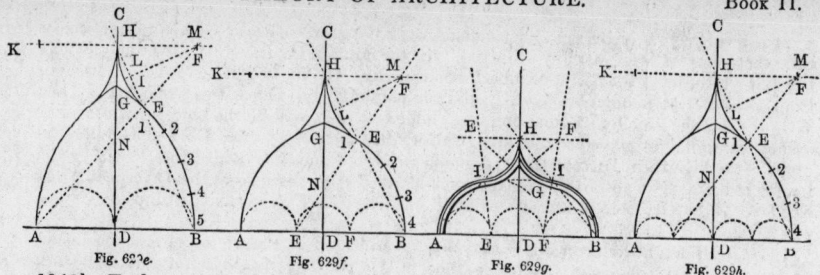

Fig. 629e.   Fig. 629f.   Fig. 629g.   Fig. 629h.

1943h. *To draw an ogee arch of four points* (*fig.* 629h.). Bisect the span, draw the centre line, fix

the four points, and describe the arcs AG, GB; then divide GB into *four* parts, and proceed as above indicated. But a difference is taught by an illustration adduced by Viollet le Duc, to show another feature of mediæval art. In *fig.* 629i. it will be observed that the arch GA is divided into *five* portions, and that the line AH is drawn through the second division. The line F2 produced, cuts the horizontal line JH in M; or 2H may be bisected, and a perpendicular obtained meets in the point M, for the ogee line 2H. A centre N has been assumed for the line RR; and also another centre, O, for the line PP, both lines being drawn each way from I; from which arrangement it results that the lines A2H, RIR, and PIP, are not parallel for their whole lengths. In some cases the line of work must be the centre of a fillet or of a

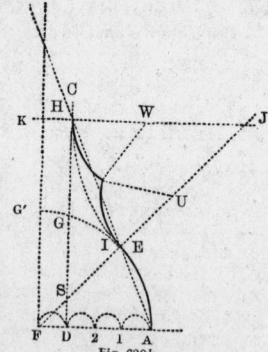

Fig. 629i.

boltel. It should be noticed that some very good decorated work of the middle of the 14th century, uses five-eighths of the space for the radius, and finds the centre of the ogee curve upon a line drawn from that central point of radius at an angle of 45° with the horizontal springing line.

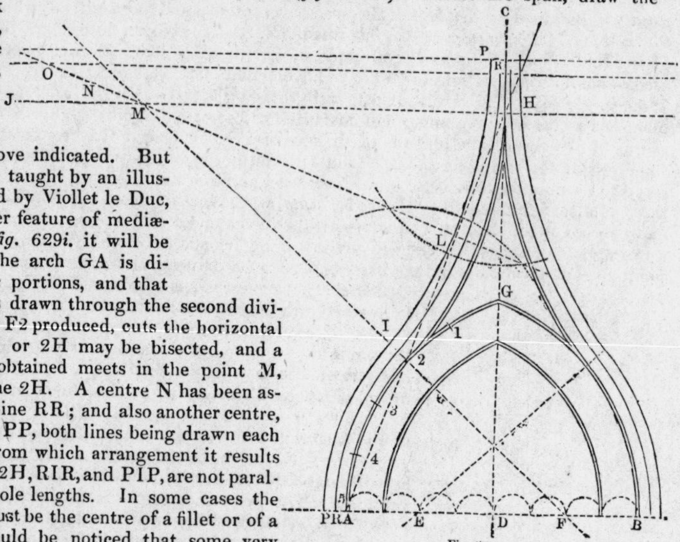

1943i. *To draw a cusped ogee arch* (*fig.* 629k.). Proceed as above described for an arch of one point as far as the construction of the horizontal line JK. Then from the centre F through E draw a line, and thereon make IU equal to IS, being so much of IF as is intercepted by the centre line of the pointed arch; and then on the horizontal line JK make WH equal to IS: thus are obtained the two centres for the cusp. But Viollet le Duc appears to prefer another mode, which very slightly differs in result. He draws SI produced at an angle of 45° with the base line; on this he marks G'U, which is the half of a semicircle, equal to GA, fixing IU, and continuing the process as in the former method.

1944. II. OF THE CONSTRUCTION OF INTERSECTING VAULTS OR GROINS. The forms of vaults may be so adapted to one another that the lines of intersection shall be in planes,

Fig. 629k.

and these planes the diagonals of the plan of the intersecting part of the vaults; if, however, they be not so adapted, the lines of intersection will be curved on the plan, and these curves it is necessary to ascertain in making both the moulds and the centerings for executing the work.

1945. *To determine the form of a vault to intersect with a given one in the plane of the diagonal, and also to find the diagonal rib for the centering.* Let the given vault be EIF (*fig.* 630.) and AC and BD the diagonals, crossing in *f*. Draw *f* I perpendicular to EF, cutting EF in *c*. In the arc IF take any number of points *ab*, and draw *ag*, *bh* parallel to I*f*, cutting EF in *d*, *e*, and the diagonal AC in *g*, *h*. Draw *fp*, *gq*, *hr* parallel to EF, cutting the base GH at *m*, *n*, *o*. Make *mp*, *nq*, *or*, each respectively equal to *c*I, *du*, *eb*. Draw *f*l', *gk*, *hl*, perpendicular to AC, and make *f*l', *gk*, *hl* respectively equal to *c*I, *da*, *eb*. Make

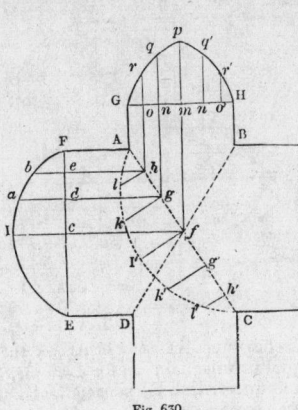

Fig. 630.

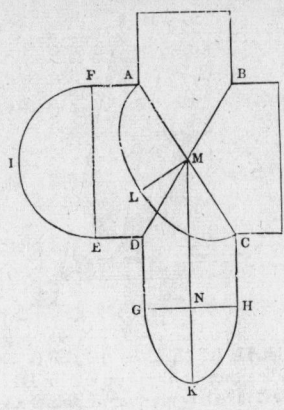

Fig. 631.

fg', fh' each respectively equal to fg, fh. Draw $g'k'$, $h'l'$ parallel to fl'. Make $g'k'$ equal to gk, $h'l'$ equal to hl; also make mn', $m'o'$ each respectively equal to mn, mo. Draw the arcs pqr, $p'q'r$, as also $l'kl$, $l'k'l'$; then, through the points thus found, draw the curves upon their bases AC and GH, and that on GH is the form of the intersecting vaults, and that on AC is the form of the angle rib. If the form of the given arch be that of a semicircle EIF (*fig.* 631.), let ABCD be the angular points of the plan, AC and DB the diagonals, cutting each other at M. Draw MK parallel to GD, or CH cutting GH in N. Draw ML perpendicular to AC, and make ML equal to the radius of the semicircle. Then, with the transverse axis AC, and semi-conjugate axis ML, describe a semi-ellipse, which will be one of the angle ribs, as required. Also make NK equal to the said radius; then with the lesser axis and the semi-greater axis NK describe the semi-ellipse GKH, which is the form of the other vault.

1946. The same method applies in *fig.* 632., where the narrow opening is a semi-circle

Fig. 632.

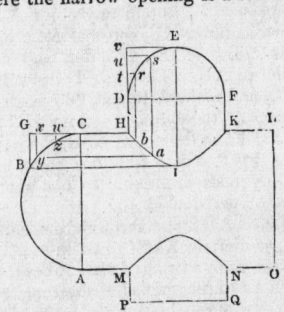

Fig. 633.

and the wide one, consequently, a semi-ellipse, having its minor axis vertical and its major axis horizontal.

1947. *When two circular-arched vaults of different heights intersect, to determine the plan of the arrisses in which the arches meet.* Let ABC (*fig.* 633.) be the arch of the main vault, and DEF that of the lesser vault; ACLO the plan of the main vault, and DPQF that of the lesser vault; and let the two vaults intersect each other at the points HKNM. Also, let E be the middle point of the lesser semi-circular arc DEF. Produce HD to v, and in the arch DE take any number of points rs, and draw rb, sa, EI parallel to DH. Draw rt, su, Ev parallel to DF, cutting Dv at the points tuv, and produce HC to G. In CG make Cw, Cx, CG respectively equal to Dt, Du, Dv, and draw wz, xy, GB parallel to AC, cutting the semi-circle ABC in the points zyB. From the points Byz draw BI, ya, zb, parallel to CL. Then through the points Iab draw a curve, which will be one half of the plan of the arris. The other half will be found in the same manner.

1948. The method of tracing the plan of the groins is the same (see *fig.* 634.) when the vaults intersect obliquely.

1949. *To find the plan of the intersections of two arches of the same height, and either of the same or different species.* Let the sections of the two arches be ABC and DEF (*fig.* 635.), the arcs AB, BC being equal to each other, and the arcs DE, EF equal to each other;

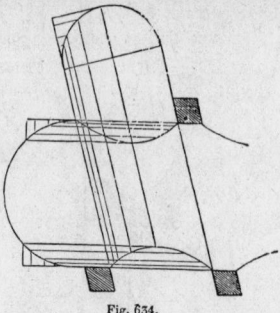

Fig. 634.

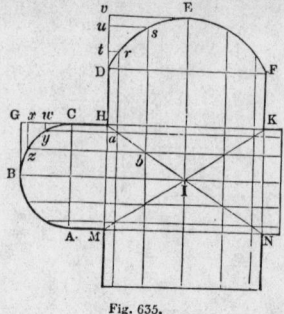

Fig. 635.

and let H, K, N, M be the points where the two arches intersect each other on the plan. Divide either of the arcs BC or DE into parts, equal or unequal; as, for example, in the arc DE take any number of points r, s at pleasure, and draw ra, sb, EI perpendicular to DF. Produce HD to v, and draw rt, su, Ev, parallel to DF, cutting Dv in t, u, v. Produce HC to G, and make Cw, Cx respectively equal to Dt, Du; and as the arches are equal in height, CG will be equal to Dv. Draw wy, xz, GB, parallel to AC, cutting the arc BC in the points y, z, and touching it in B. Draw ya, zb and BI parallel to HK, and through the points HabI draw the curve HabI, which will be half the plan of the groin as required. The other half IN and the other groin MK will be found in the same manner.

1950. *To find the plan of the groins produced by the intersection of a cylindric and a conic vault, the angle of position of the axis, the diameter of the cylinder, and the plan of the conic vault being given.* Let AB (*fig.* 636.) be the axis of the cylinder, CD that of the cone, C being the apex, and D the point through which the base passes. Through any point A in AB draw EF perpendicular to AB, and make AE and AF each equal to the radius of the cylinder, and draw EH and FI parallel to AB. Through D draw KM perpendicular to CD, and make DK and DM each equal to half the diameter of the cylinder. Join KC and MC, cutting EH and FI in the points N, O, P, Q. Divide the semicircles FGE and KLM into parts, whereof the corresponding ones are equal to one another. From the points of division in the semicircle EGF draw lines parallel to AB; and through the corresponding points in the semicircle KLM draw lines perpendicular to the diameter KM, cutting KM. From the points of section draw lines to the apex C of the cone, cutting the former drawn through the points in the semicircumference FGE. Through each set of corresponding points draw a curve, and the two curves will represent the arrises of the groin on the plan. If in an octagonal ground vault the octagonal range be cylinders, and the cross vaults, which tend to the centre, diminish to a line of the height of the vault, the following construction applies : — Let EFGHI (*fig.* 637.) be the exterior side of the vault, which is both equilateral and equiangular, and let JKLMN be the line of the exterior surface of the inner wall; so that the lines EJ, FK, GL, HM, IN, which pass through every two corresponding angles, may tend to the centre O of the ground vault. Let the sections of the given ribs be PQR and STU, so that PR of the rib PQR may stand at right angles to the sides EF and JK and the side SU of the rib STU on the middle of the side FG. Divide the two bases PR and SU in the same proportion, and through the joints of division in SU draw lines from the centre O of the ground vault to meet the curve STU; and

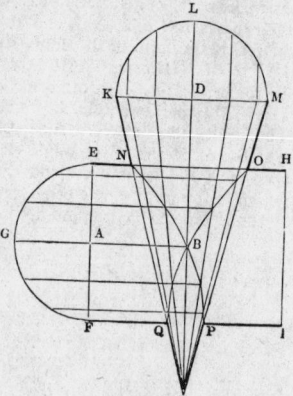

Fig. 636.

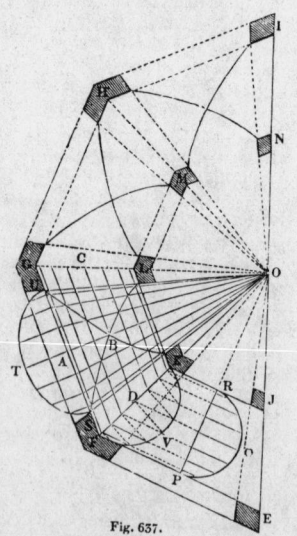

Fig. 637.

through the points of division in the base PR of the cross rib PQR draw lines parallel
to EF, to terminate in the line FK, and in the semicircle PQR. From the points where
these lines meet FK, draw perpendiculars on one side of FK, and make the heights of
these perpendiculars respectively equal to the ordinates of the arc PQR; and through the
ends of these perpendiculars draw a curve FVK, which will be the angle rib. From the
points of meeting in the line FK draw lines parallel to FG, and through the points of
division in SU draw lines to the centre O, intersecting the former lines drawn from the
points of division in FK; through the corresponding points of intersection draw the
curves SBL and KBU, which will form the plan of the angle.

1951. In single groins the centres are made for the widest avenue, and are covered over
with boards (*fig.* 638.), so that the top of the boards may form the surface required for

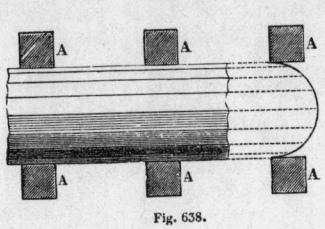

Fig. 638.

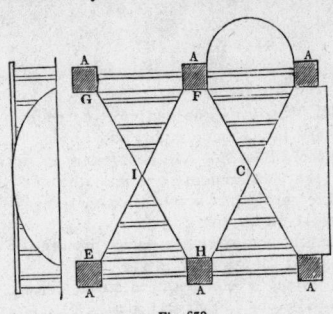

Fig. 639.

turning the arch upon the intersections; or the angles are found by the following practical
method. The groins meet in the points I, C (*fig.* 639.), upon the boarding of the two
groins. Place the straight edge of a board upon the point I, so as to range over the line
GH on the plan. Then set up another straight edge upon the point H, so as to be vertical,
and the straight vertical edge will meet the horizontal edge; then apply a third straight
edge to each of the other two straight edges, so that it may also come in contact with
the boarding. After this draw a line along this third straight edge upon the boarding as
far as may be found convenient; shift the moveable or third straight edge, and apply it in
the same manner to another adjoining portion of the surface of the boarding. Proceed in
the same manner until the whole line be completed on the surface. By this means, the
necessity of laying down lines for the covering is avoided. The lines being thus drawn,
ribs for the cross vaults are fixed on the top of the boarding; so that, making proper
allowance for the thickness of the same, its surface, when fixed, may form the true surface
of the other cross vault. The ribs fixed upon the boarding to form the cross vaults are
called *jack ribs.*

1952. The mode of constructing the curves by lines is shown for a rectangular groin in
fig. 640., in which A is the plan, B the elevation.
Here, to find the pliant moulds for forming the
groins on the surface of the boarding, and working
the arch-stones, describe a semicircle on one of its
sides, and divide it into any convenient number
of equal parts. Draw lines perpendicular to the
base or diameter, the semicircle being supposed to be
within the piers; the ordinates will cut the diagonals; but if it be laid down on the outside, the ordinates must be produced until they cut the diagonals. From the points where the ordinates cut the
curve, draw lines parallel to the other side of the
groin, and produce the side on which the diameter
of the semicircle is placed, and extend the semicircular arc with its divisions upon any convenient part
of the line thus produced. Through the points of
division draw perpendiculars, so as to intersect with
the former parallel lines; then through the points of
intersection draw the curve, as shown at C, which
will be the mould required.

1953. Sometimes several vaults meet in one common centre, as in *fig.* 641., which exhibits the plan
of an equiangular and equilateral groined vault,
constructed of semicircular arches.

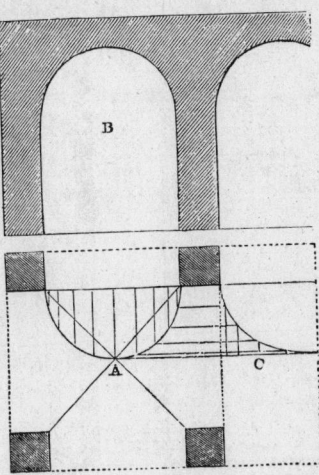

Fig. 640.

Fig. 641.

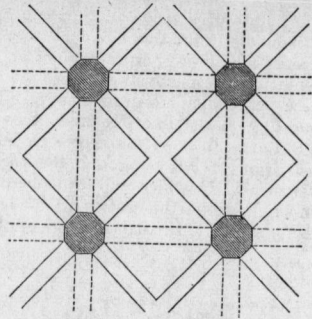

Fig. 642

1954. Where the piers supporting groins (*fig.* 642.) are made octangular, the angles of the groins should be cut off or arched as ribs, by which they are rendered much stronger than when they are square. In stone groins, where the arch is cut off, there is no advantage in point of strength, and rather a defect in point of appearance, to the groined angles.

1955. Arches intersecting a coved ceiling are similar to groins. Such arches are called *lunettes*, and are generally practised for semicircular-headed windows piercing the coves in the ceiling: *fig.* 643. exhibits a plan and section of such arches.

1956. A dome is a solid, which may be conceived to be generated by the figure of the base diminishing as it rises, till it becomes a point at the summit ; and when a dome has a polygonal base, the arches are plain arches, and the construction is similar to that of a groin. A domed ceiling of this kind upon a rectangular plan is shown in plan B (*fig.* 644.); the sections A A being elliptical in the top, and with lunette windows. C shows the geometrical construction.

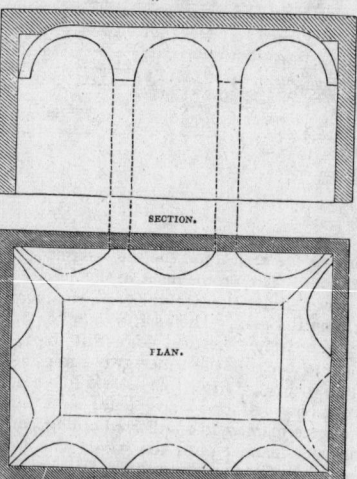

SECTION.

PLAN.

Fig. 643.

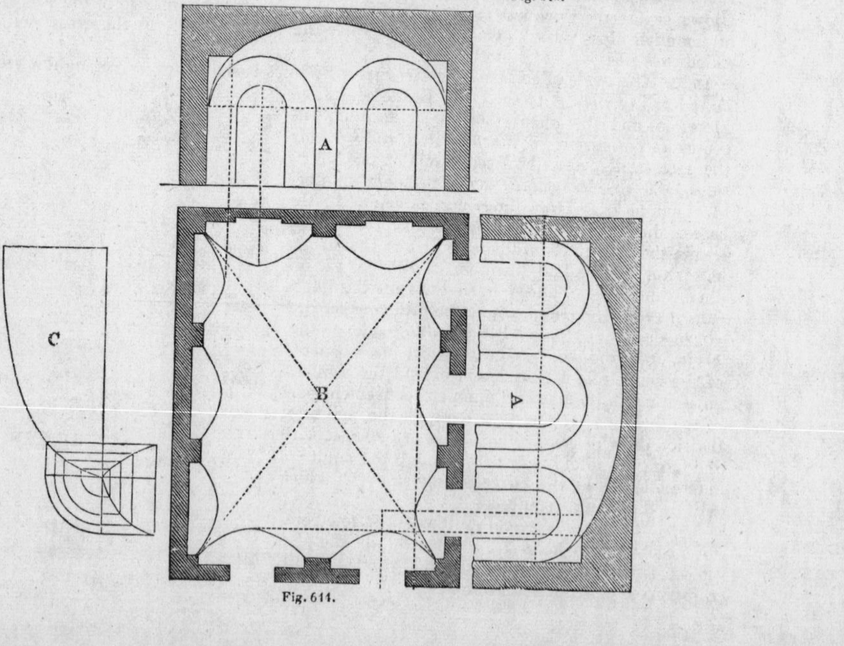

Fig. 644.

1957. *When arches intersect an inclined vault, and the projections of the arrisses cross each other at right angles, and the angle of elevation of one of the semicircular vertical ribs of the ascending avenue or opening is given to obtain the geometrical construction; so that the cross arches may be cylindrical surfaces.*

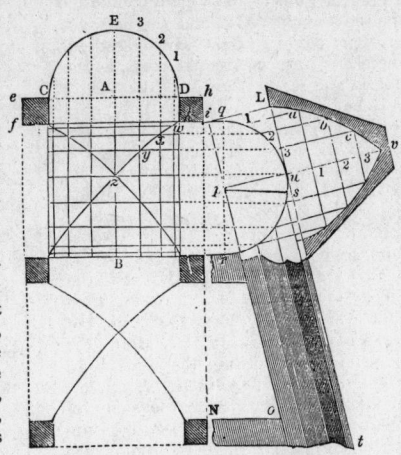

Draw the straight line AB (*fig.* 645.) to represent the axis of the inclined vault, and draw CD perpendicular to AB. Produce CD to *e* and *h*; make AC and AD each equal to the radius which forms the edges of the ribs; draw *h*N parallel to AB, and make the angle N*ho* equal to the inclination of the axis represented by its plan AB. In the line *ho* take any point *p*, and draw *qr* parallel and *ps* perpendicular to *h*N. Make *ps* equal to AC or AD, and through *s* draw L*t* parallel to *ho*. Draw *pu* perpendicular to L*t*, cutting it in *u*. Produce *pu* to *v*. Set the circumference of the inclined vault from *u* to *v*, divided into the equal parts *u*, 1, 1, 2; 2, 3; 3*v*, at the points 1, 2, 3. Divide each of the quadrants *qs*, *sr*, into the same number of equal parts at the points 1, 2, 3, and through these points and in *uv* draw 1*a*, 2*b*, 3*c* parallel to *vt*, and through the points 1, 2, 3, in the curve *qs*, draw *i*L, 1*a*, 2*b*, 3*c*, parallel to *pu*. Through all the points

Fig. 645.

L, *a*, *b*, *c* draw the curve L*abcv*, and this will be the pliable mould for forming the angle or groin over the plan, and for working the arch stones. Draw D*k* parallel to A*z*. Let E divide the circumference CED into the two equal parts EC, ED; divide the arcs DE, EC into the same number of equal parts as *uv* at the points 1, 2, 3, and draw 1*w*, 2*x*, 3*y*, E*z*, parallel to AB; also through the points 1, 2, 3 in the quadrant *qu* draw *gk*, 1*w*, 2*x*, 3*y*, *uz*, perpendicular to *y*N; then through the points *k*, *w*, *x*, *y*, *z*, draw a curve, which will be the plan of the groin whereof the stretch-out is L*abcv*. In the same manner the other half of the plan will be found, as also the whole of the other parts.

1958. *The form of an arch crossing an inclined groined vault at right angles, and the plan of the diagonal ribs being given ; to find the arch of the level vault.* Let AB, BC (*fig.* 646.)

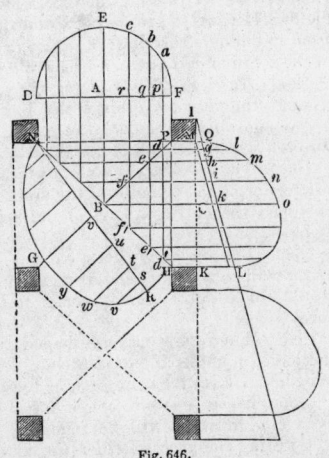

be the plan of the axis of the vaults. Through any point A in AB draw DF perpendicular to AB, and make AD and AF each equal to the horizontal breadth of the vault. Draw DG and FH parallel to AB; draw also any line LK parallel to AB, cutting BC in C, and make the angle KIL equal to the inclination of the axis represented by its plane AB. Make CM and CK equal to the breadth of the level vaults; draw KG and MN parallel to BC, and let MN cut DG in N, and FH in P. Draw the diagonals PG and NH. Produce GK to cut IL in L, and NM to cut IL in Q. In the curve DEF take any number of points *a*, *b*, *c*, and draw *ad*, *be*, *cf* parallel to AB, cutting DF in the points *p*, *q*, *r*, and the diagonal GP in *d*, *e*, *f*, and the diagonal HN in the points *d'*, *e'*, *f'*. Produce BA to E, draw *dl*, *em*, *fn*, B*o* parallel to BC, cutting QL in the points *g*, *h*, *i*, *k*; make *gl*, *hm*, *in*, *ko* equal respectively to *pa*, *qb*, *rc*, AE; then through the points *l*, *m*, *n*, *o*, draw the curve Q*o*L. Draw HR perpendicular to NH, and make HR equal to KL, and join NR; then will HR be the line of ramp for

Fig. 646.

the diagonal rib over its plan HN. Perpendicular to HN, draw *d'v*, *e'w*, *f'y*, BG cutting the line of ramp RN in the points *s*, *t*, *u*, *v*. Make *sv*, *tw*, *uy*, *v*G respectively equal to *pa*, *qb*, *rc*, AE. Then through all the points *v*, *w*, *y* draw a curve, which will be the angle rib standing over HN, and which will also serve for the angle rib standing over GP. All the groined vaults continued in the same range may be constructed by the same moulds.

1959. *To make the working drawings for a semicircular arch with a straight face, and to describe the moulds for the voussoirs.* This simple case will serve as a rule for those following; hence the explanation should be perfectly understood, as all the other cases differ

from it only according to the different kinds of arches to be constructed; such as the *bevelled arch*, that in a *battering* or *sloping wall*, and that on a *circular wall*.

1960. Draw two lines (*fig.* 647.) perpendicular to and crossing each other, as BA, GD

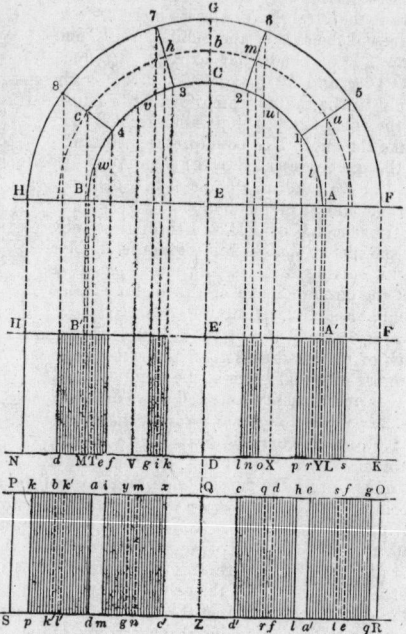

From the point E, as a centre, describe the sofite curve ACB, and the extrados or upper curve FGH. Divide each of these arcs into two equal parts, as the dotted arc *abc*. Draw LM parallel to AB, and make the distance A′L equal to the thickness of the wall wherein the arch is to be constructed. Draw the outer and inner lines of the plan F′K, A′L, B′M, HN parallel to CD. Divide the arc ACB into the proper number of equal parts for the arch stones or voussoirs, suppose five, by the joint lines 1, 2, 3, 4; from the point E draw the joints 1—5, 2—6, 3—7, 4—8; then from every point where the joints cut the arcs ACB, FGH, &c. draw the perpendiculars cutting the line K N, as 8*d*, *c*M, 4*f*, 7*g*, *hi*, 3*k*, 2*l*, *mn*, 6*o*, *p*, *a*L, and 5*s*. Divide the sofite of each voussoir A1, 1—2, 2—3, &c. into two equal parts *t*, *u*, *v*, *w*, from which also let fall the perpendiculars *t*Y, *u*X, *v*V, *w*T.

1961. *To draw the moulds of the sofite* below NK. Draw the line OP parallel to the line KN; prolong ED to Z and make the distance QZ equal to ED. Through Z draw RS parallel to OP, and on each side of QZ lay off the distances C3, 3*v*, *v*4, 4*w*, and *w*B respectively on Q*x*, *xy*, *ya*, *ab*, and *b*P. On the other side lay off C2, 2*u*, *u*1,

Fig. 647.

1*t* and *t*A on Q*c*, *cd*, *de*, *ef*, and *f*O. Through the points O, *e*, *c*, *x*, *a* let fall on RS the perpendiculars OR, *ea′*, *cd′*, *xc′*, *ad*, PS, and through the points *f*, *d*, *y*, *b* let fall the perpendiculars from the middle sheetings *fe′*, *df′*, *yg′*, *bh′*; the distances of the dark lines give the breadth of the sofite of each stone in the sofite curve.

1962. *To draw the moulds of the joints:* lay off the distance 1—5 on *eg*, *ch*, *xi*, *ak*, and through the points *ghin* draw the lines *gq*, *hl*, *im*, *kp*, parallel to QZ. To find the middle of the joint divide the distances *eg*, *ch*, *xi*, *an*, each into two equal parts, as in *k′*, *m′*, *g′*, *s*, through which draw the lines *k′l′*, *m′n′*, *q′r′*, *s′t* parallel to QZ.

1963. The elevation is a section of a hollow cylinder, of which the concave or interior surface forms the intrados of the arch, and the convex or exterior surface the extrados, and of which the cutting plane of the section is perpendicular to the common axis of the cylinder.

1964. The angles of the stone are found from the angle which the arc of this section makes with any joint, and the curving of the sofite of the stone is found by a ruler or mould, the edge of which is made to the curve. The ends of the sofite are found by its developement.

1965. When the stones are shaped according to the moulds, and joined together in consecutive order, the whole mass, thus united, will form the solid arch as required.

1966. These separate operations being properly attended to, every difficulty will be removed, and no confusion will arise during the process, which can, in any degree, tend to perplex the delineator.

1967. *To find the bevels and moulds for the joints and sofites of an elliptical arch cutting obliquely through a straight wall, the joints radiating to the centre of the opening.* Draw the axis EN of the arch (*fig.* 648.), and therein take any point E, through which draw AB perpendicular to EN; make EA and EB each equal to half the space of the extrados or centre line of the arch; also make EC and ED each equal to half the span of the inner arch. Produce the diameter NE to G;

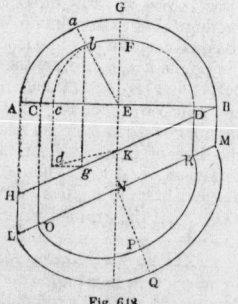

Fig. 648.

make EF equal to the height of the inner arch and EG equal to the height of the outer arch. On the major axis AB, and semi-minor axis EG, describe the semi-ellipsis AGB, which is the extrados of the arch. Also, on CD as the major axis, and EF the semi-minor axis, describe the semi-ellipsis CFD.

1968. Make the angle ABH equal to the angle which the wall makes with the right section of the arch, and let BH cut the axis in K. Draw ML at such a distance from BH that they may comprehend between them the thickness of the wall, and let ML cut the axis in N. The intrados of the arch on the one side of the wall is OPR, and the extrados is LQM; they are both ellipses respectively of the same height as the intrados and extrados of the right arch, but with the axes OR and LM.

1969. *To find the bevel of the angle of the arch stones corresponding to the joint ab tending to the centre E.* Describe the arc *bc* from E with the radius E*b* cutting AB in *c*. Draw *bg* parallel to EN cutting BH in *g*, and draw *cd* parallel, and *gd* perpendicular, to EN, and join K*d*: then EK*d* is the angle or bevel required (*fig.* 648.)

1970. The sofite of the arch is drawn according to the general principles of developement

1971. *To make the working drawings for an arch in a sloping wall, as, for instance, an arch in a terrace wall.* To draw the elevation; from any convenient point *o* in the line AB (*fig.* 649.), describe the arc of the intrados *aPf* and the arc of the extrados AQB: divide each of these arcs into odd numbers of equal parts (for the arch stones in this example five), and draw the joints *bg, ch, di, ek*. For the plan of the arc of the intrados draw AR perpendicular to AB, and draw the line of slope or *batter* AS. In the arc of the intrados take any number of points *bcd*, &c. and draw the lines *bb, cc*, intersecting AR in the points 1, 2, &c. and meeting the line of batter AS in the points *bc*. Draw CD parallel to AB, and at any convenient distance from it draw *aubvcw* perpendicular to CD, intersecting it in the points *e, l, m, n,* &c. Find the points *b′, c′, d′* in the straight lines *bv, mw, nx*, such that the distance of those points from the line ED may be respectively equal to the intervals 1*b*, 1*c*, &c. between the perpendicular AR and the line of batter AS, and draw the curve *a′ b′ c′ d′ e′ f′*, which will be the plan of the arc of the intrados. In the same manner the curve E*g′h′ik*D may be described; which being done, the plan of the arc of the extrados will be obtained.

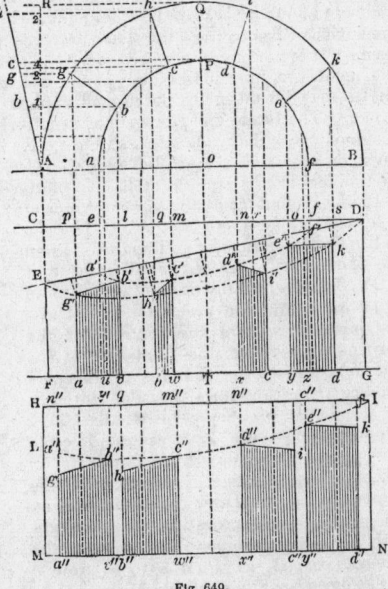

Fig. 649.

1972. *To find the moulds of the sofites and beds.* Draw any straight line HI in a separate place, and extend the arc of the intrados *abcdef* upon the line HI from H to I; divide it into the same number of parts that the arc *aPf* of the intrados is divided into (in this instance five), and mark the points of division *l′, m′, n′, c′*. Transfer the distances *ea′, lb′, mc′* between the line CD and the plan of the arc of the intrados, to the perpendiculars *n″a″, l″b″, m″c″, n″d″, c″e″*, and through the points *a″b″c″d″e″f″* draw a curve, which will be the developement of the arc of the intrados. Produce the lines *l″b″, m″c″, n″d″*, to *v″, w″, x″*, and transfer the distances *b′v, c′w, d′x* from the plan to the sofite on the lines *b″v″, c″w″, d″x″*. Draw *ga″, hb″, ic″, kd″* perpendicular to HI; transfer the distances *g′a, h′b, i′c* from the plan to the sofite upon *ga″, hb″, ic″*, and join *a″v″, b″w″, x″c″*, which will complete the moulds of the joints.

1973. *To make the drawings for an oblique arch by an abridged method.* The following method is said to be abridged, because, by one very short operation the moulds of the sofites and joints are found within the plan of the arch ABDC (*fig.* 650.). Divide AB in E into two equal parts, and draw EF parallel to AG. From the point A draw AG perpendicular to AC; prolong DB to G; divide AC into two equal parts in the point H. From H, as a centre, describe the arc AFG, which divide into voussoirs, and draw the joints from the centre H. Draw lines from each sofite parallel to EF, and below the line CD; the moulds for the sofites are comprised between the parallels of the key, and those of the joints are traced on the sides of the plan, as follows : —

1974. *To find the moulds of the sofites.* Through the point Q draw QN parallel to GH. To find on RS the point N, through the point K draw KL also parallel to GH. To find on QT the point M, and on RS the point L, draw the front line of the second sofite

MN, and the front line of the first IL. The back of this sheeting sofite is found by the same operation below the plan. The mould of the key is formed by two lines RS, QT, and the front and back lines of the plan AB, CD; the two moulds of the sofites NMTS and LIXV serve to trace the two stones on each side, observing only that the lower arrisses of the sofite on the side AC become those of the top on the side BD; or that the under arriss of one side may be that on the other side by reversing the mould, which will have the same effect.

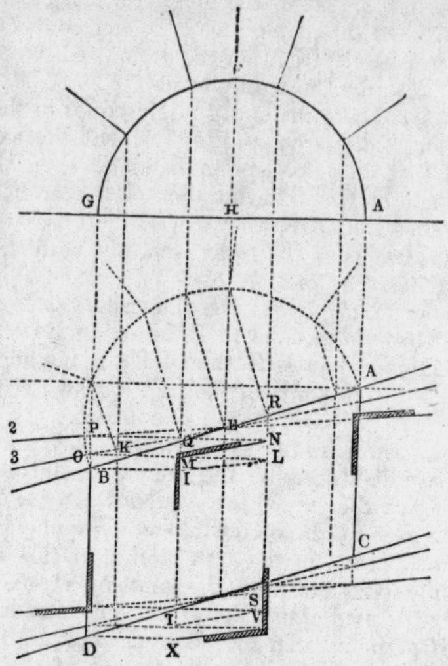

1975. *To find the moulds of the beds or joints.* Prolong NQ to meet DG, to find the point P, and through it and the point E draw the front of the second joint P2; prolong LM to GD to find O, through which and the point E draw the front of the joint O3. Proceed in the same manner to find the backs of the other joints, which are sufficient also to trace the stones by reversing them. It is not absolutely necessary to cut out the moulds of the sofites and joints, but the angles may be taken by bevels and applied to stones. The heads are prepared, as usual, with the moulds of the heads of the straight arc. It must be observed, that in this arch the face or front differs from a straight arch, being formed by different sections of a cylinder.

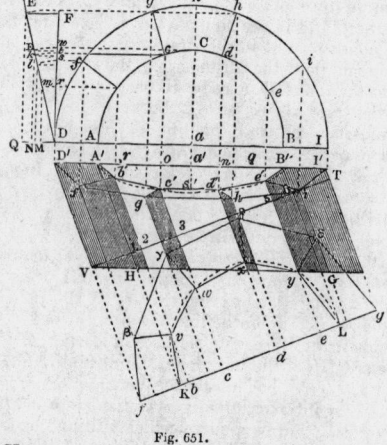

Fig. 650.

1976. *To find the moulds for an oblique arch, whereof the front slopes and the rear are perpendicular to the axis.* Let A'B'GH (*fig.* 651.) be the plan of the imposts. From the point *a*, as a centre, describe the arcs ACB, DRI, which divide into five or more equal parts for the arch stones. Draw the joint lines from the centre, and the perpendiculars from the joints below the line AB. From the summits of the perpendiculars, draw lines parallel to AB, to terminate in the perpendicular DF. From the point D, as a centre, describe arcs from the points which terminate in DF, to meet the line of slope DE in the points *m*, *l*, *k*, E. Draw the lines *mr*, *ls*, *kt*, EF parallel to AB, meeting the perpendicular DF in the points *rst*F; transfer the distances *rm*, *tk*, *u*P from *n* to *b'*, from *o* to *c'*, from *a'* to *s'*, and through the points A'*b'c'd'e'*B' draw the curve. Find the extrados or outer line D*fghi* in a manner similar to that in which the inner curve has been found. Draw the points *b'f'*, *c'g'*, *d'h*, *e'i*. Prolong AH and BG to K and L, and draw the lines *b'b*, *c'c*, *d'd* parallel to AK.

Fig. 651.

1977. *To make the straight arches.* Draw KL perpendicular to A'K, and produce KL to *f'* and *g'*. Transfer the distances between the points *m*, *l*, *k*, E, and the line QD to the ordinates of the lower arc from *b* to *v*, from *c* to *w*, from *d* to *x*, and from *e* to *y*, and draw the curve K*vwxy*L. Also find the outer curve in the same manner, and draw VT at right angles to AH.

1978. *To find the moulds of the sofites.* Draw the line WX (*fig.* 652.) in any convenient surface, and lay the breadths of sofite, not from the arc ABC as before, but from those of the right arc K*vwxy*L, that is, transfer the distance K*v*, *ww*, *wx*, *xy*, *y*L to the line WX upon W*a*, *ab*, *bc*, *cd*, and *d*X. Through the points W*abcd*X, draw the lines *dy*, *ei*, *fk*, *gl*, *hm*, *yz*, perpendicular to

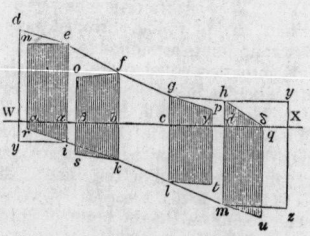

Fig. 652.

WX.   Transfer the distances 1A, 2b', 3c', 4d', 5e' upon the perpendiculars to WX: that is, from a to e, from b to f, from c to g, from d to h, and from X to y, and join de, ef, fg, gh, hy.   In the same manner draw the line yiklmz, which will complete the sofites.

1979. *To find the moulds of the joints.*   Transfer the distances vβ, wγ, xδ, yε, to the line XW from a to α, from b to β, from c to γ, and from d to δ, and through the points, α, β, γ, δ draw the lines nr, os, pt, δu perpendicular to WX.   Find the points n, o, p, q, as also, r, s, t, u, as in the preceding examples; then the moulds of the joints will be *eirn, fkso, ptlg, hδum.*   It must be observed that the boundaries, or extrados and intrados, DRI, ACB of the ring of the arch, do not stand in a plane perpendicular to the plan, but are supposed to be the lines which are drawn on the wall itself; and this is the reason why arcs are described between the perpendiculars DF and the line of slope DE.   It must also be observed, that the voussoirs of this arch must be cut by the moulds of the heads of the straight arch, and the moulds of the sofite must be applied on the voussoirs before the sofite is hollowed. Thus, let the first voussoir on the right hand be cut by the head mould on that face of the stone intended for the sofite; apply the first sofite mould, and its upper bed the first joint mould, and on its under bed the plan of the impost.   Then cut the two heads according to these moulds, and hollow the sofite square to its arrisses, using for this purpose the curved bevel.

1980. *To find the moulds for executing a semicircular-headed arch in a mass of masonry, of which one of its faces is a battering plane upon an oblique plan, and the other opposite face a portion of a cylindric surface.*   Describe

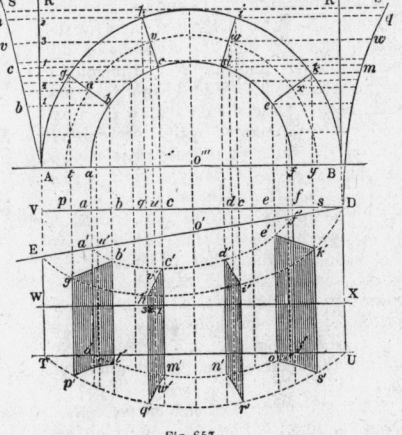

Fig. 653.

the intrados and extrados of the elevation; draw the joints and describe the plan a'b'c'd'e'f' of the intrados (*fig.* 653.), and the plan Eg'h'i'k'D of the extrados. Draw BR' perpendicular to AB, and draw BS', the portion of the cylindric surface.   From the arc BS' draw the plan a'l'm'n'o'f' of the intrados upon the line TU, and the plan Tp'q'r's'U of the extrados in the same manner from the arc BS, as the plan of the plane face was drawn from the line of slope AS.

1981. *To find the plan of any joint,* as that for the line or joint ch in the elevation.   Bisect ch in v, draw cm', vw', and hq' perpendicular to AB, intersecting the line VD in the points quc.   From the points cvh, in the joint ch, draw cc, vv, hh, meeting the line AS in the points cvh, and intersecting the line AR in the points 1, 3, 2 by three intervals, 1c, 3v, 2h.   Find the places hvc of the three points hvc on the elevation.   In the same manner find the places q'w'm' of the three corresponding points; then will c'v'h'q'w'm' be the plan of the joint required.   The plans of the other joints will be found in the same manner.

1982. *To find the joint mould itself.*   Draw the line HI (*fig.* 654.) equal in length to the developement of the intrados, and let Hc be the developement of the arc ac; draw cm'' perpendicular to HI.   Draw any line WX in the plan parallel to VD, intersecting the lines c'm', v'w', h'q', in the points 1, 2, 3.   Draw W'X' in the developement or sofite parallel to HI, and at the same distance from HI that WX is from VD in the plan, and let WX intersect the line c''m'' in 1.   Make the distances 1—2, 2—3 respectively equal to cv, vh, in the joint ch in the elevation, and through the points 1, 2, 3, just found, draw VW, h''q'', parallel to C'm''.

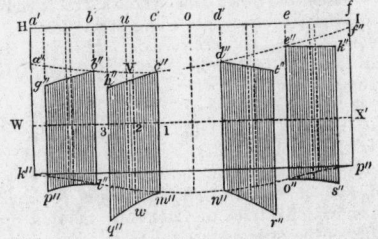

Fig. 654.

From the plan transfer the distances 2v', 2w', 3h', 3q'' to the sofite from 2 to V, and from 2 to W; also from 3h'' and from 3 to g the points cvp'' will be in a straight line, because they correspond to the straight face of the wall, and the points m'', w, q'' will be in a curve, because they correspond to the cylindric surface.   Draw, therefore, the straight line c''h'', and draw the curve line m''wq'', which will be a portion of an ellipsis, differing in its curvature but in a very small degree from that of a circle drawn through the same three points.   However, if more exactness be required, we may find as

many points in the joints of the surface of the wall and in the cylindric surface as we please; then $c''m''p''h''$ is the joint required, which serves for the upper and under beds of the two stones that unite together in that joint.

1983. Find all the other joint moulds $b''l''p''g''$, $d''n''v''t''$, $e''o''s''k''$, in the same manner, and find the points $a''f''$ in the developement. Through the points $a''b''c''d''e''f''$ draw a curve line by hand, or by a ruler bent to the points, and this will be the front curve of the sofite. Find the points $k''p''$ in the developement corresponding to the points a' and f on the plan, and through the points corresponding to the points a' and f on the plan, and the points $k''l''m''n''o''p''$, draw another curve, which will be the developement of the other side of the sofite. The developements of each of the parts of the sofite and of the two adjacent joint moulds give the three moulds for working one stone and the adjacent joints of the stone on each side of it. The angle which each of these joints makes with the sofite is found by making a bevel with one of its edges, circular for the intrados of the arc of the elevation, and the other to coincide with the joint line adjacent.

1984. *To find the moulds for executing a gateway in the quoin of a sloping wall.* Let ABCD (fig.655.) be the plan of the angle in which the arch is to be constructed, whereof AB is the span. Draw the centre line EL, to which draw the perpendicular FG. Prolong the line CA to F, and DB to G; then from the point L, as a centre, describe the sofite FHG and its extrados. Divide these arcs into equal parts for the arch stones, and from the divisions let fall perpendiculars, and also from the middle of the sofites to EC, ED. From the summits of the perpendiculars draw lines parallel to FG terminated by the lines of slope Set off the slope at the different heights $a1$, $a2$, $a3$, $a4$ respectively at right angles to the lines on the plan, on $d1$, $b2$, $d3$, $b4$, $K5$; also on the opposite side lay $a2$, $a4$ on $d2$, $b4$; then on one side draw the curve $AbbK$, and on the other, to abridge the work, join Bb, bb, bK. Again, for the outer curve, or extrados, set off $c1$, $c2$, cG on di, $d2$, $N3$. On both sides draw the curve $MddO$ on the one side, and to abridge the labour, draw the straight lines Od, dd, dN.

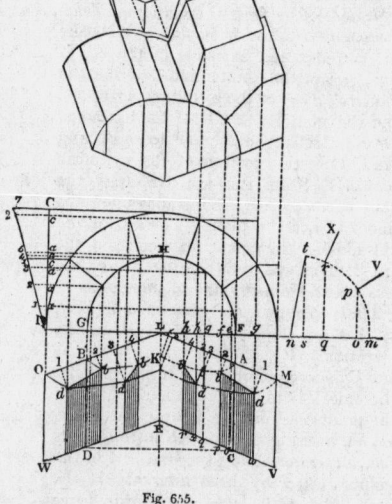

1985. *To find the moulds of the sofites.* Draw the line PQ (fig.656.), on which lay the arc of the sofite FHG in the usual manner, making the points 1, 2, 3, which correspond to the points dividing such arc into equal parts; then on the lines of the sofite lay the distances FA, fb, gb, hb, LK, on PR, $1k$, $2l$, $3m$, $4m$, QS, and trace the front curve of the sofite $RklmnS$. Also repeat the same on the other side where there is only a straight line drawn from one sofite curve to another.

Fig. 655.

1986. *To find the back curve of the sofite.* Lay the distances eo, fp, gq, kr, LE on PT, $1o$, $2t$, $3u$, $4v$, QU, and trace the curve TotuvU.

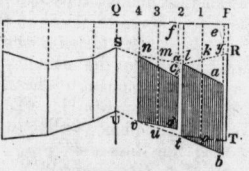

1987. *To find the moulds of the beds or joints.* The sofite lines to which the beds belong are $2t$ and $4v$. Draw the straight lines eb, fd parallel to QU, respectively distant from $2t$, $4v$ by the breadth GI of the joint, and let the lines be, fd meet PQ in e and f; make ea equal to gd, and ab equal to dw, and join al, bt; make fc equal to hd, and cd equal to dx, and join nc, vd. To trace the stones by moulds, prepare the voussoirs with the head of the moulds of the straight arch FHG. The sofite should be hollowed in each voussoir by its particular mould: the rest is done as usual; but it must be observed, that if the sofite moulds are made with straight lines in front and near the sofite, it must not be hollowed till the last. The voussoirs may be worked by bevels, preparing the stones by the plans ACVM, BDWO, as for common imposts. Although the arch in each front be not absolutely necessary here, we shall give the method of constructing it. Let the line mn be drawn apart, on which lay the distances L5, L4, L2, LA on the lines ns, nq, no, nm square to mm. Draw the perpendiculars op, qr, st, on which lay the heights of the joints of the straight arch taken on the line of slope; that is, lay I2, on op, I4 on qr, I5 on st, and

Fig. 656.

draw the line *nt*, which is the slope. Then draw the curve *mprt*, and from the point *n* draw the joint lines *pv* and *r*X. The centre of this gate is represented (in the upper part of the diagram) with voussoirs, and the keystone placed behind to show the mitre of the centre. The sofite moulds serve for curving the ends of the stone where the intrados meets the surface of the two walls. It must, however, be observed, that, previous to the application of the sofite mould, the concave surface of the intrados must be formed by a mould with a convex edge, and then the sofite mould or moulds of developement must be bent into the hollow, so that the two parallel edges may coincide with the corresponding edges of the stone. The angles which the intrados makes with the joints are taken from the elevation of the face of the arch. This elevation is no more than a section of the arch perpendicular to the axis of the cylinder which forms the intrados.

1988. *To construct a semicircular-headed arch in a round tower or circular wall.* Let ABDC (*fig.* 657.) be the plan of the tower. Bisect the arc AB, and through the point of bisection draw EF parallel to the jamb line AC or BD. Through any point *a* in EF draw GH perpendicular to EF. Produce the lines CA and DB to meet GH in the points G, H, and GH will be bisected in *a*. From *a*, as a centre, and with the radius *a*G or *a*H, describe the semicircular arc GFH. Also describe the arc of the extrados and divide the arcs each into five equal parts, and let fall the perpendiculars of the joint lines, and those of the middles of the sofite curves to the inside circular line CED of the tower. Having extended the arcs of the intrados curve on the line IK, and having drawn the lines of the sofites and those in the middle of each sheet as before directed, lay off the distances between the right line GH and the circular outside line A*b*B, viz. GA on IX and on KZ, *cd* on *ef*, V*g* on *hi*, S*k* on *lm*, M*n* on *op*, *ab* on *qr* ; then trace the front curve on the sofite X*r*Z. To find the rear curve, lay GC on IY, *c*C on *e*S, &c., by which the rear curve will be obtained.

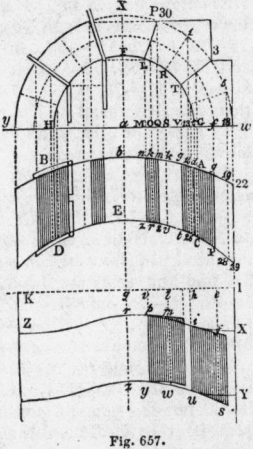

Fig. 657.

1989. We do not consider it necessary to pursue the construction of the moulds, the operations being very similar to those already given in the previous examples.

1990. *To find the moulds for an oblique semicircular arch in a circular tower.* The construction of this differs from the preceding only in the bevel or obliquity of the tower; hence it requires no particular description ; only observing, that the bevel causes the mould to be longer on one side than on the other (see *fig.* 658.), as is evident from the plan ; therefore the distances taken between the right line AB and the circular line of the tower CDE, being unequal, must be transposed each on its particular line of the mould and joint to which it corresponds in the sofite, that is, the distance AC must be laid on FG, BE on HI, and so of the rest. To work the stones, dress the beds, then apply the proper moulds and cut the head and tail circular as before. Trace the breadth of the sofite on the upper bed, then hollow the sofite, and cut the joints by the bevel.

1991. *To construct an oblique arch in a round sloping tower intersecting a semicircular arch within it.* This is nearly the same as the two preceding cases. On one side draw the line of slope (*fig.* 659.) AB, and on the other the arc CD. Draw parallels from the divisions of the sofites and their middles, as in the figure, in order to cut the line of slope and arc. To work for the slope, set off all the retreats comprised between the perpendiculars AH and the line of slope AB on the perpendiculars of the sofite, square to the front line of the tower F 19 G, as follows : Transfer the retreat 9—10 on 19—20 by placing the compasses so that the line 19—20 would pass

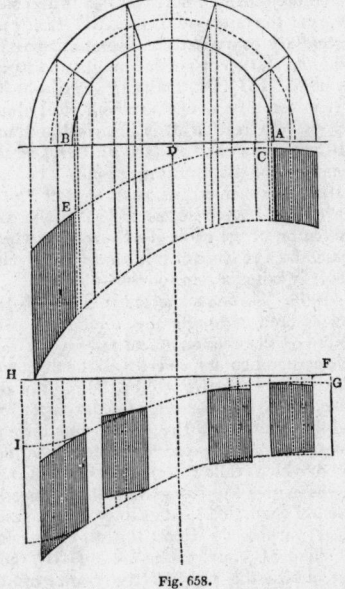

Fig. 658.

through the centre of the tower, and the point 20 fall on the centre of the gate O—75, and 7—8 on 17—18, and on 21—22 in the same manner (only terminated by the lines

from the sofite instead of the centre line of the arch), set also 5—6 on 15—16, and on 23—24, 3—4 on 13—14 and on 25—26, and lastly 1—2 on 11—12 and on 27—28, and through these points trace the sofite 28—20 —11. The extrados is found in like manner, and the middles of the joints 47, 49, 53; which done, draw the plan of the joints 14—47—35, 18—19—37, 22—51—39, and 26—53—41.

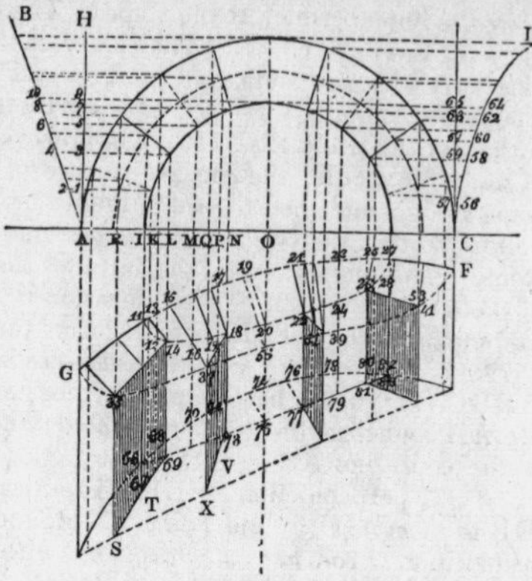

1992. *To find the curve of the plan which terminates the tails of the moulds.* Set the projections of the buttress of the semicircular arc at right angles to the inside line of the tower; viz. 64—65 on 74—75; 62—63 on 72—73 and on 76—77; 60—61 on 70—71, and on 78—79, 58—59 on 68—69. and on 80—81; 56—57 on 66—67 and on 82—83; then trace by hand the curve 83—75—66. The curves of the extrados and joints are found in the same manner.

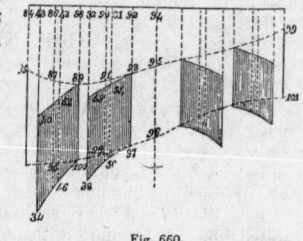

Fig. 659.

1993. *To find the moulds of the sofite.* Draw the line of direction 94—84 (*fig. 660.*) as before, below which set off the distances I—11 or 84—85, K—12 on 86—87, L—14 on 88—89, M—16 on 90—91, N—18 on 92—93, O—20 on 94—95, and then trace the front of the sofite moulds 85—95—99. To find the rear, set I—66 on 84—33, K—67 on 86—36, L—69 on 88—100, M—71 on 90—98, N—73 on 92—97, O—75 on 94—96, and trace the rear curve of the mould 101—96—33.

1994. *To find the moulds of the joints.* Transfer P—19 on 31—54, Q—37 on 32—48, I—47 on 42—52, R—35 on 43—40, and through these points trace the front joint or bed moulds 93—54—48, 89—92—40. To find the rear, make 31—50 equal to PV, 32—38

Fig. 660.

equal to QX, 42—46 equal to IT, and 43—34 equal to RS; which done, trace the curve lines 97—50—38 and 100—46—34. The two other joints are found by the same method. We do not consider it necessary further to multiply examples of the kind here given: the latter sort, especially, rarely occur in practice; and if they should, all that will be necessary to master the operations will be the application of a little thought and study.

1995. III. Of Dome Vaulting. In whatever direction a hemispherical dome is cut, the section A is always the same. B represents one half (see *fig. 661.*) of the same in the plane of projection. The construction is sometimes such that the plan is only a semicircle, as B, as in the termination of the choir of a church: in which case the French call it a *cul-de-four*; with us it is called a semi-dome.

1996. Through the extremities of the joints, and through the middle of each sofite of the section A, let fall on the line *ab*, perpendiculars, whereof all the distances *dc* from the centre *c* will be the radii of the arcs, which will serve for the developement of the sofites, of the joints, and for the construction of the arch stones. The method which follows, though it will not perhaps give the sofites and joints strictly accurate, will do so sufficiently for all practical purposes. Upon the developement C make SC equal to the arc MDGC, then set out to the right of the points of division the parts ST equal to *st* on the plan B; then raise through the points T upon the line SC perpendiculars equal

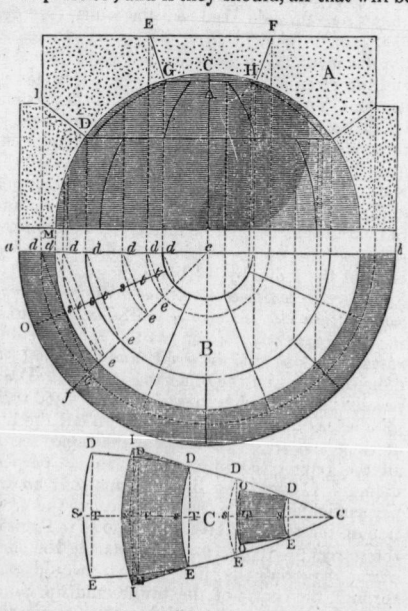

Fig. 661.

to the correspondents *e, t, d* of the plan B, and draw the curve ESD through the points so found.

1997. The sofites are terminated by four curves, whereas the joints have two right sides, as DI, EI, and DO, EO, and two curved sides, as II, DE, and OO, DE; the widths DI, DO of the joints are equal to DI, GE of the section; in one direction they are curved only one way, but as respects their sofites they are so in every way. The heights of the voussoirs are given by the section A, their bases on the plan B Thus G, I, in the voussoir next the keystone, being the most opposite points, the base of it on the plan will be comprised between the two arcs *dte*, which answer to the perpendiculars let fall from G and I. The base of the first voussoir, according to the first method, will be equal to the surface comprised between the arc *aof* and the arc *dse*, which answers to the perpendicular let fall from the point D.

1998. EF and GH are the diameters of the upper and lower bases of a truncated cone, whose lower surface is hollowed out spherically. After working the voussoirs, so as to make their bases such as we have just indicated, they must be worked to sofite moulds for giving them the hemispherical form of the section; after which the angles of the moulds are joined by arcs parallel to the arrisses of each stone, or by applying a general mould of the form of the section, that is, circular, of the radius of the dome.

1999. *For the pendentives formed in an hemispherical dome.* The piers D and E are supposed those of half the dome pierced by the pendentives. If we suppose the face or

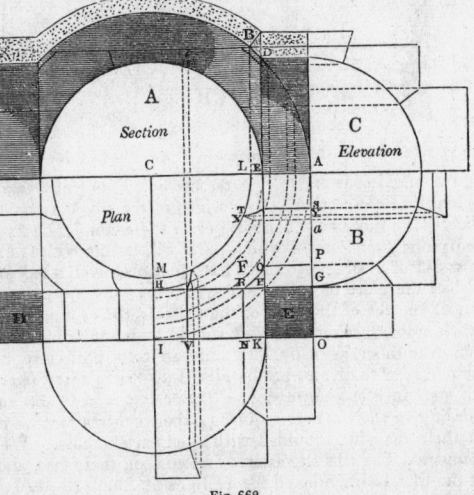

elevation B (*fig.* 662.) to make one quarter of a revolution about the point A, we obtain the elevations B and C. Through the points of division on the elevation C draw to the arc AD right lines perpendicular to CA. On the extremities of these lines upon CA, and from C, as centre, describe arcs in the plan F, by which the plan of the projection on F is obtained, whose intersections with the right lines drawn from B will give the joints and faces for the level beds. The lines HF, FE, ED are right lines. The spaces GAEF, FHIK are pieces of cylindrical vaulting, so that the only difficulty is in joining to each of their voussoirs their correspondent parts in ELMHFE.

Fig. 662.

2000. The elevation B gives the height of the voussoirs; their bases, as seen in the preceding example, will be OPQRNO, GSTUVKFG. The length of the keystone will be XY, and *a*—A will be half its width.

2001. The part FQR is the plan of the springing stones of the pendentive in the elevation A. The remaining parts of the construction are sufficiently shown by the lines of the diagram, which will be understood by the student if he has previously made himself acquainted with the previous portions of this section.

2002. We should willingly have prolonged this part of our labours, if space had permitted us to do so without sacrificing other and important objects. If the subject be one in which more than the ordinary practice of the architect is called upon to put into execution, we refer him to Simonin, *Coupe des Pierres*, Paris, 1792, and Rondelet's *Art de Bâtir*, which we have used with much freedom, and in which many more interesting details will be found than we have thought it absolutely necessary here to introduce, though we believe we have left no important point in masonry untouched. We cannot close this section without paying our tribute of respect to the masons of this country, who are among the most intelligent of the operative builders employed in it. A very great portion of them are from the north of the island, and possess an astuteness and intelligence which far exceeds that of the other classes of artisans. We must not, however, altogether do this at the expense of those employed in carpentry, which will form the subject of our next section, among whom there will be found much skill and intelligence, when the architect takes the proper means of drawing it out; and we here advise him never to be ashamed of such means.

2002a. IV. Of Caissons in Cylindrical and Hemispherical Vaulting. — The method of setting out the *caissons* or sunken panels in cylindrical vaults and domes, is a process required almost in every building of importance, and imparts great beauty to the effect of the interior when properly introduced: it is, indeed, one of the elements in composing them, and must therefore be well understood before the student can succeed in developing his ideas.

2002b. In setting out the ribs of cylindrical vaulting, the vertical ones are supposed as falling on supports below the springing; but if such supports fall too wide apart, the caissons themselves will be too wide, and the space must be divided into a greater number; in which case, if practicable, an odd number is to be preferred, taking care that the caissons are not too much reduced in width. This, however, is only for the purpose of ascertaining roughly how many caissons may be used in the circuit of the vault; and it is to be remembered that they must be of an odd number, because a tier of caissons should always extend along the crown of the vault. *Fig.* 662a. is an example of a cylindrical vault wherein the

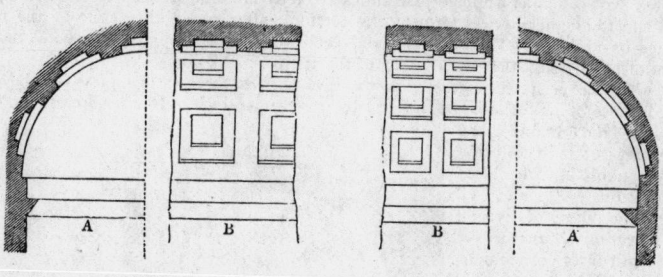

Fig. 662a.   Fig. 662b.

number of caissons is five. A is one half of its transverse section, and B a small portion of the longitudinal section. The width of the ribs between the caissons is one third of them; hence, if the number of caissons, as in the example, be five, the arch must be divided into twenty-one parts, one of which parts will be the width of a rib, and three will be given to the width of a caisson. As we have just observed, a caisson is always placed in the centre; we shall therefore have the half-arch $= 1\frac{1}{2} + 1 + 3 + 1 + 3 + 1 = 10\frac{1}{2}$ and $10\frac{1}{2} \times 2 = 21$. The vertical lengths of the sides of the caissons thus found will regulate the horizontal lengths of their sides, inasmuch as they should be made square. If the caissons in the vault be seven in number, as in *fig.* 662b., the sofite or periphery must be then divided into twenty-nine parts; if their number be nine, into thirty-seven parts; and so on, increasing by eight each step in the progression. The caissons may be single or double sunk, or more, according to the richness required; their centres may be moreover decorated with *fleurons*, and their margins moulded with open enrichments. Where the apartment is very highly ornamented, the ribs themselves are sunk on their face, and decorated with frets, guilloches, and the like, as mentioned for ceilings in Book iii., c. i., s. xxiv. Durand, in his *Cours d'Architecture*, regulates the width of the caissons entirely by the interaxes of the columns of the building; but this practice is inconvenient, because the space may in reality be so great as to make the caissons extremely heavy, which is, in fact, the case in the examples he gives.

2002c. In the case of dome or hemispherical vaulting, the first point for consideration is the number of caissons in each horizontal tier of them; and the student must recollect that allowing, as before, one third of the width of a caisson as the width of a rib, the number of parts into which the horizontal periphery (whereof $e'e'$ on the plan A is one quarter, and its projected representation at ee on the section B) is to be divided (*fig.* 662c.) must be multiples of 4, otherwise caissons will not fall centrally on the two axes of the plan. Thus,

A dome having 16 caissons in one horizontal tier must be divided into 64 parts.

—	20 ditto	-	-	-	-	-	80 ditto.
—	24 ditto	-	-	-	-	-	96 ditto.
—	28 ditto	-	-	-	-	-	112 ditto.
—	32 ditto	-	-	-	-	-	128 ditto.

and so on increasing by 16 for each term in the progression. In the figure, the number of caissons is sixteen. The semi-plan is divided into thirty-two parts, three whereof are given to each caisson, and one and a half to each half-caisson on the horizontal axis of the plan. From the divisions thus obtained lines are carried up to the section ab, ab, cd, cd. As the projected representations of the great circles of a sphere are ellipses, if from b, b, d, d, we construct a series of semi-ellipses whose transverse diameters are equal

to the semi-diameter of the sphere, and their conjugate axes determined from the points of intersection $b, b, d, d,$ we shall have the vertical sides of the caissons. The next part of the process is to ascertain the ratio of diminution in the heights of the tiers of caissons as they rise towards the vertex, so that they may continue square in ascending. Upon a vertical line CC', whose length is equal to the developed length of the line of dome ef, or in other words, whose length is equal to one quarter of the length of a great circle of the sphere, to the right and left of C set out at g and g the half width of the caisson obtained from the plan, and make hg, hg equal to one third of the caisson for the width of the ribs on each side. Draw lines to the vertex of the development from hh and gg. A diagonal hi being then drawn, the horizontal line ik will determine the lower edge of the next caisson upwards. Proceed in this way for the next from l and so on. The heights of the caissons thus obtained, being transferred to the section on the quadrant ef, will give the proportionate diminution thereon of the caissons as they rise. They are discontinued, and the dome is left plain, when they become so small as to lose their effect from below, and indeed they could not beyond a certain limit be executed.

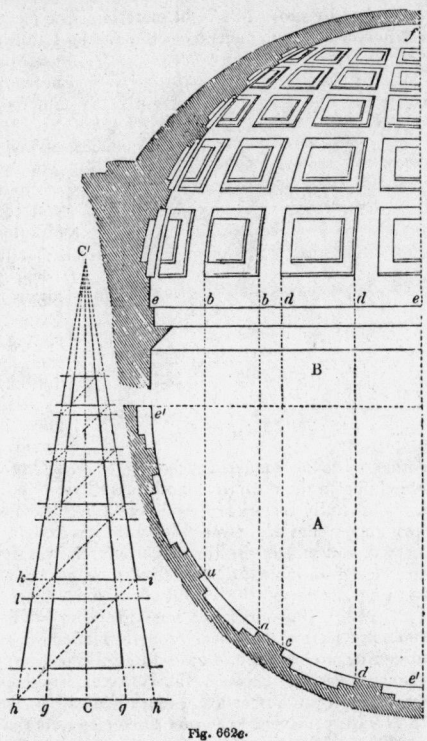

Fig. 662c.

2002d. V. Of Gothic Vaulting.—Professor Willis, in his valuable essay *On the Vaults of the Middle Ages*, printed in the Transactions of the Institute of British Architects, 1842, states that every rib should spring as a separate and independent arch, and that the elliptic curves produced by the method of obtaining the form by ordinates from those of the transverse ribs, are totally at variance with the characteristic forms of the Gothic style. De Lorme first taught this method, and others followed him, but it was never intended by them to be applied to Gothic rib-vaulting. This author shows (ch. viii.) that every rib is perfectly independent of the other in its curvature; each rib consists of a single arc of a circle whose centre is *upon the impost level*, and they cannot be therefore connected by projections. They all form pointed arches of different proportions, with the exception of the diagonal arch, which is very nearly a semicircle. "This," says Willis, "may have been the genuine French method, but in our English examples the centres are commonly placed without respect to the impost level, and the general forms of the vault are different from those which are produced in this manner." Dérand, writing later than De Lorme, says, "that in this style the ribs are always made arcs of circles, elliptical or other curves being inadmissible" (p. 177). Willis, later, however, allows certain ribs in a vault to be "semi four-centred arches," the others being arcs of circles. (See 1943a.)

2002e. "In the early stage of *rib-vaulting*," remarks Professor Willis, "the ribs consist of independent and separate voussoirs down to the level course from which they spring. The separate stones were roughly jointed at the back, instead of being each got out of a single stone, as in later structures. The back of these ribs is concentric with the soffite. The transverse rib of the north-east transept of Canterbury Cathedral consists of about one hundred richly-moulded stones, but the workmanship is exceedingly rude."

2002f. "The rough construction of the spandril, in the early instances, was followed at once by a more artificial structure, bespeaking a great advance in the art of masonry; and it remained with very slight change to the very latest period of rib-vaulting. This system is shown in *fig.* 662d. The junction of the solid mass L to N with the clearstory wall, is bounded by parallel vertical lines D, and this mass is always built of solid masonry bonded into the wall and forming part of it; the French name for this block of masonry is *tas de charge*. It is from the level of N that the real rib and panel work of the vault begins, for separate ribs are erected upon the surface of this solid, and

connected by vaults of a light material. The decorative construction, however, of the vault, exhibits the rib and panel from the abacus L, upwards. The point N is commonly at about

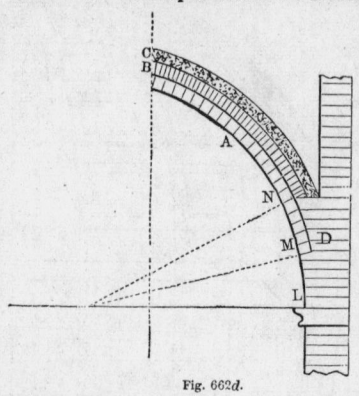

Fig. 662d.

half the vertical height of the arch, and is not necessarily guided by the impost of any clear-story rib adjoining. M is the general position where the mouldings of the several ribs run clear of one another at the divergence of the ribs. The solid part LM is built of horizontal courses of masonry, generally each of a single stone, and its level beds cut the curved mouldings obliquely in front."

2002g. Moller, *Memorials*, &c., translation 1836, p. 154, notices that, at Cologne, the lower part of the vaulting of the cathedral is formed by horizontal courses of stone projecting from the wall, consequently the actual span of the vaulting is proportionally diminished, while, on the other hand, the abutment is in the same degree strengthened. Still more deserving of attention is the manner in which the essential parts are so linked together as to be rendered incapable of thrusting or giving way, and therefore of necessity remaining in their original position. Price, in his work on *Salisbury Cathedral*, 1753, p. 25, quaintly remarks: "And here I beg leave to make a conjecture, that is, that all the springing stones of the vaultings were inserted into the walls at the time of their being erected, and so left till the whole church was roofed and covered in; and then being defended from rains, &c., they fixed their principal ribs and groins, and turned over the vaultings, as having the weight of the superstructure to act instead of a buttment."

2002h. "Above M," continues Professor Willis, "the ribs are each built separately of voussoirs, having their beds properly inclined to meet the axis of curvature of the rib, and these ribs are backed and united by solid masonry which connects them with the wall, and which, appearing between the rib, seems to be a portion of the light vaulting surface, really employed higher up. From the upper surface N, each rib A is still built as from M to N with voussoirs, but upon these ribs rests the light thin vault or panel-work."

2002i. "It is remarkable that the courses of the vaults are not laid level, but are in most cases made to incline downwards upon the diagonal rib. The reason for it is not easy to explain, but it is very common, especially in the earlier examples. These courses, in the transepts at Westminster Abbey, are of a light coloured stone, probably chalk, interrupted at regular intervals by a course of a darker stone; and the ridge, which has no rib, is also formed entirely of this darker stone, laid in a serrated manner. These dark courses are rather broader than the light ones, and there are four or five courses of the light between each of the dark. The surface of the panel between each rib is also made slightly concave or domical (probably to preserve the effect of being level, as seen from below it), and may therefore have been laid without any centreing, since each course would support itself. These peculiarities may all be found with some variations in other vaults of the same age."

2002k. "The architect of Leon cathedral," remarks Mr. Street, in his work on *Gothic Architecture in Spain*, p. 110, "filled in the whole of the vaults with a very light tufa, obtained from the mountains to the north of Leon; so at least I was assured by the superintendent of the works at the cathedral. Some of the material I saw was no doubt tufa; but some of it seemed to me to be an exceedingly light kind of concrete. The vaulting of Salisbury Cathedral is similarly constructed. I do not know whether at Beauvais the same expedient was adopted to lessen the weight." Both at Beauvais and Leon the construction in every part was too light.

2092l. Over the vaults was *commonly* laid a thick irregular course of rubblework, which again is also often covered with a kind of concrete. The vaults of the western compartments of Westminster, and of the south transept and tower of Hereford, are left bare on the upper surface: and these vaults, instead of being built with small brick-like stones, are composed of long thin slabs. The ribs themselves are, in some later examples, formed of a few long bar-shaped voussoirs instead of the small and numerous pieces of the earlier examples. Thus, in the transept at Westminster, L to N consists of 13 or 14 stones; but at the west end of the nave of 6 only.

2002m. Price notices (p. 24) that at Salisbury, "The groins and principal ribs are of Chilmark stone, but the shell, or vaulting between them, is of hewn stone and chalk mixed, on top of which is laid a coat of mortar and rubble of a consistence, probably ground in a kind of mill, and poured on hot, while the lime was bubbling; because by this, the whole is so cemented together, as to become all of one entire substance. This composition is

very remarkable, somewhat resembling the pumice-stone, being porous and light, by which it contributes prodigiously to the strength of the whole, and at the same time the least in weight of any contrivance that perhaps was ever used."

2002n. "The early moulded *ribs* are formed as *fig.* 662f. from St. Saviour's Church, Southwark, the vaulting or panel-work resting only on their backs; but the ribs of later date are rebated for the reception of this work, as shown in *fig.* 662e."

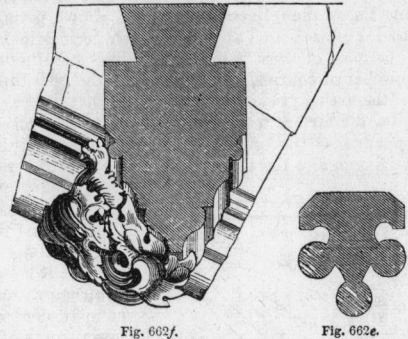

Fig. 662f.   Fig. 662e.

2002o. As early as 1225–50, the square plans for vaults were superseded by oblong ones, which allowed the *cross-rib*, the *groin-rib*, and the *wall-rib* to arrive at nearly one level. In the new system the groin-ribs were portions of circles, and the cross-ribs were struck with the same radius; but these vaults were soon considered to be weak, and the cross-ribs were heightened while the groin-ribs were either stilted or (subsequently) sharper pointed.

2002p. As soon as mediæval builders admitted the principle that the strength of arch-stones, like that of beams, is more dependent on the depth than on the width, they reduced the width as much as they could in order not to require a large abacus to the capital. The next step was to resolve all thrusts upon that support into a force acting directly upon it; and consequently to endeavour to make the various pressures, which the pillar has to bear, combine in a point in a stone that should be fully as large in plan as the abacus, and perhaps rest upon others of the same character.

2002q. The operation of deciding the form and place of this stone is very simple after the size of the arch-stones has been determined. Supposing that the work is, as in a cloister, bounded by a wall, and with-out wall-ribs, there will only be a cross-rib and two groin-ribs to be heeded. A line AB (*fig.* 662g.) showing the face of the wall is to be cut in O by another line CD representing the centre of the cross-rib; and the plan of the arch-stones for that rib is to be projected by the aid of these lines. It gives at the wall a centre O, and in its length OE *on the central line* a radius with which a semicircle may be described (as shown by the dotted line); a couple of parallel lines, FG and HK, will now show the thickness of the cross-rib. To proceed with a groin-rib, a line from O must be laid down at the correct angle made by the groin with the wall; and the plan of the groin-rib must be so projected that, with this line for an inside line, the front of the arch-stone shall touch the semicircle. A couple of parallel lines MN and PQ will now show the thickness of the groin-rib; and the plan of the abacus of the pillar may be designed, even so as to allow of wall-ribs if they should be intended.

2002r. The use of the semicircle is not an indispensable, but is a naturally convenient step, because the equal quantities so taken by it from all the spans of the ribs leaves undisturbed in general result all calculations founded upon lines drawn from mathematical points that are taken as centres in a plan made to a small scale; but the plans of the groin-ribs may be placed anywhere upon their respective centre-lines,

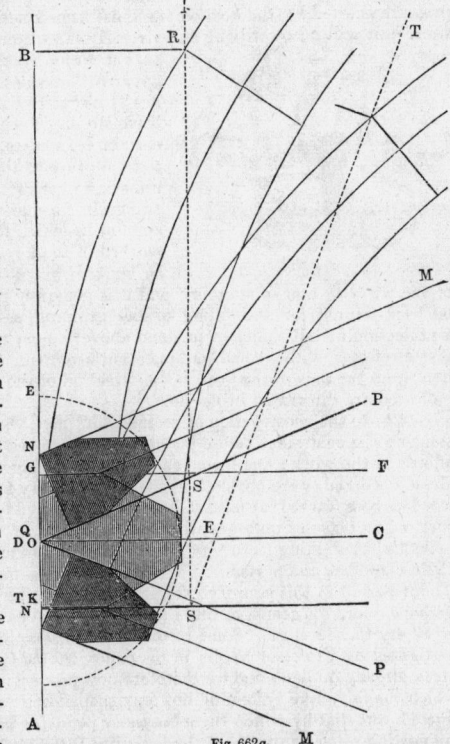

Fig. 662g.

so long as the intersection or junction of the neighbouring lines of the widths of the ribs is secured at some point. This intersection is not an absolute necessity, but it is the means of reducing the size of the abacus; and the point of junction S is that beyond which (working from the wall) the two ribs will be distinct. Taking this point S as fixing a line for the springing, the elevations of the two arches are to be drawn on the intersecting lines; then lines SR and ST drawn perpendicular to the springings, will cut the extrados of each arch at points which decide the level of the top bed of the horizontal work. The mass of work between this bed and the capital will be divided into a convenient number of courses, and the plans of the beds thus fixed are easily drawn from the elevations of the arches; when it will be seen that, if the groin-ribs are less in depth than the cross-ribs, the former will give a good starting-place for the material which is to form the spandrils of the vaults. In a similar manner, the intersections of any number of ribs may be found, and the tertiary and secondary ribs may be successively suppressed in favour of

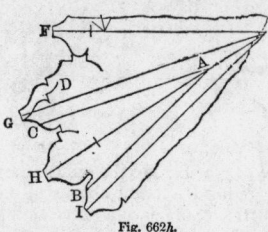

Fig. 662h.

the primary principal ones. Viollet le Duc, *Dictionnaire*, s.v. Construction, p. 96. Prof. Willis gives the following illustration (*fig*. 662h.) showing the method of setting out mouldings for vaulting, belonging to the perpendicular period; it is taken from one of the spandrils of a complex vault which formerly covered the extreme north-western compartment of the nave of Canterbury Cathedral, the lower storey of the so-called Lanfranc's tower. The number of ribs being seven required two stones in each of its upper courses at least; *fig*. 662h. being only a portion of the spandril, contains but four of them. It also shows that the stone had been scored, then rejected, and another set of lines drawn, and actually employed. AB, AC, are the rejected centres, and D a portion of the first outline. EF, EG, EH, and EI are the true lines drawn, each parallel to its own rib. The average thickness of the courses is about 10 inches.

2002s. The *key-stone* or *boss-stone* was adopted by the mediæval architects as a necessary appendage to groin-ribs, because the solidity of the vaulting depends greatly upon the pressure exerted by the key, which must consequently be heavier than any of the arch-stones; it will necessarily be an extremely large stone, allowing a great part of its mass to

Fig. 662i.

be cut away by the sculptor in order to diminish its apparent heaviness. This stone should generally be nearly circular in plan; for if the ribs diverge enough to leave any large space between them, a fracture is almost certain. In cases of such divergence, it is best to design the sculpture so that a mass may occupy the space. This remark, of course, does not apply where there are only two groin-ribs meeting at right angles; but it governs the amount to which the groin-rib should be allowed to be worked in the key-stone. No part of the boss ought to be sunk within a horizontal line connecting the intrados of one rib with that of another; and it is generally desirable that, whether or not the ribs be back-jointed for the filling of the groining, as *fig*. 662f., the key-stone should have a projection or tail sufficient to stand above the back of the filling. " Every boss-stone," says Professor Willis, " had its upper surface made horizontal, on which were drawn the lines from the axis of the boss in the direction of the respective ribs." The principles here indicated are illustrated in *fig*. 662i.

2002t. In the construction of groined vaulting it has been considered best to fix the key-stone on the centreing, before laying the arch-stones, for the sake of the guidance which it affords in the work; the inconveniences of working a boss in its place, and of setting it if already worked, were obviated in the 13th century by leaving its breast smooth, so that a wooden boss, carved at leisure, might be fastened to it with hooks. In the 15th century such a boss was not unfrequently of stone instead of wood.

2002u. A striking feature of the Flamboyant style is the frequent use of *pendents* in the vaulted roofs of the period. These, however, are not confined to the Continent, for the Tudor period in this country exhibits many splendid instances of their employment, none, perhaps, more gorgeous, or more interesting as regards its construction, than the Chapel of Henry the Seventh. Some of the various examples that exist have been scientifically investigated by Professor Willis, in his paper *On the Construction of the Vaults of the Middle Ages*, already quoted; and we therefore now proceed merely to indicate the principles upon which the fairy-like system of not only suspending vast bosses from the ceiling was conducted, but that by which these bosses or pendents became in their turn the springers for supporting other vaults, as in the beautiful little Lady Chapel at Caudebec in Normandy, and many other examples. A plan is given in the section on Principles of Proportion.

2002v. This chapel is hexagonal on plan, about 23 feet in span, or from side to side.

Fig. 662k. shows the mode by which, from the key-stone of an arch approaching a semi-circular form, and suspended or elongated beyond its ordinary depth, support is given for the springing of the vaults of the different bays.   On this practice Philibert De Lorme observes, " Les ouvriers ne font seulement une clef au droict de la croisée d'ogives, mais

Fig. 662*k*.   LADY CHAPEL AT CAUDEBEC.

aussi plusieurs quand ils veulent rendre plus riches leurs voûtes, comme aux clefs où s'assemblent les tiercerons et liernes, et lieux où ils ont mis quelquefois des rempants, qui vont d'une branche à l'autre, et tombent sur les clefs suspendues, les unes étant circulaires, les autres en façon de soufflet, avec des guymberges, mouchettes, claire-voyes, feuillages, crestes de choux et plusieurs bestions et animaux : qui étoient trouvés fort beaux du temps qu'on faisoit telles sortes de voûtes, pour lors appelées des ouvriers (ainsi que nous avons dict) voûtes à la mode françoise."

2002*w.* We have shown above the mode of suspending the pendent in a polygonal building.   The *fig.* 662*l.*, by a little consideration, will explain the mode of suspending pendents not centrically situate, as in the case of the ceiling of Henry the Seventh's Chapel, whose date runs coincident with the Flamboyant period.   The figure is a transverse section and plan of the vaulting of the building, in which one of the main arches, on which the whole construction depends, springs just below A, and reaches its summit at B.   The voussoirs or arch-stones whereof it consists are marked in their order.   The dotted interval from *a* to *b* is not to be considered as an interruption of the formation of the arch by the pendent, but may be supposed an imaginary line passing through it, or rather through the arch-stone or voussoir C, whose general form is marked by the bounding letters *c d e f b a* ; so that, in fact, the pendent is nothing more, as in the case of the Lady Chapel at Caudebec, than a voussoir, a large part whereof hangs down below the face of the vaulting.   The voussoirs are out of blocks about 3 feet 6 inches deep ; but a considerable portion of the solid below the soffite of the arch is cut away to form the lobes of the cinquefoils.   The arch D serves, by its connection with the walls, to stiffen and give weight to the arch where it would be most required, that is, towards the springing.   The pendent or voussoir E, on the same block with C, being thus established in its place, serves at, or towards its foot, as a springer for the ribs of a fanwork tracery shown on the plan, whose ribs are, in fact, ribs of a dome, and in construction do not differ from it.   Their section is shadowed somewhat lighter than the pendent voussoir.   The fanwork round each affords the means of introducing another pendent at its meeting at F in the plan.   (This pendent is shown at F in the two sections given in PRINCIPLES OF PROPORTION.)   The *fan* vault is very properly distinguished by Prof. Willis from what he calls the *stellar* vault, which is formed of ribs that may be, and indeed frequently are, of different curvature, and the rays of the star of different lengths ; whereas the fan vault consists of ribs of the same curvature and height, and the summit of the fan is bounded (see the *fig.*) by a horizontal circular rib, instead of the ends of lozenges forming the points of the star.   " The effect of the fan is that of a solid of revolution, upon whose surface panels are sunk : the effect of the star is that of a group of branching ribs."   It is manifest that the constructive details of these two sorts of vaulting are vastly different.   In the one, the dependence is upon ribs which support, by rebates on them, the filling-in panels ; while in the other the principle is similar to that of dome-vaulting.   This will be immediately perceived by reference to the plan G, in which the courses are marked, as also in the part of the section marked H.   The plan I shows the tracery of the soffite of the vault.   The author above quoted observes, " The construction of these fan vaults is in all examples so nearly the same, that they seem to have proceeded from the same workshop ; and it is remarkable that, at least as far as I know, there are no

Continental examples of them; whereas, of the previous vaults, there are quite as many on the Continent as in England.   In France, indeed, the lierne " (ribbed) " vaults are not

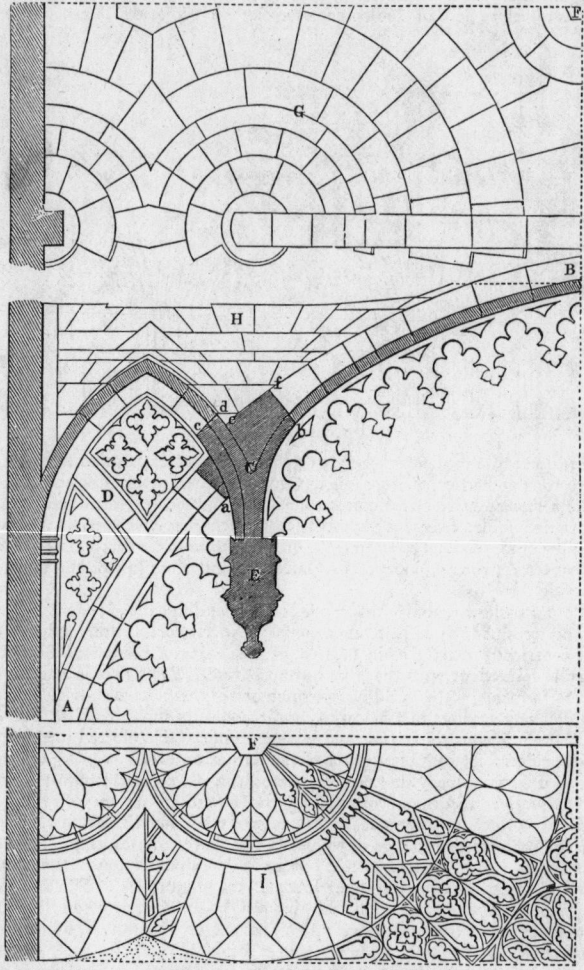

Fig. 662l.   HENRY THE SEVENTH'S CHAPEL, WESTMINSTER.

very numerous; they are confined to small chapels, and their patterns are in general simple. But in Germany and in the Netherlands there is an abundance of them, distinguished, certainly, from ours by local peculiarities, but nevertheless of similar mechanical construction, and requiring the same geometrical methods."

2002x. The introduction of fan vaulting seems to have occurred in the beginning of the 15th century.   The first instance wherein the span was considerable is the Dean's Chapel attached to the north-west transept of Canterbury Cathedral.   In St. George's Chapel at Windsor, the aisle and central compartment only have fan vaults, the principal vault not being fanwork.   The chief works of this kind, of known date (about 1500), are Henry the Seventh's Chapel at Westminster, King's College Chapel at Cambridge, the central tower of Canterbury, and Bath Abbey church.   (See PRINCIPLES OF PROPORTION.) In the church of St. Etienne du Mont at Paris, we find a remarkable example of the style of the renaissance contending with the expiring flamboyant style.   In short, the whole of the interior is a mass of interesting incongruities.   The church is cruciform, and at the intersection of the cross is a pendent key-stone, most elaborately wrought, and more than 13 feet deep.   It is obvious, in respect of these pendents, that there is no mechanical difference between their pendency and their being insistent, as lanterns are, on domes.

Sect. IV.

CARPENTRY.

2003. Carpentry is the science of framing or letting into each other an assemblage of pieces of timber, as are those of a roof, floor, centre, &c. It is distinguished from joinery in being effected solely by the use of the *axe*, the *adze*, the *saw*, and the *chisel*, which are the carpenter's tools; whereas joinery requires the use of the *plane*. See 2102, *et seq.*

2004. Though necessarily of high antiquity, the very scanty information which Pliny and Vitruvius have left us on the subject would merely show that the science was known by the ancients. The roofs of Egypt present us with no more than flat coverings of massy stone; a pediment roof, therefore, would seem to have been among the first efforts of constructive carpentry; and upon the pitch which this, then and since, has received in different countries, we shall hereafter have to speak. The Greeks appear to have used carpentry in the construction of their floors and some other purposes; but in a country abounding with stone and marble, it is not likely that wood was much used in the interiors of their buildings, unless where lightness, as in doors, for instance, required its employment. With the Romans it was much more commonly used; and from all that can be gathered, we may consider them as the fathers of the science.

2005. Among the moderns it has been very successfully cultivated; and, with very few exceptions, we may almost assert that the works of Palladio, Serlio, De Lorme, Sir Christopher Wren, Perronet, and a few others, exhibit specimens which have scarcely been surpassed in later times, notwithstanding the scientific form it has assumed in the present age.

2006. To the mechanical principles of carpentry we have, in Chap. I. Sect X. of this book, directed the attention of the student; and to the section now under our pen we should have added the words *Descriptive* and *Practical* to *Carpentry*, but that much of what could have been said on that head has already been anticipated in the section on Descriptive Geometry. Hence, in what follows, that which comes under such predicament will be only given in particular cases, for the purpose of saving time and trouble to the reader in the application of its principles to them. We must, here, also remind the reader, that under the section Beams, &c., and Timber, have been described the different sorts of timber used for building purposes, their strengths, and the strains to which they are subject and which they are capable of resisting; and that therefore this section is confined simply to putting pieces of timber together, so as to form the assemblage of timbers under which we have commenced by defining the science. To do that properly requires great skill and much thought. Considerable waste, and consequent expense to the architect's employer, result from that ignorance which assigns to the scantlings of timber larger dimensions than are absolutely necessary for the office of each piece; insufficient scantlings will bring the architect into trouble and responsibility; and the improper connection of the pieces will be equally ruinous to his reputation. The principles of practical carpentry are, nevertheless, simple; and though to form new combinations and hazard bold and untried experiments in practice will require all the skill and science of a talented artist, the ordinary routine of carpentering is to be learnt by a little application and a due exercise of common sense.

2007. After these observations, we must introduce the student to the first operation which in practice may arise. It is not every where that timber can be obtained in sufficient lengths to stretch across the void he has to cover; and it will in such cases be necessary for him to know how one piece of timber may be so joined to another, for the purpose of lengthening it, that the two pieces, when joined, may be as nearly as possible equal in strength to one whole piece of timber of the same dimensions and length. This operation is of great service to the builder, and is technically called *scarfing*. To perform it, the joints are indented, and bolts are passed through the pieces within the length of the indents, such bolts being confined above and below by means of nuts and screws. In *fig. 663.* four ways are exhibited of accomplishing the object in question. A and B are the methods usually employed for joining together plates, lintels, and ties, in which bolts

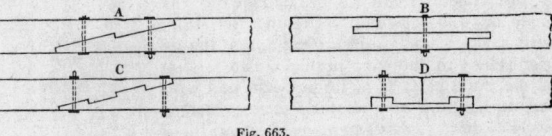

Fig. 663.

are rarely necessary; but if such a method is used for scarfing beams, bolts must be employed. The stronger forms, which only should be used for beams, shown in C and D, are not only in that respect such as should, on that account, be used for beams, but are executed without loss of length in the pieces of timber. The length of the joints of the scarfing may be increased at pleasure; the diagrams are merely given to show the mode of doing what was required. With fir, however, when bolts are used, about four times

the depth of the timber is a usual length for a scarf. Scarfing requires great accuracy in execution; for if the indents do not bear equally, the greater part of the strength will be lost: hence it is improper to use very complicated forms for the indents.

2008. Pieces of timber are framed into and joined to one another, by the aid of *mortices* and *tenons*, and by iron straps and bolts; and on the proper placing of these depends the soundness of the work. If a piece of framing is to stand perpendicularly, as in the case of partitions, without pressure from either side, the mortice and tenon should be in the centre of the wood. But in the case of framing floors, in which the pressure is on the upper surface, and entirely on one side, the mortices and tenons ought to be nearest the side on which the pressure is, by which the timber will not be so much weakened; and hence it is the constant practice to cut the mortices and tenons as in *figs.* 664, 665. By the method shown in the last-named figure, the tenon obtains more strength from an additional bearing below, which is further increased by the inclined butment above, called a *tusk*.

Fig. 664.

Fig. 665.

2009. The method of framing wall plates together at an angle, for the reception of the hip rafter on the *dragon beam*, and the angle ties for retaining the wall plates in their places, is shown in *fig.* 666., wherein A B is the mortice cut for the tenon of the hip rafter

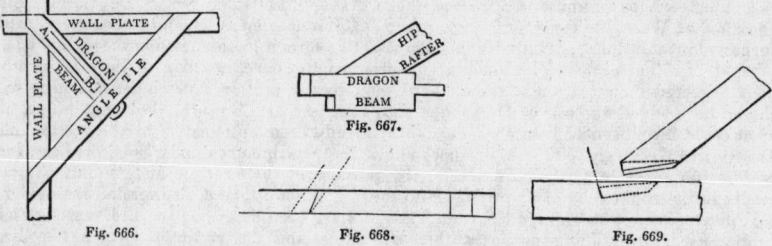

Fig. 667.

Fig. 666.   Fig. 668.   Fig. 669.

shown in *fig.* 667. *Fig.* 668. is one of the wall plates, showing the halving to receive the other plate, and the cutting necessary for dovetailing the angular tie. *Fig.* 669. shows the method of cutting the mortices and tenons of principal and hip rafters; another method being given in *fig.* 670., and to be preferred where a greater resistance to thrust is sought, because by it a double *butting* is obtained on the tie beam. Inasmuch, however, as in this last case the beam is cut across the grain to receive the rafter, the part left standing to receive the heel of the rafter may be easily split away; to obviate which, the socket may be cut, as at A, parallel to the grain of the wood. *cd* is the iron strap for securing the rafter's foot to the tie beam, and keeping it in its place. A plan of the upper part of the tie beam is given at B, showing the socket and mortice of the section A in the last figure. C exhibits the mode in which a principal rafter is strapped to a tie-beam, with the *joggling*.

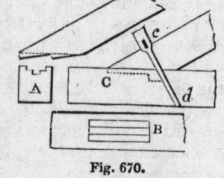

Fig. 670.

2010. The most approved method of forming butments (*fig.* 671.) for the *struts* or *braces, aa*, which are joggled into the king-post, is to make their ends, which act against the joggle, perpendicular to the sides of the brace; they will thus be kept firmly on their butments, and have no tendency to slide. C is a section of the king-post and tie beam, showing the mode of wedging and tightening the strap, with a single wedge, in order to draw the tie beam close to the king-post. D is a section of the same parts to a larger scale, and with the introduction of a double wedge, which is easier to drive than a single one, because there is less action upon the cross grain of the wood.

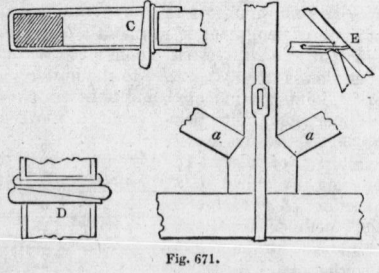

Fig. 671.

2011. Straps in carpentry should be sparingly used. Professor Robison has very properly observed, that "a skilful carpenter never employs many straps, considering them as auxiliaries foreign to his art." The most important uses of them are, that of suspending the tie beam to the king-post, and of securing the feet of the principal rafters to the tie beams in roofs.

2012. Bolts are sometimes used for the last-named office, with *washers* and heads and screw nuts, in which case the washers, nuts, and heads should be well painted, though

even then they are liable to rust. Wherever the iron work used for securing a system of framing is exposed to the humidity of the atmosphere, it should be rendered durable by frequent painting. Price (*British Carpenter*, 1759) observes thus : " There is one particular that had liked to have escaped my notice, concerning the placing of iron straps on any truss, thereby meaning to help its strength, which is by turning the end square (as shown at E, *fig.* 671.). This method embraces the timber in such a manner, to make it like a dovetail, *which cannot draw from its place ;* another observation is, to bolt on your straps with square bolts, for this reason : if you use a round bolt, it must follow the auger, and cannot be helped ; by this helping the auger-hole, that is, taking off the corners of the wood, you may draw a strap exceeding close, and at the same time it embraces the grain of the wood in a much firmer manner than a round pin can possibly do." The example given by Price, however, for turning square the strap, is injurious to the rafter, which must be partially cut to admit of it.

FLOORS.

2013. The assemblage of timbers in a building, used for supporting the flooring boards and ceiling of a room, is, in carpentry, called *naked flooring*, whereof there are three different sorts, viz. *single flooring, double flooring,* and *double-framed flooring.* But before entering on the particulars of either of the sorts, we will make some general observations on the construction of floors, which require the architect's attention. First, the wall plates, that is, the timbers which lie on the walls to receive the ends of the girders or joists, should be sufficiently strong and of sufficient length to throw the weight upon the piers. Secondly, if it can be avoided, girders should not lie with their ends over openings, as doors or windows ; but when they do, the strength of the wall plates must be increased. To avoid the occurrence in question, it was formerly very much the practice in this country, and indeed is still partially so, to lay girders obliquely across rooms, so as to avoid openings and chimneys, the latter whereof must indeed be always attended to. Thirdly. Wall plates and templets must be proportionately larger as their length and the weight of the floor increases. Their scantlings will, in this respect, vary to 4½ by 3 inches, up to 7½ by 5 inches. Fourthly. The timbers should always be kept rather higher, say half to three quarters of an inch higher, in the middle than at the sides of a room, when first framed, so that the natural shrinking and the settlement which occurs in all buildings, may not ultimately appear after the building is finished. Lastly, when the ends of joists or girders are supported by external walls whose height is great, the middles of such timbers ought not at first to rest upon any partition wall that does not rise higher than the floor, but a space should, says Vitruvius (lib. 7. c. 1.), be rather left between them, though, when all has settled, they may be brought to a bearing upon it. Neglect of this precaution will induce unequal settlements, and, besides causing the floor to be thrown out of a level, will most probably fracture the corners of the rooms below.

2014. Single Flooring is constructed with only one series of joists (as shown in *fig.* 672.). In this way of framing a floor, if a girder is used, it should be laid as nearly as possible over the centre of the apartment. A *single* floor containing the same quantity of timber as a double floor is much stronger ; but the ceiling of the former is liable to crack, and cannot be got to so

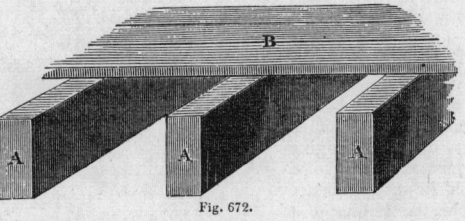

Fig. 672.

good a surface when finished. Hence, where the bearings are long, it is much better to use double flooring.

2015. The scantlings of fir joists for single flooring are exhibited in the subjoined table, and are founded on our own practice. The weight of a square varies from 11 to 18 cwt.

Length in Feet.	Width in Inches.	Depth in Inches.
6	2	6
8	2¼	7
10	2½	7½
12	2½	8
14	2½	9
18	2½	12
20	3	12

These scantlings may be varied if wanted, according to the laws laid down in the section Beams, Pillars, &c. ; 1622. *et seq.*

2016. In *fig.* 672. A A A are the joists, and B the floor boards. The laths for the ceiling are nailed to the under side of the joists A A A.

2017. In most floors, on account of the intervention of flues, chimney openings, and occasionally other causes, it will so happen that the ends of the joists cannot have a bearing on the wall. In such cases a piece of timber called a *trimmer* is framed into two of the nearest joists (then called *trimming joists*) that have a bearing on the wall. Into the trimmer, which is parallel to the wall, the ends of the joists thus intercepted from tailing into the wall are mortised. The operation is called *trimming*. The scantlings of trimmers and trimming joists may be the same as those hereafter given for binding joists; or if to the width of the common joists an eighth of an inch be added for each joist supported by the trimmer, the depth being the same, the scantling will generally be sufficient.

2018. When the bearing of a single joist floor exceeds 8 feet, a row of strutting pieces should be introduced between the joists, by which they will be prevented from horizontal twisting, and the floor will be stiffened. If the bearing be more than 12 feet, two rows of stiffening pieces or struts should be introduced, and so on for each increase of 4 feet in bearing. They should be put in, in continued rows, and be well fitted. Beyond a bearing of 15 feet it is not advisable to use single flooring, neither ought it in any case to be used where it is required to prevent the passage of sound.

2019. A *double floor* consists in its thickness of three tiers of timbers, which are called *binding joists* (these perform the office of girders), *bridging joists*, and *ceiling joists*. From an inspection of *fig.* 673. the construction will be easily understood. A A are the binding joists, which are the principal support of the floor on the upper side, whereon BB, the bridging joists are notched; which is the best method,

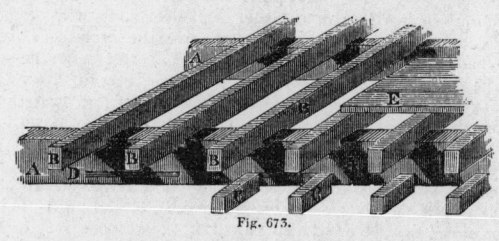

Fig. 673.

though sometimes they are framed between with *chased mortices*. The binders, of course, run from wall to wall; and as for carrying the floor, the bridging joists, as their name imports, are *bridged* on to them; so the lower tier of timbers, called the *ceiling joists*, are either notched to them, or are what is called *pulley mortised* into them; that is, a chase D is cut in the binder long enough to allow tenons of the ceiling joists C being obliquely introduced into them, and driven up to their places. The scantlings of timbers used in this method are the same as those for double-framed flooring. of which, indeed, it is but a species.

2020. The *double-framed floor* differs only from the last-named by the binding joists, instead of going from wall to wall, being framed into large pieces of timber called *girders* (as shown in *fig.* 674.), wherein A is the girder, B a binding joist, C a bridging joist, D a ceiling joist, E the pulley mortice for the ceiling joist

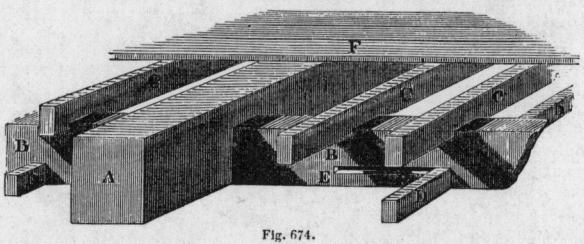

Fig. 674.

D, and F is the floor. The great advantages of this sort of flooring are, that it prevents the passage of sound between the stories, and enables the architect to make a solid ceiling.

2021. As in a double-framed floor the girders are the chief supports, it is exceedingly important that they should be sound and free from shakes. The distances between one girder and another, or the wall, should not exceed 10 feet, and their scantlings as in the following table: —

Girders of the length of 10 feet should be 9 inches deep, 7 inches wide.

12	—	10	8
14	—	11	9
16	—	12	10
18	—	12	11
20	—	13	11
22	—	14	12
24	—	15	12
26	—	16	12
28	—	16	13
30	—	16	14

2021*a*. Girders or beams whose bearing exceeds 24 feet are difficult to be procured of sufficient depth, in which case an expedient is put in requisition to strengthen a less depth. The principles it involves are explained under the head of roofs, namely, those of *trussing* them (2031, *et seq.*), an operation that converts the beam within its own thickness into a piece of framework, for the purpose of preventing the bending, or, as it is technically called, its *sagging*, which produces an injurious horizontal thrust on the walls. This operation is represented in *fig.* 675, in two different ways. No. III represents the plan.

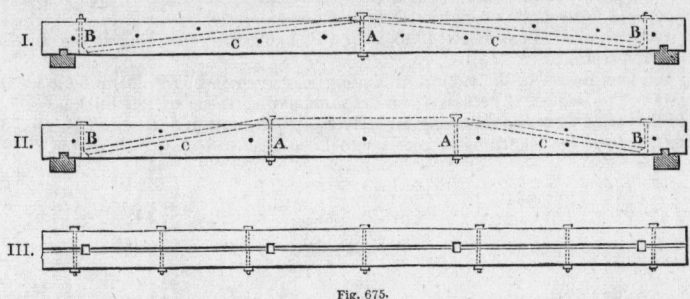

Fig. 675.

The beam is cut into two halves in the direction of its depth and length, between and into which the truss is inserted, as shown. It is better that the *truss posts* A, and *abutment pieces* B, should be of wrought iron; the *struts* C may be of oak, or some stiffer wood than the beam itself. In I. and II., the whole, or nearly the whole of the timber, is in a state of tension.

2021*b*. This operation is further developed by trussing the beam *below* itself, an arrangement considered to be safer and stronger than that above described. No. IV. has a wrought iron tension rod, with a stay in the V. centre, which takes the whole of the tension, whilst the timber is thrown entirely into compression. No. V. is the same with IV. two stays. By these systems a beam, rafter, purlin, &c., which will barely sup-

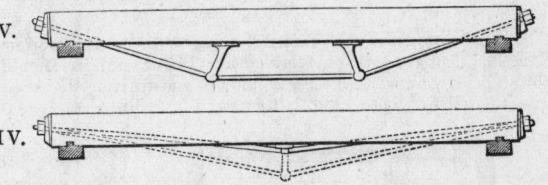

port its own weight safely, may be made to carry a load of many tons without sensible deflection. The tension rod is useful in proportion to its distance from the beam (evidently within certain limits). If it be immediately under, or concealed *within* the under edge, it becomes nearly useless, especially in a cast iron beam with a wrought iron rod, where the beam is much less extensible than the rod. In such a case, the beam would break and fall before the rod has been brought into action. The respective size or sectional area of the rod and beam is regulated by the respective strength of the materials, as it is useless to apply a rod capable of sustaining double the tensile force that the beam can resist of crushing force, and *vice versâ*; it is merely adding weight (Warr, *Dynamics*, page 259.). The flitch girder is described in par. 1629*u*.

2021*c*. The resistance of beams of soft wood may be considerably increased by strengthening the centre of gravity. Du Hamel, *Force des Bois*, took twenty-four sticks, cut from young willows, of equal strength. Each stick was 3 feet (French) long, and 1½ inch square. Six of these broke in the middle with an average weight of 566·48 lbs. In two other pieces he made a cut *across it* ⅓ inch deep in the centre, and filled it out with a piece of oak; these broke with an average weight of 594·73 lbs. Two more were cut ½ inch deep, and treated in the same manner; they broke with 585 lbs. Five were cut ¾ inch deep, and broke with 572·78 lbs. All the trials showed that the piece of harder wood increased the strength of the beam.

2021*d*. Laves's girder is a simple and effective contrivance for strengthening a beam. The piece of timber having been cut nearly from end to end (*fig.* 675*a.*), is bound at each termination with an iron strap. Blocks are driven in the cut so as to separate

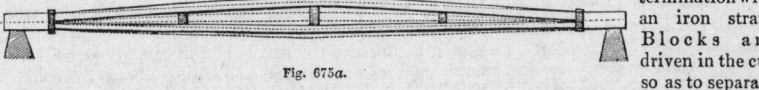

Fig. 675*a*.

the severed pieces to several inches distance in the middle of the length, thereby throwing

the material farther above and below the neutral axis. A solid beam, 40 feet long, $9\frac{1}{4}$ inches deep, and $7\frac{1}{4}$ inches wide, deflected $5\frac{1}{4}$ inches with a load of 1,700 lbs. When a similar beam had been cut to 3·6 inches of each end, making the upper part 5 inches deep and the lower part $4\frac{1}{4}$ inches, and separated by blocks until the parts were as wide asunder as half the depth of the beam, the beam suffered a less deflection by $1\frac{3}{4}$ inch. A greater strength was obtained by separating the parts to the whole depth of the beam, when it deflected 3 inches less than the solid beam ; and when separated to $1\frac{1}{2}$ times the depth, it deflected 4 inches less than the solid beam. The greatest strength is obtained by giving a section to the upper and lower parts proportional to the power of the material to resist tension and compression (*Civil Engineer* for 1840, page 161, being the paper read at the Institute of British Architects).

2022. We now return to the subject of binding joists, which ought not to be more than 6 feet apart. The depths, if necessary, for accommodating them to the thickness of the floor, may be varied from the following table by the rules given under section BEAMS, &c.

Binding joists of the length of 6 feet should be 6 inches deep, 4 inches wide.

8	—	7	$4\frac{1}{2}$
10	—	8	5
12	—	9	$5\frac{1}{2}$
14	—	10	6
16	—	11	$6\frac{1}{2}$
18	—	12	7
20	—	13	$7\frac{1}{2}$

The scantlings of bridging joists are similar to those already given for single flooring. These, as well as ceiling joists, whose scantlings are subjoined, should not be more than 12 inches apart, and they require to be scarcely thicker than is necessary to bear the nails of the laths fixed to them, for which 2 inches is quite sufficient.

Ceiling joists of the length of 4 feet should be $2\frac{1}{2}$ inches deep, $1\frac{1}{2}$ inch wide.

6	—	$3\frac{1}{2}$	$1\frac{1}{2}$
8	—	4	2
10	—	5	2
12	—	$5\frac{1}{2}$	$2\frac{1}{2}$

The weight of a square of framed flooring with counter flooring varies from 22 to 36 cwt.

2023. Though, perhaps, more curious than useful, we should not perform our duty to the student, were we to omit a method of constructing floors with short timbers, where long ones are not to be procured. Suppose it be required to floor the room ABCD (*fig.* 676.)

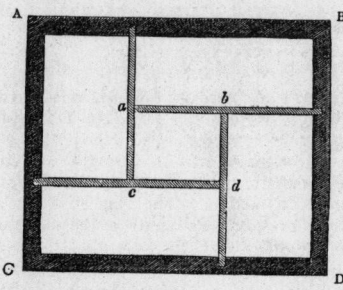

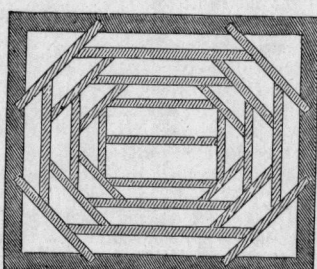

Fig. 676.   Fig. 677.

Let four joists, as in the figure, be mortised and tenoned at *abcd*, as there shown. Now it is evident that these joists will mutually support each other, for each is supported at one end by the wall, and at the other by the middle of the next joist. *Fig.* 677. shows another mode of accomplishing the same object ; and many other forms would immediately suggest themselves to the experienced architect. The expedient is of ancient origin, inasmuch as our old master (so we delight to call him, notwithstanding the new lights that modern critics have found to guide them), Serlio, has described the expedient without any difference. In the fourth volume of Rondelet (*Art de Bâtir*), an author to whom we are under infinite obligations, is described a floor executed at Amsterdam for a room 60 feet square, of exceedingly singular construction, inasmuch as it is without joists at all. Each side of the room is provided with very strong wall plates, whose angles are secured with iron straps, and are rebated to receive the flooring, which consists of three thicknesses of $1\frac{1}{2}$ inch boards. Of these thicknesses, the first is laid diagonally across the opening, its ends resting on the rebates of the wall plates, and rising about $2\frac{1}{2}$ inches towards the centre of the room. The next (second) thickness is laid diagonally at right angles to the first thickness, and the two are well nailed together. In the third thickness,

the boards are laid down parallel to one of the sides of the room, and form the upper side of the floor, being, however, well nailed to those below. The whole of them are *grooved* and *tongued* together, forming a solid floor 4½ inches thick. In this example is an instance well worthy the study of the architect, as respects a scientific connection of parts, and the great advantage of a well-disposed bond. The floor in question is, in fact, a thin plate, well supported round the edges, the strengths of the plates being directly as the squares of their thicknesses, equally strong to bear a weight in the middle, whatever their bearing; though if the load be uniformly distributed, the strength will be inversely as the area of the space.

2023*a*. The flooring of the Middle Ages, as used for upper rooms, were constructed with large square timbers resting on wood plates, which formed the cornice to the rooms ; sometimes they had stone cornices under them. Occasionally the under sides of the joists were covered with boarding, and this was divided into panels by small ribs, with bosses at the intersections, carved with foliage, or with shields of arms, or other ornaments. An example of the 15th century exists at Wingham, in Kent; Parker, *Dom. Arch.* iii. 127. These were usually coloured in distemper. The ceiling of the nave and of the eastern part of St. Alban's Abbey church is a remarkable example of a fine flat *ceiling* of early date, as is also that in the tower of the church at St. Cross, in Hampshire, and that of the library, 15th century (and formerly in the chapel) of Merton College, Oxford. In England, in the 13th century, the ceilings (which were of wood) were frequently painted the same as on the wainscot, in green and gold, and were sometimes also decorated with historical subjects and with gilded bosses.

2023*b*. The joists that came upon a beam were placed upon it, and, being cut, were pinned into corresponding blocks. If the beam took two sets of joists, the blocks might be made long enough to connect the ends of the two sets. But by the 14th century the system of girders, binders, and joists was perfected; boarding one inch and a half thick, rebated on both edges, was laid with the wider face downward, and connected by rebated battens, fixed upon stop-moulded joists, and these were dovetailed for half their depth into moulded binders, that were dovetailed three-fifths of their depth into moulded girders, the backs of all being flush for the boarding, which received the mortar and tile floor.

2023*c*. Whether in oak or fir, this latter system was apparently never enriched with painting, but moulded and carved ; indeed the inevitable towel decoration makes its appearance in panels formed by moulded strutting. These panels are let into rebates on the back of the struts and joists and binders, so as to leave a space between the panels and the flush floor, receiving the plaster or the tiles upon plastering. Another effective practice was to rebate the backs of the joists sufficiently deep to allow the apparent *ceiling* to consist of short pieces of board that were decorated on the two edges, laid close together, forming a pattern of circles, diamonds, foils, &c., cut in open work, with a ground formed by laying a plank over the whole length between the joists; over this came the finished one, or three coated floor. In the 15th and 16th centuries, pendentives hanging by keys to timber ceiling-joists, between binders, formed an entirely new arrangement of decoration, which rivalled in its complexity of drops and coffers the most elaborate works of Saracenic ceilings. In the time of Henry VIII., the ceilings were commonly of plaster, with a great variety of patterns stamped in them. The ceiling of the chapel of the Savoy Palace in the Strand is a rich example of panelling only.

2023*d*. Some of the timber houses built in Troyes at the commencement of the 15th century afford good specimens of the manner in which the construction of the floors was rendered ornamental. The studs of the framing carry the usual head-piece, which is moulded; and on this are notched down the ceiling joists, which have their ends cut as cantilevers: upon these rests a board, or plank, having its edge moulded, which is kept in place by the chantlates at the feet of the rafters. At other times the sill is separated from the joists ; because they rest upon stanchions, upon which are planted brackets carrying the ends of the joists : between the ends, which are grooved, there is a piece of carved woodwork, so that the ends of the joists, in conjunction with a moulded plate resting upon them and receiving the tie beams or ceiling joists, form a sort of corbel-table. (*Fig.* 701*l*.)

2023*e*. Another method of forming a floor, with its ceiling, into decorated construction, is due to the 15th century. This consisted in cutting balks of timber diagonally and laying them with the angles downward close together. The ends were notched into the girders or binders, leaving flush backs. If not sightly enough, triangular fillets were put in between them ; and the sharp angle might even be taken off the arris or under edge of the balks. Floors were also composed of brick segment arches (the bricks being set herring-bone) between balks of timber laid with one corner upwards, so as to form a skew-back for the arches.

2023*f*. For these few remarks we are indebted to Viollet le Duc's admirable *Dictionnaire*. As the systems therein shown will scarcely be adopted in England in general practice, the student will do well to refer to the work should he require any illustrations. A very

suggestive late example, richly moulded and carved, as it existed before 1843 at Fontainebleau, when it appears to have been reused and somewhat altered, is given in that work
among many others.

2023g. *Timber groined ceilings* are to be met with in the choir and lady chapel at St.
Albans'; in Warmington Church, Northamptonshire, of the Early English period ; in the
cloisters at Lincoln and Gloucester; in the towers at Exeter; in the lantern at Peterborough ; the lantern at Ely, and the choir at Winchester, cathedrals ; in the choir at
Selby Abbey Church, Yorkshire ; in the nave of Boston Church, Lincolnshire, where it
unfortunately occupies 22 feet of height; the chapel of St. Mary's College, Winchester ;
and the entire roofing of York Minster.   The vaults spring from stone-work carried up as
high as required to free the ribs from the wall ; there is no special mark of division at the
point where the stonework ceased and the woodwork commenced.   The boarding was let
into a groove in the sides of the ribs, or laid on a rebate.   The eastern part of the chancel of
the 13th century church at Uffington, in Berkshire, is evidently groined or prepared for
groining in this way, for whilst the walls and buttresses were insufficient to resist the
thrust of a vault even filled in with chalk, the stone springers exist.   "There seems to be
no good reason," continues Mr. Street, from whose lecture on *Woodwork* we are quoting,
"why this kind of ceiling should be condemned, as it has been by some writers, as though
it were unreal, or in any way a sham.   It is nothing of the kind, and no attempt was
made to make the wood look like stone.   The boarding was frequently feather-edged, and
grooved and tongued, and thus obviously of wood.   (*Fig.* 780*f.*)   It may be introduced in
buildings not calculated to resist the thrust of a stone vault; and it may be carried far up
into the roof and above the top of the walls, which in stone vaults is always, within a
little, the limits of internal height attainable."

PARTITIONS.

2024. The framework of timber used for dividing the internal parts of a house into
rooms is called a *partition* or *quartered partition*.   It is commonly lathed and plastered ;
when the spaces between the timbers or quarters are bricked up, it is called a *bricknogged
partition*.   The weight of a square of common partition is rarely less than from 13 to
18 cwt. ; hence it becomes necessary to take care that partitions should not be set upon the
floor, without taking due precaution to relieve it of the weight, either by struts, braces, or
the formation of a truss in it.   When a partition occurs in an upper story, under a strongly
trussed roof, it may be often advantageously suspended from the roof, and its weight thus
taken off from the floor below.   If it have a solid bearing throughout its length, it
requires nothing but struts between the quarters ; but these are not absolutely required.
The scantlings of the timbers of a quarter partition should vary according to the extent
of bearing.   Where that does not exceed 20 feet, 4 by 3 inches will be sufficient ; and where
it is as much as 40 feet, the quarters should not be under 6 by 4 inches, that is, supposing
it to bear only its own weight.   When it has to bear more, the scantling must, of course,
be increased accordingly.

2025. *Fig.* 678. represents a design for a trussed partition, with a doorway in the centre

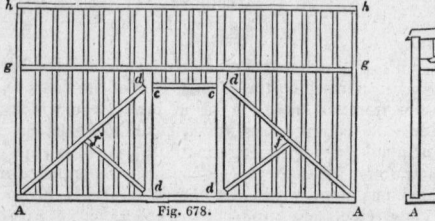 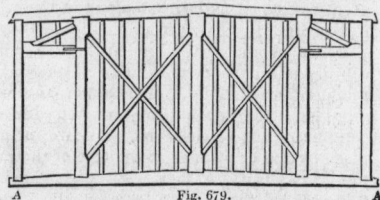

Fig. 678.   Fig. 679.

of it : in which *hh* is the head, and A A the sill ; *dc, dc* the doorposts ; *gg* the *intertie,*
A*d,* A*d* the braces ; *fd, fd* struts.   *Fig.* 679. shows a method of trussing a partition in
which the doors are at the sides.   It is obvious that additional strength may also be gained,
when wanted, by introducing a truss between the intertie and head of a partition.   The
angle of inclination of braces should be about 40° with the horizon.

CARRIAGE OF STAIRS.

2026. The framed timbers which support the steps of a staircase are called the *carriage.*
They generally consist of two pieces inclined to the pitch of the stairs, called the *rough
strings*.   When geometrical stairs consist of two alternate flights with a half-pace between
them, the carriage of the half-pace is constructed with a beam parallel to the risers of the

steps, whose joists are framed into the beam for the support of the flooring. This beam is called the *apron piece*, and that which sustains the rough strings at the upper end is called the *pitching piece*. The joists of the half-pace are sometimes turned into the pitching piece, and sometimes bridge over it ; but the steps of both flights are always supported by string pieces, as before. The upper ends of the string pieces at the landing rest upon an horizontal piece of timber, called, as above, an apron piece. The scantlings of the strings, of course, vary with the length of the inclined part. The depth given to joists of similar length will be more than sufficient.

ROOFS.

2027. The first obvious consideration in constructing a roof is the slope to be given to it, which depends on the climate against which it is to serve as a protection, and on the materials to be employed in covering it. In hot countries, rain more rarely falls than in temperate ones ; but when it comes, it descends very abundantly, which, added to the temperature of the air, makes it unnecessary to give a great slope to the roof, from which the water immediately runs, and the air dries it almost at the instant of the rain's cessation. In cold countries the rain is more searching, the air is more impregnated with moisture, and snow often lies for a long time on a roof; circumstances which require a greater proportional slope to be given to it. Again, roofs covered with lead, zinc, or copper, do not require so great a slope as those covered with tiles or slates. (See ROOFING, in Glossary.)

2028. Though among architects there does not appear to have been any fixed principle by which the slope should be determined, we find that in different climates suitable slopes have been adopted for similar materials. Thus in the southern parts of Europe we find the roofs very flat; whilst as we proceed into its northern parts the roof acquires a very considerable elevation. We shall here transfer to our pages the notice of this subject in the *Encyclopedie Methodique*, which we consider extremely important and interesting, inasmuch as it shows that necessity was the parent of beauty in the inclination of the roofs of the ancients ; and in the times of the middle ages it had some influence even in the production and developement of the lancet arch.

2029. The researches and observations made respecting the roofs of a great many ancient and modern buildings, situate in different countries, satisfy us that the slopes of roofs which have lasted best are always proportioned to the temperature of the climate. Before entering into the consideration of any law for determining the slope of a roof, it will be proper to comprehend the meaning of the word climate as here introduced, which we shall use in the same way as it is understood by geographers. According to them, the climates of the globe are comprised under belts or bands, of unequal size, parallel to the equator. Of them there are twenty-four between the equator and the polar circle, each of half an hour ; that is, the length of the longest day of a place situated at the beginning of the climate is always shorter by half an hour than that of the place situated at the extremity of the same climate, or at the beginning of the succeeding one, proceeding from the equator towards the polar circle. This difference in the length of the day, caused by the greater or less obliquity of the tropic with the horizon, is one reason of the different degrees of temperature of countries corresponding to the different climates. We are not, however, to assume that the temperature will be exactly the same for all places under the same climate, since there are many circumstances which tend to make a place more or less damp, in which cases the slope of the roof should rather have a relation to a more northern spot. In the roofs of the Continent covered with the hollow tile, as in the south of France for instance, less slope is required than with the Roman tiles (see the word TILE in Glossary), which are in sections alternately flat and circular; and these, again, require less slope than the common plain tile or slate. From the observations that have been made, we find that the slope of roofs covered with hollow tile, ⌒⌒⌒ thus, of the south of France, should be after the rate of three degrees for every climate, beginning from the equator and proceeding northward, and that when the Roman tile is used, an addition of three degrees should be made to such inclination; an addition of six degrees, if covered with slates; and of eight degrees, if covered with plain tiles. According to this law, the table which will be presently subjoined has been constructed, and a comparison of it with ancient buildings gives a remarkable corroboration of its value. Thus, at Athens, situated about the middle of the sixth climate, the slope of a pediment would be about $16\frac{1}{2}°$; and that of the Parthenon is actually about $16°$; that of the temple of Erectheus, $15\frac{1}{2}°$; of Theseus, $15°$. In Rome, which is about one third of the way up the seventh climate, the Roman tile requires an inclination of $22°$. The actual slope of the pediment of Septimius Severus is $23°$; those of the temples of Concord and Mars Ultor, $23\frac{1}{2}°$; of Fortuna Virilis and the Pantheon, $24°$; and, of more modern date, the slope of the roof of St. Paolo fuorì le murà was $23°$.

2030. We shall now give the reader the table above mentioned. The argument at the head of each column will render its further explanation unnecessary.

City.	Country.	Climate.	Length of longest Day.		Covered with			
			h.	m.	Hollow Tiles. deg. min.	Roman Tiles. deg. min.	Slates. deg. min.	Plain Tiles. deg. min.
Carthagena -	Spain - -	VI.	14	42	16 12	19 12	22 12	24 12
Palermo -	Italy - -	—	14	48	16 48	19 48	22 48	24 48
Lisbon -	Portugal -	—	14	50	17 00	20 00	23 00	25 00
Toledo -	Spain - -	—	14	58	17 48	20 48	23 48	25 48
Madrid -	Spain - -	—	15	00	18 00	21 00	24 00	26 00
Naples -	Italy - -	VII.	15	2	18 12	21 12	24 12	26 12
Constanti-nople -	Turkey -	—	15	4	18 24	21 24	24 24	26 24
Barcelona -	Spain - -	—	15	8	18 48	21 48	24 48	26 48
Rome - -	Italy - -	—	15	10	19 00	22 00	25 00	27 00
Pau - -	France -	—	15	20	20 00	23 00	26 00	28 00
Florence -	Italy - -	—	15	22	20 12	23 12	26 12	28 12
Avignon -	France -	—	15	24	20 24	23 24	26 24	28 24
Genoa - -	Italy - -	—	15	28	20 48	23 48	26 48	28 48
Bologna -	Italy - -	—	15	28	20 48	23 48	26 48	28 48
Bordeaux -	France -	—	15	30	21 00	24 00	27 00	29 00
Piacenza -	Italy - -	VIII.	15	32	21 12	24 12	27 12	29 12
Turin and Venice -	Italy - -	—	15	34	21 24	24 24	27 24	29 24
Milan - -	Italy - -	—	15	36	21 36	24 36	27 36	29 36
Lyons - -	France -	—	15	40	22 00	25 00	28 00	30 00
Geneva -	Switzerland	—	15	44	22 24	25 24	28 24	30 24
Dijon - -	France -	—	15	52	23 12	26 12	29 12	31 12
Zurich - -	Switzerland	—	15	54	23 24	26 24	29 24	31 24
Munich -	Germany -	—	15	58	23 48	26 48	29 48	31 48
Vienna -	Germany -	—	16	00	24 00	27 00	30 00	32 00
Strasbourg -	France -	IX.	16	2	24 12	27 12	30 12	32 12
Paris - -	France -	—	16	6	24 36	27 36	30 36	32 36
Ratisbon -	Germany -	—	16	8	24 48	27 48	30 48	32 48
Rheims -	France -	—	16	10	25 00	28 00	31 00	33 00
Nuremberg -	Germany -	—	16	12	25 12	28 12	31 12	33 12
Manheim -	Germany -	—	16	12	25 12	28 12	31 12	33 12
Havre -	France -	—	16	12	25 12	28 12	31 12	33 12
Mayence -	Germany -	—	16	18	25 48	28 48	31 48	33 48
Frankfort (Maine) -	Germany -	—	16	18	25 48	28 48	31 48	33 48
Cracow -	Poland -	—	16	20	26 00	29 00	32 00	34 00
Valenciennes	France -	—	16	22	26 12	29 12	32 12	34 12
Brussels -	Belgium -	—	16	26	26 36	29 36	32 36	34 36
Cologne -	Germany -	—	16	28	26 48	29 48	32 48	34 48
Antwerp -	Belgium -	—	16	30	27 00	30 00	33 00	35 00
London -	England -	X.	16	34	27 24	30 24	33 24	35 24
The Hague -	Holland -	—	16	40	28 00	31 00	34 00	36 00
Warsaw -	Poland -	—	16	42	28 12	31 12	34 12	36 12
Berlin - -	Germany -	—	16	46	28 36	31 36	34 36	36 36
Hamburg -	Germany -	—	16	58	29 48	32 48	35 48	37 48
Dresden -	Germany -	—	17	00	30 00	33 00	36 00	38 00
Dantzic -	Poland -	XI.	17	8	30 48	33 48	36 48	38 48
Moscow -	Russia -	—	17	22	32 12	35 12	38 12	40 12
Copenhagen -	Denmark -	—	17	28	32 48	35 48	38 48	40 48
Edinburgh -	Scotland -	XII.	17	32	33 12	36 12	39 12	41 12
Stockholm -	Sweden -	XIII.	18	30	39 00	42 00	45 00	47 00
Petersburgh	Russia - -	XIV.	18	44	40 24	43 24	46 24	48 24
Bergen -	Norway -	—	18	44	40 24	43 24	46 24	48 24

" There is no article," says Ware in his *Body of Architecture*, " in the whole compass of the architect's employment that is more important or more worthy of a distinct consideration than the roof. The great caution is," continues our author " that the roof be neither too massy nor too slight. Both extremes are to be avoided, for in architecture every extreme is to be shunned, but of the two the overweight of roof is more to be regarded than too much slightness. This part is intended not only to cover the building, but

to press upon the walls, and by that bearing to unite and hold all together. This it will not be massy enough to perform if too little timber be employed, so that the extreme is to be shunned. But in practice the great and common error is on the other side ; and he will do the most acceptable service to his profession, who shall show how to retrench and execute the same roof with a smaller quantity of timber ; he will by this take off an unnecessary load from the walls, and a large and useless expense to the owner."

2031. We shall now proceed to a popular view of the strains exerted by the timbers of roofs, referring the reader back to the section on BEAMS, PILLARS, &c., for a more extended and scientific view of them. Suppose (*fig.* 680.), in the simplest form of roof, the rafters (shown by dotted lines) AB, CB to pitch upon the walls A*a*, C*c*. Let the rafters be supposed to be connected together at B as by a hinge, as also similarly connected with the walls at A and C. Now if the effective weight of the walls be not sufficient to resist the thrusts of the rafters, as respects the height, thickness, and situation of the centre of gravity of such walls, taken as solid masses and moveable on the points X and Y, it is manifest the rafters by their own gravity will descend, and the walls will spread and be thrown out of an upright, as in *ab* and *cd*, and the rafters will take the places shown in the figure. It has already been shown (par. 1633) that the horizontal thrust of a pair of rafters thus

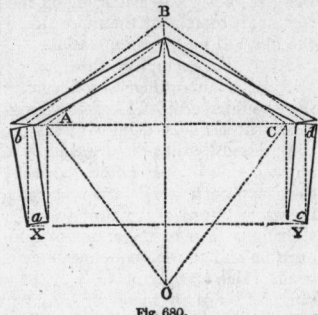

Fig. 680.

meeting each other, is proportional to the length of a line drawn perpendicularly from the rafter's foot until it intersects a vertical line drawn from its apex. As the roof therefore becomes flatter, the length of the perpendicular increases. Hence, if AB and BC be the rafters, and their weights be represented by their lengths, the weight or power of thrust exerted by the rafter AB in the direction of its length will be represented by BO, and the horizontal thrust by AO ; AO being perpendicular to AB. To secure, then, the walls in their perpendicularity, which the thrust of the rafters tends to derange, a system of framing becomes necessary. Thus, in *fig.* 681.,

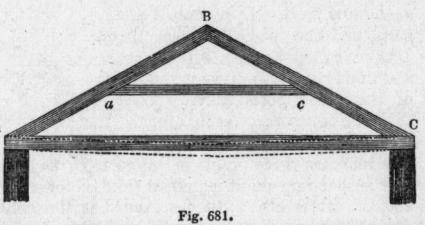

Fig. 681.

a beam AC, which from the office it performs of tying or confining the feet of the rafters is called a *tie beam*, is introduced across the opening, and into this beam the rafters are framed. If the tie is introduced above the level of the walls, it is called a *collar beam*, as *ac*. It is manifest that these beams exert their power in the same way that a string would, that is, that the principal strain which they have to perform is in the direction of their length, and hence, that for such especial purpose, if they be prevented from *sagging* or bending, a small size or scantling will be sufficient, for we have already seen that the cohesive power of timber is very great in the direction of its length. To take care that the tie beam thus introduced should be strained only in the direction for which it is used, we are now led to another expedient. The beam by its own gravity, especially in a large opening, would have a tendency to sag or bend in the middle, and the more so if its scantling be simply proportioned to its office of a tie. To prevent this a fresh tie is introduced called a *king-post* DB (*fig.* 682.), by which the beam is tied or slung up to the apex of

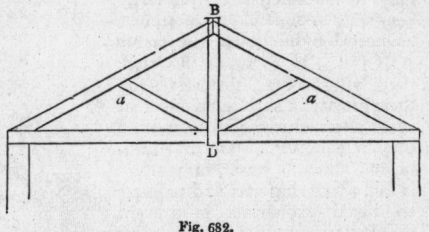

Fig. 682.

the principal rafters ; and this combination of a pair of rafters, a tie beam and a king-post, is called a *truss*, and is the most important of the assemblages which the carpenter produces. When the rafters are of such length that they would be liable of themselves to sag down, supports *aa* are introduced at the points where such failures would occur, and these supports are called *struts*, because their office is to strut up the rafter, which they should do as nearly as the case will admit in a direction perpendicular to the slope of the rafters.

2032. It is clear that out of this last case a fresh system of trusses may arise as in *fig.* 683., for from those points procured by the struts against the rafters, new rods may

be slung for increasing the stiffness of the tie beam *ad infinitum* in theory, but not in practice, because the compressibility of the fibres of timber is considerable in lines perpendicular to their direction, and the contraction and expansion of metal places a limit to its use. This compression of tim-

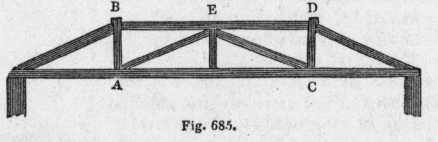

Fig. 683.

ber deserves great attention on the part of the architect. We may lay down as a rule in respect to it that the more the weights or pressures act in the direction of the fibres, the less will be the compression.

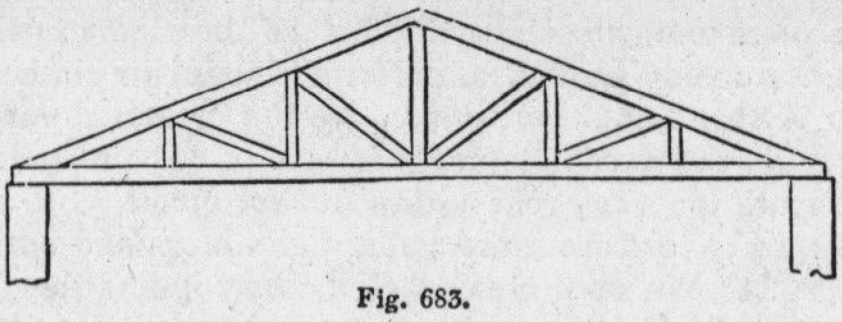

2033. To exemplify this, *fig.* 684. shows in No. 1. the principal rafters of a roof butting in an ordinary roof, against the shoulders AB, CD of the king-post, whose fibres, being vertical, are compressed by the pressure against it, on each side of the rafters, whereby they approach each other, causing the whole figure of the roof to suffer a change. For by the action of com-

Fig. 684.

pression and its consequence the kingpost must descend, and with it, consequently, the tie beam which is slung up to it. To remedy the inconvenience in roofs constructed of fir, the kingpost is often made of oak, which is less compressible, a practice which should be observed in all roofs of consequence. But cast iron kingposts are the best substitute where the expense can be justified. In No. 2. the end is accomplished much more economically by *housing* the rafters in the head of the kingpost at the angle in which the rafters meet, by which the fibres of the rafters butt against each other, bringing the compression nearer to that which takes place in a post according as the rafters are less inclined to each other, and the beam is then literally suspended from the vertical planes of the rafters at their junction.

2034. When a roof (*fig.* 685.) is trussed by two upright suspending posts, which become necessary in increased spans, such posts, AB, CD, are called *queen-posts*, and the piece between them, BD, is called a *collar*, which acts as a *straining piece* to prevent the heads of the queen-posts moving out of their places towards each other. It will on mere inspection be seen that

Fig. 685.

this roof has three points of support, B, E, and D; for by means of the struts AE, EC, a new suspending point is gained from E for sustaining the tie beam between the points A and C. It is also to be observed that the collar or straining piece BD performs in this assemblage an office exactly the reverse of that which it does in *fig.* 681.

2035. The *Mansard* roof, so called from its inventor's name, and with us called a *Curb roof*, frequently used for the purpose of keeping down the height of a building, and at the same time of obtaining sleeping or other rooms in it, is shown in *figs.* 686 and 687. It may be considered as primarily consisting of four pieces of timber connected by hinges at the points ABCDE. If these be inverted, they will arrange themselves by their gravity in such a manner that when returned to their first position they remain in a state of equilibrium, which, however, in practice is but a tottering one, and requires additional expedients to prevent the whole assemblage thrusting out the walls; and, moreover, to prevent the upper rafters from acting by their thrust to displace the lower ones. To obtain these ends the first object is to introduce the tie

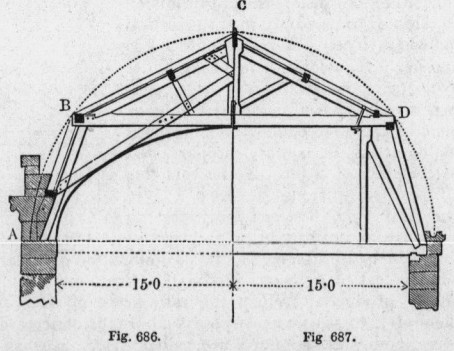

Fig. 686.   Fig 687.

AE; and, secondly, the tie BD. It is to be understood that means are to be used, when needed from their length, to prevent these beams from bending, similar to those already directed in the cases of simple trusses. *Fig.* 686 is an example selected from Krafft, (*Art. de la Charpente*, fol. 1805), having an arched ceiling to give additional height to

some large or public room. This form of roof has been frequently adopted in the palaces of France and Germany. *Fig.* 687 is a king-post Mansard roof, affording a wide space over the tie beam available as an apartment. *Fig.* 698 is an example of the principles adopted for a much wider spanned roof.

2035a. We have thus far endeavoured to explain in the simplest way the conduct to be pursued for obtaining stability in the construction of a roof; but before we proceed to the scantlings of the timbers to be employed, the reader must be informed that the trusses to roofing, with whose nature he has now become acquainted, are placed only at certain intervals (which should not exceed 10 feet) apart, and are thus made to bear the *common rafters* and the weight of the covering, as well as to perform the office of suspending the tie beam by which the walls are kept together. Hence the rafters so framed in a truss are called principal rafters; and by the means of a *purline* A (*fig.* 688.), which lies horizontally throughout the roof's length on the principal rafters, they are made to bear all the superincumbent load. The purlines are in various ways made fast to the principal rafters, and upon it the common rafters are usually notched down. Their bearings are thus lessened, and less scantlings suffice for them.

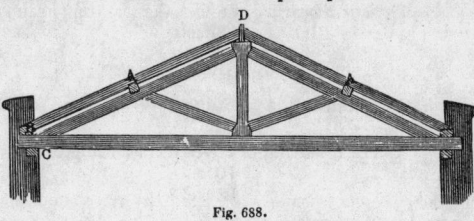

Fig. 688.

They are received at their feet on a piece of timber (B in the figure), which runs longitudinally along the sides of the building. This piece of timber is called a *pole plate*, from being the uppermost plate in a building; at their summits they abut against a *ridge piece* D. When a roof slopes each way, the space enclosed between the intersection of the slopes is called a hip (*fig.* 689.); and the longest rafters in it, which are those at the angles, are

Fig. 689.

called *hip rafters*, and the shorter ones are named *jack rafters*, as A, A, A, &c.

2036. We have, at the beginning of this section (2007.), observed, that the use made of bolts must be always in a direction as nearly as possible counter to the strain which the pieces exert; the method, therefore, of introducing them will, on due consideration, be sufficiently obvious.

Before proceeding to lay before the reader some few examples of roofs suitable to different spans, as well as of some of magnitude which have been executed, it may be as well to complete this portion of our labour, by giving some information on the scantlings of timber for roofing, in which a medium, founded on our own practice, is introduced between ignorant overloading, and fanciful theory.

2037. For roofs whose spans are between 20 and 30 feet, no more than a truss with a king-post and struts will be necessary, in which case the scantlings hereunder given will be sufficient.

For a span of 20 feet, the tie beam to be 9 in. by 4 in. ; the king-post, 4 in. by 4 in. ; principal rafter, 4 in. by 4 in. ; struts, 4 in. by 3 in.

For a span of 25 feet, the tie beam to be 10 in. by 5 in. ; the king-posts, 5 in. by 5 in. ; principal rafter, 5 in. by 4 in. ; struts, 5 in. by 3 in.

For a span of 30 feet, the tie beam to be 11 in. by 6 in. ; the king-post, 6 in. by 6 in. ; principal rafter, 6 in. by 4 in. ; struts, 6 in. by 3 in.

2038. For roofs whose spans are between 30 and 45 feet, a truss with two queen-posts and struts will be required, and a straining piece between the queen-posts. Thus —

For a span of 35 feet, the tie beams to be 11 in. by 4 in. ; queen-posts 4 in. by 4 in. ; principals, 5 in. by 4 in. ; straining piece, 7 in. by 4 in. ; struts, 4 in. by 2 in.

For a span of 40 feet, the tie beams to be 12 in. by 5 in. ; queen-posts, 5 in. by 5 in. ; principals, 5 in. by 5 in. ; straining piece, 7 in. by 5 in. ; struts, 5 in. by 2½ in.

For a span of 45 feet, the tie beams to be 13 in. by 6 in. ; queen-posts, 6 in. by 6 in. ; principals, 6 in. by 5 in. ; straining piece, 7 in. by 6 in. ; struts, 5 in. by 3 in.

2039. For roofs whose spans are between 45 and 60 feet, two queen-posts are required, and a straining piece between them; struts from the larger to the smaller queen-posts, and struts again from the latter.

For a span of 50 feet, tie beams, 13 in. by 8 in. ; queen-posts, 8 in. by 8 in. ; small queens, 8 in. by 4 in. ; principals, 8 in. by 6 in. ; straining piece, 9 in. by 6 in. ; struts, 5 in. by 3 in.

For a span of 55 feet, tie beams, 14 in. by 9 in. ; queen-posts, 9 in. by 8 in. ; small queens, 9 in. by 4 in. ; principals, 8 in. by 7 in. ; straining-piece, 10 in. by 6 in. ; struts, 5½ in. by 3 in.

For a span of 60 feet, tie beams, 15 in. by 10 in. ; queen-posts, 10 in. by 8 in. ; small queens, 10 in. by 4 in. ; principals, 8 in. by 8 in. ; straining piece, 11 in. by 6 in. ; struts, 6 in. by 3 in.

2040. The scantlings of purlines are regulated principally by their bearing ; and though we have subjoined scantlings for bearings of 12 feet, such should be avoided by not allowing the distances between the trusses to exceed 10 feet. Thus —

> For a bearing of 6 feet, the scantling of the purline should be 6 by 4.
> 8 feet,   —   7 by 5.
> 10 feet,   —   8 by 6.
> 12 feet,   —   9 by 7.

For common rafters the scantlings are as follow ; 12 feet should be the maximum of the bearing.

> For a bearing of 8 feet the scantling of the rafter should be 4 by 2½.
> 10 feet,   —   5 by 2½.
> 12 feet,   —   6 by 2½.

2040a. To determine the size of a rafter for a roof to support the covering of slate, the distance between the supports being 6 feet, and the weight of a superficial foot, including the stress of the wind, being 56 lbs. ; the deflection not to exceed $\frac{1}{40}$th of an inch for each foot in length ; the formula becomes:—56 lbs. × 6 feet = 336 lbs., and $\frac{336 \text{ lbs.} \times 40 \times 6^3}{\text{E} = 3072 \times 6}$ = 157·5 of which take $\frac{5}{8}$ths for uniform load = 98·44. If the breadth be made 2½ inches, then $\frac{98 \cdot 44}{2 \cdot 5}$ = 39·3, and the cube root of 39·3 is 3·4 inches, the depth required. These are the rules given by Barlow (page 179.), who, in the several editions of his work on *Strength of Materials*, put the "reduced tabular value" for Riga fir, E = 96, and 32 times E became 3072 ; and for English oak E = 105. In the edition of 1851, this has been altered to E = 192, and 16 times E = 3072 also, for fir ; or for oak E = 210. The reason of this change has been explained in Beams and Pillars, par 1630m.

2040b. Another element in the calculation for timbers above-named, is the weights of the different materials used in covering buildings ; these are roughly stated to be as follows :—

A square of	pantiling	about	7¼ cwts.,		650 lbs.	$\frac{2}{3}$
„	plain tiling	„	14½ „		1780 „	$\frac{2}{4}$
„	stone slating	„	— „		2380 „	$\frac{2}{7}$
„	slating, a mean	„	6½ „		— „	—
„	„ common	„	— „	also put at	500 to 900 „	$\frac{1}{4}$
„	„ large	„	— „		1120 „	$\frac{1}{3}$
„	lead	„	5 „		700 „	$\frac{1}{48}$
„	zinc, 15 ounce	„	1 „		— „	$\frac{1}{48}$
„	copper	„	— „		100 „	$\frac{1}{48}$
„	thatch	„	— „		— „	$\frac{1}{3}$

The last column shows what the height of the roof, in parts of the span, is usually made. As the timbers employed are of course less in dimension as the weight decreases, it follows that a much less quantity of timber is requisite where the metals can be employed. On *flats* it will be necessary to consider the weight of the number of persons who may be probably standing on it at a time. The force of the wind has been considered in par. 1592a. When the rise or pitch is $\frac{1}{6}$th of the span, the angle formed is 18°25″ ; $\frac{1}{4}$ is 26°35″ ; $\frac{1}{3}$ is 33°42″ ; $\frac{1}{2}$ is 45° ; $\frac{2}{3}$ is 53° ; $\frac{3}{4}$ is 56°20″ ; when equilateral, 60° ; a whole pitch is 63°30″.

2041. By a study of the roofs which follow as examples, the architect will be led to other expedients and modifications of the forms submitted to his notice, as circumstances may call forth his ingenuity and talents. We have, we trust, already said enough to lead him on. Where economy must be consulted, the roof shown in *fig.* 690. may be used ; it is only fit for a small building, and the span of such a one should not exceed 25 feet. The left end of the collar beam exhibits what is called the *carpenter's boast*, but it partakes somewhat of the rule joint, being worked out to a centre. But in roofs above 25 feet span it is not well to omit the king-post and tie beam, though, if particular strains are to be provided

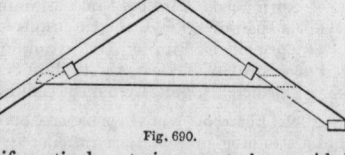

Fig. 690.

against, even in such small spans the struts should not be omitted, and the form shown in *fig.* 691. should be adopted, which will answer for spans at least up to 35 feet. In this and

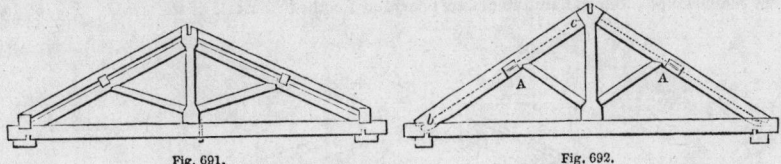

Fig. 691.   Fig. 692.

other cases of larger span, it is often desirable that the common rafters should not stand above the principals, and then the purlines are framed by mortices and tenons into the principals, as shown at A, *fig.* 692., wherein the line *bc* shows the underside of the common rafters notched on to the purlines.   This is a usual practice in Gothic roofs.

2042. From 35 to 45 feet, the tie beam should be suspended from at least three points, or it will be unnecessarily heavy ; and this suspension of the tie beam, so that it may be really a tie unsusceptible of altera-
tion in form, is the
true cause of this
introduction   of
king and queen
posts, as before ex-
plained.   Indeed,
as a general rule,
it is well that the
distance between
such points of sup-
port for a tie beam
should not exceed

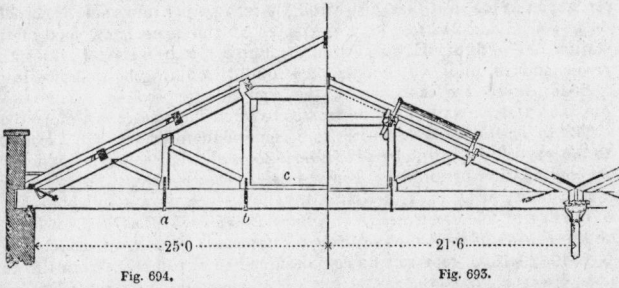

Fig. 694.   Fig. 693.

13 to 15 feet, without expedients being used to prevent intermediate sagging. *Fig.* 693. is a queen-post roof of a span of 43 feet, over the railway workshops at Worcester, showing the introduction of skylights. The trusses are placed 15 feet apart. The principal rafters are 8 by 8 ; tie beam, 12 by 8 ; queen-post, 8 by 6 ; struts, 4½ by 4½ ; straining beam, 9 by 8 ; common rafters, 4½ by 2 ; purlines, in two flitches each (trussed with stirrup pieces and iron ties), 9 by 3. The tie beams are carried on iron shoes. *Fig.* 694. is a queen-post truss for a span of 50 feet, which leaves a considerable space free in the middle. The tie beam will probably be scarfed, which will be best made between *a* and *b*. The straining sill *c*, strapped to the tie beam, will add materially to its strength.

2043. For spans above 60 feet we have not given scantlings of timber in the preceding tables ; but such do not greatly increase beyond 60 feet with practicable spans, and enough has been already said to make the reader acquainted with that part of the subject. *Fig.* 695. is the truss of the parish church of Elgin, de-signed by A. Simpson, of Aberdeen. The trusses are placed 6 feet 6 inches from centre to centre. The tie beam is in two flitches, each 13 by 5½ ; prin-cipal rafters, 11 inches deep at lower end, 8 inches at top, and 6 inches thick ; collar beam, 7 by 5½ ; king-

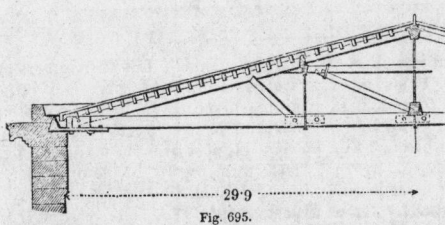

Fig. 695.

post struts, 5 by 5½ ; struts, 5 by 4½ ; horizontal rafters, 4½ by 2½, placed 13 inches apart, and covered with inch grooved and tongued deal, and 7 lbs. lead. This is similar to the Italian system intimated in Specifications, par. 2285. The tie beams have cast iron shoes at each end, with abutments formed for the rafters, and secured with ⅞ inch diameter bolts with nuts and washers. The wrought iron suspending rods are inch square, and have abutment pieces for the rafters and struts.

2043*a*. *Fig.* 695*a*. is the truss of a roof for a span of 45 ft., with cast iron shoes as abut-ments for the timbers acting as struts. The end of the tie beam has a cast iron shoe, which also takes the foot of the principal rafter. The sole plate of the shoe is prolonged inwards, to admit of its being secured by bolts to the tie beam. The head of the principal rafter *a*, and the end of the straining beam *a b*, are inserted into a cast iron socket, shown in detail in *fig.* A. The suspension rod passes through the solid part of the socket ; it has a head at its upper end, and at its lower end it is screwed and secured by a nut. On the side of the socket is cast a rest, *c*, for the side of the purline. To avoid cutting the principal

rafters, the other purline at B is also carried in a cast iron rest bolted to the rafter. The centre suspending rod passes through a cast iron socket, which serves as an abutment to the main struts. Similar abutments are provided for the lower end of the struts. *Fig. 695b.*,

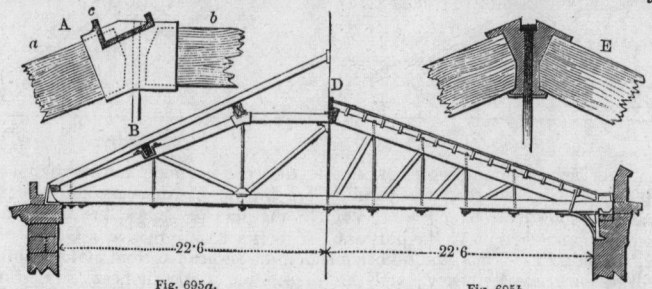

Fig. 695a.   Fig. 695b.

for a span of 45 feet, has also wrought iron suspension rods. A roof of this description, 54 feet span and 212 feet long, is erected at the passengers shed of the Croydon railway station. The figure E is a section through a cast iron socket taking the heads of the principals, and through which passes a wrought iron king bolt, shown in position at D.

2044. In all the cases given, the roof is supposed to receive no support from any but the external walls, and the trusses to be in most cases not more than 10 feet apart.

2045. The reader who desires to become acquainted with other examples, is recommended to the works by Krafft, *Art de la Charpente*, and *Charpenterie*; Rondelet, *L'Art de Bâtir*, and its continuation by Blouet; Emy, *Art de la Charpenterie*; Tredgold, *Carpentry*; Newland, *Carpenter's and Joiner's Assistant*, to which work we are indebted for the above new examples: and *The Doctrines of Carpentry Explained—of a Roof*, by Lieut.-Col. Waddington, in the Papers of the Corps of Royal Engineers, 1849, x. 71–152.

2046. *Fig.* 696. represents a roof designed by J. Gibbs. From the centres of columns the

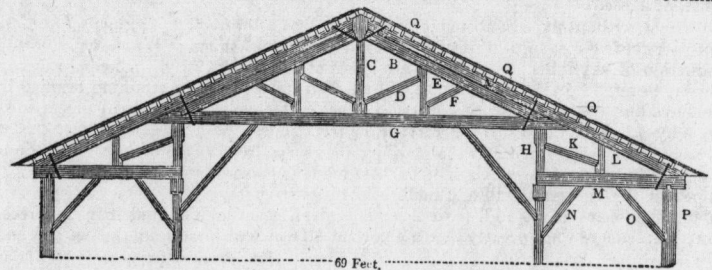

Fig. 696.   ST. MARTIN'S-IN-THE-FIELDS, WESTMINSTER.

middle aisle is 39 ft. 11 in. The roof is well contrived and framed; but the timbers are stronger than they need have been. The scantlings are as follow:—A, principal rafter, 13 in. by 10 at bottom, and 11 in. by 10 at top; B, straining brace, 14 in. by 10 at bottom, and 11 in. by 10 at top; C, king-post, 9 in. by 9; D, strut, 7 in. by 7½; E, queen-post, 8 in. by 9½; F, strut, 7 in. by 7; G, tie-beam, 14 in. by 9½; H, post over the column, 14 in. by 9½; I, brace, 7 in. by 7; K, brace, 7 in. by 7; L, post, 8 in. by 9; M, hammer beam, 14 in. by 9½; N, brace, 8 in. by 8; P, post in the wall; QQQ, purline rafters, 4 in. by 6.

2047. *Fig.* 697. is the section of a roof by James Stuart, about 1785. The span is 51 ft., and as a variation from the general forms of roofs, it is worth the student's attention. The

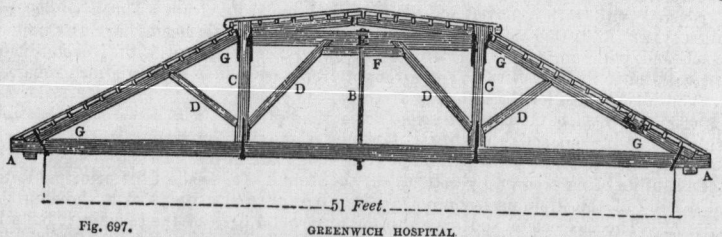

Fig. 697.   GREENWICH HOSPITAL.

scantling of the timbers are subjoined. The distance between the trusses is about 7 ft. All the joints are well secured with iron straps. AA, tie-beam, whose whole length is 57 ft., 51 ft. clear between the walls, 14 in. by 12 in.; B, an iron king-post, 2 in. square; CC,

queen-posts, 9 in. by 12; DDDD, struts, 9 in. by 7; E, straining beam, 10 in. by 7; F, straining piece, 6 in. by 7; GG, GG, principal rafters, 10 in. by 7; *hhhh*, &c. purline rafters for boarding upon instead of rafters; H, a camber beam, supporting the platform.

2048. *Fig.* 698. exhibits the roof of the old Drury Lane Theatre, which was built in

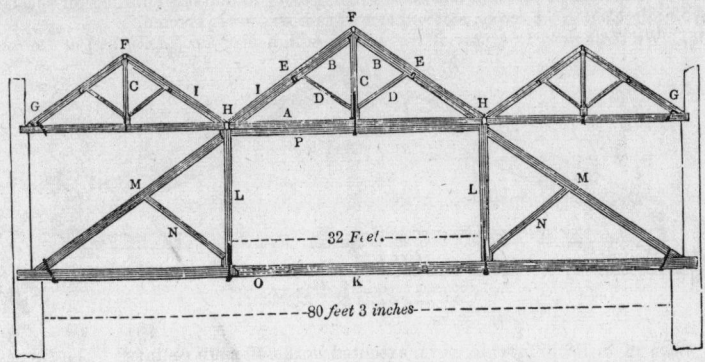

Fig. 698.

1793. It possesses great merit, from the simplicity of its composition and the accommo-dation afforded in the middle space for the carpenters and painters. By dividing the breadth of the building into three parts, the roof was kept low, and the scantlings much reduced in size. The span is 80 ft. 3½ in., the trusses were 15 ft. apart, and the whole length of the roof was 200 ft. It was destroyed by fire on the 24th of February, 1809. The scantlings of the timbers were as follow : — A, beams, 12 in. by 7; B, principal rafters, 7 in. thick ; C, king-posts, 12 in. by 7; D, struts, 5 in. by 7; E, purlines, 9 in. by 5 ; F, ridge pieces, 1½ in. thick ; G, pole plates, 5 in. by 5 ; H, gutter plates framed into beams, 12 in. by 6 ; I, common rafters, 5 in. and 4 in. by 2½; K, beams, 15 in. by 12; L, posts, 15 in. by 12 : M, principal braces, 14 in. by 12 and 12 ; N, struts, 8 in, by 12 ; O, oak trusses to the middle bearing of beams, 5½ in. by 4½; P, straining beams, 12 in. by 12.

2049. The last example we shall present is of the method in which the external dome of St. Paul's is framed (*fig.* 699.). The internal dome A*a* is of brickwork, two bricks thick, having, at every five feet, as it rises, a course consisting of bricks eighteen inches long, which serves to bind the whole thickness together. This dome was turned upon a centre, which rested upon the projection at its springing, without any support from below, and was afterwards left for the use of the painter. It was banded together with iron at the springing. Exterior to the brick dome (which has indeed, nothing immediately to do with the subject) is a cone of brickwork BB*b*, 1 foot 6 inches in thickness, plastered and painted, part whereof is seen from the pavement under the cupola through the opening *a*. On this cone BB*b* is supported the timber work which carries the external dome, whose hammer beams CC, DD, EE, FF are tied into the corbels G, H, I, K with iron cramps, which are well bedded into the corbels with lead, and bolted to the hammer beams. The stairs which lead to the Golden Gallery on the top of the dome are carried between the trusses of the roof. The dome is boarded from the base upwards, hence the ribs are fixed horizon-tally at near distances to each other. The scantling of the curve rib of the truss is 10 in. by 11½ at the bottom, and 6 in. by 6 at the top. The sides of the dome are segments of circles, whose centres are not marked in the figure ; and which, if continued, would

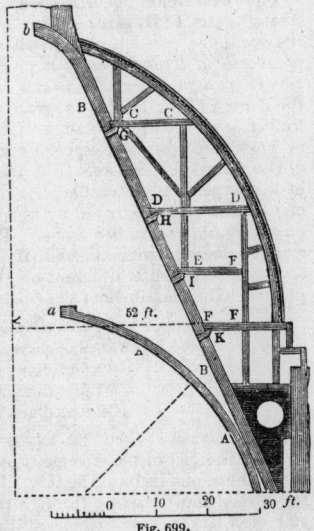

Fig. 699.

meet at top, and form a pointed arch. Above the dome rises a lantern of Portland stone, about 21 feet in diameter, and 64 feet high, standing on the cone. The whole of this construction is manifest from the figure, which exhibits the inner and outer domes with the cone between them. The combination is altogether an admirable example of the mathe-matical skill and judgment of Sir C. Wren.

2050. The largest timber roof perhaps ever projected, was over a riding-house at Moscow, in 1790, for Paul I. Emperor of Russia, the representation of which may be seen in Krafft, *Recueil de Charpente.* The span is 235 feet, and the slope with the horizon about 19°. The external dimensions of the building were 1920 feet long by 310 feet wide. It was lighted by a lantern at top, and had an interior gallery round the building for spectators. Cresy, in his *Civil Engineering*, states that this roof was never erected.

2051. We shall close this part of the section with a diagram (*fig.* 700.) of the roof of

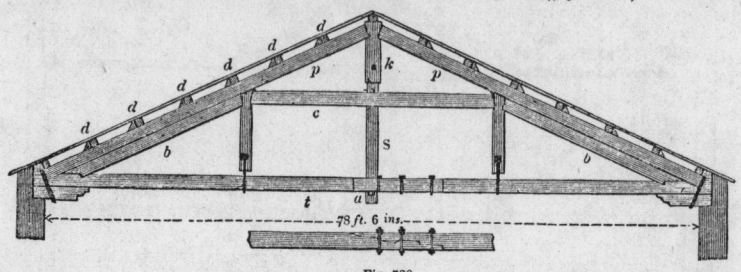

Fig. 700.

the basilica of S. Paolo fuorì le murà, executed in the fifteenth century. The trusses are double, each consisting of two similar frames, nearly 15 inches apart, at intervals from each other of about 10 feet 6 inches. The principal rafters abut on a short-king post *k*. Between the trusses a piece of timber S is placed and sustained by a strong key of wood passing through it and the short king-posts. This piece sustains the beams by means of another strong key at *a*. The tie beams are in two lengths, and scarfed together, the scarf being held together by three iron straps. The scantlings of the timbers are as follow : beams *t*, 22¼ in. full by nearly 15 in. ; principal rafters *p*, 21¾ in. by nearly 15 in. ; auxiliary rafters *b*, full 13¾ in. by full 13¼ in. ; straining beam *c*, near 15 in. by full 12¾ in. ; purlines *d*, 8½ in. square and 5 ft. 7 in. apart ; common rafters, full 5¼ in. by 4¼ in., and 8½ in. apart. The roof, which is constructed of fir, is nearly 78 ft. 6 in. span, and is covered with the Roman tile, the exact dimensions and form whereof will be found, under the head TILE, in the Glossary appended to this work. The roof is ingeniously and well contrived, and, with a different covering, would suit other climates. It was consumed by fire in the month of July, 1823. (275.)

Philibert Delorme, in his work entitled " *Nouvelles Inventions pour bien bâtir a petits Frais,*" Paris, 1561, gives a mode of constructing domes without horizontal cross ties, when the springing of each rib is well secured at the foot. It is a very simple method, and of great use in domes, even of large diameter, the principle being that of making the several ribs in two or more thicknesses, which are cut to the curve in lengths not so great as to weaken the timber, and securing these well together by bolts or keys, and observing especially to *break* the joints of the several thicknesses. This method was adopted in the large Halle aux bleds at Paris, which was many years since destroyed by fire, and has been replaced by an iron-ribbed dome. The *fig.* 701. will explain the construction ; and, if necessary, an iron hoop passed round at different heights will add much to the strength.

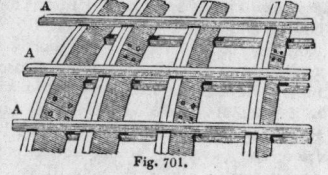

Fig. 701.

2052. The scantlings of the ribs, as given by Delorme, are as under : —

For domes of	24 feet diameter, the ribs to be	8 in. deep, and 1 in. thick.
	36 feet diameter, —	10 in. deep, and 1½ in. thick.
	60 feet diameter, —	13 in. deep, and 2 in. thick.
	90 feet diameter, —	13 in. deep, and 2¼ in. thick.
	108 feet diameter, —	13 in. deep, and 3 in. thick.

For small spans of about 24 to 30 ft., the inch plank is about 4 ft. long by about 8 in. wide. The feet of the ribs are tenoned into the wall plates ; the shoulders of the tenons being about one inch. The ties A, placed about 2 feet distant, are 4 in. by 1 in. ; they are sometimes shown passing through the planks pinned with keys 1 in. thick and 1⅓ in. wide, and of a length nearly the width of the plank ; this method tends materially to weaken the ribs ; that shown in the cut is a better mode. The wall plates, 10 or 12 inches wide and 8 or 9 inches thick, have mortices 2 inches wide, 3 inches deep and 6 inches long, sunk at 2 feet apart, to receive the ends of the ribs. In a roof where the span was 64 feet, the scantling was increased to 13 inches wide and 1½ inches thick. The ties were alternately double and single, and were 3 inches by 1½ ; and each rib was double tenoned into the wall plate. This system, with many modifications, was extensively adopted in the

construction of the nave and side erections of the building for the Exhibition of 1862; and also for some of the passages, &c., of the Horticultural Society, where they still exist, and deserve examination. It is also adopted for temporary sheds of large spans.

2052a. This work by De Lorme deserves the study of every one that seeks to be an architect, though in these unfortunate days for the art the reward of study and reading is very doubtful.

2052b. Since the period of De Lorme, another system, arising out of it, has been extensively adopted for large buildings. Colonel Emy, having been called upon in 1819 to design a roof of 60 feet span, succeeded in composing one in which, while timbers of a greater length might be used, the necessary solidity, with the lightness and economy of the system of De Lorme, might be combined. This he carried out in 1825 and 1826. The workmanship is less than in De Lorme's roofs, as the wood is all in straight pieces, and is within the power of the ordinary carpenter. An arch is composed of a series of long and thin planks, laid flatways, the flexibility of which permits them to be easily and quickly bent without the aid of heat; and their rigidity, properly regulated, maintains the form given and destroys the thrust. *Fig.* 701a. is a portion of the base of one arc, which will illustrate the system. The details are best learnt from Emy's own work, as it would require much space to do justice to them. The vertical pieces A are $7\frac{3}{4}$ inches thick, and placed about 4 inches from the wall. The three first radial pieces B are prolonged beyond the uprights, and enter recesses in the wall to steady the frames. The plates C, breaking joint well with one another, compose the arc, and are $1\frac{3}{8}$ inch thick, $5\frac{1}{10}$ inches broad, and about 40 feet long, bolted together, the bolts being driven tightly into accurately made holes, and are further firmly tied together by iron straps; the bolts are $\frac{7}{10}$ inch diameter, and about 2 feet 6 in. apart; the principal rafters are $5\frac{1}{4}$ in. thick; the trusses are placed 9 feet 10 in. apart.

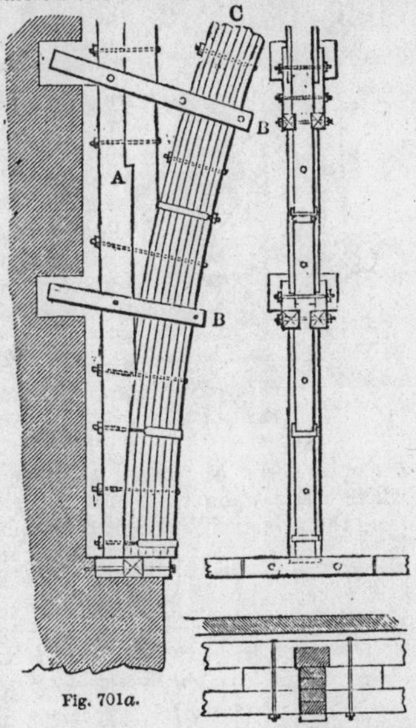

2052c. Upon an experiment that was made by Emy to test the strength and thrust of this arch, he found it necessary to add a supplementary plate to a part of the extrados, and two plates to a part of the intrados. The following is the proportion of the number of plates and their width, which he adopted as a rule:—

Fig. 701a.

		ft.	in.	
From the springing to radial (B) No. 1 -	- 7 plates,	1	3	wide
From radial No. 1 to the tie placed between radials Nos. 6 and 7 - - - - -	- 8 „	1	7	„
From this tie to radial No. 6 - -	- 6 „	1	0	„
From radial No. 9 to the king-post -	- 5 „	nearly 0	11	„

These supplementary plates were of oak, and of the same thickness as the others. These roofs are also given with sufficient detail in Newlands' work above-mentioned.

2052d. Mediæval Roofs.—In the south of France the few Romanesque roofs did not differ from the common king-post roof, except in two points, viz., that the tie-beam and the king-post were stop-chamfered; and the strain of the purlines upon the principal rafter was counteracted by a nearly upright strut from the tie-beam. This system left the principal rafter with a false bearing, if the walls were not extremely thick in proportion to the width of the apartment which they enclosed. As a remedy, the late Romanesque builders tenoned the purline into the principals, and, moreover, laid it with its wider side to the rafters, in order that the backs of the common rafters should be flush with those of the principal rafters (similarly to *fig.* 692.). The next step was to put proper struts from the foot of the king-post. At the present day the purline is placed on edge for economy of material.

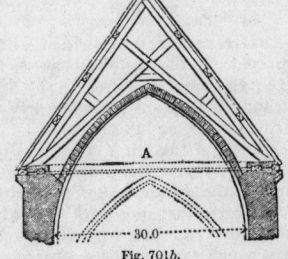

Fig. 701b.

2052f. In the north of France there was difficulty in roofing over the vaulting; either the main walls had to be carried as high as the ridge-rib, or else the frame of the roof had to be similar in principle to that shown in *fig.* 701b. Experience proved that the

latter scheme resulted in letting the principal rafters draw the tenons of the braces, and so destroy all idea of a tie connecting the two walls; hence the mediæval builders were obliged to raise the walls sufficiently high to allow the tie-beams to pass over the back of the ridge-rib, as would be the case at A.   This was expensive, and, moreover, it was scarcely practicable where the walls were little thicker than was necessary for the backing to the formerets of the vaulting over the arches of windows.   It is to these facts, rather than to any influence of climate, that may be attributed the adoption of the high-pitched roof, a system which required neither great width of footing nor large scantling of timber, for the purlines were discarded, and the weight was distributed among the rafters and trusses of each bay.   The details of such a roof are simple.   Two plates A (*fig.* 701c.) are placed with their widest sides on the wall, and are strutted between from

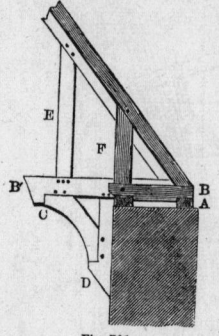

the feet of the trusses to the centre of the bay. Upon these plates, tassels or short hammers B, are cocked down at intervals between the tie-beams, which are cocked down and dove-tailed, to take not only the feet of the common rafters, but also the nearly upright stud or ashlar rafter F, which serves to give a wider base to the principal and to the rafter.   All these vertical pieces are double-tenoned and pinned into the other portions of the work.

2052g. The racking motion to which large roofs are liable, soon showed that this was not the manner in which to make them secure.   The purlines had been discarded, but the need of their service remained; the necessity was obviated by erecting a sort of trussed partition under the ridge.   If the king-post was *not* carried by the tie-beam, the whole roof depended upon the strength of the head of the king-post, into which the ridge was tenoned, and the manner in which it was connected with the ends of the principal rafters.   It therefore appears to be more probable that the king-post was supposed to be carried by the tie-beam; indeed,

Fig. 701c.

examples occur of trussed partitions (*fig.* 701d.) to ridges, supported by king-posts A, which stand upon tie-beams that ride in queen-stirrups, B, where the stirrups are hung from the principal rafters at three-quarters of the height of the roof.   Care has been given

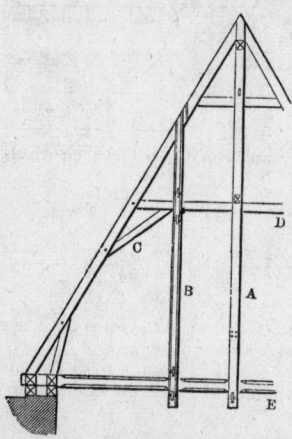

to this detail of the practice, because it seems to have been entirely mistaken by Viollet le Duc, *Dict.* : for example, the braces C, to the collars D, are supposed by him to exercise a favourable effect in preventing the flexure of the rafter outwards, whereas the fact would seem to be that the brace has to hold up the collar D and with it the stirrup B, and with them the tie-beam E, *for the collar is tenoned into the king-post and rafter.*   That author defers dating the period of the perfection of mediæval carpentry (as well as of joinery) until the end of the 15th and the beginning of the 16th century.

2052h. The framing of cradle roofs, with king-posts carried upon (*not carrying,* as Viollet le Duc supposes) the tie-beams, became a practice that in France was general from the latter part of the 12th until the end of the 16th century, and which continued the same peculiarities of construction that are above indicated.   The distinction between the stirrup and the post is less easy in the truss shown in *fig.* 701e., but still it must be reckoned as a post; this example from the *préfecture,* formerly the episcopal palace, at

Fig. 701d.   AT AUXERRE.

Auxerre, covers a hall which is 30 feet wide; the trusses are placed 13 feet apart from centre to centre.   The scantlings are as follows:—King-posts, 5 by 5, and principal rafters $5\frac{1}{4}$ by $4\frac{3}{4}$; the common rafters, 5 by $4\frac{3}{4}$, are shown in *fig.* 701f., and are trussed in a different manner; they are placed nearly 2 feet apart.   The roof appears to be boarded on the inside to the circular form.

2052i. Although Viollet le Duc is of opinion that the tie-beams to the fine cradle roof, 57 feet 3 inches span, constructed at the beginning of the 16th century, over the great hall of the *Palais de Justice,* at Rouen (*fig.* 247.), have been cut away, it may not be unfair to suggest that the work might have stood as well if, in its construction, it had resembled the older and fine roof of the château at Sully-sur-Loire, which he so well illustrates, but which want of space prevents our also doing.   The student has, perhaps, no cause for regret, as its construction can scarcely be recommended for imitation in the present day.   It is about 36 feet span.

2052k. The absence of a ridge-roll and the position of the ridge-piece in the majority

of mediæval roofs deserve notice. As soon as the purlines were discarded, it seems that builders relied upon the king-post to carry a ridge-piece upon which rested the ends of the rafters; these were halved and spiked together above it. Excepting in a few cases the ridge-piece was rather a purline at the top of the roof than an abutment. Much of the bolt and strap work applied in the visible frames of roofs is not always the most judicious as regards the conversion of construction into decoration. For example, if it were calculated that a tie-beam would sag, instead of increasing its scantling, or of trussing it, the mediæval carpenter would very probably hang it up to his truss, as in *figs.* 701*g.* and 701*h.* At a later period (say the 14th century) with some spikes. *Fig.* 701*k.* illustrates the method of forming the junction of post, beam, and strut in a roof; and *fig.* 701*l.* that of beams and posts in the timber framing of houses.

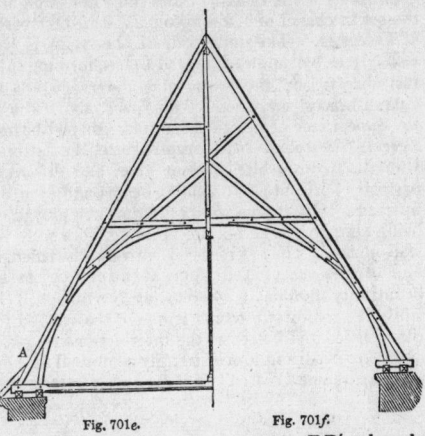

Fig. 701*e.*   Fig. 701*f.*

2052*l.* It will be at once perceived, by *fig.* 701*c.*, that the *hammer-beam* BB′ takes the place of the tie-beam, the middle part of which may have been cut away. The tinted portion shows the foot of the rafters in a cradle roof; and the lighter portion the position and form of the hammer-beam, the outer end of which is tenoned and pinned on to the wall

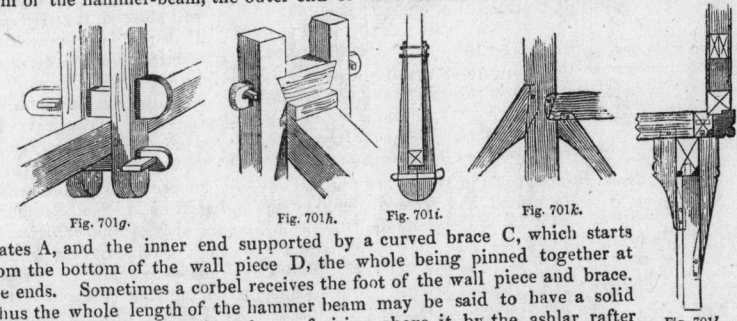

Fig. 701*g.*   Fig. 701*h.*   Fig. 701*i.*   Fig. 701*k.*

plates A, and the inner end supported by a curved brace C, which starts from the bottom of the wall piece D, the whole being pinned together at the ends. Sometimes a corbel receives the foot of the wall piece and brace. Thus the whole length of the hammer beam may be said to have a solid bearing equal to supporting the roof rising above it, by the ashlar rafter or strut E, and at the same time forming a part of that structure. When   Fig. 701*l.* the whole is put together securely, it has been considered almost impossible for hammer-beam roofs to spread, as from the stiffening action of the braces, it would require a very heavy force to push out the walls. But "the absence of that curved brace which distinguishes the Westminster example, makes these roofs much more likely to exert a thrust upon the walls, and, accordingly, it is notorious that in very many cases this has occurred. In the fine example at Croxton, the strain was so great as absolutely to break short off the perfectly sound heart of oak pins, nearly an inch in diameter, with which it was held together; and it is to be feared that many of the finest of these examples are similarly in a dangerous condition." So writes Mr. Street, in his *English Woodwork*, read at the Institute of British Architects in 1865, a paper which should not be neglected by the student. The principle of the construction of these roofs has perhaps not yet been satisfactorily elucidated.

2052*m.* The timber roofs in England may be divided into five classes:—I. Roofs with tie-beams; II. Roofs with trussed rafters, or single framed roofs; III. Roofs with braces with or without collars; IV. Roofs framed with hammer-beams; and V. Aisle roofs. The first are more general and better treated in France. The others are more peculiar to England, in which country elaborate examples of these forms are to be found, especially on the hammer-beam system.

2052*n.* *Pitch.*—These roofs are for the most part acutely pitched, though this was by no means their invariable characteristic. An angle of 90° was perhaps the ordinary elevation of Norman roofs, and in the early English period, though generally acutely pointed, roofs are nevertheless found of an equilateral pitch or angle of 60°, though this is of rare occurrence. In this and the succeeding style, examples are found of so low a pitch as to equal the flattest specimens of the perpendicular period. The roof, of the decorated

style, over the larger south aisle of St. Martin's Church, Leicester, has a span of 21 feet, with a rise of only 4 feet. (See *par.* 2040*b.*).

2052*o.* I. The *tie-beam* bears the whole weight of a low pitched roof. The roof over the south chapel of Kiddington Church, Oxfordshire, is of rather a steeper pitch than that at Leicester. The under side of the beam is well moulded, and is connected with the wall-pieces by moulded curved braces forming a very obtusely pointed arch; the purlines rest directly on the beam, and the ridge is supported on it by a post, and by short curved braces, the whole of the space above the tie-beam being filled up so as to give it the appearance of a solid triangular shaped beam. The naves of Raunds and of Higham Ferrers Churches, Northamptonshire, the latter of decorated date, and of Wimmington Church, Bedfordshire, present good and differing examples. The tie-beam is rarely left perfectly horizontal; the collar-beams and even the hammer-beams will be found to incline upwards. Tie-beams were sometimes employed quite independently of the other timbers, being simply laid across the building from wall to wall, notched down, and pinned to the wall plates. They were never entirely discarded, as they are to be met with in each of the four usually accepted divisions of the style. At Southfleet Church, Kent, the tie-beam is beautifully moulded; whereas, at Northfleet, it is left in almost its natural roughness, while the roof itself, which is one of the trussed rafter kind, is panelled, and has moulded ribs with carved bosses at the intersections.

2052*p.* An example of a strongly cambered tie-beam, with an ornamented king-post, is seen in Swardestone Church, Norfolk, and it is by no means uncommon in the counties of Kent

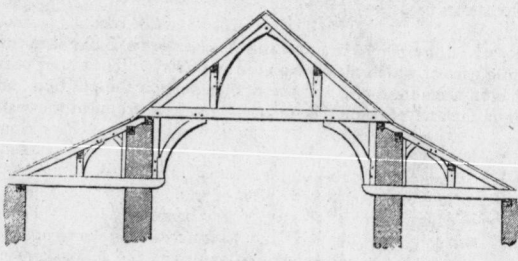

and Sussex. The tie-beam of the roof over the aisle of North Walsham Church, Norfolk (*fig.* 701*m.*), passes through the nave wall, the end forming a corbel for the wall pieces of the nave roof. This roof also presents a practice which became almost universal in roofs of later date, viz., an intermediate truss between the tie-beams, in consequence of the extreme width between

Fig. 701*m.*   NORTH WALSHAM, NORFOLK.

the main trusses, to support the ridge and purlines, by the adoption of double rafters on each side, strongly united and framed together, springing from a small hammer-beam over the apex of the arches. In roofs of high pitch, various endeavours were made to retain the arched shape in conjunction with the tie-beam. At Pulham Church, Norfolk, and Morton Church, Leicestershire, the beam divides the arch into two, with a bad result.

2052*q.* II. *Single-framed roofs* sometimes have only diagonal braces connecting the rafters. These occur generally where the span is small, as over a porch. In wider spans, even without tie-beams, each pair of rafters was framed with a collar-beam, and was stiffened by braces crossing at times above the collar, and at others the braces being tenoned into its under side; when the latter was the case, a second

Fig. 701*n.*   WIMBOTSHAM, NORFOLK.

collar was generally introduced above the first. Such roofs were very frequently boarded underneath, forming thus a polygonal barrel vault, and moulded ribs were applied, dividing the boarding into panels, with carved bosses at the intersections. The above details will be found combined in the examples of the decorated period from the nave of Wimbotsham Church, Norfolk (*fig.* 701*n.*). The angle of the roof is 78°. The span is 21 feet 9 inches; the rafters and collars are 4½ inches by 4 inches. The former are placed 1 foot 9 inches apart between the centres. The nave roof of Reedham Church, Norfolk, 31 feet span, is framed on the same principle. The hall at Sully-sur-Loire is a fine example.

2052*r.* III. Roofs constructed with *braces* may be divided into two classes: I. Those with collar-beams and braces; and II. Those without collar-beams. An example of the former is seen in the roof of the nave at Pulham Church (*fig.* 701*o.*), which is formed at an angle of 105°, with a span of 20 feet 5 inches. Wall pieces A, are used, pinned into

the underside of the principal rafters, descending low down on the wall; the arched brace springs directly from this to the collar-beam, uniting them both with the principal. It is held that it would be impossible for this roof to spread until it had broken the curved

braces. The various timbers are all effectively moulded. The principal rafters, 12 inches by 10 inches; common rafters, 6 inches by $3\frac{1}{2}$ inches; collar-beam, 14 inches by $8\frac{1}{2}$ inches; ridge piece, 8 inches by 8 inches; purline, 8 inches by $6\frac{1}{2}$ inches; wall piece, 10 inches by $8\frac{1}{2}$ inches. Width between centres of trusses, 6 feet 2 inches; and depth of cornice 3 feet 2 inches. Of class II. is the roof over the nave of Starston Church, Norfolk (*fig.* 701*p.*). The angle formed is 100°. At the apex of the roof is a strut B, about 9 inches square, which hangs down 2 feet; its four sides are morticed, two to receive the ends of the braces where they are pinned, thus preventing the possibility of its dropping; and the other two on the opposite sides, to receive the arched ridge braces, as shown at C. This arrangement tends to prevent the roof either spreading outwards, or rocking from east to west. The span is 21 feet 10 in. The principal rafters are 10 in. by 9 in.; common rafters, 6 in. by 4 in.; wall piece, 10 in. by $7\frac{1}{4}$ in.; purline, $6\frac{1}{2}$ in. by $5\frac{1}{2}$ in.; and cornice, 11 in. by 10 in.

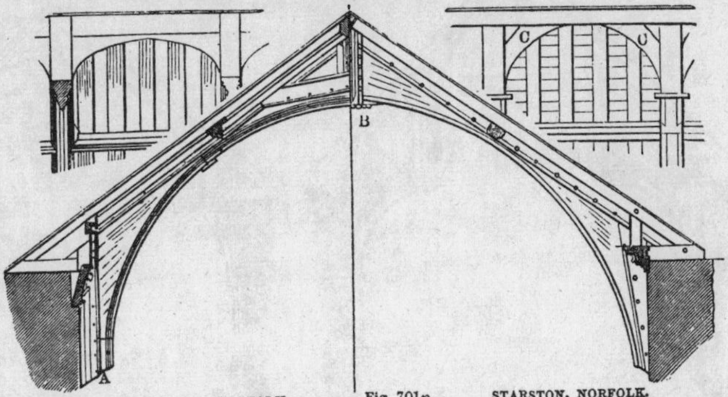

Fig. 701o.   PULHAM, NORFOLK.   Fig. 701p.   STARSTON, NORFOLK.

2052s. IV. *Hammer-beam roofs* are always double-framed roofs, the rafters being supported by a skeleton framing of purlines and ridge, resting on, or framed into, the principal trusses. Among the many varieties of this description of roof may be noticed:—(1) Those with collar-beams and no struts, the collars, principals, and hammer-beams being united with curved braces; (2) Those in which the collar-beam is omitted, the curved braces being carried up almost to the ridge, and framed at the apex of the arch into a strut, which receives also the upper ends of the principals; (3) Those with no collars or struts, the whole of the truss being connected together and stiffened with curved braces only; in this instance the arched braces are formed of three pieces of timber, one on either side of the roof, tenoned into the hammer-beam and principal, and reaching up as far as the purline, the centre piece forming the apex of the arch, being tenoned into each principal, itself acting as a brace, and to a certain extent as a collar beam; and (4) Those having hammer-beams, collars, and struts, connected together with curved braces. (See *par.* 2052*l.*)

2052t. An example of the first sort is the roof of Capel St. Mary's Church, Suffolk (*fig.* 701*q.*). The angle formed is 87°, and it is very seldom that a hammer-beam roof has a steeper pitch. The span is 18 feet 3 inches. The principal rafter is 10 inches by

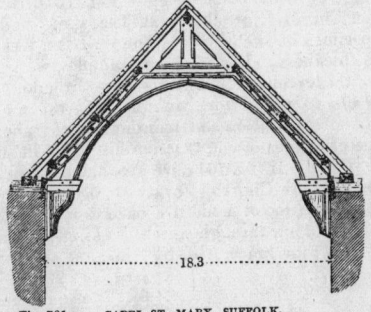

Fig. 701q.   CAPEL ST. MARY, SUFFOLK.

8 inches; common rafter, 6 inches by 3 inches; hammer-beam, 10 inches by 8 inches; collar-beam, 10 inches by 8 inches; purlins, 6 inches by 5 inches; ridge piece, 6 inches by 6 inches. The trusses are 6 feet apart from centre to centre. The second sort is shown in *fig.* 701*r.*, the nave roof of Trunch Church, Norfolk. The intermediate trusses are the same, except that instead of the long wall-piece and brace, the wall-piece is stopped at the crown of the arch of the clearstory window, and a very depressed brace connects it with the hammer-beam. The spandrils are filled in with perforated tracery. The span is 19 feet. The principal rafter is 10 inches by 9 inches; common rafter, 6 inches by 4 inches; hammer-beam, 10 inches by 10 inches; purline, 8 inches by 5 inches; ridge piece, 10 inches by 10 inches. The trusses are 5 feet 6 inches apart. The third sort is shown in *fig.* 701*s.*, from the nave of Wymondham Church, Norfolk. The hammer-beams project rather more than a quarter the width of the nave, and are carved into figures; the intermediate trusses have also similar figures, but made subordinate to those of the main trusses. At the intersections of the purlines and ridge braces are large carved flowers standing out in bold relief. Of the

fourth sort, the most noted examples are those of Westminster Hall, 68 feet span (*fig.* 196.); Hampton Court, 40 feet span; Eltham Palace, 36 feet 3 inches; Beddington Hall;

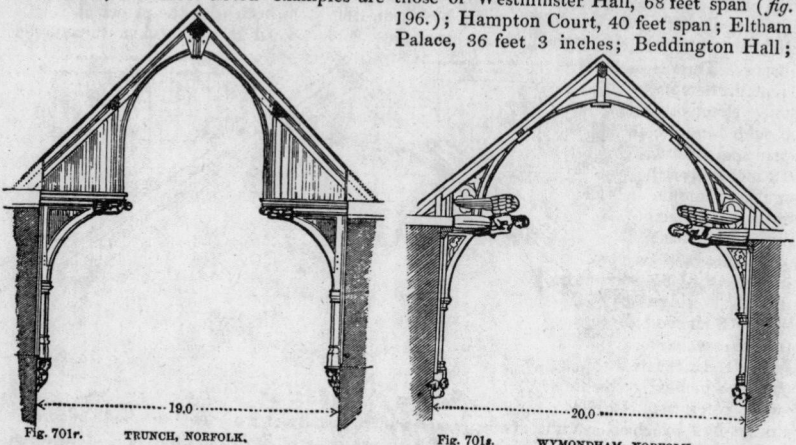

Fig. 701r.   TRUNCH, NORFOLK.   Fig. 701s.   WYMONDHAM, NORFOLK.

South Wraxhall, 19 feet 9 inches; Croydon, 37 feet 9 inches, &c. It will be well to notice, what is not usually known, or shown, in the sections of the Westminster roof, that the main purlines over the strut, are upheld with the collar-beam by an intermediate rafter of great strength.   Mr. S. Smirke has observed (*Archæologia*, xxvi. page 417–18), that "this roof is the common collar-beam roof, and of extremely simple construction; the whole pressure is carried by the straight lines of the principal rafter, and (curved) brace, above alluded to, directly into the solid wall, where it *ought* to be." The examples of lesser importance, as regards span, are not all of the same elegance as that of Westminster, which, at the same time that it is the largest and best, is also the earliest (1397) of the series.   Some examples present double hammer-beams, forming a sort of corbelling over up to the ridge or to the collar-beam. *Fig.* 701t., from Knap-ton Church, Norfolk, is 32 feet span, and is a fair specimen of such roofs. The wall is 2 feet 10 inches in thickness. For all these examples, we are indebted to the excellent publication by Brandon, *Mediæval Roofs*, to which work we must refer the reader for de-

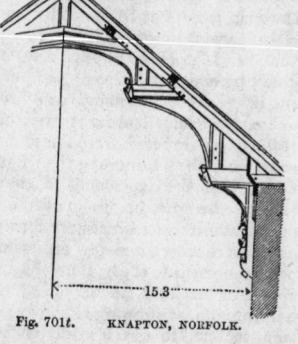

Fig. 701t.   KNAPTON, NORFOLK.

tails of decoration and painting, as the above figures are only here introduced to show the principles of construction displayed in such roofs.

2052u.   In *fig.* 701u, we give the modern roof, of 31 feet 2 inches span, over the nave of Bickerstaffe Church, Yorkshire, designed by Sydney Smirke, R. A., as a good specimen of the adaptation of modern science to mediæval structures. The collar-beam is double, each 9 in. by 3 in., through which the king-post is tenoned and strapped. The purlines are 7 in. by 4 in.; the brace, 9 in. by 7 in.; and the corbels are 11 in. wide, being also tailed in 11 in.

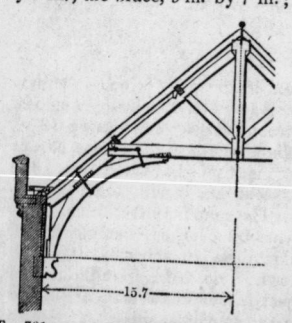

Fig. 701u.   BICKERSTAFFE, YORKSHIRE.

2052v. V. *Aisle*, or *Lean-to, roofs*, may be described as usually consisting of strong timbers, answering the pur-pose of principal rafters, laid at each end on plates, the lower plate resting on the external wall, the upper one either supported on corbels projecting from the nave wall, or inserted therein. Wall-pieces are tenoned into the upper and lower extremities of the principals, and curved braces springing from the feet of these meet in the centre of the principal, forming a perfect arch, having the spandrils generally filled in with tracery. A purline is usually framed into the principal, and on this and the plates the common rafters are supported (see also *fig.* 701o.). In aisle roofs the whole of the timbers, even to the common rafters, were frequently found more richly moulded than those of the nave, possibly from being nearer the eye of the spectator.

2053. The following instructions relative to the lines necessary to be found in the framing of roofs are from Price's *British Carpenter*; and although published nearly 100 years, few subsequent works on this subject give more complete information. Let *abcd* (*fig.* 702.)

be a plan to be inclosed with
a hipped roof, whose height
or slope is Cb. Divide the
plan lengthwise into two
equal parts by the line *ef*,
which produce indefinitely
at both ends. Make *ag*
equal *ea*, and *dk* equal to
df; and through *k* and *g*,
parallel to *ab* or *cd*, draw
lines indefinitely *mo*, *lp*.
With the distance dc or Cc,
either of which is equal to
the length of the common
rafters, set off *qe*, as also from
h to *p*, from *i* to *o*, and from
f to *n*; from *k* to *m*, and from
g to *l*. Make *ts* equal to Cb,
and *ab* equal to *ta*, which

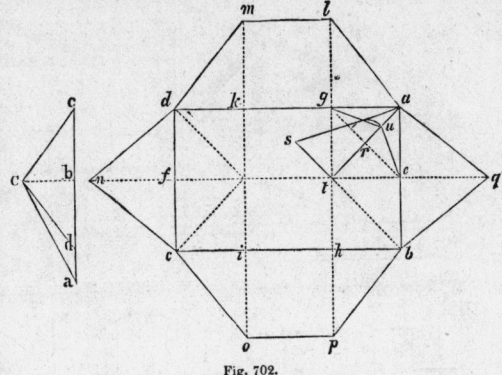

Fig. 702.

points join; then either a C or *as* represents the length of the hip rafter, and joining the
several lines *aqb*, *bpoc*, *cnd*, and *dmla*, they will be the *skirts* of the roof.

2054. To find the back of the hip. Join *ge*, and from *r* as a centre describe an arc
touching the hip *as*, and cutting *at* in *u*. Then join *gu* and *ue*, and *gue* is the back of the
hip rafter required.

2055. *Fig.* 703. represents, in *abcd*, the plan of a building whose sides are bevel to each
other. Having drawn the
central line *ef* indefinitely,
bisect the angle *rag* by the
line *ae*, meeting *ef* in *e*.
From *e* make *eg* equal to *re*,
and *rg* perpendicular to *ea*;
then, if e a be made equal
to *ea*, ra or *aq*, it will be the
length of the hip rafter from
the angle *a*. Through *e*
and *f*, perpendicular to the
sides *db*, *ca*, draw the lines
np, *mq* indefinitely; and from
a, as a centre with the radius
aq, describe an arc of a circle, cutting *mq* in *q*, and *er*
(perpendicular to *ba*) produced in *l*. By the same
kind of operation *oc* will be

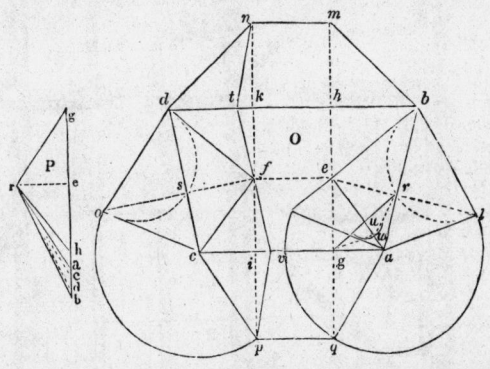

Fig. 703.

found, as also the other parts of the skirts of the roof.   The lines *nt*, *tfv*, and *vp* are introduced merely to show the trouble that occurs when the beams are laid bevel. The angle of
the back of the hip rafter, *rwg*, is found as before, by means of *u* as a centre, and an arc of a
circle touching *aq*. The backs of the other hips may be found in the same manner.

2056. *Fig.* 704., from Price's *Carpentry*, is the plan of a house with the method of placing
the timbers for the roof with the upper part of the elevation above, which, after a perusal of
the preceding pages, cannot fail of being understood. The plan F is to be prepared for a
roof, either with hips and vallies, or with hips only. The open spaces at G and H are
over the staircases: in case they cannot be lighted from the sides, they may be left to be
finished at discretion. The chimney flues are shown at I K L M N O. Then, having laid
down the places of the openings, place the timbers so as to lie on the piers, and as far as
possible from the flues; and let them be so connected together as to embrace every part of
the plan, and not liable to be separated by the weight and thrust of the roof. P is a
trussed timber partition, to discharge the weight of the roof over a salon below.

2057. Q is the upper part of the front, and R a pediment, over the small break, whose
height gives that of the blank pedestal or parapet S. Suppose T to represent one half of
the roof coming to a point or ridge, so as to span the whole at once, " which," as Price
truly observes, " was the good old way, as we are shown by Serlio, Palladio," &c., or
suppose the roof to be as the other side U shows it, so as to have a flat or sky-light over the
lobby F, its balustrade being W; or we may suppose X to represent the roof as spanning the
whole at three times. If X be used, the valley and hip should be framed as at Y; if as T,
the principal rafters must be framed as at Z, in order to bring part of the weight of the roof
and covering on the partition walls. The remainder needs not further explanation.

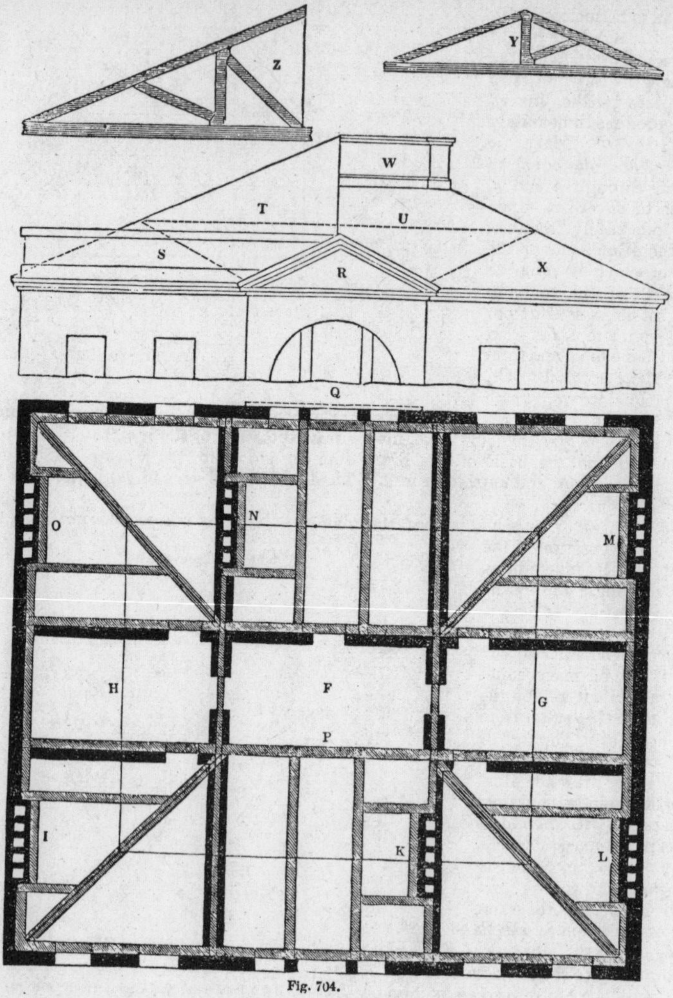

Fig. 704.

RIBS FOR GROINS, ETC.

2058. We shall now proceed to the method of forming the ribs for groined arches, niches, &c. The method of finding the shape of these is the same, whether for sustaining plastering or supporting the boarding of centres for brick or stone work, except that, for plaster, the inner edge of the rib is cut to the form, and, in centering, the outer edge. Groins, as we have already seen, may be of equal or unequal height, and in either case the angle rib may be straight or curved; and these conditions produce the varieties we are about to consider.

2059. *To describe the parts of a groin where the arches are circular and of unequal height, commonly called* Welsh Groins. We here suppose the groin to be right-angled. Let AB (*fig.* 705.) be the width of the greater arch. Draw BD at right angles to AB, and in the straight line BD make CD equal to the width of the lesser arch. Draw DF and CE perpendicular to BD and EF parallel to BD. On AB describe the semicircle B*ghi*A, and on EF describe the semicircle E*qro*F. Produce AB to *p*, and FE to *m*, cutting A*p* in *y*. Through the centre *x* of the semi-

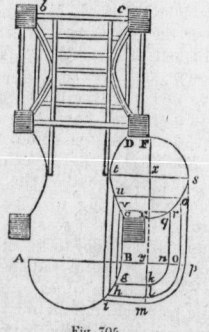

Fig. 705.

circle Eqrs F draw ts perpendicular to BD, cutting the circumference of the semicircle in s. Draw sp parallel to BD. From the centre y, with the distance yp, describe the quadrant pm. Draw mi parallel to AB, cutting the semicircle described upon AB in the point i. In the arc Bi take any number of intermediate points g, h, and through the points ghi draw it, hu, gv, parallel to BC. Also through the points ghi draw gk, hl, im parallel to AB, cutting FE produced in k and l. From the centre y describe the arcs kn, lo, cutting AB produced in mo. Draw nq, or, parallel to BD, cutting the lesser semicircular arc in the points q, r. Through the points q, r, s draw qv, ru, st parallel to AB; then through the points tuv draw the curve tuvc, which will be the plan of the intersection of the two cylinders. The other end of the figure exhibits the construction of the framing of carpentry, and the method in which the ribs are disposed.

2060. To describe the sides of a groin when the arches are of equal height and designed to meet in the plane of the diagonals. Let af and al (fig. 706.) be the axes of the two vaults, meeting each other in a, perpendicular to af. Draw AB cutting af in w, and perpendicular to al, draw BG cutting al in b. Make wA and wB each equal to half the width of the greatest vault, and make bB and bG each equal to half the width of the lesser vault. Draw AH and BE parallel to af, and draw BH and DF parallel to al, forming the parallelogram DEHF. Draw the diagonals HD, FE. On the base AB describe the curve BcdefA, according to the given height wf of the required form, which must serve to regulate the form of the other ribs. Through any points cde in the arc BcdefA draw the straight lines cq, dr, es cutting the diagonal HD at q, r, s. Draw qh, ri, sk parallel to al cutting the chord BG at the points x, y, z, b. Make xh, yi, zk, bl each respectively equal to tc, ud, ve, wf, and through the points Ghikl to B, draw the curve GhiklB. Draw qm, rn, so, ap perpendicular to HD. Make qm, rn, so, ap respectively equal to tc, ud, ve, wf, and through the points D, m, n, o, p, H draw a curve, which will be the angle rib of the groin to stand over HD; and if the groined vault be right-angled, all the diagonals will be equal, and consequently all the diagonal ribs may be made by a single mould.

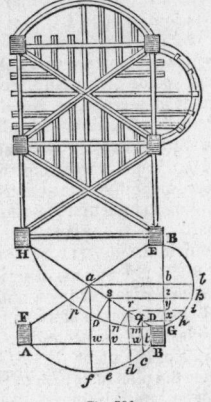

Fig. 706.

2061. The upper part of the above figure shows the method of placing the ribs in the construction of a groined ceiling for plaster. Every pair of opposite piers is spanned by a principal rib to fix the joists of the ceiling to.

2062. The preceding method is not always adopted, and another is sometimes employed in which the diagonal ribs are filled in with short ribs of the same curvature (see fig. 707.) as those of the arches over the piers.

2063. The manner of finding the section of an aperture of a given height cutting a given arch at right angles of a greater height than the aperture is represented in fig. 708.

2064. When the angle ribs for a square dome are to be found, the process is the same as for a groin formed by equal arches crossing each other at right angles, the joints for the laths being inserted as in fig. 707.; but the general construction for the angle ribs of a polygonal dome of any number of sides is the same as to determine the angle rib for a cove, which will afterwards be given.

2065. When a circular-headed window is above the level of a plane gallery ceiling, in a church for example, the cylindrical form of the window is continued till it intersects the plane of the ceiling. To find the form of the curb or pieces of wood employed for completing the arris, let dp (fig. 709.) be the breadth of the window in the plane of the ceiling. Bisect dp in h, and draw h4 perpendicular to dp. Make h4 equal to the distance the curb extends from the wall. Produce 4h to B. Make

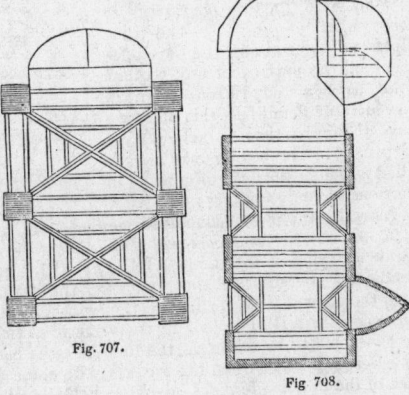

Fig. 707.

Fig 708.

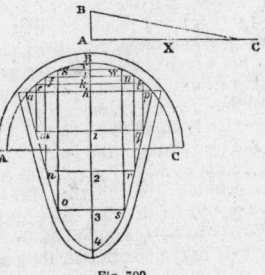

Fig. 709.

*h*B equal to the height of the window above the ceiling, and through the three points *d*, B, *p* describe the semicircle ABC for the head of the window. Divide *h*B into any number of equal parts, as 4 at the points *k*, *l*, *v*; and *h*4 into the same number of equal parts at the points 1, 2, 3. Through the points *klv* draw the lines *et*, *fu*, *gw* parallel to *dp*, and through the points 1, 2, 3 draw the lines *mg*, *nr*, *os*. Make 1*m*, 2*n*, 3*o* respectively equal to *ke*, *lf*, *vg*; as also 1*q*, 2*r*, 3*s* equal to *kt*, *lu*, *vw*; that is, equal to *ke*, *lf*, *vg*. Then through the points *dmno*4, and also through *pqrs*4, draw a curve which will form the curb required. In the section X of the figure, AC shows the ceiling line, whereof the length is equal to *h*4, and AB is the perpendicular height of the window; hence BC is the slope.

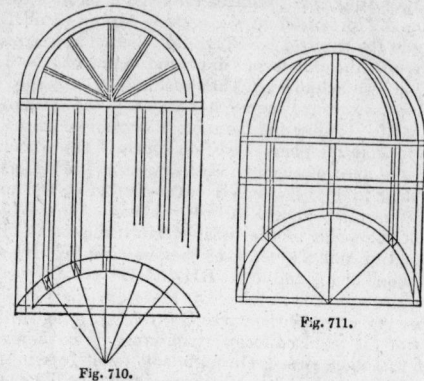

Fig. 711.

Fig. 710.

2066. The construction of a niche, which is a portion of a spherical surface, and stands on a plan formed by the segment of a circle, is simple enough; for the ribs of a niche are all of the same curvature as the plan, and fixed (*fig.* 710.) in planes passing through an axis corresponding to the centre of the sphere and perpendicular to the plane of the wall. If the plan of the niche be a semicircle (*fig.* 711.) the ribs may be disposed in vertical planes.

2067. In the construction of a niche where the ribs are disposed in planes perpendicular to the horizon or plan, and perpendicular to the face of the wall, if the niches be spherical all their ribs are sections of the sphere, and are portions of the circumferences of different circles. If we complete the whole circle of the plan (*fig.* 712.), and produce the plan of any rib to the opposite side of the circumference, we shall have the diameter of the circle for that rib, and, consequently, the radius to describe it.

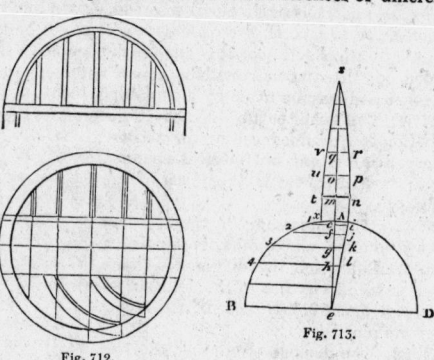

2068. *Of forming the boards to cover domes, groins, &c.* The principles of determining the developement of the surface of any regular solid have already been given in considerable detail. In this place we have to apply them practically to carpentry. The boards may be applied either in the form of gores or in portions of conic surfaces; the latter is generally the more economical method.

Fig. 712.   Fig. 713.

2069. *To describe a gore that shall be the form of a board for a dome circular on the plan.* Draw the plan of the dome ABD (*fig.* 713.), and its diameter BD and A*e* a radius perpendicular thereto. If the sections of the dome about to be described be semicircular, then the curve of the vertical section will coincide with that of the plan. Let us suppose the quadrant AB to be half of the vertical section, which may be conceived to be raised on the line A*e* as its base, so as to be in a vertical plane, then the arc AB will come into the surface of the dome. Make A*i* equal to half the width of a board and join *ei*. Divide the arc AB into any number of equal parts, and through the points of division draw the lines 1*i*, 2*j*, 3*k*, 4*l*, cutting A*e* in the points *efgh* and *ei* in the points *ijkl*. Produce the line *e*A to *s*, and apply the arcs A1, 12, 23, 34 to A*m*, *mo*, *oq* in the straight line A*s*. Through the points *mnoq* draw the straight lines *tn*, *up*, *vr*, and make *mn*, *op*, *qr*, as also *mt*, *ou*, *qv*, respectively equal to *ei*, *ff*, *gk*; then through the points *inpr* to *s*, and also through the points *xtuv* to *s*, draw two curves from the points *x* and *i* so as to meet each other in *s*; and the curves thus drawn will include one of the gores of the dome, which will be a mould for drawing the boards for covering the surface.

2070. In polygonal domes the curves of the gore will bound the ends of the boards; as, for example, in the **octagonal** dome

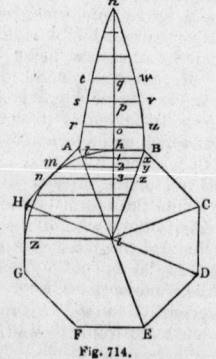

Fig. 714.

(*fig.* 714.), the plan being ABCDEFGH.   Let *i* be the centre of the circle in which the octagon may be inscribed.   Draw the half diagonal *i*A, *i*B, *i*C perpendicular to any side AB of the plan.   Draw the straight line *ih*, cutting AB in *h*.   Let *hlmZ* be the outline of one of the ribs of the dome, which is here supposed to be the quadrant of a circle.   Divide the arc *hZ* into any number of equal parts from *h* at the points *lmn*, and through these points draw *lx*, *my*, *nz*, cutting B*i* at the points *xyz*, and *ih* at the points 1, 2, 3.   Extend

the arcs *hl*, *lm*, *mn*, on the line *hn*, from *h* to *o*, from *c* to *p*, from *p* to *q*, and through the points *opq* draw the straight lines *ru*, *sv*, *tw* perpendicular to *hn*. Make *ou*, *pv*, *qw*, as also *or*, *ps*, *qt*, respectively equal to 1*x*, 2*y*, 3*z*; then through the points A*rst* draw a curve, and through the points *uvw* draw another curve, meeting the former one in the point *n*. Thus will be formed the gore or covering of one side of the octagonal dome.

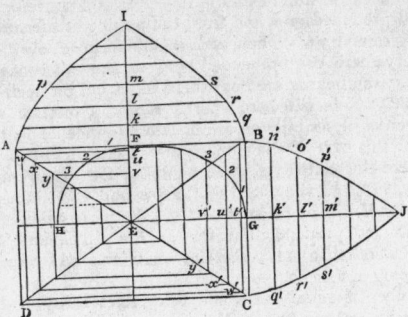

Fig. 715.

2071. When the plan of the base is a rectangle, as *fig.* 715., draw the plan ABCD and the diagonals AC and BD, cutting each other in E.   Through E draw EI perpendicular to AB cutting AB in F, and through E draw EJ perpendicular to BC, cutting BC in G.   Let the height of the dome be equal to half its breadth, and the section over the straight line EF a quadrant of a circle; then from the centre E describe the arc FH, its base being EF, and with the straight line EG as half the major axis of an ellipsis, and EF the minor axis, describe the quadrant GF of an ellipsis. Produce EF to I, and EG to J.   Divide the arc of a quadrant FH from F into any number of equal parts, and extend the parts on the line FI to *klm*, through which draw. the lines *kq*, *lr*, *ms*, &c. perpendicular to FI.   Through the points 1, 2, 3, &c. draw *wt*, *xu*, *yv*, &c., cutting AE in *w*, *x*, *y*, and FE at *t,u,v*.   Make *k'n'*, *l'o'*, *m'p'*, also *kq*, *lr*, *ms*, respectively equal to *tw*, *ux*, *vy*, and through the points *n'o'p'* draw a curve, also through the points *qrs* draw another curve meeting the former in I; then these two curves with the

line AB will form the gore or boundary of the building of two sides of the dome.   Also in the elliptical arc GF, take any number of points 1, 2, 3, and draw the lines 1*w'*, 2*x'*, 3*y'*, parallel to BC, cutting EC in the points *w'x'y'*, and GE in the points *t'*, *u'*, *v'*.   Extend the arcs G1, 12, 23 from G*k'*, *k'l'*, *l'm'*, upon the straight line GJ, and through the points *k'l'm'* draw the lines *n'q'*, *o'r'*, *p's'*.   Make *k'n'*, *l'o'*,

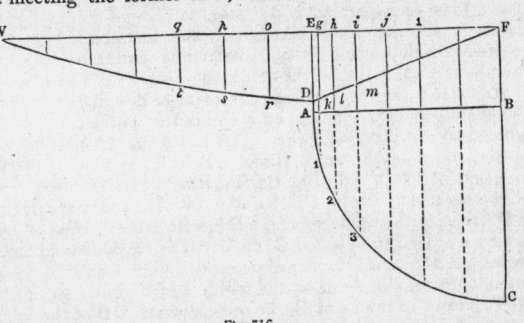

Fig. 716.

m'p', also *k'q'*, *l'r'*, *m's'* respectively equal to *t'w'*, *u'x'*, *v'y'*, and through the points B*n'o'p'* draw the curve BJ, and through the points C*q'r's'* draw the curve CJ; then BJC will be the gore required, to which the boards for the other two sides of the dome must be formed.

2072. A general method of describing the board or half gore of any polygonal or circular dome is shown in *fig.* 716.   Let DE be half either of the breadth of a board or of one of the sides of a polygon, EF the perpendicular drawn from the centre. Draw the straight line AB parallel to EF, and draw EA and FB perpendicular to EF; then upon the base AB describe the rib AC of the vertical section of the dome.   Divide the curve AC into the equidistant arcs A1, 12, 23, and through the points of division draw the lines 1*g*, 2*h*, 3*i* perpendicular to AB cutting EF at *ghi* and DF at *klm*.   Produce FE to V and extend the arcs A1, 12, 23 upon the straight line EV from E successively to the points *opq*.   Through the points *opq* draw the lines *or*, *ps*, *qt* parallel to ED.   Make *or*, *ps*, *qt* respectively equal to *gk*, *hl*, *im*; then through the points *r s t* draw a curve, and DEV will be the half arc or half mould of the boarding.

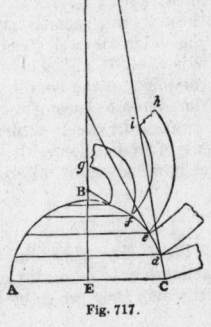

Fig. 717.

2073. *To cover a hemispherical dome by boards moulded to portions of conic surfaces.* Draw a vertical section of the dome ABC (*fig.* 717.) and divide the circumference into equal arcs C*d*, *de*, *ef*. Through the centre E draw EB perpendicular to AC. Draw the chords C*d*, *de*, *ef*, and produce all these chords till they meet the line EB, which they will produced in a convenient space; but those chords that are next to the bottom AC will require a distance too remote from AC; and for the present confining our attention to those chords which, when produced, would meet the line EB at a convenient distance from AC, let *ef* meet the axis EB produced in *g*, and from the point *g* as a centre with the distances *ge* and *gf* describe the arcs *eh* and *fi*. Then *efih* is the form of the board, so that its breadth is everywhere comprehended between the two concentric circles *eh* and *fi*, and when the boards are bent their edges fall on horizontal planes.

2074. We will here shortly repeat a method which has previously been given of describing an arc of a circle independent of its centre, as connected with this part of the subject, and useful in cutting out the boards of a dome where the centre is inaccessible or too distant for convenience. Let AB (*fig.* 718.) be the chord of the arc and CD its height in the middle. In this case AB will be bisected at C by the perpendicular CD. Draw the half chord AD, and perpendicular thereto draw AE, and through the point D draw EF parallel to AB; also draw AG and BH perpendicular to the chord AB cutting EF in the points G and H. Divide AC and ED each into the same number of equal parts, and draw lines through the corresponding points of division; these lines will converge, and if produced with the lines EA and FB, would all meet in one point. Divide AG into the same number of equal parts as the lines AC, ED, and from the points of division draw lines to the point D to intersect the former. A curve drawn through the points of intersection will form the arc of a circle. The other part DB is found in the same manner; and this is a convenient method, because any portion of a circle may be described within the width of a board.

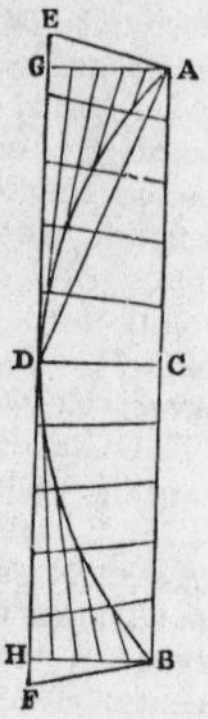

2075. To find the relation between the height and the chord of the arc. Let *abc*, &c. (*fig.* 719.) be the middle points of the boards in the arc, and from *a* draw a line parallel to the base to meet the opposite curve; also from these points draw lines to the opposite extremity of the base; then each parallel is the base, as *fa*, and the distances *eg* intersected between it, and the point where the oblique line from its extremity cuts the middle vertical is the height of the segment.

2076. It is, however, more convenient to describe the curvature of the board by a continued motion, which may be done as follows. Let AB (*fig.* 720.) be the chord of the arc. Bisect AB at C by the perpendicular CD, and make CD equal to the height of the segment. Draw DE parallel to AB, and make DE a little larger than AD; then form an instrument ADE with laths or slips of wood, and make it fast by a cross slip of wood GH. By moving the whole instrument, so that the two edges DA and DE may slide on two pins A and D, the angular point D of the instrument will describe the segment of a circle, and if the pin be taken out of A and put in the point B, the other portion DB of the segment ADB will be described in the same manner.

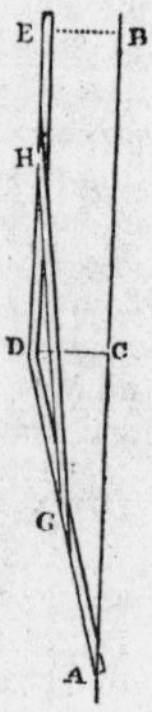

2077. The covering of an elliptical dome is formed by considering each part a portion of the surface of a cone. ABC (*fig.* 721.) is a vertical section through the greater axis of the base; the other vertical section through the axis at right angles being a semicircle; the joints of the boards therefore fall in the circumference of vertical circles.

2078. In the same manner the covering of an annular vault whose section is semicircular is found, being on the same principles as now shown for a horizontal dome, which will be evident from an inspection of *fig.* 722.

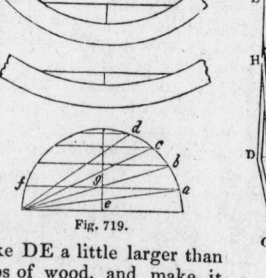

Fig. 718.

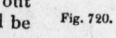

Fig. 719.

Fig. 720.

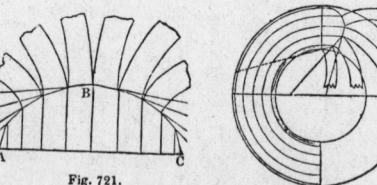

Fig. 721.

Fig. 722.

BRACKETING.

2079. The pieces of wood which sustain the laths of cornices, coves, and the like, are called *brackets*, and they take in form the general outlines as nearly as possible of the forms to which they are to be finished.

2080. *A cornice bracket of any form being given, to make another similar one, or one that shall have the same proportions in all its parts.* Let ABCDEF (*fig.* 723.) be the given bracket. Draw lines from the angular points CDE, and let A*b* be the projection of the required bracket. The lines AC, AD, AE, being drawn, draw *bc* parallel to the edge BC, cutting AC in *c*; draw *cd* parallel to CD, cutting AD in *d*. Draw *de* parallel to DE, cutting AE in *e*, and draw *ef* parallel to EF, cutting AF in *f*. Then A*bcdef* is the bracket required.

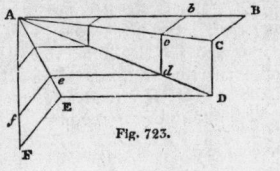

Fig. 723.

2081. *To form an angle bracket to support the plastering of a moulded cornice.* Let *fig.* 724. X be the plan of the bracket. Draw the straight line AE equal to the projection *ab* of the bracket on the plan X, and A*a* perpendicular to AE, to which make it equal. Join E*a*, and on AE describe the given form AFGHIKLE of the bracket which stands perpendicular to the line of concourse of the wall and the ceiling. From the angular points FGHIKL, draw the lines F*a*, G*b*, I*c*, H*c*, K*d*, L*d*, cutting AE in the points BCD, and *a*E in the points *a*, *b*, *c*, *d*. Draw *af*, *bg*, *ci*, *dk*, perpendicular to *a*E. Make *af*, *bg*, *ch*, *ci*, *dk*, *dl*, each respectively equal to AF, BG, CH, CI, DL, DK. Join *fg*, *gh*, *hi*, *ik*, *kl*, *l*E. Then *afghikl*E is the angle bracket required.

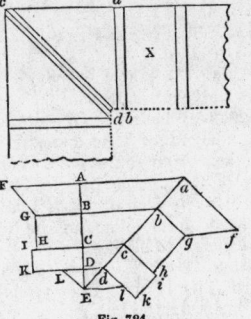

Fig. 724.

2082. An angle bracket for a cove (*fig.* 725.) may be described in exactly the same manner.

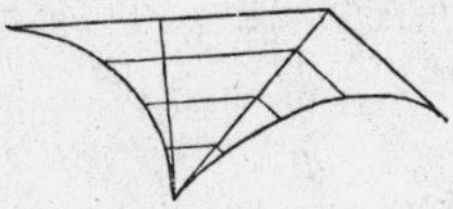

Fig. 725.

2083. When cove brackets have different projections, the method of describing the angle one is shown in *fig.* 726. Let AB, BC be the wall lines. Draw any line GD perpendicular to AB and HF perpendicular to BC. Make GD equal to the projection of the bracket from the wall represented by the line AB, and make HF equal to the projection of the bracket from the wall represented by BC. Then, as one of the brackets must be given, we shall suppose the bracket GAD described upon GD. Draw DE parallel to AB, and FE parallel to BC, and join BE. In the curve AD take any number of points Q, S, and draw QP, SR cutting GD in P, R and BE in *p*, *r*. From the points *p*, *r* draw the lines *pq*, *rs* parallel to BC, cutting HF in the points *p*, *r*. Draw *pq*, *rs* perpendicular to BE. Make *pq*, *rs* also *pq*, *rs* respectively equal to PQ, RS, &c. B*a* and HC equal to G*a*, then through the points *aqs*, &c. draw a curve which forms the bracket for the angle. Also through the points C, *q*, *s* draw another curve, and this will form the cove bracket.

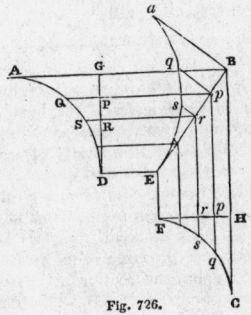

Fig. 726.

2084. The angle bracket of a cornice or cove may be formed by the method shown in X and Y (*fig.* 727.), whether the angle of the room or apartment be acute or obtuse, external or internal. Let ABC be the angle. Bisect it by the line BE. Draw GF perpendicular to BC, and make GF equal to the projection of the bracket, GC equal to its height, and FC the curve of the given bracket or rib. In the curve FC, take any number of points PQ, and parallel to BC draw the lines P*r*, Q*s*, cutting BE in the points *r*, *s*, and GF in the points R, S. Draw *rp*, *sq* perpendicular to BE, and make the ordinates *rp*, *sq* respectively equal to RP, SQ, and through all the points *pq*, draw a curve, which will be the bracket as required.

2085. When the angle is a right angle, it may be drawn as at *fig.* 728., which is an ornamental bracket for the string of a stair, and traced in the same manner as that on a right-angled triangle.

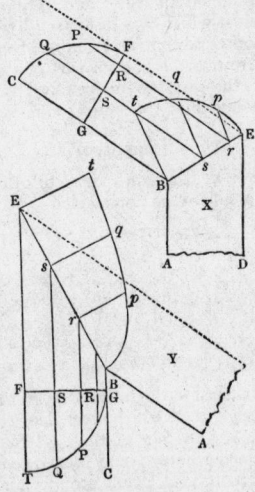

Fig. 727.

2086. In coved ceilings, the coves meeting at an angle are of different breadths, and the plan of the angle is a curve to construct the brackets. Let ABC (*fig.* 729.) represent the angle formed by the walls of the room, and let B*defg* be the plan of the bracket in the angle of a curvilinear form. Draw HM, and thereon describe the bracket HOPQ intended for that side, and in the curve HOQ take any number of points NOP, and draw the lines NR, OS, PT perpendicular to AB, cutting it in the points R, S, T. Let MQ be the height of the bracket, and draw QA perpendicular to BA, and through the points NOPQ draw the straight lines N*d*, O*e*, P*f*, cutting HM at IKLM. Draw *hm* perpendicular to BC. Make *hr*, *hs*, *ht*, *ha* respectively equal to HR, HS, HT, HA, and draw *rn*, *so*, *tp*, *aq* perpendicular to BC; also from the points *defg* draw the lines *dn*, *eo*, *fp*, *gq*, and through the points *hnopq* draw a curve, which will form the other bracket required.

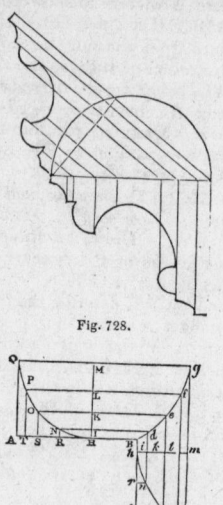

Fig. 728.

2087. Whether brackets occur in external or internal angles, the method of describing them is the same, and when the brackets from the two adjacent walls have the same projection, one of them must be given to find the angle bracket. When the brackets from these walls have unequal but given projections, then the form of one of the brackets must be given in form to find the angle bracket.

2088. *To form a bracket for a moulded cornice.* On the drawing of such cornice, draw straight lines, so as to leave sufficient thickness for the lath and plaster, which should in no case be less than three-fourths of an inch. Thus the general form of the bracketing will be obtained.

Fig. 729.

DOMES.

2089. We have, in a foregone page, mentioned a method of constructing domes with ribs in thicknesses. We here present to the reader two designs for dome-framing, wherein there is a cavity of framed work between the inner and outer domes; with moderate spans, however, simple framing is all that is required. *Fig.* 730. A is a design for a domical roof. B exhibits the method of framing the curb for it to stand upon, the section of the curb being shown upon *fig.* A. The design here given is nearly the same as that used for the dome of the Pantheon in Oxford Street, which was destroyed by fire. C is another design for a domical roof, which is narrow at the bottom part of the framing, for the purpose of gaining room within the dome.

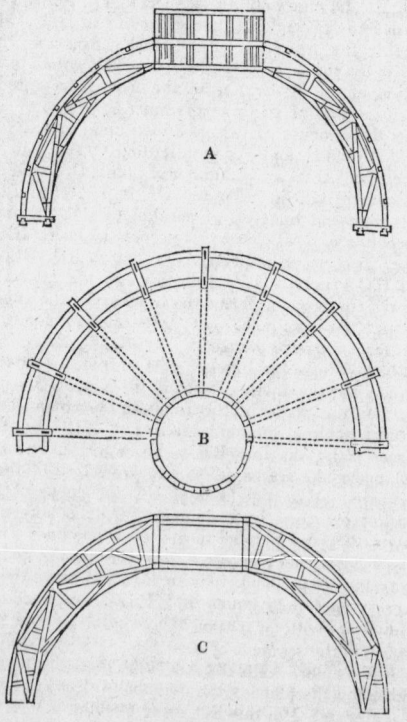

PENDENTIVES.

2090. If a hemisphere, or other portion of a sphere, be intersected (*fig.* 731.) by

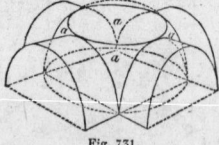

Fig. 731.

cylindrical or cylindroidal arches, vaults *aa* are formed, which are called *pendentives*. The termination of these at top will be a circle, whereon may be placed a dome, or an upright drum story, which, if necessary, may be terminated by a dome.

Fig. 730.

The reader will immediately perceive that many varieties may be formed. Our object here is merely to show how the carpenter is to proceed in making his *cradling*, as it is called, when pendentives are to be formed in wood.

2091. *To cove the ceiling of a square room with conical pendentives.* Let ABC (*fig.* 732.) be half the plan of the room, and DFE the half plan of the curb, at whose top the ribs are all fixed. The hyperbolical arches *agb*, *bhc* on each of the four sides are of equal height. The straight ribs *bf*, *ik*, *lm*, &c. are shown on the plan by FB, IK, LM, &c. The method of finding the hyperbolical curves *agb*, *bhc* will be explained in the following figure.

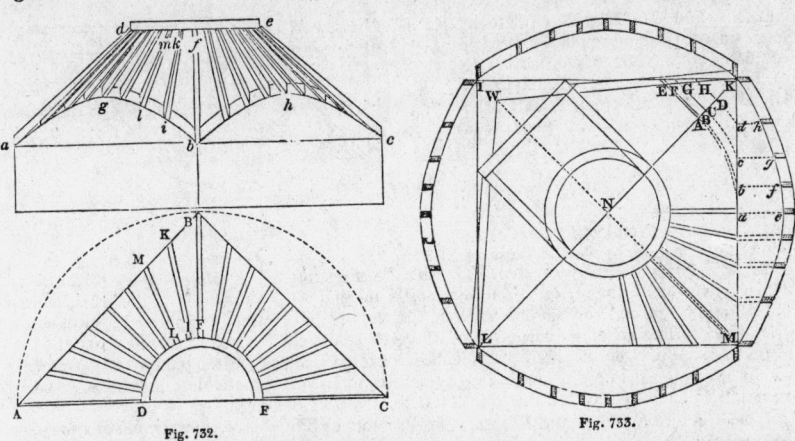

Fig. 732.   Fig. 733.

2092. *To find the springing lines of the preceding pendentives, the section in one of the vertical diagonal planes being given.* Bisect the diagonal LK (*fig.* 733.) at the point N by the perpendicular NW, which make equal to the height of the cone, and draw the sides LW and KW. Bisect the side MK of the square at *a*, and on N, with the radius N*a*, describe an arc *a*A, cutting the diagonal LK at A. Then take any points B, C, D, between A and K, and with the several radii NB, NC, ND, describe the arcs B*b*, C*c*, and D*d*, cutting KM at the points *d*, *c*, and *b*. From the points A, B, C, and D, draw AE, BF, CG, and DH perpendicular to the diagonal KL, cutting the side WK of the section of the cone at E, F, G, H. At the points *abcd* erect perpendiculars *ae*, *bf*, *cg*, and *dh* to the side ML, making each equal to their corresponding distances AE, BF, CG, and DH, which will be one half of the curve for that side from which the other may be traced. The dark parts show the feet of the ribs.

2093. *Fig.* 734. shows the method of coving a square room with spherical pendentives, which a few words will sufficiently describe. CD, DE are two sides of the plan; AFB is half the plan of the curb. In the elevation above is shown the method of fixing the ribs (which, in projection, are portions of ellipses) on two sides of the plan. *ab* is the elevation of the curb AFB; *cfd* and *dge* are ribs on each side of the plan supporting the vertical ribs that form the spherical surface, which vertical ribs support the curb *afb*. On *afb* may, if necessary, be placed a lantern or skylight; or, if light be not wanted, a flat ceiling or a dome may be placed. This pendentive is to be finished with plaster; hence the ribs must not be farther apart than about 12 inches.

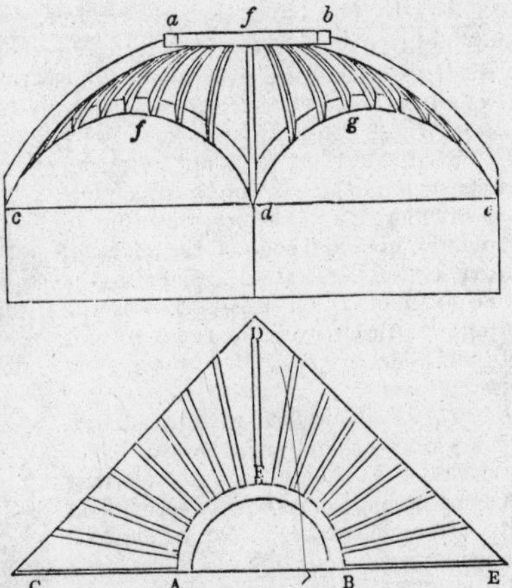

2094. For finding (*fig.* 735.) the intersection of the ribs of a spandrel dome, whose section is the segment of a circle, and whose plan is a square ABCD. Let DEFB be the section on the plane of the diagonal. First plan one quarter of the ribs, as at UC, TN, SL, RI, and QG, this last being parallel to DC or AB, the sides of the square; on V, with the radii VG, VI, VL, VN, and VC, describe the arcs GP*g*, I*ti*, L*ul*, N*vn*, &c. cut-

Fig. 734.

ting the base DB of the angular rib in g, i, l, and n. Draw gh, ik, lm, and no, each perpendicular to DB, cutting the diagonal rib at h, k, m, and o. Then making the distances GH, IK, LM, and NO equal to the corresponding distances gh, ik, lm, and no, through the points H, K, M, O draw a curve which will be the under edge of that for the bottom of the ribs QG, RI, SL, TN, and UC, shown complete on each side of the square plan. If each of the circular segments on each side of the square plan be turned up at right angles to the plan ABCD, the ribs will then stand in their true position.

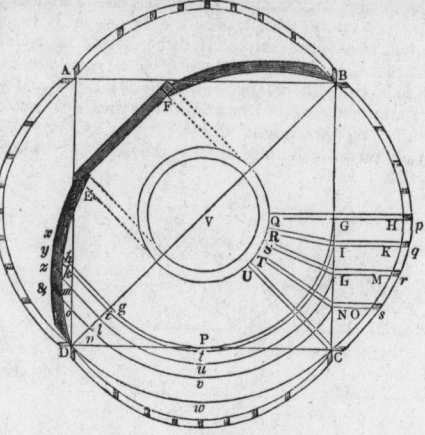

Fig. 735.

BRIDGES.

2095. We shall in this work confine ourselves to the simplest forms of timber bridges, which, as well as those of stone, will be found fully treated of in the *Encyclopædia of Engineering*, by Mr. Cresy, which forms one of the series. As they mostly depend on the principle of the truss, where the span is large, and this combination of timbers we have already explained; so in stone bridges the principle of construction of the arch is the chief matter for consideration, and to that a large portion of this work has been devoted; hence, on the part of the architect, we do not resign his pretension to employment in such works, for which, indeed, as respects design, his general education fits him better than that of the engineer.

2096. The bridge over the Brenta, near Bassano, by Palladio, is an example of a wooden bridge (*fig.* 736.), which is not only elegant as a composition, but one which is economical

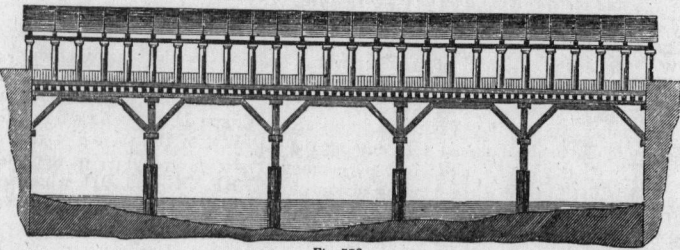

Fig. 736.

and might be employed with advantage where it is desirable that the piers should occupy a small space, and the river is not subject to great floods. The same great architect, in his celebrated *Treatise on Architecture*, has given several designs for timber bridges, the principles of whose construction have only been carried out further in many modern instances He was the earliest to adopt a species of construction by which numerous piers were rendered unnecessary, and thus to avoid the consequences of the shock of heavy bodies against the piers in the time of floods. Of this sort was the bridge he threw over the rapid torrent of the Cismone (*fig.* 737.) whose span was 108 feet.

2097. Palladio has given a design for a timber bridge (*fig.* 738.) which is remarkable as having been the earliest that has come to our knowledge, wherein the arrangement is in what may be called framed voussoirs, like the arch stones of a bridge, a principle in later days carried out to a great extent, and with success, in iron as well as timber bridges.

Fig. 737.

Fig. 738.

2098. We shall conclude our section on practical carpentry with a method of constructing timber bridges proposed by Price in his *Treatise on Carpentry*, and one not dissimilar in principle to the method of Philibert de Lorme, before mentioned. The bridge (*fig.* 739.) is supposed to consist of two principal ribs *ik*. The width of the place is spanned at once by an arch rising one sixth part of its extent. Its curve is divided into five parts, "which," says Price, "I purpose to be of good seasoned English oak plank, of 3 inches thick and 12 broad. Their joint or meeting tends to the centre of the arch. Within this rib is another, cut out of plank as before, of 3 inches thick and 9 broad, in such sort as to break the joints of the other. In each of these ribs are made four mortices, of 4 inches broad and 3 high, and in the middle of the said 9-inch plank. These

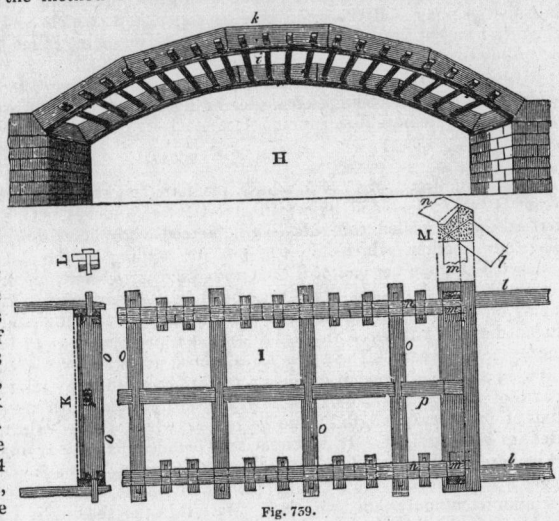

Fig. 739.

mortices are best set out with a templet, on which the said mortices have been truly divided and adjusted. Lastly, put each principal rib up in its place, driving loose keys into some of the mortices to hold the said two thicknesses together; while other help is ready to drive in the joists, which should have a shoulder inward, and a mortice in them outward; through which keys being drove keep the whole together. On these joists lay your planks, gravel, &c.; so is your bridge compleat, and suitable to a river, &c. of 36 feet wide."

2099. "In case the river, &c. be 40 or 50 feet wide, the stuff should be larger and more particularly framed, as is shown in part of the plan enlarged, as I. These planks ought to be 4 inches thick and 16 wide; and the inner ones, that break the joints, 4 inches thick and 12 broad; in each of these are six mortices, four of which are 4 inches wide and 2 high; through these are drove keys which keep the ribs the better together; the other two mortices are 6 inches wide and 4 high; into these are framed the joists of 6 inches by 12; the tenons of these joists are morticed to receive the posts, which serve as keys, as shown in the section K, and the small keys as in L; all which inspection will explain. That of M is a method whereby to make a good butment in case the ground be not solid, and is by driving two piles perpendicularly and two sloping, the heads of both being cut off so as to be embraced by the sill or resting plate, which will appear by the pricked lines drawn from the plan I and the letters of reference." Price concludes: " All that I conceive necessary to be said further is, that the whole being performed without iron, it is therefore capable of being painted on every part, by which means the timber may be preserved; for though in some respects iron is indispensably necessary, yet, if in such cases where things are or may be often moved, the iron will rust and scale, so as that the parts will become loose in process of time, which, as I said before, if made of sound timber, will always keep tight and firm together. It may not be amiss to observe, that whereas some may imagine this arch of timber is liable to give way, when a weight comes on any particular part, and rise where there is no weight, such objectors may be satisfied that no part can yield or give way till the said six keys are broke short off at once, which no weight can possibly do."

SECT. V.

JOINERY.

2100. Joinery is that part of the science of architecture which consists in framing or *joining* together wood for the external and internal finishings of houses, such as the linings of walls and rough timbers, the putting together of doors, windows, stairs, and the like.

It requires, therefore, more accurate and nicer workmanship than carpentry, being of a decorative nature and near the eye. Hence the surfaces must be smooth and nicely wrought, and the joints must be made with great precision. The smoothing of the wood is called *planing*, and the wood used is called *stuff*, which consists of rectangular prisms roughly brought into shape by the saw, such prisms being called battens, boards, and planks, according to their breadth and thickness.

2101. We shall give but a succinct account of the joiner's tools; an acquaintance with their forms and uses being sooner learnt by mere inspection over a joiner's bench than by the most elaborate description.

TOOLS.

2102. The first is the *bench*, whose medium height is about 2 feet 8 inches, its length about 10 or 12 feet, and its width about 2 feet 6 inches. One side is provided with a vertical board, called the *side board*, pierced with holes ranged at different heights in diagonal directions, which admit of pins for holding up the object to be planed, which is supported at the other end of it by a *screw* and *screw check*, together called the *bench screw*, acting like a *vice*. The *planes* used by the joiner are the *jack plane*, which is used for taking off the roughest and most prominent parts of the stuff, and reducing it nearly to its intended form. Its *stock*, that is, the wooden part, is about 17 inches long, 3 inches high, and $3\frac{1}{2}$ inches broad. The *trying plane*, whose use is nearly the same as that last described, but used after it, the operation being performed with it by taking the shaving the whole length of the stuff, which is called *trying up*, whereas with the jack plane the workman stops at every arm's length. The *long plane*, which is used when a piece of stuff is to be tried up very straight. It is longer and broader than the trying plane, its length being 26 inches, its breadth $3\frac{5}{8}$ inches, and depth $3\frac{1}{8}$ inches. The *jointer*, which is still longer, being 2 feet 6 inches long, and is principally used for obtaining very straight edges, an operation commonly called *shooting*. With this the shaving is taken the whole length in finishing the joint or edge. The *smoothing plane*, which, as its name imports, is the last employed for giving the utmost degree of smoothness to the surface of the wood, and is chiefly used for cleaning off finished work. It is only $7\frac{1}{2}$ inches long, 3 inches broad, and $2\frac{3}{4}$ inches in depth. The foregoing are technically called *bench planes*.

2103. The *compass plane* which in size and shape is similar to the smoothing plane, except that its under surface or *sole* is convex, its use being to form a concave cylindrical surface. Compass planes are therefore of various sizes as occasion may require. The *forkstaff plane* resembles the smoothing plane in size and shape, except that the sole is part of a concave cylindric surface, whose axis is parallel to the length of the plane. The form is obviously connected with its application, and, like the last named, it is of course of various sizes. The *straight block* is employed for shooting short joints and mitres, instead of the jointer, which would be unwieldy: its length is 12 inches, its breadth $3\frac{1}{8}$ inches, and depth $2\frac{3}{4}$ inches.

2104. There is a species of planes called *rebate* planes, the first whereof is simply called the *rebate plane*, being, as its name imports, chiefly used for making rebates, which are receding planes formed for the reception of some other board or body, so that its edge may coincide with that side of the rebate next to the edge of the rebated piece. The length of the rebate plane is about $9\frac{1}{2}$ inches, its depth about $3\frac{1}{2}$ inches, and its thickness varies according to the width of the rebate to be made, say from $1\frac{3}{4}$ to $\frac{1}{2}$ inch. Rebate planes vary from bench planes in having no *tote* or handle rising out of the stock, and from their having no orifice for the discharge of the shavings, which are discharged on one side or other according to the use of the plane. Of the sinking rebating planes there are two sorts, the *moving fillister* and the *sash fillister*, whereof, referring the reader to the tool itself, a sight of which he can have no difficulty in procuring, the first is for sinking the edge of the stuff next to the workman, and the other for sinking the opposite edge, whence it is manifest that these planes have their cutting edges on the under side. Without enumerating many other sorts which are in use, we shall mention merely the *plough*, a plane used for sinking a cavity in a surface not close to the edge of it, so as to leave an excavation or hollow, consisting of three straight surfaces forming two internal right angles with each other, and the two vertical sides two external right angles with the upper surface of the stuff. The channel thus cut is called a *groove*, and the operation is called *grooving* or *plowing*. This species will vary according to the width from the edge; but it is generally about $7\frac{3}{8}$ inches long, $3\frac{5}{8}$ inches deep.

2105. *Moulding planes* are for forming mouldings, which, of course, will vary according to the designs of the architect. They are generally about $9\frac{3}{8}$ inches long, and $3\frac{3}{8}$ inches deep. When mouldings are very complex, they are generally wrought by hand; but when a plane is formed for them they are said to be *stuck*, and the operation is called *sticking*.

2106. The *bead plane* is used very frequently in joinery, its use being for sticking mouldings whose section is semicircular; when the bead is stuck on the edge of a piece of stuff to form a semi-cylindric surface to the whole thickness, the edge is said to be

beaded or rounded. When a bead is stuck so that it does not on the section merely fall in with its square returns, but leaves a space   , thus, between the junctions at the sides, it is said to be *quirked*. The beads or planes vary from very small sizes up to the $\frac{3}{4}$ inch and $\frac{7}{8}$ bead. They may however be larger, and are sometimes stuck double and triple. The *snipebill plane* is one for forming the *quirk*, whereof we have spoken ; but we do not think a detailed description of it necessary, more than we do of those which are made for striking *hollows* and *rounds*.

2107. The *stock and bit* is the next tool to be mentioned. Its use is for boring wood, and the iron, which varies as the size of the bore required, is made in a curve on its edge of contrary flexure so as to discharge the wood taken out. It fits into what is called the stock, which has a double curved arm working on spindles, the end opposite to the bit being pressed by the body, whose weight against the whole instrument is the power whereby the operation is performed. The bit is also called a *pin*, or *gouge bit*. It is an important tool, and much used. (See Auger in *Glossary*.)

2108. *Countersinks* are bits for widening the upper part of a hole in wood or iron for the head of a screw or pin, and are formed with a conical head. *Rimers* are bits for widening holes, and are of pyramidal form whose vertical angle is about $3\frac{1}{2}$ degrees. The hole is first pierced by means of a drill or punch, and the rimer then cuts or scrapes off the interior surface of the hole, as it sinks downwards, by pressing on the head of the stock. According to the metal on which they are to be used they are differently formed.

2109. The *taper shell bit* is conical both within and without. Its horizontal section is a crescent, the cutting edge being the meeting of the interior and exterior conic surfaces. Its use is for widening holes in wood. Besides the above bits, there are some which are provided with a screw-driver for sinking small screws into wood with more rapidity than the unassisted hand will accomplish.

2110. The *brad awl*, the smallest boring tool, is so well known, that it would be waste of space to do more than mention it, the commonest of instruments in the science of construction.

2111. The variety of *chisels* is great. They are well known to be edge tools for cutting wood by pressure on it, or by percussion with a mallet on its handle. The *firmer chisel* is a tool used by the carpenter as well as the joiner for cutting away superfluous wood by thin chips. Those are best which are made of cast steel. If much superfluous wood is to be cut away, a strong chisel, with an iron back and steel face, is first used with the aid of the mallet, and then a slighter one with a very fine edge. The first is the *firmer* first mentioned, and the last is called a *paring chisel*, in the use whereof the force employed is from the shoulder or hand.

2112. The *mortice chisel*, whose use is for cutting out rectangular prismatic cavities in stuff is made of considerable strength. The cavity it so cuts out is called a *mortice*, and the piece which fits into it a *tenon*, whence the name of the tool. This chisel is one acted on only by the percussion of the mallet.

2113. The *gouge* is used for cutting concave forms in stuff. It is, in fact, a chisel whose iron is convex.

2114. The *drawing knife* is an oblique-ended chisel, or old knife, for drawing in the ends of tenons by making a deep incision with the sharp edge, guided by that of the tongue of a square, for which purpose a small part is cut out in the form of a triangular prism. The use of this excavation is to enter the saw and keep it close to the shoulder, and thus make the end of the rail quite smooth, for by this means the saw will not get out of its course.

2115. There are many species of the *saw*, which is a thin plate of steel, whose edge is indented with teeth for cutting by reciprocally changing the direction of its motion. The varieties are—the *ripping saw*, which is used for dividing or splitting wood in the direction of the fibres ; its teeth are large, the measure being usually to the number of eight in 3 inches, such teeth standing perpendicularly to the line which ranges with the points : the length of the *plate* or *blade* of this saw is about 28 inches. The *half ripper* is used also for dividing wood in the direction of the fibres : the plate of this saw is as long as of that last described, but it has only three teeth in an inch. The *hand saw*, whose plate is 26 inches long, contains fifteen teeth in 4 inches ; it is used for cross cutting, as in the direction of the fibres ; for which purposes the teeth recline more than in the two former saws. The *panel saw* has about six teeth in an inch, the length of its plate being the same as the last ; but in this and the hand saw thinner than in the ripping saw : it is used for cutting very thin wood, either with or across the fibres. The *tenon saw* is most used for cutting wood transverse to the fibres, as the shoulders of tenons. The plate of a tenon saw is from 14 to 19 inches long, having eight to ten teeth in an inch. This saw not being intended to cut through the whole breadth of the wood, and the plate being too thin to make a straight kerf, or to keep it from buckling, it has a thick piece of iron fixed on the edge opposite to the teeth, called the back. From the opening for the fingers through the

handle of this and the foregoing saws being enclosed all round, it is called a double handle. The *sash saw* is used for forming the tenons of sashes; its plate is 11 inches in length, having about thirteen teeth to the inch. It is sometimes backed with iron, but more frequently with brass. The *dovetail saw* is used for cutting the dovetails of drawers and the like; its plate is backed with brass, it contains fifteen teeth in about one inch, and is about 9 inches long. The handles of this and the last saw are only single. The *compass saw*, for cutting wood into curved surfaces, is narrow, thicker on the cutting edge as the teeth have no set, and is without a back; the plate, near the handle, is about an inch broad, and about a quarter of an inch at the other extremity, having about five teeth to the inch; the handle is single. The *keyhole*, or *turning saw*, in its plate resembles the compass saw, but the handle is long, and perforated from end to end for inserting the plate at any distance within the handle; there is a *pad* in the lower part of the handle, through which is inserted a screw for fastening the plate therein. As its name implies, it is used for turning out quick curves, as keyholes, and is therefore frequently called a keyhole saw.

2116. The teeth of all saws, except turning and keyhole saws, are bent alternately on the contrary sides of the plate, so that all the teeth on the same side are alike bent throughout the length of the plate, for the purposes of clearing the sides of the cut made in the wood by it. The saw is a tool of great importance in every case where wood is to be divided, for by its means it can be divided into slips or scantlings with no more waste than a small slice of the wood, whose breadth is equal to the depth of the piece to be cut through, and the thickness of it equal to no more than the distance of the teeth between their extreme points on the alternate sides of the saw measured on a line perpendicular to them; whereas, by any other means, such as the axe for instance, large pieces of timber could only be reduced in size by cutting away the superfluous stuff, which would be no less a waste of labour than of the material used; and even then it would have to be reduced to a plane surface.

2117. Joiners use the *hatchet*, which is a small axe, for cutting away the superfluous wood from the edge of a piece of stuff when the part to be cut away is too small to be sawed.

2118. The *square* consists of two rectangular prismatic pieces of wood, or one of wood, and the other, which is the thinnest, of metal, fixed together, each at one of their extremities, so as to form a right angle both internally and externally; the interior right angle is therefore called the inner square, and the exterior one the outer square. Squares are, for different applications, made of different dimensions. Some are employed in trying up wood, and some for setting out work; the former is called a trying square, and the latter a setting out square. To prove a square it is only necessary to reverse the blade after having drawn a line on the surface to which it is applied: if the line of the blade on reversal do not coincide with that first drawn, the square is incorrect.

2119. The bevel consists, like the square, of a blade and handle; but the tongue is moveable on a joint, so that it may be set to any angle. When it is required to try up many pieces of stuff to a particular angle, an immoveable bevel ought to be made for the purpose; for unless very great care be taken in laying down the moveable bevel, it will be likely to shift.

2120. The *gauge* is an instrument used for drawing or marking a line on a piece of stuff to a width parallel to the edge. It consists generally of a square piece with a mortice in it, through which runs a sliding bar at right angles, called the stem, furnished with a sharp point or tooth at one extremity, projecting a little from the surface; so that when the side of the gauge next to the end which has the point is applied upon the vertical surface of the wood, with the toothed side of the stem upon the horizontal surface, and pushed and drawn alternately by the workman from and towards him, the tooth makes an incision from the surface into the wood at a parallel distance from the upper edge of the vertical side on the right hand. This line marks precisely the intersection of the plane which divides the superfluous stuff from that which is to be used. When it is required to cut a mortice in a piece of wood, the gauge has two teeth in it, and is called a *mortice gauge*, one tooth being stationary at the end of the stem, and the other moveable in a mortice between the fixed tooth and the head; so that the distances of the teeth from each other, and of each from the head, may be set at pleasure, as the thickness of the tenon may require.

2121. The *side hook* is a rectangular prismatic piece of wood, with a projecting knob at the ends of its opposite sides. The use of the side hook is to hold a board fast, its fibres being in the direction of the length of the bench, while the workman is cutting across the fibres with a saw or grooving plane, or in *traversing* the wood, which is planing it in a direction perpendicular to the fibres.

2122. The *mitre box* consists of three boards, two, called the sides, being fixed at right angles to a third, called the bottom. The bottom and top of the sides are all parallel; the sides of equal height, and cut with a saw in two directions of straight surfaces at right angles to each other and to the bottom, forming an angle of 45 degrees with the sides. The mitre box is used for cutting a piece of tried up stuff to an angle of 45 degrees with two

of its surfaces ; or at least to one of the arrises, and perpendicular to the other two sides, or at least to one of them, obliquely to the fibres.

2123. The *straight edge* is a slip of wood made perfectly straight on the edge, in order to make other edges straight, or to plane the face of a board straight. It is made of different lengths, according to the required magnitude of the work. Its use is obvious, as its application will show whether there is a coincidence between the straight edge and the surface to which it is applied. When joiners wish to ascertain whether the whole surface of a piece of wood lies in the same plane, they use two slips, each straightened on one edge, with the opposite edge parallel, and both pieces of the same breadth between the parallel edges ; whence each piece has two straight edges or two parallel planes. To find, therefore, whether a board is twisted, one of the slips is placed across one end and the other across the other end of the board, with one of the straight edges of each upon the surface. The joiner then looks in a longitudinal direction over the upper edges of the two slips, until his eye and the said two edges are in one plane ; or otherwise the intersection of the plane passing through the eye and the upper edge of the nearest slip will intersect the upper edge of the farthest slip. If it happen as in the former case, the ends of the wood under the slips are in the same plane ; but should it happen as in the latter, they are not. In the last case, the surface is said to *wind ;* and when the surface is so reduced as for every two lines to be in one plane, it is said to be *out of winding,* which is the same as to say it is a perfect plane. From the use of these slips, they are denominated *winding sticks.*

2124. The *mitre square,* an instrument so called because it bisects the right angle or mitres the square, is an immoveable bevel, for the purpose of striking an angle of 45 degrees with one side or edge of a piece of stuff upon the adjoining side or edge of the said piece of stuff. It consists of a broad thin board, let or tongued into a piece on the edge called the fence or handle, which projects equally on each side of the blade, whereof one of the edges is made to contain an angle of 45 degrees with the nearest edge of the handle, or of that in which the blade is inserted. The inside of the handle is called the guide. The handle may be about an inch thick, 2 inches broad ; the blade about $\frac{3}{16}$ to $\frac{1}{4}$ of an inch thick, and about 7 or eight inches broad. The *arris* of a piece of stuff is the edge formed by two planes.

MACHINERY.

2124a. In many of the operations of the joiner, where numerous copies of the same thing have to be produced, accuracy is ensured by introducing the principle of the *guide,* either to direct the tool over the work, or the work over the tool. The *mitre box,* *shoot blocks,* and the various kinds of *fences* and *stops,* are examples. The principle of the *guide* is also applied to simple sawing and planing, and to grooving, tonguing, morticing, tenoning, and shaping. The *circular saw* was introduced about the end of the last century into England, and attempts to construct a *planing machine* were made about 1776 and 1791 (G. L. Molesworth, *On the Conversion of Wood by Machinery,* read at the Institute of Civil Engineers, November 17, 1857). When Sir S. Bentham was in Russia previous to 1790, he had made considerable progress in contriving machinery for shaping wood, such as all the parts of a highly finished sash window ; another for preparing all the parts of a wheel, so that the joiner or wheelwright in that case had only to put the several pieces together. In 1802 Bramah patented machinery for producing straight, parallel, and curvilinear surfaces on wood. In 1807 Brunel's famous block machinery was set in motion in Portsmouth dockyard. Thomson's machinery for sawing, gauging, grooving, and tonguing floor boards was in operation in 1826 ; and, in 1827, Muir of Glasgow patented a machine for working floor boards, which has since served as a model for others. This machine has approached perfection in that of MacDowall of Johnstone. A rack circular saw bench, for round or square timber, quickly converts a log or balk into square timber.

2124b. For the ordinary workshop, where the trade is limited and much varied, the simpler American machines are more suitable. The *saw bench* occupies little space and can be applied in plain and bevel sawing, and ripping, mitring, tenoning, rebating, &c. It is only 3 feet 2 inches long, 2 feet 2 inches wide, and 3 feet $6\frac{1}{2}$ inches high ; the saw is 8 inches in diameter and makes $15\frac{1}{2}$ revolutions for each turn of the handle. A crank may be acted on by a treadle when the stuff is thin, but in ordinary cases the machine requires two operators. We cannot satisfactorily describe the details, without illustrations, of the many operations which this handy bench aids in performing with accuracy and dispatch. In Furness's patent wood working machine for planing, moulding, morticing, sawing, squaring, tenoning, boring, rebating, and grooving, the stuff is operated upon by cutters, held by horizontal arms fixed to a vertical shaft, in which it resembles the Bramah's machine of 1802, but it is much simpler and less expensive. Worssam's " general joiner " for the same purposes will, it is said, with a 2 horse-power, do the work of at least fifteen skilled joiners. Perin's patent French *band saw blades* are made from $\frac{1}{16}$th of an inch to 8 inches in width and up to 50 feet in length.

2124c. In machines with revolving cutters the general opinion is, that the greater the speed of the cutting tool the better will be the quality of the work. The practical limit,

however, appears to be between 2,500 and 3,500 revolutions per minute. A higher velocity heats the bearings, destroys the balance, and causes injurious vibrations. To produce a good result the travel of the work should be very slow relatively to the travel of the cutters. In some of the planing machines the cutters revolve with a velocity of 7,000 feet per minute, while the work advances at the rate of only 30 feet, but as a general rule the work travels about $\frac{1}{20}$th of an inch for each stroke of the cutters. To withstand this high velocity the framing of the machine requires to be perfectly constructed; the bearings made of a hard alloy, and precautions taken for obviating the wear of them. Newlands' work gives illustrations and detailed descriptions of some of the machinery.

2124d. Mention must be made, though space prevents a description, of Jordan's patent wood and stone carving machine invented about 1843, and worked by Pratt in 1845 to 1850 on a large scale. It roughed out the material according to the design, leaving but little labour to be received from the hands of the carver. The invention has been again taken up. Moulded work was also for some time obtained by burning away the wood by applying red hot iron moulds to it. This system has quite exploded.

2125. In joiner's work executed during the 13th, 14th, and 15th centuries, the wood has neither warped, split, nor shrunk in the tenons and at other joints. This excellence is ascribed to the practice of seasoning the wood for at least six years after it was sawn; by first leaving it in damp places or even in water, and then stacking it on open piles under cover, when it was often turned and sometimes smoked; after such treatment the wood, when worked, has a tendency to acquire in the course of time the appearance of Florentine bronze.

2125a. As very old timber is likely to show shakes and to be worm-eaten, the mediæval joiners felled oak from two to three hundred years old; i.e., timber which, at a yard from

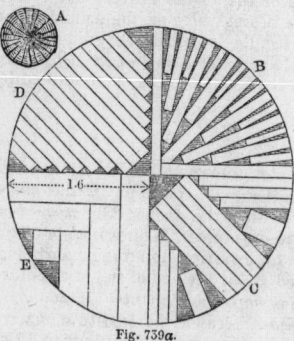

Fig. 739a.

the ground, measured from 66 or 72 to 120 or 126 inches in girt without the albumen, and commenced its conversion by marking it with one diameter crossing another at right angles. The cuts on these lines having been made, the quarters were sawn in various ways, regard being had, as much as possible, to the texture of the wood. An unseasoned log of oak splits as shown at A, *fig.* 739a. because the inner concentric circles are harder and more compact than the outer ones; therefore the latter, being the most extensive in surface as well as the most porous, contain a greater quantity of moisture, and shrink more than the inner ones in drying, thus causing splits or shakes leading to the centre. If timber be converted without regard to this result of dryness, the stuff will not only split, but will be so affected by changes of weather as to twist. If the cuts be made in lines converging, or even tending to the centre, the stuff may shrink in width but will neither split nor warp. Although oak is formed like other exogenous trees by a succession of layers, these are united and solidified in this particular wood by the medullary rays which form a sort of natural dowel.

2125b. The best method of converting oak for the use of the joiner is shown at B, *fig.* 739a., in which there is no waste, as the triangular portions form feather-edged laths for tiling and other purposes. The next best method is that at C; that at D is inferior; but the most economical method, where thickness is required, as for planks or for moulded work, is that marked E. The resemblance to a watered silk, which is sometimes called the feather, or flower, or curl, or pattern, of wainscot, is due to the medullary rays, which show most when the saw follows the chink-grain as in B; in C and D the silky appearance does not exist, as most of the rays are cut across; very slight examination will show which course has been followed, especially in the case of the quarter-grain stuff produced by the method E. It is probable that the cross-cuts will follow the line of a layer, called the felt-grain, in the plan marked B, which is that adopted in Holland on timber furnished in great part from Champagne (whence, simply, the superiority of Dutch wainscot), and in all cases of split oak for lathing and for park paling. (Viollet-le-Duc).

2125c. The wood principally used for joinery is of three sorts, pine, and white and yellow deal; the two first for panelling, and the last for framing. Of late years much American wood has been used, both for panels and frames. It works easily, is soft, free from knots, but more liable to warp than white deal. But joinery is not of course limited to the use of a particular sort of wood. When the exporter cuts a log, the first thing done is to get one good deal or more for the London market; the residue is then converted to supply other markets. Many deals 3 inches thick are sent to France, perhaps as large a proportion as those of 2 inch and $1\frac{1}{4}$ inch, but they are not of so good a description as those sent to London. France is the great mart for all deals that will not suit the London

market. The following are the modes which have been and are at present practised to obtain deals for both markets. In 739b. (the mode practised until the French market

improved), are obtained an English deal, A, 9 in. by 3 in , and two battens, B, 7 in. by 2½ in., making 62 feet superficial. In 739c., the old mode of cutting, gave two English deals, C, 9 in. by 2½ in., and two English battens, D, 7 in. by 2¼ in., making 80 feet superficial. In 739d., the present mode of cutting, gives two

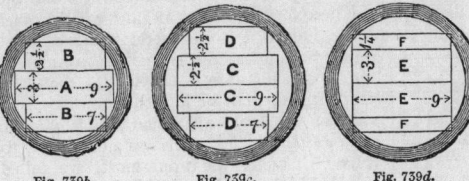

Fig. 739b.　　　　　Fig. 739c.　　　　　Fig. 739d.

English deals, E, 9 in. by 3 in., and two French deals, F, 9 in. by 1¼ in., making 76½ feet superficial. This communication has been obligingly furnished by Mr. T. A. Britton, as obtained at the Docks.

2125d. *Glue* is a material extensively used in joinery; see GLOSSARY, and Addendum.

MOULDINGS.

2126. When the edge of a piece of wood is reduced to a cylindrical form, it is said to be *rounded*, which is the simplest kind of moulded work. (*Fig.* 740.) When a portion of the arris is made semicylindrical, so that the surface of the cylindrical part is flush both with the face and the edge of the wood, with a groove or sinking made in the face only, the cylindrical part is called a bead, and the sinking a quirk; the whole combination (*fig.* 741.) being called a *quirked bead*.

2127. If a quirk is also formed on the other or returning face, so as to make the rounded part at the angle three fourths of a cylinder, the moulding (see *fig.* 742.) is called a *bead and double quirk*.

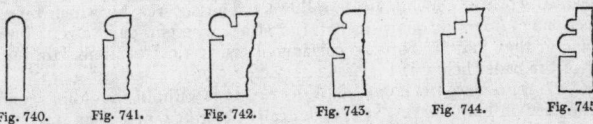

Fig. 740.　　Fig. 741.　　Fig. 742.　　Fig. 743.　　Fig. 744.　　Fig. 745.

2128. If two semicylindrical mouldings both rise from a plane parallel to the face, and one comes close to the edge of the piece and the other has a quirk on the further side, and its surface flush with the face of the wood, as in *fig.* 743., the combination is called a *double bead* or *double bead and quirk*, wherein the bead next to the edge of the stuff is much smaller than the other.

2129. Mouldings are usually separated from one another, and often terminated by two narrow planes at right angles (*fig.* 744.) to each other : these are called *fillets*, and show two sides of a rectangular prism. The different pieces of the combination of mouldings are called *members*. A semicylindrical moulding, rising from a plane parallel to the face, and terminated on the edge by a fillet (*fig.* 745.), is called a *torus*. In the figure there are two semicylindrical mouldings, whence that is called a *double torus*. The reader must observe that the distinction between torus mouldings and beads in joinery is, that the outer edge of the former always terminates with a fillet, whether the torus be single or double; whereas a bead never has a fillet on the outer edge. A repetition of equal semicylindrical mouldings, springing from a plane or cylindrical surface, is called *reeds*. In joinery, the ∫, *cima recta*, and ∫, *cima reversa*, are called respectively the *ogee* and *ogee reverse*. The ovolo), so named from its egg-like form, and the *quarter round*, the fourth part of a cylindrical surface, are the remaining of the principal mouldings used in joinery. When the margin of any framing terminates on the edges next to the panel, with one or more mouldings, which both advance before and retire from the face of the framing to the panelling, the mouldings thus introduced are called *bolection mouldings*. (See *fig.* 759.) Mediæval mouldings will be treated in the chapter PRACTICE OF ARCHITECTURE.

DOORS.

2130. We shall now more particularly address ourselves to the subject of doors and their mouldings. The most inferior sort of door used in building is the *common ledged door*, in which five or six or seven vertical boards are held together usually by three horizontal pieces called ledges, to which the vertical ones are nailed. Sometimes there is an outer framing, consisting of the top rail and the two outside stiles, but still having ledges as

before; these are called *framed and ledged doors*. A door, properly made, is formed by framing and fitting pieces of stuff together of the same thickness; those which are horizontal (*fig*. 746.) AAAA being called *rails*, and those which are vertical BBBB being called *stiles*. These form a skeleton into which *panels*, usually of a less thickness, are fitted. And this, indeed, is the general practice in all systems of framed joinery. In doors, the upper rails are called *top rails*; the next in descending, *frieze rails*; the next, which are usually wider than the two first, are called the *lock* or *middle rails*; and the lowest, from their situation, are called *bottom rails*. The stiles on the flanks are called *outside stiles*, and those in the middle are called *middle stiles*. The panels are also named from their situations on the door; thus CC, being the uppermost, are called *frieze panels*; the next DD are called *middle panels*, and EE *bottom panels*. The rails and stiles are wedged together, being previously morticed and tenoned into each other. The student should, however, to obtain a clear comprehension of the method adopted, see a door put together at the bench. The varieties and forms of doors are dependent upon the will of the architect, from whom the design of the whole emanates; it will be, therefore, here sufficient to mention the three sorts, viz. the *common door*, just described; the *jib door*, which is made with the same finishings and appearance as the room in which it is placed, so as not to have the appearance of a door; and, lastly, *folding doors*, which open from the centre of the doorway, and are used for making a wider communication between two apartments than a common door will permit, or, in other words, to lay two rooms into one.

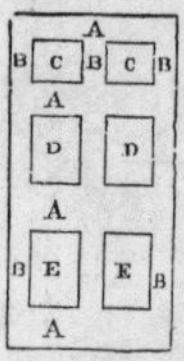

Fig. 746.

2131. Though the panelling of framed work is generally sunk within the face of the framing, it is for outside work sometimes made flush. In the best flush work, the panels are surrounded with a bead formed on the edge of the framing, and the work is called *bead and flush*. In the commoner kind of flush framing, the bead is run only on the two edges of the panel in the direction of the fibres, and is called *bead and butt*.

2132. The different denominations of framed doors, according to their mouldings and panels and framed work in general, are as follows. The figures by which they are represented are sections of doors through one of the stiles, wherein only a small part of the panel is shown, or they may be equally considered as vertical sections, through the top rail and part of the panel below it.

2133. *Fig*. 747. represents the commonest door. It is without mouldings, and the panel is a straight surface on both sides. It is technically described, first mentioning the number

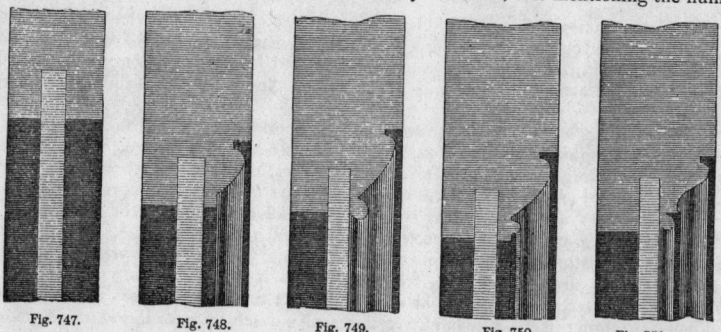

Fig. 747.   Fig. 748.   Fig. 749.   Fig. 750.   Fig. 751.

of panels intended in it, as a *door square and flat panel on both sides*. We shall not, in the following, repeat the observation as to the number of panels, that being always supposed as mentioned, but it will be found carried out under SPECIFICATIONS.

2134. *Fig*. 748. represents the rail and panel of a door, with a quirked ovolo and a fillet on one side, but having no mouldings on the other. The panel flat on both sides, it is described as a *door with quirked ovolo, fillet and flat with square back*.

2135. *Fig*. 749. only differs from the last in having a bead instead of a fillet, and is described as *quirked ovolo, bead and flat panel with square back*.

2136. *Fig*. 750., with an additional fillet on the framing, is described as *quirked ovolo, bead fillet and flat panel with square back*. The back, in the foregoing and following cases, is described as square, because of its having no mouldings on the framing, and of the panel being a straight surface on one side of the door.

2137. In *fig*. 751. the framing is formed with a quirked ogee, and a quirked bead on one side and square on the other, the surface of the panel being straight on both sides, and the door is described as *quirked ogee, quirked bead and flat panel with square back*.

2138. *Fig*. 752. only differs from the last in the bead being raised above the lower part of the ogee and a fillet. It is described as *quirked ogee, cocked bead and flat panel with square back*.

2139. *Fig.* 753. is described as a door with *cove, cocked bead, flat panel and square back.*

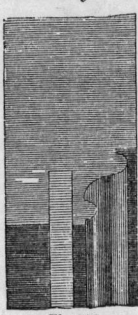
Fig. 752.

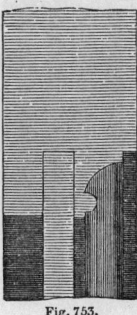
Fig. 753.

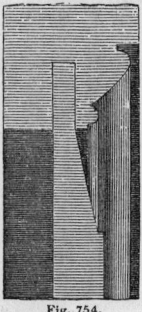
Fig. 754.

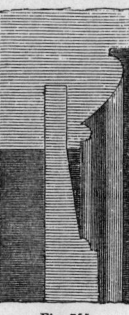
Fig. 755.

2140. *Fig.* 754. is a combination, by which much strength is imparted to the door, and it is therefore much used for external doors. It is, however, often in the interior of houses, and is described, *quirked ovolo, bead fillet and raised panel on front and square back.* It is from the raising of the panel that the additional strength is acquired.

2141. *Fig.* 755. resembles the last in general appearance, the difference being in the ovolo on the raised panel. It is described, *quirked ovolo, bead and raised panel, with ovolo on the raised panel and square back.* When an external door has raised panels, they are always placed towards the exterior.

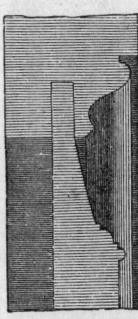
Fig. 756.

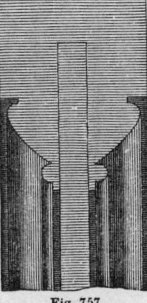
Fig. 757.

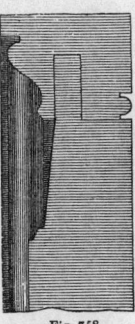
Fig. 758.

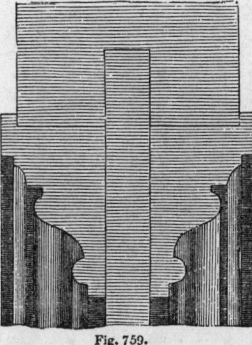
Fig. 759.

2142. In *fig.* 756. there are more mouldings than in the last on the raised panel. It is described, *quirked ogee, raised panel with ovolo and fillet on the rising and astragal on the flat of panel in front and square back.*

2143. *Fig.* 757. is described, *quirked ovolo, bead fillet and flat panel on both sides.* This description of doors is used where a handsome appearance is to be equally preserved on both sides of the door, as between rooms, or between halls or principal passages and rooms.

2144. *Fig.* 758. is a combination used, as all bead butt and bead flush work is, where strength is required. The form here given is described, *bead and flush front and quirked ogee, raised panel with ovolo on the rising, grooved on flat panel on back.*

2145. The series of mouldings are, as we have before mentioned, called *bolection* mouldings (*fig.* 759.), and are laid in after the door is framed square and put together. They project beyond the framing on each side. When bradded on through the sides of the quirks, the heads of the brads will be entirely concealed ; but it is to be observed that, in driving the brads, they must not be directed towards the panels, but into the solid of the framing. The form of these bolection mouldings is of course varied according to the pleasure of the architect.

2145a. *Mediæval Doors,* of a simple sort, were formed

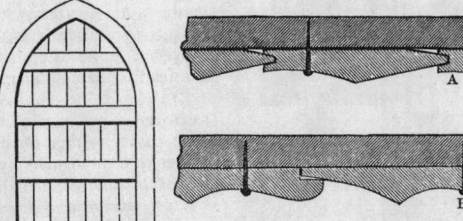
Fig. 759a.

of planks placed upright, grooved or feather-tongued at the edges, and generally secured

together by plain band-hinges, or more or less ornamented, or with scroll work. These planks are further nailed to a skeleton framing. *Fig.* 759a. gives a sketch of the back of the door at Bidborough Church, Kent, with its planking at A; and B is a section of the same at Staplehurst Church, Kent; the place for the nails is only indicated. These examples were supplied to the *Dictionary of Architecture* by Professor Lewis. Larger doors were made up of frames and rails, strutted or braced, on the same principle as the modern ledged doors and coach-house gates. Viollet le Duc's *Dictionnaire* has many examples of this mode of framing, all the timbers being stop-chamfered, and the planks bolted through the braces.

2145b. The head of a door enriched with panelling; the door, with the planks carved with panelling, running ornament, and niches with figures; an early English door, with

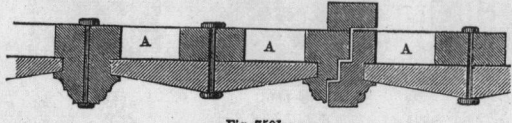

Fig. 759b.

two foliated band hinges; of the same period with three hinges; of the decorated period, the panelled and enriched headed door at Holbeach Church, Lincolnshire, of which the construction (a framing of square panels, AA) is shown in *fig.* 759b., rising from a plain plank 14½ inches high; with other examples, are all given in Brandon, *Analysis*, etc. together with one of the perpendicular period, wherein the face has panelled planks, and square panel framing at back.

2145c. The framework is sometimes placed externally and ornamented, as in *fig.* 759c., from the west door of the Church of San Pietro; and *fig.* 759d., from a door in a courtyard opposite that of Sta. Maria Antica, both at Verona. The sizes are 9½ inches and 12 inches respectively, from centre to centre of panels. These cuts are taken from the plates of the *Dictionary.* The very elaborate moulded and carved door from the Norman portion (12th century) of the Palazzo Reale, at Palermo, is given in the illustrations of the *Dictionary of Architecture,* from careful measurements by the late J. M. Lockyer. In the doors of cedar or deal, but covered with paint, at the chapels of St. Martin and St. Giles at Notre Dame le Puy (cir. 1043–53.),

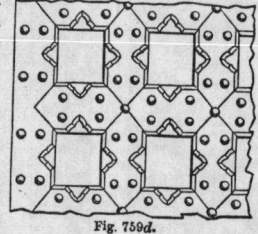

Fig. 759d.

9½

Fig. 759c.

the subjects, inscriptions, and borders are all obtained simply by sinking the ground 3-16ths of an inch. Gates of the same description are said to exist in the churches of Chamalières and Lavoûte-Chilhac in the same district. The wood doors, having iron plates beaten up into a pattern, and nailed with large brass nails, at Huesca Cathedral, may date about 1400–1515, the era of the erection of the west entrance. (Street.)

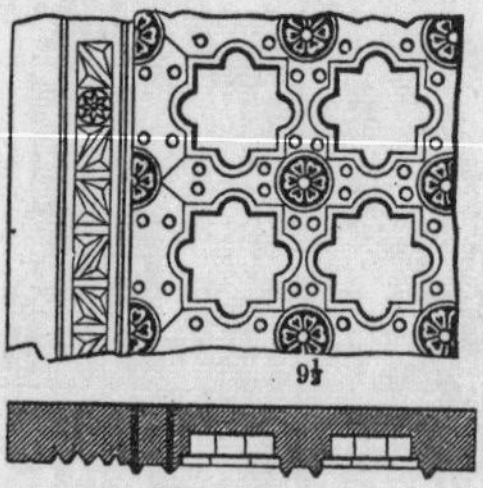

SHUTTERS.

2146. *Shutters,* which are the doors of window openings, are framed upon the same principles as doors themselves; but their backs are very often flush. In the better sort of buildings they are folded into recesses called *boxings,* whereof we shall give a figure below as an example of the ordinary method; but as the extent and different forms of windows vary, the ingenuity of the architect will be often required to contrive his shutters within a very small space. Into minutiæ we cannot enter in a work of this nature; however, in all their shapes, they are dependent on the leading principles given.

2147. *Fig.* 760. is a plan of the shutters, architrave, sash-frame, and part of the sash of common shutters. The cavity which forms the *boxing* into which the sashes fold is formed by the ground B (upon which the architrave A is nailed), the *back lining* F of the boxing, and the *inside lining* G of the sash-frame, whereof H is the *inside bead.* L is the *outside lining* of the sash-frame, M the *back lining* of it, and K the *parting bead,* so called from parting the upper and

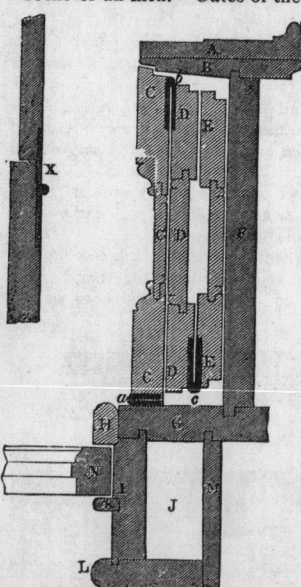

Fig. 760.

lower sash. The vacant space J, between the pulley piece I and M, is a cavity which contains the weights for balancing the sashes; N shows the plan of one of them. The shutters, when stretched out in their different folds, are supposed to cover one half of the window, another series being supposed to be placed on the other side of it.   The *front shutter* CCC is hung by hinges at *a* to the inside lining G of the sash-frame.   The inner shutters DDD and EE are called the *back flaps*, the former of which is hinged on to the front shutter at *b*, and the latter is hinged on to DDD at *c*. It will be immediately seen that these three will thus altogether turn upon the hinges at *a*, and cover, in one straight line, from both sides, the whole of the light of the window.   When the boxes are scanty, the hinge, called a *back flap hinge*, may be placed as shown in X attached to the figure.

2148. In ordinary cases, this example will sufficiently exhibit the method to be adopted. When it is not applicable, the architect must apply himself to the work *pro re natâ*, in which, with very little attention, he will not find insurmountable difficulty.

2148a. The *boxings* of a window are further described in the Glossary and Addendum. Besides the *lifting shutters* commonly used in houses of a lower rate, which in their construction is simply a repetition of the sash-frame, we must notice briefly the many *revolving shutters* for inside and outside purposes, whether of iron, steel, or wood, laths.   The latter were first made at Ipswich, some twenty years since, and were wound up and down by a winch and upright rod working a toothed wheel. They were soon afterwards made of iron, also worked by machinery. Within the last few years, their great convenience has led to many improvements, and the greater use of wood; instead of machinery, counterbalance weights were introduced.   Later, they were "constructed of laths of wood rebated together, having numerous mortices, through which pass a series of tempered steel bands, causing the shutter to be *self-coiling*." Iron laths were also used. Lately, they "are made of steel, in one sheet, without either chains, links or rivets, or pins; the steel being corrugated transversely gives them the appearance of laths, and enables them to be coiled into a small space." We avail ourselves of some illustrations issued by Clark and Co., showing the adaptability of this shutter to various places, as windows, shops, doors, fireplaces, &c.   *Fig.* 760a. shows the head and foot of an ordinary house window.   At A, it is fitted with the shutter inside, and to pull down.   At B, it is fitted also inside, and to lift up, the coil being placed in a boxing forming a step *on* the floor.   When the position of the joists admit of so doing, the coil may be placed *in* the flooring, as at C; and occasionally it may be more convenient to place it even *under* the ceiling, at D.   *Fig.* 760b. is the plan of a window frame, showing the groove, *a*, for the shutter, which is 1 inch deep by ⅞ths wide.

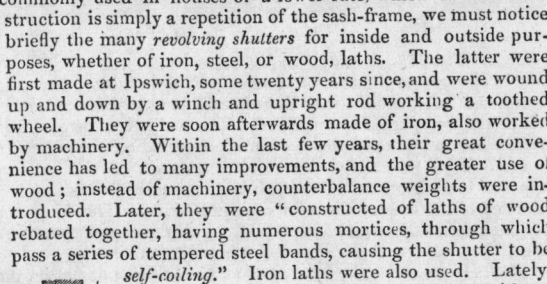

Fig. 760b.

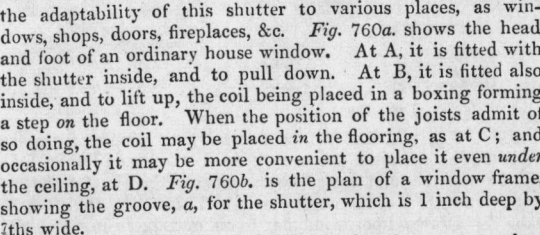

Fig. 760a.

2148b. A great improvement in securing the common shop shutters without a shutter-bar is one of the early inventions introduced by Jennings; these *shutter shoes* are so much advertised with illustrations that further notice of them herein is needless.

HINGEING.

2149. A very essential consideration in the neatness and beauty of joiners' work, is the formation of the joints on which are placed the hinges of doors and shutters. They ought to be so continued as to preserve the uniformity of the door or shutter on both sides, and as much as possible to be close enough to exclude a rush of air between the edges of the bodies to be hinged together, which, in this cold climate, is essential.   In these joints, both angles of one of the bodies is usually beaded, to conceal the open space, which would otherwise be seen; and for preserving the appearance of the work, the hinges are made of such a curvature towards the eye, as to seem, when painted, a part of the bead itself on that side where the knuckle is placed, so that when hung the whole may appear to be one bead.

2150. The section of a door style, and part of the *hanging style* at the joint, are represented in A and B (*fig.* 761.), wherein the centre of the bead on each side is in the line of the straight part of the joint from the opposite side. In this figure, C is the centre of the bead, AG part of the joint in a line with its edge. Joining AC, draw AB perpendicular thereto.   The other part BH is perpendicular to EF, which

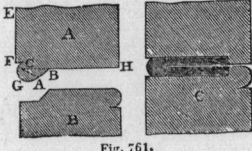

Fig. 761.

is the face of the door or hanging style. This is a joint suitable for many purposes, and may be made with common hinges. If crooked, it will assist in excluding the current of air, a point of no mean importance.

2151. In *fig.* 762. A and B exhibit a plane joint, beaded similarly on both sides. In this case, the plane of the joint is a tangent to the cylindrical surfaces of the two beads; and as the margin on each side is alike, no check to the rush of cold air is afforded. The hinge, moreover, is such that it cannot be made in the usual manner, but must be formed as at C.

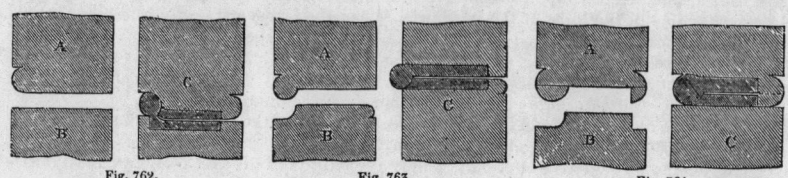

Fig. 762.   Fig. 763.   Fig. 764.

2152. *Fig.* 763. A and B represent a hinging wherein the plane of the joint from one side is directed to the axis of the bead on the other. The principle in it is the same as that in *fig.* 761., and it may therefore be hinged with common hinges, as shown in C, in which the two parts are conjoined. The methods shown in this and *fig.* 761. are useful in cases wherein a part of the margin is concealed on one side of the door.

2153. *Fig.* 764. A and B exhibit the beads of similar size on each side, and exactly opposite to each other, the joint being broken by indenting a part terminated by a plane directed to the axis of the two opposite beads. The hinges are required merely of the common form, the arrangement is strong, and the apartment rendered comfortable by their use. In C the parts are shown as hinged together.

2154. In *fig.* 765. the beads are on both sides, but not on the same piece, as in the last figure. The appearance is uniform, but the bead, which projects the whole of its thickness, is weakened. The junction is seen in the representation at C.

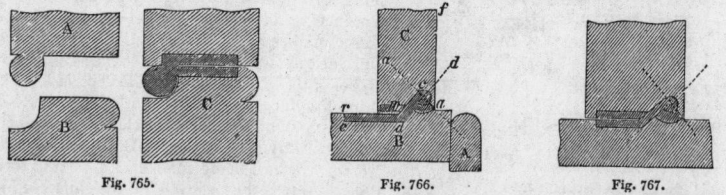

Fig. 765.   Fig. 766.   Fig. 767.

2155. *Fig.* 766. is a method that has been adopted for concealing the hinges of shutters. A is the inner bead of the sash-frame, B the inside lining, C the style of the shutter. For the form of the joint, let *af* be the face of the shutter, perpendicular to *ar* the face of the inside lining. Let the angle *f a r* be bisected by the straight line *aa*, and in the centre take *c*. Draw *dd* perpendicular to *aa*, cutting it in *c*, which is the centre of the hinge. From *c*, as a centre, describe the arc *am*, which must be hollowed out from the inside lining of the sash through the height of the shutter. In order to make room for the opening and shutting of the hinge, the internal right angle of the shutter must be cut out of its edge to the breadth of the hinges. The *toils* of the hinge are here for the purpose of strengthening them, represented of different lengths.

2156. In *fig.* 767. the hinges, which are for a door, are concealed, as the door allows it in the thickness of the wood, the ends of the hinges being of equal lengths.

2157. *Fig.* 768. shows the common method of hingeing shutters, a mode wherein the whole thickness of the hinge is let into the thickness of the shutter, the inside lining being assumed as too thin to afford sufficient hold for the screws employed to fasten them.

2158. *Fig.* 769. exhibits the hanging of a door with the centres concealed. Let *ad* be the side of the jamb in contact with the edge of

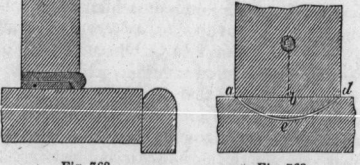

Fig. 768.   Fig. 769.

the door; bisect it in *b*, and draw *bc* perpendicular to *ad*, make *bc* equal to *ba* or *bd*, and join *ac* and *cd*; from *c*, as a centre, describe the arc *aed*, which will show the portion to be hollowed out of the jamb. The centres are fixed to the upper and under parts of the door, and the former is to be so constructed as to allow its being taken out of the socket to unhang the door when required.

2159. Shutters are usually hung in the way represented in *fig.* 770., wherein the centre

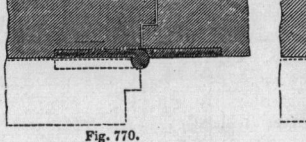

Fig. 770.

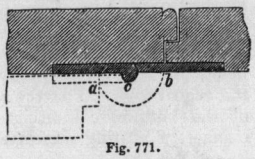

Fig. 771.

of the knuckle of the hinge is exactly opposite to the perpendicular part of the rebate. The dotted lines exhibit the flap when folded back.

2160. When the axis of the knuckle cannot be disposed so as to fall opposite to the joint, the hinge is to be placed as shown in *fig. 771*. Thus, *ab* being the distance of the edge of the flap from that of the shutter, bisect it in *c*, which will be the point opposite whereto the centre of the hinge is to be placed. This arrangement is necessary, both when the shutters are not square at the ends, and when the boxing is restricted in space; the principle being to place the centre of the knuckle of the hinge at half the distance of the edge of the flap from the rebate on the edge of the shutter. In *fig. 772.* the two parts are shown hinged together.

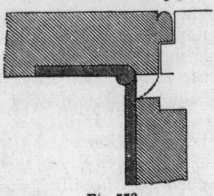

Fig. 772.

2161. When a door has attached to it any projection, and, when open, it is requisite to bring it parallel to its place when shut, the knuckle of the hinge (*fig. 773.*) must project at least as far as the projection in question. An inspection of the diagram, wherein the dotted lines show the situation of the door when folded back, will sufficiently convey the mode of conducting this expedient.

2162. *Fig. 774.* is the representation of what is called a *rule joint*, which is used when the piece to be hung is not required to open to more than a right angle. In this case, the centre of the hinge is necessarily in the centre of the arc. In *fig. 775.* the expedient shows the method turned to a right angle.

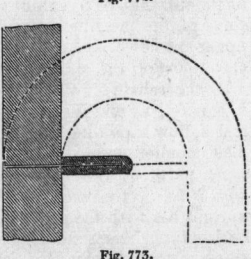

Fig. 773.

2163. The various methods of hingeing to suit every possible case would occupy a very large space, were we to enter into them; and even after

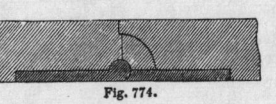

Fig. 774.

exhausting all the cases that we may have imagined, others would arise to which no example given might be applicable; we therefore leave this portion of the subject of joinery, under an impression that the principles have been sufficiently developed to enable the student to pursue from them the application to any case that he may be called upon to put in practice.

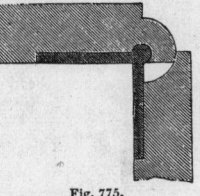

Fig. 775.

SASH-FRAMES AND SASHES.

2164. In *fig. 760.* the connection between the shutters and sash-frame has been fully explained; we may now, therefore, proceed to the detail of a common sash-frame with its sashes, supposing them to be hung so as to be balanced by weights, suspended by sash-lines running over pulleys, capable of balancing those of the sashes themselves. On the case of *French sashes*, which open like doors, we do not think it necessary to dilate. They are, in fact, nothing more than glazed doors; and the principal object for attainment in their construction, is to prevent the rain from penetrating into the apartments they serve, as well where they meet in the middle as at their sills, which is a subject requiring much care and attention.

2165. In *fig. 776.* is shown the construction of a sash-frame, and the method of putting together the several parts, wherein R is the elevation of the frame, of which ABCD is the outer edge. The thinner lines at EF, GH, FG, are grooves whose distances from the edges of the sash-frame LM and KI are equal to the depth of the boxing, together with three-eighths of an inch more that is allowed for margin between the face of the shutter, when, in the boxing, and the edges ML and KI of the sash-frame next to the bead. S is a horizontal section of the sides, whereon is shown also the plan of the sill. T is a vertical section of the sill and top, in which is shown the elevation of the pully style *m* and *n*, and the pullies let into the pully piece. U is the horizontal section of the sides, showing also a plan of the head of the sash-frame. V the elevation of the outer side of the sash-frame; the outside lining being removed for the purpose of showing the work within the sash-frame. In this *fg* is the *parting strip* fastened by a pin; *ed* one of the weights connected to the sash by means of a line going over the pulley *c*, the other end being fixed to the edge of the sash.

The weight *de* is made equal to one half the weight of the sash. W is the head of the sash-frame before put together, and X shows the edge of W. Y is the edge of the bottom, exhibiting the manner of putting the styles in it, and Z is the plan of Y. *Fig.* 777., Nos. 1. and 2., are sections of the sills of sash-frames, with sections of the under rail of the sash, showing the best method of constructing them, in order to prevent rain from driving under the sash-rail. In each of these, A is the section of the bottom rail, B a section of the bead tongued into the sill, C a section of the sill. *Fig.* 778. exhibits sections of the meeting rails of the upper and lower sashes, with side elevations of the upright bars ; C is the rebate for the glass, D a square, E and F an astragal and hollow moulding, G a fillet. The smaller letters mark the same parts of the under sash. *Fig.* 779. is the section of an upright bar with the plans of two horizontal bars, showing the *franking* or manner in which they are put together to keep the upright bars as strong as possible. The thickness of the tenon in

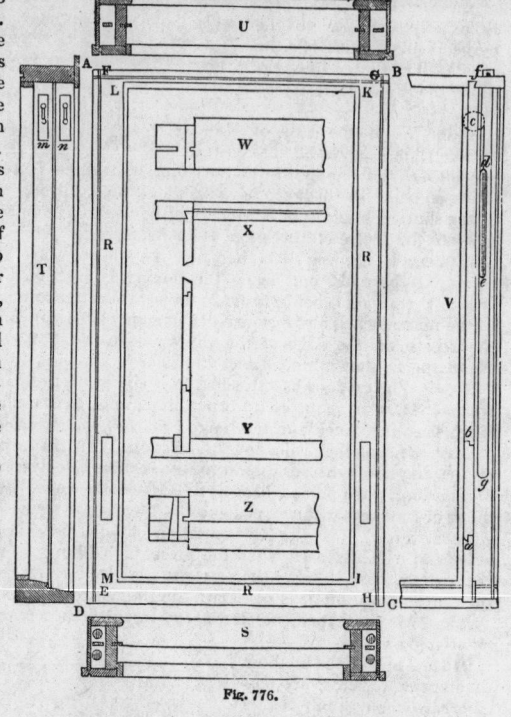

Fig. 776.

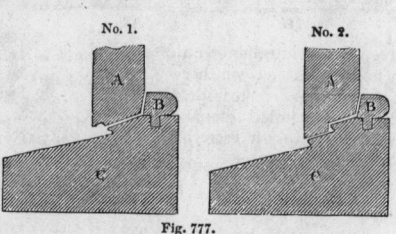

Fig. 777.

Fig. 778.

general is about one sixteenth of an inch to the edge of the hollow of the astragal, and close to the rebate on the other side. *hh* is a dowel to keep the horizontal bars still firmer together. In this diagram the letters refer to the same parts as in the preceding figure ; and it is also to be observed, that no rebate is made for the glass on the inside meeting rail, a groove being made to answer that purpose. *Fig.* 780. exhibits four sections of sash bars. But their forms, as in the case of mouldings, generally depends on the taste of the architect.

2165a. Several patents have been taken out, of late years, for hanging sashes so that they may be removed from the frames for cleaning or repairing without taking down the inside beads, an operation which always results in at least

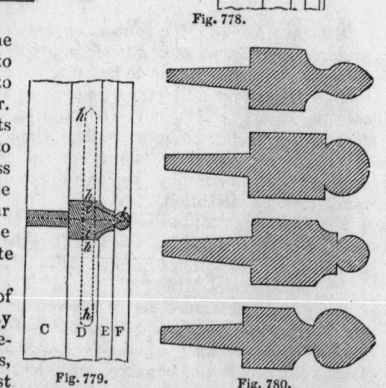

Fig. 779.

Fig. 780.

damaging them in a few years. They are not always satisfactory. Gurman's *sash pocket and fittings*, and Gribbons' *sash mountings*, were introduced about 1858. Other inventions have been made for hanging them so that the upper and lower sashes shall open with the same action. William M‘Adam's " Imperishable material applied to sash and other pulleys, economical sash weights, and improved methods of hanging windows," comprises

a material for pulleys of vitrified stoneware, proof against the action of the weather. For window weights he substitutes a cheap material manufactured out of various kinds of refuse; and suggests an improvement in the mode of hanging windows whereby one weight can be made to answer the same purposes as two applied in the usual way. For sash lines see the GLOSSARY, Addendum.

2165*b.* The *French casement window*, or *sash door* as it is called when it opens down to the ground, is a feature commonly introduced even into English town houses. Its most ordinary form for small apertures is that of two leaves opening inwards or outwards, meeting in the centre of the opening; one leaf being secured to the frame by a bolt at top and bottom, and the other, when closed, is fastened to the first by a handle, fixed on the second leaf, and turning over a staple fixed on the first. When the casement is high, this second leaf may require a bolt also at top and bottom to prevent the wind bending it (when inwards), and so admitting cold air and wet. When placed towards an exposed quarter,

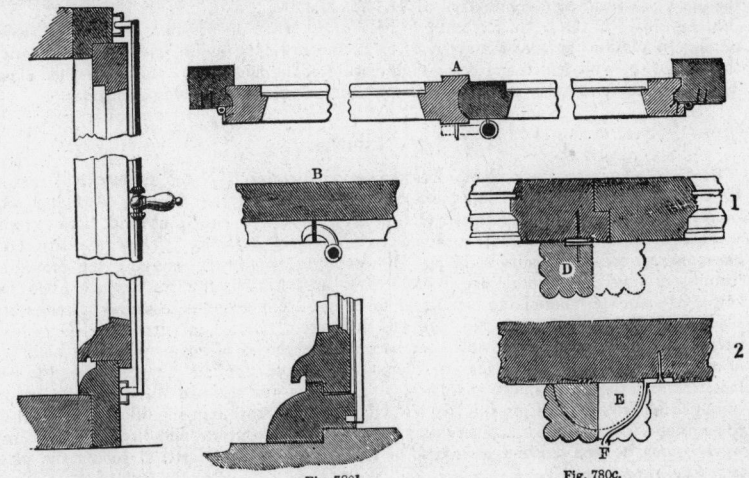

Fig. 780*a*.　　　　　　Fig. 780*b*.　　　　　　Fig. 780*c*.

and subject to driving rains, it becomes necessary to take extra precautions to prevent the wet being blown through the joints at the bottom and the sides. To effect this object, the stiles, rails, and frames are beaded and sunk in various manners; some are shown in *figs.* 780*a.* and 780*b.*, sills and bottom rails. For the latter, a *water bar* is now much used.

2165*c.* The next improvement is perhaps that of affixing to the leaf which is first opened an upright bar, which turns, and on being closed, fits against the other leaf, and by a hook at top and bottom effectually fastens both leaves. A similar method is shown in *fig.* 780*c.*, adopted at Pisa, as given in the *Papers* of the Royal Engineers, x. 187. The upright square reeded bar D, is moved to or from the sash, as the window is required to be opened or shut; the top and bottom of the bar being rounded, as shown at E, so as to slide into two segmental plates F, secured

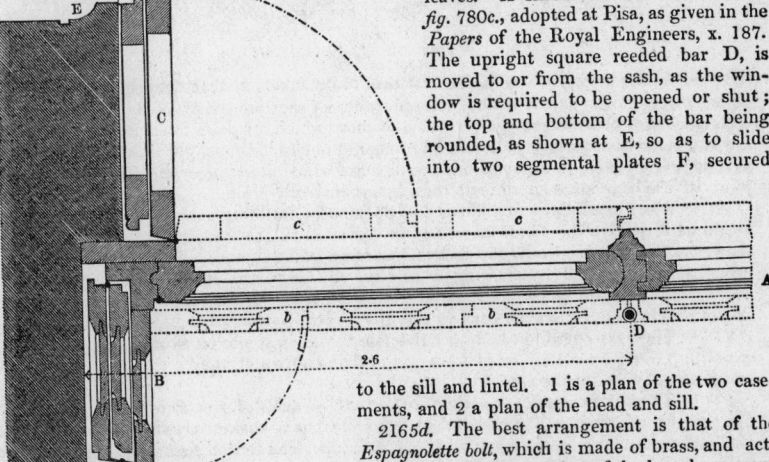

Fig. 780*d*.

to the sill and lintel. 1 is a plan of the two casements, and 2 a plan of the head and sill.

2165*d.* The best arrangement is that of the *Espagnolette bolt*, which is made of brass, and acts in the same manner as that of the bar above mentioned. There are several other contrivances of a similar kind to effect the object, but the above

are those in most general use. There is also a late invention for forming the bolt into a plate, and setting it in a groove in the *edge* of the meeting stile, a corresponding groove being formed in the other stile to receive its half of the plate when moved forward by the handle in closing the casement. This, at the same time, forms a weather bar. (See *par.* 2259.)

2165e. The *fig.* 780*a.* is a section of an ordinary arrangement in France for a casement. A is the plan, taken across the middle of the height, near the handle; and B the plan of the hooks at top and bottom of the rod, working into a staple fixed in the head and in the sill, with the movement of the rod by its handle. The round and hollow joint in the middle of the casement necessitates the two leaves being closed together and pressed into the frame when shutting the leaves, thus securing all the joints from admitting air or water.

2165f. *Fig.* 780*d.* is a plan of the elaborate but usual French casement, as lately put up to the stone-fronted houses in the Rue de la Victoire, at Paris. It is given by Daly, in the *Revue Generale de l'Architecture* of 1858. A shows the casements when shut; B the shutters closed in the boxings; and *b b* the shutters when opened out. C the *persiennes* or outside blinds shut against the stone reveals; the ordinary mode is for them to shut on the face of the wall, which spoils the architecture of the façade; *c c* the same when closed; D the espagnolette bolt; E the outside architrave; and F the inside architrave.

GROUNDS.

2166. *Grounds* are formed of pieces of wood-forming skeleton frames, and attached to walls, around windows, doors, or other openings, for the facility of fixing architraves or other mouldings upon them. For doorways the front and back grounds were connected by a third, specified as *dovetailed backing.* They are disused in common work, the grounds being the wrought woodwork carrying the mouldings, forming a single or double faced architrave, and having the jamb space filled by a single or a double rebated and beaded jamb lining. The grounds served as screeds for the plastering, for which purpose the edge was chamfered, rebated, or grooved. Grounds or *narrow grounds* were those to which the bases and surbases of rooms were fastened; slips of wood now receive the skirtings of rooms. All these appliances were secured to wood bricks, which themselves have given way to plugs or wedges. In all cases the grounds ought to be fixed vertical on the face and edge, and the workman should take especial care to fix them firm and solid in every part; for, without accuracy and firmness, the inside work cannot be well finished, as it is to be recollected that in plastered rooms the plaster is worked to them.

2167. In fixing window grounds, the sash-frame must be first carefully placed so as to stand perfectly vertical; and then the face of the ground must stand quite parallel to the face of the sash-frame, and project about three quarters of an inch from the face of the naked brickwork, so as to leave a sufficient space for the thickness of the plaster. The edge of the ground should be in the same plane with the edge of the sash-frame, or, as the workmen term it, "out of winding." The edge of the architrave, when finished, in ordinary cases, will stand about three-eighths of an inch within the inner edge of the sash-frame, so that a perpendicular line down to the middle of the grounds would stand exactly opposite to a perpendicular line down to the middle of the sash-frame.

FLOORS OR FLOOR BOARDS.

2168. In the laying of floors, the first care to be taken is that they be perfectly level, which, owing to the nature of the materials whereof they are constructed, is a difficult task. The chief sorts of floors may be divided into those which are *folded,* that is, when the boards are laid in divisions, whose side vertical joints are not continuous, but in bays of three, four, five, or more boards in a bay or fold; and those which are *straight joint,* in which the side joints of the boards are continuous throughout their direction.

As soon as the windows are fixed, the floors of a building may be laid. The boards are to be placed on their best face, and put to season till the sap is quite exhausted, when they may be planed smooth, and their edges shot and squared. The opposite edges are brought to a breadth by drawing a line on the face parallel to the other edge with a flooring guage, after which the common guage is used to bring them to a thickness, and they are rebated down on the back to the lines drawn by the guage.

2169. The next operation is, to try the joints, which, if not level, must be brought so, either by *furring up* if they be hollow, or by adzing down if they are convex, the former being more generally the case.

2170. The boards used for flooring are battens, or deals of greater breadth, whose qualities are of three sorts. The best is that free from knots, shakes, sapwood, or cross-grained stuff, selected so as to match well with one another. The second best is free of shakes and sapwood, and in it only small sound knots are permitted. The third, or most common sort, are such as are left after taking away the best and second best.

2171. The joints of flooring-boards are either quite square, ploughed and tongued, rebated, or dowelled; and in fixing them they are nailed on one or both edges, when the joints are plain and square without dowels. When they are dowelled, they may be nailed on one or both sides; but in the best dowelled work the outer edge only is nailed, by driving the brad through the edge of the board obliquely, without piercing its surface, which, when the work is cleaned off, appears without blemish.

2172. In laying the floor-boards, they are sometimes laid one after the other, or one is first laid, then the fourth, at an interval of something less than the united breadth of the second and third together. The two intermediate boards are then laid in their places with one edge on the edge of the first board and the other upon that of the fourth board, the two middle edges resting against each other, rising to a ridge at the joint. In order to force these boards into their places, two or three workmen jump upon the ridge till they have brought the under sides of the boards close to the joints; they are then fixed in their places with brads. This method is that first mentioned under this head, and in it the boards are said to be folded. We have here mentioned only two boards, but four boards are most commonly folded at a time, and the mode is always resorted to when a suspicion exists that the boards are not sufficiently seasoned, or they are known not to be so. The headings of these folds are either square, splayed, or ploughed and tongued. If a heading occurs in the length of the floor, it should be invariably made to fall over a joist, and one heading should not meet another.

2173. In dowelled floors, the dowels should be placed over the middle of the interjoist rather than over the joists, so that the edge of one board may be prevented from passing that of the other. When the boards are only bradded upon one edge, the brads are concealed by driving them in a slanting direction through the outer edge of every successive board, without piercing the upper surface. In adzing the under sides of floor-boards over each joist, great care should be taken to chip away the stuff straight, and also to avoid taking away more of the stuff than is necessary, in which case the soundness of the floor will not be compromised.

2173a. The practice of joining the edges of *boards* by means of rebates, or of tongued grooves, does not appear to have existed before the 15th century. Previously to that period, the use of ledges dovetailed to the whole or part of their depth into chases, of dovetailed wooden cramps, or of wood or iron pins or dowels, was general. In the cathedral at Messina the boarding under the tiling is in two thicknesses that cross each other; and, in the cradle roofs, it

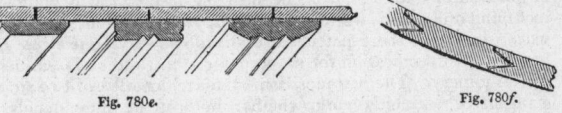

Fig. 780e.   Fig. 780f.

was usual to groove and tongue the wainscoting, and also to cover those joints with moulded fillets, as shown in the examples in *fig.* 780e. The thickness of this wainscoting, which was oak split, not sawn, was only three-eighths of an inch (barely more or less), and it was frequently put together in the manner shown in *fig.* 780f.

2173b. *Parquetry, &c.* Floors of principal rooms of the better class of houses are now being finished with parquetry. It is composed of different pieces of some four or five coloured and hard woods, arranged in regular geometrical figures, for the whole of a room, corridor, or gallery; or applied as borders round carpets, to treads and risers of stairs and landings; and even as dadoes, panellings, friezes, &c. Parquetry is kept clean by sweeping and periodical waxing. It is made *solid*, one inch thick, grooved, tongued, and keyed at the back and corners. When the woods are applied only as a veneer, they are liable to warp and separate by heat. " Wood tapestry (Howard's patent) for covering walls, ceilings, and other surfaces with real wood at a less cost than painting and graining," is a late invention. " Ornamental pyrographic woodwork," for panels and in cabinet work, being a process for burning-in ornament upon wood, is now in operation.

2173c. *Marquetry*, or the inlaying of coloured woods, became very general at the latter end of the 16th century. Oak was inlaid with ebony ornaments in the panels and stiles of wainscoting; and the framing of doors, windows, and shutters, was sometimes made of dark coloured woods, the panels being of light colours, inlaid with ornaments, profiles of heads, &c. This process is applied greatly to furniture, where it is imitated by paint. A new method has been introduced, of applying a printed pattern to the prepared wood, as in the Tunbridge ware, and then varnishing it as usual.

FRAMING.

2174. In *fig.* 781. are shown several methods for framing angles in dadoes, skirtings, troughs, and other objects, whereof A exhibits the method of mitring a dado on exterior angles in an apartment. In fixing this together, brads may be driven from each side. B is a method of framing used for troughs or other rectangular wooden vessels. C is a method of putting a dado or skirting together at any interior angle of a room. This mode

is also employed for water-trunks, or troughs. In D is shown the manner of fixing and finishing two pieces of framing together, with a bead at their meeting, by which the joint is concealed. It is used only in common finishings. In those of a better sort the angle is kept entire, and only a three-eighth bead used at the joint. It is of great importance in all joiner's work to preserve the sharpness of the angles of the work, and many prefer to employ the method shown in F, without any bead at the joint. In this the joint is made as close as possible, and is well glued together. If additional strength be required, blockings may be glued in the interior angle, which will make it quite firm. The method, by a simple mitre at E, is not so good as at A, because it has no abutment.

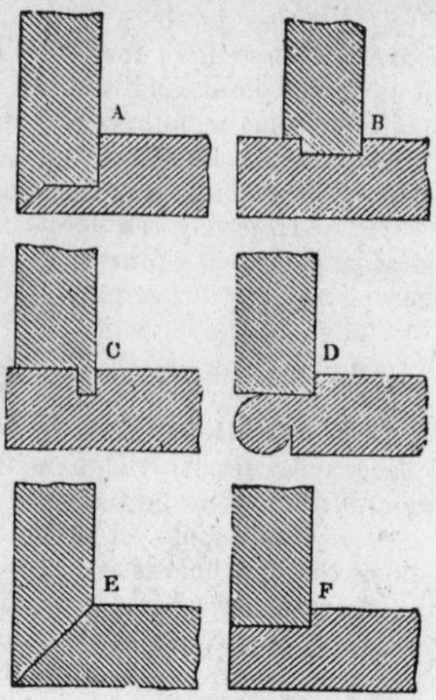

2175. When it is required to glue up large work, those edges which are to receive the glue should be well warmed at a fire, and then, while warm, and the glue as hot as possible, they should be united, inasmuch as glue never holds well when it is chilled or cold.

Fig. 781.

2175a. In studying mediæval *framing*, much attention should be given to the modes in which the junction of pieces was effected ; there are two which are chiefly important. The first is a characteristic in the work of the carpenter as well as of the joiner, viz., the shoulder, either solid or applied (*figs.* 701*k.* and 701*l.*). In the first case, it is not economical of material, which was a great point of consideration ; and therefore it is rarely seen except on short pieces, such as the posts of doorways : but as an applied means of strength it is almost as common in good work as a corbel in masonry. The second is the use of the mortice and tenon with trenails ; and the extreme care which was given to this part of the work is scarcely to be expected in these days of speed and cheapness. It may be predicted that no truly mediæval work will now be ever reproduced except in the fancy-work of the cabinet-maker and the smith.

2175b. Another peculiarity is the use of stops to all chamfers and mouldings at points of junction of framing : it is not until the last phase of pointed art, that the stop of the moulding of a stile is worked in the rail, or that the corner of a panel is rounded : it is only in the dawn of the renaissance that the *four-panel quirk ogee front and square back* can be portion of a specification for a door ; for a mitre-joint is eminently not a feature of mediæval joinery. The juxtaposition, even accidentally, of two stop-chamfered edges, suggests a means of enriching work, whether in open or close panels. The avoidance of work against the grain, and of large hollows, is also mentioned as a characteristic of joiner's work in pointed art ; but this disappears in the course of the 15th century. The mediæval joiner, depending sometimes upon halving his work together, more frequently thought time less valuable than material, and did not repent a profusion of morticing and tenoning, to which he added the trouble of fastening with wooden trenails or iron pins. As large an amount of rebating and of grooving, however, was done in framing by the joiner as could be expected by those who were accustomed to the back-jointed and the grooved work of the mason.

2175c. Perhaps the most defective part of the joinery of the middle ages is that which consisted in planting one thickness upon another. The contrivances in glueing and dovetailing were not of themselves sufficient ; and recourse was obliged to be had to nails. The absence of screws and nails, except where nail heads could be made decoration, is another characteristic of mediæval joinery. It was not until the beginning of the 14th century that the transition from planted work to panel work can be said to have appeared in any strength. At the end of that century, an architect might have specified a door as *nine-panelled, beaded three edges, chamfered bottom, and raised panel both sides* ; but his beads would have been stuck in the solid, and not applied : during the whole of the 14th century planted work was commonly introduced, as in screens, closets, and shutters, where perhaps a sham buttress serves to conceal the wide joint made by the work in consequence of the inaccurate finish of the hingeing. A curious method, which must have been laborious before the introduction of the plane, of attaching the planted work, consisted in running in the ground a chase wide enough to take the whole breadth of the planted stuff, and then to run a couple of grooves in that chase ; of course the back of the planted stuff had to be worked to match, with two tongues to enter the grooves.

2175d. The size of the materials was restricted. Three inch stuff for the thickness of rails and stiles, with a not much wider face ; inch and a half stuff for mouldings to be planted ; panels not more than eight inches wide, and three-quarters of an inch thick ; may be quoted as usual dimensions for joiner's work. The observance of this restriction constitutes an essential characteristic of mediæval work,

STAIRS.

2176. *Stairs* and their *handrails* are among the most important objects of the joiner's skill. The choice of situation, sufficiency of light, and easy ascent, are matters for the exercise of the architect's best talent.

2177. There are some leading principles which are common to all staircases, of whatsoever materials they may be constructed. Thus it is a maxim that a broad step should be of less height than one which is narrower; and the reason is sufficiently obvious, because in striding, what a man loses in breadth he can more easily apply in raising himself by his feet. Now, as in common practice it is found that the convenient rise of a step 12 inches in width is $5\frac{1}{2}$ inches, it may be assumed as some guide for the regulation of other dimensions. Thus $12 \times 5\frac{1}{2} = 66$, which would be a constant numerator for the proportion. Suppose, for instance, a step 10 inches in breadth, then $\frac{66}{10} = 6\frac{3}{5}$ inches would be the height; and this agrees very nearly with the common practice. The breadth of steps in the commonest staircase may be taken at 10 inches at a medium. In the best staircases the breadth of the step should not be less than 12 inches, neither should it be more than 18 inches. (See 2814.)

2178. Having adjusted the proportions of the steps, our next consideration is to ascertain the number of risers which will be necessary to carry us from one floor to another. Suppose, for example, the height from the top of one floor to that of the next be 15 feet = 180 inches; here, if the steps are each of 6 inches rise, we have $\frac{180}{6} = 30$, which is the number of risers necesssary to ascend from floor to floor. If the height divided by the rise of each step should not give an exact number of risers, it is better to add one rather than diminish the number. Thus, suppose the distance from floor to floor be 13 feet 2 inches = 158 inches, then $\frac{158}{7} = 22\frac{4}{7}$. Here it would be better to take 23 risers, for the steps must be equal in height.

2178a. An easy mode of proportioning steps and risers may be obtained by the annexed method. Set down two sets of numbers, each in arithmetical progression; the first set showing the width of the steps, ascending by inches, the other showing the height of the riser, descending by half inches. It will readily be seen that each of these steps and risers are such as may suitably pair together. (Newland, *Carpenter's and Joiner's Assistant*, 1860, p. 197.) It is seldom, however, that the proportion of the step and riser is exactly a matter of choice—the space allotted to the stairs usually determines this proportion; but the above will be found a useful standard. In first-class buildings the number of steps is considered in the plan, which it is the business of the architect to arrange in accordance with the style of the edifice.

Treads. inches.	Risers. inches.
5	9
6	$8\frac{1}{2}$
7	8
8	$7\frac{1}{4}$
9	7
10	$6\frac{1}{2}$
11	6
12	$5\frac{1}{2}$
13	5
14	$4\frac{1}{2}$

2179. The width of the better sorts of staircases should not be less than 4 feet, to allow of two persons freely passing each other; but the want of space in town houses often obliges the architect to submit to less in what is called the *going* of the stair.

2180. The parts of every step in a staircase are one parallel to the horizon, which is called the *tread* of the step, terminated on the edge by a moulded or rounded *nosing*, and the other perpendicular to the horizon, which is called the *riser* of the step.

2180a. A curious instance of economy of material is given in *fig.* 781a., which shows the mode of getting six steps out of round timber 30 inches in diameter, being a saving of about ten per cent. upon the attempt to cut up square timber. Such solid steps were housed into the carriage; A showing the under side of it in relation to the step B. In straight flights the system of carrying solid newels from bottom to top of the staircase is one which has since been repeated successfully in iron construction. The ingenuity of the mediæval joiner in this subject is seen best treated in Viollet le Duc's dictionary. (See *par.* 2185.)

2181. Stairs have many varieties of structure, dependent on the character, situation, and destination of the building. We shall now, therefore, describe the method of carrying up *dog-legged, bracket,* and *geometrical stairs.*

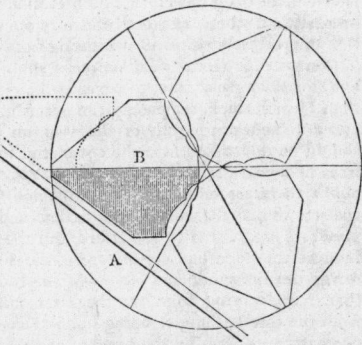

Fig. 781a.

2182. A Dog-legged Staircase is one which has no opening or well-hole, and in which the rail and balusters of the progressive and returning flights fall in the same vertical planes. The steps in it are fixed to strings, newel, and carriages, the ends of the steps of the inferior kind terminating only upon the side of the string without any housing. Y and Z in *fig.* 782, are the plan and elevation of a staircase of this kind; AB is the lower newel whereof the part BC is turned. On the plan, *a* is the seat of this newel. DE and FG in Y are the lower and upper string boards framed into newels, KL is a joist framed into the trimmer I. The lines on the plan represent the faces of the steps in the elevation without the nosings. MO and FQ are called the upper and lower ramps, the method of drawing

which is as follows: — In the upper ramp, for example, produce the top of the rail HM to P; draw MN vertical, and produce the straight part ON of the pitch of the rail to meet it in N, making NO equal to NM. Draw OP at a right angle to ON. From P, as a centre, describe the arc MO, and then the other contrary curve, which will complete the ramp required. The *story rod* RS is in the fixing of all staircases a necessary instrument; for in fixing the steps and other work by a common measuring rule, bit by bit, the chances are that an excess or defect will occur, to make the staircase faulty; which cannot be the case if the story rod is applied to every riser, and such riser be regulated thereby.

2183. A Bracket Staircase is one which has an opening or well, with strings and newels, and is supported by landings and carriages. The *brackets* are mitred to the end of each riser, and fixed to the string board, which is usually moulded like an architrave. In this sort of staircase the same methods are to be observed in respect of dimensions and laying off the plan and section as in a dog-legged staircase. Nothing is to be done without the story rod just described, which must be constantly applied in making and setting up the stairs. The method of forming the ramps and knees has been touched upon in the preceding article, and the few particulars we intend to give respecting scrolls and handrailing will be reserved for a subsequent page. In bracket stairs the internal angle of the

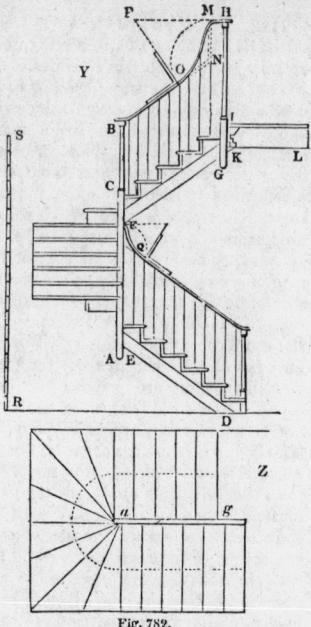

Fig. 782.

steps is open to the end, and not closed by the string, as in common dog-legged stairs; the neatness also of the workmanship is as much attended to as in geometrical stairs. The balusters should be nicely dovetailed into the ends of the steps by twos, and the face of each front baluster is to be in a plane with the front face of the riser, and all the balusters being equally divided, the face of the middle one must of course stand in the middle of the face of the riser of the preceding step. The treads and risers are previously all glued up and blocked together, and when put in their places the under side of the step is nailed or screwed into the under edge of the riser, and then rough bracketed to the strings, as in a dog-legged staircase, in which the pitching pieces and rough strings are similar.

2184. A Geometrical Staircase is one whose opening is down its centre, or, as it is called, an open newel, in which each step is supported by one end being fixed in the wall or partition, the other end of every step in the ascent having an auxiliary support from that immediately below it, beginning from the lowest one, which, of course, rests on the floor. The steps of a geometrical staircase should, when fixed, have a light and clean appearance, and, for strength's sake, the treads and risers, when placed in position, should not be less than $1\frac{1}{8}$ inch thick, supposing the going of the stair or length of the step to be 4 feet. For every 6 inches in length of the step an eighth of an inch should be added. The risers should be dovetailed into the cover, and in putting up the steps, the treads are screwed up from below to the under edges of the risers. The holes for sinking the heads of the screws ought to be bored with a centre bit and fitted closely in with wood well matched, so that the screws may be entirely concealed, and appear as a uniform surface without blemish. Brackets are mitred to the risers, and the nosings are continued round; but this practice induces an apparent defect, from the brackets, instead of giving support, being themselves unsupported, and actually depending on the steps, being indeed of no other use than merely tying together the risers and treads of the internal angles of the steps; and from the internal angles being hollow, except at the ends, which terminate by the wall at one extremity, and by the bracket at the other, there is an appearance of incomplete finish. The cavetto or hollow is carried all round the front of the slip, returned at the end, and again at the end of the bracket, thence along the inside of it, and then along the internal angle at the back of the riser.

2185. The ancient mode, however, was the best, in which the wooden was an imitation of the method of constructing geometrical stairs in stone, which will be found under Masonry, in the previous Section III.; that is to say, the making of the steps themselves solid, and in section of the form of a bracket throughout their length. This is a more expensive method, but it is a solid and good one, and is still practised on the Continent, especially in France. (See also par. 2180a.)

2186. In *fig.* 783. X is the plan and Y the elevation, or rather **section**, of a geometrical staircase. AB in X is what is called the *cur-tail step* (curved like the tail of a cur dog), which must be the first step fixed. CCC are the *flyers* supported from below by rough carriages, and partly from the string board DHEF in Y. The ends next the wall are sometimes housed into a notch board, and the steps then are made of thick wood and no carriages used. GGG are *winders* fixed to bearers and pitching pieces, when carriages are used to support the flyers. The winders are sometimes made of strong stuff firmly wedged into the wall, the steps screwed together, and the other ends of the steps fixed to the string DEHF. In all cases of wooden geometrical stairs their strength may be greatly augmented by a flat bar of wrought iron coinciding with the under side and screwed to the string immediately below the steps. HIK in Y is the line of

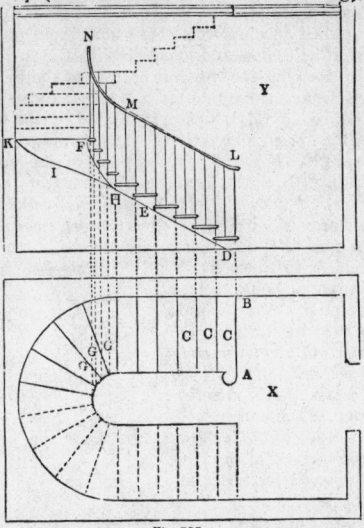

Fig. 783.

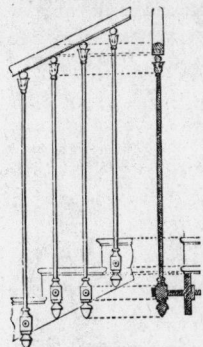

Fig. 784.

the soffite of the winding part of the stairs, and LMN part of the rail supported by two balusters upon every step. Where the space of the going of the stairs is confined, the French have long since introduced, as in *fig.* 784., the practice of placing the balusters outside the steps, which affords more room for persons ascending and descending.

HANDRAILS AND CUR-TAIL STEP.

2187. The upper part of the fence formed by capping the balusters of stairs is called the *handrail*, whose use, as its name imports, is for a support to the hand in the ascent and descent of stairs. The hand, for support to the body, should glide easily over it without any strain, whence it is evident, that to be properly formed, it must necessarily follow the general line of the steps, and be quite smooth and free from inequalities. It must be obvious to the reader who has thus far followed us throughout the different previous portions of our labours, that the chief principle of handrailing will be dependent on the methods of finding sections of cylinders, cylindroids, or prisms, according to three given points in or out of the surface, or, in other words, the section made by a plane through three given points in space. The cylinder, cylindroid, and prism are hollow, and of the same thickness as the breadth of the rail, or the horizontal dimension of its section; and their bases, their planes or projections on the floor. Thus is formed the handrail of a staircase of a portion of a cylinder, cylindroid, or prism whose base is the plane of the stair, for over this the handrail must stand, and is therefore contained between the vertical surface of the cylinder, cylindroid, or prism. As the handrail is prepared in portions each whereof stands over a quadrant of the circle, ellipse, or prism of the base which forms the plane, such a portion may be supposed to be contained between two parallel planes, so that the portion of the handrail may be thus supposed to be contained between the cylindrical, cylindroidal, or prismatic surfaces and the two parallel planes. The parts to be joined together for forming the rail must be so prepared that in their place all the sections made by a vertical plane passing through the imaginary solid may be rectangular: this is denominated *squaring the rail*, and is all that can be done by geometrical rules. But handrails not being usually made of these portions of hollow cylinders or cylindroids, but of plank or thicknesses of wood, our attention is naturally drawn to the consideration of the mode in which portions of them may be formed from planks of sufficient thickness. The faces of the planks being planes, they may be supposed to be contained between two parallel planes, that is, the two faces of the plank. Such figures, therefore, are to be drawn on the sides of the plank as to leave the surfaces formed between the opposite figures, portions of the cylindrical, cylindroidal, or other surfaces required, when the superfluous parts are cut away. A mould made in the form of these figures, which is no more than a section of them, is called the *face mould*.

2188. The vertical, cylindrical, or cylindroidal surfaces being adjusted, the upper and lower surfaces must be next formed; and this is accomplished by bending another mould

round the cylindrical or cylindroidal surfaces, generally to the convex side, and drawing lines on the surface round the edge of such mould. The superfluous wood is then cut away from top to bottom, so that if the piece were set in its place, and a straight-edge applied on the surfaces so formed, and parallel to the horizon directed to the axis of the well-hole, it would coincide with the surface. The mould so applied on the convex side for forming the top and bottom of the piece, is called the *falling mould*. For the purpose of finding these moulds it is necessary to lay down the plan of the steps and rail; next, the falling mould, which is regulated by the heights of the steps; and lastly, the face mould, which is regulated by the falling mould, and furnishes the three heights alluded to.

2189. *Fig.* 785. exhibits two of the most usual forms of handrails. The upper part, A and B of the figure, are sections of the rail and mitre cap of a dog-legged staircase. Vertical lines are let fall from the section of the rail A, to the mitre in B; from thence, in arcs of circles, to the straight line passing through the centre of the cap at right angles to the former straight lines; then perpendiculars are set off and made equal in length to those in A.

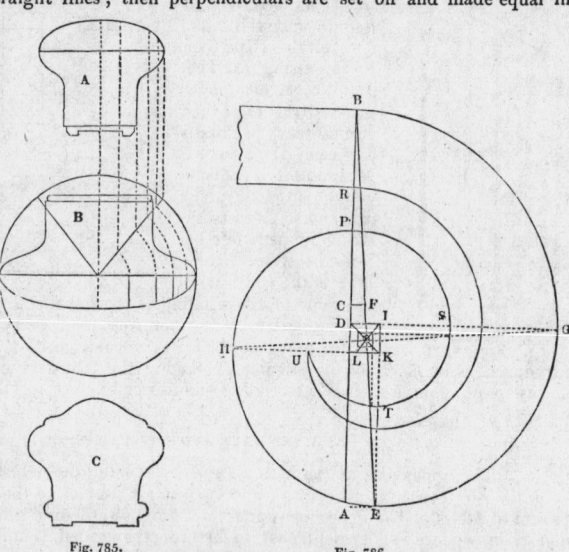

A curve being traced through the points gives the form of the cap. C is called a *toad's back rail*, and is used for a superior description of staircases.

2190. *Fig.*786. shows the method of drawing the scroll for terminating the handrail at the bottom of a geometrical staircase. Let A B be the given breadth; draw A E perpendicular to A B, and divide it into eleven equal parts, and make A E equal to one of them. Join B E, bisect A B in C and B E in F. Make C D equal to C F and draw D G perpendicular to A B. From F, with the radius FE or FB, describe an

Fig. 785.   Fig. 786.

arc cutting D G at G. Draw G H perpendicular to B E cutting B E at O. Draw the diagonals D O K and I O L perpendicular to D O K. Draw I K parallel to B A; K L parallel to I D, and so on to meet the diagonals. From D as a centre, with the distance D B, describe the arc B G. From I as a centre, with the distance I G, describe the arc G E. From K as a

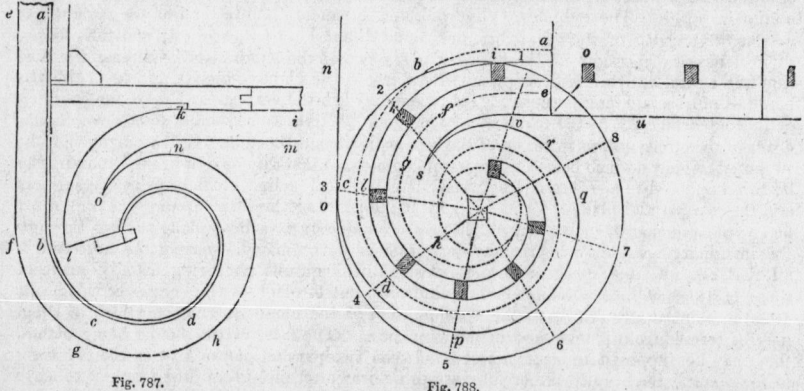

Fig. 787.   Fig. 788.

centre, with the distance K E, describe the arc E H. From L as a centre, with the distance L H, describe the arc H P. Proceed in the same manner and complete the remaining three quarters, which will finish the outside of the scroll. Make B R equal to the breadth of the rail; namely, about two inches and a quarter. Then with the centre D and distance

DR describe the arc RS, with the centre I and distance IS describe the arc ST, and with the centre K and distance KT describe the arc TU, and the scroll will be completed.

2191. *Fig.* 787. gives the construction of the cur-tail step, or that which lies under the scroll, *abcd* is the veneer that covers the riser ; *efgh*, the nosing of the cover or horizontal part of the step ; *ikl* the face of the string board, and *mno* the projection of the nosing.

2192. In *fig.* 788 is shown the cover board for the cur-tail step, *abcd* and *efgh* in dotted lines represent the plan of the scroll ; *opqrs*, the nosing of the cur-tail step ; *t, u, v, s,* the nosings and ends of the risers.   The circle 1, 2, 3, &c. is described from the centre of the scroll, and divided into equal parts equal to the distances of the balusters from centre to centre, and lines are drawn to the centre of the scroll in order to ascertain the middle of the balusters, by giving a regular gradation to the spaces.   The whole of the spiral lines in this and the previous figure are drawn from the same centres as the scroll.

BENCHES.

2192a. " It must be confessed," says Denison, in his *Lectures on Church Building,* 1856, page 242, " that our ancestors did not offer much temptation to people to come to church by the comforts they provided for them when they got there.   Nothing, indeed, can be better for sitting in than some of the old stalls, such as those in King's College Chapel, where the back has a slope of one to four ; but most of the common old church seats are frightfully uncomfortable—the back of the seat ought to be inclined, especially when it rises as high as the shoulders.   It is not of so much consequence when the seat backs are low, but even in them it is better to have a little inclination, about one in eight ; and above all things, the top rail ought *not* to project.   The seats ought never to be less than 13 inches wide with a sloping back, or 14 inches with an upright one, and they will be all the better if they are an inch or two more.   Nothing under 2 feet 10 inches at the very least will allow proper room for sitting, standing, and kneeling, especially if there are any divisions under the seats to prevent people from kicking their neighbours' hats, or appropriating their hassocks.   Where it is necessary to save room in every possible way, it is not a bad plan to make the division under the seat only come down to 3 or 4 inches from the floor ; and never in any case ought there to be (what there often is) a thick rail or bar of wood lying along the floor and taking off an inch or more from the space for the feet. The book boards are best not sloping, which is of no use, but flat and narrow, just wide enough to lay a book upon shut, and to put the arms upon in kneeling.   As regards the difficulty of finding a good place and proper height for the pulpit and reading desk, I know of no better advice to give upon the subject than to try various places before you finally fix upon any one, unless the construction of the church is such that there is one place marked out by nature (as we may say) as the proper one."

2192b. Examples of benches and bench ends are represented in so many publications that it is deemed unnecessary to give any illustration.   Some cappings to benches, and edges to divisions, are shown in the section WOOD MOULDINGS in Book III.   Those shown in Brandon's *Analysis*, and Bury's *Woodwork*, give the following dimensions :—

Name of Church.	Height.	Width.	Seat.	Opening.	
Comberton, Cambridge - -	2. 9	3. 4	1. 0	1. 6	
Bentley, Suffolk - - -	2. 5	2. 10	0. 11½	1. 6	
Great Waltham, Essex, 1420 -	3. 1	2. 6	1. 2	1. 1	
Bishops Lydeard, Somerset -	2. 10¼	{ 2. 3½ } { 2. 7½ }	0. 11	{ 1. 0 { 1. 4	
Westonzoyland, Somerset -	3. 3	2. 9½	—	1. 7	{ end { 1. 4
Atherington, Devon - -	3. 9	—	0. 11½	—	
Ickleton, Cambridge - -	2. 4½	—	0. 10½	—	1. 10
Stalls, Bridgewater, Somerset -	—	—	0. 11½	centre to centre	} sitting { 2. 3
„ Wantage, Berks - -	—	3. 5	—	1. 4½	1. 10

The rules of the Incorporated Society for Promoting the Building of Churches state, that " the distance from the back of one seat to that of the next must depend in great measure on the height of the backs.   Where the funds and space will admit, convenience will be best consulted by adopting a clear width of 3 feet ; but a width of not less than 2 feet 8 inches from centre to centre will be allowed if the back of the seat is not more than 2 feet 8 inches in height.   If a greater height be adopted, the distance from back to back must be increased one inch at least for every additional inch in height ; but under no circumstances must it exceed 3 feet.   There must not be any projecting capping on the top of the backs.   Facilities for kneeling in all cases to be provided.   The width of the seat boards for adults to be not less than 13 inches.   20 inches in length must be allowed for each adult, and 14 inches for a child.   Children's seats must be at least 26 inches from

back to front, and must have backs." Her Majesty's Commissioners for building new churches allow 20 inches by 34 inches for each sitting; free seats 20 inches by 27 inches, and 14 inches for children. Benches for free sittings are to be 3 feet, 4 feet 6 inches, or 6 feet long. The allowance made for each sitting in St. Paul's Cathedral is, as nearly as possible, 20 inches by 33 inches. From 4 to 5 square feet of floor is not too much space to be calculated for each person, allowing for gangways, communion table, &c.

2192c. Cloisters, porches, canopies, over-doors, stall-work, lych-gates, windows, staircases, bell-wheels and carriages, luffer or louvre boards, fencing, screens, pulpits, desks, lecterns, chests, tables, *cum multis aliis*, are amongst the many other productions of the joiner, being far too numerous to be described in detail herein.

FORMATION OF BODIES BY JOINING THEM WITH GLUE.

2193. The way in which bodies are glued up together for different purposes will be given below, and with them will close this section.

2194. *Fig.* 789. shows at A a section of two boards glued up edge to edge. At B the face of the same is seen. C shows the section of two boards glued edge to edge, each piece being grooved, and a *tongue* inserted at their junction. By similar means a board may be increased to any width, be the pieces whereof it is composed ever so narrow. D shows two boards fixed at right angles, the edge of one being glued on the side of the other. A block for the purpose of strengthening the joint is fitted and glued to the interior side.

Fig. 789.   Fig. 790.

2195. *Fig.* 790. A is a section of two boards to be joined at an oblique angle. They are mitred and glued together with a block at the angle. B shows the inner sides of the boards so fixed. It is by repeating this operation that columns are glued up.

2196. *Fig.* 791. A is the section of an architrave. The moulding is usually, if not always, glued to the board; the vertical line therefore, showing the extreme boundary of the moulded part, is the section of the piece to be glued, B is the face of the architrave, C and D a section and front of it before it is moulded, E a section of it with the button and nail to show the way in which the two parts are glued together, and F shows the back of the architrave with the buttons which are used for the purpose of bringing the two surfaces to be glued together in contact, till after they are set and fully held together, being knocked off when the glue has become hard, and then the moulding shown at A and B is stuck.

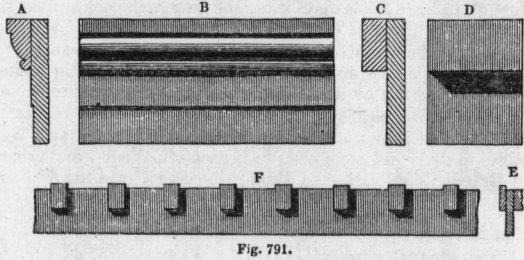

Fig. 791.

2197. *Fig.* 792. exhibits the method of gluing up a solid niche in wood where A is the elevation. The work is performed in the same way as if it were stone or brick, except that the joints are all parallel to the plane of the base, because of the difficulty of making a joint with curved surfaces, which would necessarily be the case if they all tended to the centre of the sphere. B and C are the two bottom

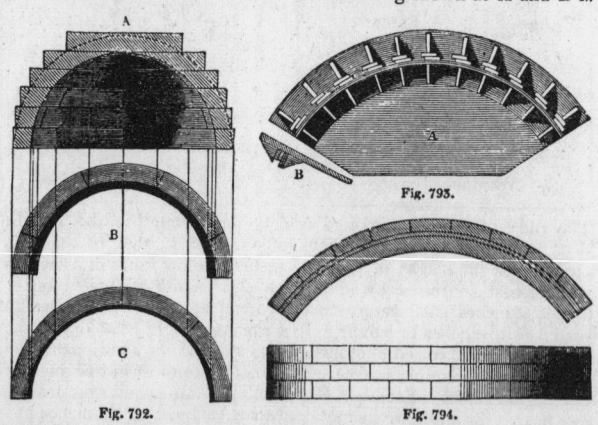

Fig. 792.   Fig. 794.

Fig. 793.

courses, where the vertical joints are made to break, as seen in the elevation A.

2198. In *fig.* 793. is exhibited the mode in which veneers are glued together for the purpose of forming cylindrical surfaces. Brackets with their faces upwards are nailed to

a board. Their ends are perpendicular, and a cavity is left between them sufficient to receive the veneers and wedges. In A the thin part in the form of an arc shows the veneers as in the state of glueing, the wedges being on the convex side. B is a section of the board and bracket. The work when putting together should be dry and warm, and the glue should be hot. When this last has set hard, the wedges must be slackened, and the veneers, which now form a solid, taken out.

2199. *Fig.* 794. is a strong method of forming a concave surface by laying the veneer upon a cylinder, and backing it with blocks in the form of bricks, which are glued to the convex side of the veneers and to each other. The fibres of the blocks are to be as nearly as possible parallel to the fibres of the veneers. A is the section of the cylinder veneer and blocks, and B shows the convex side of the blocks.

2200. *Fig.* 795. is another mode of glueing veneers together with cross pieces screwed to a cylinder, the veneers being placed between the former and the latter.

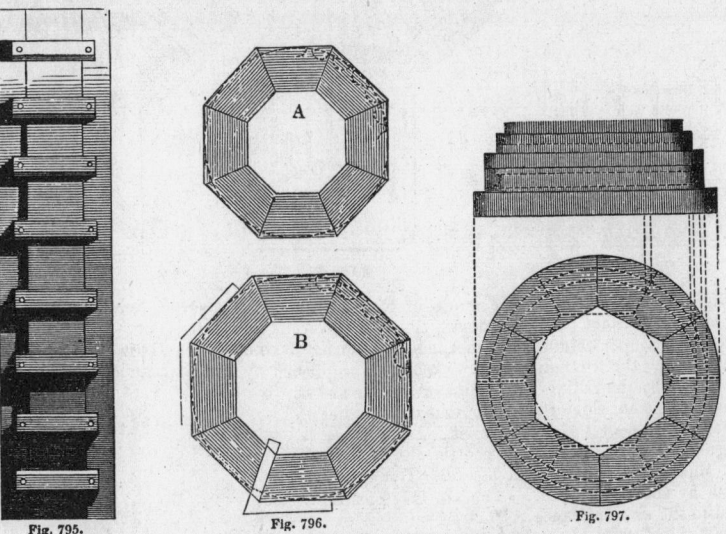

Fig. 795.   Fig. 796.   Fig. 797.

2201. In *fig.* 796. is shown the method of glueing up columns in pieces, which here are eight in number, each being glued to the other after the manner of *fig.* 790. The workman should be careful to keep the joints out of the flutes, when the columns are to be fluted, by which the substance will be more likely to prevent the joints giving way. A is a section of the column at top, and B at the bottom. After glueing together, the octagons and mitres should be correctly laid down for the true formation of the joints. In B are shown two bevels, one for trying the mitres, and the other for trying the work when put together.

2202. *Fig.* 797. is the mode of glueing up the base of a column. It is formed in three courses, the pieces in each of which are made to break joint over one another. The horizontal joints of the courses must be so adjusted as to fall at the junction of two mouldings, forming a re-entering angle. After the glue is set quite hard, the rough base is sent to the turner, by whom it is reduced into the required profile. The fibres of the wood should lie horizontally, in which direction the work

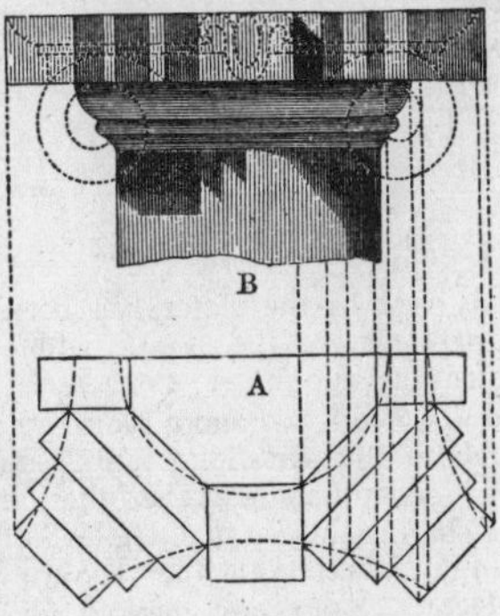

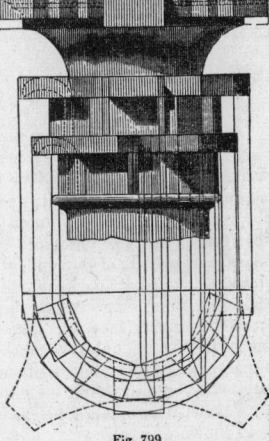

Fig. 798.

Fig. 799.

will stand much better than when they are vertical.   A is the plan of the base inverted, and B is the elevation.

2203. The formation of a modern Ionic capital is given in *fig.* 798., wherein A is the plan inverted, showing the method of placing the blocks; and B is the elevation.

2204. *Fig.* 799. is the method of glueing up for the leaves of the Corinthian capital, A is the plan inverted, and B is the elevation.   The abacus is glued up in the same manner as in the preceding example.

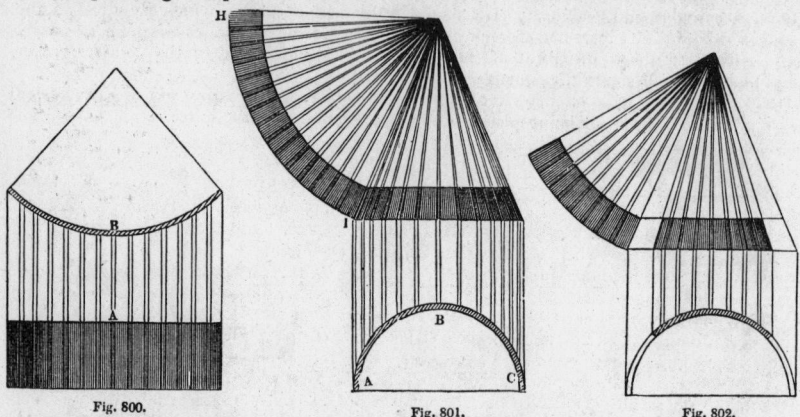

Fig. 800.   Fig. 801.   Fig. 802.

2205. *Fig.* 800. exhibits the mode of forming a cylindrical surface without veneers, by means of equidistant parallel grooves, A is the elevation, and B the plan.

2206. *Fig.* 801. exhibits the method of covering a conic body.   It is, in fact, no more than covering the frustum of a cone, and is accomplished by two concentric arcs terminated at the ends by the radii.   The radius of the one arc is the whole slant side of the cone, that of the other is the slant side of the part cut off.   In this case, the grooves are directed to the centre, and filled in with slips of wood glued as before.   The plan is shown by the circle ABC.   The arc HI must be equal to the circumference ABC.

2207. *Fig.* 802. shows the same thing for a smaller segment.

2208. *Fig.* 803. shows the manner of glueing up a globe or sphere by the same method.   A is the face of the piece; B the edge showing the depth of the grooves; C shows the mould for forming the piece to the true curvature; and D the faces of two pieces put together.

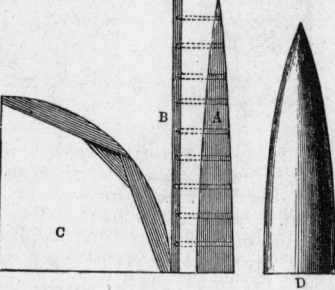

Fig. 803.

Sect. VI.

SLATING.

2209. An account of the materials used by the slater has been detailed in Chap. II. Sect. IX.   The tools used by this artificer are the *scantle*, which is a gauge by which slates are regulated to their proper length; the *trowel*; the *hammer*; the *zax*, an instrument for cutting the slates; a small *handpick*, and a *hod* and a *board* for mortar.   The *zax* is an instrument made of tempered iron, about 16 inches long and 2 inches wide, like a large knife bent a little at one end, with a wooden handle at the other, and having a projecting piece of iron on its back, drawn to a sharp point, to make holes in the slates for the nails, the other side being used to chip and cut the slates to their required size, as when brought from the quarry they are not sufficiently square and cleaned for the slater's use.   The places for the nail holes are marked usually on the slate where they have to be punched, with a gauge, and then the iron of the *zax* is struck through the slate.   Each slate has two holes; large slates require three.   A better mode of obtaining the place for the holes is to mark a plank with two small pieces of wood across it, at the distance required; the position is thus shown at once.

2210. Slating is laid in inclined courses, beginning from the eaves and working upwards, the courses nearest the ridge of the roof being less in width than those below. The *lap* of one slate over another is called its *bond*, and it is the distance between the nail of the under slate and the lower end of the upper slate. The *bed* of a slate is its under side, and the upper side is called its *back*. The part of each course which is exposed to the weather is called its *gauge, bare*, or *margin*. The slates are nailed to close or open boarding, lying on the back of the rafters, with nails, which should be of copper or zinc. If iron nails are used they should be well painted. The operation of cutting or paring the side and bottom edges of the slates is called *trimming* them; but the head of the slate is never cut. In that part the holes were formerly pierced by which the nails pass to the boarding. This boarding (or *sarking*, as it is called in the north of Great Britain) is usually $\frac{3}{4}$ inch to $1\frac{1}{4}$ inches thick, rough, of equal thickness, and well secured to the common rafters. A good practice obtains of bedding slates in mortar, on boarding, which gives them a sound bearing, especially if the roof will have to stand much wear from persons passing along the gutters, or over the ridge, for repairs and other purposes.

2210a. Another method of forming a roof, as lately employed by some architects, consists in slating on boards fixed to purlin-rafters, without any common rafters, as shown in *figs.* 695a. and 697. The purlins are placed somewhat closer than when rafters are used; the boards are $1\frac{1}{4}$ inches thick, usually placed diagonally. It makes very sound work, and saves height, where that may be an object. Another method, as noticed in par. 2285, is to nail the boarding on to common rafters laid as purlins, as shown in *figs.* 695 and 696.

2210b. The common method of slating is to nail the slates to laths or battens, as in tiling, but a house so done is more liable to be affected with the various changes from heat to cold than by the other system. These laths are cut to boards of 20, 25, 30 or 36. Thus a board 12 × 9 × 3, cut 3 deep and 4 flat, equals 1 board 20. If cut 4 deep and 4 flat, equals 1 board 25. If cut 4 deep and 5 flat, equals 1 board 30. If cut 5 deep and 5 flat, equals 1 board 36. Slating laid on battens, at places on the sea coast, and as usual in work in Ireland, is either wholly "rendered" with lime and hair on the under side, or only the under edges and laths are thus secured. Without this precaution the slates rattle, and the driving winds get under them, tending to strip the roofs. Rendering, properly done, lasts as long as the slates exist in a perfect state.

2210c. Open or ventilated slating, which is nearly equally as waterproof as the usual method of slating, will save one-third of the quantity per square.

2210d. *Felt.* Slate is also laid on *felt*, on $\frac{3}{4}$ inch boarding. Croggon's patent *asphalte roofing felt* is impervious to rain, snow, and frost, and is a non-conductor. From its anti-corrosive properties, it is of service when placed between iron and wood and between metals. It is manufactured of any required length, by 32 inches wide. There is some risk of dry rot occurring, however, by using it thus; the better plan is to lay the felt on boards, and then to batten for the slates over the felt, so as to leave an air space between the felt and the slates. Its general weight is about 42 lbs. per square. *Non-conducting felt* is formed entirely of hair, and is used for covering boilers, steam-pipes, &c., for the purpose of preventing the radiation of heat. When applied to boilers, a cement of 2 parts of white lead, $1\frac{1}{2}$ parts of red lead, 4 parts of whiting, is mixed with boiled linseed oil; after being spread over the felt, the whole is patted down on the boiler, and in a short time the felt firmly adheres. No cement is needed for steam-pipes, the felt being wrapped round and secured by twine. Sheets of this felt are made 32 inches by 20 inches; and of the following weights:—No. 1, 16 oz.; No. 2, 24 oz.; No. 3, 32 oz.; No. 4, 40 oz.; No. 5, 48 oz. This dry hair or inodorous felt is also useful for deadening sound, by cutting it into 2 or $2\frac{1}{2}$ inch strips, and laying it on the joists under the floor boards; also as lining to walls and floors; and for iron houses to equalise the temperature.

2210e. Felt is also applied for forming roofs of temporary buildings. It has been suggested for permanent buildings, but to that employment of it we must withhold our approval. The rafters may be about 3 inches by $1\frac{1}{4}$ inches, placed 20 to 24 inches apart, laid at a pitch of 2 or 3 inches to the foot, and covered with $\frac{1}{2}$ inch boarding. The felt is to be stretched tight, overlapping one inch at the joints, nailed with twopenny fine clout nails, first heated and cooled in grease, about $1\frac{1}{2}$ inches apart; copper nails are preferable. The whole roof is then to have a good coating of hot coal tar and lime, in the proportion of 2 gallons of the former to 6 pounds of the latter, well boiled together, put on with a common tar mop, and while it is soft some coarse sharp sand sifted over it. The gutters are made of two folds, cemented together with the boiling mixture. The coating to the roof must be renewed every fourth or fifth year, according to the climate. The felt is found to last better, if it be not made to adhere by any mixture to the boarding.

2210f. Felt for sheds, or occasional purposes, may be put up without boarding; the rafters in this case would not exceed 3 inches by $1\frac{1}{4}$ inches, placed at a distance of 30 inches apart. To prevent the felt bagging, battens, or slighter rafters, of about 2 inches by 1 inch, are placed between the others. To such roofs the felt must be laid from eaves to eaves, nailing through the overlap into the main rafter. The pitch of this roof should be about 6 inches to the foot. The "ventilated" slating will bear an economical contrast, provided the smaller size of slates be used, and is more durable.

2210*g*. Slating is sometimes laid lozengewise, but it is much less durable than when laid in the usual method. It is introduced for the sake of ornamental effect. The ends of the slates are also rounded, or cut angleways to a point, or the angles only cut off; or, if the slates be of a small size, they are set angleways over courses with square ends. These are all shown in an excellent article in Viollet le Duc's *Dictionnaire*, s.v. Ardoise. Slating is also made to have a decorative effect by forming zigzag patterns with red coloured slates among blue slates; or a few courses of the one above a larger number of the other.

2210*h*. Several years ago, a patent was obtained for forming roofs with slate slabs without boarding or battens. In this the slates were all reduced to widths equal to the distance between centre and centre of the rafters. On the backs of these last they are screwed by two or three strong inch and half screws at each of their ends. Over the junctions of the slates, on the backs of the rafters, fillets of slates about two and a half or three inches wide, bedded in putty, are screwed down, to prevent the entrance of rain. The handsome regular appearance of this sort of slating gained it at first much celebrity; but it was soon abandoned, on account of the disorder it is liable to sustain from the slightest partial settlement of the building, as well as from the constant dislodgement of the putty, upon which greatly depended its being impervious to rain.

2211. Subjoined is a succinct account of the different sorts of slates brought to the London market, and enumerated in the order of their goodness and value.

2211*a*. *Westmoreland slates.* These are from 3 feet 6 inches to 1 foot in length, and from 2 feet 6 inches to 1 foot in breadth. They should be nailed with not less than sixpenny and eightpenny copper or zinc nails (iron nails should never be used); and a ton in weight of sized slates will usually cover about two squares and a quarter. The weight of the coarsest Westmoreland slates is to that of common tiling as 36 to 54.

2211*b*. *Welsh rags* are next in goodness, and are nearly of the same sizes as those last mentioned; but a ton of these will cover only from one square and a quarter to one square and three quarters.

2211*c*. Table of the Names and usual Sizes of Slates,

With the squares a thousand (1200) will cover according to their size, and the gauge at which they are laid, as stated in various works. * Denotes best Welsh roofing sizes.

Name.	Size. Inches.	Cover about Squares.	Cover about Squares.	Weight per 1200. Cwts. 1st quality.	Weight per 1200. Cwts. 2nd quality.
Queens	32, 34, 36 × 16, 17, 18	-	-	-	-
Princesses	30 × 15	16¾	-	115	
Ditto	28 × 14	14½	-	97	
Ditto	*24 × 14	12¾	12¼	70	90
Empress	26 × 16	-	-	95	
Ditto, small	26 × 14	-	-	90	
Duchesses	*24 × 12	11	10	60	80
Ditto, small	*22 × 12	-	-	55	
Marchionesses	22 × 12	9½	9	55	70
Ditto	*22 × 11	9	8	50 / 47½	60
Countesses	*20 × 10	7¾	7	40	54
Ditto	20 × 12	-	-	50	
Ditto, small	*18 × 10	-	-	36	
Viscountesses	18 × 10	6¾	6⅛	36	47
Ditto	*18 × 9	6	5½	33 or 31	40
Ladies, wide	*16 × 10	-	-	30	42
Ditto	16 × 9	5¼	-	28	
Ditto	*16 × 8	4¾	4½	25	33
	14 × 12	-	-	33	44
Small Ladies	*14 × 8	3¾	3½	22	26
Ditto	14 × 7	3½	3⅛	19 or 20	22
Doubles	13 × 10	-	4	25	31
Ditto	*13 × 7	-	2½	16·18	21
Ditto, small	*12 × 6	2½	-	13·14	14
Ditto	12 × 8	-	-	-	22
	11 × 5½	-	2½	18	12
Singles	-	-	1	-	-
Headers	*12 × 6	-	-	14	
Ditto	*14 × 12	-	-	33	
Ditto	*13 × 10	-	-	26	

During last century, when building works were executed with more regard to durability, a thousand duchesses were said to cover 9 squares; countesses, 6 squares; ladies, 3 squares; and doubles, 2 to 2¼ squares.

2211*d*. Slates are now split so thin, that in specifications it is desirable to state the weight per square of the slating required. The scientific journals have lately noticed that at the Rhiwboyfdir Slate Company's quarries, sheets of slate 8 feet long and ³⁄₃₂nd part of an inch were obtained, the length being generally 16 inches. The grain must, of course, be very fine to permit of so thin a cleavage.

2211*e*. The strength of slate 1 inch thick is considered equal to that of Portland stone 5 inches thick. A foot superficial weighs from 11¼ to 14 lbs. Slates of the usual thickness will not bear much heat before cracking; the thicker the slate the more readily does it crack with heat; and they will fly at once if cold water be poured suddenly upon them when in a heated state.

2211*f*. The *Tavistock slates* were sold by the thousand of ten hundred, which quantity covered about three squares and forty feet.

2211*g*. Horsham slate, obtained in Essex, is a limestone, and is found to have no limit to its durability; but being very heavy, proper preparation is needed for it, as timbers of much greater scantling than usual are required.

2211*h*. French slates, formerly used in London to some extent, are very light, and must therefore only be used on boards; otherwise the wind would act upon them. In France they are bedded in plaster on the boarding.

2211*i*. The ridge, hips, and valleys of a slated roof were formerly always covered with lead. The valleys are still usually so formed, but slate has been introduced for the two former. The pieces require to be cut truly square, screwed to the boarding, and the joints and heads secured with putty or white lead. For hips and ridges, *slate roll ribbing* is often employed (*fig.* 803*a*.). Shorter slates, A, are first nailed to each side of the ridge-piece, C, or of the hip rafter, to form the saddle; and then the slate roll B is put on and secured by screws through the top. This roll is made also with rebated joints, but it is obviated by the roll breaking joint with the saddle. The roll, as shown in the figure, is sometimes attached to one side of the saddle, which must be made according to the pitch of the roof. The 3-inch diameter roll has a 7-inch width of saddle on each side; the 2½-inch a 6-inch; and the 2-inch a 5½-inch saddle. There are 175, 225, and 320 feet in a ton of the ribbing; and 400, 560, and 700 feet of the ribbing.

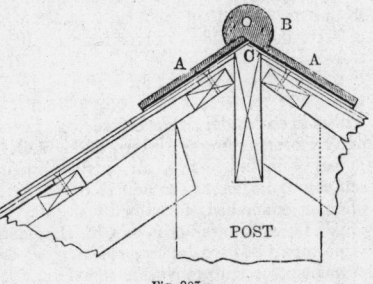

Fig. 803*a*.

2211*k*. The edges of the slates next a wall, either at the head or sides of a roof, have to be protected. This, in the best work, is effected by lead flashings (*par.* 2214.). In the former case, it is laid on the head of the slate for about 5 to 7 inches, and then turned up against the wall for about the same height, and secured by holdfasts; it may also be either turned over into a course of bricks, and the brickwork continued up, or the turned up edge is protected by a lapping of lead inserted in the brickwork. This lapping, in commoner work, is replaced by cement. At the edge of the roof against a wall, lead is likewise placed in a similar manner; but as the lapping cannot be laid in a straight joint, it is cut in a zigzag form, called "stepping," to each course of bricks. Of late years this lead flashing is entirely replaced by filleting of lime and hair-plaster; of gauged stuff, being lime and cement mixed; or of cement and sand. But as these materials crack and fall away in a few years, the filleting has to be looked to periodically or whenever damp makes its appearance. Zinc also takes its place, but is not so effective, as it is more difficult to dress it to the surface of the slates.

2211*l*. In exposed situations, where filleting cannot be trusted, and lead is too expensive, various contrivances have been made for preventing the entrance of wet. One of these consists in forming a small gutter between two rafters, lining it with lead, turning one side of the lead under the slates, and turning up the other side against the wall, and cementing over it. Another good method is to cement a row of tiles against the wall above the slates, and when dry to cover the tiles and wall with cement, tucking it well into all the crevices.

2211*m*. The mediæval method of easing the line of tiling at the foot of the framing deserves some notice; thus, as shown in *fig.* 701*e*., it appears that the use of chantlates, A, frees the tie-beams, tassels, and other timber, except plates, from all contact with the masonry; and, as a matter of course, from any consequent tendency to rot. This method seems more advantageous than that of beam-filling, which is altogether prevalent at the

present time, in order to keep out draughts, but it requires care in closing the work. Tiling has been already described in the section Bricklaying.

2211n. In many churches with open roofs, the solid rafters, without any under panelling or boarding, may be seen covered with rough slabs of boarding, having large fissures through which the lead is visible. Great inconvenience is often felt in roofs so constructed during the autumn and winter months, when, upon sudden alteration of temperature, condensation takes place under the lead, and the drops of water fall in almost a shower. This defect has been the cause for ceiling many open roofs. A space of two inches left between the inner boarding and the outer covering has been found to be sufficient to obviate this discomfort. Felt (par. 2210d.) is also sometimes used, to assist in remedying the evil.

2211o. In Pembrokeshire, slate is used for everything. For posts and rails of the same scantling as if for wood. The walls of buildings are of square blocks, rough casted. A range of stabling might be erected of rough blocks, with the door and window-frames of worked slate. A prejudice exists against the use of squared blocks without plastering them, on the ground that they admit damp. It was found that if there was the smallest perforation in the slate ; or if, as was often the case from the want of absorption, the joints were not perfectly close, the damp is driven through. The defect might, perhaps, be obviated by laying every block with the bed slightly inclining outwards.

2211p. Slabs of slate, sawn, self-faced, and planed, are now extensively manufactured at all the large quarries. They are usually in $\frac{1}{2}$, $\frac{3}{4}$, 1, $1\frac{1}{4}$, $1\frac{1}{2}$, $1\frac{3}{4}$, 2, $2\frac{1}{2}$, and 3 inch thicknesses. A quarter of an inch is required for each face planed from the rough, and they are sanded in addition afterwards. The best quality Bangor slabs can be obtained in sizes varying from 4 to 6 feet long, or from 2 to 3 feet wide ; and from 6 to 8 feet long, or from 3 to 3 feet 6 inches wide. The second quality slabs, quarry planed, are under 6 feet long or 3 feet wide.

2211q. The purposes for which slate slabs are now used are multifarious. Amongst them are: cisterns (Plumbery) from $\frac{3}{4}$ inch to 2 inches thick ; sinks of inch slate, 4 inches deep inside, either bolted together as cisterns, or with flush ends, planed both sides, and screwed ; troughs ; filters, baths, 2 feet wide, 2 feet high, 4 feet 9 inches at bottom and 5 feet 9 inches at top, all outside dimensions, of plain slate, sanded inside, or enamelled self-colour inside, or enamelled Siena marble inside, and so on ; urinal back and divisions, plain or enamelled, fitted with angular earthenware basin, flat back basin, hollow back cradle basin, square basin, or with slate apron only ; linings to damp walls ; panels of doors ; table tops ; billiard tables ; shelving to dairies and pantries ; fittings for wine bins, with permanent or with moveable shelves and ledges ; steps ; and landings.

2211r. Enamelled slate, as it is called, is worked for chimney-pieces, to represent marbles ; for covers to stoves and hot water coils, besides many other decorative purposes. The process, which is simply painting dried at a great heat, requires to be well done to be really lasting. There are, of course, imitations of the process, but these are defective in that quality.

2211s. Thatching is an admirable covering for securing warmth in winter, and coolness in summer ; but it is subject to injury by birds, and to risk from fire. It was much used for churches in Norfolk and Suffolk (fig. 701n.). The thatcher requires a common stable fork, to toss up the straw together before being made into bundles ; a thatcher's fork, to carry the straw from the heap up to the roof ; a thatcher's rake, to comb down the straw straight and smooth ; a knife, or eaves' knife, to cut and trim the straw to a straight line ; a knife to point the twigs ; a half glove of leather, to protect the hand when driving in the smaller twigs or spars ; a long flat needle ; a pair of leathern gaiters to come up above the knees, used when kneeling on the rafters ; and a gritstone to sharpen the knives. Wheat straw lasts from 15 to 20 years ; and oat straw, about 8 years. Reed thatching, as done in the West of England, is the truss after the ears have been cut off, leaving the clean, sound pipe straw, of which a thickness of 3 inches is laid on the common thatching with spars only. The materials required are straw or reeds, laths, nails, withes and rods. A load of straw, laid on about 12 to 16 inches in thickness, will do a square and a half ; a bundle of oak laths, $1\frac{1}{4}$ inches wide, and from $\frac{1}{4}$ to $\frac{3}{8}$ths thick, nailed about 8 inches apart, 1 square ; a hundred of withes, 3 squares ; a pound of rope yarn, 1 square ; 100 of rods, 3 squares ; and $2\frac{1}{2}$ hundred of nails, 1 square. The fish house at Meare, Somersetshire, of about the middle of the 14th century, still retains its thatched roof. Probably thatched roofs were ornamented by a species of cresting, for in some parts of the country the withes or willow twigs that bind the thatch are sometimes arranged on the tops of ricks and cottages in an interlacing manner, terminating with a spike with a rudely formed cock. Viollet le Duc alludes to the custom of forming the ridge in mud, in which plants and grasses were inserted to prevent the earth being dissolved and washed away by the rain.

Sect. VII.

PLUMBERY.

2212. The plumber has but few working tools, for the facility with which the metal in which he works is wrought does not render a variety necessary. The principal are—a heavy iron *hammer*, with a short but thick handle. Two or three different sized wooden *mallets*, and a *dressing and flatting tool*, which is made of beech wood, usually about 18 inches long and $2\frac{1}{2}$ inches square, planed smooth on one side, and rounded on the other or upper side. It is tapered and rounded at one of its ends for convenient grasping by the workman. Its use is to stretch and flatten the sheet lead, and dress it into the shape required for the various purposes whereto it is to be applied, by the use of its flat and round sides as wanted. The *jack and trying planes*, similar to those used by carpenters, for planing straight the edges of their sheet lead when a regular and correct line is requisite. They also use a line and roller called a *chalk line*, for lining out the lead into different widths. Their cutting tools are *chisels* and *gouges*, of different sizes, and *cutting knives*. The latter are for cutting the sheet lead into strips and pieces to the division marked by the chalk line. They use also *files* of different sizes for making cistern heads to pipes, for pumpwork, &c. For the purposes of soldering, they have a variety of different sized *grozing irons*, which are commonly about 12 inches long, tapered at both ends, the handle end being turned quite round to allow of its being held firmly in the hand whilst in use. The opposite end is spherical, or more usually spindle-shaped, and proportioned to the different situations for which they are required. The *grozing iron* is heated to redness when in use. The *iron ladles* are of three or four sizes, and used for the purpose of melting lead or solder. The plumber's *measuring rule* is 2 feet long, in three parts, each of 8 inches. Two of the legs are of box-wood, and the third of steel, which is attached to one of the box legs by a pivot whereon it turns, and shuts into the other legs in a groove. The steel leg is useful for passing into places which the plumber has to examine, into which anything thicker would not easily enter, and it is often used also for removing oxide or other extraneous matter from the surface of the heated metal. The plumber moreover is provided with *centre bits* of all sizes, and a stock to work them in, for perforating lead or wood where pipes are to be inserted, as well as with *compasses*, for striking out circular portions of lead. *Scales and weights* are also in constant requisition, as nothing done by the plumber is chargeable till the lead is weighed.

2213. The method most commonly adopted in laying *sheet lead* for terraces or flats, is to place it on a surface as even as possible, either of boarding or plastering. If boards are employed, they should be sufficiently thick to prevent warping or twisting, which, if it occur soon, causes the lead to crack or to become unsightly. As sheets of lead are not more than about 6 feet in width, when the area to be covered with them is large, joints become necessary, which are contrived in various ways to prevent the wet from penetrating. To do this, the best method is that of forming *rolls*, which are pieces of wood about 2 inches square extending in the direction of the joint, planed and rounded on their upper side. These being fastened under the joints of the lead between the edges of the two sheets which meet together, one is dressed up over the roll on the inside, and the other over both of them on the outside, whereby all entry of the water is prevented. No fastening is required other than the adherence of the lead by close hammering together and down on the flat: indeed, any fastening would be injurious, as by it the lead would not have free play in its expansion and contraction from heat and cold. When rolls are used, the rule should be specially enforced of turning the open sides or laps from the south-west, west, or south, wherever practicable, so as to ensure the lap from being forced up by the wind, and thereby the water consequently blown in. If *rolls* are not employed, which from their projection are in some cases found inconvenient, *seams* are substituted for them; but they are by no means equal to the roll either for neatness or security. They are formed by merely bending up the two edges of the lead, and then over one another, and then dressing them down close to the flat throughout their length. Though some solder the joints, it is a bad practice, and no good plumber will do it, for the same reason as that just given in respect of fastenings in flats. A lead *flat*, as well as a gutter, should be laid with a fall to keep it dry. A quarter of an inch in a foot is sufficient inclination for lead, if the sheets be 20 feet long, so that in this case they will be 5 inches at one end higher than at the other. This *giving a current*, as it is called, is usually provided for by the carpenter previous to laying the lead.

2214. Round the extreme edges of flats and gutters where lead is used, are fixed pieces of milled lead which are called *flashings*. When the lead work is bounded by a wall of

brick or stone work, the flashings are passed on one edge into and between a joint of the work, and the edges of the flat or gutter being bent up, the other edge of the flashing is dressed over it. If there be no joint into which the flashing can be inserted, it is fastened on that side with wall hooks (*par.* 2211*k.*). *Drips* in flats and gutters are used when the length of the gutter or flat is greater than the length of the sheet of lead, or sometimes for convenience, or to avoid joining lead by soldering it. Some architects place them every 6 or 8 feet, which however good in a box or parallel gutter, it raises an ordinary gutter too much, and causes great width of lead at the head. They are formed by raising one part above another, and dressing the lead round, as has been described for rolls. No sheet should be laid in greater length than 10 or 12 feet without a *drip*, to allow of expansion and contraction. Small *cisterns* are often sunk in gutters to collect the water before passing off into the head of the down pipe. The cistern has usually over it a perforated lead *rose*, to prevent dirt, leaves, &c. passing down with the water.

2215. The work of the plumber is estimated by its weight and the time employed in fixing it.

2215*a.* The thickness of sheet lead varies from 5 to 12 lbs. in weight to the superficial foot, and is used in covering large buildings, in flats or slopes, for gutters, the hips, ridges, and valleys of roofs, the lining of cisterns, &c. Thus 7lb. lead is commonly used for roofs, flats, and gutters; it is the least thickness in which *bossing* can be properly done. 8lb. lead is a better quality for all these purposes. 6lb. lead is used for hips and ridges; this is the thinnest quality for such purposes. 5lb. lead is used for flashings. It is said that 16lb. lead was used on the earlier mediæval churches. The following thicknesses, obtained from Hurst, *Surveyors' Handbook*, may be compared with the Birmingham Wire Gauge given in *par.* 2254, Sect. **x.**

TABLE I. OF THE THICKNESS AND WEIGHT OF LEAD, PER SUPERFICIAL FOOT.

Thickness or Decimal of an Inch	$\frac{1}{16}$ ·0625	$\frac{1}{8}$ ·125	$\frac{3}{16}$ ·1875	$\frac{1}{4}$ ·25	$\frac{5}{16}$ ·3125	$\frac{3}{8}$ ·375	$\frac{7}{16}$ ·4375	$\frac{1}{2}$ ·5
Pounds	3·708	7·417	11·125	14·833	18·542	22·250	25·958	29·667
Thickness or Decimal of an Inch	$\frac{9}{16}$ ·5625	$\frac{5}{8}$ ·625	$\frac{11}{16}$ ·6875	$\frac{3}{4}$ ·75	$\frac{13}{16}$ ·8125	$\frac{7}{8}$ ·875	$\frac{15}{16}$ ·9375	Inch. 1·0
Pounds	33·375	37·083	40·792	44·500	48·208	51·917	55·625	59·333

TABLE II. OF THE WEIGHT AND THICKNESS OF LEAD, PER FOOT SUPERFICIAL.

Weight in Pounds.	Thickness in inches.	Weight in Pounds.	Thickness in inches.	Weight in Pounds.	Thickness in inches.
1	0·017	6	0·101	11	0·186
2	0·034	7	0·118	12	0·203
3	0·051	8	0·135		
4	0·068	9	0·152		
5	0·0 5	10	0·169		

2215*b.* Lead is generally cast about 7 feet wide and about 33 feet in length, but its width and length depend upon the margin which is cut off after casting, as the scum, &c., is driven to those parts. This may reduce it about 6 inches in width and 18 to 24 inches in length. Lead is now cast to the above-named weights, and also "bare," according to the directions of the contractor. The architect, to do justice to his employer, should carefully ascertain for himself the weight and size of the sheet of lead from which the piece is cut. It is usually marked or painted upon it. A small piece is not a true test either for weight or gauge, and the edge is sometimes cut on a bias. The best direction is that it should weigh over the weight specified.

2216. A hundred weight of sheet lead will usually cover on a platform, roof, gutter, &c. at 4 lbs. = 28 ft.; 5 lbs. = 22 ft. 5 ins.; 6 lbs. = 18 ft. 8 ins.; 7 lbs. = 16 ft.; 8 lbs. = 14 ft.; 9 lbs. = 12 ft. 6 ins.; and 12 lbs. = 9 ft. Old lead weighed for recasting has generally a deduction made of 6 lbs. per cwt. for waste, &c.

2217. Lead is used to fasten iron cramps, posts, and bars into masonry by filling up the cavities between them. Sheets of thin lead are sometimes placed between the drums of columns (par. 1925*a.*), as well as in the bed joints of wrought stone arches, to distribute

the pressure between the stones. Lead work treated ornamentally for ridges, and hips of roofs, knobs, vanes, &c., as during the Mediæval period, is superseded in the present day by cast and wrought iron, and by zinc work. See essay in *Builder*, 1856, p. 410.

2218. We do not think it necessary to describe at length the machinery of a *water closet*. Every one knows that the principle on which it is formed is that of a head of water in a cistern placed above it, which by means of a lever attached to a valve in the cistern allows a body of water to rush down and wash the basin, whose valve is opened for the discharge of the soil at the same moment that the water is let down from the cistern. Various instruments for this purpose have been contrived and patented, but we are not aware of any better than those which were made by the late Mr. Bramah, almost as soon as the subject formed a matter of inquiry. The reader will obtain by the inspection of one a far better notion than words or diagrams will convey. The apparatus of a water closet has also been made self-acting, either by opening the door of the closet ; by lifting the lid of the seat of the closet ; or by depressing the seat itself. One of the most simple and efficient pans is that called by Messrs. Doulton the *enamelled stoneware closet pan, figure D*, which with pan and trap complete, is sold at 3s. 9d. each. A cistern is described in par. 2223f.

2218a. In opposition to *water* closets, *earth* or *dry soil* closets have lately been much advocated. The deposits are at once deodorised by coal ashes or earth, which absorbs the ammonia and other fertilizing properties, for removal to the garden or field. It may be considered more serviceable where there is a deficient water supply or a want of proper drainage, and in country, rather than in town, localities.

2218b. The importance of good stench traps to drains is not to be overrated. The usual iron *bell trap*, as supplied to a sink, or let into a pavement, is sufficient as long as the bell remains perfect. Tye and Andrews have patented a useful *syphon trap* for the same services ; and Cottam has also a cast iron trap or " effluvium interceptor." Beard and Dent have patented a *cast lead pipe trap* of 2 and 4 inches diameter, and claim for it that it is of pure and solid lead without solder or seam of any kind ; as clear inside and out as any pipe made by hydraulic pressure ; of a perfectly regular substance throughout ; and that being composed of one metal, it is not subject to expansion, nor liable to be affected by the gases, which tend to destroy the ordinary trap. All these traps will only continue effective as long as water remains either in the cup or at the syphon bend, a fact which is either not known to, or forgotten by very many housekeepers, who complain of bad smells from the drains in summer time, or after some days of dry weather.

WATER SUPPLY.

2219. As it is a branch of the plumber's trade to find and fix the pumps for the supply of water to a dwelling, we think it right to furnish a description of the three sorts commonly used, which are the *lifting*, the *common*, and the *force pump*.

2220. *Fig.* 804. is a diagram of a *lifting pump*, in which ABCD is a short cylinder submerged in the well or other reservoir, whence the water is to be raised. In this cylinder a valve is placed at *x*, above which the pipe or tube CE is carried upwards as high as is requisite for the delivery of the water. In the cylinder AD a water-tight piston moves vertically, being worked by rod or framework as seen in the diagram. To this piston is fixed a valve at *v* opening upwards. On the descent of the piston the pressure against the water opens the valve *v*, and the cylinder between the two valves is filled with the water. When the piston is then raised, the water between the valves being pressed upwards against the valve *x*, opens it, and is driven into the tube CE, from which, on the renewed descent of the piston, its return is intercepted by the valve *x*. The water follows the piston in its ascent by the hydrostatic pressure of the water on the reservoir outside the cylinder ; and on the next descent of the piston the water will again pass through the valve *v*, and will be driven through the valve *x* on its next ascent. It is manifest from inspection that the valve *x* relieves the valve *v* from the pressure of the column of water in the tube CE during the descent of the piston ; for if the valve *v* were subject to that pressure during the descent of the piston, it could not be opened by the pressure of the water in the well, inasmuch as its level is necessarily below the level of the water in the pipe CE. The valve *v* prevents the

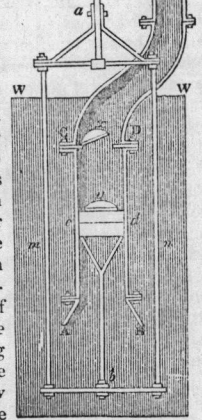

Fig. 804.

return of the water through the piston during its ascent. In raising the piston a force is required sufficient to support the entire column of water from the valve *v* to the surface of the water in the tube CE. To estimate this, we must take the weight of a column of water whose base is equal to the area of a section of the piston,

and whose height is equal to that of the surface of the water above the valve v in the tube CE. Hence, after each stroke of the pump, the pressure on the piston and the force necessary to raise it, will be increased by the weight of a column of water whose base is the horizontal section of the piston, and its height equal to the increase which the elevation of the column in CE receives from the water driven through the valve x. In the figure cd is the piston, the bottom of whose rod is at b; m and n are rods which connect it with the upper part of the work, and WW is the level of the water in the well.

2221. The common, or as it is usually called, *suction pump* (shown in *fig.* 805.), is nothing more than a large syringe connected with a tube whose lower extremity is plunged in the well from which the water is to be raised. The tube is called a *suction pipe* (SO), and its end in the well is represented at O, which, for the purpose of preventing the ascent of solid impurities, that might choke the pipe and impede its action, is pierced with holes like a strainer. At the upper end of this suction pipe is placed the valve x opening upwards. At this place the tube is connected with another, BC, which acts as a great syringe, and in which works a piston having a valve at v, also opening upwards. The piston is worked alternately upwards and downwards in common pumps by a lever called the *brake*, but it may be worked in many ways. In the figure, W is the level of the water, CD the *flange*, where the lower valve is fixed, cd the piston, ab the piston rod, and MN the cistern into which the water is raised and delivered by its gravity at the *nozzle* of the pump e. At the commencement of the operation the water in the suction tube stands at the same height as the water in the well, being equally subject to the atmospheric pressure; but as soon as the syringe BC exhausts the air by the upward and downward action of the piston cd, the pressure of the air in SO being diminished and rendered less than that on the surface of the water in the well, will rise in SO by the atmospheric pressure; and as the air becomes more completely exhausted in the column of water in the tube SO below the valve x, so will its pressure on the surface of the column be diminished, and whilst that diminution goes on, the height of the column will increase. If the air could be entirely withdrawn from the tube SO, and a

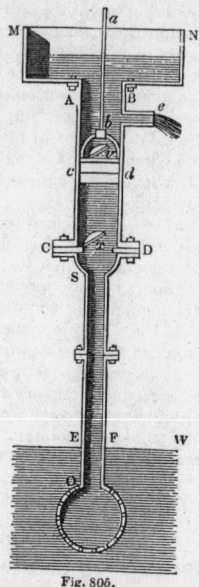

Fig. 805.

perfect vacuum created beneath the valve x, similar to that existing above the mercury in a barometer, then the atmospheric pressure, acting with undiminished effect on the surface of water in the well, would, in the tube SO, sustain a column of water equal to a column of mercury of the same base and of the same height as the mercury in the barometer. Now, the specific gravity of mercury being $13\frac{1}{2}$ times greater than that of water, a force capable of sustaining a column of mercury 30 inches high, would sustain a column of water equal to 30 inches $\times 13\frac{1}{2} = 405$ inches $= 33\frac{9}{12}$ feet. But an absolute vacuum is never formed, and, moreover, in this country, as the barometric column varies between 28 and 31 inches in height, the valve x should on no account be more than 28 feet above the level of the water in the well, taking into consideration all the attendant circumstances.

This is the construction and principle upon which the common household pump is formed, and in it no other aid is derived from atmospheric pressure than what we have already stated; hence the pump requires as much force to work it as, in general terms, is equal to the weight of all the water in it at any time, the atmospheric pressure affording no aid to the workman. The cistern at the top is placed for the purpose of affording an unintermitted discharge of the water by holding more than the whole accumulation of water which is contrived to be greater than the spout or nozzle will discharge.

2222. The *forcing pump* whose construction is shown in *fig.* 806., is a combination of the common suction and lifting pump. CEFD is a suction pipe descending into the well, and at its top is the valve V opening upwards. The pump barrel ABCD is furnished with a solid piston cd, whose rod is ab, without any valve. From the side of the barrel, just above the suction valve, a pipe proceeds, communicating with an upright cylinder GH, carried to such height as the water is intended to be raised. At the bottom of this cylinder is placed the valve V' opening upwards. At the commencement of working, the suction pipe CE and the

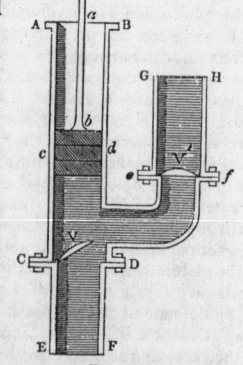

Fig. 806.

chamber between the piston and valves are filled with air. When the piston descends to the valve V, the air enclosed in the latter chamber becomes condensed, and opening,

therefore, the valve V', a part of it escapes through it. On raising the piston the air below it becomes partially exhausted, and that in the suction pipe, opening the valve V by its greater pressure, expands into the upper chamber. A part of this is expelled when the piston next descends, by means of the valve V'. This action is similar to that of an air pump or exhausting syringe. When by the repetition of this action the air is sufficiently exhausted, the atmospheric pressure upon the water in the well causes the water to rise therefrom through the suction pipe and the valve V, into the chamber between the piston and the valves. When the piston next descends it presses on the surface of the water, and the valve V closing prevents the return of the water into the suction pipe, while the pressure of the piston being transmitted by the water to the valve V', opens it, and as the piston descends, the water passes into the force pipe GH. On the next ascent of the piston more water is allowed to pass through the valve V, and the next descent forces this water through the valve V' into the force pipe. By repeating the action the quantity of water in the force pipe increases, receiving equal additions at each descent of the piston. It is obvious that the position of the force pipe is a matter of no moment; it may be perpendicular, oblique, or horizontal; for in each case the water will be propelled through it. When the piston is pressed downwards, and the valve V' is opened, it is necessary that the force working the piston should balance the weight of the column of water in the force pipe, for this weight is transmitted by the water between the piston and force pipe to the bottom of the piston; the height, therefore, of the column of water in the force pipe will measure the intensity of the pressure against the base of the piston when the valve V' is open. A column of water suspended 34 feet in height in the force pipe will press on the base of the piston with a force of about 15 pounds for each square inch; and the pressure at other heights will be proportional to this. Thus the force necessary to urge the piston downwards may always be calculated. The valve V' is closed in drawing up the piston, and it then relieves the piston from the weight of the incumbent column. If the valve V is opened, the piston is subject to the same pressure as in the suction pump, and this has already been seen to be equal to the weight of a column of water raised above the level of the water in the well. From this it follows, that when the height of the force pipe is equal to the length of the suction pipe, the piston will be pressed upwards and downwards with equal forces; but when the height of the force pipe is greater or less than the length of the suction pipe, the downward pressure must be greater or less, in the same proportion, than the force which draws the piston up.

2223. The supply of water by the force pipe through the valve V' is evidently intermitting, being suspended during the ascent of the piston; hence the flow from the point of discharge will be subject to the same intermission if means be not taken to counteract such effect. A cistern at the top of the force pipe, as already shown, for the suction pump, would answer the purpose; but it is found more convenient to use an apparatus called an *air vessel* (see *fig.* 807.), in which immediately above the valve V' a short tube communicates with a strong close vessel of sufficient capacity, through the top whereof the force pipe GH passes, and descends to near the bottom. When the pump is in action the water is forced into the vessel MN, and when its surface, as at *ww*, rises above the mouth H of the force pipe, the air in the vessel MN is confined above the water; and as the water is gradually forced in, the air, being compressed, acts with increased elastic force on the surface of the water. This pressure forces a column of water into the pipe HG, and maintains it at an elevation proportional to the elastic force of the condensed air. When the air in the vessel MN is reduced to half its original bulk it will act on the surface of the water *ww* with double the atmospheric pressure; meanwhile, the water in the force pipe being subject to merely once the atmospheric pressure, there is an unresisted force upwards equal to the atmospheric pressure which sustains the column of water in the tube, and a column 34 feet high will thus be sustained. If the air is reduced to one third of its original bulk, the height of the column sustained will be 68 feet, and so on. If the force pipe were made to terminate in a ball pierced with small holes so as to form a *jet d'eau*, the elastic pressure of the air on the surface would cause the water to spout from the holes.

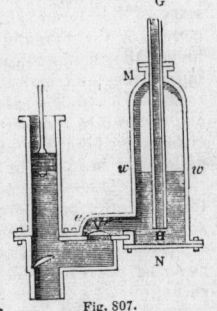

Fig. 807.

2223a. In the formation of all pumps the parts should be nicely fitted, and as air-tight as possible, otherwise, in using them, much of the power employed will be lost. All expedients which tend to this great desideratum are of value; indeed, any arrangement adapted to insure the perfect action of a pump is of the utmost importance for the comfort and convenience of small, no less than large, dwellings. The joint CD, *figs.* 805 and 806, is especially liable to leak if not well fitted. The variety of pumps now made is very great, although they are all formed on the principles first explained. The architect had best select the manufacturer, and learn of him the make and powers of his articles. Among

these inventions are : Pumping apparatus for public thoroughfares with cast iron cased well-engine frames, with fly wheel and with one or two handles; pillar well-engine frame and single or double cranks; the same with wheel and pinion to decrease labour; rotary action, fixed on plank; horse wheel frame, for horse power, and others applied to steam power; pumps for artesian wells; lift-pump; vibrating standard lift-pump; and rotary action lift-pump, all on planks; &c.

2223b. Another mode of obtaining a supply of water is by the *hydraulic ram*. It is more available in the country on account of the noise caused by the continual clicking of the valve. It is a simple self-acting machine for raising water into a cistern or tank where a fall of water can be secured from a stream, or other source. Once set in motion it will continue to work as long as it is supplied with water or until the wearing of the iron valve disables it. A fall of only 5 feet to the ram will enable it to supply a tank 60 feet higher than the source and 2,000 yards distant. Much of our present information on the subject of supply of water was known to the Romans, and is carefully described by Vitruvius in Book VIII. of his work.

2223c. Having obtained the source of a water-supply, a *tank* for a collection for a farm, or a *cistern* for the supply of a house, are requisite. The former may also be required to retain the rain water from the wood, lead, or zinc gutters of the buildings; water from copper gutters is poisonous. The *tank* is usually formed of brick or stone built in cement, and cemented inside, and when of a small size it is domed over, with a man-hole for access. If of large size, iron girders supporting slate or stone slabs will form a flat covering to it. These should be well jointed to prevent dirt falling in. Painting the cement with a solution of silicate of potash, is said to prevent the soft rain water becoming hard in a new tank. Such a system as the following would be found very serviceable on many farms having clay lands.

2223d. In Venice, the rain water is collected from the roofs and led into the court-yard, where it undergoes a regular system of filtration before it reaches the tank, whence it is raised by buckets. The construction to effect this consists of—I. A water-tight enclosure, II. A well of dry brickwork in the centre of, III. A wall of sand, filling up the remainder of the enclosure round the well, and serving partially as a reservoir, and partially as a filter; care being taken that no water enters the well but what passes through the sand. The system is shown in the *Allgemeine Bauzeitung* for 1836, pl. 556; and in the *Transactions* of the Institute of British Architects, 1842, p. 187.

2223e. Another and more simple method is described in the *Building News*, 1862, p. 127. A large hole is dug about 9 feet deep; the sides are supported by an oaken framework of a square truncated pyramid, the wide base being turned upward. A coating of compact clay, 1 foot thick, is applied on the frame with great care to stop the progress of the roots of plants, as also to prevent the pressure of the water. A large circular stone, partly hollowed out like the bottom of a kettle, is placed therein with the cavity upwards, and on this as a foundation a cylinder of well baked bricks is constructed having no intersectices except a number of holes in the bottom row. The large vacant space left between the sides of the pyramid and the cylinder is filled with well scoured sea sand. At the four corners of the pyramid a stone trough is placed covered with a stone lid pierced with holes; they communicate with each other by means of a small channel made of bricks resting on the sand, and the whole is then paved over. The rain water is led from the roof to these four sink stones, and penetrating into the sand through the channels, filters down and passes into the filter itself by the small hole left in the bottom row of bricks. These cisterns get filled five times a year, and the distribution of water is at the rate of about 312 gallons per head. The annual average rainfall is 31 inches.

2223f. The *cistern* for a house was originally placed outside, and made entirely of lead, the front of it being frequently decorated with devices, either cast with it, or secured by *paleing*, i.e., the soldering on of embossed figures. Lead cisterns are still in use, but they are cased with wood, and placed where most wanted for the supply. They should never be put where the sun can act upon them, as vegetation in the water sometimes ensues.

2223g. Such a cistern is usually made of 2 inch memel fir, lined with 6 lb. lead. A cover should always be provided. This metal lining is now much superseded by one of zinc, on account of the deleterious effects arising by the action of pure water on the lead; but zinc can only be trusted as a temporary resource. Slate is a better material for all collections of water or other liquids in general use. Care must be taken that a porous quality be not supplied; and it should not be placed where mild damp air will meet and condense on its cold surface, and consequently run down in drops. As it is so unyielding to the expansion of ice, its position in the house in that respect is an important consideration, and in case the joints become leaky from that or any other cause. Cisterns are supplied with water by a main service or feed pipe sufficiently large to allow of its filling during the time the water is turned on. The flow of water is regulated by a *ball cock*. The cistern to supply a water-closet should properly be distinct from that for domestic purposes; and when it is placed in a confined spot, necessitating smallness of dimensions, one of an

upright form is essential to provide the head of water for flushing the basin. *Fig.* 807a. shows an apparatus fitted to a lead cistern for supplying water to the pan.   A, the ball valve pulled down by the wire B, and thus lifting by the wire C, the valve D, which admits the water into the lead service-box E, soldered into the bottom, F, of the cistern.   The air-pipe G lets out the air from the box forced into it by the pressure of the water rushing through the down pipe, H.   A waste pipe for emptying the cistern, or for carrying off the surplus water when being over filled, must always be provided.   When a cistern supplies the house, a service pipe is required from it, the outlet having a *rose.*   For a slate cistern, a brass flange, (*fig.* 807b.) fitted with screws and nuts, is soldered to the lead service-box, and then secured to the slate.   A "round closet valve with union fly-nut," and air-pipe (*fig.* 807c.) is occasionally used in lieu of the above contrivances; or a spindle valve with union, fly-nut and air pipe.

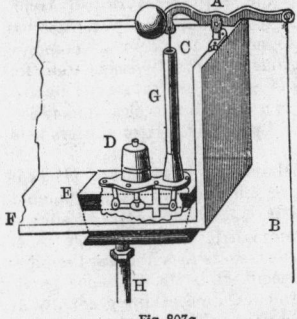

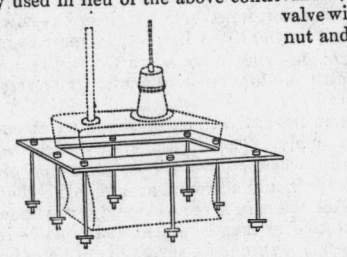

Fig. 807a.   Fig, 807b.   Fig. 807c.

2223h. Wrought iron tanks and cisterns made of plate iron riveted, plain or galvanized, are made to any shape or size; as also of a small size in stoneware.   With the constant supply system now being introduced in many towns, service cisterns are said to be unnecessary; but it will be well to form one near any office requiring a good supply of water, as the house is occasionally cut off for a day or two from the mains, during repairs or cleaning. In some towns, the company insist upon a small cistern being placed in each water-closet, to prevent waste of water.   The main service pipes may be of smaller bore than for the intermittent supply.

2223i. One cube foot of cistern will hold nearly $6\frac{1}{4}$ gallons of water; and a cube foot of water weighs 62·321 lbs.; a gallon weighs 10 lbs.; a cylinder inch, ·02842 lbs.; and a cylinder foot, 49·1 lbs.   The supply for each man, woman, and child in a house is reckoned at 15 gallons per day, though it is considered no one really uses much more than 6 gallons; or about 12 gallons, as calculated by Sir W. Clay, by a family in London.   An imperial gallon per man per day, appears to be the allowance on board a vessel.   In stables, each horse should be provided with 16 gallons, four of which is consumed with his food.   Each four-wheeled carriage takes about 16 gallons.   Each two-wheeled carriage about 9 gallons. To wash a paved court or passage, a gallon of water may be provided for each superficial yard.   The supply of water to London has been calculated at from 30 to 40 gallons per head, or about 150 gallons per house per day, for all purposes.   The available rainfall from roofs in England is estimated at 18 inches per annum; and if the source of supply be only rainfall, a tank capable of holding 4 months' collection should be provided.   (Hurst, *Surveyors' Handbook.*)

2223k. Filters are used for purifying water for towns, or purposes for which large quantities are required.   They are usually formed in England of several layers of sand and gravel, gradually increasing in the volume of its particles in descending; and in the lowest course of gravel, perforated tiles are laid, through which the water flows into the reservoirs. The water is supplied on the top, so as to stand at a depth of from 4 to 6 feet over the sand and other filtering media.   At the Lambeth Water Works, these media consist of: I. A layer of sand 3 feet thick; II. A layer of clean sea-shells 6 inches thick; III. Fine gravel 6 inches thick; IV. Coarser gravel 6 inches thick; V. Very coarse screened and washed ballast 6 inches thick; and VI. Pierced tiles covering the drains.   At the Southwark Water Works the filtering media are rather thicker.   At Hull the sand is 2 feet thick, and the gravel 16 inches thick.   At York the sand is 4 feet thick, and the gravel 4 feet thick.   At Paisley the sand is 2 feet thick, and the gravel only 6 inches; but the upper part of the sand is mixed with animal charcoal.   Local conditions must regulate the proportion of these materials, for the thickness of the sand must be increased according to the impurity of the water.   When the water is at all turbid, it is advisable to make settling reservoirs by the side of the filtering basins, to collect the impurities.   The usual yield of filtered water from a basin established under the preceding conditions, is about 80 to 100 gallons per foot superficial per day.

2223l. In some places both the chemical and mechanical impurities may be eliminated from water by dividing the tank by a cross wall of a filtering stone.   Such a stone will

filter about 60 gallons per foot superficial per day. Chemically, this could be effected by causing the water to pass through a diaphragm or cross wall, composed of two slabs of filtering stone, placed at a small distance from one another, and filled in with animal charcoal or with magnetic oxide of iron. The latter material appears to be the best for such water as is collected from roofs, because it parts with its oxygen with great rapidity to the rain water, and is susceptible of rapid revivification; it is also cheaper than charcoal. A double wall thus formed ought to pass 100 gallons per foot superficial per day. Ransome's patent siliceous stone is the best material of the kind ordinarily obtainable in England. Filters of porous sandstone, as made at Halifax, are recommended as effective and durable. A paper on the subject of filtration, read at the Institute of British Architects, 1850–51, by Mr. G. R. Burnell, and given in the *Builder*, ix. 404, deserves attention. Household filters, whether for occasional use or for a system of domestic filtration of water as it flows from the cistern, is now a serious subject of consideration for each tenant and landlord. A few drops of permanganate of potass, put into water tasting and smelling of decaying organic matter, will render it in a few minutes clear and sweet. A small quantity of alum tends to render water very pure, by freeing it from matters held in suspension.

2223m. From the cisterns *pipes* are required to convey the water to the several places it is destined to supply. Those of lead are either cast round, or soldered. In casting, a mould is made of brass, wherein down the middle a core of iron is loosely supported, at such a distance from the mould all round as is equal to the contemplated thickness of the pipe. When this is set, the core is removed and the cylinder opened, so as to withdraw the pipe, which is much thicker than is needed, and must be lengthened, while its substance is reduced, by *drawing* it through a succession of holes in steel plates, diminishing gradually in diameter, similarly to the method employed in drawing iron rods. This machinery became gradually improved in its construction, so that it was of rare occurrence to meet with an imperfect pipe. Lately, the manufacture of lead pipes has been further improved by casting them under hydraulic power. A quantity of lead is placed in a box, and forced through the mould at a certain rate, which gives the metal time to cool, so that it is pressed out gradually in a complete state, and wound round a wheel ready for use, its length being made within the limits of carriage. When pipes are made by soldering, a core of wood is provided, round which the sheet lead is rolled, and the edges are brought together and joined with *solder*.

2223n. The *pipes* used for the purposes of building are proportioned to their uses. Those, for instance, called *soil pipes*, for carrying away the soil from a water closet; or those for conveying water from roofs, called *water pipes*; and from sinks, are, of course, of larger diameter than those called *service pipes*, which are merely, as their name implies, for laying on water to a house, those of somewhat larger diameter being called *main service pipes*.

Table I. of the Weight of Lead Pipes per Foot Lineal, as now usually Made.

| Bore in Inches. | Thickness of metal in parts of an inch. | | | | | [Hurst. |
	$\frac{1}{16}$	$\frac{1}{8}$	$\frac{3}{16}$	$\frac{1}{4}$	$\frac{5}{16}$	$\frac{3}{8}$
$\frac{3}{16}$ lbs.	·243	·607	1·092	1·699	2·427	3·277
$\frac{1}{4}$,,	·303	·728	1·273	1·942	2·730	3 641
$\frac{5}{16}$,,	·364	·850	1·456	2·184	3·034	4·004
$\frac{3}{8}$,,	·425	·971	1·638	2·427	3·337	4 369
$\frac{7}{16}$,,	·485	1·092	1·820	2·670	3·640	4·733
$\frac{1}{2}$,,	·546	1·214	2·013	2·913	3·944	5·097
$\frac{9}{16}$,,	·607	1·335	2·184	3·155	4·248	5·460
$\frac{5}{8}$,,	·667	1·520	2·366	3·398	4·551	5·825
$\frac{11}{16}$,,	·728	1·578	2·548	3·641	4·853	6·189
$\frac{3}{4}$,,	·789	1·699	2·731	3·873	5·157	6·553
$\frac{13}{16}$,,	·851	1·820	2·913	4·126	5·461	6·917
$\frac{7}{8}$,,	·910	1·942	3·095	4·368	5·764	7·281
$\frac{15}{16}$,,	·971	2·063	3·276	4·611	6·067	7 646
1 ,,	1·032	2·184	3·457	4·854	6·371	8·009
$1\frac{1}{4}$,,	1·274	2·670	4·186	5·825	7·585	9·466
$1\frac{1}{2}$,,	1·517	3·155	4·915	6·796	8·796	10·923
$1\frac{3}{4}$,,	1·760	3·641	5·642	7·768	10·013	12·375
2 ,,	2·001	4·127	6·372	8·734	11·223	13·833
$2\frac{1}{4}$,,	2·245	4·607	7·096	9·707	12·436	15·290
$2\frac{1}{2}$,,	2·489	5·100	7·829	10·683	13·654	16·762
$2\frac{3}{4}$,,	2·729	5·583	8·554	11·650	14·869	16·762
3 ,,	2·971	6·066	9·286	12·492	16·080	19·660

TABLE II. OF THE WEIGHT OF LEAD PIPES IN THEIR LENGTHS, AS VARIOUSLY CAST.

Bore in Inches.	Length in Feet.	Weight of length in pounds of various makers.										
		Common. Per foot.			Middling. Per foot.				Strong. Per foot.			
$\frac{1}{2}$	15	15	16	1·07	17		22	0	22		26	0
$\frac{5}{8}$	15	17	-	-	20		-	-	24			
$\frac{3}{4}$	15	24	24	1·6	28	27	28	1·8	32	36	30	2·0
1	15	30	30	2·0	42		40	2·6	50	46	42	2·8
$1\frac{1}{4}$	12	36	36	3·0	42		44	3·7	52		53	4·4
$1\frac{1}{2}$	12	48	48	4·0	56		56	4·7	64	70	66	5·6
$1\frac{3}{4}$	12	76	-	-	84		-	-	96			
2	10	50	56	5·0			70	6·0			83	7·0
$2\frac{1}{2}$	10	-	70	7·0			86	8·6			100	10·0

2223o. *Solder* is a mixture of two parts of lead with one part of tin. In soldering, portions of the lead must first be scraped, and when finished they are then done over with a black paint. This solder is used also for tin plates and zinc work.

2223p. *Earthenware pipes*, like iron mains, are employed underground. At the beginning of this century, machinery was invented for forming *stone* pipes, which were used for some time, but did not supersede those in use formed of timber. Near Lincoln have been found circular earthenware tiles, 6 inches diameter and 22 inches long, set in a thick casing of cement, so as to exclude air entirely, and to strengthen and protect the piping, which conveyed the water for about a mile and a half. It is always necessary to have some outlets for letting off the air which accumulates in any length of such tubing. When water is first allowed to enter a long length of new piping, a quantity of very fine sand or dust should be put into it to fill up any cracks or spaces left in the joints. This is also recommended to be done for new iron boilers, iron water tanks, &c., as it tends to make the joints watertight. A well made stoneware pipe of 4 inches diameter will bear a pressure of from 75 to 100 lbs. per square inch.

2223q. *Iron water pipes* for the service of a house are objectionable in case of their bursting in winter, but this is remedied by placing a stop-cock at the entrance of the pipe into a house, to shut off the supply for repairs, or in anticipation of a frost. Some wrought iron pipes are lined and coated with hydraulic mortar; others are *enamelled* in the interior. These latter have been found, both for gas and water purposes, absolutely incorrodible; in the former case preventing the great loss from leakage, and in the latter case conveying the water in perfect purity. For a high service hot water supply, a galvanized wrought iron hot water cistern, with main hole screwed down, is supplied. It is usually 2 feet 6 inches long, 2 feet wide, and 18 inches deep. Cast iron pipes are naturally very porous; so much so, that water when very forcibly compressed as in an hydraulic machine, will make its way through the thick cast iron cylinder in a sort of perspiration on the external surface. Oxidation, to a certain extent, will close the pores of the metal, and prevent this escape of water or of gas; and it is recommended that all new gas pipes be proved with a solution of sal ammoniac, which being forced into the body of the metal effectually oxidizes it, and to a great extent cures the evil. Patent welded wrought iron tubes and fittings, and malleable iron fittings, are made for gas, or low pressure steam, and cast iron pipes for water, of from $\frac{1}{8}$ to 4-inch bores; such pipes are also made for high pressure steam or water, and proved to a pressure of 200 lbs. per square inch. The ordinary gas pipe is proved to 75 lbs. on the square inch.

2223r. *Gutta Percha.* On account of the injurious effects of water on lead cisterns and piping, this material has been recommended as a substitute for it in both cases, since its general introduction about 1849. But it is uncertain whether the material can be guaranteed as a lining; and some soils appear to affect it when buried underground. It is also attacked by a fungus. Experiments made at the Birmingham Water Works, on the strength of gutta percha, showed, that tubes made $\frac{3}{4}$ inch diameter and $\frac{1}{8}$ inch thick, attached to the iron main, and subjected for two months to a pressure of 200 feet head of water, were not in the slightest degree deteriorated. They were afterwards subjected to a proof of 337 lbs. per square inch. The material being slightly elastic, the tubes expanded, but recovered their former size on the pressure being withdrawn. At Stirling, $1\frac{1}{2}$ inch tubing bore a pressure of about 450 feet, without the slightest injury, whilst the same pressure upon strong leather hose scattered the rivets in all directions.

2223s. Pipes to cisterns are supplied with ball cocks and valves, both round way and square way, of various forms and sizes, too numerous to be here described. For sinks, or the usual supply taps, bib-cocks having a " T key" or a "spanner" or other key, are required; these are of different makes, and produce a recoil. "Screw-down" or "valves"

are used where the high pressure system is adopted, the "T key" then screws down the valve. A "stop-cock" or "valve" shuts off the water in a length of pipe, and is serviceable in shutting off the service from the main pipes, as above noticed, and for reducing the pressure of the water on the "screw-down" valves in a constant service. This system is described in Cresy, *Encyclopædia*, pages 1655–57.

2223*t*. *Lavatories* are fitted up with an apparatus for supplying the basin with hot and cold, and for taking off the waste, waters. *Baths* are supplied from a boiler either placed at the back of a kitchen range, or set in the fireplace of the bath room, or of an adjoining chamber. They are also heated by a gas boiler adjoining the bath, having a flow and return pipe; or by ranges of lights under the bath itself. A five-feet bath is said to be heated to 100° in half-an-hour by gas, at a small cost. A bath generally contains about 60 gallons of water, and requires about 20 gallons of boiling water to heat it.

2223*u*. The bath itself is sometimes formed of marble, cast iron enamelled, opalized glass, glazed earthenware, and glazed porcelain tiles (Rufford's), the weight of which is 7 cwt.; while zinc, lead, copper, galvanized iron, and slate (par. 2211*p*.) all require a coating of light coloured paint, so as to render easily apparent any want of purity of the water. If not painted, all metal baths require considerable friction to appear clean. The difficulty of making a bath with joints that shall not leak is self-evident. Tylor's pattern-book gives several descriptions of their baths (par. 2288*a*).

2223*v*. With water raised to a high level great power is gained for various purposes, domestic and otherwise. The *hydraulic lift*, lately introduced into banks and hotels, is the saving of much trouble and time. The general details for hotels have been described by J. Whichcord, in a paper read at the Institute of British Architects, 18th January, 1864, and given in the *Transactions*. A small lift, to be worked by hand, is readily arranged for raising a scuttle of coals, or other package, from the bottom to the top of a building. Water applied to a turbine is capable of producing a small motive power, useful for organ blowing, turning a fan to effect ventilation, and other such purposes, without wasting the water so employed.

2223*w*. It will be useful to note the *non-compressibility of water*. It is often necessary, before re-melting cast iron, to reduce the large masses into smaller pieces. This by the ordinary method is both troublesome and difficult. A simple and ingenious mode of producing the required fracture has been recently employed in France. It consists in drilling a hole in the mass of cast iron for about one-third of its thickness, and filling the hole with water, then closing it with a steel plug, fitting very accurately, and letting the ram of a pile-driver fall on the plug. The first blow separates the cast iron into two pieces.

COPPER.

2224. Many of the uses to which copper is put have already been noticed in the paragraphs 1787 to 1791. The nave of Chartres Cathedral was roofed in 1836–41 with iron ribs covered with copper plates; in 1853 the latter had so much oxidised as to require removal. It is said that if strips of the best zinc, about 8 inches by 2 inches, be screwed on each course of copper, galvanic action would prevent the oxidation of the latter material. Iron cramps encased and brazed in copper, or gun metal cramps, in lieu of iron merely, the exfoliation of which bursts and demolishes stonework, is a precaution now generally adopted in good work. In the Indies, copper gutters decay after twenty years' use, not lasting longer than shingles; the heat and moisture of the climate converting the metal into red oxide of copper: iron nails decay there very fast from the same cause.

2224*a*.   TABLE I. OF THICKNESS OF COPPER SHEETS.

Number of wire gauge Weight of one foot super. in pounds	1 14·5	2 13·9	3 12·75	4 11·6	5 10·1	6 9·4	7 8·7	8 7·9	9 7·2	10 6·5
Number of wire gauge Weight of one foot super. in pounds	11 5·8	12 5·08	13 4·34	14 3·6	15 3·27	16 2·9	17 2·52	18 2·15	19 1·97	20 1·78
Number of wire gauge Weight of one foot super. in pounds	21 1·62	22 1·45	23 1·3	24 1·16	25 1·04	26 0·92	27 0·83	28 0·74	29 0·64	30 0·55 Hurst.

No. 1 is equal to $\frac{5}{16}$ths of an inch thick; No. $4=\frac{1}{4}$; No. $7=\frac{3}{16}$; No. $11=\frac{1}{8}$; No. $16=\frac{1}{16}$; and No. $22=\frac{1}{32}$; Nos. 22 to 28, or 18 to 12 ounces per foot superficial were used formerly

for gutters. As the plates of copper are made of an uniform size, 4 feet long by 2 feet wide, the weight determines the thickness; thus, 70 lb. plates are $\frac{3}{16}$ths thick; 46½ lbs.= $\frac{1}{8}$; 23 lbs.= $\frac{1}{16}$; 11¼ lbs.= $\frac{1}{32}$; 6 lbs. = $\frac{1}{64}$th of an inch.

2224b. TABLE II. OF THE WEIGHT OF A LINEAL FOOT OF ROUND AND SQUARE COPPER, IN POUNDS.

Inches -	$\frac{1}{4}$	$\frac{3}{8}$	$\frac{1}{2}$	$\frac{5}{8}$	$\frac{3}{4}$	$\frac{7}{8}$	1	$1\frac{1}{8}$	$1\frac{1}{4}$	$1\frac{3}{8}$	$1\frac{1}{2}$	$1\frac{5}{8}$
Square -	·24	·54	·96	1·50	2·16	2·94	3·84	4·86	6·00	7·27	8·65	10·15
Round -	·188	·424	·755	1·17	1·69	2·31	3·02	3·82	4·71	5·71	6·79	7·94

Inches -	$1\frac{3}{4}$	$1\frac{7}{8}$	2	$2\frac{1}{8}$	$2\frac{1}{4}$	$2\frac{3}{8}$	$2\frac{1}{2}$	$2\frac{5}{8}$	$2\frac{3}{4}$	$2\frac{7}{8}$	3	
Square -	11·77	13·52	15·38	17·36	19·47	21·69	24·03	26·50	29·08	31·79	34·61	
Round -	9·21	10·61	12·08	13·64	15·29	17·03	18·87	20·81	22·84	24·92	27·18	

The table given in Hurst's *Handbook*, is a slight increase on the above; from that Tables I. and II. have been derived.

2224c. TABLE III. OF THE WEIGHT OF COPPER, PER SUPERFICIAL FOOT, IN POUNDS.

Thickness - - -	$\frac{1}{16}$	$\frac{1}{8}$	$\frac{3}{16}$	$\frac{1}{4}$	$\frac{5}{16}$	$\frac{3}{8}$	$\frac{7}{16}$	$\frac{1}{2}$
Weight - - -	2·891	5·781	8·672	11·563	14·453	17·344	20·234	23·125
Thickness - - -	$\frac{9}{16}$	$\frac{5}{8}$	$\frac{11}{16}$	$\frac{3}{4}$	$\frac{13}{16}$	$\frac{7}{8}$	$\frac{15}{16}$	1
Weight - - -	26·016	28·906	31·797	34·688	37·578	40·469	43·359	46·250

2224d. Solder for copper, iron, and brass, is composed of an alloy of zinc and copper; pewter, for an alloy of tin, lead, and bismuth.

2224e. *Wetterstedt's patent metal* should be laid by a good plumber. The flats are formed with rolls and drips similar in every respect to lead, but the latter should be formed with a gradual descent. The rolls need not be more than 1 to 1¼ inch diameter, tapered at the ends, and brought close up to the edge of the drip. Circular and sloping roofs may be laid either with rolls or welts, the ends of the sheets being joined by a welt or overlap of 6 inches. The metal should be laid free, and nails avoided as much as possible, but if used they should be of wrought copper. Soldering is to be avoided, but to secure the metal as against an upright face, a solder dot over a screw is the best means to adopt.

2224f. *Muntz's metal* is used as a coating for iron vessels under water; to prevent galvanic action a band of vitreous sheathing is attached for some distance below and above the water line. This sheathing consists of small plates of iron covered with a preparation of glass, and is intended to be an anti-fouling as well as a protective agent.

ZINC.

2224g. The common sheets in general use are 12, 14, 16, 18, and 20 ounces to the foot superficial; and as 18 thicknesses of 16 ounces to the foot are half an inch thick, the following show the thicknesses of the different weights:—

Plates or sheets of 10 ounces to the foot are 0·01736 inch thick.

12	—	0·02083 „
14	—	0·02430 „
16	—	0·02777 „ = $\frac{1}{36}$ of an inch.
18	—	0·03125 „
20	—	0·03472 „

It is employed for water-cisterns and baths, rain-water pipes—in short, for almost all purposes where lead has been hitherto employed. Latterly it has been formed into sash-bars for skylights and ornamental sashes; for which purposes, strength excepted, it is superior to iron, as not being liable to rust, and loosen the putty and glass. It is, in every respect, equal to copper, and not more than one-third the cost of it. The discovery of the electro process was said to have introduced the application of zinc to cast and wrought iron, so as to prevent its oxidation or rust, but such has not been the case (see galvanized and zinked IRON).

2224*h.* About 1861, the Vieille Montagne Zinc Mining Company took steps to improve the mode of laying zinc roofs, and to prevent the use of thin gauges of sheet zinc, which are unfit for the purpose. This Company recommend that for roofs and flats on boards no gauge thinner than No. 13 be used : a medium thickness, No. 14, for roofs, flats, and gutters; for best work and for roofs without boards, Nos. 15 or 16. The Company is preparing thicker zinc, Nos. 17 and 18, principally for gutters. Steel cut gauges notched for roofing numbers only, are supplied whereby to test the thickness. The weight of No. 13 gauge is 19 oz. 10 drs. ; No. 14 is 21 oz. 13 drs ; No. 15 is 24 oz. ; and No. 16 is 26 oz. 3 drs., per square foot.

2224*i.* Good zinc, properly laid, has been proved by long experience in France, Belgium, Germany, and Italy, to be a secure, durable, and economical covering. No detrimental effects from any particular climate are to be feared, so that care be taken to adopt the proper mode of laying, and to select the proper gauges, of the best quality of zinc. Even good zinc badly laid will prove a failure. Screws or embossed holes on the surface of good zinc work are not required. As the prescribed mode for laying zinc, illustrated by diagrams, can be obtained on application to the agents of Devaux's Vieille Montagne Zinc Company, and to the agents for the supply of the Improved roofing zinc, we do not consider it necessary to describe it here in detail.

2224*k. Stamped ornamental zinc,* for dormers, Mansard roofs, vanes, finials, moulding, and enrichments, has been used on the Continent for many years with good effect. In London it is hardly known, but has been employed lately at the Charing Cross Hotel; at the Langham Hotel; and at No. 114 Piccadilly. The steeple of Ripple Church, Kent; the Victoria Railway Station, Pimlico; and many other public and private buildings throughout the kingdom, now show the employment of this useful material.

2224*l. Perforated zinc* for various sizes of perforations or in patterns, is extensively employed in filling up squares in sashes, or panels in partitions, to assist ventilation by breaking the force of the current of air.

BRASS.

2224*m.* Table of the Weight of a superficial Foot of a Plate of Brass, in Pounds.

(Molesworth, *Formulæ.*)

Thickness, parts of an inch	$\frac{1}{16}$	$\frac{1}{8}$	$\frac{3}{16}$	$\frac{1}{4}$	$\frac{5}{16}$	$\frac{3}{8}$	$\frac{7}{16}$	$\frac{1}{2}$	$\frac{9}{16}$	$\frac{5}{8}$	$\frac{11}{16}$	$\frac{3}{4}$	$\frac{13}{16}$	$\frac{7}{8}$	$\frac{15}{16}$	1
Weight in pounds	2·7	5·5	8·2	11	13·7	16·4	19·2	21·9	24 6	27·4	30·1	32·9	35·6	38·3	41·2	43·9

Sect. VIII.

GLAZING.

2225. Glazing, or the business of the glazier, consists in fitting glass in sashes, frames, and casements, either in putty or lead. It may be classed under the heads of sashwork, leadwork, and fretwork. Glass, as a material, has been already described in Chap. II. Sect. XII. of this Book.

2226. The tools necessary for sashwork are—a *diamond,* polished to a cutting point, and set in brass in an iron socket, to receive a wooden handle, by which it is held in a cutting direction. The top of the handle goes between the root of the forefinger and middle finger, and the under part between the point of the forefinger and thumb. In general, there is a notch on the side of the socket, which should be held next the lath. Some diamonds have more *cuts* than one. Plough diamonds have a square nut on the end of the socket next the glass, which, on running the nut square on the side of the lath, keeps it in the cutting direction. Glass benders have their plough diamonds without long handles, as they cannot make use of a lath in cutting, but direct them by the point of their middle finger. The *ranging lath* should be long enough to extend beyond the boundary of the table of glass. *Ranging* of glass is the cutting it in breadths, and is best done by one uninterrupted cut from one end to the other. A *short lath* is used for stripping the square to suit the rebate of the sash, as in ranging they are generally cut full. A *square,* for the more accurate cutting at the right angles from the range. The carpenter's *chisel* is used in paring away some of the rebate of the sash when the glass does not lie so flat as to allow a proper breadth for front putty. The *glazing knife* is used for laying in the putty on the rebates, for bedding in the glass, and finishing the front putty. A *bradding hammer* is made with a head in the form of a small parallelopiped, with a socket for the handle, using it at an obtuse angle from the middle of one of its sides. The square edges of the head drive

the brads in a horizontal direction, and with this tool there is less liability to accident than with any other. Some use the basil of the chisel for the purpose. *Brass points* are considered the best for bradding; *small cut brads* are also used. All new work should be bradded, to prevent the glass being moved out of its bed. The *duster* is a large brush for brushing the putties, and taking the oil from the glass. The *sash tool* is used wet, for taking the oil from the inside after the back putties are cleared off. The *hacking knife* is for cleaning out the old putty from the rebates where squares are to be stopped in. The use of the *glazier's rule* needs no explanation : it is 2 feet long, doubling in four different pieces.

2226a. The *putty* in which the glazier beds the glass is of four sorts. *Soft putty*, which is composed of flour, whiting, and raw linseed oil; *hard putty*, composed of whiting and boiled linseed oil ; *harder putty*, the same ingredients as the last, with the addition of a small quantity of turpentine for more quickly drying it ; *hardest putty*, composed of oil, red or white lead, and sand. The first of these putties is the most durable, because it forms an oleaginous coat on the surface, but it requires a long time for drying. The hard sorts are apt to crack if not soon well painted, and the hardest of them renders it difficult to replace a pane when broken ; hence it is altogether unfit for hothouse and greenhouse work. (See 2227a.).

2226b. To remove glass from old sashes, a mixture of 3 parts of American potash with 1 part of unslaked lime, laid on both sides with a stick, and allowed to remain for twenty-four hours, will soften the putty enough to cut out easily. This mixture will also take off paint, and even tar.

2227. Leadwork for fixed lights is used in ecclesiastical buildings, often in inferior offices, and frequently in country buildings. Frames made with crossbars receive these lights, which are fastened to *saddle bars*. Where openings are wanted, a casement is introduced of wood or iron. Sometimes a sliding frame is used, particularly for house windows.

2227a. Probably the best manner of fixing glass and glazed frames in stone mullions, is with a mixture of Bath stone dust and linseed oil, made up similarly to putty. Its elasticity allows of any slight settlement if the work be new, and it is more of a waterproof cement than Portland, as it is not nearly so liable to crack : that cement, without a large proportion of sand, will almost invariably burst glass or stone after a few months ; and it also stains freestones, Corsham Down stone especially, giving it the appearance of having been burnt. (*Builder*, 1864, p. 796.)

2228. The *glazier's vice* is for preparing the leaden slips called *cames* with grooves, &c., to fit them for the reception of glass. The German vices are the best, and turn out a variety of lead in different sizes. There are *moulds* belonging to these vices in which bars of lead are cast ; in this form the mill receives them, and turns them out with two sides parallel to each other, and about $\frac{3}{8}$ of an inch broad, and a partition connecting the two sides together, about $\frac{1}{8}$ of an inch wide, forming on each side a groove near $\frac{3}{16}$ by $\frac{1}{8}$ of an inch, and 6 feet long. The *setting board* is that on which the ridge of the light is worked, and divided into squares, and struck out with a chalk line, or drawn with a lath, which serve to guide the workman. One side and end is squared with a projecting bead or fillet. The *latterkin* is a piece of hard wood pointed, and so formed as to clear the groove of the lead, and widen it, for the more readily receiving the glass. The *setting knife* is a blade with a round end, loaded with lead at the bottom of the blade, and having a long square handle. The square end of the handle serves to force the squares home tight in the lead ; being loaded with lead, it is of greater weight, and also cuts off the ends of the lead with greater ease, as in the course of working these lights the lead is always longer than is necessary till trimmed.

2229. The resin box contains powdered resin, which is put on all the joints previous to soldering. *Clips* are for holding the irons. All the intersections are soldered on both sides except the outside joints of the outer side, that is, where they come to the outer edge. These lights should be cemented, which is done by thin paint being run along the lead bars and the chasm filled with dry whiting. After it has stood a short time a small quantity of dry red or white lead is dusted over it, which will enable it to resist the weather well.

2229a. Fretwork is the ornamental part of lead-light work, and consists in working ground or stained glass into different patterns and devices, as may be seen in the old stained glass windows. The leads used until the middle of the seventeenth century, are nearly of one uniform width, and are much narrower in the *leaf* than the common modern leads. That this was the case, can be proved not only by the existence of the original leads themselves, but more satisfactorily perhaps by the black lines drawn upon the glass, with which the glass painters were accustomed sometimes to produce the effect of leads without unnecessarily cutting

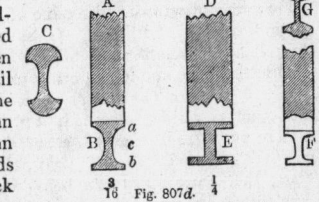

$\frac{3}{16}$ Fig. 807d. $\frac{1}{4}$

the glass. A in *fig.* 807*d.* represents an ancient lead of the usual width ; B its section, consisting of the *leaf*, *a* and *b*, and the *core c.* C is the section of a German lead of the early part of the 14th century. D is a piece of modern *fret lead* of the ordinary width, and which is now considered (1847) as being very narrow ; and E its section. The process of compressing the lead between rollers to the proper dimension makes them more rigid than the old leads. It is the practice at the present day to surround each *glazing panel* with a *broad lead*, that is, a lead three-quarters of an inch broad in the leaf, to strengthen the work (page 27.). Leads somewhat narrower than these were very extensively employed. An entire window, at Stowting Church, Kent, probably of the early part of the reign of Edward IV., was leaded with leads as F. The other lead, G, is of the early part of the reign of Henry VI., and is from Mells Church, Somersetshire, where similar lead is commonly used. This mode of strengthening the lead without increasing its width was not confined to the decorated period. Both these specimens had all the appearance of being cast in a mould. One of the faces in each is narrower than the others ; these were placed outside, and the difference probably arose from decomposition of the metal. A still narrower lead may be occasionally met with in heraldry and other minute mosaic work of the 15th and 16th centuries. It is hardly necessary to observe that the greater the number of leads employed, the weaker the work individually may they be made (page 259–61.). The width of the leads must be proportionate to that of the lines usually painted on the glass, for the leaden outlines will easily be detected if they are much stronger than the painted ones. The effect of the increased width of modern leads, E, although so trifling, is very perceptible.

2229*b. Saddle bars* in ancient windows will be found to be usually placed from 8 to 9 inches apart, which seems to be the most agreeable distance, though one of 6 inches does not appear too little in some cases. The great object is to avoid, as much as possible, causing the light to appear as if it were divided into a number of square compartments, by making the height too nearly the width of the glass. Amongst the advantages resulting from the use of saddle bars at short intervals, is the opportunity it affords the glazier of carrying a horizontal lead across the light immediately in front of each saddle bar, the opacity of which hides the lead. This method of concealing lead work was carried to such perfection during the first half of the 16th century, that a person ignorant of it would find it difficult to conceive how some of the works of that period were constructed.

2229*c. Iron standards* or *stancheons*, in ancient windows put through the saddle bars, should be retained in pattern windows, which they improve, and do not appear to be out of place in picture windows whenever they do not happen to pass immediately behind the head of the principal figure. They seem also on the whole to improve the effect of the architecture from without. (WINSTON, *Inquiry into Style in Glass Painting*, 8vo. 1847.)

2229*d.* It is stated that at Cologne Cathedral the glass is strong ; the different pieces are joined together with lead, and soldered with tin, both inside and outside, which gives the whole great strength. The panes are fastened upon iron frames, which are again fastened upon rods. In the interior the panes are screwed upon iron bars, half an inch thick, which are let into the masonry.

2230. In London a large portion of the glazier's business consists in cleaning windows.

2231. *Glazed partitions* formed of wood, or of iron frames with the lower panels filled in with slate, are now very usual in warehouses, banks, and counting-houses. If sound be desired not to pass through such fittings, they must be glazed with extra thick glass ; but double sheets or squares, placed about half an inch or more apart, and carefully puttied, is best. This method will also conduce to the warmth of the room. Double windows to the fronts of houses are common fittings to effect both the above purposes.

2231*a.* Glass has been introduced for a variety of building purposes. Thus, Lloyd and Summerfield's patent crystal *window bars*, for windows, shop fronts, and cases, are not uncommon. They are fitted with arched heads and spandrils of glass, having patterns, silvered or gilt, on a coloured ground. Glass *tiles* and *slates* are a useful auxiliary to a roof where a small modicum of light is required. Lockhead's *perforated glass ventilator* can either be set in the sash, or fixed outside of it in a frame for the whole width of the opening, air being admitted by moving the sash. For the like purpose are such inventions as Moore's louvre ventilators in a sash pane ; Boyle's draughtless window ventilators, being a fine gauze of wire set in a pane of glass, and used with or without a glass cover ; and the glass revolving ventilator. Glass *balusters* and *handrails* ; pilasters for chimney-pieces ; door handles, knobs, and plates ; mirror frames ; trays for dairies ; and cut crystal and opal letters, are among the other useful inventions in this material.

2231*b. Coloured or stained glass.* We can only here name the varieties. There are three modes of colouring glass : I. Pot metal glass, in which the colour is mixed up with the molten mass. II. Flashed, covered, or coated, glass, formed by uniting a thin layer of coloured glass with another layer, either of a different colour or colourless. III. Painted glass, the white substance being painted on, and then the colour or pigment burnt in. The colouring materials are in all cases metallic substances. Such are the methods by which all coloured glass windows are produced.

2231c. For ornamental purposes, besides *coloured* glass, glass may have a *ground* surface, which is obtained by grinding it with a stone, or by the use of fluoric acid. *Embossed glass*, which permits the application of devices, according to the fancy of the designer or intention of the manufacturer, is effected by covering the square of glass with a varnish, except where the device is intended. An acid is then poured on which eats away the uncovered glass for a small depth. The varnish is then cleaned off, and the general surface is ground as usual. Its imitation is obtained by covering the plate with a varnish, a lace or stencil pattern placed on it, then dusted over with a colouring matter in the state of fine powder, and the plate thus treated sufficiently heated to vitrify and fix the dusted varnish to the glass. Messrs. Chance, and other manufacturers, sell various enamelled stencilled patterns, as *white enamelled, enamelled and flocked, embossed repeated pattern, stained enamelled*, and *double etched glass, self shadowed glass, patent polychromatic glass, printed glass, stamped in colours*, and many other kinds, all which are better seen at the factories than described.

2231d. The compressive strength of glass, that is, its resistance to a force tending to crush it, is about 12¼ tons per square inch. This is nearly equal to one quarter the strength of cast iron. Glass has three times the specific gravity of iron. In the form of bars, a favourable shape for developing a highly tensile strength, one ton per square inch of area is the highest amount to be assumed for it.

2231e. Mosaic work. This durable manner of decoration in glass, requires a short notice. The *Roman mosaic* is composed of pieces of enamelled glass, thus rendered opaque, sometimes called *smalto* and sometimes *paste*, made of all kinds of colours and of every different hue. For large pictures they take the form of small cakes. For small works they are produced as threads, varying in thickness from that of a piece of string to the finest cotton thread. The *Venetian mosaic* pictures are formed of pieces of very irregular shapes and sizes, of all colours and tones of colours; the ground tint almost invariably prevailing is gold. The manner of execution is always large and coarse, and rarely approaches any neatness of joint or regularity of bedding. *Opus Grecanicum* consists in the insertion, into grooves cut in white marble to a depth of about half an inch, of small cubes of these coloured and gilded *smalto*, and in the arrangement of these forms in such *geometrical combination* as to compose the most elaborate patterns. It was customary to combine the bands of this mosaic work with large slabs of Serpentine, Porphyry, Pavonazzetto, and other valuable marbles, and to use it in the decoration of ambones, cancelli, &c.; its use externally was comparatively rare. The hexagon, triangle, square, and octagon, form the usual bases of most of the specimens of this ingenious art to be found in Italy. Patterns of accumulating intricacy are seen at Palermo, and at Monreale. Illustrations in colour are given in the useful work on *Mosaics*, by M. D. Wyatt.

2231f. *Coloured enamels* are made of a vitreous *paste* (or glass), to this are added other mineral substances, which, when properly prepared and fused together, impart to the paste its density and extreme hardness, and also its colour; the better the manufacture, the more satisfactory the appearance and the greater the durability of the mosaic work. In an imperfect manufacture, the mosaic is liable to be injured by damp, smoke, and all atmospheric changes; when well produced, they can be made to give precisely the same effect as the painting.

2231g. *Gold and silver enamels* were introduced: these are made of the precious metals, but in such thin sheets that their use is comparatively inexpensive. The process is a difficult one, for, to produce true gold and silver enamels, great knowledge and experience are necessary. On a ground of thick glass or enamel, according as it is desired to render the gold enamel transparent or opaque, or to impart to it a warm or variegated colour, there is laid a leaf of gold or silver, which is attached principally by the action of fire; then a film of the purest glass is spread over it, and this may either be perfectly colourless or of any tint that may be required. When well manufactured, these thin layers, after being fused, become perfectly united with each other, and form a homogeneous body, and the metal is for ever protected against all possibility of injury from any cause except actual violence.

2231h. Stevens has produced a new kind of glass mosaic, executed at about one third the price of the ancient manufacture of this kind. The glass is stained or gilt, and the method is adapted for many purposes. Messrs. Rust are working in gold, silver, and enamel mosaics of their own invention; and Dr. Salviati employs his "indestructible system of Venetian enamel-mosaic, in works, in a comparatively inexpensive and expeditious manner." At the Wolsey tomb-house, at Windsor, the entire ceiling, consisting of 2,100 feet, was decorated in the space of ten months, including the time of the transit of the mosaics from Venice; and was executed, with the scaffolding, at the price of 4,725l. It was also employed at St. Paul's Cathedral, for the figure of the prophet Isaiah, covering 250 feet, which was executed and fixed in two months, at the price of 600l. (Lecture read at Leeds, by A. Salviati, 1865.)

2231i. The cements used are of three sorts. The first, for large tesseræ in forming floors, is composed of pitch, mixed with a black earth. The second, for stones of a mid-

dling dimension, is made of tufa and oil. The third, for the more delicate mosaics of pieces of glass, is made of white of lime, pounded bricks, gum andragan, and the white of eggs. The ancients are said to have used 1 part of slaked lime and 3 parts of pounded marble, made up with water and white of egg. But as this is considered to harden too quickly, a mixture of 1 part of slaked lime, and 3 parts of powdered travertine stone, mixed up with linseed oil, and kept stirred every day, is used, adding oil as it dries. The mass is ready sooner in warm weather than in cold, varying from 20 to 30 days, when it is like a smooth ointment. For the larger works, Keene's, Portland, or other similar cements might be used.

Sect. IX.

PLASTERING.

2232. In the finishing of our dwellings, the decoration owes much of its effect to the labours of the plasterer : it is in his department to lay the ceilings, and to give, by means of plaster, a smooth coat to the walls, so as to hide the irregularities left by the bricklayer and mason, and make them sightly and agreeable. He also, in the better sort of buildings, furnishes plain and decorated mouldings for the cornices and ceilings; and in the external parts, where stone is expensive or not to be procured, covers the exterior walls with stucco or other composition imitative of stone.

2233. The plasterer's tools are—a *spade* or *shovel* of the usual description; a *rake* with two or three prongs bent downwards from the line of the handle, for mixing the hair and mortar together ; *stopping* and *picking out tools ;* rules called *straight edges ; wood models ;* and *trowels* of two sorts and various sizes, namely, the *laying and smoothing tools,* consisting of flat pieces of hardened iron, about 10 inches long, and 2½ inches wide, very thin, and ground to a semicircular shape at one end, but square at the other. Near the square end on the back of the plate a small iron rod is rivetted, with two legs, whereof one is fixed to the plate, and a round wooden handle is adapted to the other. All the first coats of plastering are laid on with this tool, as is also the last, or *setting,* as it is technically called. The other sorts of trowels are of three or more sizes, and are used for *gauging* the *fine stuff* and plaster for cornices, mouldings, &c. The length of these trowels is, the largest about 7 inches in length on the plate, and the smallest 2 or 3 inches : they are of polished steel, converging gradually to a point, with handles of mahogany adapted to the heel or broad end with a deep brass ferrule.

2234. The stopping and picking out tools are of polished steel, of various sizes, about 7 or 8 inches long and half an inch broad, flattened at both ends, and somewhat rounded. They are used for modelling and finishing mitres and returns to cornices, as also for filling up and finishing ornaments at their joinings. There is also used a small instrument, which is a piece of thin fir 6 or 7 inches square, called a *hawk,* with a handle vertical to it, for holding small quantities of plaster.

2235. The composition used by the plasterer is a groundwork of lime and hair, on which, for the finish, a coating of finer material is laid. The sorts of it are various ; as, for instance, white lime and hair mortar on bare walls ; the same on laths as for partitions and plain ceilings ; for renewing the insides of walls, roughcasting on laths ; plastering on brickwork with finishing mortar, in imitation of stone work, and the like upon laths. For cornices and the decorations of mouldings, the material is plaster of Paris, one which facilitates the giving by casts the required form and finish to the superior parts of his work. The plasterer uses it also for mixing with lime and hair, where the work is required to dry and set hard in a short time. For inside work, the lime and hair, or *coarse stuff,* is prepared, like common mortar, with sand ; but in the mixing, hair of the bullock, obtained from the tanners' yards, is added to it, and worked in with the rake, so as to distribute it over the mass as equally as possible.

2236. What is called *fine stuff* is made of pure lime, slaked with a small quantity of water, and afterwards, without the addition of any other material, saturated with water, and in a semi-fluid state placed in a tub to remain until the water has evaporated. In some cases, for better binding the work, a small quantity of hair is worked into the composition. For interior work, the fine stuff is mixed with one part of very fine washed sand to three parts of fine stuff, and is then used for *trowelled* or *bastard stucco,* which makes a proper surface for receiving painting.

2237. What is called *gauge stuff* is composed of fine stuff and plaster of Paris, in proportions according to the rapidity with which the work is wanted to be finished. About four-fifths of fine stuff to one of the last is sufficient, if time can be allowed for the setting. This composition is chiefly used for cornices and mouldings, run with a wooden mould. We may here mention that it is of the utmost importance, in plasterers' work, that the lime should be most thoroughly slaked, or the consequence will be blisters thrown out upon the work after it is finished. Many plasterers keep their stuffs a considerable

period before they are wanted to be used in the building, by which the chance of blistering is much lessened.

2238. When a wall is to be plastered, it is called *rendering;* in other cases the first operation, as in ceilings, partitions, &c., is *lathing*, nailing the laths to the joists, quarters, or battens. If the laths are oaken, wrought iron nails must be used for nailing them, but cast iron nails may be employed if the laths are of fir. The lath is made in three and four foot lengths, and, according to its thickness, is called *single*, something less than a quarter of an inch thick, *lath and half*, or *double*. The first is the thinnest and cheapest, the second is about one-third thicker than the single lath, and the double lath is twice the thickness. When the plasterer laths ceilings, both lengths of laths should be used, by which, in nailing, he will have the opportunity of breaking the joints, which will not only help in improving the general *key*, (or plastering insinuated behind the lath, which spreads there beyond the distance that the laths are apart,) but will strengthen the ceiling generally. The thinnest laths may be used in partitions, because in a vertical position the strain of the plaster upon them is not so great; but for ceilings the strongest laths should be employed. In lathing, the ends of the laths should not be lapped upon each other where they terminate upon a quarter or batten, which is often done to save a row of nails and the trouble of cutting them, for such a practice leaves only a quarter of an inch for the thickness of the plaster; and if the laths are very crooked, which is frequently the case. sufficient space will not be left to straighten the plaster.

2239. After lathing, the next operation is *laying*, more commonly called *plastering*. It is the first coat on laths, when the plaster has two coats or set work, and is not scratched with the scratcher, but the surface is roughed by sweeping it with a broom. On brickwork it is also the first coat, and is called rendering. The mere laying or rendering is the most economical sort of plastering, and does for inferior rooms or cottages.

2240. What is called *pricking up* is the first coat of three-coat work upon laths. The material used for it is coarse stuff, being only the preparation for a more perfect kind of work. After the coat is laid on, it is scored in diagonal directions with a *scratcher* (the end of a lath), to give it a key or tie for the coat that is to follow it.

2241. *Lath layed* or *plastered and set* is only two-coat work, as mentioned under laying, the setting being the guage or mixture of putty and plaster, or, in common work, of fine stuff, with which, when very dry, a little sand is used; and here it may be as well to mention, that *setting* may be either a second coat upon laying or rendering, or a third coat upon *floating*, which will be hereafter described. The term finishing is applied to the third coat when of stucco, but setting for paper. The setting is spread with the smoothing trowel, which the workman uses with his right hand, while in his left he uses a large flat-formed brush of hog's bristles. As he lays on the putty or set with the trowel, he draws the brush, full of water, backwards and forwards over its surface, thus producing a tolerably fair face for the work.

2242. Work which consists of three coats is called *floated :* it takes its name from an instrument called a *float*, which is an implement or rule moved in every direction on the plaster while it is soft, for giving a perfectly plane surface to the second coat of work. Floats are of three sorts : the *hand float*, which is a short rule, that a man by himself may use ; the *quirk float*, which is used on or in angles; and the *Derby*, which is of such a length as to require two men to use it. Previous to floating, which is, in fact, the operation of making the surface of the work a perfect plane, such surface is subdivided in several bays, which are formed by vertical styles of plastering, (three, four, five, or even ten feet apart,) formed with great accuracy by means of the plumb rule, all in the same plane. These styles are called *screeds*, and being carefully set out to the coat that is applied between them, the plaster or floating laid on between them is brought to the proper surface by working the float up and down on the screeds, so as to bring the surface all to the same plane, which operation is termed *filling out*, and is applicable as well to ceilings as to walls. This branch of plastering requires the best sort of workmen, and great care in the execution.

2243. *Bastard stucco* is of three coats, the first whereof is roughing in or rendering, the second is floating, as in trowelled stucco, which will be next described; but the finishing coat contains a small quantity of hair behind the sand. This work is not hand-floated, and the trowelling is done with less labour than what is denominated trowelled stucco.

2244. *Trowelled stucco*, which is the best sort of plastering for the reception of paint, is formed on a floated coat of work, and such floating should be as dry as possible before the stucco is applied. In the last process, the plasterer uses the hand float, which is made of a piece of half-inch deal, about nine inches long and three inches wide, planed smooth, with its lower edges a little rounded off, and having a handle on the upper surface. The ground to be stuccoed being made as smooth as possible, the stucco is spread upon it to the extent of four or five feet square, and, moistening it continually with a brush as he proceeds, the workman trowels its surface with the float, alternately sprinkling and rubbing the face of the stucco, till the whole is reduced to a fine even surface. Thus, by small portions at a

time, he proceeds till the whole is completed. The water applied to it has the effect of hardening the face of the stucco, which, when finished, becomes as smooth as glass.

2245. From what has been said, the reader will perceive that mere laying or plastering on laths, or rendering on walls, is the most common kind of work, and consists of one coat only; that adding to this a setting coat, it is brought to a better surface, and is two-coat work; and that three-coat work undergoes the intermediate process of floating, between the rendering or pricking up and the setting.

2245*a*. This plain plastered surface has received an improvement in a method of stamping or incising it, while wet, the invention, in 1857, of Mr. Benj. Ferrey, architect. "It is well known that the external rough-casting on old timber houses was stamped or wrought in small devices, known by the term *pargetting*; but it never assumed the importance of extensive wall decorations. The plan now proposed is to impress the common stucco with geometrical or other forms, and applied according to taste, either under string courses, around arches, in spandrils, soffites, or in large masses of diapering; and texts may be imprinted on the plaster instead of being simply painted on the walls. If colour be desired, it can be effected by mixing the desired colour with the coat forming the groundwork, then by laying the stencilled pattern against it, and filling in the solid portions of the device with the ordinary stucco or plaster." The process does not pretend to do more than enliven wall surfaces, but for this purpose it is very effective. Whippingham Church, in the Isle of Wight, is decorated in this manner, with devices in different colours.

2246. Ceilings are *set* in two different ways; the best work is where the setting coat is composed of plaster and lime putty, commonly called *gauge stuff* (2237). Common ceilings are formed with plaster without hair, as in the finishing coat for walls set for paper. The deflection of $\frac{1}{40}$th of an inch for each foot in length is not injurious to ceilings; indeed, the usual allowance for settlement is about twice that quantity. Ceilings have been found to settle about four times as much without causing cracks, and have been raised back again without injury. (Barlow, p. 179.)

2246*a*. In Dublin, the designations in plasterers' work are different to those we have named above. Work to ceilings is described as "Lath scratched, floated, and coated;" while to walls it is described as "scratched, floated, and coated." *Skimming*, to plasterers' work, is a very thin coat of white (i.e. lime) put on float work to smoothen it, and to leave a clean face; *coated* is the term for better work of the same character.

2246*b*. *Wirework*, in place of *lathing*, for forming ceilings and other plaster surfaces, patented in 1841 by L. Leconte, had been previously adopted in the building of the Pantechnicon, near Belgrave Square.

2246*c*. Nickson and Waddingham have patented a *slate ground for plaster*, by using, instead of laths, those slates which do not turn out in the quarries sufficiently wide for sized roofing slates; an immense number of them being necessarily thrown aside daily, although of the best quality. The slates are fixed with the rough side towards the plaster, and $\frac{1}{4}$ in. apart; the plaster to be $\frac{3}{4}$ in. thick, of well haired stuff, which keys itself between the slates and into perforations, two or more being made in each slate according to its size; they run from 12 to 17 in. long and upwards. The system has been worked for about four years at Manchester, and has many other useful qualities.

2247. *Pugging* is plaster laid on boards, fitted in between the joists of a floor to prevent the passage of sound between two stories, and is executed with a coarse stuff made of lime and hay chopped into lengths of about 2 inches.

2248. The following materials are required for 100 yards of render set; viz. $1\frac{1}{2}$ hundred of lime, 1 double load of river sand, and 4 bushels of hair; for the labour, 1 plasterer 3 days, 1 labourer 3 days, 1 boy 3 days; and upon this, 20 per cent. profit is usually allowed. For 130 yards of lath plaster and set—1 load of laths, 10,000 nails, $2\frac{1}{2}$ hundred of lime, $1\frac{1}{2}$ double load of river sand, 7 bushels of hair; for the labour, 1 plasterer 6 days, 1 labourer 6 days, 1 boy 6 days; and upon this, as before, 20 per cent. is usually allowed.

	inch	$\frac{7}{8}$	$\frac{3}{4}$ in.	$\frac{5}{8}$	$\frac{1}{2}$ in.
1 bushel of Portland or Roman cement will cover, yards super.	$1\frac{1}{7}$	$1\frac{3}{4}$	$1\frac{1}{2}$	$2\frac{1}{2}$	$2\frac{1}{4}$
1 ditto, and 1 of sand	$2\frac{1}{4}$	$2\frac{3}{4}$	3	4	$4\frac{1}{2}$
1 ditto, and 2 ditto	$3\frac{1}{3}$	$4\frac{1}{4}$	$4\frac{1}{2}$	6	$6\frac{3}{4}$
1 ditto, and 3 ditto	$4\frac{1}{2}$	$5\frac{1}{2}$	6	8	9
1 cwt. of mastic and 1 gallon of oil . . .			$1\frac{1}{2}$		$2\frac{1}{2}$

1 cubic yard of chalk lime, 2 yards of sand, and 3 bushels of hair, will cover 75 yards of render set on brickwork; 70 yards on lath; or 65 yards plaster; or render two coats and set on brick; and 60 yards on lath. Floated work requires about the same as two coats and set. A bundle of laths and 500 nails will cover about $4\frac{1}{2}$ yards superficial. Two hundred laths, 4 feet long, are required for a square. A bundle of laths contains 500 feet nominally.

2249. In the country, for the exterior coating of dwellings and out-buildings, a species of plastering is used called *roughcast*. It is cheaper than stucco or Parker's cement, and

therefore suitable to such purposes. In the process of executing it, the wall is first pricked up with a coat of lime and hair, on which, when tolerably well set, a second coat is laid on of the same materials as the first, but as smooth as possible. As fast as the workman finishes this surface, another follows him with a pailful of the roughcast, with which he bespatters the new plastering, so that the whole dries together. The roughcast is a composition of small gravel, finely washed, to free it from all earthy particles, and mixed with pure lime and water in a state of semi-fluid consistency. It is thrown from the pail upon the wall, with a wooden float, about 5 or 6 inches long, and as many wide, formed of half-inch deal, and fitted with a round deal handle. With this tool, while the plasterer throws on the roughcast with his right hand, in his left he holds a common whitewasher's brush dipped in the roughcast, with which he brushes and colours the mortar and the roughcast already spread, to give them, when finished, an uniform colour and appearance.

2249a. *Gypsum* or *plaster of Paris* is largely used in France for the construction of walls, both internally and externally, as well as for rendering them afterwards. We adopt the following method of working it, as explained by G. R. Burnell : " The coarser kinds of plaster are used for rendering ; the finer qualities for ceilings, cornices, and decorative works. For walls, the plaster must be gauged stiff for the first coats, and more fluid for the setting coat. For cornices worked out in the solid, the core is made of stiffly gauged plaster, which is floated with finer material, and lastly finished off with plaster laid on by hand, about the consistence of cream. Practice only can ascertain the precise degree of stiffness to be given, as every burning yields a different quality of plaster. When walls are to be rendered, they require to be first jointed, and then wetted with a broom. The surface is then covered with a coat of thinly gauged stuff, laid on with a broom, or at least worked with a trowel in such a manner as to leave sufficient hold for the next coat. This is gauged stiff, and is laid on with a trowel ; it is floated with a rule, but the face is finished with a hand trowel ; the surfaces, however, are never so even, or the angles so square and true, as in the usual plasterers' work adopted in England. The ceilings are lathed about 3 to $3\frac{1}{2}$ inches from centre to centre, and the plaster poured in from above on to a sort of flat centering, leaving about an inch for the thickness of plaster ; the ceiling coat is added after the centering is removed. The better descriptions are made with laths 4 inches from centre to centre, the space between ceiling and floor filled up with light work, and the under and upper surfaces rendered to receive the ceiling and tiles."

2249b. With gypsum, only about $\frac{3}{8}$ths of the evaporation arises as from ordinary plastering. A series of experiments made in 1850, proved that the cost of ordinary works need not exceed in any sensible proportion, if at all, those usually called " render set ; " and that they are strictly the same as " render float and set." A room was begun and finished in thirty hours, whilst a common lime and hair rendering coat would have required, properly speaking, about a month. French plaster must never be used in any position where moisture is likely to affect it for any length of time. It is very hygrometric, and soon decays if kept moist. If it be used as mortar, as in brick-nogged partitions, to be covered over immediately, a space for its expansion must be allowed. In France, a small space is left between the wall and partitions ; this is filled in by the plastering coat. The same observation applies to floors with plaster pugging, and even to cornices with a large body of that material, the mitres and returns being executed some time after the straight mouldings.

2250. In forming the coves and cornices which are applied below the ceilings of rooms, it is of the greatest importance to make them as light as possible, for the plaster whereof they are formed is heavy, and ought not to depend merely on its adhesion to the vertical and horizontal surfaces to which it is attached. Hence, when cornices run of large dimensions, bracketing, as has already been described in the section JOINERY (2079, *et seq.*) must be provided, of the general form of the cornice or cove, or other work, and on this the plastering is to be formed. On this, when roughed out, the work is run with wooden moulds, having zinc or copper edges, so as to give the general outline of the cornice. If enrichments are used in it, they are cast in plaster of Paris, and afterwards fixed with that material in the spaces left for them to occupy. These enrichments are previously modelled, and from the model a matrix is formed, as for all other plaster casting. Great nicety is required in all the operations relative to the moulding and fixing of cornices, and most especially that the ornaments be firmly fixed by screws or other means, that they may not be detached from their places by partial settlements of the building, and cause accidents to the occupiers of the rooms where they are used.

2250a. In 1862 Mr. Westmacott patented a new plaster, made by combining lime with unburnt limestone or chalk, suitably ground or reduced to powder. When using very good lime, 2 measures of unburnt chalk or limestone to 1 of lime can be taken as the proportion. This compound may be employed alone, or combined with sand, plaster of Paris, clay, or other materials, according to the circumstances under which it is to be used. Some experiments were made on this plaster by a Committee of the Institute of British

Architects, in 1863. The quick stucco for rendering ceilings consisted of 2 parts of un-slaked lime to 1 of chalk, with sand, mixed together before adding the water; it occu-pied twenty minutes in making and setting, and was followed in an hour by ordinary gauged stuff, and stood without cracking. For outside work, the proportions to be used are 1 part of slaked grey lime to 2 of chalk, used as cement or common mortar. This is to be treated like lime, and therefore must be used directly. The difference between this and the internal or quick stucco, is that the latter material has been dry slaked before being gauged. When placed on the wall, it hardens and sets at once throughout its mass; whilst the other, slaked like mortar, hardens gradually from the surface. When required for common mortar, the lime is slaked, and ground chalk mixed with it to form a cream; then sand is added in the usual manner. This is used at once, but it will improve with age if kept damp; it indurates gradually, varying, according to the weather and amount of sand it contains, from a sixteenth to an eighth of an inch per week. For rendering plaster, the sand may be mixed with the lime and chalk before adding water, the difference being that whereas in the first form the mortar gradually indurates, in this it can be placed upon the laths before the lime slacks, which generally takes place in an hour, and it often sufficiently hardens to be followed by the second coat in the same day. It does not eventually indurate to an equal strength with the first method, yet it forms a plaster harder and stronger, without hair, than is generally obtained with that material combined. It is not liable to crack. An external stucco, in which a highly hydraulic lime is used, is formed of one part of lime, two of chalk, and two of sand; this stucco indurates quickly through the mass. A specimen of seven months old, and formed of 1 part of grey lime and 2 parts of chalk, which had been placed for that period exposed to atmospheric in-fluences, showed great hardness. This plaster will take a good polish in about three minutes. By the addition of a little plaster of Paris, a good internal cement is produced, which dries quickly, and is much harder than plaster of Paris.

2250b. A *rendering plaster* for superseding the use of lime and hair mortar in the plastering of walls and ceilings, has been brought forward by A. G. Barham, of Bridg-water. It is stated to be very tough and strong, not liable to crack or swell, and is applied without hair, direct to brick walls or lathwork. The surface dries and hardens rapidly, and it can be painted or papered at once, as there is nothing in the plaster to injure either of the processes. When dry it is of itself a good grey in colour. For outside stucco, it is also stated to be a safe material, and is likewise free from vegetation and colouring.

2250c. Stucco is a species of plastering which is sometimes subsequently worked to resemble marble. There are two sorts of *stucco*, those made of limes, and those made of plaster. The former are often classed under the name of cements, but their disagreeable colour prevents their being used for ornamental decoration. They serve, however, to form the foundations for the better class whenever humidity is to be feared. The latter are generally made of lime, mixed with calcareous powder, chalk, plaster, and other substances, in such a manner as to obtain in a short time a solid surface, which may be coloured, painted, and polished with such perfection as to allow of its being used instead of more expensive materials.

2250d. The Italians usually execute their stuccos in three coats; the first is very coarse, to form the rendering. The second is much finer, and contains a larger proportion of lime, bringing the work up to a very even close grain. The last is made of rich lime, which has been slaked and run through a very fine sieve; it is allowed to stand from four to five months, in order that every particle may be reduced to a hydrate. If the lime cannot be kept for so great a length of time, the slaking may be assisted by beating it up very fre-quently. When great perfection is required, pounded white Carrara marble is mingled with it; gypsum and alabaster are used for enclosed situations. Colours are obtained by mixing with the lime such metallic oxides, &c., as the case may require. The excellence of the work consists in the care with which the effects of the natural marbles are imitated.

2250e. When plaster is used instead of lime, it is gauged with lukewarm water, in which size or gum has been dissolved, so as to fill up the pores, to give more consistency, and to render it susceptible of receiving a better polish. Any colours used should be previously dissolved in the size water. When the whole of the stucco is perfectly dry, the surface is then rubbed with grit stone and polished up with rubbers much in the same way as real marble. The thickness of a coat of stucco varies from one-sixth to one-eighth of an inch.

2250f. *Stucco work*, as it is called, and as executed daily in Ireland for outside work, consists of their *roche lime*, slaked for three or four months previously, as above described, mixed with sand, and worked up with the trowel. It stands the weather as perfectly as Roman cement. The term is also given to the interior moulded and cast work.

2250g. The manufacture of *Scagliola* work, an imitation of real marbles, is described in the Glossary. It has generally been assumed as a mystery. We shall, in this place, only notice some of its uses. Scagliola is so easily put up in a building, and requires so small an amount of time and expense for renovation and repair, compared with repainting and

varnishing, that those who are induced to go to the expense of plastering the walls with mastic, to be ready for immediate painting, marbling, and high polishing, might be justified in expending a further sum and adopt scagliola at once. For the walls of the staircase in the building formerly called Crockford's Club House, St. James's Street, the scagliola was prepared upon slabs of slate half an inch thick, sawn on the surface with cuts about one-eighth of an inch deep, to form a key for the plaster groundwork. When the slabs were fit for polishing they were secured with battens fixed to the wall. The scagliola to the staircases at the Reform Club House is worked upon the walls; they are richly panelled, moulded and inlaid. The fluted columns, in the same building, to the gallery and skylight of the saloon are done upon stone. The three-quarter columns in the drawing and coffee rooms were cast in three lengths, and each backed with tiles bedded in coarse plaster. Some black and gold columns, worked in Keene's cement on stone, and two twisted columns in plaster, are placed in Wilton Church, Wiltshire. When Parian cement is used, the groundwork is formed of wet cement of the coarse quality, the veneer being of the same thickness as common scagliola; but one half of the quantity of colours will produce the same depth of colouring as in the common scagliola. For polishing, the same process is to be followed as for walls, as described in par. 2251i.

2250h. Scagliola *floors* exist at Sion House, Isleworth; at the entrance hall at the Athenæum Club House, London; and at Crewe Hall, Cheshire. Many other examples of the employment of scagliola work will be found named in an excellent article in the *Builder* for 1863, p. 840, one of the best on the subject; and another in February 1845. A very inferior imitation of scagliola is too often to be seen.

2250i. A material has been lately prepared for similar decorative purposes, at the Patent Marble Works, in which all the advantages of the real material are said to be obtained. It is manufactured in slabs from $\frac{3}{4}$ to 1 inch thick, of any size, for the lining of halls and rooms, as well as for moulded work. The prices are stated to be under those for enamelled slate.

2251. In the present time, the use of ornaments made of *carton-pierre*, a species of *papier maché*, has been reintroduced for cornices, flowers, and other decorations. The basis of it is paper reduced to a pulp, which, having other ingredients mixed with it, is pressed into moulds, and thus ornaments are formed of it. They have not all the delicacy of the plaster cast, and there is the want of that nicety which a good cornice workman in plaster exhibits; but their lightness, and the security with which they can be fixed with screws, render them often preferable to plaster ornaments. The "Critic" newspaper in 1863 stated that in Bergen, in Prussia, there is a church capable of holding 1,000 persons, constructed entirely, statues and all, of papier maché. Probably, however, the material is that used to a very great extent in Norway and Sweden for forming the roofs of houses, and said to be incombustible. It appears to be in many respects similar to the *Fibrous slab*, the manufacture of which, by Bielefeld, was discontinued a few years since, after much success; though the dust penetrated through it, showing the marks of the joists, as in plaster work. The ceiling of the reading room at the British Museum was lined with it. Another material, superseding *carton-pierre* and papier maché, is Desachy's *Fibrous plaster*, which is formed of a thin coat of plaster of Paris, run upon a backing of coarse canvas. It is of great lightness, not inflammable, and is ready to be painted immediately after it is made. It is adapted for the speedy and economical production of any coffered or circular work; and for wagon-headed ceilings, as but little bracketing is necessary, it being fixed to the joists direct; for fluted or ornamented columns, panelled dadoes, &c., for the lining of walls and ceilings, and for all purposes of ornamental plaster work. Mr. Owen Jones has extensively used this material for his interior decorations.

CEMENTS.

2251a. We have already adverted to the cements used in plastering. Parker's, Atkinson's, and Portland, cements, are the principal ones for the outside coating of buildings, and the process of laying them on is so similar to that of other plasterer's work, that it will not be necessary to say much respecting them. The best mode, perhaps, of using these natural cements is to employ them purely in works under water, or where a great crushing weight is to be brought upon them at once. For foundations in damp situations, where rapidity of execution is desired, the mixture may be 2 parts of sand to 3 of cement; and also for cornices or coatings exposed to the weather. For upright faces, the proportion is of 3 parts of sand to 1 of cement. Care must be taken that no fissures are formed such as will admit water, as the action of frost will destroy it. The brickwork in mortar, to be covered, should be thoroughly dry, or the expansion of the water will throw off the cement; the brickwork itself must, however, be wetted before a coat is applied, to prevent the absorption of the moisture before the coat sets, or it will not harden. With slow setting cements, it is too often the custom to allow the filling out, and even plain faces, to become partially set, when the adhesion of the next quantity will be found imperfect and unsound.

All work requires to be finished off at once for a good result. Dirty sand causes the cement to be crumbly. Cement once set, or even partially so, should not be worked up in a fresh mixture, or it will form rotten work. Like lime in the setting coat in plastering, cement facings and mouldings are not so liable to show fire-cracks on the face if a small quantity of sand be mixed up with it.

2251b. In using *Portland cement*, plasterers should use thicker screeds, and finish their work in one coat with the screed-rule, instead of working all the water used in gauging to the surface with the hand-float and trowel, spoiling the thinner coat whilst they lay it on. This cement has an advantage over others, that it can, with good management, be worked in winter, while other cements cannot be so used without great risk of the frost injuring them before they are dry. More cement added to make a coat set quicker, causes it to crack and burst. This cement is best when used of a uniform thickness of ⅜ths of an inch, any dubbing out being done with pieces of brick and Roman cement. A proportion of Portland cement mixed in the usual plastering coat affords a quicker drying material for finishing with Portland or with Martin's cement. The coarse quality of Martin's cement takes the place of plastering, and all the delays consequent on its use.

2251c. However much we may regret employing cements to cover the coarse brick and rubble stone of our buildings, it must be acknowledged that they are in a far better condition than many of those in which the stones, commonly used during late years, have been introduced.

2251d. For *interior* embellishments, the cements known as Martin's, Keene's, and Parian, are largely adopted. *Martin's cement* is manufactured in three qualities, coarse fine, and superfine. The coarse quality presents a whitish speckled surface, and is supplied in red, light red, and grey, colours. The fine is whiter; the superfine is a cream colour. It is said to cover 20 per cent. more surface, at half an inch in thickness, at a less cost than an equal quantity of any other cement for internal use, and to be 35 per cent. cheaper than such cements. For walls, 1 part of coarse cement is used with 1½ of clean dry sharp sand, for the under coat of half an inch thick, finished with ⅛ inch thick of pure cement. It is of a fireproof character, and preserves to some extent the building from damp: the cement is supposed to continue to indurate with age, and therefore to be very durable. When adopted for floors, skirtings, and other finishings, whether plain or ornamental, in lieu of wood, the cost is stated to be less than similar work executed in that material, while in appearance it is very much superior, as it takes a fine polish. It can be painted upon within twenty hours after having been worked on old brickwork, and in twelve hours when on lathed work; but all three qualities are as well without paint. Plaster of Paris must not be mixed with it, or Roman or Portland cement used as an undercoat.

2251e. *Keene's cement* is said to show on its face the lines of any woodwork which it may be carried across. If required, it can be painted upon in twenty-four hours after the coat on old brickwork is completed. Skirtings, flooring, and internal stucco are worked in this material, on account of its superior hardness. This cement will mix with any of the metallic oxides, &c., to produce a coloured cement.

2251f. *Parian cement* (Keating's patent), for internal stucco, has been used throughout the Westminster palace. It does not effloresce, takes paint or paper in forty-eight hours, and makes a very hard and beautiful scagliola. It sets in four or five hours. It must not be treated as common plastering, by being hand-floated up with water, as for all purposes as little water as possible is to be used with it. This material must not come in contact with green lime, or with limewater in any of the operations. On *brickwork*, it is first floated about ½ in. thick, with equal parts of clean washed sharp sand, and the surface slightly dragged. The next day a setting coat, ³⁄₁₆ in. thick, of net cement, may be worked, laid down with a beech float and slightly trowelled. If intended to be painted or papered, the first coat of paint should be applied from twenty to twenty-four hours after. The paint is to be mixed, for the first coat, only one-fourth oil and three-fourths turpentine, and with a very small portion of red lead and gold size. The succeeding coats of paint are to be mixed in the usual manner. On *lathing*, the laths may be closer than usual; the first coat of equal parts of clean washed sharp sand and cement, broomed while soft, and floated the next day with cement as before; the setting coat to be followed up next day, and finished as described for brickwork. The three coats will be ¾ in. in thickness.

2251g. *Damp walls* require a first coat of Portland cement ¾ in. thick; when dry, a coat of ½ part of Parian cement mixed with ¼ part of washed sand, gauged very stiff, rubbed in hard, and dragged before it sets. When hard, a floating coat without sand is to be applied; to be set as before on the following day, and painted on the succeeding morning, without fail.

2251h. For *floors*, the cement mixed with ⅓ part of Bath stone dust, ¾ in. thick, is to be laid on a solid bottom of Portland concrete, in one body ¾ in. thick. On *common plastering*, where the ordinary time is allowed for finishing the works, the plaster is to be laid fair, and dragged and left to dry; the cement to be mixed with an equal part of washed sharp sand and floated ½ in. thick. The next day a thin coat of cement having ⅛ of sand is laid down and trowelled as before. If required to be *papered*, it must first have two coats of

paint. In patching, when required to be painted or distempered on immediately, the edge of the old plastering is to have first a coat of paint.

2251i. For *polished work* on walls, the floating coat is mixed with equal parts of sharp sand and cement. The setting coat is ¼ in. in thickness, of fine net cement, rubbed down with grit stones and water; the grit is to be then well washed off, and when the water is gone, a stopping of fine cement mixed up stiff in a pan is to be applied and well rubbed in. This is then to be scraped off with a wood scraper, and the stopping repeated until a proper face is obtained, leaving a scum on the face to be taken off by the next grinding, which should be done with finer grit stones. The stopping is to be repeated and finally finished with snake stone, putty powder, and clean cloths. Three or four weeks' time is required before a good polish can be obtained, it being essential that each successive stopping of fine cement should be allowed several days to harden before the surface is again scraped.

2251k. For *casting* work, the cement is to be mixed stiff and dubbed in the moulds with a brush, and then left until thoroughly set. Such are the instructions for all these several processes issued by Messrs. Francis, the manufacturers of this cement, which was applied to the walls of the wards, corridors, and staircases of Middlesex Hospital, in 1849, from its non-absorbing qualities.

2251l. A very good specimen of plain decorative work is to be seen in the booking-office of the London, Chatham, and Dover Railway Company, at the Victoria Station. The walls, piers, &c., were executed in this cement, then painted in flat tints, and varnished and polished several times.

2251m. Cement *floors* may be made in an economical manner, by first forming a bed of concrete to prevent damp rising, then placing on it a coat 1½ in. thick of Atkinson's cement, mixed with three of clean fine sand; or in Roman cement; or in Portland cement, with four of sand, floated in by a rule on screeds, care being taken to prevent the joints setting. If the cement set slow, it may be trowelled down while soft, but not when it is setting, or the face will be injured. If the cement sets very quick, a rough key is to be formed. and then covered with fine mortar ⅛ in. thick, trowelling it gently before it begins to set. If rising damps be not anticipated, the floor may be first paved with clean hard brickbats in lieu of concrete, and covered an inch thick with good cement.

2251n. Portland cement floors have answered perfectly in several instances, but it is an uncertain material; therefore, where the floors were not to be covered, or where a slight defect was of consequence, it has been considered better to use other cements, such as Keene's, as employed at the Metropolitan Convalescent Asylum, Walton-on-Thames. A good floor for common purposes is made of a concrete formed of 6 parts of clean gravel to 1 of ground lias lime: this is generally impervious to damp and vermin.

2251o. The *bituminous cements* are used for paving, and for covering the extrados of arches to prevent the percolation of water through them. In all new constructions, there are always movements which crack the coatings executed in limes and natural cements, which are also subject to unequal shrinkage, producing crevices; and from these united causes, it is very rare to find such coatings impermeable. The bituminous cements are more elastic; it may happen that small crevices, so to speak, solder themselves, and if any serious repairs are required they are much easier to be executed than in those works executed with limes. When asphalte is to be used, it is placed in a quantity of nearly boiling *mineral pitch* to secure its melting. Colonel Émy found the following proportions as the best for the asphalte of Gaugeac, and it may be taken for the others of this class of cements, when used as a coating for arches: —

2⅛ pints (wine measure) of pure mineral pitch.
11 lbs. avoirdupois of bitumen or asphalte.
17 pints of powdered stone dust, wood ashes, or minion.

It is advisable to lay this mixture upon a bed of concrete or mortar; and as much as possible in slabs of 2 feet 6 inches to 3 feet in width. It should be evenly spread and compressed with a trowel, well rubbed, and reduced to a uniform close surface. When all the bubbles have been expelled, a fine sand is sprinkled over the surface, and worked in with the trowel, observing never to fill the crevices formed by the air-bubbles with sand, but only with asphalte. The thickness for coating any arches is not more than from three-fifths to half-an-inch. The quantity of cement thus employed to cover a yard square is about 4½ lbs.

2252. It is scarcely within the branch of the plasterer's practice, but as we shall have no other place for adverting to it, we may as well here mention what are called "composition" ornaments, seldom used in cornices, but principally for the decoration of chimney-glasses, frames, and to woodwork generally. The composition is very strong when dry, of a brownish colour, consisting of about 2 pounds of powdered whiting, 1 pound of glue in solution, and half a pound of linseed oil mixed together in a copper, heated and stirred with a spatula till the whole is incorporated. After heating it is laid upon a stone covered with powdered whiting, and beaten to a tough and firm consistence, when it is laid by for use, covered with wet cloths to keep it fresh. This composition is then put into moulds and pressed. Later inventions have nearly caused its disuse in architectural decoration.

SECT. X.

SMITHERY AND IRONMONGERY.

2253. Smithery is the art of uniting several lumps of iron into one lump or mass, and forming them into any desired shape. The operations necessary for this are primarily performed in the forge, and on the anvil with the hammer; but for finishing, many other implements and tools are necessary. These, however, we do not think useful to particularise, a course we have pursued in the other trades, because the expedients introduced by the engineer and machinist have of late years, except in rough work, superseded many of them. It is now, for instance, easier to plane iron to a perfect surface than it was a few years ago to file or hammer to what was then always an imperfect one. Formerly a man would be occupied as many minutes in drilling a hole as by machines it now takes seconds to perform.

2254. We have, in a previous section, given all the particulars relating to the produce of the metal from the ore; in this section we propose little more than to enumerate the different objects which the smith and ironmonger furnish in the construction of buildings; and introductory to that it will be convenient to subjoin tables of the weights of round and bar iron, and also of the weights of 1 foot of close hammered bar iron of different thicknesses; remembering that a cube foot of close hammered iron weighs about 495 lbs., of common wrought iron about 480 lbs., and of cast iron 450 lbs., whence may be derived the weight of other solids whose cubic contents are known.

TABLE SHOWING THE WEIGHT OF ONE FOOT IN LENGTH OF A SQUARE IRON BAR.

Side of Square in inches.	Weight in lbs. avoirdupois.	Side of Square in inches.	Weight in lbs. avoirdupois.
1/4	0·1875	2 1/8	15·0625
3/8	0·4687	2 1/4	16·8740
1/2	0·8125	2 3/8	18·8125
5/8	1·2812	2 1/2	20·8125
3/4	1·8740	2 5/8	22·9687
7/8	2·5625	2 3/4	25·1875
1	3·3125	2 7/8	27·7500
1 1/8	4·2187	3	30·0000
1 1/4	5·1875	3 1/8	32·5312
1 3/8	6·3125	3 1/4	35·1875
1 1/2	7·5000	3 3/8	37·9687
1 5/8	8·8125	3 1/2	40·7812
1 3/4	10·1875	3 5/8	43·7812
1 7/8	11·7187	3 3/4	46·8740
2	13·3125	3 7/8	50·0520
		4	53·3125

TABLE SHOWING THE WEIGHT OF ONE FOOT IN LENGTH OF A ROUND IRON BAR.

Diameter in inches.	Weight in lbs. avoirdupois.	Diameter in inches.	Weight in lbs. avoirdupois.
1/4	0·1562	2 1/8	11·8125
3/8	0·3750	2 1/4	13·2500
1/2	0·6562	2 3/8	14·7500
5/8	1·0000	2 1/2	16·3437
3/4	1·4687	2 5/8	18·0000
7/8	2·0000	2 3/4	19·7812
1	2·5937	2 7/8	21·6250
1 1/8	3·3125	3	23·5625
1 1/4	4·0937	3 1/8	25·5625
1 3/8	4·9375	3 1/4	27·6562
1 1/2	5·9375	3 3/8	29·8125
1 5/8	6·9052	3 1/2	32·0625
1 3/4	8·0000	3 5/8	34·4062
1 7/8	9·1875	3 3/4	36·8125
2	10·4607	3 7/8	39·3116
		4	41·8740

These tables give a little less weight than some others now in use. To convert into weight of other metals, multiply the numbers, for cast iron by ·93; for steel by 1·01; for copper by 1·15; for brass by 1·09; for lead by 1·48; and for zinc by ·92.

TABLE I. OF THE WEIGHT OF HOOP IRON, according to the customary width and thickness, by the Birmingham Wire Gauge, per 100 feet lengths (Hurst).

Mark. No.	Width in Inches.	Weight in Pounds.	Mark. No.	Width in Inches.	Weight in Pounds.
11	2 3/4	115·78	15	1 1/2	36·37
11 (1/8)	3	126·30	15	1 3/8	33·34
12	2 1/2	91·78	16 (1/16)	1 1/4	26·52
12	2	73·42	17	1 1/8	20·84
13	2 1/4	71·23	18	1	16·17
13	2	63·32	19	7/8	12·38
14	1 3/4	47·15	20	3/4	8·84
14	1 1/2	40·41	21	5/8	6·95

TABLE II. OF THE WEIGHT AND THICKNESS OF A SUPERFICIAL FOOT OF SHEET IRON, by the Birmingham Wire Gauge:—

Mark. No.	Decimals of an Inch Thick.	Pounds Weight.	Mark. No.	Decimals of an Inch Thick.	Pounds Weight.	Mark. No.	Decimals of an Inch Thick.	Pounds Weight.
00000 ($\frac{1}{2}$)	·500	20·	10	·137	5·62	24	·022	1·00
0000	·450	18·	11 ($\frac{1}{8}$)	·125	5·00	25	·020	0·90
000 ($\frac{7}{16}$)	·4375	17·50	12	·109	4·38	26 ($\frac{1}{64}$)	·018	0·80
00 ($\frac{3}{8}$)	·375	15·	13	·094	3·75	27	·016	0·72
0	·340	13·60	14	·080	3·12	28	·014	0·64
1 ($\frac{5}{16}$)	·3125	12·50	15	·072	2·82	29	·013	0·56
2	·284	12·00	16 ($\frac{1}{16}$)	·0625	2·50	30	·012	0·50
3	·261	11·00	17	·055	2·18	31 ($\frac{1}{128}$)	·010	0·40
3–4 ($\frac{1}{4}$)	·250	10·00	18	·048	1·86	32	·009	0·36
5	·222	8·74	19	·042	1·70	33	·008	0·3 2
6	·208	8·12	20	·035	1·54	34	·007	0·28
7 ($\frac{3}{16}$)	·1875	7·50	21 ($\frac{1}{32}$)	·0312	1·40	35	·005	0·20
8	·166	6·86	22	·029	1·25	36	·004	0·16
9	·158	6·24	23	·025	1·12			

TABLE III. OF THE WEIGHT OF A SUPERFICIAL FOOT OF PLATE IRON IN POUNDS.

Thickness, parts of an Inch	$\frac{1}{16}$	$\frac{1}{8}$	$\frac{3}{16}$	$\frac{1}{4}$	$\frac{5}{16}$	$\frac{3}{8}$	$\frac{7}{16}$	$\frac{1}{2}$
Weight in pounds	2·526	5·052	7·578	10·104	12·630	15·156	17·682	20·208

Thickness, parts of an Inch	$\frac{9}{16}$	$\frac{5}{8}$	$\frac{11}{16}$	$\frac{3}{4}$	$\frac{13}{16}$	$\frac{7}{8}$	$\frac{15}{16}$	1
Weight in pounds	22·734	25·260	27·786	30·312	32·839	35·365	37·891	40·417

TABLE IV. OF THE WEIGHT OF ORDINARY ANGLE IRON IN POUNDS PER LINEAL FOOT.

Breadth in inches	$1\frac{1}{4}$	$1\frac{1}{2}$	$1\frac{3}{4}$	2	$2\frac{1}{4}$	$2\frac{1}{2}$	$2\frac{3}{4}$	3	$3\frac{1}{4}$	$3\frac{1}{2}$
Weight per pound	1·8	2·7	3·3	3·9	5·0	6·5	8·3	10·4	11·7	14·0

TABLE V. OF WEIGHT OF IRON BOLTS AND NUTS. (Mulholland, in *Builder*, IV. 22.)

Diameter of Bolt, inch.	$\frac{1}{4}$	$\frac{3}{8}$	$\frac{1}{2}$	$\frac{5}{8}$	$\frac{3}{4}$	$\frac{7}{8}$	1	$1\frac{1}{8}$	$1\frac{1}{4}$	$1\frac{3}{8}$	$1\frac{1}{2}$	$1\frac{5}{8}$
Weight per foot of round Iron, pounds	·2	·4	·7	1·0	1·5	2·0	2·7	3·4	4·2	5·0	6·0	7·0
Weight per inch of round Iron	·016	·033	·058	·083	·125	·166	·225	·283	·350	·416	·500	·583
Weight either of Head or Nut	·021	·062	·145	·260	·468	·729	1·125	1·77	2·187	2·86	3·75	4·74

2254a. Bolts are now often made with square heads, so that these being let into the timber, the stem cannot turn while the nut is being screwed up. Machinery has been brought to bear for the manufacture of bolts, rivets, spikes, and other like articles; "the motions are so arranged that no attention is required beyond entering the bars into the feed rolls and cleaning the pieces of the ends of the iron out of the dies."

TABLE SHOWING THE WEIGHT OF *close-hammered* FLAT BAR IRON, FROM ONE INCH WIDE AND AN EIGHTH OF AN INCH THICK TO FOUR INCHES WIDE AND ONE INCH THICK.

Inches, and their Parts in breadth.	Thickness in Parts of an Inch, and Weight in Pounds averdupois.							
	1/8	1/4	3/8	1/2	5/8	3/4	7/8	1
1	0·429	0·859	1·289	1·718	2·148	2·578	3·007	3·437
1 1/8	0·484	0·968	1·503	1·937	2·422	2·905	3·383	3·868
1 1/4	0·539	1·078	1·639	2·148	2·682	3·226	3·758	4·305
1 3/8	0·593	1·187	1·773	2·368	2·953	3·547	4·133	4·726
1 1/2	0·648	1·289	1·937	2·579	3·218	3·867	4·508	5·156
1 5/8	0·695	1·398	2·093	2·789	3·492	4·187	4·890	5·585
1 3/4	0·750	1·500	2·250	3·008	3·758	4·508	5·266	6·016
1 7/8	0·804	1·609	2·414	3·218	4·281	4·835	5·641	6·445
2	0·859	1·699	2·578	3·437	4·297	5·156	6·016	6·874
2 1/8	0·913	1·828	2·742	3·356	4·562	5·476	6·391	7·305
2 1/4	0·948	1·937	2·897	3·867	4·835	5·805	6·766	7·734
2 3/8	1·023	2·039	3·062	4·148	5·101	6·125	7·148	8·164
2 1/2	1·069	2·148	3·218	4.297	5·375	6·445	7·547	8·594
2 5/8	1·125	2·250	3·383	4·516	5·641	6·766	7·897	9·023
2 3/4	1·179	2·366	3·500	4·726	5·905	7·093	8·273	9·443
2 7/8	1·234	2·468	3·721	4·937	6·180	7·414	8·648	9·882
3	1·289	2·578	3·867	5·156	6·445	7·734	9·023	10·312
3 1/8	1·344	2·687	4·031	5·375	6·734	8·055	9·398	11·742
3 1/4	1·398	2.789	4·187	5·609	6·984	8·375	9·773	11·172
3 3/8	1·443	2·905	4·335	5·805	7·250	8·703	10·156	11·601
3 1/2	1·500	3·007	4·508	6·016	7·516	9·039	10·503	12·031
3 5/8	1·562	3·117	4·672	6·226	7·789	9·344	10·905	12·461
3 3/4	1·609	3·218	4·860	6·445	8·062	9·664	11·281	12·890
3 7/8	1·630	3·328	5·000	6·656	8·328	9·992	11·656	13·320
4	1·718	3·437	5·156	6·874	8·593	10·312	12·031	13·750
8	3·436	6·874	10·312	13·748	17·186	20·624	24·062	27·400
12	5·156	10·312	15·469	20·625	25·781	30·937	36·094	41·250
If of Cast Iron.								
12	4·835	9·664	14·500	19·336	24·172	29·000	33·836	38·672

2255. For the carcass of a building the articles furnished by the SMITH are, wrought iron *columns with caps and bases* for the support of great superincumbent weights; cast iron *columns* and *stancheons* are now preferred both for economy and stiffness; as was also that material for *girders, beams, joists,* and *bressummers,* until the introduction of *plate iron* and *rolled iron;* all which have been treated in previous sections. *Cast, blister, shear,* and *spring steel; charcoal sheets* and *plates; boiler, tank,* and *flitch plates; galvanized* and *tinned sheets; chequered floor plates, buckled plates; flat bars* up to 12 in. wide, *round bars* up to 8 in. diameter, *square bars* up to 5 in.; *angle,* T, and *trough irons.* Ties of all descriptions, *straps, bolts, nuts* and *screws, plates, washers,* and the like, employed in connecting pieces in framing where the strain is greater than the mere fibres of the wood will resist. *Half-round, bevelled, oval, octagon, hexagon, moulding,* and *fancy irons; hoop iron, nail rods,* and *sash iron; shoes* for piles, when that mode of obtaining a foundation is adopted; *cramps* for holding blocks of stone together, but those of cast iron are better, as less likely to be subject to oxidation; while those of copper or gun metal are still better; *area gratings* and *window bars* for securing openings, now generally superseded for those of cast iron, especially when of an ornamental character, as are *balusters* and *railings* for stairs and balconies; and, among other things, *chimney bars,* which are wide, thin, bent bars or plates of wrought iron (see SPECIFICATIONS), to relieve the weight of brickwork over a chimney opening; in kitchens and rooms where a large opening is required, and two bars may not be sufficiently strong, a wrought or cast iron *cradling* is necessary. The liability to expansion and contraction from the varying temperature often produces fractures about the chimney jambs, but on the whole they produce a security which sanctions their use. The Metropolitan Building Act requires that, if the breast project more than 4 1/2 in. from the face of the wall, and the jamb on either side is of less width than 17 1/2 in., the abutments must be tied in by an iron bar or bars, turned up and down at the ends, and built into the jambs for at least 8 1/2 in. on each side.

2255a. The advantage of now being able to procure *wrought iron flitches* of a good

length and depth has obviated the necessity of *welding* two or more lengths together by the sledge hammer, which has not a sufficient impetus to reach the very core of the metal, and thus the joint became weaker than the remainder of the flitch or bar. In 1864 experiments were made at Paris, on the effect of welding by hydraulic pressure; two bars, each $1\frac{1}{2}$ in. square, were thus welded together with great ease, and the machine was stopped when the part welded was brought down to the thickness of the bar. After cooling, the welded part was cut through, and the inside was found perfectly compact.

2255*b*. *Boiler plate* is made of rolled or wrought iron. They are termed *sheets* when under $\frac{1}{4}$ inch in thickness; *plates* from a $\frac{1}{4}$ inch to 2 inches thick; and *slabs* when more than 2 inches thick. They are named according to the quality of the iron, or the locality where they are manufactured. The sizes of those most in use are from 6 feet to 9 feet long, 2 feet to 4 feet wide, and from a $\frac{1}{4}$ to $\frac{3}{4}$ of an inch in thickness.

2255*c*. *Corrugated iron* is sheet iron which has been rolled into the form of a series of waves. It is in that state frequently used for a covering for temporary purposes; between joists to carry concrete, &c.; and for fencing, the corrugation giving a thin sheet great capability for carrying a heavy weight, or for stiffening framework. The flutes are generally about $5\frac{1}{4}$ or 6 inches from centre to centre. Sheets of Nos. 16, 18 and 20 wire gauge are made from 6 feet by 2 feet, to 8 feet by 3 feet; and of Nos. 22, 24 and 26, from 6 feet by 2 feet, to 7 feet by 2 feet 6 inches. In calculating the measure for fixed roofing, add $\frac{1}{10}$ to the weight per square for lapping. The sheets should overlap each other about 6 inches, and be double riveted at the joints. About 3lbs. of rivets are required for a square of roofing. In roofs, the iron sheets are best used in a curved form.

2255*d*. *Wrought iron casements* are still introduced into buildings; this has given rise to several improvements upon the old method of manufacture for making them wind and water tight. Those now generally advertised are, the patent *wrought iron windows*, by the General Iron Foundry Company (Limited); Burt and Potts' patent *wrought iron water-tight window and frame*; Gibbons and White's *wrought iron weather-tight casements and frames* for stone mullions; and casements for wood mullions, as designed by Mr. G. Devey, architect. All these are fitted with *casement stays and fastenings*. Connected with this purpose are Smith's (of Princes Street, Leicester Square) "patent weather-tight *water-bar*," for French casements, formed in the sill; and one of another make, by a manufacturer of the same name (formerly of Queen Street, Oxford Street).

2255*e*. The usual dimensions, outside of frames, of fire proof wrought iron doors and frames, and gates, may be usefully inserted here:—5 ft. 9 in. high by 2 ft. 3 in. wide; 6 ft. by 2 ft. 4 in.; 6 ft. 2 in. by 2 ft. 6 in.; 6 ft. 6 in. by 2 ft. 6 in.; 6 ft. 2 in. by 2 ft. 8 in. ; and 6 ft. 4. in. by 3 ft.

2255*f*. Iron *shop fronts* are introduced in many towns. They are made from 12 feet by 6 feet to 14 feet by 10 feet, generally at one shilling per superficial foot. "Whole brass" and "half brass" sash bars, of nearly every form and size, are manufactured, as well as brass, copper, and zinc beads. Metal "stall board plates" hardly come within our province, except to notice them. With this subject is connected the varieties of *revolving shutters* in iron, wood, or steel, and with or without machinery; and made to lift up, or down, or to move sideways. A revolving safety shutter in one sheet of steel, is probably the last invention; it requires no machinery. Where the old method of putting up shutters exists, Jennings's *shop-shutter shoes* secure them as they are each put up, without the necessity of any shutter bar.

2255*g*. Wrought iron *wine bins*, and new registered iron bins adapted for small quantities of wine, placed in a sitting or other room, and with or without doors, will be found a useful addition in small houses.

2255*h*. The ornamental portion of SMITH's work has been largely introduced, of late years especially, in wrought iron shaped by hand into various devices and patterns, more especially according to the several periods of mediæval architecture. The taste is chiefly developed in gates, railings, altar and staircase standards, screens, grilles and gratings, tombs, hinge fronts, the band finishing either in a fleur de lys or trident, reaching to about three-fourths of the width of the door, and of $\frac{3}{8}$ths iron; or in some scrollwork, which curls and scrolls over the entire face of the door ; shutter hinges, common door hinges; gable crosses, terminals, vanes, and hipknobs; ridge crestings; drop handles with plates, closing rings and plates ; lock plates and escutcheons, knockers, keys, latches and bolts, bell pulls, levers and plate pulls; umbrella stands; scrapers; fenders and fire-irons; dog grates; lecterns and book rests; candlesticks, gas, lamp, and candle pendants and brackets, desk lights, and standards; coronælucis, lanterns, and pillars. It is almost unnecessary to add that many of these articles are to be had in polished brass, and that many of them are imitated in cast iron. Wrought and cast iron, as in panelled work to gates, are sometimes employed together, the wrought parts enclosing the panels.

2255*i*. As iron has now neither the tenacity nor the ductility which it gained by the old process of being repeatedly forged, the modern smith can scarcely hope to emulate the fine works which were produced in mediæval times, unless the iron be made for the

purpose. It is not easy to repeat the mediæval operations of slotting a bar, so as to get the eyes at equal distances, without a machine; or of fastening hot (or, as in later times, cold) clips; or of cutting slits into a bar from the edge, and then curling the splintered parts; yet these were common work for the smith in the 12th century. It is equally difficult to produce the twisted work which was easy to the mediæval smith, whose chief care in the 13th and 14th centuries was bestowed in welding, stamping, and chiselling; the file was scarcely ever used. In welding he was careful to fire the two parts separately, getting the upper one to a white heat, the lower part to a red heat, and hammering the joint lightly at first, but harder as the iron grew colder. He disguised the uneven state of the upper part by punching on it separate dots, or else close ones, forming a sort of incised line.

2255j. In very large specimens of ancient work, some parts are additions entirely welded, others are additions confined at the ends by bands, which are welded across the groundwork. To imitate work of the 13th century, such as a grille, requires a drawing at full size, and a matrix for each leaf or bud, with an anvil cut to each section which a bar or a band is to assume; this last seems, with regard to the bar, to have been overlooked by M. Viollet le Duc. Then, when a bar has been rounded (if needful), and the end stamped, the curl is given and the smith has a stalk with a foot. Two of these must be applied to the drawing to have the point of junction marked, and the feet are to be welded together. If the sprigs then made are to be combined into branches, the larger stem is to be prepared; and, if moulded on the face, this was passed between the hammer and the cut anvil by a process equivalent to rolling the bar. After the sprigs are welded with the branch, the poverty of the joint is perhaps to be masked: usually the mask was a moulded band, to which an ornament, e.g. a cup of foliage, was sometimes added; but frequently the band was superseded by a stamped button. After the feet of the branches are welded to the trunk or main stem, bands are laid over the junction, are welded, and are finished with the chisel. The whole has to be riveted to the framework. The size and weight of the pieces at the last times of welding were difficulties that were partly obviated after 1250 by omitting the welded bands.

2255k. These operations were superseded by the introduction of sheet iron, in England before 1300, in Germany before 1400, and in France soon afterwards, which was cut and bossed to a remarkable extent, sometimes stamped, and frequently welded, but later was riveted. In work of the 15th century the bars are neither stamped nor chased, and the sheets are riveted instead of being welded; but later they are either planted or housed. Finally, the mediæval smith returned to the slots, mortises, and short bars of the earlier periods, and used clips which were closed cold with rivets of soft iron.

2255l. The founder, now more especially, is employed to supply ornamental fancy gates, sashes and frames, rain water pipes in 6 feet lengths, 2 to 8 in. in diameter, with their cistern heads, offsets, elbows, branch pieces, shoes, union sockets, and ears plain and ornamental. Square rain water pipes, $2\frac{1}{3}$ in. square; 3 in. by $2\frac{1}{2}$ in., 3 in. square; $3\frac{1}{4}$ in. by 2 in.; $3\frac{1}{2}$ in. by $2\frac{1}{2}$ in., $3\frac{1}{2}$ in. by $3\frac{1}{4}$ in., ; 4 in. by $2\frac{1}{2}$ in., 4 in. by 3 in., $4\frac{1}{2}$ in. by 3 in., 4 in. square, and 5 in. by $3\frac{1}{2}$ in. with branch pieces, shoes, ears, &c. Rain water gutters of all shapes and sizes, plain and moulded, roof gutters between slopes, square, angular, and square and angular. Pavement gutters, air or stench traps, scrapers, and coalplates, with many, if not all, of the articles required for "stable fittings" either plain, enamelled, or galvanized, as advertised by Varnel; Cottam and Hallen; the St. Pancras Iron Work Company; Musgrave, at Belfast; and others.

2256. The chief articles furnished by the ironmonger are for the joiner's use, and, except in particular cases, are kept in store by that tradesman for immediate supply as required.

2257. They consist in screws made in brass, copper and iron, whose common sizes are from three quarters of an inch up to 4 inches in length. They are sold by the dozen. Self-boring wood screws, the thread being made at a particular angle, are supplied in lengths of $\frac{1}{2}$, $\frac{5}{8}$, $\frac{3}{4}$, 1, $1\frac{1}{4}$, $1\frac{1}{2}$, $1\frac{3}{4}$, 2, $2\frac{1}{2}$, 3, $3\frac{1}{2}$, and 4 inches. Nails are now both wrought, cut, and cast, and made of iron, copper, and zinc. They are called by a variety of names according to their special uses. See Glossary, s. v. nail and adhesion. The weight of flooring brads (wrought and cut) per 1000 (rarely exceeding 900 nails) is—

Wrought.		Patent Cut.		Thickness of floors.
Length.	Weight.	Length.	Weight.	
2 inch.	8 lb.	2 inch.	8 lb.	$\frac{3}{4}$ inch.
$2\frac{1}{4}$,,	10 ,,	$2\frac{1}{4}$,,	10 ,,	Inch.
$2\frac{1}{2}$,,	12 ,,	$2\frac{1}{2}$,,	12 ,,	Inch.
$2\frac{3}{4}$,,	16 ,,	$2\frac{3}{4}$,,	15 ,,	$1\frac{1}{4}$ inch.
3 ,,	20 ,,	3 ,,	18 ,,	$1\frac{1}{2}$,,

Tacks are tinned over; and all nails can be galvanized to prevent their rusting. Nails for ornamental purposes, and likewise screws, are made with *brass heads*, and the latter also with *gilt heads.*

2258. *Butt hinges,* whose name is probably derived from butting close surface to surface when closed, are used for hanging doors and shutters, and made of wrought and cast iron and brass, the former varying in size from $1\frac{1}{4}$ to 4 inches in length; the latter from 1 inch to 4 inches. These, as well as all other hinges, are in size necessarily proportioned to the magnitude and consequent weight of the shutters or doors they are to carry; and it is to be observed, that for the well-hanging of a door or shutter, the size of the hinge should be rather on the outside of enough than under the mark. There is a species of hinge used for doors called the *rising joint hinge,* a contrivance in which the pivot, having on it a short portion of a spiral thread, and the part to which the door is fixed having a correspondent mass, the door in opening rises, and clears the carpet or other impediment usually placed on the floor. The *projecting brass butt* is used when the shutter or door is required to clear some projection, and thus, when opened, to lie completely back in a plane parallel to its direction when shut. All hinges are sold by the pair, including the necessary screws.

2258a. Besides these hinges, there are *cross garnets,* whose form is like the letter ⊢ sidewise. These are only used on the commonest external doors, and are made from 10 to 12 inches, varying in their dimensions by differences of two inches. H *hinges* are of the shape of the letter H, showing their form as well as the origin of their name; and in their sizes range from 4 to 12 inches by differences of an inch. HL *hinges* (H and L conjoined), whose form is implied by their name, and whose sizes are from 4 to 14 inches, proceed by inches. *Parliament hinges* are to allow a shutter to open back upon a wall, and are made of cast and wrought iron, from $3\frac{1}{2}$ to 5 inches, proceeding in size by half inches.

2258b. Redmund's patent hinges consist of, iron rising butts; or in brass with moulded burnished knuckles and concealed joints; iron and brass projecting butts with moulded burnished knuckles, flaps and concealed joints, in three sizes of proportional strength, from $1\frac{1}{4}$ to $4\frac{1}{2}$ inches projection; *pew hinges,* in iron and brass, projecting 1, $1\frac{1}{2}$, and 2 inches. Rising *spring hinges* in iron; and not rising spring hinges, in brass, iron, and patent malleable iron, and of single and double action; these are made flush, the knuckle being made to suit the bead of the architrave; rising swing hinges, which rise and act each way; gate hinges of many descriptions, &c.

2258c. Collinge's patent spherical hinges run from 2 to 6 inches, in plain brass, ornamental brass, and cast iron. The gate or strap hinge, from 1 foot 6 inches to 3 feet 6 inches, in steps of three inches. Improved gate springs with hardened joints. Spring hinges, and also to open both ways, are made light, strong, and extra strong, for $1\frac{1}{2}$, 2, $2\frac{1}{4}$, and $2\frac{1}{2}$ inch doors, in iron and brass.

• 2258d. Among other useful hinges are, swing centres, double action, to open both ways, known as Smith's patent, Redmund's, and Gerish's, chiefly for 2 and $2\frac{1}{2}$ inch doors. Hart's iron rod door springs, from 15 to 42 inches, called No. 1, No. 2, No. 3, and No. 4 qualities, also brass mounted. Circular door springs. Rising and not rising door back springs; spiral door springs; and patent climax door springs for single and double action doors, must also be noted for closing doors.

2259. *Rough rod bolts* are those in which there is no continued barrel for the bolt, and are for the most common service. Their sizes begin with a length of 3 inches, and proceed by inches up to a length of 10 inches; such, at least, are their common sizes. *Bright rod bolts* run of the same sizes as the last; and, as the name indicates, the bolt is polished and finished, so as to make them a better fastening, as far as appearance is concerned. The *spring plate bolt* is contrived with a spring to keep the bolt up to its work, but one which so soon gets out of order that we wonder it is now manufactured or used. It is made of lengths from 3 to 8 inches, by variations of an inch in size. *Barrelled bolts* are those in which the whole length of the bolt is enclosed in a continued cylindrical barrel, and are superior to all others in use, as well as the most finished in their appearance. Their common sizes are from 6 to 12 inches, varying by steps of an inch. All the bolts above mentioned are sold per piece by the ironmonger, as are those called *flush bolts,* a name given to such as are let into the surface to which they are applied, so as to stand flush with it. They are mostly made of brass, and are of two different thicknesses, viz. half and three quarter inch. Their lengths vary from $2\frac{1}{2}$ to 12 inches, and occasionally, as circumstances may require, as in book-case doors and French sashes, to a greater length. But for French casements, what is called the *Espagnolette bolt,* a contrivance whose origin is French, though much improved in its manufacture here, is now more generally in use. Smith's *patent weather tight casement fastenings for French windows,* consists of a plate formed in the edge of one door, which when shut is forced half its width into a groove in the other door. This acts in lieu of the Espagnolette bolt above mentioned. Smith's patent *water bar* for casements has been mentioned in pars. 2165b. and d, and 2255b. Jackson's patent *mortise bolt* appears to be a late improvement upon the round or the flush bolt.

2260. *Pullies,* for hanging sashes and shutters, are made of iron and of brass, and with

brass sheaves and brass axles. Their sizes are from one inch and a half to two inches and a half in diameter. M'Adam's pulleys for window sashes, of porcelain or vitreous material, are considered to be exempt from damp and rust through which cords may become rotten. He adds to them a method of hanging double sashes with a single weight on each side of the window. Austin's imperial patent sash and blind lines are made of flax, in four qualities. A common description is made from jute, but this sort has not the strength or durability of flax, and is not so good as the common cord lines. Newall's patent *copper wire cord* and *wire strand* are extensively used for window sash line, hothouses, lightning conductors, picture cord, clock cord, tent ropes, clothes lines, &c. The advantages, as reported, being that they are cheaper, much more durable, equally flexible, and one-sixth part the bulk. Newall's patent improved *iron wire rope*, we do not detail.

Table I. of Newall's Copper Cords.

Number . .	0 1	1¼	1½	1¾	2	3	4	5	6	7	8	9	10
Diameter, inch .	$\frac{3}{8}$				$\frac{1}{7}$	$\frac{1}{8}$	$\frac{1}{10}$						
	Lightning Conductor	For Window Sash Line, Hothouse, &c.							Picture Cord, &c.				
Breaking strain, lbs.	1260	960	690	480	300	180	125	45	90	120	128	130	300
Working load, in lbs.	336	224	168	112	75	45	31	11	22	30	32	50	80

Brass axle pulleys, and hothouse pulleys, are supplied to suit.

Table II. of Iron Cords—Galvanized and Plain.

Number	1	1¼	1½	1¾	2	3	4
Breaking strain, in pounds . . .	2520	1920	1380	960	600	360	250
Working load, in pounds	672	448	326	224	150	90	60

Wire strand, 4 and 6 wire, of No. 3, 4, 5, 6, and 7 qualities; galvanized and ungalvanized.

2261. The varieties of locks, their contrivances for security, and their construction, are so many, that to describe them minutely would require almost a work of itself. All that the architect has to deal with, for common purposes in building, we shall mention. For fastening places where particular security is requisite, as strong closets for plate or cash, some of the patented locks should be used, and we must leave this matter for inquiry in the hands of the architect. Every patentee says his invention is the best. We nevertheless believe, notwithstanding the boasts of all the inventors, that no lock has appeared which an expert locksmith acquainted with its construction will not be able to pick. The locks in common use are *stock locks*, whose box is usually of wood, and whose sizes vary from 7 to 10 inches. *Dead locks*, whose sizes are from 4 to 7 inches, and so called from the key shooting the bolt home *dead*, without a spring. *Cupboard locks* of 3, 3½, and 4 inches in size. *Iron rim locks*, whose box or case is made of iron, and which are fitted on to one of the sides of a door, and whose sizes are from 6 to 8 inches. Of those made of the last-named size, there are some, as also of 9 inches, which are used for external doors, called *iron rim drawback locks*. For the doors of all well-finished apartments, *mortise locks* are used. These take their name from being mortised into the thickness of the door, and being thus hidden. Gerish's patent cylindrical mortise lock, Barron's patent locks, Bramah's patent locks, Chubb's patent locks, Hobbs' patent locks "are made for all purposes, from the smallest cabinet to the largest fortress gate." To these either plain or fancy *furniture*, that is, *knobs* and *escutcheons*, are affixed. Pitt's patent *self-adjusting spindle*, with his new patent *mount and spindle*, and Ager's patent *adjusting spindle*, all command a large sale. They are all fitted with knobs and plates, from china, plain white and buff, to gold lines, gold bands, flowers, &c., and in hard woods, as ebony, maple, satin, rose, mahogany, wainscot, and walnut; the knobs in many shapes: also with plain and fancy brass, brass and china combined, and buffalo horn furniture. Also with glass furniture, crystal and amber, of varying shapes and cutting, with green, black, and opal cut octagons. Above and below them *finger plates* are generally directed to be fixed, to prevent the door being soiled in the places where it is mostly caught.

2262. The different sorts of latches in use are the *thumb latch*, which receives its name from the thumb being placed on the lever to raise its latch; the *Norfolk-latch*, which is sunk, and requires a pressure on the lever to raise the latch; the *Suffolk-latch*; the four-inch *bow latch* with brass nobs; the brass *pulpit latch*; the *mortise latch*; and Gothic latches.

2262*a*. Adams and Son's *electric bells* for domestic use, has M. Breguet's (of Paris) patent indicator system, with a dial which shows when the bell is ringing. In Thomson and Co's patent *electric bells, electric fire alarms*, and *alarms for windows and doors*, the battery is con-

tinuous, requiring to be replenished but once (and at only a small cost) in twelve months. The wires can be covered with silk or cotton of the same colour as the decorations, to be practically invisible. Moseley's patent electric bells are fixed on the system of the battery not being in use when the bell is not ringing, therefore the wires cease to be, as in the French system, charged with electricity. The price appears to be, for a number of bells, from 25s. and upwards per pull. The ordinary crank system is noticed in Specifications, par. 2292. Wishaw's registered improved *telekouphonon* for speaking pipes, consists of a whistle mouthpiece of ivory, wood, or metal, with an indicator attached to point out from which one of two or more tubes the whistle proceeds.

2263. Besides the articles already mentioned, *spikes* of 5, 6, and 7 inch lengths, *hold-fasts*, *wall hooks*, *door springs* of various sorts, *door chains* and *barrels*, *thumb screws* and other shutter and sash fastenings and shutter bars, *brass turn buckles*, *closet knobs*, *brass flush rings*, *brass rollers*, *bars with latchets*, *shelf brackets*, *drawer handles*, *sash weights*, besides many other articles, are furnished by the ironmonger.

2263a. In treating on Specifications, in a subsequent section, it will be seen how the several articles of smithery and ironmongery are applied.

2264. Bolts, straps, and other exposed iron work are preserved from the action of moisture on them by the following mixture :—To two quarts of boiling oil add half a pound of litharge, putting in small quantities at a time, and cautiously. Let it simmer over the fire two or three hours ; then strain it, and add a quarter of a pound of finely-pounded resin and a pound of white lead, keeping it at a gentle heat till the whole is well incorporated. It is to be used hot. A composition of oil and resin and finely levigated brickdust is found useful in preserving iron from rust. It is to be mixed, and used as a paint of the usual consistence (see par. 1780, *et seq.*). Wrought iron ornamental work exposed to the weather, has been cased with copper and gilt, as much for decoration as for preservation.

GAS FITTER.

2264a. The works of this artizan may be placed under the head of this section, although his trade is now kept distinct. The main distribution of gas is effected through cast iron pipes with sockets and spigot ends, whenever the diameter exceeds 2 inches. The various formulæ for calculating the velocity and the pressure of the effluent gas are to be found in Clegg, *Treatise on Gas Lighting*. The most economical working pressure is equivalent to the weight of a column of water on the outlet, of about 1 inch. The formula for calculating the quantity discharged is $q = 1350d^2 \sqrt{\frac{h\,d}{s\,l}}$; in which $q =$ the quantity sought in cubic feet per hour ; d, the diameter of the pipe ; h, the working pressure in inches ; l, the length of the pipe in yards ; and s, the specific gravity of the gas compared with atmospheric air as unity.

Table of the Delivery per Hour through Pipes of the Diameters named.

Size. diameter.	Thickness.	Length.	Weight.	Delivery.	Cost of Laying.
ins.				cubic ft.	
¼				90	See Lockwood's
⅜	wrought			160	*Price Book*, 1862,
½	iron.			250	art. Gas Fitter.
¾				380	
⅞					
1	inch.	feet.	cwt. qr. lbs.	500	
2	5-16ths	6	0 1 24	2,000	
3	11-32nds	6	1 0 3	4,500	
4	3-8ths	9	1 1 24	8,000	
5	13-32nds	9	1 3 24	12,500	
6	7-16ths	9.	2 2 2	18,000	
7	15-32nds	9	3 0 14	24,500	
8	1-half	9	3 3 5	32,000	
9	17-32nds	9	4 2 2	40,500	
10	9-16ths	9	5 1 6	50,000	
12	5-8ths	9	7 0 5	72,000	

2264b. In the details of house fittings, wrought iron pipes are used when the diameter is, and exceeds, half an inch ; ¾ in. is the least size recommended to be used, even for supplying upper rooms. For pipes of smaller diameters, and where abrupt bends have to be made, tin or composition pipes are fixed. For occasional use, flexible pipes are employed, such as those made of gutta percha, caoutchouc, with or without a wire coil inside,

and caoutchouc coated with varnish.   This last is the safest of the flexible pipes; the other, though safer when used with a wire core, is not impermeable to gas, though a coat of linseed oil may render it so.   The first-named is not only permeable, but causes an unpleasant smell, and is liable to contraction at any junctions with metal work, allowing of the escape of gas.   Under no circumstances whatever should either iron or composition pipes be let into the plastering, as is too constantly done, or into solid brick or stone work; for the salts in the latter are liable to affect the pipes in a serious manner, and the contraction and expansion of their materials may injure the joints; whilst it must always be difficult to trace a leakage.   When placed in a partition, the gas escaping fills all the spaces between the studs, and between the joists of the floors, so that when it comes in contact with a light the whole ignites, and the force of the explosion may cause the entire destruction of the house.   The police regulations of Paris require that gas-pipes in houses should be visible throughout their length, excepting when they traverse floors, partitions, &c., when the pipe conveying the gas is required to be enclosed in a larger one, projecting beyond the floor or partition, so as to ensure ventilation round it.   Copper pipes should never be used, for after a short time a detonating substance is formed in their interior by the action of the gas on the metal.

2264c. The form of *burner* which yields the best economical results is the argand; the bat's wing is the next best; and the fish-tail the worst.   A number of small burners dispersed will give a better light than collections of them.   For lighting large rooms, where it is not necessary to throw the light upon any particular space, the solar or sun-light arrangement is agreeable, and it is now fitted so as to promote the ventilation of the room. It is very costly, not only in its first establishment, partly from the necessity of securing the burners and pipes from setting fire to the surrounding timbers, but also in the subsequent consumption of gas.   In rooms of moderate height, the heat to the occupants is objectionable.   The argand burner, with 15 holes, will burn about $5\frac{1}{2}$ to 8 feet per hour, according to the pressure; ordinary street lamps, having the bat's wing, burn 3 to 8 feet per hour, and are usually contracted for at the rate of $5\frac{1}{2}$ feet.

2264d. As illustrations of the mode of *lighting* public buildings may be cited: I. The concert room at Liverpool, designed and executed by Mr. A. King; it is effected principally by carrying a pipe in the cove of the ceiling, which pipe is pierced with numerous holes for fish-tail burners.   II. St. James's Hall, London, and the great hall of the Reform Club, which are admirable illustrations of the use of the stellar and of the solar lights.   III. The new theatre du Chatelet, at Paris, where the lighting is effected by 1,300 burners placed above a vault of ground glass, and under a large enamelled reflector; the glass vault forms, in fact, the ceiling of the body of the house, so that the burners themselves are entirely hid.   This arrangement was also employed for a few years at the picture gallery in Suffolk Street, London.   And IV. The various passages and rooms of the Houses of Parliament, which are lighted and ventilated under Faraday's principle.

2264e. A notice was issued in January 1862, from the London Fire Engine Establishment, stating that, " It appears absolutely necessary that some steps should be taken to caution owners of property, particularly in large wharves and warehouses, as to the position and protection of the dangerous gas lights.   These remarks may not be considered unnecessary when it is remembered that in many of the most valuable buildings in the metropolis moveable gas brackets are placed within 20 inches of the ceiling without the slightest protection whatever.   It may be laid down as a rule that the jet on the outer arm of the bracket should never be less than 36 inches from the ceiling over it, and that it should be protected on the top by a hanging shade, and on the sides by stops on the swivel joints, which should prevent the brackets moving beyond a safe distance.   Attention might, perhaps, also be called to the very common and dangerous practice of nailing tin or iron on the adjoining timbers.   This has long proved to be no protection, and it has the disadvantage of allowing the timber to be charred completely through before it is known."   In some places gas lights are used within 15 inches of the ceiling, and when the glass shade has been broken and not replaced, the heat has been known to ignite the floor timbers over the plastering.

2264f. It will not be necessary here to do more than mention the use of gas in the kitchen for boiling water, or for baking and roasting; the baths heated by gas, so readily adaptable in places where a coal stove cannot be used; or the several gas stoves for warming buildings and rooms.

2264g. The urgency of efficient *ventilation* when gas is burnt in a room habitually, is a subject of immediate importance.   It is principally to the neglect of this precaution that the bulk of the injurious effects said to attend the use of gas may indeed be attributed. In the case of libraries, the destruction of book bindings may be assigned more justly to the heat than to the chemical action of the products of combustion.   No doubt the bisulphide of carbon, which is present in even the most carefully purified gases, must give rise to the formation of minute quantities of sulphurous acid: and this, in its turn, must be destructive to some descriptions of leather—especially Russian (as noticed in the

Builder, vi. 89); but a rapid removal of the products of combustion would almost entirely obviate this effect. It seems, however, that the excessive dryness and the heat of the air in the upper part of rooms where gas is burnt, may occasion the injury quite as much as the chemical reactions supposed to take place ; the books which suffer most being always those placed above the level of the lamps. Under any circumstances, ventilation should take place close to the plane of the ceilings. Even when provision is made for ventilation over gas burners, a stratum of heated air is often allowed to stagnate over the openings, close under the line of the ceiling ; and the area of the openings is rarely sufficient to allow the escape of the decomposed gases. Again, if any sulphurous acid should be produced, it will be found also to tarnish the colours of tapestry and hangings, and to turn imitation gold ; hence none but the best leaf-gold should be employed in rooms where gas is burnt. The injury caused by the use of such gas as is supplied in London, Paris, Bruxelles, &c., is very small compared with the brilliance of the light ; and the gas of Liverpool, Edinburgh, Manchester, and some other places having, bulk for bulk, a higher illuminating power than that of London, is even less injurious. Mr. Spencer has reported that the quantity of gas leaking from London gas pipes is not less than 9 per cent., or between six and seven million cubic feet per annum, which causes the stinking black earth of the London street subsoil: no such leakage occurs at Liverpool or Manchester, where the joints of the pipes are bored, turned, and fitted to each other, like ground stoppers in glass bottles ; whereas in London the pipes are jointed with tow and lead, so that after expansion and contraction in summer and winter the perfection of the joints is destroyed. The gas then acting upon the subsoil forms sulphuretted carbon, which corrodes not only the gas pipes, but the water mains also, and converts them in ten years almost entirely into a sort of plumbago, although in pure London subsoil they last a century.

2264*h*. Wrought iron welded tubing for gas is made from 2 in. diameter, $1\frac{1}{2}$ in., and then down by each $\frac{1}{4}$ in. to $\frac{1}{2}$ in., then $\frac{3}{8}$, $\frac{1}{4}$, and $\frac{1}{8}$ in. diameter, in lengths of from 4 to 12 feet, from 2 to 4 feet, and shorter pieces under 2 feet; together with all their connecting pieces, cocks, taps, screws, &c. We have availed ourselves of G. R. Burnell's contribution to the *Dictionary of Architecture* for much of the information upon this subject here laid before the reader.

Sect. XI.

FOUNDERY.

2265. The very general use of cast iron by the architect induces us to give a succinct account of the common operations of foundery, or the art of casting metal into different forms. To gain a proper knowledge of the operations, the student should attend a few castings at the foundery itself, which will be more useful to him than all the description we could detail of it; however, we give a few particulars not noticed in the previous section on Iron. Some of the articles cast are noticed in par. 2255*k*.

2265*a*. Those manufacturers who will attend to the good quality of the irons they sell, can generally command their own price. Thus, the Low Moor and the Bowling bar irons continue in possession of the market at nominally high prices, whilst the ordinary irons are hardly saleable at remunerative ones. The Welsh iron, known as the SC brands, or the Staffordshire mitre iron, are of at least equal quality to the above, and there are others as good. The average price of Welsh bars is usually 1*l*. per ton below that of the Staffordshire bars, and the latter are sold at about 10*s*. per ton below the price of the Yorkshire bars, a tolerably fair indication of their respective values. Another test is the mean average prices of pig iron at the furnaces throughout the kingdom, which for the year 1858, were about 3*l*. 2*s*. per ton. Locally, the prices at the furnaces varied as follows:—

	£	s.	d.		£	s.	d.
Scotch pig, mixed numbers -	2	17	3	Yorkshire, mixed numbers -	3	5	0
Durham „ - -	3	3	0	Staffordshire „ - -	2	17	0
Cleveland „ - -	2	14	6	Welsh „ - -	3	15	0

2265*b*. Staffordshire, Shropshire, and Derbyshire, afford the best irons for castings. The Scotch iron is much esteemed for hollow wares, and has a beautifully smooth surface, which may be noticed in the stoves and other articles cast by the Carron Company. The Welsh pig iron is principally used for conversion into bar iron. Almost all irons are improved by admixture with others, and therefore, where superior castings are required, they should not be run direct from the smelting furnace ; but the metal should be remelted in a cupola furnace, which gives the opportunity of suiting the quality of the iron to its intended use. Thus, for delicate ornamental work, a soft and very fluid iron will be required, whilst for girders and castings exposed to cross strain, the metal will require to be harder and more tenacious. For bed plates and castings, which have merely to sustain a compressing

force, the chief point to be attended to is the hardness of the metal. Various mixtures of different qualities of iron have been recommended as materials for large castings (see Fairbairn's *Application of Iron, &c. 65.*). Most engineers are agreed in considering that the best course for an engineer to take, in order to obtain iron of a certain strength for a proposed structure, is, not to specify to the founder any particular mixture, but to specify a certain minimum strength which the iron should exert when tested by experiment.

2265c. As noticed in a previous chapter, the ores are smelted by cold and hot air blasts. The latter iron makes very fine castings, but is deficient in tenacity, and requires great care in its application to the purposes of machinery, and for girder castings, by employing it as second runnings from the cupola, and mixing third-class pig iron with the first. On account of some defects in it, hot blast iron should be excluded from all such works as girder bridges, machinery castings, &c., and from the preparation of bar iron where great strength in the metal is required. It appears that there are no means of detecting hot or cold blast irons in pig castings. Whenever great strength is required, air furnaces instead of cupolas should be used, and where it is not connected with too great an expense, loam instead of green sand should be used for moulding.

2265d. TABLE OF THE WEIGHT OF CAST IRON PER FOOT SUPERFICIAL. (Hurst.)
The weight of a cubic foot is put at 456 lbs. and 460 lbs.

Thickness in inches -	$\frac{1}{16}$	$\frac{1}{8}$	$\frac{3}{16}$	$\frac{1}{4}$	$\frac{5}{16}$	$\frac{3}{8}$	$\frac{7}{16}$	$\frac{1}{2}$
Weight in pounds -	2·34	4·68	7·03	9·37	11·72	14·06	16·40	18·75
Thickness in inches -	$\frac{9}{16}$	$\frac{5}{8}$	$\frac{11}{16}$	$\frac{3}{4}$	$\frac{13}{16}$	$\frac{7}{8}$	$\frac{15}{16}$	1
Weight in pounds -	21·09	23·44	25·78	28·12	30·47	32·81	35·16	37·50

2265e. Collinson's Mansfield moulding sand has a wide reputation among the modellers of the finest brass and iron castings, arising, no doubt, partly from its exquisite fineness of grain, but more particularly from its clay-like adhesiveness and plaster quality, combined with a total freedom from any coarse or gritty particles. It is found under a deep deposit of coarse sand, ordinarily known as building sand, and within a short distance of the well-known white and red Mansfield stone quarries, in Nottinghamshire. The Isle of Wight sands are also used for the purpose. The sand usually employed in casting is of a soft yellow and clammy nature, over which, in the mould, charcoal is strewed. Upon the sand properly prepared, the wood or metal models of what is intended to be cast are applied to the mould, and pressed so as to leave their impression upon the sand. Canals are provided for the metal, when melted, to run through. After the frame is finished, the patterns are taken out by loosening them all round, that the sand may not give way. The other half of the mould is then worked with the same patterns, in a similar frame, but having pins which, entering into holes that correspond to it in the other, cause the two cavities of the pattern exactly to fall on each other. The frame thus moulded comes now under the care of the melter, who prepares it for the reception of the metal.

2265f. In making patterns for cast iron, an allowance is always made of about one-eighth of an inch per foot for the contraction of the metal in cooling. And it may be also requisite that the patterns should be slightly bevelled, that they may be drawn out of the sand without injuring the impression ; for this purpose, $\frac{1}{16}$ of an inch in 6 inches is sufficient.

2265g. All castings should be kept as nearly as possible of the same bulk, in order that the cooling may take place equably. It is of importance to prevent air-bubbles in castings, and the more time there is allowed for cooling the better, because, when rapidly cooled, the iron does not become so tough as when gradually cooled. It is important in any casting to have the metal as uniform as possible, and not of different sorts, for different sorts will shrink differently, and thus will be caused an unequal tension among the parts of the metal, which will impair its strength ; and, beyond this, an unevenness is produced by such mixture on the surface of the casting, for different sorts can never be perfectly blended together.

2265h. Castings should show on the outer surface, a smooth, clear, and continuous skin, with regular faces and sharp angles. When broken, the surface of fracture should be of a light bluish grey colour, and close-grained texture, with considerable metallic lustre ; both colour and texture should be uniform, except that near the skin the colour may be somewhat lighter and the grain closer ; if the fractured surface is mottled, either with patches of darker or lighter iron, or with crystalline patches, the casting will be unsafe ; and it will be still more unsafe if it contains air-bubbles. The iron should be soft enough to be slightly indented by a blow of a hammer on an edge of a casting. Castings are tested for

air-bubbles by ringing them with a hammer all over the surface. Iron becomes more compact and sound by being cast under pressure; and hence cannon, pipes, columns, &c., are stronger when cast in a vertical than in a horizontal position, and stronger still when provided with a *head* or additional length, whose weight serves to compress the mass of iron in the mould below it. The air-bubbles ascend and collect in the head, which is broken off when the casting is cool. Care should be taken not to cut or remove the skin of a piece of cast iron at those points where the stress is intense.

2265i. *Malleable cast iron* is made by embedding the castings to be made malleable in the powder of red hæmatite. They are then raised to a bright red heat, which occupies about twenty-four hours, maintained at that heat for a period varying from three to five days, according to the size of the casting, and allowed to cool, which occupies about twenty-four hours more. The oxygen of the hæmatite extracts part of the carbon from the cast iron, which is thus converted into a sort of soft steel; and its tenacity, according to experiments by Messrs. A. More and Son, becomes more than 48,000 lbs. per square inch. (*Rankine.*)

2266. The foundery of statues, which is among the most difficult of its branches, belongs exclusively to the sculptor, and is usually carried on in bronze. The execution of the bronze castings, made by the firm of Barbedienne of Paris, is attributed mainly, after the skill of the modeller, to the fineness of the sand, which can only be obtained at Fontenay-aux-Roses, in France. When new it is yellow in colour, but on account of its cost it is mixed in well-ascertained proportions with the old sand, which has become black, the mixture forming a good combination for the mould; other sands are considered to have too much silex in them, whereas the Fontenay sand has exactly the proportion necessary for the fineness of the work.

SECT. XII.

PAINTING, GILDING, PAPER-HANGING, ETC.

2267. Painting is the art of covering the surfaces of wood, iron, and other materials with a mucilaginous substance, which acquiring hardness by exposure to the air, protects the material to which it is applied from the effects of the weather. The processes employed in house painting were described by the editor at the Institute of British Architects, *Transactions*, Nov. 1857.

2268. The requisite tools of the painter are—*brushes of hog's bristles*, of various sizes suitable to the work; a *scraping or pallet knife; earthen pots* to hold the colours; a *tin can* for turpentine; a *grinding stone and muller*, &c. The stone should be hard and close-grained, about 18 inches in diameter, and of sufficient weight to keep it steady. The knots, especially of fir, in painting new work, will destroy its good effect if they be not first properly *killed*, as the painters term it. The best way of effecting this is by laying upon those knots which retain any turpentine a considerable substance of lime immediately after it is slaked. This is done with a stopping knife, and the process dries and burns out the turpentine which the knots contain. When the lime has remained on about four and twenty hours, it is to be scraped off, and the knots must be painted over with what is called *size knotting*, a composition of red and white lead ground very fine with water on a stone, and mixed with strong double glue size, and used warm. If doubts exist of their still remaining unkilled, they may be then painted over with red and white lead ground very fine in linseed oil, and mixed with a portion of that oil, taking care to rub them down with sand paper each time after covering them when dry; so that they may not appear more raised than the other parts. When the knotting is completed, the *priming colour* is laid on. The priming colour is composed of white and a little red lead mixed thin with linseed oil. One pound of it will cover from 18 to 20 yards. When the primer is quite dry, if the work is intended to be finished white, mix white lead and a very small portion of red with linseed oil, adding a little quantity of spirits of turpentine for second colouring the work. Of this second primer, one pound will cover about 10 to 12 square yards. The work should now remain for some days to harden; and before laying on the third coat, it should be rubbed down with fine sand paper, and stopped with oil putty wherever it may be necessary. If the knots still show through, they should be covered with silver leaf, laid on with japanned gold size. The third coat is white lead mixed with linseed oil and turpentine in equal portions, and a pound will cover about 8 square yards. If the work is not to be finished white, the other requisite colour will of course be mixed with the white lead, as in the case of four coats being used. When the work is to be finished with four coats, the finishing coat should be of good old white lead as the basis, thinned with bleached linseed oil and spirits of turpentine; one of oil to two of turpentine. If the work is to be finished *dead white*, the very best old lead must be used, and thinned entirely with spirits of turpentine.

2269. When stucco is to be painted, it will require one more coat than wood-work; the

last coat being mixed, if the work is as usually executed, with half spirits of turpentine and half oil, for the reception of the finishing coat of all turpentine or *flatting*. If the work be not flatted, the finishing coat should be with one part oil and two of turpentine. It would be impossible to enter into the details which are to be observed in painting walls of fancy colours ; all that can be said on this point in instruction to the architect is, that when fancy colours, as they are called, which in these days a painter construes as anything but white and a tinge of ochre or umber, each coat must incline, as it is laid on, more and more to the colour which the work is intended to bear when finished.

2270. In repainting old work, it should be well rubbed down with dry pumice stone, and then carefully dusted off, and when requisite, the cracks and openings must be well stopped with oil putty. After this, a mixture of white, with a very small portion of red lead, with equal parts of oil and turpentine, is used to paint the work, which the painters technically call second colouring old work. After this, the work being dry, a mixture of old white lead, adding a small portion of blue black in a medium of half bleached oil and half turpentine, is used for finishing, or, if flatting be intended, the former preparation will be suitable for receiving dead white or any fancy colour. The same process will serve for stuccoed walls, observing that, if more coats be required, the mixture of half oil and half turpentine is proper.

2271. In respect to outside work, the use of turpentine is to be avoided, for turpentine is more susceptible of water than oil, and thence not so well calculated to preserve work exposed to the weather. Oil, however, having from its nature a natural tendency to discolour white, that is necessarily finished with a portion of half oil and half turpentine; but in dark colours this is not necessary, and in such cases, boiled oil, with a little turpentine, is the best, or indeed boiled oil only.

2271a. When linseed oil is clarified and cleansed by means of sulphuric acid, much of the cohesion in the vegetable property of the oil is destroyed, preventing its forming that perfect pellicle which it invariably does upon exposure to the atmosphere during drying. White lead should be ground with linseed oil in its pure state ; this oil is now largely adulterated with oils of resin and pine, as those oils are very much cheaper. Oils are thus clarified that the lead, when ground, may appear at once as white as possible ; whereas, if ground in pure linseed oil which has had the refuse cast down by means of ivory black or powdered litharge, it will at first have a yellow tinge, which is only to be got rid of by time ; and hence arises the value of old ground white lead. (*Builder*, xiv).

2271b. The blackness which in the winter frequently shows itself upon exterior painted work probably arises from the outer skin of the oil having been rendered porous by the sulphuric acid, and the foul, or hydrogen gas, readily fastens itself to the unprotected lead, for which it has an affinity, and hence results the mottled appearance of such work.

2271c. The best linseed oil is obtained from good Baltic and Bombay linseed, crushed. Mineral turpentine is sometimes used as an adulteration of that article ; the paint made with it dries, and then softens, becoming sticky even under a coat of sugar of lead and varnish. Woodwork prepared with bad linseed oil for being stained, prevents the varnish from drying : good size is all that is required. To distinguish the good and bad qualities, states a writer in the *Builder*, xxi. p. 919, pure vegetable turpentine, upon exposure to the air, always loses in bulk by evaporation, but gains in weight by absorption of oxygen, which makes it more binding in its properties. This peculiarity none of the mineral substitutes possess ; on the contrary, the mineral is so extremely volatile that, upon exposure, the spirit all flies off, leaving the oil without anything to assist it to harden, and of course increases the evil of the bad oil, instead of counteracting it. The use of varnish in white lead work cannot be sufficiently reprehended, on account of the ultimate defect of the work.

2271d. Nut oil has been stated to be more durable, and to stand the weather much longer than any other oil in paint.

2272. White lead, which is the principal basis of all stone colours, is carbonate of lead, generally containing hydrated oxide of lead, which is sometimes combined in the proportion of one atom of hydrated oxide to two of carbonate of lead. It is usually made either by precipitation, as when carbonic acid or a carbonate is used to decompose a soluble salt, or a subsalt of lead : or by exposing plates of cast lead to the joint action of the vapour of acetic acid air and carbonic acid. It is by the latter process only that the resulting carbonate of lead is obtained of that degree of density, opacity, and perfect freedom from crystalline texture, which fits it for paint. The last, called the Dutch process, was introduced into England about 1780. White lead is often largely adulterated with sulphate of baryta, which may be detected by insolubility in dilute nitric acid, whereas pure white lead is entirely dissolved by it. Fine lead is now made from *slag lead*, which is treated with nitrate of soda, thus oxidising all impurities except copper. The same effect is accomplished by calcining the lead in an improving furnace, especially when the lead contains much antimony. The copper is next removed by a process not yet published, and finally the lead is crystallised by Pattinson's process. The resulting metal is remarkable for its fine crystalline surface and bold columnar fracture. Lead containing even only $2\frac{1}{4}$ ounces

of copper per ton communicates a pink tint to the corrosions of white lead, which it is important to remove.

2272a. The ill effects on the constitution of persons engaged both in the manufacture and use of the article, have recently (since the publication of the first edition of this work) induced the French chemists to find some less deleterious substitute for it, and M. de Ruolz has discovered two substances which fulfil the required conditions—viz., combination with oil, good colour, property of concealing, &c. The first is an arsenical compound (product) hitherto little known, which M. de Ruolz does not describe, because, although inoffensive, it may be made by very simple chemical reaction, to retake its poisonous qualities, and be employed criminally. The second, which he considers well adapted for use, is the oxide of antimony, and possesses the following properties : its colour is a very pure white, rivalling the finest silver white, it is very easily ground, and forms with oil an unctuous and cohesive mixture; comparatively with the white lead of Holland as 46 to 22; mixed with other paints it gives much clearer and softer tones than white lead. It may be obtained directly from the natural sulphuret of antimony, and at one-third of the cost of ordinary white paint. (See *Literary Gazette*, Nov. 25, 1843.) If the finishing colour is white, nothing but white lead should be employed.

2272b. The other metallic white paint used is Hubbuck's patent *zinc white*, known for its intense whiteness, its resistance to sulphurous and other deteriorating causes, and its harmless qualities to the painter and the inmates of the house under decoration. It is requisite that the oil used should be as white as possible, that the brushes and pots should not have been used for white lead, or else have been cleaned with spirits; and that driers and colours with a lead basis should not be mixed with it. *Zinc white* possesses less body than white lead, and great care is requisite that the colour when ground in oil is of sufficient consistence to be laid on a flat surface without showing through; for in that state any oil in excess will form a slight glutinous coating on the surface, retaining every particle of dust brought in contact with it, until it has evaporated. Proper drying oils will cause zinc white to dry as quickly as the other colour. With these precautions, a few trials will enable any painter who is willing to work zinc white to overcome the difficulties which appear at first to condemn the invention. It is asserted that in consequence of the great durability of the colour of this material, a house painted with it may be washed for a succession of three, four, or even five years; and that after each successive washing, the surface will be found as clear and bright as when fresh painted. The effect, in appearance, of this paint is perhaps better when it is applied as a finish to a coat of pure white lead; generally it looks better on new work than on old, as some specimens prove that it was then apt to turn black. An American discovery consists in subjecting the oxide of zinc, in its dry state, to the combined action of friction and pressure, by which means its bulk is greatly reduced, and it is enabled to be ground with a reduced quantity of oil, while a greater body is given to the paint. Hubbuck states that 2 cwt. of his paint, with 6 gallons of oil, covers as much surface as 3 cwt. of white lead and 12 gallons of oil; and that it is cheaper also than white lead.

2272c. Lead colours are formed by a mixture of white lead with lamp black ; all colours, however, that are called *fancy colours*, have white lead for their basis, chocolates, black, brown, and wainscot only excepted. The *fancy colours* are drabs, French greys, peach blossom, lilac, light greens, patent greens, blues, vermilion, lake, &c.

2273. There is a process used by painters termed *clear-coleing*, which is executed with white lead ground in water, and mixed with size. This is used instead of a coat of paint; but it has not sufficient body usefully to answer the end for which it is usually employed. It prevents the oil paint sinking into the wood; it scales off, and in damp situations its colour almost immediately changes. The only occasions wherein it is useful, are where the work is greasy and smoky, in which the use of it prepares better for the reception of paint. It should, however, never be employed upon joiner's work or cornices to ceilings, where much enrichment is found; for, of all things, it destroys the sharpness and beauty of the ornaments. Painters are very fond of using it; but their endeavours to persuade the architect should always be resisted, except in cases of absolute necessity, namely, that in which a fair appearance cannot otherwise be given to the work. The old work should be well cleaned and dried, and then the mixture above stated applied. For finishing, the white lead is mixed in half linseed oil and half turpentine, and used as stiff as possible ; blue black, or some colour, and a little drier, are requisite.

2273a. Various prepared paints are employed. One of the oldest is Carson's *Anticorrosion paint*, used for out-door work only, such as farm buildings, implements, fencing, &c., all kinds of iron work, brick, stone, compo, &c. It is stated to be lower in price and as lasting twice as long as the best white lead. The powder, in which state it is supplied, is composed of ground glass bottles, scoriæ from lead works, burnt oyster shells, and the required matter for the colour that may be chosen. 112 lbs. of this paint requires 7 gallons of raw linseed oil and 1 gallon of turpentine ; to be mixed over-night ; 2 coats are required on paint, 3 on new work ; 3 or 4 on brick, compo, &c. ; everything to be well scraped first,

and the paint rubbed in well. It is thus more laborious to put on than common paint ; it wears out the brushes in a very short time. and as it lasts so long, painters will seldom use it. The appearance of a surface painted with it is rough, resembling that of unrubbed cast iron or freestone. It will blunt the edges of carpenters' tools when being sawn or cut through.

2273b. *Oxide of iron paint,* of various colours, is a ferruginous paint, for iron and wood, made at Matlock. Messrs. Peacock and Buchan have successfully applied their *improved coating composition* to many iron vessels and life boats, for many years, and it is found to preserve the plates, keep the iron cleaner, and to stand the sea air and salt water much better than most, if not all, other paints. The *Pure Carbon paint* protects iron from rust, and is valuable for all outside work. When *tar* is used as a paint, about a pint of spirits of turpentine is put to a gallon of tar as driers, or a larger quantity if it be required to dry quickly. The addition of yellow ochre will change the black to several shades of brown.

2273c. The *Bideford and mineral black paint* has been exclusively used in H. M. dockyards, &c., for the last forty years. " Its superiority is observable in the preservation of wood, iron, and canvas; it covers the work well, dries quick and hard, is more durable, and does not blister like other blacks, and has a body inferior only to white lead." The *Torbay iron paints,* made at Brixham, in Devonshire, have been much used in dockyards, &c , for coating materials under water, or in a position to be affected by damp. Their peculiar characteristics are, great covering properties, 62 lbs. effectually coating as large a surface as 112 lbs. of lead paint; economy, durability, protection of iron from corrosion, arresting oxidation at any stage, and resistance to sulphurous and other gases. (Hunt, *Handbook,* 1862. *Builder,* xx. 527.)

2273d. The *Iron minium paint,* by A. de Cartier, manufactured at Auderghem, near Bruxelles, is a pure oxide of iron mixed with about one-fourth its weight of siliceous clay, and not containing any acids. It is now extensively used in this and other countries for painting the ironwork of ships, gas-holders, &c., superseding red lead and other pigments for such purposes. It is said to be solid, durable, cheap, and, above all, to preserve iron from oxidation, and of hardening wood. It is a dark brown in colour, but mixes easily with other colours, such as black, yellow, green, &c. To test its purity, it is said to be sufficient to dilute it with a small-quantity of water, spreading it on paper, when, if pure, the edges of the paper will preserve the special tint of the iron minium. If a change of tint is perceived, an adulteration has been effected.

2273e. Warner's *Silicate of iron paint* is sold prepared in genuine boiled linseed oil, of a great variety of colours, for painting iron work. It is said to stand extreme heat and damp, and not to be affected by the strongest acid, sea water, sulphuretted hydrogen, or ammonia ; and to be equally well adapted for iron or wood. It adheres so tenaciously, that sheet iron may be bent until it breaks, without the paint coming off. The powder, when boiled up with tar, is a very cheap preservative for iron or wood.

2273f. When visiting Paris in 1860, the present editor was much struck with the appearance of the margins of the stairs at the hotel. On examination, they proved to be covered with a thickish coat of a hard compound, having rather a glossy surface, and somewhat of a light orange tinge. A water-closet which had been out of order on one morning was not only repaired, but the seat and riser, the floor, and the wall to a height of three feet, covered with this mixture, and ready for use by the next day. The tiled floor of the manuscript room at the library of St. Généviève, which had been covered with the same mixture, was then in various stages of obliteration according to the traffic. The attendant there spoke very highly in favour of its cleanliness. It is believed to be composed of 10 lbs. of purified yellow wax, 10 lbs. of linseed oil, 8 lbs. of spirits of turpentine, and 5 lbs. of common resin. The wax is dissolved separately in the linseed oil, and the resin in the spirits of turpentine by heat, and are subsequently intimately mixed, when they form a pasty compound. In this condition it is used as priming, being nearly colourless after application. Pigments ground up in oil in the usual way are added in the proportion of one-third of the vehicle, and then spirits of turpentine added in quantity sufficient to produce the desired amount of liquidity. So soon as the turpentine has evaporated, the coat of paint will support rubbing, if not too hard, without damage, but it takes some time to become *completely* hard. It is put on in one coat, without apparently any of the smell or inconveniences attending the ordinary process of painting.

2273g. The use of *distemper* is older than that of oil and varnish. *Whitewashing* is a kind of distemper, especially when size is used with it. Common distemper colour for walls is Spanish white, or *whiting,* broken into water, to which is added strong size whilst warm, and then allowed to cool, when it should appear a thin jelly ; two coats are generally necessary. The old work should be first washed by a brush with water. This process in old publications is called, " painting in water colours." It is much used for ceilings, and always requires two, and sometimes three, coats, to give it an uniform appearance. It is not generally known that walls which have been distempered cannot afterwards be *limewhited,* in consequence of the lime when laid on whiting turning yellow ; oil colours, however, can be applied, and then white lead is used as the vehicle. Papered rooms

coloured in this manner, especially over flock papers, look well, as the raised pattern can be seen through the coats of colour. Rooms may be distempered and dry again in a day, with little dirt. When wood is covered with distemper, it is liable to swell with the damp. Rooms that are to be afterwards *varnished* are prepared in two ways : I. By applying the intended distemper colour, and then covering it with as many coats of varnish, coloured or uncoloured, as may be required; but if the wood be not dry, the colour becomes hardened and flakes off. II. The colour is ground and mixed up with varnish, which produces a better result. If the last coat of varnish be applied colourless, it then forms a glazing to the under tints, and its brilliancy will be greater. The use of size here, again, produces a considerable saving of varnish. For new plaster work a coating of size is desirable.

2273h. *Distemper*, and *fresco painting*, are subjects we do not think well to treat in this section, as they would come under " Decorative painting," a higher branch of artistic skill.

2274. Some colours dry badly, black especially, and in damp weather they require a *drier*, as it is called, which may be made from equal parts of copperas and litharge, ground very fine, and added according to circumstances. Drying oil is made as follows :—To 1 gallon of linseed oil, put 1 lb. of red lead, 1 lb. of umber, and 1 lb. of litharge, and boil them together for two or three hours. Great care must be taken that the oil does not boil over, on account of the danger to which the premises would be thereby exposed. Thus, in a pot capable of holding fifteen gallons, it would not be prudent to boil more than one-third of that quantity.

2275. Painters' putty is made of whiting and linseed oil, well beaten together.

2276. *Graining* (or *combing*, as it is termed, in some late specifications) and *marbling*, or the imitation of real woods and marbles, is done by the painter. *Mahogany grained* in 1798 is the earliest notice the writer on the subject in the Architectural Publication Society's *Dictionary*, had found ; *grained wainscot* appeared in 1815. Imitation *wainscot* is obtained by giving the painted work a coat *in oil* of a brownish tone, the colour being thicker than usual ; this is then scratched over by combs of bone, with blunt points, and of various degrees of coarseness, leaving the ground visible. The cross white veins or *champs* are next taken out with the corners of a piece of soft leather doubled up. The next process, which in cheap work is omitted or carelessly done, is *over-veining*; this is effected with a wide flat brush, the hairs of which are long and slender, dipped in transparent colour, when the hairs stick together in a sort of lock; the cross veins of the wood are dexterously imitated with this tool, and show the other veins below. Other expedients have been devised to imitate knots, veins, mottles, &c., of various woods. The little dark spots with a lighter shade round them in maple wood, are imitated by dexterous touches with the tips of the fingers on the wet pigment. Almost every other wood, as well as wainscot, is imitated in distemper, for which small beer and water, mixed with Vandyke brown and burnt sienna, according to the tint required, is found to be sufficiently glutinous without the aid of size, to prevent it smearing during the application of the coat of copal varnish which follows soon afterwards. Graining operations are always done after the wood has been painted ; in best work, indeed, the coats are thicker than usual to afford a good ground for the combing. Taken with the subsequent varnishing, grained work is considered to be more lasting than painted work. Certain tools have been invented for performing this work ; the grain has been imitated by machinery ; and grained papers have been printed from the grain of the wood itself. To save the delay consequent on painting and all its annoyances, the editor of this edition explained, in 1857–8, his system of graining on the wood itself, whereby only a preparatory sizing is necessary; the result is that scarcely any smell of paint is perceived ; a greater brilliancy in effect is attained ; and the woodwork may be left to dry until the last moment.

2276a. *Marbling* is painting on a prepared painted surface, an imitation of the material as exact as the talent of the painter will admit, and requires no detailed explanation.

2276b. *Varnishing*, a subsequent operation to both of the above processes, requires much care and the use of good material, the best copal varnish, to bring out the colours of the work. Many qualities of varnish are manufactured, as ;—finest copal for imitation woods, &c. ; copal oak, for grained interior work ; mahogany varnish, being darker in colour ; fine hard-drying oak varnish, drying in about 8 hours, and used for seats in churches, &c.; dark hard-drying oak varnish, used after deal has been stained ; paper varnish, for paper-hangings, &c. Where expense is not an object, two or three coats are applied, especially to marbling, each coat being well rubbed down to obtain an even surface and a high degree of polish. To restore the gloss of varnished graining, of marbling, or of varnished paper, the whole must be well cleaned, then sized afresh, and revarnished. But the original colour of the work can never be fully reproduced, as the varnish darkens by time. Bruns-wick black varnish, a quick drying jet black, is used for grates, iron work, &c. Copal cabinet varnish, and a white, and a brown, hard varnish, and French polish, are used for cabinet-makers' work. A water flatting varnish renders paperhangings washable without imparting a gloss. These varnishes are all as made by Mander, Brothers, Wolverhampton.

2276c. To clean varnished work, soap and water applied carefully with a sponge, and

the use of warm woollen cloths to dry the work, is very efficacious. The steps of wooden staircases, painted, grained, and varnished, last a very long time, and neither dust nor dirt adhere so easily to such work, as to paint. Real woods, especially wainscot, are prepared for receiving coats of varnish, by being first sized to prevent the rise of the grain which ensues when the slightest quantity of water touches it. When to be polished, they are well smudged over a short time previously, with Russian tallow. A preparation called *Lethicium* is said to remove paint from wood in twenty minutes, doing away with the necessity for burning it off. A *hypo-nitro kali* has been introduced for the same purpose.

2276d. *Sand paper, glass paper, emery paper,* and *emery cloth,* of various degrees of fineness are employed to rub down work to a surface. It is made by the pulverized material being placed in fine sieves, and by a gentle motion, distributing it by hand over the paper or cloth prepared for its reception.

2276e. *Stains,* as substitutes for paint, the tints resembling oak, mahogany, rosewood, walnut, and satinwood, cause the natural grain of the deal on which they are applied, to appear. The wood is then sized and varnished; their durability is stated to be at least three times that of paint in interior work, and only at half the cost. This is Stephen's preparation. Naylor's *stain* is said not to require sizing, and to stand exposure to the weather. Swinburn's *Transparent staining and anti-dry rot fluids* are chemically prepared, and show the natural grain and feathery appearance of the wood. When sized and the proper varnish used, they are said not to fade or blister by exposure to the weather.

2277. In the outside work and stairs, the process of *sanding* is frequently adopted. It is performed with fine sand thrown on the last coat of paint while wet. Cement work is generally *coloured* with its own cement mixed up with water. Roman cement or black cement, as it is sometimes called, must have a wash or two; and while Portland cement is declared not to require any colouring, certain it is, that in London, not many years pass over before its dirty look urges a colouring or painting process. The process of painting the artificial cements, such as Parian, &c., is noticed in par. 2251f.

2277a. *Gilding* is of two kinds, burnished, and mat or dead, gilding. The former is seldom used in architectural decoration. The latter is done in oil-size on woodwork; in water-size on plastering. The gold leaf of various thicknesses, but generally about $\frac{1}{282000}$ of an inch, is called "single," "double," and "thirds," and of tints, is furnished in books of 25 leaves, each leaf being $3\frac{1}{8}$ by 3 inches, or in the book 18 inches and $\frac{6}{8}$ of an inch superficial, covering about 1 foot of plain work. It should not be too thin nor have too much alloy. Gilding on metal is effected by first giving it a coat of paint or some other substance to prevent oxidation. Gold, absolutely pure and of extra thickness was applied to the ironwork of the great tower at Westminster; and double gold leaf, pure, was used in the reading room of the British Museum. It has been stated, that if just before commencing to gild, each leaf of the book be *slightly* rubbed over with wax, sufficient only to cause the adhesion of the gold, that gilding in the open air, even in windy weather, may be done without the loss of a leaf, as the stickiness of the gold-size will overcome that of the wax, and no part be blown away, as is generally the case.

2277b. A *gold paint,* patented by H. Bessemer, is now much used, which, by the highly improved manufacture of bronze powder, has greatly reduced its price in England, although very much is still purchased from the German dealers. As an impalpable metallic powder, its application to plaster, wood, &c., is effected by using a camels' hair brush, which is dipped into a little of the powder and rubbed up in a small portion of transparent gummy varnish, by which it adheres to the surface. For all outdoor works it requires to be varnished over for better preservation.

2278. With painting is often connected the practice of *paper-hanging* by the same artificer. The various sorts of paper used for lining walls it would be useless to describe. We have only to mention that papers are printed 12 yards in length, such a length being called a *piece,* and 1 foot 8 inches wide; hence, 1 yard in length contains 5 feet superficial; therefore, any number of superficial feet divided by 60 (the length 36 × 1 ft. 8 ins.) will give the number of pieces wanted for the work; 1 piece in 7 or 8 is allowed for cutting and waste to common papers, and any odd yards are allowed as a piece. French papers contain about $4\frac{1}{2}$ yards superficial per piece, being of various widths. In best papers this allowance for waste is not enough. Borders are 12 yards or 36 feet in each length, each being technically a *dozen.* A ream of printed paper of 20 quires of 24 sheets to the quire, is equal to 28 pieces of paper, or each piece contains 17 sheets. Arsenical green in printed papers is considered injurious to health, from its flaking off in light particles, and floating in the air, when it is taken into the lungs while breathing. This colour may be at once detected by placing a few drops of ammonia on it, whereby the green will be changed into a deep blue. The methods of manufacturing marble, granite, and wainscot wall papers, is well described in the *Builder* for 1865, page 912, and which need not be here entered upon. Satin papers should be hung over a *lining paper.* The paperhanger has to provide and hang materials required for covering damp walls.

2278a. Walls of rooms should *always be stripped* before the new paper be put up, a process

usually attempted to be shirked, even when charged in the estimate. In bad common plasterer's work, the setting coat often comes off in parts with the paper and has to be repaired. The walls are usually prepared for papering by a coat of *clearcole*.

Sect. XIII.

SPECIFICATIONS.

2279. The importance of an accurate specification or description of the materials and work to be used and performed in the execution of a building, is almost as great as the preparation of the designs for it. The frequent cost of works above the estimated sum, and its freedom from extra charges on winding up the accounts, will mainly depend on the clearness, fulness, and accuracy of the specifications; though it is but justice to the architect to state that extras arise almost as often from the caprice of his employer during the progress of the work, as from the neglect or carelessness of the architect in making the specification. A specification should be made in all cases of new designs, additions, or alterations in reference to designs, which, the more they are given in working drawings by the architect, the better will it be for his employer, no less than for the artificer.

2280. It is impossible to frame a set of directions which shall be applicable in all cases. What we here propose to do is, to give something like a list or skeleton of the component parts of buildings, from which the architect may select such as are suitable to the particular case whereon he may be engaged. We have not carried this into the repairs and alterations of houses, because, with difference of application, we apprehend what we are placing before the student will enable him to carry the system forward in such cases without any difficulty. The works of each artificer are as follow : —

2281. Excavator. To take down any old buildings and impediments that may be on the site of the new works. If any old materials are to be used again, he is to clean, sort, and stack them for re-using in such parts of the premises as may be directed. The rubbish, as well from these as from any superfluous earth that may come out of the basement and foundations, if not wanted for raising the ground or for other purposes, he is to cart away, either wholly, or to such part of the premises as may require it, on direction to that effect, as well as all rubbish that may accumulate in executing the works.

To dig out for basement story (where one is to be) for the foundations, areas, drains, floors, and all other works requisite. To beat down to a solid consistence the ground forming the beds of the trenches for receiving the foundations and walls, and after they are in, he is to fill in and ram down the ground with wooden rammers ; to level, and to do such other rough groundwork as may be necessary for forming the sectional ground lines shown upon the drawings. In basements no earth is to be left nearer than 9 inches to any floor or other timbers, such cavities being by the specification to be filled in with dry lime core. And, finally, he is to leave the ground altogether free from all useless soil or other materials.

To bale out or pump out and remove all soil and water which may be necessary for laying the foundations, whether arising from springs, drains, cesspools, rain, or otherwise, and to be answerable for all accidental damage that may occur whilst the foundations and walls are carrying up, as also, when buildings adjoin, for all damage that may occur to neighbouring buildings.

2282. Bricklayer. The brickwork is to be executed with the very best hard well-burnt *grey stocks* (*or kiln-burnt red stock bricks, if the others are not to be had*), to be laid in flat joints, and so that every four courses shall not exceed 11½ inches in height.

When better bricks are used for *facing* external walls, they are to be specified as *best marle stocks, second marle stocks,* or *Suffolk white bricks,* as the case may be, in which case it must be specified that no headers of the facing are to be cut off, except where absolutely necessary to form good bond. Fronts so faced must be described to be either carried up with a neat flat parallel ruled joint, or to be afterwards tuck-joint pointed if a very finished face is wanted, though the latter is not altogether a very sound practice. In old work the joints may be described to be raked out, the brickwork washed, stained, and tuck-joint pointed.

No *place* or *samile* bricks to be allowed in any part of the work, under a penalty of two shillings for every such brick that may be detected to have been used.

The *mortar* is to be compounded of stone lime and sharp clean drift sand (if the work be of importance), to be ground in a pug-mill, or otherwise to be well tempered and beaten with wooden beaters, and to be in the proportion of one heaped bushel of lime to two of sand.

BRICKLAYER. (2282a.)

When the foundations are bad *concrete* should be provided, and is thus described : it is to be formed in the proportion of six parts of Thames or other unscreened clean ballast, and one part of fresh-burnt Dorking (or other) *stone* lime, beaten to powder on the premises, and unslaked.   They are to be thoroughly mixed in small quantities at a time, the lime at mixing being slaked with as small a quantity of water as possible.   The concrete, after mixing, is to be dropped from a stage to be formed by the contractor, so as to fall into the trench provided for its reception from a height of at least 12 feet.   The thickness of the concrete thus executed may vary from 4 feet to 18 inches in height, according to the badness or goodness of the foundation.

English bond should be directed, and the work should be specified to be flushed up at every course with mortar.   No bats to be allowed except for closures ; and for sound work every fourth course to be *grouted* with liquid mortar, and in the foundations every course, or at least every second course.   The walls, chimneys, their shafts and other works are to be carried up of the height and thicknesses and in the manner shown and figured on the several plans and drawings, together with all brickwork requisite for the completion of the house.   If the architect prefers, he may particularise these, but the drawings will show his meaning better.   When the work is within the metropolitan district, and not required to be of particularly great solidity it will be sufficient to describe that the thicknesses of the walls, their heights above the roofs, &c., shall be conformable to the regulations contained in the Building or other Act of the locality where one exists.

When the work is to appear without a stone or plaster facing, there must be described *rubbed* and *gauged arches* for all the external openings that will be seen in the principal fronts, of 9 or 14 inches in depth (or more according to their span), accurately cut, and set closely in front, in back, and on their sofites.   To the other openings the arches are to be described plain arches, closely set ; those which appear externally to be tuck-pointed on their outside faces.   Over all lintels, too, in external walls, the specification should provide uncut accurately formed arches.

When *fascias* are formed of brick, they must be described with their projections, as also all cornices formed by the arrangements of bricks, whereof the heads may be required to show as modillions ; but a drawing should, for the latter, always appear on the drawing or specification.

When the shafts of chimneys are carried up above the roof, out of the common way, they must be referred to drawings ; otherwise what relates to them and their flues is merely described as follows : — *Turn, parget,* and *core* the chimney flues, and finish the shafts with salient courses 6 inches in height, with *double plaintile creesing* thereto, and for each flue provide and fix a large-sized chimney mould ; the upper courses of the shafts above the creesing to be laid in Parker's cement.   In most cases, now, the flues are covered with square chimney moulds, cast of Parker's cement, and may be described as plain or moulded, and otherwise ornamented.

When parapets are not to be coped with stone or cement, they must be described as finished with double plaintile creesing, and a brick on edge thereover, all laid in Parker's cement.

Generally, where weather is to be provided against in upper courses and elsewhere, the laying in Parker's cement must be described.

Turn *trimmers* of 4-inch brickwork to all the fire-places for receiving the hearths throughout the building, except where the hearths lie on ground in basement stories.

Where there are basement stories, or the story is on the ground.   Describe piers 9 inches square, or continued walls 9 inches thick, to carry the sleepers whereon the joists of the floor or the courses of paving stone are to lie ; in either case the cavity is to be filled, for at least 9 inches in height, with dry lime core.

Bed in mortar all bond timber, wall or other plates, lintels, wood bricks, templets, stone, or other work connected with the brickwork.   All the door and window frames to be bedded in and pointed round with lime and hair mortar.   Execute all requisite beam filling.

When the building is faced with stone, or stone dressings are used ; to the above must be added — back up and fill in solid with brickwork all the stone work and iron work that is set in the brickwork.

If cornices, fascias, &c. are to be run in Parker's cement, or other sort of plaster, the instruction is — Prepare and fix brickwork, and such Yorkshire stone slabs and other materials as may be necessary for forming the several external cornices, pediments, strings, sills, and dressings to openings, in Parker's cement, or other cement, as the case may be, as shown on the drawings.

Turn arches in cement (if wanted) for carrying entrance or other steps.   Provide all brickwork for stone steps.   Turn vaults of brickwork (describe thickness not less

BRICKLAYER. (2282b.)

than 9 inches) over the intended cellars, according to the drawing, and properly cut all groins of intersections. The spandrels to be filled in with solid brickwork up to the level of the internal crown of the vaulting, the whole grouted with liquid mortar. When the centering is struck, the sofites of the vaultings are to be evenly and fairly cleaned off, and pointed.

Construct round the building a dry drain, as shown on the drawings, the top of the wall thereof to be level with the sections of the ground. Ram down the ground at the back thereof as the work is carried up, and provide such stone stays from the building as may be necessary for maintaining such wall in its place.

To execute proper barrel drains for draining the premises, as shown on the plans, to fall into a main sewer, or cesspool, as the case may be. The principal drains to be 1 ft. 6 in. and the smaller ones 12 inch barrelled drains, with half-brick rims, and the lower half of each drain composed with pure Parker's cement. At the foot of all rain-water, soil, and waste pipes, proper brick funnels are to be formed to lead down to the drain, the same to be constructed in Parker's cement. From all sink-stones funnels and drains to be formed to lead to the principal drains. N.B. We have here described the sizes of drains as for a moderate-sized mansion. We might say that 30 inches is the maximum diameter likely to be required for a large building, and none should be made less than 9 inches wide with half-brick sides, three courses high, curved top and bottom.

When a portico is designed, provide and execute walls for carrying the columns of portico, as shown on the plan, all piers or cross walls for receiving the landings, and brickwork to receive the steps. If the portico be of large size, describe discharging arches above the architrave in the space over intercolumniations, and from return columns to main walls. If a pediment, back up with brickwork behind the tympanum of pediment quite up to under side of raking cornice of pediment.

Wells, when above 6 feet in diameter, should be described to be steaned in a thickness of one brick, and when less than that size, in half a brick.

When water cannot be carried off to a public sewer or running stream, *cesspools* must be formed to receive it, and allow, if possible, its absorption by the earth. They are usually 3 feet 6 inches to 5 feet clear diameter, and are to be described as circular on plan, steaned round with hard stocks, in half a brick thick, laid dry till within 18 inches of the top, which 18 inches are to be laid in Parker's cement. If there be privies or water-closets far apart, each must be provided with a cesspool. Cesspools are sometimes domed over in brickwork, with a circular stone let into the eye or opening at the top of the dome; or they may be described to be covered with Yorkshire stone.

If any fence walls are required, their footings, thicknesses, heights, and lengths are to be mentioned, and of what bricks they are to be built. If any thing peculiar in their form, a section and elevation should be given.

Bricknogged partitions, which in practice ought, if possible, to be avoided, and are only to be justified where room is an object, are described as with bricks laid flat, or on edge, filled in between the quarters, ties, &c. of the partition.

Strong closets for plate or deeds require merely description of thickness of walls and brick arch, and usually 4-inch walls brought up for holding the requisite number of shelves. The same of wine cellars, whose bin walls must be mentioned.

Paving with bricks is described to be either of stocks, paving bricks, malm paviors, or clinkers, which may be laid flat or on edge in sand, mortar, or cement, and either straight-coursed or herring-bone.

Paving with tiles is usually in mortar; the tiles may be either 10 or 12 inches square.

All splays, ramps, and *chases* are to be cut where wanted; the two former to be rubbed where necessary, and the latter to be pargetted

Brick ovens (one 10 feet wide and 8 feet 6 inches deep will bake twelve bushels of bread, and one 8 feet wide and 7 feet deep will bake eight bushels, and so in proportion) are to be constructed with Welsh lumps or fire bricks for fire-place, domed over, and hooped with iron hoops. The bricklayer is to provide the bars, plate door, bar to the archway of door, and other ironwork, and to carry up a proper flue from the fire.

Iron ovens. The bricklayer is to set in proper brickwork an iron oven capable of baking two bushels of bread.

Coppers and stewing stoves to be set neatly in brickwork, the latter in guaged brickwork with tile top, and proper flues carried up therefrom.

Columns to porticoes or fronts which are to be coated with cement must be described of such diameters as the drawings for finishing require, with entablature, &c., as the case may be, carried up in Parker's cement.

In describing stables, besides what may be applicable from the foregoing directions, two *air-flues* are to be constructed to each stall and loose box, 9 inches square, and

BRICKLAYER.   (2282c.)

carried up over the racks within the thickness of the brickwork, communicating at their tops with the external air by curved tops to secure them from the penetration of the rain. *Dung-pit walls*, whose dimensions depend on the size of the stables. *Lime white* walls of stables.

If roofs are covered with tiles, either pan or plain. The description for the former will be either laid dry, or bedded in lime and hair, or pointed outside or inside, or on both sides; or if glazed pantiling, to be so described, laid to a 10-inch guage on stout fir laths, with hip, ridge, and valley tiles, filleting cutting to splays, beam filling, painted T nails, hip hooks, &c.   *Plain tiling* is described as laid to a close guage on heart of oak double laths, with all the plaintiles pegged. The hip and ridge tiles to be set in Parker's cement, with T nails dipped in melted hot pitch in all the joints.   Strong, similarly pitched, wrought iron hip hooks.   Filletings of Parker's cement, with strong cast iron nails for forming a key driven into the walls or other brickwork at intervals, close enough to secure the same.

In cases of underpinning the bricklayer is to cut all holes for the needles, and to remove the old work, and to bring up the work in Parker's cement on concrete foundation; and, finally, drive the cast iron wedges for bringing the work to a solid bearing.

Where inverted arches are used in foundations they must be shown on the drawings.

Provide, according to the extent of the job, a certain number of rods of brickwork for such extras as may be ordered by the architect; and if the whole or any part thereof should not be wanted, a deduction to be made on settling the accounts for so much thereof as shall not have been used, at a price per rod to be named.

To build all the walls level, except otherwise directed; to be answerable for all damage that may occur to the work, by settlements or otherwise, during the time of building, and to make good the same as the architect shall direct; and, further, to perform all such jobbing work as shall be necessary for completely finishing the building.   To provide good sound and sufficient scaffolding, which is to remain for the use of the mason, carpenter, and other artificers that may have occasion to use the same.

To pay the proper fees to the district, sewer, and paving surveyors, and to give the necessary notices and obtain the proper licences in their departments for executing the works. This only applies in the metropolitan district, where there are such officers.

2283. SLATER. To cover the roofs with the best strong Westmoreland, Tavistock, Welsh rag, imperial, queen, duchess, countess, ladies, or double slating, (as the architect may think most appropriate, each being named in the order of the value and quality,) securely fixed with best strong copper nails.   Every part to be properly bonded, especially at the eaves and heading courses thereof, with slates cut to keep the bond uniform.   No slates to be laid lengthwise.

Fillets against the brickwork, where requisite, of Parker's cement; such fillets to be formed with nails driven at proper intervals to form a hold for the cement (where lead step flashings are intended the fillets need not be described).   Fillets of brick or stone may be built up with the wall, level or raking; and if they should be preferred by the architect, they must be described in the bricklayer's or mason's works.

All the slating is to be rendered up perfect on completing the building, and all jobbing work to be performed that may become necessary as the work is carried on.

If the slating is required to be rendered as air-tight as possible, it must be described to be pointed on the inside with stone lime mortar, with a proper quantity of hair therein; but the pointing of either slates or tiles, from the constant expansion and contraction arising from heat and cold, soon falls out and becomes useless. Slater to be answerable twelve months for his work.

If slate skirtings and cisterns are intended about the building, they must be particularly described.

2284. MASON. The stone to be used in a building generally depends of course on the place where it is to be built, unless, without regard to expense, the employer determines on the use of any particular sort; in which case the account of the different quarries of the provinces, given in Chap. II. Section II. of this Book, will furnish the architect with the means of describing the best of its sort. For the choice, therefore, where it is left to the architect to decide, we must refer him to that account.   In the neighbourhood of London that from the island of Portland is most used. Granite is chiefly used where great strains and pressures occur, or where wear and tear and the action of the weather indicate its employment.

Having described the sort of stone selected to be of the best quality, free from all vents, shakes, &c., the next direction is, that it shall be throughout laid in the direc-

MASON.   (2284a.)

tion of its natural bed in the quarry; and if the whole building is of stone, many of the following particulars will be unnecessary,—which of them will immediately speak for themselves. Where the building is only faced with stone, the specification will run as follows: — The . . . fronts (describing them) are to be faced with Portland (or other, as the case may be) stone ashlaring in courses to fall in with the courses of brickwork, carried up after the manner of Flemish bond. The stretchers of such ashlaring being 4½ inches deep and the headers 9 inches, with bond stones running through the whole thickness of the wall in the proportion of $\frac{1}{15}$ of the face, to be introduced where the piers allow. No quoins to show a thickness of less than 12 inches. The whole to be cramped with cramps to the satisfaction of the architect, the mason finding the same, and properly running them with lead.

In cases where the building is of brick with stone dressings, the specification will run thus: — To provide and set a Portland stone (or other stone or granite) plinth all round (or part, as the case may be) the building, . . . feet . . . inches high and 8½ thick, in stones not less than 3 feet in length, the vertical joints to be cramped with T cramps not less than 12 inches long. Describe whether joints are to be close or channelled, and whether ashlar is to be rusticked (rockworked). To provide and fix at the angles of the building, as shown upon the drawings, solid quoins of Portland (or other, as the case may be) stone [here describe whether close, chamfered, or channelled joints, and whether rusticked (rockworked)] of the length and height shown.

To provide and fix, as shown, string courses, scantling . . . inches by . . . . inches, throated and bevelled on the upper face, and the joints plugged with lead.

To provide and fix, as shown on the drawings, a cornice and blocking course, scantling . . . by . . ., moulded according to the drawings, the bed to be such that the weight of each block of stone in the projecting part shall not be equal to that on the bed by one fourth of its cubic contents. The same to be executed according to the drawings; to have proper sunk water joints, and to be channelled and plugged with lead at all the joints.

Blocking course, as shown on the drawings, . . . inches high, . . . thick on the bed, and . . . on the top, plugged with lead at all the joints, with solid block at the quoins returned at least 24 inches.

Balustrades (if any) to be provided of the heights and sizes shown on the drawings and section thereof. The balusters to be wrought out of stone, allowing at least 1 inch of joggle at their ends into the plinth and impost. All the vertical joints to be well plugged with lead; the impost to be cramped with cast iron (or bell metal), and the whole to be securely fixed. The half balusters to be worked out of the same block of stone as their adjoining pedestal.

Columns and pilasters (if any), with pedestals, capitals, bases, plinths, &c., and entablature, to be provided and fixed as shown on the drawings. The columns and pilasters not to be in courses of more than . . . blocks of stone. The architraves to be joggled from those resting on the columns or pilasters themselves, and these as well as the frieze and cornice to break joint over the architrave. The architraves, if blocks of stone can be supplied large enough, to be in one block from centre to centre of column, with return architraves in like manner. The whole of the entablature (as well as the pediment, if any) to be executed with all requisite joggles and cramps (and if a pediment be projected, the apex to be in one stone) as shall be approved by the architect. The pilasters (if any) to be bonded not less than . . . inches into the wall, against which they are placed in every other course. The sofites of the portico to be, as shown on the plan and sections, formed into panels and ornamented. Provide and let into the top of the architrave good and sufficient chain bars, with stubs on the under side for letting into every stone composing the architrave.

If the portico be very large, it is not necessary to make the frieze solid, but concealed arches should be turned in the space from column to column to support the superincumbent weight of the cornice and pediment. If the columns are fluted, it must be mentioned.

When a pediment, the tympanum may be described to be faced with ashlaring.

To construct and fix dressings and sills to the external windows and doors, as shown on the drawings, with all such throated, sunk, moulded, carved, rebated, and other works as may be necessary.

If a portico is shown, to provide and fix of solid . . . stone . . . steps round the portico scantling . . . by . . ., properly back-jointed and worked all over; and within the portico to provide and fix a complete landing of stone, at least 4 inches thick (or less, if a small portico), in slabs, as shown. The joints of the steps and landings are to be joggled and run with lead.

Mason. (2284b.)

All ornaments, carving, enrichment of capitals, of columns and pilasters, and of such as may be shown in the entablature, is to be executed in an artist-like good style. Models from the working drawings are to be made at the contractor's expense, and the whole to be executed to the satisfaction of the architect.

The order may be described if the working drawings are not sufficiently made out.

Provide and fix plinths and base mouldings to the portico, as shown on the drawings, to be worked out of (describe stone) . . . stone of . . . by . . . scantling.

Finish the chimney shafts with mouldings as shown in the drawings, or with sunk moulded and throated copings, . . . inches wide and . . . inches thick.

To describe sills generally, take the following : —

Sills to . . . windows of Portland stone, 9½ by 6 inches.

Sills to . . . windows moulded and of Portland stone, 14 by 8 inches.

Sills to . . . windows of Aberdeen granite, finely tooled, scantling 14 inches by 9 inches.

Sills to . . . windows of Portland stone, 9 by 5 inches.

All window sills are to be properly sunk, weathered, and throated, and at each end to be 4 inches longer than the opening.

To provide and lay to all the walls Yorkshire stone 3 inches thick and 4 inches on each side wider than the several lowest footings, in slabs of one length across the width of the footing.

If balconies to a house, describe thus : — A balcony landing of Portland stone . . . . inches thick, moulded on the edges and the pieces joggled together, and run with lead, to be provided with holes cut therein for the iron railing. The said balcony is to be tailed into the wall, and securely pinned up.

Steps to doorways must be described as to scantlings. All external steps should be weathered.

Where story posts are used in a front, it is well to place along the front two pieces of parallel square Aberdeen or other good granite curb scantling, 12 inches by 9 inches, cut out to receive the bases of the columns and story posts.

For a back staircase, carry up and construct a staircase from the basement to the principal floor, with solid Yorkshire quarry steps 13 inches wide and 6½ inches high, properly back-jointed and pinned into the brickwork; cut holes for the iron balustres. N. B. This sort of staircase of Portland will serve also for back stairs of upper flights. That from the basement may also be made of granite street curb, 12 by 7 or 8 inches. A staircase may, for cheapness, be made of Yorkshire stone paving 3 inches thick, wrought with fair tooled edges, and securely pinned into the brickwork.

Principal stairs to be of Portland stone (as may be), to extend from principal to . . . floor, with steps and square (or semicircular, as may be) landings, entirely of solid stone, tailed 9 inches into the brickwork, with moulded nosings and returned nosings, and also at the back. The sofites to be moulded to the shapes of the ends of the steps. The landings to be 6 inches thick, with moulded nosings and joggled joints, run with lead, to be inserted at least 4 inches in the walls, but such as tail into the walls, as steps, must go at least 9 inches into the walls.

When the under sides of the steps of the geometrical staircase are not moulded, the nosings are returned so as to fall beyond the upright line of the succeeding tread; in this case the sofite or string is plain wrought.

Pave the entrance hall and principal staircase, together with (any apartments wished) with the best . . . marble, and border according to the pattern drawn.

The back staircase (and such other parts as require it) is to be paved with Portland stone 2 inches thick, laid in squares, and with a border 8 inches square.

Dairy, if any, to be paved with . . . . stone, in regular courses . . . . inches thick. Provide a shelf or dresser round the said dairy of veined marble 1 inch thick, and a skirting round it 6 inches high. The dresser to go into the wall 1 inch, and to be supported on veined marble piers 4 inches square.

Pave the scullery, larder, pantry, passages, lobbies (and such other places as may require mention), with rubbed Yorkshire stone 2½ inches thick, laid in regular courses with close rubbed joints.

Pave the bottom of the air drain with Yorkshire paving.

Yards may be paved with 2½-inch Yorkshire paving, or such other as the place affords, as in common use. The same to basement stories.

To fit up the wine cellar with bins, as per drawing, with 3-inch Yorkshire stone shelves (some prefer slate), fairly tooled, and set in Parker's cement.

To provide and fix a warm bath of veined marble; rendered waterproof by being properly set in Dutch tarras, and plugged and cramped with copper at the joints, with all requisite finishing. A marble step round two sides of the bath. Cut all holes

Mason. (2284c.)

necessary for laying on the water. A bath may be similarly made of slate, which is of course much cheaper.

Where iron girders are used, describe . . . . pieces of granite street curb, each . . . . feet long, to receive the ends of the cast iron girders.

Where chimneys project without support from below, corbels must be described proportioned to the weight they have to carry. The best corbel, however, is the gradual projection of the work by inverted steps, which, if there be height to hide them, should always be the mode of execution.

Cellar doorways should have in each of them three pieces of Portland or other such stone, 18 inches wide, 18 inches long, and 9 inches high, cut out to receive the hinges and rim of the lock.

All fire-places should have back hearths of 2½-inch rubbed Yorkshire stone.

The commonest chimney-pieces that can be described are of 1¼-inch Portland, jambs, mantels, and shelves, 6 inches wide; slabs of 2-inch Portland stone, 20 inches wide.

For butler's and housekeeper's rooms drawings are usually given. They may be of Portland stone slabs, 2 inches thick, 4 feet long, and 1 foot 8 inches wide.

For a kitchen chimney, describe jambs and mantle of 2-inch Portland stone, 10 (or 12) inches wide, with a slab of 2½-inch rubbed Yorkshire stone. The mantel to be in one piece.

For the several rooms where marble chimney-pieces are to be placed, chimney-pieces are described to be provided of a given value, varying in the less important to the best apartments, from eight or ten up to 100 guineas or more in value, of such marble as the employer may select : but if the working drawings have been fully prepared, this is a matter which need not be left in uncertainty.   It must always be provided in the specification that the slabs are included, and that the price is or is not (as the case may be) to include the carriage and fixing.

Sinks of Portland or other stones, 7 inches thick (describing the size required), to be provided and fixed as shown in the drawings, with holes cut for the grating and socket pipe, and fixed with all requisite bearers complete.

Sink stones to be provided where shown on the plan.   The joints generally are to be where exhibited on the drawings, and the work is to be left perfectly cleaned off, all necessary joggles, joints, rebates, moulded, sunk, weathered and throated works, grooves, chases, holes, back joints, and fair edges, that may be necessary in any part of the work, and all jobbing, though not particularly mentioned under the several heads, is to be done that may be requisite for the execution of the building, and all the work is to be well cleaned off before delivering it up. The whole of the work is to be warranted perfect, and any damage that may occur to it by reason of frost or settlement within two years after the completion of the building is to be repaired, under the architect's direction, at the sole expense of the contractor.

All mortar is to be of the same quality as that described in the bricklayer's work.

The contractor is to provide lead to run the cramps and joints.

In works within the metropolitan district, the contractor is to pay the expense, under the commissioners of sewers or paving, as the case may be, of making good the street paving to the areas, plinths, and steps abutting thereon.

To provide and fix under the contract . . . . cubic feet of . . stone, including plain work and setting thereto, also . . . . superficial feet of 2½-inch Yorkshire paving, laid in regular courses ; and in case the whole or any part of either or both should not be wanted, the quantity not used or directed shall be deducted from the amount of the consideration of the contract after the rate of . . . . per foot of cubic stone and . . . . per foot superficial for the Yorkshire paving, including the workmanship and fixing thereof.

In stables, granite should be provided to receive the heel-posts if cast iron be not employed, and at the piers of gates, hinge and spur stones, the latter, of granite, if to be had, should be described. The caps and bases of the last can be described only with reference to the drawings of them.

The paving of stables and their courts is described thus : Prepare the ground for paving (stating where) with good and sufficient hard materials, and pave it with Aberdeen granite paving, properly dressed and sorted, 8 inches deep and 5 inches wide at the top and bottom thereof. The whole to be laid with good currents upon a layer 4 inches at least in thickness of good rough gravel, the joints of the surface to be run with stone lime and river sand grouting. It is to be well rammed, and the contractor is to relay, at his own expense, all such parts as may sink within eighteen months of the work being completed.

Where the work is within the metropolitan district, or within a town, a sufficient hoarding must be erected for enclosing the premises during the execution of the

Mason. (2284d.)

works, which is to be removed and carried away when they are complete. So, also, all shoring is to be provided, if the works be alterations, or the adjoining buildings may be injured by carrying them into effect. The shoring is to be performed in a safe, scientific, and workmanlike manner, of the fronts, floors, or otherwise, as the case may be.

2285. Carpenter and Joiner. Where the extent of the works requires a clerk of the works : a direction must be given to provide, erect, and maintain, during their performance, a temporary office for the clerk of the works, with all appurtenances complete, with stool, table, and all other requisite furniture.

All materials requisite for completion of the buildings according to the drawings are to be provided by the contractor. The oak is to be of English growth ; the timber not specified of oak is to be of the best Dantzic, Riga, or Memel yellow fir. No American, Swedish, or Scotch fir to be used in any part of the building. All the floors and joiner's work are, except where otherwise directed, to be of the best Christiana deals. The timbers and deals are to be cut square, entirely free from sapwood, shakes, large knots, and all other defects. If any part or parts of the joiner's work should shrink or fly within eighteen months from the finishing and fixing the same, the contractor is to take down, refix, and make good the same, together with all works that may be affected thereby, at his own expense.

No joists, rafters, or quarters are in any case, unless particularly so directed, to be more than 12 inches clear distance from one another.

To provide and fix, ease, and strike all centering and turning pieces for the vaults, arches, trimmers, and other works. Provide all temporary shores that may be necessary. Fix all iron-work of every description. Provide and fix all necessary templets, linings, blocks, stops, casings, beads, springing fillets, angle staffs, grounds, linings, backings, furrings, cappings, and other finishings incident to carpenters' and joiners' works, together with all necessary grooving, rebating, framing, tonguing, housing, beading, mitring, framing, and other workmanship necessary for completing the works.

To provide good and secure casing for all the stone dressings, to protect the same from injury during the execution of the works ; and any accident arising from neglect in this respect is to be made good at the expense of the carpenter.

Bond timber.　One tier is generally enough for basement story.
　　　　　　　　Two tiers in the other floors, unless very lofty.
　　　　　　　　One tier in the upper story.

4 inches by 2½ inches all around the walls, except where intercepted by the chimneys, to be lapped together, where joints occur, at least 6 inches, and to be properly spiked together. Party walls may be bonded with iron hooping, if thought proper, for a greater security against fire.

To find and fix all wood bricks for fixing the finishings to.

Provide and fix all lintels, and filling in lintels that may be necessary to the several openings : each to be 4 inches high, of the width of the brick work, and 16 inches longer than the opening.

Two small lintels will do if the width of the sofite be considerable, and arches as directed in the bricklayer's work be turned.

For ground or rather basement floors, walls are brought up for receiving oak sleepers, 5 by 3 inches ; on which fir joists 4½ by 2½ are generally the scantlings employed.

For other floors.　Wall plates 6 by 4 are described.

　　　　　　Girders　　-　　　-　　　⎤ All which, with their requisite
　　　　　　Joists of all descriptions, according ⎬ scantlings, will be found in
　　　　　　　　to the kind of floor　-　　⎥ Practical Carpentry. (2013, et
　　　　　　Trimmers and trimming joists　⎦ seq.)

　　　　　　Cradling to the girders and such parts as may be necessary to form panels and coffers on the under side for the ceiling, if such be practised.

Where it is necessary to truss the girders, that must be stated.

Cock down all girders on the wall plates. Pin bridging joists to binders with ¾-inch oak pins.

For roofs, wall plates should be at least 6 inches by 6 inches.

　　　　For the different timbers of the several sorts of roofs, the reader will refer to the section on Practical Carpentry, where they are described, and scantlings given of works that have been executed. (2027, et seq.) Ceiling joists also to be described.

　　　　To what is there found, we may add, that hips and ridges rounded for lead ought to be 10 by 2.

Carpenter and Joiner. (2285a.)

Where close boarding is used, it should not be less than $\frac{3}{4}$ to an inch thick.   If battens for slating, they should be $2\frac{1}{2}$ inches wide; the first should be nailed with eightpenny nails.   Provide lear boards.

We prefer, on many accounts, and, indeed, ourselves usually adopt, the Italian method of laying the rafters horizontally as so many purlines.   For the boarding not lying lengthwise towards the gable, any wet that may find its way on to it from defective slates or lead, is not apt to lodge against and rot the edges.

Flats are described with wall plates usually 6 by 6.   Trimmers and trimming joists against chimneys, and where skylights occur; and $1\frac{1}{4}$-inch yellow deal boarding, listed, free from sapwood, laid with a current of $1\frac{1}{2}$-inch to 10 feet lineal, with $2\frac{1}{4}$ drips to heading joints, of lead rolls to longitudinal joints, and inch yellow deal risers not less than 4 inches wide next the gutter

Gutters to the roof or roofs are to be as shown on the plan, with inch yellow deal bottoms on strong fir bearers, and laid with a current of $1\frac{1}{4}$ inches to every 10 feet; $2\frac{1}{4}$ rebated drips, and at the sides to have $\frac{3}{4}$-inch deal lear boards, 9 inches wide. Gutter boards are rarely more than $1\frac{1}{4}$ inch thick.

Gutter plates, if any, to be described, but they should never be used without support from below.

Trim for trap doors, if any, leading to the roof, and provide and fix dormers with all necessary framing.

Cheeks, doors, beaded stops and linings, and ironmongery.   Boarding for slating or lead to top and cheeks, as the case may be.

Dormers may be similarly described for windows in the roof.

Quartered partitions, where shown on the plan, with heads and sills 4 inches by 4 inches.   Ties above the doors 4 inches by 5 inches.   Posts 4 inches by $3\frac{1}{2}$ inches. Braces or struts 3 inches square.   Quarters 4 inches by 2 inches, and three tiers of interties, 1 inch by $2\frac{1}{2}$ inches.   In cases where partitions are to be trussed for carrying either their own or some additional weight, reference must be made to drawings.

To put to .... floors (or to the whole if desired) *sounding boarding* of $\frac{3}{4}$-inch deal, chopped and fixed upon fillets to receive the pugging.

All external walls should be described to be battened.   The thickness of the battens is usually from $\frac{3}{4}$-inch to $1\frac{1}{4}$-inch, their widths $2\frac{1}{4}$ inches, and they are placed from 7 to 12 inches apart.   If no bond timber to nail them to, plugs must be let into the walls.

Bracketing and cradling is usually, for cornices, coves, &c., $1\frac{1}{4}$ inch thick; for entablatures, circular sofites, and waggon-headed ceilings, $1\frac{1}{2}$ to 2 inches thick.

All bearers to be fixed and provided as shall be necessary.

Weather boarding of the best sort is described as 3-inch yellow deal, wrought, or wrought and beaded.

Luffer boarding ought to be of 1-inch deal, wrought two sides and splayed.

Warehouse posts must be described with their relation to the weight they are to carry (see Beams and Pillars, 1635, *et seq.*), the caps to them should be long, so that they may not press into the girders, and, if practicable, iron dowels should pass through the girders to catch the bases of the posts in the floor above.

In ordinary cases fir story posts are about 9 inches square.   Oak caps 3 feet long, with splayed ends 9 by 6.   Floors are usually rough, not less than $1\frac{1}{2}$-inch deal. rebated.

Water trunks are made of sizes from 4 to 6 inches or more square, of $\frac{3}{4}$-inch to $1\frac{1}{4}$-inch deal.   They are always to be described as pitched and fixed complete, with hopper heads and shoes, wall hooks, holdfasts, &c.

Park paling is of the following varieties, and must be described accordingly : —

4-feet oak cleft pales, 2 arris rails and oak posts.
5-feet oak cleft pales, 2 arris rails and oak posts.
6-feet oak cleft pales, 3 arris rails and oak posts.

If there is to be an oak plank at the bottom, and oak capping at top, they must be specially mentioned.

To provide and fix ... cubic feet of Baltic yellow fir timber, with all labour thereto, beyond the quantity necessary for the work herein described, to be used in such additional works as may be directed by the architect; and if the whole or any part thereof should not be ordered, the same shall be deducted from the amount of the consideration of the contract, after the rate of ... per foot cube.   All additional fir, if any should be ordered, is to be taken at the like price of ... per foot cube.

The varieties of *floors* are as follow, each set of thicknesses being enumerated in the order of their increasing value.   Batten floors are for better rooms.

Carpenter and Joiner. (2285*b*.)

¾-inch *white* deal, rough, with edges shot.
¾-inch *white* deal, wrought, and laid folding.
¾-inch *yellow* deal, rough, with edges shot.
¾-inch *yellow* deal, wrought, and laid folding.
¾-inch *white* deal batten floor, wrought, and laid folding.
¾-inch *yellow* deal batten floor, wrought, and laid folding.
1-inch *white* deal, rough edges shot.
1-inch *white* deal, wrought, and laid folding.
1-inch *white* deal, wrought, and laid straight joint and splayed headings.
1-inch *yellow* deal, rough edges shot.
1-inch *yellow* deal, wrought, and laid folding.
1-inch *yellow* deal, wrought, and laid straight joint and splayed headings.
1-inch *white* deal batten floor, wrought, and laid folding.
1-inch *white* deal batten floor, wrought, and laid straight joint and splayed headings.
1-inch *yellow* deal batten floor, wrought, and laid folding.
1-inch *yellow* deal batten floor, wrought, and laid straight joint and splayed headings.
1¼-inch *white* deal, rough edges shot.
1¼-inch *white* deal, wrought, and laid folding.
1¼-inch *white* deal, wrought, straight joint, and splayed headings.
1¼-inch *yellow* deal, rough edges shot.
1¼-inch *yellow* deal, wrought, and laid folding.
1¼-inch *yellow* deal, wrought, straight joint, and splayed headings.
1¼-inch *white* deal batten floor, straight joint, and splayed headings.
1¼-inch *white* deal batten floor, straight joint edge nailed, and splayed headings.
1¼-inch *yellow* deal batten floor, straight joint, and splayed headings.
1¼-inch *yellow* deal batten floor, straight joint, edge nailed, and tongued headings.
1½-inch *white* deal batten floor, edge nailed, and tongued headings.
1½-inch *yellow* deal batten floor, edge nailed, and tongued headings.
1¼-inch *yellow* deal batten floor, dowelled with oak dowels, with mitred and glued borders.
1¼-inch *yellow* deal, clean batten floor, dowelled with oak dowels, with mitred and glued borders.

Warehouse floors are of
1½-inch *yellow* deal, rough edges shot.
1½-inch *yellow* deal, wrought, and laid folding.
1½-inch *yellow* deal, wrought, and straight joint, and splayed headings
2-inch *yellow* deal, rough edges shot
2-inch *yellow* deal, wrought, and laid folding.
2-inch *yellow* deal, wrought, and laid straight joint and splayed headings.
All these last may be ploughed, rebated, and feather-tongued.

The floors of inlaid or *parquetry* work must form, when to be provided, special subjects of specification; they must be described according to drawings, on which are to be marked the different woods to be used in their formation.

The varieties of *skirtings* are classed as under, beginning with the commonest sort: —
½-inch deal square skirting.
¾-inch deal square skirting.
¾-inch deal torus skirting.
1-inch deal square skirting.
1-inch deal square skirting, rebated and backed plinth, with fillet nailed to floor.
1-inch deal torus skirting.
1¼-inch deal square skirting.
1¼-inch deal torus skirting.
1¼-inch deal torus skirting, rebated and backed plinth, with fillet nailed to floor.

If any of these, as to stairs for instance, are raking, and to be scribed to steps, they must be so described, and so if any of them are to be ramped, and similarly if they are to be scribed to moulded nosings, as also if they be circular on the plan.

Dados in their varieties are as follow, premising that they are nailed to grounds which should be mentioned.
¾-inch deal keyed.
1-inch deal keyed.
1¼-inch deal keyed.
1¼-inch deal keyed, ploughed, and tongued.
1¼-inch deal keyed, feather-tongued.

Carpenter and Joiner. (2285c.)

Scribed to steps, circular on plan, and wreathed, or ramped : those matters must be mentioned.

Of *wainscotting* with fascia and skirting, the different kinds are subjoined in the order of their quality.

1-inch deal, square framed
1-inch deal, square framed dwarf
1¼-inch deal, square framed
1¼-inch deal, square framed, dwarf   The number of panels high to be specified.
1¼-inch deal, bead butt or moulded
1¼-inch deal, bead butt
1¼-inch deal, bead flush

When any of these are raking, or to have a beaded or moulded capping, or both or either, such must be specified.

Partitions of deal for the division of rooms are only used in taverns and the like; but where they are wanted, as for a mere separation in servants' rooms, they may be employed. Their varieties are —

1-inch deal board, and braced with ½-inch panels.   These are scarcely to be em-
1¼-inch deal, braced with ¾-inch panels.   ployed.
1¼-inch deal, rough, and ledged edges shot.
1½-inch deal, wrought both sides, and ploughed.
1½-inch deal, wrought both sides, tongued, and beaded.
1¼-inch, square framed.
1½-inch, square framed.
1½-inch, bead butt, moulded and square.
1½-inch, bead flush and square.
1½-inch, moulded on both sides.
2-inch, square framed.
2-inch, bead butt or moulded and square.
2-inch, bead flush and square.
2-inch, moulded on both sides.
2-inch, moulded and bead flush.
2-inch, bead flush and bead butt.
2-inch, bead flush on both sides.

These, as well as any preceding and following parts of a specification, will, of course, have reference to what is wanted in the design which it is the architect's object to describe in such specification.

Grounds. — We have mentioned grounds generally (2166.); but it may be as well here to insert their several sorts: for instance, —

Those of ¾-inch deal, of 1-inch deal, of 1¼-inch deal, of 1½-inch deal, and whether circular; also 1-inch, 1¼-inch, and 1½-inch skeleton grounds, which it is, perhaps, for security against extras, as well to repeat.

Door cases are usually employed on basement stories, and should be of oak, though fir is constantly used for them. They fit into the brickwork, and are usually about 5 by 5 inches, and they should be tenoned (the tenon being well pitched or set in white lead) into the stone step, on which they ought to be placed; for the sill, into which it is the practice to place them, soon rots, however good the material.

Door linings and their sofites. — These are either plain or framed, the former being of the commoner sort, and the latter for better work and places. They may be enumerated as follow : —

1-inch deal, single rebated.
1-inch deal, double rebated (that is, so that the door may hang on either side).
1¼-inch deal, single rebated.
1¼-inch deal, double rebated.
1½-inch deal, single rebated.
1½-inch deal, double rebated.

Either of the foregoing, if to be beaded on the edge, must be so described. Of framed linings and sofites for doors there are —

1¼-inch, square framed in one panel and double rebated.
1¼-inch, square framed in one panel and double rebated, bead butt or moulded.
1¼-inch, square framed in one panel and double rebated, bead flush.
1½-inch, square framed in one panel and double rebated.
1½-inch, square framed in one panel and double rebated, bead butt, or moulded.
1½-inch, square framed in one panel and double rebated, bead flush.

If the panels in the linings are to be raised, to correspond with panels of doors, they must be so described.

Carpenter and Joiner.   (2285d.)

Framed back linings are as follow : —
  1-inch deal, two panel square.
  1-inch deal, two panel square, bead butt.
  1-inch deal, three panel square.
  1-inch deal, three panel square, bead butt.
  1-inch deal, four panel square.
  1-inch deal, four panel square, bead butt.
If there be more than four panels, or they are splayed on the plan, or if bead flush, or of a greater thickness, they must be so specified.

Backs, *elbows*, and *sofites* to windows are described as —
  1-inch deal, keyed.
  1-inch deal, keyed, framed square.
  1¼-inch deal, framed square.
  1¼-inch deal, framed square, moulded, or bead butt.
  1¼-inch deal, framed square, bead flush.
  1¼-inch deal, square framed sofite, with one edge circular. ⎫ Applicable to bay win-
  1¼-inch deal, square framed sofite, with two edges circular. ⎭ dows.
  1¼-inch deal, square framed sofite, moulded, or bead butt.
  1½-inch deal, framed square.
  1½-inch deal, framed square, moulded, or bead butt.
  1½-inch deal, framed square, moulded, or bead flush.
If any of these are splayed, fancy moulded, and with cappings, when also they are circular on the plan, they must be so particularly specified, inasmuch as the price is thereby enhanced.

Boxings for shutters are of the following varieties : —
  1-inch deal, splayed boxings.
  1-inch deal, proper boxings.
  1¼-inch deal, splayed boxings.
  1¼-inch deal, proper boxings.
  1¼-inch deal, boxings with circular head.
  1-inch deal, boxings for sliding shutters, with pulley pieces, beads, fillets, and grooves, complete.
  1¼-inch deal, boxings for sliding shutters, with pulley pieces, beads, fillets, and grooves, complete.
These, if to be double hung, must be so described.

Window shutters. — As in the foregoing parts of a specification, we shall proceed from the common to the better sorts.
  ¾-inch deal, ledged or clamped.
  ¾-inch deal, ledged, or clamped, in two heights.
  1-inch deal, clamped.
  1-inch deal, clamped in two heights.
  1-inch deal, clamped in two heights, one panel, bead butt, and square.
  1-inch deal, clamped in two heights, one panel, bead flush, and square.
  1-inch deal, clamped in two heights, one panel, bead flush, and bead butt.
  1¼-inch deal, two panels square.
  1¼-inch deal, two panels square, in two heights.
  1¼-inch deal, two panels square, in two heights, moulded, or bead butt, and square.
  1¼-inch deal, two panels square, in two heights, bead flush, and square.
  1¼-inch deal, two panels square, in two heights, bead flush, and bead butt.
These may be described of 1½-inch deal ; but the back flaps need not be more than one inch, and the additional panels in height, projecting mouldings, if any, and other variations from the general description, must be mentioned.

Sliding shutters are to be described in their varieties, as follow : —
  1-inch deal, two panels square, hung with lines and weights.
  1¼-inch deal, two panels square, hung with lines and weights.
  1¼-inch deal, bead butt and square, hung with lines and weights.
  1¼-inch deal, bead flush and square, hung with lines and weights.
  1¼-inch deal, bead butt and moulded, hung with lines and weights.
  1¼-inch deal, bead flush and bead butt, hung with lines and weights.
These, if of 1½-inch deal, and if more panels in height, must be so described ; so also if they are circular on the plan ; and if patent lines are to be used for the hanging, they must be mentioned.

Outside shutters, now rarely used, even in the provinces, except for shop fronts, must be mentioned, to make our description complete ; they are of
  1¼-inch deal, three panels, bead butt and square.
  1¼-inch deal, three panels bead flush and square.

CARPENTER AND JOINER.   (2285e.)

1¼-inch deal, three panels, bead flush and bead butt.
1¼-inch deal, three panels, bead flush on both sides.
1¼-inch deal, three panels, bead butt and square.
1½-inch deal, three panels, bead flush and square.
1½-inch deal, three panels, bead flush and bead butt.

If these are circular on the plan, or contain more than three panels in height, the specification must so state.

Staircases are described as under, beginning with the commonest.

1-inch yellow deal, steps, risers, and carriages.
1¼-inch deal, steps, inch risers, and carriage.
1¼-inch deal, steps and risers glued up and blocked to close string moulded nosings, and two fir carriages.
1¼-inch deal, steps and risers mitred to cut string, and dovetailed to balusters.
1¼-inch deal, steps to winders, mitred to cut string, and dovetailed to balusters, one end circular.
1¼-inch deal, steps to winders, mitred to cut string, and dovetailed to balusters, both ends circular.

If the risers are to be tongued to the steps, if feather jointed, or if of clean deal, such must be stated in the specification.

1½-inch deal, wrought steps, risers, and strong carriage.
2-inch deal, wrought steps, risers, and strong carriage.
1¼-inch oak, treads and risers mitred to string and dovetailed with fir carriage (with solid quarter ends to steps if required), also curtailed step and riser (2187, *et seq.*), returned moulded and mitred nosings, circular, if necessary, with cut plain (and circular) brackets.

Housings to ends of steps and winders, and the same to moulded nosings and circular ends, are to be specified.

String boards to staircases to receive the ceilings of stairs (or strings as they are called), are —

1-inch deal, framed.
1-inch deal, framed, rebated, and beaded.
1¼-inch deal, framed string board.
1¼-inch deal, framed string board, sunk and beaded.
1¼-inch deal, framed string board, sunk, beaded, and moulded.
1¼-inch deal, framed string board, sunk, beaded, moulded, and mitred to risers.
1½-inch deal, wreathed outside, string glued upright, rebated, and beaded.
1½-inch deal, wreathed outside, string glued upright, rebated, beaded, and sunk.
1½-inch deal, wreathed outside, string glued upright, rebated, beaded, sunk, and moulded.

If the string is to be glued up in thicknesses, that must be specified, as also all plain or moulded circular cuttings or ramps.

1-inch deal, plain wall string.
1¼-inch deal, plain wall string.
1½-inch deal, plain wall string.
2-inch deal, plain wall string.

If moulded, to be so described.

Handrails to staircases are described as —

1¼-inch deal, plain wreathed.
1½-inch deal, plain wreathed.
2-inch deal, plain wreathed.

If moulded, state so.

Deal moulded 2½-inch handrail.
Deal moulded 2½-inch handrail, ramped (or circular where required).
Deal moulded 2½-inch handrail, wreathed and twisted.
Honduras mahogany or wainscot moulded handrail.   To be described if necessary with ramps, circular and twist, or with scroll and twist to the curtail step.
Spanish mahogany handrail is also similarly described.

If grooved for balusters, circular, or sunk for iron cores, mitred and turned caps, such to be mentioned.

Balusters and newels are described —

Deal square framed newels.
Deal square framed newels, chamfered.

Single and double turnings to newels to be mentioned, as also pendent drops, when used.

Deal square bar balusters.
Deal square bar balusters, dovetailed.

CARPENTER AND JOINER. (2285*f.*)

Turned balusters according to drawing, when necessary.

Planceer rounded on both edges, or moulded, as the case may be.

Fix all iron balusters and stays.

Sash frames are of great variety, whereof the following is a list : —

Deal cased frame for 1½-inch sashes, oak sunk sill with brass pulleys for single hanging.

Ditto, for double hanging.

Ditto, ditto, with circular head.

Ditto, circular on plan (and with circular head, when required).

Deal cased frames for 2-inch sashes, oak sunk sills with brass pulleys prepared for single hanging.

Ditto, prepared for double hanging.

If circular on head and plan, or either, such to be specified.

Deal-cased frames for 2-inch sashes, oak sunk sills with wainscot pulley pieces and beads, brass axle pulleys prepared to hang double.

•If circular on head and plan, or either, such to be specified.

Deal cased frames for 2-inch sashes, oak sunk sills, mahogany pulley pieces and beads with brass axle pulleys, prepared to hang double.

The same description holds for 2½-inch sashes.

If, as before, circular on head and plan, or either, such to be mentioned.

Venetian frames are described as —

Deal cased frames for 1½-inch sashes, oak sunk sills, and prepared to hang single or double, as the case may be.

If circular on plan and head, or either, specify the same.

The above description for 1½-inch serves also for 2-inch and 2½-inch sashes.

If wainscot or mahogany, they must be so described.

Casement frames for French casements : —

Fir solid wrought frames for 1½-inch French casements, with oak sunk sills (plain or circular on the plan, as the case may be).

Fir solid wrought frames for 2-inch French casements and oak sunk sills (as before).

Fir solid wrought frames for 2-inch French casements and oak sunk sills (as before), with wainscot or mahogany styles and beads as may be correspondent with the sashes.

The same for 2½-inch sashes.

Fanlight frames over doors, which have nearly lost their employment from square lights having superseded them, are of —

1½-inch deal frames, square framed.

Ditto, semicircular head.

2-inch deal, square framed.

Ditto, semicircular head.

If elliptical, so describe them.

Sashes are to be described as follows : —

1½-inch deal ovolo (describe whether with circular head or circular on plan, if so).

2-inch deal ovolo (ditto).

2-inch deal astragal and hollow (ditto).

2½-inch deal astragal and hollow (ditto).

The above, if of wainscot, Honduras or Spanish mahogany, are to be so described, as also that they are to be hung single or double, as the case may be, with patent lines and iron weights, and patent sash-fastenings complete.

French casements are usually decribed as follows : —

2-inch deal ovolo casements. If with marginal lights or circular on plan, or both, describe them so; or if with astragal and hollow.

The same of 2½-inch, with the same modifications as in preceding article.

If either of the above be of wainscot, Honduras or Spanish mahogany, let them be so described.

It is usual to describe with these the hanging, which is commonly with 4-inch iron or brass butt hinges, and the species of fastening which it is common to place, at a sum varying from five to twenty shillings. When the turning Espaniolette fastenings are used, they must be particularly specified.

Shop-window sashes vary so much that we shall merely observe of their thicknesses, they are from 1½ to 2½ inches, and in the present extravagant rage for novelty among tradesmen, there is no end to the forms of their horizontal sections ; — nothing, however *outré*, would be considered too extravagant for these people, and all that we can do is to say that, after describing their thickness, they are to be executed according to the drawings. In subjects of this kind, too, the *stall*

Carpenter and Joiner. (2285g.)

board, and other fittings of the like nature, are to be specified in all, whereof the best way is to describe with reference to such drawings.

Friezes and cradling for cornices should always be referred to drawings, specifying generally their height.

Skylights, now usually made of metal; but if not, describe as follows : —

1½-inch deal ovolo skylight (if hipped, and with cross bars, state such).
2-inch deal ditto   (ditto).
2½-inch ditto   (ditto).

If astragal and hollow, or if of oak, such to be specified.

Kerbs for skylights are to be described —

1½-inch deal kerbs to circular skylights in two thicknesses, bevelled and chamfered.
2-inch ditto   ditto.
2½-inch ditto   ditto.

If elliptical, to be so specified.

Doors we shall, as in the preceding articles, describe, beginning with the commonest sort, for out-houses and the like.

¾-inch ledged wrought deal door.
Ditto, ploughed, tongued, and beaded.
1-inch wrought deal ledged ditto.
Ditto, ploughed, tongued, and beaded.
1¼-inch wrought deal ledged ditto.
Ditto, ploughed, tongued, and beaded.

1½-inch and 2-inch deal ledged doors are similarly described.

These doors may be hung with **H L** or cross garnet hinges or with butt hinges, and with bolts, locks, latches, and other fastenings, as the case may require. External doors with 4-inch butts, if that be the sort used, and internal ones with 3½-inch butts.

Gates and coach-house doors are specified as —

2-inch deal, framed and braced, filled in with 2-inch deal, and ploughed, tongued, and beaded.
The same, filled in with battens.
2½-inch deal, framed and braced, filled in with 1-inch deal, ploughed, tongued, and beaded.
Ditto, filled in with battens.

If filled in with whole deal, it must be so specified.

2-inch deal bead butt and square gates, in eight panels.
2-inch deal bead butt and square gates, beadflush and square.
2-inch deal bead butt and square gates, bead flush on both sides.

If with more panels, or framed with a wicket, such must be specified.

The hanging of gates, and their hinges and fastenings, may be inserted according to the occasion of the work, at from 10*l*. to 15*l*. or even 20*l*., which may be declared in the specification as to the value at which they are to be provided.

1-inch deal 1-panel square doors.
1-inch deal 1-panel square doors, folding.

The above are rarely used : we shall now, therefore, proceed by the number of panels, up to 6-panel doors, beyond which they are to be so particularly specified, or with reference to drawings.

1¼-inch, 2 panels, square.
1¼-inch, 2 panels, bead butt and square.
1¼-inch, 2 panels, bead flush and square.
1¼-inch, 2 panels, moulded and square.
1¼-inch, 2 panels, bead butt on both sides.
1¼-inch, 2 panels, bead butt and bead flush.
1¼-inch, 2 panels, bead butt and moulded.
1¼-inch, 2 panels, bead flush on both sides.
1¼-inch, 2 panels, bead flush and moulded.
1¼-inch, 2 panels, moulded on both sides.

When hung folding, to be so specified.

1½-inch deal, 2 panels, square.
1½-inch deal, 2 panels, bead butt and square.
1½-inch deal, 2 panels, bead flush and square.
1½-inch deal, 2 panels, moulded and square.
1½-inch deal, 2 panels, bead butt on both sides.
1½-inch deal, 2 panels, bead butt and bead flush.
1½-inch deal, 2 panels, bead butt and moulded.
1½-inch deal, 2 panels, bead flush on both sides.

CARPENTER AND JOINER.   (2285*h*.)

1¼-inch deal, 2 panels, bead flush and moulded.
1½-inch deal, 2 panels, moulded on both sides.
2-inch deal, 2 panels, square.
2-inch deal, 2 panels, bead butt and square.
2-inch deal, 2 panels, bead flush and square.
2-inch deal, 2 panels, moulded and square.
2-inch deal, 2 panels, bead butt on both sides.
2-inch deal, 2 panels, bead butt and bead flush.
2-inch deal, 2 panels, bead butt and moulded.
2-inch deal, 2 panels, bead flush on both sides.
2-inch deal, 2 panels, bead flush and moulded.
2-inch deal, 2 panels, moulded on both sides.
2½-inch deal, 2 panels, square.
2½-inch deal, 2 panels, bead butt and square.
2½-inch deal, 2 panels, bead flush and square.
2½-inch deal, 2 panels, moulded and square.
2½-inch deal, 2 panels, bead butt on both sides.
2½-inch deal, 2 panels, bead butt and bead flush
2½-inch deal, 2 panels, bead butt and moulded.
2½-inch deal, 2 panels, bead flush on both sides.
2½-inch deal, 2 panels, bead flush and moulded.
2½-inch deal, 2 panels, moulded on both sides.

All these, as well as the following, must be specified as to be hung folding, if the nature of the work so requires.

1½-inch deal, 4 panels, square.
1½-inch deal, 4 panels, bead butt and square.
1½-inch deal, 4 panels, bead flush and square.
1½-inch deal, 4 panels, moulded and square.
1½-inch deal, 4 panels, bead butt on both sides.
1½-inch deal, 4 panels, bead butt and bead flush
1½-inch deal, 4 panels, bead butt and moulded.
1½-inch deal, 4 panels, bead flush on both sides.
1½-inch deal, 4 panels, bead flush and moulded.
1½-inch deal, 4 panels, moulded on both sides.
2-inch deal, 4 panels, square.
2-inch deal, 4 panels, bead butt and square.
2-inch deal, 4 panels, bead flush and square.
2-inch deal, 4 panels, moulded and square.
2-inch deal, 4 panels, bead butt on both sides.
2-inch deal, 4 panels, bead butt and bead flush.
2-inch deal, 4 panels, bead butt and moulded.
2-inch deal, 4 panels, bead flush on both sides.
2-inch deal, 4 panels, bead flush and moulded.
2-inch deal, 4 panels, moulded on both sides.
2½-inch deal, 4 panels, square.
2½-inch deal, 4 panels, bead butt and square.
2½-inch deal, 4 panels, bead flush and square.
2½-inch deal, 4 panels, moulded and square.
2½-inch deal, 4 panels, square, beat butt on both sides.
2½-inch deal, 4 panels, square, bead butt and bead flush.
2½-inch deal, 4 panels, square, bead butt and moulded.
2½-inch deal, 4 panels, square, bead flush on both sides.
2½-inch deal, 4 panels, square, bead flush and moulded.
2½-inch deal, 4 panels, square, moulded on both sides.
1½-inch deal, 6 panels, square.
1½-inch deal, 6 panels, bead butt and square.
1½-inch deal, 6 panels, bead flush and square.
1½-inch deal, 6 panels, moulded and square.
1½-inch deal, 6 panels, bead butt on both sides.
1½-inch deal, 6 panels, bead butt and bead flush.
1½-inch deal, 6 panels, bead butt and moulded.
1½-inch deal, 6 panels, bead flush on both sides.
1½-inch deal, 6 panels, bead flush and moulded.
1½-inch deal, 6 panels, moulded on both sides.

If the panels of 1½-inch doors are raised, or if double marginal doors, so describe them.

Carpenter and Joiner. (2285i.)

Wainscot doors are usually as follow : —

$1\frac{1}{2}$-inch wainscot, 2 panels, square.
$1\frac{1}{2}$-inch wainscot, 2 panels, bead flush and square.
$1\frac{1}{2}$-inch wainscot, 2 panels, moulded and square.
$1\frac{1}{2}$-inch wainscot, 2 panels, bead flush on both sides.
$1\frac{1}{2}$-inch wainscot, 2 panels, bead flush and moulded.
2-inch wainscot, 2 panels, square.
2-inch-wainscot, 2 panels, bead flush and square.
2-inch wainscot, 2 panels, moulded and square.
2-inch wainscot, 2 panels, bead flush on both sides.
2-inch wainscot, 2 panels, bead flush and moulded.
$2\frac{1}{2}$-inch wainscot, 2 panels, square.
$2\frac{1}{2}$-inch wainscot, 2 panels, bead flush and square.
$2\frac{1}{2}$-inch wainscot, 2 panels, moulded and square.
$2\frac{1}{2}$-inch wainscot, 2 panels, bead flush on both sides.
$2\frac{1}{2}$-inch wainscot, 2 panels, bead flush and moulded.
$1\frac{1}{2}$-inch wainscot, 4 panels, square.
$1\frac{1}{2}$-inch wainscot, 4 panels, bead flush and square.
$1\frac{1}{2}$-inch wainscot, 4 panels, moulded and square.
$1\frac{1}{2}$-inch wainscot, 4 panels, bead flush both on sides.
$1\frac{1}{2}$-inch wainscot, 4 panels, bead flush and moulded
$1\frac{1}{2}$-inch wainscot, 4 panels, moulded on both sides.
2-inch wainscot, 4 panels, square.
2-inch wainscot, 4 panels, bead flush and square.
2-inch wainscot, 4 panels, moulded and square.
2-inch wainscot, 4 panels, bead flush on both sides.
2-inch wainscot, 4 panels, bead flush and moulded.
2-inch wainscot, 4 panels, moulded both on sides.
$2\frac{1}{2}$-inch wainscot, 4 panels, square.
$2\frac{1}{2}$-inch wainscot, 4 panels, bead flush and square.
$2\frac{1}{2}$-inch wainscot, 4 panels, moulded and square.
$2\frac{1}{2}$-inch wainscot, 4 panels, bead flush on both sides.
$2\frac{1}{2}$-inch wainscot, 4 panels, bead flush and moulded.
$2\frac{1}{2}$-inch wainscot, 4 panels, moulded on both sides.
2-inch wainscot, 6 panels, square.
2-inch wainscot, 6 panels, bead flush and square.
2-inch wainscot, 6 panels, moulded and square.
2-inch wainscot, 6 panels, bead flush on both sides.
2-inch wainscot, 6 panels, bead flush and moulded
2-inch wainscot, 6 panels, moulded on both sides.
$2\frac{1}{2}$-inch wainscot, 6 panels, square.
$2\frac{1}{2}$-inch wainscot, 6 panels, bead flush and square.
$2\frac{1}{2}$-inch wainscot, 6 panels, moulded and square.
$2\frac{1}{2}$-inch wainscot, 6 panels, bead flush on both sides.
$2\frac{1}{2}$-inch wainscot, 6 panels, bead flush and moulded.
$2\frac{1}{2}$-inch wainscot, 6 panels, moulded on both sides.
2-inch wainscot *sash-doors*, with diminished stiles, lower panel moulded, bead flush, with astragal and hollow sash.
2-inch wainscot sash-doors, with diminished stiles, lower panel moulded, bead flush, with astragal and hollow sash, moulded on both sides.
$2\frac{1}{2}$-inch wainscot sash-doors, diminished stiles, lower panels moulded, and bead flush, with astragal and hollow sash.
$2\frac{1}{2}$-inch wainscot sash-doors, diminished stiles, lower panels moulded, and bead flush, with astragal and hollow sash, moulded on both sides.

If any of these are to be hung folding, double margined, or moulded on the raising, such must be specified.

Mahogany doors as follows : —

2-inch Honduras mahogany doors, 2 panels, moulded and square.
2-inch Honduras mahogany doors, 2 panels, moulded on both sides.
2-inch Honduras mahogany doors, 4 panels, moulded and square.
2-inch Honduras mahogany doors, 4 panels, moulded on both sides.
2-inch Honduras mahogany doors, 6 panels, moulded and square.
2-inch Honduras mahogany doors, 6 panels, moulded on both sides.
$2\frac{1}{2}$-inch Honduras mahogany doors, 4 panels, moulded and square.
$2\frac{1}{2}$-inch Honduras mahogany doors, 4 panels, moulded on both sides.
$2\frac{1}{2}$-inch Honduras mahogany doors, 6 panels, moulded and square.

CARPENTER AND JOINER. (2285k.)

2½-inch Honduras mahogany doors, 6 panels, moulded on both sides.

If any of these are hung folding, with projecting mouldings, or with double margins, it must be so specified. The last set of doors, if required to be of a better description, may be specified of the best Spanish mahogany.

2-inch Honduras mahogany sash-door, astragal and hollow, bottom panel moulded and square.

2-inch Honduras mahogany sash-door, astragal and hollow, bottom panel moulded on both sides.

2½-inch Honduras mahogany sash-door, astragal and hollow, bottom panel moulded and square.

2½-inch Honduras mahogany sash-door, astragal and hollow, bottom panel moulded on both sides.

If hung folding, or with double margin, or diminished stiles, to be so specified.

External doors are of varieties, as follow : —

2-inch deal, 4 panels, the lower panels bead butt and square, and the upper panels square both sides.

2-inch deal, 4 panels, the lower panels bead butt and square, and the upper panels bead butt on the back.

2-inch deal, 4 panels, the lower panels bead butt and square, and the upper panels bead flush on the back.

If the panels have raised mouldings, specify them.

2½-inch deal, 4 panels, the lower panels bead butt and square, upper panels square on both sides.

2½-inch deal, 4 panels square, bead butt on the back.

2½-inch deal, 4 panels square, bead flush on the back.

Specify raised mouldings, if any.

2-inch deal, 6 panels, lower panels bead butt and square, upper panels square both sides.

2-inch deal, 6 panels, lower panels bead butt and square, upper panels square, bead butt on the back.

Specify raised mouldings, if any.

2½-inch deal, 6 panels, the lower panels bead butt and square, and the upper panels square both sides.

2½-inch deal, 6 panels, the lower panels bead butt and square, and the upper panels square, bead butt on the back.

2½-inch deal, 6 panels, the lower panels bead butt and square, and the upper panels square, bead flush on the back.

If with raised mouldings, so describe them ; also, if double margined, &c.

Any of these external doors, if hung folding, or with circular or curved heads, must be so specified.

Sash doors are of the following varieties : —

1½-inch deal, 2 panels, square, diminished stiles, and ovolo sash.

1½-inch deal, 2 panels, bead butt and square, diminished stiles, and ovolo sash.

1½-inch deal, 2 panels, bead flush and square, diminished stiles, and ovolo sash.

1½-inch deal, 2 panels, moulded and square, diminished stiles, and ovolo sash.

1½-inch deal, 2 panels, moulded and bead butt, diminished stiles, and ovolo sash.

1¼-inch deal, 2 panels, moulded and bead flush, diminished stiles, and ovolo sash.

1½-inch deal, 2 panels, moulded on both sides, diminished stiles, and ovolo sash.

2-inch deal, 2 panels square, diminished stiles, and ovolo sash.

2-inch deal, 2 panels, bead butt and square, diminished stiles, and ovolo sash.

2-inch deal, 2 panels, bead flush and square, diminished stiles, and ovolo sash.

2-inch deal, 2 panels, moulded and square, diminished stiles, and ovolo sash.

2-inch deal, 2 panels, moulded and bead butt, diminished stiles, and ovolo sash.

2-inch deal, 2 panels, moulded and bead flush, diminished stiles, and ovolo sash.

2-inch deal, 2 panels, moulded on both sides, diminished stiles, and ovolo sash.

2½-inch deal, 2 panels, square, with diminished stiles, and ovolo sash.

2½-inch deal, 2 panels, bead butt and square, diminished stiles, and ovolo sash.

2½-inch deal, 2 panels, bead flush and square, diminished stiles, and ovolo sash.

2½-inch deal, 2 panels, moulded and square, diminished stiles, and ovolo sash.

2½-inch deal, 2 panels, moulded and bead butt, diminished stiles, and ovolo sash.

2½-inch deal, 2 panels, moulded and bead flush, diminished stiles, and ovolo sash.

2½-inch deal, 2 panels, moulded on both sides, diminished stiles, and ovolo sash.

If hung folding, or with marginal lights, to be so described.

It is the practice in describing joiner's work, to specify the ironmongery used with it, that is, the hinges, locks, fastenings, and furniture ; and we have accordingly mentioned the hanging and fastening of common doors, and gates, and coach-house doors

Carpenter and Joiner.   (2285*l.*)

Common framed 4-panel doors are usually hung with 3½-inch butts and 7-inch iron rim stock locks.   Better doors are hung with 4-inch iron or brass butts, mortice locks and brass nob furniture.   Folding doors, if heavy, should have 4½ or 5-inch brass butts, and if necessary to clear mouldings, they should be hung with projecting brass butts, and should moreover be provided with flush and other bolts, and mortice locks and furniture.   Doors of dining, drawing, and other rooms, where they are required to clear the carpet by rising as they open, should have 4 or 4½-inch rising joint butts. For closet doors, 3½-inch butts are usually described with brass tumbler locks and keys.   External doors require the provision of larger locks, which are usually iron rim locks with 10 or 12-inch bright rod bolts, chains, staples, &c.   Shutters when hung are with butts, which for the back flaps are of a less size, and spring bar fastenings should be specified to them.   Brass nobs to the front flaps.

Moulded architraves to doors and windows are described by their width.

Columns and pilasters are usually described —

1¼-inch deal diminished columns, . . . inches diameter.

1½-inch deal diminished columns, . . . inches diameter.

Pilasters similarly specified.   Both one and the other to be glued up and blocked. If fluted, to be mentioned ; as also necking grooves to columns.   Caps and bases according to the order, carved or of papier maché, as the expense will allow.

Entablatures got out of deal, as per drawing, provide glued, blocked, and fixed with all necessary brackets and grounds.

Water-closets are fitted up with 1-inch clean deal (wainscot or mahogany), seats, risers, and clamped flaps, square skirtings, all requisite bearers and pipe-casing ; and the joiner is to attend on the plumber while fixing the basins and other work.   *Privies* are described as to seats and risers the same as water-closets.

Cisterns, internal and external, must have their cistern cases proportioned in thickness to their sizes ; thus one about 3 or 3 feet 6 inches long, and 2 feet 9 inches deep, will do on 1¼-inch deal dovetailed · it should be described with requisite bearers, and a cover of ¾-inch deal with a wood handle.   For a good-sized external cistern, we should specify, provide and fix a wrought and dovetailed 2-inch deal cistern case, . . . feet long, . . . feet wide, and . . . feet deep in the clear.   Find and fix all necessary bearers for the same, together with all other requisite fittings, and further provide a ¾-inch deal strongly ledged cover, with saddle-back fillets and water channels at each joint, as shall be directed.

Cisterns for water-closets.

Each to have cistern cases of 2-inch deal capable of containing 36 cubic feet of water, fixed with strong bearers and ledged covers of ¾-inch yellow deal tongued and beaded.

Sinks, describe as under, when wooden ones lined with lead are used.

1½-inch dovetailed sink, enclosed with 1¼-inch deal square-framed front, and door hung with 3-inch butts and other necessary ironmongery.

Warm bath.

To be fitted up (of the best Spanish mahogany) with riser, frame, and clamped flap, provided and fixed with all requisite bearers and other fittings and appurtenances. The flap to be moulded in front, and hung with 3½-inch butt hinges, and the riser panelled and moulded as shown in the drawings.

Dressers.   The following is a specification for a good house.

Provide and fix a dresser in the kitchen, of 2-inch deal, with cross-tongued top 10 feet long and 2 feet 9 inches wide, supported on strong framed legs and bearers. 1-inch deal pot-board and bearers.   Six 1¼-inch sunk shelves, whose widths are to average 7 inches.   Back of the shelves to be of 1-inch deal, wrought, beaded, grooved, and cross-tongued.   1-inch deal top, 14 inches wide, with moulded cornice. Five drawers with bottoms and dovetailed rims of ¾-inch deal.   The fronts to be of 1-inch deal, beaded.   A brass drop handle and a good patent tumbler lock to each drawer, together with all slides, runners, bearers, and other requisite appurtenances.

Dresser top for scullery, 1½-inch clean deal, 2 feet 6 inches wide and 6 feet long, cross-tongued and fixed upon strong wrought and framed legs and bearers.

Plate-rack for scullery to be provided over the sink, and of the same length.   Sink as above described.

Spit-rack to be provided over the kitchen chimney, or other convenient place, as may be directed.

Dwarf closets, if any are used, may be of 1-inch deal, square framed and moulded in front, the doors to be hung with 2½-inch butts, and to have tumbler locks.

Pipe casings, wrought and framed, to be provided where necessary, to hide lead pipes of all descriptions, and fronts to unscrew for coming at the pipes in case of defects therein.

Carpenter and Joiner. (2285m.)

Fittings for larder, as follow: —

Provide a clean deal dresser top, $1\frac{1}{2}$ inch thick, 2 feet 6 inches wide, and . . . feet long, to be feather-tongued and fixed on strong framed legs and rails. Two meat rails, 6 feet long, of wrought fir, $3\frac{1}{2}$ by 2 inches, suspended from wrought iron stirrups. Provide also a hanging shelf, 6 feet long, 10 inches wide, and $1\frac{1}{4}$ inch thick, to be similarly suspended by wrought iron stirrups.

Laundry to be fitted up with $1\frac{1}{2}$-inch clean white deal washing troughs, wrought two sides, and splayed and put together with white lead, as shown on drawing. $1\frac{1}{4}$-inch deal ironing board, wrought both sides and clamped, properly hung with hinges to a hanging stile. Provide two clothes racks, hung with pullies and ropes to the ceiling to raise and lower the same.

Dust bin, with proper slides, where shown on the plan, to contain 30 feet cube, the whole to be of oak.

Arris gutters to eaves should never be of wood: zinc or copper are better materials, and we do not therefore think it necessary to describe them.

Fittings to shops are so various that no general description can be given. They must be referred to drawings, and on them the specification should be written. So of *shop fronts*.

Stable fittings are specified as follow: —

Mangers, &c. 2-inch deal bottoms and $1\frac{1}{2}$-inch deal sides. Wrought oak manger-rails, 4 by 3 inches. Wrought, rebated, and rounded oak manger post, 6 by 4 inches, wrought and framed with bearers thereto. Oak heel-posts, wrought, 6 by 5 inches, and groove for partitions. Oak top rails, 5 by 4 inches, grooved and rounded at the top. Oak bottom rails, wrought, 4 by 4 inches, grooved and arris rounded off. $1\frac{1}{2}$-inch deal partitions, wrought on both sides, ploughed, tongued, and beaded. $1\frac{1}{4}$-inch deal rails on each side, board wide, and the arrisses rounded off.

Fronts to hay-racks. Oak standard, 4 by 4 inches, wrought and framed into oak bearer under the manger. $1\frac{1}{4}$ inch deal fronts framed for the reception of cast-iron hay-racks well secured. Fix fir bearers and 1-inch deal partitions at each end of hay-racks, with fir arris rails 3 inches apart at the bottom of each rack.

Dressings over stalls connected with heel-posts. 1-inch deal frieze, wrought joints, feather-tongued, and backings thereto, segmental sofites and keystone in centre of arches. Impost moulding at the springings and moulded cornice to girt about 10 inches.

Line the walls to the height of 5 feet with 1-inch yellow deal, wrought, ploughed, tongued, and beaded, with a $\frac{5}{8}$-inch beaded capping thereon.

Churches. To give general directions for the specification of a church would be impossible. The principles of its timbering may be collected from what has preceded. *Pewing* is executed as planned on the drawings, of whole deal (generally) square-framed partitions two panels high; $1\frac{1}{2}$-inch framed doors and enclosures one or two panels high, with stiles, munnions, and top rails 3 inches wide, and bottom rails 6 inches wide. The panels of the doors and enclosures should not be more than a board in width, and the framework round them chamfered. The doors are hung with 3-inch butt hinges, and should have brass nob pulpit latches. Capping to the whole of the pewing, grooved and moulded according to drawing. *Pew fittings* are, $1\frac{1}{2}$-inch wrought and rounded seats 12 inches wide, with proper bearers and $1\frac{1}{4}$-inch cut brackets not more than 3 feet apart. Seats rounded next the pew doors. *Flap-seats* in the galleries to have strong joints. All the pews to have $\frac{3}{4}$-inch book boards 6 inches wide, with $\frac{1}{2}$-inch rounded capping bearers, and $\frac{1}{2}$-inch cut brackets thereunder, not more than 2 feet 6 inches apart, and the ends rounded next the pew doors. If there be an organ, its enclosure and the free seats adjoining it should correspond with the pew enclosures. *Free seats* of $1\frac{1}{4}$-inch deal, as shown in the drawings. The seats to be 11 inches wide, rounded in front. Backs framed with stiles, munnions, and rails, $3\frac{1}{2}$ inches wide, and the standards, ends, and bearers, according to the drawings. *Children's seats* to be of $1\frac{1}{4}$-inch deal, with brackets same thickness, not more than 2 feet 6 inches apart; at least 8 inches wide, and the flap seats, where they occur, to be hung with strong butts. *Pulpits and reading desks* are usually of $1\frac{1}{4}$-inch deal, framed according to drawings, with $1\frac{1}{4}$-inch doors, hung with brass hinges and pulpit latches. Whole deal floors on bearers, 1-inch book boards, cappings and bearers. 1-inch clean deal or wainscot steps and risers, moulded returned nosings, $1\frac{1}{4}$ inch, beaded, sunk and cut string boards, strong bracketed carriages. 1-inch square framed sofite under pulpit floor and stairs, mahogany or wainscot moulded handrail, with caps turned and mitred; square bar balusters with one in ten of iron; turned newels to block steps; seats of $1\frac{1}{4}$-inch deal, 13 inches wide, and proper bearers thereto, together with all appurtenances and requisite fittings for executing the drawings.

Carpenter and Joiner. (2285n.)

The carpenter and joiner is to provide all such jobbing work, in following or preceding the other artificers engaged on the works and their appurtenances, as may be requisite for the completion thereof in every respect, without any extra charge.

2286. Founder, Smith, and Ironmonger. For describing cast iron girders and columns, reference must be had to Chap. I. Sect. X. (1628e, et. seq.), wherein will be found the method of determining their scantlings—for which no rule can be given that is not dependent on the results there laid down. Having determined the weight to be borne, no girder (and such should be inserted in the specification) should be allowed to be used, that has not been previously tested by *weighting* it at the foundery.

Cast iron cradles are sometimes used for openings, which must be described for the particular occasions as they occur.

Chimney bars are described usually as follows : —
Provide and fix to kitchen chimney two wrought iron cradle bars, each 2 inches wide and ¾-inch thick, long enough to extend to the outside of the chimney jambs, and turned up and down at each end. The other chimneys are to have wrought iron chimney bars 3 inches wide and ½ inch thick.

Straps, stirrup irons, nuts, bolts, screws, and washers, together with all other wrought iron work for the roofs and partitions, to be provided, as may be requisite for tying in and securing all carpentry, and the smith is to deliver to and assist the carpenter in fixing or attaching the same.

Where the quantity is uncertain, a given weight beyond the above general direction should be provided in the contract, such part thereof as may not be wanted to be deducted from the accounts after the rate of . . . per cwt.

Provide all necessary cramps of cast and wrought iron, as may be directed, for the mason, the former to be used where the works are exposed to the air.

Wrought iron doors to be provided for strong room (or if opening in a party wall), folding, and of the best quality, as shown in drawing ; with hinges and proper fastenings, of the value at least of 25l.

If *cast iron sashes* are used in any part of a building, they are to be provided with reference to drawings.

Wedges for underpinning must be described with reference to the thickness of walls they are to catch : each pair must be at least as long as the wall is thick.

Balusters to a buck stone staircase and landings are described —
Wrought iron balusters, ¾ inch square, with turned wrought iron newel equal to 1½ inch diameter, with rounded handrail of wrought iron 1½ by ½ inch. The balusters and newel are to be riveted into the handrail at top, and at the bottom let into the stone work and run with lead.

Balusters to a principal staircase are described —
Ornamental cast iron balusters, as shown on the drawings, with top rail of wrought iron 1¼ by ½ an inch, let into and firmly screwed to the mahogany (or wainscot) handrail. The balusters and newels are to be riveted into the iron rail, and at the bottom they are to be let into the stonework and run with lead

Balusters of wrought iron to be provided for strengthening the principal staircase when not of stone. Every tenth baluster to be of wrought iron, properly fastened.
Provide and fix . . . knockers for . . . doors to . . . .

Air bricks of cast iron to be provided and fixed in the brickwork for the ventilation of the floors.

Air gratings, . . . in number, to be provided, 9 inches square, and fixed round the lower part of the walls of the house.

Area gratings, . . . to each area (if any there be), to be prepared and fixed of cast iron, with bars 1½ inch by ¾ of an inch, and not more than 1½ inch apart. Frames 1½ inch by 1 inch, and with strong flanges to let into the surrounding stone-work.

Window guards of wrought iron to the windows of . . ., and . . . bars to be 1 inch square and 4 inches apart, with framework of iron of the same substance securely fixed to the brickwork.

Cast iron rain-water pipe, for a large size stack, is described —
6 inches diameter, to lead from the roof down into the drain, with head and shoe complete.

Coal plates (if more than one) of cast iron, with proper fastenings to be fixed over the coal shoot.

Cast iron ornamental railing, as per drawing, to the windows, or to the stone balcony in front of the house, as the case may be.

Air traps of cast iron to all communications of surface water with drains to be of appropriate size, and provide all gully-hole gratings that may be necessary.

To provide for the carpenter's and joiner's works, and use and fix thereto, besides that

FOUNDER, SMITH, AND IRONMONGER. (2286a.)

which has been already described, all requisite spikes, nails, screws, and other proper ironmongery, and all requisite brass work, both to be of the very best quality.

Provide a copper, . . . inches diameter, and stewing stoves as shown on the drawings, with all requisite bars and iron work.

For fittings to stables describe —

No. . . . Cast-iron hay-racks, 3 feet wide and 2 feet high in the clear. 1¼-inch round staves, about 3 inches apart, the frames 1¼ by ¾ of an inch, with the arris rounded off next the staves. Provide and fix two manger rings in each stall.

Cast iron coping to the walls of the dung-pit of the thickness of ⅞ of an inch, and returned on each side 4 inches down at the least.

Cast iron gratings to stable yards are usually described as of the weight of 1 cwt.

For church and chapel work, the founder's, smith's, and ironmonger's work is so dependent on the design, that no general instructions for specifications can be given. The following are the only peculiarities : —

Provide *cast iron saddle bars* for the windows ⅝ by 1¼ inch, 12 inches longer than the clear width of each window, laid into and worked up with the brickwork, at the height shown on the drawings.

Provide to each window wrought iron framework for a hopper casement, as shown on the drawings, and fit up the same complete, with patent lines, brass pulleys, and all other requisite appurtenances.

2287. PLASTERER. To *lath, plaster, float,* and *set* all the ceilings and strings of staircases, and the quartered partitions of the . . . chambers (such as servants' rooms) on attic stories.

To *render, float,* and *set* all brickwork in attic stories.

To plaster all sides of the kitchen offices and office passages with best floated rough stucco, lathed where requisite.

All the remainder of the sides of the interior throughout is to be executed with the very best floated stucco, lathed where requisite. Stucco of offices (or office buildings if any) to be finished with rough surfaces; all the rest of the stucco to be troweled quite smooth.

All the arched, groined, panelled, and coffered work, and the bands and architraves, to be executed in guaged stuff, in the best and most accurate manner.

To run plaster cornices round the several rooms, lobbies, passages, and other parts of the building, with enrichments thereto accurately modelled according to the drawings (the enrichments, if so wished, to be described as of papier maché). A centre flower to each room on the ground and one-pair floor, where marked, securely fixed to the ceiling. These are, on all accounts, better for security in the papier maché, as they can be then screwed to the ceiling.

Basement or ground story (or both, as the case may be) is to be run round in all the rooms, lobbies, passages, &c. with *skirtings of Parker's cement,* 10 inches high, 1¼ inch thick, whited when soft, and finally washed of stone colour.

The plasterer is to execute all necessary beads, quirks, and arrisses. To stucco all internal and external reveals, to dub out where the work may require it, so as to bring out all extra thicknesses and projections, and to counter-lath the work over large timbers and elsewhere, as may be necessary.

The lathing throughout is to be performed with lath-and-half heart of fir laths, free from sap. Enrichments to be carefully trimmed and finished off, and where heavy leaves or embossed work may require it, to be screwed with strong copper screws.

The ceilings on the two principal floors are to be distempered by the painter. All the rest of the ceilings, strings, and mouldings are to be whitened.

The sides of the rooms in the attic or garret (as the case may be) stories, as well as the lobbies, closets, passages, &c., are to be finished of such stone colour tints as the architect may direct.

Lime-white stables and coach-house walls, larders, sculleries, cellars, including vaulting under sides of floors where open, &c.

When Parker's cement is used for external works, describe as under : —

To stucco in the very best manner with Parker's cement, jointed to imitate masonry, the whole (or part, if such be the case) of the exterior of the building, with columns, pilasters, plinths, entablatures, strings, mouldings, labels, jambs, reveals, chimneys, chimney moulds, decorations, enrichments, and appurtenances of every kind, as shown on the drawings and profiles. Such works to be subject to such further instructions from the architect as he may think proper, and to be ,roughly coloured as each portion is executed, and finally coloured when the architect shall so direct, with weather-proof colour-

PLASTERER. (2287*a.*)

ing, fixed with Russia tallow, beer grounds, tar, and the other proper ingredients.

Where desired, decorative chimney pots, of Parker's or other cement, and of the value of two guineas, to be provided for each flue.

Pugging. To fill in upon the sounding boarding between the joists, where so provided, with good lime and hair pugging mortar, laid throughout 1 inch in thickness.

Roughcasting. For the mode of describing this, see Plastering, Sect. IX. (2249.)

2288. PLUMBER. To lay the *flats and gutters* with milled lead of 8 lbs. to the foot superficial. Where against walls, to be turned up 7 inches; where against slopes, as rafters, to turn up 10 inches. Rolls not to exceed 27 inches apart.

Work *flashings* of milled lead in the walls of 5 lbs. to the foot, and to turn down over gutters and flats. Where flashings adjoin the slopes of a roof, they should be described to be laid stepwise into the brickwork, and of an average width of 12 inches.

Hips and ridges to be covered with milled lead 6 lbs. to the foot, and at least 18 inches wide, well secured with lead-headed nails.

Where eaves gutters are used, describe as follows: —

To put round the eaves at the curb plate 4-inch copper (or zinc) guttering, fixed complete with bands and brackets, with copper (or zinc) pipes . . . . inches diameter, with neat heads and appropriate shoes to lead into the gutter or drain.

Domes should be covered with lead from 6 to 8 lbs. to the foot superficial, according to their size, and must be well secured with proper seams or rolls thereto.

For coverings of *zinc* the reader is referred to Sect. VIII. Chap. II. (1792, *et seq.*) and Sect. VII. Chap. III. (2224*g.*) of this Book.

Tops and sides of dormers to be covered with 5-lb. milled lead, turned down all round full 8 inches. A flashing of 5-lb. milled lead 30 inches wide, to be fixed over the sill of the dormer door or window, as the case may be.

Aprons of 6-lb. milled lead, and 10 inches wide, should be described to sky-lights.

External mouldings of wood should be covered with 6-lb. milled lead, to turn up 6 inches, and to have flashings of 4-lb. milled lead let into the brickwork, and to be turned down 5 inches.

To fix . . . . *stacks of rain-water pipes* from the gutters to the drains, of (5) inches bore, turned up from milled lead of 8 lbs. to the foot superficial, and securely fixed with ornamental cistern heads as shall be approved by the architect, and 2-inch strong overflow discharging pipes. Similar description for conveying water from a portico. A lead rose is often placed over water pipes to prevent stoppage.

No pipes but of lead or zinc should be used against stone buildings. Cast iron pipes should only be used to offices.

In London, it is usual to specify that the water should be laid on for the service of the house in the following manner: —

To lay on from the main of the . . . . Company water with $\frac{3}{4}$-inch strong cast lead pipe to the cistern of the upper water-closet, with ball-cock complete. Similarly to lower water-closet and to such other cisterns as are provided, with ball-cocks, &c. complete, and to pay all official fees.

Line the sinks in the scullery and butler's pantry (and other small ones, if any) with 6-lb. milled lead, and fix thereto 2-inch waste pipes, with brass bell traps complete to go into the drains.

Line the kitchen cistern with milled sheet lead, bottom 9 lbs. and sides 6 lbs. to the foot, with all soldering thereto. To provide to the same a 1¼-inch waste pipe. Line the kitchen sink with lead of 8 lbs. to the foot, to turn well over the woodwork and to have a 2-inch strong waste pipe to lead into the drain, with brass bell grate complete. A $\frac{3}{4}$-inch service pipe and brass cock to be provided from the cistern for supplying water to the sink.

Roses pierced with holes of sufficient dimensions to be provided of 10-lb. lead to gutters and rain-water cesspools.

Water closets to be constructed and fitted up in every respect complete, with blue basin, and the very best patent valve apparatus. Soil pipe of 4½-inch bore out of 8-lb. lead, to lead into drain with strong D trap, lead service box, 10 inches by 7, and 6 inches deep, of 10-lb. milled lead; 5-lb. lead safe under pan, with 2-inch swan-necked waste pipe. 1-inch supply pipe to the basin, and all other pipes, wires, cranks. handles, and other proper fitments. The *cistern* is to be lined, bottom with 8-lb. cast lead, and sides with 5-lb. milled lead. 1¼-inch waste pipe, soldered in below the dip, with washer and waste complete.

Inferior water closets to be provided with strong cast iron trapped pan (or stoneware syphon pan) with water laid on, and in all respects to be fitted complete.

Provide all stench-traps that may be requisite where the pipes communicate with the drains.

PLUMBER. (2288a.)

For a cold bath provide and fix a . . . feet . . . inches bath of copper of 16 ounces to the foot superficial, tinned on the inside, and painted in japan to imitate marble, or as may be directed. Lay on the water with strong 1¼-inch lead pipe, with brass cock, and fix 2½-inch strong lead waste pipe, with brass washer and plug, thereto.

If the hot bath be not of marble, the following clauses will describe the several positions and varieties of the boilers by which a supply of hot water is obtained in the present day : —

I. Provide a Tylor and Sons' 5-feet 2-inch taper oval-end copper (or galvanized tinned iron) bath, white marbled inside, with copper pipes, mounted in wood cradle, with 1¼-inch deal framing panelled with French polished Honduras mahogany top. Three of Tylor and Sons' inch roundway bath taps, S. B., with socket keys and handsome levers, hot, cold, waste. A Tylor and Sons' patent bath boiler, with stove front to fit opening of fireplace, with doors and damper (no setting required). Inch lead pipe from cold water cistern to boiler, ¾-inch lead pipe to relieve boiler up to and turned over top of cistern (or any convenient outlet). Inch lead pipe for hot, cold, waste, and overflow pipes to bath. Lead safe with waste under cocks, and leave the work perfect; as estimated, at 39l. 0s. 9d., exclusive of carriage and any bricklayer's, plasterer's, or carpenter's work, cutting away for pipes and making good, fixing bath framing, and graining and varnishing it. A galvanized tinned iron bath is 6l. less.

II. Tylor and Sons' 22-gallon copper chimney boiler, with wrought iron band, with bolts and nuts to carry ditto, and stove front to fill up opening in fireplace, with sliding blower, revolving damper, soot door, and bars; as estimated at 38l. 0s. 9d.

III. Tylor and Sons' copper saddle boiler with unions, a stove front to suit ditto, with sliding blower, revolving damper, soot door and bars. A galvanized wrought iron cistern, close top, with manhole screwed down, to be fixed with two lines of inch wrought iron pipe from boiler to hot cistern, inch ditto to supply cold water to hot cistern, ¾-inch ditto to relieve hot cistern, inch hot, cold, waste, and overflow pipes to bath, &c. ; as estimated at 47l. 4s. 3d.

IV. Provide a 5-feet (larger or smaller, as deemed necessary) strong best make improved kitchen range, with strong wrought iron back boiler with close top, wrought iron oven, and line fireplace with panelled covings. A galvanized wrought iron hot water cistern, &c. ; as estimated at 61l. 3s. 9d.

V. The range fitted with two boilers, one for the bath, the other for domestic use; where a fire is kept sufficiently large to work two boilers, they are recommended. Estimate 4l. extra to No. IV.

VI. A range with partially closed fire instead of one with open fire. 4l. 15s. extra to No. IV.

VII. Tylor and Sons' 22-gallon copper dome-top boiler, with furnace iron work, doors, bars, and damper, and continue as No. I. This boiler may be fixed in the basement, and will supply a hot bath in any apartment below the level of the cold water cistern. As estimated, 43l. 15s. 3d.

NOTE. In I., the bath and boiler may be fixed in the same or separate apartments; open or close fire at pleasure. All the estimates are framed presuming on a cold water cistern and a rain water pipe, or a drain, being within 10 feet of the room. In III., the hot water cistern is placed over the fireplace in the room. In IV., the hot cistern is supposed to be 25 feet above the boiler. In VII., the cold cistern is supposed to be 25 feet above boiler. The waste pipe from the bath to the drain should always have as great a fall as possible, and never be laid to so small a fall as allowed by placing it within the depth of the floor.

Common pumps are generally described as 3-inch pumps, with neat cast iron cases fixed complete, with proper lead suction pipe to bring sufficient supply of water from well, and all other appurtenances. The manufacturer's stock to be seen if others be required.

To provide and fix (this where the water is not laid on, as in London), a 3½-inch lifting engine pump, with brass barrel; and provide from the well . . . feet of 1½-inch strong suction pipe. Service pipes to the cisterns, with all cocks and joints that may be necessary.

Provide all wrought copper and zinc nails that may be wanted for laying the metal works.

To provide in the contract . . . . cwt. extra of cast sheet lead, including labour and all proper materials as may be wanted and directed by the architect; and if the same or any part thereof should not be used, there shall be a deduction made for the same on making up the accounts, after the rate of . . . . per cwt. for such portion thereof as shall not have been used. Also extra of milled lead.

2289. GLAZIER. To glaze all the windows with best crown glass; the offices with second crown glass. To glaze all the front windows with best sheet glass; or with best flattened sheet; or with patent plate; or with British plate; as the case may be, and according to the weight to be specified. For varieties of glass and glass for other purposes, see Chap. II. Sect. XII. *par.* 1870, *et seq.* The architect very often names the manufactory from which the glass is to be procured, to ensure the proper quality being supplied.

All the glazing is to be properly bedded, stopped in, sprigged, and back-puttied, the convex side outwards (of crown and sheet glass), to be free from specks, blisters, or other blemish; and to be left whole and clean, on the works being rendered up as complete.

The whole of the windows, including the hopper ventilators and the diamond shaped ventilator (of the church, robing room, &c.), are to be glazed with . . . . glass, in strong lead quarries, firmly soldered at the angles, and tied to the saddle bars. The lights to be fixed into the grooves and stopped in with white lead.

2290. PAINTER. To knot (with silver leaf in best work), to pumice down and smooth, to stop, and otherwise to properly prepare all the wood and other works intended for painting.

To paint four times in oil, or till they bear out, with the best oil and colour, all the internal and external wood and iron works, all the stucco, and all other works that are usually painted.

The walls of the principal staircase, lobbies, and entrance hall are to be imitations of marbles, jointed like masonry, in blocks of sizes as shall be directed, and twice varnished with the best copal.

The doors, shutters, dadoes, skirtings, boxings, architraves, and other dressings on the ground and one-pair floors (and others if required), are to be grained wainscot (or other wood as may be specified), in an artist-like manner, and sized, and varnished twice with best copal varnish.

If any of the mouldings of doors and shutters are to be gilt, specify the same.

Distemper the ceilings (or as follows) :—

The ceilings and cornices on ground and one-pair floor to be painted four times in oil, and flatted and picked in with such extra colours as may be directed.

To flat extra, of such tints as may be directed, all the rest of the stucco work and wood work on the principal and one-pair floors.

Sashes to be finished on the outside of . . . . colour. The plain painting to be of tints of brown, drab, or stone colour, as may be directed.

To French polish in the best manner the handrail of the staircase, the mahogany work of the bath and water closet, and other parts (if any).

2291. PAPERHANGER. To prepare and bring to a proper face all the walls and surfaces intended for papering.

To hang with figured paper, value . . . . per yard, the rooms (to be described) on the . . . . floor, with borders (as may be desired).

The remainder of the rooms to be hung with paper . . . . per yard, with or without borders.

Where satin paper is to be put up, or any of the more expensive descriptions, then to underline, or line the walls, with lining paper, and hang with . . . . paper of . . . . shillings per piece, the rooms on the . . . . floor. Borders also, if thought desirable, must be specified.

To paper the entrance passage or hall, staircase, and landings, up to . . . . with Siena marble (or other) paper, value . . . . per yard, hung in blocks, or hung horizontally and lined to sized blocks with brown lines (or black pencil), twice sized, and varnished (once or twice) with best copal.

Provide and fix with needle points a ¾-inch gilt . . . . moulding round the dressings, and along the top and bottom of the . . . . room, or . . . . rooms.

All the patterns are to be approved by the architect or his client.

2292. BELLHANGER. To provide and fix with all necessary wires (concealed or otherwise), pulls, cranks, and every other appendage, bells from the following places :—[Here enumerate the places.].

It is usual to mark the place both up and down stairs where the bells are to be hung; and where there are many of them together they are sometimes described to be so tuned as to form a musical scale.

The electric bell system will depend upon the patent selected.

2293. EXCAVATOR. Cover over the spaces under paved or tiled floors (except where the tiles are laid on joists) with broken bricks well rammed and grouted with liquid mortar. This layer is to be made of sufficient thickness to receive 6 inches of concrete, which is to be properly rammed and covered with a layer of 2 inches of fine concrete, finished with a level surface.

2293a. BRICKLAYER. Foundations to piers of arches to be in brickwork of hard bricks, laid in cement, and every course throughout the foundations to be well grouted.

When the building is to be heated with hot air or hot water, then;—build furnace room where shown on plan, with flues as necessary: or, build channels for hot water pipes under floors; the channels to be 2 feet high by 12 inches wide in the clear, resting upon 3 inches of concrete and a double course of Bangor duchess slates to form channel floors; the sides to be half a brick thick in mortar.

Build 9-inch sleeper walls to support ends of joists of wood floors abutting upon paved floors (as in a church), and build half-brick honeycomb sleeper walls on one brick footings, 4 feet apart, under all wood floors in basement, or on ground floor when not excavated under.

Lay in drains of glazed socketed stoneware pipes of Lambeth (or other) manufacture, as shown on drawings, of the clear internal diameters there figured, and at the depths below the surface as figured. Provide all necessary bends and junctions. All the pipes to be jointed in cement, and the drains to be properly connected with the sewer (or cesspool). The outlet of the drain to have a galvanized iron flap to shut flush all round.

Insert a damp-proof course of Bangor slates in cement in all walls throughout their entire thickness 3 inches lower than the general level of the ground floor (and where else as needed). See Chap. III. Sect. I. par. 1886b, et seq. for other methods of obviating the rise of damp.

The moulded bricks to be carefully made in accordance with the detail drawings, and to be trimmed up before they are placed in the kiln. They are to be made a little thicker than the other bricks, so that the beds and joints may be rubbed true before they are laid; they are to be set in fine mortar, and (before the scaffolding is struck), they are to be rasped, rubbed with gritstone, and the arrises to be made as straight and true as stonework.

Work into the exterior and interior faces of the walls (if required), crosses, diapers, zigzags, or other patterns; and form bands, string-courses, &c., with white, black, red, or other bricks, as shown on the elevations, &c. The red and black bricks are to be laid in blue-black mortar, or the joints to be raked out and pointed with the same.

Brick relieving arches that are visible, are to be formed of three or four courses of red and black bricks, alternately or otherwise, as shown, or as the architect may hereafter direct.

A specimen brick of every description, splayed, moulded, for facing, &c. to be submitted to the architect for his approval before the commencement of the work.

Hollow walls for exposed situations. The external walls above the plinth line are to be built with a hollow cavity in the middle of about 3 inches, having courses of bonders or through stones not more than 1 foot apart in height, and of various widths, but never more than 2 feet 6 inches apart. At the level of the top of the plinth, a course of thick slates, or of thin stones, is to be worked on the walls, closely bedded in strong mortar under all the voids or flues thus formed, and a small aperture, 9 inches by 6 inches, is to be made for the admission of air and to carry off any moisture that may have been driven in; openings into each of these flues are also to be made between the joists of the different floors for ventilation. Other methods of building such walls are described in Chap. III. Sect. II. par. 1902c.

2293b. MASON. All cramps to be of copper; iron cramps not to be allowed (see par. 2284a.). Lead joggles, and slab slate dowels to be inserted in the joints where directed.

The quoins, jambs, string-courses, hoodmoulds, buttress weatherings, copings, and dressings generally, to be strictly worked according to detail drawings, and to be dragged, chopped, tooled, or rubbed (according to the quality of the stone) so as to be truly worked in every particular.

All the tracery and mouldings to be set out full size, and cut and set to the right jointing as approved by the architect or the clerk of the works.

The caps and bases to piers to be in large stones. The caps and bases to dwarf shafts

MASON (2293*b*).

(if any), and the corbels under wall pieces or other roof timbers, to be well pinned into walls, and sunk and dowelled to receive shafts or timbers.

The tower and spire to be carefully carried out in accordance with detailed drawings. The spire to spring from squinch arches or from the solid broaches (or as the case may be), and gradually reduced towards the top, each stone to be wrought and cut to its through bed and inclination of its plane, the parts (as shown) to be in solid ashlar and carefully tailed and bonded. The bands, mouldings, cornices, strings, &c., to be worked as shown, and continued round ; the storm lights to be formed with solid sills, heads, &c. ; the vane to drop through the finial and to be securely fixed. The windows of the tower and the storm lights of the spire, to be grooved for louvres of wood or slates (or to be filled in with thin slabs of stone with ornamental piercings).

Turn relieving arches over all arches of nave, chancel, &c., formed of different coloured stones, arranged as directed, and form bands, diapers, crosses, &c., of same where shown. The stones for parti-coloured work to be Pennant, Caen, Temple Quiting, Red Forest of Dean, Silver Grey Forest of Dean, Red Mansfield, Whinstone, or Blue Warwickshire, stone (or local stone, if of suitable colour).

Provide shafts where shown of Derbyshire, Devonshire, Purbeck, or other marble, or of alabaster, serpentine, Aberdeen or Peterhead granite (or other as may be selected), to be well polished ; and to be sunk, dowelled, and secured into caps and bases. Shafts in angles of doorways (if any) to be of any suitable dark stone (if necessary) to contrast with the jamb.

Pave the entrance hall, passage, &c. ; or if a church, pave the passages, porches, &c., where coloured on plan, with Minton's (or other) encaustic tiles, one third (or more or less) being figured, combined with chocolate and black tiles, value . . . . per yard superficial, manufacturers' prices. Pave the chancel (usually with richer tiles) with tiles value . . . . per yard superficial.

Face the walls of . . . . with Minton's glazed (or other) tiles, value . . . . per yard superficial, to be secured with cramps of stout copper wire inserted in holes in edges of the tiles.

All the tiles to be of the best quality, free from blemishes ; to be set in Roman cement, and to have all cement removed from their face after the work is finished ; the edges of the tiles to be rubbed, where necessary, to ensure neatness of workmanship, and care is to be taken that they are not injured by the workmen after they are laid.

The steps to the sanctuary and chancel to be of rubbed Portland, Red Mansfield, Robin Hood, Craigleith, or other hard stone or marble, in lengths of not less than 10 feet, very carefully set and bedded, pinned, joggle jointed, and run and plugged with lead, and back-jointed to receive tile paving.

The base mouldings of the tower, jambs and arches of the windows and doors throughout the building, and whatsoever parts are tinted . . . . upon the elevations, are to be of tooled or dragged masonry.

The plinths, eaves, string courses, and the labels over the windows and doors, are to be of Ketton (or other suitable) stone, finished with a dragged or tooled face.

Regularity in the quoin stones is not desired, but they may be worked and set in any reasonable scantling so as best to bond in, and harmonise with, the intermediate rubble. The upper beds of the stones to be laid with a slight inclination outwards, and as close as their nature will allow. Every precaution is to be taken to avoid risk of the settling of the work from imperfect beds and open joints. The work is to be carried up regularly all round the building. In the case of a church with a tower, the walls of the latter are to be specified, to be built up very slowly and without being bonded into those of the church, but are to have slip joints or chases worked in them for forming the connection ; this is in all cases to be so free as to allow for the settlement of the masonry without injury to the work in the church walls : with this exception, no part of any wall is at any time to be raised more than three feet higher than another, during the progress of the works.

The walls of the tower of a church are to be built quite solid, and inverted arches are to be turned under all the large apertures therein. All flat headed apertures are to be covered with York (or other) lintels, of thickness proportionate to the width of the opening.

The coping of the gables to be of Bramley Fall or other stone that is not porous, worked as shown, and the apices of the (here enumerate which) gables to be surmounted by crosses worked in Ketton or other stone, according to drawing, set with copper dowels.

Walls with concrete cores. The external face to be built up in courses of hammered, scabbled, or sawn stone. The internal face to be built up in sawn (or other) ashlar,

Mason (2293*b*).

or in rough brickwork, in English bond, or rubble if it is to be plastered. The body of the walls to be filled in with strong concrete, composed of 1 part of ground stone lime and 6 parts of clean sharp gravel, filling in interstices. At every 2 feet 6 inches in height a double course of bricks is to be set in mortar ; and at every 8 feet 6 inches in height, a bonding through stone, from 10 inches to 1 foot 3 inches deep, is to be fixed. Stone chippings may be mixed with the gravel forming the concrete.

Kentish Rag. The Kentish rag to be of the best quality, from the quarries at Boughton, sound and free from hassock, laid in random courses, gulletted and pointed with dark mortar. A sufficient number of bond stones to be built in, one through stone (at least) to each yard superficial.

Bath Stone. To be the best Bath stone from Sumpsion's, Pictor's, or Randall and Saunder's Combe Down quarries (no Farleigh Down stone to be used), to be laid on its natural bed in all cases, and cleaned off when set. All plinths, bases, and other work for a height of 4 feet above the ground level to be of Box Ground stone.

Flint work. (Flint walling is of the following descriptions :—Rough, or as the flints are dug ; random, or broken without any regard to regularity ; split, so that they are true on the face and oval in form ; or, split and squared, by which neat and square work is produced.) The walling is to be built in the soundest manner with . . . . flints (state which of the four descriptions is to be used), laid in mortar compounded of quick-setting stone lime and coarse sharp sand, free from loam ; bricks, tiles, pebbles, &c., may be bedded in the centre or core of the wall. The long flints to be selected and laid as through stones, and the string-courses, &c., to be laid entirely through the thickness of the wall, so as to give additional bond. The work to be kept as dry as possible during the construction, to be protected by boards in wet weather, and to be covered in as soon as possible after completion. No grouting to be used. If the walling is faced with half-flints, care is to be taken in laying them to keep their upper surfaces as level as possible, to prevent rain driving into the centre of the wall ; firmly pin up the lower bed with fragments.

Random walling of local stone. The stone for the walls generally is to be brought from . . . . (state the quarry), that for the foundations (unless brickwork is used for them) to be of large size ; all those in the visible surface of the walls are to be carefully hammered, scabbled, or sawn (as the quality of the stone and nature of the work may require). All stone used in the main walls of the building to be of good scantling, and no very thin stone will be allowed in any part.

2293*c*. Carpenter and Joiner. The trusses of roofs are to be framed as shown, and of timbers of the scantlings respectively figured, or as here specified. They are to be mortised, tenoned, arched, notched, moulded, chamfered, and stopped, as shown on the detail drawings ; and to be bolted and strapped with wrought iron straps, forged with ornamental ends ; all bolts to have washers and nuts, notched as shown.

The curved ribs (if any) are to be put together in (three) thicknesses, so as to break joint, to be wrought all over, and the joints to be tongued. These (three) thicknesses are to be screwed close together with long screws, and bolted with ½-inch bolts between each joint. The centre thickness to be tenoned into the timbers on which it abuts. Tongue a bold 3-inch bead to underside of same.

The hammer-beams (if any) are to be cogged down upon the wall plates, and framed to the ribs, and bolted, as shown. The principals are to be notched and tenoned to the hammer-beams, and well spiked to ribs, and tenoned together and pinned at top. The collars (if any) are to be firmly tenoned into and spiked to principals. The purlins are to be notched down and housed into the principals on each side, and spiked. The king-post or queen-posts are to be framed in the usual manner.

All the timbers of the roofs exposed to view are to be wrought, and the angles moulded, or chamfered, or stop chamfered.

All roofs (if exposed to view) to be boarded above the rafters with ⅞-inch wrought matched V jointed boarding, laid diagonally, and securely nailed to rafters and covered with (asphalted) felt (or specify, to lath on the top of rafters and plaster between the same). Lay battens 3 inches by 1 inch over the boarding or laths, on the back of every rafter, and on the battens lay 3 inch by 1 inch slating battens (or double oak tiling laths if the roof be tiled), fixed to a proper gauge for the sized slates required.

In churches, the floors under the seats are usually of wood, and require rebated and chamfered oak margins, 6 inches by 4 inches, laid flatwise, where they abut upon paved floors. These margins are to be mortised or dowelled to receive bench ends, and the wood floors to be kept 3 inches above the tile floors on which they abut.

CARPENTER AND JOINER (2293c).

The whole of the seating throughout to be formed as detail drawings, of good, well-seasoned, English oak (or otherwise), to be wrought, chamfered, and stopped, or moulded and cut, as shown or required; to be carefully framed and put together. The bench ends to be (at least) 3 inches thick, tenoned and pinned to the chamfered oak sill. The backs to have solid moulded oak capping. The seats to be $1\frac{1}{4}$ inches thick, and the book-boards to be 2 inches thick (fixed flat or sloping), edges chamfered, all to be well housed and cut into bench ends. Fix cut brackets not more than 4 feet apart, under the seats; and cut brackets, not more than 3 feet apart, under the book-boards. All the seats to be kept clear of the piers (if any).

Doors. Those on the exterior are to be 2 inch wrought, ledged, framed, and braced, folding (or other) doors, with stop chamfered, arched heads, stiles, rails, and braces, covered on the outside with $\frac{3}{4}$-inch wrought, tongued, and V jointed, oak boarding, hung to solid oak frame (or on hinge-hooks let into stone jambs), with strong, heavy, wrought iron mediæval hinges, and fastened with best rim dead lock cased with oak, and a heavy wrought iron latch with bold ornamental drop handle and plate, key-plate, &c., all wrought according to detail drawing (or a price to be stated for each article). The frames to be of oak, 6 inches by 4 inches, wrought, double rebated, stop chamfered, grooved, &c., tenoned into stone steps, and to have extra strong hooks on plates screwed to same.

For a dwelling house; the principal entrance door to be of deal $1\frac{1}{2}$ inches thick, framed flush, with V joints inside; the exterior to be cased with $\frac{3}{4}$-inch oak boards, with moulded fillets over the joints, the same to return round the head, and to die at bottom on an oak rail, 9 inches deep, sometimes having sunk quatrefoils, &c. The door to be hung on wrought iron ornamental hinges to hooks let into the jambs (or screwed to frames); an 8-inch rim lock and ornamental drop handle, escutcheon, and key-plate, and two 8-inch barrel bolts.

The back, or side entrance, door to be $1\frac{1}{4}$-inch, framed, ledged, and braced, covered with $\frac{3}{4}$-inch wrought oak boarding with chamfered joints, nailed on with rose nails driven through and clenched; hung on hinges and fastened with lock and bolts, similar to those specified for front entrance.

The internal doors may be of the following varieties:—

$1\frac{1}{2}$-inch four-panelled, with hollow on the room side, and $\frac{3}{4}$-inch diagonal V boarding next the hall or passage; to be hung with fleur-de-lys or ornamental wrought iron hinges, made to clasp the door so as to show on both sides, and fastened with wrought iron latches and ornamental drop rings.

$1\frac{1}{2}$-inch four-panelled, square framed, stop chamfered, filled in with upright or diagonal V jointed boarding, and hung on hinges as previously specified.

Cupboard fronts to correspond with the doors of their respective rooms, hung on ornamental S, HL, or other similar hinges, fastened with small tumbler locks, wrought iron key plates, and small twisted or other drop handles.

The *ceilings* of the principal rooms;—after they are plastered, to be divided into square panels about . . . feet square, by nailing thereon hollowed fillets $2\frac{1}{2}$ inches by 1 inch (or more), neatly scribed at intersections, with staff beads 1 inch (or more) diameter, nailed along the centre of the same, mitred at intersections, and conveyed round walls as a cornice. Care is to be taken in laying the joists so that they may form nailing points for these panel ribs.

The principal *staircase* to have $1\frac{1}{4}$-inch pitch pine (or other) treads, with rounded nosing and hollow moulding under same, and inch risers, glued and blocked to fir carriages; the ends of the steps to be housed into $1\frac{1}{4}$-inch wall strings, and 2-inch outer string boards, sunk and staff beaded, and finished at the top with a boldly moulded capping, framed at the bottom and corners into 6-inch square newels, with moulded finials, bases, and pendents, as drawing. Boldly moulded oak handrail, 4 inches wide and 6 inches deep, with $1\frac{1}{2}$-inch square oak balusters, stop chamfered.

The *landings* to be formed by joists resting upon boldly moulded stopped beams, as shown on sections.

The *tiled floor* (when laid on joists):—spike fillets to joists, at 3 inches below their upper surfaces; fill in between the same with inch rough boarding. The vacuity to be filled up with pugging of concrete flush with the upper surface, finished with a layer inch thick of Roman cement smoothly floated to receive the tiles.

2293d. PLASTERER. If the walls of a church are to be plastered, the stone jambs to windows and doors are usually specified to project one inch beyond the face of wall, so as to form a stop for plaster, and afterwards cleaned off and left flush.

Lath for, and plaster to, the spaces between the rafters (unless the boarding is intended to be left visible).

2293e. SLATER OR TILER.   Cover the *ridges* with socketed roll Staffordshire ridge tiles set in cement ; the tiles to be grooved for cresting (if any).   Cover the *hips* with proper lapping hip tiles or rolled hip tiles.   Provide ornamental *tile cresting* (if any), and fix same on ridges where shown on elevations.

Cover the roofs with good sound plain tiles, combined with ornamental tiles, to form patterns, as shown ; every tile to be pegged with a good English oak peg, and laid in mortar to a 3-inch lap.

Cover the roofs with best Bangor slates ; the bands and diapers to be formed of Carnarvon or Westmoreland green, or other coloured slates ; or courses to be laid of slates cut to a notched pattern.

The slater to provide slates to form damp-proof course in walls ; and for the bottoms of hot water pipe channels (if any).

2293f. SMITH.   Provide and fix ½-inch square saddle bars to all the windows, with lead lights ; to be fixed on an average 12 inches apart.

Provide and fix to outside of windows, where necessary, 1-inch square stancheons, not more than 6 inches apart, with ornamental heads forged to drawing, let into (frames or) stone sill at bottom, and passed through saddle bars with mortises formed thereon.

For church windows with tracery heads, provide and build in across the springing of the arch of all windows of 3 lights and upwards, wrought iron bars 2 inches by ½-inch, corked, and well turned up 2 feet from jambs, on each side ; these bars to be well galvanized, and fixed with play for expansion or strain, in notches through the mullions.

Provide . . . . wrought iron hopper (or other) casements, and fix one to each light of each window (or as many as necessary).   If hoppers are used they are to rest on the sill, and be hinged next to it, so that when closed the exterior glazing may be flush, and to be fitted with opening racks and fastenings.

Provide all requisite straps, bolts, nuts, and washers for the various roofs.   Where visible, the straps are to be worked to detail drawings ; and the washers and nuts to be notched and stamped as directed.

Provide and fix according to drawing, the wrought (or cast) iron vanes, crosses, ridge cresting, guards to areas, balconies, &c. ; all to be securely fixed ; the vanes and gable crosses to have stems as long as possible, and to be leaded into the stone or screwed to the roof timbers, as the case may be.

Provide and fix ornamental wrought iron hinges, latches, key-plates, closing rings, &c., on doors, as specified in carpenter's work, all to be strictly worked according to detail drawings.

Provide and fix an ornamental cast iron grating to pattern, to cover hot water pipe channels.

Provide and fix to all overhanging eaves 4-inch cast iron eaves gutter, with all necessary angle pieces, valley pans to internal angles, swan-necks, and socket pipes cast on the gutter to lead into heads of rain water pipes.   The gutters to be fixed on strong wrought iron brackets screwed to the feet of the rafters, and the joints to be screwed together and bedded in red lead putty.   Rectangular down pipes are now frequently used, with ornamental ears or bands.

Provide and fix Newall's (or other) copper wire lightning conductor with point, properly secured, to . : . . (the highest portion of the building), and brought down with all requisite insulators ; the end to be carried into the earth for a depth of 3 feet from the surface.

2293g. GLAZIER.   Glaze all the windows (of the church) and tracery heads (if any) with quarries and borders in strong church lead ⅜-inch wide.   The lead to be secured to the saddle bars and stancheons with strong copper wire, soldered to lead, and securely twisted round the saddle ; the glazing to be properly cemented, to be let into the grooves of stonework, and neatly pointed with lime and stone dust.

The glass to be Powell's quarries, or Hartley's patent rough cathedral glass, ⅛-inch thick.   The quarries to be of one tint, and the borders of another tint (as for instance, green and yellow).

Skylights and windows, in exposed situations, where much light is not required, may be glazed with Hartley's rough plate glass, ¼-inch thick, or less.

Water-closet and similar windows (where privacy is desired), with Hartley's patent rough plate glass, ⅛-inch thick ; with fluted glass ; or with diapered, or with embossed glass.

Any other windows to be glazed with ribbed, enamelled, embossed, or stained glass must be enumerated.

Provision to be made in window sills and skylights (where practicable), for conveying condensed water to the exterior of the building.

2293*h.* Painter. Stop with coloured stopping, twice oil with linseed oil, and twice varnish with best copal varnish, the exterior doors and frames.

Stop with stained stopping, and knot with coloured knotting, the wrought woodwork of roofs ; brush the whole twice with boiled oil, and once varnish the same. Pick out the chamfers and mouldings in roofs with vermillion, cobalt blue, chocolate, pale yellow, and white, in two oils, and stencil patterns thereon, according to drawing.

Deal seats, or benches, are to be knotted with stained knotting, stained with . . . . stain (approved by the architect), and twice varnished with tackless varnish.

In a dwelling house ;—all the wrought woodwork (except the floors, and the work executed in oak) to be stained with . . . . stain, once coated with linseed oil, and twice varnished with the best copal varnish. Or, if the deal has been picked, it may be left plain, and only varnished. Or, if selected with much care, the deal and pine may be polished. Inside *oak* work is best left to obtain an effect by use, but where immediately desirable, it may be once or twice oiled.

Pick out the ornamental ironwork on doors, roofs, screens, &c., in black or dark blue. A pattern or diaper is sometimes done in gold leaf upon it.

All paint and varnish to be of the best quality ; sizing and mineral turpentine will not be allowed.

2293*i.* Bellhanger. The front (and side) entrance doors to have bold pendant mediæval wrought iron pull, according to detail drawing.

The pulls in the principal rooms to be bronze or iron lever pulls of mediæval character, and very strong ; the wire of strong copper, to be conveyed in zinc secret tubing ; the cranks to be best horn cranks. Floor boards over bell wires to be screwed (not nailed) down for ready removal.

2293*j.* Gas Fitter. Lay on from the main, strong wrought iron welded tubing of the necessary diameter, with all necessary bends ; junctions, stopped ends, T pieces, &c.

Provide and fix in each of the principal rooms a pendent corona of . . . lights, value . . *s.* each, fitted with balance weights and a ball and socket joint. Fix bronzed (or brass) bracket burners in passages (or where else required), value . . *s.* each.

Church lights of wrought iron, bronze, or brass, standards, coronæ, brackets, &c., according to their situations, for gas or for candles (specify value of each).

All lights to be fitted with argand, fish-tail, or batswing burners. Ground glass, or figured glass globes, where stated, are sometimes included by the architect.

2293*k.* We now close this general outline of a specification (which has been submitted as nothing more than a skeleton for filling up as different cases may require) by adding a general form of a contract, with the usual conditions. This requires as much variation to meet each particular case, as does the specification.

2294. Conditions. That all the works shall be executed in the best and most workmanlike manner, to the satisfaction of [Here add employer's name], or his architect, without reference thereon to any other person. If any alterations should hereafter be made by order of (*the employer*), or his architect, by varying from the plans or the foregoing specification, either in adding thereto or diminishing therefrom, or otherwise however, such alterations shall not vacate the contract hereby entered into, but the value thereof shall be ascertained by the said architect, and added to or deducted from the sum hereinafter mentioned, as the case may be ; nor shall such alterations, either in addition, diminution, or otherwise, supersede the condition for the completion of the whole of the works, but the contractor shall, if such alterations, of whatever sort, require it, increase the number of his workmen, so that the same, as well as the works contained in the above particulars, shall be completely finished, and so delivered up to   (*the employer*), on or before the day of   , in the year   , on failure whereof the contractor shall forfeit and pay to   (*the employer*), the sum of   for every day that the work remains unfinished and undelivered as aforesaid, which sum the said   (*the employer*) shall be allowed to stop as liquidated damages out of any moneys that may be due and owing to the said contractor on account of the works.

If any doubt or doubts should arise during the execution of the works, or at measuring the extras should occur, or at making out the accounts as to any extras or other works for which the contractor may consider he may have a claim, over and above the sum hereinafter mentioned, the admission and allowance of any such claim or claims shall be judged of, determined, and adjusted solely by the architect to   (*the employer*), without reference in any way to any other person ; it being the intention of these conditions that all such works of every kind that may be necessary for completely finishing the works proposed, for the rectification of any failure from whatever cause arising, and the well maintaining, sustaining, and supporting the whole of the works, as well as alterations and additions, should such be made, so that the whole may remain sound and firm, are implied in the foregoing specification, although the same may not therein be specifically expressed.

If the contractor shall neglect or refuse to carry on the works with such dispatch as is thought proper by the architect, it shall be lawful for   (*the employer*) or his architect, and either of them is hereby empowered to employ such other person or persons as (*the employer*) or his architect, or either of them, may think fit or necessary, to finish and complete the several unfinished works, after having given notice thereof in writing six days before employing such person or persons, such notice to be left either at the contractor's shop, counting-house, or usual place of abode, without effect, and the amount or amounts of the bill or bills of any artificers that may be so employed shall be deducted out of any moneys that may be due and owing to the said contractor, or any part thereof, as the case may be.

It is hereby agreed, this   day of   , in the year   , between (*the employer*), on the one part, and   (*the contractor*) on the other part, that he, the said   (*the contractor*), for his executors, administrators, and assigns, doth hereby promise and agree to and with the said   (*the employer*), to do and perform all the works of every kind mentioned and contained in the foregoing particulars, and according and subject to the conditions above recited, and according to the plans prepared and referred to, at and for the sum of   pounds ; and the said   (*the contractor*) doth hereby agree to abide by and be subject to the several clauses, conditions, and penalties hereinbefore mentioned and contained.

In consideration whereof the said   (*the employer*) doth hereby promise and agree to pay to the said   (*the contractor*), on the certificate of the architect, the aforesaid sum of   pounds, in   separate payments, it being agreed that neither of the said payments, except the last, shall amount to more than two-thirds of the value of the work done at the time of such certificate being given.

In witness whereof the said parties have hereunto set their hand, the day and year above written.

Witness, E. F.   A. B. (the employer.)
                          C. D. (the contractor.)

Sect. XIV.

MEASURING AND ESTIMATING.

2295. The practice of measuring is dependent on rules already given under Mensuration, in Sect. VI. Chap. I. of this Book (1212, *et. seq.*), in which are described the methods of ascertaining the superficial and solid contents of any figure. The application of them to architecture, in the practice of measuring and estimating the different parts of a building, forms the subject of this section.

2296. For the purposes of measuring, the common instruments are a pair of 5-feet rods, divided into feet, inches, and half inches, and a 2-feet rule divided into inches and eighths and twelfths of inches, beyond which subdivision, measurements are rarely carried in this country.

2297. The mode of what is called squaring dimensions, as usually practised by duodecimals, will be now explained.

2297a. Duodecimals are a series of denominations beginning with feet, wherein every inch in the lower denomination makes twelve in that next above it; they form a series of fractions, of which the denominations are understood, but not expressed. The dimensions are taken in feet, inches, and twelfths of an inch, but not nearer, except in works of the greatest nicety. Feet and inches are marked with their initial letters, but twelfths or seconds by a double accent, thus 2″, and thirds by a triple accent, thus 5‴.

2297b. To multiply duodecimals together, write down the two dimensions to be multiplied in such way that the place of feet may stand under the last place of the multiplicand ; begin with the right hand denomination of the multiplier, and multiply it by every denomination of the multiplicand, throwing the twelve out of every product, and carrying as many units as there are twelves to the next. Placing the remainders, if any, under the multiplier, so that the like parts in the product may be under like parts of the multiplicand, proceed with every successive figure of the multiplier towards the left, in the same manner, always placing the first figure of the product under the multiplier. Then the sum of these partial products will be the whole product. In duodecimals there will be as many denominations below feet as in both the factors taken together.

Example 1.—Multiply 7 ft. 5 in. by 3 ft. 4 in.

$$7 : 5$$
$$4$$
$$\overline{2 : 5 : 8}$$
$$22 : 3$$
$$\overline{24 : 8 : 8}$$

Example 2.—Multiply 24 ft. 8 in. 8′ by 3 ft. 7 in.

$$24 : 8 : 8$$
$$3 : 7$$
$$\overline{14 : 5 : 0 : 8}$$
$$74 : 2 : 0$$
$$\overline{88 : 7 : 0 : 8}$$

2297c. In example I. there is only one place of duodecimals in each factor; there are therefore two places in the product. In the second example there are two places of duodecimals in the multiplicand and one in the multiplier, which make, together, three; there are therefore three denominations in the product. This method of placing the denominations of the factors gives the correct places of the product at once; since like parts of the product stand under like parts of the multiplicand. It also shows the affinity between duodecimals, decimals, and every series or scale of denominations whereof any number divided by the radix of the scale makes one of the next towards the left hand. The consideration is, moreover, useful in discovering readily the kind of product arising from the multiplication of any two single denominations together.

2297d. When the number of feet runs very high in the factors, it will be better to write down the product of each multiplication, without casting out the twelve, and add together those of each denomination beginning on the right, and divide by 12, to carry to the next higher place, then add these, and so on, as often as there are places in the whole product.

Example.—Multiply 262 ft. 5 in. by 54 ft. 8 in.

$$262 \ : \ 5$$
$$54 : 8$$

$$2099 : 4$$
$$1048 \ : \ 20$$
$$13100 \ : \ 250$$

$$197 = \frac{2369}{12}$$

$$14345 \ : \ 5 \ : \ 4$$

Thus, under inches, the products being set down and added, they amount to 2369, which, divided by twelve, gives 197 to carry to the place of feet, and 5 remainder. Then adding the feet together with the quantity carried, it gives the whole number of feet; while the operation is extremely simple and free from the troubles of either side operations or useless stress on the memory.

2297e. The division of the foot into 12 parts renders the application of the rules of *practice* very valuable in the computation of duodecimals. The practical rule is to set down the two dimensions one under the other, that is, feet under feet and inches under inches, and multiply each term in the multiplicand by the feet in the multiplier, beginning at the lowest; and, if the numbers be large, put down the inches without carrying 1 for every 12 from inches to feet. Then, instead of multiplying by the inches, take such aliquot parts of the multiplicand as the inches are of a foot; after which add the lines together, carrying 1 for every 12 inches.

Example 1.—Multiply 7 ft. 5 in. by 3 ft. 4 in.

$$4 \text{ in.} = \tfrac{1}{3}. \quad 7 : 5$$
$$3 : 4$$

$$22 : 3$$
$$2 : 5 : 8$$

$$24 : 8 : 8$$

Example 2.—Multiply 262 ft. 5 in. by 54 ft. 8 in.

$$8 = \tfrac{2}{3}. \quad 262 : \quad 5$$
$$54 : \quad 8$$

$$1048 : 270$$
$$1310$$
$$87 : \quad 5 : 8$$
$$87 : \quad 5 : 8$$

$$23 = \frac{281}{12} : 4$$

$$14345 : \ 5 : 4$$

The same examples have been used to show the relative advantages of the two methods.

2297f. Thus far we have treated of the squaring of dimensions to obtain the superficies of work. To learn the solidity of certain materials, such as timber, stone, and some others, the dimensions have to be cubed. The process is similar to the above, and is continued a further step. One example will suffice to explain the method, and we will take the figures given in the above system.

Example.—What is the cube of a block of stone, 7 ft. 5 in. wide, 3 ft. 4 in. thick, and 12 ft. long?

$$7 : 5$$
$$3 : 4$$

$$22 : 3$$
$$2 : 5 : 8$$

$$24 : 8 : 8 \text{ super.}$$
$$12$$

$$296 : 8 : 0 \text{ cube.}$$

2297g. The abridgment of the labours of practical men is always a matter of importance—being identical with the saving of time which is lost in calculation, and which with the architect is of the utmost importance, when it is recollected what multifarious duties he has to discharge. Hence the following table of squares, cubes, and roots of numbers, up to 1000, will be most acceptable to him. The first column of the table shows the number, the second the square of such number, the third exhibits its cube. In the fourth column is found the square root of the number, and in the fifth its cube root. Thus, looking to the number 61 in the first column, its square is found to be 3721, its cube 226981, its square root 7·8102497, and its cube root 3·936497. Again, taking the number 784, we find its square to be 614656, its cube 481890304, its square root 28, and its cube root 9·220872.

No.	Square.	Cube.	Square Root.	CubeRoot.	No.	Square.	Cube.	Square Root.	CubeRoot.
1	1	1	1·0	1·0	64	4096	262144	8·0	4·0
2	4	8	1·4142136	1·259921	65	4225	274625	8·0622577	4·020726
3	9	27	1·7320508	1·442250	66	4356	287496	8·1240384	4·041240
4	16	64	2·0	1·587401	67	4489	300763	8·1853528	4·061548
5	25	125	2·2360680	1·709976	68	4624	314432	8·2462113	4·081656
6	36	216	2·4494897	1·817121	69	4761	328509	8·3066239	4·101566
7	49	343	2·6457513	1·912933	70	4900	343000	8·3666003	4·121285
8	64	512	2·8284271	2·0	71	5041	357911	8·4261498	4·140818
9	81	729	3·0	2·080084	72	5184	373248	8·4852814	4·160168
10	100	1000	3·1622777	2·154435	73	5329	389017	8·5440037	4·179339
11	121	1331	3·3166248	2·223980	74	5476	405224	8·6023253	4·198336
12	144	1728	3·4641016	2·289428	75	5625	421875	8·6602540	4·217163
13	169	2197	3·6055513	2·351335	76	5776	438976	8·7177979	4·235824
14	196	2744	3·7416574	2·410142	77	5929	456533	8·7749644	4·254321
15	225	3375	3·8729833	2·466212	78	6084	474552	8·8317609	4·272659
16	256	4096	4·0	2·519842	79	6241	493039	8·8881944	4·290841
17	289	4913	4·1231056	2·571282	80	6400	512000	8·9442719	4·308870
18	324	5832	4·2426407	2·620741	81	6561	531441	9·0	4·326749
19	361	6859	4·3588989	2·668402	82	6724	551368	9·0553851	4·344481
20	400	8000	4·4721360	2·714418	83	6889	571787	9·1104336	4·362071
21	441	9261	4·5825757	2·758923	84	7056	592704	9·1651514	4·379519
22	484	10648	4·6904158	2·802039	85	7225	614125	9·2195445	4·396830
23	529	12167	4·7958315	2·843867	86	7396	636056	9·2736185	4·414005
24	576	13824	4·8989795	2·884499	87	7569	658503	9·3273791	4·431047
25	625	15625	5·0	2·924018	88	7744	681472	9·3808315	4·447960
26	676	17576	5·0990195	2·962496	89	7921	704969	9·4339811	4·464745
27	729	19683	5·1961524	3·0	90	8100	729000	9·4868330	4·481405
28	784	21952	5·2915026	3·036589	91	8281	753571	9·5393920	4·497942
29	841	24389	5·3851648	3·072317	92	8464	778688	9·5916630	4·514357
30	900	27000	5·4772256	3·107232	93	8649	804357	9·6436508	4·530655
31	961	29791	5·5677644	3·141381	94	8836	830584	9·6953597	4·546836
32	1024	32768	5·6568542	3·174802	95	9025	857375	9·7467943	4·562903
33	1089	35937	5·7445626	3·207534	96	9216	884736	9·7979590	4·578857
34	1156	39304	5·8309519	3·239612	97	9409	912673	9·8488578	4·594701
35	1225	42875	5·9160798	3·271066	98	9604	941192	9·8994949	4·610436
36	1296	46656	6·0	3·301927	99	9801	970299	9·9498744	4·626065
37	1369	50653	6·0827625	3·332222	100	10000	1000000	10·0	4·641589
38	1444	54872	6·1644140	3·361975	101	10201	1030301	10·0498756	4·657010
39	1521	59319	6·2449980	3·391211	102	10404	1061208	10·0995049	4·672330
40	1600	64000	6·3245553	3·419952	103	10609	1092727	10·1488916	4·687548
41	1681	68921	6·4031242	3·448217	104	10816	1124864	10·1980390	4·702669
42	1764	74088	6·4807407	3·476027	105	11025	1157625	10·2469508	4·717694
43	1849	79507	6·5574385	3·503398	106	11236	1191016	10·2956301	4·732624
44	1936	85184	6·6332496	3·530348	107	11449	1225043	10·3440804	4·747459
45	2025	91125	6·7082039	3·556893	108	11664	1259712	10·3923048	4·762203
46	2116	97336	6·7823300	3·583048	109	11881	1295029	10·4403065	4·776856
47	2209	103823	6·8556546	3·608826	110	12100	1331000	10·4880885	4·791420
48	2304	110592	6·9282032	3·634241	111	12321	1367631	10·5356538	4·805896
49	2401	117649	7·0	3·659306	112	12544	1404928	10·5830052	4·820284
50	2500	125000	7·0710678	3·684031	113	12769	1442897	10·6301458	4·834588
51	2601	132651	7·1414284	3·708430	114	12996	1481544	10·6770783	4·848808
52	2704	140608	7·2111026	3·732511	115	13225	1520875	10·7238053	4·862944
53	2809	148877	7·2801099	3·756286	116	13456	1560896	10·7703296	4·876999
54	2916	157464	7·3484692	3·779763	117	13689	1601613	10·8166538	4·890973
55	3025	166375	7·4161985	3·802953	118	13924	1643032	10·8627805	4·904868
56	3136	175616	7·4833148	3·825862	119	14161	1685159	10·9087121	4·918685
57	3249	185193	7·5498344	3·848501	120	14400	1728000	10·9544512	4·932424
58	3364	195112	7·6157731	3·870877	121	14641	1771561	11·0	4·946088
59	3481	205379	7·6811457	3·892996	122	14884	1815848	11·0453610	4·959675
60	3600	216000	7·7459667	3·914867	123	15129	1860867	11·0905365	4·973190
61	3721	226981	7·8102497	3·936497	124	15376	1906624	11·1355287	4·986631
62	3844	238328	7·8740079	3·957892	125	15625	1953125	11·1803399	5·0
63	3969	250047	7·9372539	3·979057	126	15876	2000376	11·2249722	5·013298

No.	Square.	Cube.	Square Root.	CubeRoot.	No.	Square.	Cube.	Square Root.	CubeRoot.
127	16129	2048383	11·2694277	5·026526	190	36100	6859000	13·7840488	5·748897
128	16384	2097152	11·3137085	5·039684	191	36481	6967871	13·8202750	5·758965
129	16641	2146689	11·3578167	5·052774	192	36864	7077888	13·8564065	5·768998
130	16900	2197000	11·4017543	5·065797	193	37249	7189057	13·8924440	5·778996
131	17161	2248091	11·4455231	5·078753	194	37636	7301384	13·9283883	5·788960
132	17424	2299968	11·4891253	5·091643	195	38025	7414875	13·9642400	5·798890
133	17689	2352637	11·5325626	5·104469	196	38416	7529536	14·0	5·808786
134	17956	2406104	11·5758369	5·117230	197	38809	7645373	14·0356688	5·818648
135	18225	2460375	11·6189500	5·129928	198	39204	7762392	14·0712473	5·828476
136	18496	2515456	11·6619038	5·142563	199	39601	7880599	14·1067360	5·838272
137	18769	2571353	11·7046999	5·155137	200	40000	8000000	14·1421356	5·848035
138	19044	2628072	11·7473444	5·167649	201	40401	8120601	14·1774469	5·857765
139	19321	2685619	11·7898261	5·180101	202	40804	8242408	14·2126704	5·867464
140	19600	2744000	11·8321596	5·192494	203	41209	8365427	14·2478068	5·877130
141	19881	2803221	11·8743421	5·204828	204	41616	8489664	14·2828569	5·886765
142	20164	2863288	11·9163753	5·217103	205	42025	8615125	14·3178211	5·896368
143	20449	2924207	11·9582607	5·229321	206	42436	8741816	14·3527001	5·905941
144	20736	2985984	12·0	5·241482	207	42849	8869743	14·3874946	5·915481
145	21025	3048625	12·0415946	5·253588	208	43264	8998912	14·4222051	5·924991
146	21316	3112136	12·0830460	5·265637	209	43681	9123329	14·4568323	5·934473
147	21609	3176523	12·1243557	5·277632	210	44100	9261000	14·4913767	5·943911
148	21904	3241792	12·1655251	5·289572	211	44521	9393931	14·5258390	5·953341
149	22201	3307949	12·2065556	5·301459	212	44944	9528128	14·5602198	5·962731
150	22500	3375000	12·2474487	5·313293	213	45369	9663597	14·5945195	5·972091
151	22801	3442951	12·2882057	5·325074	214	45796	9800344	14·6287388	5·981426
152	23104	3511808	12·3288280	5·336803	215	46225	9938375	14·6628783	5·990727
153	23409	3581577	12·3693169	5·348481	216	46656	10077696	14·6969385	6·0
154	23716	3652264	12·4096736	5·360108	217	47089	10218313	14·7309199	6·009244
155	24025	3723875	12·4498996	5·371685	218	47524	10360232	14·7648231	6·018363
156	24336	3796416	12·4899960	5·383213	219	47961	10503459	14·7986486	6·027650
157	24649	3869893	12·5299641	5·394690	220	48400	10648000	14·8323970	6·036811
158	24964	3944312	12·5698051	5·406120	221	48841	10793861	14·8660687	6·045943
159	25281	4019679	12·6095202	5·417501	222	49284	10941048	14·8996644	6·055048
160	25600	4096000	12·6491106	5·428835	223	49729	11089567	14·9331845	6·064126
161	25921	4173281	12·6885775	5·440122	224	50176	11239424	14·9666295	6·073177
162	26244	4251528	12·7279221	5·451362	225	50625	11390625	15·0	6·082201
163	26569	4330747	12·7671453	5·462556	226	51076	11543176	15·0332964	6·091199
164	26896	4410944	12·8062485	5·473703	227	51529	11697083	15·0665192	6·100170
165	27225	4492125	12·8452326	5·484806	228	51984	11852352	15·0996689	6·109115
166	27556	4574296	12·8840987	5·495865	229	52441	12008989	15·1327460	6·118032
167	27889	4657463	12·9228480	5·506879	230	52900	12167000	15·1657509	6·126925
168	28224	4741632	12·9614814	5·517848	231	53361	12326391	15·1986842	6·135792
169	28561	4826809	13·0	5·528775	232	53824	12487168	15·2315462	6·144634
170	28900	4913000	13·0384048	5·539658	233	54289	12649337	15·2643375	6·153449
171	29241	5000211	13·0766968	5·550499	234	54756	12812904	15·2970585	6·162239
172	29584	5088448	13·1148770	5·561298	235	55225	12977875	15·3297097	6·171005
173	29929	5177717	13·1529464	5·572054	236	55696	13144256	15·3622915	6·179747
174	30276	5268024	13·1909060	5·582770	237	56169	13312053	15·3948043	6·188463
175	30625	5359375	13·2287566	5·593445	238	56644	13481272	15·4272486	6·197154
176	30976	5451776	13·2664992	5·604079	239	57121	13651919	15·4596248	6·205821
177	31329	5545233	13·3041347	5·614673	240	57600	13824000	15·4919334	6·214464
178	31684	5639752	13·3416641	5·625226	241	58081	13997521	15·5241747	6·223083
179	32041	5735339	13·3790882	5·635741	242	58564	14172488	15·5563492	6·231678
180	32400	5832000	13·4164079	5·646216	243	59049	14348907	15·5884573	6·240251
181	32761	5929741	13·4536240	5·656652	244	59536	14526784	15·6204994	6·248800
182	33124	6028568	13·4907376	5·667051	245	60025	14706125	15·6524758	6·257324
183	33489	6128487	13·5277493	5·677411	246	60516	14886936	15·6843871	6·265826
184	33856	6229504	13·5646600	5·687734	247	61009	15069223	15·7162336	6·274304
185	34225	6331625	13·6014705	5·698019	248	61504	15252992	15·7480157	6·282760
186	34596	6434856	13·6381817	5·708267	249	62001	15438249	15·7797338	6·291194
187	34969	6539203	13·6747943	5·718479	250	62500	15625000	15·8113883	6·299604
188	35344	6644672	13·7113092	5·728654	251	63001	15813251	15·8429795	6·307992
189	35721	6751269	13·7477271	5·738794	252	63504	16003008	15·8745079	6·316359

No.	Square.	Cube.	Square Root.	Cube Root.	No.	Square.	Cube.	Square Root.	Cube Root.
253	64009	16194277	15·9059737	6·324704	316	99856	31554496	17·7763888	6·811284
254	64516	16387064	15·9373775	6·333025	317	100489	31855013	17·8044938	6·818461
255	65025	16581375	15·9687194	6·341325	318	101124	32157432	17·8325545	6·825624
256	65536	16777216	16·0	6·349602	319	101761	32461759	17·8605711	6·832771
257	66049	16974593	16·0312195	6·357859	320	102400	32768000	17·8885438	6·839903
258	66564	17173512	16·0623784	6·366095	321	103041	33076161	17·9164729	6·847021
259	67081	17373979	16·0934769	6·374310	322	103684	33386248	17·9443584	6·854124
260	67600	17576000	16·1245155	6·382504	323	104329	33698267	17·9722008	6·861211
261	68121	17779581	16·1554944	6·390676	324	104976	34012224	18·0	6·868284
262	68644	17984728	16·1864141	6·398827	325	105625	34328125	18·0277564	6·875343
263	69169	18191447	16·2172747	6·406958	326	106276	34645976	18·0554701	6·882388
264	69696	18399744	16·2480768	6·415068	327	106929	34965783	18·0831413	6·889419
265	70225	18609625	16·2788206	6·423157	328	107584	35287552	18·1107703	6·896435
266	70756	18821096	16·3095064	6·431226	329	108241	35611289	18·1383571	6·903436
267	71289	19034163	16·3401346	6·439275	330	108900	35937000	18·1659021	6·910423
268	71824	19248832	16·3707055	6·447305	331	109561	36264691	18·1934054	6·917396
269	72361	19465109	16·4012195	6·455314	332	110224	36594368	18·2208672	6·924355
270	72900	19683000	16·4316767	6·463304	333	110889	36926037	18·2482876	6·931300
271	73441	19902511	16·4620776	6·471274	334	111556	37259704	18·2756669	6·938232
272	73984	20123648	16·4924225	6·479224	335	112225	37595375	18·3030052	6·945149
273	74529	20346417	16·5227116	6·487153	336	112896	37933056	18·3305028	6·952053
274	75076	20570824	16·5529454	6·495064	337	113569	38272753	18·3575598	6·958943
275	75625	20796875	16·5831240	6·502956	338	114244	38614472	18·3847763	6·965819
276	76176	21024576	16·6132477	6·510829	339	114921	38958219	18·4119526	6·972682
277	76729	21253933	16·6433170	6·518684	340	115600	39304000	18·4390889	6·979532
278	77284	21484952	16·6733320	6·526519	341	116281	39651821	18·4661853	6·986369
279	77841	21717639	16·7032931	6·534335	342	116964	40001688	18·4932420	6·993191
280	78400	21952000	16·7332005	6·542132	343	117649	40353607	18·5202592	7·0
281	78961	22188041	16·7630546	6·549911	344	118336	40707584	18·5472370	7·006796
282	79524	22425768	16·7928556	6·557672	345	119025	41063625	18·5741756	7·013579
283	80089	22665187	16·8226038	6·565415	346	119716	41421736	18·6010752	7·020349
284	80656	22906304	16·8522995	6·573139	347	120409	41781923	18·6279360	7·027106
285	81225	23149125	16·8819430	6·580844	348	121104	42144192	18·6547581	7·033850
286	81796	23393656	16·9115345	6·588531	349	121801	42508549	18·6815417	7·040581
287	82369	23639903	16·9410743	6·596202	350	122500	42875000	18·7082869	7·047208
288	82944	23887872	16·9705627	6·603854	351	123201	43243551	18·7349940	7·054003
289	83521	24137569	17·0	6·611488	352	123904	43614208	18·7616630	7·060696
290	84100	24389000	17·0293864	6·619106	353	124609	43986977	18·7882942	7·067376
291	84681	24642171	17·0587221	6·626705	354	125316	44361864	18·8148877	7·074043
292	85264	24897088	17·0880075	6·634287	355	126025	44738875	18·8414437	7·080698
293	85849	25153757	17·1172428	6·641851	356	126736	45118016	18·8679623	7·087341
294	86436	25412184	17·1464282	6·649399	357	127449	45499293	18·8944436	7·093970
295	87025	25672375	17·1755640	6·656930	358	128164	45882712	18·9208879	7·100588
296	87616	25934336	17·2046505	6·664443	359	128881	46268279	18·9472953	7·107193
297	88209	26198073	17·2336879	6·671940	360	129600	46656000	18·9736660	7·113786
298	88804	26463592	17·2626765	6·679419	361	130321	47045881	19·0	7·120367
299	89401	26730899	17·2916165	6·686882	362	131044	47437928	19·0262976	7·126935
300	90000	27000000	17·3205081	6·694328	363	131769	47832147	19·0525589	7·133492
301	90601	27270901	17·3493516	6·701758	364	132496	48228544	19·0787840	7·140037
302	91204	27543608	17·3781472	6·709172	365	133225	48627125	19·1049732	7·146569
303	91809	27818127	17·4068952	6·716569	366	133956	49027896	19·1311265	7·153090
304	92416	28094464	17·4355958	6·723950	367	134689	49430863	19·1572441	7·159599
305	93025	28372625	17·4642492	6·731316	368	135424	49836032	19·1833261	7·166095
306	93636	28652616	17·4928557	6·738665	369	136161	50243409	19·2093727	7·172580
307	94249	28934443	17·5214155	6·745997	370	136900	50653000	19·2353841	7·179054
308	94864	29218112	17·5499288	6·753313	371	137641	51064811	19·2613603	7·185516
309	95481	29503629	17·5783958	6·760614	372	138384	51478848	19·2873015	7·191966
310	96100	29791000	17·6068169	6·767899	373	139129	51895117	19·3132079	7·198405
311	96721	30080231	17·6351921	6·775168	374	139876	52313624	19·3390796	7·204832
312	97344	30371328	17·6635217	6·782422	375	140625	52734375	19·3649167	7·211247
313	97969	30664297	17·6918060	6·789661	376	141376	53157376	19·3907194	7·217652
314	98596	30959144	17·7200451	6·796884	377	142129	53582633	19·4164878	7·224045
315	99225	31255875	17·7482393	6·804091	378	142884	54010152	19·4422221	7·230427

No.	Square.	Cube.	Square Root.	Cube Root.	No.	Square.	Cube.	Square Root.	Cube Root.
379	143641	54439939	19·4679223	7·236797	442	195364	86350888	21·0237960	7·617411
380	144400	54872000	19·4935887	7·243156	443	196249	86938307	21·0475652	7·623151
381	145161	55306341	19·5192213	7·249504	444	197136	87528384	21·0713075	7·628883
382	145924	55742968	19·5448203	7·255841	445	198025	88121125	21·0950231	7·634606
383	146689	56181887	19·5703858	7·262167	446	198916	88716536	21·1187121	7·640321
384	147456	56623104	19·5959179	7·268482	447	199809	89314623	21·1423745	7·646027
385	148225	57066625	19·6214169	7·274786	448	200704	89915392	21·1660105	7·651725
386	148996	57512456	19·6468827	7·281079	449	201601	90518849	21·1896201	7·657414
387	149769	57960603	19·6723156	7·287362	450	202500	91125000	21·2132034	7·663094
388	150544	58411072	19·6977156	7·293633	451	203401	91733851	21·2367606	7·668766
389	151321	58863869	19·7230829	7·299893	452	204304	92345408	21·2602916	7·674430
390	152100	59319000	19·7484177	7·306143	453	205209	92959677	21·2837967	7·680085
391	152881	59776471	19·7737199	7·312383	454	206116	93576664	21·3072758	7·685732
392	153664	60236288	19·7989899	7·318611	455	207025	94196375	21·3307290	7·691371
393	154449	60698457	19·8242276	7·324829	456	207936	94818816	21·3541565	7·697002
394	155236	61162984	19·8494332	7·331037	457	208849	95443993	21·3775583	7·702624
395	156025	61629875	19·8746069	7·337234	458	209764	96071912	21·4009346	7·708238
396	156816	62099136	19·8997487	7·343420	459	210681	96702579	21·4242853	7·713844
397	157609	62570773	19·9248588	7·349596	460	211600	97336000	21·4476166	7·719442
398	158404	63044792	19·9499373	7·355762	461	212521	97972181	21·4709106	7·725032
399	159201	63521199	19·9749844	7·361917	462	213444	98611128	21·4941853	7·730614
400	160000	64000000	20·0	7·368063	463	214369	99252847	21·5174348	7·736187
401	160801	64481201	20·0249844	7·374198	464	215296	99897344	21·5406592	7·741753
402	161604	64964808	20·0499377	7·380322	465	216225	100544625	21·5638587	7·747310
403	162409	65450827	20·0748599	7·386437	466	217156	101194696	21·5870331	7·752860
404	163216	65939264	20·0997512	7·392542	467	218089	101847563	21·6101828	7·758402
405	164025	66430125	20·1246118	7·398636	468	219024	102503232	21·6333077	7·763936
406	164836	66923416	20·1494417	7·404720	469	219961	103161709	21·6564078	7·769462
407	165649	67419143	20·1742410	7·410794	470	220900	103823000	21·6794834	7·774980
408	166464	67917312	20·1990099	7·416859	471	221841	104487111	21·7025344	7·780490
409	167281	68417929	20·2237484	7·422914	472	222784	105154048	21·7255610	7·785992
410	168100	68921000	20·2484567	7·428958	473	223729	105823817	21·7485632	7·791487
411	168921	69426531	20·2731349	7·434993	474	224676	106496424	21·7715411	7·796974
412	169744	69934528	20·2977831	7·441018	475	225625	107171875	21·7944947	7·802453
413	170569	70444997	20·3224014	7·447033	476	226576	107850176	21·8174242	7·807925
414	171396	70951944	20·3469899	7·453039	477	227529	108531333	21·8403297	7·813389
415	172225	71473375	20·3715488	7·459036	478	228484	109215352	21·8632111	7·818845
416	173056	71991296	20·3960781	7·465022	479	229441	109902239	21·8860686	7·824294
417	173889	72511713	20·4205779	7·470999	480	230400	110592000	21·9089023	7·829735
418	174724	73034632	20·4450483	7·476966	481	231361	111284641	21·9317122	7·835168
419	175561	73560059	20·4694895	7·482924	482	232324	111980168	21·9544984	7·840594
420	176400	74088000	20·4939015	7·488872	483	233289	112678587	21·9772610	7·846013
421	177241	74618461	20·5182845	7·494810	484	234256	113379904	22·0	7·851424
422	178084	75151448	20·5426386	7·500740	485	235225	114084125	22·0227155	7·856828
423	178929	75686967	20·5669638	7·506660	486	236196	114791256	22·0454077	7·862224
424	179776	76225024	20·5912603	7·512571	487	237169	115501303	22·0680765	7·867613
425	180625	76765625	20·6155281	7·518473	488	238144	116214272	22·0907220	7·872994
426	181476	77308776	20·6397674	7·524365	489	239121	116930169	22·1133444	7·878368
427	182329	77854483	20·6639783	7·530248	490	240100	117649000	22·1359436	7·883734
428	183184	78402752	20·6881609	7·536121	491	241081	118370771	22·1585198	7·889094
429	184041	78953589	20·7123152	7·541986	492	242064	119095488	22·1810730	7·894446
430	184900	79507000	20·7364414	7·547841	493	243049	119823157	22·2036033	7·899791
431	185761	80062991	20·7605395	7·553688	494	244036	120553784	22·2261108	7·905129
432	186624	80621568	20·7846097	7·559525	495	245025	121287375	22·2485955	7·910460
433	187489	81182737	20·8086520	7·565353	496	246016	122023936	22·2710575	7·915784
434	188356	81746504	20·8326667	7·571173	497	247009	122763473	22·2934968	7·921100
435	189225	82312875	20·8566536	7·576984	498	248004	123505992	22·3159136	7·926408
436	190096	82881856	20·8806130	7·582786	499	249001	124251499	22·3383079	7·931710
437	190969	83453453	20·9045450	7·588579	500	250000	125000000	22·3606798	7·937005
438	191844	84027672	20·9284495	7·594363	501	251001	125751501	22·3830293	7·942293
439	192721	84604519	20·9523268	7·600138	502	252004	126506008	22·4053565	7·947573
440	193600	85184000	20·9761770	7·605905	503	253009	127263527	22·4276615	7·952847
441	194481	85766121	21·0	7·611662	504	254016	128024064	22·4499443	7·958114

No.	Square.	Cube.	Square Root.	Cube Root.	No.	Square.	Cube.	Square Root.	Cube Root.
505	255025	128787625	22·4722051	7·963374	568	322624	183250432	23·8327506	8·281635
506	256036	129554216	22·4944438	7·968627	569	323761	184220009	23·8537209	8·286493
507	257049	130323843	22·5166605	7·973873	570	324900	185193000	23·8746728	8·291344
508	258064	131096512	22·5388553	7·979112	571	326041	186169411	23·8956063	8·296190
509	259081	131872229	22·5610283	7·984344	572	327184	187149248	23·9165215	8·301030
510	260100	132651000	22·5831796	7·989569	573	328329	188132517	23·9374184	8·305865
511	261121	133432831	22·6053091	7·994788	574	329476	189119224	23·9582971	8·310694
512	262144	134217728	22·6274170	8·0	575	330625	190109375	23·9791576	8·315517
513	263169	135005697	22·6495033	8·005205	576	331776	191102976	24·0	8·320335
514	264196	135796744	22·6715681	8·010403	577	332929	192100033	24·0208243	8·325147
515	265225	136590875	22·6936114	8·015595	578	334084	193100552	24·0416306	8·329954
516	266256	137388096	22·7156334	8·020779	579	335241	194104539	24·0624188	8·334755
517	267289	138188413	22·7376340	8·025957	580	336400	195112000	24·0831892	8·339551
518	268324	138991832	22·7596134	8·031129	581	337561	196122941	24·1039416	8·344341
519	269361	139798359	22·7815715	8·036293	582	338724	197137368	24·1246762	8·349125
520	270400	140608000	22·8035085	8·041451	583	339889	198155287	24·1453929	8·353904
521	271441	141420761	22·8254244	8·046603	584	341056	199176704	24·1660919	8·358678
522	272484	142236648	22·8473193	8·051748	585	342225	200201625	24·1867732	8·363446
523	273529	143055667	22·8691933	8·056886	586	343396	201230056	24·2074369	8·368209
524	274576	143877824	22·8910463	8·062018	587	344569	202262003	24·2280829	8·372966
525	275625	144703125	22·9128785	8·067143	588	345744	203297472	24·2487113	8·377718
526	276676	145531576	22·9346899	8·072262	589	346921	204336469	24·2693222	8·382465
527	277729	146363183	22·9564806	8·077374	590	348100	205379000	24·2899156	8·387206
528	278784	147197952	22·9782506	8·082480	591	349281	206425071	24·3104916	8·391942
529	279841	148035889	23·0	8·087579	592	350464	207474688	24·3310501	8·396673
530	280900	148877000	23·0217289	8·092672	593	351649	208527857	24·3515913	8·401398
531	281961	149721291	23·0434372	8·097758	594	352836	209584584	24·3721152	8·406118
532	283024	150568768	23·0651252	8·102838	595	354025	210644875	24·3926218	8·410832
533	284089	151419437	23·0867928	8·107912	596	355216	211708736	24·4131112	8·415541
534	285156	152273304	23·1084400	8·112980	597	356409	212776173	24·4335834	8·420245
535	286225	153130375	23·1300670	8·118041	598	357604	213847192	24·4540385	8·424944
536	287296	153990656	23·1516738	8·123096	599	358801	214921799	24·4744765	8·429638
537	288369	154854153	23·1732605	8·128144	600	360000	216000000	24·4948974	8·434327
538	289444	155720872	23·1948270	8·133186	601	361201	217081801	24·5153013	8·439009
539	290521	156590819	23·2163735	8·138223	602	362404	218167208	24·5356883	8·443687
540	291600	157464000	23·2379001	8·143253	603	363609	219256227	24·5560583	8·448360
541	292681	158340421	23·2594067	8·148276	604	364816	220348864	24·5764115	8·453027
542	293764	159220088	23·2808935	8·153293	605	366025	221445125	24·5967478	8·457689
543	294849	160103007	23·3023604	8·158304	606	367236	222545016	24·6170673	8·462347
544	295936	160989184	23·3238076	8·163309	607	368449	223648543	24·6373700	8·466999
545	297025	161878625	23·3452351	8·168308	608	369664	224755712	24·6576560	8·471647
546	298116	162771336	23·3666429	8·173302	609	370881	225866529	24·6779254	8·476289
547	299209	163667323	23·3880311	8·178289	610	372100	226981000	24·6981781	8·480926
548	300304	164566592	23·4093998	8·183269	611	373321	228099131	24·7184142	8·485557
549	301401	165469149	23·4307490	8·188244	612	374544	229220928	24·7386338	8·490184
550	302500	166375000	23·4520788	8·193212	613	375769	230346397	24·7588368	8·494806
551	303601	167284151	23·4733892	8·198175	614	376996	231475544	24·7790234	8·499423
552	304704	168196608	23·4946802	8·203131	615	378225	232608375	24·7991935	8·504034
553	305809	169112377	23·5159520	8·208082	616	379456	233744896	24·8193473	8·508641
554	306916	170031464	23·5372046	8·213027	617	380689	234885113	24·8394847	8·513243
555	308025	170953875	23·5584380	8·217965	618	381924	236029032	24·8596058	8·517840
556	309136	171879616	23·5796522	8·222898	619	383161	237176659	24·8797106	8·522432
557	310249	172808693	23·6008474	8·227825	620	384400	238328000	24·8997992	8·527018
558	311364	173741112	23·6220236	8·232746	621	385641	239483061	24·9198716	8·531600
559	312481	174676879	23·6431808	8·237661	622	386884	240641848	24·9399278	8·536177
560	313600	175616000	23·6643191	8·242570	623	388129	241804367	24·9599679	8·540749
561	314721	176558481	23·6854386	8·247474	624	389376	242970624	24·9799920	8·545317
562	315844	177504328	23·7065392	8·252371	625	390625	244140625	25·0	8·549879
563	316969	178453547	23·7276210	8·257263	626	391876	245314376	25·0199920	8·554437
564	318096	179406144	23·7486842	8·262149	627	393129	246491883	25·0399681	8·558990
565	319225	180362125	23·7697286	8·267029	628	394384	247673152	25·0599282	8·563537
566	320356	181321496	23·7907545	8·271903	629	395641	248858189	25·0798724	8·568080
567	321489	182284263	23·8117618	8·276772	630	396900	250047000	25·0998008	8·572618

No.	Square.	Cube.	Square Root.	Cube Root.	No.	Square.	Cube.	Square Root.	Cube Root.
631	398161	251239591	25·1197134	8·577152	694	481636	334255384	26·3438797	8·853598
632	399424	252435968	25·1396102	8·581680	695	483025	335702375	26·3628527	8·857849
633	400689	253636137	25·1594913	8·586204	696	484416	337153536	26·3818119	8·862095
634	401956	254840104	25·1793566	8·590723	697	485809	338608873	26·4007576	8·866337
635	403225	256047875	25·1992063	8·595238	698	487204	340068392	26·4196896	8·870575
636	404496	257259456	25·2190404	8·599747	699	488601	341532099	26·4386081	8·874809
637	405769	258474853	25·2388589	8·604252	700	490000	343000000	26·4575131	8·879040
638	407044	259694072	25·2586619	8·608752	701	491401	344472101	26·4764046	8·883266
639	408321	260917119	25·2784493	8·613248	702	492804	345948408	26·4952826	8·887488
640	409600	262144000	25·2982213	8·617738	703	494209	347428927	26·5141472	8·891706
641	410881	263374721	25·3179778	8·622224	704	495616	348913664	26·5329983	8·895920
642	412164	264609288	25·3377189	8·626706	705	497025	350402625	26·5518361	8·900130
643	413449	265847707	25·3574447	8·631183	706	498436	351895816	26·5706605	8·904336
644	414736	267089984	25·3771551	8·635655	707	499849	353393243	26·5894716	8·908538
645	416025	268336125	25·3968502	8·640122	708	501264	354894912	26·6082694	8·912736
646	417316	269586136	25·4165301	8·644585	709	502681	356400829	26·6270539	8·916931
647	418609	270840023	25·4361947	8·649043	710	504100	357911000	26·6458252	8·921121
648	419904	272097792	25·4558441	8·653497	711	505521	359495431	26·6645833	8·925307
649	421201	273359449	25·4754784	8·657946	712	506944	360944128	26·6833281	8·929490
650	422500	274625000	25·4950076	8·662301	713	508369	362467097	26·7020598	8·933668
651	423801	275894451	25·5147016	8·666831	714	509796	363994344	26·7207784	8·937843
652	425104	277167808	25·5342907	8·671266	715	511225	365525875	26·7394839	8·942014
653	426409	278445077	25·5538647	8·675697	716	512656	367061696	26·7581763	8·946180
654	427716	279726264	25·5734237	8·680123	717	514089	368601813	26·7768557	8·950343
655	429025	281011375	25·5929678	8·684545	718	515524	370146232	26·7955220	8·954502
656	430336	282300416	25·6124969	8·688963	719	516961	371694959	26·8141754	8·958658
657	431649	283593393	25·6320112	8·693376	720	518400	373248000	26·8328157	8·962809
658	432964	284890312	25·6515107	8·697784	721	519841	374805361	26·8514432	8·966957
659	434281	286191179	25·6709953	8·702188	722	521284	376367048	26·8700577	8·971100
660	435600	287496000	25·6904652	8·706587	723	522729	377933067	26·8886593	8·975240
661	436921	288804781	25·7099203	8·710982	724	524176	379503424	26·9072481	8·979376
662	438244	290117528	25·7293607	8·715373	725	525625	381078125	26·9258240	8·983508
663	439569	291434247	25·7487864	8·719759	726	527076	382657176	26·9443872	8·987637
664	440896	292754944	25·7681975	8·724141	727	528529	384240583	26·9629375	8·991762
665	442225	294079625	25·7875939	8·728518	728	529984	385828352	26·9814751	8·995883
666	443556	295408296	25·8069758	8·732891	729	531441	387420489	27·0	9·0
667	444889	296740963	25·8263431	8·737260	730	532900	389017000	27·0185122	9·004113
668	446224	298077632	25·8456960	8·741624	731	534361	390617891	27·0370117	9·008222
669	447561	299418309	25·8650343	8·745984	732	535824	392223168	27·0554985	9·012328
670	448900	300763000	25·8843582	8·750340	733	537289	393832837	27·0739727	9·016430
671	450241	302111711	25·9036677	8·754691	734	538756	395446904	27·0924344	9·020529
672	451584	303464448	25·9229628	8·759038	735	540225	397065375	27·1108834	9·024623
673	452929	304821217	25·9422435	8·763380	736	541696	398668256	27·1293199	9·028714
674	454276	306182024	25·9615100	8·767719	737	543169	400315553	27·1477439	9·032802
675	455625	307546875	25·9807621	8·772053	738	544644	401947272	27·1661554	9·036885
676	456976	308915776	26·0	8·776382	739	546121	403583419	27·1845544	9·040965
677	458329	310288733	26·0192237	8·780708	740	547600	405224000	27·2029410	9·045041
678	459684	311665752	26·0384331	8·785029	741	549081	406869021	27·2213152	9·049114
679	461041	313046839	26·0576284	8·789346	742	550564	408518488	27·2396769	9·053183
680	462400	314432000	26·0768096	8·793659	743	552049	410172407	27·2580263	9·057248
681	463761	315821241	26·0959767	8·797967	744	553536	411830784	27·2763634	9·061309
682	465124	317214568	26·1151297	8·802272	745	555025	413493625	27·2946881	9·065367
683	466489	318611987	26·1342687	8·806572	746	556516	415160936	27·3130006	9·069422
684	467856	320013504	26·1533937	8·810868	747	558009	416832723	27·3313007	9·073472
685	469225	321419125	26·1725047	8·815159	748	559504	418508992	27·3495887	9·077519
686	470596	322828856	26·1916017	8·819417	749	561001	420189749	27·3678644	9·081563
687	471969	324242703	26·2106848	8·823730	750	562500	421875000	27·3861279	9·085603
688	473344	325660672	26·2297541	8·828009	751	564001	423564751	27·4043792	9·089639
689	474721	327082769	26·2488095	8·832285	752	565504	425259008	27·4226184	9·093672
690	476100	328509000	26·2678511	8·836556	753	567009	426957777	27·4408455	9·097701
691	477481	329939371	26·2868789	8·840822	754	568516	428661064	27·4590604	9·101726
692	478864	331373888	26·3058929	8·845085	755	570025	430368875	27·4772633	9·105748
693	480249	332812557	26·3248932	8·849344	756	571536	432081216	27·4954542	9·109766

No.	Square.	Cube.	Square Root.	Cube Root.	No.	Square.	Cube.	Square Root.	Cube Root.
757	573049	433798093	27·5136330	9·113781	820	672400	551368000	28·6356421	9·359901
758	574564	435519512	27·5317998	9·117793	821	674041	553387661	28·6530976	9·363704
759	576081	437245479	27·5499546	9·121801	822	675684	555412248	28·6705424	9·367505
760	577600	438976000	27·5680975	9·125805	823	677329	557441767	28·6879766	9·371302
761	579121	440711081	27·5862284	9·129806	824	678976	559476224	28·7054002	9·375096
762	580644	442450728	27·6043475	9·133803	825	680625	561515625	28·7228132	9·378887
763	582169	444194947	27·6224546	9·137797	826	682276	563559976	28·7402157	9·382675
764	583696	445943744	27·6405499	9·141788	827	683929	565609283	28·7576077	9·386460
765	585225	447697125	27·6586334	9·145774	828	685584	567663552	28·7749891	9·390241
766	586756	449455096	27·6767050	9·149757	829	687241	569722789	28·7923601	9·394020
767	588289	451217663	27·6947648	9·153737	830	688900	571787000	28·8097206	9·397796
768	589824	452984832	27·7128129	9·157713	831	690561	573856191	28·8270706	9·401569
769	591361	454756609	27·7308492	9·161686	832	692224	575930368	28·8444102	9·405338
770	592900	456533000	27·7488739	9·165656	833	693889	578009537	28·8617394	9·409105
771	594441	458314011	27·7668868	9·169622	834	695556	580093704	28·8790582	9·412869
772	595984	460099648	27·7848880	9·173585	835	697225	582182875	28·8963666	9·416630
773	597529	461889917	27·8028775	9·177544	836	698896	584277056	28·9136646	9·420387
774	599076	463684824	27·8208555	9·181500	837	700569	586376253	28·9309523	9·424141
775	600625	465484375	27·8388218	9·185452	838	702244	588480472	28·9482297	9·427893
776	602176	467288576	27·8567766	9·189401	839	703921	590589719	28·9654967	9·431642
777	603729	469097433	27·8747197	9·193347	840	705600	592704000	28·9827535	9·435388
778	605284	470910952	27·8926514	9·197289	841	707281	594823321	29·0	9·439130
779	606841	472729139	27·9105715	9·201228	842	708964	596947688	29·0172363	9·442870
780	608400	474552000	27·9284801	9·205164	843	710649	599077107	29·0344623	9·446607
781	609961	476379541	27·9463772	9·209096	844	712336	601211584	29·0516781	9·450341
782	611524	478211768	27·9642629	9·213025	845	714025	603351125	29·0688837	9·454071
783	613089	480048687	27·9821372	9·216950	846	715716	605495736	29·0860791	9·457799
784	614656	481890304	28·0	9·220872	847	717409	607645423	29·1032644	9·461524
785	616225	483736025	28·0178515	9·224791	848	719104	609800192	29·1204396	9·465247
786	617796	485587656	28·0356915	9·228706	849	720801	611960049	29·1376046	9·468966
787	619369	487443403	28·0535203	9·232618	850	722500	614125000	29·1547595	9·472682
788	620944	489303872	28·0713377	9·236527	851	724201	616295051	29·1719043	9·476395
789	622521	491169069	28·0891438	9·240433	852	725904	618470208	29·1890390	9·480106
790	624100	493039000	28·1069386	9·244335	853	727609	620650477	29·2061637	9·483813
791	625681	494913671	28·1247222	9·248234	854	729316	622835864	29·2232784	9·487518
792	627264	496793088	28·1424946	9·252130	855	731025	625026375	29·2403830	9·491219
793	628849	498677257	28·1602557	9·256022	856	732736	627222016	29·2574777	9·494918
794	630436	500566184	28·1780056	9·259911	857	734449	629422793	29·2745623	9·498614
795	632025	502459875	28·1957444	9·263797	858	736164	631628712	29·2916370	9·502307
796	633616	504358336	28·2134720	9·267679	859	737881	633839779	29·3087018	9·505998
797	635209	506261573	28·2311884	9·271559	860	739600	636056000	29·3257566	9·509685
798	636804	508169592	28·2488938	9·275435	861	741321	638277381	29·3428015	9·513369
799	638401	510082399	28·2665881	9·279308	862	743044	640503928	29·3598365	9·517051
800	640000	512000000	28·2842712	9·283177	863	744769	642735647	29·3768616	9·520730
801	641601	513922401	28·3019434	9·287044	864	746496	644972544	29·3938769	9·524406
802	643204	515849608	28·3196045	9·290907	865	748225	647214625	29·4108823	9·528079
803	644809	517781627	28·3372546	9·294767	866	749956	649461896	29·4278779	9·531749
804	646416	519718464	28·3548938	9·298623	867	751689	651714363	29·4448637	9·535417
805	648025	521660125	28·3725219	9·302477	868	753424	653972032	29·4618397	9·539081
806	649636	523606616	28·3901391	9·306327	869	755161	656234909	29·4788059	9·542743
807	651249	525557943	28·4077454	9·310175	870	756900	658503000	29·4957624	9·546402
808	652864	527514112	28·4253408	9·314019	871	758641	660776311	29·5127091	9·550058
809	654481	529475129	28·4429253	9·317859	872	760384	663054848	29·5296461	9·553712
810	656100	531441000	28·4604989	9·321697	873	762129	665338617	29·5465734	9·557363
811	657721	533411731	28·4780617	9·325532	874	763876	667627624	29·5634910	9·561010
812	659344	535387328	28·4956137	9·329363	875	765625	669921875	29·5803989	9·564655
813	660969	537367797	28·5131549	9·333191	876	767376	672221376	29·5972972	9·568297
814	662596	539353144	28·5306852	9·337016	877	769129	674526133	29·6141858	9·571937
815	664225	541313375	28·5482048	9·340838	878	770884	676836152	29·6310648	9·575574
816	665856	543338496	28·5657137	9·344657	879	772641	679151439	29·6479325	9·579208
817	667489	545338513	28·5832119	9·348473	880	774400	681472000	29·6647939	9·582839
818	669124	547343432	28·6006993	9·352285	881	776161	683797841	29·6816442	9·586468
819	670761	549353259	28·6181760	9·356095	882	777924	686128968	29·6984848	9·590093

No.	Square.	Cube.	Square Root.	Cube Root.	No.	Square.	Cube.	Square Root.	Cube Root.
883	779689	688465387	29·7153159	9·593716	942	887364	835896888	30·6920185	9·802803
884	781456	690807104	29·7321375	9·597337	943	889249	838561807	30·7083051	9·806271
885	783225	693154125	29·7489496	9·600954	944	891136	841232384	30·7245830	9·809736
886	784996	695506456	29·7657521	9·604569	945	893025	843908625	30·7408523	9·813198
887	786769	697864103	29·7825452	9·608181	946	894916	846590536	30·7571130	9·816659
888	788544	700227072	29·7993289	9·611791	947	896809	849278123	30·7733651	9·820117
889	790321	702595369	29·8161030	9·615397	948	898704	851971392	30·7896086	9·823572
890	792100	704969000	29·8328678	9·619001	949	900601	854670349	30·8058436	9·827025
891	793881	707347971	29·8496231	9·622603	950	902500	857375000	30·8220700	9·830475
892	795664	709732288	29·8663690	9·626201	951	904401	860085351	30·8382879	9·833923
893	797449	712121957	29·8831056	9·629197	952	906304	862801408	30·8544972	9·837369
894	799236	714516984	29·8998328	9·633390	953	908209	865523177	30·8706981	9·840812
895	801025	716917375	29·9165506	9·636981	954	910116	868250664	30·8868904	9·844253
896	802816	719323136	29·9332591	9·640569	955	912025	870983875	30·9030743	9·847692
897	804609	721734273	29·9499583	9·644154	956	913936	873722816	30·9192497	9·851128
898	806404	724150792	29·9666481	9·647736	957	915849	876467493	30·9354166	9·854561
899	808201	726572699	29·9833287	9·651316	958	917764	879217912	30·9515751	9·857992
900	810000	729000000	30·0	9·654893	959	919684	881974079	30·9677251	9·861421
901	811801	731432701	30·0166620	9·658468	960	921600	884736000	30·9838668	9·864848
902	813604	733870808	30·0333148	9·662040	961	923521	887503681	31·0	9·868272
903	815409	736314327	30·0499584	9·665609	962	925444	890277128	31·0161248	9·871694
904	817216	738763264	30·0665928	9·669176	963	927369	893056347	31·0322413	9·875113
905	819025	741217625	30·0832179	9·672740	964	929296	895841344	31·0483494	9·878530
906	820836	743677416	30·0998339	9·676301	965	931225	898632125	31·0644491	9·881945
907	822649	746142643	30·1164407	9·679860	966	933156	901428696	31·0805405	9·885357
908	824464	748613312	30·1330383	9·683416	967	935089	904231063	31·0966236	9·888767
909	826281	751089429	30·1496269	9·686970	968	937024	907039232	31·1126984	9·892174
910	828100	753571000	30·1662063	9·690521	969	938961	909853209	31·1287648	9·895580
911	829921	756058031	30·1827765	9·694069	970	940900	912673000	31·1448230	9·898983
912	831744	758550528	30·1993377	9·697615	971	942841	915498611	31·1608729	9·902383
913	833569	761048497	30·2158899	9·701158	972	944784	918330048	31·1769145	9·905781
914	835396	763551944	30·2324329	9·704698	973	946729	921167317	31·1929479	9·909177
915	837225	766060875	30·2489669	9·708236	974	948676	924010424	31·2089731	9·912571
916	839056	768575296	30·2654919	9·711772	975	950625	926859375	31·2249900	9·915962
917	840889	771095213	30·2820079	9·715305	976	952576	929714176	31·2409987	9·919351
918	842724	773620632	30·2985148	9·718835	977	954529	932574833	31·2569992	9·922738
919	844561	776151559	30·3150128	9·722363	978	956484	935441352	31·2729915	9·926122
920	846400	778688000	30·3315018	9·725888	979	958441	938313739	31·2889757	9·929504
921	848241	781229961	30·3479818	9·729410	980	960400	941192001	31·3049517	9·932883
922	850084	783777448	30·3644529	9·732930	981	962361	944076141	31·3209195	9·936261
923	851929	786330467	30·3809151	9·736448	982	964324	946966168	31·3368792	9·939636
924	853776	788889024	30·3973683	9·739963	983	966289	949862087	31·3528308	9·943009
925	855625	791453125	30·4138127	9·743475	984	968256	952763904	31·3687743	9·940379
926	857476	794022776	30·4302481	9·746985	985	970225	955671625	31·3847097	9·949747
927	859329	796597983	30·4466747	9·750493	986	972196	958585256	31·4006369	9·953113
928	861184	799178752	30·4630924	9·753998	987	974169	961504803	31·4165561	9·956477
929	863041	801765089	30·4795013	9·757500	988	976144	964430272	31·4324673	9·959839
930	864900	804357000	30·4959014	9·761000	989	978121	967361669	31·4483704	9·963198
931	866761	806954491	30·5122926	9·764497	990	980100	970299000	31·4642654	9·966554
932	868624	809557568	30·5286750	9·767992	991	982081	973242271	31·4801525	9·969909
933	870489	812166237	30·5450487	9·771484	992	984064	976191488	31·4960315	9·973262
934	872356	814780504	30·5614136	9·774974	993	986049	979146657	31·5119025	9·976612
935	874225	817400375	30·5777697	9·778461	994	988036	982107784	31·5277655	9·979959
936	876096	820025856	30·5941172	9·782946	995	990025	985074875	31·5436206	9·983304
937	877969	822656953	30·6104557	9·785428	996	992016	988047936	31·5594677	9·986648
938	879844	825293672	30·6267857	9·788908	997	994009	991026973	31·5753068	9·989990
939	881721	827936019	30·6431069	9·792386	998	996004	994011992	31·5911380	9·993328
940	883600	830584000	30·6594194	9·795861	999	998001	997002999	31·6069613	9·996665
941	885481	833237621	30·6757233	9·799333	1000	1000000	1000000000	31·6227767	10·0

2297*h*. A *power* is that number which is obtained by multiplying a number several times by itself. A square is the number multiplied by itself; a cube by multiplying it twice by itself. The square is called the second power; the cube is called the third power; when multiplied again by itself it becomes the fourth power, which is commonly called the *bi-quadrate*; and so on :—

Power,	Of No. 2.		Of No. 3.		Number.	4th Power.	5th Power.
I.		2		3	1	1	1
II.	or square	4	or square	9	2	16	32
III.	or cube	8	or cube	27	3	81	243
IV.		16		81	4	256	1,024
V.		32		243	5	625	3,125
VI.		64		729	6	1,296	7,776
VII.		128		2,187	7	2,401	16,807
VIII.		256		6,561	8	4,096	32,768
IX.		512		19,683	9	6,561	59,049
X.		1,024		59,049	10	10,000	100,000
XI.		2,048		177,147	11	14,641	161,051

2297*i*. We shall now at once proceed to the general principles on which the measurement and estimation of work in the several artificers' departments are conducted.

2298. DIGGING is performed by the solid yard of twenty-seven cubic feet (that is, 3 feet × 3 feet × 3 feet = 27 feet). Where the ground is soft in consistence, and nothing more is necessary beyond cutting with a spade, a man may throw up a cubic yard per hour, or 10 cubic yards in a day; but if of firmer quality, *hacking* becomes necessary, and an additional man will be required to perform the same work; if very strong gravel, more assistance will be required. If, therefore, the wages of a labourer were 2*s*. 6*d*. per day, the price of a yard would be 3*d*. for cutting only, without profit to the contractor; 6*d*. for cutting and hacking, and 9*d*. if two hackers be necessary. In sandy ground, where wheeling becomes necessary, three men will remove 30 cubic yards in a day to the distance of 20 yards, two for filling and one for wheeling. But to remove the same quantity in a day to a greater distance, an additional man for every 20 yards will be required.

2299. The method of ascertaining the quantity of excavation will, of course, be obvious; the quantity is the length multiplied into the depth and width. In the cases of trenches merely dug for the reception of walls, which, of course, are sloped to prevent the earth falling in on the excavators, a mean width is to be taken. Thus, suppose an excavation 24 feet long, 4 feet wide at top, and 2 feet at the bottom (average width therefore 3 feet), and 5 feet deep, we have for the quantity of yard $\frac{24 \times 3 \times 5}{27} = 13 \cdot 33$ cube yards.

2300. BRICKWORK. In measuring and estimating the value of brickwork, the following points must be remembered. A rod of brickwork is a mass 16½ feet square; hence the quantity of superficial feet which it contains is 272¼ feet (16·5 × 16·5), but the ¼ of the foot is too trifling to make it worth while to embarrass calculations with it, and consequently 272 feet is universally taken as the superficial standard content of a rod. Its standard thickness is one brick and a half (or 13½ inches). Hence it follows, that a cubic rod of brickwork would be 272 feet × 13½ inches = 306 feet cube. The allowance for the number of bricks is taken on an average at 4500. Much, however, depends on the closeness of the joints and the nature of the work. In walling, a reduced foot is generally taken as requiring 17 bricks; a foot superficial in Flemish bond, laid in malm facing, about 8 bricks; and a foot superficial of gauged arches, 10 bricks. In paving, a yard requires 82 paving bricks, or 48 stock bricks, or 144 Dutch clinkers laid on edge, or 36 bricks laid flat.

2301. In tiling, which is measured by the square of 100 superficial feet, a square will require 800 at a 6-inch gauge, 700 at a 7-inch gauge, and 600 at an 8-inch gauge. The gauge necessarily regulates the distance of the laths, and, at the same time, must be dependent on the slope of the roof, which, if flat, should not be less than 6 inches, as for instance, above the kerb in a kerb roof; and not more than 8 inches in any case. A square of plain tiling requires about on an average a bundle of laths, two bushels of lime, and five of sand, and at least a peck of oak pins. The laths are sold in bundles of 3, 4, and 5-feet lengths. A bundle of the 3-feet contains eight score, the 4-feet six score, and the 5-feet five score to the bundle. The nails used are fourpenny; they are purchased by the long hundred, that is, of six score, and, in day work, are charged by the bricklayer 5-score to the hundred. The name of nails, as fourpenny, fivepenny, &c., means fourpence, fivepence, &c. per hundred. The number of nails required for a bundle of 5-feet and 6-feet laths, are 500 and 600 respectively.

2302. A square of pantiling requires 180 tiles laid at a 10-inch gauge, and a bundle of 12 laths 10 feet long.

2303. In lime measure, what is called a hundred is 100 pecks, or 25 striked bushels (old measure).

2304. In sand measure, 18 heaped bushels, or 21 striked bushels, equal to 1 yard cube, is a single load, and about 24 cubic feet 1 ton.

2305. In mortar 27 cubic feet make 1 load, which on common occasions contains half a hundred of lime with a proportional quantity of sand. Eleven hundred and thirty-four cubic inches make a hod of mortar; that is, a mass 9 inches wide, 9 inches high, and 14 inches long. Two hods of mortar are nearly equal to half a bushel. The following measures and weights it may be also useful to remember : —

23½ cubic feet of sand = 1 ton; hence 1 cubic foot weighs 95·3 lbs.

17½ cubic feet of clay = 1 ton; hence 1 cubic foot weighs about 130 lbs.

18 cubic feet of common earth = 1 ton; hence 1 cubic foot weighs nearly 124 lbs.

306 cubic feet of brickwork = 13 tons; hence 1 cubic foot is equal to full 95 lbs.

2306. In the measurement of brickwork, from the surface being 272 feet and the standard thickness 1½ brick, it will be immediately seen that nothing more is requisite than, having ascertained the thickness of each part of the work, to reduce it to the standard thickness above stated, and this will be found sufficiently easy in almost all cases. Where, however, this cannot be done, we can always ascertain with sufficient accuracy the cubic contents in feet of any mass of brickwork ; and dividing by 306 we have the number of rods.

2307. We here present an illustration in a wall of the most common occurrence (*fig.* 808.), which we will suppose 20 feet long without reference to any wall which might return from it, and thus diminish its length in measuring therewith a *returning wall*. The following is the method of entering and calculating the dimensions.

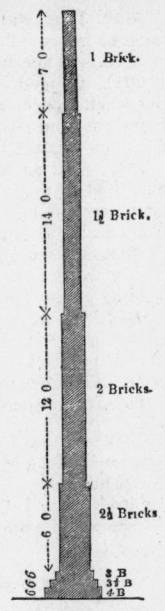

Fig. 808.

	Length multiplied by the Height.	Area.	Number of Bricks in Thickness.	Factors to reduce the Area to Standard of 1½ Brick.	Thickness reduced to 1½ Brick in Feet sup.
Footings 6 courses	20·0 6 ———	10·0	4	2⅔	26·8
	20·0 6 ———	10·0	3¼	2⅓	23·4
	20·0 6 ———	10·0	3	2	20·0
Basement wall -	20·0 6·0	120·0	2¼	1⅔	200·0
Ground-floor wall	20·0 12·0	240·0	2	1⅓	320·0
One-pair wall -	20·0 14·0	280·0	1½	1	280·0
Two-pair wall -	20·0 7·0	140·0	1	⅔	93·4
					963·4

Therefore the total is 963·4 superficial feet 1½ brick thick, and $\frac{963}{272}$ = 3 rods, 147 feet.

2308. Upon this principle the measuring and estimation of brickwork is conducted, and having the price and quantity of bricks in a rod, and the lime, sand, and labour, which will presently be given, we may come to a pretty accurate knowledge of its value. But there are other articles which will require our attention, to which we shall presently advert. Before proceeding, however, we may as well observe that the above result of 3 rods 147 feet might have been similarly obtained by cubing the mass of brickwork and dividing the whole mass by 306, but with much more labour.

2309. In measuring walls faced with bricks of a superior quality, the area of such facing must be measured, or allowance extra is made in the price per rod of the brickwork.

2310. All apertures and recesses from any of the faces are deducted.

2311. Gauged arches are sometimes deducted and charged separately, sometimes not; but whether deducted or not does not signify, as the extra price must be allowed in the latter case and the whole price in the former. Rubbed and gauged arches, of whatever form, are measured and charged by the superficial foot.

2312. The angles of groins, outside and inside splays, bird's mouths, bull's noses, are measured by the lineal or running foot; but cuttings are measured by the foot superficial. Chimneys are measured solid to allow for the trouble of forming and pargetting the flues. The opening at bottom, however, is to be deducted.

2313. Quarters in bricknogging are measured in, as are all sills, stone strings, and timber inserted in walls. Two inches are also allowed in the height of brickwork for bedding plates if no brickwork be over them.

2314. Ovens, coppers, &c. are measured as solid work, deducting only the ash holes; but all fire stone, Welsh lumps, tiles, &c., though measured alone, are not to be deducted out of the brickwork. Pointing, colouring, &c. to fronts, is measured by the foot superficial. Plantile creasing by the foot lineal.

To estimate the value of a rod of brickwork, the method is as under: —

	£	s.	d.
4500 stocks, at　　per thousand - - - - - -	0	0	0
1½ hundred of lime=37½ striked bushels containing 27 feet cube to the hundred - - - - - - - -	0	0	0
2 loads of sand - - - - - - - -	0	0	0
Labour and scaffolding - - - - - - -	0	0	0
	0	0	0
Per cent. profit - - - - - -	0	0	0
Per rod - - - - - - -	0	0	0

2315. In measuring and estimating all sorts of artificers' works, the method usually adopted for saving labour in making out the account is to arrange in separate columns each sort of work, and then to add them up and carry the total to the bill. In brickwork, where walls are of different thicknesses, these with their deductions are arranged in separate columns, and then all are reduced to the standard thickness.

2316. The common measure for tiling is a square of 10 feet, containing therefore 100 feet superficial. Claims are made for the eaves to the extent of 6 inches; but in pantiling this ought not to be allowed, as a claim not founded in justice, though custom is pleaded for it.

2317. The following table shows the number of bricks necessary for constructing any number of superficial feet of walling from 1 to 90,000, and from half a brick to 2½ bricks thick; and thence, by addition only, to any thickness or number required, at the rate of 4500 bricks to a reduced rod. Thus, if it be required to find the number of bricks wanted to build a piece of work containing 756 feet super. of walling 1½ brick thick, we find by inspection for 700 feet 11580 bricks; for 50 feet, 827 bricks; and for 6 feet, 99 bricks; in all, 11580 + 827 + 99 = 12506.

TABLE SHOWING THE REQUISITE QUANTITY OF BRICKS FOR A GIVEN SUPERFICIES OF WALLING.

Area of Wall in Feet.	No. of Bricks to Thicknesses of				
	½ Brick.	1 Brick.	1½ Brick.	2 Bricks.	2½ Bricks.
1	5	11	16	22	27
2	11	22	33	44	55
3	16	33	49	66	82
4	22	44	66	88	110
5	27	55	82	110	137
6	33	66	99	132	165
7	38	77	115	154	193
8	44	88	132	176	220
9	49	99	148	198	248
10	55	110	165	220	275
20	110	220	330	441	551
30	165	330	496	661	827

Area of Wall in Feet.	No. of Bricks to Thicknesses of				
	½ Brick.	1 Brick.	1½ Brick.	2 Bricks.	2½ Bricks.
40	220	441	661	882	1102
50	275	551	827	1102	1378
60	330	661	992	1323	1654
70	386	772	1158	1544	1930
80	441	882	1323	1764	2205
90	496	992	1488	1985	2481
100	551	1102	1654	2205	2757
200	1102	2205	3308	4411	5514
300	1654	3308	4963	6617	8272
400	2205	4411	6617	8323	11029
500	2757	5514	8272	11029	13786
600	3308	6617	9926	13235	16544
700	3860	7720	11580	15441	19301
800	4411	8823	13235	17647	22058
900	4963	9926	14889	19852	24816
1000	5514	11029	16544	22058	25753
2000	11029	22058	33088	44117	55147
3000	16544	33088	49632	66176	82720
4000	22058	44117	66176	88235	110294
5000	27573	55147	82720	110294	137867
6000	33088	66176	99264	132352	165441
7000	38602	77205	115803	154411	193014
8000	44117	88235	132352	176470	220588
9000	49632	99264	148896	198529	248161
10000	55147	110294	165441	220588	275735
20000	110294	220588	330882	441176	551470
30000	165441	330882	496323	661764	827205
40000	220588	441176	661764	882352	1102940
50000	275735	551470	827205	1102940	1378675
60000	330882	661764	992646	1323528	1654410
70000	386029	772053	1168087	1544116	1930145
80000	441175	882352	1323528	1704704	2205080
90000	496323	992646	1468969	1985292	2481615

2318. The next table which we submit for use exhibits the number of reduced feet to superficial feet from 1 to 10,000, the thicknesses being from ½ to 2½ bricks.

Area of Wall in super-ficial Feet.	Reduced Quantity in																			
	½ Brick.				1 Brick.				1½ Brick.				2 Bricks.				2½ Bricks.			
	Rods.	qrs.	ft.	in.	Rods.	qrs.	ft.	in.	Rods.	qrs.	ft.	in.	Rods.	qrs.	ft.	in.	Rods.	qrs.	ft.	in.
1	0	0	0	4	0	0	0	8	0	0	1	0	0	0	1	4	0	0	1	8
2	0	0	0	8	0	0	1	4	0	0	2	0	0	0	2	8	0	0	3	4
3	0	0	1	0	0	0	2	0	0	0	3	0	0	0	4	0	0	0	5	0
4	0	0	1	4	0	0	2	8	0	0	4	0	0	0	5	4	0	0	6	8
5	0	0	1	8	0	0	3	4	0	0	5	0	0	0	6	8	0	0	8	4
6	0	0	2	0	0	0	4	0	0	0	6	0	0	0	8	0	0	0	10	0
7	0	0	2	4	0	0	4	8	0	0	7	0	0	0	9	4	0	0	11	8
8	0	0	2	8	0	0	5	4	0	0	8	0	0	0	10	8	0	0	13	4
9	0	0	3	0	0	0	6	0	0	0	9	0	0	0	12	0	0	0	15	0
10	0	0	3	4	0	0	6	8	0	0	10	0	0	0	13	4	0	0	16	8
11	0	0	3	8	0	0	7	4	0	0	11	0	0	0	14	8	0	0	18	4
12	0	0	4	0	0	0	8	0	0	0	12	0	0	0	16	0	0	0	20	0
13	0	0	4	4	0	0	8	8	0	0	13	0	0	0	17	4	0	0	21	8
14	0	0	4	8	0	0	9	4	0	0	14	0	0	0	18	8	0	0	23	4
15	0	0	5	0	0	0	10	0	0	0	15	0	0	0	20	0	0	0	25	0
16	0	0	5	4	0	0	10	8	0	0	16	0	0	0	21	4	0	0	26	8
17	0	0	5	8	0	0	11	4	0	0	17	0	0	0	22	8	0	0	28	4

Area of Wall in superficial Feet.	Reduced Quantity in									
	½ Brick.			1 Brick.			1½ Brick.			2 Bricks.			2½ Bricks.

Area of Wall in superficial Feet.	½ Brick. Rods. qrs. ft. in.	1 Brick. Rods. qrs. ft. in.	1½ Brick. Rods. qrs. ft. in.	2 Bricks. Rods. qrs. ft. in.	2½ Bricks. Rods. qrs. ft. in.
18	0 0 6 0	0 0 12 0	0 0 18 0	0 0 24 0	0 0 30 8
19	0 0 6 4	0 0 12 8	0 0 19 0	0 0 25 4	0 0 31 8
20	0 0 6 8	0 0 13 4	0 0 20 0	0 0 26 8	0 0 33 4
21	0 0 7 0	0 0 14 0	0 0 21 0	0 0 28 0	0 0 35 0
22	0 0 7 4	0 0 14 8	0 0 22 0	0 0 29 4	0 0 36 8
23	0 0 7 8	0 0 15 4	0 0 23 0	0 0 30 8	0 0 38 4
24	0 0 8 0	0 0 16 0	0 0 24 0	0 0 32 0	0 0 40 0
25	0 0 8 4	0 0 16 8	0 0 25 0	0 0 33 4	0 0 41 8
26	0 0 8 8	0 0 17 4	0 0 26 0	0 0 34 8	0 0 43 0
27	0 0 9 0	0 0 18 0	0 0 27 0	0 0 36 0	0 0 45 0
28	0 0 9 4	0 0 18 8	0 0 28 0	0 0 37 4	0 0 46 8
29	0 0 9 8	0 0 19 4	0 0 29 0	0 0 38 8	0 0 48 4
30	0 0 10 0	0 0 20 0	0 0 30 0	0 0 40 0	0 0 50 0
31	0 0 10 4	0 0 20 8	0 0 31 0	0 0 41 4	0 0 51 8
32	0 0 10 8	0 0 21 4	0 0 32 0	0 0 42 8	0 0 53 4
33	0 0 11 0	0 0 22 0	0 0 33 0	0 0 44 0	0 0 55 0
34	0 0 11 4	0 0 22 8	0 0 34 0	0 0 45 4	0 0 56 8
35	0 0 11 8	0 0 23 4	0 0 35 0	0 0 46 8	0 0 58 4
36	0 0 12 0	0 0 24 0	0 0 36 0	0 0 48 0	0 0 60 0
37	0 0 12 4	0 0 24 8	0 0 37 0	0 0 49 4	0 0 61 8
38	0 0 12 8	0 0 25 4	0 0 38 0	0 0 50 8	0 0 63 4
39	0 0 13 0	0 0 26 0	0 0 39 0	0 0 52 0	0 0 65 0
40	0 0 13 4	0 0 26 8	0 0 40 0	0 0 53 4	0 0 66 8
41	0 0 13 8	0 0 27 4	0 0 41 0	0 0 54 8	0 1 0 4
42	0 0 14 0	0 0 28 0	0 0 42 0	0 0 56 0	0 1 2 0
43	0 0 14 4	0 0 28 8	0 0 43 0	0 0 57 4	0 1 3 8
44	0 0 14 8	0 0 29 4	0 0 44 0	0 0 58 8	0 1 5 4
45	0 0 15 0	0 0 30 0	0 0 45 0	0 0 60 0	0 1 7 0
46	0 0 15 4	0 0 30 8	0 0 46 0	0 0 61 4	0 1 8 8
47	0 0 15 8	0 0 31 4	0 0 47 0	0 0 62 8	0 1 10 4
48	0 0 16 0	0 0 32 0	0 0 48 0	0 0 64 0	0 1 12 0
49	0 0 16 4	0 0 32 8	0 0 49 0	0 0 65 4	0 1 13 8
50	0 0 16 8	0 0 33 4	0 0 50 0	0 0 66 8	0 1 15 4
60	0 0 20 0	0 0 40 0	0 0 60 0	0 1 12 0	0 1 32 0
70	0 0 23 4	0 0 46 8	0 1 2 0	0 1 25 4	0 1 48 8
80	0 0 26 8	0 0 53 4	0 1 12 0	0 1 38 8	0 1 65 4
90	0 0 30 0	0 0 60 0	0 1 22 0	0 1 52 0	0 2 14 0
100	0 0 33 4	0 0 66 8	0 1 32 0	0 1 65 4	0 2 30 8
200	0 0 66 8	0 1 65 4	0 2 64 0	0 3 62 8	1 0 61 4
300	0 1 32 0	0 2 64 0	1 0 28 0	1 1 60 0	1 3 24 0
400	0 1 65 4	0 3 62 8	1 1 60 0	1 3 57 4	2 1 54 8
500	0 2 30 8	1 0 61 4	1 3 24 0	2 1 54 8	3 0 17 4
600	0 2 64 0	1 1 60 0	2 0 56 0	2 3 52 0	3 2 48 0
700	0 3 29 4	1 2 58 8	2 2 20 0	3 1 49 4	4 1 10 8
800	0 3 62 8	1 3 57 4	2 3 52 0	3 3 46 8	4 3 41 4
900	1 0 28 0	2 0 56 0	3 1 16 0	4 1 44 0	5 2 4 0
1000	1 0 61 4	2 1 54 8	3 2 48 0	4 3 41 4	6 0 34 8
2000	2 1 54 8	4 3 41 4	7 1 28 0	9 3 14 8	12 1 1 4
3000	3 2 48 0	7 1 28 0	11 0 8 0	14 2 46 0	18 1 36 0
4000	4 3 41 4	9 3 14 8	14 2 56 0	19 2 29 4	24 2 2 8
5000	6 0 34 8	12 1 1 4	18 1 36 0	24 2 2 8	30 2 37 4
6000	7 1 28 0	14 2 56 0	22 0 16 0	29 1 44 0	36 3 4 0
7000	8 2 21 4	17 0 42 8	25 2 64 0	34 1 17 4	42 3 38 8
8000	9 3 14 8	19 2 29 4	29 1 44 0	39 0 58 8	49 0 5 4
9000	11 0 8 0	22 0 16 0	33 0 24 0	44 0 32 0	55 0 40 0
10000	12 1 1 4	24 2 2 8	36 3 4 0	49 0 5 4	61 1 6 8

2319. The following table exhibits the value of a rod of brickwork (allowing 4500 bricks to a rod) at the prices from 30s. to 60s. per thousand for the bricks, and for labour, mortar, and scaffolding the several sums of 3l. 5s., 3l. 10s., 3l. 15s., 4l., 4l. 5s., and 4l. 10s. per rod.

Bricks per Thousand.	Labour, Mortar, &c. per Rod, 3l. 5s.			Labour, Mortar, &c. per Rod, 3l. 10s.			Labour, Mortar, &c. per Rod, 3l. 15s.			Labour, Mortar, &c. per Rod, 4l.			Labour, Mortar, &c. per Rod, 4l. 5s.			Labour, Mortar, &c. per Rod, 4l. 10s.		
s.	£	s.	d.	£	s.	d.	£	s.	d.	£	s.	d.	£	s.	d.	£	s.	d.
30	10	0	0	10	5	0	10	10	0	10	15	0	11	0	0	11	5	0
32	10	9	0	10	14	0	10	19	0	11	4	0	11	9	0	11	14	0
34	10	18	0	11	3	0	11	8	0	11	13	0	11	18	0	12	3	0
36	11	7	0	11	12	0	11	17	0	12	2	0	12	7	0	12	12	0
38	11	16	0	12	1	0	12	6	0	12	11	0	12	16	0	13	1	0
40	12	5	0	12	10	0	12	15	0	13	0	0	13	5	0	13	10	0
42	12	14	0	12	19	0	13	4	0	13	9	0	13	14	0	13	19	0
44	13	3	0	13	8	0	13	13	0	13	18	0	14	3	0	14	8	0
46	13	12	0	13	17	0	14	2	0	14	7	0	14	12	0	14	17	0
48	14	1	0	14	6	0	14	11	0	14	16	0	15	1	0	15	6	0
50	14	10	0	14	15	0	15	0	0	15	5	0	15	10	0	15	15	0
52	14	19	0	15	4	0	15	9	0	15	14	0	15	19	0	16	4	0
54	15	8	0	15	13	0	15	18	0	16	3	0	16	8	0	16	13	0
56	15	17	0	16	2	0	16	7	0	16	12	0	16	17	0	17	2	0
58	16	6	0	16	11	0	16	16	0	17	1	0	17	6	0	17	11	0
60	16	15	0	17	0	0	17	5	0	17	10	0	17	15	0	18	0	0

2320. The following is a table of the decimal parts of a rod of reduced brickwork.

Feet.	Dec. Parts.	Feet.	Dec. Parts.	Feet.	Dec. Parts.	Feet.	Dec. Parts.	Feet.	Dec. Parts.
1	·00367	41	·15073	81	·29779	121	·44485	161	·59191
2	·00735	42	·15441	82	·30147	122	·44852	162	·59559
3	·01102	43	·15809	83	·30515	123	·45220	163	·59926
4	·01470	44	·16176	84	·30882	124	·45588	164	·60294
5	·01838	45	·16544	85	·3125	125	·45956	165	·60662
6	·02206	46	·16912	86	·31617	126	·46323	166	·61029
7	·02573	47	·17279	87	·31985	127	·46691	167	·61397
8	·02941	48	·17647	88	·32353	128	·47059	168	·61765
9	·03309	49	·18015	89	·32720	129	·47426	169	·62132
10	·03676	50	·18382	90	·33088	130	·47794	170	·625
11	·04044	51	·1875	91	·33456	131	·48162	171	·62867
12	·04412	52	·19117	92	·33823	132	·48529	172	·63235
13	·04779	53	·19485	93	·34191	133	·48897	173	·63604
14	·05147	54	·19852	94	·34559	134	·49265	174	·63971
15	·05515	55	·20221	95	·34926	135	·49632	175	·64338
16	·05882	56	·20588	96	·35294	136	·5	176	·64706
17	·0625	57	·20956	97	·35662	137	·50637	177	·65073
18	·06617	58	·21323	98	·36029	138	·50735	178	·65441
19	·06985	59	·21691	99	·36397	139	·51102	179	·65809
20	·07353	60	·22059	100	·36765	140	·51470	180	·66176
21	·07721	61	·22426	101	·37132	141	·51838	181	·66544
22	·08088	62	·22794	102	·375	142	·52206	182	·66912
23	·08456	63	·23162	103	·37867	143	·52573	183	·67279
24	·08823	64	·23529	104	·38235	144	·52941	184	·67647
25	·09191	65	·23897	105	·38604	145	·53309	185	·68015
26	·09559	66	·24265	106	·38970	146	·53676	186	·68382
27	·09926	67	·24632	107	·39338	147	·54044	187	·6875
28	·10294	68	·25	108	·39706	148	·54412	188	·69117
29	·10662	69	·25367	109	·40073	149	·54779	189	·69485
30	·11029	70	·25735	110	·40441	150	·55147	190	·69853
31	·11397	71	·26103	111	·40809	151	·55515	191	·70221
32	·11765	72	·26470	112	·41176	152	·55882	192	·70588
33	·12132	73	·26838	113	·41544	153	·5625	193	·70956
34	·125	74	·27206	114	·41912	154	·56617	194	·71323
35	·12867	75	·27573	115	·42279	155	·56985	195	·71691
36	·13235	76	·27941	116	·42647	156	·57353	196	·72059
37	·13604	77	·28309	117	·43015	157	·57721	197	·72426
38	·13970	78	·28676	118	·43382	158	·58088	198	·72794
39	·14338	79	·29044	119	·4375	159	·58456	199	·73162
40	·14706	80	·29412	120	·44117	160	·58823	200	·73529

Feet.	Dec. Parts.	Feet.	Dec. Parts.	Feet.	Dec. Parts.	Feet.	Dec. Parts.	Feet.	Dec. Parts.
201	·73897	216	·79412	231	·84926	245	·90073	259	·95221
202	·74265	217	·79779	232	·85294	246	·90441	260	·95588
203	·74632	218	·80147	233	·85662	247	·90809	261	·95956
204	·75	219	·80515	234	·86029	248	·91176	262	·96323
205	·75367	220	80882	235	·86397	249	·91544	263	·96691
206	·75735	221	·8125	236	·86765	250	·91912	264	·97059
207	·76103	222	·81617	237	·87132	251	·92279	265	·97426
208	·76470	223	·81985	238	·875	252	·92647	266	·97794
209	·76838	224	·82353	239	·87867	253	·93015	267	·98162
210	·77206	225	·82721	240	·88235	254	·93382	268	·98529
211	·77573	226	·83088	241	·88604	255	·9375	269	·98897
212	·77941	227	·83456	242	·88970	256	·94117	270	·99265
213	·78309	228	·83823	243	·89338	257	·94485	271	·99632
214	·78676	229	·84191	244	·89706	258	·94853	272	1·00000
215	·79044	230	·84559						

2321. The subjoined table shows the number of plaintiles or pantiles required to cover any area from 1 to 10,000 feet.

Feet superficial.	Plaintiles. Gauges.			Pantiles. Gauges.		
	6 inches.	6½ inches.	7 inches.	11 inches.	12 inches.	13 inches.
1	7½	7	6½	1⅔	1½	1⅓
2	15	14	13	3⅓	3	2⅔
3	22½	21	19½	5	4½	4
4	30	28	26	6⅔	6	5⅓
5	37½	35	32½	8⅓	7½	6⅔
6	45	42	39	10	9	8
7	52½	49	45½	11⅔	10½	9⅓
8	60	56	·52	13⅓	12	10⅔
9	67½	63	58½	15	13½	12
10	75	70	65	16⅔	15	13⅓
20	150	140	130	33⅓	30	26⅔
30	225	210	195	50	45	40
40	300	280	260	66⅔	60	53⅓
50	375	350	325	83⅓	75	66⅔
60	450	420	390	100	90	80
70	525	490	455	116⅔	105	93⅓
80	600	560	520	133⅓	120	106⅔
90	675	630	585	150	135	120
100	750	700	650	166⅔	150	133⅓
200	1500	1400	1300	333⅓	300	266⅔
300	2250	2100	1950	500	450	400
400	3000	2800	2600	666⅔	600	533⅓
500	3750	3500	3250	833⅓	750	666⅔
600	4500	4200	3900	1000	900	800
700	5250	4900	4550	1166⅔	1050	933⅓
800	6000	5600	5200	1333⅓	1200	1066⅔
900	6750	6300	5850	1500	1350	1200
1000	7500	7000	6500	1666⅔	1500	1333⅓
2000	15000	14000	13000	3333⅓	3000	2666⅔
3000	22500	21000	19500	5000	4500	4000
4000	30000	28000	26000	6666⅔	6000	5333⅓
5000	37500	35000	32500	8333⅓	7500	6666⅔
6000	45000	42000	39000	10000	9000	8000
7000	52500	49000	45500	11666⅔	10500	9333⅓
8000	60000	56000	52000	13333⅓	12000	10666⅓
9000	67500	63000	58500	15000	13500	12000
10000	75000	70000	65000	16666⅔	15000	13333⅓

The use of the foregoing tables it can scarcely be necessary to explain, They are such as to indicate, on inspection, their value; and we shall therefore leave them without further comment for their application.

2322. When work is performed by the day, or the materials used are to be numbered, as ofttimes necessarily occurs, fire bricks, red rubbers, best marle stocks for cutters, second best ditto, pickings, common bricks, place bricks, paving bricks, kiln-burnt bricks, and Dutch clinkers are charged by the thousand.

2323. Red rubbers, kiln and fire-burnt bricks, are also charged by the hundred. Foot tiles and ten inch tiles are charged either by the thousand or hundred.

2324. Sunk foot tiles and ten-inch tiles with five holes, now never used in the south of England, are charged by the piece.

2325. Pantiles, plaintiles, and nine-inch tiles are charged by the thousand.

2326. Oven and Welsh oven tiles, Welsh fire lumps, fire bricks, and chimney pots are also sold by the piece.

2327. Sand, clay, and loam are charged by the load; lime sometimes by the hundred weight; but the *hundred* of 100 pecks is the more usual measure in and about the metropolis. Dutch terras is charged by the bushel, which is also sometimes the measure of lime. Parker's cement is similarly charged.

2328. Pantile and plaintile laths are charged by the bundle or load; hair and mortar by the load; hip hooks and T tiles by the piece.

2329. Neither here, nor in the following pages, is it intended to convey to the reader more than the principles on which an estimate is founded. The prices of materials are in a state of constant fluctuation; and though when we come to the consideration of the prices of joiner's work, we intend, from the ingenious computations of Mr. Peter Nicholson, to give something approaching a constant value from the known performance of a good workman, it is to be recollected by the student, that cases so vary as to make it impossible to give a list of prices and value, that would be of any value at the period of a month from the time of his reading this paragraph. The details of prices he must constantly watch if he intends to do justice to his employer.

CARPENTRY AND JOINERY.

2330. The works of the CARPENTER are the preparation of piles, sleepers, and planking, and other large timbers, formerly much, but now rarely, used in foundations; the centering on which vaults are turned; wall plates, lintels, and bond timbers; naked flooring, quarter partitions, roofing, battening to walls, ribbed ceilings for the formation of vaulting, coves, and the like in lath and plaster, posts, &c.

2331. In large measures, where the quantity of materials and workmanship is uniform, the articles are usually measured by the square of 100 feet. Piles should be measured by the foot cube, and the driving by the foot run according to the quality of the ground into which they are driven. Sleepers and planking are measured and estimated by the foot, yard, or the square.

2332. Plain centering is measured by the square; but the ribs and boarding, being different qualities of work, should be taken separately. The dimensions are obtained by girting round the arch, and multiplying by the length. Where groins occur, besides the measurement as above, the angles must be measured by the foot run, that is, the ribs and boards are to be measured and valued separately, according to the exact superficial contents of each, and the angles by the linear foot, for the labour in fitting the ribs and boards, and waste of wood.

2333. Wall plates, bond timbers, and lintels are measured by the cubic foot, and go under the denomination of *fir in bond*.

2334. In the measurement and valuation of naked flooring, we may take it either by the square or the cube foot. To form an idea of its value, it is to be observed, that in equal cubic quantities of small and large timbers the latter will have more superficies than the former, whence the saving is not in proportion to the solid contents; and the value, therefore, of the workmanship will not be as the cubic quantity. The trouble of moving timbers increases with their weight, hence a greater expenditure of time; which, though not in an exact ratio with the solid quantity, will not be vastly different, their sections not varying considerably in their dimensions. As the value of the saving upon a cube foot is comparatively small to that of the work performed by the carpenter, the whole cost of labour and materials may be ascertained with sufficient accuracy when the work is uniform.

2335. When girders occur in naked flooring, the uniformity of the work is thereby interrupted by the mortices and tenons which become necessary; thus the amount arising from the cubic quantity of the girders would not be sufficient at the same rate per foot as is put on the other parts, not only because of the difference of the size, but because of the mortices which are cut for the reception of the tenons of the binding joists. Hence, for

valuing the labour and materials, the whole should be measured and valued by the cubic quantity, and an additional rate must be put upon every solid foot of the girders; or, if the binding joists be not inserted in the girders at the usual distances, a fixed price must be put upon every mortice and tenon in proportion to their size. The binding joists are not unfrequently pulley or chase-morticed for the reception of the ceiling joists; sometimes they are notched to receive the bridging joists on them, and they should therefore be classed by themselves at a larger price per foot cube, or at an additional price for the workmanship, beyond common joisting. All these matters must be in proportion to the description of the work, whether the ceiling joists be put in with pulley mortices and tenons, or the bridgings notched or adzed down.

2336. Partitions may be measured and estimated by the cube foot; but the sills, top pieces, and door heads should be measured by themselves, according to their cubic contents, at a larger price; because not only the uniform solidity, but the uniform quantity, of the workmanship is interrupted by them. The braces in trussed partitions are to be taken by the foot cube at a larger price than the common quartering, on account of the trouble of fitting the ends of the uprights upon their upper and lower sides, and of forming the abutments at the ends.

2337. All the timbers of roofing are to be measured by the cubic foot, and classed according to the difficulty of execution, or the waste that occurs in performing the work. Common rafters, as respects labour, are rated much the same as joists or quarters; purlins, which require trouble in fitting, are worth more, because on them are notched down the common rafters. The different parts of a truss should, to come accurately at the true value, be separately taken, and the joggles also separately considered, including the tenons at the ends of the struts; morticing tie beams and principals, forming the tenons of the truss posts, morticing and tenoning the ends of the tie beams and principals, are in another class. The strapping is paid for according to the number of the bolts. Common or bridging rafters' feet are also to be considered; the size and description of the work being always matter for the consideration of the architect.

2338. It is usual and fair to measure the battening of walls by the square, according to the dimensions and distances of the battening.

2339. Ribbed ceilings are taken by the cubic quantity of timber they contain, making due allowance for the waste of stuff, which is often considerable. The price of their labour is to be ordered by the nature of the work, and the cubic quantity they contain.

2340. Trimmers and trimming joists are so priced as to include the mortices and tenons they contain, and also the tenons at the extremities of the trimmers. But to specify all the methods required of ascertaining the value of each species of carpenter's work would be impossible, with any respect to our limits. They must be learned by observation; all we have to do is with the principles on which measuring and estimating is conducted.

2341. When the *carcass* of the building is completed, before laying the floors or lathing the work for receiving the plastering, the timbers should be measured, so that the scantlings may be examined and proved correct, according to the specification; and in this, as a general rule, it is to be remembered that all pieces having tenons are measured to their extremities, and that such timbers as girders and binding joists lie at least 9 inches at their ends into the walls, or ⅓ of the wall's thickness, where it exceeds 27 inches. In the measurement of bond timber and wall plates, the laps must be added to the net lengths. If a necessity occur for cutting parallel pieces out of truss posts (such as king or queen-posts), when such pieces exceed 2 feet 6 inches in length, and 2¼ inches in thickness, they are considered as pieces fit for use, deducting 6 inches as waste from their lengths.

2342. The boarding of a roof is measured by the square, and estimated according to its thickness, and the quantity of boards and the manner in which they are jointed.

2343. Where the measurement is for labour and materials, the best way is, first, to find the cubical contents of a piece of carpentry, and value it by the cubic foot, including the prime cost, carting, sawing, waste, and carpenter's profit, and then to add the price of the labour, properly measured, as if the journeyman were to be paid. It is out of the question to give a notion of any fixed value, because it must necessarily vary, as do materials and labour; hence no tables or price-books are ever to be depended upon; they gull the unwary, and mislead the amateur who consults them. The only true method of forming a proper estimate is dependent on the price of timber and deals, for which general tables may be formed, and some will be presently given.

2344. It is, perhaps, unnecessary to repeat that a load of fir timber contains 50 cube feet: if, then, we know the price of the load in the timber merchant's yard, we may approximate the value of a cube foot as under. We will suppose the price to be, at the moment of estimating, 4*l.* 10*s.* per load. We shall then have —

		£	s.	d.
Prime cost of a load of fir		4	10	0
Suppose the cartage (dependent on distance)		0	5	0
Sawing into necessary scantlings		0	10	0
		5	5	0
Waste in converting equal to 5 feet, at $2\frac{1}{10}$ s. per foot, the load being 105s.		0	10	6
		5	15	6
20 per cent. profit on 5l. 15s. 6d.		1	3	0
		£6	18	6

2345. Now, $\dfrac{6l.\ 18s.\ 6d.}{50} = 2\cdot77$ shillings, or 2 shillings and 9 pence and nearly 1 farthing per foot cube.

2346. It is only in this way that we can arrive at the value of work; and it is much to be regretted that from no species of labour of the carpenter have been formed tables capable of furnishing such a set of constants as would, by application to the rate of a journeyman's wages, form factors, or, in other words, furnish data for a perpetual price-book. As we have before hinted, the best of the price-books that have ever been published are useless as guides to the value of work. The method of lumping work by the square is as much as possible to be avoided, unless the surfaces be of a perfectly uniform description of workmanship; as, for instance, in hipped roofs, the principal trouble is at the hips, in fitting the jack rafters, which are fixed at equal distances thereon; hence such a price may be fixed for the cubic quantity of hips and valleys as will pay not only for them, but also for the trouble of cutting and fixing the jack rafters. Such parts, indeed, as these should be separately classified; but the analysis of such a subject requires investigation of enormous labour; and as it must depend on the information derived from the practical carpenter, is, we fear, not likely to be soon, if ever, accomplished.

2347. Mr. Peter Nicholson, a gentleman to whom the architect as well as the practical man are more indebted than to any other author on this subject, is the only person who has attempted to promulgate a system founded on the scientific basis to which we have just alluded; and we have much pleasure in here alluding to the value of his labour, and of placing before the reader the extent to which he carried it, regretting much that he did not further pursue an investigation, which we have carried to a greater extent, though not now so complete as we could have wished.

2348. It is manifest that if the average time of executing each species of work were known, no difficulty could exist in fixing uniform rates of charge for it; but, as we have observed, the parties who could best instruct us on the subject are those most interested in withholding such information as would be required for the purpose. We shall now proceed to the question, premising that, for the present, we are only dealing with the cost of labour, that of the materials being a simple affair, as we have already seen in the case of ascertaining the value of a cubic foot of fir, and as we shall hereafter see in ascertaining the value of superficial feet of deals of any thickness.

2349. In the subjoined tables, the price is represented by the days, or decimal parts of a day, in which one man can perform the quantity of that sort of work, against which such price is affixed. Hence, knowing the rate per day of such man's wages, it forms a factor by which the value of the labour of such quantity of work will be estimated. We begin by centering.

Centering.

For plain cylindric vaults, fixed per square	2·033 days.
For groins of cylindric vaults, fixed per foot super.	·057
For guaged brickwork, per foot super.	·073
For brick trimmers bridgewise, per foot super.	·041
For coach-head trimmers, per foot super.	·057
For apertures, per foot run	·02

2350. To apply this to practice, we will take the first article in the table, that of the centering of a cylindric vault, a square whereof, we see, will occupy a man 2·033 days to make and fix. Now, supposing such man's wages to be 5s. per diem, we have only to multiply 2·033 by 5s. = 10·165, or nearly 10s. 2d. for a square of such work. The other items being similarly used, will give the results whereof we are in search.

The next table is one composed of several miscellaneous articles, and is as follows:—

Fir in bond and wood bricks, at per foot run	·008 day.
Fir in templates, lintels, and turning pieces, at per foot run	·025
Planing fir, from the saw, per foot super.	·017
Rebating fir up to 2 in. by $\frac{3}{4}$	·025
Rebating fir from 2 in. by $\frac{3}{4}$ to 3 in. by $1\frac{1}{4}$	·041

Single beading, up to ¾ inch - - - - - - ·008 day.
Single quirk beading, from ¾ inch to 1¼ - - - - - ·012
Return beads, worth double.
The next table is for quarter partitions : —
Common 4-inch, per square - - - - - - 1·033 days
Common 5-inch, per square - - - - - - 1·113
Common 6-inch, per square - - - - - · 1·307
Common 6-inch, circular plan, per square - - · 1·888
Common trussed frame, with king-post, per square - - 1·743
Common trussed frame, with king and queen-posts, per square 2·226
The subjoined is a table for naked flooring : —
Ceiling floor, framed with tie beams, binding and ceiling joists, fixed
   per square - - - - - - - - - 1·355 days.
Ceiling floor, with tie beams and ceiling joists only, fixed per
   square - - - - - - - - - 1·065
Ceiling joists only, fixed per square - - - - ·646
Single-framed floor, trimmed to chimney, and well holes less than
   9 inches deep, fixed per square - - - - - 1·355
The same, above 9 inches deep, fixed per square - - - 1·646
The same, if trimmed to party walls, add extra per square, ·388.
Single-framed floor, with one girder, fixed per square - - 1·936
Strutting to be paid for extra.
Single-framed floor-case and tail-bays, fixed per square - - 2·130
For every extra bay, add per square, ·484.
Framed floors, with girders, binding and ceiling joists, fixed per
   square - - - - - - - - - 3·581
Ground joists, bedded, fixed per square - - - ·775
Ground joists, framed to chimneys, fixed per square - - ·968
Ground joists, pinned down on plates and framed to chimneys, fixed
   per square - - - - - - - - 1·065
Girders reversed and bolted, per foot run - - - ·097
Truss girder braces, 4 by 4, per foot run - - - - ·194
If any of the above works be executed in oak, add one third.
The following table is for roofing of various sorts : —
Common shed roofing, one story high, fixed per square - - ·968
Common shed roofing, two stories high, fixed per square - - 1·033
Common shed roofing, three stories high, fixed per square - - 1·113
Single span roofing, one story high, fixed per square - - 1·065
Single span roofing, two stories high, fixed per square - - 1·113
Single span roofing, three stories high, fixed per square - - 1·210
If the above are with purlins, add ·194 per square.
If purlins are framed diagonally, add ·388 per square.
Hips and valleys, per foot run - - - - - ·08
   In common kerb roofing, add extra per square, when one
     side is kerbed - - - - - - ·194
   When three sides - - - - - - ·357
   When four sides - - - - - - ·516
Girt of roofing, with framed principals, collar beams, and purlins,
   fixed per square - - - - - - 2·323
Framed with principals, beams, king-posts, purlins, and common
   rafters, fixed per square - - - - - 3·484
If the principals and rafters are framed flush, and the purlins housed
   in, add ·387 day to the above.
Framed with principals, beams, king-posts, queen-posts, and common
   rafters, three stories, fixed per square - - - 4·549 days.
The same, four stories, fixed per square - - - 4·84
Hips and valleys, per foot run - - - - - ·145
Hip and ridge rolls, fixed in iron, per foot run - - - ·048
Bedded plates to common span roofing, per foot run - - ·008
Bedded plates to framed roofing, as above, per foot run - - ·028
Diagonal and dragon pieces, per foot run - - - ·065
Angular ties and struts, per foot run - - - - ·032
Rafters' feet and eaves bond, per foot run - - - - ·032
The table for guttering is as follows : —
Inch or inch and quarter deal and bearers, including 6-inch layer
   board, per foot super. - - - - - ·057
The same in kerb roofs, per foot super. - - - - ·073

For furrings and battenings, table as follows : —

If the stuff be ¾ by 1½ inch, fixed per square - - -	·872 day.
If it has also to be cut out, add ·146 per square.	
Battenings with quarters, 3 by 2 inches, fixed per square - -	·92
Battenings to quarters, 3 by 2 inches to window piers, fixed per square - - - - - - - -	1·355
If the battens be fixed to plugs, add ·29 per square.	

When any of the above are circular on the plan, half as much more must be added to the price of the work.

Table for bracketing, including plugging, is as under : —

To straight cornices, fixed per foot super. - - - -	·089 day.
To coved straight cornices, fixed per foot super. - - -	·065
If circular on the plan, add one half more.	
To groins in passages less than 4 feet wide, fixed per foot super.	·162
To the same above 4 feet, fixed per foot super. - - -	·121

2351. The works of the Joiner consist in the preparation of boarding, which is measured and estimated by the foot superficial. Of this there are many varieties; as, edges shot; edges shot, ploughed, and tongued; wrought on one side and edges shot; the same on both sides and edges shot; wrought on both sides and ploughed and tongued. Boards keyed and clamped; mortice clamped, and mortice and mitre clamped. The value per foot increases according to the thickness of the stuff. When longitudinal joints are glued, an addition per foot is made; and if feather-tongued, still more.

2352. The measurement and estimation of floors is by the square, the price varying as the surface is wrought or plain; the method of connecting the longitudinal and heading joints, and also on the thickness of the stuff; as well as on the circumstance of the boards being laid one after another or folded; or whether laid with boards, battens, wainscot, or other wood. Skirtings are measured by the foot super., according to their position, as whether level, raking, or ramping. Also on the manner of finishing them, as whether plain, torus, rebated, scribed to floors or steps, or whether straight or circular on the plan.

2353. The value of every species of framing must depend on the thickness of the stuff employed, whether it is plain or moulded; and if the latter, whether the mouldings be struck on the solid, or laid in; whether mitred or scribed, and upon the number of panels in a given height and breadth, and also on the form of the plan.

2354. Wainscotings, window-linings, as backs and elbows; door linings, such as jambs and sofites; back linings, partitions, doors, shutters, and the like, are all measured and valued by the foot super. The same mode is applied to sashes and their frames, either together or separately.

2355. Skylights, the prices whereof depend on their plans and elevations, are also measured by the foot super. Framed grounds, by the foot run.

2356. The value of dado, which varies as the plan is straight or circular, or being level or inclined, is measured by the foot super.

2357. In the measurement of staircases, the risers, treads, carriages, and brackets are, after being classed together, measured by the foot super., and the string board is sometimes included. The value varies as the steps may be flyers or winders, or from the risers being mitred into the string board, the treads dovetailed for balusters and the nosings returned, or whether the bottom edges of the risers are tongued into the step. The curtail step is valued by itself, and returned nosings are sometimes valued at the piece; and if they are circular on the plan, they are charged at double the price of straight ones. The handrail, whose value depends upon the materials and diameter of the well hole, or whether ramped, swan-necked, level, circular, or wreathed; whether got out of the solid, or in thicknesses glued up together, is measured by the foot run. The scroll is charged by itself, as is the making and fixing each joint screw, and 3 inches of the straight part at each end of the wreath is measured in. The deal balusters, as also the iron ones and the iron columns to curtail, housings to steps and risers, common cut brackets, square and circular on the plan, together with the preparing and fixing, are valued all by the piece. Extra sinking in the rail for iron balusters is valued by the foot run, the price depending on the rail as being straight, circular, wreathed, or ramped. The string board is measured by the foot super., and its value is greater or less as it is moulded, straight, or wreathed, or according to the method in which the wreathed string is constructed by being properly backed upon a cylinder.

2358. The shafts of columns are measured by the foot super., their value depending upon the diameter, or whether it be straight or curved on the side, and upon its being properly glued and blocked. If the columns be fluted, the flutes are taken in linear measure, the price depending on the size of the flutes, whose headings at top and bottom are charged by the piece. Pilasters, straight or curved in the height, are similarly measured, and the price taken by the foot super. In the caps and bases of pilasters, besides the mouldings, the mitres are charged so much each, according to the size.

2359. Mouldings, as in double-face architraves, base and surbase, or straight ones struck by the hand, are valued by the foot super. Base, surbase, and straight mouldings wrought by hand, are generally fixed at the same rate per foot, being something more than double-faced architraves. When the head of an architrave stands in a circular wall, its value is four times that of the perpendicular parts, as well on account of the extra time required to fit it to the circular plan as of the greater difficulty in forming the mitres. So all horizontal mouldings on a circular plan are three or four times the value of those on a straight plan, the trouble being increased as the radius of the circle upon which they are formed diminishes. The housings of mouldings are valued by the piece. The value of mouldings much depends on the number of their quirks, for each whereof the price increases. It will also, of course, depend on the materials of which they are formed, on their running figure, and whether raking or curved.

2360. Among the articles which are to be measured by the lineal foot are beads, fillets, bead or ogee capping, square angle staffs, inch ogees, inch quirk ogee, ovolo and bead, astragals and reeds on doors or shutters, small reeds, each in reeded mouldings, struck by hand up to half an inch, single cornice or architrave, grooved space to let in reeds and grooves. And it must be observed, that in grooving, stops are paid extra; if wrought by hand, still more; and yet more if circular. Besides the foregoing, narrow grounds to skirting, the same rebated or framed to chimneys, are measured by the foot run. Rule joints, cantilevers, trusses, and cut brackets for shelves are charged by the piece.

2361. Water trunks are valued according to their size by the foot run, their hopper heads and shoes being valued by the piece. Moulded weather-caps and joints by the piece. Scaffolding, where extra, must be allowed for. Flooring boards are prepared according to their length, not so much each; the standard width is 9 inches; if they are wider, the rate is increased, each board listing at so much per list. Battens are prepared in the same way, but at a different rate.

2362. The following memoranda are useful in estimating : —

1 hundred (120) 12-feet-3-inch deals, 9 inches wide (each deal containing, therefore, 2 feet 3 inches cube), equal 5⅔ loads of timber.

1 hundred (120) 12-feet-2½-inch deals, 9 inches wide (each deal containing, therefore, 1 foot 10 inches cube), equal 4¼ loads of timber.

1 hundred (120) 12-feet-1½-inch deals equal 1 reduced hundred.

1 load of 1½-inch plank, or deals, is 400 feet superficial.

1 load of 2-inch plank, or deals, is 300 feet superficial.

And so on in proportion.

Twenty-four 10-feet boards, at a 5-inch guage, will finish one square.

Twenty 10-feet boards, at 6-inch guage, will finish one square.

Seventeen 10-feet boards, at a 7-inch guage, will finish one square.

Fifteen 10-feet boards, at an 8-inch guage, will finish one square.

Thirteen 10-feet boards, and 2 ft. 6 in. super, at a 9-inch guage, will finish one square.

Twelve 10-feet boards, and 2 ft. 6 in. super., at a 10-inch guage, will finish one square.

Twenty 12-feet boards, at a 5-inch guage, will finish one square.

Sixteen 12-feet boards, at a 6-inch guage, will finish one square.

Fourteen 12-feet boards, at a 7-inch guage, will finish one square.

Twelve 12-feet boards and 4 feet super., at an 8-inch guage, will finish one square.

Eleven 12-feet boards, and 1 foot super., at a 9-inch guage, will finish one square.

Ten 12-feet boards, and 1 foot super., at a 10-inch guage, will finish one square.

Battens are 6 inches wide.

Deals are 9 inches wide.

Planks are 11 inches wide.

Feather-edged deals are equal to ¾-inch yellow deals; if white, equal to slit deal.

A reduced deal is 1½-inch think, 11 inches wide, and 12 feet long.

2363. It may here be useful to advert to the mode of reducing deals to the standard of what is called a reduced deal, which evidently contains 1 ft. 4 in. 6 parts cube; for 12 ft. × 11 in. × 1½ in. = 1 : 4·46, or in decimals, 12 ft. × ·91666 ft. × ·125 ft. = 1·375 cube ft. nearly. Hence the divisor 1·375 will serve as a constant for reducing deals of different lengths and thicknesses. Thus let it be required to find how many reduced deals there are in one 14 feet long, 10 inches wide, and 2½ inches thick. Here 14 ft. × ·8333 ft. (or 10 in.)

× ·20833 (or 2½ in.) = 2·43042 cube feet, and $\frac{2\cdot43042}{1\cdot375}$ = 1·767 reduced deal.

2364. The table which is now subjoined exhibits the prices of deals and parts thereof calculated from 30l. to 95l. per hundred, a range of value out of which it can rarely happen that examples will occur, though it has fallen within our own experience during the late war to see the price of deals at a very extraordinary height. This, however, is not likely to happen again. The elements on which it is based are —

First. Price of deals, each being 12 feet long, three inches thick, 10 inches wide. Then from $\frac{30l.}{120}$ we have the prime cost of each deal **5·00**

Second. Profit on prime cost, 15 per cent. - - - - **0·75**

Third. Planing both sides and waste, the former a constant depending on the price of labour (say 5s. per day used in the table), and the latter a variable, increasing with the cost price of the material - **0·8333**

6s. 7d. as in the table for a 12 feet deal = **6·5833**

In the third element a *constant* (the planing) being involved and a *variable* (the waste) increasing with the cost of the material, the latter was eliminated by experiment and found equal to ·4166 shilling for every 10l. upwards of the price per hundred of the deals.

The width of the running foot is 9 inches. For instance at 45l. per cent. the cost of a foot super. (=144 in.) = 1·25s. = 1s. 3d. and of a foot run ·9375 shilling = 11½d. ∴ $\dfrac{144 \times ·9375}{\frac{1·25}{12}}$ = 9 inches.

Price per hundred.	Thickness.	10 feet long each.	12 feet long each.	14 feet long each.	Per foot run.	Per foot super.	Price per hundred.	Thickness.	10 feet long each.	12 feet long each.	14 feet long each.	Per foot run.	Per foot super.
	In.	s. d.	s. d.	s. d.	s. d.	s. d.		In.	s. d.	s. d.	s. d.	s. d.	s. d.
£30	½	1 4¾	1 8	1 11¼	0 2	0 2¼	£65	½	2 7¼	3 1½	3 7¾	0 3½	0 4⅜
	¾	1 7¼	1 11½	2 3	0 2½	0 3		¾	3 1½	3 9½	4 5	0 4¼	0 5½
	1	2 0½	2 5¼	2 10½	0 3	0 3¾		1	3 11¼	4 11	5 1½	0 5¾	0 7½
	1¼	2 6¼	3 0½	3 6¼	0 3½	0 4½		1¼	5 0½	6 0½	7 0½	0 7	0 9¼
	1½	2 11¾	3 6¼	4 1½	0 4½	0 5¼		1½	6 0	7 2½	8 5	0 8¼	0 11
	2	3 11	4 7	5 4	0 5½	0 7		2	7 9¾	9 4½	10 11¼	0 11	1 2¼
	2½	4 8¼	5 8¼	6 7¼	0 6½	0 8⅝		2½	9 9	11 8¼	13 7¼	1 1½	1 6
	3	5 5¾	6 7	7 8¼	0 7½	0 10		3	11 6½	13 10½	16 2¼	1 4	1 9¼
£35	½	1 6¾	1 10½	2 2¼	0 2¼	0 3	£70	½	2 9¼	3 4	3 10½	0 3¾	0 5¼
	¾	1 10½	2 2½	2 7½	0 2½	0 3½		¾	3 4½	4 0½	4 8½	0 4½	0 6¼
	1	2 4	2 9½	3 3½	0 3½	0 4¼		1	4 4½	5 3	6 1½	0 6	0 8
	1¼	2 10½	3 5¼	4 0½	0 4	0 5¼		1¼	5 5	6 6	7 7	0 7½	0 10
	1½	3 5	4 1	4 9	0 4½	0 6¼		1½	6 5½	7 8½	9 0	0 9	1 0
	2	4 3¾	5 2	6 0½	0 6	0 8		2	8 5½	10 2½	11 10½	0 11¾	1 3¾
	2½	5 4½	6 5¾	7 6¼	0 7¼	0 10		2½	10 6½	12 8	14 9½	1 2½	1 7¾
	3	6 4¼	7 7½	8 10¼	0 9	0 11¾		3	12 5	14 11	17 5	1 5	1 11
£40	½	1 8¾	2 1	2 5¼	0 2½	0 3¼	£75	½	2 11½	3 6½	4 1¼	0 4	0 5½
	¾	2 0½	2 5¾	2 10½	0 3	0 3¾		¾	3 7¼	4 3½	5 0½	0 5	0 6¾
	1	2 7¼	3 2	3 8¼	0 3¾	0 5		1	4 8½	5 7¼	6 6½	0 6½	0 8½
	1¼	3 3	3 10¾	4 6¼	0 4¾	0 6		1¼	5 9½	6 11	8 1½	0 8	0 10½
	1½	3 10	4 7½	5 4½	0 5¼	0 7		1½	6 10½	8 3	9 7½	0 9½	1 0¾
	2	4 11¾	5 11¼	6 11¾	0 7	0 9¼		2	9 1	10 11½	12 9	1 0½	1 5
	2½	6 2	7 5	8 8	0 8¼	0 11¾		2½	11 3½	13 7	15 10½	1 3½	1 9
	3	7 2¾	8 8	10 1¼	0 10	1 1½		3	13 3½	15 11½	18 7½	1 6¼	2 0¼
£45	½	1 11	2 3¼	2 8	0 2¾	0 3½	£80	½	3 1½	3 9	4 4½	0 4¼	0 5¾
	¾	2 3¼	2 9	3 2½	0 3	0 4¼		¾	3 9½	4 6½	5 3½	0 5¼	0 7
	1	2 11¼	3 6¼	4 1½	0 4	0 5½		1	4 11¼	5 11½	6 11½	0 6½	0 9
	1¼	3 7½	4 4	5 0¾	0 5	0 6¾		1¼	6 1½	7 4½	8 7½	0 8¼	0 11½
	1½	4 3½	5 1½	5 11¾	0 6	0 8		1½	7 3½	8 9¼	9 2¾	0 10	1 1½
	2	5 6¾	6 8½	8 11	0 7¾	0 10¼		2	9 7½	11 6½	13 5¼	1 1¼	1 5¾
	2½	6 11	8 3½	9 8	0 9¼	1 1½		2½	13 11½	14 4½	16 9½	1 4	1 9½
	3	8 1	9 8½	11 4	0 11¾	1 3		3	14 2	17 0	19 10	1 7½	2 2½
£50	½	2 1¼	2 6	2 11	0 3	0 4	£85	½	3 4	4 0½	4 8	0 4½	0 6
	¾	2 6¼	3 0	3 6	0 3¼	0 4¾		¾	4 0½	4 10	5 7¾	0 5¼	0 7½
	1	3 2¼	3 10½	4 6	0 4½	0 6		1	5 3¼	6 3½	7 4½	0 7	0 9¼
	1¼	3 11½	4 9	5 6½	0 5½	0 7½		1¼	6 6	7 9	9 1	0 8¾	1 0
	1½	4 8½	5 7¾	6 7	0 6½	0 8½		1½	7 9	9 3½	10 10	0 10½	1 2¾
	2	6 2¼	7 5	8 7½	0 8½	0 11½		2	10 2	12 2	14 3	1 2	1 6
	2½	7 7½	9 2	10 8½	0 11½	1 2		2½	12 8	15 2½	18 0	1 5¼	1 11½
	3	8 11¾	10 9	12 6½	1 0½	1 4½		3	14 11½	18 0½	21 0½	1 8½	2 3¾
£55	½	2 3	2 8½	3 3	0 3½	0 4¼	£90	½	3 5½	4 2	4 10½	0 4¾	0·6¼
	¾	2 8½	3 3½	3 9½	0 3½	0 5		¾	4 2½	5 1	5 11¼	0 5½	0 7¾
	1	3 6¼	4 2½	4 11½	0 5	0 6½		1	5 6½	6 7½	7 9	0 7¼	0 10¼
	1¼	4 4	5 2	6 1	0 6	0 8		1¼	6 10¼	8 2	9 6½	0 9¼	1 0½
	1½	5 1¼	6 2¼	7 3½	0 7½	0 9½		1½	8 2½	9 9½	11 5¼	0 11¼	1 3¼
	2	6 8½	8 1	9 5¼	0 9¼	1 0½		2	10 9	12 11	15 0½	1 3	1 8
	2½	8 4¼	10 10½	11 8	0 11½	1 2¾		2½	13 4½	16 0½	18 9	1 6½	2 0⅜
	3	9 10	11 9½	13 9	1 1½	1 6¼		3	15 11	19 1	22 3	1 10	2 5¼
£60	½	2 5	2 11	3 5	0 3½	0 4¾	£95	½	3 7½	4 4½	5 1¼	0 5	0 6⅝
	¾	2 11½	3 6¼	4 0½	0 4	0 5¼		¾	4 5½	5 4½	6 3	0 6	0 8
	1	3 9¼	4 7	5 4½	0 5½	0 7		1	5 10	7 0	8 2	0 8	0 10¾
	1¼	4 8½	5 7¾	6 7	0 6½	0 8½		1¼	7 2¾	8 8	10 1¼	0 10	1 1½
	1½	5 6¾	6 8½	7 9¾	0 7½	0 10¼		1½	8 7½	10 4	12 0	1 0	1 4
	2	7 3¼	8 9	10 2¼	0 10½	1 1		2	11 4½	13 7½	15 10½	1 3¾	1 9
	2½	9 1½	10 11	12 8½	1 0	1 4¼		2½	14 1½	16 11½	19 9¼	1 7½	2 2¼
	3	10 8½	12 10	14 11¼	1 2¼	1 7¼		3	16 9¼	20 1½	23 5¼	1 10¾	2 6

2365. The above table we cannot suppose will require explanation; but as we wish to be quite explicit, we will merely take one example for illustrating its use, premising, that if deals are at a price between, above, or below that stated in the first column, the rules of arithmetic must be applied for the intermediate prices. Suppose deals, then, to be at 45*l*. per hundred; an inspection of the table shows that the value of 1½-inch deal is 8*d*. per foot super., or 6*d*. run; that a 12-foot deal 2 inches thick is worth 6*s*. 8¼*d*.; and that a foot run of 3-inch deal 11 inches wide, which is the standard width, is worth 11¼*d*. The preceding table, which is applicable purely to joinery, is all that can be given in general terms as to the prices of work; for that which follows we are again indebted, partly to Mr. Peter Nicholson, and partly to our own industry. The information is not all that could be desired on the subject, nor, as we have before said, can constants of labour be easily obtained for every article in a building; but, as far as they go, they must be considered valuable, though they seem not to have met with the reception they deserved. The value of the labour is given as before, in parts and decimal parts of a man's labour in each description of work per diem, so that the factor to be applied to each is the rate per diem at which the journeyman is engaged. The first table subjoined is one for doors, and in the first article of it, by way of application, suppose the wages of the joiner be 5*s*. 6*d*. per diem, that =5·5 shillings will be the factor, and the price, therefore, of the labour on a 1¼-inch door, both sides square, will be 5·5 × ·06 = ·330 shillings, or nearly 4*d*. per foot, without fitting and hanging. If to this be added the price of the quantity of deal used in it, from the foregoing table, we shall arrive at a result not far from its value. We proceed, then, in giving the constants of doors according to their most common descriptions.

Doors, 1¼ Inch thick.

2-panel, both sides square - - - - - per foot super.	·06
4-panel, both sides square - - - - -	·07
6-panel, both sides square - - - - -	·08
2-panel, quirk ovolo and bead, and square back - - -	·1
4-panel, quirk ovolo and bead, and square back - - -	·11
6-panel, quirk ovolo and bead, and square back - - -	·12
2-panel, bead and flush front, and square back - - -	·1
4-panel, bead and flush front, and square back - - -	·11
6-panel, bead and flush front, and square back - - -	·12
2-panel, bead and butt front, and square back - - -	·09
4-panel, bead and butt front, and square back - - -	·1
6-panel, bead and butt front, and square back - - -	·11
2-panel, quirk ovolo and bead on both sides - - -	·14
4-panel, quirk ovolo and bead on both sides - - -	·15
6-panel, quirk ovolo and bead on both sides - - -	·16
2-panel, bead and butt on both sides - - - -	·12
4-panel, bead and butt on both ends - - - -	·13
6-panel, bead and butt on both ends - - - -	·14
2-panel, bead and flush on both sides - - - -	·14
4-panel, bead and flush on both sides - - - -	·15
6-panel, bead and flush on both sides - - - -	·16

2366. In applying the above table to other thicknesses, for every additional thickness of one quarter of an inch the rate per foot super. must be increased ·005.

2367. When the panels are raised on one side, ·002 must be added, and double that (·004) when raised on both sides. If an astragal or ovolo is on one of the rising sides, ·003 must be added, and double that (·006) if such occur on both sides. Generally, if the number of panels be given, and the price per foot square on one side, with extra work on the other side, its price is one of the same number of panels, and the same number of panels on both sides minus the rate of the first from that of the last. But adding the difference of the second, we have the rate extra on both sides. Thus the rate is ·06 for 1¼-inch two-panel door, square on both sides, and for a two-panel door, square on one side, with quirk ovolo and bead upon the other, it is ·1. The difference is ·04, which added to ·1 = ·15 for the rate of 1¼-inch two-panel door, with ovolo and bead on both sides.

2368. We now turn to another of the items to be considered in measuring and estimating works, that of linings, wherein the difference of labour between square-framed door linings, backs, elbows, sofites, or wainscotings, and door square on both sides, where the panels and thicknesses are alike, arises only from planing the panels and the framing on the other side of the door. If the difference, therefore, per foot, on the rate of a door square on both sides, and one square on one side, with any extra work on the other side, be added to the rate of door-linings, backs, elbows, sofites, or wainscoting framed square, we shall have the rate per foot for door-linings, window-linings, or wainscoting, taking the extra work as above considered. The rails and stiles are taken in the rates as not rebated, and

. the framed linings for walls or apertures are supposed as made of stuff one quarter of an inch thinner than the doors.   Linings are uusually about an inch thick, being stiffened by fixing to the wall ; but this depends on the distance of the panel's recess from the framing, and on the depth of the moulding employed.

FRAMED INCH LININGS.

1-panel, square as in backs   -   -   -   -   - per foot super. ·051
3-panel, square as in backs, and elbows measured together   -   ·071
4-panel, square as in backs, and elbows and sofites   -   -   ·061
3-panel, moulded as in backs, and elbows together   -   -   ·087
4-panel   ditto   and sofites measured together   -   ·077
3-panel, quirk moulded as in backs, and elbows measured
  together   -   -   -   -   -   -   -   ·095
4-panel, quirk moulded as in backs, and sofites measured
  together   -   -   -   -   -   -   -   ·085
Semicircular moulded sofites in two panels seven times the straight.   For each additional quarter of an inch add ·005 to the foot super.
     N.B. In the above table the backs, elbows, and sofites, though numbered as of 3 and 4 panels, are only of one panel each, the number being collected.

INCH AND A QUARTER DOOR-LININGS, ONE PANEL HIGH.

Rebated   -   -   -   -   -   - per foot super. ·051
Rebated and beaded   -   -   -   -   -   -   ·058
Double rebated, not exceeding 7 inches wide   -   -   -   ·067
Double rebated, not exceeding 7 inches wide, and one edge beaded   ·071
Double rebated, not exceeding 7 inches wide, and both edges beaded   ·075
If the plan be circular, the price increases as the diameter diminishes.
Semicircular heads straight on the plan are worth five times as much as straight.

SHUTTERS, two panels in height, either shutters or flaps, inch framed, uncut.   If mouldings are described, they are considered as to be laid in, but if stuck on the framing, add ·012 to the rate.   Add ·016 to the rate for every extra panel, and ·012 for any extra height, and ·008 if they are quirk moulded.

Square   -   -   -   -   -   -   - per foot super. ·071
Bead butt and square -   -   -   -   -   -   ·1
Bead flush and square -   -   -   -   -   -   ·111
Bead flush and bead butt   -   -   -   -   -   ·131
Two panels in height, inch and quarter, uncut, adding for extras, as in the heading above.
Moulded and square   -   ·1   -   -   -   - per foot super. ·1
Moulded bead butt   -   -   -   -   ·   -   ·111
Moulded bead and flush   -   -   -   -   -   ·135
Moulded on both sides -   -   -   -   -   -   ·111
Ovolo and bead, or quirk ogee front, and square back   -   -   ·103
Ovolo and bead, or quirk ogee front, with bead and butt back   -   ·123

WAINSCOTING, 1¼-inch, two panels high, with square fascia, framed up to ceiling.

Square   -   -   -   -   -   -   - per foot super. ·039
Moulded   -   -   -   -   -   -   -   ·055
Quirk moulded   -   -   -   -   -   -   ·063
Bead and butt -   -   -   -   -   -   ·051
Bead and flush -   -   -   -   -   -   -   ·059
Bead and flush, with three reeds   -   -   -   -   ·075
Should either of these be framed with raised mouldings, add ·008 to the rate, or framed with more, ·006 is to be added for each additional panel in height.

WAINSCOTING, 1¼-inch dwarf, one panel high, including square skirting.

Square   -   -   -   -   -   -   - per foot super. ·047
Moulded   -   -   -   -   -   -   ·063
Quirk moulded   -   -   -   -   -   -   ·071
Bead and butt -   -   -   -   -   -   ·059
Bead and flush -   -   -   -   -   -   ·067
Bead and flush, with three reeds   -   -   -   ·083
If dwarf wainscoting be framed with two panels in height, add ·016 to the rate, as in full wainscoting.   When raked to stairs, ·023 extra, and when with raised mouldings, ·007.   All cappings are measured run, and the skirtings of stairs must be taken separately from their wainscoting.

THREE-QUARTER-INCH or SLIT DEAL, from the bench.

Edges shot - - - - - - - per foot super.	·004
Wrought on one side - - - - - - -	·016
Wrought on one side, grooved, tongued, and beaded - -	·028
Wrought on two sides, and edges shot - - -	·028
Wrought on two sides, grooved, tongued, and beaded - -	·04
When joints glued, add per foot ·004.	

INCH AND QUARTER DEAL.

Wrought on one side, and edges shot - - - - per foot super.	·02
Wrought on both sides, and edges shot - - - -	·032
Wrought on one side, and ploughed and tongued - -	·036
Wrought on two sides, ploughed, tongued, and beaded - -	·052
With glued joints, add ·004 to the rate.	

INCH AND HALF DEAL.

Edges shot - - - - - - - per foot super.	·008
Ploughed and tongued - - - - - - -	·024
Wrought on one side, with edges shot - - - -	·02
Wrought on both sides, with edges shot - - -	·036
Wrought on both sides, ploughed and tongued - - -	·052
With glued joints, add ·012 to the rate.	

TWO-INCH DEAL, from the bench.

Edges shot - - - - - - - per foot super.	·02
Ploughed and tongued - - - - - -	·036
Wrought on one side - - - - - -	·028
Wrought on both sides - - - - -	·044
Wrought on both sides, ploughed and tongued - - -	·056
With glued joints, add ·016 to the rate.	

TWO-AND-HALF-INCH DEAL, from the bench.

Edges shot - - - - - - per foot super.	·028
Ploughed and tongued - - - - - -	·048
Wrought on one side - - - - -	·048
Wrought on both sides - - - - -	·063
Wrought on both sides, ploughed and tongued - -	·083
With glued joints, add ·016 to the rate.	

THREE-INCH DEAL.

Edges shot - - - - - - per foot super.	·032
Ploughed and tongued - - - - -	·056
Wrought on one side - - - - -	·056
Wrought on both sides - - - - -	·08
Wrought on both sides, ploughed and tongued - -	·103
With glued joints, add ·016 to the rate.	

INCH BOARDING, one side planed.

Ploughed and tongued - - - - - - per foot super.	·24
Glued joint - - - - - - -	·03
Clamped - - - - - - -	·056
Mortice clamped - - - - - -	·063
Laid with straight joint in floors - - - -	·02
Keyed dado - - - - - -	·044
Keyed in backs and elbows - - - -	·056
Wrought on both sides, ploughed and tongued - -	·036
Wrought on both sides, glued joint - - - -	·04
Groove-clamped flaps to shutters, in one height - -	·053
Clamped flaps to shutters, in two heights - -	·071
Inch mortice, clamped, outside shutters - - -	·063
Ledged doors, with plain joint - - -	·044
Ledged doors, ploughed, tongued, and beaded - -	·056

PREPARING FLOORING BOARDS, guaged to a width, and rebated to a thickness not more than 9 inches wide.

Inch deals, 10 feet long - - - - - for each board	·063
Inch deals, 12 feet long - - - - -	·075

PREPARING FLOORING BOARDS.
Inch deals, 14 feet long   -   -   -   -   - for each board ·087
Inch and quarter deals, 10 feet long   -   -   -   -   ·071
Inch and quarter deals, 12 feet long   -   -   -   -   ·083
Inch and quarter deals, 14 feet long   -   -   -   -   ·1
Inch and quarter battens, 10 feet long -   -   -   -   ·044
Inch and quarter battens, 12 feet long -   -   -   -   ·056
Inch and quarter battens, 14 feet long -   -   -   -   ·075

MOULDINGS, from the bench.
Double-faced architraves   -   -   -   -   - per foot super. ·111
Base and surbase   -   -   -   -   -   ·127
When above 4 inches girt, struck by hand   -   -   -   ·127
In a combination of mouldings, with more than two quirks, add 016 for each.

INCH AND INCH AND QUARTER FRAMED GROUNDS TO DOORS, from the bench.
Both edges square   -   -   -   -   -   - per foot run ·028
One edge square, and the other rebated and beaded   -   -   ·032
Rebated on one edge, and beaded on both edges   -   -   .036
Framed to a circular plan with flat sweeps, the head to be thrice the rate of straight,
    but the smaller the sweep the greater the rate.

RUNNING ARTICLES.
Beads and fillets   -   -   -   -   -   - per foot run ·004
Bead or ogee capping   -   -   -   -   -   ·016
Inch ogee   -   -   -   -   -   -   ·016
Inch quirked ogee, or ovolo and bead   -   -   -   -   ·023
Square angle staff, rebated   -   -   -   -   ·028
Angle staff, rebated and beaded   -   -   -   -   ·048
Single cornice or architrave   -   -   -   -   ·048
Small reeds in reeded mouldings, stuck by hand to ½ an inch   -   ·004
Reeds above ½ an inch, stuck by hand, including grooved space   -   ·008
Grooves in ornamental work   -   -   -   -   ·004
Narrow ground to skirting   -   -   -   -   ·011
Narrow ground to skirting, rebated or grooved   -   -   ·016
Narrow ground, framed to chimneys   -   -   -   ·032
Double-beaded chair rail   -   -   -   -   ·023
Plugging is included in the above rates.   Such of the articles as are circular on
    plan, to be double rate.
Legs, rails, and runners to dressers   -   -   -   per foot run ·055
Rule joints to shutters   -   -   -   -   ·063

STAIRS, inch and quarter nailed steps, with carriages.
Flyers   -   -   -   -   -   -   - per foot super. fixed ·08
Winders   -   -   -   -   -   -   ·111
Flyers, moulded and glued, with close string board   -   ·103
Winders, moulded and glued, with close string board   -   ·135
Moulded planceer under steps   -   -   -   -   ·04
Housings to flyers   -   -   -   -   each ·127
Housings to winders   -   -   -   -   ·2
Common cut brackets to flyers   -   -   -   ·143
Common cut brackets to winders   -   -   -   ·286
Fancy brackets to be paid for extra, according to their value

HANDRAIL, 2 inches deep and 2¼ inches broad.
Deal, moulded   -   -   -   -   -   - per foot run fixed ·111
Deal, moulded and ramped   -   -   -   -   ·495
Deal, moulded, level, circular   -   -   -   -   ·413
Deal, moulded, wreathed   -   -   -   -   1·2
Mahogany, moulded, straight   -   -   -   -   ·263
Mahogany, moulded, ramped   -   -   -   -   ·831
Mahogany, moulded, ramped, swan-necked   -   -   -   ·927
Mahogany, moulded, level, circular   -   -   -   1·08
Mahogany, moulded, wreathed, from 12 in. and above   -   1·6
Mahogany, moulded, wreathed, under 12 in.   -   -   1·8
Mahogany, moulded, wreathed, not less than 12 in. opening -   2·8
Mahogany, moulded, wreathed, under 12 in. opening   -   3·4

HANDRAIL.

Extra sinking to rail, for iron balusters - - - per foot run fixed ·032
Extra sinking to rail, in ramp or wreath - - - ·1
Mahogany moulded cap, wrought by hand, each - - ·495
Mahogany moulded cap, turned and mitred, each - - ·4
Mahogany scroll, each - - - - - 1·8
Making and fixing each joint with joint screw - - ·231
Making model and fixing iron balusters - - - 2·095
Making model and fixing iron columns to curtail, each - 2·142
Preparing and fixing deal bar balusters, each - - ·04
Preparing and fixing deal bar balusters, dovetailed to steps - ·056

Every half rail is measured two-thirds of a whole one; and all rails are measured 3 inches beyond the springing of every wreath or circular part.

All cylinders used in rails, glued up in thicknesses, to be paid for extra.

The following have not been before computed : —

FRENCH CASEMENT FRAMES.

Plain solid frames, oak sunk sills, weathered and throated for
1½ inch French casements, quarters not exceeding 4 by 3 - per foot super. fixed ·043
Ditto, for 2-inch French casements, quarters 4 by 4 - ·057
Deal-cased frames, oak sunk sills, with wainscot stiles and
beads, for 2-inch French casements - - - ·086
Circular head, measured square - - - - ·258
Circular circular head, curve ½ inch to a foot - - ·727
If with mahogany stiles and beads, add on the wainscot - ·021
If any of the above are for 2½-inch sashes or casements, add
on the deal - - - - - - ·014
If any on the wainscot - - - - - ·021
If any on the mahogany - - - - - ·028
Extra grooves or beads, add - - - - per foot run ·014
Circular on plan, flat sweep, once and a half the straight.
Quirk on plan, double.

SASHES AND FRAMES, fitted and hung.

Deal cased frames, oak sunk sills, 1½-inch ovolo sashes, single
hung brass pulleys, best white lines, and iron weights - per foot super. ·086
Ditto, double hung - - - - - ·100
Ditto, double hung, circular head, measured square - - ·257
Ditto, circular on plan, flat sweep - - - ·143
Deal cased frames, oak sunk sills, 2-inch ovolo sashes, single hung,
brass pulleys, best white lines, and iron weights - - ·100
Ditto, double hung - - - - - ·107
Ditto, double hung, circular head, measured square - - ·272
Ditto, double hung, circular on plan, flat sweep - - ·157
Circular circular head, ½ inch to the foot - - ·770
Deal cased frames, oak sunk sills, wainscot pulley pieces and
beads, 1½-inch wainscot astragal sashes, brass axle pulleys, single
hung with patent lines - - - - - ·121
Ditto, double hung - - - - - ·143
Deal cased frames, oak sunk sills, wainscoat pulley pieces and
beads, 1½-inch wainscot astragal sashes, brass axle pulleys with
patent lines, circular on plan, flat sweep - - - ·172
Circular circular head, ½ inch to the foot - - ·866
Deal cased frames, oak sunk sills, wainscot pulley pieces and
beads, 2-inch wainscot astragal sashes, brass axle pulleys, double
hung with patent lines - - - - - ·143
Ditto, circular head, measured square - - - ·342
Ditto, circular on plan, flat sweep - • - - ·214
Circular circular head, ½ inch to the foot - - ·909
Deal cased frames, oak sunk sills, mahogany pulley pieces and
beads, 1½-inch Spanish mahogany astragal sashes, brass pulleys
and patent lines, single hung - - - - ·157
Ditto, double hung - - - - - ·171
Ditto, circular head, measured square - - - ·371
Ditto, circular on plan, flat sweep - - - ·257
Circular circular head, ½ inch to the foot - - ·98
Deal cased frames, oak sunk sills, mahogany pulley pieces and

Sashes and Frames.

beads, 2-inch Spanish mahogany astragal sashes, brass pulleys
and patent lines   -   -   -   -   -   - per foot super. ·178
Ditto, circular head, measured square   -   -   -   -   ·399
Ditto, circular on plan, flat sweep   -   -   -   -   ·272
Deal cased frames, oak sunk sills, mahogany pulley pieces and
beads, 2½-inch Spanish mahogany astragal sashes, brass axle
pulleys and patent lines   -   -   -   -   -   ·243
Ditto, circular on plan, flat sweep   -   -   -   ·315
Circular circular head ¼ inch to the foot   -   -   -   1·123
If Honduras mahogany, deduct from the straight   -   -   ·029
If Honduras mahogany, deduct from the circular   -   -   ·043
If lamb's tongue, or other modern modelled bar, add on the
astragal   -   -   -   -   -   -   -   ·014

Venetian and Palladian Sashes and Frames, fitted and hung.

Venetian deal cased frames, oak sunk sills, 1¼ inch ovolo sashes,
brass pulleys, double hung with best flax line and iron weights, per foot super. ·111
Ditto, with 2-inch sashes   -   -   -   -   -   ·129
Ditto, circular on plan, flat sweep   -   -   -   -   ·172
Palladian head, measured square   -   -   -   -   ·286
Circular Palladian head, measured square   -   -   -   ·866
Venetian deal cased frames, wainscot pulley pieces and beads,
1½-inch wainscot astragal sashes, brass pulleys and patent lines,
double hung   -   -   -   -   -   -   ·157
Ditto, with 2-inch sashes   -   -   -   -   -   ·172
Ditto, circular on plan, flat sweep   -   -   -   -   ·200
Ditto, Palladian head, measured square   -   -   -   ·342
Circular Palladian head, measured square   -   -   -   ·952
If any of the above are in 2½-inch wainscot, add on the 2-inch
straight   -   -   -   -   -   -   -   ·014
Ditto, on the circular   -   -   -   -   -   -   ·028
Ditto, on the circular circular   -   -   -   -   -   ·043
If in Spanish mahogany, add on similar article in straight wainscot   ·043
Ditto, on the circular   -   -   -   -   -   -   ·114
If lamb's tongue, add on the astragal   -   -   -   -   ·007
When any of the above sashes are with a bevelled bar up to the
rebate, add on the astragal   -   -   -   -   -   ·014

French Casements, fitted and hung.

1½-inch deal ovolo   -   -   -   -   -   - per foot super. ·057
2-inch deal ovolo   -   -   -   -   -   -   ·064
2½-inch deal ovolo   -   -   -   -   -   -   ·071
1½-inch wainscot   -   -   -   -   -   -   ·078
2-inch wainscot   -   -   -   -   -   -   ·086
2½-inch wainscot   -   -   -   -   -   -   ·100
1½-inch Honduras mahogany   -   -   -   -   -   ·086
2-inch Honduras mahogany   -   -   -   -   -   ·100
2½-inch Honduras mahogany   -   -   -   -   -   ·114
1½-inch Spanish mahogany   -   -   -   -   -   ·100
2-inch Spanish mahogany   -   -   -   -   -   ·114
2½-inch Spanish mahogany   -   -   -   -   -   ·129
If with margin lights, add on the deal   -   -   -   -   ·018
If with margin lights, add on the wainscot   -   -   -   ·029
If with margin lights, add on the mahogany   -   -   -   ·036
If in two heights, add   -   -   -   -   -   ·021
If in two heights add, on the wainscot   -   -   -   -   ·029
If in two heights, add on the mahogany   .   -   -   ·043
Circular on the plan, flat sweep, once and a half the straight, and
exceeding ½ inch to the foot, double.
If astragal and hollow lamb's tongue, or other modern bar, add -   ·014
If with bevelled bars up to the rebate, add on the astragal and
hollow   -   -   -   -   -   -   -   ·007
Extra rebated edges, grooves, or beads, in deal -   -   - per foot run   ·014
Extra rebated edges, grooves, or beads, in wainscot   -   -   ·021
Extra rebated edges, grooves, or beads, in mahogany   -   -   ·028

Skylights, fixed.

1½-inch deal ovolo   -   -   -   -   .   -   - per foot super. ·043

SKYLIGHTS.

2-inch deal ovolo	-	-	-	-	-	- per foot super. ·050
2-inch oak ovolo	-	-	-	-	-	·071
If astragal and ovolo, add	-	-	-	-	-	·007

DADO.

¾-inch deal, keyed	-	-	-	-	-	- per foot super. ·043
1-inch deal keyed	-	-	-	-	-	·050
Raking and scribed to steps, add	-	-	-	-	-	·012
If ploughed and tongued, add	-	-	-	-	-	·007
If feather-tongued, add	-	-	-	-	-	·012
Circular on plan, flat sweep	-	-	-	-	-	·143
Circular on plan, quirk sweep	-	-	-	-	-	·229
If 1¼-inch deal, add on the straight	-	-	-	-	-	·007
If 1¼-inch deal, add on the circular	-	-	-	-	-	·014
Narrow dado grounds	-	-	-	-	-	·018
Narrow dado grounds, circular flat sweep	-	-	-	-	-	·043

2369. We have now enumerated the principal articles of joinery in use. If further information be sought, and the reader have not the means of tracing the value in the way by which the constants already given have been obtained, he may refer to some of the price books, whereof we consider Skyring's to be as well digested as any of those that are annually published.

2370. SLATER. The work of the slater is measured and estimated by the square of 100 feet superficial. Of the different sorts of slate, and how much a given quantity of each will cover, we have already spoken in Chap. II. Sect. IX. (1798, *et seq.*) To measure slating, in addition to the nett measure of the work, 6 inches are allowed for all the eaves, and 4 inches by their length for hips; such allowance being made in the first-named case because the slates are there double, and in the latter case for the waste in cutting away the sides of the slates to fit. When rags or imperial slates are used an additional allowance of 9 inches is made for the eaves, because those slates run larger than the other sorts.

2371. MASON. Solid works, such as pilasters, cornices, coping, stringings, and other solid works, should be first measured to ascertain the cubic quantity of stone they contain as going from the *banker* to the building; and on this, work, as it may happen to be the plain work, sunk work, moulded or circular work, must be measured in superficial feet and separately valued. It is usual to allow a plain face to each joint, but no more than one should be taken to a 3-feet length. In staircases the flyers should be taken where splayed on the back, their full length and width by three fifths of the depth of the riser, to allow for waste in getting two of the steps from the same block of stone. The measurement for the winders seems to be most properly conducted by ascertaining the nett cubic contents of them, and then making the allowance for waste. Indeed this is a more proper and satisfactory mode for the flyers. The top of the treads are then taken on the superficies as plain work, and the fronts and ends of the risers as moulded work. In an open staircase, the under side of the flyers is measured as plain work; the under side of the winders as circular plain work; the rebates, cuttings out, pinnings in, &c., as they are found. Cylindrical work, such as of columns, after the cube quantity is ascertained, is measured as equal to plain work twice taken. In Portland dressings to chimneys, wherever edges appear, it is customary to add an inch to the dimensions for extra labour; to marble, ¾ of an inch; or to take the running dimensions of the edges.

2372. Paving slabs and stones under 2 inches thick are taken by superficial measure. Cornices are measured by obtaining their girt, and multiplying by their length for the quantity of moulded work in them.

2373. The following are a few constants of the chief articles of labour in mason's work, applicable, as before mentioned, in the carpenter's and joiner's works.

Plain work	-	-	-	-	- per foot super. ·166
Plain work, rubbed to face	-	-	-	·18
Plain work, tooled	-	-	-	-	·208
Sunk work	-	-	-	-	·222
Moulded work	-	-	-	-	·278
Moulded work, stopped	-	-	-	-	·333
Gothic moulded work	-	-	-	-	·445
Gothic moulded work, stopped	-	-	-	·528
Gothic moulded work, circular	-	-	-	·556
Circular plain work	-	-	-	-	·264
Circular sunk plain work	-	-	-	·333
Circular moulded plain work	-	-	-	·361
Circular, plain moulded work, stopped	-	-	·416

2374. FOUNDER. The proper mode of estimating cast iron is by the ton or cwt. Moulds for the castings, when out of the common course, are charged extra. Very often, too, cast iron pipes and gutters are, according to their sizes, charged by the yard. (See 1754, *et seq.*)

2375. SMITH and IRONMONGER. Wrought iron for chimney bars, iron ties, screw bolts, balusters with straps, area gratings, handrails and balusters, hook-and-eye hinges, brackets for shelves, chains for posts, wrought iron columns with caps and bases, fancy iron railing, casements, shutterbars, and the like, are charged by the pound, at various prices, according to the nature of the work. In the ironmonger's department nails and brads are charged by the hundred, though sold by weight, seldom exceeding 900 to the 1000. Screws, which take their names from their length, are charged by the dozen. Cast, and also wrought butts and screws, cast and wrought back flaps, butts and screws, side or ⊢ hinges, with screws, by the pair. All sorts of bolts with screws, of which the round part of the bolt determines the length, by the inch. ⊢ hinges and cross garnet hinges, by the pair. Other hinges and screws by the piece. Locks by the piece. Pulleys according to their diameters. On all ironmongery 20 per cent. is charged on the prime cost. (See 2253, *et seq.*)

2376. PLASTERER. The work of the plasterer is measured, generally, by the yard. The most usual way of measuring stucco partitions and walls is, to take the height from the upper edge of the ground to half way up the cornice, the extra price of the stucco making good for the deficiency of floated work under it. In ceilings and other work, the surface under the cornice is often taken, because there is no deficiency but in the setting, and that is compensated for by the labour in making good. Cornices are measured by the foot, and estimated according to the quantity of mouldings and enrichments they contain. Where there are more than four angles in a room, each extra one is charged at the price per foot run extra of the cornice. Stucco reveals are charged per foot run, and according to their width of 4 or 9 inches or more. Quirks, arrisses, and beads by the foot run, as are margins to raised panels, small plain mouldings, &c. In the case of enriched cornices and mouldings, and flowers to ceilings, they must be considered with reference to the size and quantity of ornament. For these, the papier maché ornaments, (see 2251.) which are much lighter, are coming now into very general use, and from the ease and security with which they are fixed, will, we have no doubt, within no very distant period, supersede all use of plaster ornaments. In subsection 2248 will be found some information useful in the investigation of the value of plasterers' work, and which might form the basis for a set of constants under that head. But we have not been able to obtain sufficient data for carrying them completely out; which, from the minor importance of this branch of building, is perhaps of no very great consequence.

2377. PLUMBER. The work of this artificer is charged by the cwt., to which is added the labour of laying the lead. Water pipes, rain-water pipes, and funnel pipes are charged by the foot, according to their diameter; so also are socket pipes for sinks, joints being separately paid for. Common lead pumps, with iron work, including bucket, sucker, &c., at so much each; the same with hydraulic and other pumps, according to their diameters. In the same manner are charged water-closets, basins, air traps, washers and plugs, spindle valves, stop-cocks, ball-cocks, &c. (See 2212, *et seq.*)

2378. GLAZIER. The work of the glazier is measured and estimated by the superficial foot, according to the quality of the glass used; it is always measured between the rebates. (See 2225, *et seq.*)

2379. PAINTER. In the measurement and estimation of painting, the superficial quantity is taken, allowing all edges, sinkings, and girths as they appear. When work is cut in on both edges it is taken by the foot run. The quantity of feet is reduced to yards, by which painting is charged for large quantities. In taking iron railing the two sides are measured as flat work; but if it be full of ornament, once and a half, or twice, is taken for each side. Sash frames are taken each, and sash squares by the dozen. On gilding we have already spoken in Sect. XII. (2267, *et seq.*) Cornices, reveals to windows and doors, strings, window sills, water trunks and gutters, handrails, newels, &c., are taken by the foot run. Many small articles by the piece. Plain and enriched cornices by the foot run, according to the quantity of work in them. Work done from a ladder is paid for extra. The price depends on the number of times over that the work is painted; and the labour is usually considered as one third of the price charged. Imitations of woods and marbles are also charged extra.

2380. PAPERHANGER. In common papers the price varies according to the colours or quantity of blocks used in printing the pattern. Embossed and other papers are of higher prices. These, as well as lining paper, are charged by the piece, containing 63 feet super. The hanging is charged separate, and borders, mouldings, &c. by the yard run. (See 2278.)

CHAP. IV.

MEDIUM OF EXPRESSION.

Sect. I.

DRAWING IN GENERAL.

2381. Under this section it is not our intention to enter into the refinements of the art, but merely to make the attempt of directing the student to the first principles of a faithful representation of ordinary and familiar objects, with all their imperfections; or, in other words, of transferring to a plane surface what the artist actually sees or conceives in his mind. This power is of vital importance to the architect, and without it he is unworthy the name.

2382. The usual mode of teaching drawing now in use is, as we conceive, among the most absurd and extravagant methods of imparting instruction that can be well conceived. The learner is usually first put to copying drawings or prints, on which he is occupied for a considerable time. Much more would he learn, and much more quickly, by following the course which the following lines will prescribe. *Outline* is the foundation of all drawing; the alphabet of graphic art. As soon as the student has attained the use of the pencil and the pen in drawing purely geometrical figures, he is prepared to receive the rudiments of perspective. As shown in the following section, the representations of all geometrical solids is dependent upon mechanical means; and these may, if it be desirable, be shadowed truly by the methods given in Sect. III.; but what is now called free-hand drawing is the matter for our present consideration.

2383. Outline, as we have stated above, is the foundation of all drawing, the alphabet of graphic art. Every representation of an object, or series of objects, however complicated, is in reality but a set of outlines composed of straight or curved lines. The knowledge, or rather the power of forming these lines, is essential to the student, and in the same manner that he was obliged to form pothooks and hangers before he proceeded to ellipses when he was taught to write, he should begin his study of free-hand drawing by practising himself in the production of straight lines, proceeding to segments, and then to curves of contrary flexure. It is a good plan to compare the copy with the pattern; and, inasmuch as all formal diagrams that are set as patterns should be perfect, it is desirable that the standards for straight lines, segments, and contrary flexures should be drawn by the teacher himself from rulers; these rulers can be subsequently applied to the copies, and are sometimes the only evidence upon which to make a mutinous pupil conscious of his errors. The student ought not to proceed to the elliptical and oval forms until the hand, first turning one way, can draw a tolerably correct circle; and then, turning in the other direction, can make another equally good. The next step will be to acquire the power of drawing spiral lines in one direction, and of repeating them in another; which will be followed by that of drawing lines either parallel or slowly approximating.

2383a. After this, the student is sufficiently advanced to attempt to repeat all these stages with copies of a size larger or less than the patterns; and he will be ready to learn the mechanical use of chalk. This branch of his tuition needs only such examples as the prints, which have been prepared for that purpose, of purely geometrical forms: in this stage the rudiments of shadow are implanted, and the use of the brush may be acquired.

2383b. The student will then be ready to learn the mode of obtaining local colour, and of blending his materials so as to obtain tints and shades of the different colours. The next steps would be to draw in chalk, in ink, or in colour, the simplest architectural ornaments, such as a chevron or an ovolo; and to proceed through a course of architectural foliage from prints. The result of such training is usually a confidence in the eye; and, what is sometimes highly important, a judgment so sound as to be able to reproduce any part of a subject that may have been destroyed.

2383c. Aptitude of the pupil must be a consideration, but in general a year of steady application may be sufficient so to imbue the mind with the grammar of architectural ornament, as to enable the hand to represent it; after which the student ought to be capable of inventing for himself. Indeed, it is only by such a course that originality in designing ornament can be obtained. The study of natural foliage, first as seen, and then as conventionalized, may be carried out at the same time.

2383*d*. It is very remarkable that all the inferences are false, which usually are derived from the assertion that he who can draw the human figure will be able to draw any other object that is submitted to him for representation. The few men who can *faultlessly* draw the human figure as they see it, may doubtlessly have eyes keen enough and hands true enough to repeat the minutest details so accurately that any comparison of a particular detail with the original shall be creditable to them; but these men have spent years in obtaining, besides delicacy of handling, that knowledge of anatomy which reminds them at every stroke of the pencil that such a muscle is in such a place, that here it overlaps another, that there it dies into a bone, and that consequently they have to mark the curves and angles which occur, for instance, six or seven times between the elbow and the wrist, and to determine how many can be omitted if the scale be less than that of life.

2384. The majority of men who can draw the figure tolerably well can draw nothing else equally correctly: for the reason that their attention has been given to the mechanism of the human form solely; the representation, by our best portrait-painters, of the accessories which they introduce into their pictures, especially of architectural details, is almost without an exception ludicrously inaccurate. Every person who has tried to apply his power of representing geometric forms to the task of copying in chalk from a mask, must be aware of the enormous facility which he acquires by previously studying the usual methods of expressing the totality of the eye, the ear, the nose, and the lips. In a similar manner, the artist who wishes to give the effect of a suite of mouldings, or of a carved ornament, requires to know previously all the parts which compose the work. In other words, some men can pretend to sketch distant rocks and yet miss the very features by which the outlines intimate the geological character.

2385. Such are the reasons which have for many years led to the conviction that the architect's course of drawing should leave the figure alone until he has made one or more studies from carving in each style of art that opportunity presents to him; this is affirmed to be the only method of obtaining a satisfactory appreciation of the minute characteristics which sometimes constitute the differences between styles; and the only method of making a royal road to the object, which some teachers pretend is the easiest, but is truly the most difficult, in art. Having acquired the power of accurate representation of ornament, which involves dexterity in the use of his materials, the student may commence his operations with the figure.

2386. The method proposed in the following pages is old, at least in principle, yet it has been of late years published as new in Paris, by M. Dupuis. ("*De l'Enseignement du Dessin sous le point de vue industriel*," 1836.) The principles of the work, however, are perhaps better expressed and arranged, in some respects, than we might have presented them to the reader: and we shall not, therefore, apologise for the free use we make of it, premising, however, that in respect to the whole figure and the application of the method to landscapes, what follows is not found in the work of M. Dupuis.

2387. Between the ancient mode of teaching the student (we will take the head, for instance, shown in *fig.* 809. as the first roughing of the leading lines of that which in *fig.* 812. has reached its completion) and the method practised by M. Dupuis, the only difference is this, that M. D., instead of letting the student form the rough outline at once from the finished bust, roughing out on paper the principal masses, provides a series of models roughly bossed out in their different stages, which he makes the student draw. The system is ingenious; but as the greatest artists have been made without the modification in question, we do not think it material; at all events, the principles are the same. M. Dupuis, for this purpose, has a series of sixteen models, the first of each four of the series are quite sufficient to show the old as well as his own practice. Thus, in

Fig. 809.   Fig. 810.

fig. 809., the general mass of the oval of the head is given, in which it is seen that the profile is indicated by an obtuse angle, whose extreme point corresponds with the lower part of the nose, and the lines at one extremity terminate with the roots or commencement of the hair, and at the other with the lower jaw. The form of the rest of the head is the result of combining the most projecting points of it by curved lines, in short, of supposing a rough mass, out of which the sculptor might actually, in marble or other material, form the head.

2388. The next step is exhibited in *fig.* 810., with the four principal divisions: the occipital to the beginning of the hair, the forehead to the line of the eyes, the projection of the nose, and the inferior part of the face, with some indication of the mouth.

2389. In *fig.* 811. it will be seen that another step is gained.   The eyes (here only one appears, but we speak with reference to the subject, being less in profile), the mouth, the chin, and the ear are more clearly marked out, with some sort of expression of the whole work, but still without details, though sufficiently indicating that little more is necessary to bring the rude sketch of *fig.* 809. to a resemblance.

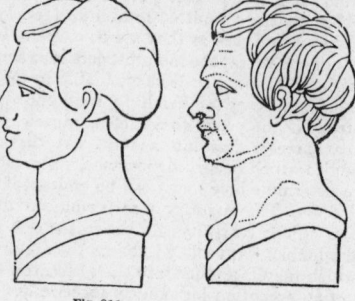

Fig. 811.   Fig. 812.

2390. In *fig.* 812. this is obtained; but still, according to the degree to which an artist considers finishing necessary, to be further pursued and carried through to make a perfect drawing; all that is here intended being to show the principles upon which the matter is conducted, and upon which we shall presently have further observations to make.   It will be observed, that on the shadowing and finishing in this way the drawings the student may make we set no value: when he can draw, if those matters be of importance to him, they will not be difficult of acquisition.

2390a. Having accomplished the art of drawing, with tolerable correctness, the figure, the architect will have little difficulty in drawing the most complex productions of nature. The principles are precisely the same; but we wish here to impress upon him the necessity of recurring to nature herself for his ornaments: a practice which will always impart a freshness and novelty to them which even imitation of the antique will not impart.

2391. The port crayon, whether carrying chalk or a black lead pencil of moderate weight and size, say full seven inches long, is the best instrument to put into the hands of the beginner.   The first object he must consider in roughing the subject, as in *fig.* 809., is the relation the height of the whole bears to its width; and this determined, he must proceed to get the general contour, without regard to any internal divisions, and thus proceed by subdivisions, bearing the relative proportions to each other of the model, comparing them with one another and with the whole.   We will now show how the port crayon assists in this operation.   Let the pupil be supposed seated before the model, at such a distance from it that at a single look, without changing the position of his head upwards, downwards, or sideways, his eye takes in the whole of it.   The strictest attention to this point is necessary, for difficulties immediately present themselves if he is too near, as well as if he is too far from it.   And here let it be observed that the visual rays (see *fig.* 813.) upon every object

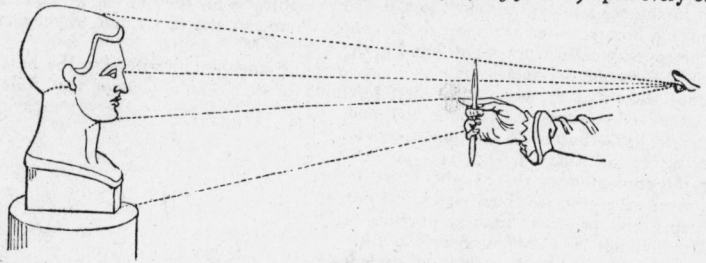

Fig. 813.

may be compared to the legs of a pair of compasses, which open wider as we approach the object and close as we recede from it.   This is a law of perspective well known, and which the student may easily prove by experiment, keeping the head of the compasses near his eye, and opening the legs to take in, in looking along them, any dimension of an object. He will soon find that as he approaches such object he must open the legs wider in order to comprise within them the given dimension.   Hence every diameter or dimension, separately considered, is comprised in the divergence of the visual rays.   It is on this account that, being at a proper distance, any moveable measure which with a free motion of his body he can interpose upon some one of the points of the distance between his eye and the model, may, though much less than the model itself, take in the whole field of view, reach the extremities of the dimension, and consequently become of great assistance in certain mathematical measures.   For by applying such a measure to one division only of the model, we shall obtain, as it were, an integer for finding a great many others into which the model may be subdivided.

2392. Thus, taking *fig.* 809., which is profile, and supposing the width at the neck unity, if this is twice and a half contained in the general height of the bust, we have immediately the proportions of one to two and a half, which may be immediately set out on the paper or canvas.   This is not all; the integer or unity obtained by the diameter of the

neck serves also for measuring the horizontal diameter of the head, and also of the bust; whence new proportions may be obtained. So much for the first casting of the general form. Now, in the entire bust, as respects the head only, suppose we wish to obtain the proportions of the principal divisions, — for example, from the base of the bust to the base of the chin, — we may establish another integer to measure other parts; as, if from the point of view, the distance from the base of the bust to the base of the chin is the same as from the last to the summit of the head, the learner would have nothing more to do in that respect than to divide the whole height into two equal parts. On the same principle, passing from divisions to subdivisions, the distance between the base of the chin and the point whence the nose begins to project, may be found a measure for the height of the nose, and from thence to the top of the cranium. We are here merely showing the method of obtaining different integers for measuring the different parts mentioned; others will in practice occur continually, after a very little practice. We do not suppose our readers will believe that we propose to teach drawing by mathematical rules; we now only speak of obtaining points from which undulating and varying lines are to spring and return, and which none but a fine and sensitive eye will be able to express. But to return to the port crayon, which is the moveable measure or compasses whereto we have alluded, and requires only skilful handling to perform the offices of compasses, square, plumb rule, and level. By interposing it (see *fig.* 813.) on the divergence of the visual rays between the eye and the object, we may estimate the relative proportions; since in the field of view the learner may apply it to the whole or any of the parts, and make any one a measure for another. For this purpose he must hold it, as shown in the figure, steadily and at arm's length. Any portion of it that is cut by the visual rays between any two parts of the object, becomes the integer for the measurement of other parts whereof we have been speaking. This in the drawing will be increased according as the size is greater or less than the portion of the port crayon intercepting the visual rays. This process may be easily accomplished by making, upon one and the same line of the visual ray, the extreme point of the port crayon to touch one of the extremities of the proportion sought upon the model, so that they may exactly correspond. Then at the same time fixing the thumb or fore-finger where the visual ray from the other extremity is intercepted, we shall find any equal length by moving the port crayon with the thumb and fore-finger fixed to any other part we want, as to size, to compare with the first, or by using the same expedient to other parts, other integers may be found. The different integers, indeed, which may be thus obtained is infinite. The port crayon will also serve the purpose of a plumb bob by laying hold of it by the chalk, and holding it just only so tight between the fingers as to prevent its falling, so that its own gravity makes it assume a vertical direction.

Doing so, if it then be held up to intercept the visual rays, we may discover the proportion in which a line swells whose directon approaches the vertical, as also the quantity one part projects before another in the model; and comparing this again with the integer, obtain new points for starting from. Again, by holding it before the eye in an horizontal direction, we shall obtain the different parts of the model that lie before the eye in the same horizontal line. By degrees we shall thus soon find the eye become familiarised with the model it contemplates; judgment in arranging the parts supervenes; the hand becomes bold and unhesitating, and the leading forms are quickly transferred to the paper or canvas to be subdivided to such extent as is required by the degree of finish intended to be bestowed upon the drawing.

2393. The process that we have considered more with relation to the bust is equally applicable to the whole figure. In *fig.* 814. we have more particularly shown by the dotted lines the horizontal and vertical use of the port crayon; but the previous adjustment of some measure of unity for proportioning the great divisions to each other is also applied to it as already stated. In the figure, EE is the line of the horizon, or that level with the eye; it will be

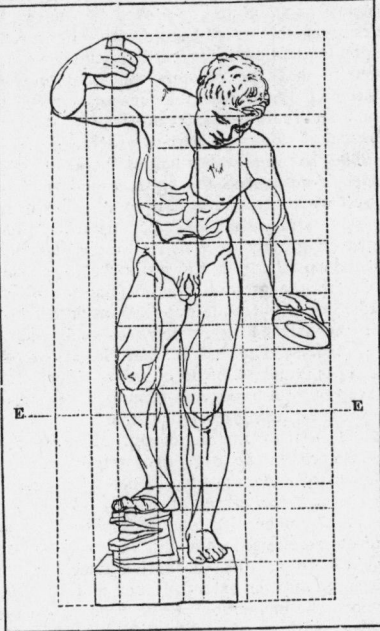

Fig. 814.

seen passing through the knee of that leg upon which the principal weight of the body is thrown.

2394. Though our object in this section is to give only a notion of the way of transferring to paper or canvas such objects as present themselves, we think it proper to hint at a few general matters which the student will do well to consider, and these relate to the balance and motion of the human figure. Geometry and arithmetic were with the painters of antiquity of such importance that Pamphilus the master of Apelles declared, without them art could not be perfected. Vitruvius particularly tells us the same thing, and, as follows, gives the proportions of the human figure: — "From the chin to the top of the forehead, or to the roots of the hair, is a tenth part of the height of the whole body; from the chin to the crown of the head is an eighth part of the whole height; and from the nape of the neck to the crown of the head, the same. From the upper part of the breast to the roots of the hair, a sixth; to the crown of the head, a fourth. A third part of the height of the face is equal to that from the chin to the under side of the nostrils, and thence to the middle of the eyebrows the same: from the last to the roots of the hair, where the forehead ends, the remaining third part. The length of the foot is a sixth part of the height of the body; the fore-arm, a fourth part; the width of the breast a fourth part. Similarly," continues our author, "have the other members their due proportions, by attention to which the ancient painters and sculptors obtained so much reputation. Just so, the parts of temples should correspond with each other and with the whole. The navel is naturally placed in the centre of the human body; and if a man lie with his face upwards, and his hands and feet extended, and from his navel as the centre, a circle be described, it will touch his fingers and toes. It is not alone by a circle that the human body is thus circumscribed, as may be seen (*fig.* 815.) by placing it within a square. For, measuring from the feet to the crown of the head, and then across the arms fully extended, we find the latter measure equal to the former; so that the lines at right angles to each other, enclosing the figure, will form a square."

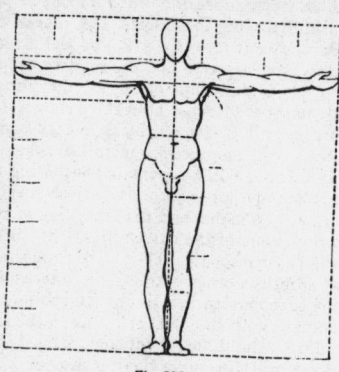

Fig. 815.

2395. "How well," says Flaxman (*Lectures on Sculpture*), "the ancients understood the balance of the figure, is proved by the two books of Archimedes on that subject; besides, it is impossible to see the numerous figures, springing, jumping, dancing, and falling, in the Herculaneum paintings, on the painted vases, and the antique basso-rilievos, without being assured that the painters and sculptors must have employed geometrical figures to determine the degrees of curvature in the body, and angular or rectilinear extent of the limbs, and to fix the centre of gravity." Leonardo da Vinci has illustrated the subject in his *Trattato di Pittura*, a perusal of which cannot fail of being highly beneficial to the student.

2396. As in all other bodies, the centre of gravity of the human figure is that point from which, if suspended, the figure would remain at rest when turned round upon it. Flaxman, by some strange mistake, has described the centre of gravity as "an imaginary straight *line*, which falls from the gullet between the ankles to the ground, when it (the figure) is perfectly upright, equally poised on both feet, with the hands hanging down on each side." (*Fig.* 816.). The fact is, that the centre of gravity is found to be in a line so drawn, or rather removed backwards from it, in a vertical plane returning from that line.

2397. Motion implies change of position; for instance, in *fig.* 817., the weight of the figure is thrown on one leg, hence a line passing through the centre of gravity falls from

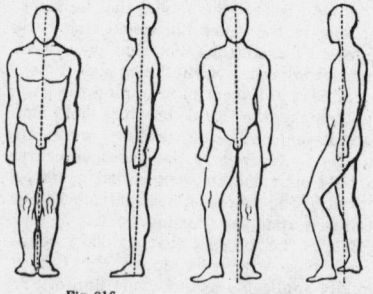

Fig. 816.   Fig. 817.

the gullet on one leg, on which side also the shoulder becomes lowered, and that on the opposite side raised; the hip and knee sinking below those on the side supporting the weight. In *fig.* 818. the dotted lines terminated by the letters ABCD represent lines of motion, as also the extent of such motion. The same are also shown in *fig.* 819., wherein A shows the inclination of the head to the breast; B the extreme bend of the back over the legs, without changing their position; C that of the back bent backwards, the legs

remaining in the same position. If the back be bent as far as D, the thighs and legs will project as far as E.

2398. Referring back to *fig.* 817. for comparison, as the commencement of motion, with *fig.* 820., we shall immediately see that the preparation for running consists in throwing the balance beyond the standing foot; and that when the centre of gravity, which is now about to take place, falls out of the common base, the hinder leg must be out, and off the ground, to balance the fore part of the figure, which would otherwise fall.

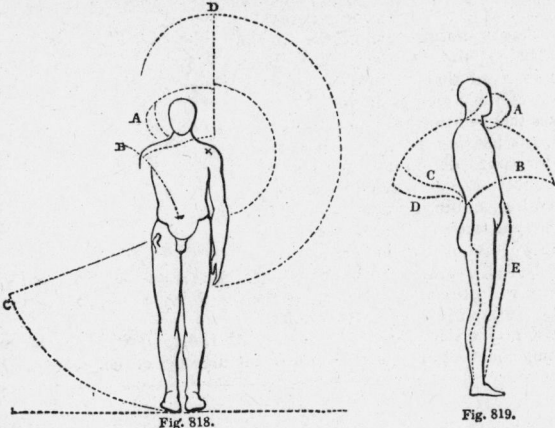

Fig. 818.   Fig. 819.

2399. In preparing to strike (*fig.* 821.), the figure is thrown back at the beginning of

Fig. 820.   Fig. 821.

the action to give force to the blow: the dotted line shows the extent of the springing forward, in which the action is ended by the fall of the blow upon the object.

2400. In *fig.* 822., bearing a weight, the combined centres of gravity of the figure and

Fig. 822.   Fig. 823.   Fig. 824.

the weight to be borne must be found; and through it the line falls between the feet, if the whole weight rests equally on both, or on the supporting foot, if the weight is thrown upon one. Flaxman, who was a finer artist than a geometrician, has, in his lectures, fallen into another mistake on this head, by saying the centre of gravity is the centre of the incumbent weight, which is absurd; because the figure has not only to balance the weight itself, but also its own weight.

2401. In leaping (*fig.* 823.), the body and thighs are drawn together to prepare for the spring; the muscles of the leg draw up the heel, and the figure rests on the ball of the foot; the arms are thrown back to be ready immediately for swinging forward, and thus assisting in the impulse. When the figure alights, the arms, at the instant of alighting, will be found raised above the head; and a line dropped from the centre of gravity will be found to fall near the heels.

2402. In leaning (*fig.* 824.), if on more than one point, the greatest weight is about that point on which the figure chiefly rests.

2403. *Fig. 825.* is a flying, and *fig.* 826. a falling figure, both where- of being in motion through the air rest on no point. In the first it will be observed that the heaviest por- tion of the figure is bounded by lines inclined upwards; as in fall- ing the heaviest portion of it has a downward direction. We have thought these elements would be useful, as exhibiting those leading principles without the comprehen- sion whereof no motion or action

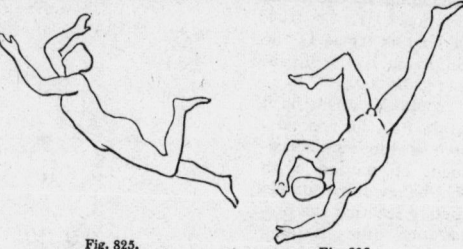

Fig. 825.   Fig. 826.

can be well expressed. "Every change," says Flaxman, "of position or action in the human figure will present the diligent student with some new application of principles, and some valuable example for his imitation."

2404. We shall close this section with the application of the principles detailed in the management of the port crayon to the drawing of landscapes. The subject of *figs.* 827.

Fig. 827.

Fig. 828.

and 828. is from a spot a little way out of Rome, the tower of Cæcilia Metella being seen in the distance.

2404a. In *fig.* 826. the masses are roughed in from the objects themselves; and the principal mass *abc*0l*d* on the left side is first very carefully drawn by itself, being, as respects leading lines and thicknesses, corrected until the eye is satisfied of the truth of its general form. The eye is as high as E and E, which therefore show the height of the horizontal line, and are also, in fact, the vanishing points for the wall on the right-hand side of the picture, and the house on the same side a little beyond it. Holding the port crayon level, and taking on it with the thumb or forefinger the distance 0l, we shall find that twice that measure in 2 and 3 will give the junction of the wall with the pier; and that a line continued horizontally from *d* cuts the top of the plinth of the gate pier. The picture happens to be divided into two equal parts by a vertical line drawn through the break in the city wall in the distance. *d*l, continued upwards, determines one side of the house on the right-hand side of the road, and from a point at a break in the foreground intersects the projecting wall at *e* : a vertical line determines the left side of the tower. The remaining horizontal lines, it will be seen, determine other points and lines; and thus it is manifest that the whole arrangement has been accomplished by making the mass *abc*0l*d* a measure or unit for ascertaining the size and relative position of the other parts. In *fig.* 828. the detail is filled in, and brought to a higher state of finish.

2404b. There is a mechanical method of obtaining the exact relative sizes of objects, and their positions in making drawings from nature or casts, which we will endeavour to explain. If the draftsman take a pair of pretty large sized compasses, and, fastening a piece of string at the joint end of them, hold the points open before his eye, so as to take in the extent of space his drawing is intended to occupy; then tie a knot in the string to keep it between his teeth, so that the compasses' points may be kept in any plane always equally distant from the eye; he may, for the various parts of his drawing, by opening or closing the compasses, have their exact relative heights, widths, and positions, to be at once transferred to the drawing.

Sect. II.

PERSPECTIVE.

2405. A perspective delineation is the linear representation of any object or objects, as it or they appear to the eye, and is such a figure of an object as may be supposed to be made by a plane making a section of the body or pyramid of visual rays directed from the eye to the different parts of the object. A delineation so made, being properly coloured and shadowed, will convey a lively idea of the real object, and at the same time indicate its position and distance from the eye of the observer.

2406. DEFINITIONS. — 1. *An original object* or *objects* is or are an object or number of objects proposed to be delineated : for instance, a house, a ship, a man, or all or any of them together. In *fig.* 829. the house ABCDFHK is the original object.

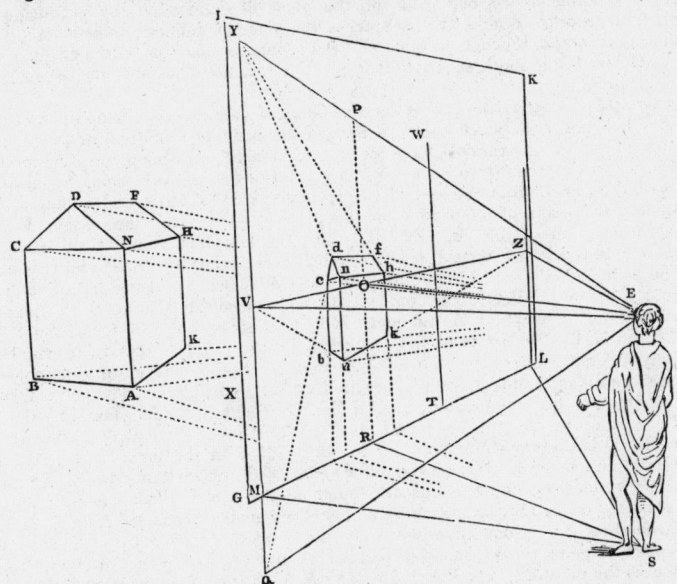

Fig. 829.

2. *Original lines* are any lines that are the boundaries of original objects, or of planes in those objects. The lines AB, BC, CD are original lines, being partly the boundaries of the original object ABCDFHK.

3. The *ground plane* is that upon which the objects to be drawn are placed, and is

always considered a boundless level plane. The plane X in the figure is the ground plane, upon which is placed the object ABCDFHK.

4. *The point of view* or *point of sight* is the fixed place of the eye of the observer, viewing the object or objects to be delineated : E in the figure is such point.

5. *The station point* is a point on the ground plane, perpendicularly under the point of sight or eye of the observer, and expresses on the plan the station whence the view is taken. S is the station point in the figure, being a point on the ground plane vertically under the eye of the observer at E.

6. *The plane of delineation* or *the picture* is the canvas or paper whereon it is intended to draw any object or number of objects. Thus, in the figure, the plane GIKL is the plane of delineation; but, in the extensive sense of the word, the plane of delineation is considered a boundless plane, however circumscribed may be the delineation made thereon.

7. *The horizontal line* or *the horizon* is a line on the plane of delineation in every part level with the eye of the observer or point of view. VZ is the horizontal line on the plane of delineation GIKL. It is supposed to be obtained by the intersection of a plane passing through the eye of the observer, parallel to the ground plane, produced till it touches the plane of delineation.

8. *The centre of the picture* is a point perpendicularly opposite the eye of the observer, or point of view, and is consequently always somewhere in the horizontal line. O in the horizontal line VZ is the centre of the picture, being perpendicularly opposite to the eye at E.

9. *The vertical line* is a line drawn through the centre of the picture perpendicular to the horizon. In the figure PR is the vertical line. It is here worthy of notice that the vertical line determines how much of the view lies to the right and how much to the left of the eye of the artist.

10. *The distance of the picture* is a direct line from the eye to the centre of the picture. EO is the distance of the picture, or plane of delineation, GIKL.

11. *The ground line* is that where the ground plane intersects the plane of delineation, as GL in the figure.

12. *An intersecting point* is one made on the plane of delineation, by producing a line in an original object till it touches the plane of delineation. Thus, T is the intersecting point of the original line BA.

13. *An intersecting line* is one made on the plane of delineation, by producing any plane in an original object till it touches the plane of delineation, or where, if produced, it would touch it. Thus WT is the intersecting line of the original plane ABCDN, being the line, where that plane, if produced, would touch the plane of delineation.

14. *A vanishing point* is that point on the plane of delineation to which two or more lines will converge, when they are the perspective representations of two or more parallel lines in an original object, whose seat is inclined to the plane of delineation. The point V in the figure is the vanishing point of the line AB, being found by the line EV, drawn from the eye of the spectator parallel to it, and produced till it touches the plane of delineation in the point V. For a similar reason, V is the vanishing point of the line CN; it is also the vanishing point for any other line parallel to the line CN, as BA; all parallel lines having the same vanishing point. The point Z is the vanishing point of the line AK, being obtained by a line drawn from the eye parallel to the line AK, and produced till it touches the plane of delineation. The point Z, moreover, is the vanishing point of the original lines DF and NH. And it is to be recollected by the student, that there will be as many different vanishing points of lines in the delineation of an original object as there are different directions of lines in that original object. The point Y is the vanishing point of the parallel original lines DN and FH, being found by the line EY being drawn from the eye parallel to them till it touches the plane of delineation. So also Q is the vanishing point of the line CD. In the process of perspective delineations, as we shall presently see, the plan of the object being drawn, the places of the various vanishing points are found on the ground line, whence they are transferred to the horizontal line by means of perpendiculars raised from them.

15. *A vanishing line* is one supposed to be made on the picture by a plane passing through the eye of the observer parallel to any original plane produced till it touches the picture. The line VZ is the vanishing line of an horizontal plane, and of all horizontal planes, being found by the intersection of a plane passing horizontally through the eye, or parallel to an horizontal plane. The vertical line YVM is the vanishing line of the original vertical plane, ABCDN being the line where a plane passing the eye of the spectator parallel to that plane would touch the plane of delineation. There will be as many different vanishing lines on the plane of delineation as there are different positions of planes in the object or objects; and

all parallel planes will have the same vanishing line. Similarly, all lines lying in the same plane will have their vanishing points in the vanishing line of that plane. All planes or lines in an original object which are situated parallel to the plane of delineation can have no vanishing lines or vanishing points on the plane of delineation.

16. *A visual ray* is an imaginary right line, drawn from the eye to any point of observation. EA and EY, &c. are visual rays, being right lines drawn from the eye to the points A and Y. Hence a number of visual rays directed to every part of an object will form a pyramid of rays, whereof the eye is the apex, and the object the base.

17. *A perspective delineation*, then, is the section of a pyramid of rays producing a perspective projection, and is most commonly considered as being made between the object and the eye. But the section of rays may be taken when they are extended beyond the object; in which case such a section is called a *projected* perspective representation of the object.

2407. It will then be seen that a knowledge of perspective is, as Addison has said, a knowledge of " the science by which things are ranged in picture, according to their appearance in their real situation."

2408. The situation of the objects being given with the plan and position of the plane of delineation and the height and distance of the eye of the observer, the delineation of such objects is truly determinable by rule. The mechanical operations necessary for this purpose form the subject of what follows. It is however necessary, before proceeding to lay them before the reader, to premise that he must thoroughly study and understand the preceding definitions before he can proceed with profit to himself, and we recommend a repeated perusal of them until that be effectually accomplished.

2409. Example I. In *fig.* 830., No. 1., we have the plan of the original object

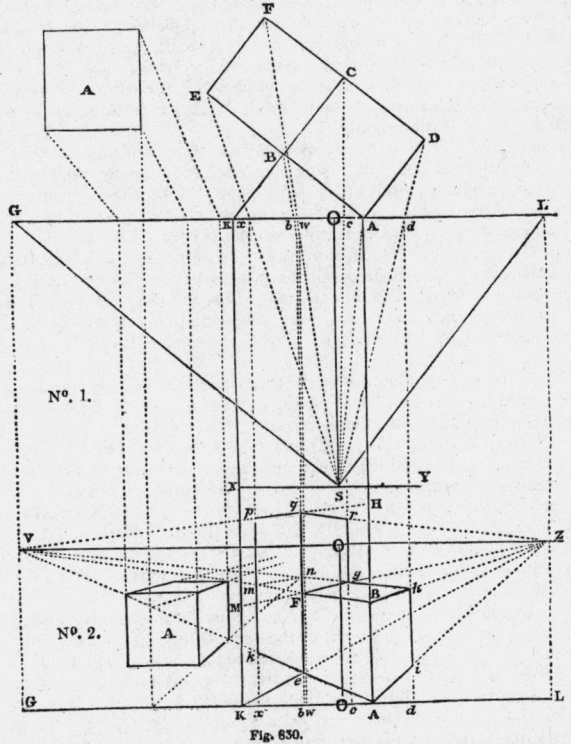

Fig. 830.

EBADCF, whereof ABCD is a cube, and BCEF a double cube, that is, twice the height of CBAD. GL is the plan of the ground line; S, the station point. Through S draw XY parallel to the plane of delineation GL, and draw SG and SL respectively parallel to the sides EA and AD of the united cubes ABCD and BCFE; and these produced to meet

the plane of delineation will determine the vanishing points (Def. 14.) of the horizontal lines AE and AD, and of all other horizontal lines parallel to them. Draw the line SO perpendicular to GL, which line being the direction of the eye perpendicular to the plane of the picture determines the point thereon to which the eye should be directly opposite to view it when completed, showing also how much of the object is on one side, and how much on the other of the point of view. We have now to draw the visual rays SA, SB, SE, SF, SC, SD, cutting the plane of the picture or delineation in b, x, w, c, and d; the point A of the nearest cube touching, itself, the picture at that point. The preparation on the plan is now completed.

2410. The picture (No. 2.) or plane of delineation is to be prepared as follows : — First draw the ground line GL, and to such ground line transfer, by dropping verticals, the points KxbwcA and d. Above, and parallel to GL, at such convenient height as may be necessary to show more or less of the upper surfaces of the cubes or otherwise, as desired, draw the horizontal line VZ ; mark on such horizontal line the point O, to which the eye is supposed to be perpendicularly opposite for viewing the delineation when completed. All the other preparations are obtained from the plan, and may be obtained as follows : — First set off on the horizontal line VZ the points V and Z, which are the vanishing points of the sides AE and AD respectively. As A, the nearest angle of the object, touches the plane of delineation, it is manifest that a line vertically drawn from that point will be of the same height as the object itself, that is, as the figures are cubes, equal to AB or AD in the plan No. 1. Take, therefore, AB No. 2. of the height required, and draw the lines BV and AV, also AZ and BZ, which being crossed by verticals carried up from xbwcd will determine the points ke and i at the bottom, and in f AE and h at the top, and pq and r in the part where the cube is double the height. Drawing hV it is intersected by the verticals from the visual rays at c and w, cutting in g and n. The line KK forms another line of heights, if desired, for finding the height Fq; indeed, by continuing any line BC (No. 1.) to K, intersecting the picture, a line of height may be obtained. The representation of the cube marked A will be understood without difficulty, if what has preceded be well comprehended. As by Definition 15. we have seen that all planes or lines in an original object situated parallel to the plane of delineation have no vanishing lines or points in the plane of delineation, so two of the sides of the cube will be bounded by horizontal and vertical lines, inasmuch as those sides lie parallel to the plane of delineation. The vanishing points for the other lines will of course be found in O, which passes through the picture at right angles to it from S, the station point.

2411. Example II. To find the representation of a quadrangular building, situated inclined to the picture, covered with a single spanned roof, having a gable at each end.

2412. Let the rectangle ABCD (No. 4.) (fig. 831.) be the plan of the building, the line EF will be the place of the ridge of the roof extending from end to end. Let the line QL be the place of the plane of delineation, and let S be the station point.

2413. Find O the centre of the picture, also the points Q and L, the vanishing points of the lines AB and AD, and their parallels, by lines drawn from S parallel to such lines, and intersecting the picture. Produce the face of the building AD to I for an intersection with the picture, and draw the visual rays intersecting the ground line of the picture in the points beaf and d. These need not, however, be drawn beyond the plane of delineation.

2414. Prepare the picture (No. 5.) by drawing the horizontal and ground lines VZ and GR at any distance from each other at pleasure ; fix upon the centre of the picture O, and draw the vertical line OO; set off the distances of the vanishing points OV and OZ, equal the distances of the vanishing points OQ and OL in No. 4. Draw the intersecting line IL (No. 5.), and all the visual lines, through the points beaf and d, taken from their respective places and distances beaf and d (No. 4.), and proceed as follows : —

2415. On the intersecting line IL (No. 5.) set up the height IK equal to the height of the building BC or HG (Nos. 1. and 2.), and draw the lines KZ and IZ, determining the plane gmop for the front of the building. Draw the lines mV and gV, determining the end of the building ghim. It now remains to place the roof, which is readily done, but which, however, requires some circumspection in the process.

2416. Place the height of the roof XD (No. 1.) on the intersecting line at IL (No. 5.), and draw LZ, which will give the height of the roof on the angular line of the building gm at r ; from which spot it may readily be transferred to its proper place in the visual line ek by the line rV, which cuts the line ek in the point k, the point required. From the point k draw the lines ki and km, completing the gable end of the building. Draw the ridge of the roof kZ, cutting the end visual line, in the point n ; and lastly, draw the line no, completing the whole linear delineation of the building ghiknop. It is to be observed, that whatever original plane is produced to the picture to obtain an intersection, such intersection serves only to obtain heights in the direction of that plane ; whence they may be transferred to other planes in contact with it, as in the present instance. The intersecting line IL (No. 5.) is the intersecting line of the plane gmop ; hence any original height set up

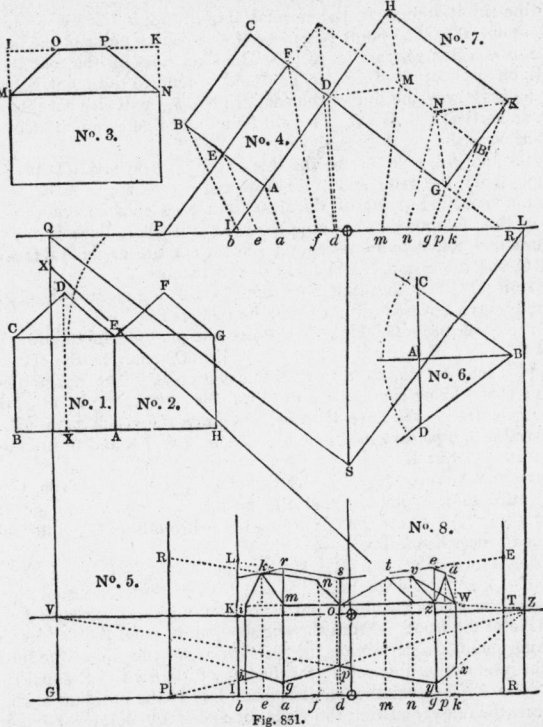

Fig. 851.

thereon can only be transferred throughout the direction of that plane. Thus the height of the roof 1L was transferred by the line LZ along that plane to its other extremity s; but the line rs is not the place of the ridge of the roof, which lies in the middle of the plane $ghikm$, proceeding from the point k; but any height on the angular line gr is easily transferred along that plane by means of its horizontal vanishing point V, by which means the height of the roof was obtained by the line rV at k. If, instead of the plane over the line AD (No. 4.) being produced for an intersection, the plane of the middle of the house in the direction of the ridge of the roof had been drawn, and the height of the roof had been set up on that line, it would at one application be transferred to its proper place.

2417. Let the line FE (No. 4.) be produced to P for an intersection, set off the distance OP at OP (No. 5.), and draw the intersecting line PR. On PR set up the height of the ridge of the roof equal XD (No. 1.), and draw the ridge line RZ, and it determines the exact ridge of the roof between the proper visual lines, and will be found to correspond exactly with the ridge obtained by the former process.

2418. The roof may, however, be found by another process, thus:—The slant lines of the roof have their vanishing points on the picture as well as any other direction of lines in the same object. The line km (No. 5.) being in the vertical plane $ghikm$, will have its vanishing points somewhere in the vanishing line of that plane. (Def. 15.) A vertical line drawn through the horizontal vanishing point V will be the vanishing line of the plane $ghikm$; therefore the vanishing point of the lines km, ki, and of all lines parallel to them, will be somewhere in the vertical GVXQ.

2419. Two lines drawn from the eye parallel to any two lines in an object, finding their vanishing points, will make the same angle at the eye as the lines in the object make with each other; for the two lines in the one instance are respectively parallel to the two lines in the other.

2420. The line SQ is drawn from the station S parallel to the line AB (No. 4.), and a line drawn from the station S, making the same angle with SQ as ED does with EC, (No. 1.), will find the vanishing point of the line ED, and this point must be evidently somewhere in a vertical line through the point Q. To obtain this point in practice, take the distance of the vanishing line it is in, that is, the length from S to Q in the compasses, and set off the same in the horizon (No. 5.) from V. to W. At the point W make an angle VWX equal to the inclination of the roof, that is, equal to the angle CED (No. 1.), and

produce the line till it intersects the vertical line through the vanishing point V in the horizon in the point X. The point X will be the vanishing point of the line of the roof *km* (No. 5.), and of the line *no*, parallel to it. The slant lines of the roof *km* and *no*, already obtained, will, on application of a ruler, be found to tend to the point X, as above stated.

2421. In the same way the line of the roof *ki* (No. 5.) will also have its vanishing point, and in the same vertical line GVQ. It will be found to be as much below the horizontal vanishing point V as the point X is above it. (Def. 14.)

2422. Let the line AB (No. 6.) be the line of the horizon, and CD the vanishing line of a vertical plane, being the gable end of a house, and let the angle ABC be that of inclination, finding the vanishing point of the slant lines of a roof in one direction. Let the line BD be the line, finding the vanishing point of the slant lines in the other direction, having the same inclination to an horizontal line; then the angle ABD will be equal to the angle ABC, and the distance AD equal to the distance AC.

2423. Example III. To find the representation of a quadrangular building situated inclined to the picture, covered with a single hipped roof.

2424. Let the quadrangle GDHK (No. 7.) be the plan of the building; the line MN will represent the ridge of the roof. The former line QL may be the place of the plane of delineation, and it may be viewed from the same station S. The position and direction of the lines of this object being the same as those of the last example, the preparatory lines will also answer for this. We have then only to draw the visual rays MS, NS, CS, PS, and KS, intersecting the picture in the points *m, n, g, p*, and *k*, and to produce the line DG for an intersecting point at R.

2425. Prepare the picture (No. 8.); let the line VZ be the horizon, GR the ground line, O the centre of the picture, and the points *m, n, g p*, and *k* coresponding with *m, n, g, p* and *k*. (No. 7.) Draw the visual line lines through those points and the intersecting point R, and proceed as follows: —

2426. On the intersecting line RE set up the height RT, equal the height of the object HG (No. 2.), and draw the lines TV and RV, cutting the visual lines of the front of the building in the points *z* and *o, y* and *p*, determining the plane *ypoz* for the representation of the plane of the front. From the angular points *z* and *y* draw the lines *zw* and *yx* to their vanishing point Z determining the plane *yzwx* for the end of the building.

2427. On the intersecting line set up the height of the roof TE equal the height NK (No. 3.), and draw EV cutting the angular visual line of the building in the point *e*, from which point draw the line *ez*, cutting the visual line *pa* in the point *a*, the point of direction of the ridge of the roof. Draw the line *a*V, which, cutting the visual lines through the points *m* and *n* in the points *t* and *v*, determines the exact position of the ridge of the roof *tv*, which is the representation of OP (No. 3.), or of the ridge MN (No. 7.); draw the lines *to, vz*, and *vw*, which will complete the whole representation required. In No. 8., if the lines *az* and *aw* be drawn, they will form a gable end *yzawx*, of which the point *a* is the point of the gable, and will answer for the direction of the ridge, whether it be a gable end or a hipped roof, for in both cases it lies in the middle of the breadth of the house; wherefore the line *a*V answers as well the edge of a hipped roof as of a gable end.

2428. In examining the plans (Nos. 4. and 7.) of the two buildings, it will be seen that they are placed at right angles to each other, and in contact at the point D, so that the second example might have been easily accomplished from the first, without the aid of another intersection and other preparatory lines, than the additional visual rays from the angles, which the student will have surely no difficulty in carrying through, without the necessity of encumbering these pages with the detail.

2429. Example IV. In *fig.* 832. No. 1. is the general plan of a church similar to many country churches. ABCD is the main body of it; EFGH its tower; IKLM and MLNO subordinate parts of the building, and *abcd* the porch. No. 2. is its geometrical elevation; the ends and measurements, AB and BC, answering to IM and MO in No. 1., and the points of the roofs D, E, and F. (No. 2.) answering to the lines of the ridges QR, TV, and PL, No. 1. To find the perspective representation of this building on the plane of delineation YZ, the station being at S, the following is, perhaps, the readiest process.

2430. Find the vanishing points Y and Z of the horizontal lines of the building by the lines SY and SZ being drawn from the station parallel to them. O is the centre of the picture. Draw the visual rays from the visible angles of the object in direction to the station S, to intersect the plane of delineation.

2431. When a complicated object, that is, one composed of many parts, is to be drawn, it requires, of course, a great number of visual rays for the precise determination of those parts, and the whole together forms an apparently confused number of lines. The eye, however, which views them properly, does not perceive that confusion; and, if it perplex the student, different coloured inks, or of different shades of depth, may be used to particularise different parts. In the delineation of such an object as the present example, the most important consideration is the choice of a proper intersection; for though any inter-

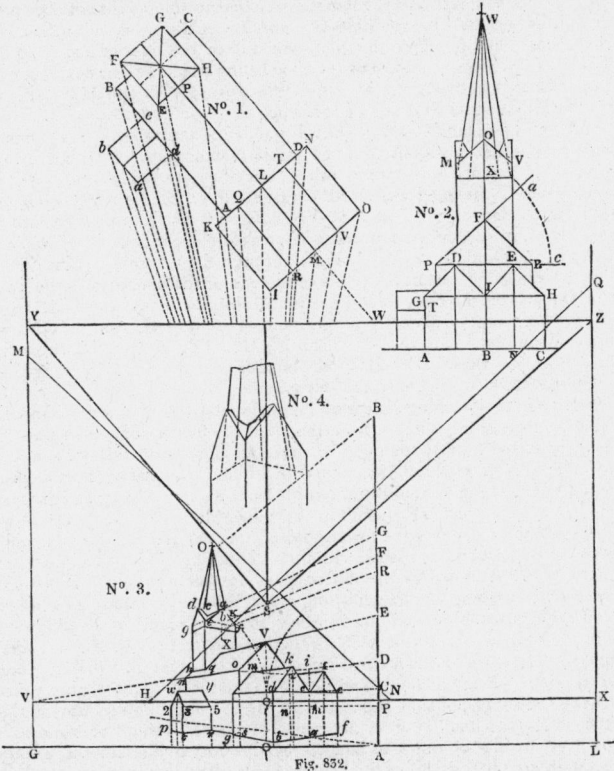

Fig. 852.

section will do, that should be chosen which unites most parts in its direction with the greatest exactness and the least trouble. In the case under consideration, none seems more eligible than the direction of the roof PLM, which produce to W.

2432. In the picture No. 3., GL is the ground line, GV the height of the horizon, the line VX being then the horizontal line. O in the horizon is then the centre of the picture, from which, place the distances of the horizontal vanishing points OV and OX equal OY and OZ, No. 1. AB (No. 3.) is the intersecting line, and all the visual lines on the plane of delineation are drawn conformably to their intersections on the ground line in the plan. On the intersecting line the height AC is made equal to the height AG of the elevation No. 2.; and the lines Cc and Aa, being drawn in direction to the vanishing point V, determine the height ac; being the height of that part of the building on the visual line answering to the ray from the point M in the plan No. 1. Through the points a and c draw the lines de and bf to their vanishing point X, determining the plane bdef, the representation of the plane AGHC, No. 2.; the visual lines bd and fe answering to the rays from the points I and O in the plan. Draw the lines dh and bg tending to their vanishing point V, to the ray from K in the plan completing the plane bghd. On the intersection make the height AD equal to the height of the roof NE of the elevation No. 2., and draw Di in direction to V. Through i draw the line kl to the vanishing point X, touching the visual lines of the roofs in the points k and l. Draw the lines km, mh, kd, kc, lc and le, which will complete the whole of the structure over the plan IKNO, No. 1.

2433. The height of the roofs of the low buildings is equal to the height of the upright walls of the body of the building, as shown by the line PR in the elevation No. 2.; hence, the line mo, and the return line on, may be drawn to the visual lines corresponding with the intersections from the angles A and B of the plan From the angle g the line gs may also be drawn, which will determine the lines sr, rt, and tp of the porch. Make AE on the intersection equal to the height of the roof BF in the elevation, and draw the line EV determining the ridge of the roof between the two visual lines from the points P and L of the plan. Draw the lines of the gable end ·vo and vz, the point z being obtained by the line om drawn to its vanishing point X, cutting the visual line from the angle D of the plan in the point z.

2434. Make AG and AF on the intersection equal to the heights of the tower BO and BM of the elevation, and draw the lines GV and FV cutting the visual line from P in the plan, in the points a and b; through which points draw the lines ac and ef to their vanishing point X; and the lines cd and eg to their vanishing point V; the points g, e, and f being in the proper visual lines from the angles of the tower F, E, and H in the plan. The tower will be completed by drawing the lines dg, de, ae, and af.

2435. This example elucidates the general practice of vanishing points, which are as well to be obtained of other positions of lines as horizontal ones. It is not always that the vanishing points of inclined lines are required, but they are often useful, and sometimes absolutely necessary. In the geometrical elevation No. 2. the lines MO, PF, GD, IE are all parallel lines, as also are the lines OV, FR, EH, and DI, and though situated in different, yet they are in parallel planes, and will therefore have a common vanishing point. A line drawn perpendicularly to the horizon through the vanishing point X (*fig.* 3.), as LQ, will be the vanishing line of the plane of the end of the church over the line IO of the plan, also of the end of the body AD, likewise of the side of the tower EH; and a line drawn through the point V (No. 3.) perpendicularly to the horizon, as GM, will be the vanishing line of the planes over the lines (No. 1.) IK, AB, ab of the porch, and FE of the tower, and all lines in those planes, or the boundaries of those planes, will have their vanishing points somewhere in those vanishing lines.

2436. To obtain the vanishing points of the inclined lines of the roofs and tower, take the distance of the vanishing point Z from the station S in the compasses, and apply it on the horizon from X to H. At the point H make an angle with the horizontal line equal the angle of the roofs aPc (No. 2.); the curve KI and the distance of it from the centre H being equal to the curve ac, and distance of it from its centre P: then is the angle KHI equal to the angle of the roof aPc (No. 2.). Produce the line HK to Q; Q will be the vanishing point of the line ea of the tower, also of the parallel lines ov, dk, and cl, which, though obtained by a different process, will all be found, by application of a ruler, to tend truly to that point, as is shown by the dotted lines in the example. Proceeding in the same way with the distance of the vanishing point Y from the station S, we obtain the vanishing point of the same inclination of lines in the other planes of the object. Take the length SY in the compasses, and set it off on the horizon from V to N. At the point N make an angle INT on the horizon equal the angle KHI, that is, equal the angle of inclination of the roof aPc (No. 2.). The line NT produced to M in the vanishing line GM will be the vanishing point of the line de of the top of the tower, also of the lines $w3$ and $y5$ of the porch (the inclination of the roof of the porch being the same as the other roofs of the body of the church), as shown by the dotted lines in the example. The walls of the porch are obtained from the height AP on the intersection, equal the height AT, No. 2., Pm being drawn to the vanishing point V, and mn to X, give the lines $n5$, 53, and 32. We may observe that the inclined lines af, le, kc, and vz have a common vanishing point, which, if required, may be obtained; it will be in the same vanishing line with the point Q, and as much below the horizontal vanishing point X as the point Q is above it, to which point, were it obtained, the lines already drawn will be found exactly to tend. It is seldom absolutely necessary to have both those points; in this instance one only of them, the point Q, is obtained, which answers every end required of both; for, supposing it were left to that vanishing point for finding the inclined lines, the visual lines being drawn, and the heights of the upright walls being found, the line dk being drawn in direction to the vanishing point Q determines one side of the gable end at the visual line in the middle; the other is accomplished by joining the points k and c together. So of the other gable, cl being drawn, le is also had by joining together the points l and e.

2437. To complete the whole, draw the line xq on the tower from the point x to the angle of the tower, in direction to the vanishing point Q; then draw the lines qh and nh to their proper visual lines and vanishing points V and Q. The putting on of the spire requires some consideration, and in it we must proceed with some thought and care. The base of it is intended to be a regular octagon. If the two external lines in the geometrical elevation of the spire be continued till they touch the sides of the tower, as is done at K and L (No. 2.), and an octagon be there constructed, extending the square of the tower, it will be the base of the spire. Set up the height of the spire BW (No. 2.) on the intersection (No. 3.) at B; also the height of the base line KL at R, and draw the lines BV and RV; the first, cutting the visual line through the centre of the tower in the point O, determines the height of the spire; the other, cutting the tower in the point u, determines its base. Through the point u draw a line round the lower, and find the points of the octagon in the middle of each face of the tower, to which let lines be drawn from the top O, and the whole will be completed, as shown in the example.

2438. Thus have we gone through the process of finding the representation of rather a complicated object with as little confusion of lines as possible; but one thing succeeding another, and each being required to remain for the student's observance, the whole unavoidably becomes intricate. Indeed, it is not now so perfectly executed but that

something remains for the student to complete, which must result from his own study or occupy more space than all we have already written on it. We allude to the intersections that take place at the lodgment of the spire on the top of the tower, to elucidate which it is drawn to a larger scale at No. 4., the mere inspection whereof will convey a full and, we hope, satisfactory idea of what we advert to. The student has been left to complete the base of the octagon, a process so simple that we cannot, if he retain what he has read, believe he will find difficulty in accomplishing, either by visual rays or otherwise. It is next to an impossibility to describe intricate matters like these so as to leave nothing for the exercise of the reader's judgment; for, however copious the instruction, there will always remain sufficient unexplained to keep his mind in action, and afford him the opportunity of exercising his own ingenuity.

2439. Example V. In *fig.* 833. the objects X and Y are plans of columns with bases

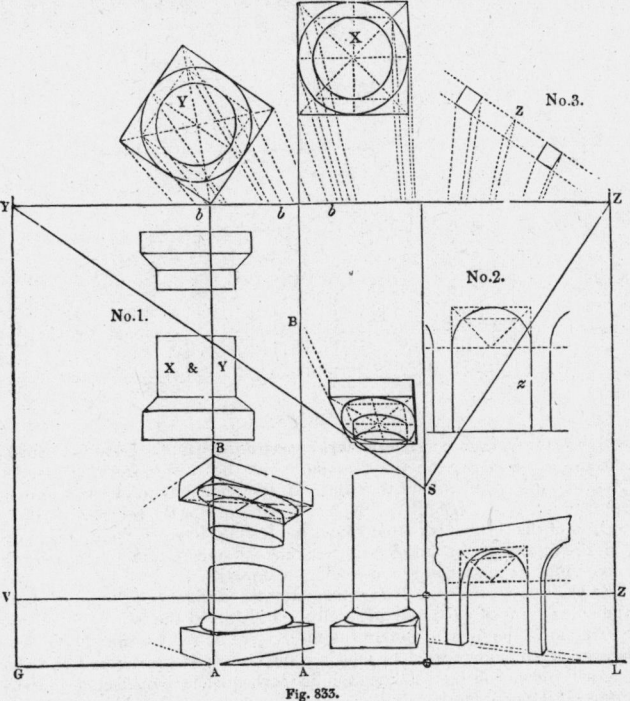

Fig. 833.

and capitals, whose general forms are shown at X and Y (No. 1.). YZ, as before, is the plane of the picture, S the station point. The picture, as previously, is prepared with the vanishing points VZ, and the ground line GL. OO is the central line of the picture, and BA, BA are, it will be seen, lines of height.

2440. In the squares X and Y the dotted lines show the diagonals and boundaries of squares inscribed in the circles, by which so many more lines are gained for obtaining the curves which the circles form in the perspective representations. The visual rays are drawn as in the preceding examples, and transferred to the picture, the process being, in fact, nothing more than making squares following the profiles, which, at the different heights, guide the formation of circles within and around them, of which the upper ones only, for preventing confusion, are shown in the perspective representation. In each series, the extreme width of the appearance of the circle may be obtained by visual rays, as at *b, b, b.*

2441. At Z and *z* (Nos. 3. and 2.) are the plan and elevation of an arcade, from which it will be seen that the principle of inscribing squares and diagonals is equally applicable to the vertical representation of circles. Presuming that we have sufficiently described the diagram to enable the student to proceed in drawing the examples at large, we shall now submit an example of general application.

2442. Example VI. In *fig.* 834. YZ is the plane of delineation, and the plan of the building, with its projections, roof, and chimneys, is shown in No. 1. In practice, this is generally made on a separate drawing board, to enable the draughtsman to make his perspective

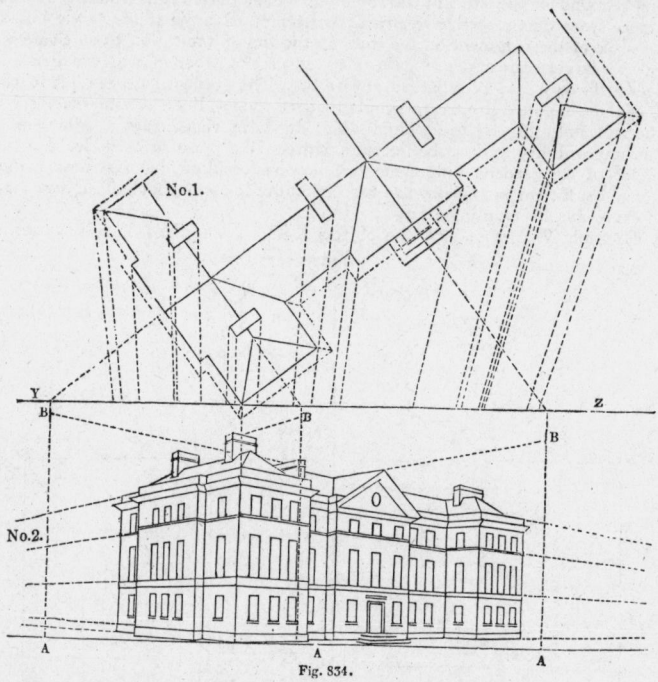

No.1.

Y   Z

No.2.

A   A   A

Fig. 834.

outline without injury from constantly working over the paper. Here the vanishing points are too distant to be shown on the diagram; but the reader, from the tendency of the several lines, will easily find where they lie. In the same manner, he will find whereabout the station point is placed. BA, BA, BA, No. 2., are lines for the transference of the heights. The projection of the cornice is dotted round the leading lines of the building on the plan. The rest of the figure cannot fail of being understood and put in practice by the student who has made himself master of the preceding examples.

2443. We shall now turn to a point whereon much difference of opinion has prevailed, namely, the adjustment of what may generally be considered the best angle of vision, within which objects should be seen to obtain the most agreable representation of them. For as this angle is enlarged or decreased by viewing the objects at greater or less distances, their appearance will vary, and their delineation, in consequence, be affected thereby, and distortion of the objects will be the result.

2444. By the angle of vision or angle of view is understood the expansion of the lines proceeding from the eye, by the two extreme visual rays embracing the whole extent of the view, and this whether it consists of one object or of many. Let A (*fig.* 835.) represent the plan of a mansion; let B be the outhouse contiguous to the mansion, and let the places of trees be at CCC and DDD. Let S be the station or point of view from which the whole is seen. Considering the mansion A as a lone object, the extreme visual rays Sa Sb form at the eye the angle aSb; then aSb is the angle of view under which that object is seen, Sa and Sb being the two extreme visual rays embracing the whole extent of the object. Again, if the outhouse B be taken as a single object, then will the extreme visual rays cS and dS form, at the eye, the angle cSd, being the magnitude of the angle under which that object is seen. So of any object, the visual rays that embrace its whole extent form the angle of view under which it is said to be seen. It is then manifest that the angle of view will be either large or small, as the eye is near to or remote from the object. Suppose both the objects A and B are to be taken into the view, with the ad-

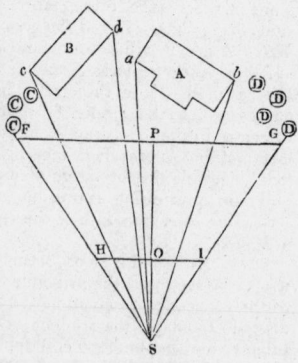

Fig. 835.

dition of the trees to their right and left. Let visual rays be drawn from the trees on both sides to the station S. The angle CSD is the angle of view under which the whole extent is seen, and the rays CS and DS are denominated the extreme visual rays of the view.

2445. Objects may not only be placed too near the eye for comfortably viewing them, but they may be so nearly placed to the eye as to give it pain. The eye only contemplates a small portion at a time; it is only by its celerity and continual motion that it becomes perfectly sensible of a whole and of the many forms whereof it is composed. But when an object, or many objects, widely extended, are placed too near, the traverses of the eye in viewing the whole become painful. Every one must have experienced that this is so, and why so we must leave to others to account for. When the eye is removed to an agreeable distance, the extent of the view to be delineated is at once seen without turning the head to one side or the other, so that all the objects are at once comprehended.

2446. In taking a view, the turning of the head is to be avoided. The view should on no account comprise a greater extent than can be taken by a *coup d'œil*, or than can be viewed by the traverse of the eye alone; and this necessarily confines the extent of that with which we have to deal, and brings the angle of view within certain limits. What the eye can contemplate without trouble it views with pleasure, and beyond a certain extent the eye becomes distracted.

2447. Smallness of object has no relation to the angle of view; a die, or the smallest possible object, may be brought so near the eye as to give pain in looking at it, and a large extent of view may be contemplated with as much ease as a small one, by merely placing the larger one at a greater distance. If the place of the plane of delineation be at FG, then FSG will be the angle of view. If a section of the same visual rays be taken at HI, then HI will be the extent of the picture, and the angle HSI is the angle of view; but the angles FSG and HSI are the same, therefore the eye views both with equal satisfaction: but in this case one must be placed at the distance SO, and the other at the distance SP.

2448. The attempt to select an angle suitable to all the cases that may occur, as the best angle of view, would be as vain as it would be absurd. Different subjects require different treatment. External subjects differ from internal ones; and the last from each other, according to circumstances. Some authors on the subject have laid it down as a rule, that the greatest distance of the eye from the picture should not exceed the width of the picture laterally, which makes the angle of view about 53 degrees; others have insisted that the distance should be less, requiring that the angle of view should not be smaller than 60 degrees; and others allow of a still larger angle. The elder Malton, and his son, to whom we are indebted for all that is valuable in this section, and whose (both of them) experience in the matter was very extended, advise that the angle of view should never exceed from 53 to 60 degrees; the former recommending an angle of 45 degrees as the best, because neither too large nor too small. The elder Malton advises to keep between the one and the other, that is, not to let the angle of view exceed 60 degrees, nor be less than 45, the first being likely to distort the objects, and the last rendering them too tame in the outline. We can add, from our own experience, that the advice is sound; for though, under very particular circumstances, it may be necessary to use a larger angle of view than 60 degrees, such a case does not frequently occur. Much must always be left to the discretion of the artist in respect to points which are to guide the angle of view he adopts. After a little experience, he will find that angle best suited to the circumstances under which his drawing is to exhibit the object or objects.

2449. Example VII. The principles upon which we delineate any of the interior parts of a building are in no wise different from those used for the representation of their external views, for it is of course immaterial whether we represent the external faces of their sides, or those which form their internal faces; the only difficulty which arises in making an internal view being that which arises from the inability, on account of the restricted distance under which they are in reality viewed, of placing the station point at such a distance as to take in a sufficient quantity of the objects to be represented. A person placed in a room can of course only see the whole of one and part of another wall; in short, in every direction he cannot see comfortably more than, as we have above mentioned, forty, or, at the most, fifty, degrees of the objects around him. On this account, and for the purpose of showing more than in reality can be seen, it is customary, and perhaps justifiable, in order to give a more comprehensive view of the interior to be delineated, to place the station point of the spectator out of the room or place, supposing one or more of its sides to be removed. This is, in fact, a delusion, as is every view of an interior possessing any merit that has come under our notice. But for picturesque delineation, it is not only one which is necessary, but one without the practice whereof no satisfactory representation can be given of an interior whose dimensions are not very extended. The section whereon we are now engaged is not supposed to be a treatise on Perspective, but merely a concise developement of its principles so as to give the reader such a general knowledge of the subject as may enable

him to pursue it, if he please, from the hints it affords.   With this apology for not producing to him a more complicated, though not less useful subject, we proceed.

2450. *Fig.* 836. (No. 1.) represents the plan of a staircase one third the size used for the

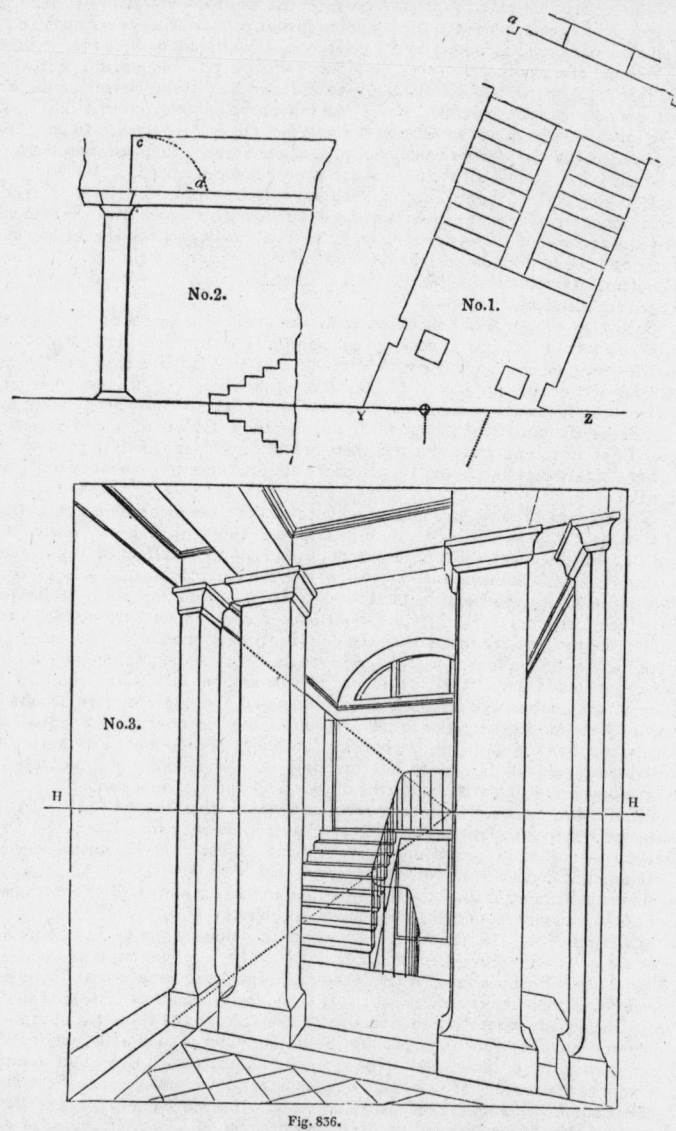

Fig. 836.

purposes of the delineation ; YZ (No. 1.) is the plane of the picture, O is its centre.   From
the data, therefore, there will be no difficulty of obtaining the vanishing points of the sides
Y*a* and *ab*.   The diagram is not encumbered with the visual rays necessary for the delineation, which we are to suppose drawn and transferred to their proper places on No. 3.,
wherein HH is the horizontal line.   No. 2. is a longitudinal section of the staircase, wherein
are shown the rising and descending steps, and the dotted line *cd* gives the section of the
vaulted ceiling over the staircase.   It will be immediately seen that the ends of the steps
will be determined by visual lines, notwithstanding the ascent and descent of them, because
either is determined by referring to any lines of height, which may be obtained from the
plan and section, by which the portions seen of the flights will be immediately found and

transferred to their respective places on the picture. With these observations we leave the diagram for the exercise, on a larger scale than here given, of the ingenuity of the student.

2451. Example VIII. The last perspective example to be submitted is that of a cornice

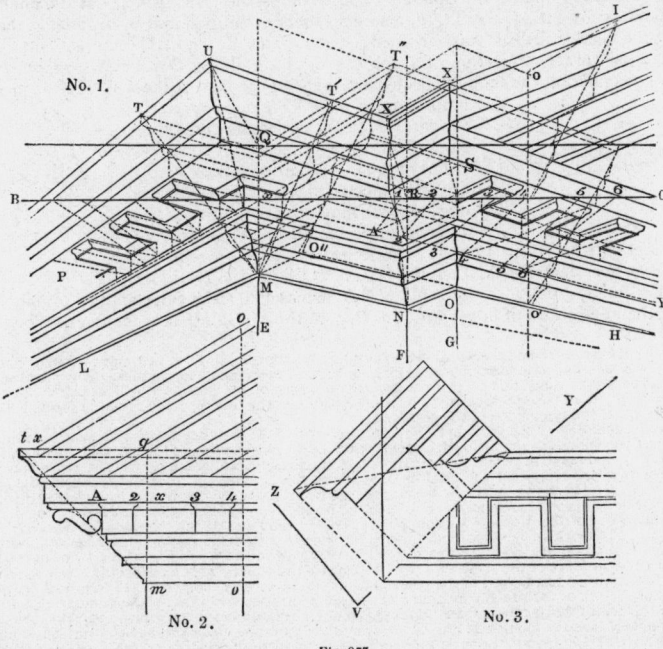

Fig. 837.

(*fig. 837.*), wherein the contrivance of the elder Malton is used for finding the places of the modillions and the other parts.

2452. Let EM, FN, GO (No. 1.) represent the angles of a building in perspective, LMNO being the lower horizontal line of the cornice, whose geometrical elevation and profile are shown in No. 2. Make MQ equal to *mq* the depth of the cornice, supposing the edge EQ to be in the plane of projection; draw PQRS, &c., the lines of the top of the cornice, to their respective vanishing points. Make QT, QT′ in RQ, PQ, produced equal to the perspective projection of the cornice *qt*. Then place the depths of the various mouldings along MQ, and fix the lengths of their projections on the lines drawn to the vanishing points through those in EQ, an operation which may be much facilitated by drawing MT, MT′, by which, in many places, the points of the mouldings are at once determined, as in the case of the top and bottom of the fillets of the ovolo; and very often, if the drawing is not on a very large scale, *mt* and its perspective images MT, MT′, &c. will enable the eye to proportion the mouldings. Thus the perspective projections MQT, MQT′ of the sections of the cornice by the planes of the sides EN, EL, supposed to be prolonged or extended, may be found; and it is manifest that lines through the points of these sections to the proper vanishing points will give the perspective forms of the cornice mouldings as they would appear.

2453. The lines found will by their intersections supply the mitre MQU; but where the scale is large, it is better to obtain mitre sections at each principal angle of the building as shown by the lines MQU, NRX, &c. The planes of the mitres form, of course, angles of forty-five degrees with the sides of the building itself, consequently the vanishing points of QU, RX, &c. may be found by bisecting perspectively the right angles found, or by drawing on the plan lines parallel to the diagonal lines or mitres from the station point to intersect the picture. If these, indeed, are found in the first place, there would be no necessity to draw the square sections MQT, MQT′, inasmuch as lines drawn from the mouldings intersecting the mitre sections to the vanishing points will at once form the perspective representation of the cornice. In practice, this is the usual mode of proceeding, because a skilful draughtsman can pretty well proportion by his eye most mouldings as seen in perspective; but where great accuracy is required, the method of proceeding by square sections is recommended, because, from the great foreshortening of the diagonal line, the smallest inaccuracy of intersection on it will cause very large errors in the mouldings.

When the diagonal sections alone are used, it is clear that the geometrical profile, No. 2., will not be the same as that formed by the oblique section of the cornice: this last must therefore be obtained from a plan and elevation of the mouldings as shown in No. 3.

2454. Instead of finding the square section made by the plane FNGO at the angle OG, it may be drawn on the plane TQM, where it is more readily found by producing the lines whereby the section TQM was obtained; so the lines T'T'', MO'' are set out in perspective equal to the projection of the break of the building ON: moreover by the line T''O'' we may obtain the mouldings of the cornice on the face of the wall GH as produced

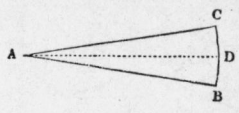

or prolonged to T''O'', and conversely the cornice in perspective may be drawn from this imaginary section, if it be previously found. Where vanishing points are at an inconvenient distance in drawings, a mode may be adopted to obviate the inconvenience, the principle whereof

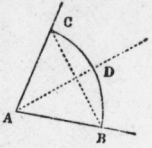

Fig. 837. a.

Fig. 837. b.

is this. Let A (*fig.* 837 a.) be the vanishing point, CDB a segment of a circle whose centre is A; then if CB be bisected in D, AD will be a vanishing line for such bisection; and if CD be bisected, and a ruler applied to join CD, it will, by the application of a square on CD, give the vanishing line for the new bisection. *Fig.* 837. b.

2455. Our next care is to find the vanishing point of the raking mouldings, which may be found from what has already been said, and a perspective section must be made of these mouldings by means of any vertical plane where most convenient; but the best place is through the apex of the pediment, which, as it could not, for want of room, be done in the present example, is taken through the line oo, No. 2., passing through the extreme left angle of the tympanum of the pediment.

2456. As the mouldings of the pediment (*fig.* 837.) here are of the same depth and projection as in the horizontal parts, they will not, when inclined, coincide with the diagonal section of the horizontal cornice at OS; hence that section, if found in perspective at OS, cannot be used for drawing the perspective representation of the pediment cornice, except for the bead or fillet above the corona, which, from the construction of the pediment, will coincide at this mitre, as we may see in No. 2.; whence it may also be seen that the point x does not coincide with t. X'x cannot, therefore, in the perspective representation, be drawn through X, the point answering to t in the diagonal section NRX. OO' in the line OH is to be made in perspective equal to mo, No. 2., and the whole depth oo, and those of the several mouldings on the oblique section, being set upon EQ produced, they are to be transferred to OO' by means of the vanishing points. The distance O'I is the perspective distance of the projection qt of the cornice as before, and is most readily obtained from the section O''T'', which is transferred to the plane O'I, and will be easily comprehended from the figure; the quantity of projection of each raking moulding of the pediment is equal to that of the same moulding where horizontal. Thus the perspective representation of an oblique section made by a plane passing through oo, No. 2., is obtained, and the mouldings are then drawn to the vanishing point through the various points, the line IX' cutting T''X in the point corresponding to x, No. 2. As to the modillions, their representations are found with less confusion by planning them apart and using visual rays; but if no plan is used, the following method, invented by the elder Malton, may be adopted: —

2457. Draw BC, the line intersecting the plane of the sofite of the corona, Nos. 2. and 3., through the proper point x in MQ at right angles to it, and draw xy to the vanishing point. Produce the line corresponding to A in No. 3. to A in xy, and transfer A to 1 in BC, so as to be proportional to it in respect of the whole extent. Then set off the proportional widths and intervals of the modillions, as shown on Nos. 2. and 3. on BC, and transfer them by means of the same proportioning point by which x was transferred to 1; and from the points 2, 3, 4, 5, 6, &c. in xy thus obtained, draw on the perspective of the sofite by the use of the vanishing point the lines representing the tops of the modillions corresponding to 2, 3, 4, &c., No. 2. The cymatium round them and the inner angle of the sofite may be drawn by the eye, or where great accuracy is required, the mitre or diagonal sections may be determined as for the principal mouldings already described. At the backs of the modillions the verticals are to be determined either by means of visual rays from a plan, or through the medium of intersections of the perspective lines of the upper parts of them on the sofite, which is as much as can be requisite for guiding us to a correct delineation. The same process is to be used for the modillions on the other sides.

The following is an easy method for dividing vanishing lines in perspective. Let AB, CD be the perspective representation of two parallels, no matter in what plane. It is required to divide the given portion of AB on one of them so that its parts shall be the perspective representation of equal portions of the real line (or in any assigned ratio). Draw BE parallel to CD and equal to AB, and divide it into the required number of equal parts or of parts in the desired proportion beginning at E. Join AE and produce it to meet CD in F. From F draw lines to each of the points of division PQRS of the line AE, and they will cut AB in the required points of subdivision $p\ q\ r\ s$.

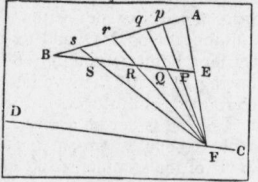

Fig. 837. c

Sect. III.

SHADOWS.

2458. Sciography, or the doctrine of shadows, is a branch of the science of projection, and some preparation has been made for its introduction here in Sect. VI. Chap. I. (1110, *et. seq.*) on Descriptive Geometry, which, if well understood, will remove all difficulty in comprehending the subject of this section.

2459. The reader will understand that in this work, which is strictly architectural, the only source of light to be considered is the sun, whose rays, owing to his great distance, are apparently parallel and rectilineal. It is moreover to be premised, that such parts of any body as may be immediately opposed to the rays of light are technically said to be *in*

light, and the remaining parts of such body are said to be *in shade*. But when one body stands on or before another, and intercepts the sun's rays from the latter, which is thereby deprived of the action upon it of the rays of light, the part so deprived of the immediate action of the light is said to be *in shadow*. It seems hardly necessary to observe, that the parts of any body nearest the source of light will be the brightest in appearance, whilst those furthest removed from it will, unless under the action of reflected light, be the darkest.

2460. It has been the practice, in architectural drawings, to represent the shadows of their objects at an angle of forty-five degrees with the horizon, as well on the elevations as on the plans. The practice has this great convenience, namely, that the breadth of the shadow cast will then actually measure the depth of each projecting member which casts it, and the shadowed elevation may be thus made to supply a plan of the external parts of the building. Now, if in the elevation the shadows be cast at an angle of forty-five degrees, it will on a little consideration be manifest, that, being only projections of a more lengthened shadow (for those on the plan are at an angle of forty-five degrees), the actual shadow seen diagonally must be at such an angle as will make its projection equal to forty-five degrees upon the elevation; because all elevations, sections, and plans, being themselves nothing more than projections of the objects they represent, are determined by perpendicular, horizontal, or inclined parallel lines drawn from the points which bound them to the plane of projection, and similarly, a shadow in vertical projection, which forms an angle of forty-five degrees with the horizon, can only be the representation on such projection of an angle, whose measure it is our business now to determine.

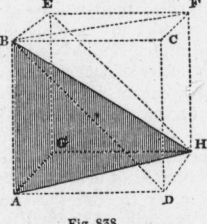

Fig. 838.

2461. In the cube ABCDEFGH (*fig.* 838.) the line BD, forming an angle of forty-five degrees with the horizon, is a projection or representation of the diagonal AH on the vertical plane ABD; and our object being to find the actual angle AHB, whereof the angle ADB is the projection, we have the following method. Let each side of the cube, for example, = 10. Then (by 907.) $AD^2 + DH^2 = AH^2$.

That is, $10 \times 10 + 10 \times 10 = 200 = AH^2$, consequently $AH = 14 \cdot 142100$.

As BAH is a right angle, we have by Trigonometry, using a table of logarithms, —

$$\begin{array}{lcr}
\text{As AH } (= 14 \cdot 14142100) \text{ or Ar. Co. Log.} & . & 9 \cdot 8494850 \\
\text{To tangent } 45^\circ & . \quad . \quad . & 10 \cdot 0000000 \\
\text{So AB } (= 10 \cdot 00000000) \text{ log.} & . \quad . & 1 \cdot 0000000 \\
\end{array}$$

$$\text{To tangent of angle FHB} = 35^\circ \ 16' . \quad . = 9 \cdot 8494850$$

The angle ABH is therefore $54^\circ \ 44'$.

Hence it follows, that when shadows are projected on the plan as well as on the elevation, at an angle of forty-five degrees, the height of the sun which projects them must be $35^\circ \ 16'$.

2462. It is of the utmost importance to the student to recollect this fact, because it will be hereafter seen that it will give him great facility in obviating difficulty where confusion of lines may lead him astray, being, in fact, not only a check, but an assistance in proving the accuracy of his work.

2463. We now proceed to submit to the student a series of examples, containing the most common cases of shadowing, and which, once well understood, will enable him to execute any other case that may be presented to his notice.

2464. In *fig.* 839. we have on the left-hand side of the diagram the common astragal fillet and cavetto occurring in the Tuscan and other pilasters, above in elevation and below in plan. The right-hand part shows the same connected with a wall, whereon a shadow is cast by the several parts. LL is a line showing the direction of the light in projection at an angle of forty-five degrees. It will on experiment be found, by a continuation of the line, or by one parallel to it, to touch the side of the astragal at a, whence an horizontal line drawn along it will

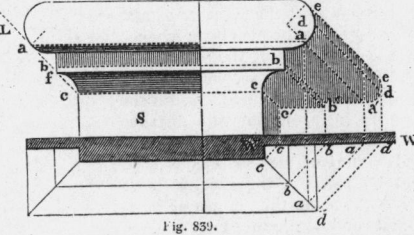

Fig. 839.

determine its line of shade. We here again repeat, to prevent misunderstanding, that in the matter we are now attempting to explain we are not dealing with reflected light, nor with the softening off of shadows apparent in convex objects, but are about to

determine the mere boundaries of *shade* and *shadow* of those under consideration. The rest must be learned from observation, for the circumstances under which they are seen must constantly vary. This, however, we think, we may safely state, that if the boundaries of shade and shadow only be accurately given in a drawing (however complex), the satisfaction they will afford to the spectator will be sufficient, without further refinement. But it is not to be understood from this that we discountenance the refinement of finish in architectural subjects ; all that we mean to say is, that it is not necessary. To return to the diagram : it is manifest that if the boundary of *shade* be at a from that point parallel to the direction of the light a line ab will determine the boundary of *shadow* on the fillet at b, and that from the lower edge of such fillet at f a line again parallel to the direction of the light will give at c the boundary of the shadow it casts upon the shaft S. As, in the foregoing explanation, a was the upper boundary of shade, so by producing the horizontal line which it gave to a on the right-hand side of the diagram we obtain there a corresponding point whence a line aa' parallel to the direction of the light is to be drawn indefinitely ; and on the plan a line *aa*, also parallel to the direction of the light, cutting the wall WW whereon the shadow is cast at a. From the point last found a vertical line from a, where the shadow cuts the wall on the plan, cutting aa' in a', will determine the point a' in the shadow. The point e, by a line therefrom parallel to the direction of the light, will determine similarly the situation e' by obtaining its relative seat on the diagonal cd, which perhaps will be at once seen by taking the extreme point d of the projection of the astragal, and therefrom drawing dd' parallel to the direction of the light. From the line dd, drawn similarly parallel to the direction of the light, and cutting WW in d, we have the boundary of the shadow on the plan, and from that point a vertical dd being drawn, the boundary of shadow of the extreme projection of the astragal is thus obtained. The boundary of shadow of the fillet on the right-hand side at b, similarly by means of bb, and by the vertical bb', gives the boundary point of the shadow from b. The same operation in respect of cc gives the boundary of shadow from c to c' in the latter point. We have not described this process in a strictly mathematical manner, because our desire is rather to lead the student to think for himself a little in conducting it ; but we cannot suppose the matter will not be perfectly understood by him even on a simple inspection of the diagram.

2465. In the diagram (*fig.* 840.) is represented a moulding of common occurrence in architectural subjects, and, as before, the right-hand side is the appearance of its shadow on the wall WW on the plan. It will be immediately seen that LL being the projected representation of the rays of light, the line aa determines the boundary of shadow on the ovolo, and that at b, the boundary of its shade, is also given by a line touching that point parallel to the rays, or rather projected rays, of light. On the right-hand side of the figure oo', drawn indefinitely parallel to the direction of the light,

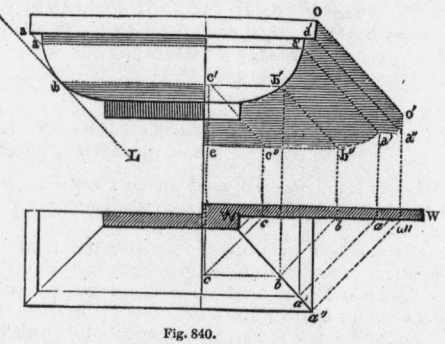

Fig. 840.

and determined by a vertical from a", the intersection by a"a" with the wall, will give o'a", the line of shadow of oa'. The line aa determines the shadow on the ovolo, and this continued to a' horizontally gives also a like termination to a" in the shadow ; b, the boundary upwards of the ovolo's shade, is represented to the right by b', and to the right on the plan by b, whence by a vertical cutting the line b'b" in b", the boundary of shadow which b' will cast is obtained. cc on the plan is in projection the distance of the line of shade c' from the wall whereon the shadow is cast, and its place in the shadow is at c", ee"b" being the length of horizontal shadow produced by the circumstances.

In *fig.* 841., which, it will be seen, is a common fillet and cavetto, LL is, as before, the direction of the

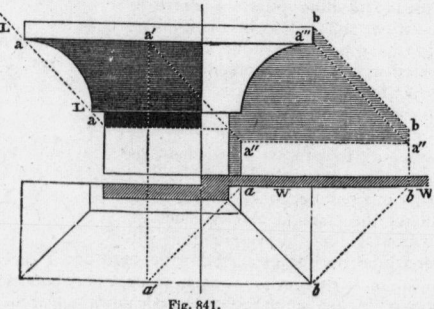

Fig. 841.

light, and aa gives the boundary of shadow, as well of the fillet's lower edge as of the lower edge of the cavetto itself. In respect of the right-hand side of the figure, a′a′ is a line showing in profile the extent of projection of the fillet before the wall line WW, and from a′ a line drawn indefinitely parallel to the direction of the light, and terminated by the intersection of a vertical from a′ in a″, will give the point a′ in the shadow. So is bb found through a vertical from b on the wall, by a line drawn parallel to the direction of the light from b on the plan. The several points being connected by lines, we gain the boundaries of the shadow, wherein a′a‴ is represented by a″a″.

2466. *Fig.* 842. exhibits a fillet and cyma reversa or ogee, wherein, as before, LL is the direction of the light at a similar angle to that used on the plan. From the lower edge of the fillet, parallel to the direction of the light, is obtained the point a on the ogee, and from b a similarly parallel line gives the boundary of shadow in c. A line from o in direction of the light, drawn indefinitely, intercepted by a vertical line from d′, its projection on the plan in d determines o′d, the boundary of the shadow of the fillet on the wall WW. cc‴ is the line of profile of the projecting boundary in elevation, of the shade of the ogee before the wall, whereon its shadow is terminated from c and c″ by a vertical c‴ c″. bb′, the boundary of shade of the

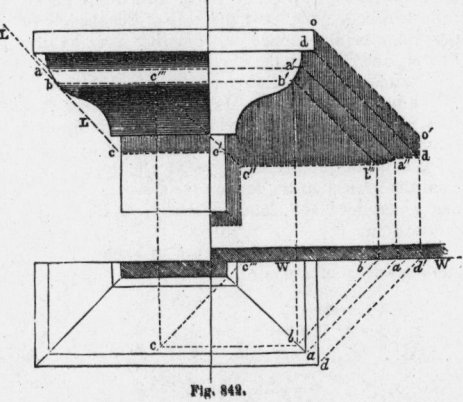

Fig. 842.

ogee itself, is found in shadow by the line b′b‴ drawn indefinitely parallel to the direction of the light, and terminated by a vertical from b′, the point on the wall correspondent to b on the plan, the place of the shade's point in the elevation. By the junction of the lines so found, we shall have the outline of the shades and shadows cast. It is here to be observed, that the portion of light a′b′ which the moulding retains is represented in the shadow by a″b‴, all the other parts of its curved form being hidden, first by the projection of the fillet, and secondly by the line of shade bb″, which acts in the same way as the fillet itself in producing the line aa′, for the moment the light is intercepted, whether by a straight or curved profile, shadow must follow the shade of the moulding, whatever it be; and this is by the student to be especially observed.

2467. *Fig.* 843. exhibits the mode of obtaining the shadows and shade in the cyma recta. LL is the direction of the light, parallel whereto the line ab determines the line of horizontal shadow cast by the lower edge of the fillet upon the cyma, and cd that of the under part of the cyma itself upon the fillet at d. cc′ is the upper boundary of the shade of the cyma, and e the point for determining the shadow of the lower fillet, the points abcd corresponding with abcd on the plan. WW on the right hand is the face of the wall, whereto the lines e′e″, d′d″, c′c″, b′b″, and a′a″ are drawn parallel to the direction of the light. From e″d″c″b″a″ vertical being drawn, cutting the indefinite lines oo′, a′a″, &c. parallel to the direction of the light in e″, d‴, c″, b″, and a″, we have the

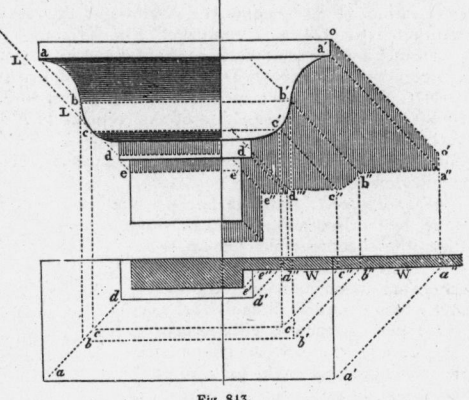

Fig. 843.

form of the shadow in elevation. The part from b′ to c′ of the cyma being in light, its shadow will be the curve c″b″, wherein, if it be required on a large scale, any number of points may be taken to determine its form by means of correspondent points on the plan as for the parts already described.

2468. *Fig.* 844. is the plan and elevation of some steps, surrounded by a wall, and P in the plan is a square pillar standing in front of them. It will be seen that the line AB

corresponds with ab on the plan, as do the points
E, F, G, H with efgh, from which verticals determine them in the elevation. The projection of the
plinth on the lower step is found by KI and a
corresponding line and vertical, which, to prevent
confusion, is not shown on the plan. The shadow
of the square pillar P is found in a similar manner
by the line CD corresponding to cd on the plan, the
shadows on the steps being also determined by the
points L, M, N, O, through the medium of verticals
from l, m, n, o. The left-hand side of the shadow of
the pillar is determined in a similar way by the
line pq, and QR in the elevation is given by qr in
the plan, and is the line representing the back ps
of the top of the pillar. It will be observed that
we have not described any of the preceding diagrams in a strict way, neither shall we do so in
those that follow, presuming that the reader has,
from the perusal of the section on Descriptive Geometry acquired sufficient knowledge to follow the
several lines.

2469. The *fig.* 845. is a sort of skeleton plan
and elevation of a modillion cornice, but deprived

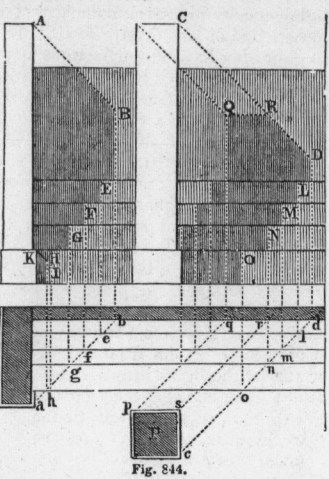

Fig. 844.

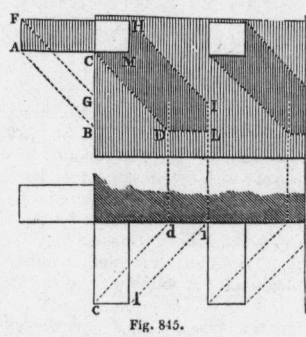

Fig. 845.

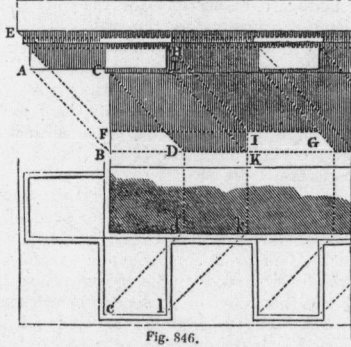

Fig. 846.

of a corona, so as to show the shadows of the modillions, independent of any connection
with other parts of the assemblage. FG, HI, and AB parallel to the direction of the light
determine, by means of verticals from d and i, the points of shadows from the correspondent points c, l, the points D, L, and I, whereof L is the point of shadow of M.

2470. In *fig.* 846. we approach a little nearer to the form of a modillion cornice. The
line EF determines the shadow of the corona, and AB by means of the lines cd, Ik, and the
verticals dD, kK, the boundary of the side HL of the modillions. A line also drawn
horizontally from B will give the under sides of their shadows. FG is a line representing
the shadow of the corona.

2471. *Fig.* 847. gives the finished modillion, and the lines Aa, Bb, Cc, Dd will determine, by horizontal lines drawn from
them, the shadows which we are seeking. The auxiliary lines, to which no
letters are attached, cannot fail of being
understood ; but if difficulty arise in
comprehending them, it will be removed
by planning the several points, and
therefrom drawing on the plan, to meet
what may be called the frieze, vertical
lines to intercept those from the correspondent points in the elevation, and the
operation will be facilitated, perhaps,
by projecting the form of the curved
lines (as seen in the figure) whereof
the modillion is formed.

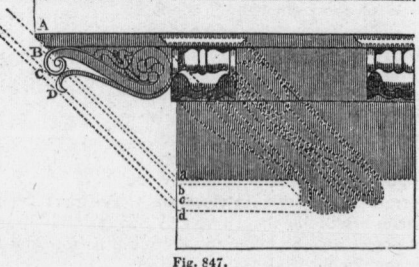

Fig. 847.

2472. *Fig.* 848. will scarcely require a description. It is a geometrical elevation of the

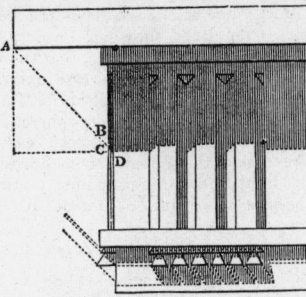

Fig. 848.

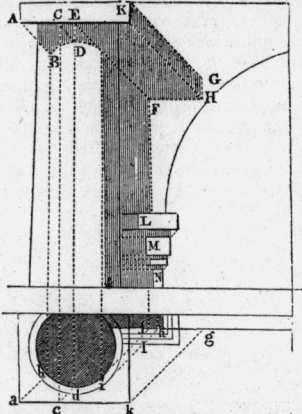

Fig. 849.

Doric triglyph and frieze, with the usual accessories. AB gives the boundary of shadow on
the femora of the triglyph, AC the boundary of
shadow on the light sides of the glyphs, and AD
of the shadow of the corona on the frieze.

2473. *Fig.* 849. is a skeleton representation
of a three-quarter column, forming part of an
arcade. The abacus is the mere block of material AK. In the plan ab shows the
length of the line of shadow AB, and is determined by the vertical bB. In the same way,
CD is found by cd and the vertical dD. KG is
the representation of kg on the plan, and by a
vertical from g the line GH is also determined;
H giving also by the horizontal line FH, in which
H is already found, the situation of shadow of the
point E of the abacus, as also by a vertical from
f. LMN are places of the shadow of the column
on the impost moulding of the arch, whereof two
correspondent points are seen in l and n.

2474. The form of shadow of the console in
fig. 850. will be seen on inspection to have been
found from the lines aa, cc, dd, &c. on the elevation, corresponding with *aa*, *cc*, *dd*, &c. on the
section, all which are parallel to the direction of
the light, and sufficiently explain themselves.

2475. *Fig.* 851. is the elevation and section of
a hemispherical niche, wherein are shown the
shadows cast thereon by the vertical wall in which
it is placed. Through the
centre O draw DD at right
angles to the direction of the
light, and from O draw OA
parallel to the direction of the
light: A will be found the point
in the wall casting the longest
shadow. Produce AO indefinitely; and from a, the corresponding point in the section
to A on the elevation, draw aa′,
parallel to it, which will cut
the surface of the niche in a′.
Draw the horizontal line a′ a″
cutting AO produced in a‴,
and a″ will represent in the
shadow the point A in the circumference. Take any other

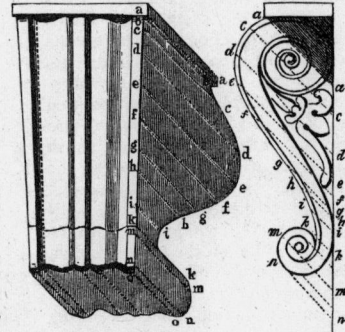

Fig. 850.

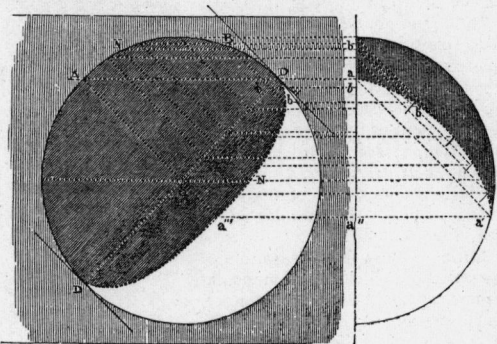

Fig. 851.

point B in the edge of the niche, and by means of a line drawn therefrom horizontally we
have the correspondent point b of B in the section. From B draw in the direction of the
light the line Bb‴ b″, cutting DD on the diameter in b‴; transfer the point b‴ in the
elevation to b in the section, and draw bb′ in the direction of the light indefinitely.
Then with Bb‴ as a radius from b as a centre, describe an arc cutting bb′ in b′; and
from b′ draw the horizontal line b′ b″, cutting Bb‴ produced in b″, and b″ will be the
point in the shadow corresponding to B in the elevation. To avoid the confusion which

would follow the description of the remainder of the operation, we have not encumbered the diagram with more letters of reference; the lines showing, on inspection, similar applications of the process for all parts of the curve. The fact is, that the whole of the shadow may be completed by taking the line DD as the transverse axis of an ellipsis, and finding the semi-conjugate axis Oa by the mèans above described, for Da″D is a semi-ellipsis in form, inasmuch as it is the projection of a section of a hemisphere. This example is applicable to the shadow of a cylindrical niche with a hemispherical head. The line NN shows the shadow of the portion of the head, and the remainder is obtained by the mere intersection of lines in the direction of the light from different points to the left of N, of which enough has been already given in the previous examples to make the application intelligible.

2476. *Fig. 852.* is the representation of a pediment wherein the section A is that of the

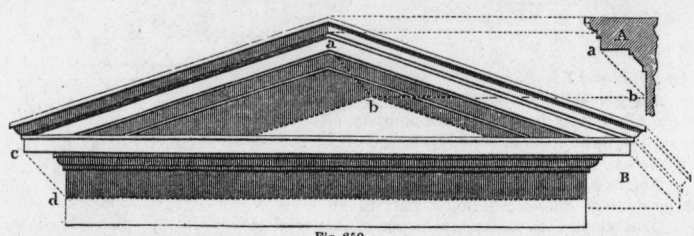

Fig. 852.

mouldings of the pediment at its apex. In the section, ab drawn from the projection a of the corona in the direction of the light, determines the point b therein, wherefrom the horizontal line intercepted by the line ab in the elevation, also drawn parallel to the direction of the light, gives the point b in the elevation. A line from b, parallel to the inclined sides of the pediment on the left, will give the shadow of the corona on the tympanum on that side, and similarly the line of shadow from b on the right side. cd determines the line of shadow on the frieze, and B is the section of the shadow of the assemblage of mouldings on the right.

2477. In *fig. 853.* is given the plan, elevation, and section of a square recess, covered with a cylindrical head. The lines AA, BB, CC of the elevation are determined by aa, bb, and cc of the plan; and in the section c′c′ is the representation of the line cc of the plan. D, the point at which the direction of the light begins to touch the circular head, is d′ in the section.

2478. *Fig. 854.* is the elevation of an arch, below which is its plan and the shadow cast by it on the plane upon which it stands. AA is shown by aa on the plan, the corresponding points in the rear of the arch being a′ a′, and a″ a″ the points in the shadow. In a similar way, by BB corresponding with bb′ on the plan the points b″ b″ are obtained in the shadow.

2479. *Fig. 855.* is the plan and elevation of the upper part of a house,

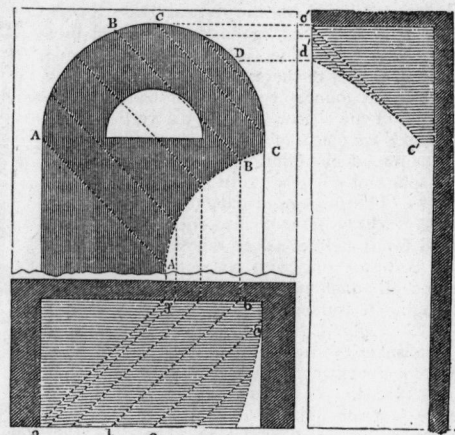

Fig. 853.

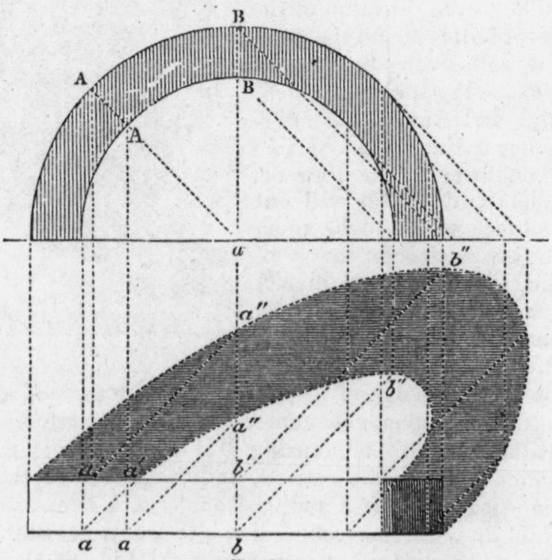

Fig. 854.

wherein the upper story is occupied by an attic in the centre, against which, on each flank, the sloping roof is terminated. aa on the plan in the direction of the light, produced to intersect the hip at b, gives, by a vertical to B on the elevation, the direction BB of the shadow thereon ; and BB cut by AA in the direction of the light, the length BA of the line of shadow, which may, by letting fall the vertical Aa, determine the length aa on the plan. The line of shadow ac is determined by letting fall a vertical from C, where the line of shadow is intercepted by the hip of the roof; and from c the shadow will be found on trial to return as shown in the diagram. E and D on the elevation are found,

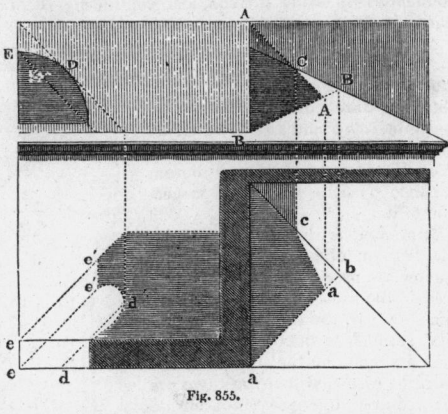

Fig. 855.

as seen in previous examples, in ee, and d on the plan, and their shadows at e'e' and d'.

2480. What is called an attic base is given in plan and elevation by *fig. 856*. The method of obtaining the shadows thereof in plan and elevation is now to be explained. It is an example which constantly occurs in architectural subjects, and should be well studied and understood. The operations requisite for obtaining a representation of the lines of shadow of the different mouldings in this example depend upon the principles developed in the preceding subsections. The lower portion of the figure exhibits the plan, and the middle portion the elevation of the attic base in question. The uppermost portion of it presents three sections of the mouldings of the base in question cut in three different places parallel to the direction of the light. This last portion of the figure is not absolutely necessary, inasmuch as the profiles in question might have been obtained upon the elevation ; but we have preferred keeping it separate to prevent a confusion of subsidiary lines. There is moreover another advantage in thus separating the parts from each other, namely, that of immediately and more distinctly seeing the lines at each selected place, in which the rays of light separate the parts actually in light from those in shadow; and where the student is likely to meet with

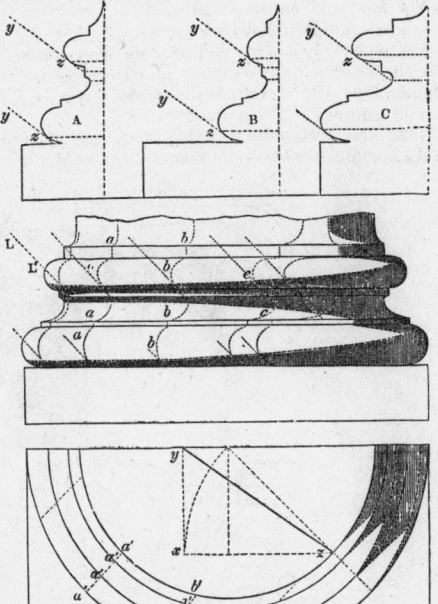

Fig. 856.

matters of perplexity, nothing should be left untried to save his time, and, what is often more important, his patience. The mode to be adopted is as follows : —

Make on the plan any number of sections $a'a'a'a'$, $b'b'b'b'$ in the direction of the light, and draw on the elevation the corresponding sections *aaaa, bbbb*. LL being the direction of the light, draw parallel thereto tangents to the curves of the convex mouldings, and the boundaries of their shades will be obtained, as will also those of their shadows, by continuing them from such boundaries till they cut the other parts in each section, as will be more especially seen at *cc*. It will be recollected that in our first mention of the projected representation of the line of light and shadow we found that it was an angle of 54° 44' of the diagonal of a cube. This angle is set out in *xyz* on the plan. We have therefore another mode of finding the boundaries of shade and shadow on the moulding, by developing the sections $a'a'a'a'$, $b'b'b'b'$, &c., as at A, B, and C, and drawing tangents *yz* to the convex mouldings for

boundaries of shade thereon, and continuing them, or otherwise, for the other parts, as shown in the diagram.

2481. In *fig.* 857., which represents the capital of a column, a similar method is used to that last mentioned for obtaining the shades and shadows, by means of *a'a'a'a'* and *b'b'b'b'*, which are shown on the elevation by *aaaa* and *bbbb*. We apprehend this will be understood by little more than inspection of it.

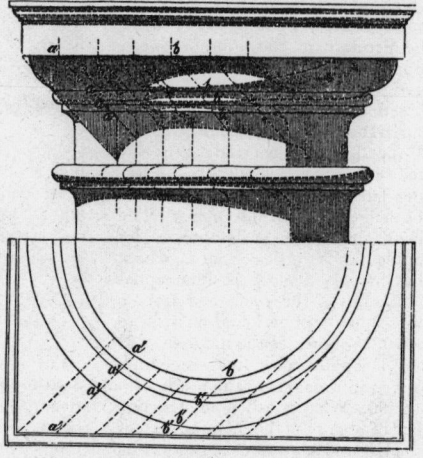

It is obvious that the means here adopted for obtaining the lines of shadow are precisely similar to those used in the preceding example. In this, however, the sections of the capital parallel to the direction of the light are made on the elevation, and it will be seen that many of them are not required to obtain an accurate boundary of the lines of shadow sought; for after having obtained those points from which the longest shadow falls, and on the other side those where the line of shadow com-

Fig. 857.

mences, a curve line of an elliptical nature connects the points found. If the drawing to be made be on a large scale, it may then be worth the architect's while to increase the number of points wherefrom the shadow is to be projected, so as to produce the greatest possible accuracy in the representation.

2482. The shadows of an Ionic capital are given in *fig.* 858. The shadow of the volute on the column is obtained by any number of lines AA, BB, CC, &c. from its different

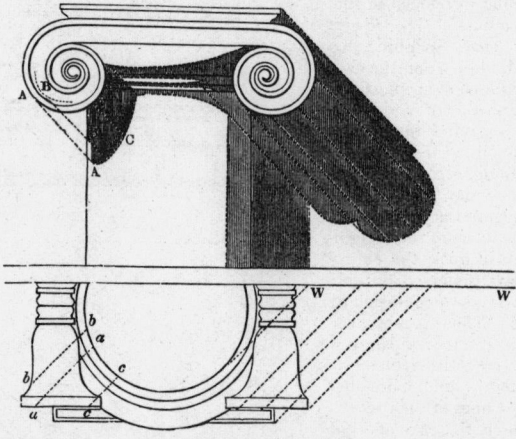

Fig. 858.

parts and verticals from their corresponding ones *aa, bb, cc,* &c. on the plan, and similarly the shadow of the capital on the wall. In this example, as in those immediately preceding, the employment of sectional lines parallel to the direction of the light is again manifest. The use of them is most especially seen in the example of the Corinthian capital which follows. As a general rule, it may be hinted to the student of sciography, that in the difficulties that may occur, they will be most expeditiously and clearly resolved by the use of the sectional lines, whereon we have thought it proper so much to dilate.

2483. The Corinthian capital in *fig.* 859. will require little more than inspection to understand the construction of its sciography; and all that we think necessary to particularise are the developed projections A, B, C, D, E, F of the abacus and the leaves, whereon the termination of the shadows at angles of 54° 44', as explained in *fig.* 856., give their respective depths on the elevation.

There is another method of arriving at the result here exhibited, by drawing sectional lines parallel to the direction of the light through the different parts and leaves of the

Fig. 859.

capital on its elevation, as in *fig.* 857., and such was the mode we were formerly in the habit of adopting.   It however induces such a confusion of lines, that we have long since abandoned it, and have no hesitation in recommending the process here given as the best and most likely to avoid confusion.   It is of course unnecessary, in making drawings, to project more than the shadow of one capital, as in a portico, or elsewhere, similar capitals, similarly exposed to the light, will project similar shadows, so that the projection on one serves for the projection on all of them.

2484. For instruction upon the mode in which reflected light acts upon objects in shade and shadow, we must refer the learner to the contemplation of similar objects in relief. The varieties of reflexes are almost infinite ; and though general rules might be laid down, they would necessarily be so complicated, that they would rather puzzle than instruct, and under this head we recommend the study of nature, which will be found the best instructress the student can procure.

<hr />

Sect. IV.

GENERAL PRINCIPLES OF COMPOSITION.

2485. The end of architecture, without whose aid no other art can exist, is not merely to please the eye, but so to provide against the changes of the seasons as to be serviceable to man.   Pleasure to the eye may, however, result from the useful, well combined with the beautiful modifications whereof it is susceptible.   It is in combining thus that the genius of the architect is exhibited.   The art of decorating a well-proportioned edifice is a very secondary and comparatively easy part of his work, though requiring, of course, the early cultivation of his taste and an intimate acquaintance with the parts, whereof this may be taught and that acquired ; but the distribution and arrangement of the several portions on the plan, upon which every accessory is dependent, requires great knowledge and considerable experience.   And in this is involved not only the general convenience and effect of the building, but what is of much consequence to the proprietor, the cost of the work.   None but those practically conversant with the planning of a building would believe the saving that may be produced by proper distribution.   In the case of many external breaks, for instance, much addition arises in the length of walls enclosing the edifice, without generally increasing the convenience of the interior, but always when the elevation comes to be adapted to the plan, with the certainty of breaking up the masses, and destroying the simplicity of the effect.   This is mentioned merely as an instance of simplicity of plan always producing simplicity of section and elevation.

2486. All ornament in architecture is non-essential, inasmuch as the pleasure received by the eye is not its end. To public and private utility, the welfare and comforts of individuals, which are the ends of the art, every other point must be sacrificed; and it is only when these have been accomplished that we are to think of decoration. An anecdote is related of a certain nobleman, who, having boasted to a friend of the beauty of the façade of his house, which within was exceedingly ill contrived, was told that he thought the peer would do well to take the house opposite, that he might be thus always able to look at it. Those who make the internal parts of an edifice subservient to the project of a façade, and adjust their plan and section to the elevation, must be considered as making the end of less importance than the ornament of the building. Those who work in this mode produce little variety in their designs, which, numerous though they be, consist of but few different combinations, whilst those that result from the natural order of making the façade subservient to the internal parts, which the plan and section impose, are susceptible of infinite variety and decoration.

2487. It is not, however, to be supposed that we are, in what has been said, sanctioning the student's neglect of careful composition and adjustment of the façades. Upon the adaptation of the different fronts of the building to sort with the internal convenience, the greatest care should be bestowed. It is from these his reputation is likely to flow, because they are the parts most susceptible of comprehension by the public. The architect will, upon every succeeding day's experience, find that the two objects are not incompatible; but if such a case, which is possible, arise, he had far better sacrifice the façade, considering first the comforts of those who are to inhabit the house, and then the gratification of those who are only to look at it.

2488. Durand has well observed that compositions conducted on the above principles must please. "Has not nature," says that author, "attached pleasure to the satisfaction of our wants, and are our most lively pleasures other than the satisfaction of our most pressing wants? These wants are better satisfied in the interior distribution of a building than in the exterior." Who leaves the Pantheon without more satisfaction than he expected from the view of the portico, fine though it be? Again, faulty as are both St. Peter's and St. Paul's, will any one who understands the subject aver that he has received more pleasure from their respective façades than from their noble interiors? The pleasurable sensations produced by both are entirely dependent on their interior distribution. But when we find that in the former of these buildings there is no mockery of a dome, the interior and exterior being as far dependent on each other as the circumstances of construction would permit, whilst the dome of the latter is worse than a mockery, the interior and exterior domes having nothing in common with each other, the last being no more than a timber leaded appurtenance to the fabric, Wren, with all his greatness, for great he was, shrinks into nothingness by the side of Michael Angelo, although the external form of the dome of London be more elegant than that of the Vatican. This is a strong but not a forced illustration of our opinions, the good sense whereof must be left for appreciation to our readers, who, we doubt not, on a little reflection, will concur with us.

2489. In ninety-nine cases out of a hundred the student will find that a good distribution of his plan leads him, with anything like ordinary tact, to the composition of good sections and good elevations, far better, indeed, than he could arrive at by pursuing an opposite course. In domestic Gothic architecture, this is notorious, for in that a regular distribution of the openings would often produce the tamest and least picturesque effect. The Gothic architects placed windows internally where only they would be serviceable, letting them take their chance in the exterior. It is not to be understood, because such would be rather *outré*, that this method will exactly suit the principles of composition in Italian architecture; but it is well known to practical men that a required opening in a particular place, instead of being a blemish, may be converted on many occasions into a beauty. Indeed, it is incontrovertibly true that distribution and disposition are the first objects that should engage the architect's attention, even of him whose great aim is to strike the attention by ornament, which can never please unless its source can be traced to the most convenient and economical distribution of the leading parts. Theorists may be laughed at, but it does not move us, nor diminish our regret to see many architects without any other theory than that whereon, in an inverted position, their own wild fancies are grafted. If what we have stated be true, and from the nature of things we cannot imagine a controversy can arise upon our observations, the talent of the architect is to be estimated, as Durand properly observes, according to his solution of the two following problems: —

First. For a given sum, as in private buildings, to erect the most convenient and suitable house for his employer.

Second. The requisites in a building being given, as in public buildings, to erect it at the smallest possible expense.

2490. An investigation of all the modes of accomplishing these desiderata can only be fully effected in a work of much larger extent than this; but we have, in the practical parts of our volume, so prepared the reader, that he will not generally be at a loss in respect of the construction of a building, whatever its nature or destination.

Sect. V.

DRAWINGS NECESSARY IN COMPOSITION.

2490a. For the thorough comprehension of a projected edifice, at least three drawings are necessary, the *plan*, the *section*, and the *elevation*. The first is a horizontal section of it, the second the vertical section, which shows the building as if it were cut in half, that half nearest the spectator being removed from its plan, so as to permit the inner parts to become visible, and the third is the geometrical appearance of the front represented as if viewed from an infinite distance, in which no convergence of the lines would be seen.

2490b. In making a design, it is always better to put the general idea together on a single sheet of paper, and consequently, in most cases, on a small scale. This, in afterwards making the drawings, is, as may be necessary, increased in size. The three parts being drawn under one another, as shown in *fig.* 895a., wherein the middle diagram is the plan, the lower one the section, and the upper one the elevation. By thus beginning on a single sheet, in which the whole is before the eye, the corresponding lines are more readily transferred from one part to another. Having drawn through the middle of the paper the vertical AA, cut at right angles by the horizontal line BB, draw the required centres or axes of the walls CC and DD, and supposing the building is to be square, with the same opening of the compasses set out the axes of the return walls EE and FF. Having determined the thickness of the walls, one half may be set out on each side the axes, as in *ee*, *ff*, *cc*, and *dd*, and then the lines showing the thicknesses of the walls may be drawn. The width of openings in the walls may be next set out, half on each side the axes BB and AA, first drawn towards *bb* and *aa*, and the lines drawn to their places. Having thus proceeded, we shall discover that not only has the plan been drawn, but at the same time a considerable portion of the section and elevation. To distinguish the voids from the solids, the latter should be coloured or hatched, and then the next step will be as follows : — Parallel to the principal axis BB, draw the ground lines GG and GG. From these lines the heights of the building, its cornice and openings, may be set up in the section and elevation ; and afterwards, the height of the roof and projection of the cornice having been determined, they may be set out and drawn. In the section, as in the plan, it is usual either to colour or hatch the solid parts, as we have done in the figure.

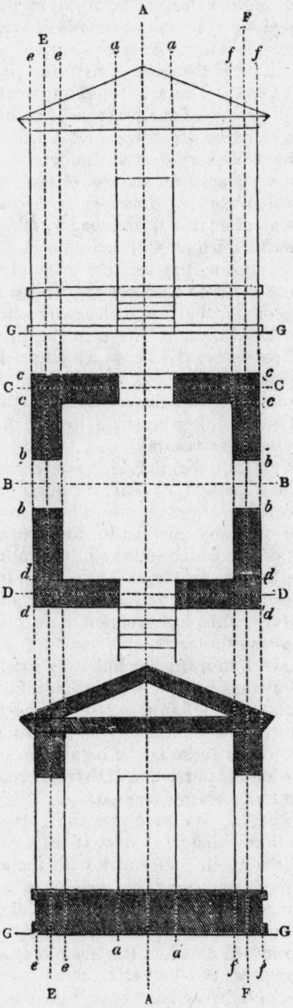

2490c. Simple as the above process may be, it contains the whole elementary part of the mechanical process necessary for making a design. It might have been conducted on a more complicated mass, but had we done so, it would not have been so well understood, and we therefore deprecate any observations on the simpleness of our process by those who have been brought to know these things by practice and experience. We do not, however, feel we should discharge our duty before closing this section, without a censure on the attempt to convert drawings of *geometrical* elevations and sections into picturesque representations, because such

Fig. 859a.

practice is not only injurious to the art, but is dishonest, and has a tendency to mislead the architect's employer ; and we are sorry to say that it is not unfrequently done with such a view. We denounce it, and without hesitation aver that the casting of shadows on a design is only admissible for the purpose of showing the relative depths of projecting parts ; and when so admitted, the medium should be confined to Indian ink or sepia, and thrown in merely in masses, the apertures being just slightly filled in with the same colour.

2491. Working drawings are those made of the parts at large for executing the works, which could not be well done from drawings on a small scale, wherein the small parts would not be either sufficiently defined, or could not be figured so as to enable the workman to set out his work with accuracy. They are generally in outline, except the sectional parts, which are frequently tinted to bring the profiles more readily before the eye.

2491a. It is obvious that though drawings made to a twelfth or a twenty-fourth part of their real size may well enough supply the wants of the workman where there is no complication in the distribution and arrangement, and where there is a simple treatment of regular forms, of right angles and the like; yet in all cases wherein we have to deal with the minor details of architecture, and in construction, where the variety of forms used is infinite from the variety of the circumstances, nothing short of drawings of the full, or at the least of half, the size will safely guide the workman.

2491b. The art of making working drawings, which must have been well understood at all periods of the practice of architecture, involves a thorough knowledge of projection, or descriptive geometry, and consists in expressing by lines all that occurs for the development of every part of the details of a building, in plan, elevation, and profile, each part being placed for the use of the workman with clearness and precision. All the rules by which working drawings are wrought are dependent on the matter in this work already communicated to the reader, excepting only those details of the orders, and some other matters, which will be found in Book III. But we shall here, nevertheless, briefly replace before him the leading principles whereon working drawings are to be prepared. And first, he is to recollect that solids are only represented by the faces opposite to the eye; secondly, that the surfaces by which solids are enclosed are of two sorts, that is, rectilinear or curvilinear. Those bodies in which these properties are combined may be divided into three sorts: 1. Those which are bounded by plane surfaces, such as prisms, pyramids, and generally all straight work. 2. Those in which there is a mixture of straight and curved lines, as cylinders, cones, or portions of them, voussoirs of vaulting, and the like; and 3. Those solids wherein a double flexure occurs, as in the sphere, spheroid, and in many cases of voussoirs.

2491c. We should, however, unnecessarily use our limited space by further entering on these matters, on which enough has been said in previous sections. The plain truth is, that working drawings are to be so made for the use of the artificer as to embody on a scale, to prevent any mistake, all the information which this work has already given on construction, and that which follows in the more refined view of architecture as a fine art.

2491d. In works whose magnitude is not of the first class, the drawing of every part, both in construction and in those which involve the work as one of art, should be given of the full size whereof it is proposed to be executed. Where the building is large, as also the parts, this may be dispensed with; but then it becomes (the detail being drawn on a smaller but fully intelligible scale) the duty of the architect to see that the drawings he furnishes are faithfully drawn out to the full size by the artificer on proper moulds. Often it is useful—never, indeed, otherwise—to *offer up*, as it is called, small portions of mouldings on the different parts of a building, to ascertain what the effect may be likely to be at the heights fixed for their real places. In these matters he should leave no means untried to satisfy himself of the effect which his first drawings *in small* is likely to produce when executed.

2491e. We have presumed that the architect is so far educated as to have acquired a full knowledge of all that rules can teach, and that, strictly speaking, he has proportioned his work in conformity with them. Still, in real practice, there are constantly so many circumstances which concur in making it almost necessary to depart from established rules, such as surrounding buildings, where it is of importance to give predominance to a part for the purpose of making it a feature, that the expedient of trying a portion of the proposed detail in the place it is actually to occupy, is a matter that we would advise every architect to adopt after he has made and studied the working drawings whereof we treat.

2491f. We have not alluded to the matters of carpentry and joinery, in which it is often necessary to give the artificer information by means of working drawings; but the methods of trussing in carpentry, and of framing in joinery, often require working drawings. What has already been exhibited under those heads (2031, *et seq.*) will prevent his being left uninstructed, and will, moreover, have afforded such information as to prepare him, by the exercise of his own ingenuity, for such cases as may not have been specially given in the examples herein contained. We therefore here close our observations under this section by an intimation to the student, that the proper preparation of working drawings for the use of the artificer tests his acquaintance with the theory and practice of the art, and is of the utmost importance to the pocket of the employer, which it is his duty as a gentleman incessantly to protect.

BOOK III.

PRACTICE OF ARCHITECTURE.

CHAP. I.

GRECIAN AND ITALIAN ARCHITECTURE.

Sect. I.

BEAUTY IN ARCHITECTURE.

2492. THE existence of architecture as a fine art is dependent on *expression*, or the faculty of representing, by means of lines, words, or other media, the inventions which the architect conceives suitable to the end proposed.   That *end* is twofold; to be useful, and to connect the use with a pleasurable sensation in the spectator of the invention.   In eloquence and poetry the end is to instruct, and such is the object of the higher and histo- rical classes of painting; but architecture, though the elder of the arts, cannot claim the rank due to painting and poetry, albeit its end is so much more useful and necessary to mankind.   In the sciences the end is utility and instruction, but in them the latter is not of that high moral importance, however useful, which allows them for a moment to come into competition with the great arts of painting, poetry, and eloquence.   It will be seen that we here make no allusion to the lower branches of portrait and landscape painting, but to that great moral and religious end which fired the mind of Michael Angelo in the Sistine Chapel, and of Raffaelle Sanzio in the Stanze of the Vatican and in the Cartoons. Above the lower branches of painting just mentioned, the art whereof we treat occupies an exalted station.   In it though the chief end is to produce an useful result, yet the ex- pression on which it depends, in common with the other great arts, brings each within the scope of those laws which govern generally the fine arts whose object is beauty.   Beauty, whatever difference of opinion may exist on the means necessary to produce it, is by all admitted to be the result of every perfection whereof an object is susceptible, such perfec- tions being altogether dependent on the agreeable proportions subsistent between the several parts, and those between the several parts and the whole.   The power or faculty of inventing is called *genius*.   By it the mind is capable of conceiving and of expressing its conceptions.   *Taste*, which is capable of being acquired, is the natural sensation of a mind refined by art.   It guides genius in discerning, embracing, and producing beauty.   Here we may for a moment pause to inquire what may be considered a standard of taste, and that cannot be better done than in the words used on the subject by Hume (Essay xxiii.): "The great variety of tastes," says that author, "as well as of opinion, which prevails in the world, is too obvious not to have fallen under every one's observation.   Men of the most confined knowledge are able to remark a difference of taste in the narrow circle of their acquaintance, even where the persons have been educated under the same government and have early imbibed the same prejudices.   But those who can enlarge their view to con- template distant nations and remote ages are still more surprised at the great inconsistence and contrariety.   We are apt to call *barbarous* whatever departs widely from our own taste and apprehension, but soon find the epithet of reproach retorted on us, and the highest arrogance and self-conceit is at last startled on observing an equal assurance on all sides, and scruples, amidst such a contest of sentiment, to pronounce positively in its own favour."   True as are the observations of this philosopher in respect of a standard of taste, we shall nevertheless attempt to guide the reader to some notion of a standard of taste in architecture.

2493.   There has lately grown into use in the arts a silly pedantic term under the name of Æsthetics, founded on the Greek word ᾽Αισθητικὸς, one which means having the power of perception by means of the senses; said to be the science whereby the first principles in all the arts are derived, from the effect which certain combinations have on the mind as con- nected with nature and reason: it is, however, one of the metaphysical and useless additions

to nomenclature in the arts, in which the German writers abound, and in its application to architecture of least value; because in that art form is from construction so limited by necessity, that sentiment can scarcely be said to be further connected with the art than is necessary for keeping the subordinate parts of the same character as the greater ones under which they are combined; and, further, for thereby avoiding incongruities.

2494. It is well known that all art in relation to nature is subject to those laws by which nature herself is governed, and if we were certain that those rules of art which resulted from reason were necessarily and actually connected with sensation, there would be no difficulty in framing a code of laws whereon the principles of any art might be firmly founded. "Principles in art," as well defined by Payne Knight, "are no other than the trains of ideas which arise in the mind of the artist out of a just and adequate consideration of all those local, temporary, or accidental circumstances upon which their propriety or impropriety, their congruity or incongruity, wholly depend." By way of illustrating the observation just made, we will merely allude to that maxim in architecture which inculcates the propriety of placing openings over openings and piers over piers, disallowing, in other words, the placing a pier over an opening without the exhibition of such preparation below as shall satisfy the mind that security has been consulted. There can be no doubt that a departure from the maxim creates an unpleasant sensation in the mind, which would seem to be immediately and intimately connected with the laws of reason; but there is great difficulty in satisfying one's self of the precise manner in which this operates on the mind, without a recurrence to the primitive types in architecture, and thence pursuing the inquiry. But in the other arts the types are found in nature herself, and hence in them no difficulty occurs in the establishment of laws, because we have that same nature whereto reference may be made. We shall have to return to this subject in the section on the Orders of Architecture, to which we must refer the reader, instead of pursuing the subject here.

2495. Throughout nature beauty seems to follow the adoption of forms suitable to the expression of the end. In the human form there is no part, considered in respect to the end for which it was formed by the great Creator, that in the eye of the artist, or rather, in this case the better judge, the anatomist, is not admirably calculated for the function it has to discharge; and without the accurate representation of those parts in discharge of their several functions, no artist by means of mere expression, in the ordinary meaning of that word, can hope for celebrity. This arises from an inadequate representation having the appearance of incompetency to discharge the given functions; or, in other words, they appear unfit to answer the end.

2496. We are thus led to the consideration of *fitness*, which, after all, will be found to be the basis of all *proportion*, if not proportion itself. Alison, in his *Essay on Taste*, says, "I apprehend that the beauty of proportion in forms is to be ascribed to this cause," (fitness) "and that certain proportions affect us with the emotion of beauty, not from any original capacity in such qualities to excite this emotion, but from their being expressive to us of the fitness of the parts to the end designed." Hogarth, who well understood the subject, concurs with Alison in considering that the emotion of pleasure which proportion affords does not resemble the pleasure of sensation, but rather that feeling of satisfaction arising from means properly adapted to their end. In his *Analysis of Beauty* that great painter places the question in its best and truest light, when, speaking of chairs and tables, or other common objects of furniture, he considers them merely as fitted from their proportions to the end they have to serve. In the same manner, says Alison, "the effect of disproportion seems to me to bear no resemblance to that immediate painful sensation which we feel from any disagreeable sound or smell, but to resemble that kind of dissatisfaction which we feel when means are unfitted to their end. Thus the disproportion of a chair or table does not affect us with a simple sensation of pain, but with a very observable emotion of dissatisfaction or discontent, from the unsuitableness of their construction for the purposes the objects are intended to serve. Of the truth of this every man must judge from his own experience." We cannot refrain from continuing our extracts from this most intelligent author. "The habit," he says, "which we have in a great many familiar cases of immediately conceiving this fitness from the mere appearance of the form, leads us to imagine, as it is expressed in common language, that we determine proportion by the eye, and this quality of fitness is so immediately expressed by the material form, that we are sensible of little difference between such judgments and a mere determination of sense; yet every man must have observed that in those cases where either the object is not familiar to us or the construction intricate our judgment is by no means speedy, and that we never discover the proportion until we previously discover the principle of the machine or the means by which the end is produced."

2497. The nature of the terms in which we converse shows the dependence of proportion on fitness, for it is the sign of the quality. The natural answer of a person asked why the proportion of any building or machine pleased him, would be, because the object by such proportion was fit or proper for its end. Indeed, proportion is but a synonyme of fitness,

for if the form be well contrived, and the several parts be properly adjusted to their end, we immediately express our opinion that it is well proportioned.

2498. There is, however, between proportion and fitness, a distinction drawn by our author, which must be noticed. " Fitness expresses the relation of the whole of the means to the end ; proportion, the proper relation of a part or parts to their end." But the distinction is too refined to be of importance in our consideration ; for the due proportion of parts is simply that particular form and dimension which from experience has been found best suited to the object in view. " Proportion," therefore continues Alison, " is to be considered as applicable only to forms composed of parts, and to express the relation of propriety between any part or parts and the end they are destined to serve."

2499. Forms are susceptible of many divisions, and consequently proportions; but these are only subordinate to the great end of the whole. Thus, for instance, in the constantly varying forms of fashion, say in a chair or table, the merely ornamental parts may bear no relation to the general fitness of the form, but they must be so contrived as to avoid unpleasant sensation, and not to interfere with the general fitness. If we do not understand the nature of its fitness, we cannot judge of the proportion properly. " No man," says Alison, " ever presumes to speak of the proportions of a machine of the use of which he is ignorant." When, however, we become acquainted with the use or purpose of a particular class of forms, we at the same time acquire a knowledge which brings under our view and acquaintance a larger circle of agreeable proportions than the rest of the world understand ; and those parts which by others are regarded with indifference, we contemplate with pleasure, from our superior knowledge of their fitness for the end designed. The proportions of an object must not in strength be carried beyond what is required for fitness, for in that case they will degenerate into clumsiness, whilst elegance, on the contrary, is the result of the nicest adjustment of proportion.

2500. Fitness cannot exist in any architectural object without *equilibrium* in all the parts as well as the whole. The most complete and perfect notion that can be conceived of *stability*, which is the result of equilibrium, may be derived from the contemplation of an horizontal straight line ; whilst, on the contrary, of instability nothing seems more expressive than a vertical straight line. These being, then, assumed as the extremes of stability and instability, by carrying out the gradations between the two extremes, we may, extending in two parts the vertical line, obtain various forms, more or less expressive of stability as they approach or recede from the horizontal line. In *fig.* 860. we have, standing on the same base, the general form of the lofty Gothic spire ; the pleasing, solid, and enduring form of the Egyptian pyramid ; and that of the flat Grecian pediment : which last, though in its inclination adjusted on different grounds, which have been examined in Book II. Chap. III. subsect. 2027, *et seq.*, is an eminent instance of stability.

Fig. 860.

The spire, from its height and small base, seems to possess but a tottering equilibrium compared with the others.

2501. Stability is obviously dependent on the laws of gravitation, on which, under the division of statics, not only the architect, but the painter and sculptor, should bestow considerable attention. We cannot for a moment suppose it will be disputed that at least one of the causes of the beauty of the pyramid is a satisfactory impression on the mind of the state of rest or stability it possesses. Rest, repose, stability, balance, all meaning nearly the same thing, are then the very essential ingredients in fitness; and therefore, in architectural subjects, instability, or the appearance of it, is fatal to beauty. Illustrations of this exist in the famous Asinelli and Garisendi towers at Bologna, and at Pisa in the celebrated leaning Campanile.

2502. It may be objected to what we have written, that fitness alone will not account for the pleasure which arises in the contemplation of what are called the orders of architecture, and Alison seems very much to doubt whether there be not some other cause of beauty. It will, however, be our business to show how the ancients, their inventors, considered principally their fitness ; and upon these grounds to show, moreover, how the proportions in ancient examples varied, and may be still further varied, without infringing upon the principles which guided them in the original invention. Payne Knight has well observed, " that the fundamental error of imitators in all the arts is, that they servilely copy the effects which they see produced, instead of supplying and adopting the principles which guided the original artists in producing them ; wherefore they disregard all those local, temporary, or accidental circumstances upon which their propriety or impropriety, their congruity or incongruity, wholly depend." " Grecian temples, Gothic abbeys, and feudal castles were all well adapted to their respective uses, circumstances, and situations ; the distribution of the parts subservient to the purposes of the whole ; and the ornaments and decorations suited to the character of the parts, and to the manners, habits, and employments of the persons who were to occupy them : but the house of an English noble-

man of the 18th or 19th century is neither a Grecian temple, a Gothic abbey, nor a feudal castle; and if the style of distribution or decoration of either be employed in it, such changes and modifications should be admitted as may adapt it to existing circumstances, otherwise the scale of its exactitude becomes that of its incongruity, and the deviation from principle proportioned to the fidelity of imitation." This is but another application of the principle of fitness which we have above considered, the chief foundation of beauty in the art. We have shown how it is dependent on stability as a main source of fitness, and here subjoin some maxims which will lead the student to fitness in his designs, and prevent him from running astray, if he but bring himself to the belief that they are reasonable, and founded upon incontestable grounds, which we can assure him they are.

First.   Let that which is the stronger part always bear the weaker.
Second.   Let solidity be always real, and not brought to appear so by artifice.
Third.   Let nothing be introduced into a composition whose presence is not justified by necessity.
Fourth.   Let unity and variety be so used as not to destroy each other.
Fifth.   Let nothing be introduced that is not subordinate to the whole.
Sixth.   Let symmetry and regularity so reign as to combine with order and solidity.
Seventh.   Let the proportions be of the simplest sort.
Eighth.   Let him recollect that nothing is beautiful which has not some good and useful end.

If, after having made his design, he will scrupulously test it by these maxims *seriatim*, and will strike out what is discordant with the tenor of them, he will have overcome a few of the difficulties which attend the commencement of his career.

2503. We are not of the same opinion with those who, on a geometrical elevation of a building, draw lines from its apex, which, bounding the principal parts of the outline, find a pyramidal form, and thence infer beauty of general outline. If those who favour such a notion will but reflect for a moment, they must see that this cannot be a test of its effect, inasmuch as the construction of a geometrical elevation of any edifice supposes it to be viewed at an infinite distance, whereas, in fact, it is most generally viewed under angles which would puzzle the most learned architect, without full investigation, to discover the primary lines which they assume to be the causes of its beauty. The obscurations and foreshortenings that take place are at points of view near the building itself; and, however judicious it may be to form the general masses in obedience to such a system, so as to produce an effect in the distance that may be in accordance with the principle, it would be extremely dangerous to lay the principle down as a law. The finest view of St. Paul's is perhaps a little east of Fetter Lane, on the northern side of Fleet Street; but it would puzzle any one to discover its pyramidal form from that point of view.

2504. The beauty of the proportions of architecture in the interiors of buildings is dependent on those which govern the exteriors. Much has been said on proportions of rooms, which, hereafter, we shall have to notice: we mean the proportions of their length to their breadth and height. That these are important, we cannot deny; but whether the beauty of a room is altogether dependent on the due adjustment of these, we have some doubts; that is, under certain limits. We here address ourselves more particularly to that fitness which, in ornamenting a ceiling, for example, requires that the beams which appear below the general surface should invariably fall over piers, and that in this respect corresponding sides should be uniform. In the study of this point, Inigo Jones is the great English master who has left the student the most valuable examples of this branch of the art.

2505. It may, perhaps, be useful to observe generally that the bare proportions of the interiors of apartments depend on the purposes for which they are intended, and according to these we seek immediately for the expression of their fitness. This point, therefore, involves on the part of the architect so general an acquaintance with the most refined habits of his employers, that we should be almost inclined to agree with Vitruvius on the multifarious qualifications necessary to constitute a good one. Certain it is that no instructions he can receive for building a mansion will qualify him without an intimate acquaintance with the habits of the upper classes of society.

2506. We have already stated that it is hopeless to arrive at a fixed standard of taste. That considered worthy of the appellation will not be so considered in another. "The sable Africans," says Knight, quoting from Mungo Park, "view with pity and contempt the marked deformity of the Europeans, whose mouths are compressed, their noses pinched, their cheeks shrunk, their hair rendered lank and flimsy, their bodies lengthened and emaciated, and their skins unnaturally bleached by shade and seclusion, and the baneful influence of a humid climate." In the countries of Europe, where some similarity of taste may be expected, the tyranny of fashion, no less than that of habit and circumstance, has, and always will have, its influence on the arts. Within the short space of even a few months we have seen what is called the *renaissance* style of architecture imported from France, drawing into its vortex all classes of persons, many of them among the higher

ranks, possessed of education to have patronised better taste; and in architecture, and some other arts, no one solves the question of what is really right by saying that there have been errors in the tastes of different ages.

2507. The specimens of Greek sculpture, whose beauty is founded in nature herself, will throughout all time excite the admiration of the world; because in this case, the standard or type being nature, mankind generally may be supposed to be competent judges of the productions of the art. But it is very different in architecture, whose types in every style are, as respects their origin, uncertain; and when we are asked whether there be a real and permanent principle of beauty in the art, though we must immediately reply in the affirmative, we are at the same time constrained to refer it to the quality of fitness. If this were not the case, how could we extend our admiration to the various styles of Egyptian, Grecian, Roman, Gothic, and Italian architecture? These at first appear, compared with each other, so dissimilar, that it seems impossible to assign beauty to one without denying it to the rest. But on examination each will be found so fitted to its end, that such cause alone will be found to be the principal source of the pleasure that an educated mind receives from each style; and that thence it arises, rather than from any certain or definable combinations of forms, lines, or colours that are in themselves gratifying to the mind or agreeable to the organs of sensation. If this be true, what becomes of the doctrine of the German æsthetical school, so vaunted of by self-constituted critics and reviewers, who pass their judgment *ex cathedrâ* on works they have never seen, and, strange to say, are tolerated for a moment by the public? The truth is, the public rarely give themselves the trouble to judge; and unless led, which is easily done by the few, do not undertake the trouble of judging for themselves. That the Egyptian pyramid, the Grecian and the Roman temple, the early Christian basilica, the Gothic cathedral, the Florentine palace, the Saracenic mosque, the pagoda of the East, are all beautiful objects, we apprehend none will dispute; but there is in none of them a common form or standard by which we can judge of their beauty: the only standard on which we can fall back is the great fitness of them, under their several circumstances, for the end proposed in their erection.

2508. We are thus unavoidably driven to the conclusion that beauty in its application to architecture changes the meaning of the word with every change of its application; for those forms which in one style are strictly beautiful on account of their fitness, applied to another become disgusting and absurd. By way of illustrating this, let us only picture to ourselves a frieze of Grecian triglyphs separating the nave and clerestory of a Gothic cathedral. From what we have been taught to consider the type of the Doric frieze connected with its triglyphs an idea of fitness immediately arises in the mind; but we cannot trace its fitness in a dissimilar situation, neither can we comment on such an incongruity better than in the oft-quoted lines of Horace: —

> " Humano capiti cervicem pictor equinam
> Jungere si velit, et varias inducere plumas
> Undique collatis membris, ut turpiter atrum
> Desinet in piscem mulier formosa supernè;
> Spectatum admissi risum teneatis amici?"

The influence of circumstances in every age has imparted to each style of architecture its peculiar beauty and interest; and until some extraordinary convulsion in society give the impetus to a new one, we are constrained to follow systems which deprive us of other novelty than those of changes which are within the spirit of the universally established laws of the art. Turn to the Gothic churches of the present day, — the little pets of the church commissioners and clergy. What objects of ineffable contempt the best of them are! The fact is, the religious circumstances of the country have so changed that they are wholly unsuitable in style to the Protestant worship. Had, with the scanty means afforded to the architects, such a model as St. Paul's, Covent Garden, been adopted, we might have seen a number of edifices in the country, though

> " Facies non omnibus una
> Nec diversa tamen,"

that might have been an honour to the age in which we live, and suitable to the circumstances of the times.

2509. Unity and harmony in a work necessarily enter into that which is beautiful; and it will not therefore require any argument to show that from a mixture of styles in any building incongruity and unfitness, and consequently a want of unity and harmony, must be the result. Hence we cannot agree with those wise reviewers who advocate the possibility of amalgamating the arch with the severe Grecian style. We leave them to their dreams, and trust that before we give them credence we may have some proof of their practical power in this respect.

2510. Symmetry is that quality which, as its name imports, from one part of an assemblage of parts enables us to arrive at a knowledge of the whole. It is a subordinate, but nevertheless a necessary, ingredient in beauty. It is necessary that parts performing the same office in a building should be strictly similar, or they would not *ex vi termini* be

symmetrical; so, when relations are strictly established between certain parts, making one the measure of another, a disregard of the symmetry thus induced cannot fail of destroying beauty. But here again we have to say, that for want of attention to the similarity of the parts, or neglect of the established relations on which the whole is founded, they have lost their symmetry, and have thus become *unfit* for their purpose; so that thus again we return to fitness as the main foundation of beauty.

2511. Colour abstractedly considered has little to do with architectural beauty, which is founded, as is sculpture, on fine form. We are here speaking generally, and are not inclined to assert that the colour of a building in a landscape is unimportant to the general effect of that landscape, or that the colours used on the walls of the interior of a building are unessential considerations; but we do not hesitate to say that they are of minor consequence in relation to our art. We believe it would be difficult to paint (we mean not in the sense of the artist) the interior of the banqueting room at Whitehall, were it restored to its original destination, and divested of the ruinous accessories which from its original purpose have turned it from a banqueting room into a chapel,—we believe, we say, that it would be difficult to paint it so as to destroy its internal beauty. But as we intend to be short under this head, we shall quote a brochure touching on this subject published by us in 1837.

2512. One of the beauties tending to give effect to the edifices of Greece has been, on the testimony of almost all travellers, the colour of the materials whereof they are composed. Dr. Clarke observes that a warm ochreous tint is diffused over all the buildings of the Acropolis, which *he* says is peculiar to the ruins of Athens. " Perhaps," says the author, " to this warm colour, so remarkably characterising the remains of ancient buildings at Athens, Plutarch alluded" (*In Vita Pericles*) "in that beautiful passage cited by Chandler, where he affirmed *that the structures of Pericles possessed a peculiar and unparalleled excellence of character; a certain freshness bloomed upon them and preserved their faces uninjured, as if they possessed a never-fading spirit, and had a soul insensible to age.*" It is singular that recent discoveries have incontestably proved that this species of beauty at all events did not originally exist in them, inasmuch as it is now clearly ascertained that it was the practice of the Greeks to paint the whole of the inside and outside of their temples in party colours. It had been some time known that they were in the habit of painting and picking out the ornaments on particular parts of their buildings; but M. Schaubert, the architect of the King of Greece, found on examination that this fell far short of the extent to which this species of painting was carried, and M. Semper, another German architect, has fully corroborated the fact in his examination of the Temple of Theseus. The practice was doubtless imported into Greece from Egypt, and was not to be easily abandoned, seeing the difficulty of falling away from the habits of a people whence it seems certain the arts of Greece more immediately came. It is by no means uncommon for a person to be fully alive to all the beauties of form, without at the same time having a due feeling or perception of the beauty resulting from harmony in colouring. It is therefore not to be assumed that the Greeks, though given to a practice which we would now discourage, possessed not that taste in other respects which has worthily received the admiration of posterity. The practice of painting the inside and outside of buildings has received the name of *polychromatic* architecture, and we shall here leave it to the consideration of the student as a curious and interesting circumstance, but certainly without a belief that it could add a charm to the stupendous simplicity and beauty of such a building as the Parthenon.

2513. After all that we have said of fitness, it will be expected that in *decoration* it shall form a principal ingredient. By the term decoration we understand the combination of objects and ornaments that the necessity of variety introduces under various forms, to embellish, to enrich, and to explain the subjects whereon they are employed. The art of decoration, so as to add to the beauty of an object, is, in other words, that of carrying out the emotions already produced by the general form and parts of the object itself. By its means the several relations of the whole and the parts to each other are increased by new combinations; new images are presented to the mind whose effect is variety, one great source of pleasure. From these observations two general rules may be deduced in respect of decoration. *First*, that it must actually be or seem to be necessary. *Second*, that such objects must be employed in it as have relation to the end of the general object of the design. We are not to suppose that all parts of a work are susceptible of ornament. Taste must be our guide in ascertaining where decoration is wanted, as well as the quantity requisite. The absence of it altogether is in many cases a mode of decoration. As in language its richness and the luxuriance of images do not suit all subjects, and simplicity in such cases is the best dress, so in the arts of design many subjects would be rather impoverished than enriched by decoration. We must therefore take into consideration the character of the building to be decorated, and then only apply such ornament as is necessary and suitable to that character. We may judge of its necessity if the absence of it causes a dissatisfaction from the void space left; of its suitableness, by its developing the character. History has recorded the contempt with which that decorator was treated who

ornamented the senate house with statues of wrestlers, and the gymnasium with statues of senators.

2514. By some the art of architecture itself has been considered nothing more than that of decorating the buildings which protection from the elements induces us to raise.

2515. The objects which architecture admits for decoration result from the desire of producing *variety, analogy*, and *allegory*. We here follow Quatremère de Quincy. (*Encyc. Method.*) The first seems more general than the others, as being common among all nations that practise building. It is from this source we have such a multitude of cut-work, embroidery, details, compartments, and colours, more or less minute, which are found in every species of architecture. It would be useless for the most philosophical mind to seek for the origin of these objects in any want arising out of the mere construction, or in any political or superstitious custom. Systems of conjecture might be exhausted without arriving one point nearer the truth. Even in the most systematic of the different kinds of architecture, namely, that of the Greeks, we cannot avoid perceiving a great number of forms and details whose origin is derived from the love of variety, and that alone. In a certain point of view, thus considered, an edifice is nothing more than a piece of furniture, a vase, an utensil, the ornaments on which are placed more for the purpose of pleasing the eye than any other. Such, for instance, are the roses of caissons in ceilings and sofites, the leaves round the bell of the Corinthian capital, the Ionic volutes, and many others, besides universally the carving of mouldings themselves. These ornaments, drawn from the store-house of nature, are on that account in themselves beautiful; but it is their transference to architecture, which in the nature of things can have but a problematical and conjectural origin, that seems to indicate a desire to vary the surface. Unless it was the desire of variety that induced them, we know not what could have done so.

2516. It has been well observed by the author we have just quoted, that though the art has been obliged to acknowledge that many of its decorations depend in their application on such forms as necessity imposes, and in the formation of them on chance, caprice, or whatever the love of variety may dictate, yet in the disposition of them there must reign an order and arrangement subordinate to that caprice, and that at this point commences the difference between architecture as an art subservient to laws which are merely dependent on the pleasure imparted to the eye, and those which depend on the mere mechanical disposition of the building considered as a piece of furniture. Architecture, of all the arts, is that which produces the fewest emotions of the minds of the many, because it is the least comprehensible in regard to the causes of its beauty. Its images act indirectly on our senses, and the impressions it seems to make appear reducible chiefly to magnitude, harmony, and variety, which after all are not qualities out of the reach of an architect of the most ordinary mind, and therefore not — at least the first and last — unattainable where economy does not interfere to prevent the result to be attained.

2517. Analogy, the second of the objects by which decoration is admitted into architecture, seems to be resultant from the limited nature of all human inventions in the arts, and the power of being unable to invent except by imitation and alteration of the forms of objects pre-existent. It is most difficult to discard altogether what have been considered types in architecture, and that difficulty has so prevailed as to limit those types to their most probable origin in the case of the orders.

2518. The reader will begin to perceive that our analogy in decoration tends upon trees for columns, the ends of beams for triglyphs, and the like. Whatever truth there may be in this analogy, it is now so established as to guide the rules of decoration that are involved in it; and it must be conceded, that if we are desirous of imitating the peculiar art of any country, we have no hope of success but by following the forms which the construction in such country engenders; and we must admit that, as far as external circumstances can direct us, the architecture of Greece, which, modified, has become that of. the whole of Europe, and will become that of America, seems so founded on the nature of things, that, however we may doubt, it would not be prudent to lead the reader away from the consideration, and perhaps from a belief, that such is the truth. Without holding ourselves bound by the analogy of the types of the tree and the cross beam, which appear to have guided the architects of Greece, we can without hesitation assert, that whenever those have been abandoned the art has fallen on the most flagrant vices; witness the horrors of the school of Borromini, where the beams are broken, pediments, which are the gables of roofs, are broken into fantastic forms, and none of the parts seem naturally connected with each other. The works of the school in question seem indeed so broken up, that the study of them would almost convince an impartial and competent judge that the converse of its practice is sufficiently beautiful to establish the truth of the types whereon we have here and before expressed our scepticism. "Sitôt," says De Quincy, "que le génie decorateur s'est cru libre des entraves de l'analogie, toutes les formes caractéristiques se sont contournées, perverteés, et dénaturées, au point qu'il y a entr'elles et celle de la bonne architecture, plus de distance qu'entre celles-ci et les types de la primitive construction."

2519. In the decoration of architecture, neither of the other two means employed are

more important than that ocular language which architecture occasionally employs in its ornaments. By its use architecture is almost converted into painting, and an edifice becomes a picture, or a collection of pictures, through the aid of the sculptor. We shall refer to no other building than the Parthenon to prove the assertion. Here the history of the goddess is embodied in the forms of the building, and to the decoration thus introduced the subordinate parts of the sculpture, if it be not heresy so to call them, is kept so under that we are almost inclined to cry out against their not having been principals instead of accessories. This is the true principle upon which buildings should be decorated to impress the mind of the spectator with the notion of beauty, and the principle which, carried out, no matter what the style be, will insure the architect his most ample reward, reputation. The matter that is supplied by allegory for decoration in architecture may be considered under three heads — *attributes, figures,* and *paintings.*

2520. The first takes in all those foliages, plants, flowers, and fruits, which from their constant use in sacrifices were at last transferred from the altar to the walls of the temple. The garlands, festoons, chaplets, and crowns which we find sculptured on temples seem to have had their origin from the religious ceremonies performed in them; as do the instruments of sacrifice, vases, the heads of the victims, pateræ, and all the other objects employed in the worship of the ancients. Thus, in architecture, these have become conventional signs, indicating the destination of the buildings to which they are applied. From the particular application of some ornaments on temples we derive in the end a language in the arts of imitation. It was thus that the eagle grasping in his talons the attribute of Jupiter, came to represent eternity and omnipotence; the myrtle and dove of Venus, the passion of love; the lyre and laurel of Apollo, to point to harmony and glory; the spear and helmet of Mars, to represent war. Palms and crowns became the emblems of victory, as did the olive the emblem of peace. In the same way the ears of corn of Ceres, the serpent of Esculapius, the bird of Minerva, and the cock of Mercury were equivalent to the expression of abundance, science, and vigilance. Instruments of the arts, sciences, in short, all objects useful to the end for which an edifice is erected, naturally become signs of that edifice; but applied otherwise become absurd. What, for instance, could be more ridiculous than placing ox sculls and festoons on the frieze of a Protestant church? — and yet this has been done in our own days.

2521. Figures of men and animals come under the second head. The application of these may be seen to their highest perfection in the Parthenon, to which we have already alluded. They may be introduced in low, high, or full relief. In the last case their situation is usually that of a niche. We shall say no more on the subject of figures than that of course they must have relation to the end for which the edifice is erected, and if not in that respect perfectly intelligible are worse than useless.

2522. The walls of Pompeii furnish ancient examples of the decoration obtained by the aid of painting, as do the loggie of the Vatican and the ceilings of the Farnesina modern examples of it. Herein the moderns have far surpassed anything we know of the ancient application of painting. Sculpture, however, seems more naturally allied to architecture than painting, and, except in purely decorative painting on walls and ceilings, the introduction of it seems bounded within narrow limits. The rules as to fitness of the subjects introduced, applicable to the first two heads, are equally so under that of painting.

Sect. II.

THE ORDERS.

2523. An order in architecture is a certain assemblage of parts subject to uniform established proportions, regulated by the office that each part has to perform. It may be compared to what organisation is in animal nature. As from the paw of a lion his dimensions may be deduced, so from a triglyph may be found the other parts of an example of the Doric order, and from given parts in other orders the whole configuration may be found. As the genus may be defined as consisting of *essential* and *subservient* parts, the first-named are the column and its entablature, which, as its name imports, is as it were the tabled work standing on the column. The subservient parts are the mouldings and detail into which the essential parts are subdivided, and which we shall hereafter separately consider. The species of orders are five in number, Tuscan, Doric, Ionic, Corinthian, and Composite, each of whose mass and ornaments are suited to its character and the expression it is intended to possess. These are the five orders of architecture, in the proper understanding and application whereof is laid the foundation of architecture as an art. The characters of strength, grace, and elegance, of lightness and of richness, are distinguishing features of the several orders, in which those characters ought to be found not only in the column employed, but should pervade the whole composition, whereof the

column is, as it were, the regulator. The mode of setting up, or, as it is technically termed, profiling an order, will be given in a subsequent part of this section. Here we shall merely observe that the entablature is subdivided into an architrave, which lies immediately upon the column, a frieze lying on the architrave, and a cornice, which is its uppermost subdivision. The height of these subdivisions together, that is, the whole height of the entablature, is one fourth that of the column according to the practice of the ancients, who in all sorts of entablatures seldom varied from that measure either in excess or defect. " Palladio, Scamozzi, Alberti, Barbaro, Cataneo, Delorme, and others," says Sir William Chambers, " of the modern architects, have made their entablatures much lower in the Ionic, Composite, and Corinthian orders than in the Tuscan or Doric. This, on some occasions, may not only be excusable but highly proper; particularly where the intercolumniations are wide, as in a second or third order, in private houses, or inside decorations, where lightness should be preferred to dignity, and where expense, with every impediment to the conveniency of the fabric, are carefully to be avoided ; but to set entirely aside a proportion which seems to have had the general approbation of the ancient artists is surely presuming too far."

2524. As rules in the fine arts which have obtained almost universal adoption are founded on nature or on reason, we may be pretty certain that they are not altogether empirical, albeit their origin may not be immediately apparent. The grounds on which such rules are founded will, however, in most cases become known by tracing them to first principles, which we shall here endeavour to do in respect of this very important relation of height between the column and its entablature. We were first led into this investigation by the perusal of a work by M. Lebrun, entitled *Théorie de l'Architecture Grecque et Romaine deduite de l'analyse des Monumens antiques*, fol. Paris, 1807 ; but our results differ very widely from those of Lebrun, as will be seen on reference to that work.

2525. One of the most obvious principles of proportion in respect of loads and supports, and one seemingly founded on nature herself, is, that a support should not be loaded with a greater mass or load than itself; or, in other words, that there should be an equality between weights and supports, or, in the case in point, between the columns and entablature. In respect of the proportion of the voids below the entablature between the columns or supports, a great diversity of practice seems to have prevailed, inasmuch as we find them varying from 1·03 to 2·18, unity being the measure of the supports. Lebrun makes the areas of the supports, weights, and voids equal to one another, and in what may be termed the monumental examples of the Doric order, such as the Parthenon, &c., he seems borne out in the law he endeavours to establish ; but in lighter examples, such as the temple (Ionic) of Bacchus at Teos, where the supports are to the voids as 1 : 2·05, and in the temple of Minerva Polias, where the ratio is as 1 : 2·18, he is beyond all question incorrect : indeed there hardly seems a necessity for the limitation of the voids he prescribes, seeing that, without relation separately to the weight and support, stability would be obtained so long as the centre of gravity of the load fell within the external face of the support. If it be admitted that, as in the two examples above mentioned, the voids should be equal to the supports jointly, we have a key to the rule, and instead of being surprised at the apparently strange law of making the entablature one fourth of the height of the column, we shall find that no other than the result assumed can flow from the investigation.

2526. In fig. 861. let AB be the height of the column, and let the distance between the columns be one third of the height of the column = CD. Now if AB be subdivided into four equal parts at *a, b*, and *c*, and the horizontal lines *ad, be*, and *cf* be drawn ; also, if CD be divided horizontally into four equal parts, and lines be drawn perpendicularly upwards intersecting the former ones, the void will be divided into sixteen equal parallelograms, one half whereof are to be the measure of the two whole supports BC and DE ; and DE being then made equal to one half of CD, it will be manifest, from inspection, that the two semi-supports will jointly be equal to eight of the parallelograms above mentioned, or one half of the void. We have now to place the entablature or weight AGHI upon the supports or columns, and equal to them in mass. Set up from A to F another row of parallelograms, each equal to those above mentioned, shown on the figure by AFKI. These will not be equal to the supports by two whole parallelograms, being in number only six instead of eight ; dividing, therefore, 8, the number in the supports, by 6, the number already obtained, we have 1·333, &c., which is the height to be assigned to AG, so that the weight may exactly equal the

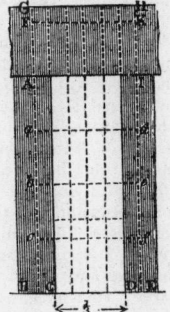

Fig. 861.

supports, thus exceeding one quarter of the height of the support (or column) by $\frac{333}{1000}$ of such quarter, a coincidence sufficient to corroborate the reason on which the law is founded.

2527. From an inspection of the *figs.* 861, 862, 863, it appears that when the void is one third the height of the supports in width, the supports will be 6 diameters in height; when one fourth of their height, they will be 8 diameters high; also that the intercolumniation, called systylos or of two diameters, is constant by the arrangement. When the surface of the columns, as they appear to the eye, is equal to that of the entablature, and the voids are equal to the sum of those surfaces, the height of the entablature will always be one third of that of the columns. Thus, let the diameter of the columns be $= 1$, their height $= h$, their number $= n$. Then the surface of the columns is nh; that of the entablature the same. As the surface of the voids is double that of the columns, the width of the intercolumniations is double the width of the columns, that is, $2n$ diameters, which, added to the n diameters of the columns, gives $3n$ diameters for length of the entablature; therefore, the surface of this entablature is nh, and its length being $3n$, its height must be $\frac{nh}{3n} = \frac{h}{3}$ exactly.

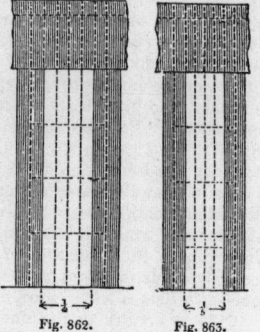

Fig. 862.   Fig. 863.

2528. Trying the principle in another manner, let *fig.* 864. be the general form of a tetrastyle temple wherein the columns are assumed at pleasure 8 diameters in height.

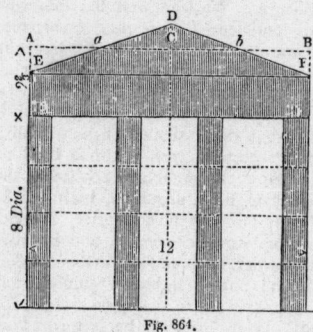

Fig. 864.

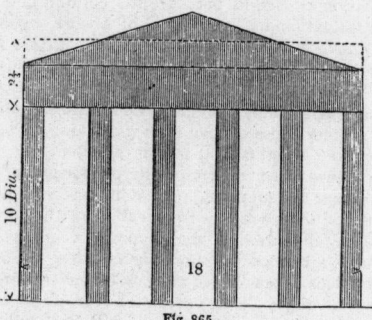

Fig. 865.

Then $4 \times 8 = 32$ the areas of the supports; and as to fulfil the conditions the three voids are equal to twice that area, or 64, they must consequently be in the aggregate equal to 8 diameters, for $\frac{64}{8} = 8$, and the whole extent will therefore be equal to 12 diameters of a support or column. To obtain the height of the entablature so that its mass may equal that of the supports, as the measures are in diameters, we have only to divide 32, the columns, by 12, the whole extent of the facade, and we obtain two diameters and two thirds of a diameter for the height of the entablature, making it a little more than one quarter of the height of the column, and again nearly agreeing in terms of the diameter with many of the finest examples of antiquity. If a pediment be added, it is evident, the dotted lines AC, CB being bisected in *a* and *b* respectively, that the triangles AE*a*, *b*FB are respectively equal to CD*a* and D*b*C, and the loading or weight will not be changed.

2529. Similar results will be observed in fig. 865., where the height is ten diameters, the number of columns 6, the whole therefore 180, the supports being 60. Here $\frac{60}{18} = 3\frac{1}{3}$ diameters will be the height of the entablature. This view of the law is further borne out by an analysis of the rules laid down by Vitruvius, book iii. chap. 2, ; — rules which did not emanate from that author, but were the result of the practice of the time wherein he lived, and, within small fractions, strongly corroborative of the soundness of the hypothesis of the voids being equal to twice the supports. Speaking of the five species of temples, after specifying the different intercolumniations, and recommending the eustylos as the most beautiful, he thus directs the formation of temples with that interval between the columns. " The rule for designing them is as follows: — The extent of the front being given, it is, if tetrastylos, to be divided into $11\frac{1}{2}$ parts, not including the projections of the base and plinth at each end; if hexastylos, into 18 parts; if octastylos, into $24\frac{1}{4}$ parts. One of either of these parts, according to the case, whether tetrastylos, hexastylos, or octastylos, will be a measure equal to the diameter of one of the columns." . . . . " The heights of the columns will be $8\frac{1}{4}$ parts. Thus the intercolumniations and the heights of the columns will have proper proportion." In the same chapter he gives directions for setting out aræostyle, diastyle, and systyle temples, which directions it is not here necessary to investigate, and our limits do not indeed permit us so to do. We

will therefore now examine the directions quoted. The tetrastylos is $11\frac{1}{2}$ parts wide and $8\frac{1}{2}$ high; the area therefore of the whole front becomes $11\frac{1}{2} \times 8\frac{1}{2} = 97\frac{3}{4}$. The four columns are $4 \times 8\frac{1}{2} = 34$, or a very little more than one third of the whole area; the remaining two thirds, speaking in round numbers, being given to the intercolumns or voids.

2530. The hexastylos (see *fig.* 865.) is 18 parts long and $8\frac{1}{2}$ high; the whole area therefore is $18 \times 8\frac{1}{2} = 153$. The six columns will be $6 \times 8\frac{1}{2} = 51$, or exactly one third of the whole area; the voids or intercolumns occupying the remaining two thirds.

2531. The octastylos is $24\frac{1}{2}$ parts in extent and $8\frac{1}{2}$ in height. Then $24\frac{1}{2} \times 8\frac{1}{2} = 208\frac{1}{4}$. The eight columns will be $8 \times 8\frac{1}{2} = 68$, being a trifle less than one third of the area, and the voids or intercolumns about double, or the remaining two thirds.

The average of the intercolumns in the first case will be $\dfrac{11\frac{1}{2} - 4}{3} = 2\frac{1}{2}$ diameters.

In the second case — — — — $\dfrac{18 - 6}{5} = 2\frac{2}{5}$ diameters.

In the third case — — — — $\dfrac{24\frac{1}{2} - 8}{7} = 2\frac{357}{1000}$ diameters.

A discrepance between practice and theory, unless extremely wide, must not be allowed to interfere with principles, and we have therefore no hesitation in candidly submitting a synoptical view of some of the most celebrated examples of antiquity in which a comparison is exhibited between the voids and supports; certain it is that in every case the former exceed the latter, and that in the earlier examples of Doric, the ratio between them nearly approached equality. In comparing, however, the supports with the weights, there is every appearance of that part of the theory being strictly true; for in taking a mean of the six examples of the Doric order, the supports are to the weights as $1 : 1\cdot16$; in the five of the Ionic order as $1 : 1\cdot05$; and in the four of the Corinthian order as $1 : 1\cdot04$, a coincidence so remarkable, that it must be attributed to something more than accident, and deserves much more extended consideration than it has hitherto received.

Building.	Order.	Number of Columns.	Supports.	Weights.	Voids.
Temple of Jupiter Nemeus - -	Doric	6	1·00	0·79	1·03
Parthenon - - -	—	8	1·00	1·07	1·04
Temple at Bassæ - - -	—	6	1·00	1·14	1·16
Temple of Minerva at Sanium -	—	6	1·00	1·40	1·17
Temple of Theseus at Athens -	—	6	1·00	1·13	1·21
Temple of Jupiter Panhellenius -	—	6	1·00	1·45	1·36
Temple of Erectheus - - -	Ionic	6	1·00	0·89	1·24
Temple of Fortuna Virilis at Rome -	—	4	1·00	1·15	1·71
Temple on the Ilyssus - -	—	4	1·00	0·96	1·72
Temple of Bacchus at Teos - -	—	8	1·00	1·35	2·05
Temple of Minerva Polias, Athens -	—	4	1·00	1·01	2·18
Portico of Septimius Severus -	Corinthian	6	1·00	0·93	1·37
Maison Carrée at Nismes - -	—	6	1·00	0·93	1·58
Temple at Jackly - - -	—	6	1·00	0·90	1·62
Pantheon Rome - - -	—	8	1·00	1·43	1·84

If instead of taking the apparent bulk of a column, that is, as a square pier, we take its real bulk, which is about three quarters ($\frac{3}{4}$) that of a square pier of the same diameter and height; the height of the entablature will be one fourth of the height of the column; for $\frac{3}{4}$ of $\dfrac{h'}{3} = \dfrac{h}{4}$.

There is a curious fact connected with the hypothesis which has been suggested that requires notice; it is relative to the area of the points of support for the edifice which the arrangement affords. In *fig.* 866. the hatched squares represent the plans of quarter piers of columns in a series of intercolumniations every way, such intercolumniations being of two diameters, or four semidiameters. These, added to the quarter piers, make six semidiameters, whose square 36 is therefore the area to be covered with the weight. The four quarter piers or columns=4, hence the points of support are $\frac{4}{36}$ of the area =0·111. Now in the list (1583.) of the principal buildings in Europe the mean ratio is 0·168, differing only 0·057 from the result here given; but if we select the following buildings, the mean will be found to differ much less.

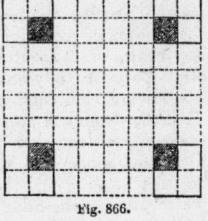

Fig. 866.

Temple of Peace - 0·127
S. Paolo fuori le Murà - 0·118
S. Sabino - - 0·100
S. Filippo Neri - - 0·129 Sum = 0·474. Mean $\dfrac{0\cdot474}{4} = 0\cdot118$.

MOULDINGS.

2532. The subservient parts of an order, called mouldings, and common to all the orders, are eight in number. They are—1. The *ovolo, echinus,* or *quarter round.* (*Fig.* 867.) It is formed by a quadrant, or sometimes more, of a circle, but in Grecian examples its section is obtained by portions of an ellipse or some other conic section. This latter observation is

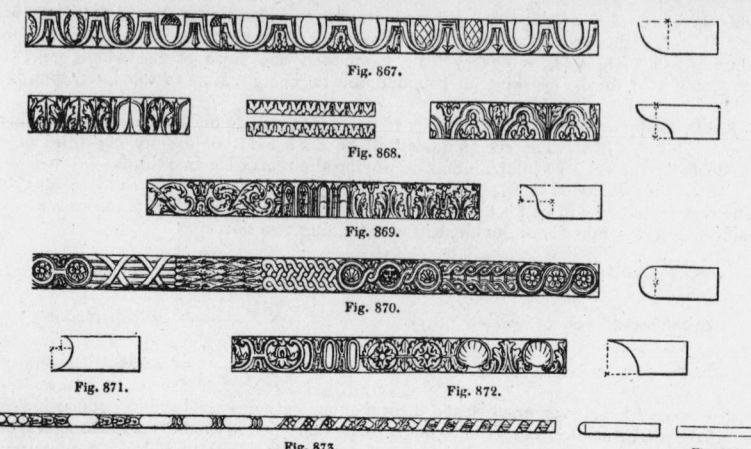

Fig. 867.

Fig. 868.

Fig. 869.

Fig. 870.

Fig. 871.   Fig. 872.

Fig. 873.   Fig. 874.

applicable to all mouldings of Greek examples, and we shall not repeat it in enumerating the rest of them. It is commonly found under the abacus of capitals. The ovolo is also almost always placed between the corona and dentils in the Corinthian cornice: its form gives it the appearance of seeming fitted to support another member. It should be used only in situations above the level of the eye. 2. The *talon, ogee,* or *reversed cyma* (*fig.* 868.) seems also, like the ovolo, a moulding fit for the support of another. 3. The *cyma, cyma recta,* or *cymatium* (*fig.* 869.) seems well contrived for a covering and to shelter other members. The cyma recta is only used properly for crowning members, though in Palladio's Doric, and in other examples, it is found occasionally in the bed mouldings under the corona. 4. The *torus* (*fig.* 870.), like the astragal presently to be mentioned, is shaped like a rope, and seems intended to bind and strengthen the parts to which it is applied; while, 5. The *scotia* or *trochilos* (*fig.* 871.), placed between the fillets which always accompany the tori, is usually below the eye; its use being to separate the tori, and to contrast and strengthen the effect of other mouldings as well as to impart variety to the profile of the base. 6. The *cavetto, mouth,* or *hollow* (*fig.* 872.) is chiefly used as a crowning moulding, like the cyma recta. In bases and capitals it is never used. By workmen it is frequently called a *casement.* 7. The *astragal* (*fig.* 873.) is nothing more than a small torus, and, like it, seems applied for the purpose of binding and strengthening. The astragal is also known by the names of *bead* and *baguette.* 8. The *fillet, listel,* or *annulet* (*fig.* 874.) is used at all heights and in all situations. Its chief office is the separation of curved mouldings from one another.

2533. Sir William Chambers observes on these different mouldings that their inventors meant to express something by their different figures, and that the destinations above mentioned " may be deduced not only from their figures, but from the practice of the ancients in their most esteemed works ; for if we examine the Pantheon, the three columns in the Campo Vaccino, the temple of Jupiter Tonans, the fragments of the frontispiece of Nero, the basilica of Antoninus, the forum of Nerva, the arches of Titus and Septimius Severus, the theatre of Marcellus, and indeed almost every ancient building, either at Rome or in other parts of Italy and France, it will be found that in all their profiles the cyma and cavetto are constantly used as finishings, and never applied where strength is required. That the ovolo and talon are always employed as supporters to the essential members of the composition, such as the modillions, dentils, and corona ; that the chief use of the torus and astragal is to fortify the tops and bottoms of columns, and sometimes of pedestals ;" . . . "and that the scotia is employed only to separate the members of bases, for which purpose the fillet is likewise used not only in bases but in all kinds of profiles." It is the fitness of these forms for their ends in their several situations that gives them a positive and natural beauty, which is immediately destroyed by their change of position, as primary forms of architecture ; and the author just quoted well observes, " that Palladio erred in employing the cavetto under the corona in three of his orders, and in making such frequent use through all his profiles of the cyma as a supporting member. Nor has Vignola been more judicious in finishing his Tuscan cornice with an ovolo ; a moulding extremely improper for the purpose, and productive of a very disagreeable effect; for it gives a mutilated air to the whole profile, so much the more striking, as it resembles exactly that half of the Ionic cornice which is under the corona."

2534. The simplest method of describing the contours of mouldings is to form them of

quadrants of circles. Those of the ovolo, talon, cyma, and cavetto being equal to their height, and those of the curve parts of the torus, and astragal equal to half their height. Circumstances, however, often justify a variation from the rule; and if that be the case, the ovolo, talon, cyma, and cavetto may be either described from the summits of equilateral triangles, or be composed of portions of the ellipsis, which latter was almost constantly used by the Greeks. By means of it also the scotia may be produced, as well as by quadrants of circles; but the curved part of the torus and astragal is always semicircular in form, and if more projection is wanted it is obtained by the use of straight lines.

ORNAMENTS OF MOULDINGS.

2535. In ornamenting the profile of an order, repose requires that some mouldings should be left plain. If all were enriched, confusion instead of variety would result. Except for particular purposes, the square members are rarely carved. There are but few examples in the best age of the art in which the corona is cut; indeed at this moment the only one that occurs to us wherein work is in fine style is that of the three columns in the Campo Vaccino. So where the ovolo above and talon below it are carved, the dentil band between them should be uncut. Scamozzi, in the third chapter of his sixth book, inculcates that ornaments should be neither profuse nor abundant, neither are they to be too sparingly introduced. Thus they will be approved if applied with judgment and discretion. Above all things, they are to be of the most beautiful forms and of the exactest proportions; ornaments in buildings, being like the jewels used for the decoration of princes and princesses and persons of high rank, must be placed only in proper situations. Neither must variety in ornaments be carried to excess. We have to recollect that, being only accessories, they must not obtrude upon but be kept subordinate to the main object. Thus ornaments applied to mouldings should be simple, uniform, and combining not more than two distinct forms in the same enrichment; and when two forms are used on the same moulding they should be cut equally deep, so that an uninterrupted appearance may be preserved. Mouldings of the same form and size on one and the same profile should be similar; and it is moreover a requisite of the greatest importance, so to distribute the centres of the ornaments employed that the centre of one may fall exactly over the centres of those below, of which the columns of the Campo Vaccino form an example for imitation in this respect. Nothing is more offensive than, for example, to see the middle of an egg placed over the edge of a dentil, and in another part of the same moulding to see them come right, centre over centre, and the like negligent and careless distribution. This may always be avoided by making the larger parts regulate the smaller. Thus where there are modillions they must be made to govern the smaller ornaments above and below them, and these smaller ones should always be subdivided with a view to centring with the larger parts. The larger parts are dependent on the axes of the columns and their intercolumniations; but all these must be considered in profiling the order. It will of course be necessary to give the ornaments such forms as may be consistent with the character of the order they enrich. The enrichment of a frieze depends upon the destination of the building, and the ornaments may have relation to the rank, quality, and achievements of the proprietor. We do not agree with Chambers in condemning the introduction of arms, crests, and cyphers, as an unbecoming vanity in the master of the fabric. These may often be so introduced as to indicate the alliances of the family, and thus give a succinct history of its connections. In Gothic architecture we know the practice induced great beauty and variety. We have before observed, in Sect. I. of this Book (2520.), that the instruments and symbols of pagan worship are highly indecorous, not to say ludicrous, on edifices devoted to the Christian religion.

2536. In carving ornaments they must be cut into the solid, and not carved as if they were applied on the solid, because the latter practice alters their figure and proportion. In fact, every moulding should be first cut with its contour plain, and then carved, the most prominent part of the ornament being the actual surface of the moulding before carving, observing that all external and re-entering angles are kept plain, or have only simple leaves with the central filament expressed on or in the angle. In the circular temple of Tivoli the principle of cutting the ornament out of the solid is carried out so far, that the leaves, as usual in most examples of the Corinthian order, instead of being mere appliquées to the bell of the capital, are actually cut out of it.

2537. The degree of relief which ornaments ought to have is dependent on their distance from the eye and the character of the composition: these matters will also regulate the degree of finish they ought to possess. There are some mouldings whose profile is indicative of bearing weight, as the ovolo and talon, which by being deeply cut, though themselves heavy in character, are thereby susceptible of having great lightness imparted to them, whilst such as the cyma and cavetto should not be ornamented deep in the solid. The imitation from nature of the objects represented should be carefully observed, the result whereof will impart beauty and interest to the work on which such attention is bestowed.

CHARACTERS OF THE ORDERS.

2538. In the First Book of this work, Sect. XI. (133, *et seq.*) we have considered the history of the five orders of architecture; we shall here offer some general observations upon them before proceeding to the detail of each separately. The orders and their several characters and qualities do not merely appear in the five species of columns into which they have been subdivided, but are distributed throughout the edifices to which they are applied, the column itself being the regulator of the whole composition. It is on this account the name of orders has been applied to the differently formed and ornamented supports, as columns, which have received the names of the Doric, Ionic, Corinthian, Tuscan, and Composite orders, whereof the three first are of Grecian origin, and the two last, it is supposed, of Italian or Roman origin. Each of these, by the nature of its proportions, and the character resulting from them, produces a leading quality, to which its dimensions, form, and ornaments correspond. But neither of the orders is so limited as to be confined within the expression of any single quality. Thus the strength indicated in the Doric order is capable of being modified into many shades and degrees of that quality. We may satisfy ourselves of this in an instant by reference to the early compared with the later Doric column of the Greeks. Thus the columns of the temple at Corinth are only four diameters high, while those of the portico of Philip are six and a half.

2539. As the Doric seems the expression of strength, simplicity, and their various modes, so the Ionic, by the rise in height of its shaft and by the slenderness of its mass, as well as by the elegance of its capital, indicates a quality intermediate between the grave solidity of the Doric and the elegant delicacy of the Corinthian. Bounded on one side by strength, and by elegance on the other, in the two orders just named, the excess of elegance in the Corinthian order ends in luxury and richness, whereof the character is imprinted on it.

2540. We cannot here refrain from giving, in the words of the excellent Sir Henry Wotton, a quaint and homely, but most admirable description of these five orders, from his *Elements of Architecture*. "First, the *Tuscan* is a plain massive rural pillar, resembling some sturdy, well-limbed labourer, homely clad, in which kind of comparisons, Vitruvius himself seemeth to take pleasure." (Lib. iv. cap. 1.) . . . "The *Dorique order* is the gravest that hath been received into civil use, preserving, in comparison of those that follow, a more *masculine aspect* and little trimmer than the *Tuscan* that went before, save a sober garnishment now and then of *lions' heads* in the *cornice*, and of *triglyphs* and *metopes* always in the *frize*." . . . "To discern him will be a piece rather of good *heraldry* then of *architecture*, for he is knowne by his place when he is in company, and by the peculiar ornament of his *frize*, before mentioned, when he is alone." . . . "The *Ionique order* doth represent a kind of feminine slendernesse; yet, saith Vitruvius, not like a light housewife, but, in a decent dressing, hath much of the *matrone*." . . . "Best known by his trimmings, for the bodie of this *columne* is perpetually *chaneled*, like a thick-pleighted gowne. The *capitall* dressed on each side, not much unlike women's wires, in a spiral wreathing, which they call the *Ionian voluta*." . . . "The *Corinthian* is a columne lasciviously decked like a courtezan, and therefore in much participating (as all inventions do) of the place where they were first born, *Corinth* having beene, without controversie, one of the wantonest towns in the world." . . . "In short, as plainness did characterise the *Tuscan*, so, much delicacie and varietie the *Corinthian* pillar, besides the height of his rank." . . . "The last is the *compounded order*, his *name* being a briefe of his *nature* : for this pillar is nothing in effect but a *medlie*, or an *amasse* of all the precedent *ornaments*, making a new kinde by stealth, and though the most richly tricked, yet the poorest in this, that he is a borrower of his beautie." Each of the orders, says De Quincy, is, then, in the building to which it is applied, the governing principle of the forms, taste, and character of that system of moral order met with in Grecian architecture which alone seems to have suited the physical order of proportions with each part, so that what is agreeable, ornate, and rich is equally found in the whole as in the parts.

2541. On the two Latin orders we do not think it necessary to say more than that they will be fully described in following pages. The invention of new orders must arise out of other expressions of those qualities which are already sufficiently well and beautifully expressed; hence we consider, with De Quincy, to attempt such a thing would be vain. Chambers thus expresses himself on this subject, without the philosophy of De Quincy, yet with the feelings of a learned and experienced architect: "The ingenuity of man has, hitherto, not been able to produce a sixth order, though large premiums have been offered, and numerous attempts been made, by men of first-rate talents to accomplish it. Such is the fettered human imagination, such the scanty store of its ideas, that Doric, Ionic, and Corinthian have ever floated uppermost, and all that has ever been produced amounts to nothing more than different arrangements and combinations of their parts, with some trifling deviations, scarcely deserving notice; the whole tending generally more to diminish than to increase the beauty of the ancient orders." Again: "The suppression of parts of

the ancient orders, with a view to produce novelty, has of late years been practised among us with full as little success ; and though it is not wished to restrain sallies of imagination, nor to discourage genius from attempting to invent, yet it is apprehended that attempts to alter the primary forms invented by the ancients, and established by the concurring appro-bation of many ages, must ever be attended with dangerous consequences, must always be difficult, and seldom, if ever, successful.   It is like coining words, which, whatever may be their value, are at first but ill received, and must have the sanction of time to secure them a current reception."

2542. In the progress of the five orders, from the Tuscan up to the Composite, taking seven diameters for the height of the Tuscan column, and eleven for that of the Composite, if the entablature be taken of the same absolute height in all, and at the same time in height one quarter of that of the column, we shall have the height of the entablature in terms of the diameter of the column, as follows : —

In the Tuscan order . $\frac{1}{4}$ of $\frac{7}{1}$ = $1\frac{3}{4}$ entablature diameters high.
In the Doric order   . $\frac{1}{4}$ of $\frac{8}{1}$ = 2 entablature diameters high.
In the Ionic order   . $\frac{1}{4}$ of $\frac{9}{1}$ = $2\frac{1}{4}$ entablature diameters high.
In the Corinthian order $\frac{1}{4}$ of $\frac{10}{1}$ = $2\frac{1}{2}$ entablature diameters high.
In the Composite order $\frac{1}{4}$ of $\frac{11}{1}$ = $2\frac{3}{4}$ entablature diameters high.

HEIGHT AND DIMINUTION OF COLUMNS.

2543. Vitruvius tells us that the ancients were accustomed to assign to the Tuscan column seven of its diameters for the height ; to the Doric, eight ; to the Ionic, nine ; and to the Corinthian and Composite, ten.   Scamozzi, the leader of the moderns, adopts similar proportions.   But these are not to be considered as more than an approximation to the limits, nor as relating to the proportions between the heights and diameters of the ancient Doric examples, whereof in our First Book we have examined certain specimens. This work cannot be extended to a representation of the variety under which the orders have appeared in their various examples of each order.   The works in which they are contained must be consulted for particulars of detail in this respect.   Our intention is to give general information on the subject, and to follow, with few exceptions, in that respect, the precepts of Vignola, as tending to the most generally pleasing results, and as being also those which have been adopted on the Continent for general instruction in the art.

2544. We have already spoken (2524, et seq.) of the general proportion of the height of the entablature to that of the column as one fourth, and, without returning to the discussion of the propriety of that proportion, will only here incidentally mention that Scamozzi, Bar-baro, Alberti, and Palladio have not assigned so great a height to their entablatures, chiefly, it appears, because they seemed to consider the slenderness of the columns in the more deli-cate orders unsuited to the reception of heavy burdens.   If, however, the reader will bear in recollection what has been said at the beginning of this section relative to the supports and weights, it will directly occur to him that the practice these great masters sanctioned is not founded upon just deductions.   Chambers seems to have had a glimpse of this theory, but without any notion of its developement, when he says, " It must be remembered that, though the height of an entablature in a delicate order is made the same as in a massive one, yet it will not, either in reality or in appearance, be equally heavy, for the quantity of matter in the Corinthian cornice A (fig. 875.) is considerably less than in the Tuscan cornice B, and the increased number of parts composing the former of these will of course make it appear far lighter than the latter."   He was, however, nearer the exact truth where he speaks in a previous passage of the possibility of increasing the intervals between the columns.

2545. The diminution or tapering form given to a column, whereof all the authors find the type, whether truly or not, in that of the trunk of a tree, in the ancient examples, some-times commences from the foot of the shaft. sometimes from a quarter or one third of its height, in which case the lower part is a perfect cylinder.   Though the latter method has been mostly adopted by modern artists, the former seems more to have prevailed among the ancients.   Of the method of entasis, that is, of swelling columns as they rise, we have already spoken in the First Book (144.).   A curve of diminution, if we may so term it, in which the lower part does not much vary from the cylinder, but never much exceeding its boundary for the height of one third upwards, is the best, and to something like that we now come. Blondel (Resolution des quatre principaux Problemes d'Architecture) says, that the best and simplest instrument for the diminution of columns is that invented by Nicomedes for describing the first conchoid, which, applied at the bottom of the shaft, gives, by continued motion, both the swelling and the diminution.   Vignola had not strictly anticipated Blondel in this method, which, it is said, was that used for the columns in the Pantheon ; but the old master had come so near to it that we shall first describe Vignola's method, and then that proposed by Blondel.   Vignola having already spoken of the common practice, says,

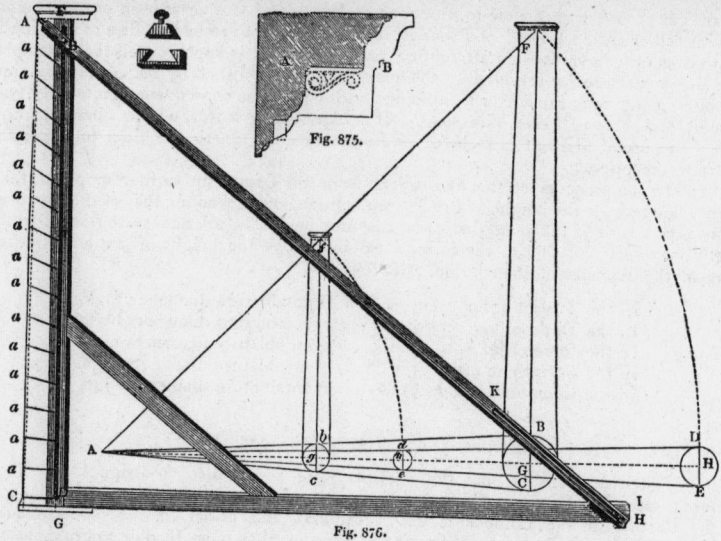

Fig. 875.

Fig. 876.

(Stampani's **edit.** *Dei cinque Ordini d'Architettura*, Roma, 1770, cap. 7. p. 51.), " In respect of this second mode, it is my own discovery, and will be soon understood by the figure, though not so well known as the first named.   The measures of the column having been fixed, namely, the height of the shaft and its upper and lower diameters, from C (*fig.* 876.), draw an indefinite line through D perpendicular to the axis of the column.   From A, the extreme point of the upper semi-diameter, to B, a point in the axis, set off CD the lower semidiameter.   Through B from A draw the line ABE, cutting the indefinite line CD in E, and from the point of intersection E and through the axis of the column draw any number of rays, as EB*a*, whereon, from the axis towards the circumference, setting off the interval CD, any number of points *aaa* may be found, and through them a curve being drawn gives the swell and diminution of the shaft.

2546. This method is so far defective as to require the curve to be drawn by hand on the application of a flexible ruler through the points found.   To remedy the defect, Blondel, who on investigation of the curve found it to be a conchoid, applied the instrument of Nicomedes for the purpose, the description of which instrument here follows.   The height of the shaft and the upper and lower diameters of the column having been determined, as also the length (*fig.* 876.) of the line CDE, take three rulers, FG, ID, and AH, of which let FG and ID be fastened together at right angles in G.   From top to bottom let a dovetail groove be cut down the middle of FG, and at E on the ruler ID, whose length from the centre of the groove in FG is the same as that of the point of intersection from the axis of the column, fix a pin.   On the ruler AH set off the distance AB equal to the lower semidiameter of the column CD, and at the other end of the ruler cut a slit through it from H to K, the length whereof must at least be equal to the difference in length between EB and ED, and its breadth sufficient to admit the pin fixed at E to pass through the slit, and allow the ruler to slide thereon.   Now, the middle of the groove in the ruler FG being placed exactly over the axis of the column, the ruler AH in moving along the groove will with its extremity A describe the curve A*aa*C, which curve is the same as that produced by Vignola's method, except that the operation is performed by the continued motion of the ruler AH.   If the rulers be of an indefinite size, and the pins at E and B be made to move along their respective rulers, so as to be able to increase or diminish at pleasure the lengths AB and DE, the instrument will answer for drawing columns of any size.

2547. The diminution of the column as respects quantity is rarely in ancient examples less than one eighth of the lower diameter of the column, nor often more than one sixth, as will be seen in the subjoined examples.   One sixth is the diminution recommended by Vitruvius, and followed by Vignola, in all his orders, except the Tuscan.   In the following table the first column contains the order; the second, the example; the third, the height of the column in English feet and decimal parts of a foot; the fourth column shows its diameter in similar terms; and the fifth the ratio of diminution.   The dimensions are from Perrault, reduced here from French to English feet.

Order.	Examples.	Height of Column in English Feet.	Diameter of Column in English Feet.	Ratio of Diminution.
Doric	Theatre of Marcellus	22·386	3·198	0·200
—	Coliseum	24·384	2·865	0·077
Ionic	Temple of Concord	38·376	4·485	0·182
—	Temple of Fortuna Virilis	24·340	3·109	0·125
—	Coliseum	24·518	2·909	0·166
Corinthian	Temple of Peace	52·400	6·041	0·111
—	Portico of Pantheon	38·998	4·796	0·106
—	Altars of Pantheon	11·548	1·465	0·133
—	Temple of Vesta	29·226	3·109	0·111
—	Temple of the Sybil at Tivoli	20·254	2·487	0·133
—	Temple of Faustina	38·376	4·796	0·133
—	Columns of Campo Vaccino	39·975	4·840	0·111
—	Basilica of Antoninus	39·442	4·752	0·106
—	Arch of Constantine	23·097	3·435	0·117
—	Interior of Pantheon	29·314	3·642	0·133
—	Portico of Septimius	39·442	3·632	0·125
Composite.	Baths of Diocletian	37·310	3·553	0·200
—	Temple of Bacchus	11·371	1·443	0·111
—	Arch of Titus	17·056	2·102	0·117
—	Arch of Septimius Severus	23·097	2·877	0·117

2548. The recommendation of Vitruvius (lib. iii. c. 2.) to give different degrees of diminution to columns of different heights has been combated by Perrault in his notes on the passage; and we are, with Chambers, of opinion that Perrault is right in his judgment, inasmuch as the proper point of view for a column fifty feet high (*fig.* 876. unshaded part) ought not to be at the same distance as for one of fifteen, the point being removed more distant as the column increases in height, and therefore the apparent relation between the upper and lower diameters would appear the same. For supposing A to be a point of view whose respective distance from each of the columns *fg* FG, is equal to the respective heights of each, the triangles *f*A*g* FAG will be similar; and A*f*, or A*h*, which is the same, will be to A*g*, as AF, or its equal AH, is to AG: therefore, if *de* be in reality to *bc* as DE is to BC, it will likewise be apparently so: for the angle *d*A*e* will then be to the angle *b*A*c*, as the angle DAE is to the angle BAC; and if the real relations differ, the apparent ones will likewise differ. " When, therefore," observes Chambers, "a certain degree of diminution, which by experience is found pleasing, has been fixed upon, there will be no necessity for changing it, whatever be the height of the column, provided the point of view is not limited; but in close places, where the spectator is not at liberty to choose a proper distance for his point of sight, the architect, if he inclines to be scrupulously accurate, may vary; though it is, in reality, a matter of no importance, as the nearness of the object will render the image thereof indistinct, and, consequently, any small alteration imperceptible." Our author afterwards adds: " It must not, however, be imagined that the same general proportions will in all cases succeed. They are chiefly collected from the temples and other public structures of antiquity, and may by us be employed in churches, palaces, and other buildings of magnificence, where majesty and grandeur of manner should be extended to their utmost limits, and where, the composition being generally large, the parts require an extraordinary degree of boldness to make them distinctly perceptible from the proper general points of view."

SUBDIVISION OF ENTABLATURES.

2549. We have spoken of the entablature as the fourth part of the height of the column. In general terms, its subdivisions of architrave, frieze, and cornice are obtained by dividing its height into ten equal parts, whereof three are given to the architrave, three to the frieze, and four to the cornice; except in the Roman Doric order, in which the whole height of the entablature is divided into eight parts, of which two are given to the architrave, three to the frieze, and three to the cornice. From these general proportions variations have been made by different masters, but not so great as to call for particular observation. They deviate but little from the examples of antiquity; and the ease with which they may be recollected render them singularly useful.

MODE OF MEASURING THE ORDERS.

2550. Several methods have been used for forming the scale of equal parts, by which the orders are measured; but they are all founded on the diameter of the column at the bottom of the shaft; for those that use the module or semi-diameter as the measuring unit (which all have done in the Doric order) must still recur to the diameter itself. The authors have also usually divided it into thirty parts, but all concur in measuring by an unit founded on the diameter. We shall follow the practice of Vignola in describing the orders, that master dividing the diameter into two equal parts, of which each is the unit of the scale for

profiling the order. The *module* for the two first orders, the Tuscan and Doric, is divided into twelve parts or *minutes*; and for the Ionic, Corinthian, and Composite orders into eighteen parts, by which minute fractions are avoided.

2551. For drawing or *profiling*, as it is called, an order, the proper way is to set out the height of the leading parts and their projections, and then proceed to the subdivisions of each. As a general rule, we may mention that it is usual to make projections of cornices nearly or quite equal to their heights.

APPLICATION OF THE ORDERS.

2552. The application of the orders among the ancients was exceedingly extensive. Porticoes abounded about their cities; their temples were almost groves of columns, with which also were profusely decorated their theatres, baths, basilicæ, and other public buildings, as were no less the courts, vestibules, and halls of their private dwellings. The moderns have in a great measure imitated their example, and their use has very much exceeded the limits of propriety. The maxim of Horace, " Nec Deus intersit," has in no case been more violated by architects than in the unnecessary introduction of the orders on the façades of their buildings. The test of fitness being applied to their employment is the best that the young architect can adopt.

Sect. III

THE TUSCAN ORDER.

2553. The reader, in *fig.* 877., has before him the geometrical representation of the Tuscan order and its details. A shows the plan of the sofite of the cornice, and B is a plan of the capital. The example is from Vignola's profile, whereon we consider it proper to remark, in conformity with an opinion before expressed (2532, 2533.), that the ovolo which crowns the cornice is an improper moulding for the situation it occupies. The substitution for it of a fillet and cyma recta would have been much more suitable, and would have also been more pleasant in effect.

2554. " The Tuscan order," says Chambers, " admits of no ornaments of any kind; on the contrary, it is sometimes customary to represent on the shaft of its column rustic cinctures, as at the Palace Pitti in Florence, that of the Luxembourg in Paris, York Stairs in London, and many other buildings of note. This practice, though frequent, and to be found in the works of many celebrated architects, is not always excusable, and should be indulged with caution, as it hides the natural figure of the column, alters its proportions, and affects the simplicity of the whole composition. There are few examples of these bandages in the

Fig. 877.

remains of antiquity, and in general it will be advisable to avoid them in all large designs, reserving the rustic work for the intercolumniations, where it may be employed with great propriety, to produce an opposition which will help to render the aspect of the whole composition distinct and striking." Our author proceeds to observe, that " in smaller works, of which the parts being few are easily comprehended, they may be sometimes tolerated, sometimes even recommended, as they serve to diversify the forms, are productive of strong contrasts, and contribute very considerably to the masculine bold aspect of

the composition." Le Clerc allows their propriety in the gates of citadels and prisons, and also considers them not out of place for gates to gardens or parks, for grottoes, fountains, and baths.   Delorme made abundant use of them in several parts of the Thuilleries, covering them with arms, cyphers, and other enrichments.   They are to be found in the detail of the Louvre, with vermiculated rustics.   De Chambrai, who banishes the Tuscan order to the country, nevertheless admits that the Tuscan column may be consecrated to the commemoration of great men and their glorious actions, instancing Trajan's column, one of the proudest monuments of Roman splendour, as also the Antonine column.

2555. Having adjusted the size of the module with its subdivisions of twelve parts, so that the paper or other material on which the order is profiled may contain the whole of the order, it always being understood that the representation for practical purposes need not include the whole height of the shaft of the column, whose minutiæ of diminution may form the subject of a separate drawing, the first step is to draw a perpendicular line for the axis of the column.   Parallel to the base lines are then to be drawn, according to the dimensions (parts of the module) given in the table subjoined ; and the beginner, as well as the more practised man, is recommended not to set up these as they are given separately, but in every case to add the succeeding dimensions to those preceding rather than to set them off one by one, which, on a small scale, causes minute errors in reading off from the scale to become in the end large in amount.   By the adoption also of such a practice the work corrects itself as it proceeds.   As the heights are set up, the projection of each member from the axis of the column is to be set off, and this should be always done on both sides at the same time, by which *gulling* of the paper from the point of the compasses, and errors in other respects, are avoided.   The *fig.* 878. is

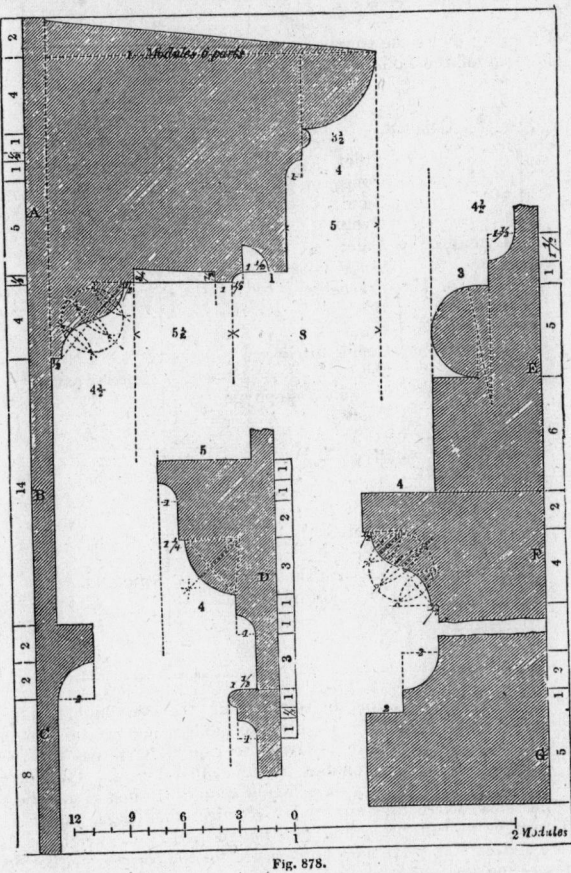

Fig. 878.

but the detail on a larger scale of the general representation exhibited in that preceding The measures of each part are given in the following table.

Table of the Parts of the Tuscan Order.

Mouldings whereof the Parts are composed.			Heights of Mouldings in Parts of a Module.	Projection from the Axis of Column in Parts of a Module.
Entablature.				
Cornice A, 16 parts.	Cymatium, and parts.	Quarter round - -	4	27½
		Astragal - - -	1	
		Fillet - - - -	½	23½
		Congé, or cavetto - -	1	22½
		Corona - - -	5	22½
		Drip - - - -	1	21½
		Sinking from corona, or hollow - - -	½	19½
		Fillet - - - -	½	14
	Bed moulding Ogee - - -		4	13½
Frieze B, 14 parts.	- - - - - -		14	9½
Architrave C, 12 parts.	Fillet.	Fillet, or listel - -	2	11½
	Fascia.	Congé, or small cavetto -	2	9½
		Fascia - - - -	8	9½
The height of the drip under the corona is taken on that member, and that of the hollow in the height of the fillet.				
Column.				
Capital D, 12 parts.	Abacus.	Fillet - - - - -	1	14½
		Congé, or cavetto - -	1	13½
		Band - - - - -	2	13½
	Cymatium.	Ovolo - - - - -	3	13¼
		Fillet - - - - -	1	10½
		Congé, or cavetto - -	1	9½
	Neck, or Hypotrachelion - -		3	9½
Shaft, 12 modules.	Astragal, or necking.	Bead - - - - -	1	11
		Fillet - - - - -	½	10½
		Congé, or cavetto - -	1	9½
	Shaft.	Shaft - - - - -	11 mod. 8 parts.	9½
		Congé, or apophyge -	1½	12
Base, E, 12 parts.	- -	Fillet - - - - -	1	13½
		Torus - - - - -	5	16½
		Plinth - - - - -	6	16½
Pedestal.				
Cornice G, 6 parts.	Cymatium.	Listel - - - - -	2	20½
		Ogee - - - - -	4	20
Die F, 44 parts.	- -	Die, or dado - -	3 mod. 4 parts.	16½
		Congé, or apophyge -	2	16½
Base, 6 parts.	- -	Fillet - - - -	1	18½
		Plinth - - - - -	5	20½

2556. Vitruvius in this order forms the columns six diameters high, and makes their diminution one quarter of the diameter. He gives to the base and capital each one module in height. No pedestal is given by him. Over the capital he places the architrave of timber in two thicknesses connected together by dovetailed dowels. He however leaves the height unsettled, merely saying that their height should be such as may be suitable to the grandeur of the work where they are used. He directs no frieze, but places over the architrave cantilevers or mutuli, projecting one fourth part of the height of the column, including the base and capital. He fixes no measure for the cornice, neither does he give any directions respecting the intercolumniations of this order. The instructions are not so specific as those which he lays down for the other orders, and there have been various interpretations of the text, which unfortunately cannot in any of the suppositions be tested

on ancient remains. The whole height, according to the measuring unit which we have adopted from Vignola, is 16 modules and 3 parts.

2557. Palladio makes the height of his Tuscan column 6 diameters, and diminishes the shaft one fourth of a diameter. The height of the base and capital are each half a diameter. He provides no pedestal, but, instead thereof, places the base of the column on a zoccolo, or lofty plinth, whose height is equal to the diameter of the column. He leaves the inter-columniation unsettled, merely hinting that as the architraves are of timber, they, the intercolumniations may be wide. The whole height by him assigned to the order is 9 diameters and three quarters of the column. The whole height according to our scale is 19 modules and 6 parts.

2558. Serlio makes the column of the order 5 diameters exclusive of base and capital, each of which are half a diameter in height, and his diminution is one quarter of the diameter. He gives half a diameter to the height of the architrave, and an equal height to the frieze and to the cornice. His pedestal is with a plinth and base, a die, and cymatium, the whole being a third of the height of the column. He gives no rules for the intercolumniations, though in book 4. he inserts a diagram wherein intercolumns appear, merely saying that they are equal to 3 diameters. The total height according to our measure is 19 modules and 3 parts.

2559. Scamozzi makes the shaft of his column 6 diameters, and diminishes it one fourth part of its diameter. The heights of the base and capital are each half a diameter. To the entablature he assigns for height one fourth of the height of the column, including its base and capital, less half its diameter. He places a sort of triglyph in the frieze, which arises from a misconception of the text of Vitruvius. The height of his pedestal is a fourth part of that of the column, with base and capital, less half a diameter. The whole height in our measure is 21 modules and 9 parts.

Sect. IV.

THE DORIC ORDER.

2560. The Doric order of the moderns is of two sorts: mutular and denticular, the former is represented in *fig.* 879. A is a plan of the sofite of the corona; B, a plan of the

Fig. 879.

capital; and C, a plan of the base. In the frieze the channelled projections are called *triglyphs*, and the spaces between them *metopæ*, which should in breadth be equal to their

height, which is that of the frieze. The shaft is usually channelled with twenty *flutes*. Over the triglyphs are distributed *mutules* or modillions, and another peculiarity is the introduction of *guttæ* or *drops*, which decorate the sofite of the cornice and the feet of the triglyphs.

2561. Daviler, speaking of the two Doric entablatures given by Vignola, admires the elegance of their composition, and scarcely knows which of them to select as the most beautiful. "The first" (or denticular), hereafter immediately subjoined, says Chambers, following that author, "which is entirely antique, is the lightest, and consequently properest for interior decoration or objects intended for near inspection ; the other, composed by Vignola himself from various fragments of antiquity, being bolder, and consisting of larger parts, seems better calculated for outside works and places where the point of view is either distant or unlimited. On polygonal plans, however, the mutule cornice must be avoided, because the sofites of the angular mutules would form irregular and very disagreeable figures : neither should it be employed in concaves of small dimensions, for the same reason ; nor in places where frequent breaks are requisite, it being extremely difficult, often impossible, to prevent the mutules from penetrating and mutilating each other in various unsightly manners ; and wherever this cornice is used on a convex surface, the sides of the mutules must be made parallel, for it would be both disagreeable and unnatural to see them broader, and consequently heavier in front than where they spring out of the mutule band." We have elsewhere observed that there is very great difficulty in distributing the parts of the Doric entablature, on account of the intervals between the centres of the triglyphs, which necessarily confine the composer to intercolumniations divisible by three modules, thus producing spaces which are often too wide or too narrow for his purposes.

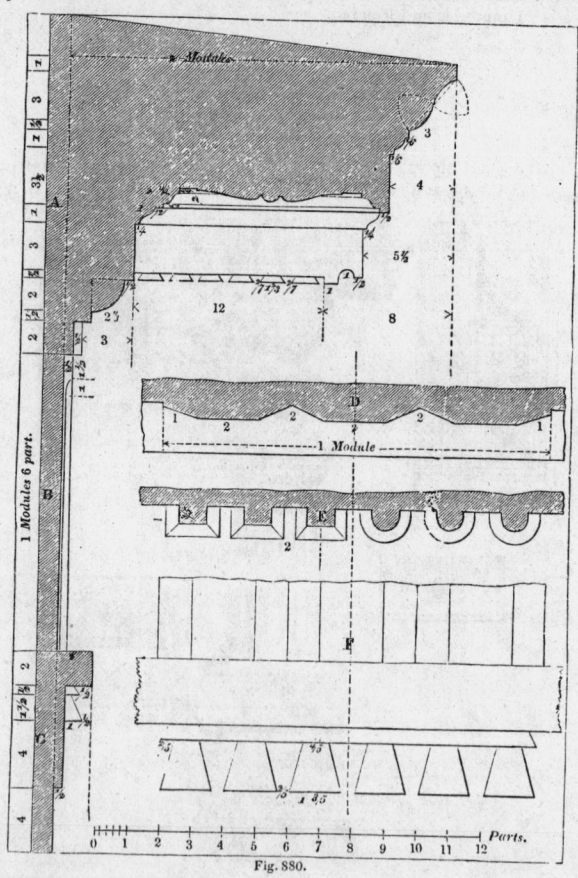

Fig. 880.

2562. In *fig.* 880. the entablature of the mutular Doric order is given to a larger scale than that of the preceding figure ; and we subjoin, as in the Tuscan order, —

TABLE OF PARTS OF THE ENTABLATURE OF THE MUTULAR DORIC.

Mouldings whereof the Parts are composed.		Heights of Mouldings in Parts of a Module.	Projections from Axis of Column in Parts of a Module.
Cornice A, 18 parts.	Fillet of the corona - - -	1	34
	Cyma - - - - -	3	31
	Fillet - - - - -	$\frac{1}{2}$	31
	Cyma reversa - - -	1	$30\frac{3}{4}$
	Corona - - - -	$3\frac{1}{2}$	30
	Cyma reversa - - -	1	$29\frac{1}{2}$
	Mutule - - - -	3	$28\frac{1}{2}$
	Drip - - - - -	$\frac{1}{2}$	28
	Gutta of the mutule - -	$\frac{1}{2}$	26
	Echinus, or quarter round - -	2	$13\frac{1}{2}$
	Fillet - - - -	$\frac{1}{2}$	$11\frac{1}{4}$
	Capital of the triglyph - -	2	11
Frieze B, 18 parts.	Triglyph - - - -	18	$10\frac{1}{2}$
	Metope - - - -	18-	10
Architrave C, 12 parts.	Listel - - - -	2	12
	Capital of the guttæ - -	$\frac{1}{4}$	$11\frac{1}{2}$
	Guttæ - - - -	$1\frac{1}{2}$	$11\frac{1}{4}$
	First fascia - - - -	6	$10\frac{1}{2}$
	Second fascia - - - -	4	10

D is the plan of a triglyph to double the scale.
E is the plan of the round or square guttæ.
F is the elevation of the triglyph and its guttæ.

2563. To obviate the difficulties mentioned in 2561. relative to the triglyphs, they have often been omitted and the entablature left plain, as in the Coliseum at Rome, the colonnades of St. Peter's of the Vatican, and in many other buildings. This, says Chambers, is an easy expedient; but as it robs the order of its principal characteristic distinction, the remedy is a desperate one, and should only be employed as a last resource.

2564. The Doric order was used by the ancients in temples dedicated to Minerva, to Mars, and to Hercules. In modern buildings, Serlio (lib. iv. c. 6.) recommends it in churches dedicated to saints remarkable by their suffering for the Christian faith. Le Clerc suggests its use for military buildings. "It may," says Chambers, "be employed in the houses of generals, or other martial men, in mausoleums erected to their memory, or in triumphal bridges and arches built to celebrate their victories."

2665. As the difference between the mutular and denticular Doric lies entirely in the entablature, we give in the following table the whole of the details of the order,

Fig. 881.

observing, that from the capitals downwards, the measures assigned to them are the same for each. *Fig.* 881. represents the entablature of the denticular Doric and its parts,

which, with those of the capital, base, and pedestal, are in *fig.* 882. given to a larger

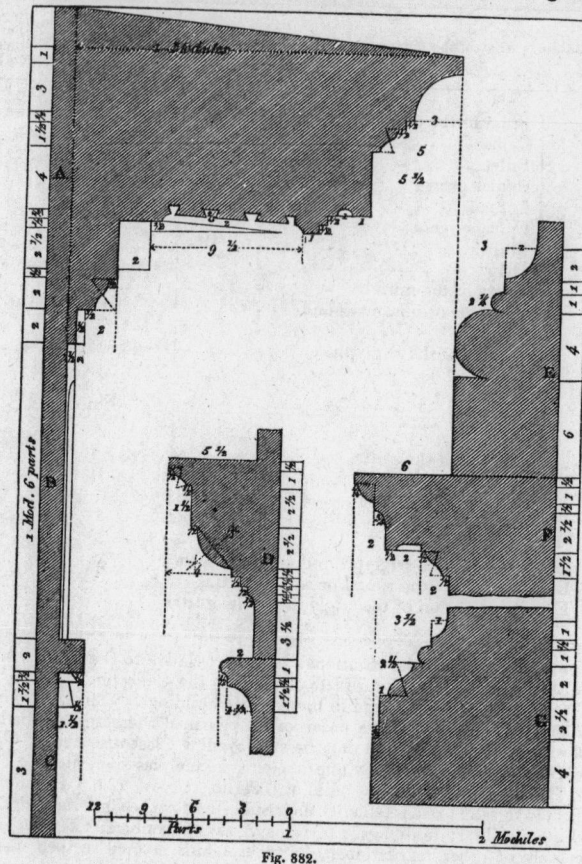

Fig. 882.

scale, as we have before represented the parts of the Tuscan order.　The general table is subjoined : —

	Members composing the Order.				Heights in Parts of a Module.	Projections in Parts of a Module from Axis of Column.
	ENTABLATURE.					
	Fillet of corona	-	-	-	1	34
	Cavetto	-	-	-	3	31
	Fillet -	-	-	-	$\frac{1}{2}$	26
	Cyma reversa -	-	-	-	$1\frac{1}{2}$	30
	Corona	-	-	-	4	$28\frac{1}{2}$
A, Cornice,	Drip -	-	-	-	$\frac{1}{2}$	$27\frac{1}{2}$
18 parts.	Fillet -	-	-	-	$\frac{1}{2}$	25
	Gutta under the corona	-	-	$\frac{1}{2}$	$24\frac{1}{2}$
	Dentil	-	-	-	3	15
	Fillet -	-	-	-	$\frac{1}{2}$	13
	Cyma reversa -	-	-	-	2	$12\frac{1}{2}$
	Capital of triglyph	-	-	-	2	11
B, Frieze,	Triglyph	-	-	-	18	$10\frac{1}{4}$
18 parts.	Metope	-	-	-	18	10

Members composing the Order.			Heights in Parts of a Module.	Projections in Parts of a Module from Axis of Column.
C, Architrave, 10 parts.	Listel		2	$11\frac{1}{2}$
	Capital of guttæ		$\frac{1}{2}$	11
	Guttæ		$1\frac{1}{2}$	11
	Fascia		10	10
COLUMN.				
D, Capital, 12 parts.	Listel		$\frac{1}{2}$	$15\frac{1}{2}$
	Cyma reversa		1	$15\frac{1}{4}$
	Band		$2\frac{1}{2}$	14
	Echinus or quarter round		$2\frac{1}{2}$	$13\frac{3}{4}$
	Three annulets		$1\frac{1}{2}$	$11\frac{1}{2}$
	Neck of capital		4	10
	Astragal	Ovolo	1	12
		Fillet	$\frac{1}{2}$	$11\frac{1}{2}$
		Congé	$1\frac{1}{2}$	10
SHAFT OF THE COLUMN, 14 modules.				
E, Base, 12 parts.	Apophyge or congé		2	12
	Fillet		$\frac{2}{3}$	14
	Astragal		$1\frac{1}{3}$	$14\frac{3}{4}$
	Torus		4	17
	Plinth		6	17
PEDESTAL.				
F, Cornice, 6 parts.	Listel		$\frac{1}{2}$	23
	Echinus		1	$22\frac{3}{4}$
	Fillet		$\frac{1}{2}$	$21\frac{3}{4}$
	Corona		$2\frac{1}{2}$	21
	Cyma reversa		$1\frac{1}{2}$	$18\frac{1}{2}$
DIE OF THE PEDESTAL, 4 modules.				
G, Base, 10 parts.	Congé		1	17
	Fillet		$\frac{1}{2}$	18
	Astragal		1	$18\frac{3}{4}$
	Inverted cyma		2	19
	Second plinth		$2\frac{1}{2}$	21
	First plinth		4	$21\frac{1}{2}$

2566. Vitruvius, with more clearness than in the others, describes the Doric order (book iv. chap. iii.). In order to set out its proportions, he tells us, though not giving a direct rule, that its pedestal is composed of three parts, the cymatium or cornice, the die, and the base; and that the base and cimatium are composed of many mouldings, whose individual proportions, however, he does not give. He assigns no particular base to the Doric order; but, nevertheless, places under half a diameter in height the attic base, whose members are the plinth, small fillet, scotia, and the upper torus with its superior and inferior fillets, together with the apophyge of the column. He gives to the projection of the base a fifth part of the diameter of the column. The height of the shaft he makes of 6 diameters, and its diminution a sixth part of the diameter. The capital's height he makes equal to half a diameter, and divides it into three parts, one for the abacus and its cymatium, another for the echinus and its fillets, the third for the hypotrachelium. To the architrave he assigns the height of one half diameter of the column, and to the frieze 50 parts of the module (semidiameter divided into 30 parts), including the fascia, forming the capital of the triglyphs. His cornice consists of 30 parts of the module, and its projection 40. The whole height which he gives to the order is, in the measure here adopted, 17 modules and 20 parts.

2567. Palladio makes the Doric pedestal rather less than $2\frac{1}{2}$ diameters of the column, dividing it into three parts, the base, die, and cymatium. To the die he assigns nearly a diameter and one third of the column. To the cymatium a little more than one third of the diameter. He uses the attic base to the order, but, for the sake of carrying off the water, turns the plinth into an inverted cavetto (*guscio*), ending in the projection of the

cymatium of the pedestal.   To the shaft of the column he assigns various proportions, directing that if accompanied with pilasters, it should be of the height of 8$\frac{1}{2}$ diameters, and if entirely isolated, 7 or at most 8 diameters high.   He cuts the shaft into 24 flutes, and diminishes it the tenth part of its diameter.   The height of his capital is half a diameter, and, like the annotators on Vitruvius, he decorates the neck or frieze, as they both call it, with roses, adding, however, other flowers, and making its projection a little more than a fifth part of the diameter.   To the architrave, frieze, and cornice he gives a little more than one fourth part of the height of the column, so that the whole height of his order is in our measure 24 modules and a fraction above 2$\frac{1}{4}$ parts.

2568. Serlio makes the height of the pedestal of his column a little less than 3 diameters, with its base, die, and cymatium.   The height of the die is set up equal to the diagonal of a square, formed on the plinth of the column.   The height of the cymatium, according to the strict text of Serlio, should not be less than that of the base; but he altogether omits any mention of its projection.   His base is the attic base, to which he assigns a projection of a quarter of a diameter.   The column is 6 diameters high, and has 20 flutes.   His capital differs only from that of Vitruvius in its projection, which is rather more.   The architrave and frieze do not much differ from those already described.   The projection given to the cornice is equal to its height.   The whole height in our measures amounts to 23 modules and 5 parts.

2569. The Doric order as described by Scamozzi is not very dissimilar to those already described.   The pedestal is by him made 2 diameters and a little more than a quarter, with a base, die, and cymatium, and the projection barely a quarter of the diameter of the column, to which he gives the attic base.   His column is 7$\frac{1}{2}$ diameters high, and the diminution a fifth part of the diameter.   There are 26 flutes on the shaft, separated from each other by fillets, whose width is one third of the flute.   This author gives three different sorts of capitals for the order : the first has three annulets ; the second has only the lower annulet, the two upper ones being changed to an astragal ; the third, instead of the two lower annulets, has a cyma reversa.   Lastly, above the corona he places a cyma reversa, and in the other parts does not vary much from the preceding authors, especially in the frieze and architrave, except that in the last he uses two fasciæ.   To the cornice he assigns the projection of five sixths of a diameter of the column.   His whole entablature is a little less than one fourth the height of the column, including base and capital.   The whole height of the order in our measures is 23 modules and 8 parts.

2570. In *fig.* 883. the profile of the Grecian Doric from the Parthenon at Athens is given.   Though very different to those we have already described of this order, the resemblance is still considerable.   Its character is altogether sacred and monumental, and its application, if capable of application to modern purposes, can scarcely be made to any edifice whose general character and forms are not of the severest and purest nature.   The various absurd situations in which the Grecian Doric has been introduced in this country, has brought it into disrepute ; added to which, in this dark climate the closeness of the intercolumniations excludes light, which is so essential to the display of architecture under the cloudy skies with which we are constantly accompanied in high latitudes.   The diameter of the columns in the original is 6 feet 2·7 inches.

2571. Lest we may be reproached with neglecting to submit to the student in this place (and the remark equally applies to the following section on the Ionic order) more examples of the Grecian Doric, we would here observe that this work is not to stand in place of a parallel of the orders.   Nothing would have been easier than to have placed before him an abundance of examples; but they must be sought elsewhere,

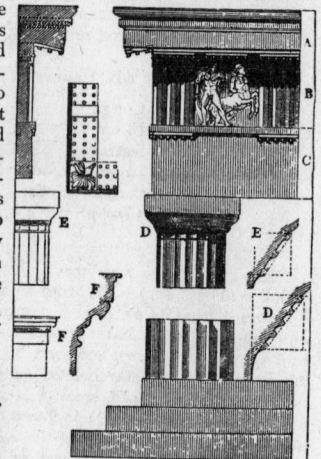

Fig. 883.

inasmuch as the nature of our labours requires general, not special, information in this respect.   We have not, however, refrained in the first book (142, *et seq.*) from entering into details respecting the Grecian Doric, which we consider much more valuable to the reader than would be the exhibition of a series of profiles of its principal examples.   We have, moreover, at that place, suggested some criteria of their comparative antiquity.   We do not think the nice copying of a profile into a modern work any other than a disgraceful exhibition of the want of ability in the man, we cannot call him artist, who adopts it, and shall be much better pleased to leave the student in doubt, so that he may apply himself *pro re natâ* to the matter which calls his genius into play.   From what we have said on *the orders* in Sect. II. of this Book, (2523, *et seq.*), relative to the order, and on *mouldings*

(2532, *et seq.*), it must be quite clear that the variety of every order, keeping to first principles, has not been yet exhausted, neither is it likely to be so.

TABLE OF THE PARTS OF THE GRECIAN DORIC (PARTHENON).

Members composing the Order.		Heights in Parts of a Module and Decimals.	Projections in Parts of a Module from Axis of Column.
ENTABLATURE.			
A, Cornice, 15·32 parts.	Fillet - - - - -	0·60	22·10
	Echinus - - - -	3·12	20·40
	Fillet, with sunk cyma reversa -	2·20	
	Corona - - - -	4·88	18·98
	Fillet - - - - -	1·10	18·80
	Capital of mutules - -	1·10	
	Mutules - - -	0·32	18·66
	Bead and capital of triglyphs -	2·00	11·46
B, Frieze, 14·88 parts.	Frieze (in metope) - -	15·12	
	Triglyph - - - -	14·88	11·40
C, Architrave, 17·10 parts.	Fillet - - - -	1·50	12·50
	Cap of guttæ - - -	1·00	12·40
	Guttæ - - - -	0·20	
	Architrave below guttæ -	14·40	11·20
COLUMN.			
D, Capital, 11·16 parts.	Abacus - - - -	4·40	12·90
	Echinus - - - -	3·60	12·60
	Fillets and hollows, with cavetto -	0·80	
	Neck - - - -	2·20	9·44
	Groove or sinking - -	0·16	
	Shaft - - - - -	20·30 { at top 9·38 / at bottom 12·00 }	
	First step or plinth - -	6·90	12·80
	Second step or plinth - -	6·70	21·80
	Third step or plinth - -	6·90	30·84

2572. The minutiæ of the Grecian Doric, as we have just observed, cannot be given in a general work of this nature. In its smaller refinements it requires plates on a much larger scale than this volume allows. The reader, therefore, must be referred to *Stuart's Antiquities of Athens* (original edition), and the publications of the Dilettanti Society, for further information on the subject of the Grecian Doric. All that was here possible was to give a general idea of the order. In the figure, E is the section of the capitals of the inner columns of the temple on a larger scale. DD relate to the principal columns. F is a section of one of the antæ or pilasters to double the scale of the capital. The centre intercolumniation 4 modules 55/100, from axis to axis of columns. The principal Grecian Doric examples are — the Parthenon, the temple of Theseus, the propylæum and the portico of the Agora at Athens; the temple of Minerva at Sunium; the temple at Corinth; of Jupiter Nemæus, between Argos and Corinth; temple of Apollo and portico of Philip in the island of Delos; the temple of Jupiter Panhellenius at Egina, and of Apollo Epicurius at Phigalia; the two temples at Selinus; that of Juno Lucina and Concord at Agrigentum; the temple at Egesta, and the three temples at Pæstum. (See 142, *et seq.*)

SECT. V.

THE IONIC ORDER.

2573. Of the Ionic order there are many extant examples, both Grecian and Roman; and, except the debased later examples of the latter, there is not that wide difference between them that exists between the Grecian and Roman Doric. The Ionic has been considered as deficient in appearance as compared with the other orders, on account of

the irregularity of its capital, which, on the return, presents difficulties in use. These difficulties are not obviated by the practice of the Greeks, who made an angular volute on each extremity of the principal façade, and then returned the face of the capital. With all our respect for Greek art, we think the expedient, though ingenious, a deformity ; albeit, in the case of the type being a timber architrave, we must admit that the face of the capital should lie in the direction of the superincumbent beam.

2574. In the example given (*fig.* 884.) we have, as in the examples of the preceding

Fig. 884.

orders, selected the profile of Vignola as the most elegant of the moderns ; and the reader will here recollect that in the Ionic, Corinthian, and Composite orders, the module or semi-diameter of the column is divided into 18 parts.   In the figure, A is a plan of the sofite of the cornice, and B a plan of the capital.   The method of tracing the volute will be given in a subsequent figure : previous to which, as in the orders already given, we subjoin a table, showing the heights and projections of the parts of the order.

Members composing the Order.		Heights in Parts of a Module.	Projections from Axis of Column in Parts of a Module.
ENTABLATURE.			
A, cornice, 34 parts.	Fillet of cyma - - -	$1\frac{1}{2}$	46
	Cyma recta - - - -	5	
	Fillet - - - - -	$\frac{1}{2}$	41
	Cyma reversa - - -	2	$40\frac{1}{2}$
	Corona - - - -	6	$38\frac{1}{4}$
	Fillet of the drip - - -	1	$29\frac{1}{4}$
	Ovolo - - - -	4	$28\frac{1}{4}$
	Astragal - - - -	1	25
	Fillet - - - -	$\frac{1}{2}$	$24\frac{1}{2}$
	Dentel fillet - - - -	$1\frac{1}{2}$	21
	Dentels - - - -	6	24
	Fillet - - - - -	1	20
	Cyma reversa - - -	4	$19\frac{1}{2}$
B,	Frieze - - - - -	27	15

Members composing the Order.		Heights in Parts of a Module.	Projections from Axis of Column in Parts of a Module.
C, Architrave, 22½ parts.	Listel	1½	20
	Cyma reversa	3	19⅔
	First fascia	7½	17
	Second fascia	6	16
	Third fascia	4½	15
D,	Capital on the side	19	20
	Capital on the coussinet, or cushion	16	17½
	COLUMN.		
E, Capital, 17 parts.	Fillet	1	20
	Cyma reversa	2	19½
	Listel	1	17½
	Channel of the volute	3	17
	Ovolo	5	22
	Astragal: Bead	2	18
	Astragal: Fillet	1	17
	Astragal: Congé, or cavetto	2	15
	Shaft of the column above	16 mod. 6 parts.	15
	Shaft of the column below		18
	Apophyge	2	18
F, Base, 19½ parts.	Fillet	1½	20
	Torus	5	22½
	Fillet	¼	20½
	Scotia	2	20
	Fillet	¼	22
	Two beads	2	22½
	Fillet	¼	22
	Scotia	2	21
	Fillet	¼	24
	Plinth	6	25
	PEDESTAL.		
G, Cornice, 11¾ parts.	Fillet	⅔	35
	Cyma reversa	1⅓	34¾
	Corona	3	33½
	Fillet of the drip	½	30
	Ovolo	3	29½
	Bead	1	27
	Fillet	1	26¼
	Congé	1¼	25
	Die, 4 modules	12¾	1 mod. 7.
H, Base, 10 parts.	Congé	2	25
	Fillet	1	27
	Bead	1⅓	28
	Cyma reversa	3	27½
	Fillet	⅔	31⅔
	Plinth	4	33

The flutes in this order are separated by a listel.

2575. The letters to the leading divisions of the above table refer to the *fig.* 885., wherein the parts are drawn to a larger scale, and wherein I is the eye of the volute, presently to be described.

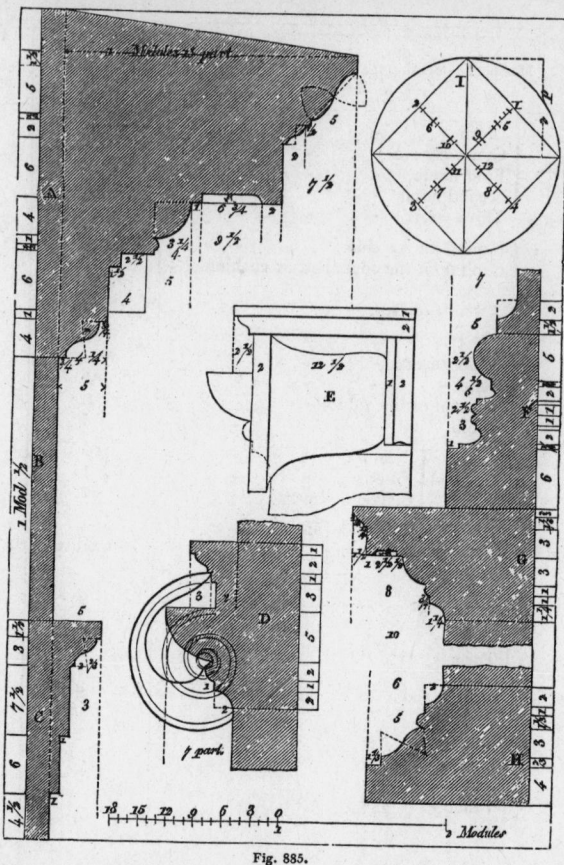

Fig. 885.

2576. *Fig.* 886. shows the method of drawing the volute, the centre of whose eye, as it is called, is found by the intersection of an horizontal line from E, the bottom of the

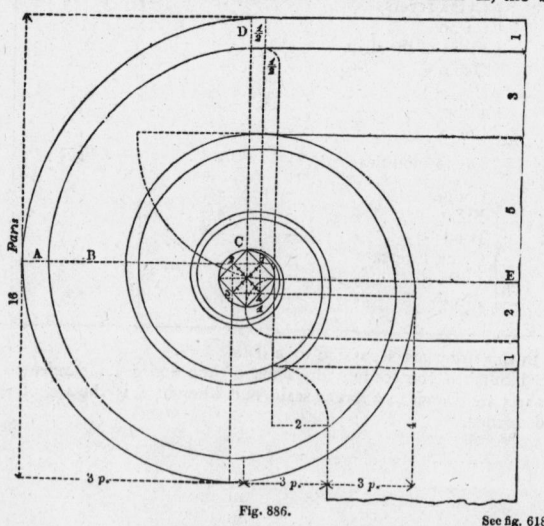

Fig. 886.

See fig. 618c.

echinus, with a vertical from D, the extremity of the cyma reversa. On the point of intersection, with a radius equal to one part, describe a circle. Its vertical diameter is called the *cathetus*, and forms the diagonal of a square, whose sides are to be bisected, and through the points of bisection (see I, *fig.* 885.) the axes 1, 3 and 2, 4 are to be drawn, each being divided into 6 equal parts. The points thus found will serve for drawing the exterior part of the volute. Thus, placing the point of the compasses in the point 1, with the radius 1 D, the quadrant D A is described. With the radius 2 A another quadrant may be described, and so on. Similarly, the subdivisions below the points used for the outer lines of the volute serve for the inner lines. The total height of the volute is 16 parts of a module, whereof 9 are above the horizontal from E, and 7 below it.

2577. Vitruvius, according to some authors, has not given any fixed measures to the pedestal of this order. Daniel Barbaro, however, his commentator, seems to think otherwise; and, on this head, we shall therefore follow him. The height of the pedestal is made nearly a third part (including its base and cymatium) of the height of the column. To the base of the column he assigns half a diameter, and to the shaft itself nearly 8 diameters, its surface being cut into 24 flutes, separated by fillets from each other. His method of describing the volute is not now thoroughly understood; and it is, perhaps, of little importance to trouble ourselves to decypher his directions, seeing that the mode of forming it is derived from mathematical principles, as well understood now as in the days of the author. The architrave he leaves without any fixed dimensions, merely saying that it must be larger or smaller according to the height of the columns. He prescribes, however, that the architrave, frieze, and cornice should together be somewhat less than a sixth part of the height of the column, with its base and capital. The total height he makes the order, according to our measures, is 25 modules and nearly 9 parts.

2578. Palladio gives to the pedestal 2 diameters and nearly two thirds of the height of the column. He adopts the attic, though without rejecting the Ionic base, and makes it half a diameter high, adding to it a small bead, which he comprises in the height of the shaft, which he makes 8 diameters in height. To the architrave, frieze, and cornice, taken together, he assigns a little less than one fifth of the height of the column, including its base and capital, and makes the projection of the cornice equal to its height. The total height of the order, in our measures, is, according to him, 27 modules and nearly 8 parts.

2579. Serlio, in this order more than any of the others, varies from Vitruvius. To the pedestal he gives, including base, die, and cymatium, a little more than a third part of the height of the column, with its base and capital. To the shaft of the column he gives 7 diameters, and diminishes it a sixth part of its diameter. His capital is that of Vitruvius, as far as we can understand that master. His mode of constructing the volute differs from other authors. His directions are, that having found the cathetus, which passes through the centre of the eye, it must be divided into eight parts, from the abacus downwards, one whereof is to be the size of the eye of the volute, four remain above the eye, and three below that part comprised below the eye. The cathetus is then divided into six parts, properly numbered by figures from 1 to 6. With one point of the compasses in 1, and the other extended to the fillet of the volute, he describes a semicircle, and so on with semicircles consecutively from 2 to 6, which will ultimately fall into the eye of the volute. We cannot speak in high terms of Serlio's method, and therefore have thought it unnecessary to accompany the description with a figure. It is rather a clumsy method, and we fear, if exhibited in a figure, would not satisfy our readers of its elegance. The height of his architrave, frieze, and cornice together is a little less than a fourth part of the height of the column, including the base and capital. The whole height of his order, in our measures, is 25 modules and 6 parts.

2580. Scamozzi directs that the pedestal shall be with its base and cornice two diameters and a half of the column. He uses the attic base, and, like Palladio, gives an astragal above the upper torus. To the shaft of the column he assigns a height of little less than 8 diameters, and makes its diminution a sixth part of the diameter. He adopts the angular capital, something like the example of that in the temple of Fortuna Virilis. The height of his architrave, frieze, and cornice is a little less than a fifth part of the height of the column, with its base and capital. The total height of his order, in our measures, is 26 modules.

2581. The principal examples of the Grecian Ionic are in the temples of Minerva Polias, of Erectheus, and the aqueduct of Hadrian, at Athens; in the temple of Minerva Polias at Priene; of Bacchus at

Fig. 887.

Teos; of Apollo Didymæus at Miletus; and of the small temple on the Ilyssus, near Athens, whereof in *fig.* 887. the profile is given, and below, a table of the heights and projections of the parts. It is to be observed, that in the Grecian Ionic volute the fillet of the spiral is continued along the face of the abacus, whilst in the Roman examples it rises from behind the ovolo. Some of the Athenian examples exhibit a neck below the echinus, decorated with flowers and plants. The entablatures of the early Ionic are usually very simple. The architrave has often only one fascia, the frieze is generally plain, and the cornice is composed of few parts. In Book I. Chap. II. (153, *et seq.*) we have already examined the parts of the Grecian Ionic, and thereto refer the reader.

TABLE OF THE PARTS OF THE GRECIAN IONIC IN THE TEMPLE ON THE ILYSSUS.

Members composing the Order.	Heights in Parts of a Module and Decimals.	Projections in Parts of a Module from Axis of Column.
ENTABLATURE.		
Cornice, supposed height 18·33 parts. { Fillet - - - - -	restored.	restored.
Cyma recta - - - -	restored.	restored.
Fillet - - - - -	restored.	restored.
Echinus - - - -	2·040	34·440
Corona - - - -	6·240	33·960
Drip - - - - -	4·680	
Cyma reversa - - -	2·700	20·520
Fillet - - - - -	0·720	
Echinus - - - -	1·260	18·360
Frieze - - - - -	29·901	17·400
Architrave, 33·66 parts. { Fillet - - - - -	1·920	30·520
Echinus - - - -	2·520	20·100
Bead - - - - -	1·200	17·880
Fascia - - - -	27·600	17·160
COLUMN.		
Capital, 19·32 parts. { Echinus - - - -	2·040	19·860
Fillets, or beads of volutes - -	1·050	
Channel - - - -	7·320	
Fillets, or beads of volutes - -	1·050	
Channel - - - -	0·600	
Cathetus - - - -	- -	17·550
Echinus - - - -	4·650	18·960
Bead - - - - -	1·080	17·250
Fillet - - - - -	0·450	15·720
Congé - - - -	1·080	
Shaft - - - - -	17 mod. 7·110	{above 15·360 {below 18·000
Base, 33·27 parts. { Apophyge - - - -	1·080	
Fillet - - - - -	0·450	18·960
Bead - - - - -	1·080	19·320
Horizontally fluted torus - -	6·120	22·500
Fillet - - - - -	0·450	22·500
Scotia - - - -	6·000	21·840
Fillet - - - -	0·450	23·640
Torus - - - -	5·760	24·960
Plinth - - - -	11·880	26·520

The height from the top of the echinus to the centre of the eye of the volute is 15·72 parts.

Total projection of the volute from axis of column, 27·90.

The flutes are elliptical on the plan (see *fig.* 887.), and the distance between axes of columns, 6 modules 3·24 parts.

THE CORINTHIAN ORDER.

2582. For the Corinthian order, we must seek examples rather in Rome than in any part of Greece.   The portico at Athens, and the arch of Hadrian at Athens, do not furnish us with specimens of art comparable with the three columns in the Campo Vaccino, belonging, as is generally supposed, to the temple of Jupiter Stator.   Those in the temple near Mylassa, and the Incantata, as it is called, at Salonica, do not satisfy the artist, as compared with the examples in the remains of the temple of Mars Ultor at Rome, the temple of Vesta at Tivoli, and others, for which the reader may refer to Desgodetz.

2583. The reader is again here reminded that the module or semidiameter is to be

Fig. 888.

divided into eighteen parts.   In *fig.* 888. is a representation of the Corinthian order, whose measures are given in the following table : —

Members composing the Order.		Heights in Parts of a Module.	Projections from Axis in Parts of a Module.
	ENTABLATURE.		
	Fillet of cornice - - - -	1	53
	Cyma recta - - -	5	53
	Fillet - - - -	$\frac{1}{4}$	48
	Cyma reversa - - -	$1\frac{1}{2}$	$45\frac{1}{2}$
	Corona - - - -	5	46
	Cima reversa - - - -	$1\frac{1}{2}$	$45\frac{1}{2}$
A, cornice,	Modillion - - - -	6	$44\frac{1}{2}$
38 parts.	Fillet (remainder of modillion band) -	$\frac{1}{2}$	$28\frac{1}{2}$
	Ovolo - - - -	4	28
	Bead - - - -	1	25
	Fillet - - - -	$\frac{1}{2}$	$24\frac{1}{4}$
	Dentils - - - -	6	24
	Fillet - - - - -	$\frac{1}{2}$	20
	Hollow or congé - - -	3	$19\frac{2}{3}$

	Members composing the Order.	Heights in Parts of a Module.	Projections from Axis in Parts of a Module.
B,	Frieze, 1 mod. $7\frac{1}{2}$ parts high	- -	15
C, architrave, 27 parts.	Fillet	1	20
	Cyma reversa	4	$19\frac{2}{3}$
	Bead	1	17
	First fascia	7	$16\frac{1}{2}$
	Cyma reversa	2	$16\frac{1}{3}$
	Second fascia	6	$15\frac{1}{2}$
	Bead	1	$15\frac{1}{2}$
	Third fascia	5	15
	Column.		
D, capital, 42 parts. (*fig.* 890.)	Echinus	2	diagonally 36,
	Fillet	1	on plan $33\frac{1}{3}$,
	Lower member of abacus	3	
	Inverted echinus of the bell	2	$22\frac{2}{3}$
	Large volutes	6	$31\frac{1}{3}$
	Upper small leaves	4	
	Large leaves	12	at top, $24\frac{1}{2}$
	Lower leaves	12	at top, $20\frac{1}{2}$
Shaft, 17 modules $1\frac{1}{2}$ part.	Astragal	2	18
	Fillet	1	17
	Congé	$2\frac{1}{4}$	
	Shaft — Upper part	- -	15
	Shaft — Lower part	- -	18
	Apophyge	2	20
	Fillet	$1\frac{1}{2}$	$21\frac{5}{8}$
E, base, $14\frac{1}{2}$ parts.	Torus	3	22
	Fillet	$\frac{1}{4}$	$20\frac{1}{2}$
	Scotia	$1\frac{1}{2}$	20
	Fillet	$\frac{1}{4}$	$21\frac{3}{8}$
	Two beads	1	22
	Fillet	$\frac{1}{4}$	$21\frac{5}{8}$
	Scotia	$1\frac{1}{2}$	$21\frac{1}{8}$
	Fillet	$\frac{1}{4}$	23
	Torus	4	25
	Plinth	6	25
	Pedestal.		
F, Cornice, $14\frac{1}{4}$ parts.	Fillet	$\frac{2}{3}$	$33\frac{1}{2}$
	Cyma reversa	$1\frac{1}{3}$	$33\frac{1}{4}$
	Corona	3	32
	Throat	$1\frac{1}{4}$	$30\frac{3}{4}$
	Bead	1	$26\frac{1}{2}$
	Fillet	$\frac{3}{4}$	$25\frac{3}{4}$
	Frieze	5	25
	Bead	$1\frac{1}{4}$	$26\frac{7}{8}$
Die, $91\frac{1}{2}$ parts.	Fillet	$\frac{3}{4}$	$26\frac{1}{4}$
	Congé	$1\frac{1}{2}$	25
	Die	$87\frac{1}{4}$	25
	Fillet	$1\frac{1}{2}$	25
	Congé	$\frac{3}{4}$	$26\frac{1}{4}$
G, Base, $14\frac{1}{4}$ parts.	Bead	$1\frac{1}{4}$	$27\frac{1}{4}$
	Inverted cyma reversa	3	$26\frac{3}{8}$
	Fillet	1	$30\frac{3}{4}$
	Torus	3	$32\frac{1}{2}$
	Plinth	6	$32\frac{1}{2}$

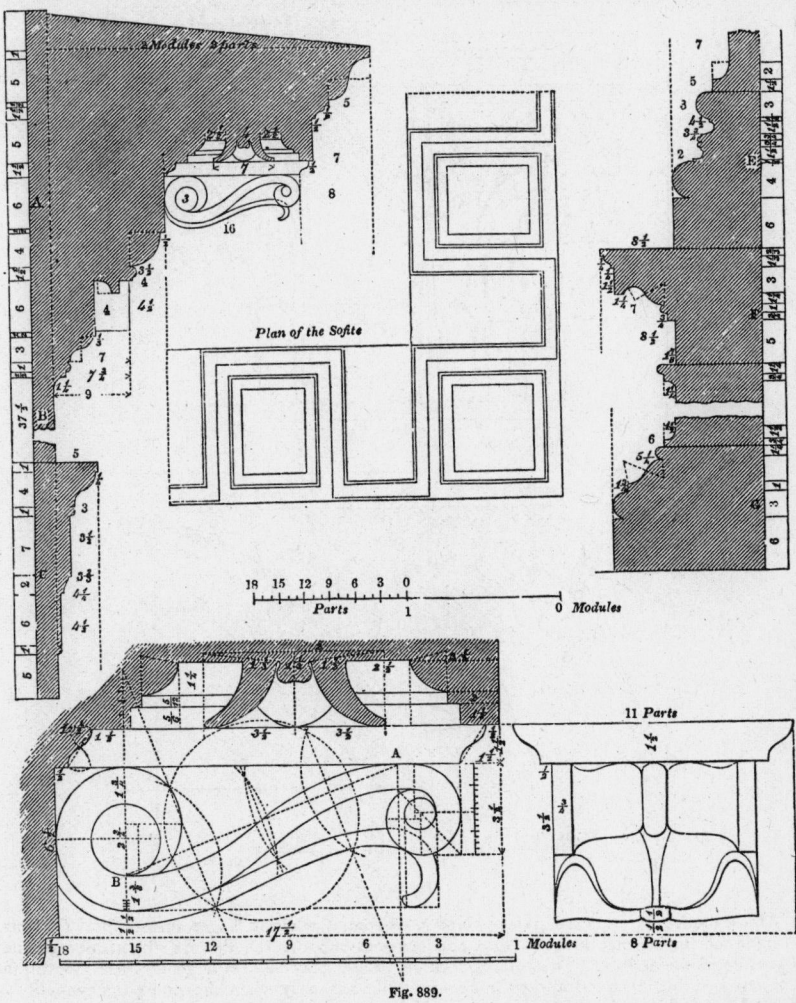

Fig. 889.

2584. *Fig.* 889. shows the details of the entablature, &c. and also the profile and front of the Corinthian modillion to a larger scale. On the profile is shown the caisson or sunk panel on the sofite of the corona. The height is six parts, and the projection sixteen. As seen in the figure, a distance equal to three parts and a half is taken for the height of the smaller volute, and on this distance a scale of sixteen equal parts is made; the figure shows the dimensions to be given to the small squares, whose angles serve as centres to describe the curves. Having drawn the line AB, it is divided into four equal parts by lines perpendicular to it, which, meeting vertical lines from A and B, give the points, which serve as centres for striking the curve of the modillions. The acanthus leaf which supports it, as well as the curves which form the profile of the roses in the caisson, are also struck by compasses.

2285. In *fig.* 890., which exhibits the method of drawing the Corinthian capital, one half of the plan shows the capital in plan, and the other half of it laid down diagonally. Having drawn the axis of the plan correspondent to the axis of the elevation of the capital, with a radius equal to two modules, describe a circle, which divide into sixteen equal parts. Their lines of division will each correspond to the centre of each leaf. The vase of the capital is determined by a circle whose radius is 14½ parts. The figure shows the circles which bound the leaves upwards on the vase.

2586. The elevation shows the heights whereon are carried the projections of the plan.

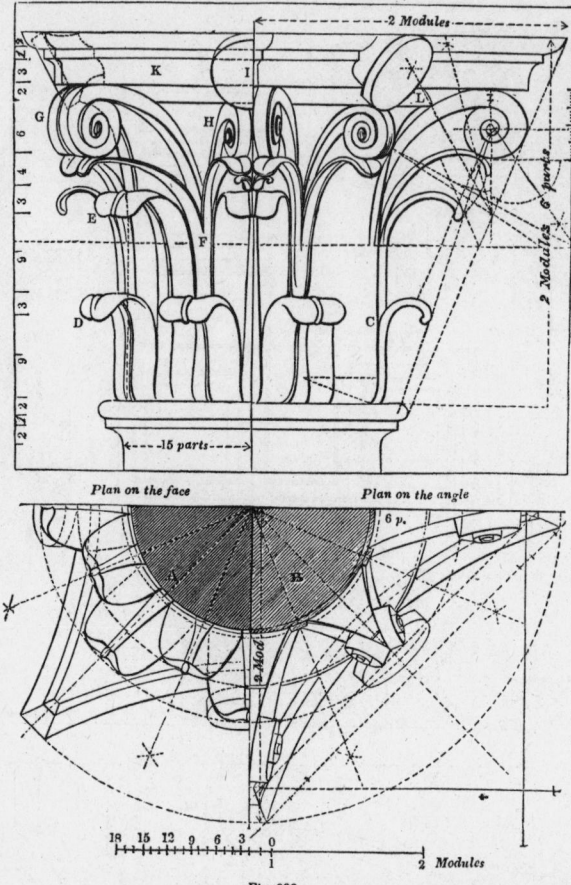

Fig. 890.

Above the leaves come the sixteen volutes, whereof the eight larger ones support the four angles of the abacus, and the eight smaller ones support the flowers which decorate the middle of the abacus. The volutes seen in profile may be drawn geometrically with the compasses, but they are always more agreeable and easy when drawn by the eye with a hand which feels the contours.

The different parts of the capital are as follow: A, plan of the leaves and abacus; B, plan of the larger and smaller volutes; C, the vase or body of the capital; D, the first tier of leaves; E, the second tier of leaves; F, the caulicolus; G, the larger volute; H, the smaller volute; I, the flower; K, the abacus; L, the lip of the vase.

2587. Vitruvius is scanty in the information he gives on the Corinthian order, and what he says respecting it relates more to the origin of the capital and the like than to the proportions of the detail. He makes the capital only 1 diameter high, and then forms upon the plan a diagonal 2 diameters long, by means whereof the four faces are equal according to the length of the arc, whose curve will be the ninth part in length and its height the seventh part of the capital. He forms the order with a pedestal, with base and cornice, as Daniel Barbaro would have it. The whole height given to it in our measures is about 27 modules and 2 parts.

2588. Palladio uses the pedestal with its ordinary subdivisions, making it between a third and fourth part of the height of the column, including its base and capital. To the base he gives 1 module, the shaft of the column a little less than 8 diameters, and places twenty-four flutes upon it, which two thirds downwards are channelled, and on the other or lower third neatly fitted with convex pieces of segments of cylinders called *cablings*. He makes the capital 1 diameter and a sixth in height, giving it two tiers of leaves, caulicoli, and abacus. To the architrave, frieze, and cornice he assigns a little less

than a fifth part of the column, including the base and capital.   The whole height given to the order by this author is about 27 modules and 10 parts of our measures.

2589. Serlio makes his pedestal pretty nearly as the rest.   To the base of the column he assigns half a diameter for the height, when that is about level with the eye, but when much above it he directs all the members to be increased in height accordingly, as where one order is placed above another, he recommends the number of parts to be diminished.   To the shaft of the column he gives a little more than 7 diameters, and to the capital the same height as that given by Vitruvius, whom, nevertheless, he considers in error, or rather that some error has crept into the text, and that the abacus ought not to be included in the height.   The height of the architrave, frieze, and cornice he makes a little less than a fourth part of the column, including its base and capital.   The whole of the order, according to him, is 28 modules and a little more than 1 part of our measures.

2590. Scamozzi gives to the pedestal of this order the height of 3 diameters and one third, composing it with the usual parts of base, die, and cornice; to the base of the column the same height and mouldings as Palladio.   To the shaft of the column he assigns the height of 8 diameters and one third, and diminishes it on each side an eighth part of its thickness at bottom.   The capital is of the same height as that by Palladio.   The architrave, frieze, and cornice he directs to be a little less than a fifth part of the height of the column.   By our measures the whole height of his order is 30 modules and 20 parts.

Sect. VII.

THE COMPOSITE ORDER.

2591. The Composite order, as its name imports, is a compound of others, the Corinthian and Ionic, and was received into the regular number of orders by the Romans. Philander, in his notes on Vitruvius, has described its proportions and character.   Its capital consists, like the Corinthian, of two ranges of acanthus leaves distributed over the surface of a vase, but instead of the stalks or branches, the shoots appear small and as though flowering, adhering to the vase and rounding with the capital towards its middle.   A fillet terminates the vase upwards, and over the fillet an astragal is placed, and above that an echinus, from which the volutes roll themselves to meet the tops of the upper tier of leaves, on which they seem to rest.   A large acanthus leaf is bent above the volutes, for the apparent purpose of sustaining the corner of the abacus, which is dissimilar to that of the Corinthian order, inasmuch as the flower is not supported by a stalk seemingly fixed on the middle of each face of the abacus.   The principal examples of

Fig. 891.

the order are at Rome, in the temple of Bacchus, the arches of Septimius Severus, of the Goldsmiths, and of Titus; also in the baths of Dioclesian.

2592. *Fig.* 891. (see preceding page) is a representation of Vignola's profile of the order. Its measures are subjoined in the following table: —

Members composing the Order.		Heights in Parts of a Module.	Projections from Axis in Parts of a Module.
ENTABLATURE.			
A, Cornice, 36 parts.	Fillet of cornice	$1\frac{1}{2}$	51
	Cyma recta	5	51
	Fillet	1	46
	Cyma reversa	2	$45\frac{1}{4}$
	Bead	1	$43\frac{3}{4}$
	Corona	5	43
	Cyma under the corona	$1\frac{1}{2}$	41
	Fillet	1	33
	Cyma reversa	4	$32\frac{1}{4}$
	Fillet of the dentils	$\frac{1}{2}$	28
	Dentils	$7\frac{1}{2}$	29
	Fillet	1	23
	Ovolo	5	22
B, Frieze, 27 parts.	Bead	1	17
	Fillet	$\frac{1}{2}$	$16\frac{1}{4}$
	Congé	$\frac{3}{4}$	15
	Upright face	$17\frac{1}{4}$	15
	Apophyge	7	22
C, Architrave, 27 parts.	Fillet	1	22
	Cavetto	2	$20\frac{1}{4}$
	Ovolo	3	20
	Bead	1	$17\frac{3}{4}$
	First fascia	10	17
	Cyma reversa	2	$16\frac{2}{3}$
	Second fascia	8	15
COLUMN.			
Capital, 42 parts.	Echinus and fillet	2	$20\frac{2}{3}$
	Lower member of abacus	4	diagonally $32\frac{1}{2}$
	Volute	12	diagonally $30\frac{2}{3}$
	Bend of upper leaves	3	24
	Upper leaves	9	$22\frac{1}{4}$
	Bend of lower leaves	3	$20\frac{2}{3}$
	Lower leaves	9	$19\frac{1}{3}$
Column, 16 mod. 12 parts.	Astragal	2	$17\frac{1}{2}$
	Fillet	1	$16\frac{1}{2}$
	Congé	2	$15\frac{1}{2}$
	Shaft { Above	- -	15
	Shaft { Below	16 mod. 12 parts. - -	18
	Apophyge	2	20
	Fillet	$1\frac{1}{2}$	20
E, Base of column, 18 parts.	Congé	2	20
	Fillet	$1\frac{1}{8}$	20
	Torus	3	22
	Fillet	$\frac{1}{4}$	$20\frac{1}{2}$
	Scotia	$1\frac{1}{2}$	20
	Fillet	$\frac{1}{4}$	$21\frac{1}{3}$
	Bead	$\frac{1}{2}$	$21\frac{3}{4}$
	Fillet	$\frac{1}{4}$	$21\frac{1}{3}$
	Scotia	2	$20\frac{2}{3}$
	Fillet	$\frac{1}{4}$	23
	Torus	4	25
	Plinth	6	25

Members composing the Order.						Heights in Parts of a Module.	Projections from Axis in Parts of a Module.
	PEDESTAL.						
	Fillet	-	-	-	-	$\frac{2}{3}$	33
	Cyma reversa	-	-	-	-	$1\frac{1}{3}$	$32\frac{3}{4}$
	Corona	-	-	-	-	3	$31\frac{1}{2}$
F, Cornice,	Cyma recta	-	-	-	-	$1\frac{1}{3}$	$28\frac{1}{2}$
14 parts.	Fillet	-	-	-	-	$\frac{1}{2}$	$26\frac{1}{4}$
	Cavetto	-	-	-	-	1	$25\frac{1}{4}$
	Frieze	-	-	-	-	5	25
	Bead	-	-	-	-	1	27
	Fillet	-	-	-	-	1	$27\frac{1}{4}$
	Congé	-	-	-	-	$1\frac{1}{4}$	25
Die, 94 parts.	Die -	-	-	-	-	$88\frac{3}{4}$	25
	Apophyge	-	-	-	-	2	27
	Fillet	-	-	-	-	1	27
	Bead	-	-	-	-	1	$27\frac{3}{4}$
	Inverted cyma reversa		-	-	-	3	$30\frac{1}{4}$
G, Base,	Fillet	-	-	-	-	1	$31\frac{1}{4}$
12 parts.	Torus	-	-	-	-	3	33
	Plinth	-	-	-	-	4	33

2593. The flutes in this order are separated by a fillet between them, and are, when used, twenty-four in number.

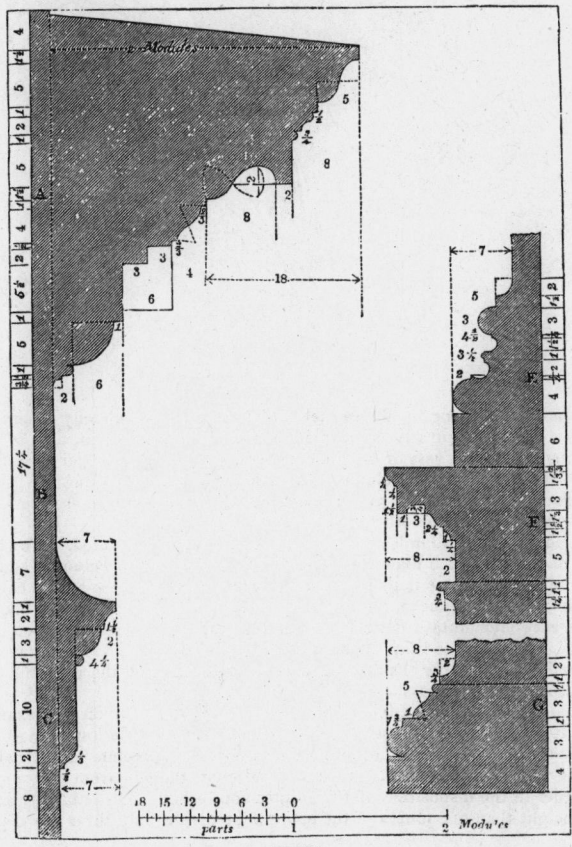

Fig. 892.

2594. *Fig.* 892. (see preceding page) shows the parts of the entablature, base, and pedestal to a larger scale, and *fig.* 893. gives, similarly, a more intelligible, because larger, represent-

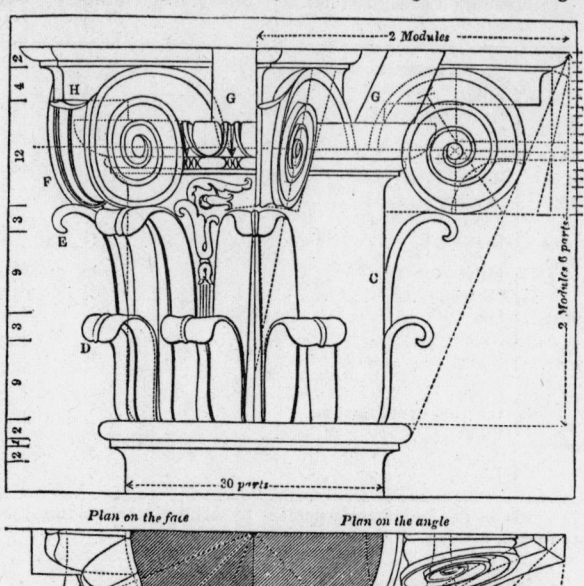

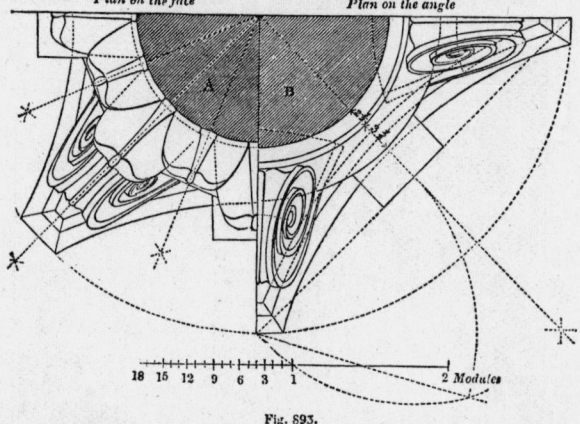

Fig. 893.

ation of the mode of setting up the capital, which, as we have already observed, has only eight volutes. In this figure A is the plan, as viewed frontwise; B, that of the capital, viewed diagonally; C, the vase or body of the capital; D, the first tier of leaves; E, the second tier of the same; F, the volutes; G, the flower; H, the abacus.

2595. Vitruvius has not given any instructions on this order; we are therefore obliged to begin our parallel, as in the other orders, with —

2596. Palladio, whose examples of it are light and much decorated. To the pedestal's height this master assigns 3 diameters and three eighths of the column, adding to it a lower plinth of the height of half a diameter. He makes the base of the column half a diameter in height, and assigns to the shaft 8 diameters and a little more than one fourth, and cuts on it twenty-four flutes. The height of this capital is 1 diameter and a sixth, his volutes being very similar to those he prescribes for his Ionic. The architrave, frieze, and cornice he makes a little less than a fifth part of the height of the column. The whole height of his profile in our measures is 30 modules and 12 parts.

2597. Serlio seems to have founded his profile of this order upon the example in the Coliseum at Rome. He makes the height of the pedestal a little less than 4 diameters of the column. To the shaft of the column he assigns 8 diameters and a half. To the height of the capital he gives 1 diameter, differing therein from his profile of the Corinthian order in the disposition of the volutes and leaves. His entablature, which is a little less in height than one fourth of the column, he divides into three equal parts for the

architrave, frieze, and cornice. The total height of his profile in our measures is 32 modules and 9 parts, being much higher than that of Palladio.

2598. Scamozzi's profile greatly resembles that of Palladio. His pedestal is 3 diameters, and the base of his column half a diameter in height. The shaft of his column without base or capital, is 8 diameters and one twelfth high, and the capital 1 diameter and a sixth. The entablature is one fifth part of the column in height, and the whole of the profile in our measures is nearly 29 modules and 7 parts.

Sect. VIII.

PEDESTALS.

2599. We think it necessary to devote a small portion of our labour to the consideration of pedestals, on account of the great difference which exists in the examples of the orders, and this we shall place in a tabular form, previous to the general remarks it will be necessary to make.

TABLE SHOWING THE HEIGHT OF PEDESTALS IN ANCIENT AND MODERN WORKS.

		Plinth in Minutes.	Mouldings above Plinth in Minutes.	Die in Minutes.	Cornice in Minutes.	Total Height in Minutes.
Doric	Palladio	26	14	80	20	140
	Scamozzi	30	15	$68\frac{4}{7}$	$22\frac{1}{2}$	$136\frac{1}{14}$
Ionic	Temple of Fortuna Virilis	44	$19\frac{3}{4}$	$93\frac{3}{4}$	$23\frac{1}{4}$	$180\frac{3}{4}$
	Coliseum	$33\frac{1}{4}$	$9\frac{1}{2}$	$81\frac{5}{6}$	17	$141\frac{1}{2}$
	Palladio	$28\frac{2}{3}$	$14\frac{1}{3}$	$97\frac{3}{4}$	$21\frac{1}{2}$	$162\frac{1}{4}$
	Scamozzi	30	15	$82\frac{1}{2}$	$22\frac{1}{2}$	150
Corinthian	Arch of Constantine	$17\frac{1}{2}$	29	153	$29\frac{1}{2}$	228
	Coliseum	23	$11\frac{1}{2}$	78	$19\frac{1}{4}$	$131\frac{3}{4}$
	Palladio	$23\frac{1}{2}$	$14\frac{1}{2}$	93	19	150
	Scamozzi	30	15	$132\frac{1}{2}$	$22\frac{1}{2}$	200
Composite	Arch of Titus	55	30	141	29	255
	Arch of the Goldsmiths	46	$25\frac{1}{4}$	$144\frac{1}{2}$	$25\frac{1}{4}$	241
	Arch of Septimius Severus	30	$30\frac{5}{8}$	$140\frac{1}{2}$	$29\frac{5}{8}$	$182\frac{1}{8}$
	Palladio	33	17	133	17	200
	Scamozzi	30	15	$112\frac{1}{2}$	$22\frac{1}{2}$	180

2600. The minutes used in the above table are each equal to one sixtieth of the diameter of the shaft.

2601. Whether the pedestal is to be considered a component part of an order is of little importance. There are so many cases that arise in designing a building, in which it cannot be dispensed with, that we think it useful to connect it with the column and entablature, and have consequently done so in the examples already given of the several orders. Vitruvius, in the Doric, Corinthian, and Tuscan orders, makes no mention of pedestals, and in the Ionic order he seems to consider them rather as a necessary part in the construction of a temple than as belonging to the order itself.

2602. A pedestal consists properly of three parts, the base, the die, and the cornice. "Some authors," says Chambers, "are so very averse to pedestals, and compare a column raised on a pedestal to a man mounted on stilts, imagining they were first introduced merely through necessity, and for want of columns of a sufficient length. "It is indeed true," he continues, "that the ancients often made use of artifices to lengthen their columns, as appears by some that are in the baptistery of Constantine at Rome ; the shafts of which, being too short for the building, were lengthened and joined to their bases by an undulated sweep, adorned with acanthus leaves ; and the same expedient has been made use of in some fragments which were discovered a few years ago at Nismes, contiguous to the temple of Diana. Nevertheless, it doth not seem proper to comprehend pedestals in

the number of these artifices, since there are many occasions on which they are evidently necessary, and some in which the order, were it not so raised, would lose much of its beautiful appearance. Thus, within our churches, if the columns supporting the vault were placed immediately on the ground, the seats would hide their bases and a good part of their shafts; and in the theatres of the ancients, if the columns of the scene had been placed immediately on the stage, the actors would have hid a considerable part of them from the audience; for which reason it was usual to raise them on very high pedestals, as was likewise necessary in their triumphal arches; and in most of their temples the columns were placed on a basement or continued pedestal (*stylobata*), that so the whole might be exposed to view, notwithstanding the crowds of people with which these places were frequently surrounded. And the same reason will authorise the same practice in our churches, theatres, courts of justice, or other public buildings where crowds frequently assemble. In interior decorations, where, generally speaking, grandeur of style is not to be aimed at, a pedestal diminishes the parts of the order, which otherwise might appear too clumsy; and has the farther advantage of placing the columns in a more favourable view, by raising their base nearer to the level of the spectator's eye. And in a second order of arcades there is no avoiding pedestals, as without them it is impossible to give the arches any tolerable proportion. Sometimes, too, the situation makes it necessary to employ pedestals, an instance of which there is in the Luxembourg at Paris; where, the body of the building standing on higher ground than the wings, the architect was obliged to raise the first order of the wings on a pedestal, to bring it upon a level with that of the body or *corps de logis* of the building, which stands immediately on the pavement."

2603. The dies of pedestals are occasionally decorated with tablets or with sunk panels whose margins are moulded; but, generally speaking, such practices are to be avoided. In very large pedestals the surface may be thus broken, as in single monumental columns, which, at best, are but paltry substitutes for originality. Habit has reconciled us to view with pleasure the Trajan and Antonine columns, the monument of London, and the column of Napoleon in the Place Vendôme at Paris, in each of which the pedestals are ornamented in some way or other, so as to tell in some measure the story of the person in whose honour they were erected, or, as in the basso-relievo of the London column, the event which it records. But care must be taken when inscriptions are used to preserve a rigid adherence to truth, and not to perpetuate a lie, as was the case in the monument just named, against a most worthy portion of the people of the British empire.

2604. As respects the employment of pedestals, we should advise the student, except under very extraordinary circumstances, to avoid the use of them under columns which are placed at a distance from the main walls of an edifice, as, for example, in porches peristyles, or porticoes, — a vice most prevalent in the Elizabethan architecture, or rather the cinque-cento period, which the people of this day are attempting with all its absurdities to revive. Here we must again quote our author, Sir William Chambers, whose excellent work we have used above, and on which we shall continue to draw largely. "With regard," he says, "to the application of pedestals, it must be observed, that when columns are entirely detached, and at a considerable distance from the wall, as when they are employed to form porches, peristyles, or porticoes, they should never be placed on detached pedestals, as they are in some of Scamozzi's designs, in the temple of Scisi (Assisi) mentioned by Palladio, and at Lord Archer's house, now Lowe's hotel, in Covent Garden; for then they indeed may be compared to men mounted on stilts, as they have a very weak and tottering appearance. In compositions of this kind, it is generally best to place the columns immediately on the pavement, which may be either raised on a continued solid basement, or be ascended to by a flight of fronting steps, as at St. Paul's, and at St. George's Bloomsbury; but if it be absolutely necessary to have a fence in the intercolumniations, as in the case of bridges or other buildings on the water, or in a second order, the columns may then, in very large buildings, be raised on a continued plinth, as in the upper order of the western porch of St. Paul's, which in such case will be sufficiently high: and in smaller buildings, wherever it may not be convenient or proper to place the balustrade between the shafts, the columns may be placed on a continued pedestal, as they are in Palladio's designs for Signor Cornaro's house at Piombino, and at the villa Arsieri, near Vicenza, another beautiful building of the same master." The same author continues: "The base and cornice of these pedestals must run in a straight line on the outside throughout, but the dies are made no broader than the plinths of the columns, the intervals between them being filled with balusters, which is both really and apparently lighter than if the whole pedestal were a continued solid." The author quoted then proceeds to caution the student against the employment of triangular, circular, and polygonal pedestals, and such as are swelled and have their die in the form of a baluster, or are surrounded by cinctures.

These extravagances were rife in the age of Louis XV., but notwithstanding the zeal of the jobbing upholsterers and decorators of the present day, who are the curse of all architectural art, we hope they will never be permanently revived in this country, though their introduction has already proceeded to a considerable extent.

2605. An intercolumniation is the clear distance between two columns measured at the lower diameter of their shafts. This distance must depend principally on the order employed: in the Tuscan, for example, the nature of its composition allows a greater width between columns than would be admissible in the Corinthian order, independent of what has already been stated in Sect. II. (2524, *et seq.*) in respect of supports and loading; and this because of the enrichments of the several orders requiring that they should take their departures (to use a phrase borrowed from another science) from the axes of their respective columns. The ancient names (which are still preserved) of the different intercolumniations are described by Vitruvius in his second and fourth books. They are — the *pycnostyle*, wherein the space between the columns is 1 diameter and a half, as its etymology from πυκνος and στυλος imports (thick in columns), an intercolumniation used only in the Ionic and Corinthian orders; the *systyle* (συστυλος, with columns a little more apart), wherein the interval between the columns is a little greater; the *eustyle* (ευστυλος, or well-contrived interval), wherein the intercolumniation is of 2 diameters and a quarter; the *diastyle* (διαστυλος, with a more extended interval between the columns), having an intercolumniation of 3 diameters; and the *aræostyle* (αραιοστυλος, with few columns), wherein the interval is 4 diameters. In the Doric order the triglyphs necessarily regulate the intercolumniations, inasmuch as the triglyph should fall over the axis of the column; hence the intercolumniations in this order are either systyle monotriglyph (that is, with a single triglyph in the intercolumniation), or 1½ diameter; diastyle, or of 2¾ diameters; or aræostyle, which will make the interval 4 diameters, as will be immediately understood on reference to *fig.* 894.; wherein A is the systyle monotriglyph intercolumniation of 3 modules; B, that of the diastyle, or 6 modules; and C, the aræostyle, or of 8 modules. The intercolumniation marked D serves for

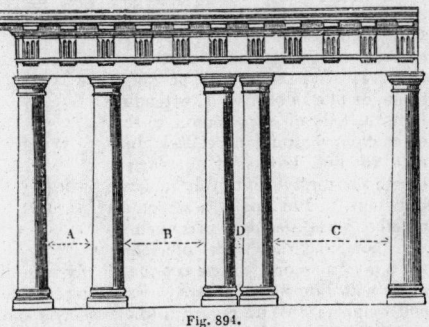

Fig. 894.

the application of coupled columns, wherein the rule seems necessarily to be that the space between the columns may be increased, so that the requisite number of supports according to the order and intercolumniation is preserved.

Fig. 895.

2606. The intervals of the Tuscan order are indicated in *fig.* 895., wherein A shows the intercolumniation called eustyle of 4½ modules; B, the diastyle of 6 modules; and C, the aræostyle of 8. D, of 1 module, is the space of coupled columns.

The intercolumniations in this order are scarcely susceptible of rules other than those we have indicated in our previous discussion on the orders generally in Sect. II. (2523, *et seq.*), wherein we have entered on the subject at such length that we refrain from saying more in this place. We may, however, observe, that the application of the principles there mentioned are so intimately connected with this section, that the separation of one from the other would destroy all our scheme for keeping the student in the right path. Hereafter the principles in question will be applied to and tested on arcades.

2607. In *fig.* 896., of Ionic inter-columniations, A is the eustyle arrangement; B, that of the diastyle; C, that of the aræostyle; and D, that of coupled columns.

2608. *Fig.* 897. is a similar application of the intercolumniations to the Corinthian order, wherein also A exhibits the eustyle; B, the diastyle; and C, the aræostyle intervals: D also showing the space used of 1 module for coupled columns.

2609. Sir William Chambers, for whose observations we have much respect, — and, indeed, to whose valuable labours we acknowledge ourselves much indebted, — seems to have had a distant glimpse of the doctrine of equal weights and supports, but knew not exactly how to justify his notions on the subject. He therefore avoids the main question by attributing the pycnostyle intercolumniation rather to necessity than choice; observing, that "as the architraves were composed of single stones or blocks of marble, extending from the axis of one column to that of another, it would have been difficult to find blocks of a sufficient length for diastyle intervals in large buildings." But this is a reason altogether unsatisfactory, inasmuch as we know that they were sufficiently

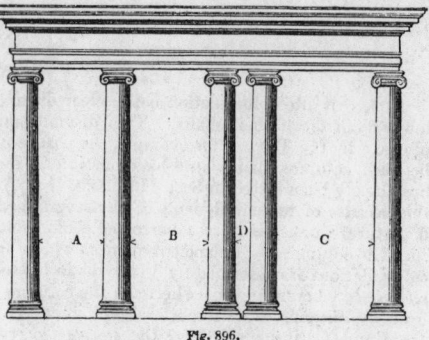

Fig. 896.

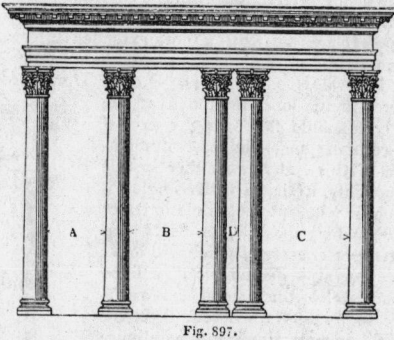

Fig. 897.

masters of masonry to have conquered any such difficulty. We are much more inclined to agree with him when he says (always, however, reverting to the principle of equal supports and weights), "With regard to the aræostyle and Tuscan intercolumniations, they are by much too wide either for beauty or strength, and can only be used in structures where the architraves are of wood, and where convenience and economy take place of all other considerations: nor is the diastyle sufficiently solid in large compositions." These considerations, however, may be always safely referred to the doctrines laid down in Section II. of this Chapter, already alluded to; and, indeed, that reference is justified by the instructions of Vitruvius in the second chapter of his third book, wherein he directs that the thickness of the column should be augmented in an enlarged intercolumniation: as, for example, supposing the diameter of a column in the pycnostyle species to be taken one tenth of the height, it should in an aræostyle be one eighth; arguing, that if in an aræostyle the thickness of the columns exceed not a ninth or tenth part of their height, they appear too slender, and in the pycnostyle species the column at one eighth of its height is clumsy and unpleasant in appearance. Upon this passage Chambers observes, "that the intention of Vitruvius was good, but the means by which he attempts to compass it insufficient. His design was to strengthen the supports in proportion as the intervals between them were enlarged; yet according to the method proposed by him this cannot be effected, since one necessary consequence of augmenting the diameter of the column is enlarging the intercolumniation proportionably. Palladio and Scamozzi have however admitted this precept as literally just, and by their manner of applying it have been guilty of very considerable absurdity." We are not at all inclined to admit the truth of the opinion of Chambers; for, again reverting to the doctrine of the supports and loading, which was unknown to him, it is to be remembered that increase in the space of the intercolumniation immediately involves increase of weight in the load or entablature, and therefore seems to demand increase of diameter to the supports. Palladio and Scamozzi were not therefore guilty of the absurdity laid to their charge.

2610. Among the other reasons for our adopting the practice of Vignola is that he has observed so much uniformity in his intercolumniations, except of the Doric order, wherein the triglyphs prevent it, aware as we are that the practice has by many able writers been much condemned. Chambers even says that his practice in this respect is "preferable to any other, as it answers perfectly the intention of Vitruvius, preserves the character of each order, and maintains in all of them an equal degree of real solidity."

2611. With the exception of the Doric order, wherein the most perfect arrangement of the detail results from the interval produced by the ditriglyph, there can be no doubt that, abstractedly considered, the diastyle and eustyle intercolumniations are very convenient in use, and may be employed on most occasions, except, as just mentioned, in the Doric order.

2612. In setting out the intervals between columns especial care must be taken that the centres of modillions, dentils, and other ornaments in the entablature fall over the axes of the columns.   It is on this account that Vignola gives about two diameters and a third to the intervals in all the orders except the Doric, instead of two diameters and a quarter, as required by Vitruvius; an alteration which removes the difficulty and greatly simplifies the rules.

2613. Cases from many circumstances often occur where greater intercolumniations than the eustyle and diastyle are too narrow for use, and the moderns, headed by Perrault, have adopted an interval which that master has called aræosystyle.   This disposition is obtained without infringing on the law of weights and supports, to which we have already so often alluded.   In it the columns are *coupled*, as shown in the preceding figures, the interval being formed by swo systyle intercolumniations, the column separating them being, as Chambers observes, "approached towards one of those at the extremities, sufficient room being only left between them for the projection of the capitals, so that the great space is 3½ diameters wide, and the small one only half a diameter."   One of the finest examples of this practice is to be seen in the façade of the Louvre, (see *fig.* 176.) which in many respects must be considered as the finest of modern buildings.   The objections of Blondel to the practice are not without some weight, but the principal one is the extra expense incurred by it; for certain it is that it requires nearly double the number of columns wanted in the diastyle, besides which it cannot be denied that it causes considerable irregularities in the entablatures of the Doric, Corinthian, and Composite orders, which, however, are not apparent in the other two.   It is, nevertheless, so useful in cases of difficulty which constantly arise, that we should be sorry to exclude the practice altogether, though we cannot recommend it for unlimited adoption.

2614. A great many expedients have been employed to obviate the irregularity of the modillions in the Corinthian and Composite orders, arising from the grouping of columns. We, on this head, agree with Chambers, whose instructions we subjoin in his own words : " The simplest and best manner of proceeding is to observe a regular distribution in the entablature, without any alteration in its measures, beginning at the two extremities of the building, by which method the modillions will answer to the middle of every other column, and be so near the middle of the intermediate ones, that the difference will not easily be perceivable.   The only inconvenience arising from this practice is, that the three central intercolumniations of the composition will be broader by one third of a module than is necessary for eleven modillions: but this is a very trifling difference, easily divided and rendered imperceptible if the extent be anything considerable."   In the Doric order, the grouping of columns is not so easily managed, and therein our author recommends the expedient employed by Palladio, in the Palazzo Chiericato, and in the Basilica at Vicenza. In the last-named, the coupled columns are only 21 minutes apart, thus making the space between the axes 2 modules and 21 minutes, that is, 6 minutes beyond the breadth of a regular metope, and 2 half-triglyphs.   To conceal the excess, the triglyphs are 31 minutes broad, and their centres are carried 1 minute within the axis of the column, and the metope is 3 minutes broader than the others.   These small differences are not perceptible without a very critical and close examination of the distribution.   In this arrangement the attic base of Palladio should be employed, because of its small projection, and the larger intercolumniation must be aræostyle.

2615. Intercolumniations should be preserved of equal width in all peristyles, galleries, porticoes, and the like ; but in loggias or porches, the middle interval may be wider than the others by a triglyph, a modillion or two, and a few dentils, that is, if there be no coupled columns at the angles nor groupings with pilasters, in which cases all the other intervals should be of the same dimensions.   It has been observed by Blondel, that on occasions where several rows of columns are used, as, for instance, in the curved colonnades of the piazza of St. Peter's, the columns ought as much as possible to be in straight lines, because otherwise the arrangement can only be understood by viewing it from the centre of the figure employed.   The observation is well worth the student's consideration, for the resulting effect of a departure from this rule, as Chambers has properly observed, is "nothing but confusion to the spectator's eye from every point of view."   The same author condemns, and with justice, though in a smaller degree, the use of "engaged pilasters or half columns placed behind the detached columns of single, circular, oval, or polygonal peristyles, as may be seen in those of Burlington House.   Wherefore," he says, "in buildings of that kind, it will perhaps be best to decorate the back wall of the peristyle with windows or niches only."   We can hardly suppose it here necessary to caution the student against the use of intercolumniations without reference to the absolute

size of them : they must not be less than three feet even in small buildings, because, as Sir William Chambers seriously says, " there is not room for a *fat* person to pass between them."

2616. Before leaving the subject which has furnished the preceding remarks on inter-columniations, we most earnestly recommend to the student the re-perusal of Section II. of this Book. The intervals between the columns have, in this section, been considered more with regard to the laws resulting from the distribution of the subordinate parts, than with relation to the weights and supports, which seem to have regulated the ancient practice : but this distribution should not prevent the application generally of the principle, which may without difficulty, as we know from our own experience, be so brought to bear upor it as to produce the most satisfactory results. We may be perhaps accused of bringing a fine art under mechanical laws, and reducing refinement to rules. We regret that we cannot bind the professor by more stringent regulations. It is certain that, having in this respect carried the point to its utmost limit, there will still be ample opportunity left for him to snatch that grace, beyond the reach of art, with the neglect whereof the critics are wont so much to taunt the artist in every branch.

Sect. X.

ARCADES AND ARCHES.

2617. An arcade, or series of arches, is perhaps one of the most beautiful objects at-tached to the buildings of a city which architecture affords. The utility, moreover, of arcades in some climates, for shelter from rain and heat, is obvious; but in this dark climate, the inconveniences resulting from the obstruction to light which they offer, seems to preclude their use in the cities of England. About public buildings, however, where the want of light is of no importance to the lower story, as in theatres, courts of law, churches, and places of public amuse-ment, and in large country seats, their introduction is often the source of great beauty, when fitly placed.

2618. In a previous section (2524.) we have spoken of Lebrun's theory of an equality between the weights and sup-ports in decorative architecture : we shall here return to the subject, as applied to arcades, though the analogy is not, per-haps, strictly in point, because of the dissimilarity of an arch to a straight lintel. In *fig*. 898. the hatched part AEMFDCOB is the load, and ABGH, CDIK the supports. The line GK is divided into six parts, which serve as a scale to the diagram, the opening HI being four of them, the height BH six, NO two, and OM one. From the exact quadrature of the circle being unknown, it is impossible to measure with strict accu-racy the surface BOC, which is necessary for finding by sub-traction the surface AEMFDCOB ; but using the common method, we have

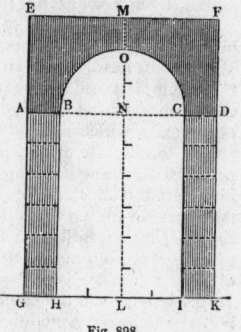

Fig. 898.

$$AD \times AE - \frac{BC^2 \times \cdot 7854}{2} = \text{ to that surface; or, in figures,}$$
$$6 \times 3 - \frac{4 \times 4 \times \cdot 7854}{2} = 11 \cdot 72.$$

Now the suports will be IK × IC × 2 (the two piers) = the piers; or, in figures,
$$1 \times 6 \times 2 \qquad\qquad = 12 \cdot 00.$$

That is, in the diagram the load is very nearly equal to the supports, and would have been found quite so, if we could have more accurately measured the circle, or had with greater nicety constructed it. But we have here, where strict mathematical precision is not our object, a sufficient ground for the observations which follow, and which, if not founded on something more than speculation, form a series of very singular accidents. We have chosen to illustrate the matter by an investigation of the examples of arcades by Vignola, because we have thought his orders and arcades of a higher finish than those of any other master ; but testing the hypothesis, which we intend to carry out by examples from Palladio, Sca-mozzi, and the other great masters of our art, not contemplated by Lebrun, the small differences, instead of throwing a doubt upon, seem to confirm it.

2619. In *fig*. 898. we will now carry, therefore, the consideration of the weights and supports a step further than Lebrun, by comparing them with the void space they sur-round, that is, the opening HBOCI ; and here we have the rectangle HBCI = HB × HI, that is, $6 \times 4 = 24$, and the semicircle BOC equal, as above, to $\frac{4 \times 4 \times \cdot 7854}{2} = 6 \cdot 28.$ Then $24 + 6 \cdot 28 = 30 \cdot 28$ is the area of the whole void, and the weight and support being $11 \cdot 72 +$

$12 = 23 \cdot 72$, are a little more than two thirds the areas of the whole void; a proportion which, if we are to rely on the approval of ages in its application, will be found near the limits of what is beautiful.

2620. We shall now refer to the examples of Vignola alluded to; but to save the repetition of figures in their numbers, as referred to, each case is supposed in what immediately follows as unconnected with the entablatures which they exhibit, it being our intention to take those into separate consideration.

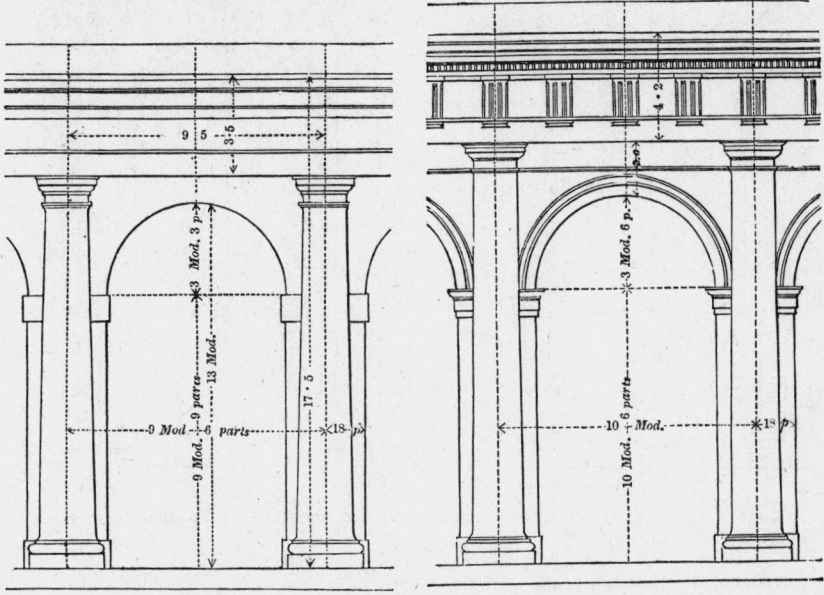

Fig. 899.   Fig. 900.

2621. Suppose the Tuscan example (*fig.* 899.) without an entablature, we have the

$$\text{Supports, } 9 \cdot 75 \times 3 \quad = \qquad 29 \cdot 25$$
$$\text{The whole of rectangle above them, } 4 \cdot 25 \times 9 \cdot 5 = 40 \cdot 375$$
$$\text{Less semi-arch, } \frac{6 \cdot 5 \times 6 \cdot 5 \times \cdot 7854}{2} = 16 \cdot 6$$
$$\underline{\qquad\qquad 23 \cdot 775}$$
$$\underline{\qquad\qquad 53 \cdot 025 \text{ solid parts.}}$$

The area of the void is $16 \cdot 6 + \overline{9 \cdot 75 \times 6 \cdot 5} = 79 \cdot 97$, whereof $53 \cdot 025$, the portion of solid parts, is not widely different from two thirds.

In Vignola's Doric example, (*fig.* 900.), again without the entablature, we have

$$\text{Supports, } 10 \cdot 5 \times 3 \quad = \qquad 31 \cdot 50$$
$$\text{The whole rectangle above them, } 5 \cdot 5 \times 10 \cdot 0 = 55 \cdot 00$$
$$\text{Less semi-arch, } \frac{7 \times 7 \times \cdot 7854}{2} = 19 \cdot 24$$
$$\underline{\qquad\qquad 35 \cdot 76}$$
$$\underline{\qquad\qquad 67 \cdot 26 \text{ solid parts.}}$$

The area of the void is $19 \cdot 24 + \overline{10 \cdot 5 \times 7} = 92 \cdot 74$, whereof $67 \cdot 26$, the portion of solid parts, is not much different from two-thirds.

In the Ionic example (*fig.* 901.), still without considering the entablature, the following will result : —

$$\text{Supports, } 12 \cdot 64 \times 2 \cdot 66 = \qquad 33 \cdot 61$$
$$\text{The whole rectangle above them, } 10 \cdot 88 \times 5 \cdot 2 = 56 \cdot 57$$
$$\text{Less semi-arch, } \frac{6 \cdot 4 \times 6 \cdot 4 \times \cdot 7854}{2} = 16 \cdot 08$$
$$\underline{\qquad\qquad 40 \cdot 49}$$
$$\underline{\qquad\qquad 74 \cdot 10 \text{ solid parts.}}$$

The area of the void is $16 \cdot 08 + \overline{12 \cdot 64 \times 7 \cdot 1} = 105 \cdot 82$, whereof $74 \cdot 10$, the portion of solid parts, differs little in amount from two thirds of the void.

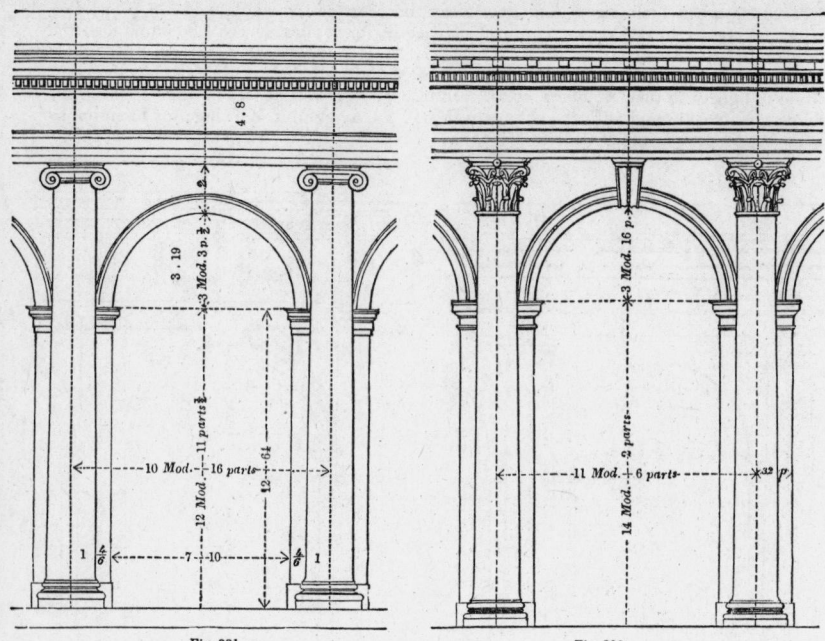

Fig. 901.   Fig. 902.

In the Corinthian example (*fig.* 902.), not taking into consideration the entablature, the following is the result: —

$$\text{Supports, } 14{\cdot}11 \times 3{\cdot}55 = \qquad 50{\cdot}09$$
$$\text{The whole rectangle above them, } 11{\cdot}33 \times 5{\cdot}88 = 66{\cdot}62$$
$$\text{Less semi-arch, } \tfrac{7{\cdot}76 \times 7{\cdot}76 \times {\cdot}7854}{2} = 23{\cdot}65$$
$$= 32{\cdot}97$$
$$\overline{\qquad\qquad} \text{ 83·06 solid parts.}$$

The area of the void is $23{\cdot}65 + \overline{14{\cdot}111 \times 7{\cdot}76} = 133{\cdot}15$, whereof $83{\cdot}06$, the portion of solid parts, is somewhat less than two thirds of the void.

2622. The result which flows from the above examination seems to be that, without respect to the entablature, the ratio of the solid part to that of the void is about ·666. Bearing this in mind, we shall next investigate the ratio of the supports and weights, considering the entablature above the arcade as a part of the composition; and still following Vignola, whose examples, as we have above stated, do not so much differ from those of other masters as to make it necessary to examine those of each, we will begin with that architect's Tuscan arcade, without pedestals, exhibited in *fig.* 899. on the preceding page. In this example, from centre to centre of pier,

$$\text{The whole area, in round numbers, } 17{\cdot}5 \times 9{\cdot}5 \quad - \quad - \quad - =166{\cdot}2$$
$$\text{Area of semi-arch, } \tfrac{6{\cdot}5 \times 6{\cdot}5 \times {\cdot}7854}{2} \quad - \quad - =16{\cdot}6$$
$$\text{Rectangle under it, } 9{\cdot}75 \times 6{\cdot}5 \quad - \quad - =63{\cdot}3$$
$$\text{Total void, therefore, } =79{\cdot}9$$

$$86{\cdot}3$$
$$\text{Entablature, } 9{\cdot}5 \times 3{\cdot}5 \quad - \quad - \quad - \quad - \quad - =33{\cdot}2$$
$$\text{Leaves for the supporting parts} \quad - \quad - \quad - \quad - \quad - \quad 53{\cdot}1$$

In this example, therefore, the supporting parts are 53, those supported 33, and the voids 79. The ratio between the solid and void parts = ·9, and the ratio of the supports to the weights is $\frac{33}{33} = {\cdot}62$.

The distance between the axes of the columns is 9 modules and 6 parts; the height of the semi-arch, 3 modules and 3 parts; and between the crown of it and the under side of the architrave is 1 module; the whole height, including entablature, being 17 modules and a half.

2623. Following the same general method, we submit the Doric arcade (*fig.* 900.) without pedestal. Measuring, as before, from centre to centre of piers,

The whole area, in round numbers, $20 \cdot 2 \times 10$ -   -   - $= 202 \cdot 0$

Area of semi-arch $\dfrac{7 \times 7 \times \cdot 7854}{2}$ -   -   - $= 19 \cdot 2$

Rectangle under it, $10 \cdot 5 \times 7$ -   - $= 73 \cdot 5$

Total void, therefore, $= \quad 92 \cdot 7$

$109 \cdot 3$

Entablature, $10 \times 4 \cdot 2$ -   -   -   -   - $42 \cdot 0$

Leaves for the supporting parts -   -   -   - $67 \cdot 3$

In this example, therefore, the supporting parts are 67, those supported 42, and the voids 92. The ratio between the solid and void parts is ·85, and the ratio of the supports to the weights is $\frac{42}{67} = \cdot 63$.

The distance between the axes of the columns is 10 modules, the height of the semi-arch is 3 modules and 6 parts, and between the crown of it and the underside of the architrave is 2 modules; the whole height, including the entablature, being 20 modules $3\frac{1}{2}$ parts.

2624. The Ionic arcade, without pedestal, is shown in *fig.* 901. The measurements, as above, from centre to centre of pier,

The whole area, $22 \cdot 64 \times 10 \cdot 88$ in round numbers -   -   - $= 246 \cdot 3$

Area of semi-arch, $\dfrac{6 \cdot 4 \times 6 \cdot 4 \times \cdot 7854}{2}$ -   - $= 16 \cdot 1$

Rectangle under it, $12 \cdot 64 \times 7 \cdot 1$ -   - $= 89 \cdot 7$

Total void, therefore, $= 105 \cdot 8$

$140 \cdot 5$

Entablature, $10 \cdot 88 \times 4 \cdot 8$ -   -   -   -   -   - $52 \cdot 2$

Leaves for the supporting parts -   -   -   - $88 \cdot 3$

Hence, in the example, the supporting parts are 88, those supported 52, and the voids 105; so that the ratio of the voids to the solids, in this order, is ·8, and the ratio of the supports to the weights does not materially differ from the other orders, being $\frac{52}{88} = \cdot 6$.

The distance between the axes of the columns is 10 modules 16 parts, the height of the semi-arch is $3\frac{1}{4}$ modules 3 parts, and between the crown of it and the under side of the architrave is 2 modules; the whole height, including the entablature, being 22 modules $13\frac{1}{2}$ parts.

2625. *Fig.* 902. represents the Corinthian arcade without pedestal. The measurement, as before, is from centre to centre of pier.

The whole area, $25 \cdot 2 \times 11 \cdot 33$, in round numbers -   - $= 288 \cdot 5$

Area of semi-arch, $\dfrac{7 \cdot 76 \times 7 \cdot 76 \times \cdot 7854}{2} = \quad 23 \cdot 6$

Rectangle under it, $14 \cdot 11 \times 7 \cdot 76 = 109 \cdot 5$

Total voids, therefore, $= 133 \cdot 1$

$155 \cdot 4$

Entablature, $10 \cdot 36 \times 5 \cdot 6$ -   -   -   -   -   - $58 \cdot 0$

Leaves for the supporting parts -   -   -   - $97 \cdot 4$

In the Corinthian example, therefore, the supporting parts are 97, those supported 58, and the voids 133. The ratio between the solid and void parts $= \cdot 8$, and the ratio of the supports to the weights $\frac{58}{97} = \cdot 59$. The distance between the axes of the columns is 11 modules and 6 parts, the height of the semi-arch is 3 modules 16 parts, and between the crown of it and the under side of the architrave is 2 modules $3\frac{1}{2}$ parts; the whole height, including the entablature, being 25 modules $3\frac{1}{2}$ parts.

2626. The laws laid down by Chambers for regulating arcades are as follow : — " The void or aperture of arches should never be much more in height nor much less than double their width; the breadth of the pier should seldom exceed two thirds, nor be less than one third of the width of the arch, according to the character of the composition, and the angular piers should be broader than the rest by one half, one third, or one fourth." . . . " The height of the impost should not be more than one seventh, nor need it ever be less than one ninth of the width of the aperture, and the archivolt must not be more than one eighth nor less than one tenth thereof. The breadth of the console or mask, which serves as a key to the arch, should at the bottom be equal to that of the archivolt, and its sides must be drawn from the centre of the arch. The length thereof ought not to be less than one and a half of its bottom breadth, nor more than double."

2627. The ratios that have been deduced by comparing the void and solid parts, if there be any reason in the considerations had, show that this law of making arches in arcades of the height of 2 diameters is not empirical, the following being the results of the use of the ratios in the arcade without, and that with pedestal, of which we shall presently treat. Thus in the

	Diameters.	Diameters.
Tuscan arcade without pedestal,	$\frac{13\cdot5 \text{ height}}{6\cdot5 \text{ width}} = 2\cdot0$; with pedestals,	$\frac{17\cdot5}{9\cdot5} = 1\cdot84$
Doric arcade without pedestal,	$\frac{14\cdot0}{7} = 2\cdot0$ —	$\frac{20\cdot0}{10\cdot0} = 2\cdot00$
Ionic arcade without pedestal,	$\frac{15\cdot83}{7\cdot10} = 2\cdot2$ —	$\frac{22\cdot0}{11\cdot0} = 2\cdot00$
Corinthian arcade without pedestal,	$\frac{18\cdot00}{7\cdot76} = 2\cdot3$ —	$\frac{25\cdot0}{12\cdot0} = 2\cdot08$

2628. In the examples of the arcades with pedestals, we shall again repeat the process by which the results are obtained, first merely stating them in round numbers. *Fig.* 903. is a

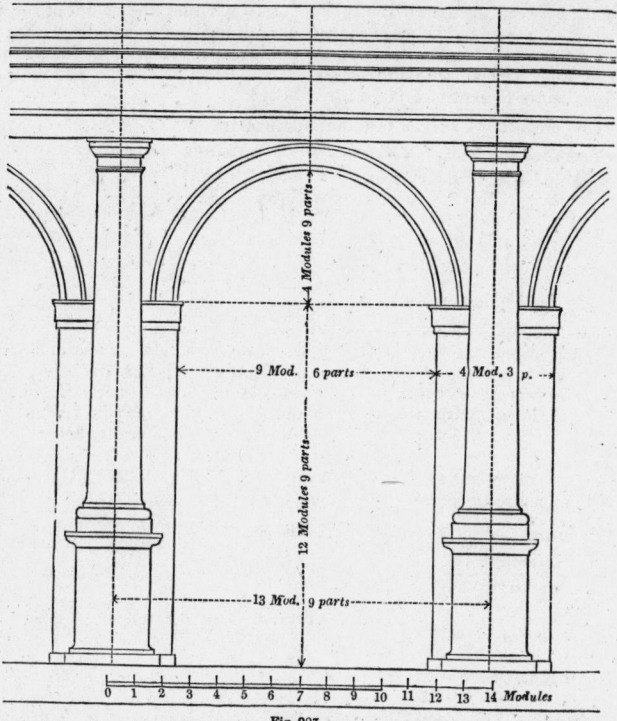

Fig. 903.

Tuscan arcade from Vignola's example, as will be the following ones. In this the whole area is 306, omitting fractions, the area of the void is 156, that of the entablature 50, and the supports 100. The ratio of the supported part (the entablature), therefore, is $\frac{50}{100} = \cdot5$, and the supports and weights are very nearly equal to the void. The height of the pedestal is almost 3 modules and 8 parts, the opening 9 modules 6 parts, and the width of the whole pier 4 modules and 3 parts.

The detail of the above result is as follows : —

The whole area, $22\cdot30 \times 13\cdot75$		$= 306\cdot62$
Area of semi-arch, $\frac{9\cdot5 \times 9\cdot5 \times \cdot7854}{2} = 35\cdot43$		
Below that, $12\cdot75 \times 9\cdot75$	$= 121\cdot12$	
	Total voids, therefore,	$= 156\cdot55$
		$150\cdot07$
Entablature, $13\cdot75 \times 3\cdot66$		$= 50\cdot32$
Leaves for supporting parts		$99\cdot75$

It will be seen that we have taken the numbers in the preceding paragraph without supplying strictly the decimal parts that arise from the multiplication and subtraction of the several portions compared. The coincidence of the hypothesis with the apparent law is no less remarkable in this example than it will be found in those that follow ; and, sceptical as we at first were on the appearances which pointed to it, we cannot, after the examination here and hereafter given, do otherwise than express our conviction that, in carrying out the principles, no unpleasant combination can result.

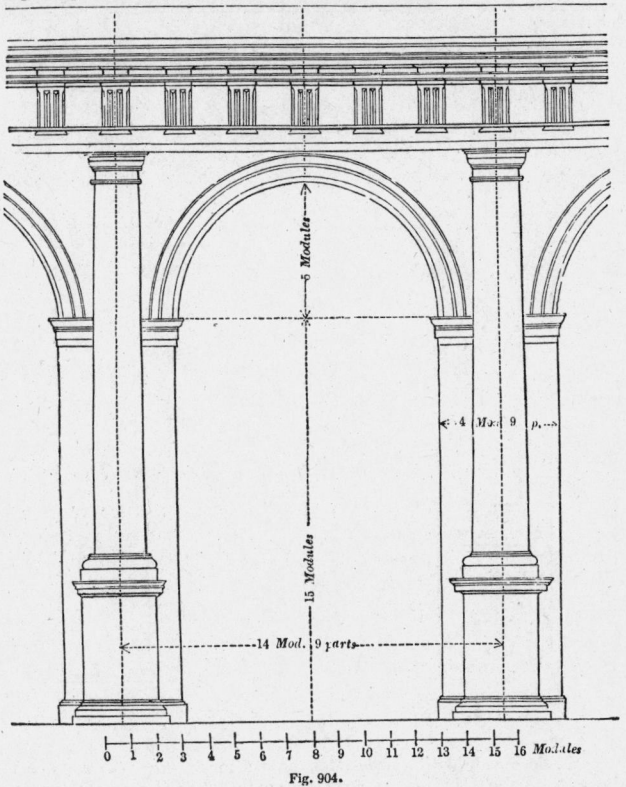

Fig. 904.

2629. *Fig.* 904. exhibits the Doric arcade, whose whole area from centre to centre of columns is 374. The area of the void is 189, that of the entablature 62, and of the supporting parts 112. The ratio of the entablature to the supports is therefore $\frac{62}{112} = \cdot 55$, and that of the supports and weights to the voids $\cdot 9$. The height of the pedestal is almost 5 modules and 4 parts, the opening 10 modules, and the width of a pier 4 modules and 9 parts.

As in the preceding example, we think it will be useful to detail the process by which the general results stated have been arrived at. It is curious and interesting to observe the similarity between the cases. It is scarcely possible to believe that accident could have produced it. May not the freemasons of the middle ages have had some laws of this nature which guided their operations? But we will now proceed to the calculation.

The whole area, $25 \cdot 4 \times 14 \cdot 75$ -   -   -   - $= 374 \cdot 65$

Area of semi-arch, $\dfrac{10 \cdot 0 \times 10 \cdot 0 \times \cdot 7854}{2} = 39 \cdot 27$

Below that, $12 \cdot 75 \times 9 \cdot 75$ - $= 150 \cdot 00$

Total voids, therefore,   - $= 189 \cdot 27$

$185 \cdot 38$

Entablature, $14 \cdot 75 \times 4 \cdot 25$ -   -   -   -   - $= 62 \cdot 68$

Leaves for supporting parts -   -   -   -   - $122 \cdot 70$

Herein, as before, the general result in the preceding paragraph has been given in round

numbers, that the mind of the reader may not be distracted from the general proportions. The detail again corroborates the hypothesis, as in the preceding subsection was predicated, and the further we proceed, as will be presently seen, its truth becomes more manifest.

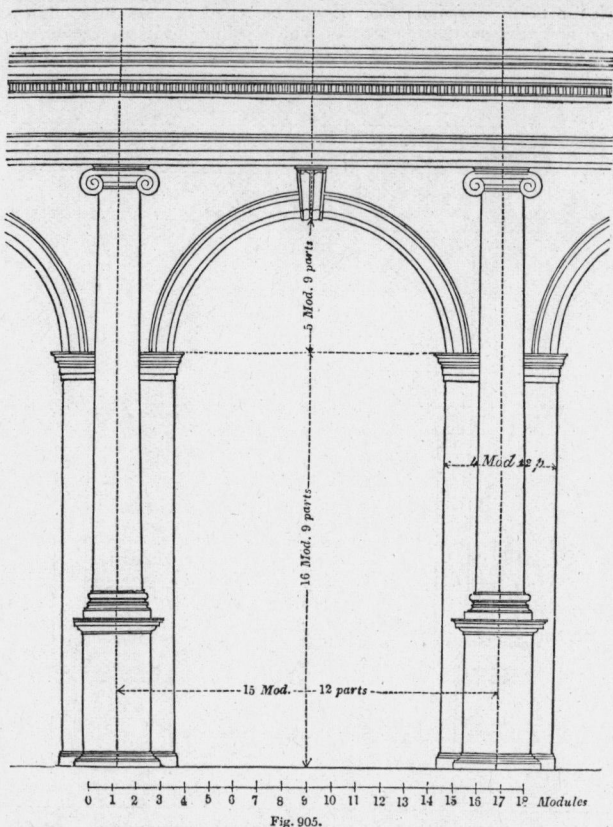

Fig. 905.

2630. The Ionic arcade with a pedestal is shown in *fig.* 905. The whole area is 448 between the axes of the columns; that of the void, 228. The entablature's area is 73, and the supporting parts 146. The ratio, therefore, of the load to the support is $\frac{73}{146} = \cdot 5$, and supports and weights are very nearly equal to the void. The height of the pedestal is 6 modules, the opening 11 modules, and the width of a pier 4 modules and 12 parts.

Once more returning to the detail on which the above proportions are based, and which in this as in the following example we think it better to supply, observing, as before, that the numbers above stated are given roundly, we shall have in the Ionic arcade,

Whole area, $28 \cdot 66 \times 15 \cdot 66$ -   -   -   -   - $= 448 \cdot 81$
Area of semi-arch, $\dfrac{11 \times 11 \times \cdot 7854}{2} = 47 \cdot 01$
Below it, $16 \cdot 5 \times 11$ - $= 181 \cdot 50$

           Total area of voids, therefore, $= 228 \cdot 51$

           $220 \cdot 30$

Entablature, $15 \cdot 66 \times 4 \cdot 7$ -   -   -   -   - $= 73 \cdot 50$

Leaves for supporting parts -   -   -   -   - $146 \cdot 80$

Whence it will be seen that the round numbers first given are shown to be sufficiently accurate for exemplification of the law, and that the further we examine the hypothesis the more closely we find it connected with the theory of weights and loads that has occupied a very considerable portion of this Book, and which we hope may not have had the effect of exhausting the reader's patience. We trust we shall have his pardon for pursuing the course we have taken.

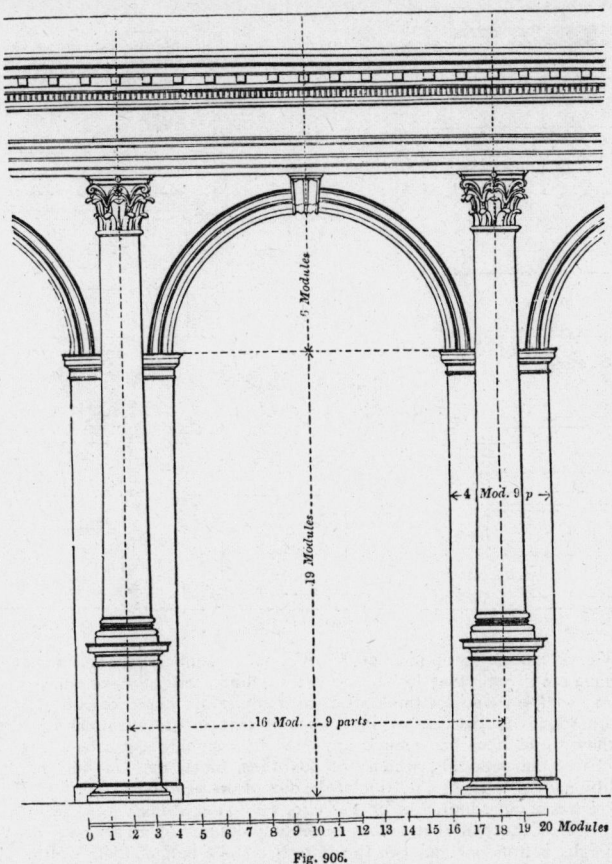

Fig. 906.

2631. *Fig.* 906. is an arcade with pedestals of the Corinthian order. Its total area is 528, that of the void 284, the area of the entablature 84, and that of the supporting parts 159. Hence, the ratio of the load to the support is $\frac{84}{159} = \cdot 52$, and the supports and weight are equal in area to the void within a very small fraction. The height of the pedestal is $6\frac{1}{2}$ modules, the opening is 12 modules wide, and the width of a pier is 4 modules and 9 parts.

We here close the curious proofs of a law whose existence, we believe, has never been suspected by modern architects. It was clearly unknown to Rondelet, and but for the work of Lebrun already quoted, we might never have been led to the investigation of it. That author himself, as we believe, did not entertain any notion of it.

In the Corinthian arcade with pedestal we have

Whole area, $32 \times 16 \cdot 5$ - - - - - -		$= 528 \cdot 00$
Area of semi-arch, $\dfrac{12 \times 12 \times \cdot 7854}{2} = 56 \cdot 05$		
Below it, 19×12 - $= 228 \cdot 00$		
	Total area of voids, therefore,	$= 284 \cdot 05$
		$243 \cdot 95$
Entablature, $16 \cdot 5 \times 5 \cdot 09$ - - - - -		$= 84 \cdot 10$
Leaves for supporting parts - - - - -		$159 \cdot 85$

Thus, again, the law seems to be borne out, and to prove that the assumptions we have been making are not those of empiricism.

2632. In *fig.* 907. are collected the imposts and archivolts used in the arcades of the diffrrent orders.

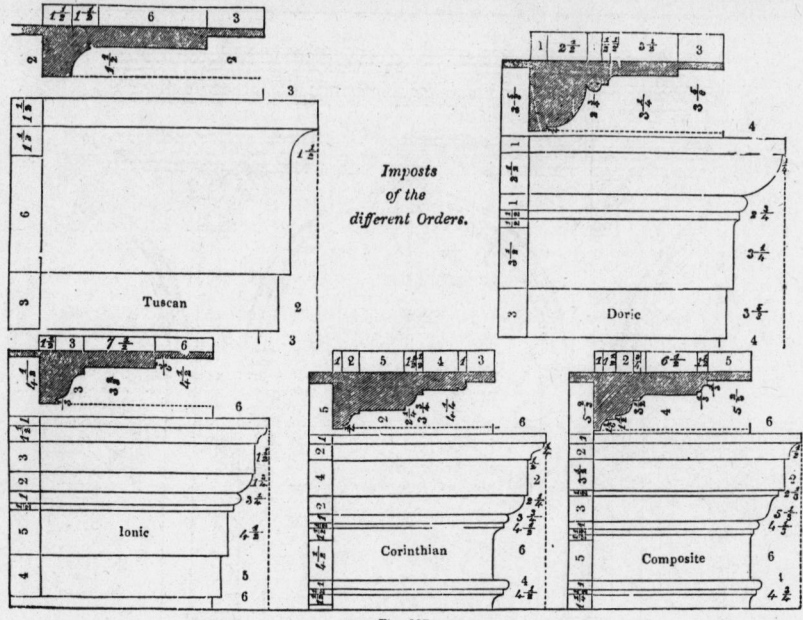

Fig. 907.

2633. We are not of the opinion of Sir William Chambers in respect of the arcades which Vignola has given; that author had not, we think, critically examined their composition, and we confess we do not think his own examples are improvements on those of the master in question; but we are willing to admit that in the examples of arcades with pedestals, they would have been much improved by assigning a greater height generally to the plinths of the pedestals, which are, doubtless, much too low, and might be well augmented by adding to them a portion of the dies of the pedestals.

2634. Great as is our admiration of Palladio, we do not think it necessary to say more relative to his arcades, than that he has given only designs of arches with pedestals, and that their height is from one and two thirds to two and a half of their width. His piers are generally $3\frac{3}{4}$ modules, except in the Composite order, wherein they are $4\frac{1}{4}$ modules.

2635. Scamozzi makes his Tuscan arch a little less than double its width, increasing the height gradually to the Corinthian arch with pedestals to nearly twice and a half the width. He diminishes his piers as the delicacy of the order increases, his Corinthian piers being only $3\frac{3}{4}$ modules in width. We do not, however, think it necessary to dwell longer on this part of the subject, and shall close it by observing that the impost of the arch should not much vary from half a module in height, and that the width of the archivolt, which should touch the shaft of the column or pilaster in the geometrical elevation, at its springing, is necessarily prescribed by the width of pier left after setting out the column upon it. Where columns are used on piers, their projection must be such that the most prominent member of the impost should be in a line with the axis of the column on the transverse section. In Ionic, Composite, and Corinthian arcades, however, it may project a little beyond the axis of the columns, to avoid the disagreeable mutilations which are otherwise rendered necessary in the capitals. Arcades should project not less than their width from the front of the wall which backs them." With regard to their interior decoration," says Chambers, " the portico may either have a flat ceiling or be arched in various manners. Where the ceiling is flat, there may be on the backs of the piers, pilasters of the same kind and dimensions with the columns on their fronts; facing which pilasters there must be others like them on the back wall of the portico. Their projection as well as that of those against the back of the piers may be from one sixth to one quarter of their diameter. These pilasters may support a continued entablature, or one interrupted and running across the portico over every two pilasters to form coffers; or the architrave and frieze only may be continued, while the cornice alone is carried across the portico over the pilasters as before, and serves to form compartments in the ceiling, as is done in the vestibule of the Massini palace at Rome, and in the great stable of the King's mews, near Charing Cross," — no longer in existence, having been destroyed to make way on its site for the execrable mass of absurdity to which the government who sanctioned it have facetiously

given the name of National Gallery.   Chambers thus continues : — " Where the portico is arched, either with a semi-circular or elliptical vault, the backs of the piers and the inner wall of the portico may be decorated with pilasters, as is above described, supporting a regular continued entablature, from a little above which the arch should take its spring, that no part of it may be hid by the projection of the cornice.   The vault may be enriched with compartments of various regular figures, such as hexagons, octagons, squares, and the like, of which, and their decorations, several examples are given among the designs for ceilings."   Of these we shall hereafter give figures in the proper place.   " But when the vault is groined, or composed of flats, circular or domical coves, sustained on pendentives, the pilasters may be as broad as are the columns in front of the piers, but they must rise no higher than the top of the impost, the mouldings of which must finish and serve them instead of a capital, from whence the groins and pendentives are to spring, as also the bands or *arcs-doubleaux* which divide the vault."

2636. In the examples of arcades, we have followed those given by Chambers, as exhibiting a variety which may be instructive to the student, and at the same time afford hints for other combinations.   *Fig.* 908. is one of the compositions of Serlio, and is an

Fig. 908.   Fig. 909.

expedient for arching in cases where columns have been provided, as in places where the use of old ones may be imposed on the architect.   The larger aperture may be from 4½ to 5 diameters of the column in width, and in height double that dimension.   The smaller opening is not to exceed two thirds of the larger one, its height being determined by that of the columns.   Chambers thinks, and we agree with him, that this sort of disposition might be considerably improved by adding an architrave cornice or an entablature to the column, by omitting the rustics and by surrounding the arches with archivolts.   It is not to be inferred, because this example is given, that it is inserted as one to be followed except under very peculiar circumstances.   Where an arrangement of this kind is adopted, care must be used to secure the angles by artificial means.

2637. *Fig.* 909. is given from the cortile of the castle at Caprarola by Vignola, a structure which in the First Book of this work we have (346.) already mentioned.   The height of the arches is somewhat more than twice their width.   From the under side of the arch to the top of the cornice is one third of the height of the arch, the breadth of whose pier is equal to that of the arch, and the aperture in the pier about one third of its breadth.

2638. A composition of Bramante, executed in the garden of the Belvedere at Rome, is given at *fig.* 910.   The arch in height is somewhat more than twice its width, and the

Fig. 910.   3 I   Fig. 911.

breadth of the pier equal to the opening. By dividing the latter into twelve parts we have a measure which seems to have prevailed in the mind of the architect, inasmuch as two of them will measure the parts of the pier supporting the archivolts, four for the space for the two columns, two for the intervals between the niche and the columns, and four for the niche. Half the diameter of the arch measures the height of the pedestal; the columns are of the height of ten diameters, and their entablature one quarter of the height of the columns. The impost and archivolt are each equal to half a diameter of the column.

2639. *Fig.* 911. is an example whose employment is not uncommon in the designs of Palladio, and was considered by our great countryman Inigo Jones to be worthy of his imitation. The arch may be taken at about twice its width, and the pier not less than one nor more than two thirds of the width of the aperture.

Fig. 912.

Fig. 913.

2640. The example in *fig.* 912. is from the hand of Vignola, and was executed for one of the Borghese family at Mondragone, near Frascati. In it the arch is a little more in height than twice its width, and the breadth of the pier columns supporting the arch includes a little less than the width of the arch itself. We are not quite satisfied in having here produced it as an example, though, compared with the following one, we scarcely know whether we should not on some accounts prefer it.

2641. The last example (*fig.* 913.) is one by that great master, Palladio, from the basilica at Vicenza. From the figure it is impossible to judge of its beauty in execution, neither can any imitation of it, unless under circumstances in every respect similar, produce the sensation with which the building itself acts on the spectator; yet in the figure it appears meagre and nothing worth. We can therefore easily account for the conduct of the critics, as they are called, who, never having seen this master's works, indulge in ignorant speculations of the pictorial effects which his compositions produce. Though not entirely agreeing with Chambers in his concluding observations on arcades and arches, we may safely transfer them to these pages. "The most beautiful proportion," he observes, "for compositions of this kind is, that the aperture of the arch be in height twice its width; that the breadth of the pier do not exceed that of the arch, nor be much less; that the small order be in height two thirds of the large columns, which height being divided into nine parts, eight of them must be for the height of the column, and the ninth for the height of the architrave cornice, two fifths of which should be for the architrave and three for the cornice. The breadth of the archivolt should be equal to the superior diameter of the small columns, and the keystone at its bottom must never exceed the same breadth."

Sect. XI.

ORDERS ABOVE ORDERS.

2642. Vitruvius, in the fifth chapter of his book "On the Forum and Basilica," in both which species of buildings it is well known that orders above orders were employed, thus instructs his readers: — "The upper columns are to be made one fourth less than those below" (*quarta parte minores quam inferiores sunt constituendæ*), "and that because the latter, being loaded with a weight, ought to be the stronger; because, also, we should follow the practice of nature, which in straight-growing trees, like the fir, cypress, and pine, makes the thickness at the root greater than it is at top, and preserves a gradual diminution throughout their height. Thus, following the example of nature, it is rightly ordered that bodies which are uppermost should be less than those below, both in respect of height and thickness." It is curious that the law thus given produces an exactly similar result to that

laid down by Scamozzi, p. 2. lib. v. cap. ii., whereon we shall have more presently to speak. Galliani, Chambers, and others have considered the above-quoted passage of Vitruvius in connection with another in chap. vii. of the same book, which treats of the portico and other parts of the theatre, wherein the author states, after giving several to this question unimportant details, " The columns on this pedestal" (that of the upper order) " are one fourth less *in height*" (quartâ parte minores *altitudine* sint) "than the lower columns." The reader will here observe the word *altitudine* is introduced, which does not appear in the passage first quoted ; and we beg him, moreover, to recollect that the last quotation relates entirely to the scene of the ancient theatre, in which liberties were then taken with strict architectural proportion as much as they are in these later days. Those who think that because Vitruvius interlarded his work with a few fables, he is therefore an author not worth consulting, as ephemeral critics have done in respect of that great master of the art, Palladio, may opine we have wasted time in this discussion ; but, adopting the old maxim of Horace, " Non ego paucis offendar maculis," we shall leave them to the exposure which, with the instructed architect, their own ignorance will ultimately inflict on them, and to the enjoyment of the felicity attendant on a slight knowledge of the subject a person is in the habit of handling.

2643. We will now place before the student our own reading and explanation of the passage of Vitruvius relative to the use of orders above orders, and attempt to show what we conceive to be its real meaning. In *fig.* 914. the diagram exhibits an Ionic placed above a Doric column : the entablature (which however does not belong to the consideration) being in both cases one fourth of the height of the column. Inasmuch as in our previous rules (following Vignola) it will be recollected that the module of the Doric order is subdivided into twelve, whilst that of the Ionic is subdivided into eighteen parts, we must, for the purpose of obtaining an uniformity of measures in both orders, reduce those of either to the other to obtain similar dimensions. Instead, therefore, of measuring the upper order by itself, which would not afford the comparison sought, we shall have to reduce its established measures to those of the lower one, or Doric, and this, as well as the measurement of the lower order itself, is taken in modules and decimal parts of its semidiameter. Thus, the lower order being 2 modules at its bottom diameter and 1·666 modules at its upper diameter, the mean, without descending to extreme mathematical nicety, may be taken at 1·833, which multiplied by the height, 18 modules = 32·994, the area of a section through the centre of the column. Now if the upper columns are to be the same thickness at the bottom as the lower ones are at the top, that is, 1·666 module of the lower order, their upper diameters will be 1·387 (that is, five sixths of the lower diameter), and the mean will be 1·526, which, multiplied by 16, the height, = 24·416 the area of a section down the centre of the column, and just one fourth less than that of the lower column. The investigation tends to show us that we should not lightly treat the laws laid down by Vitruvius and his followers at the revival of the arts, for we may be assured that in most cases they are not empirical, but founded on proper principles. We cannot, however, leave this point without giving another reason, which is conclusive against Chambers's construction of the passage ; it is, that supposing the upper column's lower diameter to be the same or nearly so as the lower column's upper diameter,

Fig. 914.

if the *fourth* part had relation to the height instead of the bulk, we should have had the absurdity in the illustration above given, of an Ionic column in the second order only six and three quarters diameters high, whilst the lower or Doric is nine diameters in height.

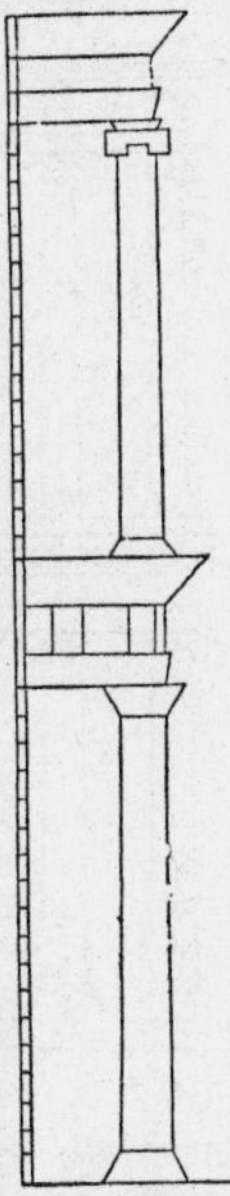

2644. Scamozzi, we doubt not, thought as we have expressed ourselves on this subject, and we here translate the words he uses in the eleventh chapter of his sixth book (second part). " Hence it is more satisfactory, and they succeed better and are more pleasing to the eye, when these columns (the upper ones) are made according to their proper diminution, so that the lower part of the upper column may be just the thickness of the upper part of the lower one, and so from one to the other, as may be seen in the Ionic order of the Theatre of Marcellus and other edifices; and this is the reason and natural cause that it is the same as though out of a long and single tree the shafts were cut out one after the other."

2645. The laws of solidity seem to require that where more than one order is used, the strongest is to occupy the lower situation ; thus the Doric is placed on the Tuscan, the Ionic on the Doric, the Corinthian on the Ionic, and the Composite on the Corinthian; though, with respect to the last, we find examples of importance wherein the reverse has been the case. Two tiers of columns should not be of the same order, neither should an intermediate order be omitted ; such, for instance, as placing the Ionic on the Tuscan column, or the Corinthian on the Doric ; for by this practice many irregularities are introduced, especially in the details of the members.

2646. Frontwise the axes of the upper and lower columns must be in the same vertical plane, but viewed in flank this is not absolutely necessary; they should not, however, deviate too much from it.   In the theatre of Marcellus the axes of the upper columns are nearly a foot within those of the Doric below them ; but circumstances required this, and there is no great objection to the practice if the solidity of the structure be not lessened by it. Chambers observes that the retraction should never be greater than at the theatre of Marcellus, where the front of the plinth in the second order is in a line with the top of the shaft in the first.   When the columns are detached, they should be placed centrally over each other, so that the axes of the upper and under ones may form one continued line, by which means solidity is gained as well as a satisfactory result to the eye.   As to the false bearings of the bases of the upper order on the profile, this is a matter neither really affecting stability nor the appearance of the design.

2647. In England there are not many examples of orders above orders, while on the Continent the practice has not been uncommon ; but it is always a matter of great difficulty so to arrange them as to avoid irregularities where triglyphs and modillions in the same design meet in the composition. We have used the figures of Chambers for our illustration here, because they are nearly coincident with the rules of Vitruvius and Scamozzi, and we shall now place them before the reader, observing that the irregularities alluded to are almost altogether avoided.

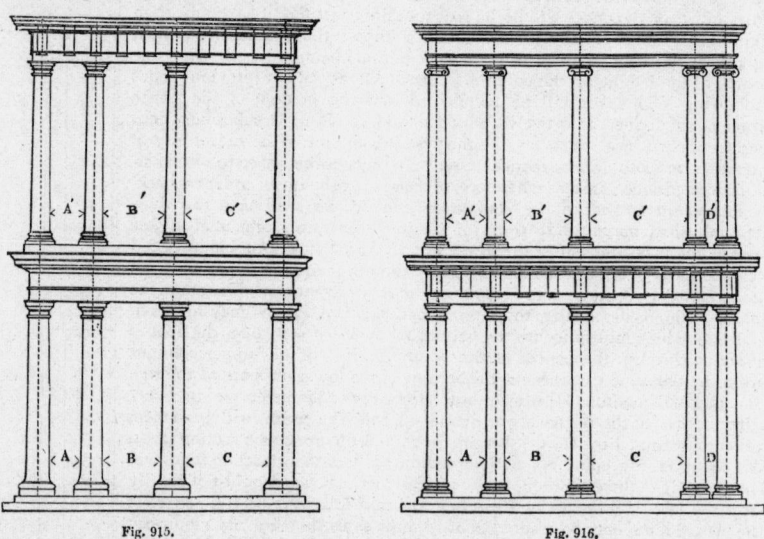

Fig. 915.   Fig. 916.

2648. *Fig.* 915. exhibits the Doric over the Tuscan order.   The intervals A, B, and C are respectively 2⅜, 4¼, and 6⅛ modules ; and A′, B′, and C′, 3, 5½, and 8 modules of their order.   The entablature of the lower order is 3⅓ modules, the column, including base and capital, being 14 modules high ; and the entablature of the upper order is 4 modules high, the column with its base and capital being 16 modules in height.

2649. The distribution of the Doric and Ionic orders is given in *fig.* 916., wherein the intervals A, B, and C are respectively 3, 5⅓, and 8 modules ; D, ·7 module ; and A′, B′, C′, and D′ respectively 4, 7, 10, and 1¼ modules.   The Doric order in this example is 20 modules high, whereof 4 are assigned to the entablature; the Ionic 22 modules high, whereof 4 belong to the entablature.

2650. In *fig.* 917. is represented the Corinthian above the Ionic order ; the intervals A, B, C, D are respectively 5, 6, 7, and 1 modules, and those of A′, B′, C′ D′ respectively 6·4, 7·6, 8·8, 1·6 modules ; the lower order is 22½ modules high, 18 being given to the column with its base and capital ; and the upper or Corinthian order is 24½ modules high, whereof 20 belong to the height of the column, including its base and capital.

2651. The last (*fig.* 918.) is of the Corinthian order above and Composite below.   In the lower order the intervals A, B, C, D are 4⅔, 6, 7, and 1 modules respectively, and A′, B′, C′, and D′, in the upper order, 6, 7·6, 8·8, and 1·6 modules respectively.   The whole height of the Corinthian order is 25 modules, whereof 5 are given to the entablature; the Composite order here is 24½ modules, of which 20 belong to the column, including the base and capital.

2652. We insert the observations of Chambers relative to the above four figures, which,

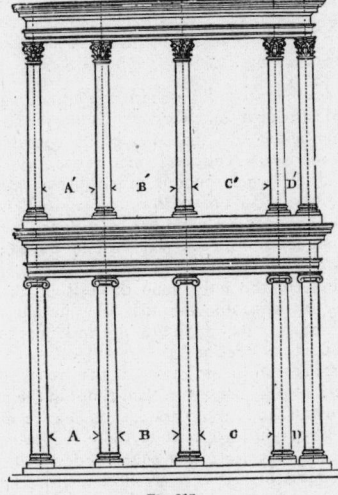

Fig. 917.

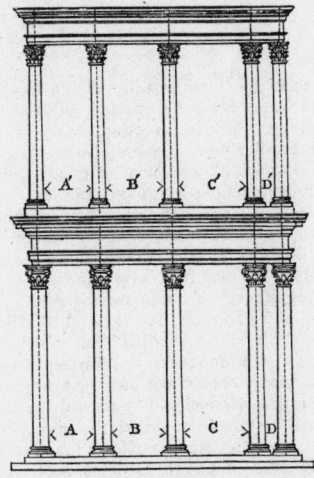

Fig. 918.

as we have adopted them, shall be in his own words. " Among the intercolumniations there are some in the second orders extremely wide, such as the Ionic interval over the Doric áræostyle ; the Composite and Corinthian intervals over the Ionic and Composite aræostyle, which, having a weak meagre appearance, and not being sufficiently solid, excepting in small buildings, are seldom to be suffered, and should seldom be introduced. The most eligible are the eustyle and diastyle for the first order, which produce nearly the diastyle and aræostyle in the second." Speaking of the use of pedestals in orders above orders, the author thus proceeds : — " Many architects, among which number are Palladio and Scamozzi, place the second order of columns on a pedestal. In compositions consisting of two stories of arcades this cannot be avoided, but in colonnades it may and ought ; for the addition of the pedestal renders the upper ordonnance too predominant, and the projection of the pedestal's base is both disagreeable to the eye and much too heavy a load on the inferior entablature. Palladio, in the Barbarano palace at Vicenza, has placed the columns of the second story on a plinth only, and this disposition is best ; the height of the plinth being regulated by the point of view, and made sufficient to expose to sight the whole base of the column. In this case the balustrade must be without either pedestals or half balusters to support its extremities, because these would contract and alter the form of the column ; its rail or cap must be fixed to the shafts of the columns, and its base made level with their bases ; the upper torus and fillet of the columns being continued in the interval, and serving as mouldings to the base of the balustrade. The rail and balusters must not be clumsy ; wherefore it is best to use double-bellied balusters, as Palladio has done in most of his buildings, and to give the rail a very little projection, that so it may not advance too far upon the surface of the column, and seem to cut into it. In large buildings the centre of the baluster may be in a line with the axis of the column ; but in small ones it must be within it, for the reason just mentioned. The height of the balustrade is regulated in a great measure by its use, and cannot well be lower than three feet, nor should it be higher than three and a half or four feet. Nevertheless, it must necessarily bear some proportion to the rest of the architecture, and have nearly the same relation to the lower order, or whatever it immediately stands upon, as when a balustrade is placed thereon chiefly for ornament. Wherefore, if the parts are large, the height of the balustrade must be augmented, and if they are small it must be diminished ; as is done in the Casino at Wilton, where it is only two feet four inches high, which was the largest dimension that could be given to it in so small a building. But that it might, notwithstanding its lowness, answer the intended purpose, the pavement of the portico is six inches lower than the bases of the columns, and on a level with the bottom of the plat-band that finishes the basement."

We must here leave this subject, recommending the student to an intimate acquaintance with the various examples that have been executed, and further advising him to test each of the examples that may fall under his notice by the principles first adverted to in this section, as the only true means of arriving at a satisfactory result.

Sect. XII.

ARCADES ABOVE ARCADES.

2653. As the disposition of one arcade upon another is, under certain regulations, subject to the same laws of voids and solids as the simple arcade of one story, which has formed the subject of a previous section, we shall no further enter into the rules of its combination than to offer a few general observations on the matter in question; and herein, even with the reproach of a want of originality, we shall draw largely on our much-quoted author, Chambers, whose language and figures we are about to use. So sound, indeed, is the doctrine of Chambers in this respect, and so well founded on what has been done by those whom we consider the greatest masters, that we should not be satisfied without transferring his dicta to these pages, and that without any alteration.

2654. "The best," says Chambers, "and, indeed, the only good disposition for two stories of arcades, is to raise the inferior order on a plinth, and the superior one on a pedestal, as Sangallo has done at the Pallazzo Farnese; making both the ordonnances of an equal height, as Palladio has done at the Basilica of Vicenza."

2655. "Scamozzi, in the thirteenth chapter of his sixth book, says that the arches in the second story should not only be lower, but should also be narrower, than those in the first; supporting his doctrine by several specious arguments, and by the practice, as he says, of the ancient architects in various buildings mentioned by him. In most of these, however, the superior arches are so far from being narrower, that they are either equal to or wider than the inferior ones. In fact, his doctrine in this particular is very erroneous, entirely contrary to reason, and productive of several bad consequences; for if the upper arches be narrower than the lower ones, the piers must of course be broader, which is opposite to all rules of solidity whatever, and exceedingly unsightly. The extraordinary breadth of the pier on each side of the columns in the superior order is likewise a great deformity; even when the arches are of equal widths it is much too considerable. Palladio has, in the *Carità* at Venice, and at the Palazzo Thiene in Vicenza, made his upper arches wider than the lower ones, and I have not hesitated to follow his example; as by that means the weight of the solid in the superior order is somewhat diminished, the fronts of the upper piers bear a good proportion to their respective columns, and likewise to the rest of the composition."

2656. "In a second story of arcades there is no avoiding pedestals. Palladio has, indeed, omitted them at the Carità, but his arches there are very ill proportioned. The extraordinary bulk and projection of these pedestals are, as before observed, a considerable defect; to remedy which in some measure they have been frequently employed without bases, as in the theatre of Marcellus, on the outside of the Palazzo Thiene, and that of the Chiericato in Vicenza. This, however, helps the matter but little; and it will be best to make them always with bases of a moderate projection, observing at the same time to reduce the projection of the bases of the columns to ten minutes only, that the die may be no larger than is absolutely necessary; and in this case particular care must be taken not to break the entablature over each column of the inferior order, because the false bearing of the pedestal in the second order will by so doing be rendered far more striking, and in reality more defective, having then no other support than the projecting mouldings of the inferior cornice. There is no occasion to raise the pedestals of the second order on a plinth, for as they come very forward on the cornice of the first order, and as the point of view must necessarily be distant, a very small part only of their bases will be hid from the eye."

2657. "The balustrade must be level with the pedestals supporting the columns; its rail or cornice and base must be of equal dimensions, and of the same profile with theirs. It should be contained in the arch and set as far back as possible, that the form of the arch may appear distinct and uninterrupted from top to bottom; for which reason, likewise, the cornice of the pedestals must not return nor profile round the piers, which are to be contained in straight perpendicular lines from the imposts to the bases of the pedestals. The back of the rail may either be made plain or sunk into a panel in form of an open surbase, for so it will be most convenient to lean upon, and it should be in a line with or somewhat recessed within the backs of the piers. The back part of the balustrade may be adorned with the same mouldings as the bases of the piers, provided they have not much projection; but if that should be considerable, it will be best to use only a plinth crowned with the two upper mouldings, that so the approach may remain the more free."

2658. In *fig.* 919. is a Doric above a Tuscan arcade, from the example given by Chambers, whereon, before giving the dimensions of the different parts, we shall merely observe of it that the voids or arcades themselves are in round numbers to the solids as 295 to 205, being vastly greater. We are inclined to think that the voids in this case are rather too great in volume, and that, had they been reduced to one half their height exactly, the

proportions would have been somewhat more pleasing. It is true that a trifling irregularity would have been introduced into the triglyphs of the upper order, or rather the metopæ between them; but that might have been easily provided against by a very trifling alteration in the height of the frieze itself. This fault of making the voids too large pervades Chambers's examples, and but that we might have been thought too presuming we should have slightly altered the proportions, little being requisite to bring them under the laws which we have thought to be founded on reason and analogy. We have indeed throughout this work refrained from giving other than approved examples, preferring to confine ourselves to observations on them when we have not considered them faultless.

Fig. 919.

2659. In the figure the clear width of the lower arcade is $7\frac{2}{3}$, and its height $14\frac{1}{2}$ modules. The width of each pier is 1 module. Of the upper arcade the width is $9\frac{1}{2}$, and the height 18·233 modules. The width of the piers is $1\frac{1}{4}$ module each. The height of the plinth of the lower order is $1\frac{1}{2}$ module, that of the column, including base and capital, $14\frac{1}{2}$ modules, the entablature $3\frac{1}{2}$. The height of the pedestal of the upper order is 3·733 modules, of the column with its base and capital 16, and of the entablature 3·733 modules. In the proportions between the voids and solids above taken the balustrade is not considered as a solid, because, in fact, it is nothing more than a railing for the protection of those using the upper story. As we have expressed our desire to give the examples of others rather than our own, we feel bound to recommend the student to set up the diagram in question, with the simple alteration of reducing the solids nearly to an equality with the voids, which may be done with sufficient accuracy by assigning to the lower arcade a module less in width than Chambers has done; and we venture to say that he will be surprised at the difference, as regards grace and elegance, which will result from the experiment. It is to be understood that no change is proposed in the other dimensions of the ordonnance, the width of piers, orders, entablatures, all remaining untouched.

2660. In *fig.* 920. we give another example from Chambers, which, in our opinion, requires a rectification to bring it into proper form. Herein the Ionic is used above the Doric arcade, and the voids to the solids are as 3·33 to 2·98, being much more than equal to them. In this, as in the former example, we should have preferred a greater equality between the solids and voids, though in that under consideration there is a nearer approximation to it.

2661. In the figure the clear width of the lower arch is $8\frac{1}{2}$, and its height $16\frac{1}{6}$ modules; the width of each pier is 1 module. Of the upper arcade the width is $10\frac{1}{2}$, and the height $20\frac{1}{2}$ modules. The width of the piers is $1\frac{1}{4}$ module each. The height of the plinth of the lower order is $1\frac{1}{2}$ module that of the column, including the base and capital, $16\frac{1}{6}$ modules, and of the entablature 4 modules. The height of the pedestal of the upper order 4 modules, of the column, including base and capital, 18 modules, and of the entablature 4, and of the balustrade above it $3\frac{1}{5}$.

2662. The dimensions of the Ionic and Corinthian arcades in *fig.* 921. are as follow: — Clear width of lower arch 9 modules, its height $18\frac{1}{6}$ modules. The width of each pier is 1 module. Of the upper arcade the width of an arch $15\frac{3}{5}$ modules, and its height 23 modules. The width of

Fig. 920.

Fig. 921.

the piers is 1¼ module each. The height of the plinth to the lower order is 1⅔ module;
of the column, including base and capital, 18 modules; the
entablature 4½ modules. The pedestal of the upper order
is 4½ modules high; column, including base and capital, 20
modules; entablature 4½ modules; and, lastly, the balustrade is 3⅜ modules in height.

2663. *Fig.* 922. is an arrangement adopted by Palladio
in his basilica at Vicenza, being the dimensions, or nearly,
of the arcades on the flanks. The intermediate ones are
much wider. In the basilica, however, the entablature
breaks round the columns of the orders. The width
between the axes of the columns of the lower order is 15
of their modules. The arch is 15 modules high and 7⅝
wide. The order wherefrom the arch springs is 10⅝ modules
high; from axis to axis of the small columns in the lower
arcade is 9 modules. The height of the plinth is 1½ module,
of the principal columns, including bases and plinths, 16¼
modules, and of their entablature 4 modules. In the upper
arcade the distance between the axes of the principal
columns is 18 of their modules. Their pedestals are 4
modules high, the columns, including bases and capitals, 18
modules, and entablature 4 modules high. The width of the
arch is 9⅔ modules, and its height 20⅝ modules. The height
of the small columns is 11·733 modules high, including
their entablature.

2664. The use of arcades above arcades seems from its
nature almost confined to public buildings, as among the
ancients to their theatres and amphitheatres. In the in-
terior quadrangles or courts of palaces they have been much employed on the Continent,
and in the magnificent design made by Inigo Jones for the palace at Whitehall are to
be found some very fine examples.

Fig. 922.

Sect. XIII.

BASEMENTS AND ATTICS.

2665. When the order used for decorating the façade of a building is placed in the middle
or second story, it is seated on a story called the *basement*. The proportion of its height to
the rest must in a great measure depend on the use to which its apartments are to be
appropriated. " In Italy," observes Chambers, " where their summer habitations are very
frequently on that floor, the basements are sometimes very high. At the palace of Porti,
in Vicenza, the height is equal to that of the order placed thereupon; and at the Thiene,
in the same city, its height exceeds two thirds of that of the order, although it be almost
of a sufficient elevation to contain two stories; but at the Villa Capra, and at the Loco
Arsieri, both near Vicenza, the basement is only half the height of the order; because in
both these the ground floor consists of nothing but offices." It may hence be gathered that
no absolute law can be laid down in reference to the height of a basement story. Yet we may
state, generally, that a basement should not be higher than the order it is to support, for it
would in that case detract from the principal part of the composition, and, in fact, would be
likely to interfere with it. Besides which, the principal staircase then requires so many steps
that space is wasted for their reception. " Neither," says Chambers, " should a basement
be lower than half the height of the order, if it is to contain apartments, and consequently
have windows and entrances into it ; for whenever that is the case the rooms will be low,
the windows and doors very ill formed, or not proportional to the rest of the composition,
as is observable at Holkham : but if the only use of the basement be to raise the ground
floor, it need not exceed three, four, or at the most five or six feet in height, and be in the
form of a continued pedestal."

2666. Basement stories are decorated generally with rustic work of such various kinds,
that we fear it would be here impossible to describe or represent their varieties. Many
are capriciously rock-worked on their surface, others are plain, that is, with a smooth surface. The height of each course, including the joints, should on no account be less than
one module of the order which the basement supports ; their length may be from once and
a half to thrice their height. As respects the joints, these may be square or chamfered
off. When square joints are used, they should not be wider than one eighth part of the

height of the rustic itself, nor narrower than one-tenth, their depth not exceeding their width. When the joints are chamfered, the chamfer should be at an angle of forty-five degrees, and the whole width of the joint from one third to one fourth of the height of the rustic.

2667. The courses are sometimes (often on the Continent) laid without showing vertical joints; but, as Chambers says, this "has in general a bad appearance, and strikes as if the building were composed of boards rather than of stone. Palladio's method seems far preferable, who, in imitation of the ancients, always marked both the vertical and the horizontal joints; and whenever the former of these are regularly and artfully disposed, the rustic work has a very beautiful appearance." We shall presently make a few remarks on the subject of rustics; but here, to continue and finish that more immediately under consideration, have to add, that when a high basement is used, it is not uncommon to crown it with a cornice, as may be seen in *fig.* 909.; but the more common practice is to use a platband only (as in *fig.* 911.), whose height should not be greater than that of a rustic exclusive of the joint. Of a similar height should be made the zoccolo or plinth; but this may, and ought, perhaps, to be somewhat higher. When arches occur in basements, the platband, which serves for the impost, should be as high as a course of rustics, exclusive of the joint; and if the basement be finished with a cornice, such basement should have a regularly moulded base at its foot; the former to be about one thirteenth of the whole height of the basement, and the base about one eighteenth, without the plinth.

2668. The Attic — which is used instead of a second order where limits are prescribed to the height of a building, examples whereof may be seen at Greenwich Hospital, and in the Valmarano palace, by the great Palladio, at Vicenza — should not exceed in height one-third of the order whereon they are placed, neither ought they to be less than one quarter. Bearing some resemblance to a pedestal, the base, die, and cornice whereof they are composed may be proportioned much in the same way as the respective divisions of their prototypes. They are sometimes continued without, and sometimes with, breaks over the column or pilaster of the order which they crown. If they are formed with pilasters, such ought to be of the same width as the upper diameter of the order under them, never more. In projection they should be one quarter of their width at most. They may be decorated with sunk moulded panels if necessary; but this is a practice rather to be avoided, as is most especially that of using capitals to them — a practice much in vogue in France under Louis XV.

2669. We now return to the subject of the rock-worked rustic, whereof, above, some notice was promised. The practice, though occasionally used by the Romans, seems to have had its chief origin in Florence, where, as we have in a former Book (329.) observed, each palace resembled rather a fortification than a private dwelling. Here it was used to excess; and if variety in the practice is the desire of the student, the buildings of that city will furnish him with an almost infinite number of examples. The introduction of it gives a boldness and an expression of solidity to the rustics of a basement which no other means afford. In the other parts of Italy it was sparingly applied, but with more taste. Vignola and Palladio seem to have treated it as an accident productive of great variety rather than as a means of decoration. The last-named architect has in the Palazzo Thiene carried it to the utmost extent whereof it is susceptible. Yet, with this extreme extent of application, the design falls from his hands full of grace and feeling. To imitate it would be a dangerous experiment. De Brosse failed at the Luxembourg, and produced an example of clumsiness which in the Palazzo Pitti does not strike the spectator.

2670. Rustics and rockwork on columns are rarely justifiable except for the purpose of some particular picturesque effect which demands their prominence in the scene, or street view, as in the gateway at Burlington House in Piccadilly, — a splendid monument of the great talent of Lord Burlington.

Sect. XIV.

PILASTERS.

2671. Pilasters, or square columns, were by the Romans termed *antæ*, by the Greeks *parastatæ*. This last word implies the placing one object standing against another, a sufficiently good definition of the word, inasmuch as in ninety-nine cases out of a hundred they are engaged in or backed against a wall, or, in other words, are portions of square columns projecting from a wall.

2672. It is usual to call a square column, when altogether disengaged from the wall, a *pillar* or *pier*; and we are inclined to think, notwithstanding the alleged type of trees, that the primitive supports of stone buildings were quite as likely to have been square

as round, and that the inconvenience attendant upon square angles may have led the earliest builders to round off the corners, and gradually to bring them to a circular plan. Isolated pillars are rarely found among the examples left us by the ancients; the little temple at Trevi furnishes, indeed, an example, but not of the best period of the art. The principal points to be attended to in their use are their projection, diminution, the mode of uniting the entablature over them with that of their columns, and their flutings and capitals.

2673. In respect of the projection of pilasters, Perrault says they should project one half, and not exceed that by more than a sixth, as in the frontispiece of Nero, unless circumstances require a different projection. The pilasters of the Pantheon project only a tenth part of their width ; and sometimes, as in the forum of Nerva, they are only a fourteenth part. But when pilasters are to receive the imposts of arches against their sides, they are made to project a fourth part of their diameter ; and this is a convenient proportion, because in the Corinthian order the capital is not so much disfigured. Hence, when pilasters are made to form re-entering angles, they should project more than half their diameter. Many and various opinions have been formed on the propriety of diminishing pilasters. Perrault, with whom we incline to agree, thinks that when one face only projects, pilasters should not be diminished. Those at the flanks of the portico of the Pantheon are without diminution. But when pilasters are on the same line as columns, we want to lay the entablature from one to the other without any projection, in which case the pilaster must be diminished in the same degree as the column itself, speaking of the front face, leaving the sides undiminished, as in the temple of Antoninus and Faustina. When the pilaster has two of its faces projecting from the wall, being on the angle, and one of those faces answers to a column, such face is diminished similarly to the column, as in the portico of Septimius, where the face not corresponding to the column receives no diminution. There are, however, ancient examples where no diminution is practised, as in the interior of the Pantheon, where it is so small as not to be very apparent, being much less than that of the column, as is also the case in the temple of Mars Ultor, and in the arch of Constantine. In these cases, the custom of the ancients is sometimes to place the architrave plumb over the column, which brings it within the line of the pilaster. This may be seen in the temple of Mars Ultor, in the interior of the Pantheon, and in the portico of Septimius. Sometimes this excess is divided into two parts, one whereof goes to the excess of projection of the architrave above the column, and the other half to the deficiency of extent above the pilaster, as in the forum of Nerva. The whole matter is a problem of difficult solution, which Chambers has avoided, but which, with reference to the examples we have cited, will not be attended with difficulty to the student in his practice.

2674. We have above seen that pilasters, when used with columns, are subject to the form and conditions of the latter. As to their flutings we are left more at liberty. In the portico of the Pantheon we find the pilasters fluted and the columns plain. This, however, may have been caused by the difficulty of fluting the latter, which are of granite, whilst the pilasters are of marble. On the other hand, we sometimes find the columns fluted and the pilasters plain, as in the temple of Mars Ultor, and the portico of Septimius Severus. Generally, too, it may be observed that when pilasters project less than half their diameter, their return faces are not fluted. In respect of the number of the flutes, if the examples of the ancients were any guide, there could have been no fixed rule ; for in the portico of the Pantheon, the arch of Septimius Severus, and that of Constantine, seven flutes only are cut on the pilasters, whilst the flutes of the pilasters in the interior of the Pantheon are nine in number. This, however, is to be observed, that the flutes must always be of an odd number, except in re-entering pilasters, wherein four are placed instead of three and a half, and five instead of four and a half, when the whole pilaster would have nine. This is done to prevent the ill effect which would be produced in the capital by the bad falling of the leaves over the flutes.

2675. We shall hereafter give from Chambers some representations of pilaster capitals, which, except as regards their width, resemble those of the order they accompany. The practice of the ancients in this respect was very varied. Among the Greeks the form of the pilaster capital was altogether different from that of the column, seeming to have no relationship to it whatever ; but on this point the student must consult the works on Grecian antiquities, an example whereof will be found in fig. 883.

2676. A pilaster may be supposed to represent a column and to take its place under many circumstances ; and, notwithstanding all that was said on the subject by the Abbé Laugier, many years ago, against the employment of pilasters altogether, we are decidedly of opinion that they are often useful and important accessories in a building. It would be difficult to enumerate every situation wherein it is expedient to use pilasters rather than insulated or engaged columns. In internal apartments, where the space is restricted, a column appears heavy and occupies too much room. The materials, morever, which can be obtained, often restrict the architect to the use of pilasters, over which the projections of the entablature are not so great ; indeed, as the author in the *Encyclopedie Methodique* ob-

serves, a pilaster may be considered as a column in bas-relief, and is thus, from the diminished quantity of labour and material in it, simpler and more economical in application. That in houses and palaces of the second class the decoration by pilasters is of great service may be amply shown by reference to the works of Bramante, San Gallo, Palladio, and the other great masters of Italy, no less than in this country to those of Jones, Wren, and Vanbrugh.

2677. In profiling the capitals of Tuscan and Doric pilasters there can of course arise no difficulty ; they follow the profiles of those over the columns themselves. In the capitals, however, of the other orders, some difficulties occur : these are thus noticed by Chambers. " In the antique Ionic capital, the extraordinary projection of the ovolo makes it necessary either to bend it inwards considerably towards the extremities, that it may pass behind the volutes, or, instead of keeping the volutes flat in front, as they commonly are in the antique, to twist them outwards till they give room for the passage of the ovolo. Le Clerc " (*Traité d'Architecture*) " thinks the latter of these expedients the best, and that the artifice may not be too striking, the projection of the ovolo may be considerably diminished, as in the annexed design " (*fig.* 923.), " which, as the moulding can be seen in front only, will occasion no disagreeable effect."

2678. " The same difficulty subsists with regard to the passage of the ovolo behind the angular Ionic volutes. Le Clerc therefore advises to open or spread the volutes sufficiently to leave room for the ovolo to pass behind them, as in the design " (*fig.* 924.) " annexed ; which may be easily done, if the projection of the ovolo is diminished. Inigo Jones has in the Banqueting House made the two sides of the volutes parallel to each other, according to Scamozzi's manner, and at the same time has continued the ovolo in a straight line under them, so that the volutes have an enormous projection ; which, added to the other faults of these capitals, renders the whole composition unusually defective and exceedingly ugly."

Fig. 923.   Fig. 924.

2679. " What has been said with regard to the passage of the ovolo behind the volutes in the Ionic order is likewise to be remembered in the Composite ; and in the Corinthian the lip or edge of the vase or basket may be bent a little inwards towards its extremities, by which means it will easily pass behind the volutes. The leaves in the Corinthian and Composite capitals must not project beyond the top of the shaft, as they do at San Carlo in the Corso at Rome, and at the Banqueting House, Whitehall; but the diameter of the capital must be exactly the same as that of the top of the shaft. And to make out the thickness of the small bottom leaves, their edges may be bent a trifle outwards, and the large angular leaves may be directed inwards in their approach towards them, as in the annexed design " (*fig.* 925.), " and as they are executed in the church of the Roman college at Rome. When the small leaves have a considerable thickness, though the diameter of the capital is exactly the same as that of the shaft, in each front of the Composite or Corinthian pilaster capital, there must be two small leaves with one entire and two half large ones. They must be either of olive, acanthus, parsley, or laurel, massed, divided, and wrought, in the same manner as those of the columns are, the only difference being that they will be somewhat broader."

Fig. 925.

2680. It is desirable to avoid the use of pilasters at inward angles penetrating each other, because of the irregularity such practice produces in the entablatures and capitals. One break is quite as much as should be ever tolerated, though in many of the churches in Rome they are multiplied with great profusion of mutilated capitals and entablatures; " than which," observes Chambers, " nothing can be more confused or disagreeable."

2681. Neither should columns be allowed to penetrate each other, as they do in the court of the Louvre, inasmuch as the same irregularity is induced by it as we have above noticed in the case of pilasters.

Sect. XV.

CARYATIDES AND PERSIANS.

2682. The origin of caryatides we have in the First Book (165, *et seq.*) so far as regards our own opinions, explained, and in that respect we shall not trouble the reader. Our object in this section is merely to offer some observations on the use of them in modern practice. The figures denominated Persians, Atlantes, and the like, are in the same category, and we shall not therefore stop to inquire into their respective merits; indeed, that has already been sufficiently done in the book above alluded to. The writer of the article in the *Encyclopedie Methodique* has, we think, thrown away a vast deal of elegant writing on the subject of caryatides; and using, as we have done, to some extent, that extraordinary work, we think it necessary to say that we cannot recommend anything belonging to that article to the notice of the reader, except what is contained in the latter part of it, and with that we do not altogether agree.

2683. The object, or apparent object, in the use of caryatides is for the purpose of support. There is no case in which this cannot be better accomplished by a solid support, such as a column, the use of the attic order, or some other equivalent means. But the variety in quest of which the eye is always in search, and the picturesque effect which may be induced by the employment of caryatides, leads often to their necessary employment. The plain truth is, that they are admissible only as objects necessary for an extreme degree of decoration, and otherwise employed are not to be tolerated. There can, as we imagine, be no doubt that the most successful application of these figures as supports was by Jean Gougeon in the Louvre; as was the most unfortunate in the use of them in a church in the New Road, which at the time of its erection was much lauded, but which we hope will never be imitated by any British architect.

2684. As to the use of what are called Persians or male figures, originally in Persian dresses, to designate, as Vitruvius tells us, the victory over their country by the Greeks, the observations above made equally apply, and in the present day their application will not bear a moment's suspense in consideration.

2685. We have been much amused with the gravity wherewith Sir William Chambers, not with his usual sound sense, treats the claims of the personages whose merits we are discussing: he says, "Male figures may be introduced with propriety in arsenals or galleries of armour, in guard-rooms and other military places, where they should represent the figures of captives, or else of martial virtues; such as strength, valour, wisdom, prudence, fortitude, and the like." He writes more like himself when he says, "There are few nobler thoughts in the remains of antiquity than Inigo Jones's court" (in the design for the great palace at Whitehall), "the effect of which, if properly executed, would have been surprising and great in the highest degree." (See *fig.* 207.)

2686. What is called a *terminus*, which is, in fact, nothing more than a portion of an inverted obelisk, we shall not observe upon further than to say that it is a form, as applied to architecture, held in abhorrence. For the purpose, when detached and isolated, of supporting busts in gardens, it may perhaps be occasionally tolerated: further we have nothing to say in its favour. Those who seek for additional instruction on what are called termini, may find some account of them, as the boundary posts of land among the Romans, in books relating to the antiquities of that people.

2687. We shall now proceed to submit some examples of caryatides for the use of those whose designs require their employment. *Fig.* 926. is from a model of Michael Angelo

Fig. 926   Fig. 927.   Fig. 928.   Fig. 929

Buonarotti, and is extracted from the *Treatise on Civil Architecture*, by Sir William Chambers, as are the succeeding examples.

2688. *Figs.* 927. and 928. are also designs by Michael Angelo, which, though not designed for a building, are well adapted for the purpose under certain conditions.

2689. *Fig.* 929. is the design of Andrea Biffi, a sculptor of Milan, in the cathedral of which city it is one of the figures surrounding the choir. The statue possesses mucn grace, and was admirably suited to the edifice wherein it was employed.

2690. *Fig.* 930. comes from Holland, having been executed by Artus Quellinus in the judgment-hall of the Stadthouse at Amsterdam.

Fig. 930.   Fig. 931.   Fig. 932.   Fig. 933.   Fig. 934.

2691. *Fig.* 931. is by Michael Angelo, and is at the Villa Ludovisi at Rome.

2692. *Fig.* 932. is from the design by the last-named master for the monument of Pope Julius, whereof we have had occasion already to make mention in the First Book of this work. (335.)

2693. *Fig.* 933. is a representation of one of the celebrated caryatides by Jean Gougeon in the Swiss guard-room of the old Louvre at Paris, and does not deserve less admiration than it has received. The scale on which this and the preceding figures are given does not admit of so good a representation as we could wish.

2694. *Fig.* 934. is from the arch of the goldsmiths at Rome, being thereon in basso rilievo, but considered by Chambers as well as ourselves a suitable hint for carrying out the purpose of this section.

SECT. XVI.

BALUSTRADES AND BALUSTERS.

2695. A baluster is a species of column used as an ornamental railing in front of windows, or in arcades, or on the summit of a building, whose professed object is the protection of its inhabitants from accidents: analogously, too, it consists of a capital, shaft and base.

2696. The baluster is not found in the works of the ancients, and we believe it owed its introduction in architecture to the restorers of the arts in Italy, in which country a vast variety of examples are to be found. They made their first appearance in the form of stunted columns, not unfrequently surmounted by a clumsily-shaped Ionic capital. The term is said to have had its rise (with what truth we cannot pronounce) from the Latin *balaustium*, or the Greek βαλαυστιον, the flower of the wild pomegranate, to which in form the architectural baluster is said by some to bear a resemblance. The writer in the *Encyclopedie Methodique* has taken the opportunity, in the article " Balustre," of launching his anathema against the use of it, but we by no means agree with him; and instead of calling it, as he does, " *une invention mesquine*," we incline to think that it was almost the only invention of the modern architects that deserves our admiration. It is true that the form has been abused in every possible shape; but we are not, in art more than in morals, to arrive at the conclusion that anything is bad because it has been abused and inisapplied. Such, then, being the case, we shall proceed in a serious vein to consider its proportions, founded on the best examples that have come to our hands. We must first premise with J. F. Blondel, that balusters and balustrades, which last are a series of the first, should in form and arrangement partake of the character of the edifice. They have even been in their species so subdivided as to be arranged under as many classifications as the orders themselves, a distinct sort having been assigned for employment with each order. We are not quite certain that such an arrangement is necessary, but are rather inclined to think it fanciful; though we are quite willing to allow that where the lighter orders are employed,

the balustrades to be used over them are susceptible of a more minute and lighter sub-division of their parts.

2697. The general rules to be observed in the use of the balustrade are, that its balusters be of an odd number, and that the distance between them should be equal to half their larger diameter, from which will result an equality between the open and solid spaces. Blondel disapproves of a half baluster on the flanks of a subdivision of a balustrade: in this we dissent from him, and would always recommend its adoption if possible. In respect of the detailed proportions of the balusters themselves, we are to recollect that the subdivisions are of the capital, the shaft or vase of the baluster, and its base. For proportioning these to one another, Chambers (and we think the proportions he uses not inelegant) divides the whole given height into thirteen equal parts, whereof the height of the baluster is eight, that of the base three, and of the cornice or rail two. If the baluster is required to be less, he divides the height into fourteen parts, giving eight to the baluster, four to the base, and two to the rail. He calls one of these parts a module for the measurement of the rest, and that measure we think convenient for adoption in this work. The module he divides into nine parts.

2698. Balusters intended for real use in a building, as those employed on steps or stairs, or before windows, or to enclose terraces, should not be less than three feet in height, nor more than three feet six inches; that is, sufficiently high to give security to the persons using them: but when merely used as ornamental appendages, as in crowning a building, they should bear some proportion to the parts of the building. Chambers says that their height never ought to exceed four fifths of the height of the entablature on which they are placed, nor should it ever be less than two thirds, without counting the zoccolo or plinth. the height of which must be sufficient to leave the whole balustrade exposed to view from the best point of sight for viewing the building. We can scarcely admit these rules to pass without noting the examples in Palladio's works, which give a much greater latitude for variety. When balusters fill in between the pedestals, as in the façade of the Palace Chiericato at Vicenza, the balustrade's height is of course regulated by that of the pedestal itself; but in the court of the Porti palace the crowning balustrade is not higher than the cornice of the entablature on which it stands. The same proportion is observed in the atrium of the Carità at Venice. In the Valmarana palace the height of the balustrade is equal to that of the entablature of the small order. It is true that in a few instances this master made the height of the balustrade equal to that of the whole entablature, and Inigo Jones has in some instances followed his example; but this was not the general practice either of the one or the other.

2699. We have already said that the baluster generally varies in form, so as to be appropriate to the order over which it is used. It is moreover to be observed that the baluster is susceptible of a pleasing variety of its form by making it square instead of circular on the plan, whereof examples are given in *figs.* 938, 939, and 940.; but when the situation requires an expression of solidity, almost all the circular examples we submit to the reader may be changed from a circular to a square form on the plan, and thus as required we may obtain the character suitable to their respective situations. These changes, from one to another form in details of this description, are in their adoption much more the index to the capacity and genius of the architect than the restless and capricious longing after variety recently exhibited in some of the latest works produced in the city of London, works which reflect no credit on the age in which we live. In *fig.* 935. is given a baluster

Fig. 935.　　　　　　Fig. 936.　　　　　　Fig. 937.

suitable to the Tuscan order; and using the module of nine parts above mentioned, the following is a table of its dimensions:—

Members.		Heights in Parts of a Module.	Projections in Parts of a Module from Centre of Baluster.
Rail, 2 modules.	Fillet - - - -	3	27½
	Corona - - - -	8⅔	24⅓
	Quarter round - - -	4⅔	
	Fillet - - - -	1⅔	
Baluster, 8 modules.	Abacus - - - -	5⅔	11½
	Cyma reversa - - -	4	
	Neck - - - -	5	5¼
	Astragal } Fillet } - - - -	3⅓	
	Centre of belly - - -	27	13
	From same to astragal - -	9	
	Astragal } Fillet } - - - -	2⅓	10½ fillet
	Inverted cyma - - -	6⅓	
	Plinth - - - -	7⅓	13
Pedestal, 3 modules.	Inverted cavetto - - -	5	
	Fillet - - - -	2	
	Astragal - - - -	5	
	Plinth - - - -	15	24

2700. In *fig.* 936. is given the form of a baluster suited to the Doric and Ionic orders, of which also the table of dimensions is subjoined: —

Members.		Heights in Parts of a Module.	Projections in Parts of a Module from Centre of Baluster.
Rail, 2 modules.	Fillet - - - -	2	27
	Cyma reversa - - -	3⅔	
	Corona - - - -	7	22
	Quarter round - - -	4	
	Fillet - - - -	1⅓	
Baluster, 8 modules.	Abacus - - - -	5⅔	11
	Echinus - - - -	3⅓	
	Fillet - - - -	1	
	Neck - - - -	5	5
	Astragal } Fillet } - - - -	3	
	Centre of belly - - -	27	12½
	From same to astragal - -	9	
	Astragal - - - -	2	
	Fillet - - - -	1	
	Inverted cavetto - - -	6	10 (upper part)
	Fillet - - - -	2⅔	
	Plinth - - - -	7⅓	12½
Pedestal, 3 modules.	Fillet - - - -	1⅓	
	Inverted ogee - - -	5	
	Fillet - - - -	1⅔	
	Astragal - - - -	4⅓	
	Plinth - - - -	15	23½

2701. A suitable baluster for the Corinthian or Composite order is exhibited in *fig.* 937., whereof the measures are as follow: —

Members.					Heights in Parts of a Module.	Projections in Parts of a Module from Centre of Baluster.
Rail, 2 modules.	Fillet -	-	-	-	$1\frac{2}{3}$	$26\frac{1}{2}$
	Echinus -	-	-	-	$2\frac{2}{3}$	
	Fillet -	-	-	-	1	
	Corona -	-	-	-	$6\frac{1}{3}$	$21\frac{1}{2}$
	Cyma reversa -	-	-	-	$3\frac{2}{3}$	
	Astragal ⎫ -	-	-	-	$2\frac{2}{3}$	
	Fillet ⎭					
Baluster, 8 modules.	Abacus -	-	·	-	5	$10\frac{1}{2}$
	Echinus -	-	-	-	3	
	Fillet ⎫					
	Cavetto ⎭ -	-	-	-	$2\frac{1}{3}$	
	Neck -	-	-	-	5	$4\frac{3}{4}$
	Astragal ⎫ -	-	-	-	$2\frac{2}{3}$	
	Fillet ⎭					
	Centre of belly -	-	-	-	27	12
	From same to astragal -	-	-	9	
	Astragal ⎫ -	-	-	-	$2\frac{2}{3}$	
	Fillet ⎭					
	Scotia -	-	-	-	$4\frac{2}{3}$	$4\frac{3}{4}$ (at top)
	Fillet -	-	-	-	1	
	Astragal -	-	-	-	$3\frac{2}{3}$	
	Plinth -	-	-	-	6	12
Pedestal, 3 modules.	Fillet ⎫ -	-	-	-	$2\frac{2}{3}$	
	Astragal ⎭					
	Inverted cyma recta -	-	-	$4\frac{1}{3}$	
	Fillet -	-	-	-	1	
	Astragal -	-	-	-	4	
	Plinth -	-	-	-	15	23

2702. The Tuscan baluster (*fig.* 938.) is suitable for terraces and basements: its rail

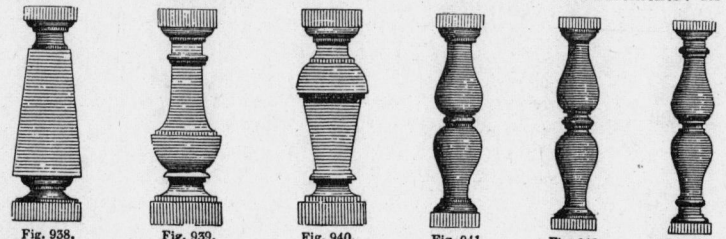

Fig. 938.   Fig. 939.   Fig. 940.   Fig. 941.   Fig. 942.   Fig. 943.

and pedestal may be the same height as in the *fig.* 935. Its principal measures being as follow : —

Members				Heights in Parts of a Module.	Projections in Parts of a Module from Centre of Baluster.
Baluster 5 modules.	Abacus -	-	-	3	6
	Cyma reversa -	-	-	2	
	Neck ⎫				
	Fillet ⎭ -	-	-	4	{ 3
	Rustic belly { at top ⎫ -	-	-		$4\frac{1}{2}$
	{		27	
	{ at bottom ⎭ -	-	-		$7\frac{1}{2}$
	Bottom of belly ⎫				
	Fillet ⎭ -	-	-	$2\frac{1}{2}$	
	Inverted cavetto and fillet -	-	3	3
	Plinth -	-	-	$3\frac{1}{2}$	$7\frac{1}{2}$

Other forms of Tuscan balusters are given in *figs.* 939. and 940., but it is not necessary to give the detail of the parts, as the proportions are sufficiently preserved in the figures.

2703. The double-bellied baluster is used in situations where greater lightness is required from the smallness of the parts and the delicacy of the profiles. The proportions for the bases and rails need not vary from those already given. Perhaps they need not be quite so large.

2704. *Fig.* 941. is an example of a double-bellied baluster, suitable to the Doric order. Its parts are as follow : —

Members.		Heights in Parts of a Module.	Projections in Parts of a Module from Centre of Baluster.
Baluster, 8 modules.	Abacus - - - -	4½	8
	Echinus } Fillet } - - -	4½	
	Upper part - - - -	24¾	{ 4 neck { 8 belly
	Middle part - - - -	4½	6 centre
	Lower part - - - -	24¾	{ 8 belly { 4 neck
	Fillet } Inverted echinus } - - -	4½	
	Plinth - - - -	4½	8

2705. In *fig.* 942. we give an example of the double-bellied baluster for the Ionic order, and its measures are subjoined : —

Members.		Heights in Parts of a Module.	Projections in Parts of a Module from Centre of Baluster.
Baluster, 10 modules.	Abacus - - - -	4½	9
	Fillet and cyma reversa - -	4½	
	Upper part - - - -	30½	{ 4½ neck { 9 belly
	Middle part - - - -	9	7½ centre
	Lower part - - - -	30½	{ 9 belly { 4½ neck
	Inverted cyma and fillet - -	4½	
	Plinth - - - -	4½	9

2706. The last example we shall give of the double-bellied baluster (*fig.* 943.) is suitable to the Corinthian order. The measures are as follow : —

Members.		Heights in Parts of a Module.	Projections in Parts of a Module from Centre of Baluster.
Baluster, 12 modules.	Abacus - - - -	5	11
	Echinus and fillet - - -	4	
	Neck - - - -	5½	5½
	Astragal and fillet - - -	3½	
	Upper part - - - -	29	{ 5½ at top { 11 at belly
	Middle - - - -	6	
	Lower part - - - -	29	{ 11 at belly { 5½ at bottom
	Fillet and astragal - - -	3½	
	Neck - - - -	5½	5½
	Fillet and inverted echinus - -	4	
	Plinth - - - -	5	11

2707. We do not deem it necessary to give any examples of the scroll and Guiloche balustrades, which were so much in vogue during the reigns of Louis XIV. and Louis XV., though the present taste seems almost to require it. As that taste has been mainly generated by house decorators, as they are called, and upholsterers, these gentry will soon find out another means of amusing the public, by driving them out of fashion and finding all that is beautiful in some renovated and equal absurdities.

2708. We have already observed that the intervals between balusters should not be more than half the diameter of the baluster at its thickest part; to this we may here add, that they should not be less than one third of that diameter. The pedestals for supporting the rail ought neither to be too frequent nor too far apart; for in the first case they impart a heavy appearance to the work, and in the last the work will seem weak. Seven or nine balusters are good numbers for a group, besides the two half ones engaged in the pedestals. The disposition, however, and number of the pedestals depend on the places below of the piers, columns, or pilasters, for over these a pedestal must stand; and when, therefore, it happens that the intervals are greater than are required for the reception of nine balusters, the distance may contain two or three groups each, flanked with half balusters, and the width of the dies separating the groups may be from two thirds to three quarters the width of the principal pedestals. The rail and base should not be broken by projections, but run in unbroken lines between the pedestals.

2709. When the principal pedestals stand over columns or pilasters, their dies should not be made wider than the top of the shafts, and on no account narrower; indeed, it is better to flank them on each side when the ranges are long with half dies, and give a small projection to the central pedestal, and to let the base and rail follow the projection in their profiles. This practice will give real as well as apparent solidity to the balustrade.

2710. *Fig.* 944. shows the application of a balustrade to a portion of a staircase, and herein the same proportions are observed as on level ranges. Some masters have made the mouldings of the different members of the baluster, follow the *rake* or inclination of the steps; but the practice is vicious: they should preserve their horizontality, as exhibited in the figure, in which, at A and B, is also shown the method in which the horizontal are joined to the inclined mouldings of the base and rail. In the balustrades of stairs the spaces between the balusters are usually made narrower than they are on level beds; and Le Clerc recommends that the height of the plinth should be equal to that of the steps; but this is not absolutely required, though it must on no account be less.

2711. The bulbs or bellies of balusters and their mouldings may be carved and otherwise enriched: indeed, in highly decorated interiors, this seems requisite.

Fig. 944.

2712. The following observations as to the height of statues placed upon balustrades are from Sir William Chambers: — "When statues are placed upon a balustrade their height should not exceed one quarter of the column and entablature on which the balustrade stands. Their attitudes must be upright, or, if anything, bending a little forwards, but never inclined to either side. Their legs must be close to each other, and the draperies close to their bodies, for whenever they stand straddling with bodies tortured into a variety of bends, and draperies waving in the wind, as those placed on the colonnades of St. Peter's, they have a most disagreeable effect, especially at a distance, from whence they appear like lumps of unformed materials, ready to drop upon the heads of passengers. The three figures placed on the pediment of Lord Spencer's house, in the Green Park, which were executed by the late ingenious Mr. Spang, are well composed for the purpose."

2713. "The heights of vases placed upon balustrades should not exceed two thirds of the height given to statues," says the same author. We are not altogether averse to the application of either statues or vases in the predicated situations, but we think the greatest discretion is required in their employment. When it is necessary to attract the eye from an indispensably obtrusive roof, they are of great value in the composition; but we shall not further enter on this point of controversy, for such it is, inasmuch as many object to their use altogether, and have considerable reason on their side. We must, however, briefly state the ground of objection, and Chambers's answer as respects statues. There are, he says, some "who totally reject the practice of placing statues on the outsides of buildings, founding their doctrine, probably, upon a remark which I have somewhere met with in a French author, importing that neither men, nor even angels or demi-gods, could stand in all weathers upon the tops of houses or churches."

2714. "The observation is wise, no doubt," (we doubt the wisdom of it,) "yet, as a piece of marble or stone is not likely to be mistaken for a live demi-god, and as statues, when properly introduced, are by far the most graceful terminations of a composition, one of the most abundant sources of varied entertainment, and amongst the richest, most

durable, and elegant ornaments of a structure, it may be hoped they will still continue to be tolerated." We fear that if the only reasons for their toleration were those assigned by the author, their doom would soon be sealed.

Sect. XVII.

PEDIMENTS.

2715. A pediment, whose etymology is not quite clear, consists of a portion of the horizontal cornice of the building to which it is applied, meeting two entire continued raking cornices, and enclosing by the three boundaries a space which is usually plain, called the *tympanum*. It is not, however, necessary that the upper cornice should be rectilinear, inasmuch as the cornice is sometimes formed by the segment of a circle. The arrangement in question was the Roman *fastigium*, and is the French *fronton*. The Greeks called pediments αετοι, or eagles; why, this is not the place to inquire. The origin of the pediment, according to authors, seems to have arisen from the inclined sides of the primitive hut. This is a subject, however, which in the First Book (subsec. 5.) has been already considered, and we shall therefore in this section confine ourselves to its employment in the architecture of the day.

2716. Of the varied forms which, by masters even of acknowledged talent, have been given to the pediment, whether polygonal, with curves of contrary flexure, with mixed forms, broken in the horizontal part of the cornice or in the raking parts of it, or reversed in its office with two springing inclined sides from the centre, we propose to say no more than that they are such abuses of all rules of propriety, that we shall not further notice them than by observing that in regular architecture no practice is to be tolerated where the pediment is composed otherwise than of two raking unbroken and one horizontal unbroken cornice, or of the latter and one continued flexure of curved line. To these only, therefore, we now apply ourselves.

2717. Generally, except for windows and doors, the pediment ought not to be used, but as a termination of the whole composition; and though examples are to be found without number in which an opposite practice has obtained, the reader, on reflection, will be convinced of the impropriety of it, if there be the smallest foundation for its origin in the termination of the slant sides of the hut.

2718. The use of the pediment in the interior of a building is, perhaps, very questionable, though the greatest masters have adopted it. We think it altogether unnecessary: if the pyramidal form is desirable for any particular combination of lines, it may be obtained by a vast number of other means than that of the introduction of the pediment. Hence we are of opinion that the attempted apology for them in Sir William Chambers's work, is altogether weak and unworthy of him, and only to be explained by that master's own practice.

2719. Vitruvius ordains that neither the modillions nor dentils which are used in the horizontal cornice should be used in the sloping cornices of a pediment, inasmuch as they represent parts in a roof which could not appear in that position: and the remains generally of antiquity seem to bear him out in the assertion; but the Roman remains seem to bear a different testimony to the validity of the law, and to our own eyes the transgression affords pleasure, and we should recommend the student not to feel himself at all bound by it; for, as Chambers most truly observes, "The disparity of figure and enrichment between the horizontal and inclined cornices are such defects as cannot be compensated by any degree of propriety whatever, and therefore to me it appears best, in imitation of the greatest Roman and modern architects, always to make the two cornices of the same profile, thus committing a trifling impropriety to avoid a very considerable deformity."

2720. Different sized pediments in the same façade are to be avoided; but as respects their forms in ranges of windows and niches a pleasing variety is often obtained by making them alternately curved and rectilinear, as in the temple at Nismes and in the niches of the Pantheon at Rome.

2721. In the horizontal part of a cornice under a pediment the two upper mouldings are always omitted, and the intersection of the inclined with the horizontal lines, supposing the inclined members of the cornice to be of the same height as those which are horizontal, will not fall into the profile (*fig.* 945.) whereof AB and BC are the leading lines. To obviate this inconvenience, some architects have made a break in the cymatium and fillet, as shown

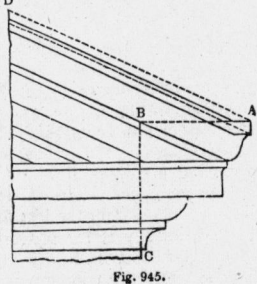

Fig. 945.

in the figure. But this is a bad practice, and to it we prefer either making the cyma and fillet higher, as the dotted line AD indicates, or altogether lowering the height of the cyma on the horizontal line. If the inclined cornice is joined on each side by horizontal ones, the best expedient is to give only such small projection to the cyma as that it may meet the inclined sides.

2722. The heights of pediments should be regulated by their lengths, independent of the consideration of climate. (See Book II. Chap. III. Sect. IV. 2027.) Thus, when the base of the pediment is short, the height of the pediment may be greater; and when long, it should be diminished; for in the former case the inclined cornice leaves but scanty space for the tympanum, and in the latter case the tympanum will appear overcharged. From one fifth to one quarter of the length appears to have been agreed on as the limits; but we subjoin, from a work by Stanislas L'Eveillé (*Considerations sur les Frontons*, 4to. Paris, 1824), the method which we consider the best for determining the height of a pediment, observing, by the way, that a strict adherence to the ordinary rules for finding the height may produce the absurdity of a pediment higher than the columns by which it is borne, a condition which would not at all accord with the view we have taken of the orders in Sect. II.

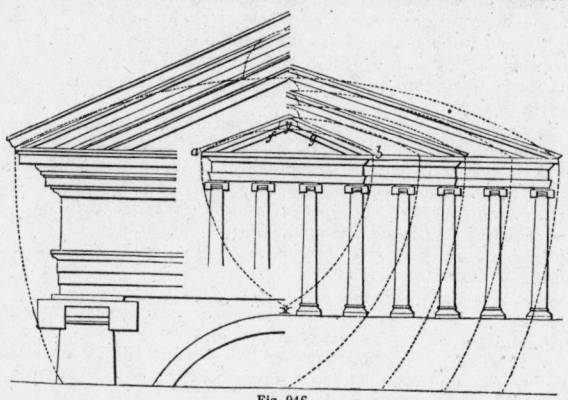

Fig. 946.

Chap. I. of this Book. In fig. 946. we have a synoptical view of pediments of various extents, and as the letters applied to the central pediment will apply to all the rest, we shall restrict our description to that. Suppose the points a and b to be the extremities of the fillet of the corona. Then, with a radius equal to ab, from the points a and b, describe the arcs ax, bx, and from their intersection x with the same radius let the arc ayb be described. From y, as a centre, with a radius equal to the height of the horizontal part of the cornice, describe the portion of the circle fg, and from a and b draw thereto tangents intersecting in y. Then yb and ya will be the proper inclination of the fillet of the corona to which the other members of the inclined parts will necessarily be parallel.

2723. We conclude this section by the words of Chambers. "The face of the tympan is always placed on a line perpendicular with the face of the frieze; and when large, may be adorned with sculpture, representing the arms or cypher of the owner, trophies of various kinds, suited to the nature of the structure, or bas-reliefs, representing either allegorical or historical subjects; but when small it is much better left plain."

Sect. XVIII.

CORNICES.

2724. In many cases the façades of buildings are erected without any of the orders appearing in the design, other, perhaps, than those which are applied as the dressings of windows, niches, or doors. The palaces of Florence and Rome abound with such examples, in most of which the edifice is crowned with a cornice, which adds dignity to the building, producing a play of light and shadow about it of the utmost importance as regards its picturesque effect. The moderns have generally failed in this fine feature of a building, and it is only within the last few years, in this country, that a return to the practice of the old masters, a practice properly appreciated by Jones, Wren, Vanbrugh, and Burlington, has manifested itself. If a building be entirely denuded of pilasters and columns, and there are very few common instances that justify their introduction, it seems rational to

deduce the proportion of the height and profile of its cornice from the proportions that would be given to it if an order intervened.

2725. If we consider the height of the crowning cornice of a building in this way, and as the portion of an entablature whose height is, as in the case of an order, one fifth of that of the building, we should immediately obtain a good proportion by dividing the whole height into 25 parts and giving two of them to the height of the cornice. For the

entablature being one fifth of the whole height, and its general division being into 10 parts, four whereof are given to the cornice, we have for its height the $\frac{4}{10}$ of $\frac{1}{5} = \frac{4}{50} = \frac{2}{25}$, or the twelfth and a half part of the total height of the building $= 0\cdot08$. Now there are circumstances, such as when the piers are large, and in other cases when the parts are not very full in their profiles, which may justify a departure from the strict application of this rule; but it will be seen that in the following ten well-known examples the practice has not much differed from the theory, nearly the greatest deviation being in the celebrated cornice of the Farnese palace, which is here placed (*fig.* 947.) as an extraordinary work of art in connection with the building it crowns. The examples alluded to are as follow, and we shall begin with those of earlier date,

Fig. 947.

the diminution in height being almost a chronological table of their erection, with the exception of those by Palladio: —

In the Spannocchi palace, at Siena, the cornice is $\frac{81}{1000}$ of the whole height of building, or $\frac{3}{37} = \cdot081$.

In the Picolomini palace, at Siena, the cornice is $\frac{74}{1000}$ of the whole height of building, or $\frac{2}{27} = \cdot074$.

In the Pojana palace, built by Palladio, at Pojana, in the Vicentine territory, the cornice is $\frac{71}{1000}$ of the whole height of building, or $\frac{1}{14} = 071$.

In the Strozzi palace, at Florence, the cornice is $\frac{69}{1000}$ of the whole height of building, or $\frac{2}{29} = \cdot069$.

In the Pandolfini palace, at Florence, by Raffaelle, the cornice is $\frac{69}{1000}$ of the whole height of building, or $\frac{2}{29} = \cdot069$.

In the Villa Montecchio, by Palladio, the cornice is $\frac{69}{1000}$ of the whole height of building, or $\frac{2}{29} = \cdot069$.

In the Villa Caldogno, by Palladio, the cornice is $\frac{69}{1000}$ of the whole height of building, or $\frac{2}{29} = \cdot069$.

In another villa by Palladio, for the family of Caldogno, the cornice is $\frac{66}{1000}$ of the whole height of building, or $\frac{1}{15} = \cdot066$.

In the Farnese palace, at Rome, the cornice is $\frac{59}{1000}$ of the whole height of building, or $\frac{1}{17} = \cdot059$.

In the Gondi palace, at Florence, the cornice is $\frac{57}{1000}$ of the whole height of building, or $\frac{2}{35} = \cdot057$.

From these examples it appears that the mean height of the cornices under consideration is something more than one fifteenth of the height of the building, and experience shows that, except under particular circumstances, much more than that is too great, and much less too little, to satisfy an educated eye. The grace beyond the reach of art is, if we may use an Hibernicism, in the power of few, but the bounds have been passed with success, as is testified in the Farnese palace. It may be objected to the system that we have generally adopted in this work, that we are too much reducing the art to rules. But this is a practice of which the painter is not ashamed in the proportions of the human figure, and we must remind our reader and the student that all rules are more for the purpose of restraining excess than bounding the flights of genius.

2726. *Fig.* 948. is an entablature by Vignola, which possesses great beauty, and has been often imitated in various ways for crowning a building; this must be con-

Fig. 948.

sidered more in relation to a building than a mere cornice, and requires rustic quoins, if possible, at the angles when used. Chambers, speaking of this example, says, that "when it is used to finish a plain building, the whole height is found by dividing the height of the whole front into eleven parts, one of which must be given to the entablature, and the remaining ten to the rest of the front." We suspect that the smallness which is assigned by this author to its height has been induced by some error, and that a better rule would be induced by assigning to the cornice its proper height, according to the laws above hinted at, and proportioning the rest of the entablature from the cornice thus obtained.

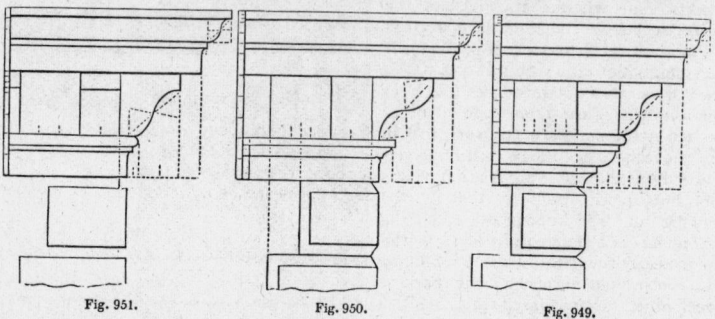

Fig. 951.   Fig. 950.   Fig. 949.

2727. In *figs.* 949, 950, and 951. are given three examples of block cornices (the second being by Palladio), whose proportions the figures sufficiently show without here giving a detail of their parts. The height of either should not be less than one fifteenth of the height of the building.

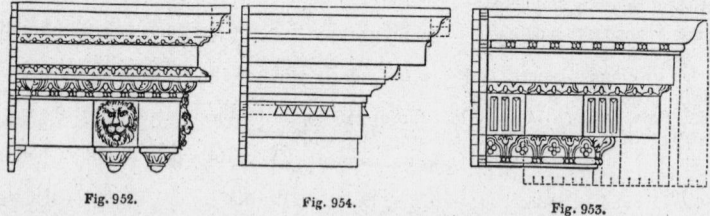

Fig. 952.   Fig. 954.   Fig. 953.

2728. *Figs.* 952. and 953. are block cornices, which we have adopted from Chambers, the first being from a palace at Milan, and the other, by Raffaelle, in a house in the Lungara at Rome. The height of these, says the author, and we agree with him, need not exceed one sixteenth part of the whole front, nor should either be less than one eighteenth. *Fig.* 954. is what is called an architrave cornice, which was frequently employed by the old masters. It seems well adapted to the entablatures of columns bearing arches, being rather in the nature of an impost; but it is useful, changing it to suit the order in cases where the height does not admit of the whole of the entablature being used over the order.

Sect. XIX.

PROFILES OF DOORS.

2729. One of our objects in this work has been to impress throughout on the minds of our readers that architecture does not depend on arbitrary laws; and though we may not have proved satisfactorily to the student that the precise laws have been exactly stated, we trust we have exhibited sufficient to show and convince him that there was a method and limit in the works of the ancients which in the best times prevented the artists from falling on either side into excess.

2730. In *fig.* 955. we give a door with its architrave, frieze, and cornice, without relation to mouldings, but merely considered in the masses. Its proportions correspond with those most usually adopted; that is, its height is twice its width, the entablature is one fourth of the height of the opening, and the architraves on each side, together, two sixths of the width. The opening, therefore, measuring it in terms of the width of the architrave, will be 6 parts wide and 12 high, and its area consequently 72 parts. Now

it will be found that the solid parts of this are exactly on their face two thirds of this area; for up to the top of the opening each architrave being equal to 12, the sum will be 24; and the entablature being 8 wide and 3 (one fourth of twelve) high, $8 \times 3 = 24$; which added to 24 for the architraves gives 48 for the solids, and $\frac{48}{72} = \frac{2}{3}$, as above stated. The same analogy does not seem to hold in respect of doors and windows, of making the voids equal to the supports and weights, as in intercolumniations; nor indeed ought we to expect to find it, for the conditions are totally different, inasmuch as no door can exist except in a wall, whereas the office of columns is connected with the weight above only. We trust, therefore, we have shown enough to keep the reader's mind alive to some such law as above developed, without insisting very strongly on a minute attention to it in detail.

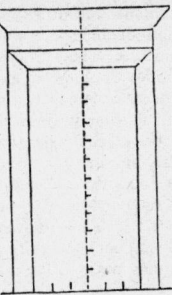

Fig. 955.

2731. We shall now, before submitting any examples of doorways to the reader, touch upon some important points that must be attended to; the first of which is, that all gates and doors, independent of all other considerations, must be of sufficient size for convenient passage through them. Hence internal doors must never be reduced under 2 feet 9 or 10 inches, and their height must not be under 6 feet 10 inches or 7 feet, so as to admit the tallest person to pass with his hat. These are minimum dimensions for ordinary houses in the principal floors; but for houses of a superior class, which are provided with what may be called state apartments, widths of 4, 5, and 6 feet, folding doors and the like, will not be too great for the openings, and the heights will of course be in proportion. The entrance doors of private houses ought not to be under 3 feet 6 inches, nor ordinarily more than 6 feet in width; but in public buildings, where crowds of people assemble, the minimum width should be 6 feet, and thence upwards to 10 or 12 feet. No gate should be less than 9 feet wide; and when loaded waggons or carts are to pass through it, 11 or 12 feet will not be too much. As a general observation we may mention that all doors should open inwards, for otherwise the person entering pulls the door in his face, which is an inconvenient mode of entering a room. Also when the width of a door is greater than 3 feet 8 inches it should be formed in two flaps, by which three advantages accrue: first, that the door will not occupy so much space for opening; second, that each door will be lighter; and, third, that the flaps will more nearly fold into the thickness of the wall. Chambers properly says, "That in settling the dimensions of apertures of doors regard must be had to the architecture with which the door is surrounded. If it be placed in the intercolumniation of an order, the height of the aperture should never exceed three quarters of the space between the pavement and the architrave of the order; otherwise there cannot be room for the ornaments of the door. Nor should it ever be much less than two thirds of that space, for then there will be room sufficient to introduce both an entablature and a pediment without crowding; whereas if it be less it will appear trifling, and the intercolumniation will not be sufficiently filled. The apertures of doors placed in arches are regulated by the imposts, the top of the cornice being generally made level with the top of the impost; and when doors are placed in the same line with windows, the top of the aperture should be level with the tops of the apertures of the windows; or if that be not practicable without making the door much larger than is necessary, the aperture may be lower than those of the windows, and the tops of all the cornices made on the same level."

2732. To say that the principal door of a building should if possible be in the centre of the front would seem almost unnecessary; but it is not so, perhaps, to inculcate the necessity of its being so situated in connection with the internal arrangement of the building as to lead with facility to every part of it, being, as Scamozzi observes (Parte Secunda, lib. vi. c. 4.), like the mouth of an animal placed in the middle of the face, and of easy communication with the *inside*. In the internal distribution the doors should as much as possible be opposite one another on many accounts, not the least whereof is the facility thus given to ventilation; but such a disposition also gives the opportunity of a far better display of a series of rooms, which on occasions of fêtes imparts great magnificence to the apartments. In this climate it is well to avoid too great a number of doors, and they should never, if it can be avoided, be placed near chimneys, because of subjecting to draughts of air those who sit near the fire. Generally the doors in a room should be reduced to the smallest number that will suit the distribution, and the practice of making feigned or blank doors, though sometimes necessary, should if possible be excluded.

2733. The ornaments with which doors are decorated must of course depend on the building in which they are used; and as this is a matter in which common sense must direct the architect, it is hardly necessary to say that the ornaments applied to them in a theatre would ill suit a church.

2734. The composition and designing of gates and their piers must of necessity suit the occasion, as well as the folding gates attached to them, for the enclosure of the parks,

gardens, and other places they are to serve.   There are few finer examples in the higher class of this species of design than the celebrated gates at Hampton Court.

2735. The evil days on which we have fallen in this country, in respect of the arts, precludes the hope of again seeing the doors of our buildings ornamented with bassi relievi and bronze ornaments, a practice common among the ancients no less than among the revivers of the arts; witness the doors of St. Peter's, and, above all, those monuments of the art, the doors of the baptistery at Florence by Lorenzo Ghiberti, wherein art rises by being made only subservient to the holy purpose to which it is the mere handmaid.   In the mention of doors those of San Giovanni Laterano at Rome must not be omitted; they have the credit of having been the enclosures to the temple of Saturn in the ancient city.

2736. The manufacture of doors has been already sufficiently noticed in the Second Book; and it therefore only remains for us to subjoin a few examples, which, we think, among many others, deserve the attention of the student.

Fig. 957.   Fig. 956.   Fig. 958.

2737. Fig. 956. is an external doorway designed and executed by Vignola, at Caprarola, not a great distance north of Rome; it must speak for itself: if the reader be of our mind, he will see in it a beautiful handling of the subject; but we cannot further answer for our opinion, knowing as we do that some of the reviewers of these days may find out that it possesses no *æsthetic* beauties.   There are cases where imitation has been permitted; and the sanction for our opinion is, that it has been imitated by one whom we and all others hold in reverence at Greenwich Hospital, though, as we think with Chambers, for the worse.   "The aperture is in the form of an arch, and occupies somewhat more than two thirds of the whole height.   It is adorned with two rusticated Doric pilasters and a regular entablature.   The height of the pilasters is 16 modules, that of the entablature 4. The width of the aperture is 7 modules, its height 14, and the breath of each pier is 3 modules."   To the detail of Chambers we have to add that the void in this example, which has no analogy to that which as a general rule we gave in the commencement of the section, is about one third of the area of the whole design, the void being to such area as 7·57 to 20·88.

2738. *Fig. 957.* is a design by the last-mentioned master, in which the void is as nearly as possible equal to one third of the area, the supports another, and the weights the other third: in other terms, the aperture occupies two thirds of the whole height and one half of the whole breadth, being, in fact, a double square.   Its entablature has an alliance with the Tuscan order, and the cornice is equal to one fifteenth of the whole height of the door. These two examples are especially external; those which follow are from their nature applicable in general form to either external or internal doorways.

2739. *Fig. 958.* is a doorway in the Cancellaria at Rome, and is from the design of Vignola. The width is one half the height, and the height of the entablature is equal to one third of the height of the aperture.   The breadth of the architrave is one fifth of the aperture's width, and the pilasters below the consoles are half as broad as the architrave. It is heavy, as might have been expected from the proportion between the voids and the solids.

2740. *Fig. 959.* is a design by Michael Angelo Buonarotti, and its aperture may be twice its height,

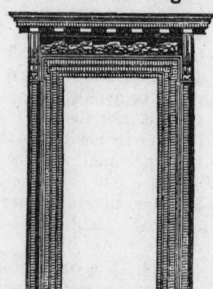

Fig. 959.   Fig. 960.

the whole entablature a quarter of its height, and the architrave one sixth of the width of the aperture.   The face of the pilasters or columns at the sides must be regulated by the lower fascia of the architrave, and their breadth is to be a semidiameter.

2741. *Fig.* 960. is by Vignola, and is in the Farnese palace at Rome. The opening is twice the width in height, and the entablature is three elevenths of the height of the aperture, one of the foregoing elevenths being given to the architrave.   The whole of the ornament on the sides is, including architraves and pilasters, equal to two sevenths of the width of the aperture.   The cornice is Composite, with modillions and dentils, and the frieze is enriched with a laurel band.

2742. *Fig.* 961., another of the examples given by Chambers, is believed to be by Cigoli.   The void is rather more in height than twice its width.   The impost of the arch is equal to half a diameter, the columns are rather more than nine diameters high, and rusticated with five square cinctures.   The entablature is not so much as one quarter of the height of the column, and its tablet is equal to the width of the aperture.

Fig. 961.   Fig. 962.   Fig. 963.

2743. *Fig.* 962. is by Inigo Jones, and the aperture may be twice as high as it is wide. The architrave may be a sixth or seventh of the width of the aperture, the top of it being level with the astragal of the columns, which are Corinthian, and ten diameters in height. They must be so far removed on each side from the architrave as to allow the full projection of their bases.   The entablature may be from two ninths to one fifth of the column, and the pediment should be regulated by the rules given in Sect. XVII. (2722.).

2744. *Fig.* 963. is by Serlio.   The aperture may be a double square, or a trifle less ; the diameter of the columns a quarter of the width of the aperture, or a trifle less ; their height 8 to 8½ diameters ; the entablature about a quarter of the height of the columns, and the pediment should be drawn in conformity with the directions in Sect. XVII.

Sect. XX.

WINDOWS.

2745. Windows, of all the parts of a building, are those which require the greatest nicety in adjustment between the interior and exterior relations of them.   The architect who merely looks to the effect they will produce in his façades has done less than half his work, and deserves no better name or rank than that of a mere builder.   It seems almost useless to observe that the windows of a building should preserve the same character, that those in each story must be of the same height, and that the openings must be directly over one another.   Blank windows are, if possible, to be avoided : they always indicate that the architect wanted skill to unite the internal wants of the building with its external decoration.   Windows, moreover, should be as far removed as the interior will permit from the quoins of a building, because they not only apparently, but really, weaken the angles when placed too near them.

2746. Vitruvius, Palladio, Scamozzi, and Philibert de l'Orme, besides many other masters, have given different proportions to them as connected with the apartments to be lighted.   That these should be different is indicated by the different places in which those masters have written.   Nothing, indeed, seems so much to disallow general laws as the proportion of windows to an apartment ; according to the climate, the temperature, the

length of the days, the general clearness of the sky, the wants and customs of commerce and of life generally. In hot climates the windows are always few in number and small in dimension. As we approach those regions where the sun has less power and the winter is longer, we observe always an increase in their size and number, so as to enable the inhabitants to take as much advantage as possible of the sun's light and rays. It seems, therefore, almost impossible to give general rules on this subject. We shall on this account endeavour, in the rules that this section contains, to confine ourselves to the sizes which seem suitable in this climate, as respects the proportion of light necessary for the comfort of an apartment.

2747. It is a matter of experience that the greatest quantity of light is obtained for an apartment when lighted by an horizontal aperture in the ceiling. Of this a very extraordinary verification is to be found in the Pantheon at Rome. This edifice, whose clear internal diameter is 142 feet 6 inches, not including the recesses behind the columns, is nearly 74 feet high to the springing of the dome, which is semicircular. The total clear number of cubic feet in it may therefore be taken in round numbers at 1,934,460 cubic feet. Those who have visited it well know that it is most sufficiently and pleasingly lighted, and this is effected by an aperture (the *eye*, as it is technically called,) in the crown of the dome, which aperture is only 27 feet in diameter. Now the area of a circle 27 feet in diameter being rather more than 572 feet, it follows that each superficial foot of the area lights the astonishing quantity of nearly 3380 cubic feet. Independent of all considerations of climate, this shows the amazing superiority of a light falling vertically, where it can be introduced. But in a majority of cases the apertures for light are introduced in vertical walls; and the consequence is, that a far greater area of them for the admission of light becomes necessary. In considering the question it must be premised that a large open space is supposed before the windows, and not the obstructed light which it is the lot of the inhabitants of closely-built streets to enjoy. Again, it is to be recollected that in the proportioning of windows it is the apartments on the principal floor that are to be considered, because their width in all the stories must be guided by them, the only variety admissible being in the height. In this country, where the gloom and even darkness of wet, cloudy, and foggy seasons so much prevails, it is better to err on the side of too much rather than too little light, and when it is superabundant to exclude it by means of shutters and blinds. We are not very friendly to the splaying of windows, because of the irregularity of the lines which follows the practice; but, it must be admitted, it often becomes necessary when the walls are thick, and in such cases a considerable splay on the inside increases the light in effect by a great diminution of shade. It is well, if possible, to have an odd number of windows in an apartment: nothing wherein contributes more to gloom than a pier in the centre.

2748. We do not think it necessary to advert to the rule of Palladio for the dimensions of windows given in the first book of his work, chap. 25.; because, were it true for the climate of northern Italy, it would not be so for that of Great Britain; neither are we at all satisfied with that which in his practice Sir William Chambers says he adopted, and which is as follows, in his own words:—" I have generally added the depth and height" we suppose width " of the rooms on the principal floor together, and taken one eighth part thereof for the width of the window; a rule to which there are few objections: admitting somewhat more light than Palladio's, it is, I apprehend, fitter for our climate than his rule would be." This rule is empirical, as indeed is that on which we place most dependence, and to which we shall presently introduce the reader, being ourselves inclined to the belief that in the lighting a room there is a direct relation between the area of the aperture admitting the light and the quantity of cube space in the room. Indeed the law which we are about to give is one founded on the cubic contents of the apartment; and if the results bore a regular ratio to that quantity, the discussion would be at an end, for we should then have only to ascertain the cubic contents, and, knowing how much an area of light one foot square would illuminate, the division of one by the other would supply the superficies of windows to be provided. Our own notion on this subject is, that 1 foot superficial of light in a vertical wall, supposing the building free from obstruction by high objects in the neighbourhood, will in a square room be sufficient for 100 cube feet if placed centrally in such room. It will, however, immediately occur to the reader, that this rule cannot in many cases satisfy the requirements of an apartment as respects the quantity of light necessary for its proper illumination. The subject is beset with numerous difficulties, which to overcome requires the greatest skill. In the case of an apartment, long as compared with its width, it is well known to every practical architect that windows of the same collective area at either of the narrow ends of such apartment will light it much more effectively than if the same area of light were admitted on either of the long sides, and most especially so, if it should happen that on such long side there were a pier instead of a window in the centre of such side. In illustration of what we mean, let us refer the reader to the ball room at Windsor Castle, an apartment 90 feet long, 34 feet wide, and 33 feet high. This room is lighted from the northern narrower side by a window nearly occupying the

width, and is supplied by an abundance of light.   But had the same quantity of light been admitted from either of the long sides of the room, so many masses of shadow would have been introduced through the interposition of piers, that its effect would have differed most widely from the cheerful and airy aspect it now presents.   We have taken this as an example that more presently occurs to us, but the reader from his observation will have no difficulty in supplying instances in corroboration of our impressions on this subject.

But we shall now proceed to give, in the author's own words, the rules of which we have spoken.   That author is Robert Morris, and the work quoted is *Lectures on Architecture, consisting of Rules founded on Harmonick and Arithmetical Proportions in Building.* London, 8vo. 1734.   " There are rules, likewise, for proportioning of light according to the magnitude of the room by which any room may be illuminated, more or less, according to the uses of them, and at the same time preserve an external regularity ; which, as it is on an uncommon basis, I shall explain to you as well as I conveniently can.   Let the magnitude of the room be given, and one of those proportions I have proposed to be made use of or any other ; multiply the length and breadth of the room together, and that product multiply by the height, and the square root of that sum will be the area or superficial content in feet, &c. of the light required."

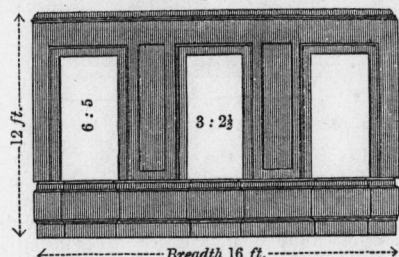
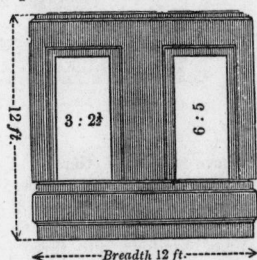

Fig. 964.   Fig. 965.

2749. " Example.   Suppose a room (*fig.* 964.), whose magnitude is the arithmetical proportion of 5, 4, and 3, and is 20 feet long, 16 feet broad, and 12 feet high, the cube or product of its length, breadth, and height multiplied together is 3840, the square root of which sum is 62 feet.   If the height of the story is 12 feet as before mentioned, divide that 62 feet into three windows ; each window will contain 20 feet 8 inches of superficial light, and those will be found to be 3 feet 2½ inches broad, and 6 feet 5 inches high, which are windows of two diameters."

2750. " Let us now suppose another room on the same range whose height is 12 feet, as the preceding example is, and its proportion (*fig.* 965.) shall be the cube.   The product of that cube is 1728, and its root is 41 feet 4 inches, or thereabouts : divide that 41 feet 4 inches in two parts for two windows, and each will be 20 feet 8 inches of superficial light, and those will be two diameters in height, and the magnitude the same as the preceding room."

2751. " For example sake, I will only suppose one more room (*fig.* 966) upon the same range, and 12 feet in height, whose proportion shall be the arithmetical of 3, 2, and 1 ; that is, its height being 12 feet, the breadth will be 24 and length 36, the product of those numbers multiplied together will be 10368, and its root 101 feet 8 inches, or thereabouts : divide this room into five windows, each window will have 20 feet 4 inches superficial light, and the magnitude will be near or equal to

Fig. 966.

the others, and if the proportion be 6, 4, and 3, and coved, the light is the same."

2752. " There is," says the author, rather perhaps simply, " but one objection to this rule to make it universal for all kinds of proportioned rooms on the same floor, and that is, the square root doth not always happen to be exact enough for to make them alike ; but as the variation will be so small, it may be made use of ; and if the area something exceeds the standard of the principal room, that room may be converted to a use which requires more than standard light, and the necessities of families sometimes require it.   But, however, the rule will serve for the purpose near enough for any practice."

2753. " If you extend the rule to larger rooms, the same methods will be preserved even if the height be continued through two stories, if the upper windows be made square,

Fig. 967.

and to have two tire " (tiers) " of windows. Let us suppose the room (*fig.* 967.) with two tire of windows in height, to be 50 feet long, 40 feet wide, and 30 feet high, the arithmetical proportion of 5, 4, and 3, the product of those numbers multiplied together will be 60000, the square root of which sum is 245 superfical feet; divide that sum for the tire " (tiers) " of windows into three parts, or take one third of it, and that makes the attic or square windows 81 feet 8 inches superficial light; divide this into 5 windows, and they are 4 feet and half an inch square, and the five lower windows, consisting of 163 feet 4 inches superficial light, being what remains out of the 245 feet, the root, each of these windows is 4 feet and half an inch by 8 feet 1 inch, or two diameters, which 245 feet, the whole sum of the square root of the room, will sufficiently illuminate the same."

2754. The extreme piers should not, if possible, be less than half the width of the principal piers. This cannot always be obtained, but a much less width causes great irregularity, and that more especially when one of such end piers falls opposite a chimney breast, besides causing a great mass of shadow on the other side of the chimney, which has a tendency towards making the room dark and gloomy.

2755. Windows in the same story should be similar. There may be an occasional deviation for a great central window, but such deviation must be used with much caution. Another practice, most properly reprobated by Chambers, is that of intermitting the architrave and frieze of an order in the intervals between the columns to make room for windows and their enrichments, as on the flanks of the Mansion House in the city of London; a practice from which Sir Christopher Wren was, unfortunately, not exempt, as may be noticed in St. Paul's Cathedral.

2756. What are called Venetian windows are occasionally allowable, when so ranged and introduced as not to interfere with the composition, — a task often difficult to effect. They should not be much repeated, as in the front at Holkham, where they become actually disgusting. Though in the examples which follow there be two which are composed with semicircular-headed centres, we do not approve of the general use of examples designed on such principles, and would advise the student rather to study the composition of the Venetian window, when required, as in *fig.* 968., which we do not present as one of beauty, but rather of propriety, where the want of light to the apartment renders a Venetian window expedient. The method of making sashes, shutters, and the other accessories of windows has been described in a previous section; we therefore proceed to offer a few of the most celebrated examples of windows. It is not necessary, after the investigation relative to the voids and solids of doors, to pursue the inquiry into the relative proportions of windows as respects that part of the subject. They are, in a measure, in regard to windows, subject to the same principles, and this, by trial, will be immediately apparent to the student; and we therefore shall not stop for such investigation.

Fig. 968.

2757. *Fig.* 969. is after the lower story of windows at St. Peter's at Rome, by Michael Angelo, and is rather less than the double square in height. The architrave is one seventh

Fig. 969.   Fig. 970.

of the aperture's width, being the same as that of the pilasters. The length of the consoles is one third of the width of the aperture, and the entablature one quarter of its height.

2758. *Fig.* 970. is from the Mattei palace at Rome, and is the design of Bartolomeo Ammanati. It possesses, though rather heavy, considerable beauty, and well deserves the attention of the student. Chambers, from whom we have selected many of our examples in this and others sections, says, "the parts made somewhat less would succeed better, as would also a pediment instead of the sloped covering at top:" but we entirely disagree with him, and are of opinion that what he proposes would ruin the design.

Fig. 971.   Fig. 972.

2759. *Figs.* 971. and 972. are the compositions of Bernardo Buontalenti. The apertures are a double square, or something less, the architraves a sixth or seventh of the apertures, and the pilasters may be about the same. The height of the entablature should not be more than a quarter that of the aperture, nor much less. The greatest length of the consoles should not exceed half the width of the aperture, nor should their least length be less than one third of it.

2760. *Fig.* 973. is from the old Louvre at Paris, and is by the celebrated Pierre Lescot,

abbot of Clugny in the reigns of Francis I. and Henry II.   Its proportions are not much dissimilar from the two last examples.

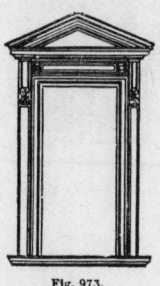

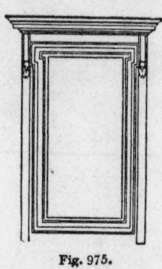

Fig. 973.   Fig. 974.   Fig. 975.

2761. *Fig.* 974. is a window constantly used by Palladio.   The opening is a double square, the breadth of the architrave equal to one sixth of the aperture, and the frieze and cornice together equal to double the height of the architrave.   The breadth of the consoles equal to two thirds the width of the architrave.   The breaks over the consoles in the bed mouldings of the cornice are perhaps not strictly correct, but are deviations from propriety which may be tolerated.   The breaks in the upper vertical parts of the architrave would perhaps be better omitted.   The practice generally should be avoided, except in cases where a greater length of cornice is wanted for the purpose of filling the bare walls to which the windows are applied.

2762. *Fig.* 975. is from the Banqueting House at Whitehall, by Inigo Jones.   The aperture is a double square, the entablature one fourth of its height, and the architrave somewhat more than one sixth of its width.

2763. *Fig.* 976. is by Michael Angelo, and executed at the Farnese palace at Rome.   It possesses all the wildness and fancy of the master, and though abounding with faults, is redeemed by its grandeur and originality.

2764. In *fig.* 977. is given the design by Ludovico da Cigoli of a window from the ground floor of the Renuccini palace in Florence.   It can scarcely be properly estimated without its connection with the façade, to the character whereof it is in every respect suitable.

2765. *Fig.* 978. is a design of Palladio, nearly resembling that executed in the Barbarano palace at Vicenza.   It has been imitated by Inigo Jones, and perhaps improved on by him, in the flanks at Greenwich Hospital.

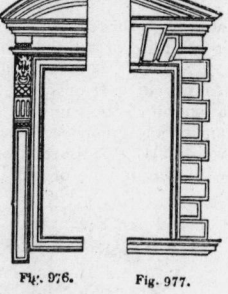

Fig. 976.   Fig. 977.

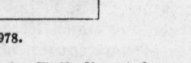

Fig. 978.   Fig. 979.

2766. *Fig.* 979. is also by Palladio, and executed by him in the Porto palace at Vicenza.
2767. *Fig.* 980. is the design of Raffaelle Sanzio, and worthy of the reputation of that

great painter and architect.   It is executed in the Pandolfini palace at Florence, on the principal floor.   The height of the aperture is a very little more than twice its width, the architrave is one seventh the width of the aperture.   The columns, which are Ionic, are

Fig. 980.   Fig. 981.

9 diameters high, and should be as much detached from the wall as possible.   The distance of them from the architrave of the window is a quarter of a diameter, which is also the distance of the entablature from the top of the same architrave.   The total height of the entablature is two ninths of that of the column, and the height of the pediment is one quarter of its base or somewhat less.   The pedestals are one quarter of the height of the whole order.

2768. *Fig.* 981. is one of the windows of the Bracciano palace at Rome, by Bernini. The aperture is more than a double square, and the architrave about one sixth the width of the aperture.   The entablature is only one fifth of the height of the columns, including their sub-plinths, and the pediment is less in height than one quarter of its extent.

Fig. 982.   Fig. 983.

2769. *Fig.* 982. is from the principal floor of the Palazzo Thiene at Vicenza.   The aperture is two and two tenths of its width in height ; the columns are nine diameters high, and one quarter engaged in the wall.   The under sides of the Ionic capitals are level with the top of the aperture, having angular volutes with an astragal and fillet below the volute. The bases are Tuscan, and there are on each shaft five rustic dies of an equal breadth.

whose inner sides are on a line with the sides of the aperture, and their projection equal to that of the plinth of the base, that is, one fifth of a diameter of the column. The keystones incline forwards towards the top, and they are hatched, only the surface being left rough, as are likewise the dies on the columns, except at their angles, which are rubbed smooth. The entablature is Ionic, the architrave consisting of only two fasciæ, the frieze swelled, and the dentil band placed immediately on the frieze, without any intervening mouldings, a practice not very unusual with Palladio. The pedestals are rather more than one third the height of the columns. The dies and balusters stand on the platband of the basement, which was done to diminish the projection.

2770. *Fig.* 983. is a design by Inigo Jones, which has been much used in this country. It is rather higher than a double square. The width of the architrave is one fifth that of the aperture, and the rustics are a trifle less than the third of it. The entablature is two ninths of the height of the opening, and the height of the pedestal is $\frac{27}{100}$, or nearly so, of the height of the aperture and pedestal taken together.

Fig. 984.　　　　　　　　　　　　　　　　　Fig. 985.

2771. *Fig.* 984. is the design of a Venetian window by Colin Campbell, the compiler of the three first volumes of the *Vitruvius Britannicus ;* and

2772. *Fig.* 985. is very similar to the Venetian windows in the west façade of the Horse Guards, executed by Kent. It is perhaps as favourable an example of this species of window as can be produced.

Sect. XXI.

NICHES AND STATUES.

2773. A niche is a recess constructed in the thickness of a wall for the reception of different objects, such as statues more especially, but occasionally also for that of busts, vases, and tripods. Vitruvius makes no mention of niches, and but for an inscription published by Visconti in the *Monumenti Gabini* we should not have known that they were by the ancients called *zothecæ*, or places for the reception of a figure. Our English word niche is evidently derived from the Italian *nicchio*, a shell.

2774. In the early Greek temple the niche is not found; at a later period, as in the monument of Philopappus, we find a circular and two quadrangular-headed niches occupied in the time of Stuart by statues; and it does not seem improbable that in the Gymnasia, Agora, Stadia, &c. of the nation mentioned, the use of the niche was not uncommon. But the different forms of the ancient tomb, and the early methods of sepulture, would soon suggest to the Greeks and Romans the use of the niche, especially in such tombs as were devoted to the use of a particular family. These sepulchres, whose subdivisions were called *columbaria*, had their walls ornamented with small niches for the reception of cinerary urns, or those containing the ashes of the dead. In these, a large-sized niche occupies the principal place in the apartment, and in this was deposited the urn or sarcophagus of the head of the family.

2775. The small temples (*ædicula*) of the Romans are often found decorated with niches; and in the small building on the Lake of Albano, generally supposed to have been a Nympheum, we find each side of the interior dressed with six niches, whose height sufficiently indicates that they were provided for the reception of statues. In the temple of Diana, commonly called the *maison carrée*, at Nismes, which, however, is usually considered to

have been a building sacred to the Nymphs, the interior has two sides decorated with six Corinthian columns, and in the wall between each intercolumniation is a niche of the sort called tabernacles by the moderns. Each is placed on a pedestal, and is finished on the sides by pilasters alternately surmounted by segmental and triangular pediments. We do not, however, consider it necessary to enumerate the various Roman works wherein the niche finds a place, and shall therefore do no more than refer the student to the Pantheon, the temple of Peace, the arch of Janus, at Rome, and to its exuberant employment at Palmyra, Baalbek, and Spalatro. The buildings cited will furnish him with examples of all sorts and characters.

2776. The dresses of niches seem to bear an analogy to those of windows and doors in their form and decoration; the niche may really be considered as an opening in a wall, and indeed there are, in the arch of Claudius Drusus, now the Porta Maggiore, at Rome, openings used as niches, in which an object placed may be seen from either side of the wall. It therefore appears not improper to dress the niche with the ornaments which custom has sanctioned for doors and windows. The author of the article " Niche " in the *Encyclopedie Methodique*, has divided niches into three classes. The first are such as are square on the plan, and either square or circular-headed. These are the simplest, and are without dressings of any sort. Second, such as are square on their plans, and with square heads, but ornamented with dressings, or crowned with a simple platband supported by two consoles. In the third class are included all niches whose plan and heads are semicircular, either ornamented with festoons, or with dressings, or with columns and entablature. These, says the author, are to be introduced into buildings according to their several characters, from simple to highly enriched, as requisite.

2777. Some architectural authors have laid down positive rules for the proportions of niches. According to others the proportion is found in a niche twice and a half its width in height; and indeed this produces a proportion not inelegant. But in considering the classes separately, they have divided the width of the niches invariably into twelve parts. To a niche of the first class they give twenty-eight of such parts; to one of the second class, thirty; and to one of the third class, thirty-one parts. This reduction, however, of the proportions of a niche seems to us to partake of empiricism; and we would rather always trust to an educated eye than to rules which seem to have no basis on fitness and propriety. It is, moreover, to be recollected that all rules of art can be considered only as *mean terms*, serving more as approximations than positive laws for the guidance of the artist in the different combinations he imagines.

2778. The use of tiers of niches over each other is condemned by J. F. Blondel, unless separated by a line of entablature between them, which may seem to indicate the existence of a floor; otherwise, he observes, one figure seems to stand on the head of another. This, however, is an abuse of reasoning; not that it is to be understood that we think the practice very allowable. The recommendation of this master in respect of the relation between niches and the statues that are to occupy them is worthy of attention. He opposes, and we think with great propriety, the placing a statue without a plinth in the niche. The plinth is, indeed, necessary to the good effect of every statue; and to pretend that the imitation in marble could or ever was intended to be mistaken for the object it imitates, would be to leave behind all those matters of convention in art for which the spectator is well prepared. In architectural decoration, no less than in the abstract imitation of the objects of sculpture, no one is desirous of believing them natural and living, but only as models of imitation.

2779. The following observations are from Chambers, relative to the size of the statues used in niches. " The size of the statue depends upon the dimensions of the niche; it should neither be so large as to seem rammed into it, as at Santa Maria Maggiore, in Rome, nor so small as to seem lost in it, as in the Pantheon, where the statues do not occupy above three quarters of the height of the niche, and only one half of its width. Palladio, in arched niches, makes the chin of his statues on a level with the top of the impost (springing), so that the whole head is in the coved part. In the nave of St. Peter's, at Rome, the same proportion has been observed, and it has a very good effect. The distance between the outline of the statue and the sides of the niche should never be less than one third of a head, nor more than one half, whether the niche be square or arched; and when it is square, the distance from the top of the head to the soffite of the niche should not exceed the distance left on the sides. The statues are generally raised on a plinth, the height of which may be from one third to one half of a head; and sometimes, where the niches are very large in proportion to the architecture they accompany, as is the case when an order comprehends but one story, the statues may be raised on small pedestals, by which means they may be made lower than usual, and yet fill the niche sufficiently, it being to be feared lest statues of a proper size to fill such niches should make the columns and entablature appear trifling. The same expedient must also be made use of whenever the statues in the niches, according to their common proportions, come considerably larger than those placed at the top of the building. A trifling disparity will not be easily perceived, on ac-

count of the distance between their respective situations; but if it be great, it has a
very bad effect; and therefore this must be well attended to and remedied, either by the
above-mentioned method, or by entirely omitting statues at the top of the building, leaving
the balustrade either free, or placing thereon vases, trophies, and other similar ornaments."
Further on in the same work, the author says that "niches, being designed as repositories
for statues, groups, vases, or other works of sculpture, must be contrived to set off the
things they are to contain to the best advantage; and therefore no ornaments should ever
be introduced within them, as is sometimes injudiciously practised, the cove of the niche
being either filled with a large scollop shell, or the whole inside with various kinds of projecting rustics, with moulded compartments, either raised or sunken, or composed of different coloured marbles, for all these serve to confuse the outline of the statue or group.
It is even wrong to continue an impost within the niche, for that is of considerable disadvantage to the figures, which never appear so perfect as when backed and detached on a
plain smooth surface. An excess of ornaments round the niche should likewise be avoided,
and particularly masks, busts, boys, or any representation of the human figure, all which
serve to divide the attention, and to divert it from the principal object."

2780. "The depth of the niche should always be sufficient to contain the whole statue,
or whatever else it is to contain, it being very disagreeable to see statues, or any other
weighty objects, with false bearings, and supported on consoles or other projections, as is
sometimes done, and in the case of niches, the side views become exceedingly uncouth; for
in these a leg, an arm, a head, in short, those parts alone which project beyond the niche,
appear and look like so many fragments, stuck irregularly into the wall." We trust we
shall be excused for this and many other long quotations from Chambers, on account of the
strong common sense with which they abound, though not always expressed in the most
elegant language that might have been selected.

2781. We conclude the section with a few examples of niches, whose general proportions are sufficiently to be derived from the figures which represent them, and which,
therefore, will not require our more minute description in this place, the diagrams themselves being the more useful mode of submitting the subject to the student.

 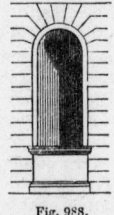 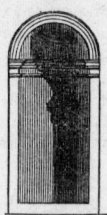

Fig. 986.　　　　　Fig. 987.　　　　　Fig. 988.　　　　　Fig. 989.

2782. *Fig.* 986. is the simple niche, square and circular in the head and in the plan; in
the latter we have before, as a general rule, given the proportion of its height as twice and a
half that of its width; but the former, or the square-headed one, may be a double square,
yet it never should exceed in height twice and a half its width.

2783. *Fig.* 987. is a common form of using the niche where the opening of windows
with which it is accompanied requires a correspondent square recess for the niches, as also
in interiors where the leading lines may require such an expedient.

2784. *Fig.* 988. shows the method of introducing niches in a rusticated basement, which
is often requisite. The rustics are received on a flat ground, in which the niche is formed.
The reader is not to understand that any of the
figures are intended as models for imitation, but
merely as modes on which, in using them, he may
so work as to reduce them to his own views in
the design whereon he is engaged.

2785. *Fig.* 989. is from the plate of Palladio's
Egyptian Hall, and exhibits the violation of Chambers's excellent maxim of not allowing the impost
to be continued round the springing of the niche.
If niches are merely introduced for play of light
and shadow without reference to their reception
of statues, the practice of this abuse may be tolerated; but certainly not in cases where statues
are to be placed in them.

2786. *Fig.* 990. is the niche accompanied by
entablature, pediment, architraves, consoles, and
pedestals, as in the windows which have already

Fig. 990.　　　　　Fig. 991.

been given, and their proportions will serve as a guide in this; the only difference being, that a niche is inserted within the architrave of the opening.

2787. *Fig.* 991. is imitated from one of the niches of the Pantheon, for the details whereof the reader may refer to Desgodetz.

Sect. XXII.

CHIMNEY PIECES.

2788. It is not our intention to devote much of a space, necessarily restricted, to the consideration of designs for chimney pieces; not because we consider them unworthy of the serious attention of the student, nor because the ever-varying fashion of the day seems to create a desire for new forms, but because they come under the category of doors and windows (strange as it may seem) in respect of the relation of the void to the solid parts. We are not aware that any view of this nature has heretofore been involved in the consideration of them, but we are not the more on that account to be driven from our hypothesis. The examples of chimney pieces that have been given by Chambers, and, before him, by old Serlio, were but fashions of their respective days; and if it be possible to establish something like a canon on which they might be designed, we apprehend it would be useful to the student.

2789. A chimney piece is the ornamental decoration applied to the aperture of a chimney opening, and it seems but reasonable that in its general distribution it should be subject to those laws which regulate the ornaments of other openings. The forms and fancies into which this ornament of a room may be changed are infinite, and we therefore consider that if its appendages can be drawn into a consistent shape we shall be of service in the few

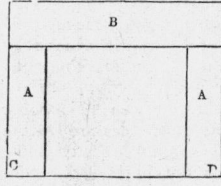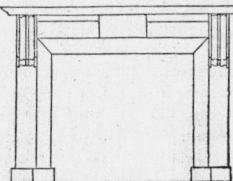

Fig. 992.   Fig. 993.   Fig. 994.

remarks subjoined. In *fig.* 992. the chimney opening to be decorated is 4·0 wide and 3 feet 6 inches high; its area is therefore equal to $4 : 0 \times 3 : 6 = 14$ feet. The principle here recommended is to make the two supporting pieces equal to one half of that area, or seven feet, and the supported piece B equal to the other half. Now, as the height is 3 : 6, we shall have $\frac{7}{3 \cdot 5} = 2$ for the width of the two piers, that is, each will be one foot wide. By the addition of these to the width of the opening, the dimension becomes six feet; and as B is to contain seven feet superficial, it follows that $\frac{7}{6} = 1\frac{1}{6}$ is the height of B that it may contain 7 feet.

2790. In *fig.* 993. we have shown the method of developing the principle; in it the supports, load, and void bear the same relation to each other as in the preceding figure. The entablature is divided into three equal parts for the architrave, frieze, and cornice, and trusses are placed on the pilasters by the sides of the architrave. The tablet is of course not absolutely required, and the trusses may be formed of leaves instead of being plain, as here shown.

2791. *Fig.* 994. is another mode of using the proportions given in *fig.* 992., and upon it, as well as that last given, we have only to observe, they are not introduced as specimens of design, but solely with the view of illustrating a principle. The projection of chimney-pieces should not generally be greater than the whole width of the support, nor less than half.

2792. We wish we could give some rule for adjusting the size of a chimney opening to that of the room it is to warm. Morris, in his *Lectures on Architecture*, before quoted, imagined that he had found out one, and he speaks with confidence on the results which follow its use; but we confess we are not satisfied with them. We nevertheless should be wrong in omitting it, and therefore give his words for the consideration of the student. The first rule is as follows: — " To find the height of the opening of the chimney from any given magnitude of a room, add the length and height of the room together, and extract the square root of that sum, and half that root will be the height of the chimney." The second rule is as follows: — " To find the breadth of a chimney from any given magnitude

of a room, add the length, breadth, and height of the room together, and extract the square root of that sum, and half that root will be the height of the chimney." The third rule he gives is, " To find the depth of a chimney from any given magnitude, including the breadth and height of the same, add the breadth and height of the chimney together, take one fourth of that sum, and it is the depth of the chimney." His fourth and last rule is, " To find the side of a square or funnel proportioned to clear the smoke from any given depth of the chimney, take three fourths of the given depth, and that sum is the side of the square of the funnel. Observe, only, that in cube rooms the height is equal to the breadth, and the foregoing rules are universal." The rules given by Chambers are extremely vague and general. He says that " in the smallest apartments the width of the aperture is never made less than from three feet to three feet six inches ; in rooms from twenty to twenty-four feet square, or of equal superficial dimensions, it may be four feet wide ; in those of twenty-five to thirty, from four to four and a half ; and in such as exceed these dimensions, the aperture may be extended to five or five feet six inches ; but should the room be extremely large, as is frequently the case of halls, galleries, and salons, and one chimney of these dimensions neither afford sufficient heat to warm the room nor sufficient space round it for the company, it will be much more convenient, and far handsomer, to have two chimney pieces of a moderate size than a single one exceedingly large, all the parts of which would appear clumsy and disproportioned to the other decorations of the room." It is well so to place the chimney as that persons on entering a room may at once see it. In this climate a cheerfulness is imparted by the sight of a fire ; but it is not to be so placed as to be opposite a door, neither ought it, if possible to be avoided, to be so placed as to have a door on either side of it. There are, however, circumstances under which even the last-named category cannot be avoided, but it is always well if it can. The fact is, that the further the door can, generally speaking, be removed from a chimney, the better ; and the architect must, if the plan admit it (and he ought so to distribute his parts), avoid all cross draughts of air in a room. Angular chimneys are only admissible in small rooms where space and other considerations permit no other means of introducing a chimney. We can hardly think it necessary to say, with Chambers, that " whenever two chimneys are introduced in the same room they must be regularly placed, either directly facing each other, if in different walls, or at equal distances from the centre of the wall in which they both are placed. He observes, however, with a proper caution to the student, that " the Italians frequently put their chimneys in the front walls, between the windows, for the benefit of looking out while sitting by the fire ; but this must be avoided, for by so doing that side of the room becomes crowded with ornaments, and the other sides are left too bare ; the front walls are much weakened by the funnels, and the chimney shafts at the top of the building, which must necessarily be carried higher than the ridges of the roofs, have, from their great length, a very disagreeable effect, and are very liable to be blown down." All these objections, however, may be easily answered, and the funnels collected, or shafts, as they then become, be, with skill, made even ornamental to a building. It is in cases like these that the power of the architect above the artisan is manifest.

2793. Where the walls of a building are sufficiently thick, their funnels rise within the thickness of the walls, but in walls of a mean thickness this cannot be accomplished, for under such circumstances the walls and chimney pieces will necessarily project into the rooms, and if the break be great, the effect is unpleasant ; but this may always be obviated by making arched recesses on each side, which, in commoner rooms, may be occupied by presses or closets, thus enabling the architect to carry the cornice unbroken round the room, a point which should never be forgotten, inasmuch as by the cornice or entablature of the apartment being carried round it without a break, which gives the ceiling an unbroken and regular form, a regularity is preserved infinitely more satisfactory to the eye than the disagreeable appearance of a broken, and, we may say, disjointed cornice.

2794. Of the materials employed in the construction of chimney pieces, nothing more is requisite than to say that the costliness of the material must follow the wealth of the founder of the building. Marble, however, is the material usually employed, and the various sorts known are not unfrequently intermixed, so as to produce a pleasing effect. When the aid of the sculptor is called in, much latitude is allowed in the proportions ; but on this head we hope we may, without prejudice, deliver our opinion, that the effect has never amounted to anything like what might have been expected from his extraneous aid ; and the solution is easy : his object is not to produce a work in harmony with the apart-ment, but rather to exhibit his own powers.

2795. In the external appearance of chimney shafts, so as to group them with the building to which they belong, no architect can be put in competition with Sir John Van-brugh. Those of Blenheim, Castle Howard, and other of his buildings, exceed all praise, and deserve the closest investigation of the student. They become in his works, as they always should do, parts of the building, inseparably connected with it, and their removal would detract from the majesty of the structure with which they are connected. On this point we are certain that the best advice that can be given to the student is a constant

contemplation of the works of Vanbrugh. In these days there seems to be a return to good feeling in this respect; and we hope it will, for the credit of the English school, be followed up.

Sect. XXIII.

STAIRCASES.

2796. A staircase is an enclosure formed by walls or partitions, or both, for the reception of an ascent of stairs, with such landings as may be necessary. Of the construction of stairs we have treated in previous sections; this will be confined to general observations on them and their enclosures.

2797. Scarcely any subdivision of a building is of more importance, as respects the character of the architect and the comfort and pleasant occupancy of it by his employer, than its principal and subordinate staircases. There is, moreover, no part, perhaps, in which more room is left for architectural and picturesque display. In our own country there are some extraordinary examples of great beauty produced in staircases on comparatively small scales; whence the student may learn that without great space he may produce very imposing effects. One of these may be still seen, though in a very neglected state, as are most of the buildings attached to the collegiate church of Westminster, at one of the prebendal houses there built by our great master Jones. It is a specimen of his consummate skill as an artist, and well worth the attention of the student, if he can obtain admittance to view it; but if he cannot, we may refer him to some plates executed from drawings made by us many years since, and published in the first and best edition of *Illustrations of the Public Buildings of London* (Lond. 1828). The extreme space occupied by the staircase in question does not exceed 24 by 23 feet; and within these small dimensions he contrived a staircase fit for a palace. So highly did the late Sir John Soane think of this bijou that he had a series of drawings made to illustrate its parts, and exhibited them in his lectures at the Royal Academy.

2798. It is almost unnecessary to impress upon the student that an excess rather than a deficiency of light is requisite in a staircase, and that it should be easily accessible from all parts of the building. Those laws upon which the ease of persons ascending and descending depend will form the subject of two subsections shortly following (2804. and 2814.), to which we particularly recommend the reader's attention. They are of the utmost importance, and we record with surprise that they have not been attended to by architects generally of late years. We have crept up staircases in houses of consequence, which deserved little more than the name of ladders, and we are sorry to say that this defect is found even in the works of Chambers himself; but never in those of Jones and Wren. We shall with these remarks proceed to further observations on the subject, which has already been partially touched upon in 2176. *et seq.*

2799. We know little of the staircases of the Greeks and Romans, and it is remarkable that Vitruvius makes no mention of a staircase, as an important part of an edifice; indeed his silence seems to lead to the conclusion that the staircases of antiquity were not constructed with the luxury and magnificence to be seen in more recent buildings. The best preserved ancient staircases are those constructed in the thickness of the walls of the pronaos of temples for ascending to the roofs. Of this sort remains are found in several peripteral temples. That of the temple of Concord at Agrigentum is still entire, and consists of forty-one steps. According to Pausanias, similar staircases existed in the temple of the Olympian Jupiter at Elis. They were generally winding and spiral, like the inside of a shell, and hence are called *scale a lumaca* by the Italians, and by the French *escaliers en limaçon*. Sometimes, as in the Pantheon at Rome, instead of being circular on the plan, they are triangular; so were they in the temple of Peace, and in the baths of Dioclesian.

2800. Very few vestiges of staircases are to be seen in the ruins of Pompeii; from which it may be inferred that what there were must have been of wood, and, moreover, that few of the houses were more than one story in height. Where they exist, as in the building at the above place called the country house, and some others, they are narrow and inconvenient, with steps sometimes a foot in height. Occasionally, too, we find private staircases mentioned, as in the description of Pliny's Tusculan villa, where one was placed by the side of the dining room, and appropriated to the use of the slaves who served the repast.

2801. The author of the article "Escalier" in the *Encyc. Method.* observes that the magnificence of the staircase was but tardily developed in modern architecture, and that it owed much of its luxury to the perfection to which a knowledge of stereotomy brought the science of masonry. The manners too and the customs of domestic life for a length of time rendered unnecessary more than a staircase of very ordinary description. Thus in the earliest palaces the staircases seem to have been constructed for the use of the inha-

bitants only, possessing in fact no more beauty than we now give to a back staircase. They are for the most part dark, narrow, and inconvenient. Even in Italy, which in the splendour of its buildings preceded and surpassed all the other nations of Europe, the staircase was, till a late period, extremely simple in the largest and grandest palaces. Such are the staircases of the Vatican, Bernini's celebrated one being comparatively of a late date. The old staircases of the Tuilleries and of the Louvre, though on a considerable scale, are, from their simplicity, construction, and situation, little in unison with the richness of the rest of these palaces. And this was the consequence of having the state apartments on the ground floor. When they were removed to a higher place, the staircase which conducted to them necessarily led to a correspondence of design in it.

2802. It will be observed that our observations in this section are confined to internal staircases. Large flights of steps, such as those at the *Trinità de' Monti* and *Araceli* at Rome, do not come within our notice, being unrestricted in their extent, and scarcely subject to the general laws of architectural composition. In these it should however be remembered that they must never rise in a continued series of steps from the bottom to the summit, but must be provided with landings for resting places, as is usually the case in the half and quarter spaces of internal stairs. An extremely fine example of an external flight of stairs may be cited in those descending from the terrace to the orangery at Versailles. For simplicity, grandeur, design, and beauty of construction, we scarcely know anything in Europe more admirable than this staircase and the orangery to which it leads.

2803. The selection of the place in which the staircase of a dwelling is to be seated, requires great judgment, and is always a difficult task in the formation of a plan. Palladio, the great master of the moderns, thus delivers the rules for observance in planning them, that they may not be an obstruction to the rest of the building. He says, " A particular place must be marked out, that no part of the building should receive any prejudice by them. There are three openings necessary to a staircase. The first is the doorway that leads to it, which the more it is in sight the better it is; and I highly approve of its being in such a place that before one comes to it the best part of the house may be seen, for although the house be small, yet by such arrangement it will appear larger : the door, however, must be obvious, and easy to be found. The second opening is that of the windows through which the stairs are lighted ; they should be in the middle, and large enough to light the stairs in every part. The third opening is the landing place by which one enters into the rooms above ; it ought to be fair and well ornamented, and to lead into the largest places first."

2804. " Staircases," continues our author, " will be perfect, if they are spacious, light, and easy to ascend ; as if, indeed, they seemed to invite people to mount. They will be clear, if the light is bright and equally diffused ; and they will be sufficiently ample, if they do not appear scanty and narrow in proportion to the size and quality of the building. Nevertheless, they ought never to be narrower than 4 feet " (4 feet 6 inches English *), " so that two persons meeting on the stairs may conveniently pass each other. They will be convenient with respect to the whole building, if the arches under them can be used for domestic purposes ; and commodious for the persons going up and down, if the stairs are not too steep nor the steps too high. Therefore, they must be twice as long as broad. The steps ought not to exceed 6 inches in height ; and if they be lower they must be so to long and continued stairs, for they will be so much the easier, because one needs not lift the foot so high ; but they must never be lower than 4 inches." (These are Vicentine inches.) " The breadth of the steps ought not to be less than a foot, nor more than a foot and a half. The ancients used to make the steps of an odd number, that thus beginning to ascend with the right foot, they might end with the same foot, which they took to be a good omen, and a greater mark of respect so to enter into the temple. It will be sufficient to put eleven or thirteen steps at most to a flight before coming to a half-pace, thus to help weak people and of short breath, as well that they may there have the opportunity of resting as to allow of any person falling from above being there caught." · We do not propose to give examples of other than the most usual forms of staircases and stairs; their variety is almost infinite, and could not even in their leading features be compassed in a work like this. The varieties, indeed, would not be usefully given, inasmuch as the forms are necessarily dependent on the varied circumstances of each plan, calling upon the architect almost on every occasion to invent *pro re natâ*.

2805. Stairs are of two sorts, straight and winding. Before proceeding with his design, the architect must always take care, whether in the straight or winding staircase, that the person ascending has what is called *headway*, which is a clear distance measured vertically from any step, quarter, half-pace, or landing, to the underside of the ceiling, step, or other part immediately over it, so as to allow the tallest person to clear it with his hat on; and this is the minimum height of headway that can be admitted. To return to the straight and winding staircase, it is to be observed, that the first may be divided into two *flights*, or be

* The Vicentine foot is about 13·6 inches English.

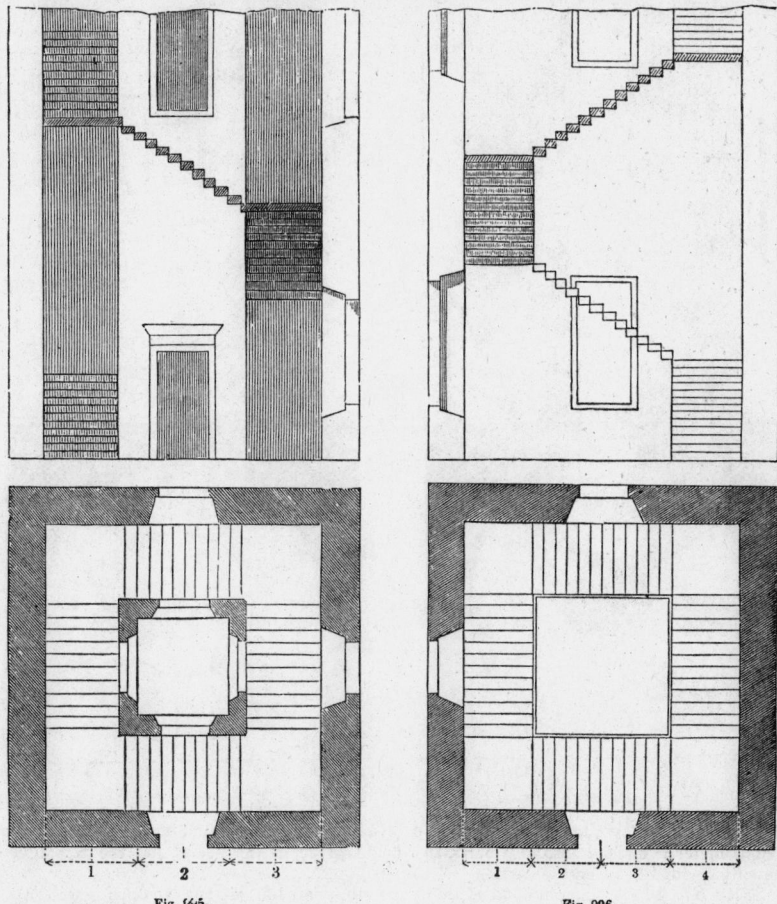

Fig. 995.   Fig. 996.

made quite square, so as to turn on the four sides round a close or open newel, as in *fig.* 995. in which the former is the case, light being obtained by windows in the walls which enclose the newel; or, as in *fig.* 996. : in which case, the newel is open, and the light may be received either from a vertical light above, or from side windows in the walls. Palladio says these two sorts of stairs were invented by Sig. Ludovico Cornaro, a gentleman of much genius, who erected for himself a magnificent palace at Padua.

2806. Of winding or spiral stairs, some are circular on the plan, either open or with a solid newel; others elliptical, also with open or solid newels. Those with the open newel are preferable, because of their allowing the staircase to be lighted additionally, if requisite, by the light obtainable from above; besides which, persons passing up and down may see each other. Palladio thus directs the setting out of spiral staircases. "Those," he says, "which have a newel in the middle are made in this manner. The diameter being divided into three parts, two are given for the steps, and the third is for the newel; or, otherwise, the diameter may be divided into seven parts, three of which are for the newel and four for the steps. "Thus," he says, "was made the staircase of the column of Trajan at Rome; and if the stairs are made circular," (that is, the treads segments of circles on the plan,) "they will be handsomer and longer" (of course) "than if made straight."

2807. "But as it may happen that the space will not give room for these measures, the diameter may be reduced and divided according to the plates." The essence of these plans, omitting the step whose plan is segmental, we here subjoin.

2808. *Fig.* 997. is a plan and section of a staircase with a solid newel, in which the whole diameter is divided into twelve parts, and of these four are given to the newel, and the remainder divided equally between the steps.

Fig. 997.　　　　　　　　　　　　　Fig. 998.

2809. *Fig.* 998. is the plan and section of a spiral staircase with an open newel, wherein the diameter is divided into four parts, two being given to the newel, and the remainder equally divided between the steps.

2810. *Fig.* 999. is the plan and section of an elliptical staircase with an open newel. The conjugate diameter is divided into four parts, whereof two are given to the conjugate diameter of the newel, and the remainder one on each side to the steps.

2811. In *fig.* 1000. the same staircase is given, but with a solid newel, and of course requiring many openings on the sides to light it.

2812. It is not the difficulty of multiplying the examples of staircases which prevents our proceeding on this head, but the space into which our work is to be condensed. Enough of example has been given, by using portions of the examples, to meet every case, the decoration being dependent on the design of the architect, and the distribution on his good sense in the application of what we have submitted to him.

2813. There is, however, one important point in the construction of a staircase to which we must now advert, and that is easiness of ascent. Blondel, in his *Cours d'Architecture*, was, we believe, the first architect who settled the proper relation between the height and width of steps, and his theory, for the truth whereof, though it bears much appearance of it, we do not pledge ourselves, is as follows.

2814. Let x = the space over which a person walks with ease upon a level plane, and z = the height which the same person could with equal ease ascend vertically. Then if h be the height of the step, and w its width, the relation between h and w must be such that when $w = x$, $h = 0$, and when $h = z$, $w = 0$. These conditions are fulfilled by equations of the form $h = \frac{1}{2}(x - w)$ and $w = x - 2h$. Blondel assumes 24 (French) inches for the value of x, and 12 for that of z. We are not sufficiently, from experiment, convinced that these are the proper values; but, following him, if those values be substituted in the equation $h = \frac{1}{2}(24 - w)$, and $w = 24 - 2h$: if the height of a step be 5 inches, its width should be $24 - 10 = 14$ inches, and it must be confessed that experience seems to confirm the theory, for it must be observed, and every person who has built a staircase will know the fact, that the merely

Fig. 999.   Fig. 1000.

reducing the height of the risers without giving a correspondent width of tread to the step is inconvenient and unpleasant.

Sect. XXIV.

CEILINGS.

2815. Economy has worked so great a change in our dwellings, that their ceilings are, of late years, little more than miserable naked surfaces of plaster. This section, therefore, will possess little interest in the eye of speculating builders of the wretched houses erected about the suburbs of the metropolis, and let to unsuspecting tenants at rents usually about three times their actual value. To the student it is more important, inasmuch as a well-designed ceiling is one of the most pleasing features of a room.

2816. There is, perhaps, no type in architecture more strictly useful in the internal distribution of apartments than that derived from timber-framing ; and if the reader has understood our section on floors, he will immediately see that the natural compartments which are formed in the carpentry of a floor are such as suggest panels and ornaments of great variety. Even a single-framed floor with its strutting or wind-pieces between the joists, gives us the hint for a ceiling of coffers capable of producing the happiest effect in the most insignificant room. If the type of timber-framing be applied to the dome or hemispherical ceiling, the interties between the main ribs, diminishing as they approach the summit, form the skeletons of the coffers that impart beauty to the Pantheon of Agrippa. We allude thus to the type to inculcate the principle on which ornamented ceilings are designed, being satisfied that a reference to such type will insure propriety, and bring us back to that

fitness which, in the early part of this Book, we have considered one of the main ingredients of beauty. If the panels of a ceiling be formed with reference to this principle, namely, how they might or could be securely framed in the timbering, the design will be fit for the purpose, and its effect will satisfy the spectator, however unable to account for the pleasure he receives. Whether the architrave be with plain square panels between it and the wall, as in the temples of the Egyptians, or as at a later period decorated with coffers, for instance in the Greek and Roman temple, the principle seems to be the same, and verifies the theory. The writer of the article " Plafond " in the *Encyc. Meth.* has not entered into the subject at much length, nor with the ability displayed in many other parts of that work ; but he especially directs that where a ceiling is to be decorated on the plane surface with painting, the compartments should have reference to the construction. With these preliminary observations, we shall now proceed to the different forms in use. Ceilings are either flat, coved, that is, rising from the walls with a curve, or vaulted. They are sometimes, however, of contours in which one, more, or all of these forms find employment. When a coved ceiling is used, the height of the cove is rarely less than one fifth, and not more than one third the height of the room. This will be mainly dependent on the real height of the room, for if that be low in proportion to its width, the cove must be kept down ; when otherwise, it is advantageous to throw height into the cove, which will make the excess of the height less apparent. If, however, the architect is unrestricted, and the proportions of the room are under his control, the height of the cove should be one quarter of the whole height. In the ceilings of rooms whose figure is that of a parallelogram, the centre part is usually formed into a large flat panel, which is commonly decorated with a flower in the middle. When the cove is used, the division into panels of the ceiling will not bear to be so numerous nor so heavy as when the ceiling appears to rest on the walls at once, but the same sorts of figures may be employed as we shall presently give for other ceilings. If the apartment is to be highly finished, the cove itself may be

Fig. 1001.   Fig. 1002.   Fig. 1003.

Fig. 1004.   Fig. 1005.   Fig. 1006.

decorated with enriched panels, as in the *figs.* 1001, 1002, 1003, 1004, 1005, 1006. In all ceilings it is desirable to raise the centre panel higher than the rest, and the main divisions representing the timbers in flat ceilings should, if possible, fall in the centre of the piers between the windows.

2817. *Fig.* 1007. shows the ceiling of a square room in two ways as given on each side of the dotted line, or it may be considered as representing the ends of a ceiling to a room whose form is that of a parallelogram. The same observation applies to *figs.* 1008. and 1009. The sofites of the beams should in all cases approach the width they would be,

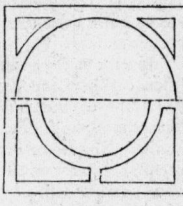
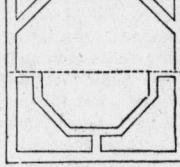
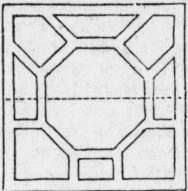

Fig 1007. Fig. 1008. Fig. 1009.

considered as the sofites of architraves of the columns of the order to which the cornice belongs, and they may be decorated with guiloches, as in *fig.* 1010., or with frets. (See the word "Fret" in Glossary.)

Fig. 1010.

2818. In the two following figures (1011. and 1012.) are given four examples of rooms which are parallelograms on the plan, and above each is a section of the compartments.

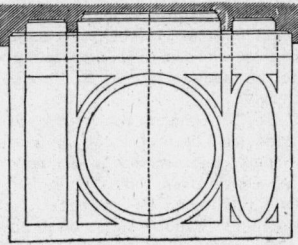

Fig. 1011 Fig. 1012.

2819. As to the proportion of the cornice, it ought in rooms to be perhaps rather less than in halls, salons, and the exterior parts of a building; and if the entablature be taken at a fifth instead of one fourth of the height, and a proportional part of that fifth be taken for the cornice, it cannot be too heavy. Perhaps where columns are introduced it will be better to keep to the usual proportions. Chambers, if followed, would make the proportions still lighter than we have set them down. He says that if the rooms are adorned with an entire order, the entablature should not be more than a sixth of the height nor be less than a seventh in flat-ceiled rooms, and one sixth or one seventh in such as are coved; and that when there are neither columns nor pilasters in the decoration, but an entablature alone, its height should not be above one seventh or eighth of those heights. He further says that in rooms finished with a simple cornice it should not exceed one fifteenth nor be less than one twentieth, and that if the whole entablature be used its height should not be more than one eighth of the upright of the room. In the ceilings of staircases the cornices must be set out on the same principles; indeed in these, and in halls and other large rooms, the whole of the entablature is generally used. In vaulted ceilings and domes the panels are usually decorated with panels similar to those in *figs.* 1001, 1002, 1003, 1004, 1005, 1006., but in their application to domes they of course diminish as they rise towards the eye of the dome. (See 2837.)

Sect. XXV.

PROPORTIONS OF ROOMS.

2820. The use to which rooms are appropriated, and their actual dimensions, are the principal points for consideration in adjusting the proportions of apartments. Abstractedly considered, all figures, from a square to the sesquialteral proportion, may be used for the plan. Many great masters have carried the proportion to a double square on the plan; but except the room be subdivided by a break the height is not easily proportioned to it. This objection does not however apply to long galleries which are not restricted in length,

on which Chambers remarks, " that in this case the extraordinary length renders it impossible for the eye to take in the whole extent at once, and therefore the comparison between the height and length can never be made."

2821. The figure of a room, too, necessarily regulates its height. If a room, for example, be coved, it should be higher than one whose ceiling is entirely flat. When the plan is square and the ceiling flat the height should not be less than four fifths of the side nor more than five sixths; but when it leaves the square and becomes parallelogramic, the height may be equal to the width. Coved rooms, however, when square, should be as high as they are broad; and when parallelograms, their height may be equal to their width, increased from one fifth to one third of the difference between the length and width.

2822. The height of galleries should be at least one and one third of their width, and at the most perhaps one and three fifths. " It is not, however," says Chambers, " always possible to observe these proportions. In dwelling-houses, the height of all the rooms on the same floor is generally the same, though their extent be different; which renders it extremely difficult in large buildings, where there are a great number of different-sized rooms, to proportion all of them well. The usual method, in buildings where beauty and magnificence are preferred to economy, is to raise the halls, salons, and galleries higher than the other rooms, by making them occupy two stories; to make the drawing-rooms or other largest rooms with flat ceilings; to cove the middle-sized ones one third, a quarter, or a fifth of their height, according as it is more or less excessive; and in the smallest apartments, where even the highest coves are not sufficient to render the proportion tolerable, it is usual to contrive mezzanines above them, which afford servants' lodging-rooms, baths, *powdering-rooms*," (now no longer wanted!) " wardrobes, and the like; so much the more convenient as they are near the state apartments, and of private access. The Earl of Leicester's house at Holkham is a masterpiece in this respect, as well as in many others: the distribution of the plan, in particular, deserves much commendation, and does great credit to the memory of Mr. Kent, it being exceedingly well contrived, both for state and convenience."

2823. In this country, the coldness of the climate, with the economy of those who build superadded, have been obstacles to developing the proper proportions of our apartments; and the consequence is, that in England we rarely see magnificence attained in them. We can point out very few rooms whose height is as great as it should be. In Italy, the rules given by Palladio and other masters, judging from their works, seem to be sevenfold in respect of lengths and breadths of rooms, namely, — 1. circular; 2. square; 3. the length equal to the diagonal of the square; 4. length equal to one third more than the square; 5. to the square and a half; 6. to the square and two thirds; or, 7. two squares full. As to the height of chambers, Palladio says they are made either arched or with a plain ceiling: if the latter, the height from the pavement or floor to the joists above ought to be equal to their breadth; and the chambers of the second story must be a sixth part less than them in height. The arched chambers, being those commonly adopted in the principal story, no less on account of their beauty than for the security afforded against fire, if square, are in height to be a third more than their breadth; but when the length exceeds the breadth, the height proportioned to the length and breadth together may be readily found by joining the two lines of the length and breadth into one line, which being bisected, one half will give exactly the height of the arch. Thus, let the room be 12 feet long and 6 feet wide, $\frac{12+6}{2} = 9$ feet the height of the room. Another of Palladio's methods of proportioning the height to the length and breadth is, by making the length, height, and breadth in sesquialteral proportion, that is, by finding a number which has the same ratio to the breadth as the length has to it. This is found by multiplying the length and breadth together, and taking the square root of the product for the height. Thus, supposing the length 9 and the breadth 4, the height of the arch will be $\sqrt{9 \times 4} = 6$, the height required; the number 6 being contained as many times in 9 as 4 is in 6.

2824. The same author gives still another method, as follows: — Let the height be assumed as found by the first rule ($=9$), and the length and breadth, as before, 12 and 6. Multiply the length by the breadth, and divide the product by the height assumed; then $\frac{12 \times 6}{9} = 8$ for the height, which is more than the second rule gives, and less than the first.

CHAP. II.

PRINCIPLES OF PROPORTION.

Sect. I.

GENERAL REMARKS.

2825. In undertaking to point out some of the mechanical methods of obtaining proportions of length, breadth, and height, in plans and elevations, as traceable upon geometric representations of the design, we would recall the reader's attention to the admirable remarks on the true nature of proportion made by the author of this Encyclopædia in Sect. I of the first chapter in this book.

2826. But, however just those remarks may be, they do not, any more than any of the mechanical means, result in success in the building as executed and seen in perspective. The ever varying relation between the sides of a mass, such as a Greek temple, can hardly be supposed to be at every moment equally beautiful in proportion, and the finest mediæval structure equally owes the satisfactory effect which it produces to the spectator's judicious choice of his point of view. Some very judicious observations on the rectification of proportions according to the position of the spectator are given by James Pennethorne, in his *Elements and Mathematical Principles of the Greek Architects*, 8vo., London, 1844.

2827. Before the probable effect in execution of an intended design can be ascertained, the designer must have well mastered the routine of drawing, as explained in the several sections on Drawing, Perspective, and Shadows, given in this work. He should likewise have familiarised himself with the varying effects of the changes resulting from points of view and alteration of light upon some building of which he may have opportunities to make studies in the usual Geometric Drawings (explained 2490a. *et seq.*), so as to become imbued with that sense of general fitness of parts to the whole, which is meant by having the "compasses in one's eye."

2828–2837. The simpler such a building may be, the easier it will be at first to begin to acquire the power of anticipating correctly the effect in a design if it be executed: that power can then be applied to designs of more complicated character resulting from the various methods, which we are about to point out, of obtaining proportions.

Sect. II.

HORIZONTAL AND VERTICAL COMBINATIONS OF BUILDINGS.

2838. The different elements of a building are ranged by the side of or above each other, and in designing an edifice both these combinations must be kept in mind, though in the study of the subject, in order to lighten the labour, they may be separately considered. The two species of disposition are horizontal, as in plans, and vertical, as in sections and elevations.

2839. As respects horizontal disposition of the elements of a fabric, beginning with columns, their distance in the same edifice should be equal, but that distance may be varied as circumstances require. In buildings of small importance, the number is reduced as much as possible, on the score of economy, by increasing the distance between them; but in public buildings they should be introduced in greater number, as contributing to the greater solidity of the edifice by affording a larger number of points of support. They ought not, however, to be at all introduced except for the formation of porticoes, galleries, and the like subdivisions. The least distance at which they can be properly placed from a wall is that which they are apart from one another. This distance, indeed, suits well enough when the columns are moderately wide apart; but when the intercolumniations are small compared with their height and the diameter of the columns, their distance from the walls in porticoes must be increased, otherwise these would be much too narrow for their height, affording shelter neither from the sun's rays nor from the rain. On this account, under such circumstances, they may be set from the walls two or three times the distance between the axes of the columns. From this arrangement will result an agreeable and suitable proportion between the parts.

2840 The ceiling of a portico may be level with the under side of the architrave, or it

may be sunk the depth of the architrave, which may return in a direction towards the walls, thus forming sunk panels in the ceiling, or the sinking of the panels may be as much as the whole height of the entablature, whose mouldings should then be carried round them. When several ranks of columns occur in a portico the central part is sometimes vaulted, the two central columns of the width being omitted. The method of disposing pilasters in respect of their diminution has been treated of in a former part of this work. (2671, *et seq.*)

2841. The exterior walls which enclose the building should run as much as possible in straight continued lines from one angle to another; a straight line being the shortest that can be drawn. The internal walls, which serve for subdividing the building into its several apartments, should, as much as may be, extend from one side to the opposite one. Where they are intercepted by openings, they should be connected again above by lintels or other means.

2842. In *fig.* 1013. is shown the method of forming a plan or horizontal distribution, and combining it with the vertical distribution in the section and elevation. The thing is so simple that it can hardly want explanation. The equidistant parallel axes being drawn and cut at right angles by similarly equidistant ones, the walls, according to the required accommodations, are placed centrally upon the axes; and the columns, pilasters, &c. upon the intersections of the axes. The doors, windows, niches, and the like are then placed centrally in the interaxes, which must be bisected for that purpose. Above and below the horizontal combination the section and plan are to be drawn. These vertical combinations are infinite, and from every plan many sections and elevations may be formed. The figure exhibits a building of one story only, with a central apartment occupying the height of two stories. But on the same plan a building of two or more stories may be designed. These may have two tiers of porticoes, one above the other, or one only on the ground story, forming by its covering a terrace on the first floor; or a portico might receive on its columns the walls of the next story, and thus become recessed from the main front. So, again, the stories may be equal in height, or of different heights, as circumstances may require. The most usual practice is, above a basement to make the succeeding story higher; but above a principal floor the height of succeeding ones is diminished. The method of placing orders above orders does not require that any addition should be made to what has been said on that subject in Chap. I. Sect. 11. of this Book, and by the same methods arcades over arcades may be conducted.

2843. Not the least important of the advantages resulting from the method of designing just submitted to the reader is the certain symmetry it produces, and the prevention, by the use of these interaxal lines on each floor, of the architect falling into the error of false bearings, than which a greater or more dangerous fault cannot be committed, more especially in public buildings. The subterfuge for avoiding the consequence of false bearings is now a resort to cast iron, a material beneficially enough employed in buildings of inferior rank; but in those of the first class, wherein every part should have a proper point of support, it is a practice not to be tolerated. Neither should the student ever lose sight, in respect of the ties he employs in a building, of the admirable observation of Vignola on the ties and chains proposed by Tibaldi, in his design for the baptistery at Milan: "Che le fabbriche non si hanno da sostenere colle stringhe;"—Buildings must not depend on ties for their stability. The foregoing figure is from Durand's *Precis d'Architecture.* We now submit, in *fig.* 1018., an illustration of the principles of interaxal division from the celebrated and exquisite Villa Capra, near Vicenza, by Palladio, wherein it will be seen, on comparing the result with what has actually been executed, how little the design varies from it. It will from this also be seen how entirely and inseparably connected with

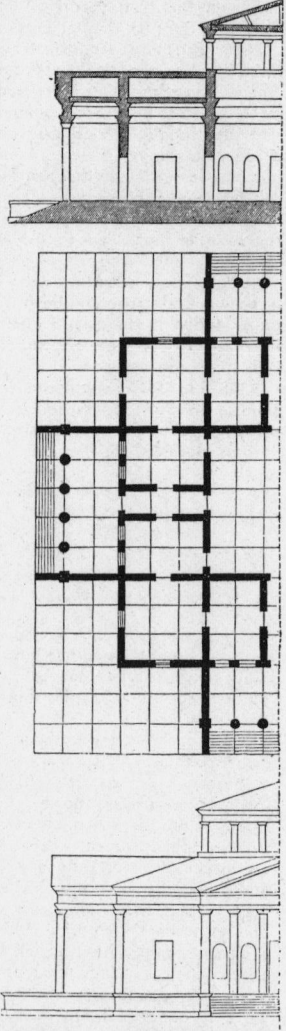

Fig. 1013.

the horizontal are the vertical combinations in the section and elevation, the voids falling over voids, and the
solids over solids.   Whatever the extent of the building, if it is to be regular and symmetrical in its composition, the principles are applicable, and that even in
buildings where no columns are used ; for, supposing
them to exist, and setting out the design as though
they did exist, the design will prove to be well proportioned when they are removed.   The full application of the principles in question will be seen in
the works of Durand, the *Précis* and *Cours d'Architecture*, which we have used freely ; and where we have
had the misfortune to differ from that author, we have
not adopted him.

2844. The student can scarcely conceive the infinite
number of combinations whereof every design is susceptible by the employment of the interaxal system
here brought under his notice ; neither, until he has
tested it in many cases, will he believe the great
mastery in design which he will acquire by its use.
In the temples and other public buildings of the ancients, it requires no argument to prove that it was the
vital principle of their operations, and in the courts,
cavædia, &c. of their private buildings it is sufficiently
obvious that it must have been extensively used.   That
its use in the buildings of those who are called the
Gothic architects of the middle ages was universal, a
glance at them will be sufficient to prove.   The system
of triangles which appears to have had an influence on
the proportions of the early cathedrals may be traced
to the same source (see the early translation of Vitruvius by Cæsar Cesarianus), and indeed, followed up to
that source, would end in the principle contended for.

2845. It is impossible for us to prove that the
interaxal system was that upon which the revivers of
our art produced the astonishing examples many
whereof are exhibited in our First Book ; neither
can we venture to assert that it was that upon which
our great master Palladio designed the example above
given, unquestionably one of his most elegant works ;
but, to say the least of the coincidence which has been
proved between the actual design and the theory upon
which it appears to have been founded, it is a very
curious, and, if not true, a most extraordinary circumstance.   Our belief, however, is, that not only Palladio but the masters preceding him used the system
in question, and that is strengthened by the mode
(not strictly, we allow, analogous) in which Scamozzi,
in the tenth chapter of his third book, directs the
student to adopt in buildings seated on plots of ground
whose sides are irregular.

2846. To Durand, nevertheless, the public is
greatly indebted for the instruction he has imparted
to the student in his *Précis d'Architecture* more especially, and we regret that in our own country the art
is treated by its professors too much in the manner
of a trade, and that the scramble after commissions
has prevented their occupation upon works similar to
those which have engaged the attention of professors
on the continent.   The fault, however, is perhaps not,
after all, so much attributable to them as to a government, whatever the party in power, till within the last

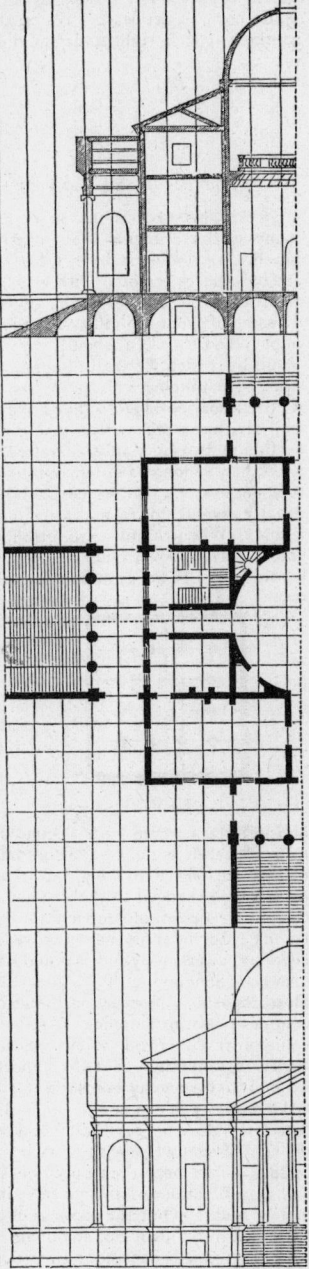

Fig. 1014.

five years (nay perchance even now) totally indifferent to the success of the fine arts, whose
palmy days here were under the reign of the unfortunate Charles.   Our feelings on this subject, and love for our art, betray us perchance too much into expressions unsuitable to the
subject under consideration, and thereon we entreat, therefore, the patience of our readers,
knowing " we have a good conscience."

2847. Our limits preclude the further enlargement on this part of the subject, which in

detail would occupy the pages of a separate work, and which, indeed, from its nature, could not be exhausted. We trust, however, enough has been given to conduct the student on the way to a right understanding of this part of the laws of composition.

Sect. III.

SUBDIVISIONS AND APARTMENTS OF BUILDINGS AND THEIR POINTS OF SUPPORT.

2848. The subdivisions, apartments, or portions whereof a building consists are almost as many as the elements that separately compose them: they may be ranked as porticoes, porches, vestibules, staircases, halls, galleries, salons, chambers, courts, &c. &c. All these are but spaces enclosed with walls, open or covered, but mostly the latter, as the case may require. When covered, the object is accomplished by vaults, floors, terraces, or roofs. In some of them, columns are employed to relieve the bearing of the parts above, or to diminish the thrust of the vaulting. The horizontal forms of these apartments — a general name by which we shall designate them, be their application what it may — are usually squares, parallelograms, polygons, circles, semicircles, &c.; their size, of course, varying with the service whereto they are applied. Some will require only one, two, or three interaxal divisions; others, five, seven, or more. It is only these last in which columns become useful; and to such only, therefore, the system is usefully applied. The parts whereof we speak may belong to either public or private buildings: the former are generally confined to a single story, and are covered by vaults of equal or different spans; the latter have usually several stories, and are almost invariably covered with roofs or flats.

2849. When columns are introduced into any edifice to diminish the action of the vaults and increase the resistance to their thrust, the choice of the species of vault must be well considered. If, for example, the vault of a square apartment (*fig.* 1015.) of five interaxal

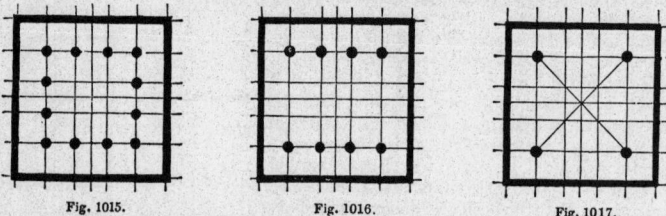

Fig. 1015.   Fig. 1016.   Fig. 1017.

divisions be covered with a quadrangular dome, or, in other words, a quadrantal cove, mitred at each angle, twelve columns would be required for its support. If the vault were cylindrical (*fig.* 1016.) eight columns only would be necessary; but if the form of the covering be changed to the groined arch (*fig.* 1017.), four columns only will be required. Supposing a room of similar form on the plan contained seven interaxal divisions each way, twenty columns must be employed for the coved vault, twelve columns for that whose covering was semi-cylindrical, and still but four for the groined vault. It is obvious, therefore, keeping economy in mind, that the consideration and well weighing of this matter is most important, inasmuch as under ordinary circumstances we find it possible to make four columns perform the office of twelve and even twenty. Here, again, we have proof of the value of the interaxal system, whose combinations, as we have in the previous section observed, are infinite. But the importance of the subject becomes still more interesting when we find that economy is inseparable from that arrangement whose adoption insures stability and symmetry of the parts. These are considerations whereof it is the duty of the architect who values his reputation and character never to lose sight. If honour guide him not, the commission wherewith he is intrusted had better have been handed over to the mere builder, — we mean the respectable builder, who will honestly do his best for his employer.

2850. What occurs in square apartments occurs equally in those that are oblong, for the first or square is but the element of the last. If it happen that from the interaxal divisions contained in the length of an oblong or parallelogram, the subdivisions will not allow of three bays of groins, it does not follow that the arrangement must be defective, for one may be obtained in the middle bay. In subdivisions of width, allowing five interaxes, at least four columns would be saved, and in those of seven interaxes eight columns might be dispensed with. (See *fig.* 1018.)

2851. When the subdivisions on the plan, supposing it not square, take in five interaxes which in the longitudinal extent of the apartment include several bays of groins, whose number must always be odd, one column is sufficient to receive each springing of the arch, but in those of seven interaxal divisions two columns will be necessary. (See *fig.* 1019, A.)

2852. If the vaulting be on a large scale, its weight and thrust are necessarily increased,

and the columns may be changed into pilasters connected with the main walls, as in *fig.* 1020., or as II in the preceding figure.

2853. The height of the apartment from the floor to the springing of the arches will be found three interaxes in apartments whose horizontal combination is of five interaxes, and four and a half for the height to springing of such as are of seven interaxal divisions on the plan. Where the combinations are different in the adjoining apartments the heights just mentioned afford the facility of lighting the larger one above the crown of the lower one, as at B in *fig.* 1019.

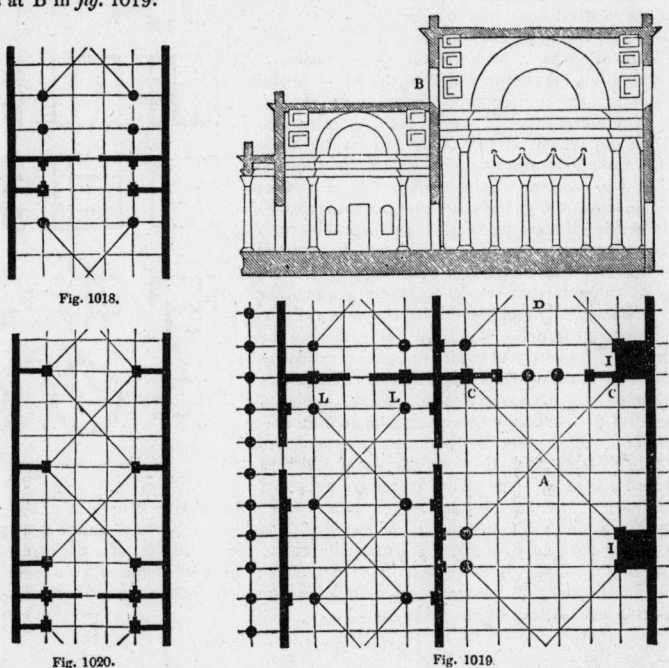

Fig. 1018.

Fig. 1020.   Fig. 1019

2854. Sometimes the springing is from the walls themselves, as at C, *fig.* 1019., instead of from the columns as at L. The first of these arrangements should be permitted only when *en suite* with the apartment there is another, D, wherein the springings are from columns. When the apartment is the last of the suite, the springings must be from piers or columns, one interaxis at least from the wall. If all these matters are well understood, as also the sections upon the orders, and upon the different elementary parts of a building, a graphic combination has been established by which we shall be much aided in the composition or design of all sorts of buildings, and enabled, with little trouble, and in a much shorter period of time than by any other process, to design easily and intelligently. To do more distinguishes the man of genius from the man who can be taught only up to a certain point.

Sect. IV.

COMBINATION OF THE PARTS IN LEADING FORMS.

2855. Having shown the mode whereby the parts of a building are horizontally and vertically combined in the several apartments, which may be considered the grammar of composition, we shall now show its application in the leading forms or great divisions of the plan. Keeping in mind the advantage, upon which we have before touched, of arranging the walls of buildings as much as possible in straight lines, we should also equally endeavour to dispose the principal apartments on the same axes in each direction. Upon first thoughts the student may think that a want of variety will result from such arrangement, but upon proper reflection he will in this respect be soon undeceived. The combinations that may be made of the different principal axes are, as above stated, numberless, that is, of those axes whereon the parts may be advantageously placed so as to suit the various purposes to which the building is destined, paying also due regard to the nature of the ground whereon the fabric is to be erected.

2856. Let us, for example, take a few only of the combinations which may be formed from the simple square, as in the first sixteen diagrams of *fig.* 1021., by dividing it in both directions into two, three, and four parts. The thick lines of the diagrams may be considered as representing either walls or suits of apartments, in which latter case the open spaces between them become courts. In reference also to the vertical combinations connected with the dispositions in question, some parts of them may consist of one, other parts of two and three stories, as well for additional accommodation of the whole building to its purpose as for producing variety of outline in the elevation. If, as in some of the diagrams, we omit some of the axes used for the division, such omissions produce a new series of subdivisions almost to infinity. By this method large edifices may be most advantageously designed; it enables us to apply to the different leading axes the combinations suitable to the destination of the building. Considered however as merely an exercise for the student, the use of it is so valuable that we do not believe any other can be so beneficially employed by those masters who profess to teach the art. We have not gone into the subdivisions of the circle in detail, contenting ourselves with the two most obvious dispositions. These are susceptible of as great variety as the square, observing however that the leading axes must be concentric.

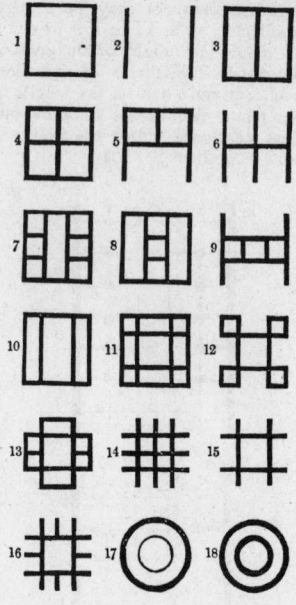

Fig. 1021

2857. Following up the method just proposed, let us imagine a design consisting of a certain number of similar and dissimilar parts placed in certain relations to each other. Now, having fixed clearly in our mind the relative situations of the several parts and the mode by which they are connected with each other, we shall have a distinct perception of the work as a whole. We may abbreviate the expression of a design by a few marks, as in *fig.* 1022., wherein the crosses represent square apartments, and the simple lines are the expressions of parallelograms, whose relative lengths may be expressed by the lengths of the lines. The next step might be to expand these abbreviations into the form given in *fig.* 1023., on which we may indicate by curves and St. Andrew's crosses, as dotted in the diagram, the way in which the several apartments are to be covered.

2858. We may now proceed with the design; but first it will be well to consider one of the apartments, for which let one of the angles B be taken (see *fig.* 1024. and 1025.). Suppose it, for instance, to be five

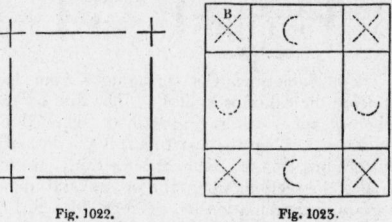

Fig. 1022.　　　　　　　Fig. 1023.

or any other number of interaxal parts square. This, then, will be the width of the apartments whose forms are that of a parallelogram; and inasmuch as in this apartment the diameter of the vault will be diminished by two interaxes, which results from the use of the four angular columns, the groined vault will be of the width of three interaxes, and the same arrangement will govern the rest of the apartments. In the centre an open court is attendant on the disposition, as indicated by the diagram. The section which is the result of the combination, subject however to other regulation in the detail, is given under the plan of the figure, and the elevation above it entirely depends upon, and is regulated by, the joint combination of the plan and section. The example is given in the most general way, and with the desire of initiating the student in the theory of his art. The building here instanced might serve some public purpose, such as a gallery for the reception of painting or sculpture, or at least give the hint for one; but our object is not to be misunderstood, — we seek only to give the tyro an insight into the principles of composition.

2859. It is not our intention to enter further on the variety which follows the method of designing, of which the foregoing are only intended as hints; but we cannot leave the subject without submitting another example for the study of the reader. Our desire is that of establishing general principles, whereof *fig.* 1026. is a more complete illustration than those that have preceded it. The abbreviated form of the horizontal disposition is shown at A, and in B it is further extended, and will be found to be very similar to that of No. 15. in *fig.* 1021. In the example the interaxal divisions are not drawn through the

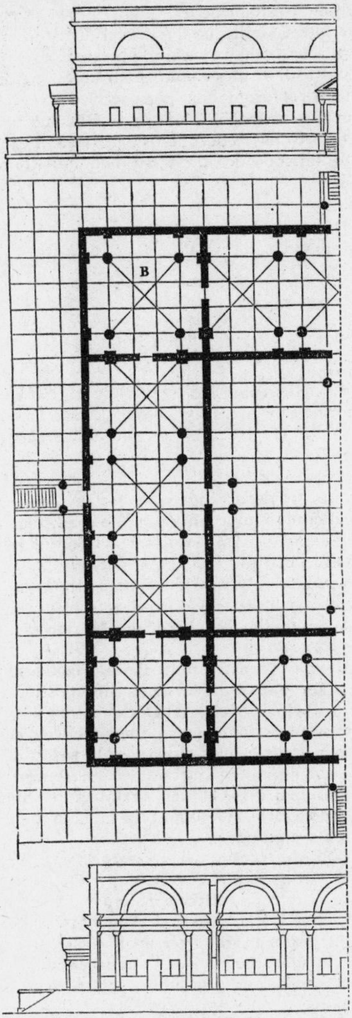

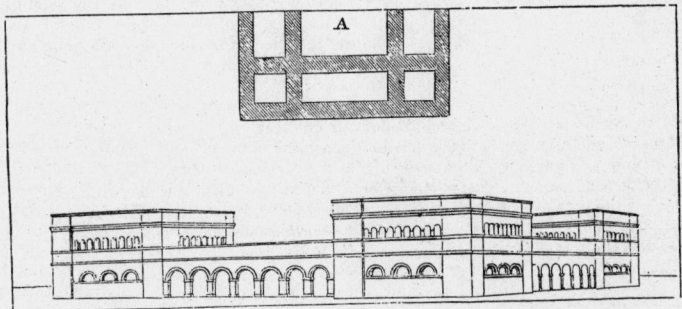

Fig. 1024. 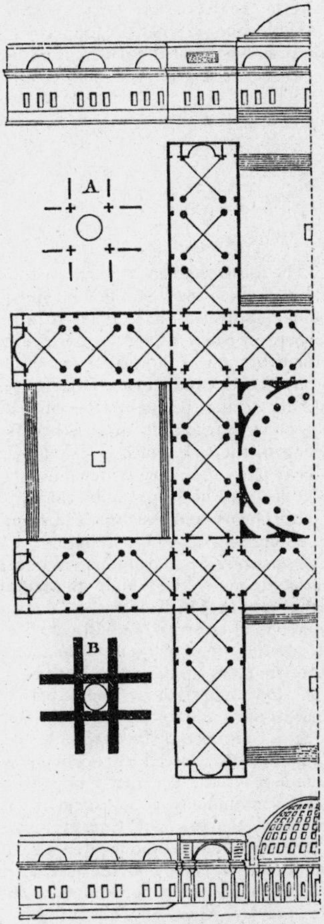   Fig. 1025.

plan, but it will be immediately seen that the space allotted to the whole width of the apartments is three in number.   In the centre a circular apartment is introduced and covered with a dome, which might have been raised, in the vertical combination, another story, and thus have added more majesty to the elevation.   And here we repeat, that in

Fig. 1026.

designing buildings of more than one story, (for it cannot be too often impressed on the mind of the student), the combination of the vertical with the horizontal distribution will suggest an infinite variety of features, which the artist may mould to his fancy, although it must be so restrained as to make it subservient to the rules upon which fitness depends.

2860. We close this portion of the subject with an example in perspective from Durand. The general plan, A, *fig.* 1026., will be found similar to No. 11 in *fig.* 1021., and the distribution may be a good practice for the student to develope.   It is an excellent example for exhibiting of what plastic nature are the buildings which the vertical combinations will admit as based on those which are horizontal.

Sect. V.

GENERAL PRINCIPLES OF PROPORTION.

(The following pages of this section were originally compiled by the late Edward Cresy for his *Encyclopædia of Civil Engineering,* published by Messrs. Longmans, who have now deemed it preferable to place it in this edition of Gwilt's *Encyclopædia of Architecture,* as being in every respect a more suitable place for it.)

That branch of the principles of architecture which is most intimately connected with the architect's practice, the *proportioning of masses,* or the arrangements for the supports of an edifice, must be the objects of his unwearied study and attention.   We shall, therefore, here endeavour to point out, as briefly as possible, the general features which in this respect belong to the two oldest divisions, viz. the Greek, and the Roman, architecture.

That part of Greece which lies to the south of Thessaly, near the foot of Mount Othrys, is supposed to have contained the capital of Hellen, who left his kingdom to his three sons Æolus, Dorus, and Xuthus, the second son becoming the founder of the Dorian race, and the youngest that of the Ionian.

Architecture can hardly be said to have existed as a science until the Dorians perfected that style, which we find in the temples and other buildings scattered throughout those islands and countries in the Mediterranean Sea which received Doric colonies.   The dwellings of these early civilisers of mankind were plain and simple ; the laws of Lycurgus forbade the use of any carving or decoration, their doors being fashioned only with the saw, and their roofs by the axe ; but in their temples and public edifices, they were encouraged to bestow more labour and superior workmanship : the Dorian architecture appears never to have undergone any great change ; the same style, and almost the same proportions, are found in most of the examples that have been spared us.

These people spread a knowledge of the arts of construction wherever they settled ; and we find them at a very early period in the northern districts of Greece, under the Olympian chain of mountains, in the island of Crete, on the eastern side of the northern coast, on which is situated the town of Cnossus with its harbours, Heracleum and Apollonia, at which latter places their religious rites were celebrated.   After having overrun Thessaly, they sent from thence a colony to the district of Driopis, called the Doric Tripolis, between Œta and Parnassus, from the union of the three cities Bæum, Cytinium, and Erineus, and, subsequently, when Acyphas was added, Tetrapolis.

The country next occupied by the Doric tribes extended from the river Sperchius beyond Œta to Parnassus and Thermopylæ, but the most important of their migrations was that called the Return of the Heraclidæ.   After this period they were for a short time driven into Attica, where they received protection from Theseus, and when again settled in the Peloponnesus, they sent out colonies to Rhodes, Cnidus, and Cos, led by princes of the Heraclidæ from Argos and Epidaurus.   Another colony from Trœzen was established at Halicarnassus.   The towns which composed the Tripolis of Rhodes, together with Cnidus, Cos, and Halicarnassus, formed the Doric league called Hexapolis, but after the separation of the latter place, Pentapolis : this league met on the Triapian promontory to celebrate the rites of Apollo and Ceres.   A colony was sent from Lindos to Telos ; others from Cos, Nisyrus and Calydna ; from Argos to Carpathus, now the island of Scapanta ; from Cnidus to Syme, a town of Asia Minor ; from Megara a migration took place, which settled at Astypalea, one of the Cyclades ; and others to Anaphe, Thera, Phalegandros, Melos, Myndus, Mylasa, Cryassa, Synnada, and Noricum in Phrygia.

The Rhodians founded Gagæ, and Corydalla in Lycia, on the shores of Asia Minor ; Phaselis on the confines of that country ; Pamphylia ; and Soli in Cilicia.   According to Thucydides, about 713 years before Christ, Antiphemus led a colony from Lindus, and founded the town of Gela in Sicily.

Corinth sent out numerous colonies from Lechæum in the Cresæan Gulf, which founded Syracuse about 760 years before Christ; Molycrion, Chalcis, towns of Æolia; Salicum in Acarnania; Ambracia and Anactorium in Epirus; Leucadia, now the island of St. Maura, which was formerly joined to the continent by a narrow isthmus; Corcyra, on the coast of Epirus; Epidamnus in Macedonia; Apollonia Potidæa, with several others.

Issa, an island in the Adriatic, was peopled from Syracuse. Megara, situated between Corinth and Athens on the Sinus Saronicus, after it became a part of the territory of the Heraclidæ, sent colonies to Astacus in Bithynia and Chalcedon, another city in that province opposite to Byzantium, Selymbria in Thrace, and Heraclea in Pontus, celebrated for its naval power.

Megara also colonised Hybla in Sicily, famous for its wild thyme and honey, which people founded Selinus. Sparta founded Tarentum about 700 years before Christ, which at one time comprised thirteen tributary cities within its government, and could muster 100,000 foot and 3000 horse.

From Gela, which was colonised from Lindus in the Island of Rhodes, originated Agrigentum, a place of considerable importance at the time the Cretan Phalaris obtained the sovereignty; indeed Crete and Rhodes jointly may be said to be the founders of Agrigentum.

In following the progress of the Heraclidæ along the shores of the Mediterranean to the Pillars of Hercules, we find wherever they settled those beautiful examples of construction in masonry which we can never be weary of admiring and studying. The temples in the Doric style in Sicily are of great beauty, and they may be some years anterior to those now remaining in Greece, but the difference cannot be very great: those at Syracuse and Agrigentum were constructed from the spoils obtained when Hiero defeated the Carthaginian general Hamilcar at Himera, and those at Athens were not built till some time after the defeat of Xerxes; but by some of the historians it is said that both battles were fought on the same day, that whilst Hiero was obtaining his independence, the Persians were overthrown at Salamis. Some time, however, elapsed after these victories before the Athenians and other states of Greece which had been engaged in the war recovered their prosperous condition; and it was not until the time of Pericles, which is nearly 50 years after the building of the temples at Agrigentum and Syracuse, that the restoration of the Parthenon and other public buildings throughout Greece was undertaken. The temples at Selinus are said to have been built when the city was founded, 620 years before Christ, and it is asserted they were entirely destroyed when the inhabitants deserted the city 250 years after its foundation: could this be proved, they would rank among the first erected.

The Propylea at Athens was built by Mnesicles in the 85th Olympiad; and a few years afterwards, when Pericles governed, Ictinus completed the Parthenon, and probably the temple of Theseus. The temples at Sunium and Phygalia were also the work of that renowned architect, and are deservedly ranked for their proportions and execution among the most graceful productions of Greek architecture. The temple of Jupiter Panhellenius in the Island of Egina was founded by Eacus before the Trojan war, but the ruins we now admire no doubt may be referred to the time of Pericles.

The source of those beautiful effects which have received the almost instinctive admiration of every age and country can only be traced by correct measurement, and a careful observation of the proportions of the masses, which will almost irresistibly convince us that in temples and fronts of porticoes one general law prevailed, and was applied to all tetrastyle, hexastyle, and octastyle arrangements, based upon the proportion of a cube. This is found to govern most of the designs executed from the time of Pericles to the death of Alexander, the golden age of Greek art, when sculptors, painters, architects, and engineers were called forth to vie with each other in their several branches, and workmen of skill and ingenuity were found to embody the suggestions of their imagination; and the results would lead us to suppose that the acme of perfection was attained, for since that period none of the productions either in sculpture or architecture have equalled those of the Greeks in the simple elegance of their design, or the excellence of their execution.

Tetrastyle Porticoes with four columns exhibit the simplest, and perhaps the earliest, application of the Doric order; the entire façade is comprised within a square, the height being divided into three portions, the upper constituting the entablature, and the other two-thirds being divided equally between the supports and their three intercolumniations, making the latter a little more than a diameter. We may imagine the square divided in its height and width by 8, making altogether 64 compartments of equal area; the upper 8 devoted to the pediment will have, when the inclined sides are set out, a diminution of one-half their area, four whole squares being rejected in those parts above the pediment, the area of the tympanum being only equal to four. The entire mass is thus reduced to the area of 60 of these squares, which are thus disposed of; 20 are given to the supports, or 5 cubes to each column, 20 are divided between the three intercolumniations, and the remaining 20 constitute the load supported; the columns are 5 diameters in height, and bear no more than their own weight, a due harmony being obtained through-

out ; the eye is satisfied that the load cannot distress its supports, and the spaces between the supporting masses are again proportioned and made equal to either, so that we have a triple division,—one, the perpendicular arrangements of the supports, another their just distribution or equal distances, and the third, the entablature proportioned to the strength that is to carry it, all of which are comprised within the boundary of a square. The tetrastyle porticoes that remain are not numerous, and none are perfect ; three have been selected, which will enable us to test the idea we have attempted to define. First, that at Eleusis, the entire width of which is 20 feet 6 inches, the height 21 feet 6 inches ; and if we reject half the height of the pediment we shall have a square : the united diameter of the columns only varies 5 inches in width from those of the intercolumniations.

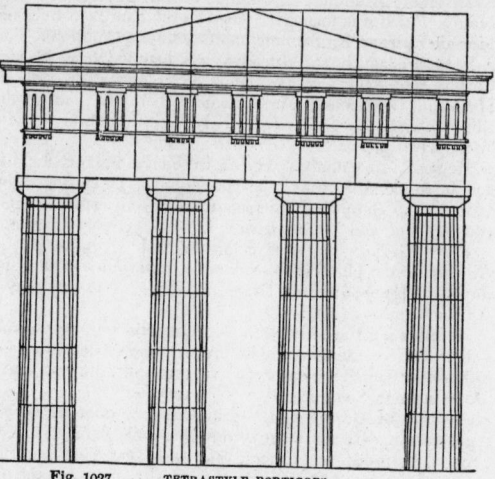

Fig. 1027.   TETRASTYLE PORTICOES.

If we divide the height into three, rejecting, as already observed, half the pediment, which in this case is 1 foot 1½ inch, we have for the height of the square 20 feet 4 inches, whilst the entire width is 20 feet 6 inches, a difference not very great : this divided into three, and giving two-thirds to the height of the columns, would make them only 13 feet 6 inches and 8 seconds, whilst they really are 14 feet 2½ inches in height. In this example the entire height, which we may call 21 feet 5½ inches, is divided into three, two parts of which constitute the height of the columns.

In the Temple of Themis at Rhamnus, the width is 20 feet 11 inches, and the height the same, the diameters of the columns being in excess 3 inches only above the width of the intercolumniations.

In the Doric Portico at Athens, the entire height equals nearly the width.

Hexastyle Porticoes. — The practice of the Dorian architects, in setting out a temple with six columns in front, appears sometimes to have been to divide the width into twelve parts, the height without the pediment being made equal to eight of them ; thus forming a façade within a parallelogram or a square and a half : as the ninth division in height cuts the pediment in half, we have thirty-six squares for the entablature or mass supported, being the same quantity found in the six columns and the five intercolumniations ; at other times we find the entire width divided into nine parts, and six given to the height, one of which indicates the pediment, thus rising a ninth : if a circle be described in the tympanum, and a horizontal line drawn through the centre, cutting off a twelfth of the height, the remaining 11½ being divided into three equal parts, the upper third, or entablature, being the part supported, the remaining ⅔ are divided between the columns and their interspaces ; thus making the columns equal to ⅔ of the height comprised between the centre of the tympanum and the platform upon which they were placed.

If we take each of these nine parts as 5 feet, we have 45 feet for the width, 30 for the height, including the 5 feet for the rise of the pediment, which if we divide by the horizontal line, to obtain its true area or quantity, we shall have 2 feet 6 inches for its mean height, and 6 feet 8 inches for that of the level entablature : for as we have observed, these two dimensions, which make 9 feet 2 inches, must be equal to half the height of the columns, or the whole will not be divided into three parts ; or, which is the same thing, the height from the centre of the pediment must be divided into three parts, and the upper division taken for the entablature. These proportions are exceedingly simple in their application ; if it were intended that the columns and the spaces between them should be equal, half the width of the façade, or 22 feet 6 inches, should be distributed among the intercolumniations, and the other half divided among the columns.

The Temple of Theseus at Athens is one of the best preserved as well as the most admired, and was probably erected soon after the Parthenon ; it is of Pentelican marble, adorned with admirable sculptures. The total width of its hexastyle portico is 45 feet, and its height, instead of 30, is 31 feet ; the extra foot, which prevents it being an exact square and a half, is given to the pediment, which probably has undergone some change, as it rises much more than the ninth of its whole extent.

Fig. 1028.　　　　HEXASTYLE PORTICOES.

	Feet.	In.
The height of the pediment is - - - -	5	9·75
level cornice - - - -	1	0·45
frieze - - - - -	2	8·55
architrave - - - -	2	8·9
columns - - - -	18	8·8
and of the entire façade - - -	31	0·4

	Feet.	In.
half the pediment - - - -	2	10·875
the level entablature - - -	6	5·9
making together a dimension nearly equal to half the height of the } columns.	9	4·775

The façade of this beautiful temple is divided equally into three parts ; ⅓ is given to the entablature, and the other two to the columns and their intercolumniations. The outer columns are 3 feet 4·85 inches in diameter, and all the others 3 feet 3·4 inches. The middle intercolumniation is 5 feet 3·95 inches, the next two each 5 feet 4·05 inches, and those towards the angles 4 feet 6·35 inches. The diameters taken together are 20 feet, and the intercolumniations 25 feet, so that the columns and their spaces are not in equal proportions: the former would have required a diameter of 3 feet 9 inches, which would have made them nearly five diameters in height, instead of what they are; they would have been heavier, it is true, but more in accordance with the early examples.

The *Hexastyle Temples at Rhamnus, Sunium, Egina, Eleusis,* and *Phygalia,* are not sufficiently perfect to enable us to decide whether our principles would apply to them : but from the judgment we can form from their remains, they appear to have been all comprised in a square and a half, and their entablatures and pediments in the proportion of a third of the whole.

The *Hexastyle Temple at Segesta in Sicily* is sufficiently perfect to enable us to judge of its entire proportions.

	Feet.	In.
Its total length is - - - - - -	76	0
and height - - - - - -	50	8

or the whole façade is bounded by a square and a half.

	Feet.	In.
The height of the columns is - - -	31	0
entablature - - -	11	4
pediment - - - -	8	4
Total	50	8

	Feet.	In.
Half the height of the pediment is - - - -	4	2
entablature - - - -	11	4
Total height of superincumbent mass - - -	15	6

which is exactly one-half of 31 feet, the height of the columns; so that we have, as far as height is concerned, $\frac{1}{3}$ for the superincumbent mass or entablature, and $\frac{2}{3}$ for the columns and their intercolumniations.

	Feet.
The columns have their united diameters - - -	37
The intercolumniations ditto - - - - -	39

so that they are not in exact equality, although the difference is not considerable.

At Agrigentum are the remains of four Hexastyle Temples.—That of Juno Lucina is without its cornice and pediment : the diameter of the columns is 4 feet 6 inches, and the entire width is 55 feet. The united diameter of the six columns is 26, and of the five intercolumniations 29 feet.

The Temple of Concord is in width 57 feet, and in height 38 ; or it is comprised within a square and a half.

	Feet.	In.
The height of the columns is - - -	23	0
entablature - - -	8	0
pediment - - -	7	0
	38	0

	Feet.	In
Half the height of the pediment is - - -	3	6
The height of the entablature - - -	8	0
which is equal to half the height of the column -	11	6

Thus one-third of the entire height is given to the entablature or mass supported. The united diameter of the columns is 28 feet, and that of the intercolumniations 29 feet, the latter being a little in excess.

Temple of Hercules.— The total width is 84 feet, and height 56, which is a square and a half.

	Feet.	In.
The height of the columns is - - - -	33	6
entablature - - - -	13	0
pediment - - - -	9	6
Making a total height of - - - -	56	0

The united diameter of the columns is 43 feet, and that of the intercolumniations 41 feet. The height of the entablature and half pediment is in this case 17 feet 9 inches, instead of 16 feet 9 inches, as it should have been to have equalled half the height of the columns.

Temple of Castor and Pollux is imperfect, but the total width is 45 feet, of which the diameters of the six columns occupy 24 feet, and the intercolumniations 21. The height of the columns is about 20 feet, and that of the entablature 8 feet, as measured on the flank. This temple nearly agrees in width with the temple of Theseus at Athens, but its proportions vary ; there is not sufficient remaining to judge of its entire form.

At Selinus are the remains of five hexastyle temples. In one the total extent is 51 feet, of which the united diameters of the columns occupy 24, and that of the five intercolumniations 27 feet. The height of the entablature is about 11 feet, but that of the columns and pediments has not been yet ascertained.

The second temple is in width 77 feet 6 inches, the diameters of the columns occupying 37 feet, and the five intercolumniations 40 feet 6 inches ; the height is 50 feet 8 inches, so that the whole façade is included in a parallelogram, having a height not quite equal to two-thirds its extent, or a square and a half.

	Ft.	In.
The height of the columns is - - - -	29	4
entablature - - - -	13	4
pediment - - - -	8	0
In all - - - -	50	8

which is a foot less than the required height.

In this example there is not an exact correspondence between the columns and what they support : the entablature and pediment occupy 13, the intercolumniation 12, and the

columns 11 parts out of the whole number, 36, into which the parallelogram may be supposed to be divided.

The third temple is not sufficiently measured to enable us to examine into its proportions; the total width is 79 feet, of which the united diameters of the six columns occupy 36 feet, and the five intercolumniations 43 feet.

The fourth temple is in width 84 feet 9 inches, and in height 56 feet 6 inches or a square and a half.

	Feet.	In.
The height of the columns being - - -	34	0
entablature - - -	11	6
pediment - - -	11	0
In all the height is - - -	56	6

	Ft.	In.
The height of half the pediment is - - - -	5	6
the level entablature - - - -	11	6
Making a height equal to half that of the columns, viz. -	17	0

Thus the heights are in just proportion, one-third being given to the entablature and pediment, and the other two-thirds to the columns and their intermediate spaces, which are in the proportions of 44 feet 9 inches for the columns, and 40 feet for the five intercolumniations.

The fifth temple is 81 feet in front, the six columns occupying 37 feet 8 inches, and the five intercolumniations 43 feet 4 inches. The height of the column is 31 feet, and the entablature 15 feet 6 inches, or one-half the height of the column, so that, without the pediment, the entablature in this example would constitute a third; and if the pediment had only risen 7 feet 6 inches, to make the general proportion a square and a half, these columns would have had more to sustain than any other example we have yet referred to.

Octastyle Temples.— We will now apply these principles to a façade with eight columns, and endeavour to follow the same system. We have already had a square, and a square and a half, as the form or figure within which the design was comprised; the portico of four columns being circumscribed by the one, and that of six by the other; and as in the octastyle there are double the number of columns contained in the first, a double square is required to comprise it, that the same relative proportions may be obtained.

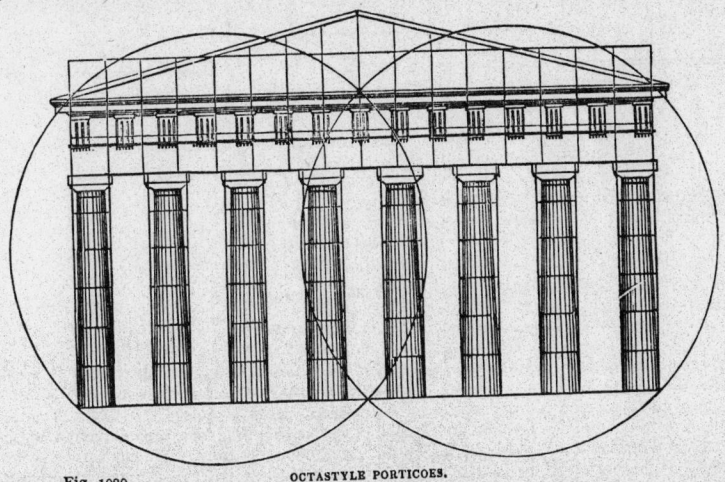

Fig. 1029.　　OCTASTYLE PORTICOES.

After the width of the façade is determined, it is divided into sixteen parts, and ten are set out for the height to the top of the tympanum of the pediment; which generally rising a ninth of the extent, two divisions will serve to denote it, and if a circle be inscribed in the tympanum, and a horizontal line drawn through the centre, we shall have a parallelogram 16 squares in width, and 9 in height.

Six squares in height will determine the under side of the entablature, which, if divided equally between the columns and their intercolumniations, would give 48 squares to each, which are precisely the proportions of the example we are about to examine.

The Parthenon or Temple of Minerva at Athens is admitted to have the most beautiful proportions of all octastyle Greek examples; its entire width, measured in the front of the columns at the base, is 100 feet 9 inches, and its height to the centre of the tympanum, from the level of the platform on which the columns are placed, 51 feet 2½ inches, 20 inches only beyond what it should be to accord with the rules laid down. Dividing this height into three parts, we have in round numbers 17 feet 1 inch for each: the height of the entablature and half pediment is 17 feet, and that of the columns 34 feet 2 inches, precisely one-third of the height being devoted to the entablature, the lower two-thirds being divided between these and their intercolumniations; adding all the diameters together, we have 49 feet 6 inches; the intercolumniations being 51 feet 3 inches, or only 1 foot 9 inches in excess for the latter: hence if a parallelogram or double square be divided into 40¾ squares, and 13½ be given to the columns, the same quantities to the intercolumniations, the entablature and its pediment, we should have the general proportions of the Parthenon, the difference before alluded to being too slight to produce any effect on the eye in so large a mass. The height to the centre of the pediment is 51 feet 2½ inches, consequently the width to make it an exact double square should have been 102 feet 5 inches, instead of 100 feet 9 inches; and this difference may have been occasioned by the difficulty of setting out the triglyphs, or from the idea that the width, as measured along the corona, should have some consideration, and a mean be established.

As we have before observed that the Parthenon is considered perfect both in its design and execution, a more detailed account of its construction and mouldings will be the best illustration that can be offered on the subject of Greek masonry, premising that in the present instance it is all of the finest marble from Pentelicus.

The Doric Column varies considerably in its proportions, some not being more than four diameters in height, whilst in other examples they are from that to six and a half: those we are now considering are formed of twelve blocks; on the upper and lower bed of each are described two circles, the circumference of the outer being 9 inches from the edge, whilst the inner circle is only 20 inches in diameter. The space between these is not polished, but left rough as from the chisel, and a little sunk for the purpose of retaining

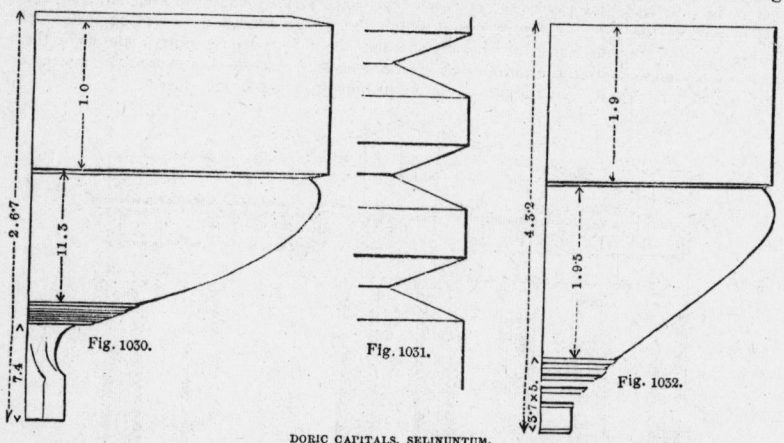

Fig. 1030.   Fig. 1031.   Fig. 1032.

DORIC CAPITALS, SELINUNTUM.

a fine mortar or cement. In the centre of each block is a square hole, measuring 5½ inches on each side, sunk 3 inches in depth; in these were inserted pieces of hard wood, 6 inches in length, to steady the blocks, and keep them from being displaced, particularly at the time the flutes were worked, or the exterior was undergoing the process of polishing. The outer columns are 6 feet 3$\frac{6}{10}$ inches in diameter at bottom, and the others 6 feet 1$\frac{8}{10}$ inch, the upper diameter of the latter being 4 feet 9¾ inches: their total height is 34 feet 2$\frac{8}{10}$ inches, or nearly five diameters and a half; the diminution is not regular, there being at a certain height a swelling or entasis, which improves the outline, and destroys that meagreness which is the result of a straight line. The angular column is a little more in diameter, that it may not appear less than the others, which are not so surrounded by air.

The shafts have generally twenty flutes, uniting in an arris, and not with a square fillet between them, as in the other orders; they are elliptical in some examples, as at Pæstum, where their number is 16 and 24; the heads are variously finished. The capital of this order varies in its height from ½ to ⅔ of the lower diameter of the columns, and the

abacus is sometimes more than ¼ longer than that width, all these proportions depending more upon the height of the column than upon its lower diameter.

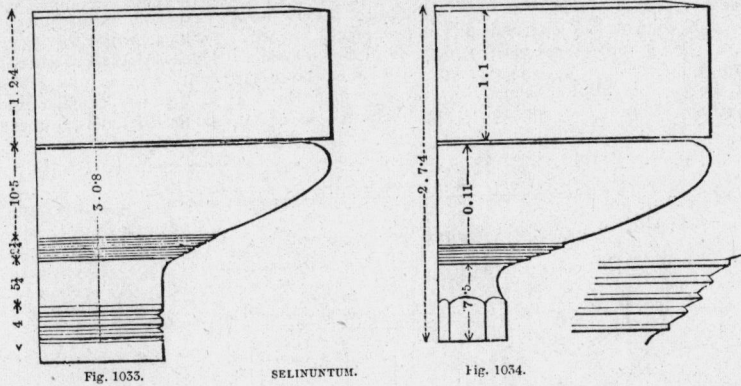

Fig. 1033. SELINUNTUM. Fig. 1034.

Under the abacus is the *echinus* or *ovolo*, which is beautifully turned, or cut like the bell or profile of a flat cup, under which are usually from 3 to 5 annulets. The contour

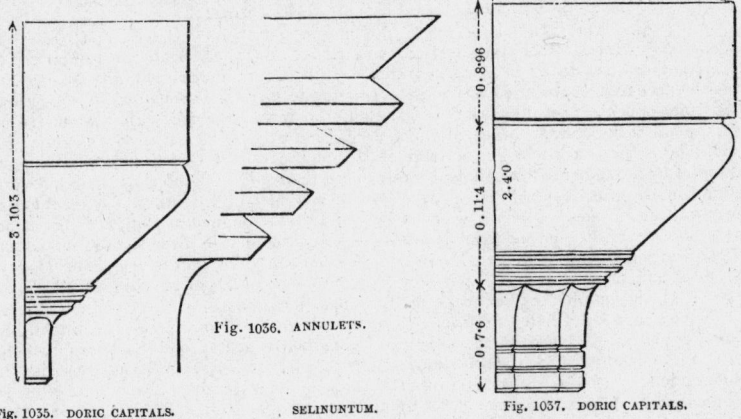

Fig. 1036. ANNULETS.

Fig. 1035. DORIC CAPITALS. SELINUNTUM. Fig. 1037. DORIC CAPITALS.

or profile of the echinus is a portion of a curve formed by the section of a cone. Where the capital is placed on the column is another sinking, and sometimes three; and the true and delicate manner in which these lines are cut gives a charm that more elaborate sculpture fails in attaining.

The architrave of the Parthenon, which extends from the centre of one column to that of the other, is in three thicknesses, showing two joints on the soffite. The frieze is admirably contrived not to overload the architrave : the triglyphs are each in a single block, 3 feet wide and 2 feet 3 inches in thickness. On each side is a perpendicular groove 1½ inch deep, into which the sculptured metopes are slipped, the clear width between the triglyphs being 4 feet 3¹⁵⁄₁₀₀ inches, and the angular one 3 inches less : at the back of the metopes, and between the triglyphs, is a hollow space, from 8 to 14 inches deep. The metope is held to the back of the frieze by a metal cramp in the form of an H, 2 feet long, and attached on each side to the adjoining triglyph by others 17 inches in length. The cornice is in one thickness; the angular block covers two mutules, each of the others one space and a mutule. For further particulars of the construction of the Parthenon, and for several dimensions omitted by Stuart, the writer must refer to some notes he added a few years after his return from Athens to his wife's (Mrs. Cresy) translation of " The Lives of celebrated Architects, ancient and modern, by Francesco Milizia," 2 vols. 8vo. 1826.

In the Doric Order we may trace a reason for the direction given to the several lines, whether perpendicular or horizontal; and although there is great variety in the form of the members, yet when examined in detail, nothing will be found to disturb the unity

of the design. The voids are nicely adjusted to the solids, and all those parts, as the columns and triglyphs, intended as supports, are striated perpendicularly, whilst those supported are decorated with members and mouldings running horizontally, and indicating rest or repose. The inclined lines of the pediment are the only exception to this rule, and they are composed of longitudinal members, placed consistently with their use, viz. that of throwing off the water from the roof: so well-combined a whole, consisting of parts all expressing their utility, deserves our admiration: even the annulets under the echinus of the capital indicate so many cinctures to bind the tops of the perpendicular flutes together, before the elegant tazza or cup-like vase is placed between the shaft and the abacus.

Fig. 1058.　　IONIC CAPITAL.

Ionic Proportions. — This style seems very nearly coeval with the Doric: it is supposed by some commentators to be of Achaic origin, by others of Persian; both Greeks and Persians may have contributed to its formation; the term Ionic was applied to it by Vitruvius, from its being first used by the inhabitants of Ionia; the few perfect examples remaining are of the greatest beauty, both in design and execution.

The shores of Asia Minor, in the reign of Medon, the son of Codrus, were taken possession of by a number of Greeks, who commenced their migration about a thousand years before Christ; after they had passed from Attica, they first mixed with the inhabitants of Caria and the Leleges. Helen the son of Deucalion, who reigned in Phthia, situated between the rivers Peneus and Asopus, having left his kingdom to his eldest son, the others sought for settlements elsewhere: Dorus established himself in the neighbourhood of Parnassus and Xuthus in Attica, where he married the daughter of Erechtheus, the sovereign of Athens, and had by her two sons Achæus and Io.

Io with a number of followers from Athens went into the Peloponnesus and established himself at Ægialus, a place on the sea-shore lying between Elis and Sicyonia; here he married the daughter of Selinuntus, king of that district, at whose death he succeeded to his dominions; Io built Helice, and called the inhabitants Ionians. Some time after Io was recalled to Athens to command the troops in a war against the Thracians, over whom he obtained a victory: the Athenians in consequence designated themselves Ionians. Attica was divided by Io among four tribes, the Geleontes, the Argades, the Ægicores, and the Hopletes, the names of his four sons, or according to Strabo, labourers, artisans, priests, and guards.

When Erechtheus died, Cecrops, his eldest son, succeeded, and Xuthus, his other son, was driven out of Attica; in the country he afterwards inhabited he built four towns, Œnoe, Marathon, Probalinthus, and Tricorythus, after which he died at Ægialus; his son Achæus then passed into Laconia and Thessaly, when he recovered his father's dominions; his two sons Archandar and Architeles went into Argos, where they married two daughters of Danaus, one of the royal family of Argos. The Lacedæmonians and Ægeans were called after Achæus Achæans, until the return of the Heraclidæ, when they were driven out, and obliged to flee to Ægialus and into Attica, where the Ionians again received them on account of their common origin.

At the death of Codrus, his youngest son Nileus embarked with all the Ionians into Asia, where they occupied eight of the Ionian cities, viz. Miletus, Ephesus, Myus, Teos, Priene, Lebedos, Erythræ, and Clazomene; the other four founded by the Ionians were Colophon, Phocæa, Samos, and Chios. The Ionians formed themselves into twelve states, because, according to Herodotus, they were previously so divided in the Peloponnesus; the names of the cities from whence they were ejected were Pellene near Sicyon, Ægira and Ægæ, Bura, Helice, Ægium, Rypæ, Patræ, Pharæ, Olenus, Dyme and Tritæa, the last being an island.

The inhabitants of Athens who migrated from the Prytaneum were the most noble

among the Ionians, though all who celebrated the Aplurian festival, from which alone the Ephesian and Colophonians were excluded, were afterwards called Ionians.

The appellations Doric, Ionic, and Corinthian are derived from Vitruvius: but it appears doubtful whether these terms were current among the Greeks: that author asserts that the first is the most ancient; "for Dorus, the son of Hellen, and the nymph Orseis, built the temple of Juno at Argos of this order when he reigned over the whole of Achaia and Peloponnesus: that many temples afterwards erected throughout Greece were of the Doric order, but by command of the Delphic oracle in a general assembly of the different states of Greece, thirteen colonies were sent into Asia, who built the cities before mentioned, and erected temples; among the first they dedicated was one to Apollo Panionios, having Doric proportions, and another to Diana, in which some variations was made. The first was of a masculine proportion, the other feminine, and the latter was the invention of the Ionian settlers, and afterwards called from them Ionic.

But if it be difficult to trace the Ionic order to its origin, we may analyse its proportions, and compare them with that order which prevailed so universally in Greece, which will lead us to remark that a very great change took place when the rules that guided the Doric builders were laid aside: at no other period were such material alterations made in the proportions of the masses, the columns, entablatures, and intercolumniations; to the Corinthian, so universally used in later times by the Romans, the feminine proportions were applied which are stated by Vitruvius to have commenced with the Ionians.

There is of course much fable in all the accounts that have reached us upon these important changes, but among them is one which seems to carry with it some semblance of truth, and which is as follows:—"when Hermogenes was employed to erect the temple of Bacchus at Teos, according to Vitruvius, the marble was prepared for one in the Doric style; but the architect changed his mind, from the idea that other proportions, afterwards called Ionic, were more suitable for the purpose, almost inducing the inference that Hermogenes was the inventor of those delicate proportions; he appears unquestionably to have displayed great skill and ingenuity in all his designs, and to have entertained the opinion that sacred buildings should not be constructed with Doric proportions, as they obliged the adoption of false and incongruous arrangements."

To obtain more delicate proportions, without sacrificing the great principle of making the weight supported equal to its supports, would seem at first difficult: in the example of the Doric order we have seen this practice universally adopted, and it is equally evident in the Ionic, though not exactly after the same method; the columns and their entablatures, or what they carry, agree in quantity, but their distribution is different. The square or figure which bounds the Ionic façade is divided into four parts, one of which is given to the entablature, a second to the columns, and the other two, or one half, are distributed among the intercolumniations.

In the quantity of material for constructing the two varieties of temples there is a considerable difference, the Doric requiring one-third more than the Ionic; for example, in a Doric tetrastyle portico where the area was 12, four parts would be given to the entablature, four to the columns, and four to the intercolumniations. In the Ionic three parts would be required for the entablatures, and three for the columns, six being allowed for the intercolumniations; thus one temple would have eight, and the other six parts solid out of twelve, consequently, with a given quantity of materials, two very different porticoes might be built, without making any change in the proportions which the columns bear to their entablatures. Hermogenes could construct with the same material a much larger temple in the Ionic style than in the Doric; and supposing the dimensions already decided upon, there would be a saving of labour and material: from the imperfect state of the Ionic temples remaining, it is scarcely possible to enter into a thorough examination of their proportions; that on the Ilissus at Athens, measured by Stuart, no longer exists, but its dimensions, given by that very accurate delineator, may serve our purpose as an example of a tetrastyle portico. Its entire width was 18 feet 7¾ inches, and height to the top of the level cornice in front 18 feet 4⅔ inches, to which must be added that of the tympanum of the pediment: multiplying the width by the height of the entablature and half the pediment, which together is 5 feet 7 inches and 10 parts, we have for the area of the portions supported 105 feet 4 inches and 9 parts: the quantity contained in the four columns is found by multiplying their united diameters, 7 feet 1 inch and 7 parts, with their height, 14 feet 9 inches and 4 parts, giving a product of 105 feet 4 inches and 9 parts as their area. The united intercolumniations in this example are 11 feet 6 inches and 2 parts, which multiplied by the height of the columns is 170 feet 1 inch and 9 parts for the area; 40 feet 7 inches and 9 parts less than it would have been had it equalled the quantity contained in the columns and their entablature, or been one-half the entire area of the façade.

The portico of this elegant example of Ionic was nearly a square without the pediment, and the supports and supported are in exact accordance as to quantity, whilst the intercolumniations are about 1¾ times the quantity contained in the columns, instead of double. Departing a little from the proportions before us, let us endeavour to set out a

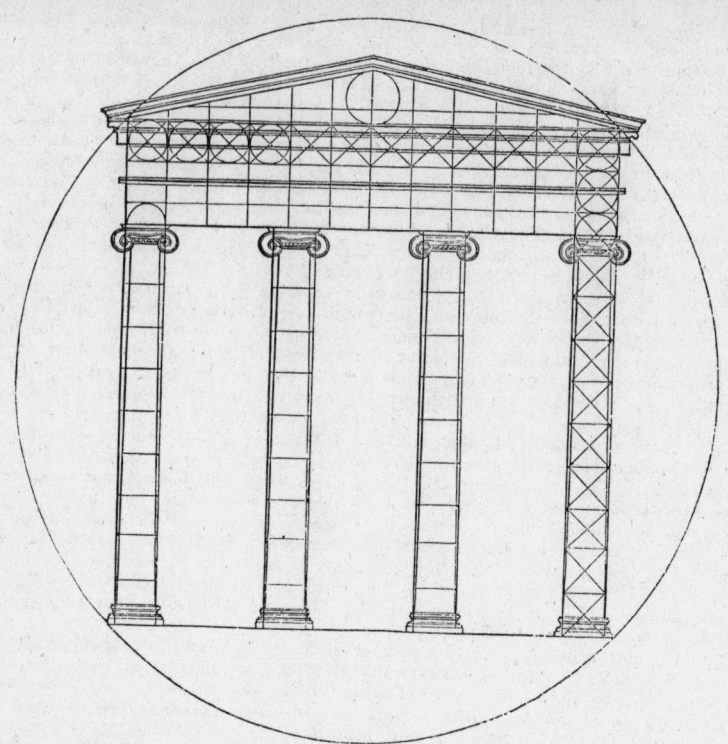

Fig. 1059. IONIC TETRASTYLE TEMPLES.

portico, as already done for the Doric order, having the same number of columns, and like the tetrastyle eustyle of Vitruvius, divide each side of the square which circumscribes it into 11¼ parts, premising that the pediment rises a ninth and one side of the square passes through its centre. The side of the square being divided into 11¼ parts, 1 is given to the diameter of the columns, 3 parts to the middle intercolumniation, and 2¼ to each of the others; thus the sites for the columns are obtained: dividing the upright sides of the square into the same number of parts, 8¼ are given to the height of the column, and the remaining 3 to the entablature and half pediment.

Multiplying 11¼ by the same, we have for the entire area 132¼, which if divided into 4 is 33 and a fraction for the columns, the same for the entablatures, and double that for the intercolumniations: the columns being four in number and 8¼ diameters in height, their area will be 34 parts; the intercolumniations being 7½ in their united width, that multiplied by 8¼, their height, gives 63¾ for their area, and the entablature being 3 high and 11¼ in width, we have for its contents 34¼ parts, giving a result of nearly a fourth for the entablature as well as for the columns, and a half for the intercolumniations. By making some allowance for the diminution of the columns, an exact agreement between the quantities might be obtained; those in the intercolumniations would then be found equal to those in the entablature and its supports, or half the entire square devoted to solid and the other half to voids: had the columns of the temple on the Ilissus been about 1 inch less in diameter, its proportions would have been in close accordance with those of the figure, where the 4 columns occupy 38 squares, the entablature the same number, and the intercolumniations 76.

Ionic Hexastyle. Temple of Erechtheus at Athens.—This highly-enriched example, executed in the finest marble, is in height without the pediment 26 feet 6¾ inches, and in width, measured along the front of the corona, 40 feet 6 inches, so that this portion is comprised within a square and a half or nearly so: the lower diameter of the columns is 2 feet 3⁵⁄₁₀ inches, and the upper 1 foot 11⁷⁄₁₀ inches, giving a mean of 2 feet 1⁵⁄₁₀ inches; their collected diameters are 12 feet 9 inches, whilst that of the intercolumniations at the same level is 23 feet 1⁵⁄₁₀ inches, nearly double the space occupied by the columns. The height of the entablature without the pediment is 4 feet 11¼ inches, and its superficial content on the face 190 feet, and adding 85 feet for the area of the tympanum, we have altogether 275 feet.

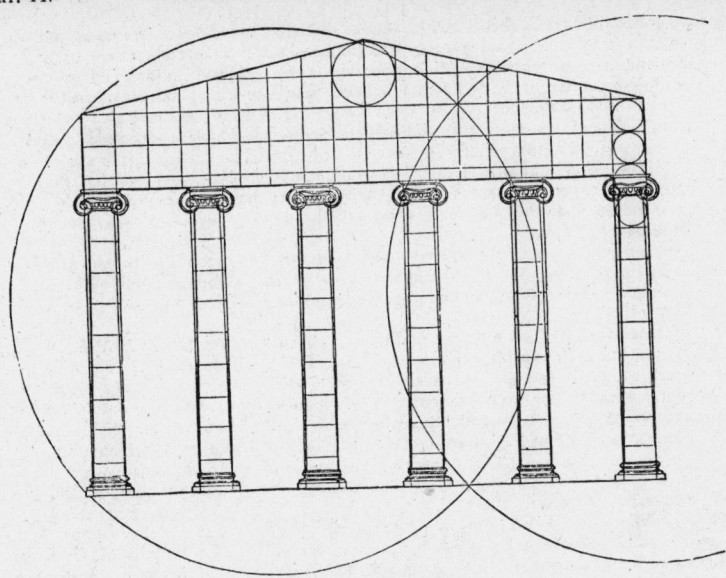

Fig. 1040.

IONIC HEXASTYLE TEMPLES.

supposing the tympanum to rise a ninth of its base; the height of the columns is 21 feet
7¼ inches, and their united mean diameter 12 feet 9 inches, which being multiplied together
produce 275 feet 8 inches, or nearly equivalent to the area of the mass they support. To
obtain the exact quantity of mass and void, the mean diameters of the columns as well
as of the intercolumniations should be taken; the greater the probable delicacy of execution, the greater is the necessity for the architect to balance his quantities exactly. In
the subject now under consideration the whole is comprised within a square and a half; the
supports and the entablature are equal, and the intercolumniations as much as the two together or one-half the whole.   The height of the architrave is 2 feet $1\frac{5}{100}$ inches; that
of the frieze 1 foot $11\frac{3}{4}$ inches, and the level part of the cornice $10\frac{45}{100}$ inches.

Roman Tetrastyle.   Ionic Temple of Fortuna Virilis.—The width is 33 feet 6 inches, and
height, including half the pediment, 37 feet 1 inch, comprising an area of 1242 feet 4 inches,
one quarter of which, 313 feet 1 inch, nearly agrees with the quantity contained in the
entablature as well as in the columns which support it; their height is 27 feet, and their
united diameters 12 feet 4 inches, which multiplied together produce 333 feet for the area of
the supports.   The height of the entablature with half the pediment is 10 feet 1 inch: this
multiplied by its width, 33 feet 6 inches, gives 337 feet 10 inches for the area of that supported:
the intercolumniations are together 21 feet 2 inches, which multiplied by their height, 27 feet,
gives 571 feet 6 inches for their area, about 100 feet less than the quantity comprised in
the columns and entablature.

Without the pediment this façade is nearly square; its proportions rank very high in
the estimation of all admirers of Roman architecture; it has, however, undergone many reparations before the stucco was put upon the columns; they were lighter, as was the entablature, the upper members of the cornice being somewhat heavier than is usual in the
early examples of this order; if divested of these additions, and giving a trifle more to the
intercolumniations, we shall obtain half the area for the columns, and a quarter for each of
the other divisions; at present the columns equal in quantity the mass they carry.

If it be required to draw a tetrastyle portico in exact accordance with the rules laid
down, after forming the square each side should be divided into 12 parts, or 144 squares,
arranged like those of an abacus: one of these divisions on the base would become the diameter of the column, and nine their height, the other eight on the base would be devoted to
the intercolumniations, and the upper three of the height to the entablature. The columns, 9
diameters in height, would thus comprise 36 squares, the intercolumniations 72, and the
entablature and half pediment 36; consequently the columns and entablature would be
equal in quantity, and the intercolumniations half the whole, or equal to the contents of
the supports and supported.

Roman Hexastyle.   Corinthian, Maison Carrée at Nismes. — This beautiful temple has
undergone several restorations; its entire width and height to the apex of the pediment is
43 feet 8 inches, from whence it has derived its name.   The height of the columns, includ-

ing base and capital, is 29 feet 6 inches, that of the entablature 6 feet 9 inches, and of the pediment 7 feet 5 inches ; taking away half the height of the pediment, we have 39 feet 11 inches and 6 parts, which may be considered as 40 feet ; this multiplied by the width produces for the entire area 1746 feet 8 inches.   The superficial content of pediment and entablature, 456 feet 8 inches, is obtained by multiplying the entire width by 10 feet 5½ inches, the height of the entablature and half the pediment, which superficies is only 20 feet 2 inches more than a quarter of the whole.   The united diameter of the six columns is 17 feet 6 inches, and that of the intercolumniations 26 feet 2 inches, so that they are in the proportions to each other of 2 and 3, the whole being 5, one having an area of 515 feet 9 inches, the other 772 feet ; when added together they are nearly three times the area of the part supported.

The proportion between the columns and intercolumniations of the temple at Assissi is also similar, the height of the columns is 32 feet 10 inches, and the total width of the six 52 feet, which dimensions multiplied together produce 1707 feet 4 inches, one-fifth being 341 feet 6 inches nearly.

The area of the columns is 684 feet, and that of the intercolumniations 1023 feet 4 inches, giving a proportion of two-fifths and three-fifths.   The entablature, pediment, and pedestals upon which the columns are placed seem to have undergone a change since their erection. If the whole extent of an hexastyle portico be divided into 18 parts, and one be called the diameter, to obtain the same proportions as those laid down for a tetrastyle portico, the height up to the centre of the pediment must include 12 only of those parts, which would give a portico of a square and a half, comprising 216 squares ; the 6 columns, each 9 diameters in height, would require 54 ; the 5 intercolumniations, double that number, or 108, and the entablature and half pediment 54.

Roman Octastyle. — The Pantheon at Rome, which has a portico of 8 columns, is one of the best examples that can be selected for examination.   The total width is 109 feet 10 inches ; the diameters of the eight columns 39 feet 5 inches, and the seven intercolumniations 70 feet 5 inches, or nearly in the proportion of 1 to 2.   The height of the columns is 46 feet 5 inches, and that of the entablature and half pediment 23 feet 2½ inches, together 69 feet 7½ inches, nearly a square and a half, the area of which is 7647 feet 2 inches.

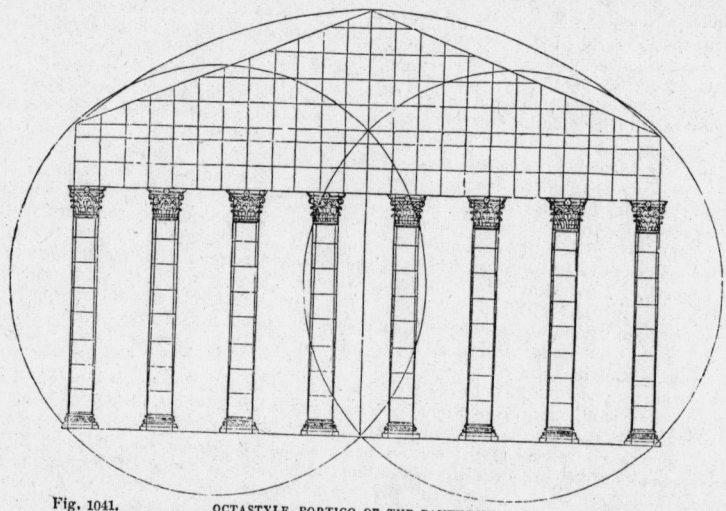

Fig. 1041.   OCTASTYLE PORTICO OF THE PANTHEON.

The united diameter of the columns, 39 feet 5 inches, multiplied by their height, gives 1829 feet 7 inches, and the collected intercolumniations multiplied by the same height will be 3268 feet 6 inches : multiplying 109 feet 10 inches by 23 feet 2½ inches, we obtain for the area of the entablature and pediment 2549 feet, which, rejecting parts of an inch, will, when added to the two other calculations, make up a sum agreeing with the entire area.

			Feet.
The supported is	-	-	2549
The area of columns	-	1829·7 ⎤	
of intercolumniations	-	3268·6 ⎦	5098
Together	-	-	7647

A line drawn through the centre of the pediment, another at half the height of the columns, and a third under the entablature, would divide the height into three equal portions, proving that, in this example, the Romans made the part supported one-third of the whole, and divided the other two between the columns and their intercolumniations. The shaft of each column is cut out of a single block of granite ; they are not sufficiently delicate to be exactly in the proportion of half the quantity contained in the intercolumniations ; but if allowance be made for their diminution, the difference is not very great. The whole width being 109 feet 10 inches, the third, 36 feet 7 inches and 4 parts, is nearly a mean between the collected diameters of the top and bottom of the shaft, making the intercolumniations double the quantity contained in the supports, or equal to that of the supports added to the mass they·carry. The whole would then be divided into four, as in the previous examples of the Ionic, and two portions given to the intercolumniations.

The Pantheon Portico is a double square without the pediment, or nearly so, the length of the level cornice, which crowns the entablature, being double the height of the order : this, no doubt, was the outline of the proportions before the heavy pediment was placed upon it, which in all probability was heightened beyond the ordinary rise of a ninth, for the purpose of concealing the wall behind it. The Roman proportions are frequently made independently of the pediment ; the tetrastyle porticoes are a square, the hexastyle a square and a half, and the octastyle, as in this instance, a double square without it.

To set out an octastyle portico, in which half the pediment should be comprised within the double square, after dividing the width into 24 and the height into 12, which multi-plied produce 288 squares, 72 are given to the column, the same to the entablature and half pediment, and double that, or 144, to the intercolumnations, or proportions similar to those laid down for the tetrastyle and hexastyle porticoes. The columns in such a case would be nine diameters in height, the entablature and half pediment three : supposing the latter to rise a ninth of the span, the remainder would be distributed among architrave, frieze, and cornice.

We have endeavoured to show the proportions required in a tetrastyle, hexastyle, and octastyle portico among the Dorians, the Ionians, and their followers the Romans : the square and a half, or the double square, were the outlines or boundary figures from whence the other proportions were deduced.

The great difference of character in the Doric and Ionic designs arises from the distance at which the columns are placed, which affects the proportions of the entablature laid upon them, as well as that of the columns themselves ; where these are six diameters in height or consist of six cubes, they are made to carry the same quantity, whatever may be their distance apart, and where drawn out to nine diameters, they have only their own weight to support ; but the form given to this weight, or the proportions of architrave, frieze, and cornice, vary, as the intercolumniations are of one or more diameters.

It has been too generally considered that the orders derived their proportions from the lower diameter of the columns, without reference to their application : this has produced a variety of design, but at the same time occasioned a great departure from the true principles, and led to very important errors. The Tuscan, the Doric, the Ionic, the Corinthian, and Composite orders have been laid down in modules or measures of various kinds, which the young architect has adopted as mere isolations, regardless of the many other considerations which have stamped beauty on his model ; hence we have imitations, but soul is wanting.

The Doric order is treated of as so many diameters in height according to its age, and the entablature is said to be heavy or light, as it was of early or late execution ; the other orders have been chronicled in a similar manner, and architecture has been fettered, and its great principles lost, or at least neglected : it is true that the outline which bounds the figure has undergone but few changes, but the subordinate parts or the filling-in are sus-ceptible of interminable variety. An object inscribed within a circle is perhaps the most easily compassed by the eye, next that within the square, and when a building is vast, and distance is necessary to comprise a view of the whole, the double square ; beyond this the ancients seem seldom to have gone for the proportions of their façades, or of a portico intended to be seen in front. After the masses were proportioned, their de-corations were more various than the buildings themselves ; no two are perfectly alike, but the great difference is in their ornaments and enrichments, or in the number of diameters contained in the height of the columns.

The Parthenon and Pantheon porticoes are both octastyle, each admitted to be as beau-tiful as they can be — one the perfection of sober grandeur, the other of cheerful lightness ; one Greek Doric, the other Corinthian, both comprised within a double square, and having their columns equal in quantity to the mass of entablature they support : where, then, is the difference between the two examples? It results, as we have already seen, from the mate-rial in the one occupying two-thirds, and in the other only half the entire area. In the façade of the Parthenon the eye has one-third void only to contrast with the solid matter, and in the Pantheon half, which proportions seem to have been established by the Ionians, and usually adopted by the Romans.

In proportioning the architrave, frieze, and cornice, care must be taken that no more is laid upon the columns than their own bulk: when the latter are one diameter apart, this quantity will be greater in height than when they are further distant; so that the greater the intercolumniation, the lighter in appearance will be the entablature, the columns still bearing the same weight, nor need they be increased after it is ascertained that they are competent to their duty: to do so would be to employ material in excess, which it should be the aim of an architect to avoid.

If we now examine the portico of the Pantheon, we cannot fail to perceive the agreement existing between the parts supported and their supports.

						ft.	in.
The mean diameter of the columns is	-	-	-	-	-	4	7
Their height, including capital and base	-	-	-	-	-	46	5
The solid content of each	-	-	-	-	-	765	10·6
Consequently the cube of the whole 8 is	-	-	-	-	-	6027	0

						ft.	in.
The mean width of the architrave and frieze is	-	-	-	-	-	4	3
Their height	-	-	-	-	-	-	6	8·3

The solid contents of the entire length, 110 feet, is	-	-	-	3125	11
The mean width of the cornice is 7 feet, length 114 feet, height 3·6 feet, and its cubical contents	-	-	-	-	-	2793	0

The solid content of entablature   5918   11

which leaves little more than 100 cubical feet of difference between one and the other; and if the crown moulding returned on the flank be comprised, the quantity contained in the entablature would equal that of the eight columns.

The pediment is omitted altogether in this calculation, it being in reality, though not in appearance, an additional load for the eight columns beyond their regular entablature, which is of marble, and weighs probably 452 tons; the granite columns with their marble bases and capitals are something more than that quantity, and these, including the entablature and pediment, probably contain upwards of 1000 tons of material.

The Capitals of the Columns of the Pantheon are admitted to rank among the best examples found in Rome: though not so highly and elaborately worked as those which decorate the columns of the temple of Jupiter Stator, yet they are remarkable for the elegant

Fig. 1042.   CAPITALS OF THE PANTHEON.

arrangement of the ornaments : further details will be found in the Architectural Antiquities of Rome, whence this has been selected.

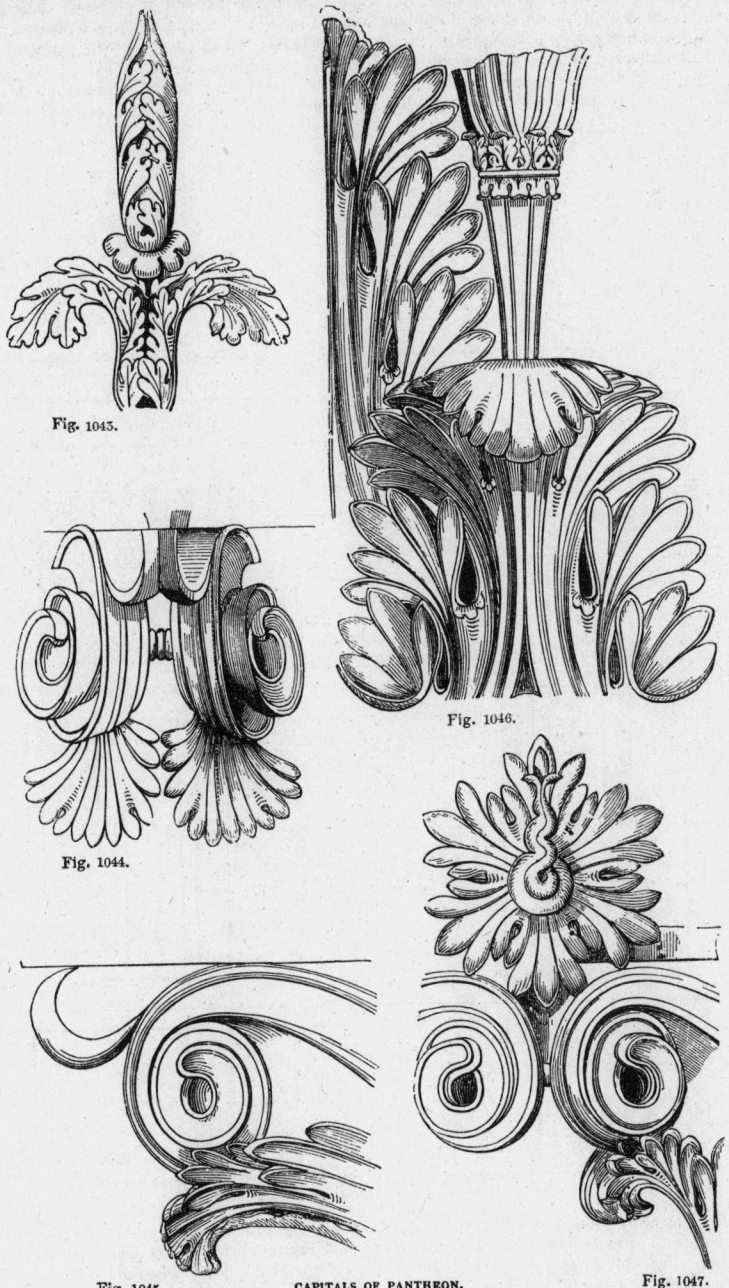

Fig. 1043.

Fig. 1046.

Fig. 1044.

Fig. 1045.　　　CAPITALS OF PANTHEON.　　　Fig. 1047.

Although the Romans did not improve the arts which the Greeks had spread among them, by the introduction of the arch they materially altered the character of the architecture practised before the time of the Republic: this feature alone produced entirely

different construction, and the several changes it has since undergone in form have served
to establish a variety of styles, as we shall afterwards find.

Sewers, aqueducts, bridges, theatres, amphitheatres, baths and triumphal arches, all
exhibit the arch in its most useful application, and as did the halls of the baths vaulting
of stupendous span; the dome of the Pantheon being 142 feet 6 inches in diameter internally, covered by a hemispherical dome.

Symmetry, as understood by Vitruvius, seems to relate more to the proportions of the
façade than to those of the detail; but he doubtless intended it to be understood that

Fig. 1048.   ARCHWAY, IN THE "SONGE DE POLIPHILE."

perfect harmony should subsist between them as well as between each particular member,
however subordinate; as in the well-formed human figure, all the limbs being in due proportion, the whole when combined produces true symmetry : and the same author insists very
strenuously on a careful study of the rules upon which this is founded, proving that the
effect desired cannot be produced by a mere effort of fancy, or what is commonly called
taste.

A building, though entirely devoid of ornament, may be rendered beautiful by the justness of its proportion, and the richest edifice wanting in this never can excite admiration : façades having but height and breadth, these two dimensions must be equal to each other, if we adopt the symmetrical proportions prescribed by Vitruvius, for he observes " the square includes the human figure either lying down or standing in an erect posture, the arms being stretched out." Temples, triumphal arches, and other buildings left us by the Greeks and Romans were decidedly designed upon this principle, as were most of the façades of the religious structures erected since the fall of the Roman empire.

In the " Songe de Poliphile," originally published in Italian by Aldus in the year 1499, are some observations on setting out a façade, which convey some idea of the principles adopted for the formation of a perfect and harmonious design on the revival of Roman architecture.

" Draw a square figure, divided by three perpendicular and three horizontal lines, at equal distances from each other, forming sixteen squares ; on the top of the square add a half square, which, similarly divided, makes altogether twenty-four squares : in the lower square draw two diagonals, crossing eight squares in the same manner ; then form a lozenge above the great square, tracing within it four lines on the four principal points that separate the four sides of the void."

After understanding this figure, I thought within myself what can modern architects do, who esteem themselves so learned without letters or principles ? They neither know rules nor dimensions, and therefore corrupt and deform all sorts of buildings, both public and private, despising nature, who teaches them to do well if they would imitate her : good workmen, besides their science, may enrich their work either by adding to or diminishing therefrom, the better to please the eye, but the mass should remain entire, with which all should be made to harmonise. By the mass is understood the body of the edifice, which, without any ornament, shows the knowledge and spirit of the master, for it is easy to embellish after any invention ; the distribution and arrangement of the parts is also a matter of consideration ; hence we may conclude that any workmen or their apprentices know how to ornament a work, but to invent lies only in the heads of the wise.

Taking from the square and a half, the lozenge and the diagonal lines leaves the three perpendicular and the three horizontal, except that in the middle, which terminates in the centre of the perpendicular, cutting it into four parts or portions ; by this rule will be found two perfect squares, one above and one below, each containing four small squares, which form the opening or doorway ; now if you take the diagonal of the lower square, it will show you what thickness must be given to the centre of the portico ; if you carry it straight, the line will serve to denote the architrave : and the point of the centre of the upper square will rest on the centre of the arch or curve to be given to the door ; turning a semicircle it will rest on the transverse line, which cuts the square and a half into two equal parts ; but if done by any other means I do not esteem it perfect. This method was invented by ancient and expert masons, and observed in their arches and vaults, to give them both grace and solidity ; the pedestal on which the columns rest commences at the level of the pavement by a plinth, and the whole is a foot high, furnished with mouldings ; one portion is divided into architrave, frieze, and cornice, the latter being something more than the others ; that is to say, if the architrave and frieze contained five parts, the cornice should be six. The whole twenty-four squares form a square and a half ; then divide the upper half into six parts by five horizontal and five perpendicular lines, and draw a line from the centre of the fifth transverse to the corner of the great perfect square, where the architrave commences ; then draw it perpendicular on the key of the archivolt, and it will show you the height to be given to the frontispiece above, the extremities of which should unite and relate to the projection of the cymatium and its mouldings.

General Principles.— It would appear that all the principal Roman triumphal arches with single openings were a square, either comprising or excluding their attics : that the centre from whence the archivolt was struck was the centre of the square, or if the façade was more than a square, as the arch of Trajan at Ancona, then where the two diagonals crossed the centre was fixed. The width of the opening is generally half the entire extent, sometimes three parts out of seven.

These triumphal arches were generally surmounted by a group of figures, or the car and horses of the conqueror, accompanied by his companions in arms and the trophies obtained from the enemy ; these, as shown on several medals, appear to be equal in height to $\frac{1}{3}$ of the entire edifice upon which they are placed, the attic and entablature representing $\frac{1}{3}$, and the columns and pedestals the other $\frac{2}{3}$; and as the former are nearly equal in their height, it follows that the horse and his rider, or the car and its triumphant hero, were double the height of the pedestal on which they were placed, for so we may consider the attic which contained the inscription, the body of the arch being a perfect square, and in correct proportion, without the attic. The depths of these arches varied ; that of Constantine at Rome is nearly the same as the width of the great centre opening ; many of the others are less than that proportion ; but it seems that the cube was the measure that

bounded the proportions, as shown in fig. 2995. The several Roman examples selected differ in arrangement, but not in principle, from the description given by Poliphile: take away the pedestals on which the columns are placed, and then four squares in height include half the tympanum, and eighteen squares the entire figure, 6 of which may be considered as devoted to the arch, and the other 12 to supports: or, if we comprise the whole façade in 20 squares, and abstract the 8 which belong to the opening between the pedestals, we have 4 for each pier or support, and 4 for the en-

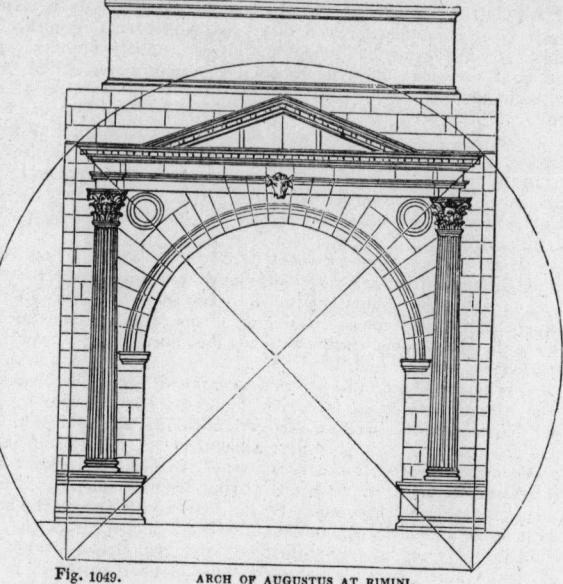

Fig. 1049.   ARCH OF AUGUSTUS AT RIMINI.

tablature, the supported being only ½ the quantity contained in the two supports: resistance to the arch, or its thrust, requires a different arrangement from that of a portico, but we nevertheless find definite proportions made use of, and a double quantity given to masses which have to bear weight as well as resist thrust.

The Arch of Augustus at Rimini has the height of its order determined by the length of the frieze.

The Arch of Augustus at Aosta resembles that of Titus in arrangement; it is a perfect square comprising the attic.

Fig. 1050.   ARCH OF AUGUSTUS, AT AOSTA.

The Arch of Sergius at Pola is a perfect square, without attic, like that of Titus.

The Arch of Titus at Rome, raised by the senate and Roman people to commemorate the conquest of Judæa, is one of the best examples of proportion that remain: built of white marble, it is a monument of constructive art, some of the blocks being 9 feet square, and 2 feet thick; the arch is composed of eleven voussoirs 16 feet deep. For a detailed account of its construction and ornament the reader is referred to the "Architectural Antiquities of Rome."

The proportions are a square, as is the opening of the archway, up to the springing; and not a double square, as described by Serlio. The pedestals are in height nearly half the opening of the archway, which Palladio observes was the ordinary proportion

Fig. 1051.   ARCH OF SERGIUS AT POLA.

given by the ancients. The entire length of the upper member of the cornice in this example is 48 feet, which dimension corresponds with the entire height, almost to a fraction: the width of the opening is 17 feet 6 inches, a trifle more than one-third of the entire width: bounding the façade by a parallelogram, excluding the attic, and drawing two diagonals, we obtain the centre from which the arch is struck, which rule will apply to the other

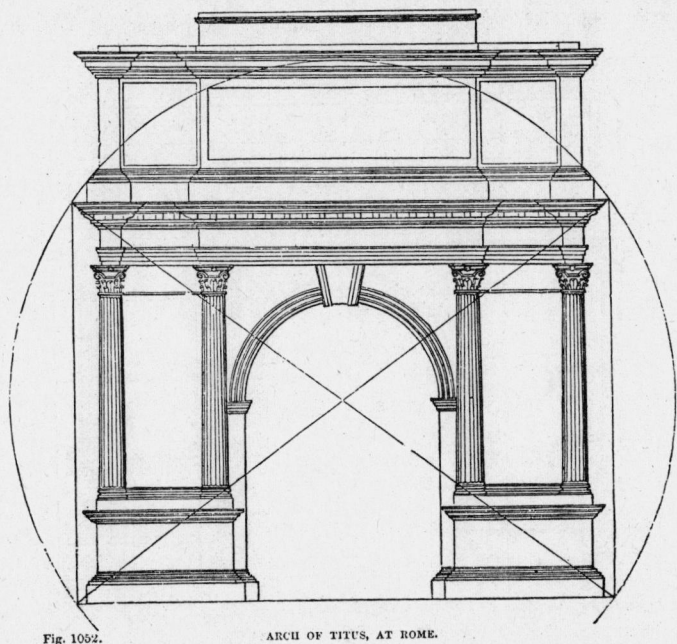

Fig. 1052.   ARCH OF TITUS, AT ROME.

triumphal arches with a single opening, though varying materially from the principles laid down by Poliphile, and adopted by Serlio and other architects at the revival of Italian architecture. The Arch of Titus is a square comprising its entire façade; that of Poliphile a square up to the under side of the entablature; consequently, the opening of the triumphal way is in width half the height to the top of the impost upon which the archivolt rests, while in the more ancient the entire aperture without the arch is a square.

In the Arch of Poliphile the entablature and pediments are nearly equal in quantity to each of the piers upon which they are carried; and the piers themselves are in width only one quarter of the whole breadth of the façade: it will be found, however, that nearly the same proportions exist between supports and supported in both examples.

The Arch of Augustus at Susa has a single arch: proportion a square to the top of the entabla-

Fig. 1053.   ARCH OF AUGUSTUS AT SUSA.

ture, opening a square to the springing: width divided into four, two given to the opening and one to each pier, which has a three-quarter column at the angle: attic as high as piers are wide.

In arches with three openings, as those of Septimus Severus and Constantine, these

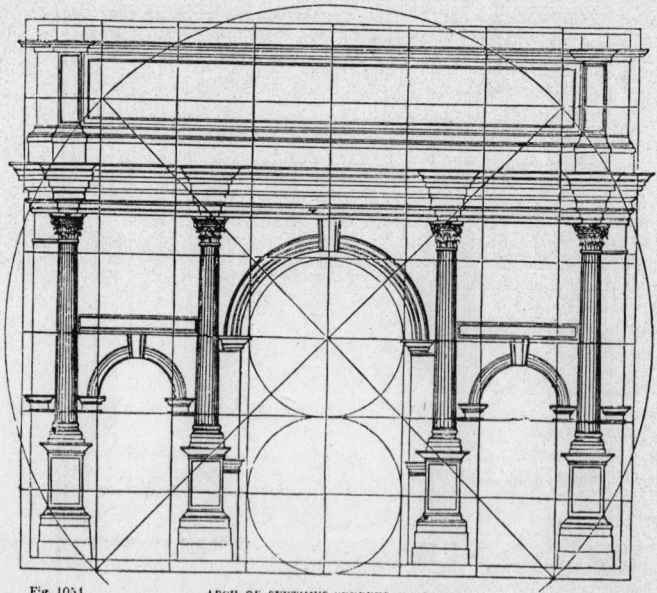

Fig. 1051.   ARCH OF SEPTIMUS SEVERUS, AT ROME.

occupy one-half the width, and the piers the other: where the diagonals of the figure cross is the centre, from which the principal arch is struck.

The Arch of Trajan at Beneventum. — Circle struck from the centre which describes the archivolt ; comprises all within it except the attic : division of width into seven, two for each pier, three for centre ; attic half the height of the order.

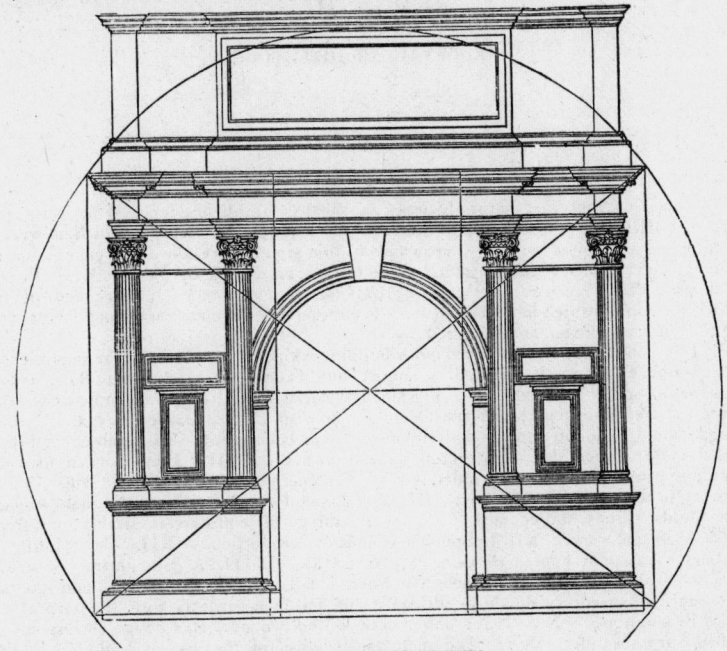

Fig. 1055.   ARCH OF TRAJAN AT BENEVENTUM.

In the foregoing examples, we have attempted to show that the beauty which belongs to form in architecture rests upon one principle based on the laws of nature, and that the first element in a good design is the proportion of the parts as well as the whole : nothing has more misled the critics upon this subject, as well as architects themselves, than implicitly following the rules laid down for drawing the orders. In treating upon the antique, they have frequently been right as far as regards the letter, but essentially wrong in the spirit. The laws of nature do not vary, nor do our organs of sense or perception, and what was apparently fit and proper in the opinions of the Greeks is equally so at the present day : in their sculptures we never find a man represented carrying more than his own weight, and such laws ought to be our guide.

After the destruction of the Roman empire, the character impressed upon architecture by the Greeks was lost : other styles arose in succession, which have been designated as Byzantine, Romanesque, Lombardic, Saxon, Norman, Saracenic, and Pointed. The five first retained the semicircular arch, and only differed in the quantity of material employed : for examples of the three first-mentioned we must refer to a work entitled " Architecture of the Middle Ages at Pisa," by Edward Cresy and G. L. Taylor, containing measurements made in 1817.

CHAP. III.

MEDIÆVAL ARCHITECTURE.

Sect. I.

THE STYLE IN GENERAL.

The question that first naturally arises is, What is Gothic or Mediæval architecture? Although Rickman, in his essay mentioned on page 929, gave a sketch in which he wished to show the differences between Classic and Gothic architecture, the first real attempt at defining the character of Mediæval art seems to have been made by the late A. W. Pugin, who, in his *True Principles of Pointed or Christian Architecture*, 1841, enunciated the following principles, which have formed the keynote for the various works and lectures on the subject since written and delivered : —

I. There should be no features about a building which are not necessary for convenience, construction, or propriety. II. All ornament should consist of enrichment of the essential construction of the building. III. The smallest detail should have a meaning or serve a purpose. IV. The construction itself should vary with the material employed. V. The design should be adapted to the material in which it is executed. VI. Pointed architecture does not conceal her construction, but beautifies it. VII. Plaster, when used for any other purpose than coating walls, is a mere modern deception. VIII. A flat roof is contrary to the spirit of the style. IX. A splayed form is necessary for piers, arches, basemoulds, strings, and copings. X. All mouldings of jambs are invariably sunk from the face of the work. XI. Large stones destroy proportion. XII. The jointing of masonry should not appear to be a regular feature. XIII. A joint in tracery should always be cut to the centre of the curve where it falls. XIV. The external and internal appearance of an edifice should be illustrative of, and in accordance with, the purpose for which it is destined. XV. It is a defect to make the two sides of a design correspondent if their purposes differ. XVI. The picturesque effect of the ancient buildings results from the ingenious methods by which the old builders overcame local and constructive difficulties. XVII. The elevation should be subservient to the plan. XVIII. Details are multiplied with the increased scale of the building.

These principles, with the addition of the subject mentioned in the next paragraph, seem to form the creed of the most advanced foreign archæologists, such as M. Viollet le Duc, for the consideration of the spirit of the style has been neglected in favour of an investigation of details by French and German writers on architecture.

"Internal altitude," writes Pugin in the same work (p. 66.), "is a feature which would add greatly to the effect of many of our fine English churches, and I shall ever advocate its introduction, as it is a characteristic of foreign pointed architecture of which we can avail ourselves without violating the principles of our own peculiar style of English Christian architecture, from which I would not depart in this country on any account. I once stood on the very edge of a precipice in this respect, from which I was rescued by the advice and arguments of my respected and revered friend Dr. Rock, to whose learned researches and observations on Christian antiquities I am highly indebted, and to whom I feel it a bounden duty to make this public acknowledgment of the great benefit I have received from his advice. Captivated by the beauties of foreign pointed architecture, I was on the verge of departing from the severity of our English style, and engrafting portions of foreign detail and arrangement. This I feel convinced would have been a failure; for although the great principles of Christian architecture were everywhere the same, each country had some peculiar manner of developing them, and we should continue working in the same parallel lines, all contributing to the grand whole of Catholic art, but by the very variety increasing its beauties and its interest."

This author claimed for pointed architecture the merit of its having been the only phase of art in which the "principles" had been carried out, and is supported, with some reservations, by Viollet le Duc. Our space is too limited to discuss that assertion ; the student who desires to investigate the subject must refer to Pugin's publication for his arguments, and must guard against being captivated by the one-sided illustrations given as "contrast." For an assertion of the same general principles in regard of Classic and Modern architecture, the reader is referred to the chapter on BEAUTY IN ARCHITECTURE, in the present work

(*par.* 2492, *et seq.*), written, we are inclined to consider, before the publication of Pugin's propositions.

A more strictly architectural definition of the term *Gothic architecture* has been deduced from the writings of various investigators, as being that combination of art and science in building which followed the adoption, during the middle ages, of broken arches for vaults, openings, and ornaments, in lieu of the previously existing arches of continuous lines. The term Gothic architecture, according to such writers, does not acknowledge as its legitimate productions any structures that are point vaulted and point arched, point vaulted but not arched, point arched but not vaulted, or neither arched nor vaulted, unless they conform to rules approved by the builders in north-western Europe (and especially in England) during the middle ages.   These regulations are, in effect, nine :—I. Daylight must not fall upon any apparently *horizontal plane surface*, however small, except pavements, steps, seats, and tables. II. Every *arch* must be moulded within a chamfer, or at least be chamfered. III. Every *impost* must follow the plan of the arch or arches which it receives. IV. Every *pillar* must be an assemblage of juxtaposed shafts or mouldings. V. Every *pier* must be polygonal, or at least circular in plan. VI. Every *base* must follow the plan of the pillar or pier to which it belongs, or at least be either polygonal (preferably octagonal), or cylindrical if under a shaft. VII. All *decoration* must be worked within the plane of the walling to which it belongs, except in the cases of bases, bands, capitals, cornices, copings, and dripstones. VIII. *Roofs* of high pitch and flying buttresses, spires, and pinnacles, tracery and foliation, are incidental, rather than peculiar, features. IX. The *continuous arch* may be exceptionally employed when it, with the rest of the building in which it occurs, exhibits submission to the preceding regulations.

These regulations were observed to the north of the Loire and of the Alps, which was the seat of what may be designated *original Gothic.*   South of those boundaries we have to deal with what may be designated *imitative Gothic*, to which, as a matter of course, appends itself one of the two divisions, Christian and Mahomedan, of *Pointed* art. We take it for granted that the reader is already convinced that the Romanesque and Byzantine perfect developments of Roman construction do not become transitional to *original* or *imitative Gothic* architecture merely by the introduction of the pointed arch as a mere form, independent of the regulations above enumerated. On the contrary, they become new *styles*, with their own periods of transition and development; which, by those writers who do not feel that the architecture of the Mahomedans has been as consistent as that of north-western Europe, are at present considered as mere solecisms, deserving to have the epithets of *pointed Romanesque* and *pointed Byzantine* given to them.

These regulations, therefore, define the difference between *Gothic* and *Pointed* architecture.   They exclude from the title of *Gothic* those branches of the transition from Romanesque art which, in Germany, Italy, and the Spanish peninsula, were, whatever the period might be, merely imitation Gothic ; as they also exclude any branch of the pointed Byzantine school, which was employed by the Normans in Sicily, or by other Christian communities.

The readers who are desirous of considering this subject more in detail are referred to Freeman, *History of Architecture*, 1849, wherein Chapter I. Part II. treats upon the " Definition and Origin of Gothic Architecture ; " and concludes with the observation : " We may then define Gothic architecture as a style whose main principle is verticality, a principle suggested by the pointed arch, and carried out in its accompanying details." A writer in the *Archæological Journal*, for February 1847, has expressed his notion that " it would be very possible to build a *thoroughly good* Gothic church, taken entirely from ancient examples, without a single pointed arch throughout ; " a principle which would astonish most of the talented practitioners of the present day.

An eminent amateur has written a very studied and elaborate explanation of what he considers to constitute Gothic architecture. " I believe," says Mr. Ruskin, in *Stones of Venice*, Vol. II. Chap. VI., after a short inquiry into the mental power or expression, " that the characteristic or moral elements of Gothic are the following, placed in the order of their importance :—I. Savageness ; II. Changefulness; III. Naturalism ; IV. Grotesqueness ; V. Rigidity; and VI. Redundance.   These characters are here expressed as belonging to the building.   As belonging to the builder they would be thus expressed :— I. Savageness, or rudeness; II. Love of change; III. Love of nature ; IV. Disturbed imagination; V. Obstinacy; and VI. Generosity. The withdrawal of any one, or any two, will not at once destroy the Gothic character of the building ; but the removal of a majority of them will."   He then proceeds to examine them in their order ; but our limited space prevents our following him word for word, and we have found it necessary to curtail some of the following paragraphs.

In defining its outward form, he states that the most striking feature is that it is composed of pointed arches. " I shall say then, in the first place, that Gothic architecture is that which uses, if possible, the pointed arch for the roof proper ;" and subsequently adds, " Our definition will stand thus : Gothic architecture is that which uses the pointed arch

for the roof proper, and the gable for the roof mask."—" All good Gothic is nothing more than the development in various ways, and on every conceivable scale, of the group formed by the *pointed arch for the bearing line* below, and the *gable for the protecting line* above (*fig.* 1056.). The subject of the masonry of the pointed arch has been discussed in Chapter XI. of Volume I. (of his work), and the conclusion deduced, that of all possible forms of the pointed

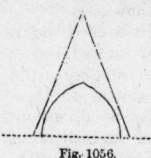

arch (a certain weight of material being given), that generically represented in *fig.* 1057. is the strongest. But the element of foliation *must* enter somewhere, or the style is imperfect; and our final definition of Gothic will, therefore, stand thus :—Foliated architecture, which uses the pointed arch for the roof proper, and the gable for the roof mask."

Fig. 1056.

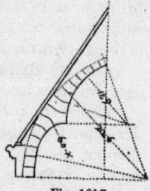

Fig. 1057.

The figure 1057, though of the outline as given by Mr. Ruskin, really exhibits the stone arch erected in granite across the chancel of the Bruen Testimonial Church at Carlow, designed by the late J. Derick (*Builder*, 1854, p. 34.). The trefoiled arch exercises a force within the building neutralising the outward thrusting force of the lancet arch, the two forces producing a state of rest.

" A few plain and practical rules," continues Mr. Ruskin, " will determine whether a given building be good *Gothic* or not, and if not Gothic, whether its architecture is of a kind which will probably reward the pains of careful examination :—I. Look if the roof rises in a steep gable, high above the walls. If it does not do this, there is something wrong ; the building is not quite pure Gothic, or has been altered. II. Look if the principal windows and doors have pointed arches, with gables over them. If not pointed arches, the building is not Gothic; if they have not any gables over them, it is either not pure or not first-rate. If, however, it has the steep roof, the pointed arch, and gable all united, it is nearly certain to be a Gothic building of a very fine time. III. Look if the arches are cusped, or apertures foliated. If the building has met the first two conditions, it is sure to be foliated somewhere ; but, if not everywhere, the parts which are not unfoliated are imperfect, unless they are large bearing arches, or small and sharp arches in groups, forming a kind of foliation by their multiplicity, and relieved by sculpture and rich mouldings. If there be no foliation anywhere, the building is assuredly imperfect Gothic. IV. If the building meets all the first three conditions, look if its arches in general, whether of doors and windows, or of minor ornamentation, are carried on true shafts with bases and capitals. If they are, then the building is assuredly of the finest Gothic style. It may still, perhaps, be an imitation, a feeble copy, or a bad example, of a noble style ; but the manner of it, having met all these four conditions, is assuredly first-rate. If its apertures have not shafts and capitals, look if they are plain openings in the walls, studiously simple, and unmoulded at the sides. If so, the building may still be of the finest Gothic, adapted to some domestic or military service. But if the sides of the window be moulded, and yet there are no capitals at the spring of the arch, it is assuredly of an inferior school."

" The next tests to be applied are in order to discover whether the building be *good architecture* or not ; for it may be very impure Gothic, and yet very noble architecture ; or it may be very pure Gothic, and yet, if a copy, or originally raised by an ungifted builder, very bad architecture :—I. See if it looks as if it had been built by strong men; if it has the sort of roughness, and largeness, and nonchalance, mixed in places with the exquisite tenderness, which seems always to be the sign-manual of the broad vision and massy power of men who can see *past* the work they are doing, and betray here and there something like disdain for it. If it has not this character, but is altogether accurate, minute, and scrupulous in its workmanship, it must belong to either the very best or the very worst of schools: the very best, in which exquisite design is wrought out with untiring and conscientious care, as in the Giottesque Gothic; or the very worst, in which mechanism has taken the place of design. On the whole, very accurate workmanship is to be esteemed a bad sign. II. Observe if it be irregular, its different parts fitting themselves to different purposes, no one caring what becomes of them so that they do their work. III. Observe if all the traceries, capitals, and other ornaments, are of perpetually varied design. IV. Lastly, *Read* the sculpture. Preparatory to reading it, you will have to discover whether it is legible (and, if legible, it is nearly certain to be worth reading). The criticism of the building is to be conducted precisely on the same principles as that of a book ; and it must depend on the knowledge, feeling, and not a little on the industry and perseverance of the reader, whether, even in the case of the best works, he either perceives them to be great, or feels them to be entertaining."

" The *variety* of the Gothic schools," says Mr. Ruskin, in another portion of the same work, " is the more healthy and beautiful, because in many cases it is entirely unstudied, and results, not from mere love of change, but from practical necessities. It is one of the

chief virtues of the Gothic builders, that they never suffered ideas of outside symmetries and consistencies to interfere with the real use and value of what they did.   If they wanted a window they opened one ; a room, they added one ; a buttress, they built one; utterly regardless of any established conventionalities of external appearance.   Every successive architect employed upon a great work built the pieces he added in his own way, utterly regardless of the style adopted by his predecessors.   These marked variations were, however, only permitted as part of the great system of perpetual change which ran through every member of Gothic design, and rendered it as endless a field for the beholder's inquiry as for the builder's imagination ; change, which in the best schools is subtle and delicate, and rendered more delightful by intermingling of a noble monotony, in the more barbaric schools is somewhat fantastic and redundant; but, in all, a necessary and constant condition of the life of the school.   Sometimes the variety is in one feature, sometimes in another: it may be in the capitals or crockets, in the niches or the traceries, or in all together, but in some one or other of the features it will be found always.   If the mouldings are constant, the surface sculpture will change ; if the capitals are of a fixed design, the traceries will change ; if the traceries are monotonous, the capitals will change ; and if ever, as in some fine schools, the early English for example, there is the slightest approximation to an unvarying type of mouldings, capitals, and floral decoration, the variety is found in the disposition of the masses, and in the figure sculpture."

SECT. II.

PERIODS OF GOTHIC ARCHITECTURE.

The divisions of Gothic architecture in England, as made by King, Dallaway, Millers, and others, have been used in Book I. Chap. III. ; but their subdivisions and nomenclature have been discarded by later investigators ; and many tables have been put forward of divisions and subdivisions.   Thus, Britton's nomenclature (1807) was, English 1189–1272; decorated English 1272–1461 ; highly decorated, or florid, English 1461–1509; debased English 1625.   Millers's division (1807) was early English 1200–1300; ornamented English 1300–1460 ; and florid English 1460–1537, as adopted herein in Book I.   E. Sharpe classifies the style as, *Romanesque*—Saxon period until 1066 ; Norman 1066–1145 , *Gothic*—transitional 1145–1190; lancet 1190–1245 ; geometrical 1245–1315 ; curvilinear 1315–1360 ; and rectilinear 1360–1550.

The following table introduced by Rickman, *Attempt to Discriminate, &c.*, shows his nomenclature and the duration of the periods ; these names have maintained themselves, in consequence of their general appropriateness, from 1819 to the present time : —

Kings.	Date.	Name of Period.	Remarks.
William I. William II. Henry I. Stephen. Henry II.	1066 1087 1100 1135 1154 to 1189	NORMAN.	Prevailed little more than 124 years ; no remains really known to be more than a few years older than the Conquest.
Richard I. John. Henry III. Edward I.	1189 1199 1216 1272 to 1307	EARLY ENGLISH.	Prevailed about 118 years.
Edward II. Edward III.	1307 1327 to 1377	DECORATED ENGLISH.	Continued perhaps 10 or 15 years later ; prevailed little more than 70 years.
Richard II. Henry IV. Henry V. Henry VI. Edward IV. Edward V. Richard III. Henry VII. Henry VIII.	1377 1399 1413 1422 1461 1483 1483 1485 1509 to 1546	PERPENDICULAR ENGLISH.	Prevailed about 169 years. Few, if any, whole buildings executed in this style later than Henry VIII. This style used in additions and re-buildings, but often much debased, as late as 1630 or 1640.

The reign of Richard I. was the chief period of the transition from the Norman to the early English style; that of Edward I. for the change from the early English to the decorated style (the Eleanor crosses belonging rather to the latter, than to the former, style) ; while in the latter part of the long reign of Edward III. the transition to the perpendicular style commenced, and was almost completed by the time of the accession of Richard II.

Similar tables of the duration of styles in foreign countries have been given in the section
Pointed Architecture, in Book I.

Rickman, in describing the style to which he gives the name " decorated," especially
classes under that style the tracery in which " the figures such as circles, trefoils,
quatrefoils, &c., are all worked with the same moulding, and do not always regularly
join each other, but touch only at points; this," he says, " may be called geometrical
tracery." The Rev. G. A. Poole, *Ecclesiastical Architecture*, 1848, remarks that " a very
large proportion of the buildings in which this kind of tracery is used, belongs to
the previous period, called early English. The examples which might have been supposed to clear up the difficulty only make it greater. Thus, in speaking of the chapter-
house at York, which has splendid geometric tracery, he says, " The chapter-house
is of *decorated* character ; " yet the chapter-house is clearly of a character which prevailed
during a considerable part of that period which Rickman assigns to the early English
style. The general tendency has likewise been, of late, to range with the early English
by far the greater proportion of those examples which answer to Rickman's definition of
geometrical decorated; a few of the later examples only being treated as transition from
early English to decorated. The mouldings, it is true, are generally of perfectly early
English character, and so are the clusters of foliage, the bosses, and other ornamental
appendages. Instances occur in which the simple early English lancet was used during
the period of the geometrical tracery. How, then, are the two styles, if they be two, to be
separated, in a system which is in part chronological? How are they to be united, in a
system which is also in part founded on similarity of parts?

" It is, however, perhaps the most perfect of all the styles ; for its tracery has the completeness and precision of the perpendicular, without its license and exuberance; while its
minor details partake of the boldness and sharpness of the early English, which need not
fear to be compared with the ornamental accessories of any subsequent style. Besides the
intrinsic beauty of this style, it is important as affording the first full development of tracery
and of cusping, with all their power of enriching large windows, and of bringing together
several lights as one whole."

" In pursuing the study of mediæval architecture, it may be held as an axiom," writes
Brandon, *Analysis of Gothic Architecture*, " that personal inspection of the old churches of
England is the *only means* by which it can be possible now, either to appreciate the genius of
our mediæval architects, or to sympathise with the spirit which animated them. But it is
probable that even experienced observers may sometimes be misled by a practice of occasionally assimilating work in a later style to some already existing portion of an incomplete
general design. Indeed it forms a strongly marked exception to the usual practice ; for it
was a general rule with the builders of the middle ages never to fall back upon a past
era of their art, even when engaged in completing structures of a bygone age." He then
describes the proceedings in this respect at St. Alban's Abbey Church, at Westminster
Abbey, and at Fotheringay Church, Northamptonshire.

The early English character of Westminster Abbey Church has been so well preserved
throughout, that in many cases it requires a close inspection before it is possible to detect
the presence of decorated or of perpendicular work. Thus the windows in the aisles
erected by Henry V. are very decidedly of early decorated character ; the customary
octagonal and moulded cap of the perpendicular period occupy the place of the corresponding circular and foliated members, which, had the windows really been erected some
hundred years earlier, would assuredly have surmounted the boltels placed in their jambs.

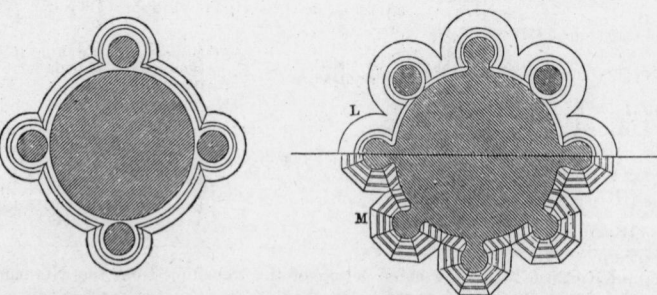

Fig. 1058. WESTMINSTER ABBEY ; TRANSEPT   Fig. 1059. WESTMINSTER ABBEY ; PILLARS OF NAVE (L, EASTERN
  AND CHOIR. EARLY ENGLISH.   BAYS, DECORATED—M, WESTERN BAYS, PERPENDICULAR.)

In the earlier plans of the nave piers four shafts stand clearly detached from the main
body of the pier, *fig.* 1058. ; but subsequently the pier was worked with eight shafts,
fig. 1059. (L) ; and, later still, with eight shafts, *fig.* 1059. (M) all attached to the central

mass, indicative of the altered fashion of the day, in which detached shafts, once such a favourite feature, were entirely discarded.   In the piers they worked the bands of the 13th century (N) with the mouldings peculiar to the 15th (O).   *Figures* 1060, both drawn to the same scale, show how they departed both from the outline and size of the original.   In the triforia, the early English design is equally apparent in the earlier and later portions of the work ; but the mouldings in each are true to their styles.

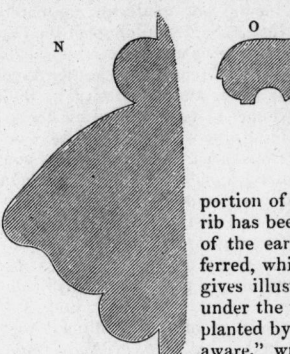

Fig. 1060.
WESTMINSTER ABBEY.

Although the groining is tolerably in keeping throughout, in the aisles and in the later portion of the vaulting, the original spring and height of the ridge rib has been preserved, while to the elegant acutely pointed lancet of the earlier groining an obtusely pointed arch has been preferred, which, consequently, it has been necessary to stilt.   Brandon gives illustrations of the early English and perpendicular arcades under the windows, a feature which, though long disused and supplanted by a system of panelling, is yet followed out.   " I am not aware," writes the Rev. J. L. Petit, " whether sufficient attention has been given to the attempts occasionally made by the mediæval architects to assimilate their work to the portions erected in an earlier style.   In some instances, as in the choirs at Ely and Lincoln, this is done without sacrificing any of the distinctive features of the style then in use ; but in Beverley Minster, and in Whitby Abbey, the case is different.   In the latter, the whole of the early English arrangement of the choir, as regards its lancet windows, is continued in the transept, though the ornaments with which it is enriched show that this part clearly belongs to the decorated period.   The triforium in the former is uniform throughout the whole church, for the same is continued in the decorated work, except the disuse of marble in the shafts."

The same system of using previous ideas, but working them out with later details, is exemplified in the *Sketch Book* of Wilars de Honecort, an architect of the middle of the 13th century.   In comparing his sketches with drawings from the original works, their extreme inaccuracy and contempt of detail is evident.   He sketched them because he saw there was something in the general arrangement which, with alterations, might become useful.   He therefore drew each with his own improvements to it.   As to the details, Wilars did not want them, for he was perfectly convinced that those of his own time were better than anything previously executed.   The reader will find reviews of this work in the *Builder* for 1858, with some woodcuts of the illustrations.

Besides this question of assimilation of style, there arises that of *similarity of work* in different buildings, resulting from the superintendence or design of one master mind ; but this is so extensive a subject that in our limited space we dare not do more than name it for the attention of the student or reader.   Another interesting important point is that of the *transition* from one period into another, such as the decorated into the perpendicular. A curious example of this exists in the church at Edington, in Wiltshire, an account of which, with woodcuts, is given by Parker, in the 6th edition of Rickman's *Attempt,* 1862.

Sect. III.

MOULDINGS.

It will probably surprise many of our readers that even so late as 1845, the statement was made that " but little acquaintance with mouldings is evinced in the works of most modern architects."   Such was the opinion expressed by F. A. Paley, when he published his very useful *Manual of Gothic Mouldings.*   " Viewed as an inductive science," he writes, " the study of Gothic mouldings is as curious and interesting in itself as it is important in its results.   Any one who engages actively in it will be amply repaid, if only by the enlarged views he will acquire of the ancient principles of effect, arrangement, and composition.   But the curves, the shadows, and the blending forms, are really in themselves extremely beautiful, and will soon become the favourites of a familiar eye ; though viewed without understanding they may seem only an unmeaning cluster of holes, nooks, and shapeless excrescences.   Perhaps few are aware that any group can be analysed with perfect ease and certainty ; that every member is cut by rule, and arranged by certain laws of combination.   The best work on Gothic mouldings which could possibly be written will do no more than set him in the right way to obtain a knowledge of the subject by his own research.   The look of a moulding is so very different in section, projected in a reduced size

on paper, from its appearance in perspective reality, that the same form seen in the one may scarcely be recognised in the other.

" Gothic architecture revelled in the use of mouldings ;—and yet, mouldings are merely the ornamental adjuncts, not the essentials, of architecture. Some buildings of the best periods were quite devoid of them, whence it is evident that they are not necessary even to a perfect design. Boldness and simplicity produce effects, different indeed in their kind, yet not less solemn and striking than richness of detail. If the uniformity in their use had not been very strict and close, it had been a hopeless task ever to master the subject; indeed, if there had not been a *system* of moulding, there would have been nothing to investigate. But so little did the mediæval masons depart from the fixed conventional forms, that we often find a capital, a base, or an arch mould of perfectly the same profile in an abbey or a cathedral which we had copied in our note-book from a village church at the other end of the kingdom, so that we might almost suspect that the very same working drawing had been used for both."—Thus far we have quoted from Paley, to whose work we shall again have recourse in the further development of this section; but in so condensed a form, that it should not prevent the student from himself possessing so invaluable a work, of which a third edition was issued in 1865, with an accession of illustrations.

We must now attempt to give some idea of the *nomenclature* of mediæval mouldings. " The most complete specimen," writes Professor Willis, in his *Architectural Nomenclature of the Middle Ages*, 1844, " is that preserved to us by William of Worcester, or Botoner," who was born in Bristol, in 1415, and is now best known by a manuscript note book remaining in the library of Corpus Christi College, Cambridge; it was printed in 1778 by Nasmith. Two of its pages contain lists of technical words attached to roughly drawn outlines of jamb mouldings, the one showing the *north* door of St. Stephen's Church, the other the west door of St. Mary's Redcliffe Church, both at Bristol. These doors are still in existence; on comparison, the former agrees perfectly with the mouldings of the *south* porch of the church in question, except that two little boltels have been scraped clean off. The west door of Redcliffe Church has undergone a much severer *skinning*. *Fig.* 1061. represents the outline of the former door ; " the names given to the mouldings by Botoner are, A, a cors wythoute ; B, a casement, C, a bowtelle ; D, a felet ; E, a double ressaunt ;

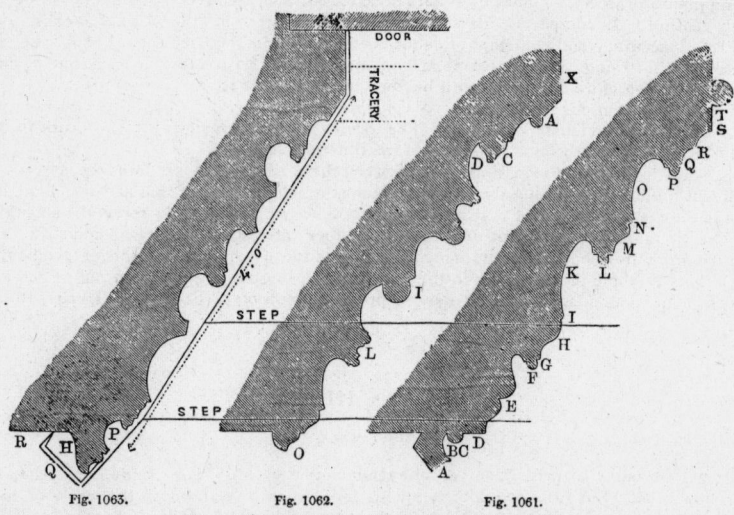

Fig. 1063.   Fig. 1062.   Fig. 1061.

ST. MARY'S REDCLIFFE; AND ST. STEPHEN'S; BRISTOL.

F, a boutel ; G, a felet ; H, a ressant ; I, a felet ; K, a casement wyth Levys ; L, a felet, a boutel, a felet ; M, a ressant ; N, a felet ; O, a casment wyth trayler of Levys ; P, a felet, a boutell, a filet ; Q, a casement ; R. a felet ; S, a casement ; T, a felet ; U, yn the myddes of the dore a boutelle." Of these terms (which display his various modes of spelling) perhaps the only ones needing remark are K and O, which are identical, and have square leaves or flowers in them of the usual form, set at regular intervals, forming a long continuous train. " Benet le Ffremason" appears to have worked the original mouldings.

The section of the mouldings of the west door of Redcliffe Church is shown in *fig.* 1062., to which the names were also attached, the additional terms obtained being " A, a chamfer ; C, a double Ressant wyth a filet ; O, a Ressant lorymer ; M, a lowryng casement ; and I, a grete bowtelle." " I cannot help pointing out," writes Professor Willis, " how imperfect

a nomenclature must be, which can make no stronger distinction between the combinations E and C, than by calling one a 'double ressant,' and the other a 'double ressant with a fillet.' The universal moulding O, in fig. 1062, is a 'ressant lorymer.'" *Fig.* 1063. is an outline of the jamb mouldings as they appear at present, engraved from a drawing made expressly for us by Mr. T. S. Pope, of Bristol, and exhibits the skinning they have undergone.

Mouldings of an arch or jamb are said to be *grouped* when they are placed in combination as they are generally found ; but a *group* is a branch of mouldings or separate members, standing prominent or isolated, either on a shaft, or between two deep hollows. An arch of two or more *orders* is one which is recessed by so many successive planes or retiring arches (see *fig.* 1065. &c.), each placed behind or beneath the next before it, reckoning from the outer wall line. The accompanying figures exhibit both groups and orders.

We have adopted the usual architectural system of exhibiting the mouldings in the manner of a mould or pattern, and it likewise carries out the principle of this work. It is also preferred to the popular way of engraving sections, that is, by an apparently perspective representation of a stone cut out of an arch. The several sets of figures are all drawn to scale. The examples selected are, Fountains Abbey, Yorkshire, for the transition and for the early English period ; Tintern Abbey, Gloucestershire, for the geometric period ; Howden Church, Yorkshire, for the late decorated period ; and Henry VII.'s Chapel, Westminster, for the perpendicular period. For those from the three first buildings, we have to express our grateful acknowledgment to E. Sharpe's *Architectural Parallels*, 2 vols. fol. 1845–48, a work combining technical precision, without which it would be useless to the *architect*, with artistic character, by which it will recommend itself to every one interested in such antiquities. The illustrations of Tintern are valuable examples of the geometric period. The work contains many geometrical plans, elevations, and sections of 14 buildings, with all the principal mouldings to a large scale (those herein are all reduced, and therefore less useful), with an additional valuable volume of the mouldings engraved full size. For the illustrations of the fourth period we are indebted to Cottingham's work on the Chapel, fol. 1822–29, perhaps the only perfect monograph of a large structure yet published in England.

One reason for selecting the illustrations in this manner has been that, with the very limited space at our disposal for so extensive a subject as the detail of Gothic architecture, we could not emulate either the very satisfactory work which now, with its useful illustrations, passes as Rickman's *Attempt to Discriminate the Styles of Architecture in England*, 8vo. 1865, 6th edit., or Brandon's *Analysis of Gothic Architecture*, which is full of examples of detail drawn to scale. Another reason was, to give the means of comparing the use of details in similar parts of edifices of nearly the same general dimensions; otherwise we could merely have given the prettiest selection that it had been possible to have made for the purpose.

" During the period in which the so-called *Anglo-Saxon* architecture prevailed, little decorative work was done. The very rude carvings are extremely shallow, being such as could be worked with the hammer or pick, and without the chisel. In some doors and larger arches there is a regular impost at the springing, having a rude resemblance to Roman mouldings; otherwise the jambs and arch stones are merely returned square. The tower of Sompting Church possesses early carved work, and boltels at the angles of the window openings, and also a very peculiar ornamented string course. The chancel arch at Wittering Church, Northamptonshire, is among the early attempts at moulding observed in this country, being rough and coarsely chiselled members, generally semi-cylindrical. A square-edged reveal soon became a boltel, by first chamfering, and then removing indefinitely the angles. Thus, a square-edged arch with its sub-arch or soffit rib, was either worked into rounds at each angle or into pointed rolls; or some edges were chamfered, others worked into rolls, and the sub-arch cut away into a broad semi-cylindrical rib.

" The *Norman* architects never got much beyond the plain semi-cylindrical roll (*fig.* 1064. does not show even so much work). They paid more attention to surface sculpture

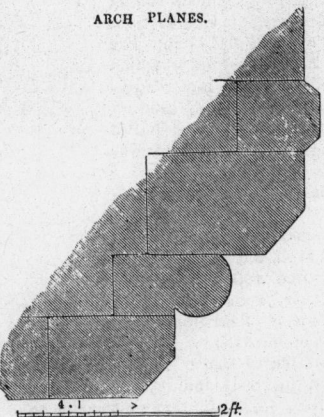

ARCH PLANES.

Fig. 1064.   FOUNTAINS ABBEY; NAVE.

and shallow ornamental work in the archivolts and soffits. Some of the early mouldings and ornaments are illustrated in *fig.* 188., in Book I.

" The invention of the pointed boltel, contemporaneously with the pointed arch, opened the way to a great number of new forms, all more or less referable to this common origin, in varying the members of complex *early English* groupings. The first and by far the most important of these is the *roll and fillet*, as A in *figs.* 1065. and 1066. It is the keynote of almost all the subsequent formations. The characteristics of the mouldings of this style may be defined to be, deep undercut hollows between prominent members, which comprise a great variety of pointed and filleted boltels, clustered, isolated, and repeated at certain intervals, a great depth or extent of moulded surfaces, and the general arrangement in rectangular faces. The hollows, giving the effect of a series of detached arches or ribs, rising in succession, are seldom true circles (A, *fig.* 1067.) ; and, like the projecting parts, they assume a great number of capricious forms. They are not always arranged in exact *planes* ; the student must be fully prepared to find great irregularity in this respect.

" Early English mouldings may be said to comprise the following members :—I. The plain boltel or edge roll ; II. The pointed boltel ; III. The roll and fillet ; IV. The scroll moulding (rare) ; and V. Angular forms, consisting of chamfered ridges and intervening projections of irregular character. The other forms chiefly consist of capricious modifications of the roll and fillet. The *roll and triple fillet* (of which B, *fig.* 1067., is a modification), is much used in the more advanced buildings of the style, and was the favourite form during the reigns of Edwards I. and II. Sometimes only one side has a fillet attached, as at C, and others. Three pointed rolls, placed together somewhat in the shape of a fleur-de-lis, form

ARCH PLANES.

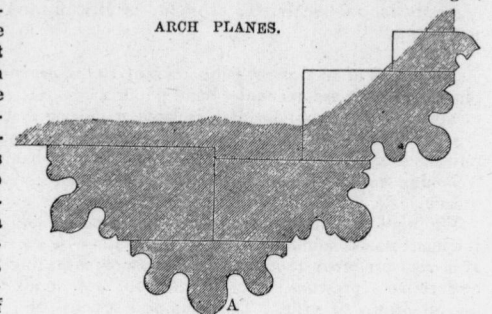

Fig. 1065. FOUNTAINS ABBEY ; CHOIR.

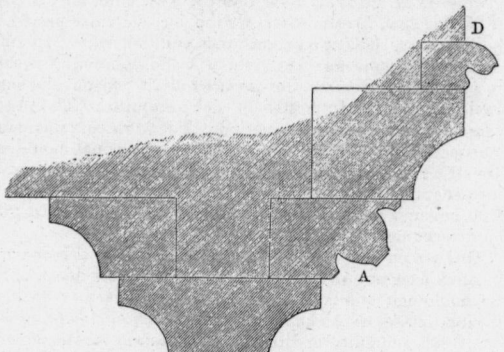

Fig. 1066. TINTERN ABBEY ; NAVE.

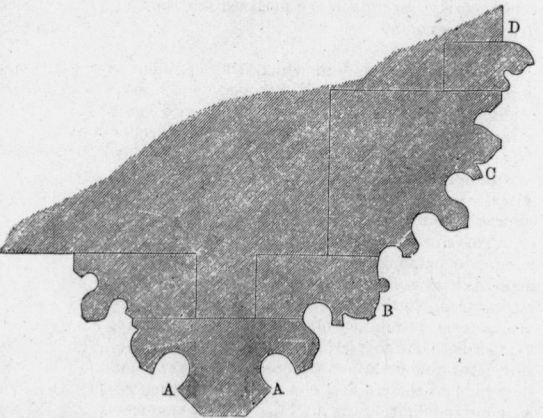

Fig. 1067. TINTERN ABBEY ; CHOIR.

a combination of very frequent occurrence (as *figs.* 1097. and 1104.), with many minor varieties of shape. The fillet is almost always a narrow edge line. The irregular shape and the freely undulating curve of the roll and fillet moulding has been commonly preferred. Almost every conceivable modification of the plain roll, peaked, depressed, elliptical, grooved at the end, throated, isolated, and combined, might be found and catalogued by a careful observer. The *scroll* moulding, also called *edge* moulding or *ressant lorymer*, as O in *fig.* 1062. and D in the above figures, was used in advanced early English work ; it is

so called from its resemblance to a roll of thick paper, the outer edge of which overlaps the side exposed to view. It was extensively used in the decorated period."

The exquisite skill, taste, and patient labour invariably evinced in the working of early English mouldings, are truly admirable. The deepest hollows are all as clearly and perfectly cut as the most prominent and conspicuous details; and as much so in the village church as in the cathedral. Some examples (of doorways) occur at Bolton and Furness Abbeys, whose arch mouldings extend 5 to 6 feet in width.

" The details of *decorated* mouldings are for the most part identical with those of the preceding style, with the addition of some new members, and several important modifications of grouping. The latter will be found to produce an entirely different effect, though in description the distinction may appear very trifling. Much greater geometrical precision in drawing both the hollows and the projecting members prevailed. Segments of circles, both convex and concave, were much used, with an avoidance of strong contrasts of light and shade, which imparted a more pleasing, though much less striking, effect. The perfection of moulding, as of all architectural detail, is considered by many to have been attained in this period; yet rich mouldings in it are of rather rare occurrence. Very often plain chamfers are used in all the windows, doorways, and pier arches, while minor parts, such as bases, sedilia, and the like, have fine and elaborate details.

" There appear to be three distinct kinds to which decorated mouldings may be generally referred:—I. The plain or hollow chamfer of two or more orders, which, properly speaking, is only the step preparatory to moulding. II. Roll and fillet mouldings, and fillets with hollows between each group. III. A succession of double ogees, or double ressants, divided by hollows of three-quarters of a circle. Sometimes the mouldings of II. are combined with those of III. The mouldings of class II. are generally borne by jamb shafts, now engaged in, and not detached, from the wall. Those of III. are almost always continuous, except in pier arches, where they constantly occur. Four or five of these together give a very deep and rich effect to a doorway. One member of a double ogee is often considerably larger than the other, or those of one order of different size from the others.

" The principal forms found in decorated work are:—I. The roll and fillet, the fillet being extremely broad, often as much as 3 and 4 inches. II. The roll and triple fillet, invariably producing a fine effect. Its edge lines are sharp and delicate, and the profile beautifully relieved by the deep side hollows with which it is necessarily connected. III. The ogee. IV. The double ogee, or *double ressant.* V. The scroll moulding, or *ressant lorymer.* VI. The wave moulding, which may be called the *undy-boltel* (A in *fig.* 1068.), from its gently undulating surface: scarcely any method of moulding is so common in, or so characteristic of, this period, as two orders of the wave moulding, with a hollow between them: all the varieties of this moulding appear to occur without any definite distinction throughout the decorated and perpendicular periods; it is wider and shallower in early than in late work; the wavy line is even at times very faint. VII. The plain,

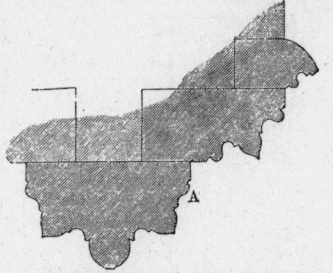

Fig. 1068. HOWDEN CHURCH; CHOIR.

or hollow, chamfer; and VIII. The sunken chamfer. The boltel, or three-quarter round, is used very sparingly. The hollows are usually of larger size than those of the early English; and there is this general difference in their use, that *in this style they divide groups, in the early English, individual members.* A few exceptional instances occur of a tongue-shaped member projecting from the inner side of the principal roll and fillet; this is a very characteristic detail of the class II.

" In windows, the plane in which the mouldings of the jamb lie is seldom coincident with that on which the side of the mullion is arranged, for this would in most cases give too great thickness to the latter. The difference of inclination may be very slight, but it requires attention.

" In mouldings of the *perpendicular period,* a comparatively meagre save-trouble method of working them is perceived. Large and coarse members, with little of minute detail; wide and shallow hollows; hard wiry edges in place of rounded softened forms, are all conspicuous characteristics. Their general arrangement on the chamfer plane (*figs.* 1061. and 1062.), which is a marked feature of this period, gives a flatness unpleasing to the eye in comparison with the rectangularly recessed grouping of the two preceding styles. Three peculiarities are so common, that their absence almost forms the exception to the general usage. These are:—I. A wide shallow hollow, usually occupying the centre of the group, and equal to about one third of the entire width. When the hollow is deep and narrow, it is generally a mark of early work; of late, when wide and shallow; and of debased, when sunken but little below the chamfer plane. One or both ends of the hollow are sometimes returned in a kind of quasi-boltel (as I. *fig.* 1062.). The boltel is often

formed from a plane by sinking a channel on each face; and occasionally it stands like an excrescence on the surface of a plane (as in *figs.* 1061. and 1062.); but this is a departure from the usual practice, as well as from the principle of mouldings. II. The constant use of boltels, or beads, of three-quarters of a circle, resembling small shafts. And III. The frequency of the double ogee, and some varieties of it peculiar to the period, as shown in the figures above-named. This double ogee appears to be composed of a semi-circular hollow continued in a boltel. All varieties may be considered distinctive criteria of the period. The *double ressant* is sometimes of a large and clumsy size. The roll and fillet was not extensively used; its form is that of B, *fig.* 1071.

"Rich and good perpendicular mouldings are not very common, most examples consisting but of three or four very ordinary members, offering nothing either novel or interesting to the view. The doorways are, however, often very deeply recessed, and the engaged jamb shafts bear isolated groups of considerable delicacy. The distinction of the *orders* is often completely lost in this period, while it is seldom undefinable in the previous one. The chamfer plane in many cases is either more or less than an angle of 45°. Sometimes two parallel chamfer planes are taken for the basis of the arrangement of the mouldings."

Among the characteristics of the tertiary French style, or the Flamboyant, which has been described and illustrated in *pars.* 546, *et. seq.*, is that called by Professor Willis, in a most ingenious and valuable paper, read in 1840 before the Institute of British Architects, *penetration* or *interpenetration* of the different mouldings and parts. The French antiquaries have called the system in question *moulures prismatiques*. Neither of these terms seem satisfactory, but of the two we are inclined to prefer the first as most significant. In the paper above mentioned, he observes that the practice is very rarely to be seen in English buildings, but produces an instance of it in the turrets of King's College chapel, at Cambridge (*fig.* 1069.), where the cornice A of the pedestal seems to pierce the plinths of the angle buttresses, and appears at B. This is, however, by no means a capricious, but rather an indispensable arrangement, by

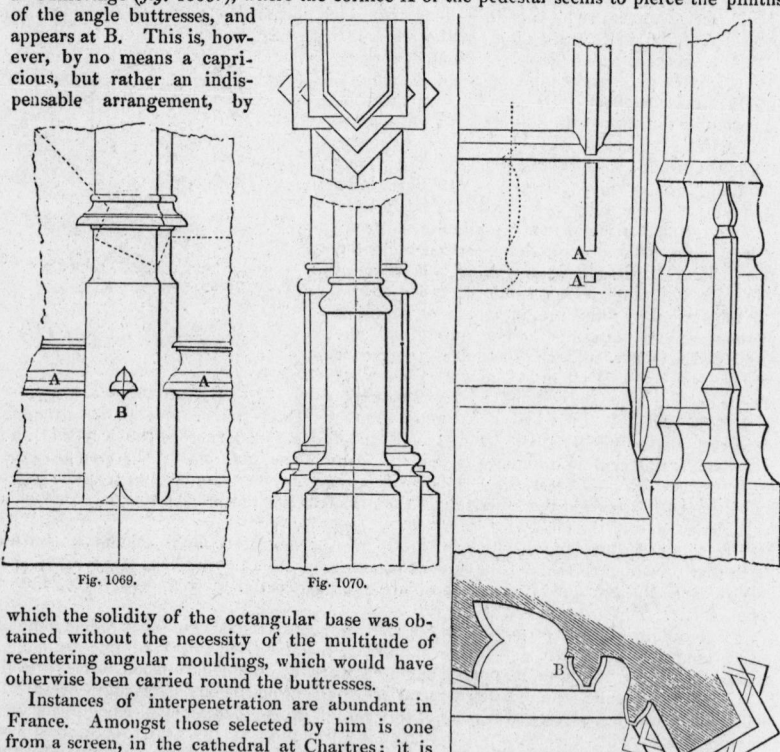

Fig. 1069.　　　　　　　Fig. 1070.

1 : 5　³/₁₆

Fig. 1071.

which the solidity of the octangular base was obtained without the necessity of the multitude of re-entering angular mouldings, which would have otherwise been carried round the buttresses.

Instances of interpenetration are abundant in France. Amongst those selected by him is one from a screen, in the cathedral at Chartres; it is given here geometrically (*fig.* 1070.). *Fig.* 1071. is from the stone cross at Rouen, in which the interpenetration principle is displayed in many of the vertical as well as horizontal members of the structure. The parts A A, mark where the fillet of the mullion pierces the chamfered and moulded parts of the sill. "In many Flamboyant examples, small knobs and projections may be observed, and on a superficial

view might pass for mere unmeaning ornaments, but will be found explicable upon this system of interpenetration." *Fig.* 1072, " is a window from a house near Roanne, at the base of whose mullions, knobs may be observed, which really represent the Gothic base of a square mullion on the same plinth with the hollow chamfered mullion, and interpenetrating with it." The Professor also states that, " it may perhaps be found that this character belongs to one period, or one district, of the Flamboyant style ; " but from our own observation, we are inclined to believe it to have been universal from the middle of the fifteenth century to the period when the style of the Renaissance superseded it. The principles on which it is conducted certainly prevailed

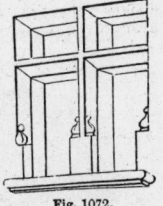

Fig. 1072.

in Germany and in the Low Countries, as Professor Willis afterwards states. A notion to what extent it proceeded may be perceived by *fig.* 1073, taken from Möller's *Denkmäler der Deutschen Bau-kunst*, 1821, and exhibits on the plan a series of interferences contrived with great ingenuity and a consummate acquaintance with practical geometry. The subject is the plan of a tabernacle, or canopy, such as is not unfrequent in churches on the Continent. It shows, says Möller, how the simple and severe architecture of the 13th and 14th centuries had been debased. The square BCDE is the commencing figure.

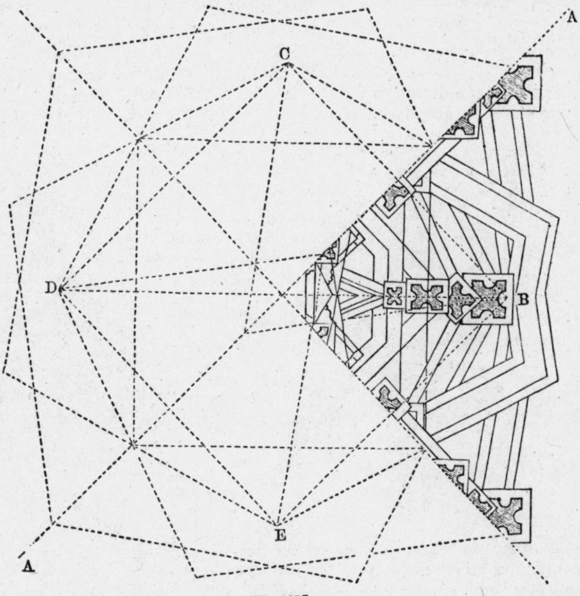

A comparison of English and French mouldings has been made, with illustrations, by the Rev. J. L. Petit, in his work, *Architectural Studies in France*, 8vo. 1854,

Fig. 1073.

page 141. Of course Viollet le Duc's *Dictionnaire* has now become a well of information on this as on many other details. Some few examples are given at the end of the ensuing chapter of this Book. Venetian details have been carefully elucidated by J. Ruskin, in *Stones of Venice*, Vol. III , 1853, wherein pp. 221–249 are devoted to the examination in succession of the bases, doorways and jambs, capitals, archivolts, cornices, and tracery bars, of Venetian architecture. We do not, however, perceive that any scale or dimension is given to the examples illustrated, the absence of which materially lessens the usefulness of the examples. German details may be sought in Möller's work before quoted ; in King, *Study Book of Mediæval Architecture and Art*, 1860 ; in Statz, Ungewitter, and Riechensperger, *Gothic Model Book*, 1859 ; and in Hoffstadt, *Gothisches ABC buch*, 1840.

Sect. IV.

PIERS AND COLUMNS.

The general plans of the piers supporting the principal arches are either simple or compound : simple, when composed of one plain member ; and compound, when consisting of a core surrounded by smaller shafts, detached or engaged. Piers of the earliest period for carrying walls were square, as at the cathedral at Worms. These were relieved by engaged shafts, as in *fig.* 1074. In the 12th century the shaft begins to take the form on its plan of a Greek cross (*fig.* 1075.), with engaged columns in its angles as well as on its principal faces.

For the benefit of those making surveys of buildings, we think it useful to subjoin the following recommendation from the " Remarks" of Professor Willis :—" In making

architectural notes, the plan of a pier should always be accompanied with indications of the distribution of its parts to the vaulting ribs and arches which it carries. The mere plan of the pier by itself conveys but small information; for it often happens that the identical pier may be distributed in many different ways, and that these differences constitute the only characters that distinguish the practice of one age or

Fig. 1074.

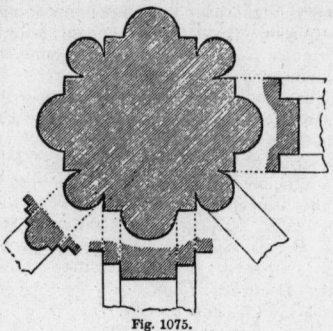

Fig. 1075.

country from another. *Fig.* 1075a. shows one way in which the plan alone may be made to convey these particulars. The dotted lines, drawn from the respective members of the pier, mark the direction of the ribs and arches; and upon each of these, at a small distance from the pier, are placed vertical sections of these ribs, as at ABCD."

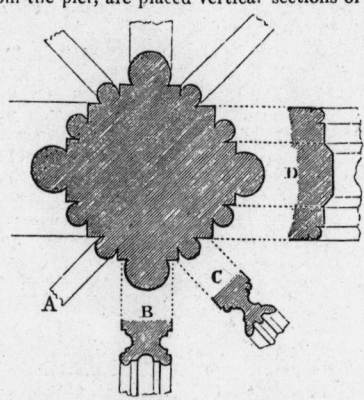

Fig. 1075a.

Fig. 1076.   FOUNTAINS ABBEY; NAVE.

Norman piers are, in their earlier form, mostly masses of wall, with rectangular nooks containing attached shafts, as at Winchester, *figs.* 1267 and 1268. The circular (*fig.* 1076.) and octagonal columns seem to have been introduced about the time of the transition; and continued common in ordinary parish churches throughout the early English and decorated periods. Complex early English piers are so varied in arrangement that it would be impossible here to do more than notice their general characteristics, which consist principally in the number of smaller isolated shafts clinging to a central column, to which they are at intervals attached, in reality as well as in appearance, by moulded bands or fillets (Westminster Abbey, *fig.* 1278.), wherein a circular shaft is found, with four detached colonnettes (*fig.* 1058.), and with eight small detached shafts at Ely. *Fig.* 1077. is a gracefully designed pier. One without the colonnettes, and with broader fillets, is a very common form in the early English and decorated periods, with some varieties.

Geometric and decorated piers have their shafts engaged (*figs.*

Fig. 1077.   FOUNTAINS ABBEY; CHOIR.

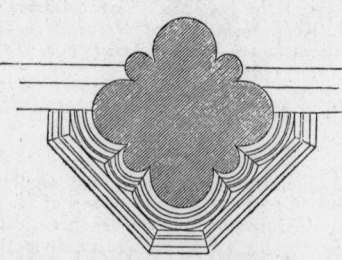

Fig. 1078.   TINTERN ABBEY; PIER.

1078. and 1079.), so that a clustered column is formed by working out the surfaces of the mass in lines and hollows. The example (*fig.* 1059.), from Westminster Abbey, has four detached, and four attached, colonnettes to the central shaft, but the reason for this exceptional arrangement has been explained. It would require a volume to set forth the richness

and extent of the great piers in cathedrals and abbeys.   Piers in the perpendicular period are generally of oblong or parallelogrammic plan, the longitudinal direction extending

from north to south (*fig.* 1316.).   On the east and west sides half shafts are attached, which bear the innermost order or soffit mouldings of the arch; the rest, including the great hollow, being usually continuous, without the interruption of any impost.   The plan of the pier in Henry VII.'s Chapel is a fine example (*fig.* 1324.) of such an arrangement; and *fig.* 1059. shows the continued adoption of the decorated piers in the later portion of the nave of Westminster Abbey.   Sometimes the ground plan is a square, set angleways (as in the nave of Canterbury Cathedral, *fig.* 1299., and at Bath Abbey Church, *fig.* 1320.), and each angle may have an engaged shaft of a

Fig. 1079.   HOWDEN CHURCH.   circular or ogee form.

SECT. V.

CAPITALS.

The mouldings of capitals and bases are more definitely marked in the various periods than any other kind of mouldings.   "It is by no means impossible, even for an experienced eye, to mistake the details of a decorated for those of a perpendicular arch ; but no one moderately acquainted with the subject could hesitate in pronouncing the style of a capital or base, provided it possessed any character at all.   In the Norman period, when the shaft was round, the highest and lowest members only were square, the parts immediately next them being rounded off to suit the shape of the shaft (*fig.* 1266.).   This is seen in the ordinary form of the *cushion capital.*   We may observe the lingering reluctance to get rid of the square plinth, in the tongue-shaped leaves or other grotesque excrescences which are often seen to issue from the circular mouldings of transition Norman bases."   *Fig.* 1080. is a curious example of the square form in front (N), and the circular moulded form in rear, of the shaft, shown on plan, *fig.* 1076.   As soon as a sub-arch was introduced the corners of the capitals were either cut off or cut out : the former process produced the octagonal form ; the shape of the shaft produced

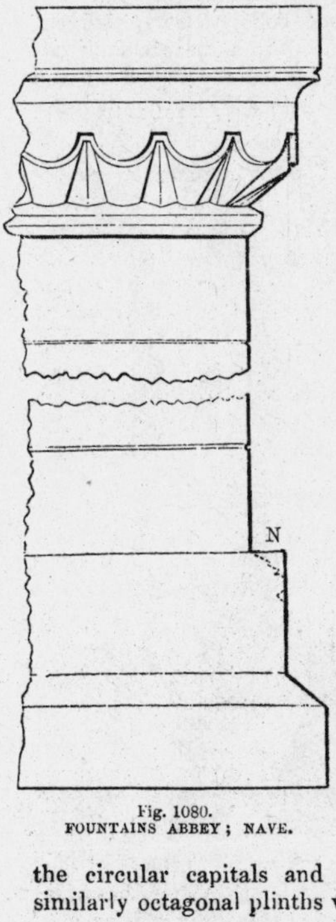

Fig. 1080.
FOUNTAINS ABBEY ; NAVE.

Fig. 1081.
FOUNTAINS ABBEY ; CHOIR.
Scale, the same as to fig. 1064.

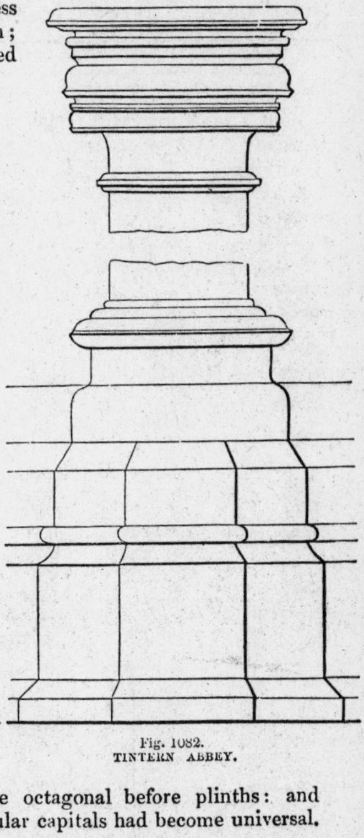

Fig. 1082.
TINTERN ABBEY.

the circular capitals and base.   But capitals became octagonal before plinths : and similarly octagonal plinths were retained long after circular capitals had become universal.

Fig. 1081. is the front face of the shaft shown in *fig.* 1077., as is also *fig.* 1082. of that of *fig.* 1078., &c.

"Capitals may be divided into moulded and floriated. In the latter, the foliage in the transition Norman and early English period is arranged vertically, in the decorated it

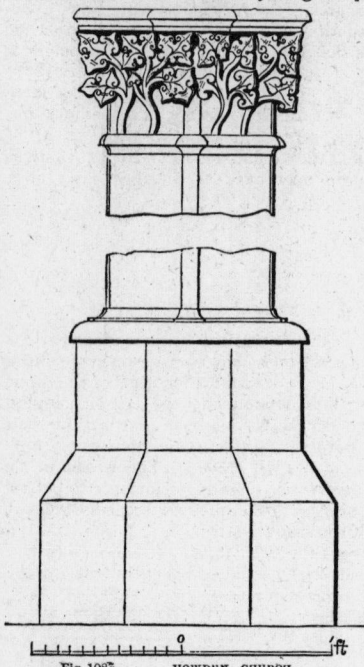

twines horizontally, or rather transversely, round the capital (*fig.* 1083.). In the perpendicular, more frequently small leaves or pateræ are set like studs at intervals round the shaft above the neck. The capital consists of three parts, the abacus, the bell, and the neck. In the early English period the abacus is almost invariably undercut. In the decorated it consists of the scroll moulding with a cylindrical roll of less size below it. The bell, in early English caps, is sometimes double, with a very handsome effect, while in decorated work it is seldom so deeply undercut. It is also much more varied by elaborate and capricious forms, as by a number of fine edge lines ; and the underpart of the bell is often composed of a roll and fillet. The necking forms an important detail in judging of the dates of the work. In the early English it is usually of a bold annular outline ; or a semihexagon. The neck during the decorated period is almost always the scroll moulding, but many other forms will be found to occur. Even a practised eye may occasionally be deceived in the date of capitals of the two early periods.

"The capitals in the perpendicular period present such marked features that they are seldom liable to be mistaken. The mouldings are large, angular, meagre and few. Neither abacus nor bell is clearly defined. The latter is reduced to a meagre slope, al-

Fig. 1083.   HOWDEN CHURCH.

though it sometimes still remains. The upper part of the abacus is usually sloped off to a sharp edge, and the section of the moulding below resembles the letter S inverted, being a

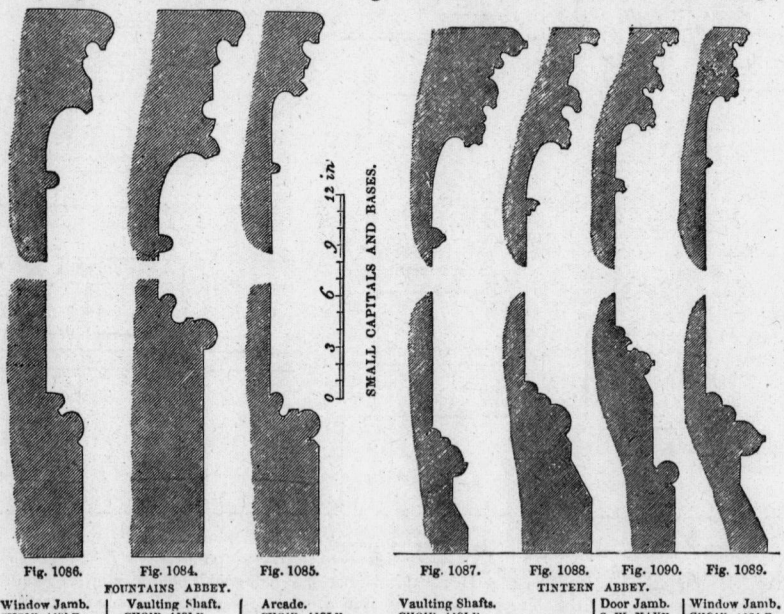

SMALL CAPITALS AND BASES.

| Fig. 1086. | Fig. 1084. | Fig. 1085. | | Fig. 1087. | Fig. 1088. | Fig. 1090. | Fig. 1089. |

FOUNTAINS ABBEY.   TINTERN ABBEY.

Window Jamb. | Vaulting Shaft. | Arcade. | | Vaulting Shafts. | Door Jamb. | Window Jamb.
CHOIR AISLE. | CHOIR AISLE. | CHOIR AISLE | | CHOIR AISLE. | S. W. NAVE. | CHOIR AISLE.

mere corruption of the decorated scroll moulding; *above all*, the capital is octagonal, while that of the preceding styles is round. The shaft, however, is circular in the perpendicular work, while octagonal capitals most generally occur in the other styles in the case of large single columns of the same shape. The base in the

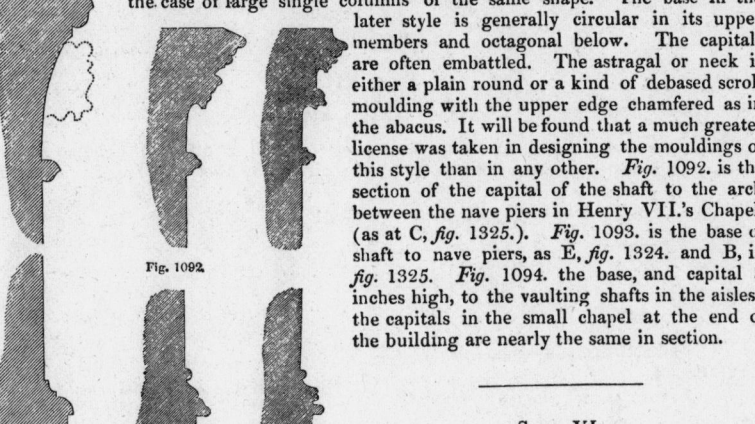

later style is generally circular in its upper members and octagonal below. The capitals are often embattled. The astragal or neck is either a plain round or a kind of debased scroll moulding with the upper edge chamfered as in the abacus. It will be found that a much greater license was taken in designing the mouldings of this style than in any other. *Fig.* 1092. is the section of the capital of the shaft to the arch between the nave piers in Henry VII.'s Chapel, (as at C, *fig.* 1325.). *Fig.* 1093. is the base of shaft to nave piers, as E, *fig.* 1324. and B, in *fig.* 1325. *Fig.* 1094. the base, and capital 8 inches high, to the vaulting shafts in the aisles; the capitals in the small chapel at the end of the building are nearly the same in section.

Fig. 1092.

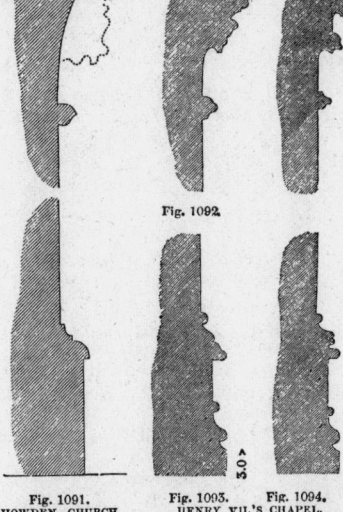

Fig. 1091.
HOWDEN CHURCH.
Vaulting Shaft,
CHOIR AISLE.

Fig. 1093.   Fig. 1094.
HENRY VII.'S CHAPEL.
Scale, the same as to Fig. 1085.

Sect. VI.

BASES.

The bases of the shafts in the 11th and 12th centuries are often chamfered and frequently moulded in the Attic form, more or less modified and debased. In the latter period the Attic base is sometimes found almost pure. In early work the base consists of the plinth or lower step, of solid masonry, generally square (*fig.* 1080. see the curious modifications of it in the plan *fig.* 1076.), but in early English often octangular (*fig.* 1077. and 1081.); and the base mouldings, a series of annular rolls, slopes, or hollows, taking the form of the column. In decorated and perpendicular columns, the plinth is apparently omitted, and the base is divided into heights, stages, or tables, by gradually spreading courses, each separated from the next by a plain, or by a moulded, order. The lower part of the base is sometimes octagonal or polygonal. A cavetto above a quarter round is a very common form in early work. A bold annular roll, quirked on the under side, often divides the shaft from the plinth.

The early English base is very similar to the Attic form, the chief peculiarity consisting in the hollow being cut downwards and extended from half to three quarters of a circle, so that it is capable of containing water (*figs.* 1081., 1084., and 1085.). The earlier the base is in the period, the shallower, as a general rule, is this water-holding hollow (*fig.* 1086.). A common form is obtained by omitting the hollow altogether, and thus bringing the rolls into contact (like *fig.* 1088.). In very rich early English bases there are often double hollows between filleted rolls, and below these occur other bold annular rolls, single, double, and even triple, as at the beautiful Galilee porch at Ely, where the bases are worked out of Purbeck marble and were polished. The spread of the base in the uppermost members generally equals that of the capital, or nearly so. By far the commonest decorated base is that shown in *fig.* 1087. and *fig.* 1089., the number of rolls being generally three, but often only two. A few modifications may be perceived, but they are seldom very complex. The large spreading roll is worked out of the block, with which it usually stands flush, and is separated by a quirk or angular nook. This is also observable in the previous style. A simple form of base is shown in *fig.* 1091.

The prevailing characteristic of the bases of perpendicular columns is a large bell-shaped spread in the upper part, often double, forming the contour of a double ogee in section, as *fig.* 1093.; and is one of the ordinary kind. The lower part is almost invariably octagonal, the upper being generally round, but also frequently octagonal, irrespective of the shape of the shaft (*fig.* 1300.). It has either one or more stages sloping off by a hollow chamfer, or by a second bell-shaped slope. The first member of the base is always an annular roll, resembling the neck of capitals; this is often in the form of the debased roll and fillet. Edge lines scarcely ever occur. Other examples of bases are given in the last section of this book. The usual distribution of the table mouldings of a late base consist of a plain slope F (*fig.* 1320.), reckoning upwards from the ground line C, a flat surface E and a projecting moulding D. In more elaborate structures, the number of these base tables

and intermediate *champs* or *fasciæ* is increased, and the latter are often carved in panels, &c. Thus a second table, B, is introduced above the ground line G. Professor Willis applies the term "ground table, grass table, or earth table," to the slope B, and states that to such tables as D the term " ledgement tables " were probably applied.

Sect. VII.

VAULTING SHAFTS AND RIBS.

When the main shaft supporting the clerestory had an attached circular shaft in front, the latter was often carried up as a shaft to the roof (*fig.* 1266.) The point

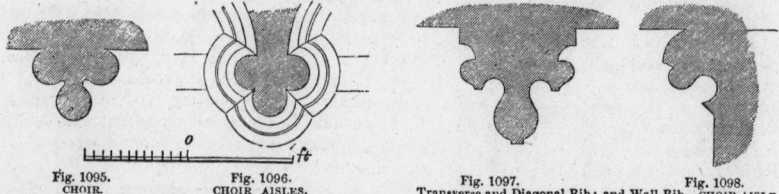

Fig. 1095.
CHOIR.
Fig. 1096.
CHOIR AISLES.
FOUNTAINS ABBEY. VAULTING SHAFTS.

Fig. 1097.
Transverse and Diagonal Rib; and Wall Rib—CHOIR AISLE.
FOUNTAINS ABBEY. VAULTING RIBS.
Fig. 1098.

has not yet been settled whether this shaft in some early buildings was, or was not, so carried up to receive the cross-rib of a vault, or simply to bear the beam of the roofing. When vaulting became more general, the purpose of the shaft was undisguised (*fig.* 1278.), and being made correspondent with the vaulting ribs, the groups of the latter were received on a colonnette or on small columns. The vaulting ribs at St. Saviour's (Southwark) Church, are given in *fig.* 662e. In the latter part of the 15th century engaged colonnettes for receiving the vault ribs rise from corbels placed on or above the capitals of the shafts, and sometimes the ribs themselves spring from the corbels (*figs.* 1274. and 1275.), and later, or in the perpendicular period,

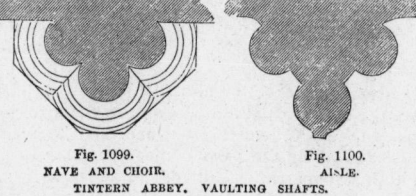

Fig. 1099.
NAVE AND CHOIR.
Fig. 1100.
AISLE.
TINTERN ABBEY. VAULTING SHAFTS.

the older form was, as it were, reverted to, and the attached circular shaft was carried up to, and received the vaulting ribs, as in *figs.* 1302., 1307., 1314., 1317., and 1325.

CORBELS very frequently supplied the place of capitals both for the springing of arch mouldings and for vaulting. These corbels were either moulded or carved to correspond with the capitals (*fig.* 1109.), or they were fashioned into a mass

Fig. 1101.
NAVE AND AISLES.
Aisles, Transverse Rib, and Diagonal.
Fig. 1102.
Wall Rib.
Fig. 1103.
NAVE AND CHOIR.
Transverse Rib and Diagonal.
TINTERN ABBEY. VAULTING RIBS.

of foliage, into heads of males and females, or of animals. Even whole figures were introduced, occasionally deformed if not purposely so carved for admission within the

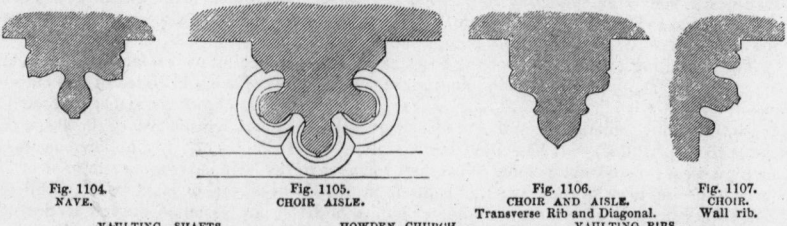

Fig. 1104.
NAVE.
Fig. 1105.
CHOIR AISLE.
Fig. 1106.
CHOIR AND AISLE.
Transverse Rib and Diagonal.
Fig. 1107.
CHOIR.
Wall rib.
VAULTING SHAFTS. HOWDEN CHURCH. VAULTING RIBS.

space. In the vaulted sacristy at Winchester College, its " springers present an archbishop in benediction, a bishop, and a king, and over the door a guardian angel. Bosses of

oak leaves and roses alternately, carved with great taste and 'subtilitè,' enrich and cover the junction of the ribs.—The uncouth and

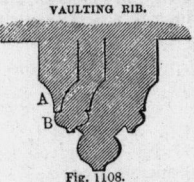

VAULTING RIB.

Fig. 1108.
A and B, Ribs for groining.
HENRY VII.'S CHAPEL; AISLE.

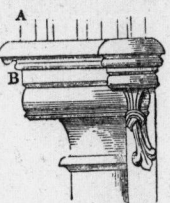

Fig. 1109.   WESTMINSTER ABBEY CHURCH; NORTH AISLE OF CHOIR.

barbaric heads in the corbels which surround the principal figures contrast with their graciousness, and form that antithesis which the great masters in fine arts of the succeeding centuries employed so abundantly. The virgin patroness presides over the western pinnacle of the chapel; the angel Michael at the other termination of the building menaces with his flaming falchion the several demons which might approach the hall, refectory, cellar, and kitchen; the angel Raphael points out the entrance to the house of prayer at New College; the king and the bishop support the label of the gateways to the college at Winchester, and the entrance of the chapel; and as the appointed guardians and supporters of temporal and spiritual things, they sustain alternately the corbels or springers of the ceiling of the chapel. At the entrance of the hall and kitchen, the recreating psaltery and bagpipes are affixed; over the kitchen window is 'excess,' a head vomiting; and opposite is 'frugality' in the figure of a bursar with his iron-bound money chest. Over the master's windows are the pedagogue instructing, and a listless scholar, scarcely attentive to the book he holds in his hand. Elsewhere we recognise the soldier, the scholar, the clergyman, &c., as suggesting the various professions in which the inmates may occupy themselves in after life. The inept substitutions for these significant and appropriate ornaments are amongst the most palpable evidences of the insufficiency and inaptness of our mimicry of this style, in most instances in the present day; and they betray great ignorance of the poetical mind and spirit of mediæval sculpture."— Cockerell, *The Wykeham Buildings*.

Sect. VIII.

HOOD MOULDINGS AND STRING COURSES.

" The strings consist of projecting ledges of stones carried below windows, both within and without a building, round buttresses, and other angular projections, and to cornices, parapets, tower stages, and other parts of edifices, being used as dividing lines. Though subordinate, they are of the greatest possible importance in imparting a character to a building. They at once relieve naked masonry, and bind into a whole the seemingly detached portions of a rambling or irregular construction. In most cases, especially to windows, a string course forms a real drip or weathering, and adapts its upper surface especially to this end, thus becoming what is termed a hood moulding, which when used

Fig. 1110.   Fig. 1110a.   Fig. 1110b.   Fig. 1110c.   Fig. 1113.   Fig. 1114.   Fig. 1111.   Fig. 1112.
                                                                                       FOUNTAINS ABBEY.
                        NORMAN PERIOD.   CHOIR AISLES.   NAVE CLERESTORY.   AISLE.

internally, cannot be said to have any real use; but they form a decorative finish of too important a kind to be neglected with impunity."

Norman string courses are generally full of edges or hard chamfered surfaces (*fig.* 1110.). In most cases they have some sculptured decoration of the style, as the billet, the chevron,

Fig. 1115.   Fig. 1116.   Fig. 1117.   Fig. 1118.   Fig. 1119.   Fig. 1120.
        TINTERN ABBEY; NAVE, ETC.   HOWDEN CHURCH; CHOIR.
CLERESTORY.   AISLE.   AISLE.   TRIFORIUM.   AISLE.   AISLE.
        The scale of the last ten Sections is the same as that attached to fig. 1085.

the hatched or serrated moulding, or the like (*fig.* 188.). *Figs.* 1111. and 1112. are among the simplest, being the latest in the period. The commonest early English strings are like *figs.* 1114. and 1115.; the under-cutting giving a bold projection is a striking feature

of this moulding as of all others of the style. The most frequent decorated form is *fig.* 1116. That shown on *figs.* 1179. and 1181. is also very common. The scroll, with a half-round next below it, *fig.* 1115., is very characteristic. The rounded form of the upper side, or weathering (*fig.* 1118.), is peculiar to the two first styles; the angular or chamfered, of the last (*figs.* 1119. and 1120.). String courses follow the principle of the abacus of the capitals, from which indeed they are often continued along the wall of the building.

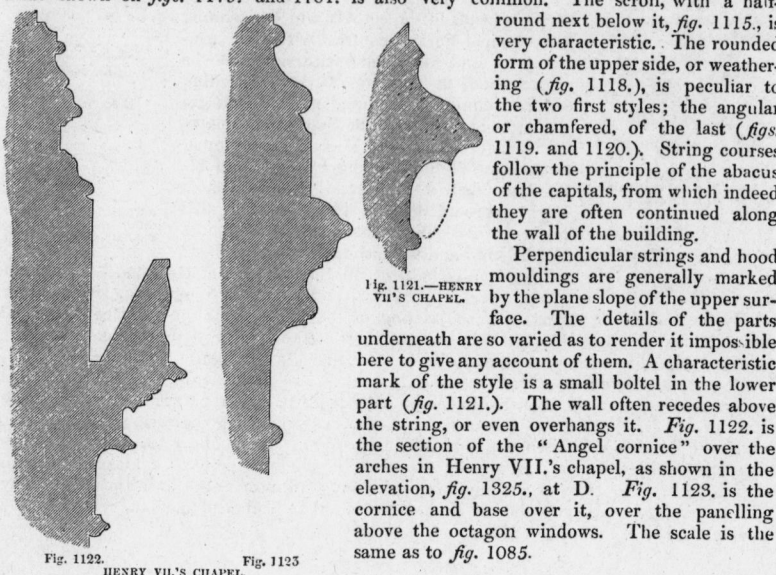

Perpendicular strings and hood mouldings are generally marked by the plane slope of the upper surface. The details of the parts underneath are so varied as to render it impossible here to give any account of them. A characteristic mark of the style is a small boltel in the lower part (*fig.* 1121.). The wall often recedes above the string, or even overhangs it. *Fig.* 1122. is the section of the " Angel cornice " over the arches in Henry VII.'s chapel, as shown in the elevation, *fig.* 1325., at D. *Fig.* 1123. is the cornice and base over it, over the panelling above the octagon windows. The scale is the same as to *fig.* 1085.

Fig. 1121.—HENRY VII'S CHAPEL.

Fig. 1122.   Fig. 1123.
HENRY VII.'S CHAPEL.

SECT. IX.

BASE COURSES OR PLINTHS.

This term is applied to that series of mouldings formed at the base of a wall, which leads the eye from the upright face gradually into the ground. The lowest course of them is even called the " earth table." The early examples are very plain, consisting of one or of more chamfered set-offs at various heights, as *fig.* 1124.

In the early English period, the roll moulding was introduced at the upper edge of a deep chamfer, as *figs.* 1125. and 1272., and with one or two

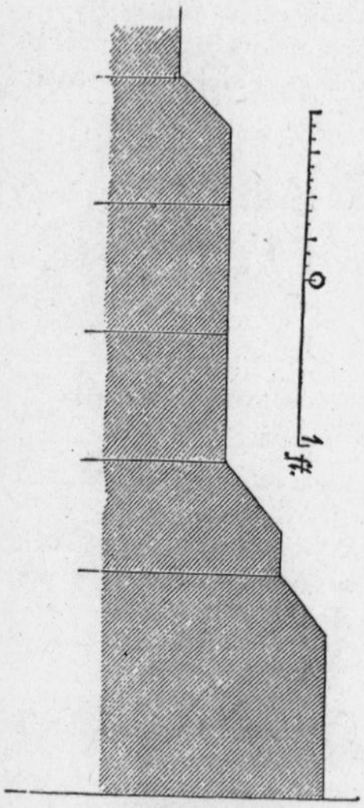

Fig. 1124.
FOUNTAINS ABBEY.
NAVE.

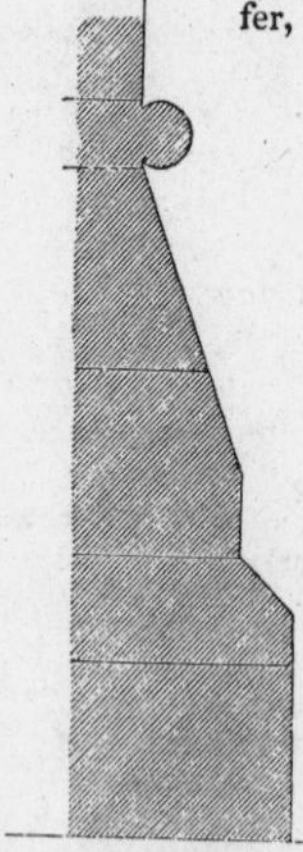

Fig. 1125.
FOUNTAINS ABBEY.
CHOIR.

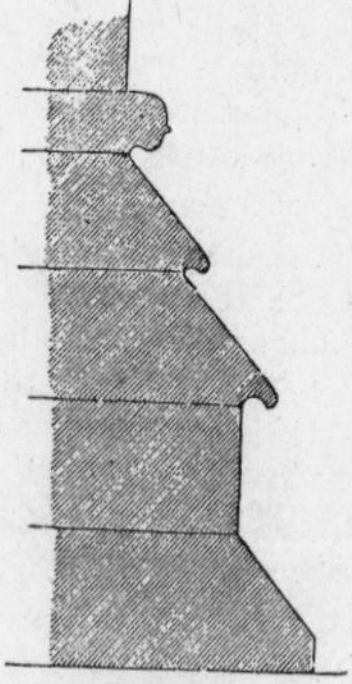

Fig. 1126.
TINTERN ABBEY.
NAVE, ETC.

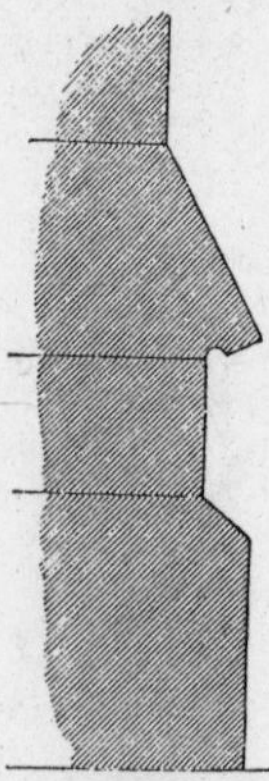

Fig. 1127.
HOWDEN CHURCH.
CHOIR.

chamfered set-offs. They then became very similar, as in the transepts of Beverly Minster, to *fig.* 1126., of the geometric or decorated period, in which the tablet or slope took a curved or ogee outline, and was generally only one in number, finished at top by a scroll moulding, with occasionally a string above it, as at Ewerby. The height of

fig. 1126 is very small for so large a building. The basement to Lichfield Cathedral is not much more defined. *Fig.* 1277. is a richer example.

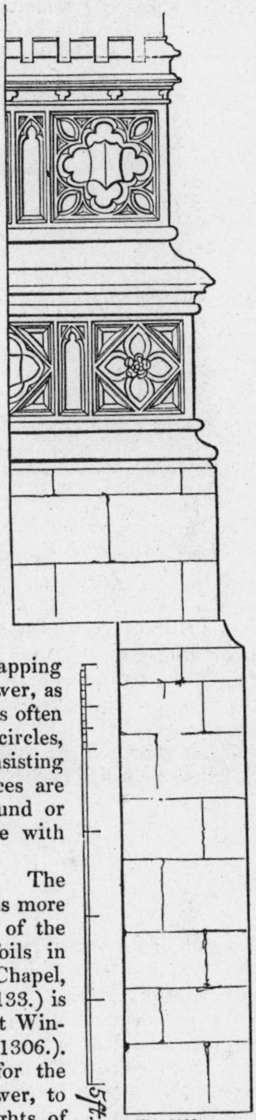

The basement in the perpendicular period is one of the glories of the style. That shown in *fig.* 1306. from Winchester, may be considered very plain, as is also that at Bath, *fig.* 1319. Reversed ogees and hollows, variously disposed, are the principal members. *Fig.* 1128. being the basement round the outside of Henry VII.'s chapel, will afford some idea of the work bestowed upon this feature. Yelvertoft Church, Northamptonshire, has four rows of diagonal, square, and circular panelling, one above the other (Rickman, page 213., 6th edit.). In Norfolk, where flint work was used in the erection of the building, it was introduced in upright panelling in the lowest face, above an ogee moulding (*ibid*, page 214.).

SECT. X.

PARAPETS.

The Norman period may be said not to have exhibited any parapet, the roof being finished by the tiles or lead work projecting over the wall and supported by a corbel blocking.

During nearly the whole of the early English period, the parapet in many buildings was often plain, as *figs.* 1129. and 1126.; or with a series of arches and panels; or with quatrefoils in small panels, as *fig.* 1277., which is of the next period; or plain, with a rich cornice under it.

In the decorated period it was still plain but with moulded capping and cornice, as *figs.* 1130. and 1131., and with the ball flower, as in *fig.* 1128., but also closer and connected by tendrils; it is often pierced in various shapes, of which quatrefoils (*fig.* 1277.), in circles, or without that enclosure, are very common; but another, consisting of a waved line, is more beautiful and less usual; the spaces are trefoiled. Pierced battlements are very common, with a round or square quatrefoil. The plain battlement most in use is one with small intervals, and the capping moulding only horizontal.

They continued to be used in the perpendicular period. The trefoiled panel with waved line is seen, but the dividing line is more often straight, making the divisions regular triangles. One of the finest examples of a panelled parapet, consisting of quatrefoils in squares with shields and flowers, is that at the Beauchamp Chapel, Warwick. The pierced parapet on Henry VII.'s Chapel (*fig.* 1133.) is a fine example, with its angle pinnacle. That on the choir at Winchester Cathedral consists of upright panelling only (*fig.* 1306.). Early period *battlements* frequently have quatrefoils either for the lower compartments or on the top of the panels of the lower, to form the higher. The later examples have often two heights of panels, or richly pierced quatrefoils in two heights, forming an inducted battlement. They have generally a running cap moulding carried round the indentations.

Fig. 1128.
HENRY VII.'S CHAPEL.

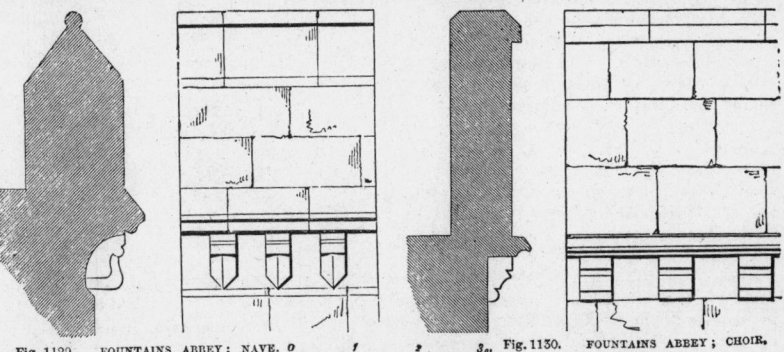

Fig. 1129.   FOUNTAINS ABBEY; NAVE.    Fig. 1130.   FOUNTAINS ABBEY; CHOIR.

In a few late buildings the capping is ornamented, somewhat like a cresting : and in a few instances figures resembling soldiers on guard have been carved on the battlements.

Plain battlements have been divided into four descriptions. I. Of nearly equal divisions, having a plain capping running round the outline. II. Of nearly equal intervals,

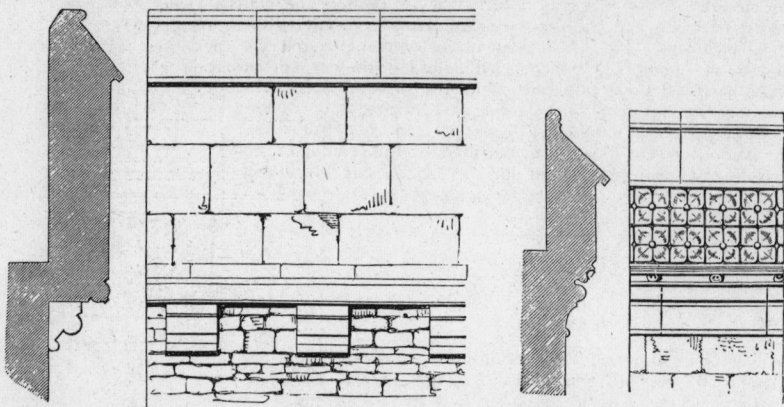

Fig 1131.   TINTERN ABBEY ; CHOIR.   Fig. 1132.   HOWDEN CHURCH ; CHOIR.

and sometimes with large battlements and small intervals, the capping being only placed on the top, and the sides cut plain. III. Like the last, but with a moulding running round the outline, the horizontal capping being set upon it. And IV. The most common late battlement, with the capping broad, of several mouldings running round the outline, often narrowing the intervals (Rickman). It is seldom that the battlements will tell the age of the building, as they have been so often rebuilt. A small battlement differing to these four descriptions, is shown in *fig.* 1128., under the windows of Henry VII.'s chapel. A few more words may be said in the section TOWERS AND SPIRES.

Sect. XI.

MOULDINGS IN WOODWORK.

" If this kind of work be attentively examined, it will be seen that it was wrought altogether on the same principles as the corresponding sculpture in stone. We see the thoroughly conventional early school, the naturalesque middle-pointed school, and the again conventional third-pointed school of carvers, succeeding each other in exactly the same way, the main difference between the two being that the work in wood is ordinarily very much more thin, flat, delicate, and sharp, than the work in stone ; that it has always some limits set to its exuberance by the nature of the framework in which it was wrought. In carpenter's work, it was always the rule only to mould the useful members, and so it was also as regards the carving. It was not useful or convenient to put on to a piece of oak framing a mass of oak to be carved as a boss or a stopping to a label (this sort of device was reserved for the ingenuity of nineteenth century architects), and so it will be found that most of the old wood-carving is so contrived as to be wrought out of the same plank or thickness as that which is moulded. or else is a separate piece of wood —in a spandril, for instance, enclosed within the constructional members. The spandrils in the arcades behind the stalls at Winchester Cathedral are an admirable example ; they are carved in thin oak, perforated in all directions, and then set forward about half-an-inch in advance of the back panelling. The effect of this is, as may be supposed, to give the

Fig. 1133.   HENRY VII.'S CHAPEL.

carving the most distinct relief ; and it is an effect strictly lawful, because it was impossible in other material, and yet natural in woodwork. The same attention to the material will be found exemplified very remarkably in all old wooden mouldings. The accompanying illustrations (*figs.* 1134. and 1135.) will show how extraordinarily minute, delicate, and sharp they were. In the stalls at Selby we see an elabo-rate cap, only 1¾ inches high ; at Winchester, a band ⅞ths of an inch in height, and yet consisting of four distinct members, and showing in elevation as many as eight

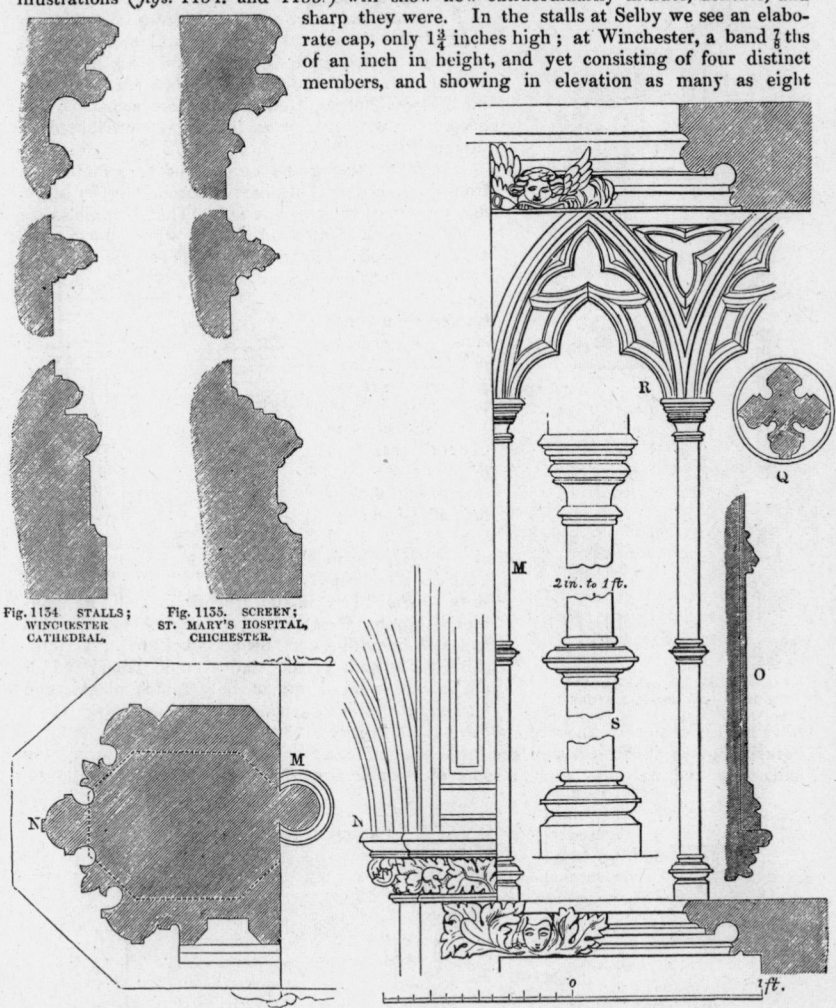

Fig. 1134. STALLS ;
WINCHESTER
CATHEDRAL.

Fig. 1135. SCREEN ;
ST. MARY'S HOSPITAL,
CHICHESTER.

2 in. to 1 ft.

R

Q

M

S

O

N

M

N

Fig. 1137.　　Scale 2 in. to 1 ft.

Fig. 1136.　　SCREEN ; NORTHFLEET.

distinct lines. The finish of the wall plates in the porch at Horsemonden, and the carving of the miserere seat, so curiously preserved in the midst of woodwork some three hundred years later in date, in Henry VII.'s chapel, are fair illustrations of the goodness of the earlier sculpture.'

" The whole of the early mouldings are sharp, delicate, minute, and quaintly undercut. They are very often unlike any stone mouldings, just as many wooden traceries (e.g. those of the screen at St. Mary's hospital, at Chichester (*fig.* 1135.), and the stalls at Lancaster), are quite unlike what could conveniently be executed in stone. In spite of a bad fashion which obtains just now," among some of the present mediæval architects, " of ignoring the value of mouldings, I maintain that they prove conclusively the existence of a school of art in this country of almost unsurpassable excellence." Street, *On English Woodwork in the 13th and 14th centuries,* read at the Royal Institute of British Architects, 20th February, 1865.

As an example of early work we give *figs.* 1136. and 1137., from Bury, *Woodwork,* being the details of the screen in Northfleet Church, Kent. M, in the first figure, is the first column (the details being given to a larger scale at S) in the screen abutting upon the

centre opening, the arch of which is shown at N. The corresponding positions on plan are exhibited in *fig.* 1137. The section O, represents the face of the buttress P, while the plan Q is that of the arch mouldings at R.

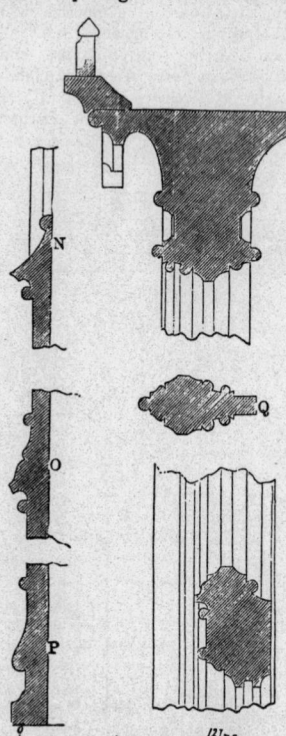

Fig. 1138. is a section of the screen on the south side of the chancel at Lavenham Church, Suffolk, wherein the details N, O, and P, are those belonging to the buttress Q, which even in late mediæval carpentry was not omitted, though somewhat out of accordance with the "true principles" attributed to design in that style.

Fig. 1139, being the capital and base mouldings from the screen in Aldenham Church, Hertfordshire, are of the perpendicular period. These examples are all further illustrated in Bury's work above-mentioned, as well as *figs.* 1140. to 1144., showing the general style of mouldings adopted for seats and bench ends, as noticed in *par.* 2192*b*. *Fig.* 1140. is the rail of the bench ; *fig.* 1141. the division under the seat ; and *fig.* 1142. the section of the arm of the stall and of a bench end, all at Bridgenorth Church, Somerset-

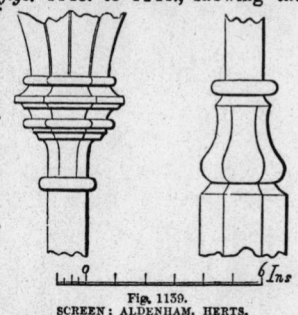

Fig. 1139.
SCREEN; ALDENHAM, HERTS.

Fig. 1138. LAVENHAM, SUFFOLK.

shire. *Fig.* 1143. is the arm of the stalls at Wantage Church, Berkshire ; and *fig.* 1144. the rail and stall mouldings at Swinbrook Church, Oxfordshire. The ends of the stall even in Henry VII.'s chapel are worked out of only 3-inch planks, and formed into three attached shafts, similar to *fig.* 1143.

Other notices of the thickness of stuff are given in *par.* 2175*d*.

Having given illustrations of the principles of constructing timber roofs during the mediæval period, we now append some of their details, which, on comparison with the

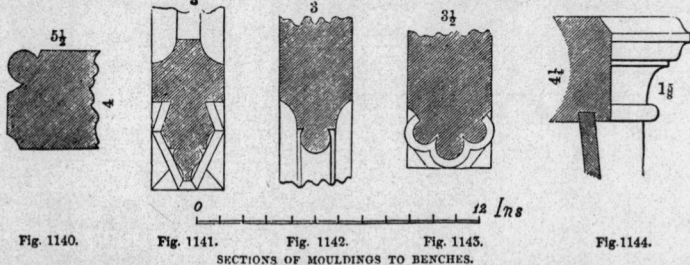

Fig. 1140. Fig. 1141. Fig. 1142. Fig. 1143. Fig.1144.
SECTIONS OF MOULDINGS TO BENCHES.

figures just given, will tend to show the mode in which the rougher and larger timbers were ornamented, especially those so much further from the sight than screens and other

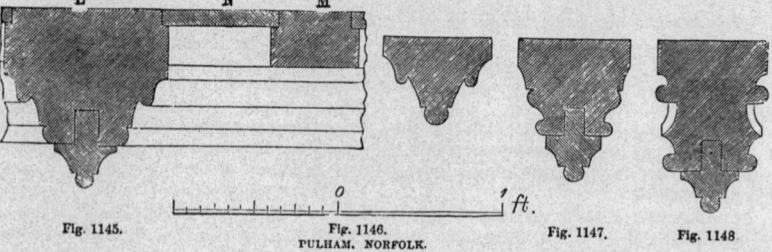

Fig. 1145. Fig. 1146. Fig. 1147. Fig. 1148
PULHAM. NORFOLK.

like decorative work. *Fig.* 1145. shows the rafters used at Pulham Church, Norfolk (*fig.* 701*o*.), L being the main, and M the common, rafters, with the boarding N sunk

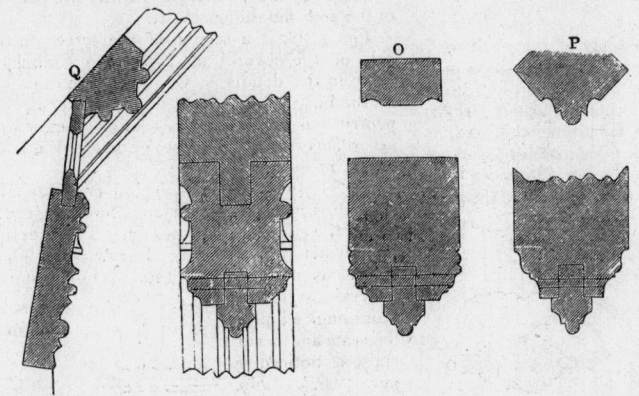

Fig. 1151.   Fig. 1150.   Fig. 1149.   Fig. 1152.
                              CAPEL ST. MARY, SUFFOLK.

in between them. *Fig.* 1146. is the purline; *fig.* 1147. the wall piece; and *fig.* 1148. the collar-beam. *Fig.* 1149. illustrates the rafters in the church at Capel St. Mary,

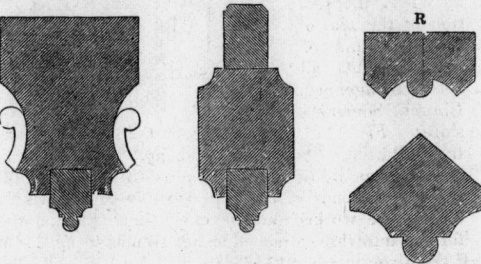

Suffolk (*fig.* 701*q*.), O being the section of the common rafter. *Fig.* 1150. is the collar-beam with the arched truss under it; and P the ridge piece; *fig.* 1151. shows the moulded cornice abutting upon the hammer-beam, *fig.* 1152., and Q the lower purline. *Fig.* 1153. gives the details of the roof of late work at Knapton Church, Norfolk (*fig.* 701*t*.), being the section of the lower hammer-beam; *fig.* 1154. the post abutting upon it; *fig.* 1155. the ridge piece; and R

Fig. 1153.   Fig. 1154.   Fig. 1155.
                   KNAPTON, NORFOLK.

the purline. These will all be found to a larger scale, with the other details, in Brandon's *Analysis.* All the illustrations from *figs.* 1145. to 1155. are drawn to the same scale.

The following sections represent the roof timbers in the south aisle of Lavenham Church,

Fig. 1156.   Fig. 1157.   Fig. 1158.   Fig. 1159.   Fig. 1160.   ST. ALBAN'S.
                        LAVENHAM, SUFFOLK.

Suffolk, from which building the screen in *fig.* 1138. was also derived. *Fig.* 1156. is the cornice; *fig.* 1157. the wall strut, and *fig.* 1158. the purline. *Fig.* 1159. is the cornice in the chancel aisle. These are likewise derived from Bury, *Woodwork.*

Sect. XII.

WINDOWS.

In the body of the work we have, under each period of Gothic architecture, given a description in general terms of the windows prevailing at the several times. The examples here brought together, are inserted merely for the purpose of showing the gradual change in their forms and combinations, which are almost infinite in number, and yet that the latter are far from exhausted, is conclusively shown by R. W. Billings, in his work on *Geometric Combinations* ; and by E. Sharpe, in *Decorated Window Tracery.*

The earliest windows are extremely small, always semi-circular headed, or nearly so, and without moulded archivolts. They are usually with a single light (*fig.* 1266.), except in belfry towers, where we often find them divided into two by a shaft with a capital, as in the tower at St. Alban's (*fig.* 1160.). The simple plain head, however, in the latter part of the early period, was more or less ornamented with the chevron or zigzag, and other orna-

Fig. 1161.   BEAUDESERT.   Fig. 1162. CANTERBURY.   Fig. 1163.   SALISBURY.

ments of the time, as in *fig.* 1161. One of the greatest and most striking changes brought in by the pointed style was that of introducing, from the suddenly elongated dimensions of its windows, a blaze of light into its edifices, which, from the low and narrow sizes of their predecessors, were masses of gloom. From the beginning of the 12th century we see them lengthened in a surprising manner, and terminating with a lancet-head, which sometimes became occasionally cusped. An instance of the simple lancet-head is given in *fig.* 1162., from the Trinity Chapel at Canterbury Cathedral. Sometimes an elegant combination is obtained by grouping lancet-headed windows under one hood, the centre rising above the side ones, as at Salisbury Cathedral (*fig.* 1163.), where the spaces between the heads are ornamented, or have a sunk panel or device. These spaces are frequently pierced with foliated circles, or with trefoils or quatrefoils not enclosed. In an example at Lincoln (*fig.* 1164.), the height of the group is equal, but the light of the centre being wider than the two side lights, the curvature of the arches of the latter

Fig. 1164.   LINCOLN.

is necessarily much less than that to the former, and the effect is not satisfactory. There were, however, many other arrangements in designing these lancet-headed windows than the single and triple ones just mentioned. Two, four, and five, lights occasionally form the group. Of the last-named, are windows at Irthlingborough, in Warwickshire, and at Oundle, in Northamptonshire, in which the lights on the sides gradually rise up to the centre one. In the latter part of the period, heads finish with trefoils ; the mullions are moulded and finished, both inside and outside, with shafts or colonettes, from the capitals of which spring the mouldings of the subdivisions.

The finest and largest group of early English lancets in the kingdom is the five, commonly called 'the five sisters,' in the north transept at York Cathedral, completed 1250. They are each about 5 feet 7 inches wide, and nearly 60 feet high, and in the interior have a beauty altogether their own, not surpassed, if it be equalled, by any decorated or perpendicular window in the kingdom. The rich effect of the arrangement of the two stories, each having three lights, at the east end of Southwell Minster, is well deserving of attention. Ely cathedral has internally five lights over three, while externally three more are observed over the five.

At Kilkenny Cathedral there are three huge early English lancets, the centre one being

62 feet high and 8 feet wide.   The detached shafts are filleted in four rows ; the mouldings over are formed into trefoil arches.   In the south side of the choir of St. John's Priory, in the same city, is a continuous arcade of 54 feet of lancets, the largest pier being only 9 inches wide.

These filleted bands are an interesting work, as they are found in many parts both of Ireland and England.   Perhaps the most remarkable example in England is that at Walsoken Church, near Wisbeach, where the chancel arch has four small shafts in each pier, all banded five or six times.   It is additionally striking from its greater antiquity than any of the Irish examples, being, as at St. Alban's, romanesque.   These banded columns and roll mouldings find their counterpart at Margam Abbey, in Glamorganshire, the west front of which shows a fine triplet, and a doorway below banded in this peculiar manner.   *Transactions* of the Institute of British Architects, 1865–66, pp. 80–86.

The *foliations* seen in windows belonging to the earlier examples of this style in England are not generally cut out of the same stone as the head of the arch to which they belong,

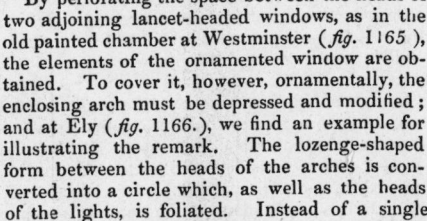

but form the tracery, in small pieces, and these enter into the class of *plate tracery*, i.e. they belong to the flat soffit, and not, like *bar tracery*, to the outer mouldings.

By perforating the space between the heads of two adjoining lancet-headed windows, as in the old painted chamber at Westminster (*fig.* 1165), the elements of the ornamented window are obtained.   To cover it, however, ornamentally, the enclosing arch must be depressed and modified ; and at Ely (*fig.* 1166.), we find an example for illustrating the remark.   The lozenge-shaped form between the heads of the arches is converted into a circle which, as well as the heads of the lights, is foliated.   Instead of a single

Fig. 1165.
PAINTED CHAMBER.

Fig. 1166.
ELY.

circle inserted in the head of the window, we then have them with three foliated circles, as

Fig. 1167.   MERTON COLLEGE.   Fig. 1168.   CATHEDRAL, OXFORD.   Fig. 1169.   ST. OUEN, ROUEN.

at Lincoln, one above and two below ; the same cathedral furnishing an example in the east window of its upper part having one large circle inclosing seven smaller foliated ones, besides its containing similar ones in the heads of the two leading divisions below.   The windows just described belong to a transitional style between the early English Gothic and the decorated ; but the ornamented windows of the 14th century exhibit in their general form and details a vast variance from them in the easy unbroken flow of the tracery with which they abound.

In the next stage come the examples shown by *fig.* 1167., Merton College Chapel, and *fig.* 1168., the Cathedral, both at Oxford ; the latter whereof has a tendency towards the Flamboyant style, which has been before mentioned, and which, in the 14th century, had thoroughly established itself in France, as may be seen in the windows of the church of St. Ouen, at Rouen, exhibited in *fig.* 1169. It may be observed that the principal lights are seldom divided by transoms ; when they, however, occur they are mostly plain, and rarely embattled.   Though the ogee head is often found, the usual form is that of the simple-pointed arch.   In the clerestory, square-headed windows are often seen, but more often in other parts of the edifice.   In the preceding, as well as in this period, occurs the window bounded by three equilaterally segmental curves foliated more or less as the date increases.   The arrangement of the tracery of

Fig. 1170.   CAWSTON.

windows has, by the French antiquaries, been divided into two classes —*rayonnant* and

flamboyant. Their *rayonnant,* so called on account of the great part the circle plays in it, and on whose radii its leading forms are dependent, was flourishing throughout the 14th century in France. The *flamboyant* or tertiary pointed style followed it. We have already observed that the Continent preceded us in each style as much as half a century.

After this comes the Florid style, in which the edifices seem to consist almost entirely of windows, and those of the most highly ornamented description. It is scarcely necessary to do more than exhibit the figures for a comprehension of the nature of the change which

took place; in short the introduction of the Tudor arch alone was sufficient hint for a totally new system. In the example (*fig.* 1170.) of a window at Cawston Church, Norfolk, we may observe the commencement of the use of transoms, which at length were repeated

Fig. 1171.   NORWICH.

Fig. 1172.   AYLSHAM.

twice and even more in the height of the window, and indeed became necessary for affording stays to the lengthy mullions that came into use. *Fig.* 1171. is an example of the square-headed window of the period, and *fig.* 1172. of a Tudor-headed window at Aylsham Church, Norfolk. Another example may be referred to in *fig.* 200., and in the several illustrations given under the section PRINCIPLES OF PROPORTION, at the end of this chapter.

Mullions appear to have been introduced about the end of the 12th century as substitutes for iron frames, and were at first built in courses that corresponded with the other work of the wall in which they stood, or were in small pieces. But as early as 1235 they were *face-bedded* stones dowelled with iron. As the oxidation of the metal

proved injurious, iron was superseded, after the end of the 14th century, by dowels made from the bones of sheep or from the horns of deer. *Fig.* 1173., from the west windows in the tomb-house at Windsor, temp. Henry VII., illustrates the arrangement usually adopted in drawings to show the distance from centre to centre, as at M, N and O, that is to be allowed in forming the length of radius employed in striking the curves for the tracery. Other examples of such sections are given from the clerestory of the nave of Winchester Cathedral, *fig.* 1303.; Rouen Cathedral, *fig.* 1290.; King's College Chapel, *fig.* 1312.; St. George's Chapel, Windsor, *fig.* 1316.; and from Amiens Cathedral, *fig.* 1329.

The simplest *mullion* or *monial* or *tracery bar* would be a plain rectangular block of stone. The next, with the edges chamfered, varied by substituting a hollow for a plain chamfer; by giving an ogee form to the chamfer; and by cutting out a hollow in the chamfer with receding angles instead of a receding curve; this last is perhaps peculiar to the early decorated style. The hollowed

Fig. 1173.   WINDSOR.

chamfer is the only moulding ordinarily made to carry the ball flower ornament of the 14th century, and the four-leaved flower of the 15th century. When the tracery becomes at all elaborate, the subordination of the parts is effected by giving to the jambs and mullions, or perhaps to some of the mullions only, and to some of the tracery bars, an additional *order of mouldings.* Then the fillet or boltel of the outer moulding (N, in *fig.* 1173.) describes the greater lines; that of the inner moulding (O) the smaller lines of the tracery and the whole of the cusping. In like manner a third order is

Fig. 1174.   Fig. 1175.

FOUNTAINS ABBEY. CHOIR.

often added by the same means and for the same purpose (as M). Each of these orders

may be as varied as was the first. Perhaps the most common form for the first is the hollowed chamfer, and for the second and third, the ressant with a fillet. In a very few instances, the outer fillet becomes a sharp edge, i.e. the mullion is chamfered to an arris.

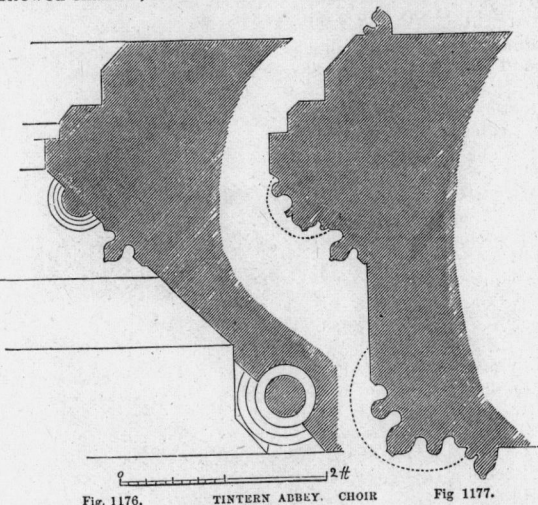

Fig. 1176.   TINTERN ABBEY. CHOIR   Fig 1177.

"Nothing is more essential to the good effect of windows (except where the mullions are treated as shafts under a mass of tracery without glazing), and nothing is so much neglected by modern architects, as making the mullions of adequate thickness," writes Mr. Denison, in *Church Building*. "The modern works are very seldom more than ⅛th of the width of the lights; probably about 4 inches in the ordinary side windows, and sometimes less, and perhaps a few as much as 7 or 8 inches in large east and west windows. In the east window of Tintern Abbey, which has eight lights (*fig.* 1178.), the principal mullion is 15 inches thick, and the two secondary ones are 11 inches, and the four smallest very nearly 8 inches. At Guisborough Priory, of the geometrical period, a window of only seven lights had two principal mullions, both as thick as the middle one at Tintern. The great mullion of the east window at Lincoln is about 2 feet thick. Even the two small east windows of Guisborough, with only three lights, has 9-inch mullions, and those at Tintern 7-inch. Some four-light windows at Whitby have the middle mullions about 13 inches, and the short clerestory windows of Bridlington are above a foot thick. No mullion ought to be much less than one-third of the width of the adjacent light. The *lights* of the small Guisborough windows are exactly three times the width of the mullions; the aisle windows of Selby are about the same;

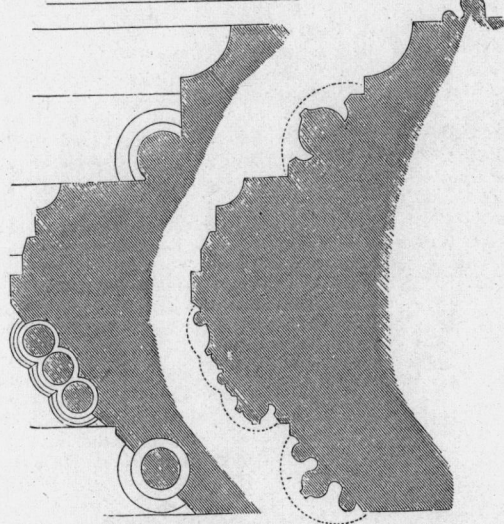

Fig. 1178.   TINTERN ABBEY. EAST WINDOW.   Fig. 1179.

where there are more lights than these, and therefore two or more classes of mullions are required, the larger ones must be considerably more than this. In all cases the depth from back to front ought to be at least twice the width or thickness from side to side. There are a few old geometrical windows, with 'thin' mullions, but they are exceptions, and do not look well.

"The difference between good and bad windows, strikingly exhibited in the same church, may be seen in the north aisle of the choir at Selby, where a set of windows of no more than three lights, and those rather short ones, having tracery of the simplest possible pattern, only three quatrefoils in the head, are perhaps the most beautiful windows of the size to be found anywhere. Above them in the clerestory are windows of four lights and much more elaborate tracery, and yet almost as ill-looking as any modern ones. The reason is that the lower ones are deep set, and have thick mullions and tracery, and high arches, whereas the others are very shallow, on account of the passage in the wall; the mullions are thin, and the arches are low."

Sect. XIII.

WINDOW JAMBS AND ARCH PLANES.

The following details of window jambs and mouldings, are reduced from those given in the valuable publication already mentioned, namely Sharpe's *Architectural Parallels.* *Fig.* 1174. is the plan of the jambs, and *fig.* 1175. of the mouldings of the arch over them, to the early English choir at Fountains Abbey, Yorkshire. *Figs.* 1176. and 1177. are the similar portions to the geometric choir at Tintern Abbey, Monmouthshire. The same publication gives, amongst its numerous details, the elaborate grouping of mouldings to the magnificent east (*figs.* 1178. and 1179.) and west (*figs.* 1180. and 1181.) windows of this building, which is somewhat transitional to the decorated period, and of very great beauty. *Fig.* 1182. is the jamb mouldings to the decorated east window at Howden Church, Yorkshire, showing a passage in the wall, which materially deteriorates from the good effect of the window.

The following illustrations are from Henry VII.'s Chapel. *Fig.* 1183. is the wall jamb to the first cant of the angular windows to the aisles. *Fig.* 1184. is the first angle mullion of the circular or bow windows; it also shows the arrangement for the mullions or monials, and (L) the mitring

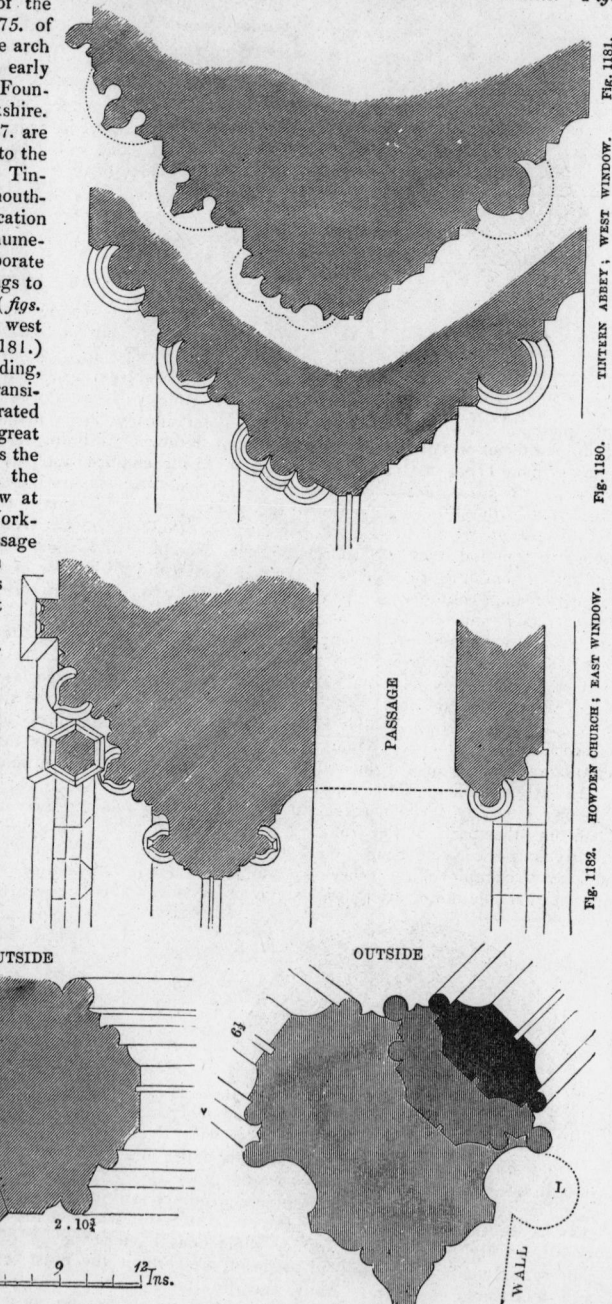

Fig. 1181.

TINTERN ABBEY; WEST WINDOW.

Fig. 1180.

HOWDEN CHURCH; EAST WINDOW.

Fig. 1182.

PASSAGE

OUTSIDE

OUTSIDE

WALL

2 . 10¾

0   3   6   9   12 Ins.

WALL

L.

Fig. 1183.   HENRY VII.'S CHAPEL.

Fig. 1184.   HENRY VII.'S CHAPEL.

with the wall-work inside. *Fig.* 1185. is the jamb mouldings of the upper range, or the clerestory windows. These are all reduced from Cottingham's work on this building, and are, to some extent, shown in the interior elevation of the bay, given in *fig.* 1325.

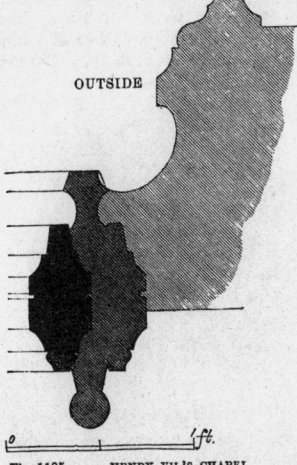

OUTSIDE

Fig. 1185.　　HENRY VII.'S CHAPEL.

The section of the jambs to the windows of the clerestory at Winchester Cathedral is given in *fig.* 1303. ; to the windows of King's College Chapel, Cambridge, in *fig.* 1312. ; to those of St. George's Chapel, Windsor, in *fig.* 1316. ; and to those in the clerestory at Amiens Cathedral, in *fig.* 1329.

The arch planes worked in the same buildings, have been placed on pages 929., 930., and 931., while the series of mouldings to the arches of Henry VII.'s Chapel will be found very poor in comparison, as may be observed in *fig.* 1325.

SECT. XIV.

CIRCULAR WINDOWS.

The large circular windows so frequently seen in the transepts of churches, and sometimes at the west ends of them, and going by the general name of rose windows, seem to have originated from the *oculi* with which the tympana of the ancient basilicæ were pierced, and which are still observable in monuments of the 11th century. For the study of this species of window the edifices of France furnish the most abundant means, many of them being of exquisite composition, and in our opinion far surpassing any elsewhere to be seen. Many of these, from Rouen, Beauvais, and Amiens, will be found illustrated in the following chapter of this work.

It is scarcely previous to the 12th century that they can be fairly called *rose* windows ; before that period they are more properly denominated *wheel* windows, the radiating mullions resembling the spokes of a wheel and being formed of small columns regularly furnished with bases and capitals, and connected at top by semicircular arches or by trefoils. By many the more decorated circular window has been called the *marigold* window, but we scarcely know why that should have been done. The rose windows are used in gables, but their dimensions are then generally smaller and they are often enclosed in segmental curves whose versed sines form an equilateral triangle or a segmental square.

An early specimen of the wheel window is in Barfreston Church (*fig.* 180.), wherein it is manifestly later than the other parts of the front. The example from Patrixbourne Church, Kent (*fig.* 1186.), is a curious and early example of the wheel window ; herein, and indeed in all the minor examples, a single order of columns is disposed round the centre ;

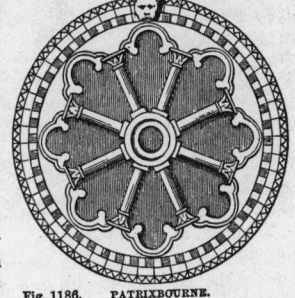

Fig. 1186.　　PATRIXBOURNE.

Fig. 1187　　YORK.

Fig 1188.　　ST. DAVID'S.

but in the south transept at York Cathedral we have a noble instance of this species (*fig.* 1187.)—a double order of columns being employed, connected by foliation above the capitals of the columns; this example is of the 13th century. As the early style came in, the columns would of course give place to the mullion, as in the elegant specimen from St. David's, shown in *fig.* 1188. The two following examples (*figs.* 1189. and 1190.) from Westminster, and Winchester Palace, Southwark, are both of the 14th century. The first

Fig. 1189.   WESTMINSTER ABBEY CHURCH.   Fig 1190.   WINCHESTER PALACE, SOUTHWARK.

is not the original window, but we have reason to believe it was accurately remade from the original one. The latter is a most elegant arrangement flowing from the continued sides

Fig. 1191.   ST. OUEN, ROUEN.

of the central hexagon, and consequently forming a series of equilateral triangles decorated with foliation. It was placed in the gable of the great hall of the palace, which hall was spanned by a timber roof of very beautiful and ingenious construction, a few years since destroyed by fire, after which the wall containing the window was taken down.

During the period of the three last examples in this country, the French were making rapid strides towards that era in which their flamboyant was to be stifled and extinguished by the introduction of the renaissance style, about which we have already submitted some remarks, and produced some examples. In the church of St. Ouen, at Rouen, the circular window (*fig.* 1191.), middle of the 14th century, exhibits the extraordinary difference between French and English examples of the same date. Beautiful as many of the English examples undoubtedly are, we know of none that is equal to this for the easy and elegant flow of the tracery composing it. The leading points it will be seen are dependent on the hexagon, but, those determined, it appears to branch off from the centre with unchecked luxuriance, preserving, nevertheless, a purity in its forms quite in character with the exquisite edifice it assists to light. The details of this window may be advantageously studied in Pugin's *Antiquities of Normandy*, and in the larger woodcut given in the subsequent chapter.

Besides these examples of circular windows, others will be found of varying patterns, forming the centre pieces in the heads of large windows, as at the churches of Easby, Howden, Wellingborough, and at St. Alban's Abbey.

SECT. XV.

TRACERY OF WINDOWS.

As the perpendicularity of the style changed, at the beginning of the 13th century, from that which might be termed horizontal, so did the comparatively rude and clumsy form of its ornament assume a lightness founded on a close observation of nature. Its sculpture is endowed with life, and its aspiring forms are closely connected with the general outlines bounding the masses. The models used for decoration are selected from the forest and the meadow. Among the flowers used for the angular decorations of pinnacles and spires,

on crockets, and in similar situations, an ornament very much resembling the *Cypripedium calceolus*, or lady's slipper, and the iris, are of constant occurrence. The former plant, however, appears to be found only in the woods in the north of England, and now, at any rate, it is very rare.

These models, however, though closely and beautifully imitated (says Ramée), are submitted to reduction within such boundaries as brought them to a regular and geometrical form. Thus is found every conceivable description of ornament brought within the limits of circles, squares, and triangles, as well as within the more varied forms of the many-sided polygons; the latter, as in the marigold and rose windows, being again subject to the circumscribing circle; these polygonal subdivisions having always reference to the regulating subdivisions of the apsis, as will be further referred to in Chap. IV.

The circle obviously presents a boundary for a very extended range of objects in nature. In the vegetable world, a flower is scarcely to be found which, within it, cannot be symmetrically arranged. Its relations afford measures for its subdivisions into two, three, four, and six parts, and their multiples, by the diameter and radius alone; the last being an unit, upon which the equilateral triangle and hexagon are based; moreover, as the interior angles of every right-lined figure (*Euclid*, prop. 32. b. 1.), together with four right angles, are equal to twice as many right angles as the figure has

Fig. 1192.

Fig. 1193.

sides, it will be immediately seen that the interior angles in the equilateral triangle, the pentagon, the hexagon, the nonagon, and the dodecagon, are divisible by the sides so as to clear the result of fractions. Thus, in the equilateral triangle, the number of degrees subtended by the sides is 60°. In the pentagon the number is 108°; in the hexagon, 120°; in the nonagon, 140°; and in the dodecagon, 150°. (See *par.* 1219.). Independent, therefore, of the service of the circle in construction, we are not to be surprised at

Fig. 1194.

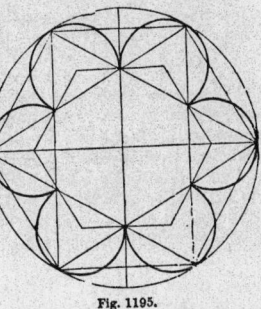

Fig. 1195.

its being so favourite a figure in architecture, from the period at which the art was to become truly serviceable to mankind.

In respect of the pentagon (*fig.* 1194.), if lines be drawn from each angle so as to connect every two of its sides, the pentalpha results; a figure in much esteem in the 13th and 14th centuries, and used among the Pythagoreans as a symbol of health, centuries and centuries before.

The heptagon and undecagon, whose interior angles are not divisible without a fraction or remainder, were rarely used by the Freemasons; an instance of either does not occur to us.

An inspection of *figs.* 1192. to 1198. will show the mode of generating from the several polygons the lobes of circular windows, as also the way of obtaining the centres for the lobes in a simple and symmetrical manner. In *fig.* 1192. the basis of formation is the equilateral triangle, and three lobes are the result. Those of four lobes, or quatrefoils (*fig.* 1193.), originate from the square; and the Cruciferæ, or cruciform plants, Tetradynamia of Linnæus's system, seem to be their types in nature.

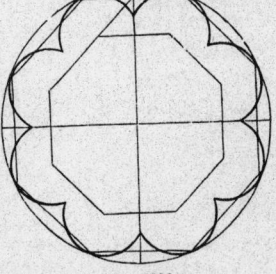

Fig. 1196.

For those of five lobes, resulting from the pentagon (*fig.* 1194.), types are found in the

classes Pentandria, Decandria, and Icosandria, of Linnæus. They comprise the rose, the apple, cherry, and medlar blossoms; those of the strawberry, the myrtle, and many others. For circular windows consisting of six lobes, and based on the hexagonal formation (*fig.* 1195.), the class Hexandria seems to furnish the type, under which are found almost all the bulbous-rooted flowers, pinks, &c. These observations might be extended to a

Fig. 1197.

Fig. 1198.

great length; but the writer does not feel inclined to pursue the system to the extent to which it has been carried by a German author (Metzger), who bases the principles of all pointed architecture on the formations of the mineral and vegetable kingdoms. In *fig.* 1196. the octagon is the base; in *fig.* 1197. the nonagon; and in *fig.* 1198.

the dodecagon. Beyond the last, the subdivision is very rarely, if ever, carried. It was not that all these types were selected from a mere desire of assimilating to nature the decorations of the 13th century, but it sprung from that deep impression of the utility of

Fig. 1199.　　　　Fig. 1200.

geometrical arrangement, which sought in the vegetable kingdom, and elsewhere, such forms as fell in with the outlines adopted. Similar formations based upon the arrangement of squares, triangles, and polygons, are exhibited in *figs.* 1335. to 1339., in the latter portion of this chapter, as obtained from the decorations of Amiens Cathedral.

Mr. Denison comments upon a particular figure in window tracery, which appears to him to be very bad, and often adopted. He calls it the "broken-backed cusp," (*fig.* 1199.) because it gives the feeling that it is always going to break (like *fig.* 1205., doorway). By it,

the cusps are made a principal instead of an accessory; the proper way being to make a sub-arch at the back of the lower pair of cusps (*fig.* 1200.), and to thicken the trefoil above until it looks like a piece of solid stonework, and having a real bearing on each other, and capable of resisting pressure.

Few attempts have been made to point to the origin of tracery and its ramifications. As the spaces of window openings went on increasing, until at last they became gigantic, in several instances exceeding 40 feet, a construction of stone framework became absolutely necessary. This framework, as we find in examples of the early decorated period, was at first unornamented—mere pillars or mullions below, with segmental curves, crossing each other, to fill the arch. But by degrees these curves changed their character, and assumed all the infinite variety we now know under the term tracery. From great windows, this class of decoration descended to the minor parts of buildings; and at last we find that light, fragile, screen-work, to be the great depository of this kind of knowledge. Fixed geometric forms, rather than mere fancy, as the foundation of composition, are ever to be preferred as of the utmost importance to the designer, if he wishes or intends to arrive at a successful result.—Billings, *Infinity of Geometric Design.*

Our limited space warns us to refrain from the further elucidation of this subject; but before quitting it, we can refer to the many illustrations of the further development of

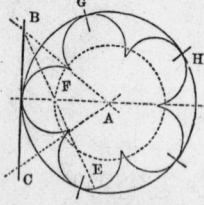

Fig. 1201.

"tracery and geometric forms," forming a portion of the PRIN-CIPLES OF PROPORTION, treated hereafter, wherein examples are given from Westminster Abbey, Beauvais, Rouen, and other cathedrals.

To aid in the formation of tracery a perfect knowledge of practical geometrical drawing is requisite; we therefore refer the reader to that section in Book II. where, commencing at *par.* 1007., he will find other more useful problems that will assist him in his designs. We append another application of the problem "to inscribe a circle in a given triangle," as being one

of those more generally required in circular forms, and perhaps a quicker method than those above described. If a five-lobed figure be required, as in *fig.* 1201., obtain the triangle A B C from the five divisions, on a base line B C at a tangent to the circle; bisect B C and join A D. Bisect the angle A B C by a line B E, and

where it crosses the line A D, as at F, will be the centre of the required circle or lobe. A circle with the radius A F being drawn, the other centres on the lines of division. as A G, A H, &c., are readily found.

Another usual geometrical problem in tracery work consists in finding the centre of a circle placed in the head of an arch. This has been eluci-dated by E. W. Tarn, in the *Builder* for 1863, p. 221. Let A B C in *fig.* 1202. be an equilateral arch, and the width A B be divided into three equal portions A'D E B. Let the arches D F and E G be drawn with the same radius as those of A and B, as D H. Then it is re-quired to find the centre of the circle which shall touch the four arcs. Make E I equal to ⅙th of E B, and with the centre A and radius A I draw an arc cutting the perpendicular or centre line of the window in K; then K is the required centre, and K L the radius of the circle.

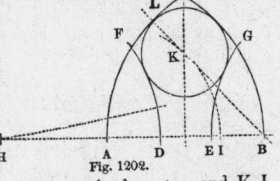
Fig. 1202.

SECT. XVI.

DOORWAYS.

It is almost needless to observe that through the several changes of style the door-ways followed their several. forms; our duty will, therefore, be to do little more than present the representations of four or five examples to the notice of the reader. The Prior's entrance at Ely (*fig.* 187.) is a fine specimen of a highly decorated Norman doorway. The earlier Norman doorways had but little carving. They are, as in *fig.* 1203., generally placed within a semicir-cular arch, borne by columns recessed from the face of the wall, and the whole sur-mounted with a dripstone. In *fig.* 187. it will be seen that the semicircular head of the door is filled in level with the springing, and sculptured with a figure of our Saviour in a sitting attitude; his right arm is raised, and in his left is a book. What is termed the *vesica piscis* surrounds the composition, which is supported by an angel on each side. These representations are frequently met with in Norman doorways. Many examples are composed of a series of recesses, each spanned by semicircular arches springing from square jambs, and occupied by insu-lated columns; though sometimes the columns are wanting and the recesses run down to

Fig. 1203.   WYKEN CHURCH, WARWICKSHIRE.

Fig. 1204.   LICHFIELD.

Fig. 1205.   ST. NICHOLAS, LYNN.

the plinth. The arches are very often decorated with the chevron, zigzag, and other Norman ornaments.

The early English doorways have the same character as the windows of the period; the smaller ones are often recessed with columns, from which a pointed arch is twined with a cut moulding on it and a dripstone over it. The more important doors, however, are mostly in two divisions, separated by a pier column, and with foliated heads. These are generally grouped under one arch, springing from clustered columns on each side, and the

Fig. 1206. TATTERSHALL CASTLE.

Fig. 1207. ST. GEORGE'S CHAPEL.

space over the openings is filled in, and decorated with a quatrefoil, as in the doorway to the chapter-house at Lichfield (*fig.* 1204.). Sculpture often occurs in the arrangement. The door to the chapel of St. Nicholas, at Lynn (*fig.* 1205.), is a curious example of the latter part of the decorated period. *Fig.* 1206., from Tattershall Castle, Lincolnshire, belongs to the Florid English or perpendicular period, whose simplest doorways usually had the depressed or Tudor arch, and without the square head which appears in the example. The more ornamental ones were crocketed, and terminated with finials, as appears in the face of the porch at King's College Chapel, Cambridge (*fig.* 1208.). The doorway at St. George's Chapel, Windsor (*fig.* 1207.), though later in date, is more simple than the last, notwithstanding the exuberance of ornament and tracery which had then very nearly reached its meridian.

Sect. XVII.

PORCHES.

The porch is a distinguishing feature both in ecclesiastical and domestic architecture throughout northern Europe during the whole of the mediæval period. In the case of the smaller churches it was usually attached to the north and south doors. When to the north, it was generally built of stone, while the south porch was more often of timber. In France the porches are usually of very grand proportions and of elaborate structure.

A Norman porch, with an upper story or *parvise*, a chamber which appears to have been variously appropriated, occurs on the north side of Southwell Minster, Nottinghamshire, and is arched (Rickman, p. 81.); and another at Sherborne, Dorsetshire, which is groined. The example at Malmesbury Abbey Church is perhaps the finest of the few that exist of this period. An early English porch with a chamber remains on the north side of St. Cross Church, Hampshire. The porch at Felkirk, in the West Riding of Yorkshire, of late early English or early decorated date, has a roof formed of stone ribs 1 foot in breadth by 10 inches in depth, plain chamfered at the angles, placed about 18 inches apart, springing from a string or impost about 4 feet from the floor. A complete illustration of this interesting example is given in Robson, *Mason's Guide.* The same simple plan is followed in those at Barnack, Northamptonshire, and at Middleton Cheney, Northamptonshire. The south porch at St. Mary's Uffingdon, Berkshire, is groined. This feature was extensively used in this period, as at Salisbury and Wells.

A beautiful example of a vaulted roof to a shallow porch occurs in the decorated church at Higham Ferrars, Northamptonshire (Rickman, p. 111.), also giving a plain vault with richly moulded door jambs at the west porch of Raunds Church, Northamptonshire). Stone ribs are employed in the vestry or chapel at Willingham Church, Cambridgeshire (Rickman, p. 179., decorated); the chapel is 14 feet 1 inch long, and 9 feet 9 inches wide, as shown in Lysons' *Cambridgeshire*, p. 285. In this, and in the following, periods, the groined roof became common, and partook of all the varied enrichment exhibited in larger roofs. The porches exceed in profuseness of decoration those of the preceding style: they were almost universally adopted. The south porch of Gloucester, and the south-west porch of Canterbury are beautiful examples. In the former, canopied niches occupy the front over the doorway, the front being crowned with an embattled parapet of pierced panelling, and at the quoins are turrets embattled and finished with crocketed pinnacles.

The example here given of the shallow porch at King's College Chapel, Cambridge (*fig.* 1208.), is beautiful in design and in proportion. The north porch at Beverley Minster rises somewhat higher than the aisle, the upper part forming a *parvise*. The door has a fine feathered straight-sided canopy, over one of ogee form, both crocketed. It is flanked with niches, buttresses, and pinnacles; the whole front is panelled and crowned with a lofty central pinnacle, having a niche. An idea of it will be gained from the illustration given as a frontispiece to the present edition. The south porch of Leverington Church, Cambridgeshire, is groined, and also has carved bosses. Over it is a *parvise* 10 feet 1 inch wide and 14 feet 4 inches in length. The covering (of slabs of stone?) is supported by six arched stone ribs, placed 2 feet 1 inch apart, and 9 feet 5 inches span; the rib is 4 inches wide, 6 inches in depth, and chamfered on the lower edge. It has a richly perforated stone ridge ornament. The section and details are given in *Builder* for 1848, p. 91, which also (iii. 598.) illustrates the south porch at North Walsham Church, Norfolk, which is lofty and open to the roof, it not having been divided into stories. It is a specimen of the mixture of flint

Fig. 1208.   KING'S COLLEGE CHAPEL, CAMBRIDGE.

with stone details. The south porch of a church near Evesham, in Worcestershire; the sacristy, also at Felkirk; and the porches at the churches of Strelly, in Nottinghamshire; of All Saints, at Stamford; and of Arundel, in Sussex, have interesting stone roofs.

In the case of domestic buildings, the porch, as at Wingfield Manor House, Derbyshire, has a story over the entrance, differing from those at Eltham, Croydon, Cowdray (which has an elaborate groined stone roof), and many others, having only one story. That at Porchester Castle hall was the whole height of the building, having a room above the entrance to the hall, which was elevated on a basement story, and was reached by a flight of steps occupying the lower story of the porch. At Dartington Manor House, Derbyshire, and at East Barsham, Norfolk, there are two stories above the entrance, an arrangement frequently observed in similar erections, as at Thorpland Hall, Norfolk, and at Eastbury House, Essex, erected cir. 1572. From the architectural prominence given to this feature in domestic buildings, the designation "porch house" was often employed.

Fig. 1209.   PORCH, AT LUBECK.

So very exceptional is the use of *brickwork* in England in mediæval work, at any rate until the common brick porches, which were added in the 17th century, that we are induced to notice one of the many examples in this material executed abroad, in Germany especially. The north porch of Lübeck Cathedral (*fig.* 1209.), is described by G. E. Street, as "a 13th century addition, of two bays in depth, with groining piers of clustered shafts with sculptured capitals, and a many-shafted doorway of the best character. Its interior is probably mainly of stone, but the exterior is all of brick. The archway is boldly moulded, and above it is a horizontal arcaded corbel table, stepped up in the centre to admit the arch. The gable is boldly arcaded upon shafts, and has a stepped corbel table, with a double line of moulded bricks above it next to the tiles. A couple of simple open

arches are pierced in each side wall, and there are flat pilasters at the angles. In the gable, enclosed within the arcading, are some circular openings, one of which is cusped with small foliations formed of brick. The moulded bricks in the main arch are of two kinds only, one a large boltel, the other a large hollow, and these arranged alternately with plain square-edged bricks, produce as much variety as is needful. The jamb of the doorway is of plain bricks, built with square recesses, in which detached stone shafts are placed. The capitals throughout are of stone, and carved with simple foliage. Perhaps no other example is more completely all that it should be in the use of its materials. The exterior is simple in all its details, yet sufficiently enriched by their skilful arrangement to be thoroughly effective; whilst in the interior, where more adornment was naturally required, brick is frankly abandoned, and the richly moulded and sculptured ribs and archivolts are all of stone, though I have no doubt the vaulting and walls are, as on the outside, of brick. The only tracery which can be properly executed in brick is in fact the simplest *plate tracery* (and even this requires great skill and care in its execution), or that simple fringe of cusping round an opening which occurs in the porch, and which may be executed with ease with a single pattern of moulded brick often repeated." *Church Builder*, 1863, p. 56. We have somewhat altered the arched entrance as shown in Mr. Street's sketch, understanding that this porch has been lately restored in this manner.

SECT. XVIII.

TOWERS AND SPIRES.

Europe has been considered by J. H. Parker, *Transactions* of the Institute of British Architects, to be indebted to Caen and its neighbourhood for that very interesting feature, the Gothic spire of stone. He has also traced its history from the low pyramid of Thaon

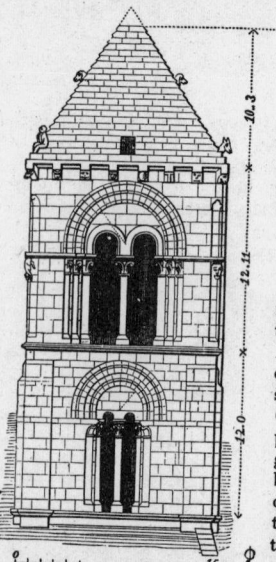

Fig. 1211.
SECTION OF SPIRE.

Fig. 1210. THAON, NORMANDY.

Church, Normandy, dating about the end of the 11th century, shown in *fig.* 1210., whereof the stones are left rough within and overhang one another, while at the base a large piece of timber was introduced as if to bind the whole together (*fig.* 1211.), which has now entirely decayed. The apex has also decayed or been removed. The spires of Comornes near Bayeux; Basly near Caen, middle of 12th century; and Rosel, are of the same character, and are followed by those at Huppeau near Bayeux, which is considerably taller, but of about the same date; Vaucelles, near Caen; St. Loup, near Bayeux; St. Contest, near Caen; and Bougy, which is of a fine transitional character, as is that at Douvres; the small square spires at the east end of St. Stephen's at Caen; and the elegant lofty octagonal spire with square pinnacles at Ducy, which is a little earlier than the elegant western spires of St. Stephen's at Caen. On that building are altogether eight spires, varying in date from one of about the middle of the 12th century on a stair turret; the two pairs of early Gothic work of the choir; to the light western spires which possess pinnacles of open work at the angles and in the centre of each face; these date about 1230. The fine spire on St. Peter's Church, at Caen, dates at the beginning of the 14th century, and is commonly quoted as the perfection of a spire (*figs.* 1212. 1213.). It is octagonal, with openings pierced in the flat sides. That of St. Saviour's is later and not so good. Nearly all the spires in this district have the surface of the stone cut to imitate shingles, a clear proof of their having had a timber prototype. The spires at Bayeux Cathedral were probably being built at the same time as those at St. Stephen's Church, which they resemble. Secqueville Church has one of nearly the same date.

Of later date are the spires at Bretteville, Bernières, and Langrune, coming up to the middle of the 13th century. They are all of elegant design, and light construction. After these are the unfinished spires of Norrey and Audrieu, closing the century. Illustrations of several of these buildings will be found in Britton's *Normandy*. Mr. Fergusson considers that the spire took its origin from the gable termination seen in some early foreign towers.

A chronological sketch of the gradual development of the spire in Germany, has lately been attempted by W. H. Brewer, in the *Builder* for 1865, to which we can here only refer the reader, as well as for its very peculiar illustrations.

Fig. 1212. Fig. 1213.
ST. PETER'S AT CAEN.

Fig. 1214. WARMINGTON.

In England, during the Norman period the west end of the larger churches sometimes had towers terminating the aisles. Another tower rose from the intersection of the cross (the smaller churches had but this one), while it was only of sufficient elevation to break the long line of nave, choir, and transepts, all of equal height. The roofs of the towers were of but little higher pitch than the rest. The nearest approach to spires, in form if not in height, were found in the pinnacles surmounting the angle buttresses in the larger churches. During the early English period, towers rise to a greater elevation, and are very generally finished with a spire, sometimes of great height. The most frequent spire is that called a *broach* when it does not rise from within parapets, but is carried up on four of its sides from the top of the square tower, the diagonal faces resting on *squinches*, or arches thrown across the corners within, and finished on the outside in a slope, as shown in *fig.* 1214. of Warmington Church, Northamptonshire, which has been published in detail by W. Caveler. A great many spires consisted of wooden frames, covered with lead or with shingles; and these in general, as well as stone spires in a few instances, were connected with the tower in a different way; the spire itself being at first only four-sided, and the angles being canted off a little above the base, to form the octagon. The early English spire, completed in 1222, to Old St. Paul's Cathedral was the highest in Europe, being 520 feet high, according to Stow's account.

In the decorated period, Heckington Church, Lincolnshire, one of the most beautiful and perfect models in the kingdom shows, says Rickman, "a very lofty tower and spire situated at the west end (*fig.* 1215.), the four pinnacles which crown the tower are large and pentagonal. This unusual shape has, at less cost, an effect fully equal to an octagon, and the pinnacles are without crockets, but have rich finials; the spire is plain, with three tiers of windows on the alternate sides. The whole arrangement of this steeple is peculiarly calculated for effect at a distance." The details of this work are given in Bowman and Crowther's useful publication. The elaborately arranged octagon at Ely Cathedral, the design of Alan de Walsingham, is of this period. The work entitled *Churches of the Archdeaconry of Northamptonshire*, 1849, illustrates in small pictorial views several of the fine lofty west towers and spires of this and the succeeding period, erected in that locality.

The perpendicular period is distinguished by the splendour and loftiness of its towers and spires. That at Salisbury, for example, rises to the height of about 387 feet. That at Norwich, rebuilt soon after 1361, is 318 feet high. St. Michael's spire, at Coventry, built 1373-95, is the most beautiful one in the kingdom; it does not rise, like those at Salisbury and Norwich, from the centre of a transeptal church, but from the ground; and its flying buttresses and extremely taper form, give it great advantage over every spire which rises from within battlements. The *broach* is not unfrequent in this style, and examples are chiefly to be found in Northamptonshire. Of other remarkable spires of

this style we should name Whittlesea, in Cambridgeshire (*fig.* 1216.); Rushdon, in Northamptonshire; the two spires of St. Mary and St. Alkmund, at Shrewsbury; Iaughton-en-le-Morthen, in Yorkshire; Chester-le-Street, in Durham; and finally, Louth, in Lincolnshire, of which latter structure the building accounts are given in the *Archæologia*, vol. x., showing its completion between 1501 and 1518.

The spire of the tower of St. Nicholas Church, at Newcastle-upon-Tyne, from its peculiarity of standing on arched ribs, holds a high place in the series; it is the type of which there are various imitations. The best known are St. Giles's, at Edinburgh; the church at Linlithgow; the college tower at Aberdeen, and its modern imitation by Sir C. Wren, at St. Dunstan's-in-the-East Church, in London. Of another class of towers of this period, that of Fotheringay Church is the type. The ordinary square tower is surmounted by an octagonal lantern of much smaller dimensions, connected with the tower, in composition,

Fig. 1215. HECKINGTON.   Fig. 1216. WHITTLESEA.

Fig. 1217. ALL SAINTS', DERBY.

by flying buttresses from the bases of the angle pinnacles. The tower of All Saints' Church, at Derby, has deservedly a very high reputation (*fig.* 1217.). It is late in the style; as is also the fine detached campanile at Evesham. The tower of St. Peter Mancroft, at Norwich, is a good specimen of flint building with stone panels. The most remarkable of the perpendicular towers, both in itself and for its influence in the ecclesiastical architecture of a large district, is that of Gloucester, erected about 1455. This noble tower rises above 200 feet from the ground and about 100 feet above the roof of the choir. It is surmounted by a crenellated parapet flanked by four turret-like pinnacles, all of delicate open work, to the very finials, of a light and graceful character almost beyond the natural capacity of stonework. Among the more important imitations of it are St. John's, at Glastonbury; St. Stephen's, at Bristol; St. Mary, at Taunton; and that at North Petherton; the two last are said to have been designed by the same architect.

Beacons were sometimes added to towers; such is the lantern of All Saints' Pavement, at York, which is an octagon erected upon the tower. Hadleigh Church, in Essex, has a beacon in an iron framework placed on the top of an angle turret.

By far the finest west front, comprising two towers of the perpendicular period, is that of Beverley Minster. What the west front of York is to the decorated style, this is to the perpendicular, with the addition, that in this front nothing but one style is seen—all is harmonious. (See frontispiece, *fig.* 1218.) Each of the towers has four large and eight

small pinnacles, and a very beautiful battlement. The whole front is panelled, and the buttresses, which have a very bold projection, are ornamented with various tiers of niche-work of excellent composition and most delicate execution. We may here incidentally notice that the east front is fine, but mixed with early English, which style extends to the transepts, while the nave and aisles are decorated, terminating with perpendicular, and finished with the west façade above noticed.

In concluding this portion, we cannot withhold naming the most elaborate work on the subject of this section, published from drawings made by C. Wickes, in 3 vols. fol. 1853–59. Its chief drawback is that the illustrations are pictorial and not geometric, which might have been obviated by a plan and section to each. Our sketch of the varieties of towers and spires will be found filled up, in Rev. G. A. Poole's *History of Ecclesiastical Architecture.*

In Ireland, the Dominican Abbey, commonly called the Black Abbey, at Kilkenny, had a tower placed on the south of the altar in a most singular way. At the Franciscan Church, the tower was placed at the east end of the nave, with a chancel at the end; the tower was much narrower than the nave, but exactly the width of the lofty arch support-ing it, so that now the roof has gone, the construction appears extremely bold and hazard-ous. This building was one of a numerous class. Except the round towers, which ceased to be built when the English went to Ireland, and the low Cistercian towers, the Irish churches up to that period were almost towerless. In a few instances other towers could be named, as the fine massive one of the Trinitarian Friary, at Adare; but sud-denly, in the 15th century, it became the practice to build to the Franciscan and Domin-ican structures these lofty and slender additions. The nave was shut out from the choir by two transverse walls placed close together and pierced each with a narrow arch; above them rose the slender tower, standing as it were on the apex of the gables, instead of spreading over the width of the nave. They were finished with a peculiar battlemented parapet. There is no instance of two western towers to the mediæval churches in Ireland; and a mediæval spire is not known to exist in that country.

In Scotland, the spires are chiefly of the middle pointed period, but not erected until about the middle of the 15th century. Short octagonal stone spires form a very common termination to towers of late date; they generally carry small pedimental headed lights either on all or on the cardinal faces, and are for the most part plain, though, as at Cors-torphine, at Aberdeen, and at Crail, in Fifeshire, they are banded by two or three em-battled strings or coronæ into stages. Sometimes, as at the two former places, there are small pinnacles at the angles; while at Corstorphine, and St. Andrew's at Aberdeen, a lumpish semi-pyramidal abutment on the angles is extremely suggestive of the *broach.*

The *construction* of the tower and spire is of such importance as to require much attention. A tower built for the reception of bells intended to be rung, should have a solid founda-tion, not merely four arches nearly as wide as the tower itself, leaving four piers not much bigger than the thickness of the wall which they support. Bells require a tower to them-selves, for it is known that they will spoil the best clock ever fixed. In Sir C. Wren's towers, and others built by his imitators, the substance of the walls was concentrated at the angles, leaving a moderate sized arch on each side, and only the same internal area as would exist in the case of four straight walls. This is sound construction, and is well displayed in the tower of Antwerp Cathedral. Such an arrangement also admits of a staircase being carried up in the substance of the wall, without diminishing strength, besides, a desirable object in some large towers, doing away with the necessity for but-tresses. The tower, if thus carried up its whole height, will be more fit to support an octangular or circular spire or lantern. The mean internal area should be half the external area, and then, if well built and of good materials, the tower will safely bear as many bells as can be hung on one level.

There should be an offset to support the ringing floor and the bell floor, so that no timber be run into the wall to act as battering rams. Neither should a bell be hung on cross beams resting on the walls, but always in a trussed cage. As regards sound, one level of bells is considered better than two tiers. It is wonderful that some of the early brick or stone cones or pyramids (shown in *fig.* 1211.) have stood, for they were evidently built in level but gathering courses, even in the 11th century, around a light frame of timber, which was either removed or left to decay. As soon as the principle of diminution up-ward was acknowledged, two systems of construction presented themselves; the first is direct carriage of the upper storey from the basement floor; the other is a false-bearing; the weight being, in either case, thrown as much as possible upon the angles, even to the extent upon each floor of an opening in the centre of each side, which is the weakest part of a blank tower. In the first case there are two varieties, one being the pyramidal roof square on plan; the other being the pyramidal roof octagonal on plan. The latter, whether completed externally as a *broach* or otherwise, requires to be carried as low down the tower for support as possible; and in some cases, as at St. Léonard, in France, the octagon is more judiciously placed with four angles over the centres of the sides of the

tower, than with four faces over the corners of the tower, which then require to be loaded by pinnacles. These are set diagonally more advantageously than when square with the tower, because they thus have a larger base. The greater height given in the middle of the 12th century to the spire rendered such precaution inevitable; and at the same time it became evident that if the spire were to be no longer square on plan, it must not seem to rise abruptly out of a square.

Octagonal steeples, with octagonal spires not built through, but resting upon them, seem to be considered now as dangerous experiments in construction. Yet one at Guebwiller, in France, is a central steeple of four stages, including the pendentives. At Schelestadt is another of the same kind. This plan does not seem to have been in favour after the commencement of the 13th century.

When the French architects determined to trust their octagonal spires to the upper storeys of their steeples, they seem to have been careless about allowing the pendentives to approach points of weakness. The student will gather a good lesson on this point from the section of the steeple at the Abbaye de la Trinité, at Vendôme, given in Viollet le Duc's *Dictionnaire*. In the steeple of the cathedral at Chartres, the pendentives of the octagon sit upon the four pinnacles, which are thus each obliged to take a part of the weight of the spire; the other part being thrown upon the four faces of the octagonal drum, which are weighted by heavy gables. At the bottom the spire is 31½ in. thick, and at top 11¾ in. in a length of 156 ft. 8 in., built of hard Berchère stone. The roofs of the pinnacles are 19¾ in. thick. It is to be noticed that the danger of a fall, which was so imminent as to cause the destruction of the steeple at St. Denis, is attributed in great part to the increase of weight given to it during a course of restoration, by using the stone of St. Pierre instead of that of Vergelé. Some French spires have a very curious effect, due to the presence of a simulated hip in the centre of their sides for the whole or part of the height: but still more extraordinary were the slits in that of St. Denis, and the slit with two transoms in that of St. Nicaise, at Reims.

The spire of the church at Langrune, near the sea-coast, north of Caen, in Normandy, has at its base in the interior, a sort of buttress of thin stone resting on the thicker walls of the tower, which runs up for a great height to each of the angles and sides of the spire. They are pierced so as to afford a free passage all round at the base of the spire; and may have been provided to assist in strengthening it on account of its exposed position. It has been drawn by Rev. J. L. Petit in his *Architectural Studies*.

It will be found that the stone spires of the 12th century were high in regard to the rest of the steeple. The *proportions* at St. Denis were 38½ to 35; those at Chartres are 60 to 42; but in time these proportions were altered so much that the spires of St. Nicaise at Reims (end of 13th century), and those of the front of the cathedral in that city, are scarcely half the height of the tower instead of equal or superior to it. Murphy, in his account of the *Batalha*, remarks that no settled proportion seems to have been observed in the dimensions in general; they varied from four times the width of the base to eight times.

As regards the jointing of the stones of which spires are composed, their security seems to be wholly the result of an accurate working of the beds and vertical joints, and the adhesion of naturally good and properly applied mortar. In modern work it is questionable whether such aids as dowelling and cramping should be altogether dispensed with. Iron must not be used, for reasons given in an earlier portion of this work. One method used at present to steady and tie in the spire, is that of the insertion of an intermediate stage or floor of timber framing. Sir C. Wren, when rebuilding the upper portion of the (former) spire of Chichester Cathedral which had been forced out of the upright, placed two intermediate stages connected with a pendent beam of timber about 80 feet in length attached to the finial stone; each stage was about 3 inches less in diameter than the spire at their levels; these restored the spire if it departed from the upright. A similar pendulum, with two stages, to act in like manner, has been introduced by Gibbs in his spire of St. Martin's in the Fields, London. Iron rods have of later years been used to effect this purpose.

When the beds of the stones are horizontal, one course of binders secured with dovetailed dowels will perhaps be enough in the height; but when the beds are inclined, two or three of these courses in its height would be an effectual means of preventing its spread. It has been considered that a spire is stronger when the beds are set at right angles to the face, but if not well set, water gets in, and sudden frosts do much injury. It is probable, however, that a large number of steeples would, were examination possible, be found to have been well chained with timber or with metal. The former material appears to have been employed in the church at Châteauneuf (Sâone et Loire).

The spire, built *cir.* 1315, of St. Aldate's Church, Oxford, had to be taken down in 1865. The tower is about 56 feet high; the spire, about the same height to the weathercock, was for 10 feet down from it of solid stone, similarly to that shown in *fig.* 1213. The cause of its failure was that a 1½-inch iron bar coupled at the angles and inserted in

the first course of stone 7 inches thick at the base of the spire, had rusted, in some places entirely through, bursting the stone inside and out. The angle pinnacles alone sustained the spire for many years.

Nearly all the spires of Normandy are said to have been executed in thin slabs of stone ; they are all about 7 inches thick at the bottom, and about 4 inches thick at the top, and are almost all executed in the Creuilly stone. In Caen, especially, that stone was employed in the steeples, though it had to be brought about 12 or 14 miles. The joints are (probably) set at right angles to the face of the stone. The spire at Batalha is about 7 inches thick, independent of the carved work, though almost a fourth part of its superficies is perforated : its stones are said to be keyed together by means of dovetailed pieces of pine wood (Murphy). The slender stone ribs of the octagonal spire of Freiburg Cathedral are girded together at intervals of about 15 feet by means of double horizontal ribs or bands of limestone ; in the middle of each of these bands an iron cramp is inserted, so that one half of the thickness of the metal is fixed in the under course of the stone-work, and the other half in the upper course, in order to prevent all thrust. The space between the rib and the horizontal bands is filled up with perforated tracery, so that the appearance of great lightness, united with great boldness, is imparted to the whole. Plate XI. of Moller's work shows a careful representation of the joints, explaining in what manner the stones are connected together, both in the principal members and the ornamental parts. The spires of Strasburg and Constance Cathedrals, and that of St. Stephen's Church at Vienna, present other examples of open work spires. The thickness of the decorated spire to the staircase in the north tower of the west front of Peterborough Cathedral, is about 11 inches at 2 feet above the wall of the tower, where the octagon commences, and is about 10 feet diameter (shown in Robson, *Masons' Guide*). The methods adopted of strengthening Salisbury spire and tower, are related by Price in his work published in 1750, who states that it is 400 feet high from the pavement to the extreme top, but to the top of the capstone or ball only 387 feet as previously noticed. It is only 9 inches thick at the bottom, diminishing to 7 inches.

The outline of a tower in elevation should be a parabolic curve, for strength as well as appearance, as it will not then present a top-heavy appearance. The difficulty in designing a tower and spire in the Roman or Italian style is to prevent a telescopic effect ; and in the mediæval style the appearance of an extinguisher is too often obtained. The entasis to the spire, and due diminution of the tower (though the former is usually held not to have existed, some spires being formed of two and even three lines at different angles), are desirable both for appearance and strength. They are common features in Essex and Middlesex, and the absence of them may be noticed by any one going from Essex into Suffolk, the round towers in which county have the entasis, but not those of later date. The tower of All Saints' Church, Colchester, possesses it, and diminishes from 21 feet to 19 feet, having internally an offset at each floor and at the roof, so that no timbers run into the walls.

A mathematical method of setting out the entasis for a spire was furnished by Mr. Thomas Turner, of Hampstead, to the *Builder* for 1848, through the late Professor Cockerell, R.A. But as he states that the ordinates may be obtained very nearly true by taking a thin lath and bending it to the extent required, we do not consider it necessary here to do more than to refer to the paper. In the reconstruction of the spire to St. Stephen's Church, at Vienna, an iron framework was introduced to support the light stone ribs, until near to the summit, which was made wholly of iron.

The iron spires at Rouen, Bruxelles, and Auxerre, are the only three we have noted.

CHAP. IV.

MEDIÆVAL PROPORTION.

SECT. I.

EFFECT OR USE OF NUMBERS.

The introduction into this work of the investigation of the principles of proportion, as propounded by the late E. Cresy, renders it necessary that some preliminary details should be considered, before the student passes on to those pages. These details will consist of the result of the use of numbers, as given by the late Mr. Gwilt and appended to the previous editions, and of the enquiry by modern investigators into the use of the *triangle* and of the *square* during the mediæval period. The subject is interesting, and a very enticing

one, and we regret that our limited space will not allow us to do more than merely enter upon it. We would warn the student that should he feel inclined to devote any time to this subject himself, he must not be content with the measurements he may usually find in publications, but must found his theories on those taken by himself to be in any degree certain of his deductions.

The plan on which the earlier Christian churches were constructed, wrote Mr. Gwilt, was that of a cross : he omitted to notice, however, the Italian basilican plan and the domical Greek plan; but he justly observes that (in western Europe) after the 10th century it would perhaps be difficult to find a cathedral deviating from a cruciform plan. At

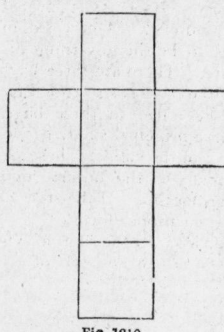

the beginning of the 9th century, in an inauguration (of a church) sermon, the preacher observes, "In dextro cornu altaris quæ *in modum crucis* constructa est ; " and again, " In medio ecclesiæ quæ est instar *crucis constructa*." (Acta SS. Benedict.) Round churches, as at Aix la Chapelle, in Germany, Rieux and Merinville, in France, with Little Maplestead, Cambridge, Northampton, and the Temple Church, London, in England, are not enough in number to affect the rule. It was in the 13th century that the termination of the choir was changed from a circular to a polygonal form. The general ordonnance of the plan was, however, not changed, and seems almost to have sprung from the laws and proportions upon which surfaces and solid bodies are dependent. The square and its diagonal, the cube and its sides, appear, at least the latter or the side of the former (*fig.* 1219.), to furnish the *unit* on which the system is based. Hence the

Fig. 1219.

numbers 3, 5, and 7, become the governing numbers of the different parts of the building. The unit in the Latin cross, placed at the intersection of the nave, gives the development of a perfect cube, according to the rules of descriptive geometry. Here are found the number 3, in the arms of the cross and the centre square ; the number 5, in the whole number of squares, omitting the central one ; and the number 7, counting them in each direction. The foot, however, of the cross was, in time, lengthened to repetitions of five and six, and even more times. In monumental churches, formed on such a system, there necessarily arises an unity of a geometrical nature ; and the geometrical principles emanating therefrom guided not only their principal, but their secondary, detail. Even before the 13th century there seems to have been some relation between the number of bays into which the nave was longitudinally divided, and the exterior and interior divisions whereof the apsis consisted; but after the introduction of the pointed style, this relation became so intimate, that from the number of sides of the apsis the number of bays in the nave may be always predicated, where the work has been carried out as it was originally designed. From the examination of many, indeed most, of the churches in Flanders, this circumstance had been long known to us; but for its first publicity, the antiquary is indebted, we believe, to M. Ramée, in 1843.

The connection of the bays of the nave with the terminating polygon of the choir was such, that the polygon is inscribed in a circle, whose diameter is the measuring unit of the nave, and generally of the transepts, and forms always the side of the square intercepted

by them. It is most frequently octagonal (*fig.* 1220.), and generally formed by three sides of the octagon. When this is used, the governing number will be found to be 8, or some multiple of it. Thus, in the Abbaye aux Hommes, at Caen (this, however, is previous to the 13th century), the termination of the choir is by a double octagon, and the number of bays in the nave is eight. The same occurs at St. Stephen's, at Vienna ; in the Church of St. Catherine, at Oppenheim ; at Lichfield Cathedral ; at Tewkesbury Abbey, and at almost every example that is known.

Fig. 1220.

It may be well here to observe, that English cathedrals, partly from their great deficiency in symmetry, on account of their not having been finished on their original plans, do not afford that elucidation of the theory that is found in those on the Continent. In twenty-four instances of them we have sixteen in which the terminations are *square* instead of polygonal ; when polygonal, the rule seems to have been always followed. It must be noted, however, that in contradistinction to the rest of Europe, England kept steadily, as a rule, to a square east end ; and though at Canterbury and Tewkesbury, and a few other noted examples, the circular form appears, yet often, as at Peterborough and Westminster, the curved apse was capped with a rectilinear addition, protesting, as it were, against the foreign element.

An eastern termination of the choir in three bays may be produced from the octagon, by omitting the sides in the direction of the length of the building, as in *fig.* 1221. In *fig.* 1222. the three sides will be found to be those of a hexagon ; and in this case the number 6

governs the other parts. Examples of this arrangement are, the minster at Freiburg-im-
Breisgau ; the cathedral at Cologne, where the apsis is do-

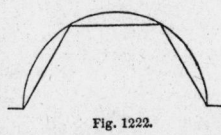

decagonal, and there are six bays in
the nave; and the abbey at Westminster, where the eastern end is
hexagonal, and there are found
twelve bays in the nave. In respect of a nonagonal termination,

Fig. 1221.

Fig. 1222.

the most extraordinary instance of a coincidence with the above-mentioned rules occurs
in the duomo of Milan, commenced at the end of the 14th century. Its apsis is formed
by three sides of a nonagon, and the bays in the nave are nine in number. One third of
the arc contained under the side of an equilateral triangle seems to be the governing dimension. The number 3, submultiple of 9, pervades the structure. There are three bays
in the choir, and the like number in the transepts. The vault of the nave is subtended by
an equilateral triangle. The lower principal windows are each designed in three bays.
The plan of the columns in the nave in each quarter contains three principal subdivisions,
and, in a transverse section of the nave, the voids are just one-third of the solids. These are
curious points, and much more worthy of investigation than many of the unimportant
details which now-a-days so much occupy the attention of archæologists. If the stem of
the plant is right, the leaves and fruit will be sure to grow into their proper forms.

Figs. 1223. and 1224. show the decagonal terminations of an apsis. In the first, a side
of the polygon faces the east ; in the second, the angle of the polygon is on the axis of the

church. The last case is of rare
occurrence. Examples of it are,
however, found in the church at
Morienval, and in the choir of
the dom-kirche of Naumburg.
The first case is illustrated by
a variety of examples—such are

Fig. 1223.

Fig. 1224.

the cathedrals at Reims, Rouen, Paris, Magdeburg, and Ulm, with the churches of Ste.
Elizabeth at Marburg, that at St. Quentin, &c., and, in this country, the cathedral at Peterborough; all of which have either five or ten bays in the nave. The dodecagon, as a
termination, is subject to the same observations as the hexagon : indeed they were anticipated by the mention of the cathedral at Cologne. Under the figure of the heptagon must
be classed the magnificent cathedral of Amiens, wherein seven chapels radiate round the choir
end, and there are as many bays in the nave (*fig.* 237.). The choir at Beauvais is terminated
by a double heptagon ; and, had the church been completed, it would doubtless have had
seven or fourteen bays in the nave. At Chartres, the choir is also terminated by a double
heptagon, and the nave contains seven bays. In the duomo at Florence, the eastern
termination is octagonal, and there are four bays in the nave; this is an example of the
expiring Gothic style in Italy.

On an examination of the principal churches on the Continent, in and after the 13th
century, it would appear that the practice of regulating the details was dependent on the
number of sides in the apsis, or of bays in the nave. Thus, if the choir is terminated by
three bays, formed on an octagonal plan, we find 3, or a multiple of it, is carried into the
subdivision of the windows. So, if the number 5 is the dominant of the apsis, that
number will be found transferred to the divisions of the windows ; and in like manner the
remainder is produced. There are two or three other matters affecting the monuments of
art erected in and after the 13th century. The aisles are usually half the width of the
nave, though instances occur where the width is equal. Many churches have two apsides—
such are the cathedrals at Nevers, and at St. Cyr; and in Germany, St. Sebald at Nuremberg ; the dom-kirche at Mayence ; the abbey church at Laach ; the cathedrals of Bamberg, Worms, and others. So far Mr. Gwilt.

" It remains to observe," writes Professor Cockerell, in the *Archæological Journal*, 1845,
" upon the mysterious *numbers* employed by Wykeham in the plans of his chapels at Winchester and Oxford, which are divided longitudinally by 7, and transversely by 4, equal
parts. In the first, the chapel consists of 6 of these parts, and the ante-chapel of 1 ; in
the second, the chapel consists of 5, and the ante-chapel of 2 ; the width being equal to
4, corresponding with the entire figure of the *vesica piscis.*"

The recurrence of the number 7, " a number of perfection," is constant ; accordingly we
find it employed in the following remarkable instances, sometimes in the nave, and sometimes in the choir. In the cathedrals of York, Westminster, Exeter, Bristol, Durham,
Lichfield, Paris, Amiens, Chartres, and Evreux ; in the churches of Romsey, Waltham,
Buildwas, St. Alban's (Norman portion), and Castle Acre ; and in St. George's Chapel,
at Windsor, Roslyn Chapel, and many others. See also the notice on page 969.

The idea is now generally sanctioned, that the mediæval architects had some settled system of proportioning their designs either by simple geometric forms or by combinations of them. It will be our endeavour to indicate the sources whence the facts on this subject can be drawn, and to notice such of the details as our space will permit.

The knowledge of geometry previous to, and in, the 12th century has been commented upon in par. 309, *et seq.* The *Album* of Wilars de Honecort, an architect living in the middle of the 13th century, exhibits the use of geometry in various ways. This manuscript was published in facsimile by M. Lassus in 1858, and an English translation was edited by Professor Willis in 1859. The sketches also show a certain mastership of figure drawing, besides many designs of portions of buildings. Some original drawings still exist of Reims Cathedral, known to be before 1270, thus of the same period as those of Wilars, and two of them have been published in the *Annales Archéologiques*, vol. v. page 92. The drawings were traced with a masterly line; they only showed how the design was to be arranged; and by means of *axial lines only*, the whole was set out as regularly as could be done for the most classical building. Scarcely any of the later original drawings still existing in many continental cities show the use of geometric figures (see *fig.* 1073.). Yet, on the 14th of February, 1321, during the erection of the cathedral at Siena, five persons who had been appointed for the purpose reported that "the *new* work ought not to be proceeded with any further, because if completed as it had been begun, it would not have that measure in length, breadth, and height, which the rules for a church require." The *old* structure, it also appears, "was so justly proportioned, and its members so well agreed with each other in breadth, length, and height, that if in any part an addition were made to it under the pretence of bringing it to the right measure of a church, the whole would be destroyed." Della Valle, *Lettere Sanesi,* ii. p. 60; noticed in Hawkins, *Gothic Architecture,* 1813, p. 183. This statement would seem to prove that some system had existed.

In *par.* 620, we have already mentioned the disputes on the great question of proportioning the cathedral at Milan, 1387–1392, by the foreign system of *squares,* or by the native theory of *triangles.* The first notice in England of this unique instance of a dispute appears to have been taken by J. W. Papworth, who presented in 1854 to the Institute of British Architects some extracts from the Records of the Board of Works for Milan Cathedral, published by Giulini, *Memorie di Milano,* 4to. Milan 1776, part 2, pp. 448–60 of the *Continuazione.* These notes further condensed show, that on the 1st of May, 1392, fourteen of the artists employed upon the works made affidavit of their opinion on ten points submitted to them, on the part of the German Enrico di Gamondia, who was one of the number. On the third point, thirteen declared that the said church, not including the intended cupola, should be raised *non al quadrato ma fino al triangolo,* that is to say, on the triangular proportion. The same opinion is given on the fifth point as to the versed sine of the vaulting. Enrico, who on all the points held a contrary opinion to the thirteen, was thereupon dismissed. Another meeting of similar character, held 26th of March, 1401, of thirteen artists employed on the building, and two amateurs, was not so nearly unanimous upon the question of the alterations proposed by the Frenchman Giovanni Mignotto, and upon that occasion Guidolo della Croce (one of those employed) declared that the alterations were correct, and that Mignotto was a *verus operarius geometra,* because his ratios were like those of the dismissed *maestro* Enrico. The dismissal of this Jean Mignot, 13th of October, 1401, was accompanied by a charge for the expense of pulling down the work that he had erected during two years. Although the chronicle makes the curious mistake that the magister Enricus and the magister Annex (i.e. Johann von Fernach, 1391–92), also a German, had advocated the *triangular* system, it rightly adds that the triangular system prevailed over that of the square; and the lines may be supposed to have been truly given by Cesare Cesariano. The conclusion we have arrived at in the matter is that the plan was designed on the principle of the *square* (exhibited in *fig.* 1231.), while the elevation was designed on that of the *triangle* (shown in *fig.* 1232.).

Cesare Cesariano, the first translator of *Vitruvius,* Como, 1521, terms the geometric principle of design, "Germanic symmetry," and "rule of the German architects." Rivius, who translated this work (Nur. 1548), names the order resulting from the *triangle* as "the highest and most distinguished principle of the stonemasons." One principle rested on the arrangement of the *square,* or of the octagon which proceeds from it, in the same way as that of the equilateral *triangle* was based upon the hexagon or dodecagon which resulted from it. On this law of the *square* is founded the work by M. Roriczer, *On the Ordination of Pinnacles,* 1486, which was printed by Heideloff, in *Die Bauhütte des Mittelalters in Deutschland,* Nuremberg, 1844; and also by Reichensperger, who translated it into

modern German, Trier, 1845.   It was noticed in the *Journal* of the Archæological Institute of Great Britain, 1847; and translated in a concise manner by J. W. Papworth for the Architectural Publication Society, *Detached Essay*, 1848, with woodcuts.   An appendix follows *On the Construction of a Canopy*, which was also given in Heideloff's publication.

The *square*, or octagon system, maintained itself among the German stonemasons until the commencement of the 19th century.   Heideloff relates that the *chef-d'œuvre* of Kieskalt, the last city architect of Nuremberg (1806), was founded on the rules used in Roriczer, and those in the book of instructions written 1506 by Laurenz Locher, architect of the Count Palatine, on the art of the stonemason, *nach des Choresmaass und Gerichtigkeit*, "according to the measure and ordination of the choir."

"The system depending on the equilateral *triangle* for its variety of form," states E. Cresy, *Stone Church*, 1840, "continued in use till the beginning of the 15th century in France, when it underwent a great and important change by the introduction of the isosceles triangle and its compound the pentagon.   A pupil of Berneval, the designer of the Church of St. Ouen at Rouen, proved that these figures could furnish novelties in design.   We can well imagine how displeasing this innovation must have been to the whole fraternity of masons; their mystery was invaded."   Pommeraye, in his *History* of the Abbey of St. Ouen, mentions that the master was so incensed at the clergy preferring the rose window of the northern transept (*fig.* 1293.) executed by his pupil, where this innovation was first introduced, to that of the south (*fig.* 1288.), of his own execution, upon the ancient triangular system, that in a fit of jealousy he killed his rival, and was himself condemned to be hanged.   (See page 994.)

In the year 1525, Albert Duerer published in German his *Geometrical Elements*, showing therein clustered columns, and a few other details of Gothic architecture.   In 1532 a Latin edition was published at Paris, entitled Albertus Durerus, *Institutionum Geometricarum*; and in 1606 a second edition was printed at Arnheim.   It is this author who first brings to our notice the use of a figure called the *vesica piscis*, which is explained in Sect. III.   In 1589 Spenser published his *Faëry Queene*, and in it allusion is made to the proportion of a building in words which deserve attention (b. 2, canto 9, v. 21).   In 1593 Sir Thomas Tresham erected the curious lodge at Rushton Hall, Northamptonshire, entirely constructed on the equilateral triangle; it contains one room of an hexagonal form; the upper windows are mostly triangular openings (*Builder*, iii. 538. 550.).

Stieglitz, in *Altdeutscher Bauhunst*, 4to. Leipzig, 1820, records the possession of a manuscript *Treatise on Architecture*, giving the rules and instructions according to which the ancient *werkmeisters* and *steinmetzen* worked.   Judging from the character of the handwriting, it must belong to the middle of the 17th century, and this is also indicated by the drawings which exhibit the Italian style of that epoch.   But the rules for the construction of churches belong to a more remote period, and the author of the manuscript states that these rules were never described, but were transferred in a traditional way to, and kept by, the artists, who called them, like the ancients, Measure of the Choir and Justice.   It seems to be the *only* written directions for a building which has come down to us.   The drawings in it, which are only shaded, are finely executed by a steady and practised hand.   They show the formation of the several cornices, mouldings, jambs for doors and windows, plinths, and arches, and also the formation and the arches of the vaulting.   The building is proved to have strict rules and an established module, according to which all the members are regulated by the ensemble of the structure, and the whole is again regulated by the members.   The choir is considered as the key, and after its breadth is regulated, the thickness of the enclosure-wall, and also all the dimensions for the cornices and other members are obtained.   Thence the saying, "Measure of the Choir and Justice."

At first, from a given circle an octagon is to be constructed, and according to it, the ground-plan and the pentagonal projection of the choir are to be devised.   Should the choir contain 20 feet in the clear, its wall would be 2 feet thick; and if 30 feet wide, then 3 feet.   The pillars of the choir are commonly $2\frac{1}{2}$ feet thick at their base, exclusive of the ground table (*schrägesims*), and the depth is double of the thickness.   The width of the windows is regulated by the space between the columns, which is divided into 5 parts: 3 are given to the window in the clear, together with the mullions.   If the choir be very extensive, and therefore the lights of the windows be too wide, in such case intermediate mullions are introduced; but small windows have only one main or two subsidiary mullions.

The nave and aisles are regulated after the manner of the choir, being made equal to it in width, yet in such a manner that the pillars, although equal in thickness to the wall of the choir, do not run in the same line of the opening, but project with three sides of their octagonal form.   The breadth of the choir being divided into 3 equal parts, 2 are to be given to each aisle, including the wall of the choir.   The same dimension of two such parts is applied to the pillars from one centre to the other, which shows at the same time the space for the buttresses on the enclosure-wall.   As, in consequence of the aisles, the nave portion requires a wider vaulting than the choir, the enclosure-wall of the nave ought to

be constructed one-third thicker than that of the choir. The buttresses are the same in thickness and breadth as for the choir. The windows are kept of the same width throughout the whole structure. The transept projects as far as the breadth of the aisles, and its wall has the same thickness as the wall of the choir. The length of the church is for the most part regulated according to the requirements of the population.

The towers, erected on both sides of the façade, are devised from the width of the inner shafts and external pillars, which width formed into a square gives the external enclosure-line of the towers. If only a single tower be constructed, it ought to be regulated after the choir, and agree with the same. The thickness of the tower-wall is regulated by the height of the tower itself. Thus for every 100 feet of height, 5 feet in thickness is required for the wall. Then, to this thickness one half more is to be given for the foundation. But if the ground be firm and good, this thickness need only be kept as far as the base, and thence gradually reduced. The formation of the groining is not so clearly developed by the editor, and we therefore omit it.

The outline and elevation of the choir are also calculated from its width. A choir which is 20 feet broad, ought to be one and a half or twice as high. The latter height was called the real height. An ordinary choir requires only four tables or strings. The ground table (*schrägesims*) rises from the floor or ground to a height equal to the thickness of the counterforts. The string course (*kaffsims*) above is placed as high as the distance between the pillars. The supporting string (*tragesims*) ought not to rise higher than the capital of the pillars in the interior of the choir. The top, or roof-cornice (*dachsims*) ought to be placed at least half a foot higher than the vaulting. The pillar-cornice is measured by taking the thickness of the pillars twice down from the top-cornice. A choir of greater height requires more cornices and decorations. The height of the nave portion is fixed by taking twice the width of the choir, and this is measured from the ground-table to above the top-cornice. The ground floor of the tower ought to be as high as the whole tower is broad, and the upper floors to be regulated accordingly. We have only to add that the form given to the towers by the author of the MS. shows the Italian style of his epoch, whilst the church itself is constructed in German fashion, that is, with high pointed-arched windows and buttresses, which are drawn without any mouldings.

Sect. III.

THE VESICA PISCIS.

If on the diameter of a circle (*fig. 1225.*), with an axis perpendicular to it, an equilateral triangle be described, whose vertical height shall be equal to the semi-diameter of such circle, and from the angles of the triangle on the diameter, with a radius equal to one side of the triangle, arcs of circles be described cutting each other superiorly and inferiorly, the figure described is that which is called the *vesica piscis*, or fish's bladder.

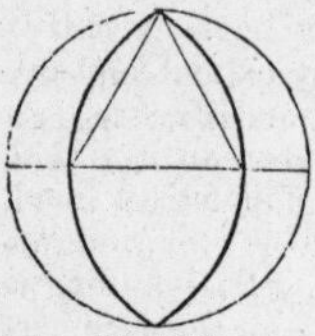

Fig. 1225.

The Greek word ἰχθὺς, signifying a fish, seems to have been in early ages a mystical word, under which Christ was denominated, "Eò quod in hujus mortalitatis abysso, velut in aquarum profunditate, sine peccato esse potuerit, quemadmodum nihil salsedinis a marinis aquis pisci afficiatur ;" that is, Because in the unfathomed deep of this mortal life he could exist without sin, even as a fish in the depths of the sea is not affected by its saltness. The term, too, at a very early period, furnished an anagram, whose parts were expanded into the expression, Ἰησοῦς Χριστὸς Θεοῦ Υἱὸς Σωτήρ. The initials of these words were, in their turn, expanded into a long acrostic (to which reference may be had, *sub voce Acrostichia*, and also under the term *Ichthys*, in Hoffmann's incomparable Lexicon) on the Day of Judgment, said to have been delivered, *divino afflatu*, by the Erythrean sybil, but much more resembling the hard-spun verses of a learned and laborious man than the extemporaneous effusions of a mad woman. This acrostic is recognised by Eusebius, and by St. Augustine, *Civ. Dei.*, &c. There is nothing, declared Mr. Gwilt, to afford any proof of the connection of this monogram with the form and plan of the churches erected during the mediæval period of the art. Apology, perhaps, would be due for any digression upon it, had it not been for an opinion in favour of its use expressed by the late Professor C. R. Cockerell, whose talents and learning deservedly ranked high in the eyes of the public, in his essay on the *Architectural Works of William of Wykeham*, read 1845, before the Archæological Institute of Great Britain and Ireland. Ramée, in his *Histoire*, has also gone more at length into this subject. Professor Cockerell likewise noticed that the writers of the 16th century, Cesariano 1521, Caporali 1536, and De Lorme 1576, recommend this figure, chiefly as that geometrical rule by which "two lines may be drawn on the ground at right angles with each other in any scale, according to the conception of Euclid's mind."

From an early time the *triangle* seems to have been associated with as much mystery and veneration as the number 3. Without here touching on symbolism, in its use, whether equilateral or isosceles—we cannot but perceive, both in one and in the other, a tendency to the production of the pointed arch. The geometrical law for describing it is, as every one knows, founded on the intersection of two circles of the same radius (*fig.* 1226.) The Pythagoreans called the equilateral triangle, Tritogeneia. It was, according to Plutarch, the symbol of justice. The subdivision of the arcs bounding an equilateral triangle by other arcs of equal radius, gives other modifications of the pointed arch, and by their intersections are obtained the skeleton lines of ornamented windows of an early period, which, at a later date, branched out into the most luxuriant forms. Mrs. Jameson, in *Sacred and Legendary Art*, 3rd edition, 1857, vol. i. p. 93, gives a drawing from an ancient Greek picture, wherein the upper part of the representation of the Infant Christ is placed in a figure formed of four equilateral triangles (which produce the dodecagon). The head of the infant may be supposed to occupy in the diagram the site of a chancel, the body in the place of a nave, and the hands, being held forth, assume the place of the transepts.

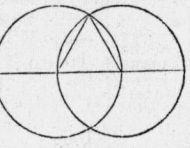

Fig. 1226.

Sect. IV.

MODERN INVESTIGATIONS.

Among the investigators early in the present century was C. L. Stieglitz, who published his *Altdeutschen Baukunst,* 1820, as already mentioned. Therein he states that, "with regard to the ground-plans of churches, it seems that two sorts have been employed. With the first, the nave of the church was in *breadth* equal to that of each of the aisles. With the second, if, for instance, such a breadth be taken as an unit, the breadth of the nave would be the diagonal line of the square, and the breadth of each aisle an unit. The length of the interior of the churches of these two sorts, measured from the entrance to the choir, contains usually nine units. The church of St. Stephen, at Vienna, is an illustration of the first system; and the Münster at Strassburg of the second. The cathedral at Cologne is a variety of the first plan. In this instance the nave is the breadth of its aisle, but each aisle is divided into two by a row of columns in the middle. The fore-part of the church has usually three diagonals of the square for its breadth, wherefrom the unit, should it be unknown, can easily be deduced. According to this principle, if the whole inner breadth of the church be considered as the root of a square, the diagonal of the same will be equal to the whole breadth of the front on the outside.

In the first sort of plan, the nave of the church is raised either to an equal height with the aisles or a little higher. In the second, however, the nave is constructed far higher. Owing to the first disposition, both the nave and the aisles are brought under a single roof, as in St. Stephen's at Vienna. In those of the second sort, the nave and the choir (which was equal in breadth to the nave) had each, as well as the aisles, a separate roof. The wall of the nave and of the choir, on account of its small thickness, comparatively with its height, required some support at the sides, and this was provided for by arched counter-forts or flying buttresses from the enclosure-wall of the aisles. The cathedral at Cologne shows a similar disposition, although the nave is equal in breadth to one of the aisles, wherefore the aisles are divided into two rows by pillars, for the purpose of giving to this portion of the vault (when it will be finished), on account of its smaller arching, a less height than the one intended for the vault of the nave and of the choir. The ground-plan of this cathedral is a Latin cross. The aisles surround the choir, which rises high above them, and therefore the enclosure-wall of the choir is connected with the pillars of the outer wall by means of arched buttresses. According to Boecker's observations, the number 7, consecrated by religion and philosophy, is applied all over the parts of this edifice, not only in the measures of length, in the proportions of height, in the pillars of the nave, as well as in those of the choir, but also in the decorations and details."

The inner height of the choir is stated to be 161 feet; the height to the gable, corresponding to the entire width of the west front, is 231 feet; the (proposed) height of the towers is equal to the entire length of the building, 532 feet; the height of the side aisles 70 feet, and so forth. In a similar manner, at the entrances on either side, are pedestals for seven statues; in each of the entrances as many spaces for statues; there are 14 corner tabernacles on the southern tower; and with attention, the same combination may be traced in all the details. Twenty years appear to have elapsed, and then Hoffstadt published the *Gothisches ABC Buch,* Frankfort, 1840, which enters fully into the formation of details by a geometric system.

In England, the subject was not thoroughly taken up until 1840, when R. W. Billings published his *Attempt to Define the Geometric Proportions,* &c. He therein considers that

during the Norman period, no intricate figures were used for regulating the proportions of the various parts of buildings. He exhibits the early simplicity of proportion, in the elevation of a compartment of the Norman nave of Gloucester Cathedral, as in the annexed *fig.* 1227. Something of the same sort of equality may be perceived at Winchester Cathedral, as shown in *fig.* 1266., where the width K L gives the heights I M and M N ; the diagonal of this square gives the height L O ; and O P is a square in height ; but we are at a loss to regulate the upper part, unless the triangle be used, when P Q will give the upper point at R, the centre of the head of the semicircular window.

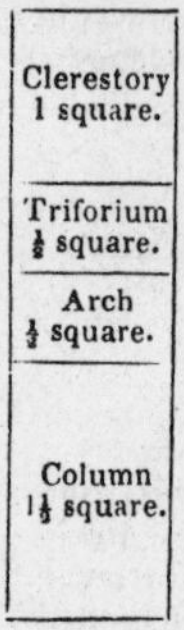

Clerestory	1 square.
Triforium	⅔ square.
Arch	½ square.
Column	1½ square.

Fig. 1227.

In the projection of the plans of the nave and choir of Carlisle Cathedral (*fig.* 1228.), the architect, says Mr. Billings, was guided by the repetition of a *circle* whose diameter in the first or Norman part was the extreme width of the building; and in the second part, erected 200 years subsequently, it was the width between the internal walls. The distribution and even the substance of the columns was regulated by some recognisable subdivision of the circle; and a circle, or arc of a circle regulated by the width of each compartment thus formed, was the basis upon which the heights of the different portions of the interior were framed. The woodcut must suffice to show this principle as regards the plan. The precise divisions will not probably answer in any other building, but must be modified. The east wall, it will be perceived, is included within the boundary lines; this is also the case at the Temple Church, London. From the result of calculations, the scale for the *choir* was made 8 parts of the radius of the principal circle, or 1/16 th of the diameter; this sixteenth part is equal to 4 feet 6 inches (or a yard and a half),

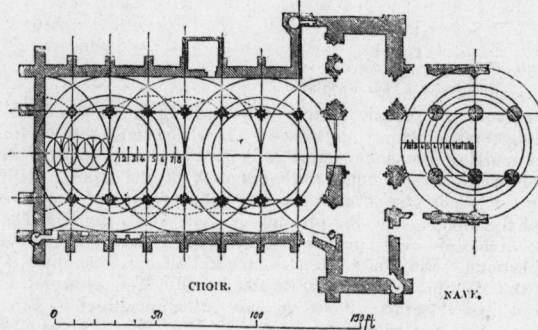

CHOIR.   NAVE.

Fig. 1228.   PLAN OF CARLISLE CATHEDRAL.

and the dimensions of the building may be calculated therefrom. In the nave, the piers are exactly 5 feet 8 inches, or 1/12 th of the diameter, and it was this exact division, states Mr. Billings, which induced the application of the scale of twelve parts to the diagram of that end of the building.

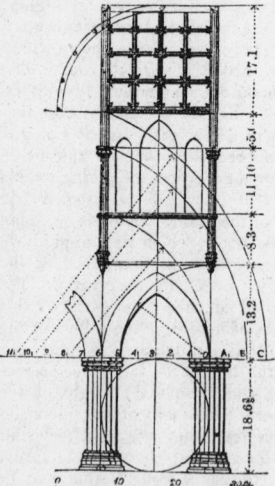

Fig. 1229.   BAY IN CHOIR; CARLISLE.

In every portion of the elevation of a compartment of the choir (*fig.* 1229.), there is evidence of its geometric formation. The student must have recourse to the publication itself for the further detailed development of the system in connection with this figure, but it is necessary to state that from the dimensions of the arch Mr. Billings divided the width between the centres of the piers into 6 parts for a scale; this gives all the remaining proportions. The same scale of 6 parts of the width was applied by Mr. Billings to a bay of the presbytery of the choir at Worcester, and finding it satisfactory, though totally at variance in its proportions, with the exception of the principal arch, it was considered as confirmatory of the theory. These two examples are of nearly the same period in the style.

In 1846 Mr. Billings published his *Architectural Antiquities of the County of Durham*, and in collecting the measurements of its churches he was led to compare their proportions. The result is given by him in two tables, proving a groundwork of *squares*, and this he states "would at once account for the non-existence of ancient working drawings, for the designer would only have to communicate a rough diagram of his plan, bounded by series of equal squares, and give the dimensions of one, to be properly understood by a practical man. Most singularly, the measure is in each case one square yard (as above noticed). No less than six of the chancels are 15 feet; three others are 18 feet; and three of 21 feet. At Houghton, the widths of the chancel, of the transept, and the distance between the columns of the nave, are all 15 feet."

The next investigator was the late Prof. Cockerell, R.A., who, in his essay before noticed (pages 965 and 968), considers that Cesare Cesariano "may be said to have done to a great extent in that style what Vitruvius did in the Greek, namely, in discovering many of its fundamental doctrines and principles. More especially does he reveal the estimation in which Vitruvius was held during the middle ages; and the interpretations of his rules attempted by the architects and commentators of that period." Thus, the church in the Castle of Nuremburg, built by Barbarossa in 1158, and the Frauenkirche, probably of later date, in the centre of that city, are exact illustrations of the temple "in Antis" of Vitruvius, as given by Cesariano, lib. iii. fol. 52. The use of the work of Vitruvius, about 1284, is also recorded in Galiani's edition of the author, by an amusing story connected with the building of the Castel Nuovo at Naples.

"It is needless to produce any further proofs of resemblance," writes J. S. Hawkins, in his *History of the Origin of Gothic Architecture*, 1813, p. 223, "than to say that, in every Gothic cathedral as yet known, the extent from north to south of the two transepts, including the width of the choir, if divided into ten, as Vitruvius directs (for Tuscan buildings, lib. iv. cap. 7), would exactly give the distribution of the whole. Three arches form the north and three the south transept; the other four give the breadth from one transept to the other. One division of the four being taken for each of the side aisles of the nave, and two left for its centre walls, the complete distribution of the nave is also given. Of the proportion of one-third of the whole width as the height of the columns, the cathedral of Milan is a decided instance. The two transepts together are 110 cubits, the breadth of the choir 28, making together 138; and the height of the columns is 46 cubits."

The rules named by Cesariano occur in his *Commentary*, fols. xiv. and xv., and he illustrates them by the plan and section, of Milan Cathedral, which was commenced in 1386. The figures are entitled "ichnographia,"—"orthographia,"—"scenographia,"—"sacræ Ædis Baricephalæ, Germanico more, a Trigono ac Pariquadrato perstructa," and, "secundum Germanicam symmetriam," and again, "per symmetriæ quantitatem ordinariam ac per operis, decorationem ostendere, Germanico more," &c.

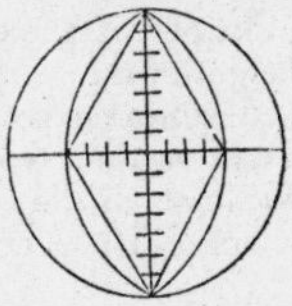

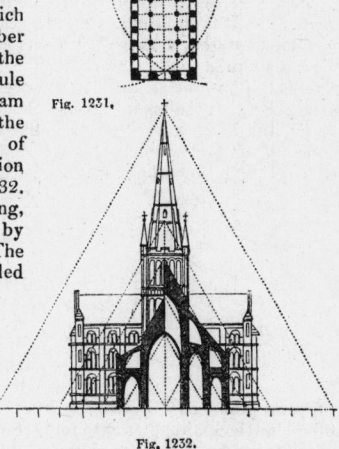

Fig. 1230.

The first rule, "a Trigono," establishes the respective proportions of the length and breadth of the cross, which are included within the two arcs of 102°, constructed according to the first proposition of Euclid. The *fig.* 1230. has been commented upon (page 968) as involving the *vesica piscis.* Mr. Cockerell continues his remarks by noticing Mr. Kerrich's paper in the *Archæologia*, xix. p. 353–61, wherein that author uses the figure but does not confess his debt. In all the examples given by him the vesica is applied to the internal length and breadth.

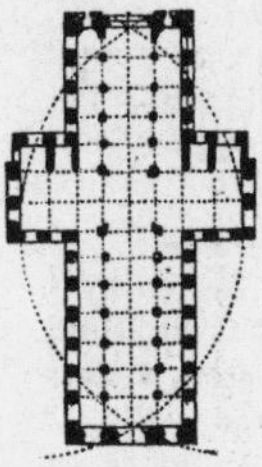

The second rule, "a Pariquadrato," is effected by dividing the area comprehended in the *vesica*, into commensurate squares or bays, on the intersections of which the columns and buttresses are placed. The number of them will be determined by the extent of the plan. *Fig.* 1230. represents the illustration of the rule in which 14 by 8 are used; in the chapels of Wykeham we have 7 by 4. The plan, *Fig.* 1231., explains the determination (by the symbol of the *vesica piscis*) of the length and breadth of a church; the subdivision into squares, the position of its piers, &c. *Fig.* 1232. explains the rule by which the heights of the vaulting, the roof, the spire, &c., are determined, namely, by equilateral *triangles* erected upon the plan. The woodcut exhibits both a single and a double aisled church.

Fig. 1231.

This important fundamental rule will be found to be applicable to cathedrals in England, as at York, Winchester, Worcester, Lichfield, Hereford, Salisbury, Norwich, Exeter, Westminster, Romsey, and others: in Italy, in the church of San Petronio at Bologna, and in most of the works of the architects Lombardi, as San Zaccaria and San Salvatore, at Venice: in France, in the cathedral at Rouen, and in others: and in Germany, in those at Prague, and others. But it is to be noted, continues Professor Cockerell, that another rule of distribution (not yet discovered) is more frequent in the latter countries.

Fig. 1232.

The third rule, also "a Trigono," is orthographic, and establishes the normal heights in

the elevations and sections by equilateral *triangles*, according to Cesariano, fol. 15. " The

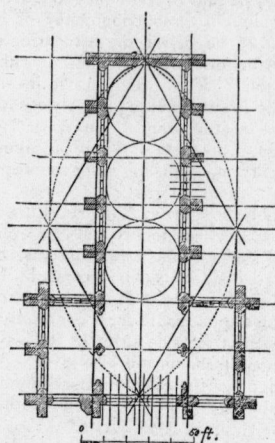

application of the first and second rules in New College Chapel is exact ; the whole and the parts are commensurate, as well in the bays or squares as in the subdivision of the bays of the windows ; of the flanks, as also of the west end. While in All Souls' and Magdalene Chapels, the two copies of the former, the divergences are extreme. *Fig.* 1233. is the plan and its subdivisions of New College Chapel, Oxford. To our author's own work we must refer the student for the apt remarks and comparison of the three plans, merely adding that the first is three diameters long, while the other two are less than three diameters, by which Professor Cockerell apprehends that the rule had been lost, or was disregarded, although Chichele's chapel was built by " the King's masons." The chapel at Winchester is upon the same principle, the number 7 including the vestibule, which only occupies one of the divisions instead of two, as at New College ; the relation of three diameters is obtained without making the diagram, as in New College Chapel, inclusive of the walls.

Fig. 1233. PLAN; NEW COLLEGE CHAPEL; OXFORD.

" The application of the third, the orthographic rule, is not traced so distinctly in the elevations and interior of New College Chapel, though more exactly in that of Winchester, and we also perceive the value of the principle of the extension of these squares laterally, for the purpose of establishing the height of the ceiling, and of the pinnacles in the east and west fronts."

The next exponent of this instructive subject was R. D. Chantrell, who in 1847 read a paper on the *Geometric system*, before the Institute of British Architects. It was printed, with cuts of the two chief keys of the system, in the *Builder* for the same year. He first refers to Mr. Kerrich's use of the *vesica piscis*, explaining it, as in *fig.* 1234. Where the

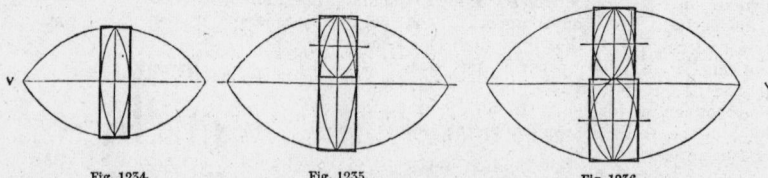

Fig. 1234.   Fig. 1235.   Fig. 1236.

chancel is separated by an arch, the plan is subdivided by taking the breadth as radius (*fig.* 1235.), as at Routh Church, near Beverley, the *vesica* coming sometimes within the walls and western arch, and at others extending to the western face of the arch in the nave, in many works of the 13th century. The apse is sometimes included in, and sometimes excluded from, the *vesica*. Where the nave and chancel vary in breadth, the base of the triangles equal the breadth of the chancel (*fig.* 1236.), its length being determined by the *vesica*, and in each of these cases the breadth of the nave is obtained by framing a similar *vesica* upon the remaining length.

The Anglo-Norman church at Adel, in Yorkshire, is defined upon the extreme length internally, as shown in *fig.* 1237., and subdivided by the proportions of smaller *vesicæ* and other proportions.

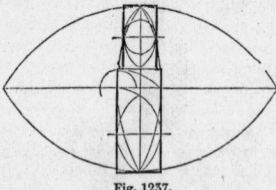

The *equilateral triangle* alone has been tried, but no great variety, he considers, can be produced, as, like the former system, it is but a minor portion of the great system in which most others will be found combined.

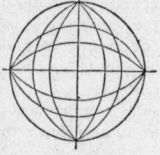

He notices that in 1830, J. Browne,

Fig. 1237.   Fig. 1238.

of York, produced a system on the circle. By placing a square or cross on the centre of the circle, dividing it into four equal parts, centres are obtained for *vesicæ* (*fig.* 1238.) of different proportions to those formed by the double triangles. By striking these radial lines upon each of the four points on the circumference, centres are produced in abundance for quatrefoils, crosses, and other figures applying more especially to tracery. The first *vesica* gives the proportions of the naves and their aisles of the cathedrals at Durham, Ely, Peterborough, Canterbury and Salisbury, but no others, and cannot therefore be considered an universal system.

In 1842 Mr. Chantrell developed a system which includes that of Kerrich's. Its formation is detailed in the journal named, to which we must refer the investigator, as the essay
has not otherwise been published. *Fig.* 1239. will at once show the principle, and if it

be drawn out to a very
much larger scale it
will not appear so com-
plex. Besides the tri-
angles, the points are
obtained for many po-
lygons. The six divi-
sions, A A, B B, from
the semidiameter are
first obtained; and
straight lines drawn to
each alternate one give
triangles. On their in-
tersections, as C C, if
lines be continued to
the circumference, six
centres are given, D D,
F F, upon which, with
the first radius A B
(or of the semi-diame-
ter), strike a second
series of segments, and
a third set of 12 cen-
tres is obtained. The
second centres will give
two intersecting tri-
angles, completing the
first part of the design.
Upon the 24 points of
the intersecting *inner*
arcs, a circle inscribed

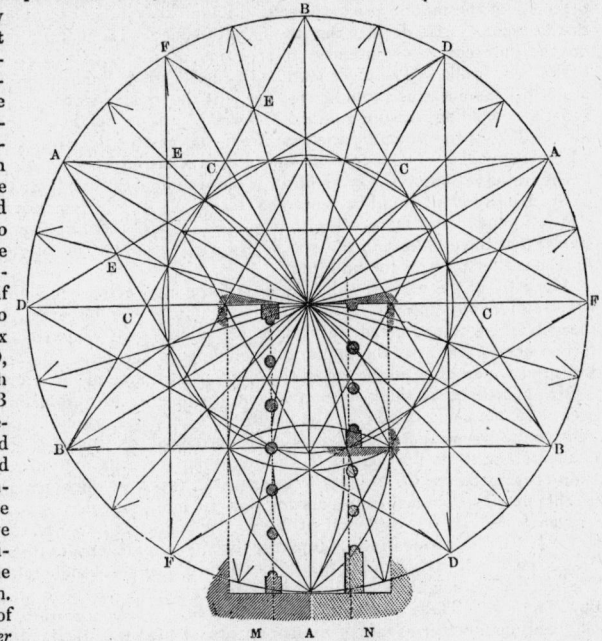

Fig. 1239.   MR. CHANTRELL'S SYSTEM.

will determine the inner triangles upon the centres of the first, and the diagram is perfected.
For more complex forms, an additional number of centre lines may be drawn upon the
remaining intersections.

The number 10 was, according to Vitruvius, Plato's perfect number; but the anti-
Platonists, with their 6 or the radial division of the circle (A to B, *fig.* 1239.), could, by the
working of their centres, without the necessity of dividing with the compasses, produce the
10, showing that they were the more perfect, as their system combined with all others.
The examples named by Mr. Chantrell, in which "the system is clearly exhibited," are
the rose window in the south transept of York Cathedral; that of Winchester Palace in
Southwark (*fig.* 1190.), but slightly varied and almost undisguised; and the east window
of Hawkhurst Church, Kent. Walkington Church, near Beverley, using the entire diagram,
affords a simple illustration; whereas Kerrich's plans are proportioned upon the second
radial figure produced by the division of the circle, they should be placed upon the base of
the great triangle, thus facilitating the operation of giving proportion to a plan. In the
composition of the cathedrals at Ely, Lincoln, Canterbury, Norwich, Salisbury, Worcester,
Durham, Peterborough, and Winchester, the general proportion is determined by the first
of the 24 subdivisions on each side of the centre intersecting the great triangle. The
abbeys are all produced on the intersections of the triangles and their centres, and the
subdivisions for the piers are found in the centre portion of the diagram, with this occasional difference, that transversely the radial lines may either pass through the *centres of the
piers* or *come on the outer or inner faces*, to conceal the principle on which they were based.
Thus M (*fig.* 1239.) is part of the plan of the nave of Boston Church, Lincolnshire,
arranged on the former principle, while N is part of that of Middleton-on-the-Wolds
Church, Yorkshire, where the lines come on the inner face of the piers.

"For the elevation, proceeding with the double spherical triangle upon the centres
longitudinally, and the variations before noticed, transversely, the various heights were
obtained for the pillars; and the subdivisions by the spherical triangles upon them gave
arches, capitals, and bases, triforia, tracery, mouldings of every description, and due
proportion to each feature. I have every reason to believe," concludes Mr. Chantrell,
"that this system will apply to the works of all ages that can be tested by sound geometric
principles."

The results of the investigations published by E. Cresy in 1847 are added in Sect. VI.

F. C. Penrose, in his investigations at Lincoln Cathedral in 1848, for the Archæological

Institute of Great Britain and Ireland, urges that " the tendency towards the system of designing on the *square*, with greater or less degree of approximation, is found to occur in so many churches that it is a law which had great authority with, at least, the more orthodox of the middle age architects, although they did not scruple to modify it when they saw occasion." He decides that the nave of Lincoln Cathedral was formed on this system on the intersection or intended intersection of the piers, and coinciding with the *outside* of the main walls. The choir seems to be built upon the true system of squares, which are of the same size as those of the nave, but the greater width of the former allows of the squares coinciding with the *inside* of the walls. " The height of the choir appears to be obtained, as is so frequently the case, from that of an equilateral *triangle*, whose base lies within the walls. The height of the nave is obtained by a square placed within the same limits, which, though less symbolical, is more commensurate." He thinks that if the length of St. Hugh's choir could be recovered, the whole length from east to west was then such that it included the transepts within a *vesica piscis.* He also conceives (for reasons he states) that the architect to the presbytery had access to the original drawings prepared for the earlier parts of the building.

The ratio of the voids to solids appears to be more remarkable than is to be found in any vaulted building in Europe, at least among the larger structures. Very careful measurements taken immediately above the plinths give voids 1056, supports 107, or the former nearly ten times the supports, including in the latter, the external buttresses and walls ; and including in the voids, the clear internal area of the church.

Mr. Penrose gives the measurements of the heights of various parts taken by him with great exactness, and this height he divides into 26 parts, which will be found " to agree in an exceedingly accurate manner with the principal divisions of the bays. In Bourges Cathedral, he states the height of the vaults agrees with that of an equilateral triangle whose base occupies the breadth from centre to centre of the external walls. Some of the heights may be obtained from parts of this triangle, and others from integral numbers of French feet. In the cathedral at Metz, the height is 130 French feet = 138·6 English feet. If this be divided into 300 parts, various proportions of them determine heights. The cathedral of Ratisbon appears to be founded on the triangle taken as that at Bourges. The ratio of its height to length is as 3 to 8 ; and is 104·2 English feet high, or 110 Bavarian feet. These results are well worth further consideration, from the well-known conscientious habit of taking measurements adopted by Mr. Penrose.

The next investigator appears to be W. P. Griffith, who published 1850–52, various essays on this subject, as named in the list of books in the Glossary addendum. He exhibits

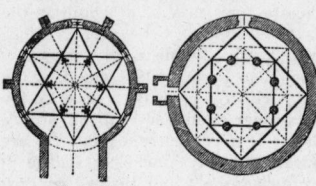

the adaptation of the *square*, set square and diagonally, one upon another (as in *fig.* 1073.) to the church of the Holy Sepulchre at Cambridge, *fig.* 1240.; and also of the *triangle*, for early churches, as at Little Maplestead, *fig.* 1241. Westminster Abbey Church, and the cathedrals at Salisbury, Winchester, and Rochester, are based upon a triangle whose base being the width of the nave, including the walls, is placed upon the centre of the central tower, and three of these triangles will include the length of the nave. Ely Cathedral, Redcliffe Church,

Fig. 1241.   Fig. 1240.
CHURCH AT LITTLE   CHURCH OF THE HOLY
MAPLESTEAD.   SEPULCHRE, CAMBRIDGE.

Bristol, and Bath Abbey Church, are proportioned in a similar manner. " We must insist," he writes, " after a primary figure of form or unit has been given, that each part produced shall bear a proportion to each other, and to the original unit.—Although the equilateral triangle dictated the general proportions, the square and pentagon were found very useful in the details. The chapter houses of Wells, York, Salisbury, and Westminster, are proportioned by joint squares forming an octagon; and those of Lincoln, Westminster, Worcester, and others, by two conjoint pentagons, forming a decagon." He illustrates the formation of the plan of Salisbury Cathedral, both on the *square* and on the *triangle*; but, as noticed respecting Milan Cathedral, although the square appears to suit best for the plan, the elevations appear to have been set out upon the *triangle*. Fig. 1242. shows the system applied by him to the plan of Sefton Church, Lancashire.

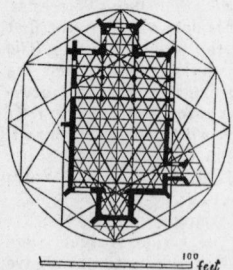

Fig. 1242.   SEFTON.

A comparison of the number of equilateral triangles, as named by Mr. Griffiths, in fixing the *height* of buildings, will be as follows, viz., Westminster Abbey, 6 ; King's College Chapel, 4 ; Lincoln, 3½ ; Hereford Cathedral, 4 ; Peterborough; 3½ ; Lichfield, 3½ ; Exeter, 4 ; Worcester, 3½ ; Bristol, 3. The loftiness of Westminster Abbey is attributed to the cause that the cloisters adjoining (similar to double aisles, as originally intended) being included in the

base of the triangle of the transverse section, therefore the height of the abbey is *more* than the cathedrals. The chancel of Bristol Cathedral has no triforium, and is accordingly *less* in height. These buildings having been based upon the equilateral triangle, that figure will alone be a key to them, and it will be futile to try the square. In Westminster Abbey that figure mostly abounds (in trefoils, hexafoils, dodecafoils, &c.); while Salisbury Cathedral, being based on the *square*, that figure and its products will be found chiefly employed (in tetrafoils, octafoils, &c.). This building is 4 squares high.

Dr. Henszlmann, in his *Remarks* on his alleged discovery of the constructional laws of mediæval church architecture, read at the Institute of British Architects, 1852, states that "the architects of old did not employ much reckoning in their constructions, but used geometric forms.—In studying the churches, I became persuaded that out of a ground-line or sum, considered as a basis, there can be developed, either by a geometrical or algebraical method, between 30 and 60 sums or lines, corresponding to the size, age, and importance of the building, and there is, with very few exceptions, not a structural member, be it large or small, the proportions of which are not defined by one of these lines or sums, or exceptionally by their multiples or divisions." He published the first portion of his elaborate system in 1860; this, together with the extensive system put forward by D. R. Hay, of Edinburgh, must be left to the reader to investigate from the books themselves.

The last of the investigators with whose system we shall trouble the student is W. White, who published it in the *Ecclesiologist* for 1853. He has perceived that each architectural period has its own appropriate order of rules, and this in minute accordance with an intelligible system of development. Thus, in the Norman period, the general proportions of the plan are reducible to the *square*, and the relative proportions and positions of the minor parts chiefly by the equilateral *triangle*. As architecture progressed the square disappeared, and to the outline and detail was applied the *triangle*. In the middle of the 14th century, as art declined, the triangle was forgotten, and a system of a diagonal square was taken up. Since then mathematical proportions have been chiefly employed, especially that of the diagonal of the square, *fig.* 1243.

"The figures applicable to the setting out of mediæval buildings are these: 1. the square; 2. the equilateral triangle; and 3. certain arcs described upon diagonals and

I.   II.   III.   IV.   V.

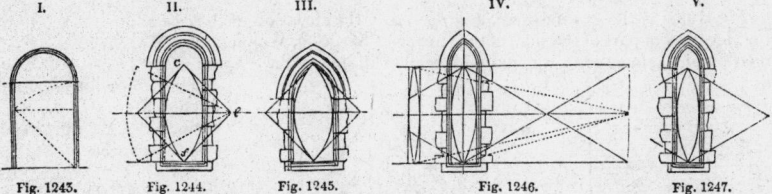

Fig. 1243.   Fig. 1244.   Fig. 1245.   Fig. 1246.   Fig. 1247.

bases of the same." Thus, in Norman work, the proportion of a square placed lozengeways from the ends of which a *vesica piscis* is struck (*fig.* 1244.) is in common use. In first

VI.

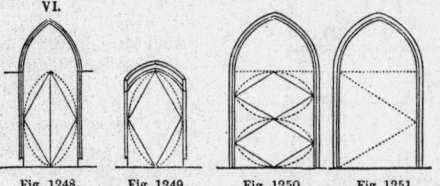

Fig. 1248.   Fig. 1249.   Fig. 1250.   Fig. 1251.

pointed work, the proportion is that of a square touching the head and sill (*fig.* 1245.). The system shown in *fig.* 1246. seems chiefly used in lancet windows and works of that period, the height being first determined. The proportion in *fig.* 1247. is used in traceried first pointed, the *vesica*, giving the width, being obtained from the apex of an equilateral triangle. The proportions *figs.* 1248. to 1251. predominate in middle pointed; those of II. and V. the same, only in the latter period the rule is applied to the determining of the lights or bays instead of the whole opening, and is applied to the centres of the mullions and not to the sides only. All these proportions appear to have been equally well known in all early times, but in the middle pointed period they gradually became more complicated, and are consequently more difficult to trace out. In third pointed they can hardly be found, and in obtuse third pointed they quite

VII.

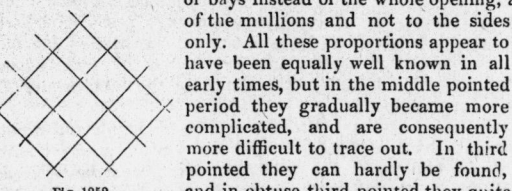

Fig. 1252.

VIII.

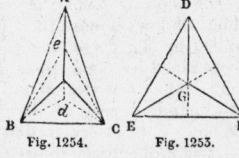

Fig. 1254.   Fig. 1253.

disappear, the proportions shown in *figs.* 1243. and 1252. taking their place. The equilateral triangle of 60°, D E F (*fig.* 1253.) used to obtain one point, is often accompanied by the angle formed of 30°, E F G, to obtain another relative point; each equal subdivision

F D and F G; F G and F E, having the corresponding angles of each equal; whereas in other triangles (as *fig.* 1254.) this is not the case.

We give one of his illustrations of the theory as applied to Steyning Church, Sussex, a Norman building. The plan (*fig.* 1255.) is set out by equal *squares*, and also the exterior (*fig.* 1256.) to some extent. The interior (*fig.* 1257.) is set out by squares and triangles. The diagrams will explain themselves. The diameter of the columns is determined similar to *c e f* in Rule II. The lower window is set out by II. and the upper one by VI.

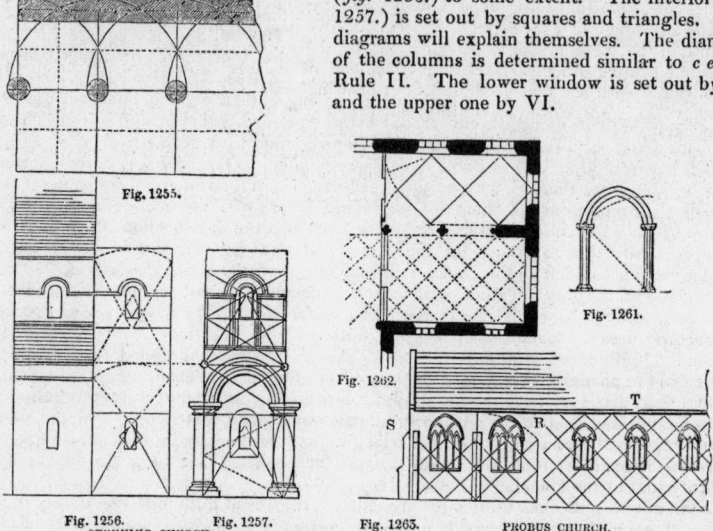

Fig. 1255.

Fig. 1261.

Fig. 1262.

Fig. 1256.   Fig. 1257.
STEYNING CHURCH.

Fig. 1263.   PROBUS CHURCH.

Fig. 1258. is the ground-plan, and *fig.* 1259. the elevation of the east end ; and *fig.* 1260. the elevation of part of the side, of the church of St. John, Wappenbury, Warwickshire. The relation of the lines one with another is well exhibited in the diagrams. At Itchenor Church,

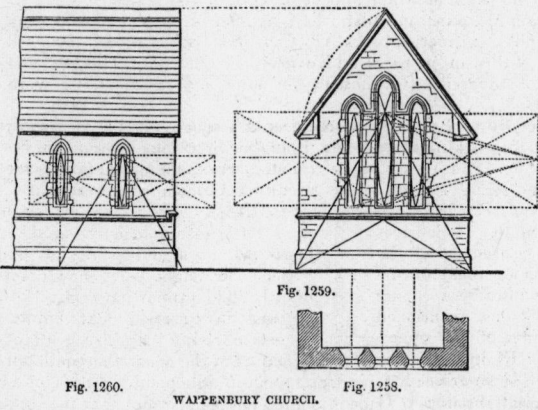

Fig. 1259.

Fig. 1260.   Fig. 1258.
WAPPENBURY CHURCH.

Sussex, the width is divided externally. In the west window of the north aisle of the church of St. Andrew's at Ewerby, the centres of the mullions obtained on the plan by squares diagonally divided, exactly coincide with the same points on the elevation as developed according to Rule VI. This system is shown in *figs.* 1287. and 1303. *Figs.* 1262. and 1263. explain the method of setting out the proportions for third pointed work ; the height of the bay (R) being first determined by the diagonal of a square.

The example is the church at St. Probus, Cornwall. The windows S are a square wide to the outer edge of the moulding, and are fixed by a square on the base of the bays. The windows T have their points fixed much in the same way, but their width is determined by the diagonal of a square. The height of the arches in the interior are also determined by the diagonal of a square (*fig.* 1261.).

" No one," writes Mr. White, " seems to have carried out upon the equilateral triangle any definite theory of design, or to have reduced the application of it to any tangible shape.—The theory is that the several parts of a perfect building must be in certain relative proportions to each other,—so that all parts may be brought into an entire and unmistakable harmony with each other,—hence it is not a definite application of these principles that is insisted on, but only a systematic observance of them in some way or other.—In secular and domestic buildings, we do not look for the same amount or kind

of beauty, nor is the same exactness of proportion of equal importance as in an ecclesiastical building, where every line ought to be in its proper place, and every form distinctly marked to convey an idea of perfection. In common dwelling-houses, where it is directly evident that the external form is entirely dictated by certain requirements of internal arrangement, a sort of natural beauty always results, and so there is not the same need to have recourse to exactness of proportion to produce some degree of good effect.

"The advantage of a mechanical process for defining proportions and forms would be immense in the mere practical carrying out of the work ; for by its means we could, by taking one leading dimension, transcribe, reduce, or enlarge drawings with the greatest accuracy, and with less than half the labour of using scales and compasses. A large body of men, working apart from each other, but under certain and very rigid restrictions, must produce diversity as well as similarity. Their works must all possess the same general character, though the details and form in the application of them must vary in every instance with the circumstances of the case and the workings of the different minds."

This system is developed by Mr. White, on numerous plans, details, towers, &c. taken from his own dimensions.

Sect. V.

PROPORTIONS OF MOULDINGS.

To enable us to decide that mouldings may have been also designed according to a measure, there is a very interesting notice recorded by Llaguno, *Noticias de los Arquitectos y Arquitectura de España*, edited by Cean-Bermudez, 1829, wherein, under the life of Pascual Iturriza, he states that that architect designed, 8th of May, 1541, the *capilla mayor* to the parish church at Plasencia in Guipuzcoa. While the work was in hand, complaints arose from the townspeople, voters, that he was decorating it with work that was too minute and could not be seen from the floor. To this assertion he replied, according to an entry in the archives of the town, that they might bring some persons, *peritos en la gimetria*, who could give a judgment in the matter. Such skilled persons were brought to the building and approved the work in debate. Whereon the town council requested the vicar, as being a person who was always in the building, to oversee the remainder of the work. The church is in the Gothic style, with a nave and chancel only, and is executed in cut stone. Iturriza was further employed at Santa Marina de Oxirondo in 1559.

We have given in the section Masonry an illustration (*fig.* 662h.) of a mode of setting out the ribs for vaulting, found on an incised block of stone. Such specimens of mediæval work are very rare. Prof. Willis, in his paper on *Vaulting*, gives another example, and perhaps only two more could be quoted. But these do not show how the mouldings were proportioned.

We insert from the appendix to Roriczer's work, quoted on page 966, the method of making the template or mould for working the mouldings for a canopy. The directions are :— In a given square A B C D (*fig.* 1264.) inscribe a circle and draw the diagonal and centre lines. With the centre Z, and a radius equal to the given line A B, describe a circle, and

therein inscribe a square E F G H parallel to the diagonals of the first square. This gives the size of the horizontal measurement of the four leaves of the great flower or finial of the canopy. In the same circle inscribe a square I K L M of equal size to the last mentioned square, but parallel to the sides of the square A B C D, and let the line I K intersect the line F G in N, and the line F G intersect K L in O, and the line K L intersect the line G H in P, and the line G H intersect the line L M in Q. Bisect the line B K in R, and with the centre B and the radius B R describe a circle ; and with the same radius describe a similar circle about the centre C. With the centre G, and the same radius, cut off from the line G Z a portion G T, and through the point T draw

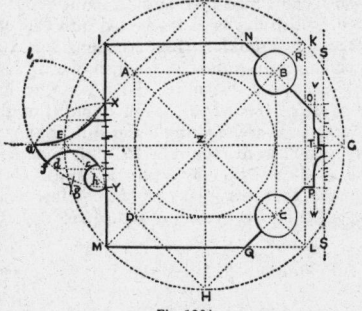

Fig. 1264.

a line S S of indefinite length ; and from the points O and P draw lines perpendicular to the line S S and joining it. This gives the outline of the template for the arched mouldings ; for M Q will be the internal face of the wall, Q P the external splay, with one hollow moulding C therein ; the rectangular parallelogram under P O will contain the jamb mouldings from which the template of the mullion is found, &c.

The jamb and hood mouldings are not described by Roriczer, but probably the back of the hood is obtained by the radius X Y cutting Z E at *a*, and from *a* and X the same radius will give the point *b*, from whence the curve X *a* is obtained. The curved line Y *a* is obtained from X. Divide X Y into 5 equal parts, and at 1 draw a line parallel to Z *a*. The length *af* will be equal to the diameter *e* Y. With a radius equal to *d e*, and the centres *f* and Y, describe arcs of circles intersecting in the point *g*, and with the centre *g* and the same radius describe the arc *f* Y. The roll moulding appears to be formed by the length *e* Y on the line E Y, cutting the line Y X at 1.

The jamb moulding is probably obtained by dividing the line S S into 8 equal parts; a radius equal to one of the parts struck from 2 and 6 will give the point, and the line V W. T *r* will be equal to half T 4, and the jamb is completed. For the remainder of the construction of the canopy we must refer the reader to the publication in question.

" It is in vain," states Cresy, *Stone Church, Kent*, 1840, " that we attempt to imitate the tracery or mouldings belonging to this (the 13th century) style correctly, unless we consider them to emanate from some simple figure. However numerous the mouldings, they never appear confused, which entirely arises from the order observed in their arrangement." This he illustrates by the mouldings forming the trefoil arches round the chancel. " The points of intersection of the two equilateral triangles are the centres for the hollows, and the more prominent parts of the moulding are set out with the same radius at the points of the triangles ; or, in other words, four circles are encircled within a circle, and by omitting each alternate one the figure is formed."

Fig. 1265. is from Mr. White's essay, and represents his system applied to a cap and base of the porch doorway at the church of St. Andrew, at Heckington, in Lincolnshire. The mouldings are reduced from full size drawings whereon the diagrams coincide very accurately with the several

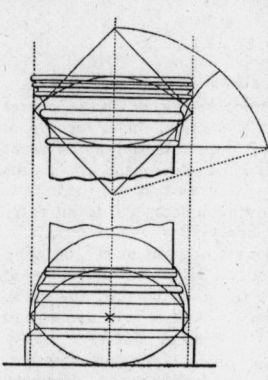

Fig. 1265*a*.   CAP AND BASE AT STEYNING.

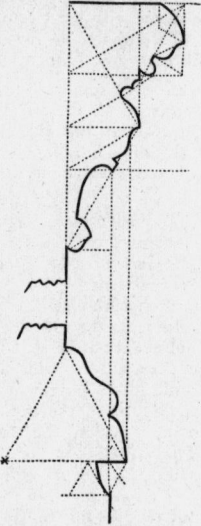

Fig. 1265.   HECKINGTON.

members, the whole being set out by subdivisions of the equilateral triangle, or angles of 30° and 60° &c. (as *fig.* 1253.). *Fig.* 1265*a*. illustrates another cap and base from Steyning church, previously selected as an example. The cap of the columns is formed on the principle of Rules II. and III., and the base upon that of VI.

A remarkable circumstance connected with this subject is, that although the German archæologists appear to have reduced the proportioning of mouldings and details to a system, as illustrated and explained by Hoffstadt, *Gothisches A B C Buch*, Frankfort, 1840, which has been translated into French by T. Aufschlager, *Principes du Style Gothique*, Paris and Frankfort, 1847, no one has translated it into English, or prepared a corresponding publication on English work (certainly not since the well-conceived but lamentably produced system by Batty Langley in 1742), not even the author of the *Analysis of Gothic Architecture*, from whom it might have been expected. In fact, a true system of mediæval architecture being still unknown in England, designs are made at random, and the school, in disregard of its professed principles, continues disunited. For the satisfaction of those who may desire to subject the mouldings given in Chap. III. to a system, we add that the plans of Fountains, Tintern, and Henry VII.'s Chapel, appear to be designed on the system of the square ; that of Howden on the triangle.

Sect. VI.

PRINCIPLES OF PROPORTION.

The following portion of the elucidation of this subject was originally published in 1847 by E. Cresy in his *Encyclopædia*, as referred to at page 900 of this work, who noticed, while introducing it, that " our attention must not be directed to the decorative portions of the style, but to the construction, from the study of which some valuable lessons may be deduced."

The Saxon manner of Building. — A division of the transept of the cathedral at Winchester has been selected as the best authenticated example of the style in use previous to the Norman Conquest. In a paper read before the British Archæological Association at their second annual congress, held at Winchester in August, 1845, the author gave his reasons for supposing it to be the work of St. Athelwold, for which the reader is referred to its " Transactions."

Arches upon arches enabled the Saxons to continue their walls to a considerable height, the openings between the piers being proportioned as those of the Roman buildings in the time of the emperors. The plans of the piers differ from those previous to the introduction of Christianity : in Britain both the Greek cross and the circle are applied to them.

At Winchester Cathedral the columns of the triforium recede within the pier, and are set round a circle, (fig. 1267.); the passage in the walls of the clerestory is shown at the side ; in another portion of the same building is a similar arrangement in less massive piers. (fig. 1268.)

The Saxon churches were generally divided into three tiers or stories, viz. a lower arcade, a triforium, and clere-story above ; and such was the solidity and thickness of the walls, that buttresses were altogether omitted, the outer face of their buildings in this particular bearing a closer resemblance to the Roman than the Norman, although the workmanship was rude, and the decoration scanty.

The proportions found in Saxon buildings are the same as in the Roman, which, without doubt, they took for their models. The circular temple of the Pantheon at Rome, 142 feet 6 inches diameter internally, and 183 feet 8 inches externally, contains the proportions of two-fifths wall and three-fifths void ; the area of the latter being 15,948 superficial feet, and of the former 26,493 superficial feet ; the difference of these areas giving 10,545 feet for the area of the walls.

We have already seen that in the Coliseum at Rome the points of support are about one-sixth of the entire area of the plan ; and the proportions of both these buildings have been admired for nearly 2000 years, the one vaulted, the other uncovered.

Generally the walls and piers of our Saxon cathedrals occupy from one-third to two-fifths of the entire area ; in their sections one-third is devoted to walls and piers, and the remainder divided between the nave and side aisles.

The division of the cathedral at Winchester exhibits very perfectly the Saxon manner of building ; the piers that support the lower arches are 10 feet wide, and the clear openings between them 12 feet 1 inch. The nave and transepts retain their original construction ; in the former under the casing executed by William of Wykeham, and in the latter it is seen in its full purity. The choir stands over the crypts built by St. Athelwold, and though

Fig. 1266. WINCHESTER CATHEDRAL.

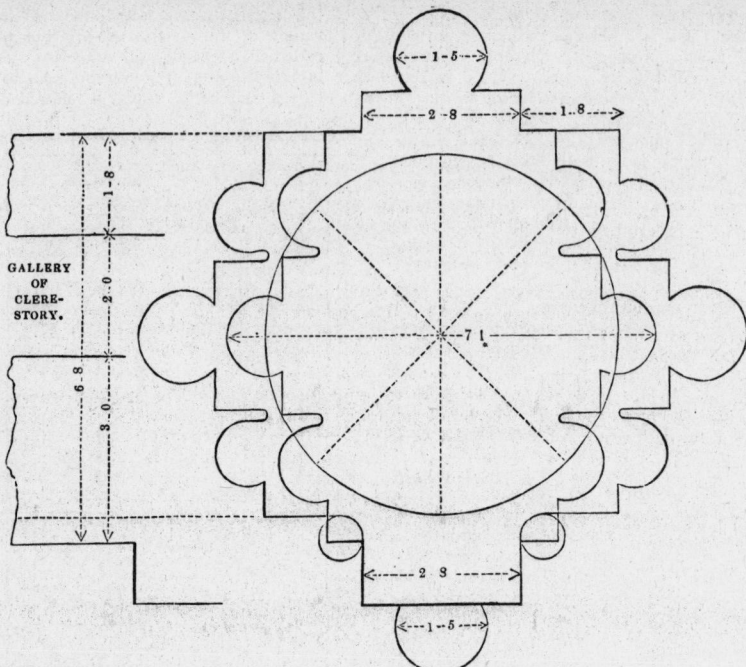

Fig. 1267.　　　PIER IN NAVE AT WINCHESTER CATHEDRAL.

somewhat changed by the Normans, it yet retains the dimensions given to it by its
celebrated Saxon constructor.

The small piers, one of
which, in the south transept,
is nearly perfect, are set out
with great regularity, and
measure 9 feet 8 inches from
west to east, and 8 feet 2
inches from north to south;
their form is that of the Greek
cross, composed of five cubes,
each 2 feet 7 inches in width,
with large and small columns
placed around them to receive
the mouldings that decorate
the arches: six of these columns have their centres on
the same circle: it is evident
that the hexagon, or the duplication of the equilateral
triangle, was applied, and
that the whole was set
out by one conversant in
geometry, and acquainted
with the proportions of the
cube. The Greek cross, which
defines the solid mass, is continued through the triforium
and clerestory up to the timber

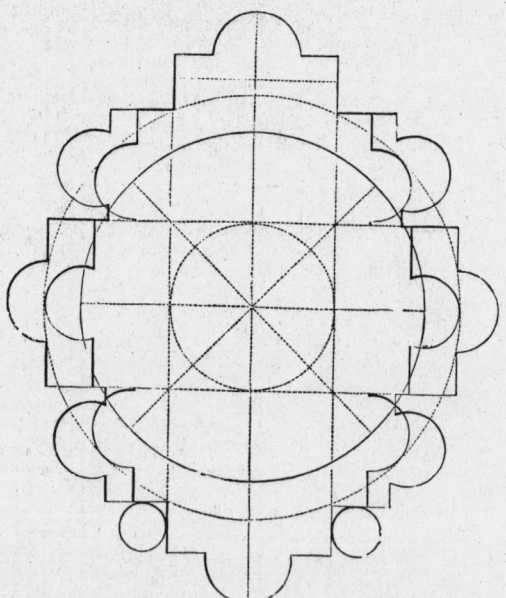

Fig. 1268.　　PIER AT TRANSEPT AT WINCHESTER CATHEDRAL.

roof. The columns of the triforium, set round the inner circle, are partly cut into
the lateral arms of the Greek cross, but the face of the shafts of the columns are in a line

with its outer side. The centre of the pier is preserved throughout, and so placed as always to balance the masses around it equally. The circular shafts at Gloucester Cathedral, Tewkesbury Abbey Church, and several others, were probably of earlier date than pillars formed of several shafts; those in the church of Saint Germain des Prez, at Paris, are delicate examples of the former style.

That aisles, galleries, and passages, belonged to the construction of a Saxon church, we have sufficient evidence in the accounts left us by contemporary historians; but the present subject is almost conclusive on this point, there being a preparation for a wall 6 feet 8 inches in thickness, containing the passage 2 feet in width, indicated by the plan of the pier at fig. 1267. The arrangement of the columns shows that there was no intention of vaulting the side aisles, for the two which carry the cross springers appear to have been added some time after the original construction, as were also those in the pier, fig. 1268.

Athelwold is supposed to have executed the whole of this work before the year 980: the mouldings throughout are rudely cut, the capitals of the main pillars being the only portions which are at all enriched by sculpture, and they are very simply carved.

The Norman manner of Building can scarcely be said to differ from the Saxon, though the masons employed after the Conquest certainly acquired a superior knowledge in their art. The ornaments which we find in Norman buildings had all been previously used by the Saxons; hence the difficulty of distinguishing the works of one from the other: where written authority is not handed down to us, we can only judge by the difference of the workmanship; it cannot be denied that there were many very able masons among the Saxons, who were qualified to raise buildings and enrich them with sculptured ornament.

The finest examples of Norman work may be seen at Caen and its neighbourhood, and have been engraved from measurements taken by the late Mr. Pugin.

In England the same style prevailed throughout our religious structures; there is a great similarity of arrangement, and little variety of ornament. The Norman style was generally adopted after the Conquest, but that named by the monkish historians the "Opus Romanum" was continued in many of our parish churches, as well as in some larger buildings. The Norman pillar was sometimes composed of a cylinder with four small half columns attached, as at Amiens, which is 7 feet 2 inches diameter.

For the Saracenic or Arabian Styles we must refer to the beautiful work recently published by Mr. Owen Jones, where the decorative parts of this curious and highly ornamented

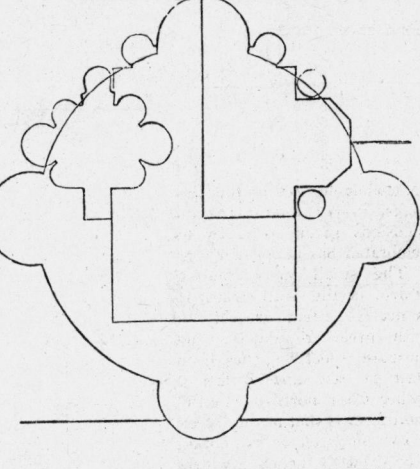

Fig. 1269.   PIER AT AMIENS.

architecture are admirably given, and proceed to the description of the principles which guided the constructors of pointed architecture.

The Lancet Style succeeded the Norman, and we find it well defined in many churches and cathedrals as early as the year 1180; in it decoration was sparingly introduced, and throughout every part of the design there was simple uniformity, and a display of a considerable knowledge of geometry: the heads of the windows and doors were formed of a pointed arch, constructed upon an equilateral triangle; all the mouldings which surrounded those apertures were delicately formed, and had both capitals and bases; this style was practised till 1230, when it was followed by another, which by some writers has been termed

The Early English or the Geometric Style, from the manner in which the several portions of a building were set out; and we find it adopted generally up to the year 1280.

Salisbury Cathedral, founded by Bishop Richard Poore, in the year 1220, was finished in 1260. Its plan is that of a Greek or patriarchal cross, the extreme length being 480 feet, that of the great transept from north to south 232 feet, and that of the lesser transept 172 feet: the stone used for the external walls and buttresses was brought from the quarries at Chelmark, which lies about 12 miles distance, westward from the city. The middle

of the walls is filled in with rubble, and the shafts of the columns are of marble, from the Purbeck quarries.   At the intersection of the nave with the great transept rises a noble stone tower and octagonal spire, the total height of which is 400 feet; the stone of the spire is in thickness about 2 feet to the height of 20 feet above the tower, after which it is only 9 inches in thickness to the summit: this spire, though braced and strengthened throughout by timbers and ironwork, has declined from the perpendicular 22¼ inches; but since 1681, when the observation was made, there has been no further declination.

The walls, after they were carried up to the floor of the triforium, appear to have been increased by corbelling, as if it had been doubted whether, as originally set out, there would be sufficient strength to carry the cross springers of the vaulted nave; the total width is exactly 100 feet. The clear width of the nave, as measured on a level with the triforium, is 33 feet 3 inches, and that of each side aisle half that dimension, or 16 feet 9 inches; had this last been 16 feet 7½ inches only, the proportions shown by a section would have been exactly one-third for walls and two-thirds for voids; after appropriating the third of the 100 feet to the walls, half the remainder is given to one side, and half to the other; we also find that each of these dimensions of 16 feet 8 inches is divided into three, two parts of which are given to the outer wall and buttress, and the other to the main pillar that divides the nave and side aisles, or nearly so.

The inclination of the arched buttresses is not such as to resist the spreading of the vault at its base; the knowledge of their use not having then been attained. The height of the vaulting of the nave from the pavement is 81 feet.

Wells Cathedral has some peculiarities in its construction, particularly in the application of its arched buttresses: they pitch against a stone corbel inserted below the springing of the

Fig. 1270.   PLAN OF CLERESTORY.   Fig. 1271.   PLAN OF TRIFORIUM.

Fig. 1272.   SECTION OF WELLS CATHEDRAL.

middle vault, and a tangent drawn at the back of the vault and elongated determines the inclination of the top of the flying buttress: here some improvement is shown upon those

at Salisbury. The masonry of the arches is admirably constructed, and the joints all radiate to a common centre.

The total width of this cathedral from face to face of the buttress is 86 feet 5 inches, and that of the nave 31 feet 10 inches, instead of 28 feet 9½ inches, as it would have been if a third had been adopted; the side aisles are also diminished in consequence, being only 13 feet 7¼ inches in the clear; they are, however, equal to the buttress, outer wall, and main pillar added together, the first projecting 2 feet 8 inches, the second or outer wall being 6 feet in thickness, and the piers 5 feet diameter; whilst the width of the side aisle measures 13 feet 7¼ inches, an approximation sufficiently near to suppose that the proportions of thirds was still adopted in practice. The nave has been increased at the expense of the side aisles, and its height is 68 feet 9 inches to the top of the vaulting from the pavement.

Fig. 1273. TRIFORIUM, INSIDE.

Fig. 1274. DIVISION OF WELLS CATHEDRAL.

Chapter House at Wells, erected between the years 1293 and 1302, is an octangular building of great beauty. A section through the buttresses shows that two equilateral triangles crossing each other have determined the mass and void, which are in the proportion of one to two, or the thickness of the two walls is equal to one-third the entire diameter: the base line of the triangle, on which the supports of the crypt are placed, clearly indicates this arrangement. Of the twelve equilateral triangles comprised in the parallelogram formed by uniting the bases of the two larger, each outer wall and buttress occupy two, or the two walls and their buttresses four of the twelve divisions, leaving eight for the space between them.

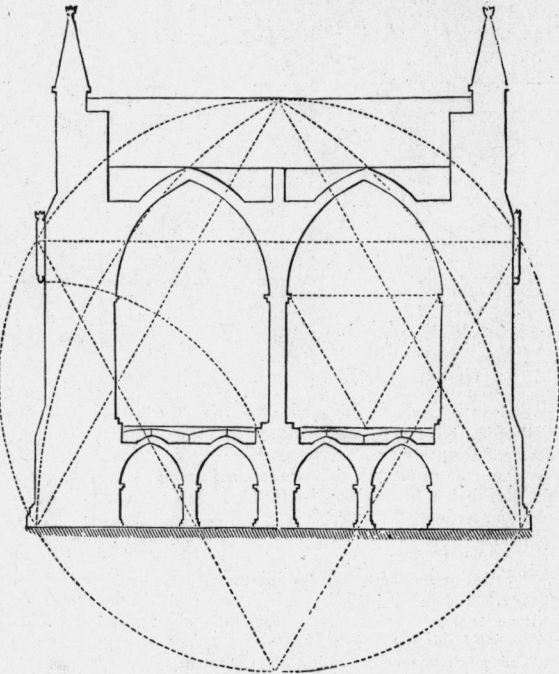

Fig. 1275. CHAPTER-HOUSE AT WELLS.

Where it is determined that the walls shall occupy one-third of the section of a building, no figure is so well calculated for such a distribution as the equilateral triangle; it enables the architect at once to limit and fix the proportions of his design; hence its universal application: and the mysterious qualities attached to it by the freemasons no doubt arose from the extraordinary facility it afforded them in setting out their several works. What can be more simple or more beautiful than the distribution of this edifice? Within a circle a hexagon is set out, the perpendicular sides of which mark the outer faces of the buttresses; the junctions of the angles, by forming a base to every two sides, produce the two equilateral triangles, which sub-divided not only enable us to arrange the other portions accurately, but also to measure with the greatest nicety their relative dimensions. The quantities of material employed in construction can be estimated by such means much more easily than by measuring each portion separately, cubing it, and adding the numerous dimensions so obtained together; there is decidedly more simplicity in the former than in the latter system: the area of one triangle being found, we at once know that of all the rest.

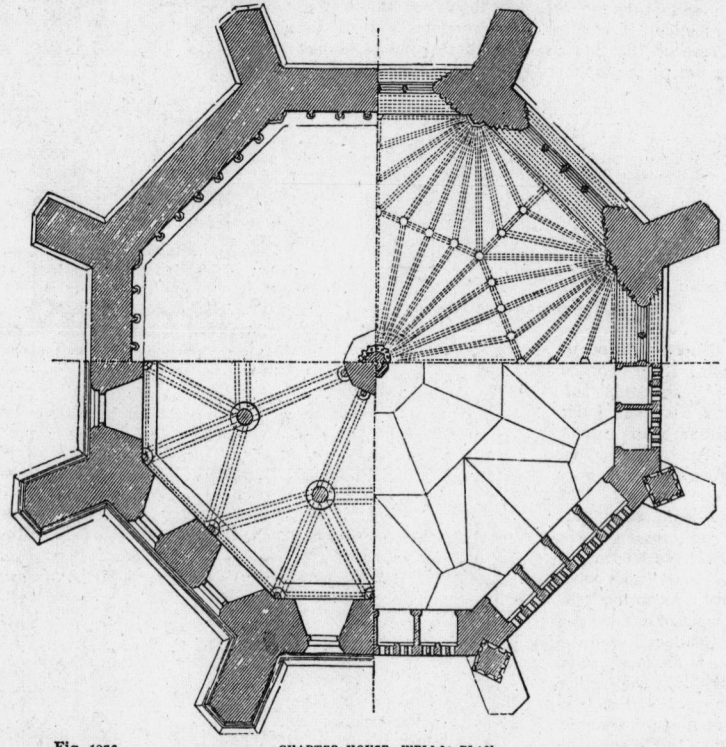

Fig. 1276.   CHAPTER-HOUSE, WELLS: PLAN.

or of any portion. In the subject before us the distance from the middle of one buttress to that of the other is 31 feet 6 inches, and the diameter taken through them at this level is 92 feet; omitting the buttresses, the outer side measures 26 feet, and the inner 21 feet 6 inches, the respective radii of the circles which comprise the octangular outer walls and the void being 38 feet and 31 feet 5 inches. Hence we find that the entire area of the

building without the buttress is   -   -   -   -   3264 feet.
The area of the void -   -   -   -   -   -   2176 feet.

And of the walls or points of support -   -   -   -   1088 feet.

At the level of the crypt, above the outer plinth, we have these regular proportions, two-thirds void and one-third walls.

The height of the entire building, from the pavement to the top of the parapet, is 72 feet 6 inches, and to the top of the pinnacles 92 feet, the total height being equal to the extreme diameter taken above the plinth moulding on the outside. The interior of this chapter-

house exhibits the most perfect proportions as well as appropriate decorations; the eight windows, divided into four days, have their heads filled in with circles set out upon equilateral triangles; the vaulted stone roof rests partly upon the octangular central pillars, 3 feet in diameter, surrounded by sixteen small columns, one at each angle and another between; the height of the pillar is 22 feet 8 inches.

Thoroughly to comprehend the expression, as well as use of the various members found in the architecture of the middle ages, we must trace the progress made in vaulting, and observe the changes it underwent, from the simple cylindrical to the more complex and difficult display of fan tracery or conoidal arches. The ridge ribs, or *liernes*, as they are termed, in the crypt of the Chapter-house at Wells, pass from the centre of the building to the middle of each buttress; the diagonals, or *croissées*, mitre into them as well as into the *formerets* or ribs against the outer walls.

In the vaulting of the Chapter-room, we have evidence of greater refinement, and an

Fig. 1277.   CHAPTER-HOUSE AT WELLS: SECTION.

improvement in the decoration, by the addition of a number of intermediate ribs terminating against the octangular one in the middle.

At a later period we find transverse ribs made use of, then others between; but although the design may seem complicated, yet when laid down the plan will assume the greatest simplicity, as shown in the division representing the groining of the crypt.

When this system had been carried out to a considerable extent, the fan tracery was introduced, and although apparently more difficult of execution, it is far more scientific in its application and arrangement, evincing a higher knowledge of mathematical principles and geometry, and is another evidence of the gradual progress of the mind towards perfection in this style of architecture.

Westminster Abbey, commenced in the year 1245, is in that style which for many years prevailed in France: the fine church at St. Denys, near Paris, is exactly similar in all its detail. The windows are wide, divided by mullions, and have their heads filled in with plain circles, the origin of the cusp, or that kind of decoration which every pointed arch afterwards received. This style, which succeeded the Lancet, is found throughout England, and many of the parish churches exhibit fine examples of it. Stone Church, in Kent, of which the writer has published an account, may be cited as one of the best; its ornament shows the skill and taste that prevailed among the freemasons at that period. Salisbury, Wells, and York Cathedrals abound with rich foliage and sculptures of the highest merit executed at the same time, and it is wonderful to observe to what a state of perfection the artists of this country had arrived. The effects of the chisel of the Pisan school were displayed upon marble, but our sculptors worked upon an inferior material; yet the draperies of their figures, as seen in the front at Wells, and elsewhere, are quite equal to those wrought by the pupils of Italian masters at the same time. The circle and its intersections at this period were alone employed for the plans of piers, sections of mouldings, and the filling in of windows and doorways: from them we trace the origin of the style which immediately succeeded.

The cathedrals of Cologne, Amiens, Beauvais, the Sainte Chapelle at Paris, and numerous other examples on the continent, exhibit the same proportions and style with that of Westminster; the lofty pointed arches, which rest upon the main cluster, are decorated with numerous small mouldings; the triforium, in some instances glazed, have their pointed arches filled in with trefoils, cinquefoils, or sexfoils, and the clerestory, carried up to the very apex of the vaulting, is similarly adorned. Westminster Abbey is one of the finest examples of building executed in the thirteenth century.

Tracery and Geometric Forms.—To comprehend thoroughly the principles which directed the freemasons of the middle ages in the execution of all their works would require far greater illustration than can be bestowed upon the subject in the present volume: it must be sufficient if we point out a few which influenced the design of some of their best examples, and show that it is a perfectly erroneous opinion to suppose they were executed without a thorough knowledge of certain rules, originating with themselves, and perfected by a constant study of what was not only useful, but productive of the best effect. Those who inquire into this subject must collect the data upon which an opinion can be formed, for it is scarcely possible, without positive measurement, to arrive at any conclusion upon the matter: the admirer of the Greek, or the commentator upon Vitruvius, alone can scarcely hope to be successful: it is true that in one of the early printed Italian editions of the valuable author quoted, there are several diagrams which seem to point to the subject, but the student will find only the nucleus around which the lovers of geometry in the middle ages

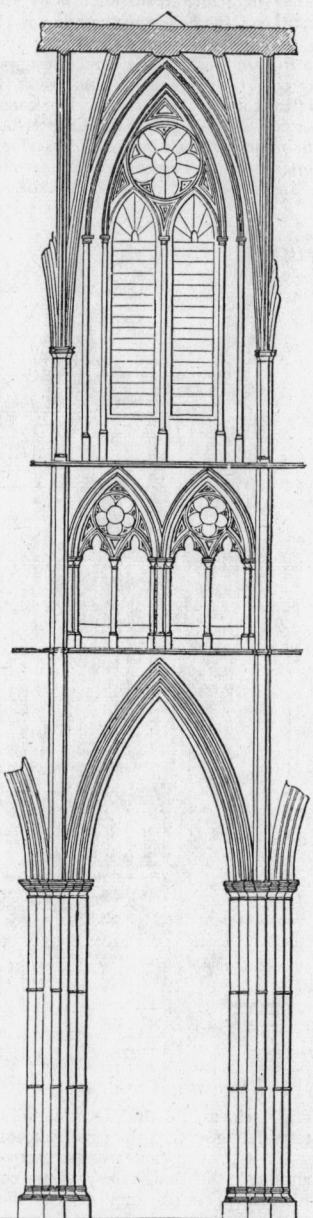

Fig. 1278.   WESTMINSTER ABBEY.

arranged their varying and beautiful forms; this is the equilateral triangle, and by inclosing the plan, section, or elevation of a building within it, the several proportions can be accurately measured, and if sub-divided into a number, either of the triangles would show the proportion it bore to the whole area.

In one of the tracery heads of the windows in the cloister at Westminster, the date of which is about 1348, we have two figures that resemble the plans given to clustered pillars, indicating at once that the same principles were applied to the setting out of both windows and points of support. When the circumference of a circle is divided into twelve equal parts, the points which divide them form the termination of four equilateral triangles, and we have at their intersections, not only the centres of the circles that constitute the filling in, but also the several mitres and other portions of the figure.

Fig. 1279.   CLOISTERS AT WESTMINSTER ABBEY.

These rules were evidently applied to windows, and to tracery of every description, executed at the end of the thirteenth and commencement of the fourteenth centuries; also to the plans of the main cluster of pillars in many cathedrals and churches. For nearly a century, circles and their intersections formed the ornamental portions of every kind of panel and window head; they were afterwards blended into other figures, and apparently set out upon different principles; but the hexagon and equilateral triangles were necessary to produce the flowing lines which succeeded. The change which took place in design no doubt arose from the facility which had been attained by the practice of this method, and if it were possible to exhibit each variety in England alone, there would be ample evidence of the inventive power of the freemasons, and the progressive improvement in their school for depicting form. The quatrefoil in fig. 1279. is met with in the panels of several altar tombs, in the spandrills of the arches of doorways, and it is worthy of observation that all the mitres, where the figures change their form, are perfect for each: had these considerations been neglected, we should not have had the graceful flowing lines found in these designs: no other triangles crossing are so universally applicable, or require less skill in their adoption. The student of the present day might occupy a life in the collection of these subjects, and they are most excellent models for the application of the rules of theoretical geometry to practice.

Fig. 1280.   CLOISTERS AT WESTMINSTER ABBEY.

Windows of three Days or Divisions are met with, having heads of singular beauty, inclosed within an equilateral triangle, and so numerous are the designs, that it is rare to meet with two exactly similar. In

Fig. 1281.

the more simple of three days or lower divisions, the head is occupied by three circles, each of which contains a trefoil constructed upon the crossing of either three or four equilateral triangles.

A very extraordinary design, composed of intersecting circles, is to be seen at the east end of the chancel of the church at Sutton, at Hone, in Kent; although much dilapidated, it still preserves many of its original flowing lines, all struck from the same radius, through points previously determined by crossing the primitive circle by four equilateral triangles.

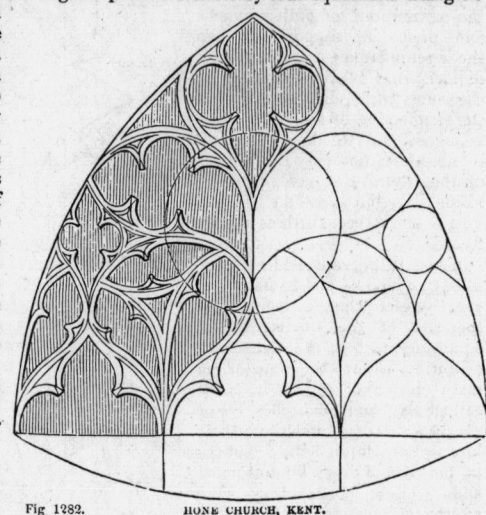

At half the height of the head of the window a horizontal line may be supposed to be drawn from one side to the other, on which are three circles: the two outer touching, are crossed by the third, struck from the point of their junction; with the same radius several spherical triangles are struck from the points of intersections, producing the lines, which unite and divide the window head into several compartments, differing in pattern and dimension. After the circles were struck, the lines that did not play into each other were left out, and those only retained which flowed on gracefully; by these nice considerations and just application of principles, the masons were certain of producing a perfect effect, without rigidly adhering to any particular form.

Fig 1282.   HONE CHURCH, KENT.

Windows of four Days or Divisions. — Among the heads of a more simple character are those which contain one large circle, subdivided by three equilateral triangles, each

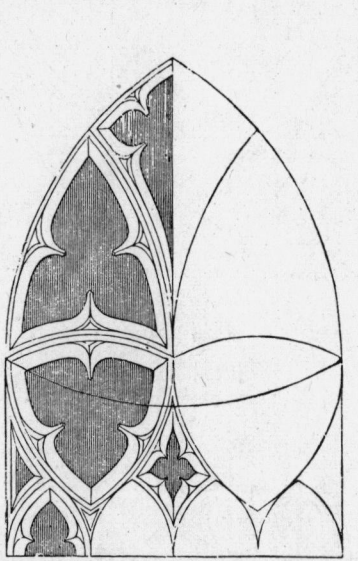

Fig. 1283.

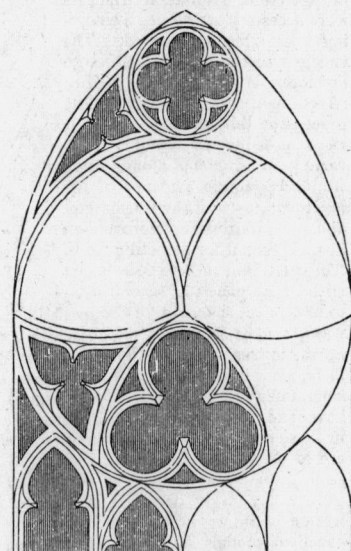

Fig. 1284.

inclosing a trefoil. Others contain, in addition to the one great equilateral triangle, two smaller, constructed upon the points of its base, and dropping into the space comprised between the heads of the divisions below.

Windows of Six Divisions are far more complicated, and, though exhibiting greater skill in geometry, are set out precisely upon the same principle. The two equilateral triangles inclosed within the great circle mark out the prominent features of the design, and their terminations are the centres of as many spherical triangles, which, by their crossing, constitute the elaborate filling in.

In some examples, above the two main lower divisions is a circle divided by several others, the twelve which are indicated in the figure serving to proportion the tracery of this compartment.

At the latter end of the fourteenth century, these designs were so multiplied that almost every cathedral and church had its peculiar windows: in Amiens cathedral, the chapels constructed at this same time receive their light from windows, the heads of which are filled in with tracery exceedingly varied, but the general principles of setting out the work are preserved; the circle and the equilateral triangle were subdivided almost to infinity, and at no period of the arts do the inventive faculties appear so fertile as in that we are now considering. The great west window of York Cathedral is the finest example of the improvement made in this mode of decoration; the geometric forms are there so concealed by the blending of the several curves, as to produce continued flowing lines, which is partly shown in fig. 1282. : they are, however, all set out in the same manner, and the centres upon which they are struck are established by the crossing of equilateral triangles.

During the episcopacy of John Grandisson, from the year 1327 to 1369, Exeter Cathedral was undergoing an entire change in its architecture.

Fig. 1285.

Fig. 1286.

To this bishop we are indebted for the great west window, of nine days, and several smaller of four and five, in which are introduced tracery showing a great variety of design : some are composed of equilateral triangles, each containing a trefoil, some of circles with six turns, others have four and three ; but the heads of all, varied as they are, belong to the same school as fig. 1285.

The great east window at Bristol Cathedral is another fine example of nine days,

executed about the middle of the 14th century; the centre of the head of the window, or rather the nucleus to the tracery, is an octagon, six sides of which are retained, the other two being suppressed, to allow of a better combination with the three centre divisions of the lower part.

The equilateral triangle also defined the form and magnitude of the several mullions, as shown by *fig.* 1287., constructed upon measurement of the windows of the clerestory of the nave at Winchester: a line drawn from the apex of one mullion to the other is the base of the triangle, and the space inclosed by the two is divided into ten other equilateral triangles, two of which agree in dimensions and form with each mullion. Of the twelve equilateral triangles embracing two half mullions, ten are given to the day or space to admit the light, and two, or one-sixth of the whole, is comprised by the mullion; such appears to have been the manner of proportioning the parts of windows in the middle ages.

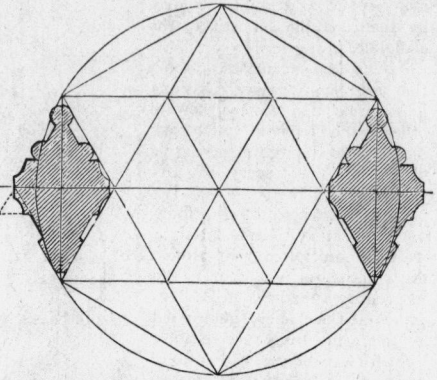

Fig. 1287.   See also fig. 1303.   WINCHESTER.

Rose Windows in the West Transept of the Church of St. Ouen at Rouen is 29 feet 6 inches in diameter, and composed of seven equal circles, one of which occupies the centre: each of those, which surround it, are again subdivided by others; two only of the outer six are preserved in the figure, and form the quatrefoils, whilst the intersections of the others serve as centres to the rest of the design.

Fig. 1288.   ST. OUEN AT ROUEN.

Rose Window of the South Transept of the Cathedral at Rouen is 23 feet in diameter, measured to the centre of the large bead, which comprises the figure. A portion only of

this beautiful example is given, for the purpose of exhibiting the principle upon which it is set out : it will be evident that the nucleus of the design is composed of two equilateral triangles, and the sides of each continued, constitute the alternate divisions.

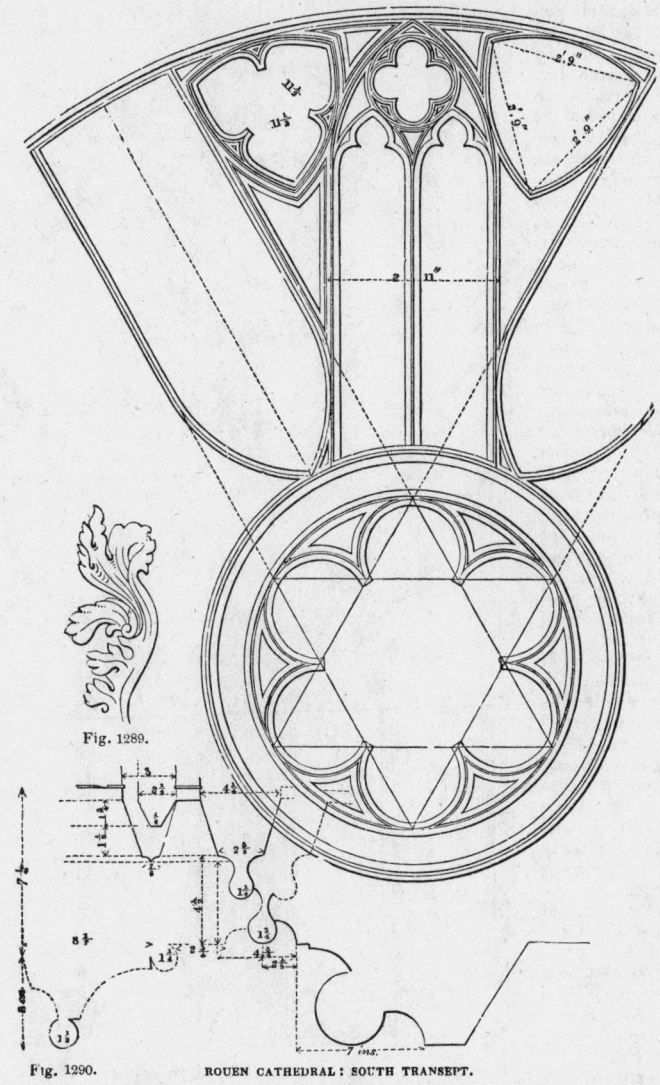

Fig. 1289.

Fig. 1290.   ROUEN CATHEDRAL : SOUTH TRANSEPT.

The internal hexagon has its parallel sides prolonged, to mark the position of the four divisions that have their pointed heads attached to the small circle, which forms the eye of the pattern ; and the length of these prolonged lines is limited to the extent of the sides of an equilateral triangle, which is again divided regularly, the triangular spaces between being filled in with trefoils. The small mullions are in width 2½ inches, the next size 3 inches, and those which mark out the figure and have a bead for their termination are 4½ inches : another bead and bold projecting label, or rim, circumscribe the whole rose window, the hollow around which is enriched with a curved leaf. On each side of the internal hexagon an equilateral triangle is constructed, around which a circle is struck, uniting elegantly with the next, and forming the six turns which characterise the filling in of

circles at this period; these were the principal decorations after the Lancet style was abandoned, and were continued until succeeded by more flowing and varied designs.

Rose Window of the South Transept at Beauvais, 34 feet 4 inches in diameter, is composed of six large circles and their intersections.

To set out this window the great circle expressed by the outer bead is divided into twelve parts, each being equal to half the radius; twelve equilateral triangles are then inscribed, the points of which touch each of the divisions, and where they cross nearest to the outer circle, the twelve pointed arches that surround the figure are struck; the other points of intersection of the triangles are centres, from which the other curves are drawn. It must at once be evident, that in a circle so divided, or by any other equal number of equilateral triangles, the portions contained between the smaller angles must be equal to each other; the six circles around the centre have their curves blended into the outer, and if it be required to fix centres for each of these flowing lines, they can only be obtained by covering the entire rose window with lines in the manner already described. The radius being equal to the side of a hexagon, and that figure being composed of two equilateral triangles, was probably the chief reason of its first preference over all others; it certainly affords the most extraordinary powers of combination,

Fig. 1291.   BEAUVAIS CATHEDRAL: SOUTH TRANSEPT.

and there is scarcely a moulding or form in the architecture of this period but is set out from it. The mullions that bound the divisions are all portions of this figure, as are the mouldings, which sweep round the arches of the buildings themselves. Nothing can surpass the brilliant effect of these marigold windows when glazed with rich colours, and exposed to either a rising or setting sun; in the example now described, this effect is still further heightened by making nearly the whole end of the southern transept a continuation of the same design, the glass descending almost to the tops of the doors which afford access to the cathedral. The construction of such works must excite our highest admiration, for it appears scarcely possible to excel the perfect manner in which the parts are put together and worked off, the execution being in every particular worthy the design.

The Rose Window in the South Transept at Amiens, 29 feet 6 inches in diameter, is set out upon two squares, which cross each other diagonally.

Fig. 1292.   AMIENS CATHEDRAL : SOUTH TRANSEPT.

Sixteen divisions are employed in this figure, and by crossing as many squares, we arrive at the method by which it is set out ; each side of the square is equal to the radius by which the master line on the outer bead or circle is struck : where the squares cross each other are the divisions of the pattern, and their several points are the centres upon which the pointed arches are struck, which surround the outer portion of the rose.

Where the lines of the squares cross, in the interior of the figure, the smaller divisions are established, and their points of intersection serve for centres to strike the lesser curves ; to show this clearly the whole must be set out, and drawn to a large scale.

The architecture of France underwent a material change after the thirteenth century ; the heads of the windows were no longer filled with tracery composed of six foils, generally three in each window, but branched out into a more running pattern, as practised in several parts of England. The fourteenth century not only exhibits windows of more difficult design, but an apparent absence of the principles by which the several parts were proportioned to each other. Before the Perpendicular style appeared, great progress had been made in the groining of the spacious vaults of the naves, as well as those of the side aisles. After the fan tracery was substituted in England, the windows had straight mullions ascending till they intersected the arch ; and we have no further display of the varied figures that everywhere prevailed before : geometry was now exercised upon the intricacies which their surprising vaults exhibited. It is somewhat singular that we never find the beauties of a previous era retained, and blended with that which succeeded.

For the 300 years during which the Pointed style continued to flourish, each half century gave to it a new character ; hence we have seldom any difficulty in establishing its date : all these changes resulted from an improved knowledge in the art of construction. The lodges of freemasons were gradually approaching the principles which directed the efforts of the architects of the Byzantine school, and which were found too refined and delicate to be practised out of Italy after the eleventh century.

The Rose Window in the Northern Transept of the Church of St. Ouen at Rouen, 28 feet 6 inches in diameter, is an example of the pentagonal setting out.

Fig. 1295.   ST. OUEN AT ROUEN.

When the sides of a pentagon are prolonged, they unite and form five isosceles triangles, each having for its base a side of the original pentagon. The equilateral triangle, the square, and the pentagon may have been adopted by different confraternities of freemasons; the first can be formed into hexagons, duodecagons and their multiples; the squares, by crossing diagonally, into octagons; they may be also tripled and quadrupled: the mitre of the equilateral triangle is in the direction of its centre of gravity, as is that of the square and the isosceles triangles; consequently to unite the mouldings around either, the plummet would indicate the direction of the line, when dropped from the angles and suffered to cross, the point of intersection being the centre of gravity common to the several lines.

In the chapel of St. Cecile is the monument of Alexander Berneval, the master mason of the works at St. Ouen, at the time the rose window was executed by his pupil, whom it is reported he murdered from jealousy: such an application of triangles was then called the *pentalpha.*

The foundations of this church were laid by Marcdargent, about 1318, by whom it was built as far as the transept; but probably the rose window of the northern transept was not inserted till many years after, for the memorial of Berneval bears the date of 1440: this monumental stone is 8 feet 6 inches in length, and 4 feet in width, and in it is represented the architect and his pupil, each employed tracing with his compasses his respective design; these beautiful brasses with their rich tabernacle work were in the highest state of perfection when the writer was last at Rouen, and around the master figure was inscribed in German letters : —

Cy gist Maistre Alexandre de Berneval, Maistre des oeuvres de Maconnerie du Roy, notre Sire, du Baillage de Rouen, et de ceste Eglise, qui trespassa, l'an de grace mil. ccccrl. le v jour de Januier.

Priés Dieu pour l'ame de luy.

The date of the pupil's death is not commemorated, which has led some to imagine the tale of his murder untrue, and that he erected the monument to his master with the intention of being buried by his side.

The North Rose Window at Amiens, 37 feet 8 inches in diameter, is a magnificent example of the application of the pentagon, with 5 isosceles triangles around it.

This window, probably executed in the fourteenth century, has a great resemblance to the last described; the fan tracery, of which we have early specimens in the cloisters at Gloucester, required the same knowledge of geometry to perfect their design. In 1482 Euclid was first printed at Venice from the Greek text; but geometry had been studied in England from the time that Adhelard, in 1130, had introduced a translation of that author from the Arabic versions which he met with during his travels in Spain. In 1256 Campanus of Navarre translated Euclid, who seems to have been commented upon by several eminent writers, and no doubt it was the text-book of the freemasons, who diligently applied the problems it contained to every purpose of their art. In 1486 the Editio Princeps of Vitruvius appeared, and the commentaries of Cæsare Cæsariano followed in 1521; the latter author published three plates of the Cathedral at Milan, covered with equilateral triangles, which have not been described so as to be useful or understood.

Fig. 1294.   AMIENS: ROSE WINDOW.

The compartments which have the flat sides of the original pentagon for their base, and parallel sides throughout till they terminate in the pointed arch, have their mullions proportioned to their opening, the larger being double the size of the smaller, whilst the latter are equal to half the open space between them: the mullions in these examples, which divide two spaces, 6 inches in width, are usually 3 inches in thickness, and the others are in the same proportion. The next sized mullion is 4¼ inches, with a bead of 1¼ inch diameter, which runs round the whole pattern of the figure, the centre of which may be called the master line, by which all the rest are set out; the several mullions are all twice as much in depth as in width.

Baptistery of Pisa. — The internal diameter of this circular building is 100 feet, and the thickness of its outer walls and columns 10 feet 6 inches; its external diameter is 121 feet, the area of which is 11,499 superficial feet, that of the interior being 7854; if we deduct from it what is occupied by the four piers and eight columns, or 188 feet, we have 7666 feet for the void, exactly two-thirds of the entire area. To find these proportions in an edifice commenced about the middle of the twelfth century in Italy, is a curious corroboration of the opinions already advanced, the same rules as those described for the Chapter House at Wells being apparently followed: the conical brick dome was the work of an after period, and may have been the prototype for that of St. Paul's at London; the pointed architecture belonging to the exterior of this edifice, of the same character as that which adorns the crosses of Queen Eleanor in England, was added in the fourteenth century.

The section shows how the equilateral triangle governs the proportions of this celebrated building; the extreme diameter is the base, and its apex the level on which the

more recent conical and hemispherical domes are placed: the intersection of the two
great triangles fixes the diameter to be given to the internal void, around which the side
aisle, its walls and pillars should be formed. The circle which has its diameter comprised between the apex of the two equilaterals determines the clear width between the

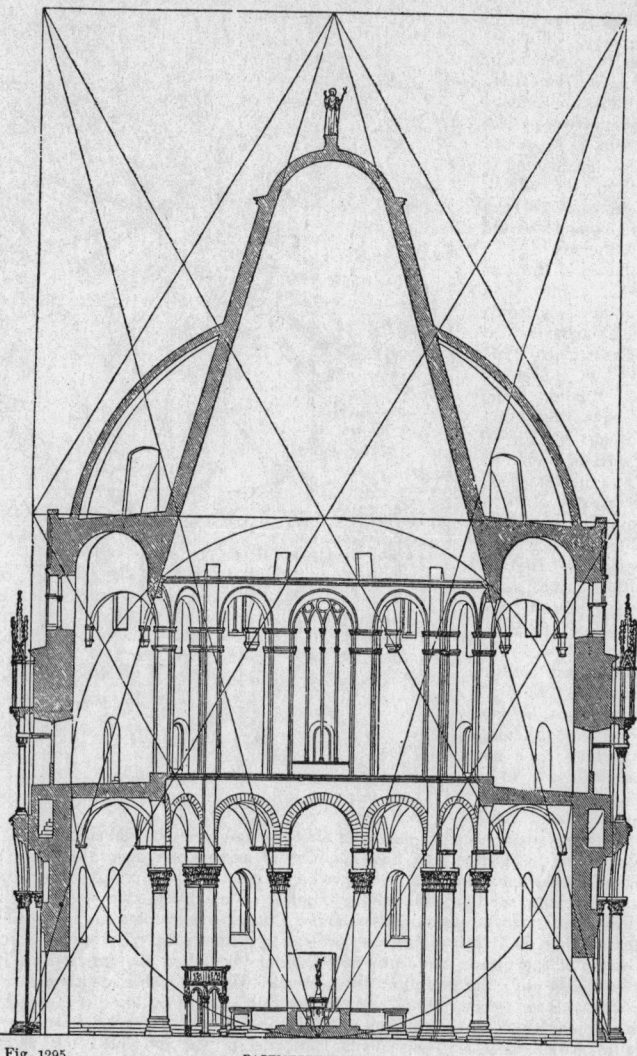

Fig. 1295. BAPTISTERY OF PISA.

outer walls. That the architects of those days delighted in the forms produced by the
several intersections of the circle in combination with the equilateral triangle, we are
assured by viewing the several designs they have left us in mosaic upon the walls of the
Duomo, and at the cathedrals of Florence, Sienna, and elsewhere.

Roslyn Chapel, Scotland, commenced about the year 1446, has its buttresses well
suited to give aid to the walls, and to enable them to resist the thrust of its nearly semicircular vault, which they receive below the springing. The extreme width from face
to face of the buttresses is 48 feet 4 inches; the span of the nave is 15 feet 8 inches,
being 5 inches less than the proportion of a third; the two side aisles together

are 15 feet, or within a few inches of the width of the nave; consequently the walls and piers in this beautiful example are 17 feet 8 inches, or 15 inches more in extent than they would have been if the proportion of one-third had been adopted. The height from the pavement to the under side of vault is 41 feet 10 inches.

After the examples described, we cannot doubt of the great proficiency that had been made in the application of the rules of geometry to architecture; every feature, whether the simple moulding or the most elaborate tracery, was set out either upon the equilateral triangle, square, or pentagon, and these regular figures seem to have been chosen on account of the facility by which they are subdivided. From the introduction of the style each fifty years that succeeded brought with them new and improved principles, and at the very commencement of the fourteenth century, we see the clustered pillar and

Fig. 1296.　　　ROSLYN CHAPEL.　　　Fig. 1297.

Fig. 1298.　　　SECTION OF ROSLYN CHAPEL.

its many moulded arches yielding to a style that combined greater simplicity with a more thorough knowledge of construction, which will be evident upon an examination of St. Stephen's Chapel, Westminster, (now destroyed,) begun in 1348, the nave of Canterbury and Winchester Cathedrals, and several others. In these examples we have elegantly formed arches resting on well-proportioned piers, the mouldings of which so combine that they form a perfect figure, and show that the points of support were designed to carry all that is placed above them; the same contour of moulding that surrounds the pier performs its useful part in the upper portions of the building, constituting one entire whole. This style, simple as well as elegant, was executed by masons fully qualified to advance it to the greatest perfection, and deserves both our study and admiration.

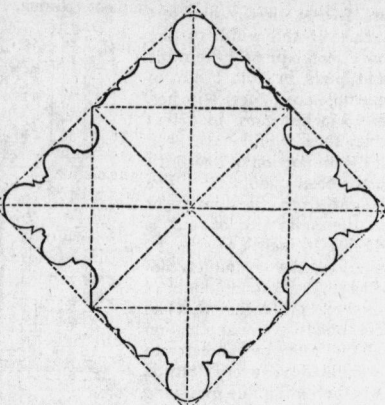

Fig. 1299.   CANTERBURY CATHEDRAL.

Canterbury Cathedral exhibits every variety of style found in mediæval architecture; its history has been published by Mr. Britton: to that work, to which the writer contributed some measurements in 1820, he must refer for a detailed and elaborate account of the several changes made in the decoration of the edifice. It is only to the pillars of the nave we are desirous of drawing the attention, and that merely to show their simple form, and the manner of setting them out: four squares are so placed that their diagonals and sides are united in the centre, thus constituting a form capable of the greatest resistance at the four points of the entire pier, where the several thrusts and pressures are received: the O G mouldings of the piers run round the arches, whilst the columnar mouldings towards the aisle and nave support the ribs of their respective vaults. Greater simplicity can hardly be obtained, and every line and indentation of the plan has its use and appropriation: there is no profusion, or member for the sole purpose of decoration; in this arrangement we have the commencement of good taste, and the indication of a more harmonious and perfect style.

Fig. 1300.   CANTERBURY CATHEDRAL.

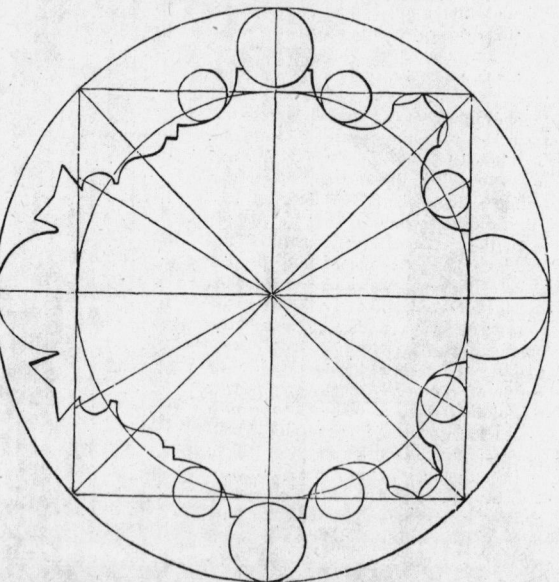

Fig. 1301.   ST. OUEN AT ROUEN.

In the Church at St. Ouen at Rouen, we have a very different arrangement, and by no means so solid a form.

Winchester Cathedral. — One division of the nave has been selected to show the peculiar style practised at the latter end of the fourteenth century, and also the skill exhibited in changing the form of a Saxon edifice, and giving it its present character.   The plan, fig. 1303. is that of the pillar, as well as of the mouldings and walls of the triforium and clerestory above.   When William of Wykeham effected the changes in the nave of this cathedral, he preserved all above the arches of the triforium, cutting away only the masonry of each division below that level which intervened between the main pillars; he then caused the whole to be cased with an ashlar, so that the original Saxon masonry and proportions of the mass remain within the casing.   The dotted semicircular arch is the same as that in fig. 1266., and in the roofs above the groining the Saxon walls are traceable, — another proof that when any alteration was made in a building by our mediæval masons, they did not think it necessary entirely to demolish it.   We have in this example the decorative character which belongs to the architecture of the latter end of the fourteenth century, though somewhat heavy in its proportions, which arises from the mass constituting the original fabric being preserved, or having undergone so little change.   The thickness of these pillars from north to south is 10 feet 8 inches, and from east to west 10 feet, whilst the width of the opening from east to west is only 14 feet.

If we examine the area of one severy of the nave, as left by Wykeham, and calculate the points of support, we shall see that the proportions are not those found in the nave at Canterbury, or in other cotemporary buildings; comprising the space between the buttresses, the entire area of the parallelogram contained between lines drawn through the middle of the piers from north to south is 2228 feet; while the points of support within that area are 557 feet, or one-quarter of the whole.

On the section, shown at fig. 1304., the buttresses on the north side project 6 feet; the north wall is 5 feet 6 inches in thickness, the half piers attached project internally 2 feet 1 inch; the north aisle is in width 13 feet 1 inch, the pier 10 feet 8 inches; the clear width of the nave 32 feet 5 inches; the pier 10 feet 8 inches; the south aisle 13 feet 1 inch, the half-pier which projects from the south wall 2 feet 1 inch, and the thickness of the south wall 7 feet 2 inches; there are no buttresses, as the cloister, now removed, served their purpose.   The width from east to west, measured from the centres of the piers, being 22 feet 1 inch, and the width of

Fig. 1302.   NAVE OF WINCHESTER CATHEDRAL.

buttresses outside 3 feet 2 inches.
The cathedral or duomo at Pisa
presents a very different result;
the total width of the nave is
113 feet 6 inches, and the width
of a severy 17 feet 1 inch, the
area of which is nearly 1930 feet,
the points of support being only a
twelfth of that quantity on the
plan, and one-sixth as regarded
upon the section. Hence we see
the necessity of ascertaining the
proportions of mass and void in a
building, before we can accurately
judge of its merits as a style, each
having its peculiar quantity, which
marks its character.

The section or rather plan of
the walls, on the level with the
gallery of the triforium, shows
the method adopted to proportion
the openings to the mass. The
thickness of the clerestory walls is
included within the eight equilateral triangles, and where their
sides cross, the position of their
mullions is established. In fig.
1287. the circle which comprises
the two that divide the window
into three days shows their proportion and their size, which
in this example is one-third
of the opening: in a window
of three days we have six triangles
for space, and three for mullions:
the splays at the sides of these
windows, uniting them with
the faces of the wall, are cut
parallel with the sides of the
several triangles. The main pier
is set out by uniting the bases of
two equilateral triangles with
perpendicular lines, or forming
the whole into the figure of a
hexagon. By a comparison of
this plan with that of fig. 1267.,
the additions made by William of
Wykeham to the original Saxon
pillar will be readily perceived.

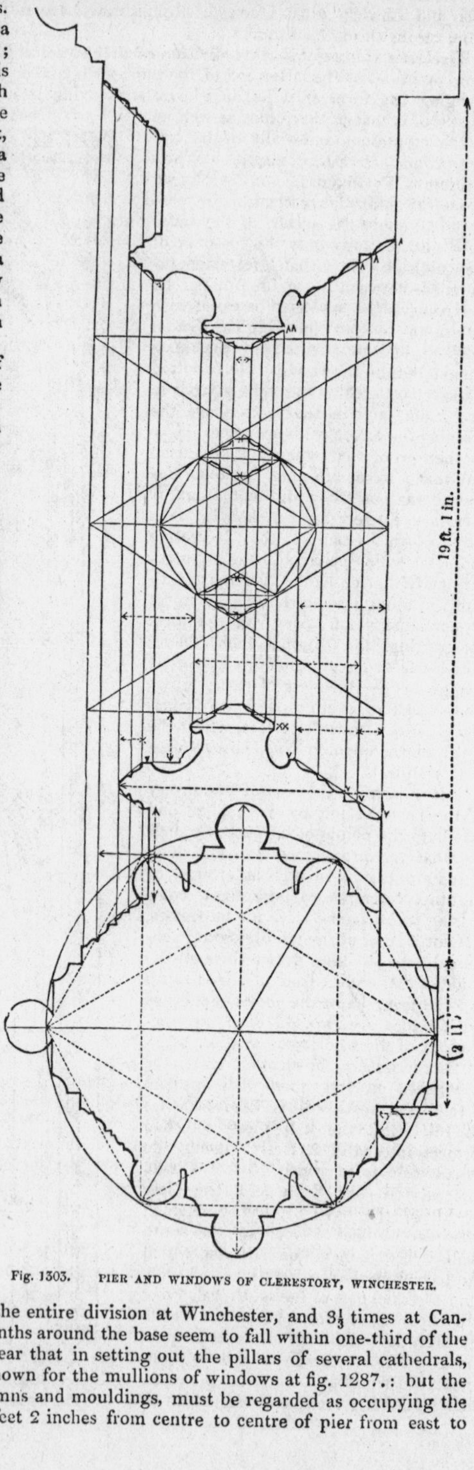

The width of one of the divisions of the nave at Winchester,
measured from the centres of the
piers from west to east, is 22 feet
1 inch, and the same dimension
taken in the nave at Canterbury
is 20 feet only. In the former
example the opening between the
piers is 12 feet 1 inch, and in the
latter 14 feet; there is consequently no comparison, with regard to lightness, in these two
works of the same period; the

Fig. 1303.　　PIER AND WINDOWS OF CLERESTORY, WINCHESTER.

pier being comprised 2⅔ times in the entire division at Winchester, and 3⅓ times at Canterbury, or on the pavement the plinths around the base seem to fall within one-third of the
entire width. It would almost appear that in setting out the pillars of several cathedrals,
the same system was practised as shown for the mullions of windows at fig. 1287.: but the
plinths, and not the cluster of columns and mouldings, must be regarded as occupying the
third. Bath Abbey church is 20 feet 2 inches from centre to centre of pier from east to

west, and the clear width between the plinths about two-thirds of that dimension, and this is the case with many examples.

The Section through the Nave of Winchester Cathedral is highly deserving of our attention: the clear width of the side aisles is 13 feet 1 inch, and that of the nave 32 feet 5 inches; the clear width of the building between the outer walls is 80 feet, the thickness of the walls 16 feet 10 inches, the projection of the buttress 6 feet, and the thickness of the piers 10 feet 8 inches, making for the entire width from north to south 102 feet 8 inches.

The width between the walls forms the base of an equilateral triangle, the apex of which determines the height of the vaulting of the nave; a semicircle struck upon this base, with a radius of 52 feet, determines the intrados of the arches of the flying buttresses on each side, which are admirably placed to resist the thrust opposed to them.

On this section we have endeavoured to apply the principles of *Cesare Cesariano*, before referred to, to the measurement of mass and void by a method far more simple than that usually adopted.

By covering the design with equilateral triangles we see the number occupied by the solids, and can draw a comparison with those that cover the voids: to prevent confusion in the diagram a portion only of three of the triangles has been subdivided, to show with what facility the quantities of the entire figure might be measured, if the several large equilaterals were subdivided throughout in a similar manner.   The band which extends

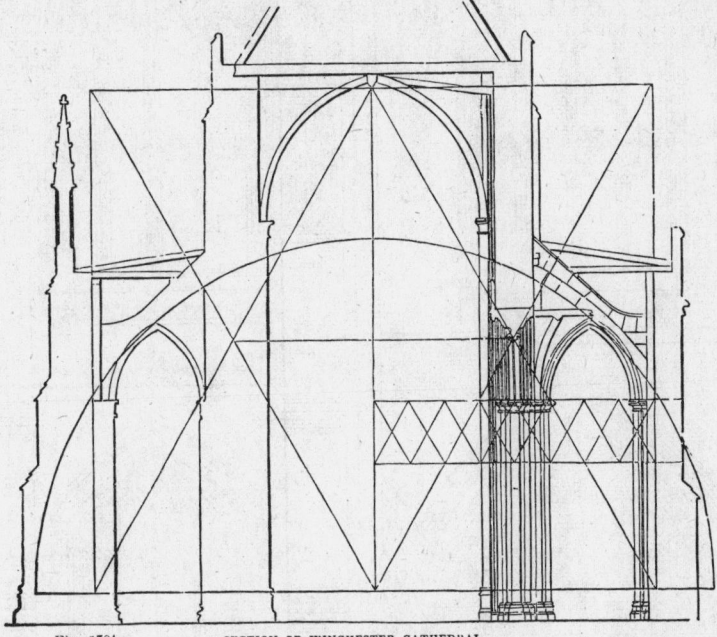

Fig. 1304.   SECTION OF WINCHESTER CATHEDRAL.

from the face of the outer buttress to the centre of the section contains 36 small equilateral triangles, six of which cover the pier; consequently it occupies on the section one-sixth of that quantity; no further calculation is requisite to find the proportion it bears to the whole: in like manner the other parts of the section may be compared.   Such was the use of equilateral triangles in the middle ages for ascertaining quantity.

The two equilateral triangles which occupy the nave and a portion of the piers are comprised within the figure called a Vesica Piscis; if the horizontal line drawn at half the height, uniting the base of the upper and lower triangles, be taken as a radius, and its extremities as centres, it will be evident that parts of circles may be struck, comprising the two triangles within them.   Euclid has shown that a perpendicular may be raised or let fall from a given line by a similar method, the space between the segments being called afterwards a nimbus; and there can be no doubt that from time immemorial all builders have used it: the bee adopts for its honied cell a figure composed of six equilateral triangles, and this is proved to be the most economical method of construction; the sides of each hexagon are all common to two cells, and no space is lost by their junction.   The nearer the boundary line of a figure approaches the circle, the more it will contain in proportion to it,

but circles could not be placed above and under each other, or side by side, without interstices occurring, and the equilateral triangle, or a figure compounded of it, is the only form that will admit of it being so arranged.

The interior and exterior division of the choir at Winchester exhibits two styles; the latter is a fine example of the decorated elegance to which architecture had arrived at the commencement of the sixteenth century.

Fig. 1305.   WINCHESTER CATHEDRAL: CHOIR.   Fig. 1306.

King's Colleye Chapel, Cambridge, has no side aisles, but in lieu of them are small chapels between the buttresses, which are not interrupted in their depth, their whole strength being requisite to maintain in equilibrio the highly wrought stone vault; this they have hitherto perfectly done, to the admiration of all who have studied its principles of construction. The chapel is divided in its length into twelve equal divisions or severies, each of which is formed of four quadrants of a concave parabolic conoid standing on their apex, and is bounded by a main rib or arch of masonry which has its abutments secured by the weighty buttresses added to the outer walls. The width of each severy from centre to centre is 24 feet, the thickness of the buttresses being 3 feet 7 inches, and the length of the chapel between them 20 feet 6 inches; their depth is 13 feet 6 inches in the clear.

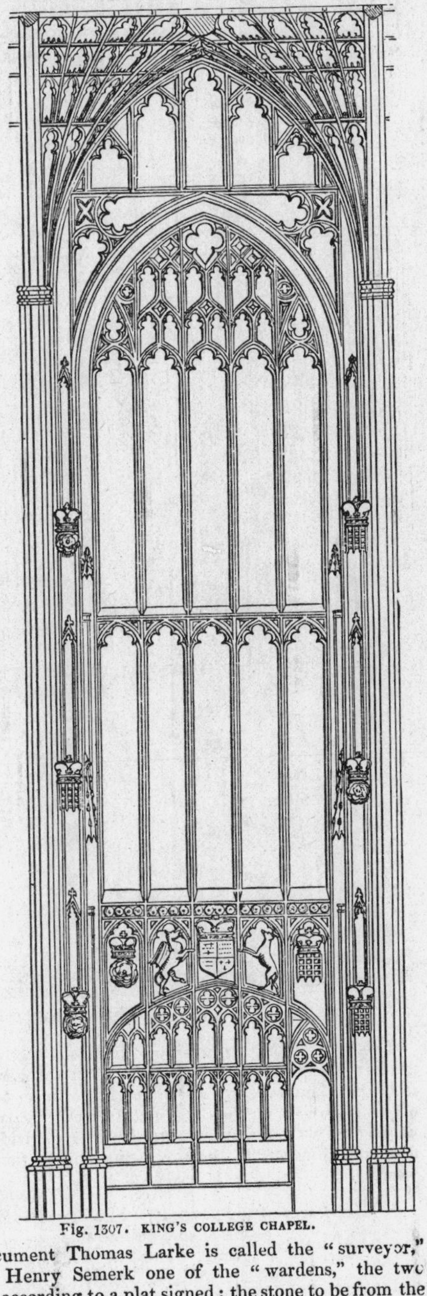

The transverse section shows more particularly the proportion of mass and void, which are here equal: the total extent or width from the face of one buttress to that of the other is 84 feet, and the clear width 42 feet; the height from the pavement to the top of the stone vault is 80 feet 1 inch, though this varies from the pavement being out of the level; the thickness of the walls at top is 5 feet 7½ inches; in it is a gallery 2 feet 1½ inch wide, and 7 feet high, communicating entirely around the building.

The height of the cluster column, whose capital receives the points of the inverted cones, is 59 feet 3 inches, so that the arch, which is struck from four centres, does not rise more than 18 feet 6 inches, and the intersections take place at one quarter of the span when the height is 15 feet 6 inches: this arch or stone rib is 2 feet in depth and 18 inches in breadth, formed of twelve voussoirs on each side, the joints radiating to the centres respectively; it abuts at its extremities against the ponderous buttresses, and remains steadfast and immovable, dividing, as before stated, the vault into several severies.

The plan of the main piers shows that there has been no after-thought grafted upon the original design, which, in all probability, was commenced soon after the year 1446, as we find that a stone quarry at Haselwode, and another at Huddlestone, in Yorkshire, were granted, for the works to be carried on here. The stone roof does not appear to have been commenced till about 1512, the indenture concerning it bearing date the fourth year of King Henry VIII.; in this document Thomas Larke is called the "surveyor," John Wastell the "master mason," and Henry Semerk one of the "wardens," the two latter agreeing to set up a sufficient vawte, according to a plat signed; the stone to be from the Weldon quarries: the contracting parties were also to provide "lyme, scaffoldyng, cinctores, moles, ordinaunces," and "every other thyng required for the same vawting: the timbers

Fig. 1307. KING'S COLLEGE CHAPEL.

of two severies of the "great scaffolding" were given them for the removal of the whole; and they were to have the uses of all "gynnes, whels, cables, hobynatts, saws, &c.;" they were to pay for the stone, and to have 100*l.* for each severy, or 1200*l.* for the whole, money being advanced for wages as the works proceeded: the "chare roff," as the vault is called was to be sufficiently buttressed, and the whole performed in a perfect manner.

Fig. 1308. SECTION OF KING'S COLLEGE CHAPEL.

The extreme width, measured from the face of one buttress to that of the other, is 84 feet, and from north to south, from the centre of one pier to that of the other, 24 feet; thus the area comprised in a severy, or space between two lines drawn through the centres of the buttresses on the plan, is 2016 feet, exactly double the area of one of the severies of St. George's Chapel, Windsor: the extreme width is the same, but the difference arises from the divisions in the one being double that of the other, as measured from east to west.

					Feet.
The area of the nave, 42 × 24 -	-	-	-	-	1008
of the chapel on one side	-	-	-	-	336
ditto on the other	-	-	-	-	336
of the walls on one side	-	-	-	-	168
ditto on the other	-	-	-	-	168

Hence we have for the areas of the space or void on the plan 1680 feet, and for the walls and pier 336 feet, or one-sixth of the whole 2016 feet, similar proportions to those which we

shall afterwards find in St. George's
Chapel, Windsor. In King's College
the nave comprises half the entire
area of a severy, and the remaining
half is divided into three, one of
which is given to each of the chapels,
and the other divided between the
points of support: in this beautiful
building, with its majestically contrived roof of stone, the lightest
construction is adopted. The catenarian curve exhibits the direction of
the thrust of the vault, which falls
within the base.

The stone roof we are now examining differs somewhat from that
of Henry VII.'s chapel at Westminster; the area of the points of
support is only one-half of those in
the latter elegant example; in no
instance have we so much effect produced by the mason's art, with so
small a quantity of material: it is
evident that the gradual changes
made in the architecture of the mediæval period led at last to the
greatest perfection, beyond which
it seems impossible for us to advance.

In selecting a style of any one
period, it may be fairly asked whether
the principles found in the latter, or
the economy adopted in the constructions of the 15th century, might
not be applied to it, and the same
effect produced,—the section of the
chapter-house at Wells, for instance,
lightened of half its material: undoubtedly it might, for the lofty
pointed arch, not having the thrust
which the latter, struck from four
centres, had, would exert less thrust,
and be in favour of such a change.

But at the present day, when copies
are rigidly made of the finest examples of each style, it would seem a
bold innovation to suggest such an
adoption; still it might be introduced,
and probably would have been, had
the freemasons continued an operative
fraternity, and been required to build
in the Lancet or other style, which
superseded it. The same decorations and form of arch may be used

Fig. 1309. VAULTING OF KING'S COLLEGE CHAPEL.

in the later styles as in the earlier, as far as construction is concerned, and we have evidence of sufficient strength in the example before us; the principles are the same in each,
though they may differ in form ; there would be no more difficulty in transforming one
style to that of another, than was experienced by William of Wykeham, when he changed
the Saxon nave of Winchester to the Perpendicular.

On the section shown at *fig.* 1308. a line is drawn exhibiting the catenarian curve, for
the purpose of showing that the abutment piers are set out in correspondence with its
principles; it is not contended that a knowledge of this curve guided the freemasons in
proportioning their piers, or that their flying buttresses were always placed within it ;
but it is singular that in those structures where their true position seems to have been
decided, the catenarian passes through them.

Bath Abbey section (*fig.* 1319.) is an example which exhibits this most perfectly; and by
a comparison of its section with that at Wells (*fig.* 1272.), it will be perceived that the struts
are differently placed, and that the earlier example is defective : *fig.* 1298. represents Roslyn

Chapel, in which there is evidently some improvement; but at the time of its construction perfect knowledge on this subject had not been attained. In a catenarian chain formed of links of equal length, every side is a tangent to the curve, and the direction of each link is at right angles to it, acting in a direction perpendicular to the line it forms in the catenaria; and hence its useful application to the science of construction. It is quite clear that wherever the curve passes through the section of a building, stability is obtained; and where it does not, it is doubtful: certainly the best application of flying buttresses is that which can be tested by this principle.

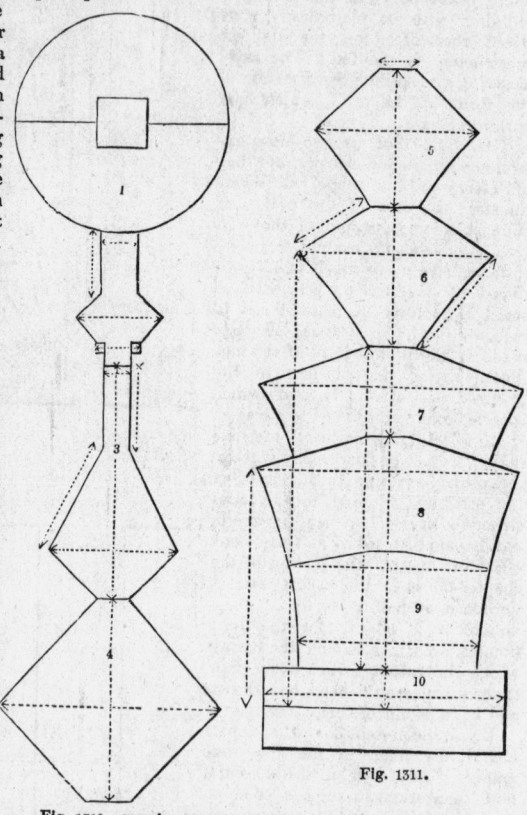

The main arches of the roof abut against the outer buttresses, and spring from a cluster of mouldings set round a circular pier; the situation of the small columns and hollows which decorate it being determined by the crossing of equilateral triangles. The ribs of each severy abut in the centre upon a circle 3 feet 6 inches in diameter, formed of two stones, and indicated by No. 1.: in the middle is a mortise-hole 9 inches square; No. 2. is in width 17 inches in the widest part; No. 3. is 2 feet 2 inches; No. 4., 3 feet 8 inches; No. 5., the same; No. 6., 3 feet 3 inches; No. 7. 4 feet 3 inches; No. 8., the same; No. 9., 3 feet 2 inches, and No. 10., which abuts against the outer wall, 4 feet.

By a reference to the plan on fig. 1312., it will be understood how the several rings of voussoirs which compose the quarter of the parabolic conoid abut and are locked one into the other: the construction of this vault is somewhat similar to that adopted by Soufflout at the Church of St. Geneviève at Paris, although his manner of applying it materially differs.

Fig. 1311.

Fig. 1310. KING'S COLLEGE CHAPEL: RIBS OF VAULT.

The buttress in the present example has an area of 56 feet, equal to that of the piers, to which it is attached; or the two piers and buttresses together have an area of 224 feet: it is curious to find that of the 336 feet before given to the points of support, one-sixth should be applied to the piers, one-sixth to the buttresses, and the other portion to the walls between; for 55 ft. 6 in. × 6 = 336 feet — the area of the points of support taken on both sides; so equally are the parts even distributed.

When the Normans first used flying buttresses, as at the Cathedral at Chartres, the Abbaye aux Hommes at Caen, and several other buildings, they abutted them against the ordinary outside wall; but it was soon discovered that a greater resistance was necessary to oppose the thrust, and prevent the abutments from yielding. Salisbury Cathedral was probably one of the earliest where flying buttresses were used; and the opinion of Sir Christopher Wren is worthy of quoting upon this subject, as it applies more particularly to the first constructed, and not so immediately to those erected in the fourteenth or fifteenth centuries. " Almost all the cathedrals of the Gothic form are weak and defective in the poise of the vault of the aisles; as for the vaults of the nave, they are on both sides equally supported and propped up from spreading by the bowes or flying buttresses, which rise from the outward walls of the aisles: but for the vaults of the aisles, they are indeed supported on the outside by the buttresses; but inwardly, they have no other stay but the pillars themselves, which, as they are usually proportioned, if they stood alone, without the weight above, could not resist the spreading of the aisles one minute: true, indeed, the great load above of the walls and vaulting of the nave should seem to confine the pillars

in their perpendicular station, that there should be no need of butment inwards, but experience hath shown the contrary, and there is scarce any Gothic cathedral, that I have

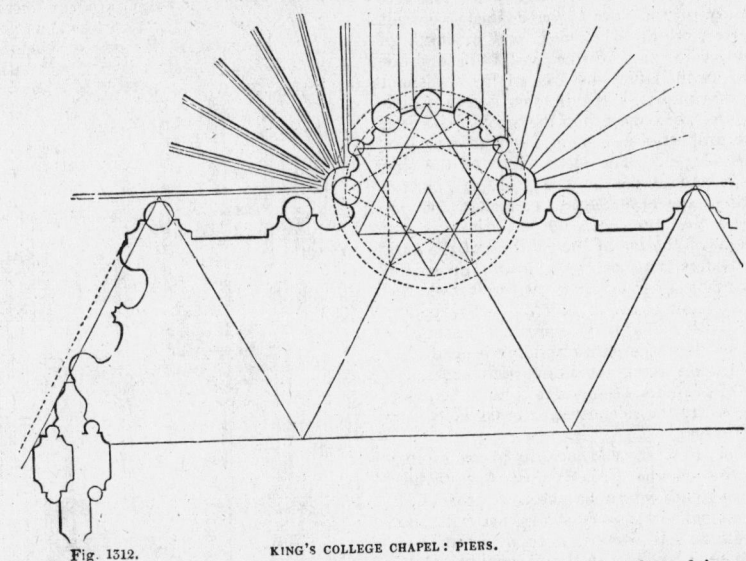

Fig. 1312.   KING'S COLLEGE CHAPEL: PIERS.

seen at home or abroad, wherein I have not observed the pillars to yield and bend inwards from the weight of the vault of the aisle; but this defect is the most conspicuous upon the angular pillars of the cross, for there not only the vault wants butment, but also the

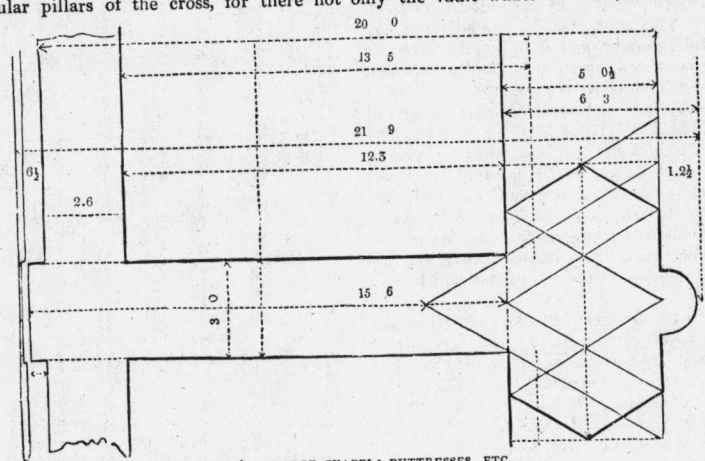

Fig. 1313.   KING'S COLLEGE CHAPEL: BUTTRESSES, ETC.

angular arches that rest upon that pillar, and therefore both conspire to thrust it inwards towards the centre of the cross."

At King's College chapel, flying buttresses are dispensed with, and happily the knowledge of construction had arrived at such perfection, when its astonishing vault was projected, that we have no evidence whatever of its yielding in any part.

It may seem extraordinary that the Pointed style made so little progress in Italy, the Byzantine being always preferred: the architects of that country were probably unwilling to relinquish a mode of construction so economical, half only of the material employed in the lightest, and a quarter in the earliest of the Gothic style, being required for the basilica: for example, where 100 rods of stonework would be used in the latter, 200 would be necessary for the style practised at King's College, St. George's Chapel, and Bath Abbey Church, and 400 for that of the Chapter-house at Wells; this result would lead to the conclusion, that no style is so well adapted for the wants of the present day as the Byzantine.

St. George's Chapel, Windsor. — If we suppose a line on the plan to pass through the centre of the buttresses and piers, and one severy of the nave to be defined, we shall have a width of 12 feet, and a length of 84 feet, the area of which is 1008 feet: after this we shall find the area of the walls and piers comprised within this severy to be 168 feet, or one-sixth of the whole; such are the proportions of mass and void found in this chapel. The clear width of the side aisles between the columns is 11 feet 9 inches; that of the nave 34 feet 10 inches, and between the outer walls 69 feet 2 inches: the height of the top of the vaulting of the nave is 54 feet 2 inches. The height up to the springing line of the great vault over the nave being equal to half the entire width, it is evident that two squares must comprise within them the entire building beneath this line; upon setting them out we find the nave and its pillars occupy one, whilst the other is given to the side aisles, external walls, and buttresses.

The Rev. John Milner, in his admirable treatise on the Ecclesiastical Architecture of England, which has been the text-book for all modern writers, states that "its rise, progress, and decline, occupy little more than four centuries in the chronology of the world: as its characteristic perfection consisted in the due elevation of the arch, so its decline commenced by an undue depression of it. This took place in the latter part of the 15th century, and is to be seen, amongst other instances, in parts of St. George's Chapel, Windsor, commenced by Edward IV. in 1482; in King's College Chapel, Cambridge, and in the Chapel of Henry VII. at Westminster. It is undoubtedly true that the architects of these splendid and justly admired erections, Bishop Cloose, Sir Reginald de Bray, &c. displayed more art and more professional science than their predecessors had done; but they did this at the expense of the characteristic excellence of the style itself which they built in."

"In St. George's Chapel we have the work covered with tracery and carvings of the most exquisite design and execution, but which fatigue the eye, and cloy the mind by their redundancy:" but we have also a building constructed with one-half the materials that would have been employed had the style practised in the chapter-house of Wells been adopted. The admirers of the Pointed style have not sought for the true principles which mark its several changes; they have not examined into its constructive arrangements; had they done so, they would have perceived that, as the skill of the freemasons advanced, and their workmanship improved, they economised material, constructed more solidly, and produced a richer and more harmonious effect, without sacrificing any of the principles which governed their practice; the improvements they made were as great as those noticed when the

Fig. 1314. ST. GEORGE'S CHAPEL, WINDSOR.

Doric proportions were changed to the Ionic.   In the Doric we had two-thirds mass, one-third void ; in the Ionic half mass, half void ; at Wells Chapter-house one-third mass, two-thirds void ; in St. George's Chapel, one-sixth mass and five-sixths void.

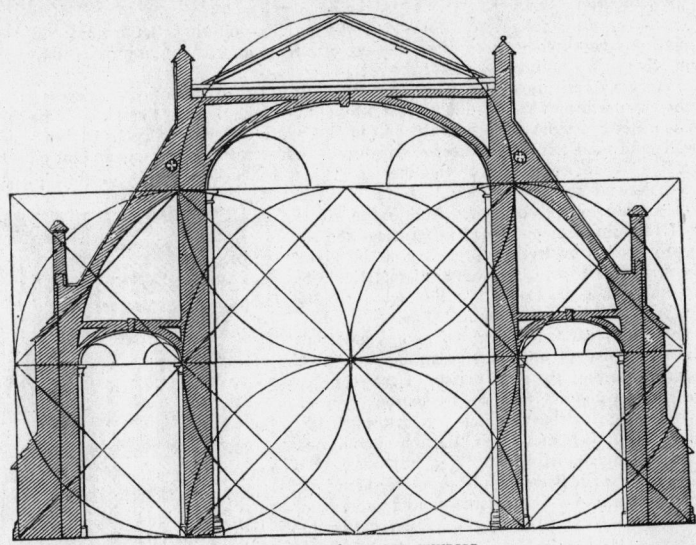

Fig. 1315.   ST. GEORGE'S CHAPEL, WINDSOR.

The plan of the pillars is that of a double square, or parallelogram, the diagonals of which latter figure become the sides of equilateral triangles that serve for the setting out

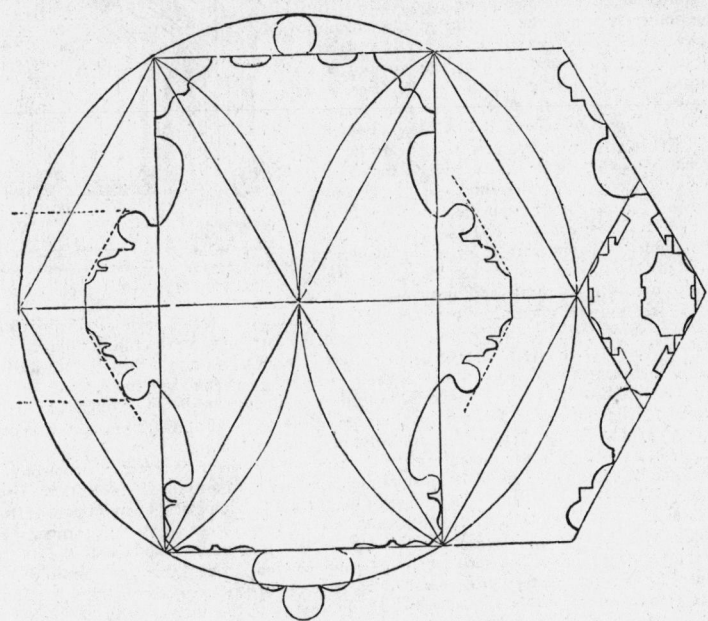

Fig. 1316.   PIER OF ST. GEORGE'S CHAPEL, WINDSOR.

the splays, upon which the several mouldings are cut : from east to west these piers are 3 feet 1 inch, from north to south 3 feet 6 inches, not comprising in this last dimension the three

small columns on the fall towards the nave, or the single column on that towards the side aisles, the first of which projects 6¼ inches, and the latter 4 inches.

The mouldings around the windows and their mullions are shown at the side of the pier in their proper position.

Division of the Nave of St. George's Chapel. — The mouldings set around the plan of the pier are continued up to the vaulting of the roof, without any other interruption except where they are mitred round the arches.

Bath Abbey Church is 89 feet 5 inches in width from cut to cut measured across the nave, and the clear width of the nave is 29 feet 10 inches, or one-third of the whole, and each of the side aisles is a trifle more than the half of the width of the nave, being 15 feet 8 inches ; the walls and piers added together are not quite equal to a third, as they amount only to 14 feet 2 inches on each side, or together to 28 feet 4 inches, the difference being given to increase the side aisles.

The section of this beautiful building presents to us all the improvements made in vaulting, and the right proportions as well as directions to be given to the flying buttresses : in the first application of those supports, as at Salisbury, they are evidently misapplied, but in the example before us we find that the constructors had arrived at a knowledge of the principles of the catenarian curve, which is traceable through the solid masses of the section : it was by slow degrees that the freemasons arrived at a knowledge of the peculiar properties of this figure ; had it been known at the first commencement of the introduction of flying buttresses, we should have had a better application of them ; in several instances we find them adopted where no advantage, or very little, could be derived from them.

Division in Bath Abbey Church differs from all other examples of this period, by the height given to the clerestory and the omission of the triforium : the judicious and excellent arrangement of the flying buttresses permits of the greater display of glass, which in the sixteenth century had arrived at its most gorgeous state, rich in every colour, and beautiful from the drawing of the patterns, and figures with which it was covered.

Bishop King commenced this building about the year 1500, on an entirely new site, near the old church : from the centre of one pier to that of the other is 20 feet 1 inch ; the thickness of the outer buttresses 3 feet, and their projection 4 feet ; one severy of building contains 1650 feet, and the area of the points of support is 275 feet, or one-sixth. The pillars are square, though set diagonally, their width from north to south and from east to west being 5 feet, and the opening of the arches between them 15 feet 1 inch ; half their plan and base is shown at fig. 1320. : the height from the pavement to the top of the capitals, where the sculptured angel is placed, is 56 feet 3 inches, and to the top of the vaulting 73 feet 6 inches, within 7 feet as much as the clear width between the outer walls.

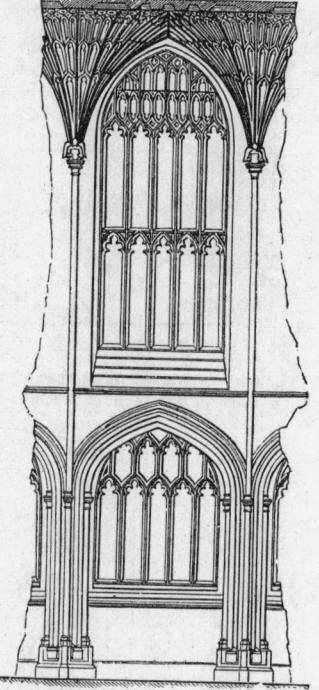

Fig. 1317. BATH ABBEY CHURCH.

Fig. 1321. shows the plan of the stone vaulting, which is perfectly geometrical in its setting out ; the cloisters at Gloucester, the aisle at the east end of Peterborough cathedral, and St. George's Chapel, Windsor, have vaults of a similar kind.

The thickness of the stone which comprises the vaults of fan tracery varies according to its position, but in no instance is it considerable, or more than absolutely necessary to resist crushing.　The spire of Salisbury, 180 feet in height, of an octangular form, measures from east to west internally 33 feet 2 inches, and from north to south 6 inches more ; the thickness of the spire at bottom is only 2 feet, or the area of its base is half that of the void, the void containing two parts, and the solid around it one ; this spire diminishes in thickness for the first 20 feet, after which it is 9 inches in thickness throughout ; at about 30 feet from the summit is a hole, by which an exit from the interior may be made, and by means of the crockets and irons on the outside the top of the spire may be attained : in 1816 the writer examined the position of the vane, and the manner in which the capping stone was placed, and descended astonished at the perfection of the masonry, and the thinness of the stone with which it was constructed.

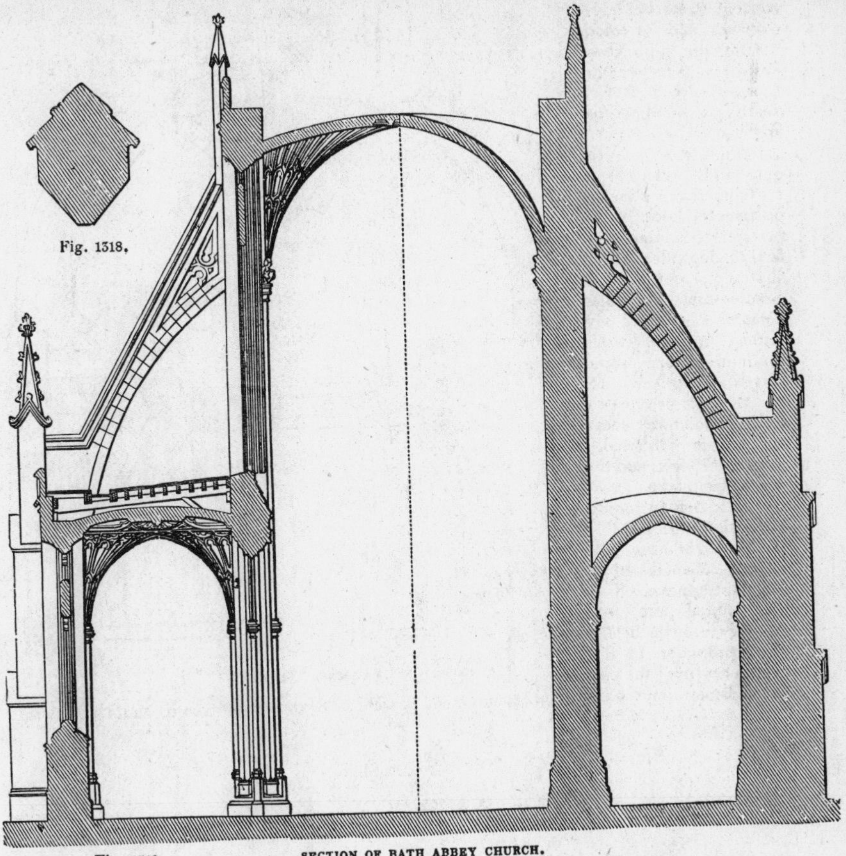

Fig. 1318.

Fig. 1319.　　　SECTION OF BATH ABBEY CHURCH.

Fig. 1320.　PIER.　　　Fig. 1321.　GROINING.

Caudebec Sacristy, near Rouen, in Normandy, exhibits the manner of suspending a keystone by locking it between the voussoirs of a strong semicircular arch. The length of this

pendent stone is 17 feet 6 inches, and its thickness at the top, where locked, is 30 inches : the voussoirs are 3 feet in depth ; the small pointed arches or ribs that form the groining of the hexagonal vault spring from the side walls and the ornamental knob of the pendentive, and are perfectly independent. The abutments of the semicircular arch, which has a radius of 12 feet, are formed by solid walls continued for some length in the direction of its diameter. This sacristy is hexagonal ; each side internally measures 12 feet, and the height from the pavement to the springing of the ribs is 18 feet.

Henry the Seventh's Chapel, Westminster. — The first appearance of the pointed arch was probably a little before the termination of the twelfth century ; the pillars and mouldings which

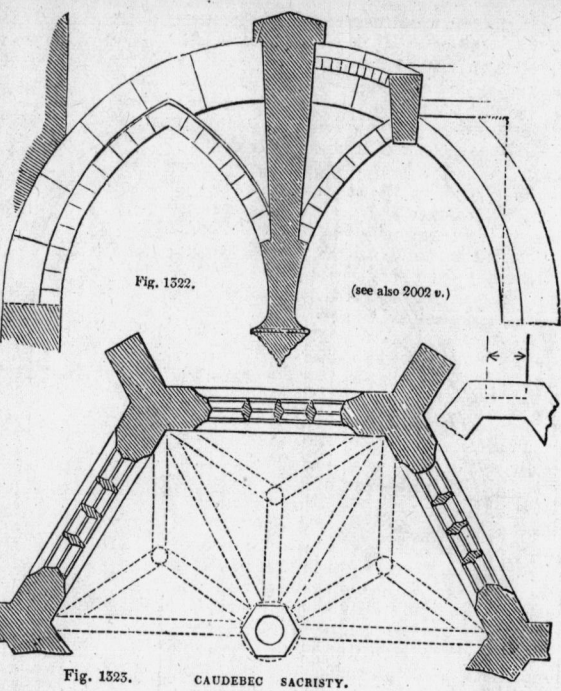

Fig. 1322.

(see also 2002 *v.*)

Fig. 1323. CAUDEBEC SACRISTY.

then accompanied it were of Saxon origin : to its acute form was

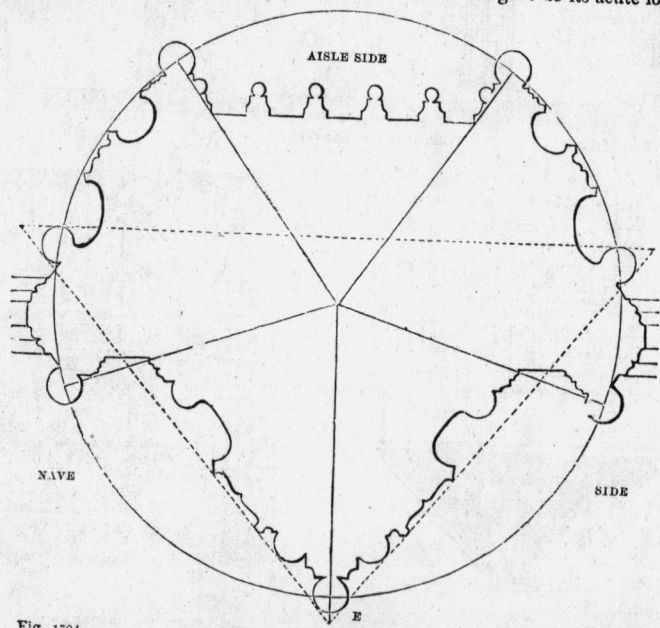

AISLE SIDE

NAVE

SIDE

E

Fig. 1324. PIER OF HENRY VII.'S CHAPEL.

afterwards added the slender Purbeck columns and simple groining, producing that unadorned majesty which reigns throughout the cathedral of Salisbury. This style underwent several changes, and was succeeded at the latter end of the thirteenth century by another, in

which the arch was struck from more than two centres: the naves of York, Canterbury, and Winchester Cathedrals have been cited as among the best examples. But we have now to describe the principles of a style founded upon the others, and applied to all buildings in England from the middle of the fifteenth to the middle of the sixteenth century; it is not met with on the continent, the Italian or revived classic architecture having there been generally introduced and preferred.

The variety exhibited in groined vaults, progressing from simple ribs to those of an intricate and net-like arrangement, no doubt led the masons of the time to the construction of the cloisters at Gloucester, King's College, and Henry the Seventh's Chapel at Westminster, which works are the best evidences that can be adduced of the improvements made in professional science, and which could only result from a continued perseverance in the study of the subject: an examination of the several styles will prove that they must have been produced by the same school or fraternity, and that neither Sir Reginald Bray nor William of Wykeham could have become acquainted with the mysteries of the craft, unless they had been instructed by the freemasons; and that to them, and not to any individual, nor to the clergy as a body, ought we to attribute the construction of these scientific and highly decorated works.

The Division of Henry the Seventh's Chapel bears a strong resemblance in its general proportions to that of St. George's at Windsor, although it is rendered more ornamental by the multitude of figures enshrined in delicate tabernacle-work, which covers almost the entire walls. The mouldings of the main piers (fig. 1324.) that separate the middle from the side aisles are enclosed within a circle divided into a pentagon—a form the best adapted to receive the weight of the ribs, and the flying buttresses that were to resist their force.

The Rev. James Dallaway, whose discourses upon the architecture of England, created so many admirers of this interesting subject, observes, that " here the expiring Gothic seems to have been exhausted by every effort. The pendentive roofs, never before attempted on so large a scale, are prodigies of art." But it is not to the profusion of sculptured angels, statues, royal heraldic devices, &c., that we are desirous of drawing the attention, so much as to the extraordinary construction that prevails throughout this master-piece, in which we have the strongest evidence that theory and practice went hand in hand; that the knowledge of geometry had advanced to its highest pitch in the constructive arts, and that not only were the principles of the arch thoroughly understood, but considerable advance made in the application of the properties belonging to the cone.

The section of this beautiful chapel is 78 feet in width; the buttresses and outer walls together are 6 feet 9 inches, the side aisles 11 feet 3 inches; the piers from north to south 4 feet

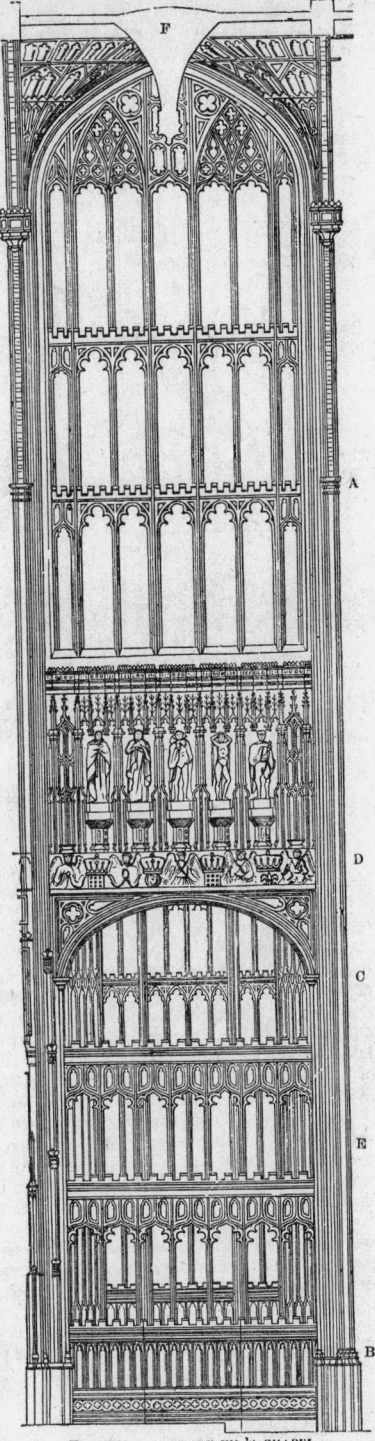

Fig. 1325.   HENRY VII.'S CHAPEL.

Fig. 1526.   SECTION OF HENRY VII'S. CHAPEL.

6 inches, and the clear width of the nave 33 feet.   The entire width, at the basement or level of the pavement of the crypt, is 79 feet : 26¼ feet, or ⅓, is devoted to points of support, and 52⅔ feet, or ⅔, to the side aisles and nave ; the area of a severy shows ⅓ applied to walls and piers, and ⅔ to the void, which proportions accord with the early rather than with the late examples ; the great weight of the vaulting, which is 62 feet high from the pavement of the chapel, requiring additional strength, the proportions of St. George's Chapel at Windsor would not have been equal to the necessary resistance.   (See *par.* 2002*w.*)

Our limits will not permit a more extended inquiry into the principles of proportion, the study of which is calculated to produce an important improvement in the noble art, for the practice of which the young architect must prepare himself by careful measurement, not only of the ruins of the Acropolis and of the Capitol, but of all that remains of mediæval architecture : he must be a pilgrim seeking after truth, not bowing before any favourite shrine, but returning with a devotion as enlarged as his subject.   The stupendous works which antiquity has transmitted to us, it is hoped, may excite the attention of the general reader, nor will his interest be diminished by the contemplation of the astonishing development of modern industry.   The writer cannot but feel the importance and variety of his subject, and, while he is conscious of his own imperfections, he must often accuse the deficiency of his materials : but the results of his labour, however inadequate to his own wishes, he finally delivers to the candour of the public.

The Figure of the Cube has from time immemorial been selected by the architect and engineer as best suited for every variety of edifice; and it is remarkable that the multiplying of the cube constitutes the design of the Greek temple, the Gothic cathedral, and the modern iron structure at Sydenham, the variety of effect depending upon the mode of its application. Reviewing the temples of the ancients, we find that those composed of a portico of four columns, and six intercolumniations on the flank, or seven columns; that the whole constituted a double cube, or two cubes side by side. A cube of 32 feet 4 inches in height, breadth, and length, placed behind another of the same dimensions, would represent the entire mass of the temple of Fortuna Virilis at Rome.

The temple of six columns, or the Hexastyle, is composed of nine half cubes, or three entire, placed one behind the other, with the addition of three half cubes against the sides of the first, making altogether four cubes and a half.

The Octastyle temple is composed of nine whole cubes, or four cubes and a half in depth, repeated twice, placed side by side. The Parthenon is thus formed of cubes, whose sides each measure 50 feet 6 inches; two occupy the front, of 101 feet; the depth of the four and a half cubes are a trifle more than 227 feet, the true extent being 227 feet 7 inches.

Six cubes, placed one above the other, form the design of the Campanile, at Florence, commenced by the celebrated Giotto in the year 1334; and on the breaking up of these cubes into ornament, the perpendicular lines are lengthened out, whilst in the Greek temple the horizontal are made to preponderate; repose in the latter, and lofty aspiration in the former, marks the distinction between them.

The *Tower of Rochester Castle*, usually supposed to be of Norman construction, perfectly resembles the far-famed Coliseum at Rome, in the manner in which the spiral vaults are executed, and in the general method adopted in carrying up the massive walls. The cement employed was evidently manufactured on the spot, as it is entirely composed of the materials found close at hand, and the stone such as could be brought down the Medway, and quarried on its shores. If this enduring structure was the work of Gundulph in the 12th century, we have the strongest evidence that the Roman arts of construction were continued without any change either in the art or mystery of building up to that period at least.

The building is a cube and a half nearly, being about 74 feet square without the entrance porch, and its height to the top of the angular turrets is 112 feet. A square divided into twenty-five equal squares exhibits its plan; the sixteen outer squares represent the thickness of the walls, in which are galleries, recesses, and contrivances necessary for its protection against an enemy; the nine inner squares of the plan are divided into two spacious rooms, one being 45 feet by 19 feet, the other 45 feet by 21 feet; the wall that divides them is 5 feet 6 inches in thickness. The height comprises a basement story and three others beneath its roof, which has been vaulted, and which is 90 feet to the top of the battlement, and 112 feet to the top of the turrets.

Rules adopted by the Freemasons in setting out their Buildings, from the Tenth to the Fifteenth Century:—

In the foregoing remarks on Proportion some general rules have been suggested as to mass and void, and more particularly the principles of setting out the windows and tracery of the English and French cathedrals. On referring again to this interesting subject, the writer was led to inquire why the structures of the latter country should be so uniformly larger than those of the former, from which they differed but little in style, preserving the same relative proportions, though differing in dimensions. Guided by the supposition that the buildings of the above period were the works of fraternities of freemasons, it seemed conclusive that they should have some standard of measurement, either of their own or peculiar to each country; and, on testing the measurements with that view, it resulted that those of England were set out with the English perch of 16 feet 6 inches, and no doubt by an English lodge; while in those of France the French perch royal, of 22 *pieds du roi*, equal to 23·452 English feet, was employed; the few exceptions at Bayeux, Caen, St. George Bocherville, and some others with round arches, and the elegant church of St. Ouen at Rouen, in the flamboyant style, are set out with the English perch of 16 feet 6 inches, and are universally attributed to English constructors; they certainly most curiously agree in proportion and dimension with the English cathedrals, which have two cubes given to the nave, producing on the plan a Latin cross, instead of the Greek so usually found in France. It would seem that the standard measures referred to were well and wisely chosen, as if intended to apply to all times and all varieties of structure; for it is singular how nearly the dimensions of the cubes of the fairy palace at Sydenham, 24 feet, correspond to 23 feet 6 inches of the royal French perch.

To illustrate this subject fully is not within our present narrow limits; a very few examples must suffice, out of the numbers which might be adduced in support of the proposition; and it is earnestly hoped that the young architect may be sufficiently inte-

rested to test the theory practically, that while he admires their picturesque beauties, he will examine by measurement their plans and sections.

Of the French Cathedrals, we must be content to refer to Chartres, Reims, and Amiens as those most admired, and which serve as examples of the application of the French perch in setting out their various parts as well as the whole.

Chartres Cathedral, in which the pointed arch first appears, is a structure of the 11th century, and one of the most remarkable, as well as beautiful, erected after the first introduction of the pointed style by those who had journeyed with the Crusaders, and had an opportunity of studying their craft in the East.

The proportions are simple in the extreme. A cube is devoted to the nave, two to the transept, one to the choir; in addition to which, at the eastern extremity, is a semicircular termination with six polygonal chapels attached, forming on the plan a Greek cross of admirable design.

The nave, comprising six divisions of pointed arches on each side, is in its length and width six royal perches, the distribution of which will enable the reader to comprehend the setting out of the entire plan, which he can refer to in several publications.

The clear width of the nave is two royal perches between the clerestory walls; each side aisle is one royal perch, and the distance from the middle of one pier to that of the other, from west to east, is also a royal perch.

The entire width of the nave from out to out, that is to say, from the face of the exterior buttresses, is six royal perches, four perches being given to the two side aisles and nave for their clear widths, and the other two to the projection of the buttresses, thickness of the two outer walls, and those of the clerestory of the nave.

If the royal perch be divided into three, one part constitutes the diameter given to the pillars, and another the thickness of each of the walls of the side aisles.

The internal height of the nave is the same as its clear internal width with side aisles; so justly is all proportioned that the perch royal, and its division into three, enables us to comprehend the dimensions of the parts, as well as that of the entire mass of construction.

Reims Cathedral was similarly set out. The clear width of the nave is two royal perches, and each of the side aisles is one perch. The extreme width of the nave, comprising the projection of the buttresses, is six royal perches; the diameter of the piers, one-third of a royal perch, as in the example of Chartres.

It must be observed that the dimensions do not apply to the clear distances between the pillars, but to the space between the walls, which in the clerestory are peculiar for the contrivances of a gallery, which usually continues around the entire cathedral, and which will be better understood when we treat upon Amiens Cathedral, reserved for a fuller description. That the perch was the standard of measurement there can be no doubt; for in the smaller churches of Great Britain, as that of Roslyn, for example, the nave is a single perch in width, and the side aisles half a perch; the proportions of the parts being also those of the third of an English perch.

Salisbury Cathedral, a contemporary structure with Amiens, is set out with the English perch, and affords the best commentary upon the two standard measures made use of in the same century by the French and English freemasons.

The Nave of Amiens Cathedral is usually admired for its elegant proportions, and by several eminent critics has been cited as the *beau idéal* of that style of architecture so universally practised during the middle ages, or after the Romanesque had been discontinued. It is one of the most simple in its arrangement, though at first sight, removing all idea of simplicity, and appearing so complicated from its variety of parts, as to defy the application of any ordinary rules; the numerous arcades, the narrow and lofty compartments, the vaulted divisions, the diagonal and curved lines, blending one into the other, and apparently without limit, it is some time before the eye can acquiesce in the idea that such an edifice can be brought under the same laws as a Greek temple, or that the cube could be the measure of its parts or its whole. In taking the measurements, however, of this rare example, the dimension of 23 feet 6 inches so frequently occurred that it seemed to denote a standard by which to arrive at the length, breadth, and height of the whole, and that, if considered after the manner of Sebastian Serlio, where he describes Bramante's plan of St. Peter's, we might arrive at something like a clue to the whole design.

It is curious to note, in the work of the above mentioned architect, several allusions to the cube, in the defining the parts as well as the whole of a design, and there can be little doubt that this simple figure served as the means of measuring the quantities, of either solid or void, in every period of the constructive arts; certainly none presents to the architect a better means of comprehending or of measuring quantity, and none is more readily subdivided, or rendered subservient to the taste of the designer, whatever may be the architecture he is anxious to imitate.

Within an isometrical cube may be placed the entire nave of Amiens Cathedral; and the better to understand its proportions, we must suppose each square or cube into which it is

divided to measure 23 feet 6 inches each side, or the isometrical figure to contain 216 such cubes; the total height, width, and length being 141 feet, or six times the 23 feet 6 inches. (See *fig.* 1327.)

On the plan are six divisions in length and width, or altogether 36 squares; each measure 23 feet 6 inches on each of their sides. The six outer divisions of the principal figure are devoted to walls and buttresses; the adjoining six on each side show the situation

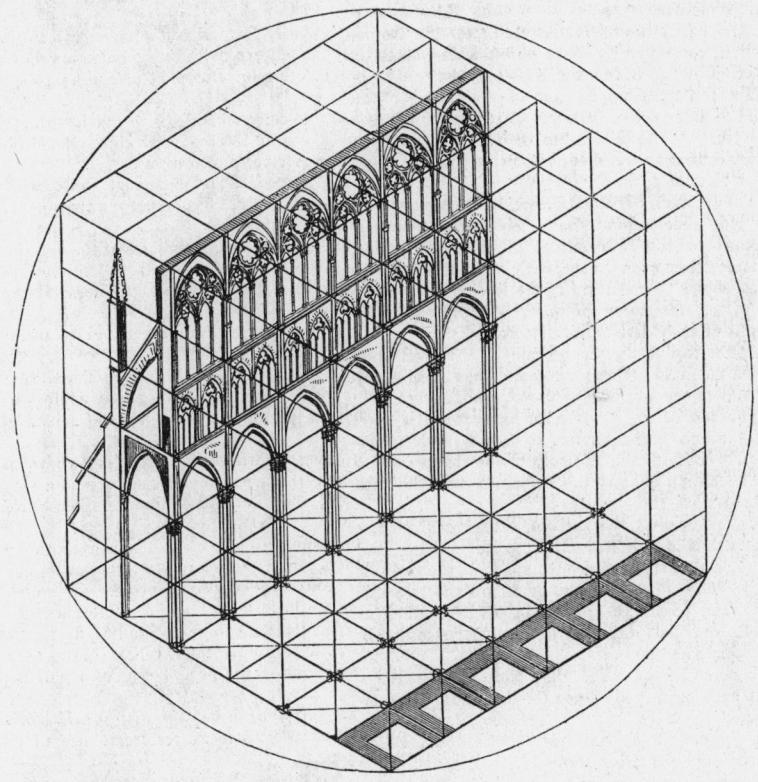

Fig. 1327.   NAVE OF AMIENS CATHEDRAL.

of the side aisles; and the two middle divisions that of the nave. The two side aisles occupy together 12 squares, as does the nave; the remaining 12 being devoted to outer walls and their buttresses.

The entire area, therefore, has 24 squares to represent its interior distribution, and half that number its external walls; or one-third walls, two-thirds void. Such are the general arrangements of its plan, and its extreme simplicity has enabled the constructors to execute the vaulting of the side aisles and that of the centre nave by diagonal ribs, which in the former extend over one square, and in the latter two, thus giving to the nave its due proportion of height, without changing the principle of its construction.

The freemasons of the middle ages were so perfectly acquainted with geometry that there is seldom any defect in their vaulting; it is evident that they laid down their plans for its execution before they decided upon the form of their main piers; in their setting out, every part had its due function; and the column, which was intended to be connected with the vaulting, either of nave or side aisle, was peculiarly adapted by its position for its use.

The master mason Robert de Luzarche commenced the building of this nave about the year 1220, the founder being Bishop Evrard. The pillars of the nave were raised to the height of their capitals in 1236, but it was not till 1236 that the vaulting was completed; and about eight or nine years afterwards the lateral chapels were added.

To the top of the battlement of the nave there is not quite so much height as the outer wall of the Coliseum at Rome, which is 157 feet; but it is curious to observe that one division of this renowned building does not differ very materially in its proportions from that at Amiens; the division of the ampitheatre being seven cubes in height; the piers occupy one third of the width of a compartment, as is usual in Roman structures of the same period. The masonry of Amiens Cathedral is executed after the Roman models, consequently the pointed arch makes the chief difference between the two styles.

To render the application of the theory of the cube to the nave of Amiens Cathedral more evident, or how the 216 cubes which the isometrical figure contains are placed, somewhat more of detail must be entered into.

The six main divisions shown in the figure, with the side aisle behind them, have their points of support at the four angles of each of the six squares; then each square, with its 23 feet 6 inches sides, shows the position of the lowest cube of the six placed one above the other, forming the entire height of each division or severy.

At the top of the second cube is the level upon which the main arches spring, and that upon which the ribs of the vaulting of the side aisles rest.

The top of the third cube indicates the level upon which the triforium is based, and consequently contains the vaulting of the side aisle.

The fourth cube is the triforium, and the fifth and the sixth the clerestory.

On examining the section, the side aisles are three cubes in height, including the vaulting, and the nave six; the entire open space of the interior has 18 cubes for each aisle, or 36 for the two side aisles, and 72 for the nave; in all 108 cubes, or exactly one half the entire number contained in the isometrical cube.

It must be remarked that considerable alterations have been made since the building was constructed; between the buttresses, chapels have been formed, and the original windows, which lighted the side aisles, removed to the extent, or somewhat beyond the outer face of buttresses, as represented. The interior is therefore increased materially in width, and its effect greatly improved, making the entire internal width and height more in conformity with each other, or each 141 feet.

In the elevation of the divisions the boundary of each of the six cubes is more clearly marked. The width from centre to centre of each pillar, indicated by the seven circles (*fig.* 1328.) is 23 feet 6 inches; to the top of the capitals from the pavement A B, the height is twice that dimension; to the bottom of the bases of the column of the triforium B C, the same; thence to the bottom of the glass of the clerestory windows C D, the same; to the tops of the capitals or spring of the arches D E, the same; and above that line to the underside the vaulting E F, the same; thus, six times 23 feet 6 inches, or 141 feet, is the total height from the pavement, of the division represented in *fig.* 1328.

As the groined vaults of the side aisles are set out upon a square, and the width from the centres of piers is the same as those towards the

Fig. 1328.   ELEVATION OF NAVE; AMIENS.

nave, we have three perfect cubes of 24 feet in each severy up to the bottom of the triforium story, and the same number from thence to the top of the vaulting of the nave.

The main pillars are 7 feet, and 7 feet 2 inches in diameter, composed of a large cylindrical column, with others attached for the support of the vaulting. Towards the nave there are three columns which are carried up to the height of about the middle of that of the clerestory windows; on the capitals which terminate them rest the cross springers and diagonal ribs of the vaulting. The arches of each division are 4 feet 9 inches in thickness, and rest on the side columns, of 18 inches diameter. The faint line on the plan *fig.* 1329. represents the pier and mullions of the division of the clerestory window.

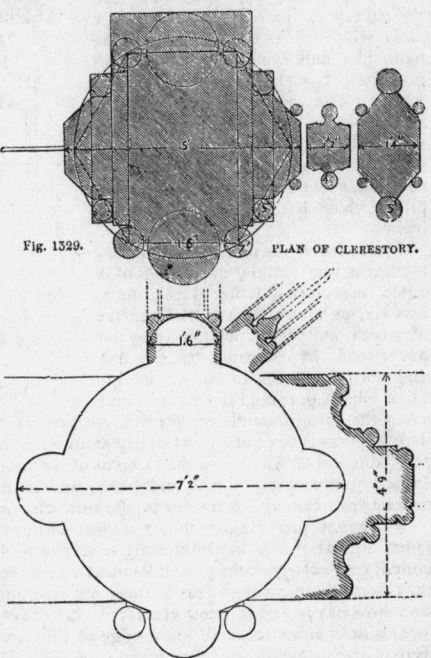

Fig. 1329.   PLAN OF CLERESTORY.

The seven circles shown in *fig.* 1328. exhibit the proportion each pier bears to the opening, namely, that of two-sevenths for piers, and five-sevenths for the space between them. The dimensions vary a little as taken throughout the six severies, as in some instances the diameter of the piers varies as above stated.

It may be remarked that the contour of the torus and scotia in the base, are not sections of cylinders or their portions, but partakes of the elliptical. The mouldings below, are contoured differently to those above, the eye, and consideration is given to their position, to produce proper effect.

Fig. 1330.   PLAN OF COLUMNS; AMIENS.

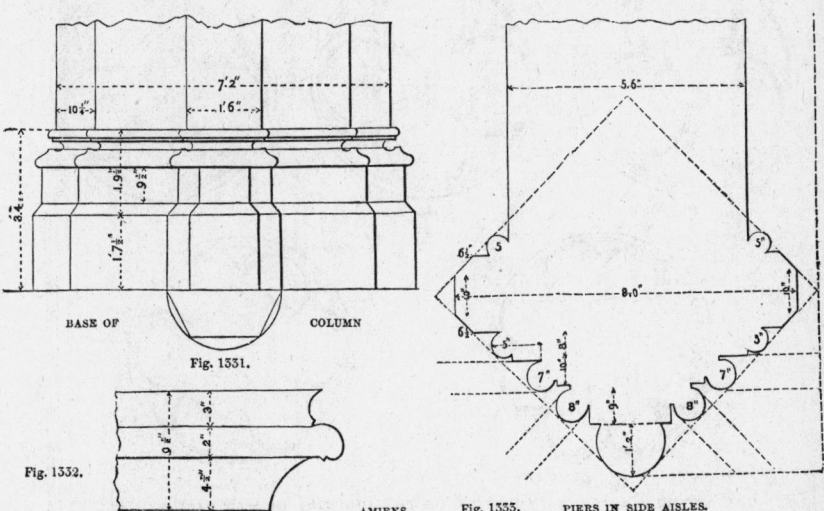

BASE OF   COLUMN

Fig. 1331.

Fig. 1332.

AMIENS.   Fig. 1333.   PIERS IN SIDE AISLES.

The base and capital of the main pillars, as here shown with their dimensions, is the same as the front view towards the nave, with the exception that the two 7-inch columns at the side of that in the middle are omitted.

The piers that divide the side chapels, and the original outer buttresses, have been changed probably from their original design; they are now 8 feet wide.

The clerestory window with its piers and mullions being already given (*fig.* 1329.) it remains to show the plan of the piers and mullions of the triforium, and its gallery or passage, which has a clear width of 20 inches between the main pier and the outer wall, which is about 10 inches in thickness (*fig.* 1334.) The middle mullion, or that which divides the triforium into two principal arches, is 2 feet 6 inches in width, and composed of seven small columns, as shown attached to the main pillar, which has a depth of 6 feet 8 inches.

The ordinary decoration in this cathedral is very simple, consisting of a circle, comprising either three, four, five, six, or eight others; the centres of which and their portions may be understood by reference to the five diagrams *figs.* 1335. to 1339. Sculptured foliage occurs in the capitals and

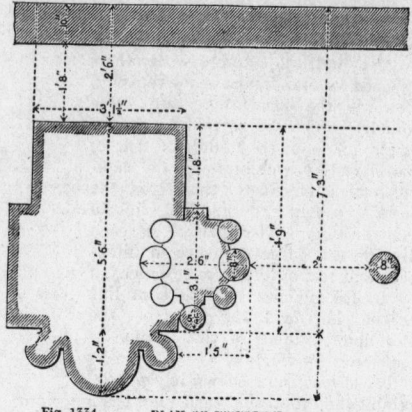

Fig. 1334.   PLAN OF TRIFORIUM.

along the string mouldings; figures, however, of the most elaborate execution and design decorate the exterior, and particularly around the chief entrances; perhaps few buildings excel the Cathedral of Amiens in the richness of these portions, or the magnificence of its porches. In describing the *figs.* 1292. and 1294., an attempt was made to convey an idea of the geometrical style of the tracery in the rose windows, as well as those of the side chapels.

We cannot quit this part of our subject without regretting the want of further space for the treatment of this very interesting reference to the arts as displayed by the builders of this period, particularly as the principles upon which they practised are so little known. Simple as they were, their system seems to have been forgotten after the lodges of the freemasons were broken up, and the new era appeared. The *renaissance,* or the return to the Greek models, at once set aside all knowledge of that architecture which had attained such perfection in Europe for four centuries.

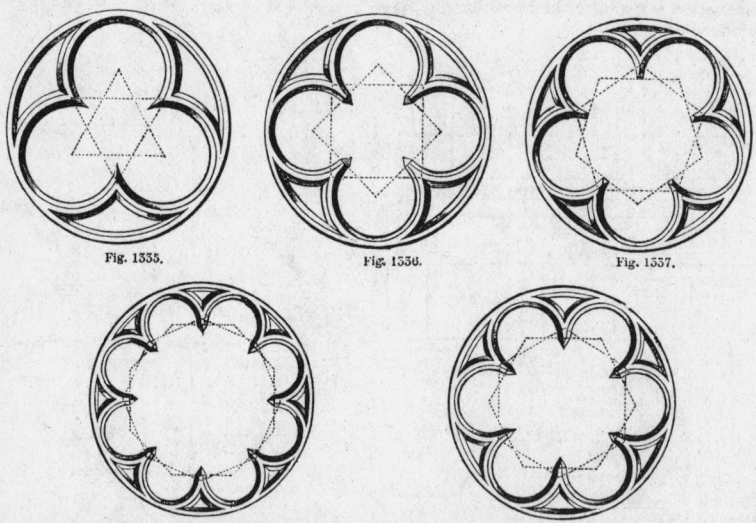

Fig. 1335.   Fig. 1336.   Fig. 1337.

Fig. 1338.   Fig. 1339.

THE BUILDING FOR THE EXHIBITION OF THE INDUSTRY OF ALL NATIONS, 1851.

This building was stated to have been suggested to the Society of Arts in June 1845 by his Royal Highness Prince Albert, and it was not long ere the plan for its adoption was developed. The public quickly responded to an appeal by subscribing 75,000*l.* to enable the commissioners to erect a suitable building, to be completed by the 1st of May 1851; the site being granted by Her Majesty, on the south side of Hyde Park; and all that was required of the exhibitors was, to deliver their various specimens of art and

manufacture at the building which would be provided for them.   Mr. Paxton, after some other designs had been set aside, submitted a design composed chiefly of glass and iron, which Messrs. Fox, Henderson, & Co. tendered to construct for 79,800*l.*   This was immediately carried into effect.

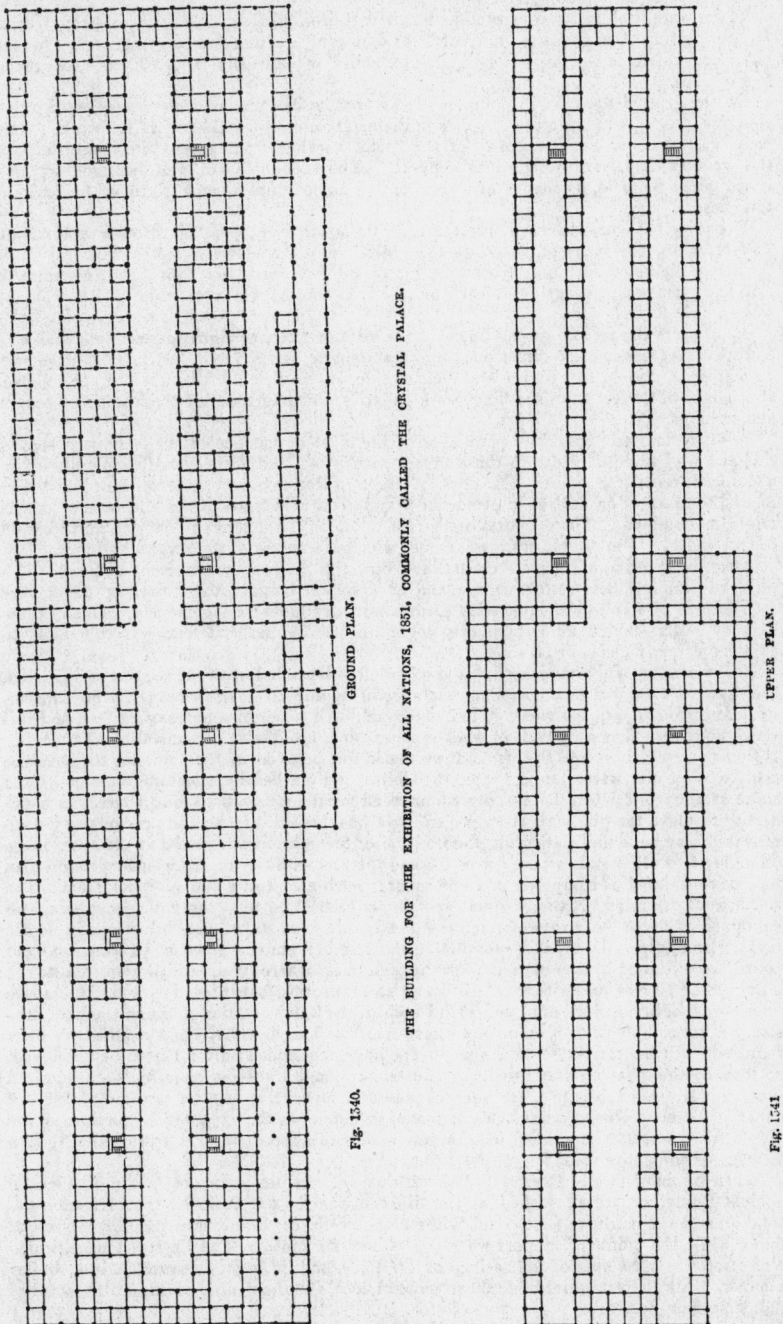

GROUND PLAN.

UPPER PLAN.

THE BUILDING FOR THE EXHIBITION OF ALL NATIONS, 1851, COMMONLY CALLED THE CRYSTAL PALACE.

Fig. 1540.

Fig. 1541.

The site for the building contained about 26 acres, being 2,300 feet in length, and 500 feet in breadth; the principal front extending from west to east. The total area of the ground-floor was 772,784 superficial feet, and that of the galleries 217,100 square feet. The length of these galleries extended nearly a mile. The cubical contents of the building were estimated at 33,000,000 feet.

There were used in its construction 2,300 cast iron girders, 358 wrought iron trusses for supporting the galleries and roof, 30 miles of gutters for carrying water to the columns which served as water-pipes, 202 miles of sash-bars, and 900,000 superficial feet of glass.

On the ground-floor, 1,106 columns of cast iron, rested on cast iron plates, based upon concrete; these columns were 8 inches in diameter, and 18 feet $5\frac{1}{2}$ inches in height; they were cast hollow, the thickness of the metal varying from $\frac{3}{8}$ to $1\frac{1}{8}$ in., according to the weights they were destined to support. The sectional area was increased by four broad fillets or faces, $3\frac{1}{2}$ inches in width, and a little more than a sixth of an inch in thickness.

The principal entrance was in the centre of the south side; passing through a vestibule 72 feet by 48, the transept was entered, which was covered by a semi-cylindrical vault 72 feet in diameter, springing from a height of 68 feet from the floor; and this vault of iron and glass was in length 408 feet from north to south. On each side of the transept was an aisle 24 feet wide.

Standing in the middle of the transept, the vista or nave, at right angles, extended east and west 900 feet in each direction; the total length being 1,848 feet. This nave was 72 feet wide, and 64 feet high; and on each side was an aisle 24 feet in width; and above, at a height of 24 feet from the floor, were galleries which surrounded the whole of the nave and transept.

Beyond these side aisles and parallel with them, at a distance of 48 feet, were second side aisles, of an equal width to those already mentioned, and also covered with galleries on a similar level to the others. Bridges of communication were made at convenient distances, to allow of an unbroken promenade, and from which a view of the several courts might be obtained. These courts were roofed in, at the height of 2 stories, and were 48 feet in width. Ten double staircases 8 feet wide gave access to the several galleries.

After the transept and nave were marked out, the general arrangement consisted of a series of compartments 24 feet square, and as much in height; these bays or cubes were each formed of 4 columns, supporting girders put together very ingeniously. One of these bays or gallery-floors, 24 feet square, containing 576 superficial feet, was calculated to support as many cwts., or 30 tons.

The symmetry and strength of this vast building depended upon the accuracy with which the simple plan was drawn out, and much credit is due to Mr. Brounger, who superintended this portion of the work. He had to establish a series of squares of 24 feet, and this was admirably effected by rods of well-seasoned pine, fitted with gun-metal cheeks.

Stakes were driven into the ground to mark the position of the columns, their precise centres being afterwards found by the theodolite, and marked by a nail on the top of the stake or pile; and when the digging commenced for the foundations, and there was a necessity to move the pile, a right-angled triangle was formed in deal, and previous to the removal of a stake, a nail indicating the position of the column was placed at the apex of the triangle; two other stakes were driven in, and the first withdrawn. The entire ground plan may be considered as composed of 1,453 squares, each containing 576 superficial feet. The south front occupied 77, the east and west fronts each 17, so that the entire parallelogram contained 1,309 of these squares; on the north side were 48 others, 3 divisions in depth, making an additional 144, thus completing the number stated. The nave, transept, and courts were formed by the omission of the columns, where their width required to be either 48 or 72 feet, and girders of sufficient strength were substituted to span the space where such columns were omitted. Had each of the 1,387 squares of which the plan consists had its complement of columns to have perfected each cube, 1,502 would have been required; but the formation of the wider openings occasioned only 1,106 to be employed, so that, by the omission of a third, the courts, nave, and transepts acquired their admired proportions. Each of the 1,387 squares was 576 superficial feet, or a total of 798,912 superficial feet. The columns being 8 inches in diameter, the area of the section of the whole 1,106 was 380 superficial feet, or the points of support were a trifle more than a 2,000th of the entire area, for $\frac{798912}{380} = 2,102$.

When we compare the Crystal Palace with one of the lightest constructed basilicas of ancient Rome, we are astonished at the difference in the proportions. For instance, the total area of the basilica of St. Paul without the walls of Rome, was 108,000 superficial feet; while the points of support were 12,000, or one ninth. The Crystal Palace, which was seven times the area of the basilica of St. Paul, had it been constructed in a similar manner, would have required 84,000 superficial feet for the points of support, instead of 380 superficial feet.

In the Saxon cathedrals, one third of the entire area was employed for walls and piers; in the Pantheon at Rome, one quarter; in St. Paul's, London, one sixth; and in most of the cathedrals constructed from the 12th to the 15th century, the same proportions are practised; but we have never hitherto seen any attempt to lessen the proportions of the supports beyond a twentieth of the entire area, when the ordinary building materials, as brick or stone, have been employed, whilst in this instance iron columns are found sufficiently strong, when they have the proportion of a 2,000th part of the whole, or are one hundred times less in section than their points of support, estimated as a twentieth of the whole, and which we have considered as the lightest of the constructions hitherto practised; the round Temple of Claudius at Rome being the example. Tredgold calculated that an iron column of cast iron 8 inches in diameter, and 24 feet high, will carry nearly 50 tons, or 1,106, 55,300 tons; so that, if each of 1,387 squares had to sustain 30 tons, there would be ample strength, this not amounting to more than 41,610 tons.

In preparing the foundations for the columns, great care was taken to arrive at the gravel, upon which a bed of concrete was thrown; and it was estimated that a pressure per superficial foot of $2\frac{1}{2}$ tons should be provided for. The concrete varied in depth from 3 to 4 feet, and was finished by covering the top with a surface of fine mortar, worked even and with a level face. On this was laid a base plate for each column, the lower part consisting of a horizontal plate having attached to it a vertical tube of the form of the column it was to carry. The length of these base plates was from north to south, so that the water brought down by the columns from the roof might run in the direction from east to west. Into the sockets, cast iron pipes 6 inches in diameter were inserted, for the purpose of conveying the water into the cisterns and tanks provided to receive it.

At the upper portion of the base plate four holes were cast, in as many projections, which answered to others at the foot of the column to be placed upon it, which, when fixed, was secured by nuts. Between the shaft and its base, pieces of canvas dipped in white lead were introduced before the joints were secured, which were thus rendered watertight. The columns were 8 inches in diameter, and those on the ground floor 18 feet $5\frac{1}{2}$ inches in height, being cast hollow to allow of a current for the rain water; the strength of these columns was increased by four projecting ribs, and by the form of angular additions made to receive the nuts and screws.

The Crystal Palace at Sydenham had also the *simple cube* as the nucleus of which this vast

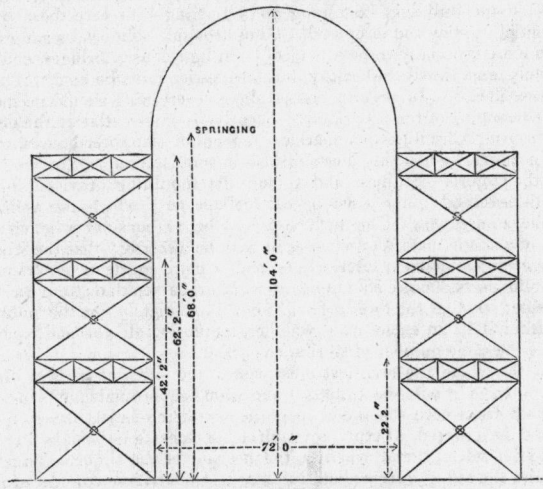

Fig. 1342.　　SECTION OF THE CRYSTAL PALACE, SYDENHAM.

edifice was composed; and the simplicity of its form enabled the constructors, by a small variety of castings, to execute the whole. The perfection of the work, as it was delivered to the artificer to be put together, abridged much of his labours, and enabled him to perform an apparent quantity of work in a very small space of time. It was to this locality that the materials of the Hyde Park building were removed and readapted to a much more extensive erection. The same dimensions of the cube were adopted. Three of these cubes, placed one on the other, formed the side galleries, as seen in the section *fig.* 1342.

The omission of six such cubes measures the width and height of the nave to the level of the springing of the arched covering; such are the simple proportions composing this vast structure.

On the ground-floor is laid boarding $1\frac{1}{2}$ inches in thickness, $\frac{1}{2}$ an inch apart, upon joists 7 inches by $2\frac{1}{2}$ inches, which rest upon sleepers 13 inches by $3\frac{1}{4}$ inches, placed 8 feet apart.

The second tier of columns are 16 feet $7\frac{1}{4}$ inches long, with connecting pieces 3 feet $4\frac{1}{2}$ inches deep, and a similar girder to those below. The third tier of columns and connecting pieces in every case are the same as the second.

CHAP. V.

PUBLIC AND PRIVATE BUILDINGS.

Sect. I.

GENERAL OBSERVATIONS.

2861. This chapter will be devoted to such remarks on public and private buildings as may be necessary to guide the architect in their general composition. To enter into a detail of each would be impossible, neither indeed could it be useful, for there are rarely two buildings destined to the same purpose which could be erected exactly similar. More or less accommodation may be required in one than another. The site may not be suitable for the reception of similar buildings. A city will require very different buildings as to magnitude from those necessary for a town, besides many other considerations which will immediately occur to the reader.

2862. In designing public and private buildings the first object of the architect is to make himself acquainted with the uses for which the building is destined, and the consequent suitableness of the design for its purpose. He must enter into the spirit which ought to pervade the building, examining and adjusting with care those qualities which are most essential to the end proposed. Thus, though solidity be an essential in all buildings, it is more especially to be attended to in lighthouses, bridges, and the like. In hospitals, not only must the site be healthy, but the interior must be kept wholesome by ventilation and other means. In private houses almost everything should be sacrificed to the convenience and comfort of the proprietor. Security is an essential in the design and construction of prisons. Cleanliness in markets and public slaughter-houses, which we hope will, on every account, be ultimately established in suburbs, and not in the heart of every great town of the empire. Stillness and tranquillity should be provided for in places of study; cheerfulness and gaity must be the feelings with which the architect arranges places of public amusement. The next step will be to consider whether the building should consist of a single mass, and whether it will be necessary that the whole should be solid, or whether it should open interiorly on one or more courts or quadrangles; whether the different solid parts should communicate with or be separate from each other. He must also consider whether the building will abut immediately on the public way, or be placed away from it in an enclosure; whether, moreover, all the solid parts should or should not have the same number of stories.

2863. From the whole the architect must pass to the different parts or divisions, determining which of them should be principal and which subordinate; which should be near and which distant from each other, and consequently their relative places and dimensions; how they should be covered, whether by vaulting or flooring; if the former, what species of vault should be selected, and whether the bearing of the timbers or the extent of the vault will require the aid of intermediate columns. Under these considerations, the sketch being made, the interaxal divisions of each apartment set out and written thereon, the architect may add them together, and thus ascertain the whole number of interaxal divisions, so that he may see that they can be contained on the given site. This done, he should take care that none of the interaxes are too wide or too narrow compared with the scale. Should that be the case, the number of interaxal divisions must be increased or diminished accordingly, either throughout or in those parts wherein the arrangement is defective.

2864. As the number of interaxes is greater or less in the apartments, so we may now determine the order to be used below the springing of the arches. On a sketch thus

conducted we shall have little more to do than to determine the profiles, ornaments, and other detail that the edifice requires. The student, by pursuing the course thus pointed out, will soon find his progress much advanced in the facility and success of designing. It is the course indicated by common sense as much in the study of the art as in the composition of designs, both of which are but an uninterrupted series of observations and reasonings.

Sect. II.

BRIDGES.

2865. Unless the design for a bridge be triumphal (a species now quite out of use), the composition can scarcely possess too much simplicity. If, indeed, in the design of a bridge we strictly adhere to the principles which regulate its convenience, stability, and economy, it will possess every beauty that can be desired. It is clear, therefore, that all applications of columns to the piers of bridges will fall under our severest censure. They can be of no service to the fabric, and are therefore unsuitable and absurd; their use moreover is a great waste of money, hence they are violations of an economical disposition in the design. We may, for illustration sake, point to the last bridge of importance erected in this country, viz. London Bridge, which is well and properly designed in comparison with Waterloo Bridge, which, though not behind the other in the requisites of strength and solidity, is inferior in the unfortunate application of columns to its piers. Had they been omitted, the deserved reputation of the engineer under whose designs it was executed would have been greatly increased, were his reputation and well-earned fame in jeopardy. The same comparison may be made between the bridge at Neuilly and that of Louis XVI., now the bridge *de la Concorde*. In the last decoration is attempted, in the former it is avoided: the last is hideous, the first agreeable.

2866. There are certain rules respecting bridges which must not be lost sight of, whereof the principal one is, that their direction must, if possible, be at right angles to the stream, and in the line too of the streets which they connect on the opposite banks of the stream. From a want of regard to these points many unfortunate blunders have been committed, which a prodigal expenditure of public money will not afterwards rectify, as we have seen in the operations consequent on the rebuilding of London Bridge. We allude to this point without the intent of blaming the parties concerned, but rather as a beacon to warn future authorities of the rock on which they may be wrecked.

2867. We had almost determined not to have introduced the section now under our pen, from the circumstance of the course of employment of the architect having latterly been so changed in favour of the engineer; but on reflection we have thought it proper, however short the notice, to say at least a little on the subject, which may be useful, from the engineer, strictly speaking, having but rarely the views in his designs of an accomplished artist; and we say this without the smallest feeling against or disrespect to the very able body of men called engineers in this country. On the equilibrium of arches and their piers, which are the chief parts of a bridge, we have in a previous part of the work already spoken, and so far explained our views on those points as to render further discussion here unnecessary. In most of the bridges of the ancients the arches were semicircular, in those of modern date they have been segmental or semi-elliptical. The last two forms are very much more suitable, because of the freer passage of the stream, especially in the case of floods.

2868. In the bridge at Pavia, over the Ticino, which is of an early period, and also a covered bridge, (a practice useless perhaps, but not uncommon in Italy and other parts of the Continent,) the arches are pointed; a form very favourable in every respect, and most especially so in rivers subject to sudden inundations, but unfavourable certainly in cases where the span of the arch is required to have a large width in proportion to its height. But the bridge just named has no common comparison with the ancient bridge. The effect resultant from its disposition is nevertheless satisfactory and magnificent, which abundantly proves that forms and proportions have less influence in producing beauty than have the qualities of propriety and simplicity.

2869. The position of a bridge should be neither in a narrow part nor in one liable to swell with tides or floods, because the contraction of the waterway increases the depth and velocity of the current, and may thus endanger the navigation as well as the bridge itself. It is the common practice, except under extraordinary circumstances, to construct bridges with an odd number of arches, for the reason, among many others, that the stream being usually strongest in the middle, egress is there better provided by the central arch. Further, too, if the bridge be not perfectly horizontal, symmetry results by the sides rising towards the centre, and the roadway may be made one continued curve. When the roadway of a bridge is horizontal, the saving of centring for the arches is considerable because two sets of centres will be sufficient for turning all the arches. If, however, the bridge be

higher in the middle than at the extremities, the arches on each side of that in the centre must diminish similarly, so that they may be respectively symmetrical on each side of the centre. From this disposition beauty necessarily results, and the centring for one of the sides equally suits the other. A bridge should be constructed with as few arches as possible, for the purpose of allowing a free passage for the water, as well as for the vessels that have to pass up and down the stream, not to mention the saving of materials and labour where the piers and centres are fewer in number. If the bridge can be constructed with a single arch, not more should be allowed. The piers must be of sufficient solidity to resist the thrust of the arch, independent of the counter thrust from the other arches; in which case the centring may be struck without the impendent danger of overturning the pier left naked. The piers should also be spread on their bases as much as possible, and should diminish gradually upwards from their foundations. The method now usually employed for laying the foundations is by means of coffer-dams, which are large enclosures formed by piling round the space occupied by the pier so as to render it water-tight, after which the water is pumped out, and the space so enclosed kept dry till the pier is built up to the average level of the water. When, however, the ground is loose, to the method mentioned recourse cannot so well be had; and then caissons must be employed, which are a species of flat-bottomed boat, wherein the pier is built up to a certain height and then sunk over the place where it is intended to remain, the bed of the river having been previously dredged out to receive it, or piles driven on which it may lodge when the sides of the chest or caisson are knocked away. The centre should be so constructed as to be unsusceptible of bending or swerving while the arches are in the course of construction, or its form will be crippled. We have diverged a little from the limits by which this section should have been circumscribed, because no other place in the work allowed us to offer the practical observations here submitted to the reader.

Sect. III.

CHURCHES.

2870. The churches whereof we propose speaking are not such as the present commissioners for building churches in this country sanction, but true good churches, such as appeared here under the reign of Queen Anne; true honest churches, one whereof is better than a host of the brick Cockney-Gothic things that are at present patronised, wherein the congregations are crammed to suffocation and not accommodated. These, therefore, we shall leave to the care of the peculiar school in which they originated, and the society to which they more properly belong, to speak of buildings that deserve the name. Neither do we think it useful to inquire into the designs of the temples of the ancients, seeing that paganism has passed away, never to return. The largest of these temples compared to the cathedrals of the moderns was but a small affair.

2871. The early Christian worship, attended by large congregations, required for its exercise edifices whose interiors were of great extent and well lighted. Nothing was so well adapted for the purpose as the basilicæ, which, bearing the name from their resemblance to the ancient courts of justice, were raised for the purpose. Such was that of St. Paul without the walls of Rome (*figs.* 141. and 142.), the ancient St. Peter's, and many others. That of S. Giovanni Laterano was divided by four ranks of columns, which supported the walls, carrying the roofs of five aisles formed by the ranks of columns, the middle one or nave being wider and higher than the others. Each aisle being lower than that adjoining parting from the centre, admitted lights to be introduced in the several walls. The direction of the length of the nave and aisles was from east to west, and was crossed by a transverse nave called a transept from north to south. In front an ample porch or portico was provided for the assembling of the people, and for their shelter from the seasons. The distribution we have just described was, as we have mentioned in an earlier part of this work, the type of the Gothic cathedral, though it passed through two or three steps before the adaptation assumed the magnificence that would have been displayed in the church at Cologne had that structure ever been completed.

2872. The portico we consider essential to any building which deserves the name of a church, not less on account of the beauty it imparts to the edifice than for its use.

2873. The use of the modern church being the same as that of the first Christian basilicæ, it may be doubted whether for extremely large assemblies a better disposition could be chosen. The desire, however, of novelty, says Durand, induced Bramante to imitate the temple of Peace in the design for the new church of St. Peter, although that building was less a temple than a public depôt or treasury destined by Vespasian to receive the spoils from Judea. The desire, moreover, continues that author, of surpassing the ancients, by gathering into a single edifice the beauties of several, induced the same architect to

crown the edifice imitated from the temple of Peace with another, imitated from the Pantheon; and in this country the same sort of thing was done by Wren in St. Paul's.

2874. It is easy to perceive that these buildings are not so well calculated for worship as the ancient basilicæ. The obstruction to seeing and hearing caused by the large piers of the modern churches is a great defect when compared with the little obstruction that the columns of the basilica present. But this is not the only blemish in the cathedral of Italian origin, as may be shown from the fact of basilicæ of the time of Constantine being still in existence; whilst the church of St. Peter, erected long posterior to that period, would in this day have been a heap of ruins, but for the enormous repairs constantly bestowed on the fabric, and the iron chains with which the dome has been girt. The cost is another serious objection to them, most especially in the construction of their domes, which are, with their tambours, buildings deficient in real solidity, from the large portion of false bearing they must involve; creating a very different sensation to that experienced in viewing the lantern of a Gothic cathedral, as at Peterborough and Ely, to which, without being insensible to the beauties of St. Peter's, St. Paul's, and other buildings of the class, we do not hesitate to give the preference.

2875. The facilities of designing a church on the principle of the basilica will be obviously those of interaxal divisions, and will not require further developement. The same method will be useful in designing the smaller parish church, with its nave and an aisle on each side, which is not only the most economical, but the best form. It was that which best pleased Sir C. Wren, whose churches are generally so planned; and we shall here give a short account of one of his best of this form, that of St. James's, Westminster, whose interior is worthy of all praise. It is an excellent example of Wren's love of harmony in proportions; the breadth being half the sum of its height and length, its height half its length, and its breadth the sesquialtera of its height: the numbers are 84, 63, and 42 feet. The church is divided transversely into three unequal parts, by a range of six columns on each side the nave, forming aisles which are each one fifth of the whole breadth, the remaining three fifths being given to the breadth of the nave. The roof is carried on these columns, and is as great a proof of the consummate skill of the architect as any portion of the fabric of St. Paul's, on account of its extreme economy and durability. It is not further necessary to describe the building; but the observations of the architect upon it are of the utmost value, emanating from such a man, to the church-builders of the present day, if it be possible to reclaim them from their pasteboard style. " I can hardly think it possible." says our architect, " to make a single room so capacious, with pews and galleries, as to hold above two thousand persons, and all to hear the service, and both to hear distinctly and see the preacher. I endeavoured to effect this in building the parish church of St. James's, Westminster, which, I presume, is the most capacious, with these qualifications, that hath yet been built; and yet at a solemn time, when the church was much crowded, I could not discern from a gallery that two thousand were present. In this church I mention, though very broad, and the middle nave arched up, yet as there are no walls of a second order, nor lanterns, nor buttresses, but the whole roof rests upon the pillars, as do also the galleries, I think it may be found beautiful and convenient, and, as such, the cheapest of any form I could invent." On the place of the pulpit in a church of this class, the same architect continues: " Concerning the placing of the pulpit, I shall observe, a moderate voice may be heard fifty feet distant before the preacher, thirty feet on each side, and twenty behind the pulpit; and not this, unless the pronunciation be distinct and equal, without losing the voice at the last word of the sentence, which is commonly emphatical, and if obscured spoils the whole sense. A Frenchman is heard further than an English preacher, because he raises his voice, and not sinks his last words. I mention this insufferable fault in the pronunciation of some of our otherwise excellent preachers, which schoolmasters might correct in the young, as a vicious pronunciation, and not as the Roman orators spoke: for the principal verb is in Latin usually the last word; and if that be lost, what becomes of the sentence?" Speaking of the dimensions of a church, the following are Wren's own words, after stating that a proposed church may be 60 feet broad, and 90 feet long, " besides a chancel at one end, and the belfry and portico at the other." " These proportions," he says, " may be varied; but to build more room than that every person may conveniently hear and see, is to create noise and confusion. A church should not be so filled with pews, but that the poor may have room enough to stand and sit in the alleys, for to them equally is the gospel preached. It were to be wished there were to be no pews, but benches; but there is *no stemming the tide of profit*, and the advantage of pew-keepers; especially, too, since by pews in the chapels of ease the minister is chiefly supported." We shall close the section by the following quotation from the same admirable artist. Quaint though the language now seem, and simple as the mind of the writer, it is of great value, and would be respected by any but commissioners for building churches. " As to the situation of the churches, I should propose they be brought as forward as possible into the larger and more open streets, not in obscure lanes, nor where coaches will be much obstructed in the passage. Nor are we, I think, too nicely to observe east or west in the position, unless it falls out

properly: such fronts as shall happen to lie most open in view should be adorned with porticoes, both for beauty and convenience; which, together with handsome spires or lanterns, rising in good proportion above the neighbouring houses, (of which I have given several examples in the city, of different forms,) may be of sufficient ornament to the town, without a great expense for enriching the outward walls of the churches, in which plainness and duration ought principally, if not wholly, to be studied." Such are the common-sense remarks of a man of whom this country has to be proud, but who died neglected, the common fate of all artists who do not minister to the vanity of their employers.

2876. Churches are usually constructed on the plan of a *Greek cross*, which is that wherein the length of the transverse part, or transept, is equal to that of the nave; of a *Latin cross*, wherein the nave is longer than the transept; *in rotondo*, where the plan is a circle; *simple*, where the church has only a nave and choir; *with aisles*, when a subdivision occurs on each side of the nave; and those with aisles, as we have above seen, may have more than one of such aisles on each side of the nave.

Sect. IV.

PALACES.

2877. We regret that in this country we can offer no model of a palace for the student. Windsor Castle, with all its beauties, which however consist more in site and scenery than in the disposition of a palace, will not assist us. A palace is properly an edifice destined not only for the residence of the sovereign or prince, but for the reception also of persons who have the privilege of public or private audience. It being impossible for the whole of the parties to be present together, besides the apartments which are occupied by the sovereign and his family, there must be ample room and apartments for the attendants in waiting of every degree, and the consequent accessories. A palace should be disposed with porticoes, vestibules, galleries, halls of waiting suited to every season, wherein those to be admitted may wait with convenience and comfort till their turn of admission arrives. It is evident that, from the nature of such an edifice, much magnificence should be displayed in it. The palaces of the Escurial, Versailles, and the Tuileries are, though extremely spacious, and consequently imposing, but ill disposed and imperfect examples of a palace. Perhaps the most perfect in Europe is that of the King of Naples at Caserta, commenced in 1752, which is described by Milizia as follows:—" The plan of this palace is a vast rectangle, 731 feet long from east to west, 569 from north to south, and 106 feet in height. The interior is divided into four courts, 162 feet by 244. The depth of building that surrounds these courts, in which are the apartments, passages, &c., is 80 feet, including the thickness of the walls, which are in some instances 15 feet. The two principal façades have five stories besides that below the ground, and each contains thirty-seven windows. There are three entrances, one in the centre, and the others at equal distances between it and the extreme angles, where, as well as in the centre, the building breaks forward a little, is carried up to the height of 60 feet, and formed into pavilions by columns 42 feet high. Thus the whole height of the building is 102 feet from the foundation to the top of the pavilion, at the angles 162 feet, and in the centre 190 feet. The basement, which is rusticated, comprises the lower offices, the ground floor and its mezzanine. Above is placed an Ionic order of columns and pilasters, which contains the two ranges of state apartments; the lower windows are ornamented with pediments; in the frieze are introduced the windows of the upper mezzanine. The centre entrance leads to a superb portico, which traverses the building from north to south, and is sufficiently spacious to allow carriages to pass under from either façade to the centre of the building, where is a large octangular vestibule, which unites the arms of the cross produced by dividing the plan into four courts: two sides of the octagon are open to the portico, four to the four courts, one to the grand staircase, and the eighth is occupied by a statue of Hercules crowned by Virtue, with this inscription :—

'Virtus post fortia facta coronat.' "

2878. " The grand staircase, which is on the right, is lighted by twenty-four windows, and decorated in a beautiful style. At the first landing it is divided into two flights; the hundred steps of which it is composed are 18 feet long, and each of one piece of marble; it is lighted also from the top by a double skylight. The upper vestibule is also octangular, and surrounded by twenty-four columns of yellow marble 18 feet high. Four doors lead from thence to the apartments, the one opposite the landing to the chapel, that to the right to the apartments of the king, which comprehend the south-west angle of the building overlooking the sea and the plains of Naples and Capua. To the left are the apartments of the queen, occupying the north-west angle, the remainder of these floors being occupied by the princes. The chambers throughout are vaulted, and admirably arranged; the

apartments of the king and queen are separated by a gallery 138 feet long, 42 wide, and 52 high. The palace contains a small elegant theatre, on a circular plan, divided into nine compartments, with four tiers of boxes. The chapel is rectangular in its plan, with the end terminated semicircularly, and decorated with isolated Corinthian columns on pedestals, with an entablature, in which the cornice is not omitted. The marbles and sculptures throughout are of the richest kind; the apartments generally well arranged and distributed, of magnificent dimensions, and of various forms. The whole is a rare assemblage of vastness, regularity, symmetry, richness, ease, and elegance. The multiplicity of windows may certainly be a little at variance with propriety.

" But the most wonderful part of this grand work has not as yet been described. There are ranges of aqueducts of a great height, and of sufficient length to unite the two Tifati mountains near the Furche Caudine. The waters on the mountains are collected into a canal for the purpose of supplying these aqueducts, and conducted to various lakes and fountains of every description. To the embellishments," adds Milizia, " of this royal residence are added a convenience and solidity that throw into shade all that has been done before or since." The plans, &c. of this palace may be referred to in Durand's *Parallele des Edifices.*

2879. Great as this work is, it would not have eclipsed the palace at Whitehall projected by Inigo Jones, and published in Kent's *Designs,* (see *fig.* 207., *supra,*) had the edifice, whereof the banqueting-house is not the hundredth part, been carried to completion. This palace has already been described in the First Book of this work, in turning to which the reader will find that the proposed palace consisted of six courts, and, with greater beauties of composition, would have occupied a much larger site than the palace at Caserta.

2880. We have been diffuse in the description of the last-named palace, because it contains the leading, and, indeed, governing principles, upon which the palace for a sovereign should be constructed; and from the description, the student might almost be at once led to the design of such an edifice.

2881. The designs which Bernini made at the request of Louis XIV., instigated, no doubt, by his minister Colbert, (for they were both of them lovers and patrons of the fine arts,) for uniting the Tuileries and Louvre, would, had they been executed, added another palace to which the student might have been referred for information on the subject of palaces. They may be seen in Durand's " Parallel " above mentioned, and, we think, will bear out the propriety of reference; and we fully agree with Le Grand, except in the inflated language he adopts, that " Le gouvernement qui attachera son nom a cette execution sera proclamé grand dans la posterité; il honorera la nation par les arts en reunissant ainsi les beautés eparses, incomplétes de ces deux palais, pour n'en former qu'un seul, il s'assuréra la gloire d'effacer par cette merveille celles dont, excepté les pyramides d'Egyptes l'existence n'est plus que dans l'histoire."

2882. It is almost unnecessary to observe, that the site on which a palace is to be seated must be open and free in every respect, that a large expanse of gardens should be attached to it for the use of the public as well as the sovereign, in which respect the palaces of the Tuileries and Versailles are unparalleled. All should have a royal bearing, parsimony being inadmissible in works of this nature.

Sect. V.

GOVERNMENT OFFICES.

2883. The offices of government should be designed consistently as regards their distribution and magnificence, with some respect to the power and importance of the nation for whose use they are to be constructed. Whilst on the Continent, and especially in Paris, some of the finest examples of art provide for the convenience of the different departments, the only building that can be named here in this respect are the offices at Somerset House, built by the late Sir W. Chambers. And herein so mean and indifferent to the arts has of late been every set of ministers in this country, that but for the appropriation of the eastern part of the site to a joint-stock college, it is probable the river front would never have been finished.

2884. The nature of the disposition of government buildings must of course depend on the particular department for which the building is destined, full information on which must be had in every particular before the architect can begin to imagine the building to be designed. The most ample space should be allotted to them, and no rooms for the performance of the duties attached to the department should be allowed above the first story over the ground floor. The public, indeed, ought not to have to ascend or descend even one flight of steps. The access to the different apartments should be spacious and easy;

the quadrangles, where they are necessary, should be ample, so as to afford abundance of light and air; porticoes should be provided for the shelter of the public who have to transact business, and the façades should be in a broad simple style.

2885. Without intending any affection for the fanciful style adopted by their architect, we would, in this country, point to the mode in which the offices at the Bank of England were disposed and planned by the late Sir John Soane, and the beautiful method of lighting, as highly valuable studies for the architect. The skill here exhibited by him, if not obscured by his successors, and the restless desire of change that the directors seem to exhibit, will be lasting monuments of that architect's ability, however disfigured his designs may have been by the caprice of their ornaments.

2886. The splendour of the government offices in this country seems, in every case, to be in an inverse ratio to the renown of the department. Thus, let the Admiralty be the example for consideration, and it would be difficult to decide which was worst, the interior or the exterior. On the Treasury jumble of buildings, it would be difficult to bestow a serious word. If the country be too poor to accomplish all the works at once which would be necessary for putting us in possession of buildings worthy the country, surely designs on a proper scale for rebuilding all these edifices might be made, and rigidly adhering to the designs approved after due consideration, portions might be annually executed, so as to distribute the outlay over a series of years. But we regret to say that we fear any hints under this section will be thrown away, while political parties are contending for power, and consider the comfort of the public and the promotion of the fine arts subjects of comparative insignificance. The source of the evil is in the nature of the constitution; and though, speaking as Englishmen, we do not wish to see that changed, yet we think a little more absolute power, under which there is invariably less jobbing, would be in some measure beneficial to the arts.

2887. We have hinted that there is no government building to which we should wish to refer the reader, Somerset House excepted. In Paris he will find an abundance of examples. The Admiralty there, a recent building of the most simple exterior, on which there are neither dolphins, tridents, nor anchors, as in that near Charing Cross, is a stupendous mass of building, well calculated for the narrow street in which it stands, to which it imparts unmeasured dignity. The *Garde Meuble*, as it was formerly called, in the Place de la Concorde (formerly de Louis XV.) is one of the most beautiful compositions in Europe. This is, perhaps, an example rather too florid for imitation (we do not mean in lines, but in spirit) in this country, though it is known that a well and richly-designed building costs little, if any, more than a bad, ill-digested one. The Mint of Paris is another of the French government offices worthy of the nation. But we need not multiply the instances, Paris being now almost as well known to the Englishman as London itself. It is, however, to be recollected that in France all the government buildings are of as much interest to the government in the provinces as in its metropolis, and that the great hospital at Lyons, by Soufflout, is not surpassed in Europe. In England, we know not one that approaches it.

Sect. VI.

COURTS OF LAW.

2888. A court of law in this country, speaking in more senses than one, but chiefly, here, to preserve the gravity of our work architecturally, is a building in which every one, whose business unfortunately leads him to it, sits in pain, the judges and counsel excepted. Attorneys, witnesses, jury, and audience, or public, are equally doomed to be pent up and cramped like the poor sheep at Smithfield, or a sailor in the bilboes, if that punishment be still in existence. The practice is infamous and inexcusable; it originates not with the architect, but with the government, which affords neither space nor money for the erection of courts suitable to the administration of justice, though the public are, by a pleasing assumption of the administrators of the laws, supposed to know all the decisions that take place in them, and treated by an answer to those that plead ignorance, which, but from the little of their proceedings that oozes out by that useful organ, the public press, would really be the case — " Ignorantia non excusat legem." It came out in evidence before a committee of the House of Commons on the late rebuilding of the courts at Westminster, that Sir John Soane, their architect, was told by a chief of one of the courts then proposed to be built and since executed, that *his* court, as planned, would be quite large enough to hold all *that had any business there;* rather a strange dictum for a personage whose duty, sitting on the judgment-seat, was to tell the people that their unaffected ignorance of the laws he was sworn to administer was no excuse for violating the law which might bring them before him.

2889. We have thus prefaced our short observations on this section for the purpose of impressing on the mind of the architect who may be called on to furnish designs in the provinces (for in London there is not much chance of his employment on such an occasion), that there are other persons who have equal right to as good accommodation as the judges and the bar, who are extremely well paid for the duties they perform; the parties to which we allude being the jury who are to decide upon the evidence, the witnesses from whom such evidence is derived, the attorneys whose instructions to counsel are from instant to instant necessary for the proper conduct of a case, and, though last not least, the public, who have an undoubted right to be present, not only because they are entitled to instruct themselves, as the axiom requires, that they may not be ignorant of the law, but because, in this country, the conduct of the judge himself may be open to public opinion, and his character properly transmitted to posterity, and estimated by the public.

2890. After the foregoing remarks, we apprehend it will be scarcely necessary to impress on the mind of the architect the importance of providing an ample space for the audience or public, rooms for jurymen in waiting, and full space for the latter when they are placed in what is called their *box*, so that the pain of the body may not distract the mind from the evidence of the witnesses and the charge of the judge. The artist, therefore, must be careful to supply such accommodation as shall render the office of all parties engaged a pleasing duty rather than an irksome task.

2891. To every court of law should be attached a large vestibule or salon, sufficiently large to afford a promenade for those of all classes engaged in the courts. In Westminster, bad as the courts are, this is well provided in the magnificent room called Westminster Hall, to which had the courts that open on it been in character our opening observations had been spared. It is almost needless to observe that apartments and accommodation are to be provided for the robing and occasional refreshment of the judges, the bar, and the different officers attached to the court. In courts for the trial of felons it may be necessary, if the prison has no communication with the court, to add some few cells for securing criminals. This, however, will be dependent on the circumstance mentioned, and should be provided accordingly.

2892. In these, as in other buildings where there is often congregated a great number of persons, the entrances, and at the same time outlets, should be increased in number as much as convenience and the situation will permit; and another indispensable requisite is, that the court itself should be so placed in the design that no noise created on the outside of the building may be heard in the interior, so as to interfere with the attention of those engaged on the business before them.

2893. In the provinces the observations we have made may be of some use to the student, and on this ground we have thought it our duty to offer them.

Sect. VII.

TOWN HALLS.

2894. The town hall of a city or town will necessarily vary with their extent and opulence. In towns of small extent it should stand in the market-place; indeed, in a large proportion of the towns of this country the ground floor is usually on columns, and forms the corn market of the place, the upper floor being generally sufficiently spacious for transacting its municipal business. Where the sessions and assizes, as in cities, are held in the town hall, it is necessary to provide two courts, one for the civil and the other for the criminal trials; and in this case the observations on courts of law in the preceding section equally apply to this in that respect.

2895. In cities and corporations where much municipal business occurs, the number of apartments must of course be increased to meet the exigencies of the particular case; and, if possible, a large hall should be provided for the meetings of the corporation. A certain appearance of its being the property of the public is the character to be imparted to it, and this character must be stamped on the disposition as well as the elevation. Thus, on the ground floor of the first class of town halls, courts, porticoes, or arcades, and spacious staircases should prepare for and lead to the large apartments and courts of law on the first floor. Every means should be employed in providing ample ingress and egress to the persons assembling. Fire-proof rooms, moreover, should be always provided for the records and accounts belonging to the town. The exterior of the building should not be highly decorated, but designed with simplicity, yet with majesty, as it is an index to the wealth and importance of the place for whose use it is erected.

2896. For the disposition of these buildings the student may turn with profit to the examples abroad, in which, generally, apartments are provided for every branch of the

government of the city. Durand, in his *Parallèle des Edifices*, has given several examples. We have chosen the Belgian examples, as most splendid, to remark upon, but it is not to be understood that fine specimens are only to be found in that country. France and Germany (see *Builder* for 1866) abound with such edifices, and a very voluminous work might be produced on the subject.

2896a Of the four principal hôtels de ville, that of Bruges is the earliest. Its date is 1377, and it is chiefly remarkable for the original wooden roof to the great hall. The Hôtel de Ville of Brussels is, as an edifice, the first of the class, whether considered by itself, or as the dominant feature of a *place* surrounded by buildings of the most unique and varied appearance, the most interesting that we recollect anywhere to have contemplated. It appears to have been completed in 1445. *Fig.* 1343. is a view of the east façade. An ancient building which occupied this site, has not been entirely removed ; for in the northern

Fig. 1343.   HOTEL DE VILLE; BRUSSELS.

side from the tower, the piers of the loggia, which on the basement extends along the front, consist, at least three of them, of columns whose date is evidently a century earlier, and which it is probable were left when the main front of the building was carried up. Indeed, it seems highly probable that when the architect Jean van Ruysbroeck undertook the tower, his part of the work, the hôtel was in existence as high as the one-pair floor. The whole of the tower seems rather later than the date above given, which accords well enough with the northern wing. The authorities we have looked into scarcely, however, admit us to doubt its correctness. As the building stands executed, taking one of the bays on the northern side as a measuring unit, there are three measuring the central space for the tower, ten for the north wing, and eleven for the south wing; the height, to the top of the parapet, nine ; to the ridge of the roof, thirteen ; to the top of the spire, thirty-three. The tracery on the spire is very elegant, and is pierced throughout. It is 364 feet high, and crowned with a copper gilt colossal statue of St. Michael, the patron of the city, 18 feet high, which is so well balanced upon the pivot on which it stands that it is susceptible of motion with a very gentle wind. The interior of the edifice has a quadrangular court, with two modern fountains, statues of river gods with reeds and vases, as usual in

such cases. Besides the *Grande Salle*, there are many interesting apartments, some whereof possess ceilings of great beauty. This fine monument is perhaps the most admirable example of the adaptation of the style to secular architecture that can be quoted.

2896*b*. Smaller in plan, but more beautiful and symmetrical, is the hôtel de ville of Louvain. It is the most perfect, in every respect, of this class of buildings in Europe. Nothing can surpass the richness and delicacy of the tracery upon it. Like that at Brussels, it consists of three stories, but has no tower. Commenced in 1448, it was not completed till 1463 by De Layens. It stands on a site of about 85 feet by 42 feet; so that it derives little advantage from its absolute magnitude, and perhaps appears less than it really is, from the great height of the roof, which is pierced by four tiers of dormers or lucarnes. The angles are flanked by turrets, of which some notion may be formed by reference to *fig.* 1344., and the ridge of the roof is received at each end by another turret corbelled over from the gables. The façade towards the *Place* extends rather more than the height, and is pierced with twenty-eight windows and two doorways, being ten openings in each story, the spaces between the windows being decorated with canopies, and groups of small figures from the Old Testament. some whereof are rather licentious. This charming edifice, which in its delicate rich tracery had suffered much from time and the elements, has, at the joint expense of the town and government,

Fig. 1344.　　　　HOTEL DE VILLE; LOUVAIN.

undergone a complete renovation. This has, stone by stone, been effected with great care and artistic skill by M. Goyers. The new work being executed in very soft stone, which, however, hardens with exposure to the air, it has been saturated with oil.

2896*c*. In form, though not in features, totally different from the hôtels de ville we have just left, is that at Ghent, never completed, but exhibiting, in what was executed of the design, a choice example of the last days of the flamboyant period. It was begun in 1481; in it are all those indications of change in the sofites and curves, as well as in the lines of the foliage and tracery, that eventually proved its downfall; and the style is now out of character with the habits of the age, from which alone a real style of architecture can ever spring. The subdivision of the building as to height is into two stories as to effect, though in

reality there are more; and the transoms, which abound in the apertures, seem to reign in accordance with the horizontal arrangement of lines which was so soon to supersede the flaming curves that had prevailed for nearly half a century. The elegant turret or tribune at the corner, with the part adjoining, in the richest flamboyant Gothic, is by Eustace Polleyt, 1527–60; the other façade 1600–20 has columns of three different orders superposed.

2897. The most celebrated of town halls in Europe is that of Amsterdam, erected during the first half of the seventeenth century by Van Campen. The design is given in Durand's *Parallèle*, and also forms the subject of a volume, in folio, published in Holland; the cost of its erection was more than thirty millions of florins, and the fabric stands, they say, on 13,659 piles, which were required from the marshy nature of the ground. The plan is nearly a square; it is 282 feet long and 255 feet wide, and its height is 116 feet. To describe the disposition of the plan would be impossible; it can only be comprehended by reference to it. The ground story in the principal façade forms the basement on which rises an order of Corinthian pilasters, containing two ranges of windows; then an entablature, and above that a repetition of similar pilasters, containing two ranges of windows. The latter are simple, having no ornament except a festoon between each range. At the angles are two pavilions, ornamented with four pilasters, and in the centre one with eight, which projects forward a little. On this a pediment rises ornamented with historical bas reliefs, and thereover, more distant, is an elegant cupola for the clock. Instead of one large principal entrance there are seven small ones, alluding, as it is said, to the seven united provinces; and it is also pleasantly said that the smallness of the provinces are typical of the smallness of the doors.

2898. We cannot, however, laud the composition of this building, which, by the way, encloses the bank and public treasury. Its merit consists mainly in the disposition of the plan, the restraint in decoration, and the good construction of the work, whilst its imposing effect results from its magnitude as a mass. The use of the Corinthian and Composite orders for such a building was almost an abuse, for their proportions vary so little from each other as almost to create confusion between the two. Again, the similarity of the subdivision in the two stories, each divided into two ranks of windows, produces a cold monotony. The windows too, without architraves, have an effect as mean as the festoons which are introduced between the windows are insipid. Neither will the excuse given for the seven small doors justify the introduction of such poverty in a building whose dimensions are so great, besides their appearance seeming to give strength to the impression that they are only entrances to the basement story. The student, on the subject of town halls, may be referred also to those of Antwerp and Maestricht and Louvain. And here we cannot refrain from alluding to the works we noticed but a little time past in the restoration, and indeed completion, of the Hotel de Ville at Paris, first commenced in 1533 on the designs of François de Cortonne, in what is now called the style of the renaissance. The additions which became necessary in consequence of the extended business of the city are executing in the same style, and will present one of the most picturesque features of the city. Such an occasion as this is a legitimate one for the employment of the style of the renaissance, and not in the trumpery stuff that appears in this country, without any solid reason for its adoption. The interior of this building, with its court or quadrangle, is not without grandeur; and the interior distribution of it, with its beautiful staircase, is a sufficient proof that what the Germans and their admirers now denominate " æsthetics" in art was well understood and practised in Italy, France, and even England, on the renaissance, whilst their country, as respects architecture, was in a state of barbarism. We regret we have not the opportunity of referring to any town hall in England which meets in all respects what we deem the requisites of such a building. We do not say that none such exist, only that it has not come to our knowledge.

Since the above was written, many buildings have been erected, which would, probably, have been deemed satisfactory. Such are St. George's Hall, at Liverpool; with the town halls at Leeds and Halifax.

Sect. VIII.

COLLEGES.

2899. A college, which is an establishment for the education of young men, generally consists in this country of one or more courts or quadrangles, round which are disposed the rooms for the students, with the chapel, library, and eating hall; apartments for the head of the establishment and for the fellows; a combination room, which is a spacious apart-

ment, wherein the latter assemble after dinner; kitchen, buttery, and other domestic offices, laitrines, gardens, &c.

2900. In these particulars, we are speaking of English habits, for on the Continent the college is quite a different sort of thing. As, however, we consider the best instruction to the student will be concise information on those which exist, we shall shortly mention the most celebrated abroad and in England.

2901. At Rome, the college formerly that of the Jesuits, now the Roman College, is a very large edifice, simple in character, as this species of building seems to demand. Its length is 328 feet, and its height, without the attic, 87 feet. Two large gateways are placed in the middle compartment, and form the entrances to the building. In these there is nothing particularly to admire, nor in the façade generally, which is encumbered, from the nature of the edifice, with a great number of windows. The great quadrangle is, however, one of the finest in Rome, consisting of two stories of arcades, a distribution particularly applicable to buildings of this class, and which we are surprised has never found adoption in this country. In these galleries the different classes or lecture rooms are placed, under their divisions of literæ humaniores, rhetoric, and philosophy. Had the building been finished as Ammanati designed it, there would not have been in Italy a finer structure nor one more suitable to its destination. It has, by the alterations from the original plan, been much cut up; yet it is a magnificent pile of building, consisting of corridors, dormitories, gardens, refectories, and other accessories, which, with the church which forms a part of the plan, occupy a circuit of upwards of 1500 feet. The other buildings in Rome which pass under the name of colleges are not to be considered as establishments for education, being destined to the study of theology and other sciences: such are the Propaganda and the Sapienza, which last is one of the finest modern buildings of the eternal city.

2902. At Genoa is a magnificent college, which was formerly the palace of the Balbi family, by whom it was given to the Jesuits for a place of education; but, from the original destination of the building, it possesses nothing of the essential character which belongs to an edifice of this class.

2903. Paris, we believe, still contains nine colleges, hardly one whereof, says the author of the article " College" in the *Encyclopedie Methodique*, deserves notice. The same writer says that in England alone are found examples of what a college ought to be; and from all that we have seen on the Continent, we believe him to have come thereon to a correct conclusion.

2904. The universities of Oxford and Cambridge furnish a study for the architect in this class of building nowhere else to be found; and though the greater part of their colleges are extremely irregular in plan, they are generally convenient in disposition and highly picturesque in effect. In Oxford, the most regular in plan is Queen's College, and this is of modern construction, having been commenced as late as 1710, and in the Italian style. We are not, however, about to describe the style, which is not an example for study, but the disposition of the building. The principal front stands towards the High Street. The whole site on which the college stands is 300 feet by 220, which is divided by the chapel and hall on the right and left of the intervening building into two spacious courts. The south court, which is that nearest the street, is 140 feet long and 130 broad, having an arcade round it on the south, east, and west sides. Over that on the west side are two stories, which contain the apartments of the fellows, those of the provost, and a gallery communicating with the hall and common or combination room. The east side, which is uniform with that on the west, comprises the apartments for students of the society, and on the north side are the chapel and hall. The south side of the court or quadrangle has no dwelling in it, but is composed of a decorated wall, in whose centre is the great entrance, above whose arch an open cupola stands upon columns, and under the cupola the statue of Queen Caroline, the consort of George II. The interior court or north quadrangle is 130 feet by 90. On the north, east, and south sides are provided apartments for the members of the society, and the west is occupied by the library: the entrance to it is by a passage between the hall and chapel. The dimensions of the hall are 60 by 30 feet; those of the chapel are necessarily, as to width, the same, but it is 100 feet long. The library, which was completed earlier than the rest of the building, is 123 feet long and 30 feet broad. That the student may form an idea of the accommodation afforded on the site described, it may be taken as holding about 170 persons, including the provost and fellows, whose apartments, of course, occupy a considerable portion of the space. Hawksmoor is, as we believe, the architect; certainly, as far as we can judge, not Sir Christopher Wren, to whom some have attributed it.

2905. We have no intention to pursue the description of the colleges in either of the universities. We have selected the above as a model of disposition only, because, as we have hinted, it is in very bad taste: so bad, indeed, in that respect, as to be a model for avoidance. We shall, however, give a few more memoranda as to the parts of colleges in existence, here merely observing that a bed and sitting room, both of moderate dimensions, are as much as can be afforded to the students of the establishment.

2906. Of the colleges in Oxford, Christchurch is past question the most magnificent. Its extent, towards the street, is 400 feet. Its hall is 115 feet long, 40 feet broad, and 50 feet in height, and the entrance to it is by a very noble staircase. The chapel is the cathedral of Oxford, and is 154 feet long, and the breadth, including aisles, 54 feet. The great quadrangle is nearly 280 feet square, and this communicates with another called Peckwater quadrangle, of considerable dimensions, in which, on the south side, stands the noble library of the college, the upper room whereof is 141 feet long, 30 feet broad, and 37 feet high. At the side of and adjoining the last are the Canterbury quadrangle and Fell's Buildings, and on the other side the chaplain's quadrangle. What is called the Christ-church Meadow, attached, affords the most delightful walks for the exercise and recreation of the members, being bounded on the east by the Cherwell, on the south by the Isis, and on the west by a branch of the same river. The whole establishment is worthy of the princely founder, whose spirit seems still to reign in the conduct of those connected with it. Such a magnificent foundation cannot elsewhere be referred to.

2907. In Cambridge, the library and court of Trinity College, the former one of the finest works of Wren, and the extraordinary and beautiful chapel of King's College, are the principal features of the university. There are also some beautiful pieces of architectural composition; but as there is nothing we could select as a model for a college, which is the principal object of the section, we do not consider it necessary to detain the reader by an account of them. We may, however, mention that the chapel of King's College is 316 feet long, 84 feet broad, and 90 feet from the ground to the top of the battlements. Corpus Christi College is, perhaps, the last college in either of the universities that has been rebuilt; but in disposition, and most especially in design, it is rather an index *rerum vitandarum* than a model we should recommend to the student's attention.

Sect. IX.

PUBLIC LIBRARIES.

2908. Although a public library would seem to require a grave and simple style of treatment, it is, nevertheless, properly susceptible of much richness, if the funds admit, and it comports with the surrounding buildings to use much decoration. A public library may be considered as the treasury of public knowledge; indeed its treasures are even more important to society than the public treasures of gold and silver. It is also to be considered as a temple consecrated to study. Security against fire is the first important consideration in its construction; indeed that point ought to be deemed indispensable; and the next consideration for the accomplishment of its purpose is quietness. The first requires that no materials except stone, brick, and iron should be employed in the walls, floors, and roofs; and the last, that it should stand far removed from a public thoroughfare. Within, especially in this climate, there can scarcely be too much light, because there are always modes of excluding the excess in the brightest days of our short summers; and in the dark days of our winters no such excess can occur. Neither should the light be placed high up for the purpose of obtaining more room for the presses which are to receive the books, because even a greater space may be obtained, as in the magnificent library at Trinity College, Cambridge, by Wren, by making the presses stand against the piers at right angles with the longitudinal walls, and placing the windows between them. Moreover, the presses, when placed longitudinally against the walls, the windows being above, have the titles of the books they contain indistinct, from being too much in shadow. The library just mentioned is in every respect one of the finest works of Sir Christopher Wren. It stands on an open arcade, at the north end whereof is a vestibule, whence the ascent is by a spacious staircase to the library itself, which is 200 feet long, 40 feet wide, and 38 feet high, floored with marble, and decorated with pilasters and an entablature of the Corinthian order. Though this library is of no mean extent, we do not adduce it as an example of a large public library suited to a nation, but as a perfect model of the mode of distribution, which might be carried in principle to any extent. If the readers be very numerous, a reading room, of course, becomes necessary, which should be placed as centrally as may be to the whole mass of building, so that the labour of the attendants may be lessened, and the readers at the same time more readily served with the books wanting. The best mode of warming the apartments is by a furnace and boilers, not at all adjoining to or communicating with the building, but by carrying pipes round the apartments or in the floor, through which pipes a constant circulation of the boiling liquid is kept up, and from which a radiation of the heat takes place.

2909. The most ancient and celebrated library in existence is that of the Vatican; in the latter respect, as well on account of its size as of the number of valuable manuscripts it con-

tains: it occupies in the suite of its apartments one of the sides of the Vatican 900 feet in length. The presses containing the books are decorated with the finest specimens of Etruscan vases. The long gallery terminates at one end by the Museum Christianum and the Stanza de' Papyri, and at the other end by the new museum, with which it communicates by a marble staircase. The ante-salon to the library is about 200 feet long and about 87 wide. In the architecture or arrangement there is nothing particularly to admire, and indeed it was not originally intended for the purpose to which it has been appropriated.

2910. We do not think it necessary to stop the reader for an account of the Medicean library at Florence, though the work of Michael Angelo. Its proportions are grand, but the details are as capricious as that great man could possibly have invented; but of the library of St. Mark at Venice we entertain the greatest admiration. We have already described this in the First Book when speaking of the Venetian school. Notwithstanding the difficulties that Sansovino had to encounter in respect of its site and connection with other buildings, which restricted the design in the façade, because of the height of the adjoining *Procurazie Vecchie*, and the width of the ground; — notwithstanding all these, and the jealousy of his enemies superadded, Palladio considered the success of it to have been so great as to have made it worthy of any age.

2911. The splendid collection of books at Paris, containing 900,000 and upwards printed volumes, called the Bibliothéque du Roi, is, speaking architecturally, though of immense extent, little more than a warehouse for holding the books: that, however, of the abbey of St. Geneviève in the same city, though containing less than a quarter of the number just mentioned of printed volumes and 30,000 MSS., is a well-conceived and well-designed building, and particularly suited to its destination. The plan is that of a large Greek cross, which affords on the plan four large halls, connected by a central circular apartment crowned with a dome. (This last named structure has since been entirely rebuilt; the present ornamental edifice was designed by M. Labrouste in 1843.)

2912. Perhaps one of the most absurd distributions of plan for the buildings under consideration is to be seen in the Radcliffe Library, at Oxford. It is circular on the plan, and hence vast loss of room is experienced; but we do not think it necessary further to enter into its demerits, merely stating here that it was unworthy of Gibbs, who in most of his works exhibited great good sense.

Sᴇᴄᴛ. X.

MUSEUMS.

2913. A museum is a building destined to the reception of literary or scientific curiosities, and for that of the works of learned men and artists. The term was first applied to that part of the palace at Alexandria appropriated solely to the purpose of affording an asylum for learned men; it contained buildings and groves of considerable magnificence, and a temple wherein was a golden coffin containing the body of Alexander. Men of learning were here lodged and accommodated with large halls for literary conversations, and porticoes and shady walks, where, supplied with every necessary, they devoted themselves entirely to study. The establishment is supposed to have been founded by Ptolemy Philadelphus, who here placed his library. It was divided into colleges or companies of professors of the several sciences, and to each of such professors was allotted a suitable revenue. Museums, in the modern sense of the word, began to be established about the sixteenth century, when collections were formed by most of the learned men who studied natural history.

2914. Museums on a small scale are becoming every day more common in the principal towns of this country, and we hope the day is not distant when none will be without its collections of science, literature, and art. Where economy requires it, and the collection in each department be not too large, the whole may be properly and conveniently comprised within one building. In respect of security against fire, and quietness of the situation, the same precautions will be necessary as are indicated for libraries in the preceding section, and must always be observed.

2915. Great skill is necessary in introducing the light properly on the objects in a museum, inasmuch as the mode of throwing the light upon objects of natural history is very different from that which is required for pictures, and this, again, from what sculpture requires.

2916. Specimens illustrating natural history sculpture, vases, and the like, should, if possible, be lighted vertically; and we have seen in subsec. 2747., where reference is made to the light introduced into the Pantheon, how very small an opening in a spherical ceiling will produce abundance of light. There are subjects, nevertheless, in all these classes, (in mineralogy for example,) for which strong side lights are essential to an advantageous exhibition of them. In such cases small recesses may be practised for the purpose At the

Hotel de Monnaies at Paris, the presses which contain the collection of mineralogy form a circle which encloses a small lecture theatre, and thus become doubly serviceable. We mention this *en passant* that the student may be aware how room is to be gained when the area of a site is restricted. Picture galleries in a museum, as elsewhere by themselves, when containing large paintings, should be lighted from above. In this case the lights should be in square or polygonal tambours, whose sashes should be vertical or slightly inclined inwards, their forms following the form on the plan of the rooms. The noble pictures of Paul Veronese at the Louvre could not be seen with side lights. For small cabinet pictures side lights are well adapted to their display. Every one will recollect how miserably lighted for exhibiting the pictures is the long gallery of the Louvre; the same may be said, though not to so great an extent, of the collection of sculpture, whilst the models and other objects, paintings excepted, in the Vieux Louvre, are exhibited to perfection.

2917. Where the same museum is to contain several classes of objects the suites of rooms for the different departments should be accessible from some central one common to all: this may be circular or polygonal, as may best suit the arrangement and means; and, if possible from the site, the building should not consist of more than one story above the ground; on no account of more than two.

2918. For the objects it contains we question whether the British Museum is surpassed, as a whole, in Europe; and those of the Vatican, of the Uffizj at Florence, of Portici, and of Paris, are none of them of sufficient architectural importance to detain the reader by description; neither would they, if so described, be useful to the student as models. At Munich the Glyptotek for sculpture, and the Pinacotek for pictures, are in some respects well suited to the exhibition of the objects deposited in them, better, indeed, than is the museum at Berlin. These have all been much praised by persons of incompetent judgment as specimens of fine architecture; but we cannot recommend the study of them to any one who is desirous of acquiring a pure taste in the art, nor indeed any other works of the modern German school.

2919 In the composition of museums decoration must not be exuberant. It must be kept in the interior so far subordinate as not to interfere with the objects to be exhibited, which are the principal features of the place. With this caution we do not preclude the requisite degree of richness which the architecture itself requires. Using the shorthand of the previous chapter –○–, the Greek cross, connected by a dome in the centre, for the great hall of communication, is perhaps as good a form for a museum on a small scale as could be adopted: however, this is a matter which would form an admirable exercise for the student.

Sect. XI.

OBSERVATORIES.

2920. We had great doubts upon the admission of this section, not because of its want of importance, but because we can scarcely bring ourselves to the conviction that traversing domes for equatorial instruments and chases in a roof for fixed ones can be ever united with beauty of design. The observatory at Paris, from the designs of Perrault, is a noble building, but, we believe, is universally admitted to be very ill suited to the purposes for which it was built. Hence we shall be brief in what we have to say under this section.

2921. A *regular* observatory is one where instruments *are* fixed in the meridian, whereby, with the assistance of astronomical clocks, the right ascensions and declinations of the heavenly bodies are determined, and thus motion, time, and space are converted into measures of each other. On the observations and determinations made in such establishments they are therefore, to maritime states, of vital importance, and ought to be liberally endowed by their governments. As the subject will be better understood by a plan, we subjoin, in *fig.* 1345., a plan and elevation of the observatory at Edinburgh. The general form of the plan, as will be therein seen, is a Greek cross, 62 feet long, terminated at its feet by projecting hexastyle porticoes, which are 28 feet in front, and surmounted by pediments. The intersecting limbs of the cross at their intersection are covered by a dome 13 feet diameter, which traverses round horizontally, and under its centre a pier of solid masonry is brought up of a conical form 6 feet in diameter at the base, and 19 feet high. This is intended either for an astronomical circle or for an equatorial instrument for observations of the heavenly bodies made out of the meridian. In the eastern foot of the cross (*bb*) are stone piers for the reception of the transit instrument; *c* is the stone pier to which the transit clock is attached; and *d* is a stone piece on which an artificial horizon may be placed; when observations are taken by reflection: this is covered by a floor board when

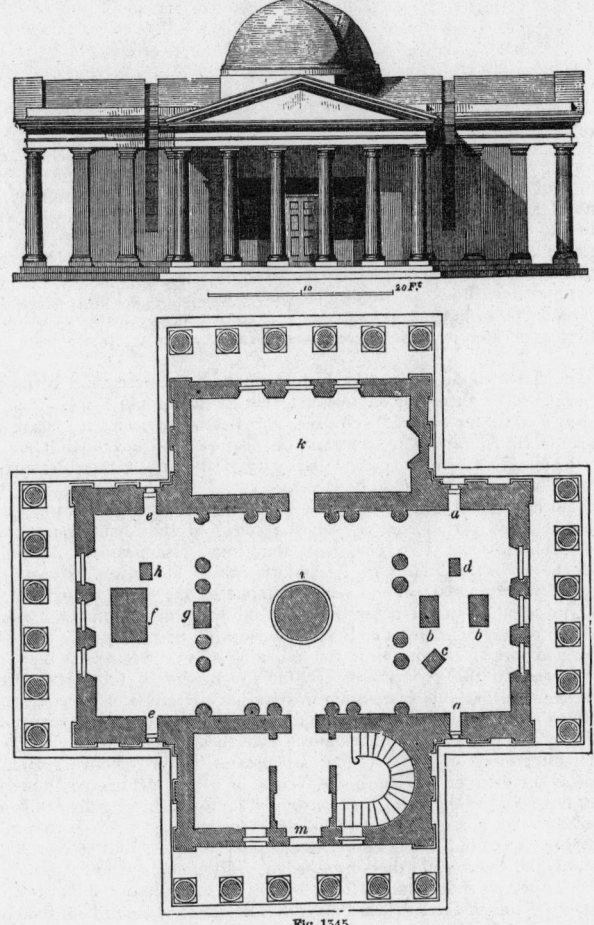

Fig. 1345.

not in use, being just under the level of the floor; *aa* are the slits or chases running through the walls and roof, but closeable by means of shutters when the observation is completed. On the western side (*ee*) are chases as in the transit room; *f* a large stone pier for the reception of a mural circle; *g* the clock pier; *h* the pier for an artificial horizon as before; *i* is the conical pier above mentioned, over which the moveable dome is placed, having an opening (*l*) in the elevation for the purpose of observation; *k* is the observer's room; and *m* the front entrance.

2922. It is to be especially observed that the piers for the reception of the instruments must not be in any way connected with the walls of the building; they should stand on the firmest possible foundation, which, if at all doubtful, must be formed with concrete, and the piers should, if possible, be out of a single block of stone; but if that cannot be obtained, the beds must be kept extremely thin; partial settlement being ruinous to the nicety of the instruments as well as to the observer's business. The observation applies also to the clock piers, all vibration and settlement being injurious also to them. At the Campden Hill observatory, near Kensington, belonging to Sir James South, there is a traversing dome 30 feet diameter in the clear.

2923. A dry situation should be chosen for the site, for, except in the computing rooms, no fire heat can be allowed; and it is important that the brass whereof the instruments are made should not be corroded by the action of moisture. In large public observatories there should be the readiest access from one part to another, and rooms for a library and computers independent of the chief astronomer's room.

Sect. XII.

LIGHTHOUSES.

2924. It may perhaps be thought that we are touching on the province of the engineer in devoting a section to lighthouses; but we cannot forego the completion of the previous section by some few observations on lighthouses, which are the handmaids to the important results which flow from observatories, being the spots which verify the course of the navigator, and serve as precautions for his guidance when near the shores of a country.

2925. The lighthouse dates from the earliest period; and without entering into the question whether the ancient lighthouses were dedicated to the gods, or whether the towers erected for the purpose of warning the mariner were nautical colleges, where astronomy and the art of navigation were perfectly taught, we may at once proceed to state that in the earliest times they appear to have consisted of a tower of masonry, sometimes of a circular form, but usually square, and consisting of various apartments, as the establishment was greater or less, wherein was a raised altar upon which the beacon was established.

2926. Those who wish to pursue the history of the lighthouse must be referred by us to Jacob Bryant, whose theory is so pleasant that to it we must apply the old Italian saying, " *Se non è vero è ben trovato*." We therefore leave the reader to consult our author on the subject of the purait or fire-towers. So also we shall not touch upon their perversion, nor the alleged dissoluteness and barbarity of the priests and priestesses who had the care of them, which we believe to be fables.

2927. Certain however it is that the whole of the ancient establishment of fire-towers or lighthouses at an early period common on the shores of the Mediterranean, the Archipelago, the Bosphorus, and Red Sea, have long since disappeared. Among the most celebrated of these was the Pharos of Alexandria, which has given its name in French and Italian to all lighthouses. It was accounted one of the seven wonders of the world, and, in history at least, has perpetuated the glory and name of its founder, Ptolemy Philadelphus. If Pliny may be relied on, it was the work of Sostratus, 300 years before the Christian æra, and bore an inscription to the following effect : " Sostratus the Gnidian, the son of Dexiphanes, to the gods preservers, for the benefit of those who use the sea." Lucian, however, says that this inscription was craftily covered with plaster, on which the name of Ptolemy was inscribed, but that the decay of the plaster left the name of Sostratus only. The story is however improbable, and is dependent entirely on the authority of the satirist. The dimensions of this building are not satisfactorily known : some have said its height was 300 cubits, or 100 times the height of a man, which would assign to it a height of 550 feet. On its top a fire was constantly kept, which, according to Josephus, was seen at the distance of three hundred stadia, equal to about forty-two British miles, which is a reasonable account; but those who have delighted in marvellous stories have made the distance one hundred miles, and others have wonderfully gone beyond the last by assigning seven hundred miles as the distance, from which the speculum used distributed light! That this work was one of extraordinary magnificence cannot be doubted; the cost has been stated at 800 talents (300,000*l.* sterling); and there is reason to suppose that it was *quasi* the parent of all others: but all we have said must be taken with great allowance, except that we believe it was a splendid monument of the time.

2928. We have thus far extended in this case our observations, not perhaps in very strict accordance with the plan of this chapter, which relates rather to principles than history; and the only excuse we offer is, that we know not where in our work they might have been more appropriately introduced. We perhaps may not better satisfy the reader in what follows; which, from the nature of the subject, must be more instructive from what has been actually executed than from the general principles upon which the construction of a lighthouse depends.

2929. The most architectural of modern lighthouses is that of Corduan on the coast of France, which stands on a large rock, or rather on a low island, about three miles from land, at the entrance of the river Garonne. Like that of Alexandria, this lighthouse seems to have been intended for the commemoration of an æra in the history of France from the eminent utility of the building and the magnificence of its structure. Founded about the year 1584, in the reign of Henry II. king of France, it was carried on under the reigns of three successive monarchs, arriving at its completion in 1610, in the reign of Henry IV. It stands upon a platform of solid masonry, and is surrounded by a parapet about 145 feet in diameter, which is equal to the height. The lightkeepers' apartments and store rooms are not in the main tower, but form a detached range of buildings on the great platform, the interior of the tower itself being finished in a style of magnificence too splendid for the use of common persons. Over the fuel cellar, which is formed in the solid masonry of the platform, is the great hall, 22 feet square, 20 feet high, with an arched

ceiling. On this floor are two wardrobes and other conveniences. Above the last-mentioned room is the king's room, 21 feet square and 20 high, with an elliptical ceiling, There are on this floor a vestibule, two wardrobes, and other conveniences. On the third floor is placed the chapel, for a priest who occasionally says mass is attached to the establishment, and this is 21 feet in diameter, domed, and 40 feet high, and lighted by eight windows. There is an eye in the dome through which is seen the ornamental roof of the room above, and that is 14 feet diameter and 27 feet high. This is used by the lightkeepers as a watch room. Over it rises an apartment, which is immediately under the light room, used for holding sufficient fuel for one night's consumption, and capable itself of being converted into a place for the exhibition of a light in case of repairs being required to any extent in the main light room, which, as we have said, is immediately over it, and is surrounded by a balcony and circular stone parapet. The height from the floor to the top of the cupola of the original lantern or light room was 17 feet, and being unglazed, the smoke was carried out on either side in the direction of the wind. The roof, moreover, formed a kind of chimney in the form of a spire, terminating with a ball. The height of the light room, which was entirely of stone, was 31 feet from the light room floor to the ball on the top of the spire. The fuel first used for the light was oak, after which pit coal was introduced; but in modern times lamps and reflectors have succeeded the last, and the light is now seen at a proper distance.

2930. In England the student may turn to the Eddystone lighthouse, by the celebrated Smeaton, not only as an object of great beauty, but of that soundness of construction, which is the most essential requisite in works of this kind. The general form is seen in fig. 1346. This is a fine illustration of fitness producing beauty. The resistance it affords against the waves arises from the beautiful curved line which leads them up it instead of being broken against it. Indeed, in stormy weather, the waves actually roll up the side, and fall in a contrary curve over the top of the lighthouse. The beds of the masonry are so laid and dovetailed and joggled into the rock itself as to become a part of it. The foundation stone of it was laid on the 12th of June, 1757, and it was first lighted on the 16th of October, 1759. A narrative of the work was published by Mr. Smeaton, to which for detail the reader is referred. The two lower stories are used as store rooms ; the next above serves for the kitchen, above which is the bedroom, over which is the light room.

2931. Thus, we see, there is no reason why lighthouses should not be beautifully formed structures, instead of absurd misshapen masses of masonry, as they generally are. The attempt to make them resemble columns is intolerable; they should possess, according to the different situations, a character peculiar to themselves : hence the application of a column for the purpose is the worst of abuses. The North Foreland lighthouse, whose plan is polygonal, would be a good example had the details been properly attended to in the design. We do not here touch upon the mode of lighting, which has of late years occupied much attention, having considered the duty of the architect performed when he

Fig. 1346.

has provided a beautiful, lasting, and secure fabric for the reception of the lights.

Sect. XIII.

ABATTOIRS OR PUBLIC SLAUGHTER-HOUSES.

2932. It may be thought unnecessary to assign a section in this work to the consideration of a species of building unfortunately unknown to this country, in which its general non-employment is truly a reproach. Among the improvements lately made in the metropolis, the removal of Smithfield market into the outskirts, has resulted in the establishment, at last, of several slaughter-houses as part of the Metropolitan Cattle Market, which was designed by the late J. B. Bunning, City architect, and opened in 1855. If to this were added the establishment of public slaughter-houses or abattoirs round London, as has long since been

done about the city of Paris, we might have another source of congratulation for its inhabitants. This is a subject that ought to be forced on the attention of the government. It ought not to be left to individuals to take charge of the comforts and security of London and its suburbs. The public cemeteries established by companies have doubtless been most useful, but such matters concern the public welfare, and should be in the hands of their rulers.

2933. The accidents arising from overdriving cattle through the narrow streets of Paris, and the infectious effluvia from the slaughter-houses often causing contagious maladies in their neighbourhood, induced the French government, in 1811, to execute a project which had been entertained for nearly a century previously, that of removing all the slaughter-houses from the heart of their capital. The result of this determination has been, not only the prevention of all cause of complaint of the former inconveniences, but has produced a set of buildings bearing a character of grandeur and magnificence proportionate to their destination. It was a worthy exercise of the power of the government; it has obviated the disgraceful sights almost every day witnessed in London, sights tending to deprive the lower classes of humanity, and to render them ferocious, to corrupt the mind, to offend the eye, and to injure the public health. Without strictly adhering to the term abattoir, which would more properly signify a slaughter-house where the cattle are slaughtered, we mean by our proposition, not only the place for killing the cattle, but an establishment where, after they are killed, under the inspection of proper officers, the skins are arranged for sale, as well as the tallow obtained from the fat, before these are distributed to the respective trades.

2934. Political economists have doubted whether an individual ought to be restricted in the exercise of his industry wherever he may think it most conducive to his interest; we are however inclined to apply to the principle the maxim of the lawyers, "sic utere tuo ut alienum non lædas," and think that disagreeable and unwholesome establishments should be removed from all large cities. The experiment however, at all events, has been most successfully made in Paris, where butchers are no longer allowed to kill their cattle, except in the public abattoirs. For the purpose five open airy spots have been selected in the outskirts of the city, corresponding in size to the demand of those parts of the town to which they are correspondent. Those of Menilmontant and of Montmartre are the most considerable and extensive; but the rest are constructed on similar plans, in which there is no difference except in the number and extent of the buildings. We shall therefore describe generally the first named, that of Menilmontant.

2935. The slaughter-house of Menilmontant at Paris is situated on a declivity, which contributes to its good drainage, and the consequent salubrity of the establishment. It stands on a site about 700 feet by about 620 feet, being insulated between four streets. Through an iron railing, about 108 feet in extent, flanked by two lodges, or *pavillons*, in which are accommodated the officers of the establishment and their *bureaux*, is the principal entrance of the edifice. On entering from this a large square space presents itself, from the centre whereof may be seen the whole of the buildings, twenty-three in number, composing the abattoir. This court is about 315 feet broad, and on its great sides about 475 feet long, and on its right and left are four double buildings, separated by a road which traverses the whole ground parallel to the principal façade. These are the slaughter-houses, each whereof is about 200 feet long by 136 feet in breadth, and they are separated by a paved court, in the direction of their length, so inclined as to carry off the filth, such court dividing them into two piles of building, each of which contains eight slaughter-houses for the particular use of the butchers. Each slaughter-house is lighted and ventilated from openings in the front walls. Above them are attics for drying the skins and depositing the tallow, and to keep them cool the flat roofs project very considerably. Behind the slaughter-houses, and parallel to them, are two sheepfolds, and at their extremities two stables, each of which contains lofts for the hay, and on each side of the court complete the two masses of building which compose the design. At the end of the court is a convenient watering place, and two folds for the first distribution of the cattle; and also two insulated buildings for melting the tallow. These are intersected by a broad corridor, giving access to four separate melting-houses, with vaulted cellars, which serve as coolers. Beyond these, parallel to the enclosing wall, are two long buildings, divided into many warehouses on the ground and first floor, and standing on cellars, in which the undressed leather is kept, the upper floor being destined for the reception of calves' and sheep skins. The last point to be noticed is a large double reservoir of water, of masonry, carried on two series of vaults, which serve as stands for carriages. A steam-engine between the two basins pumps the water into the reservoir. The basins are about 323 feet in length. Happe was the architect; and the cost was something above 120,000*l*. The rent which some years ago the five establishments yielded to the city was about 12,000*l*. per annum.

2936. The description we have given shows the general distribution of the buildings, which are the subject of the section. Although general, we apprehend that, with the particular information of which in every case the architect must possess himself, enough has been said on the subject.

Sect. XIV

EXCHANGES.

2937. An exchange is a place of meeting and resort for the merchants of a city to transact the affairs relating to their trading. We are not aware that the ancients had any edifices exactly in their destination resembling the modern exchange, as used by us in these days; there is, indeed, every reason to believe that the ancient basilica served at the same time for the accommodation of the officers of the law and for the assembling of the merchants.

2938. All modern cities with any pretension to commerce have some place appropriated to the reception of the merchant, to which at a certain hour he resorts. Sometimes we find it a place surrounded with porticoes and planted with trees. Often it is a building, including several porticos on the ground floor, surrounded by offices for the bankers and money-changers, which latter use has given among us the name of exchange to the building.

2939. The Exchange at Amsterdam seems for a long time to have prevailed as the model for all others. It was commenced in 1608, and finished in 1613, and its architect was Cornelis Dankers de Ry. It is about 271 feet long, and about 152 feet wide. The whole edifice is supported on three large arches, under which flow as many canals. On the ground floor is a portico surrounding a court, above which are halls supported on forty-six piers. The divisions which they form are numbered and assigned each to a particular nation or class of merchants. In the court, and within the enclosure, is the place of meeting for mercantile affairs. At the top is another large hall, and a warehouse for various kinds of merchandise.

2940. The exchange is, perhaps, next in importance to the cathedral of the city, and should be commensurate in appearance and accommodation with its wealth and consequence; it should, moreover, if possible, be placed in the most central part. Such was Sir Christopher Wren's idea in forming the plan of London after the conflagration. He considered the forum of the ancients to be the true model upon which a modern exchange might be engrafted, and we think he was correct. Any edifice which in appearance resembles an ancient temple is unfit in character, and shows puerility and poverty of imagination in the designer. Porticoes are the principal features of such a building, and the variety in which they may be used for the purpose is infinite, and will afford ample scope for the artist's talent.

2941. No offices or shops, as have been constructed in the new Royal Exchange, for the purpose of obtaining rent, should be connected with the fabric, save only as in Paris, for example, a *Tribunal de Commerce* with its accessories, an establishment much wanted in England; and perhaps in addition to this, in a maritime country like ours, a large hall and offices for the transaction of business relating to the shipping interest.

2942. In London and other places it has been usual to leave the court of resort open to the heavens; an absurd practice, which, we suppose, because it was so before, has been readopted in the exchange about to be rebuilt in this city. The French are wiser, and though the weather is, generally speaking, much finer in France than it is here, they build their exchange with a roof, for the comfort of those that use it. If, however, our merchants prefer exposure to the inclemency of the seasons, it is not our business to complain of the fancy.

2943. As we consider the Bourse at Paris an admirable model, both in distribution and design, we shall briefly here describe it. The edifice in question was begun in 1808, under the designs of Brongniart, and completed by Labarre at a much protracted period. The general form on the plan is a parallelogram of 212 feet by 126 feet. It is surrounded by an unbroken peristyle of sixty-six Corinthian columns, supporting an entablature and attic. The peristyle forms a covered gallery, to which the ascent is by a flight of steps extending the whole width of the western front. The intercolumniations on the walls are filled in with two tiers, one above the other, of arched windows, separated by a Doric entablature, and surmounted by a decorated frieze. The roof is formed entirely of iron and copper. In the centre of the parallelogram is the *Salle de la Bourse*, or great hall, 116 feet long and 76 feet broad, wherein the merchants and brokers assemble. The Doric order is that used with arcades round the sides, and between the arcades are inscribed the names of the principal mercantile cities in the world. The ceiling is formed by a cove, and in the centre a large skylight serves for lighting the great hall just described. It is rich in sculpture, and decorated with monochrome paintings, to imitate bassi relievi, sixteen in the whole, that is, five on each long and three on each short side. They are all allegorical. The hall conveniently contains 2000 persons. At its eastern end is a circular space railed off for the convenience of the *agens de change*: these only are admitted within it, and to it there is a communication from their hall of business. On the right are rooms for the committee

and syndicate of the *agens de change,* for the *courtiers de commerce,* and a hall of meeting for the latter. On the left is an ample staircase leading to the gallery, supported by Doric columns, and to the hall of the Tribunal de Commerce, with its several apartments and waiting rooms. From the gallery, as on the ground floor, a corridor extends round the Salle, communicating with the Chamber of Commerce, the Court of Bankruptcy, and other public offices. The cost of this very elegant and splendid building was about 326,000*l.* ; but the merchants and city of London disgrace themselves by allowing 150,000*l.* for a similar purpose here ; and even for this sum they cut up their building into little slices, to reimburse themselves by rents for the miserable outlay. So much for the spirit and liberality of the British merchant !

Sect. XV.

CUSTOM-HOUSES.

2944. It is almost unnecessary to inform our readers that a custom-house is an establishment for receiving the duties, or, as they are called, customs levied on merchandise imported into a country, as well as of regulating the bounty or drawback on goods exported. According, therefore, to the importance and wealth of a city, the building to receive it is of considerable consequence. The first point that immediately presents itself is, that it should be provided with spacious warehouses for holding the merchandise which arrives, and in which it is, as it were, impounded till the duties are paid ; and next, that there must be provided ample accommodation for the officers who are to supervise the levying of the imposts. Now, these being the data, it is manifest that there can be no building so subject to modification in every respect as a custom-house, and that that which might be well suited to a small town or city, looking to its trade, would be ridiculous either in excess or smallness in another. Yet there are general principles which should guide the student in designing the smallest as well as the largest establishment of this sort, and these are contained in the two maxims, of ample capaciousness for the merchandise to be received into the warehouses, and a panoptical view, on the part of the proper officers, of that which passes in the establishment. Without these requisites, a custom-house is an ill-planned building ; but it is not to be supposed that such an observation can apply to an establishment of this nature in a metropolis like London, the subdivisions and details of whose commerce have found as yet all the delegations of the customs in the various docks and sufferance wharfs still even too small for the commerce of the country, and have induced the government to extend the collection of the dues beyond the central establishment. We must, however, return to the custom-house calculated for a port of ordinary size, and not that of a metropolis like London, though presently we must refer to what on that has been thought necessary for our guidance in smaller matters. Security against fire must be strictly attended to. The warehouses and covered places for examining and stowing the goods should therefore be arched in brick or stone, and should, moreover, be as much as possible on the ground floor. The offices for the public and heads of the establishment may be over them on the first floor. Both of these are, of course, to be regulated in size by the extent of trade in the place. The general character should be that of simplicity ; decoration is unsuited, and should be very sparingly employed. The species of composition most suitable seems to be pointed out in arcades and arched openings. The site should be as near as may be to the river or port, so that the merchandise may be landed and housed with as little labour as possible.

2945. The following is a general view of the apartments and offices of the London Custom House. The long room, which is the principal public room for the entries &c., is 190 feet long and 66 wide. This, as well as the rooms next enumerated, are on the first or principal floor, viz. a pay office for duties, treasury, bench officers or commissioners' rooms, secretary's room, rooms for the inspector general, surveyor of shipping, registrar of shipping, surveyor of acts of navigation, strong rooms, comptrollers, outward and inward, surveyor of works ; Trinity light office, bond office, board room, chairman's room, committee room and plantation clerk's office. On the ground floor are the following offices : for minute clerks, clerk of papers, petitions, messengers, landing surveyors, wood farm office, tide waiters, tide surveyors, inspectors of river, guagers, landing waiters, coast waiters, coast office long room, coast bond office, coffee office, housekeeper, searchers, merchants and brokers' rooms, comptrolling searchers, appointers of the weighers and office for the plantation department. Besides these apartments there are warehouses for the merchandise.

2946. The above long list will give a notion of what would be wanted on a smaller scale ; but on such matters the special instructions on each case must be the guide to the architect in making his design. Many of the above offices would, of course, be unnecessary

in a small port, neither would the dimensions be so large as in the example quoted. The staircases, corridors, and halls must be spacious in all cases, the building being one for the service of the public.

Sect. XVI.

THEATRES.

2947. A taste for dramatic representations prevailed at a very early period among the people of antiquity, and this was not diminished by the introduction of Christianity, even when the temples were deserted and paganism seemed extinct. The destruction of these, however, was its concluding triumph. It would be a difficult matter to fix the precise date of the abolition of the pagan theatre, but it seems likely to have resulted rather from the falling into decay of the old theatres than from a disinclination on the part of the people to the pleasure they received at them. It is not, however, the object of this section to trace the history of the theatre; though we think it right to say a few more words on the subject. With the revival of the arts, the taste for scenic representations appeared with the literature on which they are dependent. In Italy we find, therefore, the drama at this period represented in very large enclosures, such as the amphitheatre constructed by Bramante in the large court of the Vatican, whence the taste soon spread over all the nations of Europe.

2948. The pleasure which flowed from this renewal of an ancient art was at first confined to few, and those were either men of learning or select societies, who bore the expenses, and again raised in the country a renewal of a theatre much resembling those of the ancients as respected the form and disposition. To prove this, we need only cite the example of the celebrated theatre at Vicenza, built by Palladio in 1583, and designed in imitation of the ancient theatres. Its form is a semi-ellipsis, whose transverse axis is parallel with the scene, encompassed with fourteen ranges of steps for the spectators. The greater diameter of this ellipse is 97½ feet, and the lesser, as far as the stage, about 57½ feet. At the summit is a corridor of the Corinthian order, which, from the want of ground, could not be detached all round from the external wall. The nine central and the three external intercolumniations, therefore, where the columns touch the external wall, are filled with niches and statues. The stage is designed with two tiers of Corinthian columns surmounted with an appropriate attic. In the front of the stage are three openings through which three avenues of magnificent buildings appear, and at the end of each is a triumphal arch. All these are executed in alto relievo, but are foreshortened and diminished perspectively. A full account of this building, which is well worth the student's attention, is given in *L' Origine dell' Academia Olympica, &c. Opera di Ottavio Bertotti Scamozzi.* Vicenza, 1690. For dramatic representations this theatre is no longer used, and at present it is only recognised as a monument of the extraordinary skill of the architect, and a memorial of the dramatic buildings of its period. The theatre at Parma, built by Aleotti, is another building belonging to the same class, and preserved, like the last-mentioned, as a curiosity.

2949. When, however, the taste for scenic amusements began to spread, the sovereign princes, who alone could support the expense of such establishments, began to make them a necessary part of their palaces; and the theatre, no longer a public and essential building, became what it now is, not an edifice for the reception and accommodation of the whole population of a city at certain periods, but a place which served for the habitual amusement of those who could afford it. The drama again revived, and its history is an index to the edifices that rose for its representation. Becoming thus necessary for the amusement of the better classes of society, the establishment of theatres was undertaken by individuals in almost every city, and competition was the natural consequence. Then began the division of the theatre into different parts, the entry to which was marked by different prices, and the separation of the common people from those of rank and fortune.

2950. Italy does not contain so many theatres, nor of such consequence, as might be predicated from the taste of its inhabitants. Among the earliest of consequence was that built at Bologna in 1763 by Antonio Galli Bibiena, (not to mention that built at Verona under the direction of the celebrated Scipio Maffei by Francesco Galli Bibiena,) with a noble portico in front and salons in the angles, possessing moreover great merit in its interior distribution. In the Italian theatres there is almost invariably a certain feeling of grandeur and unity about the interior little to be expected from the exterior, which in no way leads the spectator to the suspicion of a fine *Salle de Spectacle* behind it.

2951. France has the credit of having erected the first modern theatre that can be denominated an example in this species of monumental architecture. That to which we allude is the theatre at Bordeaux, which is 325 feet in length, and half that measure in width. It is surrounded by arcades, whose piers are decorated with pilasters of the Corinthian order, running up the whole height through the ground and one-pair stories. Set back, an attic

is raised, which conceals the roof, wherein the necessary accommodations which a theatre requires are disposed. Whether we consider the exterior or interior of this edifice, everything is grand; the accessories are worthy of the whole, and the richness of the interior decoration is only equalled by the fine forms whereon the decorations are used. The ingress and egress are admirable; and a splendid concert-room and magnificent staircases complete the destination, to which it is so suited, as to afford the finest model of a theatre to which we can refer the student. The plans, &c. of this work were published by the architect, under the title of *Salle de Spectacle de Bourdeaux*, atlas folio, Paris, 1782. Paris but followed Bourdeaux in improving its theatres, and latterly the metropolis of England followed in the wake.

2952. The principal points for the consideration of the architect in the composition of a theatre, may be classed under the heads of utility, suitableness for the purpose, and taste in combining them. Under the first head must be placed the accomplishment of two main objects, those of seeing and hearing what passes on the stage. These, indeed, are intimately connected with each other, and are entirely dependent on the form adopted for the plan of the interior, that is, the general form given to the boxes which surround the part before the curtain. We are not aware of any plan which, in this respect, is not based on a quadrangular, elliptical, or circular form.

2953. The quadrangular form, besides its want of beauty, is not well adapted for fulfilling the objects with which we set out. In this, the greater number of spectators or audience who occupy the side boxes, are so inconveniently placed, that, to observe what is going on, their heads must be turned sidewise, and they are hence in a false position for the object. The actor being generally the point to which all eyes are directed, the spectator opposite the proscenium will look at him in a right direction; but as the spectator removes to the extremity of the side, it is manifest that the angle in which the head must be turned becomes sharper, and the position is then painful. Besides this objection, the form is known to be unfavourable to hearing or to the propagation of sound.

2954. The truncated oval is in some measure subject to the same inconveniences on the sides as the last-mentioned figure. It removes also a large portion of the spectators to a considerable distance from the centre of the scene, besides which, in the boxes near the proscenium, their seats tend in opposite directions to the actor. It has been to remedy these faults that the form of the horseshoe has been adopted, which is a sort of mean between the quadrangular and oval forms: and where the plot of ground is much longer than it is wide, it is a suitable figure, and one which affords the opportunity of increasing the number of boxes.

2955. When, however, the circumstances concur in allowing it, the adoption of the semicircular plan is doubtless the best. It is a figure which allows each spectator to be at an equal distance from the scene, that also by which the spectators in adjoining boxes less interfere with one another, that which affords the means of all seeing equally well, that in which the sound is most equally distributed, and that whose uniformity and simplicity seems to engender the best decoration. The semi-elliptic, with the transverse axis parallel to the proscenium, has interior advantages in some respects over the semicircle; but it induces great difficulty in connecting the proscenium itself with the auditory part of the house, and, by increasing the width of the proscenium, increases the perplexity in framing the roof conveniently for the painting rooms, and securely as respects the walls.

2956. Upon the destruction by fire of Drury Lane Theatre, a pamphlet appeared, entitled "Observations on the Principles of a Design for a Theatre," by Benjamin Wyatt, London, 8vo. 1811. These observations are so well worth the notice of the student that we shall close this section by giving the substance of them. The heads for consideration, says the author, are —

2957. *First.* The size or capacity of the theatre, as governed by the width of the proscenium or stage opening; and by the pecuniary return to be made to those whose property may be embarked in the concern. *Second.* The form or shape of the theatre, as connected with the primary objects of sound and vision. *Third.* The facility of ingress and egress, as materially affecting the convenience of those who go to every part of the house respectively, as well as their lives, in cases of sudden accident or alarm. *Fourth.* Decorum amongst the several orders and classes of the visitants to the theatre, as essential to the accommodation of the more respectable part of those visitants, and consequently of great importance to the interests of the theatre. *Fifth.* Security against fire, as well with relation to the expense of insurance as with relation to the lives of individuals going to the theatre.

2958. The size or capacity will necessarily depend very much on the width of the proscenium or stage opening, inasmuch as it is from the extremities of that opening that the form of the theatre must spring. The annexed is a statement of the width of proscenium at the theatres named : —

Argentino, at Rome - - - - -	36 feet.
Old Covent Garden (burnt 1856) - - -	38 feet.

Théâtre Italien, Paris (burnt)	-	-				38 feet.
Turin	-	-	-	-	-	-	39 feet.
Bourdeaux	-	-	-	-	-	-	39 feet.
Parma	-	-	-	-	-	-	40 feet.
Milan	-	-	-	-	-	-	40 feet.
San Benedetto, at Venice	-		-	-		40 feet.
Théâtre François, at Paris	-		-	-		40 feet.
Drury Lane	-	-	-	-	-		40 feet 6 inches.

A width beyond 40 feet seems to be considered by the performers as inconvenient from the space they would have to pass over in the business of the drama. A greater width, indeed, than that stated prevents the easy and secure working of the scenes, for the machinery is increased in magnitude and weight as the height and breadth of the scenes increase. In mere *spectacle* and scenic grouping a reduction in the width of the proscenium reduces the number of extra performers, or supernumeraries as they are called, which become necessary for filling the stage. Again, every additional foot given to the stage opening increases the quantity of canvass used in the scenes, as well as the framing whereon they are fixed.

In the *Edinburgh New Philosophical Journal*, vol. xxvii., there are, by Mr. J. S. Russell, some elementary considerations of certain principles in the construction of buildings designed to accommodate spectators and auditors, well worth the architect's notice. In every large room, says the writer, a perfectly good seat is one in which, without uneasy elevation of the head or eye, without straining or stretching, we can calmly and quietly take any easy position, or variety of positions, which we may be disposed to assume, and yet may in all of them see and hear the speaker with equal clearness and repose, so as to give him patient and undisturbed attention. The object, then, is to ascertain in what manner the interior of a building for public speaking should be formed, so that throughout the whole range which the voice of a man is capable of filling, each individual should see and hear without interruption from any of the rest of the audience, with equal comfort in an easy posture,

Fig. 1347.

and as clearly as if no other individual auditor or spectator were present. (See *figs.* 1347. and 1348.) The position of the seats is first investigated. In the usual variety of station

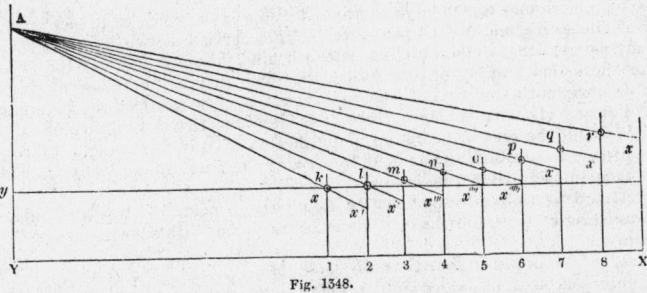

Fig. 1348.

and of position, it appears from experiments that the range required for the purpose is more than a foot and less than 18 inches, so that these may be taken as the limits; that is, over the head of the person before you there must be a clear range of 12 or 18 inches, through which the head may be moved upwards or downwards without interruption. In other words, that a straight line drawn from the speaker's head over that of the anterior spectator shall intercept the straight line which forms the back of the seat of the posterior observer, so as to cut off a height of 12 or 18 inches, within which the head of the spectator shall at

times be comprehended while sitting in a comfortab e position. Thus let S (*fig.* 1347.) be the speaker and XYZ be three successive ascents; then the line SX must fall below SY, so as to leave the space $Yx = 18$ inches $= Zy$.

2959. Applying this formula to every individual place in the room or building, we shall have the form required to satisfy the auditors. Let $2\frac{1}{4}$ feet be assumed as a constant representing the distance of one spectator behind another, measured horizontally; and $1\frac{1}{4}$ feet as the clear space, measured on the vertical line, for the mean range of comfortable vision for each. If the level of the floor, that is, of the lowest seats, be already determined, the form of the interior accommodation may be thus described. AY (*fig.* 1348.), the height of the speaker, YX the level floor. From Ay take Y$y = 4$ feet. Draw yx parallel to YX. Take Ay to yx as $1\frac{1}{4}$ to $2\frac{1}{4}$, that is, as h, the range of position of the spectator, to d, the distance between the seats. Take horizontal distances 1, 2, 3, 4, &c. $= 2\frac{1}{4}$ feet, prolong Ax to x', then the height x' to $l = 1\frac{1}{4}$ feet. Join Al and prolong it to x'', and take a distance x'' to $m = 1\frac{1}{4}$ feet. Through m draw Am, and prolong it to x''', and take $x'''n = 1\frac{1}{4}$ feet. Continue the process in the same manner to $p, q, r, s, t,$ &c., and the points will be found of the successive places which the heads of the auditors should occupy.

2960. But it is not only in receding that the back seats must rise; those too far forward may be also unpleasant. They are too low; they also should be raised: but this must be done so as not to interrupt those who are behind. It may be accomplished in a similar way; for, as formerly set off, 1, 2, 3, 4, 5, 6, &c. $= 2\frac{1}{4}$ feet (*fig.* 1349.), 1 is the first anterior point. Join A1, and let it cut the vertical line through 2 in x'', the portion downwards $x''l = 1\frac{1}{4}$ feet; then l is the point found. Join Al, make $x'''k = 1\frac{1}{4}$ feet; join Ak; and $x''''i = 1\frac{1}{4}$ feet; and so on. $g, h, i, k, l,$ are the places found which the heads of the spectators should occupy, and show the elevation to be given to the seats successively.

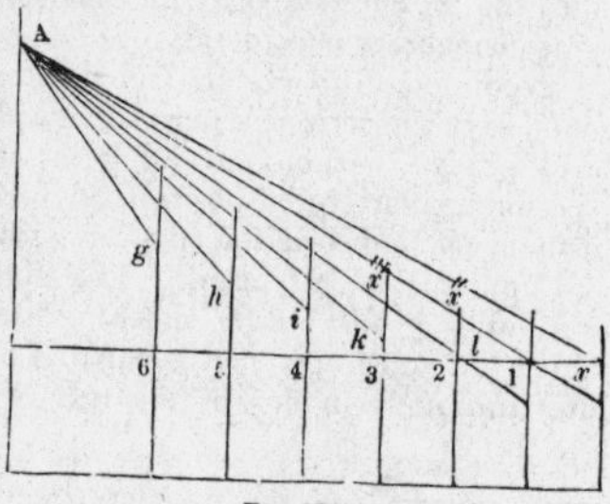

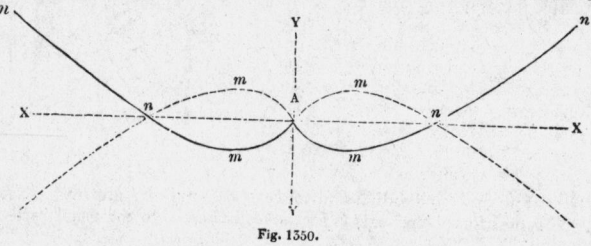

Fig. 1349.

2961. If the simple process described be accurately performed, the points which indicate the places of the spectators will lie in the branches of a very beautiful curve, which may be termed the *iseidomal* or the *isacoustic* curve, that is, *one of equal* seeing or hearing: it will be of the form in *fig.* 1350. A being the place of the speaker, and the heads of the spec-

Fig. 1350.

tators being placed on the line Amn, continued as far as the voice will reach, XAX being the axis of the curve, and YY its parameter. This curve has two branches on opposite sides of A, showing that if the building extend behind the speaker, or if the spectacle be visible or the sound audible on every side, the same may be continued all round. By means of this curve, the position of seats in a theatre may be satisfactorily determined.

2962. For any great assemblage, where it is desirable that one individual or group of individuals should be seen or heard, an amphitheatre of this form might be constructed from the surface of revolution generated by moving the curve round its axis, which would perfectly accommodate 10,000 individuals.

2963. According to the arrangement of London audiences, Mr. Wyatt calculates that a theatre consisting of three fourths of a circle on the plan, with a stage opening of 35 feet, will contain

78 boxes, in four tiers, and holding - - 1004
4 boxes of larger size, on each side next the stage - 188
A pit, capable of containing - - - 911
A two-shilling gallery - - - - 482
A one-shilling gallery - - - - 284

2869 persons, exclusive of four boxes in the proscenium, and fourteen in the basement of the theatre, immediately under the dress boxes.

2964. We have already given some general hints relative to the form; we shall here add the author's view of this matter; and thereon he very properly says that, with reference to distinct sound, the safest method is to adopt a form known to be most capable of conveying sound with facility, to construct that form of materials that are conductors of sound, and to avoid all breaks and projections on the surface of that form, because they obstruct and impede the progress of the sound. It is well known that a circular enclosure without breaks possesses the power of conveying sounds with facility, and that wood is an admirable conducting material for the purpose. Count Algarotti, in his treatise on the Opera, says, daily experience teaches us that in a box whose walls are naked, the singer's voice is reverberated in a particular manner; it sounds crude and harsh, and by no means flattering to the ear; the accents are quite lost if the box be hung with tapestry; whereas they are reflected full, sonorous, and agreeable to the ear when the boxes are only boarded, which is an obvious proof, and confirmed by experience, that the best lining for the interior part of a theatre is wood.

2965. Whatever be the form of the theatre, it ought in every part to be limited in extent to such distance as the voice will distinctly reach; and the nearer that figure conforms to the proportions wherein the natural voice is heard in each direction, the more equally will the sound be heard in every part of the theatre. The experiments tried by Mr. Wyatt proved that the reach of the voice when moderately exerted was in the proportion of about two ninths further in a direct front line than laterally; and that being distinctly audible on each side of the speaker at a distance of seventy-five feet, it will be as plainly heard at a distance of ninety-two feet in front of him, declining in strength behind him so as not to be clearly heard at much more than thirty feet. "According," says Mr. Wyatt, " to these data, it would appear that the geometrical figure, which comes the nearest to the extreme limits of the natural expansion of the voice, is a semicircle of 75 feet radius, or 150 feet in diameter, continued on each side to the extent of 17 feet, or in the proportion of

about two ninths of its lateral expansion (*fig.* 1351.) beyond the limits of the semicircle, and then converging suddenly until the two lines meet at C, behind the back of the speaker." But though the voice may be heard at these distances, it does not follow that a theatre of this extent should be erected; indeed, it would be absurd to do so, for the actor varies his place almost every moment; and as he removes from the centre, from which it has been assumed he is speaking, he would become inaudible to some parts of the audience as he receded from it. It is evident, therefore, in planning a theatre, the radius or semi-diameter must be so reduced as to bring the extreme distance at which he may in any case be placed within the space of 75 feet, that is, that when the speaker is placed at the

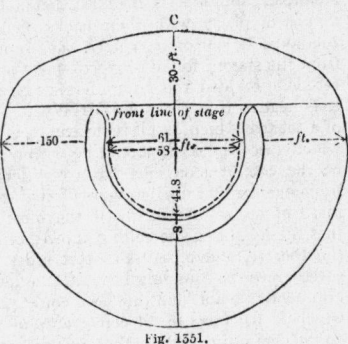

Fig. 1351.

extremity of either side of the stage, his voice may be heard by those seated on the opposite side of the house. In the diagram, the widest part of the theatre inscribed in the larger figure is 58 feet upon the level of the dress boxes; and allowing 9 feet 6 inches for the depth of the boxes on that floor, by means of a projection of 18 inches more than the boxes above, there will be 67 feet 6 inches between the extreme part of the stage on one side and the back wall of the boxes on the opposite side: but as the speaker is in no case placed at either extremity of the stage, and even if so situated, the distance between him and the opposite side of the house would be within 8 feet of the reach of his voice in its lateral direction, and 25 feet within its limits in a direct line, it hence appears that the circular is preferable to any other form; and if we fix a limit for the diameter of that form, we are in possession of the rules which limit the length of the theatre, or the distance from the front line of the stage to the boxes immediately in front of that line. Taking 75 feet for the distance at which the voice can be heard laterally, as the space between the front line of the stage and its immediately opposite boxes may occasionally be in the lateral direction of the voice, the greatest distance from the front wall of the stage to the back wall of the boxes opposite the stage should not exceed 75 feet, the limit of the voice in its lateral direction, because of the turns of head which he must often make for the business of the scene, when that which was opposite might become lateral; and thus those persons sitting in the opposite boxes would be 92 − 75 feet = 17 feet beyond the reach of his voice.

2966. The use of a semicircle without modification would, however, involve the extension of the stage opening to an inconvenient width; and Mr. Wyatt very properly considers that the whole area of a theatre should contain little more than one third of the space over

which the voice can reach; "the one," he says, "being (independently of the space behind the back of the speaker) a superficies of 11,385 feet, and the other of 4003." This, he thinks, will compensate for the absorption of sound consequent on the number of the audience, the woollen garments they wear, and the state of the atmosphere, and would ensure a good hearing in every part of the house.

2967. According to the author's statement, he recommends that the distance from the front of the stage to the back wall of the boxes immediately opposite should be about 54 feet; in the old Drury Lane it was 74 feet, and in the old Covent Garden Theatre, built about 1730, it was 54 feet 6 inches. In the Opera House, built by Vanbrugh, it was 66 feet. At Milan it is 78 feet. At the old San Carlos, at Naples, 73 feet; and at Bologna, 74 feet. The distance in the late Covent Garden Theatre was 69 feet 8 inches, or nearly 16 feet more than it ought to have been. How, then, can people wonder at not seeing and hearing in such theatres, where the cupidity of the projectors has overstepped the mark, and very much contributed to the ruin of the drama?

2968. In an opera house the band as it were sustains the voice, and the *spectacle* of the ballet is more addressed to the eye than to the understanding; but even in that the theatre is universally too large for the pleasure of those who appreciate properly what is transacted in the scene. It is satisfactory to know that the theatre which we in our introductory remarks selected as a model should coincide in the main points here in question with Mr. Wyatt's project. We are not certain whether he has visited it, but are certain that if he has he would not change his opinion.

2969. In respect of vision in a theatre, there can be no question that the semicircle gives the best chance for the whole of the audience; but the objections to it are, that it requires that either the stage opening should be of inconvenient width or that the size of the house should be too small. It is therefore, without modification, inadmissible. It is on this account that the ellipse, the horseshoe, and other flat-sided forms, have in later theatres been adopted, though it is manifest that a large proportion of the audience, says our author, " must be placed with their backs inclining towards the scene, and that in *all* of them (if the house be not of extremely *small* dimensions) the front boxes must be at a great distance from the stage; for in proportion as the sides shall approximate each other the front must recede, provided the circumference be not varied." The summing up of the question on this head is thus given by Mr. Wyatt : " There is no object connected with the formation of a theatre which, in all its bearings, is of more importance than that the part of the house which faces the scene should be within a moderate distance from the stage. Unless that be the case, it is obvious that a very large proportion of the spectators must be excluded from a clear and distinct view of that play of the features which constitutes the principal merit of the actor in many of the most interesting scenes." Mr. Wyatt does not believe that the height of the ceiling injures or affects the sound of the voice in the lower parts of the theatre, and observes that it must in every theatre "be much too high to act as reverberator or sounding board to the lower parts of the house." But we do not agree with him on this point, and think we could refer him to more than one theatre in the metropolis which is defective in the conveyance of the sound from this cause alone. Besides this, we do not feel quite certain that the diagonal line drawn from the actor to the upper tier of boxes should not be the regulating distance, instead of the horizontal one which has been mentioned above.

2970. Ingress and egress should be provided on each side of the house, so that whatever doors, passages, and staircases are placed on one side, there must be corresponding ones on the other. The spectators are thus divided, and pressure avoided. Angles should as much as possible be avoided, as well as steps in passages, for which no excuse can be offered. Doorways ought not to be less than six feet wide, nor should staircases be of less dimensions. In large staircases, which consist of a centre and two side flights, the central one should be equal in width to the side flights added together. In calculating the size, regard should in some measure be had to the number of persons which the part they serve will contain.

2971. It is only in an English theatre that the public have to complain of the admission of the most unfortunate members of the community, and of their subjection to scenes of great indecency. Nothing of this sort occurs on the Continent, whilst here the proprietors of theatres allow the admission of such persons at a reduced rate of payment if they take an admission for the season. As, in this country, it is impossible to exclude any particular class of persons, it would be well so to contrive the access to the dress circle of boxes that it may be arrived at without passing near the saloons, which are generally the resort of the class of people alluded to.

2972. With the exception of the dressings and interior ornaments of the building, and those parts of the stage and machinery which must be made of wood, it would be possible, though perhaps somewhat inconvenient, to erect a theatre, though not absolutely fire-proof, yet very secure against fire. This is, however, a subject not to be treated here; but we ought not to omit that the supply of water from large reservoirs provided in the upper parts of the

building, is a precaution which should never be omitted. Pipes may be laid on from
them to those parts, such as the carpenters' room, scene room, and painting room, where
fires would be most likely to break out, and where, if they did break out, they would
be likely to be most dangerous.

Sect. XVII.

HOSPITALS.

2973. The buildings called hospitals are destined for the reception of the sick poor, for
insane persons, and sometimes for particular diseases, among which old age may be enumerated, or disability from wounds, &c. in the public service, of which last class are the
royal hospitals of Greenwich and Chelsea. There are some for the reception and education
of foundlings, and others for the reception and delivery of pregnant women; and the term
is sometimes used to denote a building appropriated to poor persons, where they have an
allowance for their board and are lodged free; in short, what is otherwise called an almshouse.

2974. The ancients seem to have had no establishments like our hospitals for the sick;
neither do they seem to have had asylums for those who suffered in the public service,
though at Athens they were fed in the Prytaneum. In Sparta there does not appear to
have been any such establishments; neither under the kings, consuls, or emperors of Rome
does it seem there was any institution for the reception of poor sick persons. After the
establishment of Christianity many hospitals were built by the emperors at Constantinople
for poor infants, for aged persons, orphans, and strangers. To the honour of the nations of
Europe, no city in it is unprovided with one or more hospitals. In Paris there are thirty-
two hospitals, and in London, we believe, some few more. The governments of France,
Russia, Germany, and Turkey support these institutions; but in England, with the exception of Chelsea and Greenwich Hospitals, they depend upon the charity and foundations
of benevolent individuals, as at Guy's, Bartholomew's, and the other hospitals of London.
There is great reluctance often on the part of the poor to enter an hospital; and on
this account we do not think that money ill bestowed which tends to impart to it an
agreeable and cheerful exterior. It is almost unnecessary to insist upon a thorough
warming, and, what is equally important, ventilation of the edifice: no means should be
omitted to render the place wholesome, and to prevent infection spreading from one part to
another. If possible, the hospitals of a city should be seated in the least populous parts, if
the health of the city be consulted, or on each suburb; in which latter case the establishment would be nearer the quarter it is to serve, and more accessible in a short time in the
case of accidents.

2975. The plans of some of the finest hospitals in Europe are given in Durand's
Parallèle d'Edifices; among them may be mentioned that of Milan as a very fine example of
disposition. It is indeed the most celebrated in Italy. A large portion of it remains
still unfinished. The architect was Filarete, and, being commenced in 1457, it is of course
in a half-Gothic sort of style. The accommodations for the men are on one side of a very
large cloistered court, 152 feet wide and 204 feet long, and are in the form of a cross,
304 feet long on each side and 30 feet wide. In the intervals of the cross are four court
yards, on whose remaining sides are rooms for the assistants. A canal flowing at the side
answers the domestic purposes of the place, and also turns a mill for the use of the
establishment. On the opposite side of the cloistral court above mentioned are similar
accommodations for the women. And in the middle of the narrow side of the great
cloister, opposite the entrance, is a church, which serves for the whole establishment. The
cloisters of the large court and the main body of the building are in two stories, so that
they form galleries of communications. This edifice has served for model to many others;
and though it is now many years since we visited it, its excellence will not easily be
effaced from our recollection. The hospital, given by Durand in the plates above quoted,
De la Roquette, in the suburbs of Paris, designed by Poyet, was conceived on a magnificent
scale, and was admirably planned. In this design each room, as well those on one side of
the establishment for the males as those on the other side for the females, is appropriated
to one particular disease. Each of these rooms is about 32 feet wide and 30 feet 6 inches
high. Behind the beds (which are in two rows in each room) runs a passage about 3 feet
4 inches wide, which removes them so much from the walls, and allows therefore of the
necessary waiting on the invalids, and hides the wardrobe attached to each bed in the
window recesses. Above these passages, which are about 6 feet 6 inches high, is arranged
on each side a row of windows, by which ventilation as well as light is obtained. The
ground floor contains the halls and offices necessary for such an establishment. The designs for this building were made about 1788, on the instructions drawn up, after several

years' investigation, by a number of the most skilful and learned medical men of France, so as best to unite health and convenience in such an edifice. One of the conditions prescribed by their programme was the complete insulation of each apartment, as well as an easy communication by covered galleries round the building, and these were required to be of such extended dimensions that the air around should be unobstructed and circulating in every part with freedom, thus affording a wholesome promenade for the patients.

2976. The hospitals of Greenwich and Chelsea are good examples for establishments of this nature; the former, indeed, adds to its other excellencies a magnificence in the architecture worthy the object, though not so originally intended. The Hotel des Invalides at Paris is another monument worthy of all praise; and indeed we scarcely know a quadrangle more imposing than the court of this edifice with its double tier of arcades. This hospital contains 7000 veterans, and has attached to it a library of 20,000 volumes. We know not how better to close this section than with the maxims, or rather general observations, of Durand upon the subject: "Dans des hospices," says the author, "dont la disposition répondraient si parfaitement a l'importance de leur objet, on ne craindrait plus de venir chercher des secours. Leur aspect seul, si non magnifique, du moins noble et agréable, influerait sur l'efficacité des remèdes. En entrant dans des tels édifices, où tout annonce le respect que l'on porte à l'humanité, et surtout à l'humanité souffrante, on se sentirait soulagé du poids de la honte, fardeau souvent plus insupportable et plus accablant que celui du malheur même."

Sect. XVIII.

PRISONS.

2977. In considerable cities and towns, humanity, and indeed justice, demands, independent of the injury done to the morals of the public, that the same building which confines the convicted felon should not enclose the debtor and the untried prisoner, as well as him whose offence is not of an aggravated nature. Where there is a mixture of the several classes of those that have violated the laws, they that are young soon become infected by the old offenders with whom they come in contact, and return to society, after undergoing their punishment, much worse members of it than before their incarceration. In small towns, where there is only one, perhaps small, prison, the separation of the prisoners is more difficult to accomplish; but it ought always to be obtained. We hardly need say that the separation of the sexes in a prison is indispensable.

2978. For whatever class of prisoners a building is erected, salubrity and ventilation are as essential as the security of those confined. The loss of liberty is itself a punishment hard to endure, without superadding the risk of disease and death in their train, to persons who may be even innocent of the crimes with which they are charged. Besides which, the disease engendered in a gaol called the prison fever may spread into the city and carry off its inhabitants.

2979. We shall here place before the student the principal requisites which the celebrated Howard has specified for prisons. "A county gaol, and indeed every prison, should be built on a spot that is airy, and, if possible, near a river or brook. I have commonly found prisons near a river the cleanest and most healthy. They generally have not (and indeed could not well have) subterraneous dungeons, which have been so fatal to thousands; and by their nearness to running water another evil almost as noxious is prevented, that is, the stench of sewers. I said a gaol should be near a stream; but I must annex this caution, that it be not so near as that either the house or yard shall be within the reach of floods." . . . "If it be not practicable to build near a stream, then an eminence should be chosen; for as the wall round a prison should be so high as greatly to obstruct a free circulation of air, this inconvenience should be lessened by rising ground, and the prison should not be surrounded by other buildings, nor built in the middle of a town or city. That part of the building which is detached from the walls, and contains the men felons' wards, may be square or rectangular, raised on arcades that it may be more airy, and have under it a dry walk in wet weather. These wards over arcades are also best for safety; for I have found that escapes have been most commonly effected by undermining cells and dungeons. If felons should find any other means to break out of the raised ward, they will still be stopped by the wall of the court, which is the principal security; and the walls of the wards need not then be of that great thickness they are generally built, whereby the access of light and air is impeded. I wish to have so many small rooms or cabins that each criminal may sleep alone; these rooms to be ten feet high to the crown of the arch, and to have double doors, one of them iron-latticed for the circulation of air. If it be difficult to prevent their being together in the daytime, they should by all means be separated at night. Solitude and silence are favourable to reflec-

tion, and may possibly lead to repentance." . . . "The separation I am pleading for, especially at night, would prevent escapes, or make them very difficult, for that is the time in which they are generally planned and effected. Another reason for separation is, that it would free gaolers from a difficulty of which I have heard them complain : they hardly know where to keep criminals admitted to be evidence for the king ; these would be murdered by their accomplices if put among them, and in more than one prison I have seen them for that reason put in the women's ward. Where there are opposite windows they should have shutters, but these should be open all day. In the men felons' ward the windows should be six feet from the floor; there should be no glass, nor should the prisoners be allowed to stop them with straw, &c. The women felons' ward should be quite distinct from that of the men, and the young criminals from old and hardened offenders. Each of these three classes should also have their day room or kitchen with a fireplace, and their court and offices all separate. Every court should be paved with flags or flat stones for the more convenient washing it, and have a good pump or water laid on, both if possible ; and the pump and pipes should be repaired as soon as they need it, otherwise the gaols will soon be offensive and unwholesome, as I have always found them to be in such cases. A small stream constantly running in the court is very desirable. In a room or shed near the pump or pipe there should be a commodious bath, with steps, (as there is in some country hospitals,) to wash prisoners that come in dirty, and to induce them afterwards to the frequent use of it. It should be filled every morning, and let off in the evening through the sewers into the drains. There should also be a copper in the shed to heat a quantity of water sufficient to warm that in the bath for those that are sickly. There should also be an oven: nothing so effectually destroys vermin in clothes and bedding, nor purifies them so thoroughly when tainted with infection, as being a few hours in an oven moderately heated. The infirmary or sick ward should be in the most airy part of the court, quite detached from the rest of the gaol, and raised on arcades. These rooms should never be without crib-beds and bedding. In the middle of the floor of each room there should be a grate of twelve or fourteen inches square, covered with a shutter or hatch at night. The sewers or vaults of all prisons should be in the courts, and not in the passages, and (like those in colleges) close boarded between the seats up to the ceiling, the boards projecting ten inches before each seat. The infirmary and sheds will not render the court unsafe, provided the walls have parapets or small *chevaux de frise*. Debtors and felons should have wards totally separate; the peace, the cleanliness, the health and morals of debtors cannot be secured otherwise. The ward for men debtors should also be over arcades, and placed on one side of the gaoler's house. This house should be in or near the middle of the gaol, with windows to the felons' and to the debtors' courts. This would be a check on the prisoners to keep them in order, and would engage the gaoler to be attentive to cleanliness and constant washing to prevent his own apartments from being offensive. A chapel is necessary in a gaol. I have chosen for it what seems to me a proper situation. It should have a gallery for debtors or women; for the latter should be out of sight of all the other prisoners, and the rest may be separated below."

2980. The above general principles are excellent, and are followed in all gaols of modern construction. The tread-mill is also introduced for punishment, as well as occasionally workshops for trades, to avoid the idleness of the prisoners. Society owes a debt of infinite magnitude to the benevolent man from whom the foregoing quotation has been taken.

2981. One of the most celebrated prisons on a panoptical system in Europe is the celebrated house of correction at Ghent. It is situated on the north side of that city, on the Coupure canal, which is bordered by a double row of large trees. A plate of the plan is given, No. 28. Durand's *Parallèle d'Edifices*. It was begun in 1773, under the reign of Maria Theresa, and is in the form of a slightly elongated octagon, in the centre whereof is a spacious court, which communicates with the different quadrangles of the edifice. Each quadrangle or ward (eight in number) has a yard, and in the centre of that, belonging to the female ward, is a large basin of water, in which the female prisoners wash the linen of the whole establishment. Each prisoner sleeps alone, in a small but well-aired room, and is employed during the day in working at the trade or business to which he or she is competent. Of the produce of such labour, government retains one half when the prisoners are detained merely for correction, six tenths when condemned to a term of imprisonment under martial law, and seven tenths when they have been sentenced to hard labour. The remainder is divided into two portions, one given weekly to the prisoners for pocket money, the other given to them on the expiry of their imprisonment, to assist their reestablishment in society. Religious service and instruction are provided; and if prisoners are destitute of the first elements of knowledge, they are taught reading, writing, and arithmetic, besides receiving other instruction. Solitary confinement is the punishment for insubordination or refractory conduct. The shops for refreshments sold to the prisoners are strictly regulated by the officers of the institution; and the profits resulting from the

sale of the different articles are reserved for rewarding the most industrious and best-behaved prisoners. The new part of the building, which has recently been completed, has cost 40,000*l.* sterling ; and the whole edifice, when finished, and there is much still to be done, will contain 2600 prisoners. The defect in the institution lies in the reception of unfortunate and criminal persons of all descriptions, from the simple mendicant to the hardened murderer. It is true that those confined for heinous crimes are separated from those who have been guilty of misdemeanours ; but the knowledge, on the part of all its inmates, that they to a certain extent are considered in the same predicament, must necessarily so operate on their minds as to throw down the barriers between misfortune and crime, as well as between those who are only commencing a guilty course and those who have consummated their vicious career. The Penitentiary at Milbank, in London, has been erected in some measure on the principles of the house of correction at Ghent, but its inmates are such only as have received the sentence of a criminal court. Where, indeed, the population is so great as in the metropolis of England, prisons for each class of offenders should be provided, at whatever cost. It is a duty due from the government to humanity to see that this is done.

Sect. XIX.

BARRACKS.

2982. Barracks, or buildings for the reception of the military, were common with the Romans, amongst whom they were called *castra* or camps. There were many of these at Rome and in the provinces ; but the most perfect remains of Roman barracks are at Pompeii, of which sufficient remains exist to give us a general idea of their distribution. The distribution was in an oblong, and the quadrangle or parade was surrounded by a covered gallery on columns. From this gallery was the entrance to the rooms of the soldiers, but it also served as an ambulatory for exercise. Beyond the further end, opposite the entrance, was a theatre. A more perfect knowledge, however, than we have of the barracks of the ancients, would not assist us in providing better for the military in these days ; indeed, there is little required to be said in this place on the subject, inasmuch as in respect of healthy situation, perfect ventilation, and security against fire, the principles which chiefly regulate the disposition and distribution of a hospital, are equally applicable in building barracks, which are, in truth, *hospitia* for the reception of men in health instead of sick persons. Private soldiers in barracks, however, usually sleep on inclined planes, raised from the floor, and at the head abutting against the wall, instead of being provided with separate beds. In Paris there are no less than thirty buildings used as barracks. The details necessary to be provided are a canteen or public-house, for the use of the privates and non-commissioned officers ; a spacious mess-room and separate apartments for the officers, and an infirmary. In cavalry barracks, proper stabling and a riding-house of large dimensions must of course be added. For cleanliness, all the yards should be paved, and the utmost precaution taken for carrying off all filth and waste water by means of drainage into a sewer, having a considerable fall from the place. This will, as much as anything, tend to the healthiness of the building. A valuable *Report* by a Commission on this subject was issued in 1855.

Sect. XX.

PRIVATE BUILDINGS — GENERAL OBSERVATIONS.

2983. Private buildings differ in their proper character from public buildings as much as one public building differs in character from another not of the same kind. The ends in both, however, in common, are suitableness and utility. The means are the same, namely, the observance of convenience and economy. The same elements are used in the formation of one as of the other ; hence they are subject to the same principles and the same mechanical composition. Distribution, which is usually treated distinct from decoration and construction, and very improperly so, as applied to private edifices, is conducted as for public buildings, that is, as we have said, with a view to utility and economy.

2984. If the student thoroughly understand the true principles of architecture, — if he possess the facility of combining the different elements of buildings, or, in other words, fully comprehend the mechanism of composition, which it has in a previous part of this Book (III.) been our object to explain, nothing will remain for him in the composition of private buildings, but to study the special or particular conveniences required in each. There are some quaint old aphorisms of Dr. Fuller, prebendary of Sarum, which are so

applicable to all private buildings, that we shall not apologise for transferring them to our pages.

2985. " First," he says, " let not the common rooms be several, nor the several rooms common ; that the common rooms should not be private or retired, as the hall (which is a pandochæum), galleries, &c., which are to be open ; and the chambers, closets, &c. retired and private, provided the whole house be not spent in paths. Light (God's eldest daughter) is a principal beauty in a *building* ; yet it shines not alike from all parts of the heavens. An east window gives the infant beams of the sun, before they are of strength to do harm, and is offensive to none but a sluggard. A south window in summer is a chimney with a fire in it, and stands in need to be screened by a curtain. In a west window the sun grows low, and over familiar towards night in summer time, and with more light than delight. A north window is best for butteries and cellars, where the beer will be sour because the sun smiles upon it. Thorough lights are best for rooms of entertainments, and windows on one side for dormitories."

2986. " Secondly, as to capaciousness, a house had better be too little for a day than too big for a year ; therefore houses ought to be proportioned to ordinary occasions, and not to extraordinary. It will be easier borrowing a brace of chambers of a neighbour for a night, than a bag of money for a year ; therefore 'tis a vanity to proportion the receipt to an extraordinary occasion, as those do who, by overbuilding their houses, dilapidate their lands, so that their estates are pressed to death under the weight of their house."

2987. " Thirdly, as for strength, country houses must be substantives, able to stand of themselves, not like city buildings, supported and flanked by those of their neighbour on each side. By strength is meant such as may resist weather and time, but not attacks; castles being out of date in England, except on the sea-coasts, &c. As for moats round houses, 'tis questionable whether the fogs that arise from the water are not more unhealthful than the defence that the water gives countervails, or the fish brings profit."

2988. " Fourthly, as for beauty, let not the front look asquint upon a stranger, but accost him right at his entrance. Uniformity and proportions are very pleasing to the eye; and 'tis observable that freestone, like a fair complexion, grows old, whilst bricks keep their beauty longest."

2989. " Fifthly, let the offices keep their due distance from the mansion-house; those are too familiar which presume to be of the same pile with it. The same may be said of stables and barns ; without which a house is like a city without works, it can never hold out long. It is not only very inconvenient, but rather a blemish than a beauty to a building, to see the barns and stables too near the house; because cattle, poultry, and suchlike must be kept near them, which will be an annoyance to a house. Gardens ought also to be disposed in their proper places. When God planted a garden eastward, he made to grow out of the ground every tree pleasant to the sight and good for food. Sure he knew better what was proper for a garden than those who now-a-days only feed their eyes and starve their taste and smell. The same honest old dignitary (would we had some such in these days !) says, " He who alters an old house is ty'd as a translator to the original, and is confined to the fancy of the first builder. Such a man would be unwise to pull down a good old building, perhaps to erect a worse new one. But those who erect a new house from the ground are worthy of blame if they make it not handsome and useful, when method and confusion are both of a price to them."

Sect. XXI.

PRIVATE BUILDINGS IN TOWNS.

2990. The common houses of the town are not those which will engage our attention. In London, and indeed throughout the towns of England, the habits of the people lead them to prefer separate houses for each family, to one large one in which several families may be well lodged, or, in other words, they prefer rows of mean-looking buildings, with holes in the walls for windows, to the palatial appearance which results, in Paris and most of the other cities in Europe, from large magnificent buildings with courts, and capable of accommodating a number of different establishments. The section will be confined chiefly to the arrangement of a house of the first class ; and from what will be said, sufficient hints may be drawn for the composition of those in a lower class.

2991. The private buildings in a town are often in their composition beset with difficulties which do not occur in those of the country, where the extent of site is freer and ampler. These, therefore, may be isolated, and receive light from every side. Their offices may be separated from the main house, and the parts may be disposed in the simplest possible manner ; but in cities the site is generally more or less restricted, often very

irregular in form, and generally bounded by party walls. Yet, with all these obstacles, it is necessary to provide almost as many conveniences as are required in a country house; whence the disposition cannot be so simple in its application as where there is no restraint. All that can be done is to make it as much so as the nature of the spot will permit, and to produce the maximum of comfort which the site affords.

2992. Nothing must be considered below the attention of an accomplished architect, nor anything above his powers; he ought as cheerfully to undertake for the proprietor the conduct of the meanest cottage as of the most magnificent palace. Little will be requisite to be said on the common houses of London, or other cities and towns in which there are seldom more than two rooms and a closet on a floor, with an opening behind. These may be varied; but the general mode is to construct them with a kitchen in a floor sunk below the ground, and a room behind, serving for a variety of purposes; an area in front, with vaults under the street, and the same often in the rear of the house. The space opposite the descending stairs will form a dark closet; and the privies, and wine and beer cellars, with other small offices, are provided in the vaults. On the ground floor there is rarely more than a passage on one side, which conducts to a staircase; and this requiring more width than the passage itself, the best room on this floor is placed in front, and the back is a smaller room, often opening on a small light closet still further in the rear. A yard is supposed behind, by which light is obtained for the back room. On the one-pair and other floors the passage becomes unnecessary as an access; the drawing or front room therefore runs over it, and becomes larger, capable, in the upper floors, of subdivision for bedrooms, or other purposes, as may be required; and the back rooms, with their closets, if carried up, follow the form of those on the ground floor. Though little variety may be the result of the restricted space to which this species of house is usually confined, the addition of four or five feet either way will enable an intelligent architect to throw in closets and other conveniences which are invaluable, as relieving a small house from the pressure which otherwise will exist in the different apartments. But this will be obvious to the practical man, unless he walks about blindfold. The houses we have just described may stand upon a site of about twenty feet by thirty feet, independent of the vaults in front and rear, and the back light closet, which is an invaluable appendage to a house of this description; which is the scale of a second-rate house.

2993. Of the next higher rate of house the varieties are too great to be described, because the extent of the largest arrives at what would be called a palace on the continent. But, taking a mean between that just described and that last named, we may take one similar to a moderate one in Portland Place for example. In such a one we must provide, on the basement or sunk story, vaults under the street for beer, coals, wood, privies, and the like, the refuse or dust of the house. The body or corps de logis on this floor must contain housekeeper's room, servants' hall, rooms for butler and head footman, wine cellar, closets for linen, strong room for plate, with closets and other conveniences for the household. The ascending staircase must also have a space set apart for it. In the rear, under the open area behind, will be placed a kitchen, scullery, and the larder, with the other appendages of this part of the household; an area, covered, where the communication with the rest of the floor is made between the body of the house and the offices in question. Beyond the kitchen are often vaults (though the disposition is sometimes otherwise), over which the stables and coachhouses are placed, opening on the ground floor on to a mews parallel to the street in which the house is situate. The ground floor of this disposition has usually a dining-room in front, with a good-sized hall at its side, leading to a staircase which ascends in direction of the long side of the house; and this is necessary when the rooms above are to communicate by folding doors. In some old houses, however, the staircase ascends between the front and back rooms, and a back staircase is provided by the side of it. But more commonly this is placed beyond the principal stairs, to allow of throwing the drawing-rooms into one. In rear of the dining-room is often placed a library for the gentleman of the house; and beyond this, and further than the back stairs, when the lateral staircase is used, a waiting-room, at the rear of which a water-closet may be placed, with a door from it to the area over the kitchen; or there may be a communication of this sort from the waiting-room, which may serve the purpose of access to the stables. On the one-pair floor the disposition will be two drawing-rooms, a boudoir over the waiting-room, and beyond this a water-closet. On the two-pair floor two bed-rooms, each with a dressing-room, or three bed-rooms and one dressing-room, and a bath-room and water-closet. Above this four bed-rooms and closets may be obtained; and, if necessary, rooms in the roof in addition. For a good house of this class, with the offices, the plot of ground should not be much less than 100 feet by 30.

2994. Of the first class of houses, as a model may be taken the town-house, in Piccadilly, of His Grace the Duke of Devonshire, which, with the offices and court-yard in front, covers an area extending about 231 feet towards the street, and 188 feet in depth, whereof the house itself occupies a frontage of 163 feet and a depth of 188 feet, and opens on to a large garden in the rear. On the east side of the court-yard are dis-

posed the kitchen and other domestic offices, opposite whereto, on the west side, stand the coach-houses and stabling. The basement of the house contains apartments for the various persons attached to such an establishment. The principal floor to which the ascent is by an external staircase, contains an entrance-hall, 35 feet by 30 feet, and communicates to an apartment on the west side, 33 feet by 22 feet, leading to the south-western corner room, which is 20 feet square. On the north of the last is a room, making the north-west angle of the building, and this is 40 feet by 20 feet. On the east side of this last, and facing the north, is a room 33 feet by 23 feet, and in the centre of the north front, corresponding with the width of the hall, is an apartment 30 feet by 23 feet 6 inches. To the east of the last is a room 33 feet by 24 feet, and east of that, forming the north-east angle, is a small room 20 feet square. Thus far these rooms, seven in number, are all *en suite*, but this is in some measure interrupted by the remainder of the east flank, which is filled with three smaller rooms. To that of them, however, at the south, which is 20 feet square, a passage is preserved, and from that you enter another room, 23 feet by 22 feet, which once more brings you back to the hall. The staircases are between the north and south rooms on each side of the hall. Above this floor are the lodging rooms, &c. The superficial area of all the reception rooms on the principal floor, added together, amounts to 5708 feet.

2995. Burlington-house, in some respects,—for instance, in its beautiful front court,— may be considered superior to that we have just described. It can be hardly necessary to add that, in such edifices, rooms must be provided for steward, butler, housekeeper, stillroom-maid, servants' hall of good dimensions, valets, ladies' maids, &c.; for a muniment room and plate, both of which must be fire-proof. Baths also should be placed on the chamber floor, with other conveniences which will occur to the architect. The rooms for pictures, if possible, should be on the north side of the building. To Lord Burlington the English aristocracy is much indebted for the introduction of the Italian style into their dwellings; for the taste of Jones had almost passed away when the talented nobleman in question gave a new impetus to proper distribution and decoration. Plans and elevations of Devonshire-house are given in the *Vitruvius Britannicus*, which contains other town houses of importance well worth the student's attention.

Sect. XXII.

PRIVATE BUILDINGS IN THE COUNTRY.

2996. Of first-class private buildings in the country, we apprehend we cannot furnish better hints than by describing that of Kedlestone, in Derbyshire, erected for Lord Scarsdale by Robert Adam. There are others which are larger, but we do not think any superior in distribution and effect. The plans and elevations of it are to be seen in the *Vitruvius Britannicus* above mentioned. The main body of the house M (*fig.* 1352.), is about 136 feet by 105 feet; and at each angle are quadrants of communication to the four wings A, B, C, and D, which are each about 70 feet by 54 feet. On the basement story of the main building are a large and small sub-hall in the centre, the former 67 feet 3 inches by 42 feet, and the latter 42 feet by 40 feet 7 inches. On the right of these are disposed a butler's room, 22 feet 6 inches by 17 feet 9 inches; a housekeeper's room, and a steward's room, 30 feet by 21 feet 6 inches. On the left, a bath, a gun-room, 23 feet

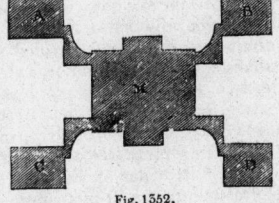

Fig. 1352.

9 inches by 23 feet 7 inches; a smoking parlour, 28 feet by 17 feet 9 inches; a boot-room, 22 feet 6 inches by 17 feet 9 inches, besides closets and staircases, &c. on either side. The wing B contains the stables, a chapel, and other apartments. C, sleeping and other rooms, eight in number, with a staircase which conducts to the corridor in the corresponding quadrant. D contains the kitchen and its requisite accessories, and a servants' hall. This wing has also a staircase to its corresponding corridor in the quadrant, which attaches it to the main body. On the principal story, the main body M has at the entrance, which is in the centre, and approached by a noble flight of steps, a magnificent hall, 69 feet 3 inches by 42 feet, at the end whereof is a saloon 42 feet diameter. To the right, entering from the hall, is the principal staircase, beyond which, laterally, is a bed-chamber 33 feet by 22 feet, with its accessories; and on its end, towards the back front, are ante-rooms, and towards the front the dining-room, whence by the corridor is access to the kitchen in the wing D, and from the ante-rooms above mentioned the corresponding corridor on that side leads to a conservatory in the back front of the wing, and the upper part of the chapel. On the left-hand side of the hall, with windows in the left flank of the main body, is the

drawing-room, 44 feet by 28 feet; at the end towards the rear is a library, which is continued in the corridor leading to the wing A, wherein is a music *gallery*, 66 feet by 18 feet, with other rooms and a staircase. On the end of the drawing-room, towards the front, is a music *room*, 36 feet by 24 feet, whence the corridor leads to Lord Scarsdale's bedroom, 18 feet square, with dressing-rooms, and the lady's library, which, on this floor, are in the wing C. The wing D is occupied by the upper part of the kitchen, a laundry, 35 feet by 18 feet, and some bedrooms, to which access is by a gallery over part of the kitchen. The main body and wings contain a story over what has been last described, chiefly for chambers. We have before (in the First Book, *figs.* 221, 222.) noticed the splendid hall and salon, which occupy the height of the whole building, and are, though somewhat faulty in detail, very finely-conceived and well-proportioned apartments. The former is 40 feet high to the top of the cove, and the latter 55 feet to the level of the eye of the dome. Though the elevations exhibit defects, we are not inclined to quarrel with them in a dwelling which deserves rather the name of a palace than of a country house.

2997. England abounds with country seats of this class: among them is Holkham, which has already been mentioned in the First Book (511.); but we know none for disposition that can claim superiority over that which we have above described at length, from which the student may derive much information on the requirenda in a mansion of the first class. It is to be understood that we here intend modern buildings. The houses of the times of Elizabeth and James are many of them magnificent structures, but the comfort introduced into houses of later date leaves them, independent of their picturesque beauty, far behind the buildings of Kent, Carr, James, and many others. Blenheim is monumental in its design, and properly so, and hence does not fall within the category of the section.

2998. There are, of course, many intervening degrees between the mansion we have just described and the villa of the retired banker or merchant: it would be impossible to state them in detail. We have given the maximum in the above case, and we shall now give the minimum for the class last mentioned.

2999. The smallest site of ground on which a villa can be well designed is, supposing it an oblong, about 80 feet by 56 to 60 feet. This on the principal floor will admit of a hall, a salon or ante-room, which may lead to the principal apartments, a drawing-room, two secondary drawing-rooms, one whereof may be appropriated to the reception of a billiard table, a good dining-room, not less than 30 feet by 20 feet, a library of equal size, with other rooms, suitable to the particular taste of the proprietor, and the conveniences and accessories which such a building requires. The ground, supposing the domestic offices to be under the principal floor, should be raised, so that they need not be much sunk below the general level of the land. If the building be seated on rising ground, a little more sinking may be allowed than under other circumstances, provided the lower story be protected by dry drains all round the building, to prevent the earth lying against the walls, because drainage, the most important of all things in a building, may then be obtained easily by the natural fall of the ground. The plot we have mentioned will admit of all the offices below, which are necessary for the service of a good-sized family, and above, with only one story above the principal one, will afford a pretty fair allowance of dormitories; but if a concealed story for servants be practised in the roof, there are few establishments on a common scale for which, on the plot, accommodation may not be provided by a skilful artist. The stables and coach-houses and the greenhouses should stand apart. Some persons like to have these communicating with the villa itself; but the practice is destructive of symmetry, and very injurious (except in the villa on an irregular plan, which then rather approaches to the *cottage orné*) to the general effect of the architecture.

3000. The villas at Foot's Cray and Mereworth, imitations of Palladio's Villa Capra, so often mentioned in this volume, and represented in *fig.* 1018., are the maxima of villas: beyond this the villa becomes a mansion, and must be treated as one on a scale more or less grand, as the means of the proprietor allow the architect to provide for his wants. All precepts, however, on this head are valueless, because the architect is regulated so much by the convenience required. He must possess himself fully of that, and, attending to the general rules given throughout the work, but especially in this Third Book, he will find little difficulty in fulfilling the commission with which he is intrusted. Among other matters let him well inform himself of what has been done, and make himself master of the points involved in domestic economy, from the lowest to the highest grade, and he cannot, using that information, fail of giving his employer that satisfaction which is the first care that should animate him.

3001. It is not our intention to touch upon the *cottage orné*, as it is called. This is a nondescript sort of building, subject only to rules which the architect chooses to impose upon himself. The only point to be attended to, after internal comfort has been provided for, is to present picturesque effect in the exterior. It is a branch of practice requiring a minimum of mind on the part of the architect, and for the successful execution of which the landscapes of Gaspar Poussin will give him enough hints to stud a province with them.

Sect. XXIII.

FARM-HOUSES.

3002. The mere building denominated a farm-house is simple enough in its distribution, and scarcely justifies a section here, because the persons engaged in agriculture have generally the best notion of the mode of suiting it to their own particular business and the nature of the farm they occupy. It is first to be considered whether it is expedient to place it close to the other buildings of the farm, such as the barns, stables, and stalls for cattle, &c. If so, it should be designed in character with them, and a large space of ground is enclosed for the formation of a farm-yard; which, notwithstanding the seemingly repulsive nature of the subject, may be made a very picturesque composition as a whole. The farm-house itself, though it must be sufficiently large to accommodate the family of the farmer, should be restricted in the size of its rooms and the extent of its plan by the magnitude of the farm, it being altogether an absurdity to plant a large house on a small farm, not only because of the original cost, which the rent of the land will not justify, but because of the cost of the annual repairs which a large building entails beyond those of a smaller one. The same observation applies to the farm buildings themselves, which in extent must be regulated by the size of the farm cultivated. It is moreover to be considered, in respect of the latter, whether the farm be grazing or arable. In the first case more provision of cattle sheds must be afforded; in the latter case more barns must be allotted to the cultivator. These, however, are matters upon which the architect receives his instructions from the proprietor, and whereon, generally speaking, he is himself incompetent to form a correct judgment.

3003. In the commonest farm-houses the external door may open to a plain passage, at the end whereof the staircase may be placed. On one side of the passage may be a common kitchen, and on the other side the better or larger kitchen, serving also as a parlour for the farmer and his family. Beyond these, on one side, may be placed the pantry, and on the other side the dairy-room, the last being much larger than the former, and being on the side of the parlour or best kitchen, not so liable to the heat. To these, as needful, may be added more rooms on the ground floor; the upper story being divided into bedchambers for the family, with garrets over them for the servants. The kitchens should be placed upon arched cellars on several accounts, not the least of which is that the farmer should have the means of preserving in good condition the malt liquor or cyder which is the principal beverage of his establishment. It is a sad mistake on the part of landed proprietors, though common enough, to think that such buildings are not only below the care of an architect, but that he is too ignorant of the wants of the farmer to be competent to the task; if, however, he will reflect for a moment, he must admit that the artist who can make the most of a large plot of ground, with numberless requirements in the accommodation, is not less able to turn to the greatest advantage for the comfort of the occupier even a small farm-house.

3004. In the erection of a larger farm-house the choice of the site, as before, must depend on the nature of the ground and the situation of the farm. Health and convenience are the primary governing matters. It must never be placed where it cannot be well drained. It should be central to the land, and as near the road as the conditions will admit. For such a building the principal door may open into a moderately wide passage, having therein a staircase to the upper rooms. On the right of the passage a common kitchen may be provided for the family, and on the left a room somewhat larger, which in very small farm-houses used to be called the best kitchen, but which in this may be really the parlour, where the family may sit retired from the servants. Under these, cellars, as above mentioned, may be provided. On the ground floor we may now add a bakehouse and scullery to the pantry and dairy provided in the first scheme, as also closets and such conveniences for the housewife. The floor above may be extended over the additional rooms just mentioned, thus giving lodging room to a larger number of persons than to those contemplated in the first scheme. "In this manner," says Ware, in his *Complete Body of Architecture*, folio, London, 1756, "the young architect will very easily see how to enlarge or contract his plan for the building of farm-houses, according to the intended bigness.". . . "They all consist of the same number of rooms, and in general of the same number of offices; this is where the bare article of convenience for farming is concerned. Where the inhabitant is grown rich, and intends to live in another manner, he may add what he pleases, which the architect may adopt.". . . "It is then no longer to be considered a farm-house, but as the house of some person of fortune, who intends to live as those independent of business do, but withal to have some farming in his eye." When the farm-house comes to this extent it trenches hard upon the condition of the villa, though not quite reaching it, because the latter includes many provisions for a refined mode of living which the yeoman, the pride of England, does not require; a class which, we fear, the manufacturing and commercial classes are fast annihilating.

Sect. XXIV.

COTTAGES.

3005. " Estates," observes Kent, (*Hints to Gentlemen of Landed Property*, 8vo. London, 1776,) " being of no value without hands to cultivate them, the labourer is one of the most valuable members of society: without him the richest soil is not worth owning." It follows, then, that his condition should be most especially considered, and it is a duty on every country gentleman to take care that the labourers on his estate are so considered as to be made at least comfortable. " The shattered hovels," says the same author, " which half the poor of this kingdom are obliged to put up with, is truly affecting to a heart fraught with humanity." . . . " The weather penetrates all parts of them, which must occasion illness of various kinds, particularly agues ; which more frequently visit the children of cottagers than any others, and early shake their constitutions." . . . " We are careful of our horses, nay, of our dogs, which are less valuable animals ; we bestow considerable attention upon our stables and kennels, but we are apt to look upon cottages as incumbrances and clogs to our property, when, in fact, those who occupy them are the very nerves and sinews of agriculture." We fear the neglect of the comfort of the cottager has given a greater impulse to poaching and other crimes than his natural propensities have induced. This, however, is not a matter for discussion here. It is not to be supposed that we mean the labourer is to be placed in an expensive dwelling ; a difference of rank must exist ; and if the whole revenue of the country were divided among the population per head, it would be seen (as M. Dupin has recently shown in a most eloquent and sound address delivered in Paris as respects France) that the division of it per day, after allowing for the expenses of the most economical government that could be devised, would be such as would not satisfy the lowest class of labourer, much less the ingenious mechanic. This is a matter so susceptible of proof, and so proper to be generally promulgated, that we have here gone a little out of our way lest we should be considered too urgent with respect to the cottager.

3006. No cottage ought to be erected which does not contain a warm, comfortable, plain room, with an oven to bake the bread of its occupier ; a small closet for the beer and provisions, two wholesome lodging rooms, one whereof should be for the man and his wife, and the other for his children. It would be well always, if possible, that the boys and girls in a cottage should be separated ; but this unfortunately entails an expense, and perhaps is not so materially necessary, because the boys find employment at an early age. A shed for fuel should be attached.

Cottages should always be placed in sheltered spots, and as near as possible to the farm where the labourer is employed. The wear and tear of a man is not very dissimilar to that of an engine, and it tends as much to the interest of the farmer as it does to the comfort of the labourer that all unnecessary fatigue be avoided.

3007. In the erection of cottages it is not only more economical, but more comfortable to the occupiers, that they should be built double, or in twos at least. In those provinces where brick or stone can be obtained they should never be constructed with timber, and tiles, if they can conveniently be had, should always supersede thatch. Further observation on this subject will be unnecessary, for we have ill delivered the principles of our art if the student be not now prepared to carry out the few hints on the subject of cottages, — buildings, in point of fact, of importance paramount to the palace which the sovereign inhabits.

The following remarks are by J. C. Loudon, and are extracted from a " Report to Her Majesty's principal Secretary of State, from the Poor Law Commissioners, on an Enquiry into the Sanitary Condition of the Labouring Population of Great Britain," 1842.

" The *essential requisites* of a comfortable labourer's cottage may be thus summed up : —

" 1. The cottage should be placed alongside a public road, as being more cheerful than a solitary situation, and in order that the cottager may enjoy the applause of the public when he has his garden in good order and keeping.

" 2. The cottage should be so placed that the sun may shine on every side of it during the day throughout the year, when he is visible. For this reason, the front of the cottage can only be parallel to the public road in the case of roads in the direction of north-east, south-west, north-west, and south-east ; in all other cases the front must be placed obliquely to the road, which, as we have previously shown, is greatly preferable to having the front parallel to the road.

" 3. Every cottage ought to have the floor elevated, that it may be dry ; the walls double or hollow, or battened, or not less than eighteen inches thick, that they may retain heat ; with a course of slate or flagstone, or tiles bedded in cement, six inches above the surface, to prevent the rising of damp ; the roof thick or double, for the sake of warmth ; and projecting eighteen inches or two feet at the eaves, in order to keep the walls dry, and to check the radiation of heat from their exterior surface.

" 4. In general, every cottage ought to be two stories high, so that the sleeping rooms may not be on the ground floor ; and the ground floor ought to be from six inches to one foot above the outer surface.

" 5. The minimum of accommodation ought to be the kitchen or living room, a back kitchen or wash-house, and a pantry, on the ground-floor, with three bedrooms over ; or two rooms and a wash-house on the ground-floor, and two bedrooms over.

" 6. Every cottage, including its garden, yard, &c., ought to occupy not less than one sixth of an acre ; and the garden ought to surround the cottage, or at all events to extend both before and behind.   In general, there ought to be a front garden and a back yard, the latter being entered from the back kitchen, and containing a privy, liquid manure tank, place for dust and ashes, and place for fuel.

" 7. If practicable, every cottage ought to stand singly, and surrounded by its garden ; or at all events not more than two cottages ought to be joined together.   Among other important arguments in favour of this arrangement, it may be mentioned that it is the only one by which the sun can shine every day on every side of the cottage.   When cottages are joined together in a row, unless that row is in a diagonal direction with reference to a south and north line, the sun will shine chiefly on one side.   By having cottages singly or in pairs, they may always be placed along any road in such a manner that the sun may shine on every side of them, provided the point given up of having the front parallel to the road, a point which in our opinion ought not for a moment to be put in competition with the advantages of an equal diffusion of sunshine.

" 8. Every cottage ought to have an entrance porch for containing the labourer's tools, and into which, if possible, the stairs ought to open, in order that the bedrooms may be communicated with, without passing through the front or back kitchen.   This, in the case of sickness, is very desirable, and also in the case of deaths, as the remains may be carried down stairs while the family are in the front room.

" 9. The door to the front kitchen or best room should open from the porch, and not from the back kitchen, which, as it contains the cooking utensils and washing apparatus, can never be fit for being passed through by a stranger, or even the master of a family, where proper regard is had by the mistress to cleanliness and delicacy.

" 10. When there is a supply of clear water from a spring adjoining the cottage, or from some other efficient source, then there ought to be a well or tank, partly under the floor of the back kitchen for drawing it up for use, as hereafter described in detail.   The advantages of having the tank or well under the back kitchen are, that it will be secure from frost, and that the labour of carrying water will be avoided.

" 11. The privy should always be separated from the dwelling, unless it is a proper water-closet, with a soil-pipe communicating with a distant liquid manure tank or cesspool. When detached, the privy should be over or adjoining a liquid manure tank, in which a straight tube from the bottom of the basin ought to terminate ; by which means the soil basin may always be kept clean by pouring down the common slops of the house.   No surface being left from which smell can arise, except that of the area of the pipe, the double flap, to be hereafter described, will prevent the escape of the evaporation from this small surface, and also ensure a dry and clean seat.

" 12. The situation of the liquid manure tank should be as far as possible from that of the filtered water tank or clear water well.   It should be covered by an air-tight cover of flagstone, and have a narrow well adjoining, into which the liquid should filter through a grating, so as to be pumped up or taken away without grosser impurities, and in this state applied to the soil about growing crops.

" 13. In general, proprietors ought not to intrust the erection of labourers' cottages on their estate to the farmers, as it is chiefly owing to this practice that so many wretched hovels exist in the best-cultivated districts of Scotland and in Northumberland.

" 14. No landed proprietor, as we think, ought to charge more for the land on which cottages are built than he would receive for it from a farmer if let as part of a farm ; and no more rent ought to be charged for the cost of building the cottage and enclosing the garden than the same sum would yield if invested in land, or, at all events, not more than can be obtained by government securities.

" 15. Most of these conditions are laid down on the supposition that the intended builder of the cottage is actuated more by feelings of human sympathy than by a desire to make money ; and hence they are addressed to the wealthy, and especially to the proprietors of land and extensive manufactories or mines."

3008. To the foregoing eighteen essential requisites we have only to add a few observations on the design for a cottage.   The plan should not be straggling, or such as to render a variety of roof-lines necessary, and although its arrangement should be compact, it should not be cramped.   Shapeless nooks and corners do not become convenient cupboards and closets or because they are enclosed and possess a door, but rather convenient hiding-places for mice and dirt.   Too many projections make a small building look smaller by

depriving it of breadth; and too great a diversity of colour gives it a vulgar appearance, and frequently destroys the effect of really good proportions. The temptation to build picturesquely and to try experiments with new materials and methods of construction, is much greater in the country than in town. Coloured bricks, bands of ornamental tiles, glazed patera, and other similar attractions, may give variety to elevations, but they must be adopted with considerable caution in small buildings. New inventions and pseudo-economical devices too often prove miserable and expensive delusions. As the details of construction, &c., which are given in the next section, are equally applicable to those in the country, this subject will be now dismissed.

3009. In the autumn of 1863 two premiums of 25*l.* each were offered through the Society of Arts for the most approved designs for cottages, to be built singly or in pairs, at a cost not exceeding 100*l.* each. It was essential that each cottage should fulfil the following requirements. On the ground floor, a living-room of about 150 feet superficial; a scullery or kitchen of not less than 70 feet superficial; with a ventilated pantry. On the upper floor, three bedrooms, one to be not less than 100 feet superficial; fire-places to be provided in two of the rooms. The height from the ground to the first floor to be 9 feet, and the bed-rooms to be 8 feet in the clear. The memorandum of the Inclosure Commissioners with respect to the substantiality of agricultural buildings to be adhered to. In the estimate, brickwork was to be taken at 8*l.* per rod reduced; Countess slates at 23*s.*; and Baltic timber at 2*s.* 3*d.* per foot cube. An allowance of 20 per cent. was to be made for contingencies and builder's profit on the cost prices of labour and materials, with 5 per cent. for superintendence. The prime cost, therefore, of each house was not to exceed 80*l.*, including not only the cottage, but the fixtures, water supply or well, fencing, paving, and all those necessary addenda which the owner must supply.

3010. An able report was drawn up on the 134 designs submitted, by the three appointed judges (given in *Builder*, 1864, p. 359), towards the conclusion of which they observe "that although good cottages may possibly be erected, under favourable circumstances, in some parts of England for a lower sum, we consider the probable average cost of a pair of cottages built with the conveniences enumerated, would be about 280*l.* to 300*l.*, and that the attempt to erect them at any considerable reduction upon this amount must result in some inferior kind of buildings, discreditable to the owner, and wanting in much of the necessary accommodation for a labourer and his family." The premiated design is given in the same volume, p. 952. On p. 295 of the following volume, six builders' estimates are given for erecting six cottages on the premiated plan, ranging from 397*l.* 13*s.* 4*d.* to 527*l.* the pair; a difference somewhat accounted for by the designer in his observations at p. 319, where he states that 260*l.* the pair would be the price of some he was then erecting, with modifications. On p. 394 is given a design estimated at 200*l.*, and tendered for at 180*l.* the pair, which is deserving of comparison.

3011. The Central Cottage Improvement Society, London, stated in 1865, that "reports from different parts of the country, of the actual cost of building, prove that on the average, each room containing 100 superficial feet, or 10 feet square, of a cottage or block of buildings, costs from 20*l.* to 25*l.*, exclusive of land; this is equivalent to 3*d.* per foot cube. In the five sets of plans published by the society, No. 1, of four rooms, has been built for 162*l.*; No. 2, slightly larger, for 168*l.*; No. 3, same as No. 1, with a scullery, for 175*l.*; and No. 4, more commodious, for an artizan, for 220*l.* per pair. The *Journal* for 1858, of the Bath and West of England Society, vol. vi., details a cottage of five rooms, built on Exmoor, for 60*l.*, with a living room 15 feet by 13 feet.

Sect. XXV.

TOWN DWELLINGS FOR THE INDUSTRIAL CLASSES.

3012. The leading features of construction and detailed arrangement, which may be considered peculiarly applicable to dwellings intended for working men whose wages range from 12*s.* to 24*s.* per week will be described herein. Workmen of this class have been hitherto strangers not only to the conveniences which render home attractive, but to the barest accommodation necessary to render social life tolerably decent. Unfortunately, the nearer an improved dwelling approaches its miserable predecessor in general aspect and character, the more popular it will be. The difficulty, therefore, in designing new homes for the poor consists in the introduction of improvements which shall lead to the gradual abandonment of injurious habits, and to give no sudden offence to jealously cherished prejudices. To do this effectively it is desirable to ascertain the leading requirements of the inhabitants of the district in which it is proposed to build.

3013. A poor man's town dwelling should consist of a living-room and bedroom; a plentiful supply of water; a water-closet, sink, and lavatory, distinct but not far removed from his tenement; a wash-house, with the means of drying clothes in any weather without artificial heat; and, when practicable, a play-ground for children.

3014. The living-room should be 12 feet by 10 feet clear of all obstructions or projections, and 8 feet high, giving 960 cubic feet at least. The rooms should be of a square form, as being easily kept clean and made comfortable. *Fig.* 1353. presents a general plan of the arrangements. The door should open into a porch or vestibule, and be placed at the end of the wall opposite to the window, so that when both are open the air in the dwelling may be effectively changed. The window should be sufficiently large to light every part of the room. It should be fitted with sashes, to insure top and bottom ventilation; and its sill should not be more than 2 feet 9 inches from the floor, to prevent high furniture being placed under it. Tolerably large panes of glass will be found to last longer than if the panes be small. The fire-place should be as near the centre of its own wall as possible, and be furnished with a range containing a

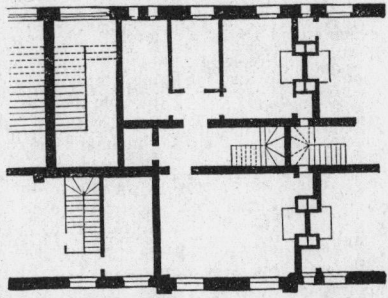

Fig. 1353. PEABODY DWELLINGS, COMMERCIAL STREET.

boiler, with a tap of the best description fixed 2 inches above the bottom; an oven; and a cooking place at least 10 inches wide from side to side, with sliding bars, flap and catch, all of which ought to be of wrought iron. The living-room should have a good serviceable closet the entire height of the room, the front flush with the chimney breast, to contain shelves for cooking utensils and crockery, &c., and a large covered box for coal; this closet should be lighted by a small window hung upon centres and to be easily opened.

3015. The bedrooms should be 12 feet by 8 feet, and 8 feet high, communicating with the living room by a door in the wall opposite to the fire-place at the end nearest to the window, so that enough wall space may be secured for the bed. As these rooms would be sufficiently warmed from the living-room, fire-places can be dispensed with where space is limited or expense of much importance.

3016. The walls should be well-built with sound stock bricks (the partitions being half a brick thick) and coloured with two coats of well sized distemper colour of a warm cheerful tint. Such walls offer no harbour for vermin; they are uninjured when nails are driven into them; and their freshness and colour are easily renewed at a trifling expense. The ceilings should be plastered, not only for a clean appearance, but also as a preventive against the spread of fire. The floor is best made of wood, though it is apt to get dirty and tolerably difficult to clean. If firewood or coal be broken upon any other floor than a wooden one the concussion is injurious to it. Tile and asphalte floors are often recommended as the best; but though they have a clean appearance, they are cold to the feet when uncovered by a carpet; are more liable to injury; and are more troublesome to repair. Asphalte and cement floors depend in a great measure upon their rigidity for their efficiency, and require iron beams and brick arches, which are expensive.

3017. As regards ventilation, beyond supplying doors that do not fit too close, windows that will open at top and bottom, and fire-places with air-channels underneath the floor, it is extremely difficult to know how to proceed further without detection. A ventilator once discovered is instantly rendered useless by being pasted over. Perforated bricks placed throughout the length of the wall in which the window is set, and in that opposite to it, causes the air to be so diffused by its passage through the narrow channels with which the bricks are provided, that the paste-brush is seldom used.

3018. The lavatory should contain a water-closet fitted with a strong galvanized iron valve; a lead trough, for washing purposes, supplied with a high-pressure loose valve cock, and an enamelled iron basin. A smaller lead trough or waste, for the discharge of dirty water, should have an inch service cock above it for supplying pails and kettles. The walls, coloured as those of the dwelling, should be well painted to the height of 18 inches above each trough, for frequent and easy washing. The floor is best covered with thick 9-inch square tiles, which bear a good deal of wear and tear and slopping in one spot without injury. The lavatory should have two windows at least, one in the external wall of the water-closet and one at the furthest end of the wall at right-angles to it.

3019. To attach a laundry to an extensive range of such dwellings becomes a positive duty. A washing tub and rinsing tub are necessary, about 3 feet 3 inches long by 1 foot 9 inches wide, with washer, plug, and chain, and a separate cold water service to each. The top of the tubs should be 3 feet 3 inches above the foot-board, or the floor, if not provided. A 10-gallon copper, with cold water service, and a tin ladle. The flue of the copper is to be carefully constructed to insure the heat being well distributed over the sides and bottom, and to afford facilities for regulating it and for cleaning. Wringing machines might be provided if hydrometers are not used; they are easily attached to the tubs. Artificial means of drying clothes, as adopted with advantage in public wash-houses,

are to be avoided in small laundries, because they cannot be maintained without considerable expense. Clothes are more easily and effectively dried when protected from rain, and suspended in strong cross currents of air.

3020. The water-cistern should be as close to the laundry as possible, in order that the piping may be short, with very few joints and bends so as to be free from the risks which attend a variety of levels. More attention is desirable to the dimensions of the iron piping, and the nature and position of the services, than they usually receive. Thus means should be provided for filling, emptying, and cleaning the cistern or tank; also for regulating the supply during the time that any portion of the piping is under repair. Every rising main should be furnished with at least two valves. The first is best fixed in the junction between the rising main and the company's street main, so as to regulate the entire supply of the building. The second should be fixed at the bottom of the rising main, so as to release the water which remains in the pipe after the cistern has been filled. In some cases an additional cock, 2 feet above each floor level, for the supply of buckets, or for the connexion of hose in case of fire, may be desirable.

3021. A few square yards of *play-ground* is of inestimable value for the labouring man's children. One large play-ground to a block of buildings is of much greater use than many small yards to as many cottages, and has tended as much as anything to ensure the success of the large blocks of dwellings in London.

3022. The drain-pipes should be of the best description, and their diameters larger than those employed under ordinary circumstances, because their liabilities to obstruction are very much greater. The main drains should be external to the building, and supplied with examination holes at intervals for repair and cleansing, and should possess the means of being regularly flushed with water. When the ground is soft, the drains, both large and small, should be laid upon beds of concrete, to preserve them in their proper falls. Soil and other pipes should be ventilated by being taken above the roof of the building.

3023. The *site* for a block of associated dwellings should be as open and in a situation as public as possible, not only to receive the advantages of light and ventilation, but that it may be easily found and readily accessible, and that its residents may have contact with neighbours whose habits and appearance are superior to their own. The ends of the site should face north and south, so that its east and west sides should have the morning and evening sun. It should offer every facility for good drainage; the nature of the subsoil should be well ascertained, and every necessary precaution taken to avoid, or to clear out, any accumulation of foul refuse that may have been carted into the vacant site. The most economical dimensions for a site within the jurisdiction of the Metropolitan Board of Works in London, are 108 feet long by 60 feet wide. This area will accommodate a building 108 feet long by 34 feet wide, and admit of a playground 26 feet deep in its rear. The multiple of 108 by $34 = 3600$ in round numbers, is the area allowed by Act of Parliament for a building containing several distinct tenements, and possessing only one entrance and staircase. The height of the building is best kept at 46 feet from the ground-line to the eaves of the roof; it admits of as many stories of dwellings as can be occupied with comfort to the tenants, and it requires no unnecessary thickness of walls. If made five stories in height it will contain 40 or 45 dwellings, about 16 water-closets, 8 lavatories, 8 wash tubs and coppers.

3024. The following paragraphs comprise a brief description of the dwellings lately built or now constructing. In the basement, only a small cellar need be provided for dust, access to it is to be obtained by a small external staircase under its first landing, but distinct, so that the dust may be removed without annoyance. The ground, first, second, and third floor plans may be divided throughout their entire length into two equal portions, by a corridor 4 feet 2 inches wide, on each side of which are arranged the dwellings (*fig.* 1354.).

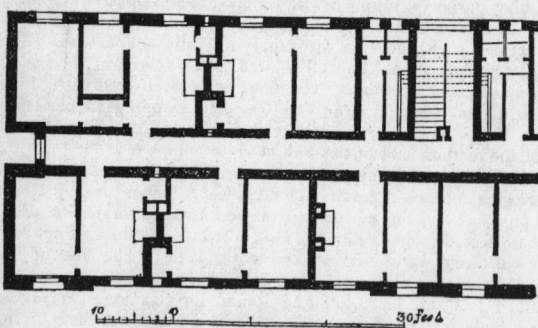

Fig. 1354   PEABODY DWELLINGS, COMMERCIAL STREET.

In the centre is the principal entrance, which is 5 feet 6 inches wide, and furnished with external and internal folding-doors under the immediate supervision of the porter whose office adjoins it. The staircase, placed immediately opposite to the entrance, is 8 feet wide, with solid square stone steps having a 10-inch tread, and an average rise of 7 inches. The side furthest from the corridor has an arch 7 feet wide, and ex-

tending from the ground-line to within a few feet of the eaves of the roof. It is separated from the corridor by two arches, whose centre pier contains a dust shaft, traversing the entire height of the building, and communicating with the cellar above named in the basement. It is 14 inches wide within, open above the roof for ventilation, and is furnished with a hopper, which receives the dust, and closing flush with the wall at each floor level.

3025. The lavatories adjoin the staircase, those for the men on one side, for the women on the other. The fourth or topmost floor contains a laundry, about 22 feet long by 12 feet wide, covered with an open timber roof, the tie-beams having standards helping to support it, and serving as clothes posts. It is lighted by a range of small casements, admitting air sufficient to remove any unpleasantness that might arise from the laundry, and to thoroughly dry the clothes. It is furnished with eight sets of wash tubs, some being separated by slate partitions, for privacy; eight 10-gallon coppers; eight wringing machines, or a patent hydrometer; trellis-framed standing boards; stools (as being better than tables) for clothes baskets; soap boxes and ladles. This floor also contains a bathroom for each sex placed over the lavatories; it is furnished with one of Rufford and Finch's stoneware baths, and has a service of cold water. Hot water is supplied from the laundry when required. A cistern lined with lead adjoins each bath-room, and also supplies the lavatories below it; this position secures a direct fall to the several services, and avoids the necessity for frequent bends and joints.

3026. The main drains are 12 or 9 inches in diameter; the smaller drains, kept as short as possible, are 6 and 4 inches, according to their requirements. The ventilation is secured by the side corridor having a window at each end of it, and by the open staircase in the middle of its length, all which forbid stagnation and remove impurities. We are indebted for the very practical observations contained in this section to the paper by H. A. Darbishire, who has designed several of the blocks of dwellings lately erected in the metropolis, as read before the Architectural Association, and given, with illustrations of those in Commercial Street, Whitechapel Road, in the *Civil Engineer*, &c., for 1864.

SECT. XXVI.

VENTILATION OF BUILDINGS.

3027. Though this and the following sections can scarcely be said to come legitimately under the heading of this chapter, the subjects are so intimately connected with each of the sections, and have been referred to occasionally in their descriptions; and as, moreover, the architect is expected to make himself fully acquainted with these subjects, the omission of any notice of them in this edition cannot be sanctioned; this place, then, appears to be the most suitable for their consideration.

3028. Whether ventilation be left to chance, or whether any special apparatus be erected for the purpose, foul or vitiated air must be got rid of; while fresh air, adapted to the purposes of respiration, must be admitted in sufficient quantity, that is, at the rate of about 4 cubic feet per minute for each individual in the apartment. The force or impetus of the incoming air ought slightly to compress the air of the room and assist the efflux of the vitiated air; and this, in its turn, ought to be so heated as to have a certain amount of ascensional power. Mechanical means are sometimes necessary to expel or withdraw the air, such as fanners, bellows, pumps, &c.; but for general purposes it is more convenient, as well as economical, to trust to the natural method of getting rid of vitiated air, that is, by making certain ventilating tubes or openings at the highest point of the room towards which the hot air tends to flow.

3029. Some authors have divided artificial ventilation into two branches, called *plenum* and *vacuum*. By the first, fresh air is forced into the interior of a building, and the vitiated air is allowed to escape by openings contrived for the purpose. By the second, vitiated air is drawn out of the building, and fresh air finds an entrance through channels adapted to the purpose.

3030. As the velocity of a falling body in a second of time is known to be eight times the square root of the height of the descent, in decimals of a foot, so the velocity of discharge per second, through vent tubes or chimneys, may be briefly stated as equal to eight times the square root of the difference in height of any two columns of air, in decimals of a foot. This number, reduced one-fourth for friction, and the remainder multiplied by 60, will give the true velocity of efflux per minute. The area of the tube in feet, or decimals of a foot, multiplied by this last number, will give the number of cubic feet of air discharged per minute. The height of a column of heated air must be calculated from the floor of the room to the top of the tube where it discharges into the open air. Where several vent tubes are employed they must all be of the same vertical height, or the highest

vent will prevent the efficient action of the lower ones, so that there might be a smaller discharge through two tubes than through one only.

3031. When several openings are made above the level of the floor of a room, the highest one may be the only one capable of acting as an abduction tube, the other lower openings often serving as induction tubes, discharging cold air into the room instead of taking it out, and, in doing so, it may lower the temperature of the hot vitiated air and prevent it from escaping, thus not only causing the bad air to be breathed over again, but filling the room with unpleasant draughts. But if the highest abduction tube be too small to carry off the requisite quantity of hot air, the tube next below it in elevation at any part of the room will act as an abduction tube. If the lower openings (to be provided with sliding valves) for the admission of fresh air be too small in proportion to those for the escape of hot air, a current of cold air will descend through one part of the hot air tube, and the hot air will ascend through another part of the same tube. In order that ventilating tubes or openings may be effective, the lower openings for the admission of fresh air must be at least as large as the upper ones, and larger if possible. Tredgold recommended that the lower should be about double the area of the upper openings, and be so subdivided as to break the current. (Tomlinson, *Warming and Ventilation, &c.*, 1850.)

3032. It must be noted that all noxious gases do not rise, and therefore that in a few exceptional cases, ventilation must be effected at the floor level. Taking atmospheric air at 60° Fahr., and under a pressure equal to 30 inches of mercury, as 1,000, then hydrogen gas equals 6,926 ; nitrogenous miasma, about 976 ; olefiant gas, 978 ; sulphureted hydrogen gas, 1,178 ; carbonic oxide, 957 ; and sulphurous acid, when anhydrous, 3,000. On the contrary, carbureted hydrogen gas, or marsh miasma, is as light as 555 ; and common coal gas ranges between 514 and 420. Thus above or below the temperature of 60° the conditions of the diffusion of gases vary in a marked manner, and it is on this account that the foul air of sewers, &c. exercises a more extended action laterally in hot weather, when it is able to diffuse itself more easily through an attenuated atmosphere, than in cold weather, when the greater density of the atmosphere, and the comparatively higher temperature of the gases given off from the receptacles mentioned, enables the foul air to rise vertically with greater ease than to spread laterally. In a room, the carbonic acid emitted by the lights and by the breath of its occupants being of greater specific gravity than atmospheric air, would, at the ordinary temperature of the air, tend to accumulate in its lower strata ; but the temperature of the products of respiration and of combustion is usually so much in excess of that of the air, that they are enabled to rise through it, and to accumulate in the upper portions of the enclosed room until some change in their temperature takes place. The foul state of the air in the lower portions of a public building on the day following a crowded meeting may be due to the change of temperature during the night, and the retention, by closed doors and windows, of the air so rendered impure. In 1865 General Morin read a paper to the Paris Academy of Sciences, again urging as a fundamental principle the exploded practice of drawing off vitiated air from the stratum nearest the floor, pure air being admitted near to the ceiling.

3033. Our limited space will not permit us to do more than to very briefly notice the chief principal methods of ventilation ; the application of any one of them must be left to the ingenuity of the architect. He will find that all public buildings, and even all private houses, from the highest to the lowest class, must be spontaneously ventilated, for if any trouble be entailed, it will be neglected. The means for ventilation must be cheap, easily procurable, always in place, self-acting, and not liable to get out of order. Such an invention is the Arnott ventilator, when placed as close to the ceiling as practicable, forming a direct communication between the room and the chimney. The chimney has been made the means of securing a ventilation by a separate and rarified air channel. Thus, besides a mere channel left in the wall adjoining a flue, Doulton's patent combined smoke and air flues, of terra cotta, for 12, 10, and 8-inch, chimneys, are effective. Boyd's patent flue plates are similar in principle. Chowne's patent air-syphon, consisting of an inverted syphon tube, acts upon the principle of the air moving up the longer leg, and of entering and descending in the shorter leg, without the necessity for the application of artificial heat to the longer leg. This, however, does not appear to be always proved in practice, for whether the current in the longer leg be ascending or descending, depends chiefly upon differences of temperature within and without a building ; but as the brickwork of chimneys often gets heated by the vicinity of the kitchen flue, or even by the sun shining upon it during the day, an ascending current is more likely to be sustained than a descending one, since brickwork will retain its heat for some hours.

3034. The system adopted by Dr. Reid, at the House of Commons, was that of admitting air into a chamber underground, where it was (and is still) purified by being washed while passing through a stream of water, and then through canvas, whereby other impurities are extracted. It then rises to the floor of the apartment, which is pierced with many thousand holes, and passing through them is then further distributed by means of a hair-cloth, ascending towards the ceiling at about the rate of one foot per minute. This

air is, in cold weather, warmed below; and in warm weather it is cooled with ice. The object is to keep the air in all seasons at a uniform temperature of 64°. The air is often cooler in the house than that outside it. From the ceiling it is carried rapidly away along a tunnel to feed the great furnace which creates this current of ventilation. The complaint is made that it carries with it from the floor the fine dust brought in by the members' feet, and being inhaled, sometimes affects those in the House. The method adopted by Dr. Reid to warm and ventilate St. George's Hall, at Liverpool, is detailed in the *Civil Engineer* for 1864, page 136. The system employed from 1736 to about 1817 at the old House of Commons, which was effectively ventilated, was by a fan placed over it for *extracting* the heated air, its rate of working being dependent upon an attendant, who received his directions from a person within the House. The common revolving wind-guard placed at the top of a chimney to induce a suction, whereby the smoke may be drawn out, is of the same system; as is also Howarth's patent revolving Archimedean screw ventilator. One of the latest systems of effecting the regularity of working such fans or screws is by the aid of the high service water supply; a flow of water impinging upon the blades of a wheel turns the extracting fan, and the water is conveyed to a lower reservoir to be used for domestic or other purposes.

3035. The opposite system, that of air being forced into apartments by mechanical means, such as the fan driven by steam power, is practised with great success at the Reform Club House, the General Post Office, and many other buildings, public and private, and especially in factories. The fan is regulated to a velocity of between 80 and 100 feet per second. Dr. Van Hecke's system of warming and ventilating, as arranged at the new French hospitals, is effected by means of a $3\frac{1}{2}$ horse power engine, working a fan, which drives the external air through long subterraneous channels into four warming apparatuses, whence it ascends into flues, which conduct it into all the wards, passing through regulating air gratings in the walls. In each ward are two or more escape flues carrying the vitiated air above the roofs.

3036. Another system prevails to some extent. The ventilation is combined with the method of warming, be it a church or other room devoted to a public purpose. This is effected by means of flues for extracting the air in the building being connected with the furnace of the apparatus. Such is the principle adopted by Messrs. Haden and Co., of Trowbridge. It has been in practice with success at the Royal Polytechnic Institution, London, for ventilating the large theatre since its erection in 1838. After the fire is once lighted, all its communications with the outer air are closed, and that of the extracting flue opened, which then supplies the fire with air brought down from the upper part of the theatre. Fresh air is admitted to the theatre only through the ordinary doors and openings.

3037. As regards ventilation by windows, or the natural method, as it is called, as no system of making a sash working upon a horizontal axis, such as French casements, can wisely dispense with stay-bars, even when made to open and shut by means of a wheel and axle, our attention may be confined to lights hung on pullies, or on hinges, or on centres. The first of these three classes is the common lifting sash. Wind-boards at top and bottom to prevent the effects of direct currents have been suggested; and machinery has been fitted to open both sashes simultaneously so as to ensure the desired circulation of air through apertures at pleasure, or that shall not be altered without a key. This improvement has lately been successfully managed by the "patent counter-balance rack slips," which also do away with the use of lines, pulleys, and weights. In double windows, however, as in the lavatories at Middlesex Hospital, a roller has been placed between the two pairs of sashes, which move reciprocally, like the double bucket action; so that when the inner top sash is lowered, the outer bottom one is raised, and the reverse; and the extension of this idea to the lights of water-closets has been advocated. It has also been suggested that in the usual windows, the horns of the upper sash styles should appear above the top rail, so that the window could never be tightly shut; but the benefit from this plan is confined to periods at which the window is not closed by shutters or by roller-blinds. The same objection applies to the use of such perforated glass and other contrivances as are mentioned in *par.* 2231a. It is stated that no draught is felt by the use of these inventions, as the air passing through the perforations is diffused equally and imperceptibly. We must notice that it will be found that the air is always passing into the apartment, and that when the wind blows towards the glass, the extra supply of air sent in is undoubtedly felt by the occupants, but sometimes not appreciated by them. Another method consists in the admittance of air either by a space left between the top beads (the horns, as before, stopping the sash from going home) and the head of the opening, or by such a space over the outer bead to communicate with the box formed by the inside lining and the architrave or other dressing, the latter being either pierced with holes or detached slightly from its grounds.

3038. Of the second class is the common hopper to a window, framed with or without side lights. In this are included all greenhouse sashes that are hung from the top, which may be made to open simultaneously by means of ratcheted stay-bars dropping into

toothed wheels fixed on a continuous axis, worked by a wheel against an endless screw. When double windows are used, as in very cold climates, or when it is desirable to shut out noises, the upper portions of them should be made to open by the action of opening the inner window. This scheme has been adopted in the hospital of the Wieden suburb, and also in the Imperial stables, at Vienna, with success; its action is not described, but the outer window is presumed to be fixed, the heads of it forming a hopper, which is opened or shut by lowering or raising the inner window.

3039. To the third class belong nearly all the modern English patents for window ventilation, which consist of one or more planes working like a jalousie lath upon a horizontal axis. Of the two principal adaptations of the system to an entire window, Hurwood's, shown in *fig.* 1355., and worked by an endless screw, is the simplest: there is another

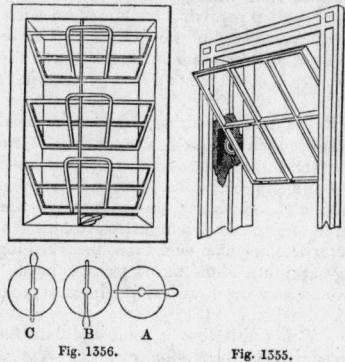

arrangement of this kind by Mackrory, where the action is similar to that of a carriage window; the sash runs in a groove, and being turned by means of a toothed pivot working against an endless screw, it can be kept at any desired height. The method indicated by *fig.* 1356., adopted at Middlesex Hospital, seems more simple and more economical. By turning the handle to the points in the plans A, B, and C, the glazed louvres are simultaneously opened or shut to those limits.

3040. Ventilation by tubes is effected on the principle of the extracting valve, as advocated by Dr. Arnott, which is a plate of metal hinged to the lower edge of a metal box next to the room, and on the other open to its chimney. The draught of the flue tends to carry away the air of the room, when the current is upward; should it be downward, a piece of cloth is driven against the plate, tending to prevent the ingress of smoke. However useful this contrivance may be, its result in cubical consumption of air is necessarily small. A cowl with vertical, or horizontal, or slanting, jalousied sides has also been employed, with or without an Archimedean screw, at the top of a flue, to exhaust the air of a room. Another well-established invention is Sheringham's ventilator. An opening is made in an external wall for the introduction of air, and a metal box inserted, which is a sort of hopper, having at its mouth a valve, so hung as to direct the current of air towards the ceiling, whereby no draught is felt by the occupants of the apartment. Somewhat similar is Hart's ventilator, the face being of perforated zinc. Such articles are also made with a box to contain charcoal as a purifier of the air before it is admitted. Looker's patent ventilator, consisting of a tubular piece of pottery fixed in the wall, into which on the inside is placed another tube, perforated all round with small holes, the inner end being closed altogether. This second tube is pushed in or out, according to the quantity of air required.

C   B   A

Fig. 1356.   Fig. 1355.

3041. Amongst the earliest of other and later systems is Watson's double-current ventilator, consisting of a tube divided by a diaphragm, and rising from the ceiling to the external air; it was intended that the air should circulate, as shown in *fig.* 1357., by an

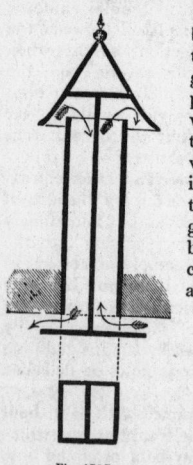

ascending and a descending current. It has been said that this result only occurs in rooms that are perfectly closed, and that the two tubes generally serve as exhausters; but our own experience is more favourable to the effective working of this invention. Somewhat similar to this is *fig.* 1358., called the Shaftesbury ventilator, which appears to have been applied in small tenements with success, probably for the very reason that the rooms in such cases are generally kept as close as possible; for it has been necessary to conceal the opening at the ceiling by an ornamental rose, and to put at G an air grate with large openings. At times,

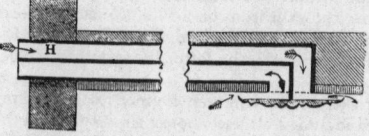

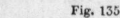

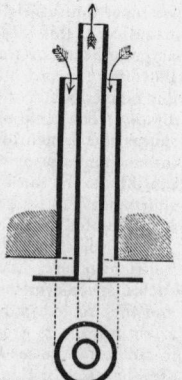

Fig. 1357.   Fig. 1358.   Fig. 1359.

however, the rush of cold air is very great through this tube into the room; to remedy

this, the end G may be connected with a horizontal tube or box about 3 feet long, and somewhat larger than the tube H; each end of this box is open, but filled with very fine wire gauze; the result then has generally proved satisfactory. A modification of the preceding invention is adopted by McKinnel. Two concentric tubes are so fixed that the inner one is longer than its envelope. This apparatus, shown in *fig.* 1359., nearly answers its purpose, according to certain authorities, and certainly gives, in some cases, a result that would be satisfactory if its regularity were not affected by atmospheric influences. A cowl is of course applicable to this machinery, which seems quite successful in its action during the winter evenings at the meeting room of the Royal Institute of British Architects, where a circle of gas lights is suspended below it. A square turret, diagonally divided, as shown in *fig.* 1360., is known as Muir's ventilator. The inventor calculates upon utilising the slightest current of air, as he supposes that when it arrives at one of the sides it will enter, descend, and force an equal quantity of foul air to discharge itself at the other sides. The report of MM. Blondel and Ser upon the London Hospitals in 1862, states broadly that none of these methods gives a satisfactory solution of the question.

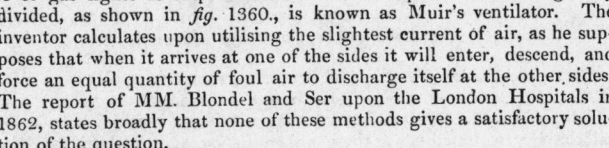
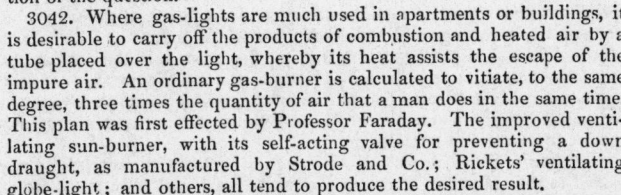

Fig 1360.

3042. Where gas-lights are much used in apartments or buildings, it is desirable to carry off the products of combustion and heated air by a tube placed over the light, whereby its heat assists the escape of the impure air. An ordinary gas-burner is calculated to vitiate, to the same degree, three times the quantity of air that a man does in the same time. This plan was first effected by Professor Faraday. The improved ventilating sun-burner, with its self-acting valve for preventing a down draught, as manufactured by Strode and Co.; Rickets' ventilating globe-light; and others, all tend to produce the desired result.

3043. The Commissioners for Barracks and Hospitals, in their *Report*, 1855, p. 65. &c., state that for such establishments, the different systems adopted in the Parisian hospitals appear to be too expensive and too complicated. Those which they approve consist of induction, and of flues for exhaustion, each of two sorts. *Induction.*—I. Openings with an air-brick in the face of the wall, and a wooden hopper near the ceiling, placed at an angle of 45°, covered with zinc pierced with holes from $\frac{1}{8}$ to $\frac{1}{8}$ inch in diameter. A plate of zinc or galvanised iron, hung at the bottom and worked by a string, regulates at pleasure the admission of air, the size of the opening being calculated at an inch square for each 60 cubic feet of space in the room, when there is not a special provision for fresh air to pass round the stove; when there is such provision the size for the opening may be one half less. II. Openings with an air-brick in the face of the wall, and a trunk or tube leading the air to a case behind the stove, so that warm air may rise in a tube to a luffer-boarded opening at the ceiling, the size of the tube being calculated at an inch square for each 100 cubic feet of space in the room.

3044. *Exhaustion.*—I. Flues of the warming apparatus extract the bottom layers of air in the room. The experiments made between 4.30 and 6.30 A.M. in April 1858, showed that the volume of air extracted was on the average 9,000 to 10,000 cubic feet by each flue, the rapidity being at the rate of 5 to 5$\frac{1}{2}$ feet; by which numbers the section of the flue would be 0·446 English feet. II. Tubes from the ceiling to the roof, the size of the opening being calculated at an inch square for each 50 cubic feet for an upper story, and for each 55 cubic feet for the story below it, and for each 60 cubic feet for the lower story. The rapidity of the current is regulated by the difference between the internal and external air, by currents, &c. When the temperatures are equal the current is feeble, when the reverse occurs it is strong. The volume extracted (under the above conditions) was 8,500 to 9,000 cubic feet, the rapidity being at the rate of 3 to 3$\frac{1}{2}$ feet. So that the greatest effect by the combined systems only takes 8,000 to 10,000 cubic feet by each flue on the average, and this irregular result is sometimes annulled; moreover, the currents may reverse the action of the flues, and enter by the exhausting tubes.

3045. *Other systems.*—In the new buildings at Guy's Hospital, as also at the Lunatic Asylum at Derby, Sylvester's method was carried out. Here the air arrives by a large inducting flue, capped by a cowl which utilises the action of currents of wind; the air passes underground in contact with hot-water pipes, rises in flues, and enters the room at the ceiling; it escapes by exhaustion holes in the skirting of the opposite walls, and rises to the roof by flues continued by plate iron tubes to an exhausting flue which surrounds the smoke flue of the warming apparatus. The inventor calculated for about 4,000 cubic feet per bed per hour, and stated that in the winter about 4,300 had been obtained generally, but that once about 2,200 only were gained.

3046. The methods of ventilation adopted in France are required to produce effects absolutely free from perceptible currents of air. The report produced by MM. Blondel and Ser, before noticed, mention Duvoir-Leblanc's system in one portion of the hôpital Lariboisière, as drawing away about 2,500 cubic feet per bed per hour, half of which is

supplied by the doors and windows : and the method of MM. Thomas and Laurens, which gives 3,200 cube feet per bed per hour, and is not found always sufficient to remove every trace of odour. They consider that Dr. Van Hecke's system, used at the Baujon and Necker hospitals, leaves much to be desired. They require 3,500 cube feet per bed per hour ; and perceive that in order to obtain anything like such a result, recourse has necessarily been had to large exhausting flues, or to mechanical means, such as the fan.

Sect. XXVII.

WARMING OF BUILDINGS.

3047. Heat, as required in architectural structures, results from raising the temperature of the air by means of various contrivances so arranged as to take advantage of the laws which govern the transmission of heat. A body capable of affording heat, gives out caloric by two methods ; these are *radiation* and *conduction*. Radiation is diffused through the air at an immense velocity without materially raising its temperature, but immediately warming solid bodies exposed to its influence, which in turn give out the acquired heat slowly; the redder the fire, the warmer is the radiant heat. When the air in a large apartment is to be raised in temperature, the method of heating by contact is employed; this is effected by volumes of air coming in contact with a heated surface, and, becoming raised in temperature, are put in motion, and communicate the heat they receive to surrounding bodies.

3048. In order to obtain full advantage of heating surfaces, their area must be proportioned to the cubic feet of air required to be warmed. A small surface, if raised to a very great temperature, will heat a large quantity of air if means are taken to pass it rapidly from contact with the heated surface. It is better, in all respects, to have a large surface maintained at a mild temperature with a gradual change of air. In general, if the temperature of the heated body is above that of boiling water, i.e. 212°, the air in contact is rendered unhealthy. Ventilation very greatly assists the endeavours to warm successfully a room or building.

3049. The method of warming classed under radiation and conduction may be further arranged under the following heads :—I. *Open fires*, including grates and stove grates of every sort, having ordinary flues or chimneys ; this is warming by radiation. Warming by conduction is effected by, II. *Close fires*, as furnaces, cokles, &c., and the Cabin, Arnott, Vesta, Gill, Chunk, Dumpy, Nott or American, laundry or ironing, caloric, ventilating, &c. stoves ; and by *gas*, as the atmopyre, asbestos, calorifere, cylinder, and gas heating apparatus; having metal or brick flues continued some distance from them for the purpose of heating. III. *Hot water* on the *low* temperature system, with pipes about 3 or 4 inches in diameter. IV. *Hot water* on the *high* temperature system, with pipes about 1 inch in diameter. And V. *Steam* both on the high and low pressure systems.

3050. The principle of erecting one chimney to serve for all the fire-places of a house is liable to very unsatisfactory results, unless such a system be carried out as that exhibited at Osmaston Manor, near Derby, by its architect H. J. Stevens, and described at the Institute of British Architects in 1851. All the rooms in Fair Oak House, Isle of Wight, are warmed by means of one shaft in the middle of the house, heated by a large open fire in the basement. Around this shaft is a thin enclosing case of brickwork, in cement, leaving a space between to receive the cool air, which is then warmed by the heated shaft, and is admitted into the several apartments through perforated cornices, the supply being regulated by a valve. Obstacles presented themselves which rendered it necessary to adopt the cornice and not the floor as the place for the admission of the warm air. The arrangements are stated to have met with a decided success ; the plan and details are given in *Builder*, 1860, p. 329. In a series of small dwellings where the one shaft system was tried, its complete failure necessitated the new formation of all the fire-places and flues.

3051. I. It scarcely enters within the province of this work to describe the best form for an open *grate*. The point has been taken up of late years by manufacturers, and very many excellent forms adopted. The result is that iron at the back and sides has been greatly discarded, and fire-lumps substituted, whereby greater heat is thrown out with the same quantity of fuel. The *fire-lump grates* for cottages, bedrooms, schools, &c., have had a large sale. But it has also been found that too large a surface of the fire-lump tends to consume the coal too quickly, consequently it is now chiefly confined to the back of the grate. A length of bar equal to about 1 inch for each foot of length of room, and the height of the front half an inch for each foot of breadth of the room, are dimensions found to produce good proportions for average purposes. The depth of the part in which the fuel is placed has

been greatly decreased, about 9 inches being ordinarily sufficient at the bottom, and enlarging upwards at the back, so as to present a good heating surface in the front, and at the top, of the fuel. The height that the lowest bar should be from the hearth is a matter of greater uncertainty; we advocate that it should be as near to 12 inches as possible, in preference to the 6 inches which the grates are now usually made. We have had grates raised from the latter to the former height with greatly increased results. Advantage has been taken of the fire-clay stoves, since the period of their invention by Count Rumford, to combine the back and sides with air flues of the same material, which, becoming heated, impart their heat to the cold air supplied from the outside, admitting warm fresh air to the apartment. These stoves were first adopted by Cundy. Radiation of the heat has been materially assisted by Sylvester's arrangement of the ends of the fire bars projecting into the room forming a hot hearth; and also by Joyce. Dr. Arnott's smoke-consuming grate; and the application of a solid bottom to a grate, producing " the Builder's fire," are points of consideration for the householder rather than for the architect.

3052. II. The varieties of close stoves are very numerous, but the principle upon which they depend for their efficiency is in all cases nearly the same. This may be stated to be the heating of metal plates by the combustion of fuel in actual contact with them. The quantity of heating surface in the room wherein the stove is placed can be materially increased, and nearly the full effects of the heated products from the fuel obtained by lengthening the smoke flue; but the longer the flue the less is the draught of the fire, which is further lessened by its becoming choked with soot; thus a 3-inch pipe attached to a small stove, burning coal and in constant use, has been found so completely filled up with soot in the course of a week that a stick half an inch in diameter could scarcely be passed through the hole left in the centre. The now common American cooking-stoves are on this principle. The principle of the Arnott stove is that of consuming the peculiar fuel recommended for its use very slowly, and the detention of the heat in the stove. The addition of a descending flue to some of these stoves is an advantage when it is desired to place the stove in the middle of a shop or warehouse. Franklin's calorifere, or the vase stove, having a descending flue, was formerly much used When this system has been adapted to flues carried under a stone floor (after the Chinese fashion) it has been found to warm most efficiently an office and principal staircase with a mere handful of fire, at a cost of about 30s., while by another apparatus the cost was 18l.; Beaumont, *Hints for preventing Damage by Fire*, 1835. This is an elaboration of the common method of warming greenhouses by the brick or smoke flue, through which the smoke and flame travels from the furnace. A fire-clay casing for the fuel is also combined with some of them.

3053. The high temperature stoves, such as the cokles, the Strutt or Belper stove, the Sylvester's, and others, all used for warming extensive spaces, consist of large metal plates or surfaces of brick or stone, heated in or by a furnace or fire, the air to be warmed being caused to impinge upon or pass between them, and then carried along in tubes to the several rooms or floors where the heat is required. The hot air pipe furnace is used for the same purposes, whereby the flame and smoke passes along the *inside* of the tubes. In Davison and Symington's furnace for obtaining heated currents of air for manufacturing purposes, the cold or fresh air is driven by a fan at a great velocity through the pipes, which are placed in contact with the flames. Any cessation of the blower may be expected to cause material injury to the pipes.

3054. A writer explaining the common American system of warming houses by hot air, says, that the whole comfort of the result depends upon *how* the atmospheric air is heated. The various plans are effected by a furnace, from the dome of which pipes are coiled and twisted about so as to gain the utmost possible radiating surface, and the air is brought in contact with them as it passes through the chamber. To get cheaply a great amount of heat, the castings are made very thin, the air chambers and hot air pipes small; whereby the result is, that a hot desiccated poisonous air is discharged into the room, injurious to the lungs, and causing headaches. Where the air chamber, however, is large, the furnace very wide and shallow, and its dome high, with the radiating surface largely extended, and the external cold air shaft spacious, this mode of heating is excellent. No apparatus of its kind ever surpassed the old Boston furnace, first invented by Chilson, and since so greatly improved by his successor in New York. In the " Boynton furnace," as it is called, the shaft bringing in the cold air is very large, frequently 4 feet wide and 2 feet or more deep, and the air chamber and tin pipes therefrom are also of considerable size. In the air-chamber a small jet of water is kept playing to restore the natural moisture to the air. Anthracite coal is used, a ton of which, for an ordinary house, would be a sufficient supply for nearly three weeks. No other fires, except that of the kitchen range, is usually seen in houses possessing this apparatus. (*Builder*, xxiii, 582).

3055. III. The circulation of hot water in pipes is caused by the unequal density of the fluid, arising from the difference of temperature in the ascending and descending columns of water connected with the heating reservoir; and its velocity is governed by the height of

the columns; Bramah, in appendix to Tredgold, *Heating*. A boiler (the " conical " boiler is considered the best form by some manufacturers, while others prefer the " saddle-back ") heats the water which, as it becomes warmed, rises and passes out through the flow pipes; these are laid at a very slight inclination, to assist the current. When the water has arrived at its furthest extent, it enters what are termed the return pipes, on its way back to the boiler, which it enters at the lowest part, to be re-heated, to rise, flow, and return as long as a fire is kept up. A rough calculation has been made that for every 50 feet of 4-inch pipe 1 square foot of boiler surface is required. The self-supplying cistern and its expansion box must be placed somewhat above the highest level at which the hot water is desired to rise, yet not so high that the pressure in the pipes will affect their joints. It should be covered, and have a pipe to allow the vapour or steam produced by over-heating to escape into the external atmosphere. With this, the low temperature system, the heat of 212°, or that of boiling water, cannot be exceeded.

3056. IV. The high temperature system was introduced by Perkins, and is frequently called by his name. Water is placed in a coil and range of piping of small diameter, hermetically closed, so as to prevent all communication with the external atmosphere. A coil, being at least one-sixth of the whole piping, is heated by the action of the fire in immediate contact with it, by which means the temperature of the water in it can be raised easily to 300° and 400°, but then the same objection applies to the air warmed by pipes so heated, as to that from high temperature stoves. As water expands with heat, allowance has to be made by the addition, at the highest point, of a larger tube to receive the surplus, which varies from 10 to 12 feet per cent.; one-tenth of the space of piping may thus be allowed for expansion. After the pipes are fixed, they are very carefully filled with water, so as to expel all air, through a filling tube situated at the bottom of the expansion tube, and when sufficiently full they are hermetically closed. The danger to be chiefly apprehended from this apparatus is, that if leakage takes place, the loss of water causes red-hot vapour to be formed, with the possibility of setting fire to any wood to which it may be attached, and thus the Metropolitan Building Act requires a clear space of 3 inches to be left between all water-pipes and woodwork. There is now no doubt but that wood, subjected to a constant current of greatly heated air, becomes very liable to combustion.

3057. When heating surfaces of great extent are required to be obtained by the application of hot water or of steam, Walker's system will probably be found to be the most effectual yet introduced. It must be sufficient here to describe it as consisting of a number of small iron blocks, each block having square perforations passing through it for the current of air from the top to the bottom, of very thin metal. The blocks are enclosed in a corresponding perforated iron box, leaving 1 inch for water or steam all round each block, which heats the metal forming the blocks. By this very compact arrangement 160 feet of heating surface may be obtained in a box measuring not more than 2 feet cube.

3058. The rules for finding the area of hot water-pipes for any sized apartment are in all respects essentially the same as will be given for steam, excepting the mean temperature of the pipes: for steam-pipes 200° is given; but 140° to 150° may be taken as that of low temperature hot water-pipes. From data obtained by Hood, *Practical Treatise*, 3rd edit., 1850, it appears that water in a pipe of 4 inches diameter loses ·851 of a degree of heat per minute, when the excess of its temperature over that of the surrounding air is 125°; and also that under the same condition, one foot of such a pipe will heat 222 cubic feet of air one degree in the same time; whence he deduces the following rule :—Multiply 125 by the difference between the maximum proposed temperature of the room and that of the external air, and divide this product by the difference between the temperature of the pipes and that proposed for the room; then the quotient is to be multiplied by the number of cubic feet of air to be warmed per minute; and the product, divided by 222, will give the number of feet, in length of pipe of 4 inches diameter, required to produce the same effect; this length is to be multiplied by 1·33 or by 2, for equivalent lengths of pipes respectively 3 and 2 inches in diameter.

3059. In making arrangements for heating by steam, we need not describe the construction of the furnace and boiler, or of the chimney, matters which are perhaps better arranged by the engineer fitting up the apparatus, as steam for warming purposes is rarely adopted except where waste steam can be brought into use, as in factories and workshops using steam power. The thicker the metal of the pipes the better for greenhouses and such like places; for buildings, the thinner the better consistent with strength; say about $\frac{3}{8}$ths of an inch in thickness. Provision must be made for the expansion of pipes, both for steam and water, of about one-eighth of an inch for every 10 feet of length. The pipes should be placed near the floor, and as close as possible to the apertures for the admission of fresh air. The pipes should be laid with an inclination to the boiler, so that condensed water from the steam shall be returned to it; and they should be carried at once to the highest part of the building and descend to the lowest.

3060. To form some idea of the requisite area of piping for any desired buildings, the quantity of cubic feet of air required per minute must first be ascertained. In order to

ascertain this, attention must be given to the loss of heat by ventilation, and the direct influence of cold external walls, glass windows, &c. From the first cause there will be a loss of heat proportioned to the quantity of air withdrawn per minute : if 4 cubic feet are supplied to each individual per minute, then "there will be for each individual 4 cubic feet of air conveying off a quantity of heat equal to the difference between the heat of the external air and that of the room." Thus, if the heat of the room be 70° and that of the external air 50°, then the withdrawal of 4 cubic feet of air per minute must lead off a quantity of heat equal to the difference between 70° and 50°, or 20°. From the second cause there will also be a loss, as heat is transmitted very quickly through glass ; the quantity of air cooled in a given time being simply proportional to the surface of the glass exposed to the external air, and, consequently, will be constant, whatever variation of temperature may take place. The rule given by Tredgold, § 67, is as follows :—" If the area of the surface of glass be multiplied by 1·5, the product will be the number of cubic feet of air per minute which will be cooled from the temperature of the room to that of the external air; " and to this loss will also be added that arising from each door and window (independently of occasionally opening and shutting the former) : this was calculated by the same author, § 65, to be equivalent to 11 cubic feet per minute, the difference of temperature between the internal and external atmosphere being 60°.

3061. From a combination of these circumstances, assisted by various experiments, Tredgold, § 68, deduced the following rule :—If the number of people the room is intended to contain be multiplied by 4 (or the quantity of air allowed per minute), and added to 11 times the number of external windows and doors (as 11 cubic feet of air is passed through each per minute on an average), added to $1\frac{1}{2}$ times the area in feet of the glass exposed to the external air, the sum obtained will be the quantity, in cubic feet, to be warmed per minute. The next operation is to find the area or surface of piping which will warm this quantity of air. The mean temperature of a steam pipe at the ordinary pressure is 200°. The temperature of the air supplying ventilation is to be known at the extreme case of cold, which for the day may be taken at 30°, but for the night may be assumed in this country at zero of Fahrenheit's thermometer ; the temperature to be maintained at the same season of cold is also to be settled. Then, Tredgold, § 44, gives the following rule :—Multiply the cubic feet per minute of air to be heated, to supply the ventilation and loss of heat, by the difference between the temperature the room is to be kept at, and that of the external air in degrees of the thermometer, and divide the product by 2·1 times the difference between 200 and the temperature of the room. This quotient will give the quantity of surface of cast iron steam pipe that will be sufficient to maintain the room at the required temperature. According to Dr. Arnott, 1 foot of superficies of heating surface is required for every 6 feet of glass ; the same for every 120 feet of wall, roof, and ceiling ; and an equivalent quantity for every 6 cubic feet of air withdrawn from the apartment by ventilation per minute. (Tomlinson, p. 124.)

3062. Regarding the danger to be apprehended from any insecurity in constructing and setting such warming apparatuses as have been described, the present editor published a small pamphlet in 1853, entitled *Notes on the Causes of Fires in Buildings*; *or, which is the safest of the various methods of warming buildings?* in order to direct the attention of the uninitiated to the defective points of each apparatus. " The Metropolitan Building Act, 1855," requires that :—I. The floor under every oven or stove used for the purpose of trade or manufacture, and the floor around the same for the space of 18 inches, shall be formed of materials of an incombustible and non-conducting nature; II. No pipe for conveying smoke, heated air, steam, or hot water, shall be fixed against any building on the face next to any street, alley, mews, or public way ; III. No pipe for conveying heated air or steam shall be fixed nearer than *six* inches to any combustible material ; IV. No pipe for conveying hot water shall be placed nearer than *three* inches to any combustible material ; and V. No pipe for conveying smoke or other products of combustion shall be fixed nearer than *nine* inches to any combustible material ; with a penalty not exceeding 20l. for non-compliance : but attention is not often paid to these clauses. The Incorporated Society for Promoting the Building, &c., of Churches, has issued a warning to churchwardens to insure such structures, in consequence of two *new* churches (uninsured) having been burnt within a twelvemonth, apparently from the overheating of the smoke flues and chimneys, arising from carelessness in their construction, and the woodwork of the seating and roofing not being properly protected. Where coal is used, the accumulation of soot is a source of very great danger, for when inflamed, the brickwork soon becomes red-hot. Facilities for the frequent cleaning of chimneys and flues should always be afforded by the introduction of soot doors. The publication of the Society, *The Church Builder* (vols. iii. 92, 167, and iv. 84, 119), gives some very useful descriptions of contrivances for warming churches.

BOOK IV.

APPENDIX.

CHAP. I.

VALUATION OF PROPERTY.

The valuations in which the architect is consulted are properly only those wherein buildings have been or may be erected; from which if he wander, the probability is that he will create difficulty for himself, tending to exhibit him as a pretender to knowledge not within the regular course of his occupation.   The general principles, therefore, on which we propose to touch, are confined to the species of property above named, as distinguished from that in which the resident valuator near the spot in the different provinces is the best adviser, from the local knowledge he possesses.   The auctioneers who with unblushing effrontery pretend to a knowledge of the value of property in the metropolis, are utterly incompetent to the duties they undertake, from an ignorance of the durability and cost of buildings, which can be attained by the practice and experience of the architect only.

Buildings may be so disadvantageously placed on their sites as to realise nothing like a proper interest on the money expended in their erection; and, indeed, so as altogether to destroy even the great value of the ground on which they are built.   Thus, to place before the reader extreme cases, which generally best illustrate a subject, let him suppose a row of hovels built in Piccadilly, and a house like Apsley House placed in Wapping High Street.   In both cases the productive value of the ground is destroyed, there being no inhabitants for such dwellings in the respective quarters of the town.

From this it must be evident that the value of town or city property, which consists principally of buildings, is divisible into two parts; namely, —

      That arising from the value of the soil or site; and

      That which arises from the value of the buildings placed upon it.

We will suppose for a house which is fairly let at a rent of 100l. per annum, no matter what the situation of it be, that it could be built for 1000l., and that the proprietor or builder would be content with 7 per cent. for the outlay of his money, a rate by no means larger than he would be entitled to claim, seeing that the letting, after it is built, is a matter of speculation, and that loss of tenants and other casualties may temporarily deprive him of the interest of his capital.   In this case, then, the rent of the mere building would be 70l. ; and as the full rent assumed is 100l.,

    $100 - 70 = 30$, which is manifestly the value of the ground or ground rent.

Thus in the cases of valuation of freeholds, wherein the gross rent can be accurately ascertained, there can be no difficulty in coming at the real value of the ground rent, because the building rent, or that arising from the expenditure of money on the soil, can be immediately ascertained by the architect, with the rate of interest on it which it is fit the builder should have.   The remainder of the rent is that inseparably attached to the value of the soil, and belongs to the ground landlord.

The reason for thus separating the two rents is this: the ground rent, attached as it is to the soil, is imperishable.   It is true that the value of ground is constantly fluctuating from the power of fashion over certain localities; but with this the valuator cannot deal.   The changes are slow; and the Lord Shaftesbury in the time of Charles II. would have little thought it possible, when he placed his residence in Aldersgate Street, that his successors would have dwelt in a house in Grosvenor Square; neither, even five and twenty years ago, did it cross the mind of the then possessor of the Grosvenor property that the Five Fields at Chelsea contained a mine of wealth in the ground rents of Belgrave and Eaton Squares.   Such are the mutations of property, with which the present question is not involved, unless the gift of foresight, in a degree not to be expected, be given to the valuator.   The other portion of the value of house property is strictly the result of the perishable part of it, namely, the building itself; and this is limited by the durability of the building, which has great relation to the time it has already existed, and to the substantiality with which it has been constructed.   The durability, then, or the number of years a building will continue to realise the rent, is the second ingredient in a valuation, and is a point upon which none but an experienced person can properly decide.

The rate of interest which the buyer is content to obtain in the investment of his money in buildings, or, in other words, in the purchase of the perishable annuity arising from the building, will necessarily vary with the value of money in the market.   In the compensation cases under public improvements, wherein it is obligatory on the owner to

part with his property, the 6 per cent. rate of the table is generally used, by which the buyer makes too little interest on the perishable part of the property. Few would be inclined to invest money in such property at so low a rate, for a rent which every year, from wear and tear, becomes less valuable. Individuals understanding the subject would scarcely be found to purchase, unless they could make at least 8 per cent. for this part of the capital. In the cases above mentioned, twenty-five years' purchase, that is, 4 per cent., is the usual price at which the ground rent is taken.

Having thus prepared the student, we will present an example of a valuation conducted on the principles named. Thus, suppose a building and the ground on which it stands to be together worth 150l. per annum, and that its durability is such that a purchaser may count on receiving that rent during a term of fifty years. We will suppose the house to stand upon a plot of ground 24 feet in frontage and 60 feet in depth; that the size of the house is 24 feet by 40 feet, and that to build a similar one would cost 1,440l., which, at a rate of 7 per cent. upon the expenditure, would produce a building rent of 100l. 16s. per annum.

	£	s.	d.	£	s.	d.
Now the total rent being - - - -	150	0	0			
The rent arising from the building itself - -	100	16	0			
The value of the mere ground must be - - -	49	4	0			

We therefore here have the imperishable part, viz. the ground, of the value of 49l. 4s. per annum, which, giving the purchaser 4 per cent. interest for his money, is twenty-five years' purchase for the fee-simple by the Fourth Table, that is   -   -   -   -   -   — 1230 0 0

An annuity (from the building) of 100l. 16s., to continue for fifty years, is, by the Fourth Table at 5 per cent., worth 18·256 years' purchase, that is   -   -   -   -   -   -   -   -   -   -   — 1840 0 11

The value of the old materials at the end of the term, if taken to be pulled down and sold for 150l., will be that sum at the end of fifty years to be received at the present time, discounting at 4 per cent. from the Second Table ·1407 × 150   -   -   -   = 21 2 0

Total value of the freehold   -   -   -   3091 2 11

In the above valuation the ground estimated by its frontage would be $\frac{49l.\ 4s.}{24\ \text{feet}} = 41s.$ per foot, and ground is usually let by the foot when demised for building. In the chief parts of great cities ground is now usually sold and let at per foot superficial.

The next case of valuation is that of a beneficial lease, in which the rent paid by the lessee is less than the actual value of the premises. The difference between them, therefore, is an annuity for the term of the lease, which is so much benefit to the lessee, and is estimated by the Fourth Table; thus—

Suppose the actual value of given premises be   -   -   -   - £100
Rent reserved by the lessor   -   -   -   -   - 50

Beneficial annuity belonging to the lessee   -   -   -   - £50

If the term of the lease be twenty-one years, such is the length of the annuity, and the question stands as under :—

An annuity for twenty-one years, discounting at 5 per cent., is by the Fourth Table worth 12·8211 years' purchase, which multiplied by 50l. = 641l. 1s.

It is to be observed that the annuities must be clear after the deduction of all outgoings which may be necessary to keep it unencumbered.

Let us take another case.

A man takes a lease of ground at 10l. per annum, and lays out 1,000l. on a sixty-one years' lease, interest being 3 per cent. How much must he receive as rent to replace the principal at the end of the term?

1000l. at 3 per cent. = 30l. + 10l. ground rent = 40l. improved rent.

1l. per annum for sixty-one years at 3 per cent. will amount to 169l. (See Third Table.)

$\frac{1000}{169} = 5l.\ 9s. =$ the sum to be laid out yearly.

And 30l. + 5l. 9s. = 35l. 9s., or 3·59, is the rate of interest to secure or replace the principal at the end of the term without consideration of repairs, loss of tenants, insurance, &c.

We now subjoin some observations on the valuation of *house property*, which claim the architectural student's attention. Inwood's *Tables for the Purchasing of Estates, &c.* have long been in general use ; they are founded on the elaborate Tables by Baily and Smart. A series are given hereafter. W. D. Biden, *Rules, Formulæ, and Tables for the Valuation of Estates, &c.*, with his smaller work, *Practical Rules for Valuers*, 1862, are useful, and have furnished the outline for the following remarks.

It is generally considered that the value of a *freehold* house ranges, according to situation, style, condition, &c., from 10 to 20 years' purchase. It naturally follows, that purchasers, and some valuators indeed, imagine that house property, as a rule, pays from 5 to 10 per cent. interest on the purchase-money. This is a great error, as many have experienced who have endeavoured to realise and to expend yearly 8 per cent. on the cost of house property. The valuation should be made at 5 per cent. (if the purchaser will be content with that interest) ; and the present value of *all* the costs, charges, and losses incident to house property should be fairly stated and deducted in the valuation, and then the purchaser will not be deluded with the idea that he is to net a very large interest, which may be spent unconcernedly. Such is the expectation of many of those who are induced to join Building Societies, and who buy, what appears to them, a bargain, as they will be receiving for years double or treble the amount of interest obtainable from the funds. A change of tenants, or other cause, soon shows the difference. Where, however, the buyer himself occupies the house, whether freehold or leasehold, he may make a very advantageous investment of his money. In the latter case, that is, of a leasehold, he must bear in mind the result of the occupation of the premises, namely, dilapidations, for which he will be called strictly to account by his landlord at the expiration of his term of lease.

Compare the following valuations, made in two ways, of a *freehold* house, which will last for about 80 years, the tenants paying the rates amounting to about £7 per annum. One valuator may make out his calculations thus :—

		£ s. d.	£ s. d.
Gross rent received by the landlord - - - -			63 0 0
Deduct Insurance - ⎫		1 10 0	
,, Land Tax - ⎬ when paid by him -		1 2 6	
,, Sewers Rate ⎭		0 15 9	
,, General repairs, 10 per cent. - - -		6 6 0	
,, Collection, &c. - - -		4 14 6	
			14 8 9
			48 11 3

(In a leasehold valuation, the ground rent would also have to be deducted.)

To pay 8 per cent., at years' purchase (Fourth Table)   -   -   12½

Presumed value of the property, according to this rough valuation   -   £607 0 8

Another valuator will make out his calculations as follows :—

	£ s. d.	£ s. d.
Gross rent - - - - - - -		63 0 0
Annual deductions, as before - - - -		14 8 9
Net rent - - - - - - -		48 11 3
But property is usually subject to various depreciating contingencies, which must be provided against by an annual reserve according to the class of building, thus :—		
Deduct for losses by bad tenants, say 1 year's rent in 6 =	10 10 0	
And, for extra repairs and expenses contingent upon such frequent changes, say an equal sum - - -	10 10 0	
Deduct a sum for rebuilding (say about £630), which, put by each year in the funds at 3 per cent. compound interest, will produce that amount at the end of the life of the house, say 80 years, i.e., £1 per annum for 80 years (Third Table) - - - - = £321·363		
2	2 0 0	
£642·726	23 0 0	
Clear income from the property - - - -		25 11 3

If the purchaser elects to have 5 per cent. for his speculation, the amount to be paid for the property will be   -   -   -   -   £512 0 0

The value of the ground in these calculations is included in the rental ; when of some importance, it must be valued upon its own merits, as shewn in the previous page.

But there may be a further expenditure for surveyors' charges, solicitors' charges for transferring the property, and loss of capital by selling out of the funds, which it may be often necessary to deduct from that amount. A matter also of consideration is whether the building is in a good state of repair, both in structure and decoration, as ready for a tenant.

When the property is *leasehold*, then, as soon as the clear income has been ascertained, it will have to be multiplied by the number of years' purchase at the rate of interest required for the term (Fourth Table), to find the amount that the property is worth. The number of years' purchase provides for the percentage and to get back the principal, the annual instalments of which must be invested at the same rate of interest to produce the total sum at the end of the term (in lieu of the rebuilding fund in the *freehold* property). Among Inwood's *Tables*, 16th edition, 1855, is one (p. 177), whereby to calculate " the present value of an income for a certain number of years, which is to pay during its continuance a given rate of interest on the purchase-money, and to replace the purchase-money at the end of the same number of years at a rate of interest to be selected."

From the former method of expressing the valuation, it would appear that a purchaser may realise 8 per cent. upon his outlay ; and so indeed he may, for a few years, if everything connected with the property be very favourable ; but the latter calculation shows exactly what may be expected, namely, that on capitalising a further sum to form a sinking fund for certain repayments, then 5 per cent. per annum may be appropriated as *income*, the remainder of the rent being set aside to supply a fund to meet exigencies of no uncommon occurrence. The real value of the property, moreover, is found to be much less than what the rough calculation would show it to be worth.

The deductions for losses depend entirely upon the class of house. First class houses in good situations let so readily to responsible tenants, who for their own comfort and display maintain the fabric, that the sums to be deducted for the occasional want of occupants and expenses of reletting are reduced to a minimum. On the other hand, a much lower class of house, together with the present unsatisfactory mode of letting houses on three years' agreements, and the still more ineligible arrangement by the year, throw so much larger amounts for repairs, decorations, and change of tenancy, upon the landlord, that the total of the sums to be deducted is raised to a very high estimate. Herein the best judgment of the valuator is called into requisition, and it requires the knowledge obtained by the practical architect to assist his judgment in such matters.

After the actual value has been ascertained, another item for consideration is the additional sum that a purchaser will be induced to give for some reason—such as the property being in a fashionable neighbourhood ; the house possessing arrangements peculiarly suited to his wishes, and so on : this amount may be called a " fancy price," and when paid had better be considered as money sunk.

For making rough calculations, according to the first instance, the value of *freehold land* in the country is generally considered worth from 30 to 33 years' purchase, being calculated on the 3 per cent. tables. In a few very exceptional cases as much as 40 years' purchase has been given ; but the difference constituted a " fancy price." For town plots from 25 to 30 years' is more usual. *Freehold houses and buildings*, 1st and 2nd class, from 18 to 20 years' purchase, or 5 per cent.; 3rd and 4th class, about 16 years' purchase, or 6 per cent.

For *Leasehold property* :—

1st and 2nd class,	from 15 to 16 years' purchase	or 6 per cent.			
2nd and 3rd „	14 to 15	„	7	„	
3rd and 4th „	12 to 13	„	8	„	
4th and 5th „	11 to 12	„	9	„	
5th and 6th „	10	„	10	„	

Freehold *Ground-rents* are valuable in proportion to the extent to which they are covered by the rack-rent and by the period of reversion. A good ground-rent ought to be six times covered, that is, five parts are brick and mortar rent, and one part ground-rent. A reversion, however, unless within forty years, is not much taken into account. Some ground-rents in the City of London (where the ground-rent is larger in proportion) have sold for $31\frac{1}{4}$ years' purchase ; those only covered by three times the rack rent, sold for 25 years' purchase. Leasehold and freehold ground-rents can only be valued according to locality, circumstances, length of holding, &c. Unsecured ground-rents are usually valued at 25 years' purchase, but those well-secured at from 30 to 33 years' purchase. *Improved ground-rents* are not worth so much as the freehold ground-rent, in consequence of the covenants of superior leases, danger of breaches of covenants, &c.

In the valuation of *leases* held on lives, the operation, after bringing the rent to a clear annuity, is conducted by means of the sixth, seventh, and eighth tables, given hereafter, as the case may require.

In the valuation of *warehouses*, the only safe method of coming at the value of a rental

is by the quantity of goods or tonnage they will contain after leaving proper gangways, and not overloading the floors. In corn warehouses, however, the grain being distributed over the surface of the floor, the squares of floor are taken to come at the contents. Goods warehoused are paid for to the warehouseman usually at a weekly or monthly rent; and it is commonly considered that the profit he should make ought to be one half of the rent he pays to the landlord, so that in fact two-thirds of the actual rent realised goes to the proprietor, and the other third to the warehouseman or lessee. Tables of the weight and space occupied by different goods are given in the GLOSSARY ADDENDUM.

We have noticed at the commencement of this chapter that valuations depending upon building or building land are essentially within the province of the architect. But as valuations for *Railway* and *Improvement compensations* ramify into one and the other, as well as into agricultural land, a portion of the subject into which we do not consider it desirable here to enter, we will only notice that, as regards the former, there are several items, beyond those already mentioned, to be taken into consideration. A man holding a property, and dispossessed against his will, has a right to be paid for his interests being so injuriously affected, hence an item for " compulsory sale " is allowed; this was formerly as much as 30 per cent. for house property, now it is only 10 per cent.; while for land, from 10 to 25 per cent. is obtained, according to circumstances. With certain exceptions, the purchase of lands compulsorily is placed under the provisions of the Statute 8 Vict. cap. 18, "The Land Clauses Act." The assessment of the items usually consists of the following heads:—I. The value of the property taken. II. Any reversionary or prospective advantage the owner may be likely to receive at any time; to be estimated in present money. III. Any advantage the owner may have by carrying on a trade, business, or profession, in a locality; whether the same would be utterly destroyed, or a portion be taken with him. IV. The cost of removing, or loss by forced sale. V. The value of the portion only of the property (if so taken), and amount of damage the remainder may sustain in consequence of the severance; this is usually called *consequential damage*. VI. If a portion only be taken, and that portion injuriously divides the remainder of the property, the estimated amount of damage is known as *severance*. VII. Compensation for loss of time, trouble, and expense, in finding a new investment; loss of interest: the parting with property to which one is attached to and has an interest in; and other losses by being forced to give up a property and seek new. This forms the item of *compulsory sale*.

CHAP. II.

CIVIL AND ECCLESIASTICAL DILAPIDATIONS.

The architect, in the course of business, may be commissioned to ascertain the extent of neglect on the part of an occupant in keeping premises in proper order according to the terms upon which the property is held by him. In civil cases it is not usual for the lessor to exercise a power, generally reserved to him in leases, of causing his architect to inspect the premises from time to time to detect dilapidation ; but it is usual for the lessor to cause such an inspection (at a reasonable period, so that the repairs may be done) before the expiration of the term : this reasonable period may vary from two to twenty-six weeks, more or less. After such inspection or survey, a notice to repair dilapidations according to its appended schedule is served upon the tenant, who may either execute the works within the term, or (unless he can compound with the lessor for a sum to be ascertained under arbitration) take the responsibility of paying the charges of the tradesmen employed by the lessor after the premises have been surrendered, to which a compensation for loss of rent is naturally added ; but this arrangement, if adopted, is a very exceptional procedure. It will be evident that in cases where a lease expires and is not to be renewed before other suitable premises can be obtained, the latter method of action may be desirable ; but generally, and especially in the case of a dwelling-house, the cheapest, if the most inconvenient, course is for the tenant to have a survey made for himself and to get the repairs executed within the term. In ecclesiastical cases the survey previous to the end of occupancy is rarely, if ever, practicable ; and a sum must be ascertained under arbitration. According to the usual tenor of leases, the lessor expects that the premises shall be delivered, at the expiration of a term, in as good condition as the *use and wear* during the time will permit, and the lessee undertakes to make good any injury which the premises may have suffered through accident, neglect, or intention ; these conditions apply, not only to what was originally demised, but to whatever may have been erected during his occupation. In ecclesiastical cases the principle, as will hereafter be explained, is rather different. It may be noticed here that the term *wear and tear* is a popular mistake which the law does not support; use and wear is legitimate, tear is dilapidation.

In civil dilapidations a tenant is bound, according to his covenant, specific or general, but never beyond maintaining and upholding, unless the conditions of repair are so bad that no measures short of reconstruction are consistent with safety, or possible from the extent of decay. His liability is not supposed to extend to such defects as only indicate age, so long as the efficiency of the part still remains. But if the effects of use or age have proceeded so far as to destroy the part, or its efficiency in the structure, the tenant is liable, it being the presumption that at the commencement of the term the tenant was satisfied that every part was sufficiently strong to last to the close. On the same presumption the degree of liability of the tenant is regulated by the actual condition of the premises at any time, as specified in his covenant, and admits of no extenuation by reason of dilapidations existing at the commencement of his term, as he is presumed to have taken the proper course to guard himself against the occurrence of undue liability. In extreme cases, the liability of a tenant extends to the rebuilding of a party wall condemned as unsafe, to reconstruction after fire, &c., unless specially excepted. In fact, under the natural and the legal favour which the lessor enjoys, the person proposing to become the lessee should employ a professional surveyor, not only to inspect the apparent, and as far as he can the hidden, state of the building, but also to check the conditions contained in the draft of the lease, which are sometimes extravagant when applied to an old and worn-out fabric, though they might be reasonable as regards a new structure.

Whatever the tenant has power to remove during the term cannot be chargeable with dilapidations. Upon this point the old rule is, that whatever is *fixed* to the freehold cannot be removed by the tenant : thus a lessee may erect barns or sheds or any building upon wooden or stone or other blocks laid on the surface of the ground, and take them down, if he please, without substituting anything in their place ; but if the barns are fixed into the ground, they immediately become the property of the lessor. There seems, however, to be an exception in respect of buildings erected for the purposes of trade : hence not only coppers and ovens may be taken away, but workshops and the like erected by the tenant for his particular trade. This exception seems at first to have applied only to wooden buildings ; but Lord Kenyon held that a brick chimney would prevent a tenant from removing a building, and decided that its being on a brick foundation would not do it. Though this opinion was not held by Lord Ellenborough, yet it was not because the buildings were of brick, but because they were erected for the purposes of agriculture, and not of trade. It is to be remembered, in all cases, that a lessee is bound to leave the premises in as good condition after the removal of fixtures as though they had never existed : thus, if a marble be substituted for a wooden chimney-piece, when the former is removed, the latter, or one of equal value, must be replaced. If a partition be put up and taken away, all damages to the adjacent work must be repaired.

The general rule for determining what injuries are considered dilapidations, is to ascertain what is *fair wear* without dilapidation arising from accident or neglect. Injury by accident is that which happens suddenly, and perceptibly differing from wear, which occurs only by lengthened use. Thus the nosing of a step worn away is not dilapidation ; but if such be broken away instead of worn, it is a dilapidation. It may be said that accident is defined here with too much latitude, inasmuch as it takes account of that which occurs without apparent reason at any particular time ; but we use the term in common language, and may cite as an example, that if the timbers of a floor decay, the floor will yield, even without a load upon it. When accident occurs, such alone does not limit the extent of the dilapidation, but also such injuries to the building as follow in its train. Thus, if the weather-boarding of a building decay from age, so long as the covering will keep out wet, it is no dilapidation ; but if broken in any part, that is a dilapidation ; and if from want of reparation any of the internal parts of the building be injured, such injury is a dilapidation : so if timber or timbers belonging to any part of a house merely decay, if it or they be still sufficient for the support of the house, no dilapidation can be chargeable ; but if such timber or timbers give way, they must be replaced, and all parts made good which suffered by their failure. *Waste,* in law, is insufferable, even in freeholds which are held for lives only. According to Woodfall (*Landlord and Tenant*), "waste may be done in houses by pulling them down or suffering them to be uncovered, whereby the rafters and other timbers of the house become rotten ; but the bare suffering them to be uncovered, without rotting the timber, is not waste : so if a house be uncovered when the tenant cometh in, it is no waste in the tenant to suffer the same to fall down." In external covering, however, it seems that decay arising from inattention to it is dilapidation, even though no accident be the cause. It is always considered that though painting neglected is not itself a dilapidation, yet where decay arises from it, it is one. Broken glass is not considered a dilapidation, unless there be more than one crack in the pane. Some, however, contend that while the glass is sufficiently entire to exclude the wind and weather, no waste is assignable. Generally it seems then to be the rule, that where accident occurs, it is a dilapidation.

In the preceding paragraph the word *neglect* has naturally occurred ; dilapidation from

neglect being very often followed by dilapidation by *accident*: the latter term is still more nearly connected with the word *misuse*, which occupies the place here given to "accident" in the Report upon Dilapidations, published in 1844 by the Royal Institute of British Architects. This Report does not define its meaning of the word *misuse*; it is clearly not the meaning in which the term is generally employed; for the Report says, "If the effects of use or age have proceeded so far as to destroy the part or its efficiency in the structure, this argues neglect or misuse." The student will find it advantageous to study the Report, and especially the specification contained therein.

This specification instructs the mason "in cases of broken nosings, or of the treads being worn to such an extent as to render the passing up and down dangerous," to piece as described the step; and also directs the joiner "to put nosings to stairs where partially defective, and treads where wholly so." There is in appearance a contradiction between these views upon worn steps and that given in the commencement of this chapter; but the practised surveyor will see that they are easily reconciled, and that his judgment must decide which is, and which is not, fair use and wear. It is to be regretted that the clear and discriminating section on dilapidations in Chambers and Tattersall, *Laws relating to Building*, 1845, contains a sweeping condemnation of this Report, which is in no way authorised by the evidence adduced.

We have added to the usual definition of dilapidation, namely any injury through *accident, misuse*, or *neglect*, the word *intention*; and the propriety of the addition, as meaning something different from wilful waste, will be obvious. The erection of a photographer's room on the top of a house in one street may be deemed an injury, and be claimed as dilapidation by a lessor, who would demand the removal of it and the restoration of the roof; while in another street, and within a few yards of this dilapidation, the same lessor might consider the same work (if judiciously executed) an improvement which he would not allow to be removed. So also a grated iron door, instead of the common wooden one, and similar alterations, may become dilapidations of intention at the pleasure of the lessor. There is another point on which surveyors have frequently differed, namely the insertion of nails and screws for the suspension of frames of pictures, &c. This may be now considered to be determined by the judgment in the case of Martin and another *v.* Roe (1857), where hot house frames, bedded in mortar on brick walls, had been removed without damage except what was unavoidable to the mortar. Lord Campbell said that, "in considering this question, we treat the removal by the plaintiff as having been in fact effected without injury to the freehold. In all cases of this kind, injury to the freehold must be spoken of with less than legal strictness. A screw or a nail can scarcely be drawn without some injury; and when all the harm done is that which is unavoidable to the mortar laid on brick walls, this is so trifling that the law, which is reasonable, will regard it as none." Among surveyors it has been held that what is nailed belongs to the freehold, but that which can be unscrewed does not, the careful withdrawal of the screw enabling the tenant to make good the hole.

Although there is a general impression that only damage of broken glass can be claimed from a yearly tenant, he is to use the building in a husbandlike manner, and is bound to fair and tenantable repairs so far as to keep it wind and water tight and to prevent waste or decay.

It used to be supposed that the judgment in the case of Wise *v.* Medcalf (1829) contained an exposition of the whole law on the subject of ecclesiastical dilapidation as far as regarded incumbents; and the decision, which is contained in the following words, should be always in the mind of the surveyor:—"Upon the whole, we are of opinion the incumbent was bound to maintain the parsonage (which we must assume upon this case to have been suitable in point of size and other respects to the benefice) and also the chancel, and to keep them in good and substantial repair; restoring and rebuilding when necessary, according to the original form, without addition or modern improvement; and that he was not bound to supply or maintain anything in the nature of ornament, to which painting (unless necessary to preserve exposed timbers from decay) and whitewashing, and papering belong." This decision is held to establish the principle that the executors of a deceased incumbent are bound to perform those repairs which are necessary to prevent decay, and to use all reasonable means for preventing any future decay. The case of Mason *v.* Lambert (1848) showed that perpetual curates were liable as incumbents for these dilapidations. We have therefore to add, in ecclesiastical cases, any provision against prospective injury; such as paint necessary to preserve exposed woodwork from decay, the insertion of ties to plates taking the feet of rafters, the underpinning of walls at cracks showing continual settlement: these might be entitled dilapidations of precaution, and ought to include the immediate destruction of any erections made by a late incumbent which were suitable to his private fortune rather than to the benefice, as seems to be indicated in the judgment given in the case of Martin and another *v.* Roe (1857), wherein it is observed that, "as to any matter of needless expense or luxury or ornament by which the present incumbent has gratified his own taste or increased his own

comfort, he is not only not bound, but he ought not, to transmit it to his successor." The principle thus stated is directly opposite to that which, as we have above observed, regulates civil cases, namely, that the occupier must keep in repair whatever may have been erected during his occupation. The judgment just cited continues in these words : " If the successor may recover damages from the executor after such things have been removed by the testator, there can be no doubt he in his turn must maintain it ; and if he maintain it he must also restore, and even rebuild when decayed ; so that the benefice might become permanently saddled with a useless burden." The duty to remove such erections does not, however, appear quite to have been thrown upon the estate of the erector : the same judgment says, " the case now supposed is that of an erection, which, if the deceased had left out of repair, his successor could not have maintained any action for dilapidations, which he himself therefore would not be bound to keep in repair, which imposes no burden on him, and which he may remove ; for it would be unreasonable to hold that he might not remove, however useless or unsuitable to the living, or even inconvenient to the occupation of the parsonage or glebe, that which for one of these reasons he was not bound to keep in repair." Finally we would quote from the same judgment : " with regard to an ecclesiastical benefice, the character and object of the building to which the chattel is attached, and the manner in which it has been so attached, seem of very great consequence in determining whether there was any intention to separate it permanently and irrevocably from the personal estate." In this case the plaintiffs (executors) were held justified in removing the framework and sashes, valued at 300*l.*, of two hot houses, and might apparently have removed also the brickwork, repairing any waste or damage to the freehold. With respect to that damage we have already referred to this case.

The real difference between civil and ecclesiastical dilapidations may be thus stated :— One man takes certain premises, engaging to pay a rent in order to derive advantages out of them, but having no interest in the freehold. The other man receives a salary to do certain services, the *use* of the house being a portion of that salary. In the latter case, if for a man's own private convenience he lays out a large sum on the freehold, that expenditure will seriously affect his successor, if he have to be burdened with large and expensive erections or decorations suitable perhaps for one of an aristocratic family, but quite foreign to the habits of a future rector of the village coming in as an ordinary occupant.

Such are the general principles of the law of dilapidations ; these, in their application, generally impose upon the out-going occupant or his representatives the payment of a sum for which special provision is rarely made during the occupancy : the misery thus entailed is sometimes evaded in civil cases by the lessee, who parts with the remainder of a lease to any one who will give something for it ; or who (if the lessor be not careful) assigns it to a man of straw.

CHAP. III.

CALCULATION OF INTEREST.

Interest, or the value of the use of money, is usually expressed *per cent*, or after the rate per hundred on the principal lent. Thus, if we put out 500 pounds sterling at 5 per cent., it signifies that for every hundred pounds the lender is to receive five pounds per annum during the continuance of the loan. The solution of this question, which is one merely of *simple interest*, is so obvious, that it is unnecessary further to detain the reader upon it ; and we therefore pass on to *compound interest*, or interest upon interest, which arises from the principal and interest taken together, as it becomes due at the end of each stated time of payment.

In the resolution of this question, we are to consider that 100*l.* at the end of a year becomes 105*l.* Let $a =$ principal. Its amount at the end of the year is found by saying, if 100 gives 105, what will a give ? and we answer $\frac{105a}{100} = \frac{21a}{20}$, which may be also expressed $\frac{21}{20} \times a$, or $a + \frac{1}{20} \times a$.

Thus, by adding its twentieth part to the original principal, we have the principal at the end of the first year ; adding to this last its twentieth, we know the amount of the given principal in two years, and so on. Hence the annual increases to the principal may be easily computed. Suppose, for instance, the principal of 1000*l.* Expressing the values in decimal fractions, it will be worth—

After 1 year - - - £1050
               52·5   One year's interest on £1050.

After 2 years - - - 1102·5
               55·125   —   1102·5

After 3 years - - - 1157·625
               57·881   —   1157·625

After 4 years - - - 1215·506
               60·775   —   1215·506

After 5 years - - - 1276·281 &c.

The method above exhibited would, however, in calculations for a number of years, become very laborious, and it may be abridged in the following manner.

Let the present principal $= a$; now, since a principal of $20l.$ will amount to $21l.$ at the end of a year, the principal a will amount to $\frac{21}{20} \times a$ at the end of that time. At the end of the following year the same principal will amount to $\frac{21^2}{20^2} \times a = \left(\frac{21}{20}\right)^2 \times a$. This principal of two years will, the year after, amount to $\left(\frac{21}{20}\right)^3 \times a$, which will therefore be the principal of three years; increasing in this manner, at the end of four years the principal becomes $\left(\frac{21}{20}\right)^4 \times a$. After a century it will amount to $\left(\frac{21}{20}\right)^{100} \times a$, and in general $\left(\frac{21}{20}\right)^n \times a$ is the amount of the principal after n years; a formula serving to determine the amount of principal after any number of years.

The interest of 5 per cent., which has been taken in the above calculation, determined the fraction $\frac{21}{20}$. Had the interest been reckoned at 6 per cent. the principal a would at the end of a year be $\left(\frac{106}{100}\right) \times a$; at the end of two years to $\left(\frac{106}{100}\right)^2 \times a$; and at the end of n years to $\left(\frac{106}{100}\right)^n \times a$. Again, if the interest be at 4 per cent. the principal a will, after n years, be $\left(\frac{104}{100}\right)^n \times a$. Now all these formulæ are easily resolved by logarithms; for if, according to the first supposition, the question be $\left(\frac{21}{20}\right)^n \times a$, this will be $L.\left(\frac{21}{20}\right)^n + L.a$, and as $\left(\frac{21}{20}\right)^n$ is a power, we have $L.\left(\frac{21}{20}\right)^n = nL.\frac{21}{20}$: so that the logarithm of the principal required is $= n \times L.\frac{21}{20} + L.a$, and the logarithm of the fraction $\frac{21}{20} = L.21 - L.20$.

We shall now consider what the principal of $1000l.$ will amount to at compound interest of 5 per cent. at the end of 100 years. Here $n = 100$. Hence the logarithm of the principal required will be $= 100 L.\frac{21}{20} + L.1000$, calculated as under : —

$$L.21 = 1 \cdot 3222193$$
$$\text{Subtracting } L.20 = 1 \cdot 3010300$$

$$L.\tfrac{21}{20} = 0 \cdot 0211893$$
$$\text{Multiply by } 100$$

$$100 \; L.\tfrac{21}{20} = 2 \cdot 1189300$$
$$\text{Add } L.1000 = 3 \cdot 0000000$$

$5 \cdot 1189300 = $ Logarithm of the principal required; from the characteristic whereof the principal must be a number of six figures, and by the tables it will appear to be $131,501l.$ In the case of a principal of $3452l.$ at 6 per cent. for sixty-four years, we have $a = 3452$ and $n = 64$. Principal at the end of the first year therefore $= \frac{106}{10} = \frac{53}{50}$. Hence the logarithm of the principal sought $= 64 \times L.\frac{53}{50} + L.3452$, which will be found to amount to $143,763l.$

When the number of years is very great, errors of considerable magnitude may arise from the logarithms not being sufficiently extended in the decimal places; but as our object here is only to show the principle on which these calculations are founded, we do not think it necessary further to pursue that subject.

There is another case which now requires our consideration; it is that of not only adding the interest annually to the principal, but increasing it every year by a new sum $= b$. The original principal a would then increase in the following manner : —

After 1 year, $\frac{21}{20}a + b$
After 2 years, $\left(\frac{21}{20}\right)^2 a + \frac{21}{20}b + b$
After 3 years, $\left(\frac{21}{20}\right)^3 a + \left(\frac{21}{20}\right)^2 b + \frac{21}{20}b + b$
After 4 years, $\left(\frac{21}{20}\right)^4 a + \left(\frac{21}{20}\right)^3 b + \left(\frac{21}{20}\right)^2 b + \frac{21}{20}b + b$
After n years, $\left(\frac{21}{20}\right)^n a + \left(\frac{21}{20}\right)^{n-1} b + \left(\frac{21}{20}\right)^{n-2} b + \dots \frac{21}{20}b + b$

This principal evidently consists of two parts, whereof the first $= \left(\frac{21}{20}\right)^n a$, and the other, taken inversely, forms the series $b + \frac{21}{20}b + \left(\frac{21}{20}\right)^2 b + \left(\frac{21}{20}\right)^3 b + \dots \left(\frac{21}{20}\right)^{n-1} b$. This last series is evidently a geometrical progression, whose exponent $= \frac{21}{20}$. Its sum, therefore, will be found by first multiplying the last term $\left(\frac{21}{20}\right)^{n-1} b$ by the exponent $\frac{21}{20}$, which gives $\left(\frac{21}{20}\right)^n b$. Subtract the first term b, and we have the remainder $\left(\frac{21}{20}\right)^n b - b$; and lastly, dividing by the ex-

ponent minus 1, that is, by $\frac{1}{20}$, we have the sum required, $=20(\frac{21}{20})^n b-20b$. Wherefore the principal sought is $(\frac{21}{20})^n a+20(\frac{21}{20})^n b-20b=(\frac{21}{20})^n\times(a+20b)-20b$.

To resolve this formula we must separately calculate its first term $(\frac{21}{20})^n\times(a+20b)$, which is $n\text{L}.\frac{21}{20}+\text{L}.(a+20b)$, for the number which answers to this logarithm in the tables will be the first term, and if from this we subtract $20b$ we have the principal sought.

Suppose a principal of 1000*l.* placed out at 5 per cent. compound interest, and to it there be annually added 100*l.* besides *its* compound interest, and it be required to know to what it will amount at the end of 25 years. Here $a=1000$, $b=100$, $n=25$; and the operation is as follows:—

$$\text{L}.\tfrac{21}{20}=0\cdot021189299$$

Multiply by 25 we have $25\,\text{L}.\tfrac{21}{20}=0\cdot5297324750$
$$\text{L}.(a+20b)=3\cdot4771213135$$
$$=4\cdot0068537885$$

The first part or number which answers to this logarithm is 10159·1*l.*; from which if we subtract $20b=2000$ we find the principal in question to be after 25 years 8159·1*l.*

If it be required to know in how many years a principal of 1000*l.* under the above conditions would amount to 1,000,000*l.*; let n be the number of years required, and since $a=1000$, $b=100$, the principal at the end of n years will be $(\frac{21}{20})^n(3000)-2000$, which sum must make 1,000,000*l.*; whence results this equation:—

$$3000\,(\tfrac{21}{20})^n-2000=1000000$$

Adding to both sides 2000 we have $3000\,(\tfrac{21}{20})^n=1002000$
Dividing both sides by 3000 we have $(\tfrac{21}{20})=334$

Using logarithms we have $n\text{L}.\frac{21}{20}=\text{L}.334$, and dividing by $\text{L}.\frac{21}{20}$, we obtain $n=\dfrac{\text{L}.334}{\text{L}.\frac{21}{20}}$. Now $\text{L}.334=2\cdot5237465$ and $\text{L}.\frac{21}{20}=0\cdot0211893$, wherefore $n=\dfrac{2\cdot5237465}{0\cdot0211893}$. If, lastly, the two terms of this fraction be multiplied by 10000000, we shall have $n=\dfrac{25237465}{211893}$, equal to one hundred and nineteen years one month and seven days, which is the time wherein the principal of 1000*l.* will be increased to 1,000,000*l.* In the case of an annual decrease instead of increase of the capital by a certan sum, we shall have the following gradations as the values of a, year after year, the interest being at 5 per cent., and, representing by b the sum annually abstracted from the principal,

After 1 year it would be $\frac{21}{20}a-b$
After 2 years   — $(\frac{21}{20})^2 a-\frac{21}{20}b-b$
After 3 years   — $(\frac{21}{20})^3 a-(\frac{21}{20})^2 b-\frac{21}{20}b-b$
After n years   — $(\frac{21}{20})^n a-(\frac{21}{20})^{n-1}b-(\frac{21}{20})^{n-2}b\ldots-(\frac{21}{20})b-b$.

This principal evidently consists of two parts, one whereof is $(\frac{21}{20})^n a$, and the other to be subtracted therefrom, taking the terms inversely, forms a geometrical progression, as follows:—

$$b+(\tfrac{21}{20})b+(\tfrac{21}{20})^2 b+(\tfrac{21}{20})^3 b+\ldots(\tfrac{21}{20})^{n-1}b$$

The sum of this progression has already been found $=20\,(\frac{21}{20})^n b-20b$; if, therefore, this be subtracted from $(\frac{21}{20})^n a$, we have the principal required after n years $=(\frac{21}{20})^n(a-20b)+20b$.

For a less period than a year, the exponent n becomes a fraction; for example, 1 day $=\frac{1}{365}$, 2 days $=\frac{2}{365}$, and so on. It often happens that we wish to know the present value of a sum of money payable at the end of a number of years. Thus, as 20 pounds in ready money amount in a twelvemonth to 21 pounds, so, reciprocally, 21 pounds payable at the end of a year can be worth only 20 pounds. Therefore, if a be a sum payable at the end of a year, the present value of it is $\frac{20}{21}a$. Hence, to find the present value of a principal a at the end of a year, we must multiply by $\frac{20}{21}$; to find its present value at the end of two years, it must be multiplied by $(\frac{20}{21})^2 a$; and, in general, its value n years before the time of payment will be expressed by $(\frac{20}{21})^n a$.

Thus, suppose a rent of 100*l.* receivable for 5 years, reckoning interest at 5 per cent., if we would know its value in present money, we have

For £100 due after 1 year, the present value is £95·239
     after 2 years   —   90·704
     after 3 years   —   86·385
     after 4 years   —   82·272
     after 5 years   —   78·355

Sum of the five terms   £432·955

So that in present money, the value is 432*l.* 19*s.* 1*d.*

But for a great number of years such a calculation would become laborious. It may be facilitated as follows:— Let the annual rent $=a$, commencing directly and con-

tinuing n years, it will be worth $a + (\frac{20}{21})a + (\frac{20}{21})^2 a + (\frac{20}{21})^3 a + (\frac{20}{21})^4 a \ldots + (\frac{20}{21})^n a$, which is a geometrical progression whose sum is to be found. We have therefore only to multiply the last term by the exponent, the product whereof is $(\frac{20}{21})^{n+1} a$, then subtract the first term, and the remainder is $(\frac{20}{21})^{n+1} a - a$. Lastly, dividing by the exponent minus 1, that is, $\frac{1}{21}$, or, which is the same, multiplying by -21, we have the sum required, $= -21(\frac{20}{21})^{n+1} a + 21a$, or $21a - 21^{n+1} a$, the value of which second term is easily calculated by logarithms.

CHAP. IV.

COMPOUND INTEREST AND ANNUITY TABLES.

As the architect is often called on to value property, we here add some practical observations on the subject, and a set of Tables for the ready calculation of such matters, which we shall at once explain.

TABLE FIRST contains the amount of $1l$. put out to accumulate at compound interest for any number of years up to 100, at the several rates of 3, 4, 5, 6, 7, and 8 per cent. The amount of any other sum is found by multiplying the amount of $1l$. found in the table at the given rate per cent., and for the given time, by the proposed sum.

Example :—Required the amount of $755l$. in 51 years, at 5 per cent.
Amount of $1l$. for 51 years, at 5 per cent. is　-　-　-　-　12·040769
Given sum　-　-　-　-　-　-　-　-　-　-　-　755
or $9090l$. $15s$. $7\frac{3}{10}d$.　　　　　　　　　　　　　　£9080·780595

TABLE SECOND contains the present value of $1l$. payable at the end of any number of years up to 100. The present value of any given sum payable at the expiration of any number of years is found by multiplying the present value of $1l$. for the given number of years, at the proposed rate per cent., by the given sum or principal.

Example:—Required the present value of $9090l$. payable 51 years hence, compound interest being allowed at 5 per cent.
By the table, the present value of $1l$. payable at the expiration of
51 years at 5 per cent. is　-　-　-　-　-　-　-　·083051
Given principal　-　-　-　-　-　-　-　-　-　9090
or $754l$. $18s$. $7\frac{4}{10}d$.　　　　　　　　　　　　　£754·933590

TABLE THIRD contains the amount of an annuity of $1l$. for any number of years, and is thus used. Take out the amount of $1l$. answering to the given time and rate of interest: this multiplied by the given annuity will be the required amount.

Example :—Required the amount of an annuity of $27l$. in 21 years, at 5 per cent. compound interest.
Annuity of $1l$. in 21 years at 5 per cent.　-　-　-　-　-　35·719251
Annuity given　-　-　-　-　-　-　-　-　-　27
or $964l$. $8s$. $4\frac{7}{10}d$.　　　　　　　　　　　　　£964·419777

TABLE FOURTH shows the present value of an annuity of $1l$. for any number of years, at 3, 4, 5, 6, 7, and 8 per cent., and is used as follows:—
First, when the annuity commences immediately. Multiply the tabular number answering to the given years and rate of interest by the given annuity, and the product will be the value required. (This table provides for the percentage and to get back the principal.)

Example:—Required the present value of an annuity of $45l$., which is to continue 48 years, at the rate of 5 per cent.
Under 5 and opposite to 48 years is (years' purchase)　-　-　18·077157
Annuity given　-　-　-　-　-　-　-　-　-　45
or $813l$. $9s$. $5\frac{4}{10}d$.　　　　　　　　　　　　　£813·472065

Second, when the annuity does not commence till after a certain number of years. Multiply the difference between the tabular numbers answering to the time of commencement and end, at the proposed rate of interest, by the given annuity, the product will be the present value required.

Example.

An annuity of 40*l.* is to commence 20 years hence, and is to continue 30 years; required its present value, the rate of interest being 4 per cent.

Under 4 per cent. and opposite to 20 is - - - - - -	13·590326
Under 4 per cent. and opposite to 50 (20 + 30) is - - -	21·482184
Difference - - - - - - - - - -	7·891858
Annuity given - - - - - - - - -	40
	£315·674320

or 315*l.* 13*s.* 5⁸⁄₁₀*d.*

TABLE FIFTH contains the annuity which 1*l.* will purchase, compound interest being allowed. The manner of using this table is obvious, from what has been said relative to the preceding tables.

Example.

What annuity for 10 years will 500*l.* purchase, the rate of interest being 5 per cent.?

Under 5 and opposite to 10 is - - - - - - -	·129504
Principal given - - - - - - - - -	500
	£64·752000

or 64*l.* 15*s.* 0³⁄₁₀*d.*

TABLES SIXTH, SEVENTH, and EIGHTH are for finding the value of annuities on single and joint lives, and were constructed by Simpson, on the London bills of mortality.

To find the value of an annuity for a single life, at a proposed rate of interest, within the limits of the table, take from Table VI. the number answering to the given age and proposed rate of interest, which multiplied by the given annuity, the product will be the value required.

Example.

What is the value of an annuity of 50*l.* upon a single life aged 40 years, according to the London bills of mortality, the rate of interest being 4 per cent. ?

The value of an annuity of 1*l.* for 40 years at 4 per cent. is - - -	11·5
Annuity - - - - - - - - - - -	50
Value - - - - - - - - - - -	£575

To find the value of an annuity of two joint lives, multiply the number in Table VII. answering to the given ages, and at the proposed rate of interest, by the given annuity, and the product will be the required value.

Example.

What is the value of an annuity of 60*l.* for two joint lives, the one being 30 and the other 40 years, interest at 4 per cent.?

The number answering to 30 and 40 years at 4 per cent. is - - -	8·8
Annuity - - - - - - - - - -	60
Value - - - - - - - - -	£528 0

To find the value of an annuity for the longest of two given lives, proceed as directed in the case immediately preceding, but using Table VIII., and the product will be the value.

Example.

What is the value of an annuity of 60*l.* for the longest of two lives, the one being 30 and the other 40 years, interest at 4 per cent.

The tabular number answering at 4 per cent. is - - - -	15·9
Annuity - - - - - - - - - -	60
Present value - - - - - - - - -	£954·0

The first five tables which follow are printed from those of Smart; the remainder are from Simpson.

The calculations involving the valuation of annuities on lives are not very frequently imposed on the architect, but it is absolutely necessary he should be capable of performing them, as in the case of valuations of leases upon lives, which sometimes occur to him.

The First Table of Compound Interest.

The Amount of One Pound in any Number of Years, &c.

Years.	3 per Cent.	4 per Cent.	5 per Cent.	6 per Cent.	7 per Cent.	8 per Cent.
$\frac{1}{2}$	1·014889	1·019803	1·024695	1·029563	1·034408	1·039230
1	1·030000	1·040000	1·050000	1·060000	1·070000	1·080000
$1\frac{1}{2}$	1·045335	1·060596	1·075929	1·091336	1·106816	1·122368
2	1·060900	1·081600	1·102500	1·123600	1·144900	1·166400
$2\frac{1}{2}$	1·076695	1·103019	1·129726	1·156817	1·184293	1·212158
3	1·092727	1·124864	1·157625	1·191016	1·225043	1·259712
$3\frac{1}{2}$	1·108996	1·147140	1·186212	1·226226	1·267194	1·309131
4	1·125508	1·169858	1·215506	1·262476	1·310796	1·360488
$4\frac{1}{2}$	1·142266	1·193026	1·245523	1·299799	1·355897	1·413861
5	1·159274	1·216652	1.276281	1·338225	1·402551	1·469328
$5\frac{1}{2}$	1·176534	1·240747	1·307799	1·377787	1·450810	1·526970
6	1·194052	1·265319	1·340095	1·418519	1·500730	1·586874
$6\frac{1}{2}$	1·211830	1·290377	1·373189	1·460454	1·552367	1·649128
7	1·229873	1·315931	1·407100	1·503630	1·605781	1·713824
$7\frac{1}{2}$	1·248185	1·341992	1·441848	1·548082	1·661033	1·781058
8	1·266770	1·368569	1·477455	1·593848	1·718186	1·850930
$8\frac{1}{2}$	1·285631	1·395672	1·513941	1·640967	1·777305	1·923543
9	1·304773	1·423311	1·551328	1·689478	1·838459	1·999004
$9\frac{1}{2}$	1·324200	1·451498	1·589638	1·739425	1·901717	2·077426
10	1·343916	1·480244	1·628894	1·790847	1·967151	2.158925
$10\frac{1}{2}$	1.363926	1·509558	1·669120	1·843790	2·034837	2·243620
11	1.384233	1·539454	1·710339	1·898298	2·104851	2·331639
$11\frac{1}{2}$	1·404843	1·569941	1·752576	1·954417	2·177275	2·423110
12	1·425760	1·601032	1·795856	2·012196	2·252191	2·518170
$12\frac{1}{2}$	1·446989	1·632738	1·840205	2·071683	2·329685	2·616959
13	1·468533	1·665073	1·885649	2·132928	2·409845	2·719623
$13\frac{1}{2}$	1·490398	1·698048	1·932215	2·195984	2·492763	2·826315
14	1·512589	1·731676	1·979931	2·260903	2·578534	2·937193
$14\frac{1}{2}$	1·535110	1·765970	2·028826	2·327743	2·667256	3·052421
15	1·557967	1·800943	2·078928	2·396558	2·759031	3·172169
$15\frac{1}{2}$	1·581164	1·836609	2·130267	2·467407	2·853964	3·296614
16	1·604706	1·872981	2·182874	2·540351	2·952163	3·425942
$16\frac{1}{2}$	1·628599	1·910073	2·236780	2·615452	3·053741	3·560344
17	1·652847	1·947900	2·292018	2.692772	3·158815	3·700018
$17\frac{1}{2}$	1·677457	1·986476	2·348619	2·772379	3·267503	3·845171
18	1·702433	2·025816	2·406619	2·854339	3·379932	3·996019
$18\frac{1}{2}$	1·727780	2·065935	2·466050	2·938722	3·496229	4·152785
19	1·753506	2·106849	2·526950	3·025599	3·616527	4·315701
$19\frac{1}{2}$	1·779614	2·148573	2·589353	3·115045	3·740965	4·485008
20	1·806111	2·191123	2·653297	3·207135	3·869684	4·660957
$20\frac{1}{2}$	1·833002	2·234515	2·718821	3·301948	4·002832	4·843808
21	1·860294	2·278768	2·785962	3·399563	4·140562	5·033833
$21\frac{1}{2}$	1·887992	2·323896	2·854762	3·500064	4·283031	5·231313
22	1·916103	2·369918	2·925260	3·603537	4·430401	5·436540
$22\frac{1}{2}$	1·944632	2·416852	2·997500	3·710068	4·582843	5·649818
23	1·973586	2·464715	3·071523	3·819749	4·740529	5·871463
$23\frac{1}{2}$	2·002971	2·513526	3·147375	3·932672	4·903642	6·101804
24	2·032794	2·563304	3·225099	4·048934	5·072366	6·341180
$24\frac{1}{2}$	2·063060	2·614067	3·304744	4·168633	5·246897	6·589948
25	2·093777	2·665836	3·386354	4·291870	5·427432	6·848475

THE FIRST TABLE OF COMPOUND INTEREST — *continued.*

The Amount of One Pound in any Number of Years, &c.

Years.	3 per Cent.	4 per Cent.	5 per Cent.	6 per Cent.	7 per Cent.	8 per Cent.
25½	2·124952	2·718630	3·469981	4·418751	5·614179	7·117144
26	2·156591	2·772469	3·555672	4·549382	5·807352	7·396353
26½	2·188701	2·827375	3·643480	4·683876	6·007172	7·686515
27	2·221289	2·883368	3·733456	4·822345	6·213867	7·988061
27½	2·254362	2·940470	3·825654	4·964909	6·427674	8·301437
28	2·287927	2·998703	3·920129	5·111686	6·648838	8·627106
28½	2·321992	3·058089	4·016937	5·262803	6·877611	8·965551
29	2·356565	3·118651	4·116135	5·418387	7·114257	9·317274
29½	2·391652	3·180412	4·217783	5·578571	7·359044	9·682796
30	2·427262	3·243397	4·321942	5·743491	7·612255	10·062656
30½	2·463402	3·307629	4·428673	5·913286	7·874177	10·457419
31	2·500080	3·373133	4·538039	6·088100	8·145112	10·867669
31½	2·537304	3·439934	4·650106	6·268083	8·425370	11·294013
32	2·575082	3·508058	4·764941	6·453386	8·715270	11·737083
32½	2·613423	3·577532	4·882612	6·644168	9·015146	12·197534
33	2·652335	3·648381	5·003188	6·840589	9·325339	12·676049
33½	2·691826	3·720633	5·126742	7·042818	9·646206	13·173337
34	2·731905	3·794316	5·253347	7·251025	9·978113	13·690133
34½	2·772581	3·869458	5·383079	7·465387	10·321440	14·227204
35	2·813862	3·946088	5·516015	7·686086	10·676581	14·785344
35½	2·855758	4·024236	5·652233	7·913310	11·043941	15·365380
36	2·898278	4·103932	5·791816	8·147252	11·423942	15·968171
36½	2·941431	4·185206	5·934845	8·388109	11·817017	16·594610
37	2·985226	4·268089	6·081406	8·636087	12·223618	17·245625
37½	3·029674	4·352614	6·231587	8·891395	12·644208	17·922179
38	3·074783	4·438813	6·385477	9·154252	13·079271	18·625275
38½	3·120564	4·526719	6·543167	9·424879	13·529303	19·355954
39	3·167026	4·616365	6·704751	9·703507	13·994820	20·115297
39½	3·214181	4·707788	6·870325	9·990372	14·476354	20·904430
40	3·262037	4·801020	7·039988	10·285717	14·974457	21·724521
40½	3·310606	4·896099	7·213841	10·589794	15·489699	22·576785
41	3·359898	4·993061	7·391988	10·902861	16·022669	23·462483
41½	3·409924	5·091943	7·574533	11·225182	16·573978	24·382927
42	3·460695	5·192783	7·761587	11·557032	17·144256	25·339481
42½	3·512222	5·295621	7·953260	11·898693	17·734157	26·333562
43	3·564516	5·400495	8·149666	12·250454	18·344354	27·366640
43½	3·617589	5·507446	8·350923	12·612615	18·975548	28·440247
44	3·671452	5·616515	8·557150	12·985481	19·628459	29·555971
44½	3·726117	5·727744	8·768469	13·369371	20·303836	30·715466
45	3·781595	5·841175	8·985007	13·764610	21·002451	31·920449
45½	3·837900	5·956853	9·206893	14·171534	21·725105	33·172704
46	3·895043	6·074822	9·434258	14·590487	22·472623	34·474085
46½	3·953037	6·195127	9·667237	15·021826	23·245862	35·826520
47	4·011895	6·317815	9·905971	15·465916	24·045707	37·232012
47½	4·071628	6·442933	10·150599	15·923135	24·873072	38·692642
48	4·132251	6·570528	10·401269	16·393871	25·728906	40·210573
48½	4·193777	6·700650	10·658129	16·878524	26·614187	41·788053
49	4·256219	6·833349	10·921333	17·377504	27·529929	43·427418
49½	4·319590	6·968676	11·191036	17·891235	28·477180	45·131097
50	4·383906	7·106683	11·467399	18·420154	29·457025	46·901612

THE FIRST TABLE OF COMPOUND INTEREST — *continued.*

The Amount of One Pound in any Number of Years, &c.

Years.	3 per Cent.	4 per Cent.	5 per Cent.	6 per Cent.	7 per Cent.	8 per Cent.
50½	4·449178	7·247423	11·750588	18·964709	30·470583	48·741585
51	4·515423	7·390950	12·040769	19·525363	31·519016	50·653741
51½	4·582654	7·537320	12·338117	20·102592	32·603524	52·640912
52	4·650885	7·686588	12·642808	20·696885	33·725347	54·706040
52½	4·720133	7·838813	12·955023	21·308747	34·885771	56·852185
53	4·790412	7·994052	13·274948	21·938698	36·086122	59·082524
53½	4·861737	8·152365	13·602774	22·587272	37·327775	61·400360
54	4·934124	8·313814	13·938696	23·255020	38·612150	63·809126
54½	5·007589	8·478460	14·282913	23·942508	39·940719	66·312389
55	5·082148	8·646366	14·635630	24·650321	41·315001	68·913856
55½	5·157817	8·817598	14·997058	25·379059	42·736569	71·617380
56	5·234613	8·992221	15·367412	26·129340	44·207051	74·426964
56½	5·312552	9·170302	15·746911	26·901802	45·728129	77·346770
57	5·391651	9·351910	16·135783	27·697101	47·301545	80·381121
57½	5·471928	9·537114	16·534257	28·515911	48·929098	83·534512
58	5·553400	9·725986	16·942572	29·358927	50·612653	86·811611
58½	5·636086	9·918599	17·360970	30·226865	52·354135	90·217273
59	5·720003	10·115026	17·789700	31·120463	54·155539	93·756540
59½	5·805169	10·315343	18·229018	32·040477	56·018925	97·434655
60	5·891603	10·519627	18·679185	32·987690	57·946426	101·257063
60½	5·979324	10·727957	19·140469	33·962906	59·940249	105·229427
61	6·068351	10 940412	19·613145	34·966952	62·002676	109·357628
61½	6·158703	11·157075	20·097493	36·000680	64·136067	113·647781
62	6·250401	11·378029	20·593802	37·064969	66·342864	118·106239
62½	6·343464	11·603358	21·102367	38·160721	68·625592	122·739604
63	6·437913	11·833150	21·623492	39·288867	70·986864	127·554738
63½	6·533768	12·067492	22·157486	40·450364	73·429383	132·558772
64	6·631051	12·306476	22·704667	41·646199	75·955945	137·759117
64½	6·729781	12·550192	23·265360	42·877386	78·569440	143·163474
65	6·829982	12·798735	23·839900	44·144971	81·272861	148·779846
65½	6·931675	13·052200	24·428628	45·450030	84·069301	154·616552
66	7·034882	13·310684	25·031895	46·793669	86·961961	160·682234
66½	7·139625	13·574288	25·650060	48·177031	89·954152	166·985876
67	7·245928	13·843112	26·283490	49·601290	93·049298	173·536813
67½	7·353814	14·117259	26·932563	51·067653	96·250943	180·344746
68	7·463306	14·396836	27·597664	52·577367	99·562749	187·419758
68½	7·574428	14·681950	28·279191	54·131713	102·988509	194·772326
69	7·687205	14·972709	28·977548	55·732009	106·532142	202·413338
69½	7·801661	15·269228	29·693150	57·379615	110·197704	210·354112
70	7·917821	15·571618	30·426425	59 075930	113·989392	218·606405
70½	8·035711	15·879997	31·177808	60·822392	117·911544	227·182441
71	8·155356	16·194483	31·947746	62·620485	121·968649	236·094918
71½	8·276782	16·515197	32·736698	64·471736	126·165352	245·357036
72	8·400017	16·842262	33·545134	66·377715	130·506455	254·982511
72½	8·525086	17·175804	34·373533	68·340040	134·996926	264·985599
73	8·652017	17·515952	35·222390	70·360378	139·641906	275·381112
73½	8·780839	17·862837	36·092210	72·440442	144·446711	286·184447
74	8·911578	18·216591	36·983510	74·582000	149·416840	297·411601
74½	9·044264	18·577350	37·896821	76·786869	154·557981	309·079203
75	9·178925	18·945254	38·832685	79·056920	159·876019	321·204529

THE FIRST TABLE OF COMPOUND INTEREST — *continued*.

The Amount of One Pound in any Number of Years, &c.

Years.	3 per Cent.	4 per Cent.	5 per Cent.	6 per Cent.	7 per Cent.	8 per Cent.
75½	9·315592	19·320444	39·791662	81·394081	165·377040	333·805539
76	9·454293	19·703064	40·774320	83·800336	171·067340	346·900892
76½	9·595059	20·093262	41·781245	86·277726	176·953433	360·509982
77	9·737922	20·491187	42·813036	88·828356	183·042054	374·652963
77½	9·882911	20·896992	43·870307	91·454390	189·340173	389·350781
78	10·030059	21·310834	44·953688	94·158057	195·854998	404·625200
78½	10·179399	21·732872	46·063822	96·941653	202·593985	420·498844
79	10·330961	22·163268	47·201372	99·807541	209·564848	436·995216
79½	10·484781	22·602187	48·367013	102·758152	216·775564	454·138751
80	10·640890	23·049799	49·561441	105·795993	224·234387	471·954834
80½	10·799324	23·506275	50·785364	108·923642	231·949854	490·469851
81	10·960117	23·971791	52·039513	112·143753	239·930794	509·711221
81½	11·123304	24·446526	53·324632	115·459060	248·186343	529·707439
82	11·288920	24·930662	54·641488	118·872378	256·725950	550·488118
82½	11·457003	25·424387	55·990864	122·386604	265·559387	572·084035
83	11·627588	25·927889	57·373563	126·004720	274·696766	594·527168
83½	11·800713	26·441362	58·790407	129·729800	284·148545	617·850757
84	11·976416	26·965004	60·242241	133·565004	293·925540	642·089341
84½	12·154734	27·499017	61·729928	137·513588	304·038943	667·278818
85	12·335708	28·043604	63·254353	141·578904	314·500328	693·456488
85½	12·519376	28·598977	64·816424	145·764403	325·321669	720·661124
86	12·705779	29·165349	66·417071	150·073638	336·515351	748·933008
86½	12·894958	29·742936	68·057245	154·510267	348·094186	778·314013
87	13·086953	30·331963	69·737924	159·078057	360·071425	808·847648
87½	13·281806	30·932654	71·460108	163·780884	372·460779	840·579135
88	13·479561	31·545241	73·224820	168·622740	385·276425	873·555460
88½	13·680261	32·169960	75·033113	173·607737	398·533033	907·825465
89	13·883948	32·807051	76·886061	178·740104	412·245775	943·439897
89½	14·090668	33·456758	78·784769	184·024201	426·430345	980·451503
90	14·300467	34·119333	80·730365	189·464511	441·102979	1018·915089
90½	14·513389	34·795029	82·724007	195·065653	456·280470	1058·887623
91	14·729481	35·484106	84·766883	200·832381	471·980188	1100·428296
91½	14·948790	36·186830	86·860208	206·769592	488·220103	1143·598633
92	15·171365	36·903470	89·005227	212·882324	505·018801	1188·462560
92½	15·397254	37·634303	91·203218	219·175768	522·395510	1235·086523
93	15·626506	38·379609	93·455488	225·655264	540·370117	1283·539564
93½	15·859172	39·139675	95·763379	232·326314	558·963196	1333·893445
94	16.095301	39·914794	98·128263	239·194580	578·196026	1386·222730
94½	16·334947	40·705262	100·551548	246·265893	598·090619	1440·604921
95	16·578160	41·511385	103·034676	253·546254	618·669747	1497·120548
95½	16·824995	42·333473	105·579125	261·041846	639·956963	1555·853315
96	17·075505	43·171841	108·186410	268·759030	661·976630	1616·890192
96½	17·329745	44·026812	110·858082	276·704357	684·753950	1680·321580
97	17·587770	44·898715	113·595730	284·884572	708·314994	1746·241407
97½	17·849637	45·787884	116·400986	293·306618	732·686727	1814·747306
98	18·115403	46·694663	119·275517	301·977646	757·897043	1885·940720
98½	18·385126	47·619400	122·221035	310·905016	783·974797	1959·927091
99	18·658866	48·562450	125·239293	320·096305	810·949836	2036·815978
99½	18·936680	49·524176	128·332087	329·559317	838·853033	2116·721258
100	19·218631	50·504948	131·501257	339·302083	867·716325	2199·761256

The Second Table of Compound Interest.

The present Value of One Pound payable at the End of any Number of Years, &c.

Years.	3 per Cent.	4 per Cent.	5 per Cent.	6 per Cent.	7 per Cent.	8 per Cent.
½	·985329	·980580	·975900	·971285	·966736	·962250
1	·970873	·961538	·952380	·943396	·934579	·925925
1½	·956630	·942866	·929428	·916307	·903492	·890972
2	·942595	·924556	·907029	·889996	·873438	·857338
2½	·928767	·906601	·885170	·864440	·844385	·824974
3	·915141	·888996	·863837	·839619	·816297	·793832
3½	·901715	·871732	·843019	·815510	·789144	·763865
4	·888487	·854804	·822702	·792093	·762895	·735029
4½	·875452	·838204	·802875	·769349	·737518	·707282
5	·862608	·821927	·783526	·747258	·712986	·680583
5½	·849953	·805965	·764643	·725801	·689269	·654891
6	·837484	·790314	.746215	·704960	·666342	·630169
6½	·825197	·774967	·728231	·684718	·644177	·606381
7	·813091	·759917	·710681	·665057	·622749	·583490
7½	·801162	·745160	·693553	·645960	·602034	·561463
8	·789409	·730690	·676839	·627412	·582009	·540268
8½	·777828	·716500	·660527	·609396	·562649	·519873
9	·766416	·702586	·644608	·591898	·543933	·500248
9½	·755172	·688942	·629073	·574902	·525840	·481364
10	·744093	·675564	·613913	·558394	·508349	·463193
10½	·733177	·662445	·599117	·542360	·491439	·445708
11	·722421	·649580	·584679	·526787	·475092	·428882
11½	·711822	·636966	·570588	·511661	·459289	·412692
12	·701379	·624597	·556837	·496969	·444011	·397113
12½	·691090	·612467	·543417	·482699	·429242	·382122
13	·680951	·600574	·530321	·468839	·414964	·367697
13½	·670961	·588911	·517540	·455376	·401161	·353817
14	·661117	·577475	·505067	·442300	·387817	·340461
14½	·651418	·566260	·492895	·429600	·374917	·327608
15	·641861	·555264	·481017	·417265	·362446	·315241
15½	·632445	·544481	·469424	·405283	·350389	·303341
16	·623166	·533908	·458111	·393646	·338734	·291890
16½	·614024	·523540	·447071	·382343	·327467	·280871
17	·605016	·513373	·436296	·371364	·316574	·270268
17½	·596140	·503403	·425781	·360701	·306044	·260066
18	·587394	·493628	·415520	·350343	·295863	·250249
18½	·578777	·484042	·405506	·340283	·286022	·240802
19	·570286	·474642	·395733	·330513	·276508	·231712
19½	·561919	·465425	·386196	·321022	·267310	·222965
20	·553675	·456386	376889	·311804	·258419	·214548
20½	·545552	·447524	·367806	·302851	·249823	·206449
21	·537549	·438833	·358942	·294155	·241513	·198655
21½	·529663	·430311	·350291	·285708	·233479	·191156
22	·521892	·421955	·341849	·277505	·225713	·183940
22½	·514235	·413761	·333611	·269536	·218205	·176996
23	·506691	·405726	·325571	·261797	·210946	·170315
23½	·499258	·397847	·317725	·254279	·203930	·165885
24	·491933	·390121	·310067	·246978	·197146	·157699
24½	·484716	·382545	·302595	·239886	·190588	·151746
25	·477605	·375116	·295302	·232998	·184249	·146017

THE SECOND TABLE OF COMPOUND INTEREST—*continued.*

The present Value of One Pound payable at the End of any Number of Years, &c.

Years.	3 per Cent.	4 per Cent.	5 per Cent.	6 per Cent.	7 per Cent.	8 per Cent.
25½	·470598	·367832	·288186	·226308	·178120	·140505
26	·463694	·360689	·281240	·219810	·172195	·135201
26½	·456891	·353684	·274462	·213498	·166467	·130097
27	·450189	·346816	·267848	·207367	·160930	·125186
27½	443584	·340081	·261393	·201413	·155577	·120461
28	·437076	·333477	·255093	·195630	·150402	·115913
28½	·430664	·327001	·248945	·190012	·145399	·111538
29	·424346	.320651	·242946	·184556	·140562	·107327
29½	·418120	·314424	·237091	·179257	·135887	·103275
30	411986	·308318	·231377	·174110	·131367	·099377
30½	·405942	·302331	·225801	·169110	·126997	·095625
31	·399987	·296460	·220359	·164254	·122773	·092016
31½	·394119	·290703	·215048	·159538	·118689	·088542
32	·388337	·285057	·209866	·154957	·114741	·085200
32½	·382639	·279522	·204808	·150507	·110924	·081983
33	·377026	·274094	·199872	·146186	·107234	·078888
33½	·371495	·268771	·195055	·141988	·103667	·075910
34	·366044	·263552	·190354	·137911	·100219	·073045
34½	·360674	·258434	·185767	·133951	·096885	·070287
35	·355383	253415	·181290	·130105	·093662	·067634
35½	·350169	·248494	·176921	·126369	·090547	·065081
36	·345032	·243668	·172657	·122740	·087535	·062624
36½	·339970	·238936	·168496	·119216	·084623	·060260
37	·334982	·234296	·164435	·115793	·081808	·057985
37½	·330068	·229746	·160472	·112468	·079087	·055796
38	·325226	·225285	·156605	·109238	·076456	·053690
38½	·320454	·220910	·152831	·106102	·073913	·051663
39	·315753	·216620	·149147	·103055	·071455	·049713
39½	·311121	·212413	·145553	·100096	·069078	·047836
40	·306556	·208289	·142045	·097222	·066780	·046030
40½	·302059	·204244	·138622	·094430	·064559	·044293
41	·297628	·200277	·135281	·091719	·062411	·042621
41½	·293261	·196388	·132021	·089085	·060335	·041012
42	·288959	·192574	·128839	·086527	·058328	·039464
42½	·284719	·188835	·125734	·084042	·056388	·037974
43	·280542	·185168	·122704	·081629	·054512	·036540
43½	·276427	·181572	·119747	·079285	·052699	·035161
44	·272371	·178046	·116861	·077009	·050946	·033834
44½	·268375	·174588	·114044	·074797	·049251	·032556
45	·264438	·171198	·111296	·072650	·047613	·031327
45½	·260559	·167873	·108614	·070563	0. 3029	·030145
46	·256736	·164613	·105996	·068537	·044198	·029007
46½	·252970	·161417	·103442	·066569	·043018	·027912
47	·249258	·158282	·100949	·064658	·041587	·026858
47½	·245601	·155208	·098516	·062801	·040204	·025844
48	·241998	·152194	·096142	·060998	·038866	·024869
48½	·238448	·149239	·093825	·059246	·037573	·023930
49	·234950	·146341	·091563	·057545	·036324	·023026
49½	·231503	·143499	·089357	·055893	·035115	·022157
50	·228107	·140712	·087203	·054288	·033947	·021321

THE SECOND TABLE OF COMPOUND INTEREST — *continued.*

The present Value of One Pound payable at the End of any Number of Years, &c.

Years.	3 per Cent.	4 per Cent.	5 per Cent.	6 per Cent.	7 per Cent.	8 per Cent.
50½	·224760	·137980	·085102	·052729	·032818	·020516
51	·221463	·135300	·083051	·051215	·031726	·019741
51½	·218214	·132673	·081049	·049744	·030671	·018996
52	·215012	·130096	·079096	·048316	·029651	·018279
52½	·211858	·127570	·077190	·046929	·028664	·017589
53	·208750	·125093	·075329	·045581	·027711	·016925
53½	·205687	·122663	·073514	·044272	·026789	·016286
54	·202670	·120281	·071742	·043001	·025898	·015671
54½	·199696	·117945	·070013	·041766	·025037	·015080
55	·196767	·115655	·068326	·040567	·024204	·014510
55½	·193880	·113409	·066679	·039402	·023399	·013963
56	·191036	·111207	·065072	·038271	·022620	·013435
56½	·188233	·109047	·063504	·037172	·021868	·012928
57	·185471	·106930	·061974	·036104	·021140	·012440
57½	·182750	·104853	·060480	·035068	·020437	·011971
58	·180069	·102817	·059022	·034061	·019757	·011519
58½	·177428	·100820	·057600	·033083	·019100	·011084
59	·174825	·098862	·056212	·032133	·018465	·010665
59½	·172260	·096942	·054857	·031210	·017851	·010263
60	·169733	·095060	·053535	·030314	·017257	·009875
60½	·167242	·093214	·052245	·029443	·016683	·009503
61	·164789	·091404	·050986	·028598	·016128	·009144
61½	·162371	·089629	·049757	·027777	·015591	·008799
62	·159989	·087888	·048558	·026979	·015073	·008466
62½	·157642	·086181	·047388	·026204	·014571	·008147
63	·155329	·084508	·046246	·025452	·014087	·007839
63½	·153051	·082867	·045131	·024721	·013618	·007543
64	·150805	·081258	·044043	·024011	·013165	·007259
64½	·148593	·079680	·042982	·023322	·012727	·006985
65	·146413	·078132	·041946	·022652	·012304	·006721
65½	·144265	·076615	·040935	·022002	·011894	·006467
66	·142148	·075127	·039949	·021370	·011499	·006223
66½	·140063	·073668	·038986	·020756	·011116	·005988
67	·138008	·072238	·038046	·020160	·010746	·005762
67½	·135983	·070835	·037129	·019581	·010389	·005544
68	·133988	·069459	·036234	·019019	·010043	·005335
68½	·132023	·068110	·035361	·018473	·009709	·005134
69	·130086	·066788	·034509	·017943	·009386	·004940
69½	·128177	·065491	·033677	·017427	·009074	·004753
70	·126297	·064219	·032866	·016927	·008772	·004574
70½	·124444	·062972	·032074	·016441	·008480	·004401
71	·122618	·061749	·031301	·015969	·008198	·004235
71½	·120819	·060550	·030546	·015510	·007926	·004075
72	·119047	·059374	·029810	·015065	·007662	·003921
72½	·117300	·058221	·029092	·014632	·007407	·003773
73	·115579	·057090	·028391	·014212	·007161	·003631
73½	·113884	·055982	·027706	·013804	·006922	·003494
74	·112213	·054895	·027039	·013408	·006692	·003362
74½	·110567	·053828	·026387	·013023	·006470	·003235
75	·108945	·052783	·025751	·012649	·006254	·003113

THE SECOND TABLE OF COMPOUND INTEREST — *continued.*

The present Value of One Pound payable at the End of any Number of Years, &c.

Years.	3 per Cent.	4 per Cent.	5 per Cent.	6 per Cent.	7 per Cent.	8 per Cent.
75½	·107346	·051758	·025130	·012285	·006046	·002995
76	·105772	·050753	·024525	·011933	·005845	·002882
76½	·104220	·049767	·023934	·011590	·005651	·002773
77	·102691	·048801	·023357	·011257	·005463	·002669
77½	·101184	·047853	·022794	·010934	·005281	·002568
78	·099700	·046924	·022245	·010620	·005105	·002471
78½	·098237	·046013	·021709	·010315	·004935	·002378
79	·096796	·045119	·021185	·010019	·004771	·002288
79½	·095376	·044243	·020675	·009731	·004613	·002201
80	·093977	·043384	·020176	·009452	·004459	·002118
80½	·092598	·042541	·019690	·009180	·004311	·002038
81	·091239	·041715	·019216	·008917	·004167	·001961
81½	·089901	·040905	·018753	·008661	·004029	·001887
82	·088582	·040111	·018301	·008412	·003895	·001816
82½	·087282	·039332	·017860	·008170	·003765	·001747
83	·086002	·038568	·017429	·007936	·003640	·001682
83½	·084740	·037819	·017009	·007708	·003519	·001618
84	·083497	·037085	·016599	·007486	·003402	·001557
84½	·082272	·036364	·016199	·007272	·003289	·001498
85	·081065	·035658	·015809	·007063	·003179	·001442
85½	·079876	·034966	·015428	·006860	·003073	·001387
86	·078704	·034287	·015056	·006663	·002971	·001335
86½	·077549	·033621	·014693	·006472	·002872	·001284
87	·076411	·032968	·014339	·006286	·002777	·001236
87½	·075290	·032328	·013993	·006105	·002684	·001189
88	·074186	·031700	·013656	·005930	·002595	·001144
88½	·073098	·031084	·013327	·005760	·002509	·001101
89	·072025	·030481	·013006	·005594	·002425	·001059
89½	·070968	·029889	·012692	·005434	·002345	·001019
90	·069927	·029308	·012386	·005278	·002267	·000981
90½	·068901	·028739	·012088	·005126	·002191	·000944
91	·067891	·028181	·011797	·004979	·002118	·000908
91½	·066895	·027634	·011512	·004836	·002048	·000874
92	·065913	·027097	·011235	·004697	·001980	·000841
92½	·064946	·026571	·010964	·004562	·001914	·000809
93	·063993	·026055	·010700	·004431	·001850	·000779
93½	·063054	·025549	·010442	·004304	·001789	·000749
94	·062129	·025053	·010190	·004180	·001729	·000721
94½	·061218	·024566	·009945	·004060	·001671	·000694
95	·060320	·024089	·009705	·003944	·001616	·000667
95½	·059435	·023621	·009471	·003830	·001562	·000642
96	·058563	·023163	·009243	·003720	·001510	·000618
96½	·057704	·022713	·009020	·003613	·001460	·000595
97	·056857	·022272	·008803	·003510	·001411	·000572
97½	·056023	·021839	·008590	·003409	·001364	·000551
98	·055201	·021415	·008383	·003311	·001319	·000530
98½	·054391	·020999	·008181	·003216	·001275	·000510
99	·053593	·020592	·007984	·003124	·001233	·000490
99½	·052807	·020192	·007792	·003034	·001192	·000472
100	·052032	·019800	·007604	·002947	·001152	·000454

THE THIRD TABLE OF COMPOUND INTEREST.

The Amount of One Pound per Annum in any Number of Years, &c.

Years.	3 per Cent.	4 per Cent.	5 per Cent.	6 per Cent.	7 per Cent.	8 per Cent.
½	·496305	·495097	·493901	·492716	·491543	·490381
1	1·000000	1·000000	1·000000	1·000000	1·000000	1·000000
1½	1·511194	1·514901	1·518596	1·522279	1·525951	1·529611
2	2·030000	2·040000	2·050000	2·060000	2·070000	2·080000
2½	2·556530	2·575497	2·594526	2·613616	2·632768	2·651980
3	3·090900	3·121600	3·152500	3·183600	3·214900	3·246400
3½	3·633226	3·678517	3·724252	3·770433	3·817061	3·864138
4	4·183627	4·246464	4·310125	4·374616	4·439943	4·506112
4½	4·742222	4·825658	4·910465	4·996659	5·084256	5·173270
5	5·309135	5·416322	5·525631	5·637092	5·750739	5·866600
5½	5·884489	6·018684	6·155988	6·296459	6·440154	6·587131
6	6·468409	6·632975	6·801912	6·975318	7·153290	7·335929
6½	7·061024	7·259431	7·463788	7·674246	7·890964	8·114102
7	7·662462	7·898294	8·142008	8·393837	8·654021	8·922803
7½	8·272855	8·549809	8·836977	9·134701	9·443332	9·763230
8	8·892336	9·214226	9·549108	9·897467	10·259802	10·636627
8½	9·521040	9·891801	10·278826	10·682783	11·104365	11·544288
9	10·159106	10·582795	11·026564	11·491315	11·977988	12·487557
9½	10·806671	11·287473	11·792767	12·323750	12·881671	13·467831
10	11·463879	12·006107	12·577892	13·180794	13·816447	14·486562
10½	12·130872	12·738972	13·382406	14·063175	14·783388	15·545258
11	12·807795	13·486351	14·206787	14·971642	15·783599	16·645487
11½	13·494798	14·248531	15·051526	15·906966	16·818225	17·788879
12	14·192029	15·025805	15·917126	16·869941	17·888451	18·977126
12½	14·899642	15·818472	16·804102	17·861384	18·995501	20·211989
13	15·617790	16·626837	17·712982	18·882137	20·140642	21·495296
13½	16·346631	17·451211	18·644307	19·933067	21·325186	22·828948
14	17·086324	18·291911	19·598631	21·015065	22·550487	24·214920
14½	17·837030	19·149260	20·576523	22·129051	23·817949	25·655264
15	18·598913	20·023587	21·578563	23·275969	25·129022	27·152113
15½	19·372141	20·915230	22·605349	24·456794	26·485205	28·707685
16	20·156881	21·824531	23·657491	25·672528	27·888053	30·324283
16½	20·953305	22·751839	24·735616	26·924202	29·339170	32·004300
17	21·761587	23·697512	25·840366	28·212879	30·840217	33·750225
17½	22·581904	24·661913	26·972397	29·539654	32·392912	35·564644
18	23·414435	25·645412	28·132384	30·905652	33·999032	37·450243
18½	24·259361	26·648389	29·321017	32·312033	35·660416	39·409816
19	25·116868	27·671229	30·539003	33·759991	37·378964	41·446263
19½	25·987142	28·714325	31·787068	35·250755	39·156645	43·562601
20	26·870374	29·778078	33·065954	36·785591	40·995492	45·761964
20½	27·766756	30·862898	34·376421	38·365801	42·897610	48·047609
21	28·676485	31·969201	35·719251	39·992726	44·865176	50·422921
21½	29·599759	33·097414	37·095243	41·667749	46·900443	52·891418
22	30·536780	34·247969	38·505214	43·392290	49·005739	55·456755
22½	31·487752	35·421810	39·950005	45·167814	51·183474	58·122731
23	32·452883	36·617888	41·430475	46·995827	53·436140	60·893295
23½	33·432385	37·838163	42·947505	48·877882	55·766317	63·772550
24	34·426470	39·082604	44·501949	50·815577	58·176670	66·764759
24½	35·435356	40·351689	46·094880	52·810555	60·669959	69·874354
25	36·459264	41·645908	47·727098	54·864512	63·249037	73·105939

THE THIRD TABLE OF COMPOUND INTEREST — *continued.*

The Amount of One Pound per Annum in any Number of Years, &c.

Years.	3 per Cent.	4 per Cent.	5 per Cent.	6 per Cent.	7 per Cent.	8 per Cent.
25½	37·498417	42·965757	49·399624	56·979189	65·916856	76·464302
26	38·553042	44·311744	51·113453	59·156382	68·676470	79·954415
26½	39·623369	45·684387	52·869605	61·397940	71·531036	83·581446
27	40·709633	47·084214	54·669126	63·705765	74·483823	87·350768
27½	41·812070	48·511763	56·513086	66·081817	77·538209	91·267962
28	42·930922	49·967582	58·402582	68·528111	80·697690	95·338829
28½	44·066433	51·452233	60·338740	71·046726	83·965884	99·569399
29	45·218850	52·966286	62·322711	73·639798	87·346529	103·965936
29½	46·388425	54·510323	64·355677	76·309529	90·843495	108·534951
30	47·575415	56·084937	66·438847	79·058186	94·460786	113·283211
30½	48·780078	57·690735	68·573461	81·888101	98·202540	118·217747
31	50·002678	59·328335	70·760789	84·801677	102·073041	123·345868
31½	51·243481	60·998365	73·002184	87·801387	106·076718	128·675167
32	52·502758	62·701468	75·298829	90·889778	110·218154	134·213537
32½	53·780785	64·438300	77·652241	94·069470	114·502088	139·969180
33	55·077841	66·209527	80·063770	97·343164	118·933425	145·950620
33½	56·394209	68·015832	82·534853	100·713639	123·517234	152·166715
34	57·730176	69·857908	85·066959	104·183754	128·258764	158·626670
34½	59·086035	71·736465	87·661596	107·756457	133·163441	165·340052
35	60·462081	73·652224	90·320307	111·434779	138·236878	172·316803
35½	61·858616	75·605923	93·044675	115·221844	143·484882	179·567256
36	63·275944	77·598313	95·836322	119·120866	148·913459	187·102147
36½	64·714374	79·630160	98·696909	123·135155	154·528824	194·932637
37	66·174222	81·702246	101·628138	127·268118	160·337402	203·070319
37½	67·655806	83·815367	104·631755	131·523264	166·345841	211·527248
38	69·159449	85·970336	107·709545	135·904205	172·561020	220·315945
38½	70·685480	88·167982	110·863342	140·414660	178·990050	229·449428
39	72·234232	90·409149	114·095023	145·058458	185·640291	238·941221
39½	73·806044	92·694701	117·406510	149·839540	192·519354	248·805382
40	75·401259	95·025515	120·799774	154·761965	199·635111	259·056518
40½	77·020226	97·402489	124·276835	159·829912	206·995708	269·709812
41	78·663297	99·826536	127·839762	165·047683	214·609569	280·781040
41½	80·330832	102·298588	131·490677	170·419707	222·485408	292·286597
42	82·023196	104·819597	135·231751	175·950544	230·632239	304·243523
42½	83·740757	107·390532	139·065211	181·644890	239·059387	316·669525
43	85·483892	110·012381	142·993338	187·507577	247·776496	329·583005
43½	87·252980	112·686153	147·018471	193·543583	256·793544	343·003087
44	89·048409	115·412876	151·143005	199·758031	266·120851	356·949645
44½	90·870570	118·193599	155·369395	206·156198	275·769092	371·443334
45	92·719861	121·029392	159·700155	212·743513	285·749310	386·505617
45½	94·596687	123·921343	164·137865	219·525570	296·072928	402·158801
46	96·501457	126·870567	168·685163	226·508124	306·751762	418·426066
46½	98·434587	129·878197	173·344758	233·697104	317·798033	435·331505
47	100·396500	132·945390	178·119421	241·098612	329·224385	452·900152
47½	102·387625	136·073325	183·011996	248·718930	341·043896	471·158026
48	104·408395	139·263206	188·025392	256·564528	353·270093	490·132164
48½	106·459254	142·516258	193·162596	264·642066	365·916969	509·850668
49	108·540647	145·833734	198·426662	272·958400	378·998999	530·342737
49½	110·653031	149·216908	203·820725	281·520590	392·531156	551·638721
50	112·796867	152·667083	209·347995	290·335904	406·528929	573·770156

The Third Table of Compound Interest—*continued.*

The Amount of One Pound per Annum in any Number of Years, &c.

Years.	3 per Cent.	4 per Cent.	5 per Cent.	6 per Cent.	7 per Cent.	8 per Cent.
50½	114·972622	156·185585	215·011762	299·411826	421·008337	596·769819
51	117·180773	159·773767	220·815395	308·756058	435·985954	620·671768
51½	119·421801	163·433008	226·762350	318·376535	451·478921	645·511405
52	121·696196	167·164717	232·856165	328·281422	467·504971	671·325510
52½	124·004455	170·970329	239·100467	338·479127	484·082445	698·152317
53	126·347082	174·851306	245·498973	348·978307	501·230319	726·031551
53½	128·724589	178·809142	252·055491	359·787875	518·968217	755·004502
54	131·137494	182·845358	258·773922	370·917006	537·316441	785·114075
54½	133·586326	186·961507	265·658265	382·375148	556·295992	816·404863
55	136·071619	191·159173	272·712618	394·172026	575·928592	848·923201
55½	138·593916	195·439968	279·941178	406·317657	596·236711	882·717252
56	141·153768	199·805539	287·348249	418·822348	617·243594	917·837057
56½	143·751734	204·257567	294·938237	431·696716	638·973281	954·334632
57	146·388381	208·797761	302·715661	444·951689	661·450645	992·264022
57½	149·064286	213·427869	310·685149	458·598519	684·701411	1031·681403
58	151·780032	218·149672	318·851444	472·648790	708·752190	1072·645143
58½	154·536214	222·964984	327·219407	487·114430	733·630510	1115·215915
59	157·333433	227·875658	335·794017	502·007717	759·364844	1159·456755
59½	160·172301	232·883583	344·580377	517·341296	785·984645	1205·433188
60	163·053436	237·990685	353·583717	533·128180	813·520383	1253·213295
60½	165·977470	243·198927	362·809396	549·381774	842·003571	1302·867843
61	168·945039	248·510312	372·262903	566·115871	871·466810	1354·470359
61½	171·956794	253·926884	381·949866	583·344680	901·943821	1408·097271
62	175·013391	259·450725	391·876048	601·082824	933·469486	1463·827988
62½	178·115498	265·083959	402·047359	619·345361	966·079888	1521·745052
63	181·263792	270·828754	412·469851	638·147793	999·812350	1581·934227
63½	184·458963	276·687318	423·149727	657·506083	1034·705480	1644·484656
64	187·701706	282·661904	434·093343	677·436661	1070·799215	1709·488965
64½	190·992732	288·754810	445·307214	697·956448	1108·134864	1777·043429
65	194·332757	294·968380	456·798011	719·082860	1146·755160	1847·248082
65½	197·722513	301·305003	468·572574	740·833835	1186·704304	1920·206903
66	201·162740	307·767115	480·637911	763·227832	1228·028021	1996·027929
66½	204·654189	314·357203	493·001203	786·283865	1270·773606	2074·823456
67	208·197622	321·077800	505·669807	810·021502	1314·989983	2156·710163
67½	211·793815	327·931491	518·651263	834·460897	1360·727758	2241·809332
68	215·443551	334·920912	531·953297	859·622792	1408·039282	2330·246976
68½	219·147629	342·048751	545·583826	885·528550	1456·978701	2422·154079
69	222·906858	349·317748	559·550962	912·200160	1507·602032	2517·666734
69½	226·722058	356·730701	573·863018	939·660263	1559·967211	2616·926405
70	230·594063	364·290458	588·528510	967·932169	1614·134174	2720·080073
70½	234·523720	371·999929	603·556169	997·039879	1670·164915	2827·280518
71	238·511885	379·862077	618·954936	1027·008099	1728·123566	2938·686479
71½	242·559431	387·879926	634·733977	1057·862272	1788·076459	3054·462959
72	246·667242	396·056560	650·902683	1089·628585	1850·092216	3174·781398
72½	250·836214	404·395123	667·470676	1122·334008	1914·241812	3299·819996
73	255·067259	412·898822	684·447817	1156·006300	1980·598671	3429·763909
73½	259·361301	421·570928	701·844210	1190·674049	2049·238738	3564·805596
74	263·719277	430·414775	719·670208	1226·366679	2120·240578	3705·145022
74½	268·142140	439·433765	737·936420	1263·114492	2193·685450	3850·990043
75	272·630855	448·631366	756·653718	1300·948679	2269·657418	4002·556624

THE THIRD TABLE OF COMPOUND INTEREST — *continued.*

The Amount of One Pound per Annum in any Number of Years, &c.

Years.	3 per Cent.	4 per Cent.	5 per Cent.	6 per Cent.	7 per Cent.	8 per Cent.
75½	277·186404	458·011116	775·833241	1339·901361	2348·243432	4160·069247
76	281·809781	467·576621	795·486404	1380·005600	2429·533437	4323·761154
76½	286·501996	477·331560	815·624903	1421·295443	2513·620472	4493·874786
77	291·264074	487·279686	836·260724	1463·805936	2600·600778	4670·662046
77½	296·097056	497·424823	857·406149	1507·573170	2690·573905	4854·384769
78	301·001996	507·770873	879·073760	1552·634292	2783·642833	5045·315010
78½	305·979968	518·321816	901·276456	1599·027560	2879·914078	5243·735551
79	311·032056	529·081708	924·027448	1646·792350	2979·497831	5449·940211
79½	316·159367	540·054688	947·340279	1695·969214	3082·508064	5664·234395
80	321·363018	551·244976	971·228821	1746·599891	3189·062679	5886·935428
80½	326·644148	562·656876	995·707293	1798·727367	3299·283628	6118·373147
81	332·003909	574·294775	1020·790262	1852·395884	3413·297067	6358·890262
81½	337·443472	586·163151	1046·492658	1907·651009	3531·233482	6608·842999
82	342·964026	598·266566	1072·829775	1964·539637	3653·227861	6868·601483
82½	348·566776	610·609677	1099·817290	2023·110069	3779·419826	7138·550438
83	354·252947	623·197229	1127·471264	2083·412016	3909·953812	7419·089602
83½	360·023780	636·034064	1155·808155	2145·496673	4044·979214	7710·634474
84	365·880535	649·125118	1184·844827	2209·416737	4184·650579	8013·616770
84½	371·824493	662·475427	1214·598563	2275·226474	4329·127759	8328·485232
85	377·856951	676·090123	1245·087068	2342·981741	4478·576119	8655·706112
85½	383·979228	689·974444	1276·328491	2412·740062	4633·166702	8995·764050
86	390·192660	704·133728	1308·341422	2484·560645	4793·076448	9349·162600
86½	396·498605	718·573422	1341·144916	2558·504466	4958·488372	9716·425174
87	402·898440	733·299077	1374·758493	2634·634284	5129·591799	10098·095609
87½	409·393563	748·316358	1409·202161	2713·014734	5306·582558	10494·739188
88	415·985393	763·631040	1444·496418	2793·712341	5489·663225	10906·943257
88½	422·675370	779·249013	1480·662269	2876·795618	5679·043337	11335·318323
89	429·464955	795·176282	1517·721238	2962·335082	5874·939651	11780·498718
89½	436·355631	811·418973	1555·695383	3050·403355	6077·576370	12243·143789
90	443·348903	827·983333	1594·607300	3141·075187	6287·185426	12723·938615
90½	450·446300	844·875732	1634·480152	3234·427556	6504·006716	13223·595292
91	457·649370	862·102667	1675·337665	3330·539698	6728·288406	13742·853705
91½	464·959689	879·670762	1717·204160	3429·493210	6960·287186	14282·482916
92	472·378851	897·586773	1760·104549	3531·372080	7200·268595	14843·282001
92½	479·908480	915·857592	1804·064368	3636·262802	7448·507289	15426·081549
93	487·550217	934·490244	1849·109776	3744·254405	7705·287396	16031·744561
93½	495·305734	953·491896	1895·267586	3855·438571	7970·902800	16661·168073
94	503·176723	972·869854	1942·565265	3969·909669	8245·657514	17315·284126
94½	511·164906	992·631572	1991·030965	4087·764885	8529·865996	17995·061519
95	519·272025	1012·784648	2040·693528	4209·104249	8823·853540	18701·506856
95½	527·499853	1033·336834	2091·582514	4334·030778	9127·956615	19435·666440
96	535·850186	1054·296034	2143·728205	4462·650504	9442·523288	20198·627405
96½	544·324849	1075·670308	2197·161639	4595·072625	9767·913579	20991·519756
97	552·925692	1097·467875	2251·914615	4731·409534	10104·499918	21815·517597
97½	561·654594	1119·697120	2308·019721	4871·776982	10452·667529	22671·841336
98	570·513462	1142·366590	2365·510346	5016·294106	10812·814912	23561·759005
98½	579·504232	1165·485005	2424·420708	5165·083601	11185·354256	24486·588643
99	588·628866	1189·061254	2484·785863	5318·271753	11570·711956	25447·699726
99½	597·889359	1213·104405	2546·641743	5475·988617	11969·329054	26446·515734
100	607·287732	1237·623704	2610·025156	5638·368058	12381·661793	27484·515704

The Fourth Table of Compound Interest.

The present Value of One Pound per Annum for any Number of Years to come, &c.

Years.	3 per Cent.	4 per Cent.	5 per Cent.	6 per Cent.	7 per Cent.	8 per Cent.
½	·489024	·485483	·481998	·478568	·475193	·471869
1	·970873	·961538	·952380	·943396	·934579	·925925
1½	1·445654	1·428349	1·411427	1·394876	1·378685	1·362842
2	1·913469	1·886094	1·859410	1·833392	1·808018	1·783264
2½	2·374421	2·334951	2·296597	2·259317	2·223070	2·187816
3	2·828611	2·775091	2·723248	2·673011	2·624316	2·577096
3½	3·276137	3·206683	3·139616	3·074827	3·012215	2·951682
4	3·717098	3·629895	3·545950	3·465105	3·387211	3·312126
4½	4·151589	4·044888	3·942491	3·844177	3·749733	3·658964
5	4·579707	4·451822	4·329476	4·212363	4·100197	3·992710
5½	5·001543	4·850854	4·707135	4·569978	4·439003	4·313856
6	5·417191	5·242136	5·075692	4·917324	4·766539	4·622879
6½	5·826741	5·625821	5·435366	5·254696	5·083180	4·920237
7	6·230282	6·002054	5·786373	5·582381	5·389289	5·206370
7½	6·627904	6·370981	6·128920	5·900657	5·685215	5·481701
8	7·019692	6·732744	6·463212	6·209793	5·971298	5·746638
8½	7·405732	7·087482	6·789448	6·510053	6·247865	6·001575
9	7·786108	7·435331	7·107821	6·801692	6·515232	6·246887
9½	8·160905	7·776425	7·418522	7·084956	6·773705	6·482940
10	8·530202	8·110895	7·721734	7·360087	7·023581	6·710081
10½	8·894082	8·438870	8·017640	7·627317	7·265145	6·928648
11	9·252624	8·760476	8·306414	7·886874	7·498674	7·138964
11½	9·605905	9·075837	8·588228	8·138978	7·724435	7·341340
12	9·954003	9·385073	8·863251	8·383843	7·942686	7·536078
12½	10·296995	9·688305	9·131646	8·621678	8·153677	7·723463
13	10·634955	9·985647	9·393572	8·852682	8·357650	7·903775
13½	10·967956	10·277216	9·649187	9·077054	8·554838	8·077281
14	11·296073	10·563122	9·898640	9·294983	8·745467	8·244236
14½	11·619375	10·843477	10·142082	9·506655	8·929756	8·404890
15	11·937935	11·118387	10·379658	9·712248	9·107914	8·559478
15½	12·251821	11·387958	10·611507	9·911939	9·280145	8·703231
16	12·561102	11·652295	10·837769	10·105895	9·446648	8·851369
16½	12·865845	11·911499	11·058578	10·294282	9·607612	8·989103
17	13·166118	12·165668	11·274066	10·477259	9·763222	9·121638
17½	13·461986	12·414902	11·484360	10·654983	9·913656	9·249169
18	13·753513	12·659296	11·689586	10·827603	10·059086	9·371887
18½	14·040763	12·898945	11·889867	10·995267	10·199679	9·489971
19	14·323799	13·133939	12·085320	11·158116	10·335595	9·603599
19½	14·602682	13·364370	12·276064	11·316289	10·466990	9·712937
20	14·877474	13·590326	12·462210	11·469921	10·594014	9·818147
20½	15·148235	13·811894	12·643870	11·619141	10·716813	9·919386
21	15·415024	14·029159	12·821152	11·764076	10·835527	10·016803
21½	15·677898	14·242206	12·994162	11·904850	10·950292	10·110542
22	15·936916	14·451115	13·163002	12·041581	11·061240	10·200743
22½	16·192134	14·655967	13·327773	12·174387	11·168497	10·287539
23	16·443608	14·856841	13·488573	12·303378	11·272187	10·371058
23½	16·691392	15·053814	13·645498	12·428667	11·372427	10·451425
24	16·935542	15·246963	13·798641	12·550357	11·469334	10·528758
24½	17·176109	15·436360	13·948094	12·668553	11·563016	10·603171
25	17·413147	15·622079	14·093944	12·783356	11·653583	10·674776

The Fourth Table of Compound Interest — *continued.*

The present Value of One Pound per Annum for any Number of Years to come, &c.

Years.	3 per Cent.	4 per Cent.	5 per Cent.	6 per Cent.	7 per Cent.	8 per Cent.
25½	17·646708	15·804192	14·236280	12·894862	11·741137	10·743677
26	17·876842	15·982769	14·375185	13·003166	11·825778	10·809977
26½	18·103600	16·157877	14·510742	13·108360	11·907604	10·873775
27	18·327031	16·329585	14·643033	13·210534	11·986709	10·935164
27½	18·547184	16·497959	14·772136	13·309774	12·063182	10·994236
28	18·764108	16·663063	14·898127	13·406164	12·137111	11·051078
28½	18·977849	16·824960	15·021082	13·499786	12·208581	11·105774
29	19·188454	16·983714	15·141073	13·590721	12·277674	11·158406
29½	19·395970	17·139385	15·258173	13·679044	12·344468	11·209050
30	19·600441	17·292033	15·372451	13·764831	12·409041	11·257783
30½	19·801912	17·441716	15·483974	13·848154	12·471465	11·304676
31	20·000428	17·588493	15·592810	13·929085	12·531814	11·349799
31½	20·196031	17·732419	15·699023	14·007693	12·590155	11·393218
32	20·388765	17·873551	15·802676	14·084043	12·646555	11·434999
32½	20·578671	18·011942	15·903831	14·158201	12·701079	11·475202
33	20·765791	18·147645	16·002549	14·230229	12·753790	11·513888
33½	20·950166	18·280713	16·098887	14·300189	12·804747	11·551113
34	21·131836	18·411197	16·192904	14·368141	12·854009	11·586933
34½	21·310841	18·539147	16·284654	14·434141	12·901632	11·621401
35	21·487220	18·664613	16·374194	14·498246	12·947672	11·654568
35½	21·661011	18·787642	16·461575	14·560510	12·992180	11·686482
36	21·832252	18·908281	16·546851	14·620987	13·035207	11·717192
36½	22·000981	19·026578	16·630072	14·679727	13·076804	11·746743
37	22·167235	19·142578	16·711287	14·736780	13·117016	11·775178
37½	22·331050	19·256325	16·790545	14·792195	13·155891	11·802540
38	22·492461	19·367864	16·86⁻892	14·846019	13·193473	11·828868
38½	22·651505	19·477236	16·943376	14·898297	13·229805	11·854203
39	22·808215	19·584484	17·017040	14·949074	13·264928	11·878582
39½	22·962626	19·689650	17·088929	14·998393	13·298883	11·902040
40	23·114771	19·792773	17·159086	15·046296	13·331708	11·924613
40½	23·264685	19·893894	17·227552	15·092824	13·363442	11·946333
41	23·412399	19·993051	17·294367	15·138015	13·394120	11·967234
41½	23·557947	20·090283	17·359573	15·181909	13·423777	11·987346
42	23·701359	20·185626	17·423207	15·224543	13·452448	12·006698
42½	23·842667	20·279118	17·485308	15·265952	13·480166	12·025320
43	23·981902	20·370794	17·545911	15·306172	13·506961	12·043239
43½	24·119094	20·460690	17·605055	15·345238	13·532865	12·060482
44	24·254273	20·548841	17·662773	15·383182	13·557908	12·077073
44½	24·387470	20·635279	17·719100	15·420036	13·582117	12·093038
45	24·518712	20·720039	17·774069	15·455832	13·605521	12·108401
45½	24·648029	20·803153	17·827714	15·490600	13·628147	12·123184
46	24·775449	20·884653	17·880066	15·524369	13·650020	12·137408
46½	24·900999	20·964570	17·931156	15·557169	13·671165	12·151096
47	25·024707	21·042936	17·981015	15·589028	13·691607	12·164267
47½	25·146601	21·119779	18·029673	15·619971	13·711369	12·176941
48	25·266706	21·195130	18·077157	15·650026	13·730474	12·189136
48½	25·385049	21·269018	18·123498	15·679218	13·748943	12·200871
49	25·501656	21·341472	18·168721	15·707572	13·766798	12·212163
49½	25·616553	21·412518	18·212855	15·735111	13·784059	12·223029
50	25·729763	21·482184	18·255925	15·761860	13·800746	12·233484

The Fourth Table of Compound Interest — *continued*.

The present Value of One Pound per Annum for any Number of Years to come, &c.

Years.	3 per Cent.	4 per Cent.	5 per Cent.	6 per Cent.	7 per Cent.	8 per Cent.
$50\frac{1}{2}$	25·841313	21·550498	18·297957	15·787841	13·816878	12·243545
51	25·951227	21·617485	18·338976	15·813076	13·832473	12·253226
$51\frac{1}{2}$	26·059528	21·683171	18·379007	15·837586	13·847549	12·262542
52	26·166239	21·747581	18·418072	15·861392	13·862124	12·271506
$52\frac{1}{2}$	26·271386	21·810741	18·456197	15·884515	13·876214	12·280131
53	26·374990	21·872674	18·493402	15·906974	13·889835	12·288431
$53\frac{1}{2}$	26·477074	21·933405	18·529711	15·928788	13·903004	12·296418
54	26·577660	21·992956	18·565145	15·949975	13·915734	12·304103
$54\frac{1}{2}$	26·676771	22·051351	18·599725	15·970554	13·928041	12·311498
55	26·774427	22·108612	18·633471	15·990542	13·939938	12·318614
$55\frac{1}{2}$	26·870651	22·164760	18·666405	16·009957	13·951440	12·325461
56	26·965463	22·219819	18·698544	16·028814	13·962559	12·332050
$56\frac{1}{2}$	27·058884	22·273808	18·729909	16·047129	13·973308	12·538390
57	27·150935	22·326749	18·760518	16·064918	13·983700	12·344490
$57\frac{1}{2}$	27·241635	22·378662	18·790390	16·082197	13·993746	12·350361
58	27·331005	22·429566	18·819541	16·098980	14·003458	12·356010
$58\frac{1}{2}$	27·419063	22·479482	18·847990	16·115280	14·012847	12·361445
59	27·505830	22·528429	18·875754	16·131113	14·021923	12·366675
$59\frac{1}{2}$	27·591324	22·576425	18·902848	16·146491	14·030698	12·371708
60	27·675563	22·623489	18·929289	16·161427	14·039181	12·376551
$60\frac{1}{2}$	27·758567	22·669640	18·955093	16·175935	14·047381	12·381211
61	27·840353	22·714894	18·980275	16·190026	14·055309	12·385696
$61\frac{1}{2}$	27·920939	22·759269	19·004851	16·203712	14·062973	12·390011
62	28·000342	22·802782	19·028834	16·217005	14·070382	12·394163
$62\frac{1}{2}$	28·078581	22·845451	19·052239	16·229917	14·077545	12·398158
63	28·155672	22·887291	19·075080	16·242458	14·084469	12·402002
$63\frac{1}{2}$	28·231632	22·928318	19·097370	16·254639	14·091163	12·405702
64	28·306478	22·968549	19·119123	16·266470	14·097635	12·409261
$64\frac{1}{2}$	28·380225	23·007998	19·140352	16·277961	14·103891	12·412687
65	28·452891	23·046681	19·161070	16·289122	14·109939	12·415983
$65\frac{1}{2}$	28·524491	23·084614	19·181288	16·299963	14·115786	12·419154
66	28·595040	23·121809	19·201019	16·310493	14·121438	12·422206
$66\frac{1}{2}$	28·664554	23·158282	19·220274	16·320720	14·126903	12·425143
67	28·733048	23·194047	19·239066	16·330653	14·132185	12·427969
$67\frac{1}{2}$	28·800538	23·229118	19·257404	16·340302	14·137292	12·430688
68	28·867037	23·263507	19·275301	16·349673	14·142229	12·433304
$68\frac{1}{2}$	28·932561	23·297228	19·292766	16·358775	14·147002	12·435822
69	28·997123	23·330295	19·309810	16·367616	14·151616	12·438245
$69\frac{1}{2}$	29·060739	23·362720	19·326444	16·376203	14·156077	12·440576
70	29·123421	23·394514	19·342676	16·384543	14·160389	12·442819
$70\frac{1}{2}$	29·185183	23·425692	19·358518	16·392644	14·164558	12·444978
71	29·246040	23·456264	19·373977	16·400513	14·168588	12·447055
$71\frac{1}{2}$	29·306003	23·486242	19·389064	16·408155	14·172484	12·449053
72	29·365087	23·515638	19·403788	16·415578	14·176250	12·450977
$72\frac{1}{2}$	29·423304	23·544464	19·418157	16·422788	14·179891	12·452827
73	29·480667	23·572729	19·432179	16·429790	14·183411	12·454608
$73\frac{1}{2}$	29·537188	23·600446	19·445863	16·436592	14·186814	12·456321
74	29·592881	23·627624	19·459218	16·443198	14·190104	12·457970
$74\frac{1}{2}$	29·647756	23·654275	19·472251	16·449615	14·193284	12·459557
75	29·701826	23·680408	19·484969	16·455848	14·196359	12·461083

The Fourth Table of Compound Interest — *continued.*

The present Value of One Pound per Annum for any Number of Years to come, &c.

Years.	3 per Cent.	4 per Cent.	5 per Cent.	6 per Cent.	7 per Cent.	8 per Cent.
75½	29·755103	23·706033	19·497382	16·461901	14·199331	12·462553
76	29·807598	23·731161	19·509495	16·467781	14·202204	12·463966
76½	29·859323	23·755801	19·521316	16·473492	14·204982	12·465326
77	29·910289	23·779963	19·532852	16·479038	14·207668	12·466635
77½	29·960508	23·803655	19·544110	16·484426	14·210264	12·467895
78	30·009989	23·826887	19·555097	16·489659	14·212774	12·469107
78½	30·058745	23·849668	19·565819	16·494741	14·215200	12·470273
79	30·106786	23·872007	19·576283	16·499678	14·217545	12·471395
79½	30·154122	23·893912	19·586495	16·504473	14·219813	12·472475
80	30·200763	23·915391	19·596460	16·509130	14·222005	12·473514
80½	30·246720	23·936454	19·606185	16·513654	14·224124	12·474514
81	30·292003	23·957107	19·615676	16·518047	14·226173	12·475476
81½	30·336621	23·977359	19·624938	16·522315	14·228153	12·476402
82	30·380585	23·997218	19·633977	16·526460	14·230068	12·477292
82½	30·423904	24·016692	19·642798	16·530486	14·231919	12·478150
83	30·466588	24·035787	19·651407	16·534396	14·233708	12·478974
83½	30·508645	24·054511	19·659808	16·538194	14·235438	12·479768
84	30·550085	24·072872	19·668007	16·541883	14·237111	12·480532
84½	30·590917	24·090876	19·676008	16·545466	14·238727	12·481267
85	30·631151	24·108531	19·683816	16·548946	14·240290	12·481974
85½	30·670794	24·125842	19·691436	16·552326	14·241801	12·482654
86	30·709855	24·142818	19·698872	16·555610	14·243262	12·483309
86½	30·748343	24·159464	19·706129	16·558798	14·244674	12·483939
87	30·786267	24·175786	19·713212	16·561896	14·246039	12·484545
87½	30·823634	24·191792	19·720123	16·564904	14·247359	12·485129
88	30·860453	24·207487	19·726868	16·567826	14·248635	12·485690
88½	30·896732	24·222877	19·733451	16·570664	14·249868	12·486230
89	30·932479	24·237968	19·739874	16·573421	14·251060	12·486750
89½	30·967701	24·252766	19·746143	16·576098	14·252213	12·487250
90	31·002407	24·267277	19·752261	16·578699	14·253327	12·487732
90½	31·036603	24·281506	19·758232	16·581225	14·254405	12·488195
91	31·070298	24·295459	19·764058	16·583678	14·255446	12·488640
91½	31·103498	24·309140	19·769744	16·586061	14·256453	12·489069
92	31·136211	24·322556	19·775294	16·588376	14·257426	12·489482
92½	31·168445	24·335712	19·780709	16·590624	14·258367	12·489879
93	31·200205	24·348612	19·785994	16·592807	14·259277	12·490261
93½	31·231500	24·361261	19·791151	16·594928	14·260156	12·490628
94	31·262335	24·373665	19·796185	16·596988	14·261006	12·490982
94½	31·292718	24·385828	19·801097	16·598989	14·261828	12·491323
95	31·322655	24·397755	19·805890	16·600932	14·262623	12·491650
95½	31·352154	24·409450	19·810568	16·602819	14·263391	12·491965
96	31·381219	24·420918	19·815133	16·604653	14·264133	12·492269
96½	31·409858	24·432164	19·819589	16·606433	14·264851	12·492560
97	31·438077	24·443191	19·823937	16·608163	14·265545	12·492841
97½	31·465881	24·454004	19·828180	16·609843	14·266216	12·493111
98	31·493278	24·464606	19·832321	16·611474	14·266865	12·493372
98½	31·520273	24·475003	19·836362	16·613059	14·267492	12·493622
99	31·546872	24·485198	19·840305	16·614599	14·268098	12·493862
99½	31·573081	24·495196	19·844154	16·616094	14·268684	12·494094
100	31·598905	24·504998	19·847910	16·617546	14·269250	12·494317
S. F.	33·333333	25·000000	20·000000	16·666666	14·285714	12·500000

The Fifth Table of Compound Interest.

The Annuity which One Pound will purchase for any Number of Years to come, &c.

Years.	3 per Cent.	4 per Cent.	5 per Cent.	6 per Cent.	7 per Cent.	8 per Cent.
1	1·030000	1·040000	1·050000	1·060000	1·070000	1·080000
1½	·691728	·700108	·708502	·716909	·725328	·733760
2	·522610	·530196	·537804	·545436	·553091	·560769
2½	·421155	·428274	·435426	·442611	·449828	·457076
3	·353530	·360348	·367208	·374109	·381051	·388033
3½	·305237	·311848	·318510	·325221	·331981	·338789
4	·269027	·275490	·282011	·288591	·295228	·301920
4½	·240871	·247225	·253646	·260133	·266685	·273301
5	·218354	·224627	·230974	·237396	·243890	·250456
5½	·199938	·206149	·212443	·218819	·225275	·231811
6	·184597	·190761	·197017	·203362	·209795	·216315
6½	·171622	·177751	·183980	·190305	·196727	·203242
7	·160506	·166609	·172819	·179135	·185553	·192072
7½	·150877	·156961	·163160	·169472	·175894	·182425
8	·142456	·148527	·154721	·161035	·167467	·174014
8½	·135030	·141093	·147287	·153608	·160054	·166622
9	·128433	·134492	·140690	·147022	·153486	·160079
9½	·122535	·128593	·134797	·141144	·147629	·154251
10	·117230	·123290	·129504	·135867	·142377	·149029
10½	·112434	·118499	·124724	·131107	·137643	·144328
11	·108077	·114149	·120388	·126792	·133356	·140076
11½	·104102	·110182	·116438	·122865	·129459	·136214
12	·100462	·106552	·112825	·119277	·125901	·132695
12½	·097115	·103217	·109509	·115986	·122644	·129475
13	·094029	·100143	·106455	·112960	·119650	·126521
13½	·091174	·097302	·103635	·110167	·116892	·123804
14	·088526	·094668	·101023	·107584	·114344	·121296
14½	·086063	·092221	·098599	·105189	·111985	·118978
15	·083766	·089941	·096342	·102962	·109794	·116829
15½	·081620	·087812	·094237	·100888	·107756	·114833
16	·079610	·085820	·092269	·098952	·105857	·112976
16½	·077725	·083952	·090427	·097141	·104084	·111245
17	·075952	·082198	·088699	·095444	·102425	·109629
17½	·074283	·080548	·087074	·093852	·100870	·108117
18	·072708	·078993	·085546	·092356	·099412	·106702
18½	·071221	·077525	·084105	·090948	·098042	·105374
19	·069813	·076138	·082745	·089620	·096753	·104127
19½	·068480	·074825	·081459	·088368	·095538	·102955
20	·067215	·073581	·080242	·087184	·094392	·101852
20½	·066014	·072401	·079089	·086064	·093311	·100812
21	·064871	·071280	·077996	·085004	·092289	·099832
21½	·063784	·070213	·076957	·083999	·091321	·098906
22	·062747	·069198	·075970	·083045	·090405	·098032
22½	·061758	·068231	·075031	·082139	·089537	·097204
23	·060813	·067309	·074136	·081278	·088713	·096422
23½	·059911	·066428	·073284	·080459	·087931	·095680
24	·059047	·065586	·072470	·079679	·087189	·094977
24½	·058220	·064782	·071694	·078935	·086482	·094311
25	·057427	·064011	·070952	·078226	·085810	·093678

The Fifth Table of Compound Interest—*continued*.

The Annuity which One Pound will purchase for any Number of Years to come, &c.

Years.	3 per Cent.	4 per Cent.	5 per Cent.	6 per Cent.	7 per Cent.	8 per Cent.
25½	·056667	·063274	·070243	·077550	·085170	·093078
26	·055938	·062567	·069564	·076904	·084561	·092507
26½	·055237	·061889	·068914	·076287	·083979	·091964
27	·054564	·061238	·068291	·075697	·083425	·091448
27½	·053916	·060613	·067695	·075132	·082896	·090956
28	·053293	·060012	·067122	·074592	·082391	·090488
28½	·052693	·059435	·066573	·074075	·081909	·090043
29	·052114	·058879	·066045	·073579	·081448	·089618
29½	·051557	·058345	·065538	·073104	·081007	·089213
30	·051019	·057830	·065051	·072648	·080586	·088827
30½	·050500	·057333	·064582	·072211	·080183	·088458
31	·049998	·056855	·064132	·071792	·079796	·088107
31½	·049514	·056393	·063698	·071389	·079427	·087771
32	·049046	·055948	·063280	·071002	·079072	·087450
32½	·048594	·055518	·062877	·070630	·078733	·087144
33	·048156	·055103	·062490	·070272	·078408	·086851
33½	·047732	·054702	·062116	·069929	·078096	·086571
34	·047321	·054314	·061755	·069598	·077796	·086304
34½	·046924	·053939	·061407	·069280	·077509	·086048
35	·046539	·053577	·061071	·068973	·077233	·085803
35½	·046165	·053226	·060747	·068678	·076969	·085568
36	·045803	·052886	·060434	·068394	·076715	·085344
36½	·045452	·052558	·060132	·068121	·076471	·085129
37	·045111	·052239	·059839	·067857	·076236	·084924
37½	·044780	·051930	·059557	·067603	·076011	·084727
38	·044459	·051631	·059284	·067358	·075795	·084538
38½	·044147	·051341	·059020	·067121	·075586	·084358
39	·043843	·051060	·058764	·066893	·075386	·084185
39½	·043549	·050788	·058517	·066673	·075194	·084019
40	·043262	·050523	·058278	·066461	·075009	·083860
40½	·042983	·050266	·058046	·066256	·074831	·083707
41	·042712	·050017	·057822	·066058	·074659	·083561
41½	·042448	·049775	·057605	·065867	·074494	·083421
42	·042191	·049540	·057394	·065683	·074335	·083286
42½	·041941	·049311	·057190	·065505	·074183	·083157
43	·041698	·049089	·056993	·065333	·074035	·083034
43½	·041460	·048874	·056801	·065166	·073894	·082915
44	·041229	·048664	·056616	·065006	·073757	·082801
44½	·041004	·048460	·056436	·064850	·073626	·082692
45	·040785	·048262	·056261	·064700	·073499	·082587
45½	·040571	·048069	·056092	·064555	·073377	·082486
46	·040362	·047882	·055928	·064414	·073259	·082389
46½	·040159	·047699	·055768	·064279	·073146	·082297
47	·039960	·047521	·055614	·064147	·073037	·082207
47½	·039766	·047348	·055464	·064020	·072932	·082122
48	·039577	·047180	·055318	·063897	·072830	·082040
48½	·039393	·047016	·055176	·063778	·072732	·081961
49	·039213	·046857	·055039	·063663	·072638	·081885
49½	·039037	·046701	·054906	·063552	·072547	·081812
50	·038865	·046550	·054776	·063444	·072459	·081742

The Fifth Table of Compound Interest — *continued.*

The Annuity which One Pound will purchase for any Number of Years to come, &c.

Years.	3 per Cent.	4 per Cent.	5 per Cent.	6 per Cent.	7 per Cent.	8 per Cent.
50½	·038697	·046402	·054650	·063339	·072375	·081675
51	·038533	·046258	·054528	·063238	·072293	·081611
51½	·038373	·046118	·054409	·063140	·072214	·081549
52	·038217	·045982	·054294	·063046	·072139	·081489
52½	·038064	·045848	·054182	·062954	·072065	·081432
53	·037914	·045719	·054073	·062865	·071995	·081377
53½	·037768	·045592	·053967	·062779	·071926	·081324
54	·037625	·045469	·053864	·062696	·071861	·081273
54½	·037485	·045348	·053764	·062615	·071797	·081224
55	·037349	·045231	·053666	·062536	·071736	·081177
55½	·037215	·045116	·053572	·062461	·071677	·081132
56	·037084	·045004	·053480	·062387	·071620	·081089
56½	·036956	·044895	·053390	·062316	·071565	·081047
57	·036831	·044789	·053303	·062247	·071511	·081007
57½	·036708	·044685	·053218	·062180	·071460	·080969
58	·036588	·044584	·053136	·062115	·071410	·080932
58½	·036470	·044485	·053056	·062052	·071363	·080896
59	·036355	·044388	·052978	·061992	·071316	·080862
59½	·036243	·044293	·052902	·061932	·071272	·080829
60	·036132	·044201	·052828	·061875	·071229	·080797
60½	·036024	·044111	·052756	·061820	·071187	·080767
61	·035919	·044023	·052686	·061766	·071147	·080738
61½	·035815	·043938	·052618	·061714	·071108	·080710
62	·035713	·043854	·052551	·061663	·071071	·080683
62½	·035614	·043772	·052487	·061614	·071035	·080657
63	·035516	·043692	·052424	·061567	·071000	·080632
63½	·035421	·043614	·052363	·061520	·070966	·080608
64	·035327	·043537	·052303	·061476	·070933	·080584
64½	·035235	·043463	·052245	·061432	·070902	·080562
65	·035145	·043390	·052189	·061390	·070872	·080541
65½	·035057	·043318	·052134	·061349	·070842	·080520
66	·034971	·043249	·052080	·061310	·070814	·080501
66½	·034886	·043181	·052028	·061271	·070786	·080481
67	·034803	·043114	·051977	·061234	·070760	·080463
67½	·034721	·043049	·051928	·061198	·070734	·080446
68	·034641	·042985	·051879	·061163	·070710	·080429
68½	·034563	·042923	·051832	·061129	·070686	·080412
69	·034486	·042862	·051787	·061096	·070663	·080397
69½	·034410	·042803	·051742	·061064	·070641	·080382
70	·034336	·042745	·051699	·061033	·070619	·080367
70½	·034263	·042688	·051656	·061002	·070598	·080353
71	·034192	·042632	·051615	·060973	·070578	·080340
71½	·034122	·042578	·051575	·060945	·070559	·080327
72	·034054	·042524	·051536	·060917	·070540	·080314
72½	·033986	·042472	·051498	·060891	·070522	·080303
73	·033920	·042421	·051461	·060865	·070504	·080291
73½	·033855	·042372	·051424	·060839	·070487	·080280
74	·033791	·042323	·051389	·060815	·070471	·080269
74½	·033729	·042275	·051355	·060791	·070455	·080259
75	·033667	·042229	·051321	·060768	·070440	·080249

The Fifth Table of Compound Interest — *continued.*

The Annuity which One Pound will purchase for any Number of Years to come, &c.

Years.	3 per Cent.	4 per Cent.	5 per Cent.	6 per Cent.	7 per Cent	8 per Cent.
75½	·033607	·042183	·051288	·060746	·070425	·080240
76	·033548	·042138	·051257	·060724	·070411	·080231
76½	·033490	·042094	·051226	·060703	·070397	·080222
77	·033433	·042052	·051195	·060683	·070384	·080214
77½	·033377	·042010	·051166	·060663	·070371	·080206
78	·033322	·041969	·051137	·060644	·070359	·080198
78½	·033268	·041929	·051109	·060625	·070347	·080190
79	·033215	·041890	·051082	·060607	·070335	·080183
79½	·033162	·041851	·051055	·060589	·070324	·080176
80	·033111	·041814	·051029	·060572	·070313	·080169
80½	·033061	·041777	·051004	·060555	·070303	·080163
81	·033012	·041741	·050979	·060539	·070292	·080157
81½	·032963	·041706	·050955	·060524	·070283	·080151
82	·032915	·041671	·050932	·060509	·070273	·080145
82½	·032868	·041637	·050909	·060494	·070264	·080140
83	·032822	·041604	·050886	·060479	·070255	·080134
83½	·032777	·041572	·050865	·060466	·070247	·080129
84	·032733	·041540	·050843	·060452	·070238	·080124
84½	·032689	·041509	·050823	·060439	·070230	·080120
85	·032646	·041479	·050803	·060426	·070223	·080115
85½	·032604	·041449	·050783	·060414	·070215	·080111
86	·032562	·041420	·050764	·060402	·070208	·080106
86½	·032522	·041391	·050745	·060390	·070201	·080102
87	·032482	·041363	·050727	·060379	·070194	·080099
87½	·032442	·041336	·050709	·060368	·070188	·080095
88	·032403	·041309	·050692	·060357	·070182	·080091
88½	·032365	·041283	·050675	·060347	·070176	·080088
89	.032328	·041257	·050658	·060337	·070170	·080084
89½	·032291	·041232	·050642	·060327	·070164	·080081
90	·032255	·041207	·050627	·060318	·070159	·080078
90½	·032220	·041183	·050611	·060309	·070153	·080075
91	·032185	·041159	·050596	·060300	·070148	·080072
91½	·032150	·041136	·050582	·060291	·070143	·080070
92	·032116	·041114	·050568	·060283	·070138	·080067
92½	·032083	·041091	·050554	·060275	·070134	·080064
93	·032051	·041070	·050540	·060267	·070129	·080062
93½	·032018	·041048	·050527	·060259	·070125	·080060
94	·031987	·041027	·050514	·060251	·070121	·080057
94½	·031956	·041007	·050502	·060244	·070117	·080055
95	·031925	·040987	·050490	·060237	·070113	·080053
95½	·031895	·040967	·050478	·060230	·070109	·080051
96	·031866	·040948	·050466	·060224	·070105	·080049
96½	·031837	·040929	·050455	·060217	·070102	·080047
97	·031808	·040911	·050444	·060211	·070098	·080045
97½	·031780	·040893	·050433	·060205	·070095	·080044
98	·031752	·040875	·050422	·060199	·070092	·080042
98½	·031725	·040858	·050412	·060193	·070089	·080040
99	·031698	·040841	·050402	·060188	·070086	·080039
99½	·031672	·040824	·050392	·060182	·070083	·080037
100	·031646	·040808	·050383	·060177	·070080	·080036
F.S.	·030000	·040000	·050000	·060000	·070000	·080000

Table VI. Showing the Value of an Annuity on one Life according to the Probabilities of Life in London.

Age.	Year's value at			Age.	Year's value at		
	3 per Cent.	4 per Cent.	5 per Cent.		3 per Cent.	4 per Cent.	5 per Cent.
6	18·8	16·2	14·1	41	13·0	11·4	10·2
7	18·9	16·3	14·2	42	12·8	11·2	10·1
8	19·0	16·4	14·3	43	12·6	11·1	10·0
9 and 10 }	19·0	16·4	14·3	44	12·5	11·0	9·9
				45	12·3	10·8	9·8
11	19·0	16·4	14·3	46	12·1	10·7	9·7
12	18·9	16·3	14·2	47	11·9	10·5	9·5
13	18·7	16·2	14·1	48	11·8	10·4	9·4
14	18·5	16·0	14·0	49	11·6	10·2	9·3
15	18·3	15·8	13·9	50	11·4	10·1	9·2
16	18·1	15·6	13·7	51	11·2	9·9	9·0
17	17·9	15·4	13·5	52	11·0	9·8	8·9
18	17·6	15·2	13·4	53	10·7	9·6	8·8
19	17·4	15·0	13·2	54	10·5	9·4	8·6
20	17·2	14·8	13·0	55	10·3	9·3	8·5
21	17·0	14·7	12·9	56	10·1	9·1	8·4
22	16·8	14·5	12·7	57	9·9	8·9	8·2
23	16·5	14·8	12·6	58	9·6	8·7	8·1
24	16·3	14·1	12·4	59	9·4	8·6	8·0
25	16·1	14·0	12·3	60	9·2	8·4	7·9
26	15·9	13·8	12·1	61	8·9	8·2	7·7
27	15·6	13·6	12·0	62	8·7	8·1	7·6
28	15·4	13·4	11·8	63	8·5	7·9	7·4
29	15·2	13·2	11·7	64	8·3	7·7	7·3
30	15·0	13·1	11·6	65	8·0	7·5	7·1
31	14·8	12·9	11·4	66	7·8	7·3	6·9
32	14·6	12·7	11·3	67	7·6	7·1	6·7
33	14·4	12·6	11·2	68	7·4	6·9	6·6
34	14·2	12·4	11·0	69	7·1	6·7	6·4
35	14·1	12·3	10·9	70	6·9	6·5	6·2
36	13·9	12·1	10·8	71	6·7	6·3	6·0
37	13·7	11·9	10·6	72	6·5	6·1	5·8
38	13·5	11·8	10·5	73	6·2	5·9	5·6
39	13·3	11·6	10·4	74	5·9	5·6	5·4
40	13·2	11·5	10·3	75	5·6	5·4	5·2

Table VI.a.   Expectation of Life.

De Moivre's Hypothesis on the duration of human life, namely, that of 86 persons born one dies every year till all are extinct, has led to an empirical rule of easy recollection for the expectation of life, namely, to subtract the age from 86 and halve the difference for an answer. In the left hand side of the subjoined table is shown the number of persons out of 10,000 who may be expected to die in the year following their attaining the age marked in the first column, according to the Hypothesis, to the Northampton and Carlisle tables, and to the Belgian one of Quetelet. The table on the right shows the values of annuities on lives at 3 per cent. in years' purchase, whence it appears that in money results the Hypothesis curiously agrees with the celebrated Northampton tables.

Age.	Hypo-thesis.	North-ampton.	Carlisle.	Belgium.	Age.	Hypo-thesis.	North-ampton.	Carlisle.
10	132	92	45	88	10	19·9	20·7	23·5
20	152	140	71	120	20	18·5	18·6	21·7
30	179	171	101	126	30	16·8	16·9	19·6
40	217	209	130	144	40	14·8	14·8	17·1
50	278	284	134	183	50	12·5	12·4	14·3
60	385	402	335	325	60	9·7	9·8	10·5
70	625	649	516	680	70	6·4	6·7	7·1
80	1667	1343	1217	1425	80	2·3	3·8	4·4

Table VII., showing the Value of an Annuity on the joint Continuance of two Lives, according to the Probabilities of Life in London.

Age of the Younger.	Elder.	Value at 3 per Cent.	Value at 4 per Cent.	Value at 5 per Cent.	Age of the Younger.	Elder.	Value at 3 per Cent.	Value at 4 per Cent.	Value at 5 per Cent.
10	10	14·7	13·0	11·6	30	55	7·9	7·3	6·7
	15	14·3	12·7	11·3		60	7·2	6·7	6·2
	20	13·8	12·2	10·8		65	6·5	6·1	5·7
	25	13·1	11·6	10·2		70	5·8	5·5	5·2
	30	12·3	10·9	9·7		75	5·1	4·9	4·7
	35	11·5	10·2	9·1	35	35	9·9	8·8	8·0
	40	10·7	9·6	8·6		40	9·4	8·5	7·7
	45	10·0	9·0	8·1		45	8·9	8·1	7·4
	50	9·3	8·4	7·6		50	8·3	7·6	7·0
	55	8·6	7·8	7·1		55	7·7	7·1	6·6
	60	7·8	7·2	6·6		60	7·1	6·5	6·1
	65	6·9	6·5	6·1		65	6·4	6·0	5·6
	70	6·1	5·8	5·5		70	5·7	5·4	5·1
	75	5·3	5·1	4·9		75	5·0	4·8	4·6
15	15	13·9	12·3	11·0	40	40	9·1	8·1	7·3
	20	13·3	11·8	10·5		45	8·7	7·8	7·1
	25	12·6	11·2	10·1		50	8·2	7·4	6·8
	30	11·9	10·6	9·5		55	7·6	6·9	6·4
	35	11·2	10·0	9·0		60	7·0	6·4	6·0
	40	10·4	9·4	8·5		65	6·4	5·9	5·5
	45	9·6	8·8	8·0		70	5·7	5·4	5·1
	50	8·9	8·2	7·5		75	5·0	4·8	4·6
	55	8·2	7·6	7·0	45	45	8·3	7·4	6·7
	60	7·5	7·0	6·5		50	7·9	7·1	6·5
	65	6·8	6·4	6·0		55	7·4	6·7	6·2
	70	6·0	5·7	5·4		60	6·8	6·3	5·8
	75	5·2	5·0	4·8		65	6·3	5·8	5·4
20	20	12·8	11·3	10·1		70	5·6	5·3	5·0
	25	12·2	10·8	9·7		75	4·9	4·7	4·5
	30	11·6	10·3	9·2	50	50·	7·6	6·8	6·2
	35	10·9	9·8	8·8		55	7·2	6·5	6·0
	40	10·2	9·2	8·4		60	6·7	6·1	5·7
	45	9·5	8·6	7·9		65	6·2	5·7	5·3
	50	8·8	8·0	7·4		70	5·5	5·2	4·9
	55	8·1	7·5	6·9		75	4·8	4·6	4·4
	60	7·4	6·9	6·4	55	55	6·9	6·2	5·7
	65	6·7	6·3	5·9		60	6·5	5·9	5·5
	70	6·0	5·7	5·4		65	6·0	5·6	5·2
	75	5·2	5·0	4·8		70	5·4	5·1	4·8
25	25	11·8	10·5	9·4		75	4·7	4·5	4·3
	30	11·3	10·1	9·0	60	60	6·1	5·6	5·2
	35	10·7	9·6	8·6		65	5·7	5·3	4·9
	40	10·0	9·1	8·2		70	5·2	4·9	4·6
	45	9·4	8·5	7·8		75	4·6	4·4	4·2
	50	8·7	7·9	7·3	65	65	5·4	5·0	4·7
	55	8·0	7·4	6·8		70	4·9	4·6	4·4
	60	7·3	6·8	6·3		75	4·4	4·2	4·0
	65	6·6	6·2	5·8	70	70	4·6	4·4	4·2
	70	5·9	5·6	5·3		75	4·2	4·0	3·9
	75	5·1	4·9	4·7	75	75	3·8	3·7	3·6
30	30	10·8	9·6	8·6					
	35	10·3	9·2	8·3					
	40	9·7	8·8	8·0					
	45	9·1	8·3	7·6					
	50	8·5	7·8	7·2					

Table VIII., showing the Value of an Annuity on the longest of two Lives.

Age of the Younger	Age of the Elder	Value at 3 per Cent.	Value at 4 per Cent.	Value at 5 per Cent.
10	10	23·4	19·9	17·1
	15	22·9	19·5	16·8
	20	22·5	19·1	16·6
	25	22·2	18·8	16·4
	30	21·9	18·6	16·2
	35	21·6	18·4	16·1
	40	21·4	18·3	16·0
	45	21·2	18·2	15·9
	50	20·9	18·0	15·8
	55	20·7	17·8	15·7
	60	20·4	17·6	15·5
	65	20·1	17·4	15·3
	70	19·8	17·2	15·1
	75	19·5	16·9	14·8
15	15	22·8	19·3	16·7
	20	22·3	18·9	16·4
	25	21·9	18·6	16·2
	30	21·6	18·3	16·0
	35	21·3	18·1	15·9
	40	21·1	17·9	15·7
	45	20·9	17·8	15·6
	50	20·7	17·6	15·4
	55	20·4	17·4	15·3
	60	20·1	17·2	15·2
	65	19·8	16·9	15·0
	70	19·4	16·6	14·7
	75	18·9	16·3	14·4
20	20	21·6	18·3	15·8
	25	21·1	17·9	15·5
	30	20·7	17·6	15·3
	35	20·4	17·4	15·1
	40	20·1	17·2	15·0
	45	19·9	17·0	14·9
	50	19·6	16·8	14·7
	55	19·4	16·6	14·5
	60	19·1	16·3	14·3
	65	18·7	16·0	14·1
	70	18·2	15·7	13·8
	75	17·7	15·3	13·5
25	25	20·3	17·4	15·1
	30	19·8	17·0	14·9
	35	19·4	16·7	14·7
	40	19·2	16·5	14·5
	45	18·9	16·3	14·3
	50	18·7	16·1	14·2
	55	18·4	15·9	14·0
	60	18·0	15·6	13·8
	65	17·6	15·3	13·6
	70	17·2	15·0	13·3
	75	16·7	14·6	12·9
30	30	19·3	16·6	14·5
	35	18·8	16·2	14·2
	40	18·4	15·9	14·0
	45	18·1	15·6	13·8
	50	17·8	15·4	13·6

Age of the Younger	Age of the Elder	Value at 3 per Cent.	Value at 4 per Cent.	Value at 5 per Cent.
30	55	17·4	15·1	13·4
	60	17·0	14·8	13·2
	65	16·6	14·5	12·9
	70	16·1	14·1	12·6
	75	15·6	13·7	12·2
35	35	18·3	15·8	13·8
	40	17·8	15·4	13·5
	45	17·4	15·1	13·3
	50	17·1	14·8	13·1
	55	16·7	14·5	12·9
	60	16·3	14·2	12·7
	65	15·8	13·8	12·4
	70	15·3	13·4	12·0
	75	14·8	13·0	11·6
40	40	17·3	15·0	13·3
	45	16·8	14·6	13·0
	50	16·3	14·0	12·7
	55	15·9	13·9	12·4
	60	15·4	13·5	12·1
	65	14·9	13·1	11·8
	70	14·5	12·7	11·4
	75	14·0	12·3	11·0
45	45	16·2	14·2	12·8
	50	15·7	13·8	12·5
	55	15·2	13·4	12·1
	60	14·7	12·9	11·7
	65	14·1	12·5	11·4
	70	13·6	12·0	11·0
	75	13·1	11·6	10·6
50	50	15·0	13·3	12·1
	55	14·5	12·9	11·7
	60	13·9	12·4	11·3
	65	13·3	12·0	10·9
	70	12·8	11·5	10·5
	75	12·3	11·0	10·1
55	55	13·6	12·4	11·3
	60	13·0	11·9	10·9
	65	12·4	11·3	10·5
	70	11·8	10·8	10·0
	75	11·3	10·3	9·5
60	60	12·2	11·2	10·5
	65	11·5	10·6	10·0
	70	10·9	10·1	9·5
	75	10·3	9·5	9·0
65	65	10·7	10·0	9·4
	70	10·0	9·4	8·9
	75	9·3	8·7	8·3
70	70	9·2	8·6	8·2
	75	8·4	7·9	7·6
75	75	7·6	7·2	6·9

A

GLOSSARY OF TERMS USED BY ARCHITECTS;

ALSO

A LIST OF THE PRINCIPAL ARCHITECTS

OF ALL TIMES AND COUNTRIES, ALPHABETICALLY ARRANGED,

AND

A CATALOGUE OF THE MOST USEFUL WORKS ON ARCHITECTURE.

[NOTE.—Further explanations, &c. of many of the terms herein will be obtained by reference to the Index.—See also the ADDENDUM.]

A.

ABACISCUS. A word sometimes used as synonymous with abacus, but more correctly applied to a square compartment enclosing a part or the entire pattern or design of a Mosaic pavement.

ABACUS. (Gr. Αϐαξ, a slab.) The upper member of the capital of a column, and serving as a crowning both to the capital and to the whole column. It is otherwise defined by some as a square table, list, or plinth in the upper part of the capitals of columns, especially of those of the Corinthian order, serving instead of a drip or corona to the capital, and supporting the nether face of the architrave, and the whole trabeation. In the Tuscan, Doric, and ancient Ionic orders, it is a flat square member, well enough resembling the original title; whence it is called by the French *tailloir*, that is, a trencher, and by the Italians *credenza*. In the richer orders it parts with its original form, the four sides or faces of it being arched or cut inwards, and ornamented in the middle of each face with a rose or other flower, a fish's tail, &c.; and in the Corinthian and Composite orders it is composed of an ovolo, a fillet, and a cavetto. The word is used by Scamozzi to signify a concave moulding in the capital of the Tuscan pedestal.

ABATE, NICHOLAS. See ARCHITECTS, list of, 240.

ABATON. (Gr. Αϐατον, an inaccessible place.) A building at Rhodes, mentioned by Vitruvius, lib. ii., entrance whereof was forbidden to all persons, because it contained a trophy and two bronze statues erected by Artemisia in memory of her triumph in surprising the city.

ABATTOIR. (Fr. Abattre, to knock down.) A building appropriated to the slaughtering of cattle.

ABBEY. (Fr. Abbaïe.) Properly the building adjoining to or near a convent or monastery, for the residence of the head of the house (abbot or abbess). It is often used for the church attached to the establishment, as also for the buildings composing the whole establishment. In such establishments the church was usually grand, and splendidly decorated. They had a *refectory*, which was a large hall in which the monks or nuns had their meals; a *guest hall*, for the reception and entertainment of visitors; a *parlour* or *locutory*, where the brothers or sisters met for conversation; a *dormitory*, an *almonry*, wherefrom the alms of the abbey were distributed; a *library* and *museum*; a *prison* for the refractory, and *cells* for penance. The *sanctuary* was rather a precinct than a building, in which offenders were, under conditions, safe from the operation of the law. *Granges*, or farm buildings, and *abbatial* residences. *Schools* were usually attached for the education of youth, with separate accommodations for the scholars. A *singing school*, a *common room*, with a fire in it, for the brothers or sisters to warm themselves, no other fire being allowed, except in the apartments of the higher officers. A *mint*, for coining, and a room called an *exchequer*. The abbey was always provided with a *churchyard*, a *garden*, and a *bakehouse*. The *sacristy* contained the garments of the priests, and the vessels, &c.; *vestiaria* or wardrobes being assigned for the monks. Many of the ordinary duties of these persons were performed in the cloisters where they delivered their lectures.

ABELE TREE. A species of white poplar, enumerated among woods by Vitruvius (book ii.

chap. ix.) as being, in many situations, serviceable from its "toughness," and also from its colour and lightness fitting it for carvings.

ABREUVOIR. (Fr.) A watering-place for horses. In masonry it is the joint between two stones, or the interstice to be filled up with mortar or cement, when either are to be used.

ABSCISS, or ABSCISSA. (Lat. Ab and Scindo.) A geometrical term, denoting a segment cut off from a straight line by an ordinate to a curve.

ABSIS. See APSIS.

ABSTRACT. A term in general use among artificers, surveyors, &c. to signify the collecting together and arranging under a few distinct heads the various small quantities of different articles which have been employed in any work, and the affixing of a price to determinate portions of each, as per square, per foot, per pound, &c., for the purpose of more expeditiously and conveniently ascertaining the amount.

ABUSE. A term applied to those practices in architecture which, arising from a desire of innovation, and often authorised by custom, tend to unfix the most established principles, and to corrupt the best forms, by the vicious way in which they are used. Palladio has given a chapter on them in his work. He reduces them to four principal ones: the first whereof is the introduction of brackets or modillions for supporting a weight; the second, the practice of breaking pediments so as to leave the centre part open; third, the great projection of cornices; and, fourth, the practice of rusticating columns. Had Palladio lived to a later day, he might have greatly increased his list of abuses, as Perrault has done in the following list: the first whereof is that of allowing columns and pilasters to penetrate one another, or be conjoined at the angles of a building. The second, that of coupling columns, which Perrault himself in the Louvre has made almost excusable; the third, that of enlarging the metopæ in the Doric order, for the purpose of accommodating them to the intercolumniations; the fourth, that of leaving out the inferior part of the tailloir in the modern Ionic capital; the fifth, that of running up an order through two or three stories, instead of decorating each story with its own order; the sixth, that of joining, contrary to the practice of the ancients, the plinth of the column to the cornice of the pedestal, by means of an inverted cavetto; the seventh, the use of architrave cornices; the eighth, that of breaking the entablature of an order over a column, &c. &c.

ABUTMENT. (According to some, from the French aboutir, to abut, among whom the learned Spelman; but according to others, from the Saxon abutan, about.) The solid part of a pier from which the arch immediately springs. Abutments are artificial or natural: the former are usually formed of masonry or brickwork, and the latter are the rock or other solid materials on the banks of the river, in the case of a bridge, which receive the foot of the arch. It is obvious that they should be of sufficient solidity and strength to resist the thrust of the arch. See p. 357, et seq., and ARCH in this glossary.

ABUTTALS. The buttings or boundings of land.

ACANTHUS. (Ακανθος, a spine.) A spiny herbaceous plant found in various parts of the Levant. Its leaf is said by Vitruvius to have been the model on which the Grecian architects formed the leaves of the Corinthian capital.

ACER. (Celt. Ac, a point; Lat. Acer, sharp.) A genus of trees comprehending the maple and sycamore, the wood whereof is not of much value. That of the acer campestre furnishes the cabinet-makers with what they call bird's-eye maple.

ACCESSES. See PASSAGE.

ACCIDENTAL POINT. In perspective, the point in which a straight line drawn from the eye parallel to another straight line cuts the perspective plane. It is the point wherein the representations of all straight lines parallel to the original straight line concur when produced. Its name is adopted to distinguish it from the principal point or point of view. See PERSPECTIVE, p. 769, et seq.

ACOUSTICS. (Gr. Ακούω, to hear.) The doctrine or theory of sounds, as applicable to buildings. See p. 1045, et seq., THEATRE.

ACROPOLIS. (Gr. Ακρος and Πολις, city.) The upper town or citadel of a Grecian city, usually the site of the original settlement, and chosen by the colonists for its natural strength. The most celebrated were those of Athens, Corinth, and Ithome, whereof the two latter were called the horns of the Peloponnesus, as though their possession could secure the submission of the whole peninsula.

ACROTERIA. (Gr. Ακρωτηριον, the extremity of anything.) The pedestals, often without base or cornice, placed on the centre and sides of pediments for the reception of figures. Vitruvius says that the lateral acroteria ought to be half the height of the tympanum, and the apex acroterium should be an eighth part more. No regular proportion, however, is observable in Grecian buildings.

The word acroterium is applied to the ridge of a building; it has also been used to signify the statues on the pedestals; but it is only to these latter that it is strictly applicable. The word has moreover been given to the small pieces of wall in balus-

trades, between the pedestal and the balusters, and again to the pinnacles or other ornaments which stand in ranges on the horizontal copings or parapets of buildings.

ACUTE-ANGLED TRIANGLE. A triangle having all its angles acute. Every triangle has at least two acute angles.

ACUTE ANGLE. A term used in geometry to denote an angle less than 90°, that is, less than a right angle.

ADAM, ROBERT. See ARCHITECTS, list of, 301.

ADAMS, ROBERT. See ARCHITECTS, list of, 244.

ADHESION (Lat. Adhæreo.) A term in physics denoting the force with which different bodies remain attached to each other when brought into contact. It must not be confounded with cohesion, which is the force that unites the particles of a homogeneous body with each other. The following is an account of some experiments recorded in the *Technical Repository* for 1824. " The insertion of a nail is accomplished by destroying the cohesion of the wood, its extraction by overcoming the force of adhesion and friction. We will consider it here solely as a case of adhesion. Fine sprigs, of which 4560 weighed one pound, $\frac{44}{100}$ of an inch long, forced four tenths of an inch into dry Christiana deals at right angles to the fibre, required a force of 22 lbs. to extract them. The same description of nail having 3200 in the pound, $\frac{53}{100}$ of an inch long, and forced $\frac{44}{100}$ of an inch into the same kind of wood, required 37 lbs. to extract it. Threepenny brads, 618 to the pound weight, one and a quarter inch long, forced half an inch into the wood, required a force of 72 lbs. to draw them out. Fivepenny nails, 139 to the pound weight, two inches long, and forced one inch and a half into the wood, required a force of 170 lbs. to extract them. The same kind of nail forced one inch and a half into the wood required 327 lbs. to draw it out. In this last experiment the nail was forced into the wood by a hammer of cast iron weighing 627 lbs. falling from a height of twelve inches, four blows of which were necessary to force the nail an inch and a half into the wood. It required a pressure of 400 lbs. to force the nail to the same depth. A sixpenny nail driven one inch into dry elm across the grain or fibres required 327 lbs. to draw it out by direct force; driven endwise into dry elm, or parallel with the grain, it required only 257 lbs. to extract it. The same sort of nail driven into dry Christiana deal was extracted by a force equal to 257 lbs., and by one of 87 lbs. from a depth of an inch. The adhesion, therefore, of a nail driven into elm across the grain, or at right angles to the fibres of the wood, is greater than when it is driven with the grain, or parallel with the fibres, in the proportion of 100 to 78, or 4 to 3. And under the same circumstances, in dry Christiana deal, as 100 to 33·8, or nearly 3 to 1. The comparative adhesion of nails in elm and deal is between 2 and 3 to 1. To extract a sixpenny nail driven one inch into green sycamore required 312 lbs.; from dry oak, 507 lbs.; and from dry beech, 667 lbs. A common screw of one fifth of an inch had an adhesion about three times as great as that of a sixpenny nail. A common sixpenny nail driven two inches in dry oak would require more than half a ton to extract it by pressure."

ADIT (Lat. Adeo), or ADITUS. The approach or entrance to a building, &c. Among the ancients the *aditus theatri*, or adits of a theatre, were doorways opening on to the *stairs*, by which persons entered the theatre from the outer *portico*, and thence descended into the seats. Upon the same principle were the adits of a circus.

ADJACENT ANGLE, in geometry, is an angle immediately contiguous to another, so that one side is common to both angles. This expression is more particularly applied to denote that the two angles have not only one side in common, but likewise that the other two sides form one straight line.

ADYTUM. (Gr. Ἄδυτον, a recess.) The secret dark chamber in a temple to which none but the priests had access, and from which the oracles were delivered. Seneca, in his tragedy of Thyestes says, —

" Hinc orantibus
Responsa dantur certa, dum ingenti sono
Laxantur adyto fata."

Among the Egyptians the *secos* was the same thing, and is described by Strabo. The only well-preserved ancient adytum that has come to our knowledge is in the little temple at Pompeii; it is raised some steps above the level of the temple itself, and is without light.

ADZE, or ADDICE. An edged tool used to chip surfaces in an horizontal direction, the axe being employed to chop materials in vertical positions. The blade, which is of iron, forms a small portion of a cylindric surface in both its sides, and has a wooden handle fixed into a socket at one of its extremities, in a radial direction, while the other extremity, parallel to the axis of the cylinder, and therefore at right angles to the handle, is edged with steel, and ground sharp from the concave side. The adze is chiefly employed for taking off thin chips from timber or boards, and for paring away irregularities at which the axe cannot come. It is also used in most joinings of carpentry, particularly when notched upon one another, scarfings, thicknesses of flooring boards opposite to the joints, &c.

Ælfric. See Architects, list of, 76.

Aerial Perspective. The relative apparent recession of objects from the foreground, owing to the quantity of air interposed between them and the spectator. It accompanies the recession of the perspective lines.

Æsthetics. (Gr. Αισθητικος, having the power of perception by means of the senses.) It is in the fine arts that science which derives the first principles from the effect which certain combinations have on the mind as connected with nature and right reason. See p. 795.

Ætherius. See Architects, list of, 60.

Ætiaioi. (Gr. Αετος, an eagle.) The name given by the Greek architects to the slabs forming the face of the tympanum of a pediment. This word occurs in the Athenian inscription now in the British Museum, brought to England by Dr. Chandler, and relating to the survey of some temple at Athens.

Ætoma, or Ætos. (Gr. Αετος.) A name given by the Greek architects to the tympanum of a pediment. It seems derived from the custom of decorating the apex or ridge of the roof with figures of eagles, and that the name thence first given to the ridge was afterwards transferred to the pediment itself.

Agamedes. See Architects, list of, 3.

Agaptos. See Architects, list of, 10.

Agnolo d', Baccio. See Architects, list of, 206.

Agnolo Gabriello. See Architects, list of, 171.

Agostino and Angelo, of Siena. See Architects, list of, 131.

Agricola. See Architects, list of, 59.

Air Drains, or Dry Areas. Cavities between the external walls of a building protected by a wall towards the earth, which is thus prevented from lying against the said walls and creating damp. They may be made with the walls battering against the ground, and covered over with paving stones, or with their walls nearly perpendicular, and arched on the top; the bottoms should be paved, and they should be well ventilated.

Air Holes. Holes made for admitting air to ventilate apartments, also for introducing it among the timbers of floors and roofs for the prevention or destruction of the dry rot.

Air Trap. A trap immersed various ways in water to prevent foul air rising from sewers or drains.

Ajutage. (Fr.). Part of the apparatus of an artificial fountain, being a sort of *jet d'eau*, or kind of tube fitted to the mouth or aperture of a vessel, through which the water is to be played, and by it determined into the form to be given to it.

Aisle, or Ala. (Lat. Ala.) A term chiefly used by the English architect to signify the side subdivisions in a church, usually separated from the nave or centre division by pillars or columns; but among different nations, as applied to architecture, it bears different significations. We are told by Strabo that among the Egyptians the alæ of the temple were the two walls that enclosed the two sides of the pronaos, and of the same height as the temple itself. The walls, he observes, from above ground, were a little farther apart than the foundations of the temple, but as they rose, were built with an inclination to each other. We do not, however, clearly understand the passage, which puzzled Pocock as much as it has ourselves. The Greek alæ, called *ptera*, were the colonnades which surrounded the cell of the temple, the monopteros temple being the only species which had columns without a wall behind them. The peripteral had one tier of columns round the cell, the dipteral two, and the pseudo or false dipteral, invented by Hermogenes, was that in which the ala was single, but occupied the same space on the sides of the cell as the dipteral, though one of the tiers of columns was left out. Thus, by metaphor, the columns were called the alæ or wings of the temple. The term is also applied to the sides of a building which are subordinate to the principal and central division, and are vulgarly called wings. In Gothic as well as many modern churches the breadth is divided into three or five parts, by two or by four rows of pillars running parallel to the sides; and as one or other is the case, the church is said to be a three-aisled or five-aisled fabric. The middle aisle is called the nave or chief aisle, and the penthouse, which joins to each side of the main structure containing the aisles, is called a wing. In Great Britain no instance occurs of a five-aisled church, except a building at the west end of the cathedral at Durham. On the Continent there are many such buildings, among which is the cathedral at Milan. It is somewhat remarkable that in Westminster Abbey and in Redcliffe Church at Bristol the aisles are continued on each side of the transept, and in Salisbury Cathedral on one side only, a circumstance not met with in any other churches in this country.

Alabaster. A white semi-transparent variety of gypsum or sulphate of lime, a mineral of common occurrence, and used for various ornamental purposes. It was much used formerly for monuments in churches and the like.

Albarium Opus. (Lat.) In ancient Roman architecture a term imagined by some to have been nothing more than a species of whitewash applied to walls, but, as we think,

incorrectly. In the passage of the tenth chapter of the fifth book of Vitruvius, where he recommends the use of the albarium opus for the ceilings of baths, he allows *tectorium opus* as a substitute; so that we think it was a species of stucco. Its employment at the baths of Agrippa, knowing as we do the extent to which luxury was carried in the baths of the ancients, seems to prove it a *superior* sort of stucco, and it is by no means improbable that it was susceptible of a high polish.

ALBERT. See ARCHITECTS, list of, 69.

ALBERTI, ARISTOTILE. See ARCHITECTS, list of, 180.

———, LEO BAPT. See ARCHITECTS, list of, 162.

ALCOCK. See ARCHITECTS, list of, 169.

ALCOVE. (Alcoba, Sp.; Elcant, Arab., a sleeping chamber.) That part of a sleeping chamber wherein the bed is placed. The use of alcoves, though not by that name, is ancient. They were frequently designed in the form of a niche; such, for instance, as those that Winkelman notices at Hadrian's villa at Tivoli, of which sort are some at Pompeii. They were often formed by enclosures or balustrades, of various heights, and by means of draperies the part was separated from the large chamber whereof it was a part. Some idea may be formed of it from many of the ancient bassi relievi, especially from the celebrated one known by the name of the *Nozze Aldobrandini*. In modern works this part of a room differs according to the rank and taste of the proprietor. In England it is rarely introduced, but in France and Italy it often forms a beautiful feature in the apartments of palaces.

ALDER. (Ang. Sax. Ellarn.) A tree belonging to the order Betulaceæ. See page 500.

ALDRICH. See ARCHITECTS, list of, 268.

ALDUN. See ARCHITECTS, list of, 79.

ALEOTTI. See ARCHITECTS, list of, 253.

ALESSI. See ARCHITECTS, list of, 215.

ALEATORIUM. In ancient Roman architecture, a room in which games at dice were played.

ALEXANDER. See ARCHITECTS, list of, 90.

ALGARDI. See ARCHITECTS, list of, 256.

ALIPTERION. In ancient Roman architecture, a room used by the bathers for anointing themselves.

ALKORANES. In Eastern architecture, high slender towers attached to mosques, and surrounded with balconies, in which the priests recite aloud at stated times prayers from the Koran, and announce the hours of devotion to worshippers. They much embellish the mosques, and are often very fantastical in form.

ALLEY. (Fr. Allée.) An aisle, or any part of a church left open for access to another part. In towns, a passage narrower than a lane. A walk in a garden.

ALMEHRAB. A niche in the mosques of the Mahometans which points towards the *Kebla*, or temple of Mecca, to which their religion directs them to bow their face in praying.

ALMONRY. Properly a closet or repository for the reception of broken victuals set apart as alms for the poor, but more generally used to denote a house near the church in abbeys or their gates, provided with various offices for distributing the alms of the convent and for the dwelling of the almoner.

ALMSHOUSE. A house devoted to the reception and support of the poor, generally endowed for a particular description of persons.

ALOISIUS. See ARCHITECTS, list of, 56.

ALONSO. See ARCHITECTS, list of, 196.

ALTAR. (Lat. Altare.) A sort of pedestal whereon sacrifice was offered. According to Servius there was among the ancients a difference between the *ara* and *altare*, the latter being raised upon a substruction, and used only in the service of the celestial and superior divinities, whereas the former was merely on the ground, and appropriated to the service of the terrestrial gods. Altars to the infernal gods were made by excavation, and termed *scrobiculi*. Some authors have maintained that the ara was the altar before which prayers were uttered, and that the altare was used for sacrifices only. There is however from ancient authors no appearance of such distinctions, but that the words were used indiscriminately. The earliest altars were square polished stones, on which were placed the offerings to the gods. Whilst the sacrifice consisted only of libations, perfumes, and offerings of that nature, the altar was small, and even portable; when man, however, began to consider he was honouring the divinity by an offering of blood, the altar necessarily expanded in dimensions. Different forms of it were adopted, according to the nature of the sacrifice, and on it the throat of the victim was cut and the flesh burnt. Of this sort is the circular altar of the Villa Pamphili at Rome, one of the largest and most elegant of the class. On it appears the cavity for holding the fire, and the grooves for carrying off the blood. The varieties of altars were suitable in form, ornament, and situation to the service to which they were appropriated: some, as we have already observed, being for sacrifices of blood, others for receiving offerings

and the sacred vessels; some for burning incense, others for receiving libations. Many were set up as mere monuments of the piety of a devotee, whilst others were raised to perpetuate some great event. They served for adjuration as well as for an asylum to the unfortunate and evil doer. In form they varied from square to oblong, and from triangular to circular. Those of metal were commonly tripodial. When of brick or stone their plan is generally square. According to Pausanius they were occasionally made of wood. They do not appear to have been of any regular standard height, for they are sometimes found on bassi relievi reaching but little above a man's knee, whereas in others they appear to reach his middle; but it seems that in proportion to its diameter the circular altar was generally the highest. Vitruvius says that they should not be so high as to intercept the statues of the gods, and he gives the relative heights of those used for different divinities. Thus, he says, those of Jupiter and the celestial gods are to be the highest; next, those of Vesta and the terrestrial gods; those of the sea gods are to be a little lower, and so on. On festivals they were decorated with such flowers and leaves as were sacred to the particular divinity. But besides this casual decoration, the ancient altars furnish us with some of the most elegant bassi rilievi and foliage ornaments that are known. According to Vitruvius, their fronts were directed towards the east, though very frequently but little regard was paid to their position, as they were occasionally placed under the peristyle of a temple, and not unfrequently in the open air. In the larger temples were often three different altars. The first was in the most sacred part, in front of the statue of the god; the second before the door of the temple; and the third (called *anclabris*) was portable, and on it the offerings and sacred vessels were placed.

The altars of the Catholic church are either attached or isolated. The former generally stand against a wall, and are so decorated as to appear quite independent of it. The decorations are either of painting or sculpture, or both. The isolated altar has no sort of connection with any part either of the building or of its decorations. The high altar is always isolated, whether placed at the end of the church or in its centre. Whatever the situation of the high altar, it should be grand and simple: it should be raised on a platform, with steps on every side. The table itself is usually in the form of an antique sarcophagus. The altar of the Protestant churches of England is generally only an oak table, covered with a white cloth, and but little ornamented either above or on the sides. In country churches we sometimes find superadded as an ornament, to show, we suppose, that painting may be tolerated in Protestant worship, the figures

> " Of Moses and Aaron stuck close by the wall,
> To hold the commandments for fear they should fall."

The fact is, the Church of England is so overawed by sectaries, that she is afraid of doing anything congenial to the feelings of a polished mind as respects the decoration of her churches, which are in the new examples built by the commissioners more than ever stript of all elegant accompaniments; a practice which turns our churches into barns rather than temples of the Most High.

The altars of the Greek church, though in other respects the religion vies in splendour with the Romish church, are destitute of painted or sculptured ornament; and in Calvinistic churches the name as well as the uses of an altar are unknown either as an appendage or a decoration.

ALTAR-PIECE. The entire decorations of an altar.

ALTAR SCREEN. The back of an altar, or the partition by which the choir is separated from the presbytery and Lady chapel. The date of its introduction into English churches we believe to have been about the close of the thirteenth century. It is generally of stone, and composed of the richest tabernacle work, of niches, finials, and pedestals, supporting statues of the tutelary saints. Those to the high altars of Winchester Cathedral, of St. Alban's Abbey, and of New College, are fine examples. Many were destroyed at the Reformation, or filled up with plaster and covered with wainscot. In all altar screens a door is placed on each side for the officiating priests, whose vestments were deposited in an apartment behind the altar screen.

ALTO RILIEVO. See RILIEVO.

ALYPIUS. See ARCHITECTS, list of, 53.

AMBITUS. A space which surrounded a tomb, and was held sacred. In descriptions of subterranean tombs, it denoted a small niche made in the wall for the reception of an urn or body. When the corpse was placed in it, to the mouth of the niche a slab was fixed, so fitted and cemented as to prevent noisome effluvia. The slabs were sometimes inscribed with the name and quality of the party. If they received an urn, either upon that or over the niche the inscription was placed. Much decoration was occasionally used in the recesses themselves.

AMBO. (Gr. ἀμβων.) The elevated place or pulpit in the early Christian churches, which, according to Ciampini, fell into disuse about the beginning of the fourteenth century.

The last erected ambo in Rome is supposed to have been that of S. Pancrazio, on which appears the date of 1249. It was an oblong enclosure, with steps usually at the two ends. Two ambones are described by Eustace in the cathedral at Salerno. They are placed on each side of the nave before the steps of the chancel. They are both of marble, and the largest is covered with mosaic and supported by twelve Corinthian granite columns.

AMBULATORY. (Lat.) A sheltered place for exercise in walking; a cloister; a gallery.

AMBULATIO. (Lat.) See PTEROMA.

AMMANATI. See ARCHITECTS, list of, 239.

AMPHIPROSTYLE. (Gr. αμφι, both or double, προ, before, στυλος, a column.) A term applied to a temple having a portico or porch in the rear as well as in the front, but without columns at the sides. This species of temple never exceeded the use of four columns in the front and four in the rear. It differed from the temple in *antis*, in having columns instead of antæ at the angles of the portico. See TEMPLE.

AMPHITHEATRE. (Gr. αμφι, about, and θεατρον, a theatre.) An edifice formed by the junction of two theatres at the proscenium, so as to have seats all round the periphery, a contrivance by which all the spectators, being ranged about on seats rising the one above the other, saw equally well what passed on the arena or space enclosed by the lowest range of seats, whose wall towards the arena was called the *podium*. The origin of the amphitheatre seems to have been among the Etruscans, to whom also are attributed the first exhibitions of gladiatorial fights. It was from this people that the Romans acquired a taste for such shows, which they communicated to every nation which became subject to their dominion. Athenæus says, " Romani ubi primum ludos facere cœperunt, huic asciti artifices ab Etruscis civitatibus fuerunt, sero autem ludi omnes qui nunc a Romanis celebrari solent sunt instituti." *Lib. iv. c.* 17. The most extraordinary edifice remaining in Rome, we may indeed say in the world, is the amphitheatre generally called the Coliseum. It was commenced by Vespatian, and completed by Titus his son. Words are inadequate to convey a satisfactory idea of its stupendous and gigantic dimensions. Ammianus says that it was painful to the eye to scan its summit : " ad cujus summitatem ægrè visio humana conscendit." Martial, in one of his epigrams, says,

" Omnis Cæsareo cedat labor amphitheatro,
　　Unum pro cunctis fama loquatur opus."

The greater axis of the ellipsis on which it is planned is about 627 feet, and the lesser 520 feet, the height of the outer wall about 166 feet, such wall being decorated by the Doric, Ionic, and Corinthian Orders, and pierced with arcades between the columns. Covering five English acres and a quarter, it was capable of containing the vast number of 87,000 persons. It has suffered much from having been used actually as a quarry for many of the modern edifices of the city; but in the present day its preservation is strictly attended to by the papal government. A description of this building has been given in p. 94, *et seq.* Besides the Coliseum, there were three other amphitheatres in Rome : the Amphitheatrum Castrense, on the Esquiline, built probably by Tiberius ; that of Statilius Taurus, and that built by Trajan in the Campus Martius. The other principal amphitheatres were those of Otricoli ; on the Garigliano, of brick : Puzzuoli, Capua, Verona, at the foot of Monte Casino, Pæstum, Syracuse, Agrigentum, Catanea, Argos, Corinth, Pola in Istria (see *fig.* 127.), Hipella in Spain, Nismes, Arles, Frejus, Saintes, and Autun. This last has four stories, in that respect like the Coliseum. That which remains in the most perfect condition is at Verona ; its age has not been accurately determined, some placing it in the age of Augustus, and others in that of Maximian ; of these, Maffei thinks the first date too early, and the latter too late. The silence of Pliny upon it seems to place it after the time of his writing. In the reign of Gallienus, it was not only built, but began to suffer from dilapidation, for many of the stones belonging to it are found in the walls of Verona, which walls were erected in the time of that emperor. Many of these were keystones, and the numbers cut upon them still remain. From the silence of authors that it was the work of any of the emperors, it seems probable that, like that at Capua, it was erected at the expense of the citizens. The length is about 514 feet, and the breadth about 410 ; the long diameter of the arena 242 feet, the short diameter 147 feet. The audience part or *visorium* contained forty-seven tiers of seats, and the building was capable of containing about 22,000 seated spectators. In the profile of the walls of this amphitheatre the diminution in thickness upwards is made on the inside, which is also the case in that at Pola. In the Coliseum, the diminution is on the outside. The amphitheatre at Nismes contained about 17,000 persons, and was about 400 feet in length and 320 feet in breadth.

The first amphitheatres, as we learn from Pliny, were constructed of wood, and usually placed in the Campus Martius, or in some place out of the city. Accidents occurring from their insecurity, they were abandoned for the more substantial species of fabric whereof we have been speaking. The first person who is said to have erected an amphi-

theatre in Rome was Caius Scribonius Curio, on the occasion of the games he gave to the people at the funeral obsequies of his father.   Determined to surpass all that had hitherto been seen, he constructed two theatres of wood, back to back, which, after the theatrical representations had been finished, were turned round with the spectators in them, leaving the stages and scenery behind.   By their opposite junction, they formed a perfect amphitheatre, in which the people were gratified with a show of gladiators.

The part in which the gladiators fought was called the *arena*, from being usually covered with sand to absorb the blood spilt in the conflicts, for which it was used.   It was encompassed by a wall called the *podium*, fifteen or sixteen feet high, immediately round which sat the senators and ambassadors.   As in the theatres, the seats rose at the back of each other ; fourteen rows back from the podium all round being allotted to the equites, and the remainder to the public generally, who sat on the bare stone, cushions being provided for the senators and equites.   Though at most times open to the sky, there were contrivances for covering the whole space with an awning.   The avenues by which the people entered and retired were many in number, and were called *vomitoria*.   The reader who wishes for further information on this subject may consult with advantage Maffei, *Degli Amfiteatri*, and the section on amphitheatres in his excellent and learned work, *Verona illustrata*.

ANAMORPHOSIS. (Gr. *ανα*, backward, and *μορφη*, form.)   A term employed in perspective to denote a drawing executed in such a manner that when viewed in the common way it presents a confused and distorted image of the thing represented, or an image of something entirely different ; but when viewed from a particular point, or as reflected by a curved mirror, or through a polyhedron, it recovers its proportions and presents a distinct representation of the object.

ANCHOR.   In decoration, an ornament shaped similarly to an anchor or arrow head.   It is used with the egg ornament (see page 806. *fig.* 867.) to decorate or enrich mouldings. By some it is called a tongue, from its supposed resemblance to the forked tongue of a serpent.   It is used in all the orders, but only applied to the moulding called the echinus or quarter round.

ANCONES. (Gr. *αγκων*, the joint of the elbow.)   The trusses or consoles sometimes employed in the dressings or antepagmenta of apertures, serving as an apparent support to the cornice of them at the flanks.   In ancient doors the ancones were sometimes broader at the top than at the bottom, and were not in contact with the flanks of the architrave, but situated a small distance from them.   The term is also used to signify the corners or quoins of walls, cross beams, or rafters.

ANDREA DI PISA.   See ARCHITECTS, list of, 130.

ANDRON. (Gr. *ανηρ*.)   In ancient architecture, the apartment appropriated to the reception of the male branches of the establishment, and always in the lower part of the house, the *gynæcia*, or women's apartments, being in the upper part.

ANDRONICUS.   See ARCHITECTS, list of, 23.

ANDROUET DU CERCEAU.   See ARCHITECTS, list of, 246.

ANGLE. (Lat. Angulus.)   The mutual inclination of two lines meeting in a point, called indifferently the angular point, vertex, or point of concourse : the two lines are called legs.   See GEOMETRY, page 262.

ANGLE BAR.   In joinery, the upright bar at the angle of a polygonal window.

ANGLE BEAD, or STAFF BEAD.   A vertical bead, commonly of wood, fixed to an exterior angle and flush with the intended surface of the plaster on both sides, for the purpose of securing the angle against accident, serving also as a guide for floating the plaster. The section of these beads is about three quarters of a circle, with a projecting part from the other quarter, by means whereof they are made fast to the wood bricks, plugging, or bond timbers.   Angle beads of wood round the intradosses of circular arches are difficult to bend without cutting or steaming them.   The former has a very unsightly appearance, and the latter method is at once inconvenient and troublesome.   The plaster itself is the best material in this case, and at the height generally placed will be out of the reach of accident.   In good finishings corner beads which are unsightly should not be used, but the plaster should be well guaged and brought to an arris.

ANGLE BRACE.   In carpentry, a piece of timber fixed to the two extremities of a piece of quadrangular framing, making it partake of the form of an octagon.   This piece is also called an *angle tie* and a *diagonal tie*.   By the use of this piece wall plates are frequently braced.   In constructing a well hole of a circular section through a roof or floor for a skylight, &c. the framing is first made in a quadrangular form ; braces are then fixed opposite to each angle, and the aperture becomes an octagon ; finally, pieces are fixed at each angle of the octagon, meeting each other in the middle of its sides, so as to transform the section of the aperture into a circle.

ANGLE BRACKET.   A bracket placed in the vertex of an angle, and not at right angles with the sides.   See BRACKETING.

ANGLE CAPITAL.   In ancient Greek architecture, the Ionic capitals used to the flank

columns which have one of their volutes placed at an angle of 135° with the planes of the front and returning frieze. As an example may be given the angle capitals of the temple of Minerva Polias at Athens. This term is also applied to the modern Ionic capital, in which the whole of the four volutes have an angular direction.

ANGLE CHIMNEY. A chimney placed in the angle of a room.

ANGLE MODILLION. A modillion placed in a direction parallel to a diagonal drawn through a cornice at its mitring. It is an abuse seen only in the buildings erected during the decline of Roman architecture, as in the ruins of Balbec and Palmyra, and in the palace of the Emperor Dioclesian at Spalatro.

ANGLE OF VISION. (See PERSPECTIVE, p. 769, *et seq.*) The angle under which an object or objects are seen, and upon which their apparent magnitudes depend. In practical perspective it should not exceed sixty degrees.

ANGLE OF A WALL. The angle contained by the vertical planes of two walls which form the angle of the building. The term is sometimes used to denote the line in which the two sides of the angle meet, which by workmen is commonly called the *arris :* the arris however is not the angle, but the line of concourse formed by the two sides or planes which contain the angle.

ANGLE RAFTER. The piece of timber in a hipped roof placed in the line of concourse of the two inclined planes forming the hip. It is more often called a hip rafter. See HIP and CARPENTRY, page 607.

ANGLE RIB. A piece of timber of a curved form placed between those two parts of a coved or arched ceiling or vault which form an angle with each other so as to range with the common ribs on each side or return part.

ANGLE STAFF. See ANGLE BEAD.

ANGLE STONES. A term used by some authors to denote *quoins*.

ANGLE TIE. See ANGLE BRACE.

ANGULAR CAPITAL. See CAPITAL.

ANNUITIES. See Book IV.

ANNULAR MOULDINGS. Generally those having vertical sides and horizontal circular sections.

ANNULAR VAULT. A vault springing from two walls each circular on the plan; such as that in the temple of Bacchus at Rome.

ANNULET. (Lat. Annulus.) A small fillet whose horizontal section is circular. The neck or under side of the Doric capital is decorated with these thin fillets, listels, or bands, whose number varies in different examples. Thus in the Doric of the theatre of Marcellus there are three, whilst in the great temple at Pæstum they are four in number, and in other cases as many as five are used.

ANTA, Æ, plur. (Lat. Anta.) The joints or square posts supporting the lintels of doors. The term antæ we think only applicable to pilasters or pillars attached to a wall, though some authors, as Perault, have thought otherwise. Vitruvius calls square pilasters when insulated *parastatæ*. There are three kinds of antæ : those of porches or jamb ornaments; angular antæ, being such as show two faces on the walls of a temple; and those on the longitudinal walls of its cell. Antæ are only found in temples as wings to the ends of the walls of the pronaos to give a finish to the terminations the ends of the walls would otherwise present. It might have been this view which led the Greeks to treat them rather as distinct objects than to assimilate their finishings to those of columns. Considered as pilasters, the reader is referred to p. 857, *et seq.*, where the diminutions and capitals are fully considered. The latter were never made by the Greeks like those of the accompanying columns. The pilasters in Roman architecture differ only from the column in being square instead of round. A rule in the use of antæ was, that their projection should always be equal to that at least of the mouldings used on them. Some beautiful examples of antæ capitals exist in the temple of Minerva Polias and the temple of Apollo Didymæus in Ionia.

ANTE-CHAMBER or ANTE-ROOM. An apartment through which access is obtained to another chamber or room. One in which servants wait and strangers are detained till the person to be spoken with is at leisure. In the distribution of many houses the peculiarity of the plan forces upon the architect the introduction of ante-rooms: in most cases, indeed, they add both elegance and dignity to a design.

ANTE-COUR. A French term, sometimes however used by English authors. It is the approach to the principal court of a house, and very frequently serves for communication with the kitchen, cellar, stables, &c.

ANTEFIXÆ. (Lat. anti and figo.) The ornaments of lions' and other heads below the eaves of a temple, through perforations in which, usually at the mouth, the water is cast away from the eaves. By some this term is used to denote the upright ornaments above the eaves in ancient architecture, which concealed the ends of the *harmi* or joint tiles.

ANTEPAGMENTA. (Lat.) In ancient architecture, the jambs or moulded architraves of a door. The lintel returning at the ends with similar mouldings down upon the antepagmenta was called supercilium.

Anterides. In ancient architecture, buttresses or counterforts for the support of a wall. The Italians call them *speroni* (spurs).

Anthemius. See Architects, list of, 61.

Anticum. (Lat.) A porch to a front door, as distinguished from posticum, which is the porch to a door in the rear of a building. It was the space also between the front columns of the portico and the wall of the cella. The word has been sometimes improperly used for *anta*.

Antique. A term applied to pieces of ancient art by the Greeks and Romans of the classical age.

Antiquarium. Among the ancients an apartment or cabinet in which they kept their ancient books and vases.

Antistates. See Architects, list of, 15.

Antoine. See Architects, list of, 306.

Antoninus. See Architects, list of, 50.

Antonio Fiorentino. See Architects, list of, 228.

Apartment. (Lat. partimentum.) A space enclosed by walls and a ceiling, which latter distinguishes it from a court or area. The distribution of apartments of a building has already been treated of in this work. See p. 792, *et seq.*

Aperture. (Lat. aperio.) An opening through any body. In a wall it has usually three straight sides, two whereof are perpendicular to the horizon, and the third parallel to it, connecting the lower ends of the vertical sides. The materials forming the vertical sides are called *jambs*, and the lower level side is called the *sill*, and the upper part the *head*. This last is either a curved or flat arch. Apertures are made for entrance, light, or ornament. In Greek and Egyptian architecture, but especially in the latter, the jambs incline towards each other. Sometimes apertures are made circular, elliptical, or portions of those figures. " Apertures," says Sir Henry Wotton, " are inlets for air and light ; they should be as few in number, and as moderate in dimensions, as may possibly consist with other due respects ; for, in a word, all opening are weakenings. They should not approach too near the angles of the walls ; for it were indeed a most essential solecism to weaken that part which must strengthen all the rest."

Apiary. (Lat. apis.) A place for keeping beehives. Sometimes this is a small house with openings for the bees in front, and a door behind, which is kept locked for security. Sometimes it is an area wherein each particular beehive is chained down to a post and padlocked.

Apodyterium. (ἀποδύσθαι, Gr., to strip oneself.) The apartment at the entrance of the ancient baths, or in the Palæstra, where a person took off his dress, whether for bathing or gymnastic exercises. In the baths of Nero, these apartments were small, but in those of Caracalla the apodyterium was a magnificent room with columns and other decorations.

Apophyge. (Gr., signifying flight.) That part of a column between the upper fillet or amulet on the base and the cylindrical part of the shaft of a column, usually moulded into a hollow or cavetto, out of which the column seems as it were to fly or escape upwards. The French call it *congé*, as it were, leave to go.

Apollodorus. See Architects, list of, 47.

Apotheca. (Gr.) A storehouse or cellar in which the ancient Greeks deposited their oil, wine, and the like.

Apron, or **Pitching Piece.** An horizontal piece of timber, in wooden double-flighted stairs, for supporting the carriage pieces or rough strings and joistings in the half spaces or landings. The apron pieces should be firmly wedged into the wall. See Staircases, p. 647, *et seq.*

Apsis, or **Absis.** (Gr., signifying an arch.) A term in ecclesiastical architecture, denoting that part of the church wherein the clergy was seated or the altar placed. It was so called from being usually domed or vaulted, and not, as Isidorus imagines, from being the lightest part (apta). The apsis was either circular or polygonal, and domed over ; it consisted of two parts, the altar and the presbytery or sanctuary. At the middle of the semicircle was the throne of the bishop, and at the centre of the diameter was placed the altar, towards the nave, from which it was separated by an open balustrade or railing. On the altar was placed the ciborium and cup. The throne of the bishop having been anciently called by this name, some have thought that thence this part of the edifice derived its name ; but the converse is the fact. The *apsis gradata* implied more particularly the bishop's throne being raised by steps above the ordinary stalls. This was sometimes called *exedra*, and in later times *tribune*.

Aqueduct. (Lat. aquæ ductus.) A conduit or channel for conveying water from one place to another, more particularly applied to structures for the purpose of conveying the water of distant springs across valleys, for the supply of large cities. The largest and most magnificent aqueducts with the existence of which we are acquainted were constructed by

the Romans, and many of their ruins in Italy and other countries of Europe still attest the power and industry of that extraordinary nation. The most ancient was that of Appius Claudius, which was erected in the 442d year of the city, and conveyed the Aqua Appia to Rome, from a distance of 11,190 Roman paces (a pace being 58·219 English inches), and was carried along the ground, or by subterranean lines, about 11,000 paces, about 190 of which were erected on arches. The next, in order of time, was the Anio Vetus, begun by M. Curius Dentatus, about the year of Rome 481. The water was collected from the springs about Tivoli ; it was about 43,000 paces in length. In the 608th year of the city, the works of the Anio Vetus and Aqua Appia had fallen into decay, and much of the water had been fraudulently abstracted by individuals, the prætor Martius was therefore empowered to take measures for increasing the supply. The result of this was the Aqua Martia, the most wholesome water with which Rome was supplied. It was brought from the neighbourhood of Subiaco, twenty miles above Tivoli, and was 61,710 Roman paces (about 61 miles), whereof 7463 paces were above ground, and the remainder under ground. A length of 463 paces, where it crossed brook and valleys, was supported on arches. To supply this in dry seasons, was conducted into it another stream of equal goodness by an aqueduct 800 paces long. About nineteen years after this was completed, the Aqua Tepula was brought in, supplied also from the Anio ; but not more than 2000 paces in length. In the reign of Augustus, Agrippa collected some more springs into the Aqua Tepula, but the latter water flowing in a separate channel, it preserved its name. This was 15,426 paces long, 7000 above ground, and the remainder of the length on arcades. To this was given by Agrippa the name of Aqua Julia. In the year 719 of the city, Agrippa restored the dilapidated aqueducts of Appius, of Martius, and of the Anio Vetus, at his own expense, besides erecting fountains in the city. The Aqua Virgo, which received its name from a girl having pointed out to some soldiers the sources of the stream from which it was collected, was brought to Rome by an aqueduct 14,105 paces in length, 12,865 whereof were under ground, and 700 on arches, the remainder being above ground. The Aqua Alsietina, called also Augusta, was 22,172 paces from its source to the city, and 358 paces of it were on arcades. The seven aqueducts above mentioned being found, in the time of Caligula, unequal to the supply of the city, this emperor, in the second year of his reign, began two others, which were finished by Claudius, and opened in the year of the city 803. The first was called Aqua Claudia, and the second Anio Novus, to distinguish it from one heretofore mentioned. The first was 46,406 Roman paces, of which 10,176 were on arcades, and the rest subterranean. The Anio Novus was 58,700 paces in length ; 9400 whereof were above ground, 6491 on arches, and the rest subterranean. Some of the arches of these are 100 Roman feet high. All the aqueducts we have mentioned were on different levels, and distributed accordingly to those parts of the city which suited their respective elevations. The following is the order of their heights, the highest being the Anio Novus, 159 feet above level of Tiber : Aqua Claudia, 149 feet ; Aqua Julia, 129 feet ; Aqua Tepula, Aqua Martia, 125 feet ; Anio Vetus, Aqua Virgo, 34 feet ; Aqua Appia, 27 feet ; and the Aqua Alsietina on the lowest level. The Tiber at Rome being 91·5 feet above the level of the Mediterranean, the mean fall of these aqueducts has been ascertained to be about 0·132 English inches for each Roman pace (58·219 English inches), or 1 in 441. Vitruvius directs a fall of 1 in 200, but Scamozzi says the practice of the Romans was 1 in 500. The quantity of water furnished by six of the aqueducts, as given by Frontinus from a measurement at the head of each aqueduct, is as follows : —

Anio Vetus	-	-	-	- 4398 quinariæ.
Aqua Martia	-	-	-	- 4690
Aqua Virgo	-	-	-	- 2524
Aqua Julia	-	-	-	- 1368
Aqua Claudia	-	-	-	- 4607
Anio Novus	-	-	-	- 4738

The whole supply is given as 14,018 quinariæ, after much fraudulent diversion of the water by individuals ; but the diminished quantity is supposed to have been 27,743,100 English cubic feet, or, estimating the population of Rome at one million of inhabitants, 27·74 cubic feet per diem for each inhabitant.

The aqueducts required constant repairs, from the nature of their construction, especially those on arches. The spaces between the piers varied much in width, and necessarily in height. Some of the arcades are as much as 27 feet in diameter.

There are remains of Roman aqueducts in other parts of Europe, even more magnificent than those we have mentioned. One, or the ruins of one, still exists at Metz, and another at Segovia in Spain, with two rows of arcades, one above the other. This last is about 100 feet high, and passes over the greater part of the houses of the city. The most remarkable aqueduct of modern times was that constructed by the order of Louis XIV. for conveying the waters of the Eure to Versailles. It is 4400 feet in length, and

contains 242 arcades, each of 50 feet span. The introduction of water pipes has now superseded the erection of these expensive structures.

ARABESQUE. A building after the Arabian style. See Moresque and Saracenic Architecture, pp. 50, *et seq.* The term is more commonly used to denote that sort of ornament in Moresque architecture consisting of intricate rectilinear and curvilinear compartments and mosaics which adorn the walls, pavements, and ceilings of Arabian and Saracenic buildings. It is capricious, fantastic, and imaginative, consisting of fruits, flowers, and other objects, to the exclusion in pure arabesques of the figures of animals, which the religion forbade. This sort of ornament, however, did not originate with the Arabians; it was understood and practised by the ancients at a very early period. Foliage and griffins, with ornaments not very dissimilar to those of the Arabians, were frequently employed on the friezes of temples, and on many of the ancient Greek vases, on the walls of the baths of Titus at Pompeii, and at many other places. To Raffaele, in more modern times, we are indebted for the most elaborate and beautiful examples of the style, which he even dignified, and left nothing to be desired in it. Since the time of that master it has been practised with varying and inferior degrees of merit, especially by the French in the time of Louis XVI. Arabesques lose their character when applied to large objects, neither should they be employed where gravity in the style is to be preserved.

ARABO-TEDESCO. (It. Arabo; and Tedesco, German.) A style consisting of a mixture of Moorish or Low Grecian with German Gothic. It is a term used chiefly by the Italians. An example of this style may be quoted in the baptistery at Pisa (*fig.* 152.), erected by Dioti Salvi in 1152. It is a circular edifice, with an arcade in the second order composed of columns with Corinthian capitals and plain round arches. Between each arch rises a Gothic pinnacle, and above it is finished by sharp pediments enriched with foliage, terminating in a trefoil. See Byzantine and Romanesque Architecture, p. 107, *et seq.*

ARÆOSTYLE. (Gr. αραιος, wide, and στυλος, column.) One of the five proportions used by the ancients for regulating the intercolumniations or intervals between the columns in porticoes and colonnades. Vitruvius does not determine precisely its measure in terms of the diameter of the column. His commentators have tried to supply the deficiency; and, following the progression observable in the intercolumniations he does describe, each of which increases by a semidiameter, the aræostyle would be three diameters and a half. Perrault, in his translation of Vitruvius, proposes that the interval be made equal to four diameters, which is the interval now usually assigned to it. It is only, or rather ought only, to be used with the Tuscan order.

ARÆOSYSTYLE. (Gr. αραιος, wide, συν, with, στυλος, a column.) A term used by the French architects to denote the method of proportioning the intervals between columns coupled or ranged in pairs, as invented by Perrault, and introduced in the principal façade of the Louvre. It was also adopted by Sir Christopher Wren in the west front of St. Paul's.

ARC. In geometry, a portion of a circle or other curve line. The arc of a circle is the measure of the angle formed by two straight lines drawn from its extremities to the centre of the circle.

ARC-BOUTANT. (Fr.) An arch-formed buttress, much employed in sacred edifices built in the pointed style, as also in other edifices, and commonly called a *flying buttress*, whose object is to counteract the thrust of the main vault of the edifice: it is also called *arched buttress* and *arched butment*. It is no invention of the moderns, as the use of it is found in the baths of Dioclesian.

ARC DOUBLEAU. (Fr.) An arch forming a projection before the sofite of a main arch or vault, in the same manner as a pilaster breaks before the face of a wall.

ARCADE. (Fr.) A series of apertures or recesses with arched ceilings or sofites. But the word is often vaguely and indefinitely used. Some so designate a single-arched aperture or enclosure, which is more properly a *vault*; others use it for the space covered by a continued vault or arch supported on piers or columns; and, besides these, other false meanings are given to it instead of that which we have assigned. Behind the arcade is generally a walk or ambulatory, as in Covent Garden, where the term piazza is ignorantly applied to the walks under the arcade instead of to the whole *place* (*piazza*) or square.

The piers of arcades may be decorated with columns, pilasters, niches, and apertures of different forms. The arches themselves are sometimes turned with rock-worked, and at other times with plain rustic, arch stones or voussoirs, or with a moulded archivolt, springing from an impost or platband; and sometimes, though a practice not to be recommended, from columns. The keystones are generally curved in the form of a console, or sculptured with some device. Scamozzi made the size of his piers less, and varied his imposts or archivolts, in proportion to the delicacy of the orders he employed; but Vignola made his piers always of the same proportion. See Book III. Chap. I. Sections 10 and 12.

ARCÆ. In ancient Roman architecture, the gutters of the cavedium; arca signifying a beam of wood with a groove or channel in it.

ARCELLA. (Lat.) In mediæval architecture, a cheese room.

ARCH. A mechanical arrangement of blocks of any hard material disposed in the line of some curve, and supporting one another by their mutual pressure. The arch itself is formed of *voussoirs* or arch stones cut in the shape of a truncated wedge, the uppermost whereof is called the *keystone*. The seams or planes, in which two adjacent voussoirs are united, are called the *joints*. The solid extremities on or against which the arch rests are called the *abutments*. The lower or under line of each arch stone is called the *intrados*, and the superior or upper line the *extrados*. The distance between the piers or abutments is the *span* of the arch, and that from the level line of the springing to the intrados its *height*. The subject of arches forms Sect. 8. Book II. Chap. I. of this work, to which the reader is referred for the theory and construction of the arch.

The forms of arches employed in the different styles of English architecture will be found described under the several heads. See p. 172, *et seq.*

ARCHIAS. See ARCHITECTS, list of, 17.

ARCHITECT. (Gr. αρχος and τεκτων, chief of the works.) A person competent to design and superintend the execution of any building. The knowledge he ought to possess forms the subject of this work; whatever more he may acquire will be for the advantage of his employers; and when we say that the whole of the elements which this work contains should be well known and understood by him, we mean it as a *minimum* of his qualifications. To this we may add, that with the possessions indicated, devotedness, faithfulness, and integrity towards his employer, with kindness and urbanity to those whose lot it is to execute his projects, not however without resolution to check the dishonesty of a builder, should he meet with such, will insure a brilliant and happy career in his profession. We here insert a

Brief Synoptical List of the principal Architects known in History, and their chief Works, from Milizia and other Authorities.

BEFORE CHRIST.

No. in Gloss.	Name of Architect.	Century.	Principal Works.
1	Theodorus of Samos.	7th.	Labyrinth at Lemnos; some buildings at Sparta and the temple of Jupiter at Samos.
2	Hermogenes of Alabanda.	—	Temple of Bacchus at Teos and that of Diana at Magnesia.
3	Agamedes and Trophonius of Delphi.	—	Temple of Apollo at Delphi; a temple dedicated to Neptune near Mantinæa.
4	Demetrius of Ephesus.	6th.	Continuation of the temple of Diana, which had been begun by Chersiphron.
5	Eupalinus of Megara.	—	Aqueduct, with many other edifices, at Samos.
6	Mandrocles of Samos.	—	Wooden bridge over the Thracian Bosphorus, erected by the command of Darius.
7	Chirosophus of Crete.	—	Temple of Ceres and Proserpine, another of the Paphian Venus, and one of Apollo; all at Tegea.
8	Pytheus of Priene.	5th.	Mausoleum of Artemisia in Caria; design for the temple of Pallas at Priene. In the former he was assisted by Statirus.
9	Spentharus of Corinth.	—	Rebuilt the temple of Apollo at Delphi, which had been destroyed by fire.
10	Agaptos of Elis.	—	Portico at Elis.
11	Libon of Elis.	—	Temple of Jupiter Olympius at Olympia.
12	Ictinus of Athens.	—	Parthenon at Athens; temple of Ceres and Proserpine at Eleusis; temple of Apollo Epicurius in Arcadia.
13	Callicrates of Athens.	—	Assisted Ictinus in the erection of the Parthenon.
14	Mnesicles of Athens.	—	Propylea of the Parthenon.
15	Antistates of Athens.	—	A temple of Jupiter at Athens.
16	Scopas of Greece.	—	One side of the tomb of Mausolus; a column of the temple at Ephesus.

BEFORE CHRIST.

No. in Gloss.	Name of Architect.	Century.	Principal Works.
17	Archias of Corinth.	5th.	Many temples and other edifices, at Syracuse.
18	Callias of Aradus.	—	Temples, &c., at Rhodes.
19	Ayclius of Aradus.	—	Temple of the Ionian Æsculapius.
20	Mnesthes.	—	Temple of Apollo at Magnesia.
21	Cleomenes of Athens.	4th.	Plan of the city of Alexandria in Egypt.
22	Dinocrates of Macedonia.	—	Rebuilt the temple of Diana at Ephesus; engaged on works at Alexandria; was the author of the proposition to transform Mount Athos into a colossal figure.
23	Andronicus of Athens.	—	Tower of the Winds at Athens.
24	Callimachus of Corinth.	—	Reputed inventor of the Corinthian order.
25	Sostratus of Gnidus.	—	The Pharos of Alexandria.
26	Philo of Athens.	—	Enlarged the arsenal and the Piræus at Athens; erected the great theatre, rebuilt by order of Adrian.
27	Eupolemus of Argos.	—	Several temples and a theatre at Argos.
28	Phæax of Agrigentum.	3d.	Various buildings at Agrigentum.
29	Cossutius of Rome.	2d.	Design for the temple of Jupiter Olympius at Athens.
30	Hermodorus of Salamis.	—	Temple of Jupiter Stator in the Forum at Rome; temple of Mars in the Circus Flaminius.
31	Caius Mutius of Rome.	—	Temple of Honour and Virtue near the trophies of Marius at Rome.
32	Valerius of Ostia.	—	Several amphitheatres with roofs.
33	Batrachus of Laconia.	1st.	These two architects built several temples at Rome. The name of the first (βατραχος), signifies a frog; and that of the latter (σαυρος) a lizard; and they perpetuated their names on some of the works by the allegorical representation of these two animals sculptured upon them. The churches of St. Eusebius and of St. Lorenzo fuori le Murà, at Rome, still contain some columns whose pedestals are sculptured with a lizard and a frog.
34	Saurus of Laconia.	—	
35	Dexiphanes of Cyprus.	—	Rebuilt the Pharos at Alexandria, at the command of Cleopatra, the other having fallen down.
36	Cyrus of Rome.	—	Architect to Cicero.
37	Postumius of Rome.	—	Many works at Rome and Naples.
38	Cocceius Auctus of Rome.	—	Grotto of Puzzuoli; grotto of Cumæ, near the lake now called Lago d'Averno.
39	Fussitius of Rome.	—	Several buildings at Rome; the first Roman who wrote on architecture.

AFTER CHRIST.

No. in Gloss.	Name of Architect.	Century.	Principal Works.
40	Vitruvius Pollio of Fano.	1st.	Basilica Justitiæ at Fano. A great writer on architecture.
41	Vitruvius Cerdo of Verona.	—	Triumphal arch at Verona.
42	Celer and	—	Golden house of Nero.
43	Severus of Rome.		

AFTER CHRIST.

No. in Gloss.	Name of Architect.	Century.	Principal Works.
44	Rabirius of Rome.	1st.	Palace of Domitian on Mount Palatine.
45	Mustius of Rome.	—	Temple of Ceres at Rome.
46	Frontinus of Rome.	2d.	He has left a work on aqueducts.
47	Apollodorus of Damascus.	—	Forum Trajani at Rome; a bridge over the Danube in Lower Hungary.
48	Lacer of Rome.	—	A bridge over the Tagus in Spain: a temple now dedicated to San Giuliano.
49	Detrianus of Rome.	—	Moles Hadriani and the Pons Aelius; now called the Castello and Ponte Sant' Angelo.
50	Antoninus, the Senator, of Rome.	—	Pantheon at Epidaurus; baths of Æsculapius.
51	Nicon of Pergamus.	—	Several fine works at Pergamus.
52	Metrodorus of Persia.	4th.	Many buildings in India, and some at Constantinople. The first known Christian architect.
53	Alypius of Antioch.	—	Employed by Julian to lay the foundation of a new temple at Jerusalem.
54	Cyriades of Rome.	5th.	A church and bridge.
55	Sennamar of Arabia.	—	Sedir and Khaovarnack, two celebrated palaces in Arabia.
56	Aloisius of Padua.	—	Assisted in the erection of the celebrated rotunda at Ravenna, the cupola of which is said to have been of one stone, 38 feet in diameter, and 15 feet thick.
57	St. Germain, bishop of Paris, of France.	6th.	Plan of the church of St. Germain at Paris, previously dedicated to St. Vincent; convent at St. Mans.
58	St. Avitus, bishop of Clermont, of France.	—	Church of Notre Dame du Port at Clermont; and that of St. Gènes at Thiers.
59	St. Agricola, bishop of Chalons, of France.	—	Cathedral of Chalons, with many other churches in his diocese.
60	Ætherius of Constantinople.	—	Part of the imperial palace, called Chalcis, at Constantinople.
61	Anthemius of Tralles, of Lydia.	—	St. Sophia at Constantinople.
62	Isidorus of Miletus.	—	Assisted Anthemius in the erection of the church of St. Sophia.
63	Chryses of Dara, of Persia.	—	Constructed the celebrated dykes along the Euripus, near Dara, to keep the river in its channel, and to keep out the sea. He was particularly excellent in hydraulic architecture.
64	Isidorus of Byzantium.	7th.	The city of Zenobia in Syria was the work of these two architects.
65	Johannes of Miletus.	—	
66	Saxulphus, abbot of Peterborough, afterwards made bishop of Lichfield, of England.	—	Built the monastery of Medeshampstede, afterwards called Peterborough.
67	Biscopius, Benedict, of England.	8th.	Conventual church of Wearmouth.
68	Egbert, archbishop of York, of England.	—	Rebuilt York Cathedral.
69	Albert, archbishop of York, of England.	—	Completed the building of York Cathedral under Egbert.
70	Eanbald, archbishop of York, of England.	—	Superintended the erection of York Cathedral, under his predecessor, Archbishop Albert.

			AFTER CHRIST.
No. in Gloss.	Name of Architect.	Century.	Principal Works.
71	Romualdus of France.	9th.	The cathedral of Rheims, the earliest example of Gothic architecture.
72	Tietland of Switzerland.	10th.	Convent of Einsidlen in Switzerland.
73	Tioda of Spain.	—	The palace of King Alphonso the Chaste, at Oviedo, now the episcopal palace; churches of St. Salvador, St. Michael, and St. Mary.
74	Ednoth, a monk of Worcester, of England.	—	Superintended the erection of the church and conventual offices of Rumsey Abbey.
75	Dunstan, archbishop of Canterbury, of England.	—	Built for himself a cell at Glastonbury Abbey, and was skilful in mechanics.
76	Ælfric, bishop of Crediton, of England.	—	Built part of Malmsbury Abbey Church, in the reign of Edgar.
77	Elphage, bishop of Winchester, of England.	—	Crypts of Winchester Cathedral.
78	Buschetto of Dulichium.	—	The cathedral or duomo of Pisa, the earliest example of the Lombard ecclesiastical style of architecture. It was built in 1016.
79	Aldhun, bishop of Durham, of England.	—	First cathedral church at Durham.
80	Pietro di Ustamber of Spain.	—	Cathedral of Chartres.
81	Lanfranc, archbishop of Canterbury, of England.	—	Choir of Canterbury Cathedral, burnt in 1174.
82	Remigius, bishop of Lincoln, of England.	11th.	Part of Lincoln Cathedral.
83	Carilepho, bishop of Durham, of England.	—	Began the cathedral church of Durham, on a plan which he had brought with him from France, when he was abbot of St. Vincent's in Normandy.
84	Walkelyn, bishop of Winchester, of England.	—	Said to have erected the oldest part of Winchester Cathedral.
85	Harlewin, abbot of Glastonbury, of England.	—	Rebuilt the abbey church of Glastonbury.
86	Mauritius, bishop of London, of England.	12th.	Built old St. Paul's, in 1033.
87	Gundulf, bishop of Rochester, of England.	—	Rochester Castle; White Tower of the Tower of London; rebuilt Rochester Cathedral.
88	Odo, prior of Croyland, of England.	—	Monastic church of Croyland. Arnold, a lay brother of the abbey, was employed under Odo as mason.
89	Ernulf, bishop of Rochester, of England.	—	Completed Gundulf's works at Rochester.
90	Alexander, bishop of Lincoln, of England.	—	Rebuilt Lincoln Cathedral.
91	Ranulf, or Ralf Flambard, bishop of Durham, of England.	—	Part of Durham Cathedral; Norham Castle.

AFTER CHRIST.

No. in Gloss.	Name of Architect.	Century.	Principal Works.
92	Henry of Blois, bishop of Winchester, of England.	12th.	A most celebrated architect; built the conventual churches of St. Cross and Rumsey in Hampshire.
93	Raimond of Montfort, of France.	—	Cathedral of Lugo.
94	Dioti Salvi of Italy.	—	Baptistery of Pisa, near the Campo Santo. His works were in the Lombard style, and were overloaded with minute ornaments.
95	Buono of Venice.	—	The tower of St. Mark at Venice, which is 330 feet high, and 40 feet square, built in 1154; a design for enlarging the church of Santa Maria Maggiore at Florence, of which the master walls still exist; the Vicaria and the Castello del' Uovo at Naples; church of St. Andrew at Pistola; la Casa della Città; campanile at Arezzo.
96	Sugger of St. Denis, of France.	—	Rebuilt the church and abbey of St. Denis, near Paris. He was distinguished by his perfection in the Gothic style.
97	Roger, archbishop of York, of England.	—	None of his works at this cathedral are now remaining.
98	Pietro di Cozzo da Limena of Italy.	—	The celebrated great hall at Padua, which is 256 feet long, 86 wide, and 72 high, built in 1172, burnt in 1420, and restored by two Venetian architects, Rizzo and Piccino; it was dismantled by a whirlwind in 1756, and again restored by Ferracina.
99	Wilhelm, or Guglielmo, of Germany.	—	The hanging tower at Pisa, built in 1174. Bonnano and Tomaso, two sculptors of Pisa, were also engaged upon it.
100	William of Sens, of England.	—	Canterbury Cathedral.
101	Sisseverne, monk of St. Alban's, of England.	—	St. Alban's Abbey Church.
102	Goldclif, Hugo de, of England.	—	St. Alban's Abbey.
103	Eversolt, Gilbert de, of England.	—	St. Alban's Abbey.
104	Baldwin, archbishop of Canterbury, of England.	—	Church at Hackinton, near Canterbury; and another at Lambeth.
105	Isembert of Xaintes, of France.	13th.	Bridges of Xaintes and Rochelle. Recommended by King John to the citizens of London as a proper person to finish London Bridge, begun by Peter of Colechurch.
106	Peter of Colechurch, of England.	—	Began London Bridge.
107	Bertram, canon of Salisbury, of England.	—	Overseer of the works of Salisbury Cathedral, under John and Henry III. Lord Orford supposes he was the same person who is called Elyas the Engineer, in a record of the reign of King John, relating to the repair of the king's houses at Westminster in 1209.
108	Fitz-Odo, Edward, of England.	—	Master of the works at Westminster under Henry III.
109	Eustachius, bishop of Ely, of England.	—	Gallery of Ely Cathedral.

AFTER CHRIST.

No. in Gloss.	Name of Architect.	Century.	Principal Works.
110	Robert of Lusarches, . of France.	13th.	Cathedral of Amiens, which was continued by Thomas de Cormont, and finished by his son Renauld.
111	Etienne de Bonneveil of France.	—	Church of the Trinity at Upsal, in Sweden, built after the model of that of Notre Dame at Paris.
112	Poore, bishop of Salisbury, of England.	—	Began Salisbury Cathedral.
113	Melsonby, bishop of Salisbury, of England.	—	Part of the cathedral of Durham.
114	Hoo, W. de, prior of Rochester, of England.	—	Choir of Rochester Cathedral.
115	Jean d'Echelles of France.	—	The portico of the cathedral of Notre Dame at Paris.
116	Pierre de Montereau of France.	—	The holy chapel at Vincennes; the refectory, dormitory, chapter-house, and chapel of Notre Dame, in the convent of St. Germain des Prez, near Paris.
117	Eudo de Montreuil of France.	—	Church of the Hotel Dieu at Paris; churches of St. Catherine du Val des Ecoliers, of St. Croix de la Bretonnerie, of Blancs Manteaux, of the Mathurins, of the Cordeliers, and of the Carthusians, at Paris. His style was unpleasing and heavy.
118	San Gonsalvo of Portugal.	—	Stone bridge at Tui.
119	San Pietro of Portugal.	—	Stone bridge called Il Ponte de Carez.
120	Lapo, or Jacopo, of Germany.	—	Convent and church of St. Francisco at Assisi; Palazzo del Barjello; and the façade of the archbishop's palace at Florence.
121	Nicola da Pisa, of Pisa.	—	Convent and church of the Dominicans at Bologna; church of San Micheli; some palaces; and the octagonal campanile of the Augustins at Pisa; the great church del Santo at Padua; church of Santa Maria at Orvietto; church de'i Fratri Minori at Venice; abbey and church in the plains of Taliacozzo, in the kingdom of Naples, built as a memorial of the victory obtained there by Charles I. over Conrad; plans of the church of San Giovanni at Sienna; of the church and convent della Santissima Trinita at Florence, and of those of the Dominicans at Arezzo, which were built by Maglione, his scholar; the repairs and alterations to the duomo at Volterra; the church and convent of the Dominicans at Viterbo. He intermixed the Gothic with the Lombard style.
122	Fuccio of Italy.	—	Church of Santa Maria sul Arno at Florence; the gates against the river Volturno at Capua; he finished the Vicaria and Castello dell' Uovo at Naples, which were commenced by Buono; he was distinguished for his skill in fortification.
123	Fenante Maglione, disciple of Nicola da Pisa.	—	Cathedral and church of San Lorenzo at Naples; the Palazzo Vecchio at Naples, in conjunction with Giovanni Benin Casa; the church and convent of the Dominicans at Arezzo.

AFTER CHRIST.

No. in Gloss.	Name of Architect.	Century.	Principal Works.
124	Masuccio of Naples.	13th.	Church of Santa Maria della Nuova at Naples; churches of S. Domenico Maggiore and S. Giovanni Maggiore; the archiepiscopal palace and Palazzo Colombrano at Naples.
125	Arnolfo Fiorentino of Florence.	14th.	The abbey and church of Santa Croce at Florence; the walls of the city, with the towers; Palazzo della Signoria, now called Il Palazzo Vecchio; model and plan of the cathedral of S. Maria del Fiore, to which the cupola was added by Brunelleschi; the church and Piazza San Micheli; Piazza dei Priori. His works were greatly admired.
126	Pietro Perez of Spain.	—	The cathedral of Toledo.
127	Robert de Courcy of France.	—	Rebuilt the cathedral at Rheims.
*128	Erwin von Steinbach of Germany.	—	Celebrated minster at Strasburg was superintended by him for twenty-eight years.
129	Giovanni da Pisa of Pisa.	—	Campo Santo, or public cemetery, at Pisa; the tribune of the Duomo in the same city; Castel Nuovo and the church of Santa Maria della Nuova at Naples; façade of the cathedral at Sienna: many churches and palaces at Arezzo and other towns in Italy. He was the first architect in the modern style of fortification, and his churches and other buildings possess great merit. He was the son and scholar of Nicola da Pisa.
130	Andrea da Pisa of Pisa.	—	Plan of the fortress della Scarperia at Mugello, at the foot of the Apennines; plan and model of the church of San Giovanni at Pistoja; the ducal Palazzo Gualtieri at Florence. He was distinguished as a military architect.
131	Agostino da Sienna, or da Pisa, of Italy. Angelo, his brother, of Italy.	—	The north and west façades of the cathedral of Sienna, as also the two gates; the church and convent of St. Francis; Palazzo de' Nove Magistrati; grand fountain in the piazza opposite the Palazzo della Signoria; hall of the council chamber, and Palazzo Publico; the church della Santa Maria in Piazza Manetti were built by him in conjunction with Angelo da Pisa, who was his brother.
132	Boyden, William, of England.	—	Chief architect to the chapel of the Virgin at St. Alban's Abbey Church, erected during the abbacy of Hugo de Eversden.
133	Bek, A. de, bishop of Durham, of England.	—	Built and enlarged Barnard Castle, and other fortresses.
134	Henry Latomus, or the stonecutter, abbot of Evesham, of England.	—	Chapter-house, dormitory, refectory, abbot's hall, and kitchen of the monastery at Evesham.
135	Helpstone, J., of England.	—	New-tower or water-tower, in the walls of Chester.
136	Eversden, Hugh de, abbot of St. Alban's, of England.	—	Lady chapel in St. Alban's Abbey Church.
137	Walter Weston of England.	—	St. Stephen's Chapel, Westminster.
138	Thomas of Canterbury, of England.	—	St. Stephen's Chapel, Westminster.

			AFTER CHRIST.
No. in Gloss.	Name of Architect.	Century.	Principal Works.
139	Giacomo Lanfrani of Italy.	14th.	Church of St. Francis at Imola; church of St. Antonio at Venice.
140	Juan Rari of France.	—	Finished the building of the church of Notre Dame at Paris.
141	William of Wykeham, bishop of Winchester, of England.	—	New College, Oxford; part of Winchester Cathedral; plan of Windsor Castle.
142	Alan de Walsingham, prior of Ely, of England.	—	Lantern Tower, and St. Mary's Chapel, at Ely Cathedral.
143	Rede, bishop of Chichester, of England.	—	An eminent mathematician; built first library at Merton College, Oxford; Amberley Castle, Sussex.
144	Andrea di Cione Orgagna, of Florence.	—	Additions to the ducal palace, and the Loggia, at Florence; his brother built the tower and gate of San Pietro Gattolini.
145	Gainsborough, or Gaynisburg, of England.	—	Employed at Lincoln Cathedral. On his monument, still existing in the cathedral, he is said to have died in June, M.CCC—, the last portion of the date being obliterated.
146	Chichele, archbishop of Canterbury, of England.	15th.	Founded All Souls College; built a monument for himself in Canterbury Cathedral; made additions to Canterbury Cathedral, Lambeth Palace, Croydon Church, and Rochester Bridge.
147	Filippo Brunelleschi of Florence.	—	Cupola of the cathedral of Santa Maria del Fiore at Florence. A council of artists was held at Florence in 1420, to consider and advise on this scheme, at which even English artists are said to have assisted; after a diversity of opinions, Brunelleschi's project was approved of and adopted. His other principal works were, the Palazzo Pitti, which was begun and half finished by him, the remainder being the work of Luca Fancelli; a great part of the church of San Spirito; the church degl' Angeli, designed and begun, but not completed, from want of money; the monastery de' Camaldosi; the fortress of Milan, and several works about that city; a model for the fortress of Pesaro; the old and new citadel at Pisa; some other works there, as well as at Trento, and in other parts of Italy. He drained the country round Mantua, and set the first example of a purer style in the architecture of Italy.
148	Michelozzo Michelozzi of Florence.	—	Palazzo di Medici, now dei Marchesi Ricardi; Palazzo Caffajiulo; convent of the Dominicans; Noviziato della Santa Croce; chapel in the church dei Servi; Palazzo della Villa Careggi; Palazzo Tornabuoni, now dei Marchesi Corsi; and several other palaces, churches, and convents at Florence; monastery of the Black Benedictines at Venice, and the Palazzo della Villa Careggi at Mujello; some buildings at Trento; a beautiful fountain at Assisi, la Citadella Vecchia at Perugia; the alterations to the palace presented by Francisco Sforza to Cosmo di Medici, whom he followed in his exile, and other great works in various parts of Italy.

AFTER CHRIST.

No. in Gloss.	Name of Architect.	Century.	Principal Works.
149	Giuliano of Majano, near Florence.	15th.	Palazzo del Poggio Reale at Naples; a Corinthian triumphal gate at the Castel Nuovo; many fountains in the same city; the Cortile S. Damaso, in the Vatican at Rome, whither he was invited by Paul II.; palace and church of San Marco at Rome; he also enlarged the church at Loreto.
150	Frowcester, Walter, abbot of Gloucester, of England.	—	Built the great cloisters of his monastery in 1400.
151	Keyes, Roger, of England.	—	Architect of All Souls' College, Oxford.
152	Horwood, W., a freemason, of England.	—	Collegiate chapel of Fotheringhay.
153	Close, or Cloos, bishop of Lichfield, of England.	—	Supposed to have designed King's College chapel, Cambridge; though, according to Hearne, his father was the architect.
154	Christobolo of Italy.	—	A mosque at Constantinople, with eight schools and eight hospitals, on the site of the church of the Apostles, by order of Mahomet II.
155	Baccio Pintelli of Florence.	—	Church and convent of Santa Maria del Popolo at Rome; the celebrated Capella Sistina in the Vatican; the hospital of S. Spirito in Sassia; Ponte Sisto; designs for the church of San Pietro in Montorio; the church of S. Sisto; the church of St. Agostino and the church of San Pietro in Vincolà at Rome; repaired the church and convent of St. Francis at Assisi; and built the palace for the Cardinal del Rovere at Borgo Vecchio; some attribute to him the palace built for the Duke Federigo Feltre at Urbino. He is said to have been the first to set the example of grandeur in the architecture of chapels.
156	Bartolomeo Bramantino of Italy.	—	Church of San Satiro at Milan, and other works in various parts of Italy.
157	Giovanni del Pozzo of Spain.	—	Dominican convent, and a great bridge over the Huexar, near Cuénça.
158	Andrea Ciccione of Naples.	—	Convent and church of Monte Oliveto; palace of Bartolomeo da Capua; and several other convents and palaces in the city of Naples.
159	Ridolfo Fioravanti of Bologna.	—	Restored the hanging tower of the church of S. Biagio, at Cento, to its perpendicular position, and built many churches at Moscow.
160	Orcheyarde, W., of England.	—	Architect of Magdalen College, Oxford, under Bishop Wayneflete.
161	Francesco di Giorgio of Sienna.	—	The ducal palace at Urbino.
162	Leone Battista Alberti of Florence.	—	Church of St. Francis at Rimini; church of St. Andrew at Mantua; the principal façade of Santa Maria Novella, at Florence, has been attributed by some to Alberti; but from the circumstance of its being Gothic, it may with much more probability be assigned to Bettini; the gate and Corinthian loggie are, however, from the designs of Alberti, as also the Doric façade of the Palazzo Rucellai, and the choir and tribune of the church della Nunziata, all at Florence. He also repaired

No. in Gloss.	Name of Architect.	Century.	Principal Works.
		AFTER CHRIST.	
			the Aqua Vergine and the fountain of Trevi, at Rome, under Nicholas V. ; the palace for the Duke Federigo Feltre at Urbino; and many other buildings in Italy.
163	Farleigh, or Ferley, W., abbot of Gloucester, of England.	15th.	Built the lady chapel of Gloucester, about 1490.
164	Beauchamp, bishop of Sarum, of England.	—	Appointed surveyor of the works at Windsor Castle by Edward IV. ; supposed to have made designs for rebuilding St George's Chapel; built a chantry chapel in Salisbury Cathedral.
165	Wayneflete, bishop of Winchester, of England.	—	Founder of Magdalen College, Oxford; overseer of the building at Windsor. Leland was informed that the greatest part of the buildings of Eton College were raised under his direction, and at his expense.
166	Kendale, John, of England.	—	Supervisor of all the king's works.
166*	Druell, J., archdeacon of Exeter, of England.	—	One of the architects employed on All Souls' College, Oxford.
167	Bramante Lazzari, or Bramante d'Urbino, of Castel Durante, near Urbino.	—	First designed and commenced the building of St. Peter's at Rome; a small model was executed after the same design for an insulated church without the walls of Todi; many works in the Vatican, particularly the library and the Belvedere court, with a magnificent design for alterations to be made in it, under Julius II.; the rotondo in the convent of San Pietro Montorio; the palaces of S. Giacomo Scosciacavalli ora de' Conti Giraud, del Duca de Sora, della Cancellaria, dell Nuovo dell' Imperiale; the churches of SS. Euloy de' Orfani, Lorenzo and Damaso; the cloisters of the monastery della Pace, &c. at Rome; the Strada Julia in that city; the ducal palace at Urbino; Palazzo Publico at Brescia; design for the church dell' Umiltà at Pistoja.
168	Ventura Vitoni of Pistoja.	—	Church dell' Umiltà at Pistoja, after the design of Bramante, whose pupil he was.
169	Alcock, J., bishop of Ely, of England.	16th.	Sepulchral chapel in Ely Cathedral; episcopal palace at Downham; supposed to have designed St. Mary's, or the University Church, Cambridge.
170	Moston, J., of Cambridge, of England.	—	Part of palace of Lambeth ; another at Canterbury ; " made a great building at Charing in Kent ;" almost the whole house of Forde. He built at Alington Park.
171	Gabriello d'Agnolo of Naples.	—	Church of S. Giuseppe ; church of Santa Maria Egiziaca ; palace of Ferdinando Orsini, duke of Gravina, at Naples.
172	Gian Francesco Normando of Florence.	—	Church of S. Severino ; Palazzo Filomarini ; Palazzo Cantalupo at Naples ; several buildings in Spain.
173	Pietro Lombardo of Venice.	—	Tomb of Dante, the poet, near the church of St. Francis at Ravenna ; church of SS. Paolo, and Giovanni, and monastery adjoining the church of Santa Maria Mater Domini ; clock-tower in the square of St. Mark ; German warehouse on the Rialto ; school della Misericordia ; cloister of Santa Giustina at Padua.

AFTER CHRIST.

No. in Gloss.	Name of Architect.	Century.	Principal Works.
174	Martino Lombardo of Venice.	16th.	School or confraternità of San Marco, and, perhaps, the church of S. Zaccaria at Venice.
175	John Cole of England.	—	Builder of Louth Spire, Lincolnshire.
176	Sir Reginald Bray of England.	—	Design of Henry VII.'s Chapel, Westminster, and of other works at St. George's Chapel, Windsor.
177	John Hylmer of England.	—	St. George's Chapel, Windsor.
178	Giuliano di San Gallo of Florence.	—	Cloister of the Carmelites di Santa Maddelena de' Pazzi at Florence; cloister for the Fratri Eremitani di S. Agostino; la Gran Fabbrica del Poggio Imperiale, fortress near the Porto a Prato, and other works, at Florence; a magnificent palace at Poggio a Cajano for Lorenzo di Medici; repaired the cupola of the church della Madonna at Loreto; restored the roof and decorations of the ceiling of the church of Santa Maria Maggiore; restored the church dell' Anima; Palazzo Rovere, near San Pietro in Vincolà at Rome; Palazzo Rovere at Savona; an unfinished palace at Milan; fortress and gate of San Marco, of the Doric order; many palaces at Pisa; fortifications at Ostia.
179	Simone Cronaca, or Pollajolo, of Florence.	—	Façade of the Palazzo Strozzi at Florence; church of S. Francis at S. Miniato, near Florence; convent of the Padri Serviti; sacristy of Santo Spirito, and the council chamber at Florence.
180	Aristotile Alberti of Bologna.	—	A bridge in Hungary; several churches in Russia.
181	Leonardo da Vinci, near Florence.	—	Aqueduct of the Adda at Milan; various machines, plans, and works on architecture.
182	Fra Giocondo of Verona.	—	Many bridges, especially that of Notre Dame at Paris; the public hall and Ponte della Pietra at Verona; fortifications at Treviso; cleansing of the Lagunes, and a design for the Ponte Rialto at Venice: after the death of Bramante, he was engaged with Rafaelle and San Gallo in erecting St. Peter's at Rome.
183	Novello da San Lucano of Naples.	—	Palace of Prince Robert Sanseverino, duke of Salerno, at Naples; and the restoration of the church of San Domenico Maggiore, which was built by Lucano.
184	Percy, John, abbot of Leicester, of England.	—	Brick buildings at Leicester Abbey.
185	Rafaelle d'Urbino of Urbino.	—	Continued the erection of St. Peter's at Rome, after the death of Bramante, his master in architecture; engaged on the buildings of the Farnese Palace; church of Santa Maria in Navicella, repaired and altered; stables of Agostino, near the Palazzo Farnese; Palazzo Caffarelli, now Stoppani; the gardens of the Vatican; the façade of the church of San Lorenzo, and of the Palazzo Uggoccioni, now Pandolfini, at Florence.
186	Bolton, W., prior of St. Bartholomew's of England.	—	Supposed to have designed Henry VII.'s Chapel, where he was master of the works.

			AFTER CHRIST.
No. in Gloss.	Name of Architect.	Century.	Principal Works.
187	John of Padua of Italy.	16th	" Deviser of buildings" to Henry VIII. of England.
188	Gibbes, W., last prior of Bath, of England.	—	Continued the building of Bath Abbey church till the dissolution of monasteries.
189	Hector Asheley of England.	—	Surveyor of buildings, employed in the erection of Hunsdon House.
190	Andrea Contucci di Monte Sansovino of Italy.	—	The beautiful chapel del Sagramento in the church di Santo Spirito; palace della Canonica at Loreto; a cloister for the monks of St. Agostino, and a little chapel without the walls of Sanseverino; some buildings at Venice, and many in Portugal.
191	Bartolomeo Buono of Bergamo, of Italy.	—	Church of S. Rocco; some parts of the Campanile di San Marco, and the Procurazie Vecchie at Venice.
192	Guglielmo Bergamasco of Bergamo, of Italy.	—	Capella Emiliana of the Camaldulenses at Murano, an island of the Lagunes; Palazzo di Calmerlinghi, near the Ponte Rialto at Venice; palace at Portagruaro, at Friuli; gate di Santo Tommaso at Treviso; gate called Il Portello at Padua.
193	Maestro Filippo of Spain.	—	Restoration of the cathedral of Seville.
194	Giovanni di Ololzago of Biscay, of Spain.	—	Cathedral of Huesca in Arragon: he blended the modern Greek style with the Gothic, in the manner called Arabo-tedescho.
195	Pietro di Gamiel of Spain.	—	Convent of S. Eugraçia at Saragossa; college of Alcala, in the Græco-Gothic style of architecture.
196	Giovanni Alonzo of Spain.	—	Sanctuary of Guadaloupe.
197	Fra Giovanni d'Escobedo of Spain.	—	Grand aqueduct of Segovia, by order of Queen Isabella.
198	Giovanni Campero of Spain.	—	Church and convent of S. Francis at Fordelaguna.
199	Antonio San Gallo of Mugello, near Florence.	—	Churches of the Madonna di Loreto near Trajan's column, of Santa Maria di Monserrato, of S. Giovanni dei Fiorentini; Palazzetto di Conte Palma; Palazzi di Santo Buono for himself, now that of the Marchesi Sacchetti; Farnese, begun by Paul III., when a cardinal; fortifications of Civita Vecchia, of Civita Castellana, of Parma, Ancona, and many other strong places in Italy; he altered the Mole of Adrian to its present form of the castle of S. Angelo; triumphal arch in the square of S. Mark at Venice; a temple to our Lady at Monte Pulciano; built the Capella Paolina del Vaticano, and assisted in the works of St. Peter's.
200	Baldassare Peruzzi of Volterra.	—	Plan and model of the cathedral or duomo at Carpi; two designs for the façade of San Petronio, and the gate of San Michele in Bosco at Bologna; fortifications at Sienna; the little palace built for Agostino Chigi, now called the Farnesina, in the Lungara; Palazzo Massimi, near the church of San Pantaleo; Villa di Papa Giulio III.; the cortile of the palace de' Duchi Altemps; casino at the Palazzo Chigi; tomb of Pope Hadrian IV. in

AFTER CHRIST.

No. in Gloss.	Name of Architect.	Century.	Principal Works.
			the church dell' Anima; Palazzo Spinosa, now the hospital degli Eretici convertiti at Rome; assisted in the erection of St. Peter's, and was buried by the side of Rafaelle, in the Pantheon. His style was good.
201	Marco di Pino of Sienna.	16th	Modernised the church della Trinità di Palazzo, and built the church and convent of Giesù Vecchio at Naples.
202	Andrea Briosco of Padua.	—	The Loggia and council house in the Piazza degli Signori at Padua, finished in 1526.
203	Ferdinando Manlio of Naples.	—	Church and hospital della Nunziata; the Strada di Porta Nolano, and di Monte Oliveto, with other streets and palaces at Naples; a bridge at Capua.
204	Giovanni Merliano of Nola of Italy.	—	Strada di Toledo at Naples; church of S. Giorgio de' Genovesi; church of S. Giacomo degli Spagnuoli; plan of the palace del Principe di San Severo, and the palace of the Duca della Torre; the Castel Capuano, altered to a court of law; a fountain at the extremity of the Mole, and some triumphal arches for the entrance of Charles V., on his return from Tunis, at Naples.
205	Giovanni Gil de Hontanon of Spain.	—	Plan of the cathedral of Salamanca, etc.
206	Baccio d'Agnolo of Florence.	—	The beautiful bell tower or campanile of Santo Spirito; lantern above the cupola of Santa Maria del Fiore, great altar and choir of which was built by his son Giuliano; palace for Giovanni Bartolini in the Piazza della Santissima Trinità; Palazzo Salvieto at Rome.
207	Giovanni Maria Falconetto of Verona.	—	Church della Madonna delle Grazie, for the Dominicans at Padua; palace in the Castel d'Usopo in the Friuli; palace for Luigi Cornaro, near the Santo; Doric gate to the Palazzo Capitano; a music hall, which was much admired by Serlio, who denominated it " La Rotonda di Padoua;" gates of SS. Giovanni and Savonarola.
208	Rodrigo Gil de Hontanon of Spain.	—	Superintended the erection of the cathedral of Salamanca; built the cathedral of Segovia.
209	Pietro de Uria of Spain.	—	Bridge of Almaraz, over the Tagus.
210	Alonzo de Cobarrubias of Spain.	—	Façade of the Alcazar at Toledo; convent and church of S. Michael at Valentia; repaired the church of Toledo, which was erected in 587, during the reign of King Riccaredo.
211	Diego Siloe of Toledo.	—	Cathedral and Alcazar at Granada; church and convent of S. Jerome in the same city.
212	Girolamo Genga of Urbino.	—	Palace of the Duke of Urbino, sul Monte dell' Imperiale; the court of the palace restored; church of San Giovanni Battista at Pesaro; façade of the cathedral and the bishop's palace at Mantua; convent de' Zoccolanti at Monte Baroccio. His son, Bartolomeo, was also an artist of considerable repute, and there are several of his works at Mondavio, Pesaro, and other parts of Italy.
213	Michele San Micheli.	—	Cathedral of Monte Fiascone; church of S. Domenico at Orvieto; numerous fortresses in

			AFTER CHRIST.
No. in Gloss.	Name of Architect.	Century.	Principal Works.
			the Venetian territory, in Corfu, Lombardy, and the ecclesiastical states, as at Legnani, Orzi Nuovo, and Castello; palaces di Canossa, dell' Gran Guardia on the Bra; Pellegrini de' Verzi; the prefecturate and façade of the Palazzo Bevilaqua at Verona; chapel Guareschi in the church of S. Bernardino; design for the campanile of the Duomo; churches of Santa Maria in Organo de' Monaci, di Monte Oliveto, di San Giorgio, and della Madonna della Campagna, in the same city; gates Nuova, del Pallio, di S. Zenone, del Palazzo Pretorio, and del Palazzo Prefettizio, at Verona; fortifications of the same city, the first instance of the introduction of triangular bastions; the first bastion, that of della Madellina, was erected in 1527.
214	Philibert de Lorme of France.	16th.	Commenced the Tuilleries; built the châteaux of St. Maur, Anet, Meudon, and many others.
215	Galeazzo Alessi of Italy.	—	The Escurial in Spain; he was much employed at Genoa.
216	Sante Lombardo of Venice.	—	Palazzo Vendramini; staircase and façade of the school of S. Rocca; palaces Trevisani and Gradenigo, at Venice.
217	Giacomo Barozzi da Vignola of Rome.	—	The magnificent palace at Caprarola for Cardinal Farnese.
218	Giulio Pippi, or Giulio Romano, of Rome.	—	Villa Madama; Palazzo Lante at San Pietro; church della Madonna del Orto; Palazzo Ciccia porci alla Strada di Banchi; Palazzo Cenci sulla Piazza S. Eustachio, near the Palazzo Lante, and other buildings in Rome; Palazzo del T. at Mantua; palace at Marmiruolo, five miles from Mantua; modernising and enlarging the ducal palaces, the Duomo, and many other buildings in the same city; façade of S. Petronio at Bologna; and some works at Vicenza. His style was agreeable.
219	Michel Angelo di Buonarroti of Florence.	—	Library of the Medici, generally called the Laurentian Library, at Florence; model for the façade of the church of San Lorenzo; second sacristy of Lorenzo, commonly called the Capella dei Depositi; church San Giovanni, which he did not finish; fortifications at Florence, and at Monte San Miniato; monument of Julius II. in the church of San Pietro in Vincolà at Rome; plan of the Campidoglio; palace of the Conservatorj; building in the centre, and the flight of steps in the Campidoglio, or Capitol, at Rome; continuation of the Palace Farnese, and several gates at Rome, particularly the Porta Nomentana or Pia; steeple of S. Michaele at Ostia; the gate to the vineyard del Patriarca Grimani; tower of S. Lorenzo at Ardea; church of Santa Maria, in the Certosa, at Rome; many plans of palaces, churches, and chapels. He was employed on St. Peter's, after the death of San Gallo.

			AFTER CHRIST.
No. in Gloss.	Name of Architect.	Century.	Principal Works.
220	Mascall or Marshall, Eustace, of England.	16th.	Clerk of the works to Cardinal Wolsey, at the building of Christchurch College, Oxford; and chief clerk of accounts for all the buildings of Henry VIII. within twenty miles of London.
221	Damiano Forment, of Valentia of Spain.	—	Façade of the church of S. Eugraçia, at Saragossa.
222	Martino de Gainza of Spain.	—	The chapel royal at Seville.
223	Alonzo Berruguette, of Parades, de Naba, of Spain.	—	Plan of the former royal palace at Madrid; gate of S. Martino at Toledo; palace of Alcala in that city; he also assisted at the erection of the cathedral of Cuença.
224	Pietro di Valdevira of Spain.	—	The beautiful chapel of S. Salvador, at Ubeda; palace in the same place; hospital and chapel of S. Jago at Baeza.
225	Pietro Ezguerra of Ojebar, of Spain.	—	Cathedral of Plasentia; church of S. Matteo de Caceres; church of Malpartida.
226	Ferdinando Riuz of Cordova, of Spain.	—	Heightened the great steeple of the cathedral of Seville, called the Torre della Giralda.
227	Machuca of Spain.	—	Royal palace of Grenada.
228	Antonio Fiorentino of Florence.	—	Church of Santa Catarina a Formello at Naples; the cupola of this church is said to have been the first that was raised of any considerable magnitude in that city.
229	Jacopo Tatti, surnamed Sansovino, of Florence.	—	Church of S. Marcello begun, and that of S. Giovanni de Fiorentini built; Loggia, on the Via Flaminia, just out of the Porto del Popolo, for Marco Coscia; Palazzo Gaddi, now del Nicolini, at Rome; church of St. Francesco della Vigna, which was finished by Palladio; Palazzo Cornari, sul Canal Grande, at San Maurizio; mint and other public buildings at Venice; church of San Fantino; church of San Geminiano, &c. His style was of the Venetian school.
230	Theodore Haveus of England.	—	Caius College, Cambridge, a good specimen of the architecture of the day.
231	Domenico Teocopoli of Greece.	—	College of the Donna Maria d'Arragona at Madrid; church and convent of the Dominican nuns; also of the Ayuntamiento at Toledo; church and convent of the Bernardine nuns at Silos.
232	Garzia d'Emere of Spain.	—	Parochial church of Valeria, near Cuença.
233	Bartolomeo di Bustamente of Spain.	—	Hospital of St. John the Baptist, near Toledo.
234	Giovan Battista di Toledo of Spain.	—	Designs for the Escurial; he assisted in planning the street of Toledo at Naples, the church of S. Jago, belonging to the Spaniards; palace at Posilippo in the same city.
235	John Thynne of England.	—	Built Somerset House in 1567.
236	Giovanni d'Herrera of Movellar, in the Asturias.	—	Continued the Escurial after the death of his master, Giovan Battista; plan of the church of S. Jago, near Cuença; bridge of Segovia at Madrid; palace at Aranjuez.
237	Pierre de Lescot of France.	—	Fontaine des Innocens, in the Rue Saint Denys, at Paris.
238	Sebastiano Serlio of Bologna.	—	Palace of Grimani at Venice; employed by Francis I. of France at Fontainebleau.

AFTER CHRIST.

No. in Gloss.	Name of Architect.	Century.	Principal Works.
239	Bartolomeo Ammanati of Italy.	16th.	Palazzo Pitti ; bridge Santissima Trinità ; Rucellai Palace at Florence ; Jesuit's college at Rome, and many other works.
240	Nicholas Abate of Modena.	—	The old château of Meudon, tomb of Francis I. at St. Denys ; decorated the apartments of the palace of Fontainebleau.
241	Andrea Palladio of Vicenza, of Italy.	—	Olympic Theatre at Vicenza ; Il Redentore at Venice ; and, perhaps, more public and private buildings than have been erected before or since by any architect.
241*	Bernardo Buontalenti of Florence.	—	Villa of Marignolle, now Casa Capponi ; the casino behind San Marco at Florence ; a palace for the Acciajuoli, now the Corvini ; the façade of the Strozzi Palace in the Via Maggiore ; the façade of the church della Santissima Trinità ; and works in many other parts of Italy.
242	Domenico Fontana of Milan.	—	Chapel of the Manger in the church of S. Maria Maggiore ; library of the Vatican, and many other works.
243	John Shute of England.	—	A painter and architect, who flourished during the reign of Queen Elizabeth, from 1558 to 1608.
244	Robert Adams of England.	—	Superintendent of royal buildings to Queen Elizabeth.
245	Louis de Foix of France.	—	The new canal of the Adour; "Tour de Cordouan," at the mouth of the Garonne.
246	Jacques Androuet du Cerceau of France.	—	Pont Neuf at Paris ; hôtels de Sully, de Mayenne, and that of the Fermes Générales ; designed the fine gallery built by Henri IV. at the Tuileries.
247	Vincenzo Scamozzi of Vicenza.	—	Supposed inventor of the angular Ionic capital ; made some additions to the library of S. Mark, finished the Olympic Theatre at Vicenza, and built a theatre at Sabionetta.
248	Jacques de Brosse of Paris.	—	Luxembourg at Paris, and other works.
249	Carlo Maderno of Lombardy.	—	Altered Michel Angelo's design for St. Peter's at Rome, from a Greek to a Latin cross; began the palace of Urban VIII.
250	John Warren of England.	17th	Architect of St. Mary's Church tower, Cambridge.
251	Sir H. Wotton of England.	—	Author of "The Elements of Architecture," published in London, 1624.
252	Inigo Jones of England.	—	Banqueting House ; chapel, Lincoln's Inn ; Surgeons' Hall ; arcade, Covent Garden, London ; and a vast number of other important works.
253	Giovanni Battista Aleotti of Ferrara.	—	Fortress at Ferrara ; many palaces, theatres, and other public buildings at Mantua, Parma, Modena, and Venice.
254	Pierre le Muet of France.	—	Plan for the grand hotel of Luynes ; hotel Laigle and Beauvilliers.
255	Francesco Borromini of Italy.	—	Author of "numerous absurdities" at Rome and Florence, nevertheless much employed.
256	Alessandro Algardi of Bologna.	—	Chiefly employed at Rome.
257	Giovanni Lorenzo Bernini of Naples.	—	The celebrated piazza, colonnade, and staircase at St Peter's ; grand fountain of the Piazza Navona.
258	François Mansard of France.	—	Abbey of Val de Grace ; Château des Maisons ; portal of the Minims in the Place Royale.

LIST OF ARCHITECTS.

AFTER CHRIST.			
No. in Gloss.	Name of Architect.	Century.	Principal Works.
259	Claude Perrault of France.	17th.	Façade of the Louvre ; chapel of Sceaux ;· chapel of Nôtre Dame in the church of the Petits Pères.
260	François Blondel of France.	—	Bridge over the Charente at Saintes ; gate of S. Denis at Paris ; repair and decorations of the gates of St. Antoine and St. Bernard.
261	Antoine le Pautre of France.	—	Wings of St. Cloud ; church of the nunnery of Port Royal ; hôtels of Gevres and Beauvais.
262	Jacques le Mercier of France.	—	Sorbonne, Palais Royal, St. Roch, Val de Grace, were erected by him after the designs of Mansard.
263	Gerard Chrismas of England.	—	Designed Aldersgate, London ; was an architect and sculptor.
264	Sir Christopher Wren of England.	—	St. Paul's ; planned the city of London after the Fire ; nearly all the churches therein ; Hampton Court, &c.
265	Robert Hooke of England.	—	The Old Bethlehem Hospital in Moorfields ; Aske's Alms-houses ; Duke of Mountague's house, afterwards the British Museum. He gave a plan for rebuilding the City of London after the Fire.
267	Jules Hardouin Mansard of France.	—	The Dome of the Hôtel des Invalides ; Gallerie du Palais Royal ; the Place de Louis le Grand ; that des Victoires, &c. He was the nephew of François Mansard.
268	Rev. H. Aldrich of England.	—	Three sides of the quadrangle of Christ's Church, called Peckwater Square, chapel of Trinity College, and church of All Saint's, at Oxford.
269	Fischer von Erlach, baron, of Germany.	18th.	Many churches and palaces.
270	Sir John Vanbrugh of England.	—	Blenheim House, Oxfordshire ; Castle Howard, Yorkshire ; Eastbury, Dorset ; King's Weston, near Bristol ; the Opera House of the time ; part of Greenwich Hospital.
270*	Filippo Ivara, or Juvara, of Sicily.	—	Buildings near Turin on the Superga ; church del Carmine ; an interior staircase to the palace at Turin ; employed on works in Portugal ; finished cupola of Sant' Andrea, Mantua ; façade of Duomo at Milan ; palace of the Count Birago di Borghe at Turin, and numberless other works.
271	Colin Campbell of Scotland.	—	Wanstead House ; Mereworth. Compiler of the " Vitruvius Britannicus," 3 vols.
272	Robert de Cotte of France.	—	He continued the Dome of the Invalides ; finished the chapel of Versailles ; and raised the new buildings at St. Denys.
273	Nicholas Hawksmoor, pupil to Wren, of England.	—	The churches of St. George, Bloomsbury ; St. Anne, Limehouse ; and St. Leonard, Shoreditch. Greenwich Hospital, &c.
274	Alexander Jean Baptiste le Blond of France.	—	L'Hôtel de Vendome, in the Rue d'Enfer at Paris. He was employed much in Russia by Peter the Great.
275	Alessandro Galilei of Italy.	—	Corsini Chapel, &c. Rome.
276	Galli da Bibiena of Italy.	—	Theatre at Verona ; theatre at Vienna. Author of two books on Architecture.

AFTER CHRIST.

No. in Gloss.	Name of Architect.	Century.	Principal Works.
277	Jacques Gabriel of France.	18th.	Buildings at Bordeaux, Rennes, Paris, &c.
278	John James of England.	—	St. George's Church, Hanover Square ; Mansion for Sir Gregory Page, Bart. at Blackheath.
279	Giacomo Leoni of Italy.	—	Lyme Hall.
280	Germain de Boffrand of Nantes, of France.	—	Much employed in Paris and Germany.
281	James Gibbs of Scotland.	—	Radcliffe's Library, Oxford ; the new church in the Strand ; St. Martin's-in-the-Fields ; King's College, Royal Library, and Senate House, Cambridge.
282	William Kent of England.	—	Temple of Venus at Stowe ; Holkham Hall in Norfolk ; staircase at Lady Isabella Finch's in Berkeley Square ; the Treasury Buildings ; and other works.
283	Thomas Ripley of England.	—	Houghton Hall ; Admiralty.
284	Edmund Bouchardon of France.	—	Many buildings at Paris.
285	Charles Labelye of Switzerland.	—	Westminster Bridge.
286	Giambattista Sacchetti of Turin.	—	Royal Palace, Madrid.
287	Sir James Burroughs of England.	—	Senate House, Cambridge.
288	Jean Nicholas Servandoni of France.	—	Part of the church of St. Sulpice at Paris ; many theatres and decorations for theatres.
289	Isaac Ware of England.	—	Foot's Cray, &c. Edited a version of Palladio. Published " A Body of Architecture."
290	George Dance, Sen. of England.	—	Mansion House, London ; the churches of St. Luke's, Old Street ; St. Leonard's, Shoreditch, &c.
291	Luigi Vanvitelli of Italy.	—	Palace at Caserta, &c.
292	Jacques François Blondel, of Rouen, of France.	—	Royal abbey of St. Louis ; a street and square opposite to the cathedral at Rouen ; many other works both there and at Strassburg.
293	Earl of Burlington of England.	—	Chiswick House ; Burlington House, Piccadilly ; and other works.
294	John Brettingham of England.	—	Holkham Hall in Norfolk, finished by, in 1764.
295	Ferdinando Fuga of Italy.	—	Palazzo Corsini at Rome ; and many works there and at Naples, &c.
296	M. Aug. Simonetti of Italy.	—	The Museo Pio Clementino in the Vatican.
297	Jacques Ange Gabriel of France.	—	The École Militaire, and Garde Meuble, Paris.
298	Jean Rodolphe Perronet of France.	—	Director of the bridges and roads of France ; bridge of Neuilly, and many others.
299	Jacques Germain Soufflout of France.	—	Hospital at Lyons ; exchange, concert-room, and theatre in the same city ; portal, nave, and towers of the church of St. Geneviève.
300	Sir William Chambers of England.	—	Somerset House ; and many other works. Author of a treatise on Civil Architecture.
301	Robert Adam of Scotland.	—	Architect to Geo. III. ; author of a work on the ruins of Spalatro ; his principal works are the Register Office at Edinburgh ; Infirmary at Glasgow ; the Edinburgh University ; Luton House ; Adelphi Terrace.

			AFTER CHRIST.
No. in Gloss.	Name of Architect.	Century.	Principal Works.
302	Sir Robert Taylor of England.	18th.	Parts of Bank of England now taken down; a great number of buildings in this country.
303	James Paine of England.	—	Mansion House, Doncaster; Wardour Castle; Worksop. Designs published.
304	V. Louis of France.	—	Theatre at Bordeaux, &c.
305	Jacques Denis Antoine of France.	—	The Mint at Paris; ditto at Berne, &c.
306	Claude Nicholas Ledoux of France.	—	Barrières at Paris; Hôtel Thelusson, &c.; and author of a splendid book on architecture.
307	Henry Holland of England.	—	Carlton House; Old Drury Lane Theatre, &c.
308	Joseph Bonomi of Italy.	—	Roseneath in Scotland; alterations at Keddlestone; and other works in England.
309	Jacques Guillaume Legrand of France.	—	Théâtre Feydeau, Paris; many other works.
310	C. G. Langhans of Germany.	—	Brandenburg Gate, &c. Berlin.
311	Robert Mylne of Scotland.	—	Blackfriars Bridge; Inverary Castle, &c.
312	Jacques Gondouin of France.	—	École de Médecine, Paris.
313	Karl Fischer of Germany.	—	Theatre, &c. Munich.
314	George Dance, Jun. of England.	—	Newgate Prison; St. Luke's Hospital; College of Surgeons, Lincoln's Inn Fields.
315	James Gandon of Ireland.	—	Custom House; Exchange; Four Courts, &c., in Dublin.
316	Sir John Soane of England.	—	Bank of England; Board of Trade; State Paper Office.
317	Charles Percier of France.	—	Architect of the Tuileries; restorations, &c. at Louvre and Tuileries; Chapelle Expiatoire. Author of " Recueil de Décorations," and other books.

ARCHITECTURE. The art of building according to certain proportions and rules determined and regulated by nature and taste. As the art, in its various parts, is the subject of this work, we do not here consider further definition necessary. For origin and progress, see Book I. Chap. I. Sect. 2; different species at early period, Book I. Chap. I. Sect. 3.

ARCHITECTURE, ARABIAN or SARACENIC, Book I. Chap. II. Sect. 10.
———— ASSYRIAN, Book I. Chap. II. Sect. 3.
———— BABYLONIAN, Book I. Chap. II. Sect. 3.
———— BRITISH, EARLY PERIOD, Book I. Chap. III. Sect. 1.
———— BYZANTINE and ROMANESQUE, Book I. Chap. II. Sect. 14.
———— CELTIC and DRUIDICAL. See DRUIDICAL.
———— CYCLOPEAN. See PELASGIC.
———— CHINESE, Book I. Chap. II. Sect. 8.
———— DRUIDICAL and CELTIC, Book I. Chap. II. Sect. 1.
———— EGYPTIAN, Book I. Chap. II. Sect. 7.
———— EARLY ENGLISH, Book I. Chap. III. Sect. 3.
———— ELIZABETHAN, Book I. Chap. III. Sect. 6.
———— ETRUSCAN, Book I. Chap. II. Sect. 12.
———— FRENCH, Book I. Chap. II. Sect. 17.
———— FLORID ENGLISH or TUDOR, Book I. Chap. III. Sect. 5.
———— OF GEORGE I. II. and III. Book I. Chap. III. Sects. 8, 9, and 10.
———— GERMAN, Book I. Chap. II. Sect. 18.
———— GRECIAN, Book I. Chap. II. Sect. 11.
———— INDIAN, Book I. Chap. II. Sect. 6.
———— ITALIAN, Book I. Chap. II. Sect. 16.
———— JAMES I. to ANNE, Book I. Chap. III. Sect. 7.

ARCHITECTURE, JEWISH, Book I. Chap. II. Sect. 5.
———————— MEXICAN, Book I. Chap. II. Sect. 9.
———————— NORMAN, Book I. Chap. III. Sect. 2.
———————— ORNAMENTED ENGLISH, Book I. Chap. III. Sect. 4.
———————— PELASGIC and CYCLOPEAN, Book I. Chap. II. Sect. 2.
———————— PERSEPOLITAN, PERSIAN, and ASSYRIAN, Book I. Chap. II. Sect 4.
———————— POINTED, Book I. Chap. II. Sect. 15 ; and Chap. IV.
———————— ROMAN, Book I. Chap. II. Sect. 13.
———————— RUSSIAN, Book I. Chap. II. Sect. 20.
———————— SPANISH and PORTUGUESE, Book I. Chap. II. Sect. 19.
ARCHITECTURE, WORKS ON. It would too far extend this work to print a list of these, but we here insert

A Catalogue of the principal and most useful Works to the Student of Architecture, arranged under the several Clauses of

1. GRECIAN ARCHITECTURE.
2. ROMAN ARCHITECTURE.
3. MISCELLANEOUS, ON ANCIENT ARCHITECTURE.
4. GOTHIC ARCHITECTURE.
5. MODERN FOREIGN ARCHITECTURE.
6. MODERN ENGLISH ARCHITECTURE.
7. RURAL ARCHITECTURE.
8. THEATRES.
9. BRIDGES.
10. ELEMENTARY AND PRACTICAL WORKS.
11. ORNAMENTS.

I. GRECIAN ARCHITECTURE,

Aberdeen, Earl of. Inquiry into the Principles of Beauty in Grecian Architecture. 8vo. London, 1822.

Aikin, E. Essay on the Doric Order. Imperial folio. London, 1810.

Antiquities (the Unedited) of Attica, comprising the Architectural Remains of Eleusis, Rhamnus, Sunium, and Thoricus. By the Society of Dilettanti, and edited by Wilkins, Gandy Deering, and Bedford. Imperial folio, 79 plates. London, 1817.

Antiquities of Ionia, by Chandler, Revett, and Pars. Imperial folio, plates, 3 vols. London, 1769–97 and 1840.

Chambers, Sir W. Decorative Part of Civil Architecture. Folio. 1759. Gwilt's edition, with an Introductory Essay on Grecian Architecture. 8vo. London, 1825.

Chandler, R. Travels in Asia Minor and Greece. 2 vols. 4to. London, 1817.

Choiseul-Gouffier. Voyage Pittoresque de la Grèce. 2 vols. folio. Paris, 1782–1809.

Cockerell, C. R. Temple of Jupiter Olympius at Agrigentum. London, 1825.

Delagardette. Les Ruines de Pæstum, ou Posidonia. Royal folio. Paris, 1799.

Donaldson, T. L. Collection of the most approved Examples of Doorways from ancient Buildings in Greece and Italy. 2 vols. 4to. London, 1833.

Gärtner, F. Monuments of Greece and Sicily. Folio. Munich, 1819.

Harris, W., and Angell, S. Metopes of the Temple at Selinus. Large 4to. plates. London, 1826.

Hittorff, J. J. Architecture Antique de la Sicile. Paris, 1825, 1830, 1837.

Le Roy. Les Ruines des plus beaux Monuments de la Grèce, considerées du coté de l'Histoire, et du coté de l'Architecture. Imp. folio, plates by Le Bas. Paris, 1758. Not a correct work.

Major, T. Ruines de Pæstum. 24 plates, large folio. 1768.

Quatremère de Quincy, A. C. Jupiter Olympien. Large folio, plates, some coloured. Paris, 1815.

———————— Restitution des Deux Frontons du Temple de Minerve à Athènes. 4to. 3 plates. Paris, 1825.

Stanhope, J. S. Olympia ; or Topography of the ancient State of the Plain of Olympia, and of the Ruins of the City of Elis. Imp. folio. London, 1824.

Stuart, James. Antiquities of Athens. 4 vols. large folio. 1762, 1787, 1794. A supplementary volume was edited by J. Woods in 1816.

Stuart, James, F.R.S., F.S.A., and Nicholas Revett's Antiquities of Athens, a second edition, with a very considerable augmentation of notes of subjects further elucidated and brought to light by Travellers since the times of Stuart and Revett, edited by W. Kinnard, architect, with a supplement of Antiquities in Greece, Sicily, &c. the result of recent Investigations, by C. R. Cockerell, W. Kinnard, T. L. Donaldson, W. Jenkins, and others, architects. 4 vols. royal folio, about 200 plates. 1825–30.
    The plates in the three first volumes of this edition are from the coppers of the French edition, by J. J. Hittorff. Folio. Paris, 1808–22.

Visconti, Chevalier. Ouvrages de Sculpture du Parthénon. 8vo. Paris, 1818.

Wilkins, W. Antiquities of Magna Græcia. Imp. folio. Cambridge, 1807.

———————— Topography and Buildings of Athens. Royal 8vo. plates. 1816.

II. Roman Architecture.

Adams, Robert. Ruins of the Palace of the Emperor Diocletian at Spalatro in Dalmatia. Folio, 61 plates. London, 1764.

Allason, T. Picturesque Views of the Antiquities of Pola. Folio, 14 plates. London, 1817.

Bartoli, P. S. Gli Antichi Sepolchri ovvero Mausolei Romani ed Etruschi. Folio, 110 plates. Roma, 1727.

——— Colonna Trajana, a P. Bellori. 128 plates.

Bellonii, J. P. Veteres Arcus Augustorum Triumphis insignes ex Reliquiis quæ Romæ adhuc supersunt per J. J. de Rubeis. Folio. Roma, 1690.

Bianchi di Lugano, P. Osservazioni sull' Arena, e sul Podio dell' Anfiteatro Flavio. Folio. Roma, 1812.

Bianconi, G. L. Descrizione dei Circhi. Folio, 20 plates. Roma, 1789.

Cameron. Baths of the Romans explained and illustrated. Folio, 75 plates. London, 1772.

Caristie, A. Plan et Coupe d'une partie du Forum Romain et des Monumens sur la Voie Sacrée. Atlas folio. Paris, 1821.

Castell, R. Villas of the Ancients illustrated. Large folio. 1728.

Ciampini, J. Rom. Vetera Monumenta. Romæ, 1747.

Cipriani, G. B. Monumenti di Fabbriche Antiche. 4to. Roma, 1796.

Desgodetz, A. Edifices de Rome, dessinées et mésurés très exactement. Folio, upwards of 300 plates. Paris, 1682.

Gell, Sir W., and J. P. Gandy. Pompeiana; the Topography, Edifices, and Ornaments of Pompeii. 2 vols. imperial 8vo. London, 1824.

Grangent, M. M., C. Durand, et S. Durant. Description des Monumens Antiques du Midi de la France. Folio, plates. Paris, 1819.

Haudebourt, L. P. Le Laurentin; Maison de Campagne de Pline le Jeune. Large 8vo. plates. Paris, 1838.

Labacco, Ant. Appartenente all' Architettura nel qual si figurano alcune notabili Antiquità di Roma. Plates, folio. Roma.

Maffei, Scipio. History of Ancient Amphitheatres. Translated by Gordon. 8vo. London, 1730.

Mazois, F., and Gau, F. C. Les Ruines de Pompei. 4 vols. folio. Paris, 1812, 1824, 1829, 1838.

Nibby, Ant. Del Foro Romano, della Via Sacra, dell' Anfiteatro Flavio, e di Luoghi adjacenti. 8vo. Roma, 1819.

Palladio, A. I Quattro Libri d' Architettura : whereof the last book is of ancient Roman Architecture. Several editions published at Venice. Figures on wood blocks.

——— Il Tempio di Minerva in Assisi confrontato colle Tavole di Giov. Antolini. Folio. Milano, 1803.

——— Les Thermes, des Romains, dessinées par O. B. Scamozzi, d'après l'Exemplaire du Lord Burlington. Folio. Vicenza, 1785.

Piranesi, Giov. Bapt. The works of (the son) subsequent to the death of John Baptist Piranesi. 29 vols. imperial folio, and double elephant folio. An abbreviated list of them is subjoined : —

Vol. 1. Ruins of ancient Edifices of Rome, with the Explanation, Aqueducts, Baths, the Forum, &c. &c.

Vol. 2. Funeral Monuments, Cippi, Vases, &c. &c.

Vol. 3. Ancient Bas-reliefs, Stuccoes, Mosaics, Inscriptions, &c. &c.

Vol. 4. The Bridges of Rome, the Ruins of the Theatres, Porticoes, &c. &c.

Vol. 5. The Monuments of the Scipios.

Vol. 6. Ancient Temples, the Temples of Vesta, of Honour and Virtue, Statue of the Goddess Vesta, Altar to Bacchus, the Pantheon of Rome, &c. &c.

Vol. 7. The Magnificence of the ancient Roman Architecture, Pedestals of the Arches of Titus and Septimius Severus, Portico of the Capitol, &c. &c.

Vol. 8. Grecian, Etruscan, and Roman Architecture, Arches of Triumph, Bridges, Temples, Amphitheatres, Prisons, &c.

Vol. 9. Fêtes and Triumphs, from the Foundation of Rome to Tiberius, Temple of Castor and Hercules, and other antique Monuments of the ancient City of Cora, &c. &c.

Vol. 10. The ancient Campo Marzio, Ruins of the Theatre of Pompeii, Portico of Octavius, Reservoir of the Virgin Water, Mausoleum of Augustus, Palace of Aurelius, the Pantheon, the Cave of the Archives of the Romans, Baths and Tombs of Adrian, Apotheosis of Antonine the Pious, Arch of Marcus Aurelius, Baths of Sallust, Plan of the Roman Senate House, &c. &c.

Vol. 11. Antiquities of Albano, Temple of Jupiter, sepulchral Attributes to the Horatii, Amphitheatre of Domitian, ancient Baths, &c.

Vol. 12. Ancient Candelabras and Vases, Urns, Lamps, &c. &c.
Vol. 13. Ancient Candelabras and Vases, Urns, Lamps, &c. &c.
Vol. 14. The Trajan and Antonine Columns.
Vol. 15. Ruins of Pæstum, Temple of Neptune, Temple of Juno, &c. &c.
Vol. 16. The principal modern Edifices of Rome, Monuments, Palaces, Fountains,
    Aqueducts, Bridges, Temples, Porticoes, Amphitheatres, Baths, &c. &c.
Vol. 17. The Principal Modern Edifices of Rome, Monuments, Palaces, Fountains,
    Aqueducts, Bridges, Temples, Porticoes, Amphitheatres, Baths, &c. &c.
Vol. 18. The principal ancient Statues and Busts of the Royal Museum of France,
    the Vatican, of the Capitol, Villa Borghese, Villa Ludovici, Farnesian Palace,
    the Gallery of Florence, &c. &c.
Vol. 19. Theatre of Herculaneum.
Vol. 20. Egyptian, Grecian, Etruscan, and Roman Chimney Pieces, Ornaments,
    &c. &c.
Vol. 21. Forty-four Plates after Guercino, by Piranesi, Bartolozzi, &c.
Vol. 22. Italian School of Painting.
Vol. 23. Twenty-four grand Subjects from Rafaelle, Volterra, Pompeii, Hercula-
    neum, &c. &c.
Vol. 24. Twelve Paintings of Rafaelle, in the Vatican, &c. &c.
Vol. 25. Fourteen Paintings of Rafaelle, in the Vatican, &c. &c.
Vol. 26. Thirteen Paintings of Vasari, after the Designs of Michael Angelo, &c. &c.
Vol. 27. The Destruction of Pompeii, its Tombs, Utensils, Ornaments, &c. &c.
Vol. 28. Antiquities of Pompeii, its Houses, Tombs, Vases, &c.
Vol. 29. Antiquities of Pompeii and Herculaneum, &c. &c.

Ponce. Description des Bains de Titus. Folio, plates. Paris, 1786.
Taylor, G. L., and Edward Cresy. Architectural Antiquities of Rome. 2 vols. folio.
London, 1820—1822.
Valadier, Gius. Raccoltà delle più insigni Fabbriche di Roma Antica e sui Adjacenze,
illustrata con Osservazioni Antiq. da F. A. Visconti, ed incise da V. Feoli. Plates.
Rome, 1810-26.
Vaudoyer, A. L. T. Description du Théâtre de Marcellus à Rome. 4to. Paris, 1812.
Vasi, Giuseppe. Magnificenze di Roma Antica e Moderna. 3 vols. Roma, 1747.
Wood, R. Ruins of Balbec and Palmyra. 2 vols. folio. London, 1753-57.

III. Miscellaneous.

Agincourt, Seroux D'. Histoire de l'Art par les Monumens. 6 vols. folio. Paris, 1823.
Arundale, F. Illustrations of the Buildings and Antiquities of Jerusalem, &c. with a
Tour in Syria and Egypt. Plates, 4to. London, 1838.
Belgrado. Architettura Egiziana; Dissertazione d' un Correspondente dell' Academia
delle Scienze de Parigi. 4to. Parma, 1786.
Cassas, L. F. le. Voyage Pittoresque de la Syrie, de la Phénicie, de la Palestine et de
la Basse-Égypte. 2 vols. folio.
Coste, P. Architecture Arabe; ou Monuments de Caire. Paris, 1824, &c.
Cousin, J. Génie de l'Architecture. 4to. 60 plates. Paris.
Daniell, T. and W. Oriental Scenery. 9 vols. folio. London, 1813.
David, F. A. Antiquités Étrusques, Grecques et Romaines. 5 vols. avec explications
par Hugues d'Hancarville. Paris, 1787.
Denon. Voyage dans la Basse et la Haute-Égypte. Translation. 4to. London, 1803.
Durand, J. N. L. Recueil et Parallèle des Édifices de tous Genres, anciens et modernes.
Elephant folio, 90 plates, and 8vo.; text by Legrand. Paris, 1801-9.
Gau, F. C. Antiquités de la Nubie; ou Monumens inédits des Bords du Nil, situés
entre la Première et la Seconde Cataracte. Folio. Paris, 1824-25.
Girault de Prangey. Monumens Arabes et Moresques de Cordoue, Seville et Grenade.
Large folio. Paris, 1840.
Jones, Owen, and Goury, J. Plans, Elevations, and Sections of the Alhambra. 2 vols.
folio. London, 1838-42.
Langles, L. Monumens, anciens et modernes, de l'Hindostan. 2 vols. folio. Paris,
1818.
Montfauçon, Bernard de. L'Antiquité expliquée et représentée en Figures. 5 vols.
folio; Supplement, 5 vols. folio, 964 plates. Paris 1729-33.
Murphy, J. Plans, Elevations, Sections, et Views of the Batalha. Large folio, plates.
London, 1795. 2nd edition, 1836.
———— Arabian Antiquities of Spain. Atlas folio, 97 plates. London, 1828.
Quatremère de Quincy, A. C. L'Architecture Égyptienne considerée. 18 plates, 4to.
Paris, 1803.
Rich, C. J. Ruins of Babylon and Persepolis. 8vo. London, 1816.
Tournefort. Voyage into the Levant. 2 vols. 4to. 1718.

Winckelman. Rémarques sur l'Architecture des Anciens. 8vo. Paris, 1783.

—— Histoire de l'Art chez les Anciens. 3 vols. 4to. Paris, 1790.

—— Monumenti Antichi inediti. 2 vols. folio, 184 plates. Napoli, 1820.

IV. Gothic Architecture.

Archæologia. A work consisting of many vols. published by the Society of Antiquaries. It contains several essays on Gothic and English architecture, and subjects connected with it, as well as on ancient and modern architecture; but, as the society are not responsible for the lucubrations which appear in it, and the papers published are therefore merely to be considered as the opinions of their writers, there are extremely few on which a student could rely with safety; and we have therefore mentioned it as a work in which it is possible some points may be found valuable for his perusal; but this opinion is confined exclusively to the art in which we have presumed that we ourselves possess some small information; many of the historical and other articles in it being of great value.

Bardwell, W. Temples, ancient and modern; or, Notes on Church Architecture. Large 8vo. London, 1837.

Bentham, J. History and Antiquities of the Church at Ely. 4to. 1771.

—— Essay on Gothic Architecture. 8vo.

Blore. Monumental Remains of noble and eminent Persons. Imp. 8vo. London, 1826.

Britton. Cathedrals, comprising Canterbury, York, Salisbury, Norwich, Oxford, Winchester, Litchfield, Hereford, Wells, Exeter, Worcester, Peterborough, Gloucester, and Bristol. 4to. 1835.

As respects the graphic part of this work, it is one of great value to the student.

Britton, J. Architectural Antiquities of Great Britain. 4 vols. 4to. London, various dates.

—— Chronological and Historical Illustrations of the ancient Ecclesiastical Architecture of Great Britain. 4to. London, 1835.

—— History and Antiquities of Bath Abbey. Royal 8vo.

—— History and Antiquities of Radclyffe Church. 4to.

Britton and Brayley. History of the ancient Palace and late Houses of Parliament at Westminster. 8vo. London, 1836.

Boisserée, Sulpice. Vues, Plans, Coupes, et Détails de la Cathèdrale de Cologne, &c. Very large folio. Stutgard, 1827. Text in 4to.

Carter, J. Ancient Architecture of England. 2 vols. folio, 1837.

Caveler, W. Select Specimens of Gothic Architecture. 4to. 80 plates. London, 1839.

Cotman, J. S. Architectural Antiquities of Norfolk. Folio, 60 plates.

—— Architectural Antiquities of Normandy. 2 vols. folio, 1820-1.

Cresy, Edw., and G. L. Taylor. The Architecture of the Middle Ages at Pisa, from Drawings and Measurements in 1817, accompanied by descriptive Accounts of their History and Construction. Imp. 4to. London, 1828-9.

Dallaway, Rev. James. Observations on English Architecture. Roy. 8vo. Lond. 1806.

—— Notices of ancient Church Architecture in the Fifteenth Century. 4to. 1824.

—— Discourses on Architecture. 8vo. London, 1833.

Ducarel. Anglo-Norman Antiquities. Plates, folio.

Dugdale, W. History of St. Paul's Cathedral in London. Folio, 1688.

Gage, J. History and Antiquities of Hengreave in Suffolk. Royal 4to. plates, 1822.

Gough. Sepulchral Monuments in Great Britain. Folio, 5 vols. London, 1796.

Grose, Captain. Essay on Gothic Architecture. 8vo.

Habershon, M. Ancient half-timbered Houses of England. 4to. London, 1836.

Halfpenny, J. Gothic Ornaments in the Cathedral of York. 4to. 105 plates, 1795.

—— Fragmenta Vetusta; or, Remains of ancient Buildings in York. Royal 4to. 34 plates, 1807.

Hall, Sir J. Essay on the Origin, History, and Principles of Gothic Architecture. 4to. 59 plates, 1813.

Hawkins, J. S. Origin and Establishment of Gothic Architecture. Plates, large 8vo. 1813.

King. Monumenta Antiqua. 4 vols. folio, plates. London, 1799.

Langlois, E. H. Description Historique des Maisons de Rouen. 8vo. with plates. Paris, 1821.

Lusson, A. L. Specimen d'Architecture Gothique; ou Plans, Coupes, Elévations de la Chapelle du Château de Neuville. Folio, 17 plates. Paris, 1839.

Mackenzie and Pugin. Specimens of Gothic Architecture, consisting of Doors, Windows, Buttresses, Pinnacles, &c. 4to. 62 plates.

Milan. Nuovo Descrizione del Duomo di Milano, &c. 8vo. plates. Milano, 1820.

Miller, G. Description of the Cathedral Church of Ely, with some Account of the Conventual Buildings. 1808.

Milner, J. Treatise on the Ecclesiastical Architecture of England. Royal 8vo. plates London, 1835.

Moller, G. Monumens de l'Architecture Allemande. Folio, Darmstadt, 1836.

Pugin, A. Specimens of Gothic Architecture, selected from various ancient Edifices in England. 4to. plates, 2 vols. London, 1823.

———— Examples of Gothic Architecture. 3 vols. 4to. 224 plates. London, 1836.

———— Examples of Gothic Ornaments. 4to. 90 plates, 1839.

———— Examples of Gothic Gables. 4to. 30 plates, 1839.

———— Specimens of Anglo-Norman Architecture. 4to. 80 plates, 1826.

Shaw, H. Series of Details of Gothic Architecture, selected from various Cathedrals, Churches, &c. Folio. London, 1823.

Smith, J. Specimens of ancient Carpentry. 4to. 36 plates.

Vetusta Monumenta: published by the Society of Antiquaries of London. 6 vols. large folio.

Warton, Rev. T. Essay on Gothic Architecture. 8vo.

Whittington, G. D. Ecclesiastical Antiquities of France. Large 8vo. London, 1811.

Wild. Cathedral Church of Lincoln. 4to. London, 1838.

Willement, T. Regal Heraldry. London, 1821.

Winkles, B. Cathedrals of England and Wales. 3 vols. London, 1836–42.

Woolnoth, W. Ancient Castles of England and Wales. 2 vols. 8vo. London, 1825.

V. MODERN FOREIGN ARCHITECTURE.

Blondel, J. B. Plan, Coupe, Elévation, et Détails, du nouveau Marché St. Germain. Folio. Paris, 1816.

Bonanni, P. P. Templi Vaticani Historia. Folio. Romæ, 1696.

Brogniart, A. T. Plans du Palais de la Bourse de Paris et du Cimétière Mont Louis. Folio. Paris, 1814.

Callet et Lesueur Architecture Italienne; ou Palais, Maisons, et autres Edifices d'Italie.

Cicognara, L. Le Fabbriche più cospicue di Venezia, misurate, illustrate, ed intagliate. 2 vols. large folio. Venez. 1815.

Clochar, P. Palais, Maisons, et Vues d'Italie. Folio, 102 plates. Paris, 1809.

Costa, G. Delizie del Fiume Brenta, espresse ne' Palazzi e Casini situate sopra le sue Sponde. Folio. Venezià, 1750.

Dumont. Œuvres d'Architecture; contenant les Détails de St. Pierre de Rome. Folio. Paris.

Duval. Fontaines de Paris. Folio. Paris.

Fontana, C. Templum Vaticanum, et ipsius Origo. Folio. Romæ, 1694.

Gauthier, M. P. Les plus beaux Edifices de la Ville de Gênes et de ses Environs. Folio. Paris, 1824—1830.

Grandjean de Montigny, A. et Famin, A. Architecture Toscane. Folio, 73 plates. Paris, 1837. New edition, 1846.

Gwilt, Joseph. Notices of the Buildings of Architects of Italy. 8vo. London, 1818.

Hittorff, J., et Zanth, L. Architecture Moderne de la Sicile. Imperial folio. Paris, 1825–39.

Klenze, L. von. Sammlung architectonischer Entwürfe. 50 plates, folio. München, 1847.

Krafft, J. C. Recueil d'Architecture civile, contenant les Plans, Coupes, et Élévations des Châteaux, Maisons de Campagne et Habitations Rurales. Folio. Paris, 1809.

Legrand, J. G., et Landon, C. F. Description de Paris et de ses Édifices. 2 vols. Paris, 1806.

Letarouilly, P. Édifices de Rome Moderne. 3 vols. folio. text 4to. Paris, 1829–55.

Moisy, M. Fontaines de Paris, anciennes et nouvelles, par Duval. Folio, 59 plates. Paris, 1812.

Palladio, A. Les Bâtimens et Desseins recueillis et illustrés, par Ottavio Bertotti Scamozzi. In French and Italian. 4 vols. folio. Vicenza, 1787.

———— L'Architettura di. Folio. Venezia, 1642.

Patte, P. Études d'Architecture. 4to. plates. Paris, 1755.

Pieraccini, F. La Piazza del Granduca di Firenze co' suoi Monumenti. Folio, plates. Firenze, 1830.

Percier, C. et Fontaine, P. F. L. Choix des plus celèbres Maisons de Plaisance de Rome et de ses Environs. 75 plates, folio. Paris, 1824. [Rome.

Rossi, G. J. Raccoltà di Fontane nel alma Città di Roma, Tivoli e Frascati. 4to.

Sanmichele, M. Porte di Città e Fortezze, Depositi Sepolchrali, ed altre principali Fabbriche pubbliche ed private, da F. Albertolli. Imperial folio. Milan, 1815.

Schinkel, C. von. Sammlung architectonischer Entwürfe. Large folio. 174 plates. Berlin, 1819–48.

Suys, F. T., et Haudebourt, L. P.   Palais Massimi à Rome ; Plans, Coupes, Élévations, Profiles, Voutes, Plafonds, &c.   43 plates.   Paris, 1818.

VI. Modern English Architecture.

Adam, W.   Vitruvius Scoticus; a Collection of public and private Buildings in Scotland.   Folio, 160 plates.   Edinburgh.

Brettingham, M.   Plans, Elevations, and Sections of Holkham, in Norfolk.   Folio, London, 1763.

Campbell, C.   Vitruvius Britannicus.   5 vols. the two last being a Continuation by Woolfe and Gandon.   Folio.   London, 1715, 1725, 1731; 1767, 1771.

Chambers, Sir W.   Plans, Elevations, Sections, &c., of the Gardens and Buildings at Kew.   Folio.   London, 1757.

Gibbs, J.   Book of Architecture, containing St. Martin's Church, &c.   Large folio. London, 1728.

———— Designs for the Radclyffe Library.   Folio.   London, 1747.

Goldicutt, J.   Heriot's Hospital, Edinburgh, the Design of Inigo Jones.   Folio, 8 plates.   London, 1828.

Jones, Inigo.   Designs for public and private Buildings, by Kent.   Folio.   London, 1770.

Lewis, James.   Original Designs in Architecture, consisting of Plans, Elevations, and Sections of various public and private Buildings in England and Ireland.   2 vols. folio, 61 plates, 1780—1797.

Mitchell, R.   Plans and Views in Perspective, with Descriptions of Buildings erected in England and Scotland.   Folio, 18 plates, 1801.

Paine, J.   Plans, Elevations, &c. of Noblemen's and Gentlemen's Houses in various Counties.   Folio, 175 plates.   London, 1783.

Richardson, G.   New Vitruvius Britannicus.   2 vols. folio.   London. 1802; 1808.

VII. Rural Architecture.

Architecture Rurale, Théorique et Pratique, à l'Usage des Propriétaires et des Ouvriers de la Campagne.   8vo. 11 plates.   Toulouse, 1820.

Aikin, E.   Designs for Villas and other Rural Buildings.   4to.   London, 1835.

Gandy, J.   Rural Architect, consisting of various Designs for Country Buildings.   4 to. 42 plates.   London, 1805.

———— Designs for Cottages, Cottage Farms, and other Buildings ; including Entrance Gates and Lodges.   4to. 43 plates.   London, 1805.

Goodwin, F.   Rural Architecture.   2 vols. 4to.   London, 1835.

———— Designs of Peasants' Cottages, Gate Lodges, small Dairy Farm Houses, &c. 4to. London, 1833.

———— Supplement to Cottage Architecture.   London, 1835.

Krafft, J. C.   Plans des plus beaux Jardins Pittoresques de France, d'Angleterre, et d'Allemagne, et des Edifices, Monumens, Fabriques, &c., qui concourent à leur Embellissement, dans tous les Genres d'Architecture.   2 vols. oblong 4to.   Paris, 1809.

Loudon, J. C.   Encyclopædia of Cottage, Farm, and Villa Architecture.   8vo. London, 1839.

Malton, J.   Essay on British Cottage Architecture.   Large 4to.   London, 1804.

Morel-Vindé, le Vicomte de.   Essai sur les Constructions Rurales Economiques ; contenant leurs Plans, Coupes, Elevations, Détails, et Devis.   Folio.   Paris, 1824.

Normand, C.   Recueil varié de Plans et de Façades Motifs pour des Maisons de Ville et de Campagne.   Folio, 53 plates.   Paris, 1815.

Papworth, J. B.   Rural Residences ; a Series of Designs for Cottages, decorated Cottages, small Villas, &c.   London, 1832.

Robinson, P. F.   Rural Architecture ; or a Series of Designs for Ornamental Cottages. 4to. 96 plates.   London, 1823.

———— Designs for Ornamental Villas.   4to.   London, 1837.

———— Designs for Village Architecture.   4to.   London, 1837.

———— Designs for Farm Buildings.   4to.   London, 1837.

Soane, J.   Sketches in Architecture; containing Plans and Elevations of Cottages, Villas, and other useful Buildings.   Folio, 43 plates.   London, 1798.

VIII. Theatres.

Arnaldi, Conte Enea.   Idea di un Teatro nelle principali sue Parti simile a' Teatri Antichi all' Uso moderno accomodato.   4to.   Vicenza, 1762.

Beccega, T. C.   Sull' Architettura Greco-Romana applicata alla Costruzione del Teatro moderno Italiano e sulle Macchine Teatrali.   Folio.   Venezia, 1817.

Bonnet, A., et J. A. Kaufmann.   Architectonographie des Théâtres de Paris, ou Parallèle

Historique et Critique de ces Edifices, considerés sous le Rapport de l'Architecture et de la Décoration. 2 vols. 8vo. 4 atlas of plates. Paris, 1837.

Borgnis, J. A. Des Machines Imitatives et des Machines Teatrales. 4to. 27 plates. Paris, 1820.

Boullet. Essai sur l'Art de construire les Théâtres, leurs Machines, et leurs Mouvemens. 4to. plates. Paris, 1801.

Descrizione del Nuovo Sipario dell' Imperiale Regio Teatro della Scala in Milano. Small folio. Milano, 1821.

Dumont. Parallèle de Plans des Salles de Spectacle d'Italie et de France, avec des Détails de Machines Teatrales. Imperial folio, 61 plates. Paris, 1774.

Fontanesi, C. F. Decorations for Theatres; or Designs for Scene Painters. Oblong folio, 24 plates, 1813.

Galliari. Décorations de Théâtre. Folio, 24 plates. Milan.

Giorgi Felice. Descrizione Istorica del Teatro di Tor di Nino. 4to. 9 plates. Rome, 1795.

Landriani, P. Osservazioni sui Defetti prodotti nei Teatri dalla cattiva Costruzione del Palio Scenico, e su alcune Inavvertenze nel dipingere le Decorazioni. 4to. 9 plates. Milano, 1815.

Louis, V. Salle de Spectacle de Bourdeaux. Atlas folio, 22 plates, containing plans of several other theatres. Paris, 1782.

Morelli, Cos. Pianta e Spaccato del nuovo Teatro d'Imola. Folio, 19 plates. Roma, 1780.

Patte, P. Essai sur l'Architecture Théâtrale. 8vo. Paris, 1782.

Saunders, G. Treatise on Theatres. 4to. 13 plates. London, 1790. Of little value.

Schinkel. Theatre at Hamburg. 6 plates, Berlin. 1828.

Ware, S. Remarks on Theatres, and on the Propriety of vaulting them with Brick and Stone. 8vo. plates. London, 1809.

Wyatt, B. On the rebuilding of Drury Lane Theatre. 4to. plates. London, 1812.

IX. Bridges.

Anselin, N. J. B. Expériences sur la Main d'Œuvres de differens Travaux dependans du Service des Ingénieurs des Ponts et Chaussées, &c. 4to. Boulogne, 1810.

Atwood, G. Dissertation on the Construction and Properties of Arches. 4to. 1801—1804.

Aubry. Mémoire sur la Construction d'un Pont de Bois de 450 Pieds d' Ouverture d' un seul Jet, &c. 4to. Paris, 1790.

Blackfriars' Bridge. 7 plates of the machines used in its construction, and the centring of the middle arch. Oblong folio.

Boistard, L. C. Recueil sur les Ponts de Nemours, &c. 4to. 19 plates. Paris, 1822.

Emmery, H. C. Pont d'Ivry en Bois, sur Piles en Pierre, traversant la Seine près du confluent de la Marne. 2 vols. 4to. plates. Paris, 1832.

Exchaquet. Dictionnaire des Ponts et Chaussées. 8vo. 12 plates. Paris, 1787.

Gauthey. Traité de la Construction des Ponts; Mémoires sur les Canaux de Navigation, &c. publié par M. Navier. 3 vols. 4to. plates. Paris, 1816

Gautier, H. Traité de la Construction des Ponts et Chaussées. 8vo. Paris, 1755.

Goury, G. Recueil d'Observations, Mémoires, et Projets, concernant la Navigation Intérieure. 2 tomes 4to. avec un atlas de planches. Paris, 1827.

Gwilt, Joseph. On the Rebuilding of London Bridge. 8vo. with 1 plate. London, 1823.

—— Treatise on the Equilibrium of Arches. 8vo. plates. London, 1826.

The editions of a later date are spurious, being without additions or corrections by the author.

Hutton, C. Principles of Bridges. 8vo. 1772.

Le Sage, P. C. Recueil de divers Mémoires des Ponts et Chaussées. 2 tom. 4to. Paris, 1810.

Milne, J. Theory and Principles of Bridges and Piers. 8vo. 36 plates. London, 1806.

Navier. Mémoire sur les Ponts Suspendus. 4to. plates. Paris, 1830.

Perronet, Œuvres de. 4to. plates, Atlas folio. Paris, 1793.

Polonceau, A. R. Notice sur la nouveau Système de Ponts en Fonte, suivi dans la Construction du Pont du Carousel. 4to. Atlas folio, plates. Paris, 1839.

Pont en Pierre a construire sur la Seine à Rouen. 4to. plates. Paris, 1815.

Prony, M. de. Nouvelle Architecture Hydraulique. 2 vols. 4to. plates. Paris, 1790.

Regemortes, M. de. Description du nouveau Pont de Pierre construit sur la Rivière d'Allier à Moulins. Folio. Paris, 1771.

Rondelet, A. Essai Historique sur le Pont de Rialto. 4to. plates. Paris, 1837.

Seaward, J. Observations on the Rebuilding of London Bridge. 8vo. plates. London, 1824.

Seguin, Ainé. Des Ponts en Fil de Fer. 8vo. plates. Paris, 1824.

Telford, T. Reports on the Holyhead Roads, Harbour, Bridges, &c. Folio, with plates. London, 1822.

Vicat. Description du Pont Suspendu construit sur la Dordogne à Argental. 4to. plates. Paris, 1830.

Ware, S. Treatise on the Properties of Arches, and their Abutment Piers. London 1809.

Wiebeking, Le Chevalier. Architecture Hydraulique fondée sur la Théorie et la Pratique. 4 vols. 4to. Atlas vol. of plates. Munich, 1814—1824.

X. ELEMENTARY AND PRACTICAL WORKS.

Alberti, Leo Bapt. Libri de Re Ædificatoria. Decem folio, 1st edit. Florence. 1485

———— Reprinted in 4to. Paris, 1512.

———— Translated into Italian by Pietro Lauro. Small 4to. Venice, 1546.

———— Translated into Italian by Cosimo Bartoli. Folio. Florence, 1556.

———— Translated into English by Leoni. Folio. London, 1726—1755 ; and Bologna, 1782.

Androuet du Cerceau. Livre d'Architecture. Folio, 50 plates. Paris, 1662.

Antoine, J. Traité d'Architecture. 4to. plates. Treves, 1768.

Aviler, d', C. A. Cours d'Architecture. 4to. Paris, 1760.

Barlow, P. Treatise on the Strength of Timber, Cast Iron, Malleable Iron, and other Materials, &c. 8vo. London, 1837. Edited by J. F. Heather, 1851.

Barozzi, Vignola di. Œuvres complètes. Folio. Paris, 1823.

———— Ordini d'Architettura Civile. 4to. 44 plates. Milano, 1814.

Bartholomew, Alfred. Specifications for Practical Architecture, preceded by an Essay on the Decline of Excellence in the Structure, and in the Science of Modern English Buildings. Large 8vo. 160 illustrations. London, 1840.

This is one of the most valuable works to the English practical architect that has ever appeared.

Blondel, J. F. Cours d'Architecture. 9 tom. 8vo. 300 plates. Paris, 1771—1777.

Borgnis, J. A. Traité Elémentaire de Construction appliquée à l'Architecture Civile. 2 tom. 4to. 30 plates. Paris, 1823.

Bruyere, L. Etudes relatives à l'Art des Constructions. Folio. Paris, 1823.

Bullet. Architecture Pratique. 8vo. plates. Paris, 1774.

———— By Mazois. Paris, 1824.

Calderari, C. Opere di Architettura. 2 tom. folio, 90 plates. Vicenza, 1800.

Chambers, Sir William. The Decorative Part of Civil Architecture, with Essay on Grecian Architecture, and other Additions by Joseph Gwilt. 2 vols. imp. 8vo. 66 plates. London, 1823.

Clerc, S. Le. Treatise on Architecture, translated by Chambers. 2 vols. 8vo. and vol. of plates. London, 1732.

Detournelle. Recueil d'Architecture. Folio, 60 plates. Paris, 1805.

Douliot, J. P. Traité special de Coupe des Pierres. 2 tom. 4to. Paris, 1825.

Durand, J. N. L. Leçons d'Architecture. 2 tom. 4to. plates. Paris, 1819.

———— Partie Graphique des Cours d'Architecture. 4to. 34 plates. Paris, 1821.

Elmes, J. On Dilapidations. 8vo. London, 1829.

Evelyn, J. Ancient and Modern Architecture. Folio. London, 1680.

———— Parallel of Ancient and Modern Architecture : translated from R. Freart. Folio, plates. London, 1723.

Farraday, Prof. On the practical Prevention of Dry Rot in Timber. 8vo. London, 1836.

Felibien, M. Principes de l'Architecture, de la Sculpture, et de la Peinture. 4to. plates. Paris, 1697.

Frezier. Théorie et la Pratique de la Coupe des Pierres et des Bois. 3 vols. 4to. plates. Paris, 1757.

Fourneau, H. Art du Trait de Charpenterie. 4 vols. folio, 87 plates. Paris, 1820.

Gauthey, E. M. Dissertation sur les Dégradations survenues aux Piliers du Dôme du Panthéon, et sur les Moyens d'y remedier. 4to. plates. Paris, 1798.

Goldman, Architecture of, by L. C. Sturms ; the text in the German language. 1714.

Gwilt, Joseph. Sciography ; or Examples of Shadows, with Rules for their Projection, for the Use of Architectural Draughtsmen, and other Artists. 8vo. 24 plates. London, 1824.

———— Rudiments of Architecture, Practical and Theoretical. Royal 8vo. plates. London, 1826.

Halfpenny, W. Architecture delineated. 4to. 45 plates. London, 1749.

———— Art of Sound Building. Folio. London, 1725.

Higgins, B. Art of composing and applying Calcareous Cements, and of preparing Quicklime. 8vo. London, 1780.

Inman, W. On Ventilation, Warming, and the Transmission of Sound; with notes. London, 1836.

Krafft, J. C. Recueil d'Architecture Civile, contenant les Plans, Coupes, et Elévations des Châteaux, Maisons de Campagne, et Habitations Rurales, &c. Folio, 121 plates. Paris, 1812.

—— Traité sur l'Art de la Charpenterie; Plans, Coupes, et Elévations, de diverses Productions. Folio. Paris, 1820.

Laugier, P. Essai sur l'Architecture. 8vo. Paris, 1755.

Ledoux, E. N. L'Architecture considerée sous le Rapport de l'Art, des Mœurs, et de la Legislation. Imperial folio, plates. Paris, 1789.

L'Eveillé, C. J. Considérations sur les Frontons. 4to. Paris, 1824.

Le Grand, Essai sur l'Histoire Générale de l'Architecture. 8vo. Paris, 1819. This is the text to Durand's Paralléle.

Lorme, Philibert de. Œuvres d'Architecture. Folio, 2 vols. in 1. Paris, 1626; Rouen, 1648.

The first edition, the Treatise on Architecture, in 9 books, was published in Paris, 1567. The tenth book on Carpentry, entitled, "Nouvelles Inventions pour bien Bâtir et à petit Frais," was published in folio. Paris, 1561—1568 and 1576.

Loudon, J. C. Architectural Magazine. 5 vols. 8vo. London, 1838.

Malton, T. Complete Treatise on Perspective. Folio, 2 vols. London, 1778.

——, J. Young Painter's Maulstick. 4to. plates. London, 1806.

Mandar. Etude d'Architecture Civile; ou Plans, Elévations, Coupes, et Détails necessaires pour élever, distribuer, et décorer une Maison et ses Dependances. Imperial folio, 122 plates. Paris, 1830.

Manetti, G. A. Studio degli Ordini d'Architettura. Folio, 25 plates. Firenze, 1808.

Mesauge, M. Traité de Charpenterie et des Bois de toutes Espèces. 2 tom. Paris, 1753.

Mitford, N. Principles of Design in Architecture traced in Observations on Buildings (published anonymously). 8vo. London, 1819.

Nicholson, P. Principles of Architecture. 8vo. 3 vols. plates. London, 1836.

—— Architectural Dictionary. 2 vols. 4to. London, 1819. Edited by Lomax, 1853.

—— Carpenter and Joiner's Assistant. 4to. London, 1815.

—— Carpenter's New Guide. 4to. London, 1819.

—— Practical Treatise on the Art of Masonry and Stone-cutting. 8vo. London, 1832.

Noble, J. Professional Practice of Architects, and that of Measuring Surveyors, and Reference to Builders. 8vo. London, 1836.

Normand, C. Nouveau Parallèle des Ordres d'Architecture des Grecs, des Romains et des Auteurs modernes. Folio, 63 plates. Paris, 1819. Translated by A. Pugin, 1829.

Nosban. Manuel du Menuisier. 2 vols. 12mo. plates. Paris, 1827.

Pasley, Col. C. W. On Limes, Calcareous Cements, Mortars, Stuccoes, Concrete, and Puzzuolanas, &c. 8vo. London, 1838. 2nd edition, part i. only, 1847.

Patte, P. Mémoire d'Architecture. 4to. Paris, 1769.

Perrault, C. Ordonnance des Cinq Espèces de Colonnes. Folio. Paris, 1683.

Pozzo, Andrea. Prospettiva di Pittori, &c. 2 vols. folio, 218 plates. Rome, 1717–37.

Price, F. British Carpenter. 4to. plates. London, 1753.

Price, R. On Reversionary Payments; by Morgan. 2 vols. 8vo. London, 1803.

Rondelet, J. Traité Théorique et Pratique de l'Art de Bâtir. 5 vols. 4to. and fol. vol. of 207 plates. Continuation by G. A. Blouet. Paris, 1858. 10th edition.

—— Mémoire Historique sur le Dôme du Panthéon François. 10 plates, 4to. Paris, 1814.

—— Mémoire sur la Réconstruction de la Coupole de la Halle au Blé de Paris. 4to. 3 plates. Paris.

Scamozzi, V. L' Idea dell' Architettura Universale. 2 vols. folio. Venetia, 1615.

Serlio, S. Architettura. 4to. Venetia, 1567.

Simonin. Traité Elémentaire de la Coupe des Pierres. 4to. Paris, 1792.

Sturm, L. C. Prodromus Architecturæ Goldmanniæ. Oblong folio. Nuremberg, 1714.

Tredgold, T. Elementary Principles of Carpentry, by Peter Barlow. 4to. 50 plates. London, 1853.

Toussaint, C. J. Traité de Géometrie et d'Architecture Théorique et Pratique simplifié. 4 vols. 4to. Paris, 1811-12.

Turnbull, W. Essay on Construction of Cast Iron Beams. 8vo. London, 1833.

Vitruve, traduit par C. Perrault. Folio, plates. Paris, 1684.

Vitruvii de Architectura notis Variorum a J. de Laet. Folio. Amst. 1649.

Vitruvio, l'Architettura di, tradotta ed comentata da B. Galiani. Folio. Siena, 1790.

Vitruvio, trad. et coment. da Barbaro. Folio, wood-cuts. Venezia, 1556.

Vitruvius, Architecture of, translated by J. Gwilt. Imperial 8vo. London, 1826.

Wiebcking, le Chevalier de.   Architecture Civile, Théorique, et Pratique, enrichi de l'Histoire descriptive des Edifices anciennes et modernes les plus remarquables. 7 vols. 4to., 260 plates, large folio.   Munich, 1823.

XI. ORNAMENTS.

Albertolli.   Corso Elementare di Ornamenti Architettonici.   Folio, 28 plates.   Milan, 1805.

Architectural Ornaments.   A Collection of Capitals, Friezes, Roses, Entablatures, Mouldings, &c. drawn on Stone from the Antique.   100 plates.   London, 1824.

Beauvallet, P. N.   Fragmens d'Architecture, Sculpture, et Peinture dans le Style Antique.   Paris, 1804.

Choix des Monumens les plus remarquables des Anciens Egyptiens, des Persans, des Grecs, des Volsques, des Etrusques, et des Romains, consistans en Statues, Bas-Reliefs, et Vases.   2 tom. fol. 244 plates.   Rome, 1788.

Colette, J.   Livre de divers Ornemens pour Plafonds, Cintres, Surbaissées, Galeries. Folio, 10 plates.   Paris.

Columbani, P.   Capitals, Friezes, and Cornices, &c.   4to.

Fowler, W.   Collection of Mosaic, Roman and Norman tesselated Pavements and ancient stained Glass discovered in different parts of England.   Elephant folio size. Published at various times.

Jalembier, C. A.   Principes d'Ornemens pour l'Architecture.   40 plates.   Paris.

Jombert, C. A.   Repertoire des Artistes; ou Recueil de Compositions d'Architecture et d'Ornemens, antiques et modernes, de tout espèce, par divers Auteurs.   2 vols. folio.   Paris, 1765.

Le Noir, A.   Nouvelle Collection d'Arabesques propres à la Décoration des Appartemens dessinées à Rome par L. Poussin.   4to.   Paris.

Le Pautre.   Œuvres d'Architecture; contenant les Frises, Feuillages, Montans ou Pilastres, Grotesques, Moresques, Parmeaux, Placarts, Trumeaux, Lansbris, Amortissemens, Plafonds, et généralement tout ce qui concerne l'Ornement.   3 vols. folio. Paris, 1751.

Moreau, C.   Fragmens et Ornemens d'Architecture dessinés à Rome d'après l'Antique. formant un Supplément à l'Œuvre d'Architecture de Desgodetz.   Large folio, 36 plates.   Paris.   1802.

Normand, C.   Nouveau Recueil en divers Genres d'Ornemens, et autres Objets propres à la Décoration.   Folio, 46 plates.   Paris, 1803.

Percier, C. et Fontaine, P. F. L.   Recueil de Décorations Intérieures, comprenant tout ce qui a rapport à l'Ameublement.   Folio, 72 plates.   Paris, 1812.

Pergolesi, M. A.   Designs for Arabesques.   Large folio, 30 plates.   1777–85.

Piroli, T.   Monumens Antiques du Musée Napoléon.   4 vols. 4to. 40 plates.   Paris, 1804.

Pompeii.   Gli Ornati delle Pareti ed i Pavimenti delle Stanze dell' Antica Pompeia. Atlas folio, 21 plates.   Napoli, 1796.

Tatham, C. H.   Grecian and Roman Ornaments.   Folio, 101 plates.   London, 1825.

Vatican.   Recueil d'Arabesques; contenant les Loges du Vatican, gravées d'après Raphael et grand Nombre d'autres Compositions du même Goût dans le Style Antique.   Large folio.   Paris, 1802.

Volpato.   Raphael's Loggie del Vaticano.   3 vols. folio.   Rome, 1772–77.

Vulliamy, L.   Examples of Ornamental Sculpture in Architecture, containing 40 plates, imp. folio.   London, 1828.

ARCHITRAVE. (Gr. Αρχειν, to govern, and Lat. Trabs, a beam.)   The lower of the three principal members of the entablature of an order, being, as its name imports, the chief beam employed in it, and resting immediately on the columns.   It is sometimes called *Epistylium*, from επι, upon, and στυλος, a column.   The height of the architrave varied in the different orders, as also in different examples of the same order.   See GRECIAN ARCHITECTURE, page 58. in the work; and, for its usual proportion, the orders from Sect. 5. to Sect. 7. Chap. I. Book III.

ARCHITRAVE CORNICE.   An entablature consisting of an architrave and cornice only, without the interposition of a frieze.   It is never used with columns or pilasters, unless through want of height.   It is, however, allowable.   See p. 870.

ARCHITRAVE OF A DOOR OR WINDOW.   A collection of members and mouldings round either, used for the decoration of the aperture.   The upper part, or lintel, is called the *traverse*, and the sides the *jambs*.   See ANTEPAGMENTA.

ARCHIVOLT. (Lat. Arcus volutus.)   The ornamental band of mouldings round the voussoirs, or arch-stones of an arch, which terminates horizontally upon the impost.   It is decorated, as to the members, analogously with the architrave, which, in arcades, it may be said to represent.   It differs in the different orders.

ARCHIVOLTUM. In mediæval architecture, an arched receptacle for filth. A cesspool or common sewer.

ARCHWAY. An aperture in a building covered with a vault. Usually an arched passage or gate wide enough for carriages to pass.

ARCUS ECCLESIÆ. In mediæval architecture, the arch dividing the nave of the church from the choir or chancel.

ARCUS PRESBYTERII. In mediæval architecture, the arch over the tribune marking the boundaries of its recess.

ARCUS TORALIS. In mediæval architecture, the lattice separating the choir from the nave in a basilica.

AREA. In Architecture, a small court or place, often sunk below the general surface of the ground, before windows in the basement story. It is also used to denote a small court even level with the ground.

AREA. In Geometry, the superficial content of any figure.

ARENA. The central space in a Roman amphitheatre, wherein the gladiators fought. See AMPHITHEATRE.

ARGELIUS. See ARCHITECTS, list of, 19.

ARMOURY. An apartment destined to the reception of instruments of war.

ARNOLFO. See ARCHITECTS, list of, 125.

ARONADE. Embattled; a junction of several lines forming indentations like the upward boundary of an embattled wall, except that the middle of every raised part is terminated by the convex arch of a circle, which arch does not extend to the length of that part.

ARRIÈRE VOUSSURE. A secondary arch. An arch placed within an opening to form a larger one; and sometimes serving as a sort of discharging arch.

ARRIS (probably abbreviated from the Ital. *a risega*, at the projection, or from the Sax. apıran, to arise). The intersection or line on which two surfaces of a body forming an exterior angle meet each other. It is a term much used by all workmen concerned in building, as the arris of a stone, of a piece of wood, or any other body. Though, in common language, the edge of a body implies the same as arris, yet, in building, the word *edge* is restrained to those two surfaces of a rectangular parallelopipedal body on which the length and thickness may be measured, as in boards, planks, doors, shutters, and other framed joinery.

ARRIS FILLET. A slight piece of timber of a triangular section, used in raising the slates against chimney shafts, or against a wall that cuts obliquely across the roof, and in forming gutters at the upper ends and sides of those kinds of skylights of which the planes coincide with those of the roof. When the arris fillet is used to raise the slates at the eaves of a building, it is then called the *eaves' board, eaves' lath,* or *eaves' catch.*

ARRIS GUTTER. A wooden gutter of this ⋁ form fixed to the eaves of a building.

ARSENAL. A public establishment for the deposition of arms and warlike stores.

ARTIFICER. (Lat. Ars and Facio.) A person who works with his hands in the manufacture of anything. He is a person of intellectual acquirements, independent of mere operation by hand, which place him above the *artisan,* whose knowledge is limited to the general rules of his trade.

ASAROTUM. In ancient architecture, a species of painted pavement used by the Romans before the invention of Mosaic work.

ASH. The Fraxinus of botanists. See TIMBER, p. 500.

ASHELFY. See ARCHITECTS, list of, 189.

ASHLAR or ASHLER. (Ital. Asciare, to chip.) Common or free-stones as brought from the quarry of different lengths and thicknesses.

Also the facing given to square stones on the front of a building. When the work is smoothed or rubbed so as to take out the marks of the tools by which the stones were cut, it is called *plain ashlar.* *Tooled ashlar* is understood to be that whereof the surface is wrought in a regular manner, like parallel flutes, and placed perpendicularly in the building. But when the surfaces of the stones are cut with a broad tool without care or regularity, the work is said to be *random-tooled.* When wrought with a narrow tool, it is said to be *chiselled* or *boasted,* and when the surface is cut with a very narrow tool, the ashlar is said to be *pointed.* When the stones project from the joints, the ashlar is said to be *rusticated,* in which the faces may have a smooth or broken surface. In superior work, neither pointed, chiselled, nor random-tooled work are employed. In some parts of the country herring-bone ashlar and herring-bone random-tooled ashlar are used. See MASONRY, p. 560, *et seq.*

ASHLERING. In carpentry, the short upright quartering fixed in garrets about two feet six inches or three feet high from the floor, being between the rafters and the floor in order to make the room more convenient by cutting off the acute angle formed by the rafters.

ASPECT. (Lat. Aspicio.) The quarter of the heavens to which the front of a building faces. Thus a front to the north is said to have a north aspect.

Asphaltum. A bituminous substance found in various places and used as a building material. See Book II. Chap. II. Sect. 11.

Assemblage. The joining or uniting several pieces together, or the union of them when so joined. Carpenters and joiners have many modes of accomplishing this, as by framing, mortise and tenon, dovetailing, &c. See Practical Carpentry and Joinery, p. 595, *et seq.*

Assemblage of the Orders. The placing of columns upon one another in the several ranges. See Orders upon Orders, Book III. Chap. I. Sect. II.

Astragal. (Gr. Αστραγαλος, a die, or huckle bone.) A small moulding of a semicircular profile. Some have said that the French call it *talon*, and the Italians *tondino*; but this is a mistake, for the term is properly applied only to the ring separating the capital from the column. The astragal is occasionally cut into representations of beads and berries. A similar sort of moulding, though not developed in its profile as is the astragal, is used to separate the faces of the architrave.

Atlantides. See Caryatides.

Atrium. In ancient Roman architecture, a court surrounded by porticoes in the interior part of Roman houses. According to Scaliger it is derived from the Greek αἴθριος, exposed to the air. By some it has been considered the same apartment as the *vestibule*, and Aulus Gellius intimates that in his time the two words were confounded. See, however, more on this head in the section on Roman Architecture in the body of the work, p. 100.

Attic, or **Attic Order.** (Gr. Αττικος, Athenian; facetiously, we supposed, derived, in the seventh edit. of Encyc. Brit. art. Architecture, from ἄτειχον, without a wall, which, if true, would transform all objects into attic things if detached from a wall.) A low order of architecture, commonly used over a principal order, never with columns, but usually with antæ or small pilasters. It is employed to decorate the façade of a story of small height, terminating the upper part of a building; and it doubtless derives its name from its resemblance in proportional height and concealed roof to some of the buildings of Greece. Pliny thus describes it after speaking of the other orders: " Præter has sunt quæ vocantur Atticæ columnæ quaternis angulis pari laterum intervallo." We, however, find no examples of square pillars in the remains of ancient art, though almost all the triumphal arches exhibit specimens of pilastral attics, having no capitals save the cornice breaking round them. In modern architecture the proportions of the attic order have never been subject to fixed rules, and their good effect is entirely dependent on the taste and feeling of the architect.

Attic Base. The base of a column consisting of an upper and lower torus, a scotia and fillets between them. It is thus described by Vitruvius, " it must be so subdivided that the upper part be one third of the thickness of the column, and that the remainder be assigned for the height of the plinth. Excluding the plinth, divide the height into four parts, one whereof is to be given to the upper torus; then divide the remaining three parts into two equal parts, one will be the height of the lower torus, and the other the height of the scotia with its fillets.

Attic Story. A term frequently applied to the upper story of a house when the ceiling is square with the sides to distinguish it from garrets. See Book III. Chap. I. Sect. 13.

Attributes. In decorative architecture, are certain symbols given to figures, or disposed as ornaments on a building, to indicate a distinguishing character: as a lyre, bow, or arrow to Apollo; a club to Hercules; a trident to Neptune; a spear to Pallas, &c.

Auger. A carpenter's and joiner's tool for boring large holes. It consists of a wooden handle terminated at the bottom with steel. The more modern augers are pointed and sharpened like a centre bit, the extremity of one of the edges being made to cut the wood clean at the circumference, and the other to cut and take away the core, the whole length of the radius.

Aula. (Lat.) In ancient Roman architecture, a court or hall.

Aviary. (Lat. Avis.) A house or apartment, set apart for keeping and breeding birds.

Avitus, St. See Architects, list of, 58.

Awning. (Fr. Aulne.) Any covering intended as a screen from the sun or protection from the rain.

Axe. (Sax. eax.) A tool with a long wooden handle and a cutting edge situate in a plane passing longitudinally through the handle. It is used for hewing timber by cutting it vertically, the edge being employed in forming horizontal surfaces. The axe differs from the *joiner's hatchet* by being much larger, and by its being used with only one hand. Axes of various sizes, depending upon the quality of the material, are used by stone-cutters and bricklayers.

Axis. The spindle or centre of any rotative motion. In a sphere a line passing through the centre is the axis.

B.

BABYLONIAN ARCHITECTURE. See Book I. Chap. II. Sect. 3.

BACK. The side opposite to the face or breast of any piece of architecture. In a recess upon a quadrangular plane, the face is that surface which has the two adjacent planes, called the sides, elbows, or gables. When a piece of timber is fixed in an horizontal or in an inclined position, the upper side is called the back, and the lower the breast. Thus the upper side of the handrail of a staircase is properly called the back. The same is to be understood with regard to the curved ribs of ceilings and the rafters of a roof, whose upper edges are always called the *backs*.

BACK OF A CHIMNEY. The recessed face of it towards the apartment, &c. See CHIMNEY.

BACK OF A HAND-RAIL. The upper side of it.

BACK OF A HIP or other RAFTER. The upper side or sides of it in the sloping plane of the side of the roof.

BACK LINING OF A SASH FRAME. That parallel to the pulley piece and next to the jamb on either side. See JOINERY, p. 641, *et seq.*

BACK SHUTTERS. Those folds of a shutter which do not appear on the face being folded within the boxing. See JOINERY, p. 638, *et seq.*

BACK OF A STONE. The side opposite to the face. It is generally rough.

BACK OF A WALL. The inner face of it.

BACK OF A WINDOW. The piece of wooden framing in the space between the lower part of the sash frame and the floor of the apartments, and bounded at its extremities right and left by the *elbows* of the window. The number of panels into which it is framed is dependent on what may be necessary for carrying out the design ; it rarely, however, consists of more than one.

BACKING OF A RAFTER or RIB. The formation of the upper or outer surface of either in such a manner as to range with the edges of the rafters or ribs on either side of it. The formation of the inner edges of the ribs for a lath and plaister ceiling is sometimes called *backing*, but improperly, since contrary to the true meaning of the word.

BACKING OF A WALL. The filling in and building which forms the inner face of the work. In this sense it is opposed to facing, which is the outside of the wall. In stone walls the backing is unfortunately too often mere rubble, while the face is ashlar.

BADIGEON. A mixture of plaster and freestone sifted and ground together, used by statuaries to repair defects in their work. The joiner applies this term to a mixture of sawdust and strong glue, with which he fills up the defects of the wood after it has been wrought. A mixture for the same purpose is made of whiting and glue, and sometimes with putty and chalk. When the first of these is used, it is allowed to remain until quite hard, after which it may be submitted to the operation of planing and smoothing. Without this precaution, it may shrink below the surface of the work.

BAGNIO. (It.) An Italian term for a bath, usually applied by the English to an establishment having conveniences for bathing, sweating, and otherwise cleansing the body. It is applied by the Turks to the prisons where their slaves are confined, in which it is customary to have baths.

BAGUETTE. (Fr.) A small moulding of the astragal species. It is occasionally cut with pearls, ribands, laurels, &c. According to M. Le Clerc, the baguette is called a *chaplet* when ornaments are cut on it.

BAILEY. See CASTLE.

BAKEHOUSE. An apartment provided with an oven and kneading troughs for baking.

BALANEIA. A Greek term for a bath.

BALCONY. (It. Balcone.) A projection from the external wall of a house, borne by columns or consoles, and usually placed before windows or openings, and protected on the extremity of the projection by a railing of balusters or ironwork. In the French theatre, the *balcon* is a circular row of seats projecting beyond the tier of boxes immediately above the pit.

BALDACHINO. (It.) An open building, supported by columns, and covered with a canopy, generally placed over an altar. Sometimes the baldachino is suspended from the roof, as in the church of St. Sulpice at Paris. It succeeded to the ancient ciborium, which was a cupola supported on four columns, still to be seen in many of the churches of Rome. The merit of its invention seems to belong to Bernini. That erected by him in St. Peter's is 128 feet high, and being of bronze weighs near 90 tons. It was built by order of the Pope Barberini, from the robbery of the Pantheon, and occasioned the bitter observation, " Quod non fecerint Barbari fecerunt Barberini."

BALDWIN. See ARCHITECTS, list of, 104.

BALECTION or BOLECTION MOULDINGS. Mouldings which project beyond the surface of a piece of framing. See p. 637.

BALKS or BAULKS. (Dutch.) Sometimes called *Dram* timber. They are pieces of whole

fir, being the trunks of small trees of that species, rough-squared for building purposes. In the metropolis the term is applied to short lengths, from eighteen to twenty-five feet, mostly under ten inches square, tapering considerably, and with the angles so left that the piece is not exactly square.

BALLIUM.   In the architecture of the middle ages, the open space or court of a fortified castle.   This has acquired in English the appellation Bailey; thus St. Peter's in the Bailey at Oxford, and the Old Bailey in London, are so named from their ancient connection with the sites of castles.

BALLOON.   A round ball or globe placed on a column or pier, by way of crowning it.   The same name is given to the balls on the tops of cathedrals, as at St. Peter's, which is 8 feet diameter, and at St. Paul's in London.

BALNEUM.   (Lat.)   A bath.

BALTEUS.   (Lat. a girdle.)   The wide step in theatres and amphitheatres, which afforded a passage round them without disturbance to the sitters.   No one sat on it; it served merely as a landing-place.   In the Greek and Roman theatres, every eighth step was a balteus. Vitruvius gives the rules for properly setting it out, in the third chapter of his fifth book.
The term balteus is also used by Vitruvius to denote the strap which seems to bind up the coussinet or cushion of the Ionic capital.

BALUSTER.   A species of small column belonging to a balustrade.   See Book III. Chap. I. Sect. 16.   This term is also used to denote the lateral part of the volute of the Ionic capital.   Vitruvius calls it *pulvinata*, on account of its resemblance to a pillow.

BALUSTRADE.   A parapet or protecting fence formed of balusters, sometimes employed for real use, and sometimes merely for ornament.   For the method of designing balustrades, and other particulars relating to them, see Book III. Chap. I. Sect. 16.

BAND.   (Fr. Bande.)   A flat member or moulding, smaller than a fascia.   The face of a band is in a vertical plane, as is also that of the fascia; the word, however, is applied to narrow members somewhat wider than fillets; and the word *fascia* to broader members. The cinctures sometimes used round the shafts of rusticated columns are called bands. In this case the column is called a *banded column*.

BANDAGES.   A term applied to the rings or chains of iron inserted in the corners of a stone wall, or round the circumference of a tower, at the springing of a dome, &c., which act as a tie on the walls to keep them together.

BANDELET, or BANDLET.   A small band encompassing a column like a ring.

BANISTER.   A vulgar term for baluster, which see.

BANKER.   A bench, on which masons prepare, cut, and square their work.

BANQUET.   (Fr.)   The footway of a bridge when raised above the carriage-way.

BAPTISMAL FONT.   A vessel raised above the ground for containing the holy water used in the administration of baptism.   Many of the fonts in Saxon churches are still in being. The plans and horizontal sections are commonly circles, octagons, or squares, and at a little later dates were elaborately decorated with mouldings and sculptures.

BAPTISTERY.   (Gr. Βαπτίζω.)   A building in the architecture of the middle ages, destined for administration of the rite of baptism.   It has been contended by some that the baptistery was at first placed in the interior vestibules of the early churches, as are in many churches the baptismal fonts.   This, however, was not the case.   The baptistery was quite separate from the basilica, and even placed at some distance from it.   Until the end of the sixth century, it was, beyond doubt, a distinct building; but after that period the font gradually found its way into the vestibule of the church, and the practice became general, except in a few churches, as at Florence, and in those of all the episcopal cities of Tuscany, Ravenna, of S. Giovanni Laterano at Rome, and some few other places.   The last mentioned is perhaps the most ancient remaining.   There was a baptistery at Constantinople, of such dimensions that, on one occasion, it held a very numerous council. That at Florence is nearly ninety feet in diameter, octagonal, and covered with a dome. It is enclosed by the celebrated bronze gates by Lorenzo Ghiberti, which Michel Angelo said were fit to be the gates of Paradise.   The baptistery of Pisa, designed by Dioti Salvi, was finished about 1160.   The plan is octagonal, about 129 feet in diameter and 179 feet high.   See p. 118.

BAR.   In a court of justice, an enclosure, three or four feet high, in which the counsel have their places to plead causes.   The same name is given to the enclosure, or rather bar before it, at which prisoners are placed to take their trials for criminal offences.

BAR.   A piece of wood or iron used for fastening doors, window shutters, &c.

BAR OF A SASH.   The light pieces of wood or metal which divide a window sash into compartments for the glass.   The *angle bars* of a sash are those standing at the intersection of two vertical planes.

BAR IRON is that made of the metal of sows and pigs, as it comes from the furnace.   The sows and pigs, as they are technically termed, pass through the forges and chaufery, where, having undergone five successive heats, they are formed into bars.   See Sect. 5.

Book II. Chap. II. For the weight of a foot of bar iron of different thicknesses, see p. 682.

Bar-posts. Posts driven into the ground for forming the sides of a field gate. They are mortised, to admit of horizontal bars being put in or taken out at pleasure.

Barbacan. A watch-tower for descrying an enemy : also the outer work or defence of a castle, or the fort at the entrance of a bridge. Apertures in the walls of a fortress, for firing through upon the enemy, are sometimes called by this name. The etymology of the word has been variously assigned to French, Italian, Spanish, Saxon, and Arabian origin. See Castle.

Barge Boards. The inclined projecting boards placed at the gable of a building, and hiding the horizontal timbers of a roof. They are frequently carved with trefoils, quatrefoils, flowers, and other ornaments and foliage.

Barge Couples. (Sax. Bẏrᵹan, to bar.) Two beams mortised and tenoned together for the purpose of increasing the strength of a building.

Barge Course. The part of the tiling which projects over the gable of a building, and which is made good below with mortar.

Barn. (Sax. Beṅn.) A covered farm-building for laying up grain, hay, straw, &c. The situation of a barn should be dry and elevated. It is usually placed on the north or north east side of a farm-yard. The barns, outhouses, and stables should not be far distant from each other. They are most frequently constructed with wooden framing of quarters, &c., and covered with weather boarding ; sometimes, in superior farms, they are built of stone and brick. The roofs are usually thatched or tiled, as the materials for the purpose are at hand ; but as the grain should of all things be kept dry, to prevent it from moulding, the gable ends should be constructed of brick, and apertures left in the walls for the free admission of air. The bays, as they are called, are formed by two pairs of folding doors, exactly opposite to each other, and, as well as for thrashing, afford the convenience of carrying in and out a cart or waggon load of corn in sheaves, or any sort of bulky produce. The doors in question must be of the same breadth as the threshing-floor, to afford light to the threshers, and air for winnowing the grain. It is a good practice to make an extensive penthouse over the great doors sufficiently large to cover a load of corn or hay, in case of the weather not permitting it to be immediately housed.

Barozzi da Vignola. See Architects, list of, 217.

Barracks. See Book III. Chap. V. Sect. 19.

Barrel Drain. One in the form of a hollow cylinder.

Barycæ or Barycephalæ. (Gr. βαρυς, low or flat, and Κεφαλη, head.) The Greek name for an aræostyle temple.

Base. (Gr. βασις.) In geometry, the lower part of a figure or body. The *base of a solid* is the surface on which it rests.

Base of a Column. The part between the shaft and the pavement or pedestal, if there be any to the order. Each column has its particular base, for which see Sections 3 to 7. on the orders. For the Attic base see under that word.

Base of a Room. The lower projecting part. It consists of two parts, the lower whereof is a plain board adjoining the floor, called the plinth, and the upper of one or more mouldings, which, taken collectively, are called the base-mouldings. In better sort of work the plinth is tongued into a groove in the floor, by which means the diminution of breadth created by the shrinking never causes any aperture or chasm between its under edge and the floor, and the upper edge of the plinth is rebated upon the base. Bed-rooms, lobbies, passages, and staircases are often finished without a dado and surbase, and indeed the fashion has extended the practice to rooms of the higher class, as drawing-rooms, &c.

Basement. The lower story of a building, whether above or below the ground. See Book III. Chap. I. Sect. 13.

Basil. Among carpenters and joiners the angle to which the edge of an iron tool is ground so as to bring it to a cutting edge. If the angle be very thin the tool will cut more freely, but the more obtuse it is the stronger and fitter it is for service.

Basilica. (Gr. βασιλευς, a king.) Properly the palace of a king ; but it afterwards came to signify an apartment usually provided in the houses of persons of importance, where assemblies were held for dispensing justice. Thus in the magnificent villa of the Gordian family on the Via Prenestina there were three basilicæ, each more than one hundred feet long. A basilica was generally attached to every forum, for the summary adjustment of the disputes that arose. It was surrounded in most cases with shops and other conveniences for traders. The difference between the Grecian and Roman basilica is given by Vitruvius in the fifth chapter of his first book. The rise and progress of the modern basilica is given, p. 109, *et seq.* The term basilica is also applied by Palladio to those buildings in the cities of Italy similar in use to our town halls.

Basis. See Base.

BASKET. A term often applied to the vase of the Corinthian capital, with its foliage, &c.

BASSE COUR. (Fr.) A court destined in a house of importance for the stables, coach-houses, and servants attached to that part of the establishment. In country houses it is often used to denote the yard appropriated to the cattle, fowls, &c.

BASSO-RELIEVO. See RELIEVO.

BASTARD STUCCO. See Sect. 9. Chap. III. Book II.

BAT. In bricklayer's work, a piece of a brick less than one half of its length.

BATH. (From the Saxon, Bað.) An apartment or series of apartments for bathing. Among the ancients the public baths were of amazing extent and magnificence, and contained a vast number of apartments. These extraordinary monuments of Roman magnificence seem to have had their origin in many respects from the gymnasia of the Greeks, both being instituted for the exercise and health of the public. The word *thermæ* (hot baths) was by the Romans used to denominate the establishment, although it contained in the same building both hot and cold baths. In later times a house was incomplete unless provided with hot and cold baths; and, indeed, it was not till the time of Augustus that public baths assumed the grandeur which their remains indicate. Different authors reckon nearly eight hundred baths in Rome, whereof the most celebrated were those of Agrippa, Antoninus, Caracalla, Diocletian, Domitian, Nero, and Titus. It appears from good authority, that the baths of Diocletian could accommodate no less than eight hundred bathers. These stupendous edifices are indicative of the magnificence, no less than the luxury of the age in which they were erected. The pavements were mosaic, the ceilings vaulted and richly decorated, and the walls encrusted with the rarest marbles. From these edifices many of the most valuable examples of Greek sculpture have been restored to the world; and it was from their recesses that the restorers of the art drew their knowledge, and that Rafaelle learnt to decorate the walls of the Vatican. See p. 96.

BATERDEAU. (Fr.) The same as coffer dam, which see.

BATRACHUS. See ARCHITECTS, list of, 33.

BATTEN. (Probably from the Fr. Bâton, from its small width.) A scantling or piece of stuff from two to six inches broad, and from five eighths of an inch to two inches thick. Battens are used in the boarding of floors and also upon walls, in order to receive the laths upon which the plaister is laid. See BOARDED FLOOR.

BATTENING. The fixing of battens to walls for the reception of the laths on which the plaster is to be laid. It also signifies the battens in the state of being fixed for that purpose. The battens employed are usually about two inches broad and three fourths of an inch thick; the thicknesses, however, may be varied according to the distances that the several fixed points are from each other. Their distance in the clear is from eleven inches to one foot. Before battens are fixed, equidistant bond timbers should be built in the wall, or the wall should be plugged at equal distances, and cut off flush with its surface. In and about London plugs are generally placed at the distance of twelve or fourteen inches from centre to centre in the length of the batten. Battens upon external walls, the ceiling and bridging joists of a naked floor, also the common joists for supporting the boarding of a floor, are fixed at the same distance, viz. from eleven to twelve inches in the clear. When battens are fixed against flues, iron holdfasts are of course employed instead of bond-timbers or plugs. When they are attached to a wall they are generally fixed in vertical lines, and when fixed to the surface of a stone or brick vault, whose intrados is generated by a plane revolving about an axis, they ought to be placed in planes tending to the axis; as in this position they have only to be fixed in straight lines, in case the intrados is straight towards the axis, which will be the case when it is a portion of a cone or cylinder; and when the intrados is curved towards the axis they will bend the easiest possible. Great care should be taken to regulate the fans of the battens, so as to be as nearly as possible equidistant from the intended surface of the plaster. Though battens are employed in floors, neither the act of laying them nor the floor afterwards formed of them is called battening; they are more commonly called *boarding*. Every piece of masonry or brickwork, if not thoroughly dry, should be battened for lath 'and plaster, particularly if executed in a wet season. When windows are boarded, and the walls of the room not sufficiently thick to contain the shutters, the surface of the plastering is brought out so as to give the architrave a proper projection, and quarterings are used for supporting the lath and plaster in lieu of battens. This is also practised when the breast of a chimney projects into the room, in order to cover the recesses and make the whole side flush, or all in the same surface with the breast.

BATTER (probably from the Fr. Battre). A term used by artificers to signify that a body does not stand upright, but inclines from a person standing before it; when, on the contrary, it leans towards a person, its inclination is described by saying it overhangs.

BATTLEMENTS. Indentations on the top of a wall, parapet, or other building. They were first used in ancient fortifications, and subsequently applied to chambers and other build-

ings as mere ornaments. Their outline is generally a conjunction of straight lines at right angles to each other, each indentation having two interior right angles, and each raised part two exterior right angles.

BATTLE-EMBATTLED. A term applied to the top of a wall which has a double row of battlements formed by a conjunction of straight lines at right angles to each other, both embrasures and rising parts being double, the lower part of every embrasure less than the upper, and therefore the lower part of each riser broader than the upper.

BAULK ROOFING. Roofing in which the framing is constructed of baulk timber.

BAULKS. See BALKS.

BAY. (Dutch, Baye.) The division of a barn or other building, generally from fifteen to twenty feet in length or breadth.

BAY. In plasterer's work, the space between the screeds prepared for regulating and working the floating rule. See SCREEDS.

BAY OF JOISTS. The joisting between two binding joists, or between two girders when binding joists are not used.

BAY OF ROOFING. The small rafters and their supporting purlins between two principal rafters.

BAY WINDOW. A window placed in the bay or bow of a window: called also an *oriel* window.

BAYS. See DAYS.

BAZAR. A species of mart or exchange for the sale of divers articles of merchandize. The word is Arabic, signifying the sale or exchange of goods or merchandize. Some of the Eastern bazars are open, like the market places of Europe, and serve for the same uses, more particularly for the sale of more bulky and less valuable commodities. Others are covered with lofty ceilings and even domes, which are pierced for the admission of light. It is in these that the jewellers, goldsmiths, and other dealers in rich wares have their shops. The bazar or *meidan* of Ispahan, one of the finest in Persia, is given in *fig.* 32.

BEAD AND BUTT WORK. Framing in which the pannels are flush, having beads *stuck* or run upon the two edges; the grain of the wood being in the direction of them. See p. 636.

BEAD, BUTT, AND SQUARE WORK. Framing with bead and butt on one side, and square on the other, is chiefly used in doors. This sort of framing is put together square, and the bead is *stuck* on the edges of the rising side of the pannel.

BEAD AND FLUSH WORK. A piece of framed work with beads run on each edge of the included pannel.

BEAD, FLUSH, AND SQUARE WORK. Framing with bead and flush on one side, and square on the other, used chiefly in doors.

BEAD AND QUIRK. A bead stuck on the edge of a piece of stuff, flush with its surface, with only one quirk or without being returned on the other surface. *Bead and double quirk* occurs when the bead appears on the face and edge of a piece of stuff in the same manner, thus forming a *double quirk*.

BEADE. (Sax. Beaðe.) A moulding whose section is circular. It is frequently used on the edge of each fascia of an architrave, as also in the mouldings of doors, shutters, skirtings, imposts, and cornices. When the bead is flush with the surface it is called a *quirk-bead*, and when raised it is called a *cock-bead*.

BEAK. A little pendent fillet left on the edge of the larmier, forming a canal behind to prevent the water from running down the lower bed of the cornice. The beak is sometimes formed by a groove or channel recessed on the soffite of the larmier upwards.

BEAM (Sax. Beam, a tie.) A piece of timber, or sometimes of metal, for supporting a weight, or counteracting two opposite and equal forces, either drawing it or compressing it in the direction of its length. A beam employed as a lintel supports a weight; if employed as a tie beam, it is drawn or extended; if as collar beam, it is compressed. The word is usually employed with some other word used adjectively or in opposition, which word implies the use, situation, or form of the beam; as *tie beam, hammer beam, dragon beam, straining beam, camber beam, binding beam, girding beam, truss beam, summer beam,* &c. Some of these are however used simply, as collar for collar beam, lintel for lintel beam, &c. That which is now called the collar beam was by old writers called *wina beam,* and strut or *strutting beam.* A beam is lengthened either by building it in thicknesses, or by lapping or splicing the ends upon each other and bolting them through, which is called *scarfing.* See CARPENTRY generally, and p. 599. Also COLLAR-BEAM.

BEAM COMPASSES. An instrument for describing large circles, and made eitner of wood or metal with sliding sockets, carrying steel or pencil points. It is used only when the circle to be described is beyond the reach of common compasses.

BEAM FILLING. The brickwork or masonry brought up from the level of the under to the upper sides of the beams. It is also used to denote the filling up of the space from the top of the wall plate between the rafters to the under side of the slating, board, or other covering.

Bearer. That which supports any body in its place, as a wall, a post, a strut, &c. In gutters they are the short pieces of timber which support the boarding.

Bearing. The distance or length which the ends of a piece of timber lie upon or are inserted into the walls or piers; thus joists are usually carried into the walls at least nine inches, or are said to have a nine-inch bearing. Lintels of an aperture should in like manner have a similar bearing, the object being to prevent any *sagging* of the piece acting on the inner horizontal quoins of the wall.

Bearing of a Timber. The unsupported distance between its points of support without any intervening assistance. A piece of timber having any number of supports, one being placed at each extremity, will have as many bearings, wanting one, as there are supports. Thus a piece of timber extended lengthwise, as a joist over two rooms, will have three supports and two bearings, the bearers being the two outside walls and the partition in the midst between them.

Bearing Wall or Partition. A wall or partition built from the solid for the purpose of supporting another wall or partition, either in the same or in a transverse direction. When the latter is built in the same direction as the supporting wall it is said to have a *solid bearing;* but when built in a transverse direction, or unsupported throughout, its whole length is said to have a *false bearing,* or as many false bearings as there are intervals below the wall or partition.

Beater. An implement used by plasterers and bricklayers for beating, and thereby tempering or incorporating together the lime, sand, and other ingredients of a cement or plaster.

Beauchamp. See Architects, list of, 164.

Beaufet. See Buffet.

Beauty. In architectural composition, see Book III. Chap. I. Sect. 1., and Chap. III.

Bed. (Sax. Beð.) The horizontal surface on which the stones, bricks, or other matters in building lie. The under surface of a stone or brick is called its *under bed,* and the upper surface its *upper bed.* In general language the beds of a stone are the surfaces where the stones or bricks meet. It is almost needless to inculcate the necessity of every stone being worked quite straight, and not dished or hollowed out, which masons are very apt to do for the purpose of making a fine joint. Stones thus worked are very liable to flush and break off at the angles, of which there are too many examples in important buildings to make it necessary that we should more particularly allude to them. See Masonry, p. 560, *et seq.*

Bed Chamber. The apartment destined to the reception of a bed. Its finishings of course depend on the rank of the party who is to occupy it.

Bed of a Slate. The under side of a slate, or that part in contiguity with the boarding or rafters.

Beds of a Stone. In cylindrical vaulting are the two surfaces intersecting the intrados of the vault in lines parallel to the axis of the cylinder. In conic vaulting, where the axis is horizontal, they are those two surfaces which, if produced, would intersect the axis of the cone. In arching the beds are called *summerings* by the workmen.

Bedding of Timbers. The placing them properly in mortar on the walls.

Beech. One of the forest trees, but not often used in building.

Beetle. (Sax. Býtel.) A large wooden hammer or mallet with one, two, or three handles for as many persons. With it piles, stakes, wedges, &c., are driven.

Bek, de. See Architects, list of, 133.

Belection Mouldings. See Balection Mouldings.

Belfry. The upper part of the steeple of a church for the reception of the bells. It is the campanile of the Italians, though amongst them a building often altogether unconnected with the body of the church. It is sometimes used more especially in respect of the timber framing by which the bells are supported.

Bell of the Corinthian and Composite Capitals. The naked vase or *corbeille* round which the foliage and volutes are arranged. Its horizontal section is every where a circle. See *fig.* 93.

Bell Roof. One whereof the vertical section, perpendicular to the wall or to its springing line, is a curve of contrary flexure, being concave at the bottom and convex at the top. It is often called an ogee roof from its form.

Belt. In masonry, a course of stones projecting from the naked, either moulded, plain, fluted, or enriched with pateras at regular intervals.

Belvedere. (It.) A raised turret or lantern raised for the enjoyment of a prospect; also a small edifice in gardens, not uncommon in France and Italy.

Bench. A horizontal surface or table about two feet eight inches high, on which joiners prepare their work.

Bench Hook. A pin affixed to a bench for preventing the stuff in working from sliding out of its place.

Bergamasco. See Architects, list of, 192.

BERNINI.　See ARCHITECTS, list of, 251.

BERRUGUETTE.　See ARCHITECTS, list of 223.

BERHAM.　See ARCHITECTS, list of, 107.

BETON. (Fr.)　A species of concrete.

BEVEL. (Lat. Bivium.)　An instrument used by artificers, one leg whereof is frequently curved according to the sweep of an arch or vault. It is moveable upon a pivot or centre, so as to render it capable of being set to any angle. The make and use of it are much the same as those of the common square and mitre, except that those are fixed, the first at an angle of ninety degrees and the second at forty-five; whereas the bevel being moveable, it may in some measure supply the office of both, and yet supply the deficiency of both, which is, indeed, its principal use, inasmuch as it serves to set off or transfer angles either greater or less than ninety or forty-five.

Any angle that is not square is called a *bevel angle*, whether it be more obtuse or more acute than a right angle; but if it be one half as much as a right angle, viz. forty-five degrees, the workman calls it a *miter*. They have also a term *half miter*, which is an angle one quarter of a quadrant or square, that is, an angle of twenty-two degrees and a half.

BILLET MOULDING. (Fr. Billet.)　A Norman moulding used in string courses and the archivolts of openings. It consists of short, small, cylindrical pieces, two or three inches long, placed in hollow mouldings at intervals equal to about the length of the billet. See p. 174.

BINDING JOISTS.　Those beams in a floor which, in a transverse direction, support the bridging joists above, and the ceiling joists below. (See CARPENTRY, p. 595.) When they are placed parallel to that side of a room on which the chimney stands, the extreme one on that side ought never to be placed close to the breast, but at a distance equal to the breadth of the slab, in order to allow for the throwing over the brick trimmer to support the hearth.

BINDING RAFTERS.　The same as purlins, which see.

BINNS FOR WINE.　The open subdivisions in a cellar for the reception of wine in bottles. The average diameter allowed for green bottles is 3·56 inches. Thus a binn 6 ft. $2\frac{3}{4}$ in. long will take twenty-one bottles. If they are laid in double tiers the depth should be 32 inches.

BIRCH.　A forest tree (*Betula*) sometimes used in building.

BIRD'S MOUTH.　An interior angle cut on the end of a piece of timber, for the purpose of obtaining a firm rest upon the exterior angle of another piece.

BISCOPIUS.　See ARCHITECTS, list of, 67.

BIT.　An instrument for boring holes in wood or any other substance, so constructed as to admit of being inserted or taken out of a spring. The handle is divided into five parts, all in the same plane; the middle and the two extreme parts being parallel. The two extreme parts are in the same straight line, one of them having a brass end with a socket for containing the bit, which, when fixed, falls into the same straight line with the other end of the stock; the further end has a knob attached, so as to remain stationary, while all the other parts of the apparatus may be turned round by means of the projecting part of the handle.

There are various kinds of bits; as *shell bits*, used for boring wood, and having an interior cylindric concavity for containing the core; *centre bits* used to form a large cylindric hole or excavation; *countersink bits*, for widening the upper part of a hole in wood or iron, to take in the head of a screw or pin, so that it may not appear above the surface of the wood; *rimer bits*, for widening holes; and *taper shell bits*, used also for the last-named purpose.

BITUMEN.　A mineral pitch used in former ages instead of mortar. The walls of Babylon are said to have been cemented with it.

BLADES. (Sax. Blæð.)　A name sometimes given to the principal rafters of a roof.

BLADE OF A CHISEL.　The iron or steel part of it as distinguised from the wooden handle.

BLADE OF A SAW.　The thin steel part on the edge of which the teeth are cut. The chief properties of a good saw are, that it should be stiff and yet bend equally into a regular curve, well tempered, equally thick on the cutting edge, and thinner towards the back edge.

BLANK DOOR.　A door either shut to prevent a passage, or one placed in the back of a recess, where there is no entrance, having, nevertheless, the appearance of a real door.

BLANK WINDOW.　One which has the appearance of a real window but is merely formed in the recess of the wall. When it is necessary to introduce blank windows for the sake of uniformity, it is much better to build the apertures like the other and real windows, provided no flues or funnels interfere; and instead of representing the sashes by painting, real sashes should be introduced with the panes of glass painted on the back.

BLINDS. Quadrangular frames of wood or metal, covered with an opaque substance, stretched between the framing, so as to cover either the whole or part of the sashes of a window. They are used for the purpose of diminishing the intense effects of the sun's rays, or of preventing passengers from seeing into the interior of an apartment.

BLOCK (Teutonic) OF WOOD. A piece of wood cut into some prescribed form for a particular purpose.

BLOCK OF STONE OR MARBLE. A piece rough from the quarry before it has received any form from the hand of the workman.

BLOCKING OR BLOCKING COURSE. In masonry, a course of stones placed on the top of a cornice forming the crown of a wall.

BLOCKINGS. Small pieces of wood fitted in and glued to the interior angle of two boards, or other pieces, for the purpose of giving additional strength to the joint. In gluing up columns the staves are glued up successively and strengthened by blockings; as also the risers and treads of stairs and all other joints that demand more strength than their own joints afford. They are always concealed from the eye.

BLOND, J. B. See ARCHITECTS, list of, 274.

BLONDEL, FR. See ARCHITECTS, list of, 260.

BLONDEL, JAC. FR. See ARCHITECTS, list of, 293.

BOARD. (Sax. Bopð.) A piece of timber of undefined length, more than four inches in breadth, and not more than two inches and a half in thickness. When boards are of a trapezoidal section, that is, thinner on one edge than the other, they are called *feather-edged boards*. Boards when wider than nine inches are called *planks*. The fir boards called *deal* (because they are *dealt* or *divided* out in thicknesses) are generally imported into England ready sawn, being thus prepared cheaper by saw mills abroad than they can be here. Fir boards of this sort, one inch and a quarter thick, are called *whole deal*, and those a full half inch thick, *slit deal*.

BOARD LEAR or LEAR BOARD. That upon which the lead work of a gutter is laid to prevent it sinking between the rafters.

BOARDS, LISTED. Such as are reduced in their width by taking off the sap from the sides.

BOARDS FOR VALLEYS or VALLEY BOARDS. Those fixed on the valley rafters, or pieces for the leaden gutters of the valley to rest on.

BOARDED FLOORS. Those covered with floor-boards. The laying of floors usually commences when the windows are in and the plaster dry. The boards should be planed on their best face and set up to season, till the natural sap is expelled. They are then to be planed smooth, shot, and squared on the edge. The opposite edges are brought to a breadth by drawing, with a flooring guage, a line on the face parallel to the other edge. After this they are guaged to a thickness, and rebated down on the back to the lines drawn by the guage. The next thing is to try whether the joists be level, and if not, either the boards must be cut on the under side to meet the inequality, or the joists must be *furred* up by pieces to bring the boards, when laid, to a level. The boards employed in flooring are either battens or deals of greater breadth. The quality of battens is divided into three sorts. The best is that free from knots, shakes, sap wood, or cross-grained stuff, well matched and selected with the greatest care. The second best is that in which only small but sound knots are permitted, but it is to be free from sapwood and shakes. The most inferior kind is that left from the selection of the other two. See p. 644.

BOARDING JOISTS. Those in naked floorings to which the boards are to be fixed.

BOARDING FOR LEAD FLATS AND GUTTERS. That which immediately receives the lead, rarely less than one inch and an eighth, or one inch and a quarter thick. It is usually laid merely with rough joints.

BOARDING LUFFER or LEVER BOARDING. Inclined boarding, with intervals between the boards, nailed in an inclined direction on the sides of buildings or lanterns, so as to admit a free current of air, and at the same time to exclude the rain.

BOARDING FOR PUGGING or DEAFENING, also called SOUND BOARDING. Short boards disposed transversely between the joists of floors to hold some substance intended to prevent sound being transmitted from one story to another. These boards are supported by *fillets* fixed to the sides of the joists about three quarters of an inch thick and an inch wide. The substance, often plaster, placed between them to prevent the transmission of the sound, is called the *pugging*.

BOARDING FOR SLATING. That nailed to the rafters for the reception of the slates, usually three quarters to seven eighths of an inch in thickness; the sides commonly rough, the edges either rough, shot, plowed and tongued, or rebated and sometimes *sprung*, so as to prevent the rain from passing through the joints. The boarding for slating may be so arranged as to diminish the lateral pressure or thrust against the walls by disposing the boards diagonally on the rafters. On the lower edge of the boarding is fixed the

eaves board, as also against all walls either at right angles to or forming an acute angle with the ridge, or a right or obtuse angle with the wall plate. The eaves board is for raising the lower ends of the lower row of slates that form the eaves. Those placed against walls are for raising the slates to make the water run off from the wall. The boarding for slates should be of yellow deal without sap.

BOARDING FOR LINING WALLS. The boards used for this purpose are usually from five eighths to three quarters of an inch thick, and are plowed and tongued together.

BOARDING FOR OUTSIDE WORK, or WEATHER-BOARDING. Boards nailed with a lap on each other, to prevent the penetration of the rain and snow. The boards for this purpose are generally made thinner on one side than on the other, especially in good permanent work. The feather-edged board is, therefore, in such cases, used, the thick edge of the upper board being laid on the thin edge of that below, lapping about an inch or an inch and a half, and the nails being driven through the lap.

BOASTER. A tool used by masons to make the surface of the work nearly smooth. It is two inches wide in the cutting part.

BOASTING IN MASONRY. The act of paring the stone with a broad chisel and mallet, but not in uniform lines.

In CARVING, it is the rough cutting round the ornaments, to reduce them to their contours and profiles, before the incisions are made for forming the raffels or minuter parts. See ASHLAR.

BODY OF A NICHE. That part of it whose superficies is vertical. If the lower part be cylindrical and the upper part spherical, the lower part is the *body* of the niche, and the upper part is termed the *head*.

BODY RANGE OF A GROIN. The wider of two vaults which intersect and form a groin.

BODY OF A ROOM. That which forms the main part of the apartment, independent of any recesses on the ends or sides.

BOFFRAND. See ARCHITECTS, list of, 280.

BOLECTION MOULDING. See BALECTION MOULDING.

BOLSTER. The baluster part of the Ionic capital on the return side. See BALUSTER.

BOLT. (Gr. βολις, a dart). In joinery, a metal fastening for a door, and moved by the hand, catching in a staple or notch which receives it. Bolts are of various sorts, whereof *plate spring* and *flush bolts* are for fastening doors and windows.

This name is also given to large cylindrical iron or other metal pins, having a round head at one end and a slit at the other. Through the slit a *pin* or *forelock* is passed, whereby the bar of a door, window shutter, or the like is made fast. These are usually called round or window bolts.

The bolt of a lock is the iron part that enters into a staple or jamb when the key is turned to fasten the door. Of these the two sorts are, one which shuts of itself when the door is shut to, called a *spring bolt;* the other, which is only acted upon by applying the key, is called the *dormant bolt.*

In carpentry, a bolt is usually a square or cylindrical piece of iron, with a knob at one end and a screw at the other, passing through holes for its reception in two or more pieces of timber, for the purpose of fastening them together, by means of a nut screwed on the end opposite to the knob. The bolt of carpentry should be proportioned to the size and stress of the timbers it connects.

BOLTEL. See BOULTINE.

BOLTON. See ARCHITECTS, list of, 186.

BOND. (Sax.) Generally the method of connecting two or more bodies. Used in the plural number, it signifies the timbers disposed in the walls of a house, such as *bond timbers, lintels,* and *wall plates.* The term *chain bond* is sometimes applied to the bond timbers placed in one or more tiers in the walls of each story of a building, and serving not only to tie the walls together during their settlement, but afterwards for nailing the finishings to.

BOND. In masonry or brickwork is that disposition of stones or bricks, which prevents the vertical joints falling over one another. See p. 551.

BOND (HEART). That bond which occurs when two stones being placed in a longitudinal position extending the exact thickness of the wall, another stone is put over the joints in the centre of the wall.

BOND MASONRY. See BOUND MASONRY.

BOND STONES. Those whose longest horizontal direction is placed in the thickness of the work.

BONEING, or BONING. (Etym. doubtful.) The act of judging of or making a plane surface or line by the eye. It is also performed by joiners with two straight edges, by which it is seen whether the work is out of *winding*, that is, whether the surface be plane or twisted.

BONOMI. See ARCHITECTS, list of, 308.

BOOTH. (British, Bwth.) A stall or standing in a fair or market. The term is also applied

to any temporary structure for shade and shelter, as also for wooden buildings for itinerant players and pedlars.

BORDERS. (Fr. Bord.) Pieces of wood put round the upper edges of any thing, either for use or ornament. Such are the three pieces of wood, to which the term in architecture is more usually applied, which are mitred together round the slab of a chimney-piece.

BORING. The act of perforating any solid. For wood the various sorts of bits are described under BIT.

BORROMINI. See ARCHITECTS, list of, 255.

BOSS. (Fr.) In sculpture, a projecting mass or prominency of material, to be afterwards cut or carved.

BOSS. Among bricklayers, a wooden vessel used by the labourers for the mortar used in tiling. It has an iron hook, by which it hangs on the laths or on the rounds of a ladder.

BOSSAGE. (Fr.) Projecting stones laid rough in building to be afterward cut into mouldings or carved into ornaments. The term is also used to signify rustic work, which seems to advance before the naked of a building, by reason of indentures or channels left at the joints. The cavities or indentures at the joints are sometimes bevelled or chamfered, and sometimes circular.

BOUCHARDON. See ARCHITECTS, list of, 284.

BOULDER WALLS. Such as are built of round flints or pebbles laid in strong mortar. This construction is used where there is a beach cast up by the sea, or where there is an abundance of flints in the neighbourhood.

BOULTINE or BOLTEL. A name sometimes given by workmen to a convex moulding, such as an ovolo.

BOUND or BOND MASONRY. That wherein the stones of each succeeding course are laid so that the joint which mounts and separates two stones always falls directly over the middle of the stone below.

BOUTANT. See ARC-BOUTANT.

BOW. (Sax. Buɡen). The part of any building which projects from a straight wall. It is sometimes circular and sometimes polygonal on the plan, or rather formed by two exterior obtuse angles. Bows on polygonal plans are called *canted bows*.

BOW. Among draughtsmen, denotes a beam of wood or brass, with three long screws that direct a lath of wood or steel to an arch. It is used in drawing flat arches of large radius.

BOW COMPASSES. Instruments for describing small circles.

BOW ROOM. A room having a bow on one or more sides of it. See BAY WINDOW.

BOW SAW. One for cutting the thin edges of wood into curves.

BOWLERS or BOLDERS. See PAVEMENT.

BOX. (Sax.) Generally, a case for holding any thing.

BOX FOR MITERING. A trough for cutting miters. It has three sides, and is open at the ends, with cuts on the vertical sides at angles of forty-five degrees with them.

BOX OF A RIB-SAW. Two thin iron plates fixed to a handle, in one of which plates an opening is made for the reception of a wedge, by which it is fixed to the saw.

BOX OF A THEATRE. One of the subdivisions in the tiers round the circle.

BOXED SHUTTERS. See BOXINGS OF A WINDOW.

BOXINGS OF A WINDOW. The cases opposite each other on each side of a window, into which the shutters are folded or fall back. The shutters of principal rooms are usually in two divisions or halves, each subdivided into others, so that they may be received within the boxings. The subdivisions are seldom more in number than three, and are so contrived that the subdivision whose face is visible, which is called the front shutter, is of the exact breadth of the boxing, and also flush with it; the next, hidden in the boxing, is somewhat less in breadth than that last mentioned, and the third still less. Suppose, for instance, a window four feet wide, standing in a two-brick or eighteen-inch wall; we may thus find the number of leaves each of the halves must have, as follows:— To the thickness of the wall add that of the plastering, say 2 inches, and we have 20 inches. Now the sash frame = 6 inches in thickness, being added to the *reveal* or distance = 4½ inches of the sash frame from the face of the wall = 10½ inches, which, subtracted from 20, the thickness of the wall and plaster, leaves 9½ inches. This will give three leaves, or subdivisions, and as it is usual to make the *back flaps*, or those folded within the boxings, less than the front shutter, whose face is visible and flush with and of the exact breadth of the boxings, the arrangement may be as follows:— Front shutter 9¼ inches, the next 8 inches, and the third 6½ inches; in all, 24 inches, the half of the opening of the window. It will be perceived that no allowance has been made for the shutters being rebated into each other, as is usually the case; and for this half an inch more must be allowed for the two rebates of the three leaves, and one eighth of an inch for the rebate at the meeting of the two principal divisions in the middle of the window, making, with the breadth of the three subdivisions, 24 + ⅝: the flaps, therefore, may be thus disposed:— Front leaf 9½

inches, second leaf $8\frac{1}{2}$ inches, and the third leaf $6\frac{5}{8}$ inches ; in all $24\frac{5}{8}$ inches, being fully the width of each principal division. To find the depth to be given to the boxings, to the thickness of each of the leaves add one sixteenth of an inch, and if there be a back lining add also the thickness of that. The second and third flaps are almost always thinner than the front leaf; thus, say front leaf $1\frac{1}{2}$ inch, second leaf $1\frac{1}{4}$ inch, and third leaf $1\frac{1}{4}$ inch ; to which add $\frac{3}{16}$ for the three leaves, and the amount will stand thus : — $1\frac{1}{2} + 1\frac{1}{4} + 1\frac{1}{4} + \frac{3}{16} = 4\frac{3}{16}$ inches for the depth of the boxings. If the walls are only a brick and a half thick, or the window very wide, the architrave is made to project before the face of the plaster, for the purpose of obtaining width for the boxings, or the plaster is brought out from the internal face of the wall by means of battening.

BOYDEN. See ARCHITECTS, list of, 132.

BRACE. (Fr. Embrasser.) An inclined piece of timber used in trussed partitions and in framed roofs, in order to form a triangle, by which the assemblage of pieces composing the framing are stiffened. When a brace is used to support a rafter, it is called a *strut*. When braces are used in roofs and in partitions, they should be disposed in pairs, and introduced in opposite directions. See ANGLE BRACE.

BRACKET. (Lat. Brachium.) A supporting piece for a shelf. When the shelf is broad the brackets are small trusses, which consist of a vertical piece, an horizontal piece, and a strut; but when narrow the brackets are generally solid pieces of board, usually finished with an ogee figure on their outer side.

BRACKETS FOR STAIRS are sometimes used under the ends of wooden steps next to the well-hole, for the sake of ornament only, for they have only the appearance of supports.

BRACKETING FOR CORNICES. The wooden ribs nailed to the ceiling, joists, and battening for supporting the cornices of rooms when too large for security, by the mere dependence on the adhesive power of plaster to the ceiling. It consists of vertical ribs whose rough outline is that of the cornice, and to which the laths are nailed for sustaining the plaster in which the mouldings are run. The bracketing for coves is only an enlargement of the scale which occurs in ordinary cornices, the operation being that of obtaining a set of ribs to which the laths may be nailed for the reception of the plastering. The ribs in question are usually out of deals, whose thickness must necessarily vary with the weight of plaster they have to support. See p. 624, *et seq.*

BRAD. (Etym. uncertain.) A thin nail used in joinery without the spreading head which other nails have, the projection of the head being only on one side. There are various sorts of brads, such as *joiners' brads* for hard woods ; others, called *batten brads*, for softer woods; and *bill*, or *quarter brads*, used for a hastily laid floor. When brads are used they are generally driven below the surface of the wood through the medium of a *punch*, and the hole is filled up with putty to prevent an appearance of the nailing.

BRAMANTE. See ARCHITECTS, list of, 167.

BRAMANTINO. See ARCHITECTS, list of, 156.

BRANCHES. The ribs of a Gothic vault, rising upwards from the tops of the pillars to the apex. They appear to support the ceiling or vault.

BRANDRITH. A fence or rail round the opening of a well.

BRASS. A metal much used in building. It is an alloy of copper and zinc, whose proportions vary according to the required colour. Four parts of copper and one of zinc form a good brass. The common process for making it is by heating copper plates in a mixture of native oxide of zinc, or calamine and charcoal.

BRASSES. Sepulchral plates, generally sunk into a flat grave-stone ; sometimes with a mere inscription, but very frequently with effigies, armorial bearings, and other devices engraved upon it.

BRATTISHING. Interpreted, we know not how truly, as the carved open work over a shrine.

BRAY. See ARCHITECTS, list of, 176.

BREADTH. The greatest extension of a body at right angles to its length.

BREAK. The recess or projection of any part within or beyond the general face of the work. In either case it is to be considered a break.

BREAK IN. In carpentry, is the cutting or breaking a hole in brickwork with the ripping-chisel for the purpose of inserting timber, or to receive plugs, the end of a beam, or the like, &c.

BREAKING JOINT. In masonry or brickwork, is the placing a stone or brick over the course below, in such a manner that the joint above shall not fall vertically immediately above those below it.

BREAST OF A CHIMNEY. The projecting or facing portion of a chimney front towards a room which projects into it, or which, from other construction, may not have a break. It is, in fact, the wall carried up over the front of a fireplace, whether projecting or not. See CHIMNEY.

BREAST OF A WINDOW. The masonry or brickwork forming the back of the recess or parapet under the window sill.

BREEZE. Small ashes and cinders used instead of coal for the burning of bricks.

Bressummer or **Breast Summer.** That is, a summer or beam placed breastwise for the support of a superincumbent wall, performing in fact the office of a lintel. It is principally used over shop windows to carry the upper part of the front, and supported by iron or timber posts, though sometimes by stone. In the interior of a building the pieces into which the girders are framed are often called summers.

Brettingham. See Architects, list of, 294.

Brewhouse. An establishment for the manufactory of malt liquors. A brewhouse is generally provided as an appendage to dwelling-houses in the country, for brewing the beer used by the family.

Brick. (Dutch, Bricke.) A sort of fictitious stone, composed of an argillaceous earth, tempered and formed in moulds, dried in the sun, and finally burnt to a proper degree of hardness in a clamp or kiln. (See Book II. Chap. II. Sect. 10.) The method pursued by the ancients in making unburnt bricks is described by Vitruvius, book ii. chap. iii. After mentioning the process, that author thus describes the different sorts in use : — "There are three sorts of bricks; the first is that which the Greeks call Didoron (δίδωρον), being the sort we use, that is, one foot long and half a foot wide. The other two sorts are used in Grecian buildings; one is called Pentadoron, the other Tetradoron. By the word Doron, the Greeks mean a palm, because the word δῶρον signifies a gift which can be borne in the palm of the hand. That sort, therefore, which is five palms each way is called Pentadoron; that of four palms Tetradoron. The former of these two sorts is used in public buildings; the latter in private. Each sort has half bricks made to suit it ; so that when a wall is executed, the course on one of the faces of the wall shows sides of whole bricks, the other face of half bricks ; and being worked to the line on each face, the bricks on each bed bind alternately over the course below. Besides the pleasant varied appearance which this method gives, it affords additional strength by the middle of a brick on a rising course falling over the vertical joints of the course thereunder." Towards the decline of the Republic, the Romans made great use of bricks as a building material. According to Pliny, those most in use were a foot and a half long, and a foot broad. This agrees nearly with the Roman bricks used in England, which are generally found to be about seventeen inches in length by eleven inches in breadth. Ancient bricks are generally very thin, being often no more than one inch and a half thick. From the article by Quatremère de Quincy in the *Encyc. Méthodique*, it appears from his researches among the antique buildings of Rome, he found bricks of the following sizes. The least were $7\frac{1}{2}$ inches (French) square and $1\frac{1}{4}$ inch thick ; the medium one $16\frac{1}{4}$ inches square, and from 18 to 20 lines in thickness. The larger ones were 22 inches square by 21 or 20 lines thick. The smaller ones were used to face walls of rubble work ; and, for making better bond with the wall, they were cut diagonally into two triangles, the longer side being placed on the outside, and the point towards the interior of the work. To make the tie more effectual between the rubble and the facing, they placed at intervals of 4 feet in height, one or two courses of large square bricks. The larger bricks were also used for the arches of openings to discharge the superincumbent weight.

Bricklayers' Work or **Bricklaying.** See Book II. Chap. III. Sect. 2.

Brickwork. Any work performed with bricks as the solid material.

Bridge. (Sax. Bρɪᵹᵹe.) A structure for the purpose of connecting the opposite banks of a river, gorge, valley, &c., by means of certain materials, forming a road-way from one side to the other. It may be made of stone, brick, iron, timber, suspended chains or ropes, or the road-way may be obtained by means of boats moored in the stream. On the general principles for the situation and construction, the reader is referred to Book III. Chap. V. Sect. 2. ; and for the principles and mode of constructing arches, to Book II. Chap. I. Sect. 9.

Bridge Board, otherwise called **Notch Board,** is a board on which the ends of the steps of wooden stairs are fastened.

Bridge-over. A term used when several parallel timbers occur, and another piece is fixed transversely over them, such piece is then said to *bridge-over* the parallel pieces. Thus in framed roofing, the common rafters bridge-over the purlins ; so, in framed flooring, the upper joists, to which the flooring is fixed, bridge-over the beams or binding-joists, and for this reason they are called *bridging-joists*.

Bridge Stone. A stone laid from the pavement to the entrance door of a house, over a sunk area, and supported by an arch.

Bridged Gutters are those made with boards supported by bearers, and covered above with lead.

Bridging Floors are those in which bridging-joists are employed.

Bridging Joists. Those which are sustained by transverse beams below, called *binding joists ;* also those joists which are nailed or fixed to the flooring-boards.

Bridgings or **Bridging Pieces,** also called **Strutting** or **Straining Pieces,** are pieces placed between two opposite beams to prevent their nearer approach, as rafters, braces, struts, &c. When a strutting-piece also serves as a sill, it is called a *straining sill.*

BRINGING-UP or CARRYING-UP.   A term used by workmen to denote building **up**.   Thus, *bringing-up* a wall four feet means building it up.

BRIOSCO.   See ARCHITECTS, list of, 202.

BROACHED WORK.   See DROVED and BROACHED.

BROAD STONE.   The same as free-stone.

BRONTEUM. (Gr.)   In ancient Greek Architecture, that part of the theatre under the floor in which brazen vessels with stones in them were placed to imitate the sound of thunder.

BRONZE.   A compound metal applied to various useful and ornamental purposes.   The composition consists of 6 to 12 parts of tin and 100 parts of copper.   This alloy is heavier and more tenacious than copper ; it is also much more fusible, and less liable to be altered by exposure to the air.

BROSSE, JACQUES DE.   See ARCHITECTS, list of, 248.

BRUNELLESCHI.   See ARCHITECTS, list of, 147.

BUDGET.   A small pocket used by tilers for holding the nails in lathing for tiling.

BUFFET. (Fr.)   A cabinet or cupboard for plate, glass, or china.   Some years back it was the practice to make these small recesses very ornamental, in the form of niches, and left open in the front to display the contents.   At present, when used, they are generally closed with a door.

BUILDER.   A person who contracts for performing the whole of the different artificers' works in a building.

BUILDING.   Used as a substantive is the mass of materials shaped into an edifice.   As a participle, it is the constructing and raising an edifice suited to the purposes for which it is erected ; the knowledge requisite for the design and construction of buildings being the subject of this work, in which it is treated under its various heads.

BUILDING ACT.   An act passed 18 & 19 Victoria, cap. 122, for regulating the construction and use of buildings in the Metropolis and its neighbourhood.

BUILDING OF BEAMS.   The same as Scarfing.

BULKER.   A term used in Lincolnshire to signify a beam or rafter.

BULL'S EYE.   Any small circular aperture for the admission of light or air.

BULL'S NOSE.   The external or other angle of a polygon, or of any two lines meeting at an obtuse angle.

BULLEN NAILS.   Such as have round heads with short shanks turned and lacquered.   They are principally used in the hangings of rooms.

BULLOCK SHEDS.   Houses or sheds for feeding bullocks, in which the main points to be observed are good ventilation, facility in feeding and cleaning the animals, perfect drainage, and a good aspect.   They ought not to be less than nineteen feet wide.

BUNDLE PILLAR.   In Gothic architecture, a column consisting of a number of small pillars round its circumference.

BUONARROTI, M. A.   See ARCHITECTS, list of, 219.

BUONO.   See ARCHITECTS, list of, 95.

BUONO, BARTOLOMEO.   See ARCHITECTS, list of, 191.

BUONTALENTI.   See ARCHITECTS, list of, 241.*

BURLINGTON, EARL OF.   See ARCHITECTS, list of, 293.

BURROUGHS.   See ARCHITECTS, list of, 287.

BUSCHETTO.   See ARCHITECTS, list of, 18.

BUSTAMENTE.   See ARCHITECTS, list of, 233.

BUT-HINGES.   Those employed in the hanging of doors, shutters, casements, &c.   They are placed on the edges with the knuckle projecting on the side in which the *closure* is to open, and the other edges stopping against a small piece of wood left in the thickness of the closure so as to keep the arris entire.   Workmen generally sink the thickness of the hinges flush with the surface of the edge of the closure, and the *tail part* one half into the jamb.   Of but-hinges there are several kinds ; such as *stop but-hinges*, which permit the closure to open only to a right angle, or perhaps a little more, without breaking the hinges ; *rising but-hinges*, which are those that turn upon a screw ; these are most employed in doors, and cause the door to rise as it opens, so as to clear the carpet in the apartment ; *slip-off but-hinges*, which are those employed where a door or window blind is required to be taken off occasionally.

BUTMENT.   The same as ABUTMENT, which see.

BUTMENT CHEEKS.   The two solid sides of a mortise.   The thickness of each cheek is usually equal to the thickness of the mortise, but it happens that circumstances arise to vary this thickness.

BUTT-END OF A PIECE OF TIMBER.   That which was nearest the root of a tree.

BUTTERY.   A store-room for provisions, which, if possible, should be on the north side of a building.

BUTTING JOINT.   That formed by the surfaces of two pieces of wood, whereof one is perpendicular to the fibres, and the other in their direction, or making an oblique angle with them, as for example, the joints made by the struts and braces with the truss posts.

Button. A small piece of wood or metal, made to turn about a centre for fastening a door, draw, or any other kind of closure. The centre is generally a nail, which should be smooth, rounded, and the head filed even.

Buttress. (Fr. Aboutir, to lie out.) A mass of brickwork or masonry to support the side of a wall of great height, or pressed on the opposite side by a bank of earth or body of water. Buttresses are employed against the piers of Gothic buildings to resist the thrust of the vaulting. See Arc Boutant, or flying buttress. The buttress called the pillared buttress is formed by vertical planes attached to the walls themselves. These sometimes form the upright terminations of flying buttresses.

C.

Cabin. (Brit. Chabin.) A term applied to the huts and cottages of poor people and to those of persons in a savage state of life.

Cabinet. (Fr.) A retired room in an edifice set apart for writing, study, or the preservation of any thing curious or valuable. The term is also applied to an apartment at the end of a gallery in which pictures are hung, or small pieces of sculpture, medals, bronzes, and other curiosities are arranged.

Cable. A moulding of a convex circular section, rising from the back or concave surface of a flute, so that its most prominent part may be in the same continued circular surface as the fillet on each side of the flute. Thus the surface of a flute is that of a concave cylinder, and that of the cable is the surface of a convex cylinder, with the axes of the cylinders parallel to each other. The cable seems to represent a rope or staff laid in the flute, at the lower part of which it is placed about one third of the way up.

Cabled Column. One in which cables, as described in the last article, are used.

Cabled Flutes. Such as are filled with cables.

Cabling. The filling of the flutes with cables, or the cables themselves so disposed. Cabling of flutes was not frequently used in the works of antiquity. The flutes of the columns of the arch of Constantine are filled with cables to about one third of the height of the shaft. Most of the columns in the ruins of Baalbec, Palmyra, and the palace of Diocletian at Spalatro, have neither flutes nor cables. In modern times an occasional abuse has been practised of cabling without fluting, as in the church della Sapienza at Rome.

Caer. A term in British antiquity, which, like the Saxon term *Chester*, denotes a castle, and is generally prefixed to the names of places fortified by the Romans.

Cage, in carpentry, is an outer work of timber inclosing another within it. Thus the cage of a stair is the wooden inclosure that encircles it.

Caisson. (Fr.) A large and strong chest of timber, water-tight, used in large and rapid rivers for building the pier of a bridge. The bottom consists of a grating of timber, contrived in such a manner that the sides, when necessary, may be detached from it. The ground under the intended pier is first levelled, and the caisson being launched and floated into its proper position, it is sunk, and the pier built therein as high as the level of the water, or nearly so. The sides are then detached, and the pier, built as described, sinks down on the foundation prepared for it. The tonnage of each of the caissons used at Westminster Bridge was equal to that of a forty-gun ship.

Caissons in Vaulting. The sunken pannels on ceilings, vaults, and cupolas. See Book III. Chap. II. Sect. 3.

Calcareous Cements. See Cement in the body of the work, p. 540, *et seq.*

Calcareous Earth. A species of earth which becomes friable by burning, and is afterwards reduced to an impalpable powder by mixing it with water. It also effervesces with acids. It is frequently met with in a friable or compact state in the form of chalk.

Caldarium. (Lat.) In ancient architecture a close vaulted room, in which persons were brought into a state of profuse perspiration. It was one of the apartments attached to ancient baths, and was also denominated *Vaporarium, Sudatorium*, and *Laconicum*.

Calffen. A place for nourishing calves. It is generally a small apartment within the cowhouse; but the practice is not to be recommended, as it keeps the cow in a restless and agitated state, and prevents her from feeding well, and giving that quantity of milk she would otherwise furnish.

Caliber. (Spanish.) The greatest extent or diameter of a round body.

Caliber Compasses. Those made with bent legs for taking the diameter of a convex or concave body in any part. See Mould.

Caliducts. (Lat.) Pipes or channels disposed along the walls of houses and apartments. They were used by the ancients to convey heat to the remote parts of the house from one common furnace.

Caliper. See Caliber.

Callias. See Architects, list of, 18.

CALLICRATES. See ARCHITECTS, list of, 13.

CALLIMACHUS. See ARCHITECTS, list of, 24.

CALOTTE. (Fr.) A concavity in the form of a cup or niche, lathed and plastered, serving to diminish the height of a chapel, alcove, or cabinet, which otherwise would appear too high for the breadth.

CAMAROSIS. (Gr.) An elevation terminated with an arched or vaulted head.

CAMBER. (Gr.) An arch on the top of an aperture or on the top of a beam. Hence camber windows.

CAMBER BEAMS. Those which form a curved line on each side from the middle of their length. All beams should, to some degree, if possible, be cambered; but the cambered beam is used in flats and church platforms, wherein, after being covered with boards, these are covered with lead, for the purpose of discharging the rain-water.

CAMERATED. (Gr.) The same as arched.

CAMES. Small slender rods of cast lead in glazing, twelve or fourteen inches long, of which, by drawing them separately through a species of vice, the glaziers make their turned lead for receiving the glass of casements.

CAMP CEILING. A ceiling whose form is convex inwardly.

CAMPANILE. (It. a bell tower.) A tower for the reception of bells, usually, in Italy, separated from the church. Many of the campaniles of Italy are lofty and magnificent structures. That at Cremona is much celebrated, being 395 feet high. It consists of a square tower, rising 262 feet, surmounted by two octagonal open stories, ornamented with columns; a conical shaft and cross terminate the elevation. The campanile of Florence, from the designs of Giotto, though in bad taste, has claims on our admiration for its richness and the superiority of the workmanship. It is 267 feet high, and 45 feet square. The most remarkable of the campaniles in the country mentioned is that at Pisa, commonly called the " Leaning Tower." It is cylindrical in general form, and surrounded by eight stories of columns, placed over one another, each having its entablature. Each column carries the springing of two arches, and there is an open gallery between the columns and the circular wall of the tower. The height of the last story of columns, in which are the bells, is set back from the general line of the elevation. The height is about 150 feet to the platform, whence a plumb line lowered falls on the leaning side nearly 13 feet beyond the base of the building.

CAMPBELL. See ARCHITECTS, list of, 271.

CAMPERO. See ARCHITECTS, list of, 198.

CAMP-SHEETING or **CAMPSHOT.** The sill or cap of a wharf wall.

CANAL. (It. Canale.) A duct for the conveyance of a fluid; thus the canal of an aqueduct is the part through which the water flows. In ancient aqueducts it was lined with a coat of mastic.

CANAL. A term sometimes used for the flutings of a column or pilaster. The *canal of the volute* is the spiral channel, or sinking on its face, commencing at the eye, and following in the revolutions of the volute. The *canal of the larmier* is the channel or groove sunk on its soffite to throw off the rain, and prevent it from running down the bed mould of the cornice.

CANCELLI. (Lat.) Latticed windows, or those made with cross bars of wood or iron. The balusters or rails which close in the bar of a court of justice, and those round the altar of a church, are also so called; hence the word chancel.

CANDELABRUM. (Lat. Candela.) A stand or support on which the ancients placed a lamp. Candelabra varied in form, and were highly decorated with the stems and leaves of plants, parts of animals, flowers, and the like. The etymology of the word would seem to assimilate the candelabrum to our candlestick; it is, however, certain that the word *candela* was but a lamp, whereof the candelabrum was the support. In the works of Piranesi some of the finest specimens are to be found. The most curious, however, as respects form, use, and workmanship, are those excavated at Herculaneum and Pompeii. They are all of bronze, slender in their proportions, and perfectly portable, as they rarely in height exceed five feet. On none of the candelabra hitherto found is there any appearance of a socket or pipe at top, from which an inference as to the use of candles could be made.

CANEPHORÆ. (Gr. Κανηφορος, bearing a basket.) Figures of young persons, of either sex, bearing on their heads baskets containing materials for sacrifice. They are frequently confounded with caryatides, from their resemblance in point of attitude and the modern abuse of their application.

CANOPY. (Gr. Κωνωπειον.) An ornamented covering over a seat of state; and in its extended signification any covering which affords protection from above. It is also the label or projecting roof that surrounds the arches and heads of gothic niches.

CANT. An external angle or quoin of a building. Among carpenters it is used as a verb, to signify the turning of a piece of timber which has been brought in the wrong way for their work.

CANT MOULDING. One with one or more bevelled, instead of curved, surfaces. The cant moulding was used at an early period of the art.

CANTALEVER or CANTILEVER. (Probably from Canterii labrum, *the lip of the rafter.*) Blocks inserted into the wall of a building for supporting a balcony, the upper members of a cornice, or the eaves of a house, and the like. They answer the same purpose as modillions, mutules, blocks, brackets, &c., although not so regularly applied. They are, in modern use, not unfrequently made of timber or cast iron, and project considerably, as in the church of St. Paul, Covent Garden, which projects one quarter of the height of the column.

CANTED COLUMN. One whose horizontal sections are polygons. In the works of the ancients it is rarely met with. The examples immediately occurring to us are the columns of the portico of Philip of Macedon and of the temple of Cora.

CANTHARUS. A fountain or basin of water in the centre of the atrium before the ancient churches, wherein persons washed their faces and hands before they entered. Among the Romans the cantharus of a fountain was the part out of which the water issued.

CANTHERS or CANTERII. In ancient carpentry the common rafters of a roof, whose ends, say some, the mutules of the Doric order represent.

CANTING. The cutting away of a part of an angular body at one of its angles, so that its horizontal section becomes thereby the portion of a polygon of a greater number of sides whose edges are parallel from the intersection of the adjoining planes.

CANTONED BUILDING. One whose angles are decorated with columns, pilasters, rustic quoins, or any thing projecting beyond the naked of the wall.

CAP. A term used in joinery, signifying the uppermost of an assemblage of parts. It is also applied to the capital of a column, the cornice of a door, the capping or uppermost member of the surbase of a room, the handrail of a staircase, &c.

CAPITAL. (Lat. Caput.) The head or uppermost member of any part of a building; but generally applied in a restricted sense to that of a column or pilaster of the several orders, to which (Sections 3, 4, 5, 6, 7. Chap. I. Book III.) the reader is referred for the differences of their capitals. The chief of the capitals of Eastern and Egyptian architecture are shown in *figs.* 58, 59, &c.

CAPITAL, ANGULAR. The modern Ionic capital, whose four sides are alike, showing the volute placed at an angle of 135° on all the faces.

CAPITAL OF A BALUSTER. The crowning or head mouldings of it.

CAPITAL OF A LANTERN. The covering by which it is terminated; it may be of a bell form, that of a dome, spire, or other regular figure.

CAPITAL OF A TRIGLYPH. The square band which projects over it. In the Roman Doric it has a greater projection than in the Grecian.

CAPREOLI. (Lat.) In ancient carpentry the joints or braces of a trussed roof. See *figs.* 91, 92.

CARACOL. A term sometimes applied to a staircase in the form of a helix or spiral.

CARAVANSERA. Among the Eastern nations a large public building or inn appropriated to the reception and lodgment of travellers by caravans in the desert. Though the caravansera serves the purpose of an inn, there is this essential difference between the two, that in the former the traveller finds nothing either for the use of himself or his cattle, but must carry all his provisions and necessaries with him. Caravanseras are also numerous in cities (see an example, *fig.* 33.), where they serve, not only as inns, but as shops, warehouses, and even exchanges.

CARCASS. The naked building of a house before it is lathed and plaistered, or the floor boards laid, &c.

CARCASS FLOORING. That which supports the boarding, or floor boards, above, and the ceiling below, being a grated frame of timber, varying in many particulars, which are described in Book II. Chap. III. Sect. 4, in the body of the work.

CARCASS ROOFING. The grated frame of timber work which spans the building, and carries the boarding and other covering. The method of framing the carcass roofing of a building in its varieties is given p. 603, *et seq.*

CARDINALES SCAPI. In ancient Roman joinery, the stiles of doors.

CARILEPHO. See ARCHITECTS, list of, 83.

CAROLITIC COLUMN. One with a foliated shaft.

CARPENTER. (Fr. Charpentier.) An artificer who practises the science of framing and fitting to each other the various pieces and assemblages of timber used in the construction of buildings. See *par.* 2003.

CARPENTER'S RULE. The instrument by which carpenters take their dimensions, and by the aid of a brass slide, which makes it a sliding rule, they are enabled to make calculations in multiplication and division, besides other operations.

CARPENTER'S SQUARE. An instrument whose stock and blade consists of an iron plate of one piece. One leg is eighteen inches long, and numbered on the outer edge from the exterior angle with the lower part of the figures adjacent to the interior edge. The other leg is twelve inches long, and numbered from the extremity towards the angle; the figures being

read from the internal angle, as on the other side. Each of the legs is about an inch broad. This instrument is not only used as a square, but also as a level and measuring rule.

CARPENTRY. (Lat. Carpentum, carved wood.) An assemblage of pieces of timber connected by framing, or letting them into each other, as are the pieces of a roof, floor, centre, &c. It is distinguished from joinery by being put together, without the use of any other edge tools than the axe, adze, saw, and chisel, whereas joinery requires the use of the plane. The leading points that require attention in sound carpentry are, — 1. the quality of the timber used; 2. the disposition of the pieces of timber, so that each may be in such direction, with reference to the fibres of the wood, as to be most capable of performing its office properly; 3. the forms and dimensions of the pieces; 4th. the manner of framing the pieces into each other, or otherwise uniting them by means of iron, or other metal. The subject of carpentry in the body of the work is treated under the head of BEAMS AND PILLARS, Book II. Chap. I. Sect. 10; and of CARPENTRY, in the same Book, Chap. III. Sect. 4.

CARRARA MARBLE. The name of a species of white marble obtained at the quarries near the town bearing that name, in the Tuscan States. It was called *marmor lunense* and *ligustrum* by the ancients, and differs from the *Parian* marble by being harder in texture, and less bright in colour.

CARRIAGE. The timber framework on which the steps of a wooden staircase are supported. See p. 602.

CARRY UP. See BRING UP.

CARTOUCH. (Fr.) A name given to the modillion of a cornice used internally. It is also used to denote a scroll of paper, usually in the form of a tablet, for the reception of an inscription. In Egyptian architecture, applied to those parts of an hieroglyphic inscription enclosed by lines.

CARVER. (Ceopran.) An artificer who cuts wood into various forms and devices. *Carving*, generally, is the art of cutting a body by recession, in order to produce the representation of an object, either in relief, or recessed within the general surface. In this sense it equally applies to the making of intaglios as to that of making cameos.

CARYATIDES. Figures used instead of columns for the support of an entablature. See Book I. Chap. II. Sect. 11., and Book III. Chap. I. Sect. 15.

CASE. The outside covering of any thing, or that in which it may be enclosed. It is also a term used to denote the carcass of a house.

CASE BAYS. The joists framed between a pair of girders in naked flooring. When the flooring joists are framed with one of their ends let into a girder, and the opposite ends let into a wall, they are called *tail-bays*. The extent of the case-bays should not exceed ten feet.

CASE OF A DOOR. The wooden frame in which a door is hung.

CASE OF A STAIR. The wall surrounding a staircase.

CASED. A term signifying that the outside of a building is faced or covered with materials of a better quality. Thus, a brick wall is said to be cased with stone, or with a brick superior in quality to that used in the inner part of the wall.

CASED SASH FRAMES. Those which have their interior vertical sides hollow, to admit the weights which balance the sashes hung between them.

CASEMATE. A hollow moulding, such as the *cavetto*, which see.

CASEMENT. A glazed frame or sash, opening on hinges affixed to the vertical sides of the frame into which it is fitted.

CASING. See LINING.

CASINO. (It. a small house.) A term applied now to a small country house; but formerly to one capable of affording defence on a small scale against an attacking force.

CASTELLA. In ancient Roman architecture, reservoirs in which the waters of an aqueduct were collected, and whence the water was conducted through leaden pipes to the several parts of a city.

CASTELLATED HOUSES. Those with battlements and turrets, in imitation of ancient castles.

CASTING. In carpentry and joinery a term synonymous with warping. It means the bending of the surfaces of a piece of wood from their original state, caused either by the gravity of the material, by its being subject to unequal temperature, moisture, or the ununiform texture of the material.

CASTLE. (Lat. Castellum, or Sax. Canrel.) A building fortified for military defence; also a house with towers, usually encompassed with walls and moats, and having a donjon or keep in the centre. The principal castles of England at present are those of the Tower of London, of Dover, Windsor, Norwich, &c. At one time those of Harwood, Spofforth, Kenilworth, Warwick, Arundel, and others, might have vied with these in importance. The characteristics of a castle are its *valla* (embankments) and *fossæ* (ditches); from the former whereof the walls rise usually crowned with battlements, and flanked by circular

or polygonal bastions at the angles formed by the walls.   These were pierced for gates, with fixed or drawbridges, and towers on each side.   The gates of considerable strength were further guarded by descending gratings, called *portcullises*.   All the apertures were made as small as they could be, consistent with internal lighting.

The component parts of the castle were — the *fosse* or *moat*, with its bridge; the *barbacan*, which was in advance of the castle, being a raised mound or tower, whose outer walls had terraces towards the castle, with their *bastions*, as above-mentioned; the *gatehouse*, flanked by towers, and crowned with projections called *machicolations*, through which heavy materials, or molten lead, were dropped on the assailants entering the gateway; the *outer ballium*, or *bailey*, or area within the castle, which was separated from the inner ballium by an embattled wall with a gatehouse, and in which the stables and other offices were usually seated; and the *inner ballium*, for the residence of the owner or governor, and his retinue; this, at one corner, or in the centre, had a *donjon*, or *keep tower*, which was the stronghold of the place, and contained a state apartment, a well, and a chapel; the former usually, and the latter frequently, are found in ancient castles.   The reader who desires detailed information on this matter is referred to King's *Mun. Antiq.* 4 vols. folio; the Archæologia, in many places; Leland's *Collect.* vol. ii. &c. &c.

CATABASION. (Gr. Καταβαινω.)   A place in the Greek church, under the altar, in which relics are deposited.

CATACOMBS.   (Gr. Κατα, against, and Κομ8ος, a hollow place.)   Subterraneous places for burying the dead.   The hypogæa, crypta, and cimeteria of the ancients were used for the same purpose.   In some cities the excavations for catacombs were of vast extent, and were used for other purposes than those of sepulture; at Syracuse, for instance, the same cavern served for a prison as well as a public cemetery.   It has been said, that in the early ages of Christianity they served as places of public worship or devotion.   The most celebrated for their extent are those of Rome, Naples, Syracuse, &c.; and the more modern ones of Paris, which have been formed by quarrying for the stone, whereof a great part of the city has been built.

CATAFALCO. (It. a scaffold.)   A temporary structure of carpentry, decorated with painting and sculpture, representing a tomb or cenotaph, and used in funeral ceremonies. That used at the final interment of Michel Angelo, at Florence, was of a very magnificent description; and, for the art employed on it, perhaps unequalled by any other before or since its employment.

CATCH DRAIN.   A drain used on the side of a larger open one, or of a canal, to receive the surplus water of the principal conduit.

CATENARY CURVE.   The mechanical curve formed by a heavy flexible cord or chain of uniform density, hanging freely from the two extremities.   Galileo first noticed it, and proposed it as the proper figure for an arch of equilibrium.   He, however, imagined that it was the same as the parabola.   It was James Bernouilli who first investigated its nature, and its properties were thereafter pointed out by John Bernouilli, Huygens, and Leibnitz.   From the first of these mathematicians, the following geometrical method of determining the relations between the parts of a catenary is translated.   The catenarean curve is of two kinds, the *common*, which is formed by a chain equally thick or equally heavy in all its points; or *uncommon*, which is formed by a thread unequally thick, that is, which in all its points is unequally heavy, and in some ratio of the ordinates of a given curve.   To draw the common catenary mechanically, suspend on a vertical plane a chain of similar and equal links of homogeneous matters, as flexible as possible, from any two points not in a perpendicular line, nor so distant from each other as the length of the chain.   Prick the plane through the links as nearly as possible in the middle of the chain, and through the points draw the catenary (*fig.* 1361.).   Let the chord FBD or Fbd be given, and the abscissa BA or bA intersecting it (*fig.* 1361,) in B or b at a given angle.

Draw the vertical line BA and FBD or Fbd at the given angle on the plane.   Fix one end of the chain at F, and from the point D or d, with another part of the chain, raise or lower the chain until the lower part coincide with A, and through points, made as before, draw the curve.

To draw a tangent to the catenary: let DBF be a horizontal line, and at right angles to BA from A draw AR equal to the curve DA, obtained as before, and draw BR, which bisect in o.   At right angles to BR draw oC intersecting BA continued in C.   Draw CR, and make the angle BDT equal to the angle ACR. DT is the tangent required, and BC equals

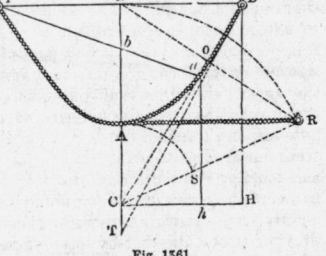

Fig. 1561.

CR; CA is the tension at the point A, or the horizontal draft, which, in a catenary, is in every point the same, and is therefore a constant quantity; as DB : BT :: CA : AR :

or as DB : BT :: the constant quantity CA : AR, equal to the length of the chain AD.

If CH be drawn through C at right angles to BC it is called the directrix, and DH drawn parallel to BC, intersecting the directrix at H, is the tension at the point D, being always equal to the sum of the abscissa and constant quantity. With the centre C and radius = the tension DH at D = CB, cut the tangent at the vertex A in R, then AR is the length of the chain AD.

AC is the semi-axis of an equilateral hyperbola, and also the radius of curvature of a circle equicurved with it and the catenary.

In the triangle CAR, when CA is the radius, then the tension equals CR, the secant of the angle ACR (= BDC). The chain AD equals AR, the tangent of the same angle and the absciss AB equals CR − CA = SR. Hence, ACR being a right-angled triangle, it is manifest that when two of the five quantities, viz. *the angle, the absciss, the length of the chain between the vertex and point of suspension, the constant quantity or tension at the vertex, and the tension at the points of suspension,* are known, the other three may be obtained geometrically, or from a table of tangents and secants.

CATHARINE WHEEL. In Gothic buildings an ornamented window or compartment of a window of a circular form, with rosettes or radiating divisions or spokes. In the cathedral at Rheims, the church of St. Ouen at Rouen, in Winchester Cathedral, and the transepts of Westminster Abbey, are specimens, among many others, of this species of ornamental window.

CATHEDRAL. (Gr. Καθεδρα, a seat or throne.) The principal church of a province or diocese, wherein the throne of archbishop or bishop is placed. It was originally applied to the seats in which the bishop and presbyters sat in their assemblies. In after times, the bishop's throne was, however, placed in the centre of the apsis, on each side whereof were inferior seats for the presbyters. In the present day the bishop's throne is placed on one side of the choir, usually on that towards the south.

CATHETUS. (Gr. Καθετος, let down.) A perpendicular line passing through the centre of a cylindrical body as a baluster or a column. It is also a line falling perpendicularly, and passing through the centre or eye of the volute of the Ionic capital.

CATTLE SHED, or CATTLE HOUSE. In agricultural buildings an erection for containing cattle while feeding, or otherwise. The cattle shed is, of course, most economically constructed when built against walls or other buildings. If cattle sheds are built in isolated situations, the expense of a double shed will be much less than that of a single one, to contain the same number of cattle. Buildings of this description should be well ventilated, and be so constructed as to require the least possible labour in supplying the food, and clearing away the dung. The stalls should be placed so as to keep the cattle dry and clean, with sufficient drains to receive the ordure. There should be good provision of air holes in the roof; and, if the building have gables, a window should be placed in each as high as possible with moveable *luffer-boards*, as in granary windows, which may be easily opened and shut by means of a rope attached to a lever connected with them. These precautions will much tend to the health of the cattle, and even preserve the timbers, which in such buildings are peculiarly apt to rot at an early period after their erection, from the constant alternations of dryness and moisture.

CATTUS. A moveable shed usually fixed on wheels.

CAULICOLÆ or CAULICOLI. (Lat. Caulis, a stalk.) The eight lesser branches or stalks in the Corinthian capital springing out from the four greater or principal caules or stalks. The eight volutes of the capital of the order in question are sustained by four caules or leaves, from which these caulicolæ or lesser foliage arise. They have been sometimes confounded with the helices in the middle, and by others with the principal stalks whence they arise. Other definitions have been also incorrectly given, but not worth notice here.

CAULKING or COCKING. The mode of fixing the tie-beams of a roof or the binding joists of a floor down to the wall-plates. Formerly this was performed by dovetailing in the following manner: — A small part of the depth of the beam at the end of the under side was cut in the form of a dovetail, and to receive it a corresponding notch was formed in the upper side of the wall-plate, across its breadth, making, of course, the wide part of the dovetail towards the exterior part of the wall, so that the beams, when laid in their notches, and the roof finished, would greatly tend to prevent the walls separating, though strained by inward pressure, or even if they should have a tendency to spread, through accidents or bad workmanship. But beams so fixed have been found liable to be drawn to a certain degree out of the notches in the wall-plates from the shrinking of the timber; a more secure mode has therefore been introduced, which obviates all hazard of one being drawn out of the other by any deficiency of seasoning in the timbers, or by any changes of weather.

CAUSTIC CURVE. (Gr. Καιω, to burn.) The name given to a curve, to which the rays of light, reflected or refracted by another curve, are tangents. The curve is of two kinds,

the *catacaustic* and the *diacaustic ;* the former being caused by reflection, and the latter by refraction.

Cavædium. (Lat.)   In ancient architecture an open quadrangle or court within a house. The cavædia described by Vitruvius are of five species : — *Tuscanicum, Corinthium, Tetrastylon* (with four columns), *Displuviatum* (uncovered), and *Testudinatum* (vaulted). Some authors have made the cavædium the same as the atrium and vestibulum, but they were essentially different.

Cave. (Lat. Cavum.)   A hollow place.   Perhaps the oldest species of architecture on record.

Caveæ. (Lat.)   In ancient architecture the subterranean cells in an amphitheatre, wherein the wild beasts were confined in readiness for the fights of the arena.   In the end the amphitheatre itself (by synecdoche) was called cavea, in which sense it is employed by Ammianus Marcellinus, lib. xxix. cap. i.

Cavetto. (Lat. Cavus.)   A hollowed moulding, whose profile is the quadrant of a circle. It is principally used in cornices.

Cedar. (Gr. Κεδρος.)   The pinus cedrus of Linnæus, a forest tree little used in this country, except for cabinet work.

Ceiling. (Lat. Cœlum.)   The upper horizontal or curved surface of an apartment opposite the floor, usually finished with plastered work.   The subject of ceilings is treated of at length in Sect. 24. Chap. I. Book III.

Ceiling Floor.   The joisting and ceiling supported by the beams of the roof.

Ceiling Joists.   Small beams, which are either mortised into the sides of the binding joists, or notched upon and nailed up to the under sides of those joists.   The last mode diminishes the height of the room, but is more easily executed, and is by some thought not so liable to break the plaster as when the ends of the ceiling-joists are inserted into *pulley mortises.*

Celer.   See Architects, list of, 42.

Cell. (Lat. Cella.)   In ancient architecture the part of a temple within the walls.   It was also called the *naos,* whence our *nave* in a church.   The part of a temple in front of the cell was called the *pronaos,* and that in the rear the *posticum.*

Cellar. (Fr. Cellier.)   The lower story of a building, when wholly or partly under the level of the ground.

Cement. (Lat. Cementum.)   The medium through which stones, bricks, or any other materials are made to adhere to each other.   The different cements for stones and bricks, the most important in building, are treated of in Book II. Chap. II. Sect. 11.

Celtic Architecture.   See Book I. Chap. II. Sect. 1.

Cemetery. (Gr. Κοιμάω, to sleep.)   An edifice or area where the dead are interred.   The most celebrated public cemeteries of Europe are those of Naples, that in the vicinity of Bologna, of Pisa, and the more modern ones of Paris, whereof that of Père-la-Chaise is the principal.   That of Pisa is particularly distinguished by the beauty of its form and architecture, which is of early Italian Gothic.   It is 490 feet long, 170 feet wide, and 60 feet high, cloistered round the four sides.

Cenotaph. (Gr. Κενὸς, empty, and Τάφος, a sepulchre.)   A monument erected to the memory of a person buried in another place.

Centering.   The temporary woodwork or framing, whereon any vaulted work is constructed, sometimes called a *centre.*   The principle upon which centering is constructed will be found under the head of Carpentry, Book II. Chap. III. Sect. 4.

Centre. (Lat. Centrum.)   In a general sense denotes a point equally remote from the extremes of a line, superficies, or body, or it is the middle of a line or plane by which a figure or body is divided into two equal parts ; or the middle point so dividing a line, plane, or solid, that some certain effects are equal on all its sides.   For example, in a circle the centre is every where at equal distance from the circumference ; in a sphere the centre is a point at the same distance from every point in the surface.

Centres of a Door.   The two pivots on which the door revolves.

Centrolinead.   An instrument for drawing lines converging to a point at any required distance, whether accessible or inaccessible.

Ceroma. (Gr.)   An apartment in the Gymnasia and baths of the ancients, where the bathers and wrestlers were anointed with oil thickened by wax, as the name imports.

Cesspool, or Sesspool.   A well sunk under the mouth of a drain to receive the sediment which might choke up its passage.

Chain Timbers.   See Bond.

Chalcidicum. (Lat.)   In ancient architecture a term used by Vitruvius to denote a large building appropriated to the purpose of administering justice, but applied sometimes to the tribunal itself.   According to Festus, the name is derived from Chalcis, a city in Eubœa.

Chalk. (Germ. Kalk.)   Earthy carbonate of lime, found in abundance in Great Britain,

and, indeed, in most parts of the world. It is insoluble in water, but decomposed by heat, and sometimes used in masonry for the same purposes as limestone.

CHAMBER. (Fr. Chambre.) Properly a room vaulted or arched, but the word is now generally used in a more restricted sense to signify an apartment appropriated to lodging. With the French the word has a much more extensive meaning; but with us the almost only use of it, beyond what is above stated, is as applied in a palace to the room in which the sovereign receives the subject, which room is called the Presence Chamber.

CHAMBER OF A LOCK. In canals the space between the gates in which the vessels rise and sink from one level to another, in order to pass the lock.

CHAMBER STORY. That story of a house appropriated for bed-rooms. In good houses it should never be less than ten feet high, in better houses from twelve feet to fifteen feet.

CHAMBERS. See ARCHITECTS, list of, 300.

CHAMBRANLE. (Fr.) An ornamental bordering on the sides and tops of doors, windows, and fireplaces. This ornament is generally taken from the architrave of the order of the building. In window frames the sill is also ornamental, forming a fourth side. The top of a three-sided chambranle is called the *transverse,* and the sides *ascendants.*

CHAMFER. (Fr. Chamfrein.) The arris of anything originally right-angled cut aslope or bevel, so that the plane it then forms is inclined less than a right angle to the other planes with which it intersects.

CHAMPAIN LINE. In ornamental carved work formed of excavations is the line parallel to the continuous line, either ascending or descending.

CHANCEL. That part of the eastern end of a church in which the altar is placed. See CANCELLI. This is the strict meaning; but in many cases the chancel extends much further into the church, the original divisions having been removed for accommodating a larger congregation. The word is also used to denote a separate division of the ancient basilica, latticed off to separate the judges and council from the audience part of the place.

CHANDRY. An apartment in a palace or royal dwelling for depositing candles and other lights.

CHANNEL. (Fr. Canal.) A long gutter or canal sunk below the surface of a body.

CHANNEL OF THE LARMIER. See CANAL OF THE LARMIER.

CHANNEL OF THE VOLUTE. See CANAL OF THE VOLUTE.

CHANNEL STONES. In paving are those prepared for gutters or channels, serving to collect and run off the rain water with a current.

CHANTRY. (Lat. Cantaria.) A little chapel in ancient churches with an endowment for one or more priests to say mass for the release of souls out of purgatory. In the fourteenth year of Edward VI. all the chantries in England were dissolved: at this period there were no less than forty-seven attached to St. Paul's Cathedral.

CHAPEL. (Lat. Capella.) A building for religious worship, erected separately from a church, and served by a chaplain. In Catholic churches, and in cathedrals and abbey churches, chapels are usually annexed in the recesses on the sides of the aisles. These are also called chantries.

CHAPITER. The same as CAPITAL, which see.

CHAPLET. (Fr. Chapelet.) A moulding carved into beads, olives, and the like. See BAGUETTE.

CHAPTER HOUSE. In ecclesiastical architecture the apartment (usually attached) of a cathedral or collegiate church in which the heads of the church or the chapter meet to transact business.

CHAPTREL. (Fr.) The same as IMPOST, which see.

CHARGED. A term used to denote that one member of a piece of architecture is sustained by another. A frieze is said to be *charged* with the ornament cut on it.

CHARNEL HOUSE. A place where the bones of the dead are deposited.

CHARTOPHYLACIUM. A recess or apartment for the preservation of records or valuable writings.

CHASE. An upright indent cut in a wall for the joining another to it, so as to hide light and exclude air.

CHASE MORTISE, or PULLEY MORTISE. A long mortise cut lengthwise in one of a pair of parallel timbers, for the insertion of one end of a transverse timber, by making the latter revolve round a centre at the other end, which is fixed in the other parallel timber. This may be exemplified in ceiling joists where the binding joists are the parallel timbers first fixed, and the ceiling are the transverse joists. See CARPENTRY, in the body of this work, p. 598.

CHEEKS. Two upright, equal, and similar parts of any piece of timber-work. Such, for instance, as the sides of a dormer window.

CHEEKS OF A MORTISE are the two solid parts upon the sides of the mortise. The thick-

ness of each cheek should not be less than the thickness of the mortise, except mouldings on the stiles absolutely require it to be otherwise.

CHEESE ROOM. A room set apart for the reception of cheeses after they are made. The walls should be lined, and fitted up with shelves with one or more stages, according to the size of the room, and proper gangways for commodious passage. In places where much cheese is manufactured, the dairy-room may be placed below, the shelf-room directly above, and lofts may be built over the shelf-room, with trap doors through each floor. This will save much carriage, and will be found advantageous for drying the cheeses.

CHEQUERS. In masonry, are stones in the facings of walls, which have all their thin joints continued in straight lines, without interruption or breaking joints. Walls built in this manner are of the very worst description; particularly when the joints are made horizontal and vertical. Those which consist of diagonal joints, or joints inclined to the horizon, were used by the Romans.

CHESNUT or CHESTNUT. The *fagus castanea*. A forest tree used in building.

CHEST. The same as *caisson*, which see.

CHEVRON WORK. A zigzag ornament used in the archivolts of Saxon and Norman arches (see *fig.* 188.). The outline of chevron work is a conjunction of right lines of equal lengths alternately disposed so as to form exterior and interior angles, and at the same time having all the angular points in the same straight line, or in the same curve line when the chevron work is used for ornamenting arches.

CHICHELE. See ARCHITECTS, list of, 146.

CHIMNEY. (Fr. Cheminée.) The place in a room where a fire is burnt, and from which the smoke is carried away by means of a conduit, called a flue. Chimneys are usually made by a projection from a wall, and recess in the same from the floor ascending within the limits of the projection and the recess. That part of the opening which faces the room is properly called the *fireplace*, the stone or marble under which is called the *hearth*. That on a level with and in front of it is called the *slab*. The vertical sides of the opening are called *jambs*. The head of the fore-plate resting on the jambs is called the *mantel*, and the cavity or hollow from the fireplace to the top of the room is called the *funnel*. The part of the funnel which contracts as it ascends is termed the *gathering*, by some the *gathering of the wings*. The tube or cavity, of a parallelogrammatic form, on the place from where the gathering ceases, up to the top of the chimney, is called the *flue*. The part between the gathering and the flue is called the *throat*. The part of the wall facing the room, and forming one side of the funnel parallel thereto, or the part of the wall forming the sides of the funnels where there are more than one, is the *breast*. In external walls, that side of the funnel opposite the breast is called the *back*. When there is more than one chimney in the same breast, the solid parts that divide them are called *withs* : and when several chimneys are collected into one mass, it is called a *stack of chimneys*. The part which rises above the roof, for discharging the smoke into the air, is called a *chimney shaft*, whose horizontal upper surface is termed the *chimney-top*.

The *covings* were formerly placed at right angles to the face of the wall, and the chimney was finished in that manner; but Count Rumford showed that more heat is obtained from the fire by reflection when the covings are placed in an oblique position. He likewise directed that the fire itself should be kept as near to the hearth as possible, and that the throat of the chimney should be constructed much narrower than had been practised, with the view of preventing the escape of so much heated air as happened with wide throats. If the throat be too near the fire, the draught will be too strong, and the fuel will be wasted; if it be too high up, the draught will be too languid, and there will be a danger of the smoke being occasionally beat back into the room.

CHIMNEY PIECE. See Book III. Chap. I. Sect. 22.

CHINESE ARCHITECTURE. See Book I. Chap. II. Sect. 8.

CHIP. A piece of any material cut by an acute-angled instrument.

CHIROSOPHUS. See ARCHITECTS, list of, 7.

CHISEL. An instrument used in masonry, carpentry, and joinery, and also by carvers and statuaries, for cutting either by pressure or by impulse from the blows of a mallet or hammer. There are various kinds of chisels; the principal ones used in carpentry and joinery are the *former*, the *paring chisel*, the *gouge*, the *mortise chisel*, the *socket chisel*, and the *ripping chisel*.

CHISELED WORK. In masonry, the state of stones whose surface is formed by the chisel.

CHIT. An instrument used for cleaving laths.

CHOIR. (Gr. Χορος.) The part of a church in which the choristers sing divine service. In former times it was raised separate from the altar, with a pulpit on each side, in which the epistles and gospels were recited, as is still the case in several churches on the Continent. It was separated from the nave in the time of Constantine. In nunneries, the choir is a large apartment, separated by a grate from the body of the church, where the nuns chaunt the service.

CHORAGIC MONUMENT. (Gr. Χορος.) In Grecian architecture, a monument erected in honour of the choragus who gained the prize by the exhibition of the best musical or theatrical entertainment at the festivals of Bacchus. The choragi were the heads of the ten tribes at Athens, who overlooked and arranged the games at their own expense. The prize was usually a tripod, which the victor was bound publicly to exhibit, for which purpose a building or column was usually erected. The remains of two very fine monuments of this sort, viz. of Lysicrates and Thrasyllus, are still to be seen at Athens. See p.69.

CHORD. In geometry, the straight line which joins the two extremities of the arc of a curve ; so called from the resemblance which the arc and chord together have to a bow and its string, the chord representing the string.

CHRISMAS   See ARCHITECTS, list of, 263.

CHRISTOBOLO.   See ARCHITECTS, list of, 154.

CHRYSES.   See ARCHITECTS, list of, 63.

CHURCH. (Gr. Κυριακον, from Κυριος, Lord.) A building dedicated to the performance of Christian worship. For the general principles on which churches are to be designed see Book III. Chap. III. Sect. 3., also in Book I. Chap. II. Sect. 14. From these latter it will be seen that the basilicæ were the first buildings used for the assembly of the early Christians. Among the first of the churches was that of St. Peter at Rome, about the year 326, nearly on the site of the present church ; and it is supposed that the first church of St. Sophia at Constantinople was built somewhat on its model. That which was afterwards erected by Justinian seems, in its turn, to have afforded the model of St. Mark's at Venice, which was the first in Italy constructed with pendentives and a dome, the former affording the means of covering a square plan with an hemispherical vault. The four most celebrated churches in Europe erected since the revival of the arts are, St. Peter's at Rome, which stands on an area of 227,069 feet superficial ; Sta. Maria del Fiore at Florence, standing on 84,802 feet ; St. Paul's, London, which stands on 84,025 feet, and St. Geneviève at Paris, 60,287 feet. The churches on the Continent are usually ranged under seven classes : *pontifical*, as St. Peter's, where the pope occasionally officiates ; *patriarchal*, where the government is in a patriarch ; *metropolitan*, where an archbishop is the head ; *cathedral*, where a bishop presides ; *collegiate*, when attached to a college ; *parochial*, attached to a parish ; and *conventual* when belonging to a convent. In this country the churches are cathedral, abbey, and parochial.

CIBORIUM. (Κιβωριον.) An insulated erection open on each side with arches, and having a dome of ogee form carried or supported by four columns. It is also the coffer or case in which the host is deposited.

CICCIONE.   See ARCHITECTS, list of, 158.

CILERY. The drapery or foliage carved on the heads of columns.

CILL. (Sax. Cill.) The timber or stone at the foot of a door, &c. *Ground cills* are the timbers on the ground which support the posts and superstructure of a timber building. The name of cill is also given to the bottom pieces which support quarter and truss partitions.

CIMBIA. A fillet string, list, or cornice.

CIMELIARCH. A name given to the apartment where the plate and vestments are deposited in churches.

CINCTURE. The ring, list, or fillet at the top and bottom of a column, which divides the shaft of the column from its capital and base.

CINQUEFOIL. An ornament used in the pointed style of architecture ; it consists of five cuspidated divisions or curved pendents inscribed in a pointed arch, or in a circular ring applied to windows and panels. The cinquefoil, when inscribed in a circle, forms a rosette of five equal leaves having an open space in the middle, the leaves being formed by the open spaces, and not by the solids or cusps.

CIONE ORGAGNA, A. DI.   See ARCHITECTS, list of, 144.

CIPPUS. A small low column, sometimes without a base or capital, and most frequently bearing an inscription. Among the ancients the cippus was used for various purposes ; when placed on a road it indicated the distance of places ; on other occasions *cippi* were employed as memorials of remarkable events, as landmarks, and for bearing sepulchral epitaphs.

CIRCLE. (Lat. Circulus.) A figure contained under one line called the circumference, to which all lines drawn from a certain point within it, called the centre, are equal. It is the most capacious of all plain figures.

CIRCULAR BUILDINGS. Such as are built upon a circular plan. When the interior also is circular, the building is called a *rotunda*.

CIRCULAR WORK. A term applied to any work with cylindric faces.

CIRCULAR CIRCULAR, or CYLINDRO-CYLINDRIC WORK. A term applied to any work which is formed by the intersection of two cylinders whose axes are not in the same direction.

The line formed by the intersection of the surfaces is termed, by mathematicians, a *line of double curvature.*

CIRCULAR ROOFS. Those whose horizontal sections are circular.

CIRCULAR WINDING STAIRS. Such as have a cylindric case or walled enclosure, with the planes of the risers of the steps tending towards the axis of the cylinder.

CIRCUMFERENCE. The boundary line of a circular body.

CIRCUMSCRIBE. (Verb.) To draw a line around a figure, or enclose it so that the enclosed shall be touched on all its angles or on its whole circumference by the line or body that encloses it.

CIRCUMVOLUTIONS. The turns in the spiral of the Ionic capital, which are usually three. but there are four in the capitals of the temple of Minerva Polias.

CIRCUS. (Lat.) In ancient architecture, a straight, long, narrow building, whose length to its breadth was generally as 5 to 1. It was divided down the centre by an ornamented barrier called the *spina*, and was used by the Romans for the exhibition of public spectacles and chariot races. Several existed at Rome, whereof the most celebrated was the Circus Maximus. Julius Cæsar improved and altered the Circus Maximus, and that it might serve for the purpose of a naumachia, supplied it with water. Augustus added to it the celebrated obelisk now standing in the Piazza del Popolo. Of this circus no vestiges remain. Besides these at Rome were the circi of Flaminius, near the Pantheon; Agonalis, occupying the site of what is now called the Piazza Navona; of Nero, on a portion whereof St. Peter's stands. Those of Antoninus and Aurelian, no longer even in ruins; but that of Caracalla, which was 738 feet in length, is at the present time sufficiently perfect to exhibit its plan and distribution in the most satisfactory manner. The spectacles of the circus were called the Circensian Games, and consisted of chariot and horse races, of both whereof the Romans were passionately fond, but particularly of the former, which in the times of the emperors excited so great an interest, as to divide the whole population of the city into factions, distinguished by the colours worn by the different charioteers. The disputes of these factions often led to serious disturbances. See page 99.

CISSOID. In geometry a curved line invented by Diocles. Its name is derived from κισσος, ivy, from the curve appearing to mount along its assymptote, as ivy climbs on the trunk of a tree. The curve consists of two infinite branches above and below the diameter of a circle, at one of whose ends a tangent being drawn, the curve approaches the tangent without ever meeting it. The curve was invented by its author with a view to the solution of the famous problem of the duplication of the cube, or the insertion of two mean proportionals between two given straight lines. Its mechanical construction may be found in Newton's *Arithmetica Universalis.*

CIST. (Gr. Κιστη, a chest.) A term used to denominate the mystic baskets used in processions connected with the Eleusinian mysteries. It was originally formed of wicker work, and when afterwards made of metal, the form and texture were preserved in imitation of the original material. When sculptured on ancient monuments, it indicates some connection with the mysteries of Ceres and Bacchus.

CISTERN. (Gr. Κιστη.) A reservoir for water, whether sunk below or formed of planks of wood above ground. In the construction of an earthen cistern, a well-tempered stratum of clay must be laid as a foundation for a brick flooring, and the bricks laid in terras mortar or Parker's cement. The sides must be built with the same materials; and if in a cellar or other place near a wall a space must be filled with clay, from the foundation to the top of the cistern contiguous to the wall, by which means it will be preserved from injury. Cisterns above ground are usually formed of wooden planks and carried by bearers; but the cistern formed of slates, now much used, is the best for adoption.

CIVIL ARCHITECTURE. The art of erecting every species of edifice destined for the use of man, the several matters necessary to the knowledge whereof forms the subject of this work.

CIVIC CROWN. A garland of oak leaves and acorns, often used as an architectural ornament.

CLAMP. In brick-making a large mass of bricks generally quadrangular on the plan, and six, seven, or eight feet high, arranged in the brick field for burning, which is effected by flues prepared in stocking the clamp, and breeze or cinders laid between each course of bricks. See Book II. Chap. II. Sect. 9.

CLAMP. In carpentry and joinery is a piece of wood fixed to another with a mortise and tenon, or a groove and tongue, so that the fibres of the piece thus fixed cross those of the other, and thereby prevent it from casting or warping.

CLAMP NAILS. See NAILS.

CLASP NAILS. See NAILS.

CLATHRI. In ancient Roman architecture, were bars of iron or wood which were used to secure doors or windows.

Clay. In ordinary language, any earth which possesses sufficient ductility to admit of being kneaded with water. Common clays may be divided into three classes, viz. *unctuous*, *meagre*, and *calcareous*. Of these the first is chiefly used in pottery, and the second and third are employed in the manufacture of bricks and tiles.

Claying. The operation of spreading two or three coats of clay for the purpose of keeping water in a vessel. This operation is also called *puddling*.

Cleam. A term used in some places with the same signification as to stick or to glue.

Clear. The nett distance between two bodies, where no other intervenes, or between their nearest surfaces.

Clear Story or **Clere Story.** The upper vertical divisions of the nave, choir, and transepts of a church. It is *clear* above the roof of the aisles, whence it may have taken its name, but some have derived the name from the *clair* or light admitted through its tier of windows. Nearly all the cathedrals and large churches have *clear stories*, or tiers of arcades, and also of windows over the aisles and triforia. There is no triforium in the priory church of Bath, but a series of large and lofty windows constitute the clear story. The choir at Bristol Cathedral has neither triforium nor clear story.

Cleats. Small wooden projections in tackle to fasten the ropes to.

Cleaving. The act of forcibly separating one part of a piece of wood or other matter from another in the direction of the fibres, either by pressure or by percussion with some wedge-formed instrument.

Clefts. The open cracks or fissures which appear in wood which has been wrought too green. The carpenter usually fills up these cracks with a mixture of gum and sawdust, but the neatest way is to soak both sides well with the fat of beef broth, and then dip pieces of sponge into the broth and fill up the cracks with them; they swell out so as to fill the whole crack, and so neatly as to be scarcely distinguishable.

Cleomenes. See Architects, list of, 21.

Cleopatra's Needles. A name given to two obelisks on the east of the palace at Alexandria. They are of Thebaic stone and covered with hieroglyphics. One has been thrown down, broken, and lies buried in the sand. The other stands on a pedestal. They were each of a single stone, about sixty feet high and seven feet square.

Clepsydra. (Gr. from Κλεπτω, to conceal, and 'Υδωρ, water). A water clock, or vessel for measuring time by the running out of a certain quantity of water, or sometimes of sand, through an orifice of a determinate magnitude. Clepsydras were first used in Egypt under the Ptolemies; they seem to have been common in Rome, though they were chiefly employed in winter. In the summer season sundials were used.

Clinching. The act of binding and driving backward with a hammer the pointed end of a nail after its penetration through a piece of wood.

Clinkers. Bricks impregnated with nitre and more thoroughly burnt by being nearer the fire in the kiln.

Cloacæ. The name given to the common sewers of ancient Rome for carrying off into the Tiber the filth of the city. The chief of these, called the Cloaca Maxima, was built by the first Tarquin of huge blocks of stone joined together without cement. It consisted of three rows of arches one above another, which at length conjoin and unite together. It began in the Forum Romanum, was 300 paces long, and entered the Tiber between the temple of Vesta and the Pons Senatorius. There were as many principal sewers as there were hills in the city.

Cloak-pins and Rail. A piece of wood attached to a wall, furnished with projecting pegs on which to hang hats, great-coats, &c. The pegs are called *cloakpins*, and the board into which they are fixed, and which is fastened to the wall, is called the *rail*.

Cloister. (Lat. Claustrum.) The square space attached to a regular monastery or large church with a peristyle or ambulatory round, usually with a covered range of building over. The cloister is perhaps, *ex vi termini*, the central square shut in or *closed* by the surrounding buildings. Cloisters are usually square on the plan, having a plain wall on one side, a series of windows between the piers or columns on the opposite side, and arched over with a vaulted or ribbed ceiling. It mostly forms part of the passage of communication from the church to the chapter house, refectory, and other parts of the establishment. In England all the cathedrals, and most of the collegiate churches and abbeys, were provided with cloisters. On the Continent they are commonly appended to large monasteries, and are often decorated with tombs and paintings in fresco.

A common appendage to a cloister was a *lavatory*, or stone trough for water, at which the monks washed their hands previous to entering the refectory.

Closer. The last stone in the horizontal length of a wall, which is of less dimensions than the rest to close the row. *Closers* in brickwork, or pieces of bricks (or *bats*), less or greater than half a brick, that are used to close in the end of a course of brickwork. In English as well as Flemish bond, the length of a brick being but nine inches, and its width four inches and a half, in order that the vertical joints may be broken at the end of the first stretcher, a quarter brick (or bat) must be interposed to preserve the con-

tinuity of the bond, this is called a *queen-closer*. A similar preservation of the bond may be obtained by inserting a three-quarter bat at the angle in the stretching course; this is called a *king-closer*. In both cases an horizontal lap of two inches and a quarter is left for the next header. See Book II. Chap. III. Sect. 2.

CLOSE STRING. In dog-legged stairs, a staircase without an open newel.

CLOSE or CLOOS. See ARCHITECTS, list of, 153.

CLOSET. A small apartment frequently made to communicate with a bed-chamber, and used as a dressing room. Sometimes a closet is made for the reception of stores, and is then called a *store closet*.

CLOUGH or CLOYSE. The same as *paddle, shuttle, sluice,* or *penstock*. A contrivance for retaining or letting out the water of a canal, pond, &c.

CLOUGH ARCHES or PADDLE-HOLES. Crooked arches by which the water is conveyed from the upper pond into the chamber of the lock of a canal on drawing up the *clough*.

CLOUT NAILS. See NAILS.

CLUSTERED. The combination of several members of an order penetrating each other.

CLUSTERED COLUMNS. Several slender pillars or columns attached to each other so as to form one. In Roman architecture the term is used to denote two or four columns which appear to intersect each other, at the angle of a building or apartment, to answer to each return.

COARSE STUFF. In plastering, a mixture of lime and hair used in the first coat and floating of plastering. In floating more hair is used than in the first coat.

COAT. A thickness or covering of plaster or other work done at one time.

COBARRUBIAS. See ARCHITECTS, list of, 210.

COB-WALLS. Such as are formed of mud mixed with straw, not uncommon in some districts of England, but the best are to be found in Somersetshire.

COCCEIUS. See ARCHITECTS, list of, 38.

COCKING or COGGING. See CAULKING.

COCKLE STAIRS. A term sometimes used to denote a winding staircase.

CŒNACULUM. (Lat.) In ancient Roman architecture, an eating or supper room. In the early period of their history, when the houses rarely consisted of more than two stories, it denoted generally the upper story. The word also signified lodgings to let out for hire, and also the upper stories of the circi, which were divided into small shops or rooms.

CŒNATIO. An apartment in the lower part of the Roman houses, or in a garden, to sup or eat in. From Suetonius it would appear that it denoted a banqueting and summer house. In the Laurentine Villa a large cœnatio is described by the younger Pliny, and it seems, from the description, that it was placed in the upper part of a lofty tower.

COFFER. (Sax. Coffne.) A sunk panel in vaults and domes, and also in the soffite or under side of the Corinthian and Composite cornices, and usually decorated in the centre with a flower. But the application of the term is general to any sunk panel in a ceiling or soffite.

COFFER DAM. A case of piling, water-tight, fixed in the bed of a river, for the purpose of excluding the water while any work, such as a wharf, wall, or the pier of a bridge, is carried up. A coffer dam is variously formed, either by a single enclosure or by a double one, with clay, chalk, bricks, or other materials between, so as effectually to exclude the water. The coffer dam is also made with piles only driven close together, and sometimes notched or dove-tailed into one another. If the water be not very deep, piles may be driven at a distance of five or six feet from each other, and grooved in the sides with boards let down between them in the grooves. For building in coffer dams, a good natural bottom of gravel or clay is requisite, for though the sides be made sufficiently water-tight, if the bed of the river be loose, the water will ooze up through it in too great quantities to permit the operations to be carried on. It is almost unnecessary to inculcate the necessity of the sides being very strong and well-braced on the inside to resist the pressure of the water.

COGGING. See CAULKING.

COIN. (Fr.) The same as *quoin*. The angle formed by two surfaces of a stone or brick building, whether external or internal, as the corner formed by two walls, or of an arch and wall, the corner made by the two adjacent sides of a room, &c.

COLE. See ARCHITECTS, list of, 175.

COLISEUM. The name given to the amphitheatre built (A. D. 72) by Vespasian. See body of the work, p. 94.

COLLAR or COLARINO. (It.) A ring or cincture; it is another name for the astragal of a column. It is sometimes called the neck, gorgerin, or hypotrachelium.

COLLAR BEAM. A beam used in the construction of a roof above the lower ends of the rafters or base of the roof. The tie beam is always in a state of extension, but the collar beam may be either in a state of compression or extension as the *principal rafters* are

with or without tie beams.   In trussed roofs, collar beams are framed into queen posts; in common roofs, into the rafters themselves.

In general, trusses have no more than one collar beam; yet, in very large roofs, they may have two or three collar beams besides the tie beam.   The collar beam supports or trusses up the sides of the rafters, so as to keep them from sagging without any other support, but then the tie beam would be supported only at its extremities.   In common purlin roofing, the purlins are laid in the acute angles between the rafters and the upper edges of the collar beams.

COLLEGE.   An establishment properly so termed for the education of youth in the higher branches of study.   See Book III. Chap. V. Sect. 8.

COLONELLI. (It.)   The Italian name for the posts employed in any truss framing.

COLONNADE. (It. Colonnata.)   A range of columns.   If the columns are four in number, it is called *tetrastyle;* if six in number, *hexastyle;* when there are eight, *octastyle;* when ten, *decastyle;* and so on, according to the Greek numerals.   When a colonnade is in front of a building it is called a *portico,* when surrounding a building a *peristyle,* and when double or more *polystyle.*   The colonnade is moreover designated according to the nature of the intercolumniations introduced as follows: *pycnostyle,* when the space between the columns is one diameter and a half of the column; *systyle,* when it is of two diameters; *eustyle,* when of two diameters and a quarter; *diastyle,* when three, and *aræostyle* when four.

COLUMBARIUM. (Lat.) · A pigeon-house.   The plural of the word (*columbaria*) was applied to designate the apertures formed in walls for the reception of cinerary urns in the ancient Roman cemeteries.

COLUMELLÆ.   A name sometimes used for balusters.

COLUMN. (Lat. Columna.)   Generally any body which supports another in a vertical direction.   For an account of the columns used in the five orders, see Book III. Chap. I. Sects. 2, 3, 4, 5, 6, and 7.   There are various species of columns, as *twisted,* *spiral,* and *rusticated.*   *Cabled* or *rudented* columns are such as have their flutings filled with cables or astragals to about one third of the height.   *Carolitic* columns have their shafts foliated.   Columns were occasionally used as monuments, as the Trajan and Antonine columns at Rome, and the Monument in London.   By the side of the Halle au Blè at Paris there is a *gnomonic* column for showing the time, erected by Catharine di Medicis.   The *Columna Bellica* at Rome was near the temple of Janus, and at it the consul proclaimed war by throwing a javelin towards the enemies' country.   The *chronological* column was rather historical, bearing an inscription to record an event.   The *cruciferal* column is one bearing a cross; the *funereal* one, an urn; the *zoophoric,* an animal; and the *itinerary* one pointed out the various roads diverging from its site.   There was among the Romans what was called a *lacteal* column, which stood in the vegetable market, and contained on its pedestal a receptacle for infants abandoned by their parents. (Juvenal, *Sat.* vi.)   On the *legal* column were engraved the laws; the *boundary* or *limitative* column marked the boundary of a province; the *manubial* column was for the reception of trophies or spoils; and the *rostral* column, decorated with prows of ships, was for the purpose of recording a naval engagement.   The *triumphal* column was erected in commemoration of a triumph, and the *sepulchral* one was erected on a tomb.   The *milliarium aureum,* or *milliary* column of the Romans, was originally a column of white marble, erected by Augustus in the Forum, near the temple of Saturn.   From it the distances from the city were measured.   It is a short column with a Tuscan capital, having a ball of bronze (formerly gilt for its finish) at top, and is still preserved in the Capitol.

COMBINATION OF THE PARTS OF BUILDINGS. See Book III. Chap. V. Sect. 1., and Book III. Chap. II. Sect. 2.

COMITIUM. (Lat.)   A building which stood in the Roman Forum, wherein assemblies of the people were held.   It occupied the whole space between the Palatine Hill, the Capitol, and the Via Sacra.

COMMISSURE. (Lat.)   The joint between two stones, or the application of the surface of one stone to the surface of another.

COMMON CENTRING.   Such as is constructed without trusses, but having a tie beam at its ends.   Also that employed in straight vaults.

COMMON JOISTS.   Those in single naked flooring to which the boards are fixed.   They are also called *boarding joists,* and should not exceed one foot apart.

COMMON RAFTERS.   Those in a roof to which the boarding or lathing is attached.

COMMON ROOFING.   That which consists of common rafters only, which bridge over the purlins in a strongly framed roof.

COMMUNICATION DOORS.   Those which, when open, throw two apartments into one.

COMPARTED. (Fr. Compartir, to divide.)   That which is divided into several parts is said to be comparted.

COMPARTITION.   The distribution of the ground plot of an edifice into the various passages and apartments.

COMPARTMENT. A subdivisional part, for ornament, of a larger division. To this alone is the term properly applicable.

COMPARTMEMT CEILING. One divided into panels, which are usually surrounded by mouldings.

COMPARTMENT TILES. An arrangement of varnished red and white tiles on a roof.

COMPASS SAW. One for dividing boards into curved pieces; it is very narrow and without a back.

COMPASSES. (Fr. Compas.) A mathematical instrument for drawing circles and measuring distances between two points. *Common compasses* have two legs, moveable on a joint. *Triangular compasses* have two legs similar to common compasses, and a third leg fixed to the bulb by a projection, with a joint so as to be moveable in every direction. *Beam compasses*, which see, are used for describing large circles. *Proportional compasses* have two pair of points moveable on a shifting centre which slides in a groove, and thereby regulates the proportion that the opening at one end bears to that of the other. They are useful in enlarging or diminishing drawings.

COMPLEMENT. The number of degrees which any angle wants of a right angle. The complement of a parallelogram is two lesser parallelograms, made by drawing two right lines parallel to the sides of the greater through a given point in the diagonal.

COMPLUVIUM. (Lat.) An area in the centre of the ancient Roman houses, so constructed that it might receive the waters from the roofs. It is also used to denote the gutter or eave of a roof.

COMPO. A name often given to Parker's cement.

COMPOSITE ARCH. The same as the pointed or lancet arch.

COMPOSITE NUMBERS. Such as can be divided by some other number greater than unity ; whereas *prime numbers* admit of no such divisor.

COMPOSITE ORDER. See Book III. Chap. I. Sect. 7., and Book I. Chap. II. Sect. 13.

COMPOSITION, ARCHITECTURAL. For general principles, see Book III. Chap. II. Sect. 1.

COMPOSITION OF FORCES. The combination or union of several forces for determining the result of the whole.

COMPOUND INTEREST. See Book IV.

COMPRESSIBILITY. The quality of bodies which permits of their being reduced to smaller dimensions. All bodies, in consequence of the porosity of matter, are compressible, but liquids resist compression with immense force.

CONCAMERATA SUDATIO. An apartment in the ancient gymnasium, between the *laconicum* or stove, and the warm bath. To this room the racers and wrestlers retired to wipe off the sweat from their bodies.

CONCAMERATE. (Lat.) To arch over.

CONCAVITY. (Lat. Concavus, hollow.) Of a curve line is the side between the two points of the curve next its chord or diameter. The concavity of a solid is such a curved surface, that if any two points in it be taken, the straight line between them is in a void space, or will coincide in only one direction with the surface.

CONCENTRIC. (Lat.) Having a common centre, as are the radii of a circle.

CONCHOID OF NICOMEDES. A name given to a curve invented by that mathematician for solving the two famous problems of antiquity — the duplication of the cube, and the trisection of an angle. It continually approaches a straight line without meeting it, though ever so far produced.

CONCRETE. (Lat. Concrescere.) To coalesce in one mass. A mass composed of stone chippings or ballast, cemented together through the medium of sand and lime, and usually employed in making foundations where the soil is of itself too light or boggy, or otherwise insufficient for the reception of the walls. See Book II. Chap. II. Sect. 11.

CONDUIT. (Fr.) A long narrow walled passage underground, for secret communication between different apartments. It is a term also used to denote a canal or pipe for the conveyance of water, and is also applied to the structure to which it is conveyed for delivery to the public.

CONE. (Gr. Κωνος.) A solid body, having a circle for its base, and terminating in a point called its vertex ; so that a straight line drawn from any point in the circumference of the base to the vertex will coincide with the convex surface. If the axis or straight line drawn from the centre of the base to the vertex be perpendicular to the base, it is termed a *right cone ;* if not, it is an *oblique cone.*

CONFESSIONAL. (Lat.) In Catholic churches the small cell wherein the priest sits to hear the confession of, and give absolution to, the penitent. It is usually constructed of wood and in three divisions, the central one whereof has a seat for the convenience of the priest.

CONFIGURATION. The exterior form or superficies of any body.

CONGE'. (Fr.) The same as APOPHYGE, which see.

CONIC SECTIONS. The figures formed by the intersections of a plane with a cone. They

are five in number : a triangle, a circle, an ellipse, a parabola, and an hyperbola; the three last, however, are those to which the term is usually applied. See Book II. Chap. I. Sect. 4.

CONICAL ROOF. One whose exterior surface is shaped like a cone.

CONISTERIUM. (Gr. Κονιστηριον.) In ancient architecture, a room in the gymnasium and palæstra, wherein the wrestlers, having been anointed with oil, were sprinkled over with dust, that they might lay firmer hold on one another.

CONJUGATE DIAMETERS. The diameters in an ellipsis or hyperbola parallel to tangents at each other's extremities.

CONOID. (Gr. Κονοειδης.) Partaking of the figure of a cone. A figure generated by the revolution of a conic section round one of its axes. There are three kinds of conoids, the *elliptical*, the *hyperbolical*, and the *parabolical*, which are sometimes otherwise denominated by the terms *ellipsoid* or *spheroid*, *hyperboloid*, and *paraboloid*.

CONSERVATORY. A building for preserving curious and rare exotic plants. It is made with beds of the finest composts, into which the trees and plants on being removed from the greenhouse, and taken from the tubs and pots, are regularly planted.

With respect to its construction, it is very similar to the greenhouse, but it must be more spacious, loftier, and finished in a superior style. The sides, ends, and roofs should be of glass, for the free admission of light, and for protection of the plants. It should be, moreover, seated on a dry spot, and so as to receive during the day as much of the sun's heat as possible. It is to be provided with flues or boiling water pipes, to raise the temperature when necessary ; there must also be contrivances for introducing fresh air when required. In summer time the glass roofs are taken off and the plants exposed to the open air; but these are restored always, if taken off, on the slightest indication of frost. The chief point in which conservatories differ from greenhouses is, that in the latter, the plants and trees stand in pots placed upon stages, whereas, in the former, they are planted in beds of earth surrounded with borders. See GREENHOUSE.

CONSOLE. The same as ANCONES, which see.

CONSTRUCTION. Literally, the building up from the architect's designs ; but amongst architects it is more particularly used to denote the art of distributing the different forces and strains of the parts and materials of a building in so scientific a manner as to avoid failure and insure durability. The second book of this work is devoted to the subjects involved in the science of construction.

CONSTRUCTIVE CARPENTRY, or PRACTICAL CARPENTRY. See Book II. Chap. III. Sect. 4.

CONTACT. (Lat. Contactus.) In geometry the touching any figure by a line or plane which may be produced either way without cutting it.

CONTENT. (Lat. Contentus.) The area or superficial quantity contained in any figure.

CONTEXTURE. (Lat. Contextus.) The inter-disposition, with respect to each other, of the different parts of a body.

CONTIGNATIO. In Roman carpentry the same as that which we term *naked flooring*.

CONTINUED. A term used to express anything uninterrupted. Thus, an attic is said to be continued when not broken by pilasters ; a pedestal is continued when, with its mouldings and dado or die, it is not broken under the columns ; so of a socle, &c.

CONTOUR. (It. Contorno.) The external lines which bound and terminate a figure.

CONTRACT. An agreement attached to a specification for the performance of certain works.

CONTUCCIO. See ARCHITECTS, list of, 190.

CONVENT. (Lat. Conventus.) A building for the reception of a society of religious persons.

CONVENTUAL CHURCH. One attached or belonging to a convent.

CONVERGENT LINES. Such as, if produced, will meet.

CONVEX. (Lat. Convexus.) A form which swells or rounds itself externally. A convex rectilinear surface, in which a point being taken, a right line passing through it can only be drawn in one direction.

COPING. (Dutch, Cop, the head.) The highest and covering course of masonry or brickwork in a wall. Coping equally thick throughout is called *parallel coping*, and ought to be used only on inclined surfaces, as on a gable, for example, or in situations sheltered from the rain, as on the top of a level wall, which it is intended to cover by a roof. Coping thinner on one edge than on the other serves to throw off the water on one side of the wall, and is called *feather-edged coping*. Coping thicker in the middle than at the edges is called *saddle-backed coping*. This, of course, delivers each way the water that falls upon it. It is commonly used on the walls of a sunk area, on dwarf walls carrying an iron railing, and in the best constructed fence walls. In Gothic architecture, coping is either inclined upon the faces or plumb ; in the former case the sides of the vertical section are those of an equilateral triangle with an horizontal base. It is sometimes in one inclined plane, terminated at top by an astragal, and at others in two inclined planes parallel to each other, whereof the upper is terminated at top by an astragal, and projects

before the lower, which, like that on one inclined plane, changes its direction at the bottom into a narrow vertical plane projecting before the level sofite before the parapet. The inclined coping is occasionally used without the astragal. The sofite of a projection is said to cope over when it slants downwards from the wall.

Copper. (Cuprum, a corruption of Cyprium, having been originally brought from the island of Cyprus.) One of the metals used in building, but not now to the extent to which it was employed a few years back. See Book II. Chap. II. Sect. 7.

Corbeil. (Lat. Corbis, a basket.) A carved basket, with sculptured flowers and fruit, used as the finishing of some ornament. The name is given to the basket placed on the heads of caryatides, under the sofite of the architrave cornice. The term is also applied to the bell of the Corinthian capital.

Corbels, in castellated and Gothic architecture, are a range of stones projecting from a wall for the purpose of supporting a parapet or the superior projecting part of the wall. Two of their sides are vertical planes perpendicular to the face of the wall; the fronts are variously moulded. They perform the same office as the modillions of an order, but the term is confined to the pointed style.

The word corbel is sometimes used to denote a niche or hollow in a wall for the reception of a statue or bust. There is also another sense in which it is used, namely, to signify a horizontal range of stones or timber fixed in a wall or in the side of a vault, serving to sustain the timbers of a floor or of a vault. In old buildings many of the timber floors or contignations were thus supported.

Corbel Steps are certain steps in the gables of old buildings.

Corbel Table. A series of semicircular intersecting arches for carrying a battlement, parapet, or cornice, and resting on corbels. Also any projection borne by corbels.

Cordon. The edge of a stone on the outside of a building.

Core. The interior part of anything. In walls of masonry there should be thorough stones at regular intervals, for strengthening the core, which is commonly composed of rubble stones, or, when they are not procurable, two bond stones lapped upon each other may be used, one from each face of the wall. Instead of each thorough stone we may lay two stones level on the upper bed, and one large stone in the core lapped upon both, observing that the tails of the two lower stones be right-angled; by this means the two sides of the wall will be completely tied together.

The core of a column is a strong post of some material inserted in its central cavity when of wood.

Corinthian Order. See Book III. Chap. I. Sect. 7., and Book I. Chap. II. Sect. 1.

Cornice. (Fr. Corniche.) Any moulded projection which crowns or finishes the part to which it is affixed. Thus, we speak of the cornice of an order, of a pedestal, of a pier, door, window, house, &c. The cornice of an order is a secondary member of the order itself, being the upper subdivision of the entablature.

Corona. (Lat.) A member of the cornice, with a broad vertical face, and usually of considerable projection. The solid, out of which it is formed, is commonly recessed upwards from its sofite, and this part by the English workmen is called the *drip*, because it facilitates the fall of the rain from its edge, by which the parts below it are sheltered. The situation of the corona is between the cymatium above, and the bed-moulding below. See Book III. Chap. I. Sect. 18.

Corps. A French term, which signifies the projecting part of a wall, and intended to form the ground for some decoration.

Corridor. (It. Corridore.) A gallery or passage round a quadrangle leading to the various apartments. Also, any gallery of communication to them.

Corsa. (Lat.) In ancient architecture, the name given by Vitruvius to any platband or square fascia whose height is greater than its projection.

Cortile. (It.) A small court or area, quadrangular or curved, in a dwelling-house, which is surrounded by the buildings of the house itself.

Cossutius. See Architects, list of, 29.

Cottage. (Sax. Cot.) A small house or dwelling for a poor person. See Book III. Chap. V. Sect. 24.

Cotte. See Architects, list of, 272.

Coucy. See Architects, list of, 127.

Counter Drain. A drain parallel to a canal or embanked water-course, for collecting the soakage water by the side of the canal or embankment to a culvert or arched drain under the canal, by which it is conveyed to a lower level.

Counterfort. (Fr.) A buttress or pier built against and at right angles to a wall to strengthen it.

Counter Gauge. In carpentry, the measure of the joints by *transferring*, as, for instance, the breadth of a mortise to the plan on the other timber, where the tenon is to be made to adapt them to each other.

COUNTER LATH. One placed between every couple of gauged ones.

COUNTERPARTS of a building are the similar and equal parts of the design on each side of the middle of the edifice.

COUNTER SINK. The sinking a cavity in a piece of timber or other material to receive a projection on the piece which is connected with it, as for the reception of a plate of iron or the head of a screw or bolt.

COUPLED COLUMNS. Those arranged in pairs half a diameter apart.

COUPLES. A term used in the north to signify rafters framed together in pairs with a tie fixed above their feet. The *main couples* answer to the trusses.

COURSE. (Lat. Cursus.) A continued level range of stones or bricks of the same height throughout the face or faces of a building. *Coursed masonry* is that therefore wherein the stones are laid in courses. The *course of the face of an arch* is the face of the arch stones, whose joints radiate to the centre. The *course of a plinth* is its continuity in the face of the wall. A *bond course* is that whose stones are inserted into the wall farther than either of the adjacent courses, for the purpose of binding the wall together. A *coursing joint* is the joint between two courses.

COURSE, HEADING, in brickwork, is that in which the bricks are laid with their short sides towards the face.

COURSE, STRETCHING, is that in which the bricks are all laid lengthwise.

COURT. (Fr. Cour.) An uncovered area before or behind the house or in the centre of it, in which latter case it is often surrounded by buildings on its four sides.

COURTS OF LAW. See Book III. Chap. V. Sect. 6.

COUSSINET. (Fr. Cushion.) A stone placed upon the impost of a pier for receiving the first stone of an arch. Its bed is level below, and its surface above is inclined for receiving the next voussoir of the arch.

The word is also used for the part of the Ionic capital between the abacus and quarter round, which serves to form the volute, and it is in the capital thus called because its appearance is that of a cushion or pillar seemingly collapsed by the weight over it, and is bound with a strap or girdle called the baltheus.

COVE. Any kind of concave moulding or vault; but the term, in its usual acceptation, is the quadrantal profile between the ceiling of a room and its cornice.

COVE BRACKETING. The wooden skeleton for the lathing of any cove; but the term is usually applied to that of the quadrantal cove, which is placed between the flat ceiling and the wall.

COVER. That part of a slate which is hidden or covered.

COVER WAY. In roofing, the recess or internal angle left in a piece of masonry or brickwork to receive the roofing.

COVING, in old buildings, the projection of the upper stories of houses over the lower ones.

COVING OF A FIRE-PLACE. See CHIMNEY.

COW-HOUSE. A building for the protection of cows from the inclemencies of the season.

COZZO, PIETRO DI. See ARCHITECTS, list of, 98.

CRAB. A species of crane much used by masons for raising large stones; it is a wheel and axle mounted on a pair of sloping legs, three or four feet apart, the legs being inserted into a frame at the base, whereon, opposite to the weight to be raised, a load may be placed for gaining so great an amount of leverage as to overcome the weight to be raised. The rope for the tackle works round the axle, which is turned by pinion wheels to gain power.

CRADLE. A name sometimes given to a centering of ribs and lattice for turning culverts.

CRADLE VAULT. A term used, but improperly, to denote a cylindric vault.

CRADLING. The timber ribs and pieces for sustaining the lathing and plastering of vaulted ceilings. The same term is applied to the wooden bracketing for carrying the entablature of a shop front.

CRAMP. An iron instrument about four feet long, having a screw at one end, and a moveable shoulder at the other, employed by carpenters and joiners for forcing mortise and tenon work together.

CRAMPERN or CRAMP IRON, usually called for shortness *cramp*, a piece of metal, bent at both extremities towards the same side, for fastening stones together. When stones are to be connected with a greater strength than that of mortar, a chain or bar of iron with different connecting knobs is inserted in a cavity, cut on the upper side of a course of stones across the joints, instead of single cramps across the joints of each two stones. Cramps are commonly employed in works requiring great solidity; but in common works they are applied chiefly to the stones of copings and cornices, and generally in any external work upon the upper surface or between the beds of the stone. All external work, liable to the injuries which weather inflicts, should be cramped. The most secure mode of fixing cramps is to let them into the stone their whole thickness, and to run them with lead; but in slight works it is sufficient to bed them in plaster, as is practised in chimney-pieces. In modern buildings iron is chiefly used. The practice is bad,

from the liability of iron to rust and exfoliate : hence cast-iron is better than wrought, and should be of somewhat larger size than when wrought iron is employed. The Romans wisely used cramps of bronze, a material far better than either cast or wrought iron.

CRAMPOONS. Hooked pieces of iron, something like double calipers, for raising timber or stones.

CRANE. (Sax. Cpan.) A machine for raising heavy weights, and depositing them at some distance from their original place. The crane may be constructed of immense power, and is generally worked by human strength.

CRANE-HOUSE. A building erected for the shelter of a crane. By the late Building Act it was most absurdly required to be of brick.

CRAPAUDINE DOORS. Those which turn on pivots at top and bottom.

CREASING or TILE CREASING. Two rows of plain tiles placed horizontally under the coping of a wall, and projecting about an inch and a half on each side to throw off the rain water.

CRENELLE. In Gothic architecture, the opening in an embattled parapet.

CRESCENT. A building, or rather a series of buildings, which on the plan is disposed in the arc of a circle.

CREST TILE. That on the ridge of a house. In Gothic architecture, crest tiles are those which, decorated with leaves, run up the sides of a gable or ornamented canopy.

CRIB. The rack of a stable ; sometimes applied to the manger. It is used also to express any small habitation ; and moreover the stall or cabin of an ox.

CROCKET. (Fr. Croc, a hook.) One of the small ornaments placed on the inclined sides of pinnacles, pediments, canopies, &c. in Gothic architecture, and most commonly disposed at equal distances from each other. The crocket seems to have had for type the buds and boughs of trees in the spring season, from the great resemblance it bears to those periodical productions : examples, moreover, of the same ornament have great resemblance to the first stage of the leaves when the buds begin to open ; sometimes, however, animals are substituted in the place of leaves.

CROMLECHS. A mass of large flat stones laid across others in an upright position. Examples of cromlechs are found in Wales, Devonshire, Cornwall, and many exposed districts of England. For a further account of the cromlech, the reader may turn to Book I. Chap. II. Sect. 1.

CROSETTES. (Fr.) The same as ancones, which see. In architectural construction the term is applied to the small projecting pieces aa in arch stones, which hang upon the adjacent stones.

CROSS. (Lat. Crux.) A figure consisting of four branches at right angles to each other, or a geometrical one, consisting of five rectangles, each side of one rectangle being common with one side of each of the other four. It is a figure more particularly used for the plans of churches than for those of other edifices. In ecclesiastical architecture, there are two kinds of plans having the form of a cross. The first is that wherein all the five rectangles are equal, or wherein each of the four wings is equal to the middle part formed by the intersection : this form is called a Greek cross. The second has only the two opposite wings equal, the other two are unequal, and the three rectangles in the direction of the unequal parts are of greater length than the three parts in the direction of the equal parts ; this is the Latin cross. The middle part in each direction is common. See ADDENDUM.

CROSS. In Gothic architecture, an erection of various kinds, which may be classed as follows : — those used for marking boundaries, those which were memorials of remarkable events, monumental or sepulchral, as that at Waltham, and others of that nature ; for preaching, as the ancient St. Paul's Cross ; and market crosses, as at Winchester, Leighton Buzzard, &c.

CROSS-BANDED. A term applied to handrailing, which is said to be cross-banded, when a veneer is laid upon its upper side, with the grain of the wood crossing that of the rail, and the extension of the veneer in the direction of its fibres is less than the breadth of the rail.

CROSS BEAM. A large beam going from wall to wall, or a girder that holds the sides of the house together.

CROSS GARNETS. Hinges having a long strap fixed close to the aperture, and also a cross part on the other side of the knuckle, which is fastened to the joint. See GARNETS.

CROSS-GRAINED STUFF. Wood which has its fibres in a contrary direction to the surface, and which consequently cannot be perfectly smoothed by the operation of the plane, without turning either the plane or the stuff. This defect arises from a twisted disposition of fibres while in the act of growing.

CROSS SPRINGERS. The ribs in the pointed style that spring from the diagonals of the pillars or piers.

CROSS VAULTING. That formed by the intersection of two or more simple vaults. When

each of the simple vaults rises from the same level to equal heights, the cross vaulting is denominated *a groin ;* but when one of the simple vaults is below the other, the intersection is called *an arch* of that particular species which expresses both the simple arches. For example, if one cylinder pierce another of greater altitude, the arch so formed is termed a *cylindro-cylindric arch ;* and if a portion of a cylinder pierce a sphere of greater altitude than the cylinder, the arch is called a *sphero-cylindric arch,* and thus for any species of arch whatever, the part of the qualifying word which ends in *o* denotes the simple vault having the greater altitude, and the succeeding word the other of less altitude.

Crow. A bar of iron used in bricklaying, masonry, and quarrying, and serving usually as a lever in its employment.

Crown. (Lat. Corona.) The uppermost member of any part. Thus, the upper member of a cornice, including the corona and the members above it, is so called.

Crown of an Arch. The most elevated line or point that can be assumed in its surface.

Crown or Joggle Post, is the same as *king post,* being the truss post that sustains the tie beam and rafters of a roof.

Crown Glass. A common sort of window glass. See Book II. Chap. II. Sect. 12.

Crowning. The part that terminates upwards any piece of architecture, as a cornice, pediment, &c.

Crypt. (Gr. Κρυπτω, I hide.) The under or hidden part of a building. It is used also to signify that part of the ancient churches and abbeys appropriated below to the monuments of deceased persons.

Crypto-Porticus. In ancient architecture a concealed portico, also one that for coolness is enclosed on every side. Some of them were sunk some way into the ground. It also is a term applied to subterranean or dark passages and galleries in the Roman villas, often used as cool sitting rooms.

Cube. (Gr. Κυβος, a die.) A solid bounded by six square sides. It is also, from its six sides, called *hexahedron.*

Cubiculum. (Lat.) A chamber. A distinction is made by Pliny between the *cubiculum* and the *dormitorium.* The name was also applied to the royal pavilion or tent which was built in the circus or amphitheatre for the reception of the emperors.

Cubit. A linear measure, in ancient architecture, equal to the length of the arm from the elbow to the extremity of the middle finger, usually considered about eighteen English inches. The geometrical cubit of Vitruvius was equal to six ordinary cubits.

Cul de Four. (Fr) A low vault spherically formed on a circular or oval plan. An oven-shaped vault.

Culmen. In ancient Roman architecture, the ridge-piece of the roof.

Culvert. An arched channel of masonry or brickwork built beneath the bed of a canal for the purpose of conducting water under it. If the water to be conveyed has nearly the same level as the canal, the culvert is built in the form of an inverted siphon, and acts on the principle of a water-pipe. The word also signifies any arched channel for water under ground.

Culver-tail. The same as Dove-tail, which see.

Cuneus. (Lat.) That part of the Roman theatre where the spectators sate.

Cupola. (It. from Cupo, hollow.) A term, properly speaking, which is confined to the *underside* or ceiling part of a dome. See Dome.

Cupboard. A recess in a wall, fitted with shelves as a receptacle for articles of the tea table.

Curb for Brick Steps. A timber nosing, generally of oak, used not only to prevent the steps from wearing, but also from being dislocated or put out of their places. When the steps are made to return, the curb also returns, but when they profile against a wall, the ends of the curb or nosing pieces house at each end into the wall.

Curb Plate. A circular continued plate, either scarfed together or made in two or more thicknesses. The wall plate of a circularly or elliptically ribbed dome is called a *curb-plate,* as likewise the horizontal rib at the top, on which the vertical ribs terminate. The plate of a skylight, or a circular frame for a well, is also called a curb-plate. The name is moreover given to a piece of timber supported in a curb roof by the upper ends of the lower rafters for receiving the feet of the upper rafters, which are thence called *curb-rafters.*

Curb Roof. One formed of four contiguous planes externally inclined to each other, the ridge being in the line of concourse of the two middle planes and the highest of the three lines of concourse. A roof of this construction (see 2035.) is frequently termed a *Mansard* roof, from the name of its inventor. Its principal advantage over other roofing arises from its giving more space in the garrets, which become attics.

Curb Stone. The stone in the foot-paving of a street, which divides it from the carriage-paving, above which they are, or ought to be, raised.

Curia. (Gr.) A Roman council-house. The city and empire contained many curiæ.

The *curia municipalis*, or *domus curialis*, seems to have, in destination, resembled our Guildhall. The *curia dominicalis* was a sort of manor house.

CURLING STUFF. That which is affected from the winding or coiling of the fibres round the boughs of the tree where they begin to shoot out of the trunk. The double iron plane is the best for working it.

CURRENT. The necessary slope of a piece of ground or pavement for carrying off the water from its surface.

CURSOR. (Lat.) The point of a beam compass that slides backwards and forwards. Also the part of a proportional compass by which the points are set to any given ratio.

CURTAIL STEP. The first or bottom step by which stairs are ascended, ending at the furthest point from the wall, in which it is placed in a scroll; perhaps taking its name from the step curling round like a cur's tail.

CURVATURE. See RADIUS OF CURVATURE.

CURVE. (Lat. Curvus.) A line that may be cut by a straight line in more points than one.

CURVILINEAR. Bounded by curve lines; thus a curvilinear roof is one erected on a curved plan, circular, elliptical, or otherwise.

CUSHION RAFTER. See PRINCIPAL BRACE.

CUSP. (Lat. Cuspis.) One of the pendents of a pointed arch, or of the arched head of a compartment of such an arch, or one of the several pendents forming what may be termed a *polyfoil*. Two cusps form a trefoil, three a quatrefoil, and so on.

CUSTOM HOUSE. See Book III. Chap. V. Sect. 15. An edifice erected for the receipt of the customs' duties payable on the importation and exportation of merchandise.

CUT. In inland navigation, the same as canal, arm, or branch.

CUT BRACKETS. Those moulded on the edge.

CUT ROOF. One that is truncated.

CUT STANDARDS. For shelves, the upright pieces supporting shelves above a dresser when cut into mouldings.

CUT STONE. Hewn stone, or that which is brought into shape by the mallet and chisel.

CUTTING PLANE. A plane dividing or cutting a solid into two parts in any direction.

CYCLOGRAPH (Gr. Κυκλος and Γραφω.) In practical geometry, an instrument for describing the arc of a circle to any chord and versed sine, but chiefly used in flat segments, or those whose curvatures approach to straight lines.

CYCLOID. (Gr. Κυκλοειδης.) A figure described by rolling a circle upon a plane along a straight edge, until the point on the circle which touches the straight edge return again to it after a revolution. The point traces the curve called the *cycloid* or *trochoid*.

CYCLOPEAN BUILDINGS. See Book I. Chap. II. Sect. 2.

CYLINDER. (G. Κυλινδρον.) A solid whose base is a circle, and whose curved surface is every where at an equal distance from the axis or line supposed to pass through its middle. Its formation may be conceived to be generated by the revolution of a rectangular parallelogram about one of its sides. The cone, sphere, and cylinder have a remarkable relation to each other, first discovered by Archimedes, namely, that the cone is one third the cylinder having the same base and altitude; and the inscribed sphere two thirds of the cylinder; or the cone, sphere, and cylinder are to each other as the numbers 1, 2, 3. It is termed a *right cylinder* when the axis is at right angles to the base, but if at an oblique angle the cylinder is said to be oblique.

CYLINDRICAL CEILING or VAULTING. Vulgarly called a *waggon-headed ceiling*. One in the shape of the segment of a cylinder. The cylindrical ceiling appears to have been first used by the Romans. It admits of being pierced by *lunettes* for the admission of light, which form cylindro-cylindric arches, and is usually formed into panels or coffers. See p. 588.

CYLINDRICAL WORK. Any kind of work which partakes of the shape of a cylinder, of whatever material it be formed.

CYLINDROID. A solid which differs from a cylinder in having ellipses instead of circles for its ends or bases.

CYMA. (Gr. Κυμα, a wave.) A moulding taking its name from its contour resembling that of a wave, being hollow in its upper part and swelling below. Of this moulding there are two sorts, the cyma recta ⌐ thus, just described, and the cyma reversa ⌐ thus, wherein the upper part swells, whilst the lower is hollow. By the workmen these are called *ogees*.

CYMATIUM. (Gr.) The name commonly applied to the upper moulding of a cornice or capping.

CYMBIA. The same as FILLET, which see.

CYPRESS. (Lat. Cupressus.) The wood of the cypress was valued for its hardness and durability by the ancient architects.

CYRIADES. See ARCHITECTS, list of, 54.

CYRUS. See ARCHITECTS, list of, 36.

CYZICENUS. In ancient architecture, a large hall decorated with sculpture.

D.

Dado. The die or part in the middle of the pedestal of a column between the base and cornice. It is of a cubic form, whence the name of die. The term is also applied to that part of an apartment between the plinth and impost moulding.

Dairy. An apartment in a house, or a separate building, for the preservation of milk, and the manufacture of it into butter, cheese, or other dairy produce. When on a small scale, where the milk is only used for butter, the dairy may be a room on the north side of the dwelling, or form one of the offices connected with the kitchen court. The temperature of a dairy should be within the range of forty-eight to fifty-five degrees of Fahrenheit, with sufficient ventilation to discharge all smells and impurities of the air. A dairy on a large scale should be a detached building, in which case it should contain a milk-room, a churning-room, and a dairy scullery, or place for scalding the utensils. If cheese be to be made, a room is required for the cheese-press, and another for drying the cheeses.

Dais. (Fr.) The platform or raised floor at the upper end of a dining-hall, where the high table stood; also the seat with a canopy open for it, for those guests who sat at the high table.

Dam, Architecturally, a fence against water. See **Coffer-dam.**

Dampness. A moisture generally attendant on buildings finished hastily, on account of the materials, not being dry, carrying up the moisture by capillary attraction. A layer of powdered charcoal mixed with pitch or resin and powdered pitcoal laid over one of the courses of the wall near the foundations will prevent the evil.

Dance, George, the elder. See **Architects,** list of, 290.

Dance, George, the younger. See **Architects,** list of, 314.

Days or Bays. In Gothic architecture, the compartments in windows formed by the transoms or horizontal pieces and mullions or vertical pieces.

Dead Shore. A piece of timber worked up in brickwork to support a superincumbent mass until the brickwork which is to carry it has set or become hard.

Deafening Sound-boarding. The *pugging* used to prevent the passage of sound through wooden partitions.

Deal. (Sax. Delan, to divide.) Properly the small thickness of timber into which a piece of any sort is cut up; but the term is now, though improperly, restricted in its signification to the wood of the fir tree cut up into thicknesses in the countries whence deals are imported, viz. Christiana, Dantzic, &c. Their usual thickness is three inches, and their width nine. They are purchased by the hundred, which contains 120 deals, be their thickness what it may, reduced by calculation to a standard thickness of one inch and a half and to a length of twelve feet. *Whole deal* is that which is one inch and a quarter thick, and *slit deal* is half that thickness. See **Board.**

Decagon. (Gr. Δεκα, ten, and Γωνια, an angle.) A geometrical figure having ten sides and ten angles. If the sides and angles are all equal, the figure is a regular decagon, and capable of being inscribed in a circle.

Decastyle. See **Colonade.**

Decimal. (Lat.) A term applied to a system of arithmetic in which the scale of numbers proceeds by tens.

Decoration. The combination of ornamental objects which the desire for varying a form or forms brings together in many ways for embellishing those subjects which are the objects of art. See Book III. Chap. I. Sect. 1.

Deliquiæ. (Lat.) A term used by Vitruvius to designate the rafters which formed the ridge of the roof and threw the water on each side.

Demetrius. See **Architects,** list of, 4.

Density. (Lat. Densus, thick.) A term used in physics to denote the quantity of matter which a body contains under a given or determinate surface; for example, a cubic foot. The quantity of matter in a body is called its mass, and is measured by the weight of the body, to which it is always proportional; hence the density of a body is great in proportion as its weight is great, and its volume small; or the density of bodies is directly as their masses, and inversely as their volumes.

Dentils or Dentels. (Lat. Dentes, teeth.) The small square blocks or projections in the bed mouldings of cornices in the Ionic, Corinthian, Composite, and occasionally Doric orders; their breadth should be half their height; and, as Vitruvius teaches, the intervals between them two thirds of their breadth. In the Grecian orders they are not used under modillions.

Description of a Building. The same as **Specification.** See Book II. Chap. III. Sect. 13.

Descriptive Geometry. That which consists in the application of geometrical rules to the representation of the figures, and the various relations of the forms of bodies, according to certain conventional forms. It differs from perspective, on account of the repre-

sentation being made in such a manner that the exact distance between the different points of the body represented can always be found, and consequently all the mathematical relations resulting from the form and position of the body may be deduced from the representation. See Book II. Chap. I. Sect. 5.

DESIGN. (Lat. Designo.) The idea formed in the mind of an artist on any particular subject, which he transfers by some medium, for the purpose of making it known to others. Every work of design is to be considered either in relation to the art that produced it, to the nature of its adaptation to the end sought, or to the nature of the end it is destined to serve; hence its beauty is dependent on the wisdom or excellence displayed in the design, on the fitness or propriety of the adaptation, and upon the utility for the end. The considerations of design, fitness, and utility will be seen at large in Book III. Chap. I. Sects. 1, 2.

DESTEMPER. See DISTEMPER.

DETAILS. A term usually applied to the drawings on a larger scale for the use of builders, and generally called *working drawings*. See Book II. Chap. IV. Sect. 6.

DETERMINING LINE. In the conic sections, a line parallel to the base of the cone; in the hyperbola this line is within the base; in the parabolic sections it forms a tangent to the base, in the elliptic it falls without it. In the intersecting line of a circle, the determining line will never meet the plan of the base to which it is parallel.

DETRIANUS. See ARCHITECTS, list of, 49.

DEXIPHANES. See ARCHITECTS, list of, 35.

DIACONICUM. A place contiguous to the ancient churches, wherein were preserved the sacred vestments, vessels, relics, and ornaments of the altar. In modern language, the *sacristy*. The sacristy is now also called the *vestry*.

DIAGONAL. (Gr. Δια, through, and Γωνια, angle.) A straight line drawn through a figure joining two opposite angles. The term, in geometry, is used in speaking of four-sided figures, but it is nevertheless properly applied with reference to all polygons whereof the number of sides is not less than four. The term diameter is used by Euclid in the same sense; but modern geometers use the term diameter only in speaking of curve lines, and diagonal when speaking of angular figures.

DIAGONAL SCALE. A compound scale formed by vertical and horizontal subdivisions with diagonals drawn across them, whereby we are enabled to measure off very small parts by means of equidistant parallels crossing others of the same kind.

DIAGRAM. (Gr. Διαγραμμα, from Δια, through, and Γραφω, I write.) The figure or scheme for the illustration of a mathematical or other proposition.

DIAGRAPH. (Gr.) A recently invented French instrument for drawing objects from nature.

DIAMETER. (Gr. Δια, through, and Μετρον, a measure.) A straight line passing through the centre of a geometrical figure, as that of a circle, ellipse, or hyperbola. The term is architecturally used to express the measure across the lower part of the shaft of a column, and is usually divided into sixty parts, called minutes, which form the scale for the measurement of all the parts of an order.

DIAMOND PAVEMENT. One disposed in squares arranged diagonally.

DIASTYLE. (Gr. Δια and Στυλος, a column.) That distance between columns which consists of three diameters, or, according to some, of four diameters. The term is sometimes used adjectively, to signify that the building is arranged with those intervals between the columns.

DIATONI. (Gr. Δια and Τονος, an extension.) In ancient architecture the angle stones of a wall, wrought on two faces, and which, from stretching beyond the stones above and below them, made a good bond or tie to the work.

DIAZOMA. (Gr. Δια, through, and Ζωμα, a cincture.) In ancient architecture, the landings or resting places which, at different heights, encircled the amphitheatre like so many bands or cinctures, whence the name.

DICASTERIUM. (Gr. Δικη, justice.) In ancient architecture, the name of a tribunal or hall of justice.

DICTYOTHETON. (Gr. Δικτυον, a net, and Τιθημι, I place.) In ancient architecture, masonry worked in courses, like the meshes of a net. Also open lattice work, for admitting light and air.

DIDORON. See BRICK.

DIE OF A PEDESTAL. That part included between the base and the cornice.

DIGGING. In soft ground, one man with a spade will throw up, per hour, a cubic yard of twenty-seven feet. If a mattock must be used, the same quantity will require two men, and in a strong gravel, three. It will require three men to wheel thirty cubic yards of gravel in a day to the distance of twenty yards.

DIGLYPH. (Gr. Δις, twice, and Γλυφω, I carve.) A projecting face, with two panels or channels sunk thereon.

Dilapidation. The state of decay and ruin into which a building has been permitted to fall. See Book IV.

Dimension. (Lat. Dimetior.) In geometry is either length, breadth, or thickness. Thus a line has one dimension, as of length; a superficies has two, length and breadth; a solid has three dimensions, length, breadth, and thickness.

Diminished Arches. Those lower or less than a semicircle, called by the French *voutes surbaissées*.

Diminished Bar of a Sash. One thinner on the edge towards the room than on that towards the glass of the window.

Diminished Column. A column whereof the upper diameter is less than the lower.

Diminishing Rule. A board cut with a concave edge, so as to ascertain the swell of a column, and to try its curvature.

Diminishing Scale. A scale of gradation used in finding the different points for drawing the spiral curve of the Ionic volute, by describing the arc of a circle through every three preceding points, the extreme point of the last arc being one of the next three. Each point through which the curve passes is regulated so as to be in a line drawn to the centre of the volute, and the lines at equal angles with each other.

Diminution of a Column. The continued contraction of the diameter of the column as it rises. Most of the modern authors make the diminution to commence from one third of the height of the column; but in all the ancient examples the diminution commences from the bottom of the shaft. See Entasis. In Gothic architecture neither swell nor diminution is used, all the horizontal sections being similar and equal.

Dining or Dinner Room. Generally one of the largest rooms in a dwelling-house. In large buildings it extends to forty or fifty feet in length, and the breadth is from half to three fourths the length. In middle-sized houses, dining-rooms run from twenty-four down to eighteen feet in length by eighteen to sixteen feet in width, and thirteen or fourteen feet in height. In houses, the largest room on the ground-floor should be appropriated to the purpose.

Dinocrates. See Architects, list of, 22.

Dioti Salvi. See Architects, list of, 94.

Dipteral. (Gr. Δίπτερος, double-winged.) In ancient architecture, a temple having a double range of columns on each of its flanks. See Temple.

Direct Radial. In perspective, a right line from the eye perpendicular to the picture.

Directing Line. In perspective, the line in which an original plane would cut the directing plane.

Directing Plane. In perspective, a plane passing through the point of sight, or the eye, parallel to the picture.

Directing Point. In perspective, that in which any original line produced cuts the directing plane.

Director of an Original Line. In perspective, the straight line passing through the directing point and the eye of a spectator.

Director of the Eye. The intersection of the plane with the directing plane perpendicular to the original plane and that of the picture, and hence also perpendicular to the directing and vanishing planes, since each of the two latter is parallel to each of the two former.

Directrix. In geometry the name given to a certain straight line perpendicular to the axes of a conic section. One of the properties of these curves is that the distance of any point of the curve from the directrix is to the distance of the same point from the focus in a constant ratio. The name is sometimes applied generally to any straight or curved line required for the description of any curve.

Discharge. (Fr. Décharger.) The relief given to a beam, or any other piece of timber, too much loaded by an incumbent weight of building. When the relief is given, the weight is said to be discharged.

Discharging Arches. Those built over wooden lintels, whereby the bearing upon them is taken off. The chords of discharging arches are not much longer than the lintel, being the segments of very large circles. A temporary arch is frequently introduced, and removed on completing the building. Sometimes the arches are built without any lintel under them.

Dishing out. The same as Cradling, which see.

Displuviatum. (Lat.) In ancient architecture, a place from which the rain is conveyed away in two channels. According to Vitruvius, a *cavædium displuviatum* was an open court exposed to the rain.

Disposition. (Lat.) One of the essentials of architecture. It is the arrangement of the whole design by means of ichnography (plan), orthography (section and elevation), and scenography (perspective view). It differs from distribution, which signifies the particular arrangements of the internal parts of a building.

DISTANCE OF THE EYE. In perspective, the distance of the eye from the picture in a line perpendicular to the plan thereof.

DISTANCE, POINT OF. In perspective, the distance of the picture transferred upon the vanishing line from the centre, or from the point where the principal ray meets it; and thus it is generally understood to be on the vanishing line of the horizon.

DISTANCE OF A VANISHING LINE. The length of a perpendicular falling from the eye perpendicular to the vanishing plane.

DISTEMPER. (Fr. Detemper.) In painting, a preparation of opaque colour, ground up with size and water.

DISTRIBUTION. (Lat.) The arrangement of the various apartments of a building.

DITRIGLYPH. (Gr. Δις, twice, Τρεις, three, and Γλυφω, I carve.) An arrangement of inter-columniations in the Doric order, by which two triglyphs are obtained in the frieze between the triglyphs that stand over the columns.

DODECAGON. (Gr. Δωδεκα and Γωνια, an angle.) A regular polygon of twelve equal sides.

DODECAHEDRON. (Gr. Δωδεκα and Έδρα, a seat.) One of the five platonic bodies, or regular solids, its surface being composed of twelve equal and regular pentagons.

DOG-LEGGED STAIRS. Such as are solid between the upper flights, or such as have no well-hole, and in which the rail and balusters of both progressive and retrogressive flight fall in the same vertical plane. The steps are fixed to strings, newels, and carriages; and the ends of the steps in the inferior kind only terminate on the side of the string without any housing.

DOME. (Lat. Domus.) The spherical, or otherwise formed, convex roof over a circular or polygonal building. A *surbased* or *diminished dome* is one that is segmental on its vertical section, a *surmounted dome* is one that is higher than the radius of its base. There is great variety in the forms of domes, both in plan and section. In the former, they are circular and polygonal; in the latter, we find them semicircular, semi-elliptical, segmental, pointed, sometimes in curves of contrary flexure, bell-shaped, &c. The oldest dome on record is that of the Pantheon at Rome, which was erected under Augustus, and is still perfect. Below is a list of the principal domes in Europe, with their dimensions; the heights in the third column are from the ground: —

Place.	Feet Diam.	Feet High.
Pantheon at Rome - - - - -	142	143
Duomo, or Sta. Maria del Fiore, at Florence -	139	310
St. Peter's at Rome - - - - -	139	330
Sta. Sophia at Constantinople - - -	115	201
Baths of Caracalla (ancient) - - - -	112	116
St. Paul's, London - - - - -	112	215
Mosque of Achmet - - - - -	92	120
Chapel of the Medici - - - - -	91	199
Baptistery at Florence - - - - -	86	110
Church of the Invalids at Paris - - -	80	173
Minerva Medica at Rome - - - -	78	97
Madonna della Salute, Venice - - -	70	133
St. Généviève at Paris (Pantheon) - - -	67	190
Duomo at Siena - - - - - -	57	148
Duomo at Milan - - - - - -	57	254
St. Vitalis at Ravenna - - - - -	55	94
Val de Grace at Paris - - - - -	55	133
San Marco, Venice - - - - -	44	

DONJON. (Fr.) The massive tower within ancient castles to which the garrison might retreat in case of necessity. It was centrally placed, and frequently raised on an artificial elevation.

DOOKS. The same as WOODEN BRICKS, which see. It is a Scotch term.

DOOR. (Sax. Dop, Gr. Θυρα.) The gate or entrance of a house or other building, or of an apartment in a house. It must be proportioned to the situation and use for which it is intended. Thus, for an ordinary dwelling-house, a door should not be less than seven to eight feet high, and three to four feet broad; but to churches and public buildings the entrance-doors should be much wider, to allow of a multitude to pass out. So in stately mansions, the doors must be from six to twelve feet in width, and of proportionate height. For the different sorts and profiles of doors, see Book III. Chap. I. Sect. 19.; for joinery of doors, Book II. Chap. III. Sect. 5.

DOOR FRAME or CASE. The wooden frame enclosing a door.

DORIC ORDER. See Book III. Chap. I. Sect. 4., and Book I. Chap. II. Sect. 4.

DORMANT TREE or SUMMER. The lintel of a door, window beam, &c. A beam tenoned into a girder to support the ends of joists on both sides of it. *Summer*, in some parts, is the common term for a girder.

DORMER. A window placed on the inclined plane of the roof of a house, the frame being placed vertically on the rafters.

DORMITORY. (Lat. Dormio, I sleep.) A large sleeping-room, capable of containing many beds.

DORON. See BRICK.

DOUBLE CURVATURE. The curvature of a curve, whereof no part can be brought into a plane, such as the cylindro-cylindric curve, &c.

DOUBLE FLOOR. One constructed of binding and bridging joists. See p. 598.

DOUBLE-HUNG SASHES. See *par.* 2165.

DOUBLE VAULTS. Two vaults of brick or stone carried up separately with a cavity between them.

DOUBLING. A term used in Scotland to denote eaves' boards.

DOUCINE. The French term for the cyma recta.

DOVE-HOUSE, or DOVE-COT. A building for keeping tame pigeons, the only essential difference between which and a common poultry house is that the entrance for the birds must be placed at a considerable height from the ground, because of the flight of pigeons being so much higher than other birds.

DOVE-TAIL (from its spreading like a pigeon's tail). A joint used by carpenters and joiners in connecting two pieces of wood, by letting one into the other, in the form of the expanded tail of a dove. It is the strongest method of joining masses, because the tenon or piece of wood widens as it extends, so that it cannot be drawn out, because the tongue is larger than the cavity through which it would have to be drawn. The French call this method *queue d'hironde*, or swallow's tail.

DOWELS. Pins of wood or iron used at the edges of boards in laying floors, to avoid the appearance of the nails on the surface. Floors thus laid are called *dowelled floors*.

DRAG. (Verb.) A term applied to anything bearing down or rubbing on another. Thus, a door is said to drag when its hinges become so loosened that the lower edge rubs upon the floor.

DRAGON BEAM or PIECE. In carpentry, a short beam or piece of timber, lying diagonally with the wall-plates at the angles of a roof for receiving the heel or foot of the hip rafter. It is fixed at right angles with another piece, called the *angle tie*, which is supported by each returning wall-plate, on which it is cocked down.

DRAIN. A subterraneous or other channel for waste water. See Book II. Chap. III. Sect. 1.

DRAUGHT. The representation of a building on paper, explanatory of the various parts of the interior and exterior, by means of plans, elevations, and sections, drawn to a scale, by which all the parts are exhibited in the same proportion as the parts of the edifice intended to be represented.

DRAUGHT. In masonry, a part of the surface of the stone, hewn to the breadth of the chisel on the margin of the stone according to the curved or straight line to which the surface is to be brought. When the draughts are framed round the different sides of the stone, the intermediate part is wrought to the surface by applying a straight edge or templet. In very large stones, when the substance needs much reduction, it is usual to make several intermediate parallel *draughts*, and thus the intermediate parts may be hewn down nearly by the eye, without much application of the straight edge or templet.

DRAUGHT COMPASSES. Those with moveable points.

DRAW BORE. (Verb.) The pinning a mortise and tenon, by piercing the hole through the tenon nearer to the shoulder than the holes through the cheeks from the abutment in which the shoulder is to come in contact.

DRAW BORE PINS. Pieces of steel in the shape of the frustrum of a cone, rather taper, and inserted in handles with the greatest diameter next to the handle, for driving through the draw bores of a mortise and tenon in order to bring the shoulder of the rail close home to the abutment on the edge of the style. When this is effected, the draw bore pins, when more than one are used, are taken out singly, and the holes immediately filled up with wooden pegs.

DRAWBRIDGE. One made with long and heavy levers to raise or let it down at pleasure.

DRAWING. See Book II. Chap. IV. Sect. 1.

   Drawing is the art of representing any object by means of lines circumscribing its boundaries. For working drawings see Book II. Chap. IV. Sect. 6.

DRAWINGS NECESSARY IN COMPOSITIONS. Book III. Chap. II. Sect. 5.

DRAWING ROOM, perhaps more properly WITHDRAWING ROOM. The apartment to which the company *withdraw* after dinner.

DRESSED. A term in masonry which expresses the operation a stone has undergone before

building it in the wall, whether by the hammer only or by the mallet and chisel, and then rubbing the face smooth. In Scotland the term is used to signify hammer dressing only.

DRESSER. A table placed against a wall in a kitchen, usually with drawers, and having shelves over it.

DRESSING ROOM. A room generally adjoining to and communicating with the sleeping room, used, as the name implies, for dressing in. It should have a separate door to open on the lobby or passage of communication.

DRESSINGS. All kinds of mouldings beyond the naked walls or ceilings are called by the general name of dressings. In joinery it is a term applied to the architraves or other appendages of apertures.

DRIFT. (Sax. Dɲɪꞃaᴅ.) The horizontal force which an arch exerts with a tendency to overset the piers from which it springs.

DRIP. See CORONA.

DRIPPING EAVES. (Dan. Dripper, to drop.) The lower edges of a roof wherefrom the rain drips or drops to the ground. By the Metropolitan Building Act dripping eaves are prohibited towards any street or public way.

DROPS. (Sax. Dɲoppaᴅ.) The frusta of cones in the Doric order, used under the triglyphs in the architrave below the tænia. They are also employed in the under part of the mutuli or modillions of the order. In the Greek examples they are sometimes curved a little inwards on the profile.

DROVED ASHLAR. A term used in Scotland for chiselled or random tooled ashlar. It is the most inferior kind of hewn work in building. What is in that country called broached work is sometimes done without being droved; but in good broached work the face of the stone should be previously droved, and then broached.

DROVED AND BROACHED. A term used in Scotland to signify work that has been roughed and then tooled clean.

DROVED AND STRIPED. Work that is first droved and then striped. The stripes are shallow grooves done with a half or three-quarter inch chisel, about an eighth of an inch deep, having the droved interstices prominent. This and the two preceding sorts of work are not much used in the southern part of England.

DRUELL. See ARCHITECTS, list of, 166. *

DRUIDICAL ARCHITECTURE. See Book I. Chap. II. Sect. 1.

DRUM. (Dan. Tromme.) The upright part under or above a cupola. The same term is sometimes applied to the solid part or vase of the Corinthian and Composite capitals.

DRY ROT. A disease of timber which destroys the cohesion of its parts; it is usually ascribed to the attacks of fungi, such as the *Polyporus destructor* and *Merulius lacrymans*, whose spawn appears upon the surface overspreading it like a tough thick skin of white leather; and there is no doubt of its being often connected with the appearance of such fungi. Dry rot is, however, in some cases to be identified with the presence of fungi of a more simple kind than those just mentioned, such as those of the genus *Sporotrichum*. See p. 506, *et seq.*

DUBBING OUT. A term used by plasterers to signify the bringing of an uneven surface in a wall to a plane, by pieces of tile, slate, or the like, before it is plastered over.

DUNSTAN. See ARCHITECTS, list of, 75.

DUODECIMAL. (Lat. Duodecim.) Proceeding by twelves. It is a term applied to an operation in arithmetic, which is explained in p. 730, *et seq.*

DWANG. A term used in Scotland to denote the short pieces of timber employed in strutting a floor.

DWARF WAINSCOTING. Such as does not reach the whole height of a room, being usually four, five, or six feet, high.

DWARF WALLS. Low walls of less height than the story of a building; sometimes the joists of a ground floor rest upon dwarf walls. The enclosures of courts are frequently formed by them with a railing of iron on the top; and indeed any low wall used as a fence is a dwarf wall.

DWELLING HOUSE. See Book III. Chap. V. Sect. 20, *et seq.*

DWELLINGS, DIFFERENT EARLY SORTS OF. See Book I. Chap. I. Sect. 3.

DYE. See DIE.

DYNAMICS. (Gr. Δυναμις, force or power.) As generally understood, the science which treats on the motion of bodies, because it is only known to us by the motion it produces in the body on which it acts. It is however usually restricted to those circumstances of motion in which the moving bodies are at liberty to obey the impulses communicated to them; the opposite cases, or those in which the bodies, whether by external circumstances or by their connection with one another, are not at liberty to obey the impulses given, being within the science of mechanics.

E.

EAGLE. (Gr. Αιετος.) A term used by the Greeks for the frontispiece or pediment of their temples.

EARS. The same as CROSETTES, which see.

EARNULPH. See ARCHITECTS, list of, 89.

EANBALD. See ARCHITECTS, list of, 70.

EAVES. (Probably Fr. Eaux.) The lowest edges of the inclined sides of a roof which project beyond the face of the walls, so as to throw the water off therefrom, that being their office.

EAVES' BOARD, EAVES' LATH, EAVES' CATCH. See ARRIS FILLET.

EBONY. The wood of a natural order of shrubby or arborescent exogens, chiefly inhabiting the tropics. Some species are remarkable for the hardness and blackness of their wood, which is principally used for furniture.

ECCENTRICITY. The difference of centre from another circle. The distance between the foci of an ellipse.

ECHEA. (Gr. Ηχεω, I sound.) In ancient architecture, sonorous vessels of metal or earth, in the form of a bell, used in the construction of theatres for the purpose of reverberating the sound of the performer's voice. They were distributed between the seats, and are described in the fifth book of Vitruvius, who states that Mummius introduced them in Rome, after the taking of Corinth, where he found this expedient used in the theatre.

ECHINUS. (Gr. Εχινος.) The same as the ovolo or quarter round, though the moulding is only properly so called when carved with eggs and anchors. (See ANCHOR.) It is the shell or husk of the chestnut, though the ornament does not seem to bear much resemblance to it.

ECPHORA. (Gr. Εκ, out, Φέρω, I bear.) A word used by Vitruvius (lib. iii. cap. 3.,) to signify the projecture of a member or moulding of a column, that is, the distance of its extremity from the naked of the column, or, according to others, from the axis.

ECTYPE. (Gr. Εκτυπον.) An object in relievo, or embossed.

EDGE. (Sax. Εσξε.) The intersection of two planes or surfaces of a solid, which therefore is either straight or curved according to the direction of the surfaces. See ARRIS. It is also that side of a rectangular prismatic body which contains the length and thickness; but in this sense of the term, the body to which it applies is generally understood to be very thin; thus we say " the edge of a door," " the edge of a board," meaning the narrow side. The edge of a tool is the meeting of the surfaces when ground to a very acute angle.

EDGE TOOLS are those which clip or shave in the operation of working.

EDGING. In carpentry, the reducing of the edges of ribs or rafters, whether externally or internally, so as to range in a plane or in any curved surface required. *Backing* is a particular use of edging, and only applies to the outer edges of ribs or rafters; but edging or ranging is a general term, and applies either to the backing or internal surface. See BACKING.

EDIFICE. (Lat. Ædificium.) A word synonymous with fabric, building, erection; the word is, however, more usually employed to denote architectural erections distinguished for grandeur, dignity, and importance.

EDNOTH. See ARCHITECTS, list of, 74.

EFFECT. (Lat. Efficio.) That quality in works of art whose nature is to give particular efficacy to other qualities, so as to bring them out and attract the eye of the spectator.

EGBERT. See ARCHITECTS, list of, 68.

EGG AND TONGUE. Ornaments used in the echinus, supposed by Quatremère de Quincy to have had their origin in the head of Isis, and, as he imagines, representing a mystical collar or necklace of the mundane egg and the tongue of the serpent of immortality; but as we think, in the representation of much more simple objects, those of nature herself. See ECHINUS.

EGYPTIAN ARCHITECTURE. See Book I. Chap. II. Sect. 7.

EGYPTIAN HALL. See ŒCUS.

ELÆOTHESIUM. (Gr. Ελαιον, oil.) In ancient architecture, an apartment in the baths wherein, after leaving the bath, the bathers anointed themselves.

ELASTIC CURVE. In mechanics, the figure assumed by an elastic body, one end whereof is fixed horizontally in a vertical plane, and the other loaded with a weight which, by its gravity, tends to bend it.

ELASTICITY. (Gr. Ελαστη, a spring, from Ελαυνω, I draw.) In physics that property possessed by certain bodies of recovering their form and dimensions after the external force which has dilated or compressed them is withdrawn. It is only perfect when the body recovers exactly its primitive form after the force to which it has been subjected has been removed, and that in the same time as was required for the force to produce the alteration. This is however a quality not strictly found in nature.

ELBOWS. (Sax. Elboʒa.) The upright sides which flank any pannelled work, as in windows below the shutters, &c.

ELEVATION. (Lat. Elevatio.) A geometrical projection drawn on a plane perpendicular to the horizon.

ELLIPSE or ELLIPSIS. (Gr. Ελλειψις, defect.) One of the conic sections produced by cutting a cone entirely through the curved surface, neither parallel to the base; nor making a subcontrary section, so that the ellipsis, like the circle, is a curve that returns into itself and completely encloses a space.

ELLIPSOGRAPH. An instrument for describing an ellipsis by continued motion.

ELLIPSOID. See CONOID.

ELLIPTIC ARCH. A portion of the curve of an ellipsis employed as an arch.

ELLIPTIC COMPASSES. The same as ELLIPSOGRAPH.

ELLIPTIC WINDING STAIRS. Such as are cased in and wind round an elliptic newel.

ELM. (Lat. Ulmus.) A forest tree occasionally used in building. See Book II. Chap. II. Sect. 4.

ELPHAGE. See ARCHITECTS, list of, 77.

EMBANKMENT. A term signifying any large mound of earth on the sides of a passage for water or other purposes; also for protection against the action of the sea. It is usually constructed of earth, and, when necessary to resist much force, cased with brick or stone.

EMBATTLED. A wall indented with notches in the form of embrasures on the top of a wall, parapet, or other building. It is sometimes called *crenelle*.

EMBATTLED ARONADE. See ARONADE.

EMBATTLED-BATTLED LINE. A straight line bent into right angles, so that if there be three sets of parts one set may be parallel to those of the other two.

EMBATTLED BUILDINGS. Those with embrasures in the parapets, resembling a castle or fortified place.

EMBOSSING or EMBOSSED WORK. (Fr. Bosse, a protuberance.) The raising or forming in relievo any sort of figure, whether performed with the chisel or otherwise. It is a kind of sculpture, in which the figures rise from the plane on which they are formed, and as they are more or less prominent they are said to be in *alto, mezzo*, or *basso relievo*.

EMBRASURE. An opening made in the wall or parapet of a fortified place. The term is also applied to an enlargement within of the sides of a window, in which sense it is the same as SPLAY, which see.

EMERE, G.d'. See ARCHITECTS, list of, 232.

EMPLECTON. (Gr. Εμπλεκω, I entangle.) Among the ancients, a method of constructing walls, in which, according to Vitruvius, the front stones were wrought fair and the interior left rough and filled in with stones of various sizes.

ENCARPUS. (Gr. Εν and καρπος.) The festoons on a frieze, consisting of fruit, flowers, leaves, &c.

END OF A STONE. The two parallel sides which form the vertical joints.

ENDECAGON. (Gr. Ενδεκα, eleven, and Γωνια, an angle.) A plain geometrical figure bounded by eleven sides.

ENGAGED COLUMNS. Those attached to walls, by which a portion of them is concealed. They never stand less than half their diameter out of the wall to which they are attached.

ENGLISH BOND. See p. 551.

ENSEMBLE. (Fr.) A term denoting the masses and details considered with relation to each other.

ENTABLATURE. (Fr. Entablement.) The whole of the parts of an order above a column. The assemblage is divided into three parts: the architrave, which rests immediately on the column; the frieze, next over the architrave, being the middle member; and the cornice, which is the uppermost part. The first and last are variously subdivided in the different orders. See the different orders, Book III. Chap. I.

ENTASIS. (Gr. Εντασις.) A delicate and almost imperceptible swelling of the shaft of a column, to be found in almost all the Grecian examples. It seems to have been adopted to prevent the crude appearance which the frusta of cones would have presented. This refinement is alluded to in the second chapter of the third book of Vitruvius, and was first in modern times observed in execution in 1814 by Mr. Allason.

ENTER. (Verb.) In carpentry and joinery, the act of inserting the end of a tenon in the mouth of a mortise previous to its being driven home to the shoulder.

ENTRESOL. (Fr.) A low story between two higher ones. See MEZZANINE.

ENVELOPE. (Verb.) The covering of a portion of the surface of a solid with a thin substance or wrapper, which in all points or parts comes in contact with the surface of such surface. To develop the surface of a solid is to find the envelopes that will cover its different parts.

EPHEBEIUM. (Gr.) A building, in ancient architecture, for the exercise and wrestling of the youth.

EPICRANITIS. (Gr.) A name given by the Greeks to the tiles forming the cyma or upper member of the cornice of their temples.

EPICYCLOID. (Gr. Επικυκλος, and Ειδος, form.) In geometry, a curve line generated by the revolution of a point in the circumference of a circle, which rolls on the circumference of another circle, either externally or internally.

EPISCENIUM. (Gr. Επι, upon, Σκηνη, a scene.) In ancient architecture, the upper order of the scene in a theatre.

EPISTYLIUM. Gr. Επι, upon, Στυλος, column.) The same as ARCHITRAVE, which see.

EPITITHEDES. (Gr. Επι, upon, Τιθημι, I place.) The crown or upper mouldings of an entablature.

EQUIANGULAR. Having equal angles.

EQUIDISTANT. At equal distances.

EQUILATERAL. Having equal sides.

EQUILIBRIUM. In mechanics, an equality of forces in opposite directions, so as mutually to balance each other. For the arch of equilibrium see Book II. Chap. I. Sect. 9.

ERGASTULUM. In ancient architecture, a name given by the Romans to a prison or house of correction, where slaves, by the sole authority of their masters, were confined for their offences and subjected to hard labour. By the Greeks these buildings were called *sophronisteria.*

ERWYN. See ARCHITECTS, list of, 128.

ESCOBEDO, D'. See ARCHITECTS, list of, 197.

ESGUERRA. See ARCHITECTS, list of, 225.

ESTIMATE. (Substantive.) The computed cost of a building before the works are commenced. See Book II. Chap. III. Sect. 14.

ESTRADE. An even or level space; a public road.

ETIENNE DE BONNEVEIL. See ARCHITECTS, list of, 111.

ETRUSCAN ARCHITECTURE. See Book I. Chap. II. Sect. 12.

EUDE DE MONTREUIL. See ARCHITECTS, list of, 117.

EUPALINUS. See ARCHITECTS, list of, 5.

EUPOLEMUS. See ARCHITECTS, list of, 27.

EURITHMY. (Gr. Ευρυθμια, justness of proportion.) The regular, just, and symmetrical measures resulting from harmony in the proportions of a building or order. Vitruvius makes it one of his six essentials.

EUSTACHIUS. See ARCHITECTS, list of, 109.

EUSTYLE. (Gr. Ευ, well, and Στυλος, column.) See COLONNADE.

EVAPORATION. (Lat.) The conversion of substances into vapour, during which process a considerable quantity of sensible heat passes into the *latent* or insensible state. The circumstances which principally influence the process of evaporation, are extent of surface, and the state of the air in respect of temperature, dryness, stillness, and density.

EVERSDEN, D'. See ARCHITECTS, list of, 136.

EVERSOLT. See ARCHITECTS, list of, 103.

EVOLUTE. (Lat. Evolvo.) In the theory of curve lines, is a curve from which any given curve may be supposed to be formed by the *evolution* or unlapping of a thread from a surface having the same curvature as the first curve. The curve thus generated is called the *involute curve.*

EXCAVATION. (Lat.) As connected with architecture is the digging out or hollowing the ground for the foundations of a building, or of a floor below the level of the ground.

EXCHANGE. See Book III. Chap. V. Sect. 14.

EXHEDRA. (Gr. Εξ, out of, and Εδρα, a chair.) In ancient architecture, a small room in the baths and other buildings appropriated for conversations.

EXOSTRA. (Gr.) In ancient architecture, a machine for representing the interior part of a building as connected with the scene in a theatre.

EXPANSION. One of the ordinary effects of heat, which enlarges the bulk of all matter. Though the expansion of solids is by increase of temperature comparatively small, it may be rendered sensible by carefully measuring the dimensions of any substance when cold and again when heated. Thus an iron bar fitted to a gauge, showing its length and breadth, will, when heated, no longer pass through the apertures. The metals are most expansible by heat and cold. The following exhibits the change which some of them undergo when heated from the freezing to the boiling point of water : —

	Temperature.	
	32°	212°
Platinum - - - -	120000	120104.
Steel - - - -	—	120147.
Iron - - - -	—	120151.
Copper - - - -	—	120204.

					Temperature.	
					32°	212°
Brass	-	-	-	-	120000	120230.
Tin	-	-	-	-	—	120290.
Lead	-	-	-	-	—	120345.
Zinc	-	-	-	-	—	120360.

EXTENSION. (Lat.) One of the general properties of matter, being the quantity of space which a body occupies, its extremities in every direction limiting or circumscribing the matter of that body. It is the magnitude, size, or bulk of a body.

EXTERNAL or EXTERIOR. A term of relation applied to whatever is on the surface or outside of a body, as opposed to *internal* or *interior*.

EXTRADOS. The exterior curve of an arch. The term is generally used to denote the upper curve of the *voussoirs* or stones which immediately form the arch.

EYE. A general term signifying the centre of any part: thus the *eye of a pediment* is a circular window in its centre. The *eye of a dome* is the horizontal aperture on its summit. The *eye of a volute* is the circle at the centre, from whose circumference the spiral line commences.

EYE, BULL'S. See BULL'S EYE.

EYEBROW. A name sometimes given to the fillet.

F.

FABRIC. (Lat.) A general term applied to a large and important building.

FAÇADE. (Fr.) The face or front of any building towards a street, court, garden, or other place ; a term, however, more commonly used to signify the principal front.

FACE MOULD. The name applied by workmen to the pattern for marking the plank or board out of which ornamental hand-railings are to be cut for stairs or other works.

FACE OF A STONE. The surface intended for the front or outward side of the work. The back is usually left rough. Stones should be faced in the opposite direction of their splitting grain.

FACETTES. (Fr.) Flat projections between the flutes of columns.

FACIA or FASCIA. (Lat. a Band.) A flat member of an order or of a building, like a flat band or broad fillet. The architrave, when subdivided for instance, has three bands called *fasciæ*, whereof the lower is called the first fascia, the middle one the second, and the upper one the third.

FACING. That part in the work of a building seen by a spectator ; but the term is usually employed to signify a better sort of material, which masks the inferior one used internally.

FACTABLING. The same as COPING, which see.

FALCONETTO. See ARCHITECTS, list of, 207.

FALLING MOULDS. The two moulds applied to the vertical sides of the railpiece, one to the convex, the other to the concave side, in order to form the back and under surface of the rail and finish the squaring.

FALSE ATTIC. An attic without pilasters, casements, or balustrades, used for crowning a building, as at the gates St. Denis and St. Martin at Paris.

FALSE BEARING. See BEARING WALL.

FALSE ROOF. That part between the ceiling of the upper floor and the covering of the roof.

FANAL. (Fr.) The French term for a lighthouse.

FANUM. (Lat.) A place consecrated to religion, including the building and ground belonging to it. Those temples erected to the memory of distinguished persons were called *fana* by the ancients.

FARLEGH. See ARCHITECTS, list of, 163.

FARM-HOUSES. See Book III. Chap. V Sect. 23.

FARRARIA. See GRANARY.

FASTIGIUM. (Lat.) See PEDIMENT.

FATHOM. (Sax.) A measure of six feet, taken from the extent of both arms when stretched out in a right line. It is chiefly used in measuring the depth of water, quarries, wells, or pits.

FEATHER-EDGED. A term applied to any thin body whose section is trapezoidal ; that is, thicker on one edge than on the other.

FEATHER-EDGED BOARDS. See BOARDS.

FEATHER-EDGED COPING. See COPING.

FEEDER. A cut or channel by which a stream or supply of water is brought into a canal. Sometimes the supply itself of the water is so called.

FEEDING HOUSE or SHED. A farm-building for stalling and fattening neat cattle. It

should be in a dry warm situation, capable of free ventilation, and supplied with proper conveniences for food and water.

FELLING TIMBER.   The cutting down a full grown tree.   Much difference of opinion has prevailed respecting the proper season for felling trees, some being in favour of mid-winter and others of midsummer.   It is however a question which principally turns upon the quantity and value of the soft or outer wood in the trunk of the tree to be felled, called *sap* by the forester and carpenter.   This sap or outer wood being the only portion of the trunk in which the sap or juices of the tree circulate, if no value be set upon it, it seems of little consequence when the tree is cut down, because the mature timber, which is the really valuable part of the wood, is impermeable to the sap in its ascent through the soft wood, and is therefore in the same state at every season of the year.   On the other hand, where much value attaches to the soft or outer wood, or where, as in the case of comparatively young trees, the greater part of the trunk consists of sap wood, they should be felled when the sap least circulates.   The season in that case is doubtless midwinter, which, *cæteris paribus*, is certainly the best season for felling timber.   The next best season seems to be midsummer, because the sap is then chiefly confined to the young shoots, to the circumference of the soft wood, and to the bark. The worst season would appear to be the spring, just before the development of the buds, when the tree is fullest of sap, and receiving fresh supplies of it from the root; and in autumn, immediately before the fall of the leaf, when there is a superabundance of sap, from its being as it were thrown out of employment by the falling of the leaf. In general all soft wood, such as elm, lime, poplar, willow, &c., should be felled during the winter.   Hard woods, like the oak, beach, ash, &c., may be felled at any time, if the trunks are of large size, and chiefly valued for their heart-wood.

FELT GRAIN.   That position of splitting timber which is cloven towards the centre of the tree, or transversely to the annular rings or plates.   The transverse position, or rather that which is in the direction of the annular plates, is called the *quarter grain*.

FELTING.   The act of splitting timber by the felt grain.

FENCE. (Lat. Defensio.)   Any sort of construction for the purpose of enclosing land, as a bank of earth, a ditch, hedge, wall, railing, paling, &c.

FENDER PILES.   Those driven to protect work, either on land or in water, from the con-cussion of a moving body.

FESTOON. (Fr.)   A sculptured representation of flowers, drapery, and foliage, looped or suspended at intervals on walls.   The festoon was much used on friezes, altars, tablets, also over or under niches, as well as in many other situations.

FETCHING THE PUMP.   The act of pouring water into the upper part of a pump to expel the air contained between the lower box or piston and the bottom of the pump.

FIGURE.   In a general sense the terminating extremes or surface of a body.   No body can exist without figure, or it would be infinite, and all space solid matter.   Figure in geometry, is any plane surface comprehended within a certain line or lines.

FILIPPO, MAESTRO.   See ARCHITECTS, list of, 193.

FILLET. (Fr. Filet.)   A narrow flat band, listel, or annulet, used for the separation of one moulding from another, and to give breadth and firmness to the upper edge of a crowning moulding, as in a cornice.   The small bands between the flutes of a column are called fillets.   See ANNULET and BAND.

FILLET.   In carpentry or joinery, is any small timber scantling equal to or less than battens.   Fillets are used for supporting the ends of boards by nailing them to joists or quarters, &c. as in *sound boarding*, and in supporting the ends of shelves.

FILLET GUTTER.   A sloping gutter, with a learboard and fillet thereon, to divert the water.

FILLING IN PIECES.   In carpentry, short timbers, less than the full length, fitted against the hips of roofs, groins, braces of partitions, which interrupt the whole length.

FINE STUFF.   Plaster used in common ceilings and walls for the reception of paper or colour.   It is composed of lime slaked and sifted through a fine sieve, then mixed with a due quantity of hair and fine sand.

FINIAL.   In Gothic architecture, the top or finishing of a pinnacle or gable, as it is now generally understood; but in ancient documents the term was used to denote an entire pinnacle.

FINISHING.   A term frequently applied to the termination of a building; but more espe-cially to the interior in the plasterer's work for the last coat, and often to the joiner's work, as in the architraves, bases, surbases, &c.

FIORAVANTI.   See ARCHITECTS, list of, 159.

FIR.   A forest tree, extensively used in building.

FIR POLES.   Small trunks of fir trees, from ten to sixteen feet long, used in rustic build-ings and outhouses.

FIR IN BOND.   A technical expression to denote lintels, bond timbers, wall plates, and all timbers built in walls.   See BOND.

Fir wrought. That planed on the edges and sides.

Fir wrought and framed. That which is both planed and framed.

Fir wrought, framed, and rebated. That which is planed, framed, and rebated.

Fir wrought, framed, rebated, and beaded. The same as the preceding article, with the addition of beading.

Fir framed. Rough timber framed, but which has not undergone the action of planing.

Fir no Labour. Rough timber employed in walls, without planing or framing.

Fire-place. See Chimney.

Fire-stone. That which resists the action of the fire. A species of it is used in joinery for rubbing away the ridges made by the cutting-edge of the plane.

Firmer Tool. A tool used by joiners.

First Coat. In plastering, the laying the plaster on the laths, or the rendering, as it is called, on brickwork, when only two coats are used. When three are used, it is called *pricking-up* when upon laths, and *roughing-in* when upon bricks.

Fischer, Von Erlach. See Architects, list of, 269.

Fischer, Carl. See Architects, list of, 313.

Fish. (Verb.) To secure a piece of wood by fastening another piece above or below it, and sometimes both, to strengthen it.

Fistuca. (Lat.) A pile-driving instrument with two handles raised by pulleys, and guided in its descent to fall on the head of a pile so as to drive it into the ground, being what is by the workmen called a *monkey*.

Fitz-Odo. See Architects, list of, 108.

Fixture. A term applied to all articles of a personal nature affixed to land. This annexation must be by the article being let into or united with the land, or with some substance previously connected therewith.

Flags. Thin stones used for paving, from one and a half to three inches thick, and of various lengths and breadths, according to the nature of the quarry.

Flake White. In painting, lead corroded by the pressing of grapes, or a ceruse prepared by the acid of grapes. It is of Italian manufacture, and for the purity of its white far surpasses the white lead of this country.

Flank. (Fr. Flanc.) That part of a return body which joins the front. In town houses the party-walls are the flank walls.

Flashing. (Probably from Fr. Flaque, a splash.) Pieces of lead or other metal let into the joints of a wall so as to lap over the gutters or other conduit pieces, and prevent the splashing of rain injuring the interior works.

Flat. That part of the covering of a house laid horizontal, and covered with lead or other material.

Flatting. In house painting, a mode of painting in oil, in which the surface is left, when finished, without any gloss. The material or paint is prepared with a mixture of oil of turpentine, which secures the colours, and when used in the finishing, leaves the paint quite dead. The process is of use where it is desirable that the surface painted should retain the colour. It is only used for inside work and in the best apartments. Nut oil may be used for the purpose, so may be poppy oil, both whereof are good media for the colour.

Flemish Bond. See p. 552.

Flemish Bricks. A species of bricks used for paving, whereof seventy-two will pave a square yard; they were originally imported from Flanders, are of a yellowish colour, and harder than common bricks.

Flexibility. (Lat. Flecto.) That property of bodies which admits of their bending. It is opposed to *stiffness* on the one hand, and *brittleness* on the other; stiff bodies being such as resist bending, and brittle those which cannot be bent without a disruption of their parts.

Flexure. The bending or curve of a line or surface. The point of *contrary flexure* is that point of a curve where the curvature alters from convex to concave, or the reverse, as respects the first direction of the curve.

Flight of Steps. In a staircase is the series of steps from one landing place to another. Thus, the same staircase between one floor and another may consist of more than one flight of steps; the flight being reckoned from landing to landing.

Flint. A material often used in inferior building. Common flints are nearly pure *silica*. They usually occur in irregular nodules in chalk. Their origin is still an unsolved geological problem.

Float. In plastering, a long rule with a straight edge, by which the work is reduced to a plane surface.

Floated Lath and Plaster. Plastering of three coats, whereof the first is *pricking-up*, see Book II. Chap. III. Sect. 9.; the second, floating or floated work; and the last, of fine stuff.

Floated Work. Plastering rendered perfectly plane by means of a Float, which see.

FLOATING SCREEDS. (The etymon. of screeds, being probably schierato, ranged.) Strips of plaster previously set out on the work, at convenient intervals, for the *range* of the floating-rule or *float*.

FLOOR. (Sax. Flope.) The pavement or boarded lower horizontal surface of an apartment. It is constructed of earth, brick, stone, wood, or other materials. Carpenters include in the term the framed timber work on which the boarding is laid, as well as the boards themselves. In carpentry, it denotes the timbers which support the boarding, called also *naked flooring* (see p. 597.) and *carcass flooring*. The term floor is, moreover, applied to the stories of a building on the same level ; thus, we have *basement floor, ground floor*, &c. When there is no sunk story, the ground story becomes the basement floor ; the expressions, *one pair, two pair*, &c., implying a story above the first flight of stairs from the ground, and so on. The *principal floor* is that which contains the principal rooms ; generally in country houses on the ground floor, but in those of the town mostly on the one pair floor.

FLOOR. FOLDING or FOLDED. One in which the floor boards are so laid that their joints do not appear continuous throughout the whole length of the floor, but in bays or folds of three, four, five, or more boards each.

FLOOR JOISTS. The joists supporting the boards of the floor ; but when the floor consists of binding and bridging joists, the bridgings are never called floor joists. For the better comprehension of the different sorts of floors in carpentry, see p. 597, *et seq*.

FLOOR. STRAIGHT JOINT. That in which the floor boards are so laid that their joints or edges form a continued line throughout the direction of their length ; in opposition to *folding floor*, wherein the joints end in *folds*.

FLOORS. See Book II. Chap. III. Sect. 4.

FLORID STYLE. In Gothic architecture. See Book I. Chap. III. Sect. 5.

FLUE. The long open tube of a chimney from the fire-place to the top of the shaft, for voidance of the smoke. See CHIMNEY.

FLUING. The same as SPLAYED, which see.

FLUSH. (Lat. Fluxus.) A term used by workmen to signify a continuity of surface in two bodies joined together. Thus, in joinery, the style, rails, and munnions are usually made flush ; that is, the wood of one piece on one side of the joint does not project or recede from that on the other.

FLUSH. In masonry or brick-work, the aptitude of two brittle bodies to splinter at the joints where the stones or bricks come in contact when contiguous in a wall.

FLUSH. (Verb.) A term to denote the complete bedding of masonry or brick-work, in the mortar or cement used for the connection of the stones or bricks, so as to leave no vacant space where the stones or bricks do not nicely fit in their places.

FLUTES or FLUTINGS. Upright channels on the shafts of columns, usually ending hemi-spherically at top and bottom. Their plan or horizontal section is sometimes circular or segmental, and sometimes, as in the Grecian examples, elliptical. The Doric column (see Book III. Chap. I. Sect. 4.) has twenty round its circumference ; the Ionic, Corinthian, and Composite (see Sections 5, 6, and 7. of the same Chapter) have twenty-four. The Tuscan column is never fluted. Flutes are occasionally *cabled*. See CABLE.

FLYERS. Steps in a flight of stairs that are parallel to each other.

FLYING BUTTRESS. A buttress in the form of an arch, springing from a solid mass of masonry, and abutting against the springing of another arch which rises from the upper points of abutment of the first. It is employed in most of the cathedrals, and its office is to act as a counterpoise against the vaulting of the nave. If flying buttresses were built solid from the ground, it is obvious that they would interfere with the vista along the aisles of the church ; hence the project of continuing a resistance by means of arches. Their stability depends on the resistance afforded by the weight of the vertical buttress, whence they spring. See ARC-BOUTANT and BUTTRESS.

FOCUS. In geometry and the conic sections, a point on the concave side of a curve, to which the rays are reflected from all points of such curve.

FODDER or FOTHER. A weight among the plumbers of London of 19½ cwt.

FŒNILIA. (Lat.) See GRANARY.

FOIX, DE. See ARCHITECTS, list of, 245.

FOLD OF A FLOOR. See FLOOR.

FOLDED FLOOR. See FLOOR.

FOLDING DOORS. Such as are made to meet each other from the opposite jambs to which they are hung ; and when they are rebated together, their edges meet folding over each other, with a bead at the joint, to give the appearance of one entire door.

FOLDING JOINT. A joint made like a rule-joint, or the joint of a hinge.

FOLIAGE. A sculptured group of the leaves of plants and flowers, so arranged as to form architectural ornaments, as in friezes, panels, &c., and in the capitals of the Corinthian and Composite orders.

FONT. A vessel, generally of stone or metal, for containing the water of baptism in the

Christian church. Some of the early fonts are extremely beautiful, and wrought with extraordinary richness of decoration. The singular inscription frequently found on the walls of baptisteries occurs also occasionally on ancient fonts : NIΨON ANOMHMATA MH MONAN OΨIN, which, reading equally well both ways, admonishes the reader to cleanse himself from sin, not less than to use the outward ceremony of baptism.

FONTANA, CARLO. See ARCHITECTS, list of, 266.

FONTANA, DOM. See ARCHITECTS, list of, 242.

FOOT. (Germ. fuss.) A measure of length, but used also in a sense which expresses surface and solidity. Thus we say, a foot *superficial* and a foot *cube*. As this term is used in almost all languages as a linear measure, it has doubtless been derived from the length of the human foot. It seems in all other countries, as in England, to be divided into twelve equal parts, or inches.

The English standard foot (31 Edw. 1.) is = 12 lineal English inches = 36 barleycorns = 16 digits = 4 palms = 3 hands = 5⅓ nails = 1⅓ spans = 1·5151 Gunter's links = ·938306 ft. of France = ·3047 met. of France. The foot is divided by geometricians into 10 digits, and each digit into 10 lines, &c. The French, as the English, divide the foot into 12 inches, and the inch into 12 lines. The foot square or superficial is a foot each way, and contains, therefore, 12 × 12 = 144 superficial inches = 2·295684 square links. The glazier's foot in Scotland = 64 square Scotch inches.

The length of the foot varies in different countries. The Paris royal foot exceeds that of England by 9½ lines. The ancient Roman foot of the Capitol consisted of 4 palms = 11 7⁄10 English inches. The Rhinland or Leyden foot, used by the northern nations of Europe, is to the Roman foot as 950 to 1000. The following table exhibits the length of the foot in the principal places of the Continent, the English foot being divided into 1000 parts, or 12 inches : —

Country.	Parts.	Ft.	In.	Lines.
London - - - - - - -	1000	0	12	0
Amsterdam - - - - - -	942	0	11	2
Antwerp - - - - - -	946	0	11	3
Bologna - - - - - -	1204	1	2	4
Bremen - - - - - -	964	0	11	6
Cologne - - - - - -	954	0	11	4
Copenhagen - - - - - -	965	0	11	6
Dantzic - - - - - -	944	0	11	3
Dort - - - - - - -	1184	1	2	2
Frankfort-on-the-Maine - - -	948	0	11	4
Lorrain - - - - - - -	958	0	11	5
Mantua - - - - - - -	1569	1	6	8
Mechlin - - - - - -	919	0	11	0
Middleburgh - - - - - -	991	0	11	9
Paris royal foot, according to Greaves - - -	1068	1	0	9·7
———— according to Bernard - -	1066	1	0	9·4
———— according to Graham, from the measure of half the toise of the Chatelet, the toise being six Paris feet - - - - - -	1065·416			
———— according to Mounier - - -	1065·351			
———— from the two last - - -	1065·4	1	0	9·4
Prague - - - - - - -	1026	1	0	3
Rhinland or Leyden - - - - -	1033	1	0	4
Riga - - - - - - -	1831	1	9	9
Rome - - - - - - -	967	0	11	6
Strasburg - - - - - -	920	0	11	0
Spanish - - - - - - -	1001	1	0	0
Toledo - - - - - - -	899	0	10	7
Turin - - - - - - -	1062	1	0	7
Venice - - - - - - -	1162	1	1	9
Greek - - - - - - -	1007	1	0	1
Old Roman, according to Greaves - - -	967	0	11	6
———— from the monument of Statilius - - - - - -	972	0	11	7

Mr. Raper (*Philos. Trans.* vol. li.), from various authorities, determines the mean of the Roman foot to be nearly 968 parts of the London foot ; and he considers that before the reign of Titus the Roman foot exceeded 970⁄1000 of the London foot, and afterwards, in

the reigns of Severus and Diocletian, it fell short of 965. Cagnazzi, from examination of the monuments of antiquity in Herculaneum and Pompeii, determines the Roman foot at ·29624 metre, which, the metre being 3·2808992 English feet, would make the old Roman foot $\frac{272}{1000}$ of the English foot.

The Scotch is to the English foot as 1·066 to 1·000, being, in fact, the French foot. See Measures.

Foot of the Eye Director. In perspective, that point in the directing line made by a vertical plane passing through the eye and the centre of the picture.

Foot of a Vertical Line. In perspective, that point in the intersecting line which is made by a vertical plane passing through the eye and the centre of the picture.

Foot Pace or Half Pace. That part of a staircase whereon, after the flight of a few steps, you arrive at a broad place on which you may take two or three paces before you come to another step. If it occur at the angle turns of the stairs, it is called a *quarter pace*.

Footing Beam. The name given, in some of the provinces, to the tie beam of a roof.

Footings of a Wall. The projecting courses at the base of a wall or building to spread the base, and give security to the wall.

Force. In mechanics, the course of motion in a body when it begins to move, or when it changes its direction from the course in which it was previously moving. While a body remains in the same state, whether of rest or of uniform and rectilinear motion, the cause of its so remaining is in the nature of the body, which principle has received the name of *inertia*. For the laws on the composition and resolution of forces, see p. 337, *et seq.*

Force Pump. See p. 661.

Forcer. In mechanics, a solid piston applied to pumps for the purpose of producing a constant stream, or of raising water to a greater height than it can be raised by the pressure of the atmosphere.

Fore Front. The principal or entrance front of a building.

Fore Plane. In carpentry and joinery, the first plane used after the saw or axe.

Foreshorten. In perspective, the diminution which the representation of the side or part of a body has, in one of its dimensions, compared with the other, occasioned by the obliquity of the corresponding side or part of the original body to the plane of projection.

Form. The external appearance or disposition of the surfaces of a body, in which sense it is synonymous with Figure, which see.

Forment. See Architects, list of, 221.

Forum. (Lat.) In ancient architecture, a public market; also a place where the common courts were held, and law pleadings carried on. The fora of the Romans were large open squares surrounded by porticoes, parts whereof answered for market-places, other parts for public meetings of the inhabitants, and other parts for courts of justice; the forum was also occasionally used for shows of gladiators. There were in Rome seventeen; of these fourteen were for the sale of goods, provisions, and merchandise, and called Fora Venalia; the other three were for civil and judicial proceedings, and called *Fora Civilia et Judicialia.* Of the latter sort was the forum of Trajan, of which the Trajan column formed the principal ornament.

Foundation. (Fr. Fondation.) The lower part of a wall on which an insistent wall is raised, than which, too, it is always much thicker. See Book II. Chap. III. Sect. 1.

Foundry. A building in which various metals are cast into moulds or shapes. See Book II. Chap. III. Sect. 11.

Fountain. (Lat. Fons.) Any natural or artificial apparatus by means whereof water springs up. In natural fountains the ascensional effect is produced by the hydrostatic pressure of the water itself; in artificial fountains, by the same sort of pressure, or by that of compressed air, and sometimes by machinery.

Fox Tail Wedging. A method of fixing a tenon in a mortise by splitting the end of the tenon and inserting a projecting wedge, then entering the tenon into the mortise, and driving it home. The bottom of the mortise resists the wedge, and forces it further into the tenon, which will expand in width, so as not only to fill the cavity at the bottom, but be firmly compressed by the sides of the mortise.

Frame and Framing. (Sax. Fpamman, to form.) The rough timber work of a house, including floors, roofs, partitions, ceilings, and beams. Generally, any pieces of wood fitted together with mortises and tenons are said to be framed, as doors, sash-frames, sashes. &c.

Franking. A term used by the makers of window-sashes, and applied to the mode of forming the joint when the cross-pieces of the frame intersect each other, no more wood being cut away than is sufficient to show a mitre.

Free Stone. Any stone which works freely, such as Portland stone, Bath stone, the limestones generally, &c.

Freeze. See Frieze.

French Architecture. See Book I. Chap. II. Sect. 17.

French Casements. Windows turning upon two vertical edges attached to the jambs, which, when shut, lap together upon the other two parallel edges, and are fastened by

means of long bolts extending their whole height. French casements are made in the form of the old English window, the two meeting styles, which lap together, forming a munnion about 4 inches in breadth. The lower part only is moveable, the upper being fixed, and having a corresponding munnion : the lower rail of the fixed part and the upper rail of the moveable part forming a transom.

FRESCO PAINTING. (It. Fresco, fresh.) A method of painting by incorporating the colours with plaster before it is dry, by which it becomes as permanent as the wall itself.

FRETTE or FRET. A species of ornament consisting of one or more small fillets meeting

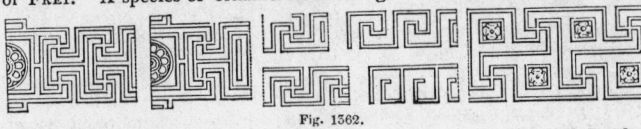

Fig. 1362.

in vertical and horizontal directions. (See *fig.* 1362.) The sections of the channels between the fillets is rectangular.

FRICTION. (Lat. Frico, I rub.) The resistance produced by the rubbing of the surfaces of two solid bodies against each other.

FRIEZE, FREEZE, or FRIZE. (Ital Fregio, adorned.) That member in the entablature of an order between the architrave and cornice. It is always plain in the Tuscan ; ornamented with triglyphs and sculpture in the Doric ; in the modern or Italian Ionic it is often swelled, in which case it is said to be *pulvinated* or *cushioned ;* and in the Corinthian and Composite it is variously decorated, according to the taste of the architect.

FRIEZE OF THE CAPITAL. The same as the HYPOTRACHELIUM, which see.

FRIEZE PANEL. The upper panel of a six-panelled door.

FRIEZE RAIL. The upper rail but one of a six-panelled door.

FRIGIDARIUM. In ancient architecture, the apartment in which the cold bath was placed. The word is sometimes used to denote the cold bath itself.

FRIZE or FRISE. See FRIEZE.

FRONT. (Lat. Frons.) Any side or face of a building, but more commonly used to denote the entrance side.

FRONTINUS. See ARCHITECTS, list of, 46.

FRONTISPIECE. (Lat. Frons and Inspicio.) The face or fore-front of a house, but the term is more usually applied to the decorated entrance of a building.

FRONTON. The French term for a pediment.

FROSTED. A species of rustic-work, imitative of ice, formed by irregular drops of water.

FROWCESTER. See ARCHITECTS, list of, 150.

FROWEY TIMBER. Such as works freely to the plane without tearing, whose grain therefore is in the same direction.

FRUSTUM. (Lat.) In geometry, the part of a solid next the base, formed by cutting off the top, or it is the part of any solid, as a cone, a pyramid, &c., between two planes, which may be either parallel or inclined to each other.

FUCCIO. See ARCHITECTS, list of, 122.

FUGA. See ARCHITECTS, list of, 295.

FULCRUM. (Lat.) In mechanics, the fixed point about which a lever moves.

FUNNEL. (Lat. Infundibulum.) That part of a chimney contained between the fire-place and the summit of the shaft. See CHIMNEY.

FURNACE. (Lat. Fornax.) An apparatus wherein is formed a cavity to contain combustible matter, which in various ways is supplied with air, to facilitate its combustion. The two classes into which furnaces are divided are air or wind furnaces and blast furnaces. In the former, the air is conducted through the fire by the draught of a funnel or chimney communicating with it ; in the latter, the action of bellows, or some other pneumatic apparatus, supplies the air. The word furnace has generally, however, a more circumscribed application, being applied usually to an apparatus for the fusion of metals, or to that used in a chemical laboratory.

FURNITURE. (Fr. Fournir, to furnish.) The visible brass work of locks, knobs to doors, window-shutters, and the like.

FURRING. (Fr. Fourrer, to thrust in.) The fixing of thin scantlings or laths upon the edges of any number of timbers in a range, when such timbers are out of the surface they were intended to form, either from their gravity, or in consequence of an original deficiency of the timbers in their depth. Thus the timbers of a floor, though level at first, often-times require to be furred ; the same operation is frequently necessary in the reparation of old roofs, and the same work is required sometimes in new as well as old floors.

FURRINGS. The pieces of timber employed in bringing any piece of work in carpentry to a regular surface when the work is uneven, either through the sagging of the timber or other causes.

FUSAROLE. (It.) A member whose section is that of a semicircle carved into beads. It is

generally placed under the echinus, or quarter round of columns in the Doric, Ionic, and Corinthian orders.

FUSSITIUS. See ARCHITECTS, list of, 39.

FUST. (Fr. Fût.) The shaft of a column or trunk of a pilaster.

FUST. A term used in Devonshire, and, perhaps, in some other counties, to signify the ridge of a house.

G.

GABLE. (Brit. Gavel.) The vertical triangular piece of wall at the end of a roof, from the level of the eaves to the summit.

GABRIEL, J. A. See ARCHITECTS, list of, 297.

GABRIEL, JACQUES. See ARCHITECTS, list of, 277.

GAGE, or GAUGE. (Sax. Læᵹᵹian, to bind or confine.) In carpentry or joinery, an instrument for drawing one or more lines on any side of a piece of stuff parallel to one of the arrisses of that side. Of this tool there are four sorts; the common gage and the flooring gage (which are both applied to the drawing of a line parallel to an arris), the internal gage, and the mortise and tenon gage.

This term is also used to signify the length of a slate or tile below the lap; also the measure to which any substance is confined. It is, moreover, used by plasterers to signify a greater or less quantity of plaster of Paris used with common plaster to accelerate its setting.

GAIN. In carpentry, the bevelled shoulder of a binding joist, for the purpose of giving additional resistance to the tenon below.

GAINSBOROUGH. See ARCHITECTS, list of, 145.

GAINZA. See ARCHITECTS, list of, 222.

GALILEE. A porch usually built near the west end of abbey churches, where the monks collected in returning from processions, where bodies were laid previous to interment, and where females were allowed to see the monks to whom they were related, or to hear divine service. The galilees of Durham and Ely are found in the situation here described. The former is highly ornamented, and is eighty by fifty feet, and divided into five aisles by clustered columns and semicircular arches. The date of its erection was towards the end of the twelfth century. That of Ely Cathedral is much smaller. It is still used as the principal entrance to the church, and is without columns or other internal support. The porch at the south end of the great transept at Lincoln Cathedral is also sometimes called a galilee. The word has been frequently used, but improperly, to designate the nave of a church. Many conjectures have been made on the origin of this term, but the most commonly received opinion, founded on a passage in the writings of St. Gervase of Canterbury, is, that when a female applied to see a monk, she was directed to the porch of the church, and answered in the words of Scripture, " He goeth before you into Galilee, there shall you see him."

GALILEI. See ARCHITECTS, list of, 275.

GALLERY. (Fr. Galerie.) An apartment of a house, for different purposes. A common passage to several rooms in any upper story is called a gallery. A long room for the reception of pictures is called a picture gallery. The platform on piers, or projecting from the wall of a church and open in front to the central space is also called a gallery. The Whispering Gallery at St. Paul's is another example of the various uses of the word. The whole or a portion of the uppermost story of a theatre is likewise called a gallery. The term is, moreover, used to denote porticoes formed with long ranges of columns on one side.

GALLI. See ARCHITECTS, list of, 276.

GANDON. See ARCHITECTS, list of, 315.

GAOL. A prison, or place of legal confinement. See Book III. Chap. V: Sect. 18.

GARDEN SHEDS. Erections for containing garden implements, flower-pots, hot-bed frames, and glass sashes, &c.; also for working in during bad weather. They are best placed on the back wall of the tool-house, and thus hold the furnaces, fuel, and other articles.

GARLANDS. (FI.) Ornaments of flowers, fruit, and leaves anciently used at the gates of temples where feasts or solemn rejoicings were held.

GARNETS, CROSS. A species of hinge used in the most common works, formed in the shape of the letter T turned thus ⊢, the vertical part being fastened to the style or jamb of the doorcase, and the horizontal part to the door or shutter.

GARRET. The upper story of a house taken either partially or wholly from the space within the roof.

GATE. (Sax. Leat.) A large door, generally framed of wood. The width of gates should be from eight and a half to nine feet, and the height from five to eight feet. The materials of gates should be well seasoned previous to use, otherwise they will be soon injured by the sun and wind. The parts should be also very correctly put together. For durability,

oak is the best; but some of the lighter woods, as deal, willow, and alder, are, on account of their lightness, occasionally used. These, however, are more for field-bar gates than close gates.

GAUGE. See GAGE.

GAVEL. The same as GABLE, which see.

GATHERING OF THE WINGS. See CHIMNEY.

GENERATING CURVE. See EVOLUTE.

GENERATING LINE or PLANE. In geometry, a line or plane which moves according to a given law, either round one of its extremities as a fixed point or axis, or parallel to itself, in order to generate a plane figure, or solid, formed by the space it has gone over.

GENESIS. (Gr.) In geometry, the formation of a line, plane, or solid, by the motion of a point, line, or plane. See GENERATING LINE.

GENGA. See ARCHITECTS, list of, 212.

GEOMETRICAL. That which has a relation to geometry.

GEOMETRICAL STAIRCASE. That in which the flight of stairs is supported by the wall at one end of the steps.

GEOMETRY. (Gr. Γη, the earth, and Μετρω, I measure.) That science which treats of the objects of figured space. Its etymology implies the object of measuring land, that, as it is said, being its first application in Egypt, where it is pretended to have been invented, for ascertaining the landmarks after the yearly recession of the inundations of the Nile, in order to mark the proper allotment of each owner. Whatever the origin, however, of the term, the occasions on which it is necessary to compare things with one another in respect of their forms and magnitudes are so numerous in every stage of society, that a geometry more or less perfect must have existed from the first periods of civilisation. See Book II. Chap. I. Sect. 1.

GEOMETRY, DESCRIPTIVE. The art of representing a definite body upon two planes at right angles with each other, by lines falling perpendicularly to the planes from all the points of concourse of every two contiguous sides of the body, and from all points of its contour, and, *vice versâ*, from a given representation to ascertain the parts of the original objects. See Book II. Chap. I. Sect. 5.

GEOMETRY, PRACTICAL. See Book. II. Chap. I. Sect. 2.

GERMAIN, ST. See ARCHITECTS, list of, 57.

GIBBS, J. See ARCHITECTS, list of, 281.

GIBBS, W. See ARCHITECTS, list of, 188.

GIBLEA CHEQUE. A term used by Scotch masons to denote the cutting away of the right angle formed by the front and returns of the aperture of a stone door-case, in the form of a rebate or reveal, so as to make the outer side of the door or closure flush with the face of the wall.

GILDING. The practice of laying gold leaf on any surface. See Book II. Chap. III. Sect. 12.

GILL. A measure equal to one fourth of a pint.

GIMBALS, GIMBOLS, or GIMBLES. (Lat. Gemellus.) A piece of mechanism consisting of two brass hoops or rings which move within one another, each perpendicularly to its plane, about two axes at right angles to each other. A body suspended in this manner, having a free motion in two directions at right angles, assumes a constantly vertical position.

GIMLET, or perhaps more properly GIMBLET. (Fr. Guimbelet.) A piece of steel of a semi-cylindrical form, hollow on one side, having a cross handle at one end and a worm or screw at the other. Its use is to bore a hole in a piece of wood. The screw draws the instrument into the wood when turned by the handle, and the excavated part, forming a sharp angle with the exterior, cuts the fibres across, and contains the core of the wood cut out.

GIOCONDO. See ARCHITECTS, list of, 182.

GIORGIO, DI. See ARCHITECTS, list of, 161.

GIOVAN BAPTISTA DI TOLEDO. See ARCHITECTS, list of, 234.

GIOVANNI DA PISA. See ARCHITECTS, list of, 129.

GIRDER. (Sax. Lýnðan, to enclose.) The principal beam in a floor, for supporting the binding or other joists, whereby the bearing or length is lessened. Perhaps so called because the ends of the joists are enclosed by it.

GIRDLE. A circular band or fillet surrounding a part of a column.

GIRT. The length of the circumference of an object, whether rectilinear or curvilinear, on its horizontal section. In timber measuring, according to some, is taken at one fourth of the circumference of the tree, and is so taken for the side of a square equal in area to the section of the tree cut through, where the perimeter is taken in order to obtain the girt.

GLASS. (Germ.) A transparent, impermeable, and brittle substance, whereof the different sorts used in building are described, Book II. Chap. II. Sect. 12.

GLASS PAINTING. A decoration frequently used in buildings, is the method of staining

glass in such a manner as to produce the effect of representing all the subjects whereof the art is susceptible. A French painter of Marseilles is said to have been the first who instructed the Italians in this art, during the pontificate of Julius II. It was, however, practised to a considerable extent by Lucas of Leyden and Albert Durer. The different colours are prepared as follows: — *Black* is produced by two thirds of iron scales or flakes, and the other third of small glass beads, or a substance called *roccagliu* by the Italians. *White* is prepared for by sand or small white pebbles calcined, pounded, and then finely ground. One fourth part of saltpetre is added, and the mixture is then again calcined and pulverised, to which a little gypsum or plaster of Paris is added. *Yellow* is formed from leaf silver, ground and mixed in a crucible with saltpetre or sulphur; then ground on a porphyry stone, and lastly, again ground with nine times the quantity of red ochre. *Red*, one of the most difficult of the colours to make, is prepared from litharge of silver and iron scales, gum Arabic, ferretta, glass beads, and bloodstone, in nearly equal quantities. Great experience is necessary to succeed in making this colour. *Green* is produced from os ustum one ounce, the same quantity of black lead, and four ounces of white lead, incorporated by the action of fire. When calcined, a fourth part of saltpetre is added, and, after a second calcination, a sixth more; after which a third coction is made before using it. *Azure, purple*, and *violet* are prepared in a similar manner to green, omitting the os ustum, and in its stead using sulphur for azure, perigueux for purple, and both these drugs for violet. *Carnations*, which are compounded colours, are calcined, and usually mixed with water. They must be finished part by part, and each with great dispatch, before the plaster dries, for there is little opportunity for blending. The lights cannot be heightened, but the shadows may, when they begin to dry, be a little strengthened. Promptitude and facility in execution are the great requisites for this method of painting.

GLASS PLATE. Glass cast in plates and polished. See p. 544.

The following is the Tariff of the Thames Plate Glass Company, Savoy Wharf, Strand, for Glass, since 1845, when the Duty was taken off: —

Feet Super.	£	s.	d.	Feet Super.	£	s.	d.	Feet Super.	£	s.	d.
1	0	3	4	31	26	2	5	61	75	6	11
2	0	8	2	32	27	8	8	62	77	5	4
3	0	15	5	33	28	13	3	63	79	4	4
4	1	3	11	34	30	0	8	64	81	3	8
5	1	12	5	35	31	11	4	65	82	18	8
6	2	1	3	36	33	0	0	66	85	3	9
7	2	12	2	37	34	9	3	67	87	4	5
8	3	3	0	38	35	16	4	68	89	0	7
9	3	12	11	39	37	6	9	69	91	2	1
10	4	3	4	40	38	17	9	70	93	4	0
11	4	17	4	41	40	9	4	71	95	4	2
12	5	13	4	42	41	18	5	72	97	7	7
13	6	8	6	43	43	11	1	73	99	7	6
14	7	4	9	44	45	4	5	74	101	10	11
15	8	2	9	45	46	18	4	75	103	14	4
16	9	0	9	46	48	9	5	76	135	0	0
17	9	19	7	47	50	4	5	77	137	15	0
18	10	18	0	48	51	16	6	78	140	10	0
19	11	18	7	49	53	8	10	79	143	5	0
20	12	18	6	50	55	5	6	80	146	0	0
21	13	19	3	51	56	19	0	81	148	15	0
22	15	0	8	52	58	12	10	82	151	10	0
23	16	2	10	53	60	11	1	83	154	5	0
24	17	5	10	54	62	6	0	84	157	0	0
25	18	9	5	55	64	1	3	85	159	15	0
26	19	13	10	56	65	17	0	86	162	10	0
27	20	19	0	57	67	17	5	87	165	5	0
28	22	2	9	58	69	14	2	88	168	0	0
29	23	9	4	59	71	11	3	89	170	15	0
30	24	14	5	60	73	4	5	90	173	10	0

The above are the prices for glazing glass. For glass to be silvered, the prices are somewhat higher. The cost of silvering is 12½ per cent. under 50l. value, and 20 per cent. above that value.

GLAZIER. An artisan whose employment is that of fitting and fixing the glass employed in a building. See Book II. Chap. III. Sect. 8.

GLUE. (from the Lat. Gluten.) A tenacious viscid matter made of the skins and hoofs of animals, for cementing two bodies together. Glue is bought in cakes, and is better the older the skin of the animal from which it is made. That which swells without dissolving when steeped in water is the best. To prepare glue it should be broken into small fragments and then steeped in water about twelve hours. It should be then heated in a leaden or copper vessel till the whole is dissolved, stirring it frequently with a stick. After this it is put into a wooden vessel and remains for use. Good glue for external work is made by grinding as much white lead with linseed oil as will just make the liquid of a whitish colour, and strong but not thick.

Glyph. (Gr. Γλυφω, I carve.) A sunken channel, the term being usually employed in reference to a vertical one. From their number, those in the Doric order are called triglyphs.

Glyptotheca. (Gr. Γλυφω, and Θηκη, deposit.) A building or room for the preservation of works of sculpture.

Gneiss. A species of granite which, from excess of mica, is generally of a lamellar or slaty texture. It is a term used by the miners of Germany.

Gnomon. (Gr. Γνωμων.) An instrument for measuring shadows, and thereby determining the sun's height. In dialling, it is the style of the dial, and its shadow marks the hour. It is placed so that its straight edge is parallel to the axis of the earth's rotation. In geometry, a gnomon is that part of a parallelogram which remains when one of the parallelograms about its diagonal is removed; or the portion of the parallelogram composed of the two complements and one of the parallelograms about the diagonal. The term is found in Euclid, but is now rarely used.

Gocciolatoio. The same as Corona, which see.

Gola, or Gula. (It.) The same as Cyma, which see.

Goldcliff. See Architects, list of, 102.

Gondouin. See Architects, list of, 312.

Goniometer. (Gr. Γωνια, an angle, and Μετρω, I measure.) An instrument for measuring solid angles.

Gonsalvo. See Architects, list of, 118.

Gorge. The same as Cavetto, which see. The *gorgerin* is a diminutive of the term.

Gorgoneia. (Gr.) Key-stones carved with Gorgons' heads.

Gothic Architecture. See Book I. Chap. II. Sect. 15 ; Book I. Chap. III. Sects. 2, 3, 4, and 5 ; and Book I. Chap. IV.

Goufing Foundations. A Scotch term, signifying a mode of securing unsound walls by driving wedges or pins under their foundations.

Gouge. A chisel whose section is of a semicircular form.

Government Offices. See Book III. Chap. V. Sect. 5.

Gradetti. The same as Annulets, which see.

Græcostasis. A hall or portico adjoining the Roman comitia, in which foreign ambassadors waited before entering the senate, and also whilst waiting the answer that was to be given to them.

Grain. In wood or stone, is the line of direction in which either may be split transversely.

Granary. (Lat. Granum.) A building for storing corn, especially that intended to be kept for a considerable time. Vitruvius calls those buildings intended for the preservation of grain, *granaria*, those for hay *fœnilia*, and those for straw *farraria*. The term *horreum* was used by the Romans for denoting buildings not only for the preservation of corn, but for various other effects.

Grand. A term used in the fine arts, generally to express that quality by which the highest degree of majesty and dignity is imparted to a work of art. Its source is, in form, freed from ordinary and common bounds, and to be properly appreciated requires an investigation of the different qualities by which great and extraordinary objects produce impressions on the mind.

Grange. A farm-yard or farmery, consisting of a farm-house and a court of offices for the different animals and implements used in farming, as also of barns, feeding houses, poultry houses, &c.

Granite. See Book II. Chap. II. Sect. 2.

Graticulation. The division of a design or draught into squares, for the purpose of reducing it to smaller dimensions.

Gravel. A term applied to a well-known material of small stones, varying in size from a pea to a walnut, or something larger. It is often intermixed with other substances, as sand, clay, loam, flints, pebbles, iron ore, &c.

Gravity. See Specific Gravity.

Grecian Architecture. See Book I. Chap. II. Sect. 11.

Greek Cross. See Cross.

Greek Masonry. The manner of bonding walls among the Grecians. See Masonry.

Greenhouse. A building for sheltering in pots plants which are too tender to endure the open air the greater part of the year. It is constructed with a roof and one or more sides of glass, and being one constructed for luxury should not be far away from the dwelling-house, so that the greatest enjoyment may be had from it. At the same time it should, if possible, be near the flower-garden, as being of similar character in use. The length and breadth can only be determined by the wealth and objects of the proprietor. The best aspects are south and south east, but any aspect may, in case of necessity, be taken, if the roof be entirely of glass, and plenty of artificial heat be supplied. In those greenhouses, however, which face the north, the tender plants do not in winter succeed

so well, and a greater quantity of artificial heat must then be supplied, and the plants should, in such case, be chiefly evergreens, and others that come into flower in the summer season, and grow and flower but little during the winter. The plants in greenhouses are kept in pots or boxes on stages or shelves, so as to be near and follow the slope of the roof, and thus made more susceptible of the action of the sun's rays immediately on passing through the glass.

An orangery, from being constructed with a ceiled roof, differs from a greenhouse; it is, moreover, chiefly devoted to plants producing their shoots and flowers in the summer season, and in the open air; the use of the orangery being merely to preserve them during the winter. The structure is more properly called a conservatory, though this term is now applied to buildings with glass roofs, wherein the plants are not kept in pots, but planted in the free soil, and wherein some are so reared as to grow and flower in the winter months.

GREY STOCKS. Bricks of the third quality of the best or malm bricks. See Book II. Chap. II. Sect. 10.

GRINDING. The act of taking off the redundant parts of a body, and forming it to its destined surface.

GRINDSTONE. A cylindrical stone, mounted on a spindle through its axis, with a winch-handle for turning it, to grind edge-tools.

GRIT STONE. One of various degrees of hardness; mostly of a grey, sometimes of a yellowish, colour. It is composed of a siliceous and micaceous sand, closely compacted by an argillaceous cement. It gives some sparks with steel, is indissoluble, or nearly so, in acids, and vitrifiable in a strong fire. It is used for millstones more than for building.

GROIN. (Sax. Lʃopʒn, to grow.) The line formed by the intersection of two arches, which cross each other at any angle. See CROSS VAULTING, and Book II. Chap. I. Sect. 8.

GROINED CEILING. One formed by three or more curved surfaces, so that every two may form a groin, all the groins terminating at one extremity in a common point.

GROOVE. (Sax. Lʃaʃan, to dig.) A sunken rectangular channel. It is usually employed to connect two pieces of wood together, the piece not grooved having on its edge a projection or *tongue*, whose section corresponds to and fits the groove.

GROTESQUE. (Fr.) A term applied to capricious ornaments which, as a whole, have no type in nature, consisting of figures, animals, leaves, flowers, fruits, and the like, all connected together.

GROUND JOISTS. Those which rest upon sleepers laid upon the ground, or on bricks, prop stones, or dwarf walls; they are only used in basement and ground floors.

GROUND LINE. In perspective, the intersection of the picture with the ground plane. See GROUND PLANE.

GROUND NICHE. One whose base or seat is on a level with the ground floor.

GROUND PLAN. The plan of the story of a house level with the surface of the ground, or a few steps above it. It is not always the lowest floor, the basement being frequently beneath it.

GROUND PLANE. In perspective the situation of the original plane in the supposed level of our horizon. It differs from the horizontal plane, which is said of any plane parallel to the horizon; whereas the ground plane is a tangent plane to the surface of the earth, and is supposed to contain the objects to be represented. The term *ground* plane is used in a more confined sense than that of original plane, which may be any plane, whether horizontal or inclined.

GROUND PLATE or GROUND SILL. The lowest horizontal timber on which the exterior walls of a building are erected. It chiefly occurs in timber buildings, or in buildings whose outside walls are formed of brick panels with timber framings.

GROUND PLOT. The plan of the walls of a building where they first commence above the foundation, though more properly it is the piece of ground selected to receive the building. For dwellings, its chief requisites are a healthy situation, a convenient supply of water, good drainage, a pleasant aspect, &c. If for trade or manufacture, it should be conveniently placed for receiving the raw material, and for exporting the articles manufactured.

GROUNDS. In joinery, certain pieces of wood attached to a wall, to which the finishings are fastened. Their surface is flush with the plastering. Narrow grounds are those whereto the bases and surbases of rooms are fastened. Grounds are used over apertures, as well for securing the architraves as for strengthening the plaster. That the plaster may be kept firm, should the wood shrink, a groove is sometimes run on the edge of the ground next to the plaster, or the edge of the ground is rebated on the side next to the wall, so that in the act of plastering the stuff is received into the groove or rebate, which prevents it from shifting when it becomes dry.

GROUPED COLUMNS or PILASTERS. A term used to denote three, four, or more columns placed upon the same pedestals. When two only are placed together they are said to be coupled.

GROUT. (Sax. Lɲuꞇ.) A thin semi-liquid mortar, composed of quicklime and fine sand, prepared and poured into the joints of masonry and brickwork, which process is called *grouting*.

GROWING SHORE. See DEAD SHORE.

GUDGEON. The axle of a wheel, on which it turns and is supported. To diminish friction gudgeons are made as small as possible in diameter, consistent with their weight. They are often made of cast iron, on account of its cheapness, but wrought iron of the same dimensions is stronger, and will support a greater load.

GUEULE. A term synonymous with CYMATIUM.

GUILLOCHE. (Fr.) An ornament in the form of two or more bands or strings twisting over each other, so as to repeat the same figure, in a continued series, by the spiral returning of the bands. The term is applied but improperly to FRETS.

GULA. Synonymous with CYMATIUM, which see.

GULIELMO. See ARCHITECTS, list of, 99.

GUNDULPH. See ARCHITECTS, list of, 87.

GUNTER'S CHAIN. One used for measuring land, and taking its name from its reputed inventor. It is 66 feet, or 4 poles, long, and divided into 100 links, each whereof is joined to the adjacent one by three rings; the length of each link, including the adjacent rings, is therefore 7·92 inches. The advantage of the measure is in the facility it affords to numerical calculation. Thus the English acre, containing 4840 yards, and Gunter's chain being 22 yards long, it follows that a square chain is exactly the tenth part of an acre, consequently the contents of a field being cast up in square links, it is only necessary to divide by 100,000, or to cut off the last five figures, to obtain the contents expressed in acres.

GUTTÆ. See DROPS.

GUTTERS and GUTTERING. Canals to the roofs of houses to receive and carry off rain-water. They are made either of lead or of tiles, which are either plain or concave; these last are called gutter tiles, and so adapted to each other as to be laid with great ease. The Romans had gutters of terra cotta along the roofs of their houses, and the rain-water from them ran out through the heads of animals and other devices placed in the angles and in convenient parts. Leaden gutters were known in the middle ages.

GYMNASIUM. (Gr. Γυμνασιον, from Γυμνος, naked.) Originally a space measured out and covered with sand for the exercise of athletic games. The gymnasia in the end became spacious buildings, or institutions, for the mental as well as corporeal instruction of youth. They were first erected at Lacedæmon, whence they spread, through the rest of Greece, into Italy. They did not consist of single edifices, but comprised several buildings and porticoes for study and discourse, for baths, anointing rooms, palæstras, in which the exercises took place, and for other purposes.

GYNÆCEUM. (Gr. Γυναικειον.) In ancient architecture, that portion of the Grecian house set apart for the occupation of the female part of the family.

GYPSUM. (Probably from Γη, earth, and Εψω, I concoct.) Crystals of native sulphate of lime. Being subjected to a moderate heat, to expel the water of crystallisation, it forms plaster of Paris, and, coming in contact with water, immediately assumes a solid form. Of the numerous species, alabaster is, perhaps, the most abundant.

H.

HACKS. In brickmaking (see p. 525.) the rows in which bricks are laid to dry after being moulded.

HACKING. In walling, denotes the interruption of a course of stones, by the introduction of another on a different level, for want of stones to complete the thickness. Thus making two courses at the end of a wall of the same height as one at the other. The last stone laid is often notched to receive the first stone of the other where the two heights commence. Hacking is never permitted in good work. The term is used more in Scotland than in England.

HALF PACE. See FOOT PACE.

HALF ROUND. A semicircular moulding, which may be a bead or torus.

HALL. (Sax. Hal.) A name applied indifferently to the first large apartment on entering a house, to the public room of a corporate body, a court of justice, or to a manor house.

Vitruvius mentions three sorts of halls: the Tetrastyle, which has four columns supporting the ceiling; the Corinthian, which has columns all round, and is vaulted; and the Egyptian, which has a peristyle of Corinthian columns, bearing a second order with a ceiling. These were called œci. In magnificent edifices, where the hall is larger and loftier than ordinary, and is placed in the middle of the house, it is called a saloon; and a royal apartment consists of a hall or chamber of guards, a chamber, an anti-chamber, a cabinet chamber, and a gallery.

HALVING. A method of joining timbers by letting them into each other. It is preferable to mortising, even where the timbers do not pass each other, as they are less liable to be displaced by shrinking.

HAM. (Sax.) Properly a house or dwelling place; also a street or village, whence it has become the final syllable to many of our towns, as Nottingham, Buckingham, &c.; hence, too, hamlet, the diminutive of ham, is a small street or village.

HAMMER BEAM. A beam acting as a tie at the feet of a pair of principal rafters, but not extending so as to connect the opposite sides. Hammer beams are used chiefly in roofs constructed after the Gothic style, the end which hangs over, being frequently supported by a concave rib springing from the wall, as a tangent from a curve, and in its turn supporting another rib, forming an arch. The ends of hammer beams are often decorated with beads and other devices.

HAND-RAIL OF A STAIR. A rail raised upon slender posts, called balusters, to prevent persons falling down the well hole, as also to assist them in ascending and descending.

HANDSPIKE. A lever for raising a weight, usually of wood, and applied to the holes in a capstan head.

HANG OVER. (Verb.) A term used to denote the condition of a wall when the top projects beyond the bottom.

HANGINGS. Linings for rooms of arras, tapestry, paper, or the like. Paper hangings were introduced early in the seventeenth century.

HANGING STILE OF A DOOR. That to which the hinges are attached.

HARLEWIN. See ARCHITECTS, list of, 85.

HARMONICAL PROPORTION. That which, in a series of quantities, any three adjoining terms being taken, the difference between the first and second is to the difference between the second and third, as the first is to the third.

HARMUS. (Gr. Ἁρμος.) In ancient architecture, a tile used for covering the joint between two common tiles.

HARNESS ROOM. A room wherein harness is deposited. It is absolutely requisite that it be dry and kept clean. Its situation should be near the stable it is destined to serve.

HASSACK. The provincial name for Kentish rag stone.

HATCHET. (Fr. Hachette.) A small axe used by joiners for reducing the edges of boards.

HAUNCHES OF AN ARCH. The parts between the crown and the springing.

HAWK. A small quadrangular tool with a handle, used by a plasterer, on which the stuff required by him is served, for his proceeding with the work in progress. He has always a boy attendant on him, by whom he is supplied with the material. The boy in question is called a Hawk-boy.

HAWKSMOOR. See ARCHITECTS, list of, 273.

HEAD. See APERTURE.

HEAD JERKIN. See JERKIN.

HEADERS. In masonry, stones extending over the thickness of a wall; and in brick-laying, the bricks which are laid lengthwise across the thickness of the wall are called headers.

HEADING COURSE. In brickwork and masonry, that in which the length of the stone or brick is across the thickness of the wall.

HEADING JOINT. In joinery, the joint of two or more boards at right angles to the fibres, or in handrailing at right angles to the back; this is so disposed with a view of continuing the length of the board when too short. In good work the heading joints are ploughed and tongued, and in dadoes are, moreover, connected with glue.

HEADWAY OF STAIRS. The clear distance, measured perpendicularly, from a given landing-place or stair to the ceiling above, allowing for the thickness of the steps.

HEADWORK. A name by which the heads and other ornaments on the keystones of arches is frequently designated.

HEART BOND. In masonry, that in which two stones of a wall forming its breadth, have one stone of the whole breadth placed over them. See BOND.

HEARTH. See CHIMNEY.

HEATHER ROOF. A covering used in Scotland, by some considered superior to straw.

HEBREW ARCHITECTURE. See Book I. Chap. II. Sect. 6.

HECATOMPEDON. (Gr.) A temple of a hundred feet in length. As applied to the Parthenon, for discovering the true length of the Greek foot. Stuart took considerable pains in the measurement of that temple. The results, (which can now be compared with those taken by Mr. Penrose,) as published by Reveley, are as follow:—

	Eng. Inches.
Length of the upper step, in front of the temple, gives for one foot -	12·139
From outside to outside of the angular columns - - -	12·095
From centre to centre of the front columns - - -	12·0982
Length of the architrave - - - - -	12·0625

HEEK. The same as RACK.

HEEL. A term used by workmen to denote a *cyma reversa.*

HEEL OF A RAFTER. The end or foot that rests on the wall plate.

HEIGHT. The perpendicular distance of the most remote part of a body from the plane on which it rests.

HEIGHT OF AN ARCH. A line drawn from the middle of the chord or span to the intrados.

HELICAL LINE OF A HANDRAIL. The spiral line twisting round the cylinder, representing the form of the handrail before it is moulded.

HELIOCAMINUS. (Gr. 'Ηλιος, the sun, and Καμινος, a furnace.) A chamber in the Roman houses which depended on the rays of the sun for warming it.

HELIX. (Gr. "Ηλιξ, a kind of ivy whose stalk curls.) A small volute or twist under the abacus of the Corinthian capital, in which there are, in every perfect capital, sixteen, called also *urillæ;* viz. two at each angle, and two meeting under the middle of the abacus, branching out of the caulicoli or stalks, which rise from between the leaves.

HELPSTONE. See ARCHITECTS, list of, 135.

HEM. The spiral projecting part of the Ionic capital.

HEMICYCLE. A semicircle ; the term is used architecturally to denote vaults of the cradle form, and arches or sweeps of vaults, constituting a semicircle.

HEMISTHERE. In geometry, the half of a globe or sphere, when divided by a plane passing through its centre.

HEMITRIGLYPH. A half triglyph.

HENRY OF BLOIS. See ARCHITECTS, list of, 92.

HENRY LATOMUS. See ARCHITECTS, list of, 134.

HEPTAGON. (Gr.) A geometrical figure of seven sides and angles.

HERMITAGE. A small hut or dwelling in an unfrequented place, occupied by a hermit.

HERMODORUS. See ARCHITECTS, list of, 30.

HERMOGENES. See ARCHITECTS, list of, 2.

HERRERA. See ARCHITECTS, list of, 236.

HERRING BONE WORK. A disposition of bricks or stones laid diagonally (see diagram in the margin), each length receiving the end of the adjoining brick or stone. See ASHLAR.

HEWN STONE. That which is reduced to a given form by the use of the mallet and chisel.

HEXAEDRON or CUBE. (Gr. 'Εξ, six, and 'Εδρα, seat.) One of the five regular solids, so called from its having six faces or seats.

HEXAGON. ('Εξ and Γωνια, angle.) In geometry, a plain figure bounded by six straight lines, which, when equal, constitute the figure a regular hexagon.

HEXASTYLE. (Gr. 'Εξ and Στυλος, column.) That species of temple or building having six columns in front. See COLONNADE.

HICK-JOINT POINTING. That species of pointing in which, after the joints are raked out, a portion of superior mortar is inserted between the courses, and made perfectly smooth with the surface. See POINTING.

HIEROGLYPHICS. ('Ιερος, sacred, and Γλυφω, I engrave.) Sculpture or picture writing, which has obtained the name from being most commonly found on sacred buildings. They consist in the expression of a series of ideas by representations of visible objects. The name is, however, more particularly applied to a species of writing used by the ancient Egyptians, which, according to Champollion, was of three different varieties of characters : — 1. The hieroglyphic, properly so called, wherein the representation of the object conveys the idea of the object itself. 2. That in which the characters represent ideas by images of visible objects used as symbols. 3. That consisting of *phonetic characters*, in which the sign does not represent an object but a sound.

HINDOO ARCHITECTURE. See INDIAN ARCHITECTURE, Book I. Chap. II. Sect. 6.

HINGES (from Hang). The metal joints upon which any body turns, such as doors, shutters, &c. There are many species of hinges, which are described in Book II. Chap. III. Sect. 5.

HIP. A piece of timber placed between every two adjacent inclined sides of a hip roof, for the purpose of receiving what are called the jack rafters.

HIP MOULD. A term used by some workmen to denote the back of the hip ; by others it is used to signify the form or pattern by which the hip is set out.

HIP or HIPPED ROOF. A roof whose return at the end of a building rises immediately from the wall plate with the same inclination as the adjacent sides. The back of a hip is the angle made on its upper edge, to range with the two sides or planes of the roof, between which it is placed. The *jack rafters* are those short rafters which are shorter than the full-sized ones to fill in against the hips.

HIP or CORNER TILES are those used at the hips of roofs ; they are ten inches long, and of appropriate breadth and thickness, and bent on a mould before burning.

HIPPODROME. (Gr. 'Ιππος, a horse, and Δοομος, a course.) In ancient architecture, a place

appropriated by the Greeks to equestrian exercises, and one in which the prizes were contended for. The most celebrated of these was at Olympia. It was four stadia (each 625 feet) long, and one stadium in breadth.

HOARD. (Sax. Hopᵭ, to keep.) A timber enclosure round a building, in the course of erection or under repair.

HOD. An utensil employed by labourers for carrying mortar or bricks.

HOLDFAST. A long nail, with a flat short head for securing objects to a wall.

HOLLAND. See ARCHITECTS, list of, 307.

HOLLOW. A concave moulding, whose section is about the quadrant of a circle; called, sometimes, by the workmen a *casement*.

HOLLOW NEWEL. An opening in the middle of a staircase. The term is used in contradistinction to solid newel, into which the ends of the steps are built. In the hollow newel, or well hole, the steps are only supported at one end by the surrounding wall of the staircase, the ends next the hollow being unsupported.

HOLLOW QUOINS. Piers of brick or stone made behind the lock gates of canals.

HOLLOW WALL. One built in two thicknesses, leaving a cavity between them for the purpose of saving materials, or for preserving an uniform temperature in an apartment.

HOMESTALL. A mansion house, or seat in the country.

HOMOLOGOUS. In geometry, the correspondent sides of similar figures. The areas and solid contents of such figures are likewise homologous.

HONTANON, GIOV. GIL. DE. See ARCHITECTS, list of, 205.

HONTANON, RODERIGO, GIL DE. See ARCHITECTS, list of, 208.

HOO. See ARCHITECTS, list of, 114.

HOOK. (Sax. Hoce.) A bent piece of iron, used to fasten bodies together, or whereon to hang any article. They are of various kinds.

HOOKE. See ARCHITECTS, list of, 265.

HOOKPINS. The same as DRAW BOREPINS, which see.

HORIZONTAL CORNICE. The level part of the cornice of a pediment under the two inclined cornices.

HORIZONTAL LINE. In perspective, the vanishing line of planes parallel to the horizon.

HORIZONTAL PLANE. A plane passing through the eye parallel to the horizon, and producing the vanishing line of all level planes.

HORIZONTAL PROJECTION. The projection made on a plane parallel to the horizon. This may be understood perspectively, or orthographically, according as the projecting rays are directed to a given point, or perpendicular to a given point.

HORN. A name sometimes given to the Ionic volute.

HORREUM. See GRANARY.

HORSE BLOCK. A square frame of strong boards, used by excavators to elevate the ends of their wheeling planks.

HORSE RUN. A contrivance for drawing up loaded wheelbarrows of soil from the deep cuttings of foundations, canals, docks, &c., by the help of a horse, which goes backwards and forwards instead of round, as in a *horse-gin*.

HORSESHOE ARCH. See p. 55.

HORWOOD. See ARCHITECTS, list of, 152.

HOSPITAL. See Book III. Chap. V. Sect. 17.

HOSTEL or HOTEL. (Fr.) Among us this word is used to denote a large inn, or place of public entertainment; but on the Continent it is also used to signify a large house or palace.

HOT HOUSE. A general term for the glass buildings used in gardening, and including stoves, greenhouses, orangeries, and conservatories. Pits and frames are mere garden structures, with glass roofs, the sides and ends being of brick, stone, or wood, but so low as to prevent entrance into them; they cannot therefore be considered as hothouses.

HOUSE. (Germ. Hause.) A human habitation or place of abode of a family. Among the nations of the east and of the south, houses are flat on the top, to which ascent is general on the outside. As we proceed northward, a declivity of the roof becomes requisite to throw off the rain and snow, which are of greater continuance in higher latitudes. Amongst the ancient Greeks, Romans, and Jews, the houses usually enclosed a quadrangular area or court, open to the sky. This part of the house was by the Romans called the *impluvium* or *cavædium*, and was provided with channels to carry off the waters into the sewers. Both the Roman and Greek house is described by Vitruvius, to whose work we must refer the reader for further information on these heads. The word house is used in various ways; as in the phrase, " a religious house," either the buildings of a monastery, or the community of persons inhabiting them may be designated. In the middle ages, when a family retired to the lodge connected with the mansion, or to their country seat, it was called " keeping their secret house." Every gradation of building for habitation, from the cottage to the palace, is embraced by the word house, so that to

give a full account of the requisites of each would occupy more space than could be devoted to the subject in this place; the reader must therefore refer to Book III. Chap. III. Sects. 20 to 24. inclusive.

HOUSING. The space taken out of one solid for the insertion of the extremity of another, for the purpose of connecting them. Thus the string board of a stair is most frequently notched out for the reception of the steps.

HOVEL. An open shed for sheltering cattle, for protecting produce or materials of different kinds from the weather, or for performing various country operations during heavy rains, falls of snow, or severe frosts.

HOVELLING. A mode of preventing chimneys from smoking, by carrying up two sides higher than those less liable to receive strong currents of air; or apertures are left on all the sides, so that when the wind blows over the top, the smoke may escape below.

HUE. In painting, any degree of strength or vividness of colour, from its greatest or deepest to its weakest tint.

HUNDRED OF LIME. A denomination of measure which, in some places, is equal to thirty-five, in others to twenty-five, heaped bushels or bags, the latter being the quantity about London, that is, one hundred pecks. The *hundred* is also used for numbering, thus deals are sold by the *long hundred*, or six score. Pales and laths are sold at five score to the hundred if five feet long, and six score if only three feet long. The *hundred weight* is 112 lbs. avoirdupois; the *long hundred weight* is 120 lbs.; so that the former is to the latter as ·93333 to 1.

HUNG, DOUBLE AND SINGLE. A term applied to sashes; the first when both the upper and lower sash are balanced by weights, for raising and depressing, and the last when only one, usually the lower one, is balanced over the pulleys.

HUT. A small cottage or hovel, generally constructed of earthy materials, as strong loamy clay, &c.

HYDRAULICS. (Gr. Ὕδωρ and Αυλος, a pipe.) That branch of natural philosophy which treats of the motion of liquids, the laws by which they are regulated, and the effects which they produce. By some authors the term *hydrodynamics* is used to express the science of the motion of fluids generally, whilst the term hydraulics is more particularly applied to the art of conducting, raising, and confining water, and to the construction and performance of waterworks.

HYDROSTATICS. (Gr. Ὕδωρ and Σταω, I stand.) The science which explains the properties of the equilibrium and pressure of liquids. It is the application of statics to the peculiar constitution of water, or other bodies, existing in the perfectly liquid form. The following is the fundamental law whereon the whole doctrine of the equilibrium and pressure of liquids is founded: when a liquid mass is in equilibrium under the action of forces of any kind, every molecule of the mass sustains an equal pressure in all directions.

HYLMER. See ARCHITECTS, list of, 177.

HYPÆTHRAL. (Gr. Ὑπο, under, and Αιθηρ, the air.) A building or temple without a roof. The temples of this class are arranged by Vitruvius under the seventh order, which had ten columns on each front, and surrounded by a double portico as in dipteral temples. The cell was without roof, whence the name, but it generally had round it a portico of two ranges of columns, one above the other. See TEMPLE.

HYPERBOLA. (Gr. Ὑπερ, over, and Βαλλω, I throw.) One of the conic sections, being that made by a plane cutting the opposite side of the cone produced above the vertex, or by a plane which makes a greater angle with the base than the opposite side of the cone makes.

HYPERBOLIC CONOID or HYPERBOLOID. A solid formed by the revolution of an hyperbola about its axis. See CONOID.

HYPERBOLIC CYLINDROID. A solid formed by the revolution of an hyperbola about its conjugate axis or line through the centre, perpendicular to the transverse axis.

HYPERTHYRUM. (Gr. Ὑπερ and Θυρα, a door.) The lintel or cross-piece of the aperture of a doorway.

HYPOCAUSTUM. (Gr. Ὑπο, under, and Καιω, I burn.) In ancient architecture, a vaulted apartment, from which the heat of the fire was distributed to the rooms above by means of earthen tubes. This contrivance, first used in baths, was afterwards adopted in private houses, and is supposed to have diffused an agreeable and equal temperature throughout the different rooms.

HYPOGÆUM. (Gr.) A term applied among the ancients to those parts of a building which were below the level of the ground.

HYPOPODIUM. A footstool used in the ancient baths.

HYPOSCENIUM. In ancient architecture, the front wall of the theatre, facing the orchestra from the stage.

HYPOTRACHELIUM. (Gr. Ὑπο, under, and Τραχηλος, the neck.) The slenderest part of the shaft of a column, being that immediately below the neck of a capital.

I.

Ice House. A subterranean depôt for preserving ice during the winter. The most important advice that can be given to the builder of an ice house is, that it be so thoroughly capable of drainage, from the lowest point of its floor, as to permit no water ever to collect upon it ; this accomplished, no difficulty will, with common precaution, prevent the preservation of the ice. The aspect of such a building should be towards the south-east, that the morning sun may expel the damp air which is more prejudicial than warmth. , If possible, it should be placed on a declivity for the facility of drainage. At the end of the drain which is to carry away the water arising from the melted ice, a perfect air trap should be placed, to prevent all communication between the external and internal air, from which trap the water should be carried off without the possibility of obstruction. With respect to the dimensions and form of the ice house, the former must depend on the size of the establishment, which, if very large, will require one of a medium diameter, from fifteen to twenty feet; if moderate, one from eight to fifteen feet will be large enough. The best form is the frustum of an inverted cone, ten to twenty feet deep, bricked round, and with double walls, a cavity of four inches being left between them. The ice is sustained on a grated floor, through which the water is rapidly carried off by the drainage first mentioned. The ice is best collected during the severest part of the frost, and should be pounded as laid in the ice house, besides being well rammed down as it is put in. Snow however, hard rammed, will answer when ice cannot be obtained.

Ichnography. (Gr. Ιχνος, a model, and Γραφω, I draw.) The representation of the ground plot of a building. In perspective, it is its representation, intersected by an horizontal plane at its base or groundfloor.

Icosaedron. (Gr. Εικοσι, twenty, and Έδρα, seat.) One of the five regular or platonic bodies, bounded by twenty equilateral and equal triangles. It may be regarded as consisting of twenty equal and similar triangular pyramids, whose vertices all meet in the same point; and hence the content of one of these pyramids, multiplied by twenty, gives the whole content of the icosaedron.

Ictinus. See Architects, list of, 12.

Image. In perspective, the scenographic or perspective representation of an object. See Perspective in the body of the work, Book II. Chap. IV. Sect. 2.

Imbow. (Verb.) To arch over or vault.

Impages. A term used by Vitruvius (lib. iv. c. 6.), which has usually been considered as meaning the rails of a door.

Imperial. (Fr.) A species of dome, whose profile is pointed towards the top, and widens towards the base, thus forming a curve of contrary flexure.

Impetus. (Lat.) In mechanics, the same with momentum or force.

Impluvium. (Lat.) In ancient architecture, the outer part of the court of a house which was exposed to the weather. In the summer time, it was the practice to stretch an awning over it.

Impost. (Lat. Impono, I lay on.) The capital of a pier or pilaster which receives an arch. It varies in the different orders; sometimes the whole of the entablature serves as the impost to an arch. The term is applicable to any supporting piece. An impost is said to be mutilated when its projection is diminished, so that it does not exceed that of the adjoining pilaster which it accompanies.

Inbond Jambstone. A bondstone laid in the joint of an aperture.

Incertum. (Lat.) A term used by Vitruvius to designate a mode of building which consisted of small rough stones and mortar, and whose face exhibited irregularly formed masonry, not laid in horizontal courses. See Masonry.

Inch. A measure of length, being the twelfth part of a foot.

Inclination. (Lat.) The approach of one line, which if continued will meet another or the same of two planes.

Inclined Plane. One of the five simple mechanical powers, whose theory is deduced from the decomposition of forces.

Incrustation. (Lat.) Anything, such as mosaic, scagliola, &c., applied by some connecting medium to another body.

Indefinite. (Lat.) Anything which has only one extreme, whence it may be produced infinitely as it is produced from such extreme.

Indented. (Lat.) Toothed together, that is, with a projection fitted to a recess.

Indian Architecture. See Book I. Chap. II. Sect. 6.

Induration. (Lat.) A term applied to the firmer consistence which a body acquires from various causes.

Inertia. (Lat. Iners.) A term applied to that law of the material world which is known to predicate that all bodies are absolutely passive or indifferent to a state of rest or motion, and would continue in those states unless disturbed by the action of some extrinsic force. Inertia is one of the inherent properties of matter.

INFINITE. (Lat. Infinitus, boundless.) In geometry, that which is greater than any assignable magnitude ; and as no such quantities exist in nature, the idea of an infinite quantity can only, and that most imperfectly, exist in the mind by excluding all notions of boundary or space.

INFIRMARY. A public building for the reception of the sick ; but the term is more generally used to denote a sick-ward or building attached to some public establishment.

INLAYING. The art of laying on some under surface a totally different kind of work to that which the original surface would present. Thus the materials are of no consequence : in stone the inlaying may be of mosaic work or in small pieces, as in wood it may be in patterns made out by different sorts of woods, which is called *marquetry*, or by some, *parquetry*. Veneering is also a species of inlaying.

INNER PLATE. The wall plate, in a double-plated roof, which lies nearest the centre of the roof ; the side of the other wall plate, called the *outer plate*, being nearer the outer surface of the wall.

INNER SQUARE. The edges forming the internal right angle of the instrument called a square.

INSERTED COLUMN. One that is engaged in a wall.

INSTRUMENTS, MATHEMATICAL. Those used for describing mathematical diagrams and drawings of every description, when the figures or elementary parts of them are composed of straight lines, circles, or portions of them. The indispensable instruments for such operations are, *a drawing pen, a pair of plain compasses,* commonly called *dividers, a pair of drawing compasses, a port crayon and pencil foot, a pair of bow, of triangular, and of proportional compasses, a protractor,* in the form of a semicircle or rectangle, graduated on the edges, *a plain scale,* and *a parallel rule.*

INSULAR or INSULATED BUILDING. Such as stands entirely detached from any other.

INSULATED COLUMN. One detached from a wall, so that the whole of its surface may be seen.

INTAGLIO. (It.) Sculpture in which the subject is hollowed out, so that the impression from it would present the appearance of a bas-relief.

INTAVOLATA. The same as CYMA, which see.

INTERCEPTED AXIS. In conic sections, that part of the diameter of a curve comprehended between the vertex and the ordinate. It is also called the *abscissa*, and forms an arch of a peculiar kind.

INTERCOLUMNIATION. (Lat. Inter, between, and Columna, a column.) The distance between two columns measured at the lower part of their shafts. It is one of the most important elements in architecture, and on it depends the effect of the columns themselves, their pleasing proportion, and the harmony of an edifice. Intercolumniations are of five species, *pycnostylos, systylos, diastylos, aræostylos,* and *eustylos,* under which several terms each is defined. The subject is also found more largely treated of in Book III. Chap I. Sect. 9.

INTERDENTELS. The space between two dentels. From a comparison of various examples, it seems that the Greeks placed their dentels wider apart than the Romans. In the temple of Bacchus at Teos, the interdentel is two-thirds the breadth of the dentel, and in that of Minerva Polias at Priene, the interdentel is nearly three-fourths. In the temple of Jupiter Stator at Rome, the interdentels are equal to half the breadth of the dentel.

INTERIOR ANGLE. An angle formed within any figure by two straight lined parts of the perimeter or boundary of the figure, the exterior angle being that which is formed in producing a side of the perimeter of the figure. The term is also applied to the two angles formed by two parallel lines, when cut on each side of the intersecting line.

INTERIOR AND OPPOSITE ANGLES. An expression applied to the two angles formed by a line cutting two parallels.

INTERJOIST. The space or interval between two joists.

INTERMODILLION. The space between two modillions.

INTERNAL ANGLE. See INTERIOR ANGLE.

INTERPILASTER. The space between two pilasters.

INTERQUARTER. The interval between two quarters.

INTERTIES. Short pieces of timber used in roofing to bind upright posts together, in roofs, in partitions, in lath and plaster work, and in walls with timber framework.

INTRADOS. The interior and lower line or curve of an arch. The exterior or upper curve is called the *extrados.* See ARCH.

INVENTION. (Lat. Invenio, I find.) In the fine arts, the choice and production of such objects as are proper to enter into the composition of a work of art. " Strictly speaking," says Sir Joshua Reynolds, " invention is little more than a new combination of those images which have been previously gathered and deposited in the memory : nothing can come of nothing : he who has laid up no materials can produce no combinations." Though there be nothing new under the sun, yet novelty in art will be attainable till all the combinations of the same things are exhausted, a circumstance that can never come to pass.

INVERTED ARCH. One wherein the lowest stone or. brick is the key-stone. It is used in foundations, to distribute the weight of particular points over the whole extent of the

foundation, and hence its employment is frequently of the first importance in constructive architecture.

INVOLUTE. See EVOLUTE.

INWARD ANGLE. The re-entrant angle of a solid. See INTERIOR ANGLE.

IONIC ORDER. See Book III. Chap. I. Sect 5.

IRON. See Book II. Chap. II. Sect. 5.

IRONMONGERY. See Book II. Chap. III. Sect. 10.

IRREGULAR FIGURE. One whose sides, and consequently angles, are unequal to each other.

ISAGON. (Gr. Ισος, equal, and Γωνια, an angle.) A figure with equal angles.

ISEMBERT. See ARCHITECTS, list of, 105.

ISIDORUS. See ARCHITECTS, list of, 62.

ISIDORUS OF BYZANTIUM. See ARCHITECTS, list of, 64.

ISODOMUM. (Gr.) One of the methods of building walls practised by the Greeks. It was executed in courses of equal thickness, and with stones of equal lengths. The other method, called *pseudisodomum*, in which the heights, thicknesses, and lengths of the stone were different. There was another mode called EMPLECTON, which see.

ISOSCELES TRIANGLE. One in which two of the sides are of equal length.

IVARA, properly JUVARA, F. See ARCHITECTS, list of, 270.*

J.

JACK ARCH. One whose thickness is only of one brick.

JACK PLANE. A plane about eighteen inches long, used in taking off the rough surface left by the saw or that of the axe, and of taking off large protuberant parts, to prepare the stuff for the trying plane.

JACK RAFTER. See HIP ROOF.

JACK RIBS. Those in a groin, or in a polygonally-domed ceiling, that are fixed upon the hips.

JACK TIMBER. Any one interrupted in its length, or cut short.

JAMB LININGS. The two vertical linings of a doorway which are usually of wood.

JAMB POSTS. Those introduced on the side of a door, to which the jamb linings are fixed. They are particularly used when partitions are of wood.

JAMB STONES. In stone walls are those which are employed in building the sides of apertures, in which every alternate stone should go entirely through the thickness of the wall.

JAMBS. (Fr.) The sides of an aperture which connect the two sides of a wall. See APERTURE and CHIMNEY.

JAMES, JOHN. See ARCHITECTS, list of, 228.

JEAN D'ECHELLES. See ARCHITECTS, list of, 115.

JERKIN HEAD. The end of a roof not hipped down to the level of the opposite adjoining walls, the gable being carried higher than the level of those walls.

JIB DOOR. A door so constructed as to have the same continuity of surface with that of the partition or wall in which it stands. Its use is to preserve an unbroken surface in an apartment where one door only is wanted nearer to one end of a room than another, and generally for the purpose of preserving uniformity.

JOGGLE. The joint of two bodies so constructed as to prevent them sliding past each other, by the application of a force in a direction perpendicular to the two pressures by which they are held together. Thus the struts of a roof are joggled into the truss posts and into the rafters. When confined by mortise and tenon, the pressure which keeps them together is that of the rafter and the reaction of the truss post. The term is also used in masonry to signify the indentation made in one stone to receive the projection in another, so as to prevent all sliding on the joints. This may be also accomplished by means of independent pieces of material let into the adjacent stones.

JOGGLE PIECE. The truss post in a roof when formed to receive a brace or strut with a joggle.

JOHANNES OF MILETUS. See ARCHITECTS, list of, 65.

JOHN OF PADUA. See ARCHITECTS, list of, 187.

JOINER. The artisan who joins wood by glue, framing, or nails, for the finishings of a building.

JOINERY. The practice of framing or joining wood for the internal and external finishings of houses; thus the covering and lining of rough walls, the covering of rough timbers, the manufacture of doors, shutters, sashes, stairs, and the like, are classed under the head of joinery. See Book II. Chap. III. Sect. 6.

JOINT. The surface of separation between two bodies brought into contact and held firmly together, either by some cementing medium, or by the weight of one body lying on another. A joint, however, is not merely the contact of two surfaces, though the nearer they approach the more perfect the joint. In masonry, the distances of the planes intended to form the joint is comparatively considerable, because of the coarseness of the particles which enter into the composition of the cement.

JOINTER. In *joinery* is the largest plane used by the joiner in straightening the face of the edge of the stuff to be prepared. In *bricklaying*, it is a crooked piece of iron forming two curves of contrary flexure by its edges on each side, and is used for drawing, by the aid of the jointing rule, the *coursing* and *vertical* joints of the work.

JOINTING RULE. A straight edge used by bricklayers for the regulation of the direction and course of the jointer in the horizontal and vertical joints of brickwork.

JOISTS. (Fr. Joindre.) The timbers whereto the boards of a floor or the laths for a ceiling are nailed. They rest on the walls or on girders; sometimes on both. When only one tier of joists is used, the assemblage is called *single-flooring*; when two, *double-flooring*.

JONES, INIGO. See ARCHITECTS, list of, 252.

JUFFERS. An obsolete term for pieces of timber four or five inches square.

JUMP. An abrupt rise in a level course of brickwork or masonry to accommodate the work to the inequality of the ground. Also *in quarrying*, one among the various names given to the dislocations of the strata in quarries.

JUMPER. A long iron chisel used by masons and miners.

K.

KEEP or KEEP TOWER. A term almost synonymous with *donjon*. See CASTLE.

KENDALL. See ARCHITECTS, list of, 166.

KENT. See ARCHITECTS, list of, 282.

KERF. The way made by a saw through a piece of timber, by displacing the wood with the teeth of the saw.

KEY. (Sax. Cæᵹe.) An instrument for driving back the bolt of a lock. The *key of a floor* is the board last laid down. In joinery generally a key is a piece of wood let into the back of another in the contrary direction of the grain, to preserve the last from warping.

KEY STONE. The highest or central stone of an arch. See ARCH.

KEYED DADO. That which has bars of wood grooved into it across the grain at the back to prevent it warping.

KEYES. See ARCHITECTS, list of, 151.

KEYS. In naked flooring are pieces of timber fixed in between the joists by mortise and tenon. When these are fastened with their ends projecting against the sides of the joists, they are called *strutting-pieces*.

KILDERKIN. A measure containing eighteen gallons of beer, and sixteen ale measure.

KILN. A building for the accumulation and retention of heat in order to dry or burn certain materials deposited within them.

KING POST. The centre post in a trussed roof. See CROWN POST.

KIRB PLATE. See CURB PLATE.

KIRB ROOF. See CURB ROOF.

KITCHEN. (Fr. Cuisine.) The apartment or office of a house wherein the operations of cookery are carried on.

KNEE. A part of the back of a handrailing, of a convex form, being the reverse of a *ramp*, which is also the back of a handrail, but is concave. The term knee is also given to any small piece of timber of a bent or angular form.

KNEE PIECE or KNEE RAFTER. An angular piece of timber, to which other pieces in the roof are fastened.

KNOTTING. The preliminary process in painting, to prevent the knots appearing, by covering them with a coat composed of red lead, then white lead and oil, and lastly, a coat of gold size. Sometimes leaf silver is also used.

KNUCKLE. The joint of a cylindrical form, with a pin as an axis, by which the straps of a hinge are fastened together.

L.

LABEL. In Gothic architecture, the drip or hood moulding over an aperture when it is returned square.

LABELYE. See ARCHITECTS, list of, 285.

LABOUR. (Lat.) A term in masonry employed to denote the value of a piece of work in consideration of the time bestowed upon it.

LABYRINTH. (Gr. Λαϐυρινθος.) Literally a place, usually subterraneous, full of inextricable windings. The four celebrated labyrinths of antiquity were the Cretan, Egyptian, Lemnian, and Italian. The first has the reputation of being the work of Dædalus to secure the Minotaur; the second is said to have been constructed under the command of Psammeticus, king of Egypt; the third was on the island of Lemnos, and was supported by columns of great beauty; the fourth is reported to have been designed by Porsenna, king of Etruria, as a tomb for himself and his successors.

LABYRINTH FRET. A fret, with many turnings, in the form of a labyrinth. See FRET.

LACER. See ARCHITECTS, list of, 48.

LACONICUM. (Lat.) One of the apartments in the ancient baths, so called from its having been first used in Laconia.

LACQUER. A yellow varnish, consisting of a solution of shell-lac in alcohol, coloured by gamboge, saffron, annotto, or other yellow, orange, or red colouring matters. The use of lacquer is chiefly for varnishing brass, and some other metals, in order to give them a golden colour and preserve their lustre.

LACTARIUM. (Lat.) Strictly a dairy-house. In ancient architecture, it was a place in the Roman herb market, indicated by a column, called the Columna Lactaria, where foundlings were fed and nourished.

LACUNAR. (Lat.) The ceiling or under surface of the member of an order. Also the under side of the larmier or corona of a cornice. The under side also of that part of the architrave between the capitals of columns. The ceiling of any part in architecture receives the name of lacunar only when it consists of compartments sunk or hollowed, without spaces or bands, between the panels; if it is with bands, it is called *laquear*.

LADY CHAPEL. The name given to a small chapel dedicated to the Virgin, generally, in ancient cathedrals, placed behind the high altar.

LANCET ARCH. One whose head is shaped like the point of a lancet, and generally applied to long narrow windows.

LANDING. The terminating floor of a flight of stairs, either above or below it.

LANFRANC. See ARCHITECTS, list of, 81.

LANFRANI. See ARCHITECTS, list of, 139.

LANGHANS. See ARCHITECTS, list of, 310.

LANTERN. (Fr. Lanterne.) A drum-shaped erection, either square, circular, elliptical, or polygonal, on the top of a dome, or on that of an apartment, to give light.

LAP. The part of one body which lies on and covers another.

LAPO. See ARCHITECTS, list of, 120.

LAQUEAR. See LACUNAR.

LARARIUM. (Lat.) In ancient architecture, the apartment in which the lares or household gods were deposited. It frequently contained also statues of the proprietor's ancestors.

LARDER. The place in which undressed meat is kept for the use of a family.

LARMIER. (Fr.) The same as CORONA, which see.

LATCH. The catch by which a door is held fast.

LATENT HEAT. That which is insensible to the thermometer, upon which the liquid and aeriform states of bodies depend, and which becomes sensible during the conversion of vapours into liquids and of liquids into solids.

LATH. (Sax. Lætta.) A thin cleft piece of wood used in slating, tiling, and plastering. There are two sorts, double and single, the former being about three-eighths of an inch thick, and the latter barely a quarter of an inch. *Pantile laths* are long square pieces of fir, on which the pantiles hang.

LATH BRICKS. A species made in some parts of England. They are twenty-two inches long and six inches broad.

LATH FLOATED AND SET FAIR. Three-coat plasterers' work; the first is called *pricking up*; the second *floating*; the third, or finishing, done with fine stuff, is the *setting* coat.

LATH LAID AND SET. Two-coat plasterers' work, except that the first is called *laying*, and is executed without *scratching*, unless with a broom. When used on walls, this sort of work is generally coloured; when on ceilings, it is whited.

LATH PLASTERED, SET, AND COLOURED. The same as lath laid, set, and coloured.

LATH PRICKED UP, FLOATED, AND SET FOR PAPER. The same as *lath floated and set fair*.

LATERAL STRENGTH. The resistance which a body will afford at right angles to its grain.

LATTICE. (Fr. Lattis.) A reticulated window, made of laths of wood, strips of iron, or other materials, and only used where air, rather than light, is to be admitted, as in cellars and dairies.

LAUNDRY. An apartment occupied by the laundress of an establishment. It should be spacious and well supplied with every convenience for mangling, drying, and ironing the linen of a family. *Horses*, or slender frames of wood, should be provided for hanging the linen upon, which should be suspended to the timbers of the ceiling by pulleys, by which they may be raised and lowered.

LAVATORY. (Lat.) See CLOISTER.

LAYER. In brickwork and masonry, synonymous with COURSE, which see.

LAYING. In plastering, the first coat on lath of two-coat work, the surface whereof is roughed by sweeping with a broom. The difference between laying and *rendering* being, that the latter is the first coat upon brick.

LAZARHOUSE or LAZARETTO. (Ital.) A hospital for the reception of the poor and those afflicted with contagious diseases. There are many in the southern states of Europe for the performance of quarantine, into which those only are admitted who arrive from

countries infected by the plague, or suspected of being so. An account of the principal lazarettos of Europe was published by the celebrated Howard.

LEAD. (Sax. Læb.) The heaviest metal next to gold, platina, and mercury, being eleven times heavier than its own bulk of water. See Book II. Chap. II. Sect. 6.

LEANTO. A building whose rafters pitch against or lean on to another building or against a wall.

LEAVES. (Sax. Læar.) Ornaments imitated from natural leaves, whereof the ancients used two sorts, natural and imaginary. The former were those of the laurel, palm, acanthus, and olive; but they took great liberties in the representations of all of them.

LEDGE. A surface serving to support a body either in motion or at rest. Ledges of doors are the narrow surfaces wrought upon the jambs and sofites parallel to the wall to stop the door, so that when it is shut the ledges coincide with the surface of the door. A ledge, therefore, is one of the sides of a *rebate*, each rebate being formed of two sides. In temporary work the ledges of doors are formed by fillets. Also the horizontal planks in common doors, to which the vertical planks are nailed. See Book II. Chap. III. Sect. 5

LEDGEMENT. The development of a surface, or the surface of a body stretched out on a plane, so that the dimensions of the different sides may be easily ascertained.

LEDGERS. In scaffolding for brick buildings are horizontal pieces of timber parallel to the walls. They are fastened to the *standards*, or upright poles, by cords, to support the *put-logs*, which lie at right angles to and on the walls as they are brought up, and receive the boards for working on.

LEDOUX. See ARCHITECTS, list of, 306.

LEGRAND. See ARCHITECTS, list of, 309.

LEGS OF AN HYPERBOLA. The two parts on each side the vertex.

LEGS OF A TRIANGLE. The sides which inclose the base.

LENGTH. (Sax. Leng.) The greatest extension of a body. In a right prism the length is the distance between the ends; in a right pyramid or cone, the length is the distance between the vertex and the base.

LENGTHENING OF TIMBER is the method of joining several beams, so as to form a long beam of any given length.

LEONI. See ARCHITECTS, list of, 279.

LESCOT. See ARCHITECTS, list of, 237.

LEVEL. (Sax. Lœrel.) A line or surface which inclines to neither side. The term is used substantively to denote an instrument which shows the direction of a straight line parallel to the plane of the horizon. The plane of the sensible horizon is indicated in two ways: by the direction of the plummet, or plumb line, to which it is perpendicular; and by the surface of a fluid at rest. Accordingly, levels are formed either by means of the plumb line, or by the agency of a fluid applied in some particular manner. They all depend, however, upon the same principle, namely, the action of terrestrial gravity.

The carpenter's level consists of a long rule, straight on its lower edge, about ten or twelve feet in length, with an upright fixed to its upper edge, perpendicular to and in the middle of the length, having its sides in the same plane with those of the rule, and a straight line drawn on one of its sides perpendicular to the straight edge of the rule. This standing piece is generally mortised into the other, and finally braced on each side, to secure it from accident, and has its upper end kerfed in three places, viz. through the perpendicular line, and on each side. The straight edge of the transverse piece has a hole, or notch, cut out on the other side equal on each side the perpendicular line. A plummet is suspended by a string from the middle kerf, at the top of the standing piece, to vibrate freely in the hole or notch when hanging at full length. When the straight edge of the level is applied to two distant points, with its two sides placed vertically, if the plummet hangs freely, and the string coincides with the straight line on the standing piece, the two points are level. If not, suppose one of the points to be at the given height, the other must be lowered or raised, as the case may require, till the string is brought to a coincidence with the perpendicular line. By two points is meant two surfaces of contact, as two blocks of wood, or the upper edges of two distant beams.

The uses of the level in carpentry are various, and need not be here detailed. The *mason's level* is formed of three pieces of wood, joined in the form of an isosceles triangle, having a plummet suspended from the vertex over a mark in the centre of the base.

LEVELLING. The art or act of finding a line parallel to the horizon, at one or more stations, in order to determine the height of one place with respect to another, for laying grounds even, regulating descents, draining morasses, conducting waters for the irrigation of land, &c. See ADDENDUM.

LEVER. In mechanics an inflexible rod, moveable about a fulcrum, or prop, and having forces applied to two or more points in it. The lever is one of the mechanical powers, and being the simplest of them all, was the first attempted to be explained. For its properties see Book II. Chap. I. Sect. 7.

LEVER BOARDS. A set of boards so fastened that they may be turned at any angle to

admit more or less light, or to lap upon each other so as to exclude all air or light through apertures.

LEWIS or LEWISSON. An instrument said to have been used in England by the builders of the middle ages to raise stones of more than ordinary weight to the upper part of a building. It was revived by a French artisan in the reign of Louis XIV., and is now generally employed. It operates by the pieces forming its dove-tail end being held in their correspondent places in the stone by a middle straight piece, kept in its situation by a pin passing through it and the dove-tail pieces at top, and the combination of the whole is effected with a large ring.

LIAS. A provincial name adopted by geologists for an argillaceous limestone, which, together with its associated bed, is characterised by peculiar fossils.

LIBON. See ARCHITECTS, list of, 11.

LIBRARY. An edifice or apartment for the reception of a collection of books. For remarks on the construction of public libraries see Book III. Chap. V. Sect. 9.

LIGHTS. A term sometimes used to denote the openings of doors, gates, and windows, and other places through which air and light have passage.

LIGHTHOUSE. A lofty building, on the top whereof artificial lights are placed to guide ships at sea. For general observations on lighthouses, see Book III. Chap. V. Sect. 12.

LIKE ARCS. In the projection of the sphere, the parts of lesser circles containing an equal number of degrees with the corresponding arcs of greater circles.

LIKE FIGURES. In geometry, such as have their angles equal, and the sides about the equal angles proportional.

LIKE SOLIDS. Those which are contained under like planes.

LIME. (Germ. Leim, glue.) A most useful earth, obtained by exposing chalk, and other kinds of limestones or carbonates of lime, to a red heat, an operation generally conducted in kilns constructed for the purpose, by which the carbonic acid is expelled, and lime, more or less pure, according to the original quality of the limestone, remains, in which state it is called *quicklime*. See Book II. Chap. II. Sect. 11.

LIMEKILN. One for the purpose of burning lime. They are constructed in a variety of ways, to save expense, or to answer to the particular nature of the fuel.

LIMESTONE. A generic term for those varieties of carbonate of lime which are neither crystallised or earthy, the former being calcareous spar, the latter chalk. When burned they yield quicklime.

LINE. (Lat. Linea.) In geometry, a magnitude having only one dimension, and defined by Euclid to be that which has length without breadth. The term is also used to denote a measure of length used formerly in France, namely, the twelfth part of an inch, or $\frac{1}{144}$ of a foot.

LINE OF DIRECTION. In mechanics, the line in which motion is communicated.

LINE, GEOMETRICAL. In perspective, any straight line in the geometrical or primary line.

LINE, HORIZONTAL. A line parallel to the horizon. In perspective, it is the vanishing line of horizontal planes.

LINE OF STATION. The intersection of a plane passing through the eye, perpendicular to the picture, and to the geometrical or primary plane with the plane itself.

LINE, VERTICAL. The intersection of a vertical plane with the picture passing along the station line.

LINE, VISUAL. A ray of light reflected from the object to the eye.

LINES OF LIGHT AND SHADE. Those in which the light and shade of a body are separated. Thus, on a curved surface, it is the line determined by a tangent to the surface in the direction of the rays of light.

LINEAR PERSPECTIVE. See Book II. Chap. IV. Sect. 2.

LINING. The covering of the surface of any body with another thin substance. Thus the lining of a wall is a wooden boarding, whose edges are either rebated or grooved and tongued. Lining is distinguished from *casing*, the first being a covering in the interior of a building, whilst the latter is the covering of the exterior part of a building.

LINING OUT STUFF. (Participle.) The drawing lines on a piece of board or plank so as to cut it into thinner pieces.

LININGS OF BOXINGS for window shutters, are the pieces of framework into which the window shutters are folded back.

LININGS OF A DOOR. Those of the sides of apertures of doors called the jambs or jamb-linings, that which covers the top or head being the sofite.

LINTEL. (Span.) A horizontal piece of timber or stone over a door, window, or other opening to discharge the superincumbent weight. If a wall be very thick, more than one lintel piece will be required, unless scanting of sufficient width be found. In some old books on carpentry lintels are classed under wall plates, but the word is now never used in this sense, unless the joisting or tie-beams rest upon it, in which case it is both a lintel and a wall plate.

LIST or LISTEL. The same as FILLET, which see.

LISTED BOARDS. See BOARDS.

LISTING. (Participle.) Cutting the sap wood out from both edges of a board.

LOAM. A soil in which clay prevails. It is called heavy or light as the clay may be more or less abundant.

LOBBY. (Germ. Laube.) An inclosed space surrounding or communicating with one or more apartments, such as the boxes of a theatre, for instance. By it also is understood a small hall or waiting room, or the entrance into a principal apartment where there is a considerable space between it and a portico or vestibule; but the dimensions, especially as regards the width, will not allow of its being called a vestibule or anti-room.

LOCK. (Sax. Loc.) A well-known instrument, consisting of springs and bolts, for fastening doors, drawers, chests, &c. A good lock is a masterpiece in smithery, requiring much art and delicacy to contrive and vary the wards, springs, bolts, and other parts whereof it is composed, so as to adjust them to the places where they are serviceable, and to the various purposes of their use. The structure of locks is so varied, and the number of inventions of their different sorts so extended, that we cannot attempt to enumerate them.

Those placed on outer doors are called *stock locks*, those on chamber doors *spring locks*, and such as are hidden in the thickness of the doors to which they are applied, *mortise locks*. The padlock is too well known to need description here.

The conditions which seem indispensable in a perfect lock are, 1. that certain parts of the lock should be variable in position through a great number of combinations, one only whereof shall allow the lock to be opened or shut; 2. that this last-mentioned combination should be variable at the pleasure of the possessor; 3. that it should not be possible, after the lock is closed and the combination disturbed, for any one, not even the maker of the lock, to discover, by any examination, what may be the proper situations of the parts required to open the lock; 4. that trials of this kind shall not be capable of injuring the works; 5. that it shall require no key; 6. and be as easily opened in the dark as in the light; 7. that the opening and shutting shall be done by a process as simple as that of a common lock; 8. that it should open *without* a key or *with* one, at pleasure; 9. that the keyhole be concealed, defended, or inaccessible; 10. that the key may be used by a stranger without his knowing or being able to discover the adopted combination; 11. that the key be capable of adjustment to all the variations of the lock, and yet be simple; 12. that the lock should not be liable to be taken off and examined, whether the receptacle be open or shut, except by one who knows the method of combination.

The above considerations involve a problem of great mechanical difficulty, which has not yet been solved, though much has been done towards it. For the locks in common use in buildings, see p. 688.

LODGE. A small house, situated in a park or domain, subordinate to the mansion. Also the cottage placed at the gate of the road leading to the mansion.

LOGARITHMS. Artificial numbers used to facilitate arithmetical calculations.

LOGHOUSE. A hut constructed of the trunks of trees.

LOGISTIC SPIRAL. One whose radii are in continued proportion, and in which the radii are at equal angles; or, in other words, a spiral line whose radii every where make equal angles with the tangents.

LOMBARDO, M. See ARCHITECTS, list of, 174.

LOMBARDO, P. See ARCHITECTS, list of, 173.

LOMBARDO, SANTE. See ARCHITECTS, list of, 216.

LONGIMETRY. A term used to denote the operation of trigonometry for measuring lengths, whether accessible or inaccessible.

LOOP. (Fr.) A small narrow window. A *loophole* is a term applied to the vertical series of doors in a warehouse, from which the goods, in craning, are delivered into a warehouse.

LORME, PHILIP DE. See ARCHITECTS, list of, 214.

LOTUS. A plant of the water-lily species much used in the architectural ornaments of the early nations, and especially in the capitals of Egyptian columns.

LOUIS. See ARCHITECTS, list of, 304.

LOZENGE. A quadrilateral figure of four equal sides, with oblique angles.

LUFFER BOARDINGS. (Fr. Louvre.) See BOARDING LUFFER.

LUNE or LUNULA. The space between two equal arcs of a circle.

LUNETTE. (Fr.) A cylindric, cylindroidic, or spherical aperture in a ceiling. As an example of the term, we may refer to the upper lights in the nave of St. Paul's Cathedral.

LUSARCHE. See ARCHITECTS, list of, 110.

LUTHERN. The same as DORMER, which see.

LYING PANELS. Those wherein the fibres of the wood, or the grain of it, lie in an horizontal direction.

LYSIS. (Gr.) A plinth or step above the cornice of the podium of ancient temples, which surrounded or embraced the stylobate, whereof an example may be seen in the temple of Fortuna Virilis at Rome.

M.

M Roof. A roof formed by the junction of two common roofs with a vallum between them. The letter Ɱ inverted represents this species of covering.

Machicolations. (Fr. Machicoulis.) In castellated architecture are, according to Grose, the projections, supported by brackets or corbels, through which melted lead and stones were dropped on the heads of assailants. They were not probably, however, projecting works, but sometimes were considered as the series of square holes in the vaultings of the portals used for the same purpose.

Machine. (Gr. Μαχανη.) In a general sense, any thing which serves to increase or regulate the effect of a given force. Machines are *simple* or *compound*. The former are the simple mechanical powers, six in number; viz. the lever, the wheel and axle, the pulley, the wedge, the screw, and the funicular machine. The latter are formed by the combination of two or more simple machines, and are classed according to the forces by which they are put in motion, as *hydraulic machines, pneumatic machines, electrical machines*, &c., or the purposes they are intended to serve, as *military* machines, *architectural* machines, &c.

Machuca. See Architects, list of, 227.

Maderno. See Architects, list of, 249.

Maglione. See Architects, list of, 123.

Magnesian Limestone. An extensive series of beds lying in geological position immediately above the coal measures; so called because the *limestone*, which is the principal member of the series, contains *magnesia*.

Magnitude. (Lat.) A term by which size, extent, or quantity is designated. It was originally applied to the space occupied by any figure; or, in other words, it was applied to objects strictly termed geometrical, and of three dimensions, length, breadth, and thickness, but it has gradually become enlarged in its signification, so as to be given to every kind of quantity that admits of mensuration, or of which greater or less can be predicated; in which sense it was used by Euclid.

Mahogany. A wood often used for doors and window-sashes. See p. 501. The Jamaica mahogany is the hardest and most beautiful, and is distinguished from that of Honduras by the chalky appearance of its fibres. Those from Honduras appear quite dark. After oiling, this distinction is not so clearly observable.

Main Couple. See Couple.

Majano. See Architects, list of, 149.

Malleability. (Lat. Malleus, a hammer.) The property of being susceptible of extension under the blows of a hammer. It is a characteristic of some of the metals, most particularly in gold. Common gold-leaf is not more a two-hundred-thousandth part of an inch in thickness. Five grains may be beaten out so as to cover a surface of more than two hundred and seventy square inches.

Mallet. (Lat.) A large kind of wooden hammer much used by artificers who work with a chisel, as masons, stonecutters, carpenters, joiners, &c.

Maltha. (Gr.) A native bitumen used by the ancients for plastering the walls of their dwellings, &c. An artificial kind was made of pitch, wax, plaster, and grease; another sort was composed of lime slaked with wine, and incorporated with melted pitch and fresh figs.

Mandrel. (Fr. Mandrin.) In machinery, a revolving shank, to which turners affix their work in the lathe.

Mandrocles. See Architects, list of, 6.

Manger. The trough in the stall of a stable wherein is placed the corn or other short food given to live stock, and more especially to horses.

Manlio. See Architects, list of, 203.

Mansard. See Architects, list of, 258.

Mansard, Jules Hardouin. See Architects, list of, 267.

Mansard Roof. (So called from the name of its inventor, François Mansard.) The same as Curb Roof, which see.

Mansion. A large house; a term more usually applied to one in the country. The origin of the word and its application is supposed to be derived from the mansiones, or stationary camps of the Roman soldiers.

Mantle Tree. See Chimney.

Marble. (Fr. Marbre.) A term limited by mineralogists and geologists to the several varieties of carbonate of lime, having more or less of a granular and crystalline texture. Among sculptors, the word is used to denote several compact or granular kinds of stone susceptible of a very fine polish; the varieties of it are extremely numerous. The most valuable sorts used by the ancients were the *Pentelican*, which was white, and was obtained from Mount Penteles in Attica. It was used in the Parthenon and other Athenian buildings, and was also in great repute among the sculptors. The *Parian marble* was, as its name imports, from the island of Paros, in which Mount Marpessus yielded the best, which was called *Marpessian*. The marble of Paros was also sometimes termed

Lychneus, because of its use in making candelabra, and *Lygdinum,* from the promontory of Lygdos. Another of the white marbles of antiquity was that of Mount Hymettus in Attica. The marbles of *Thasus* and *Lesbos* were white, and in great repute. The latter island produced also a black marble. At *Luna,* in Etruria, there was found a marble even whiter than that of Paros. Amongst the white marbles may, moreover, be mentioned the *marmor Phellense* from Mount Phellens ; the *marmor Coraliticum,* found near the river Coralios in Phrygia, and termed also *Sangarium,* from another name of the same river. The *marmor Cyzicum* was taken from the quarries of Cyzicus in Asia Minor ; the *Synnadicum,* or marmor Phrygium, was obtained from the environs of the city of Synnas in Phrygia, and was of a black ground with small circles. Another sort of marble, which resembled ivory in its colour, was called *chernites.* The marble of *Tænarus* was highly esteemed as a black marble. The *marmor Lybicum,* or *Numidian marble,* called also *marmor Luculleum,* was what the French term *noir antique.* The celebrated *marmor Chium* was excavated from the Mount Pelineus in the island of Chio, and was of a transparent chequered black colour. The *marmor obsidianum* was from Ethiopia, and of the black species, as was the *Proconnesian,* or Cyzican marble, from the island of Proconnesus. That from Mount Taygetes, called *marmor Laconicum,* was the well-known *verd antique* of antiquaries. The marble of *Carystus* was a mingled green ; that called the *Atracium,* from Mount Atrax in Thessaly, was a mixture of white, green, blue, and black. The green *Tiberian* and *Augustan* marbles were obtained from Egypt. The *marmor Ophites,* or *Memphites,* which took its first name from its resemblance to the skin of a serpent, and its second from the city of Memphis, where it was found, is the *Serpentino antico* of the Italians. The marble of *Corinth* was yellow, and the *marmor Phengites* of Cappadocia was white, with yellow spots. The *Rhodian marble* was marked with spots resembling gold ; that of *Melos* was yellow, and excavated in Mount Acynthus. The varieties of marble used in modern times are exceedingly numerous, and a classification of them would occupy a larger space than can be here given. Except the finest specimens of white marble, they are mostly opaque. Some extremely fine specimens of white marble are to be seen in the Borghese Palace at Rome, which, on being suspended by the centre on a hard body, bend very considerably. It is found that statuary marble exposed to the sun acquires, in time, this property, thus indicating a less degree of adhesion of its parts than it naturally possessed.

Almost every mountainous district of the world produces this mineral, but the finest and most valuable is from Italy. See Book II. Chap. II. Sect. 3.

MARBLE, POLISHING OF. The material is brought to an even face by rubbing with free-stone, afterwards with pumice-stone, and lastly with emery of several colours ; but white marble is finished with calcined tin. The Italians polish with lead and emery. The sawing of marble, preparatory to polishing, is by a saw of soft iron, with a continued supply of the sharpest sand and water.

MARGIN OF A COURSE. That part of the upper side of a course of slates which appears uncovered by the next superior course.

MARIGOLD WINDOW. See ROSE WINDOW.

MARMORATUM. (Lat.) A cement used by the ancients, formed of pounded marble and lime well beaten together.

MARQUETRY or PARQUETRY. (Fr. Marquetrie.) Inlaid work, consisting of different pieces of various coloured woods, of small thickness, glued on to a ground, usually of oak or fir well dried and seasoned, which, to prevent casting and warping, is composed of several thicknesses. It was used by the early Italian builders in cabinet work ; and John of Vienna, and others of his period, represented by its means figures and landscapes ; but in the present day it is chiefly confined to floors, in which the divers pieces of wood are usually disposed in regular geometrical figures, and are rarely of more than three or four species.

MASCAL or MARSHALL. See ARCHITECTS, list of, 220.

MASONRY. (Fr.) The science of combining and joining stones for the formation of walls and other parts in constructing buildings. When applied in the construction of domes, groins, and circular arches, it is difficult and complicated, and is dependent on a thorough knowledge of descriptive geometry. The subject is treated in the body of this work, Book II. Chap. III. Sect. 3.

Among the ancients, several sorts of masonry were in use, which are described by Vitruvius as follows, in the eighth chapter of his second book : — " The different species of walls," he observes, " are the *reticulatum* (net-like) (*fig.* 1363. A), a method now in general use, and the *incertum* (B), which is the ancient mode. The reticulatum is very beautiful, but liable to split, from the beds of the stones being unstable, and its deficiency in respect of bond. The incertum, on the contrary, course over course, and the whole bonded together, does not present so beautiful an appearance, though stronger than the reticulatum. Both species should be built of the smallest sized stones, that the walls, by sucking up and attaching themselves to the mortar, may last the longer : for as the stones are of a soft and porous nature, they absorb, in dry-

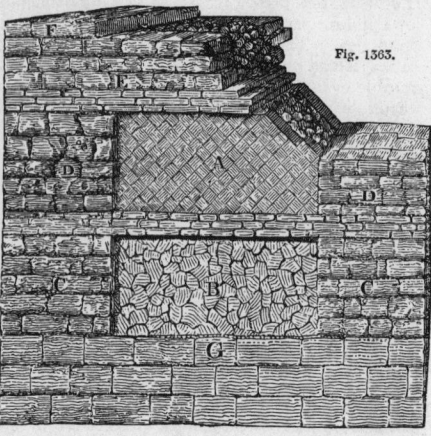

Fig. 1363.

ing, the moisture of the mortar; and this, if used plentifully, will consequently exercise a greater cementing power; because from their containing a larger portion of moisture, the wall will not, of course, dry so soon as otherwise; and as soon as the moisture is absorbed by the pores of the stones from the mortar, the lime, losing its power, leaves the sand, so that the stones no longer adhere to it, and in a short time the work becomes unsound. We may see this in several monuments about the city (Rome) which have been built of marble, or of stones squared externally, that is, on one face, but filled up with rubble run with mortar. Time in these has taken up the moisture of the mortar, and destroyed its efficacy by the porosity of the surface on which it acted. All cohesion is thus ruined, and the walls fall to decay. He who is desirous that this may not happen to his work should build his two-face walls two feet thick, either of red stone, or of bricks, or of common flint, binding them together with iron cramps run with lead, and duly preserving the middle space or cavity. The materials in this case not being thrown in at random, but the work well brought up on the beds, the upright joints properly arranged, and the face-walls, moreover, regularly tied together, they are not liable to bulge, nor be otherwise disfigured. In these respects one cannot refrain from admiring the walls of the Greeks. They make no use of soft stone in their buildings; when, however, they do not employ squared stones, they use either flint or hard stone, and, as though building with brick, they cross or break the upright joints, and thus produce the most durable work. There are two sorts of this species of work, one called *isodomum* (CC), the other *pseudisodomum* (DD). The first is so called, because in it all the courses are of an equal height; the latter received its name from the unequal heights of the courses. Both these methods make sound work; first, because the stones are hard and solid, and therefore unable to absorb the moisture of the mortar, which is thus preserved to the longest period; secondly, because the beds being smooth and level, the mortar does not escape; and the wall, moreover, bonded throughout its whole thickness, becomes eternal. There is still another method, which is called εμπλεκτον (*emplecton*) (E), in use even among our country workmen. In this species the faces are wrought. The other stones are, without working, deposited in the cavity between the two faces, and bedded in mortar as the wall is carried up. But the workmen, for the sake of despatch, carry up these casing walls, and then tumble in the rubble between them, so that there are thus three distinct thicknesses, namely, the two sides or facings, and the filling in. The Greeks, however, pursue a different course, laying the stones flat, and breaking the vertical joints; neither do they fill in the middle at random, but, by means of bond stones, make the wall solid, and of one thickness or piece. They moreover cross the wall from one face to the other, with bond stones of a single piece, which they call διατονοι (*diatoni*) (F), tending greatly to strengthen the work." We have preferred to give this account in the words of the author himself as the best description, because that of a practical architect, and though capable of some abbreviation, not sufficiently so to justify our own alteration.

MASS. (Germ. Masse.) The quantity of matter whereof any body is composed. The mass of a body is directly as the product of its volume into its density. Multiplied into the constant force of gravity, the mass constitutes the weight; hence the mass of a body is properly estimated by its weight.

MASTIC. (Gr. Μαστικη, a species of gum.) A cement of recent introduction into England, employed for plastering walls. It is used with a considerable portion of linseed oil, and sets hard in a few days. From this latter circumstance, and from its being fit for the reception of paint in a very short period, it is extremely useful in works where expedition is necessary.

MASUCCIO. See ARCHITECTS, list of, 124.

MATERIALS. (Lat. Materies.) Things composed of matter, or possessing its fundamental properties. Those used in building form the subject of the second Chapter of the second Book of this work, to which the reader is referred.

MATHEMATICS. (Gr. Μαθησις, learning.) The science which investigates the consequences logically deducible from any given or admitted relations between magnitude or numbers.

It has usually been divided into two parts, *pure* and *mixed.* The first is that in which geometrical magnitude or numbers are the subjects of investigation ; the last that in which the deductions so made are from relations obtained by observation and experiment from the phenomena of material nature. This is sometimes called *physics,* or physical science. Mathematics, as respects what is necessary for the architect, comprises ARITHMETIC, ALGEBRA, and GEOMETRY ; the latter is treated in this work, Book II. Chap. I. Sect. 1.

MATTER. (Lat. Materies.) That which constitutes substance. Of its intimate nature, the human faculty possesses no cognisance, nor either by observation or experiment can data be furnished whereon to found an investigation of it. All that we seem likely to know of it is its sensible properties, some whereof are the foundation of physical science, others of the different subordinate sciences.

MAURITIUS. See ARCHITECTS, list of, 86.

MAUSOLEUM. A term used to denote a sepulchral building, and so called from a very celebrated one erected to the memory of Mausolus, king of Caria, by his wife Artemisia, about 353 B. C. From its extraordinary magnificence, the building just mentioned was in ancient times esteemed the seventh wonder of the world. According to the account of Pliny, it was 111 feet in circumference, and 140 feet high. It is said to have been encompassed by thirty-six columns, and to have been much enriched with sculpture.

MEAN. In mathematics, that quantity which has an intermediate value between several others, formed according to any assigned law of succession. Thus, an *arithmetical mean* of several quantities is merely the *average,* found by dividing the sum of all the quantities by their number. A *geometrical mean* between two quantities, or a *mean proportional,* is the middle term of a duplicate ratio, or continued proportion of three terms ; that is, that the first given term is to the quantity sought as that quantity is to the other given term. In arithmetic it is the square root of the product of the two given terms. The *harmonical mean* is a number such that the first and third terms being given, the first is to the third as the difference of the first and second is to the difference of the second and third.

MEASURE. (Lat. Mensura.) In geometry, strictly a magnitude or quantity taken as a unit, by which other magnitudes or quantities are measured. It is defined by Euclid as that which, by repetition, becomes equal to the quantity measured. Thus, in arithmetic, the *measure of a number* is some other number which divides it without a remainder, though, perhaps, such a definition rather intimates the notion of *aliquot parts.* But that meaning on which this article is submitted is the unit or standard by which extension is to be measured. We have measures of length, of superficies, and of volume or capacity. But the two latter are always deducible from the former ; whence it is only necessary to establish one unit, namely, a standard of length. The choice of such a standard, definite and invariable, though beset with many and great difficulties, modern science has accomplished. The rude measures of our ancestors, such as the *foot,* the *cubit,* the *span,* the *fathom,* the *barleycorn,* the *hair's breadth,* are not now to be mentioned in matters of science, much more precise standards having been found, and not susceptible of casual variation. Nature affords two or three elements, which, with the aid of science, may be made subservient to the acquisition of the knowledge required. The earth being a solid of revolution, its form and magnitude may be assumed to remain the same in all ages. If this be so, the distance between the pole and the equator may be taken as an invariable quantity ; and any part, say a degree, which is a ninetieth part of it, will be constant, and furnish an unalterable standard of measure. So, again, the force of gravity at the earth's surface being constant at any given place, and nearly the same at places under the same parallel of latitude, and at the same height above the level of the sea, the length of a pendulum making the same number of oscillations in a day is constant at the same place, and may be determined on any assumed scale. Thus we have two elements, the length of a degree of the meridian, and the length of a pendulum beating seconds, which nature furnishes for the basis of a system of measures. Others have been suggested, such as the height through which a heavy body falls in a second of time, determined, like the length of the pendulum, by the force of gravity, or the perpendicular height through which a barometer must be raised till the mercurial column sinks a determinate part ; for instance, one-thirtieth of its own length ; but these are not so capable of accurately determining the standard as the terrestrial degree, or the length of the pendulum.

By an act of Parliament passed in the year 1824, it was declared, in relation to a standard which then was in the custody of the clerk of the House of Commons, whereon were engraved the words and figures *standard yard,* 1760, but which was soon after burnt in the fire of the houses of Parliament, that it should be the unit or only standard measure of extension, and that it should be called the *imperial standard yard.* The act further declared, that if at any time thereafter the said imperial standard yard should be lost, or in any manner destroyed, defaced, or otherwise injured, it should be restored by

making, under the directions of the lords of the treasury, a new standard yard, bearing the proportion to a pendulum vibrating seconds of mean time in the latitude of London, in a vacuum, and at the level of the sea, as 36 inches to 39·1393 inches. It was afterwards found that this measure, when nicely examined, was incorrect, as respected the relation of 36 to 39·1393. It seems, too, never to have been directly compared with the pendulum; neither from the difficulty of determining the lengths of the seconds pendulum, except within limits too wide for the purpose in question, could the restoration of the standard be effected with any certainty. Perhaps the only standard that can be safely referred to at the present day is that belonging to the Royal Astronomical Society.

In the English system of linear measures, the unit, as we have above seen, is the yard, which is subdivided into 3 feet, and each of those feet into 12 inches. Of the yard, the multiples are, the pole or perch, the furlong, and the mile; 5½ yards being 1 pole, 40 poles being 1 furlong, and 8 furlongs 1 mile. The pole and furlong, however, are now much disused, distance being usually measured in miles and yards. The English pace is 1⅔ yards = 5 feet. Thus, the following table exhibits the relations of the different denominations mentioned : —

Inches.	Feet.	Yards.	Poles.	Furlongs.	Miles.
1	0·083	0·028	0·00505	0·00012626	0·0000157828
12	1.	0·333	0·06060	0·00151515	0·00018939
36	3.	1·	0·1818	0·004545	0·00056818
198	16·5	5·5	1·	0·025	0·003125
7920	660·	220·	40·	1·	0·125
63360	5280.	1760·	320·	8·	1·

The measures of superficies are the square yard, foot, inch, &c., as under : —

144 square inches are equal to   -   -   - 1 square foot.
9 square feet   -   -   -   -   - 1 square yard.
2⅞ square yards -   -   -   -   - 1 square pace.
10·89 square paces   -   -   -   - 1 square pole.
40 square poles   -   -   -   -   - 1 square rood.
4 square roods   -   -   -   -   - 1 square acre.

In which it will be seen that the multiples of the yard are the pole, rood, and acre. Very large surfaces, as of countries, are expressed in square miles. The relations of square measure are given in the following table : —

Square Feet.	Square Yards.	Square Poles.	Square Roods.	Square Acres.
1·	0·1111	0·00367309	0·000091827	0·000022957
9·	1·	0·0330579	0·000826448	0·000206612
272·25	30·25	1·	0·025	0·00625
10890·	1210·	40·	1·	0·25
43560·	4840·	160·	4·	1·

The measures of solids are cubic yards, feet, and inches, 1728 cubic inches being equal to a cubic foot, and 27 cubic feet to one cubic yard. By the act of 1824, the standard measure for all sorts of liquids, corn, and other dry goods, is declared to be the *Imperial gallon*. According to the act in question, the imperial standard gallon contains ten pounds avoirdupois of distilled water, weighed in air at the temperature of 62° Fahrenheit's thermometer, the barometer being at 30 inches. The pound avoirdupois contains 7000 troy grains, and it is declared that a cubic inch of distilled water (temperature 62°, barometer 30 inches) weighs 252·458 grains. Hence the imperial gallon contains 277·274 cubic inches. The gallon is subdivided into *quarts* and *pints*, 2 pints being one quart, and 4 quarts one gallon. Its multiples are the *peck*, which is 2 gallons, the *bushel*, which is 4 pecks, and the *quarter*, which is 8 bushels. The relations of measures of volume are given in the subjoined table : —

Pints.	Quarts.	Gallons.	Pecks.	Bushels.	Quarters.
1	0·5	0·125	0·0625	0·015625	0·001953125
2	1·	0·25	0·125	0·03125	0·00390625
8	4·	1·	0·5	0·125	0·015625
16	8·	2·	1·	0·25	0·03125
64	32·	8·	4·	1·	0·125
512	256·	64·	32·	8·	1·

The old wine gallon contained 251 cubic inches, the old corn gallon 268·8 cubic inches, and the old ale gallon 282 cubic inches. Before noticing the new French, or metre, system of measures, we subjoin a few of the principal ancient ones, English inches : —

1 toise, French = 6 French feet	= 6·394665 English feet.
1 foot, do. = 12 French inches	= 12·78936 English inches.
1 inch, do. = 12 French lines	= 1·06578 English inches.
1 line, do. = 6 French points	= 0·088815 English inches.
1 point, do. = ...	= 0·0148025 English inches.

According to General Roy, an English fathom : a French toise :: 1000 : 1065·75.

In the new French system, the *metre*, which is the unit of linear measure, is the tenmillionth part of the quadrant of the meridian = 3·2808992 English feet; and, as its multiples and subdivisions are decimally arranged and named by prefixing Greek numerals, the following table exhibits each : —

Denomination.				English Feet.
Myriametres	-	- 10000 metres	=	32808·992
Kilometre -	-	- 1000	=	3280·8992
Hectometre	-	- 100	=	328·08992
Decametre -	-	- 10	=	32·808992
Metre (the unit)	-	- 1	=	3·2808992
Decimetre -	-	- 0·1	=	0·32808992
Centimetre -	-	- 0·01	=	0·032808992
Millimetre -	-	- 0·001	=	0·0032808992

The metre, therefore, is equal to 39·3707904 English inches.

The unit of superficial measure, in the French system, is the *are*, which is a surface of 10 metres each way, or 100 square metres. The centiare is 1 metre square.

Denomination.			English Square Yards.
Hectare	-	- 10000 square metres	= 11960·33
Are (the unit)	-	100	= 119·6033
Centiare	-	1	= 1·196033

The are, therefore, is equal to 1076·4297 English square feet.

The unit of measures of capacity, in the French system, is the *litre*, a vessel containing a cube of a tenth part of the metre, and equivalent to 0·22009668 British imperial gallon. Its multiples and subdivisions are as follow : —

Denomination.				Eng. Imp. Gallons.
Kilolitre	-	-	- 1000 litres	= 220.09668
Hectolitre	-	-	- 100	= 22·009668
Decalitre	-	-	- 10	= 2·2009668
Litre (the unit)	-	-	- 1	= 0·22009668
Decilitre	-	-	- 0·1	= 0·02209668

The unit of solid measure, or the *stere*, is equal to 35·31658 English cubic feet; therefore,

Denomination.				English Cubic Feet.
Decastere -	-	-	- 10 steres	= 353·1658
Stere (the unit)	-	-	- 1	= 35·31658
Decistere -	-	-	- 0·1	= 3·531658

Under the word Foot will be found the length of that measure in the principal places of Europe. We here think it right to add some further continuation of that article as drawn up by the late Dr. Thomas Young from Hutton, Cavallo, Howard, Vega, and others.

			English Feet.					English Feet.
Altdorff foot	-	-	- ·775 Hutton.	Bourg en Bresse foot	-	-	1·030 H.
Amsterdam foot	-	-	⎰ ·927 H. ⎱ ·930 Cavallo. ⎰ ·931 Howard.	Brabant ell, in Germany	-	-	2·268 Vega.
				Bremen foot	-	-	·955 H.
				Brescia foot	-	-	1·560 H.
Amsterdam ell -	-	-	2·233 C.	Brescian braccio	-	-	2·092 C.
Ancona foot	-	-	1·282 H.	Breslaw foot	-	-	1·125 H.
Antwerp foot	-	-	·940 H.	Bruges foot	-	-	·749 H.
Aquileia foot	-	-	1·128 H.	Brussels foot	-	-	⎰ ·902 H. ⎱ ·954 V.
Arles foot	-	-	·888 H.				
Augsburg foot	-	-	·972 H.	Brussels, greater ell	-	-	2·278 V.
Avignon=Arles.				Brussels, lesser ell	-	-	2·245 V.
Barcelona foot	-	-	·992 H.	Castilian vara	-	-	2·746 C.
Basle foot	-	-	·944 H.	Chambery foot	-	-	1·107 H.
Bavarian foot	-	-	·968 Beigel.	China mathematical foot	-	-	1·127 H.
Bergamo foot	-	-	1·431 H.	China imperial foot	-	-	⎰ 1·051 H ⎱ 1·050 V.
Berlin foot	-	-	·992 H.				
Berne foot	-	-	·962 Howe.	Chinese li	-	-	606·000 C.
Besançon foot	-	-	1·015 H.	Cologne foot	-	-	·903 H.
Bologna foot	-	-	⎰ 1·244 H. ⎱ 1·250 Cavallo.	Constantinople	-	-	⎰ 2·195 H. ⎱ 1·165

Measure	English Feet	Auth.
Copenhagen foot	1·049	H.
Cracow foot	1·169	H. V.
Cracow greater ell	2·024	V.
Cracow smaller ell	1·855	V.
Dantzic foot	·923	H.
Dauphiné foot	1·119	H.
Delft foot	·547	H.
Denmark foot	1·047	H.
Dijon foot	1·030	H.
Dordrecht foot	·771	H.
Dresden foot	·929	Wolfe.
Dryden ell=2 feet	1·857	V.
Ferrara foot	1·317	H.
Florence foot	·995	H.
Florence braccio	{ 1·900 / 1·910 }	Cavallo.
Franche Comté foot	1·172	H.
Frankfort=Hamburgh		H.
Genoa palm	{ ·812 H. / ·809 / ·817 }	Cavallo.
Genoa canna	7·300	C.
Geneva foot	1·919	H.
Grenoble=Dauphiné.		
Haarlem foot	·937	H.
Halle foot	·977	H.
Hamburgh foot	·933	H.
Heidelberg foot	·903	H.
Inspruck foot	1·101	H.
Leghorn foot	·992	H.
Leipzig foot	1·034	H.
Leipzig ell	1·833	H.
Leyden foot	1·023	H.
Liege foot	·944	H.
Lisbon foot	·952	H.
Lucca braccio	1·958	H.
Lyons=Dauphiné.		
Madrid foot	{ ·915 H. / ·918 How. }	
Madrid vara	3·263	C.
Maestricht foot	·916	H.
Malta palm	·915	H.
Mantua brasso	1·521	H.
Mantuan braccio=Brescia		C.
Marseilles foot	·814	H.
Mechlin foot	·753	H.
Mentz foot	·988	H.
Milan decimal foot	·855	H.
Milan aliprand foot	1·426	H.
Milanese braccio	1·725	C.
Modena foot	2·081	H.
Monaco foot	·771	H.
Montpelier pan	·777	H.
Moravian foot	·971	V.
Moravian ell	2·594	H.
Moscow foot	·928	H.
Munich foot	·947	H.
Naples palm	{ ·861 H. / ·859 C. }	
Naples canna	6·908	C.
Nuremburg town foot	{ ·996 H. / ·997 V. }	
Nuremburg country foot	·907	H.
Nuremburg artillery foot	·961	V.
Nuremburg ell	2·166	V.
Padua foot	1·406	H.
Palermo foot	·747	H.
Paris foot	1·066	H.
Paris metre	3·2808	
Parma foot	1·869	H.
Parmesan braccio	2·242	C.
Pavia foot	1·540	H.
Placentia=Parma		C.
Prague foot	{ ·987 H. / ·972 V. }	
Prague ell	1·948	V.
Provence=Marseilles.		
Rhinland foot	{ 1·023 H. / 1·030 Eytelwein. }	
Riga=Hamburgh.		
Roman palm	·733	H.
Roman foot	·966	Folkes.
Roman deto, 1-16th foot	·0604	F.
Roman oncia, 1-12th foot	·0805	F.
Roman palmo	·2515	F.
Roman palmo di architettura	·7325	F.
Roman canna di architettura	7·325	F.
Roman staiolo	4·212	F.
Roman canna dei mercanti (8 palms)	6·5365	F.
Roman braccio dei mercanti (4 palms)	{ 2·7876 F. / 2·856 C. }	
Roman braccio di tessitor di tela	2·0868	F.
Roman braccio di architettura	2·561	C.
Rouen=Paris		H.
Russian archine	2·3625	C.
Russian arschin	2·3333	Phil. Mag.
Russian verschock (1-16th arschin)	·1458	
Savoy=Chamberri		H.
Seville=Barcelona		H.
Seville vara	2·760	H.
Sienna foot	1·239	H.
Stellin foot	1·224	H.
Stockholm foot	{ 1·073 H. / ·974 Celsius. }	
Strasburg town foot	·956	H.
Strasburg country foot	·967	H.
Toledo=Madrid		H.
Trent foot	1·201	H.
Trieste ell for woollens	2·220	H.
Trieste ell for silk	2·107	H.
Turin foot	{ 1·676 H. / 1·681 C. }	
Turin ras	1·958	C.
Turin trabuco	10·085	C.
Tyrol foot	1·096	V.
Tyrol ell	2·639	V.
Valladolid foot	·908	H.
Venice foot	{ 1·137 H. / 1·140 How. / 1·167 C. }	
Venice braccio of silk	2·108	C.
Venice ell	2·089	V.
Venice braccio of cloth	2·250	C.
Verona foot	1·117	H.
Vicenza foot	1·136	H.
Vienna foot	{ 1·036 H. / 1·037 How. }	
Vienna ell	2·557	V.
Vienna post mile	24·888	V.
Vienne in Dauphiné foot	1·058	H.
Ulm foot	·826	H.
Urbino foot	1·162	H.
Utrecht foot	·741	H.
Warsaw foot	1·169	H.
Wesel=Dordrecht		H.
Zurich foot	{ ·979 H. / ·984 Phil. Mag. }	

The uncertainty respecting the ancient Greek and Roman measures had almost induced us to refrain from setting down the usually received notions on those subjects, but as we may be accused by the omission of neglect, we subjoin some few: —

SCRIPTURE LONG MEASURE.

			English Feet	Inches
1 digit		=	0	0·912
4 digits	=1 palm	=	0	3·648
3 palms	=1 span	=	0	10·944
2 spans	=1 cubit	=	1	9·888
4 cubits	=1 fathom	=	7	3·552
1½ fathoms	=1 reed (Ezekiel's)	=	10	11·328
1⅓ reeds	=1 pole (Arabian)	=	14	7·104
10 poles	=1 scœnus, or measuring line	=	145	1·104

Grecian Long Measure.

			English Paces of 5 ft.	Ft.	In.
1	dactylus, or digit	- - - - - -	= 0	0	0·7554
4	dactyli	= 1 doron, or dochme, or palesta	= 0	0	3·0218
$2\frac{1}{2}$	palestre, &c.	= 1 lichas - - -	= 0	0	7·5546
$1\frac{1}{10}$	lichas	= 1 orthodoron - -	= 0	0	8·3101
$1\frac{1}{11}$	orthodoron	= 1 spithame - - -	= 0	0	9·0656
$1\frac{1}{3}$	spithame	= 1 pous, or foot - -	= 0	1	0·0875
$1\frac{1}{8}$	pous	= 1 pygme, or cubit - -	= 0	1	1·5984
$1\frac{1}{9}$	pygme	= 1 pygons - - -	= 0	1	3·109
$1\frac{1}{5}$	pygon	= 1 pecus, or larger cubit -	= 0	1	6·13125
4	pecus	= 1 orgye, or pace - -	= 0	6	0·525
100	orgya, or paces	= 1 stadium, aulus, or furlong -	= 100	4	4·5
8	stadia, &c.	= 1 million, or mile - -	= 805	5	0

Roman Long Measure.

			English Paces.	Ft.	In.
6	scrupula	= 1 sicilicum.			
8	scrupula	= 1 duellum.			
$1\frac{1}{2}$	duellum	= 1 semniaria.			
18	scrupulas	= 1 digitus transversus -	= 0	0	0·725
$1\frac{1}{3}$	digiti	= 1 unciæ, or inch - -	= 0	0	0·967
3	unciæ	= 1 palma minor - -	= 0	0	2·901
4	palmæ	= 1 pes, or foot - -	= 0	0	11·604
$1\frac{1}{4}$	pes, or foot	= 1 palmipes - -	= 0	1	2·505
$1\frac{1}{5}$	palmipes	= 1 cubit - - -	= 0	1	5·406
$1\frac{2}{3}$	cubits	= 1 gradus - - -	= 0	2	5·01
2	gradus	= 1 passus - - -	= 0	4	10·02
2	passus	= 1 decempeda - -	= 1	4	8·04
25	passus	= 1 stadium - - -	= 120	4	4·5
8	stadia	= 1 milliare, or mile - -	= 967	0	0

Mechanics. (Gr. Μηχανη, machine.) That science in natural philosophy treating of forces and powers, and their action on bodies, either directly or by the intervention of machinery. The theory of mechanics is founded on an axiom or principle, called the *law of inertia*, namely, that a body must remain for ever in a state of rest, or in a state of uniform or rectilineal motion, if undisturbed by the action of an external cause. Theoretical mechanics consists, therefore, of two parts: — *Statics*, which treats of the equilibrium of forces; and *dynamics*, or the science of accelerating or retarding forces, and the actions they produce. (See Book II. Chap. I. Sect. 7.) When the bodies under consideration are in a fluid state, these equilibria become respectively *hydrostatics* and *hydrodynamics*.

Mechanical Carpentry. That branch of carpentry which relates to the disposition of the timbers of a building in respect of their relative strength and the strains to which they are subjected. See Book II. Chap. I. Sect. 10, Beams and Pillars.

Mechanical Powers. See Machine.

Medallion. A square, or, more properly, a circular tablet, on which are embossed figures, busts, and the like.

Mediæval Architecture. The architecture of England and the Continent during the middle ages, including the Norman and early Gothic styles.

Melsonby. See Architects, list of, 113.

Member. (Lat.) Any part of an edifice or any moulding in a collection of mouldings, as of those in a cornice, capital, base, &c.

Menagerie. (Fr.) A building for the housing and preservation of rare and foreign animals. The ancient Romans of opulence usually had private menageries, a sort of small park attached to their villa, and in them various kinds of animals were placed.

Mensuration. (Lat.) The science which teaches the method of estimating the magnitudes of lines, superficies, and bodies. See Book. II. Chap. I. Sect. 6,; as applied to measuring and estimating buildings, see Book II. Chap. III. Sect. 14.

Mercier, de. See Architects, list of, 262.

Meridian Line. A line traced on the surface of the earth coinciding with the intersection of the meridian of the place with the sensible horizon. It is therefore a line which lies due north and south. In Italy we often find these lines in large churches, as at Santa Maria del Fiore at Florence, the Duomo at Bologna, &c. They are traced on brass rods let into the pavement of the church, and marked with the signs, and otherwise graduated. A hole in the roof permits the sun's rays to fall on them at his culmination, thus marking noon as well as his height each day in the heavens.

MERLIANO. See ARCHITECTS, list of, 204.

MEROS. (Gr.)   The plane face between the channels in the triglyphs of the Doric order.

MESAULÆ. (Gr.)   Described by Vitruvius as *itinera* or passages; they were, however, smaller courts.   Apollonius Rhodius, in describing the reception of the Argonauts at the palace of Æetes, conducts them first into the vestibule, then through the folding gates into the mesaula, which had *thalami* here and there, and a portico (αιθουσα) on every side.

META. (Lat.)   A mark or goal in the Roman circus to which the chariots, &c. ran.

METAL. (Gr. Μεταλλον.)   A firm, heavy, and hard substance, opaque, fusible by fire, and concreting again when cold into a solid body such as it was before; generally malleable under the hammer, and of a bright glossy and glittering substance where newly cut or broken.   The metals conduct electricity and heat, and have not been resolved into other forms of matter, so that they are regarded as simple or elementary substances.   Modern chemists have carried the number of metals to forty-two, only seven whereof were known to the ancients; namely, — 1. *Gold,* whose symbol is thus marked ⊙; 2. *Silver,* ☽ : 3. *Iron,* ♂ ; 4. *Copper,* ♀ ; 5. *Mercury,* ☿ ; 6. *Lead,* ♄ ; 7. *Tin,* ♃ .   The *metals* of most use in building are treated of in Book II. Chap. II. Sections 5, 6, and 7.

METATOME. (Gr. Μετα, and Τεμνω, I cut.)   The space or interval between two dentels.

METOCHE. (Probably from Μετεχω, I divide.)   In ancient architecture a term used by Vitruvius to denote the interval or space between the dentels of the Ionic, or triglyphs of the Doric order.   Baldus observes that in an ancient MS. copy of that author, the word metatome is used instead of metoche.   This made Daviler suspect that the common text of Vitruvius is corrupt, and that the word should not be metoche but metatome, as it were *section.*

METOPA. (Gr. Μετα, between, and Οπη, a hole.)   The square space in the frieze between the triglyphs of the Doric order: it is left either plane or decorated, according to the taste of the architect.   In the most ancient examples of this order the metopa was left quite open, whereof notice has been taken at p. 57. in the body of the work.

METRODORUS. See ARCHITECTS, list of, 52.

MEZZANINE. (Ital. Mezzano, middle.)   A story of small height introduced between two higher ones.

MEZZO RELIEVO. See RELIEVO.

MICHELOZZI. See ARCHITECTS, list of, 148.

MIDDLE POST. In a roof, the same as KING POST.

MIDDLE QUARTERS OF COLUMNS.   A name given to the four quarters of a column divided by horizontal sections, forming angles of forty-five degrees on the plan.

MIDDLE RAIL.   The rail of a door level with the hand, on which the lock is usually fixed.

MILE. (Lat. Mille passuum, a thousand paces.)   A measure of length in England equal to 1760 yards.   The Roman pace was 5 feet; and a Roman foot being equal to 11·62 modern inches, it follows that the ancient Roman mile was equivalent to 1614 English yards, or very nearly eleven twelfths of an English statute mile.   The measure of the English mile is incidentally defined by an act of parliament passed in the 35th of Elizabeth, restricting persons from erecting new buildings within three miles of London, in which act the mile is declared to be 8 furlongs of 40 perches each, and each perch equal to 16½ feet.

MILK ROOM. See DAIRY.

MILLSTONE GRIT.   A coarse grained quartzose sandstone.   It is extracted from the group of strata which occur between the mountain limestone and the superincumbent coal formations.

MINARET. (Arab. Menarah, a lantern.)   A slender lofty turret, rising by different stages or stories, surrounded by one or more projecting balconies, common in Mohammedan countries, being used by the priests for summoning (from the balconies) the people to prayers at stated periods of the day.

MINION.   An iron ore which, mixed with a proper quantity of lime, makes an excellent water cement.

MINSTER.   A church to which an ecclesiastical fraternity has been or is attached.   The name is applied occasionally to cathedrals, as in the case of York Minster.

MINUTE. (Lat.)   A term given to the sixtieth part of the lower diameter of a column, being a subdivision used for measuring the minuter parts of an order.

MISCHIA. See SCAGLIOLA.

MITCHEL.   A name given by workmen to Purbeck stones of twenty-four by fifteen inches when squared for building.

MITER or MITRE. See BEVEL.

MITER BOX. See BOX FOR MITER.

MIXED ANGLE.   An angle of which one side is a curve and the other a straight line.

MIXED FIGURE.   One composed of straight lines and curves, being neither entirely the

sector nor the segment of a circle, nor the sector nor segment of an ellipsis, nor a parabola, nor an hyperbola.

MNESICLES. See ARCHITECTS, list of, 14.

MNESTHES. See ARCHITECTS, list of, 20.

MOAT. (Lat.) An excavated reservoir of water surrounding a house, castle, or town.

MODEL. (Lat.) An original or pattern proposed for any one to copy or imitate. Thus St. Paul's may be, though not strictly so, said to be built after the model of St. Peter's at Rome.

The word is also used to signify an artificial pattern made of wood, stone, plaster, or other material, with all its parts and proportions, for the satisfaction of the proprietor, or for the guide of the artificers in the execution of any great work. In all great buildings, the only sure method of proceeding is to make a model in relievo, and not to trust entirely to drawings.

MODILLION. (Fr.) A projection under the corona of the richer orders resembling a bracket. In the Grecian Ionic there are no modillions, and they are seldom found in the Roman Ionic. Those in the frontispiece of Nero at Rome consist of two plain faces separated by a small cyma reversa, and crowned with an ovolo and bead. In the frieze of the fourth order of the Coliseum, the modillions are cut in the form of a cyma reversa. For further information on the subject the reader may refer to p. 816. in the body of the work.

MODULAR PROPORTION. That which is regulated by a module. See MODULE.

MODULATION. (Lat.) The proportion of the different parts of an order.

MODULE. (Lat.) A measure which may be taken at pleasure to regulate the proportions of an order, or the disposition of the whole building. The diameter or semi-diameter of the column at the bottom of the shaft has usually been selected by architects as their module; and this they subdivide into parts or minutes. Vignola has divided his module, which is a semi-diameter, into 12 parts for the Tuscan and Doric, and into 18 for the other orders. The module of Palladio, Cambray, Desgodetz, Le Clerc, and others, is divided into 30 parts or minutes in all the orders. Some have divided the whole height of the column into 20 parts for the Doric, 22½ for the Ionic, 25 for the Corinthian, &c., one whereof is taken for the module by which the other parts are to be regulated.

There are two ways by which the measures or proportions of buildings may be determined. First, by a constant standard measure, which is commonly the diameter of the lower part of the column, termed a module, and subdivided into sixty parts called minutes. In the second there are no minutes, nor any certain or stated divisions of the module, but it is divided into as many parts as may be deemed requisite. Thus the height of the Attic base, which is half the module, is divided into three to obtain the height of the plinth, or into four for that of the greater torus, or into six for that of the lesser torus. Both these species of measurement have been used by ancient as well as modern architects, but the latter was that chiefly used by the ancients, and was preferred by Perrault.

Vitruvius having lessened his module in the Doric order, which in the other orders is the diameter of the lower part of the column, and having reduced the great module to a mean one, which is a semi-diameter, Perrault reduces the module to a third part for a similar reason, namely, that of determining the different measurements without a fraction. Thus, in the Doric order, besides that the height of the base, as in the other orders, is determined by one of these mean modules, that same module furnishes the height of the capital, architrave, triglyphs, and metopæ. But the smaller module obtained from a third of the diameter of the lower part of the column has uses considerably more extensive, inasmuch as by it the heights of pedestals, of columns, and entablatures in all the orders may be obtained without a fraction

MODULUS OF ELASTICITY. A term in relation to elastic bodies, which expresses the weight of themselves continued, which would draw them to a certain length without destroying their elastic power.

MOLE. (Sax.) A pier of stone for the shelter of ships from the action of the waves.

Amongst the Romans the term was applied, as in the case of the mole of Adrian (castle of St. Angelo at Rome), to a kind of circular mausoleum.

MOMENTUM. (Lat.) The impetus, force, or quantity of motion in a moving body. The word is sometimes used simply for the motion itself.

MONASTERY. A house for the reception of religious devotees, but more properly applied to one for the habitation of monks.

MONKEY. See FISTUCA.

MONOLITHAL. (Gr. Μονος, one, Λιθος, a stone.) A work consisting of a single stone; such works are found in many parts of the world.

MONOPTERAL. (Gr.) A species of temple of a round form, which had neither walls nor cella, but only a cupola sustained by columns. See TEMPLE.

MONOTRIGLYPH. (Gr.) A term applied to an intercolumniation in which only one triglyph and two metopæ are introduced.

MONTEREAU, DE.　See ARCHITECTS, list of, 116.

MONUMENT. (Lat. Moneo.)　A structure raised to perpetuate the memory of some eminent person, or to serve as a durable token of some extraordinary event.　Monuments at first consisted of stones built over the graves of the dead, on which were engraved the name and frequently a description of the actions of the persons whose memory they are to record.　Monuments were differently formed.　Thus some are pyramids, others obelisks; in some cases a square stone, in others a circular column serves the purpose.

MOORSTONE.　A species of granite found in Cornwall and some other parts of England, and very serviceable in the coarser parts of a building.　Its colours are chiefly black and white, and it is very coarse.　In some parts of Ireland immense beds of it are found.

MORESQUE ARCHITECTURE.　The style of building peculiar to the Moors and Arabs.　See ARABIAN ARCHITECTURE, Book I. Chap. II. Sect. 10.

The word Moresque is also applied to a kind of painting in that style used by the Moors.　It consists in many grotesque pieces and compartments, promiscuously, to appearance, put together, but without any perfect figure of man or animal.　The style is sometimes called *Arabesque*, and Saracenic.

MORTAR.　(Dutch, Morter.)　The calcareous cement used in building, compounded of burnt limestone and sand.　See Book II. Chap. II. Sect. 11.

MORTICE or MORTISE.　(Fr. Mortoise, probably from the Latin Mordeo, to bite.)　In carpentry and joinery, a recessed cutting within the surface of a piece of timber, to receive a projecting piece called a *tenon*, left on the end of another piece of timber, in order to fix the two together at a given angle.　The sides of the mortice are generally four planes at right angles to each other and to the surface, whence the excavation is made.

MOSAIC. (It. Mosaico.)　A mode of representing objects by the inlaying of small cubes of glass, stone, marble, shells, wood, &c.　It was a species of work much in repute among the ancients, as may be gathered from the numerous remains of it.　It is supposed to have originated in the east, and to have been brought from Phœnicia to Greece, and thence carried to Rome　The term Mosaic work is distinguished from *marquetry* by being only applied properly to works of stone, metal, or glass.　The art continues to be practised in Italy at the present day with great success.

MOSQUE. (Turk. Moschet.)　A Mohammedan temple or place of worship.　The earliest Arabian mosques were decorated with ranges of a vast number of columns, often belonging originally to other buildings.　Those of the Turks, on the other hand, are more distinguished for the size and elevation of their principal cupolas.　Each mosque is provided with a minaret, and commonly with a fountain of water, with numerous basins for ablutions.

MOSTON.　See ARCHITECTS, list of, 170.

MOULD.　A term used to signify a pattern or contour by which any work is to be wrought.

The *glazier's moulds* are of two sorts, one whereof is used for casting the lead into long rods or cames, fit for drawing through the vice in which the grooves are formed.　This they sometimes call the ingot mould.　The other is for moulding the small pieces of lead, a line thick and two lines broad, which are fastened to the iron bars of casements.

The *mason's mould*, also called *caliber*, is a piece of hard wood or iron, hollowed on the edge, answering to the contours of the mouldings or cornices to be formed.　The ends or heading joints being formed as in a cornice by means of the mould, the intermediate parts are wrought down by straight-edges, or circular templets, as the work is straight or circular on the plan.　When the intended surface is required to be very exact, a reverse mould is used, in order to prove the work, by applying the mould in a transverse direction of the arrises.

MOULDS, among plumbers, are the tables on which they cast their sheets of lead, and are simply called *tables*.　They have others for casting pipes without soldering.

The moulds for foundery are described Book II. Chap. III. Sect. 11.

MOULDINGS.　The ornamental contours or forms applied to the edges of the projecting or receding members of an order.　The regular mouldings are the *fillet, listel,* or *annulet; the astragal,* or *bead; the torus,* the *scotia,* or *trochilus;* the *echinus, ovolo,* or *quarter-round; the cyma reversa. inverted cyma,* or *ogee; the cyma recta,* the *cavetto,* or *hollow.* See p. 806.

Mouldings are divided into two classes — Grecian and Roman.　The first are formed by some conic section, as a portion of an ellipse or hyperbola, and sometimes even of a straight line in the form of a *chamfer.*　The Roman mouldings are formed by arcs of circles, the same moulding having the same curvature throughout.

For Norman mouldings see p. 174; and for Gothic mouldings, Book III. Chap. III.

MOUTH, BIRD'S.　See BIRD'S MOUTH.

MUET, LE.　See ARCHITECTS, list of, 254.

MULLION, MUNNION, or MONIAL.　In pointed architecture, the vertical post or bar which divides a window into several lights.

MUNIMENT ROOM. A strong, properly fire-proof, apartment in public or private buildings, for the keeping ,and preservation of evidences, charters, seals, &c., called muniments.

MURAL. (Lat.) Belonging to a wall. Thus a monumental tablet affixed to a wall is called a *mural monument;* an arch inserted into or attached to a wall is called a *mural arch;* and columns placed within or against a wall are called *mural columns.*

MUSEUM. (Gr. Μουσειον.) A repository of natural, scientific, and literary curiosities, or of works of art. See Book III. Chap. V. Sect. 10.

MUSTIUS. See ARCHITECTS, list of, 45.

MUTILATED CORNICE. One that is broken or discontinued.

MUTILATION. (Lat.) The defacing or cutting away of any regular body. The word is applied to statues and buildings where any part is wanting.

MUTIUS, C. See ARCHITECTS, list of, 31.

MUTULE. (Lat.) A projecting ornament of the Doric cornice, which occupies the place of the modillion in the other orders, and is supposed to represent the ends of rafters. The mutule has always been assumed as an imitation of the end of a wooden rafter; hence, say the advocates for a timber type, they are properly represented with a declination towards the front of the coronas.

MYLNE. See ARCHITECTS, list of, 311.

N.

NAIL. (Sax. Næ3el.) A small metal spike for fastening one piece of timber to another. The sorts of nails are very numerous. The principal are here enumerated. *Back nails,* whose shanks are flat so as to hold fast but not open the wood. *Clamp nails,* are for fastening clamps. *Clasp nails,* or *brads,* are those with flatted heads, so that they may clasp the wood. They also render the wood smooth, so as to admit of a plane going over it. The sorts of most common use in building are known by the names of *ten-penny, twenty-penny* and *two-shilling nails. Clench nails* are such as are used by boat and barge builders, sometimes with boves or nuts, but often without. They are made with clasp heads for fine work, or with the head beat flat on two sides. *Clout nails,* used for nailing clouts on axle-trees, are flat headed, and iron work is usually nailed on with them. *Deck nails,* for fastening decks in ships and floors nailed with planks. *Dog* or *jobent nails,* for fastening the hinges of doors, &c. *Flat points* are of two sorts, *long* and *short;* the former much used in shipping, and useful where it is necessary to hold fast and draw without requiring to be clenched; the latter are furnished with points to drive into hard wood. *Lead nails,* used for nailing lead, leather, and canvas to hard wood, are the same as clout nails dipped in lead or solder. *Port nails,* for nailing hinges to the ports of ships. *Ribbing nails,* used for fastening the ribbing to keep the ribs of ships in their place while the ship is building. *Rose nails* are drawn square in the shank. *Rother nails,* chiefly used for fastening rother irons to ships. *Scupper nails,* much in use for fastening leather and canvas to wood. *Sharp nails,* much used in the West Indies, and made with sharp points and flat shanks. *Sheathing nails,* for fastening sheathing boards to ships; their length is usually three times the thickness of the board. *Square nails* are of the same shape as sharp nails, chiefly used for hard wood. *Brads* are long and slender nails without heads, used for thin deal work to avoid splitting. To these may be added *tacks,* the smallest sort whereof serve to fasten paper to wood; the *middling* for medium work; and the *larger size,* which are much used by upholsterers. These are known by the name of *white tacks, two-penny, three-penny,* and *four-penny tacks.* See ADHESION.

NAIL-HEADED MOULDING. One common in Norman buildings, and so called from being formed by a series of projections resembling the heads of nails or square knobs. See p. 174.

NAKED. A term applied either to a column or wall to denote the face or plain surface from which the projections rise.

NAKED FLOORING. See p. 597.

NAKED OF A WALL. The remote face whence the projections take their rise. It is generally a plain surface, and when the plan is circular the naked is the surface of a cylinder with its axis perpendicular to the horizon.

NAOS or NAVE. (Gr. Naos.) See CELL.

NATURAL BED OF A STONE. The surface from which the laminæ were separated. In all masonry it is important to its duration that the laminæ should be placed perpendicular to the face of the work, and parallel to the horizon, inasmuch as the connecting substance of these laminæ is more friable than the laminæ themselves, and therefore apt to scale off in large flakes, and thus induce a rapid decay of the work.

NAUMACHIA. (Gr. from Naus, a ship, and Μαχη, a battle.) In ancient architecture, a place for the show of mock sea engagements, little different from the circus and amphitheatre, since this species of exhibition was often displayed in those buildings.

NAVE. (Gr. Ναος.) The body of a church or place where the people are seated, reaching from the rail or partition of the choir to the principal entrance. See CELL.

NEBULE MOULDING. (Lat. Nebula.) An ornament in Norman architecture, whose edge forms an undulating or wavy line, and introduced in corbel tables and archivolts. See p. 174.

NECK OF A CAPITAL. The space, in the Doric order, between the astragal on the shaft and the annulet of the capital. Some of the Grecian Ionic capitals are with necks below them, as in the examples of Minerva Polias and Erectheus, at Athens. But the Ionic order has rarely a neck to the capital.

NEEDLE. An horizontal piece of timber serving as a temporary support to some super-incumbent weight, as a pier of brickwork, and resting upon posts or *shores*, while the lower part of a wall, pier, or building is being underpinned or repaired.

NERVURES. A name given by French architects to the ribs bounding the sides of a groined compartment of a vaulted roof, as distinguished from the ribs which diagonally cross the compartment.

NET MEASURE. That in which no allowance is made for finishing, and in the work of artificers, when no allowance is made for the waste of materials.

NEWEL. The upright cylinder or pillar, round which, in a winding staircase, the steps turn, and are supported from the bottom to the top. In stairs, geometrical for instance, where the steps are *pinned* into the wall, and there is no central pillar, the staircase is said to have an open *newel*.

NICHE. (Fr. probably from Νεοσσια, a nest.) A cavity or hollow place in the thickness of a wall for the reception of a statue, vase, &c. See Book III. Chap. I. Sect. 21.

NICOLA DA PISA. See ARCHITECTS, list of, 121.

NICON. See ARCHITECTS, list of, 51.

NIDGED ASHLAR. A species of ashlar used in Aberdeen. It is brought to the square by means of a cavil or hammer with a sharp point, which reduces the roughness of the stone to a degree of smoothness according to the time employed. When stone is so hard as to resist the chisel and mallet, the method described is the only way in which it can be dressed.

NOGS. The same as WOOD BRICKS, which see. The term is chiefly used in the north of England.

NOGGING. A species of brickwork carried up in panels between quarters.

NOGGING-PIECES. Horizontal boards laid in brick-nogging, and nailed to the quarters for strengthening the brickwork. They are disposed at equal altitudes in the brick-work.

NONAGON. (Gr.) A geometrical figure having nine sides and nine angles.

NORMAL LINE. In geometry, one which stands at right angles to another line.

NORMAN ARCHITECTURE. See Book I. Chap. III. Sect. 2.

NORMAND. See ARCHITECTS, list of, 172.

NOSING OF A STEP. The projecting part of the tread-board or cover which stands before the riser. The nosing is generally rounded, so as to have a semicircular section; and in the better sort of staircases a fillet and hollow is placed under the nosing.

NOTCH-BOARD. A board which is grooved or notched for the reception and support of the ends of steps in a staircase.

NOTCHING. A hollow cut from one of the faces of a piece of timber, generally made rectangular in section.

NUCLEUS. (Lat.) In ancient architecture, the internal part of a floor, which consisted of a strong cement, over which the pavement was laid with mortar.

NYMPHÆUM. (Gr.) A name used by the ancients to denote a picturesque grotto in a rocky or woody place, supposed to be dedicated to, and frequented by, the nymphs. The Romans often made artificial nymphæa in their gardens. In Attica, the remains of a nymphæum are still to be seen decorated with inscriptions and bassi relievi, from the rude workmanship of which it may be presumed that the grotto is of very ancient date.

O.

OAK. (Sax. Ac, Æc.) A forest tree, whose timber is, from its strength, hardness, and dura-bility, the most useful of all in building. See Book II. Chap. II. Sect. 4.

OBELISK. (Probably from Οβελος, a spit, brooch, or spindle, or a long javelin.) A lofty pillar of a rectangular form, diminishing towards the top, and generally ornamented with inscriptions and hieroglyphics. The upper part finishes generally with a low pyramid, called a *pyramidion*. The proportion of the thickness to the height is nearly the same in all obelisks; that is, between one ninth and one tenth, and their thickness at top is never less than half, nor greater than three fourths, of that at bottom. Egypt abounded with obelisks, which were always in a single block of stone; and many have been removed thence to Rome and other places. The following table exhibits a list of the principal

obelisks whereof there is any record, or which are at present known, being thirty-three
in number.

Situation.	Height.	Thickness.	
		At top.	Below.
	Eng. Feet.	Eng. Feet.	Eng. Feet.
Two large obelisks, mentioned by Diodorus Siculus	158·2	7·9	11·8
Two obelisks of Nuncoreus, son of Sesostris, according to Herodotus, Diodorus Siculus, and Pliny	121·8	6·6	10·5
Obelisk of Rhameses, removed to Rome by Constantius	118·4	6·2	10·2
Two obelisks, attributed by Pliny to Smerres and Eraphius	106·0	5·9	9·8
Obelisks of Nectanabis, erected near the tomb of Arsinöe by Ptolemy Philadelphus	105·5	5·3	9·2
Obelisk of Constantius, restored and erected in front of S. Giovanni Laterano at Rome	105·5	6·2	9·6
Part of one of the obelisks of the son of Sesostris, in the centre of the piazza in front of St. Peter's	82·4	5·8	9·4
Two at Luxor	79·1	5·3	8·0
Obelisk of Augustus from the Circus Maximus, now in the piazza del Popola at Rome	78·2	4·5	7·4
Two in the ruins at Thebes, still remaining	72·8	5·0	7·5
Obelisk of Augustus, raised by Pius VI. in the Piazza di Monte Citorio	71·9	4·9	7·9
Two obelisks, one at Alexandria, vulgarly called Cleopatra's Needle, and the other at Heliopolis	67·1	5·1	8·1
Obelisk by Pliny, attributed to Sothis	63·3	4·5	5·1
Two obelisks in the ruins of Thebes	63·3	4·5	5·1
Great obelisk at Constantinople	59·7	4·5	7·2
Obelisk in the Piazza Navona, removed from the Circus of Caracalla	54·9	2·9	4·5
Obelisk at Arles	50·1	4·5	7·4
Obelisk from the Mausoleum of Augustus, now in front of the church of Sta. Maria Maggiore at Rome	48·3	2·9	4·3
Obelisk in the gardens of Sallust, according to Mercati	48·3	2·9	4·3
Obelisk at Bijije in Egypt	42·9	2·6	4·2
Small obelisk at Constantinople, according to Gyllius	34·2	3·9	5·9
The Barberini Obelisk	30·0	2·2	3·9
Obelisk of the Villa Mattei	26·4	2·2	2·7
Obelisk in the Piazza della Rotunda	20·1	2·1	2·4
Obelisk in the Piazza di Minerva	17·6	2·0	2·6
Obelisk of the Villa Medici	16·1	1·9	2·4

OBLIQUE LINE.   One which stands, in respect to another, at a greater angle than ninety
degrees.

OBLIQUE ANGLE.   One that is greater or less than a right angle.

OBLIQUE-ANGLED TRIANGLE.   One that has no right angle.

OBLIQUE ARCHES.   Such as cross an opening obliquely to the front face of them.

OBLONG.   A rectangle of unequal dimensions.

OBSERVATORY. (Fr.)   A building for the reception of instruments and other matters for
observing the heavenly bodies.   See Book III. Chap. V. Sect. 11.

OBTUSE. (Lat.)   Anything that is blunt.

OBTUSE-ANGLED TRIANGLE.   One which has an obtuse angle.

OBTUSE SECTION OF A CONE.   Among the ancient geometricians a name given to the
hyperbola.

OCTAGON. (Gr. 'Οκτὼ and Γωνία, angle.)   A figure having eight equal sides and eight
equal angles.

OCTAHEDRON. (Gr.)   One of the five regular bodies bounded by eight equal and equilateral triangles.

OCTASTYLE. (Gr. 'Οκτὼ and Στῦλος.)   That species of temple or building having eight
columns in front.   See COLONNADE.

ODEUM. (Gr.)   Among the Greeks, a species of theatre wherein the poets and musicians
rehearsed their compositions previous to the public production of them.

ODO.   See ARCHITECTS, list of, 88.

OECUS.   See HALL.

OFFICES. The appartments wherein the domestics discharge the several duties attached to the service of a house; as kitchens, pantries, brewhouses, and the like.

OFFSETS. The horizontal projections from the faces of the different parts of a wall where it increases in thickness.

OGEE. A moulding, the same as the CYMA REVERSA, which see.

OGIVE. A term used by French architects to denote the Gothic vault, with its ribs and cross springers, &c. The word is used to denote the pointed arch.

OLOLZAGO. See ARCHITECTS, list of, 194.

ONE PAIR OF STAIRS. An expression signifying the first story or floor above that floor level with, or raised only by a few steps above, the ground, which latter is thence called the ground floor.

OPÆ. (Gr. Οπη.) The beds of the beams of a floor or roof between which are the METOPÆ, which see.

OPENINGS. (Sax.) Those parts of the walls of a building which are unfilled for admitting light, ingress, egress, &c. See APERTURE.

OPISTHODOMUS. (Gr.) The same as the Roman posticum, being the enclosed space behind a temple.

OPPOSITE ANGLES. Those formed by two straight lines crossing each other, but not two adjacent angles.

OPPOSITE CONES. Those to which a straight line can be applied on the surfaces of both cones.

OPPOSITE SECTIONS. The sections made by a plane cutting two opposite cones.

OPTIC PYRAMID. In perspective, that formed by the optic rays to every point of an object.

OPTIC RAYS. Those which diverge from the eye to every part of an original object.

ORANGERY. A gallery or building in a garden or parterre opposite to the south. See GREEN-HOUSE. The most magnificent orangery in Europe is that of Versailles, which is of the Tuscan order, and with wings.

ORATORY. (Lat.) A small apartment in a house, furnished with a small altar, crucifix, &c., for private devotion. The ancient oratories were small chapels attached to monasteries, in which the monks offered up their prayers. Towards the sixth and seventh centuries the oratory was a small church, built frequently in a burial place, without either baptistery or attached priest, the service being performed by one occasionally sent for that purpose by the bishop.

ORB. (Lat. Orbis.) A knot of foliage or flowers placed at the intersection of the ribs of a Gothic ceiling or vault to conceal the mitres of the ribs.

ORCHESTRA. (Gr. Ορχεομαι.) In ancient architecture, the place in the theatre where the chorus danced. In modern theatres it is the enclosed part of a theatre. or of a music-room wherein the instrumental and vocal performers are seated.

ORCHEYARDE. See ARCHITECTS, list of, 160.

ORDER. (Lat.) An assemblage of parts, consisting of a base, shaft, capital, architrave, frieze, and cornice, whose several services requiring some distinction in strength, have been contrived in five several species — Tuscan, Doric, Ionic, Corinthian, and Composite; each of these has its ornaments, as well as its general fabric, proportioned to its strength and use. There are five orders of architecture, the proper understanding and application whereof constitute the foundation of all excellence in the art. See Book III. Chap. I. Sect. 2. on the ORDERS generally.

ORDER, COMPOSITE. See Book III. Chap. I. Sect. 7.

ORDER, CORINTHIAN. See Book III. Chap. I. Sect. 6.

ORDER, DORIC. See Book III. Chap. I. Sect. 4.

ORDER, IONIC. See Book III. Chap. I. Sect. 5.

ORDER, TUSCAN. See Book III. Chap. I. Sect. 3.

ORDERS ABOVE ORDERS. See Book III. Chap. I. Sect. 11.

ORDINATE. In geometry and conics, a line drawn from any point of the circumference of an ellipsis or other conic section perpendicular to, and across the axis, to the other side.

ORDONNANCE. (Fr. from the Lat.) The perfect arrangement and composition of any architectural work. It applies to no particular class, but the term is general to all species in which there has existed anything like conventional law.

ORGANICAL DESCRIPTION OF A CURVE. The method of describing one upon a plane by continued motion.

ORIEL or ORIEL WINDOW. (Etym. uncertain.) A large bay or recessed window in a hall, chapel, or other apartment. It ordinarily projects from the outer face of the wall either in a semi-octagonal or diagonal plan, and is of varied kinds and sizes. In large halls its usual height is from the floor to the ceiling internally, and it rises from the ground to the parapet on the outside; sometimes it consists only of one smaller window supported by corbels, or by masonry projecting gradually from the wall to the sill of the window. Milner, the learned and good Catholic bishop, in his History of Winchester,

draws a difference between the bow and oriel window. The first projected circularly, and was formerly called a compass or embowed window; whilst the projection of the last was made up of angles and straight lines forming generally the half of a hexagon, octagon, or decagon, and was better known by the name of *bay window, shot window,* or *outcast window,* a distinction, however, not generally observed.

ORIGIN AND PROGRESS OF ARCHITECTURE. See Book I. Chap. I. Sect. 2.

ORIGINAL LINE, PLANE, or POINT. In perspective, a line, plane, or point referred to the object itself.

ORLE. (Ital.) A fillet under the ovolo or quarter round of a capital. When the fillet is at the top or bottom of the shaft of a column it is called a cincture. Palladio uses the word orle to express the plinth of the bases of the columns and pedestal.

ORNAMENT. The smaller and detailed part of the work, not essential to it, but serving to enrich it; it is generally founded upon some imitation of the works of nature.

ORTHOGRAPHY. (Gr. Ορθος, right, and Γραφω, I describe.) The elevation of building showing all the parts in their proper proportions; it is either external or internal. The first is the representation of the external part or front of a building showing the face of the principal wall, with its apertures, roof of the building, projections, decorations, and all other matters as seen by the eye of the spectator, placed at an infinite distance from it. The second, commonly called the *section* of a building, shows it as if the external wall were removed, and separated from it.

In geometry, orthography is the art of representing the plan or side of any object, and of the elevation also of the principal parts : the art is so denominated from its etymology, because it determines things by perpendicular *right lines* falling on the geometrical plan, or because all the horizontal lines are straight and parallel, and not, as in perspective, oblique.

OSCULATING CIRCLE. That, the radius of whose curve at any particular point of another curve, is of the same length as that of the curve in question at that particular point. Hence it is the kissing circle, and that so closely, that there is no difference in the curvature of the two curves at that particular point.

OUTER DOORS. Those common to both the exterior and interior sides of a building.

OUTER PLATE. See INNER PLATE.

OUTLINE. The line which bounds the contour of any object.

OUT OF WINDING. A term used by artificers to signify that the surface of a body is that of a perfect plane ; thus when two straight edges in every direction are in the same plane they are said to be out of winding.

OUT TO OUT. An expression used of any dimension when measured to the utmost bounds of a body or figure.

OUTWARD ANGLE. The external or salient angle of any figure.

OVA. (Lat.) Ornaments in the shape of an egg, into which the echinus or ovolo is often carved.

OVAL. A geometrical figure, whose boundary is a curve line returning into itself ; it includes the ellipsis or mathematical oval, and all figures resembling it, though with different properties.

OVERHANG. See BATTER.

OVOLO. (Ital.) A convex moulding whose lower extremity recedes from a perpendicular line drawn from the upper extremity. See MOULDING.

P.

PADDLE. A small sluice, similar to that whereby water is let into or out of a canal lock.

PAGODA. (Corrupted from Poutgad, Pers., a house of idols.) A name given to the temples of India. See INDIAN ARCHITECTURE. Book I. Chap. II. Sect. 6.

PAINE. See ARCHITECTS, list of, 303.

PAINTER'S WORK. See Book II. Chap. III. Sect. 12.

The work of painting with different coats of oil colour and turpentine the parts of a building usually so treated.

PALACE. (Lat. Palatium.) In this country, a name given to the dwelling of a king or queen, a prince, and a bishop. On the Continent, it is a term more extensively used, almost all large dwellings and government offices being so denominated. See Book III. Chap. V. Sect. 4.

PALÆSTRA. (Gr. Παλαιω, I wrestle.) A part of the Grecian gymnasium, particularly appropriated to wrestling and other gymnastic exercises ; it was sometimes used to denote the whole building. It contained baths which were open for the use of the public. According to the authority of Vitruvius, no palæstra existed in Rome.

PALE. A small pointed stake or piece of wood used for making landmarks and enclosures placed vertically.

Palf Fencing or Pale Fence. That constructed with pales.

Palisade. A fence of pales or stakes driven into the ground, set up for an enclosure, or for the protection of property.

Palladio. See Architects, list of, 241.

Palm. A measure of length. See Measure.

Pampre. (Fr.) An ornament composed of vine leaves and bunches of grapes, wherewith the hollow of the circumvolutions of twisted columns are sometimes decorated.

Pancarpi. (Gr.) Garlands and festoons of fruit, flowers, and leaves, for the ornament of altars, doors, vestibules, &c.

Panel. (From the low Latin panellum.) A board whose edges are inserted into the groove of a thicker surrounding frame.

A panel in masonry is one of the faces of a hewn stone.

Pannier. The same as Corbel, which see.

Pantameter. A graduated bevel.

Pantiles. See Book II. Chap. II. Sect. 9.

Pantograph. An instrument for copying, diminishing, or enlarging drawings.

Paper. A substance made by the maceration of linen rags in water and spreading them into thin sheets; on this the drawings of the architect are usually made; its usual sizes being as under: —

Demy	-	-	20 inches by 15 inches.	Atlas	-	-	-	34 inches by 26 inches.
Medium	-	-	22½ — 17 —	Double Elephant	-	40	—	27 —
Royal	-	-	24 — 19¼ —	Antiquarian	-	-	53	— 31 —
Super-royal	-	-	27 — 19½ —	Extra Antiquarian		56	—	38 —
Imperial	-	-	30 — 22 —	Emperor	-	-	68	— 48 —
Colombier	-	-	34 — 23 —					

Paperhanger's Work. See Book II. Chap. III. Sect. 12.

Parabola. (Gr. Παρα, through, and Βαλλω, I throw.) In geometry, a curve line formed by the common intersection of a conic surface, and a plane cutting it parallel to another plane touching the conic surface. See Book II. Chap. I. Sect. 4.

Parabolic Assymptote. In geometry, a line continually approaching the curve, but which, though infinitely produced, will never meet it.

Parabolic Curve. The curved boundary of a parabola, and terminating its area, except at the double ordinate.

Parabolic Spiral, or Helicoid. A curve arising from the supposition of the axis of the common parabola bent into the periphery of a circle, the ordinates being portions of the radii next the circumference.

Paraboloid. See Conoid.

Parallel. (Gr. Παραλληλος.) In geometry, a term applied to lines, surfaces, &c., that are in every part equidistant from each other.

Parallel Coping. See Coping.

Parallelogram. (Gr.) Any four-sided rectilineal figure, whose opposite sides are parallel.

Parallelopiped. In geometry, one of the regular bodies or solids comprehended under six faces, each parallel to its opposite face, and all the faces parallelograms.

Parameter. (Gr. Παρα, through, and Μετρω, I measure.) In conic sections, a constant right line in each of the three sections, called also latus rectum.

Parapet. (Ital. Parapetto, breast high.) A small wall of any material for protection on the sides of bridges, quays, or high buildings.

Parascenium. Another name for the postscenium in the ancient theatre.

Parastatæ. See Antæ.

Parget. A name given to the rough plaster used for lining chimney flues, and formed of [lime and cow's dung.

Parker's Cement. See p. 540.

Parlour. (Fr.) A room for conversation, which in the old monasteries adjoined the buttery and pantry at the lower end of the hall. At the present day it is used to denote the room in a house where common visitors are received.

Parodos. (Gr.) The grand entrance of the scene of an ancient theatre that conducted on to the stage and orchestra.

Parquetry. See Marquetry. Parquetry is marquetry work applied to a floor.

Parsonage House. A building usually near the church, occupied by the incumbent of the living; in former times this sort of building was often embattled and fortified, and had various appendages, including sometimes a small chapel or oratory.

Partition. (Lat.) A wall of stone, brick, or timber, dividing one room from another. When a partition has no support from below, it should not be suffered to bear on the floor with any considerable weight, and in such cases it should have a truss formed within it, in which case it is called a trussed partition. See Truss.

Party Walls. Such as are formed between houses to separate them from each other and

prevent the spreading of fire.   The regulations prescribed for them form a large portion of the Metropolitan Building Act of 18 and 19 Victoria, cap. 122.

PARTY FENCE WALL.   A wall separating the vacant ground in one occupation from that in another.

PARVIS. (Etym. uncertain.)   A porch, portico, or large entrance to a church.   It seems also to have signified a room over the church porch, where schools used to be held.

PASSAGES.   The avenues leading to the various divisions and apartments of a building. When there is only one series of rooms in breadth, the passage must run along one side of the building, and may be lighted by apertures through the exterior walls.   If there be more than one room in breadth, it must run in the middle, and be lighted from above or at one or both ends.

PATERA. (Lat.)   A vessel used in the Roman sacrifices, wherein the blood of the victims was received.   It was generally shallow, flat, and circular.   Its representation has been introduced as an ornament in friezes and fasciæ, accompanied with festoons of flowers or husks, and other accessories.

PATERNOSTERS.   A species of ornament in the shape of beads, either round or oval, used in baguettes, astragals, &c.

PAUTRE, LE.   See ARCHITECTS, list of, 261.

PAVEMENT. (Lat. Pavimentum.)   A path or road laid or beaten in with stones or other materials.   According to the information of Isidorus, the first people who paved their streets with stone were the Carthaginians.   Appius Claudius, the founder of the Appian Way, appears to have introduced the practice into Rome, after which the Roman roads were universally paved, remains of them having been found in every part of the empire.

In the interior of the Roman houses, the pavement was often laid upon timber framing ; and the assemblages so constructed were called *contignata pavimenta.*   The pavement called *coassatio* was made of oaken planks of the *quercus æsculus,* which was least liable to warp.   The Roman pavements were also frequently of mosaic work, that is, of square pieces of stone, called tesseræ, in various patterns and figures, many of which remain in Britain to the present day.

The various sorts of paving are as follows : — 1. *Pebble paving,* of stones collected from the sea beach, mostly obtained from Guernsey or Jersey.   This is very durable if well laid.   The stones vary in size, but those from six to nine inches deep are the best, those of three inches in depth are called *bolders* or *bowlers,* and are used for paving courtyards and those places wherever heavy weights do not pass.   2. *Rag paving :* inferior to the last, and usually from the vicinity of Maidstone, in Kent, whence it bears the name of Kentish rag stone.   It is sometimes squared, and then used for paving coachtracks and footways.   3. *Purbeck pitchers,* which are square stones, used in footways, brought from the island of Purbeck.   They are useful in court-yards ; the pieces running about five inches thick, and from six to ten inches square.   4. *Squared paving,* by some called *Scotch paving,* of a clear close stone, called *blue wynx.*   This is now, however, quite out of use.   5. *Granite,* of the material which its name imports.   6. *Guernsey paving,* which, for street work, is the best in use.   It is broken with iron hammers, and squared to any required dimensions, of a prismoidal figure, with a smaller base downwards.   It is commonly bedded in small gravel.   7. *Purbeck paving,* used for footways, of which the blue sort is the best, is obtained in pretty large surfaces, of about two inches and a half thick.   8. *Yorkshire paving :* a very good material, and procurable of very large dimensions.   9. *Ryegate* or *fire-stone paving,* used for hearths, stoves, ovens, and other places subject to great heat, by which this stone, if kept dry, is not affected.   10. *Newcastle flags,* useful for the paving of offices.   They run about one and a half to two inches thick, and about two feet square, and bear considerable resemblance to the Yorkshire.   11. *Portland paving* may be had from the island of Portland of almost any required dimensions.   The squares are sometimes ornamented by cutting away their angles, and inserting small black marble squares, set diagonally.   12. *Sweedland paving :* a black slate dug in Leicestershire, useful for paving halls or for party-coloured paving. 13. *Marble paving,* of as many sorts almost as there are species of marble.   It is sometimes inlaid after the manner of Mosaic work.   14. *Flat brick paving,* executed with bricks laid flat in sand, mortar, or grout, when liquid lime is poured into the joints. 15. *Brick-on-edge paving,* executed in the manner of the last, except that the bricks are laid on edge.   16. *Herring-bone paving :* bricks laid diagonally to each other.   See HERRING-BONE WORK.   17. *Bricks laid endwise* in sand, mortar, or grout.   18. *Paving bricks,* are made especially for the purpose, and are better than stocks.   19. *Ten-inch tile paving.* 20. *Foot tile paving.*   21. *Clinker paving.*

The pavements of churches are often in patterns of several colours, of which, to shew the great variety that may be obtained from a few colours, M. Truchet (*Mém. Acad. Fran.*) has proved that two square stones, divided diagonally into two colours, may be joined together chequerwise in sixty-four different ways.

PAVEMENT (DIAMOND.) That in which the stones, flags, or bricks are laid with their diagonals perpendicular to the sides of the apartment.

PAVILION. (Ital. Padiglione.) A turret or small building, generally insulated and comprised under a single roof. The term is also applied to the projecting parts in the front of a building. They are usually higher than the rest of the building.

PEDESTAL. (Compound, apparently, of Πους, a foot, and Στυλος, a column.) The lowest division in an order of columns, called also *stylobates* and *stereobates*. It consists of three principal parts: the die, the cornice, and the base. See Book III. Chap. I. Sect. 8.

PEDIMENT. The triangular crowning part of a portico or aperture, which terminates vertically the sloping parts of the roof. In Gothic architecture, this triangular piece is much higher in proportion to its width, and is denominated a gable. The subject of pediments is fully treated of in Book III. Chap. I. Sect. 17.

PELASGIC ARCHITECTURE. See Book I. Chap. II. Sect. 2.

PENDENT. (Lat.) An ornament suspended from the summit of Gothic vaulting, very often elaborately decorated. The mode in which stone pendents are constructed, will be immediately understood by a consideration of the annexed figure. The pendent was also used very frequently to timber-framed roofs, as in that of Crosby Hall, which has a series of pendents along the centre of it. Pendents are also attached to the ends of the hammer beams in Gothic timber roofs.

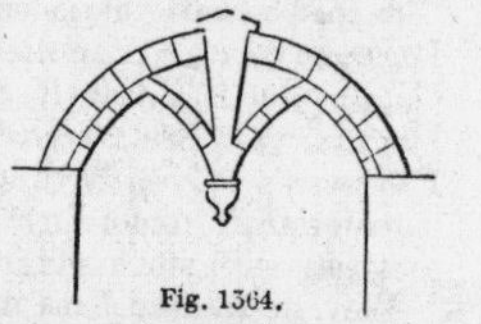

Fig. 1364.

PENDENTIVE. The entire body of a vault suspended out of the perpendicular of the walls, and bearing against the arch boutants, or supporters. It is defined by Daviler to be the portion of a vault between the arches of a dome, commonly enriched with sculpture. Felibien defines it as the plane of the vault contained between the double arches, the forming arches, and the ogives.

PENDENTIVE BRACKETING or CAVE BRACKETING. That springing from the rectangular walls of an apartment upwards to the ceiling, and forming the horizontal part of the ceiling into a circle or ellipsis.

PENDENTIVE CRADLING. The timber work for sustaining the lath and plaster in vaulted ceilings.

PENETRALE. (Lat.) The most sacred part of the temple, which generally contained an altar to Jupiter Hercæus, which appellation, according to Festus, was derived from ερκος, an enclosure, and supposed him the protector of its sanctity.

PENETRALIA. (Lat.) Small chapels dedicated to the Penates, in the innermost part of the Roman houses. In these it was the custom to deposit what the family considered most valuable.

PENITENTIARY. In monastic establishments was a small square building, in which a penitent confined himself. The term was also applied to that part of a church to which penitents were admitted during divine service. The word, as used in the present time, implies a place for the reception of criminals whose crimes are not so heinous as to deserve punishment beyond that of solitary confinement and hard labour, and where means are used to reclaim as much as possible those who have become subject to the laws by transgressing them. See PRISON, Book III. Chap. V. Sect. 18.

PENSTOCK. A small paddle, working up and down vertically in a grooved frame, for penning back water.

PENTADORON. (Gr.) A species of brick used in ancient architecture, which was five palms long.

PENTAGON. (Gr. Πεντε, five, and Γωνια, an angle.) In geometry, a figure of five sides and five angles. When the five sides are equal, the angles are so too, and the figure is called a regular pentagon.

PENTAGRAPH. See PANTOGRAPH.

PERCIER. See ARCHITECTS, list of, 317.

PERCY. See ARCHITECTS, list of, 184.

PEREZ. See ARCHITECTS, list of, 126.

PERIACTI. (Gr. Περιαγειν, to revolve.) The revolving scenes in an ancient theatre, called by the Romans *scenæ versatiles.*

PERIBOLUS. (Gr.) A court or enclosure within a wall, sometimes surrounding a temple. It was frequently ornamented with statues, altars, and monuments, and sometimes contained other smaller temples or a sacred grove. The peribolus of the temple of Jupiter Olympius, at Athens, was four stadia in circumference.

PERIDROME. (Gr. Περι, about, Δρομος, a course.) The space, in ancient architecture, between the columns of a temple and the walls enclosing the cell.

PERIMETER. (Gr.) The boundary of a figure.

PERIPHERY. (Gr. Περιφερω, I surround.) The circumference of a circle, ellipsis, parabola, or other regular curvilinear figure.

PERIPTERY. (Gr.) The range of insulated columns round the cell of a temple.

PERIPTERAL. (Gr.) A temple surrounded by a periptery, that is, encompassed by columns. See TEMPLE.

PERISTYLIUM. (Gr.) In Greek and Roman buildings, a court, square or cloister, which sometimes had a colonnade on three sides only, and therefore in that case improperly so called. Some peristylia had a colonnade on each of the four sides; that on the south being sometimes higher than the rest, in which case it was called a *Rhodian peristylium.* The range of columns itself was called the *peristyle.* See COLONNADE.

PERITHYRIDES. The same as ANCONES, which see.

PERITROCHIUM. (Gr.) A term in mechanics applied to a wheel or circle concentric with the base of a cylinder, and together with it moveable about an axis.

PERPENDICULAR. In geometry, a term applied to a right line falling directly on another line, so as to make equal angles on each side, called also a *normal line.* The same definition will hold of planes standing the one on the other. A perpendicular to a curve is a right line cutting the curve in a point where another right line to which it is perpendicular makes a tangent with the curve.

PERPEND STONE or PERPENDER. A long stone reaching through the thickness of the wall, so as to be visible on both sides, and therefore wrought and smoothed at the ends.

PERRAULT. See ARCHITECTS, list of, 259.

PERRON. A French term, denoting a staircase, lying open or without side the building; or more properly the steps in the front of a building which lead into the first story, where it is raised a little above the level of the ground.

PERRONET. See ARCHITECTS, list of, 298.

PERSIAN or PERSEPOLITAN ARCHITECTURE. See Book I. Chap. II. Sect. 4.

PERSIANS. See CARYATIDES.

PERSPECTIVE. (Lat. Perspicio.) The science which teaches the art of representing objects on a definite surface, so as from a certain position to affect the eye in the same manner as the objects themselves would. This art forms the subject of Book II. Chap. IV. Sect. 2.

PERUZZI. See ARCHITECTS, list of, 200.

PEST HOUSE. A lazaretto or infirmary where persons, goods, &c., infected with the plague or other contagious disease, or suspected so to be, are lodged to prevent communication with others, and the consequent spread of the contagion.

PETER OF COLECHUCH. See ARCHITECTS, list of, 106.

PHÆAX. See ARCHITECTS, list of, 28.

PHALANGÆ. (Gr.) A name applied by Vitruvius to a species of wooden rollers, used to transport heavy masses from one spot to another.

PHAROS. (Gr. from Φως, a light, and Οραω, I see.) The name applied to an ancient lighthouse. See Book III. Chap. V. Sect. 12.

PHEASANTRY. A building or place for the purpose of breeding, rearing, and keeping pheasants.

PHILO. See ARCHITECTS, list of, 26.

PHONICS. The doctrine of sounds, which has not yet been so reduced in its application to architecture as to have justified in this work more than its definition in this place. See the Sect. 16. Chap. V. Book III. on THEATRES.

PHOTOMETER. (Gr.) An instrument for measuring the different intensities of light.

PIAZZA. (Ital.) A square open space surrounded by buildings. The term is very frequently and very ignorantly used to denote a walk under an arcade.

PIEDROIT. (Fr.) A French term, signifying a pier or square pillar, partly hid within a wall. It differs from a pilaster in having neither base nor capital.

PIER. (Fr.) A solid between the doors or windows of a building. The square or other formed mass or post to which a gate is hung. Also the solid support from which an arch springs. In a bridge, the pier next the shore is usually called an abutment pier.

PIETRO DI GAMIEL. See ARCHITECTS, list of, 195.

PIETRO SAN. See ARCHITECTS, list of, 119.

PILASTER. (Fr.) A sort of square column, sometimes insulated, but more commonly engaged in a wall, and projecting only a fourth or fifth of its thickness. See Book III. Chap. I. Sect. 14.

PILES. (Lat.) Large timbers driven into the earth, upon whose heads is laid the foundation of a building in marshy and loose soils. Amsterdam and some other cities are built wholly upon piles. The stoppage of Dagenham Breach was effected by piles mortised into one another by dovetail joints. They are best and most firmly driven by repeated strokes; but for the saving of time, a pile engine is generally used, in appearance and effect very much like a guillotine, which, having raised the *monkey* or hammer to a certain height, lets it, by pressing the clasps which carry it up, suddenly drop down on the pile to be driven.

PILLAR. (Fr. Pilier.) A column of irregular form, always disengaged, and always de-

viating from the proportions of the orders, whence the distinction between a column and a pillar. In any other sense it is improperly used.

PIN. In carpentry, a cylindrical piece of wood driven to connect pieces of framing together. It is also called a *trenail*.

PINNACLE. (Low Lat. Pinnaculum.) A summit or apex. The term is usually applied to the ornament in Gothic architecture placed on the top of a buttress, or as the termination to the angle of the gable of a building. It is also placed on different parts of a parapet, at the sides of niches, and in other situations. Its form is usually slender, and tapers to a point.

PINNING UP. In underpinning the driving the wedges under the upper work so as to bring it fully to bear upon the work below.

The term pinning is also used to denote the fastening of tiles together with pins or pieces of heart of oak in the covering of buildings.

PINO, DI. See ARCHITECTS, list of, 201.

PINTELLI. See ARCHITECTS, list of, 155.

PIPE. A conveyance for water or soil from any part of a building, usually of lead or iron. When for the supply of water to a building it is called a *service pipe ;* when for carrying off water, a *waste pipe ;* and when for carrying off soil, a *soil pipe ;* and those which carry away the rain from a building are called *rain-water pipes.* When a cistern or reservoir is supplied in such a way that those who labour to fill it should be made aware that it is full, the pipe which discharges the overflow is called a *warning pipe.*

PIPPI. See ARCHITECTS, list of, 218.

PISCINA. (Lat.) Among the Romans this term was applied to a fish-pond, to a shallow reservoir for practising swimming, and to a place for watering horses and washing clothes. The piscina in ecclesiastical architecture was a bowl for water, generally in a niche in the wall of the church wherein the priest laved his hands. There was usually one attached to every altar for the priest to wash his hands on the performance of the sacred rites. The variety of their form is great ; some were extremely simple, others very richly decorated.

PISÈ. A species of walling, of latter years used in France, made of stiff earth or clay rammed in between moulds as it is carried up. This method of walling was however in very early use. (*Plin.* lib. xxxiv. chap. 14.)

PIT OF A THEATRE. The part on the ground-floor between the lower range of boxes and the stage.

PITCH. A term generally applied to the vertical angles formed by the inclined sides of a roof.

PITCHING PIECE. In staircasing, an horizontal piece of timber, having one of its ends wedged into the wall at the upper part of a flight of steps, to support the upper ends of the *rough strings.* See APRON PIECE.

PIVOT. (Fr.) The sharpened point upon which a wheel whose axis is perpendicular or inclined performs its revolutions.

PLACE BRICKS. See p. 526.

PLAFOND or PLATFOND. (Fr.) The ceiling of a room, whether flat or arched ; also the under side of the projection of the larmier of the cornice; generally any sofite.

PLAIN or PLANE ANGLE. One contained under two lines and surfaces, so called to distinguish it from a solid angle.

PLAIN TILES, properly PLANE TILES. Those whose surfaces are planes. See Book II. Chap. II. Sect. 9.

PLAN. (Fr.) The representation of the horizontal section of a building, showing its distribution, the form and extent of its various parts. In the plans made by the architect, it is customary to distinguish the massive parts, such as walls, by a dark colour, so as to separate them from the voids or open spaces. In a *geometrical plan*, which is that above mentioned, the parts are represented in their natural proportions. A *perspective plan* is drawn according to the rules of perspective. The *raised plan* of a building is the elevation of it.

PLANCEER. The same as the sofite or under-surface of the corona ; the word is however very often used generally to mean any sofite.

PLANE. (Lat. Planus.) A tool used by artificers that work in wood for the purpose of producing thereon a flat even surface. There are various sorts of planes, whose description will be found at p. 630.

PLANE. In geometry, a surface that coincides in every direction with a straight line.

PLANE, GEOMETRICAL. In perspective, a plane parallel to the horizon, whereon the object to be delineated is supposed to be placed. It is usually at right angles with the perspective plane.

PLANE, HORIZONTAL. In perspective, a plane passing through the spectator's eye, parallel to the horizon, and cutting the perspective plane in a straight line, called the *horizontal line.*

PLANE, INCLINED. One that makes an oblique angle with a horizontal plane.

PLANE, OBJECTIVE. Any plane, face, or side of an original object to be delineated on the perspective plane.

PLANE, PERSPECTIVE. That interposed between the original objects and the eye of the spectator, and whereon the objects are to be delineated.

PLANE TRIGONOMETRY. See Book II. Chap. I. Sect. 3.

PLANIMETRY. That branch of geometry which treats of lines and surfaces only, without reference to their height or depth.

PLANK. (Fr.) A name given generally to all timber, except fir, which is less than four inches thick and thicker than one inch and a half. See BOARD.

PLASTER AND PLASTERER'S WORK. See Book II. Chap. III. Sect. 9.

PLASTER OF PARIS. A preparation of gypsum, originally procured in the vicinity of Mont Martre near Paris. The plaster stone, or alabaster, is, however, found in many parts of England, as at Chelaston near Derby, and Beacon Hill near Newark. The former pits yield about 800 tons a year. It is ground and frequently used for manure, or rather as a stimulant for grass. It is calcined into the plaster used by the modeller, plasterer, &c. When diluted with water into a thin paste, plaster of Paris sets rapidly, and at the instant of setting, its bulk is increased. Mr. Boyle found by experiment that a glass vessel filled with this paste, and close stopped, bursts while the mixture sets, a quantity of water sometimes issuing through the cracks; hence this material becomes valuable for filling cavities, &c., when other earths would shrink. The gypsum is prepared either by burning or boiling, and loses from four to six cwt. in a ton. After burning, it is ground into powder in a mill.

PLATBAND. Any flat and square moulding whose projection is much less than its height, such are the fasciæ of an architrave, the list between flutings, &c. The platband of a door or window is the lintel, when it is made square and not much arched.

PLATE. A general term applied to those horizontal pieces of timber lying mostly on walls for the reception of another assemblage of timbers. Thus, a *wall plate* is laid round the walls of a building to receive the timbering of a floor and roof; a *gutter plate* under the gutter of a building, &c.

PLATE GLASS. See GLASS.

PLATE RACK. A fixture over the sink in a scullery for the reception of dinner plates and dishes after washing.

PLATFORM. An assemblage of timbers for carrying a flat covering of a house, or the flat covering itself. A terrace or open walk at the top of a building.

PLINTH. (Gr. Πλινθος, a brick.) The lower square member of a base of a column or pedestal. In a wall the term *plinth* is applied to two or three rows of bricks which project from the face.

PLOTTING. The art of laying down on paper the angles and lines of a plot of land by any instrument used in surveying.

PLUG. A piece of timber driven perpendicularly into a wall with the projecting part sawn away, so as to be flush with the face.

PLUG AND FEATHER, or KEY AND FEATHER. A name given to a method of dividing hard stones by means of a long tapering wedge, called the *key*, and wedge-shaped pieces of iron called *feathers*, which are driven into holes previously drilled into the rock for the purpose, and thus forcibly split it.

PLUMBING. (Lat. Plumbus.) The art of casting and working in lead and using it in building. See Book II. Chap. III. Sect. 7.

PLUMB RULE, PLUMB LINE, or PLUMMET. An instrument used by masons, carpenters, &c., to draw perpendiculars or verticals, for ascertaining whether their work be upright, horizontal, and so on. The instrument is little more than a piece of lead or plummet at the end of a string, sometimes descending along a wooden or metal ruler raised perpendicularly on another, and then it is called a level. See LEVEL.

PODIUM. (Lat.) A continued pedestal. A projection which surrounded the arena of the ancient amphitheatre. See AMPHITHEATRE.

POINT. (Lat. Punctum.) In geometry, according to Euclid, that which has neither length, breadth, nor thickness.

POINT, ACCIDENTAL. In perspective, a term used by the old writers on the science to signify the vanishing point.

POINT OF DISTANCE. In perspective, the distance of the picture transferred upon the vanishing line from the centre, or from the point where the principal ray meets it, whence it is generally understood to be on the vanishing line of the horizon. See DISTANCE.

POINT, OBJECTIVE. A point on a geometrical plane whose representation is required on the perspective plane.

POINT OF SIGHT. The place of the eye whence the picture is viewed, according to Dr. Brook Taylor, but, according to the old writers on perspective, is what is now called the centre of the picture.

POINT OF VIEW. The point of sight.

Pointed Arch. See p. 119, *et seq.*

Pointed Architecture. See Book I. Chap. IV., and Book III. Chap. III.

Pointing. The raking out the mortar from between the joints of brickwork, and replacing the same with new mortar.

Pole Plate. A plate fixed to the lower ends of a truss of a roof, to receive the ends of the common rafters.

Polishing. See **Marble.**

Pollajolo. See **Architects,** list of, 179.

Pollard. A tree which has been frequently lopped or *polled* of its head and branches, a practice very injurious to good timber.

Polygon. (Gr. Πολυς, many, and Γωνια, an angle.) A multilateral figure, or one whose perimeter consists of more than four sides and angles. If the sides and angles be equal the figure is called a regular polygon. Polygons are distinguished according to the number of the sides; thus those of five sides are called *pentagons,* those of six, *hexagons,* those of seven, *heptagons,* and so on. The subjoined is a table of the areas and perpendiculars of polygons the side being = 1.

Number of Sides.	Names of Polygons.	Area.	Perpendiculars.
3	Trigon - -	·433013	·2886751
4	Tetragon -	1·000000	·5000000
5	Pentagon -	1·720477	·6881910
6	Hexagon -	2.598076	·8660254
7	Heptagon -	3·633912	1·0382617
8	Octagon -	4·828427	1·2071068
9	Enneagon -	6·181824	1·3737387
10	Decagon -	7·694209	1·5388418
11	Endecagon -	9·365640	1·7028437
12	Dodecagon -	11·196152	1·8660254

From the above to find the area of a regular polygon, multiply one of the sides of the polygon by the perpendicular from the centre on that side, and multiply half the product by the number of sides; or, multiply the square of the given side of the polygon by the number opposite to its name under the word area.

Polygram. (Gr.) A figure consisting of many lines.

Polyhædron. (Gr.) A solid contained under many sides or planes. If the sides of a polyhædron be regular polygons, all similar and equal, it becomes a regular body, and may be inscribed in a sphere, that is, a sphere may be drawn round it, so that its surface shall touch all the solid angles of the body.

Polystyle. (Gr. Πολυς and Στυλος.) Of many columns. See **Colonnade.**

Pomel. (Lat. Pomum.) A globular protuberance terminating a pinnacle, &c.

Pontoon. (Fr.) A bridge of boats.

Poore. See **Architects,** list of, 112.

Poplar. (Lat. Populus.) A tree sometimes used in building.

Porch. (Fr.) An exterior appendage to a building, forming a covered approach to one of its principal doorways.

Porphyry. (Gr.) A very hard stone, partaking of the nature of granite. It is not so fine as many of the ordinary marbles, but far exceeds them in hardness, and will take a very fine polish. It is still found in Egypt in immense strata. It is generally of a high purple, which varies, however, from claret colour to violet. Its variations are rarely disposed in grains. The red lead coloured porphyry, which abounds in Minorca, is variegated with black, white, and green, and is a beautiful and valuable material. The pale and red porphyry, variegated with black, white, and green, is found in Arabia Petræa and Upper Egypt, and in separate nodules in Germany, England, and Ireland. The sorts best known are what the Italians call the *porfido rosso* (red), which is of a deep red with oblong white spots; the latter are of *feld spath,* which resembles *schorl.* There are two varieties of black porphyry, the *porfido nero,* or black porphyry, and that called the *serpentino nero antico.* The first has a ground entirely black, spotted with oblong white spots like the red porphyry; the other has also a black ground with great white spots, oblong, or rather in the form of a parallelopipedon, nearly resembling in colour what the French call *serpentin vert antique.* The *brown porphyry* has a brown ground with large oblong greenish spots. There are several sorts of green porphyry, which the Italians principally distinguish by the names of *serpentino antico verde,* found in great abundance and in large blocks in the neighbourhood of the ancient Ostia, of a green ground with oblong spots of a lighter shade of the same colour; and the *porfido verde,* which is of a ground of very dark green, almost approaching to black, with lighter shades of a fine grass green. The art of cutting porphyry, as practised by the ancients, appears to be now quite lost.

PORTAL. (Fr. Portail, from Lat. Porta.) The arch over a door or gate; the framework of the gate; the lesser gate, when there are two of different dimensions at one entrance. This term was formerly applied to a small square corner in a room separated from the rest of the apartment by wainscotting.

PORTCULLIS. (Fr.) A strong grated framing of timber, resembling a harrow, the vertical pieces whereof were pointed with iron at the bottom, for the purpose of striking into the ground when it was dropped, and also to break and destroy that upon which it fell. It was made to slide up and down in a groove of solid stone-work within the arch of the portals of old castles. Its introduction is supposed to have been in the early Norman castles.

PORTICO. (Lat. Porticus.) See COLONNADE.

PORTLAND STONE. A dull white species of stone brought from the island of Portland. See p. 466, et seq. and p. 478, et seq.

PORTUGUESE ARCHITECTURE. See Book I. Chap. II. Sect. 19.

POSITION. In geometry, the situation of one thing in regard to another. Speaking architecturally, it is the situation of a building in respect of the four cardinal points of the horizon.

POST. (Fr.) An upright piece of timber set in the earth. Any piece of timber whose office is to support or sustain in a vertical direction, as the *king* and *queen posts* in a roof, is so called.

POST AND PALING. A close wooden fence constructed with posts fixed in the ground and pales nailed between them. This kind of fence is sometimes called *post and railing*, though this latter is rather a kind of open wooden fence, used for the protection of young quickset hedges, consisting of posts and rails, &c.

POSTICUM. (Lat.) See CELL.

POSTSCENIUM or PARASCENIUM. (Lat.) In ancient architecture, the back part of the theatre, where the machinery was deposited, and where the actors retired to robe themselves.

POSTUMIUS, C. See ARCHITECTS, list of, 37.

POULTRY HOUSE. A building for the shelter and rearing of poultry, whereof, perhaps, the finest example is that at Winnington in Cheshire. The front is one hundred and forty feet in length, with a pavilion at each end, united to the centre by a colonnade of small cast-iron pillars, supporting a slated roof, which shelters a paved walk. In the centre of the front are four strong columns, and as many pilasters, supporting a slated roof, with an iron gate between them, from which a large semicircular court is entered, with a colonnade round it, and places for the poultry. On one side of the gate is a small parlour, and at the other end of the colonnade a kitchen.

POWER. In mechanics, a force which, applied to a machine, tends to produce motion. If it actually produce it, it is called a *moving power*, if not, it is called a *sustaining power*. The term is also used in respect of the six simple machines, viz. the *lever*, the *balance*, the *screw*, the *axis in peritrochio*, the *wedge*, and the *pulley*, which are called the *mechanical powers*.

POZZO, DEL. See ARCHITECTS, list of, 157.

POZZUOLANA. See PUZZUOLANA.

PRÆCINCTIO (Lat.) or BALTEUS. A wide seat, or rather step, round the audience part of the ancient theatres and amphitheatres. It was termed διαζωμα by the Greeks.

PREACHING CROSS. A cross erected in the highway, at which the monks and others preached to the public.

PRECEPTORY. A manor or estate of the knights templars, on which a church was erected for religious service, and a convenient house for habitation, and generally placed under one of the more eminent members of the fraternity, called the *præceptores templi*, to have care of the lands and rents of the place. The preceptories were nothing more than cells to the temple, or principal house of the knights in London.

PRESBYTERY. That part of the church reserved for the officiating priests, comprising the choir and other eastern parts of the edifice.

PRESERVING TIMBER. See p. 506.

PRICES OF WORK. See p. 741, et seq.

PRICK POST. The same as QUEEN POST.

PRIME. (Lat.) A figure in geometry that cannot be divided into any other figures more simple than itself, as a triangle in plane figures, and a pyramid in solids.

A *prime number* is one that cannot be divided by another number without a remainder.

PRIMING. In painter's work, the first colouring of the work, which forms a ground for the succeeding coats.

PRINCIPAL BRACE. One immediately under the principal rafters, or parallel to them, in a state of compression, assisting, with the principals, to support the timbers of the roof.

PRINCIPAL POINT. In perspective, a point in the perspective plane upon which a line will fall drawn from the eye perpendicular to that plane. The principal point is, in fact, the intersection of the horizontal and vertical planes, or the *point of sight*, or *of the eye*.

PRINCIPAL RAFTERS. Those whose sizes are larger than the common rafters, and framed in such a manner as to bear the principal weight of the others.

Principal Ray. In perspective, the line passing from the eye to the principal point on the perspective plane.

Priory. A building similar in its constitution to a monastery or abbey, the head whereof was called a prior or prioress.

Prism. (Gr. Πρισμα.) In geometry, an oblong or solid body contained under more than four planes, whose bases are equal, parallel, and similarly situate.

Prismoid. A solid figure, having for its two ends any dissimilar parallel plane figure of the same number of sides, and all the upright sides of the solid, trapezoids. If the ends of the prismoid be bounded by dissimilar curves, it is sometimes called a *cylindroid*.

Prison. A building erected for the confinement, or safe custody, of those who have transgressed the laws of their country, until, in due course of time, they are discharged. See Book III. Chap. V. Sect. 18.

Private Buildings. See Book III. Chap. V. Sects. 20, 21, 22.

Problem. (Gr.) In geometry, a proposition in which some operation or construction is required, as to divide a line, to make an angle, to draw a circle through three points not in a right line, &c. A problem consists of three parts: the proposition, which states what is required to be done; the resolution or solution, wherein are rehearsed the step or steps by which it is done; and the demonstration, wherein it is shown that by doing the several things prescribed in the resolution the thing required is obtained.

Prodomus. In ancient architecture, the portico before the entrance to the cell of a temple. See Cell.

Producing. In geometry, the continuing a right line to any required length.

Profile. The vertical section of a body. It is principally used in its architectural sense to signify the contour of architectural members, as of bases, cornices, &c. The profile of an order is in fact the outline of the whole and its parts, the drawing whereof is technically called profiling the order. *Profiles of doors* are given in Book III. Chap. I. Sect. 19.

Projection. The art of representing a body on a plane by drawing straight lines through a given point, or parallel from the contour and from the intermediate lines of the body, if any, so as to cut the plane. When the projection is made by drawing straight lines from a point, it is called a *perspective representation;* but if formed by parallel lines, it is called an *orthographical representation.* See Perspective, in Book II. Chap. V. Sect. 2., and Descriptive Geometry, Book II. Chap. I. Sect. 5. For the method of projecting shadows, see Book II. Chap. IV. Sect. 3.

Projecture. An out-jetting or prominence beyond the naked of a wall, column, &c. By the Greeks projectures were called εκφοραι, by the Italians *sporti*, by the French *saillés;* so our workmen called them *sailings over.*

Prolate. (Lat.) An epithet applied to a spheroid when generated by the revolution of a semi-ellipsis about its longer diameter.

Pronaos. See Cell.

Proportion. The just magnitude of each part, and of each part to another, so as to be suitable to the end in view. For the proportions of the several parts of a building, the reader is referred to Book III. Chap. I., and Book III. Chap. III.

Proportional Compasses. See Compasses.

Proportions of Rooms. See Book III. Chap. I. Sect. 25.

Propylæum. (Gr. Προ, before, and Πυλη, a portal.) Any court or vestibule before a building, or before its principal part; but more particularly the entrance to such court or vestibule.

Proscenium. (Gr.) That part in the ancient theatre whereon the actors performed in front of the scene, being what we call the stage. The Romans called this part the *pulpitum.*

Prostyle. (Gr. Προ, and Στυλος, a column.) A portico in which the columns stand in advance of the building to which they belong.

Prothyris. (Gr.) A word used in ancient architecture to signify a cross beam or overthwart rafter, as likewise a quoin or course of a wall. See Console.

Prothyrum. (Gr.) A porch at the outer door of a house; a portal.

Protractor. (Lat. Protractus.) An instrument for laying down an angle in drawing or plotting.

Pseudisodomum. See Isodomum.

Pseudodipteral or False Dipteral. A disposition in the temples of antiquity wherein there were eight columns in front and only one range round the cell. It is called false or imperfect, because the cell only occupying the width of four columns, the sides from the columns to the walls of the cell have no columns therein, though the front and rear present a column in the middle of the void. See Temple.

Pseudoperipteral or Imperfect Peripteral. A disposition in the ancient temples, in which the columns on the sides were engaged in the wall, and wherein there was no portico except to the façade in front; such are the Maison Carrée at Nismes, and the temple of Fortuna Virilis at Rome.

PTERA. See **AISLES.**

PTEROMA. (Gr. Πτερον, a wing.) The space between the wall of the cell of a temple and the columns of the peristyle, called also *ambulatio.*

PUDDLING. The filling behind a wall, filling up a cavity, or banking up with clay tempered with water, and carefully rammed down with the repeated strokes of beaters or beetles.

PUGGING. A coarse kind of mortar laid upon the sound boarding between joists, to prevent the transmission of sound from the apartment above to that below.

PUG-PILING. The same as dovetailed piling, or pile planking.

PULLEY. (Fr.) One of the five mechanical powers, consisting of a wheel or rundle, having a channel around it and turning on an axis, serving, by means of a rope which moves in its channel, for the raising of weights.

PULLEY MORTISE. The same as **CHASE MORTISE,** which see.

PULPIT. (Ital. Pulpito.) An elevated place, an enclosed stage or platform for a preacher in a church. The ancient *ambo* served the same purpose. The pulpits of the present day are generally wretched affairs, and have great affinity in form to sugar hogsheads or rum puncheons with the heads knocked out. The Catholic churches abroad almost invariably furnish fine specimens of carving and composition in their pulpits.

PULPITUM. (Lat.) See **PROSCENIUM.**

PULVINARIA. (Lat.) Cushions in the ancient temples whereon the statues of the gods were sometimes laid.

PULVINATED. See **FRIEZE.**

PUMP. See p. 661, *et seq.* where the different pumps for buildings are described.

PUNCHION. (Fr. Poinçon.) A name common to iron instruments used in different trades for cutting, inciding, or piercing a body. In carpentry it is a piece of timber placed upright between two posts whose bearing is too great, serving, together with them, to sustain some heavy weight. The term is also applied to a piece of timber raised upright under the ridge of a building, and in which are jointed the small timbers. Also to the arbor or principal part of a machine on which it turns vertically, as that of a crane.

PURBECK STONE. A species of stone obtained from the island of Purbeck in Dorsetshire, of a very hard texture. See p. 479.

PURFLED. (Fr. Pourfiler.) Ornamented work in stone, or other material, representing embroidery, drapery, or lace work.

PURLINS. Horizontal pieces of timber lying generally on the principal rafters of a roof to lessen the bearings of the common rafters. Locally called *side timbers,* and *side wavers.*

PUTEAL The marginal stone of a well. The celebrated one of Scribonius Libo was erected by order of the senate to mark the spot where a thunderbolt had fallen near the statues of Marsyas and Janus by the Comitia.

PUTLOGS. See **LEDGERS.**

PUTTY. A sort of paste consisting of whiting, with or without a small portion of white lead, and linseed oil, beaten together until it assumes a kind of tough consistency like dough. In this state it is used by glaziers for fixing in the squares of glass to sash windows, &c. and also by house-painters to stop up holes and cavities in woodwork before painting.

PUZZUOLANA. A grey-coloured earth deriving its name from Puzzuoli, whence it was originally brought. It is a volcanic matter found in many other parts of Italy, and generally in the neighbourhood of volcanoes active or extinct, from which it has been thrown out in the form of ashes. It immediately hardens when mixed with one-third of its weight of lime and water, forming an admirable water cement. See Book II. Chap. II. Sect. 10.

PYCNOSTYLE. (Gr. Πυκνος, close, and Στυλος, column.) See **COLONNADE.**

PYRAMID. (Gr. Πυρ, fire.) A solid standing on a square, triangular, or polygonal basis, and terminating at top in a point; or a body whose base is a regular rectilinear figure and whose sides are plain triangles, their several verticals meeting together in one point. It is defined by Euclid as a solid figure consisting of several triangles whose bases are all in the same plane and have one common vertex. When the base of a pyramid is but small in proportion to its height, it is called an *obelisk.* See that word. For some account of the pyramids of Egypt see Book I. Chap. II. Sect 7.

The principal properties of pyramids are as follow: — 1. All pyramids and cones standing on the same base and having the same altitude are equal. 2. A triangular pyramid is the third part of a prism, standing on the same base and of the same altitude. 3. Hence, since every multangular may be divided into triangulars, every pyramid is the third part of a prism standing on the same base and of the same altitude. 4. If a pyramid be cut by a plane parallel to its base, the sections will be similar to the base. 5. All pyramids, prisms, cylinders, &c., are in a ratio compounded of their bases and altitudes; the bases therefore being equal they are in proportion to their altitudes, and the altitudes being equal, they are in proportion to their bases. 6. Similar pyramids, prisms, cylinders, cones, &c., are in a triplicate ratio of their homologous sides. 7.

Equal pyramids, &c., reciprocate their bases and altitudes, *i. e.* the altitude of one is to that of the other, as the base of the one is to the base of the other. 8. A sphere is equal to a pyramid whose base is equal to the surface, and its height to the radius of the sphere.

PYRAMID, FRUSTUM OF A. See FRUSTUM.

PYRAMIDION. The small flat pyramid which terminates the top of an obelisk.

PYTHEUS. See ARCHITECTS, list of, 8.

Q.

QUADRA. (Ital.) A square border of frame round a basso-relievo, panel, &c.; the term is not strictly applicable to any circular border. The term is also applied to the bands or fillets of the Ionic base on each side of the scotia; and also to the plinth or lower member of the podium.

QUADRANGLE. Any figure with four angles and four sides. This term is in architecture in England applied to the inner square or rectangular court of a building, as in the college courts of Oxford, &c.

QUADRANT. (Lat.) The quarter of a circle, or an arc of it containing ninety degrees within its enclosed angle.

QUADRATURE. (Lat.) The determination of the area of a figure in a square, or even any other rectilinear form.

QUADRELS. Artificial stones perfectly square, whence their name, much used formerly by the Italian architects. They were made of a chalky or whitish and pliable earth, and dried in the shade for at least two years.

QUADRIFORES. (Lat.) In ancient architecture folding doors whose height was divided into two parts. When they opened in one height, they were termed *fores valvatæ* or *valvæ.*

QUADRILATERAL. In geometry a figure whose perimeter consists of four right lines making four angles, whence it is also called a quadrangular figure.

QUARREL, vulgarly called QUARRY. (Fr. Carré.) A square or lozenge-shaped piece of glass used in lead casements.

QUARRY. (Irish, Carrig.) A place whence stones or slates are procured. The principal stone quarries of England have been given in the body of the work, Book II. Chap. II. Sect. 1. to which place the reader is referred. The slates obtained from the different quarries in Great Britain and Ireland may be found in Book II. Chap. II. Sect. 8. The Marble quarries are described in Book II. Chap. II. Sect. 3.

QUARRYING. The operation of extracting the produce of a quarry is one which requires much practical knowledge to render it beneficial to its owner; but in respect of the details they are not required to be noticed in this work.

QUARTER GRAIN. See FELT GRAIN.

QUARTER PACE. See FOOT PACE.

QUARTER PARTITION. One consisting of quarters.

QUARTER ROUND. The same as OVOLO and ECHINUS, which see, being a moulding whose profile is the quadrant of a circle.

QUARTERING. A series of quarters, as in a partition, &c.

QUARTERFOIL. (Fr. Quatrefeuille.) A modern term denoting a form disposed in four segments of circles, and so called from its imagined resemblance to an expanded flower of four petals. It is only found in the windows, pannels, &c., of Gothic architecture. Mr. Gunn with charming simplicity, not unusual among the amateur writers on Gothic architecture, thinks that the form has no reference to any type in the vegetable kingdom, but that it was originally a representation of the *Greek cross* rounded towards the extremities. If the writings on the subject from the two universities of the country were all put in juxtaposition, they would perhaps afford more scope for mirth than was ever exhibited on any subject.

QUARTERS. Small vertical timber posts, rarely exceeding four by three inches, used instead of walls for the separation or boundary of apartments. They are placed, or ought to be, about twelve inches apart, and are usually lathed and plastered in the internal apartments, but if used for external purposes are commonly boarded.

QUARTZ. (Germ.) A mineral production better known by the name of rock crystal. It includes a variety of stones with which we have nothing here to do, and the only motive for mentioning it is its occurrence in the granites, wherein it is immediately recognised, from its glass-like appearance.

QUAY. (Fr.) A bank formed towards the sea or on the side of a river for free passage, or for the purpose of unloading merchandise.

QUEEN-POST. A suspending post where there are two in a trussed roof.

QUICKLIME. See Book II. Chap. II. Sect 10.

QUIRK. A piece taken out of any regular ground-plot or floor; thus, if the ground

plan were square or oblong, and a piece were taken out of the corner, such piece is called a *quirk*.

QUIRK MOULDING.   One whose sharp and sudden return from its extreme projection to the re-entrant angle seems rather to partake of a straight line on the profile than of the curve. Of this class are a great number of the ancient Greek mouldings.

QUOINS. (Fr. Coin.) A term applied to any external angle, but more especially applied to the angular courses of stone raised from the naked of the wall at the corner of a building, and called rustic quoins.   See RUSTIC QUOINS.

R.

RABBET.   See REBATE.

RABIRIUS.   See ARCHITECTS, list of, 44.

RACK.   The case, enclosed by bars, over the manger in a stable, wherein the hay is placed for the horses.

RADIAL CURVES.   In geometry, those of the spiral kind whose ordinates all terminate in the centre of the. including circle, and appear like so many radii of such circle.

RADIUS.   In geometry, the semidiameter of a circle, or a right line drawn from the centre to the circumference.

RADIUS OF CURVATURE.   The radius of the osculatory circle at any point in a curve.   See OSCULATORY CIRCLE.

RAFFAELLE D'URBINO.   See ARCHITECTS, list of, 185.

RAFTERS. (Quasi, Roof-trees.) The inclined timbers of a roof, whose edges are in the same plane which is parallel to the covering.   The rules and regulations that affect their disposition will be found in p. 603. *et seq.*

RAGS and RAG SLATES.   See Book II. Chap. II. Sect. 8.

RAIL. (Germ. Riegel.) A term applied in various ways, but more particularly to those pieces of timber or wood lying horizontally, whether between the panels of wainscotting or of doors, or under or over the compartments of balustrades, &c. ; to pieces, in framing, that lie from post to post in fences ; in short, to all pieces lying in an horizontal direction which separate one compartment from another.

RAIMOND.   See ARCHITECTS, list of, 93.

RAIN-WATER PIPE.   One usually placed against the exterior of a house to carry off the rain-water from the roof.

RAISING PIECE.   One which lies under a beam or beams and over the posts or punchions.   The term is chiefly used in respect of buildings constructed of timber framework.

RAKING.   A term applied to any member whose arrisses lie inclined to the horizon.

RAMP. (Fr.) In handrails, a concavity on the upper side formed over risers, or over a half or quarter pace, by a sudden rise of the steps above, which frequently occasions a knee above the ramp.   The term is also applied to any concave form, as in coping, &c., where a higher is to be joined by a continued line to a lower body.

RAMPANT ARCH.   One whose abutments or springings are not on the same level.

RANGE or RANGING. (Fr.) A term applied to the edges of a number of bodies when standing in a given plane.   Thus, if the edges of the ribs of a groin were placed in a cylindric surface, they would be said to *range*.   It is also used in respect of a work that runs straight without breaking into angles

RANULPH.   See ARCHITECTS, list of, 91.

RARI.   See ARCHITECTS, list of, 140.

RATE.   An expression formerly used in the Metropolitan Building Act to denote the particular class to which a building belonged, in order to determine the thickness of its walls and mode of building.

RAY, PRINCIPAL.   In perspective, the perpendicular distance between the eye and the perspective plane.

REBATE. (Fr. Rebattre.) A groove or channel cut on a piece of wood, longitudinally, to receive the edge of a body, or the ends of a number of bodies that are to be secured to it.   The depth of the channel is equal to the thickness of the body ; so that when the end of the latter is let into the rebate, it is in the same face with the outside of the piece.

REBATE PLANE.   One used for sinking rebates.

RECESS. (Lat. Recedo.) A cavity left in a wall, sometimes for use, as to receive a side-board, bed, &c., or to add to the quantity of floor room, and sometimes for ornament, as when formed into a niche, &c.

RECTANGLE.   In geometry, a figure whose angles are all right angles.   Solids are called rectangular with respect to their position, as a cone, cylinder, &c., when perpendicular to the plane of the horizon.   A parabola was anciently called a rectangular section of a cone.

RECTIFICATION. In geometry, the finding of a right line that shall be equal to a given curve, or simply finding the length of a curve.

RECTILINEAR. A figure whose boundaries are right lines.

REDE. See ARCHITECTS, list of, 143.

REDUCT. A quirk or small piece taken out of a larger to make it more uniform and regular.

REDUCTION of a figure, design, or draught, is the copying it on a smaller scale than the original, preserving the same form and proportions. For this purpose a pair of proportional compasses are generally used, by which the labour is much lessened.

REFECTORY. (Lat.) A room for taking refreshments. See ABBEY.

REFLEX. The light reflected from a surface in light to one in shade.

REGLET. (Fr.) A flat narrow moulding, used chiefly to separate the parts or members of compartments or panels from each other, or to form knots, frets, and other ornaments.

REGRATING. In masonry, the process of removing the outer surface of an old hewn stone, so as to give it a fresh appearance.

REGULA. (Lat.) A band below the tænia in the Doric architrave.

REGULAR. An epithet applied to a figure when it is equilateral and equiangular. A body is said to be regular when it is bounded by regular and equal planes, and has all its solid angles equal.

REGULAR ARCHITECTURE. That which has its parts symmetrical or disposed in counterparts.

REGULAR CURVES. The perimeters of conic sections, which are always curved after the same geometrical manner.

REINS OF A VAULT. The sides or walls that sustain the arch.

REJOINTING. The filling up the joints of stones in old buildings when the mortar has been dislodged by age and the action of the weather.

RELATION. The direct conformity to each other, and to the whole, of the parts of a building.

REMIGIUS. See ARCHITECTS, list of, 82.

RENDERING. The act of laying the first coat of plaster on brickwork.

REPLUM. (Lat.) In ancient architecture, the panel of the impages of a framed door.

REREDOS. (Fr. Arriéredos.) A screen or division wall placed behind an altar, rood-loft, &c., in old churches.

RESERVOIR. (Fr.) An artificial pond, basin, or cistern for the collection and supply of water.

RESISTANCE. That power which, acting in opposition to another, tends to destroy or diminish its effect. There are several sorts of resistance, arising from the various natures and properties of the resisting bodies, as the resistance of solids, fluids, air, &c.

The resistance of solid bodies is the force with which their quiescent parts retain their aggregation. Of it there are two kinds: first, where the resisting and the resisted parts are only contiguous and do not cohere, or, in other words, where they consist of separate bodies or masses. This is by Leibnitz called the *resistance of the surface*, now however called *friction*. Second, where the resisting and resisted parts are not only contiguous, but cohere, that is, are parts of the same continued body or mass. To these may be added the resistance that takes place between surfaces or solids when completely in contact, though not forming the same body, or the resistance they offer to separation. To form a notion of the resistance of the fibres of solid bodies, suppose a cylindrical body suspended vertically by one of its ends. Here the weight of the parts makes them tend downwards and endeavours to separate the body where it is weakest. The parts, however, resist this separation by the force with which they cohere. In this case, then, we see two opposite powers, viz. the weight of the cylinder, which has a tendency to break it, and the force of cohesion to resist fracture. If the base of the cylinder be increased, the length remaining the same, it is manifest that the resistance will increase as the base; but the weight will also increase in the same ratio. Hence, all cylinders of the same matter and length, when vertically suspended, have an equal resistance, whatever their bases. When the length of the cylinder is increased, the base and the resistance remaining the same, the additional weight weakens it, and it will have a greater tendency to break.

We thus learn what length a cylinder may be so as to break with its own weight, by finding what weight is just sufficient to break another cylinder of the same base and matter; for the required length must be such that its weight may be equal to that of the first, with the additional weight employed to produce the separation.

If the cylinder be fixed horizontally into a wall, and the rest thence suspended, the weight and resistance will act under different conditions, for if it broke by the action of its weight, the fracture would occur at the end fixed into the wall. In the fracture of the cylinder two forces have acted, and one has overcome the other; that is, the weight of the mass of the cylinder has overcome the resistance arising from the largeness of the base; and as the centres of gravity are points in which all the forces arising from the

weights of the several parts of the same bodies are supposed to be collected, we may conceive the weight of the whole cylinder applied in the centre of gravity of its mass, that is, in a point in the middle of the axis ; and the resistance of the cylinder applied in the centre of gravity of its base, it being the base which resists the fracture. If the cylinder breaks with its own weight all the motion is on an immoveable extremity of the diameter of the base, which extremity is the fixed point of a lever, whose arms are the radius of the base and half the axis ; hence, the two opposite forces do not only act of themselves and by their absolute, but also by the relative force derived from their distance with regard to the fixed point of the lever.

The weight required to break a body placed horizontally being always less than that required to break it when placed vertically, and being greater or less according to the ratio of the two arms of the lever, the theory is reducible to the finding what part of the absolute weight the relative weight must be, supposing the figure of the body known, which is necessary for finding the centre of gravity. But wherever the centre of gravity falls, the two arms of the lever are estimated accordingly. If the base by which the body is fixed in the wall be not circular, but, for an example, parabolical, and the vertex of the parabola be at top, the motion of the fracture will not be on an immoveable point, but on a whole immoveable line, which may be termed the axis of equilibrium, and it is with regard thereto that the distances of the centres of gravity are to be determined.

A body horizontally suspended, being such that the smallest addition of weight would break it, there is an equilibrium existing between its positive and relative weight; those two opposite powers are consequently to each other reciprocally as the arms of the lever to which they are applied. So, e converso, the resistance of a body is always equal to the greatest weight it will sustain, without breaking, in a vertical situation, that is, equal to its absolute weight. If we, therefore, substitute actual weight for the resistance, it follows that the absolute weight of a body suspended horizontally is to its relative weight, as the distance of the centre of gravity from the axis of equilibrium is to the distance of the centre of gravity of its base from the same axis. From this fundamental proposition many consequences are deducible. Thus, if the distance of the centre of gravity of the base from the axis of equilibrium be half the distance of the centre of gravity of the body, the relative weight will only be half the absolute weight.

M. Mariotte having observed that all bodies bend before breaking, considers the fibres as so many little bent springs, never exerting their whole force till stretched to a certain point, and never breaking till entirely unbent. Hence those nearest the axis of equilibrium, which is an immoveable line, are less stretched than the more distant ones, and consequently employ a less part of their force.

The following is a synopsis of the most important results that have been drawn by different writers on the subject, both practical and theoretical : —

1. The resistance of a beam or bar to a fracture by a force acting laterally is as the solid made by a section of the beam in the place where the force is applied, into the distance of its centre of gravity from the point or line where the breach will end.

2. In square beams the lateral strengths are as the cubes of their breadths and depths.

3. In cylindric beams, the resistances of strengths are as the cubes of the diameters.

4. In rectangular beams the lateral strengths are conjointly as the breadths and squares of the depths.

5. The lateral resistances of any beams whose sections are similar figures and alike placed are as the cubes of the like dimensions of those figures.

6. The lateral strength of a beam, with its narrower face upwards, is to its strength with the broader face upwards, as the breadth of the broader face to the breadth of the narrower.

7. The lateral strengths of prismatic beams, of the same materials, are as the areas of the sections and the distance of their centre of gravity directly, and as their lengths and weights reciprocally.

8. When the beam is fixed at both ends, the same property has place, except that in this case we must consider the beam as only half the length of the former.

9. Cylinders and square prisms have their lateral strengths proportional to the cubes of their diameters or depths directly, and their lengths and weights inversely.

10. Similar prisms and cylinders have their strength inversely proportional to their linear dimensions.

The relative resistance of wood and other bodies is shown in the following table : —

	Proportional Resistance.
Box, yew, plum tree, oak - - - -	11
Elm, ash - - - - - -	$8\frac{1}{2}$
Walnut, thorn - - - - -	$7\frac{1}{3}$
Red fir, holly, elder, plane, crab-tree, apple-tree -	7
Beech, cherry-tree, hazel - - - -	$6\frac{2}{3}$

	Proportional Resistance.
Alder, asp, birch, white fir, willow	6
Iron	107
Brass	50
Bone	22
Lead	6½
Fine freestone	1

The following table shows the cohesive force of a square inch of different substances from the experiments of Professor Robison: —

	lbs.
Gold when cast	20·000
Silver	40·000
Cast iron	40·000 to 60·000
Wrought iron	60·000 to 90·000
Soft steel	12·000
Razor steel	15·000
Oak and beech in the direction of their fibres from	8·000 to 17·000
Willow	12·000
Fir	8·000
Cedar	5·000
Ivory	16·000
Bone	5·000
Rope	20·000

RESOLUTION OF FORCES. See p. 337.

RESSAULT. (Fr.) The recess or projection of a member from or before another, so as to be out of the line or range with it.

RETAINING WALLS. Such as are built to retain a bank of earth from sliding down.

RETICULATED. Like the meshes of a net. The *reticulatum opus* of the ancients is described under the article MASONRY, which see.

RETURN. The continuation of a moulding, projection, &c., in an opposite direction. A side or part which falls away from the front of a straight work.

RETURN BEAD. See BEAD AND DOUBLE QUIRK.

REVEALS. (Lat. Revello.) The vertical sides of an aperture between the front of the wall and the window or door frame.

REVOLUTION. In geometry, the motion of a point or line about a centre. Thus a right-angled triangle, revolving round one of its legs as an axis, generates a cone in its revolution.

RHOMBOID. (Gr.) A quadrilateral figure whose opposite sides and angles are equal.

RHOMBUS. (Gr.) A quadrilateral figure, whose sides are all equal, and whose opposite angles are respectively equal, two being obtuse and two acute.

RIB. (Sax.) An arch-formed piece of timber for supporting the lath and plaster work of a vault.

RIBBING. An assemblage of ribs for a vault or coved ceiling.

RIDGE. (Sax.) The highest part of a roof. The term is more particularly applied to the piece of timber against which the upper end of the rafters pitch.

RIDGE TILE. A convex tile made for covering the ridge of a roof.

RIGA TIMBER. See p. 499.

RIGHT ANGLE. One containing ninety degrees.

RIGHT CIRCLE. A circle drawn at right angles with the plane of projection.

RIGHT LINE. A line perfectly straight.

RILIEVO (It.) or RELIEF. The projecture from its ground of any architectural ornament. Among sculptors there are three degrees of rilievo; namely, *alto rilievo*, when the figure stands quite out from its ground; *mezzo rilievo*, when one half of the figure projects; and *basso rilievo*, when the figures are raised from the ground in a small degree.

RIPLEY. See ARCHITECTS, list of, 283.

ROD. A measure of length equal to 16½ feet. A square rod is the usual measure of brickwork, and is equal to 272¼ square feet.

ROE STONE or OOLITE. A kind of limestone, found under chalk in various parts of England. See Book II. Chap. II. Sect. 4.

ROGER, ARCHBISHOP OF YORK. See ARCHITECTS, list of, 97.

ROLLS. Pieces of wood prepared for the plumber to turn over the lead where the sheets join, so as to protect the flat roof or edge from the admission of water. The term also signifies in Gothic architecture mouldings representing bent cylinders.

ROLLS or ROLLERS. Among workmen are plain cylinders of wood, seven or eight inches diameter and three or four feet long, used for the purpose of moving large stones, beams, and other heavy weights. They are placed successively under the fore part of the masses

to be removed, and at the same time are pushed forward by levers applied behind. When blocks of marble, or other very heavy weights, are to be moved, they use what are called *endless rolls*. These, to give them the greater force and prevent their bursting, are made of wood joined together by cross-quarters, double the length and thickness of the common rollers, and girt with iron hoops at each end. At a foot from the ends are two mortises pierced through and through, into which are put the ends of long levers, which the workmen draw by ropes fastened to the ends, still changing the mortise as the roll has made a quarter of a turn.

ROMAN ARCHITECTURE. See Book I. Chap. II. Sect. 13.

ROMAN ORDER. The same as COMPOSITE ORDER, which see.

ROMUALDUS. See ARCHITECTS, list of, 71.

ROOD. (Sax. Rode.) A cross, crucifix, or figure of Christ on the cross placed in a church. The *holy rood* was one, generally as large as life, elevated at the junction of the nave and choir, and facing to the western entrance of the church. The *rood loft* was the gallery in which the rood and its appendages were placed. This loft, or gallery, was commonly placed over the chancel screen in parish churches. In Protestant churches the organ now occupies the original place of the rood loft. The *rood tower* or *steeple* was that which stood over the intersection of the nave with the transepts.

ROOF. (Sax. Rof, Hpof.) The exterior covering of a building, for whose principles of construction and various sorts the reader is referred to p. 603, *et seq.*

ROOFING. The assemblage of timbers, and covering of a roof whose pitch in this climate, for different coverings, is shown in the following table :— (See table on p. 603.)

Species of Covering.			Inclination to the Horizon.			Height of Roof in Part of the Span.
Copper or lead	-	-	3° 50″	-	-	one-forty-eighth.
Large slates	-	-	22 0	-	-	one-fifth.
Common slates	-	-	26 33	-	-	one-quarter.
Stone slates	-	-	29 41	-	-	two-sevenths.
Plain tiles	-	-	29 41	-	-	two-sevenths.
Pan tiles	-	-	24 0	-	-	two-ninths.
Thatch	-	-	45 0	-	-	one-half.

ROOM. (Sax. Rum.) An interior space or division of a house, separated from the remainder of it by walls or partitions, and entered by a doorway.

ROOMS, PROPORTIONS OF. See Book III. Chap. I. Sect. 25.

ROSE or ROSETTE. An ornament of frequent use in architectural decorations. The centre of the face of the abacus in the Corinthian capital is decorated with what is called a rose.

ROSE WINDOW. A circular window with compartments of mullions and tracery branching from a centre, sometimes called a *catharine wheel* or *marigold window.*

ROSTRUM. (Lat.) Literally, the beak of a bird ; also the beak or fore-part of a ship ; the elevated platform in the Forum of ancient Rome, whence the orators addressed the people, so called from its basement being decorated with the prows of ships. The term is now used generally to signify a platform or elevated spot from which a speaker addresses his audience.

ROT, DRY. An extremely destructive disease incident to timber.

ROTUNDA or ROTONDO. (Ital.) A building circular on the interior and exterior, such as the Pantheon at Rome. See CIRCULAR BUILDINGS.

ROUGH-CAST. A species of plastering used on external walls, consisting of a mixture of lime, small shells or pebbles, occasionally fragments of glass and similar materials. This is usually applied to cottages.

RUDENTURE. (Lat. Rudis, a rope.) The same as CABLING, which see.

RUDERATION. (Lat. Ruderatio.) A method of laying pavements, mentioned by Vitruvius, and according to some, of building walls with rough pebbles and mortar. The mortar called *statumen* by Vitruvius was made of lime and sand.

RUIZ. See ARCHITECTS, list of, 226.

RULE. An instrument for measuring short lengths. Of rules there are various sorts, each adapted to the class of artificers for whose use they are made. Thus, there are stone-cutters' rules, masons' rules, carpenters' rules, sliding and parallel rules, &c. The sliding rule is, however, of more general use, as it solves a number of questions from the change of the position of the slider by inspection, and therefore of much importance to the less educated artisan.

RURAL ARCHITECTURE. See Book III. Chap. V. Sections 22, 23, and 24.

RUSSIAN ARCHITECTURE. Book I. Chap. II. Sect. 20.

RUSTIC ORDER. A species of building wherein the faces of the stones are hatched or picked with the point of a hammer.

RUSTIC QUOINS or COINS. The stones placed on the external angles of a building projecting

beyond the naked of the wall. The edges are bevelled, or the margins recessed in a plane parallel to the face or plane of the wall.

RUSTIC WORK. A mode of building masonry wherein the faces of the stones are left rough, the sides only being wrought smooth where the union of the stones takes place. It was a method much practised at an early period, and re-introduced by Brunelleschi at the revival of the arts. The most common sorts of rustic work are the *frosted*, which has the margins of the stones reduced to a plane parallel to that of the wall, the intermediate parts having an irregular surface; *vermiculated* rustic work, wherein the intermediate parts present the appearance of having been worm-eaten; *chamfered* rustic work, in which the face of the stones being smoothed and made parallel to the surface of the wall, and the angles bevelled to an angle of one hundred and thirty-five degrees, with the face of the stone, where they are set in the wall, the bevel of the two adjacent stones forms an internal right angle.

S.

SABLIERE. (Fr.) An obsolete word, signifying a piece of timber as long as a beam, but not so thick.

SACCHETTI. See ARCHITECTS, list of, 286.

SACELLUM. (Lat.) In ancient Roman architecture, a small inclosed space without a roof. Small sacella, too, were used among the Egyptians, attached frequently to the larger temples. In old church architecture, the term signifies a monumental chapel within a church, also a small chapel in a village.

SACOME. (Ital.) The exact profile of a member or moulding, applied by the French to the mouldings themselves.

SACRARIUM. (Lat.) A small sacred apartment in a Roman house, devoted to a particular deity; also the *cella*, *penetrale* or *adytum* of a temple.

SACRISTY. See DIACONICUM.

SADDLE-BACKED COPING. See COPING.

SAG or SAGGING. The bending of a body by its own weight when resting inclined or horizontally on its ends.

SAGITTA. (Lat. an arrow.) A name sometimes applied to the keystone of an arch. In geometry, it is often employed to signify the abscissa of a curve; and in trigonometry it is the versed sine of an arc, which, as it were, stands like a dart upon the chord.

SAIL OVER. See PROJECTURE.

SALIANT. (Fr.) A term used in respect of a projection of any part or member.

SALLY. A projecture. The end of a piece of timber cut with an interior angle formed by two planes across the fibres. Thus the feet of common rafters, and the inclined pieces which support the flying steps of a wooden stair, are frequently cut; as are, likewise, the lower ends of all inclined timbers which rest upon plates or beams.

SALON or SALOON. (Fr.) A lofty and spacious apartment, frequently vaulted at top, and usually comprehending the height of two floors with two tiers of windows. Its place is commonly in the middle of a building, or at the head of a gallery, &c. In palaces it is the state room.

SAN GALLO, ANTONIO. See ARCHITECTS, list of, 199.

SAN GALLO, G. DI. See ARCHITECTS, list of, 178.

SAN LUCANO. See ARCHITECTS, list of, 183.

SAN MICHELI. See ARCHITECTS, list of, 213.

SAND. See Book II. Chap. II. Sect. 11.

SANDSTONE. In mineralogy, a stone principally composed of grains, or particles of sand, either united with other mineral substances or adhering without any visible cement. The grains or particles of sandstone are generally quartz, sometimes intermixed with feldspar or particles of slate. When lime is the cementing matter the stone is called calcareous sandstone. The cementing matter is not unfrequently oxide of iron intermixed with alumine. The particles of sand in these stones are of various sizes, some being so small as to be scarcely visible. See Book II. Chap. II. Sect. 1.

SAP. The juice or pith of trees that rises from the earth and ascends into the arms, branches, and leaves, to feed and nourish them. Also that part of the stem or wood of the body of a tree that is soft, white, &c. The term is used also as a verb, to denote the undermining a wall by digging a trench under it.

SAPHETA. The same as SOFFITE or SOFITE, which see.

SARACENIC ARCHITECTURE. See Book I. Chap. II. Sect 10.

SARCOPHAGUS. (Σαρξ flesh, and Φαγω, to eat.) A tomb or coffin made of one stone. From Pliny it appears to have been originally applied as the name of a stone found in the Troad, which, from its powerful caustic qualities, was selected for the construction of tombs. From its frequent application to this purpose the name became at length used for the tomb itself. Sarcophagi were made of stone, marble, alabaster, porphyry, &c. The Greeks sometimes made them of hard wood, as oak, cedar, or cypress, which resisted

moisture; sometimes of terra cotta, and even of metal. The form was usually a long square, the angle being rounded. The lid varied both in shape and ornament. Those of the primitive Christians often enclosed several corpses, and were ornamented with several sets of bassi rilievi. Those of higher antiquity were frequently sculptured with great taste and beauty of design, the figures being those of the deceased, or parties connected with them, allegorical or mythological. The Egyptian sarcophagi are sculptured with hieroglyphics. Those of the Greeks and Romans sometimes represent Sleep and Death with their legs crossed, one hand supporting the head and the other holding an inverted torch; sometimes Mercury is represented conducting the Souls and Charon ferrying them over in his bark. Occasionally we find on them groups of bacchanals and bacchic scenes.

Sash. (Fr. Chassis, a frame; more probably the Dutch Sas, a gate.) A frame for holding the glass of windows, and so formed as to be raised and depressed by means of pulleys. Sashes are single or double hung; the *casement* is hung with hinges.

Sash Frame. The frame in which the sashes are fitted for the convenience of sliding up and down; when hung with hinges, to receive them after the manner of hanging a door.

Saurus. See Architects, list of, 34.

Saw. (Dutch, Sawe.) A tool made of a thin plate of steel, formed on the edge into regular teeth for cutting wood, stone, &c. Saws are of various kinds. See p. 631.

Saw-pit. A pit excavated for sawing timber. The sawing is performed by two persons called *sawyers*, one standing above and the other below. Much of the labour, however, is saved by the use of a saw-mill, or machine moving a circular saw, which by its revolutions and keeping the timber close up, performs the work quicker and better than can be done by the labour just described.

Saxon Architecture. See Book I. Chap. III. Sects. 1 and 2.

Saxulphus. See Architects, list of, 66.

Scabellum. (Lat.) A species of pedestal anciently used to support busts or statues. It was high in proportion to its breadth, ending in a kind of sheath, or in the manner of a baluster.

Scaffold. (Fr. Echaufaud.) An assemblage of planks or boards sustained by pieces of wood made fast to vertical poles, and at the other end often resting on the walls, by means whereof the workmen carry up a building, or plasterers complete their work in the interior of houses. On the Continent, scaffolds for public building are much more solidly constructed than in this country.

Scagliola. (Ital.) A species of plaster or stucco invented at Carpi, in the state of Modena, by Guido Sassi, between 1600 and 1649. It is sometimes called *mischia*, from the mixture of colours introduced in it. It was not, however, till the middle of the eighteenth century that the art of making scagliola was brought to perfection. The following is the method of making columns and pilasters:—A wooden cradle, composed of thin strips of deal or other wood is made to represent the column designed, but about 2½ inches less in diameter than the shaft is intended to be when finished. This cradle is lathed round, as for common plastering, and then covered with a pricking-up coat of lime and hair. When this is quite dry, the scagliola artist commences his operations, and, by imitating the rarest and most precious marbles, produces a work which cannot be, except by fracture or sound, discovered to be counterfeit. The purest gypsum which can be obtained is broken into small pieces, and calcined. As soon as the largest fragments lose their brilliancy, the fire is withdrawn; the calcined powder is passed through a very fine sieve, and mixed up with a solution of Flanders glue, isinglass, &c. In this solution the colours are diffused that are required to be imitated in the marble; but if the work is to be of various colours, each colour is separately prepared, and they are afterwards mingled and combined nearly in the same manner that a painter mixes the primitive colours on his palette to compose his different tints. When the powdered gypsum is prepared and mingled for the work, it is laid on the shaft of the column or other surface over the pricked-up coat of lime and hair, and it is then *floated* with proper moulds of wood, the artist during the *floating* using the colours necessary for the imitation, by which means they become mingled and incorporated with the surface. The process of polishing follows; and this is done by rubbing the surface with pumice-stone in one of his hands, while with the other he cleans it with a wet stone. It is then polished with tripoli and charcoal and fine and soft linen; and after going over it with a piece of felt dipped in a mixture of oil and tripoli, he finishes with application of pure oil.

Scale. (Sax.) A line divided into a certain number of equal parts, usually on wood, ivory, or metal, for laying down heights and distances in mathematical and architectural drawing. There are various sorts of scales; as, the *plane scale, Gunter's scale,* the *diagonal scale,* &c.; but the most generally useful scale is that wherein the objects are drawn some aliquot part of their real size, as a tenth, twelfth, twentieth, twenty-fourth, &c.

Scalene Triangle. (Σκαληνος, oblique.) In geometry, one whose sides are all unequal.

Scamilli impares. A term used by Vitruvius, which has puzzled all the commentators

It was formerly held to signify certain blocks serving to raise some of the members of a building, which from being placed below the level, or below the projection of certain ornaments, might be lost to the eye.　See GLOSSARY ADDENDUM.

SCAMILLUS.　A small plinth below the bases of the Ionic and Corinthian columns.

SCAMMOZZI.　See ARCHITECTS, list of, 247.

SCANDULÆ. (Lat.)　In early buildings of the Romans, shingles or flat pieces of wood used for covering instead of tiles.　According to Cornelius Nepos, this was the only covering used in Rome till the war with Pyrrhus in the 470th year of the city.

SCANTLING. (Fr.)　The dimensions of a piece of timber in breadth and thickness.　It is also a term used to denote a piece of timber, as of quartering in a partition, when under five inches square, or the rafter, purlin, or pole plate of a roof.　In masonry, scantling is the length, breadth, and thickness of a stone.

SCAPE or SCAPUS. (Gr.)　The shaft of a column; also the little hollow, above or below, which connects the shaft with the base, or with the fillet under the astragal.

SCAPLING.　A method of tooling the face of a stone.

SCARFING.　The joining of two pieces of timber by bolting or nailing transversely together, so that the two appear but one.

SCENE. (Gr. Σκηνη.)　Strictly an alley or rural portico for shade or shelter, wherein, according to Cassiodorus, theatrical pieces were first represented.　When first applied to a theatre, it signified the wall forming the back of the stage, but afterwards came to mean the whole stage, and is now restricted to the representation of the place in which the drama represents the action.　According to Vitruvius, the Greek scene was occupied in the middle by a great door, called the royal door, because decorated as the gate of a palace.　At the sides were smaller doors, called *hospitalia*, because representing the entrances to habitations destined for strangers, which the Greeks commonly placed on the two sides of their houses.

SCENOGRAPHY. (Gr.)　The method of representing solids in perspective.

SCHEME or SKENE ARCH.　One which is a segment of a circle.

SCHENE. (Gr.)　The representation of any design or geometrical figure by lines so as to make it comprehensible.

SCHOLIUM.　In mathematics, a remark after the demonstration of a proposition, showing how it may be done some other way, or giving some advice or precaution to prevent mistakes, or adding some particular use or application thereof.

SCIAGRAPHY or SCIOGRAPHY. (Gr. Σκια, a shadow, and Γραφω, I describe.)　The doctrine of projecting shadows as they fall in nature.　See Book II. Chap. IV. Sect. 3.

SCOPAS.　See ARCHITECTS, list of, 16.

SCOTIA. (Gr. Σκοτια, darkness.)　The hollow moulding in the base of a column between the fillets of the tori.　It receives the name from being so much in shadow.　The scotia was, from its resemblance to a pulley, called also τροχιλος.　It is most frequently formed by the junction of circular areas of different radii, but it ought rather to be profiled as a portion of an ellipsis.

SCRATCH WORK. (It. Sgraffiata.)　A species of fresco with a black ground on which a white plaster is laid, which being scratched off with an iron bodkin, the black appears through the holes, and serves for shadows.

SCREEN. (Lat. Excerno.)　An instrument used in making mortar, consisting of three wooden ledges joined to a rectangular frame at the bottom, the upper part of which frame is filled with wirework for sifting the sand or lime.　This term is used in ecclesiastical architecture to denote a partition of wood, stone, or metal, usually so placed in a church as to shut out an aisle from the choir, a private chapel from a transept, the nave from the choir, the high altar from the east end of the building, or an altar tomb from one of the public passages or large areas of the church.　In the form and ornamental detail of screens, the ancient artists appear to have almost exhausted fancy, ingenuity, and taste.

SCREW. (Dutch, Scroeve.)　One of the six mechanical powers, chiefly used in pressing or squeezing bodies close, though sometimes also in raising weights.　See Book II. Chap. I. Sect. 8.

SCRIBING.　Fitting the edge of a board to a surface not accurately plane, as the skirting of a room to a floor.　In joinery, it is the fitting one piece to another, so that the fibres of them may be perpendicular to each other, the two edges being cut to an angle to join.

SCROLL.　A convolved or spiral ornament variously introduced. Also the volutes of the Ionic and Corinthian capital.　See *fig.* 1365.

Fig. 1565.

SCULLERY.　The apartment for washing up the dishes and utensils wherein the scullion works.

SCULPTURE. (Lat. Sculpo, to carve.)　The art of imitating forms by chiselling and working away solid substances.　It is also used to denote the carved work itself.　Properly, the word includes works in clay, wax, wood, metal, and stone; but it is generally re-

stricted to those of the last material, the terms *modelling, casting,* and *carving* being applied to the others.

SEALING. The fixing a piece of wood or iron on a wall with plaster, mortar, cement, lead, or other binding, for staples, hinges, joints, &c.

SEASONING TIMBER. See p. 506.

SECANT. (Lat.) A line that cuts another. In trigonometry, the secant is a line drawn to the centre from some point in the tangent, which consequently cuts the circle.

SECOS. See ADYTUM.

SECTION OF A BUILDING. A geometrical representation of it as divided or separated into two parts by a vertical plane, to show and explain the construction of the interior. The section not only includes the parts that are separated, but also the elevation of the receding parts, and ought to be so taken as to show the greatest number of parts, and those of the most difficult construction. Of every building at least two sections should be made at right angles to one another, and parallel to the sides. A section of the flues should also be made, in order to avoid placing timbers near them.

SECTION OF A SOLID. The plane of separation dividing one part from the other. It is understood to be always a plane surface.

SECTOR. An instrument for measuring or laying off angles, and dividing lines and circles into equal parts.

SECTOR OF A CIRCLE. The space comprehended between two radii and the arc terminated by them.

SEGMENT. (Lat.) A part cut off from anything. The area contained by the arc of a circle and a chord. In the segment of a circle the chord of the arc is called the base of the segment, and the height of the arc the height of the segment.

SEGMENT OF A SPHERE. A portion cut off by a plane in any part except the centre, so that the base of such segment must be always a circle, and its surface a part of the sphere.

SELL. See CILL and APERTURE.

SEMICIRCLE. The half of a circle contained by the diameter and circumference.

SEMICIRCULAR ARCHES. Those whose arcs are semicircular.

SENNAMAR. See ARCHITECTS, list of, 55.

SEPULCHRE. (Lat. Sepelire, to bury.) A grave, tomb, or place of interment. The *cenotaph* was an empty sepulchre raised in honour of a person who had had no burial.

SERAGLIO. (Pers. Serai.) A large hall or house. The palace of an eastern prince, but more particularly that in which the females are lodged.

SERLIO. See ARCHITECTS, list of, 238.

SERPENTINE. See PORPHYRY.

SERVANDONI. See ARCHITECTS, list of, 288.

SESSPOOL. See CESSPOOL.

SETT. In piling, a piece placed temporarily on the head of a pile which cannot be reached by the monkey or weight from some intervening matter.

SETTING. The hardening of cement. The term is also used in masonry for fixing stones in walls or vaults, in which the greatest care should be taken that the stones rest firmly on their beds, and that their faces be ranged in the proper surface of the work.

SETTING-OUT ROD. One used by joiners for setting-out frames, as of windows, doors, &c.

SETTLEMENTS. Those parts in which failures by sinking in a building have occurred.

SETT-OFF. The projecting part between the upper and lower portion of a wall where it diminishes in thickness.

SEVERUS. See ARCHITECTS, list of, 43.

SEVERY. A compartment or division of scaffolding. It is also a separate portion or division of a building corresponding with the modern term compartment, being as it were severed or divided.

SEWER. A drain or conduit for carrying off soil or water from any place. See Book II. Chap. III. Sect. I.

SEXAGESIMAL. The division of a line, first into sixty parts, then each of these again into sixty, and so on, as long as division can be made. It is principally used in dividing the circumference of a circle.

SHADOWS and SHADOWING. In drawing, the art of correctly casting the shades of objects and representing their degrees of shade. See Book II. Chap. IV. Sect. 3.

SHAFT. (Sax. Sceaft.) The cylindrical part, or rather body, of a column, between the base and the capital. It is, properly, the frustum of a conoid, and is also called the *fust, trunk,* or body of the column.

SHAFT OF A CHIMNEY. See CHIMNEY.

SHAFT OF A KING POST. The part between the *joggles.*

SHAKE. A fissure or rent in timber by its being dried too suddenly, or exposed to too great heat. Any timber, when naturally full of slits or clefts, is said to be *shaky.*

SHANK. (Sax.) The space between two channels of the Doric triglyph, sometimes called the leg of the triglyph. The Romans called the shank, *femur.*

SHEET LEAD.   See Book II. Chap. II. Sect. 6.

SHELF. (Sax.)   A board fixed against a wall by its edge, the upper side being horizontal, for receiving whatever may be placed upon it.   A shelf is usually supported by brackets, or by pieces at the end, called *standards*.

SHINGLES. (Germ. Schindel.)   Small oaken boards used like slates for covering a building, from eight to twelve inches long, and about four inches broad, thicker on one edge than the other.   The process of making a roof of this kind is called *shingling*.

SHOE.   The inclined piece at the bottom of a water trunk or lead pipe for turning the course of the water, and discharging it from the wall of a building.

SHOOTING.   Planing the edge of a board straight, and out of winding.

SHOOTING BOARDS.   Two boards joined together, with their sides lapped upon each other, so as to form a rebate for making short joints.

SHORE, or SHOAR. (Sax.)   A prop or oblique timber acting as a brace on the side of a building, the upper end resting against that part of the wall upon which the floor is supported, and both ends received by plates or beams.   A *dead shore* is an upright piece built up in a wall that has been cut or broken through for the purpose of making some alterations in the building.

SHOULDER OF A TENON.   The plane transverse to the length of a piece of timber from which the tenon projects.   It should be at right angles to the length, though it does not always lie in the plane as here defined, but sometimes in different planes.

SHREAD HEAD.   The same as JERKIN HEAD, which see.

SHREDDINGS or FURRINGS.   In old buildings, short slight pieces of timber fixed as bearers below the roof, forming a straight line with the upper side of the rafters.

SHRINE. (Sax. Scpin.)   A desk or cabinet; a case or box, particularly one in which sacred things are deposited: hence applied to a reliquary and to the tomb of a canonised person.   The altar is sometimes called a shrine, and in this case its form and condition, and the annexation of a statue to it, was of importance, because such tombs had greater privileges than plainer monuments.

SHRINKING.   The contraction of a piece of timber in its breadth by seasoning, hot water, &c.   It is proportional to its breadth, the length not changing.   Hence in unseasoned timber mitred together, such as the architraves of doors and windows, the mitres are always close on the outside and open to the door, forming a wedge-like hollow on each side of the frame.   It is to avoid the effects of shrinking that narrow boards called *battens* are used in floors.

SHUTE.   See ARCHITECTS, list of, 243.

SHUTTERS.   The boards which shut up the aperture of a window.   See BOXINGS OF A WINDOW.

SIDE POSTS.   Truss posts placed in pairs, disposed at the same distance from the middle of the truss.   Their use is not only to support the principal rafters, &c., but to suspend the tie beam below.   In extended roofs two or three pair of side posts are used.

SIDE TIMBERS or SIDE WAVERS.   The same as purlins, the first term being used in Somersetshire and the last in Lincolnshire.

SIENITE.   See SYENITE.

SILL.   See CILL and APERTURE.

SILOE.   See ARCHITECTS, list of, 211.

SILT.   The muddy deposit of standing water.

SIMA.   See CYMA.

SIMILAR FIGURES.   Those whose several angles are respectively equal, and the sides about the equal angles proportional.

SIMONETTI.   See ARCHITECTS, list of, 296.

SINE.   A right line drawn from one end of an arch perpendicular upon the diameter, or it is half the chord of twice the arch.   The sine of the complement of an arch is the sine of what the arch wants of ninety degrees.   The *versed sine* is that part of the diameter comprehended between the arc and the sine.

SINGLE FRAME and NAKED FLOOR.   One with only one tier of joists.

SINGLE HUNG.   An arrangement in a pair of window sashes, in which one only is movable.

SINGLE JOISTS FLOOR.   One without binding joists.

SINGLE MEASURE.   A term applied to a door that is square on both sides.   *Double measure* is when the door is moulded on both sides.   When doors are moulded on one side and are square on the other, they are accounted measure and half.

SISSIVERNE.   See ARCHITECTS, list of, 101.

SITE. (Lat. Situs.)   The situation of a building; the plot of ground on which it stands.

SKEW BACK.   In a straight or curved arch, that part of it which recedes beyond the springing from the vertical line of the opening.

SKIRTING or SKIRTING BOARD.   The narrow board placed round the margin of a floor, which, where there is a dado, forms a plinth for its base; otherwise, it is a plinth for the

room itself. Skirting is either scribed close to the floor or let into it by a groove; in the former case a fillet is put at the back of the skirting to keep it firm.

SKIRTS. Several superficies in a plane, which would cover a body when turned up or down without overlapping.

SKREEN. See SCREEN.

SKYLIGHT. A frame consisting of one or more inclined planes of glass, placed in a roof to light passages or rooms below.

SLAB. An outside plank or board sawed from the sides of a timber tree, and frequently of very unequal thickness. The word is also used to express a thin piece of marble, consisting of right angles and plane surfaces. See CHIMNEY.

SLATE. See Book II. Chap. II. Sect. 9.

SLATERS' WORK. See Book II. Chap. III. Sect. 6.

SLEEPERS. Horizontal timbers disposed in a building next to the ground transversely under walls, ground joists, or the boarding of a floor. When used on piles they are laid upon them, and planked over to support the superincumbent walls. Underground joists either lie upon the solid earth, or are supported at various parts by prop stones. When in the former position, having no rows of timber below, these ground joists are themselves called sleepers. Old writers on practical architecture call those rafters lying in the valley of a roof, sleepers; but in this sense the word is now obsolete.

SLIDING RULE. One constructed with logarithmic lines, so that by means of another scale sliding on it, various arithmetical operations are performed merely by inspection.

SLIT DEAL. See BOARD.

SLUICE. A stop against water for the drainage or supply with water of a place. It is hung with hinges from the top edge when used merely as a stop against the water of a river; but when made for supply as well, it moves vertically in the groove of its frame by means of a winch, and is then called a penstock.

SMITHERY and IRONMONGERY. See Book II. Chap. III. Sect. 10.

SMOOTHING PLANE. See p. 630.

SNACKET. A provincial term for the hasp of a casement.

SNIPE'S BILL PLANE. One with a sharp arris for getting out the quirks of mouldings.

SOANE. See ARCHITECTS, list of, 316.

SOCKET CHISEL. A strong tool used by carpenters for mortising, and worked with a mallet.

SOCLE or ZOCLE. A square member of less height than its horizontal dimension, serving to raise pedestals or to support vases or other ornaments. The socle is sometimes continued round a building, and is then called a *continued socle*. It has neither base nor cornice.

SOFFITA, SOFFIT, or SOFITE. (Ital.) A ceiling; the lower surface of a vault or arch. A term denoting the under horizontal face of the architrave between columns; the under surface of the corona of a cornice.

SOILS. A provincial term, chiefly, however, used in the north, signifying the principal rafters of a roof.

SOLDER. A metallic composition used in joining together or *soldering* metals.

SOLID. (Lat.) In geometry, a body which has length, breadth, and thickness; that is, it is terminated or contained under one or more plane surfaces, as a surface is under one or more lines. Regular solids are such as are terminated by equal and similar planes, so that the apex of their solid angles may be inscribed in a sphere.

SOLID ANGLES. An angle formed by three or more angles in a point, and whereof the sum of all the plane angles is less than three hundred and sixty degrees, otherwise they would constitute the plane of a circle and not of a solid.

SOLID SHOOT. See WATER SHOOT.

SOLIVE. The French term for a joist, rafter, or piece of wood, either slit or sawed, with which builders lay their ceilings. The term is rarely used in the English language.

SOMMERING. See SUMMERING.

SORTANT ANGLE. The same as SALIENT ANGLE, which see.

SOSTRATUS. See ARCHITECTS, list of, 25.

SOUFFLOT. See ARCHITECTS, list of, 299.

SOUND-BOARD. The same as a canopy or type over a pulpit, to reverberate the voice of the speaker.

SOUND-BOARDING. In floors, consists of short boards placed transversely between the joists, and supported by fillets fixed to the sides of the latter for holding pugging, which is any substance that will prevent the transmission of sound from one story to another. The narrower the sound-boards the better. The fillets on which they rest may be about three-quarters of an inch thick and about an inch wide, nailed to the joists at intervals of a foot. See BOARDING FOR PUGGING.

SOUSE (Fr.) or SOURCE. A support or under-prop.

SPAN. An imaginary line across the opening of an arch or roof, by which its extent is estimated.

Span Roof. One consisting of two inclined sides, in contradistinction to *shed* or *leanto roofing.* It may be with simple rafters, with or without a collar beam, or when of increased span it may be trussed, the term only applying to the external part.

Spandrel. The irregular triangular space between the outer curve or extrados of an arch, a horizontal line from its apex, and a perpendicular line from its springing.

Spandrel Bracketing. A cradling of brackets fixed between one or more curves, each in a vertical plane, and in the circumference of a circle whose plane is horizontal.

Spanish Architecture. See Book I. Chap. II. Sect. 19.

Spar-piece. A name given in some places to the collar beam of a roof.

Spars. The common rafters of a roof for the support of the tiling or slating.

Specification. A description at length of the materials and workmanship to be used and employed in the erection of any building. See Book II. Chap. III. Sect. 13.

Specific Gravity. A gravity or weight of every solid or fluid compared with the weight of the same magnitude of rain water, which is chosen as the standard of comparison, on account of its being subject to less variation in different circumstances of time, place, &c., than any other solid or fluid. By a fortunate coincidence, at least to the English philosopher, it happens that a cubic foot of rain water weighs 1000 ounces avoirdupois; consequently, assuming this as the specific gravity of rain water, and comparing all other bodies with this, the same numbers that express the specific gravity of bodies will at the same time express the weight of a cubic foot of each in avoirdupois ounces, which affords great facility to numerical computations. Hence are readily deduced the following laws of the specific gravity of bodies: —

1. In bodies of equal magnitudes the specific gravities are directly as the weights or as their densities. 2. In bodies of the same specific gravities the weights will be as the magnitudes. 3. In bodies of equal weights the specific gravities are inversely as the magnitudes. 4. The weights of different bodies are to each other in the compound ratio of their magnitudes and specific gravities.

Thus it is obvious, that if of the magnitude, weight, and specific gravity of a body any two be given, the third may be found; and we may thus arrive at the magnitude of bodies which are too irregular to admit of the common rules of mensuration; or, by knowing the specific gravity and magnitude, we may find the weight of bodies which are too ponderous to be submitted to the action of the balance or steel yard; or, lastly, the magnitude and weight being given, we may ascertain their specific gravities.

Table of Specific Gravities
(Extracted from Davies, Lavoisier, Young, and other authentic sources).

Note. — Water at 60° is assumed 1000 specific gravity.

Mineral Productions.

Platina, purified	-	19500	Garnet, Bohemian - -	4188
——, hammered	-	20336	Sapphire of Pay - -	4076
Pure gold, cast	-	19258	Topaz, oriental - -	4010
——, hammered -	-	19361	Beryl, or oriental aquamarine	3548
Mercury -	-	13568	Diamond, rose-coloured -	3531
Lead, cast -	-	11352	——, white - -	3521
Silver, pure, cast -	-	10474	——, lightest -	3501
——, hammered	-	10510	Glass, flint - -	3329
Bismuth, cast	-	9822	——, white - -	2892
Copper, cast -	-	8788	——, bottle - -	2732
——, wire, -	-	8878	——, green - -	2642
Brass, cast -	-	8395	Fluor - -	3191
——, wire -	-	8544	Serpentine, green -	2988
Cobalt, cast -	-	7812	Mica, black - -	2900
Nickel, cast -	-	7807	Basalt, from the Giant's Causeway	2864
Iron, cast -	-	7207	Marble, white Parian -	2837
——, bar -	-	7788	Marble, green - -	2741
Steel, hard, not screwed	-	7816	——, red - -	2725
——, soft, not screwed	-	7833	——, white, of Carrara -	2716
Loadstone -	-	4800	Emerald, Peruvian -	2775
Tin, cast -	-	7291	Porphyry, red -	2765
Zinc, cast -	-	7190	Jaspar - -	2764
Antimony, cast -	-	6702	Alabaster, white -	2730
Tungstein -	-	6066	Calcareous spar, rhombic -	2715
Arsenic, cast -	-	5763	——, pyramidal -	2714
Molybdena -	-	4738	Slate - -	2671
Spar, ponderous -	-	4430	Pitch stone - -	2669
Ruby, oriental -	-	4283	Onyx, pebble - -	2664

Chalcedony, transparent	-	2664	Lapis obsidianus	- -	2348
Granite, Egyptian, red	-	2654	Selenite	- - -	2322
Rock chrystal, pure -	-	2653	Grindstone -	- -	2142
Amorphous quartz	-	2647	Salt -	- -	2130
Agate, onyx -	-	2637	Sulphur, native	- -	2033
Cornelian -	-	2613	Nitre -	- -	2000
Sardonyx -	-	2602	Brick -	- -	2000
Purbeck stone	-	2601	Plumbago -	- -	1860
Flint, white -	-	2594	Alum -	- -	1720
——, blackish	-	2581	Asphaltum -	- -	1400
Agate, oriental	-	2590	Coal, Scotch -	- -	1300
Portland stone	-	2570	——, Newcastle	- -	1270
Mill stone -	-	2483	——, Staffordshire	- -	1240
Paving stone -	-	2415	Jet -	- -	1238
Touchstone -	-	2415	Ice, *probably* -	- -	930
Porcelain, Chinese	-	2384	Pumice-stone -	- -	914

Liquids.

Sulphuric acid	-	1840	Water at 60°	- -	1000
———, Ph., London	-	1850	Sea Water -	- -	1026
Nitrous acid, Ph., London	-	1550	Muriatic acid	- -	1194
Nitric acid -	-	1217	Naphtha -	- -	708

Vegetable Productions.

Sugar, white -	-	1606	Vinegar, distilled	- -	1009
Gum Arabic -	-	1452	Bordeaux wine	- -	994
Pitch -	-	1150	Turpentine, liquid	- -	991
Malmsey, Madeira -	-	1038	Linseed oil -	- -	940
Cider -	-	1018	Asphaltum -	- -	900

Animal Productions.

Pearl -	-	2750	Milk, cow's -	- -	1032
Coral -	-	2680	Wax, white -	- -	968
Sheep's bones, recent -	-	2222	——, yellow -	- -	965
Oyster shell -	-	2092	Spermaceti -	- -	943
Ivory -	-	1917	Butter -	- -	942
Stag's horn -	-	1875	Tallow -	- -	942
Ox's horn -	-	1840	Lamp oil -	- -	923

Woods.

Pomegranate tree	-	1354	Maple -	- -	755
Lignum Vitæ	-	1333	Cherry tree -	- -	715
Box, Dutch -	-	1328	Quince tree -	- -	705
Ebony -	-	1177	Orange tree -	- -	705
Heart of oak, 60 years felled -		1170	Walnut -	- -	671
Oak, English, just felled	-	1113	Pitch pine -	- -	660
———, seasoned	-	743	Red pine -	- -	657
———, usually stated at		925	Yellow pine -	- -	529
Bog oak of Ireland -		1046	White pine -	- -	420
Teak of the East Indies	- 745 to 657		Fir of New England -	-	553
Mahogany -	1063 to 637		— of Riga -	-	753
Pear tree, trunk -	-	646	— of Mar Forest, Scotland	-	696
Medlar tree -	-	944	Cypress -	- -	644
Olive wood -	-	927	Lime tree -	- -	604
Logwood -	-	931	Filbert wood -	- -	600
Beach -	-	852	Willow -	- -	585
Ash -	- 845 to 600		Cedar -	- -	560
Yew, Spanish -	-	807	Juniper -	- -	556
——, Dutch -	-	788	Poplar, white Spanish	-	529
Alder -	-	800	———, common	-	383
Elm -	- 800 to 600		Sassafras wood -	-	482
Apple tree -	-	793	Larch of Scotland -	-	530
Plum tree -	-	755	Cork -	- -	240

SPECUS. (Lat.) In ancient architecture, the canal into which the water flowed in aqueducts raised above the surface of the ground, and constructed of hewn stones or bricks. It was covered with a vault to preserve the water from the sun, and from being mixed with rain water. The specus was sometimes covered with flat stones, laid horizontally, as in the Aqua Martia, part of the Aqua Claudia, and the aqueduct of Segovia. Sometimes the same arcade carried several of these canals one above the other.

SPERONI. See ANTERIDES.

SPHÆRISTERIUM. A building for the exercise of the ball; a tennis court. The ancients generally placed sphæristeria among the apartments of their baths and gymnasia. They were also placed in large villas, as in those of Pliny the younger.

SPHERE. (Gr. Σφαιρα.) A solid, whose surface is at every point equally distant from a certain point within the solid, which point is called the *centre of the sphere*. Every sphere is equal to two-thirds of its circumscribing cylinder, that is, it is equal to a cylinder whose ends are circles, equal to a great circle of the sphere, and whose height is equal to the diameter of the same.

SPHERICAL BRACKETING. That so formed that the surface of the plastering which it is to receive forms a spherical surface.

SPHEROID. See CONOID.

SPHEROIDAL BRACKETING. That formed to receive the plastering of a spheroid.

SPINA. See CIRCUS.

SPINTHARUS. See ARCHITECTS, list of, 9.

SPIRAL. A curve which makes one or more revolutions round a fixed point, and does not return to itself.

SPIRE. (Gr. Σπαιρα, a twisting.) In ancient architecture, the base of a column, and sometimes the astragal or torus; but among the moderns it designates a steeple diminishing as it ascends, either pyramidally or conically. See ADDENDUM.

SPLAYED. A term applied to whatever has one side making an oblique angle with the other: thus, the heading joists of a boarded floor are frequently splayed in their thickness; as are also the jambs or sides of a window. In the latter case, the practice is for the better lighting of a room. The word *fluing* is sometimes applied to an aperture, in the same sense as *splayed*.

SPRING BEVEL OF A RAIL. The angle made by the top of the plank, with a vertical plane touching the ends of the railpiece, which terminates the concave side.

SPRINGED. In boarding a roof, the setting the boards together with bevel joints, for the purpose of keeping out the rain.

SPRINGER. The impost or place where the vertical support to an arch terminates, and the curve of the arch begins; the term is sometimes used for the *rib* of a groined roof.

SPRINGING COURSE. The horizontal course of stones, from which an arch springs or rises; or that row of stones upon which the first arch stones are laid.

SQUARE. (Lat. Quadra.) A figure of four equal sides, and as many equal angles; also, an area of such form surrounded by houses, and ornamented in the centre with a lawn, shrubs, trees, &c. In joinery, a work is said to be *square framed*, or *framed square*, when the framing has all the angles of its styles, rails, and mountings square without being moulded. The word is also applied to an instrument for setting out angles square. See CARPENTER'S SQUARE. It is also a measure used in building of 100 superficial feet.

SQUARE SHOOT. A wooden trough for discharging water from a building.

SQUARE STAFF. A piece of wood placed at the external angle of a projection in a room to secure the angle, which if of plaster would be liable to be broken, and at the same time to allow a good finish for the papering.

SQUARING A HANDRAIL. The method of cutting a plank to the form of a rail for a staircase, so that all the vertical sections may be right angles.

SQUARING A PIECE OF STUFF. The act of trying it by the square, to make the angles right angles.

STABLE. (Lat.) A building for the accommodation of horses.

STACK OF CHIMNEYS. See CHIMNEY.

STADIUM. (Gr.) In ancient architecture, an open space wherein the athletæ or wrestlers exercised running, and in which they contested the prizes. It signifies also the place itself where the public games were celebrated, often formed a part of the gymnasia. The word also denotes a measure of length among the Grecians, of 125 paces.

STAFF-BEAD. See ANGLE-BEAD.

STAGE. A floor or story. In a theatre, the floor on which the performers act. The stage of a buttress is, in ecclesiastical architecture, the part between one splayed projection and the next.

STAIR. (Sax. Stæзen, to step.) A stone, or piece of other material, by which a person raises himself one step. A series of steps or stairs for ascending from the lower to the upper part of a building, when enclosed by a wall, is called a staircase.

STAIRCASE. That part or subdivision in a building containing the stairs, which enable persons to ascend or descend from one floor to another. See Book III. Chap. I. Sect. 23. for its construction.

STALK. (Sax.) An ornament in the Corinthian capital, which is sometimes fluted, and resembles the stalk of a plant; from it spring the volutes and helices.

STALL. (Sax.) A place or division in a stable wherein one horse is placed for feeding and sleeping. According to their number in a stable it is called a one-stall, two-stall, &c. stable. This word is also used to denote an elevated seat in the choir or chancel of a church appropriated to an ecclesiastic, such as the prebendal stall of a cathedral.

STANCHION. (Fr. Estançon.) A prop or support. The upright mullions or bars of a window or open screen. Also a PUNCHION, which see.

STANDARDS. The upright pieces in a plate rack, or above a dresser, to support the shelves thereover.

When the edges of standards are cut into mouldings across the fibres of the wood they are called *cut standards*.

STAPLE. A small piece of iron pointed at each end, and bent round, so that the two ends may be parallel to each other, and of equal lengths, to be driven into wood or into a wall, thus forming a loop for fastening a hasp or bolt.

STARLINGS or STERLINGS, sometimes called STILTS. An assemblage of piles driven round the piers of a bridge to give it support.

STATICS. See MECHANICS.

STATUARY MARBLE. See Book II. Chap. II. Sect. 3.

STAVES. Small upright cylinders, sometimes called *rounds*, for forming a rack to contain the hay in stables for the supply of it to the horses.

STAY. A piece performing the office of a brace, to prevent the swerving of the piece to which it is applied. The term is general, and applies to all materials.

STEEL. (Sax. Stal.) Iron united with carbon, which is accomplished in two ways, by fusion and by cementation; the former is used to convert iron into steel immediately from the ore, or from crude or cast-iron; the last-named process is effected by exposing iron, covered with charcoal, to a strong continued heat. The process for converting iron into steel was known to the ancients.

STEENING. The brickwork laid dry (that is, without mortar) used for forming the cylindrical shaft of a well or cesspool, whose office is to prevent the irruption of the surrounding soil.

STEEPLE. (Sax. Stepel.) A lofty erection attached to a church, chiefly intended to contain its bells. The word is a general term, and applies to every appendage of this nature, whether tower or spire, or a combination of the two.

STEP. The same as STAIR, which see.

STEREOBATA. See PEDESTAL.

STEREOGRAPHIC PROJECTION. That projection of the sphere wherein the eye is supposed to be placed on the surface.

STEREOGRAPHY. (Gr. Στερεος, solid, and Γραφω, I describe.) That branch of solid geometry which demonstrates the properties and shows the construction of all regularly defined solids; it explains the methods for constructing the surfaces on planes, so as to form the entire body itself, or to cover its surface; or, when the solid is bounded by plane surfaces, the inclination of the planes.

STEREOTOMY. The science of cutting solids to suit certain conditions required for their forms.

STILE. (Sax.) The vertical part of a piece of framing into which, in joinery, the ends of the rails are fixed by mortises and tenons.

STILTS. See STARLINGS.

STOA. (Gr.) In Grecian architecture, a term corresponding with the Latin *porticus*, and the Italian *portico*.

STOCK. The part of a tool for boring wood with a crank whose end rests against the breast of the workman, while with one hand he holds the boring end steady, and with the other turns the crank; the steel borers are called *bits*, and the whole instrument is called a *stock and bit*.

STONE. (Sax.) A natural indurated substance found beneath and on the surface of the earth in almost every part of the world, and which for its strength and durability has been universally employed for building purposes. See Book II. Chap. II. Sect. 1.

STOOTHINGS. A provincial term which signifies the battening of walls. See TOOTHING.

STOP-COCK. A cock used in plumbery to turn off the supply to a reservoir.

STORY. (Lat. or Sax. Stop.) One of the vertical divisions of a building; a series of apartments on the same level.

STORY POSTS. Upright timbers disposed in the story of a building for supporting the superincumbent part of the exterior wall through the medium of a beam over them; they are chiefly used in sheds and workshops, and should have either a solid wall below or stand upon a strong wooden sill upon inverted arches, or upon large stones, with their ends let into sockets.

STORY ROD. One used in setting up a staircase, equal in length to the height of the story,

and divided into as many parts as there are intended to be steps in the staircase, so that they may be measured and distributed with accuracy.

STRAIGHT JOINT FLOOR. See FLOOR.

STRAIN. (Sax. Sꞇꞃeꞃn.) The force exerted on any material tending to disarrange or destroy the cohesion of its component parts.

STRAINING PIECE or STRUTTING PIECE. A beam placed between two opposite beams to prevent their nearer approach, as rafters, braces, struts, &c. If such a piece serves also the office of a sill, it is called a *straining sill*.

STRAP. (Dutch, Stroppe.) An iron plate for the connection of two or more timbers, whereinto it is screwed by bolts.

STRENGTH OF MATERIALS. See Book II. Chap. I. Sect. 11. and Chap. III.

STRETCHED OUT. A term applied to a surface that will just cover a body so extended that all its parts are in a plane, or may be made to coincide with a plane.

STRETCHER. A brick or stone laid with its longer face in the surface of the wall.

STRETCHING COURSE. In walling, a course of stones or bricks laid with their longer dimensions in a horizontal line parallel to the face of the wall; it is exactly the contrary of a *heading course*, in which the breadths of the stones or bricks are laid in a straight line parallel to the face of the wall.

STRIÆ. (Lat.) ·The lists or fillets between the flutes of columns.

STRIATED. Champered or channeled.

STRIGES. The channels of a fluted column.

STRIKING. A term used to denote the draught of lines on the surface of a body; the term is also used to denote the drawing of lines on the face of a piece of stuff for mortises, and cutting the shoulders of tenons. Another application of the word occurs in the practice of joinery, to denote the act of running a moulding with a plane. The *striking of a centre* is the removal of the timber framing upon which an arch is built, after its completion.

STRING or STRING PIECE. That part of a flight of stairs which forms its ceiling or sofite.

STRING BOARD. In wooden stairs, the board next the well-hole which receives the ends of the steps; its face follows the direction of the well-hole, whatever the form: when curved, it is frequently formed in thicknesses glued together, though sometimes it is got out of the solid, like a hand-rail.

STRIX. (Lat.) A channel in a fluted column.

STRUCK. A term used to denote the removal of any temporary support in a building during its execution.

STRUT. See BRACE.

STRUTTING BEAM or STRUT BEAM. A term used by old writers in carpentry, for what is now called a *straining* or *collar beam*.

STRUTTING PIECE. The same as STRAINING PIECE, which see; and also BRIDGINGS and KEYS.

STUCCO. (Fr. Stuc.) A term indefinitely applied to calcareous cements of various descriptions.

STUDS. (Sax.) The quarters or posts in partitions. The term is used chiefly in the provinces.

STUFF. (Dutch.) A general term for the wood used by joiners.

STYLOBATA. See PEDESTAL.

SUBDIVISION AND APARTMENTS OF A BUILDING. See Book III. Chap. II. Sect. 3.

SUBNORMAL. The distance between the foot of the ordinate and a perpendicular to the curve (or its tangent) upon the axis.

SUB-PLINTH. A second and lower plinth placed under the principal one in columns and pedestals.

SUB-PRINCIPALS. The same as auxiliary rafters or principal braces.

SUDATIO. (Lat.) See CONCAMERATA SUDATIO.

SUGER. See ARCHITECTS, list of, 96.

SUMMER. (Perhaps from Soma, Ital.) The lintel of a door, window, &c. A beam tenoned into a girder to support the ends of joists on both sides of it. It is frequently used as a synonyme for a girder. Also a large stone laid over columns and pilasters in the commencement of a cross vault. It is, moreover, used in the same sense as BRESSUMMER, which see.

SUMMER TREE. See DORMANT TREE.

SUMMERING. See BEDS OF A STONE.

SUNK SHELVES. Such as are formed with a groove in them to prevent the plates, dishes, or other materials sliding off their upper surface.

SUPERSTRUCTURE. (Lat.) The work built on the foundation of a building. The upper part.

SUPPORT. See POINTS OF SUPPORT.

SURBASE. The series of mouldings immediately above the base of a room.

SWALLOW-TAILED. See DOVE-TAILED.

SWEDISH TIMBER. See p. 499.

Sycamore. The *acer pseudo-platanus,* a tree, whose wood is much used by turners. See p. 500.

Syenite. A stone which consists of feldspar and hornblende, of various colours, as reddish, dull green, &c., as the feldspar or hornblende may predominate. It obtained the name from its abundance of syene, and according to Pliny was at first named *pyropœcilos.* It is, in fact, a species of granite, and was the material used for Pompey's Pillar.

Symmetry. (Gr. Συν, with, and Μετρω, I measure.) A system of proportion in a building, from which results from one part the measurement of all the rest. It also conveys the meaning of uniformity as regards the answering of one part to another.

Systyle. (Gr.) See Colonnade.

T.

Tabern. A provincial term for a cellar.

Tabernacle. (Lat.) In Catholic churches the name given to a small representation of an edifice placed on the altar for containing consecrated vessels, &c.

Table. In perspective, the same as the plane of the picture, being the paper or canvas on which a perspective drawing is made, and usually perpendicular to the horizon. In the theory of perspective, it is supposed to be transparent for simplifying the theory.

Table or Tablet. (Lat. Tabula.) A flat surface generally charged with some ornamental figure. The outline is generally rectangular, and when raised from the naked of the wall, is called a *projecting* or *raised table.* When not perpendicular to the horizon, it is called a *raking table.* When the surface is rough, frosted, or vermiculated, from being broken with the hammer, it is called a *rusticated table.*

Table, Corbel. See Corbel Table.

Table of Glass. In glass works and among glaziers, a circular plate of glass, being its original form before it is cut or divided into squares. Twenty-four tables make a *case.*

Table, Water. An inclined plane where a wall sets off to a smaller projection, for the purpose of throwing off the water, principally used in buttresses and other parts of Gothic edifices.

Tablet. The same as Table.

Tabling. A term used by the Scotch builders to denote the coping of the walls of very common houses.

Tablinum. (Lat.) In Roman architecture, an apartment situated in the narrow part of the atrium, as is supposed, fronting the entrance. Its exact position is not now known, and indeed the situation of it may, under circumstances, have varied, its true place therefore must be a matter of doubt.

Tabulatum. (Lat.) A term used by the Romans not only in respect to the floors, wainscottings, ceilings, &c., which were constructed of wood, but also to balconies and other projecting parts, which latter Vitruvius calls *projectiones.*

Tacks. Small nails used for various purposes, but principally for stretching cloth upon a board.

Tænia. (Gr.) The fillet which separates the Doric frieze from the architrave.

Tail. (Verb.) A term denoting the hold of any bearing piece on that which supports it, as where the end of a timber lies or *tails* upon the wall. The expression is similar to what in joinery is called *housing,* with this difference, that housing expresses the complete surrounding of the cavity of the piece which is let in.

Tail Bays. See Case Bays.

Tail Trimmer. One next the wall, into which the ends of joints are fastened, in order to avoid flues.

Tailing. The part of a projecting stone or brick inserted in a wall.

Tailloir. (Fr.) The name which the French give to the *abacus.*

Talon. (Fr.) The name given by the French to the *ogee.*

Tambour. (Fr. a drum.) A term denoting the naked ground on which the leaves of the Corinthian and Composite capitals are placed. It signifies also the wall of a circular temple surrounded with columns, and further the circular vertical part below a cupola as well as above it.

Tangent. (Lat. Tango.) A line drawn perpendicular to the extremity of the diameter of a circle, and therefore touching it only at one point. In trigonometry it is a line drawn perpendicularly from the extremity of the diameter, at one end of the arc, and bounded by a straight line drawn from the centre through the other.

Tapering. A term expressive of the gradual approach, as they rise, of the sides of a body to each other, so that if continued they would terminate in a point.

Tarras. See Book II. Chap. II. Sect. 11. It is a strong cement, useful in water works.

Tassals, Tassels, or Torsels. (Fr.) The pieces of timber lying under the mantel tree.

Taste. See Book III. Chap. I. Sect. 1, and Book III. Chap. III. Sect. 1.

Tatti Sansovino. See Architects, list of, 229.

Tavellæ. (Lat.) Bricks in ancient Roman architecture which were seven inches long and three and a half broad.

Taxis. (Gr.) A term used by Vitruvius to signify that disposition which assigns to every part of a building its just dimensions. Modern architects have called it *ordonnance.*

Taylor, Sir Robert. See **Architects,** list of, 302.

Teaze Tenon. A tenon on the top of a post, with a double shoulder and tenon from each, for supporting two level pieces of timber at right angles to each other.

Tectorium Opus. (Lat.) A name in ancient architecture given to a species of plastering used on the walls of their apartments.

Telamones. (Gr. Tλαω, to support.) Figures of men used in the same manner as Caryatides. They are sometimes called *atlantes.*

Temones. (Gr. Τεμνος.) The places in a temple where statues were placed.

Tempered. An epithet applied to bricks which may be cut with ease, and reduced with ease to a required form. The term is also applied to mortar and other cement, which has been well beaten and mixed together.

Templa. (Lat.) Timbers in the roof of the Roman temples, which rested on the *cantherii,* or principal rafters, similar to our purlins.

Template. An improper orthography for **Templet,** which see.

Temple. (Lat.) Generally an edifice erected for the public exercise of religious worship. The subject of temples has been so fully considered in the body of the work, under the different heads of Ancient, Grecian, and Roman Architecture, that we shall here confine ourselves to the description of the different species of temples mentioned by Vitruvius. The difference between temples is by that author thus given (book iii.) : — A temple is said to be *in antis* when it has antæ or pilasters in front of the walls, which enclose the cells, with two columns between the antæ. A plan of such a temple is seen in *fig.* 1366.

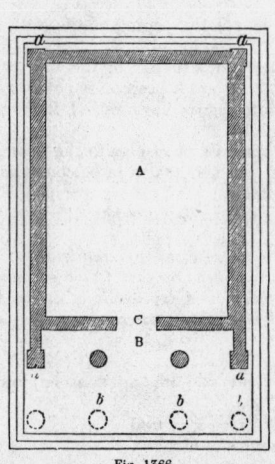

Fig. 1366.

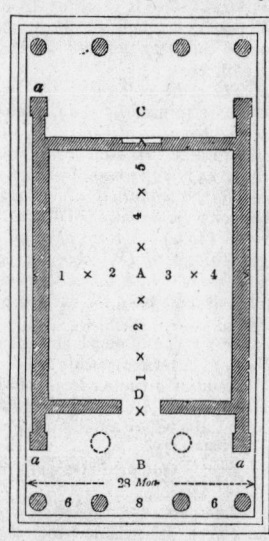

Fig. 1567.

It was crowned with a pediment, and was not dissimilar to the prostylos temple, to which we shall presently come. In the figure, A is the cell, *aa* the antæ, and if in front of them, the columns *bbbb* were placed, it would be a *prostyle* temple ; C is the door of the cell, and B the pronaos. The appearance in front of this species is the same as the *amphiprostyle* temple, which is given in *fig.* 1367., and wherein columns are also placed in front of the antæ. Of the prostyle temple, an example, that of the temple of Jupiter and Faunus, existed on the island of the Tyber at Rome. In the figure of the amphiprostyle temple, A is the cell, B the pronaos, C the posticus, D the door of the cell, and *aa* are the antæ. It will be immediately seen that the same elevation will apply (*fig.* 1368.) to both the plans just given. The amphiprostyle temple, be it observed, has columns in the rear as well as in front, and is distinguished by that from the prostylos of *fig.* 1366., wherein the columns *bbbb* (*fig.* 1367.) would make that prostylos which, but for them, would be merely a temple in antis. The *amphiprostylos* then only differs from the *prostyle* by having columns in the rear, repeated similarly to those in the front. The *fig.* 1368.

applies on double the scale of the plan to both *figs*. 1366. and 1367., and is a diastyle tetrastyle temple, that is, one whose intercolumniations (see CULONNADE) are of three diameters, and the number of whose columns is four.

Fig. 1368.

A *peripteral temple* had six columns in front and rear, and eleven on the flanks, counting the two columns on the angles (see *fig*. 1369.), and these were so placed that their

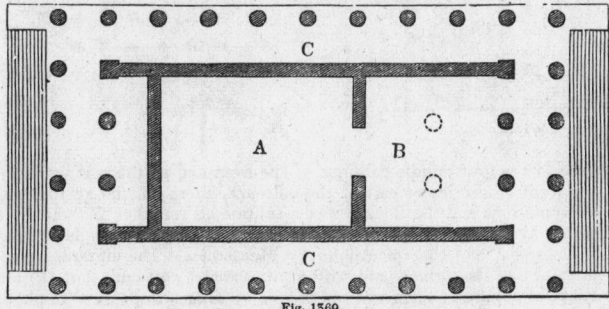

Fig. 1369.

distance from the wall was equal to an intercolumniation or space between the columns all round, and thus it formed a walk around the cell. In *fig*. 1370. is the elevation of

Fig. 1370.

the species, which is hexastyle and eustyle, that is, with six columns in front, whose intercolumniation is *eustyle*, or of two diameters and a quarter. (See COLONNADE.) In this figure, which is to a double scale of the plan, *aaa* are *acroteria*.

The *pseudo-dipteral temple* was constructed with eight columns in front and rear, and with fifteen on the sides, including those at the angles, see *fig.* 1371. The walls of the

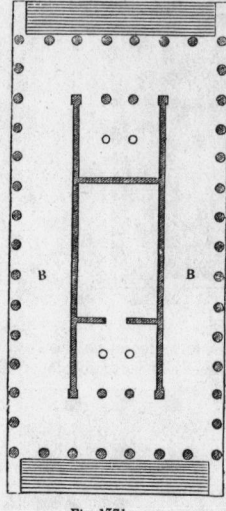

Fig. 1371.

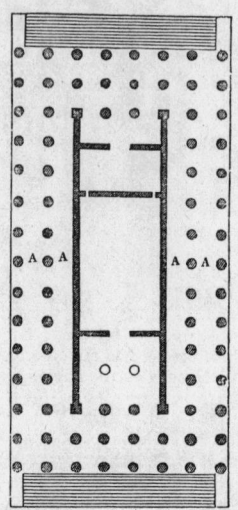

Fig. 1372.

cell are opposite to the four middle columns of the front and of the rear. Hence, from the walls to the front of the lower part of the columns, there will be an interval equal to two intercolumniations and the thickness of a column all round. No example existed of such a temple at Rome; but there was one to Diana, built by Hermogenes of Alabanda, in Magnesia, and that of Apollo by Menesthes. The dipteral temple (*fig.* 1372.) is octastylos like the former, and with a pronaos and posticum, but all round the cell are two ranks of columns: such was the temple of Diana, built by Ctesiphon. The

Fig. 1373.

elevation (*fig.* 1373.) is the same in the dipteral and pseudo-dipteral temple, and in the figure is with the systyle intercolumniation.

The *hypæthral* temple, or that uncovered in the centre, is decastylos in the pronaos and posticum; it is in other respects (see *fig.* 1374.) similar to the dipteral, except that

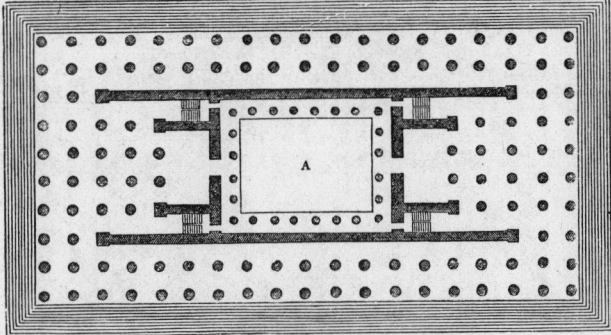

Fig. 1374.

in the inside it has two stories of columns all round, at some distance from the walls, after the manner of the peristylia of porticoes (see *fig.* 1375.), in which one half is the elevation and the other half the section of the temple.

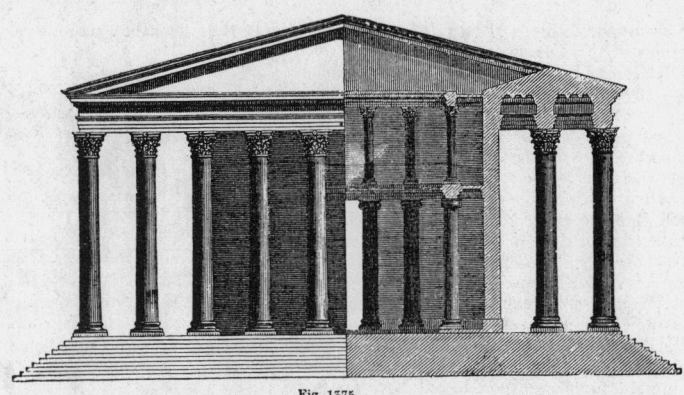

Fig. 1375.

We have described the peripteral temple, but there is still another connected with that species, though distinct, and that is the pseudo-peripteral, or false peripteral, in which there is no passage round the walls of the cell, but an appearance of surrounding columns (see *fig.* 1376.).

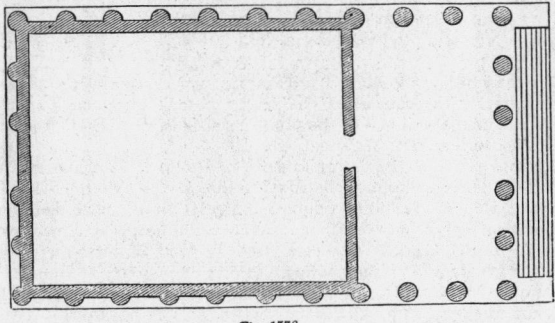

Fig. 1376.

By this arrangement more room was given to the space of the cell.

Fig. 1377.

The elevation of this is given in *fig.* 1377. Vitruvius thus describes, as follows, the proportions of the Tuscan temple :

The length of the site of the temple intended (see *fig.* 1378.) must be divided into six parts, whence, by subtracting one part, the width thereof is obtained. The length is then divided into two parts, of which the furthest is assigned to the cell, that next the front to the reception of the columns.

The above width is to be divided into ten parts, of which three to the right and three to the left are for the smaller cells, or for the alæ, if such are required; the remaining four are to be given to the central part. The space before the cells in the pronaos is to have its columns so arranged that those at the angles are to correspond with the antæ of the external walls: the two central ones opposite the walls between the antæ and the middle of the temple are to be so disposed, that between the antæ and the above columns, and in that direction, others may be placed.

Their thickness below is to be one-seventh of their height, their height one-third of the width of the temple, and their thickness at top is to be one-fourth less than their thickness at bottom. Their bases are to be half a diameter in height. The plinths, which are to be circular, are half the height of the base, with a torus and fillet on them as high as the plinth.

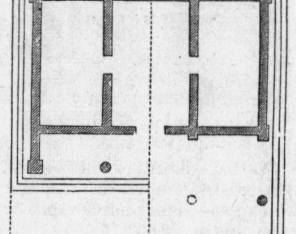

Fig. 1378

The height of the capital is to be half a diameter, and the width of the abacus equal to the lower diameter of the column. The height of the capital must be divided into three parts, whereof one is assigned to the plinth or abacus, another to the echinus, the third to the hypotrachelium, with its apophyge.

Over the columns coupled beams are laid of such height as the magnitude of the work may require. Their width must be equal to that of the hypotrachelium at the top of the column, and they are to be so coupled together with dovetailed dowels as to leave a space of two inches between them. Above the beams and walls the mutuli project one-fourth of the height of the columns. In front of these members are fixed, and over them, the tympanum of the pediment, either of masonry or timber.

Of circular temples there are two species; the monopteral (*fig.* 1379.) having columns without a cell, and the peripteral with a cell as in *fig.* 1380. In this last the clear diameter of the cell within the walls is to be equal to the height of the columns above the pedestal. Of this species was the celebrated temple at Tivoli, in the admiration whereof no dissentient from its allowed beauty has hitherto been recorded. With it situation has doubtless much to do.

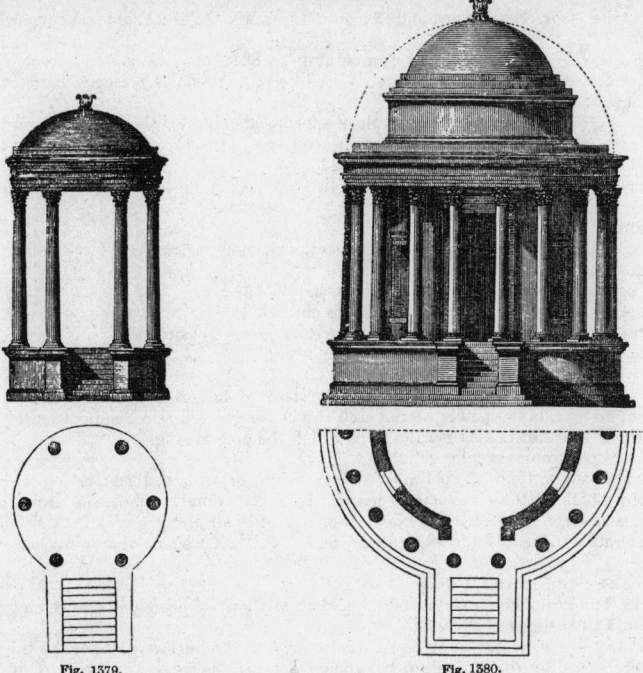

Fig. 1379.   Fig. 1380.

TEMPLET.   A mould used in masonry and brickwork for the purpose of cutting or setting
out the work.   When particular accuracy is required, two templets should be used, one
for moulding the end of the work, and its reverse for trying the face.   When many stones
or bricks are required to be wrought with the same mould, the templets ought to be
made of copper.

The term is also used to denote a short piece of timber sometimes laid under a girder,
particularly in brick buildings.

TENON.   (Fr. Tenir.)   A projecting rectangular prism formed on the end of a piece of
timber to be inserted into a mortise of the same form.

TENON SAW.   One with a brass or steel back for cutting tenons.

TENSION.   The stretching or degree of stretching to which a piece of timber or other
material is strained by drawing it in the direction of its length.

TEOCOPOLI.   See ARCHITECTS, list of, 231.

TEPIDARIUM.   (Lat.)   A name given to one of the apartments of a Roman bath.

TERM or TERMINUS.   A sort of trunk, pillar, or pedestal often in the form of the frustum
of an inverted obelisk with the bust of a man, woman, or satyr on the top.

TERRA COTTA.   (It.)   Baked or burnt earth, frequently used at an early period for the
architectural decoration of a building.   In the time of Pausanias there were in many
temples statues of the deities made of this material.   Bassi rilievi of terra cotta were
frequently employed to ornament the friezes of temples.   In modern times it has also
been much used for architectural decoration, being plastic at first, easily worked, solid,
and not expensive.

TERRACE.   An area raised before a building above the level of the ground to serve as a
walk.   The word is sometimes but improperly used to denote a balcony or gallery.

TESSELATED PAVEMENT.   A rich pavement of Mosaic work made of small square marbles,
bricks, tiles, or pebbles, called *tesselæ* or *tesseræ*.

TESSERA.   (Gr.)   A cube or die.   This name was, for what reason we are at a loss to conceive, applied to a composition used some years ago for covering flat roofs, but now,
from its failure, quite abandoned.

TESTUDO.   (Lat.)   A name given by the ancients to a light surbased vault with which
they ceiled the grand halls in baths and mansions.   Generally, any arched roof.

TETRADORON.   (Gr.)   A species of brick four palms in length.

TETRAGON.   (Gr.)   A figure which has four sides and as many angles.

TETRASPASTOS. (Gr. Τετρα, four, and Σπασσω, to draw). A machine working with four pulleys.

TETRASTYLE. (Gr. Τετρα, and Στυλος, a column.) See COLONNADE.

THATCH. The covering of straw or reeds used on the roofs of cottages, barns, and such buildings·

THEATRE. (Gr. Θεαομαι, to see.) A place appropriated to the representation of dramatic spectacles. In respect of the ancient theatres, see page 71.; and of modern theatres, Book III. Chap. V. Sect. 16.

THEODOLITE. An instrument used in surveying for taking angles in vertical or horizontal planes.

THEODORUS. See ARCHITECTS, list of, 1.

THEOREM. A proposition which is the subject of demonstration.

THERMÆ. See BATH.

THOMAS OF CANTERBURY. See ARCHITECTS, list of, 138.

THOROUGH FRAMING. The framing of doors and windows, a term almost obsolete.

THOROUGH LIGHTED ROOMS. Such as have windows on opposite sides.

THRESHOLD OF A DOOR. The sill of the door frame.

THROAT. See GORGE and CHIMNEY.

THRUST. The force exerted by any body or system of bodies against another. Thus the thrust of an arch is the power of the arch stones considered as a combination of wedges to overturn the abutments or walls from which the arch springs.

THYNNE. See ARCHITECTS, list of, 235.

TIE. (Sax. Tian, to bind.) A timber-string, chain, or iron rod connecting two bodies together, which have a tendency to diverge from each other, such as tie-beams, diagonal ties, truss-posts, &c. Braces may act either as ties or straining pieces. Straining pieces are preferable to ties, for these cannot be so well secured at the joints as straining pieces.

TIE (ANGLE). See ANGLE BRACE.

TIE BEAM. The beam which connects the bottom of a pair of principal rafters, and prevents them from thrusting out the wall.

TIERCE POINT. The vertex of an equilateral triangle. Arches or vaults of the third point, which are called by the Italians *di terzo acuto*, are such as consist of two arcs of a circle intersecting at the top.

TIETLANDUS. See ARCHITECTS, list of, 72.

TIGE. (Fr.) A term used by the French, signifying the shaft of a column.

TILE. (Sax. Tizel.) A thin piece or plate of baked clay or other material used for the external covering of a roof. See Book II. Chap. III. Sect. 10. In ancient buildings two forms of tiles were used.· The imbrex, placed in regular rows to receive the shower, and the tegula, which covered and prevented the rain from penetrating the joints. The latter were fixed at the eaves with upright ornamental pieces called antefixæ, which were also repeated along the ridge at the junction of the tiles. The present common tiles of Italy are on this principle, and are shown by *fig.* 1381.

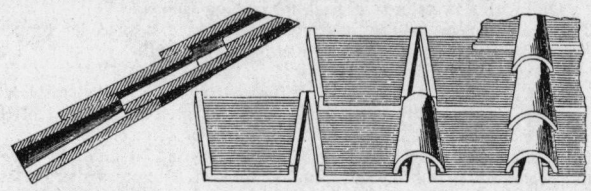

Fig. 1381.

TILE CREASING. See CREASING.

TILING. See Book II. Chap. III. Sect. 2.

TIMBER. (Sax. Timbrian, to build.) Properly denotes all such wood, either growing or cut down, as is suited to the purposes of building. A single piece of wood, similarly employed, is so called as one of the *timbers* of a floor, roof, &c. See Book II. Chap. II. Sect. 4.

TIODAS. See ARCHITECTS, list of, 73.

TOMB. (Gr. Τυμβος.) A grave or place for the interment of a human body, including also any commemorative monument raised over such a place. The word embraces every variety of grave and sepulchral monument, from the meanest grave to the most sumptuous mausoleum.

TONDINO. (It.) Same as TORUS, which see.

TONGUE. See GROOVE.

TOOLS. (Sax.) Instruments used by artificers for the reduction of any material to its

intended form. An account of those used by each set of workmen will be found under each department in Book II. Chap. III.

TOOTH. The iron or steel point in a gage which marks the stuff in its passage, or draws a line parallel to the arris of the piece of wood.

TOOTHING. A projecting piece of material which is to be received into an adjoining piece. A tongue or series of tongues. See STOOTHINGS.

TOP BEAM. The same as COLLAR BEAM, which see.

TOP RAIL. The uppermost rail of a piece of framing or wainscotting, as its name imports.

TORSEL. The same as TASSAL, which see.

TORSION. The twisting strain on any material.

TORUS. (Lat.) A large moulding whose section is semicircular, used in the bases of columns. The only difference between it and the astragal is in the size, the astragal being much smaller.

TOWER. (Sax.) A lofty building of several stories, round or polygonal.

TOWN HALL. A building in which the affairs of a town are transacted. See Book III. Chap. V. Sect. 7.

TRABEATION. Another term for ENTABLATURE.

TRABS. The Latin term for a wall-plate.

TRACERY. In Gothic architecture, the intersection, in various ways, of the mullions in the head of a window, the subdivisions of groined vaults, &c.

TRAMMEL. An instrument for describing an ellipsis by continued motion.

TRANSEPT (quasi, transseptum). The transverse portion of a cruciform church ; that part which is placed between and extends beyond those divisions of the building containing the nave and choir. It is one of the arms projecting each way on the side of the stem of the cross.

TRANSOM. A beam across a window of two lights in height. If a window have no transom it is called a clear story window.

TRANSTRA. (Lat.) The horizontal timbers in the roofs of ancient Roman buildings.

TRANSVERSE. Lying in a cross direction. The *transverse strain* of a piece of timber is that sidewise, by which it is more easily bent or broken than when compressed or drawn as a tie in the direction of its length.

TRAPEZIUM. (Gr.) In geometry, a quadrilateral figure whose opposite sides are not parallel.

TRAVERSE. A gallery or loft of communication in a church or other large building.

TREAD OF THE STEP OF A STAIR. The horizontal part of it.

TREFOIL. In Gothic architecture, an ornament consisting of three cusps in a circle.

TRELLICE. A reticulated framing made of thin bars of wood for screens ; windows where air is required for the apartment, &c.

TRESSEL or TRUSSEL. Props for the support of any thing, the under surface of which is horizontal. Each trussel consists of three or four legs attached to a horizontal part. When the tressels are high the legs are sometimes braced. Tressels are much used in building for the support of scaffolding, and by carpenters and joiners for ripping and cross-cutting timber, and for many other purposes.

TRIANGLE. (Lat.) A plane rectilineal figure of three sides, and consequently of three angles. In measuring, all rectilineal figures must be reduced to triangles, and in constructions for carpentry all frames of more than three sides must be reduced to triangles to prevent a revolution round the angles.

TRIANGULAR COMPASSES. Such as have three legs or feet by which any triangle or any three points may be taken off at once.

TRICLINIUM. (Lat.) The room in the Roman house wherein the company was received, and seats placed for their accommodation. It was raised two steps from the peristyle, and had therein a large window, which looked upon the garden. The aspect of winter triclinia was to the west, and of summer triclinia to the east. See p. 102.

TRIFORIUM. (Lat.) The gallery or open space between the vaulting and the roof of the aisles of a church, generally lighted by windows in the external wall of the building, and opening to the nave, choir, or transept over the main arches. It occurs only in large churches, and is varied in the arrangement and decoration of its openings in each succeeding period of architecture.

TRIGLYPH. (Gr. Τρεις, and Γλυφη, a channel.) The vertical tablets in the Doric frieze chamfered on the two vertical edges, and having two channels in the middle, which are double channels to those at the angles. In the Grecian Doric, the triglyph is placed upon the angle ; but, in the Roman, the triglyph nearest the angle is placed centrally over the column. The space between the channels was called a *femur*. See SHANK.

TRIGONOMETRY. (Gr. Τρεῖς, three, Γωνία, an angle, and Μέτρω, I measure.) The science of determining the unknown parts of a triangle from certain parts that are given. It is either *plane* or *spherical* ; the first relates to triangles composed of three right lines, and the

second to triangles formed upon the surface of a sphere by three circular arcs. This latter is of less importance to the architect than the former, which is, for his purpose, sufficiently explained in Book II. Chap. I. Sect. 4.

TRILATERAL. (Lat.) Having three sides.

TRIM. (Verb.) To fit to any thing; thus, to *trim up*, is to fit up.

TRIMMED. A piece of workmanship fitted between others previously executed, which is then said to be *trimmed in* between them. Thus, a partition wall is said to be trimmed up between the floor and the ceiling; a post between two beams; a trimmer between two joists.

TRIMMED OUT. A term applied to the trimmers of stairs when brought forward to receive the rough strings.

TRIMMER. A small beam, into which are framed the ends of several joists. The two joists, into which each end of the trimmer is framed, are called *trimming joists*. This arrangement takes place where a well-hole is to be left for stairs, or to avoid bringing joists near chimneys, &c.

TRINE DIMENSIONS. Those of a solid, including length, breadth, and thickness; the same as threefold dimensions.

TRIPOD. (Gr. Τρεις, and Πους, a foot.) A table or seat with three legs. In architectural ornament its forms are extremely varied, many of those of the ancients are remarkable for their elegance and beauty of form.

TRISECTION. The division of any thing into three equal parts.

TROCHILUS. (Gr. Τροχιλος, a pulley.) An annular moulding whose section is concave, like the edge of a pulley. It is more commonly called a *scotia*, and its place is between the two tori of the base of a column.

TROCHOID. (Gr. Τροχος a wheel, and Ειδος, shape.) A figure described by rolling a circle upon a straight line, such circle having a pin or fixed point in its circumference upon a fixed plane, in or parallel to the plane of the moving circle. It is also called a cycloid.

TROPHONIUS. See ARCHITECTS, list of, 3.

TROPHY. (Gr. Τροπαιον.) An ornament representing the trunk of a tree charged with various spoils of war.

TROUGH. (Sax. Τροh.) A vessel in the form of a rectangular prism, open on the top for holding water.

TROUGH GUTTER. A gutter in the form of a trough, placed below the dripping eaves of a house, in order to convey the water from the roof to the vertical trunk or pipe by which it is to be discharged. It is only used in common buildings and outhouses.

TRUNCATED. (Lat. Trunco, I cut short.) A term employed to signify that the upper portion of some solid, as a cone, pyramid, sphere, &c. has been cut off. The part which remains is called a *frustum*.

TRUNK. That part of a pilaster which is contained between the base and the capital; also a vessel open at each end for the discharge of water, rain, &c.

TRUSS. (Fr. Trousse.) A combination of timber framing, so arranged, that if suspended at two given points, and charged with one or more weights in certain others, no timber would press transversely upon another except by strains exerting equal and opposite forces. The principle of a truss is explained at p. 605.

TRUSS PARTITION. One containing a truss within it, generally consisting of a quadrangular frame, two braces, and two queen posts, with a straining post between them, opposite to the top of the braces.

TRUSSED BEAM. One in which the combination of a truss is inserted between and let into the two pieces whereof it is composed.

TRUSSING PIECES. Those timbers in a roof that are in a state of compression.

TRY. (Verb.) To plane a piece of stuff by the rule and square only.

TUBE. (Lat.) A substance perforated longitudinally; generally quite through its length.

TUMBLED IN. The same as *trimmed in*. See TRIMMED.

TUNNEL. (Fr.) A subterranean channel for carrying a stream of water under a road, hill, &c.

TURNING PIECE. A board with a circular face for turning a thin brick arch upon.

TURPENTINE. A resinous juice extracted from several trees belonging to the genus *Pinus*. All turpentine is obtained by exudation and hardening of the juice flowing from incisions into the pine trees. To obtain the oil of turpentine, the juice is distilled in an apparatus like the common still, and water is introduced with the turpentine.

TURRET. (Lat. Turris.) A small tower often crowning the angle of a wall, &c.

TUSCAN ORDER. See Book III. Chap. I. Sect. 3.

TUSK. A bevel shoulder made above a tenon, and let into a girder to give strength to the tenon.

TYMPANUM. (Gr.) The naked face of a pediment (see PEDIMENT) included between the

level and raking mouldings.   The word also signifies the die of a pedestal, and the panel of a door.

TYPE. (Gr. Τυπος.)   A word expressing by general acceptation, and consequently applicable to, many of the varieties involved in the terms model, matrix, impression, &c. It is, in architecture, that primitive model, whatever it may have been, that has been the foundation of every style, and which has guided, or is supposed to have guided, the forms and details of each.   What it was in each style is still only conjecture, and forms the ground for the various observations on them in various parts of the body of this work.

TYPE.   The canopy over a pulpit.

U.

UNDERPINNING.   Bringing a wall up to the ground sill.   The term is also used to denote the temporary support of a wall, whose lower part or foundations are defective, and the bringing up new solid work whereon it is in future to rest.

UNGULA.   The portion of a cylinder or cone comprised by part of the curved surface, the segment of a circle, which is part of the base, and another plane.

UNIVERSITY.   An assemblage of colleges under the supervision of a senate, &c.   See Book III. Chap. V. Sect. 8.

UPHERS.   Fir poles, from four to seven inches in diameter, and from twenty to forty feet in length.   They are often hewn on the sides, but not entirely to reduce them square. They are chiefly used for scaffolding and ladders, and are also employed in slight and common roofs, for which they are split.

UPRIGHT.   The elevation of a building ; a term rarely used.

URIA, DE.   See ARCHITECTS, list of, 209.

URILLA.   See HELIX.

URN. (Lat.)   A vase of a circular form, destined among the ancients to receive and preserve the ashes of the dead.

USTAMBER.   See ARCHITECTS, list of, 80.

V.

VAGINA. (Lat.)   The lower part of a terminus in which the statue is apparently inserted.

VALDEVIRA.   See ARCHITECTS, list of, 224.

VALERIUS OF OSTIA.   See ARCHITECTS, list of, 32.

VALLEY. (Lat.)   The internal meeting of the two inclined sides of a roof.   The rafter which supports the valley is called the *valley rafter* or *valley piece*, and the board fixed upon it for the leaden gutter to rest upon is called the *valley board*.   The old writers called the valley rafters *sleepers*.

VALUATIONS OF PROPERTY.   See Book IV.

VALVED.   Any thing which opens on hinges.

VANBRUGH.   See ARCHITECTS, list of, 270.

VANE.   A plate of metal shaped like a banner fixed on the summit of a tower or steeple, to show the direction of the wind.

VANISHING LINE.   In perspective, the intersection of the parallel of any original plane and the picture is called the vanishing line of such plane.   The *vanishing point* is that to which all parallel lines in the same plane tend in the representation.

VANVITELLI.   See ARCHITECTS, list of, 291.

VARIATION OF CURVATURE.   The change in a curve by which it becomes quicker or flatter in its different parts.   Thus, the curvature of the quarter of an ellipsis terminated by the two axes is continually quicker from the extremity of the greater axis to that of the lesser.   There is no variation of curvature in the circle.

VARNISH.   A glossy coat on painting or the surface of any matter.   It consists of different resins in a state of solution, whereof the most common are mastic, sandarac, lac, benzoin, copal, amber, and asphaltum.   The menstrua are either expressed, or essential oils, or alcohol.

VASE. (Lat. Vas.)   A term applied to a vessel of various forms, and chiefly used as an ornament.   It is also used to denote the bell, or naked form, to which the foliage and volutes of the Corinthian and Composite capitals are applied.   The *vases of a theatre* in ancient architecture were bell-shaped vessels placed under the seats to produce reverberation of the sound.   See ECHEA.

VAULT. (It. Volto.)   An arched roof over an apartment, concave towards the void, whose section may be that of any curve in the same direction.   Thus a *cylindric vault* has its surface part of a cylinder.   A *full-centred vault* is formed by a semi-cylinder.   When a vault is greater in height than half its span, it is said to be *surmounted* when less *surbased*. A *rampant vault* springs from planes not parallel to the horizon.   The *double vault* occurs in the case of one being above another.   A *conic vault* is formed of part of the surface

of a cone, as a *spherical vault* consists of part of the surface of a sphere. The plane of an *annular vault* is contained between two concentric circles. A vault is said to be *simple* when formed by the surface of some regular solid round one axis, and *compound* when formed of more than one surface of the same solid or of two different solids. A *cylindro-cylindric vault* is formed of the surfaces of two unequal cylinders: and a *groined vault* is a compound one rising to the same height in its surfaces as that of two equal cylinders, or a cylinder with a cylindroid. The *reins of a vault* are the sides or walls that sustain the arch. See the section on ARCHES, Book II. Chap. I. Sect. 9.

VELARIUM. (Lat.) The great awning which by means of tackle was hoisted over the theatre and amphitheatre to protect the spectators from the rain or the sun's rays.

VELLAR CUPOLA. A term used by Alberti to denote a dome or spherical surface terminated by four or more walls, frequently used over large staircases and salons, and other lofty apartments.

VENEER. A very thin leaf of wood of a superior quality for covering doors or articles of furniture which are made of an inferior wood.

VENETIAN DOOR. A door having side lights on each side for lighting an entrance hall.

VENETIAN WINDOW. One formed with three apertures separated by slender piers from each other, whereof the centre one is much larger than those on the sides.

VENT. The flue or funnel of a chimney; also any conduit for carrying off that which is offensive.

VENTIDUCT. A passage or pipe for the introduction of fresh air to an apartment.

VENTILATION. The continual supply of fresh air to an apartment, a subject which latterly has been considered so necessary, though much neglected as the moderns seem to think by their ancestors, that a volume would not hold the schemes that have been latterly proposed for that purpose. Generally it is enough for the architect to provide means for letting off the hot air of an apartment or building by apertures at the upper part of the rooms, &c. to which the hot air will ascend, without afflicting, with the currents of fresh air that are to be introduced, those that inhabit them. See Book III. Chap. IV. Sect. 26.

VERMICULATED WORK. (Lat.) A term applied to rustic-work which is so wrought as to have the appearance of having been eaten into by worms.

VERTEX. (Lat. the top.) A term generally applied to the termination of any thing finishing in a point, thus we say the vertex of a cone, &c.

VERTICAL ANGLES. The opposite ones made by two straight lines cutting each other.

VERTICAL PLANE. One whose surface is perpendicular to the horizon.

VESTIBULE. (Lat. Vestibulum.) An apartment which serves as the medium of communication to another room or series of rooms. In the Roman houses it appears to have been the place before the entrance where the clients of the master of the house, or those wishing to pay their court to him, waited before introduction. It was not considered as forming a part of the house. The entrance from the vestibulum led immediately into the *atrium*, or into the cavædium.

VESTRY. (Lat. Vestiarium.) An apartment in, or attached to, a church for the preservation of the sacred vestments and utensils. A sacristy; see DIACONICUM.

VICE. A term in old records applied to a spiral or winding staircase. In mechanics, a machine serving to hold fast anything worked upon, whether the purpose be filing, bending, riveting, &c.

VILLA. A country-house for the residence of an opulent person. Among the Romans there were three descriptions of villa, each having its particular destination, namely, the *Villa urbana*, which was the residence of the proprietor, and contained all the conveniences of a mansion in the city. The *Villa rustica*, which contained not only all that was essential to rural economy, such as barns, stables, &c., but comprised lodging apartments for all those who ministered in the operations of the farming establishment. The *Villa fructuaria* was appropriated to the preservation of the different productions of the estate, and contained the granaries, magazines for the oil, cellars for the wine, &c. See Book III. Chap. V. Sect. 22.

VINCI, DA. See ARCHITECTS, list of, 181.

VINERY. A house for the cultivation of vines. See CONSERVATORY.

VISORIUM. (Lat.) See AMPHITHEATRE.

VISUAL POINT. In perspective a point in the horizontal line in which the visual rays unite.

VISUAL RAY. A line of light supposed to come from a point of the object to the eye.

VITONI. See ARCHITECTS, list of, 168.

VITRIFICATION. The hardening of argillaceous stones by heat

VITRUVIUS POLLIO. See ARCHITECTS, list of, 40.

VITRUVIUS CERDO. See ARCHITECTS, list of, 41.

VIVO. (Ital.) The shaft of a column.

VOLUTE. A spiral scroll which forms the principal feature of the Ionic and Composite capitals.

VOMITORIUM. (Lat.) See AMPHITHEATRE.

VOUSSOIR. (Fr.) A wedge-like stone or other matter forming one of the pieces of an arch. See ARCH. The centre voussoir is called a *keystone*.

W.

WAGON-HEADED CEILING. The same as cylindric ceiling. See VAULT.

WAINSCOT. (Dutch, Wayschot.) A term usually applied to the oak or deal lining of walls in panels. The wood originally used for this purpose was a foreign oak (see p. 496); hence the name of the material became attached to the work itself.

WALKELYN. See ARCHITECTS, list of, 84.

WALL. A body of materials for the enclosure of a building and the support of its various parts. See Book II. Chap. I. Sect. 10.

WALLS OF THE ANCIENTS. *Emplecton, Isodomum, Pseudo-isodomum.* See MASONRY.

WALLS, CASED. Those faced up anew round a building, in order to cover an inferior material, or old work gone to decay.

WALNUT. A forest tree now generally used for ornamental purposes.

WALSINGHAM. See ARCHITECTS, list of, 142.

WARE. See ARCHITECTS, list of, 289.

WARREN. See ARCHITECTS, list of, 250.

WATER. See Book II. Chap. II. Sect. 11.

WATER SHOOT. See SQUARE SHOOT.

WATER TABLE. See TABLE, WATER.

WAYNEFLETE. See ARCHITECTS, list of, 165.

WEATHER-BOARDING. See BOARDING FOR OUTSIDE WORK.

WEATHER-TILING. The covering an upright wall with tiles.

WEDGE. (Dan. Wegge.) An instrument used for splitting wood or other substances; it is usually classed among the mechanical powers.

WEIGHT. (Sax. Wiht.) In mechanics, a quantity determined by the balance; a mass by which other bodies are examined. It denotes anything to be raised, sustained, or moved by a machine as distinguished from the power, or that by which the machine is put in motion.

WEIGHT, in commerce, denotes a body of given dimensions, used as a standard of comparison for all others. By an act of parliament passed in June 1824, all weights were to remain as they then were, that act only declaring that the imperial standard pound troy shall be the unit or only standard measure of weight from which all other weights shall be derived and computed; that this troy pound is equal to the weight of 22·815 cubic inches of distilled water weighed in air at the temperature of 62° of Fahrenheit's thermometer, the barometer being at 30 inches, and that there being 5760 grains in a troy pound, there will be 7000 such grains in a pound avoirdupois.

TROY WEIGHT.

24 grains = 1 pennyweight.
480 . . . = 20 . . . . . . = 1 ounce.
5760 . . . = 240 . . . . . . = 12 . . . = 1 pound.

AVOIRDUPOIS WEIGHT.

16 drams = 1 ounce.
256 . . . = 16 . . = 1 pound.
7168 . . . = 448 . . = 28 . . . = 1 quarter.
28672 . . . = 1792 . . = 112 . . . = 4 . . . . = 1 cwt.
573440 . . . = 35840 . . . = 2240 . . . = 80 . . . = 20 . . = 1 ton.

The avoirdupois pound : pound troy :: 175 : 144, or :: 11 : 9 nearly ; and an avoirdupois pound is equal to 1 lb. 2 oz. 11 dwts. 16 grains troy. A troy ounce = 1 oz. 1·55 dr. avoirdupois.

The following is a table of weights according to the new French system.

Names.	French value.		English value.
Millier,	1000 kilogrammes = 1 French ton	- =	19·7 cwts.
Quintal,	100 kilogrammes - - - - =		1·97 cwt.
Kilogramme,	{ Weight of one cubic decimeter of water of the temperature of 39° 12′ Fahrenheit.	} = {	2·6803 lbs. troy. 2·2055 lbs. avoirdupois.
Hectogramme,	$\frac{1}{10}$th of kilogramme - - - - - =	{	3·2 ounces troy. 3·52 ounces avoirdupois.
Decagramme,	$\frac{1}{100}$th of kilogramme - - - - - =		6·43 dwts. troy.
Gramme,	$\frac{1}{1000}$th of kilogramme - - - - =	{	15·438 grains troy. 0·643 pennyweight. 0·032 ounce troy.
Decigramme,	$\frac{1}{10000}$th of kilogramme - - - - =		1·5438 grain troy.

The following table exhibits the proportion of weights in the principal places of Europe to 100 lbs. English avoirdupois.

100 lbs. English	=	91 lbs.	8 oz.	for the pound of	Amsterdam, Paris (old), &c.
—	=	96	8	—	Antwerp or Brabant.
—	=	88	0	—	Rouen (the Viscounty weight).
—	=	106	0	—	Lyons (the city weight).
—	=	90	9	—	Rochelle.
—	=	107	11	—	Toulouse and Upper Languedoc.
—	=	113	0	—	Marseilles or Provence.
—	=	81	7	—	Geneva.
—	=	93	5	—	Hamburgh.
—	=	89	7	—	Frankfort, &c.
—	=	96	1	—	Leipsic, &c.
—	=	137	4	—	Genoa.
—	=	132	1	—	Leghorn.
—	=	153	11	—	Milan.
—	=	152	0	—	Venice.
—	=	154	10	—	Naples.
—	=	97	0	—	Seville, Cadiz, &c.
—	=	104	13	—	Portugal.
—	=	96	5	—	Liege.
—	=	112	$0\frac{2}{3}$	—	Russia.
—	=	107	$0\frac{1}{4}$	—	Sweden.
—	=	89	$0\frac{1}{2}$	—	Denmark.

The Paris pound (poids de marc of Charlemagne) contained 9216 Paris grains; it was divided into 16 ounces, each ounce into 8 gros, and each gros into 72 grains. It is equal to 7561 English troy grains.

The English troy pound of 12 ounces contains 5760 troy grains = 7021 Paris grains. The English avoirdupois pound of 16 ounces contains 7000 English troy grains, and is equal to 8538 Paris grains.

To reduce Paris grains to English troy grains, divide by
Or, to reduce English troy grains to Paris grains, multiply by } 1·2189.
To reduce Paris ounces to English troy, divide by
To reduce English troy ounces to Paris, multiply by } 1·015734.

WEIGHTS OF A SASH are two weights by which the sash is suspended and kept in the situation to which it is raised by means of cords passing over pulleys. The vertical sides of the sash frames are generally made hollow in order to receive the weights, which, by this means are entirely concealed. Thus, to keep the sash in suspension, each weight must be half the weight of the sash. The cords should be of good quality, or they soon fret to pieces.

WELCH GROINS. Groins formed by the intersection of two cylindrical vaults, one whereof is of less height than the other. Also called *underpitch groins.*

WELL. A deep circular pit, or sort of shaft, sunk by digging down through the different strata or beds of earthy or other materials of the soil, so as to form an excavation for the purpose of containing the water of some spring or internal reservoir, by which it may be supplied.

WELL-HOLE. In a flight of stairs, the space left in the middle beyond the ends of the steps.

WESTON. See ARCHITECTS, list of, 137.

WHEEL. (Sax.) In mechanics, an engine consisting of a circular body turning on an axis, for enabling a given power to move or overcome a given weight or resistance. This machine may be referred to the lever.

WHEEL WINDOW. In Gothic architecture, a circular window, with radiating mullions, resembling the disposition of the spokes of a wheel.

WHETSTONE. A stone of fine quality by which tools for cutting wood are brought to a fine edge, after being ground upon a gritstone, or grinding-stone, to a rough edge.

WHITE LEAD. A material forming the basis of most colours in house-painting. The common method of making it is by rolling up thin leaden plates spirally, so as to leave the space of about an inch between each coil. These are placed vertically in earthen pots, at the bottom of which is some good vinegar. The pots are covered, and exposed for a length of time to a gentle heat in a sandbath, or by bedding them in dung. The vapour of the vinegar, assisted by the tendency of lead to combine with the oxygen which is present, corrodes the lead, and converts the external portion into a white substance which comes off in flakes. These are washed and dried in stoves in lumps, and form the white lead of the painters.

WICKET. A small door made in a gate.

WILLIAM OF SENS. See ARCHITECTS, list of, 100.

WILLIAM OF WYKEHAM. See ARCHITECTS, list of, 141.

WIND-BEAM. An obsolete name for a COLLAR-BEAM. The term is now applied to a piece of wood laid diagonally under the rafters of a long roof, from the foot of one truss to the head of another to strut them, so as to prevent the roof racking with the wind.

WINDERS. The steps in a staircase which radiate from a centre, and are therefore narrower at one end than another.

WINDING. The same as *casting* or *warping*.

WINDLASS or WINDLACE. A machine for raising weights, in which a rope or chain is wound about a cylindrical body moved by levers; also a handle by which anything is turned.

WINDOW. An aperture in a wall for the transmission of light to an apartment. See Book III. Chap. I. Sect. 20.

WINE CELLAR. The apartment, generally placed on the basement story, between front and back rooms, or else formed underground, for stowing wine. The most important point in its construction is its being kept at a cool equal temperature at all times of the year. See BINNS.

WINGS OF A BUILDING. The side portions of a façade in which the centre is made prominent. A small building (such as A, B, C, and D, *fig.* 1352), attached to the centre or main portion by an arcade or passage, is also called a *wing*.

WIRE. A small flexible bar of any sort of metal, elongated by means of a machine called a draw-bench.

WITHE. (Sax.) The partition between two chimney flues. See CHIMNEY.

WOOD. (Sax.) A fibrous material much used in building, and formed into shape by edge tools. The different sorts in use form the subject of Book II. Chap. II. Sect. 4.

WOOD BRICKS. Blocks of wood cut to the form and size of bricks, inserted in the interior walls as holds for the joinery.

WORKING DRAWINGS. See Book II. Chap. IV. Sect. 6.

WOTTON, SIR HENRY. See ARCHITECTS, list of, 251.

WREATHED COLUMNS. Those which are twisted in the form of a screw, also very appropriately called *contorted* columns.

WREATHED STRING. The circular portion of a string to a stair where there is a hollow newel.

WREN, SIR CHRISTOPHER. See ARCHITECTS, list of, 264.

X.

XENODOCHIUM. (Gr. Ξένος, a guest, and Δέχομαι, to receive.) A name given by the ancients to a building for the reception of strangers.

XYSTUS. (Gr.) In ancient architecture, a spacious portico, wherein the athletæ exercised themselves during winter. The Romans called, on the contrary, their *hypæthral* walks xysti, which walks were by the Greeks called περιδρόμιδες.

Y.

YARD. A well-known measure of three feet. The term is also applied to a paved area, generally placed at the back of a house. It is also used for the ground belonging to a workshop, as a "builder's yard," &c. A long piece of timber was formerly so called.

YELLOW PINE or DEAL. The produce of the *Pinus sylvestris*, or Scotch fir. This is a better and more lasting wood than white deal, which is the produce of the *Abies excelsa* or *communis*, or Norway spruce.

Z.

ZAX. An instrument used for cutting slates.

ZIGZAG MOULDING. An ornament used in Gothic architecture. It is the same as *chevron* and *dancette*. See p. 174.

ZINC. A metal now much used in building. See Book II. Chap. II. Sect. 8.

ZOCCO, ZOCCOLO, and ZOCLE. (Ital.) The same as SOCLE, which see.

ZOPHORUS. (Gr. ζωοφόρος). The same as FRIEZE, which see.

ZOTHECA. A small room or alcove, which might be added to, or separated from, the room to which it adjoined.

GLOSSARY ADDENDUM.

ABSORPTION. The penetration of a gas or liquid into any substance; or the taking up of moisture by capillary attraction. A principle seriously affecting the durability of all building materials. The rapidity of absorption is not a criterion as to durability, but the comparative durability of stones of the *same kind* may be tested by the smallness of the weight of water which a given weight of stone is capable of absorbing. The actual absorption of water by *bricks* of various qualities has thus been stated:—Malm place brick, 62 ounces of water; white Surrey, 58 oz.; white seconds, 52 oz.; red facings, 51 oz.; pickings, 50 oz.; stocks, 27 oz.; Workman's waterproofed, 2 oz. The following table of the absorbent powers of certain *stones*, when saturated under the exhausted receiver of an air-pump, is given in the *Report* of the Commissioners on Building Stones, 1839 :—

Sandstones.		Oolites.		Magnesian Limestones.		Limestones.	
Craigleith	. 0·143	Ancaster	. 0·180	Bolsover	. 0·182	Barnack	. 0·204
Heddon	. 0·156	Bath Box	. 0·312	Huddlestone	. 0·239	Chilmark	. 0 053
Kenton	. 0·143	Portland	. 0 206	Roach Abbey	. 0·248	Ham-Hill	. 0·147
Mansfield, red	. 0·151	Ketton	. 0·244	Park Nook	. 0·249		

The *granites*, though closely granulated, take up much more than the *grauwacke*, but less than the *sandstones*; while the *grauwacke* resists the water four times that of *granite*, and thirty-six times that of *Yorkshire sandstones*.

ALURE. A gutter, passage, or gallery, as on the top of a wall or building, being one in which a person could walk. Lydgate used the word for covered walks in the streets.

ALMERY or AUMBRYE. A recess or cupboard for holding the sacred vessels, &c. used in the mass. An example, dating circa 1200, is seen in Lincoln Cathedral.

ALTAR TOMB. A tomb of a square box-like form, raised some 3 to 6 feet in height above the ground. On it is usually seen a sculptured recumbent representation of the deceased. These effigies are often placed under an arch, sometimes richly canopied.

ANGLE IRON. A plate of iron rolled into an L shape, and used for the purpose of securing two iron plates together by rivets, as Y Y in the beam of the plate girder, *fig.* 1382, and the box-beam, *fig.* 1383.

ANNULATED COLUMN. Slender shafts, clustered together or joined by bands of stone, sometimes of metal, to a central pier or to a jamb. They were much employed in early English Gothic, and were very often of Purbeck marble.

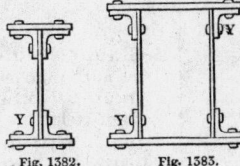

Fig. 1382.　　　Fig. 1383.

ANTEPENDIUM. The frontal hangings of the altar.

ARCADE. In Gothic architecture, an ornamental dressing to a wall, consisting of colonnettes supporting moulded arches. Sometimes they stand sufficiently forward to admit of a passage behind them.

ARCHITECT. A brief Synoptical List of the principal Architects and their chief Works (in continuation of the List given in p. 1121 to p. 1139 of the GLOSSARY).

No. in Gloss.	Name of Architect. 18th and 19th Centuries.	Principal Works.
318	James Essex of England.	The earliest in modern times who practised solely mediæval art; restoration of Ely and other Cathedrals; alterations at various colleges at Cambridge and Oxford.
319	T. Thomond of France.	The great Theatre, and the Exchange, at St. Petersburgh.
320	James Wyatt of England.	The Pantheon Assembly Rooms; Palace at Kew; Fonthill Abbey; Doddington Hall; Ashridge House; and many restorations.
321	Vincenzo Brenna of Russia.	Carried out Bazhenov's design for the Palace of St. Michael, now the School for Engineer Officers; Obelisk of black granite; the Exercising House, 540 ft. by 120 ft., at St. Petersburgh. Designs published.
322	Henry William Inwood of England.	St. Pancras New Church; St. Martin's Chapel; Regent Square Chapel; Somers Town Chapel; at London. Published " The Erechthieon at Athens."
323	Jean Nicolas Louis Durand of France.	Published " Recueil et Parallèle des Édifices," and other works.
324	Augustus Pugin of England.	Published " Specimens of Gothic Architecture," " Examples of Gothic Architecture," " Antiquities of Normandy," and other works.
325	John Nash of England.	Brighton Pavilion; Haymarket Theatre; Buckingham Palace; Regent's Park, and its terraces of dwellings; Regent Street and the Quadrant improvements.
326	Sir Jeffry Wyatville of England.	Extensively rebuilding and altering Windsor Castle.
327	William Wilkins of England.	St. George's Hospital; London University; National Gallery; University Club House; in London. Downing College, Cambridge. Published a translation of part of " Vitruvius."
328	Stefano and Luigi Gasse of Italy.	Observatory; additions to Villa Reale; Reale Edifizio di San Giacomo, or Palazzi de' Ministeri; and the Dogana; all at Naples.
329	Thomas Rickman of England.	New Court of St. John's College, Cambridge; restoration of the Bishop of Carlisle's Palace, Cumberland; upwards of twenty-five churches in the Midland Counties; several private dwellings. Published " Attempt to Discriminate the Styles of Architecture in England."
330	Carl Friedrich Schinkel of Prussia.	Hauptwache, Theatre, and Museum; Werder-Kirche (Gothic); Bauschule, and Observatory, at Berlin; Theatre at Hamburg; Schloss Krzescowice, Charlottenhof, and the Nicolai-Kirche at Potsdam. Published his designs, many of which were not executed.
331	Joseph Michael Gandy of England.	Phœnix and Pelican Assurance Offices; additions to the prisons at Lancaster; buildings at Liverpool. Published " Designs " for rural buildings. Better known for his artistic conceptions of architectural restorations.
332	Friedrich von Gärtner of Bavaria.	Façade of the Porcelain Establishment; Ludwigs-Kirche, Bibliothek, and Record Office; and many other buildings at Munich. The Befreiungshalle at Kehlheim; Pompeian House at Aschaffenburg, &c. Published his designs.
333	Sir Richard Morrison and William Vitruvius Morrison of Ireland.	Alterations of cathedral at Cashel; County Court House, Clonmel; Shelton Abbey; Kilruddery Hall; Ballyfin; Court House, Carlow; Longford Castle; &c.
334	Harvey Lonsdale Elmes of England.	Collegiate Institution; St. George's Hall; at Liverpool.
335	Peter John Gandy-Deering, of England.	Associated with Wilkins in the Club House and University. St. Mark's Church, North Audley Street; Exeter Hall, at London. Published " Pompeiana " with Sir W. Gell, and many antiquities for the Society of Dilletanti.

No. in Gloss.	Name of Architect. 19th Century.	Principal Works.
336	Jacob Gay of Russia.	Extensive fortified warehouse for grain at Novogeorgiersk, near Warsaw.
337	Augustus Welby Northmore Pugin of England.	His residences at Salisbury, and at Ramsgate with a chapel adjoining. No less than thirty-six Roman Catholic churches, including the cathedral of St. George, Southwark, and those of Killarney and Enniscorthy; the church at Cheadle; and extensive alterations at Alton Towers. Published "Contrasts," "True Principles," &c." and Designs for Metal and Timber.
338	John Haviland of United States.	Pittsburgh Penitentiary; Eastern Penitentiary at Cherry Hill; Hall of Justice, New York; Naval Asylum, Norfolk; New Jersey State Penitentiary, and many others, with gaols, asylums, and county halls.
339	Guillaume Abel Blouet of France.	Completed the Arc de l'Étoile; works at the palace at Fontainebleau. Published "Expédition Scientifique de Morée;" supplement to Rondelet's "L'Art de Bâtir;" and revised the tenth edition of that work.
340	James Gillespie-Graham of Scotland.	Culdees Castle, Perthshire; Ross Priory, Dumbartonshire; Dunse Castle, Berwickshire; and many other country residences; Victoria or Assembly Hall, at Edinburgh; chapels there and at Glasgow.
341	William Henry Playfair of Scotland.	St. Stephen's Church; Royal Institution; National Gallery; Donaldson's Hospital; Free Church College; Surgeons' Hall; all at Edinburgh.
342	John Britton of England.	Published the "Cathedral Antiquities," 14 volumes; "Architectural Antiquities," 5 vols.; "Edifices of London," 2 vols., and many others. Began the restoration of Redcliff Church, Bristol.
343	Luigi Canina of Italy.	Published many works on the History and Discoveries connected with Classic Architecture.
344	Thomas Hamilton of Scotland.	The High Schools; College of Physicians; and churches, at Edinburgh. Monument to Burns, at Ayr. Pavilion for the Grey Festival, 1834.
345	Alphonse Ricard de Montferrand of Russia.	Column to the Emperor Alexander, and Church of St. Isaac, at St. Petersburgh. Designs published.
346	Sir Charles Barry of England.	The Travellers' Club House (published); the Reform Club House; Bridgewater House; the Houses of Parliament; Privy Council Office; and Trafalgar Square, in London. The Grammar School at Birmingham. Clifden House, near Reading. Trentham Hall, Derbyshire. Three churches at Ball's Pond, Cloudesley Square, and Holloway; and St. Peter's Church at Brighton. A church, the Athenæum, and the Royal Institution, at Manchester.
347	Ernst Friedrich Zwirner of Prussia.	Restoration of Cologne Cathedral. Church at Remagen.
348	David Hamilton of Scotland.	Hutcheson's Hospital; the Nelson Monument; the Royal Exchange; the Western Club House, and other buildings, at Glasgow. Castle Toward; Dunlop House; Airth or Kier Castle; Hamilton Palace; and Lennox Castle, all in Scotland.
349	Leo von Klenze of Prussia.	The Glyptothek, and other public and private works, at Munich. The Walhalla, near Ratisbon. Buildings at St. Petersburgh. Designs published.
350	James Bunstone Bunning of England.	City of London School. Highgate and Nunhead Cemeteries; Bethnal Green Workhouse; Freemason's Orphan Schools, Brixton; the Coal Exchange; City Prison, Holloway; Billingsgate Market; Metropolitan Cattle Market, Islington; Alterations in Newgate Prison; Pauper Lunatic Asylum at Stone; with many improvements in the City of London.
351	Ludwig Förster of Austria.	Published the "Allgemeine Bauzeitung," 31 volumes (1866). Buildings in Vienna.

No. in Gloss.	Name of Architect. 19th Century.	Principal Works.
352	Charles Robert Cockerell of England.	Philosophic Institution at Bristol. Hanover Chapel, Regent Street. St. David's College, Lampeter. National Monument, Calton Hill, Edinburgh. University Library and Museum, Cambridge. Westminster Life Office, Strand. Dividend Pay Office, and the Private Drawing Office, Bank of England, and Branch Banks at Manchester, Bristol, and Liverpool. Sun Fire Assurance Office. Taylor and Randólph Galleries and Library at Oxford. Liverpool and London Insurance Buildings at Liverpool. Completion of the Fitzwilliam Museum at Cambridge; and of St. George's Hall at Liverpool.
353	Joseph Gwilt of England.	Compiler of the "Encyclopædia of Architecture." Memoir in preface.

ARCHITECTURE, WORKS ON. We here insert (in continuation of the list given in the GLOSSARY) a CATALOGUE of the principal and most useful publications to the Student of Architecture and its kindred branches, following somewhat the arrangement of the several classes previously given in pages 1140–1149.

I. GRECIAN ARCHITECTURE.

Aurès. Théorie du Module déduite du texte de Vitruve. Nismes, 1862.

Beulé, E. L'Acropole d'Athènes. 2 vols. 8vo. Paris, 1853.

Blouet, A. Expédition Scientifique de Morée. 3 vols. folio. Paris, 1826–39.

Cockerell, C. R. The Temples at Ægina and at Bassæ. Folio. London, 1860.

Donaldson, T. L. Architectura Numismatica, or Architectural Medals of Classic Antiquity. Plates, 8vo. London, 1859.

Falkener, E. Dædalus; or the Cause and Principles of the Excellence of Greek Sculpture. 8vo. London, 1860.

—— Museum of Classical Antiquities. New edition, 8vo. London, 1860.

—— Ephesus and the Temple of Diana. 8vo. London, 1862.   [Palermo, 1834–42.

Faso Pietrasanto, D.; Duca di Serradifalco. Le Antichità della Siciiia. 5 vols. folio.

Laborde, le Conte de. Athènes aux XVᵉ, XVIᵉ, XVIIᵉ siècles, d'après des documents inédits. 2 vols. 8vo. Paris, 1854.   [folio. Paris, 1833.

Luynes, le Duc de, and Debacq, F. J. Métaponte, dans la Grande Grèce. 10 plates,

Müller, K. O. Ancient Art and its Remains; or a Manual of the Archæology of Art. 2nd edition, 8vo. London, 1852.

Pennethorne, J. Elements and Mathematical Principles of the Greek Architects and Artists, &c. 8vo. London, 1844.

Penrose, F. C. Principles of Athenian Architecture; with reference to the Optical Refinements of the Ancient Buildings at Athens. 42 plates, folio. London, 1851.

Rich, A. The Illustrated Companion to the Latin Dictionary and Greek Lexicon, &c. 8vo. London, 1849.   [1848.

Smith, W. Dictionary of Greek and Roman Antiquities. 2nd edition, 8vo. London,

Stewart, J. R. Ancient Monuments still existing in Lydia and Phrygia. 26 plates, large folio. London, 1842.

Wilkins, W. Prolusiones Architectonicæ; or Essays on Subjects connected with Grecian and Roman Architecture. 2nd edition, 4to. London, 1837.

II. ROMAN ARCHITECTURE.

Bellori, J. P., and Causseo, M. A. Picturæ Antiquæ Cryptarum Romanarum et Sepulcri Nasonum delineatæ. Folio. Roma, 1750.

Canina, L. Gli Edifizi di Roma Antica cogniti per alcune importanti reliquie. 6 vols. folio. Roma, 1848–56.

—— Ricerche sull' Architettura, più propria dei Tempj Christiani, e applicazione della medesima. 2nd edition, folio. Roma, 1846.   [1827.

Cockburn, Col. J. P., and Donaldson, T. L. Pompeii Illustrated. 2 vols. Folio. London,

Davis, N. Carthage and its Remains. 8vo. London, 1860.

Dennis, J. The Cities and Cemeteries of Etruria. 2 vols. 8vo. London, 1848.

Dodwell, E. Views and Descriptions of Cyclopean or Pelasgic Remains in Greece and Italy. Folio. London, 1833.

Gutensohn, J. G., and Knapp, J. M. Denkmale der christlichen Religion &c. oder Basiliken Roms. Folio, Stuttgart, 1822–27; and folio, Roma, 1823.

Niccolini, F. and F. Le Case ed i Monumenti di Pompei. In progress. Folio. Napoli.
Paoli, P. Rovine della Città di Pesto. Folio. Roma, 1784. [1854–65.
Perret, L. Catacombes de Rome. 6 vols. 327 plates, folio. Paris, 1851.
Pistolesi, E. Antiquities of Herculaneum and Pompeii. English, French, and Italian
text. 2 vols. 4to. Naples, 1842.
Rossini, L. Le Antichità Romane. 100 large plates, atlas folio. Roma, 1820, &c.
———— Scenografia degl' Interni delle più belle Chiese e Basiliche Antiche di Roma. Folio.
Rome, 1843. [Roma, 1818.
———— I Monumenti più interessanti di Roma, dall X. sec. sino al XVIII. Folio.
Rossi, De. La Roma Sotterranea. 40 plates, folio. Roma, 1865.
Smith, R. M., and Porcher, E. A. History of the Recent Discoveries at Cyrene in 1860–
61. 60 plates, folio. London 1864.
Zestermann, A. Die antiken und christlichen Basiliken. 4to. Leipzig, 1847.

III. Miscellaneous.

Berbrugger, L. A., and others. L'Algérie historique, pittoresque et monumentale;
Algiers, Oran, Bona, and Constantine. 3 vols. folio. Paris, 1844.
Blavignac, J. D. Histoire de l'Architecture Sacrée du IVe au Xe siècle dans les anciens
évêches de Genève, Lausanne et Sion. 2 vols. 8vo. Lausanne, 1853–54.
Bonomi, J. Nineveh and its Palaces. 8vo. London, 1852.
Botta, P. E., and Flandin, E. Monuments de Ninive. 5 vols. folio. Paris, 1849–50.
Canina, L. L'Architettura Antica; Egiziana, Greca, Roma. 5 vols. plates folio, and
8vo. text. Roma, 1834–43. [Roma, 1846–49.
———— L'Antica Etruria Marittima compresa nella Dizione Pontificia. 2 vols. folio.
Dartein, F. de. Étude sur l'Architecture Lombarde. 100 plates, folio. Paris, 1866–67.
Fergusson, J. Illustrations of the Rock cut Temples of India. 19 plates, 8vo. and folio.
London, 1845. [London, 1847.
———— Picturesque Illustrations of Ancient Architecture in Hindostan. 17 plates, folio.
———— Essay on the Ancient Topography of Jerusalem. 8vo. London, 1847.
———— The Palaces of Nineveh and Persepolis restored. 8vo. London, 1851.
Flandin, E., and Coste, P. Voyage en Perse. 6 vols. folio. Paris, 1851.
Gailhabaud, J. Ancient and Modern Architecture, consisting of plans, &c. of the most
remarkable edifices in the world (4 series). 4to. Paris, 1842–52. Part translated
into English.
———— L'Art dans ses diverses branches, ou l'Architecture, la Sculpture, &c. chez tous
les peuples et à toutes les époques jusqu'en 1789. 4to. Paris, 1861.
Girault de Prangey. Essai sur l'Architecture des Arabes et des Mores en Espagne, en
Sicile et en Barbarie. 8vo. Paris, 1841. [1846–47.
———— Monuments Arabes d'Égypte, de Syrie et d'Asie Mineure. Folio. Paris,
Isabelle, C. E. Les Édifices Circulaires et les Dômes. 77 plates, folio. Paris, 1843–55.
Layard, A. H. Researches and Discoveries in Nineveh, and an Enquiry into the Arts,
&c. of the Ancient Assyrians. 4th edition, 2 vols. 8vo. London, 1850.
———— Monuments of Nineveh, from drawings made on the spot. Folio. London, 1849.
———— The Palace of Sennacherib. Folio. London, 1853.
Lenoir, A. Architecture Byzantine. 4to. Paris, 1840. [Berlin, 1849–59.
Lepsius, C. R. Denkmäler aus Aegypten und Aethiopien &c. New edition, 6 vols. folio.
———— Letters from Egypt, translated by L. and J. B. Horner. 8vo. London, 1853.
Mariette, A. E. Le Sérapéum de Memphis. Folio. Paris, 1857–63.
———— Choix de Monuments et de dessins découverts, pendant le déblacement du
Sérapéum. 4to. Paris, 1856.
Norman, B. M. Rambles in Yucatan: a Visit to the Ruins of Chi-Chen, Kabah, Zayi,
and Uxmal. 8vo. New York, 1843.
Perring, J. E., Andrews, E. J., and Vyse, Col. The Pyramids of Gizeh, from actual
survey in 1837. Folio. London, 1839–42.
Radel, P. Recherches sur les Monuments Cyclopéens, &c. 8vo. Paris, 1841.
Rossellini, I. I Monumenti dell' Egitto e della Nubia illustrati. New edition, 10 vols.
text, 8vo. 3 vols. folio. Pisa, 1835–47. [4to. Paris, 1837–40.
Roux, H., Bouchet, A., et Barré, M. L. Recueil d'Herculaneum et Pompei. 8 vols.
Salzenberg, W. Altchristliche Baudenkmale Constantinopels vom V. bis XIII. Jahr-
hundert. Folio. Berlin, 1854.
Spanish Government. Monumentos Arquitectonicos de España. French and Spanish
text. 25 parts, folio. Madrid, 1859–65.
Squier, E. G., and Davis, E. H. Ancient Monuments of the Mississippi Valley. 4to.
Washington, 1848. [York, 1853.
Squier, E. Travels in Central America, particularly in Nicaragua. 2 vols. 8vo. New
Stroganov, S., Zagoskin, M. N., Snegirev, J. M., and Veltman, A. T. History of
Architecture in Russia. Russian text. 6 vols. 4to. and folio. Moscow, 1849–53.

Taylor. L'Alhambra. 10 coloured plates by Asselineau. Folio. Paris, 1853.

Tennent, Sir J. E. Ceylon : an Account of the Island. 2 vols. 8vo. London, 1859.

Texier, C. Description de l'Asie Mineure. 3 vols. folio. Paris, 1839.

—— Description de l'Arménie, la Perse et la Mésopotamie. 2 vols. folio. Paris, 1842.

—— and Pullan, R. P. Byzantine Architecture : being a collection of Monuments of the earliest times of Christianity in the East. Folio. London, 1864.

Teynard, F. Égypte et Nubie ; Sites et Monuments. Folio. Paris (1858).

Thrupp, J. F. Antient Jerusalem. A new investigation into the History, Topography, and Plan of the City, Environs, and Temple. 8vo. Cambridge, 1855.

Verneilh, L. de. Architecture Byzantine en France ; St. Front de Périgueux et les Églises à coupoles de l'Aquitaine. Plates, 4to. Paris, 1852.

Vogüé, M. de. Les Églises de la Terre Sainte. 4to. Paris, 1860. [1864.

—— Le Temple de Jerusalem ; Monographie du Haram-ech-Chérif. Folio. Paris,

Wakeman, W. F. Handbook to Irish Antiquities, Pagan and Christian. 12mo. Dublin, 1848.

Waldeck, F. de. Voyage Pittoresque et Archéologique dans la Province d'Yucatan en 1834 et 1836. Folio. Paris, 1838. [5 vols. 8vo. London, 1837–46.

Wilkinson, Sir J. G. Manners and Customs of the Ancient Egyptians. Two series.

Williams, G. The Holy City : notices of Jerusalem ; with Professor Willis's Architectural History of the Holy Sepulchre. 2nd edition, 2 vols. 8vo. Cambridge, 1849.

IV. GOTHIC AND RENAISSANCE ARCHITECTURE.—*A*. GREAT BRITAIN AND IRELAND.

Billings, R. W. Architectural Illustrations of Carlisle Cathedral. 4to. London, 1839.

—— Illustrations of the Architectural Antiquities of the County of Durham. 4to. London, 1846. [4 vols. London, 1848–52.

—— The Baronial and Ecclesiastical Antiquities of Scotland Illustrated. 240 plates,

Blore, E. Monumental Remains of Noble and Eminent Persons. 8vo. London, 1824–26.

Boutell, C. Monumental Brasses of England. 8vo. London, 1849.

Bowman, H., and Crowther, J. S. The Churches of the Middle Ages. 2 vols. folio. London, 1845–53.

Brandon, R. and J. A. Analysis of Gothic Architecture. 2 vols. 4to. London, 1847.

—— Parish Churches ; being Perspective Views of English Ecclesiastical Structures. 8vo. London, 1848–51.

Clayton, J. Ancient Timber Edifices of England. 26 plates, folio. London, 1846.

Collie, J. Plans, &c. of Glasgow Cathedral. 34 plates, folio. London, 1835.

Colling, J. K. Details of Gothic Architecture. 2 vols. 4to. London, 1851–56.

Cottingham, L. N. Plans, &c. and Details of Henry VII.'s Chapel, Westminster. 72 plates, 2 vols. folio. 1822–29.

Dollman, F. T. Examples of Ancient Pulpits in England. 30 plates, 4to. London, 1849.

—— Examples of Ancient Domestic Architecture ; illustrating the Hospitals, Bedehouses, Schools, &c. of the Middle Ages in England. 4to. London, 1856–58.

—— and Jobbins, J. R. An Analysis of Ancient Domestic Architecture. 2 vols. 4to. London, 1861–64. [folio. London, 1848.

Hadfield, J. Ecclesiastical, Castellated, and Domestic Architecture—of Essex. 81 plates,

Ingram, J. Memorials of Oxford. 3 vols. 4to. Oxford, 1837.

Johnson, J. Outline Views of Beverley Minster. 10 plates, folio. London (1845).

—— Reliques of Ancient English Architecture. 4to. London, 1852–53.

Keux, J. Le. Memorials of Cambridge. 2 vols. 4to. Cambridge, 1845.

King, R. J. Handbook to the Cathedrals of England ; Eastern, Western, and Southern Divisions. In progress. 8vo. London (Murray), 1861–64.

Lamb, E. B. Studies of English Domestic Architecture of the times of Henry VIII. Elizabeth, and James I. Folio. London, 1846. [1844.

Mackenzie, F. Collegiate Church of St. Stephen, Westminster. 18 plates, folio. London,

Nash, J. Mansions of England in the Olden Time. 4 series, folio. London, 1839–49.

—— Views of the Interior and Exterior of Windsor Castle. Folio. London, 1848.

Paley, F. A. Illustrations of Baptismal Fonts. 8vo. London, 1844.

Petit, Rev. J. L. Remarks on the Principles of Gothic Architecture as applied to ordinary Parish Churches. 2nd edition, 2 vols. 8vo. Oxford, 1846.

Petrie, G. Ecclesiastical Architecture of Ireland ; Origin and Uses of the Round Towers of Ireland. 2nd edition, 8vo. Dublin, 1845.

Potter, J. Specimens of Ancient English Architecture. 42 plates, 4to. London, 1845–48.

Pugin, A. W. N. Treatise on Chancel Screens and Rood Lofts. 4to. London, 1851.

Richardson, C. J. Studies from Old English Mansions : their Furniture, Plate, &c. 4 series, folio. London, 1841–48. [London, 1838–40.

—— Architectural Remains of the Reigns of Elizabeth and James I. 2 parts, folio.

Scott, G. G. Gleanings from Westminster Abbey ; with appendices. 2nd edition, 8vo. London, 1863.

Sharpe, E. Architectural Parallels; or the Progress of Ecclesiastical Architecture through the 12th and 13th centuries. 121 plates, folio. London, 1845–48.

—— Supplement to ditto. 60 plates of full-sized details, folio. London, 1848.

Shaw, H. Specimens of the Details of Elizabethan Architecture. 4to. London, 1839.

Simpson, F. Series of Ancient Baptismal Fonts. 8vo. London, 1828.

Stothard, C. A., and Kempe, J. A. Monumental Effigies of Great Britain. Folio. London, 1817.

Turner, T. H., and Parker, J. H. Some Account of Domestic Architecture of England. 12th to 15th centuries. 4 vols. 8vo. Oxford, 1851–53–59.

Waller, J. G. and L. Monumental Brasses from Edward I. to Elizabeth. Folio. London.

Wickes, C. Illustrations of the Spires and Towers of the Mediæval Churches of England. 3 vols. 72 plates, folio. London, 1853–59.

Wilkinson, G. Practical Geology and Ancient Architecture of Ireland. 8vo. London, 1845.

IV. Gothic and Renaissance Architecture.—B. Other Countries.

Adler, F. Mittelalterliche Backstein-Bauwerke des Preussischen Staates. 150 plates, folio. Berlin, 1860–66. [1836–42.

Bötticher, C. G. W. Die Holz-Architectur des Mittelalters. 26 plates, folio. Berlin,

Boisserée, S. Denkmale der Baukunst vom VIIten bis zum XIIIten Jahrhundert am Nieder-Rhein. 72 plates, folio. Munich, 1833.

Bourassé, J. J. Les Cathédrales de France. 4to. Tours, 1843.

Cahier, C., and Martin, A. Mélanges d'Archéologie, &c. 4 vols. 4to. Paris, 1847–56.

Cappelletti. Le Chiese d' Italia della loro origine sino di giorni nostri. 8vo. Venezia, 1847.

—— and Ramée, D. Le Moyen Age Monumental et Archéologique. 2 vols. folio. Paris, 1840–44.

Clutton, H. Illustrations of the Domestic Architecture of France. 10 plates, folio. London, 1853–56. [Paris, 1857.

Decloux et Doury. Histoire Archéologique, etc. de la Sainte Chapelle du Palais. Folio.

Delaquérière, E. Description Historique des Maisons de Rouen. 2 vols. 8vo. Rouen, 1841.

Didron, A. N. Annales Archéologiques. 16 vols. 4to. Paris, 1844–60.

—— Lassus, J. B. A., and Duval, A. Monographie de la Cathédrale de Chartres. Text 4to. 1835. Plates folio. Paris, 1842.

Drouyn, L. La Guienne Militaire. 4to. Paris, 1863.

Essenwein, A. Norddeutschlands Backsteinbau im Mittelalter. Folio. Carlsruhe, 1863.

Escosura, P. de la, and Villa-Amil. L'Espagne Artistique et Monumentale. French and Spanish text. 3 vols. folio. Paris, 1842–59.

Förster, E. Monuments d'Architecture, de Sculpture et de Peinture, de l'Allemagne, depuis l'établissement du Christianisme jusqu'aux temps modernes. 4 vols. folio. Paris, 1859–60. [progress. Plates, folio. Paris, 1856–66.

French Government. Archives de la Commission des Monuments Historiques. In

Gailhabaud, J. L'Architecture du Moyen Age et de la Renaissance du Vᵉ au XVIIᵉ Siècle, et les Arts qui en dépendent. 400 plates, 4 vols. 4to. 1 vol. folio. 1850–59.

Gladbach, E. Der Schweizer Holzstyl in seinen cantonalen und constructiven Verschiedenheiten vergleichend dargestellt mit Holzbauten Deutschlands. Folio. Darmstadt,

Guhl, E. Der Dom zu Köln. 4to. Stuttgart, 1851. [1863.

Guilhermy, F. de, and Lassus, J. B. A. La Sainte Chapelle de Paris, après les restaurations. Folio. Paris, 1857.

Hay, R. Illustrations of Cairo and Egypt. 30 plates, folio. London, 1840.

Heideloff, C. A. von. Nürnberg Middle Age Buildings. Folio. 1843.

—— Die Kunst des Mittelalters in Schwaben. Text by F. Müller. 8 parts, 30 plates, folio and 4to. Stuttgart, 1855–64.

Hefner-Alteneck and Becker, C. Kunstwerke und Geräthschaften des Mittelalters und der Renaissance. 3 vols. 4to. Frankfurt, 1852–63.

Johnson, R. J. Specimens of Early French Architecture; selected chiefly from the Churches of the Isle de France. Folio. Newcastle-upon-Tyne, 1861–64.

Joliment, F. J. de, and Chapuy, N. M. J. Les Cathédrales de France. 115 plates, folio. Paris, 1826–31.

Jong, S. de. Contributions to the Knowledge of the Gothic or Pointed Style in the Netherlands. Folio. Amsterdam, 1847.

Jourdain, L., et Duval. Les Stalles de la Cathédrale d'Amiens. 8vo. Amiens, 1843.

Kallenbach, G. F. Geschichtsabriss der Deutschen mittelalterlichen Baukunst. 86 plates, 8vo. Berlin, 1844.

Kallenbach, G. G. Geschichtsabriss der Deutsch mittelalterlichen Baukunst. 8vo. Atlas of 86 plates entitled "Chronologie," folio. Munich, 1846.

—— and Schmitt, J. Die christliche Kirchenbaukunst des Abendlandes. 48 plates,

Kanitz. The Byzantine Monuments of Serbia. Vienna, 1862. [4to. Halle, 1850, etc.

King, T. H.   Study Book of Mediæval Architecture and Art : the Principal Monuments to uniform scales.   200 plates, 2 vols. 4to.   London, 1859.

Knight, H. G.   Saracenic and Norman Remains, to illustrate *The Normans in Sicily.*   New edition, folio.   London, 1846.

———— Ecclesiastical Architecture of Italy, from the time of Constantine to the 15th century.   Plates.   2 vols. folio.   London, 1842–44.

Kreutz, G. L.   La Basilica di S. Marco in Venezia.   57 plates, folio.   Venice, 1843–53.

Lassus, J. B. A., and Quicherat, J. E. J.   Album de Villard de Honnecourt, Architecte du XIIIᵉ Siècle : Considérations sur la Renaissance de l'Art Français au XIXᵉ Siècle.   72 plates, 4to.   Paris, 1858.   Translated with notes, by Prof. R. Willis. 4to. London, [1859.

Lenoir, A.   Architecture Monastique.   4to.   Paris, 1852–56.

Lübke, W.   Die mittelalterliche Kunst in Westfalen.   8vo. plates folio.   Leipzig, 1853.

Luynes, Le Duc de.   Recherches sur les Monumens, &c. des Normands, &c. dans l'Italie Méridionale.   Folio.   Paris, 1844.

Mallay, M.   Essai sur les Églises Romanes et Romano-Byzantines du Puy de Dôme.   Folio.   Moulins, 1838–40.   [Bruxelles, 1854.

Maquardt, C.   Monumens d'Architecture et de Sculpture en Belgique.   2 vols. folio.

Martin, P.   Recherches sur l'Architecture du Moyen Age et de la Renaissance à Lyon, &c.   Folio.   Lyon, 1863.

Mithoff, H. W. H.   Archiv für Niedersachsens Kunstgeschichte.   Folio.   Hannover, 1863.

Moller, G.   Denkmäler der Deutschen Baukunst, herausgegeben von Hessemer.   190 plates, 2 vols.   Vol. iii. edited by E. Gladbach.   New edition, folio.   Frankfurt, 1852.

Moret, S., et Chapuy, N. M. J.   Moyen Age Pittoresque.   Folio.   Paris, 1837, etc.

Nesfield, W. E.   Specimens of Mediæval Architecture in France and Italy.   100 plates, folio.   London, 1862.

Nodier, C., and Taylor, J.   Voyages Pittoresques de l'Ancienne France : Haute-Normandie ; Dauphiné ; Franche-Comté ; Auvergne ; Languedoc ; Champagne ; Picardie ; Bretagne.   14 vols. folio.   Paris, 1820-46.

Norwegian Government.   The Cathedral at Throndheim, by P. A. Munch and H. E. Schirmer.   Folio.   Christiania, 1860.

Osten, F.   Bauwerke in der Lombardei vom VIIten bis zum XVIten Jahrhundert.   French and German text.   Folio.   Darmstadt, 1846–48.

Perelle, A.   Œuvres Diverses : Recueil des plus belles Vues, &c.   2 vols. 428 engravings of castles, &c.   Folio.   Langlois, 1680, çir.

Petit, Rev. J. L.   Architectural Studies in France.   8vo.   London, 1854.

Petit, V.   L'Architecture Pittoresque ; ou Recueil des Vieux Châteaux de France des XVᵉ et XVIᵉ Siècles.   Folio.   Paris, 1854.   [folio.   Paris, 1857–60.

———— Châteaux de la Vallée de la Loire, des XVᵉ, XVIᵉ et XVIIᵉ Siècles.   2 vols.

Pollet et Roux, H.   Monumens d'Architecture Grecque, Romane, Gothique, de la Renaissance, recueillis en France ; Décorations Sculpturales, &c.   Folio.   Faris, 1840–41.

Popp, J., and Bülau, T.   Les Trois Ages de l'Architecture Gothique, à Ratisbonne.   Folio.   Paris, 1840.   [folio.   Leipzig, 1835–52.

Puttrich, L.   Denkmäler der Baukunst des Mittelalters in Sachsen.   5 vols. 387 plates,

Quaglio, A. F. von.   Denkmäler der Baukunst in Bayern.

Quast, A. F. von.   Die altchristlichen Bauwerke von Ravenna vom Vten bis zum IXten Jahrhundert.   Folio.   Berlin, 1842.

———— Denkmäler der Baukunst in Preussen.   Folio.   Berlin, 1852, etc.

Ramée, D., and Pfnor, R.   Monographie du Château de Heidelberg.   Folio.   Paris, 1859.

Revoil, H.   Architecture Romane du Midi de la France.   4to.   Paris, 1859–66.

Robb, L.   Chiese Principali d' Europa.   110 plates of eleven buildings.   Large folio.   Milan, 1824.

Runge, L.   Der Glockenthurm des Dom zu Florenz.   Folio.   Berlin, 1853.

Ruskin, J.   Stones of Venice.   3 vols. 8vo. and 1 vol. folio, plates.   London, 1851–53.

Schayes, A. G. R.   Essai sur l'Architecture Ogivale en Belgique ; Mémoire Couronne.   4to.   Bruxelles, 1840.   Translated by H. Austin in Weale's *Quarterly Papers on Architecture.*   4to.   London, 1845.

———— Histoire de l'Architecture en Belgique.   2nd edition, 4 vols. 12mo.   Bruxelles, 1853.

Schulz, H. W. von.   Denkmäler der Kunst des Mittelalters in Unter-Italien, herausgegeben von A. F. von Quast.   4 vols. 4to. 1 vol. folio.   Dresden, 1860.

Selvatico, P.   Sulla Architettura e sulla Scultura in Venezia dal medio evo sino di nostri giorni.   8vo.   Venezia, 1847.   [Folio.   London, 1858.

Shaw, R. N.   Architectural Sketches from the Continent (France, Italy, and Germany).

Simonau, C. et Fils.   Principaux Églises Gothiques de l'Europe,   Texte historique par A. Voisin.   Folio.   Bruxelles, 1843.

Stappaerts, F., and Stroobant, F.   Monuments d'Architecture et de Sculpture en Belgique.   2 vols. 63 plates, folio.   Bruxelles, 1854–55.

Statz, V., Ungewitter, G., and Reichensperger, A.   The Gothic Model-Book : a collection of Gothic Types from existing Monuments in Germany.   Folio.   London, 1859.

Stieglitz, C. L.   Altdeutschen Baukunst.   34 plates, 4to. and folio.   Leipzig, 1820.

Street, G. E.   Brick and Marble in the Middle Ages in the North of Italy.   8vo. London, 1855.

—— Some Account of Gothic Architecture in Spain.   8vo.   London, 1865.

Truefitt, G.   Architectural Sketches on the Continent.   4to.   London, 1847.

Tschischka, F.   Der St. Stephens-Dom in Wien.   New edition, folio.   Wien, 1844.

Ungewitter, G. G.   Vorlegeblätter für Ziegel- und Stein-Arbeiten.   2nd edition, folio. Leipzig, 1850.   [Renaissance. 4to. Paris, 1852–57.

Verdier, A., et Cattois, F.   Architecture Civile et Domestique au Moyen Age et à la

Viollet-le-Duc, E.   Military Architecture of the Middle Ages.   Translated from the French by M. Macdermott, with notes on English Castles, by C. A. Hartshorne.   8vo. Oxford and London, 1860.

—— et Lassus, J. B. A.   Monographie de Notre Dame de Paris et de la Nouvelle Sacristie.   63 plates, etc. folio.   Paris, 1858.   [London, 1852.

Waring, J. B.   Architectural Studies in Burgos and its Neighbourhood.   Folio.

—— Illustrations of Architecture and Ornament.   Folio.   London, 1865.

—— and Macquoid, T. R.   Examples of Architectural Art in Italy and Spain, chiefly in the XIIIth and XVIth centuries.   Folio.   London, 1850.

Whewell, W.   Architectural Notes on German Churches ; with Notes on a Tour in Picardy and Normandy.   3rd edition, with Notes on the Churches of the Rhine, by M. F. de Lassaulx.   8vo.   London, 1852.

Wiebeking, C. F. von.   Analyse Historique et Raisonnée des Monumens de l'Antiquité des Édifices les plus remarquables du Moyen Age, etc.   Text, 4 vols. 4to.   Plates folio. Munich, 1821–26 ; and 1838–40.

Wild, C.   Examples of Architectural Grandeur in Belgium, Germany, and France.   Two series, new edition.   Folio.   London, 1846.

Woillez, E.   Archéologie des Monuments Religieux de l'Ancien Beauvoisis, depuis le Vᵉ jusque vers la fin du XIIᵉ Siècle.   Folio.   Paris, 1842.

Zanotto, F.   Il Palazzo Ducale di Venezia.   New edition, 4to.   Venezia, 1846–58.

V. MODERN ARCHITECTURE.—*A.* FRANCE AND BELGIUM.

Alhoy, M., et Lurine, L.   Les Prisons de Paris.   8vo.   Paris, 1846.   [1864.

Baltard, V., et Callet, F.   Monographie des Halles Centrales de Paris.   Folio.   Paris,

Barqui, F.   L'Architecture moderne en France.   In progress.   Folio.   Paris, 1865–66.

Berty, A.   La Renaissance Monumentale en France.   Spécimens de Composition et d'Ornementation Architectoniques ;   Charles VIII à Louis XIV.   4to.   Paris, 1858–62.

Blondel, et Ser, L.   Rapport sur les Hôpitaux Civils de la ville de Londres.   Plates, 4to. Paris, 1862.

Calliat, V.   Parallèle des Maisons de Paris, de 1850 à 1860.   Folio.   Paris, 1851–64.

—— et Leroux de Lincy.   Hôtel de Ville de Paris.   44 plates, folio.   Paris, 1844. Décorations Intérieures.   New edition.   2 vols. folio.   Paris, 1860.

—— et Lance, A.   Encyclopédie d'Architecture.   12 vols. 4to.   Paris, 1851–62.

Castermans, A.   Parallèle des Maisons de Bruxelles, etc. construites depuis 1830.   Folio. Bruxelles, 1850–54.

Courlier, C.   Des Voies Publiques et des Habitations Particulières à Paris.   8vo.

Daly, C.   L'Architecture Privée au XIXᵉ Siècle ;   Maisons de Paris.   3 vols. folio. Paris, 1863–65.

—— Revue Générale de l'Architecture et des Travaux Publics.   4to.   Paris, 1839, &c.

Dédaux.   Chambre de Marie de Médicis au Palais de Luxembourg.   Folio.   Paris, 1838.

Desjardins, J.   Monographie de l'Hôtel de Ville de Lyon.   In progress.   Folio.

Goetghebuer, J. P.   Choix des Monuments, Édifices et Maisons les plus remarquables des Pays-Bas.   150 plates, folio.   Ghent, 1827.

Grantham, R. B. G.   Description of the Abattoirs of Paris.   8vo.   London, 1850.

Grim, A.   Recueil de Maisons de Ville et de la Campagne.   4to.   Paris, 1847–53.

Heré, E.   Plans, etc. de la Place Royale de Nancy.   14 plates, folio.   Paris, 1753.

—— Recueil des Plans, etc. des Châteaux, Jardins, etc. que le Roi de Pologne occupe en Lorraine.   2 vols. 64 plates, folio.   Paris, n. d.   [4to.   Paris, 1862.

Husson, A.   Étude sur les Hôpitaux, considérés sous le rapport de leur construction, etc.

Isabey, L., et Leblanc, M.   Villas, Maisons de Ville et de Campagne, composées sur les motifs des Habitations de Paris Moderne, des XVIᵉ-XIXᵉ Siècles.   Folio.   Paris, 1864.   [1821–23.

Jolimont, F. G. T. de.   Les Mausolées Français dans Père-la-Chaise.   4to.   Paris,

Normand, L., et La Croix.   Paris Moderne ; ou Choix de Maisons.   3 vols. 480 plates, 4to.   Paris, 1837–38–45.

Normand, L. M.   Monumens Funéraires choisis dans les Cimetières de Paris et des Principales Villes de France.   3 parts, folio.   Paris, 1832–36 (1847) and 1850.

Paris. Les Églises de Paris. 8vo. Paris, 1843.

Pfnor, R. Monographie du Palais de Fontainebleau. Folio. Paris, 1861.

—— Architecture, Décoration et Ameublement de l'époque de Louis XVI. Folio. Paris, 1864.

Ramée, D., et Roguet, F. Palais de Fontainebleau depuis le XVI° et XVII° Siècle. Folio. Paris, 1859–61. [Folio. Paris, 1858.

Roguet, F. Choix de Châteaux, Palais et Maisons de France du XV° au XVIII° Siècle.

Rudd, J. B. Collection de Plans, etc. des Principaux Monuments de la Ville de Bruges depuis le XIV° jusqu'au XVII° Siècle. 28 plates, folio. Bruges (1824).

Sauvageot, C. Palais, Châteaux, Hôtels et Maisons de France, du XV° au XVIII° Siècle. 2 vols. 75 plates, folio. Paris, 1866.

V. MODERN ARCHITECTURE.—B. GERMANY, ETC.

Chateauneuf, A. de. Architectura Publica. 14 plates, folio. Berlin, 1860.

Gärtner, F. von. Sammlung der Entwürfe ausgeführter Gebäude. 2 vols. folio. Munich, 1844–47.

Heideloff, C. A. von. Architectonische Entwürfe und ausgeführte Bauten im Byzantinischen und Altdeutschen Styl. 2 vols. plates, folio. Nürnberg, 1851.

Hochstetter, J. Architectonische Ausführungen. 5 parts, folio. [München, 1837.

Klenze, L. von. Anweisung zur Architectur des christlichen Cultus. 36 plates, folio.

Metzger, E. Formenlehre zur Rundbogen-Architectur. Folio. München, 1851.

Prussian Government. Vorlegeblätter für Baumeister. 4to. and folio. Berlin, 1844.

Raczynski, A. Histoire de l'Art Moderne en Allemagne. 3 vols. folio. Paris, 1836–41.

Stieglitz, C. Plans et Dessins tirés de la Belle Architecture (England and France). 113 plates, folio. Leipzig and Moscow, 1801.

Stüler, A. Das neue Museum in Berlin. Folio. Potsdam, 1850. [1847.

Titz, E. Architectonische Mittheilungen aus der Neuzeit Berlins. 2 parts, folio. Berlin,

Unger, J., and Voigt. Collection of Sketches of Private Houses and Municipal Buildings principally executed at Munich. Folio. Munich, 1850.

V. MODERN ARCHITECTURE.—C. SPAIN, ITALY, RUSSIA, ETC.

Raczynski, A. Les Arts en Portugal. 8vo. Paris, 1846.

—— Dictionnaire Historico-Artistique de Portugal, pour faire suite à l'ouvrage ayant pour titre *Les Arts en Portugal*. 8vo. Paris, 1842.

Vivian, G. Scenery of Portugal and Spain. 31 plates, folio. London, 1839.

Calderari, O. Disegni e Scritti d' Opere di Architettura. 90 plates, 2 vols. folio. Vicenza,

Cassina, F. Le Fabbriche più cospicue di Milano. Folio. Milan, 1840–44. [1808–15.

Guarino, C. G. Disegni d' Architettura. Folio. Turin, 1686.

Isabelle, C. E. Parallèle des Salles Rondes de l'Italie. 2nd edition, folio. Paris, 1863.

Parker, C. Villa Rustica ; selected from Buildings in the Vicinity of Rome and Florence, and arranged for Lodges, Dwellings, and Schools. 3 vols. 4to. London, 1849.

Price, L. Interiors and Exteriors in Venice. Folio. London, 1843.

Robb, L. Chiese Principali d' Europa. 110 plates of 11 buildings. Large folio. Milan, 1824.

Ronzani, F., e Luciolli, G. San Michele ; Fabbriche Civile, Ecclesiastiche e Militari. 147 plates, folio. Venezia, 1832.

Tosi, F. M., and Becchio, A. Altars, Tabernacles, and Sepulchral Monuments of the XIVth and XVth Centuries existing at Rome. Italian, French, and English text by Mrs. S. Bartlet. Folio. Lagny, 1843.

Valentini, A. Le Quattro principali Basiliche di Roma. 2 vols. folio. Rome, 1836–46.

Demidoff, A. de. Excursion Pittoresque et Archéologique en Russie, etc. en 1839. Folio. Paris. [1864.

Kiprianoff, V. Histoire Pittoresque de l'Architecture en Russie, etc. 8vo. Petersburg,

Ricard de Montferrand, A. Cathédrale de St.-Isaac à St.-Pétersbourg. Folio. Paris, 1846–48.

Rusca, L. Recueil des Dessins de différens Bâtimens construits à St.-Pétersbourg, etc. 180 plates, large folio. St. Petersburg, 1804–10.

Denmark. Danmark Fremstillet i Billeder. 74 plates, folio. Kjobedhaven, 1860.

Strickland, W. Public Works in the United States of America. 8vo. London, 1841.

Graffenried und Stürler, M. von. Schweizerische Architektur. French and German text. 2nd edition, folio. Berne, 1847. [Carlsruhe, 1863.

Hochstetter, J. Schweizerische Architectur in perspectivischen Ansichten, etc. Folio.

Varin, A. et E. L'Architecture Pittoresque en Suisse, ou Choix de Constructions Rustiques prises dans toutes les parties de la Suisse. 4to. 1860.

VI. Modern Architecture.—Great Britain and Ireland.

Ashpitel, A., and Whichcord, J. Erection of Fire-Proof Houses in Flats; a modification of the Scottish and Continental Systems. 8vo. London, 1855.
———————— Baths and Washhouses. 3rd edition, 8vo. London, 1852.
Baly, P. P. Baths and Washhouses. 4to. London, 1852. Appendix, 4to. London, 1853.
Barnard, H. School Architecture; with Illustrations of most approved Plans. 5th edition, 8vo. Hartford, U.S. 1854.
Brooks, S. H. Select Designs for Churches, Chapels, Schools, &c. 4to. London, 1842.
Burn, R. S. Architecture and Building; a series of Working Drawings and Designs, with Essays by eminent Architects. 55 plates, folio. Edinburgh, 1863–65.
Cape, G. A. Baths and Washhouses. 4to. London, 1854.
Clarke, J. Schools and Schoolhouses. 27 plates, folio. London, 1852.
Clayton, J. Parochial Churches of Sir C. Wren. 60 plates, folio. London, 1849–52.
Downes, C., and Cowper, C. The whole Construction of the Building for the Great Exhibition of 1851. 4to. London, 1852.   [8vo. London, 1850.
Dwellings of the Labouring Classes; their arrangement and construction; by the Society.
Foulston, J. Public Buildings erected in the West of England. 4to. London, 1839.
Fox, W. Baths and Washhouses. Folio. Liverpool, 1849.
Hakewill, A. W., Thorpe Hall. 12 plates, folio. London, 1852.
Hartshorne, C. H. System of Building Labourers' Cottages pursued on the Estates of the Duke of Bedford. 8vo. Northampton, 1849.
Hole, J. Homes of the Working Classes. 20 plates of the Model Villages of Akroydon, Copley, West Hill Park, Halifax, &c. 8vo. London, 1866,
House Planning, Grammar of; Hints on arranging and modifying Plans, &c. 12mo. London, 1864.   [Society. 1857.
Isaac, T. W. P. Essay on Labourers' Cottages, premiated by the Royal Agricultural
Jebb, R. Report on the Construction and Ventilation of Pentonville Prison. 8vo.
Jessop. Baths and Washhouses. 8vo. 1853.   [London, 1844.
Kerr, R. An English Gentleman's House; being Practical Hints for its Plan and Arrangement—containing descriptions of Houses adapted to various ranks and fortunes, from the Villa to the Palace, &c. 2nd edition, with supplement. 8vo. London, 1865.
Laing, D. Plans of Buildings executed in various parts of England, including the Custom-House. Folio. London, 1818.
Leeds, W. H. The Travellers' Club-House, by C. Barry; with Essay on Italian Architecture. Folio. London, 1839.
Lassaulx, V. de, and Elliott, J. Street Architecture; a series of Shop Fronts. London, 1855.
Morris, F. O. The Country Seats of the Noblemen and Gentlemen of Great Britain and Ireland. In progress. 4to. London, 1866.   [1818–29.
Neale, J. P. Views of the Seats of England, &c. Two series, 11 vols. 4to. London,
Papworth, J. W. and W. Museums, Libraries, and Picture Galleries; to which is appended the Public Libraries Act, 1850, &c. 8vo. London, 1853.
Prisons. Report on Construction, &c., of Convict Prisons. 8vo. London, 1851.
Pyne, W. Royal Residences. 3 vols. 100 coloured plates, 4to. London, 1819.
Radclyffe, C. W. Blenheim Palace. Folio. 1842.
Roberts, H. Dwellings for the Labouring Classes. 3rd edition, 8vo. London, 1850.
—————— Description of H. R. H. Prince Albert's Model Houses for Families. 8vo. 1851.
Starforth, J. Designs for Villa Residences. 40 plates, 4to. Edinburgh, 1866.
—————— Designs for Villa Residences and Farm Architecture. 102 plates, 4to. Edinburgh, 1866.
Thomson, J. Retreats; a series of Designs. 41 plates, 4to. London, 1833.
Truefitt, G. Designs for Country Churches. 4to. London, 1850.
Watts, W. Views of the Seats of the Nobility, &c. in England. 4to. London, 1779–90.
Whittock, N. Shop Fronts of London; their construction, decoration, &c. 4to. 1840.
(See The Civil Engineer; The Builder; The Building News; and other Illustrated Journals in Class XI.)

VII. Rural Architecture.

Andrews, G. H. Construction of Agricultural Buildings of every Description. 3 vols. 8vo. London, 1852.   [gress. London, 1865.
Blackburne, E. L. Suburban and Rural Architecture; English and Foreign. In pro-
Bogue, J. W. Domestic Architecture; Designs for Cottages and Villas. 20 plates, 4to. London, 1865.
Chateauneuf, A. de. Architectura Domestica. Folio. London, 1839–40.
Clayton, J. Ancient Half-timbered Edifices of England; selected from the Counties of Hereford, Salop, and Chester. Folio. London, 1846.

Dean, G. A.   Construction of Farm Buildings and Labourers' Cottages. 4to.   Stratford, 1849.   [1865.

Denton, J. B.   Farm Homesteads of England.   2nd edition, 65 plates, 8vo.   London.

Downing, A. J.   Architecture of Country Houses; with remarks on Furniture, &c., and Warming and Ventilating.   New edition, 8vo.   New York, 1852.   [York, 1853.

—— Architecture of Cottage Residences, with Additions, &c.   New edition, 8vo.   New

Ewart, J.   Arrangement and Construction of Agricultural Buildings.   Folio.   1851.

Farm Buildings, Models, or a Collection of Houses adapted for the Labouring Classes. Folio.   Liege, 1847.

Gray, W. J.   Rural Architecture; Plans, &c., of Farmhouses, Cottages, Schools, Gates, Railings, &c., with Specifications.   8vo.   Edinburgh, 1853.

Knightley, T. E.   Stable Architecture.   Folio   London, 1862.   [1860.

Miles, W.   General Remarks on Stables and Examples of Stable Fittings. 8vo. London,

Morton, T. C.   The Prince Consort's Farms.   4to.   London, 1863.   [London, 1847.

Pattisson, W.   Sketches for Cottages, Villas, Parsonage Houses and Lodges, &c.   Folio.

Rham, W. C.   Dictionary of the Farm, with Supplement.   Revised by W. and H. Raynbird.   3rd edition, 8vo.   London, 1853.

Starforth, J.   Architecture of the Farm; being a Series of Designs for Farmhouses, Factors' Houses, Agricultural Labourers' Cottages, and Farmsteadings.   4to.   London, 1853.

Stephens, H., and Burn, R. S.   Book of Farm Buildings: their Arrangement and Construction.   8vo.   Edinburgh, 1861.

Strickland, C. W.   Cottage Construction and Design.   18 plates, 8vo.   London, 1864.

Tattersall, G.   Sporting Architecture.   4to.   London, 1842.

Vaux, C.   Villas and Cottages: a Series of Designs prepared for Execution in the United States.   8vo.   New York and London, 1857.

Vincent, J.   Country Cottages; Designs for Improved Dwellings for Agricultural Labourers.   20 plates, 2nd edition, 4to.   London, 1860.   [1846.

Walter, T. U., and Smith, J. J.   Cottage and Villa Architecture, &c.   4to.   Philadelphia,

Weaver, H.   Hints on Cottage Architecture; Designs for Labourers' Cottages, singly, in pairs, and in groups.   2nd edition, folio.   Bath, 1850.

—— Hints on Villa Architecture; Selection of Designs for Schools, Cottages, and Parsonage Houses.   10 plates, folio.   London.

VIII. Theatres.

Bonnet, A., et Kauffmann, J. A.   Architectonographie des Théâtres de Paris. 2 vols. 4to.   Paris, 1837.

Cavos, A.   Traité sur la Construction des Théâtres.   21 plates, 4to.   Leipzig, 1849.

—— Grand Théâtre de Moscou.   1860.

Contant, C., et Filippi, J. de.   Parallèle des Principaux Théâtres Modernes de l'Europe, et des Systèmes de Machines Théâtrales Françaises, Allemandes et Anglaises.   134 plates, 2 vols. folio.   Paris, 1840–42.

Lachèz, T.   Acoustique et Optique des Salles de Réunions Publiques, Théâtres et Amphithéâtres, etc.   8vo.   Paris, 1848.

Langhans, C. F.   Das Victoria-Theater in Berlin.   4 plates, folio.   Berlin.

Semper, G.   Das königliche Hoftheater zu Dresden.   Folio.   Brunswick, 1849.

Strack, J. H.   Das altgriechische Theatergebäude, nach sämmtlichen bekannten Ueberresten.   Folio.   Potsdam, 1843.

Titz, E.   Das neue Victoria-Theater in Berlin.   24 plates, folio.   1861.

IX. Bridges.

Adhémar, J.   Traité Théorique et Pratique des Ponts Biais.   Folio.   Paris, 1857.

Bashforth, F.   Practical Treatise on the Construction of Oblique Bridges with Spiral and with Equilibrated Courses.   New edition, 8vo.   London, 1855.

Bauernfeind, C. M.   Vorlegeblätter zur Brückenbaukunde.   Folio.   Munich, 1853–54.

Blair and Phillips.   Construction of Viaducts, Bridges, &c.   8vo.   London, 1845.

Clark, E.   Britannia and Conway Tubular Bridges; with General Inquiries on Beams. 2 vols. 8vo.   London, 1850.

Cresy, E.   Practical Treatise on Bridge Building and on the Equilibrium of Vaults and Arches.   Plates, folio.   London, 1839.

Dempsey, G. D.   Malleable Iron Tubular Bridges.   Plates folio, text 4to.   London, 1850.

—— Brick Bridges, Sewers, and Culverts.   Plates folio, text 4to.   London, 1850.

Etzel, C. von.   Brücken und Thalübergänge Schweizerischer Eisenbahnen.   Folio. Basel, 1856.   Supplement, 1859.

Fairbairn, W.   Account of the Construction of the Britannia and Conway Tubular Bridges.   20 plates, 8vo.   London, 1849.

Hann, J., and Hosking, W.   Theory, Practice, and Architecture, of Bridges of Stone,

Iron, Timber, Wire, and Suspension. 4 vols. 8vo. London, 1843. Supplément, by G R. Burnell. 8vo. London, 1850.

Haskoll, W. D. Examples of Bridge and Viaduct Construction of Masonry, Timber, and Iron. Folio. London, 1864.

Haupt, H. General Theory of Bridge Construction, containing Demonstrations of the Principles of the Art, the Strains upon Chords, Ties, Braces, &c. New edition, 8vo. New York, 1853.

Hodges, J. Victoria Bridge at Montreal in Canada. Text 4to. plates folio. London, 1860.

Humber, W. Complete Treatise on Cast and Wrought Iron Bridges and Girders, as applied to Railway Structures and to Buildings generally. Plates, 4to. London, 1860.

—— Complete Treatise on Cast and Wrought Iron Bridge Construction, including Iron Foundations. 80 plates, 2 vols. 4to. London, 1864.

Latham, J. H. Construction of Wrought-Iron Bridges, embracing the Practical Application of the Principles of Mechanics to Wrought-Iron Girder Work. 8vo. Cambridge, 1858.   [Métalliques. Text 4to. plates folio. Paris, 1858.

Molinos, L., et Pronnier, C. Traité Théorique et Pratique de la Construction des Ponts

Nicholson, P. Guide to Railway Masonry, containing a complete Treatise on the Oblique Arch. 3rd edition, revised by R. Cowen. 8vo. London, 1860.

Semple, G. Treatise on Building in Water. 63 plates, 4to. Dublin, 1776.

Turnbull, W. Mathematical Investigation of Dredge's Principle for Bridges. 8vo. London, 1841.

X.—A. ELEMENTARY WORKS.

Adhémar, J. Traité de Perspective. 8vo. Paris, 1838.

Architect, The. A weekly magazine. 2 vols. 4to. London, 1849–50.   [1849–53.

Architectural Publication Society. Detached Essays, with Illustrations. Folio. London,

—— Dictionary of Architecture. K in progress. Folio. London, 1853–66.

Armengaud, C. Cours Élémentaire de Dessin Industriel à l'Usage des Écoles Premières. 4to. Paris, 1850.

—— Nouveau Cours Raisonné de Dessin Industriel appliqué principalement à la Mécanique et à l'Architecture. Folio. Paris, 1848.

Baker, T. Land and Engineering Surveying. 12mo. London, 1859.

—— Mensuration. 12mo. London, 1859.

—— Principles and Practice of Statics and Dynamics. 12mo. London, 1851.

Barr, J. Anglican Church Architecture and Furniture. 3rd edition, 8vo. Oxford, 1845.

Bartholomew, A. Specifications for Practical Architecture, preceded by an Essay on the Decline of Excellence in the Structure and in the Science of Modern English Buildings. 2nd edition, 8vo. London, 1846.

Batissier, L. Histoire de l'Art Monumental dans l'Antiquité et au Moyen Age, suivie d'un Traité sur la Peinture sur Verre. 2nd edition, revised, 8vo. Paris, 1860.

—— Éléments d'Archéologie Nationale. 8vo. Paris, 1843.

Billings, R. W. The Infinity of Geometric Design Exemplified. 4to. London, 1849.

—— The Power of Form applied to Geometric Tracery. 8vo. London, 1851.

Blenkarn, J. Architectural and Engineering Specifications of Works, Roads, and Sewers, with Agreements and Reports. 8vo. London, 1865.

Bloxam, M. H. Principles of Gothic Ecclesiastical Architecture Elucidated, with Explanation of Terms. 10th edition, 12mo. London, 1859.

Brees, S. C. Illustrated Glossary of Practical Architecture and Civil Engineering. 2nd edition, 8vo. London, 1853.   [London, 1838.

Britton, J. Dictionary of the Architecture and Archæology of the Middle Ages. 8vo.

Builder, The. A weekly magazine. 25 vols. 4to. London, 1843–66.

Building News, The. A weekly magazine. 13 vols. 4to. and folio. London, 1856–66.

Burnell, G. R. Limes, Cements, Mortars, Concretes, Masticks, and Plastering. 12mo. London, 1857.

Calliat, V., and Lance, A. Encyclopédie d'Architecture. 12 vols. 4to. Paris, 1851–65.

Castle, H. J. Treatise on Land Surveying and Levelling. 8vo. London, 1845.

Caumont, A. de. Abécédaire, ou Rudiment d'Archéologie. 3 vols. 8vo. Paris, 1851–62.

Chambers, Sir W. Treatise on the Decorative Part of Civil Architecture; with Essay on Grecian Architecture, by J. B. Papworth. The original plates. Folio. London, 1826.

Civil Engineer and Architect's Journal, The. 29 vols. 4to. London, 1837–66.

Cresy, E. Encyclopædia of Civil Engineering. With supplement, 8vo. London, 1861.

Dempsey, G. D. The Builder's Guide: a Practical Manual. 8vo. London, 1851.

Denison, E. B. Lectures on Church Building; with Remarks on Bells and Clocks. 2nd edition, 8vo. London, 1856.   [1850.

Dobson, E. Rudimentary Treatise on the Manufacture of Bricks and Tiles. 12mo. London,

—— Rudiments of the Art of Building. 12mo. London, 1849

Dobson, E. Student's Guide to the Practice of Measuring and Valuing Artificers' Work. Enlarged by E. L. Garbett. 8vo. London, 1853.

Donaldson, T. L. Architectural Maxims and Theorems. 8vo. London, 1847.

────── Handbook of Specifications, &c. ; with a Review of the Law of Contracts, by W. C. Glen. 2 vols. 8vo. London, 1860.   [London, 1866.

Edwards, Jun., F. On Smoky Chimneys ; their Cure and Prevention. 4th edition, 8vo.

Fairbairn, W. Iron, its History, Properties, and Processes of Manufacture. New edition, 8vo. Edinburgh, 1865.

Fenwick, S. Mechanics of Construction, including the Theories of the Strength of Materials, Roofs, Arches, and Suspension Bridges. 8vo. London, 1861.

Fergusson, J. Handbook of Architecture: a History and Description of all Styles. 1,212 cuts, 3 vols. 8vo. London, 1855–62.   [1849.

────── Historical Inquiry into the true Principles of Beauty in Art. 8vo. London,

Flachat, E., Barrault, A., and Petiet, J. Traité de la Fabrication du Fer et de la Fonte, &c. 3 vols. 4to. and folio. Liège, 1852.

Förster, L. Allgemeine Bauzeitung. 31 vols. 4to. and folio. Hamburgh, 1837–66.

Freeman, E. A. History of Architecture. 8vo. London, 1849.   [London, 1851.

────── Essay on the Origin and Development of Window Tracery in England. 8vo.

Gailhabaud, J. See Class III.

Garbett, E. L. Rudimentary Treatise on the Principles of Design in Architecture. 12mo. London, 1850.   [3 vols. 8vo. Oxford, 1862.

Glossary of Terms used in Grecian, Roman, Italian, and Gothic Architectures. 5th edition,

Grand, A. Le. Dessin Linéaire, basé sur la Géométrie Pratique et la Perspective. Folio. Paris 1846.   [1850–52.

Griffith, W. P. Ancient Gothic Churches, their Proportions, &c. 3 parts, 4to. London,

────── Geometrical Proportion of Architecture. 4to. London, 1843.

Harding, J. D. Elementary Art ; or the Use of the Black-lead Pencil Advocated and Explained. 28 plates, 4th edition, 4to. London, 1858.

────── Lessons on Art : displaying 140 Examples as Studies for the Student. 2 vols. 48 plates, 2nd edition, 8vo. London, 1854.

────── Principles and Practice of Art : treating of Beauty of Form, Imitation, Composition, Light, Shade, Effect, and Colour. 4to. London, 1845.   [1849.

Haskoll, W. D. Clerk of the Works and Young Architect's Guide. 12mo. London,

Hebert, L. Engineer's and Mechanic's Encyclopædia. New edition, 8vo. London, 1856–61.

Henszlmann, Dr. Théorie des Proportions appliquées dans l'Architecture depuis la XIIe Dynastie des Rois Égyptiens jusqu'au XVIe Siècle. Large folio, text 4to. Paris, 1860. Part i. only has appeared.

Higgins, W. M. The House Painter, or Decorator's Companion ; containing a Complete Treatise on the Art of House Painting, Graining, Marbling, &c. 4to. London.

Hodgkinson, E. Experimental Researches on the Strength and other Properties of Cast Iron, &c. 8vo. London, 1846.

Hoffstadt, F. Gothisches A-B-C-Buch. Text, 8vo. ; 43 plates, folio. Frankfurt, 1843–45. 1845–64. Translated into French. Folio. Paris, 1851.

Holtzapffel, C. Descriptive Catalogue of the Woods commonly employed for the Mechanical and Ornamental Arts. 8vo. London, 1843.

Hope, T. Historical Essay on Architecture. 3rd edition, 8vo. London, 1840.

Hosking, W. Architecture and Building. 4to. London, 1854.

Hutchinson, J. New Experiments in Building Materials in reference to their Conducting Power, Dryness, and Resistance to the Progress of Fire. 8vo. London, 1843.

Jousse, M. Secrets d'Architecture et des Traits Géométriques. Folio. Flèche, 1642.

Kirkaldy, D. Experimental Enquiry into the Tensile Strength, &c., of Wrought Iron and Steel. 2nd edition, 8vo. Glasgow, 1863.   [1845.

Kugler, F. Denkmäler der Kunst ; by Voit, Guhl, und Caspar. Folio. Stuttgart,

────── Handbuch der Kunstgeschichte. New edition, 8vo. Stuttgart, 1848.

────── Geschichte der Baukunst. 3 vols. 8vo. Stuttgart, 1859.

Law, H. Rudiments of Civil Engineering. 12mo. London, 1852.   [1849.

Leeds, W. H. Rudimentary Treatise on the Orders of Architecture. 12mo. London,

Lingard, J. Enquiry into the Nature and Construction of Timber ; including the Causes of Dry Rot. 2nd edition, 8vo. London, 1842.   [London, 1863.

Lloyd, W. W. General Theory of Proportion in Architectural Design. 10 plates, 4to.

Lübke, W. Geschichte der Architectur. 2nd edition, 8vo. Cologne, 1858.

Mahan, D. H. Elementary Course of Civil Engineering. Edited by P. Barlow. New edition, 4to. Edinburgh, 1846.

────── Industrial Drawing : comprising the Description and Uses of Drawing Instruments, the Construction of Plane Figures, the Proportions and Sections of Geometrical Solids, Architectural Elements, Mechanism, and Topographical Drawing ; with Remarks on the Method of Teaching the Subject, 8vo. New York, 1852.

Malton, J. Practical Treatise on Perspective. 4to. London, 1800.

Mauch, J. M. von. Neue systematische Darstellung der Architektonischen Ordnungen der Griechen, Römer und neuern Baumeister. 100 plates, 4to. Potsdam, 1850.

Minifie, W. Text-Book of Geometrical Drawing, for the use of Mechanics and Schools; with Illustrations for drawing Plans, &c., of Buildings and Machinery, Isometrical Drawing, Linear Perspective, and Shadows. New edition, 8vo. Baltimore, 1851.

Monge, G., and Brisson, M. Géométrie Descriptive; Suivie d'une Théorie des Ombres et de la Perspective. 7th edition, 4to. Paris, 1847. [1855.

Morin, A. Leçons de Mécanique Pratique. 4 vols. 8vo. Paris, 1846–50. 2nd edition, —— Fundamental Ideas of Mechanics, and Experimental Data. Translated, revised, and reduced to English Units of Measure, by J. Bennett. 8vo. New York, 1860.

Moseley, H. Mechanics applied to the Arts, including Statics and Hydrostatics. 3rd edition, 8vo. London, 1852. [London, 1855.
—— Mechanical Principles of Engineering and Architecture. 2nd edition. 8vo.

Mushet, D. Papers on Iron and Steel, Practical and Experimental. 8vo. London, 1840.

Nesbit, A. Treatise on Practical Mensuration; with Key. New edition, 12mo. 1852.
—— Practical Land Surveying. 10th edition, revised by T. Baker. 8vo. London, 1855.

Normand, L. M., et Rebout, A. E. M. Études Ombres et Lavis. Folio. Paris, 1845.

Otte, H. Handbuch der Kirchlichen Kunst-Archäologie des Deutschen Mittelalters. 8vo. Leipzig, 1854.

Oudin, J. Manuel d'Archéologie Religieuse, Civile et Militaire. 2nd edition, 8vo. Paris, 1845. [London, 1865.

Paley, F. A. Manual of Gothic Mouldings. 3rd edition, by W. M. Fawcett. 8vo.
—— Manual of Gothic Architecture. 8vo. London, 1846.

Papworth, W. Notes on the Causes of Fires; or which is the Safest of the Various Modes of Warming Buildings. 16mo. London, 1853.
—— Notes on Spontaneous Combustion. 16mo. London, 1855.

Pasley, C. W. Course of Practical Geometry and Plan Drawing. 8vo. London, 1838.

Penn, S. Tables showing the Weight of Different Lengths of Round, Square, and Flat Bar Iron, &c. 5th edition. Liverpool, 1843. [1859–61.

Percy, J. Metallurgy: the Art of Extracting Metals from their Ores. 8vo. London,

Petit, J. L. Remarks on Architectural Character. Folio. Oxford, 1846.

Poole, G. A. Churches, their Structure, Arrangement, and Decoration. 3rd edition. 18mo. London, 1852.
—— History of Ecclesiastical Architecture in England. 8vo. London, 1848.

Pratt, J. H. Mathematical Principles of Mechanical Philosophy, and their Application to Elementary Mechanics and Architecture, &c. 8vo. Cambridge, 1845. [1838.

Prout, S. Hints on Light and Shadow, Composition, &c. 20 plates, 4to. London,

Pugin, A. W. N. The True Principles of Pointed or Christian Architecture; in two lectures at S. Mary's, Oscott. 4to. London, 1841.
—— Contrasts; or a Parallel between the Edifices of the XIVth and XVth Centuries and the present day. 13 plates, new edition, 4to. London, 1841.

Pyne, G. Practical Rules on Drawing; Outline, Orders, Perspective, Light and Shade, Colour, &c. 4to. London, 1854. [Paris, 1832.

Quatremère de Quincy, A. C. Dictionnaire Historique de l'Architecture. 2 vols. 4to.

Rahn, J. R. Ueber den Ursprung und die Entwicklung des Christlichen Central- und Kuppelbaus. Leipzig, 1866. [1843.

Ramée, D. Manuel de l'Histoire Générale de l'Architecture. 2 vols. 12mo. Paris,
—— Histoire de l'Architecture en France depuis les Romains jusqu'au XVIᵉ Siècle. 12mo. Paris and Leipzig, 1846.

Rankine, W. J. M. Manual of Civil Engineering. 3rd edition, 8vo. Glasgow, 1864.
—— Manual of Applied Mechanics. 3rd edition, 8vo. Glasgow, 1864.

Reid, J. Young Surveyor's Preceptor; Art of Architectural Mensuration. 2nd edition, 4to. London, 1859.

Reusch, E. Der Spitzbogen und die Grundlinien seines Masswerks. Ein geometrischer Beitrag zur Ornamentistik des Mittelalters. 4to. Stuttgart, 1853.

Reynaud, L. Traité d'Architecture, contenant des Notions Générales sur les Principes de la Construction et sur l'Histoire de l'Art. 82 plates, folio. Paris, 1850.

Rickman, T. Attempt to Discriminate the Styles of English Architecture. 6th edition, with additions by J. H. Parker. 8vo. London and Oxford, 1862. 4th edition, 1835, contains the Topographical list of Buildings.

Roberts, J. B. Short Hints to the Student in Architecture on entering the office, making drawings, &c. 16mo. London, 1852. [Puddled Bars. 8vo. London, 1857.

Rogers, S. B. Elementary Treatise on Iron Metallurgy, up to the Manufacture of

Roy, C. F. Le. Traité de Géométrie Descriptive; suivi de la Méthode des Plans Cotés, de la Théorie des Engrenages Cylindriques et Coniques, etc. 3rd edition, 2 vols. 8vo. Paris, 1850.

Roy, C. F. Le. Traité de Stéréotomie, comprenant les Applications de la Géométrie Descriptive à la Théorie des Ombres, la Perspective Linéaire, la Gnomonique, la Coupe des Pierres et la Charpente. 2 vols. folio and 4to. Liège, 1845.

Royal Institute of British Architects. Transactions, 2 parts, 4to. London, 1837 and 1842; Sessional Papers, 14 vols. 4to. London, 1853–66.

Ruskin, J. Seven Lamps of Architecture. 8vo. London, 1849.

—— Lectures on Architecture and Painting. 8vo. London, 1852. [London, 1859.

Scott, G. G. Remarks on Secular and Domestic Architecture. 2nd edition, 8vo.

Sharpe, E. Treatise on the Rise and Progress of Decorated Window Tracery in England. 8vo. London, 1849. [1851.

—— The Seven Periods of English Architecture defined and illustrated. 8vo. London,

Simms, F. W. Principal Mathematical and Drawing Instruments. 12mo. London, 1847.

—— Principles and Practice of Levelling. 3rd edition, 8vo. London, 1856.

Smith, C. H. Lithology, or Observations on Stone used for Building. 4to. London, 1845.

Smith, J. Projection and Artistic Drawing. 2nd edition, 8vo. London, 1843.

Snell, G. Stability of Arches. 8vo. London, 1846.

Sopwith, T. Treatise on Isometrical Drawing. 2nd edition, 8vo. London, 1843.

Surveyor, Engineer, and Architect, The, by Mudie. A monthly magazine. 4 vols. 4to. London, 1840–42. [1849–50.

Terms used in Architecture, Rudimentary Dictionary of. 12mo. London (Weale),

Thiollet, F. Leçons d'Architecture, Théorique et Pratique, comprenant l'Histoire des Ordres, etc. 6 vols. 4to. Paris, 1843.

Treussart, Gen., Petot, M., and Courtois, M. Essays on Hydraulic and Common Mortars and on Lime Burning. Translated by J. G. Totten. 8vo. New York, 1842. [Paris, 1853.

Tripon, J. B. Études Progressives et Complètes d'Architecture et de Lavis. Folio.

Truran, W. The Iron Manufacture of Great Britain, theoretically and practically considered. Revised by J. A. Phillips and W. H. Dorman. 2nd edition, 84 plates, 4to. London, 1862. [1850.

Twining, H. Nature and Application of Perspective and Foreshortening. 8vo. London,

Vaudoyer, L. Patria : La France Ancienne et Moderne, Morale et Matérielle, etc.; Histoire de l'Architecture. 12mo. Paris, 1846.

Viollet-le-Duc, E. Dictionnaire Raisonné de l'Architecture Française du Onzième au Seizième Siècle. In progress, 8 vols. 8vo. Paris, 1853–66. [Paris, 1862.

Viollet-le-Duc fils, et Corroyer. Gazette des Architectes et du Bâtiment. 4 series, 4to.

Virloys, C. F. R. Le. Dictionnaire d'Architecture Civile, etc. 3 vols. 4to. Paris, 1770.

Vitruvius, Architecture of; by Poleni and Stratico. 8 parts in 4 vols. 4to. Utini, 1825–30.

—— by A. Marinio. 4 vols. folio. Rome, 1836.

—— de Perrault ; augmentée par E. Tardieu et A. Coussin. 3 vols. 4to. Paris, 1837.

—— Traduction Nouvelle, par Maufras. 2 vols. 8vo. Paris, 1847.

Walcott, M. E. C. Church and Conventual Arrangement. 8vo. London, 1861.

Walker, T. L. Essay on Architectural Practice. 8vo. London, 1841.

Warr, F. Dynamics, Construction of Machinery, Equilibrium of Structures, and the Strength of Materials. 8vo. London, 1851.

Weale, J. Quarterly Papers on Architecture. 4 vols. 4to. London, 1843–45.

Webb, B. Sketches of Continental Ecclesiology, or Church Notes in Belgium, Germany, and Italy. 8vo. London, 1848.

Webster, A. W. On the Principles of Sound ; their Application in the Construction of Public Buildings. 8vo. 1840. [1847.

Webster, T. Principles of Hydrostatics ; or Law of Fluids. 3rd edition, 8vo. London,

Whewell, W. Elementary Treatise on Mechanics. 7th edition, 8vo. Cambridge, 1847.

Whichcord, J. Kentish Ragstone as a Building Material. 8vo. London, 1846.

Wightwick, G. Hints to Young Architects. 2nd edition, 8vo. London, 1860.

Willis, R. Architectural Nomenclature of the Middle Ages. 4to. Cambridge, 1844.

Willson, H. Use of a Box of Colours : a Practical Demonstration on Composition, Light, and Shade. 8vo. London, 1842. [London, 1846.

Wilme, B. P. Handbook for Mapping, Engineering, and Architectural Drawing. 4to.

Woodbury, D. P. Treatise on the Various Elements of Stability in the Well Proportioned Arch. 8vo. New York, 1858.

Woods, J. Letters of an Architect. 2 vols. 4to. London, 1828.

Young, J. R. Mensuration in Theory and Practice. London, 1853. [1855.

—— Compendious Course of Mathematics ; Theoretical and Practical. 8vo. London,

X.—B. PRACTICAL WORKS.

Adhémar, J. Traité de Charpente. 2nd edition, 8vo. Paris, 1854.

—— Traité de la Coupe des Pierres. Text 8vo. plates folio. Paris, 1859.

Ainslie, J. Comprehensive Treatise on Land Surveying. New edition, by W. Galbraith. With plates 4to. text 8vo. Edinburgh, 1849.

Ardant, P. Sur la Charpente à Grande Portée. Folio. Paris, 1853.

Ashpitel, A. New Guide, or Book of Lines for Carpenters, geometrically explained. New edition, 4to. London, 1857. [London, 1851.

———— Handrails and Staircases ; a new and simple method of finding the lines. 4to.

Austin, J. G. Preparation, Combination, and Application of Calcareous and Hydraulic Limes and Cements, &c. 12mo. London, 1862. [1849.

Bankes, L. Joiner's Instructor in the Construction of Staircases and Handrailing. 4to.

Bernan, W. History and Art of Warming and Ventilating Rooms and Buildings. 2 vols. 8vo. London, 1846. [Edinburgh, 1851.

Bow, R. H. Treatise on Bracings, with its application to Bridges, &c. 8vo.

Braidwood, J. Fireproof Buildings. 8vo. London, 1850.

———— Fire Prevention and Fire Extinction. 8vo. London, 1865.

Brandon, R. and J. A. Open Timber Roofs of the Middle Ages. 4to. London, 1849.

Brees, S. C. Railway Practice ; a Collection of Working Plans, &c. 4 series, 4to. London, 1837, 1840, 1847.

Brun, F. M. Le. Sur l'Emploi du Béton. 4to. Paris, 1843.

Brunet, F. Dimensions des Fers de la Coupole de la Halle au Grain. 4to. Paris, 1809.

Bruyère, L. Études relatives à l'Art des Constructions. Folio. Paris, 1823–28.

Bury, T. Remains of Ecclesiastical Woodwork. 21 plates, 4to. London, 1847.

Coignet, F. Béton Aggloméré pour Fortifications, Ponts, etc. 8vo. Paris, 1862.

Colling, J. K. Details of Gothic Architecture. 2 vols. 200 plates, 4to. London, 1852–53.

Dempsey, G. D. On the Drainage of Towns and Buildings. 12mo. London, 1849.

———— Examples of Iron Roofs, spans from 20 to 153 feet. Folio. London, 1850.

Dobson, E. Rudimentary Treatise on Masonry and Stone Cutting. 12mo. Plates 4to. London, 1849.

———— On Foundations and Concrete Works. 12mo. London, 1850.

Eck, C. L. G. Traité de l'Application du Fer, de la Fonte, et de la Tôle, dans les Constructions Civiles, etc. Folio. 1841.

———— Mémoire sur la Construction de Nouveaux Planchers, destinés à rendre les Bâtimens Incombustibles. Folio. Paris, 1841. [Liège, 1845.

Émy, A. R. Traité de l'Art de la Charpenterie. 157 plates folio, and text 2 vols. 8vo.

———— Description du Nouveau Système d'Arcs pour les Grandes Charpentes. Folio. Liège, 1852.

Fairbairn, W. On the Application of Cast and Wrought Iron to Building Purposes ; with Treatise on Wrought-Iron Bridges. 3rd edition, 8vo. London, 1864.

———— Useful Information for Engineers. 1st series, 4th edition, 1864 ; 2nd series, 1860. 8vo. London. Third series, 1866.

Fontenay, T. Notice on the Construction of the Tunnels of St. Cloud and Motretout ; with General Observations on Subterranean Passages, and the Dimensions and Prices of Sixty-six Tunnels in France, England, and Belgium. 8vo. Paris, 1847.

Fox, H. H., and Barrett, G. Construction of Public Buildings and Private Dwelling-Houses on a fireproof principle, without increase of cost. 12mo. London, 1849.

Galpin, J. Joiner's Instructor, Staircasing and Handrailing. 2 vols. 4to. London, 1853.

———— Joiner's Own Book, and Builder's New Guide, showing the Improvements upon Carpentry and Joinery since the days of the late Mr. Nicholson. 39 plates, 4to. London, 1856. [York, 1863.

Gilmore. Practical Treatise on Limes, Hydraulic Cements, and Mortars. 8vo. New

Godwin, G. Nature and Properties of Concrete. 4to. London, 1836.

Goodwyn, H. Wrought-Iron Roofing, as applicable to every description of Building, and showing the modification necessary to adapt the systems to European dwellings in India, &c. 4to. Calcutta, 1844.

Hassenfratz, J. H. Traité de l'Art du Charpentier. 4to. Paris, 1804.

Hood, C. Practical Treatise on Warming Buildings by Hot Water ; and Laws of Radiant and Conducted Heat. New edition, 8vo. London, 1855.

Hosking, W. Healthy Homes: a Guide to the proper Regulation of Buildings, Streets, Drains, and Sewers. New edition, 8vo. London, 1849.

Isaacs, L. H. Practical Treatise on Sewerage and Drainage. 8vo. London, 1859.

Jousse, M. Ouverture de l'Art de Serrurier, Carpentier, etc. 2 vols. folio. Flèche, 1627.

Lasvinges, H. et L. Cathédrale de Bayeux : Reprise en sous-œuvre de la Tour Centrale ; Description des Travaux. 25 plates, 4to. Paris, 1861.

Laxton, H. Examples of Building Construction, being a Series of Working Drawings to a large Scale. 27 parts, folio. London, 1853–56. [87 plates, folio. Paris, 1866.

Mignard, B. R. Guide des Constructeurs ; Traité. 3rd edit. by A. F. Chelly. 2 vols. 8vo. ;

Morey, P., et Roux, H. Charpente de la Cathédrale de Messine. Folio. Paris, 1841. [1847.

Morin, A. Aide-Mémoire de Mécanique Pratique. 4th edition, enlarged. 8vo. Paris,

Newland, J. Carpenter's and Joiner's Assistant, &c. 2 vols. folio. Liverpool, 1860.

Oldham. Report on the Fall of the Cotton Mill. Folio. London, 1845.

Oppermann, C. A. Nouvelles Annales de Construction. In progress, folio. Paris, 1855.

Papworth, J. B. Essay on the Causes of Dry Rot in Buildings. 4to. London, 1803.

Peclet, Prof. Heat and Ventilation, considered in their various Applications. 3rd edition. 8vo. 122 plates, folio. Liège, 1845. [8vo. London, 1840.

Perkins, A. M. Improved Patent Apparatus for Warming and Ventilating Buildings.

Reid, A. Theory and Practice of Ventilation ; with Remarks on Warming, Lighting, and the Communication of Sound. 1844.

Riddle, R. Staircasing, Handrailing, Carpentry, &c. London. 1860.

Ritchie, R. A. Observations on the Sanitary Arrangements of Factories, with Remarks on the present Method of Warming and Ventilation. 8vo. London, 1844.

Roberts, T. Mode of Scarfing Timber. 8vo. Devonport, 1852.

Robson, R. Mason's, Bricklayer's, and Decorator's Guide ; containing Examples of Foundations, Domes, Lighthouses, Bridges, &c. 4to. London, 1862.

Romberg, S. A. Die Zimmerwerk-Baukunst in allen ihren Theilen. Folio. Leipzig, 1846–50.

Sganzin, J. Leçons d'un Cours de Constructions, avec des applications tirées spéciale-ment de l'Art de l'Ingénieur des Ponts et Chaussées. 5th edition, by M. Reibell. 180 plates folio, text 3 vols. 4to. Paris, 1845. [struction. 8vo. London, 1861.

Shields, F. W. Strains on Structures of Ironwork, with Practical Remarks on Iron Con-

Simms, F. W. Practical Tunnelling. Revised by W. D. Haskoll. 2nd edition, 4to. London, 1860. [1861.

Smith, T. R. Rudimentary Treatise on Acoustics of Public Buildings. 12mo. London,

Smyth, P. Method of Cooling the Air of Rooms in Tropical Climates. 4to. London, 1851.

Stone. Report and Investigation into the Qualifications and Fitness of Stone for Build-ing Purposes, more particularly for the New Houses of Parliament. New edition. 4to. London, 1845.

Stoney, B. B. Theory of Strains in Girders; with Tables of Strength of Materials, &c. 2 vols. 8vo. London, 1866. [1857–59.

Tarbuck, E. L. Encyclopædia of Practical Carpentry and Joinery, &c. 4to. London,

Thierry. Recueil d'Escaliers en Pierre, Charpente, Menuiserie et Fonte. 4to. 1844.

Tomlinson, C. Warming and Ventilation. 12mo. London, 1858.

Tredgold, T. Practical Treatise on Strength of Cast Iron and other Metals. Revised and enlarged by E. Hodgkinson. 8vo. London, 1860.

—— Principles of Warming, &c.; with Appendix, by Bramah. 8vo. London, 1836.

Trendall, E. W. Examples for Roofing, &c. for Show-Rooms, Theatres, Warehouses, Churches, Chapels, Schools, Villas, Greenhouses, &c. New edition, 4to. 1860.

Vaudoyer, L. Instruction sur les Moyens de prévenir ou de faire cesser les effets de l'Humidité dans les Bâtiments. 4to. Paris, 1844.

Ventilation and Warming of the Houses of Parliament ; Report of the Select Committee. Folio. London, 1835.

Vicat, L. J. Recherches Expérimentales sur les Chaux de Construction, les Bétons, et Mortiers Ordinaires. 8vo. Paris, 1819. Translated by J. T. Smith. 8vo. London, [1837.

Walker, T. L. Architectural Precedents. 65 plates, 8vo. London, 1841.

Watson, J. Thermal Ventilation and other Sanitary Improvements Applicable to Public Buildings. 8vo. New York, 1851.

Wyman, M. Practical Treatise on Ventilation. New edition. 8vo. New York, 1851.

XI.—A. Ornament and Decoration.

Adams, L. G. Recueil de Sculptures Gothiques d'après les plus Beaux Monuments en France depuis le XIe jusqu'au XVe Siècle. 192 plates, 2 vols. 4to. Paris, 1856.

—— Décorations Intérieures et Meubles des Époques de Louis XIII et XIV, d'après les Compositions, de C. de Passe, etc. 100 plates, folio. Paris, 1862–64.

Amé, E. Les Carrelages Émaillés du Moyen Age et de la Renaissance 4to. Paris, 1859.

Antonelli. Collezione de' Migliori Ornamenti Antichi nella Città di Venezia. 130 plates, 4to. Venezia, 1831. [Paris, 1854.

Asselineau, C. Meubles et Objets divers du Moyen Age et de la Renaissance. Folio.

Basoli, A. Raccolta di Diversi Ornamenti. 100 plates, folio. Bologna, 1838.

—— Compartimenti di Camere. 100 plates, folio. Bologna, 1827.

Blashfield, J. M. History and Manufacture of Ancient and Modern Terra Cotta, and of its Use in Architecture. 12mo. London, 1855.

Bock, translated by Suckau. Les Trésors Sacrés de Cologne. 48 plates, coloured.

Bordeaux, R. Serrurerie du Moyen Age. 4to. Paris, 1853.

Borsato, G. Opera Ornamentale ; con cenni Storici dell' Ornato Decorativo Italiano di Vallardi. 60 plates, folio. Milano, 1831.

Chapuy, N. M. J. La France Monumentale et Pittoresque. Folio. Paris, 1842, etc.

Cicognara, L.   Monumenti Sepolcrali cospicui eretti alle memorie degli Uomini Celebri in Venezia, &c.   Folio.   Turin, 1858.

Clarkson, D. A.   Ancient Ironwork from the 13th Century.   4to.   London, 1860.

Colling, J. K.   Art Foliage for Sculpture and Decoration.   72 plates, 4to.   London, 1865.

———— Gothic Ornaments of Great Britain.   200 plates, 2 vols. 4to.   London, 1848–56.

Cramer, J. O.   Ornements du Moyen Age en Italie et en Sicile.   4to.   Ratisbon, 1842.

Cutts, E. L.   Manual for the Study of Sepulchral Slabs and Crosses of the Middle Ages.   8vo.   Oxford, 1849.

Daly, C.   Motifs Historiques d'Architecture et de Sculpture d'Ornement des Monuments Français de la Renaissance à la fin de Louis XVI.   In progress.   Folio.   Paris, 1866.

Degen, L.   Constructions en Briques.   48 plates, 4to.   Paris, 1859.

———— Constructions en Bois; Motifs de Décoration et d'Ornement.   48 plates, 4to.

Destailleur, H.   Recueil d'Estampes relatives à l'Ornementation des Appartements aux XVIe-XVIIIe Siècles.   Folio.   Paris, 1865.

Didron, A. N.   Manuel des Œuvres de Bronze et d'Orfévrerie du Moyen Age; drawn by L. Gaucherel.   4to.   Paris, 1859.

Dietterlein, W.   Architectura von Ausstheilung, etc. der fünff Seulen.   Folio.   Nuremberg, 1593, 1598.   5 Büch 1655.   New edition, folio.   Liège, 1862.

Drawing-Book of the Government School of Design.   Folio.   London, 1842–43.

Duchene, Lacroix, et Seré.   Le Moyen Age et la Renaissance; Histoire des Mœurs, des Arts, etc. A.D. 500–1600.   300 plates, 5 vols. 4to.   Paris, 1848–51.

Eggert, F.   Sammlung Gothischer Verzierungen.   Plates, folio.   Munich, n.d

Eisenlohr, F.   Ornamentik in ihrer Anwendung auf verschiedene Gegenstände der Bauge-werke.   Folio.   Carlsruhe and Leipzig, 1851.

———— Mittelalterliche Bauwerke im südwestlichen Deutschland und am Rhein.

———— und Feederle, F.   Holzbauten des Schwarzwaldes, &c.   Folio.   Carlsruhe, 1854.

Feuchère, L.   L'Art Industriel; Recueil de Dispositions et Décorations Intérieures.   72 plates.   Folio.   Paris, 1839–48.   [plates, 4to   Paris, 1857.

Gaucherel, L.   Exemples de Décoration appliqués à l'Architecture et à la Peinture.   120

Heideloff, C. A. von.   Art Specimens of Nuremberg, for Turners, Pottery and Porcelain Manufacturers, Jewellers and Goldsmiths, Woodcarvers, Carpenters, &c.   4 parts, 4to.   Nuremberg, 1851.

———— and Gorgel, C.   Les Ornements du Moyen Age; (Byzantine and Gothic Styles) 144 plates, 4 parts. 4to.   Nuremberg, 1843–52.   [Berlin, 1842.

Hessemer, F. M.   Arabische und Alt-Italienische Bauverzierungen.   120 plates, large folio.

Jenkins, W., and Hosking, W.   Selection of Architectural and other Ornaments, Greek, Roman, and Italian.   25 plates, folio.   London, 1829.

Jones, O.   Grammar of Ornament.   Folio.   London, 1857.   Small edition, 1865–66.

Julienne, E.   L'Ornemaniste des Arts Industriels.   Folio.   Paris, 1840.

King, T. H.   Orfévrerie et Ouvrages en Métal du Moyen Age.   200 plates, 2 vols. folio.   Bruges, 1853–60.   [2 vols. 4to.   Paris, 1848–51.

Labarte, J.   Histoire des Arts Industriels au Moyen Age et à l'Époque de la Renaissance.

Lachave.   Nouvelle Collection de Menuiserie en Bâtiments.   Folio.   1864.

———— Serrurerie.   Recueil contenant Balcons en fer corroyé et d'autres en fonte, lits en fer, etc.   Folio.   1864.

Levy, E.   Meubles Religieux et Civils conservés dans les Principaux Monastères et Musées de l'Europe du Moyen Age et de la Renaissance.   Folio.   1863.   [Munich, 1842.

Metzger, E.   Ornaments designed from Flowers for Architects, Decorators, &c.   Folio.

Nichols, J. G.   Essay on Encaustic Tiles, with Examples.   4to.   London, 1842–45.

Normand, C.   Le Guide de l'Ornemaniste et de Décoration.   New edition, folio.   Liège, Oldham, T.   Ancient Irish Pavement Tiles.   4to.   Dublin, 1842.   [1847.

Ornament.   Collezione dei Migliori Ornamenti Antichi, sparsi nella Città di Venezia con alcune Framenti di Gotica Architettura.   Folio.   Venezia, 1843–45.

———— Cours Élémentaires de Lavis appliqué à l'Ornementation.   Folio.   Paris. 1853.

Papworth, J. W. and W.   Specimens of Decoration in the Italian Style selected from the Designs of Raffaello in the Vatican Palace at Rome.   14 plates, 4to.   London, 1844.

Petit, V.   Nouveau Portefeuille de l'Ornemaniste.   50 plates, folio.   Paris, 1864.

———— et Bisiaux.   Motifs de Décoration.   1st series, 50 plates, folio.   Paris, 1864.

Pfnor, R.   Architecture, Décoration et Ameublement de l'Époque de Louis XVI.   Folio.   Paris, 1864–65.   [London, 1846.

Pugin, A. W. N.   Glossary of Ecclesiastical Ornament and Costume.   New edition, 4to.

———— Floriated Ornament.   A Series of 31 designs.   4to.   London, 1849.

Ramée, D.   Sculptures Décoratives, Motifs d'Ornementation recueillis en France, Alle-magne, Italie, et Espagne, dans les plus Beaux Monumens élevés du XIIe au XVIe Siècle.   4to.   Paris, 1863–64.   [1844.

Reynard, O.   Ornemens des Anciens Maîtres des XVe du XVIIIe Siècles.   Folio.   Paris,

Richardson, C. J. Studies of Ornamental Design. 2 vols. folio. London, 1849–51.

Romagnesi. Recueil d'Ornemens en Sculptures. Folio. Paris, 1843. [Munich, 1849.

Rottmann, L. Ornaments from the Interiors of Celebrated Buildings of Munich. Folio.

Rouyer, E., et Darcel, A. L'Art Architectural en France depuis François Ier jusqu'à Louis XIV; Motifs de Décoration. 184 plates, 4to. Paris, 1862–65.

Runge, L. Essais sur les Constructions en Briques en Italie. Text French and German.

Schmidt, C. W. Baudenkmale in Trier und seiner Umgebung. 5 parts, folio and 4to. Treves, 1836–45.

Scott, W. B. The Ornamentist; Designs selected from the Works of Dietterlin, Berain, Blondel, Meissonier, Le Pautre, &c. 4to. Edinburgh, 1845.

Seré, F., et Louandre, C. Les Arts Somptuaires; Histoire du Costume et de l'Ameublement en Europe, et des Arts et Industries qui s'y rattachent. 4 vols. 4to. Paris, 1852–58.

Shaw, H. Handbook of Mediæval Alphabets and Devices. 8vo. London, 1853.

——— Decorative Arts of the Middle Ages. 8vo. London, 1851.

——— Specimens of Tile Pavements. 4to. London, 1852.

Silvestre, J. Collection d'Alphabets; Histoires, et Fleuronnés, tirés des Principales Bibliothèques de l'Europe. Folio. Paris, 1843.

Sommerard, A. du. Les Arts du Moyen Age, en ce qui concerne principalement le Palais de Paris; l'Hôtel de Cluny, etc. 11 vols. 8vo. and folio. Paris, 1838–46.

Thiollet, F. Modèles de Serrurerie et Fonte de Fer. Folio. Paris.

Umé, G. L'Art Décoratif; Modèles de Décoration et d'Ornementation de tous les Styles. 4to. Paris, 1862. [folio. Leipzig, 1856.

Ungewitter, G. G. Plans, &c. Meubles du Moyen Age, composés par G. U. 48 plates.

——— Sammlung mittelalterlicher Ornamentik in Geschichtlicher. Folio. Leipzig, 1863.

Viollet-le-Duc, E. Dictionnaire Raisonné du Mobilier Français de l'Époque Carlovingienne à la Renaissance. 2 vols. 8vo. Paris, 1858.

Waring, J. B. Arts connected with Architecture; Stained Glass, Fresco Ornament, Inlay, &c. during XIIIth to XVth Century in Central Italy. 41 coloured plates, folio. London, 1858. (See Class IV.) [4to. London, 1840.

Weale, J. Ornamental Ironwork, Gates, Lodges, Palisading, &c. in the Royal Parks, &c.

Westwood, G. O. Distinctive Character of the various Styles of Ornamentation employed by the Early British, Anglo-Saxon, and Irish Artists. 8vo. London, 1854.

Whitaker, H. Materials for a new Style of Ornamentation, consisting of Botanical Subjects and Compositions drawn from Nature. 4to. London, 1849.

Wilme, B. P. Manual of Writing and Printing Characters, both Ancient and Modern. 4to. London, 1845.

Wornum, R. N. Analysis of Ornament; Characteristics of Styles. 8vo. London, 1856.

Wyatt, M. D. Geometrical Mosaics of the Middle Ages. Folio. London (1848).

——— Metalwork and its Artistic Design. Folio. London, 1852. [Munich, 1842.

Zach. Ornements d'Architecture du Moyen Age d'Angleterre et de France. 4to.

Zahn, W. Die schönsten Ornamente und merkwürdigsten Gemälde aus Pompeji, Herkulanum und Stabiæ. 3 series, 250 plates, folio. Berlin, 1829–54.

——— Select Ornaments for Architects and Workmen. Folio. 1844.

——— Ornamente aller klassischen Kunst-Epochen. 100 plates, 2 vols. folio. Berlin, 1838–42, 1843–48, 1849–63.

Zanetti, G. Studj Architettonico-Ornamentali. Folio. Venezia, 1845.

XI.—B. ORNAMENT: COLOURED DECORATION, STAINED GLASS, ETC.

Adams, E. Polychromatic Ornament of Italy. 4to. London, 1847.

Arrowsmith, W. and A. House Decorator's and Painter's Guide; Designs for decorating Apartments. 4to. London, 1840.

Blackburne, E. L. History of the Decorative Painting applied to English Architecture during the Middle Ages. 4to. London, 1847.

Cahier, C., et Martin, A. Vitraux Peints de Saint-Étienne de Bourges; Recherches détachées d'une Monographie de cette Cathédrale. Verrières du XIII° Siècle. 74 plates, folio. Paris, 1841–44. [of glass, folio. Paris, 1857.

Caneto, F. Sainte-Marie d'Auch; Atlas Monographique de cette Cathédrale. 60 plates

Chevreul, M. E. De la Loi du Contraste Simultané des Couleurs, etc. 8vo. Paris, 1829. Plates, 4to. 1839. Translated by C. Martel. 8vo. London, 1854. Translated by J. Spanton. 8vo. London, 1860.

Descamps, H. P. V. et Le Maistre-d'Anstaing, I. Vitraux de la Cathédrale de Tournai, dessinés par Capronnier. 13 plates, folio. Paris, 1846–48.

Field, G. Chromatography; or a Treatise on Colours and Pigments, and of their Powers in Painting. 2nd edition, 8vo. London, 1841.

——— Rudiments of the Painter's Art; or a Grammar of Colouring. 12mo. London, 1850.

French, G. J. Hints on the Arrangement of Colours in Ancient Decorative Art. 2nd edition. 8vo. Manchester, 1850.

Girault de Prangey. Choix d'Ornemens Moresques de l'Alhambra. Folio. Paris, 1847.

Goethe, J. W. von. Theory of Colours. Translated from the German by C. L. Eastlake. 8vo. London, 1840.

Gruner, L. Fresco Decorations and Stuccoes of Churches and Palaces in Italy during the XVth and XVIth Centuries. Text by J. I. Hittorff. 4to., plates folio. London, 1844. New edition, 1854.

——— Ornamental Designs for Decorations and Manufactures. Published for the Government School of Design. Folio. London, 1848.

Hay, D. R. Nomenclature of Colours, Hues, Tints, and Shades. 8vo. Edinburgh, 1845.

——— Principles of Beauty in Colouring Systematised. 8vo. Edinburgh, 1845.

Hittorff, J. I., et Zanth, L. L'Architecture Polychrome chez les Grecs. Folio. Paris, 1852.

Jones, O. Attempt to define the Principles which should regulate the Employment of Colour in Decorative Arts. 8vo. London, 1852. (See Class XI.)

Langlois, E. H. Essai Historique Descriptif sur la Peinture sur Verre, Ancienne et Moderne, et sur les Vitraux les plus Remarquables. 8vo. Rouen, 1832.

Latilla, E. Fresco, Encaustic, and Tempera Painting. 8vo. London, 1842.

Levy, E., et Capronnier, J. B. Histoire de la Peinture sur Verre en Europe. 37 plates, folio. Bruxelles, 1860. Paris, 1865. [8vo. London, 1852.

Linton, W. Ancient and Modern Colors; with their Chemical and Artistical Properties.

Merrifield, Mrs. M. P. Art of Fresco Painting, as practised by the Old Italian and Spanish Masters. 8vo. London, 1846.

Moore, G. B. Principles of Colour applied to Decorative Art. 8vo. London, 1851.

Texier, C. Histoire de la Peinture sur Verre en Limousin. 8vo. Paris, 1847.

Warrington, W. History of Stained Glass, from the earliest Period. Folio. London, 1848.

Weale, J. Divers Works of Early Masters in Stained and Painted Glass. 2 vols. folio. London, 1846.

W(inston), C. Inquiry into the Difference of Style in Ancient Glass Paintings, especially in England; with Hints on Glass Painting. 2 vols. 8vo. Oxford, 1847.

——— Introduction to the Study of Painted Glass, with Remarks on Modern Glass Painting. 8vo. London, 1849.

——— Memoirs Illustrative of the Art of Glass Painting. 8vo. London, 1865.

XII. MISCELLANEOUS :—TABLES ; DICTIONARIES ; LAW BOOKS, ETC.

Adcock, H. Engineer's Pocket Book. 8vo. London, 1862, &c.

Addison, C. G. Treatise on the Law of Contracts, and Rights and Liabilities ex contractu. 5th edition, 8vo. London, 1862.

Amos, A., and Ferard, J. Treatise on the Law of Fixtures. 8vo. London, 1847.

Ansted, D. T. Elementary Course of Geology, &c. 2nd edition, 12mo. London, 1856.

Arnott, N. Elements of Physics. 8vo. London, 1828.

Bayldon, J. S. Art of Valuing Rents and Tillages, and Claims of Tenants upon quitting Farms. 8th edition, by J. C. Morton. 8vo. London, 1862.

Beardmore, N. Hydraulic Tables. 2nd edition, 12mo. London.

——— Manual of Hydrology. 8vo. London, 1862.

Biden, W. D. Rules, &c., for Valuations. 8vo. London, 1861.

——— Practical Rules for Valuers. 8vo. London, 1862.

Bourdais, J. Traité Pratique de la Résistance des Matériaux Appliqués à la Construction des Ponts, des Bâtiments, etc. 8vo. Paris, 1859.

Brande, W. T. Manual of Chemistry. 4th edition. 8vo. London, 1836.

Bruton, E. G. Ecclesiastical Dilapidations. 2nd edition, 12mo. Oxford, 1865.

Burn, R. S. Handbook of the Mechanical Arts in Building; with Hints on Road-making and Enclosing of Land. 2nd edition, 8vo. Edinburgh, 1860.

Campin, F. Engineer's Pocket Remembrancer. 8vo. London, 1863.

Chambers, T., and Tattersall, G. Law relating to Buildings, Fixtures, Insurance, Actions on Builders' Bills, Dilapidations. 12mo. London, 1845. [1857.

Chitty, J. Treatise on the Law of Contracts. 6th edition, by J. A. Russell. 8vo. London,

Claudel, J. Formules, etc., ou Aide-Mémoire des Ingénieurs, des Architectes, etc. 2nd edition, 8vo. Paris, 1857.

Daly, C. Revue Générale de l'Architecture. 24 vols. 4to. Paris, 1842–66.

Dean, G. A. Enfranchisement and Commutation of Copyhold Property considered with the Copyhold Enfranchisement Bill. 8vo. London, 1851.

——— The Land Steward ; Hints on Choice of Landed Estates, Principles of Drainage, Irrigation, arrangement of Farm Buildings, Walls, Roads, &c. 8vo. London, 1851.

Dilapidations. Report of Select Committee of Royal Institute of British Architects. 8vo. London, 1844.

Downing, A. J. Theory and Practice of Landscape Gardening; with a view to the Improvement of Country Residences; with Remarks on Rural Architecture. 4th edition, 8vo. New York, 1849.

Dussieux, L. Les Artistes Français à l'Étranger. 8vo. Paris, 1851.

Ecclesiastical and Architectural Topography of England; comprising Berks., Beds., Bucks., Oxon., Camb., and Hunts. 8vo. Oxford, 1851.

Elmes, J. Practical Treatise on Architectural Jurisprudence. 8vo. London, 1827.

Engineer's, Architect's, and Contractor's Pocket-Book. 8vo. London (Weale), 1863, &c.

Fownes, G. Manual of Elementary Chemistry, Theoretical and Practical. 9th edition, 8vo. London, 1863.

Ganot, A. Elementary Treatise on Physics. Translated by E. Atkinson. [8vo. London, 1863. 9th edition,

Gardissal and Tolhausen. Technological Dictionary in French, English, and German.

Gibbons, D. Law of Fixtures. 8vo. London, 1836. [3 vols.

—— Law of Dilapidations and Nuisances. New edition, 8vo. London, 1849.

—— Law of Dilapidations and Nuisances. New edition, 8vo. London, 1849.

—— Law of Contracts for Works and Services. 12mo. London, 1857.

Glynn, J. Construction of Cranes and Machinery for raising Heavy Bodies. 12mo. London, 1849. [London, 1865.

Grandy, R. E. Timber Importer's, Merchant's, and Builder's Standard Guide. 12mo.

Grier, W. The Mechanic's Calculator. 4th edition, 12mo. London, 1841.

Heideloff, C. A. Die Bauhütten. 4to. Nuremberg, 1844.

Hogg, J. Merchant and Iron Trader's Guide, &c. Tables of Weights and Measurement of Metals, Stone, and Timber. 12mo. London, 1859.

Hudson, R. Land Valuer's Best Assistant; being Tables on a very much improved plan for calculating the Value of Estates, &c., for laying out Plots of Land. New edition: 8vo. London (1859).

Hughes, J. A. Garden Architecture and Landscape Gardening. 8vo. London, 1866.

Humble, W. Dictionary of Geology and Mineralogy. 3rd edition, 8vo. London, 1840.

Hurst, J. T. Handbook for Architectural Surveyors and others engaged in Building. 32mo. London, 1865.

Ingram, T. D. Compensation to Land and House Owners. 12mo. London, 1864.

Inwood, W. Tables for the Purchasing of Estates, Freehold, Copyhold, or Leasehold; Annuities, Advowsons, &c., &c. 17th edition, by F. Thoman. 12mo. London, 1859.

Kemp, E. How to lay out a Garden; Plans, &c. New edition, 8vo. London, 1864.

Kerr, R. On Ancient Lights, and the Evidence of Surveyors thereon. 8vo. London, 1865.

Lanktree, J. Elements of Land Valuation, and Instructions as to the Qualifications and Duties of Valuators. 8vo. Dublin, 1853.

Law, T. J. Acts for Building Churches. 8vo. London, 1847.

Lea, W. Tables of Strength and Deflection of Timber. 8vo. London, 1850.

Llaguno y Amirola and Caen Bermudez. Noticias de los Arquitectos y Arquitectura de España. 4 vols. 4to. Madrid, 1829.

Loudon, J. C. Encyclopædia of Gardening, &c. New edition, 8vo. London, 1850.

Low, D. Landed Property and the Economy of Estates. 8vo. London, 1856.

Lumley, W. G. Nuisances Removal and Diseases Prevention Act, 1848; with Notes and the Amending Act: and ditto of 1855. 2nd edition, 12mo. London, 1860.

—— Law of Parochial Assessments. 4th edition, 12mo. London, 1858.

Lyell, Sir C. Elements of Geology. 5th edition, 8vo. London, 1855; and Supp., 1857.

Lyon, G. Compendium of the Law of Landlord and Tenant, as applicable both to Agricultural Leases and to those of Urban Tenements. 8vo. Edinburgh, 1848.

Mac Intosh, C. The Book of the Garden. 2 vols. 8vo. Edinburgh and London, 1852.

Major, J. Theory and Practice of Landscape Gardening. 4to. London, 1852.

Malpas, H. Builder's Pocket-Book of Reference; Tables of Strength of Timbers, Wood and Iron Beams, &c. 18mo. London, 1852.

Milizia, F. Memorie degli Architetti antichi e moderni. 2 vols. 8vo. Bassano, 1785. 4th edition, translated by Mrs. E. Cresy. 2 vols. 8vo. London, 1826.

Molesworth, G. L. Pocket Book of Useful Formulæ and Memoranda. 8th edition, with Supplement, 32mo. London, 1864.

Morris, T. Discourse upon Dilapidations. 12mo. London, 1865.

—— Clue to Railway Compensation, Value of Estates, and Parochial Assessments, &c. 2nd edit. 12mo. London, 1866.

Morton, J. L. The Resources of Estates; the Agricultural Improvement and General Management of Landed Property. 8vo.

Neville, J. Hydraulic Tables, Coefficients, and Formulæ, for finding the Discharge of Water from Orifices of all kinds. New edition, enlarged. 8vo. London, 1860.

Nightingale, F. Notes on Hospitals; with Plans. 3rd edition, 4to. London, 1863.

Papworth, J. B. Hints on Ornamental Gardening, Designs for Garden Buildings, &c. 29 plates. 8vo. London, 1823. [edition, 8vo. Glasgow, 1862.

Peddie, A. The Practical Measurer; or Wood-merchant's Assistant; with Tables. New

Peschel, C. F. Elements of Physics. Translated from the German by E. West. 2nd edition, 3 vols. 8vo. London, 1854.

Quatremère de Quincy, A. C. Histoire de la Vie et des Ouvrages des plus célèbres Architectes. 2 vols. 4to. Paris, 1830.

Raczynski, A. Dictionnaire d'Artistes, pour servir à l'Histoire de l'Art Moderne en Allemagne. 8vo. Berlin, 1842. [folio. London, 1859.

Rawlinson, R. Designs for tall Chimney Shafts, Ventilating Towers, &c. 25 plates,

Repton, H. Landscape Gardening, &c. The entire works, edited by J. C. Loudon. New edition, 8vo. London, 1842. [1849.

Rogers, F. N. Practical Arrangement of Ecclesiastical Law. 2nd edit. 8vo. London,

Rouse, R. The Practical Man, or Pocket Companion for Solicitors, Valuers, and Owners of Property. 4th edition, 8vo. London, 1841.

Ryde, E. General Text Book for the constant Use and Reference of Architects, &c.: Landed Property, by J. Donaldson. 8vo. London, 1854.

———— Hydraulic Tables, Discharge of Water through Pipes, &c. 8vo. London, 1852.

St. Leonard's, Lord. Handybook on Property Law. 7th edition, 8vo. London, 1866.

Scratchley, A. Copyhold, Life Leasehold, and Church Property. 4th edition, 8vo. London, 1859. [4th edition, 2 vols. 8vo. London, 1849.

Scriven, J. Law of Copyhold, Customary, Freehold, and Ancient Demesne, Tenure.

Siebeck, R. Art of Landscape Gardening, represented in a Plan and elucidated by the determining Motives. Translated by R. H. Westley. 6 plates, 4to. 1862.

————Picturesque Garden Plans. 24 coloured plates, folio. London, 1864.

Smith, C. H. J. Parks and Pleasure Grounds ; Practical Notes on Country Residences,

Smith, J. W. Law of Contracts. 8vo. London, 1855. [Villas, &c. 12mo. London, 1852.

———— Law of Landlord and Tenant. 8vo. London, 1860. [1852.

Standish J. and Noble, C. Practical Hints on Planting Ornamental Trees. 8vo. London,

Tate, T. Strength of Materials; containing Original Formulæ, specially applied to Tubular Bridges, Wrought Iron, and Cast Iron Beams, &c. 8vo. London, 1850.

Timber and Timber Duties; Report on, by a Commission. Folio. London, 1835.

Tomlinson, C. Introduction to the Study of Natural Philosophy. 12mo. London, 1859.

———— Mechanics. 12mo. London, 1859.

Turnbull, A. H. Tables of Compound Interest and Annuities, Yearly, Half-yearly, and Quarterly Payments. 8vo. Edinburgh, 1863.

Vasari, G. Vite de' più eccellenti Pittori, Scultori, ed Architetti. 3 vols. Bologna, 1647. 13 vols. 8vo. Firenze, 1822. Translated by Mrs. J. Forster. 5 vols. 8vo. London, 1850.

———— Le Vite ; pubblicate per cura d' una Società di Amatori delle Arti Belli. 12 vols. 12mo. Firenze, 1846-56. [1862.

Walpole, H. Anecdotes of Painting. Edited by R. N. Wornum. 3 vols. 8vo. London,

Watson, W. H. Law of Arbitration and Awards. 8vo. London, 1846. [1857.

Weir, H. F. Land Measuring Tables, showing the area of any sized plot. 8vo. Glasgow,

Wilkinson, G. Practical Geology and Ancient Architecture of Ireland. 8vo. London, 1845.

Willich, C. M. Popular Tables for ascertaining the value of Lifehold, Leasehold, and Church Property. 4th edition. 8vo. London, 1859.

Wilson, G. Chemistry. 12mo. London and Edinburgh, 1860.

Wily, W. Law of Dilapidation in Ireland. 8vo. Dublin, 1850.

Woodfall, W. Law of Landlord and Tenant. 8vo. London, 1856. [1845.

Woolrych, H. W. Law of Party Walls and Fences, with Building Act. 8vo. London,

———— Treatise of the Law of Ancient and Modern Window Lights. 12mo. London, [1864.

Yool, G. W. Waste, Nuisance, and Trespass. 8vo. London, 1863.

———— Compensation to Landowners. 8vo. London, 1864.

Young, C. F. T. Fires, Fire Engines, &c. ; with Remarks on Fireproof Construction. 8vo. London, 1866.

B.

BALL FLOWER. An ornament resembling a ball inclosed in a flower of a circular shape, the three petals of which form a cup round it. It is usually placed in a hollow moulding, and is considered one of the chief characteristics of the Decorated style of Gothic architecture.

BAR or BARRED DOOR. The term used in Scotland for a *ledged* door.

BARRY, Sir C. See ARCHITECTS, list of, 346.

BARTISAN. A turret on the summit of a tower, castle, or house, whereon was generally hoisted the standard or flag proper to the place.

BASKET HANDLE ARCH. (Fr. Anse de panier.) An arch whose vertical height is less than half its horizontal diameter, such as an elliptic arch.

BEACON TURRET. The turret of an angle of a tower, sometimes in border counties used for containing the apparatus for kindling at the shortest possible notice the *need-fire*.

BED-MOULDINGS. The mouldings under a projection, as the corona of a cornice.

BELL TURRET. A small tower formed specially for holding a bell. A "bell-gable" is a gable-like wall perforated to hold a bell.

BENATURA. The holy water vessel placed at the entrance of churches, generally on the right hand of the outer or inner porch door, or both.

BIRD'S-BEAK MOULDING. A moulding which in section forms an ovolo or ogee with or without a fillet under it, followed by a hollow. It is usual in Classic work.

BLOUET, G. A. See ARCHITECTS, list of, 339.

BOWTEL or BOLTEL. The mediæval term for a plain moulding or shaft of a circular shape. See p. 928. See BOULTINE in GLOSSARY.

BOXINGS OF A WINDOW. See GLOSSARY.

BRAZING. The union of pieces of copper by heating and hammering them. See SOLDERING and WELDING.

BRENNA, V. See ARCHITECTS, list of, 321.

BRINGING FORWARD. Priming and painting new or old work, so that the whole shall have the same appearance when finished.

BRITTON, J. See ARCHITECTS, list of, 342.

BROACH. An old English term for a spire, and still so employed. Sometimes it is used to designate a spire rising from the tower without any parapet.

BUNNING, J. B. See ARCHITECTS, list of, 350.

C.

CANINA, L. See ARCHITECTS, list of, 343.

CARBOLIC ACID. This fluid has lately been obtained from creosote by distillation. By the use of a solution of Mc Dougall's patent prepared carbolic acid, sewage is rendered imputrescible, all smell being removed, and no further decomposition possible. A solution of it (about a pint to a cartload) has lately been mixed with the water sprinkled on roads by watering carts, by which a disinfecting action takes place on the droppings of horses, decomposing dust, &c. The powder may be used in dust-bins, water-closets, in whitewashing the walls of hospitals, &c. Formed into a soap, it can be employed in washing painted work and floors, or linen. Mixed carefully with oil of vitriol, sulphurous acid gas is liberated for fumigating an apartment. It is not poisonous.

CASE-HARDENING. The process by which the surfaces of soft iron are converted into a species of imperfect steel, sufficiently hard to resist the action of an ordinary file. Hodgkinson has proved the fallacy of the assertion that if the hard skin at the outside of a cast iron bar be removed, its strength comparatively with its dimensions will be much reduced. Bars planed down on all sides to an inch square, bore a breaking-weight quite equal to those of bars cast exactly an inch square.

CHAIN MOULDING. An ornament of the Norman period, carved in imitation of a chain.

CHANTLATE. A piece of wood fastened at the end of rafters, and projecting beyond the wall, to support several rows of slates or tiles, being so placed as to throw off the rainwater from the face of the wall. See A in *fig.* 701e.

CHARCOAL. Bones or vegetable matter decomposed by heat without the free access of air. Its sanitary properties consist in its power of absorbing gases, which is most efficient when the charcoal is powdered. Animal charcoal is better than that of wood, or of peat, for the purposes of disinfection. When cleansing cesspools, the charcoal should be mixed with the soil. When used to destroy foul air, the charcoal requires to be exposed in thin films, presenting the greatest possible surface. It is essentially necessary to the proper filtration of water. It is a bad conductor of heat, but conducts electricity.

CHEVET. A term used by French architects and antiquaries to denote the surrounding aisles of the choir of a cathedral, from their resemblance on the plan to the form of a bolster.

CHRISMATORY. A recess resembling a piscina, near the spot where the font originally stood, to contain the chrism, or holy oil, with which, after baptism, infants were anointed.

CLOCK TOWER. A tower specially designed to hold a clock with its quarter and hour bells. Bells which are to be rung should properly be placed in a distinct erection, as the vibration injures the clock.

COCKERELL, C. R. See ARCHITECTS, list of, 352.

COLUMNIATION. The employment of columns in a design.

COMPOUND PIER. A term sometimes given to a clustered column.

CONDY'S PATENT FLUID. Called, from its mode of action and effectiveness, " Nature's Disinfectant," it purifies, deodorizes, and disinfects, by the agency of nascent or ozonic oxygen, its active principle. It combines powerful purifying properties with a wholesome nature.

CORBIE STEPS. See CORBEL STEPS, in GLOSSARY.

CORE. Bricks or tiles brought out for the formation of cement cornices or other projections. See GLOSSARY. It is also the interior part of a lump of lime, which has not been sufficiently burnt. In slacking lump lime these " cores " will not disintegrate, consequently they can be removed: but when lime is ground, these lumps are ground up with it; the result is an inferior mortar.

COVARRUBIAS, A. See ARCHITECTS, list of, 210.

CREDENCE. The slab whereon, in the sacrifice of the mass, the elements are deposited previous to the oblation. Sometimes a plain recess, sometimes a slab on a bracket; it is in all cases placed on the south side of the altar. The word is derived from the Italian *Credenza*, a butlery or pantry.

CRENELLATED MOULDING. A moulding used in Norman architecture, carved into a resemblance of battlements, notchings, or indentations.

CROSS. The cross, a symbol of Christianity, has very naturally been extensively used in the monuments of the middle ages. It is unnecessary to give the ornamental and profusely decorated examples, which the student everywhere finds, and we shall therefore confine ourselves to the simple forms by which each cross is distinguished. When the two branches of the cross are equal in length, as in *fig.* 1384., the cross is called a Greek cross, and when the stem is longer than the arms, as in *fig.* 1385., it is a Roman or

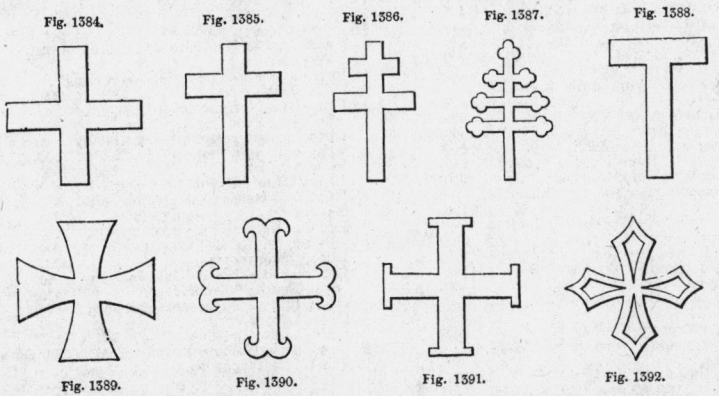

Fig. 1384.   Fig. 1385.   Fig. 1386.   Fig. 1387.   Fig. 1388.

Fig. 1389.   Fig. 1390.   Fig. 1391.   Fig. 1392.

Latin cross. When the figure has two arms, one longer than the other, as in *fig.* 1386. (the upper one meant as a representation of the inscription which was placed over the head of Christ), it is known by the name of the Lorraine cross, and has received that name from its being a bearing in the arms of the Dukes of Lorraine. By our own heralds this is called a patriarchal cross. The next cross, whose arms are triple, as *fig.* 1387., is the papal cross, and is one of the emblems of the papacy, signifying, perhaps, like the triple crown or tiara, the triple sovereignty over the universal church, the suffering church, and the triumphant church. The great majority of the western churches, with transepts, are constructed in the form of a Latin cross, those in the form of the Greek cross being very rare. Those in the form of the Lorraine cross are still rarer, and yet rarer are those constructed with triple transepts. There is another form called the truncated or *tau* cross, as *fig.* 1388., having the form of that letter, on which, as a plan, a few churches have been built. Considered as respects the contour, the cross in blason has been variously shaped and named. Thus, *fig.* 1389., in which the extremities widen as they recede from the centre, is called a cross *patée*. This is met with more frequently than any of the others. It is seen in the nimbus, on tombs, on shields, upon coins, &c. ; and is the usual form of the *dedication cross* found in religious structures. *Fig.* 1390. is by the French called *ancrée*, the extremities forming hooks, but by our own heralds it is called the cross *moline*. Crosses *flory* are those in which the ends are formed into trefoils, as is seen in *fig.* 1387., the papal cross above mentioned. *Fig.* 1391. is a cross *potent*, and *fig.* 1392. is the cross *cléchée*, as respects the outer lines of its form ; when it is *voided*, as shown by the inner lines, the ground or field is seen on which it lies.

CROWDE, CROUDE, or CROFT. The crypt of a church.

CUBIC FEET (as the quantity necessary to be allowed for health under varying circumstances). From 60 to 100 feet superficial is recommended for each bed. It is stated that a healthy man respires about 20 times in a minute, and inhales in that period about 700 cubic inches of air. Fresh air contains rather more than 23 per cent. of oxygen, and about $1\frac{1}{2}$ per cent. of carbonic acid ; by the process of respiration the oxygen is reduced, in round numbers, to 11 per cent., and the carbonic acid is increased to rather more than 8 per cent. Now, $3\frac{1}{2}$ per cent. of this gas render air unfit to support life ; so that a man, in respiring 700 cubic inches in a minute, *vitiates* about 1630 cubic inches, without taking into account the effect produced by the exhalation from the skin.

	Cubic Feet.
Fever Hospital, Islington, allows	{ 2300 per bed.
	{ 2010 „
Camp at Aldershot	. 1500 „
General Hospital, Bristol	. 1090 „
Lariboisière Hospital at Paris 1700 to 1860 „	
Vincennes Hospital . . 1200 to 1334 „	
Borough Hospital, Birkenhead . . 1430 „	
Soldiers' Hospital, Netley, 1315, 1406, 1800 „	
Herbert Hospital, Woolwich . . 1400 „	
Recently prescribed for Military Hos-	
pitals by the English Barrack and	
Hospital Commissioners,—in Great	
Britain . . . . . 1200 „	
Ditto, in hot climates . . . . 1500 „	
Ditto, in wooden hospitals, tents, and	
in permanent barracks . 400 to 600 „	
In 1858, 11 returns of Barracks from	
London, average . . . 400 „	
Ditto, 143 ditto from Ireland, average 400 „	
Ditto, 34 ditto from Scotland „ 432 „	
Ditto, 155 ditto from England „ 447 „	
Some returns were so low as . . 147 „	
Now recommended . . . 600 „	
Workhouses in Scotland . . . 480 „	
Clerkenwell Workhouse Infirmary,	
(lately) . . . . . 429 „	
St. Martin's ditto . . . . 428 „	
Greenwich ditto . . . . 450 „	
St. Leonard's, Shoreditch, ditto . 500 „	
St. George's, Hanover Square, ditto . 829 „	
Chelsea Workhouse Infirmary, highest 2260 „	
Marylebone Workhouse Infirmary,	
lowest . . . . . 206 „	
40 Metropolitan Workhouse Infirma-	
ries, average . . . . 555 „	
21 ditto, ditto, less than . . . 500 „	
City of London Workhouse Infirmary,	
average . . . . . 584 „	
East London Union, Sick Ward, aver-	
age . . . . . . 529 „	
Ditto, Infirmary, average . . . 549 „	
West London Union, Sick Ward,	
average . . . . . 639 „	
Ditto, Infirmary, average . . . 639 „	
Holborn Workhouse, Sick Ward,	
average . . . . . 495 „	
Mr. Farnall claims as a minimum . 1000 „	
Dr. Edward Smith considers ample . 500 „	

	Cubic Feet.
Minimum allowance for health in a	
sitting room . . . . . 800 per ind.	
A Meeting of Medical Officers had	
decided was sufficient in dwelling	
houses . . . . . 300 „	
London Hospital, smallest allowed . 800 per bed.	
Westminster Hospital . . . . 1100 „	
University College Hospital . . 1100 „	
Middlesex Hospital . . . . 1100 „	
St. Bartholomew's Hospital . . 1377 „	
London Hospital . . . . . 1700 „	
Guy's Hospital . . 1300 to 2000 „	
King's College Hospital . 1800 to 2068 „	

Dr. Parkes found that 2000 cubic feet per hour must be allowed in a hospital ward to keep down the carbonic acid at ·5 or ·6 per 1000 cubic feet. The normal amount being ·2 to ·5 or ·2 to ·5 volumes in 10,000. Fœtid smells were not entirely removed, if only 1200 or 1400 cubic feet were admitted.

Dr. Sankey found 800 cubic feet per hour insufficient to ventilate the wards of the Fever Hospital.

	Cubic Feet.
In registered Lodging Houses of Lon-	
don, Dublin, &c. . . 240 to 300 per bed.	
Poor Law dormitories in 1855, for	
healthy persons . . . . 300 „	
Ditto for sick persons, being used by	
day and night, rooms 10 to 12ft. high 500 „	
In modern Gaols . . 900 to 1000 „	
Surrey County Prison, each cell . 819 „	
Knutsford House of Correction, ditto 910 „	
Manchester City Prison, ditto . 844 „	
Lunatic Asylums in Scotland, gal-	
leries . . . . . 600 „	
Ditto, single rooms . . . . 1000 „	
Ditto in some crowded asylums. 2 in. 900 „	
Ditto, Devon, bedrooms . . . 470 „	
Ditto, Commissioners recommended . 550 „	
Ditto, Lanark. . . . . 800 „	
Ditto, private in Scotland . 200 to 300 „	
Cow Sheds, Holborn Board of Health 1000 per ani-	
The Cattle Plague broke out in Sheds [mal.	
allowing but . . . . 450 „	

It has been lately calculated, that the average space allowed to each person in London is 1220 square feet, while in Paris it is only 500 ditto.

Cushion capital. A capital used in very early mediæval architecture, resembling a cushion pressed down by a weight. It is also a cap consisting of a cube rounded off at its lower angles, largely used in the Norman period.

Cylinder. Table of the areas of cylinders from 9 to 15 inches' diameter. (See *par.* 1234. and **Glossary**):—

Diameter of Cylinder.	Area of Cylinder.	Diameter of Cylinder.	Area of Cylinder.	Diameter of Cylinder.	Area of Cylinder.
Inches.	Square Inches.	Inches.	Square Inches.	Inches.	Square Inches.
9	63·58	11½	103·84	13½	143·02
10	78·5	12	113·07	14	153·96
10½	86·56	12½	122·65	14½	165·04
11	95·01	13	132·66	15	176·62

Note.—The areas of cylinders are as the squares of their diameters.

D.

Dancette. The chevron, or zigzag moulding, in Norman architecture.

Deodorisation and Disinfection. The *Summary* of the "Hastings Prize Essay, 1865," on these subjects, states that:—I. For the sick room, free ventilation, when it can be secured, together with an even temperature, is all that can be required. II. For rapid deodorisation and disinfection, chlorine is the most effective agent known. III. For steady and continuous effect, ozone is the best agent known. IV. In the absence of ozone, iodine exposed in the solid form to the air, is the best. V. For that of fluid and semi-fluid substances undergoing decomposition, iodine is the best. VI. For the deodorisation and disinfection of solid bodies that cannot be destroyed, a mixture of powdered chloride of zinc or powdered sulphate of zinc, with sawdust, is the best. After this, a mixture of carbolic acid and sawdust, ranks next in order; and following on that, wood ashes. VII. For that of infected articles of clothing. &c., exposure to heat at 212° Fahr. is the only true method. And, VIII. For the deodorisation and disinfection of substances that may be destroyed, heat to destruction is the true method. Carbolic acid, Condy's fluid, Burnett's fluid, and Charcoal are among the materials supplied for this purpose.

DECIMAL EQUIVALENTS OF INCHES, FEET, AND YARDS; AND OF A SHILLING.

Fractions of an Inch.	Decimals of an Inch.	Decimals of a Foot.	Inches.	Decimals of a Foot.	Decimals of a Yard.
1	1·0000	·08333	1	·0833	0·0277
15/16	·9375	·07812	2	·1666	·0555
11/12	·9165	·07638	3	·2500	·0833
7/8	·8750	·07291	4	·3333	·1111
13/16	·8125	·06771	5	·4166	·1389
3/4 or 6/8	·7500	·06250	6	·5000	·1666
9/12	·7499	·06249	7	·5833	·1944
11/16	·6875	·05729	8	·6666	·2222
5/8	·6250	·05208	9	·7500	·2500
7/12	·5833	·04860	10	·8333	·2778
9/16	·5625	·04688	11	·9166	·3055
1/2	·5	·04166	12	1·0000	·3333
7/16	·4375	·03645			
5/12	·4166	·03472			

DECIMALS OF A SHILLING.

Fractions of an Inch.	Decimals of an Inch.	Decimals of a Foot.	d.	s.	d.	s.
3/8	·3750	·03125	1/2	·0416	6 1/2	·5416
3/12 or 1/3	·3333	·02777	1	·0833	7	·5833
5/16	·3125	·02604	1 1/2	·1249	7 1/2	·6250
1/4 or 2/8	·2500	·02083	2	·1666	8	·6666
3/16	·1875	·01562	2 1/2	·2082	8 1/2	·7083
2/12	·1666	·01388	3	·25	9	·75
1/8	·1250	·01041	3 1/2	·2916	9 1/2	·7916
1/12	·0833	·00694	4	·3333	10	·8333
1/16	·0625	·00521	4 1/2	·3750	10 1/2	·8750
			5	·4166	11	·9166
			5 1/2	·4583	11 1/2	·9583
			6	·5	12	1·0000

DECIMAL PARTS OF A POUND.

d.	Decimal.	d.	Decimal.	d.	Decimal.	s. d.	Decimal.
1/2	·00208	6	·02500	11 1/2	·04791	10 0	·5000
1	·00416	6 1/2	·02708	s. d.		11 0	·5500
1 1/2	·00625	7	·02916	1 0	·0500	12 0	·6000
2	·00833	7 1/2	·03125	2 0	·1000	13 0	·6500
2 1/2	·01041	8	·03333	3 0	·1500	14 0	·7000
3	·01250	8 1/2	·03541	4 0	·2000	15 0	·7500
3 1/2	·01458	9	·03750	5 0	·2500	16 0	·8000
4	·01666	9 1/2	·03958	6 0	·3000	17 0	·8500
4 1/2	·01875	10	·04166	7 0	·3500	18 0	·9000
5	·02083	10 1/2	·04375	8 0	·4000	19 0	·9500
5 1/2	·02291	11	·04583	9 0	·4500	20 0	1·0000

DIAPER WORK. The face of stone worked into squares or lozenges, with a leaf therein ; as over arches and between bands. It is generally done only in interior work for decorating a plain surface.

DOG-TOOTH ORNAMENT. This ornament, so greatly used in First Pointed or early English work, appears in the abacus of one of the capitals in the cloister at Monreale, in Sicily, 1182-94; and it is noted by J. G. Wigley as occurring in the jambs of the little church of the Cœnaculum at Jerusalem, now known as the mosque of the tomb of David, erected early in the Fourteenth century. He assigns the origin of the ornament, as well as of the "ball flower," to the Holy Land, the types being obtained from the *cyclamen* or gazelle's horn, and the red anemone. The use of it in Western Architecture, 1090-1187, curiously corresponds with the period of the first Crusades.

DOSSEL. See REREDOS.

DOVE-TAIL MOULDING. An ornament formed of running bands, as Example 3, *fig.* 188, and sometimes called a *triangular fret.*

DRAGGING. The operation of completing the surface of soft stone by means of a *drag*, which is a thin plate of steel with fine teeth on one edge, moved backwards and forwards by the workmen.

DRIPSTONE. The moulding in Gothic Architecture placed over an opening to throw off water. It is also called a *weather moulding* or *Hood mould* ; and *Label* when it is returned square.

DURAND, J. N. L. See ARCHITECTS, list of, 323.

E.

EARTH CLOSET. A convenience for the use of the occupants of a house, in lieu of a water closet, lately suggested by Rev. H. Moule, of Dorchester. Though adaptable to every dwelling, it is more appropriate to a country habitation. Two tubs are required, one being the store for dry common garden mould; the other, the receptacle for the deposits, over each of which is to be placed half a spadeful of the mould; this prevents any smell arising. When the tub is full, it may either be set aside for about a week or fortnight to dry, when it is then fit to be dried and re-used, or employed for garden purposes. Liquid sewage will require to be disposed of separately, as it saturates a large quantity of earth.

EARTH TABLE, or GROUND TABLE, and GRASS TABLE. The plinth, or lowest course of projecting stones immediately above the ground.

EASTER, or HOLY, SEPULCHRE. A recess for the reception of the holy elements consecrated on the Cœna Domini or Maunday Thursday, till high mass on Easter-day. The few examples in England remaining are generally shallow, under an arch of obtuse or broad ogee form, rising about three feet from the slab, and are placed on the north side of the church.

ELMES, H. L. See ARCHITECTS, list of, 334.

ENCAUSTIC WORK. An ancient mode of painting, in which the execution was accomplished by the application of heat. It would appear as if one process consisted in mixing the tints in hot wax which were then applied on the wall; and another, to coat the wall with wax after the tint had been given to the wall, rubbing in well the wax with hot cloths.

ENGLISH CATHEDRALS. The two following towns having had a cathedral formed in them, the leading dimensions are given, in continuation of the list in Book I. Chap. III. Sect. V.

MANCHESTER.—*Collegiate Church; Cathedral in* 1847.

Dates.	Founders.	Nave.	Choir.	Aisles.	Transept.	West Tower.
Circa.		L. B. H.	L. B. H.	L. B. H.		
1330	-	-	-	-	-	27 square; 140 feet high. Upper portion dates 1520.
1440 {	John Huntington	-	{ 81 25 6 — 57·6 inclusive of aisles. A crypt under it.	81 16 -	North, now St. James's Chantry, 16 by 17.	
1490 {	Bishop James Stanley -	88 29 -	110 inclusive of aisles and chapels.	88 18·6		

Length internally, 215 ft. by 112 ft.; externally, 232 ft. by 130 ft.

Lady Chapel, cir. 1330, 16 feet square. St. John Baptist or Derby Chapel, on north of north aisle of choir, cir. 1500, 80 ft. by 26 ft.; and the Chapter-house, 22 ft. by 13 ft. 6 in. having an unequal apsidal end, are both by Bishop Stanley. Jesus' Chapel, on south side of nave aisle, 1506, is 35 ft. by 25 ft. The Trafford Chapel, on south side of nave aisle, 1506, is 27 ft. by 21 ft. 6 in.; St. George's Chapel, adjoining the last, 1508, is 25 ft. by 27 ft. 6 in.; and the Bibby porch, 1520, is 13 feet square. The Strangeways Chapel, on the north side of nave aisle, 1508, is 68 ft. by 22 ft. The Oldham Chapel, opening out of the Derby Chapel, 1518, is 15 ft. by 12 ft.

RIPON.—*Collegiate Church* (by James I.); *Cathedral in* 1839.

Date.	Founder.	Nave.	Choir.	Aisles.	Transept.	3 Towers.
		L. B. H.	L. B. H.	L. B. H.	L. B. H.	
1154–81	Roger, Archbishop of York.	169 87 88	Portion of Choir.	Included.	132 36 N - 33 s -	110 feet. The spires covered with lead, now taken down, were 110 feet higher.
1288–1300	- -	-	Great repairs.			
1317–40 {	Melton, Archbishop of York.	-	101 67 79	Included.		

Whole length internally, 270 ft. 5 in.

Chapter house, 34 ft. 8 in., 29 ft. wide, by 18 ft. 8 in. high, with an apsidal end, by Archb. Thomas, 1069–1100. The Lady Chapel, 1482, is over it, a most unusual position; it is now the library. Melton extended the church eastward to twice its former length. Great east window, 25 ft. by 51 ft. high, dates at the end of 14th century. Stalls date 1404. The crypt under centre tower is 11 ft. 5 in. by 7 ft. 8 in., and 9 ft. 4 in. high; it is dedicated to the Holy Trinity.

ENTAIL or ENTAYLE. The more delicate and elaborate portions of carved mediæval decoration.

ESCUTCHEON. A shield for armorial bearings, a mode of decoration extensively used in Gothic architecture. A plate for protecting the keyhole of a door; or one to which the handle of a door is attached.

ESSEX, J. See ARCHITECTS, list of, 318.

F.

FALDSTOOL. A moveable reading desk provided with a kneeling shelf at the foot thereof.

FALL OF LAND. A measure used in Scotland, equal to 36 square yards.

FEATHERINGS. The *cusps*, plain or decorated, at the ends of a *foil* in tracery.

FEMUR. See TRIGLYPH, in GLOSSARY.

FLANGE. A projection round the edge of a pipe or other article of metal, to admit of its being fastened to a similar projection by screws, rivets, or bolts. The L-shaped pieces of wrought iron, used in girder work, are also called " flanges," and are employed for securing plates at right angles to each other, and for suspending one piece of work to another.

FLOOR CLOTH. Stout canvas covered with coarse oil paint, and then printed with a pattern, more or less elaborate. It should be thoroughly dry before being used, else it soon wears out. *Kamptulicon*, a preparation of caoutchouc and ground cork; and *Linoleum*, produced from oxidised linseed oil mixed with ground cork, and rolled on to strong canvas, are late and good substitutes for the common floor cloth.

FOIL. The small arcs in the tracery of Gothic windows or panelling. See *Cusp*.

FOLIATION. The use of small arcs or foils in forming tracery.

FOOT-STALL. The base or plinth of a building.

FORMERET. The arch rib, which in Gothic groining lies next the wall, and is consequently less than the other ribs which divide the vaulting.

FÖRSTER, L. See ARCHITECTS, list of, 351.

FREEING BEADS. The beads formed on the elbows of the boxings of a window, to allow of the shutters rising high enough to come on to the bead of the window sill.

FRET-WORK. Ornamental decoration raised in protuberances. See FRETTE in GLOSSARY.

G.

GABLET. A small gable, or gable-shaped decoration, as introduced on buttresses, &c.

GAERTNER, F. von. See ARCHITECTS, list of, 332.

GANDY, J. M. See ARCHITECTS, list of, 331.

GANDY-DEERING, P. J. See ARCHITECTS, list of, 335.

GARGOUILLE, or GURGOYLE. The carved representations of men, monsters, &c., on the exterior of a church, and especially at the angles of the tower, serving as waterspouts, being connected with the gutters for the discharge of the water from the roof.

GARRETING, or GALLETING. Inserting small splinters or chips of stone or flint, called *gallets*, in the mortar joints of rubble work, after the walls are built.

GASSE, S. and L. See ARCHITECTS, list of, 328.

GATEWAY. A passage or opening formed through an enclosure wall or fence. It is also given to a building placed at the entrance of a property, and through which access is obtained guarded by a gate, or formerly by a portcullis drawbridge.

GAUGED ARCH. One having the bricks formed radiating to a centre. The bricks have to be cut, and, in very good work, they are also rubbed, to get a fine joint.

GAUGED STUFF. In plasterer's work, stuff composed of three parts of lime putty and one part of plaster of Paris, to set quicker. In bricklayer's work, it is the same proportion of mortar and Roman or Portland cement, used for filletings and in setting chimney-pots.

GAY, P. See ARCHITECTS, list of, 336.

GEMMELS. A mediæval term for hinges.

GEOMETRY. The invention of the science has been referred to a very remote period: by some, to the Babylonians and Chaldeans; by others to the Egyptians, who are said to have used it for determining the boundaries of their several lands after the inundations of the Nile. Cassiodorus says that the Egyptians either derived the art from the Babylonians, or invented it after it was known to them. It is supposed that Thales, who died 548 B.C., and Pythagoras of Samos, who flourished about 520 B.C., introduced it from Egypt into Greece. See GLOSSARY.

GILLESPIE-GRAHAM, J. See ARCHITECTS, list of, 340.

GODROON or GADROON. An ornamented moulding, consisting of beadings or cablings.

GRASS TABLE. See *Earth table.*

GREE, GREES, GRESE, or GRYSE. An old word, signifying a step, steps, or degrees.

GWILT, J. See ARCHITECTS, list of, 353.

H.

HABITABLE ROOMS. These are required by the Metropolitan Building Act, 1855, to be not less than 7 feet in clear height. When placed in the roof they must be of that height at

least, throughout not less than one half of the area of such room. When underground, they must be of that height at least, 1 foot of which must be above the surface of the footway of the street. They must have, for their entire frontage, an open area from 6 inches below the level of the floor to the surface of the footway and 3 feet wide in every part; they must be effectually drained; have a fire-place with a proper chimney or flue; and an external glazed window of at least 9 superficial feet in area, clear of the frame, and made to open in an approved manner. There must be appurtenant to such room or cellar a water closet or privy, and an ashpit furnished with proper doors and coverings.

HAGIOSCOPE. (Gr. ἅγιος, holy, and σκοπὸς, mark.) An aperture made in the interior walls or partitions of a church, generally on the sides of the chancel arch, to enable persons in the aisles to see the elevation of the host. They are technically called *squints*, and sometimes *elevation apertures.*

HAMILTON, D. See ARCHITECTS, list of, 348.

HAMILTON, T. See ARCHITECTS, list of, 344.

HAVEUS, T. See ARCHITECTS, list of, 230.

HAVILAND, J. See ARCHITECTS, list of, 338.

HEARTH. See SLAB.

HERRING - BONE WORK. Courses of stones or bricks laid angularly in the face of a wall, so that those in each course are placed obliquely to the right and left alternately. Sometimes there is a horizontal course of stones or bricks laid between each angular course. See also in GLOSSARY.

HIP KNOB. A finial, placed at the end of the ridge piece of a roof, and against which abuts the barge board of a gable; it is often finished with a pendant.

HOOD MOULD. The projecting moulding forming a *drip* to protect the other mouldings to a door or window.

HÔTEL. The term applied on the Continent to a large house, either of a private or public nature. One of the most interesting of the former class in Paris, is that of the celebrated Hôtel de Cluny (*fig.* 1393.), now containing a museum of mediæval antiquities. It was erected at the end of the 15th century, the works being resumed in 1490 after

Fig. 1393.   HÔTEL DE CLUNY; PARIS.

some interruption, by Jacques d'Amboise, Abbé of Cluny. (See page 237.)

HURRICANE. A violent storm of wind, calculated at a velocity of from 80 to 100 miles per hour; and to exercise a force of from $31\frac{1}{2}$ to 49 lbs. per superficial foot. In places where buildings are subject to destructive hurricanes, the precautions to be observed have been described in the *Papers*, &c. of the Corps of Royal Engineers, new series, 1851, vol. i. The whole of the roof should be fixed down to the wall-plate, and the wall-plate to the wall; the wall being made strong enough to resist the powerful current of air rushing against it. Where buildings are of wood, the framework should be tied into the ground, or into stone piers fixed in the ground. During the hurricane at

Barbadoes, on the 11th August 1831, buildings having substantial partitions at short intervals, withstood the blast, whilst others without them were blown down. Inside buttresses would answer the purpose. Shutters should be made to open on pivots at top and bottom. Joists used in galleries and verandahs, when let into the wall, tend to upset it. All brickwork should be English bond well grouted throughout, the bricks having first been well saturated with water, and the mortar made of four parts of sand carefully selected, mixed with one of coral lime ; this mixture sets very strong. In the hurricane mentioned, a small building arched like a gunpowder magazine was uninjured ; and an hospital building, well tied with iron, also withstood the storm. Roofs when reconstructed had diagonal bracing inserted to stiffen the rafters ; parapet walls were found to protect roofs. Flat roofs, such as those used in the Mauritius, are perhaps the best to use.

I.

IMBRICATED TRACERY. A pattern formed like the tiles on a roof.

INTERLACING ARCHES. Arches, as in an arcade, the mouldings of which intersect each other, as frequently seen in the Norman period of Gothic architecture. Milner supposed the Pointed style to have had its origin from them.

INWOOD, H. W. See ARCHITECTS, list of, 322.

ISLE or ILE. The old way of writing *aisle* or *aile.*

J.

JETTY. The projecting part of a building, as an upper storey beyond a lower one.

JIBLET CHEEK. See GIBLET CHECK, in GLOSSARY.

JUBÉ. (Fr.) The rood loft or screen at the entrance to the choirs of French cathedrals. In England it is usually called the *chancel screen.* It is also the stand (often ending upwards in an eagle with expanded wings) on which the Gospel is placed to be read, receiving its name from the words " Jube Domne benedicere," used by the deacon when the missal is presented to him by the officiating priest at mass, previous to the reading of the Gospel.

JUVARA, F. See ARCHITECTS, list of, 270.*

K.

KAMPTULICON. An elastic covering for floors. See FLOORCLOTH.

KEBLAH or KIBLEH. The point in a mosque designating the direction of the temple of the Mahometans at Mecca.

KEEL. The fillet, raised edge, or sharp arris, formed on roll mouldings, by which the heaviness of the large ones was relieved, and diversity gained without loss of mass.

KERB and KIRB. See CURB STONES.

KERNEL or KERNELLE. See CRENELLE.

KEYSTONE. In GOTHIC VAULTING ; see PENDENT.

KLENZE, L. VON. See ARCHITECTS, list of, 349.

KNOT or KNOB. A bunch of leaves or flowers, as the bosses at the ends of a label ; at the intersection of ribs ; and in capitals.

L.

LAGGING or LAGGINS. The planks laid on the ribs forming the centreing of an arch, to carry the stones or bricks.

LANTERN. The internally polygonal tower over the intersection of the nave with the transepts of a church, as at Ely Cathedral ; St. Helen's, York ; &c. It is either formed of open work at the sides, or it is glazed.

LEAF. One side of a door, upright slab of stone, &c.

LEAR BOARD. The plank fastened on the feet of the rafters to carry the side piece of the lead of a gutter under the bottom rows of the slating or tiling.

LECETRN. The reading desk placed in the choir of mediæval churches. It was made in the shape of a pillar, with a slab for the book, and was usually of brass, sometimes elaborately carved. It was superseded by the *reading desk* after the Reformation.

LEDGMENT. A string course or horizontal moulding. *Ledgment table* is applied to any of the projections of a plinth in Gothic architecture, except the lowest or *earth table.*

LEVELLING. In the practice of levelling, it is evident that the level line, carried on by means of a spirit level or other instrument used for the purpose, is a tangent to the earth : it is therefore necessary to make an allowance for the difference between the true level B C and the apparent level B D. This difference is, of course, equal to the excess D C of the secant of the arch of distance above the radius of the earth. Hence, from station to station, accordingly, allowance must be made. The subjoined Table exhibits the corrections or values of the length C D.

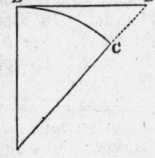

Distance or BC.	Diff. of Lev. or CD.	Distance or BC.	Diff. of Lev. or CD.	Distance or BG.	Diff. of Lev. or CD.		Distance or CB.	Diff. of Lev. or CD.	
Yards.	Inches.	Yards.	Inches.	Miles.	Feet.	In.	Miles.	Feet.	In.
100	0·026	900	2·081	$\frac{1}{4}$	0	0$\frac{1}{2}$	6	23	11
200	0·123	1000	2·570	$\frac{1}{2}$	0	2	7	32	6
300	0·231	1100	3·110	$\frac{3}{4}$	0	4$\frac{1}{2}$	8	42	6
400	0·411	1200	3·701	1	0	8	9	53	9
500	0·643	1300	4·344	2	2	8	10	66	4
600	0·925	1400	5·038	3	6	0	11	80	3
700	1·260	1500	5·784	4	10	7	12	95	7
800	1·645	1600	6·580	5	16	7	13	112	2

Lierne rib. A short rib in vaulting. See Book II. Chap. I. *fig. 590e.*

Lift or Hoist. A machine lately introduced into warehouses, to raise goods from the lower to the higher floors of the building; and worked either by manual or by hydraulic power. Lately it has been placed in large houses and in hotels, for the purpose of raising fuel, luggage, &c. to each floor: in some instances the platform has been formed into a room for the accommodation of persons while being hoisted to an upper, or lowered to an under floor, without the fatigue of walking up and down long flights of steps.

Lightning conductor. A metal rod fixed to the highest part of a building, carried down the face of it, and into the earth, for the purpose of attracting the fork of lightning and carrying it away from the other metal-work of the structure. Newall supplies copper rope of $\frac{3}{8}$, $\frac{1}{2}$. and $\frac{5}{8}$ inch diameter, with copper points and fittings. A conductor requires fixing with proper isolators and attachments, to prevent the interruption of the electric current. See p. 688. Hart and Son supply a sort of wire chain under Spratt's patent.

Locutory. An apartment in a monastery in which the monks were allowed to converse when silence was enjoined elsewhere.

Loft. An upper platform, as in Scotland, where it was applied to the gallery in a church. In modern usage it is limited to the place immediately under the rafters, as *cockloft* in a house, *hay-loft* in a stable, &c. See Solar.

Loggia. (It.) In its strict meaning, a lodge ; but usually signifying a gallery open to the air, and used for shelter, or from which to obtain a prospect.

Long and Short work. A rough sort of building, consisting of quoin stones placed flat and upright alternately. Many writers consider such masonry as a mark of 11th century work, and call it Saxon work.

Louvre, Luffer, or Lever. See Boarding Luffer in Glossary.

Louvre. A turret or lantern over a hall or other apartment with openings for the escape of smoke or steam.

Low side window. A small opening like a window, usually placed in the south chancel wall, and lower than the other windows, for what purpose is not known. It has been called a *Lychnoscope.*

Lozenge moulding. An ornament used in Norman architecture. See Example 8, *fig.* 188.

Lucarne. The same as Dormer.

Lych-gate or Corpse-gate (from the Anglo-Saxon *Leich*, a dead body). A gate at the entrance of a church-yard, where the coffin was set down for a few minutes before burial. It is generally of wood, and often thatched. Lych-gates are not of frequent occurrence in England. In Wales many of them may be seen.

M.

Manhole. An opening formed over a sewer, or by the side of it, large enough to admit a man to enter to do repairs, &c. when requisite. It is also formed on the top of large boilers, to give access to clean out the interior ; and also over a cesspool for the same purpose. A manhole has usually a close-fitting cover, well set to prevent the escape of steam, foul air, &c.

Market cross. A cross set up in a market-place. The primitive form was a long shaft with a cross stone set upon a number of steps. Subsequently it was constructed in an elaborate manner ; and later, a sort of arched structure was erected around the central pillar. In Scotland many were finished with a crowning work.

Mehrab. See Almehrab in Glossary.

Merlon. The plain parts of an embattled parapet, between the *crenelles* or embrasures.

Miserere. A small moveable seat attached on an horizontal axis to a stall in a church or cathedral. It was so contrived that if, during the performance of religious ceremonies, the occupier of it slept, he would fall on (perchance) the floor. Hence the name.

Monial. An old way of writing Mullion, and still used by some writers.

Morrison, Sir R. and W. V. See Architects, list of, 333.

MOULD STONE. One of the stones of a moulded jamb.

MUSJID. The Arabic for a mosque; the *jumma musjid* is the chief mosque of a city.

N.

NARTHEX. An inclosed space in the ancient basilica when used as a Christian church; and also of an ante-temple or vestibule outside the church; it is thus used as synonymous with *porch* and *portico*.

NASH, J. See ARCHITECTS, list of, 325.

NOTATION. In the early periods of the Roman notation, *four* was written IIII., this has been changed into IV.; *nine* was written VIIII., now IX.; *forty* was written XXXX., now XL. *Five hundred* was originally written I⊃., now D.; a *thousand* CI⊃., now M. The number I⊃ = 500, is increased in value *ten* times for every ⊃ annexed. Thus I⊃⊃ = 5,000; I⊃⊃⊃ = 50,000, and so on. The number CI⊃ = 1000 is increased in value *ten* times for every C and ⊃ prefixed or annexed to it. Thus CCI⊃⊃ = 10,000, &c. This notation is not now in use, but will be found in works of the 17th century.

NOTATION, ARCHITECTURAL. The method adopted of placing signs to figures when marking dimensions on drawings. Thus, in lieu of writing *feet, inches*, and parts of an inch, certain dashes are used, ′ for feet, ″ for inches, and ‴ for parts; or ° for feet, ′ for inches, and ″ for parts. There is no settled method for these marks.

O.

OGEE ARCH. A pointed arch, the sides of which are each formed with a double curve. (See *fig. 629g.*). It frequently appears in the decorated period of Gothic architecture, and occasionally in that of the perpendicular; chiefly in small ornamental work, as shrines and canopies; its inflected curves weaken it too much for supporting great weights. In some late work, this arch is also made to curve forward.

OILLETS or OYLETTS. Small openings or *eyelet holes*, seen in mediæval military buildings, through which missiles could be discharged without exposing the soldier.

ORIENTATION. (Lat. Oriens.) The deviation of a church from due east, it being supposed that the chancel points to that part of the east in which the sun rises on the day of the patron saint. This point, however, has not been fully investigated.

OVERISTORY. The *clear-* or *clere-story* of a building.

P.

PACE. A portion of a floor slightly raised above the general level: a *dais*. It is also applied to a landing in a staircase; its prefix, *half* or *quarter*, determines the size of it.

PARCLOSE. The screen which separates chapels (especially at the east end of the aisles) from the body of the church. They are usually of wood, but are also sometimes of stone.

PARGE WORK; PARGETTING. A particular sort of plaster work, having patterns and ornaments raised upon it or indented, much used in interior decorations, and often on the exterior of half timber houses, during the Elizabethan period.

PARVISE TURRET. The small tower which encloses the staircase to the parvise.

PAVING SLABS. Experiments made by George Rennie upon slabs 12 inches long, 2½ inches wide, and one inch thick, laid flat on bearings 10 inches apart, the weight being suspended from the middle of each, gave the following results:—

		cwts.	qrs.	lbs.
I. Green Moor and Yorkshire Blue Stone, sustained	-	2	3	27
II. Ditto ditto White Stone	-	3	0	23
III. Caithness (Scotch) Stone - - -	-	7	2	17
IV. Valentia (Irish) Stone - - -	-	7	3	3
V. Bangor Slate (Welsh) - - -	-	17	0	12

Buchanan tried specimens of stones, the weights being piled on:—

Breaking weight. lbs.

Hailes,		794
Craigleith,	3 feet long, 9 inches broad, and 3 inches deep -	1,148
Arbroath,		1,848
Caithness, 3 „ 8¾ „ 2¾ „ -		3,291

(a very hard specimen.)

PERCH. A measure for brickwork used in Ireland, in place of the ROD in England. It is 21 feet in length, by 1 foot high, and 1 foot thick. It equals 15¾ cube feet. One thousand bricks, a quarter cart of sand, and one and a quarter hogshead of lime, will serve for four and a half perches. It is also there used for masonry, as well as in some counties in England.

PEW. (Fr. Piou.) An enclosed seat in a church. Pews were in use before the Reformation.

PHOTO-LITHOGRAPHY. A process of reproducing line engravings and drawings, either

copied, enlarged, or reduced, not exceeding one-sixth, and in some cases one-tenth, of the expense by other processes.

PIEND. An arris; a salient angle; a hip. It is a northern appellation.

PIEND CHECK. The rebate formed on the *piend* or angle at the bottom of the riser of a stone step of a stair, to catch upon the angle formed at the top of the under step.

PIPE. The following rule has been given to ascertain the strength requisite to be given to a pipe of the metals named. Let $d =$ internal diameter in inches; $t =$ thickness of metal in inches; $h =$ head of water in feet required to burst the pipe; $c =$ a constant, wrought iron, 200; cast iron, 73; copper, 87; brass, 83; and lead 10. Then $c\frac{t}{d} = h$; and $\frac{dh}{c} = t$. In practice, the thickness of cast iron water pipes is taken as $= \frac{1}{3}\sqrt{\text{diameter.}}$ *Hurst, Surveyor's Hand Book.*

PLAYFAIR, W. H. See ARCHITECTS, list of, 341.

POCKET. The space in the *pulley style* of a sashed window. It is also a space closed up, or nearly so, formed out of a larger space. Pockets are often found in the flues of old houses, and form one of the great causes of fires, by accumulating the soot, which at last heats and ignites adjoining woodwork.

POLE PLATE. A plate of timber laid on the ends of the tie-beams of a roof to receive the ends of the rafters, as B, in *Fig.* 688.

POLYCHROMY. The decoration of exteriors and interiors of buildings, with colours and tints. When executed in a single colour, it is called *monochrome* painting.

POLYGON. The following Table of the Lengths of Sides of Polygons to Radius I. may be a useful addition to paragraph 1026. in PRACTICAL GEOMETRY :—

No. of sides.	Circumscribed.	Inscribed.	No. of sides.	Circumscribed.	Inscribed.
3	3·4641	1·7321	8	0·8284	0·7654
4	2·0000	1·4142	9	0·7278	0·6840
5	1·4530	1·1756	10	0·6498	0·6180
6	1·1548	1·0000	11	0·5872	0·5634
7	0·9630	0·8677	12	0·5358	0·5176

POPPY HEADS, or POPPIES. The termination of the ends of open seats, often carved as heads, foliage, &c.

POSTERN. A side door or gate, usually employed in castellated architecture.

PROTHESIS, TABLE OF. See CREDENCE.

PUGIN, A See ARCHITECTS, list of, 324.

PUGIN, A. W. N. See ARCHITECTS, list of, 337.

Q.

QUEENS. A size slate used in roofing. See *par.* 2211c.

R.

RAINFALL. To calculate the quantity of water that will accumulate over a given area, multiply the inches of rainfall by 2,323,200, which will equal the cube feet per square mile. If by 14½, it will equal millions of gallons per acre. If by 3,630, it will equal cube feet per acre. (*Molesworth.*)

RANCE. A prop or shore; a term used in Scotland.

RECIPROCALS. A term in mathematics, mostly applied to the fraction made by inverting another fraction; thus $\frac{3}{2}$ is the reciprocal of $\frac{2}{3}$, and $\frac{1}{7}$ of $\frac{7}{1}$.

REED MOULDING. A moulding formed by three or more beads worked side by side.

RE-ENTERING ANGLE. An angle returned (A), in contradistinction to a square or solid angle (B), by the former of which much space is often lost in small houses, it being sometimes adopted from its picturesque qualities.

RESPONDS. Half-piers at the east or west end of the nave, transepts, or choir. They are sometimes formed in the shape of corbels.

RICARD DE MONTFERRAND, A. See ARCHITECTS, list of, 345.

RICKMAN, T. See ARCHITECTS, list of, 329.

RIVET. RIVETING. A small bolt of metal forged with a head. When required for use in joining plates together, or a plate with an *angle iron* as in a girder, the bolt is made red hot, placed into the holes prepared for it, and maintained there by one person, whilst another hammers at the opposite end until its superabundant length has been driven flat against the plate. Such work is called *riveted.*

ROAD ROLLING MACHINE. Two steam locomotives, invented respectively by Lemoine and Ballaison, the latter having been approved as the better of the two, have been lately employed in Paris to crush and consolidate the broken granite laid on the roadways in that city. This machine has two rollers, the engine being placed between, and the boiler on one of them. With fuel and water, the weight of the Ballaison steam roller is 13½ tons with springs; and an iron framework 15¼ tons. Its strength is 10 horse-power,

and its consumption of coal about 16 lb. per horse. It does its work in half the time and at half the cost that would be required were the work done by rollers drawn by horses, besides that it is performed more rapidly and completely. Over the Pont Royal, the roadway was covered with granite at ten o'clock in the evening, the rolling continued all night, and the roadway opened for traffic in the morning, it being sufficiently levelled to allow of vehicles passing without any inconvenience.

Rococo. A debased variety of the Louis XV. style of ornament. It is also applied to anything bad or tasteless in decoration.

Roll Moulding. A moulding in the shape of a cylinder. It occurs chiefly in the Early English and Decorated periods of Gothic architecture. When it has a slight edge at one part, it is a *scroll* or *edge* moulding, or a *ressant lorymer*. See page 930. When there is a fillet, it is a *roll and fillet* moulding; this is usually seen in the Decorated period. Keel.

Rood. A measure equal to 36 square yards, by which rubble masonry is valued in Scotland. Rubble walls at and below 18 inches thick are reduced to one foot; and above 18 inches thick, to 2 feet. It is also a measure of land. See Measures.

Rybat. The Scottish term for a reveal.

S.

Saddle back roofs. A tower having a top in the form of a common roof-gable. This form appears on a few old English towers (as a Brookthorpe Church, Northamptonshire, *cir.* 1260.), and in many continental churches.

Saint. See Symbols of Saints.

Sanatory measures. Precautions taken for curing diseases.

Sancte-bell Cot. A small erection at the east end of the nave for the reception of the bell that gives notice of the *Sanctus* being commenced, and also to warn the people of the approaching elevation of the Host.

Sanitory measures. Precautions taken for preserving the health.

Sarking. Thin boards for lining, &c. Boarding for slating is so called in Scotland.

Sash lines. The rope by which a sash is suspended in its frame. They are made either of common cord, which soon untwists and breaks; the "imperial patent flax sash lines" are made in four qualities. The sash lines made of jute have neither strength nor durability.

Schinkel, C. von. See Architects, list of, 330.

Sconcheon. (Fr. ecoinçon.) The portion of the side of an aperture, from the back of the jamb or reveal, to the interior of the wall.

Screed. In plastering or cementing large spaces, a ledge of about 4 inches and of the proper thickness is carefully formed, every 4, 5, or 6 feet apart, to form a gauge for the remainder of the work, which is then applied in the panel. a long float being worked over it, forcing off the superfluous plaster, and a clear face is obtained.

Sedilia. (Lat.) Seats provided for the clergy in the sacrifice of the mass, during that part of the office in which the "Gloria" and "Credo" are sung. Their proper place is only on the south side of the altar.

Sepulchre. See Easter, or Holy, Sepulchre.

Sgraffito (Ital.) See Scratch work, in Glossary.

Shearing. The action of cutting short off, as a pair of scissors acts upon paper. It is applied to a plate of metal acting upon a bolt or rivet.

Shelf. See *Sunk shelf* in Glossary.

Shilf. Slate broken into small pieces, as employed for mending roads in Cornwall.

Shouldering. In slating, a fillet of haired lime laid under the upper edge of the smaller and thicker kinds of slates, to raise them and prevent their being open at the lap; it also makes the joint weathertight. Sometimes the whole surface under the heads of any sized slates is so done, to prevent the slates cracking when stepped on.

Skew Corbel. See Summer stone.

Slab. The *front hearth* of a fireplace. The Metropolitan Building Act, 1855, requires that " There shall be laid, level with the floor of every story, before the opening of every chimney, a slab of stone, slate, or other incombustible substance, at the least twelve inches longer than the width of such opening, and at the least eighteen inches wide in front of the breast thereof:—That on every floor, except the lowest floor, such slab shall be laid wholly upon stone or iron bearers, or upon brick trimmers; but on the lowest floor it may be bedded on the solid ground:—and That the hearth or slab of every chimney shall be bedded wholly on brick, stone, or other incombustible substance, and shall be solid for a thickness of seven inches at the least beneath the upper surface of such hearth or slab." Such precautions are too frequently neglected in country houses, to their ultimate destruction by fire. No timbers should be placed under the hearths on any account. See Timbers.

Solar, or Sollar. An upper chamber; a loft.

SOLDER. The material used for uniting two pieces of lead, or of tin. See BRAZING, and WELDING.

SPALLS. Stone broken up into shapeless lumps. "Spawled masonry," in Ireland, consists of these lumps, about 6 to 14 inches, worked up in a wall, the joints of each stone matching those of the others around it; the faces of the stones are usually rough dressed with the hammer. It is the "uncoursed rubble work" of England.

SPIRAL. See VOLUTE.

SPIRE. A spire which is octagonal, the sides facing the cardinal points being continued to the eaves which project over the lower, and the diagonal faces being intercepted at the bottom by semipyramidical projections whose edges are carried from the angles of the tower upwards, terminating in points on the corresponding oblique faces of the spire, is called a *broach*; (Fr. Broche, a spit.) See Book III. Chap. III. Sect. 18.

SPUR. Carved timberwork at the doorway of old houses, to support a projecting upper story; some fine examples of the 14th century exist in York and other old towns.

SQUINCH. A small arch, or set of arches, formed across an angle, as in a tower, to form a base, or an octagon construction above it.

SQUINT. See HAGIOSCOPE.

STILTED ARCH. In describing the cave temples at Elephanta, Freeman, *History of Architecture*, p. 56, notes, "the stilt or *dé* above the capital of the piers, and the manner in which it spreads into the roof; this would seem to be the rudest and most primitive form of the bracket capital, though it has less projection, and extends only in two directions." And in the Addenda, he says, " for this very expressive word *stilt* I am under an obligation to a paper by Professor Orlebar. It expresses a portion of masonry above the regular column, which is constructively part of the pier, but in the direction assumes the form either of a portion of the arch or of a distinct member." The first confirmed use of the stilt occurs in the Arabian buildings at Cairo, where it may have been suggested by the *dé* of the anterior Egyptian style. In p. 272 he further says, "stilted arches cannot be always avoided, where openings of different breadth are required to be of the same height."

STONEWARE. A prepared clay, burnt and glazed; as for jars, bottles, and drain pipes, &c., to prevent water soaking through it.

STOUP. See PISCINA, in GLOSSARY.

STRING COURSE. A projecting horizontal course of stone, continued along the face of a building, frequently under windows, to form a tie or bonding course. It is either plain or moulded.

STUMP TRACERY. The later or after Gothic of Germany has tracery in which the ribs are made to pass through each other, and are then abruptly cut off. This may be called *stump tracery*, according to Professor Willis.

SUMMER STONE. The lowest stone at the end of a gable, stopping the eaves of the tiling or slating. The first piece of the *tabling* is worked in the solid of the summer stone, and so becomes an abutment and support for the rest. It is also called a *skew corbel*.

SYMBOL. An attribute or sign accompanying a statue, or a picture of a personage, in allusion to some passage in the life of the person represented, and hence often used as a figurative representation of the figure itself. The symbols connected with the metals are delineated in the GLOSSARY, s. v. METALS. From the constant occurrence of symbols in the edifices of the middle ages it may be useful to insert a list of them, as attached to the Apostles and Saints, most commonly found. The Cross has been received as a symbol of Christianity.

HOLY APOSTLES.

St. Peter.—Bears a key, or two keys with different wards.

St. Andrew.—Leans on a cross, so called from him; called by heralds the "saltire."

St. John Evangelist.—With a chalice, in which is a winged serpent. When this symbol is used, the eagle, another symbol of him, is never given.

St. Bartholomew.—With a flaying knife.

St. James the Less.—A fuller's staff, bearing a small square banner.

St. James the Greater.—A pilgrim's staff, hat, and escalop shell.

St. Thomas.—An arrow, or with a long staff.

St. Simon.—A long saw.

St. Jude.—A club.

St. Matthias.—A hatchet.

St. Philip.—Leans on a spear; or has a long cross in the shape of a T.

St. Matthew.—A knife or dagger.

St. Mark.—A winged lion.

St. Luke.—A bull.

St. John.—An eagle.

St. Paul.—An elevated sword, or two swords in saltire.

St. John Baptist.—An Agnus Dei.

St. Stephen.—With stones in his lap.

SAINTS.

St. Agatha.—Her breast torn by pincers.

St. Agnes.—A lamb at her feet.

St. Aidan.—A stag crouching at his feet.

St. Alphege.—His chasuble full of stones.

St. Anagradesma.—Covered with leprosy.

St. Anne.—Teaching the Blessed Virgin to read. Her finger usually pointing to the words *Radix Jesse Floruit.*

St. Antony, Eremite.—Devil appears to him in the shape of a goat.

St. Anthony of Padua.—Accompanied by a pig.

St. Apollonia.—With a tooth.

St. Barbara.—With a tower in her hands.

St. Blaise.—With a woolcomb.

St. Boniface.—Hewing down an oak.

St. Britius.—With a child in his arms.

St. Canute.—Lying at the foot of the altar.

St. Catherine.—With a wheel and sword.

St. Cecilia.—With an organ.

St. Christopher.—A giant carrying the infant Saviour on his shoulder across a stream. A monk, or female figure, with a lantern on the further side.

St. Clement.—With an anchor.

St. David.—Preaching on a hill.

St. Denis.—With his head in his hands.

St. Dorothy.—Bears a nosegay in one hand and a sword in the other.

St. Dunstan.—Bears a harp.

St. Edith.—Washing a beggar's feet.

St. Edmund.—Fastened to a tree and pierced with arrows.

St. Edward.—Bearing in his hand the Gospel of St. John.

St. Eunuchus.—A dove lighting on his head.

St. Etheldreda, Abbess.—Asleep, a young tree blossoming over her head.

St. Eustachius, or *St. Hubert.*—A stag appearing to him, with a cross between its horns.

St. Fabian.—Kneeling at the block with a triple crown at his side.

St. Faith.—With a bundle of rods.

St. George.—With the Dragon.

St. Gertrude, Abbess.—With a loaf.

St. Giles, Abbot.—A hind with an arrow piercing her neck, standing on her hind legs, and resting her feet in his lap.

St. Gudula.—With a lantern.

St. Hilary.—With three books.

St. Hippolytus.—Torn by wild horses.

St. Hugh.—With a lantern.

St. Januarius.—Lighting a fire.

St. Joachim.—With a staff, and two doves in a basket.

St. Lawrence.—With a gridiron.

St. Magnus.—Restoring sight to a blind man.

St. Margaret.—Trampling on a dragon, a crosier in her hands.

St. Martin.—Giving half his cloak to a beggar.

St. Nicholas.—With three naked children in a tub, in the end whereof rests his pastoral staff.

St. Odilo, Abbot.—With two goblets.

St. Pancras.—Trampling on a Saracen, a palm branch in his right hand.

St. Richard.—A chalice at his feet.

St. Rosaly.—With a rock in her arms.

St. Sebastian.—As St. Edmund, but without a crown.

St. Ursula.—Surrounded with virgins much less in size than herself.

St. Vincent.—On the rack.

St. Walburga.—Oil distilling from her hand.

St. Waltheof.—Kneeling at the block, the sun rising.

St. Winifred, Abbess.—With her head in her arms.

St. Wulfstan.—Striking his pastoral staff on a tomb.

THE BLESSED VIRGIN is usually represented—

1. At the Annunciation, with an almond-tree flourishing in a flower-pot.
2. At her Purification with a pair of turtle doves.
3. In her Agony, with a sword piercing her heart.
4. In her " *Repose* " (death).
5. In her Assumption.
6. With the blessed Saviour in her lap.
7. In her Ecstasy, kneeling at a faldstool, which faces the Temple, the Holy Dove descending on her.

Martyrs hold palms; *Virgins,* lamps, or, if also Martyrs, lilies and roses; *Confessors,* lilies; *Patriarchs,* wheels.

Glories round heads are circular, except when living prelates eminent for holiness are represented, when they are square.

HUSENBETH, F. C. *Emblems of Saints.* 2nd edition, 12mo. London, 1860. TWINING, L. *Symbols and Emblems of Early and Mediæval Christian Art.* 93 plates, 4to. London, 1852.

SYMBOLISM. The remarks on this subject included by Mr. Gwilt in his Appendix are subjoined :—" Invested with much of the character of chivalry and romance, the mediæval period has been often stated to have expressed in matter its spiritual impressions. The aspiring vertical lines of its monuments have by some been considered types of aspiration after the Divinity. This may or may not have been the case, but there cannot be other than an indisposition to believe in symbolism, when there are so many forms in nature whose imitation, or the study whereof, would lead to the same results. Holding symbolism in churches as an idle conceit, not much will be said on that subject ; but a few specimens of the nonsense it induces may as well be set down. The venerable Bede, for instance, says that the walls of a church are a symbol of the Christian worshippers that frequent the edifice. ' Omnes parietes templi per circuitum omnes sanctæ ecclesiæ populi sunt, quibus super fundamentum Christi locatis, ambitum orbis replevit.' The venerable scribe, be it observed, is speaking of Solomon's temple. Again, in respect

of doors, we have ' Ostium autem templi Dominus est, quia nemo venit ad Patrem nisi per illum,' &c. As to the windows, they are symbols of the saints and spiritual worshipers; ' Fenestræ templi sunt sancti et spirituales.' To come, however, to recent symbolism, we find that the moderns have discovered that the principal entrance of a church is a symbol of our entrance into physical and moral life ; that the tympanum, or gable-like form, over the great western porch (whose origin is the Greek pediment, but raised to conform with the character of the style), is a symbol of the Holy Trinity ; the great rose window at the western end of a church is, from its circular form, accounted a symbol of Divine Providence! At Amiens, the four rose windows have been considered symbolical of the four elements! In respect of the towers, that on the left is said to represent the ecclesiastical and spiritual hierarchy, and that to the right, order, that is, the civil or temporal power! and generally, where four horizontal divisions occur, the lower one is symbolical of the curé, the next upwards of the dean or archdeacon, the third of the bishop, and the fourth of the archbishop. Should a fifth horizontal division occur, the primate is the type. So in the right-hand tower, the lowest compartment represents the mayor, and in succession upwards appear a count, a duke, a king ; and if the tower be covered with a spire, no less than an emperor appears. One is almost surprised that there is no symbol to represent the *suisse* of the continental, nor the beadle of our churches in this country. The interior of a church, according to the symbolists, affords some further curious features of mysticism. The principal entrance is at the *foot* of the Cross, because, by the use of the FEET (i.e. travelling) the Gospel was preached ! What is called *canting* heraldry surely does not equal this. The nave is said to represent the body of the faithful! The ceiling over the altar is accounted a symbol of heaven, and the chapels round the altar are said to represent the *aureola* round the head of Christ ! But it is scarcely worth while to waste more time on the consideration of such absurdity, where the things have been ingeniously fitted to the types, instead of the converse. There is, however, one other point connected with the subject, which has been recently revived, and a few words must be expended in notice of it." This is the *vesica piscis*, whose form has been noticed in Book III. Chap. III. Sect. 3.

T.

TASSELS, TORSEL, or TOSSEL. The plate of timber for the end of a beam or of a joist to rest on.

TERAM. The scroll at the end of a step.

THOMOND, T. See ARCHITECTS, list of, 319.

THROUGH or THOROUGH STONE. A bond stone ; a heading stone going through the wall.

TIE ROD. The iron rod securing the feet of the principal rafters in the manner, and in lieu, of the tie-beam.

TILTING FILLET. A chamfered fillet laid under slating or tiling, to raise it where it joins the wall, and prevent water from entering the joint.

TIMBERS. It is advisable, as directed by the Metropolitan Building Act, 1855, that no timber or woodwork be placed in any wall or chimney breast, nearer than 12 inches to the inside of any flue or chimney opening:—Under any chimney opening within 18 inches from the upper surface of the hearth of such chimney opening:—Within two inches from the face of the brickwork or stonework about any chimney or flue, where the substance of such brickwork or stonework is less than 8½ inches thick, unless the face of such brickwork or stonework is rendered :—and that no wooden plugs be driven nearer than 6 inches (not enough) to the inside of any chimney opening.

TOUCH STONE. A smooth black stone like marble. It was much used for tombs in the 16th and 17th centuries, as in that of Henry VII.

TRENAIL. A large cylindrical wooden pin, used in roof work and framing.

TRIBUNE. See APSIS.

TUCK POINTING. In old brickwork, after it has been well washed and the mortar raked out, the joints are filled with new mortar ; the face of the work is then coloured yellow or red, as desired. Lines to mark the joints are made by putting on a ridge of lime putty with the point of the trowel over the new mortar, and cutting it straight and to the required width by means of a straight edge and knife.

TUFA. A mass of volcanic earth, consolidated. *Tufo* is a mass of agglomerated sand without volcanic character. *Tufaceous*, mixed with *tufo*.

U.

UNDERCROFT. A vault under a church or chapel.

UNDERPINNING. See GLOSSARY. It is called *goufing* in Scotland.

UNDERPITCH GROIN. See WELCH GROIN, in GLOSSARY.

V.

VAULTING SHAFT. A pillar, sometimes rising from the floor, or only from the capital of a pier, or even only from a corbel, from the top of which spring the *vaulting ribs* of the groining.

Verge boards. See **Barge boards**, in **Glossary**.

Vesica Piscis. See Book III. Chap. III. Sect. 3.

Vitruvian Scroll. See **Glossary**, *fig.* 1365, *sv*, **Scroll**.

Volute. Modes of describing the spiral of the Ionic Order are given in *pars.* 1925*b*. and 2576.

W.

Washer. A flat piece of iron, or other metal, pierced with a hole for the passage of a screw, between whose nut and the timber it is placed, to prevent compression on a small surface of the timber. Also the perforated metal plate of a sink or drain, which can be removed for letting off the waste water, and thus more easily cleansing it.

Wasting. Splitting off the surplus stone from a block, with a point or a pick, reducing it to nearly a plain surface. In Scotland it is called *clouring*.

Waves. In many engineering works, the *weight of the stone* to be employed is of the utmost importance, especially for low buildings occasionally under water, where there is a rapid current, or where they are subject to the influence of powerful waves. Such circumstances will require a heavier stone to be used than may at first have been considered necessary, because all bodies immersed are reduced in weight by so much as is equal to that of the bulk of water which they displace. The force of the waves at Skerryvore lighthouse was found to be 4,335 lbs. per square foot; that at Bell Rock lighthouse, was 3,013 lbs. The highest force observed was 6,000 lbs. For weight of water, see **Weight**.

Weight of Man. For the guidance of the architect in providing sufficient strength in a floor loaded with human beings, the following weights are subjoined:—

Mean weight of a	Belgian	140·49 lbs.	Mean height,	5 feet	$6\frac{3}{4}$ inches.
„	Frenchman	136·89 „	„	5 „	4 „
„	Englishman	150·98 „	„	5 „	$9\frac{1}{2}$ „

The weight in travelling carriages usually taken is 165 lbs.

Supposing, therefore, each individual in standing to occupy 2·5 superficial feet, which would be close to one another, and indeed closer than pleasant, on a square of flooring, there would be $\frac{100}{2\cdot5}=40$ persons, and $40 \times 150\cdot98$ lbs. $=2\cdot96$ tons. The average surface of a man's body is usually considered about 15 superficial feet, which would give a cubic content of 3·95 feet, and a consequent specific gravity of 612.

Weight of Materials. As in the construction of warehouses, it is essential for the architect to know the probable weight of merchandise which his client may probably put upon the respective floors, the following tables will be found useful. The second one is taken from the *Papers of the Corps of Royal Engineers*, 1832, iii. 192, contributed by Major Harry D. Jones. The weights of many building materials have been named in the several sections of Chapter II. Book II.

Articles.	Weight of a cubic ft. lbs.	Cubic feet = one ton.	Articles.	Weight of a cubic ft. lbs.	Cubic feet = one ton.
Ashes - - - -	37	$60\frac{1}{2}$	Hay, well pressed -	8	
— 52 feet=1 chaldron.			Indigo - - -		46·6
Brimstone - - -		19·8	Iron, cast - - -	450	5
Chalk, from - -	140	$15\frac{1}{2}$	— wrought - -	487	$4\frac{5}{8}$
— to - - - -	166	$13\frac{3}{4}$	Lime, stone - -	53	$42\frac{1}{4}$
Clay, from - - -	120	$18\frac{2}{3}$	— chalk - - -	44	51
— to - - - -	135	17	Marl - - - -	120	18
Coal, Cannel - -	54	$26\frac{2}{3}$	Mortar, from (old) -	88	$25\frac{1}{2}$
— Welch - - -	58	39	— to (new) - -	119	19
— Newcastle - -	50	45	Night soil - - -		18
— Navy allowance -		48	Sand, from - - -	90	$23\frac{1}{2}$ to 25
Coals, average - -		45·3	— river - - -	118	19
— solid - - -	80		Shingle - - -	89	$25\frac{1}{2}$
Coke - - - -	47	48	Slate - - - -	180	$12\frac{1}{2}$
Cork - - - -		149·34	Straw - - - -	$3\frac{1}{2}$	Truss=36 lbs.
Concrete - - -	120	$18\frac{2}{3}$	— well pressed - -	$5\frac{1}{3}$	
Earth, from - -	95	$23\frac{1}{2}$	Sugar - - - -		69·0
— to - - - -	126	18	— hogshead 3.11 in		
Fir - - - -		65·16	middle = $15\frac{1}{2}$ cwt.		
Flint - - - -	164	$13\frac{2}{3}$	Tallow - - -		38·0
Glass, Crown - -	157	$14\frac{1}{4}$	Thames ballast - -		20·0
— Flint - - -	187	12	Tiles, average - -	112	20
— Plate - - -	184	$12\frac{1}{6}$	Oil of Turpentine -	$54\frac{3}{4}$	41
Gravel - - -	112	$21\frac{3}{4}$	— Linseed - - -	$58\frac{3}{4}$	38
— Coarse - - -	120	$18\frac{2}{3}$	— Whale - - -	$57\frac{3}{4}$	38·8
Gum - - -		24·69	Warehouse, mean for		40·0
Hay - - - -	5	Truss=56 to 60 lbs.	Shipping, ditto - -		35·0

Partitioning - - - - - - - - -	1480 to 2000 lbs. per square.
Single joisted floor without counter floor - - - - - -	1260 to 2000 lbs. „
Framed floor with counter flooring - - - - - -	2500 to 4000 lbs. „

Articles.	Description.	Weight or Number.	Articles.	Description.	Weight or Number.
Ashes - - -	Barrel -	6=1 ton	Linen, cloth -	Box - -	6=1 ton
Bleaching powders	Cask -	2¼ to 7 cwt.	,, yarn - -	Bale - -	10 cwt.
Bacon - - -	Barrel -	6=1 ton	Linseed meal -	Cask -	10 cwt.
,, - - -	Bale - -	2½ cwt.	Machinery - -	Package -	3½ cwt.
Barley - - -	Sack -	20 stone	Muriatic acid -	Carboy -	60 lbs.
,, - - -	Quarter -	4=1 ton	Oatmeal - -	Bag - -	2 cwt.
Barm - - -	Cask -	8 cwt.	Oats - - -	Sack -	24 stone
Beans - - -	Hogshead -	5¼ cwt.	,, - - -	Quarter ÷	by 6 for tons
,, - - -	Quarter -	4=1 ton	Oil - - -	Cask -	8 cwt.
Beer or Ale - -	Barrel -	3½ cwt.	Oxen - - -	Number -	5½ cwt.
,, - - -	Hogshead -	5¼ cwt.	,, - - -	Number ÷	by 3 for tons
Beef - - -	Barrel -	3 cwt. 7 lbs.	Paper - - -	Bale - -	20 lbs.
Books - - -	Case - -	1 to 5 cwt.	Peas - - -	Bag - -	2 cwt.
Bran - - -	Sack -	1 cwt.	Pork - - -	Tierce, Cask	4½ to 5 cwt.
Bread - - -	Bag - -	1 cwt.	Pigs - - -	- -	⅘ cwt. or 80 lbs.
Butter - - -	Cask -	90 lbs.	,, 1st class -	- -	5=1 ton
,, - - -	Firkin -	¾ cwt.	,, 2nd class -	- -	7=1 ton
Candles - -	Box - -	20 to 40 lbs.	,, 3rd class -	- -	15=1 ton
Cattle, 1st class -	- -	1½=1 ton.	,, 4th class -	- -	23=1 ton
,, 2nd class -	- -	2=1 ton	Poultry - -	Crate -	2 cwt.
,, 3rd class -	- -	3=1 ton	Quills - - -	Bale - -	2 cwt.
,, 4th class -	- -	4=1 ton	Rags - - -	Bag - -	2 cwt.
Coal - - -	Ton		Rum - - -	Hogshead -	56 to 58 gals.
Coffee - - -	Barrel -	2½ cwt.	,, - - -	Gallon ÷	by 224 for tons
Cotton, manufctrd	Package -	3½ cwt.	,, - - -	Cask -	8 to 32 gals.
,, - - -	Yards ÷ by	6,000 for tons.	Runnet - -	Cask -	1 cwt.
Drugs - - -	Package -	2 cwt.	Salt - - -	Bushel -	56 lbs.
Earthenware -	,, -	3½ cwt.	Silk - - -	Bale - -	1½ cwt.
Eggs - - -	Box - -	10=1 ton	,, manufactured	Yard ÷	6,000 for tons
,, - - -	Number ÷ by	28,000 for tons	Sheep - - -	Number -	60 lbs.
,, - - -	Crate or Kish	6 cwt.		,, ÷	by 33 for tons
Flax - - -	Bale - -	10 cwt. average	Sugar - - -	Hogshead -	10 cwt.
,, - - -	Bushel -	48 lbs. 1 qr.	Tallow, Irish -	Cask -	10 cwt.
Flax seed - -	Cask -	3½ cwt.	,, Foreign -	Cask -	8 to 13 cwt.
Feathers - -	Bag - -	2 cwt.	Tanners' waste -	Package -	3 cwt.
Fish - - -	Barrel -	3¾ cwt.	Timber - -	Log, 40 to	1 to 3 tons
Glass - - -	Cask -	1 cwt.		120 feet	
Glue - - -	Hogshead -	10 cwt.	Tinned plates -	Box - -	3½ cwt.
Haberdashery -	Package -	3½ cwt.	Tongues - -	Firkin -	1 cwt.
Hair - - -	Bale -	3 cwt.	Tow - - -	Bale - -	1 cwt.
Hams - - -	Barrel -	3½ cwt.	Vetches - -	Sack -	2 cwt.
,, - - -	Cask -	12 cwt.	Vinegar - -	Cask -	8 cwt.
Hardwares - -	Package -	3½ cwt.	Vitriol - -	Carboy -	60 lbs.
Hides, untanned -	Number -	40=1 ton	Wine - - -	Cask -	12 cwt.
,, - - -	Bundle -	70 lbs.	Wheat - - -	Barrel -	20 stone
Honey - - -	Cask -	½ cwt.	,, - - -	Quarter -	4 cwt.
Horses - - -	Number -	10 cwt.	Whiskey - -	Puncheon -	10½ to 12 cwt.
Horn tops - -	Hogshead -	8 cwt.	Wool - - -	Bale -	3 to 10 cwt.
Iron, wrought -	Package -	3½ cwt.			aver. 6 cwt.
Leather - -	Package -	5 cwt.	,, - - -	Package -	3 cwt.
Linen - - -	Box - -	3½ cwt.	,, - - -	Bag - -	2½ to 9 cwt.
,, - - -	Yard ÷ by	6,000 for tons	Woollen goods -	Yard ÷ by	6,000 for tons.

		Cube.	Weight.	lbs. per ft. cube.	Cube ft. per ton.
Tea, Bohea - - -	2· 9 × 1·10 × 1·8½	= 8·609	= 224 lbs.	= 26·02	= 86·09
,, Congo - - -	1·10½ × 1· 8½ × 1·4½	= 4·403	= 111 lbs.	= 25·21	= 88.87
,, Hyson - - -	1· 6½ × 1· 6 × 1·9	= 4·048	= 80 lbs.	= 19·76	=113·34
,, Souchong - -	1· 7½ × 1· 7½ × 1·7	= 4·180	= 108 lbs.	= 25·84	= 86·70
,, Twankay - -	1·11½ × 1· 6 × 1·8	= 5·140	= 104 lbs.	= 20·23	=110·70
	Mean	5·276 =		23·41	= 97·14

A heaped Bushel of Wheat=60 lbs. per foot cube, and 48·13 cube feet in a ton. A ditto of Barley=47 to 50 lbs. A ditto of Oats=38 to 40 lbs. A ditto of Coal=88 to 94 lbs.

Weight of Water:—

1 quart of water	= 69·3185 cubic inches	= 2½ lbs. weight.	
4 quarts = 1 gallon	= 277·274 cubic inches	= 10 lbs. weight.	
2 gallons = 1 peck	= 554·548 cubic inches	= 20 lbs. weight.	
4 ditto	= 1 bushel=2218·192 cubic inches	= 80 lbs. weight.	
Sea water, 1 cubic foot	= 64 lbs.; 35 cubic feet = 1 ton.		

Welding. The union of two pieces of iron by heating and hammering them. It requires great care that the joint shall be of the same strength as the remainder of the metal. See Soldering and Brazing.

Whinstone. The name by which the marl of the lower Greensand is distinguished in Western Sussex; probably of Saxon origin, remarks Mantell.

Wilkins, W. See Architects, list of, 327.

Wire gauge, Birmingham. This is given in *par.* 2254.

Wyatt, J. See Architects, list of, 320.

Wyatville, Sir J. See Architects, list of, 326.

Zwirner, E. F. See Architects, list of, 347.

INDEX.

₊ *The churches are placed under the towns in which they are situate. The figures refer to the several paragraphs, except where the letter* p. *occurs, when they refer to the page.*